Map Locator

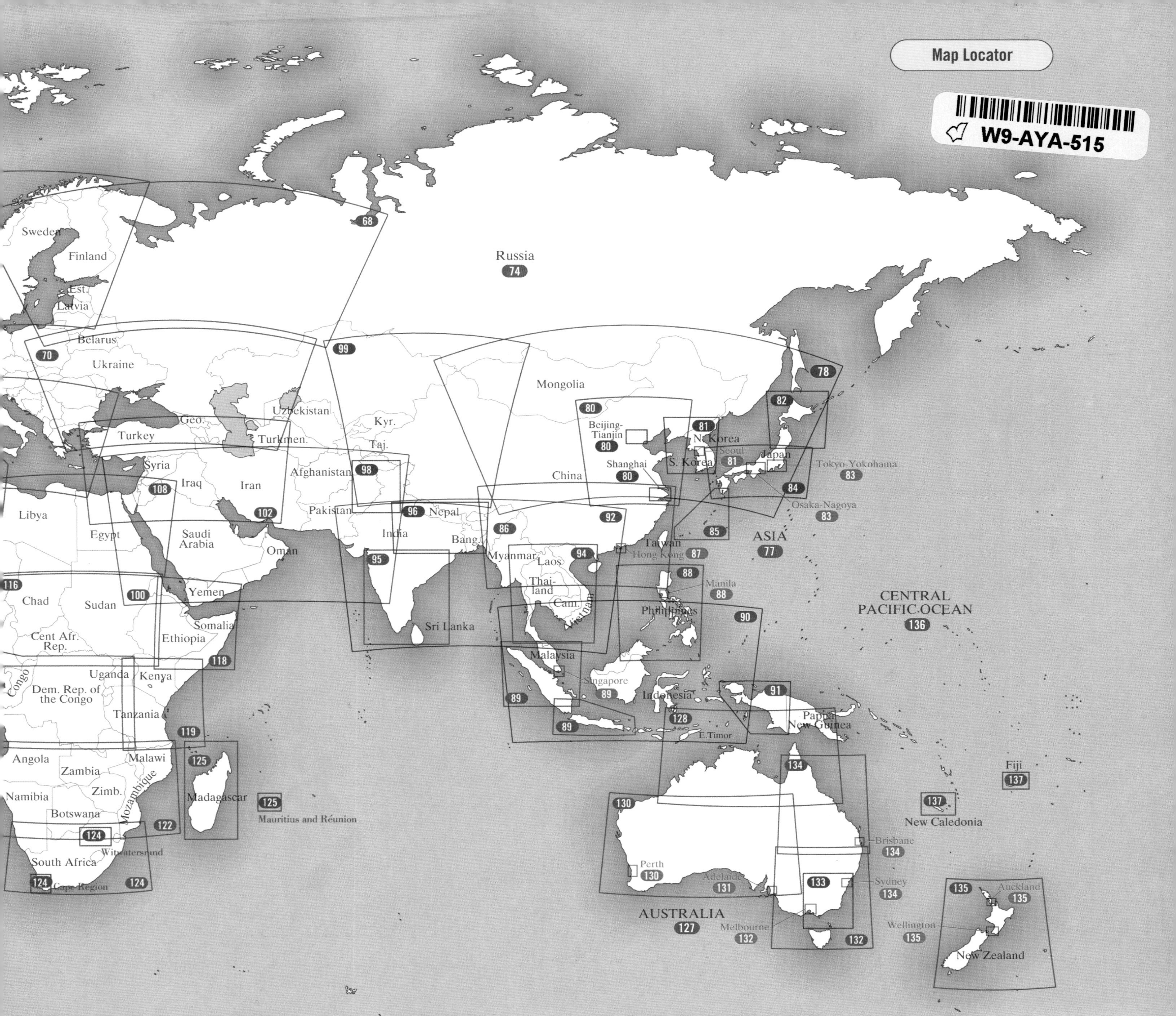

Sweden
Finland
Est.
Latvia
68
Russia
74
Belarus
70
Ukraine
99
Mongolia
78
82
80
Beijing-Tianjin
80
81
N. Korea
S. Korea
Seoul
81
Japan
Tokyo-Yokohama
83
Shanghai
80
84
Osaka-Nagoya
83
Geo.
Uzbekistan
Kyr.
Turkey
Turkmen.
Taj.
Syria
Afghanistan
98
Iraq
Iran
108
Libya
102
Pakistan
96
Nepal
China
92
Egypt
Saudi Arabia
India
Bang.
86
85
Oman
ASIA
77
Taiwan
Hong Kong
87
95
Myanmar
Laos
94
116
Yemen
100
Chad
Sudan
Thai-land
88
Manila
88
Cam.
CENTRAL PACIFIC OCEAN
136
Somalia
Philippines
90
Cent Afr. Rep.
Ethiopia
Sri Lanka
118
Malaysia
Congo
Uganda
Kenya
Dem. Rep. of the Congo
Singapore
89
Indonesia
91
Tanzania
89
128
Papua New Guinea
119
89
E.Timor
Malawi
125
Angola
Zambia
134
Fiji
137
Zimb.
Mozambique
Namibia
Madagascar
125
Mauritius and Réunion
130
137
New Caledonia
Botswana
122
124
Witwatersrand
Brisbane
134
South Africa
Perth
130
124
Cape Region
124
Adelaide
131
133
Sydney
134
135
Auckland
135
AUSTRALIA
127
Melbourne
132
Wellington
135
132
New Zealand

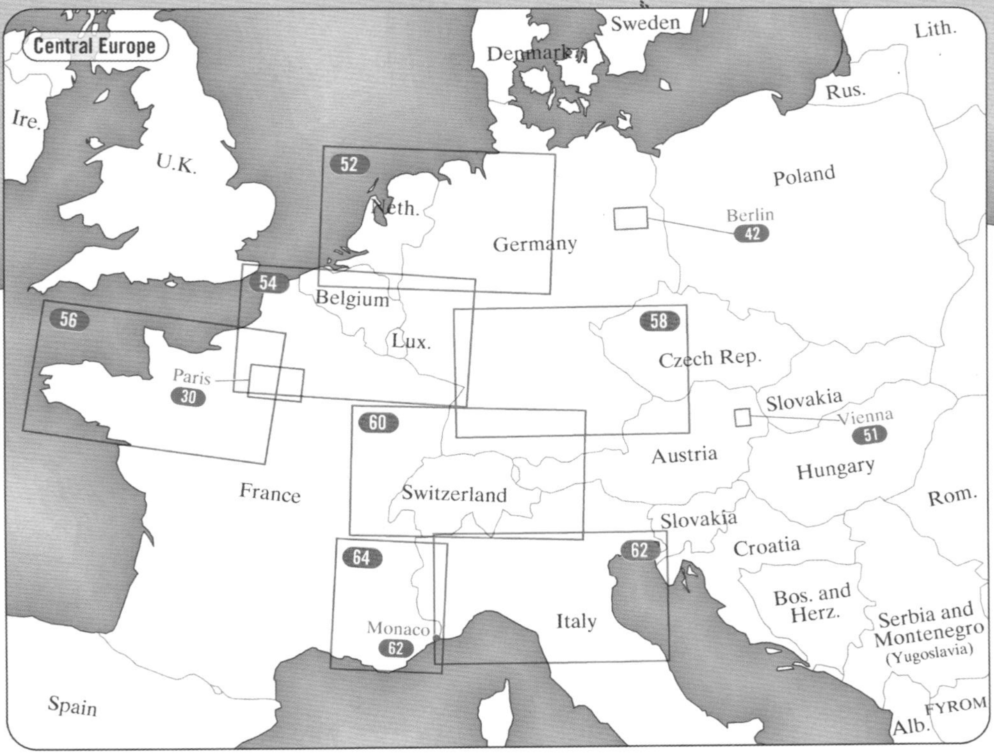

Central Europe
Sweden
Lith.
Denmark
Rus.
Ire.
U.K.
Poland
52
Neth.
Berlin
42
Germany
54
Belgium
56
58
Lux.
Czech Rep.
Paris
30
Slovakia
60
Vienna
51
Austria
Hungary
France
Switzerland
Rom.
Slovakia
64
62
Croatia
Bos. and Herz.
Italy
Serbia and Montenegro
(Yugoslavia)
Monaco
62
Spain
FYROM
Alb.

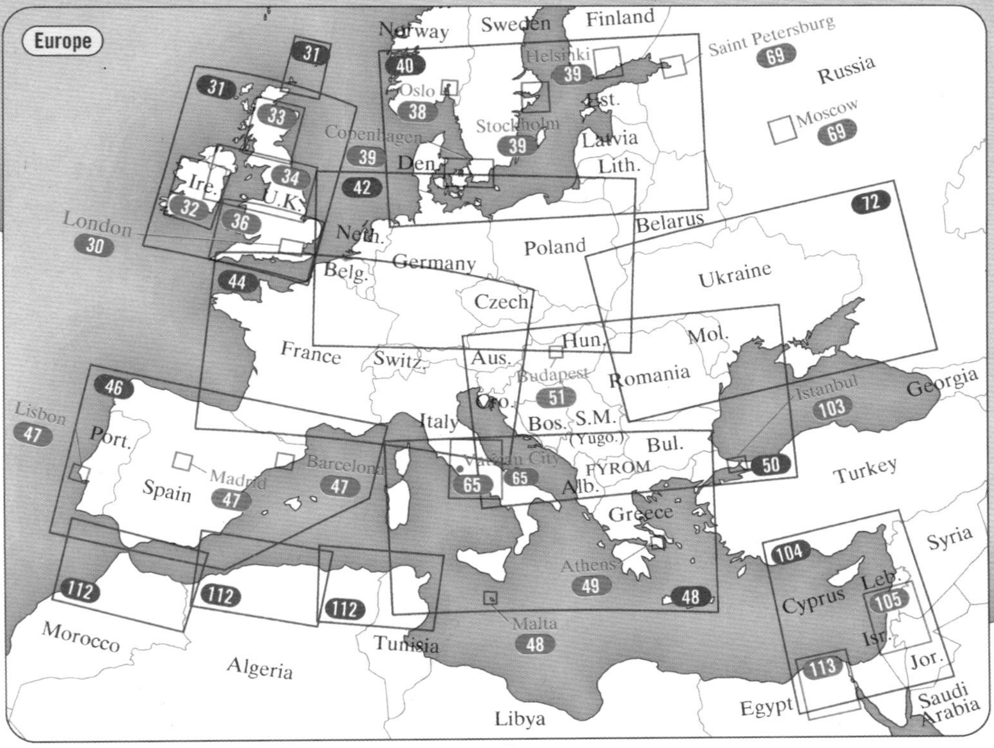

Europe
Norway
Sweden
Finland
31
Saint Petersburg
69
40
Helsinki
39
Russia
31
Oslo
38
Est.
33
Moscow
69
Copenhagen
39
Stockholm
39
Latvia
Den.
Lith.
Ire.
34
42
U.K.
32
London
30
36
Neth.
Belarus
72
Poland
Germany
Belg.
44
Ukraine
Czech
France
Switz.
Hun.
Mol.
Aus.
Budapest
51
Romania
Georgia
46
Cro.
Istanbul
103
Lisbon
47
Port.
Italy
Bos.
S.M.
(Yugo.)
Bul.
Barcelona
47
Madrid
47
Spain
65
65
FYROM
Alb.
50
Turkey
Greece
104
Syria
Athens
49
112
112
112
48
Cyprus
Leb.
105
Malta
48
Isr.
Morocco
Tunisia
Jor.
Algeria
113
Egypt
Saudi Arabia
Libya

> "What I love is near at hand,
> Always, in earth and air."

Theodore Roethke
The Far Field, 1964

HAMMOND
ATLAS OF THE WORLD

BARNES
& NOBLE
BOOKS
NEW YORK

Director of Cartography	Vera Benson
Director of Database Resources	Theophrastos E. Giouvanos
Cartography	Sudha Govindaraju Janice Hulik Walter H. Jones Jr. Sharon Lightner Harry E. Morin Andrew J. Murphy James Padykula Thomas J. Scheffer
Media and Production	Susan Miskewitz John A. DiGiorgio
Technology	Barry A. Moraller
Map Text Blocks	Helmut Vieser; Klartext Journalistenbüro, Stuttgart
Map Layout Graphics	Dipl.-Ing. (FH) Jörg Radtke

Thematic Section

Conception and Editorial Supervision Writers	Dr. Eva Maria Brugger Dr. Joachim Born, Technische Universität, Dresden Dr. Eva Maria Brugger, Heidelberg Prof. Dr. Eckart Ehlers, Universität Bonn Dr. Horst Eichler, Universität Heidelberg Dr. Gernot Gruber, Wiesbaden Prof. Uwe Jäschke, Hochschule für Technik und Wirtschaft Dresden Wolfhard Keimer, Dossenheim Prof. Dr. Wilhelm Lauer & Daud Rafiqpoor, Universität Bonn Prof. Dr. Franz-Dieter Miotke, Garbsen Prof. Dr. Stefan Rahmsdorf, Institut für Klimafolgenforschung Potsdam Prof. Dr. Theo Sundermeier, Universität Heidelberg
Layout and Composition	Matthias Hugo; Hugo Grafische Formgebung, Köln
Informational Graphics	Matthias Hugo; Hugo Grafische Fromgebung, Köln Joachim Knappe, Hamburg
Cartography	Dipl.-Ing. (FH) Jörg Radtke Dipl.-Ing. (FH) Manuela Lipp Erika Korbien

Satellite Section

Conception and Design Supervision	Dipl.-Geogr. Ellen Astor
Consultation and Photo Procurement	Dr. Lothar Beckel; GEOSPACE, Salzburg
Layout and Composition	Sigrid Hecker / doppelpack, Mannheim

Translation

German to English	John S. Southard
Editorial Assistance	Michael Venhoff Ellen Astor
Technology	Sigrid Hecker Jörg Radtke
Author of Thematic and Satellite Sections	Bibliographisches Institut & F.A. Brockhaus AG

©2003 by Hammond World Atlas Corporation.
This edition 2004 by Barnes & Noble Publishing, Inc.

ISBN 0-7607-5361-X

Printed and bound in China by Midas Printing Limited.

10 9 8 7 6 5 4 3 2

Introduction

Throughout the ages, humankind has been driven by a need to explore. From early on in our history, we recorded our explorations and marked our place in the world through the creation of maps. Although the art and science of cartography have evolved enormously, our sense of wonder at the world around us remains constant. Today, our need to know, and our demand for the latest information and sophisticated cartography, are satisfied with the help of computer technology that enables us to portray our planet with more accuracy, precision, and visual power than ever before.

The work you are holding in your hands is the definitive atlas for our new century. It describes a world of breathtaking beauty and heartbreaking devastation. A world that exists as a benefit to mankind and endures in spite of us. A world of contrasts. A world of mysteries. As you leaf through the evocative maps and fascinating text, you'll experience the excitement of exploration for yourself, of the world and of this book – the culmination of years of painstaking and dedicated labor.

At the heart of the atlas is the outstanding digital cartography. In the physical map section, realistic computer simulated relief, enhanced with naturalistic coloration, gives a vivid, 3-dimensional impression of the forms and landscapes of the Earth. Hypsometric tints for land elevations, and bathymetric tints to depict ocean depths, are used to dramatic effect in the world map section. The map image practically leaps off the page, while the clear typography of the nomenclature makes places and other features easy to identify.

If the maps are the heart of the atlas, then the extensive collection of front matter that will capture your imagination is the soul. The maps will help you find your place in the world, while the thematic text and satellite images that precede them will draw you into the planet's mysteries, wonders, and ills. Filled with intellectually stimulating information and compelling photography and graphics, the text in the thematic section guides you through fundamentals of geography and natural science and will enhance your awareness of the interrelatedness of all the living things on Earth.

The opulent satellite photography is nothing short of spectacular and further illustrates the concepts presented in the thematic text. Each of these photos, taken from the perspective of space, is accompanied by technical information and description that satisfies the intellectual curiosity of the reader. They offer a greater understanding of the technologies that allow us to explore the world in ways our ancestors never imagined.

You may have picked up this book for its utility – just to look up a place and continue on with your day. You may want to refer to it for research, study, or business. If so, the clear organization and the comprehensive index will make it easy for you to quickly find what you need. Nevertheless, when the human need to explore stirs within you, we invite you to take the time to sit back and let the beauty of the atlas inspire you on a fascinating journey of the intellect and the imagination. We are confident you will find it a rewarding experience.

Table of Contents

Map Locator
Title
Attribution
Introduction
Contents
Map and Photo Credits

Thematic Section

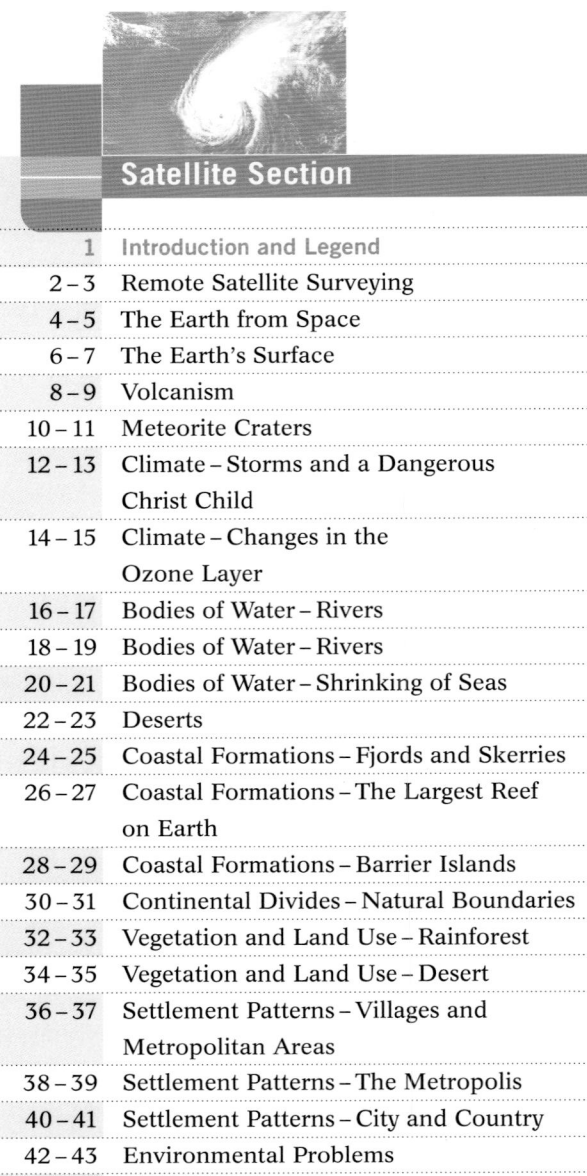

Satellite Section

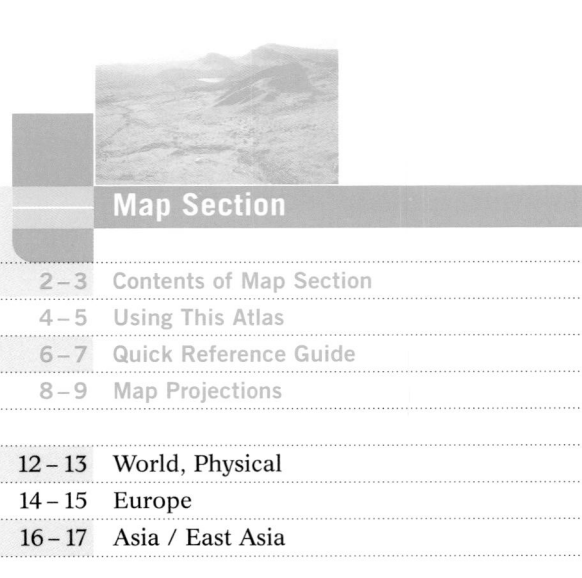

Map Section

Map and Photo Credits

Maps in the Map Section: © Hammond World Atlas Corporation 2003, Union, New Jersey

Satellite Images: © GEOSPACE, Austria, 2000, Original Data: Eurimage – © GEOSPACE / World Sat International Corp. 2000 – © Deutsches Zentrum für Luft- und Raumfahrt, Oberpfaffenhofen

Theme Section and other pages in the atlas: action press, Hamburg – aisa, Archivo iconografico, Barcelona – Archiv für Kunst und Geschichte, Berlin – theartarchive, London – Art Publishers, Durban – Astrofoto Bildagentur, Sörth – Prof. Dr. J. Bähr, Altwittenbek – Prof. Dr. W. Barthlott, Bonn – J. Bautze, Berlin – BAVARIA Bildagentur, Gauting – Berliner Missionswerk – Hans Bertram Luftbildverlag, Munich – Bibliographisches Institut & F. A. Brockhaus, Mannheim – Bibliothèque Nationale de France, Paris – Bildarchiv Preußischer Kulturbesitz, Berlin – Bilderberg, Archiv der Fotografen, Hamburg – Prof. Dr. G. Bosinski, Neuwied – Prof. Dr. G. Bräuer, Hartenholm – British Library, London – Luftbildarchiv Albrecht Brugger im Hause Fotofachlabor Schnepf, Stuttgart – R. Brugger, Königswinter – Bundesanstalt für Geowissenschaften und Rohstoffe, Hanover – J.-L. Charmet, Paris – Prof. M. Deuchler, London – Deutscher Wetterdienst, Offenbach am Main – Deutsches Museum, Munich – Digimago, Eppelheim – dpa Bildarchiv, Frankfurt am Main und Stuttgart – Dr. H. Eichler, Heidelberg – Prof. Dr. Ch. Feest, Frankfurt am Main – Photo- und Presseagentur FOCUS, Hamburg – Photo- und Presseagentur Focus, Hamburg / B. Barbey / Magnum – Photo- und Presseagentur Focus, Hamburg / J. Blair – Photo- und Presseagentur Focus, Hamburg / B. Edmaier – M. Fries, Wiesbaden – Dr. K. Gallas, München – Studio X, Gamma, Limours – Dr. G. Gerster, Zumikon, Schweiz – Dr. S. von der Heide, Cologne – Prof. Dr. K. Heine, Regensburg – D. Heunemann, Starnberg – Prof. Dr. P. Höllermann, Bonn – IFA-Bilderteam, Taufkirchen – Prof. Dr. A. Jockenhövel, Münster – W. Keimer, Dossenheim – KNA Kath. Nachrichten Agentur, Frankfurt am Main – Dr. H.-J. Kress, Fulda – Helga Lade Fotoagentur, Frankfurt am Main – laenderpress, Mainz – J. Lauré, Woodfin Camp & Associates, New York – Löppert, Optik-Foto-Dia, Munich – Dr. L. Marfaing, Hamburg – Bildagentur Mauritius, Mittenwald – P. Meyer, Frankfurt. – MEV Verlag, Augsburg – Prof. Dr. F.-D. Miotke, Garbsen – W. Müller, Ettlingen – Museum für Völkerkunde, Vienna – NASA / Earth from Space Images, Washington D.C. – NASA / JPL/RPIF/DLR – Neanderthal Museum, Mettmann – Prof. Dr. G. Niemz, Neu-Isenburg – Oberösterreichisches Landesmuseum, Linz – G. Dagli Orti, Paris – Österreichische Nationalbibliothek, Vienna – Physikalisch-Technische Bundesanstalt, Braunschweig und Berlin – Picture Press, Hamburg / Meyer-Andersen – J. Poupard – J. M. Prieto, Asunción – Dr. D. Rafiqpoor, Bonn – Prof. Dr. S. Rahmstorf, Potsdam – Agentur RAPHO, Paris – Rosgartenmuseum, Konstanz – Prof. Dr. H.-J. Sander, Bonn – K. Schlosser, Kiel – G. Schrüfer, Bayreuth – Forschungsinstitut und Natur-Museum Senckenberg, Frankfurt am Main – Silvestris Verlag, Bildarchiv, Kastl – Sipa Press, Paris – E. SLAWIK, Waldenburg – K. Stevens, USA – H. Stierlin, Genf – Dr. K.-H. Striedter, Frankfurt am Main – L. A. Thomas / Doug Peebles Photography, Hawaii – Tony Stone Bilderwelten, Munich – Uitgeverij Het Spectrum, Utrecht – Ullstein Bilderdienst, Berlin – Ulmer Museum, Ulm – Prof. Dr. W. H. Valentin, Berlin – Prof. Dr. M. Yaldiz, Berlin – ZEFA-Zentrale Farbbild Agentur, Düsseldorf – Carl Zeiss, Oberkochen

Locator maps based on MHM © 1993 Digital Wisdom, Inc.

Other graphic illustrations, maps, and drawings: Bibliographisches Institut & F. A. Brockhaus, Mannheim

Thematic Section

The Universe – Our Place in Space

"The works of incredible grandeur are as glorious as on the First Day"

Lifting our gaze upward from the earth, we look into space, but we call what we see the sky. Hung there, so it seems, are all the lights that shine upon us – the warming sun during the day, the cool moon, and the twinkling stars at night.
Ages passed before we humans abandoned the concept of an existence beneath an all-encompassing protective sky and dared to venture, intellectually at first, then through experiment, and finally in concrete steps, into the vastness of space, into the world of worlds, into the universe.

A Grain of Sand in the Desert

How can we comprehend a phenomenon like the universe, something we cannot grasp because it is too large, too small, or too far away? Modern science relies on precise observation linked with proven principles to form explanatory hypotheses. If such hypotheses stand up to all theoretical and practical attempts to refute them, they are regarded as true, and we incorporate them into our fund of knowledge.

Applying this method, we have learned that our earth is like a grain of sand in the desert in comparison to the universe. We have also come to realize that earth is not the center of the universe – indeed, that the universe has no center at all. Does that mean that the earth could as easily be somewhere else? In another solar system, another star system, or another galaxy? Theoretically, the answer is yes, but whether there would then be life on earth, or even human beings, is another question altogether.

Ordinarily, being somewhere else means being in a different place and a different environment. Modern cosmology tells us that place or position in the universe is generally inconsequential but that environment is crucial. And the heavenly bodies nearest the earth show that this must be true. Although very different from one another, the moon and our neighboring planets Venus and Mars have one thing in common which distinguishes them from the earth: As far as we know, they are devoid of life.

Galaxies – Structures of the Universe

Aside from the moon, our constant, though changeable companion, the most prominent features of the nighttime sky are stars and a nebulous, luminous band known as the Milky Way. Despite all appearances, this band of light we perceive is a system of stars to which the sun – one of millions upon millions of stars – also belongs, and with it the earth and we ourselves.

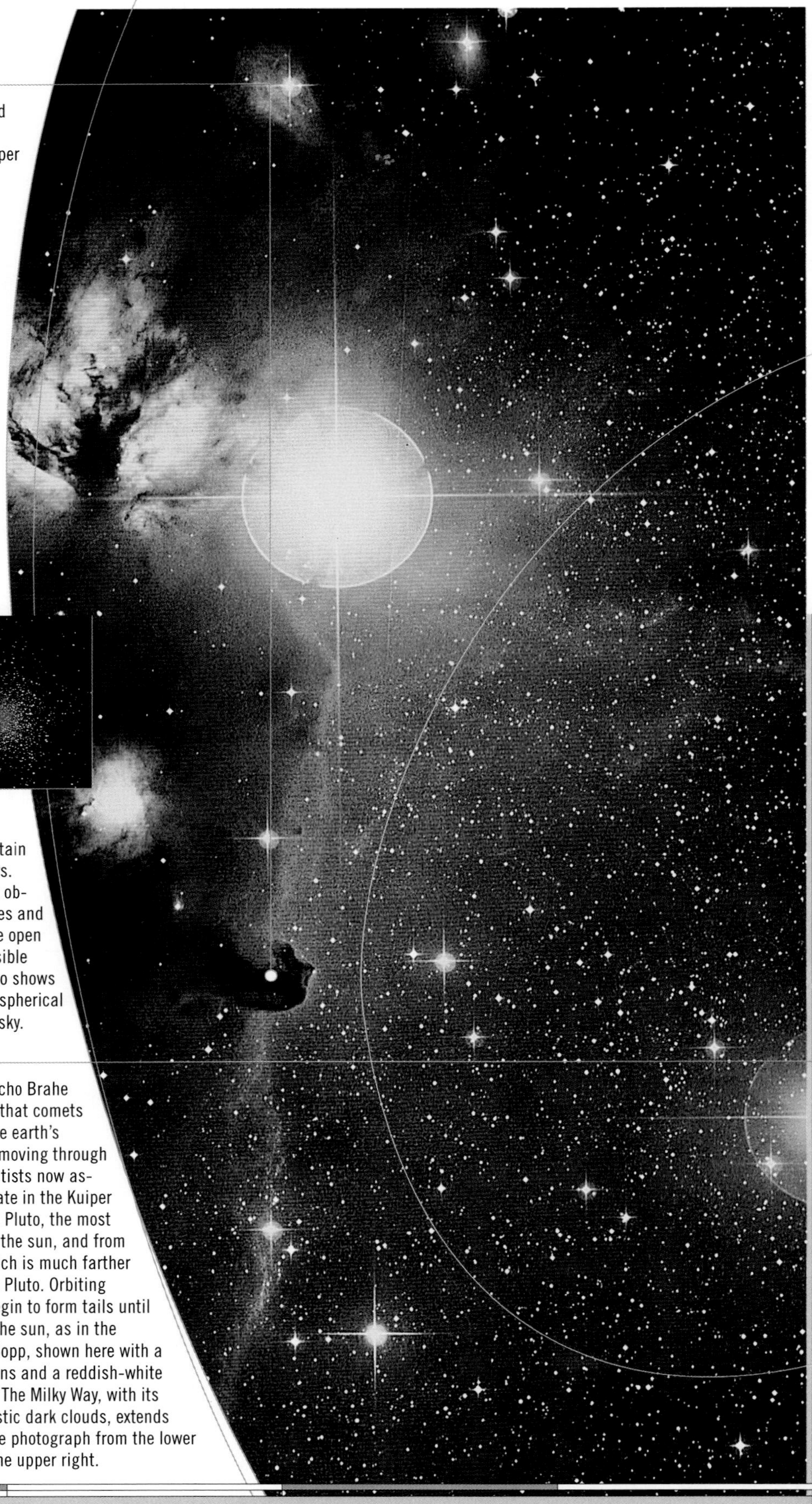

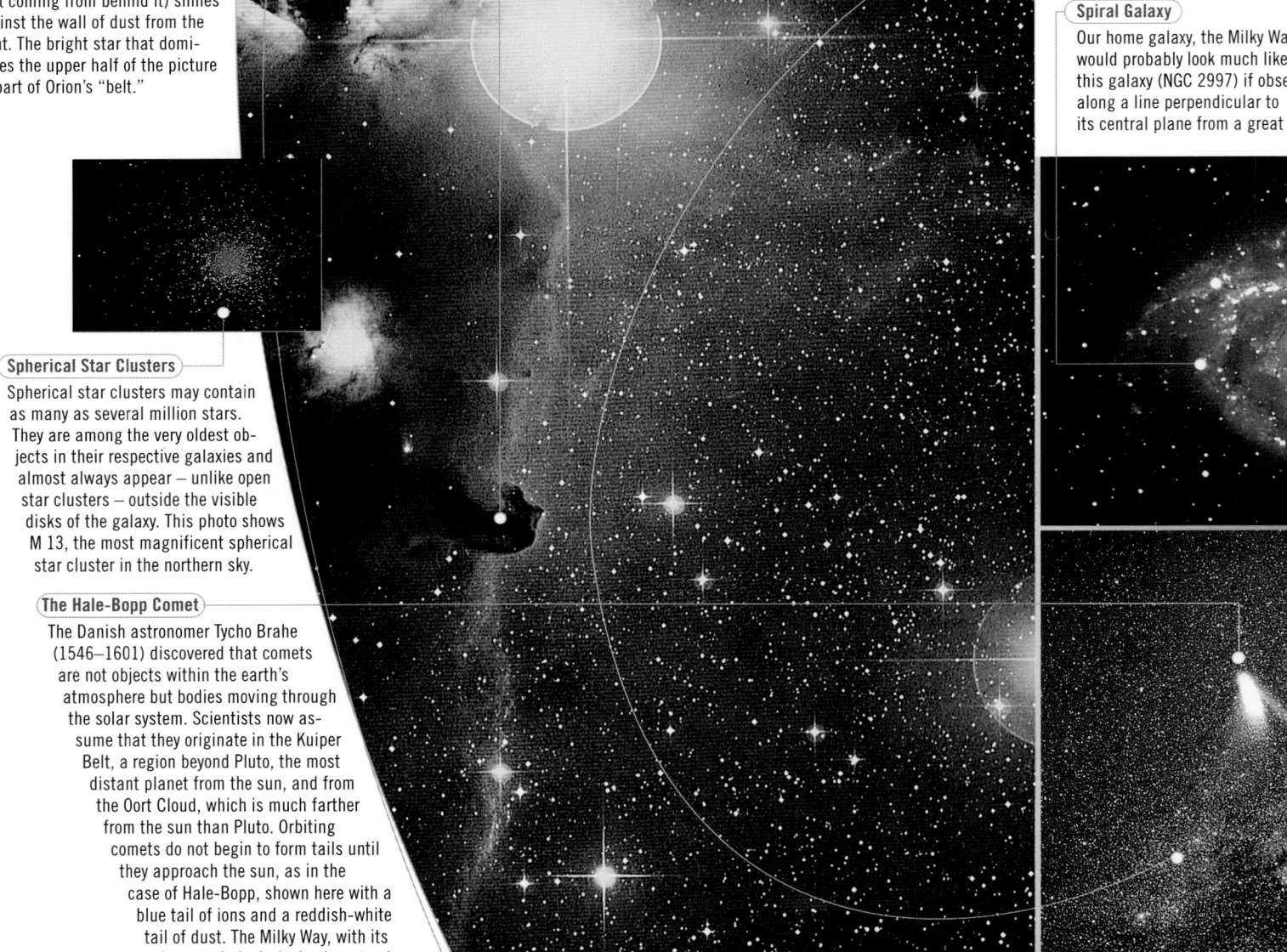

Horsehead Nebula

Named for its shape, a horsehead nebula is an extension of a huge, dark cloud of dust (seen in the upper left-hand portion of the picture) that has expanded in such a way that light from any star positioned behind it cannot penetrate it. The dark cloud covers a nebula that emits reddish light. The only stars visible in the vicinity of the dark cloud are those located in front of it. The reflective nebula of the dust cloud is visible on the left above the "horse's head," where a foreground star (which cannot be seen because it is swallowed up by the light coming from behind it) shines against the wall of dust from the front. The bright star that dominates the upper half of the picture is part of Orion's "belt."

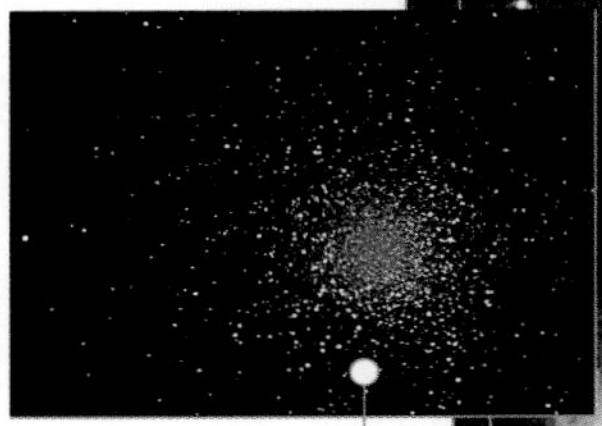

Spherical Star Clusters

Spherical star clusters may contain as many as several million stars. They are among the very oldest objects in their respective galaxies and almost always appear – unlike open star clusters – outside the visible disks of the galaxy. This photo shows M 13, the most magnificent spherical star cluster in the northern sky.

The Hale-Bopp Comet

The Danish astronomer Tycho Brahe (1546–1601) discovered that comets are not objects within the earth's atmosphere but bodies moving through the solar system. Scientists now assume that they originate in the Kuiper Belt, a region beyond Pluto, the most distant planet from the sun, and from the Oort Cloud, which is much farther from the sun than Pluto. Orbiting comets do not begin to form tails until they approach the sun, as in the case of Hale-Bopp, shown here with a blue tail of ions and a reddish-white tail of dust. The Milky Way, with its characteristic dark clouds, extends across the photograph from the lower left to the upper right.

Spiral Galaxy

Our home galaxy, the Milky Way, would probably look much like this galaxy (NGC 2997) if observed along a line perpendicular to its central plane from a great distance. Easily recognizable in its spiral arms are the arrangement of open star clusters and the distribution of interstellar dust.

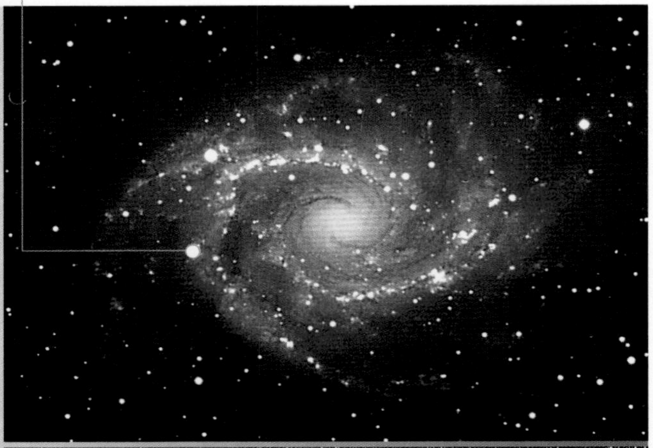

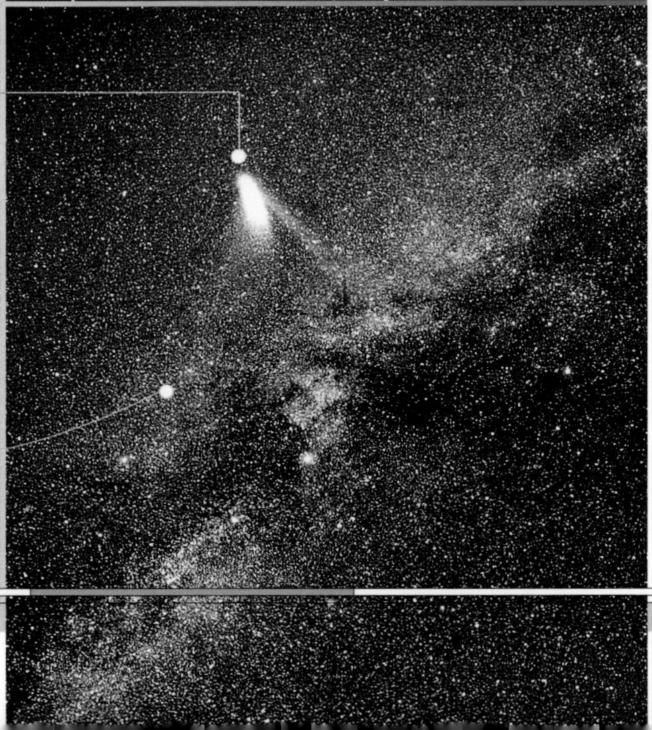

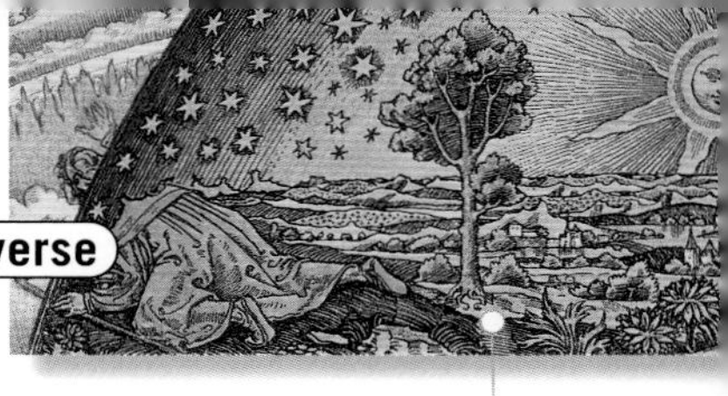

The idea that the earth and the sun are a part of the Milky Way seems somewhat more plausible if we consider that the band of the Milky Way encircles the earth completely with roughly the same intensity of light at all points. Yet it would be wrong to conclude from this observation that we are located at the center. The sun is actually far from the middle and much nearer to the edge of the system. The insight that the earth is a part of the Milky Way, the luminous band of stars we perceive, leads us to a second, valid conclusion, however: that the stars are very far apart, separated by distances much greater than that between the earth and the sun. The star closest to us, Proxima Centauri, is seven thousand times farther from the sun than Pluto, its most distant planet, which is visible to us only through a telescope.

The universe comprises a multitude of star systems of different types and sizes, generally referred to as galaxies. Astronomers estimate that there are between several hundred billion and several trillion of such galaxies. The spiral galaxy closest to earth is 2.2 million light years away. Depending upon their type and size, galaxies may consist of as few as a billion or as many as a trillion stars. Not all of these are single stars but may appear as double or multiple stellar systems and star clusters. We use the term galaxy to distinguish our home star system from all others.

The structural principle of larger objects composed of several or many similar smaller objects can be applied with respect to galaxies to derive the existence of both smaller and larger objects.

Galaxies form galactic groups and galactic clusters which may contain as many as several thousand individual galaxies, and several dozen galactic clusters may form a supercluster. Superclusters are immense cosmic structures, some of which measure more than a million light years across and are separated by equally large voids. A million light years is the distance light travels in one million years (moving at a speed of about 300,000 kilometers per second). Our galaxy and the Andromeda Galaxy are the largest members of a galactic cluster known as the Local Group.

Some stars – including our sun – have their own solar planet systems. Astronomers have determined that there are other planet systems in the Milky Way besides our solar system.

Stars and Interstellar Matter

Galactic matter appears not only in highly condensed form as stars but also as finely distributed particles in clouds of dust and gas which are observed through a telescope as luminous nebulas. There is a very close relationship between this kind of matter, which scientists refer to as interstellar matter because it is distributed between stars, and the early and late phases – the birth and death – in the development of stars. Stars form in and from interstellar matter. The greater their initial mass, the shorter their lifespans and the more forceful and violent their deaths, which often occur in explosions involving the release of huge quantities of gas and dust.

All of the stars we have observed and named as individual objects belong to the Milky Way system. To facilitate their location in the sky, ancient observers of the heavens assigned the visible stars to certain prominent celestial constellations. Since 1933, astronomers have defined constellations as specific rectangular sectors on the celestial sphere, which is divided into eighty-eight such areas.

We notice three things immediately when we gaze at the nighttime sky: that all stars twinkle, that some are brighter than others, and that they appear in different colors ranging from bluish or whitish to reddish-yellow. The twinkling effect is not produced by the stars themselves but by turbulence in the earth's atmosphere, while perceived differences in brightness depend upon the

relative distance of stars from the earth and on such factors as a star's size and temperature. The color of a star is also a function of its temperature and the direction in which it is moving – toward or away from the observer. Stars are categorized within light and spectral classes on the basis of these characteristics.

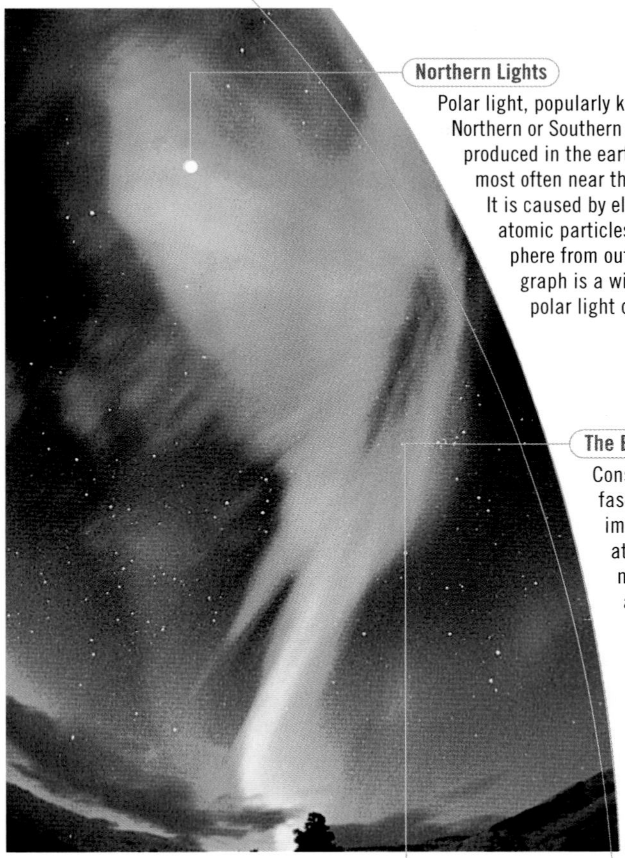

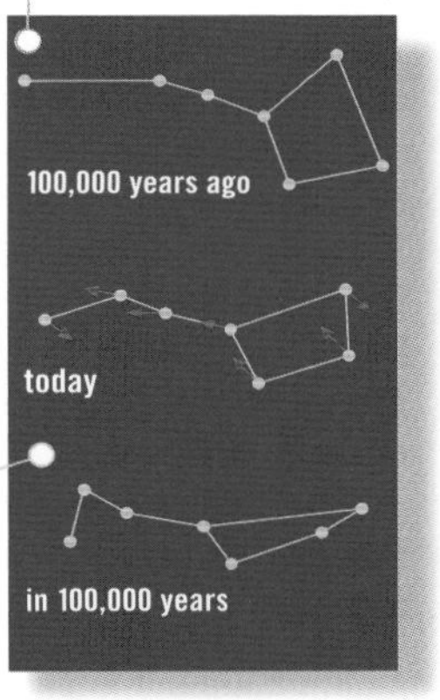

100,000 years ago

today

in 100,000 years

The fact that stars seem to hang motionless in the sky has to do with their great distance from us. They actually move through space at tremendous speeds, and their positions in the heavens change accordingly over the course of millennia. The constellation we know as the Big Dipper looked much different 100,000 years ago than it does now, and its shape will have changed again in another 100,000 years. Many stars classified as "changeable" exhibit changes in brightness over periods of several days or less, some of them, the novas or supernovas, as a result of massive explosions.

During the greater part of their lives, stars emit energy generated by nuclear fusion in their interiors at temperatures of up to several million degrees Fahrenheit.

The Unity of Nature

We are moved emotionally by the beauty of the heavens. By observing and measuring celestial bodies, we gain insight into the nature of the universe. Through thousands of years of increasingly precise observation of planets, stars, solar systems, and galaxies, we have learned that the laws of nature discovered on earth apply to the universe as well, and this principle has become very useful in the exploration of space. It was the basis for the heuristic hypothesis that the information we obtain about outer space can be explained with the aid of laws of nature discovered on earth – scientific explanation of the universe would be impossible otherwise. This is the theory of the unity of nature.

Particularly useful aids to our study of space are the laws of mechanics, the theory of gravitation, and the laws

of nuclear physics, particularly as they apply to spectral analysis. The currently accepted theory of gravitation is Einstein's General Theory of Relativity. The nature of atoms and their interaction both with one another and with electromagnetic radiation are described by various quantum theories, most notably the theory of quantum mechanics.

By applying the laws of mechanics and the theory of gravitation, we have succeeded in computing the movement of objects in the universe – both man-made and natural objects, from spacecraft to galaxies. The use of spectral analysis in combination with quantum theory has enabled us to explain cosmic structures, from elementary particles to atoms and molecules, and to describe the structures of such bodies as stars, stellar systems, and superclusters. Our capacity to describe and explain covers a broad spectrum of phenomena, beginning with the Big Bang, the earliest phase in the history of the universe, and extending practically to the origin of life on earth. We know that our solar system is five billion years old and that the Milky Way has existed for twelve billion years in a universe that is now fourteen billion years old. And we have learned that the universe and space itself have been expanding since the very first moment of their existence.

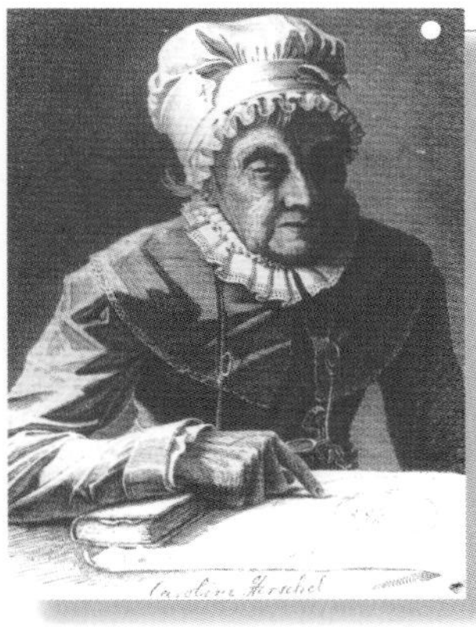

The Solar System

Our Home Star and Its Orbiting Planets

The sun is just one star among billions in our galaxy, the Milky Way. The solar system comprises the nine large planets (and their moons), Mercury, Venus, Earth (one moon), Mars (2), Jupiter (16), Saturn (17), Uranus (15), Neptune (8), and Pluto (1) as well as numerous other smaller objects, such as comets, meteorites, and asteroids. Most asteroids are less than 100 km in diameter, and nearly all of their paths pass between Mars and Jupiter. Unlike the stars, the planets, their moons, and the small celestial bodies emit no light and are visible to us only because they are illuminated by the sun.

Seen through a telescope, the planets appear as disks of various sizes. Images transmitted from spacecraft provide information about their surface features. The planets move along elliptical orbits on planes which deviate only slightly from that of the earth's orbit (e.g. 7°, Pluto 17°, Uranus nearly 0°). Puzzled by apparent reversals of direction, ancient and medieval observers were unable to explain the motions of the planets as seen from the earth.

Sizes and Distances

Because the inner, "earthlike" planets Mercury, Venus, Earth, and Mars are composed of metals and rock (rock planets), they are relatively dense. The outer, Jovian planets – Jupiter, Saturn, Uranus, Neptune – and Pluto consist primarily of gases (including hydrogen, helium, and methane) and frozen water. The asteroid belt lies between the inner and outer planets. The distribution of light and heavy matter took place during the infancy of the solar system, as lighter materials condensed in the colder outer regions of the system. With the exception of Pluto, all of the other planets (known as giant planets) are considerably larger than the earth. The diameter of Jupiter is eleven times greater than that of the earth, that of Saturn almost ten times greater. The sun's diameter is ten times larger than Jupiter's. A comparison of the masses of the objects in the solar system reveals even more marked differences. Added together, the masses of all nine planets amount to only 13 % of the sun's mass, and Jupiter alone accounts for 70 % of that total. Relative sizes and distances can be illustrated on the basis of the following example: The distance between the sun and Pluto is 5.9 billion kilometers. If the sun had a diameter of one meter, Pluto would measure two millimeters across, and the distance between the two would be four kilometers.

Born of a Cloud of Dust

Some five billion years ago, a cloud of interstellar dust began to condense, a reaction perhaps triggered by a nearby supernova. As gravitational forces increased, the core of the cloud grew increasingly dense, while the concentration of mass in the center accelerated the system's rotation. Gradually, a flat disk formed, from which the planets later emerged. Temperatures at the center of the disk approached eighteen million degrees F, generating nuclear fusion of the hydrogen atoms. The sun began to radiate. At its core, 655 million tons of hydrogen were converted into 650 million tons of helium every second, while five million tons of matter were transformed into energy. Five billion years from now, when its nuclear energy has been consumed, the sun will enter its final phase, at which point it will turn first into a red giant and later into a white dwarf.

The Earth's Reliable Heater

The sun produces temperatures of up to 27 million degrees F at its core. Pressure at that point is 200 billion times that recorded on the earth's surface. The visible surface of the sun is called the photosphere. It is about 400 km thick and has a mean temperature of 9,900 degrees F. Sunspots form where magnetic-field lines break through the surface. Granules (giant bubbles) measuring about 1,500 km in diameter form on the upper surface of the photosphere and bubble upward. Flames of gas (protuberances) shoot forth from the outer layer (the chromosphere), reaching heights up to tens of thousands of kilometers. The outer atmosphere of the sun (the corona) has very low density and temperatures around 1.8 million degrees F. It extends beyond the photosphere to heights equivalent to several times the radius of the sun.

The Inner Planets

Mercury, the second-smallest planet after to Pluto, is closest to the sun. Humans could not possibly survive its surface temperatures of 780 °F during the day and –325 °F during the night. The atmosphere (helium, argon) above the moonlike, cratered landscape is extremely thin.

The surface of Venus is not visible from the earth. Thick clouds of carbon dioxide (96 %), nitrogen (3 %), and trace amounts of water vapor and other gases reflect 65 % of the sun's rays, making Venus the third brightest object in the sky, after the sun and the moon. The greenhouse effect caused by its mantle of gases raises the surface temperatures of the planet's craters and lava fields (80 %) to temperatures in the range of 850 °F. There is no liquid water, and there are no rivers or oceans, only a few dunes.

The distance between the earth and the sun is favorable to life as we know it, and temperatures are neither too high nor too low.

People long assumed that there could be some form of life on Mars – intelligent or at least primitive life. The pattern of lines on the planet's surface thought to be a network of irrigation canals proved to be an optical illusion however, although valleys marked by meanders do suggest that rivers must have flowed through them at one time. The cold crater landscapes of the "Red Planet" (with lows at the poles approaching 300 °F) are marked by rocky deserts. The largest shield volcano on Mars is 700 km wide, 25 km high and presumably several hundred million years old.

Key Data: The Sun	
Diameter:	1,392,000 km
Mass:	333,000 x earth mass
Mean density:	1.409 g/ccm
Distance from earth:	149.6 mill. km
Time of light travel sun−earth:	8 min 20 s

Key Data: The Moon	
Distance earth−moon:	384,403 km
Mass:	0.0123 x earth mass
Mean density:	3.341 g/ccm
Daytime temp.:	265 °F
Nighttime temp.:	−240 °F

	Mass (x earth mass)	Density (g/ccm)
Mercury	0.055	5.43
Venus	0.815	5.24
Earth	1.000	5.52
Mars	0.107	3.93
Jupiter	318.0	1.33
Saturn	95.1	0.70
Uranus	14.4	1.30
Neptune	17.2	1.76
Pluto	0.002	1.7

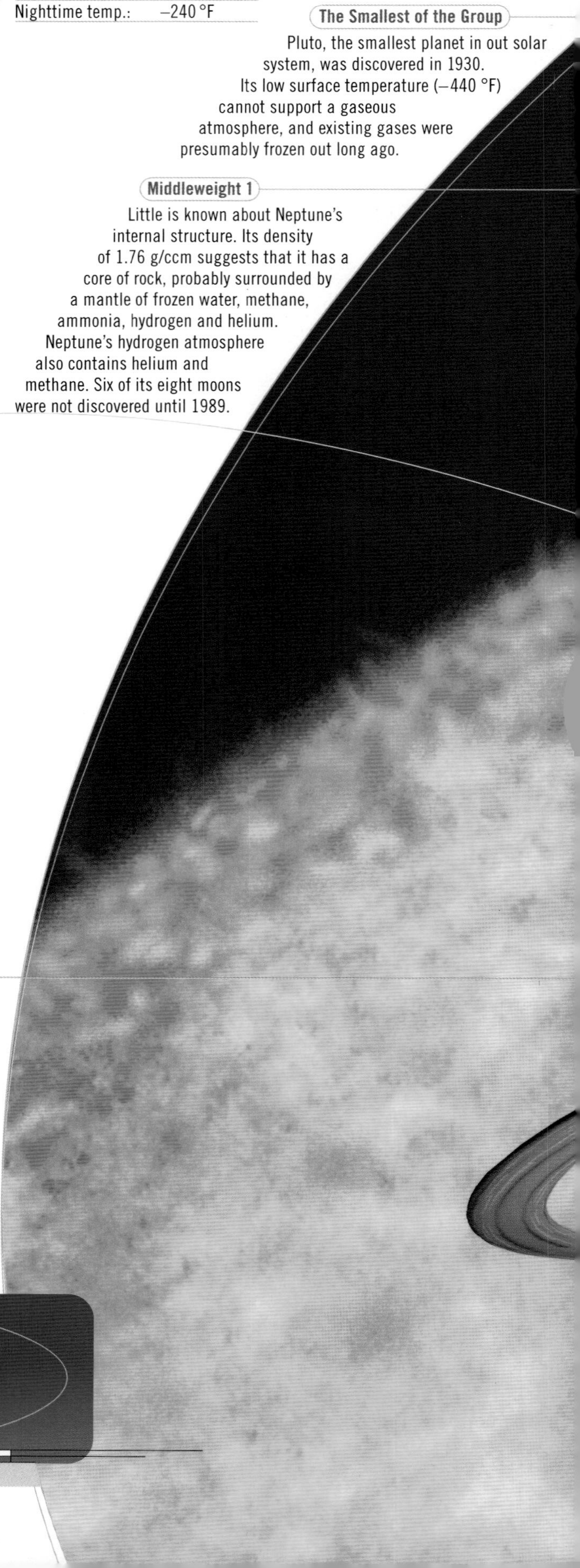

The Smallest of the Group

Pluto, the smallest planet in out solar system, was discovered in 1930. Its low surface temperature (−440 °F) cannot support a gaseous atmosphere, and existing gases were presumably frozen out long ago.

Middleweight 1

Little is known about Neptune's internal structure. Its density of 1.76 g/ccm suggests that it has a core of rock, probably surrounded by a mantle of frozen water, methane, ammonia, hydrogen and helium. Neptune's hydrogen atmosphere also contains helium and methane. Six of its eight moons were not discovered until 1989.

Predictable Relationships

The planets travel in elliptical orbits on planes which, unlike those of comet orbits, are "tilted" only slightly off the earth's orbital plane. The inner planets, Mercury, Venus, the earth, and Mars, are closest to the sun and receive more warming solar radiation than the distant outer planets, which are accordingly much colder.

Middleweight 2

Seen through a telescope, Uranus appears as a blue-green disk without visible surface features. It was not until 1986 that Voyager 2 provided a more detailed picture, revealing cloud structures, the presence of a magnetic field, and ten previously undiscovered moons. The planet's greater density indicates a composition containing metals heavier than those on Saturn. Its atmosphere consists primarily of hydrogen and helium.

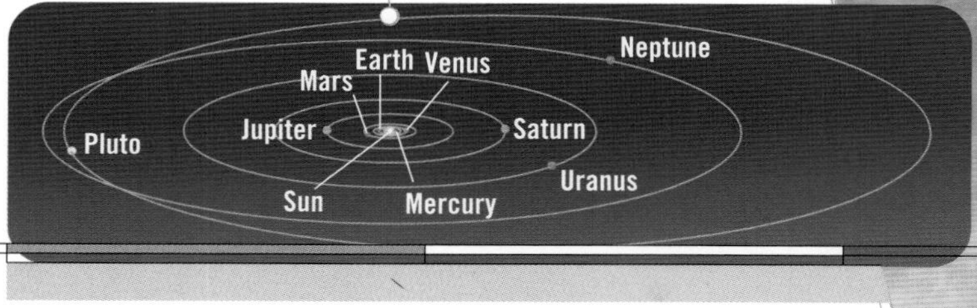

Neptune
Mars Earth Venus
Pluto Jupiter Saturn
Sun Mercury Uranus

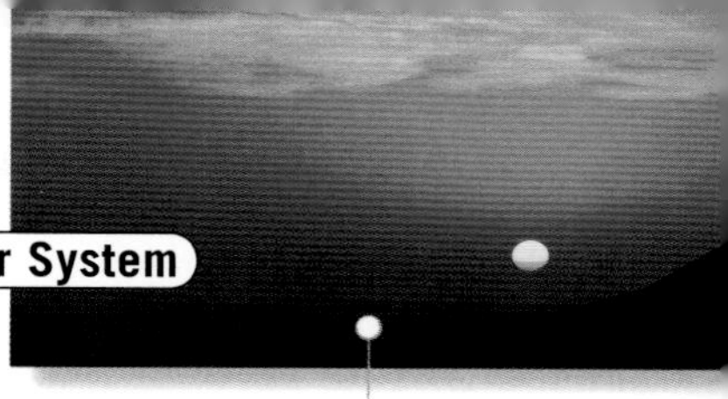

Our Moon

When Astronauts Armstrong and Aldrin took their first steps on the moon on July 21, 1969, they fulfilled an age-old human dream. Since then, plans have been in the making for a manned mission to Mars. Although that goal has yet to be achieved, a number of unmanned spacecraft have explored the depths of space as far away as Neptune.

The Blue Planet

The view from the porthole of a spacecraft shows how lost our planet is in space. Compared with the giant planets or the sun, it seems infinitely small. If mankind is to survive, we must manage our resources wisely. Viewed from outer space, our planet appears predominantly blue.

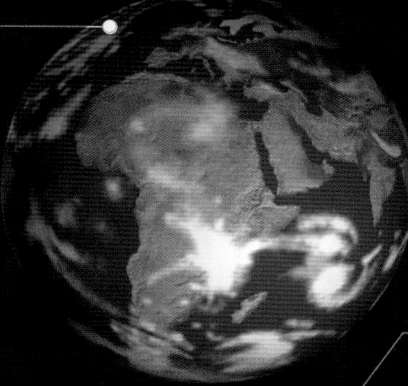

A Glaring Ball of Fire

Only when the sun is just above the horizon can we gaze at it without protecting our eyes. From this position, sunlight travels farther through the atmosphere, and the energy-laden blue rays are largely filtered out. Looking directly at the sun at midday without protection causes irreparable damage to the retina.

Giant Twins

The rings of Saturn and several of Jupiter's moons are clearly visible through even a small telescope. The giant planets Jupiter and Saturn are so large that the earth is dwarfed in comparison. Like other giant planets, Jupiter also has a system of rings, although it is not as prominent as that of Saturn. Both planets have many moons and are encircled by bands of clouds. Their atmospheres consist of hydrogen, helium and minute admixtures of methane and ammonia. Towards the interior, these gases pass through transitions from gaseous to liquid (on the planet's surface) to solid states (at their cores). The two giants have strong magnetic fields. Io, the innermost planet of Jupiter, became famous through images sent back to earth by Voyager, which provided the first opportunity to observe extraterrestrial volcanic activity. Fountains of lava expelled at speeds of up to 1,000 m/s traveled as high as 300 m above the surrounding areas covered with multi-colored lava and frozen sulfur-dioxide. No older impact craters have been identified.

Mars

Venus

Mercury

Earth

Planet Earth

... and it truly does move!

If we could look from a great distance at the supposedly firm and motionless ground on which we normally stand, we would see that it is anything but motionless. Our Earth is a dynamic celestial body which rotates on its own axis and revolves around the sun. The very point at which we stand moves along a complicated orbit through space.

Dancing on a Volcano

An entirely different kind of motion involving shifts in the positions of points on Earth relative to one another ordinarily takes place unnoticed and so slowly that extraordinarily precise instruments are required to prove that it occurs at all. Yet a time-lapse film in which 10 million years are compressed into a single second would provide striking evidence of how much the Earth's appearance has changed since prehistoric times and become the planet we know today. The key terms used to describe this process are "continental drift" and "plate tectonics." The only effects of these changes we perceive directly are the – often disastrous – earthquakes and seaquakes, frequently followed by massive tidal waves, that frequently accompany movements of the large plates in the uppermost layers of the Earth's crust.

Like our perceptions of the positions and movements of objects in the sky, much of what we experience on Earth – the alternation of day and night, the changing seasons – is caused by the motion of the Earth. The alternation of day and night would seem easy enough to explain: The Earth turns completely around its own axis every 24 hours, and thus every place on Earth experiences a sunrise and a sunset. But wait! There are regions on Earth in which the sun doesn't rise for months and doesn't set again until more months have passed: the polar zones within the Arctic and Antarctic Circles. These periods of time are referred to as polar nights and polar days.

The cause of both – and for the changing seasons everywhere on Earth – is the fact that the Earth's rotational axis is inclined 23.5 degrees to the plane of the Earth's orbit around the sun. Because the angle of the Earth's axis does not change as it revolves around the sun – its northern extension always points towards the North Star – one hemisphere is always closer to the sun: the northern hemisphere during the northern summer and the southern hemisphere during the northern winter. Only at the spring and fall equinoxes, when days and nights are equally long, are the northern and southern hemispheres exposed to the same intensity of solar radiation.

Moon – Calendar – Clock

The Earth has a constant companion on its journey around the sun – the moon. The movements of the Earth and the moon are the basis for our reckoning of time, the rhythm of our clocks, and our calendar system. The corresponding units of time are days, months, and years – the interval between one arrival of the sun at its zenith and the next; the period between full moons, and the length of time it takes the Earth to complete a full revolution around the sun. Precise astronomical observations are required to measure the lengths of these periods. Ancient astronomers discovered that neither a revolution of the Earth around the sun nor of the moon around the Earth equated to a full number of revolutions of the Earth around its own axis. There are approximately 365 ½ days in a year and about 29 ½ days in a (lunar) month. That is what makes designing a precise, reliable calendar such a difficult matter. Sophisticated correction systems are required to keep the calendar in step with the movements of the celestial bodies. Depending upon the system in use, these systems involve the addition of additional days or months to the calendar at regular intervals (in leap years, for example).

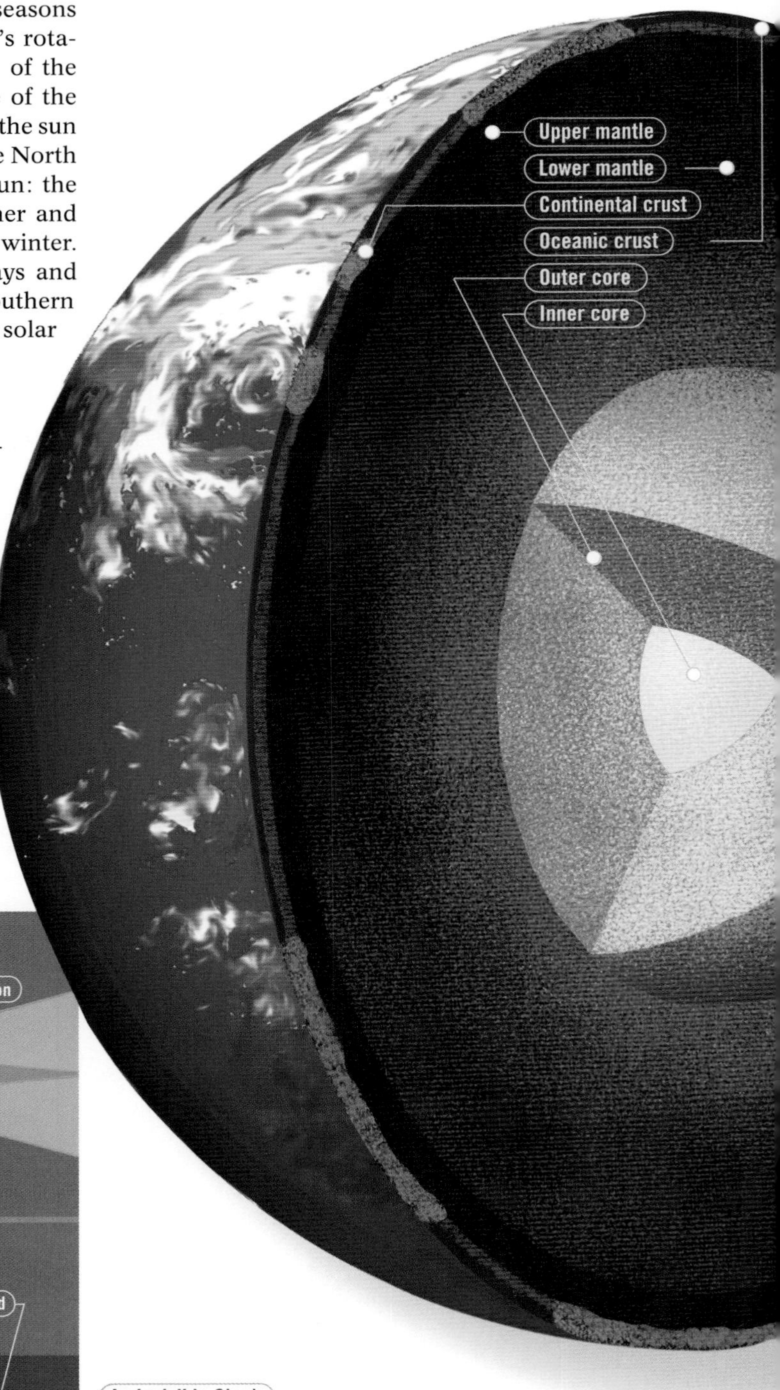

- Upper mantle
- Lower mantle
- Continental crust
- Oceanic crust
- Outer core
- Inner core

Light and Shadow

During a solar eclipse, the moon passes between the Earth and the sun, whereas a lunar eclipse occurs when the moon moves through the shadow cast by the Earth and thus grows dark. Depending upon their relative positions the sun and the moon may totally or only partially obscured. We can observe a total eclipse of the sun from a place at which the moon's umbra falls. During a total lunar eclipse, the moon is encompassed entirely within the Earth's umbra.

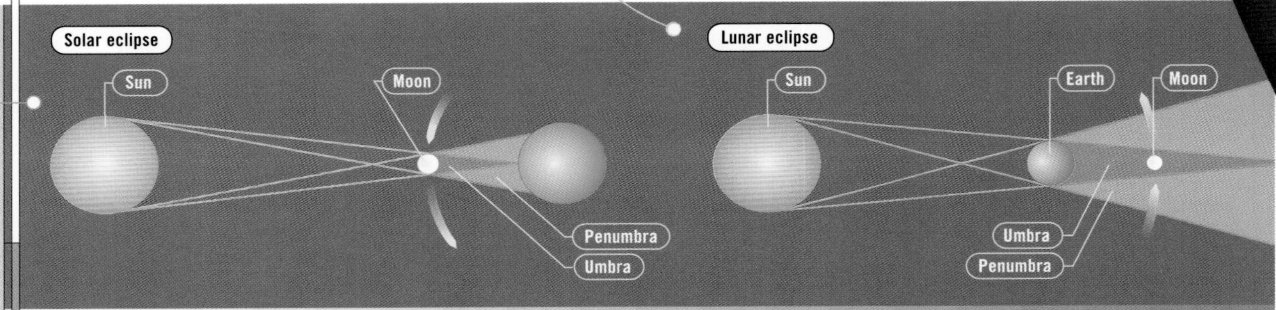

Solar eclipse

Sun — Moon — Penumbra — Umbra

Lunar eclipse

Sun — Earth — Moon — Umbra — Penumbra

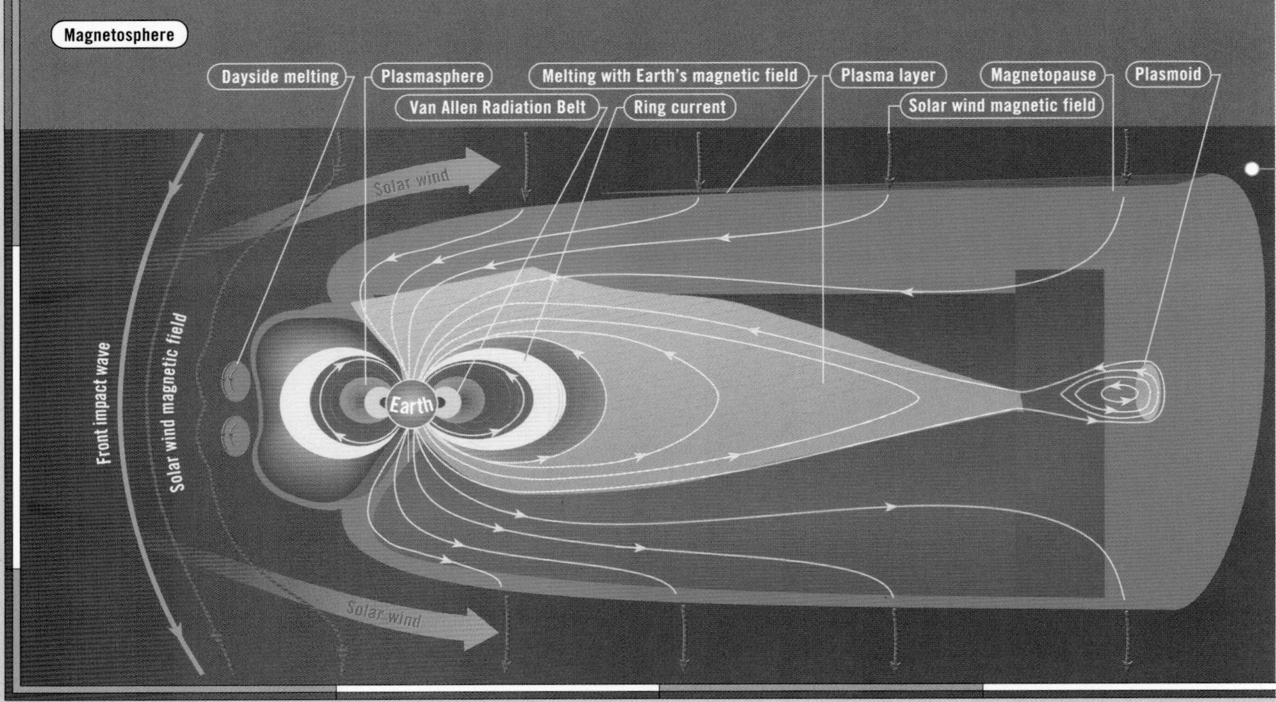

Magnetosphere

Dayside melting — Plasmasphere — Melting with Earth's magnetic field — Plasma layer — Magnetopause — Plasmoid — Van Allen Radiation Belt — Ring current — Solar wind magnetic field

Solar wind — Front impact wave — Solar wind magnetic field — Earth — Solar wind

An Invisible Cloak

Generated within the Earth's core, the Earth magnetic field is shaped and limited by solar wind, a stream of electrically charged particles emitted by the sun. The space it encloses is known as the magnetosphere. On the side of the Earth facing the sun, the magnetosphere extends to a distance equivalent to between 10 and 20 Earth radii. On the opposite side of the Earth, it pulls a tail measuring some 1,000 Earth radii in length. In the Van Allen radiation belt, electrically charged particles captured from cosmic radiation by the magnetosphere move back and forth between the Earth's magnetic poles. The term "plasma" denotes a gas consisting of positively and negatively charged particles, whose charges offset one another. Plasmoids are lumps of plasma that are cut off and catapulted from the tail of the magnetosphere.

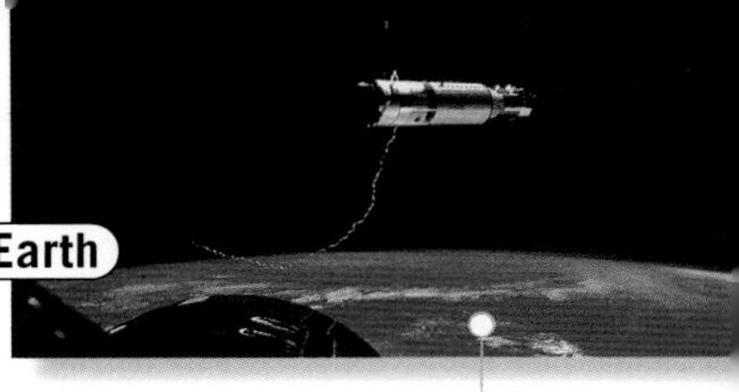

Occasional corrections to clock time are required, usually in late June and/or late December, for a different reason: the irregular rotation of the Earth. This irregularity was not discovered until the 1930s, following the invention of quarz clocks that were more exact than the Earth's own rotation. These smaller corrections involve the addition of leap seconds.

The Earth Seen from Space

Although mankind has long been aware that the Earth is an object in space, like the sun and the moon, people did not truly appreciate that fact until the age of space exploration began in the early sixties. The image shows an early docking maneuver during the Gemini 8 mission in 1966.

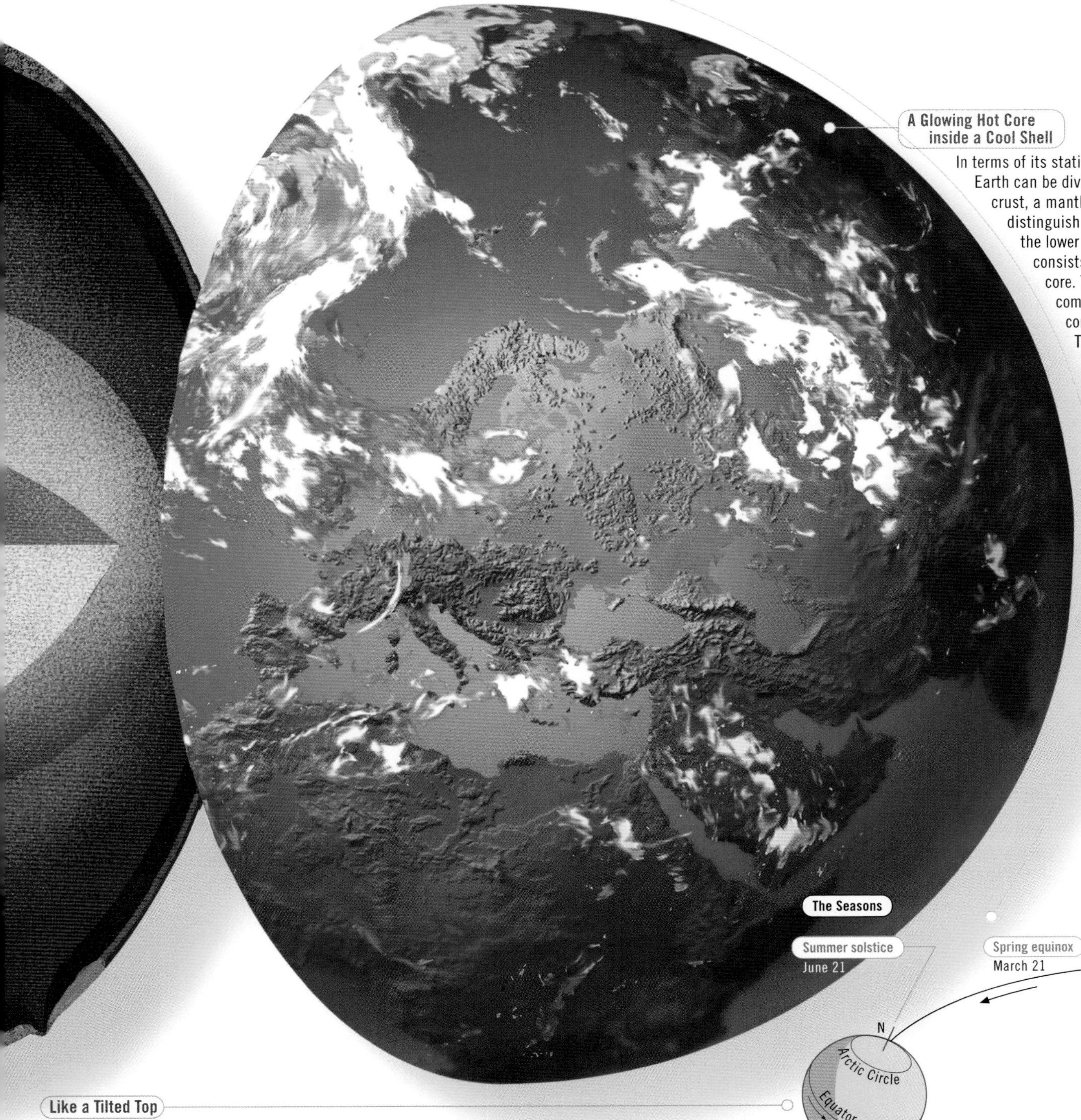

A Glowing Hot Core inside a Cool Shell

In terms of its static structure, the Earth can be divided roughly into a crust, a mantle, and a core. We distinguish between the upper and the lower mantle, while the core consists of an outer and an inner core. The crust and the mantle are composed of rock, while the core consists primarily of iron and nickel. The outer core (iron and iron oxide) is molten liquid. The inner core (iron and nickel) is solid. The continental crust is considerably thicker than the oceanic crust.

The Seasons

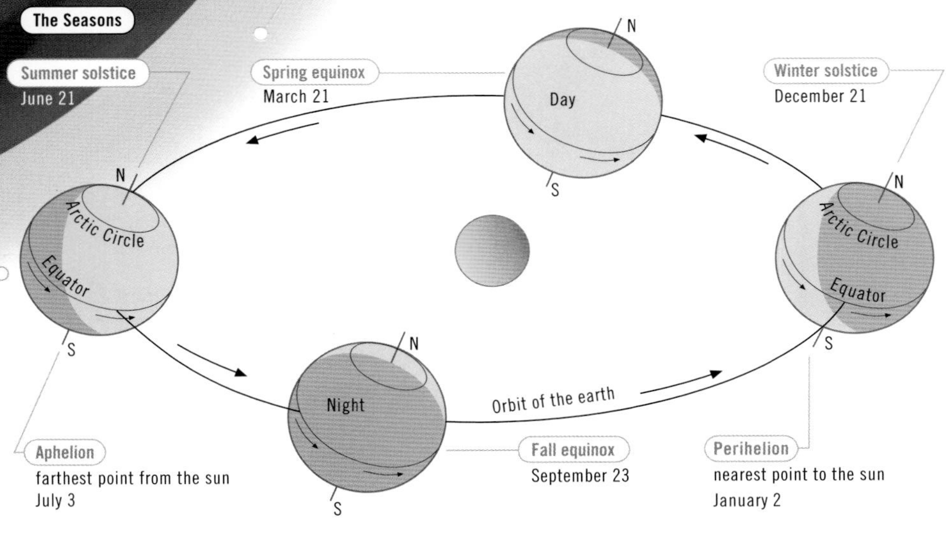

Summer solstice
June 21

Spring equinox
March 21

Winter solstice
December 21

Day

N

N

Arctic Circle

Arctic Circle

Equator

Equator

S

S

Night

Orbit of the earth

Aphelion
farthest point from the sun
July 3

Fall equinox
September 23

Perihelion
nearest point to the sun
January 2

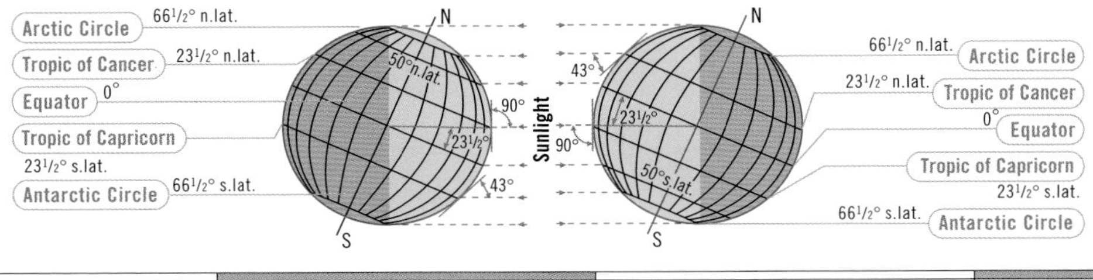

Like a Tilted Top

Seasonal temperature differences are attributable to the fact that the Earth's rotational axis is not precisely perpendicular to the plane of its orbit around the sun. As a result, the Earth tips its northern polar region toward the sun during the northern summer, while the southern polar region is inclined toward the sun during the northern winter. In the first case, the northern hemisphere is exposed to stronger solar radiation; in the second, it is the southern hemisphere that is bathed in warmer sunlight. At the spring and autumn

equinoxes, when days and nights are of equal length, the northern and southern hemispheres are exposed to the same amount of solar radiation.

The larger figures representing the Earth illustrate the distribution of sunlight at the summer solstice (around June 21st, on the left) and at the winter solstice (around December 21st, on the right).

The amount of warmth received by the various regions of the globe, and thus the temperature characteristics of the four seasons,

depend largely upon the angle at which solar radiation reaches the Earth, which is in turn a function of the time of day, geographic latitude, and the time of year.

The elliptical shape of the Earth's orbit also exerts a small influence on temperatures. At the most distant (aphelion) and the nearest points (perihelion) to the sun, the distance between the Earth and the sun is 1.7 per cent greater or smaller than its mean distance. Thus at these points, solar radiation is also nearly 3.5 per cent stronger or weaker, respectively.

Arctic Circle	$66\frac{1}{2}°$ n.lat.
Tropic of Cancer	$23\frac{1}{2}°$ n.lat.
Equator	0°
Tropic of Capricorn	$23\frac{1}{2}°$ s.lat.
Antarctic Circle	$66\frac{1}{2}°$ s.lat.

Sunlight

$66\frac{1}{2}°$ n.lat.	Arctic Circle
$23\frac{1}{2}°$ n.lat.	Tropic of Cancer
0°	Equator
$23\frac{1}{2}°$ s.lat.	Tropic of Capricorn
$66\frac{1}{2}°$ s.lat.	Antarctic Circle

Drifting Lithospheric Plates

The Evolution of Continents and Oceans

Meteorologist Alfred Wegener first presented his hypothesis of continental drift at a geologists' conference in Frankfurt in 1912. He later published a detailed discussion of his theory of continental division and drift in his book Die Entstehung der Kontinente und Ozeane (The Origins of Continents and Oceans, 1915), showing evidence of astounding similarities between geological structures, rock, fossils, and fossilized climatic evidence on both sides of the Atlantic.

Seams in the Earth

Geologist Eduard Suess had previously postulated the existence of a huge Paleozoic continent (Gondwana). Based upon the same concept, Wegener now reconstructed a supercontinent called Pangaea, which originally encompassed all of the Earth's land masses and later broke apart. His bold ideas were almost unanimously rejected by geologists, and it was not until 50 years later that studies based on new research methods confirmed his work.

Plate Tectonics, the New View of the Earth

The lithosphere consists of about twelve large plates and a number of smaller ones, all of which drift over the upper crust of the Earth. In the course of geological history, they have collided, drifted past one another, separated, and broken up into new plate segments. Beneath the continents, they are between 80 and 120 km thick, but they are much thinner under the oceans (30–70 km). The largest plate (the Pacific Plate) measures 12,000 km in diameter. Given its expansive horizontal dimensions, the lithosphere is very thin. Plates move at speeds ranging from one to 18 cm per year. Where their edges collide or overlap, the earth quakes, forming mountain ranges, faults, and volcanoes. Plates drifting apart create oceanic trenches, continental margins, and mid-oceanic ridges.

Beneath the lithosphere is the asthenosphere which in its upper region where it meets the lithosphere, is semi-plastic and near the melting point, and thus acts as a lubricant over which the plates can glide. The underlying crust is solid but not completely rigid. Slow movement is possible there under the influence of high temperatures and pressure.

Hot Currents Move Segments of the Earth's Crust

Convection currents in the mantle set the plates in motion. When one plate begins to drift, the others are moved as well. Some 500 million years ago, the continents were distributed widely over the surface of the Earth. But they later converged to form the supercontinent Pangaea. The remainder of the globe was covered by the superocean Panthalassa, which continued to expand into Pangaea north of the equator. The east-west arm of the sea (Tethys) eventually split the great land mass apart, forming Laurasia and Gondwana.

Massive mainland deposits of sandstone dating primarily from the Carboniferous and the Permian periods are found on all of the continents of ancient Gondwana. In southern Africa, they are referred to as Karoo formations (photo: western rim of the Groot Karoo). They contain fossils from a variety of climates ranging from humid to arid, as the continents have drifted through many different climate zones.

These two continents also broke apart as time passed. The present-day distribution of land and sea is only a momentary state. India has already joined Eurasia, and Africa is approaching it. "Panta rhei" (everything is in flux), declared the Greek philosopher Heraclitus with reference to this perpetual process of growth, change, and decline.

Scientists began exploring the ocean floor with the aid of sonar in 1945. The mid-oceanic ridges were discovered, along with such phenomena as seafloor spreading and subduction, the underthrusting of heavy oceanic plates beneath lighter continental plates. More recently, measurements of magnetic anomalies and radiometric rock dating techniques have shed new light on the processes involved in plate tectonics.

Disappearing Crust

When one oceanic plate slides beneath another in a process known as subduction, oceanic trenches and island chains are formed. Steeper subduction produces straighter trenches and island chains. Abrupt subduction triggers earthquakes at depths of up to 700 km. The underlying plate becomes soft and begins to melt. Cracks form in the overriding plate; parts break away and are thrust downward. The movement of the sinking plate may be blocked, forming bulges which in turn raise previously sunken volcanic islands to the surface again. Lighter oceanic sediments are not carried deep into the Earth's crust. They accumulate along with rock from the volcanic chain in deep-sea trenches, some of which are more than 10,000 meters deep. Deformed, partially folded, and thrust above the ocean surface at certain points, this chaotic mass (mélange) builds an accretionary prism that can form a chain of islands off the main volcanic chain. Volcanoes are formed by rising granodoritic magma above the area where the sinking plate begins to melt. Interarc basins, in which spread zones sink or are forced apart, are created behind the main chain. This opens channels through which lava flows to the surface.

Hot Spots and Wandering Volcanoes

In the lower crust, 2,900 m below the Earth's surface, matter along the boundary to the outer core is heated so intensely that basalt magma plumes are forced upward through the lower and upper crust. At the surface, shield volcanoes are formed above these hot spots (Hawaii is a good example). New volcanoes are created wherever oceanic crust drifts over the stationary hot spots. The extinct volcanoes in a thus created island chain are eroded and gradually submerge. Hot spots are also found beneath continents.

Building New Crust

Hot streams of magma in the crust underneath mid-oceanic ridges thrust the relatively thin oceanic plate upward, breaking it apart. Basalt lava emerges beneath the sea and closes the fissures in the crust. On both sides of the fault line, the crust drifts in the direction of the subduction zone where it is melted deep inside the Earth. Since plates drift at different speeds, transform faults emerge along the ridge. Larger volcanic islands (Iceland is an example) form at certain points. Mid-oceanic ridges can reach elevations of over 3,000 m. Oceanic crust in ocean basins is no more than 160 million years old. Only recently discovered, black smokers are hydrothermal vents – hot springs on the seafloor. They release water containing hydrogen sulphide at temperatures of over 630 °F, from which sulphide minerals precipitate in the cold water at the bottom of the ocean.

High Mountain Ranges at the Edges of Continental Plates

Deep-ocean trenches, accretionary prisms, and marginal trenches filled with sediment also form where oceanic plates subduct beneath continental plates. The continental crust is folded, broken apart, and raised in some places. Intrusions of granite magma occur, often forming magma chambers from which magma is extruded and frequently rises to the surface. High mountain chains (orogenes) topped by shield volcanoes are created at these points. Plate segments drift apart in the spread

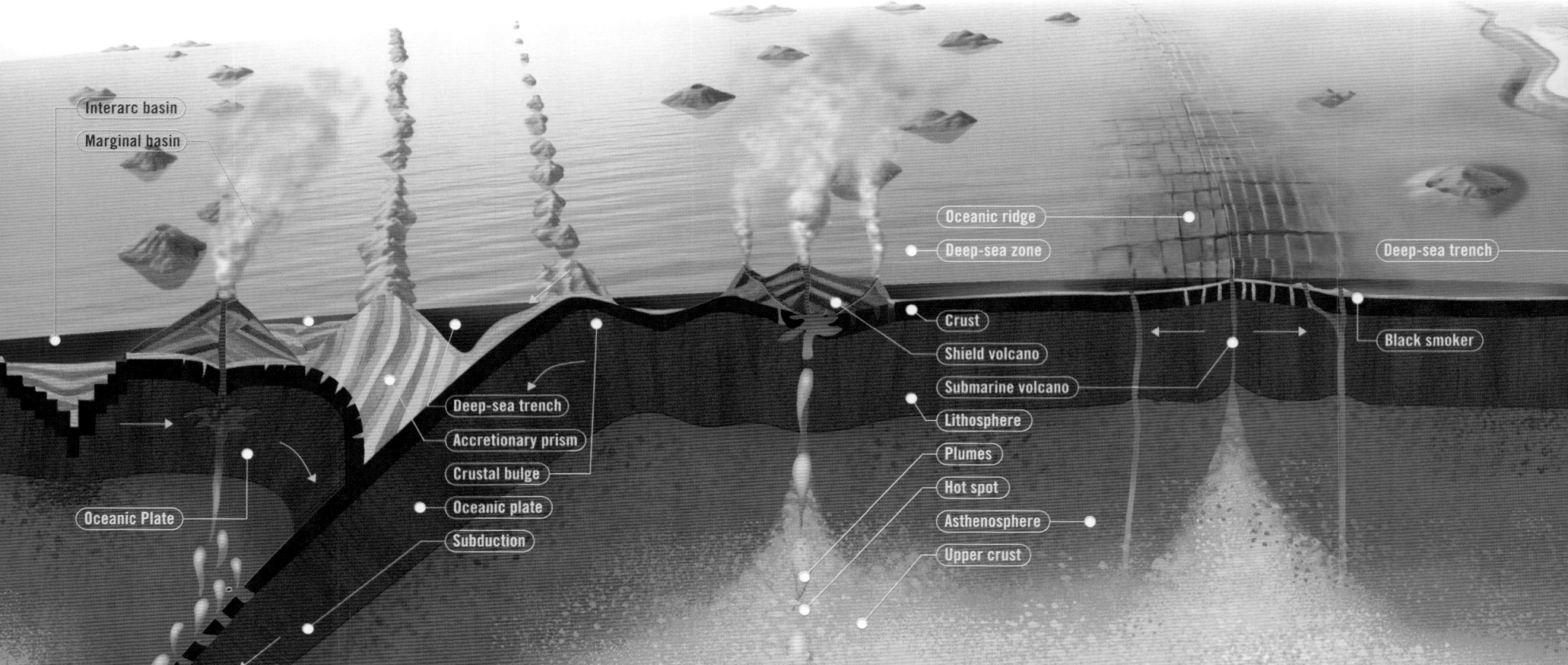

Interarc basin
Marginal basin
Oceanic ridge
Deep-sea zone
Deep-sea trench
Crust
Shield volcano
Submarine volcano
Lithosphere
Plumes
Hot spot
Asthenosphere
Upper crust
Deep-sea trench
Accretionary prism
Crustal bulge
Oceanic plate
Black smoker
Oceanic Plate
Subduction

Plates Drifting Apart in Iceland

The Mid-Atlantic Ridge rises from the sea in Iceland. The North American Plate drifts toward the west, the Eurasian Plate toward the east. A young, still active volcanic zone runs through the middle of the island. The photo shows the Thingvellir Plain at the edge of the Almannagjá Gorge.

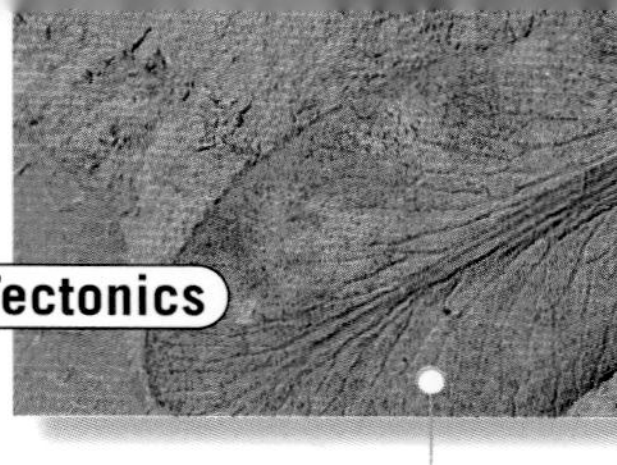

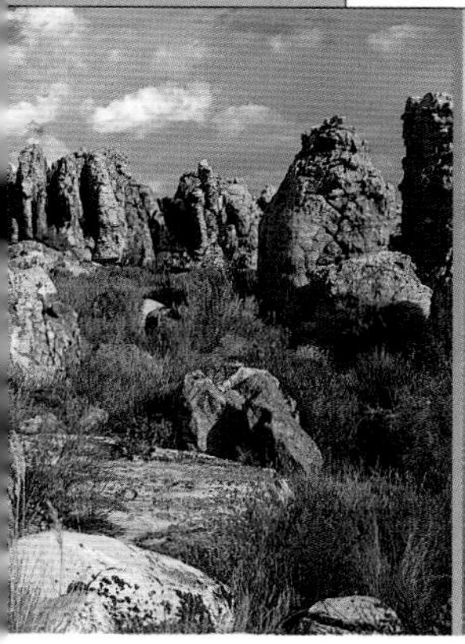

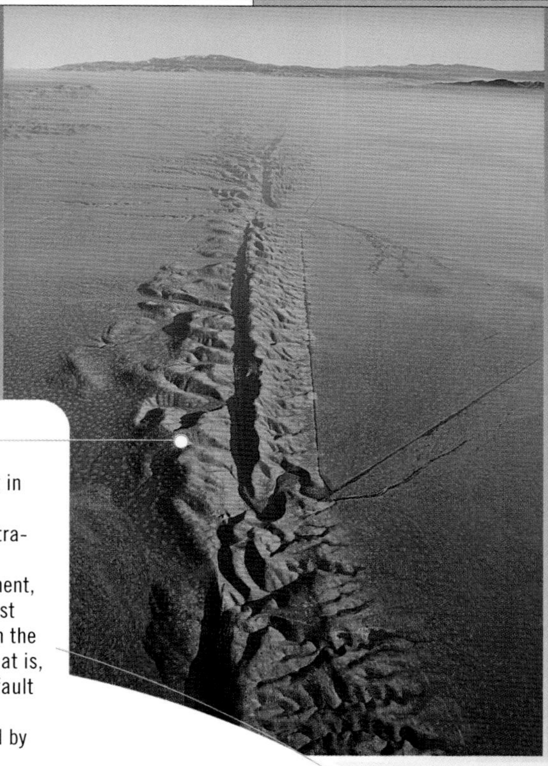

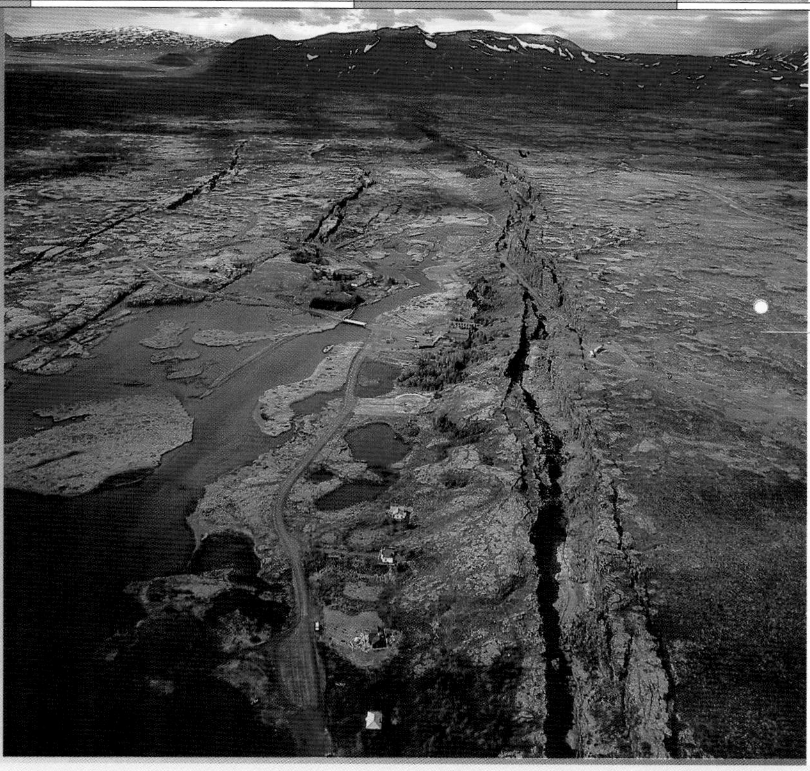

Plates Drifting Past Each Other in California

Along the San Andreas Fault in California, the Pacific Plate (right-hand side of the illustration), which forms the edge of the North American continent, is pushed horizontally against the North American Plate (on the left) towards the viewer — that is, to the northwest. Along the fault line, both plates are slightly elevated and heavily scarred by erosion.

zones in the interior of the continent, producing rift valleys. Magma rises at the rift lines, forming basalt floors and volcanoes. These basalt floors often reach massive and expansive proportions.

Young Oceans, Old Shields

Oceanic rifts eventually grow so wide that new crust is formed by magma rising from below. This marks the birth of a new ocean. The rift often fills with fresh water (e.g. the lakes of East Africa), which is later mixed with inflowing seawater. The collision of two continental plates may lead to

subduction when the rock is too light to penetrate into the heavier material of the upper crust. This causes overthrusting, which creates formations up to 80 km thick (as in the Himalayas). The continental plates have grown larger over the course of geological history. Only in the continental plates have crust segments (shields) several million years old survived as the only remaining evidence of the Earth's early history.

Continents in Motion

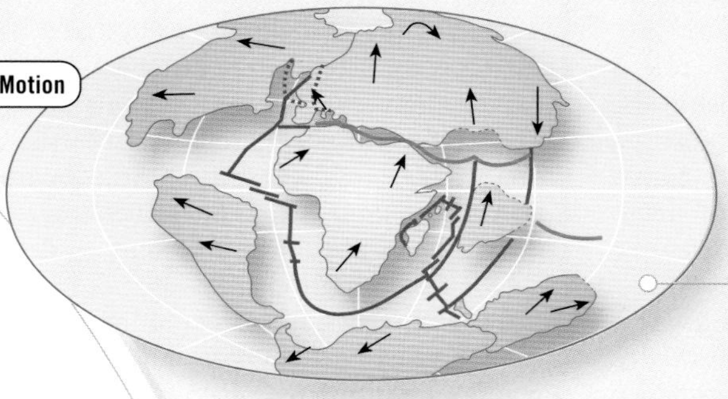

End of the Cretaceous
65 million years ago

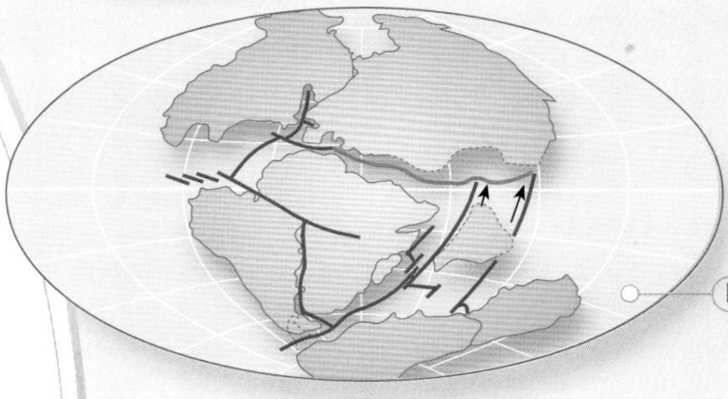

End of the Jurassic
150 million years ago

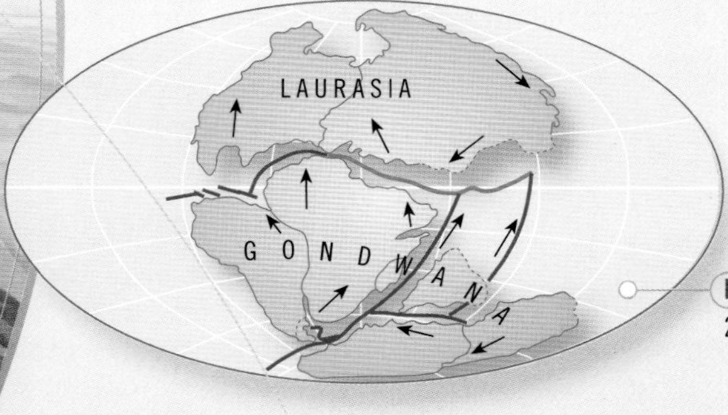

LAURASIA

GONDWANA

End of the Triassic
220 million years ago

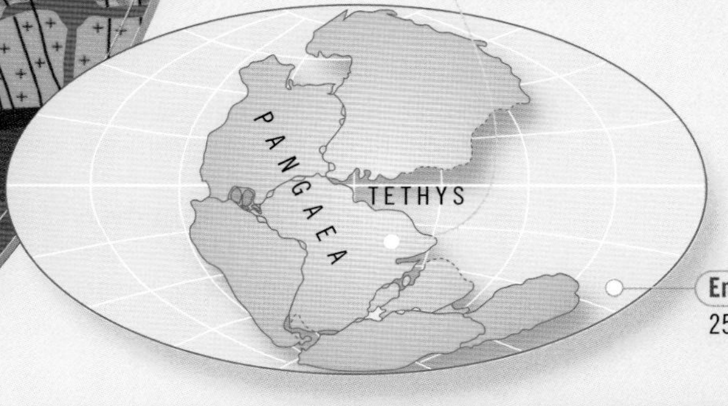

PANGAEA

TETHYS

End of the Paleozoic
250 million years ago

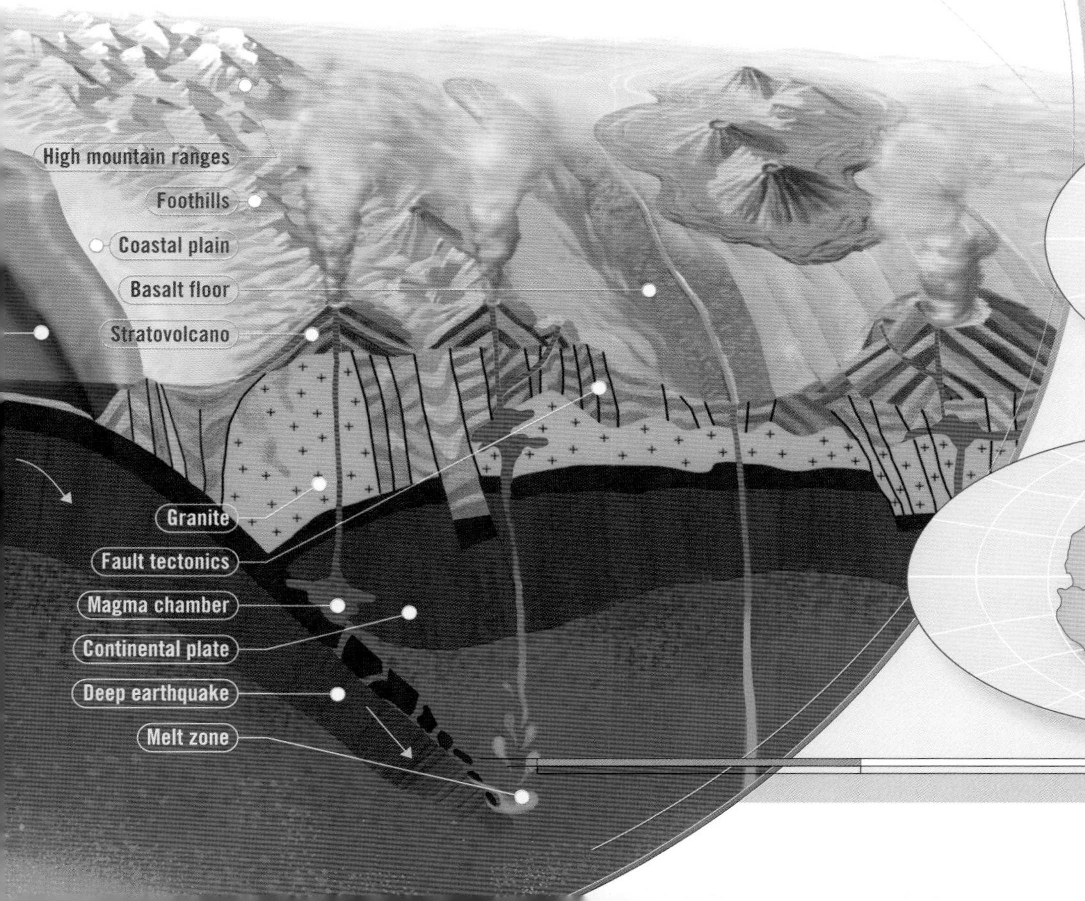

High mountain ranges

Foothills

Coastal plain

Basalt floor

Stratovolcano

Granite

Fault tectonics

Magma chamber

Continental plate

Deep earthquake

Melt zone

Earthquakes – Danger from the Depths

When the ground begins to shake beneath our feet

Well into the Middle Ages, earthquakes were regarded as the work of mythical, supernatural beings or signs of the wrath of God. The quake that destroyed Lisbon in cataclysmic waves of fire and flooding on November 1, 1775 caused many people to wonder about the validity of prevailing philosophical systems. Could anyone still look upon our world as the "best of all possible worlds," as a planet governed by reliable natural laws? And why had Lisbon, of all places, a city of churches and monasteries devoted to piety, been singled out by God for such terrible punishment? That earthquake marked the beginning of the science of seismology. The Portuguese minister Pombal had reports compiled by observers all over the country. The British engineer John Michell computed the speed of the shock waves. Questions were raised about the origin and the causes of the quake.

The Restless Earth

Although we rarely notice it, the Earth's crust is constantly moving. The oceans and atmosphere are subject to patterns of natural motion, and so are the seemingly fixed landmasses of the continents, though their movements are so slow that we do not perceive them. Much more obvious – and dangerous – are the brief (lasting less than a minute), abrupt, and rapid shifts of larger segments of crust caused by tensions inside the Earth. The amplitude of these movements of ground may amount to as much as several decimeters. The energy released in the process spreads in the form of elastic waves through the Earth's interior: longitudinal and transverse waves. Longitudinal waves (also known as P or primary waves) move faster and arrive at a given distant point sooner than transverse waves (S or secondary waves). The slowest but most highly energized waves are surface waves (L and Rayleigh waves).

The source of an earthquake, known as the focus or hypocenter, may be near the surface or deep within the Earth's crust. Based upon its distance from the epicenter, the point of greatest surface movement, seismologists distinguish between shallow, intermediate, and deep-focus earthquakes. At depths below 720 km, rock is so soft and malleable that no abrupt shifts occur.

On average, 10,000 earthquakes classified as grade 4 or higher on the Richter Scale are recorded annually. Between 10 and 15 of these cause significant damage. In 1999, more than 22,000 people died as a result of earthquakes, while the average death toll for the preceding years is about 10,000. Some 15 percent of the Earth's land area is subject to severe earthquake activity. Another 40 percent is classified as virtually risk-free.

Measuring Earthquake Energy and Effects

Earthquakes are registered and recorded in seismograms using highly sensitive measuring instruments known as seismographs. The direction, distance, and energy of an earthquake can be derived from the data in the seismogram, i.e. the amplitude of the waves generated by an earthquake. Energy is expressed as magnitude, which is computed on the basis of ground amplitude, wave duration, and a calibration function. Earthquakes are classified on the Richter Scale of Earthquake Magnitude according to the maximum amplitude measured at a distance of 100 km from the epicenter. Magnitude values range from zero to between 7.7 and 8.6, but the scale has no upper limit.

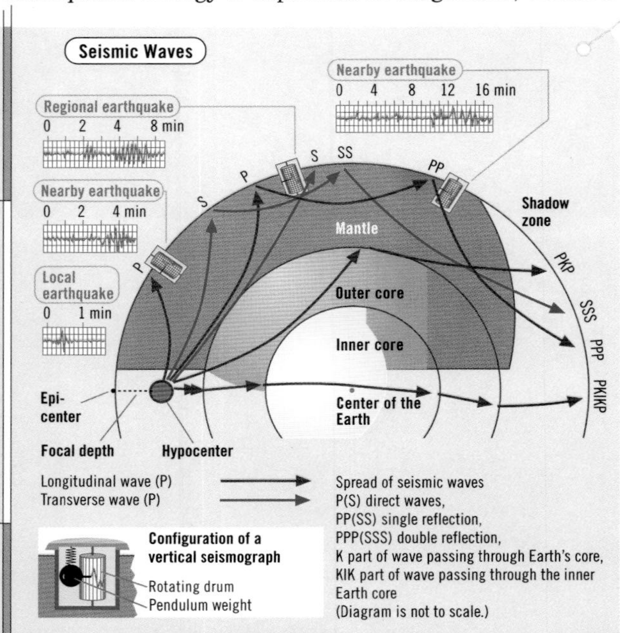

California Awaits "The Big One"

The United States Geological Survey (USGS) estimates the probability of a major earthquake in northern California by the year 2020 at 70 per cent. USGS experts anticipate a seismic event comparable to the San Francisco earthquake of 1906, which measured 8.3 on the Richter Scale and laid much of the city to waste, causing numerous fires and killing some 2,000 people. The quake in Northridge near Los Angeles in 1994 took 60 human lives, and total damage was valued at $ 30–40 billion (a U.S. record). The American West Coast is one of the most severely endangered regions in the world. The Pacific Plate thrusts against the North American Plate along several fault lines, the best known of which is the San Andreas fault. These movements are not gradual and consistent but abrupt and violent, and they are responsible for a seemingly endless series of earthquakes. Some 7,800 earthquakes are registered in California each year, although most of them can only be detected by sensitive seismographic instruments.

Seismic Waves Explore the Earth's Interior

Physical bores are mere pinpricks in the Earth's crust (at about 13 km, the deepest bore ever made reached a depth equivalent to only about 0.2 per cent of the Earth's radius). We learn a great deal more about the structure of the Earth's interior from seismic waves that penetrate to the core and beyond. This method is the basis for the shell model of the Earth, with a crust (50–70 km thick beneath the continents, 5–10 km thick below the oceans), a mantle (2,900 km thick, divided in two by a transition zone), and a core (outer core to a depth of 5,200 km, inner core to a depth of 6,371 km). Correlations between wave speeds and experimental findings generate conclusions about the density, the temperature, and the chemical and mineral composition of the different zones.

Are Earthquakes Predictable?

People in ancient China observed unusual behavior in animals immediately preceding earthquake events, although they realized this only later. Today, even seismologists disagree about whether the location, time, and magnitude of an earthquake can be predicted. Researchers have been trying to identify reliable signs for decades. Using automatic recording devices, they systematically measure changes in specific characteristics – temperature, chemical composition, gas concentration (radon) and electrical groundwater resistance, groundwater levels and spring behavior, movements at fault lines, and deformations of the Earth's surface. All of these phenomena can – but do not necessarily – indicate impending earthquake activity.

Crisis Management – Emergency Disaster Aid

In industrialized countries threatened by earthquakes, such as Japan, the U. S. (especially California), and Italy, plans have been made for responses to natural disasters. Kindergarten and school children in Japan and California learn rules for behavior when danger threatens. Public emergency disaster exercises are conducted on a broad basis in Japan. Plans are modified in response to experience gained in such emergencies. California has established a network of decentralized emergency aid stations staffed and equipped to meet specific local needs. The central Japanese authority failed to respond adequately during the Kobe earthquake.

Earthquake-Proof Construction – Only an Illusion?

The first building designed to resist earthquake shock was erected by American architect Frank Lloyd Wright in Tokyo between 1916 and 1922. It survived the earthquake of 1923 virtually undamaged. In the years since, architects have employed special methods of stable or flexible construction at locations in Japan, California, and other

---

Seismic Waves

Regional earthquake
0   2   4   8 min

Nearby earthquake
0   2   4 min

Local earthquake
0   1 min

Nearby earthquake
0   4   8   12   16 min

Mantle

Shadow zone

Outer core

Inner core

Epi-center

Center of the Earth

Focal depth   Hypocenter

Longitudinal wave (P)
Transverse wave (P)

Spread of seismic waves
P(S) direct waves,
PP(SS) single reflection,
PPP(SSS) double reflection,
K part of wave passing through Earth's core,
KIK part of wave passing through the inner
Earth core
(Diagram is not to scale.)

Configuration of a vertical seismograph

Rotating drum
Pendulum weight

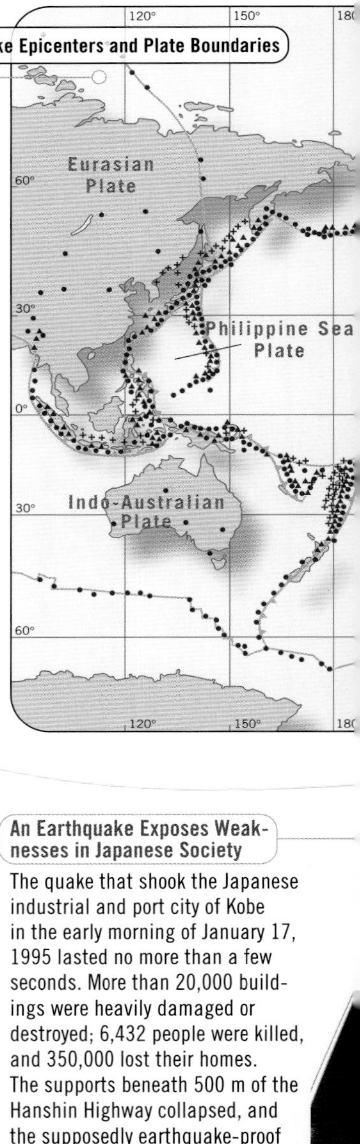

Earthquake Epicenters and Plate Boundaries

Eurasian Plate

Philippine Sea Plate

Indo-Australian Plate

Zones of Critical Seismic Activity

Ninety per cent of all earthquakes are caused by seismic activity (volcanism and collapsing hollow areas in the Earth account for the remainder). Thus the theory of plate tectonics has given rise to new insights into the causes and distribution of earthquakes. As this map of epicenters shows, seismic activity is most intense along plate margins. The Circum-Pacific Belt coincides primarily with subduction zones (these incline toward the continental interiors, which explains the locations of deep-focus earthquakes), while the Mediterranean-Transasian Belt is aligned with converging continental plates. Weaker earthquakes originate at the edges of plates moving away from another near mid-oceanic ridges.

Where the Ball Rolls – the First Seismograph

The first device used to register earthquake activity was invented in China in the first century AD. The pot-bellied vessel is adorned with eight dragon figures, each facing a crouching toad positioned on the base below. When a tremor occurs, the pendulum inside begins to swing. The mouth of the dragon on the side opposite the direction of the shock wave opens and drops a ball into the mouth of the toad beneath it. This was believed to indicate the direction of the earthquake.

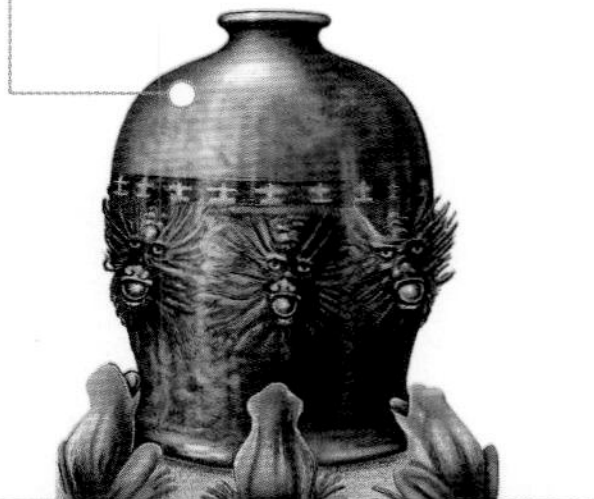

An Earthquake Exposes Weaknesses in Japanese Society

The quake that shook the Japanese industrial and port city of Kobe in the early morning of January 17, 1995 lasted no more than a few seconds. More than 20,000 buildings were heavily damaged or destroyed; 6,432 people were killed, and 350,000 lost their homes. The supports beneath 500 m of the Hanshin Highway collapsed, and the supposedly earthquake-proof elevated road crashed to the ground. The multi-story buildings nearby remained undamaged. The seemingly well-organized disaster aid and rescue system was largely ineffective.

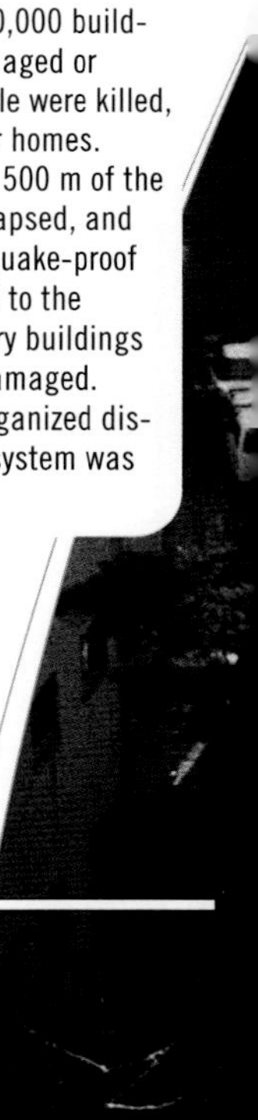

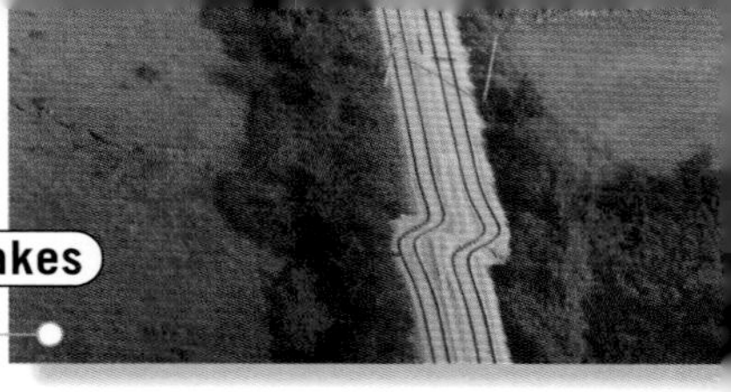

parts of the world. A number of countries have enacted corresponding building regulations in the past two years. Cellular construction techniques and "sandwich structures" comprised of steel and rubber plates built into the foundations of high-rise buildings absorb earthquake shocks. Steel structures are generally safer than stone or brick buildings. Wood-frame buildings may also offer satisfactory earthquake resistance if certain safety requirements are met. Schools, hospitals and other public buildings are subject to particularly stringent regulations. Recent experience has shown that many bridges, highway ramps, and similar structures need upgrading to meet safety requirements. Loose substrata, especially made-made fills or embankments, are very susceptible to earthquake damage. Much depends on the quality of construction – an issue of concern in developing countries. It is important to consider that the greatest damage incurred during major earthquakes (e.g. San Francisco, 1906 and Kobe, 1995) resulted from fire (broken gas lines). Although earthquakes cannot be prevented, precautionary measures reduce damage significantly.

A "Bend" in the Landscape

Only rarely are movements of the Earth's crust as obvious as in this photo: a bend of 3 to 5 meters in the railway line near Izmit, Turkey in August 1999.

Building Structure and Building Damage

With shops and underground parking areas, the basement level is the weakest part of many otherwise robust reinforced concrete structures. When it collapses, the entire building may fall. (Wufeng, Taiwan, 9/21/1999).

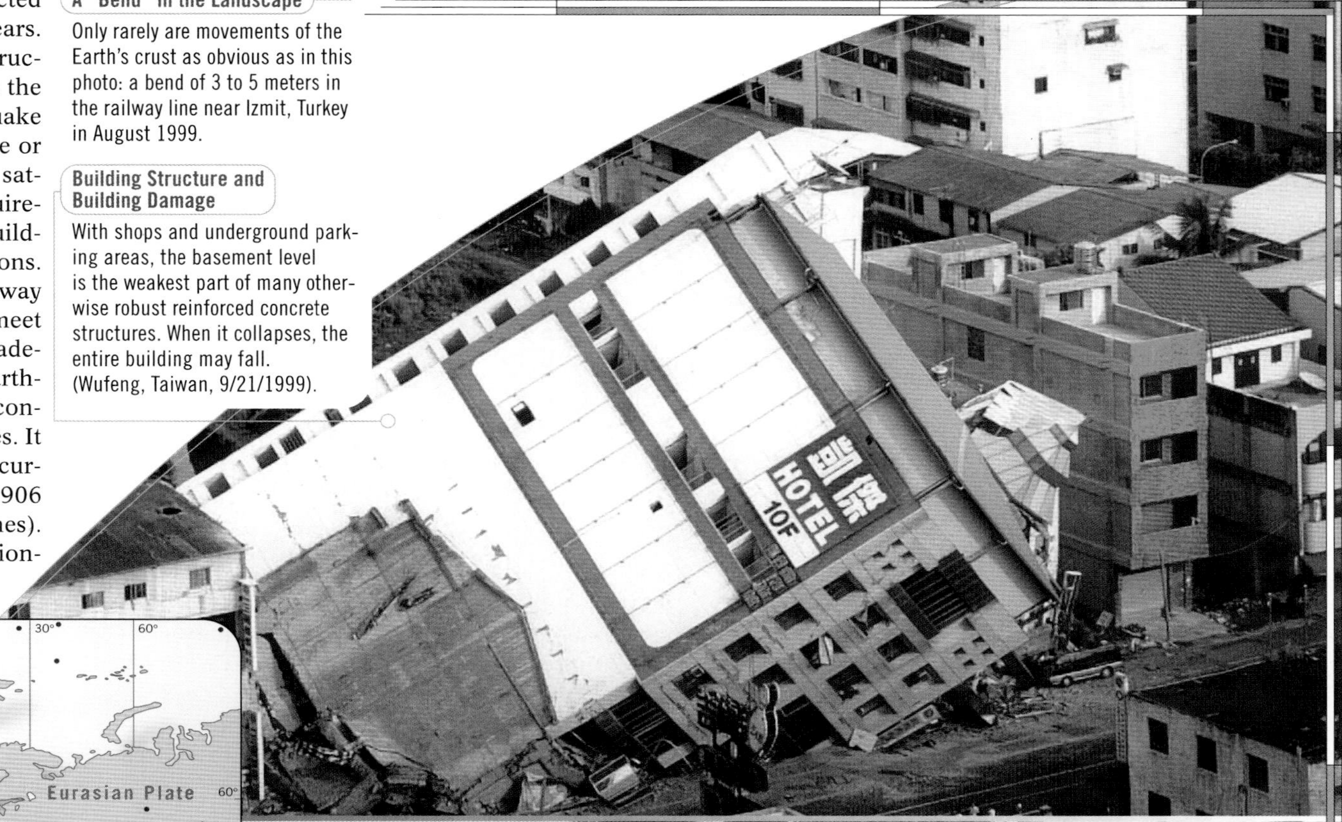

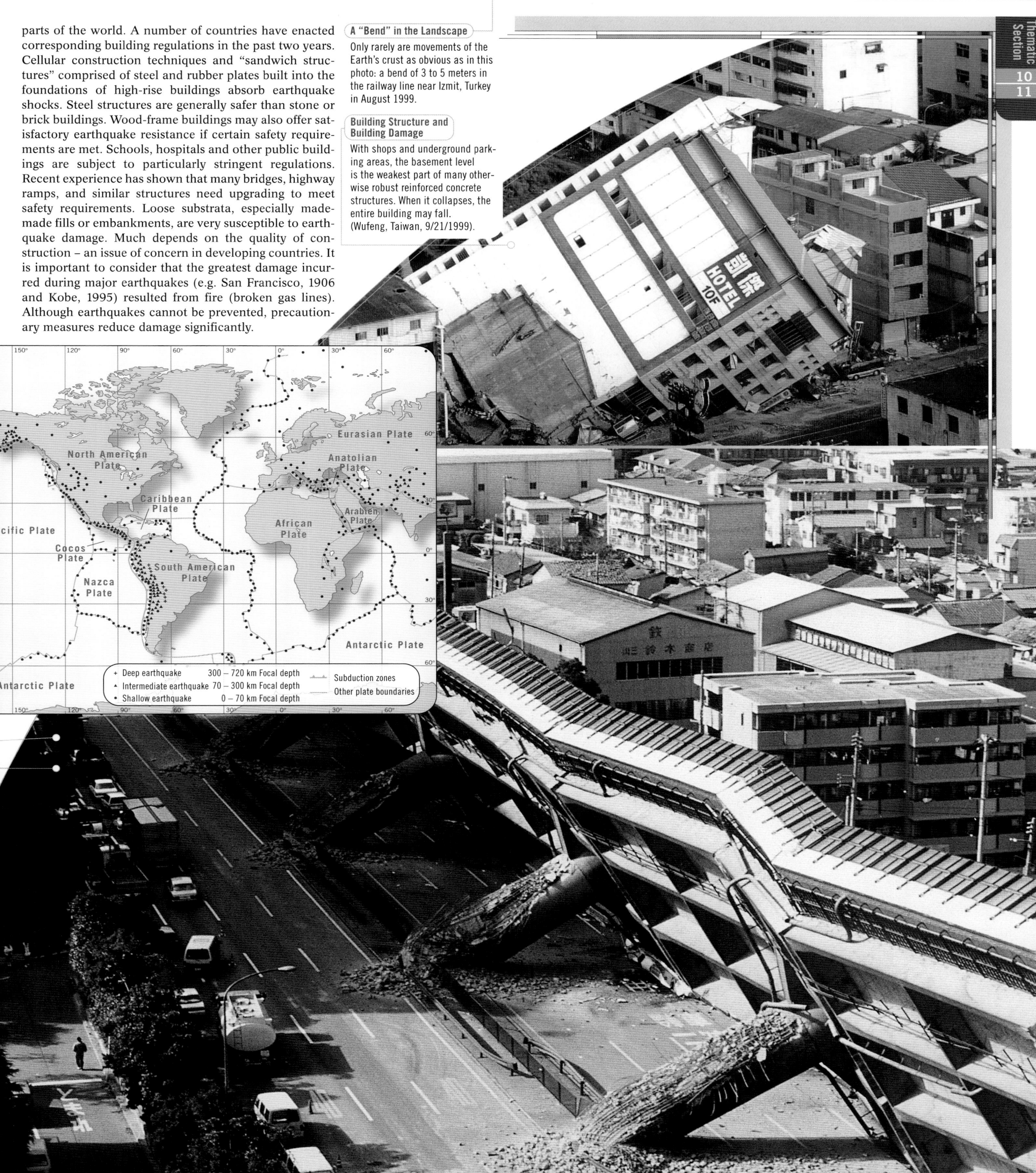

Map legend:

+ Deep earthquake   300 – 720 km Focal depth
▲ Intermediate earthquake   70 – 300 km Focal depth
• Shallow earthquake   0 – 70 km Focal depth

Subduction zones
Other plate boundaries

Plate labels: Eurasian Plate, North American Plate, Anatolian Plate, Caribbean Plate, Arabien Plate, African Plate, Pacific Plate, Cocos Plate, South American Plate, Nazca Plate, Antarctic Plate

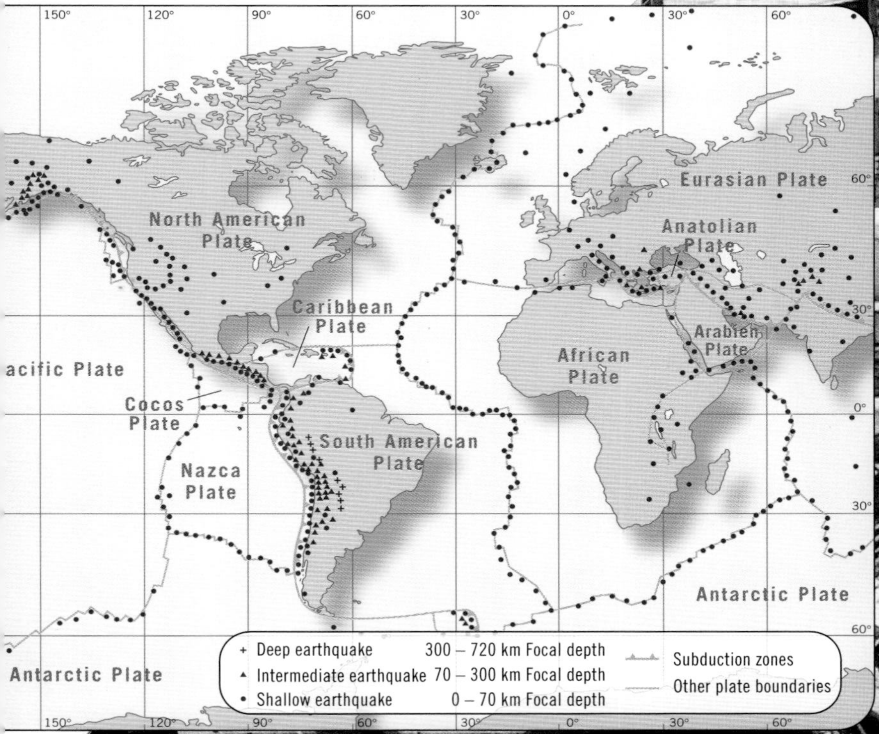

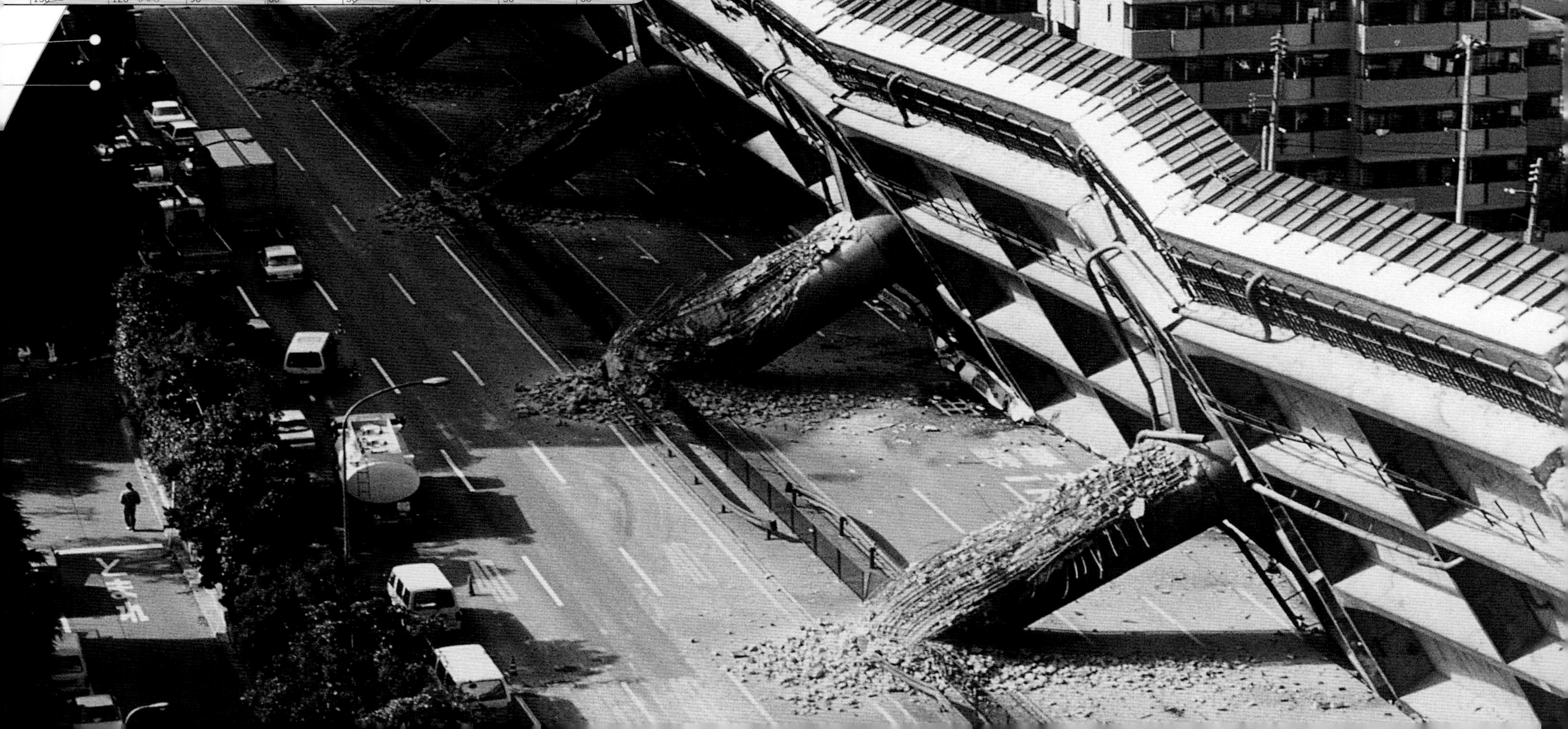

Volcanism – Unbridled Forces from the Earth's Interior

Fertile Soil – Ever-Present Danger

In the early morning hours of August 27, 1883, the small volcanic island of Krakatoa in the Sundra Strait was shaken by violent explosions which virtually blew the island paradise apart. The enormous bang was heard more than 5,000 km away, and atmospheric pressure rose by 1.45 millibars in Tokyo. Massive tremors that triggered tsunamis traveling at the speed of an airliner battered the coastlines of Java and Sumatra. Roughly 36,000 people lost their lives as a direct result of the eruptions. And this was by no means the worst volcanic disaster in history. Eruptions on the Indonesian island of Sumbawa in 1815 ejected more than 180 cubic km of lava and ash (compared to only 20 cubic km on Krakatoa). The volcano, the tidal waves, and the famine that followed were responsible for some 90,000 deaths. Dust in the atmosphere darkened the sky for weeks.

A Bubbling Inferno Beneath Us

The solid crust that floats on the hot molten rock of the upper mantle is actually very thin. Continental crust attains a maximum thickness of 70 km, while oceanic

An Eruption in Hawaii
An eruption of Kilauea in Hawaii begins with a fountain of lava lasting several hours. Escaping gas catapults the red-hot molten mass hundreds of meters into the air.

"Rushing Stream"
This is the literal translation of the Islandic word for geyser (geysir). Rainwater seeping into the hot volcanic underground is heated and ejected – often at regular intervals – through fissures in the rock. (photo: geysers in the Rotorua region of New Zealand). The process is a part of the waning phase of volcanic activity.

Volcanic Breakthrough in a Glacier
In 1996, the volcano beneath the Vatnajökull Glacier in Iceland melted a hole in the ice cap, sending clouds of ash as high as 4,000 m into the air. The lava eruptions that followed were accompanied by severe earthquakes.

Aa and Pahoehoe Lava
A skin forms on the surface of the thin, red-hot pahoehoe lava as it flows. Once it has cooled and solidified, the lava may look much like lengths of intertwining twisted ropes or strings.

A Volcanic Blessing
Geothermal energy is a readily available alternative energy source in volcanically active regions like Italy, Iceland, and New Zealand.

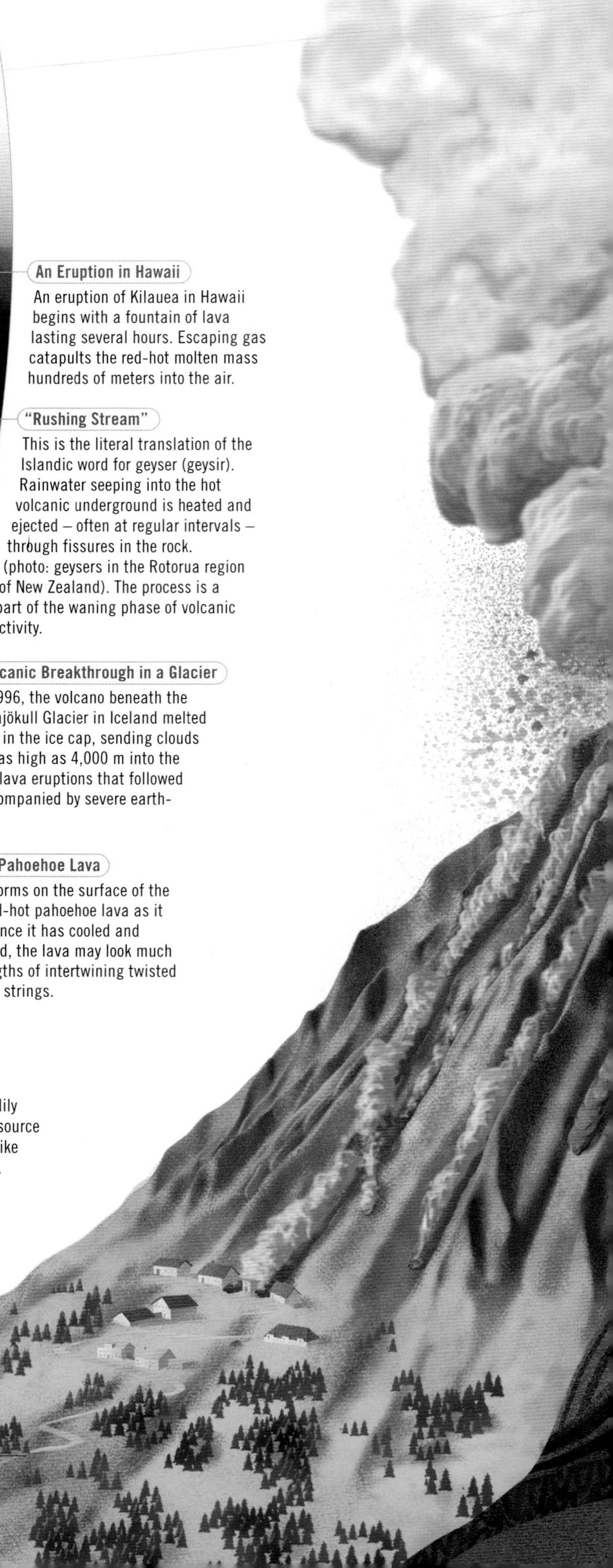

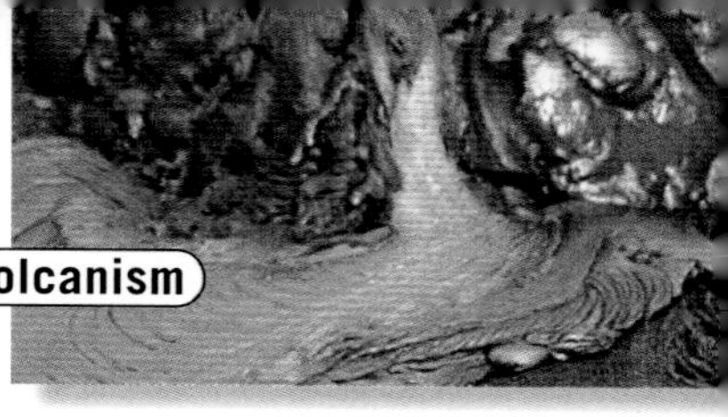

crust is ordinarily between 5 and 10 km thick. (Imagine an orange measuring 12 cm in diameter with a peel only 0.3 mm thick!). And thus it is no wonder that the Earth's thin crust is extremely fragile. Molten rock accumulates in large magma chambers beneath the surface and rises where faults or openings develop. Magma that emerges at the surface is called lava.

Harmless and Dangerous Volcanoes

The flow characteristics of lava depend on its chemical composition and gas content. Thin, basaltic lava (50 % SiO2) of the kind that erupts from Kilauea (Hawaii) is often ejected in towering fountains which then flow smoothly from the crater. Andesitic magma rich in silicic acid (60 % SiO2) is catapulted from volcanic Mount Saint Helens to heights of several kilometers. Gases escape easily from thin magma, whereas thick, highly gaseous magma builds up high pressures that are released suddenly and explosively near the surface, where outside pressure decreases rapidly. At these points, lava shoots from the volcano like champagne from a shaken bottle. Basaltic lava forms relatively flat (12 degrees) shield volcanoes like those in Hawaii, or basalt floors (Dekkan, India). Acidic lava tends to erupt violently, although it may also flow quietly down volcanic slopes. Alternating deposits of lava and tuff form cone-shaped stratovolcanoes with slopes as steep as 30 degrees. The most famous volcano of this type is Fujiama in Japan. When underground pressure has no means of escape, domes of lava form, raising the overlying layers and the Earth's surface above. The destructive power of explosive eruptions makes living in these areas extremely dangerous. The worst outbreak of this kind occurred at the Montagne Pelée on the island of Martinique in 1902. Extremely hot air (1,440° F) loaded with ash enveloped the nearby city of Saint-Pierre in a red-hot cloud, killing 29,000 people. The only survivor was found at the island prison.

Volcanoes – Gigantic Dirt Canons

Volcanic eruptions also hurl huge blocks of rock (bombs) far into the surrounding countryside. Fine particles are shot up to 10 km into the atmosphere, where they may circulate around the Earth for years. Bombs, lapilli (fragments measuring from two to 64 mm), and fine ash fall to the ground, forming volcanic tuff. Fragments that have not cooled sufficiently fuse into clinkers. Rock baked from larger masses becomes volcanic breccia. Storms among the high clouds above the volcano bring heavy rains, often causing massive mudflows that obliterate everything in their paths to the valleys below.

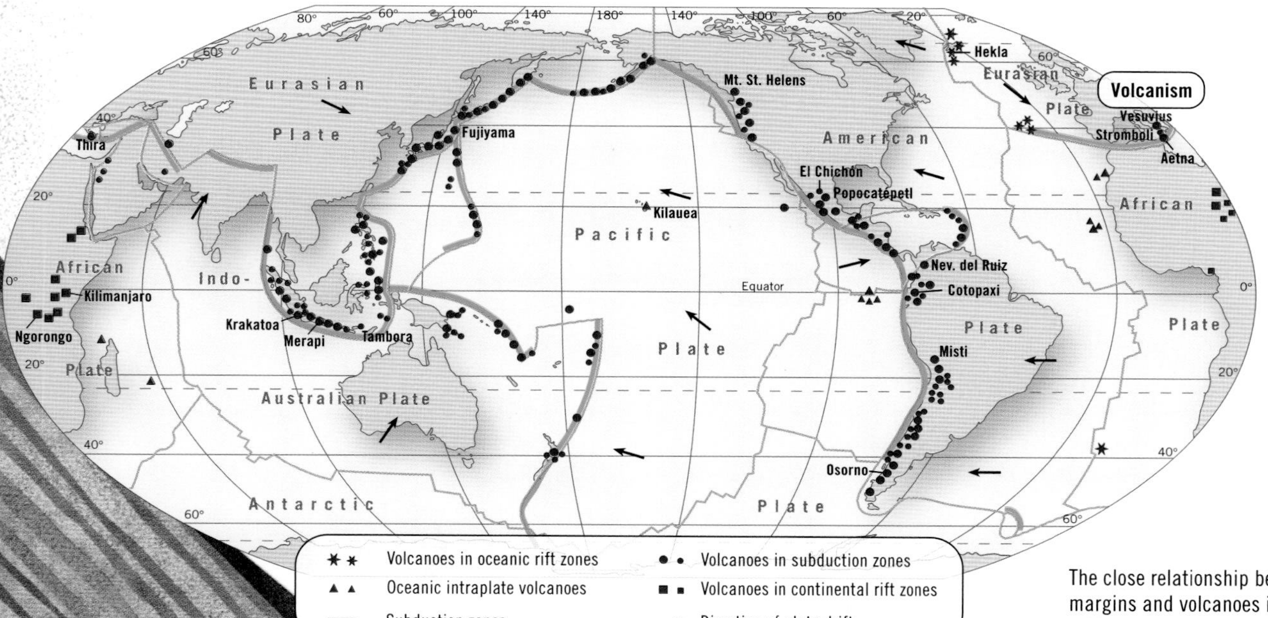

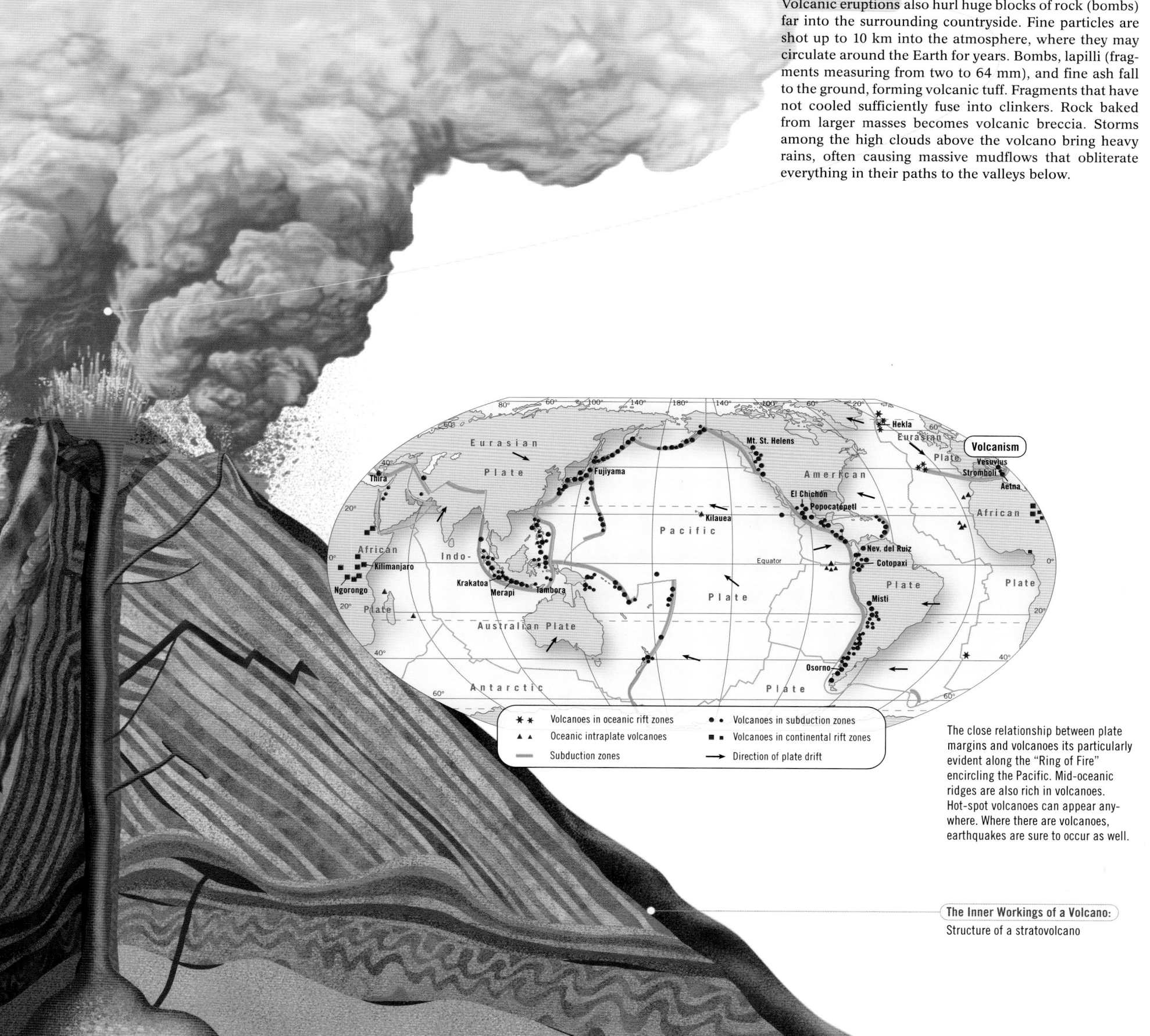

Volcanoes in oceanic rift zones • Volcanoes in subduction zones

Oceanic intraplate volcanoes ■ Volcanoes in continental rift zones

Subduction zones → Direction of plate drift

The close relationship between plate margins and volcanoes its particularly evident along the "Ring of Fire" encircling the Pacific. Mid-oceanic ridges are also rich in volcanoes. Hot-spot volcanoes can appear anywhere. Where there are volcanoes, earthquakes are sure to occur as well.

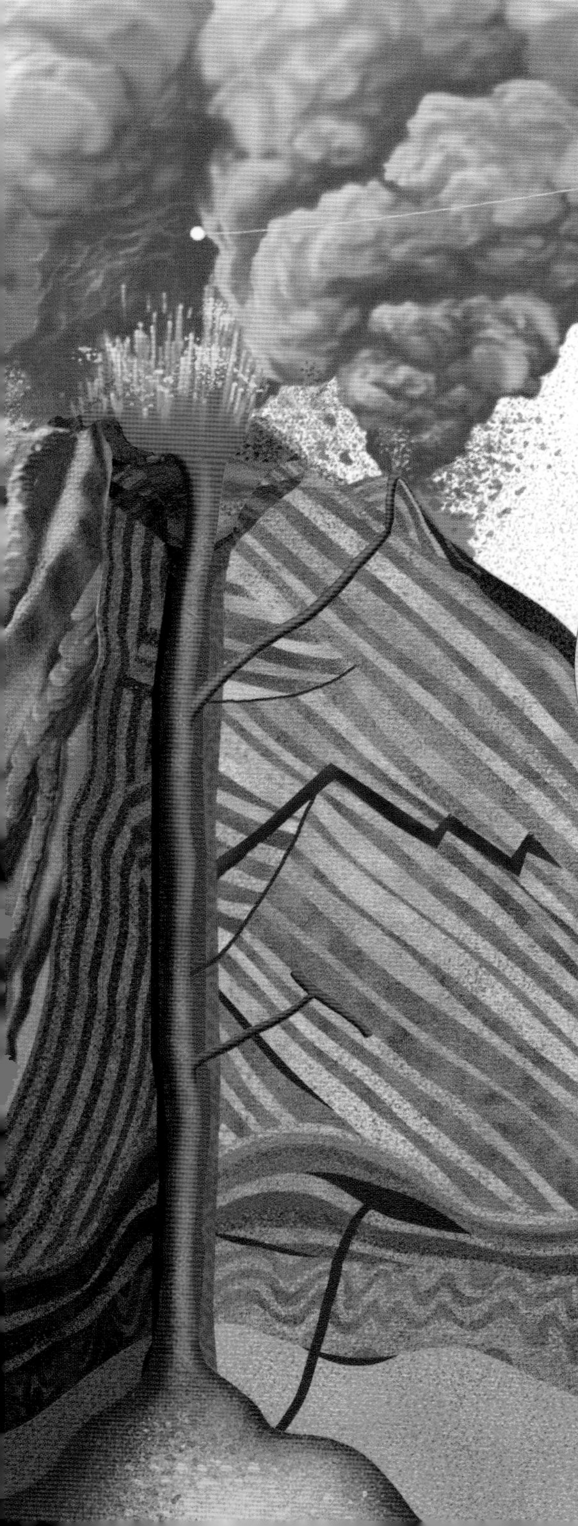

The Inner Workings of a Volcano:
Structure of a stratovolcano

Water Molds the Landscape

Water's Journey from the Sea to the Mountains and Back

Life came to Earth with water, which entered the cloud of gas that surrounds our planet in the form of gas released from molten magma. The cooling process produced the first rains, and the seas began to form. In the protective watery environment and under the influence of rising oxygen concentrations, life burst forth explosively several hundred million years ago. We come from water, and we need water to live. The human body is 70 percent water. Although we can live for weeks without food, we would die within days without water. More than half of the human race suffers from a shortage of clean drinking water. Eighty percent of the diseases responsible for millions of deaths every year are carried by water. Water is an essential, life-giving substance that is unequally distributed. Some people die of thirst, while others drown.

High into the Atmosphere and back to Earth. The Water Cycle

How does water find its way back to the sea? Raindrops falling to earth have several ways of returning to the bodies of water from which they came. They may evaporate, flow over the surface, or seep into the earth, emerging again later through springs. Water that remains on the surface reaches the sea in a matter of weeks. Yet water held captive in a freshwater lake can take years to return to the ocean. Water that falls as snow and turns to ice in cold regions of the Earth like the Antarctic, may not return to the sea for hundreds of thousands of years. Once there, it is ready to embark upon another long journey. Many water molecules take refuge at safe ocean depths, however, thus escaping the routine of constant travel.

The water cycle begins with the evaporation of liquid water, most of which takes place on the ocean surface. At a temperature of 77 °F, this process consumes 583 calories per gram of water. Molecules of water vapor transport this kinetic energy over long distances. The water condenses again only after a journey of hours or even days through the air. At this point, raindrops are formed during the transition from the gaseous to the liquid state, and evaporation heat is released again. That is how warmth from the Caribbean, for example, travels via the Gulf Stream to Norway. When raindrops freeze (changing from liquid to solid), 79.4 calories are released per gram of water. Thus, as strange as it may seem, the freezing process generates heat. Molecules move more slowly in ice than in liquid water.

Water Shapes Mountains and Valleys by Day and by Night

With rare exceptions, water flows downhill toward the sea, quickly forming drainage lines on the surface. As the kinetic energy of water rushing downhill tears away material and carries it away, long cuts form in the earth – the valleys of streams and rivers. Naturally, elevated ridges are left standing between these valleys. The product is a relief of mountains and valleys. Depending upon elevation and slope, mountains of different heights are created and cut apart by water and/or ice (glaciers). The higher the mountain range, the steeper the forms carved by the water.

A Steady Drip Hollows the Stone

Water is the most important element in the weathering process that shapes rock – just as it is when automobiles succumb to rust (corrosion). Limestone is one of the most highly soluble types of rock, and large caves and other karsts are often found in limestone formations. Apart from its corrosive effect, moving water also works mechanically to hasten the process of rock destruction.

The effects of wind, water, and salt have combined to undercut a coastal rock formation on the island of Lanzarote.

Crashing waves strike steep coastal formations with incredible force (one cubic meter of water weighs roughly a ton), wielding sand and pebbles as abrasive weapons. Although these forces are weaker in rivers, a substantial amount of material is eroded and carried away from riverbeds and banks over the course of time. Deep, V-shaped valleys and gorges offer striking evidence of the destructive power of water. Bank and bed erosion caused by flowing water forms valleys in a multitude of different shapes.

1. Cirque glacier
2. Cirque, tarn
3. Terminal moraine
4. Valley lake
5. U-shaped valley
6. Fjord
7. Trough shoulder
8. Mountain river
9. Gorge
10. Waterfall
11. Marine terrace
12. Sea cliffs
13. Beach
14. High mountain range
15. Low mountain range
16. Highland
17. Cuesta
18. Hilly upland
19. Lowlands
20. Terraced river valley
21. Oxbow lake
22. River meander
23. Delta
24. Spit, lagoon
25. Dunes
26. Strand-plain coast
27. Inshore lakes
28. Sandy heathland
29. Bay

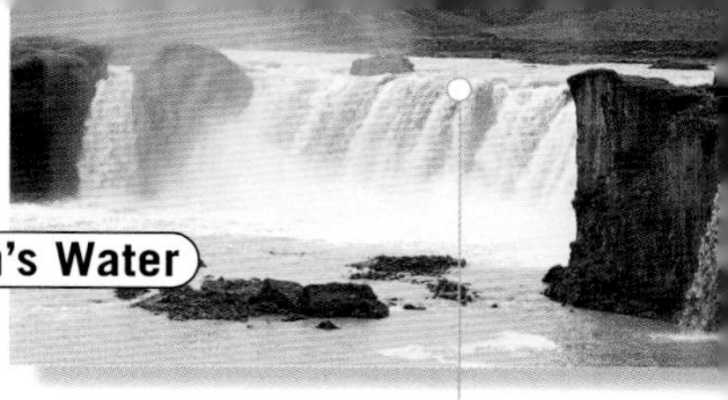

Glacial ice has even greater erosive power. The high pressure exerted by the ice causes severe erosion (detersion, exaration) even at low flow speeds. Blocks of stone the size of a house may be torn away and carried downward. This is how deep U-shaped valleys are formed. The eroded material is deposited in glacial moraines. Water and ice cover three-quarters of the Earth's surface. Although the total quantity of water on earth – some 1.4 billion square km – is almost impossible to imagine, this immense treasure is of little use to us, as 96.5 per cent of it is salty. Methods developed for desalinating seawater are too costly for most countries. And it is hardly practical to tow icebergs from the Antarctic to the arid regions of the world. We may expect future water shortages to reach life-threatening proportions in many places on Earth.

No Escape from Water

Although water is in short supply in many parts of the world, thousands die or lose their homes in water-related disasters every year. Floods, typhoons, and tsunamis ravage broad stretches of land. Melting snow and torrential rains cause rivers to swell and overflow their banks in low-lying areas. Dykes often do not hold or are simply not high enough.

When the ground freezes during the winter and is covered by a thick blanket of snow, it takes only a brief interlude of warm temperatures accompanied by heavy rainfall to melt the snow and cause severe flooding in the valleys. The frozen soil prevents water from seeping into the ground and accelerates the speed of surface runoff.

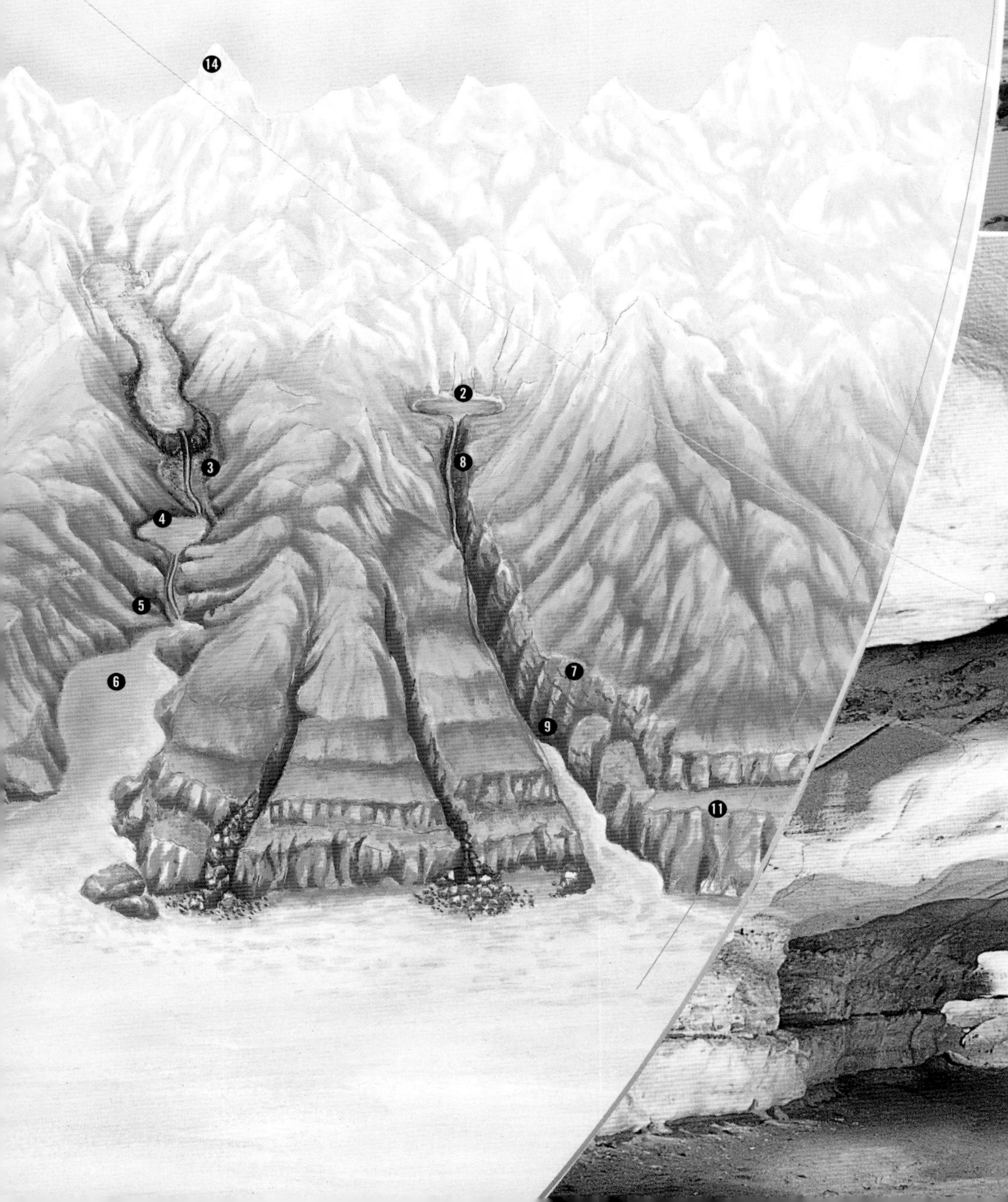

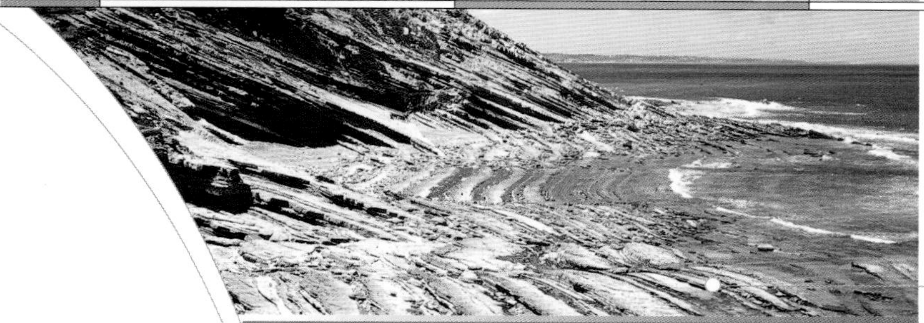

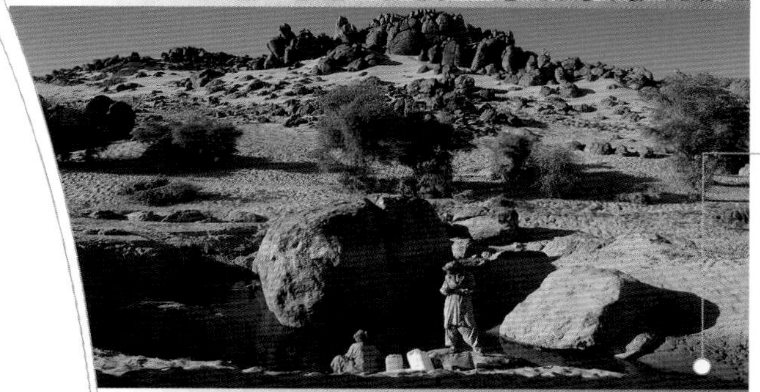

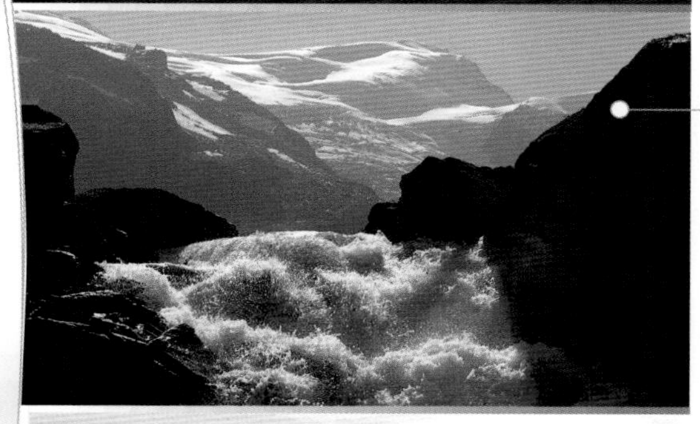

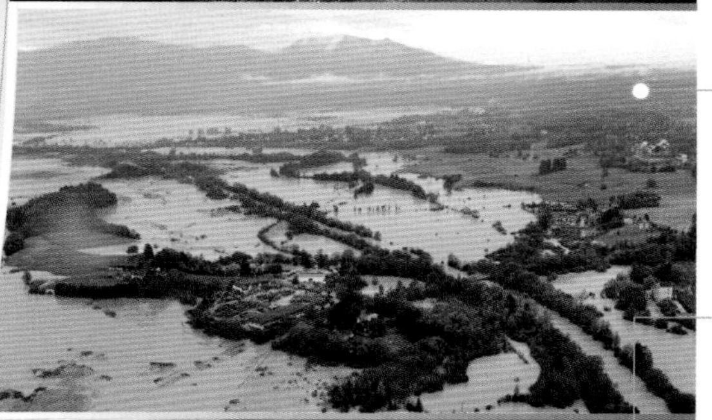

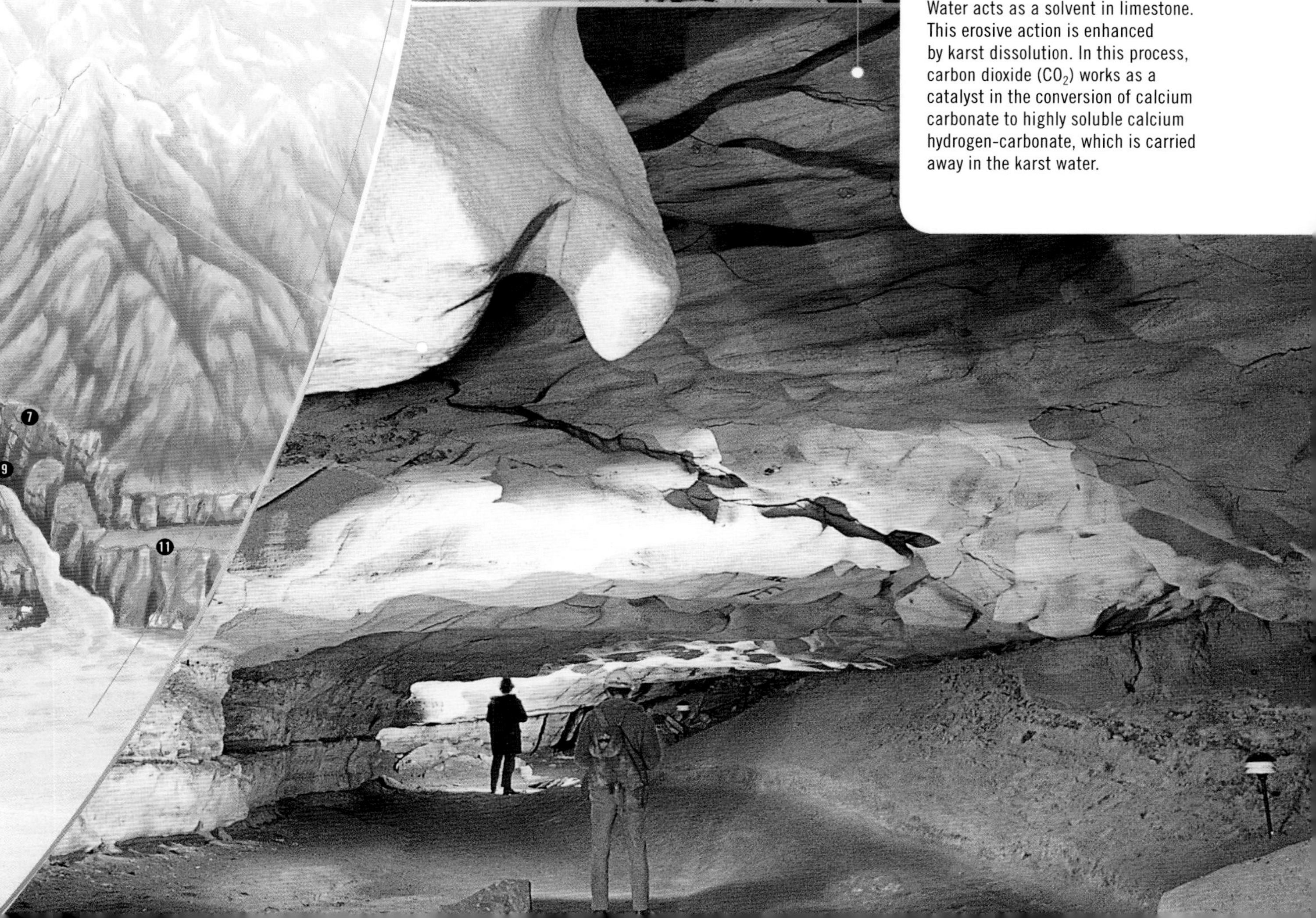

Spectacle of Nature
A thundering waterfall crashes over a steep drop in Iceland. The energy of flowing water, which mankind has not yet begun to exploit significantly, is a powerful force that here continues to erode the step in the terrain.

Planed and Leveled
The surf along the Basque coast near Saint-Jean-de-Luz has worn a flat abrasion plate in the terraced slopes of the Pyrenees.

Source of Life
Water is extremely scarce in deserts. Knowledge of the few, often hidden sources of water is crucial to survival in these extremely arid regions. Surface springs like this one in the Aïr Massif (Niger) are rare, and water must often be drawn from wells or water holes dug in the sands of dry riverbeds.

Unbridled Force
Water from melting snow and ice flows to the sea. In steep terrain, the milky glacial melt rushes unhindered to the valleys below. The fine sand dispersed in the water consists of rock material ground away under massive glacial pressure. In mountainous regions, the force of flowing water is strong enough to move even large blocks of stone.

Floods
When the snows melt in spring or rains are especially heavy in summer, flooding often occurs on the coastal plains and alpine piedmont regions of Europe.

In the Underworld
Underground erosion creates caves (photo: Wyandotte Cave, Indiana). Water acts as a solvent in limestone. This erosive action is enhanced by karst dissolution. In this process, carbon dioxide (CO_2) works as a catalyst in the conversion of calcium carbonate to highly soluble calcium hydrogen-carbonate, which is carried away in the karst water.

Natural Disasters – Human Catastrophes

Does Mankind Pose a Challenge to Nature?

The media provide news about a terrible natural disaster somewhere in the world virtually every day. Our television screens show us images of devastation and often of the dramatic events themselves as they unfold. Sober assessments of underlying causes are often overshadowed in the public mind by such sensational reports.

Yet there are several questions we cannot ignore: "To what extent are we humans at fault?" Is mankind inevitably doomed to destruction, or can we find a way to avert it?

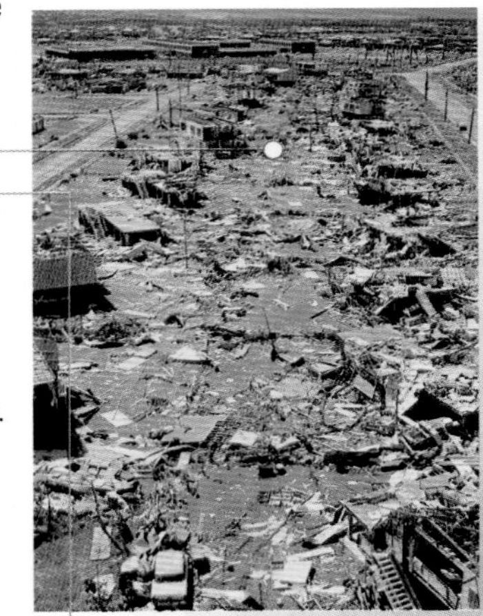

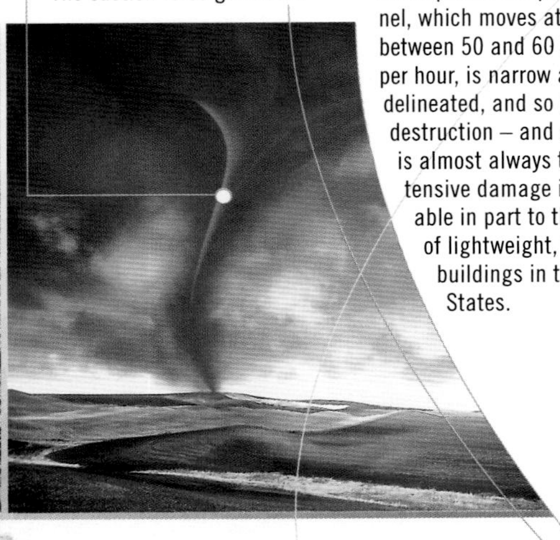

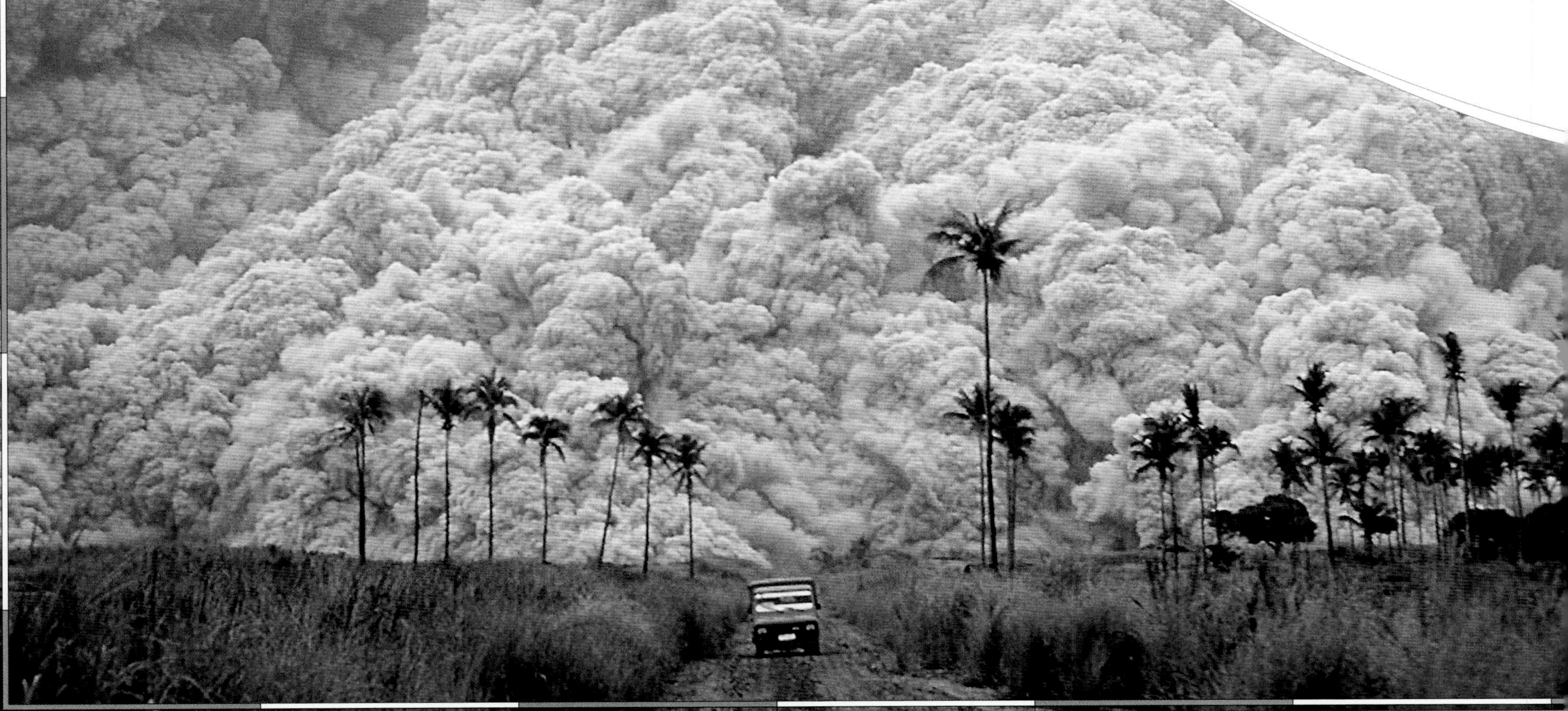

Disasters Mark the Course of the Earth's History

The history of the Earth teaches us that catastrophic events have always played a role in global and regional developments and have even impacted on the evolution of living organisms. Yet from our somewhat short-sighted present-day perspective, we tend to overlook the length of time involved in these processes. Experts continue to debate the question of whether the mass extinction of life forms some 65 million years ago was caused by a collision with an extraterrestrial body, a severe outbreak of volcanic activity, or other geological, perhaps tectonic events. Most agree, however, that the extinction of the dinosaurs (along with many other forms of animal life) paved the way for the development of mammals and thus ultimately for the origin of Homo sapiens. But when we speak of natural disasters, we are usually thinking of events that affect human beings directly.

A Devastating Christmas Present

On Christmas Day of 1974, Tropical Storm Tracy battered the city of Darwin in northern Australia. With average wind speeds of 140 kilometers per hour and gusts peaking at 260 kilometers per hour, the storm completely destroyed more than 5,000 of the 8,000 lightweight houses built on stilts. Forty-nine people died, and property damage amounted to 3 billion Australian dollars. Of Darwin's 45,000 inhabitants, 25,000 were evacuated by air, while 10,000 people fled the city by car toward the south. This was the greatest natural disaster in Australia's history.

Flight from the Inferno

In early April 1991, Pinatubo, a volcano on the Philippine island of Luzon, erupted again for the first time in human memory. In June, the mountain collapsed and lost 300 meters of elevation. Red-hot clouds spread like avalanches, covering distances of as much as 20 km. Ten cubic km of ash, gas, and other erupted matter were catapulted into the stratosphere to heights of up to 40 km. Torrential rains generated by a tropical storm turned the accumulated ash into massive streams of mud. More than 200,000 people fled the looming catastrophe; 400 lives were lost. The expulsion of ash and particles containing sulphuric acid caused average temperatures in the atmosphere near ground level to sink by as much as 0.9° F — worldwide.

Tornadoes – Dangerous Twisters

The narrow funnel of a tornado dips threateningly earthward. The air rising inside the funnel rotates at speeds that accelerate to a maximum of 200 kilometers per hour toward the inside. The suction force generated inside the funnel rips buildings apart and bursts lungs and blood vessels in human victims. Objects carried away become dangerous projectiles; dust and water are hurled high into the atmosphere. The path of the funnel, which moves at speeds between 50 and 60 kilometers per hour, is narrow and clearly delineated, and so is its wake of destruction — and destruction is almost always total. The extensive damage is attributable in part to the prevalence of lightweight, wood-frame buildings in the United States.

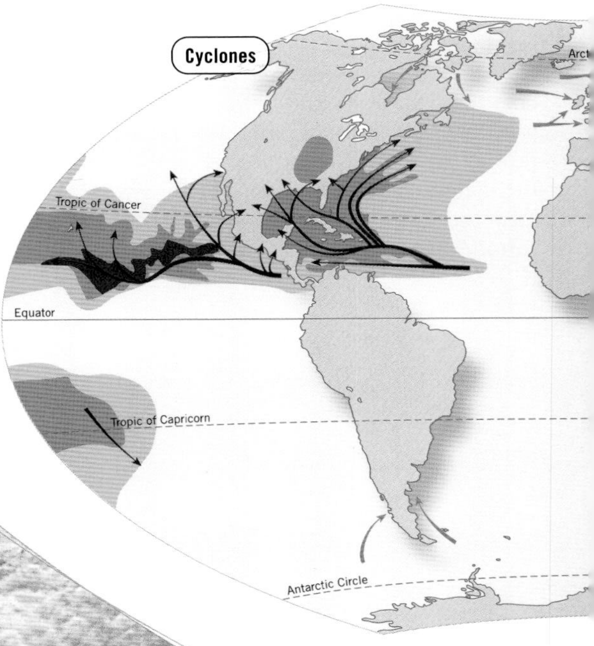

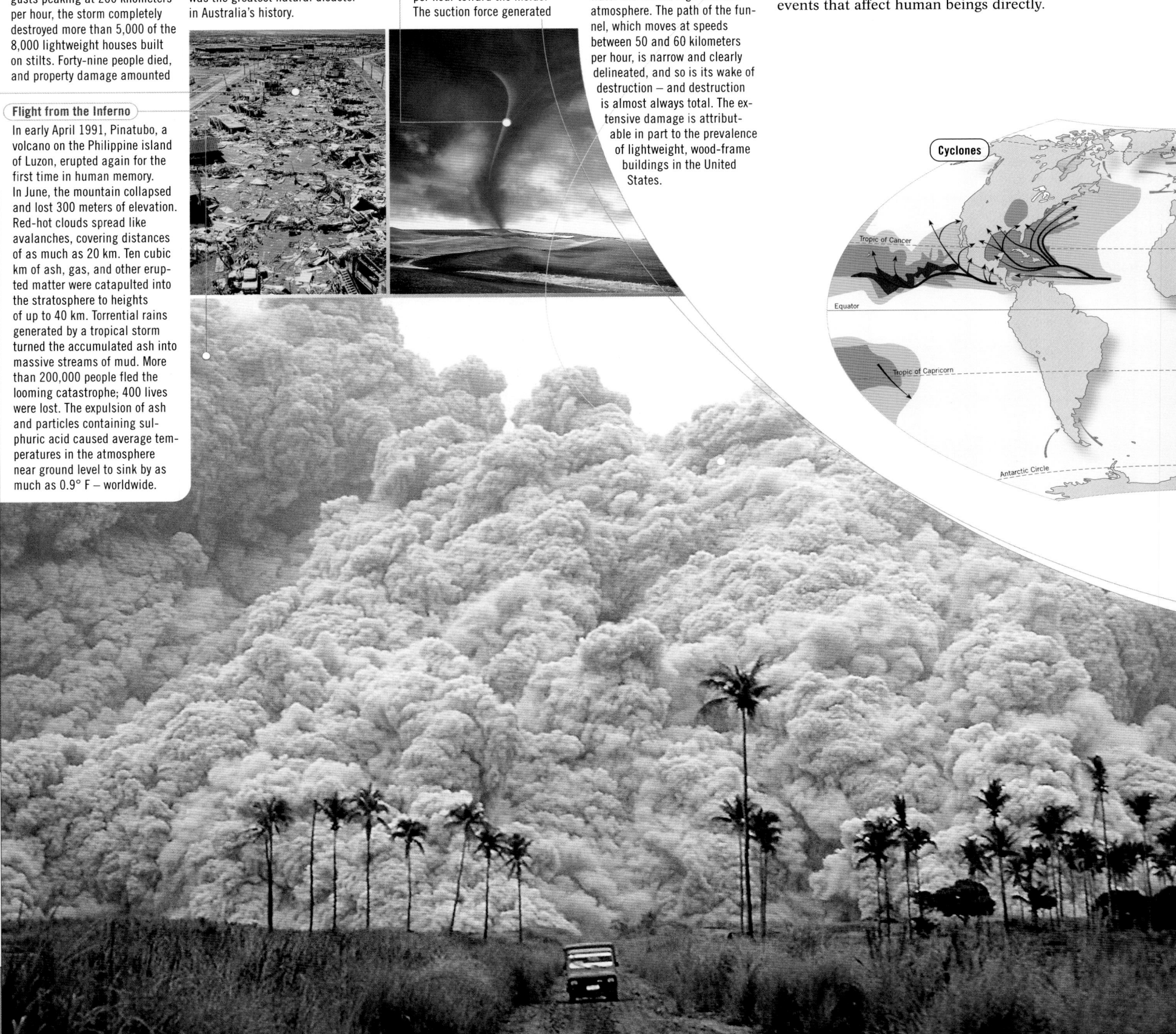

Cyclones

Tropic of Cancer

Equator

Tropic of Capricorn

Antarctic Circle

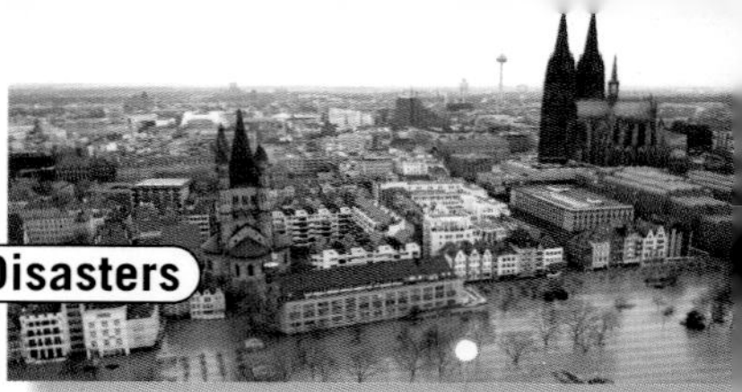

The Earth's Vast Destructive Potential

The "restless Earth" poses many dangers. Earthquakes and volcanic eruptions are concentrated in certain regions. While it is impossible to prevent such events from occurring, precautions can be taken against their consequences. The number of severe earthquakes (measuring 7.0 or above on the Richter Scale) did not increase worldwide during the twentieth century. Yet the toll in human lives and property damage has risen steadily, due to increasing population and building density, to the spread of settlements into endangered areas people once avoided, to the increasing value of property and goods (concentrated primarily in metropolitan areas) that has accompanied the rise in living standards, and to the increased susceptibility of modern societies and technologies to damage. Explosive population growth is another significant factor. The Kobe earthquake (1995) clearly showed seismic activity affects not only developing countries but often industrialized nations as well. And much the same applies to volcanism. We find ourselves in the midst of a heated debate about the dangers posed by the Earth's atmosphere and waters. Is the number of incidents rising? Are they growing in severity? And what or who is to blame – nature or mankind? A closely related issue is the question of mankind's impact on climate. Hurricanes are not the only destructive climatic phenomenon. Extended periods of heavy rain or snow storms; hail, ice, droughts; heat waves and periods of extreme cold; forest, bush, and prairie fires caused by lightning; avalanches, fog and smog all leave destruction in their wake. Excessive precipitation causes floods, landslips, and mudslides.

Stormy Times

The most dangerous storms originate in the Tropics: hurricanes along the coasts of Central and North America, typhoons over the waters off East and Southeast Asia, and cyclones in the Bay of Bengal (Bangladesh). They often wander for days over the sea in a westerly direction, only to turn suddenly north or south just before landfall. Their low pressure areas measure between 300 and 1,000 km in diameter. The center (known as the eye) of such storms is virtually cloudless and calm. It is encircled by a spiral of clouds that rotates at speeds up to 400 kilometers per hour. Torrential rain falls from massive cloud formations towering to heights of more than 15,000 meters. Storms that reach land wreak tremendous destruction, to which tidal waves also contribute, but then quickly lose intensity and dissipate. Hurricane Andrew caused $ 30 billion in damage. In Bangladesh, more than 300,000 people lost their lives in flooding caused by cyclones in 1970. The energy bundled in such storms is equivalent to that of several atomic bombs.

The tornadoes that occur frequently in the Midwestern United States are born when warm, moist air from the Gulf of Mexico is overlayered by dry, cool air from the Rocky Mountains or the Arctic. The temperature differential (between 36° and 54°F) generates incredibly high wind speeds. An average of 750 tornadoes are registered in the U.S. every year. They have costs the lives of hundreds of people – despite the well-organized warning system.

Those Who Look for Trouble …

The map divides the eastern and southeastern coasts of the United States into 58 numbered sections (each 80 km wide). Based on long-term observation, it is possible to estimate the probability of hurricane activity in a given year as a percentage value. The number of "normal" hurricanes (wind speeds higher than 33 meters per second) is entered in the inner row of boxes; "major" hurricanes (56 meters per second and higher) are listed in the outer row, which has several large gaps. Hurricane activity is most frequent in August and September.

Year in, Year out …

Floods caused by high water on the Rhine (photo: Cologne) and its tributaries are practically a regular occurrence. Data gathered at water-level measuring stations enable authorities to issue advance warnings and initiate evacuation procedures. Dykes and ad hoc precautionary measures (such as mobile protective walls) can help prevent some but by no means all flood damage. Flooding in 1993 and 1995 caused total property damage estimated at five billion dollars.

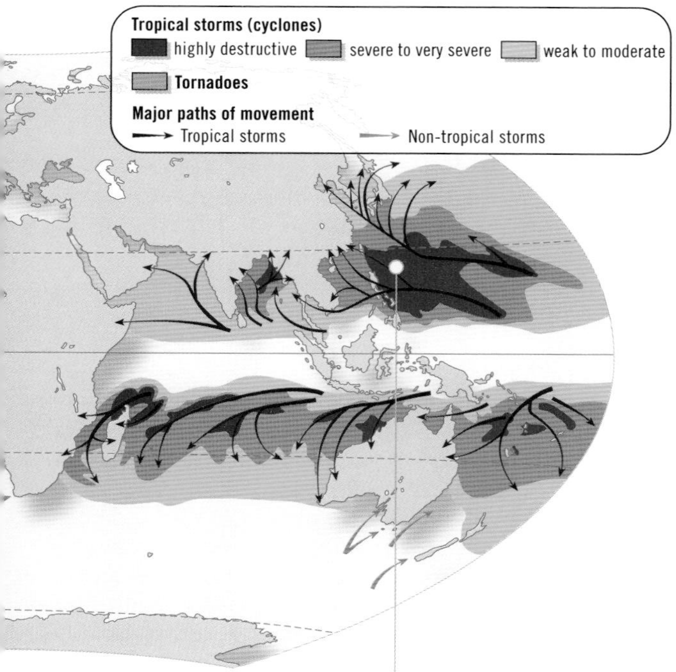

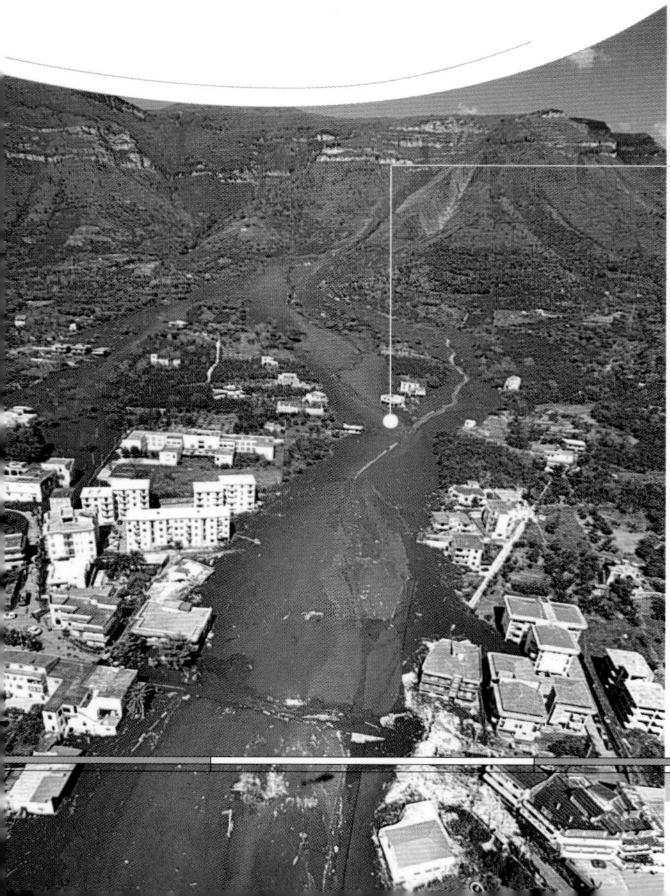

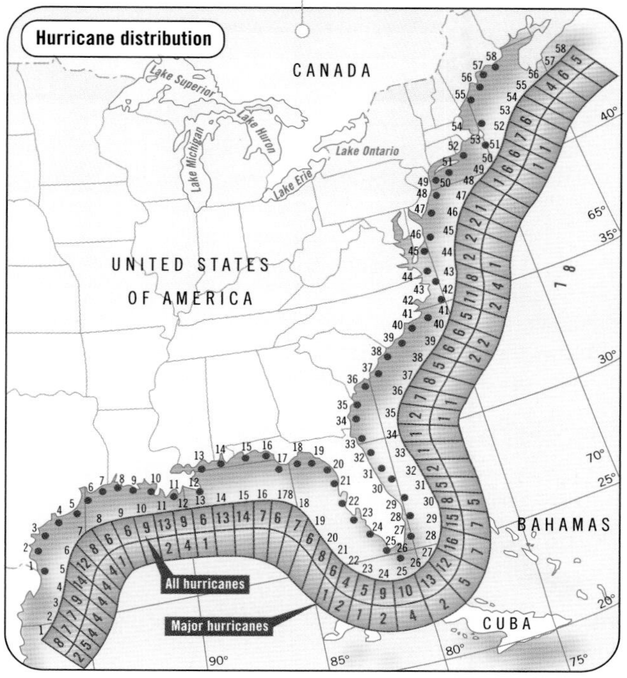

Hurricane distribution

Dangerous Tropical Storms

Tropical storms originate over waters with surface temperatures of at least 48°F in northern and southern latitudes between 5° and 30° during the late summer and early fall. A mass of moist, warm air with towering formations of cumulonimbus clouds gathers above the water. Condensation of the water vapor releases huge amounts of heat energy which accelerate the movement of rising air and the speed of the whirling mass of clouds. Tropical storms are generated by wavelike disruptions along the edge of the subtropical high-pressure belt or by the intrusion of low-pressure centers from the west-wind zone into the tropical circulation belt. Due to defrection caused by the Earth's rotation (Coriolis effect), storms spin clockwise in the southern hemisphere and counterclockwise in the northern hemisphere. Cyclonic storms do not occur near the equator, as the Coriolis effect is too weak to accelerate the rotating masses of air.

When the Earth Slides Away

Saturation of debris or "soft," porous rock on mountain slopes or hillsides by heavy, sustained rainfall or melting snow can cause extensive landslides or mudslides. When these huge masses of mud and debris are carried into the valleys below, the descending wave cuts a broad path of destruction through the landscape. Mudslides of this kind occur often in the Apennines (photo taken near Sarno, east of Mt. Vesuvius), especially in areas where slopes have been stripped of vegetation through deforestation or overgrazing.

The Great Flood Yet to Come?

High water is ordinarily caused by unusually long periods of heavy precipitation or by rapid melting of winter snows. Repeated reports of catastrophic flooding evoke the impression that these disastrous events are becoming more frequent. Are they a by-product of global climatic changes that are reflected in increasingly heavy precipitation in Central Europe and the American Midwest? Catastrophic floods have occurred often in the past, as high-water marks show, but they had less far-reaching consequences, as agriculture and housing development were much less extensive than they are today. Various human interventions in the balance of nature have accelerated runoff activity and increased the danger of flooding. Prime examples are deforestation, ground-surface sealing (roads, housing developments, etc.), soil compaction (resulting from machine plowing and the conversion of meadowlands to fields), riverbed constriction with dams and dykes, river straightening, and the draining of wetlands (along the Mississippi, Missouri, and Red Rivers, for example), in combination with ground settlement and rising riverbed levels caused by accumulating silt deposits. Awakened from their lethargy by the increasing frequency and impact of floods, experts and regulatory authorities have instituted renaturation programs for river areas. Efforts to restore natural flood plains (retention areas) often encounter stiff opposition from local farmers, however.

Tropical storms (cyclones)
highly destructive | severe to very severe | weak to moderate
Tornadoes
Major paths of movement
→ Tropical storms → Non-tropical storms

Oceans and Marine Circulation Systems

The Global Climate Pump

Seen from space, the Earth is truly a blue planet, as more than two-thirds of its surface is covered by water. No other planet in our solar system has liquid water or the life it supports. The Earth's oceans are in constant motion, as water travels in powerful currents across them and circulate between the seafloor and the surface. Our seas are stirred by eddies and gyres and moved by winds and tidal forces. Visible waves on the surface are complemented by invisible ones in the ocean depths. The dynamics of the oceans have a significant impact on our planet's climate.

Driving Forces

Three different forces prevent the seas from ever coming to rest. The first is the gravitational pull of the Moon and (to a lesser extent) the Sun, which creates tidal action beneath which the Earth passes as it rotates. As a result, the seas shift in a twelve-hour (and in some places 24-hour) rhythm within their basins, rising and falling along their coasts (tidal action). Twice each month, the Moon, the Sun, and the Earth align with one another, causing particularly strong tidal action (spring and neap tides).

The second force that moves the seas is wind. It propels the major ocean surface currents, such as the Gulf and Brazil Currents in the Atlantic and the Kuroshio and Humboldt Currents in the Pacific. Highly characteristic, constant circulation patterns are sustained by prevailing winds – the trade winds in the subtropics and the West Wind Drift in the temperate zones – which are ultimately caused by the spheroid form and rotation of the Earth. Winds affect only the surface of the seas, and thus wind-driven circulation is restricted for the most part to the top 200 meters of water. However, the average depth of the world's oceans is about 4,000 meters, and their deepest

point (the Mariana Trench in the northwestern Pacific) is more than 11,000 meters below the surface.

The third driving force results from differences in sea-water density. Water density depends upon temperature and salt content (which ranges between 3.4 % and 3.6 % in most marine waters), and thus this motion is referred to as thermohaline circulation (from the Greek word háls, for salt). The densest, heaviest water tends to sink and is found most commonly in the European North Atlantic and near the Antarctic. The sinking masses of heavier water circulate around the Earth in the depths of the oceans, while warm surface water flows into the sinking regions. In this way, all of the water in all of the oceans on the globe circulates between the seafloor and the surface and is enriched with oxygen. On average, the journey of a single water molecule from the North Atlantic to the depths of the Pacific takes about a thousand years.

The rotation of the Earth (in the form of deflection caused by the Coriolis force) plays an important role in the dynamics of marine circulation systems, causing much stronger currents along the western rims of ocean basins.

The Effects of Climate

The uppermost two meters of the ocean can store as much heat as the entire atmosphere, since water has a very high heat-retention capacity. This storage capacity works like a buffer that partially evens out seasonal temperature fluctuations. The range of these fluctuations is therefore much narrower in coastal maritime climates than in continental inland areas. The average difference between summer and winter temperatures on the East Coast of the United States is about 60 °F, but increases to 105 °F in Edmonton, Canada. In addition, ocean currents transport stored solar heat over tremendous distances, normally from the tropics to the poles. In this way, they help to narrow temperature gaps caused by the unequal distribution of solar radiation on earth.

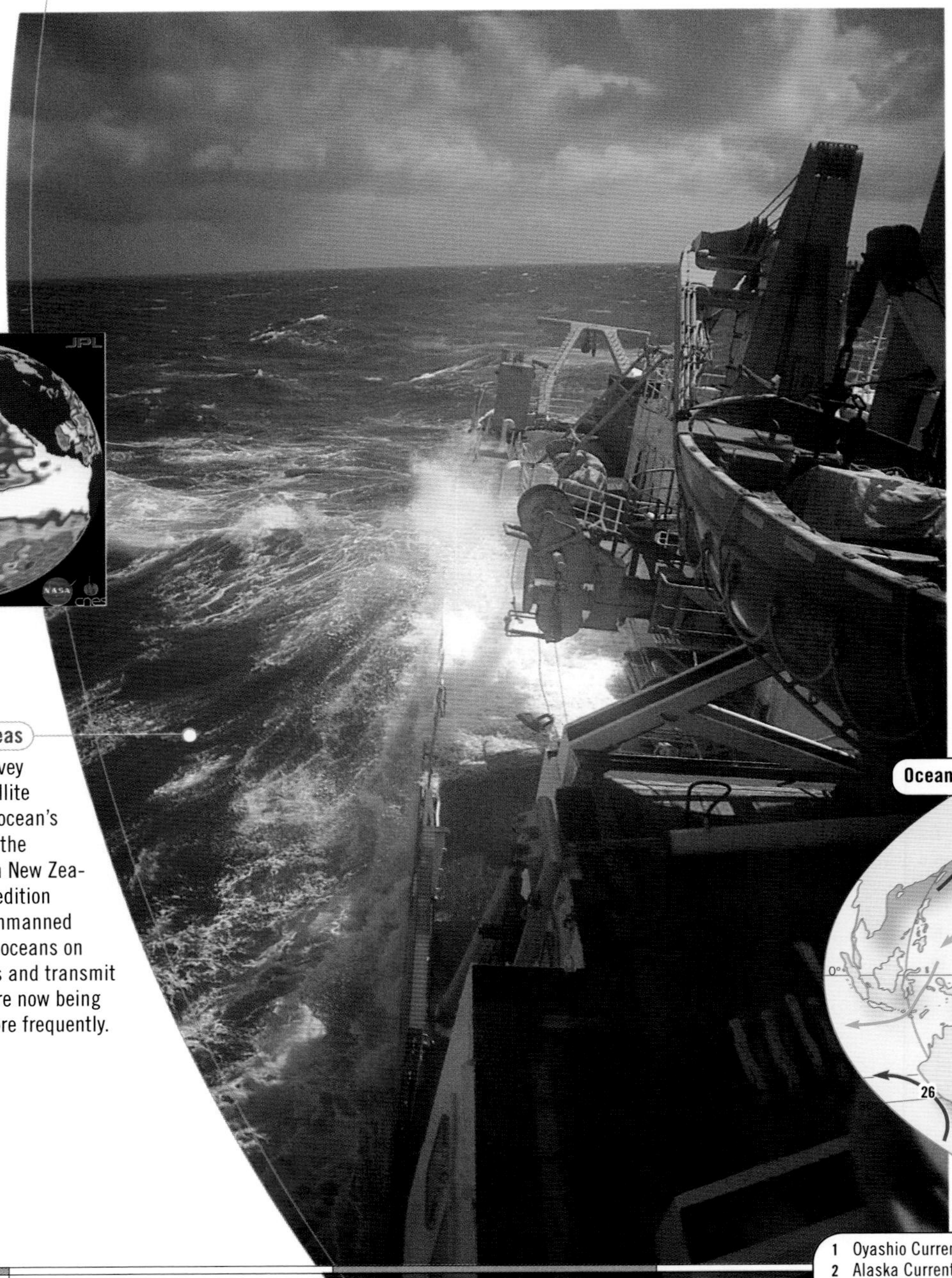

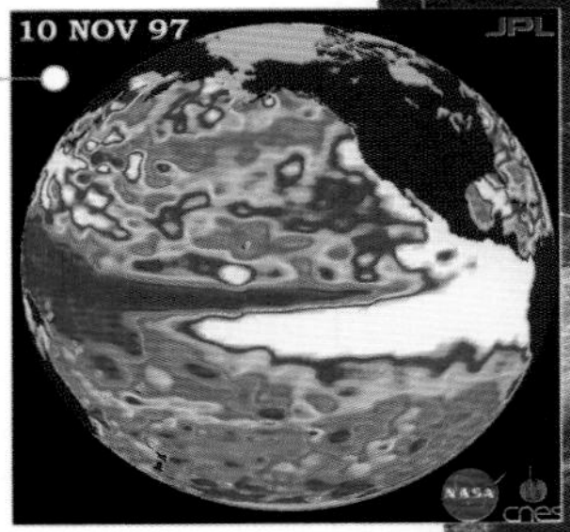

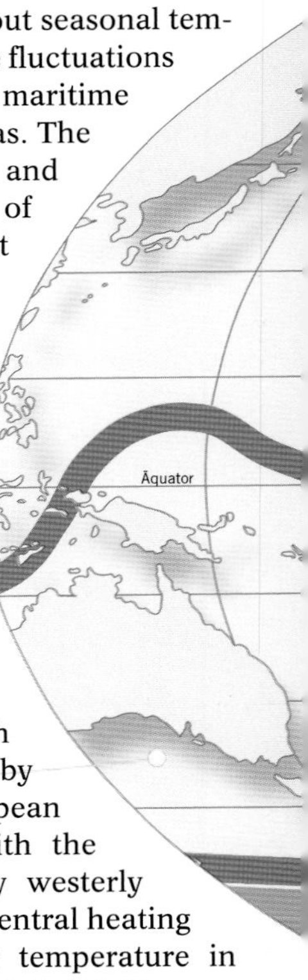

The Atlantic is unique in that heat is transported through its waters by thermohaline circulation from the southern hemisphere to regions off the coasts of Europe. There, this warmth ascends into the air, which is carried by prevailing westerly winds to the European mainland. Europeans are familiar with the mild winter temperatures brought by westerly winds from time to time. This Atlantic central heating system raises the average annual air temperature in northwestern Europe by more than 9° F (5° C) – an effect that was instrumental in the development of agriculture and the rise of northern European cultures.

El Niño, the Christ Child

The interaction of marine currents, waves, and trade winds in the Pacific tropics produces a natural climatic fluctuation known as El Niño – Southern Oscillation (ENSO). At intervals of between three and seven years, the trade winds dissipate, the cold, nutrient-rich Humboldt current slows, and unusually warm water accumulates off the Pacific coast of South America. The people of the region have named this phenomenon El Niño after the Christ Child, because the coastal waters ordinarily grow warmer around Christmas. El Niño generates waves beneath the surface of the ocean which travel across the entire Pacific along the Equator. They are reflected at its western edge and return to the east, where their arrival marks the beginning of the end of the warm phase. The reverse phase of this fluctuation – unusually cold temperatures in the eastern Pacific – is called La Niña. Occurrences of El-Niño cause massive fish death

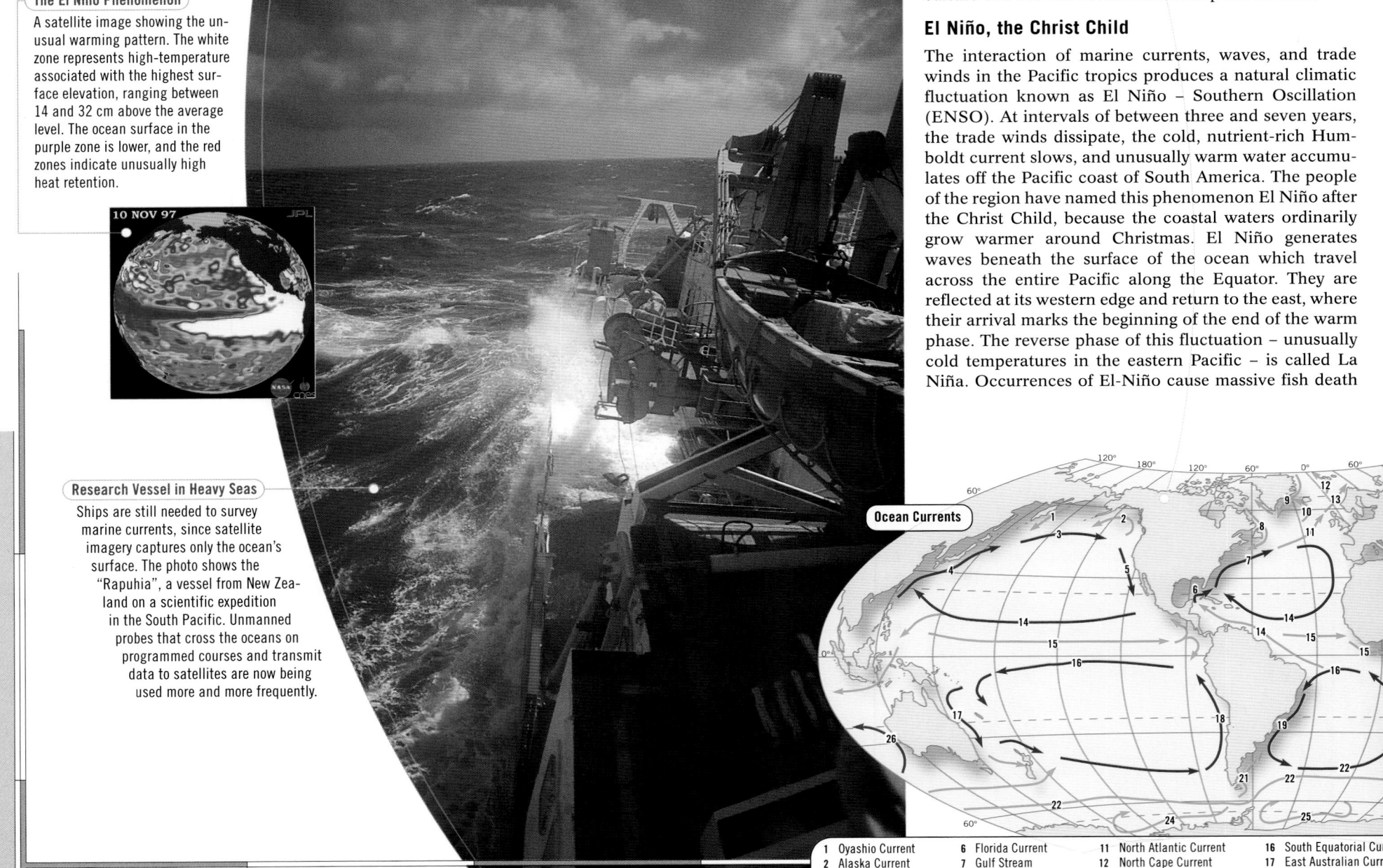

The El Niño Phenomenon
A satellite image showing the unusual warming pattern. The white zone represents high-temperature associated with the highest surface elevation, ranging between 14 and 32 cm above the average level. The ocean surface in the purple zone is lower, and the red zones indicate unusually high heat retention.

10 NOV 97   JPL   NASA

Research Vessel in Heavy Seas
Ships are still needed to survey marine currents, since satellite imagery captures only the ocean's surface. The photo shows the "Rapuhia", a vessel from New Zealand on a scientific expedition in the South Pacific. Unmanned probes that cross the oceans on programmed courses and transmit data to satellites are now being used more and more frequently.

Ocean Currents

1 Oyashio Current	6 Florida Current	11 North Atlantic Current	16 South Equatorial Current
2 Alaska Current	7 Gulf Stream	12 North Cape Current	17 East Australian Current
3 North Pacific Current	8 Labrador Current	13 Norwegian Current	18 Humboldt Current
4 Kuroshio	9 East Greenland Current	14 North Equatorial Current	19 Brazil Current
5 California Current	10 Irminger Current	15 Equatorial countercurrents	20 Benguela Current

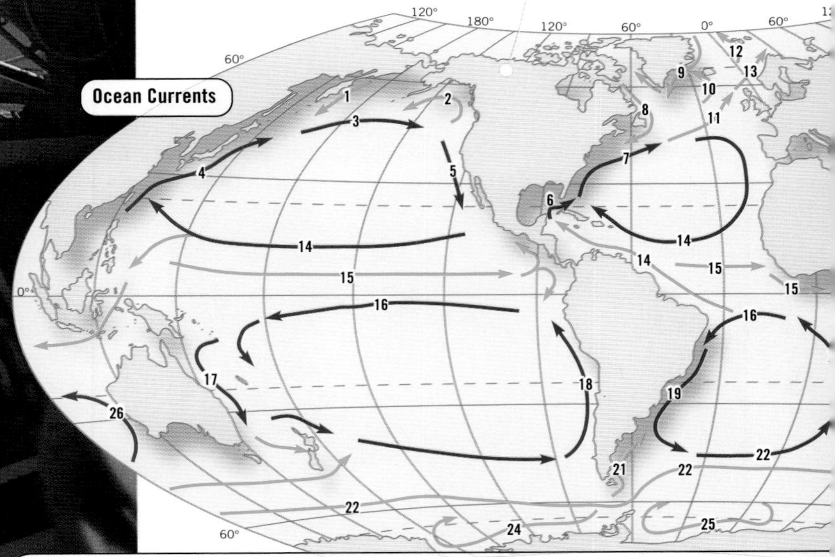

The Oceanic Climate Pump

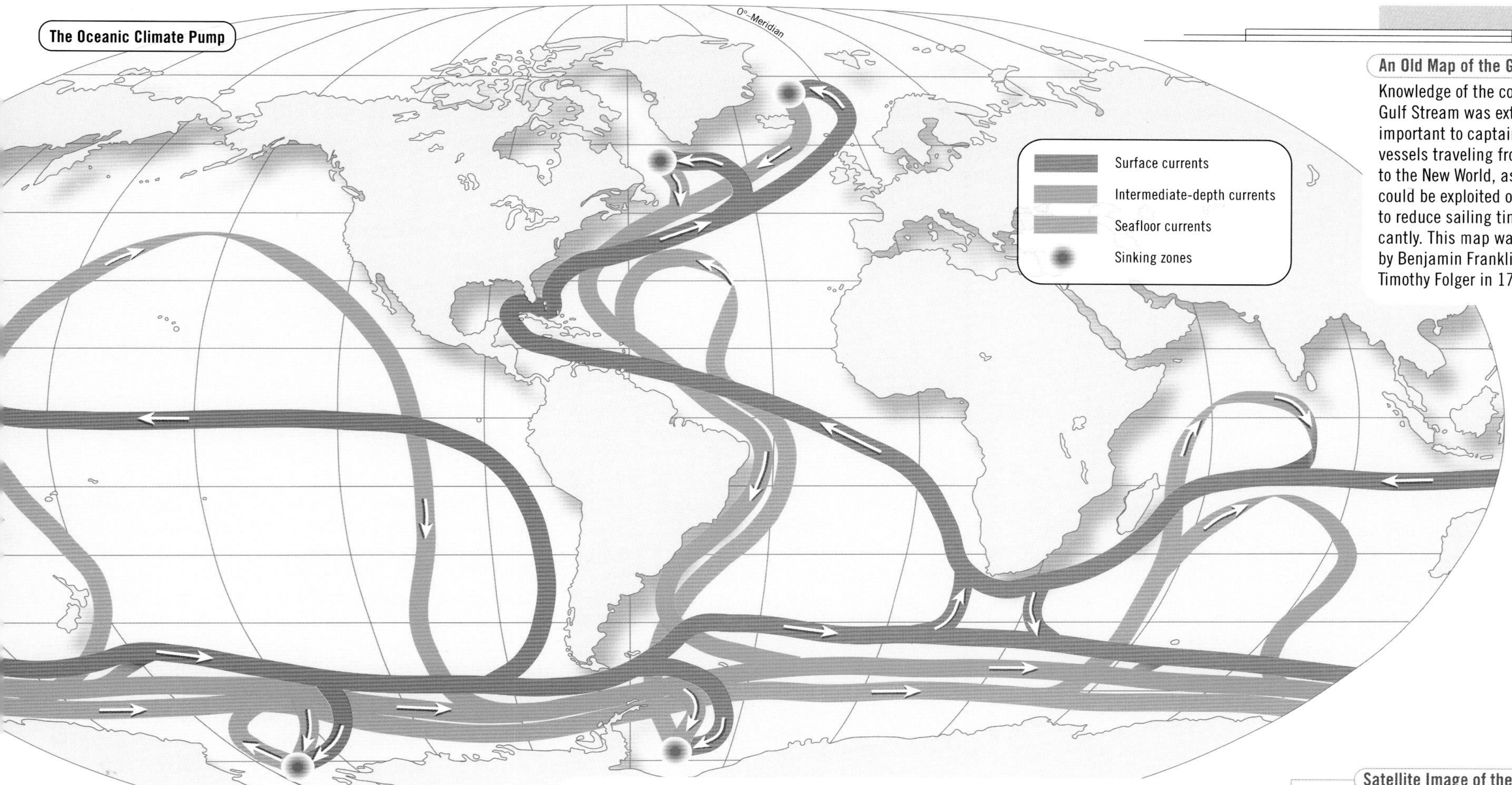

Surface currents
Intermediate-depth currents
Seafloor currents
● Sinking zones

An Old Map of the Gulf Stream
Knowledge of the course of the Gulf Stream was extremely important to captains of ocean vessels traveling from Europe to the New World, as the current could be exploited or avoided to reduce sailing times significantly. This map was compiled by Benjamin Franklin and Timothy Folger in 1769.

off the coasts of Peru and Ecuador and are responsible for weather extremes all over the globe. Today, they can be predicted several months in advance on the basis of computer simulations. If farmers respond in time, crop failures can be avoided for the most part.

Currents of Life

Ocean currents circulate vast quantities of nutrients and trace substances and supply oxygen to the depths of the sea. Thus they are essential to marine life. Without currents, the oceans of the Earth would be nearly dead. The rich fishing grounds off the coast of Peru are fed by the Humboldt Current, and thermohaline circulation promotes especially vigorous algae growth in the North Atlantic. Currents also carry carbon dioxide into the depths of the sea, thus helping rid the atmosphere of man-made emissions that contribute to global warming.

Global Thermohaline Circulation

The pattern of thermohaline circulation driven by differences in water density spans the Earth like a gigantic conveyor belt. Thus warm water near the surface of the Atlantic flows northward from the southern tip of Africa through the Benguela Current, the Gulf Stream, and the North Atlantic Current into the sinking regions in the North Atlantic (these currents overlie wind-driven circulation patterns). From there, it flows as cold water at a depth of two to three kilometers back to the south. In the process, 1015 Watts of thermal energy are transported into the North Atlantic region — the equivalent of the output of 500,000 large power plants.

Satellite Image of the Gulf Stream
In this infrared satellite image, the Gulf Stream is clearly identifiable as a warm (black and red) band. It veers from the North American coast off Cape Hatteras and breaks apart, forming meanders and gyres. Its warm water flows with the North Atlantic Stream to regions off the coasts of northern Europe.

Surface Currents

Ocean currents which flow near the surface are largely wind-driven but may also be propelled by differences in seawater density. The prevailing trade and west winds are responsible for the largest subtropical gyre, along the western edge of which the strong boundary currents (including the Gulf Stream, the Kuroshio and the Brazil Current) flow toward the poles.

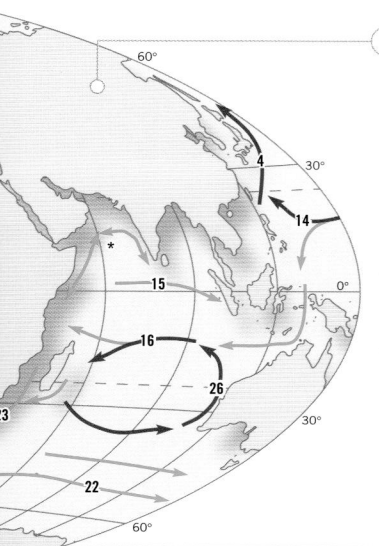

21 Falkland Current
22 Antarctic Circumpolar Current
23 Agulhas Current
24 Ross-Sea Gyre
25 Wedell Gyre
26 West Australien Current
→ Major subtropical gyres
→ Strong Currents
* Direction depends upon the season

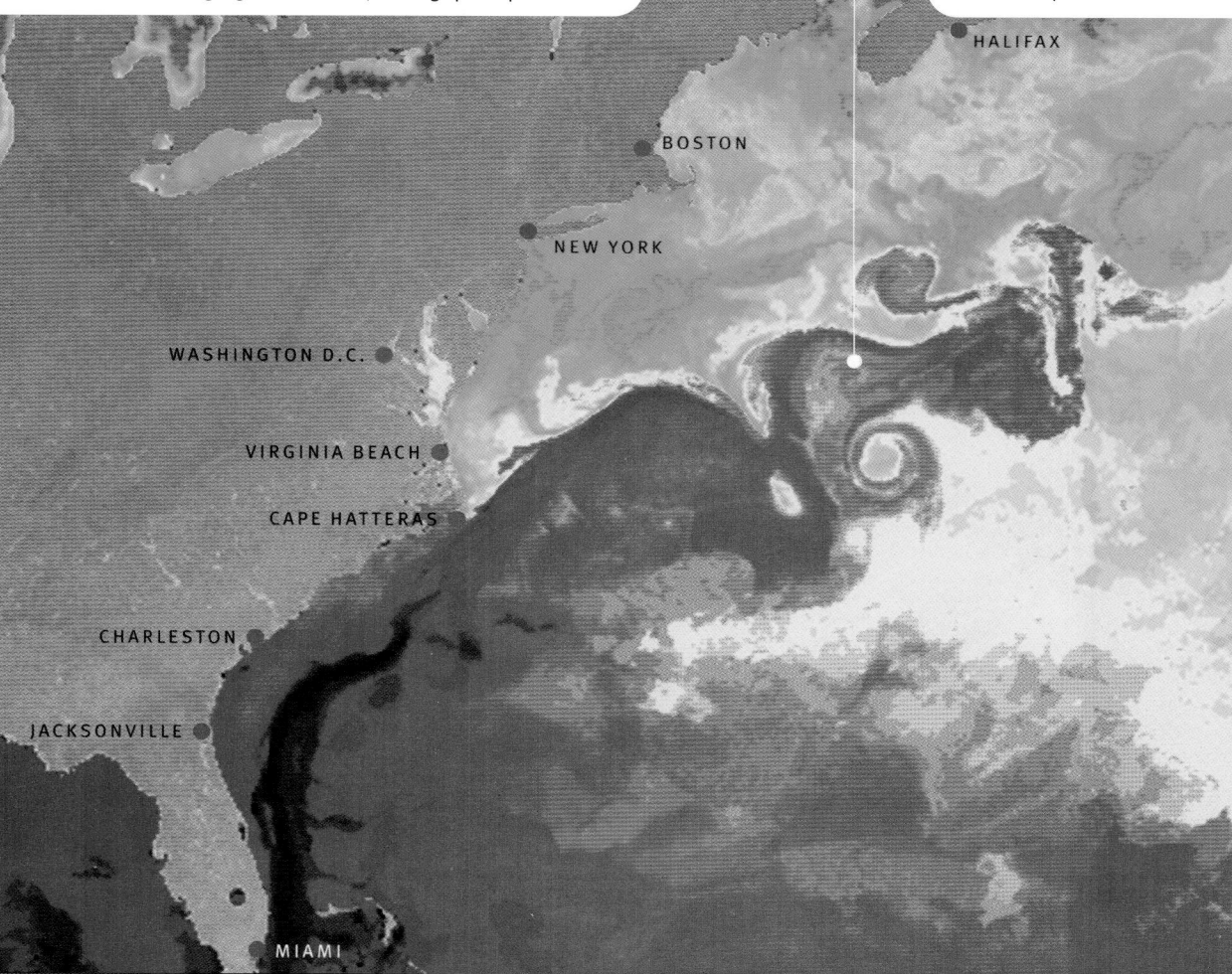

HALIFAX

BOSTON

NEW YORK

WASHINGTON D.C.

VIRGINIA BEACH

CAPE HATTERAS

CHARLESTON

JACKSONVILLE

MIAMI

The Earth's Ice – A Remnant of the Ice Age

Is Ice on Earth Melting or is a New Ice Age Coming?

Many people today are concerned that global warming will eventually melt all of the Earth's ice. Were this to happen, the sea level would rise as much as 70 meters. Coastal cities like New York, London, and Hamburg would be flooded completely. Many low-lying areas and countless islands would be submerged. On the other hand, the warming process could also produce heavier precipitation in the polar regions, adding to the existing Antarctic ice sheet. Yet the danger could come from another quarter. Oceanic warming could affect ocean currents. The Gulf Stream, our warm water heating system, could disperse, and the climate in the North Atlantic region would become much colder. Those who think in terms of geological time know that a new ice age will come sooner or later, as many warm periods lasted hardly longer than the Holocene, our own post-glacial era.

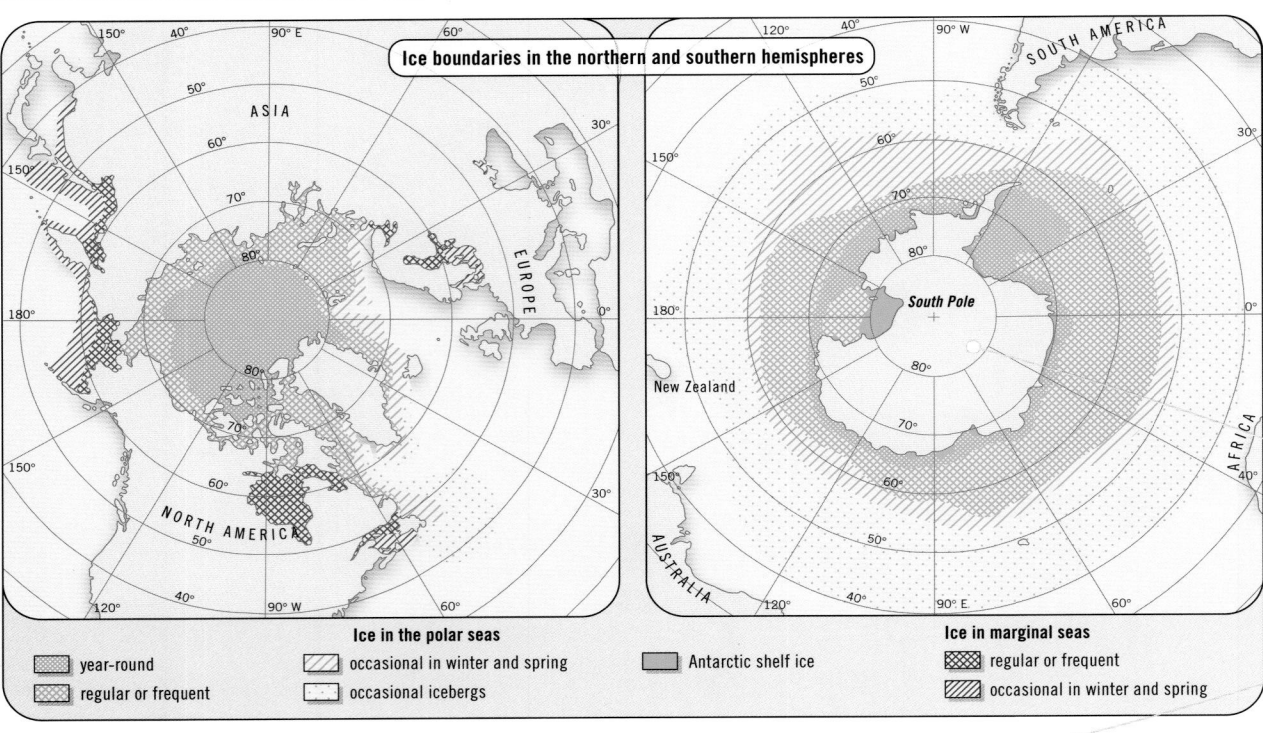

Ice boundaries in the northern and southern hemispheres

Ice in the polar seas

year-round	occasional in winter and spring
regular or frequent	occasional icebergs

Ice in marginal seas

Antarctic shelf ice	regular or frequent
	occasional in winter and spring

From Snow to Glacial Ice

Dry, fresh snow (density: 0.01–0.04 g/ccm) is 90 % air. Delicate ice crystals in snowflakes soon break down; the snow settles, melts to a certain degree, and freezes again (regelation). Developing grains of ice form firn snow (0.55 g/ccm), which contains 50 % air, and then firn ice (0.84 g/ccm), in which air bubbles account for only 30 % of total mass. The final phase is glacial ice (0.90 g/ccm), which is impermeable to air and water. Pure ice has a density of 0.917 g/ccm. In the Alps, ice grains measuring up to eight centimeters in diameter form after several years, while grains of ice at the South Pole can take 200 years to reach a diameter of one centimeter.

Ice Shapes the Topography

Although ice moves more slowly than flowing water, it exerts tremendous pressure on the underlying rock (100 to 5000 tons per square meter). Pressure and motion grind the rock away (detersion) and form roches moutonnées with flat ice-facing slopes and steeply inclined back sides. Rock fragments carried by the flow cut grooves in the smoothly ground rock, which later make it possible to trace the direction of glacial movement. V-shaped valleys carved by flowing water before the formation of ice are reshaped into U-shaped valleys. Rock debris broken away by the ice is transported to the edge of the ice flow, where it is melted out and deposited in terminal moraines. Unlike flowing water, ice is capable of moving huge boulders, which are left as erratics in the landscape after the ice recedes.

Flowing Glaciers

In contrast to rigid sea ice, glacial ice is granulated and becomes malleable and flowable under pressure. Regelation plays an important role in this process. The much colder ice in the Antarctic glides only as rigid block formations.

The Water Vapor – Ice – Water Cycle

Water evaporates from the warm oceans and rises with air currents into the high mountain regions. At these ice-cold elevations, it forms small ice crystals that fall to the ground as snow, even during the summer. This snow turns to ice, which then flows downward toward warmer areas, actually reaching the sea in some places. Icebergs are calved as inland ice slides into the sea. This cycle is driven by solar energy.

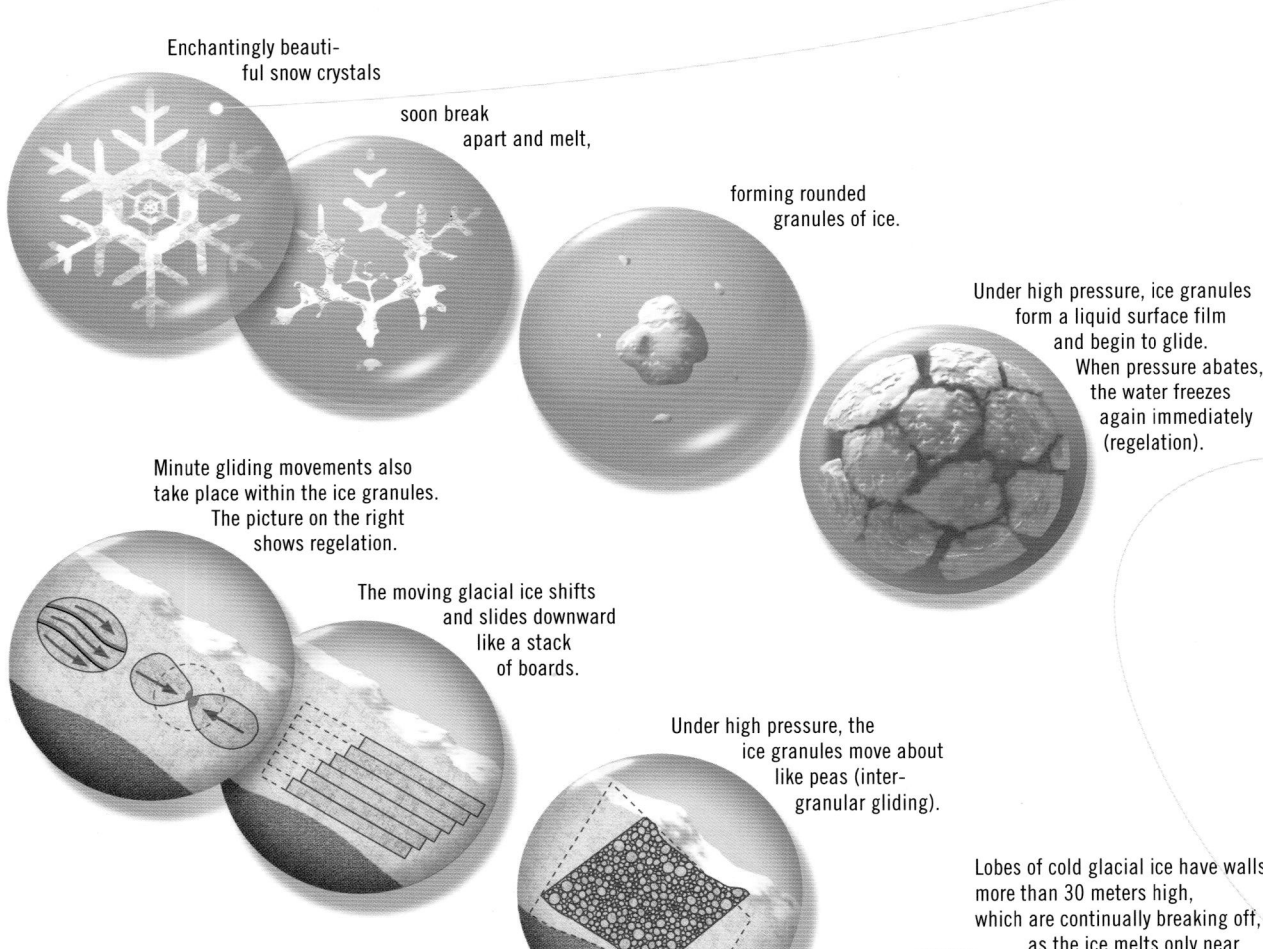

Enchantingly beautiful snow crystals

soon break apart and melt,

forming rounded granules of ice.

Under high pressure, ice granules form a liquid surface film and begin to glide. When pressure abates, the water freezes again immediately (regelation).

Minute gliding movements also take place within the ice granules. The picture on the right shows regelation.

The moving glacial ice shifts and slides downward like a stack of boards.

Under high pressure, the ice granules move about like peas (intergranular gliding).

Lobes of cold glacial ice have walls more than 30 meters high, which are continually breaking off, as the ice melts only near the sun-warmed ground. Movements of cold ice are abrupt but cause only minor glacial erosion.

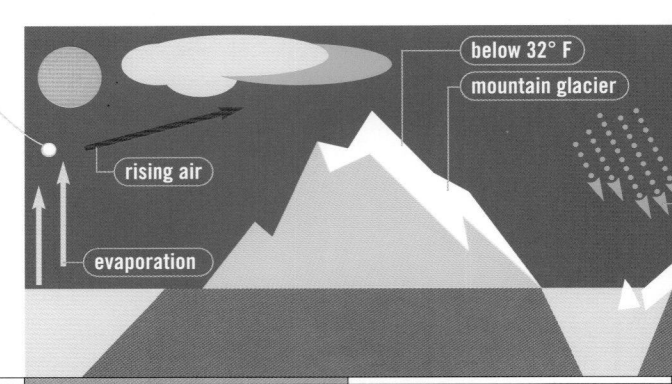

below 32° F

mountain glacier

rising air

evaporation

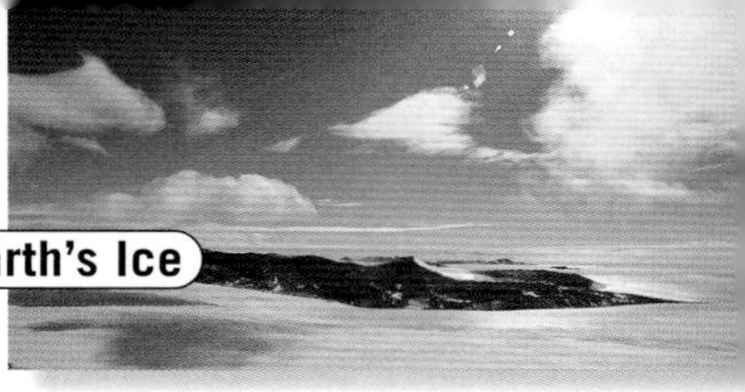

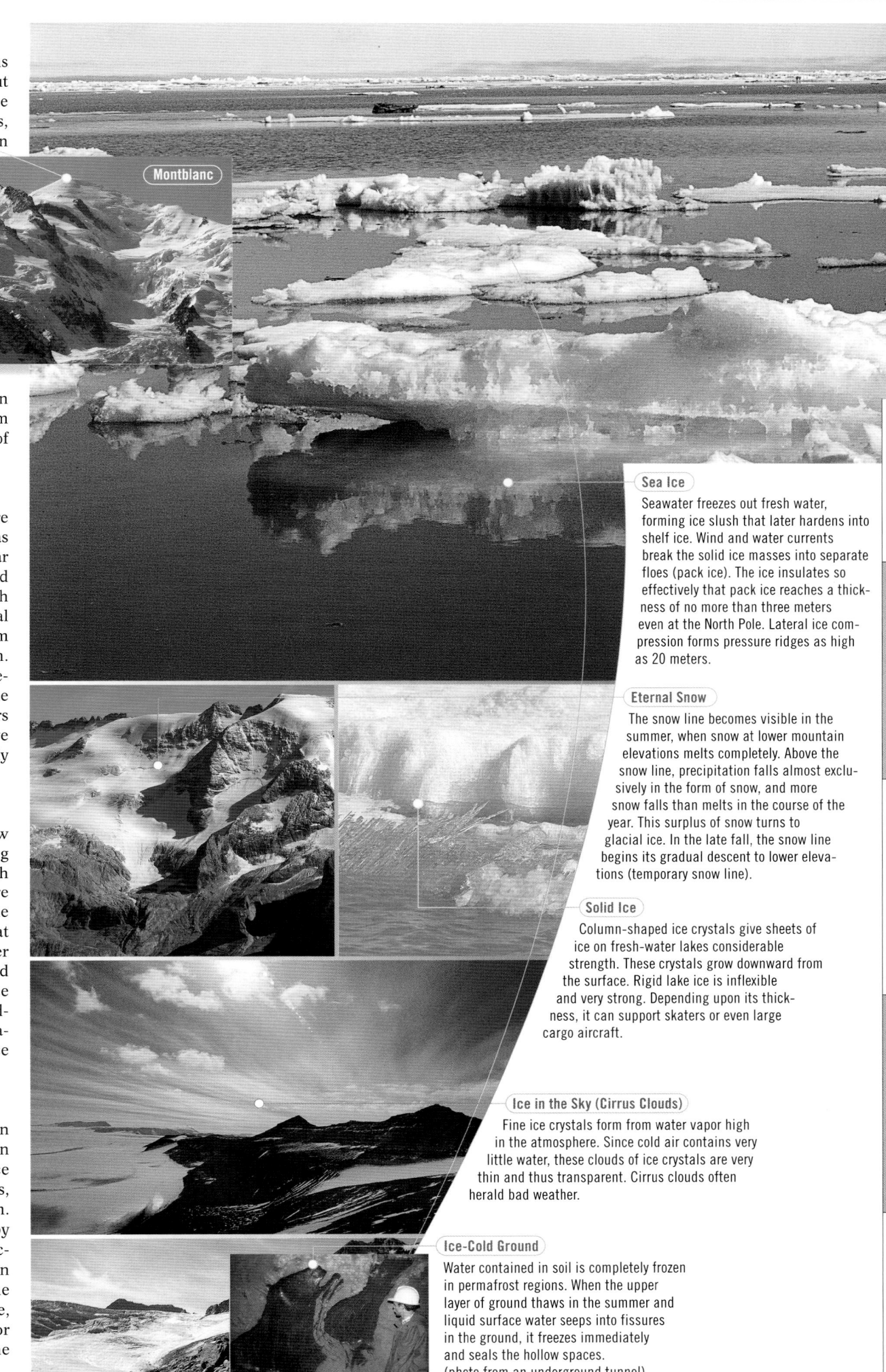

The Earth's Frozen Caps

The lower boundary of permanent ice in the mountains depends largely on the climate. The ice line lies at about 2,600 m on the northern face of the Alps, 4,800 m at the Equator, and over 6,000 m in dry subtropical regions, such as Tibet. Snow descends quickly to the valleys in avalanches from very steep terrain but forms glacial ice wherever it can accumulate.

The rocky summits of many of the world's highest mountains are hidden from view by ice caps. On steep slopes, the ice breaks apart, forming deep crevasses. Concealed by a covering of snow, these pose a particular danger to mountain climbers. Ice avalanches are common on extremely steep inclines.

There are hundreds of glaciers in northwestern Canada and Alaska. The Malaspina Glacier in Alaska, the longest valley glacier in the world, is 115 km long. Glaciers are numerous in the Rocky Mountains of the United States and the Andes in South America.

When Islands Merge with the Mainland

Global sea levels fall as increasing amounts of water are captured in ice. During the last ice age, the sea level was 135 meters lower than it is today. Many areas now far below the ocean's surface were once dry land. A land bridge across the Bering Strait connected Asia with North America. England was not an island, and coral isles rose as small mountains from the sea. During warm periods, the ice melts and sea levels begin to rise again. The Antarctic ice sheet (12.6 million square km) has presumably existed for some 20 million years. Sea ice in the Arctic (2 million square km) is only three centimeters thick and tends to melt and regelate quickly. The massive Greenland ice sheet (1.7 million square km) is relatively stable.

When Water Freezes, Everything Changes

Liquid water assumes a solid state at temperatures below 32° F. Average temperatures remain below the freezing point the year round in the polar regions and in the high mountain areas above the snow line. The polar caps are exposed to insufficient warming solar radiation, and the thin air in the alpine regions grows increasingly colder at higher elevations. Temperatures fall by up to 1.8° F per 100 meters of elevation. At heights of 5,000 meters and above, mountain slopes are covered constantly with ice and snow, even in hot, tropical inland areas. In the coldest regions of the world, the ground is frozen permanently (permafrost), though not beneath the inland ice sheets.

Ice Sheets Cover Entire Continents

During glacial periods ice may bury entire mountain ranges and expand far into the surrounding landscape. In North America, the Laurentide Ice Sheet, which once covered Canada and northern parts of the United States, covered a total area of more than 13 million square km. Today, only two parts of the world remain covered by enormous inland ice sheets: Greenland and the Antarctic. Ice in the Antarctic is some 4,800 meters thick in some places. If the 30 million cubic km of ice in the Antarctic were distributed among five million people, each of them would receive a ton of ice every minute for ten years. The same quantity of ice would cover all the dry land on earth with a layer 180 meters thick.

Snow

Inland ice sheet

Montblanc

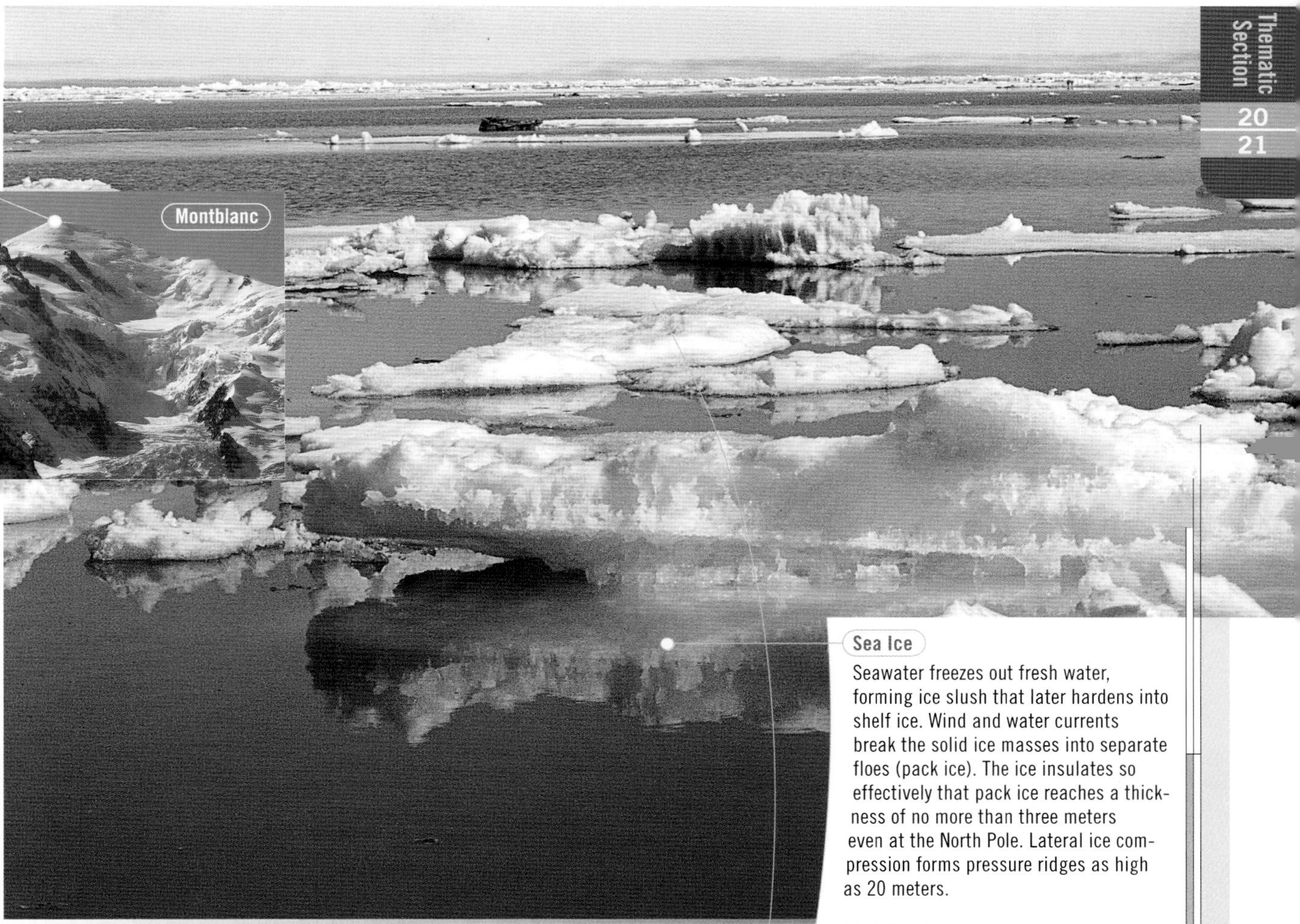

Sea Ice
Seawater freezes out fresh water, forming ice slush that later hardens into shelf ice. Wind and water currents break the solid ice masses into separate floes (pack ice). The ice insulates so effectively that pack ice reaches a thickness of no more than three meters even at the North Pole. Lateral ice compression forms pressure ridges as high as 20 meters.

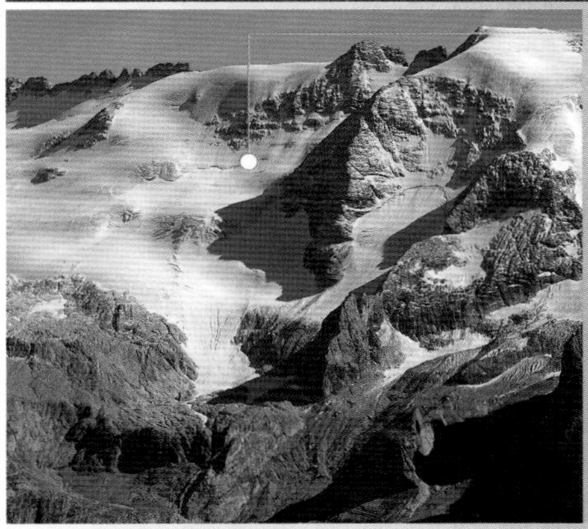

Eternal Snow
The snow line becomes visible in the summer, when snow at lower mountain elevations melts completely. Above the snow line, precipitation falls almost exclusively in the form of snow, and more snow falls than melts in the course of the year. This surplus of snow turns to glacial ice. In the late fall, the snow line begins its gradual descent to lower elevations (temporary snow line).

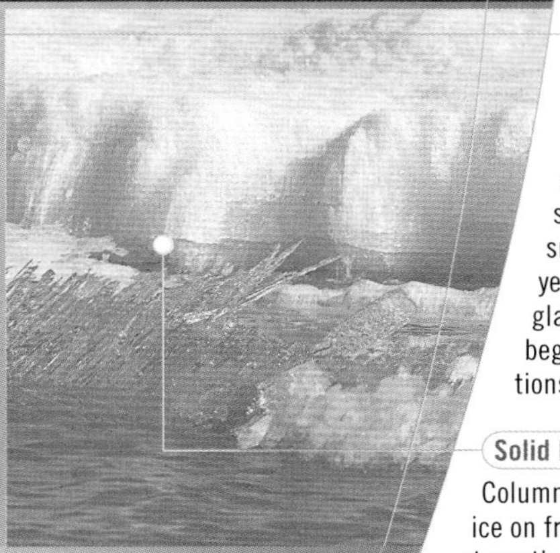

Solid Ice
Column-shaped ice crystals give sheets of ice on fresh-water lakes considerable strength. These crystals grow downward from the surface. Rigid lake ice is inflexible and very strong. Depending upon its thickness, it can support skaters or even large cargo aircraft.

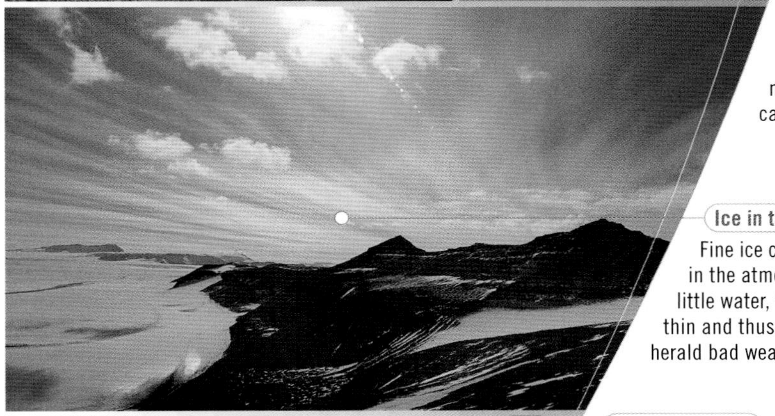

Ice in the Sky (Cirrus Clouds)
Fine ice crystals form from water vapor high in the atmosphere. Since cold air contains very little water, these clouds of ice crystals are very thin and thus transparent. Cirrus clouds often herald bad weather.

Ice-Cold Ground
Water contained in soil is completely frozen in permafrost regions. When the upper layer of ground thaws in the summer and liquid surface water seeps into fissures in the ground, it freezes immediately and seals the hollow spaces. (photo from an underground tunnel).

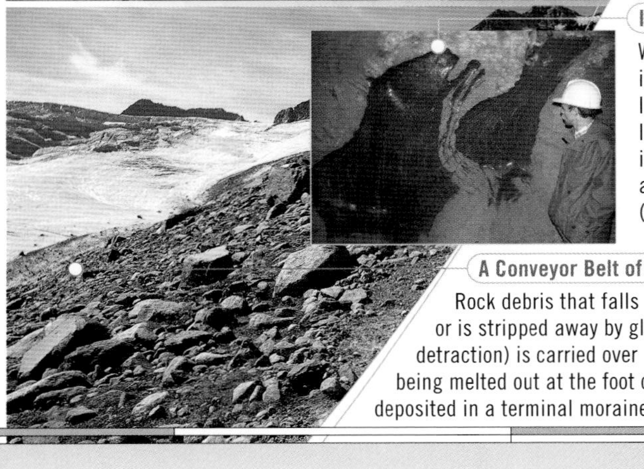

A Conveyor Belt of Ice
Rock debris that falls from mountain slopes or is stripped away by glacial ice (exaration, detraction) is carried over long distances before being melted out at the foot of the glacier and deposited in a terminal moraine.

Global Climate Zones

Stable or Constantly in Flux?

Today's climate patterns are certain to change. Just 5,000 years ago, average summer temperatures in North America were 36.5 degrees higher than today, and deciduous forests stood where conifers thrive today. The state of New Hampshire was covered by an ice sheet as recently as 18,000 years ago.

Core samples from the Greenland Ice Sheet show how abruptly climate can change. Scientists studying samples from a lake in southern Italy recently learned that local vegetation changed from dense forest to sparse steppe growth and back again within only 200 years about 75,000 years ago. The discovery came as a surprise to the many people who believed that the natural phenomenon of climate is constant over extended periods of time.

The Varying Intensity of Solar Heat

During the ice ages, plants, animals, and human beings were forced out of vast areas of the northern hemisphere. Life did not return to these regions until temperatures rose again and the ice gradually receded. We still do not know precisely what caused these drastic climatic changes, although experts agree that solar radiation is a crucial determinant of climate. Our planet is close enough to the sun to benefit from its warmth, yet far enough away that our atmosphere does not evaporate. The parallel rays of the sun strike the earth at a ninety-degree angle at the equator but reach the poles at a much flatter angle. Differences in pressure resulting from this unequal distribution of solar energy generate massive air currents. The influx of solar energy also differs from point to point depending upon the season and time of day, and this affects local weather as well. This results in part from the fact that the Earth's axis is not perpendicular to the plane of its orbit around the sun but is instead inclined at an angle of 23.5 degrees. The effects of this tilt are particularly noticeable in the polar regions (polar days and nights).

Global Respiration

Masses of air warmed in the tropics rise and drift into cooler northern or southern regions, while colder polar air flows toward the Equator. This general pattern of atmospheric circulation is a blessing that balances extremes in different climate zones. Yet a number of other factors also contribute to climate differences: elevation, topography, the distribution of land and seas, and cold or warm ocean currents. The macroclimates of specific climate zones can be broken down into mesoclimates (local weather patterns) and microclimates nearest the Earth's surface.

Launch of a weather balloon equipped with a radio sensor that transmits readings from high altitudes. Special balloons rise to altitudes of 35 km. Satellites send back data and images from as high as 36,000 km above the earth.

Weather activity takes place primarily in the troposphere, which lies beneath the stratosphere and extends to an altitude of about 13 km. The composition of our atmosphere is remarkably constant. Dry air is composed of nitrogen (78% by volume), oxygen (21%) and small amounts of argon (0.9%), carbon dioxide (0.03%), neon, helium, and other gases. It can also contain up to 4% water vapor. Terrestrial organisms have adapted to this mixture of gases. When oxygen concentration falls below 20% (at high altitudes or in poorly ventilated rooms, for example), we feel the unpleasant effects immediately.

Weather, Weather Patterns, and Climate

A look at the formations and movements of clouds in the sky tells us a great deal about local weather at any given moment. Average prevailing weather conditions at a specific location represent general weather patterns. Prevailing weather patterns that persist over long periods of time make up the climate of a particular region.

Adaptation – Creating Our Own Microclimates

Human beings depend on weather and climate more than any other living organisms. It is no coincidence that most ancient cultures had weather gods – Zeus in ancient Greece and Thor, the god of thunder in the Germanic world are just two examples. Yet unlike other living beings, humans possess the ability to protect themselves against extreme weather.

Humans have little difficulty coping with conditions in the warmer climate zones, as they adapt easily to high temperatures (due perhaps to their origin in the African savannahs). But to survive in the cold regions of the Earth, man had to gain command of fire, develop appropriate clothing, and learn to build tolerable microclimates – tents made of hides, igloos built with blocks of snow, wooden houses or urban housing developments.

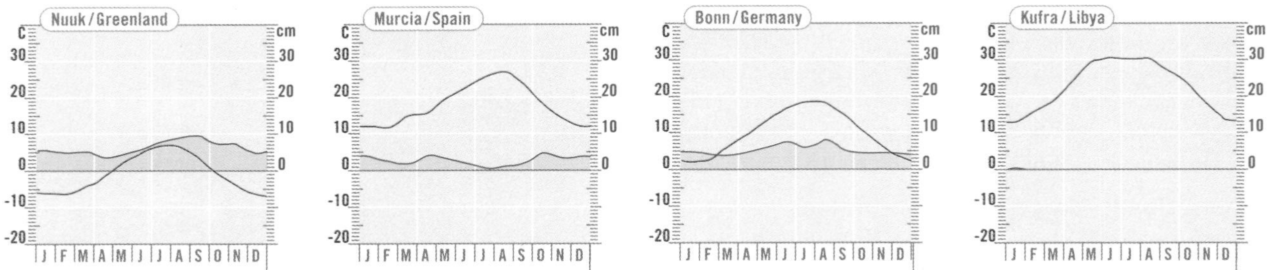

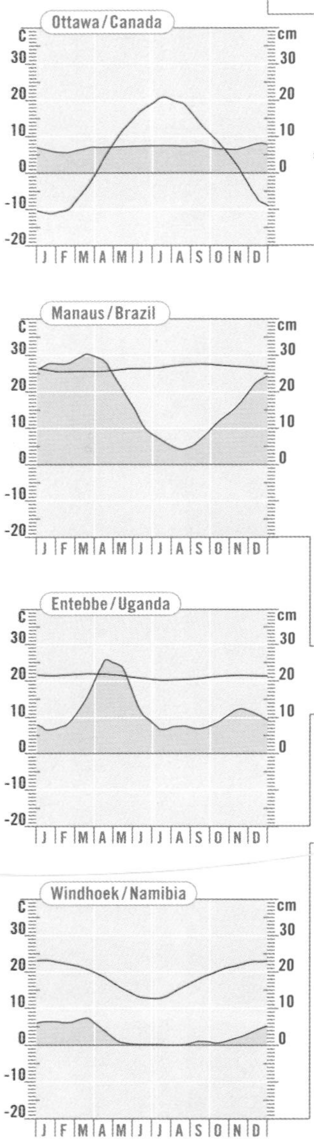

Local climate patterns can be illustrated in **climate graphs**. The graph for each station shows curves for average temperature (red) and precipitation (blue). A temperature curve that lies above the precipitation curve indicates arid conditions, while the reverse is an indicator of humidity.

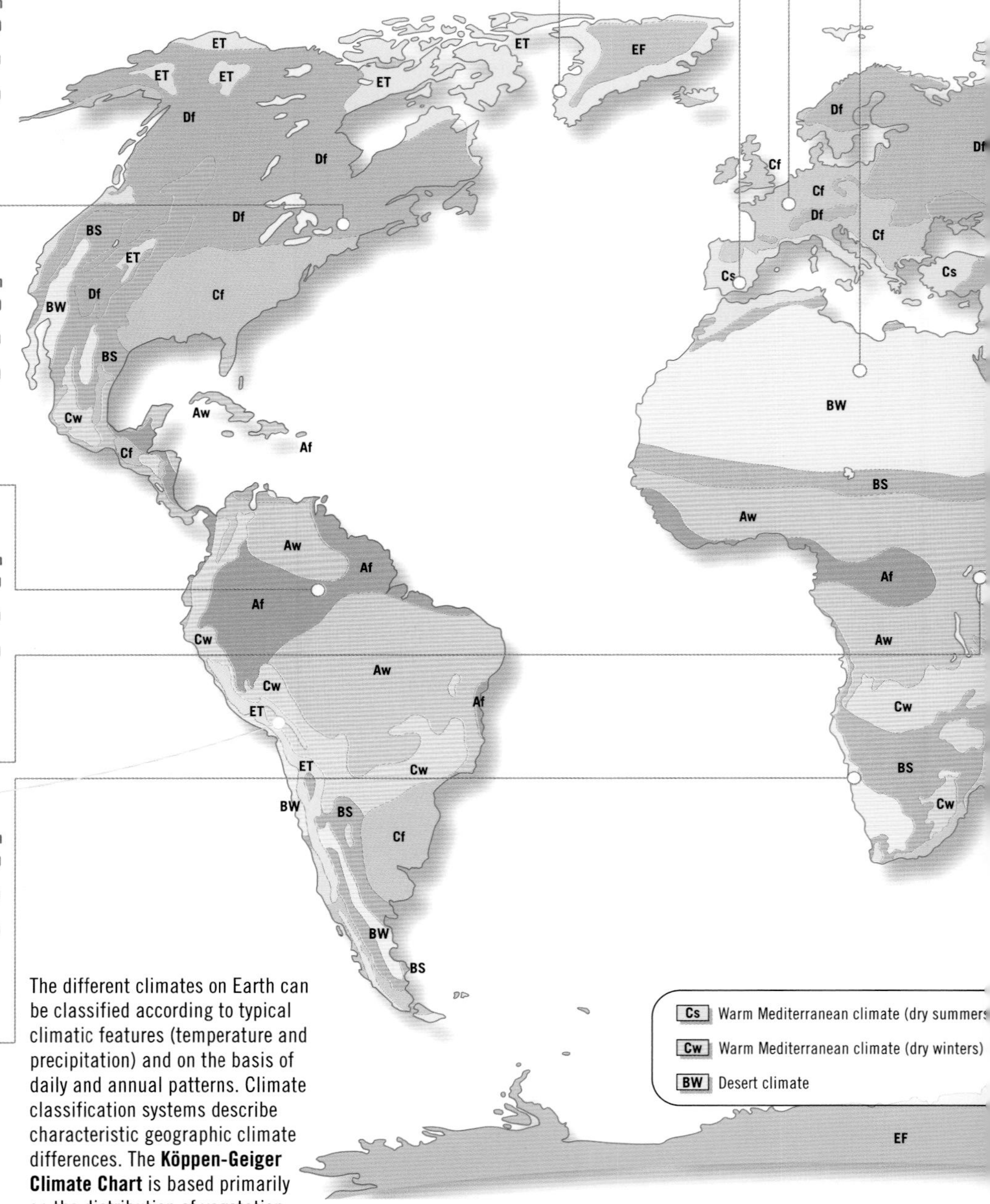

The different climates on Earth can be classified according to typical climatic features (temperature and precipitation) and on the basis of daily and annual patterns. Climate classification systems describe characteristic geographic climate differences. The **Köppen-Geiger Climate Chart** is based primarily on the distribution of vegetation. Since climate conditions are among the most important factors affecting plant growth, vegetation is a good indicator of climate at a given location.

A simplified version of Köppen-Geiger's classification scheme distinguishes among tropical wet-dry and arid climates (A), desert and steppe climates (B), humid temperate climates (C), cold wet-dry continental climates (D) and tundra and snow-and-ice climates (E).

Nuuk/Greenland

Murcia/Spain

Bonn/Germany

Kufra/Libya

Ottawa/Canada

Manaus/Brazil

Entebbe/Uganda

Windhoek/Namibia

Cs | Warm Mediterranean climate (dry summers)
Cw | Warm Mediterranean climate (dry winters)
BW | Desert climate

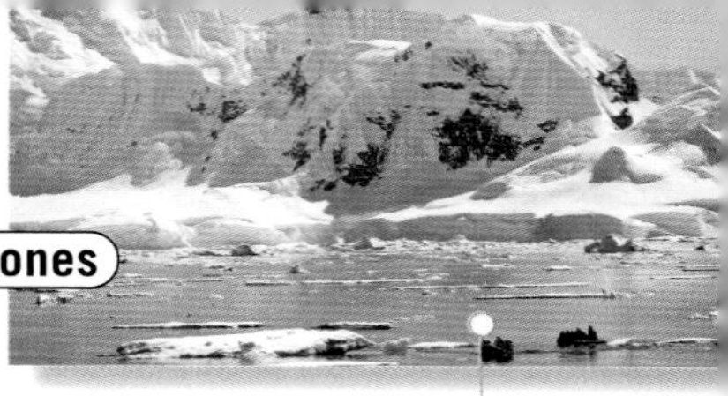

Alpine Elevation Zones

Mountain climates grow increasingly inhospitable at higher altitudes. Temperatures fall, and the air becomes moister and stormier. Vegetation is also distributed in belts at different elevations depending upon local climate conditions. The upper vegetation boundary borders on a zone of debris, snow, and ice near the summit (photo taken near Haines, Alaska). The ground is covered by snow for longer periods at higher elevations, thus shortening vegetation periods during which photosynthesis is possible. This basic heat deficit is offset somewhat by solar radiation, which is filtered only slightly by the thin atmosphere (as mountain climbers learn when they experience their first severe case of ultra-violet sunburn). Not only are air and ground temperatures lower at high altitudes, atmospheric pressure falls as well, reducing the supply of life-giving oxygen, carbon dioxide and water vapor in the air. The unfavorable conditions in the high mountain regions restrict species diversity. Summer temperatures are a crucial factor. The tree line is highest where summer solar radiation is most intense. Although plants in polar and alpine regions have much in common, they also exhibit major differences, as these climates are subject to different annual climatic shifts to which living organisms must adjust accordingly.

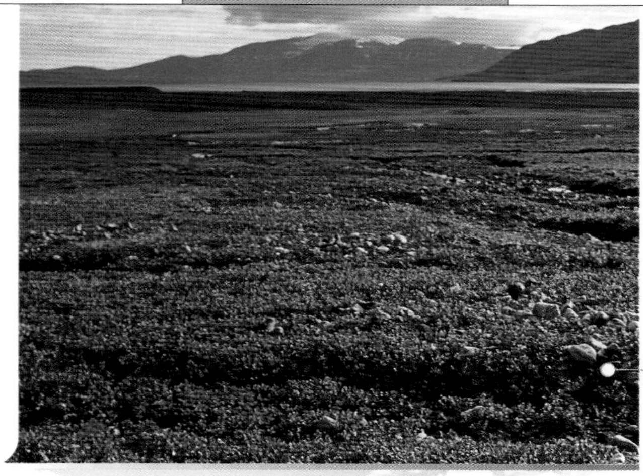

Virtually Lifeless Regions of Snow and Ice

The polar regions are not only cold, they are among the most arid areas on Earth. The capacity of air to retain water vapor diminishes as it grows colder. Thus the high Antarctic Plateau is drier than the Sahara. Human beings living here consume an average of six liters of water per day (photo: Paradise Bay, Antarctica).

Tundra Climate in the Arctic North

With average annual temperatures of about 5° F, only the uppermost layer of permafrost thaws for a few months during the summer, allowing for a vegetation period of between 30 and 90 days. The photo shows a summer carpet of alpine Veronica on Ellesmere Island.

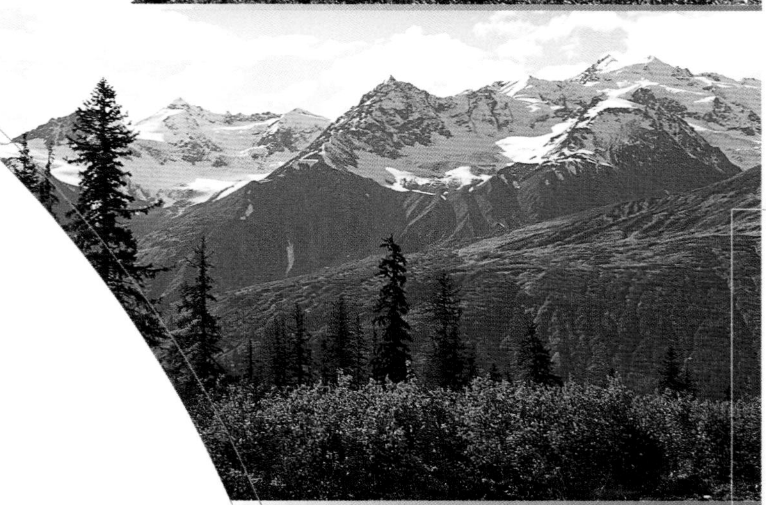

Hot, Arid Deserts with Little Vegetation

Most of the world's hot, arid zones (with less than 200 mm of precipitation per year) are found in the interiors of large continents (photo: Libyan Desert) or along the margins of cold ocean currents, where very little moisture is taken up by moving masses of air. Rainfall is also extremely sparse in trade wind belts with prevailing high pressure and on the leeward slopes of high mountain ranges.

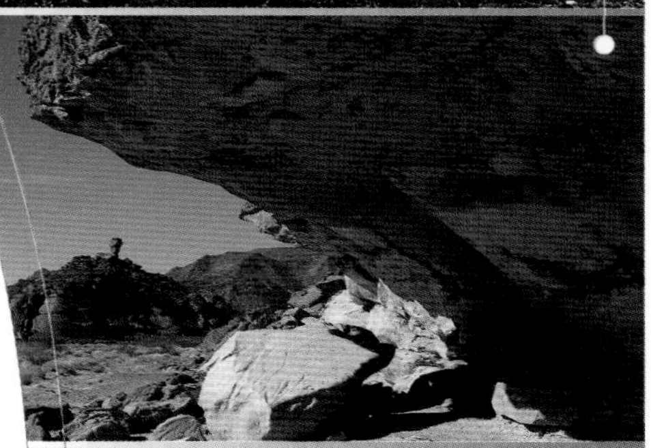

Hot Days in the Tropics

Daily temperature fluctuations in the tropics are greater than seasonal ones. It is always hot in the lowlands. Temperatures fall only slightly during rainy periods, although humidity rises to extreme levels, creating a paradise for lush plants growth (photo: eucalyptus forest in NE Australia). Tropical wet zones merge along their boundaries with semi-arid savannahs, where wet and dry periods alternate.

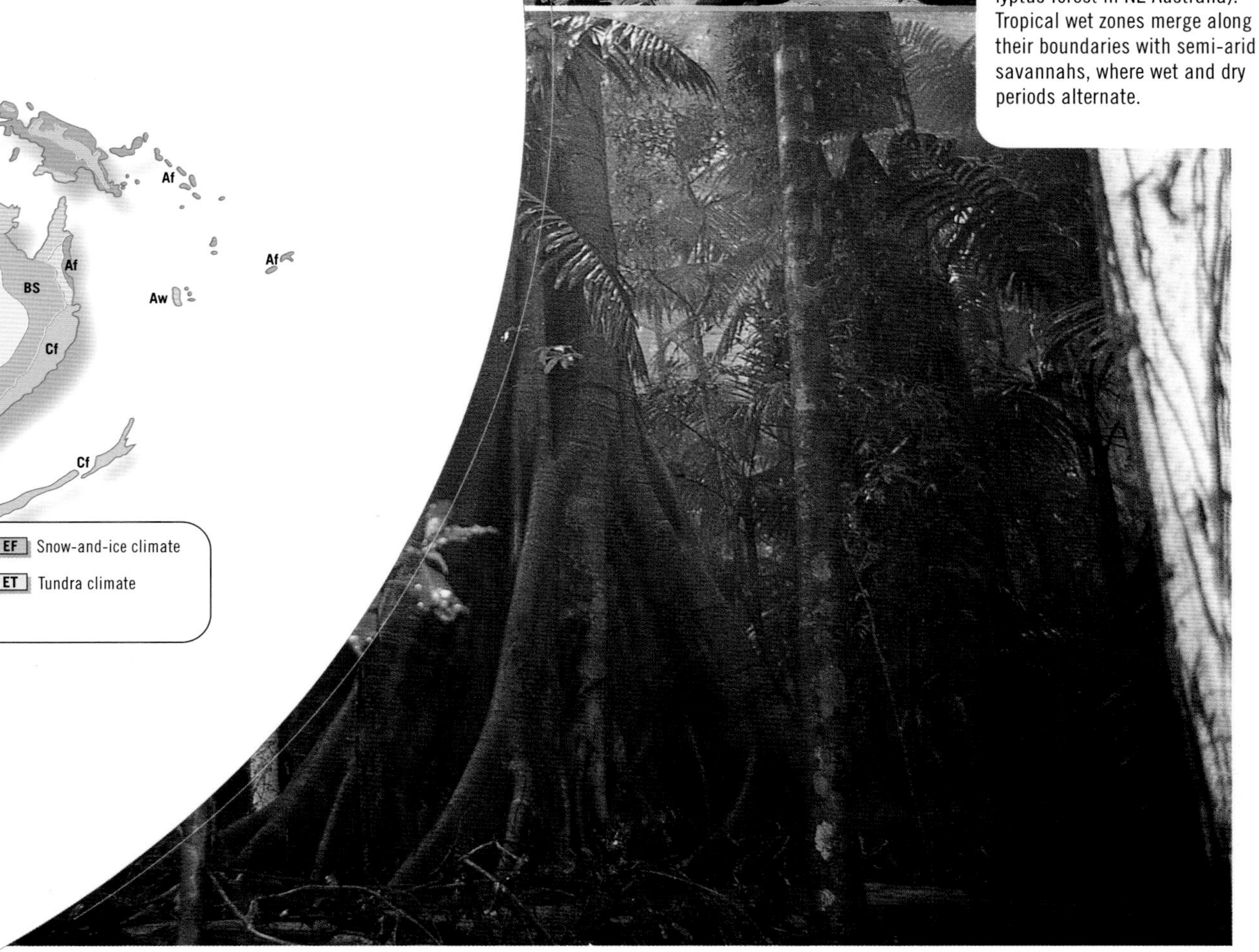

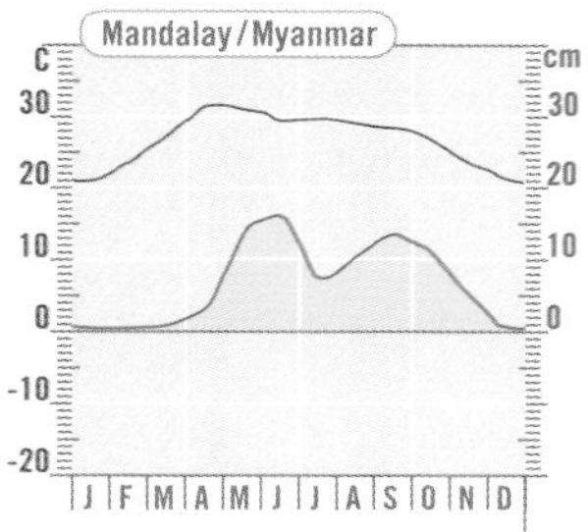

Mandalay / Myanmar

Harbin / China

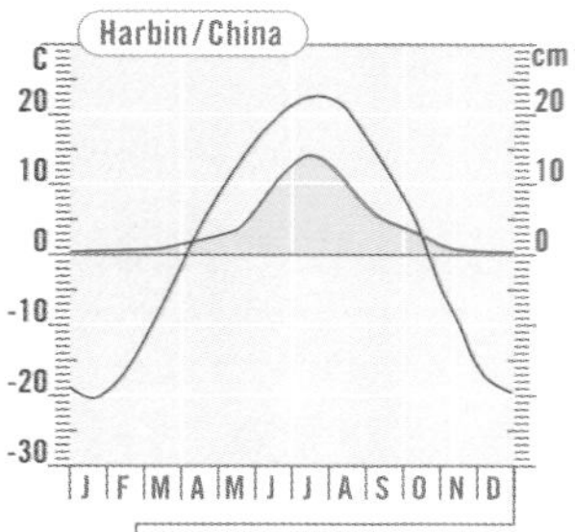

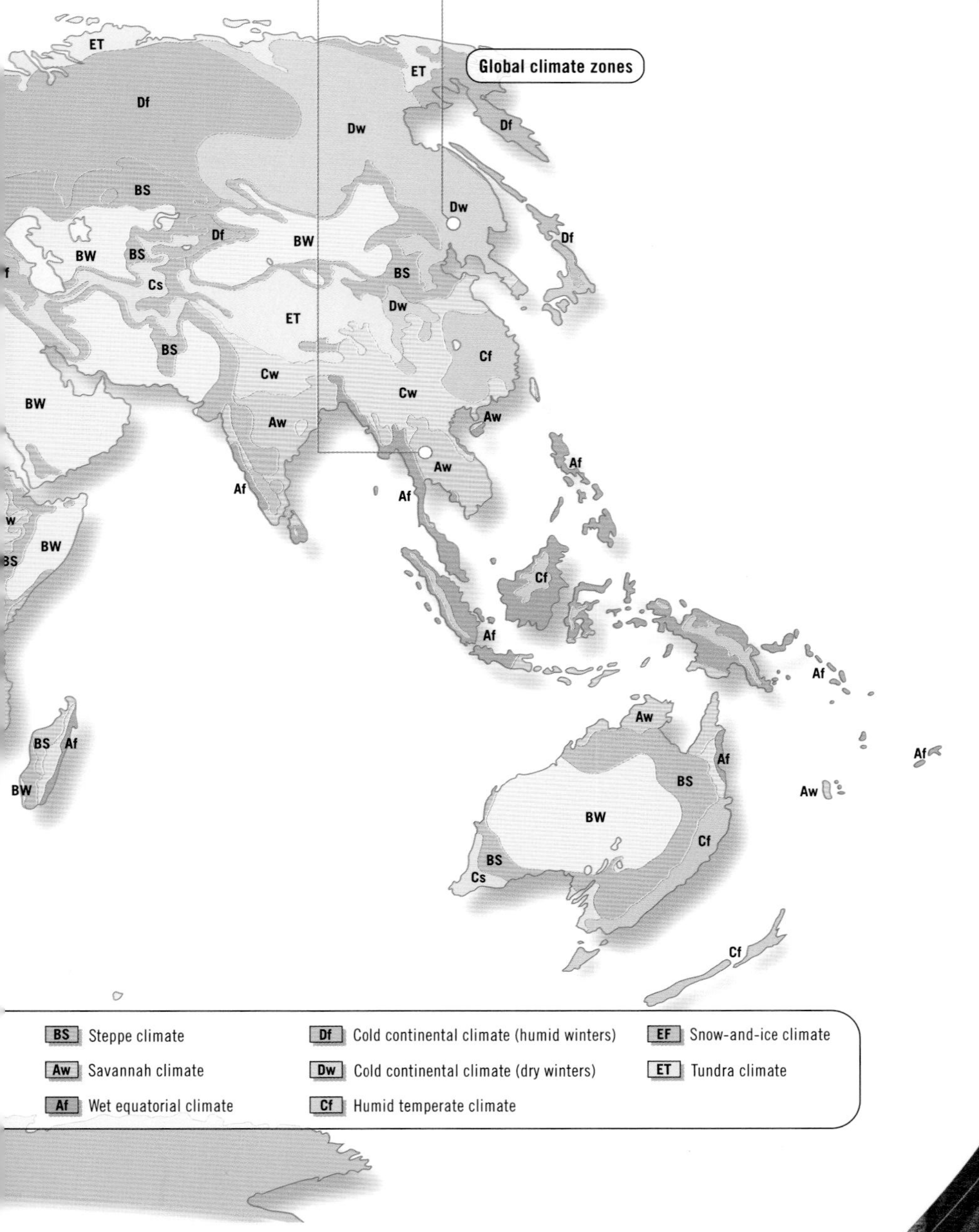

Global climate zones

BS Steppe climate	**Df** Cold continental climate (humid winters)	**EF** Snow-and-ice climate
Aw Savannah climate	**Dw** Cold continental climate (dry winters)	**ET** Tundra climate
Af Wet equatorial climate	**Cf** Humid temperate climate	

The Changing Global Climate

... and Mankind's Role in the Process

The history of the Earth's climate is one of changes, some gradual, others rapid and dramatic. Periods of relative stability and calm like the Holocene, which began some 10,000 years ago, are the exception rather than the rule. Yet it was precisely this climatic stability that allowed human civilization to develop. Today, the extent of human intervention in climatic processes is increasing. Are we merely a minor disruptive factor in the interplay of these powerful forces of nature, or does mankind pose a serious threat to the global climatic balance?

Variations in the Earth's Orbit

Some 20,000 years ago, at the peak of the last ice age, substantial portions of North America and northern Europe were covered by sheets of ice several thousand meters thick. This ice extended deep into the North American continent to the region now covered by the Great Lakes. The land south of the ice was arctic steppe, much like today's tundra regions. On the basis of bore samples taken from deposits thousands and even millions of years old, from layers of sediment on the ocean floor or from continental ice in Antarctica and Greenland, for example, it has been possible to reconstruct temperature patterns and many other characteristics of past climate. For at least two million years, the Earth's climate has been governed by relatively regular cycles. Ice ages lasting roughly 100,000 years have alternated with warm periods usually about 10,000 years long. These cycles are caused by subtle shifts in the Earth's orbit around the sun and in the inclination of the Earth's axis. These changes, known as Milankovitch variations, affect the seasonal and geographic distribution of solar radiation – although the total amount of radiation that reaches the Earth remains constant. It is not entirely clear why the Earth's climate reacts so dramatically to these changing radiation patterns. One crucial factor is apparently the intensity of summer sunlight over the continents of the northern hemisphere, for when the snows of the past winter do not melt completely, large sheets of ice begin to form. They reflect solar radiation and thus lead to further cooling. Our understanding of Milankovitch variations suggests that the Holocene is an unusually long warm phase, which would mean that a new ice age is not to be expected for several tens of thousands of years.

Abrupt Climatic Shifts

Scientists have learned only fairly recently that the last ice age was marked by a series of very abrupt and drastic changes in climate. In the course of these so-called Dansgaard-Oeschger Events (of which more than 20 are known to have occurred during the last ice age), average temperatures in the North Atlantic region rose rapidly – within only a few years – by between 11 and 14 °F. These unusually warm periods lasted several hundreds or thousands of years. Their effects were felt around the globe – even in the Antarctic. Evidently, sudden shifts in the course of marine currents played a significant role in these sudden climatic changes.

Even the Holocene, the current, relatively stable warm period, has not been free of climatic changes. Some 5,500 years ago, the Sahara was transformed from a landscape of swamps, lakes and areas of vegetation inhabited by many large animals and human beings into the desert we know today. In all likelihood, this process was set in motion by a shift in the Earth's orbit which triggered a fatal chain of events: a gradual decrease in rainfall resulting in diminished plant growth which led in turn to further reduction in precipitation.

The Radiation Budget

The Earth's temperature is regulated by a simple radiation budget. On average, the energy received from the sun is equal to the energy radiated by the Earth into space. If too much energy is received, temperatures rise and the Earth radiates more heat until balance is restored. If the Earth had no atmosphere, its average temperature would be somewhere near 0 °F. The atmosphere inhibits thermal radiation from the Earth's surface,

Frozen Lake, 1830
From the fifteenth to the eighteenth century, temperatures in Europe were 1.8 to 3.6 °F cooler than today. This cool period is known as the "Little Ice Age". Lake Constance froze over completely about every 20 years during that period but only once during the twentieth century (1963). Inhabitants of the alpine regions often experienced failed harvests and famine during the "Little Ice Age". This View of Frozen Lake Constance was painted by the local artist Nicolaus Hug in 1830.

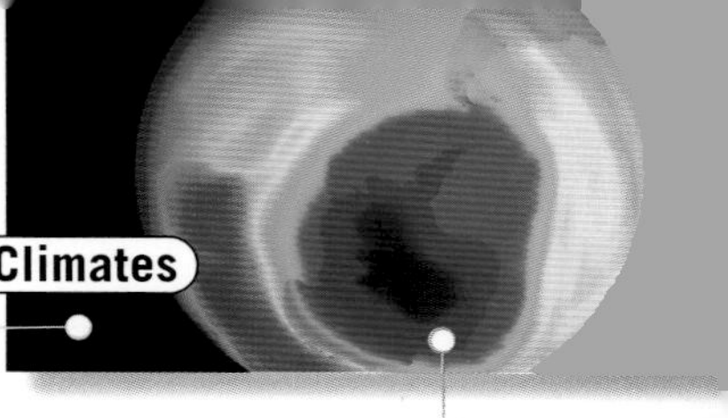

primarily due to the insulating effect of water vapor and carbon dioxide, the so-called greenhouse gases. Consequently, the Earth's surface warms until the radiation balance is restored at today's average temperature of about 59° F. It is this natural greenhouse effect that makes our planet inhabitable. Changes in the composition of the atmosphere or in the surface area of reflective ice and cloud masses can affect the radiation budget and thus raise or lower temperatures.

The Human Factor

Human impact on the global climate dates back to the Middle Ages, when people began clearing forests to make room for farmland, thereby increasing carbon dioxide levels in the atmosphere and creating lighter areas of surface that reflect more sunlight. But it was not until the Industrial Revolution in the first half of the nineteenth century that mankind developed the means to disrupt the delicate radiation balance significantly. The leading cause of these man-made changes is the use of fossil fuels – coal, petroleum, and natural gas. The fossil fuel we burn in a single year took roughly a million years to accumulate. The carbon contained in these materials oxidizes during combustion and is released into the air as carbon dioxide (CO_2). About half of it remains in the atmosphere, while the remainder is absorbed by the oceans and the biosphere. Since the beginning of the

Industrial Age, the carbon-dioxide concentration in the atmosphere has risen from 280 parts per million (ppm) to 360 ppm, and the greenhouse effect has grown stronger accordingly. Other gases released in the course of human activities intensify the greenhouse effect even further. Examples are methane and fluorocarbons, which are also responsible for the ozone hole.

Concentrations of greenhouse gases in the atmosphere have risen in recent years, raising average global temperatures by about 1.25° F – over both land and sea. Mountain glaciers are melting all over the world (total glacier volume in the Alps has already decreased by half). Artic Ice has become almost 40 per cent thinner over the past 30 years.

Using sophisticated pattern-recognition techniques, climatologists have attempted to determine the extent to which these trends are actually attributable to anthropogenic emissions and to identify other possible causes (such as fluctuations in the sun). Their findings indicate that, at the very least, the accelerated warming trend observed since 1970 is largely a man-made phenomenon.

Scientists warned as early as the late nineteenth century on the basis of simple computations that increasing concentrations of carbon dioxide in the atmosphere would lead to global warming. Today, the world's climate can be simulated with the aid of powerful computers, which make it possible both to reconstruct past climate patterns and to project scenarios for the future. If concentrations of greenhouse gases in the atmosphere continue to rise at the current pace, we can expect global temperatures to rise by between 2.7 and 9.9 degrees F over the next hundred years. Should this happen, the earth will be warmer than it has been at any time during the past 100,000 years. One consequence would be a rise in sea level of between 20 and 90 centimeters, which would persist for centuries even if the warming trend were halted. Warming would also lead to changes in precipitation patterns and thus possibly to drought and flooding, endangering many existing ecosystems in the process. Low-lying coastal regions would be threatened by flooding caused by storms, and several island nations in the Pacific would disappear beneath the sea.

In an effort to slow the process of global warming, most of the nations participating in the international conference in Kyōto, Japan in 1997 signed a Climate Treaty that obliges industrial nations to reduce emissions of greenhouse gases to five per cent below 1990 levels by the year 2012. The treaty is not yet in force, as only a few nations have ratified it, and it represents, at best, only a first small step toward effective climate protection.

The Radiation Budget and the Greenhouse Effect

Assuming a value of 100 % for the amount of solar radiation that actually effects the global radiation budget (342.5 Watts per square meter), only 45 % (on long-term, global average) actually reaches the Earth's surface. The remainder is absorbed or scattered. The total reflective capacity of the earth (including the atmosphere and clouds) is referred to as the Earth's albedo, and amounts to 30 % on a yearly average. The effective heat radiated by the Earth's surface is 18 %. This equates to the difference between 114 % – the value which would be expected if the Earth had no atmosphere – and 96 % – for radiation reflected back by the atmosphere (the greenhouse effect). The difference between incoming solar radiation and outgoing terrestrial radiation (27 %) at the surface is offset by heat currents.

Threatening Hole

In 1985, British researchers discovered a hole in the ozone layer of the upper atmosphere – our shield against dangerous cosmic radiation. One of the causes identified was the release of industrially produced fluorocarbons, such as those used in spray cans, into the atmosphere. The Montreal Protocol of 1987 called for a global ban on these gases, to be achieved in a step-by-step process. They are hardly used at all today, and scientists now predict that the ozone hole will gradually close over the next several decades. It will probably take more than 100 years to restore the ozone layer completely, however.

Global warming trends, 1976–1999

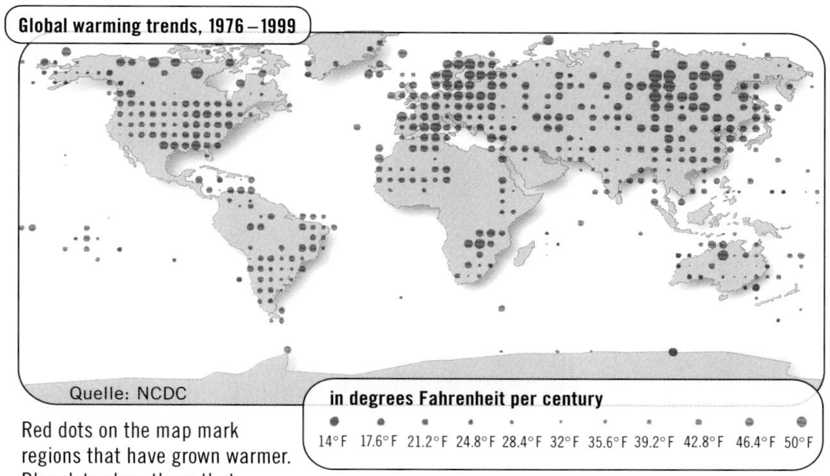

Quelle: NCDC

in degrees Fahrenheit per century

14°F 17.6°F 21.2°F 24.8°F 28.4°F 32°F 35.6°F 39.2°F 42.8°F 46.4°F 50°F

Red dots on the map mark regions that have grown warmer. Blue dots show those that have cooled. Insufficient data is available for the remaining areas.

budget and greenhouse effect

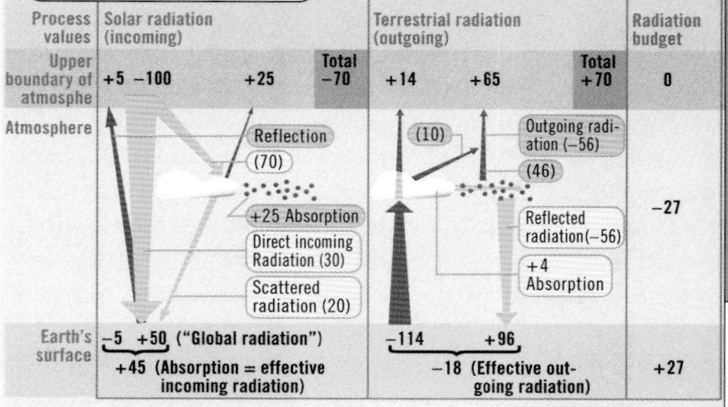

Process values	Solar radiation (incoming)			Terrestrial radiation (outgoing)			Radiation budget
Upper boundary of atmosphere	+5 −100	+25	Total −70	+14	+65	Total +70	0
Atmosphere	Reflection (70)	+25 Absorption	Direct incoming Radiation (30)	(10)	Outgoing radiation (−56) (46)	Reflected radiation (−56) +4 Absorption	−27
	Scattered radiation (20)						
Earth's surface	−5 +50 ("Global radiation") +45 (Absorption = effective incoming radiation)			−114 +96 −18 (Effective outgoing radiation)			+27

CO_2 concentration in atmosphere

Direct measurements

Computations from ice bore samples

Compensation curve   Individual readings

Year: 800 1000 1000 1400 1600 1800 2000

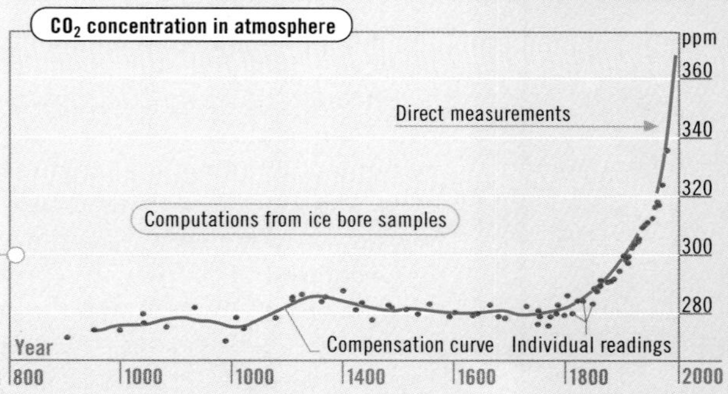

ppm: 360 340 320 300 280

100,000-year temperature curve

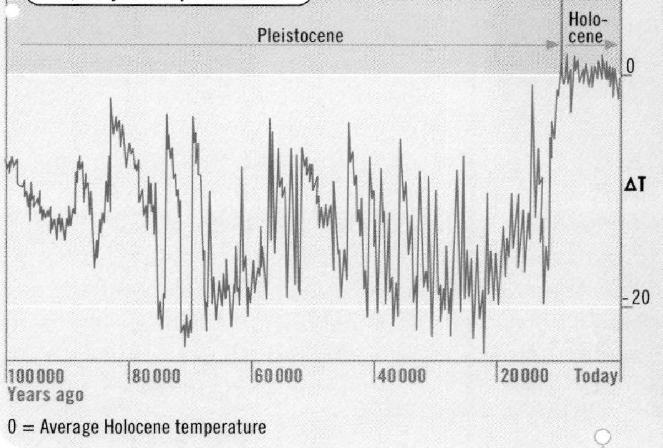

Holocene

Pleistocene

0

ΔT

−20

Years ago: 100 000 80 000 60 000 40 000 20 000 Today

0 = Average Holocene temperature

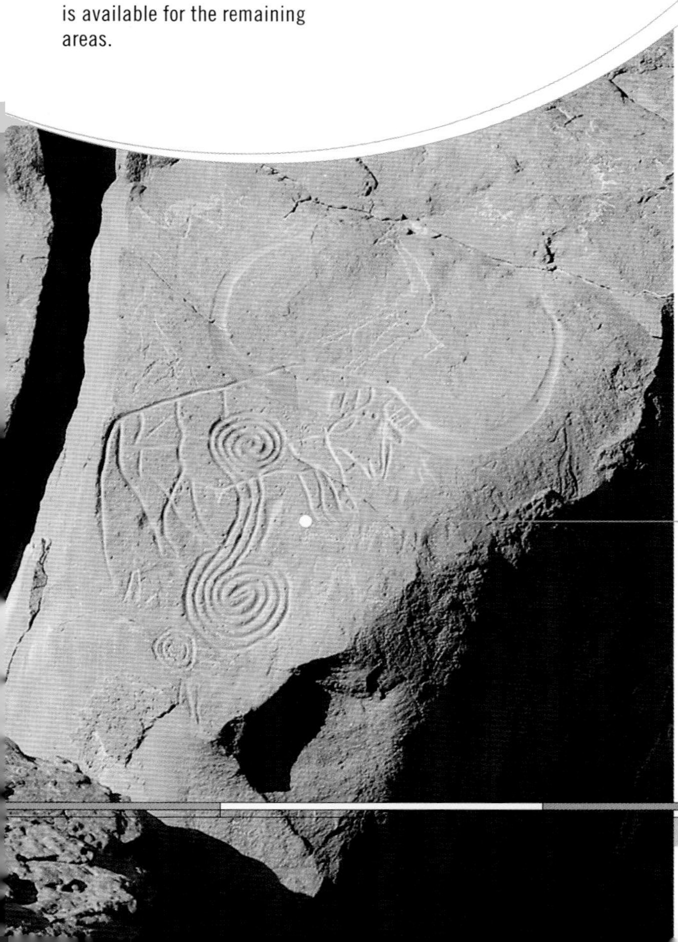

Saharan Rock Painting

Until about 6,000 years ago, the Sahara was much greener than it is today. A large number of rock drawings offer evidence of a much moister climate. The buffalo Homoioceras antiquus (Oued Djerat, Tassili n'Ajjer, Algeria) became extinct during the early Holocene.

Alarming Rise

Analyses of air bubbles in Antarctic ice and measurements taken at Mauna Loa (Hawaii) since 1957 tell us a great deal about carbon-dioxide concentration in the atmosphere: about 280 ppm during warm periods like the Holocene, 200 ppm during the ice ages, and more than 360 ppm today, thanks to our emissions.

Climate Curves for the Last 100,000 Years from Greenland Ice

This climate curve from Greenland shows the consistently warm climate of the past 10,000 years, the Holocene period. During the preceding 100,000 ice-age years, the climate was not only much colder but also subject to sudden fluctuations.

Vegetation – The Earth's Botanical Cloak

Plant and Human Life – A Reassessment

According to the Book of Genesis, God created plants on the third day, calling upon the Earth to "bring forth grass, the herb yielding seed ... and the tree yielding fruit ... and God saw that it was good." (Genesis 1:11). Mankind arrived on the scene soon afterward. By current reckoning, human beings have since destroyed about 30 % of the original 62 million square kilometers of forest on Earth, transformed much of our planet's vast grasslands into arid wastelands (desertification) through overcultivation, and altered the character of natural vegetation in many regions of the world. We have intervened in natural patterns of growth and distribution, manipulated genetic makeup through breeding experiments, and replaced local flora with secondary growth over wide areas. Yet despite this massive human intervention in the plant kingdom, more than 99 % of the Earth's biomass – about 1.8 trillion tons of organic material (300 tons for every living human being) – is vegetable matter.

The Foundation of Human and Animal Life

In his famous "Canticle of the Sun," Saint Francis of Assisi spoke of "... Earth, our Mother, who feeds us in her sovereignty and produces various fruits and colored flowers and herbs." The words of Saint Francis reflect an uncomplicated view of nature and an implicit recognition of the close and vital cosmic relationship between all living organisms (the biosphere) and the Earth's inorganic crust (the lithosphere), a mystery that was not solved by modern biological science until many years later. Biologists, ecologists and biochemists agree that animal, and thus of course human life could not exist in its present form without the Earth's botanical cloak.

Plants as Chemical Factories and Nutrient Pumps

The leaves of plants contain chlorophyll (the pigment that makes them green), which they use to convert water taken up by their roots and carbon dioxide (CO_2) absorbed from the air into glucose (sugar) with the aid of light (solar energy) captured on their surfaces in a complicated process known as photosynthesis. Through their roots, which in some plants (wheat, for example) form networks of microscopically fine fibrous tendrils with combined lengths of up to several hundred kilometers, they absorb a wide variety of elements essential to all life on Earth from the soil. These they process along with the glucose into organic matter, referred to collectively as biomass (the dry weight of organic matter).

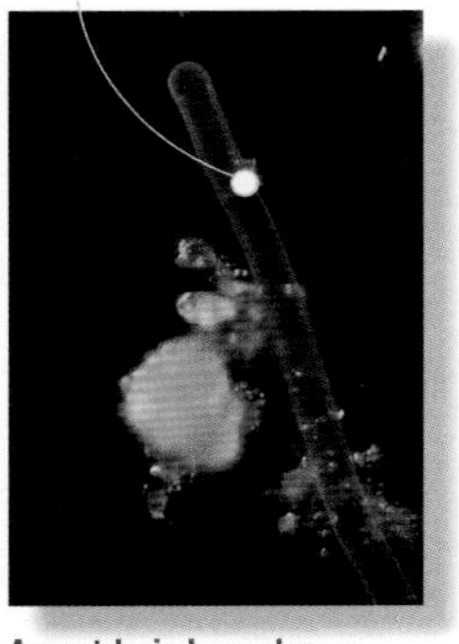

A root hair launches a biochemical attack on a calcite mineral: the first stage in the transition from mineral to chemical substance.

Through this process, a number of elements essential to many physiological processes, such as iron, phosphorus, calcium, magnesium, nitrogen, and sulfur, are incorporated into biomass and passed along through the food chain to herbivorous animal organisms and ultimately to carnivores (including humans as well, regardless of whether they actually eat meat or not, since the consumption of animal protein is virtually unavoidable for modern consumers).

In this way, the massive global nutrient pump of natural vegetation extracts more than two cubic kilometers per year – roughly six billion tons – of minerals and substances of all kinds from the Earth's crust and makes them available as sustenance to animals and human beings (approximately one ton for every living human being on Earth).

Soil-Building Vegetation

Vegetable biomass consumed by animal organisms is returned to the eternal mineral cycle as feces or in the bodies of dead organisms themselves. Unconsumed biomass is also remineralized when humus is formed through the decomposition of fallen leaves and dead plants. Mineral replacement resulting from biochemical and physical root activity, on the one hand, and the accumulation of biomass, on the other, are important soil-building processes which work within an ecological network in collaboration with such non-biological factors as the warmth and moisture of vegetation in a specific region.

Trees – Unsung "Environmental Helpers"

Trees are the largest forms of plant life. A deciduous tree between 15 and 20 meters high generates three million liters of oxygen annually (four times as much as a single human being needs in a year) through the process of photosynthesis. In one year, the same tree also filters as much as 7,000 kg of dust from the air with its foliage and extracts up to 7,000 liters of water from the soil through its root system, thus contributing significantly to the prevention of soil erosion – a problem that can assume catastrophic proportions in deforested areas. For every human being on Earth today, there are about 500 trees at work providing these important environmental services.

How Do the Little Flowers Grow, and How Do Plants Give Us Food?

The preceding description shows how very important the plant kingdom is. In light of the crucial role plants play in our lives, it is shocking to realize how little we know about them. Most people in the industrialized countries of the world can name at least 20 different makes of car but not nearly as many kinds of plants! Yet botanists have now identified more than 360,000 varieties, of which about 180,000 are blossoming plants.

It is not the species of so-called "higher plants" classified into families of trees, shrubs, flowers, and grasses that are so difficult to identify with certainty. The real difficulty and suspense begins with the attempt to establish clear scientific distinctions among the varieties of "lower plant organisms" or microflora: fungi, the various species of algae, lichens as symbiotic communities of fungi and algae, and even the types of bacteria that are classified as forms of plant life – the "little beasties" discovered and described by Antonie van Leewenhoek (1632–1723) with the aid of his home-made microscope.

Although between 10,000 and 50,000 edible varieties of plants are available for human consumption, only about 150 to 200 species (between 0.3 and 2 %) are actually used for nutritional purposes. Over 75 % of all energy consumed by human beings in the form of vegetable matter comes from only about ten crop plants (between 0.002 and 0.1 % of all edible species of plants).

The Earth's Coat of Brightly Colored Stripes

Plants have no means of locomotion, and thus the characteristics they exhibit as indicator plants at the present stage of evolutionary development are always evidence of their adaptation to prevailing conditions in their local environments (known as habitat conditions). These include such features as water-retention organs (in cactuses or agaves in arid regions), shallow, broad root systems (like those of the birch tree) in permafrost regions where soil thaws only for a few months during the summer, or a thick coat of hair as protection against evaporation in alpine regions (edelweiss is an example). Thus we understand why belts of vegetation corresponding generally to the Earth's climatic zones, communities of plants known by botanists as vegetation zones, cover the Earth like a brightly-colored striped coat. And the same explanation applies to the typical vegetation patterns in mountainous regions that reflect the increasing lack of heat at progressively higher elevations, a phenomenon described with specific reference to South America by Alexander von Humboldt as early as the late eighteenth century.

(2) Tundra Vegetation

With average annual temperatures normally below 5° F, permafrost soil thaws only briefly to a depth of a few centimeters in the summer. With a growth period of 30 – 90 days, this type of vegetation, which forms a continuous belt only in the northern hemisphere, is characterized by an extraordinary abundance of lichens (in the Arctic north) and treeless, summer-green, flower-covered meadows (in the subpolar south).

(11) Alpine Vegetation

The most impressive alpine vegetation is found in the Andes (see photographs). Here the hierarchy of vegetation levels, from the tropical rain forest to the Paramo to the high tropical grasslands (moist puna) and the frost-prone, high, cold puna at elevations of about 5,000 m, where grass is sparse but lichens are plentiful, reflect the effects of diminishing warmth at progressively higher elevations.

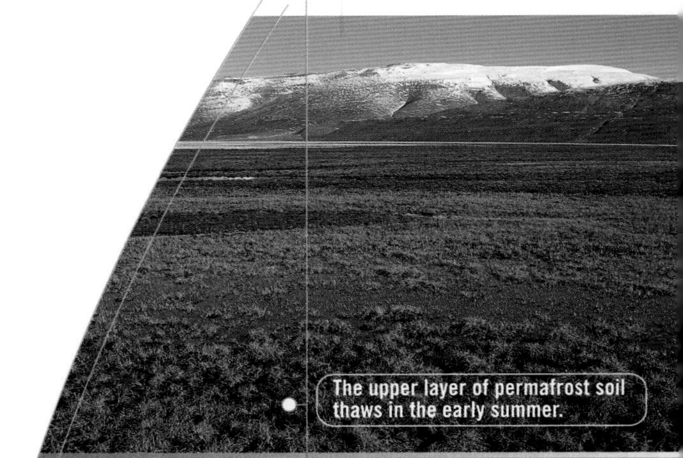

The upper layer of permafrost soil thaws in the early summer.

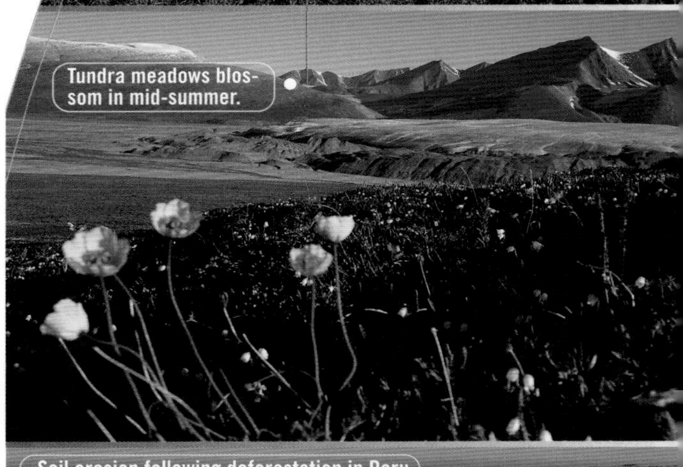

Tundra meadows blossom in mid-summer.

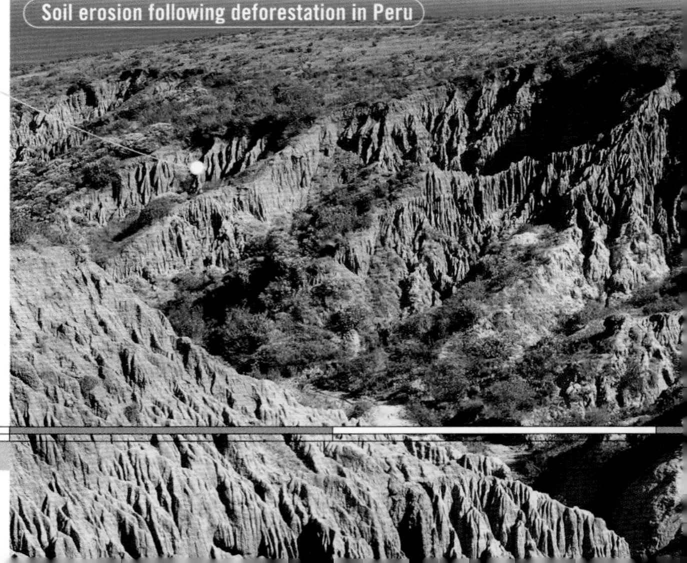

Soil erosion following deforestation in Peru

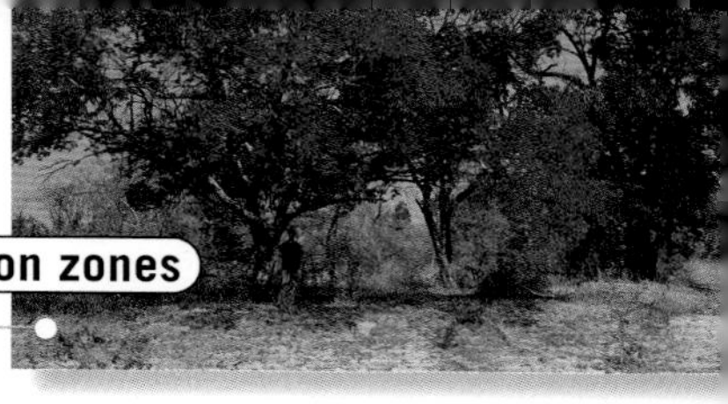

(5) Tropical deciduous forest

Despite annual precipitation often exceeding 1,000 mm, these forests of long-trunked trees that turn fully green only near their tops during the summer rainy season have a relatively short growth period, as water is scarce during the rest of the year (photo: Caprivi, Namibia). The monsoon forests of southern and Southeast Asia represent a special form of this class of vegetation.

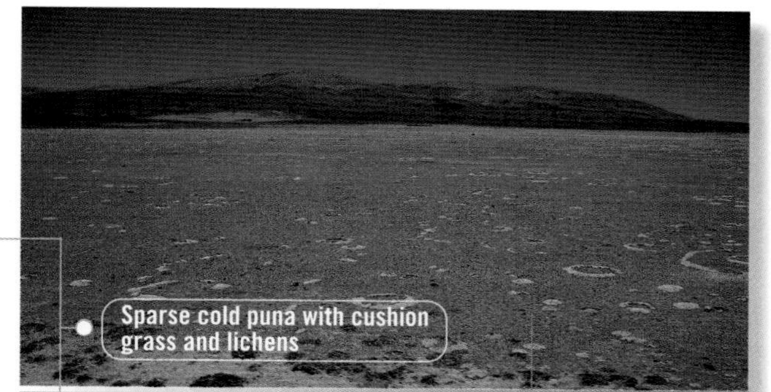

Sparse cold puna with cushion grass and lichens

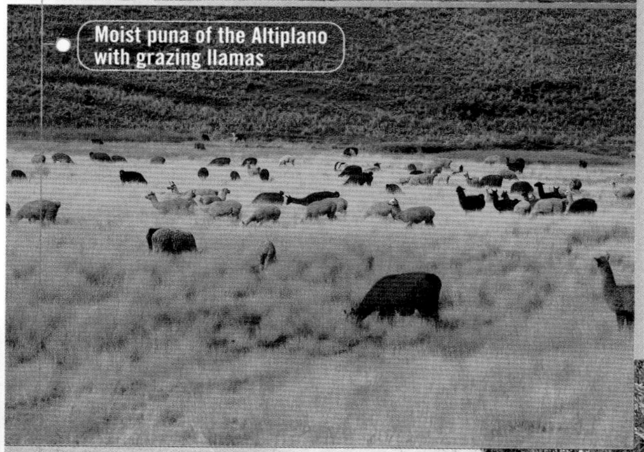

Moist puna of the Altiplano with grazing llamas

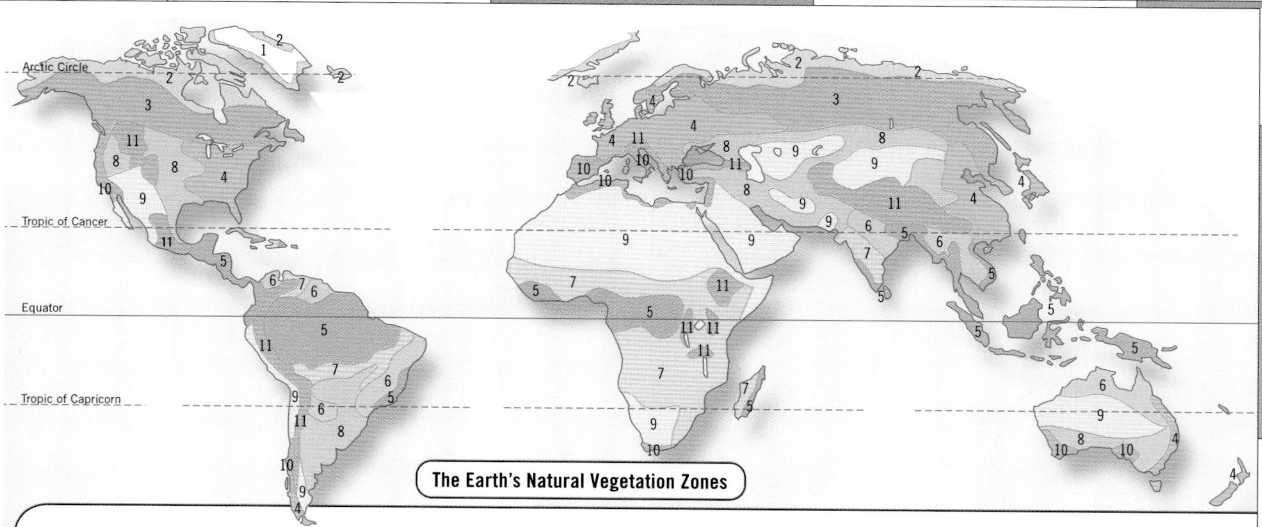

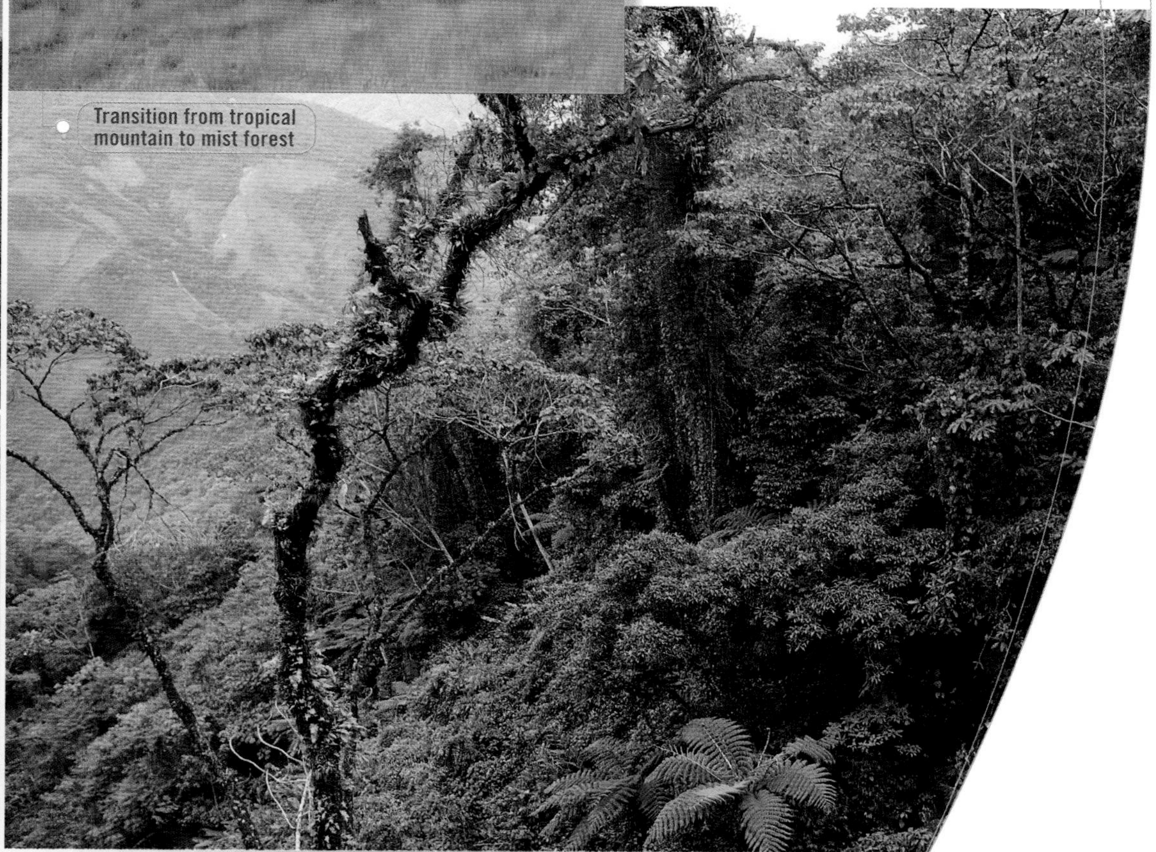

Transition from tropical mountain to mist forest

The Earth's Natural Vegetation Zones

1	Permanent ice cover	7	Tropical savanna and grassland
2	Polar barrens and Tundra	8	Subtropical grassland and steppe
3	Boreal forest, Taiga	9	Desert and semi-arid desert
4	Temperate forest and cultivated land	10	Mediterranean vegetation, sclerophyllous plants
5	Tropical rain forest	11	Alpine vegetation
6	Tropical deciduous forest		

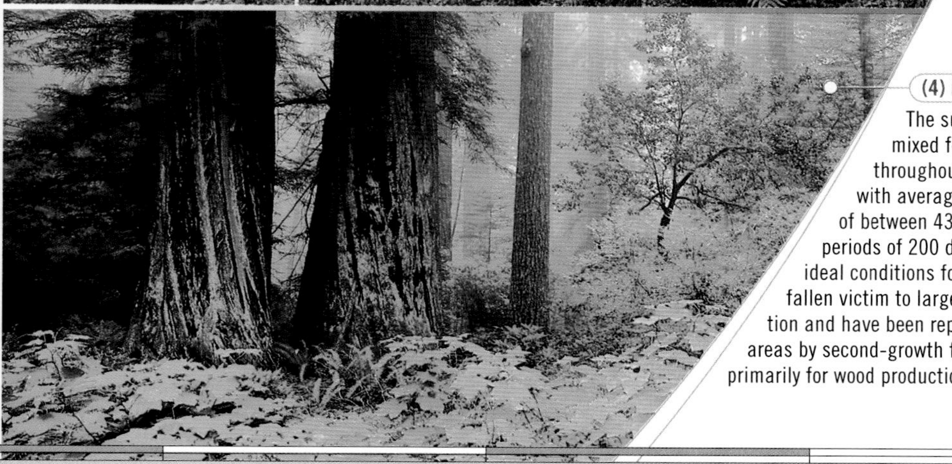

(4) Forests of the Temperate Zone

The summer-green deciduous and mixed forests that once prevailed throughout this climate zone, which with average annual temperatures of between 43 and 54° F and growth periods of 200 days or longer offers ideal conditions for agriculture, have fallen victim to large-scale deforestation and have been replaced in isolated areas by second-growth forests used primarily for wood production.

(3) Taiga – the Northern Continental Vegetation Belt

Average annual temperatures in these regions covered by boreal evergreen and summer-green coniferous forests comprising only a few species, which span the globe only in the permafrost regions of the northern hemisphere, range near 32° F. Covering some 20 million square km (about 13 % of the Earth's dry land), they represent the world's largest forest formation.

(5) Tropical Rain Forest

In the tropics, where rain falls the year round and annual precipitation often exceeds 2,000 mm, temperatures determine the character of forests. Multi-tiered, evergreen equatorial rain forest – a habitat for a wide range of species – is predominant in low-lying areas with mean annual temperatures of 72–82° F. Mountain forests with fewer species are prevalent at elevations over 1,000 m and average temperatures of 57–72° F. Mist forests characterized by beard lichens, epiphytes, and tree ferns predominate only at elevations of over 2,000 m and at average temperatures of only 40–57° F. Together, these three forest types occupy a total area of about 12.5 million square km (approximately 8 % of the dry land on Earth). They are seriously endangered, particularly at lower elevations, by logging operations and large-scale deforestation. The most common natural form of vegetation along the tropical coasts are mangrove forests, although they have now been almost totally destroyed.

(7) Savannas – Maximum Landscape Diversity

Savannas are generally thought of as expansive tropical grasslands (like the Serengeti). Actually, they display a number of different faces. Although grass is the dominant ground cover in all savanna landscapes, the spectrum of plant formations encompasses dry, thorny shrub vegetation, flourishing bush growth, densely wooded areas, and even true forests (such as the gallery forests along riverbanks or the Mopane and Miombo woodlands of southern Africa). Common to all types of savannas are summer rainy seasons and the absence of a thermal winter.

(8) Steppes – Non-Tropical Grasslands Under the Plow

Where grasslands once stretched to the horizon in climates with dry summers and often extremely cold winters (on the North American prairies or the black-earth regions of southern Russia), human beings have replaced the natural vegetation of the dry, short-grass and moister, long-grass steppes with vast grain fields. In many places, such industrial-scale farming operations have contributed to soil deterioration by clearing the way for wind and water erosion.

(9) Desert Vegetation

Vegetation in deserts and semi-arid regions (where climates are only slightly more favorable), is ideally adapted to the extreme conditions of their environments (scarcity of water, heat, nocturnal or winter frost, sand storms, etc.). Higher forms of plant life have developed appropriate survival tools: water-retaining organs, leaf coverings that inhibit evaporation, suspension of metabolic activity during extremely dry periods ("latent life") or disproportionately large (relative to above-ground biomass) underground plant organs (primarily roots). Microflora – ordinarily overlooked by human beings – is represented in abundance on the surface in the form of algae, fungi, and blankets of lichens that can even be seen in satellite images.

(10) Mediterranean Vegetation

The original natural vegetation of the Mediterranean regions, which are classified as subtropical climate zones with wet winters, was evergreen sclerophyllous forest (holm oak forests in the actual Mediterranean region). Extreme overuse by humans has caused much of this original vegetation to be replaced by meager second-growth formations such as broad-leaved shrubs and small trees (matorral, chaparral or maquis) and even poorer scrubland vegetation (garrigue).

Biodiversity – Geodiversity – Ecodiversity

Species Diversity – the Earth's Living Treasure

Why is the survival of every species so important? What prompted the authors of the Old Testament to emphasize species diversity in the story of Noah, whom God commanded to bring "of every living thing of all flesh, two of every sort . . . into the ark . . . to keep them alive?" Biological diversity is an essential aspect of life on earth. Research on biological diversity will play an important role in the future of mankind as a basis for advances in the fields of nutrition, medical care, and even tourism.

The Number of Species – an Unsolved Puzzle

The study of biodiversity involves identification and analysis of the structural diversity of communities of living organisms. The process of identifying all species of plants and animals is far from complete. About 1.7 million species have been identified thus far, yet we can only speculate as to the actual number of species on earth, drawing conclusions based on analogy. Scientists assume the existence of some 20 million species. New ones are being discovered every day.

Geodiversity – A New Concept

The term "geodiversity" refers to the wide range of geographic factors and combinations of influences that have emerged in the course of the Earth's history. It is the product of interaction between the atmosphere, the lithosphere, the pedosphere (dry land) and the hydrosphere. It determines local conditions in the biosphere (flora and fauna) and the anthroposphere (human beings). Climate and its component elements (solar radiation, temperature, precipitation, humidity, evaporation, wind) are the most important determinants of species distribution in different regions of the world. Patterns of distribution are also shaped by topography, the configuration of land masses, their position with respect to the oceans of the world, and ocean surface temperatures. Developments in the Earth's history, including the evolution of living species, have contributed significantly to present patterns of species diversity.

One important factor is floral migration, a process that has taken place in the recent geological past (mostly during periods of transition between ice ages and warm periods) along mountain ranges aligned with meridians. Thus Antarctic floras have long since moved into the tropics along the Andes in South America. Nontropical plant species have invaded the tropical regions along routes parallel to the mountain chains of Southeast Asia, enriching local flora significantly. Mountain ranges oriented along lines of latitude (the Alps, the Pyreneans, and the Himalayas) have blocked these migrations.

Diversity – a Regional View

The limited species diversity of subpolar tundra and boreal coniferous forest regions is attributable to unfavorable geographic conditions (freezing temperatures, long periods of snow cover, short annual growth periods). Diversity is similarly restricted in tropical and subtropical deserts, where high levels of solar radiation and a consistently negative radiation balance result in wide fluctuations in daily and seasonal temperatures and extreme aridity, creating a hostile living environment for flora and fauna, not to mention Homo sapiens. In the Sahara, mountain ranges (Hoggar, Tibesti, Aïr) rise up from surroundings virtually devoid of vegetation as climatically and geographically favorable zones for plant growth. Inland deserts (Atacama, Libyan Desert, Tanezrouft, Ténéré, Rub al-Chali), which receive only ephemeral precipitation at very irregular intervals, exhibit an absolute minimum of diversity. The same can be said of the subpolar regions around the Antarctic and Greenland ice sheets and the Tibetan Plateau, with its cold desert.

Generally speaking, species diversity increases from the poles to the Equator. Maximum diversity – more than 5,000 species per 10,000 square km – is found in the tropical rain and mountain forests of South America, Africa, Asia, and the Indo-Malaysian Archipelago, where tropical temperatures prevail year round and precipitation is heavy and non-seasonal. In tropical inland areas, a high degree of biodiversity is possible only in combination with maximum geodiversity. This applies in particular to tropical mountain regions where, within very small areas, topographic variations (elevation, exposure, slope steepness), mountain/valley winds, an enormous evaporation potential and high levels of latent evaporation heat, differing degrees of condensation and fog at mountain forest roofs (mist and cloud forests) favor plant diversity (Choco region in Costa Rica, eastern and western roofs of the Andes in Ecuador and

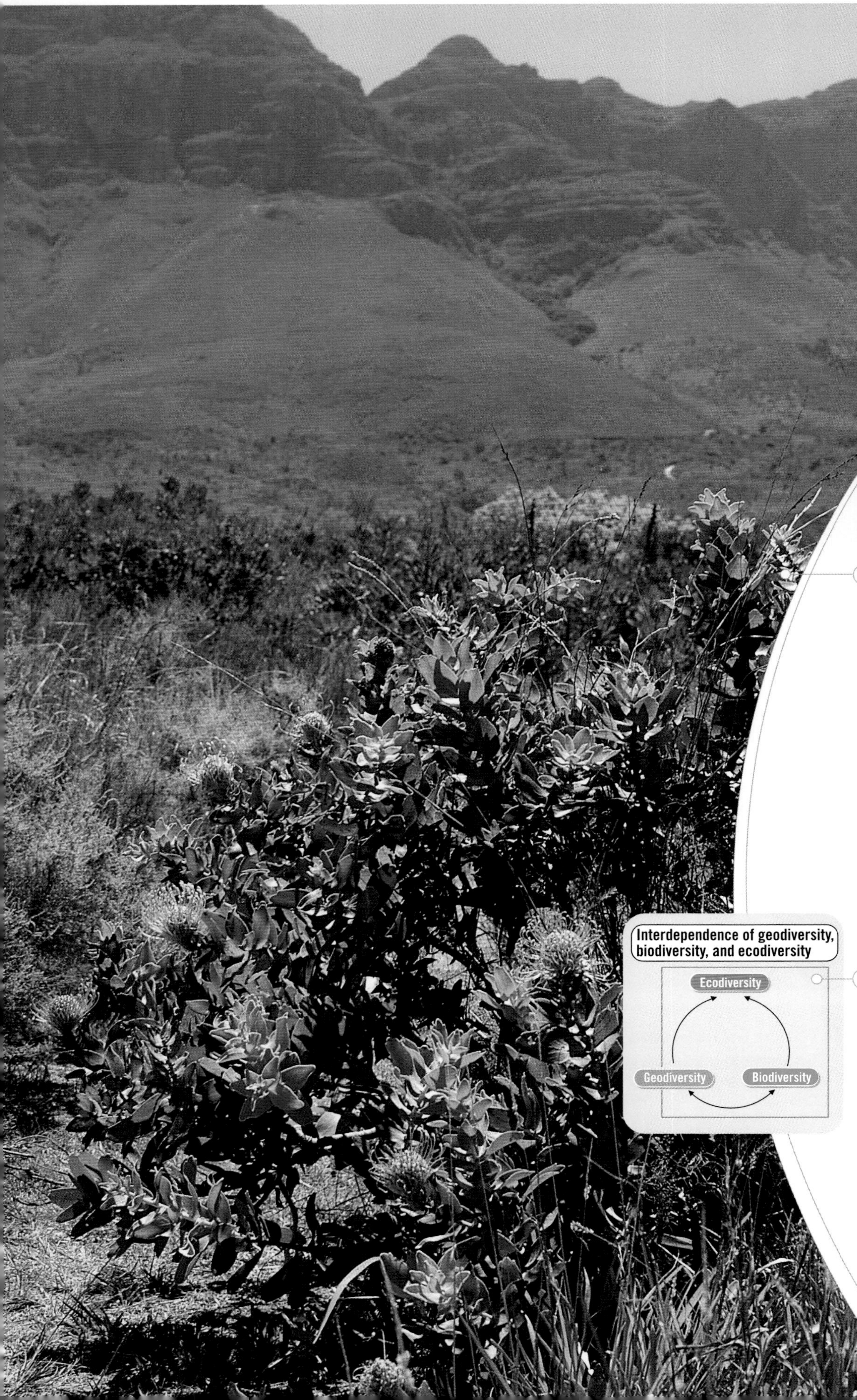

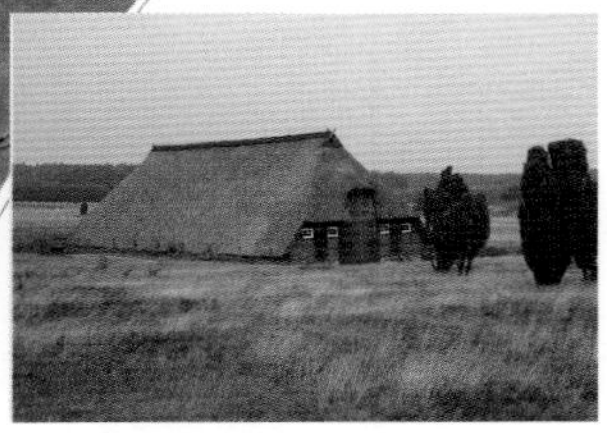

Unique Fynbos

The Cape Floral Kingdom of South Africa is home to one of the most diverse plant communities on Earth. Known as the fynbos vegetation belt, it has 8,600 plant species, 73% of which are found nowhere else on Earth. About the size of the Lüneburger Heide in Germany (photo above), it contains ten times as many plant species. Factors contributing this unusual degree of diversity include continual, relatively rapid climatic oscillations and the absence of major long-term climatic changes during the earlier geological epochs, both of which have exerted a favorable influence on evolutionary processes in this, the smallest phytogeographic kingdom on earth.

Interdependence of geodiversity, biodiversity, and ecodiversity

Ecodiversity

Geodiversity   Biodiversity

Interaction

Geodiversity and biodiversity are closely related and interdependent. Their interaction is responsible for ecodiversity.

Colombia, northeastern Brazil, eastern Himalayas / Yunnan, northern Borneo and New Guinea).

In Southeast Asia, plant diversity is supported by the monsoon-like character of the inner-tropical west wind circulation pattern, with maximum water-vapor accumulation over the warmest ocean basin of the Indo-Malaysian Archipelago. Similar conditions prevail off the western coast of Colombia and in the Gulf of Guinea.

Tropical trade wind currents blowing inland into the coastal mountain regions of the tropical-subtropical eastern continental margins (eastern Brazil, Middle America, northeastern Australia, Madagascar) also favor high levels of species diversity. In contrast, the divergent trade wind currents on the western sides of the continents tend to cause extreme aridity, although they also give impetus to the cold ocean currents. The result is a constant layer of fog over the cold ocean water, accompanied by local land/sea wind systems along the coasts. In the humid-air deserts ("fog oases"), this fog, combined with the cold ocean current, encourages the development of highly diverse flora, such as the Loma vegetation on the western coast of South America.

The subtropical regions with winter rainy seasons assume a unique status resulting from seasonal alternation of climatic factors (including most importantly rainfall) typical of tropical temperate zones. In the rainier mountainous countries, winter rains alternating with summer convection precipitation in combination with long thermal vegetation periods produce substantial phytodiversity, particularly at middle elevations, and create favorable living conditions for human beings (European Mediterranean region, Middle East, California, central Chile, the Cape Provinces of South Africa, and southwestern Australia).

Areas with high and low vascular-plant diversity are separated by transition zones. In the northern hemisphere, zones of diversity tend to run parallel to lines of latitude, much like the large landscape belts. In the southern hemisphere, they tend to align – depending upon the position and orientation of mountain ranges – concentrically in the direction of the major atmospheric currents and in response to lee/luff effects (Australia, southern Africa) or along north-south axes (South America).

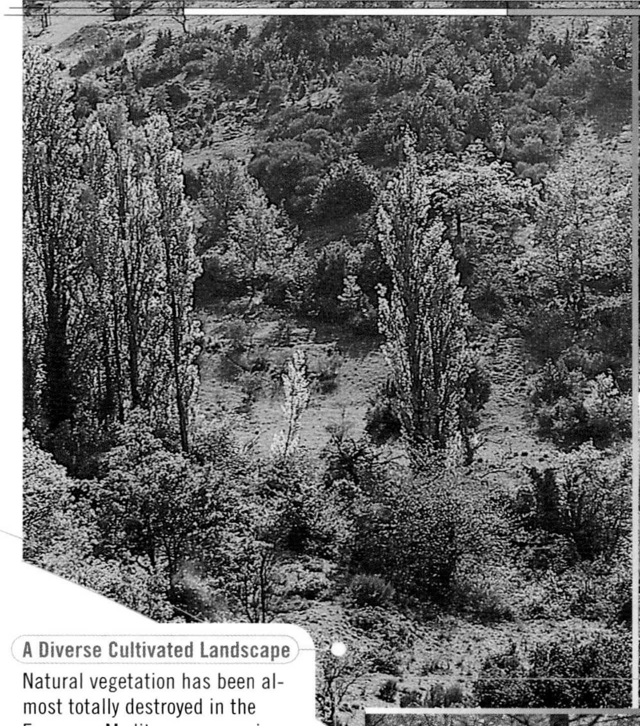

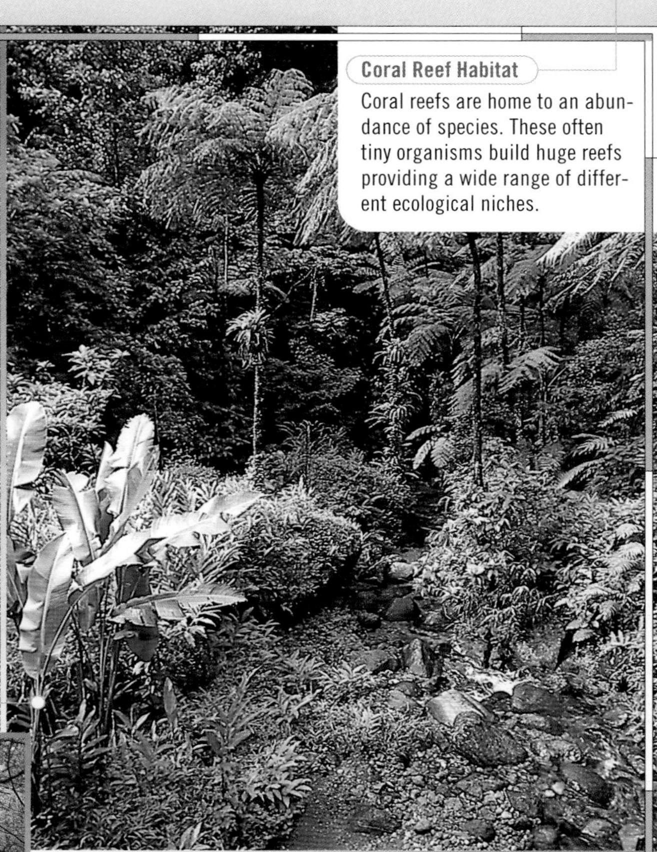

Coral Reef Habitat

Coral reefs are home to an abundance of species. These often tiny organisms build huge reefs providing a wide range of different ecological niches.

A Diverse Cultivated Landscape

Natural vegetation has been almost totally destroyed in the European Mediterranean region. Yet this rich cultivated landscape, the cradle of advanced cultures since ancient times, exhibits a high degree of species diversity thanks to its favorable climatic and edaphic influences.

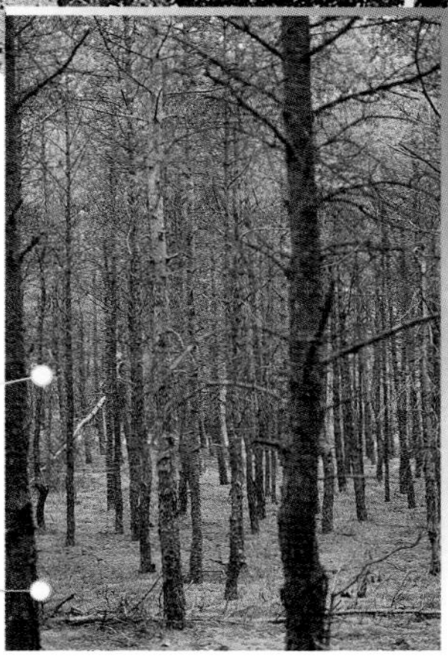

The World's Plant Reservoir

The tropics encompass regions of great species diversity. It is in the best interest of mankind to preserve them as reservoirs of new food and other crop plants.

Species-Poor Taiga

Despite their vast biomass potential, the boreal coniferous forests support only a meager selection of plant species. No more than five kinds of trees are found in the entire taiga. In the tropical rain forests, hundreds of species can be found in an area the size of that covered in the photo.

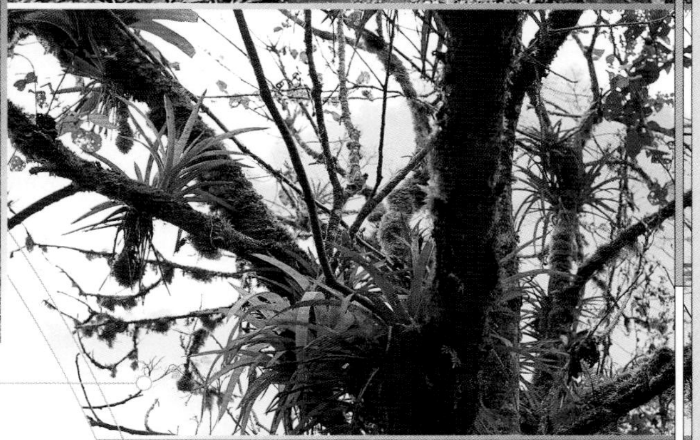

Cloud Forests

At the western roof of the Andes, trees at the cloud forest level (photo: Ecuador), are covered by an abundance of blossoming epiphytic plants.

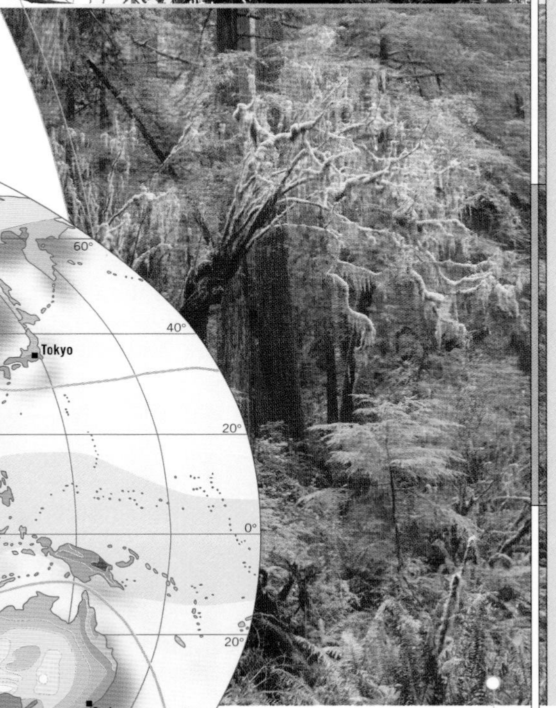

Moist Coastal Forests

Kept moist by frequent coastal fog, the mountains along the coast of northern California are densely forested. The characteristic giant redwoods (Sequoia sempervirens) are joined here by other conifers (Douglas firs, etc.) and deciduous species.

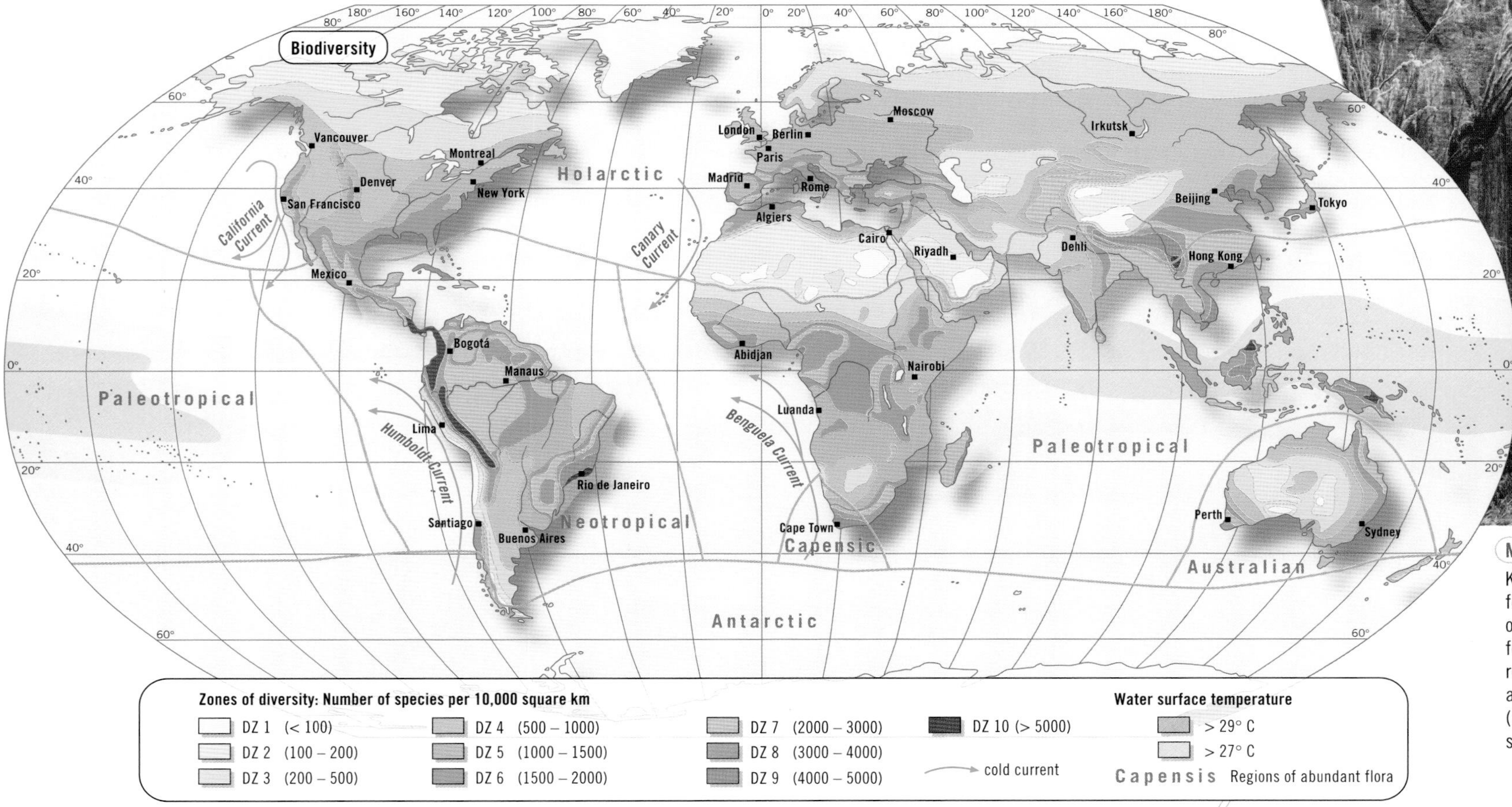

Biodiversity

Zones of diversity: Number of species per 10,000 square km

				Water surface temperature
DZ 1 (< 100)	DZ 4 (500 – 1000)	DZ 7 (2000 – 3000)	DZ 10 (> 5000)	> 29° C
DZ 2 (100 – 200)	DZ 5 (1000 – 1500)	DZ 8 (3000 – 4000)		> 27° C
DZ 3 (200 – 500)	DZ 6 (1500 – 2000)	DZ 9 (4000 – 5000)	cold current	Capensis Regions of abundant flora

Deserts and Desertification

Are We Turning the Earth into a Desert?

Public attention was first drawn to the endangered African Sahel region by the catastrophic drought and famine of 1968–1973. Steadily dwindling harvest yields and widespread livestock death cost the lives of 100,000–200,000 people. Nomads and farmers sought refuge in cities or less arid regions in the south, many of them never to return. Since then, the percentage of nomadic people among the total population of Mauritania has fallen from 70 % to 25 %. Other drought-endangered areas of the world have experienced similar fates. The UN has officially recognized the problem of "desertification," and programs have been devoted to solving it, most recently within the framework of the Agenda 21 resolution passed at the 1992 Earth Summit in Rio de Janeiro.

What is Desertification?

Desertification is a process involving natural and man-made influences by which land is transformed into desert. It affects all dry regions on Earth – not only existing deserts but especially steppes and dry savannas that could easily become or be turned into deserts. More than one-third of the dry land on our planet, and nearly a billion of its people, are threatened by desertification. The most severely endangered countries are among the poorest in the world. Between ten and fourteen million acres of farm and grazing land are lost to desertification every year.

A Constant Water Shortage

Regions with dry climates have fragile ecosystems and are thus naturally endangered. Precipitation is not only meager but seasonal as well. In tropical regions with both dry and rainy seasons, dry winters alternate with wet summers, and precipitation levels vary significantly. Dry or wet periods often last for several years. These factors influence the make-up of plant communities, determine plant survival strategies, and affect the production of vegetable biomass. Satellite images show that the southern boundary of the Sahara may drift northward or southward depending upon precipitation. Yet it is not true that the Sahara is steadily and progressively expanding. The climate in this region has not changed significantly since northern Africa began to turn arid over 4,000 years ago. The crucial factor is mankind's disruptive intervention in the delicate equilibrium of nature. Accordingly, desert-like conditions do not expand along broad fronts but tend instead to develop in spots.

Progressive Environmental Destruction

Failure to adapt land-use practices to natural circumstances in farming and grazing operations can have devastating consequences. Thus in the Sahel region, for example, the boundary of sustainable rain-fed farming (minimum precipitation of 500 mm per year in marginal tropical regions with summer rains and 300 mm in subtropical areas with winter wet seasons) was pushed into the desert during the extended humid period from 1950 to 1967 – up to 200 km in the Sahel region and 100 km in northwestern Africa. In the process, much natural vegetation, which, although sparse, was well adapted to changing moisture conditions, was thinned or eliminated entirely, causing extensive, irreparable damage. The grass cover was stripped away, and bushes and trees were cut for firewood. The destruction of vegetation accelerates the rate of evaporation; soil grows drier and is subject to wind or water erosion. Where topsoil is completely stripped away, impermeable crusts of rock may be exposed, the soil water budget can be permanently affected, and the groundwater level may sink. Sand carried away by winds may accumulate in dunes. Sandstorms originating in the Sahel and the Sahara have been known to carry material as far away as the Caribbean and South America.

Intensive farming in the Sahel region went hand in hand with shorter fallow periods (fertilizers are ordinarily not used). Nomads who had used these fields as grazing areas were forced to move to inferior land, particularly since political boundaries have made wide-ranging migration more difficult or even impossible. Deep wells were drilled in many places to secure an adequate water supply for nomads and farmers – but this, too, produced negative effects. Herds grew larger, and the groundwater level sank even further.

Where precipitation is insufficient to support cultivation, farmers must irrigate, as they have done for thousands of years in the Valleys of the Nile, the Tigris and Euphrates, and the Indus, which are fed by heavy precipitation in the mountain along their upper reaches, and along the rivers that empty into the Aral Sea in the piedmont region of Central Asia or the Tarim Basin. Due to the high evaporation rate in dry regions, however, irrigation tends to cause excessive soil salinity, as examples from ancient history show. Damage of this kind has been much more severe in recent times, however (e.g. in Pakistan and the Al-Wadi al-Jadid in Egypt).

A Global Problem

Desertification is actually a by-product of the twentieth-century population explosion brought about in part by significant improvements in medical care. Farmers and nomads rank low in the political and economic ladders of developing countries. Since colonial times, governments have consistently encouraged or decreed market-oriented production (e.g. cotton, peanuts, meat) in order to increase tax and export revenues and ensure an adequate food supply for politically significant urban populations. Increasing economic globalization and requirements imposed by the World Bank and the International Monetary Fund have put rural populations under tremendous pressure to adapt. Worldwide, desertification is responsible for production shortfalls valued at 40 billion dollars per year – more than the combined gross national products of all of the countries of the Sahel region, from Senegal to Somalia. Desertification not only jeopardizes the fulfillment of basic human needs – nutrition, health, and education – it also contributes to the spread of poverty, the dissolution of social bonds, political

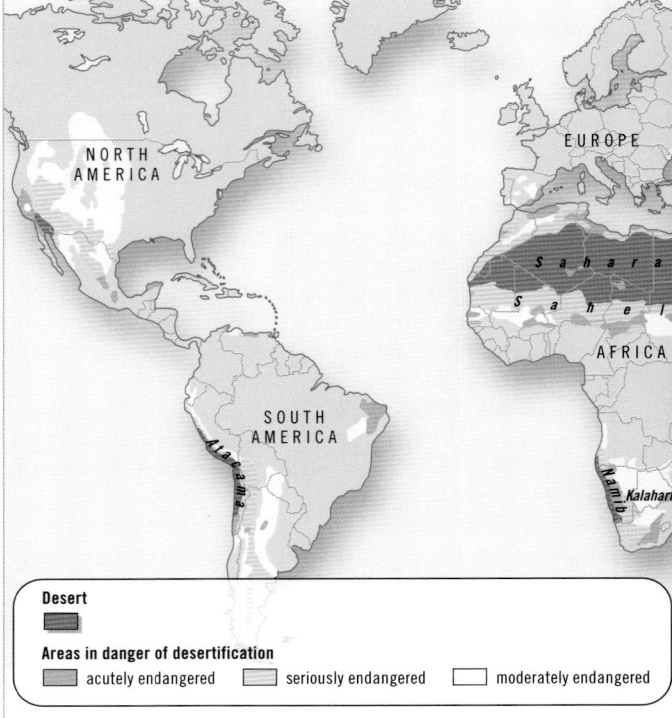

Desert

Areas in danger of desertification
acutely endangered | seriously endangered | moderately endangered

First presented at the 1977 UN Conference in Nairobi, the World Desertification Map shows that areas immediately adjacent to existing deserts are often in less danger of desertification than somewhat moister region, where the burden of cultivation and population density is greater.

Fluctuations in annual precipitation levels recorded at various measuring stations in the western Sahel region between 1901 and 1990, entered as percentage deviations from the long-term average. Older records also document similar alternating periods of precipitation deficit (1820-40) and surplus (1870-95), as do variations in the shoreline of Lake Chad.

Bread or Salt

Given sufficient water, the desert can be brought to bloom. But desert soil must be irrigated with great care, ensuring that it is well flushed in order to avoid salt accumulation. Numerous cases of excessive, irreversible soil salination have been recorded in Libya, for example, where extensive grain fields were laid out and irrigated (with long-armed rotary sprinklers) using water drawn from "fossil" reserves formed deep in the earth during wetter geological periods in the past.

The Power of Water

Where the protective cover of vegetation in dry regions has been thinned or stripped away entirely through cultivation or grazing, brief but often very heavy rains wreak havoc on the exposed soil. Rapid runoff cuts grooves, troughs, and deep gorges in the ground, as can be seen in this photo taken in the Sierra Madre del Sur, Mexico. Badland formations of this kind are especially prevalent in areas with soft sediments.

Dying of Thirst

During extended periods of drought – this photo was taken in the degraded dry Kaokoveld savanna (Namibia) in the early 1980s – water becomes so scarce that many animals die of thirst.

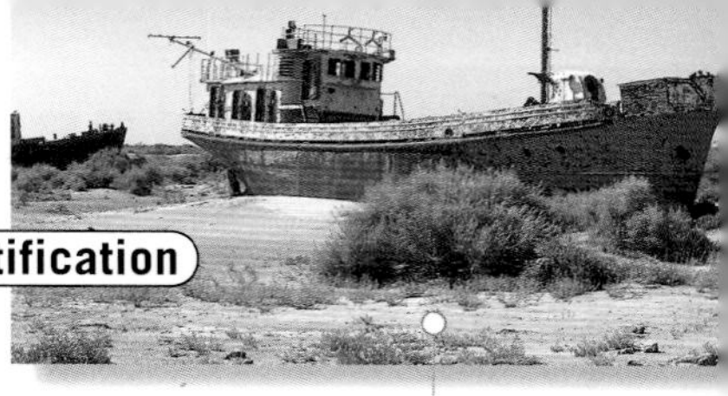

instability, and armed conflicts fueled by competition for dwindling resources. Soon, 100 million people will have joined the worldwide exodus from rural regions into the cities. The effects of this wave of migration will ultimately be felt in North America and Europe as well.

Desertification is not a new phenomenon. The ancient Romans destroyed their "granary" on the Tunisian steppe through overuse (Bedouin immigrants from Arabia reclaimed the land for grazing, and it eventually recovered, only to be converted to farmland again under French colonial rule, which hastened the process of degradation through desertification). Dust storms and soil erosion on the U.S. Great Plains ("Dust Bowl") between 1930 and 1935 (affecting 650,000 farmers and 400,000 square km of land) offered striking proof that industrialized countries are not immune to desertification. But poor countries lack the resources to overcome these problems on their own. International aid is needed, especially in light of the fact that desertification poses not only social and economic dangers but environmental ones as well. If vegetation disappears from the dry regions, huge quantities of greenhouse gases (carbon dioxide, methane), now being absorbed by plants will be released into the atmosphere – 30 times the amount of CO_2 currently emitted every year.

Can Desertification Be Stopped?

Counteractive measures need time to take effect. Once an understanding of ecological relationships is achieved, the local population must be educated and encouraged to adapt farming and grazing practices to the environment. The use of alternative forms of energy can be helpful. Other effective measures include the planting of drought-resistant crop plants, the use of appropriate agricultural methods and technologies (e.g. dams to protect against erosion, terracing, the planting of trees), and accelerated development in the non-agrarian sector.

The Aral Sea Drama

The use of water from rivers feeding the Aral Sea for irrigation caused the sea to shrink from 68,000 to 39,500 square km between 1960 and 1991. Salinity also rose to alarming levels (up to 30%), decimating the fish population. Many fishing boats were left high and dry. Salt and dust (75 million tons per year), along with accumulated toxic residues (pesticides, herbicides, fertilizers) are carried from the old seabed by winds and deposited on the surrounding fields (cotton, rice, etc.). These substances contaminate the groundwater and have led to a substantial rise in the incidence of disease, birth defects, and infant death.

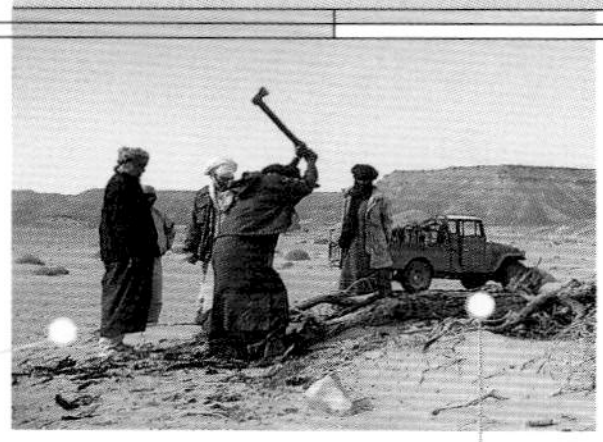

The Last Tree

In the absence of environmentally sounder energy alternatives (such as solar energy or biogas), the inhabitants of the Sahel zone, where wood is extremely scarce (photo: Tuareg tribespeople in Niger) must rely on firewood to prepare their daily meals. This results in the loss of as many as 200 savanna trees per family per year.

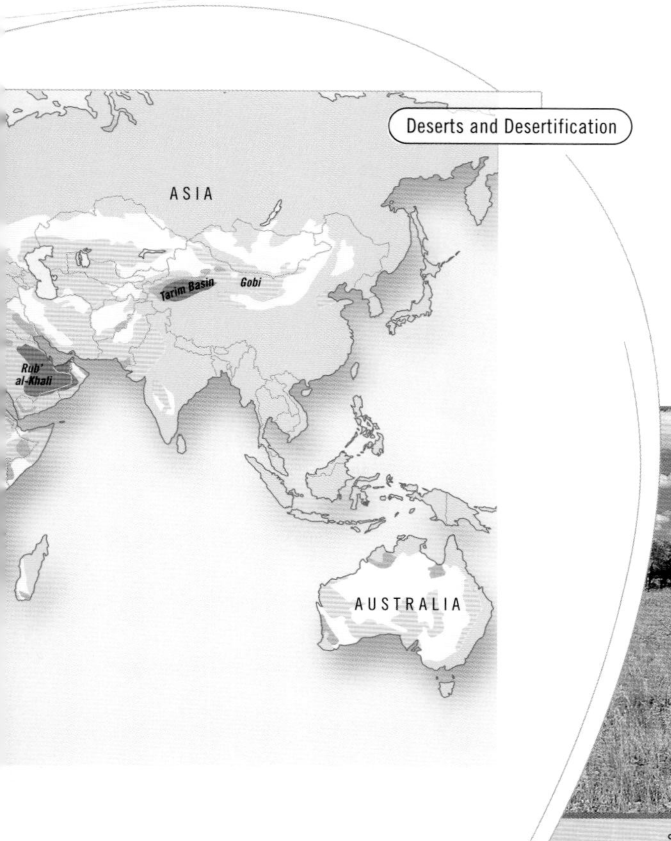

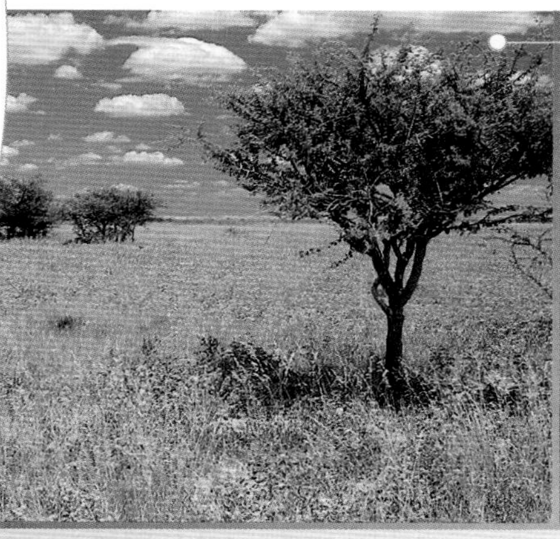

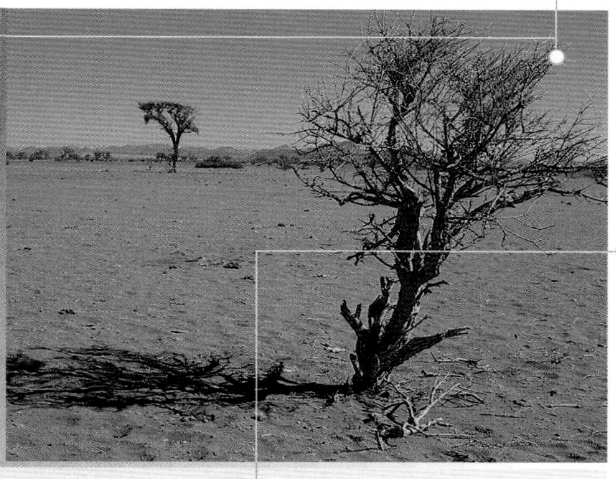

Degradation

The grass cover in the savanna is often so heavily damaged by overuse that it cannot regenerate even during the rainy season and thus leaves the bare soil exposed (left: intact or only slightly damaged savanna; right: degraded savanna). Only trees with deep roots that reach the groundwater aquifer – Acacias, for the most part – can survive.

Driven by Hunger

After several years of drought, the ground in the Sahel region along the southern rim of the Sahara is severely desiccated and covered by a network of deep cracks. Desperately searching for nourishment, these women use long poles to loosen the hard clumps of soil in the hope of finding edible plants and roots beneath them.

Deserts and Desertification

ASIA

Tarim Basin   Gobi

Rub'
al-Khali

AUSTRALIA

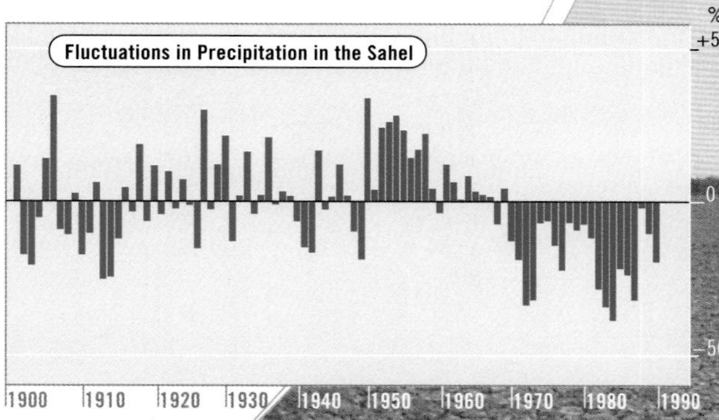

Fluctuations in Precipitation in the Sahel

%
+50

0

-50

|1900 |1910 |1920 |1930 |1940 |1950 |1960 |1970 |1980 |1990

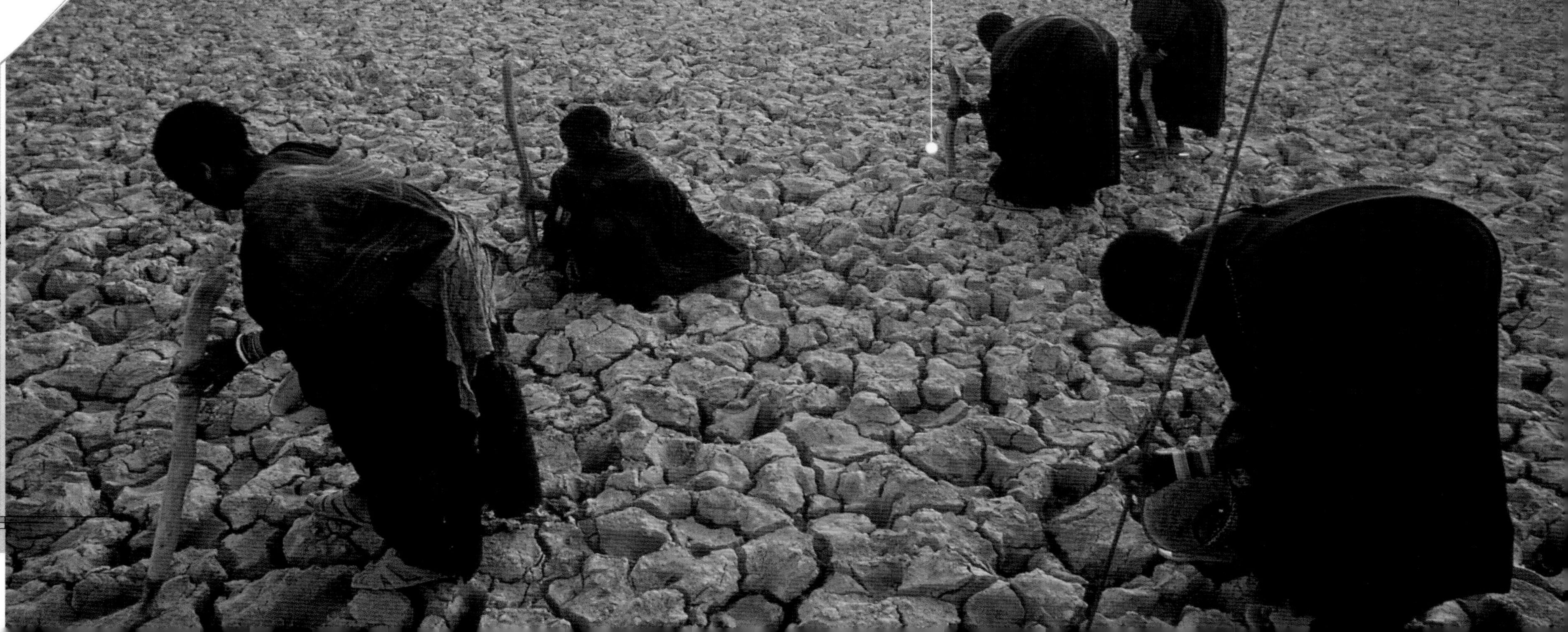

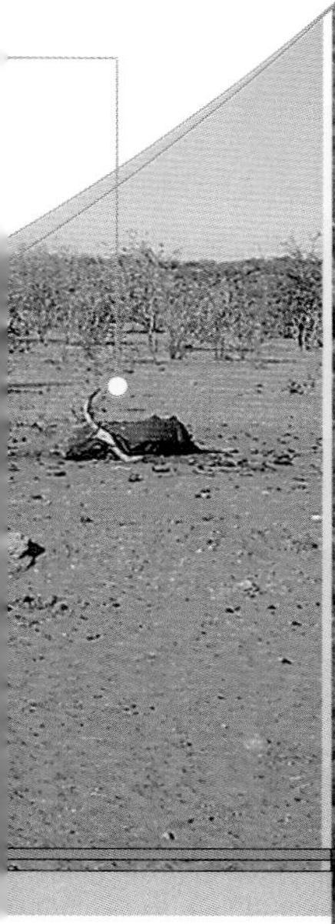

Worldwide Protection for Natural Treasures through UNESCO

Will Our Natural Heritage Be Preserved for the Next Generation?

World Natural Heritage sites are chosen for their uniqueness and outstanding universal value. Thus the goal of the UNESCO World Heritage Convention is to identify the most outstanding examples of significant natural ecosystems and landscapes and the most important geological and paleontological sites from among the many applications received. Yet some countries fear that increasing publicity will increase the pressure of tourism on already fragile landscapes and have refrained from submitting applications.

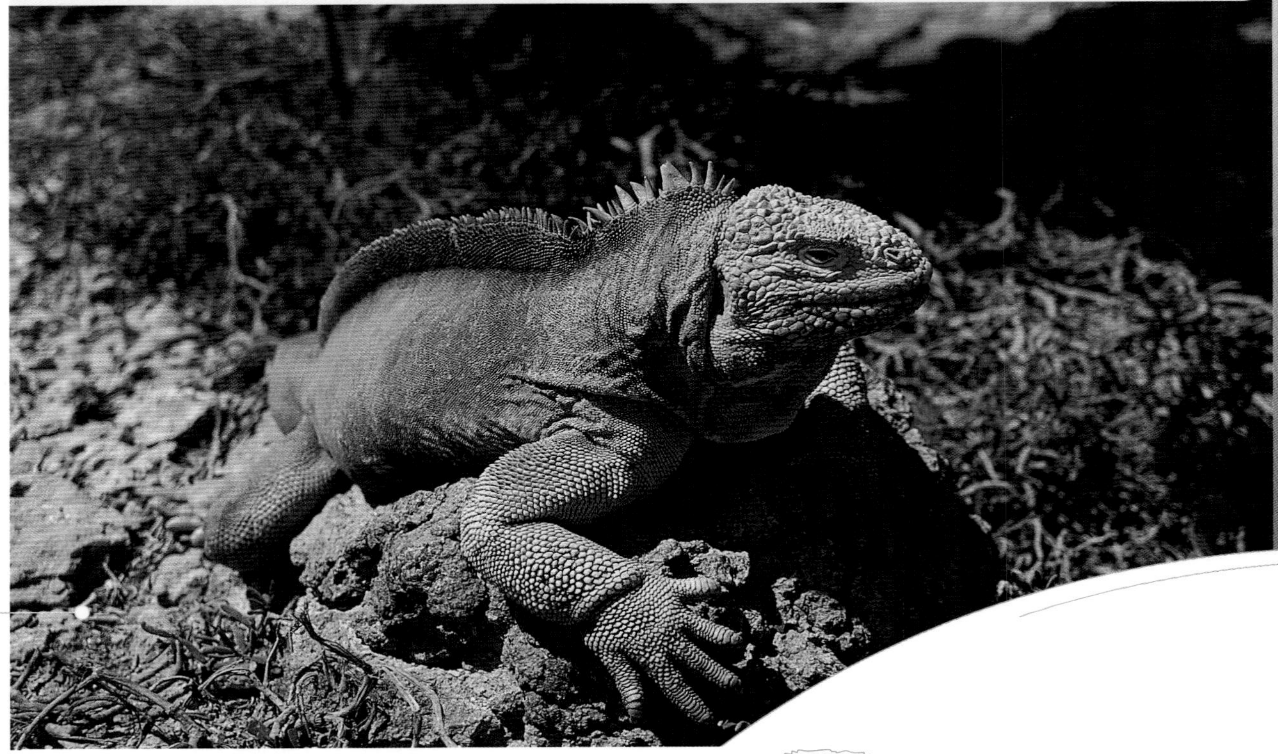

The Threat Posed by Mankind

Environmental pollution, resource depletion, population pressure! Can we truly hope to pass the heritage entrusted to us on to succeeding generations? The Convention focuses particular attention on "endangered natural heritage sites," and thus the last remaining Australian rain forests have been saved from destruction. In other cases, however, such as that of the Srebarna Danube wetlands, rescue efforts almost came too late.

Does Conservation Make Sense in Our Time?

The static concept of conservation was long the dominant guiding principle in our thinking about protecting nature. We know today that all natural systems are highly dynamic. The Agenda 21 program passed at the UN Earth Summit Conference in Rio Janeiro strongly emphasized the concept of "sustainable use and development" as a guideline for thought and action.

Home of Pele, Goddess of Fire

Kilauea is one of **Hawaii's two active volcanoes (106).** From deep in the Earth's upper mantle, the mountain brings liquid lava to the surface, where it emerges at a temperature of 2,160°F and spreads rapidly (at a speed of up to 40 km per hour) into the surrounding countryside.

Los Glaciares

The **Moreno Glacier (30)** flows eastward from the continental Patagonian ice sheet into Lago Argentino. The irregular advances of its broad tongue (more than two km wide) cause occasional flooding.

A Window on Evolution

The **Galapagos Islands (25)** were formed by a group of shield volcanoes whose peaks rise from the depth of the Pacific on both sides of the Equator. The land iguana belongs to the large group of endemic species.

Sinter Terraces

Yellowstone National Park (8) encompasses a caldera with a diameter of 79 km surrounded by high peaks in the Rocky Mountains. These sinter terraces were formed by hot springs, remnants of volcanic activity dating back 600,000 years.

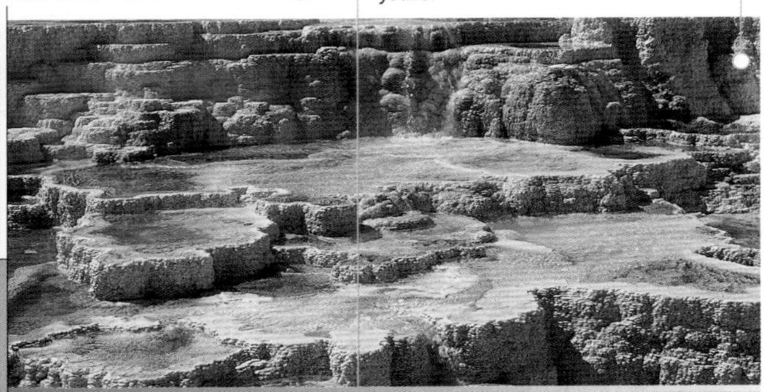

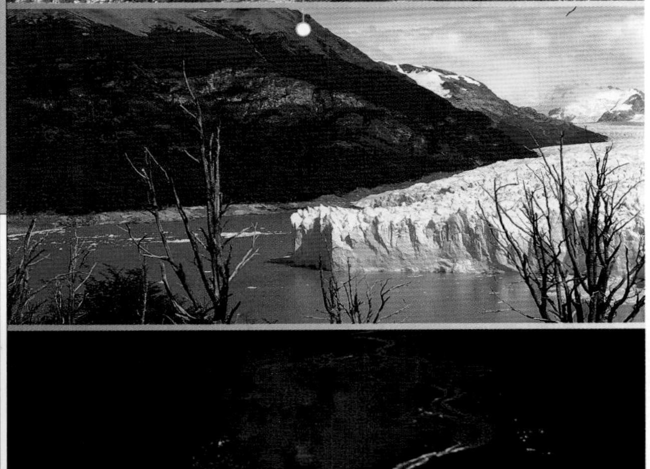

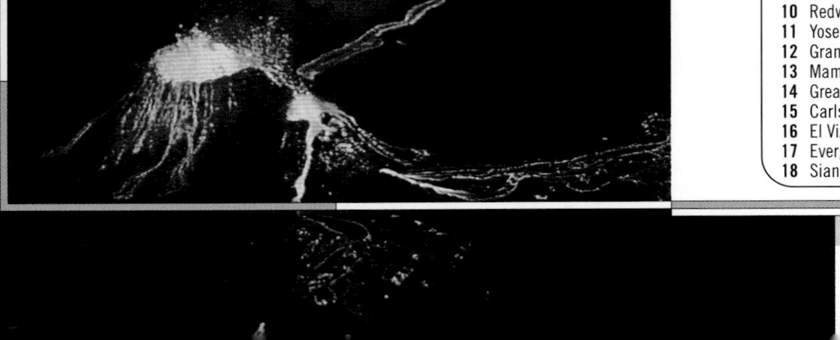

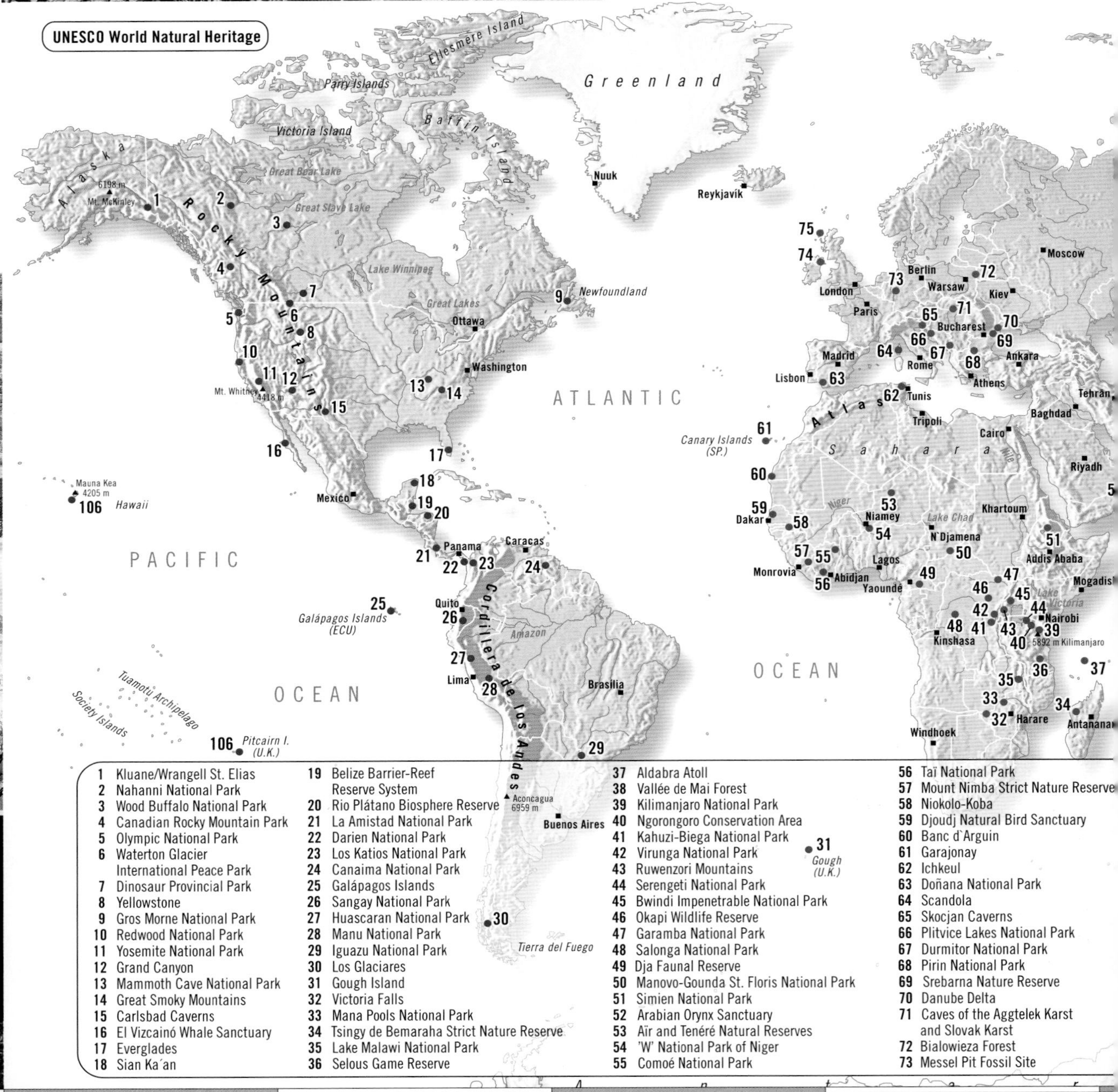

UNESCO World Natural Heritage

1 Kluane/Wrangell St. Elias Reserve System	19 Belize Barrier-Reef Reserve System	37 Aldabra Atoll	56 Taï National Park
2 Nahanni National Park	20 Rio Plátano Biosphere Reserve	38 Vallée de Mai Forest	57 Mount Nimba Strict Nature Reserve
3 Wood Buffalo National Park	21 La Amistad National Park	39 Kilimanjaro National Park	58 Niokolo-Koba
4 Canadian Rocky Mountain Park	22 Darien National Park	40 Ngorongoro Conservation Area	59 Djoudj Natural Bird Sanctuary
5 Olympic National Park	23 Los Katios National Park	41 Kahuzi-Biega National Park	60 Banc d'Arguin
6 Waterton Glacier International Peace Park	24 Canaima National Park	42 Virunga National Park	61 Garajonay
7 Dinosaur Provincial Park	25 Galápagos Islands	43 Ruwenzori Mountains	62 Ichkeul
8 Yellowstone	26 Sangay National Park	44 Serengeti National Park	63 Doñana National Park
9 Gros Morne National Park	27 Huascaran National Park	45 Bwindi Impenetrable National Park	64 Scandola
10 Redwood National Park	28 Manu National Park	46 Okapi Wildlife Reserve	65 Skocjan Caverns
11 Yosemite National Park	29 Iguazu National Park	47 Garamba National Park	66 Plitvice Lakes National Park
12 Grand Canyon	30 Los Glaciares	48 Salonga National Park	67 Durmitor National Park
13 Mammoth Cave National Park	31 Gough Island	49 Dja Faunal Reserve	68 Pirin National Park
14 Great Smoky Mountains	32 Victoria Falls	50 Manovo-Gounda St. Floris National Park	69 Srebarna Nature Reserve
15 Carlsbad Caverns	33 Mana Pools National Park	51 Simien National Park	70 Danube Delta
16 El Vizcainó Whale Sanctuary	34 Tsingy de Bemaraha Strict Nature Reserve	52 Arabian Orynx Sanctuary	71 Caves of the Aggtelek Karst and Slovak Karst
17 Everglades	35 Lake Malawi National Park	53 Aïr and Tenéré Natural Reserves	72 Bialowieza Forest
18 Sian Ka'an	36 Selous Game Reserve	54 'W' National Park of Niger	73 Messel Pit Fossil Site
		55 Comoé National Park	

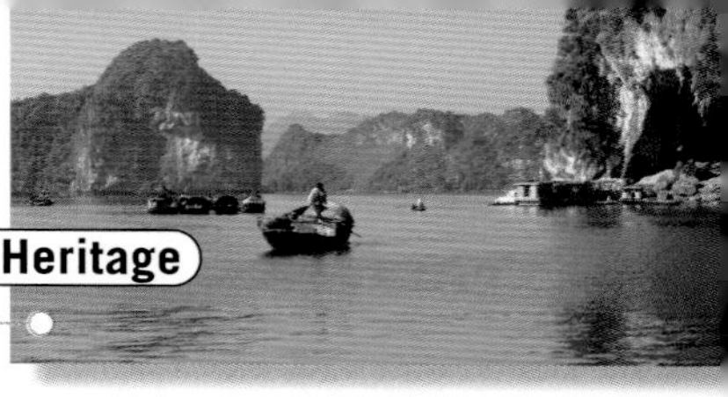

Sunken Karst Landscape

With its 1,600 islands and islets, **Ha Long Bay (82)** on the northern coast of Vietnam is one of the most beautiful examples of cone karst formations. It is the product of limestone dissolution — which began on the mainland — in a humid tropical climate. Over time, the coast has sunk, allowing the sea to inundate the karst landscape. Only the highest karst towers rise above sea level.

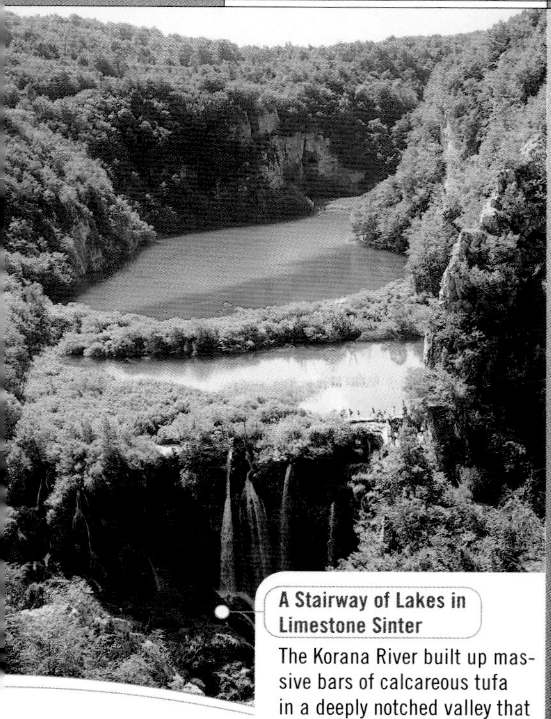

A Stairway of Lakes in Limestone Sinter

The Korana River built up massive bars of calcareous tufa in a deeply notched valley that cuts through the Croatian karst landscape, forming the **Plitvice Lakes (66)**, a stairway of 16 small and larger lakes covering a distance of 7 km. Some of the many waterfalls that spill over the sinter barriers are nearly 80 m high.

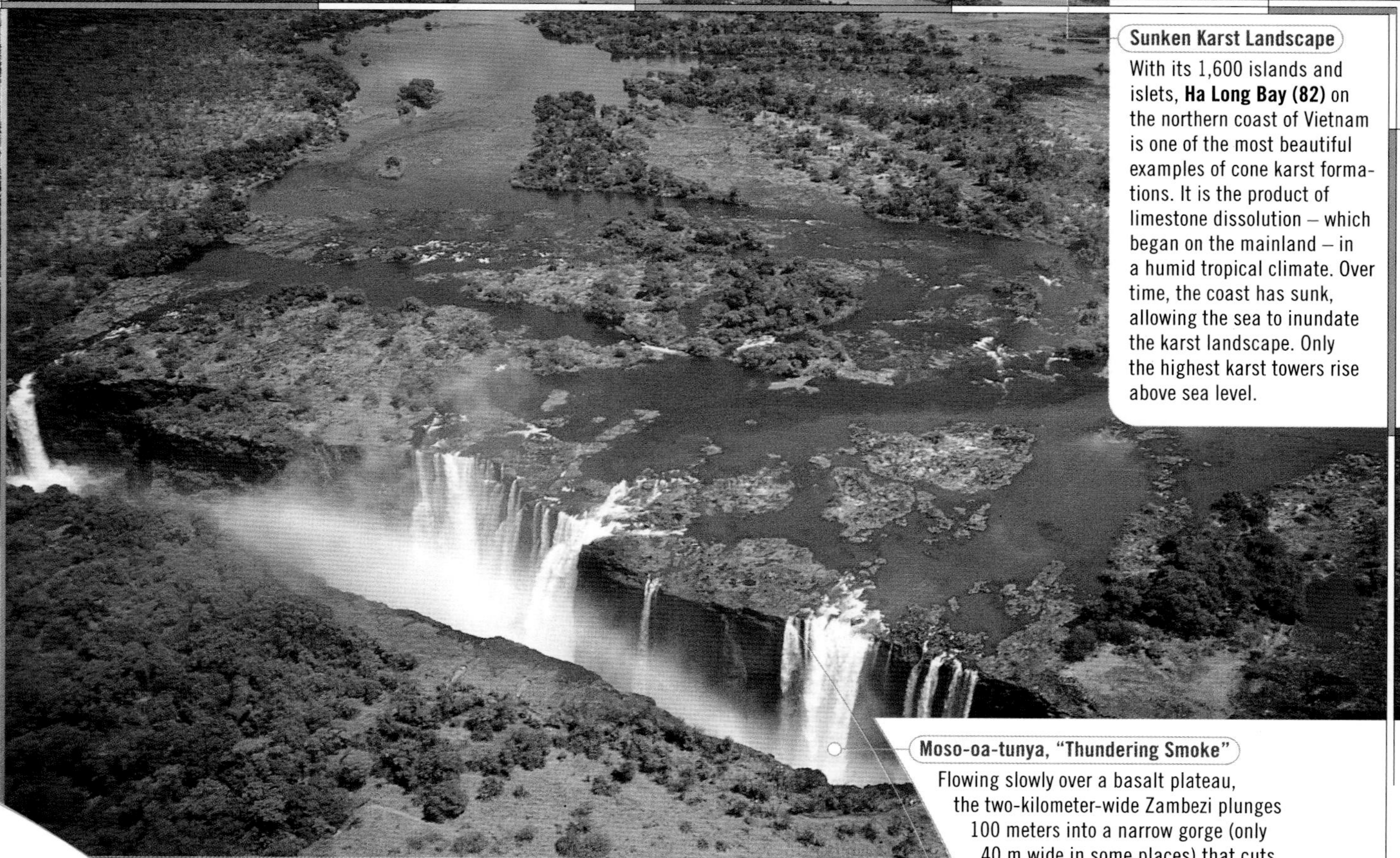

Moso-oa-tunya, "Thundering Smoke"

Flowing slowly over a basalt plateau, the two-kilometer-wide Zambezi plunges 100 meters into a narrow gorge (only 40 m wide in some places) that cuts straight across its course. The broad water curtain of the **Victoria Falls (32)** is transformed into clouds of spray and fine mist that promote rich plant growth.

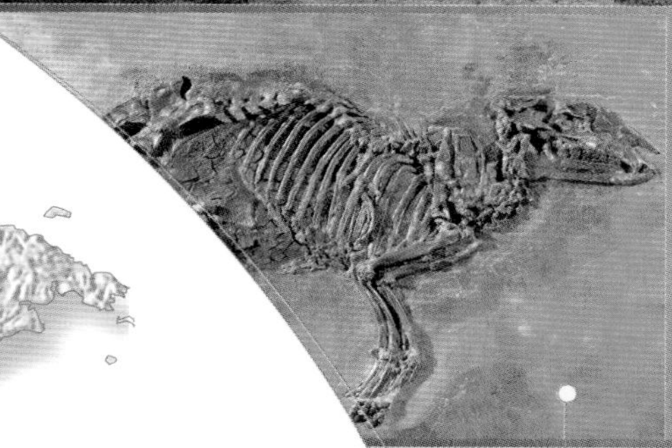

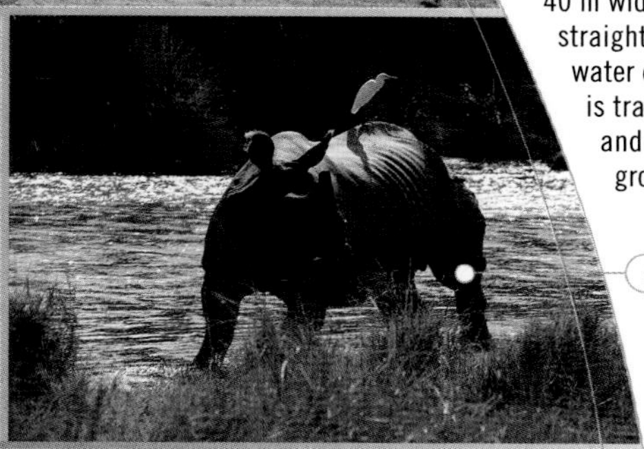

A Refuge for Rhinos

Chitwan National Park (90) in the wet lowlands of Nepal is a refuge (protected by the military) for 400 Indian Rhinos.

A Tiny Horse from a Warmer Era

Numerous fossils from the Eocene have been recovered from the oil shale layers of the **Messel Pit (73)** near Darmstadt, among them this well-preserved skeleton of the prehistoric horse Propalaeotherium parvulum. Fossil evidence of flora and fauna indicate a subtropical to tropical climate in the region some 40 to 50 million years ago.

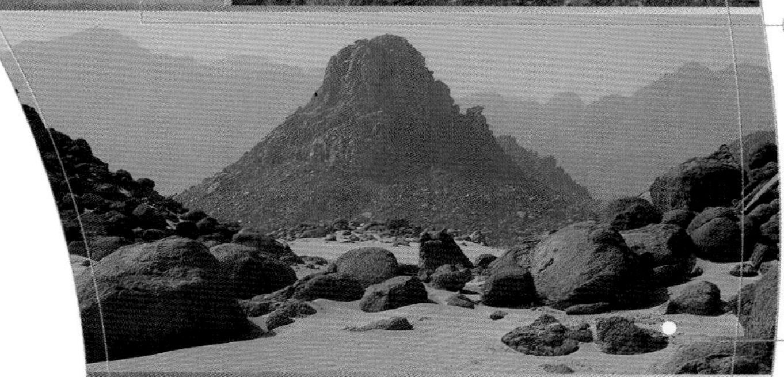

Endangered Desert Landscape

The **Aïr and Ténéré Natural Reserves (53)** comprise two different natural landscapes. The sandstone base of the Aïr desert mountain range is riddled with plutonic ring intrusions (photo: Adrar Chiriet). To the east is the Ténéré, a desolate region through which the Tuareg have traditionally driven their camel caravans, bearing salt from Bilma and Fachi to distant markets.

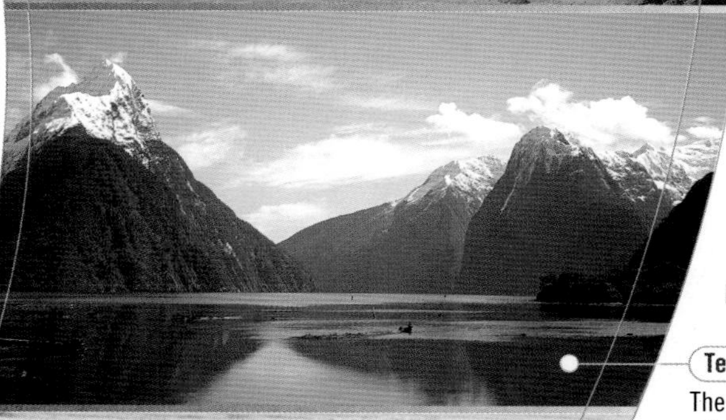

Te Wahipounamu

The **Te Wahipounamu Fiordland (103)** on the western coast of New Zealand's South Island encompasses untouched stretches of coast, 28 mountains with peaks above 3,000 m, and glaciers that descend below the tree line.

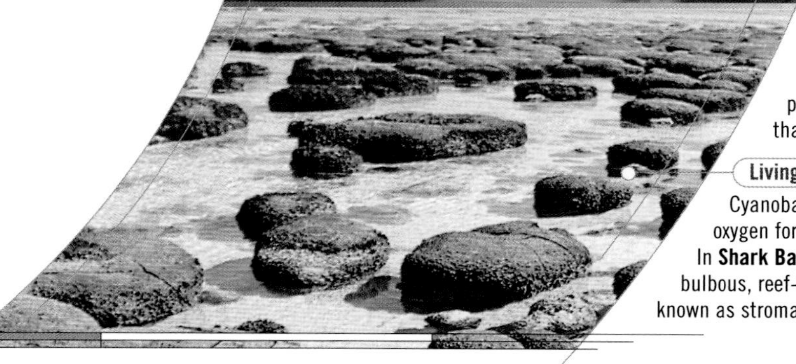

Living Fossils

Cyanobacteria have been producing oxygen for at least 2.3 billion years. In **Shark Bay (105)**, they are still forming bulbous, reef-like limestone deposits known as stromatolites today.

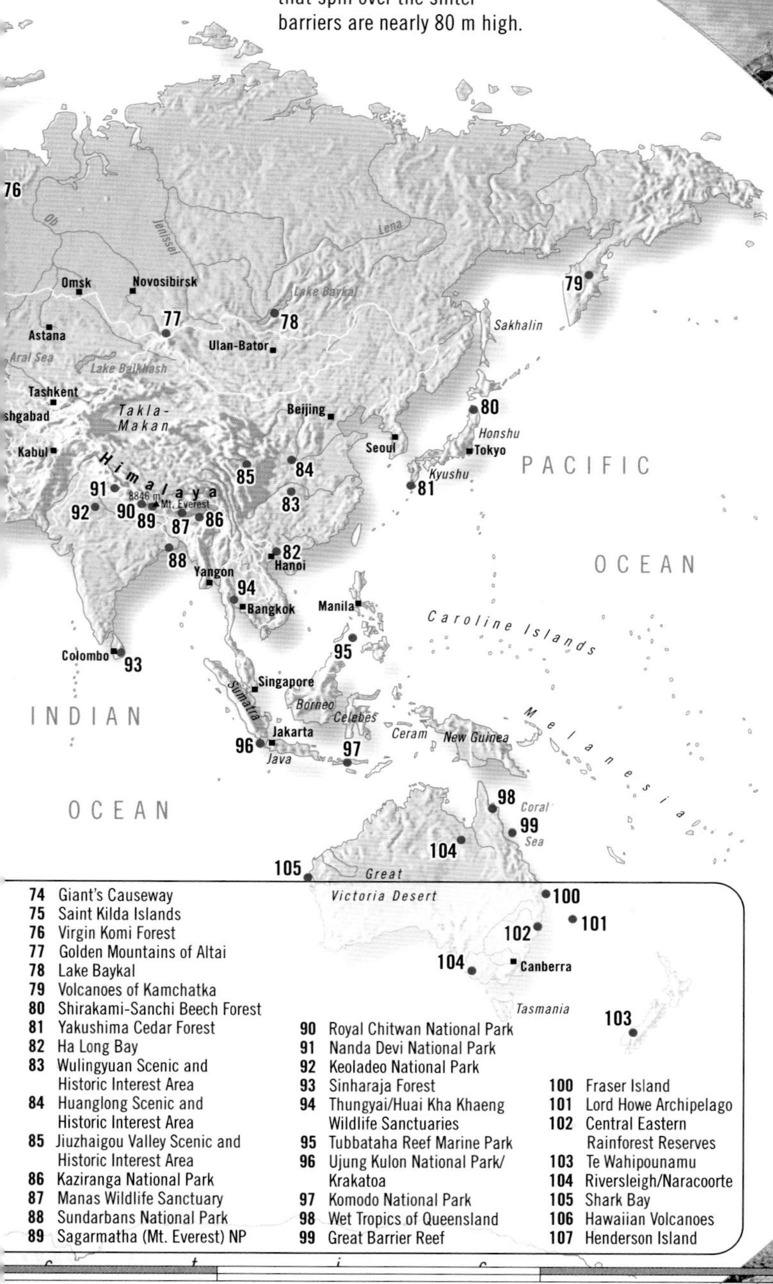

Early Human Development and Migration

Advancing to the Ends of the World

At least twice in the course of human history, our ancestors, hominids of the genus Homo, set out from Africa to conquer the world. Why did they abandon their familiar, warm, tropical homeland in the African savanna for an unknown and distant world full of surprises, challenges, and dangers – and new opportunities?
Were they forced to move – 1.8 million years ago – by population pressure, changes in climate, vegetation, or fauna, or was it curiosity and the urge to explore that drove them. Although the first sedentary communities did not appear until after the end of the last ice age 10,000 years ago, individuals are unlikely to have traveled far from their homes even long before then. Human migrations over long distances presumably took place over extended periods of time.

When Apes Came Down from the Trees –
It all began with an upright posture

The earliest phase of human evolution and migration began during a period of environmental change along the East African Rift. About six million years ago, the rain forest began to give way to expanding tree savannas, forcing tree-dwelling primates to adopt an upright posture in order to facilitate travel over greater distances. Remains of Australopithecines, hominids which first appeared about four million years ago (example: Lucy), show jawbone modifications indicating adaptation to a diet no longer comprised of soft fruit and leaves of rain forest plants but primarily of harder seeds, roots, grass, and nuts found in the savannas. An upright posture enhanced mobility. Bones of Australopithecines about 3.5 million years old have been found from Ethiopia to South Africa and in

Chad. A period of global cooling about 2.5 million years ago caused increasing aridity accompanied by changes in flora and fauna, intensifying the selective influence of the environment. The first hominids of the genus Homo (Homo habilis, Homo rudolfensis) appeared at this point. They used simple stone tools (such as scrapers) to process the harder foodstuffs and butcher animals (slain game or carrion?). The use of tools made them less dependent on their environment.

The shift to a carnivorous diet evidently favored brain development. About two million years ago, hominids with larger, more robust skeletons began to appear in Africa. The brains of these hominids were larger, more humanoid in structure, and thus indicative of higher intelligence. Homo erectus (known as Homo ergaster in its earliest form) had arrived.

Quest for Fire – Early migration from Africa

Barely 100,000 years after the period marked by the oldest finds in Africa (at Lake Turkana, 1.9 million years BC), Homo erectus had already occupied new lands in western, eastern, and southeastern Asia, presumably favoring familiar, warm biotopes (savannas or steppes) at first. The oldest remains of non-African hominids were discovered in Java (Mojokerto), China (Longgupo), Georgia (Dmanisi, all circa 1.8 million BC), and Palestine (Ubaidiya, 1.4 million BC). More recent evidence has been found in India, Vietnam, and Japan. Artifacts 800,000 years old unearthed on Flores and Timor suggest the use of boats. The dating of tools found in Europe (Andalusia, 1.6 – 1.8 million BC) is disputed. Did these ancestors migrate across the Strait of Gibraltar?

Homo erectus later advanced across the high mountain ranges of Eurasia into much cooler and more humid climes. This required a command of fire (oldest evidence discovered in Africa dating to 1 – 1,5 million BC). Fire provided warmth and light, helped keep animal predators at bay, made cooking possible, and served a social function (campfires as central gathering places). Only a few of the bone and wooden implements used alongside stone tools have survived (among them wooden lances about 400,000 years old found in Schöningen in the German state of Lower Saxony).

The oldest reliable evidence of the presence of humans in Europe (at least one million years ago) con-

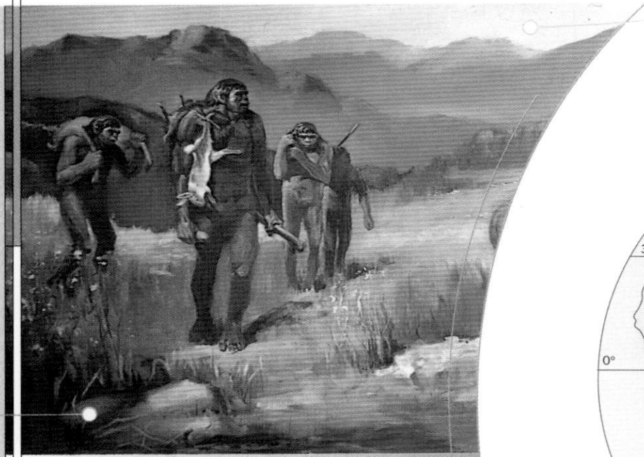

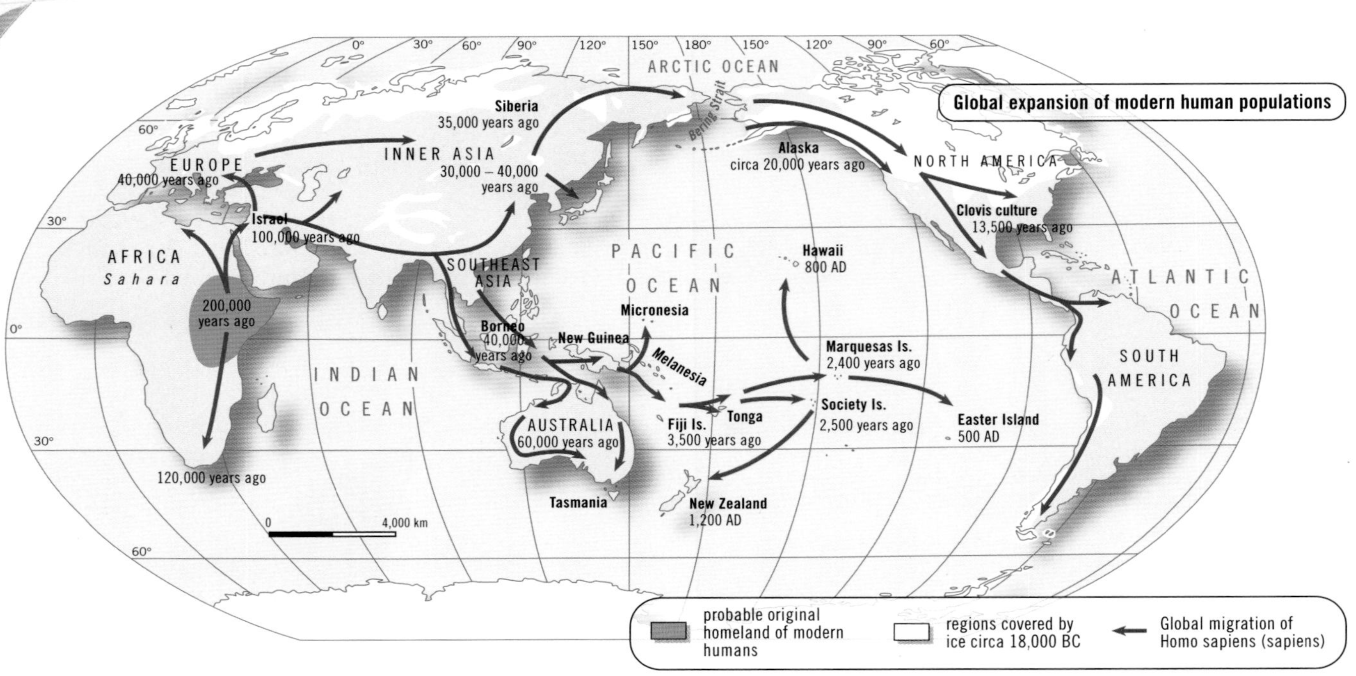

Global expansion of modern human populations

EUROPE 40,000 years ago
Siberia 35,000 years ago
INNER ASIA 30,000 – 40,000 years ago
Alaska circa 20,000 years ago
NORTH AMERICA
Clovis culture 13,500 years ago
Israel 100,000 years ago
AFRICA Sahara
200,000 years ago
SOUTHEAST ASIA
Borneo 40,000 years ago
New Guinea
Micronesia
Melanesia
Hawaii 800 AD
Marquesas Is. 2,400 years ago
SOUTH AMERICA
INDIAN OCEAN
120,000 years ago
AUSTRALIA 60,000 years ago
Fiji Is. 3,500 years ago
Tonga
Society Is. 2,500 years ago
Easter Island ~ 500 AD
Tasmania
New Zealand 1,200 AD
0   4,000 km

probable original homeland of modern humans | regions covered by ice circa 18,000 BC | Global migration of Homo sapiens (sapiens)

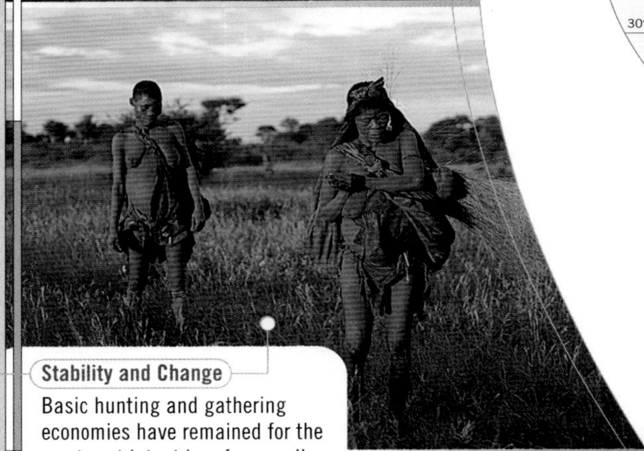

Stability and Change

Basic hunting and gathering economies have remained for the most part intact in a few small societies over a period of 1.5 million years, despite advances in weapon and tool technology, clothing, and housing. Men of the San culture (bushman) still bring their daily kill back to the community camp site just as Homo erectus (upper illustration) did ages ago. One can easily imagine early women gathering food plants with their babies strapped to their backs much like the San women (lower photo) of the Kalahari today.

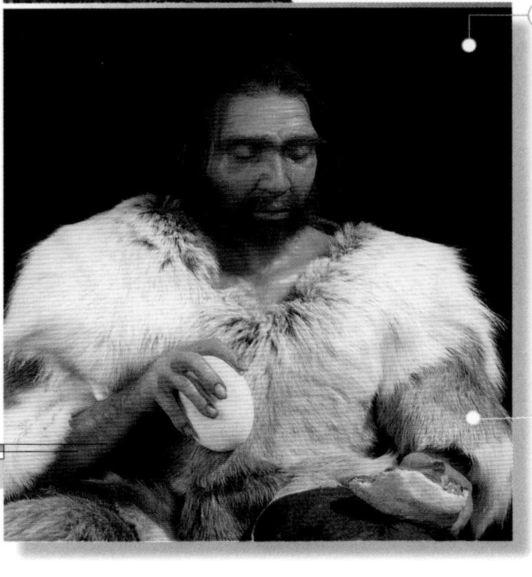

The Unjustly Maligned Neanderthal

Once considered hardly more than a "wild animal," Neanderthal Man is now regarded as an intelligent human species that adapted successfully to an inhospitable ice-age climate – either as a direct ancestor of modern Homo sapiens in accordance with the multi-regional model (parallel, independent development of modern human beings in different regions) or as an evolutionary offshoot that culminated in a dead end.

sists only of isolated artifacts (found near Nice and in the Rhine Valley). The oldest bones were found in Spain (Atepuerca, 780,000 BC). The finds uncovered in Mauer near Heidelberg (600,000 BC) and Bilzingsleben (400,000 BC) are much more recent. They have been classified along with other fossil remains as evidence of a species distinct from the humans of eastern Asia (true Homo erectus) known as Homo heidelbergensis. In general, European settlement patterns, especially in higher latitudes, reflect the influence of climatic changes associated with ice ages, which continually shifted the boundaries of inhabitable regions. It was never extremely cold south of the Alps, however. Changes in sea level impacted on settlement all over the world. During cold periods, continental shelf margins were dry and could be settled and traveled by human migrants.

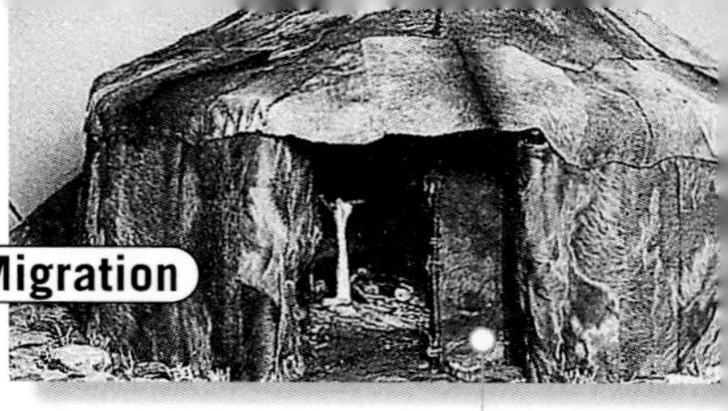

The Evolution of Homo Sapiens – Are we all Africans by descent?

Archaic Homo sapiens emerged from Homo erectus or Homo heidelbergensis in all regions of the world. This phase of evolution probably began in Africa about 600,000 years ago and in Europe around 400,000 BC.

This early human form survived longest – until about 40,000 BC – in Southeast Asia. In Europe, primarily north of the Alps, a distinct form associated with the cold periods of the Pleistocene emerged from the late archaic Homo sapiens: the Neanderthal. The "classical" Neanderthal emerged from early Neanderthals after some 200,000 years, at the beginning of the last ice age, roughly 90,000 years ago. The sturdy, stocky build typical of the late Neanderthal presumably reflects adaptation to the cold climate of the period. Neanderthal populations appeared all over Europe, from the Iberian Peninsula to Central Asia (Uzbekistan) and did not die out until about 30,000 years ago. They advanced into western Asia about 80,000 BC. Long regarded as a direct ancestor of modern man, the Neanderthal is now seen as an evolutionary dead end, since fossil remains exhibiting the anatomical features of modern Homo sapiens (sapiens) found in Africa have been dated to about 200,000 BC, and it is only there that the evolutionary process can be traced in an unbroken line.

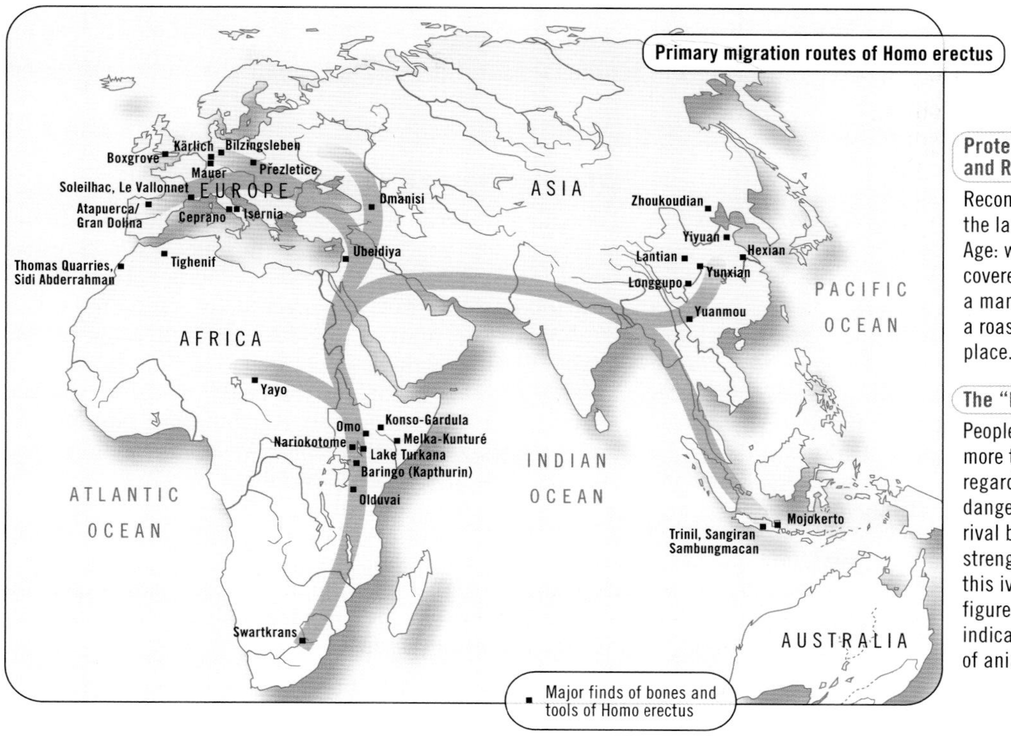

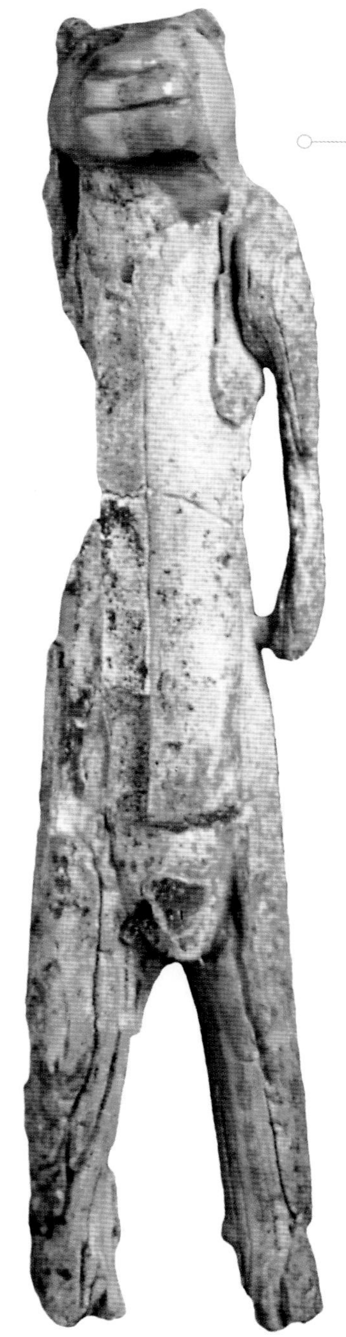

Out of Africa – Modern humans conquer the earth

As recently as 100,000 BC, modern man (as defined in anatomical terms) first appeared in western Asia, where he lived alongside Neanderthal groups for another 30,000 years. He was also a contemporary of the Neanderthal in Europe for 10,000 years, before emerging as the dominant species (Cro-Magnon People) 40,000 years ago. Isolated intermingling of the two types may have occurred.

Archaeological evidence of human settlements in Southeast Asia is dated to 40,000 BC, although humans must have arrived there much earlier, as they are known to have traveled by sea on boats or rafts to Australia more than 60,000 years ago.

Settlement in Oceania

After the settlement of New Guinea, the Bismarck Archipelago, and the Solomon Islands by forebears of the Papuans during the last ice age, Oceania – like the islands of Indonesia – witnessed an influx of Austronesian-speaking immigrants from Indochina, whose agrarian culture is identified by Lapita ceramics. The Austronesians who remained in Melanesia intermingled with the original dark-skinned population (Melanesians), and their language spread beyond the island of New Guinea. Other (light-skinned) Austronesians, who were experienced seafarers, soon moved with their food plants and domesticated animals to the islands of Polynesia. They continued to move eastward, reaching the Fiji Islands about 1,500 BC, Tonga in 1,400 BC, Samoa in 1,100 B.C, and the Society Islands in 500 BC, proceeding from there to Tahiti, Easter Island, Hawaii and New Zealand. Western Micronesia was probably settled by migrants from Indonesia or the Philippines as recently as 2,000 years ago, the remaining Micronesian islands from the south and east and the New Hebrides beginning about 1,300 BC (the Carolines were settled last, during the 3rd century AD).

The First Americans

The first humans to arrive on the American continent were anatomically modern. More than 20,000 years ago, people from hunting societies in northeastern Asia trekked over the land bridge across today's Bering Strait into the predominantly ice-free territory of Alaska.

Following the movements of game animals (mammoth, bison, reindeer), they advanced into the continental interior along an ice-free corridor between the glacial ice of the Cordilleras and the Laurentide Ice Sheet. These Paleo-Indian peoples then spread rapidly over the American continents, advancing as far as Brazil, Patagonia and Chile. Since the Monte Verde archeological site (southern Chile) is about 14,000 years old, migration into North America must have begun much earlier than the oldest finds uncovered in the region (artifacts of the Clovis Culture, named for its characteristic arrow and spear heads, from about 13,500 BC) would indicate. Was there a pre-Clovian culture whose people lived from plants and small animals and used different, more rudimentary implements? Evidence of human settlement in the Amazon Basin near the end of the last ice age points to the existence of such a culture. The significance of much older finds in South America (dating as far back as 40,000 BC) remains in dispute, however. Presumably, human populations initially spread along the coasts.

Three distinct waves of migration have been identified on the basis of linguistic and genetic evidence. The last wave brought the ancestors of the Eskimos (Inuit) to the northern regions of Canada and Greenland some 4,000 years ago. Well adapted to their arctic environment, they survived the "little ice age" that began in the 13th century BC and put an end to Viking settlements in Greenland.

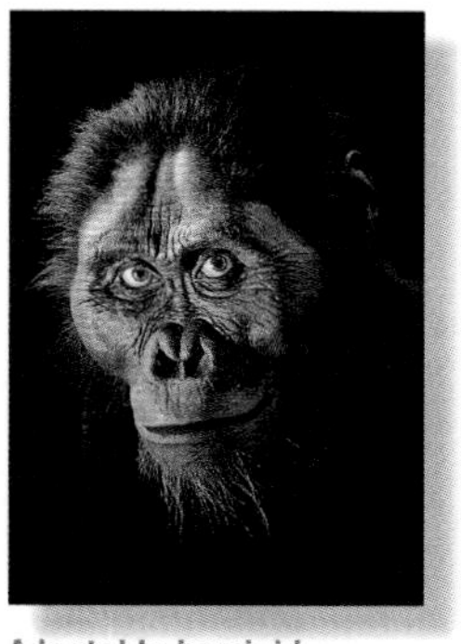

Adaptable hominid: Although the cranium of Australopithecus afarensis was no larger than that of contemporary chimpanzees, this hominid traveled on two legs through the savanna.

Map caption

Primary migration routes of Homo erectus

Kärlich · Bilzingsleben · Boxgrove · Mauer · Prezletice · Soleilhac, Le Vallonnet · Atapuerca/ Gran Dolina · Ceprano · Isernia · EUROPE · Dmanisi · ASIA · Thomas Quarries/ Sidi Abderrahman · Tighenif · Ubeidiya · Zhoukoudian · Yiyuan · Lantian · Hexian · Yunxian · Longgupo · Yuanmou · PACIFIC OCEAN · AFRICA · Yayo · Omo · Konso-Gardula · Melka-Kunturé · Nariokotome · Lake Turkana · Baringo (Kapthurin) · Olduvai · INDIAN OCEAN · ATLANTIC OCEAN · Trinil, Sangiran Sambungmacan · Mojokerto · Swartkrans · AUSTRALIA

Major finds of bones and tools of Homo erectus

Protection against Cold and Rain

Reconstruction of a house from the last phase of the Late Stone Age: walls and roof (wood) are covered with horse hides; inside, a mammoth thigh bone supports a roasting spit next to the fire place.

The "Lion King"

People living during the ice age more than 30,000 years ago regarded the lion not only as a dangerous enemy and a hunting rival but also as a symbol of strength and superiority. Does this ivory (female) human-lion figure discovered in Lonetal indicate belief in a magical unity of animal and human beings?

Evolutionary Model: "Out of Africa"

Modern Europeans	Modern Africans	Modern East Asians	Modern Australians
Cro-Magnon			
Neanderthal (archaic Homo sapiens)	Klasies people (modern Homo sapiens)	Dali people (archaic Homo sapiens)	Ngandong (archaic Homo sapiens/ late Homo erectus)
Ante-Neanderthal	African Homo erectus	East Asian Homo erectus	Indonesian Homo erectus

Exploration of the Earth's Surface

A Grand European Triumph?

The European seafarers of the 15th and 16th centuries were celebrated as great discoverers. And that they were, at least from the European perspective. Reports of their travels were circulated and analyzed by cartographers, and their knowledge was widely disseminated (with some valuable insights kept secret) thanks to the newly invented printing process. Yet other explorers had achieved great seafaring accomplishments long before. Perhaps the most ambitious adventure of all times was the settlement of Polynesia by Austronesians from Southeast Asia. The boldest of their advances took place in the 1st millennium BC and brought human settlements to Hawaii and Easter Island.

Ancient Discoveries

Egyptians are known to have voyaged to Punt (presumably Somalia) as early as 2,200 BC. Queen Hatshepsut sponsored a sea expedition to Punt in the 15th century BC. Phoenicians are believed to have circumnavigated the African continent under the flag of the Egyptian Pharaoh in the early 6th century BC. In the 5th century BC, Herodotus compiled a map of the known world on the basis of his own knowledge and accounts of voyages of exploration. The Greek seafarer Pytheas of Massalia (Marseilles) sailed the coasts of western and northern Europe in about 330 BC, and is thought to have reached Arctic drift ice.

The Arabs expanded the geographic knowledge amassed by the Greeks. In the Middle Ages, they had compiled the most detailed knowledge about Africa, western and southern Asia. The overland journeys of Ibn Battutah (14th century) took him to Timbuktu and China.

The Chinese first ventured to the shores of the Persian Gulf in the 5th century. Chinese naval exploration flourished in the 10th century and reached its zenith in the expeditions of Zheng He to East Africa in the 15th century. The European Age of Discovery began – after some forerunners like Marco Polo – with the great sea voyages of the 15th and 16th centuries. Under the leadership of Henry the Navigator, the Portuguese initially took the lead in ocean-going exploration, but were soon rivaled by the Spanish. Their goal was to eliminate Arab middlemen from the spice trade. Arab merchants had traveled as far as Southeast Asia, spreading the religion of Islam on their commercial crusades into these distant regions.

Who Discovered America?

Humans first set foot on the North American continent at least 20,000 years ago. Migrating over the land bridge between Alaska and northeastern Siberia across what is now the Bering Strait, they eventually settled the entire continent. The hunting societies on both sides of the Bering Strait remained in contact. The Vikings made a number of visits to the eastern coast of North America beginning in the 10th century AD, but their explorations had no lasting impact on early American or European societies. The arrival of Christopher Columbus had much more far-reaching consequences. The map of the known world grew larger. Europeans conquered the "New World." Native Americans were subjugated and their populations decimated in the centuries that followed.

"Show me Adam's will!"

This angry outburst by French King Francis I is indicative of the reactions of the English, Dutch, and Italians, who were compelled to look on passively while Spain and Portugal divided the world up between them, at first in the Treaty of Tordesillas in 1494 and later in the Treaty of Saragossa (1529). The nations of Europe did everything in their power to secure their share of the treasures of the "newly discovered" lands. The quest for northeast and northwest passages, short trade routes through Arctic waters to Asia, began under the English flag (Caboto) in the late 15th century.

"Replenish the earth, and subdue it!"

The "discovered" peoples might surely have posed the question of Adam's will with better reason. Why did the Europeans become the leading discoverers and conquerors? Why didn't the Aztecs or the Incas invade Spain? Why didn't the Chinese become a true sea power? A number of cultural, political, and technological factors combined to enable the Europeans to answer the biblical call to action. They were driven not only by hunger for power, gold, and riches, but also by missionary zeal and a curiosity about foreign lands that was alien to such cultures as the Chinese of the Middle Kingdom, for example.

By 1600, knowledge of geography had expanded immensely – as a by-product of exploration, so to speak. Scientific interest played an important role in the voyages of the last great seafaring explorer James Cook, and the continental explorations of Alexander von Humboldt, which also focused on vertical aspects of topography, were devoted exclusively to scientific inquiry.

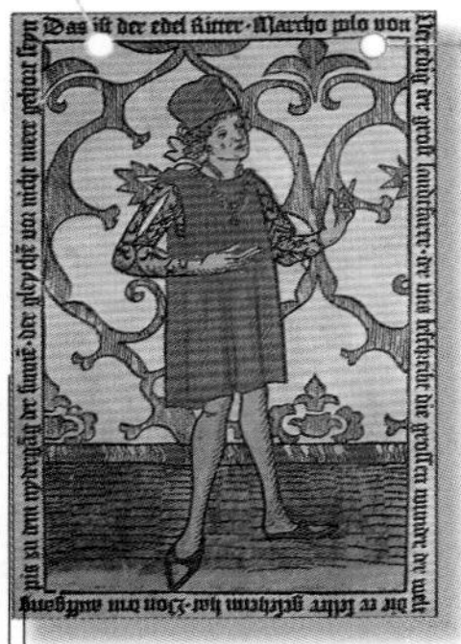

The Wonders of the Distant Orient

Members of the Polo family traveled as merchants and trade representatives to China long before the age of European expansion. Printed in many European languages, Marco Polo's Il Milione, an account of his travels, was the most important source of information about Asia in the medieval world and is known to have influenced Columbus.

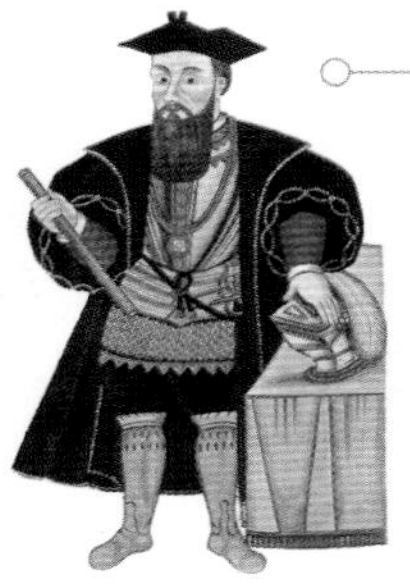

Objective Achieved

Only 28 years after the death of Henry the Navigator, Vasco da Gama discovered the sea route to India and weighed anchor off the Indian coast after a ten-month journey around Africa. He returned to Lisbon with a rich cargo of spices and jewels but with only a third of his original crew.

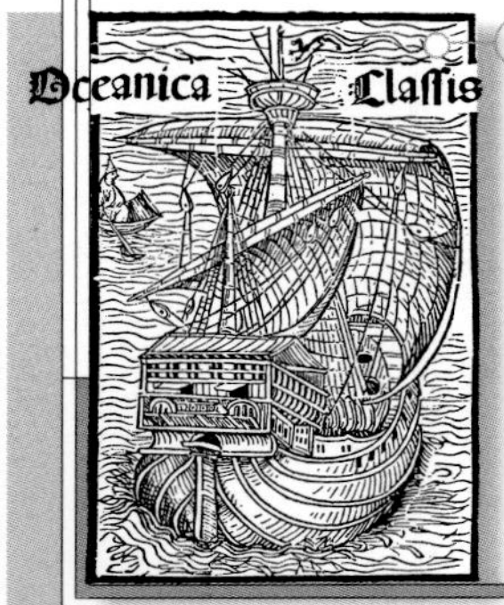

Prototype of an Explorer's Vessel

After the first voyages of discovery in small, agile caravels fitted with a triangular sail in the style of Arab dhows, explorers saw the need for larger ships capable of transporting troops, horses, cannons, and provisions. The new vessels were modeled after Nordic ships and powered by a square sail.

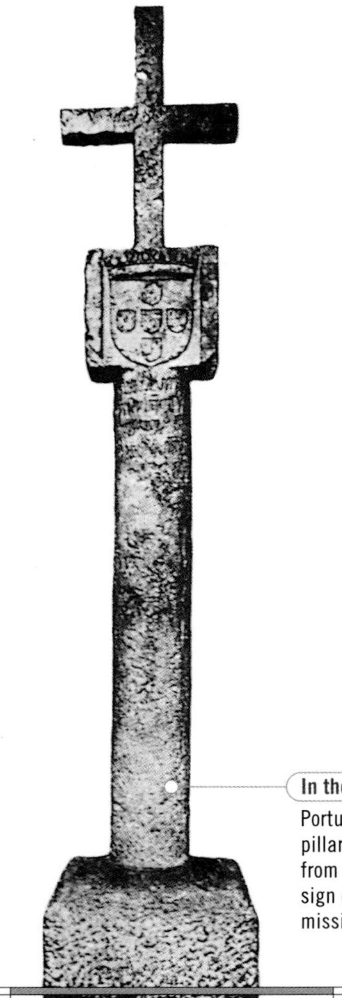

In the Name of the Cross

Portuguese seafarers placed stone pillars bearing emblems (photo from Cape Cross in Namibia) as a sign of conquest and a symbol of missionary intent.

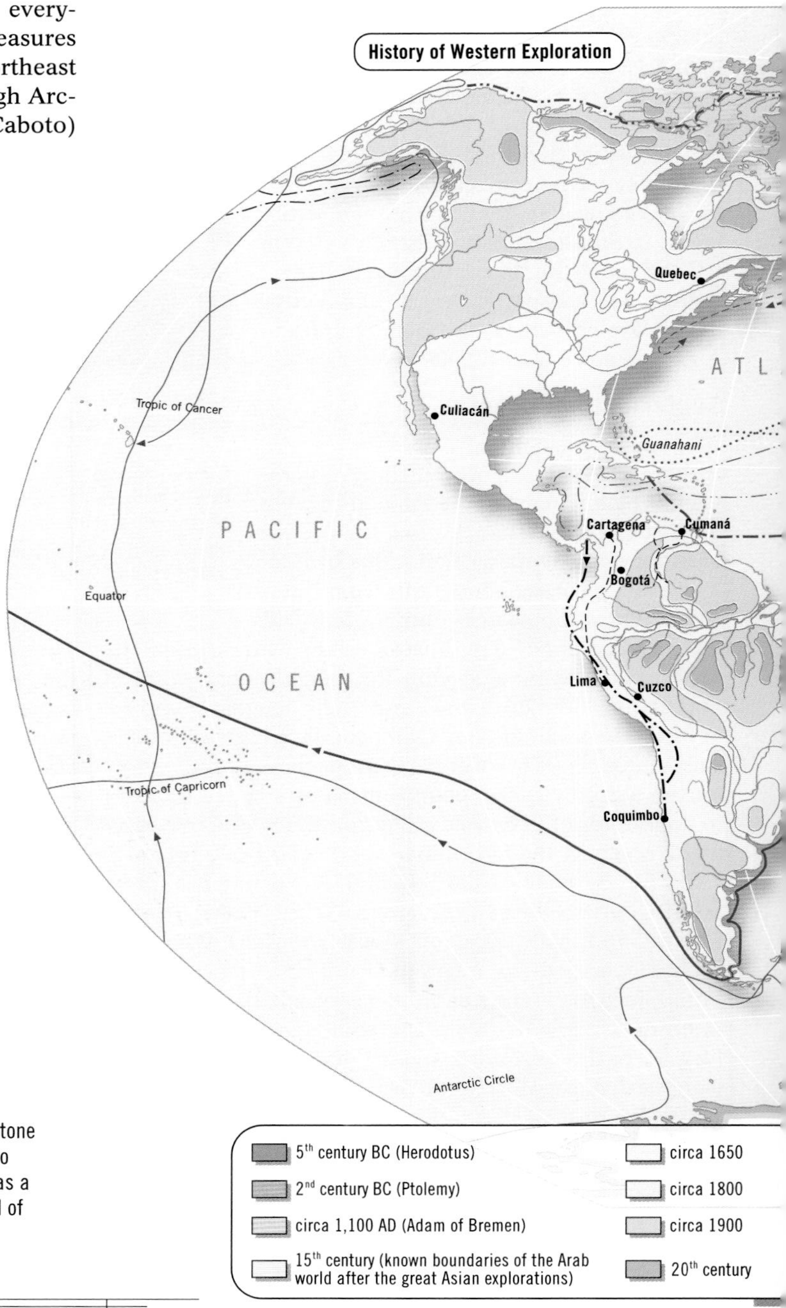

History of Western Exploration

5th century BC (Herodotus)	circa 1650
2nd century BC (Ptolemy)	circa 1800
circa 1,100 AD (Adam of Bremen)	circa 1900
15th century (known boundaries of the Arab world after the great Asian explorations)	20th century

Unveiling the Earth's surface

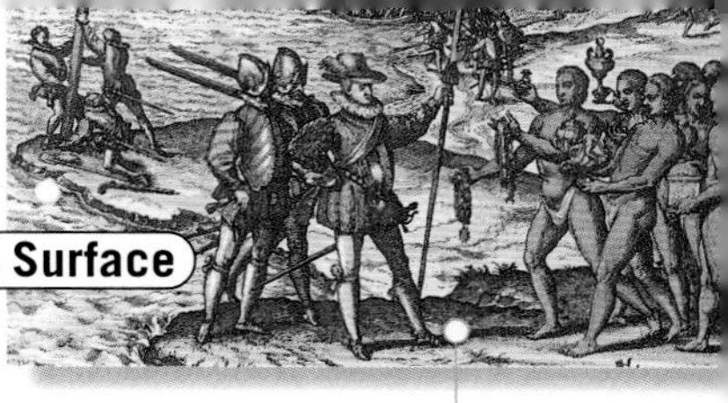

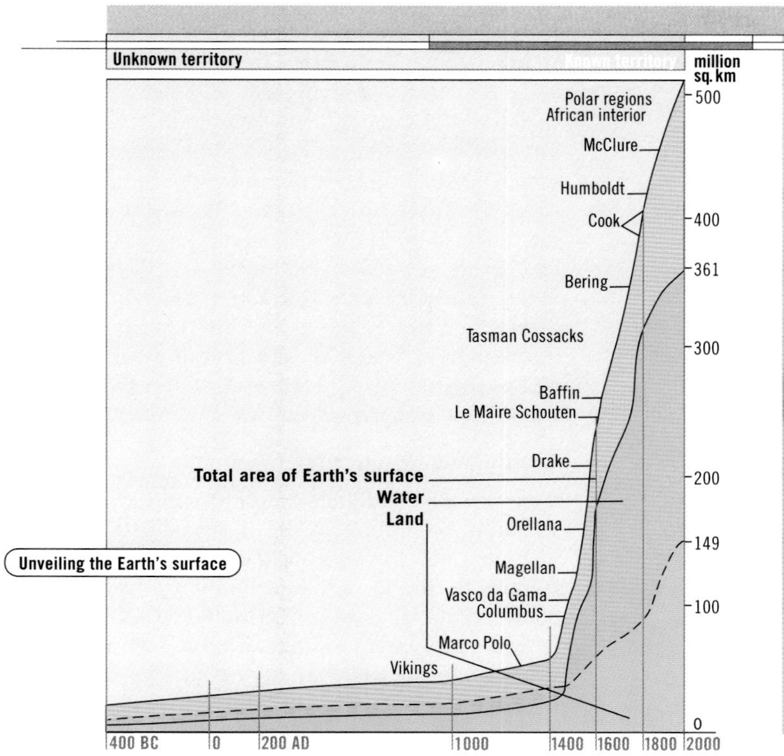

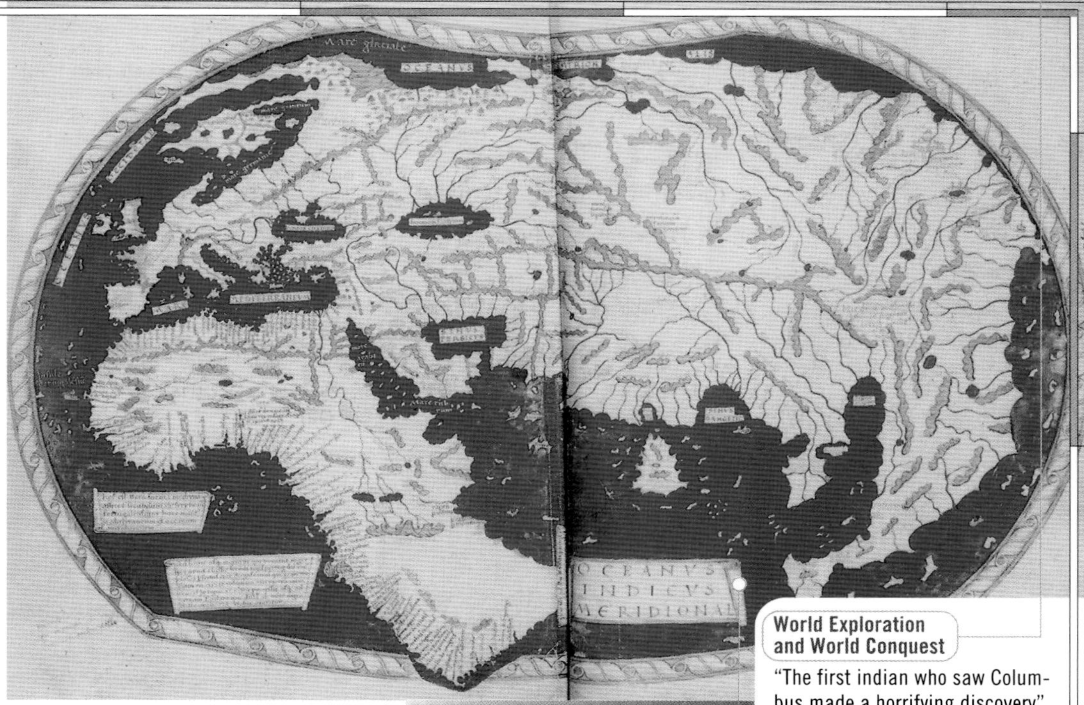

Unknown territory | Known territory

million sq. km

- 500 — Polar regions / African interior
- McClure
- Humboldt
- 400 — Cook
- Bering
- 361
- 300 — Tasman Cossacks
- Baffin
- Le Maire Schouten
- Drake
- 200 — Total area of Earth's surface / Water / Land
- Orellana
- 149 — Magellan
- Vasco da Gama / Columbus
- 100 — Marco Polo
- Vikings
- 0

400 BC | 0 | 200 AD | 1000 | 1400 1600 1800 2000

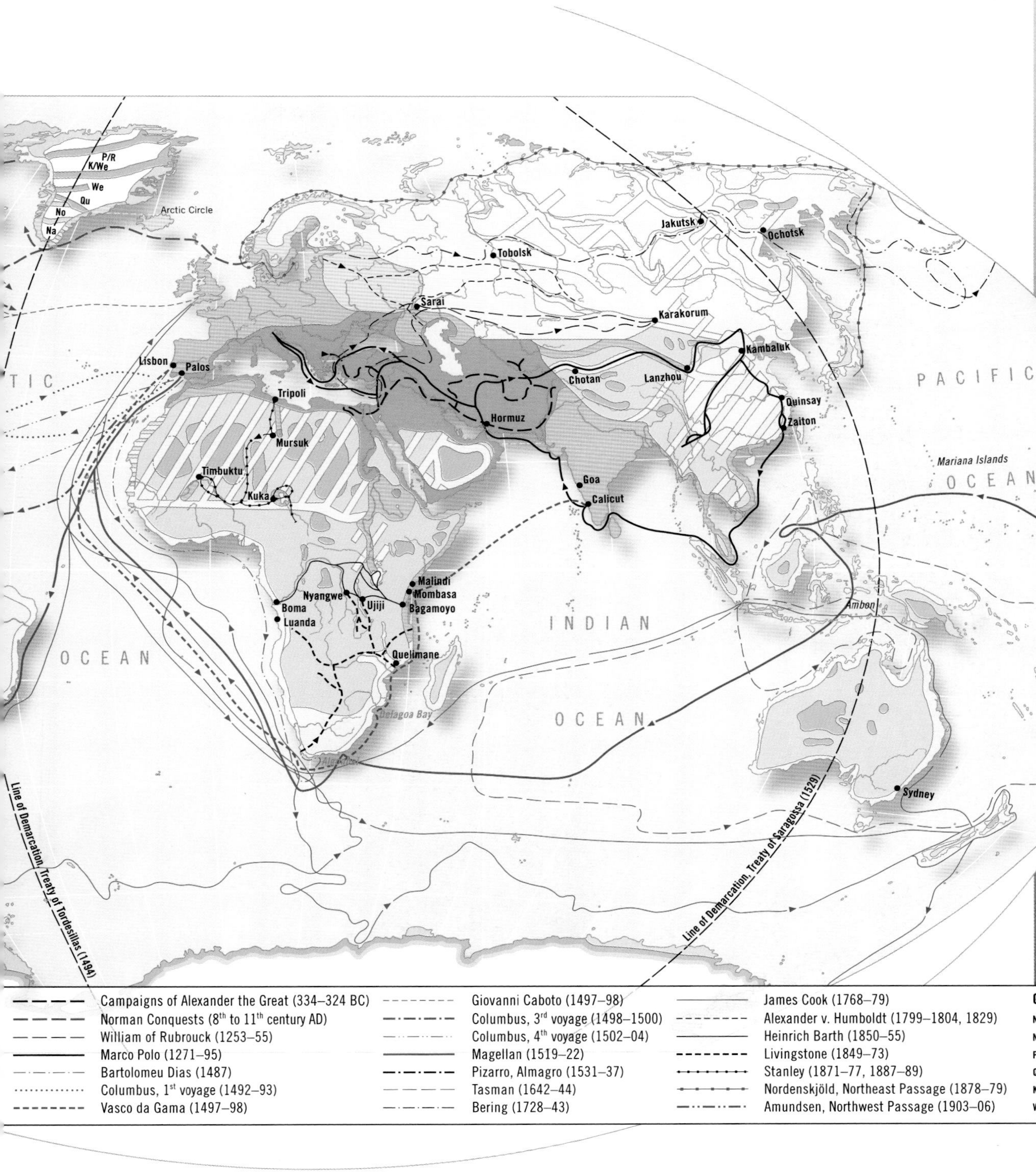

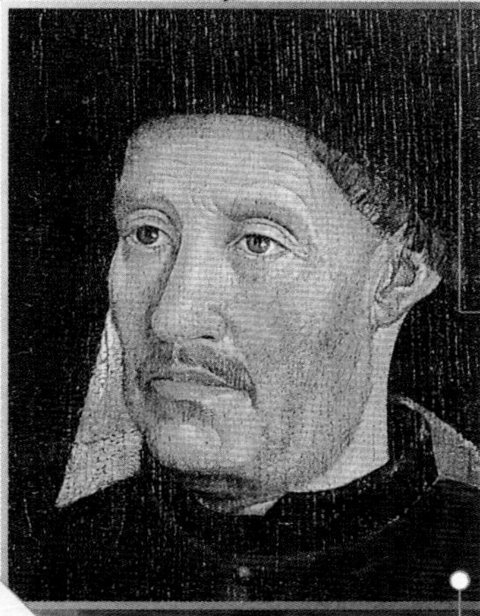

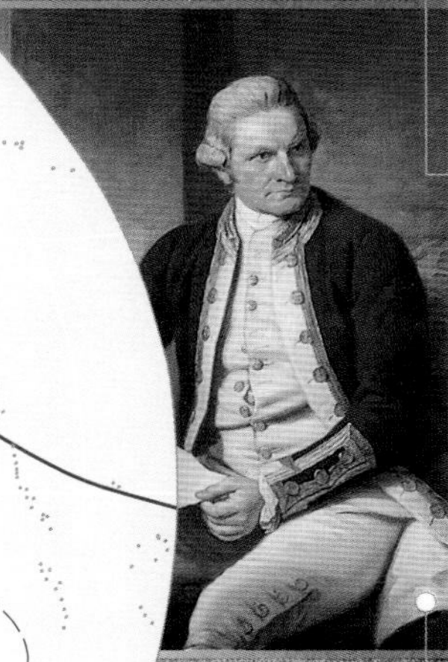

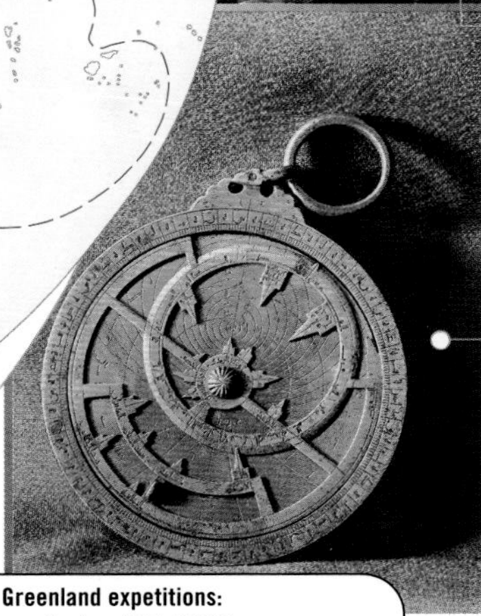

World Exploration and World Conquest

"The first indian who saw Columbus made a horrifying discovery" (G. Lichtenberg). This statement offers a view of a milestone event in world history from the other side. The painting by Johann Theodor de Bry (1594) shows indians bringing gifts while Spanish soldiers erect a cross.

The World According to Ptolemy

This 15th-century map is based on the view of the world as envisioned by the Greek astronomer and geographer Ptolemy (2nd century AD), which was generally accepted until after the rounding of the African horn (1488) and the western voyage of Columbus (1492). Africa is linked to a continent in the south, Terra australis incognita, which almost completely encloses the Indian Ocean.

A Visionary Founds a Think Tank

Known by the misleading title of "Henry the Navigator," Portuguese Prince Dom Henrique established an interdisciplinary academy of navigation in Sagres, where available geographic knowledge was compiled — and kept strictly secret. Beginning in 1418, he promoted the exploration of unknown waters in hopes of discovering a sea route to India and its spices.

Planet of Seas

The myth of the vast southern continent of Terra australis incognita was finally put to rest by James Cook. Traveling more ocean routes than all of his predecessors together, Cook shed light on the configuration of the Earth's oceans.

An Arab Innovation

Portuguese seafarers owed much of their success to nautical instruments invented by Arabs. With the aid of the astrolabe, latitude and local time could be determined on the basis of celestial measurements.

– – – –	Campaigns of Alexander the Great (334–324 BC)
– · – · –	Norman Conquests (8th to 11th century AD)
	William of Rubrouck (1253–55)
	Marco Polo (1271–95)
	Bartolomeu Dias (1487)
· · · · · ·	Columbus, 1st voyage (1492–93)
	Vasco da Gama (1497–98)

– – – –	Giovanni Caboto (1497–98)
	Columbus, 3rd voyage (1498–1500)
	Columbus, 4th voyage (1502–04)
	Magellan (1519–22)
	Pizarro, Almagro (1531–37)
	Tasman (1642–44)
	Bering (1728–43)

	James Cook (1768–79)
– – – –	Alexander v. Humboldt (1799–1804, 1829)
	Heinrich Barth (1850–55)
– – – –	Livingstone (1849–73)
· · · · · ·	Stanley (1871–77, 1887–89)
–•–•–	Nordenskjöld, Northeast Passage (1878–79)
	Amundsen, Northwest Passage (1903–06)

Greenland expeditions:
No — Nordenskjöld (1883)
Na — Nansen (1888)
P/R — Peary (1892–95), Rasmussen (1912)
Qu — Quervain (1912)
K/We — Koch-Wegener (1912–13)
We — Wegener (1930)

The Dynamic Global Population

Explosion versus Stagnation

The world's population is constantly growing. When Christ was born, some 300 million people lived on Earth. By the time Columbus discovered America, the number had risen to 500 million. In 1969, the first human to set foot on the moon looked back at a world with a population of 3.5 billion. The number has since grown to six billion and continues to rise at a rate of about 80 million every year.

Phases of Growth

Population growth has proceeded slowly but steadily since the Neolithic revolution, when human communities first adopted a sedentary lifestyle some 12,000 years ago. Growth accelerated rapidly after the Industrial Revolution, which began in Europe around 1800. Industrialization led to significant improvements in living standards, nutrition, medical care, and disease prevention and thus unleashed a veritable population explosion. The Demographic Transition Model reflects the interdependence of birth and mortality rates as a crucial parameter of population growth. As a rule, the later a country enters the third phase, the more significant – although shorter – the period of explosive growth will be.

Global Developments

Comparisons in time and place support this statement. England, birthplace of the Industrial Revolution in the waning 18th century (Malthus published his pessimistic treatise on the Principle of Population in 1803), did not achieve balance between birth and death rates until nearly 200 years later, whereas it took Japan only 40 to 50 years to do so. Today, many countries in Asia and especially in Africa are in the midst of demographic transition. Apparently growing without end, their populations double about every 25 years (Great Britain every 423 years; Austria every 2,310 years; Japan every 318 years!). Yet demographers expect that global population growth will slow to a standstill in the mid-21st century at a level of between ten and twelve billion people.

Possible Growth Scenarios

To an increasing extent, global population is concentrated in the developing nations today. In 1950, only about two-thirds of the estimated 2.5 billion people on Earth were inhabitants of these countries. By the mid-21st century, this figure will have risen to 88% of a total world population of about ten billion. Rapid growth in these regions contrasts with stagnation or extremely slow growth in the industrialized countries. Both of these tendencies pose grave dangers to human societies.

Unbridled growth in Latin America, Asia, and especially Africa not only exacerbates the social and economic disparities between north and south, it also has a severe impact on the environment in the form of uncon-

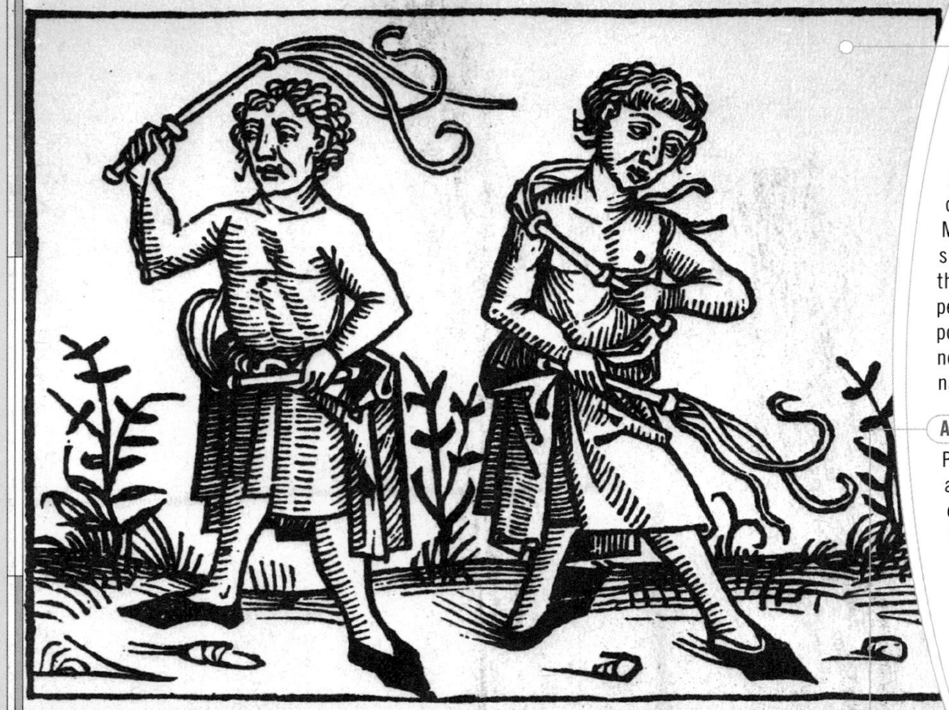

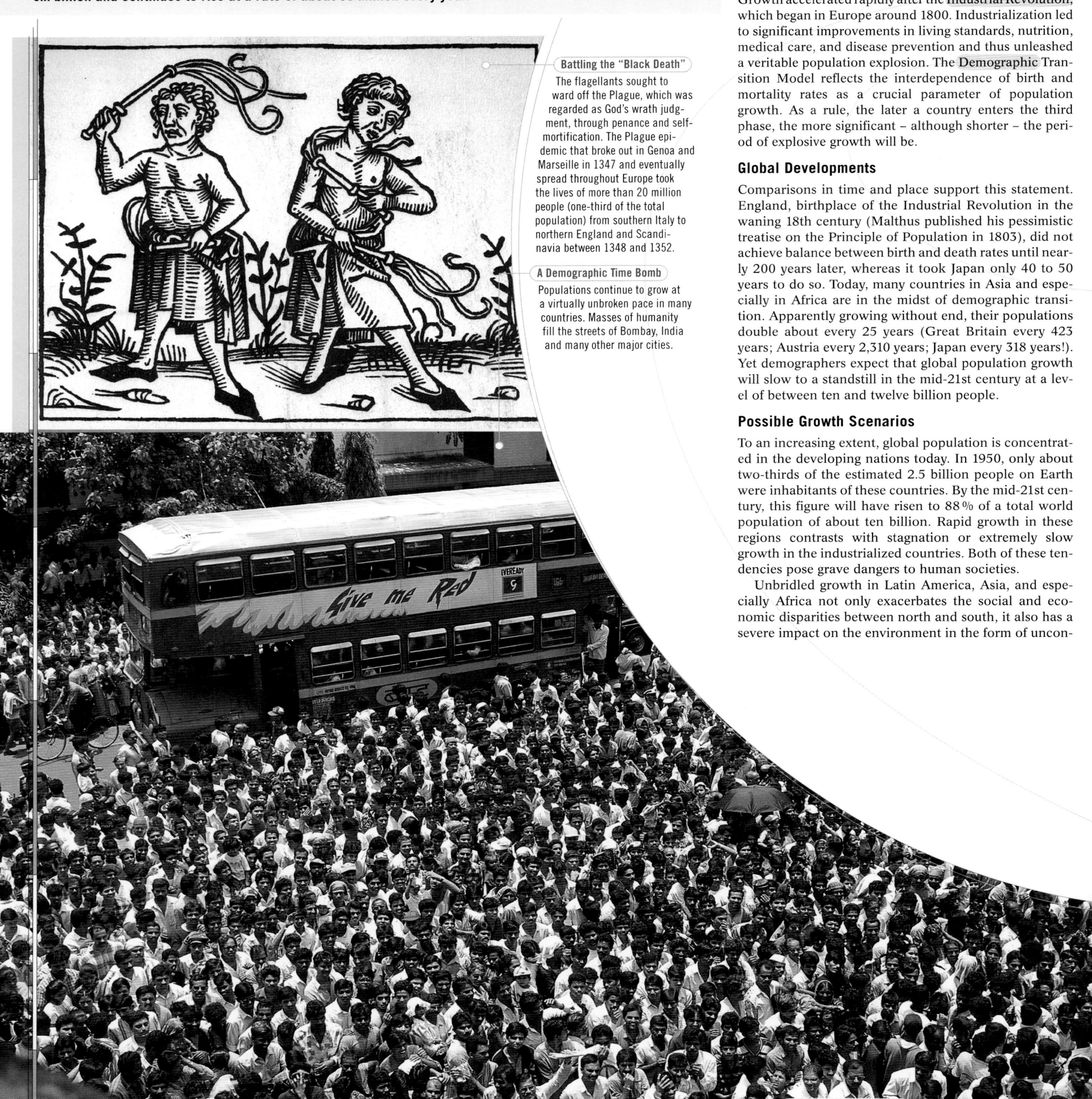

Battling the "Black Death"
The flagellants sought to ward off the Plague, which was regarded as God's wrath judgment, through penance and self-mortification. The Plague epidemic that broke out in Genoa and Marseille in 1347 and eventually spread throughout Europe took the lives of more than 20 million people (one-third of the total population) from southern Italy to northern England and Scandinavia between 1348 and 1352.

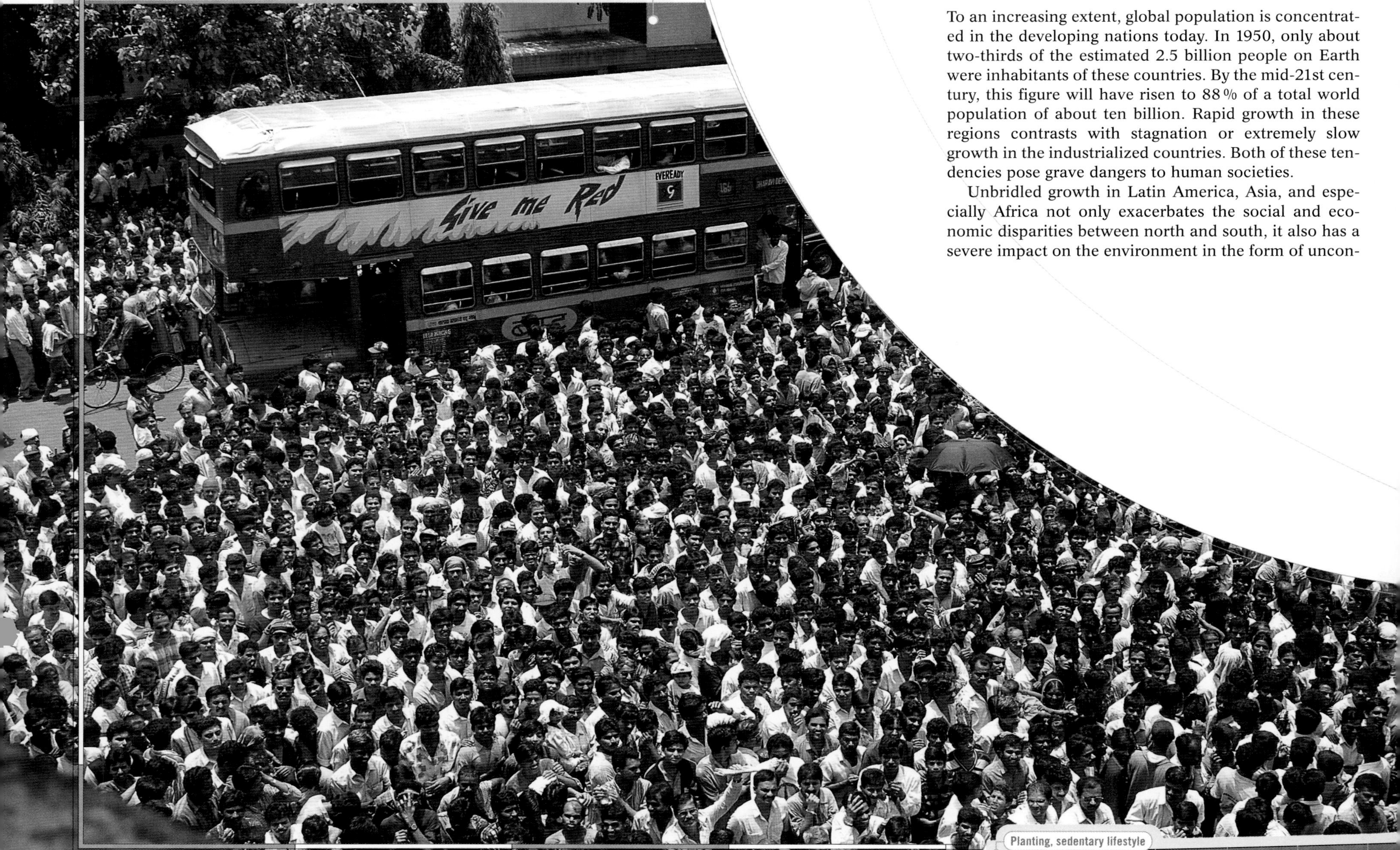

A Demographic Time Bomb
Populations continue to grow at a virtually unbroken pace in many countries. Masses of humanity fill the streets of Bombay, India and many other major cities.

Give me Red

Planting, sedentary lifestyle

| 12000 | 9000 | 8000 | 7000 | 6000 | 5000 |

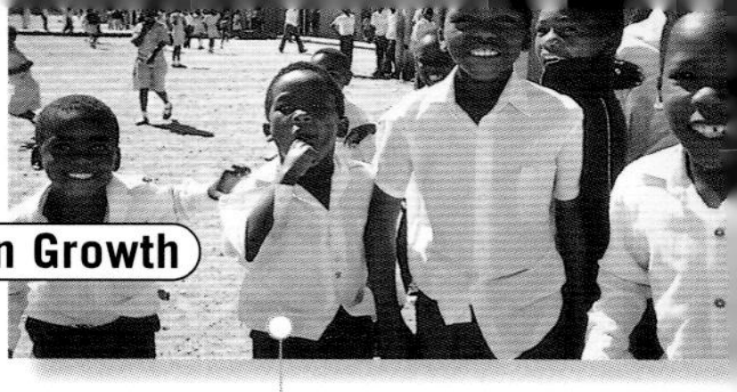

World population in 1999 — Growth and projection

	Population in millions	Birth rate per thousand	Death rate per thousand	Natural growth per cent	Population doubling (in years at current growth rate)	Projected population in 2025 (millions)	Age distribution <15	>65
World	5 982	23	9	1.4	49	8 054	31	7
Africa	771	39	14	2.5	28	1 290	43	3
North America	303	14	8	0.6	119	374	21	13
Latin America	512	24	6	1.8	38	709	33	5
Australia – Oceania	30	18	7	1.1	64	41	26	10
Asia	3 637	23	8	1.5	46	4 923	32	6
Europe	728	10	11	−0.1	–	718	18	14
Examples of extremes:								
Dem. Rep. Congo	50.5	48	16	3.2	22	105.7	48	3
Austria	8.1	10	10	0.0	2 310	8.1	17	15
Germany	82.0	10	10	−0.1	–	79.9	16	16

trolled exploitation of available land, diminishing water reserves, deforestation, and desertification. The consequences include famine, waves of refugee migration, the expansion of slums in major urban centers, increasing poverty, and the spread of disease. The devastating effects of the AIDS epidemic on societies in Africa and other parts of the world speak much louder than words.

Yet stagnation and decline (populations in several industrialized nations such as Germany and Austria are currently shrinking) pose serious problems as well. As populations dwindle, they also tend to grow older, and both trends will have a lasting impact on many areas of life – the labor market and social security systems, education and housing, public health service, commerce and transportation, to name only a few.

Limits and Dangers: Quantitative and Qualitative Population Growth

Exploding populations in some places, stagnating or declining populations in others. This disparity in a world that is becoming more closely interconnected in time and space every day poses a significant problem in itself. The situation is made worse by severe inequalities in the distribution and use of limited natural resources. The question of the Earth's ability to accommodate its inhabitants can no longer be answered simply in terms of its potential to produce food but must also be examined in the light of environmental factors. It is not necessarily the sheer numbers of people that threaten the equilibrium of System Earth. More often than not, it is the rich (we ourselves!) who jeopardize the balance through our irresponsible and insatiable urge to consume in order to satisfy what we regard as essential needs!

Demographic Transition

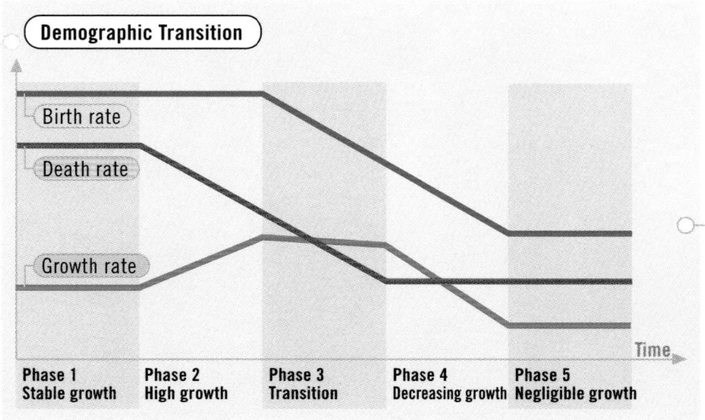

Birth rate

Death rate

Growth rate

Time

| Phase 1 Stable growth | Phase 2 High growth | Phase 3 Transition | Phase 4 Decreasing growth | Phase 5 Negligible growth |

Declining birth rates

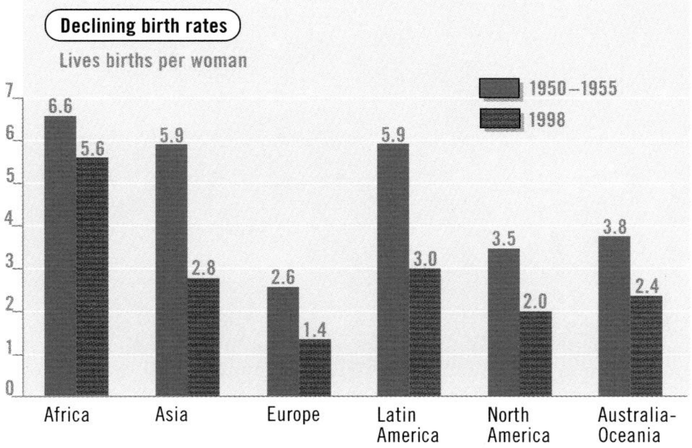

Lives births per woman

■ 1950–1955
■ 1998

Africa: 6.6 / 5.6
Asia: 5.9 / 2.8
Europe: 2.6 / 1.4
Latin America: 5.9 / 3.0
North America: 3.5 / 2.0
Australia-Oceania: 3.8 / 2.4

Future Fathers
With a growth rate of 2.3 % per annum (1990-98) South Africa is by no means the fastest-growing country on the African continent (that honor goes to Niger, with 3.9%). These school children in Johannesburg will probably be parents themselves in 15 years.

Unstoppable Growth?
The length of time it takes the global population to increase by one billion people has become increasingly shorter over the course of history. The one-billion mark was reached in 1804, and the total reached two million 123 years later. Successive billions were added at intervals of 33, 14, and 13 years, respectively. Only twelve years later – in October 1999 – world population reached six billion.

Changing Growth Rates
Demographic transition from an agrarian to an industrial society follows a predictable pattern. State 1 is characterized by high birth and death rates, with natural growth (the difference between the two) remaining relatively low. In State 2, death rates fall, birth rates remain stable, and the growth rate rises accordingly. In State 3, birth rates begin to fall as well. State 4 marks the transition from rapid to slow growth. In State 5, birth, death, and growth rates stabilize at a low level.

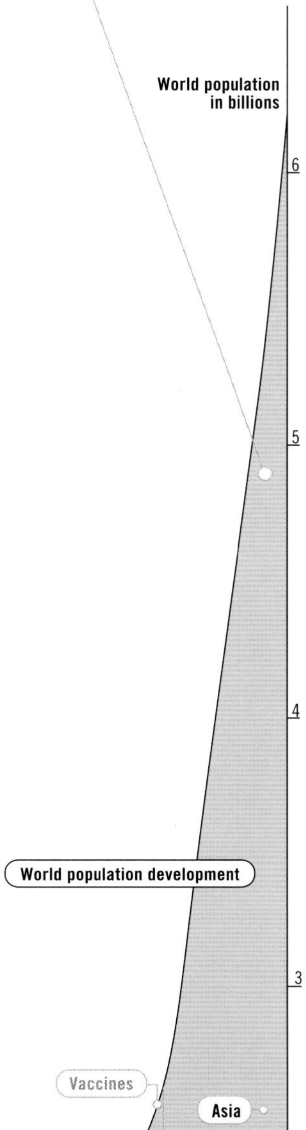

Restricted Growth
Billboards in China (photo: Beijing) appeal for acceptance of the single-child-family rule prescribed by Chinese law.

Steel Boiler, 1886
Rapid population growth began with the Industrial Revolution.

World population in billions

World population development

Vaccines

Asia

Artificial fertilizers

Americas

Industrial Revolution

Africa

Australia-Oceania

Europe

Plague epidemics

Bronze tools

Iron tools

4000 3000 2000 1000 0 1450 1500 1550 1600 1650 1700 1750 1800 1850 1900 1950 2000

6 5 4 3 2 1

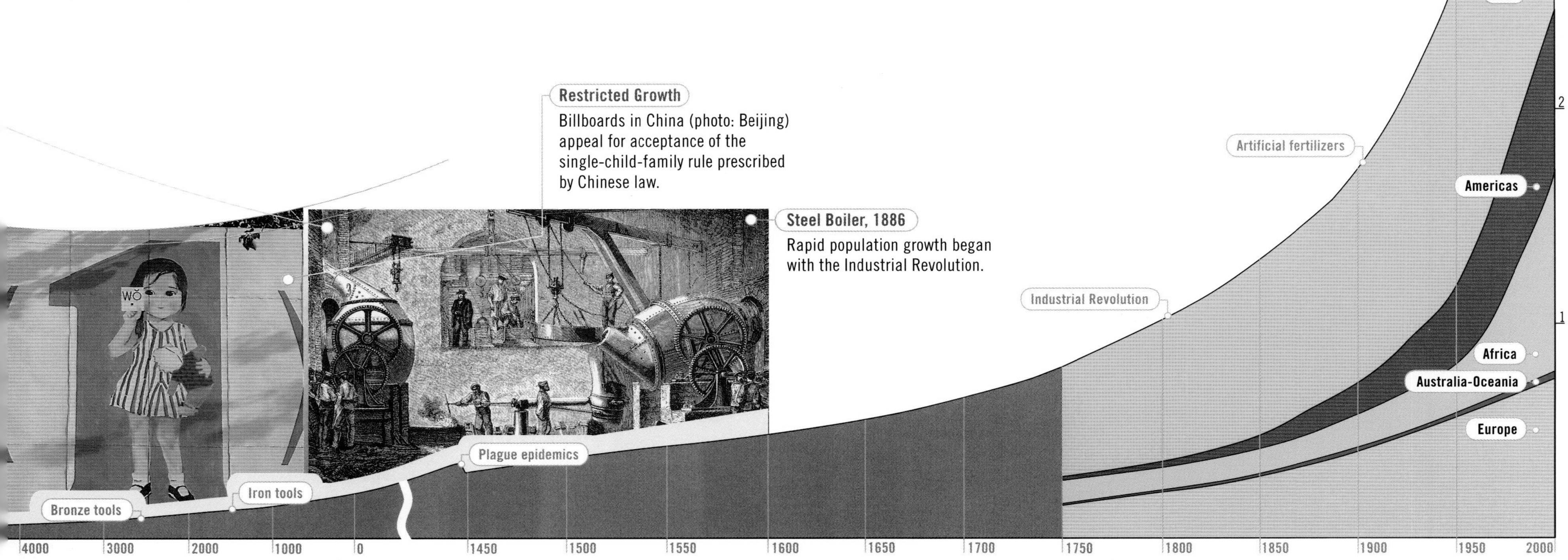

Human Migration

A Global View of Shifting Populations

The history of humanity is a history of migration – and has been since the first humans appeared on Earth. Immigrants and emigrants – invading hordes and war refugees – mass migrations: all of these terms describe aspects of a complex problem that is of crucial global importance today.

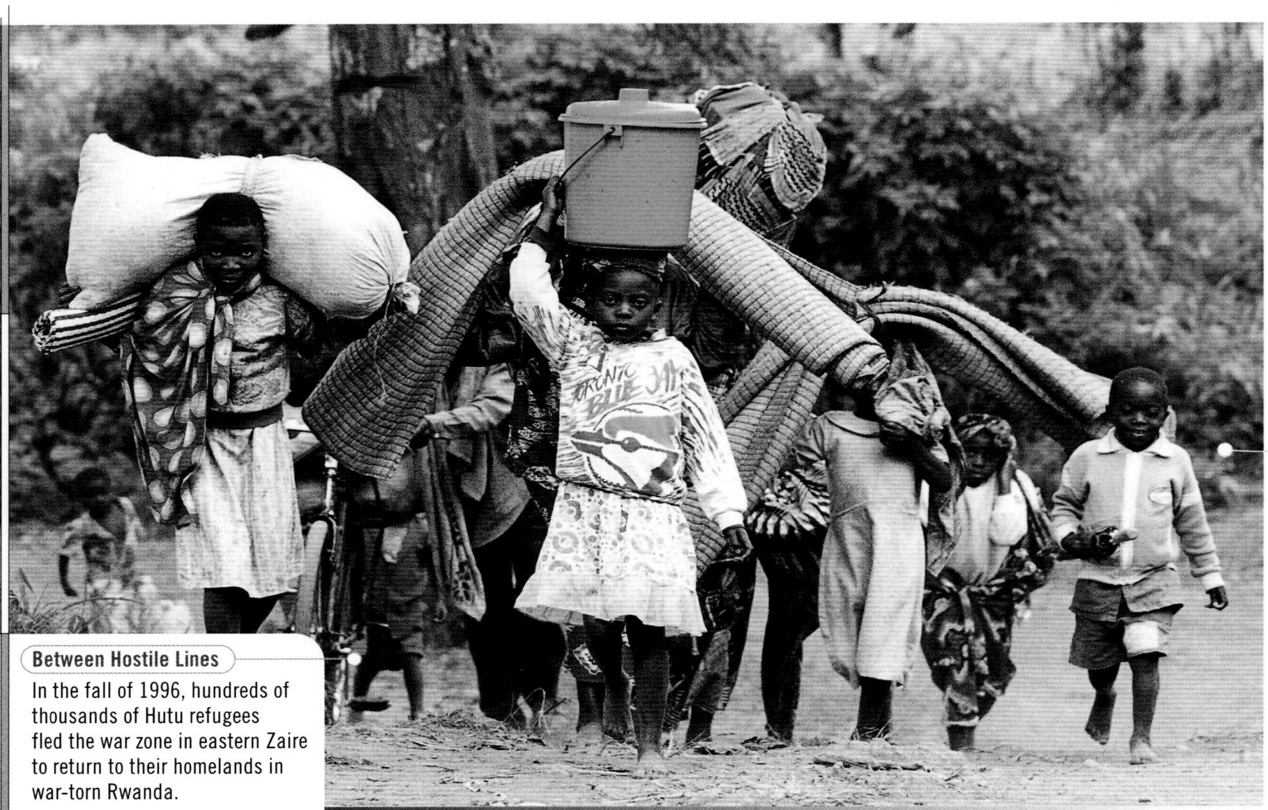

Between Hostile Lines
In the fall of 1996, hundreds of thousands of Hutu refugees fled the war zone in eastern Zaire to return to their homelands in war-torn Rwanda.

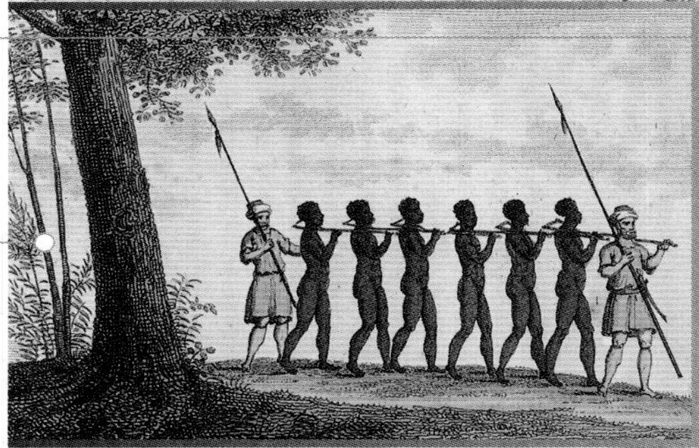

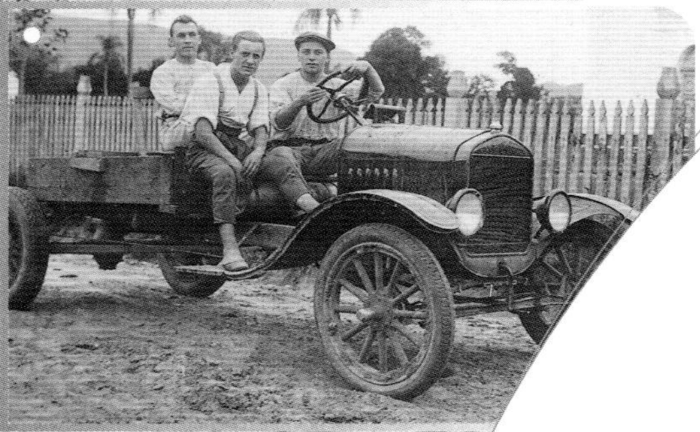

Skills Wanted Abroad
Young emigrants from Germany in Brazil (1925): automotive knowledge and skills provide the basis for a new start.

Involuntary Exile
African captives were often chained together with their hands bound to a pole during their journey into slavery.

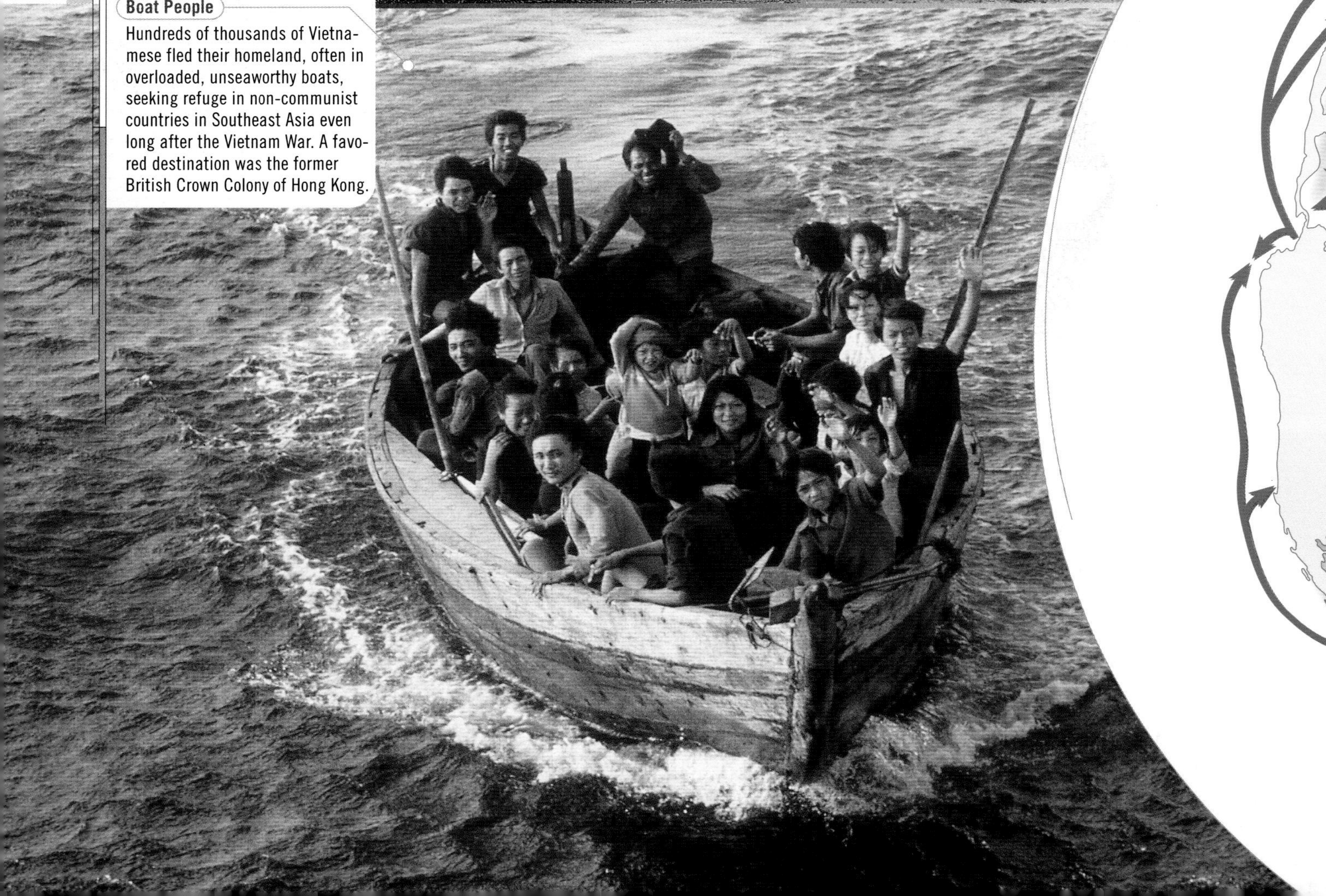

Boat People
Hundreds of thousands of Vietnamese fled their homeland, often in overloaded, unseaworthy boats, seeking refuge in non-communist countries in Southeast Asia even long after the Vietnam War. A favored destination was the former British Crown Colony of Hong Kong.

Causes of Popular Migration

In addition to the natural causes of many major population movements (floods, soil degradation, desertification, etc.), people have tended to migrate primarily for ideological and economic reasons. Aside from the many unfortunate cases of involuntary migration (banishment, deportation, flight from persecution, slavery, etc.), economic push-and-pull factors are among the most common causes of large-scale migration. Overpopulation, a shortage of work, and the corresponding economic and social misery that accompany these phenomena are and always have been important "push" factors contributing to regional migration and emigration. On the other hand, prosperity and an abundance of jobs in other countries attract workers and economic refugees, as "pull" factors, with the promise of better living conditions and opportunities for social advancement. A review of the economic and social history of the modern era clearly shows that political developments in many areas of the world have been shaped by major population movements – from the mass displacement of African slaves to the emigration of Europeans (primarily for economic or political reasons) to the New World, Australia, New Zealand, and South Africa. In the roughly one hundred years between 1830 to 1928, nearly six million Germans emigrated, about 90 % of them to the U.S., the remainder to Canada, Brazil, Australia, Argentina, South Africa, and Asia.

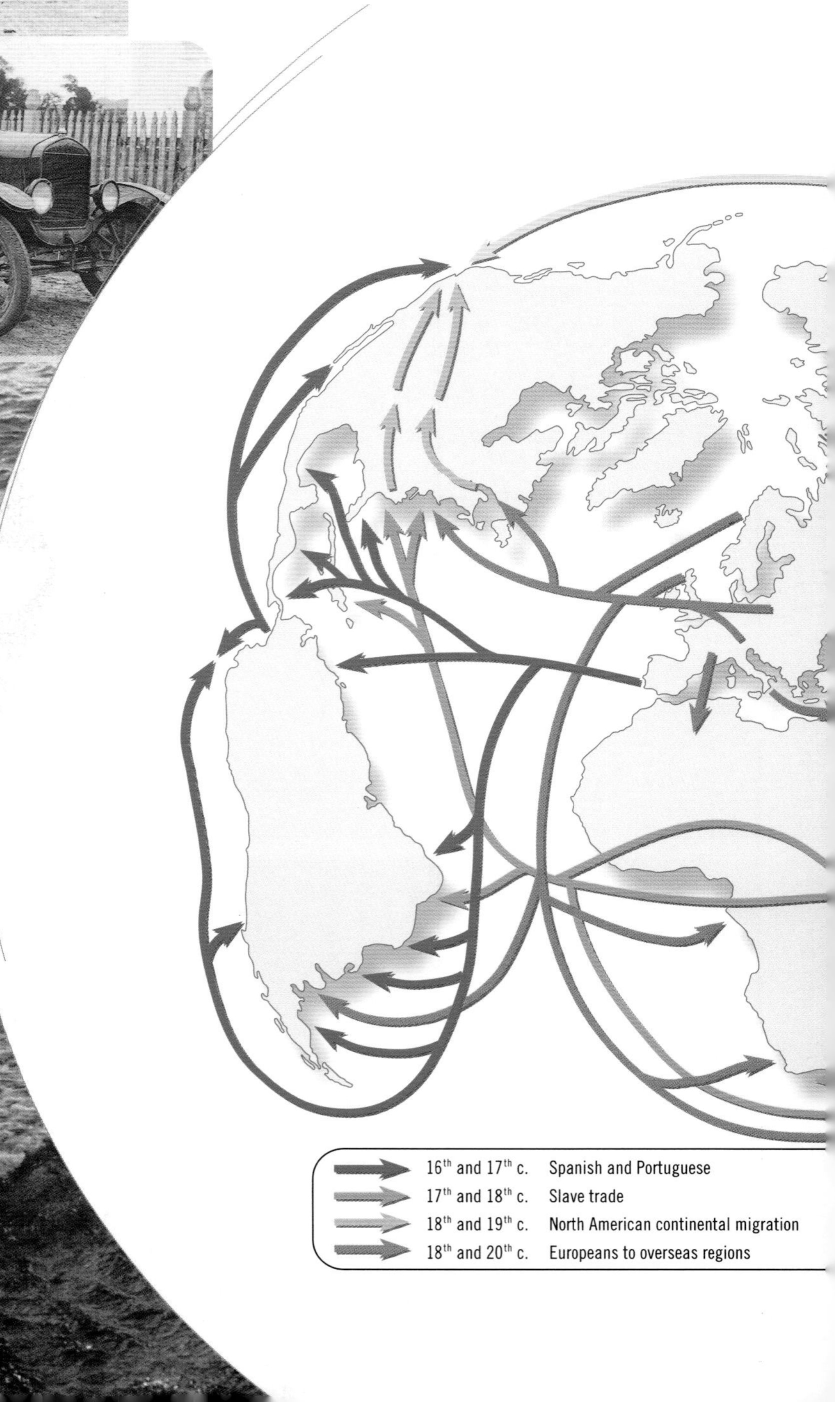

16th and 17th c.	Spanish and Portuguese
17th and 18th c.	Slave trade
18th and 19th c.	North American continental migration
18th and 20th c.	Europeans to overseas regions

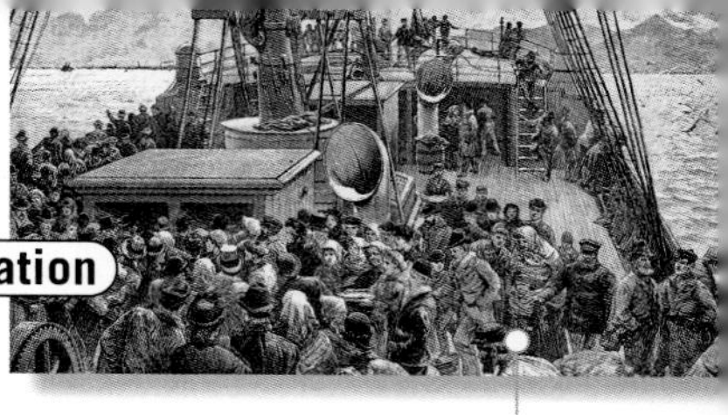

Streams of Refugees

Probably the most frequent cause of often involuntary mass migrations is war. In addition to the two World Wars, a number of more recent local wars and hostilities have caused huge groups of refugees to leave their homelands in Africa (Congo, Rwanda, the Guineas), Afghanistan, and the Middle East (where unsolved political and military conflicts between Israelis and Palestinians and problems involving Kurdish populations have persisted for decades). Striking evidence that religious and ideological differences as well as ethnic hostilities can lead to major refugee migrations can be found in the Balkan states, Southeast Asia (Christian-Moslem antagonism), and the Indian subcontinent (conflicts between Moslems and Hindus).

Environmental refugees are people who have been compelled to move away from their familiar homelands due to degradation of their natural environments and the resulting deterioration or loss of traditional foundations of life. Water shortages and water pollution, soil erosion, deforestation, desertification, and changes affecting the diversity of animal and plant species are forcing increasing numbers of people, especially in the "Third World," to abandon their native lands.

Economic refugees are prompted to leave their native lands in search of better living conditions – primarily in western industrialized countries – by worsening social and, above all, economic imbalances of regional or global proportions. Noteworthy examples include the immigration of Mexicans into the U.S., the growing stream of eastern European migrants into central and western Europe, and the rising number of Africans and Asians smuggled illegally by organized gangs into the Member States of the European Union.

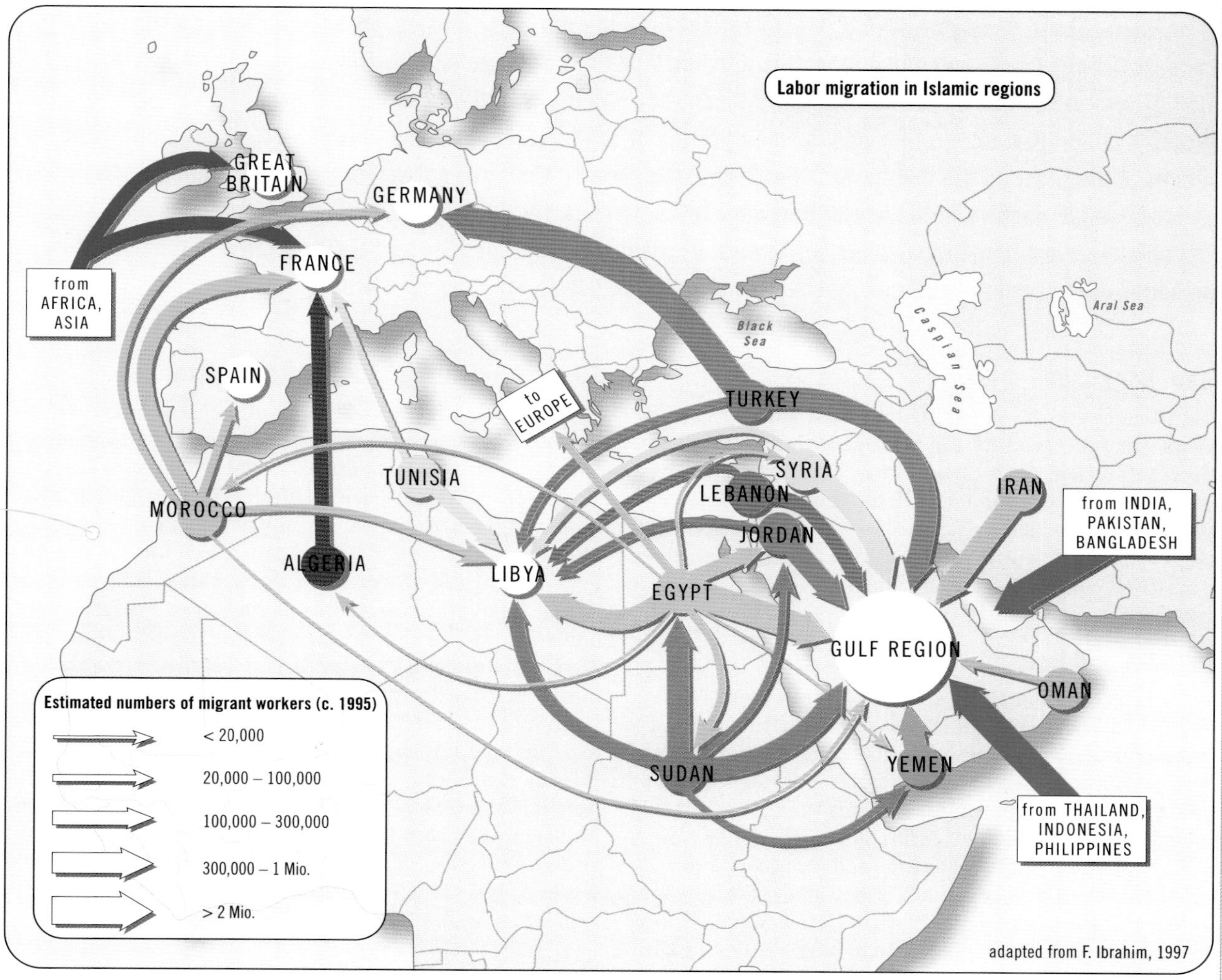

Labor migration in Islamic regions

Estimated numbers of migrant workers (c. 1995)
< 20,000
20,000 – 100,000
100,000 – 300,000
300,000 – 1 Mio.
> 2 Mio.

adapted from F. Ibrahim, 1997

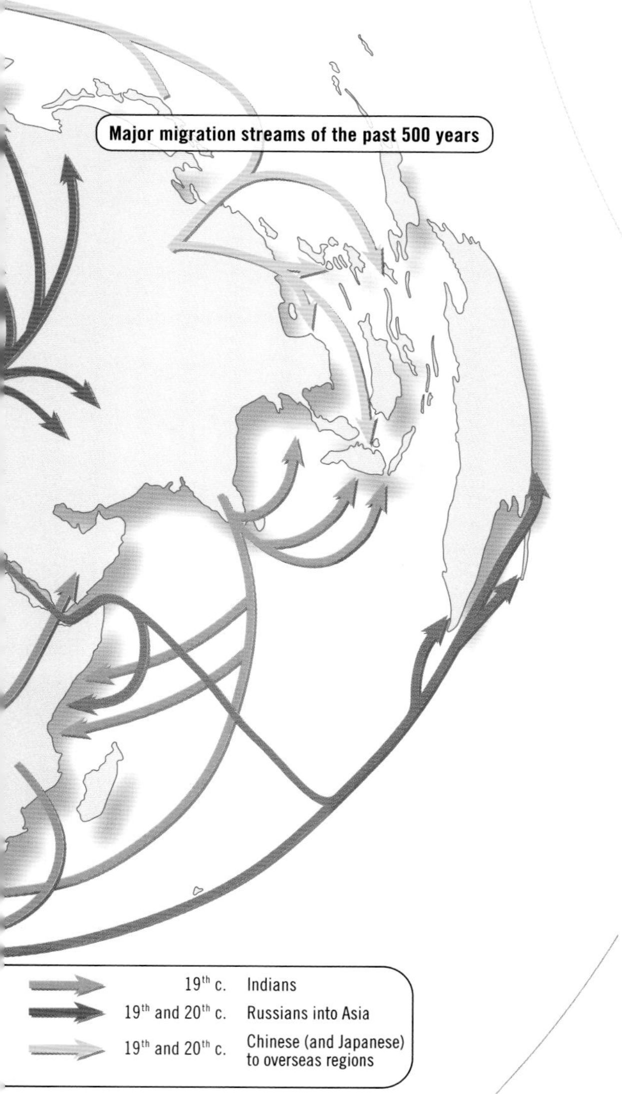

Major migration streams of the past 500 years

19th c.	Indians
19th and 20th c.	Russians into Asia
19th and 20th c.	Chinese (and Japanese) to overseas regions

Effects of disasters on world population, 1969–1993				
Type of disaster	No. of persons affected	No. of persons homeless	Death toll	No. of events
Drought and famine	57,906,000	23,000	74,000	438
Floods	47,850,000	3,178,000	12,000	1,366
Tropical storms	9,417,000	1,066,000	29,000	1,551
Earthquakes	1,765,000	224,000	22,000	640
Landslides	132,000	107,000	1,600	218
Volcanic eruptions	95,000	13,000	1,000	98
Technical accidents	53,000	8,400	600	310
Fire	33,000	88,000	3,300	583

On an Emigrant Ship

During the 19th century, thousands of Irish emigrants embarked on a quest for a better life in the New World, the majority of them fleeing during the Irish potato famine of 1845–50. This 1884 woodcut shows passengers on an emigrant ship being called to breakfast by a bell.

Labor Migration

Unlike the many and diverse groups of more or less involuntary migrants, migrants who leave their homelands in search of work ordinarily do so voluntarily on the basis of personal considerations. Two examples may serve to illustrate this phenomenon.

In North America, migrant workers are needed primarily as unskilled harvest laborers in the agricultural sector. Most of these people come from the south – from Mexico or the Caribbean. According to official estimates, there were approximately 8.5 million Mexicans living and working in the U.S. in 2001, about three million of them illegally. In most cases, these migrant workers have been smuggled into the country by organized gangs. Over the years, specific migration patterns have taken shape in the United States. A significant number of migrant laborers work as fruit pickers in Florida during the winter before moving north to the New England states to help harvest tomatoes, potatoes, and apples in the summer. A second stream of migrant workers moves from Texas into the Midwest or to the West Coast in search of jobs picking fruit, vegetables, sugar beets, or cotton. A third current flows northward along the West Coast from southern California to Washington, working during the fruit and vegetable harvests.

Migrant workers often contribute significantly to the maintenance of living standards and even to increasing prosperity, as the example of the small oil-producing countries along the Persian Gulf clearly shows. Not only do "guest laborers" account for up to 80% of their populations, social institutions and economic sectors – public services, schools, universities, hospitals, private households, national and municipal administrations, the construction business and to a certain extent even the oil industry itself – depend heavily upon foreign workers and could hardly function without them.

Prospects

Environmental catastrophes, rapid population growth, and economic stagnation in some regions; sluggish population growth accompanied by strong economic expansion in others; political disputes and regional conflicts, civil wars, and famines – all of these factors will continue to cause large-scale popular migrations and waves of refugees in the 21st century. In a global economy, hardly a single country will be spared the consequences of these developments.

Global Linguistic Diversity

One World – Thousands of Languages

Depending upon the criteria applied in distinguishing them, between 2,500 and 6,500 languages are spoken on Earth. These widely diverging figures reflect both the difficulty involved in differentiating with certainty between a dialect and a language and our lack of knowledge about many languages spoken by very small groups in regions such as the Amazon Basin, New Guinea, and the African interior.
European languages account for only a small portion of the total. Somewhere between 70 and 165 different tongues are spoken on the continent. More languages (nearly 750!) are spoken in Papua New Guinea than in any other single country in the world. Only very few countries are completely unilingual (Iceland is one). Most countries are home to speakers of several or many different tongues and their variants. A number of languages die out every year, and discoveries of new languages are rare even today.

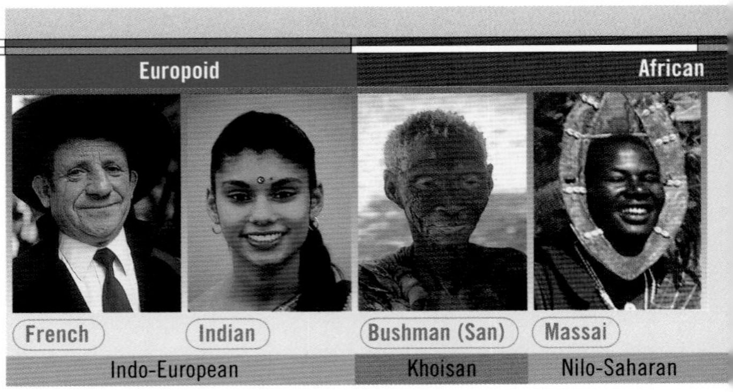

Europoid		African	
French	Indian	Bushman (San)	Massai
Indo-European		Khoisan	Nilo-Saharan

Dead Languages – Living Legacies

Some languages die out with their last speakers, while others are preserved as funds of knowledge, taught in schools (classical Arabic), used only in religious contexts (Old Hebrew), or studied as fixed points of historical reference in linguistics (Sanskrit). Still others serve as a source of new scientific terminology (Greek, Latin) or retain their vitality as literary languages (classical Chinese).

English – A Dominant World Language

Languages are affected by globalization as well. English has become the dominant language worldwide, although it ranks far behind Chinese in terms of numbers of native speakers. In sports and culture, in the high-tech world of computers and telecommunication, in the realm of travel and leisure activities, in scientific discourse and business correspondence, English has attained a degree of appeal, prestige, and influence that is unrivalled by any other language at the global level. International organizations exert considerable influence on language policy in support of other tongues. At the UN, for example, Arabic, Chinese, French, Russian, and Spanish join English as official languages. The European Union has even awarded official status to the national languages of all its member states.

Ethnic Revival – Grass Roots Resistance

The emancipation movements of the sixties and seventies led to a reassessment of the importance of language within the context of ethnic revival. Emphasis suddenly shifted from "utility" and "suitability" in a global sense to concern for linguistic diversity. "Minority" languages and tongues spoken in now independent former colonies were recognized as worthy of equal status and treatment. Languages which for centuries had been preserved and passed from one generation to the next only in oral form were systematically analyzed and described, transposed into a standardized written form, and documented in learning and reference materials such as textbooks, teachers' guides, dictionaries, and grammars (examples include Faeroese, a Germanic island language, and Swahili, the lingua franca in Africa). Bilingual or trilingual traffic and street signs, multilingual billboards, and enhanced media presence now offer striking visible and audible evidence of the new status of many once-neglected languages.

Writing Systems – Keys to Language

Human beings have employed a wide range of different writing systems to present natural, spoken language in visual form for more than three millennia. People of the ancient Egyptian, Inuit, and Maya cultures developed various forms of hieroglyphics, the Sumerians created a cuneiform system, while people of other civilizations established systems comprised of signs for words or syllables. Most forms of writing employed today make use of letters or symbols representing specific sounds. The writing systems now used in Europe and North America derive from the Phoenician alphabet developed in the 10th century BC, which also provided the basis for both the Arabic and Hebrew writing systems. Linguists have identified four major groups of alphabets: Greek (Latin, Coptic, Cyrillic, Armenian, Georgian), Semitic (Arabic, Hebrew, Ethiopian), Indian (Devanagari, Bengali, Tibetan, Burman, Thai, Khmer), and East Asian (Chinese, Japanese, Korean).

Every human has a language, but not everyone has command of its written form. Illiteracy is actually quite widespread and is particularly prevalant in the Third World. In Haiti, for example, 55% of the population cannot read or write. Illiterates account for 40% of the population of the Central African Republic, and 62% of all Yemenese are unable to read a newspaper or write even a short note. Even the rich industrialized countries of the world face the problem of illiteracy, with up to 5% of their inhabitants unable to read or express themselves in written form and thus virtually excluded from the mainstream of cultural and economic life.

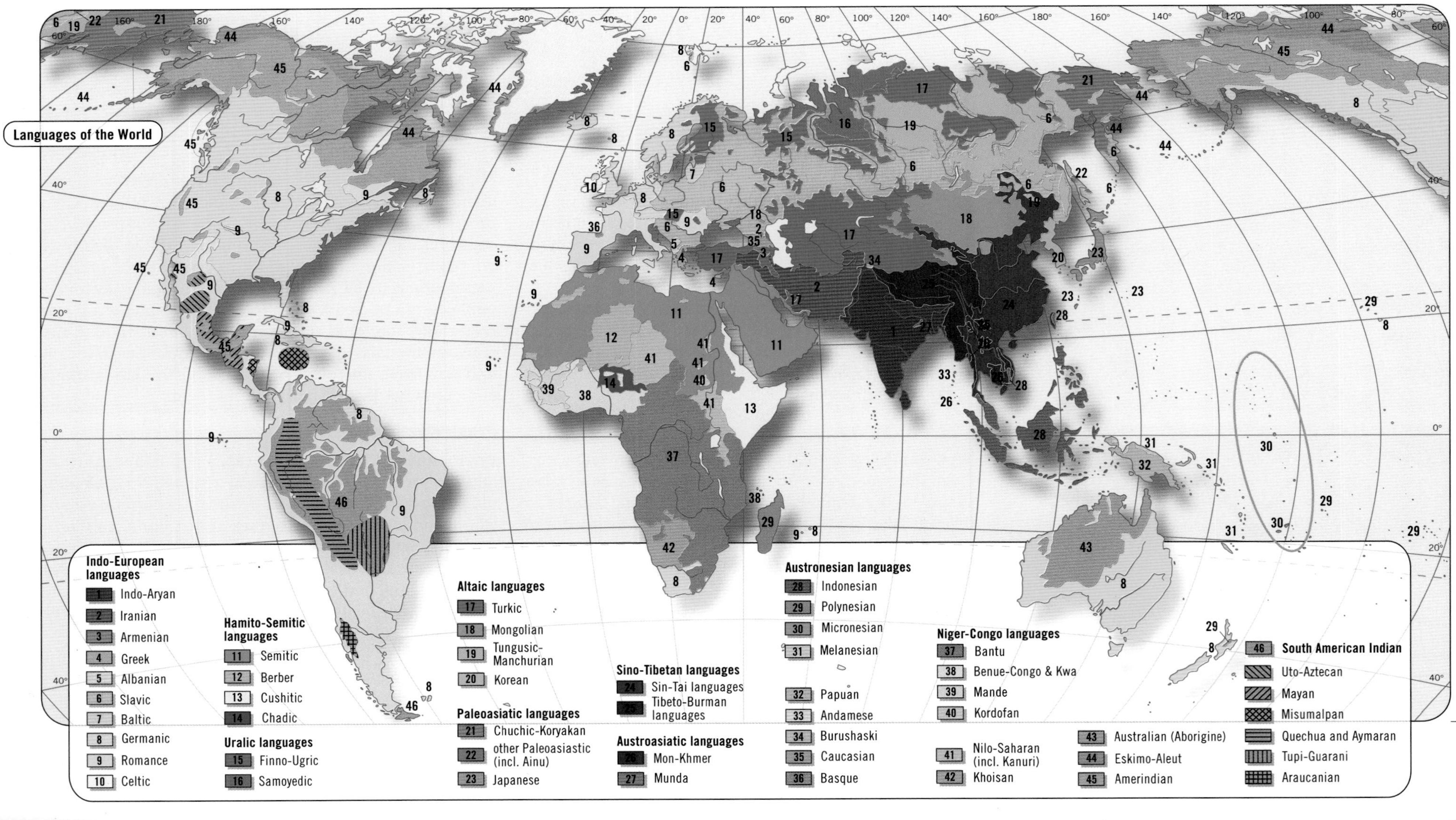

Languages of the World

Indo-European languages
1 Indo-Aryan
2 Iranian
3 Armenian
4 Greek
5 Albanian
6 Slavic
7 Baltic
8 Germanic
9 Romance
10 Celtic

Hamito-Semitic languages
11 Semitic
12 Berber
13 Cushitic
14 Chadic

Uralic languages
15 Finno-Ugric
16 Samoyedic

Altaic languages
17 Turkic
18 Mongolian
19 Tungusic-Manchurian
20 Korean

Paleoasiatic languages
21 Chuchic-Koryakan other Paleoasiatic (incl. Ainu)
22 other Paleoasiatic (incl. Ainu)
23 Japanese

Sino-Tibetan languages
24 Sin-Tai languages
25 Tibeto-Burman languages

Austroasiatic languages
26 Mon-Khmer
27 Munda

Austronesian languages
28 Indonesian
29 Polynesian
30 Micronesian
31 Melanesian
32 Papuan
33 Andamese
34 Burushaski
35 Caucasian
36 Basque

Niger-Congo languages
37 Bantu
38 Benue-Congo & Kwa
39 Mande
40 Kordofan

41 Nilo-Saharan (incl. Kanuri)
42 Khoisan

43 Australian (Aborigine)
44 Eskimo-Aleut
45 Amerindian

South American Indian
46
Uto-Aztecan
Mayan
Misumalpan
Quechua and Aymaran
Tupi-Guarani
Araucanian

East Asian		Arctic	Amerindian			Oceanian		Australian
Pygmy	Chinese	Tibetan	Inuit	Maya	Yanomami	Polynesian	Melanesian	Australian
Niger-Kordofan	Sino-Tibetan		Eskimo-Aleut	Amerindian		Austronesian		Australian

Linguistic Diversity – a Curse?
Did all humans originally speak a single language? The idea (no longer accepted) is expressed in the biblical story of the Tower of Babylon (painting by Pieter Bruegel the Elder, 1563), in which linguistic diversity is described as God's punishment for human pride and greed for power.

Linguistic Exchange – The Foreign Element

All languages have changed over the course of centuries. Apart from natural, organic evolution, languages are influenced significantly by contact among speakers of different linguistic communities – conquerors and conquered peoples, neighboring linguistic groups, etc. In this way, languages enrich one another with "foreign material" (adopted and adapted words and forms). These phenomena are referred to by historical linguistics as strata: Substrates are traces of the language of a conquered or exterminated people left behind in the language of the victors (e.g. remnants of Celtic in the Romance languages). Superstrata are elements introduced by a conquering group into the language of a subjugated people but which do not displace the original language (e.g. Franconian influences on French). Adstrata are linguistic influences which do not reflect hierarchical relationships (e.g. contacts between speakers of Germanic and Romance languages along linguistic boundaries).

The Birth of New Languages: Pidgin and Creole forms

Pidgin and Creole languages are the products of a special form of linguistic interaction which takes place primarily when speakers of different native tongues communicate with each other. Such languages have developed through trading activity and in economies significantly influenced by slavery in the New World, Africa, Southeast Asia, and Oceania. Pidgin languages are characterized by markedly simplified structures that facilitate communication but are found in neither of the original native languages involved. Pidgin languages that become established and are passed on to succeeding generations are known as Creoles. Many Creole languages have been standardized and adopted as official national languages (in Haiti, Mauritius, and the Seychelles, for example) and thus contribute to local or national identity.

The Future of Languages

Though many have predicted the eventual demise of linguistic diversity, languages have proven astonishingly resilient. Even today, there are those who hope and believe that globalization will result in the establishment of English as the worldwide medium for communication. Yet efforts have also been undertaken to have the right to speak one's native language firmly anchored in international human rights conventions. Slowly but surely, people are beginning to realize that linguistic diversity has the capacity to enrich humanity and is not, as the Bible suggests, God's punishment for human pride, vanity, and greed. In the age of technology, languages that remain open to progress and capable of integrating it into their dynamic systems will survive and ensure the preservation of linguistic diversity in the 21st century.

A Monument to Language
A prime example of a literary language developed through deliberate effort is Afrikaans, which is spoken in South Africa. The unique monument to language erected in Paarl near Cape Town commemorates the linguistic movement founded by the Boers in 1875.

The Physiognomy of Diversity
Portraits of people from selected ethnic groups and their language families (lower print bar).

Geographic distribution of languages on Earth

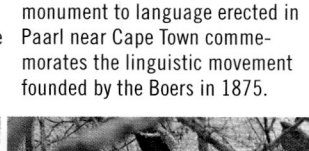

- 32% Asia
- 3% Europe
- 15% America
- 19.5% Australia & Oceania
- 30.5% Africa

Most widely spoken languages by number of speakers

as native and second language

millions	
940	Chinese
475	English
395	Hindi
375	Spanish
300	Russian
215	Arabic
200	Bengali
185	Portuguese
155	Malayan-Indonesian
125	Japanese
122	French
118	German
100	Urdu

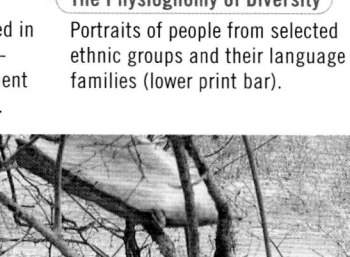

Overcoming Social Ostracism
Of the 880 million illiterates in the world, two thirds are women. 120 million children do not attend proper schools – due primarily to a lack of money. The photo shows a Massai "bush school" in East Africa.

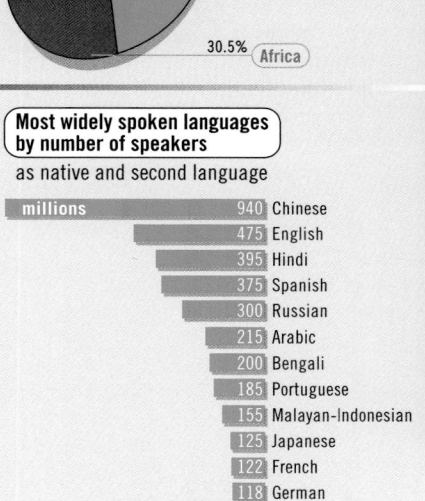

Bilingual Street Sign
Increasing attention is now being given to linguistic minorities in many countries (photo: sign in French and Occitan in Agde). Distinctions are expressed in different print sizes.

Religions the World

One Divine Power? Many Concepts of Divinity.

Religion is an expression of human responses to the experience of divinity in ritual and doctrine. It appears in different forms in different cultures and at different times, and though distinct from other manifestations of culture, it both reflects and shapes them at the same time. Religion is always community-oriented and always involves standards of ethics, although these may differ significantly from one set of beliefs and principles to another. Religion takes public form in rituals and pilgrimages, at specific places, and in the teachings of religious leaders. Religious faith informs and molds the lives of those who share it.

A Ubiquitous Phenomenon

All human societies since prehistoric times have embraced religious beliefs of some kind. We distinguish between two basic types of religion. The first is known as "primary religion." The origin and basis for all religions, it is still clearly evident today in "tribal religions" (frequently, though imprecisely and even inaccurately referred to as "natural" or "animistic" religions). These systems of belief have primarily local or regional relevance and generally govern communal life in small societies. They provide guidance and support at critical points in life – birth, puberty, marriage, death and mourning – through "rites of passage." Events marking seasonal transitions, such as planting and harvest or the winter and summer solstices, are also celebrated in rituals and serve as fixed points of reference for communal life, much like Christmas and Easter in western societies.

The second group, "secondary religions," comprises systems of belief and ritual which can be traced to the teachings or activities of founders, reformers, and charismatic leaders. They include the five major religions of the world: Judaism, Christianity, Islam, Buddhism, and Hinduism. They all pose the question of truth, which plays no role at all in primary religions, whose "natural" legitimacy is grounded in the specific societies that embrace them. Many secondary religions have sacred scriptures, which contain the basic tenets of ethics, faith, and behavior to which their adherents subscribe. Because they claim possession of universal truth, they tend to assume a missionary character, and their founders are the central focus of teaching and devotion. Buddhism, Christianity, and Islam are prime examples of this tendency. As they spread throughout the world, these secondary religions have had to come to grips with primary religions. In the process, they have adopted and adapted existing sacred rituals, places and

Christian Africa
The majority of people in most of the countries of central and southern Africa are Christians. More than one-third of African Christians are members of the Catholic Church, which actively promotes the education and development of native clerics. The "Independent Churches" embody a form of Christianity that deliberately makes room for traditional aspects of African tribal cultures.

Religion by the Book
An Ethiopian monk demonstrates the art of manuscript illumination while writing a page of the Bible in Amharic, which becomes established as the liturgical language of the Ethiopian Church.

Sacred Waters
A bath in the sacred Ganges River is believed to purify the soul of a Hindu. The ghats (bathing steps) at the pilgrimage center in Varanasi provide easy access to the Ganges.

Traditional Healer
In many African religions, misfortune, disease, and death are attributed to evil spells cast by witches. Only the healer (photo: Susa Madela, Sorcerer of Lightning, 1902–1988) can provide protection.

Islamic Pilgrimage
The Ka'bah, an empty, windowless building inside the Great Mosque in Mecca was a sacred shrine in the city even during pre-Islamic times. All Muslims are obliged to make at least one pilgrimage to Mecca in their lifetime. Pilgrims walk around the shrine seven times.

Religions of the World

Great Lakes
Salt Lake City
Tropic of Cancer
Guadalupe
ATLANTIC
PACIFIC
Equator
OCEAN
Amazon
Tropic of Capricorn

Christianity		Islam
Protestantism	Judaism	Sunni
Roman Catholicism	Significant Jewish communities	Shi'a
Eastern Orthodox Churches		
Other Christian sects		Hinduism

times, reinterpreting them and casting out whatever elements could not be reconciled with their teachings. Buddhism developed into Mahayana Buddhism in China, for example, in response to regional influences. Christianity split into an eastern (Orthodox) branch under the influence of the religions of Greece and Asia Minor and a western (Roman) form of Catholicism oriented toward the more dogmatic Roman religions. Islam adopted pre-Islamic and existing Judaic and Christian elements, as the life of Mohammed clearly shows.

When the great religions face a loss of vitality and begin to abandon their original doctrines under the influence of progressive enlightenment, modern patterns of thought, and the pressure of political systems, reformers appear, new sects are founded, and fundamentalist revival movements take shape, as we witness all over the world today. This tendency is reflected in new religious movements and sects in Japan (Tenrykyo and others), the United States (Mormons, Children of God, etc.), Latin America (Umbanda, voodoo cults), India (neo-Hinduism), and Africa (Kimbanguism, Aladura churches, etc.) as well as the emphatically pious New-Age religions.

Religion – a Source of Conflict?

All religions strive to control the lives of their members, and thus they play an important role in public life. Radical, often fundamentalist religious movements also seek to exert political influence, although they often expose themselves to manipulation by political forces as well. In view of the dangers all societies face in today's world, religions would do well to remember their humanitarian function and support the growth of a system of ethics that will enable human beings to live together in peace.

Religions of the World

Religions	Date of origin	Sacred scriptures	Number of adherents	% of world population
Christianity	30 AD	Bible	2 bn	33 % – increasing in the Third World
Islam	622 AD	Koran	1.3 bn	20 % – increasing
Hinduism and neo-Hinduism	c. 1,500 BC	Vedas, Upanishads	900 mil.	15 % – stagnant
Atheists and agnostics	–	–	900 mil.	15 % – decreasing
Buddhism	c. 530 BC	Tipitaka	360 mil.	6 % – stagnant
Chinese Religious Complex (ancestor and nature worship, Taoism, Confucianism*)	c. 1,500 BC	–	230 mil.	5 %
Tribal religions	prehistoric	Oral tradition	91 mil.	2 %
Yoruba religions: voodoo cults, Umbanda, etc.	?	–	30 mil.	< 1 %
New religious movements (Caodaism, Soka-Gakkai, Ananda Marge, etc.)	19th/20th c.	–	30 mil.	< 1 %
Sikhism	1500 AD	Adi Granth	18 mil.	< 1 %
Judaism	Babylonian exile (587 – 538 BC)	Torah, Talmud	15 mil.	< 1 %
Shamanism*	prehistoric	Oral tradition	12 mil.	< 1 %
Spiritism*	after 1800	–	10 mil.	< 1 %
Baha'i	1863 AD	The Most Holy Book	4 mil.	< 1 %
Shintō	6th c. AD	Kojiki, Nihongi, Fudoki	4 mil.	< 1 %
Jainism	6th/5th c.BC	Extensive canon in Prakrit literature	3 mil.	< 1 %
Parsiism	500 – 250 BC	Avesta	150,000	< 1 %

* not a religion in the strict sense

The Desert – Origin of all Great Religions

The Israelites were nomads, like these shepherds on the Sinai Peninsula. They are believed to have worshiped protector gods and local divinities originally. Every tribe had its own god, to whom access was gained through the tribal elders ("fathers").

Harmony and Peace

Meditation is an important religious exercise for Buddhists, as it relieves the heart of suffering and the mind of ignorance. The simple saffron-colored robe symbolizes simplicity and self-denial; the fig tree recalls the bodhi tree beneath which Buddha achieved enlightenment.

Jewish Marriage Rites

Bride and groom cover their heads with a tallit (prayer cloak) during the marriage ceremony.

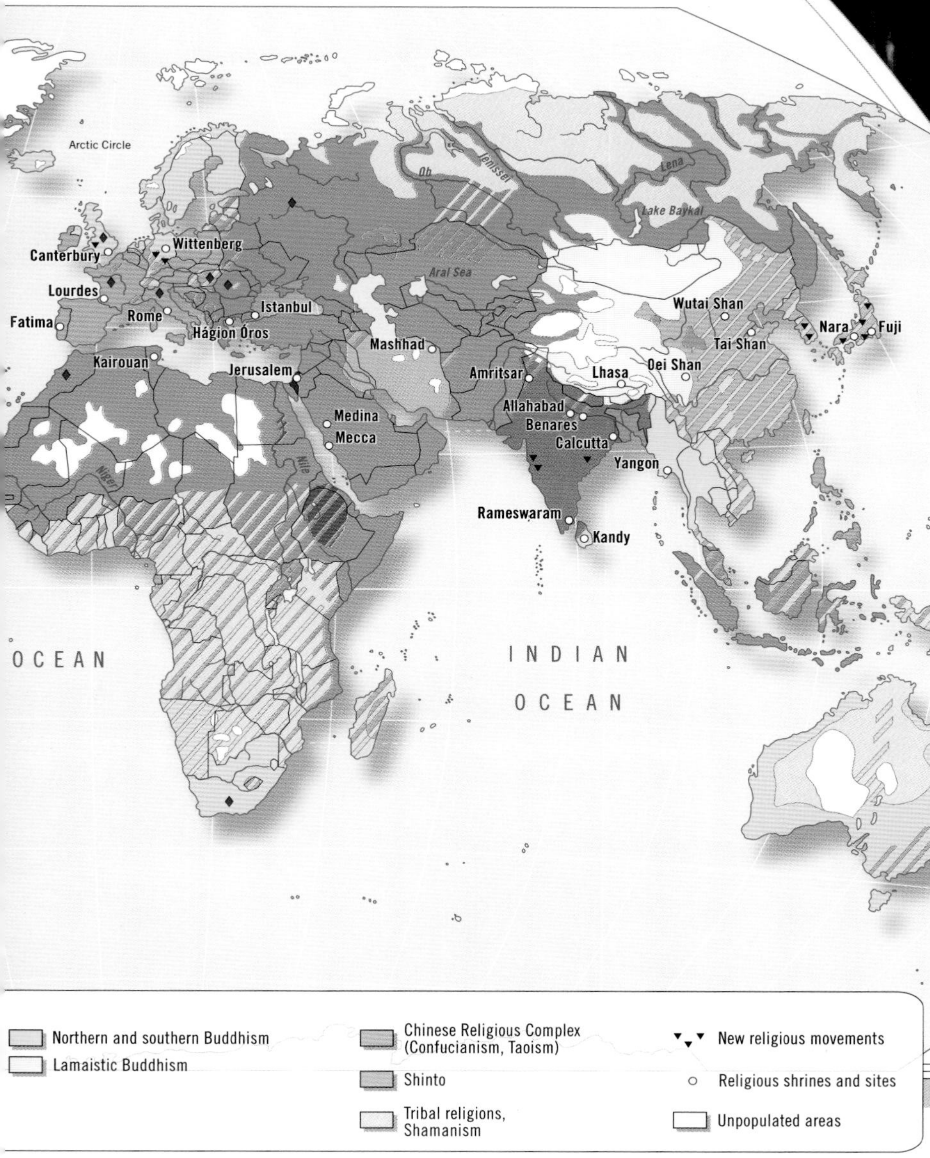

Arctic Circle

Ob · Yenisey · Lena · Lake Baikal · Aral Sea

Canterbury · Wittenberg · Wutai Shan · Nara · Fuji
Lourdes · Istanbul · Tai Shan · Oei Shan
Fatima · Rome · Hagion Oros · Mashhad
Kairouan · Jerusalem · Amritsar · Lhasa
Medina · Allahabad
Mecca · Benares
Calcutta
Yangon
Rameswaram
Kandy

PACIFIC OCEAN

INDIAN OCEAN

OCEAN

Northern and southern Buddhism	Chinese Religious Complex (Confucianism, Taoism)	New religious movements
Lamaistic Buddhism	Shinto	Religious shrines and sites
	Tribal religions, Shamanism	Unpopulated areas

UNESCO Protects the World Cultural Heritage

What is Recognition as a World Cultural Heritage Site Worth?

What does the Roman Amphitheater at Sabratha in Libya have in common with the Inca monuments of Machu Picchu in Peru, the necropolis at Thebes in Egypt with the Great Wall of China, the orthodox monastery at Rila in Bulgaria with Ayers Rock in Australia? They are all legacies of past cultures and irreplaceable treasures that belong to the global community.

The World Heritage Convention?

The Convention on Preservation of the World Cultural and Natural Heritage was passed at the UNESCO General Assembly meeting of 1972. It has since been signed by 167 nations. Signatory countries accept the obligation to protect and preserve sites, recognized as part of the World Heritage, that lie within their borders.

The underlying principle is that sites of unique and universal value – be they architectural monuments, urban districts, or cultivated landscapes – should be recognized as the common heritage of all people on Earth and afforded international protection. The value of such objects may be aesthetic, historical, or scientific in nature.

The World Heritage Committee is composed of delegates from 21 countries selected to represent all of the major cultural regions of the world. The committee convenes once each year to choose new sites for the World Heritage List from applications submitted by participating countries. The list currently contains 721 sites, of which 554 are identified as cultural legacies, 144 as natural heritage sites, and 23 as a combination of both. The Committee also makes decisions on the use of funds contributed by the signatory countries.

Differing Attitudes about the World Heritage List

As a matter of prestige, many countries are eager to have as many sites as possible entered in the list. Others regard recognition as more of a burden than an honor, as they fear a loss of control over their own national treasures.

Prehistoric Hunters

Prehistoric hunters in central North America killed game animals by driving them over high cliffs. (Photo: **Head Smashed-in Bison Jump (2)** in Alberta)

Impregnable Bastion

The fortress (16th c.) and old town of **San Juan (38)** in Puerto Rico were dominated by the massive Castillo de San Felipe del Morro. The photo shows the fortified tip of the peninsula.

Model States

A by-product of missionary work among the Guaranís, the **Jesuit Reductions (68)** were self-governing agricultural communities that survived for 160 years. (Photo: Church portal in Trinidad, Paraguay)

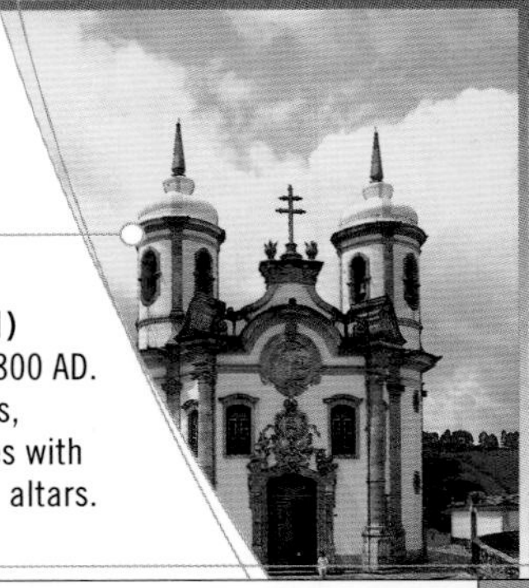

Unique Regional Baroque

A unique form of late baroque architecture emerged in the diamond and gold mining province of Minas Gerais in the 18th century. One of the most beautiful churches in **Ouro Preto (70)** is São Francisco de Assis, designed by Aleijadinho and completed in 1794.

Zoomorphic Altars

The Mayan city of **Quiriguá (41)** flourished between 500 and 800 AD. Hewn from sandstone blocks, the mythical animal figures with hieroglyphs were used as altars.

City of the Gods

Relief panels on the steps of the Quetzalcoatl Pyramid exhibit the heads of the Feathered Serpent and the god of rain or thunder. Temples erected on stepped pyramids in the ceremonial district of **Teotihuacán (22)** line both sides of the Avenue of the Dead for a distance of 2 km.

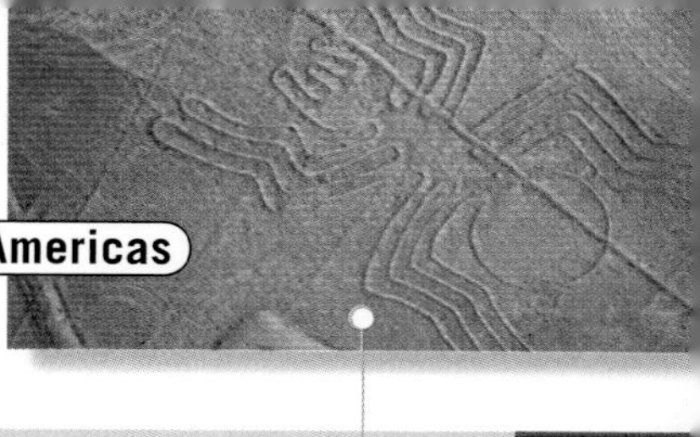

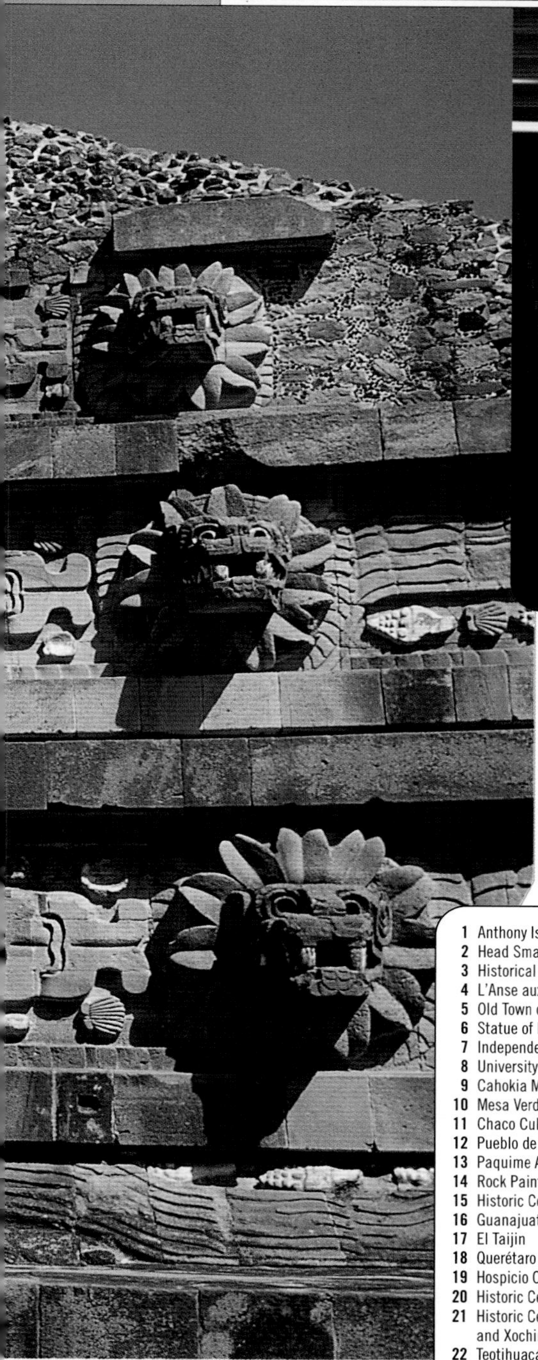

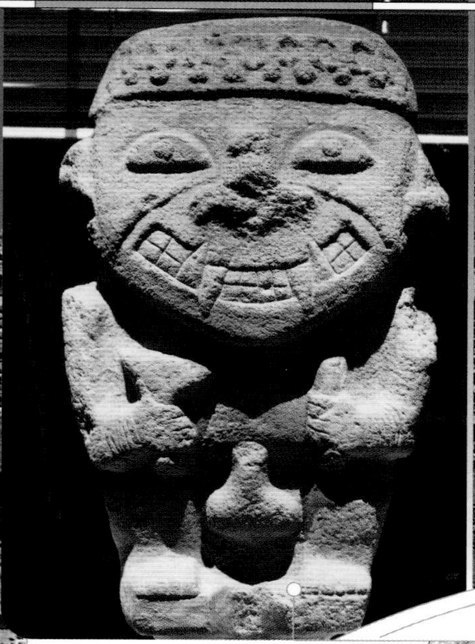

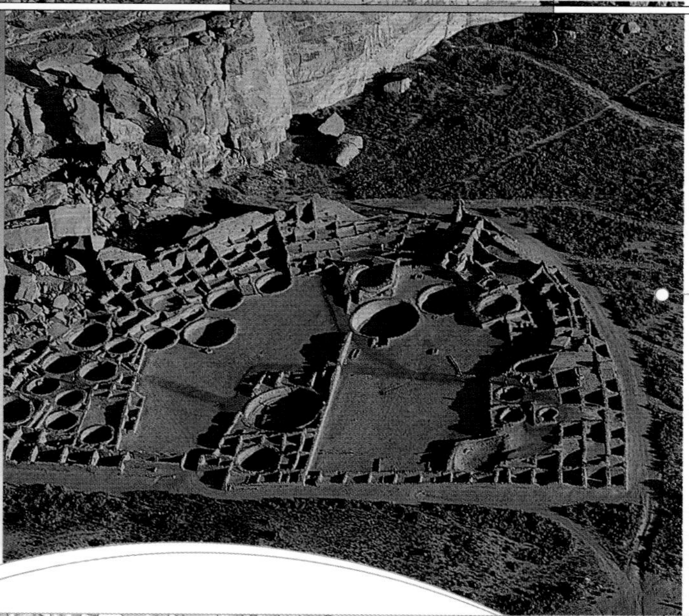

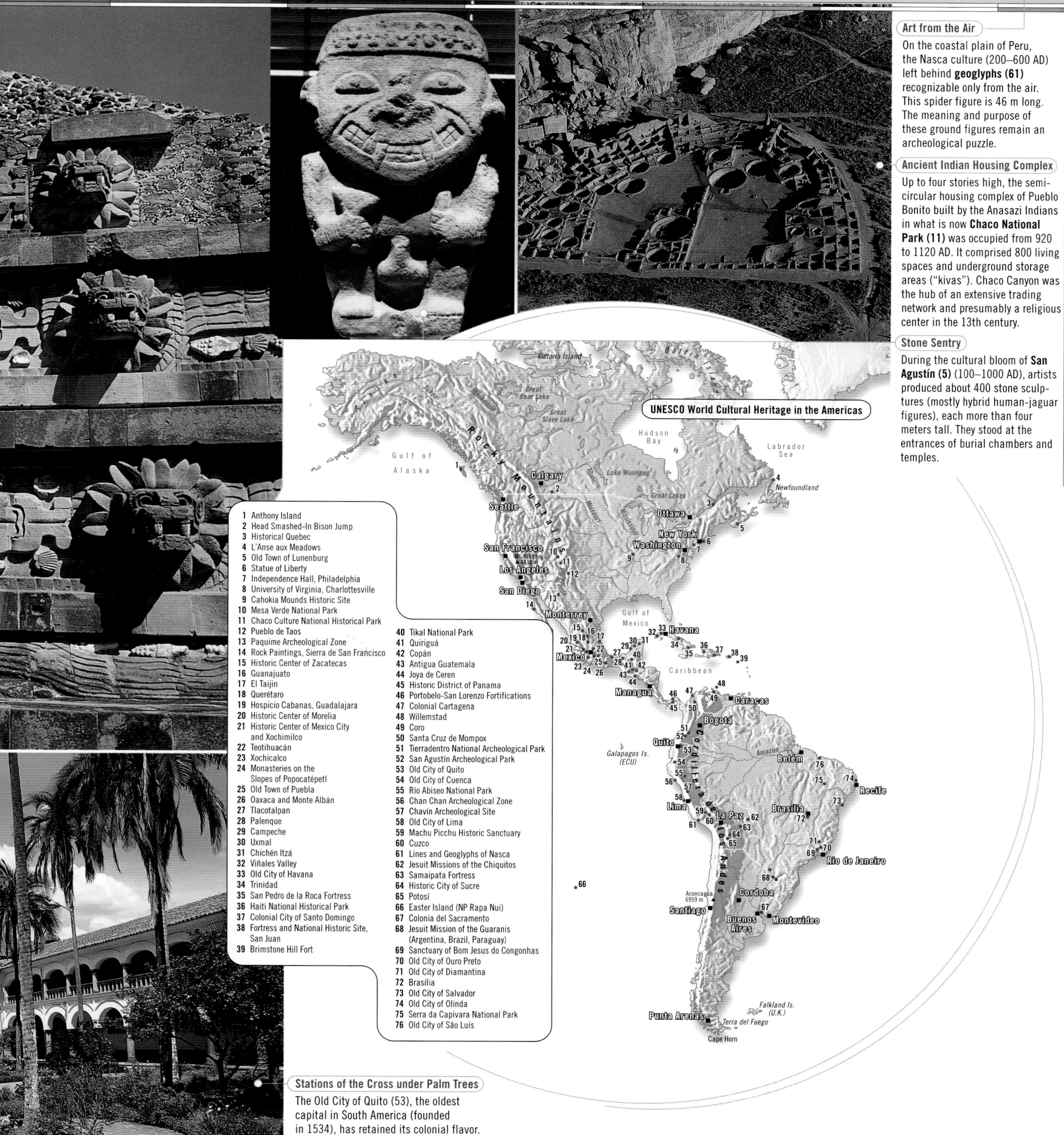

Art from the Air

On the coastal plain of Peru, the Nasca culture (200–600 AD) left behind **geoglyphs (61)** recognizable only from the air. This spider figure is 46 m long. The meaning and purpose of these ground figures remain an archeological puzzle.

Ancient Indian Housing Complex

Up to four stories high, the semi-circular housing complex of Pueblo Bonito built by the Anasazi Indians in what is now **Chaco National Park (11)** was occupied from 920 to 1120 AD. It comprised 800 living spaces and underground storage areas ("kivas"). Chaco Canyon was the hub of an extensive trading network and presumably a religious center in the 13th century.

Stone Sentry

During the cultural bloom of **San Agustín (5)** (100–1000 AD), artists produced about 400 stone sculptures (mostly hybrid human-jaguar figures), each more than four meters tall. They stood at the entrances of burial chambers and temples.

UNESCO World Cultural Heritage in the Americas

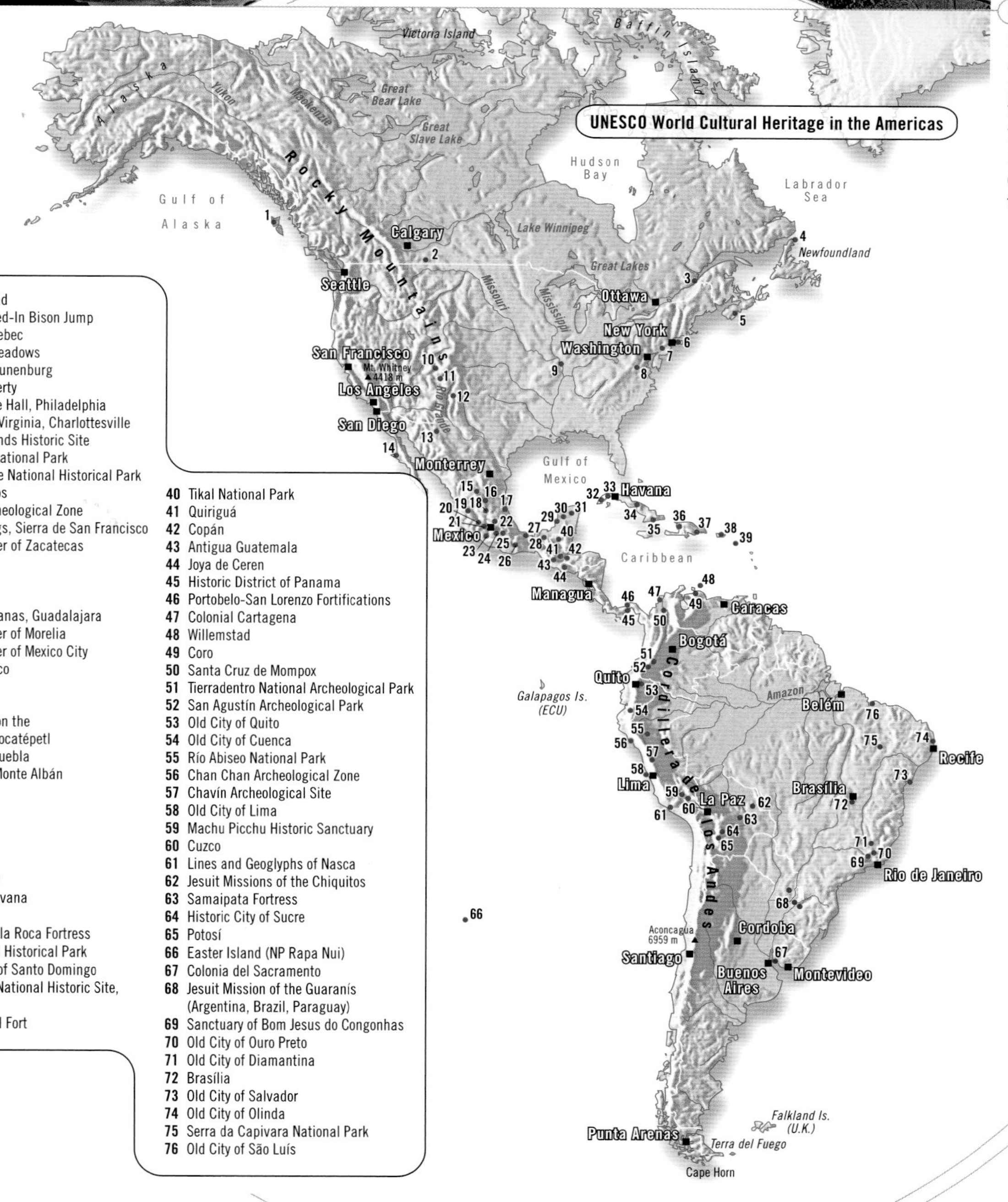

1 Anthony Island
2 Head Smashed-In Bison Jump
3 Historical Quebec
4 L'Anse aux Meadows
5 Old Town of Lunenburg
6 Statue of Liberty
7 Independence Hall, Philadelphia
8 University of Virginia, Charlottesville
9 Cahokia Mounds Historic Site
10 Mesa Verde National Park
11 Chaco Culture National Historical Park
12 Pueblo de Taos
13 Paquime Archeological Zone
14 Rock Paintings, Sierra de San Francisco
15 Historic Center of Zacatecas
16 Guanajuato
17 El Tajin
18 Querétaro
19 Hospicio Cabanas, Guadalajara
20 Historic Center of Morelia
21 Historic Center of Mexico City and Xochimilco
22 Teotihuacán
23 Xochicalco
24 Monasteries on the Slopes of Popocatépetl
25 Old Town of Puebla
26 Oaxaca and Monte Albán
27 Tlacotalpan
28 Palenque
29 Campeche
30 Uxmal
31 Chichén Itzá
32 Viñales Valley
33 Old City of Havana
34 Trinidad
35 San Pedro de la Roca Fortress
36 Haiti National Historical Park
37 Colonial City of Santo Domingo
38 Fortress and National Historic Site, San Juan
39 Brimstone Hill Fort

40 Tikal National Park
41 Quiriguá
42 Copán
43 Antigua Guatemala
44 Joya de Ceren
45 Historic District of Panama
46 Portobelo-San Lorenzo Fortifications
47 Colonial Cartagena
48 Willemstad
49 Coro
50 Santa Cruz de Mompox
51 Tierradentro National Archeological Park
52 San Agustín Archeological Park
53 Old City of Quito
54 Old City of Cuenca
55 Río Abiseo National Park
56 Chan Chan Archeological Zone
57 Chavín Archeological Site
58 Old City of Lima
59 Machu Picchu Historic Sanctuary
60 Cuzco
61 Lines and Geoglyphs of Nasca
62 Jesuit Missions of the Chiquitos
63 Samaipata Fortress
64 Historic City of Sucre
65 Potosí
66 Easter Island (NP Rapa Nui)
67 Colonia del Sacramento
68 Jesuit Mission of the Guaranís (Argentina, Brazil, Paraguay)
69 Sanctuary of Bom Jesus do Congonhas
70 Old City of Ouro Preto
71 Old City of Diamantina
72 Brasília
73 Old City of Salvador
74 Old City of Olinda
75 Serra da Capivara National Park
76 Old City of São Luís

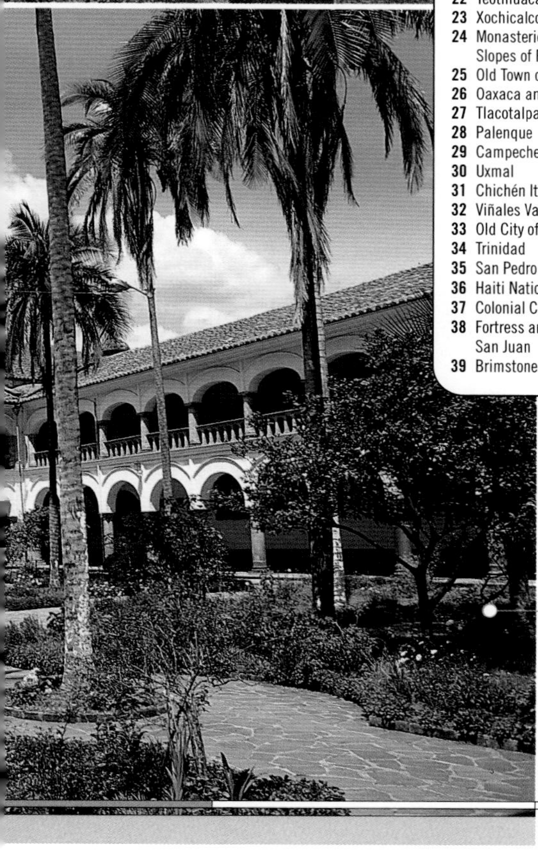

Stations of the Cross under Palm Trees

The Old City of Quito (53), the oldest capital in South America (founded in 1534), has retained its colonial flavor. The stations of the cross at the monastery of La Merced are arranged on two stories and overlook a fountain.

Criteria for Inclusion in the World Heritage List

A World Heritage Site must not only be authentic and intact, it must also be of outstanding universal value, as demonstrated by fulfillment of at least one of the following criteria:

• The site represents a unique artistic accomplishment, a masterpiece of human creative genius.

• The site has had a significant influence, over a span of time or within a cultural area of the world, on developments in architecture, monumental arts, town planning or landscape design.

• The site bears a unique or at least exceptional testimony to a cultural tradition or to a civilization which is living or which has disappeared.

• The site is an outstanding example of a type of building or architectural ensemble or landscape which illustrates a significant state in human history.

• The site is an outstanding example of a traditional human settlement or land use which is representative of a culture (or cultures), especially when it has become vulnerable under the impact of irreversible change.

• The site is directly or tangibly associated with events or living traditions, with ideas, or with beliefs, with artistic, or literary works of outstanding universal significance (this criterion should justify inclusion in the list only in exceptional circumstances and in conjunction with other criteria).

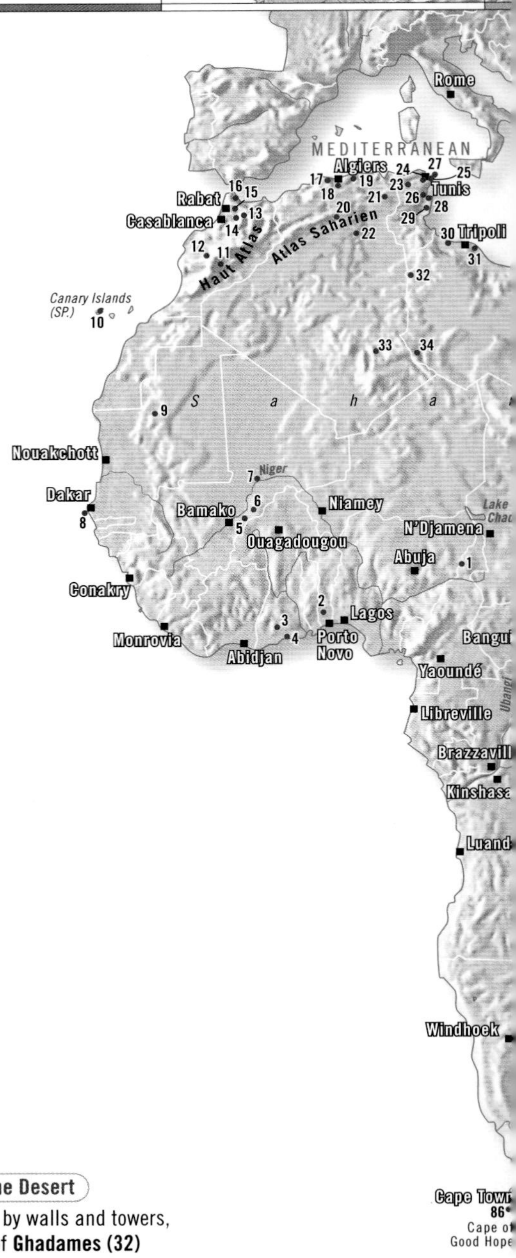

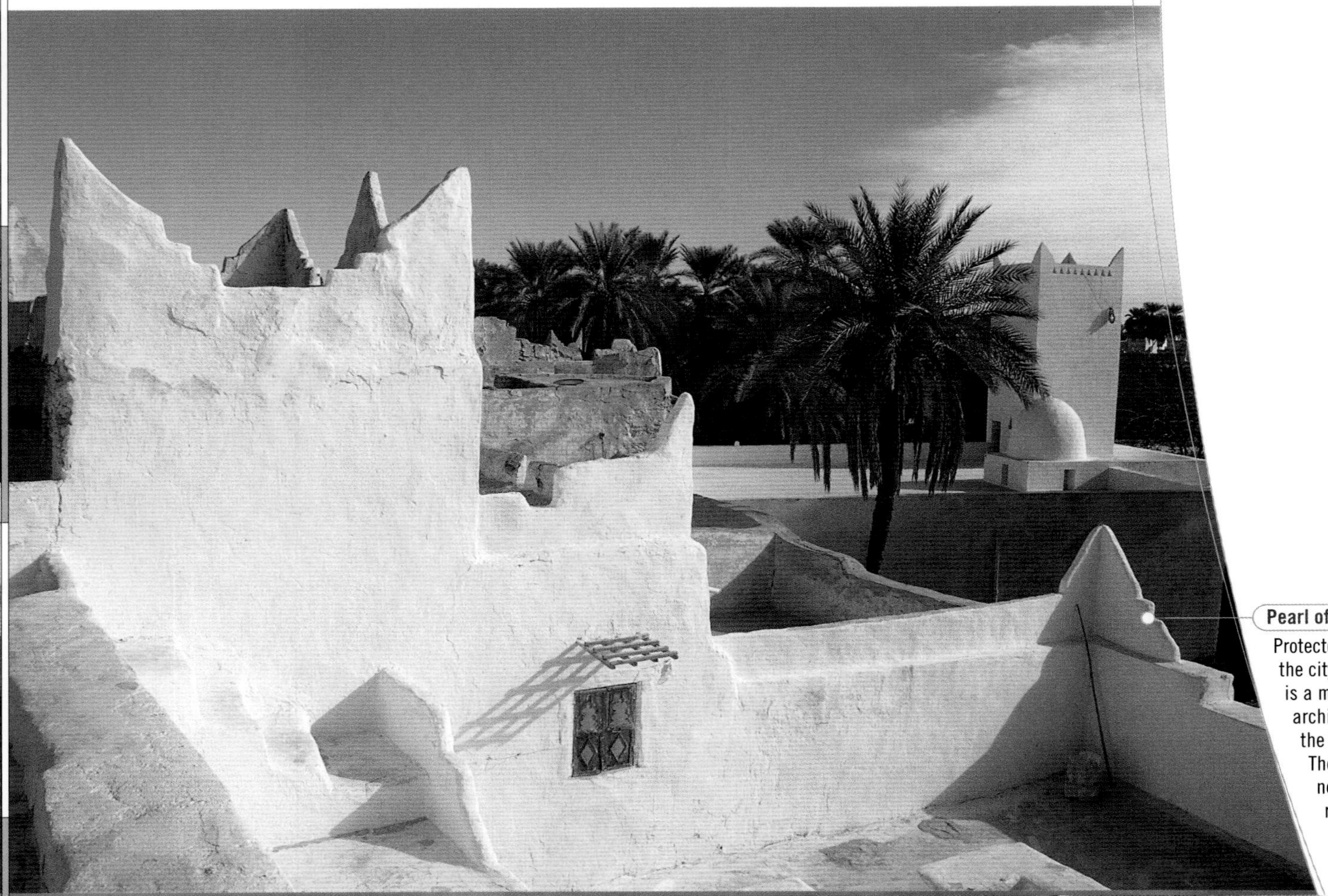

Pearl of the Desert
Protected by walls and towers, the city of **Ghadames (32)** is a masterpiece of Saharan architecture located along one of the trans-Sahara caravan routes. The three-story houses are connected by terraces — the women's realm.

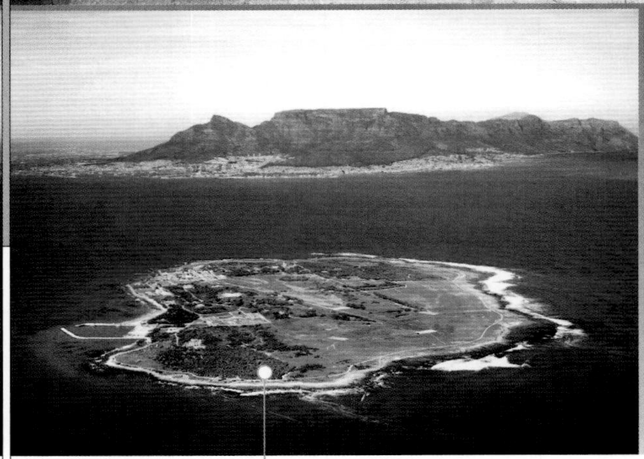

Triumph of Will
From the 17th century until 1996, **Robben Island (86)**, located eight miles from Cape Town, was used as a whaling station, a camp for lepers and the mentally ill, a military base (World War II), and a penitentiary. Nelson Mandela was confined to the maximum security wing of the prison for 18 years and forced to work in the limestone quarry. The island is now an outdoor museum of human rights and one of the most popular tourist attractions on the Cape.

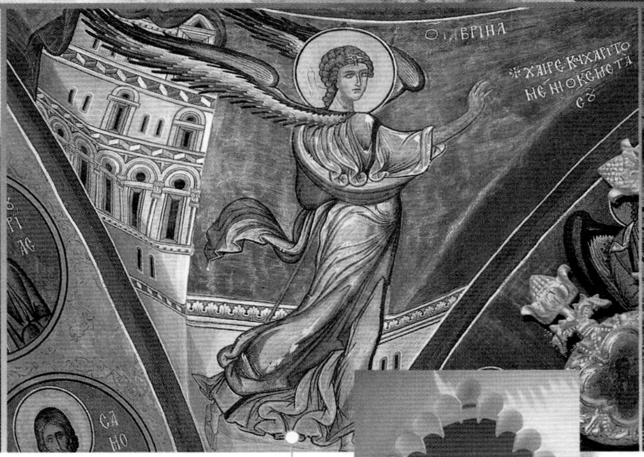

Treasures of Byzantine Art
Nowhere else are so many outstanding examples of Byzantine painting concentrated in a single region than in the **Troodos Mountains (42)** of Cyprus. The Archangel of Lagoudera (1192) is a particularly elegant work.

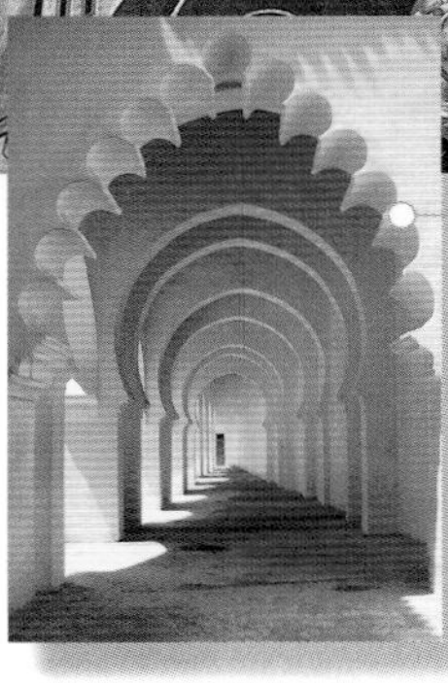

Puristic Islam
The Kutubiya Mosque (built between 1157 and 1197) is located in the pentagonal Medina of **Marrakesh (12)**. The early purism of the Almohad Dynasty is evident in the emphatic formal simplicity of the horseshoe arches in the prayer hall.

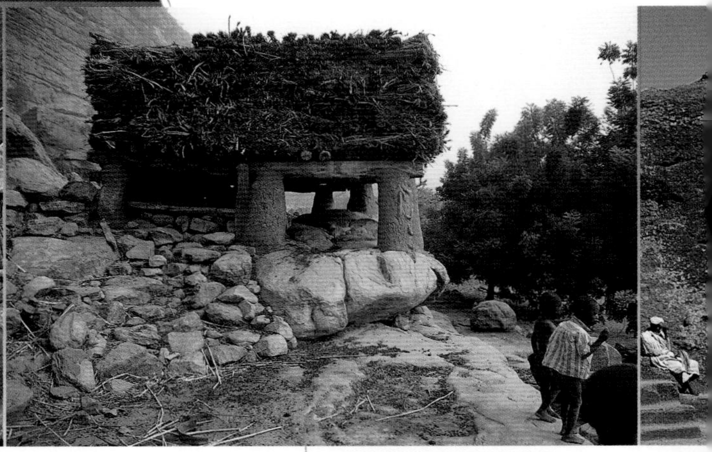

Dogon Religious Shrines
The **Cliffs of Bandiagara (6)** in Mali/Burkina Faso are home to the Dogons. Their rich cultural tradition is based upon a complex mythology of creation. Dogon shrines are built among the cliffs. The photo shows the house of the Hogon, the village religious leader.

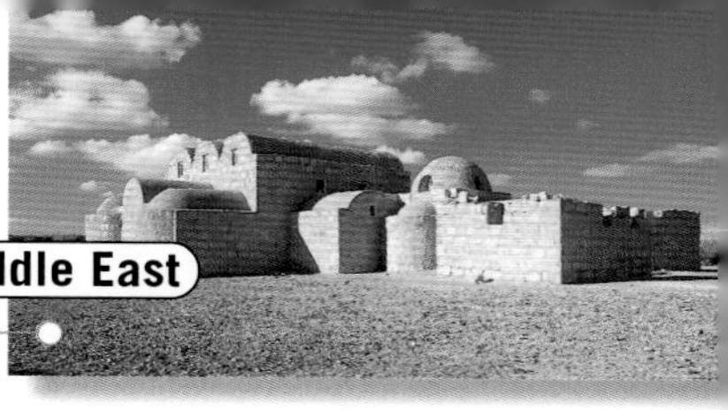

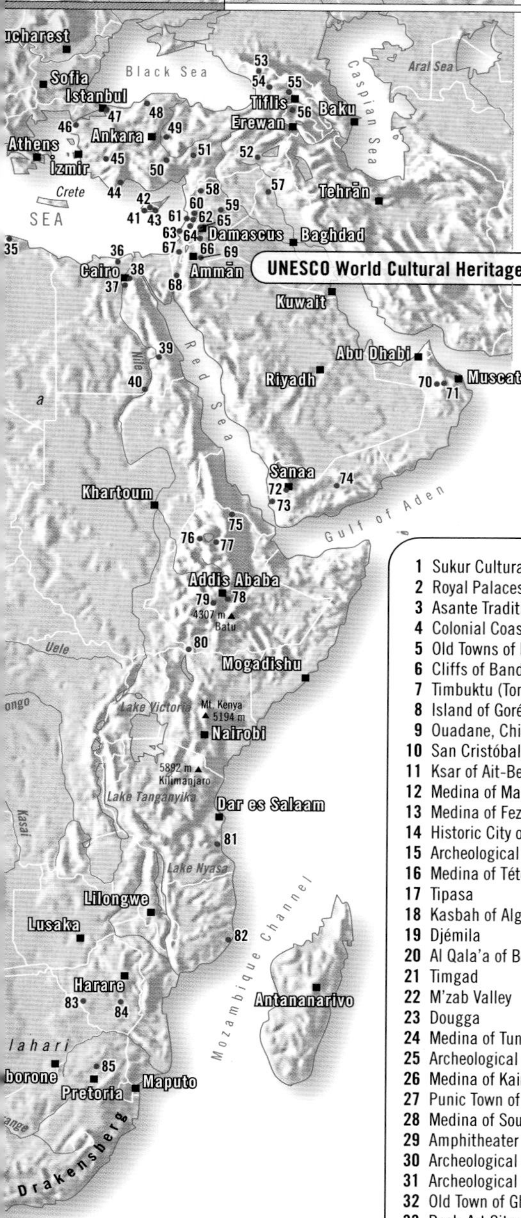

Desert Castle

The small castle of **Quseir Amra (69)** east of Amman, which dates from the Umayyad Dynasty (c. 715) features a splendidly furnished audience hall and luxurious baths.

UNESCO World Cultural Heritage Sites in Africa and the Middle East

1 Sukur Cultural Landscape	**41** Paphos
2 Royal Palaces of Abomey	**42** Painted Churches in the Troodos Region
3 Asante Traditional Buildings	**43** Neolithic Settlement of Choirokoitia
4 Colonial Coastal Forts	**44** Xanthos-Letoon
5 Old Towns of Djenné	**45** Hieropolis-Pamukkale
6 Cliffs of Bandiagara	**46** Archeological Site of Troy
7 Timbuktu (Tombouctou)	**47** Historic Areas of Istanbul
8 Island of Gorée	**48** City of Safranbolu
9 Ouadane, Chinguetti, Tichitt and Oualata	**49** Hattusha
10 San Cristóbal de La Laguna	**50** Göreme National Park and the Rock Sites of Cappadocia
11 Ksar of Ait-Ben-Haddou	**51** Great Mosque and Hospital of Divriği
12 Medina of Marrakesh	**52** Nemrut Dağ
13 Medina of Fez	**53** Mountain Villages in Svaneti
14 Historic City of Meknes	**54** Bagrati Cathedral and Gelati Monastery
15 Archeological Site of Volubilis	**55** Historic Churches of Mtskheta
16 Medina of Tétouan	**56** Monasteries of Haghbat and Sanahin
17 Tipasa	**57** Hatra
18 Kasbah of Algiers	**58** Ancient City of Aleppo
19 Djémila	**59** Site of Palmyra
20 Al Qala'a of Beni Hammad	**60** Quadi Qadisha and the Forest of the Cedars of God
21 Timgad	**61** Byblos
22 M'zab Valley	**62** Baalbek
23 Dougga	**63** Tyre
24 Medina of Tunis	**64** Anjar
25 Archeological Site of Carthage	**65** Ancient City of Damascus
26 Medina of Kairouan	**66** Ancient City of Bosra
27 Punic Town of Kerkuane	**67** Old City of Jerusalem and its Walls
28 Medina of Sousse	**68** Petra
29 Amphitheater of El Jem	**69** Quseir Amra
30 Archeological Site of Sabratha	**70** Fort of Bahla
31 Archeological Site of Leptis Magna	**71** Archeological Sites of Bat, Al-Khutm and Al-Ayn
32 Old Town of Ghadames	**72** Old City of Sanaa
33 Rock-Art Sites of Tassili n'Ajjer	**73** Medina of Zabid
34 Rock-Art Sites of Tadrart Acacus	**74** Old Walled City of Shibam
35 Archeological Site of Cyrene	**75** Aksum
36 Abu Mena	**76** Fasil Ghebbi, Gondar Region
37 Memphis and its Necropolis and Pyramids	**77** Rock-hewn Churches of Lalibela
38 Islamic Cairo	**78** Lower Awash Valley
39 Ancient Thebes (Luxor)	**79** Tiya
40 Nubian Monuments from Abu Simbel to Philae	**80** Lower Omo Valley
	81 Ruins of Kilwa Kisiwani and Songo Mnara
	82 Island of Mozambique
	83 Khami Ruins
	84 Great Zimbabwe
	85 Fossil Hominid Sites of Sterkfontein, Swartkrans and Kromdraai
	86 Robben Island

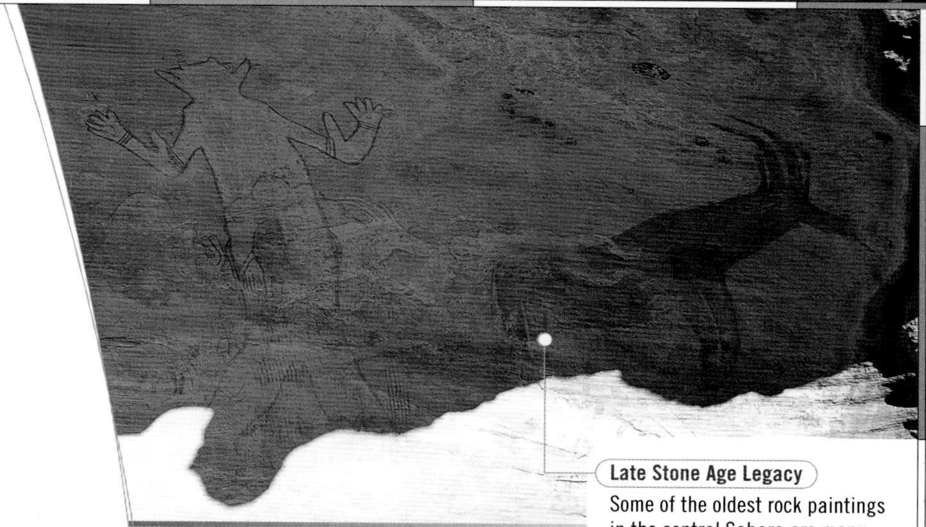

Late Stone Age Legacy

Some of the oldest rock paintings in the central Sahara are monumental works of static art. A prime example is the mysterious "Rain God Fresco" of Sefar in the **Tassili n'Ajjer (33)**.

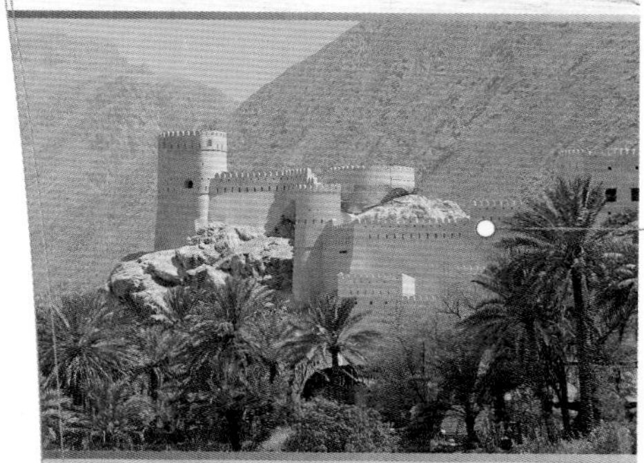

Loam Fortress

Built primarily of loam and straw, the fortress of **Bahla (70)** has towers as high as 50 m. Parts of the complex date back to pre-Islamic times. Bahla was the capital of the Sultanate of Oman at several different points in history.

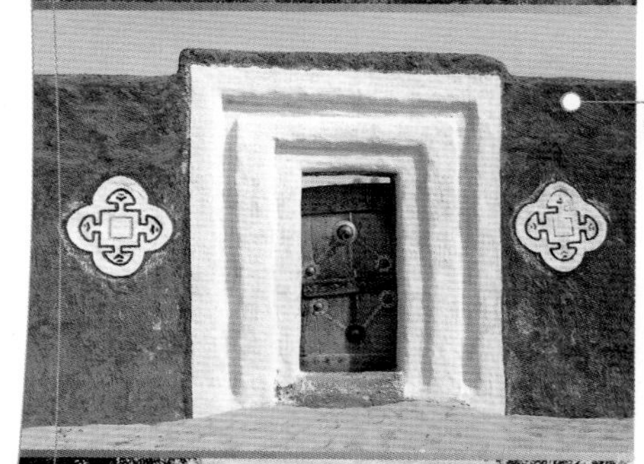

City in Ruins with a Living Artistic Tradition

A dying city today, the former trading metropolis of **Oualata (9)** on the southern edge of the Sahara is still regarded as a center of Islamic scholarship. Some of the stone buildings covered with red loam are adorned with highly symbolic ornaments.

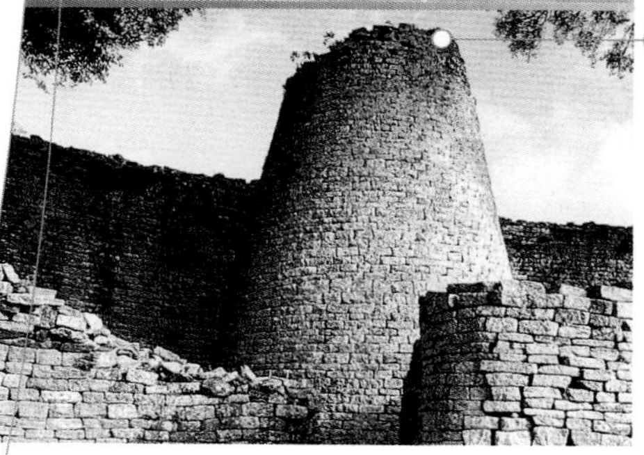

Ancient Granite Seat of Kings

The largest stone architectural complex produced by black African cultures is **Great Zimbabwe (84)**, which means "houses of stone." Built of granite blocks fitted precisely without mortared joints, the massive ring of walls bears witness to the might of the Shona Kings of the 15th century. The solid, cone-shaped stone tower resembles the grain silos used by Shona farmers.

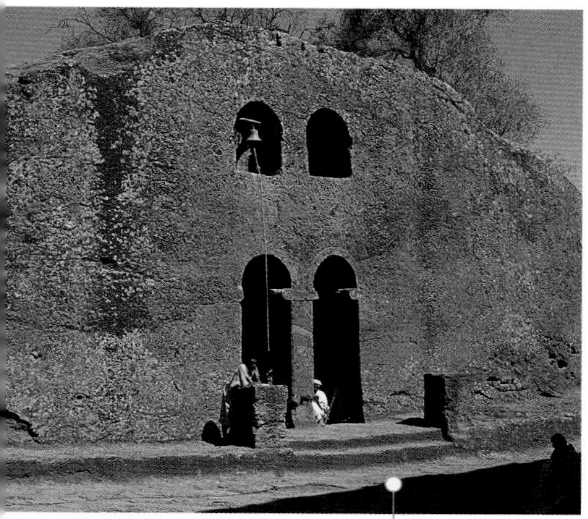

Brilliant Architecture

The **Rock Churches of Lalibela (77)** were hewn from the exposed red tuff of the Ethiopian Plateau around 1200 AD. As imitations of existing architecture, they exhibit influences from the Byzantine and ancient Aksum civilizations.

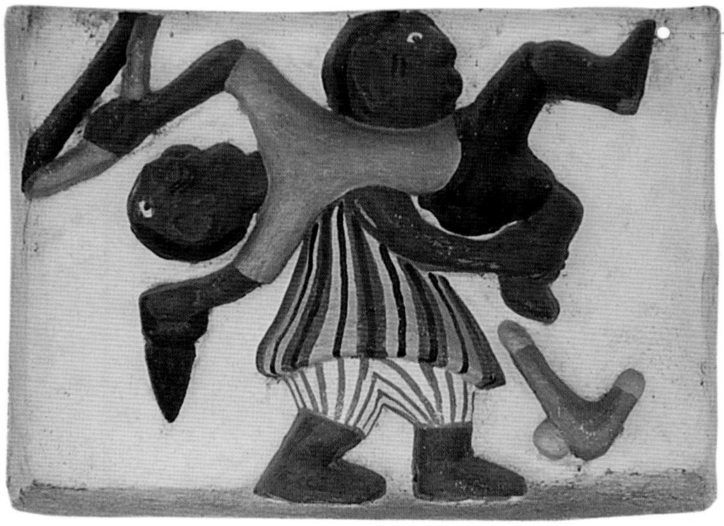

Victorious Amazons

The kingdom of Dahomey rose to affluence and power (supported by a well-trained professional army) in the 17th century. The bas-relief on the walls of the **Royal Palace of Abomey (2)** commemorates the Amazon Corps.

To What Extent Is the World Cultural Heritage Endangered? The "Red List"

In addition to the World Heritage List, the World Heritage Committee maintains a list of endangered sites – properties in need of special attention and preservation efforts. The purpose of this list is to make both governments and the pubic aware of the natural and anthropogenic dangers to which World Heritage Sites are exposed.

The list of endangered properties currently contains 27 World Heritage Sites, among them the Natural and Cultural Region of Kotor (Yugoslavia), which was shaken by an earthquake in 1979, the Royal Palace of Abomey (Benin), which suffered serious hurricane damage in 1985, the sacred temples of Timbuktu (Mali), which are beset by the destructive forces of the desert, and the monuments of Hampi (India), which are threatened by road and bridge construction.

The World Heritage Committee collaborates with individual governments in preparing an action plan for endangered sites. It provides financial support and monitors the progress of work, which usually takes considerable time. Some countries seek the Committee's help for their problems, while others tend to resent such intervention. One of the few sites that has been restored and deleted from the list is Dubrovnik (Croatia).

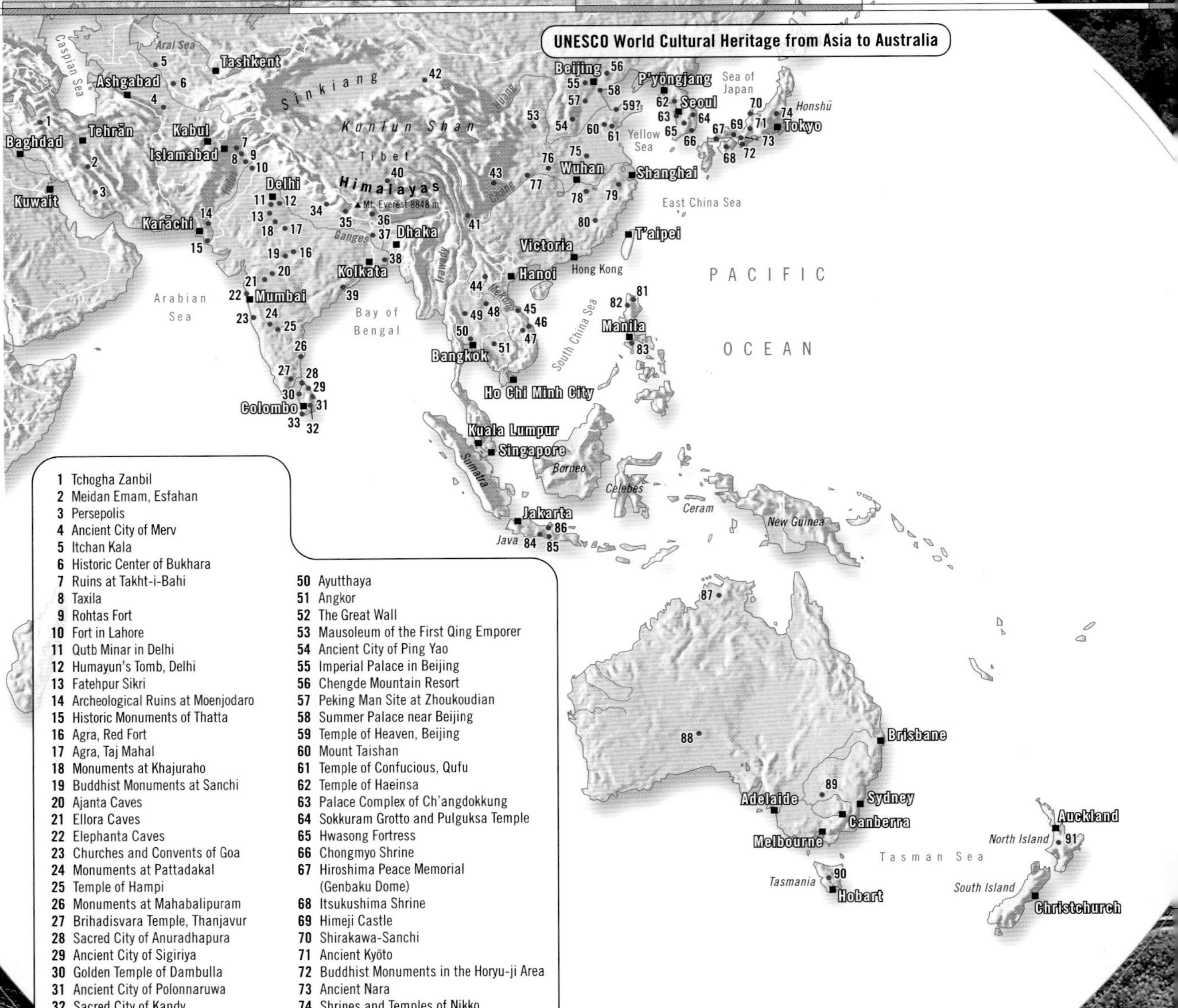

UNESCO World Cultural Heritage from Asia to Australia

1 Tchogha Zanbil
2 Meidan Emam, Esfahan
3 Persepolis
4 Ancient City of Merv
5 Itchan Kala
6 Historic Center of Bukhara
7 Ruins at Takht-i-Bahi
8 Taxila
9 Rohtas Fort
10 Fort in Lahore
11 Qutb Minar in Delhi
12 Humayun's Tomb, Delhi
13 Fatehpur Sikri
14 Archeological Ruins at Moenjodaro
15 Historic Monuments of Thatta
16 Agra, Red Fort
17 Agra, Taj Mahal
18 Monuments at Khajuraho
19 Buddhist Monuments at Sanchi
20 Ajanta Caves
21 Ellora Caves
22 Elephanta Caves
23 Churches and Convents of Goa
24 Monuments at Pattadakal
25 Temple of Hampi
26 Monuments at Mahabalipuram
27 Brihadisvara Temple, Thanjavur
28 Sacred City of Anuradhapura
29 Ancient City of Sigiriya
30 Golden Temple of Dambulla
31 Ancient City of Polonnaruwa
32 Sacred City of Kandy
33 Old Town of Galle
34 Lumbini
35 Valley of Kathmandu
36 Darjeeling Himalayan Railway
37 Paharpur
38 Historic Mosque City of Bagerhat
39 Sun Temple of Konarak
40 Potala Palace in Lhasa
41 Old Town of Lijiang
42 Mogao Caves
43 Mt. Emei Scenic Area and Giant Buddha of Leshan
44 Luang Prabang
45 Hue
46 Hoi An Ancient Town
47 My Son Sanctuary
48 Ban Chiang
49 Sukhothai
50 Ayutthaya
51 Angkor
52 The Great Wall
53 Mausoleum of the First Qing Emperor
54 Ancient City of Ping Yao
55 Imperial Palace in Beijing
56 Chengde Mountain Resort
57 Peking Man Site at Zhoukoudian
58 Summer Palace near Beijing
59 Temple of Heaven, Beijing
60 Mount Taishan
61 Temple of Confucious, Qufu
62 Temple of Haeinsa
63 Palace Complex of Ch'angdokkung
64 Sokkuram Grotto and Pulguksa Temple
65 Hwasong Fortress
66 Chongmyo Shrine
67 Hiroshima Peace Memorial (Genbaku Dome)
68 Itsukushima Shrine
69 Himeji Castle
70 Shirakawa-Sanchi
71 Ancient Kyōto
72 Buddhist Monuments in the Horyu-ji Area
73 Ancient Nara
74 Shrines and Temples of Nikko
75 Classical Gardens of Suzhou
76 Ancient Buildings in the Wudang Mountains
77 Dazu Rock Carvings
78 Lushan National Park
79 Mount Huangshan
80 Mount Wuyi
81 Rice Terraces of the Ifugao
82 Historic Town of Vigan
83 Baroque Churches of the Philippines
84 Borobudur Temple Compounds
85 Prambanan Temple Compounds
86 Sangiran Early Man Site
87 Kakadu National Park
88 Uluru-Kata Tjuta National Park
89 Willandra Lakes Region
90 Tasmanian Wilderness
91 Tongariro National Park

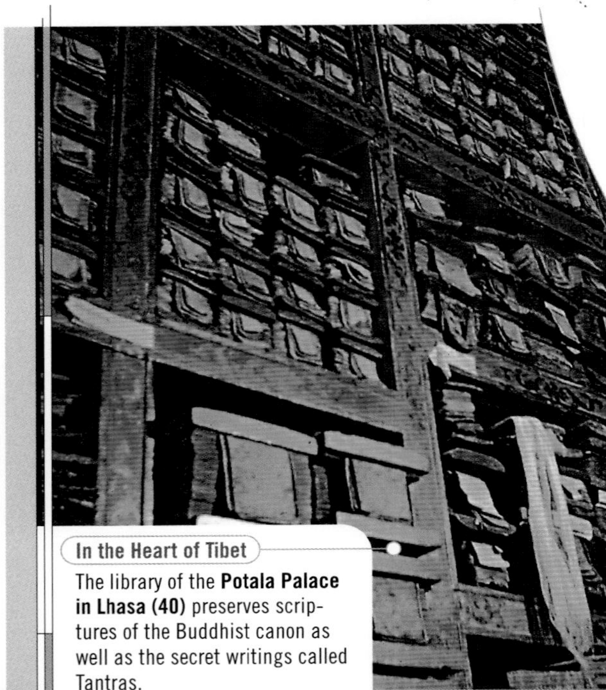

In the Heart of Tibet

The library of the **Potala Palace in Lhasa (40)** preserves scriptures of the Buddhist canon as well as the secret writings called Tantras.

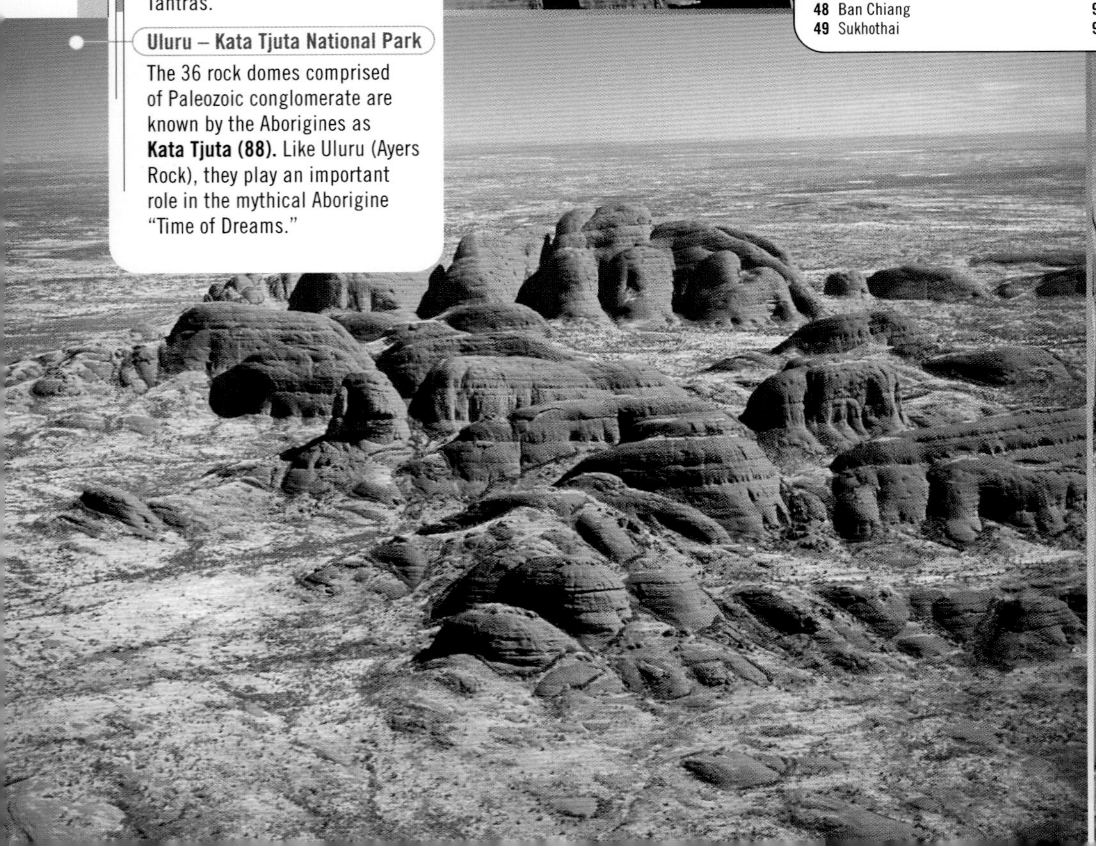

Uluru – Kata Tjuta National Park

The 36 rock domes comprised of Paleozoic conglomerate are known by the Aborigines as **Kata Tjuta (88).** Like Uluru (Ayers Rock), they play an important role in the mythical Aborigine "Time of Dreams."

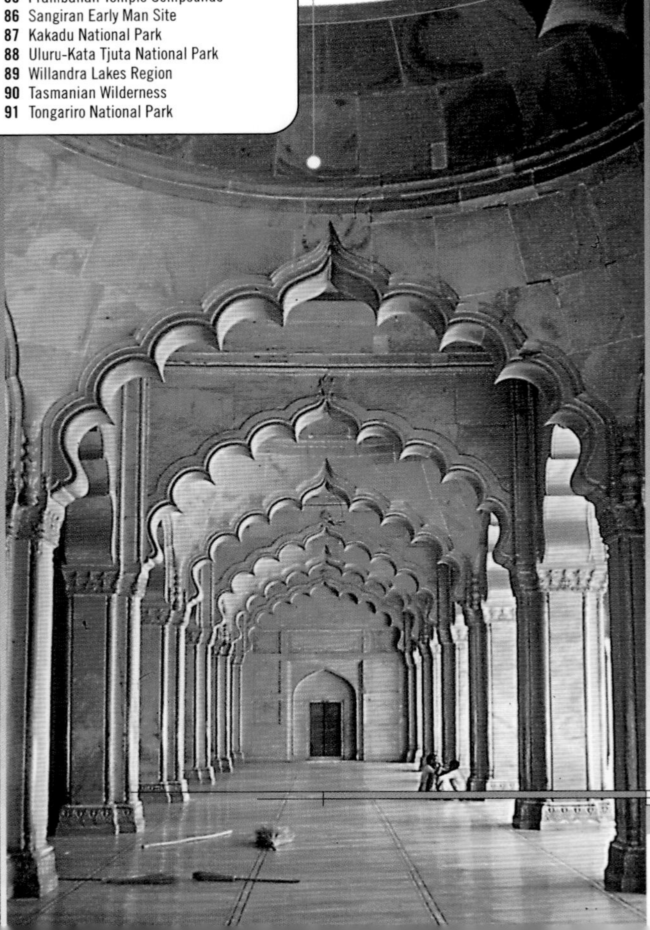

Classical Mogul Architecture

The **Red Fort (16)** of Agra comprises the Pearl Mosque (built between 1648 and 1654). The restrained decoration creates an impression of purity and clarity.

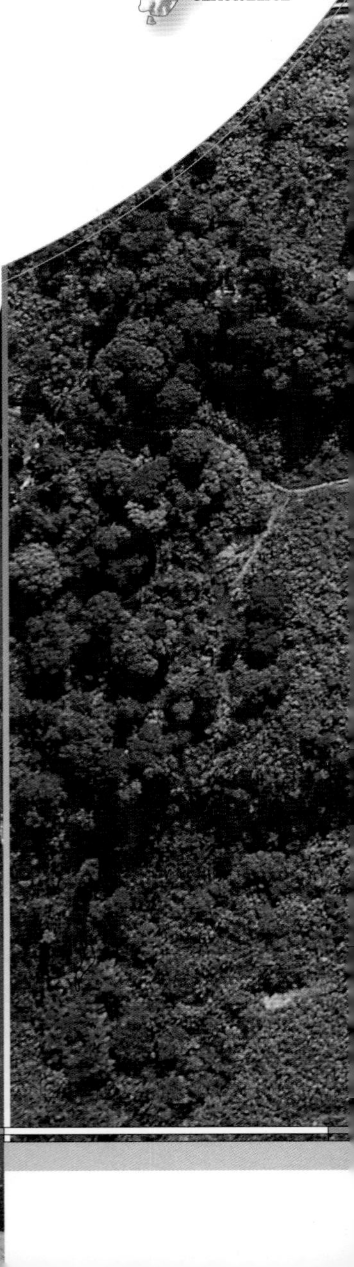

Ancient Stupa

The Dharmarajika stupa near **Taxila (8)**, originally a dome-shaped brick structure decorated with reliefs, dates to the 2nd century BC.

A Library of Wood

The repository of the **Tripitaka Koreana (62)** (13th c.) at the temple of Haeinsa near Taegu provides natural air-conditioning for the more than 81,000 wooden printing blocks, testaments of extraordinary craftsmanship.

Camels for the King

The relief on the eastern stairs of the great reception hall in **Persepolis (3)** shows Darius the Great receiving gifts.

The World's Largest Terrace System

The **Rice Terraces of the Ifugao (81)** are situated on steep mountain slopes in the northern part of the island of Luzon. Reaching heights of up to 15 meters, many of the heavy walls of stone, support terraces of only three meters wide.

Buddha Calls Upon the Earth Goddess

The sacred shrine of Wat Mahathat, containing sculptures from the 13th and 14th centuries, is located in the heart of the historic town of **Sukhothai (49).**

Ensemble of Bay, Island, and Shrine

The island of Miyajima in the Japanese inland sea is the site of a Shinto shrine built in the 6th and 7th centuries. Pilgrims arrived from the mainland (Hiroshima) at the foot of the **Itsukushima Shrine (68)** in boats. Only 160 meters from the shore, the entrance gate is submerged at high tide.

Towering Faces

The center of the Khmer Kingdom from the 9th to the 15th century, **Angkor (51)** boasted not only an unparalleled urban architecture complemented by artificial lakes but a magnificent array of ornamentation on all exterior facades.

Measured Rhythm

The majestic roofs of the halls of the **Imperial Palace in Beijing (55)** are aligned along the main axis of the palace.

Perspectives for the World Heritage Convention

Armed conflict ranks highest among the many dangers to which the cultural heritage is exposed. The impact of industrialization and urban development is also significant. Air pollution threatens building substance, tourism detracts from the authenticity of cultural sites, and the dynamics of technical and economic progress often impair the integrity of traditional cultural treasures.

Can Tourists Save the World Cultural Heritage?

Can the goal of protecting monuments of the World Cultural Heritage be achieved without neglecting the needs of people who live near them? It is not enough merely to list the necessary protective measures. It is equally important to consider marketing issues and to respond to the wishes and expectations of visitors. This applies in particular to the cultural landscape, the youngest category of the World Heritage List. The "sustainable cultural landscape" is classified as a region in which change must take place in order to ensure that its inhabitants can continue to live normal lives. But which elements of a cultural landscape can be changed without detracting from their outstanding character, and which must be preserved unaltered? The field of possibilities is broad.

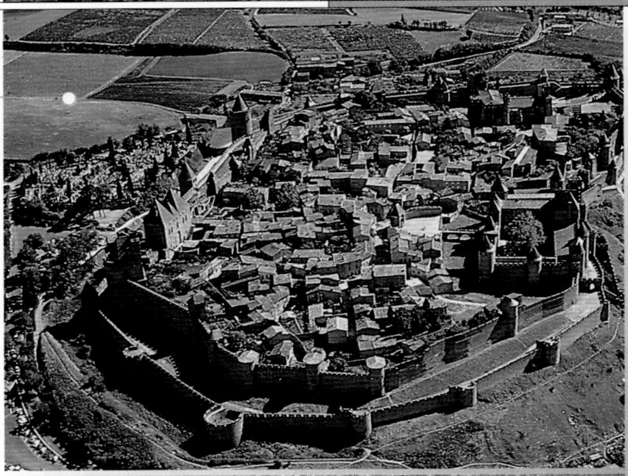

Catharist Bastion

Fortified by two rings of walls, the medieval city of **Carcassonne (38)** crowns a hill above the Aude Valley. Situated along a route from the Atlantic to the Mediterranean, its position was of strategic importance during periods of Muslim and Frankish occupation. It was captured after a long siege during the Albigensian Wars in 1209.

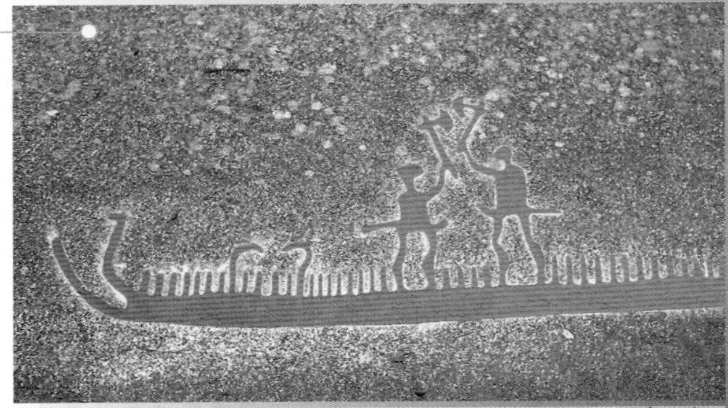

Mysterious Religious Ritual

Rock drawing of a ship and two axe-wielding warriors from the Nordic Bronze Age in **Tanum (241)**, southern Sweden.

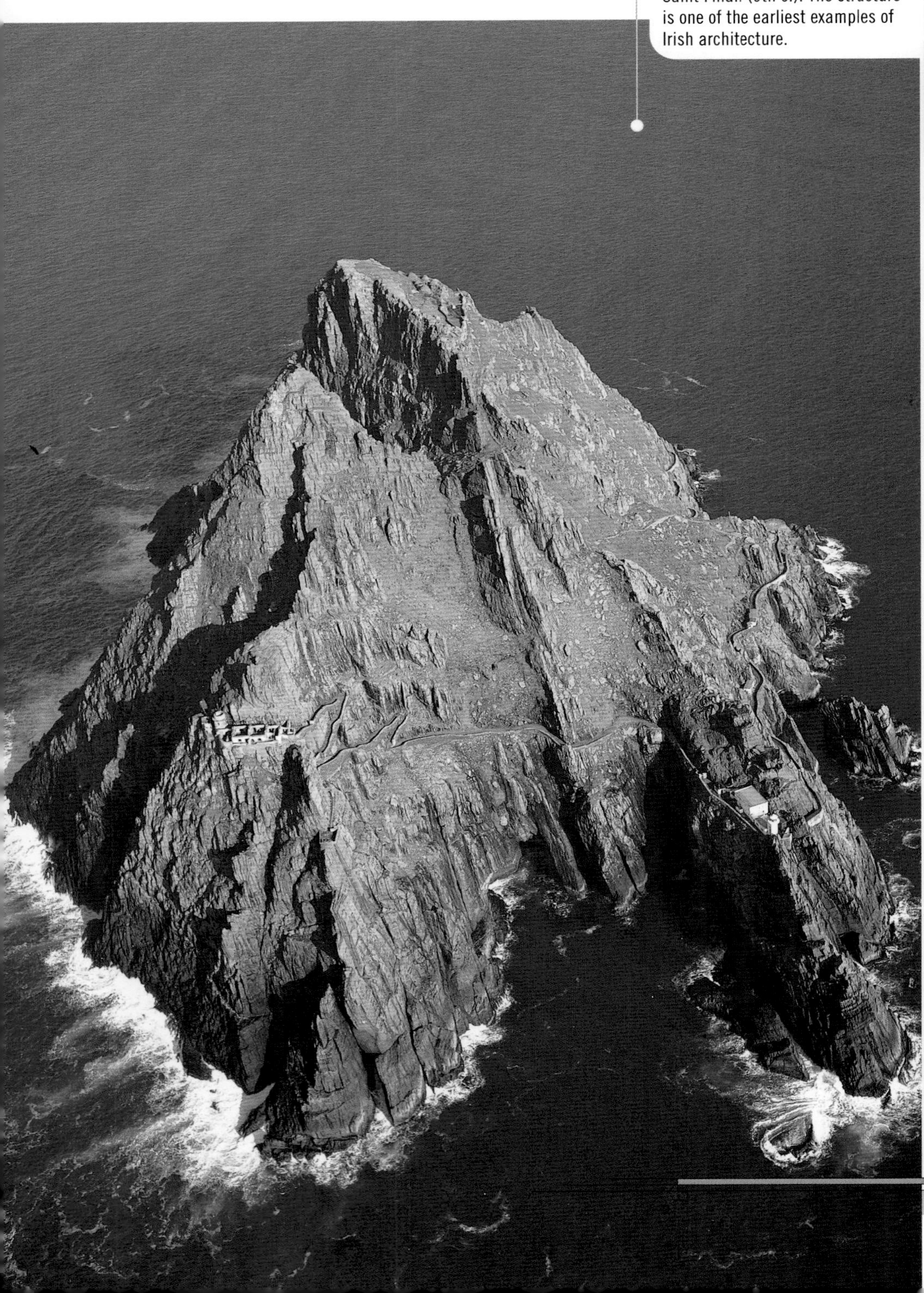

Early Christian Refuge

The rocky island of **Skellig Michael (86)** and ruins of the cloister of Saint Finan (9th c.). The structure is one of the earliest examples of Irish architecture.

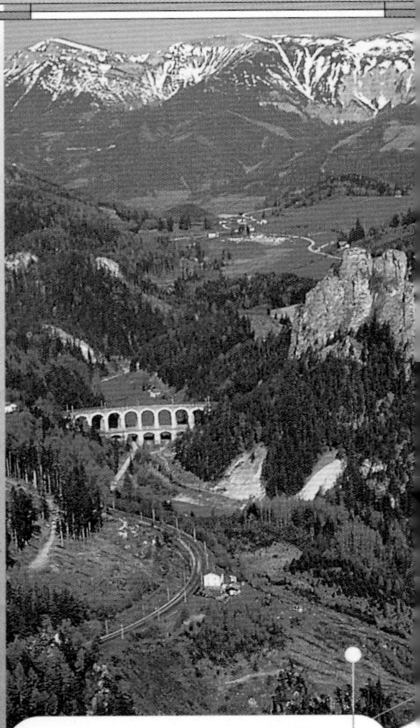

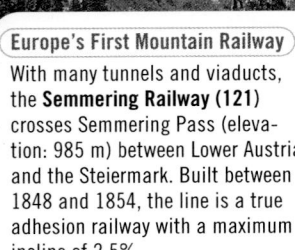

Europe's First Mountain Railway

With many tunnels and viaducts, the **Semmering Railway (121)** crosses Semmering Pass (elevation: 985 m) between Lower Austria and the Steiermark. Built between 1848 and 1854, the line is a true adhesion railway with a maximum incline of 2.5%.

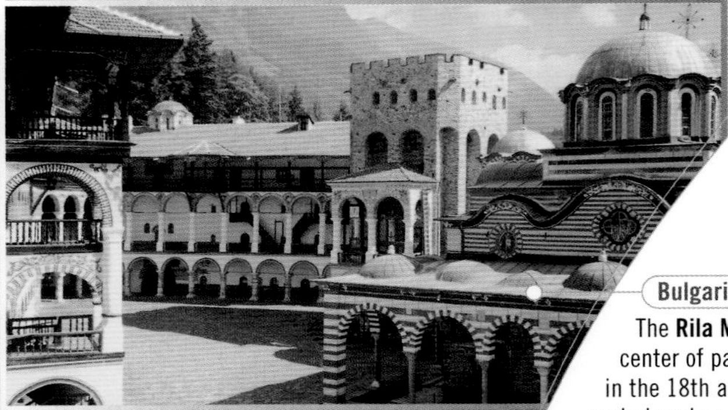

Bulgarian Renaissance Castle

The **Rila Monastery (181)** was a center of painting and literature in the 18th and 19th centuries and played an important role in the growth of a national identity. Thick, high external walls give the complex the look of a fortress.

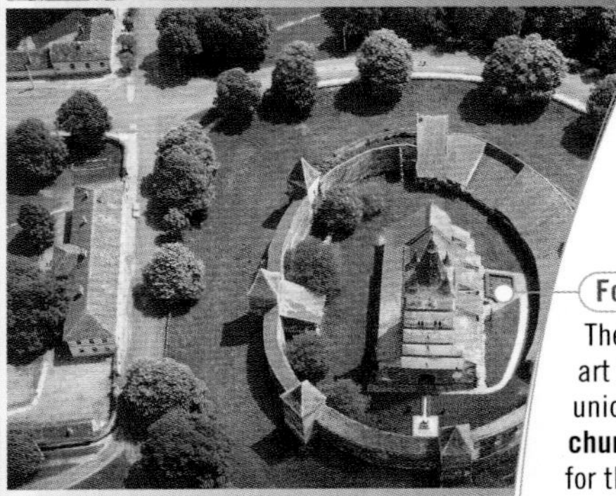

Fortified Religious Architecture

The rich heritage of Transylvanian art is represented by a number of unique churches. These **fortified churches (195)** offered protection for the "Saxons" who settled in the border region. The choir tower was the defensive core of the complex.

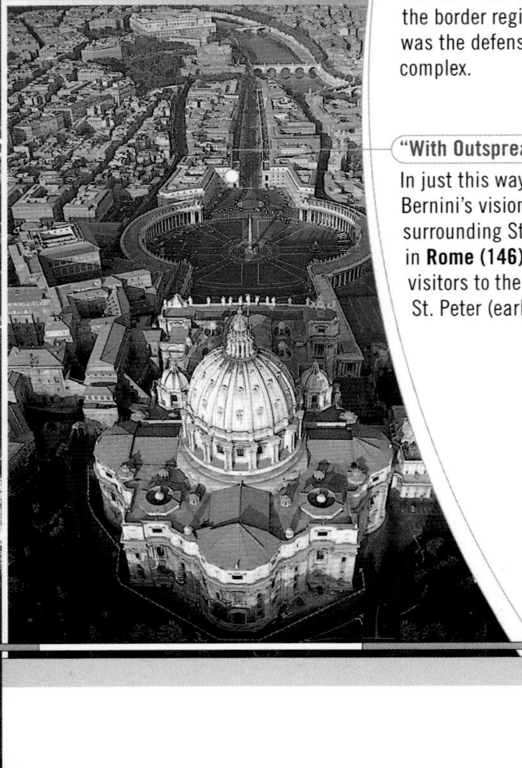

"With Outspread Arms"

In just this way, according to Bernini's vision, the collonades surrounding St. Peter's Square in **Rome (146)** were to welcome visitors to the new Basilica of St. Peter (early 17th c.).

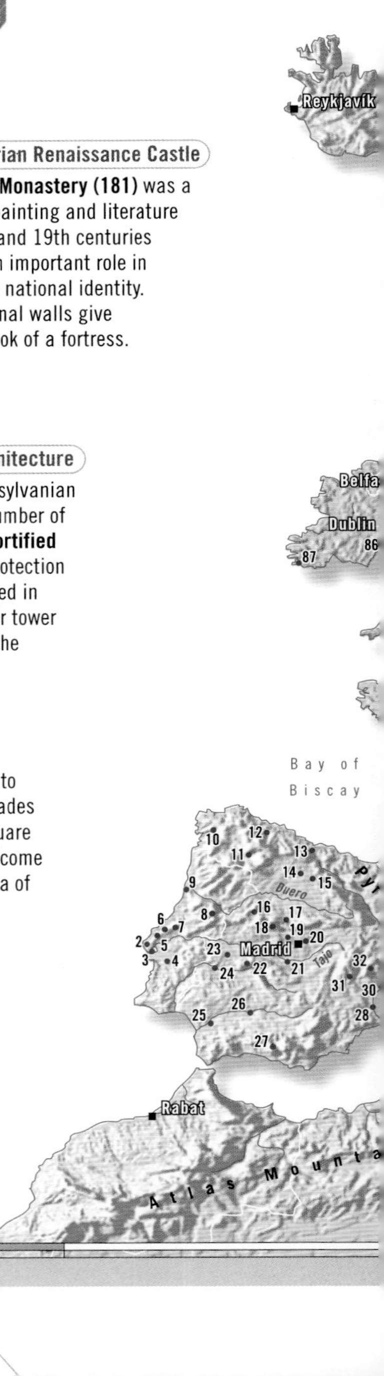

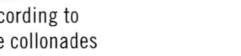

Moorish Art in Perfection

The architecture of the **Alhambra of Granada (27)** is less striking than its decorative embellishments. The intricate ornamentation of even a small niche bears witness to a tendency toward a dematerialization of objective representation.

Ancient Greek Religious Site

The Oracle of the Temple of Apollo at **Delphi (173)** was consulted by pilgrims about the prospects for success in business or political endeavors.

Northern Boundary of the Roman Empire

The borders of the empire were expanded and fortified to form a permanent defense line under Roman Emperor Hadrian. The photo shows part of **Hadrian's Wall (82)** in northern England.

Unique Silver Mines

The **Rammelsberg Mines (108)** in the Harz Mountains is the only mine complex in the world that boasts 1,000 years of continuous operation. They were closed in 1988. A shaft from the 12th century is well preserved.

UNESCO World Cultural Heritage Sites in Europe

1 City Center of Angra do Heroismo, Azores (not shown on map)
2 Cultural Landscape of Sintra
3 Hieronymite Monastery and Tower of Belem
4 Historic Center of Evora
5 Alcobaca Monastery
6 Batalha Monastery
7 Convent of Christ in Tomar
8 Rock-Art Sites in the Coa Valley
9 Historic Center of Porto
10 Historic Center of Santiago de Compostela
11 Las Medulas
12 Churches of the Kingdom of the Asturias
13 Altamira Cave
14 Cathedral of Burgos
15 San Millan Yuso and Suso Monasteries
16 Old Town of Salamanca
17 Old Town of Segovia, including its aqueduct
18 Old Town of Ávila
19 El Escorial
20 Historic Precinct of Alcalá de Henares
21 Historic City of Toledo
22 Royal Monastery of Santa Maria de Guadalupe
23 Old Town of Cáceres
24 Roman Buildings in Mérida
25 Cathedral and Alcazar in Seville
26 Mosque of Córdoba
27 Granada
28 'La Lonja de la Seda' of Valencia
29 Ibiza
30 Rock Art of the Mediterranean Basin on the Iberian Peninsula
31 Historic Walled Town of Cuenca
32 Mudejar Architecture of Aragón
33 Poblet Monastery
34 Parque Guell and Case Mila, Barcelona
35 Palau de la Musica in Barcelona
36 Mont Perdu in the Pyrenees
37 Pilgrims' Route to Santiago de Compostela
38 Old City of Carcassonne
39 Le Canal du Midi
40 Pont du Gard (Roman Aqueduct)
41 Arles
42 Papal Palace of Avignon
43 Orange (Roman Theater and Triumphal Arch)
44 Historical Monuments of Lyon
45 Decorated Grottoes of the Vézère Valley
46 Saint-Émilion
47 Church of Saint-Savin-sur-Gartempe
48 Chambord Castle
49 Cathedral of Bourges
50 Abbey Church of Vézelay
51 Royal Saltworks of Arc-et-Senans
52 Cistercian Abbey of Fontenay
53 Sites in Nancy
54 Strasbourg, Grand Ile
55 Palace and Park of Fontainebleau
56 Chartres Cathedral
57 Mont Saint-Michel
58 Palace and Park of Versailles
59 Banks of the Seine, Paris
60 Cathedral of Amiens
61 Cathedral of Reims
62 Old City of Luxembourg
63 Medieval Belfries of Flanders and Wallonia
64 Four Lifts on the Canal du Centre and Environs
65 La Grande Place, Brussels
66 Flemish Beguinages
67 Mill Network of Kinderdijk-Elshout
68 Defense Line of Amsterdam
69 Beemster Polder

70 Shokland and Environs
71 Steam Pump Plant in Wouda
72 Canterbury Cathedral
73 Royal Greenwich Park
74 Westminster Abbey and Church of St. Margaret, London
75 Tower of London
76 Stonehenge and Avebury
77 Bath
78 Blenheim Palace
79 Industrial Monuments in Ironbridge Valley
80 Fortifications of Edward I in Wales
81 Fountains Abbey
82 Hadrian's Wall
83 Castle and Cathedral in Durham
84 Edinburgh
85 Orkney Islands
86 Skelling Michael
87 Bend of the Boyne
88 Jelling Mounds
89 Roskilde Cathedral
90 Hanseatic City of Lübeck
91 Cologne Cathedral
92 Roman Monuments, Cathedral and Church in Trier
93 Castles in Brühl
94 Aachen Cathedral
95 Völklingen Ironworks
96 Speyer Cathedral
97 Abbey and Altenmünster of Lorsch
98 Maulbronn Monastery Complex
99 Pilgrimage Church of Wies
100 Residence in Würzburg
101 Old Town of Bamberg
102 Wartburg Castle
103 Classical Weimar
104 Luther Memorials in Eisleben and Wittenberg
105 Bauhaus Sites in Weimar and Dessau
106 Historic Sites in Quedlinburg
107 St. Mary's Cathedral and St. Michaels Church, Hildesheim
108 Mines of Rammelsberg and the Historic Town of Goslar
109 Palaces and Parks in Potsdam and Berlin
110 Museum Island, Berlin
111 Historic Center of Prague
112 Historic Center of Kutná Hora
113 Litomysl Castle
114 Gardens and Castle at Kroměříž
115 Lednice-Caltice Cultural Landscape
116 Pilgrimage Church at Zelen Hora in Žd'ár nad Sázavou
117 Historic Center of Telč
118 Holasovice Historical Village Reservation
119 Historic Center of Krumau
120 Palaces and Gardens of Schönbrunn
121 Semmering Railway
122 Old City of Graz
123 Salzkammergut Cultural Landscape
124 Historic Center, City of Salzburg
125 Convent of St. Gallen
126 Old City of Bern
127 Convent of St. John at Müstair
128 Rock Drawings in Valcamonica
129 Crespi d'Adda
130 Santa Maria delle Grazie in Milan
131 Residences of the Royal House of Savoy
132 Portovenere and Cinque Terre
133 Cathedral and Piazza Grande, Modena
134 Ferrara
135 Vicenza, City of Palladio and Villas on the Veneto
136 Botanical Gardens, Padua
137 Aquileia
138 Venice
139 Early Christian Monuments and Mosaics of Ravenna
140 Historic Center of Florence
141 Piazza del Duomo, Pisa
142 Historic Center of San Gimignano
143 Historic Center of Siena
144 Historic Center of Urbino
145 Historic Center of Pienza
146 Historic Center of Rome, the Properties of the Holy See, and San Paolo Fuori le Mura
147 Villa Adriana
148 Su Nuraxi di Barumini
149 Royal Palace at Caserta
150 Historic Center of Naples
151 Costiera Amalfitana
152 Archaeological Areas of Pompeii and Ercolano
153 Paestum and Certosa di Pavia
154 Castel del Monte
155 Trulli of Alberobello

156 I Sassi di Matera
157 Agrigento
158 Roman Villa of Casale
159 Megalithic Temples of Malta
160 City of Valletta
161 Hal Saflieni Hypogeum
162 Medieval City of Rhodes
163 Historical Sites, Island of Patmos
164 Island of Delos
165 Pythagoreion and Hereion of Samos
166 Monuments of Chios
167 Acropolis, Athens
168 Archeological Sites of Mycenae and Tiryns
169 Archeological Site of Epidaurus
170 Mystras
171 Temple of Apollo at Bassae
172 Archeological Site of Olympia
173 Archeological Site of Delphi
174 Meteora
175 Mount Athos
176 Monuments of Thessalonika
177 Archeological Sites of Vergina
178 Butrint
179 City and Lake of Ohrid
180 Church of Boyana
181 Monatery of Rila
182 Thracian Tomb of Kazanlak
183 Rock-hewn Churches of Ivanovo
184 Ancient City of Nessebar
185 Madara Rider
186 Thracian Tomb of Sveshtari
187 Monastery of Studenica
188 Stari Ras and Sopocani Monastery
189 Natural and Culturo-Historic Region of Kotor
190 Old City of Dubrovnik
191 Historic Complex of Split
192 Historic City of Trogir
193 Historic Center of Porec
194 Dacian Fortresses in the Orastie Mountains
195 Fortified Churches in Transylvania
196 Horezu Monastery
197 Historic Center of Sighisoara
198 Churches of Moldavia
199 Wooden Churches of Maramures
200 Hortobágy National Park
201 Benedictine Monastery of Pannonhalma
202 Budapest
203 Hollokö
204 Banska Stiavnica
205 Vlkolinec Reservation of Folk Architecture
206 Spissky Hrad and Environs
207 Historic Center of L'viv
208 Kiev
209 Old City of Zamosc
210 Wieliczka Salt Mine
211 Historic Center of Kraków
212 Kalwaria Zebrzydowska
213 Auschwitz Concentration Camp
214 Historic Center of Warsaw
215 Medieval Town of Torun
216 Malbork
217 Historic Center of Vilnius
218 Historic Center of Riga
219 Historic Center of Tallinn
220 Historic Center of St. Petersburg
221 Historic Monuments in Novgorod and Surroundings
222 Church of Anscension, Kolomenskoye
223 Kremlin and Red Square, Moscow
224 Monastery in Sergiev Possad
225 White Monuments of Vladimir and Suzdal
226 Kizhi Pogost in Lake Onega
227 Cultural and Historic Ensemble of the Solovetsky Islands
228 Verla Groundwood and Board Mill
229 Fortress of Suomenlinna
230 Old Rauma
231 Petäjävesi Old Church
232 Burial Site of Sammallahdenmäki
233 Laponian Area
234 Old City of Luleå
235 Engelsberg Ironworks
236 Skogskrykogården
237 Royal Domain of Drottningholm
238 Birka and Hovgården
239 Hanseatic Town of Visby
240 Naval Port of Karlskrona
241 Rock Carvings in Tanum
242 Bryggen, Old Hanseatic Quater of Bergen
243 Urnes Stave Church
244 Røros Mining Town
245 Rock Drawings of Alta

Global Urbanization

From Jericho to the Global City – The City as a Human Habitat?

Jericho and urban history are inseparably intertwined. Here, in the Jordan River Valley, the roots of urban culture can be traced back to the 7th millennium BC. But evidence of early city life can also be found beneath thousands of years of accumulated rubble in other parts of the world.

In the earliest phase in the history of cities, "city-dwellers" represented only a tiny segment of the world's population (estimated at roughly 80 million around the year 1000 BC). At the dawn of the third millennium AD, after nearly nine thousand years of urban history, the majority of the six billion people on earth live in urban settlements. The number of city residents is expected to rise by nearly 100% by the year 2030, increasing from 2.9 billion (48%) in the year 2000 to about five billion (about 60%) by 2030.

What is "urban" and what is "urbanity"?

Rome, the birthplace of Caesar and Cicero, has always been regarded in the western world as the prototype of the most advanced form of human communal life. During that period it was simply called "urbs" (the city) – and clearly understood as such throughout the ancient world. Rome was the capital of a world empire, a center of art and science, of architecture, of fashion and good taste – indeed of every aspect of life in all its diversity. Thus the adjective "urban" refers to the unique and specific characteristics of the city as human living space, features embodied in ancient Rome. The term "urbanity" encompasses the idea of city life as a whole. Writing in the 18th century, English author Samuel Johnson aptly described the essence of urbanity in his famous remark about the city of London: "When a man is tired of London, he is tired of life; for there is in London all that life can afford."

The Urbanization of the Earth

The invention of the steam engine (c. 1770) revolutionized the world and especially its cities. Coal began to replace water power as the most important source of energy. Nearly everywhere (but particularly in Europe), the Industrial Revolution inundated traditional urban structures with technical innovations as societies entered the Age of Industry. Massive industrial complexes spewing filth from smokestacks laid claim to both urban space and human labor. Impoverished through overpopulation, millions of people from rural areas streamed into the rapidly ballooning cities. Between 1851 and 1901, the population of London rose from 2.5 to six million, while those of Berlin and Leipzig grew by factors of four and eight, respectively, during the same period. Country people who found no room and no means of subsistence in the overcrowded cities of Europe sought refuge in the prospering urban centers of the New World (primarily in North America) in waves of migration beginning in the mid-19th century. Working class settlements and the misery endemic to them began to shape the physiognomy of

entire metropolitan areas (Manchester, Liverpool, Chicago, New York, and the Ruhr region of Germany).

In the 20th century, coal largely gave way to oil – at least in the industrialized countries of the world. The gasoline-powered automobile gained popularity rapidly, and the resulting increase in mobility was accompanied by changes in attitudes about living conditions in the urban population. New suburban developments sprang up everywhere, spreading across administrative boundaries (urban sprawl) – either invading former rural areas (suburbanization) or mixing with neighboring urban districts (to form "conurbations").

Smog is an urban environmental problem. The quality of life in densely populated metropolitan regions is often severely impaired by air pollution caused by industrial emissions and automobile exhaust – as in São Paulo (a city with over five million passenger cars).

Unreliable Statistics – Confusing Terminology

According to statistics published by the UN, there are now about 320 "urban agglomerations" (each with more than one million inhabitants) in the world. Of these, only 20 are classified on the basis of census figures for the year 1995 as "megacities" (with over 10 million inhabitants). These include the metropolitan areas of Tokyo (26.8 million), São Paulo (16.4), New York (16.3), Mexico City (15.6), Bombay (15.1), Shanghai (15.1), Los Angeles (12.4), Beijing (12.3), Kolkata (Calcutta) (11.7) and Seoul (11.6). There is no agreement among urban experts as to the precise meaning of such once commonly used terms as "city" (minimum population of 100,000 for European cities), "metropolis" (a large city with a significant central function), or "megalopolis" (urban agglomeration). Yet one thing seems clear: Global urbanization is progressing at a rapid pace – much too fast for government administrations, statisticians and urban research to follow.

The Two Faces of Development

The pattern of global urbanization mirrors the global prosperity gap between industrialized and developing countries. Urban population in the industrialized nations as a group grew at a rate of only 0.6% per year between 1995 and 2000. The figure for all developing countries for the same period was 2.9%. Demographers estimate that the statistical increase in urban population by the year 2030 will be absorbed by the urban agglomerations of the developing countries alone. This trend will result in a dramatic deterioration of urban living conditions for the latecomers, as present developments already indicate. More than half of the urban population of the developing countries now lives below the poverty line in illegal slums and hut settlements – the "favelas," "shanty towns," "squatter settlements," "barriadas," and "Bidonvilles" that have encircled existing urban structures like a constricting noose in many parts of the world. Sociologists attribute this trend to push and pull factors. Push factors such as poverty, unemployment, infrastructure deficiencies, and the generally bleak prospects of rural life turn dazzling urban behemoths into enchanting magnets that generate hopes of social and economic betterment (the pull effect). Offering ostensibly sound reasons for abandoning rural homelands, these factors have led to a general exodus from the country into the cities in the developing nations.

The Global View

At present, the urban population is growing at a rate of 2.1 per year, much faster than the total world population (1.4%). Due to climatic conditions and factors affecting transportation, the region of heaviest urban agglomeration lies within a strip of territory between 80 and 120 km wide running parallel to the coasts in the temperate zones between about 20 and 60 degrees north latitude. In other words, total urbanization of the Earth's surface is highly unlikely.

Nor has the often-cited process of economic and (in the broadest sense) cultural "globalization" eradicated the integrity and unique character of the diverse types of urban communities in the different cultural regions of

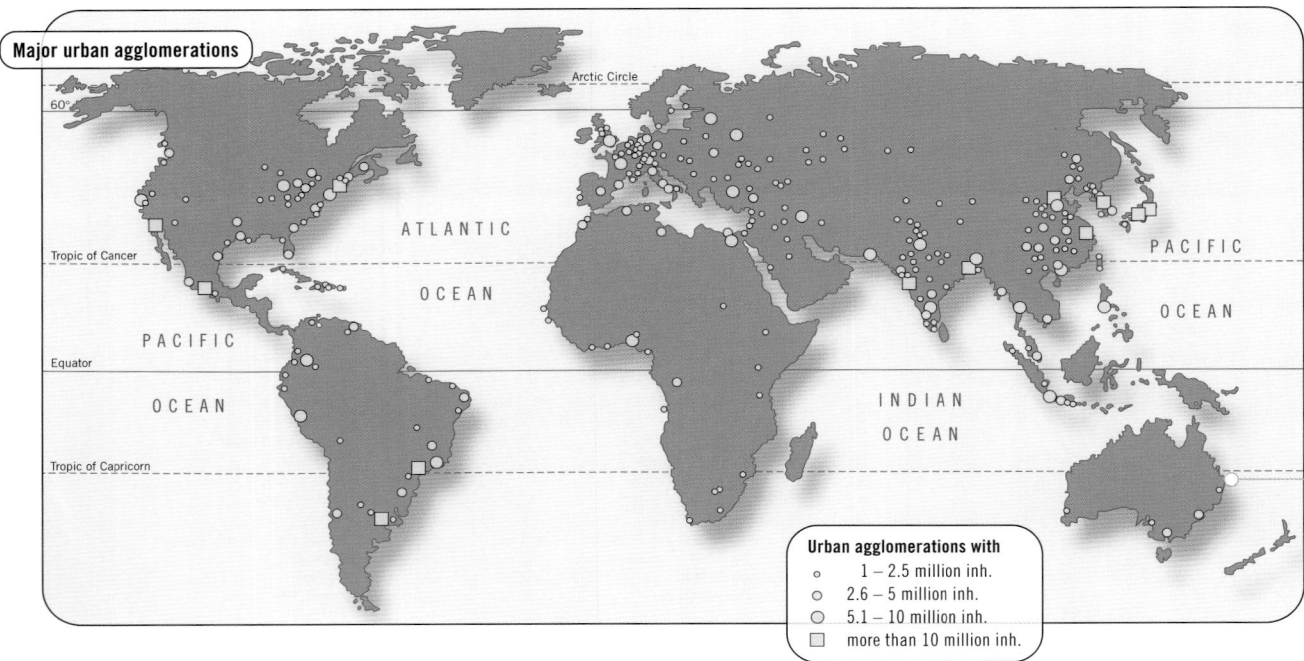

Major urban agglomerations

Arctic Circle
60°
ATLANTIC OCEAN
Tropic of Cancer
PACIFIC OCEAN
OCEAN
PACIFIC OCEAN
Equator
OCEAN
INDIAN OCEAN
Tropic of Capricorn
PACIFIC
OCEAN

Urban agglomerations with
- 1 – 2.5 million inh.
- 2.6 – 5 million inh.
- 5.1 – 10 million inh.
- more than 10 million inh.

The Dark Heart of the Continent

Satellite images of the Earth at night reveal points of light along continental coastlines – as shown in the map on the left – corresponding to major urban agglomerations. Approximately 50% of the earth's population is concentrated in regions less than 150 kilometers from the nearest coast.

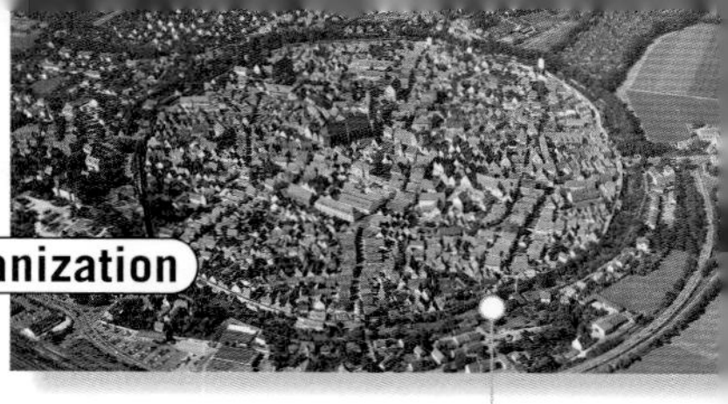

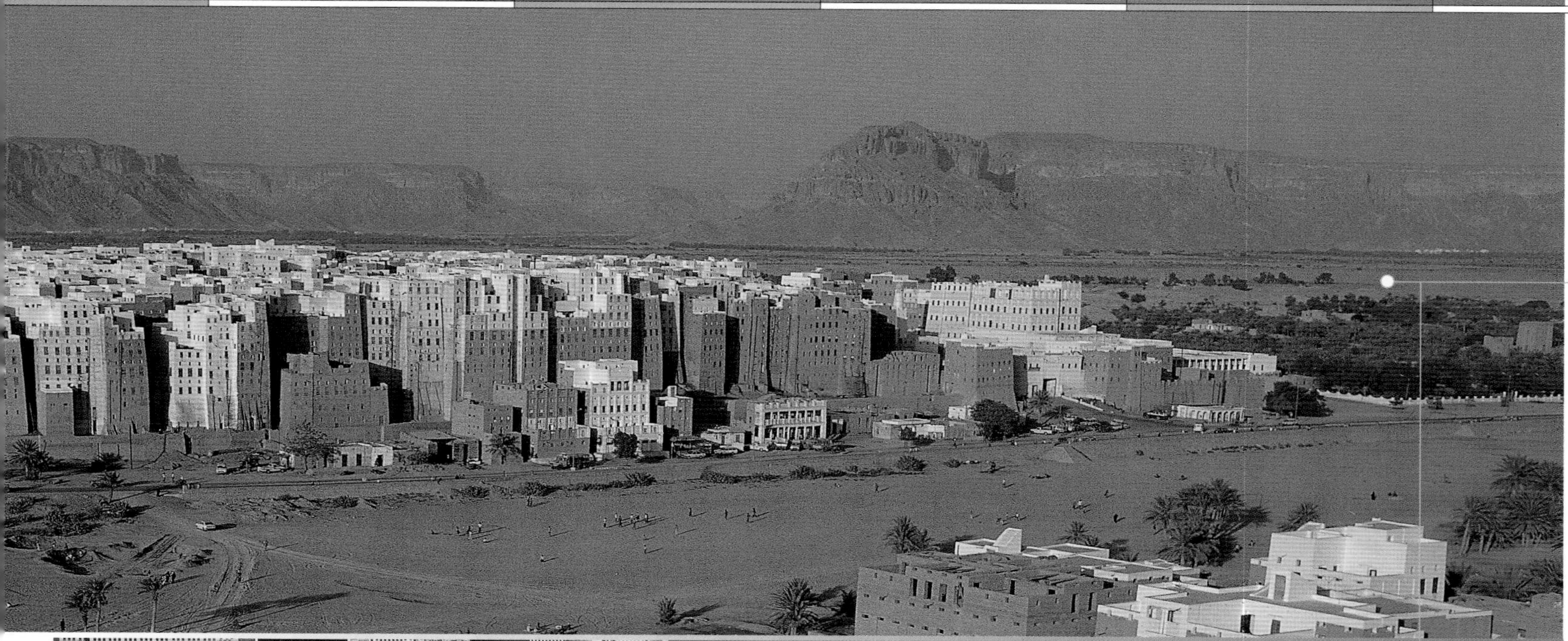

Walls, a Standard Feature of Early Urban Settlements

City walls remain a typical feature of urban architecture even in our day. The photo shows the city wall in Nördlingen, Germany – built in the 14th century and still almost entirely intact today.

Traditional Cities Resist Globalization

Many cities and urban forms have retained their distinct physiognomy in spite of the current trend. One example of a type of Portuguese colonial city that has remained virtually unchanged since the 18th century is Ouro Preto in Brazil. Shibam, the "Desert Manhattan" located in the Wadi Hadhramaut (Yemen) exemplifies a form of high-rise, loam-construction typical of oriental cities, a tradition with roots in pre-Islamic times.

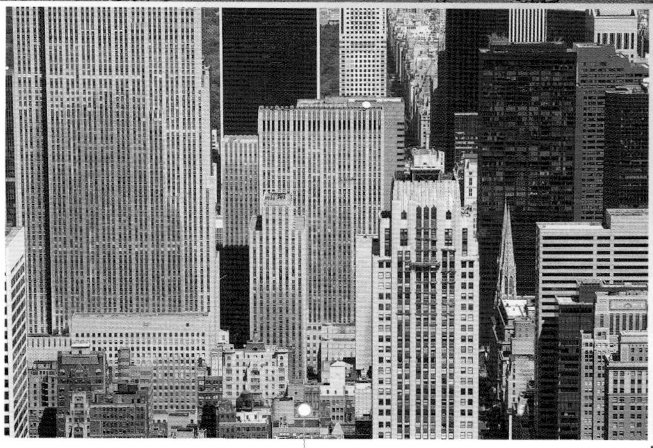

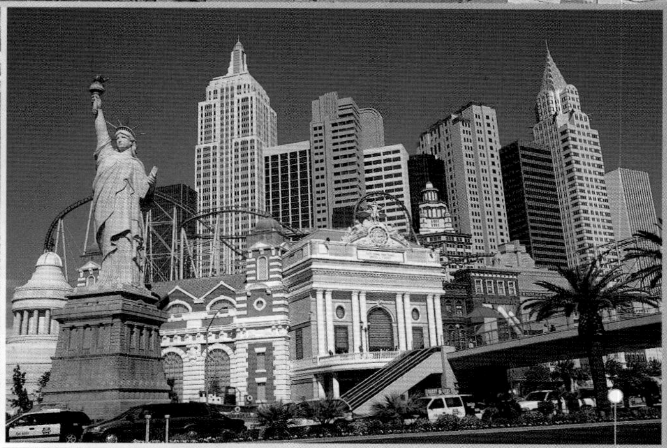

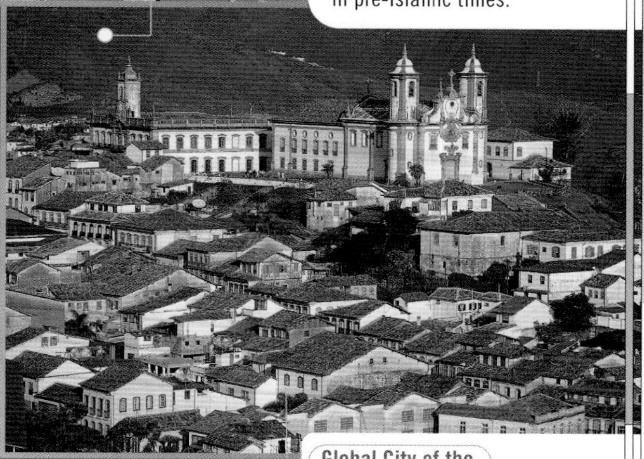

Life in the Vertical Dimension

The invention of reinforced concrete and the elevator, coupled with the high price of land, literally gave rise to upward growth in leaps and bounds in many cities in the early 20th century. Manhattan is a prime example. Skyscrapers, the modern temples of capitalism, now tower far above the church spires that once dominated the city profile.

the world (many of which are firmly rooted in historical tradition), despite the strong tendency toward uniformity in urban architecture. Only very few major metropolitan areas have achieved the status of "global cities," centers of international banking, global business management, international business and telecommunication, and world political power (those few include New York, London, Paris, Tokyo and the relative newcomers Río de Janeiro, Mexico City, Hong Kong, and Shanghai). These are the cities whose centers represent advanced forms of modern urban development almost everywhere in the world, although they often bear the indelible imprint of a randomly interchangeable physiognomy. Knowledgeable urban sociologists have identified in precisely these global control centers strong tendencies toward inner-urban polarization and signs of social and ethnic segregation. In the "global cities," the dominant entrepreneurial culture shaped by a profit-oriented, transnational urban aristocracy stands in stark contrast to the masses of urban fringe groups that depend upon low-paid, labor intensive jobs – a contrast much like that of the glittering facades of dream metropolises and their slum districts, whose ceaseless growth has devoured some eight million acres of valuable farmland worldwide (enough to produce food for ten million people) between 1980 and 2000.

Global City of the Fun Society

Cities serve their surrounding regions in many ways. Situated in the Nevada desert, Las Vegas – the wide world in a pocket-sized format – is perhaps the most bizarre manifestation of the "fun city" concept.

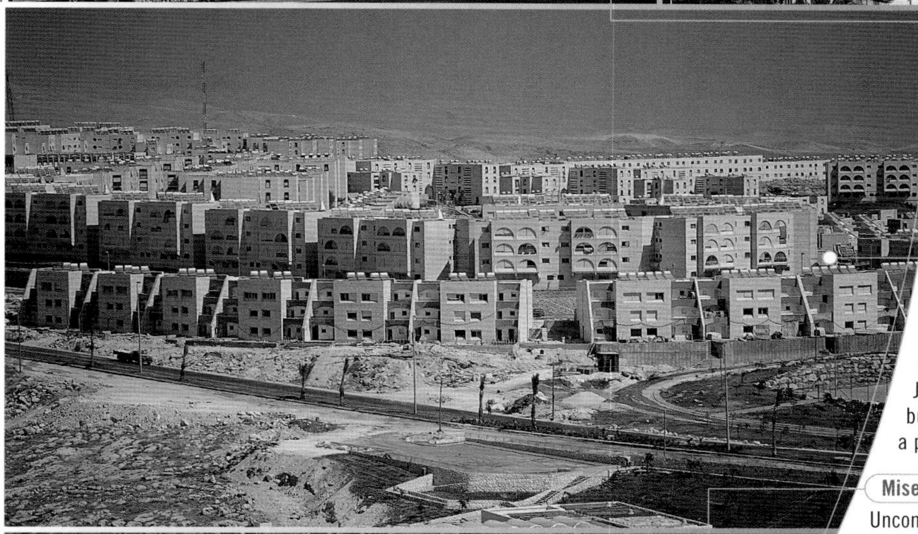

Ersatz Walls

The politically controversial Israeli settlement of Maale Adumim stands like a fortress in the desert of Judaea in the West Bank east of Jerusalem. The compact ring of buildings serves as a substitute for a protective city wall.

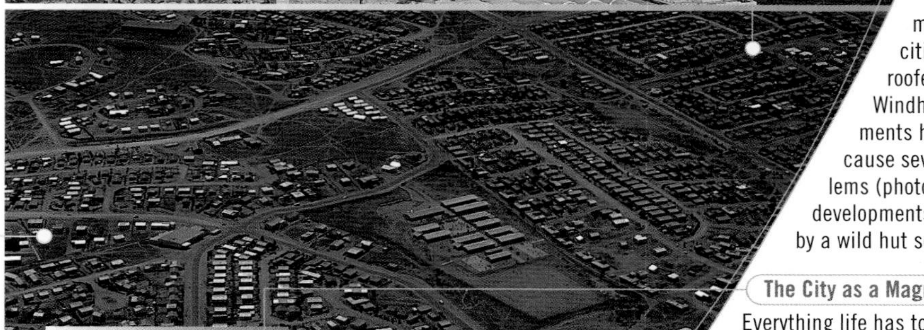

Misery on the Urban Fringe

Uncontrolled immigration creates more than a planning crisis for many cities. Visible here is the sea of tin-roofed huts in the squatter town of Windhoek (Namibia). Such settlements hinder controlled growth and cause severe environmental problems (photo: legalized, sanitized developments bordered on the right by a wild hut settlement).

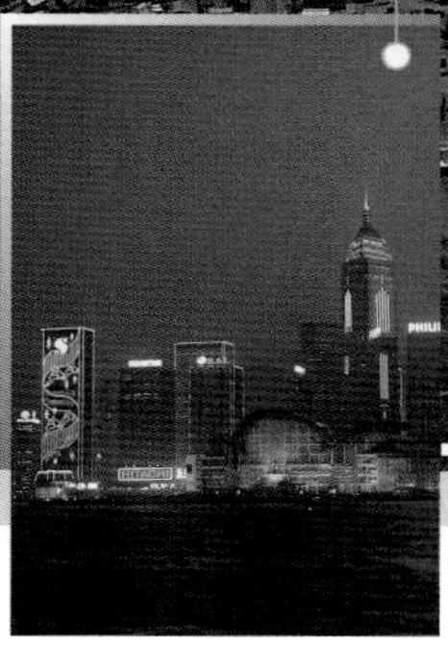

The City as a Magnet

Everything life has to offer can be found in the big city – and affects the surrounding countryside like a population magnet with a pull so strong that it can hardly be controlled with administrative means. An impassable fence along the border is the only defense against the lure of Hong Kong's nocturnal aura.

Water as a Resource and a Source of Problems and Conflicts

"Blue Gold" – Our Most Precious Resource

During the International Hydrological Decade (IHD, 1964-1974), a global effort to assess the world's water reserves was launched under the auspices of UNESCO. Based on the results, experts now agree: There is plenty of water in the world – yet not nearly enough to satisfy the needs of the entire human race in the 21st century. According to projections presented at the World Water Conference in The Hague in March 2000, some 3.3 billion people (37% of the world's population) will be directly confronted with a shortage of water by 2025 (the number has already reached two billion), because only about 0.29% of the total water supply on earth is available as fresh water suitable for human use (for drinking, hygiene, and the production of consumer goods), while the population continues to grow at a rapid pace. In the course of the 20th century, the human population grew from 1.6 billion to 6 billion people, who now share a maximum total of 4.2 million cubic kilometers of liquid fresh water – a supply that cannot be increased significantly. Thus every new addition to the world's population reduces the amount of water available to each person on earth.

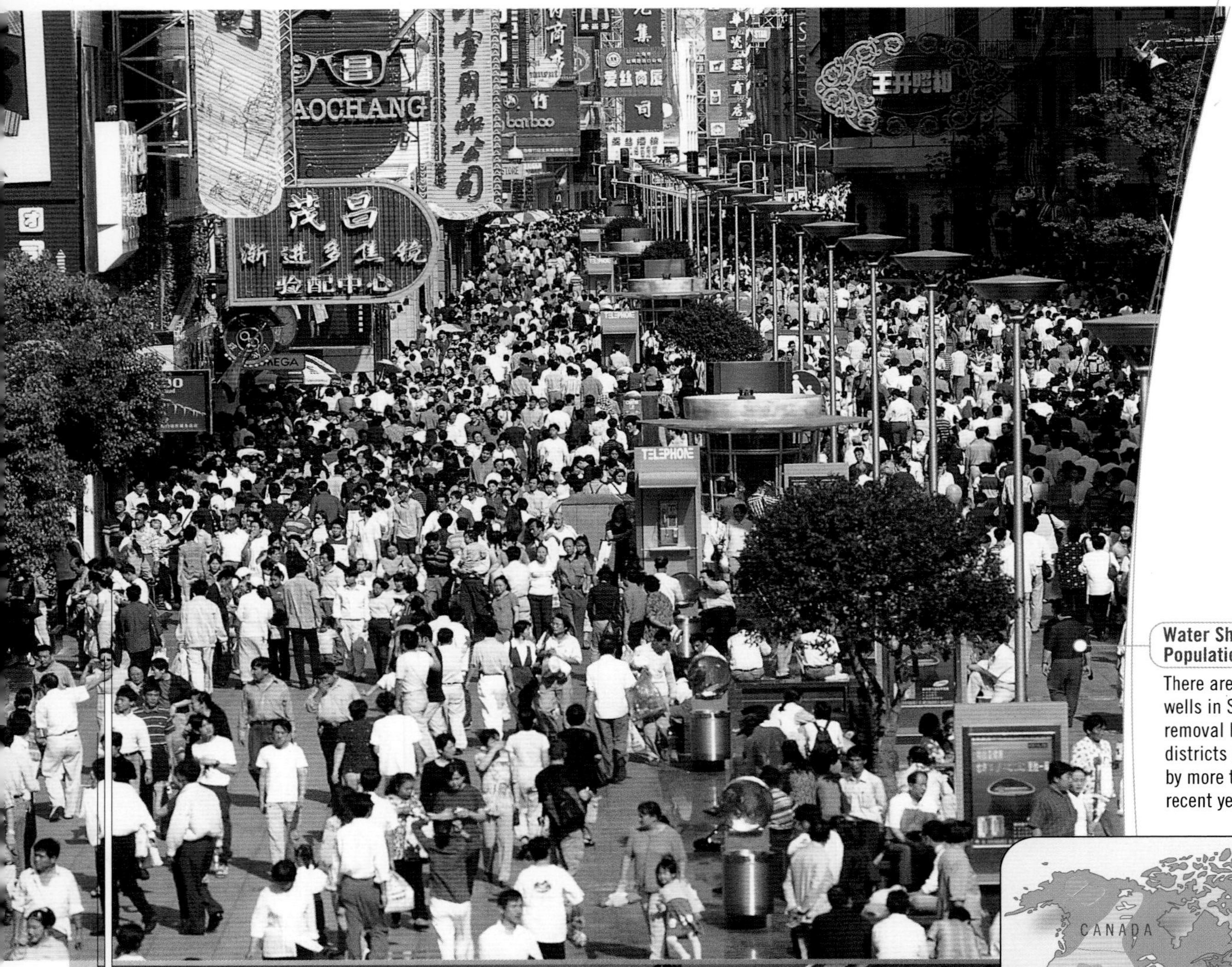

How Much Water Does a Human Being Need?

Inhabitants of temperate climate zones – North Americans, for example – need between two and three liters of water per day to satisfy their basic physical and physiological needs. People who live in hot climes require six or more liters per day. For a worker in the oil fields of Saudi Arabia, a daily ration of twelve liters of liquids is just about sufficient. If he quenches his thirst with beer, the figure of twelve liters must be multiplied by 60 (bringing the total to 720 liters), since up to 60 liters of fresh water are required to produced a single liter of beer. A scholar who stills his thirst for knowledge with three books weighing one kilogram each and places them on his bookshelf must – like the beer-drinking oil field worker – accept responsibility for the consumption of at least 750 liters of water, as it takes roughly 250 liters to produce one kilogram of paper. In light of the worldwide water shortage, the fact that between 20,000 and 30,000 liters of water are required for the production of an average passenger car should give pause for thought, especially when one considers that there are currently 750 million cars on the world's roads and that a country like China (with one-fifth of the world's population) is

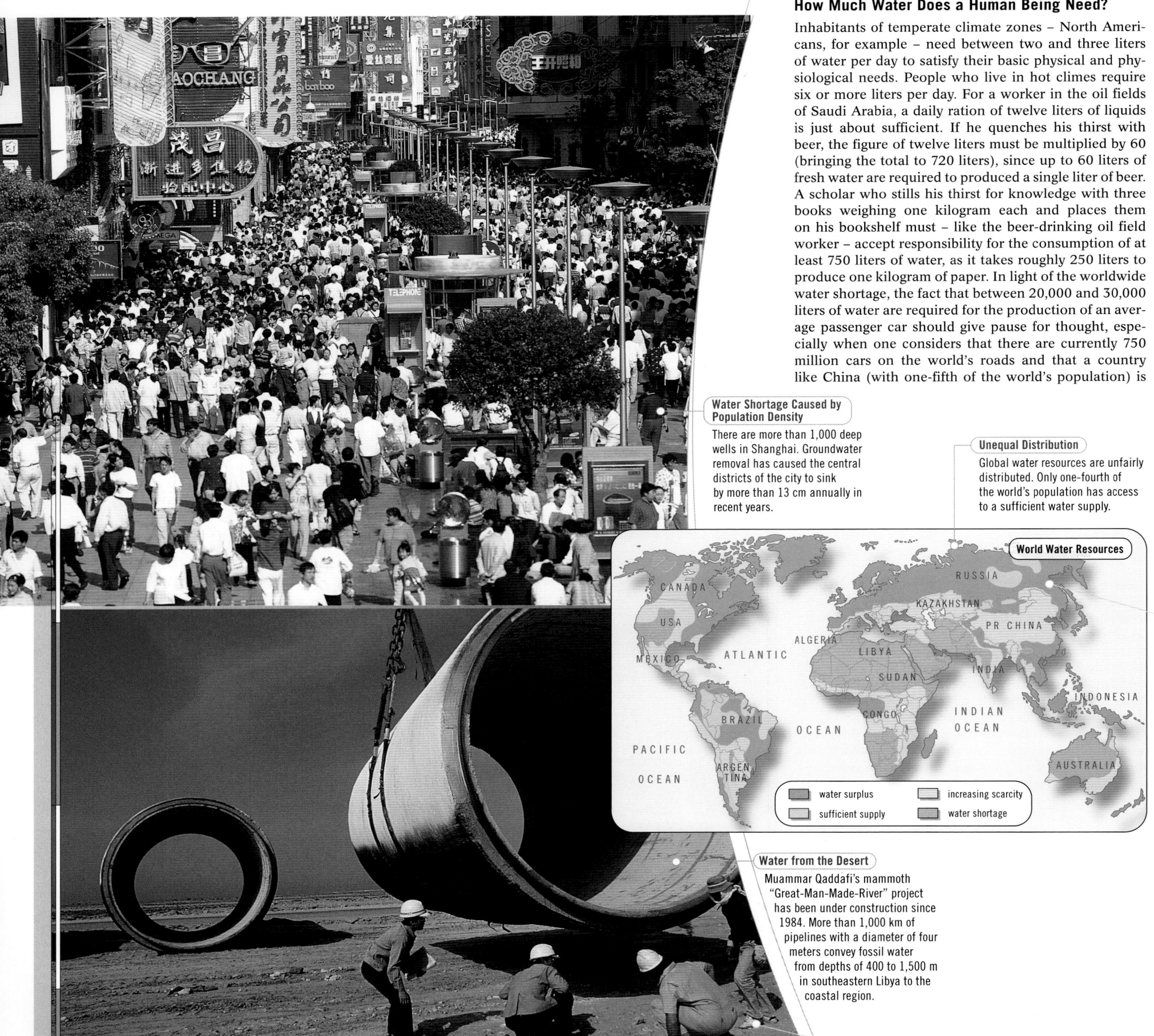

Water Shortage Caused by Population Density
There are more than 1,000 deep wells in Shanghai. Groundwater removal has caused the central districts of the city to sink by more than 13 cm annually in recent years.

Unequal Distribution
Global water resources are unfairly distributed. Only one-fourth of the world's population has access to a sufficient water supply.

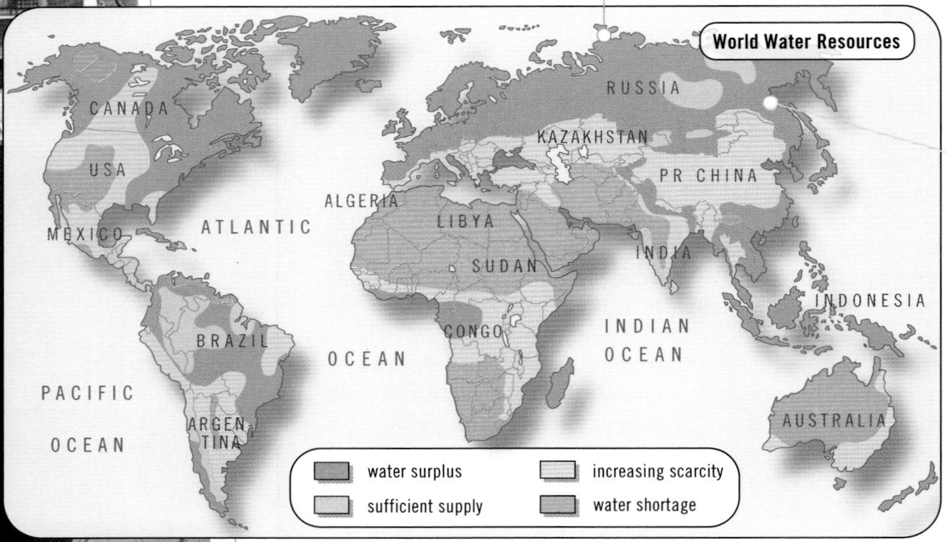

World Water Resources

CANADA
USA
MEXICO
ATLANTIC
ALGERIA
LIBYA
SUDAN
BRAZIL
OCEAN
ARGENTINA
PACIFIC
OCEAN
RUSSIA
KAZAKHSTAN
PR CHINA
INDIA
CONGO
INDIAN OCEAN
INDONESIA
AUSTRALIA

- water surplus
- sufficient supply
- increasing scarcity
- water shortage

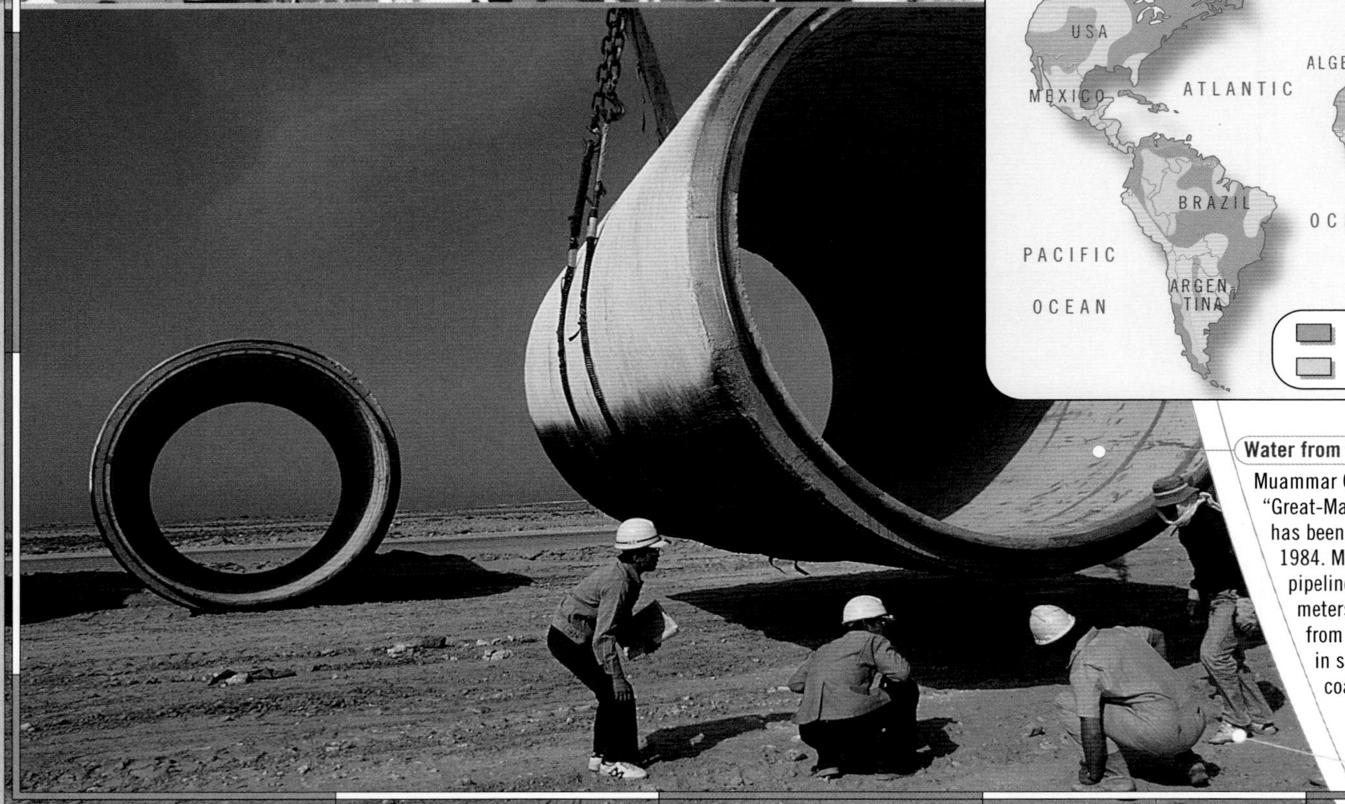

Water from the Desert
Muammar Qaddafi's mammoth "Great-Man-Made-River" project has been under construction since 1984. More than 1,000 km of pipelines with a diameter of four meters convey fossil water from depths of 400 to 1,500 m in southeastern Libya to the coastal region.

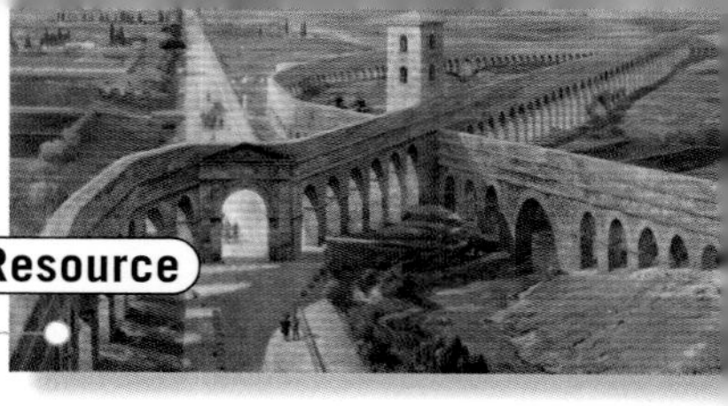

motorizing in leaps and bounds. Even more alarming is the tremendous amount of fresh water needed to ensure an adequate supply of food for the growing global population. Depending upon climate conditions, the production of one kilogram of grain requires between 1,000 and 2,000 liters of fresh water (or 1,000 to 2,000 tons of water per ton of grain). Thus our daily bread or bowl of rice – like our daily minimum ration of fresh water – is a very important factor in the calculation of per capita consumption of water, although it is seldom given sufficient consideration. The published figures for "average daily water consumption per person per day" (128 liters in Germany and about twice that amount in the U.S.) reflect only measurable household consumption and thus give a false picture of actual water use, which – particularly when viewed from a global perspective – goes far beyond daily household needs.

Who Needs and Uses How Much Water?

According to the most recent precise calculation of the global demand for fresh water (in 1990), private households, which (combined with small businesses and public consumption) account for 7.6 % of total consumption, are the smallest but most significant user group, followed in increasing size by industry (24.6 %). At 67.8 %, agriculture, in its role as the producer of food for the world, is far and away the largest consumer. In contrast to industry, which ordinarily uses water only briefly as utility or process water (which it usually returns to the water cycle as polluted waste water, however), agriculture consumes water in the production of biomass. Despite worldwide efforts to encourage economical use of water resources, the unbridled growth of the world's population is likely to make the water shortage the number-one global problem in the 21st century.

The Statistics of Scarcity

According to guidelines issued by the World Health Organization (WHO), a human being in the 21st century requires a minimum annual per capita ration of 1,000 cubic meters of fresh water (or 2,470 liters per day for food and energy production, industrial products, hygiene, education, traffic, and other purposes) to maintain a living standard appropriate in our time without endangerment to health (current per capita consumption is about 3,000 cubic meters per year in the U.S. and 1,500 cubic meters in other industrialized countries).

The water shortage is not necessarily restricted to specific climate zones. Much more important as a measure of scarcity is the quantity of renewable water resources (precipitation as well as inflowing river and groundwater) available in a given country relative to its population per year. Accordingly, countries with a fresh water supply of less than 1,000 cubic meters per person are classified as water emergency areas. Serious problems arise from water shortage where the natural supply of water falls below 1,700 – 2,000 cubic meters per person (the water stress level). Regions with renewable supplies of between 2,000 and 2,500 cubic meters and above per capita are regarded as non-critical. Africa has the largest number of water-poor countries, in which about 300 million people (one-third of the population) live under conditions of water emergency.

Reasons for Scarcity

Statistically speaking, the fresh water reserves on our "blue planet" are sufficient to serve the needs of humanity as a whole. Yet a number of factors contradict this naive statistical assessment. First of all, fresh water reserves are not equally distributed throughout the world. Nor does the presence of water in a given region necessarily mean that the other living conditions are favorable to human life. Secondly, fresh water that comes from the sky as precipitation rarely stays where it falls.

Water for Rome
Cities in the Roman Empire were supplied with water by a system of aqueducts. This painting by Zeno Diemer gives an impression of the ancient Roman water supply network.

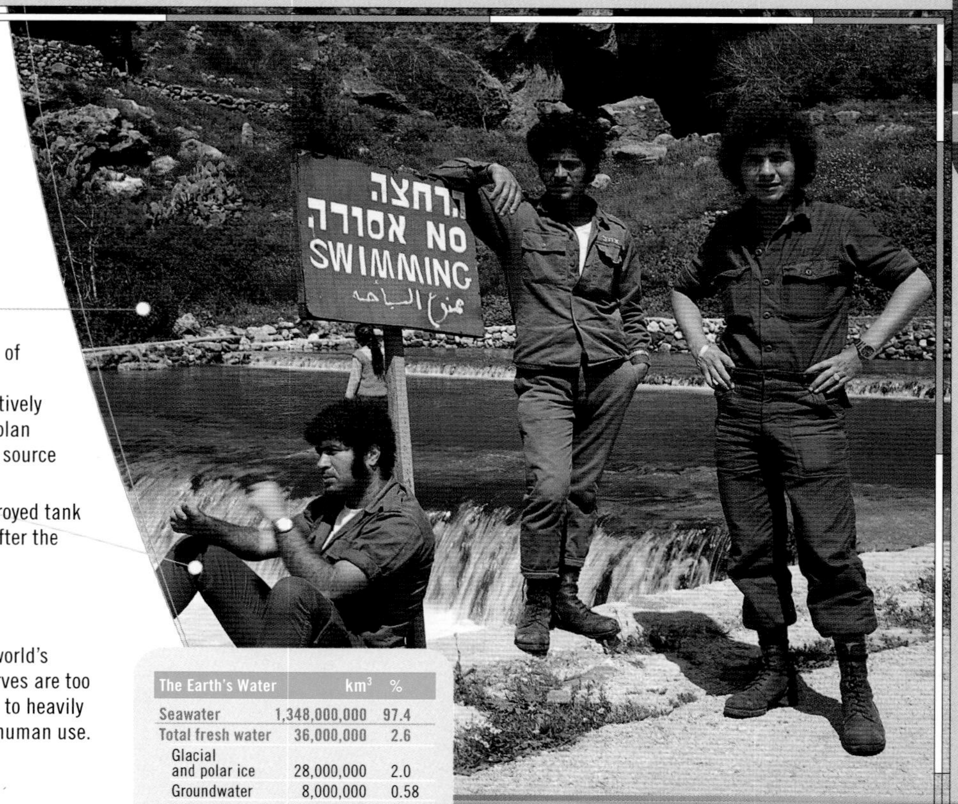

"Water War" on the Golan Heights
Israeli soldiers at the source of the Banias, a tributary of the Jordan. Blessed by relatively heavy precipitation, the Golan Heights are an important source of water for Israel.
Photo, lower right: Destroyed tank on the Golan Heights after the Six-Day War

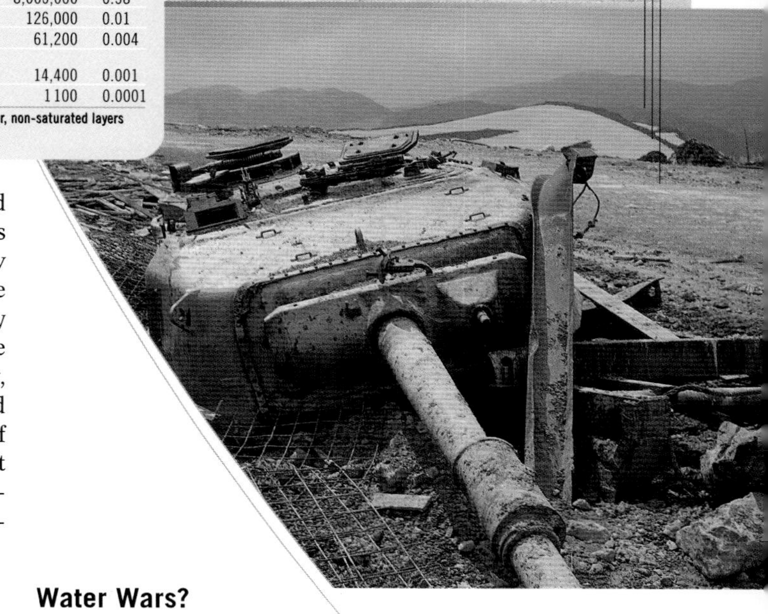

Nearly half of the world's groundwater reserves are too deep to exploit or to heavily mineralized for human use.

The Earth's Water	km³	%
Seawater	1,348,000,000	97.4
Total fresh water	36,000,000	2.6
Glacial and polar ice	28,000,000	2.0
Groundwater	8,000,000	0.58
Lakes	126,000	0.01
Soil moisture*	61,200	0.004
Atmospheric water vapor	14,400	0.001
Rivers	1 100	0.0001

* contained in the upper, non-saturated layers of soil

The nature of water – its mobility – causes it to run off, evaporate, or seep to unreachable depths in the very places it is so urgently needed by human beings and human economies. Thirdly, the global population is concentrated to an increasing degree in relatively few inhabitable regions of the Earth (about 90 % of the human race occupies four per cent of the world's dry land) and exceeds the hydrological capacity of these regions by virtue of sheer numbers alone. Finally, humans as economic beings – unlike animals and plants – tend to burden fresh water with many kinds of foreign substances (primarily chemicals) that make it unsuitable for reuse as drinking water and thus exacerbate the water shortage, particularly in densely populated urban agglomerations.

Relief Measures

Advanced cultures with large populations were forced to deal with the problem of water scarcity even in ancient times. Thus hydraulic engineering measures for the procurement and storage of scarce, life-giving water are among the oldest technical structures known to mankind. Remnants of irrigation systems from the 3rd millennium BC have been found in India, China, Yemen, and Egypt. As long ago as 1700 BC, the Babylonian King Hammurabi enacted important laws governing the use of the precious resource of water in the Code of Hammurabi.

Outstanding examples of early urban water supply systems involving technically sophisticated aqueducts are the ancient cities of Pergamum (western Anatolia) and Rome. In the 1st century AD, the Romans moved 600,000 cubic meters of water into their city daily, supplying every inhabitant with 600 liters per day. Modern water procurement systems make use of other means in addition to long-distance water conveyance via pipelines and canals (e.g. the California Aqueduct and the "Great-Man-Made-River" in Libya). Today, some 800,000 small and large dams all over the world prevent rapid water run-off, making more water available for drinking or use in farming or industrial operations than is contained in all of the rivers of the world.

Water Wars?

Experts anticipate population growth of between 30 % and 70 % in the water-poor regions of the world by the year 2025. It is highly likely that this will lead to increased competition for water, not only among cities and between agriculture and industry but between nations as well.

Forty per cent of the world's population live in regions fed by rivers that flow through more than two countries, and over 200 areas burdened by political conflict largely attributable to disputes over the use of water from such rivers clearly underscore the magnitude of the water shortage as a potential source of political conflict.

The most volatile regions of conflict over water with serious potential for armed hostilities are located along the Ganges (usage disputes between India and Bangladesh), the Tigris and Euphrates (Turkey, Syria, Iraq), the Jordan (Israel, Syria, the West Bank, Jordan), and the Nile (Egypt, Sudan, Ethiopia, Eritrea). "Real" water wars have occurred only rarely in history, but water scarcity has often been the spark that set off the powder keg of existing religious, ethnic, or territorial conflicts.

Fossil Fuels – Production and World Trade

Competition for the Earth's Energy Reserves

The recent rapid rise in prices for fuels and heating oil have reminded us how vulnerable our social and economic systems are and how dependent we are on the oil-producing countries. Our high-tech world consumes vast amounts of energy, and most industrialized countries do not have sufficient resources to cover their own needs. Cartels formed by the oil-producing countries ensure a certain degree of market stability, but they also underscore the dependence of importing countries on the suppliers of raw materials. Transnational and multinational firms operating in the raw materials markets have the power to circumvent cartel agreements more or less at will. Aside from the political and economic problems associated with fossil fuels, environmental issues are now becoming increasingly important.

The Global Oil Economy, 1999

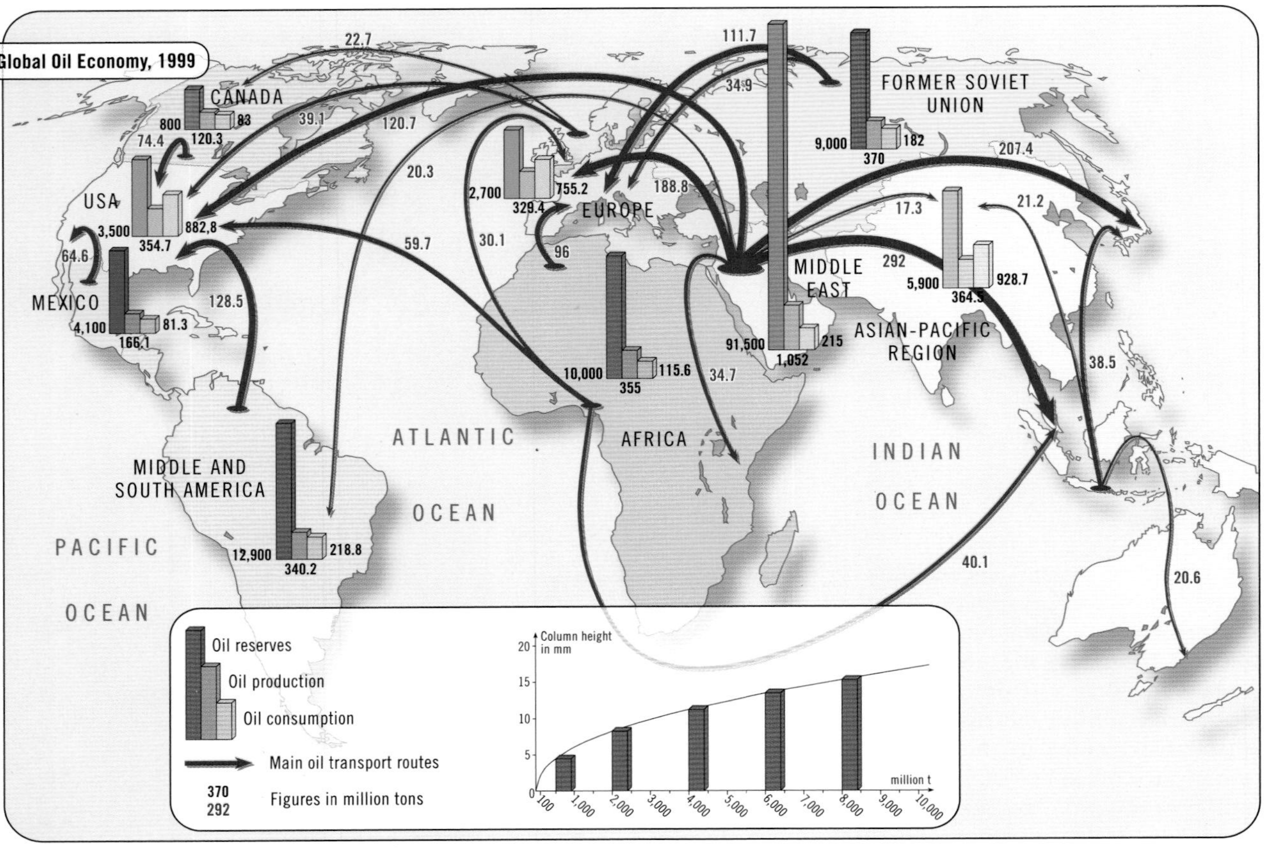

Oil reserves		
Oil production		
Oil consumption		
→ Main oil transport routes		
370 / 292	Figures in million tons	

Column height in mm — million t

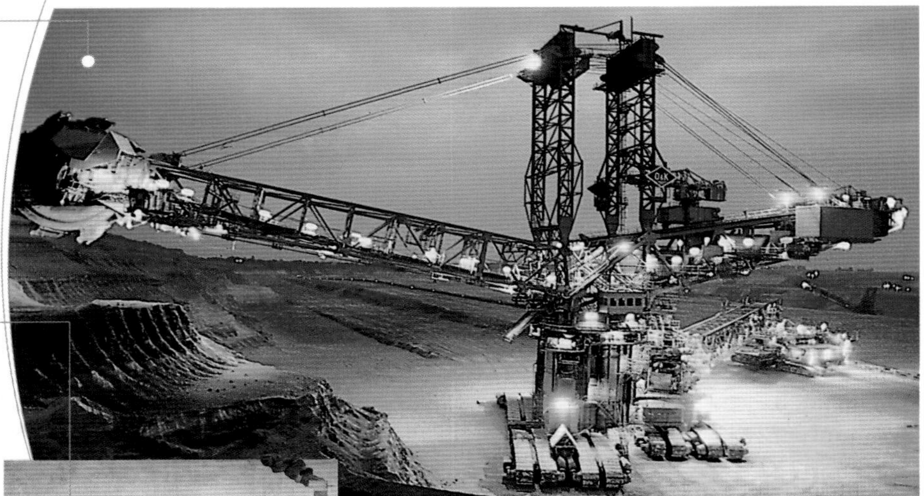

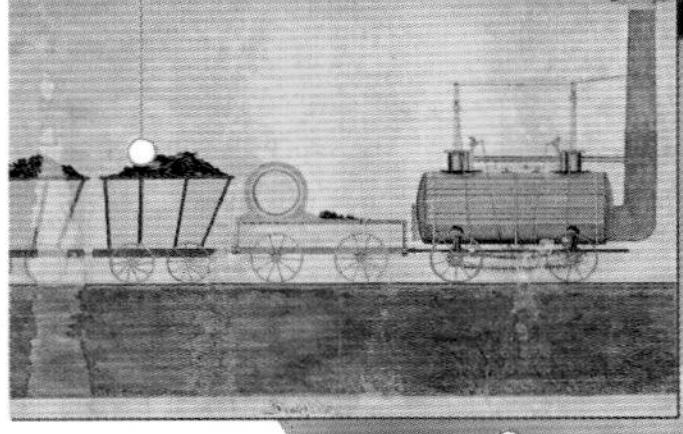

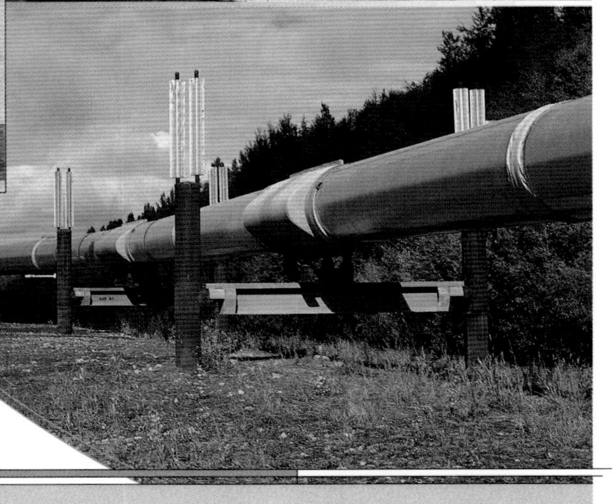

The Growing Hunger for Energy

Hunting and gathering societies met all of their energy needs with wood, a renewable source of energy. This did not change significantly during the transition to farming and animal husbandry, although wood did become scarce in heavily deforested areas. It was not until humans began processing ores to make metal implements using wood or charcoal as fuels that dependence upon renewable energy sources began to pose serious problems. Forests, which had once seemed endless, were destroyed at a pace that far outstripped their capacity to recover. Water and wind mills facilitated the processing of agricultural products and were later employed by the textile industry. The advent of industrialization and mechanized vehicles (steam locomotives) brought the need for higher-energy fossil fuels (coal). In terms of energy output, one ton of coal equated to the annual yield of two acres of forest. Electrification intensified the demand for fossil fuels and also made energy easily transportable. But this applied only to "developed countries." Around 1900, wood, wind, water, and human and animal muscle power still covered two-thirds of the world's energy needs. Only a few decades ago, wood was the only available source of heating and cooking energy for one-third of the world's population. Today, energy consumption and management prognoses must take into account the anticipated rapid rise in energy demand in the Third World.

The Underground Forest

Bituminous coal was used occasionally in ancient civilizations and to an increasing extent during the Middle Ages. Large-scale exploitation, including underground mining, did not begin until the 19th century, when coal became an indispensable source of energy. Worldwide coal production rose rapidly from twelve million tons (1820) to 1.2 billion t (1910), when 85 % of all coal produced in the world was mined in Germany, Great Britain, and the U.S.A. Although global production has stagnated in recent years (1998: 3.7 billion t) or grown only marginally, the focal points of mining activity shifted due to cost pressures. Difficult and thus expensive mining operations in the European Union (Great Britain, Germany, France) were cut back drastically in favor of cheaper coal from such countries as the U.S. The German bituminous coal-mining industry, for example, is highly subsidized, as coal costs more than $140 per ton there, while the price of imported coal is below $36. China, Australia, Colombia, South Africa, and other countries increased production, not only to cover domestic demand but for export as well. According to estimates, exploitable coal reserves amount to at least 550 billion tons of bituminous coal units, concentrated mostly in Russia, the U.S., China, Australia, and India. Due to its high water content and low energy output, brown coal is used primarily in the production of electricity and is not transported over long distances.

Petroleum, "Black Gold"

More than 140 years after the discovery of oil in Pennsylvania (1859), global economic and political developments are now more dependent than ever before on the availability of oil. This is primarily the consequence of motorization, and the rise in the use of motor vehicles to transport people and material, although petroleum is also used for heating, in power plants, and as an industrial raw material. After a modest beginning (1900: 20 million t), oil production increased dramatically following the Second World War (1950: 523 million; 1999: 4.1 billion t). Every day, nearly 10 million tons of oil are pumped from several thousand oil wells around the world. The amount of natural gas produced at the same time matches the energy value of six million tons of petroleum.

Devouring the Landscape

Brown coal deposits are usually not deep in the earth and are therefore mined almost exclusively in open pits. In the Rhenish brown-coal fields (photo), huge bucket-wheel excavators remove covering layers of sediment and mine the underlying coal. These machines can move more than 200,000 cubic meters of material a day.

Driving Force

The invention of the coal-burning steam engine launched the Industrial Revolution. The development of railroads (photo: steam locomotive built by George Stephenson, c. 1815) made it possible to transport coal, agricultural and industrial goods as well as people quickly, over long distances, and on a large scale. The loud, smoke-spewing engines gave rise to early complaints about environmental pollution.

Protection against Heat and Cold

The designers of the Alaska Pipeline (1,310 km long, 1974-77) had to find ways to protect the delicate permafrost ecosystem, in which soil thaws only near the surface in the summer and would shift if exposed to additional heat. The pipes were laid on supports above ground and equipped with automatic cooling units. But the oil entering the well-insulated pipeline at about 176° F must not cool excessively, as it would stop flowing. After four-and-a-half weeks, it arrives at the port of Valdez at about 86° F.

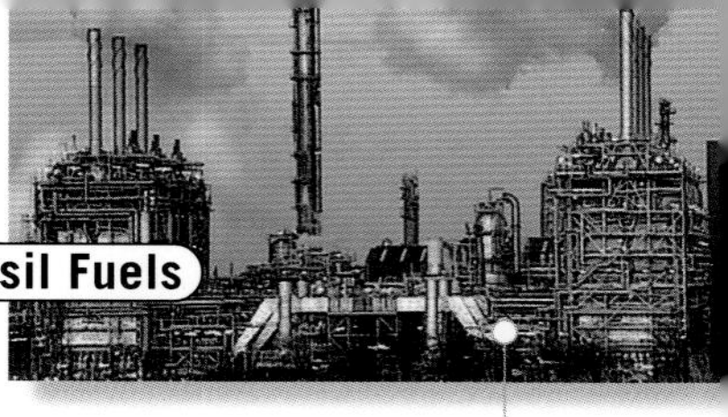

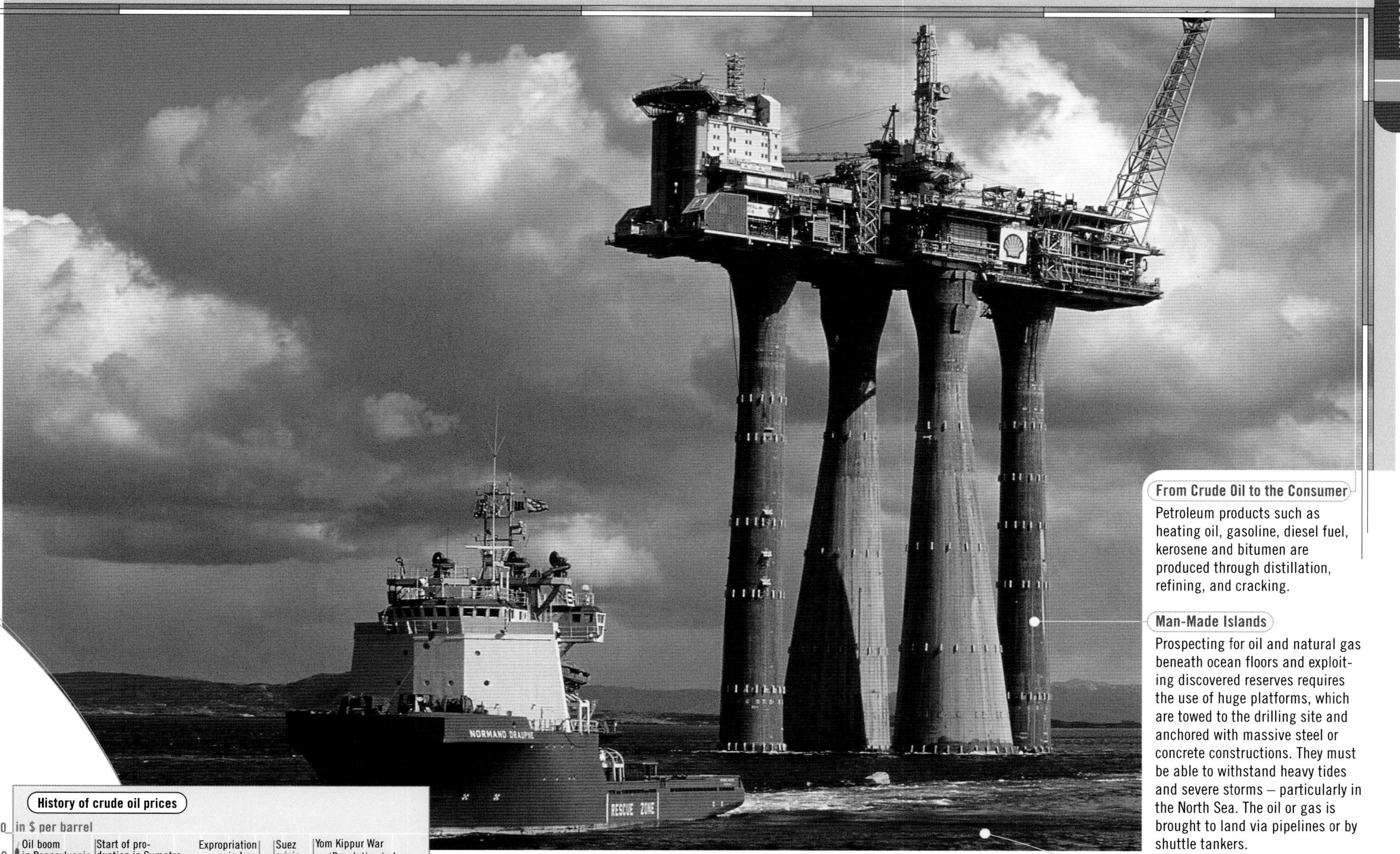

From Crude Oil to the Consumer

Petroleum products such as heating oil, gasoline, diesel fuel, kerosene and bitumen are produced through distillation, refining, and cracking.

Man-Made Islands

Prospecting for oil and natural gas beneath ocean floors and exploiting discovered reserves requires the use of huge platforms, which are towed to the drilling site and anchored with massive steel or concrete constructions. They must be able to withstand heavy tides and severe storms – particularly in the North Sea. The oil or gas is brought to land via pipelines or by shuttle tankers.

History of crude oil prices

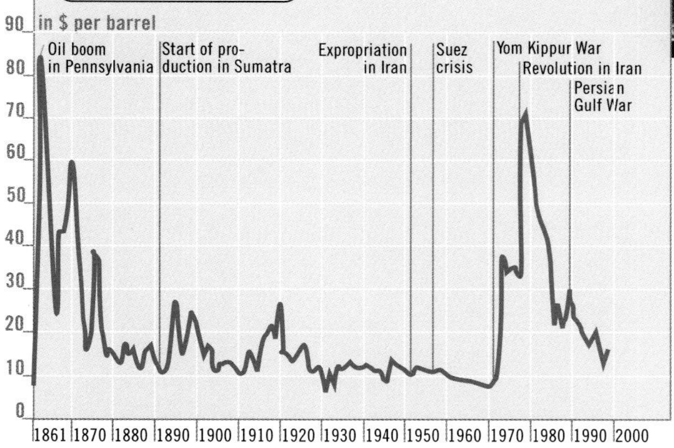

in $ per barrel

Oil boom in Pennsylvania | Start of production in Sumatra | Expropriation in Iran | Suez crisis | Yom Kippur War | Revolution in Iran | Persian Gulf War

The present tight oil supply situation and accompanying price explosion call to mind the oil crisis of 1973, when the oil price rose 600 % as the result of deliberately induced shortages in the aftermath of the Arab-Israeli War. The consequence was a worldwide economic crisis. Years before, in 1960, seven oil-exporting countries formed OPEC (Organization of Petroleum Exporting Countries, which now has eleven members), in the hope of gaining a higher share of oil revenues and exerting greater political influence as a cartel.

The end of the Oil Age predicted by the Club of Rome in 1973 did not come to pass. The sudden rise in prices made it possible to tap petroleum reserves that had previously appeared too expensive to exploit. Thanks to new fields in the North Sea and Alaska, supply rose faster than demand. The power of OPEC waned temporarily.

Natural Gas, an Increasingly Popular Fuel

The demand for natural gas has risen steadily over the past 30 to 40 years. Easily transported via pipelines, it is used to heat buildings and generate electricity. Produc-

tion is concentrated primarily in the CIS countries and the U.S. The United States, which also import natural gas from Canada and Mexico, consume more than one fourth of total world production. The largest reserves are in Russia (36 %), the other CIS countries, the Middle East, and Southeast Asia. More than 40 % are held by the OPEC states. Germany imports nearly 80 % of its natural gas (mainly from Russia, Norway, and the Netherlands).

Is an Energy Crisis Looming?

At present, 90 % of the world's energy needs are covered by fossil fuels. Industrialized countries account for nearly 60 % of total demand. Over the past 30 years, primary energy consumption has risen at a rate of 2 % per year, although the collapse of the Eastern Bloc significantly reduced the pace of growth. Increasing motorization in the developing countries could raise the rate of increase to double that figure within the next 20 years.

Half of the energy consumed by the EU countries is imported (Germany: 60 %). With only 4.5 % of the world's population, the U.S. uses 25 % of the annual production of primary energy. Europe (excluding the CIS countries) is not far behind at over 20 %.

At present consumption levels, the known reserves of petroleum (approx. 150 billion t) would last for more than 40 years, natural gas reserves (at least 150 trillion cubic meters) for over 60 years. Moreover, new technologies favor more efficient exploitation of deposits and the discovery of new ones. This could result in a doubling of known reserves. And there are also a number of as yet untapped reserves of tar sand, oil shale, and heavy crude oil. These are expensive to exploit, however, and would

raise the price of oil accordingly. Since two thirds of the easily exploitable reserves are located in the Persian Gulf region (chiefly in Saudi Arabia), the power of OPEC is likely to increase again. The OPEC countries currently hold over 75 % of known reserves and control 40 % of global production. Yet the Middle East, like the oil-rich Caspian Sea region, is politically unstable, which means that disruptions of production are likely.

Protecting the Earth's Atmosphere

Two major themes have dominated discussion with regard to global energy management in recent years: the principle of sustainability and the threat – or reality – of global warming as a consequence of a man-made greenhouse effect. The joint resolution of nearly all industrialized countries (enacted 1992 without the U.S.) calling for reduction of the burning of oil, natural gas, and coal to the 1990 level by the year 2005 has born little fruit thus far. Resistance to nuclear energy (which accounts for 7.4 % of primary energy worldwide) and the closing of nuclear power plants could actually result in higher CO_2 emissions due to the increased reliance of oil, gas, and coal. It is likely to take quite some time to achieve large-scale, effective use of renewable energy sources (currently 2.7 % of primary energy, primarily from hydroelectric power) – photovoltaic solar cells, solar heating plants, fuel cells, wind and biomass power plants, geothermal energy, heat pumps, ocean energy (wave and tide energy, ocean warmth). It will also be necessary to seek new ways of conserving energy. Regardless of the actual size of current reserves of fossil fuels, they are ultimately limited.

Division of the Globe into Time Zones

The Stock Exchange is Always Open – Somewhere on Earth!

When we want to call someone in Europe, we need to consider the time difference in order to be sure that we don't wake up our party in the middle of the night. Business people and international airlines must be constantly alert to these time differences. Stock-market speculators are happy to know that trading is possible around the clock, as there is always a stock exchange open somewhere in the world, whether in Sydney, New York, or Frankfurt am Main.

Local Time vs. Zone Time

Long ago, local times were different virtually wherever one looked. After all, it is only natural for the noon bell to ring when the sun reaches its highest point in the sky. The time difference between two towns at the same latitude separated by only 50 km is three minutes. Before the railways were built, such discrepancies were of little significance, since travel was always slow at best. Nevertheless, local mean times were introduced toward the end of the 18th century and regarded as binding for a given center and its surrounding region – Geneva time in 1780, Berlin time in 1820, Paris time in 1826, Zurich time in 1832, Pulkow and Greenwich time in 1848, Warsaw and Bern time in 1853. North Americans, in particular, lent strong support to the plan to establish a global system for measuring time. In 1873, 71 different railroad times were still in effect here. That year, Sandford Fleming, Chief Engineer of the Canadian Pacific Railway, proposed setting up a system of 24 meridians spaced at intervals of 15 degrees – a time difference of one hour – and assigning a standard time to each. That would divide the world into 24 time zones. But where was one to start? Which meridian was to get the zero label?

Ignoring the different times in effect in the many different countries of the world, seafarers had generally agreed to go by Greenwich time. But there were also zero meridians in Ferro (now Hierro), in Venice, and in many other places as well. At the Washington conference of 1884, 27 countries agreed to establish the zero meridian at Greenwich and to divide the globe into two geographic hemispheres, the western and the eastern.

Time systems were also standardized in many other European countries in response to the increasing internationalization of travel and transport. In Germany, which was still comprised of many independent states, most of them small, the railroad system could function properly only if agreement was reached on a standard time system. This was achieved with the Reichsgesetz of 1893. France did not join the system until 1911.

Most time zones are 15 degrees wide and cover a section of the globe that lies 7.5 degrees to the east and west of one of the 24 meridians. The standard time is the same everywhere within a given time zone. In some regions, time zone boundaries do not run along lines of longitude but along national borders. This is meant to ensure that the same time applies at every location within a country. Yet , many countries are too large to be accommodated within a single time zone. The U.S. is divided into four time zones, for example.

People living in Los Angeles should call their relatives on the East Coast early in the evening in order to avoid waking them during the night. TV networks must determine the best times to broadcast programs in order to reach the largest possible number of viewers. Under certain circumstances, networks accept the need to broadcast certain programs ("breaking news") at unfavorable times. Countries spanning several time zones require a system that makes it clear which time is meant when times are announced. In the U.S. times are identified by the time zone names: Eastern, Central, Rocky Mountain, and Pacific.

Which Island Will Be the First?

As the new year 2000 approached, several island countries in the Pacific set their sights on being the first to ring in the year 2000. The Fiji Islands introduced daylight saving time, turning their clocks ahead in order to be the first to celebrate. Tonga shifted the International Date Line along the eastern edge of its territory, putting itself 13 hours ahead of Greenwich. But the island kingdom had no chance against Kiribati, with its extensive ocean territory measuring 3,870 km from west to east. The eastward protrusion of the Date Line runs along the eastern border of Kiribati. Caroline Island, the easternmost atoll, was given the name Millennium Island (14 hours ahead of Greenwich).

… and the living is easy

Daylight savings time, the practice of turning the clock ahead one hour during the summer months in the northern hemisphere, has existed in Great Britain and Ireland since 1916. In the U.S., it was reintroduced in 1967 after having been used during both World Wars as a means of conserving energy by taking advantage of daylight. The desired energy-saving effect was actually never achieved, but people enjoy having an extra hour of leisure time while the sun shines and see daylight saving time as an improvement in quality of life.

One Day Too Early

People first recognized the need for an international date line when the "Victoria," a ship from Magellan's fleet, returned to Spain after circumnavigating the globe on September 6, 1522. The entries in the ship's log were a day behind the correct date. The expedition had constantly "gained time" on its westward voyage, saving an entire day by the time it had completely circled the globe.

The First Pocket Watch

Peter Henlein is believed to have invented the spring-driven watch. Beginning in 1510, he produced a series of small, portable clocks shaped like a can — the first pocket watches.

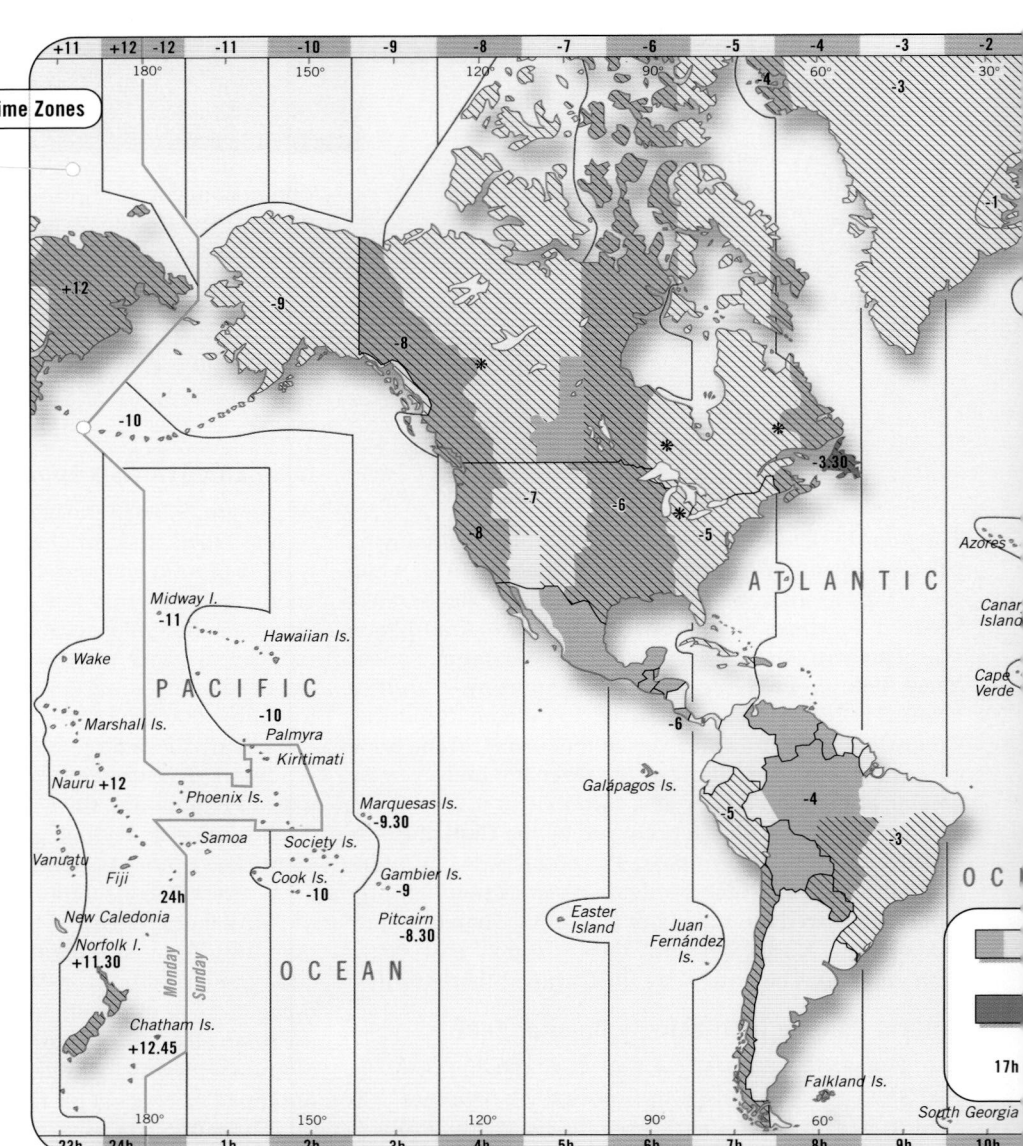

Time Zones

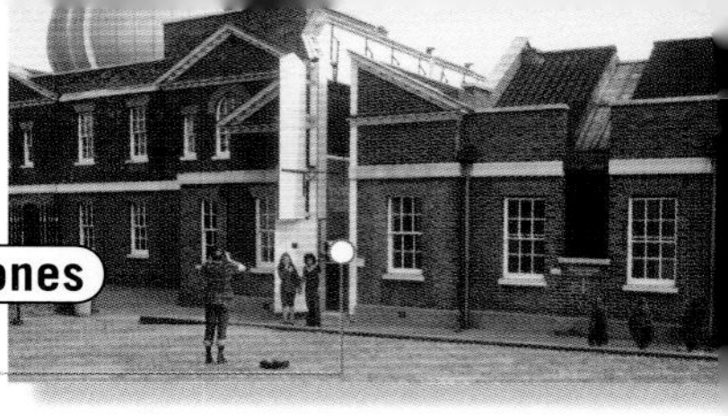

I and the Zero Meridian

The seam of our system of measuring time runs through the observatory in Greenwich (now Flamsteed House), which was established in 1675.

People who cross the International Date Line from east to west must move the calendar one day ahead. Those crossing in the reverse direction, from west to east, turn it back one day. A traveler who fails to heed this convention while circling the globe from west to east will find himself a day ahead of the local calendar upon arriving at his starting point. This happened to Phileas Fogg in Jules Verne's famous novel.

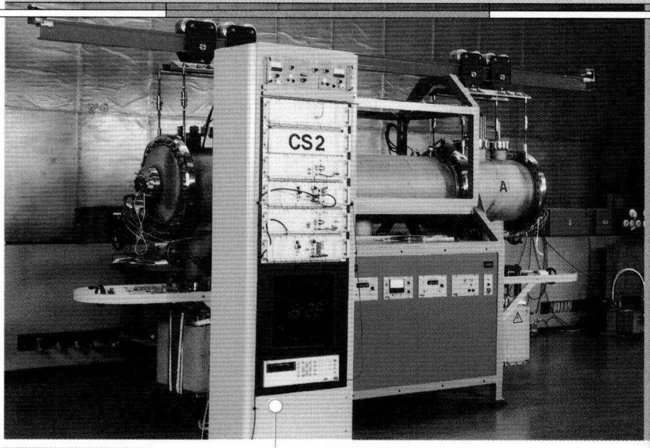

Utmost Precision

The CS 2 atomic clock at the Federal Office of Physics and Technology in Braunschweig, Germany is one of the most precise timepieces in the world. It is accurate to within a second even after two million years.

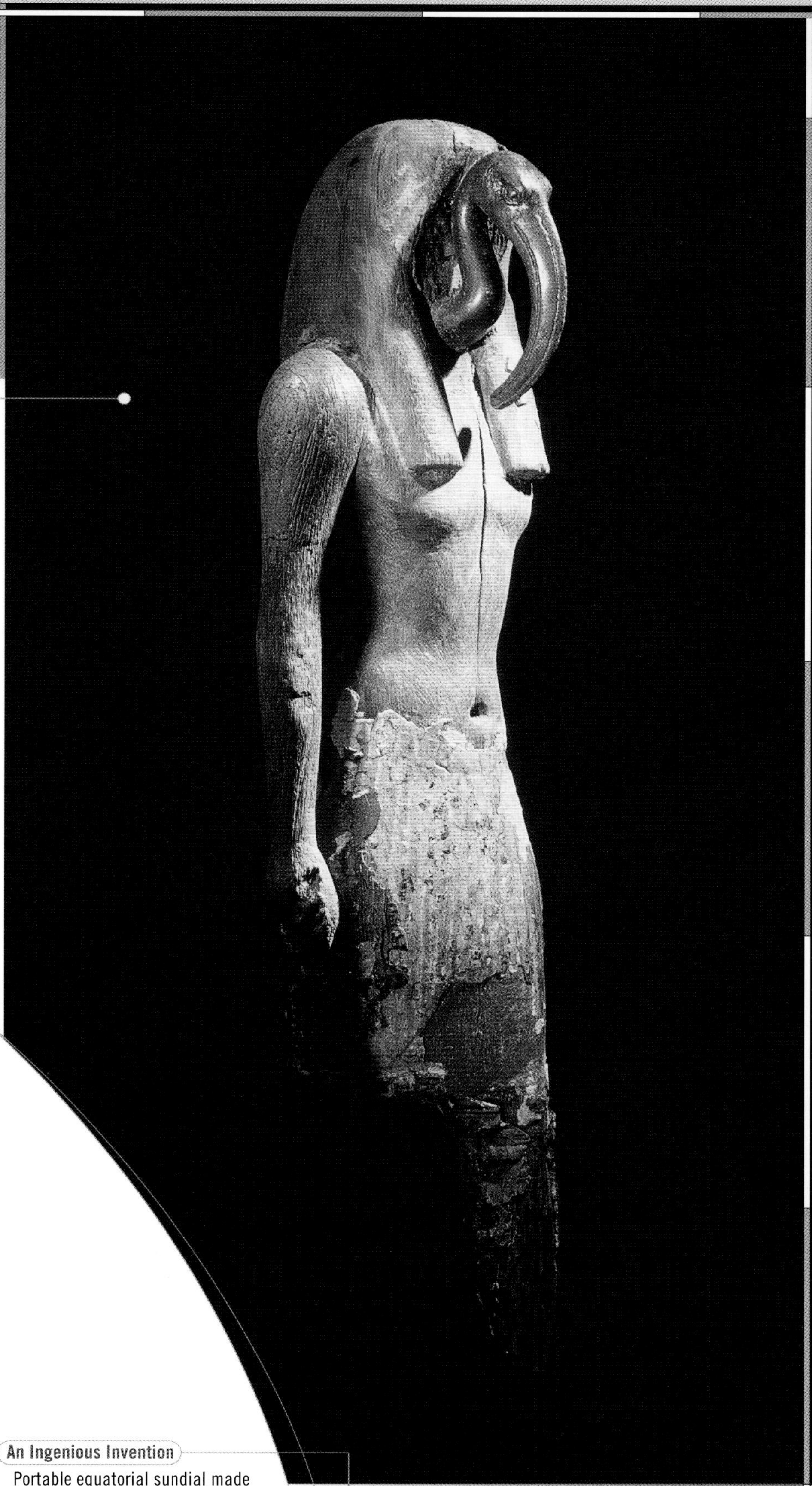

Guardian of Time

The ancient Egyptians amassed a wealth of astronomical knowledge. As early as 2750 BC, they had developed a lunar calendar and a solar calendar that divided the year into 365 days. The sciences and the calculation of time were the domain of the moon god Thot, who was often depicted as a human figure with the head of an ibis (c. 600 BC, Luxor).

International Date Line

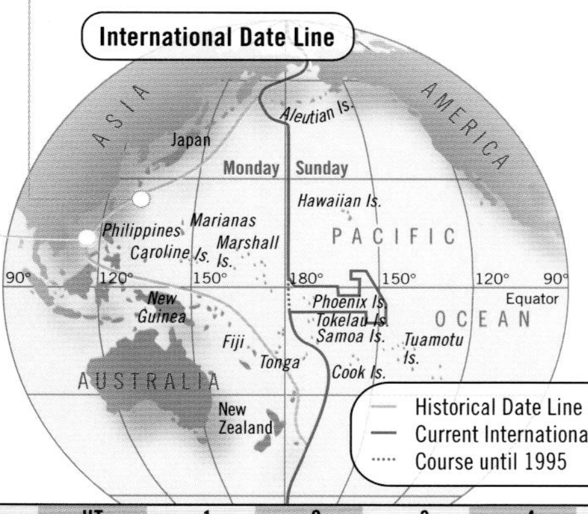

ASIA
AMERICA
Japan
Aleutian Is.
Monday | Sunday
Hawaiian Is.
Philippines
Marianas
Marshall Is.
Caroline Is.
PACIFIC
90° 120° 150° 180° 150° 120° 90°
New Guinea
Phoenix Is.
Tokelau Is.
Equator
Samoa Is.
Tuamotu Is.
OCEAN
Fiji
Tonga
Cook Is.
AUSTRALIA
New Zealand

— Historical Date Line until 1845
— Current International Date Line
⋯ Course until 1995

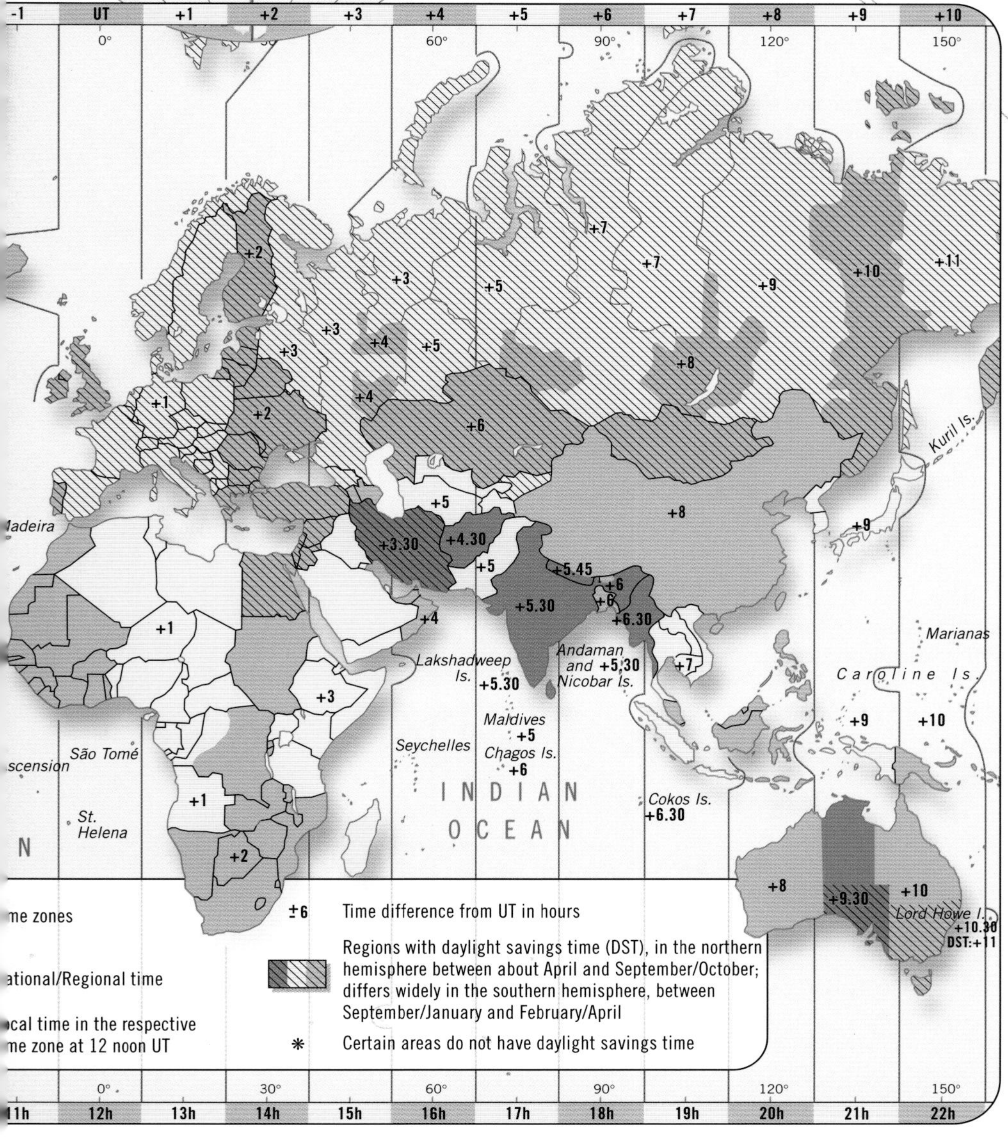

-1 | UT | +1 | +2 | +3 | +4 | +5 | +6 | +7 | +8 | +9 | +10
0° | | | | 60° | | | 90° | | | 120° | | | 150°

+2
+3
+7
+7
+10
+11
+1
+3
+3
+4
+5
+9
+10
Madeira
+4
+4
+8
+1
+6
+5
+8
+3.30 +4.30
+9
São Tomé
+5
+5.45
+6
+6.30
scension
+4
+5.30
Lakshadweep Is.
Andaman and Nicobar Is. +5.30
Marianas
St. Helena
+1
+5.30
Seychelles
Maldives +5
Chagos Is. +6
Caroline Is.
+9
+10
INDIAN OCEAN
Cokos Is. +6.30
+2
Kuril Is.
+8
+8 +9.30
+10
Lord Howe I. +10.30 DST:+11

me zones ±6 Time difference from UT in hours

ational/Regional time ▨ Regions with daylight savings time (DST), in the northern hemisphere between about April and September/October; differs widely in the southern hemisphere, between September/January and February/April

cal time in the respective me zone at 12 noon UT * Certain areas do not have daylight savings time

N

1h | 12h | 13h | 14h | 15h | 16h | 17h | 18h | 19h | 20h | 21h | 22h
0° | 30° | | 60° | | 90° | | 120° | | 150°

An Ingenious Invention

Portable equatorial sundial made by Johann Georg Vogler (1750), with an adjustable hour ring. The clock is positioned facing north with the aid of a compass; the plane of the hour ring is aligned with a point on the curved latitude scale that conforms to the latitude of the measurement site. In this way, the shadow-casting rod of the sundial is positioned parallel to the Earth's axis, so that its tip points to the north celestial pole and the hour ring is parallel to the earth's equator.

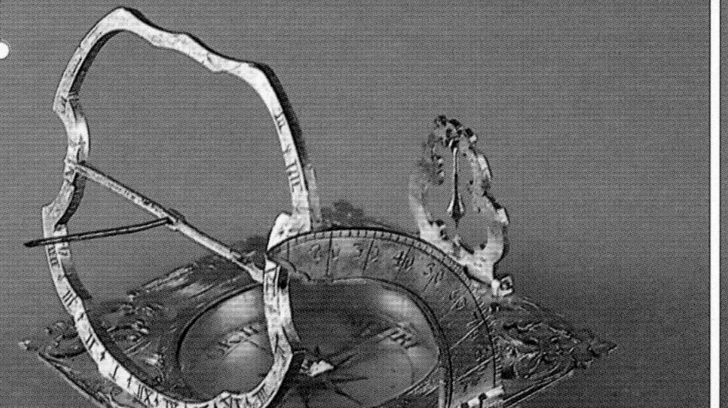

The Evolution of Cartography

Creating a Picture of the World

The first maps provided mankind with a means of creating a highly simplified, abstract image of the Earth. Long before aircraft were invented, the globe had already been depicted – from a bird's-eye view, so to speak – on a smaller, measurable scale in accordance with mathematical principles. Yet maps are never more than a reflection of social reality – of the knowledge, political visions, and religious beliefs of a given age. A map's claim to accuracy and reliability derives from the manner in which it was produced, from the degree of precision achieved by the engraver, lithographer, or draftsman, from the printer's command of his art, and from the ability of map-readers to recognize familiar aspects of their world.

Cartography

Since the mid-19th century, when the term "cartography" was first introduced, the art of map-making developed from a subdiscipline that served the needs of geodesy and geography into a science in its own right. By the early 20th century cartography had developed its own clearly defined concepts and methods.

Because of their military significance, the immense costs of making them, and the detailed nature of their contents, topographic maps remained a monopoly of the state in Europe until the latter half of the 19th century. Around the turn of the 18th to the 19th century, the nations of Europe began to establish statistical services and offices which published some of their data in topical maps intended for broad public use.

From the Disk to the Sphere

Even ancient cultures had maps of known territories showing possessions and boundaries. Excellent examples include the rock drawing of a Neolithic settlement in Çatal Hüyük dated about 6200 BC, the 3,500-year-old city map of Nippur in Babylon, and maps made by the ancient Greeks.

These early map-makers viewed the Earth as a flat disk, inhabited in the center and inaccessible at its outer edges. As knowledge increased, the disk expanded. New insights gained through the conquests of Alexander the Great and the observations of seafarers and scientists gave birth to the idea that the Earth is a sphere, for which Erastosthenes calculated a circumferences of 37,700 km (or 46,250 km, depending upon the conversion method applied) in c. 250 BC. He took his investigations a step further, projecting the three-dimensional segments of the sphere onto a flat surface and overlaying his map with a system of coordinates based upon the length and width of the Mediterranean Sea.

In the 2nd century AD, the astronomer, astrologist, and cartographer Ptolemy of Alexandria developed the first north-oriented map projection with longitudinally true lines of latitude. Ptolemy's instructions for map-making were distributed in copies, commentaries, and translations to geographers and cartographers – and along with them his most glaring error: His globe had a circumference of only 29,000 km.

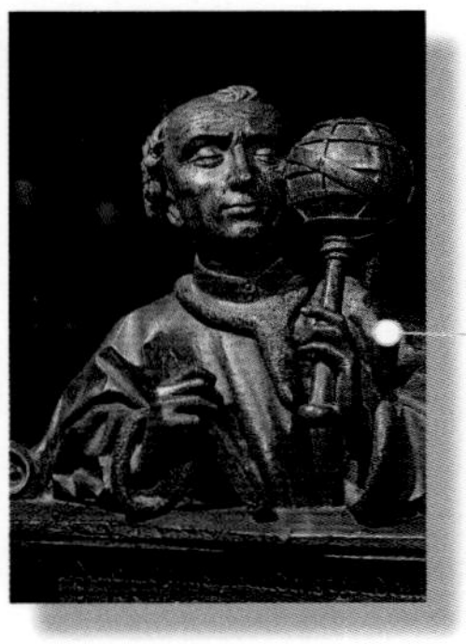

Immortalized in a Choir Loft: A wood sculpture of Claudius Ptolemaeus (Ptolemy) in the choir loft of the cathedral in Ulm (Michael Erhart, c. 1470). The publication of his Geographia in Ulm in 1482 revived the ancient concept of the shape of the world.

Mappae mundi – The Christian Image of the World

For the next several centuries, theology shaped mankind's view of the world and its representation on maps. Rome's influence waned, and the center of the new Christian world shifted to the east, to Jerusalem. Thus the maps of Christianity were oriented toward the east, and they depicted the earth once again as a flat disk. Like all works of art from this period, they proclaimed the greatness of God and the Church.

The emergence of Islam beginning in the 6th century AD posed a challenge to the dominant Christian view. Arab cartographers incorporated the ancient tradition of Ptolemy (the Earth as a sphere) into their scientific system and expanded their knowledge of the world through extensive travel and the use of astronomical instruments.

Unveiling the Earth

Maps used by seafarers and merchants were not documents of religious philosophy. Their maps were intended for practical use and were therefore as accurate as possible under the given circumstances. Portolan charts of the Mediterranean showed the coasts and major landmarks in detail, and, as studies have proven, contained only minor errors of distance.

However, maps of foreign countries and coastlines were usually kept locked away in the safes of rulers and merchants and were released for public use only after the existence of such regions had become widely known. Even Columbus lacked the most current maps on his journey of "discovery" to America. Although the Vikings had reached North America long before him, Columbus sailed westward into an "unknown" Atlantic (guided by Ptolemy's incorrect estimate of the earth's circumference) hoping to reach India. The newly discovered regions were presented on a world map made by Martin Waldseemüller as early as 1507.

Motivated by the prospect of finding new worlds beyond the horizon and by the lure of endless riches, the nations of Europe launched their campaign of worldwide exploration.

Surveying the Planet

The circumnavigation of the globe by Magellan's expedition had provided practical proof that the Earth is a sphere. Subsequent advances in science and the development of better instruments enabled cartographers to improve the accuracy and detail of their maps of the world over the course of the next several centuries. Unknown regions of the Earth were populated on maps with imaginary beings – an expression of horror vacui, the unwillingness of map-makers to reveal gaps in their knowledge to the general public. Later, they were simply entered as "white spots."

The era of cartographic precision based upon mathematical principles began in the latter half of the 18th century. In the nations of Europe, topographic surveys were carried out for military and administrative purposes, and the data obtained through these efforts serves even today as the basis for planning in modern countries.

Once it became possible to explore the Earth from space in the 20th century, the last remaining white spots disappeared from the maps of the world, and cartographers gained access to all the geographic data they could possibly need. Electronic data processing relieved map-makers of the arduous tasks of drawing and engraving maps, turning them into specialists in graphic communication.

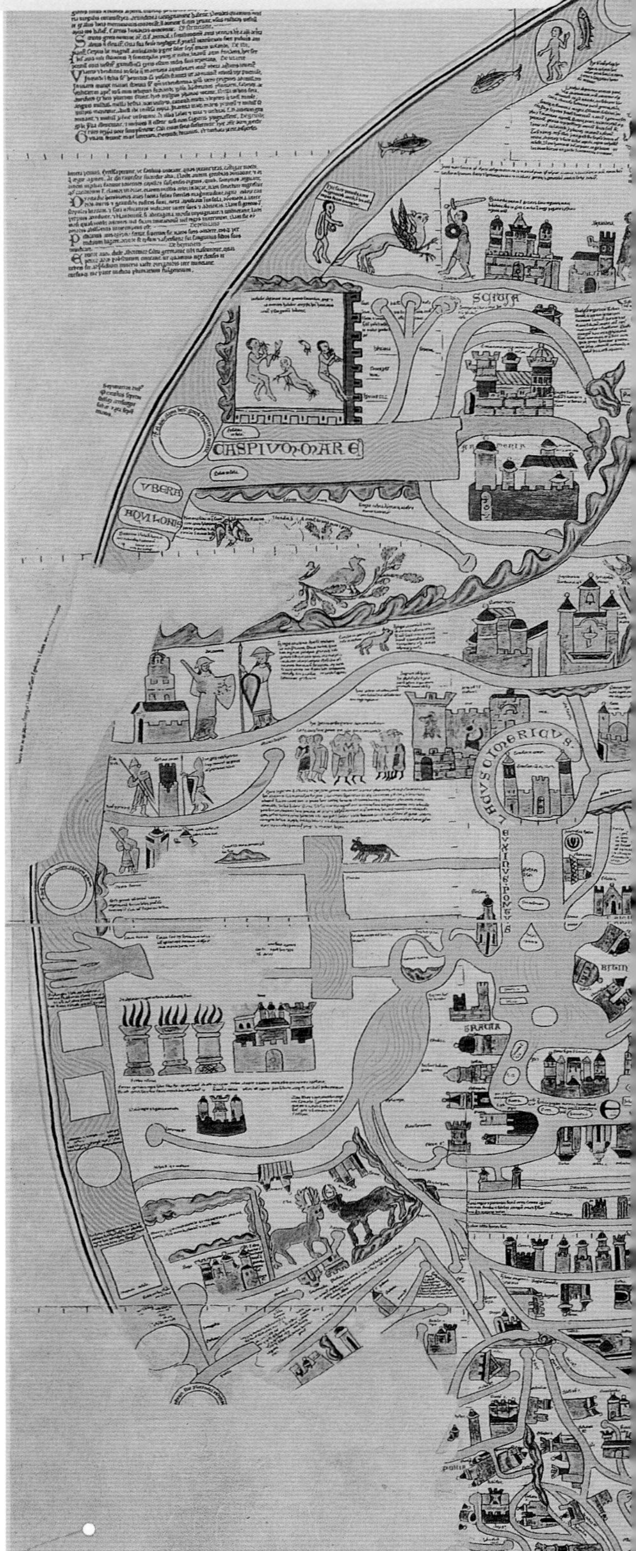

Image of the Medieval World

Produced between 1230 and 1240, the Ebstorf World Map is an example of medieval Christian cartography. Drawn in a TO configuration, it transposes the body of Christ onto the known world. Encircled by the O-shaped ocean, the Earth's landmasses are separated by the T (of the inland seas) – the symbol of Christ's death on the cross. The original map was destroyed by fire in a bombing raid on Hanover in 1943. A copy of the large map (358 x 356 cm) has survived in 30 parts.

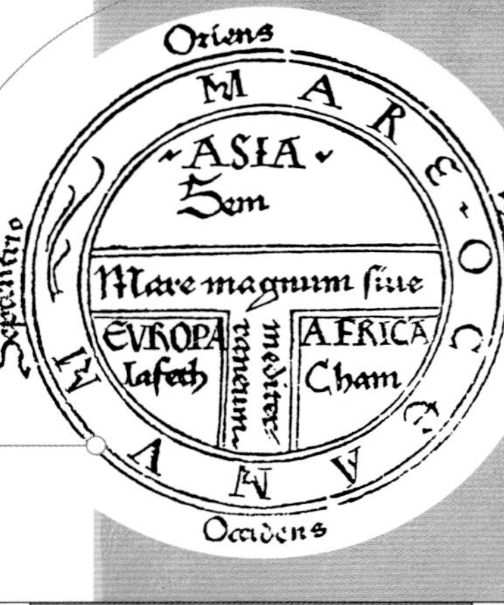

The Schematic World

Schematic world map (TO map) by Isidor of Sevilla (1472), illustrating the Christian image of the world.

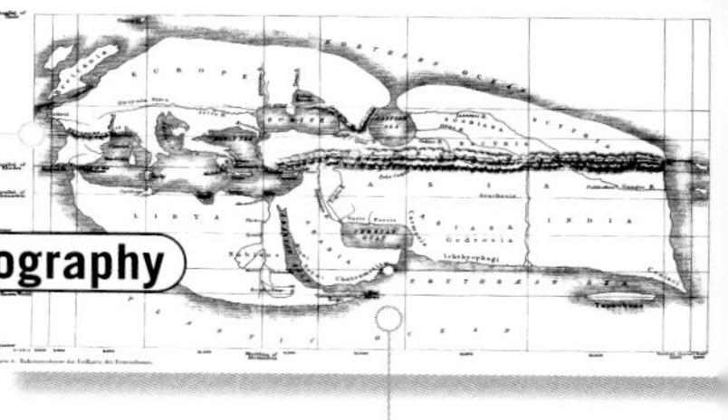

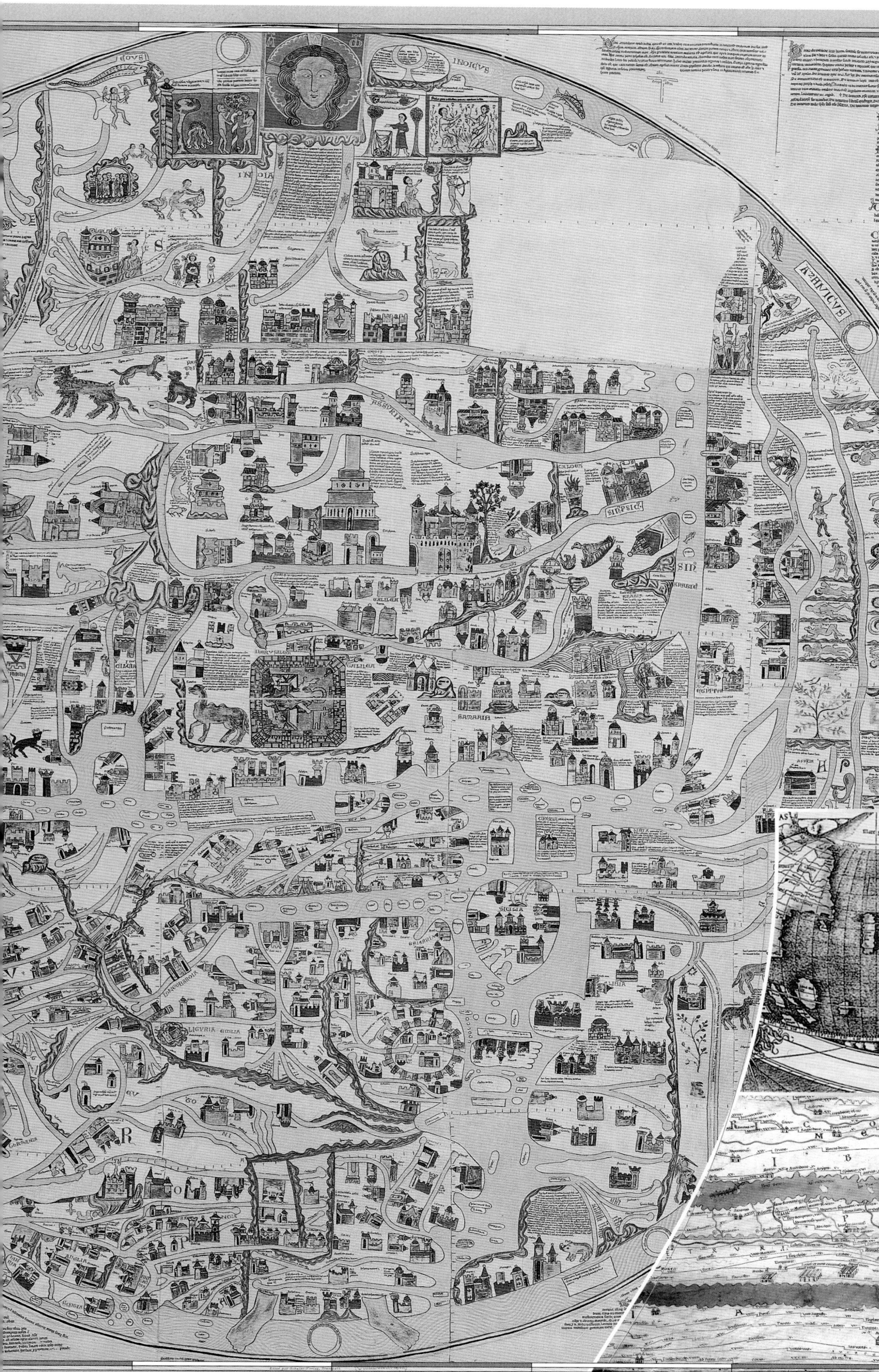

First Coordinate System

This reconstruction of a map by Eratosthenes (3rd c. BC) shows the known world in a coordinate system based upon the position of the Mediterranean Sea.

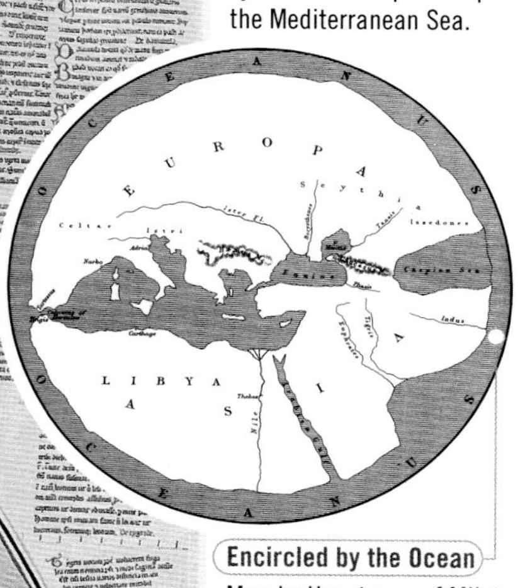

Encircled by the Ocean

Map by Hecataeus of Miletus (c.500 BC) reconstructed from texts, showing the Earth as a disk with the continents of Europe and Asia encircled by an ocean.

Roman Itinerary

The Tabula Peutingeriana illustrates the pragmatic approach of the Roman government. It depicts the network of roads as a schematic itinerary without scale, showing route markers, postal stations, and cities in signature form.

Birth of the Name "America"

Amerigo Vespucci and the regions of South America he discovered. Detail from a map by the Freiburg cartographer Martin Waldseemüller, on which the name "America" (in honor of Vespucci) appeared for the first time. The map was printed in Saint-Dié (Lorraine) in 1507.

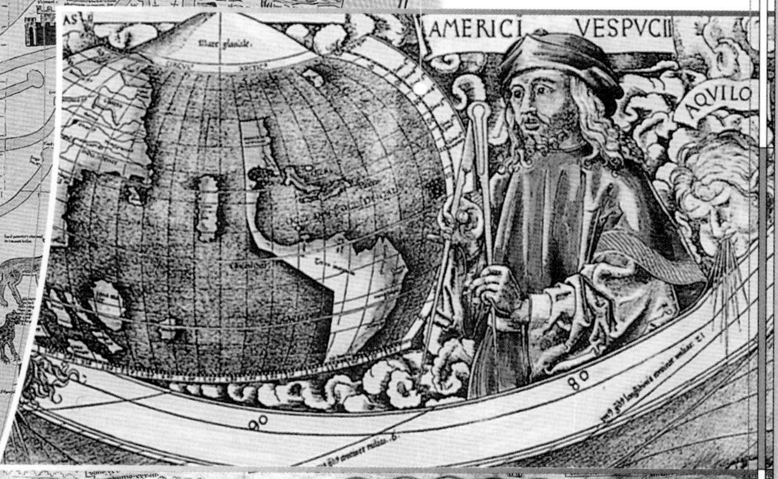

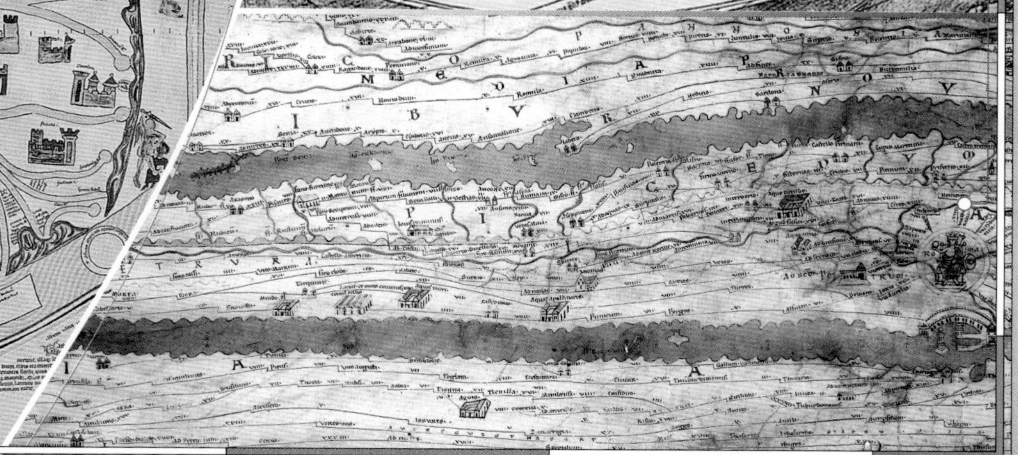

Tourism: Economics and the Environment

The Urge to Travel versus Environmental Awareness

Why do we travel, willingly accepting the costs and the risks it entails – disorientation and boredom, intestinal troubles and even malaria? Are we motivated to seek out new places less by curiosity than by the need to find ourselves? If so, the Greek philosopher Seneca reminds us that we cannot solve our problems by traveling to and fro, since "we always take ourselves along."

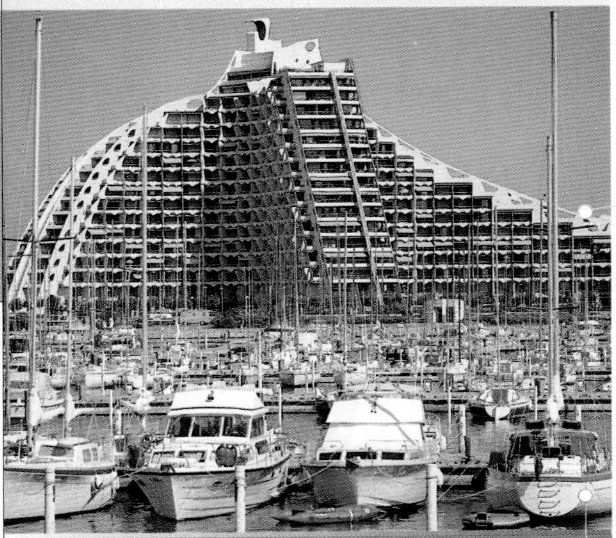

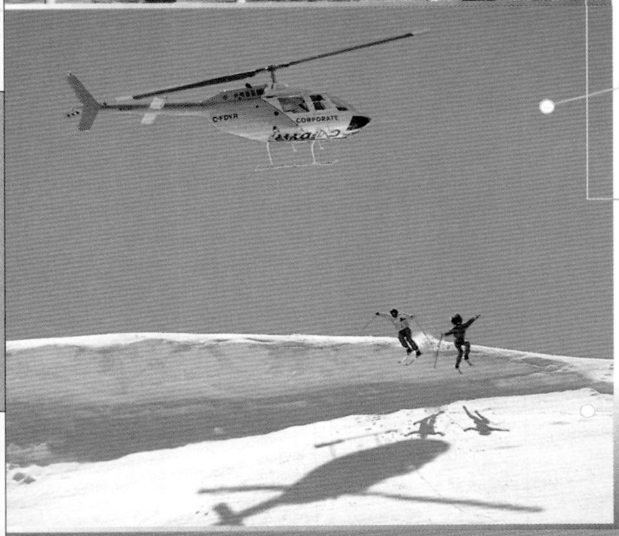

Aid or Exploitation

The tourist trade is the largest industry in the global economy in terms of both employees and investment volumes. The number of international tourists rose nearly 1000 % between 1960 (69 million) and 2000 (670 million). If we add those who travel within their own countries, the total number of tourists increases to about 5.3 billion. The Germans take the lead in world travel, while the French tend to stay at home and plan accordingly. The 180-km-long Mediterranean coast of the Languedoc-Roussillon region has been under development on a grand scale since 1963.

Many developing countries see tourism as a panacea for their economic problems but are often disappointed, as only a small portion of profits from the tourist trade actually flows into local economies.

A New Form of Colonialism?
Rebellion in Host Countries

People long believed that travel promotes better understanding of foreign cultures and thus contributes to inter-

national peace. Yet it appears that it often has the opposite effect, as old prejudices are strengthened and new ones emerge through tourism. It has become increasingly clear since the 1970s that the influx of tourists can indeed cause grave social and environmental problems. Natural landscapes are damaged (by winter sports, for example), traditional cultural landscapes are permeated by functional architecture, long-standing customs give way to behavior patterns apparently imposed by foreign visitors. Lost local and regional cultural heritage cannot be replaced. The voices of those who are no longer willing to be marketed are growing stronger in many countries. Yet the potential positive effects of globalization through tourism should not be overlooked, as contact with tourists from abroad can provide encouragement for social and economic development.

The Hard Road to Soft Tourism

In some parts of the world, indigenous communities rely on cooperation with travel companies in the hope of generating income with innovative forms of environmental tourism without placing their own cultures and environments at risk. But to what extent is this kind of sustainable tourism really possible?

It would seem to call for a new breed of traveler. Tour organizers, airlines, and publishers of tourists' guides take an optimistic view. A number of them have joined forces in support of a code of ethics for travelers.

The Most on the Coast
Built in 1967–77 according to plans by French architect Jean Marie Balladour, La Grande-Motte, a vacation area on the coast of Languedoc near Montpellier, offers the "total beach experience."

Giddy Heights
Heliskiing in virtually unexplored terrain accessible only by helicopter. There are 43 officially recognized mountain landing sites for helicopters in Switzerland, 16 of them at elevations above 3,000 m.

Meeting of Two Worlds
Oblivious to tourist photographers, the Tuareg drive their salt caravans through the Ténéré Desert (Niger), traveling for months at a time to reach their markets in Nigeria.

Adventure tours in deserts, mountains, rainforests, in polar or other regions must be judged by the respect they show for local cultures and environments.

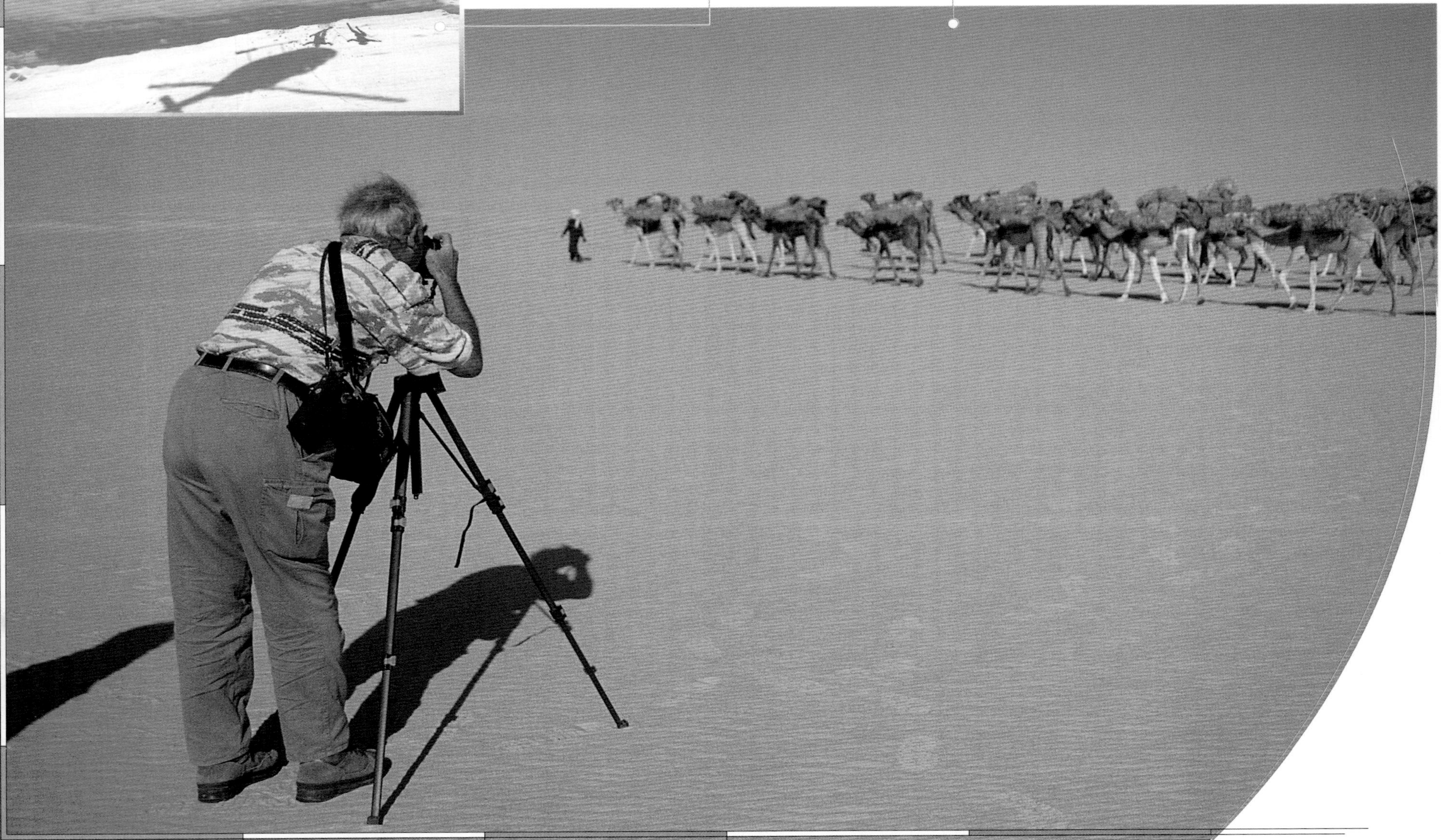

Satellite Section

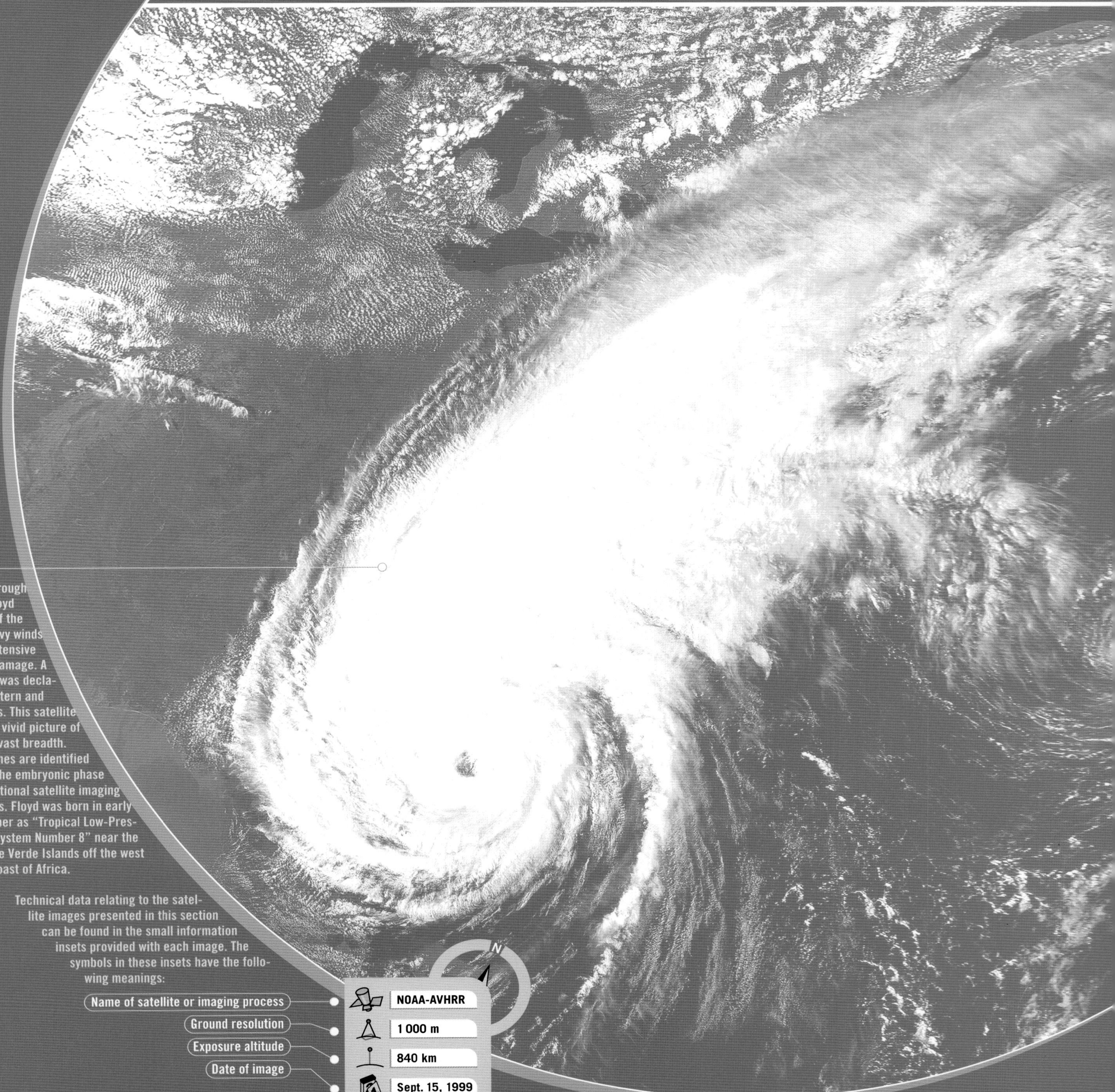

Hurricane Floyd

From September 14 through 18, 1999, Hurricane Floyd swept the East Coast of the United States with heavy winds and rains, causing extensive flooding and storm damage. A state of emergency was declared in ten southeastern and mid-Atlantic states. This satellite image provides a vivid picture of the hurricane's vast breadth. Future hurricanes are identified while still in the embryonic phase with conventional satellite imaging techniques. Floyd was born in early September as "Tropical Low-Pressure System Number 8" near the Cape Verde Islands off the west coast of Africa.

Technical data relating to the satellite images presented in this section can be found in the small information insets provided with each image. The symbols in these insets have the following meanings:

Name of satellite or imaging process	NOAA-AVHRR
Ground resolution	1 000 m
Exposure altitude	840 km
Date of image	Sept. 15, 1999

Remote Satellite Surveying

How Do Earth Survey Satellites Work?

Graphic: Imaging Techniques

Most Earth survey satellites travel around the Earth at an altitude of between 600 and 900 km in an almost circular near-polar orbit. The time it takes to complete a single orbit ranges from 90 to 120 minutes.

Depending upon the type of equipment used, satellite imaging systems scan the Earth's surface in strips varying in width from eleven to 2,000 km. Detail resolution ranges from one meter (high resolution, e.g. IKONOS) to one kilometer (medium resolution, e.g. NOAA-AVHRR weather satellites) per image pixel. The imaging sensors of some satellites can be rotated laterally or in a complete circle. This makes it possible to obtain multiple images of especially interesting regions or to produce stereoscopic images used to create digital terrain models. Image data are ordinarily transmitted by satellites to ground stations distributed around the world. Satellites also have the capacity to store image data from areas beyond the reception range of ground stations until they can be retrieved by the nearest ground receiving station.

Panoramic View of Salzburg

New perspectives for regional imaging have emerged from the combination of satellite image data with digital terrain models (DTM), which are produced either from topographic maps or stereoscopic aerial or satellite photographs. They provide elevation data on every point on the Earth's surface. Such terrain models make it possible to derive through computation a wide range of panoramic views from vertical images. They serve as the basis for virtual flights through a landscape.

The picture below is a panorama developed in this way from Landsat TM and SPOT Pan data of the Salzburg lowlands, showing the Obertrum lakes in the foreground and the regional capital of Salzburg in the center. The summits of the Hagen Mountains rise along the horizon behind the high plateau of the Tennen Mountains. Visible in the background are the Central Alps and Austria's highest peak, the Grossglockner (3,798 m).

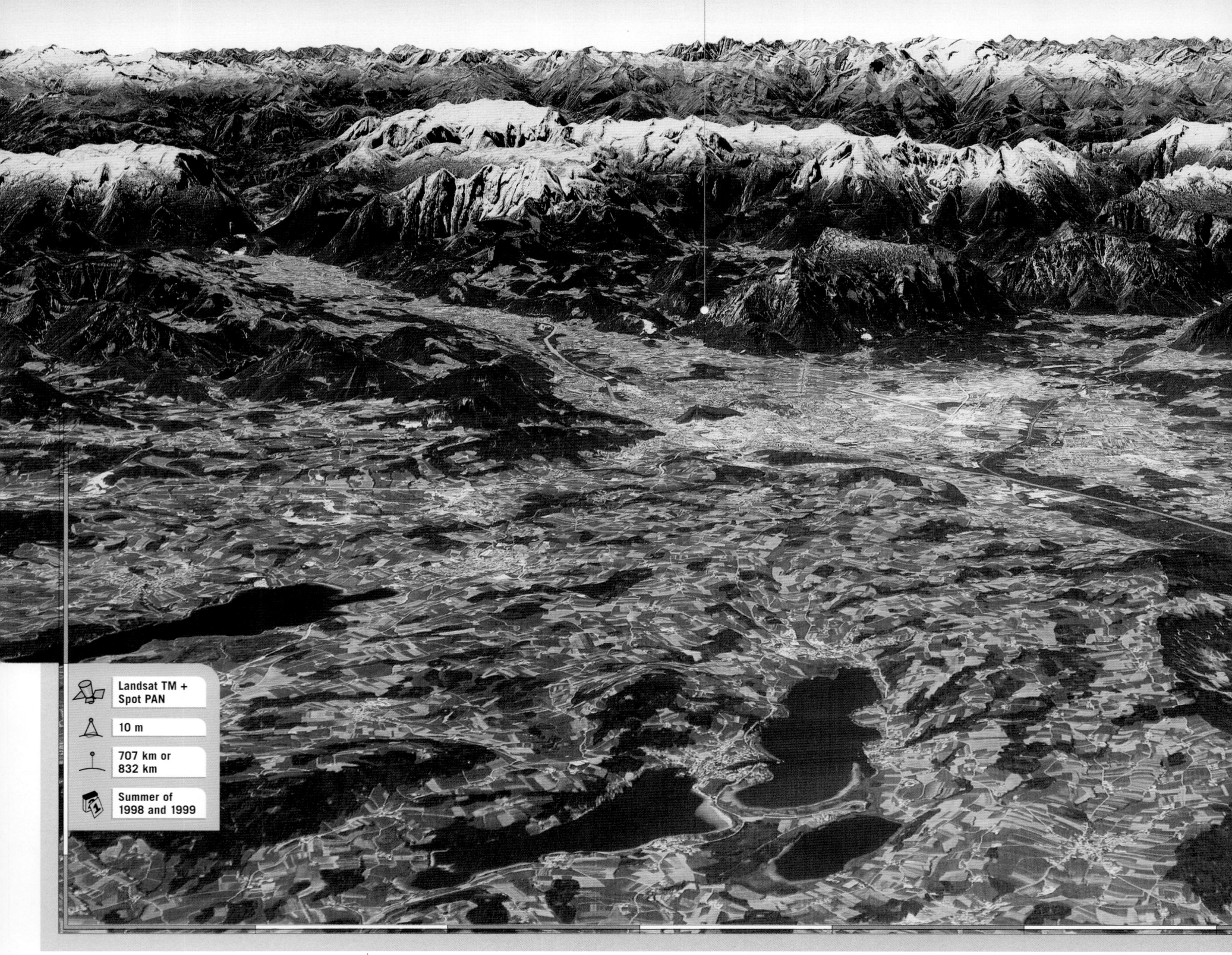

Landsat TM + Spot PAN

10 m

707 km or 832 km

Summer of 1998 and 1999

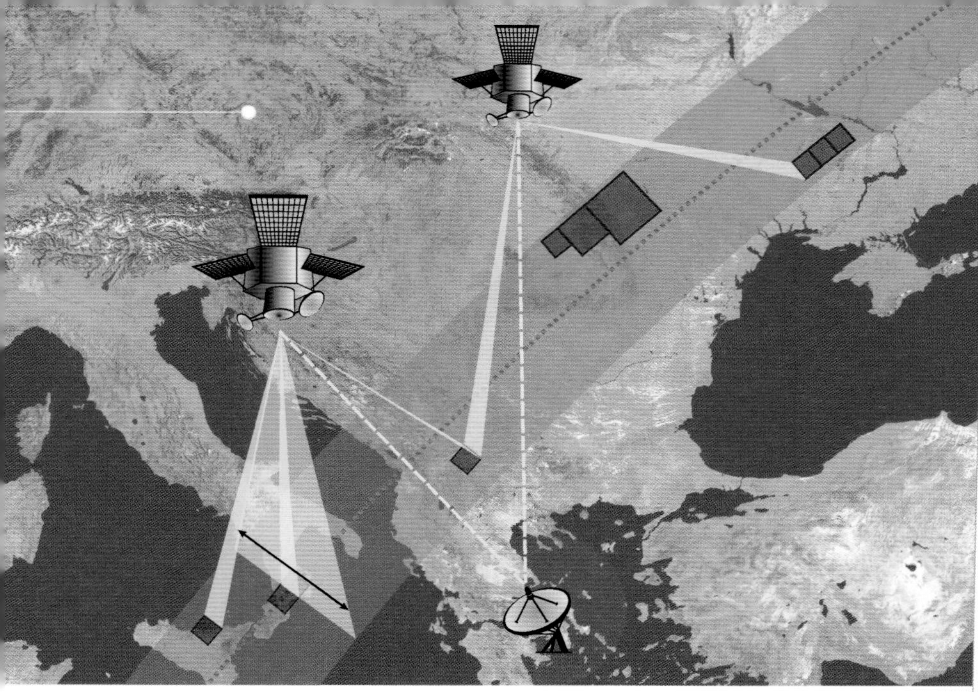

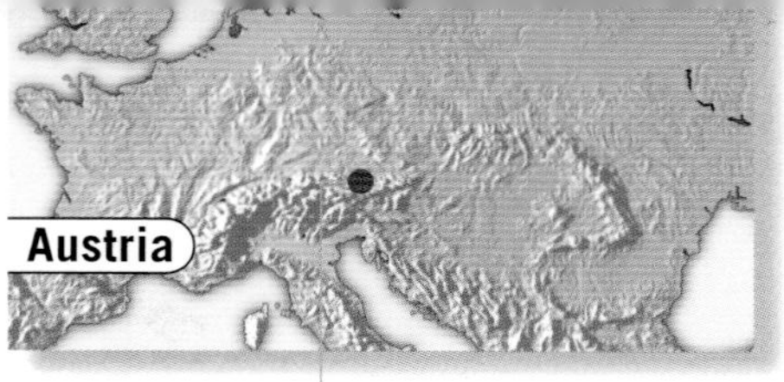

Digital Elevation Model of Cotopaxi

The Shuttle Radar Topography Mission (SRTM) achieved a new level of quality in the production of digital elevation models. In February 2000, the Space Shuttle Endeavor embarked on a mission devoted to setting up a system capable of producing a three-dimensional image of the Earth with the aid of multiple radar antennas attached to a 60-meter-long extendable mast. Using a radar interferometry technique, two radar images are taken from positions offset only slightly from one another. The differences between the two images are used to compute the elevation curves of the exposed terrain, which are then displayed on a map.

Our image shows Mount Cotopaxi in the Eastern Cordilleras of Ecuador, at 5,897 m the highest active volcano on Earth. The volcano has erupted 50 times since 1738, most recently in 1904 and 1928. The flow trenches of the cone-shaped volcano are clearly visible in the digital elevation model. As the snow line lies at an altitude of 4,000 m, the danger of mudslides in the flow trenches is great.

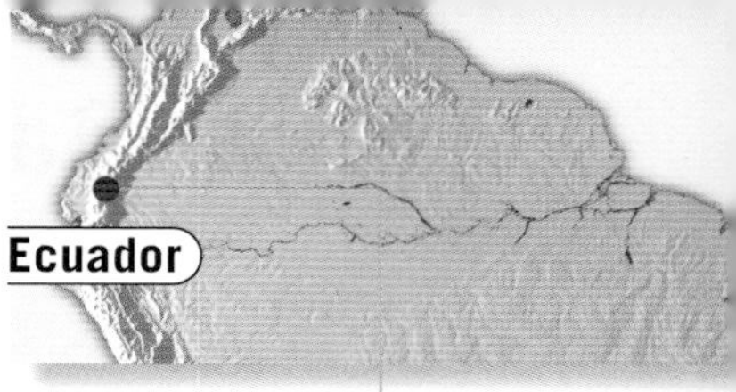

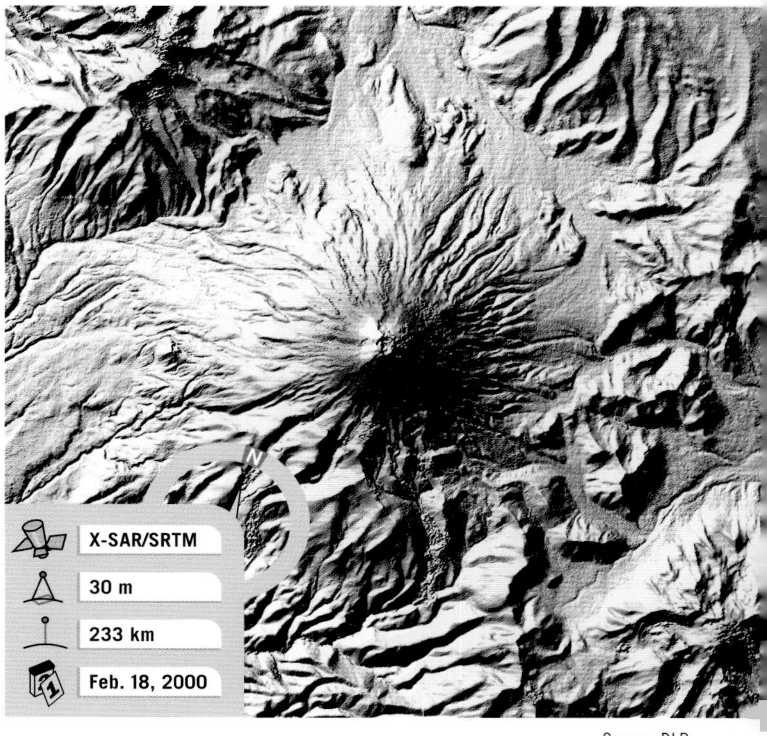

	X-SAR/SRTM
	30 m
	233 km
	Feb. 18, 2000

Source: DLR

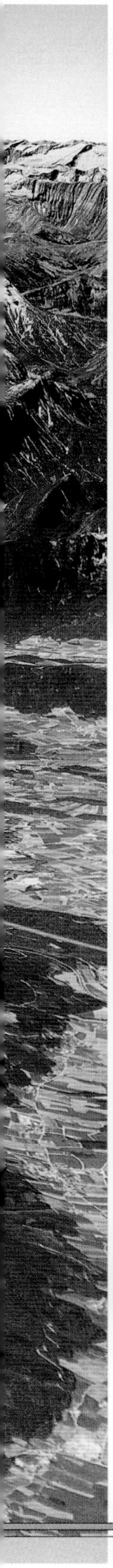

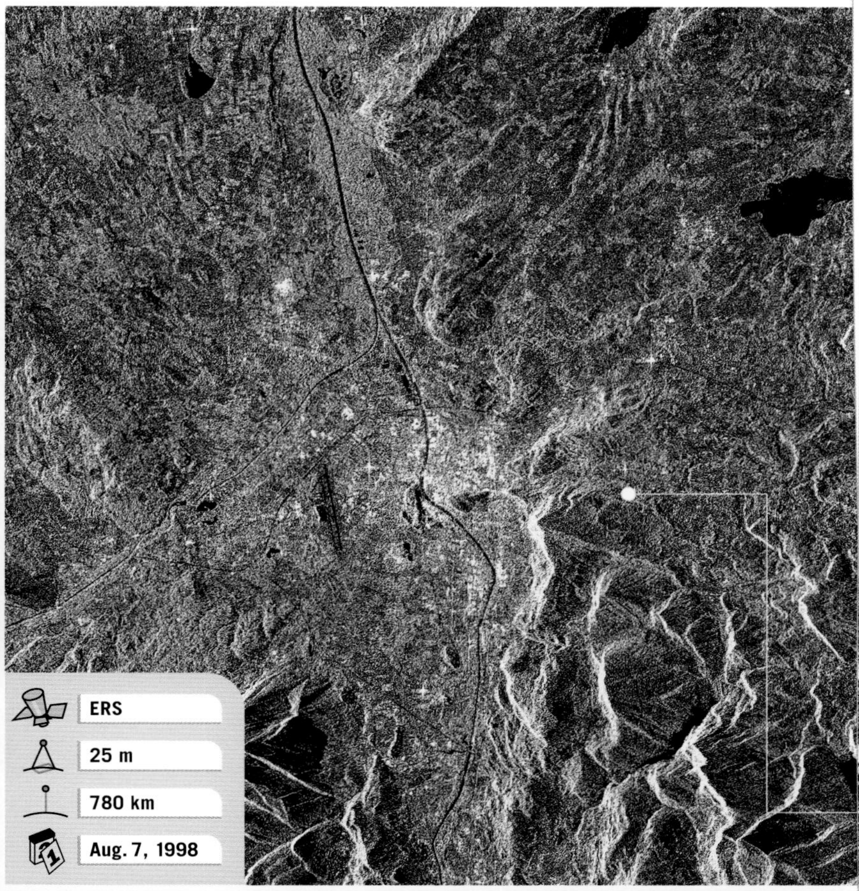

	ERS
	25 m
	780 km
	Aug. 7, 1998

Radar Image of Salzburg

Radar image of the city of Salzburg showing parts of the Flachgau and the Tennengau. While "conventional" Earth survey satellites pick up solar radiation reflected by the Earth (passive sensing systems), many radar satellites have the capacity to emit electromagnetic impulses and measure their reflection (active sensor systems), from which "images" can be computed. The strongest reflection comes from topographic ridges. Radar images can also be obtained at night or through cloud cover.

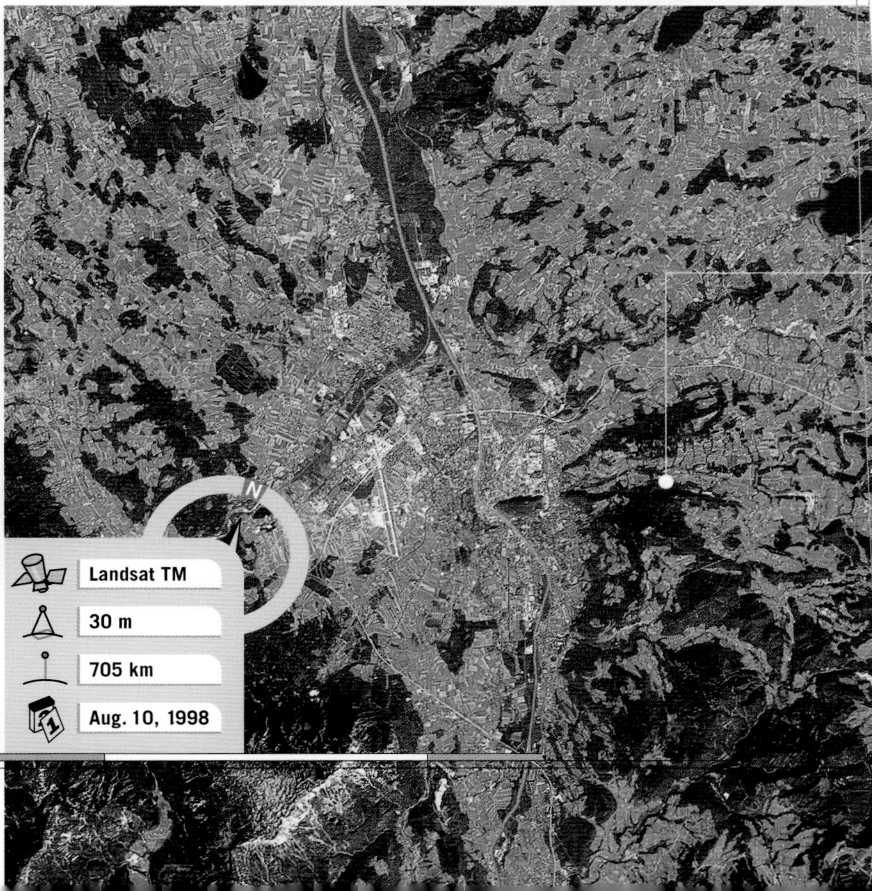

Landsat Thematic Mapper Image of Salzburg

As an example of an image produced by optical sensors, this Landsat Thematic Mapper image of Salzburg presents a much more "realistic" picture of the Earth. Optical sensors ordinarily operate in the visible, proximate infrared range. Some sensor systems produce images in the middle or thermal infrared ranges, registering in the latter the thermal radiation from the Earth's surface. The reflected radiation picked up by sensors is broken down into multiple spectral ranges (4 in SPOT, 8 in LANDSAT 7), making it possible to produce images in natural colors or in infrared or false colors (which lend themselves better to scientific analysis) from the exposures by mixing the various wavelengths. The nature of ground cover can be interpreted with the support of computer-aided imaging processes, as every surface has distinctive reflective characteristics. This facilitates recognition of water surfaces, wooded areas (deciduous, mixed, and coniferous forest), residential developments, industrial areas, etc.

	Landsat TM
	30 m
	705 km
	Aug. 10, 1998

The Earth from Space

Topographic Image

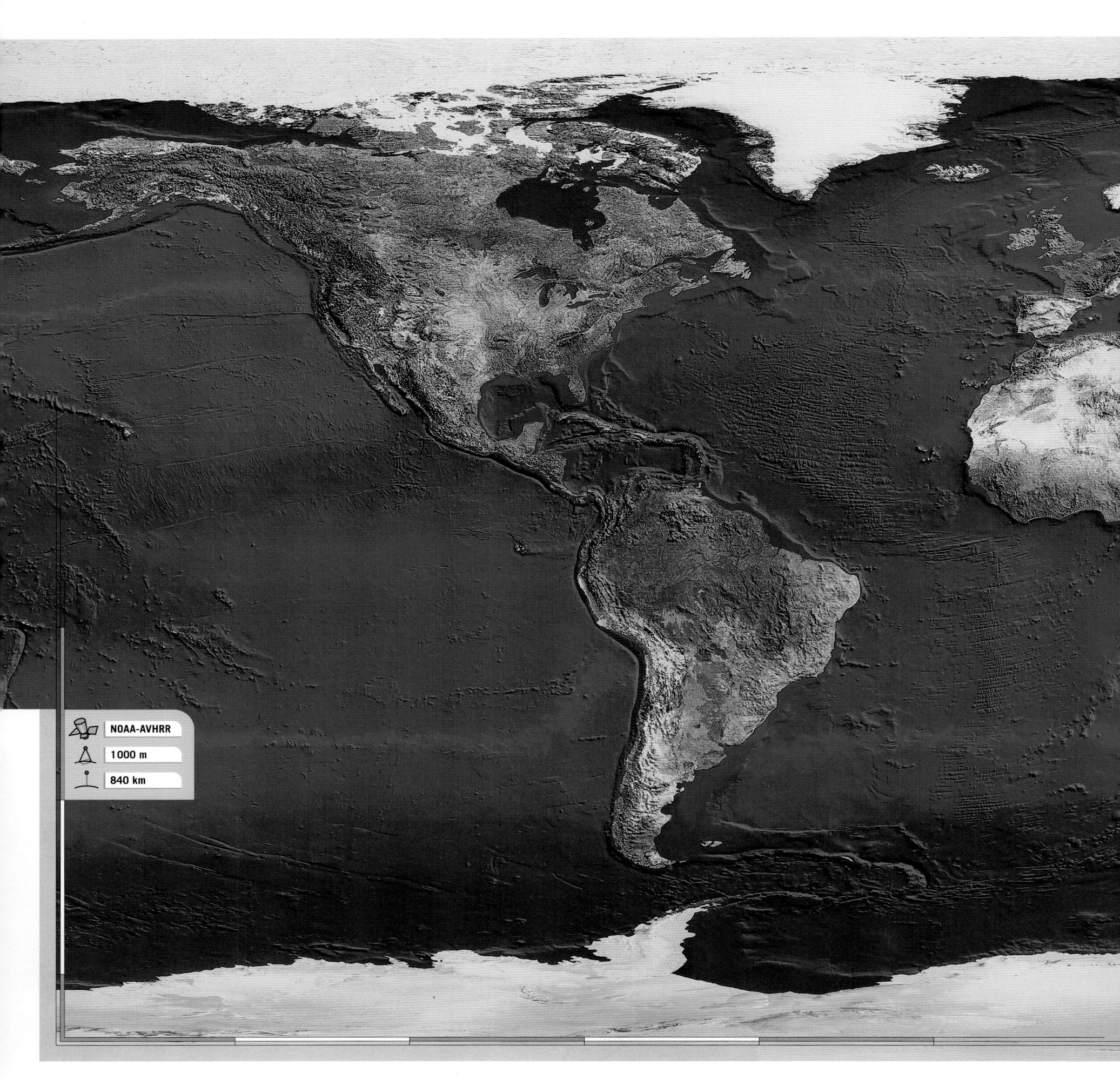

NOAA-AVHRR

1000 m

840 km

View of the Earth from Space

Several thousand images from the U.S. NOAA Satellite Series were required to compile this completely cloudless picture of the Earth.

In the projection selected for this satellite imagery map, the polar regions extend along the full length of the Equator. The continents are true to form to north and south latitudes of about 35 degrees, but distortion grows more extreme toward the poles.

This composite satellite image gives a good overview of major landscapes of the continents and their vegetation patterns. A particularly striking feature is the belt of deserts that encircles the globe.

(Copyright: GEOSPACE / World Sat International Corp. 2000)

The Earth's Surface

Land and Seafloor Topography

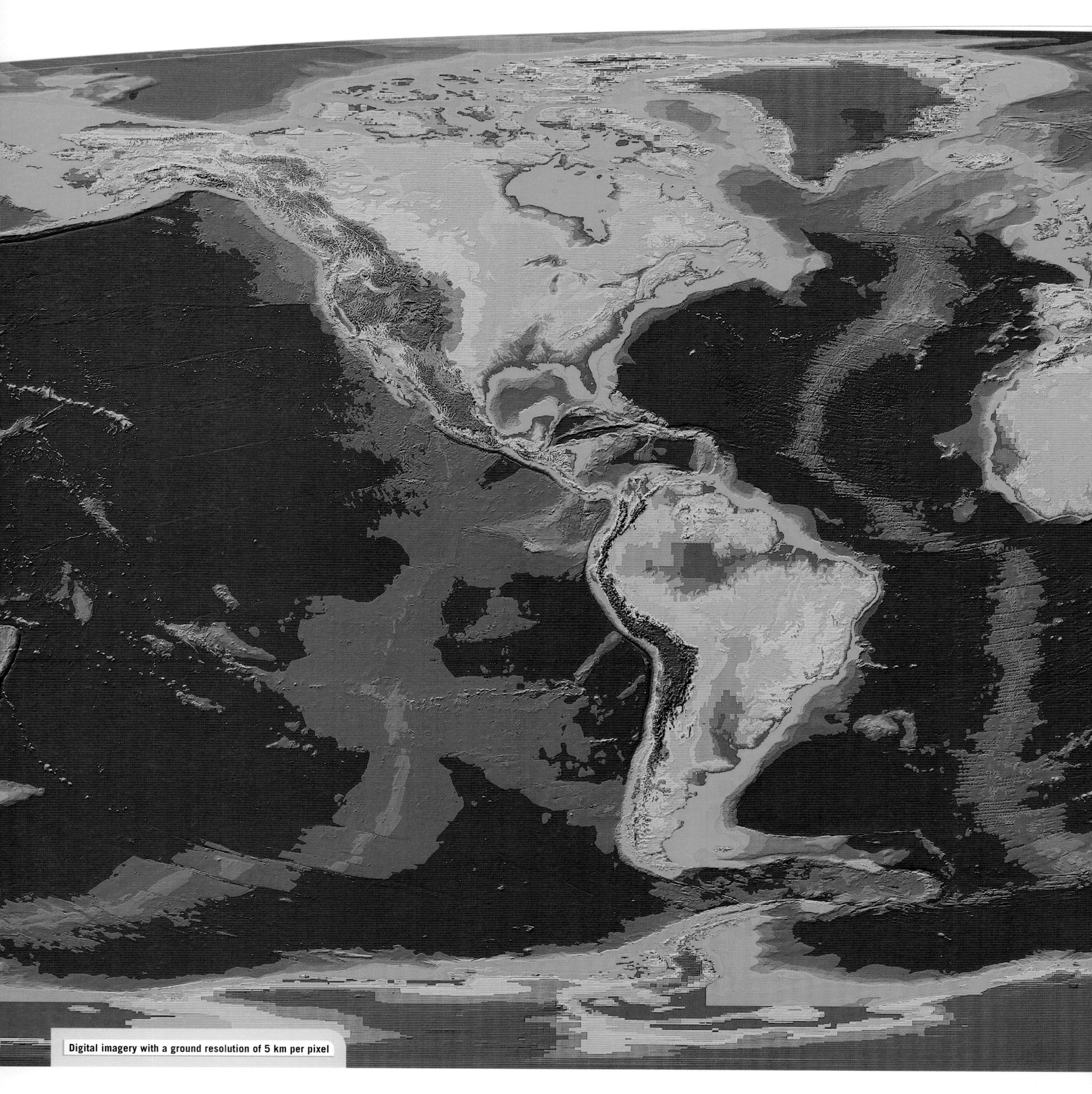

Digital imagery with a ground resolution of 5 km per pixel

The Earth's Surface

Shelf seas along the world's coastlines (light blue areas) trace the outlines of continental landmasses and highlight the topographic connections between offshore islands and their "parent" continents. The submerged oceanic ridges of the Atlantic and Indian Oceans stand out clearly as the longest continuous mountain ranges on Earth.

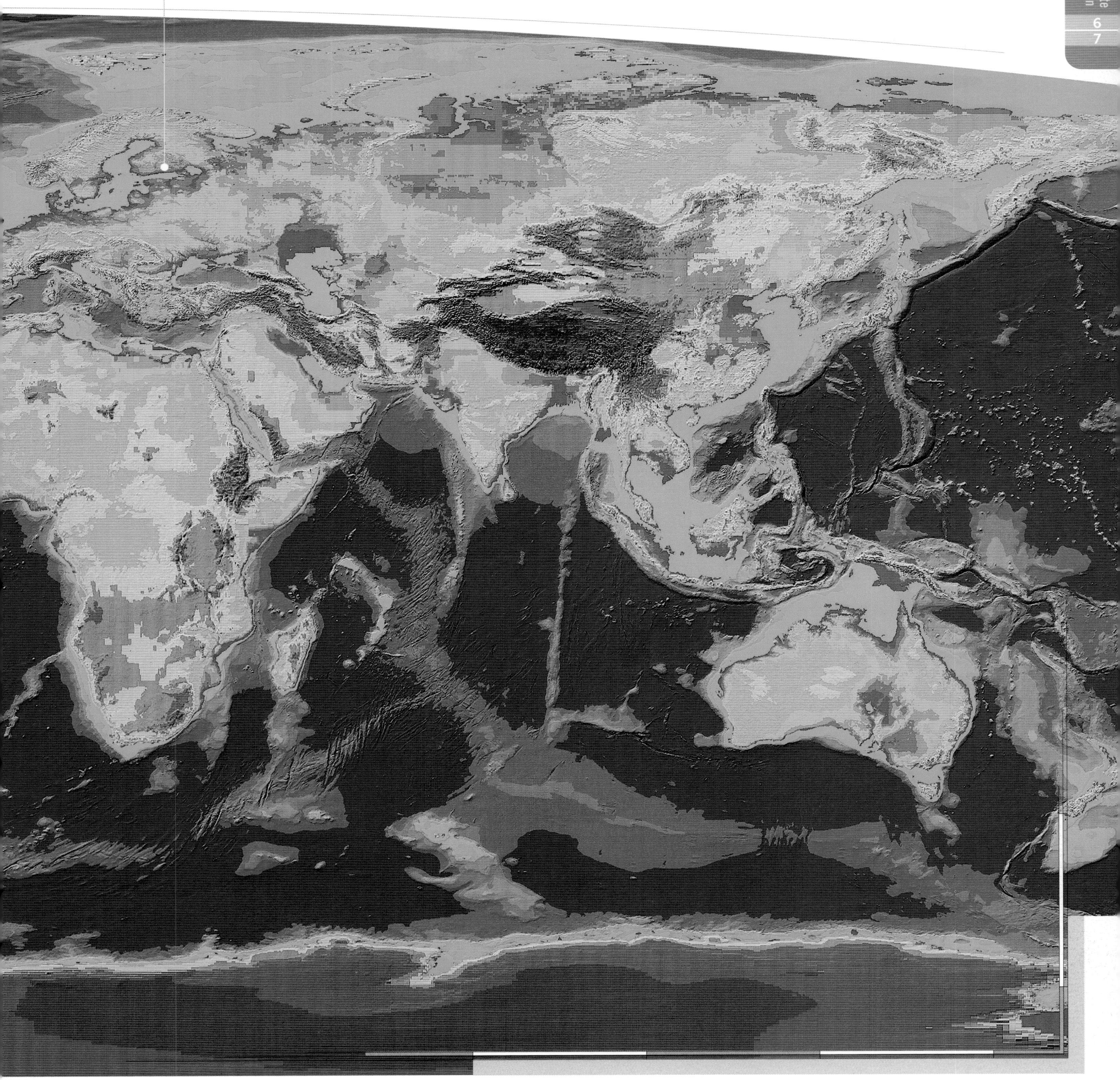

Volcanism

Living Links to the Earth's Core

Landsat TM

30 m

705 km

Aug. 20, 1986

Living Links to the Earth's Core

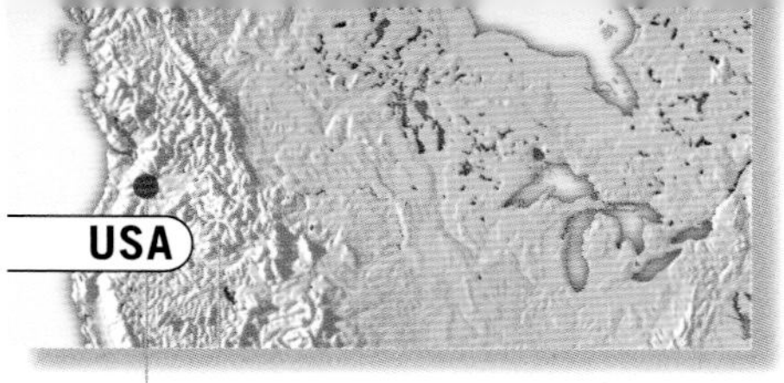

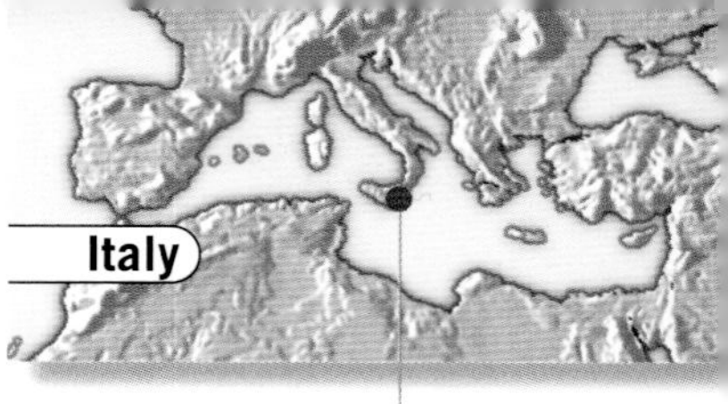

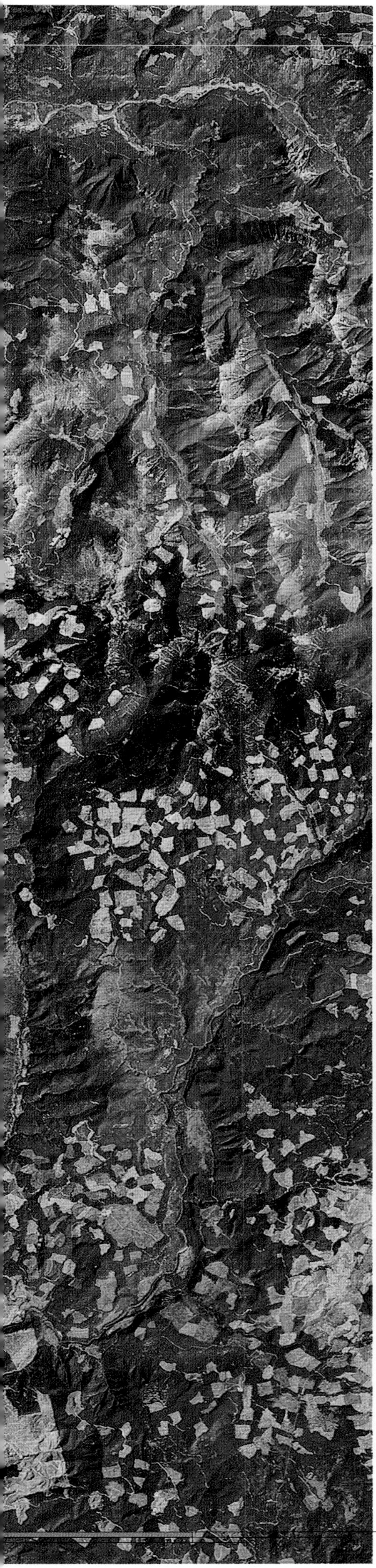

Mt. Saint Helens

One of the most spectacular natural events of the latter half of the
20th century was the eruption of Mount Saint Helens in the Cascade Range in the state of Washington. All of the active volcanoes of
North America are located in this chain of mountains that extends from
northern California to Canada. The region without vegetation in the
center of the image is the area of volcanic devastation surrounding
the collapsed oval crater (caldera) and Spirit Lake.
Originally 2,948 m high, the mountain known by the Indians as the
"Guardian of Fire" lost about 400 m of elevation during the eruption
on May 18, 1980. Avalanches of melted snow, mud, and rock debris
rushed down two river valleys, sweeping away bridges and houses and
cutting long swaths through the forests. A massive fountain of ash
rose up to 23 km into the stratosphere from the mountain's fractured
northern flank. The shockwave knocked down all trees within miles
of the cone like matches. Sixty people died in the inferno.
Less violent eruptions occurred in 1984, 1986, 1989, and 1991.

Mount Aetna

Mount Aetna, the highest active volcano in Europe, towers
above the eastern coast of Sicily between Catania and
Taormina on the shores of the Ionian Sea.
The last major eruption of Mount Aetna (present elevation:
3,350 m) occurred in 2001 and threatened the village
of Nicolosi. This thermal image shows the pattern of temperature distribution on the surface of the powerful
volcano. Red indicates areas of high temperature; blue
represents lower surface temperatures. Temperatures are
markedly influenced by solar radiation (exposed versus
shaded surfaces). Typical of Mount Aetna are its many
parasite craters – the largest of which are clearly recognizable on the western and southeastern sides of the
volcano. Also evident are the numerous fissures and
steam springs through which magma gases are released.

Landsat TM	
30 m	
705 km	
Nov. 27, 1984	

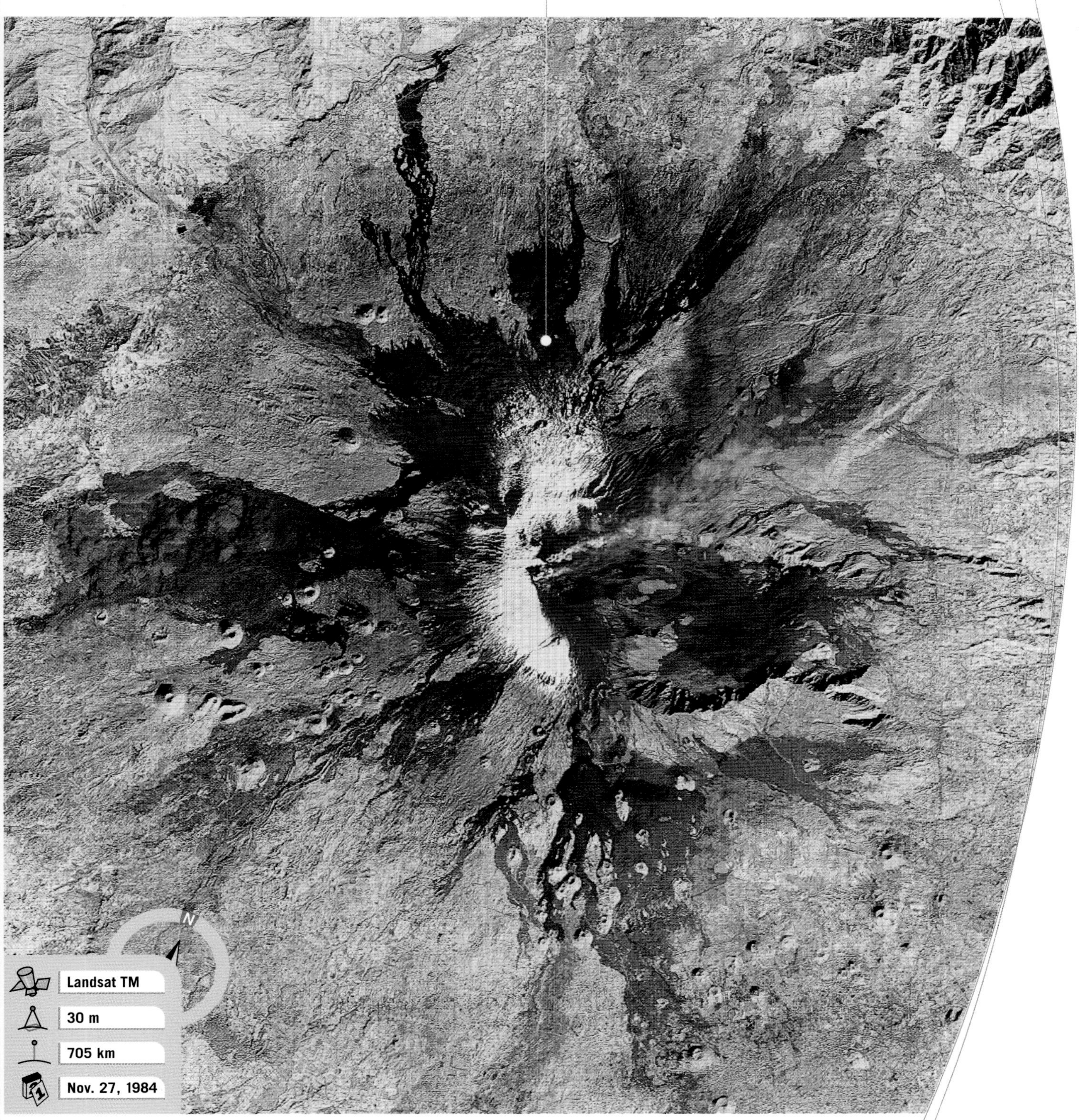

Meteorite Crater

Threat from Outer Space

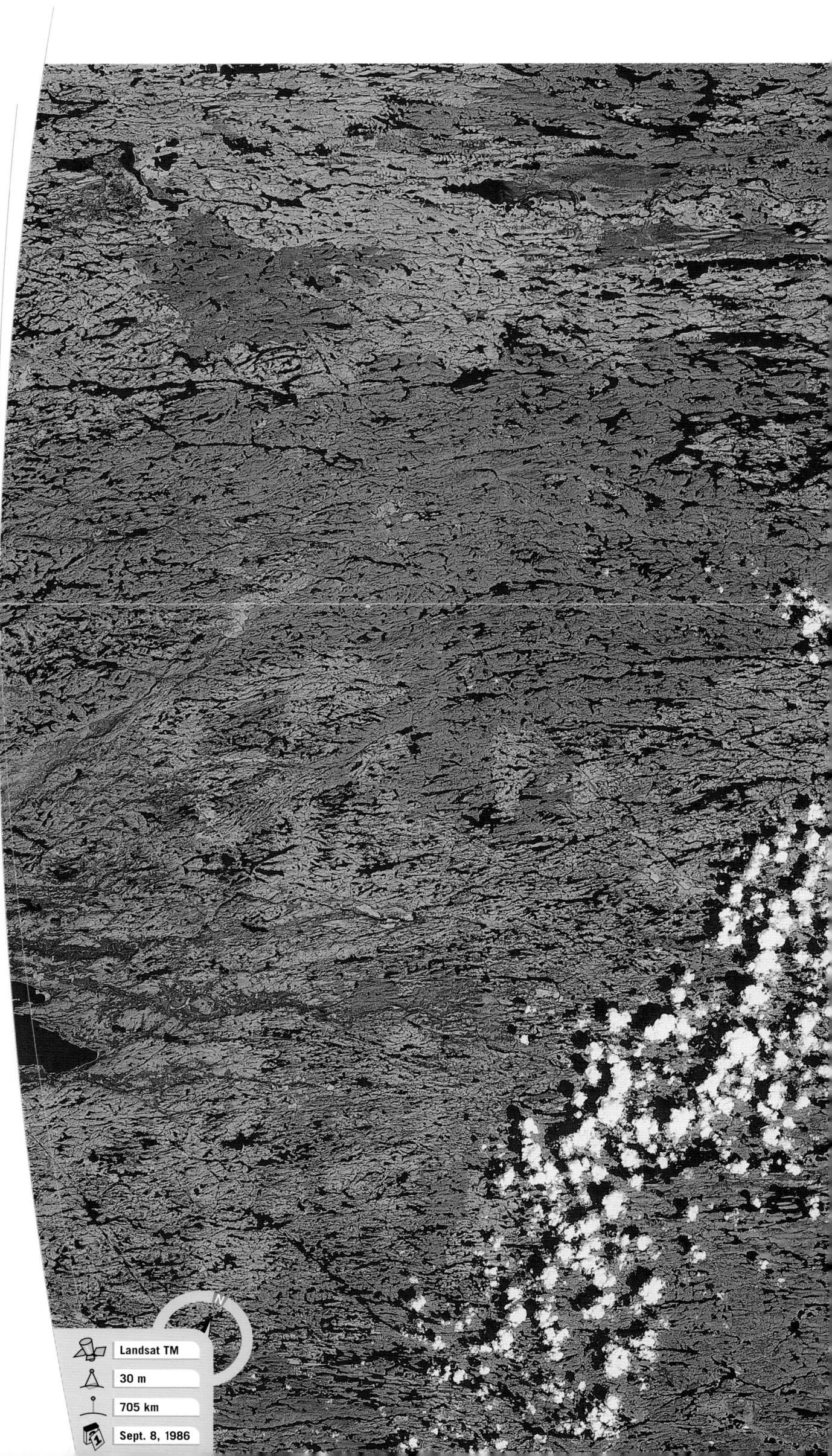

Clearwater Lake

This satellite image shows the two basins
of Clearwater Lake in the Canadian province
of Quebec. The lakebeds are the product of
an extremely rare event — the impact of "twin
meteorites" — that occurs only about once
every one million years, when two presumably
related meteorite fragments strike the earth
in succession. Complex craters formed by
impacts of large meteorites are characterized
by a central mountain formation.
The islands in the larger of the two lakes are
the visible remnants of such a central
mountain formation, left exposed after the
craters filled with water.
The impact that formed the lakes is presumed
to have occurred some 300 million years ago.

Landsat TM

30 m

705 km

Sept. 8, 1986

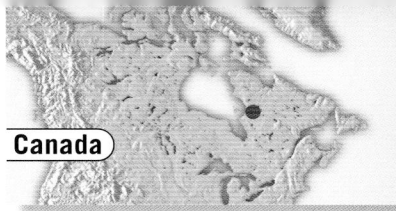

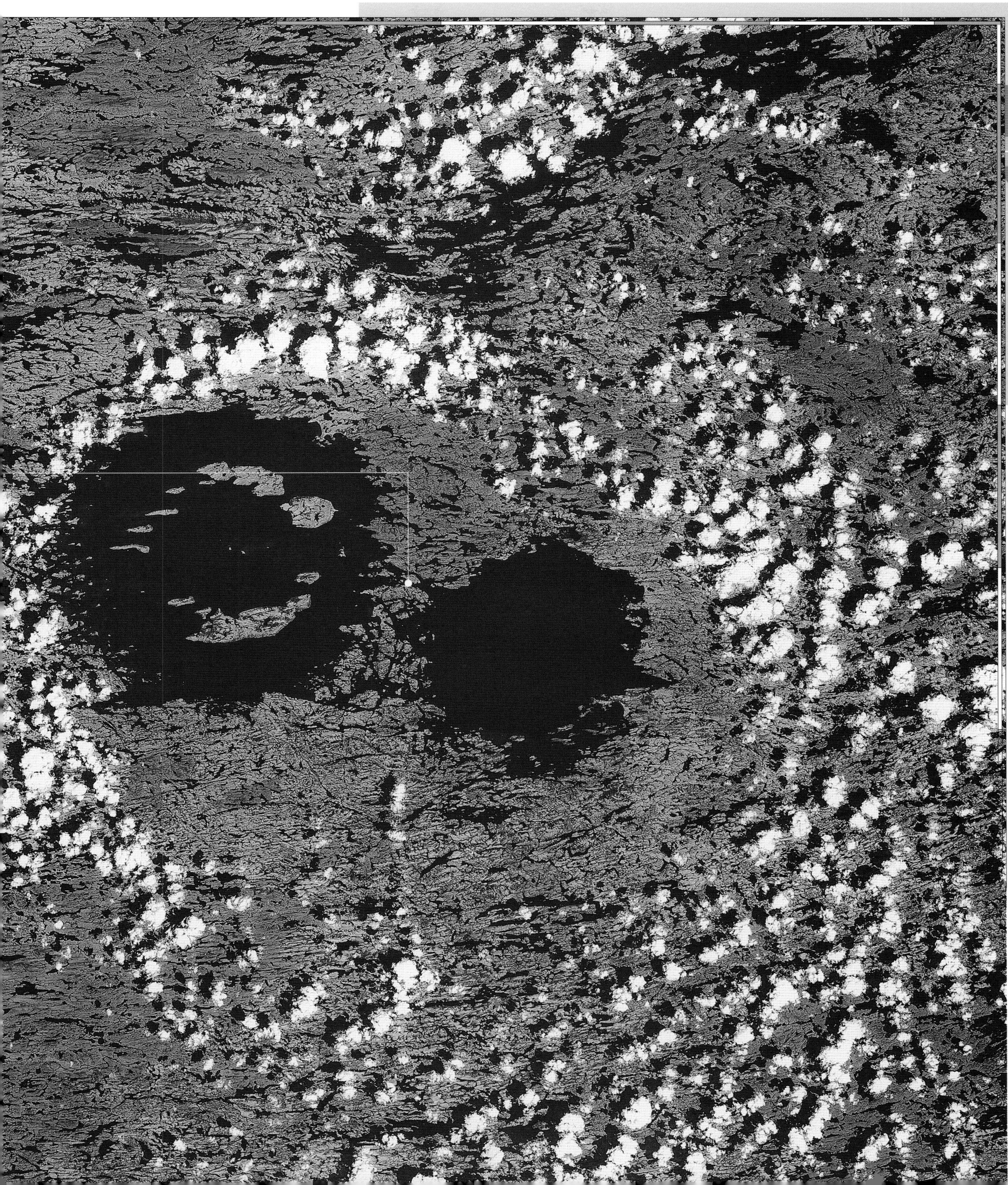

Climate

Storms and a Dangerous Christ Child

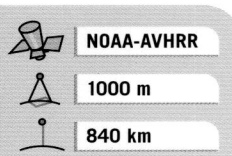

NOAA-AVHRR

1000 m

840 km

Temperature distribution
September 9, 1986

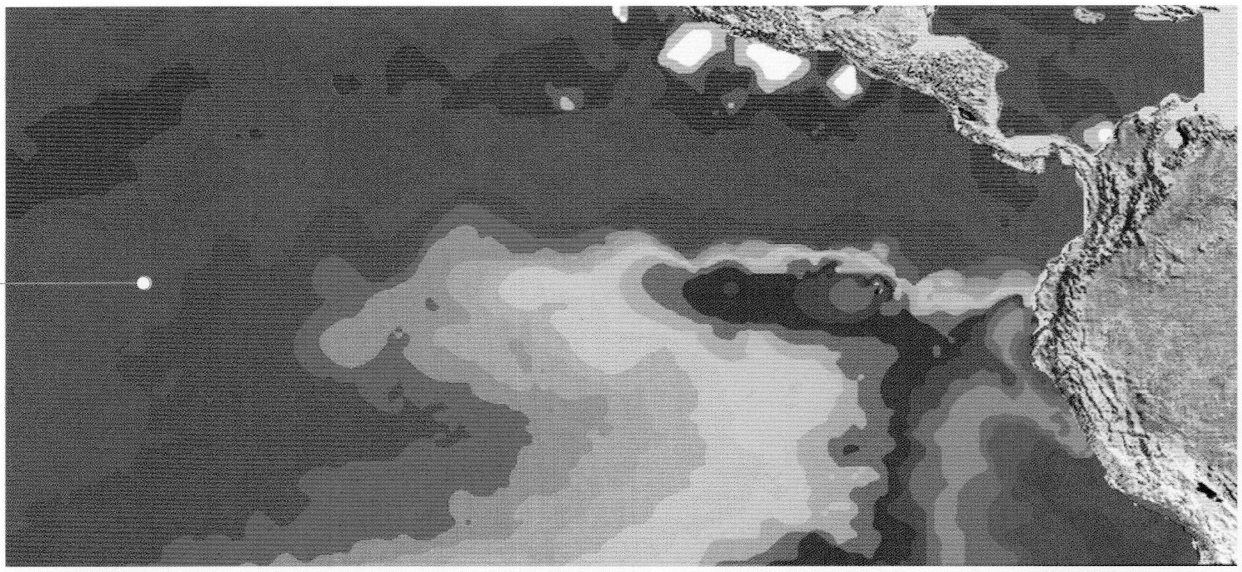

Temperature distribution
September 5, 1987

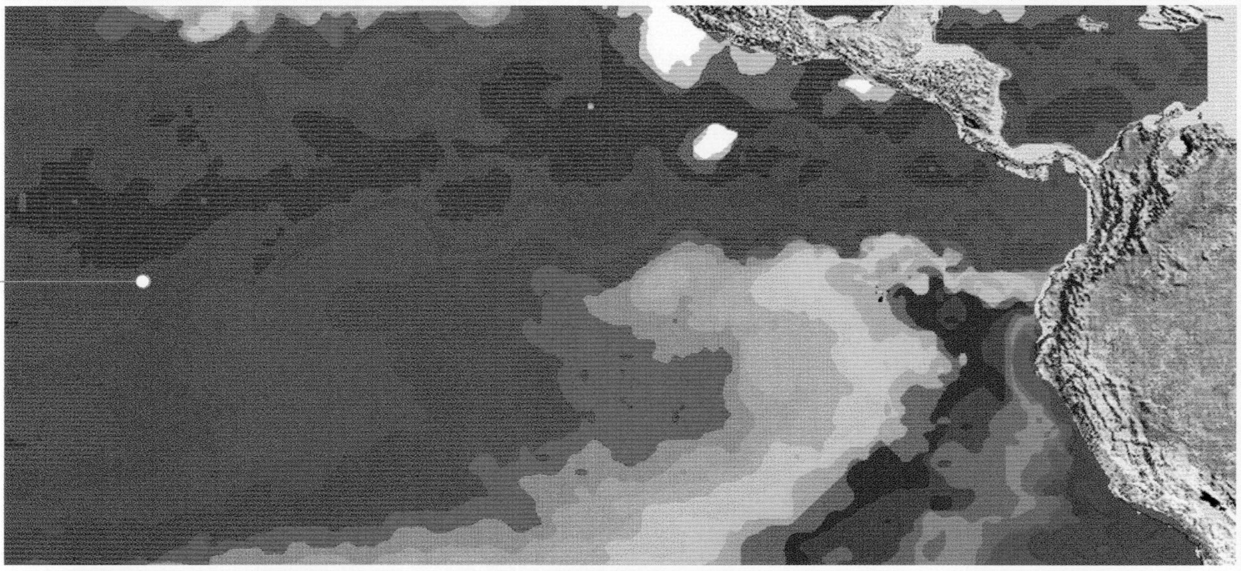

Temperature distribution
September 6, 1988

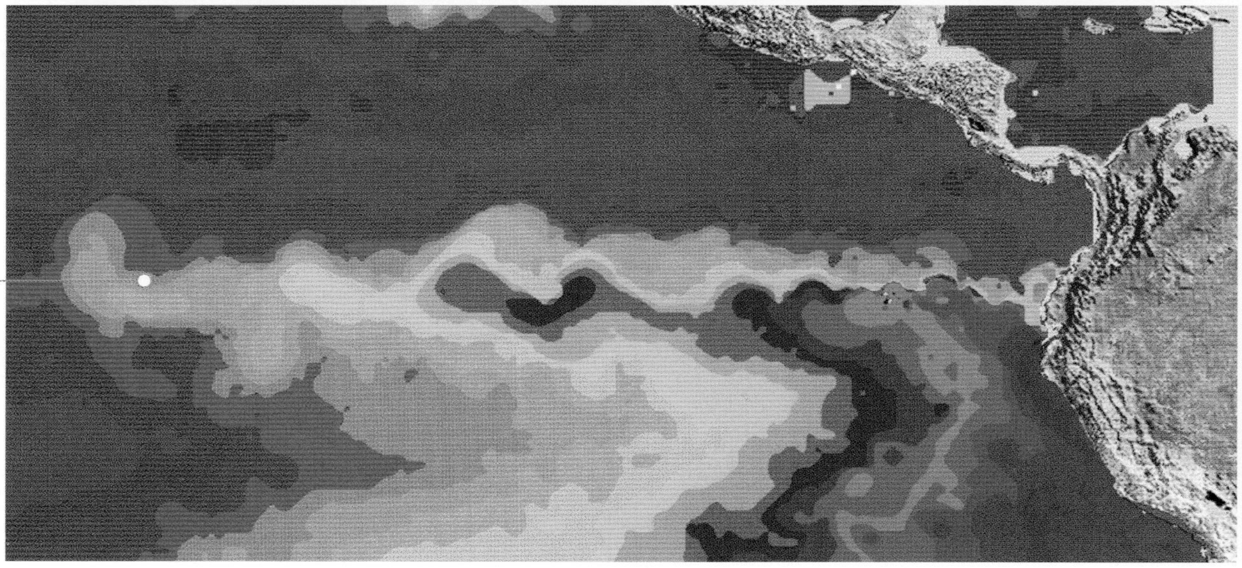

El Niño

The El Niño phenomenon appears in the Pacific around Christmas time at intervals of between four and 30 years. El Niño is Spanish for "the (Christ) Child."
It is the result of extreme pressure differences between the Australo-Asiatic low-pressure and the South Pacific high-pressure systems. These differences generate strong currents of warm water moving toward the west, which in turn produce cold reverse streams at lower depths along the path of the Humboldt current.
When the pressure differential changes, the warmed water begins to flow eastward again, heating the air above it. This leads to periods of heavy precipitation along the western coast of South America and corresponding droughts in large parts of Asia and Australia. One such El Niño year was registered in 1987. The phenomenon was particularly severe in 1997/98.
The thermal image of the Pacific shows masses of warm water (shades of yellow and red) approaching the South American coastline.

< 16.5 °C	21.0 – 21.5 °C	26.0 – 26.5 °C
16.5 – 17.0 °C	21.5 – 22.0 °C	26.5 – 27.0 °C
17.0 – 17.5 °C	22.0 – 22.5 °C	27.0 – 27.5 °C
17.5 – 18.0 °C	22.5 – 23.0 °C	27.5 – 28.0 °C
18.0 – 18.5 °C	23.0 – 23.5 °C	28.0 – 28.5 °C
18.5 – 19.0 °C	23.5 – 24.0 °C	28.5 – 29.0 °C
19.0 – 19.5 °C	24.0 – 24.5 °C	29.0 – 29.5 °C
19.5 – 20.0 °C	24.5 – 25.0 °C	29.5 – 30.0 °C
20.0 – 20.5 °C	25.0 – 25.5 °C	30.0 – 30.5 °C
20.5 – 21.0 °C	25.5 – 26.0 °C	> 30.5 °C

Landsat TM

30 m

705 km

Aug. 24, 1992

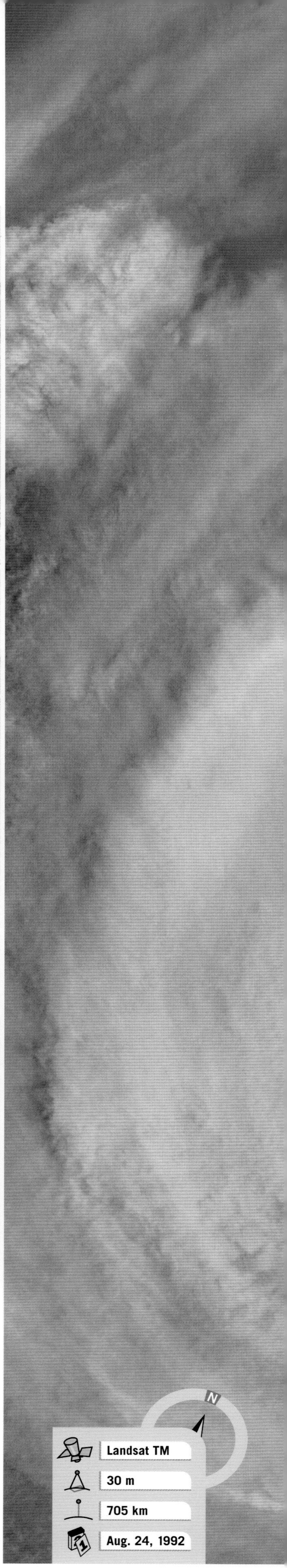

12
13

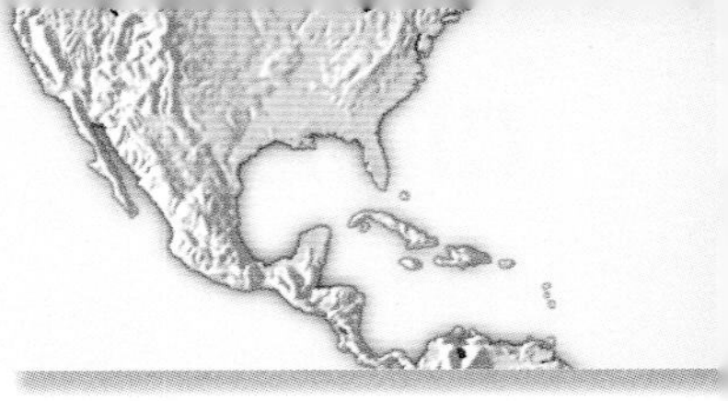

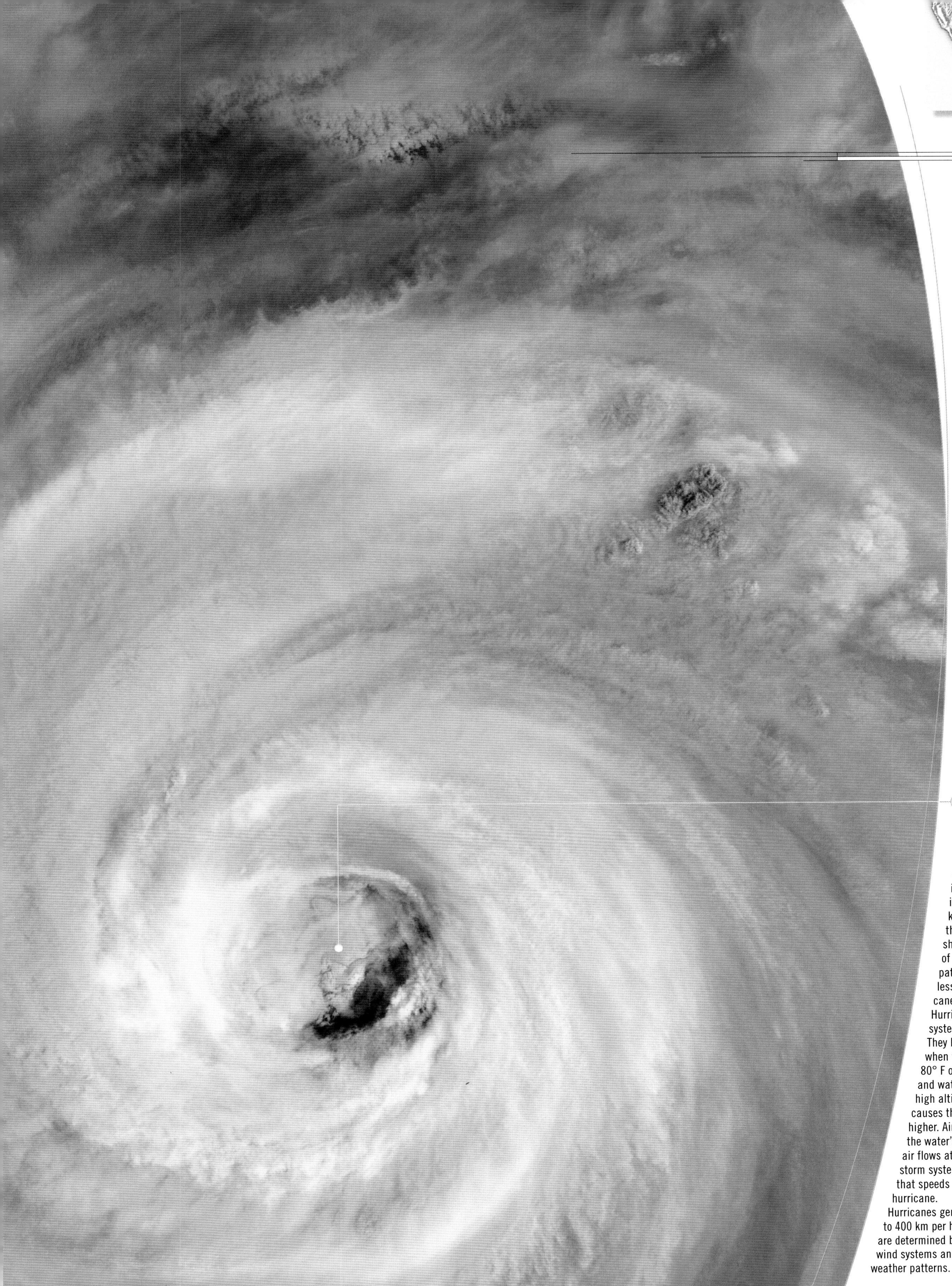

Hurricane Andrew

On August 24, 1992, Hurricane Andrew swept through the densely populated region of South Florida with peak wind speeds exceeding 270 km per hour, leaving a trail of devastation in its wake. Forty-seven people were killed, and some 350,000 lost their homes. The satellite image shows a vividly clear picture of the characteristic spiral cloud pattern and the virtually windless eye at the center of the hurricane.

Hurricanes are born as low-pressure systems formed by storm cells. They become particularly dangerous when water temperatures reach 80° F or above. Moist, warm air rises, and water vapor condenses at high altitudes, releasing heat, which causes the air column to rise even higher. Air pressure immediately above the water's surface falls, and moist air flows at an accelerated pace into the storm system — a vicious circle that speeds the development of the hurricane.

Hurricanes generate wind speeds of up to 400 km per hour. Their paths are determined by prevailing global wind systems and major regional weather patterns.

Climate   Changes in the Ozone Layer – The Ozone Hole

The large quantities of chlorofluorocarbons (CFC, used in spray dispensers and as coolants in refrigerators for example) released into the atmosphere every year produce chemical changes in the stratosphere which destroy the protective shell of the ozone layer encircling the Earth. The ozone layer absorbs some of the harmful ultra violet B radiation emitted by the Sun and helps regulate the heat budget of the atmosphere. Ozone depletion is most severe above the southern hemisphere during the months of September and October. NASA and the Ozone Research Program of the European Union have been observing changes in the ozone layer for many years. Seasonal fluctuations are illustrated in the series of images below, which show that ozone concentrations can fall to half their normal levels in certain years.

Higher atmospheric temperatures above the Arctic (as compared to the south polar region) reduce the danger of ozone depletion, although the sequence of images shows an increase here as well. The ozone veil above the Arctic is not as thin as that in the Antarctic stratosphere. However, chemical analysis has shown that the composition of the atmosphere above the north polar regions has suffered nearly the same degree of disturbance as that above the Antarctic.

Many of the consequences of atmospheric ozone depletion for mankind are well known. The increased intensity of UV radiation causes a higher incidence of sunburn and skin cancer and a general impairment of the human immune system. High UV radiation levels also have a lasting impact on plant life.

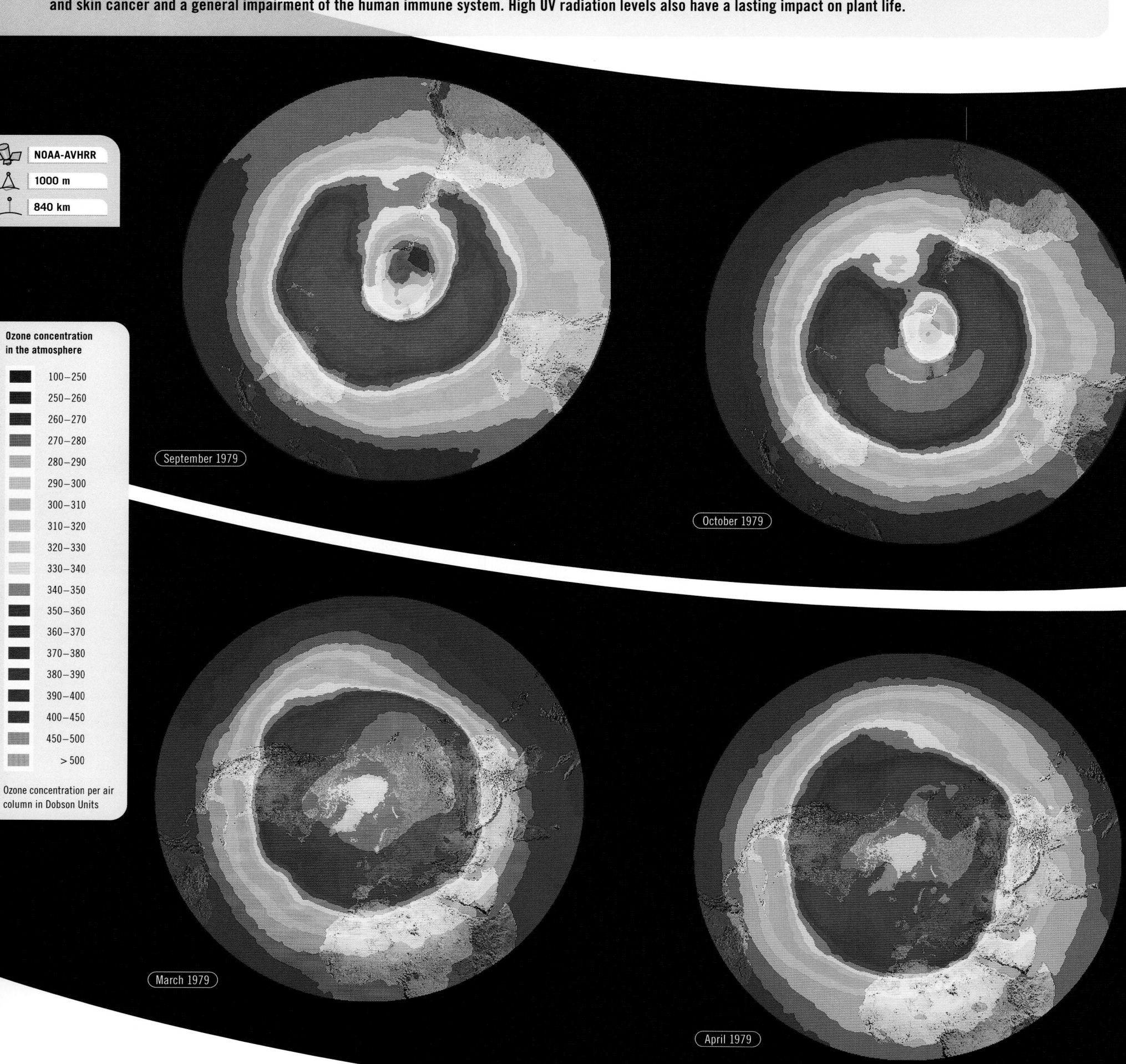

NOAA-AVHRR

1000 m

840 km

Ozone concentration in the atmosphere

	100–250
	250–260
	260–270
	270–280
	280–290
	290–300
	300–310
	310–320
	320–330
	330–340
	340–350
	350–360
	360–370
	370–380
	380–390
	390–400
	400–450
	450–500
	> 500

Ozone concentration per air column in Dobson Units

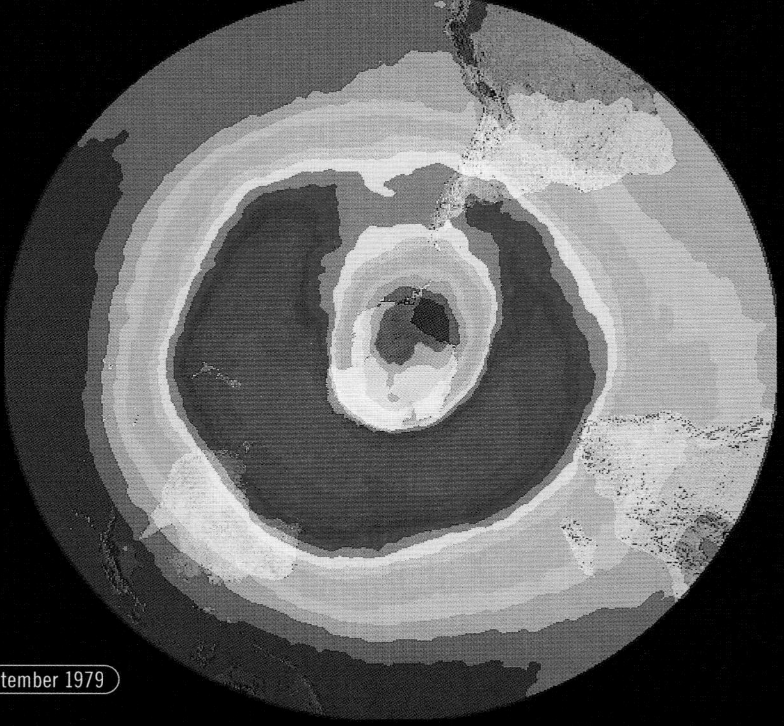

September 1979

October 1979

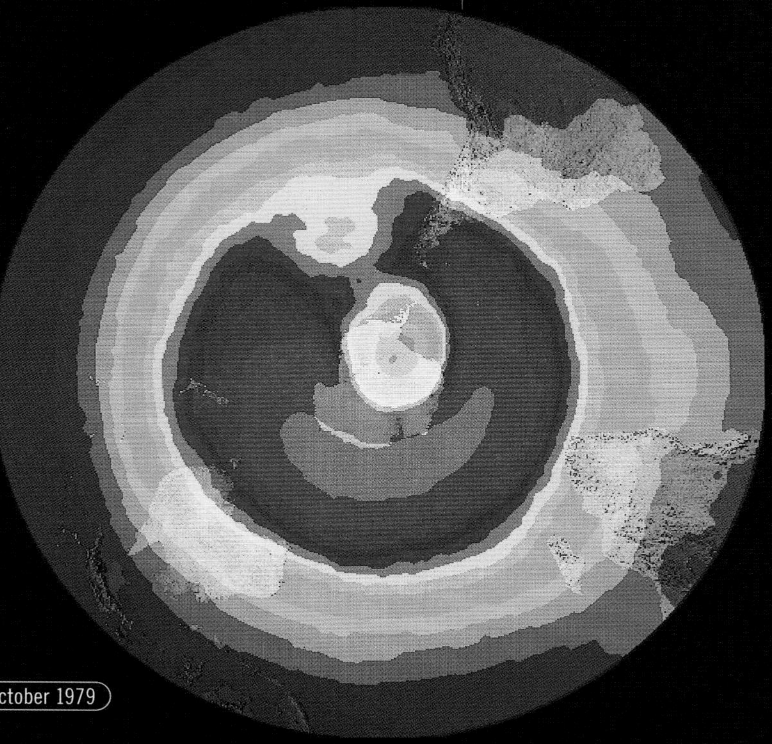

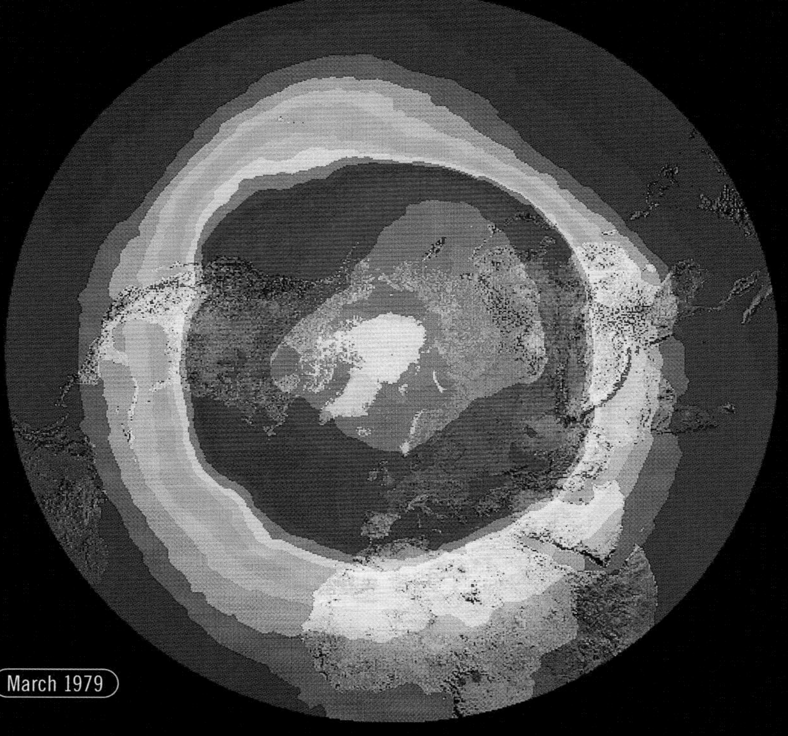

March 1979

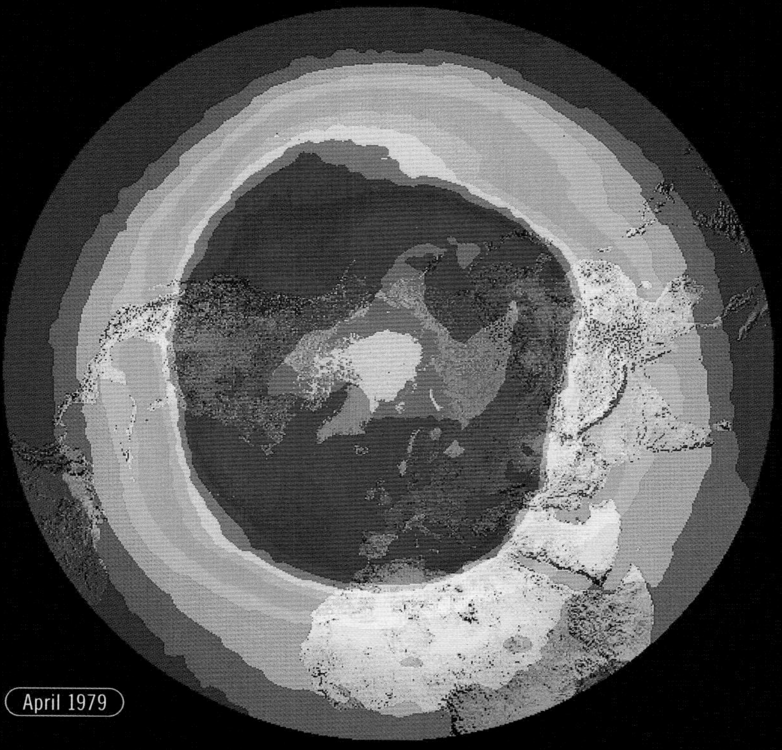

April 1979

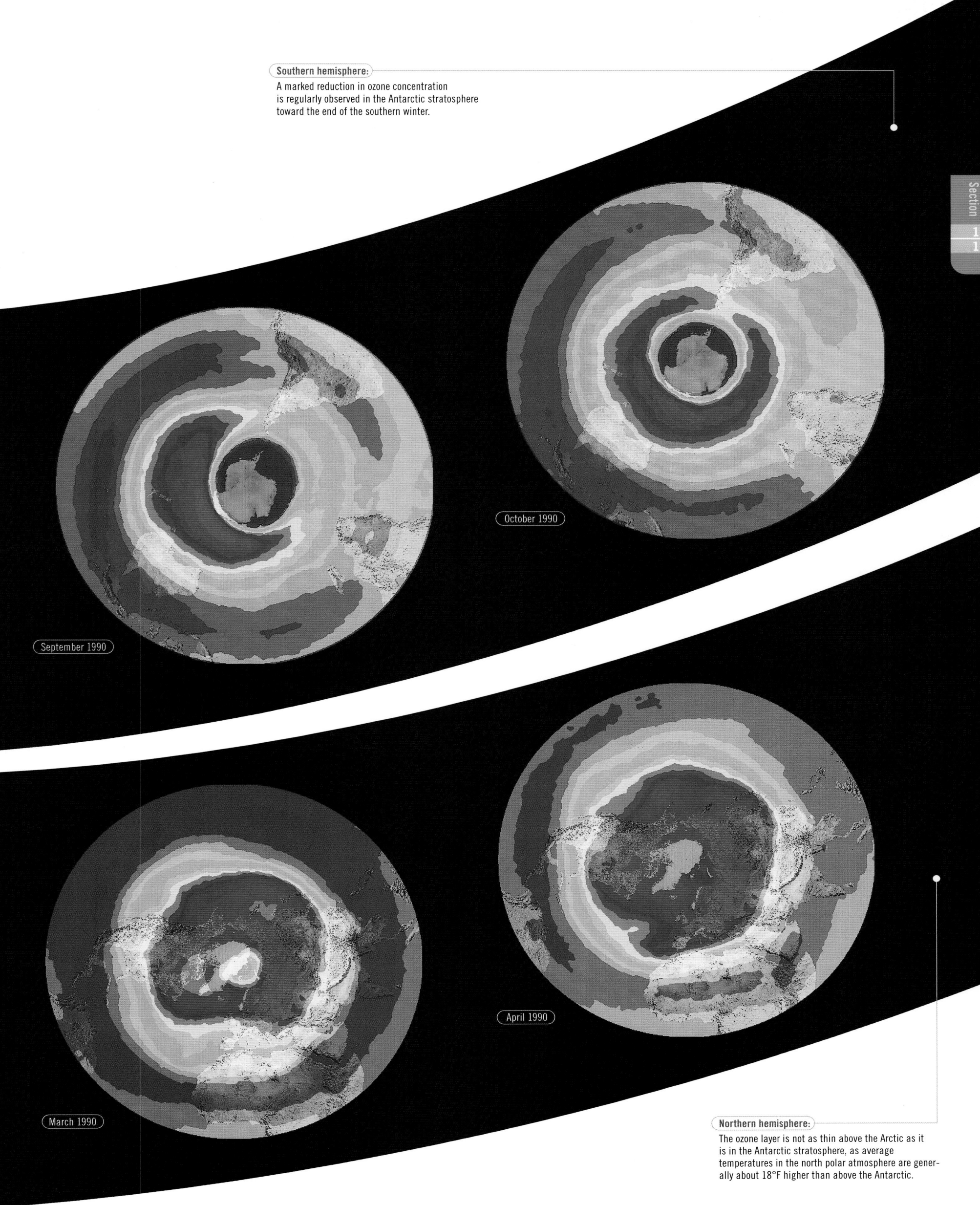

Southern hemisphere:

A marked reduction in ozone concentration is regularly observed in the Antarctic stratosphere toward the end of the southern winter.

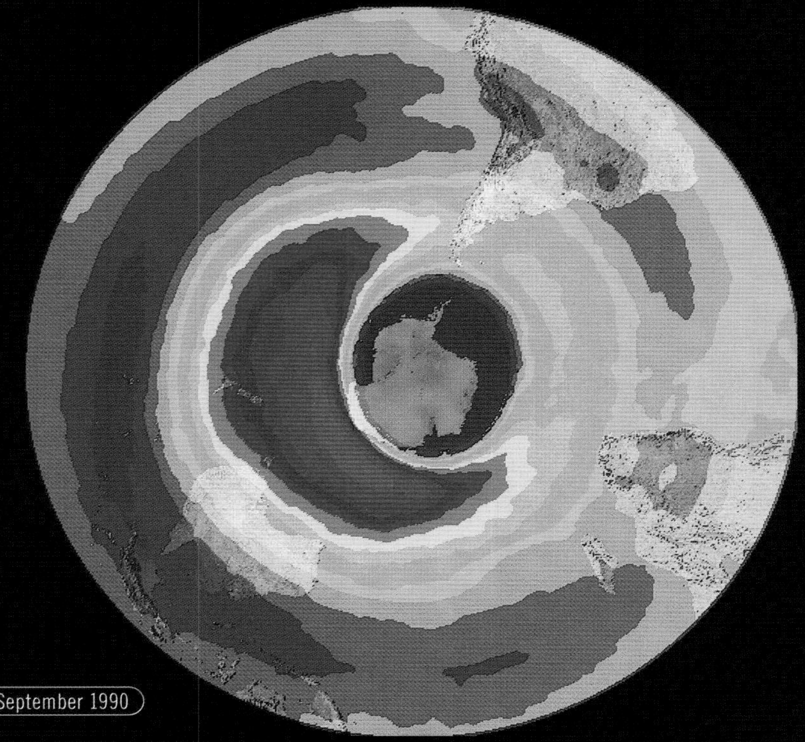

October 1990

September 1990

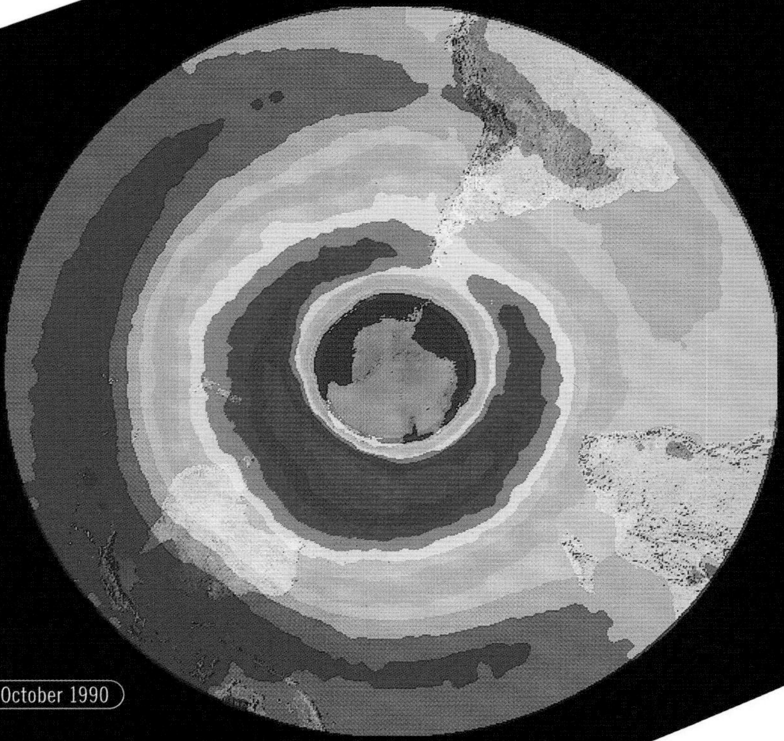

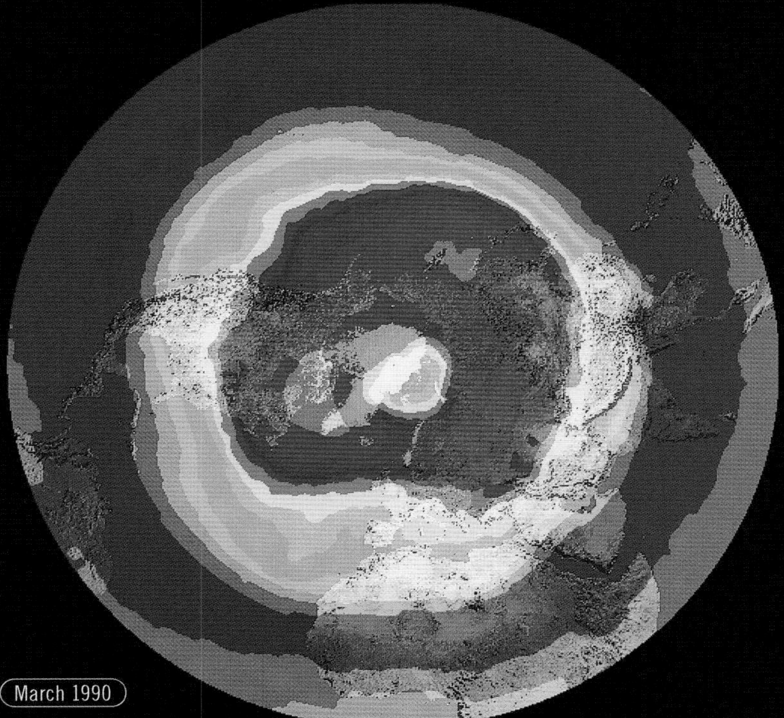

March 1990

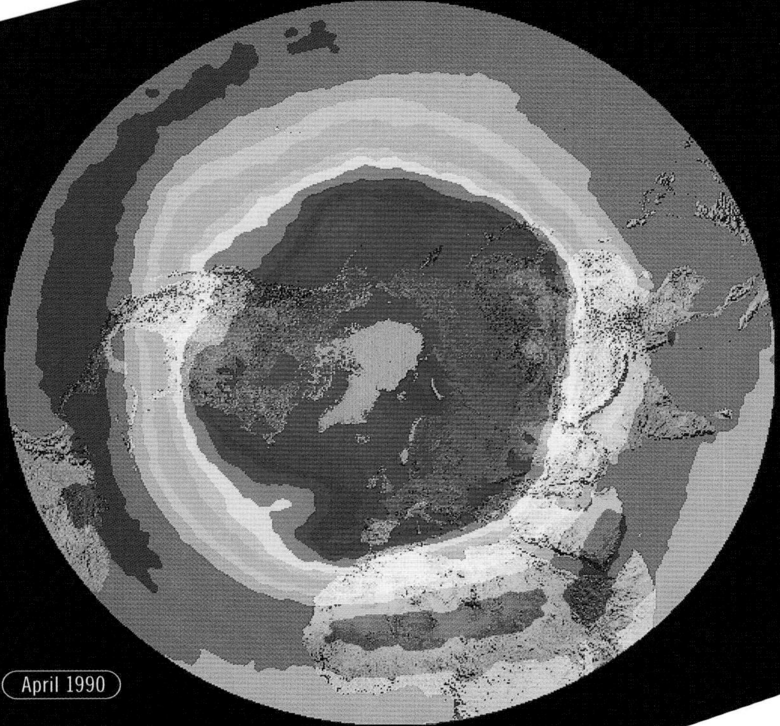

April 1990

Northern hemisphere:

The ozone layer is not as thin above the Arctic as it is in the Antarctic stratosphere, as average temperatures in the north polar atmosphere are generally about 18°F higher than above the Antarctic.

Bodies of Water

Rivers — Blood Vessels of a Country

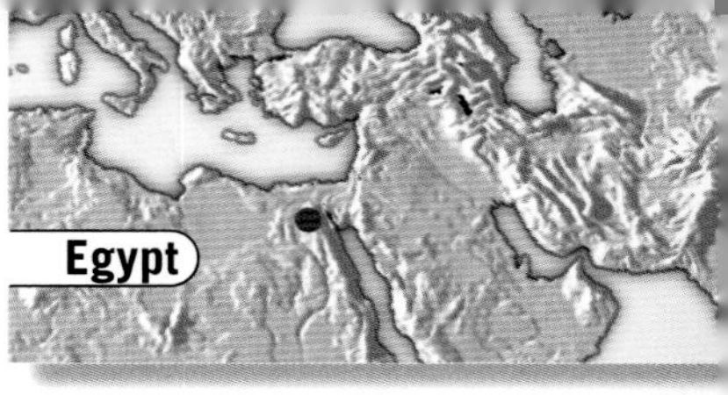

The Nile Near Cairo

The ancient Egyptian city of Cairo emerged where the Nile
Valley expands to form the Nile Delta.

With an estimated population of ten million, Cairo is the
largest city in Africa and the Arabian region. Surrounded by
Egypt's most important agricultural landscape, the city
has spread eastward into the desert at an increasingly rapid
pace over the past several decades. The nine districts of
the city are clearly delineated by their rectangular pattern of
streets. The famous pyramids of Giza are located west of
the Nile and connected to the ancient old city of Cairo by a
broad band of residential settlements.

The contrast between the uninhabited desert and the Nile Valley
could hardly be more dramatic. Measuring 6,671 km from
source to mouth, the world's second longest river flows without
tributaries in a flat-bottomed groove up to 20 km wide on
the last 2,700 km of its course between the Arabian and Nubian
deserts. Once it reaches the vast delta (24,000 sq. km),
the river forks into two branches, the Rosetta and the Damietta,
which empty into the Mediterranean Sea.

Both the Nile Valley and the Nile Delta are dotted with small
settlements positioned at regular intervals between "central"
towns. This Landsat image offers a striking picture of the
city at the point where the fertile flood plain of the river begins
to fan out into the delta.

Landsat TM

30 m

705 km

April 29, 1984

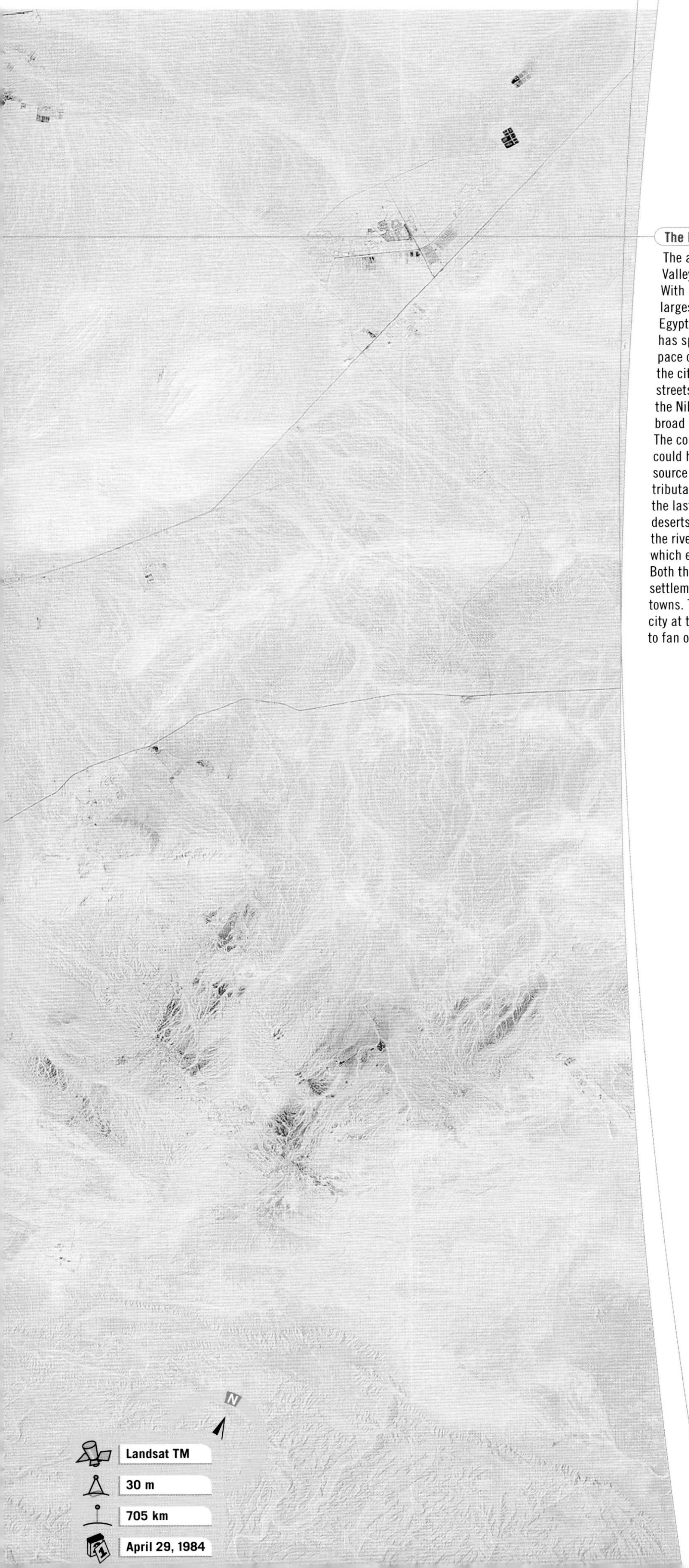

Bodies of Water

Rivers – Blood Vessels of a Country

Landsat ETM

15 m

705 km

Nov. 3, 1999

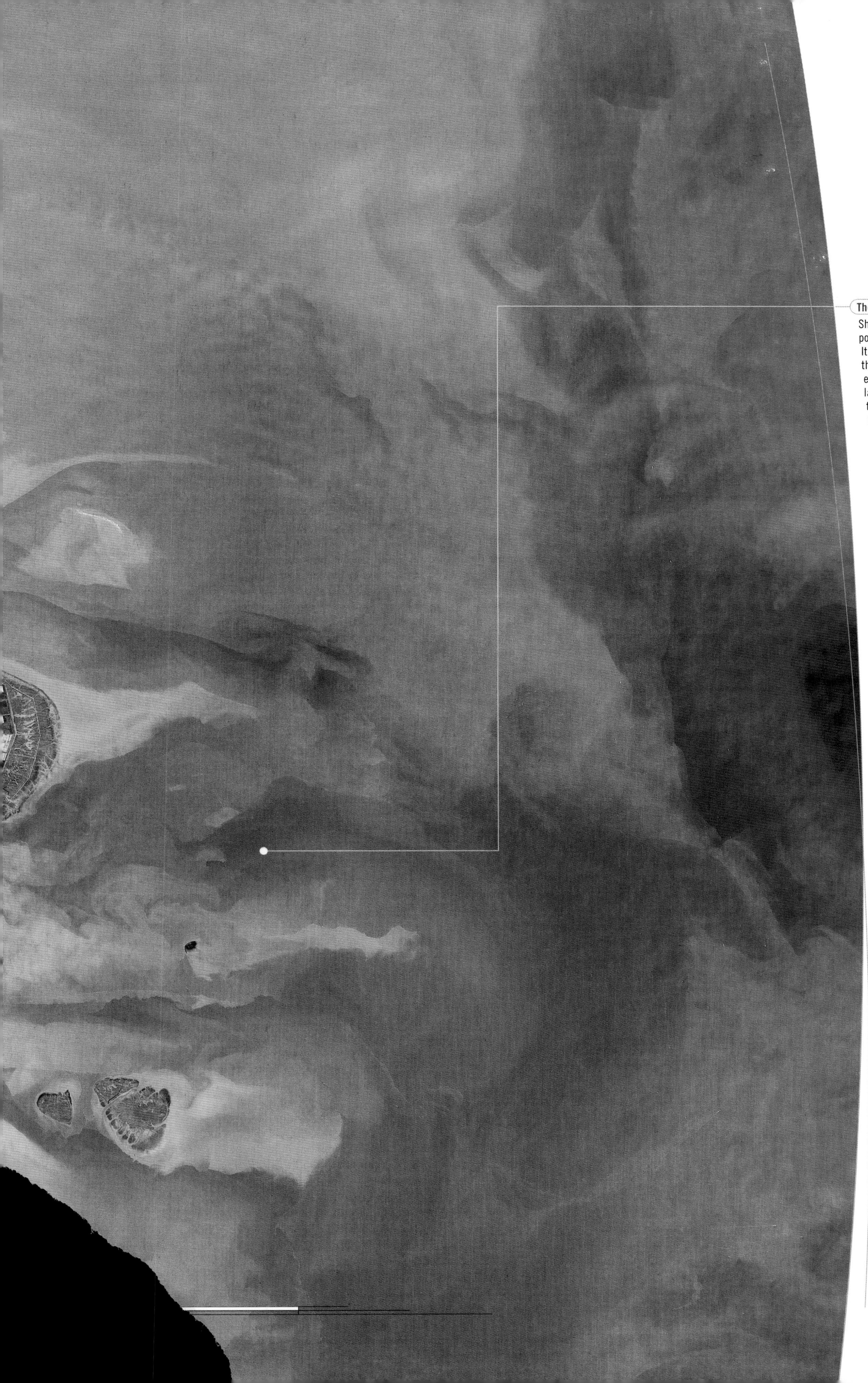

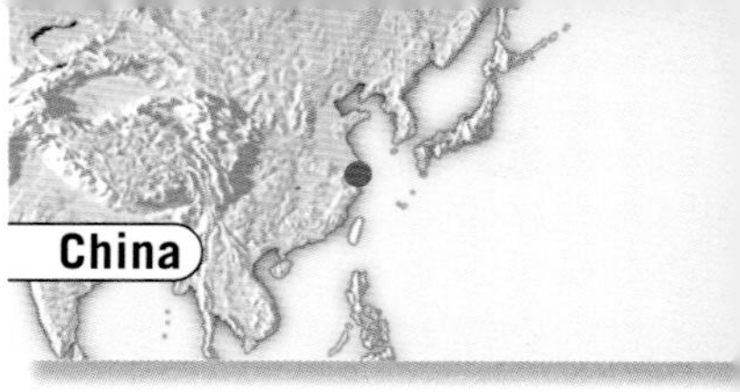

The Mouth of the Yangtze (Chang)

Shanghai is China's most important port and its largest metropolis. It radiates from the confluence of the Huang River and the Yangtze east of Tai Lake. At the turn of the last century, the city was home to some 12 million people, and nearly 20 million people live in greater metropolitan Shanghai. The opening of China to international trade has spurred rapid growth in the city in recent years, to which an expansive system of urban freeways and a number of new high-rise complexes bear witness. The amount of developed land nearly doubled between 1980 and 2000. In the process, the belt of vegetation that once encircled the city (visible in places as spots of light-green coloration in the satellite image) was obliterated. Development has been especially intensive in the Pudong district on the right bank of the Huang, where large areas of the old city were demolished and replaced by new business and industrial centers.

Bodies of Water

Shrinking of Seas

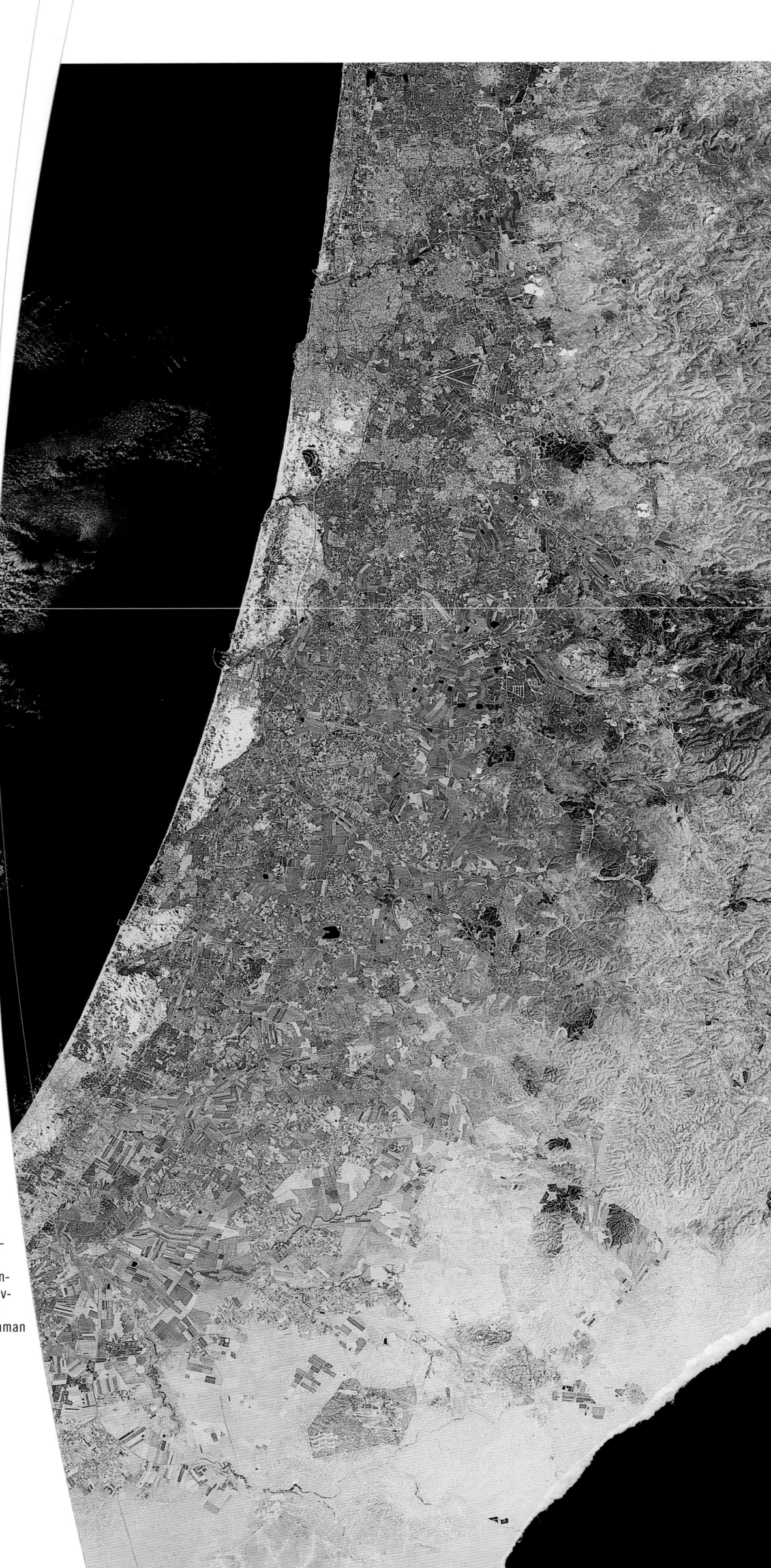

The Dead Sea

The surface of the Dead Sea, known as Yam Ha-Melah (Salt Lake) in Hebrew, lies an average of 396 m below the level of the Mediterranean, making it the lowest-lying inland sea in the world. It is 80 km long, 18 km wide, up to 794 m deep, and covers an area of 940 sq. km. As recently as the early 1970s, the Dead Sea still consisted of two bodies of water connected by a narrow channel at the tip of the Lisan Peninsula. Increasing use of water from the sea for irrigation of fields along its tributaries, coupled with industrial potassium-mining operations in the southern basin, led to higher levels of solid salt deposits and eventually divided the sea into two separate bodies of water. The sea is fed by numerous underground springs which introduce valuable minerals and trace elements, including calcium, magnesium, silicic acid, potassium, iron, bromides, and iodine. With a salinity level of 25%, the Dead Sea is totally devoid of plant and animal life. Due to the warm climate, between two and 25 mm of water surface evaporate every day, keeping salt content high despite the influx of fresh water. Potassium, bromides, and magnesium salts are collected in the evaporation basins. The industrial facilities are clearly identified by the walls of the evaporation basins.

Located in the western part of the Jordan Rift Valley are the Judaean Heights (maximum elevation 1,014 m), a region of intensive cultivation and irrigation that slopes steeply toward the Mediterranean. The capital of Israel, Jerusalem, lies at the same latitude as the northernmost shore of the Dead Sea. The Tel Aviv-Yafo metropolitan area is visible along the coast. The Jordanian capital of Amman is located northwest of the Dead Sea along the edge of the steppe.

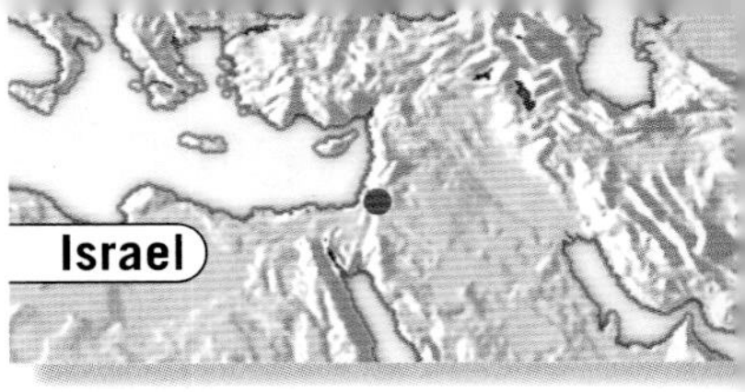

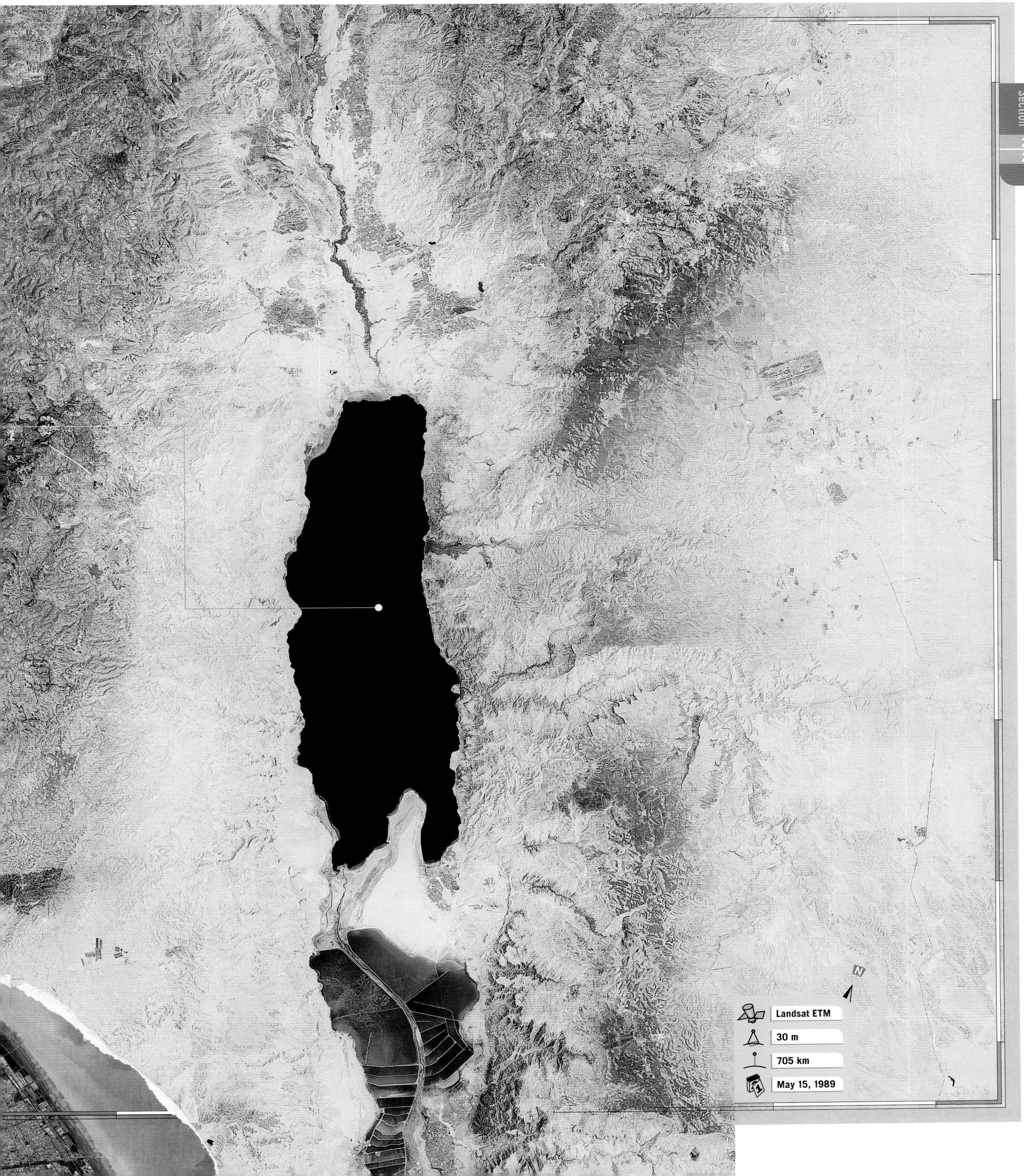

N

Landsat ETM

30 m

705 km

May 15, 1989

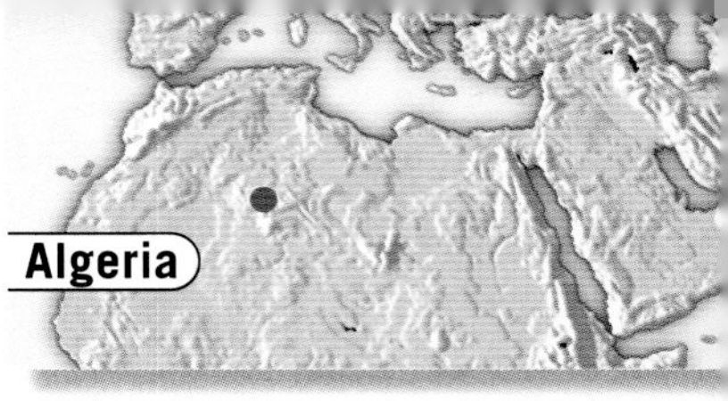

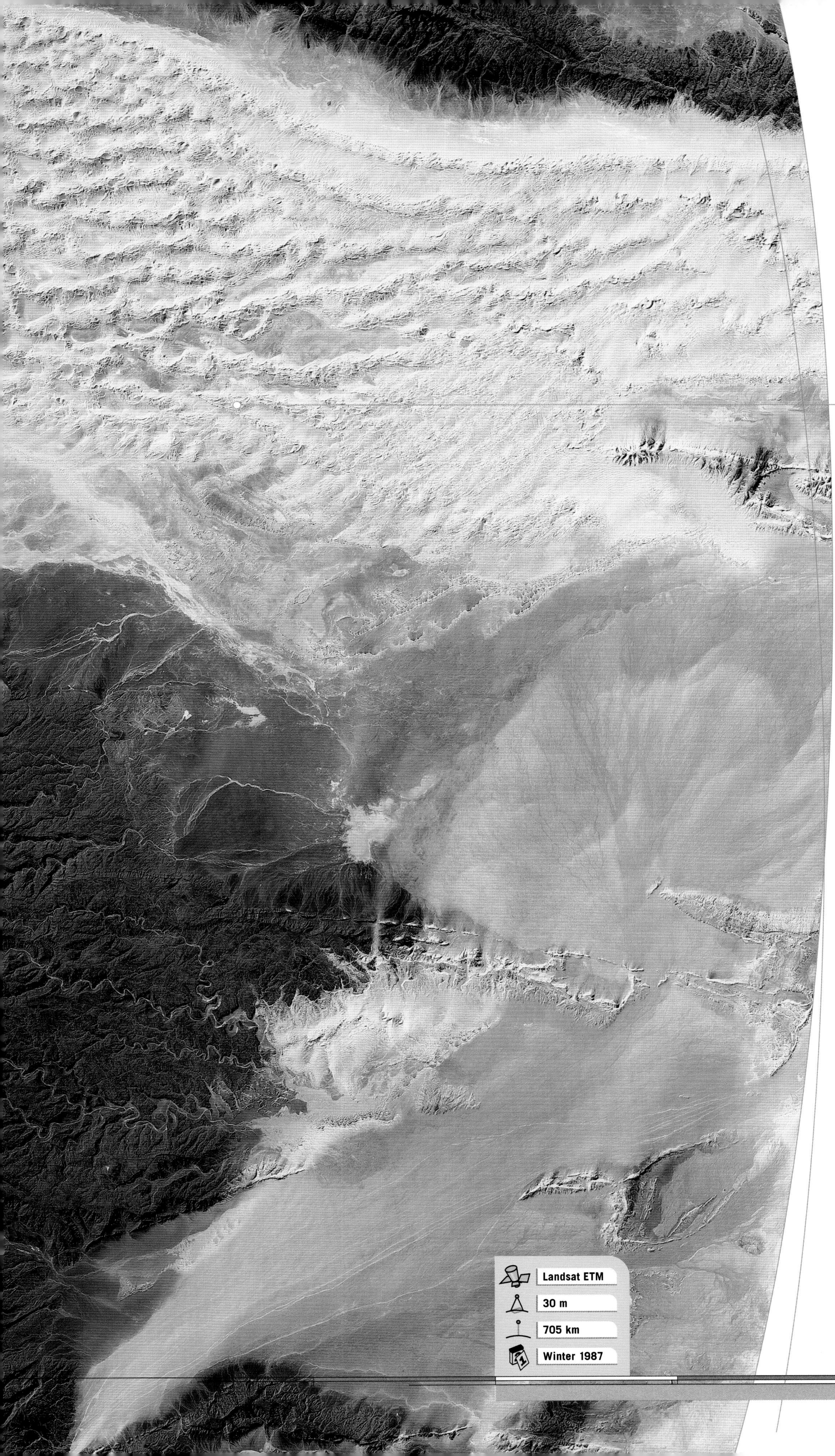

The Sahara near Amguid in Algeria

The Sahara presents a very different face in many places. Landscapes can be distinguished on the
basis of differences in surface
material – exposed rock, gravel,
sand, or salt clay. A large portion
of the image is occupied by
the debris-covered surfaces of the
Hamada de Tinrhert (light gray and
reddish brown areas). This bolder-
strewn desert is known
as Serir in Algeria. The second type
of desert in the Sahara is characterized by sand sheets and dunes.
A prominent feature of the landscape in this satellite image is the
tongue of sand in the upper portion of the picture, with its regular
pattern of star-shaped figures.
Salt clay plains (bluish-turquoise
coloration) are found in the
broad depressions where the wadis
– dry valleys through which water
flows only after heavy rains – grow
wider. The dark brown areas are
the northern fingers of the Tassili-
n-Ajjer range, with peaks as high
as 1,800 m.

	Landsat ETM
	30 m
	705 km
	Winter 1987

Coastal Formations

Fjords and Skerries

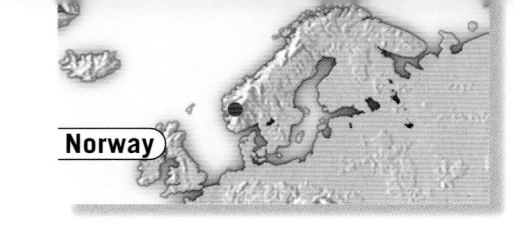

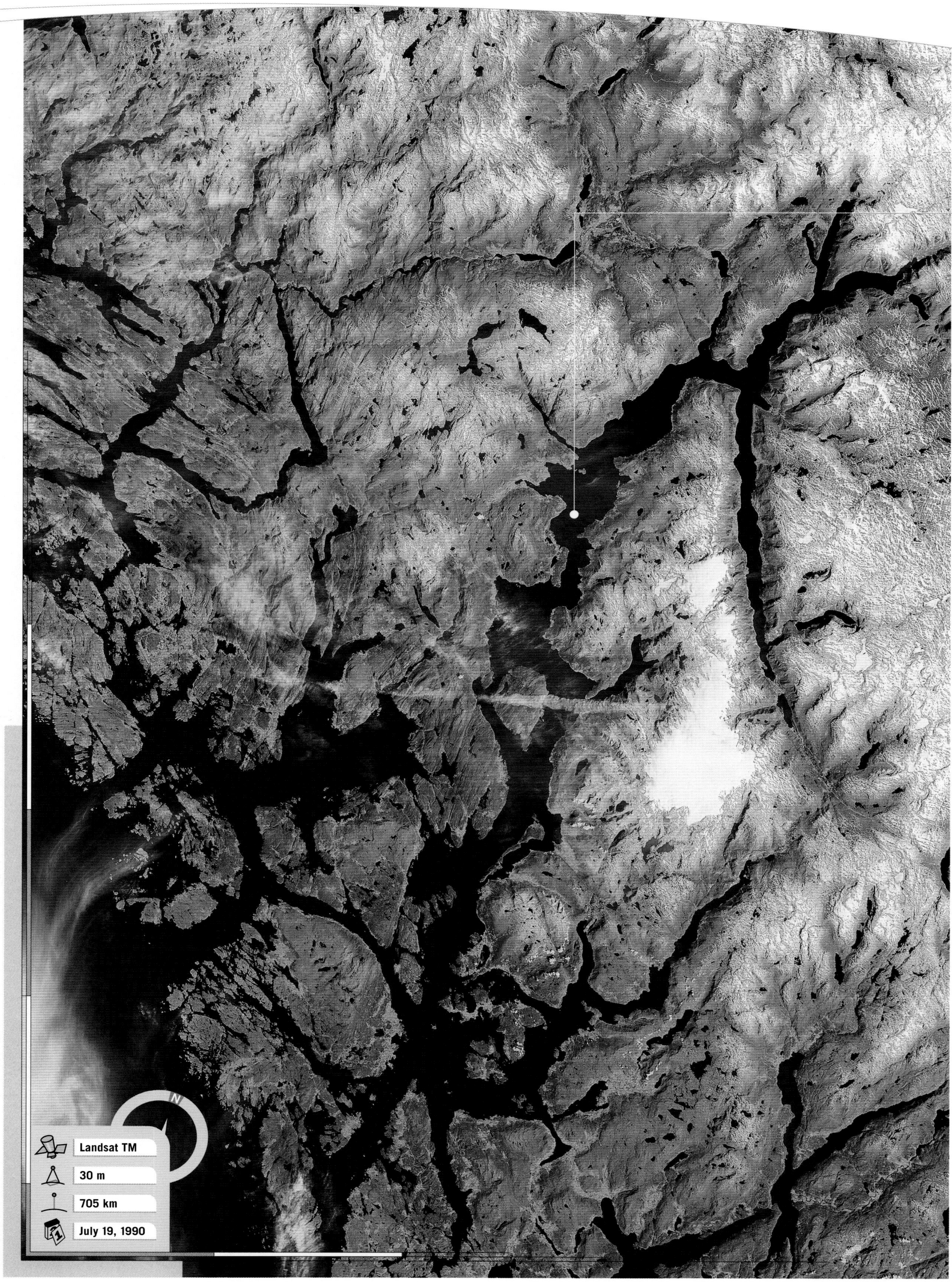

Hardangerfjorden

Framed by the Hardangerfjorden and the eastern Numedal, the snow-covered Hardangervidda in southern Norway reaches elevations of between 1,200 and 1,400 m. Covering an area of 7,500 sq. km, it is 30 times the size of the Bavarian Forest in Germany. The intricate branching network of the Hardangerfjorden extends far into the hinterland of southwestern Norway. One of the best-known fjords in the world, the Hardangerfjorden was formed during the last ice age. Huge glaciers thrust far out into the sea, pushing large volumes of debris ahead of them. When the glaciers melted, they left behind a U-shaped valley with maximum depths of more than 1,000 m, which was flooded by the sea. The debris carried by the glaciers filled the entrance to the fjord, making it relatively shallow and restricting the exchange of seawater and fresh water entering the fjord from the interior. Favored by the mild climate, large plantations of apple and cherry orchards line the shores of the Hardangerfjorden.

Landsat TM

30 m

705 km

July 19, 1990

Coastal Formations

The Largest Reef on Earth

Landsat TM	
30 m	
705 km	
July 13, 2000	

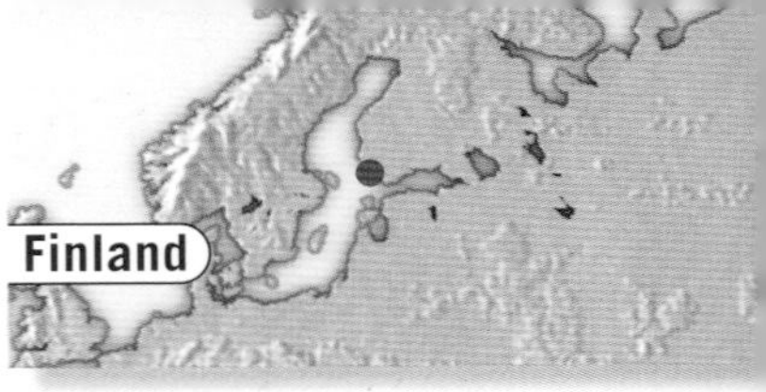

Skerry Landscape

The Åland Islands are located in the
Gulf of Bothnia between Turku
and Stockholm. The satellite image
highlights the typical features of
a skerry coast, a glacially formed
landscape of domed islets flooded by
the sea. Some of the numerous
small islands between the Åland
group and Turku are inhabited.
For generations, people have lived in
virtual isolation in the skerries.
There are very few roads, and water
routes are the most important
links to other islands and the mainland. Fishing has been the most
important source of income for centuries, although the skerry population also relies on farming, animal
husbandry, and forestry. Environmental tourism is one of the most
important sources of revenue
today.

Landsat TM	
30 m	
705 km	
May 28, 1988	

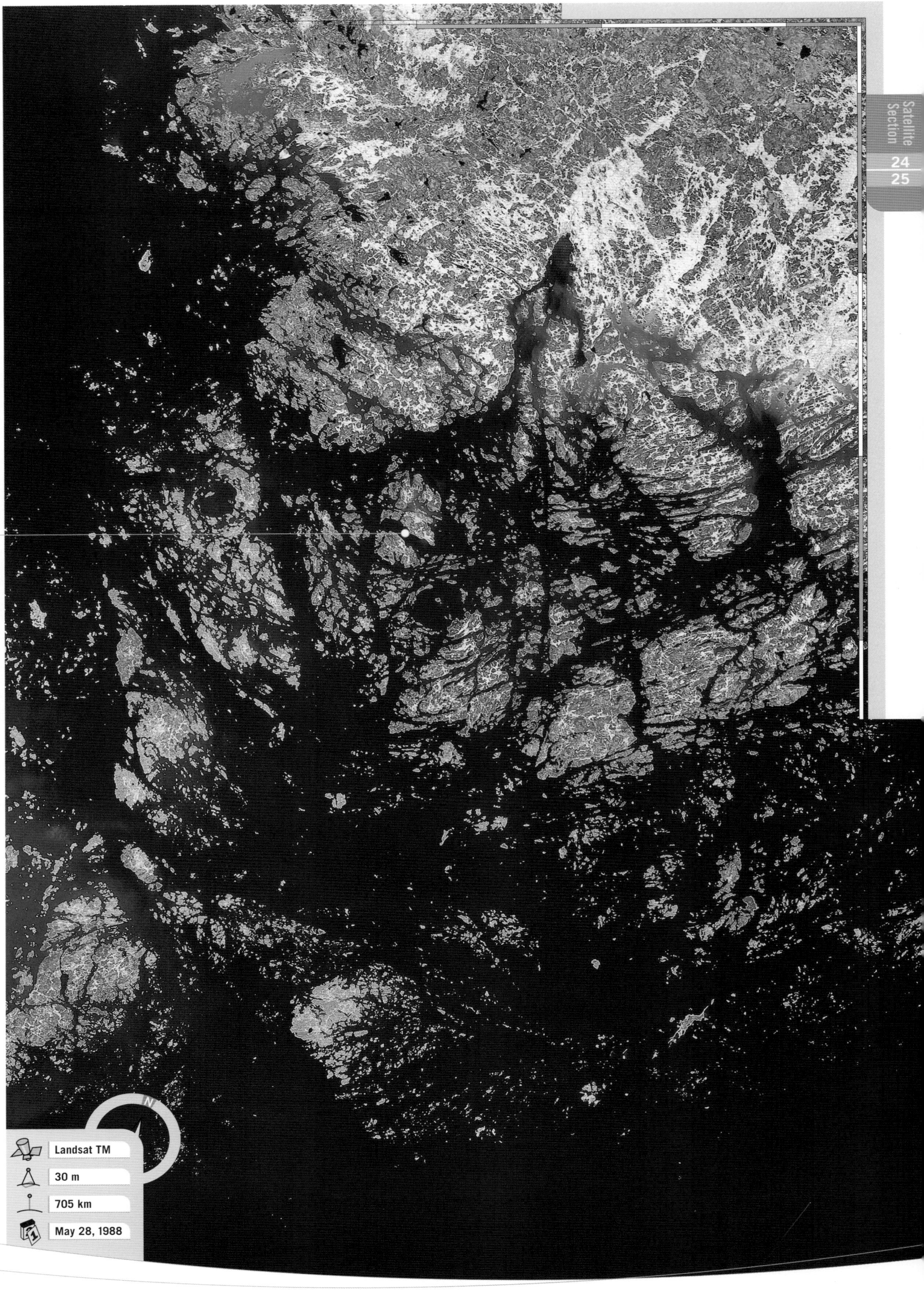

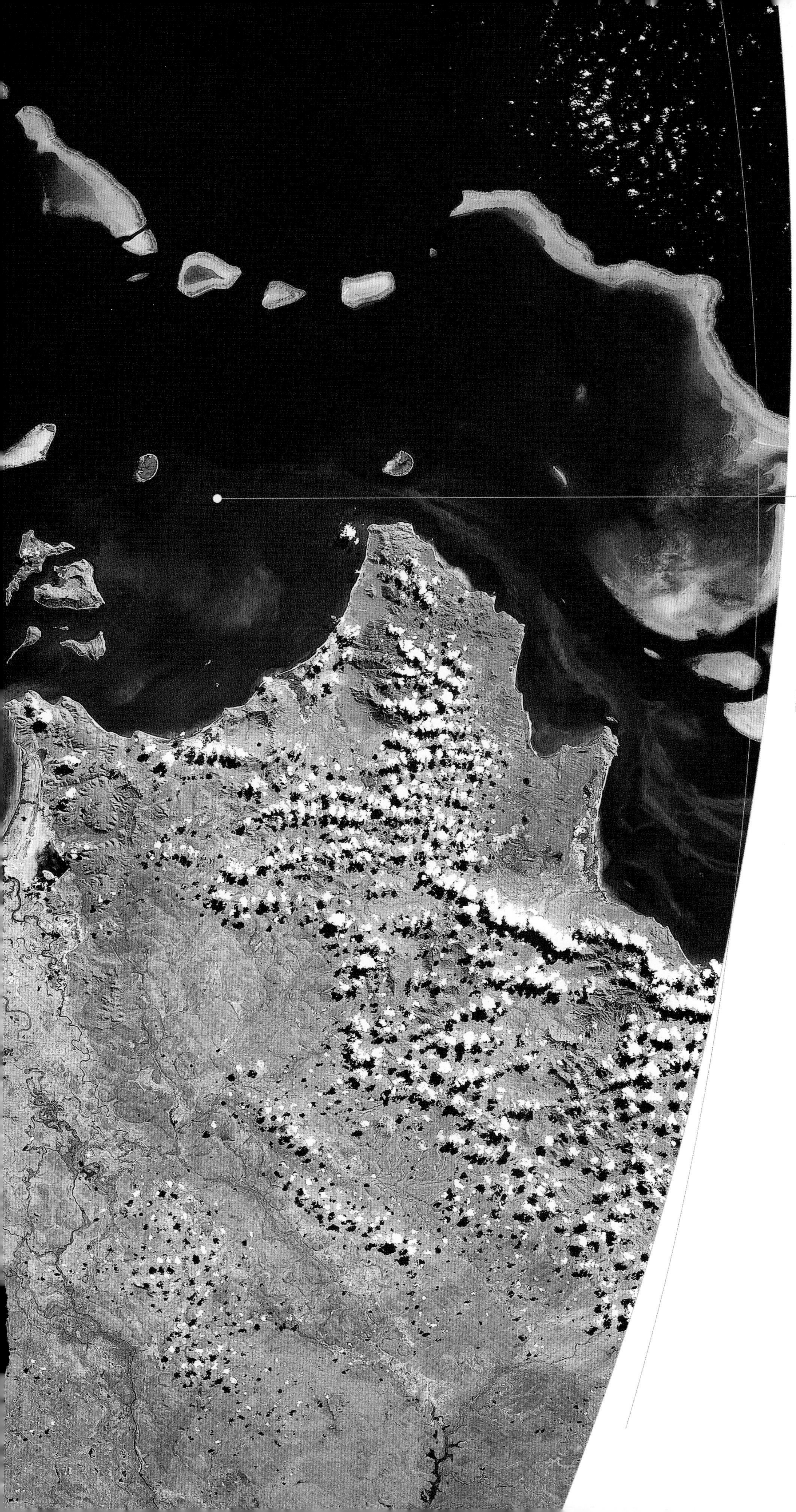

The Great Barrier Reef

The world's largest coral reef runs parallel to the coast
of Australia off the shores of Queensland. This
satellite image shows Princess Charlotte Bay on the
southern coast of the Cape York Peninsula.

The chain of elongated, oval or circular coral reefs
is discernable only from the air. Covered only by shallow
waters, they appear as turquoise and light blue
areas that stand out clearly against the deep blue of
the open sea.

The view from the air tells us something else as well. The
Great Barrier Reef is not a continuous, linear reef system
but instead comprises a large number of individual
reefs of different sizes distributed in a picturesque pattern
in the lagoon.

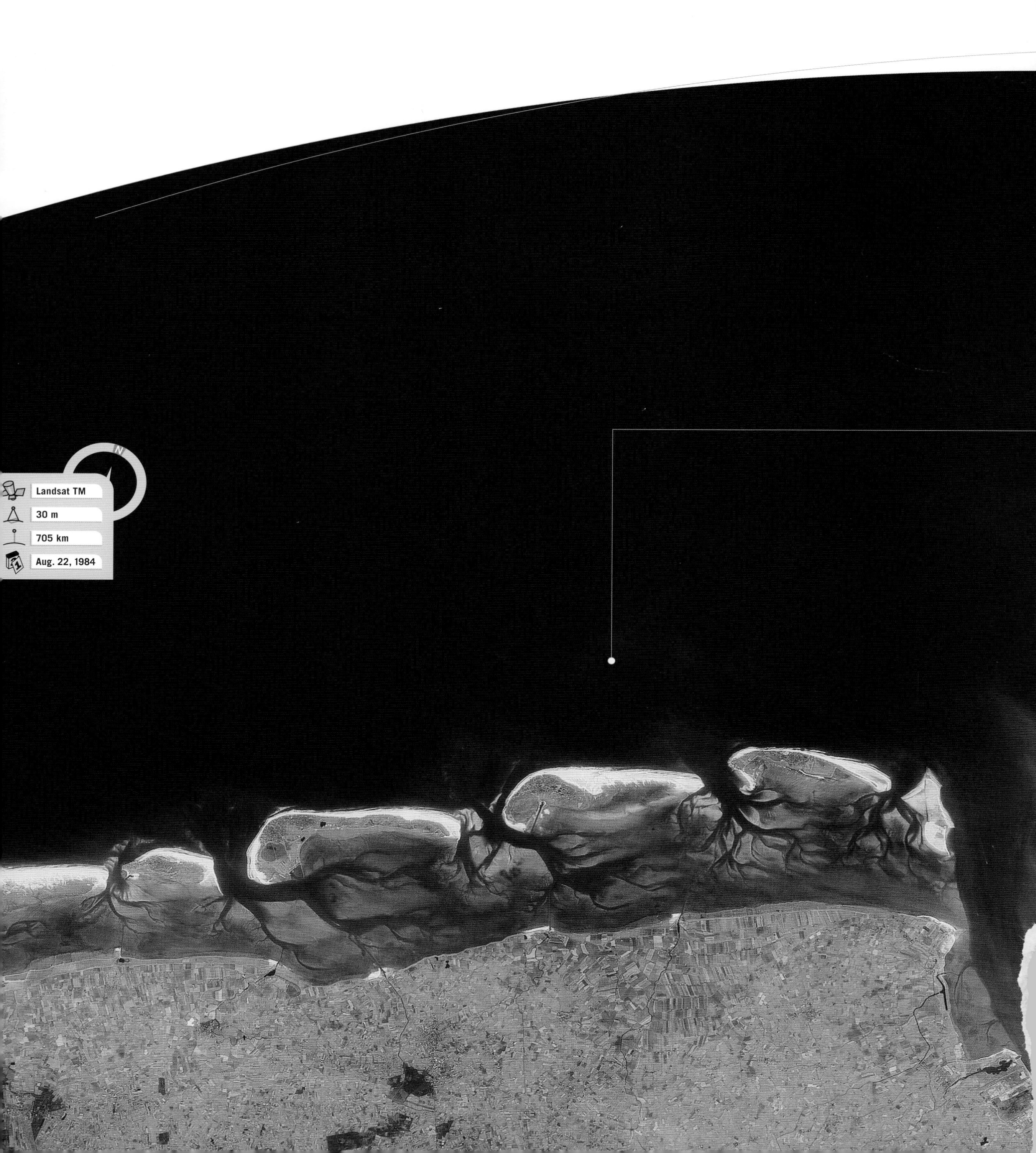

Landsat TM

30 m

705 km

Aug. 22, 1984

East Frisian Islands

The East Frisian Islands are massive dune islands built on foundations of sand. The different stages in their development are evident in this satellite image. Broad, light-colored beaches line the northern and eastern shores of the islands (rudimentary spits can be seen on the eastern side of the island of Juist). Behind them are rows of dunes – younger formations nearer the shore, older, more heavily vegetated ones farther inland. Situated inside the protective dune walls are marshlands used for grazing. Frequently flooded salt meadows lie between the beaches and the tidal flats.

The pattern of channels and flats exposed at low tide is clearly visible in this satellite image. Rising and falling by as much as 3 meters, the tides have cut gateways to depths of up to 20 meters between the islands. The tides are also responsible for the formation of arc and sickle ripples. A reddish tinge identifies the ecologically significant areas of salt meadow and tidal mud flats. The area known as the "Niedersächsisches Wattenmeer" was declared a National Park in 1986 in order to preserve this sensitive biosphere.

Hamburg

The satellite image shows the Elbe River as a complex network of waterways that wind through the city of Hamburg. Clearly visible are the extensive, branching docklands of Hamburg Harbor, one of Europe's largest and commercially most significant seaports.

The harbor and its facilities account for about 10% of the total area of Hamburg. The characteristic finger-shaped configuration of the tidal harbor results from the dredging of artificial harbor basins to allow ships to dock directly in front of the city's warehouses. Germany's largest international harbor has always been a gateway for movement of goods to and from Europe. Once primarily a transfer point for bulk and piece goods, Hamburg Harbor has since developed into a major logistics center.

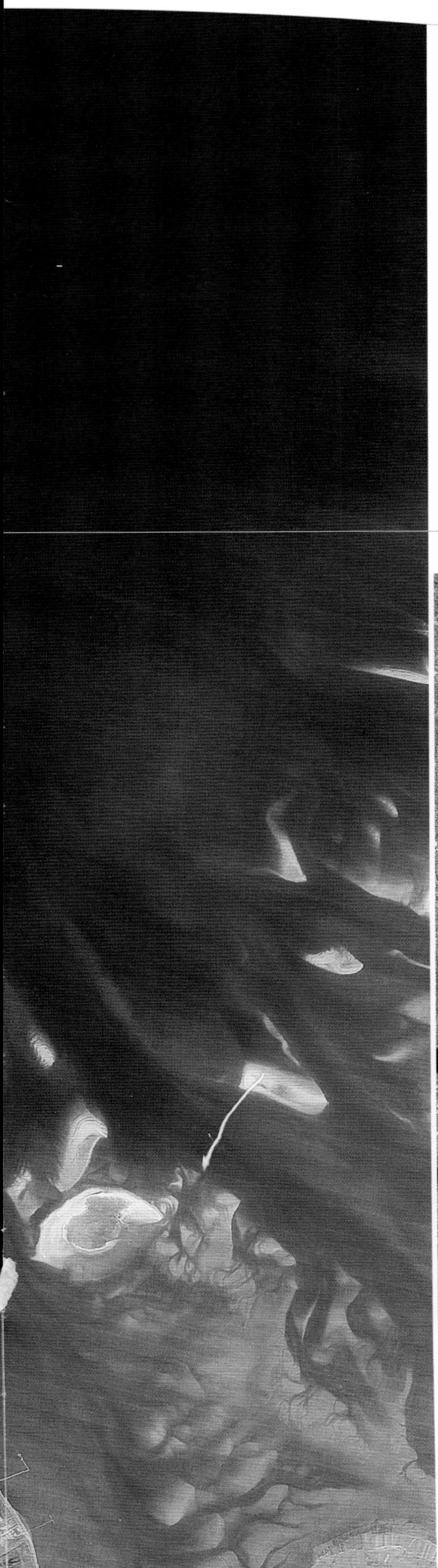

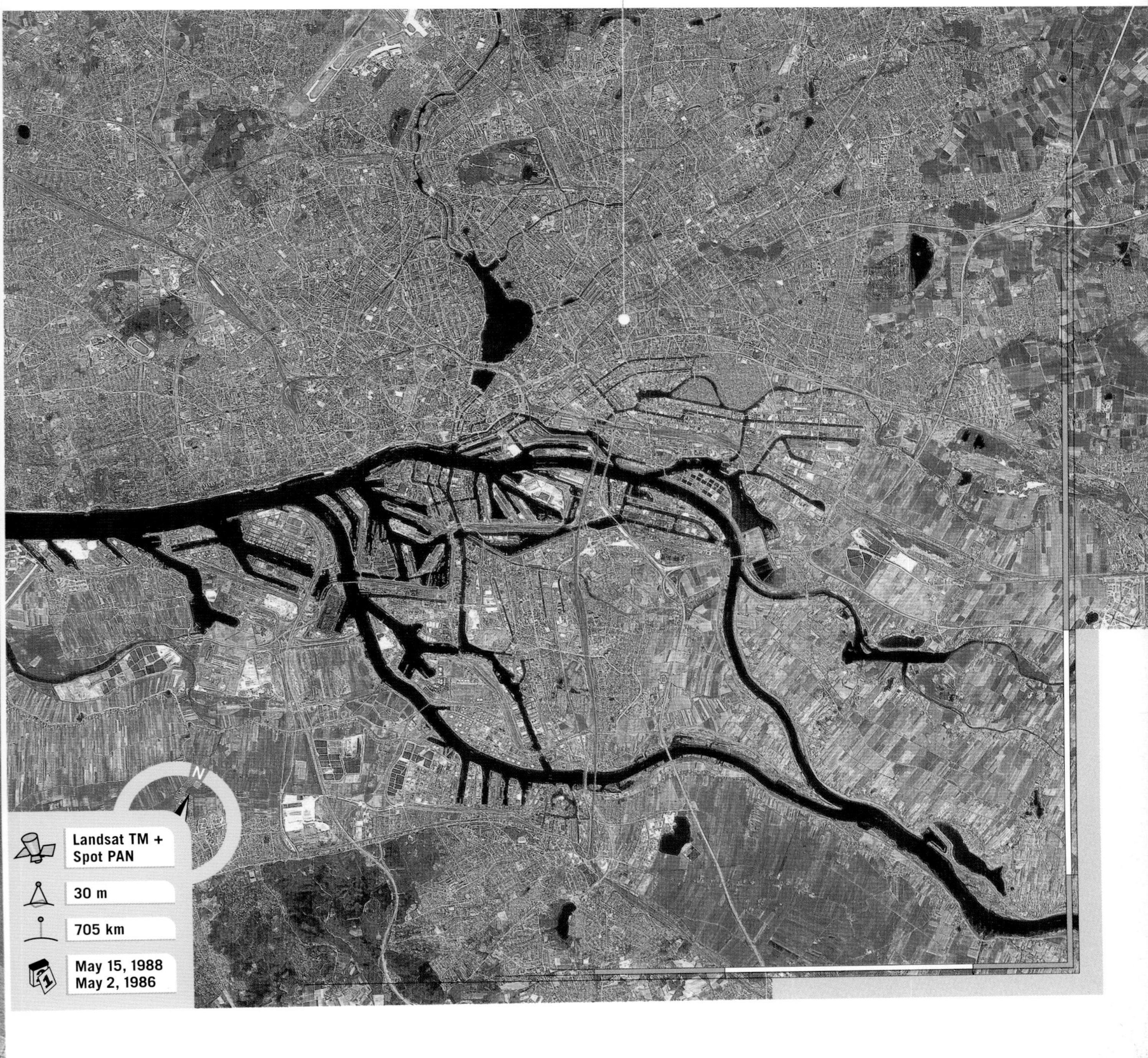

Landsat TM +
Spot PAN

30 m

705 km

May 15, 1988
May 2, 1986

Continental Divides

Natural Boundaries

Gibraltar

Roughly 60 km long, the Strait of Gibraltar narrows from west to east,
separating Spain and Morocco by only 15 km at its narrowest point.
Over the course of history, it has served as both a link between the continents
of Europe and Africa and a gateway between the New and Old Worlds.
Its strategic importance has made the Strait of Gibraltar a source of ceaseless political strife.

Landsat TM

30 m

705 km

Aug. 10, 1998

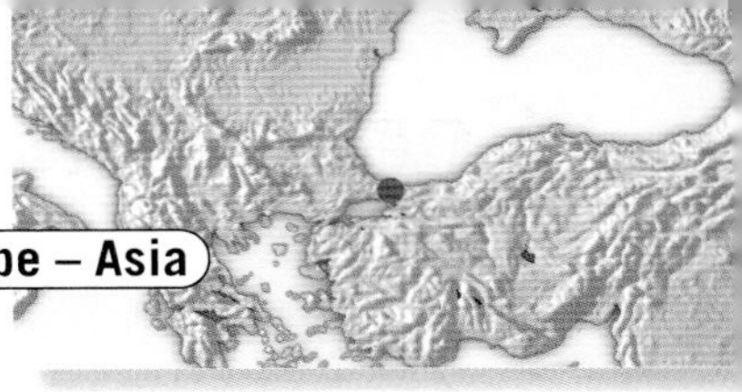

Bosporus

Measuring 31 km in length and between 660 and 3,000 m in width, the Bosporus, a narrow strait between Europe and Asia, connects the Black Sea with the Sea of Marmara. It is a flooded river valley that sank during the Würm (Wisconsin) glacial stage and eventually formed a strait linking the two seas.

The city of Istanbul sits astride the Bosporus. Like every metropolis, it is a mosaic of many different districts, each with its own distinctive character. The city center itself is divided into three parts, for which water is both a barrier and a connecting link: the Golden Horn, an arm of the sea that separates the old, formerly Greek-Byzantine Istanbul from the modern Beyoglu, and the Bosporus, which separates the European and Asian parts of the city. Although Turkey's capital was moved to Ankara in 1923, Istanbul remains the country's most important commercial and cultural center.

Suspension bridges built in 1973 and 1988 connect the European and Asian halves of the city.

Landsat ETM

15 m

705 km

Oct. 4, 1999

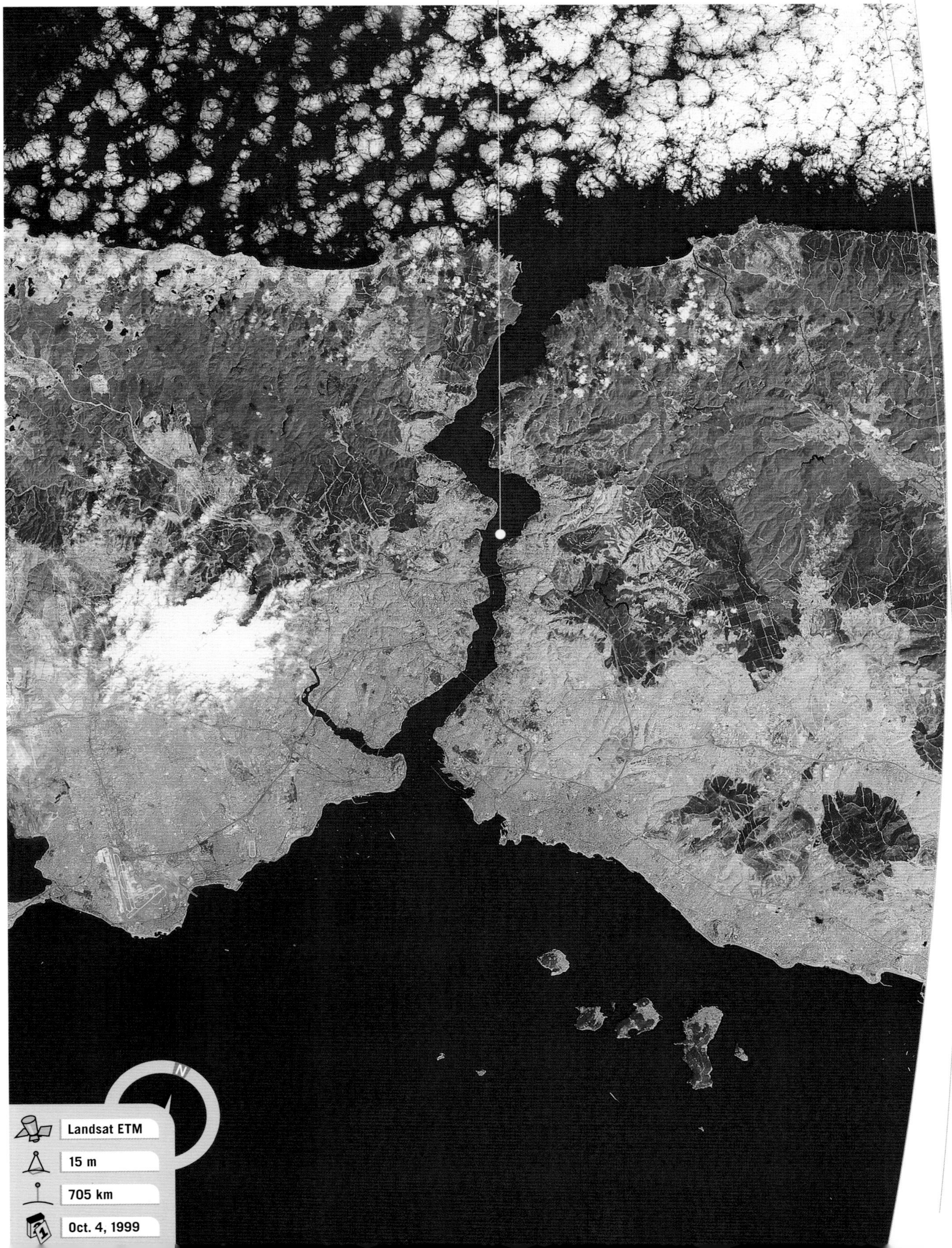

Vegetation and Land Use

Carving New Settlements from the Rainforest

Rio Paraná

In 1975, Brazil and Paraguay began constructing the world's largest dam for the Itaipú hydroelectric power plant. Itaipú means "singing stone" in the Guaraní Indian language. Since 1982, the Rio Paraná has backed up over a length of 180 km, forming a huge lake that covers an area of 1,460 sq. km. before entering a long (60 km) canyon near the city of Foz do Iguaçu. Dam projects of this magnitude have a significant impact on the environment.

The power plant went into operation at full capacity in May 1991 and now provides much of the electricity consumed in Brazil. Paraguay, which covered half of the roughly 30-million-dollar construction bill, does not need that much electrical power. The country sells 98% of its energy share to its powerful neighbor. Experts fear that silt accumulation resulting from extensive deforestation operations along the upper reaches of the river will shorten the life of the power plant.

Clearly visible in the satellite image is the sharp boundary between heavily cultivated deforested areas and the remaining virgin rain forest, which is now protected as a national park.

Landsat TM

30 m

705 km

June 25, 1987

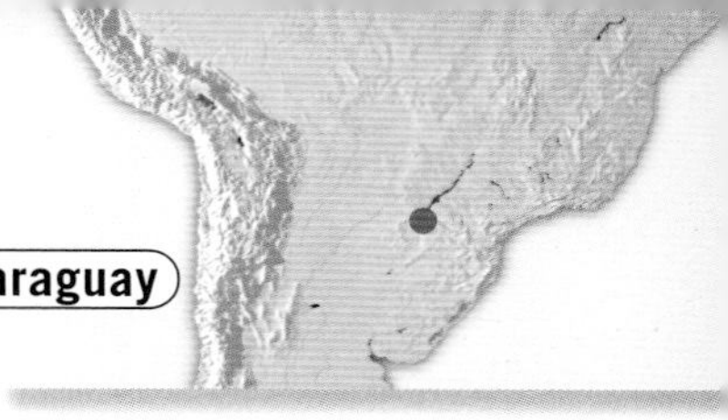

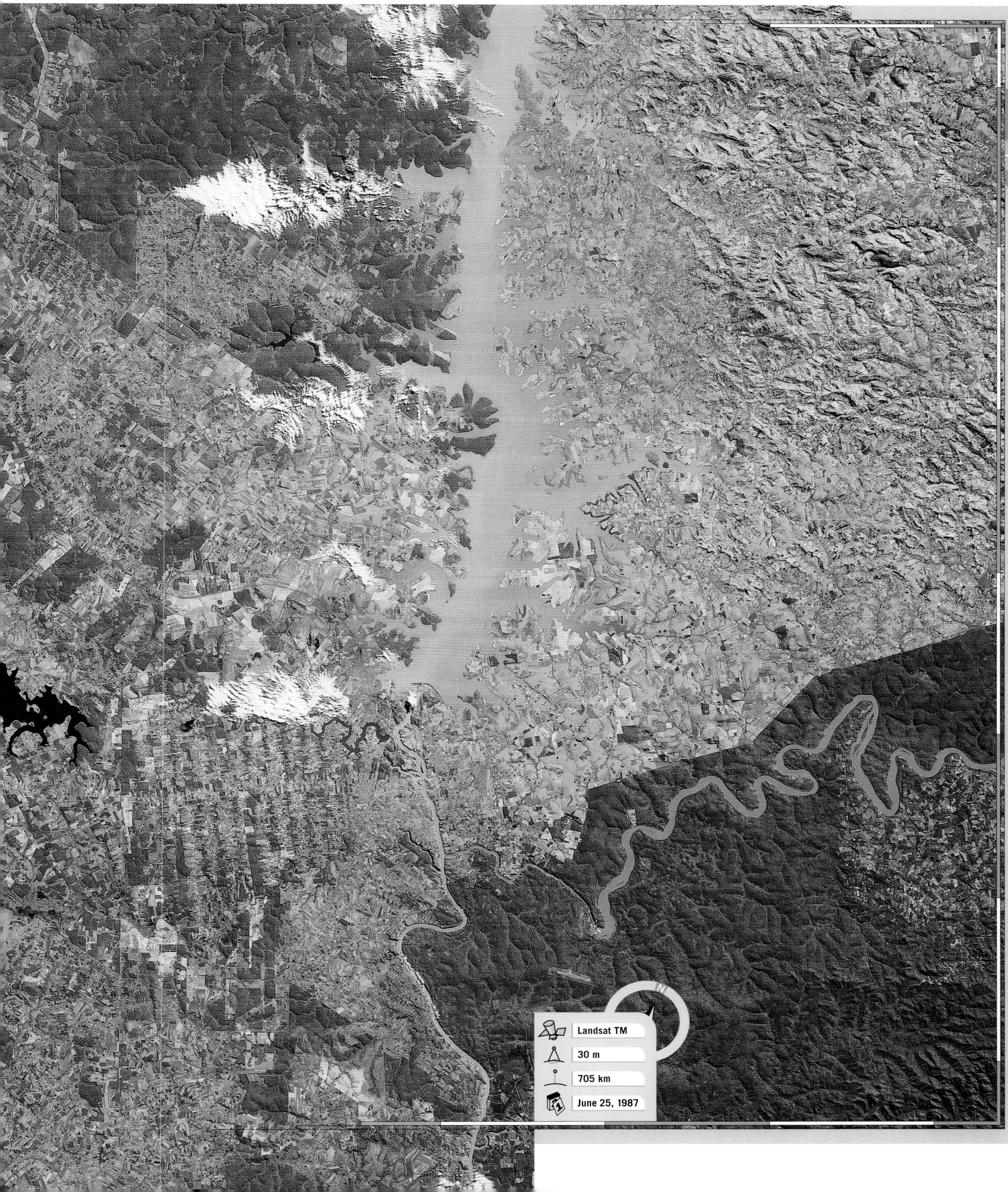

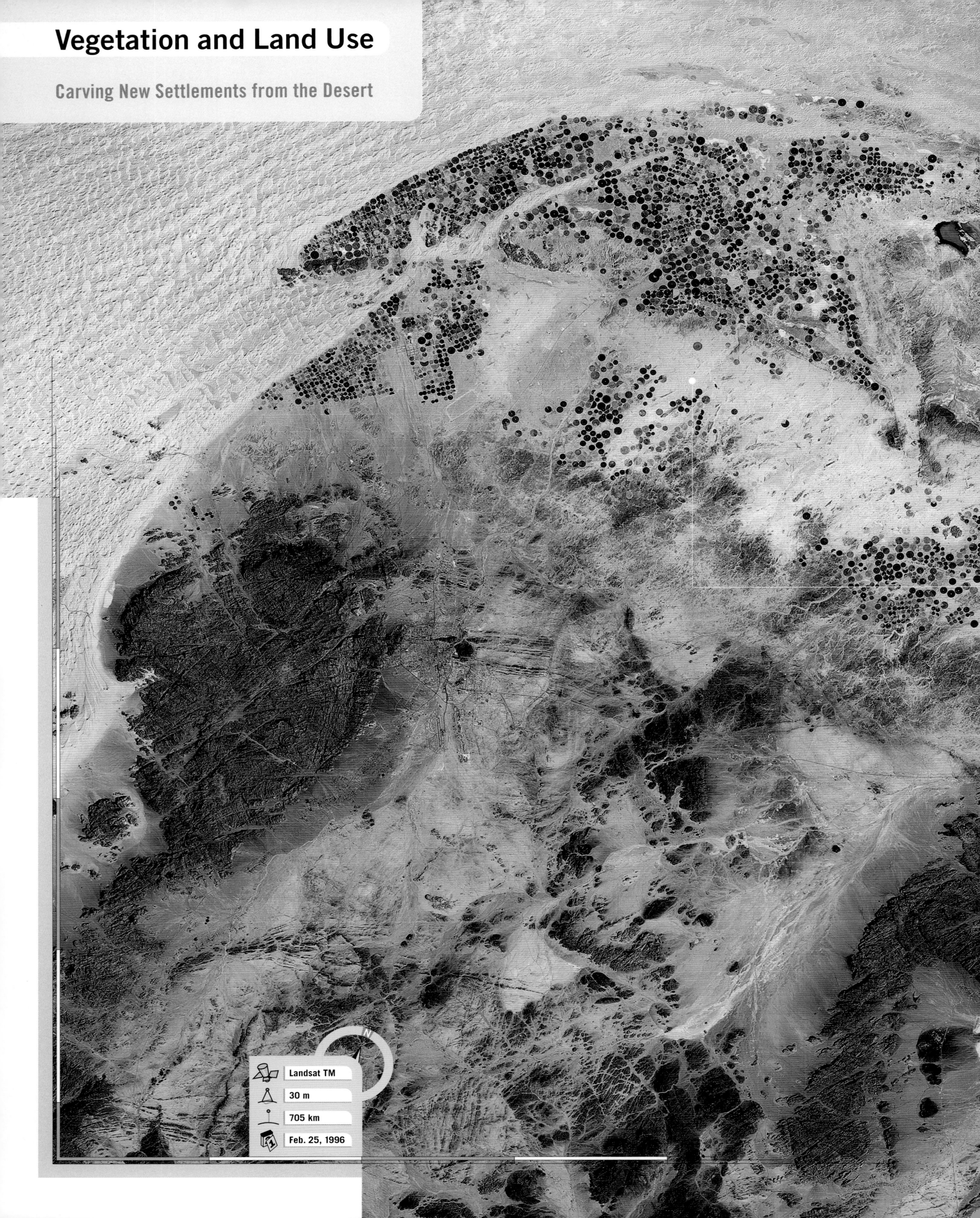

Vegetation and Land Use

Carving New Settlements from the Desert

Landsat TM

30 m

705 km

Feb. 25, 1996

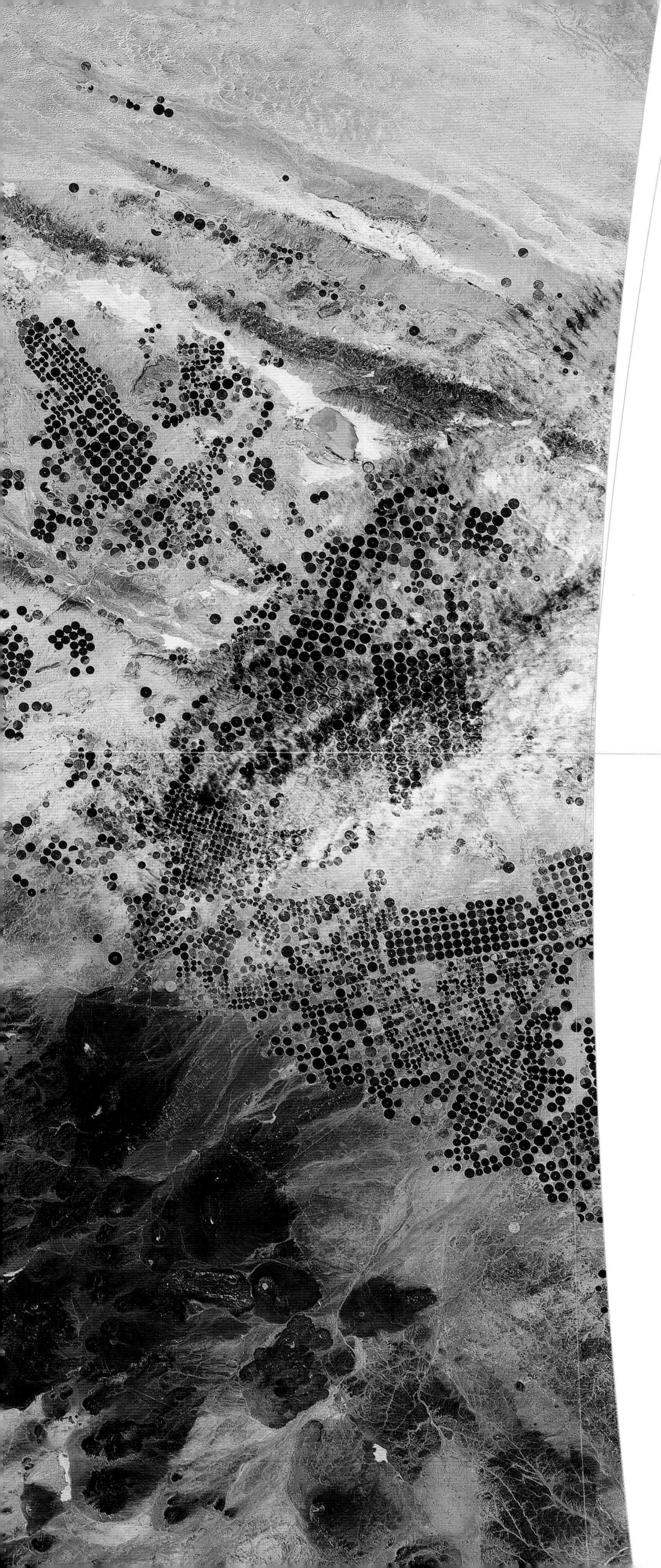

Saudi Arabia – Hā'il

Expansive plateaus irregularly interspersed with ranges of mountains and inselbergs characterize the topography of the Central Arabian Highlands. In the north, the crystalline highlands extend to the edge of the sand desert of An Nafūd. Circular patches are distributed like confetti over the yellow sand of the Wadi Ha'il — small areas of cultivation in the midst of the arid desert, irrigated with rotating sprinkler systems fed to a certain extent with fossil water. Conveyed by pumps and pipelines, the water is distributed for specified periods of time in fine veils of rain. This process enables farmers to fertilize their fields efficiently by adding plant nutrients to the water. Excessive irrigation creates swampy soil conditions, which make the fields difficult to tend. Evaporation rates are extremely high in the hot, arid regions of Saudi Arabia, and changing wind patterns can lead to unequal distribution of water vapor.

Landsat TM

30 m

705 km

Sept. 21, 1997

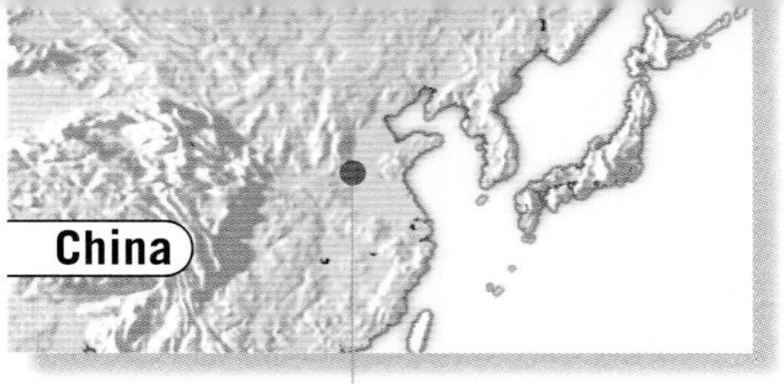

Settlement Structure in Northern China

This satellite image shows a section of the low North China Plain, where elevations range between 5 m and 50 m above sea level. The plain was formed centuries ago by frequent flooding of the Huang River and the resulting accumulation of fertile loess deposits. Extensive river regulation measures have since greatly reduced the danger of flooding. The high fertility of the region is evident in the dense, regular pattern of small rural settlements and the intensive use of land for agriculture. The most important crops in this region of northern China are wheat, corn, soybeans, peanuts, and tobacco.

San Francisco

San Francisco is famous for its location on the northern tip of the peninsula at the entrance to San Francisco Bay. The city is bordered on the west by the Pacific Ocean, on the north by the Golden Gate Strait, on the east by San Francisco Bay, and on the south by the San Bruno Mountains. The Sacramento and San Joaquin valleys open to the Bay from the northeast. Covering an area of 120 sq. km, the city encompasses Angel, Treasure and Yerba Buena islands as well as the former island prison of Alcatraz. Central San Francisco is situated on a chain of hills with elevations of up to 285 m. Cleary visible in the image is the Golden Gate, the strait (8 km long and 3 km wide) that joins the Pacific and San Francisco Bay.

Landsat TM

30 m

705 km

May 8, 1986

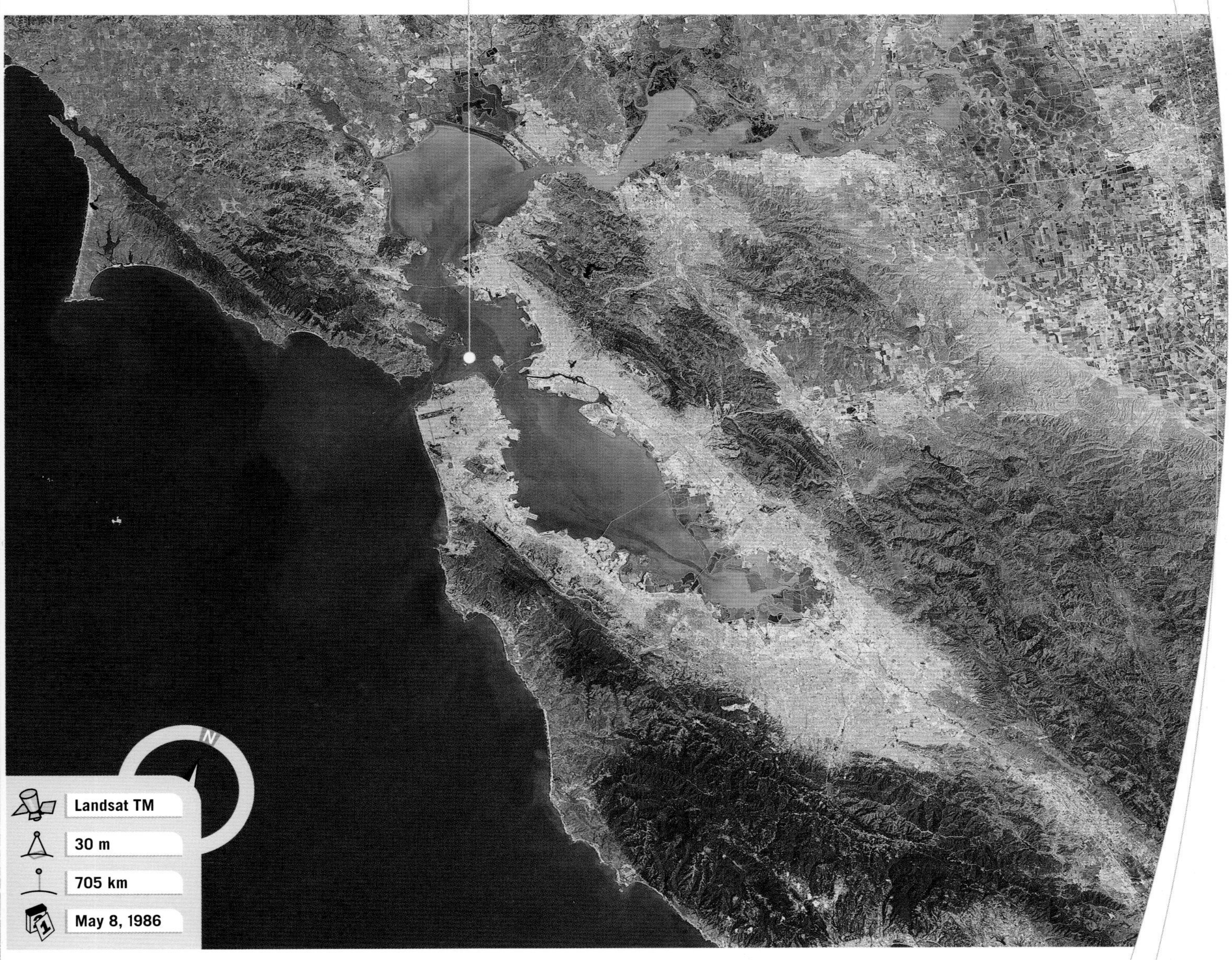

Settlement Patterns

The Metropolis

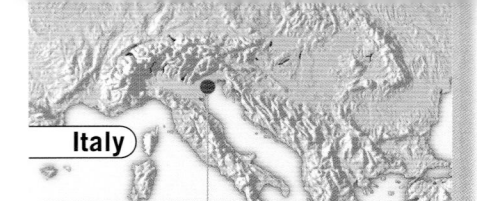

Venice

Venice was built on more than 100 small islands in the Laguna Veneta north of the Po delta. The heart of the city is St. Mark's Square, situated at the southern end of the S-shaped Canal Grande. A four-kilometer-long road and railroad bridge connects Venice to the mainland.

Venetians have lived with the threat of floods and high water for centuries. Yet flooding has grown more frequent over the past fifty years, for many different reasons. The water level in the Adriatic Sea has risen by about eight centimeters during the last one hundred years, and the city itself has sunk farther into the lagoon over the past several decades as the result of groundwater depletion on the nearby mainland.

Ikonos

1 m

682 km

Sept. 15, 2000

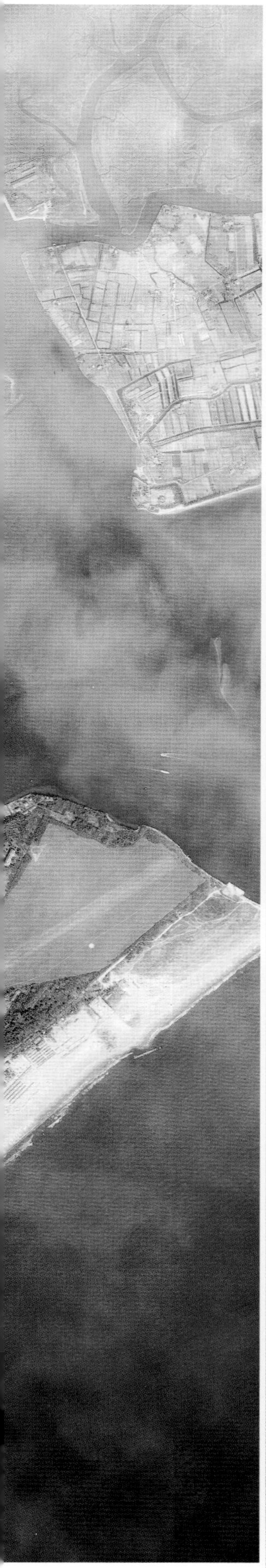

Ikonos

1 m

682 km

Apr. 4, 1996

New York

From a colonial settlement
to a modern megacity: Bordered
by the Hudson, Harlem, and
East rivers, the island of Manhattan is the heart of New
York City.
With its many skyscrapers —
concentrated heavily on
the southern tip of the island
and south of Central Park —
Manhattan is the nation's commercial and financial hub
and one of the most important
cultural centers in the world.
Defying the city's checkerboard
street pattern, Broadway,
New York's most famous thor-
oughfare, presents a changing
face along its 20-km path
from one end of the island to
the other. The proportionately
large "green island" of Central
Park is clearly visible in the
middle of Manhattan. A number
of bridges connect the island
with its neighboring boroughs.

Settlement Patterns

Landsat TM +
Spot PAN

30 m

705 km

Aug. 14, 1993
July 7, 1993

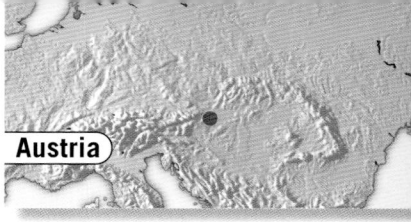

Vienna

Positioned favorably where the Alps descend to the Great Hungarian Plain at a major crossroads of traditional European trading routes from north to south, the Danube metropolis developed from a village into a world city within only few centuries.

The Danube, whose course has been artificially altered twice during the past several centuries, forms the region's natural axis. The former meanders of the Old Danube in the northern part of the satellite image serve as important urban recreation areas today.

The New Danube, which runs parallel to the river, was created in 1970 to prevent flooding. A by-product of this water-regulation measure is the Danube Island, a popular park and recreation area for the people of Vienna.

Neusiedler Lake

Despite its size – approximately 296 sq. km, including 120 sq. km of encircling reed growth, Neusiedler Lake is neither fed nor drained by a river of significant size. Its cloudy greenish-gray coloration is not caused by pollution but is a sign of the presence of billions of suspended particles that never sink entirely to the bottom of the shallow, windswept lake. The border between Austria and Hungary is vividly documented in this satellite image. The landscape in the Austrian state of Burgenland is covered by an intricate quilt of small strip parcels indicating intensive cultivation. These stand in stark contrast to the large block fields on the other side of the border – remnants of the collective farms of a bygone era.

Landsat TM +
Spot PAN

30 m

705 km

Aug. 14, 1993
Aug. 10, 1992

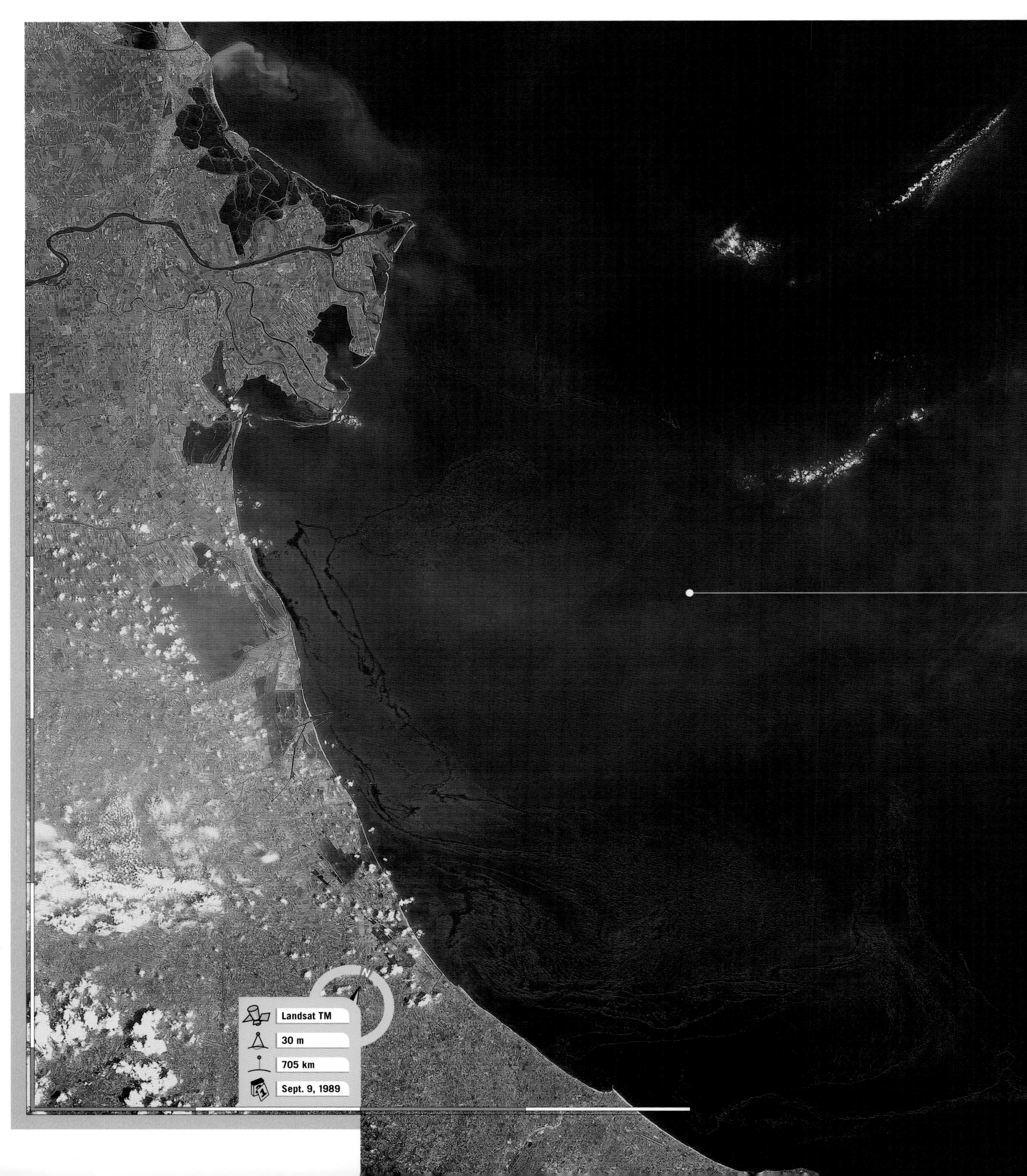

Landsat TM

30 m

705 km

Sept. 9, 1989

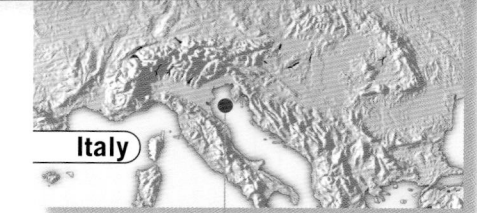
Carpet of Algae

The satellite image shows a stretch of the Italian Adriatic coastline between Chioggia in the north and Fano in the south. Particularly noticeable are the red streaks in the blue of the Adriatic Sea. Red hues indicate vegetation in the false-color image, and the streaks here represent accumulations of algae floating in the sea.

The formation of algae slime in the Mediterranean is a natural phenomenon that is intensified by long periods of good weather and placid seas. Now a common occurrence in many parts of the Mediterranean, the appearance of huge swarms of jellyfish is attributable to the influx of organic household, industrial, and agricultural waste water, which provides an abundance of nutrients for algae.

This satellite image offers impressive evidence of the expansion of the algae carpet. No other medium is capable of documenting such natural phenomena with this degree of clarity at a comparable cost.

Forest Fires on the Island of Thassos

With an area of 398 sq. km, Thassos is the second-largest island in the northern Aegean Sea and the northernmost Greek isle. The highest mountain on the rugged island is Ipsarion, which rises to an elevation of 1,203 m.

Vast areas of forest in Greece are regularly devastated by fires during the summer months. Such fires are primarily the result of dry periods that often last months at a time, although some are the work of arsonists. Disastrous forest fires on Thassos in 1985 and 1987 destroyed a large portion of the island's trees. Yet, despite the extensive damage caused by these fires, Thassos — once the most heavily forested island in Greece — has remained a green isle. The red areas visible in the southern part of the island show the regions destroyed by the fires of 1985.

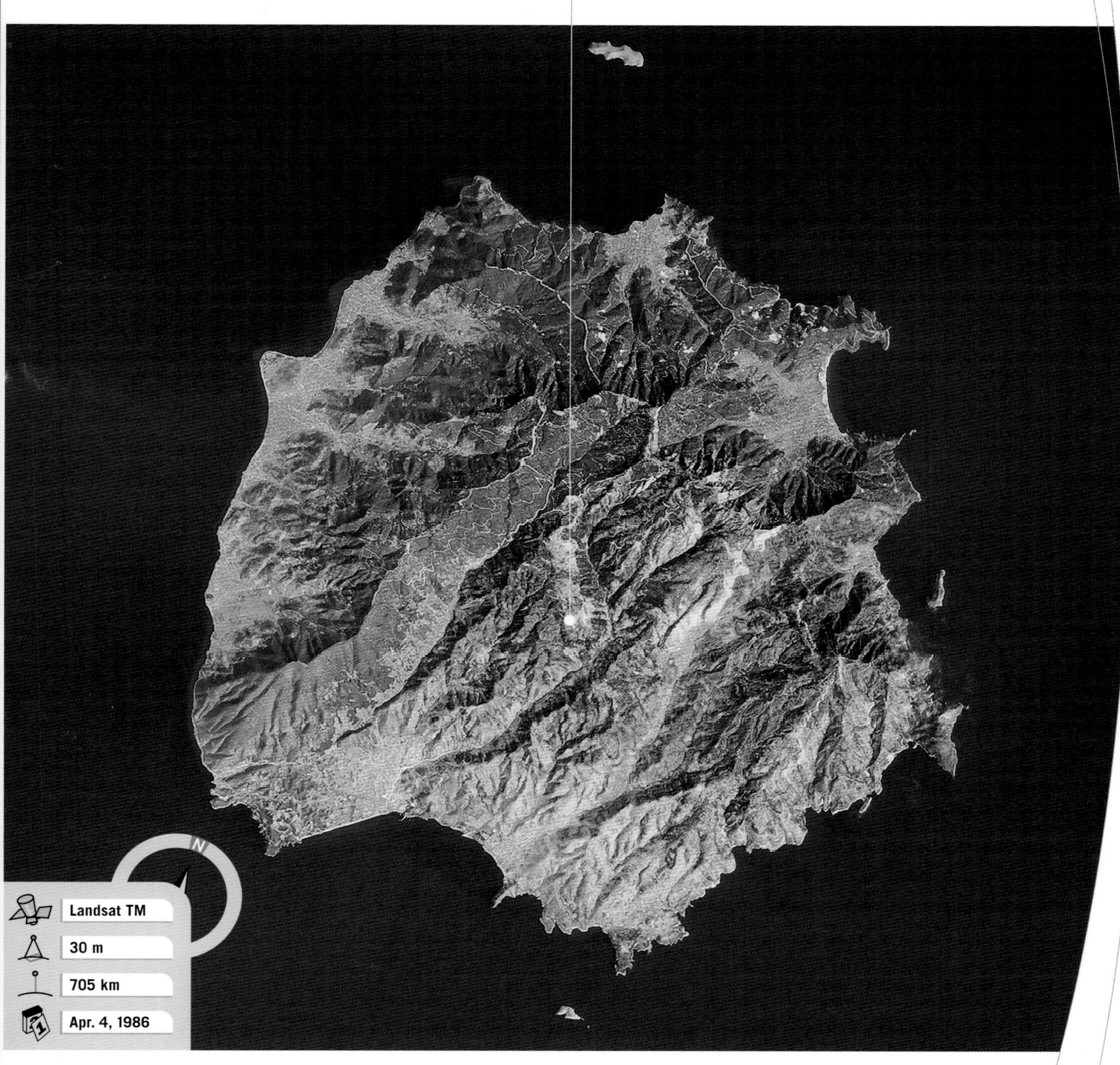

Landsat TM

30 m

705 km

Apr. 4, 1986

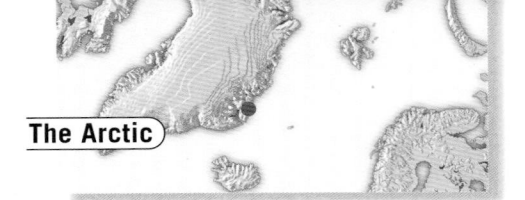

The Arctic

Landsat TM

30 m

705 km

Aug. 12, 1985

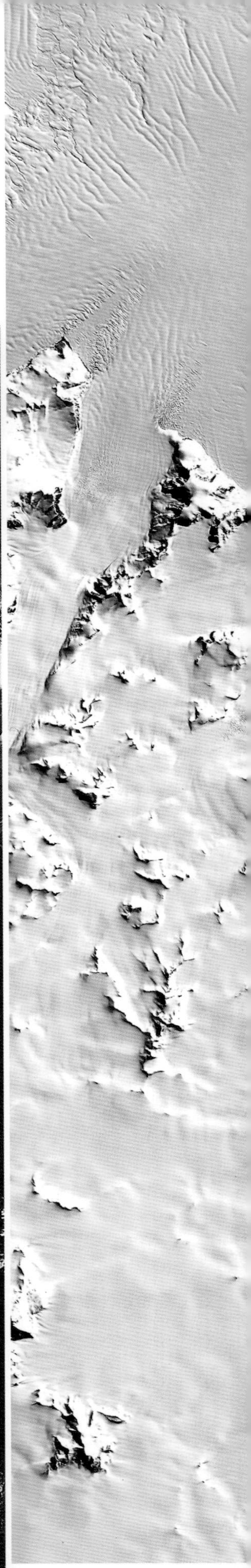

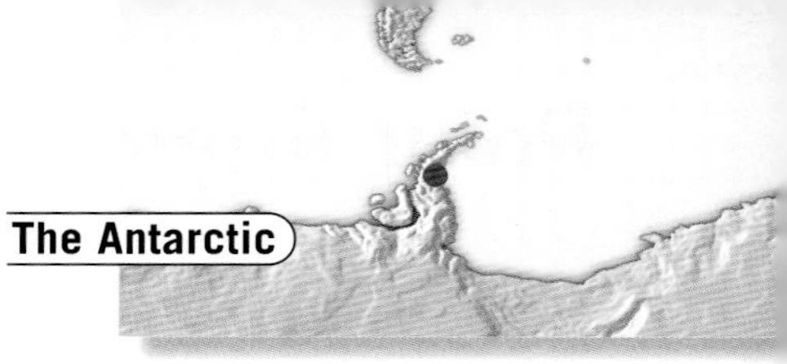

Landsat TM

30 m

705 km

Jan. 28, 1988

Larsen Ice Shelf in Antarctica

Unlike sea ice, which is created
when seawater freezes, shelf ice consists largely of frozen fresh water,
part of which is the direct, solidified
product of precipitation, although
a much larger share is contributed by
the massive flows of Antarctic inland ice.
Shelf ice reaches a thickness of up to
1,500 m at the line along which
it abuts with the Antarctic ice cap.

Arctic Eddies

Exchange between the warm water advancing from the south
and the colder masses in the polar regions is governed not
only by variations in temperature but also by differences in density
between masses of seawater with varying degrees of salinity.
The convergence of water masses with different properties — in
this case at the eastern coast of Greenland — triggers complex
interactions which in turn create marine gyres or so called eddies.

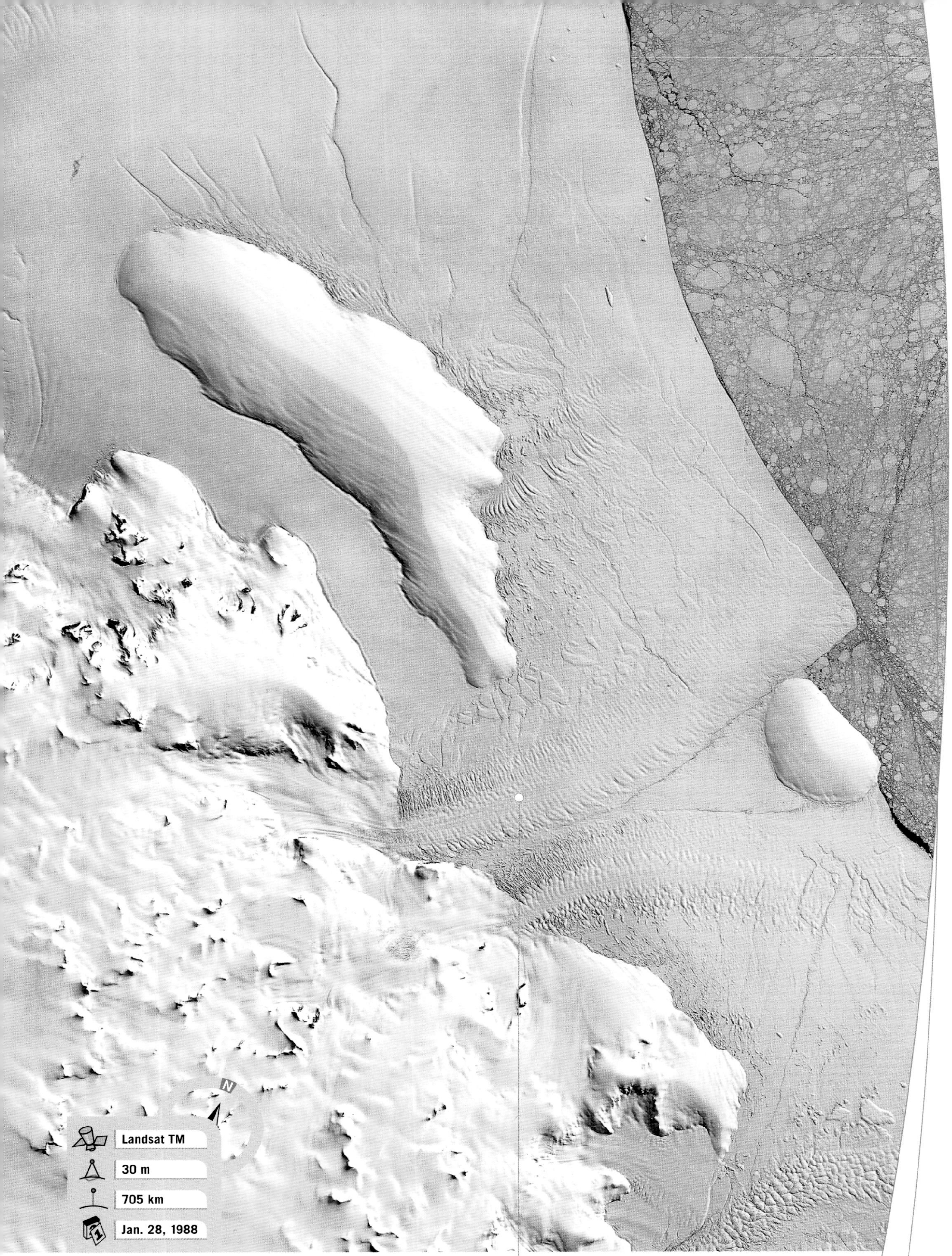

Landsat TM

30 m

705 km

Sept. 28, 1985

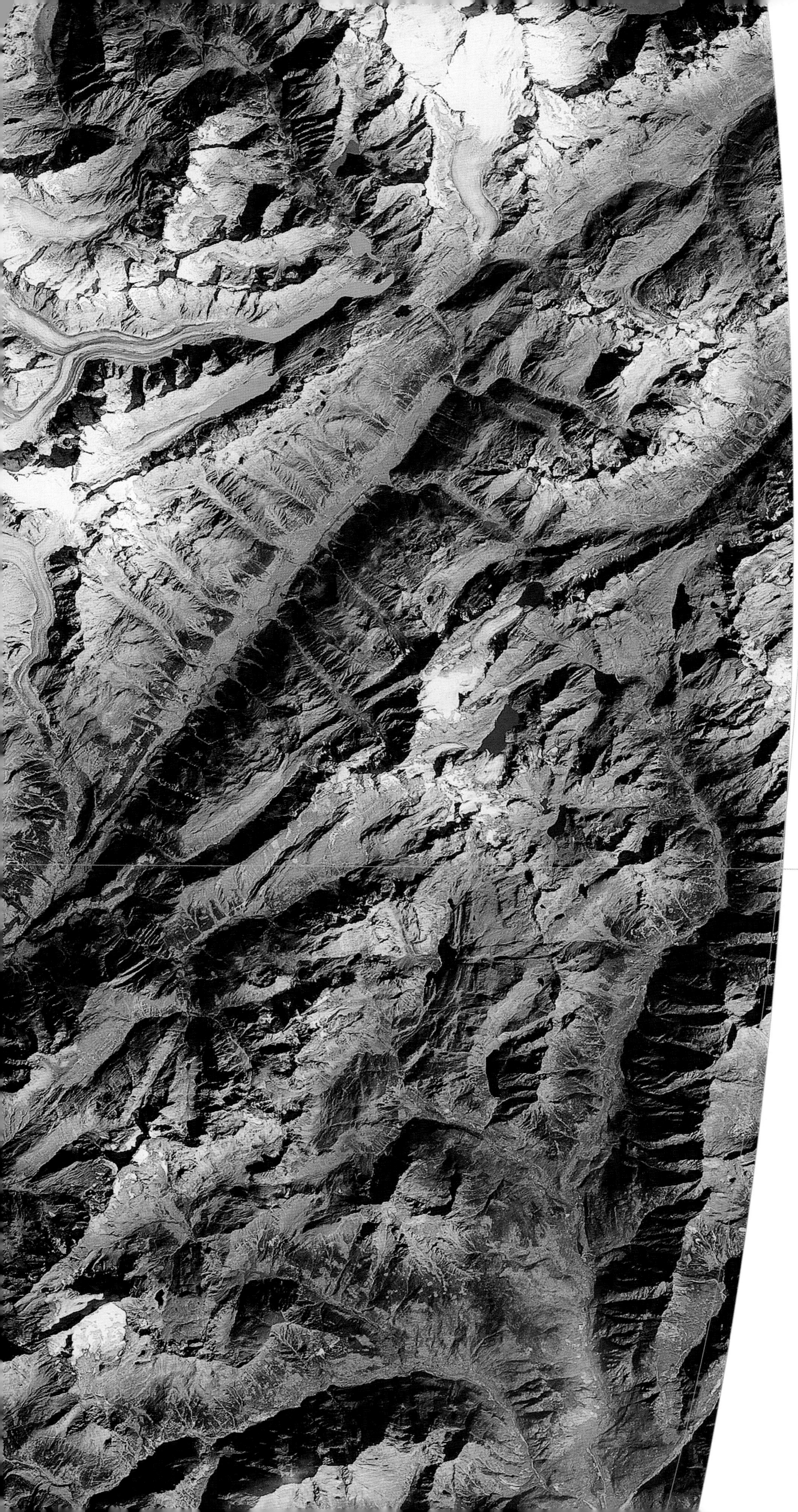

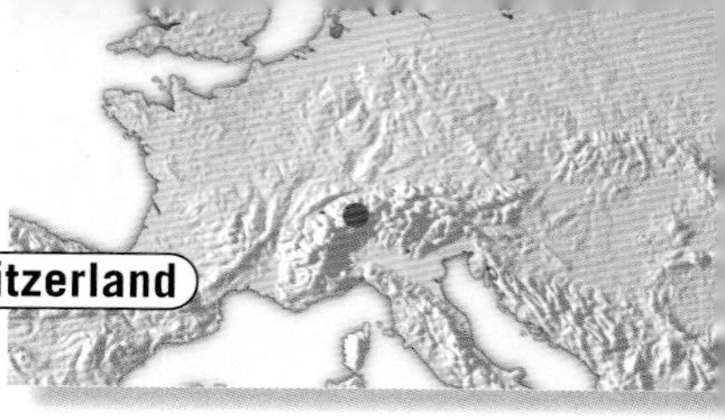

The Aletsch Glacier

The Aletsch Glacier stands out strikingly against the rugged
terrain of the Bernese Alps in this satellite image. With
a length of 24.1 km (measured in 1996) and a total area of
nearly 87 sq. km (1975), it is both the longest and the
most expansive glacier of the Alps. Known as the Great Aletsch,
the main glacier flows generally southward from the junction of several other firn fields at Concordia Platz down to the
Aletsch Forest.

Mountains

Ancient Massifs

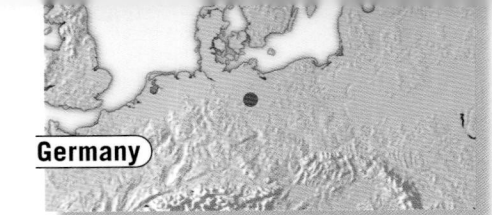
Germany

Harz

The Harz Mountain region rises like an island above
the North German Plain. A very old formation, it is
also the highest central mountain range in Germany
north of the Main River.

The numerous different types and formations of rock
make this mountain landscape an ideal laboratory
for students of geological history. Thus experts refer to
the Harz as "Silverland," emphasizing its broad
and fascinating geographic diversity. Although its ore
deposits are now nearly depleted, the richly varied
landscape, with its crystal clear mountain lakes and
massifs, is an El Dorado for professional and amateur
geologists alike.

Rugged, canyon-like valleys are interspersed among
plateaus and heaths. Parts of the Upper Harz,
including Mount Brocken, its highest peak (1,141 m),
have been set aside as National Park areas.

Landsat ETM

30 m

705 km

Aug. 31, 1989

Contents

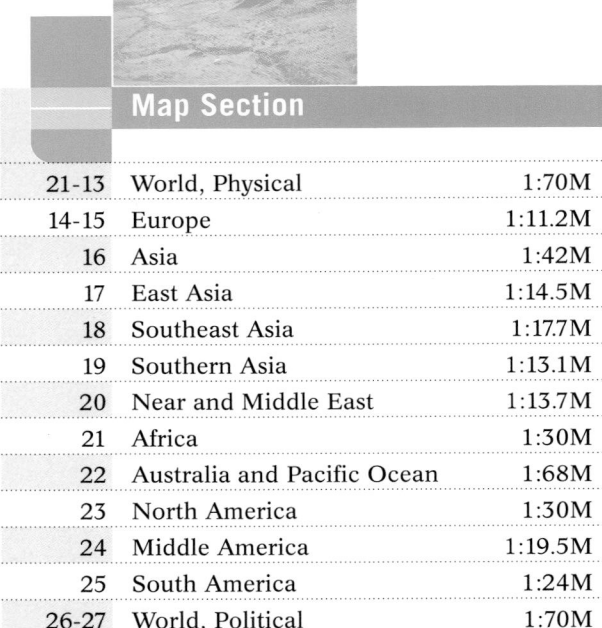

Map Section

28 Europe

76 Asia

106 Africa

126 Australia, New Zealand and Central Pacific

138 North and Middle America

178 South America and Polar Regions

193 Statistical Tables and Index

Note: M=millions, K=thousands

Using the Map Section

The Contents and Functions of Geographic Maps

Offering a broad range of features and functions, this new Atlas of the World is not only an up-to-date reference work of superior quality but an ideal and thoroughly readable guide for virtual global exploration and armchair travel. The information provided below will help you to get the most enjoyment and benefit from its use.

Relief Maps

The relief maps of the continents – on pages 12–25 of the Map Section – provide a striking impression of the character of the entire Earth's surface, from the mountains of the continental mainlands to the depths of the ocean floor. Produced with the aid of state-of-the-art computer technology, these maps offer a vividly realistic picture of the diverse structures and forms of the global terrain.

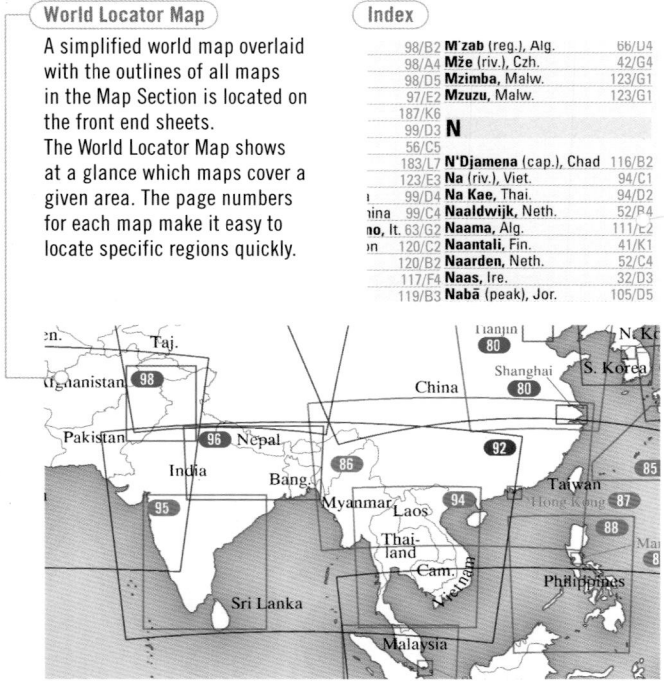

World Locator Map

A simplified world map overlaid with the outlines of all maps in the Map Section is located on the front end sheets.
The World Locator Map shows at a glance which maps cover a given area. The page numbers for each map make it easy to locate specific regions quickly.

Index

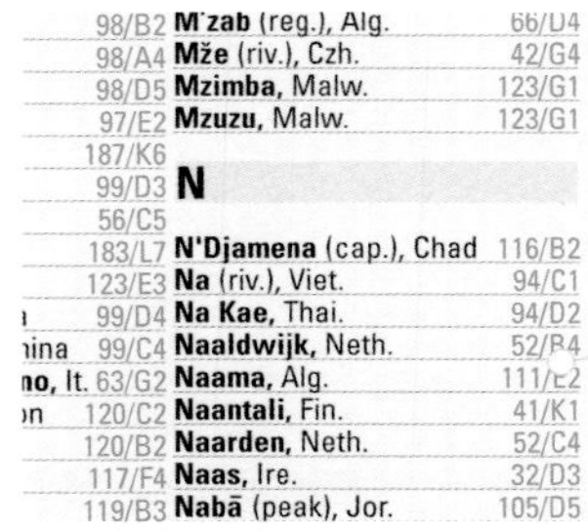

Geographic Maps

The detailed maps of all regions of the Earth are arranged by continent. The chapters for each of the continents are introduced with a stunning satellite image and a political map. The continental maps show each country in a different color in order to facilitate recognition of political divisions.

A variety of different symbols, line patterns, surface colors, and textures highlight distinctive features such as mountains, national parks, urban areas, forests, and deserts. These maps also provide a wealth of information on roadways and canals, geographic features, and political divisions. All of the geographic maps and the complex information they contain are the product of modern computer-assisted map development and compilation techniques.

Map Frames

The map frames contain a number of graphic features that make the atlas much easier to use. The page numbers of each map are entered in the blue chapter markers at the right-hand edge of each map. An additional locator map in the upper corner shows the position of the individual map section within a larger geographic area. The blue arrows along the four edges of each map refer by page number to the adjacent map sections and thus make it easy to find neighboring areas quickly in the atlas. The letters and numerals in the red squares positioned along the frame are search coordinates used to locate places and objects listed in the map index. In addition, integrated legends and introductory texts provide basic information about the region covered by each map.

Map Scales

A map's scale describes the relationship of any length on the map to a corresponding length on the Earth's surface. A scale of 1:3,000,000 means that one cm on the map represents 3,000,000 cm (30 km) in nature. Thus a scale of 1:1,000,000 is larger than 1:3,000,000, just as 1/1 is larger than 1/3.
Most regions are shown at a scale of either 1:3,000,000 or 1:6,000,000. Areas of particular interest are shown at 1:1,000,000. Selected densely populated areas are covered by maps with a larger scale. Whole continents and large regions are shown at a smaller scale.

Boundary and Name Policies

The atlas shows the internationally recognized national boundaries. Boundary disputes, armistice lines, and de facto boundaries are indicated by special symbols where appropriate. Generally, the names of places and geographic objects appear in the language of the respective country. Accepted conventional names are used for certain major foreign places names. Name usage also tends to vary depending upon cultural factors, however, and is subject to change over time, not least of all for political reasons. In several cases where, for example, a new name has not gained universal acceptance or the use of a traditional name persists, a second name has been entered in parentheses. Thus the selection of names is not entirely systematic and reflects important aspects of common usage.

Index to the Map Section

The index facilitates the search for a specific place in the atlas. It contains an alphabetical list of more than 110,000 names of places and geographic objects entered in the maps. The page numbers and coordinates listed for each index entry show the location of the desired place or object in the map corresponding coordinate grid. A list of the abbreviations used in the index is found on the first index page.

Map Components

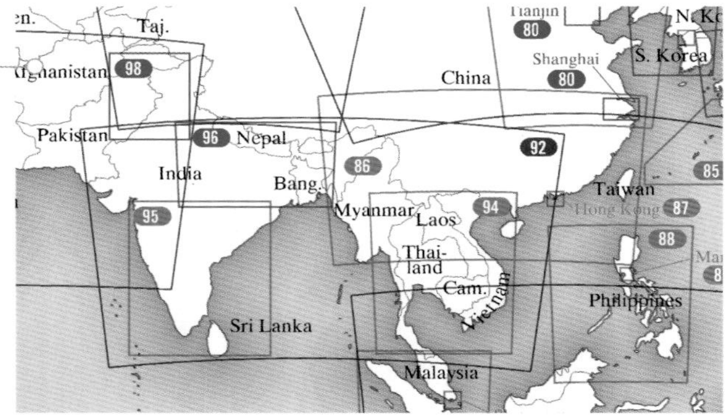

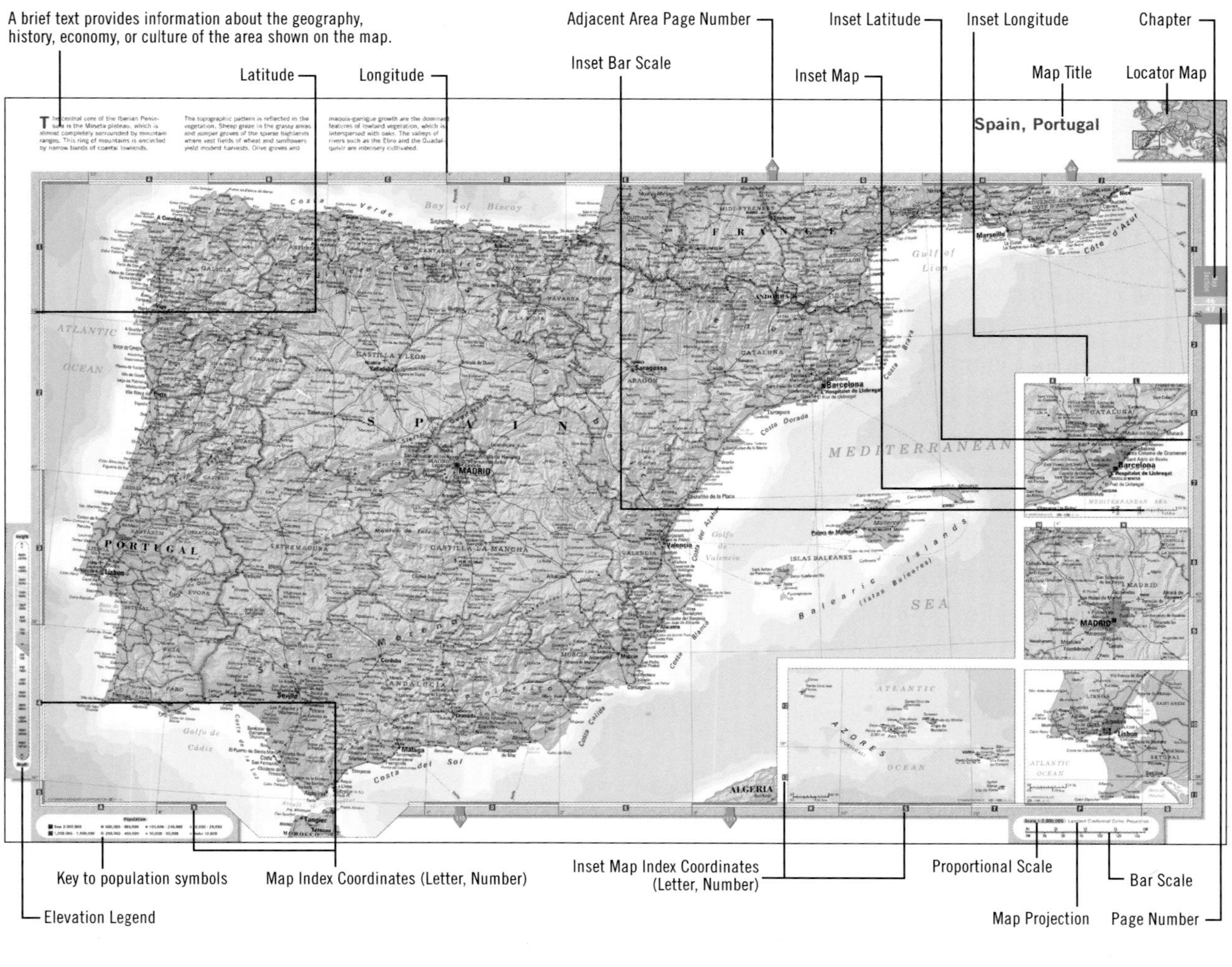

A brief text provides information about the geography, history, economy, or culture of the area shown on the map.

Adjacent Area Page Number — Inset Latitude — Inset Longitude — Chapter

Latitude — Longitude — Inset Bar Scale — Inset Map — Map Title — Locator Map

Spain, Portugal

Key to population symbols — Map Index Coordinates (Letter, Number) — Inset Map Index Coordinates (Letter, Number) — Proportional Scale — Bar Scale

Elevation Legend — Map Projection — Page Number

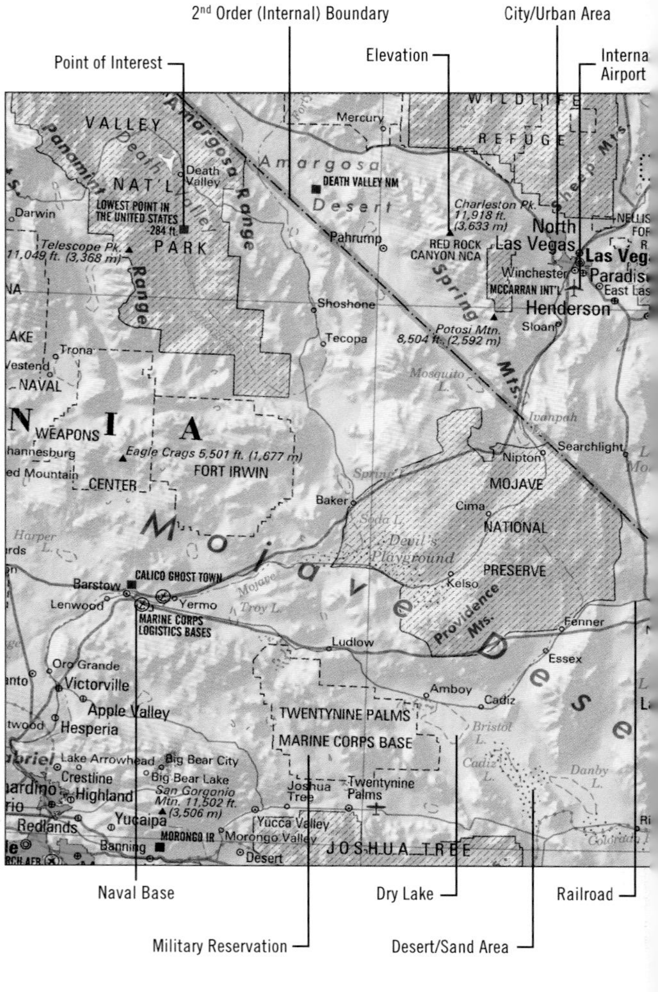

2nd Order (Internal) Boundary — City/Urban Area

Point of Interest — Elevation — International Airport

Naval Base — Dry Lake — Railroad

Military Reservation — Desert/Sand Area

Map type faces

The use of different type faces helps the reader distinguish between types of map content.

Major Political Arenas

LUXEMBOURG

Internal Political Divisions

SAXONY-ANHALT

Historical Regions

Polabská Nížina

Cities and Towns

Norfolk Sumter Smyrna

Neighborhoods

BIGGIN HILL

Points of Interest

MISSION SAN BUENAVENTURA

Water Features

L. Elsinore

Capes, Points, Peaks, Passes

Cape Horn...Pt. La Jolla
Mt. Rainier

Islands, Peninsulas

Cape Breton I.

Mountain Ranges, Plateaus, Hills

Serra do Norte

Deserts, Plains, Valleys

San Fernando Valley

The spelling of geographic names conforms to the rules of the respective official language of each country. Where the official language is written in Latin characters, local spellings, including diacritical marks and modified letters, have been used. For countries with languages written in non-Latin characters, such as China, Russia or the Arabic-speaking countries, an international standard form is used, which may deviate in some cases from conventional American usage.

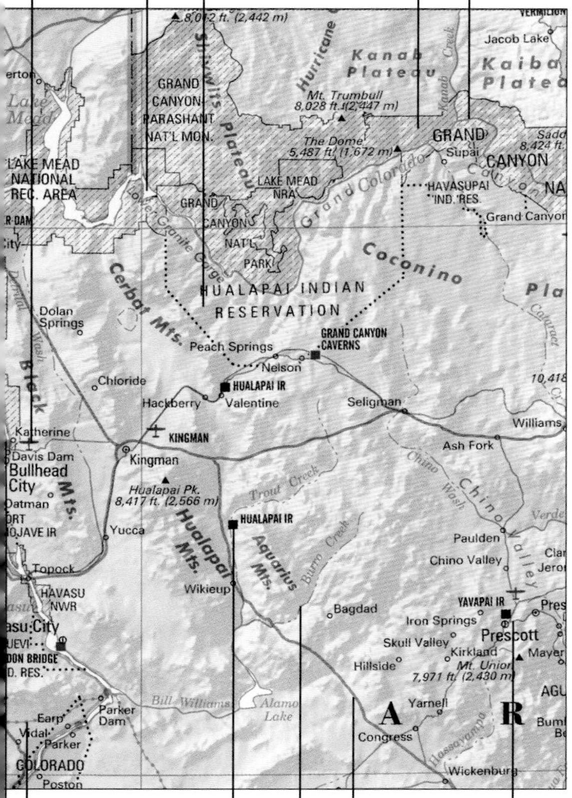

Symbols used on Maps of the World

First Order (National) Boundary

—··—··—	Demarcated Land Boundary
———	Demarcated Water Boundary
—·—·—	Disputed Boundary
————	Armistice Boundary
——	De Facto Boundary
··········	Undefined

Second Order (Internal) Boundary

—·—·—	Land/Administrative District Boundary
———	Water Boundary

Third Order (Internal) Boundary

————	Land/Administrative District Boundary
———	Water Boundary

Cities and Towns

Stockholm	First Order (National) Capital
Salt Lake City	Second Order (Internal) Capital
Manchester	Third Order (Internal) Capital
■ ⊙ ◎ ○	Towns
▣ ⊚ ◐ ○	Towns
□	City District/Neighborhood
▬	City and Urban Area Limits

Transportation

✈	International Airport
✦	Airport
———	Highways/Roads
┅┅┅	Railroads
·········	Ferries
·····	Tunnels (Road, Railroad)

Drainage Features

———	Shoreline, River
———	Intermittend River
··········	Canal
▭	Lake, Reservoir
⬚	Intermittent Lake
⬚	Dry Lake
▦	Salt Pan
≈≈≈	Swamp/Marsh

Other Physical Features

▲	Elevation
⤬	Pass
●	Falls
✳	Rapids
░	Desert/Sand Area
▒	Lava Flow
▒	Glacier/Ice Shelf

Cultural Features

⁂	Archeological Sites, Ruins
●	Dam
♣	Park
⚔	Wildlife Area
■	Point of Interest
⌣	Well
⊗	Air Base
⊘	Naval Base
———	International Date Line

⬚⬚⬚	Ancient Walls
⬚	Native Reservation/Reserve
⬚	Military/Government Reservation
▭	State Park/Recreation Area
▨	National Park/Forest/Recreation/Wildlife Area

Elevation Legend

Height

m. / ft.
6000 / 19700
4000 / 13000
2000 / 6500
1500 / 5000
1000 / 3300
500 / 1600
200 / 700
-0-
200 / 700
500 / 1600
1000 / 3300
2000 / 6500
3000 / 9800
4000 / 13000
5000 / 16400
6000 / 19700

m. / ft.

Depth

The color tints in this bar represent both elevation of land areas and depth of the oceans. The changes between colors are labeled in meters and feet. Selective shading for the land areas highlights those regions with significant relief variations. The legend is entered next to each individual map.

Abbreviations used in the maps

Abbr.	Meaning
Abor. Rsv.	Aboriginal Reserve
Admin.	Administration
AFB	Air Force Base
Amm. Dep.	Ammunition Depot
Arch.	Archipelago
Aut.	Autonomous
B.	Bay
Bfld.	Battlefield
Bk.	Brook
Br.	Branch
C.	Cape
Can.	Canal
Cap.	Capital
C.G.	Coast Guard
Chan.	Channel
Co.	County
Consv.	Conservation
Cord.	Cordillera
Cr.	Creek
Ctr.	Center
Dep.	Depot
Depr.	Depression
Des.	Desert
Dist.	District
DMZ	Demilitarized Zone
Est.	Estuary
Fed.	Federal
Fk.	Fork
For.	Forest
Ft.	Fort
G.	Gulf
Govt.	Government
Gd.	Grand
Gt.	Great
Har.	Harbor
Hist.	Historic(al)
Hts.	Heights
I., Is.	Island(s)
Ind. Res.	Indian Reservation
Int'l	International
IR	Indian Reservation
Isth.	Isthmus
Jct.	Junction
L.	Lake
Lag.	Lagoon
Mem.	Memorial
Mil.	Military
Mon.	Monument
Mt.	Mount
Mtn.	Mountain
Mts.	Mountains
Nat.	Natural
Nat'l	National
Nav.	Naval
NB	National Battlefield
NBP	National Battlefield Park
NCA	National Conservation Area
NHP	National Historical Park
NHS	National Historic Site
NL	National Lakeshore
NM	National Monument
NMEM	National Memorial
NMILP	National Military Park
No.	Northern
NP	National Park
NPP	National Park and Preserve
NPRSV	National Preserve
NRA	National Recreation Area
NRIV	National River
NRSV	National Reserve
NS	National Seashore
NWR	National Wildlife Refuge
Obl.	Oblast
Occ.	Occupied
Okr.	Okrug
Passg.	Passage
Pen.	Peninsula
Pk.	Peak
Plat.	Plateau
PN	Park National
Prom.	Promontory
Prsv.	Preserve
Pt.	Point
R.	River
Rec.	Recreation(al)
Ref.	Refuge
Reg.	Region
Rep.	Republic
Res.	Reservoir, Reservation
Sa.	Sierra
Sd.	Sound
So.	Southern
SP	State Park
Spr., Sprgs.	Spring, Springs
St.	State
Sta.	Station
Stm.	Stream
Str.	Strait
Terr.	Territory
Tun.	Tunnel
Twp.	Township
UNDOF	United Nations Disengagement Observer Force
Val.	Valley
Vill.	Village

Airport — Lake — Native Reservation — National Park Area — River — Native Reservation — Other Road — Principal Highway — Intermittent River — Canal

Quick Reference Guide

This concise alphabetical reference lists continents, countries, states, territories, possessions and other major geographical areas, including the size, population and capital or chief town of each. Blue page numbers and blue alpha-numeric reference keys (which refer to the grid squares of latitude and longitude on each map) are visible at a glance. The population figures are the latest and most reliable figures obtainable.

Place	Square Miles	Square Kilometers	Population	Capital or Chief Town	Page/ Index
A					
Afghanistan	250,000	647,500	28,717,213	Kabul	101/H 2
Africa	11,701,147	30,306,000	784,445,000	....	133
Alabama, U.S.	52,237	135,293	4,447,100	Montgomery	143/J 5
Alaska, U.S.	615,230	1,593,444	626,932	Juneau	171
Albania	11,100	28,749	3,582,205	Tiranë	49/F 2
Alberta, Canada	255,285	661,185	3,064,200	Edmonton	140/E 3
Algeria	919,591	2,381,740	32,818,500	Algiers	111/F 3
American Samoa	77	199	70,260	Pago Pago	137/T10
Andorra	174	450	69,150	Andorra la Vella	47/F 1
Angola	481,351	1,246,700	10,766,471	Luanda	107/D 6
Anguilla, U.K.	35	91	12,738	The Valley	173/N 8
Antarctica	5,500,000	14,245,000	....	....	216
Antigua and Barbuda	170	440	67,897	St. John's	173/N 8
Argentina	1,068,296	2,766,890	38,740,807	Buenos Aires	179/C 6
Arizona, U.S.	114,006	295,276	5,130,632	Phoenix	149/F 3
Arkansas, U.S.	53,182	137,742	2,673,400	Little Rock	143/H 4
Armenia	11,506	29,800	3,326,448	Yerevan	71/H 5
Aruba, Netherlands	75	193	70,844	Oranjestad	180/D 1
Ascension Island, St. Helena	34	88	1,117	Georgetown	26/J 6
Asia	17,159,867	44,444,100	3,682,550,000	....	103
Australia	2,967,893	7,686,850	19,731,984	Canberra	127
Australian Capital Territory	938	2,430	280,132	Canberra	132/D 2
Austria	32,375	83,851	8,188,207	Vienna	45/L 3
Azerbaijan	33,436	86,600	7,830,764	Baku	71/H 4
Azores, Portugal	902	2,335	241,762	Ponta Delgada	47/R12
B					
Bahamas, The	5,382	13,939	297,477	Nassau	173/F 2
Bahrain	240	622	667,238	Manama	100/F 3
Balearic Islands, Spain	1,936	5,014	796,483	Palma	47/F 3
Bangladesh	55,598	144,000	138,448,210	Dhaka	97/G 4
Barbados	166	430	277,264	Bridgetown	173/P 8
Belarus	80,154	207,600	10,322,151	Minsk	29/G 3
Belgium	11,780	30,510	10,289,088	Brussels	42/C 3
Belize	8,865	22,960	266,440	Belmopan	176/D 2
Benin	43,483	112,620	7,041,490	Porto-Novo	115/F 4
Bermuda, U.K.	19	50	64,482	Hamilton	139/L 6
Bhutan	18,147	47,000	2,139,549	Thimphu	97/G 2
Bolivia	424,163	1,098,582	8,586,443	La Paz; Sucre	179/C 4
Bosnia & Herzegovina	19,781	51,233	3,989,018	Sarajevo	50/C 3
Botswana	231,803	600,370	1,573,267	Gaborone	107/E 7
Brazil	3,286,470	8,511,965	182,032,604	Brasília	179/D 3
British Columbia, Canada	365,946	947,800	4,095,900	Victoria	140/D 3
British Virgin Islands	59	153	13,368	Road Town	173/M7
Brunei	2,228	5,770	358,098	Bandar Seri Begawan	88/A 4
Bulgaria	42,823	110,912	7,537,929	Sofia	51/G 4
Burkina Faso	105,869	274,200	13,228,460	Ouagadougou	141/E 3
Burundi	10,745	27,830	6,096,156	Bujumbura	121/G 3
C					
California, U.S.	158,869	411,470	33,871,648	Sacramento	142/C 4
Cambodia	69,900	181,040	13,124,764	Phnom Penh	94/D 3
Cameroon	183,568	475,441	15,746,179	Yaoundé	107/D 4
Canada	3,851,787	9,976,139	32,207,113	Ottawa	140
Canary Islands, Spain	2,808	7,273	1,495,000	Las Palmas; Santa Cruz	110/A 3
Cape Verde	1,556	4,030	412,137	Praia	107/J 9
Cayman Islands, U.K.	100	259	41,934	George Town	177/F 2
Celebes, Indonesia	72,986	189,034	14,946,488	Ujung Pandang	91/E 4
Central African Republic	240,533	622,980	3,683,538	Bangui	116/C 4
Chad	495,752	1,283,998	9,253,493	N'Djamena	107/D 3
Channel Islands, U.K.	75	194	147,000	St. Helier; St. Peter Port	56/C 2
Chile	292,258	756,950	15,665,216	Santiago	179/B 6
China, People's Rep. of	3,705,386	9,596,960	1,286,975,468	Beijing	77/J 6
Christmas Island, Australia	52	135	2,771	The Settlement	27/Q 6
Cocos (Keeling) Islands, Australia	5.4	14	633	West Island	27/P 6
Colombia	439,733	1,138,910	41,662,073	Bogotá	180/C 4
Colorado, U.S.	104,100	269,618	4,301,261	Denver	142/E 4
Comoros	838	2,170	632,948	Moroni	125/G 5
Congo, Dem. Rep. of the	905,563	2,345,410	56,625,039	Kinshasa	107/E 5
Congo, Rep. of the	132,046	342,000	2,954,258	Brazzaville	120/C 3
Connecticut, U.S.	5,544	14,358	3,405,565	Hartford	161/K 4
Cook Islands, New Zealand	93	240	21,008	Avarua	137/J 6
Corsica, France	3,352	8,682	260,196	Ajaccio	48/A 1
Costa Rica	19,730	51,100	3,896,092	San José	177/F 4
Côte d'Ivoire	124,502	322,460	16,962,491	Yamoussoukro	114/D 5
Croatia	22,050	56,538	4,422,248	Zagreb	50/C 3
Cuba	42,803	110,860	11,263,429	Havana	177/F 1
Curaçao, Neth. Antilles	172	445	151,498	Willemstad	173/H 5
Cyprus	3,571	9,250	771,657	Nicosia	104/C 2
Czech Republic	30,387	78,703	10,249,216	Prague	43/H 4
D					
Delaware, U.S.	2,396	6,206	783,600	Dover	143/L 4
Denmark	16,629	43,069	5,384,384	Copenhagen	40/C 4
District of Columbia, U.S.	68	177	572,059	Washington	168/B 6
Djibouti	8,494	22,000	457,130	Djibouti	118/B 2
Dominica	290	751	69,655	Roseau	173/N 8
Dominican Republic	18,815	48,730	8,715,602	Santo Domingo	173/H 4
E					
East Timor	5,743	14,874	997,853	Dili	128/B 2
Eastern Cape, South Africa	65,858	170,616	6,665,400	Bisho	124/D 3
Ecuador	109,483	283,561	13,710,234	Quito	179/B 3
Egypt	386,659	1,001,447	74,718,797	Cairo	109/F 3
El Salvador	8,124	21,040	6,470,379	San Salvador	176/D 3
England, U.K.	50,356	130,423	49,997,100	London	31/K10
Equatorial Guinea	10,831	28,052	510,473	Malabo	120/B 2
Eritrea	46,842	121,320	4,362,254	Asmara	107/F 3
Estonia	17,413	45,100	1,408,556	Tallinn	41/L 2
Ethiopia	435,184	1,127,127	66,557,553	Addis Ababa	107/F 4
Europe	4,066,019	10,531,000	728,887,000	....	55
F					
Falkland Islands & Dependencies, U.K.	4,699	12,170	2,895	Stanley	191M 8
Faroe Islands, Denmark	540	1,399	46,345	Tórshavn	29/D 2
Fiji	7,055	18,272	868,531	Suva	137/Y17
Finland	130,128	337,032	5,190,785	Helsinki	38/H 2
Florida, U.S.	59,928	155,214	15,982,378	Tallahassee	165/F 2
France	211,208	547,030	60,180,529	Paris	44/D 3
Free State, South Africa	49,963	129,437	2,804,600	Bloemfontein	124/D 3
French Guiana	35,135	91,000	186,917	Cayenne	182/C 2
French Polynesia	1,522	3,941	262,125	Papeete	137/W15
G					
Gabon	103,347	267,670	1,321,560	Libreville	120/B 3
Gambia, The	4,363	11,300	1,501,050	Banjul	114/B 3
Gauteng, South Africa	7,241	18,760	6,847,000	Johannesburg	124/Q12
Gaza Strip	139	360	1,274,868	Gaza	104/C 4
Georgia	26,911	69,700	4,934,413	T'bilisi	71/G 4
Georgia, U.S.	58,977	152,750	8,186,453	Atlanta	143/K 5
Germany	137,803	356,910	82,398,326	Berlin	42/E 3
Ghana	92,100	238,540	20,467,747	Accra	115/E 4
Gibraltar, U.K.	2.5	6.5	27,776	Gibraltar	46/C 4
Greece	50,942	131,940	10,665,989	Athens	49/G 3
Greenland, Denmark	840,000	2,175,600	56,385	Nuuk (Godthåb)	139/N 2
Grenada	131	340	89,258	St. George's	173/N 9
Guadeloupe & Dependencies, France	687	1,779	440,189	Basse-Terre	173/N 7
Guam, U.S.	209	541	163,941	Agaña	136/D 3
Guatemala	42,042	108,889	13,909,384	Guatemala	176/D 3
Guinea	94,927	245,860	9,030,220	Conakry	114/C 4
Guinea-Bissau	13,946	36,120	1,360,827	Bissau	114/B 3
Guyana	83,000	214,970	702,100	Georgetown	181/G 3
H					
Haiti	10,714	27,750	7,527,817	Port-au-Prince	177/H 2
Hawaii, U.S.	6,459	16,729	1,211,537	Honolulu	142/S10
Heard & McDonald Islands, Australia	159	412	....	....	216B/E
Honduras	43,277	112,087	6,669,789	Tegucigalpa	176/E 3
Hong Kong, China	402	1,040	7,394,170	Victoria	87/G 4
Howland Island, U.S.	0.6	1.6	....	....	137/H 4
Hungary	35,919	93,030	10,045,407	Budapest	50/D 2
I					
Iceland	39,768	103,000	280,798	Reykjavík	38/N 7
Idaho, U.S.	83,574	216,456	1,293,953	Boise	142/C 3
Illinois, U.S.	57,918	150,007	12,419,293	Springfield	143/J 4
India	1,269,339	3,287,588	1,049,700,118	New Delhi	92/C 3
Indiana, U.S.	36,420	94,328	6,080,485	Indianapolis	143/J 4
Indonesia	741,096	1,919,440	234,893,453	Jakarta	91/E 4
Iowa, U.S.	56,275	145,752	2,926,324	Des Moines	155/G 2
Iran	636,293	1,648,000	68,278,826	Tehran	103/H 3
Iraq	168,753	437,072	24,683,313	Baghdad	102/E 3
Ireland	27,136	70,282	3,924,140	Dublin	31/G10
Isle of Man, U.K.	227	588	73,489	Douglas	34/D 3
Israel	8,019	20,770	6,116,533	Jerusalem	104/C 3
Italy	116,305	301,230	57,998,353	Rome	67/F 2
J					
Jamaica	4,243	10,990	2,695,867	Kingston	177/G 2
Jan Mayen, Norway	144	373	....	....	29/D 1
Japan	145,882	377,835	127,214,499	Tōkyō	79/M 4
Java, Indonesia	48,842	126,500	121,352,608	Jakarta	89/E 4
Johnston Atoll, U.S.	1	2.8	327	....	137/J 3
Jordan	34,445	89,213	5,460,265	Amman	104/D 4
K					
Kansas, U.S.	82,282	213,110	2,688,418	Topeka	143/G 4
Kazakhstan	1,049,150	2,717,300	16,763,795	Aqmola	74/G 5
Kentucky, U.S.	40,411	104,665	4,041,769	Frankfort	162/E 2
Kenya	224,960	582,646	31,639,091	Nairobi	107/F 4
Kermadec Islands, New Zealand	13	33	....	....	136/G 8
Kiribati	277	717	98,549	Tarawa	136/H 5
Korea, North	46,540	120,539	22,466,481	P'yŏngyang	81/D 2
Korea, South	38,023	98,480	48,289,037	Seoul	81/D 4
Kuwait	6,880	17,820	2,183,161	Kuwait	103/F 4
KwaZulu Natal, South Africa	35,312	91,481	8,549,000	Pietermaritzburg	125/E 3
Kyrgyzstan	76,641	198,500	4,892,808	Bishkek	99/B 3
L					
Laos	91,428	236,800	5,921,545	Vientiane	94/C 2
Latvia	24,749	64,100	2,348,784	Riga	41/L 3
Lebanon	4,015	10,399	3,727,703	Beirut	104/D 3
Lesotho	11,718	30,350	1,861,959	Maseru	124/D 3
Liberia	43,000	111,370	3,317,176	Monrovia	114/C 5
Libya	679,358	1,759,537	5,499,074	Tripoli	108/C 2
Liechtenstein	62	160	33,145	Vaduz	61/F 3
Lithuania	25,174	65,200	3,592,561	Vilnius	41/K 4
Louisiana, U.S.	49,651	128,595	4,468,976	Baton Rouge	143/H 5
Luxembourg	999	2,587	454,157	Luxembourg	55/E 4
M					
Macau, China	6	16	469,903	Macau	87/G 4
Macedonia (F.Y.R.O.M.)	9,781	25,333	2,063,122	Skopje	49/G 2
Madagascar	226,657	587,041	16,979,744	Antananarivo	125/H 8
Madeira Islands, Portugal	307	794	245,012	Funchal	110/A 2
Maine, U.S.	33,741	87,388	1,274,923	Augusta	158/B 3
Malawi	45,745	118,480	11,651,239	Lilongwe	107/F 6
Malaya, Malaysia	50,806	131,588	18,523,632	Kuala Lumpur	89/C 1
Malaysia	127,316	329,750	23,092,940	Kuala Lumpur	90/C 2
Maldives	116	300	329,684	Male	77/F 9
Mali	478,764	1,240,000	11,626,219	Bamako	107/B 3
Malta	124	320	400,420	Valletta	48/L 7
Manitoba, Canada	250,946	649,951	1,150,000	Winnipeg	140/G 3
Marquesas Islands, French Polynesia	405	1,049	8,064	Atuona	137/M 5
Marshall Islands	70	181	56,429	Majuro	136/G 3

Place	Square Miles	Square Kilometers	Population	Capital or Chief Town	Page/ Index
Martinique, France	425	1,100	425,966	Fort-de-France	173/N 8
Maryland, U.S.	12,297	31,849	5,296,486	Annapolis	143/L 4
Massachusetts, U.S.	9,241	23,934	6,349,097	Boston	143/M 3
Mauritania	397,953	1,030,700	2,912,584	Nouakchott	107/A 3
Mauritius	718	1,860	1,210,447	Port Louis	125/T15
Mayotte, France	145	375	178,437	Mamoutzou	125/H 6
Mexico	761,601	1,972,546	104,907,991	Mexico	139/G 7
Michigan, U.S.	96,705	250,465	9,938,444	Lansing	143/J 2
Micronesia, Federated States of	271	702	136,973	Palikir	136/D 4
Midway Islands, U.S.	2	5.2	453	....	136/H 2
Minnesota, U.S.	86,943	225,182	4,919,479	St. Paul	143/G 2
Mississippi, U.S.	48,286	125,060	2,844,658	Jackson	143/H 5
Missouri, U.S.	69,709	180,546	5,595,211	Jefferson City	143/H 4
Moldova	13,012	33,700	4,439,502	Chişinău	72/E 4
Monaco	0.7	1.9	32,130	....	62/J 8
Mongolia	606,163	1,569,962	2,712,315	Ulaanbaatar	78/D 2
Montana, U.S.	147,046	380,849	902,195	Helena	142/D 2
Montserrat, U.K.	39	100	8,995	Plymouth	173/N 7
Morocco	172,414	446,550	31,689,265	Rabat	110/D 2
Mozambique	309,494	801,590	17,479,266	Maputo	123/G 3
Mpumalanga, South Africa	31,581	81,816	2,838,500	Nelspruit	125/E 2
Myanmar (Burma)	261,969	678,500	42,510,537	Yangon	93/G 2
N					
Namibia	318,694	825,418	1,927,447	Windhoek	107/D 7
Nauru	8	21	12,570	Yaren (district)	136/F 5
Nebraska, U.S.	77,358	200,358	1,711,263	Lincoln	154/D 3
Nepal	54,363	140,800	26,469,569	Kathmandu	96/D 1
Netherlands	14,413	37,330	16,150,511	The Hague; Amsterdam	52/B 5
Netherlands Antilles	371	960	216,226	Willemstad	180/D 1
Nevada, U.S.	110,567	286,367	1,998,257	Carson City	142/C 4
New Brunswick, Canada	28,355	73,440	757,100	Fredericton	158/D 2
New Caledonia & Dependencies, France	7,359	19,060	210,798	Nouméa	137/U11
Newfoundland & Labrador, Canada	156,649	405,721	533,800	St. John's	141/K 3
New Hampshire, U.S.	9,283	24,044	1,235,786	Concord	161/L 3
New Jersey, U.S.	8,215	21,277	8,414,350	Trenton	168/D 3
New Mexico, U.S.	121,598	314,939	1,819,046	Santa Fe	142/E 5
New South Wales, Australia	309,498	801,600	5,731,906	Sydney	132/C 1
New York, U.S.	53,989	139,833	18,976,457	Albany	161/J 3
New Zealand	103,736	268,676	3,951,307	Wellington	161
Nicaragua	49,998	129,494	5,128,517	Managua	177/E 3
Niger	489,189	1,267,000	11,058,590	Niamey	107/C 3
Nigeria	356,668	923,770	133,881,703	Abuja	107/C 4
Niue, New Zealand	100	259	2,124	Alofi	137/J 7
Norfolk Island, Australia	13.4	34.6	2,756	Kingston	136/F 7
North America	9,355,975	24,232,000	482,992,000	....	165
North Carolina, U.S.	52,672	136,421	8,049,313	Raleigh	163/G 3
North Dakota, U.S.	70,704	183,123	642,200	Bismarck	156/D 4
Northern Cape, South Africa	140,268	363,389	763,900	Kimberley	124/C 3
Northern Ireland, U.K.	5,459	14,138	1,697,800	Belfast	31/H 9
Northern Marianas, U.S.	184	477	80,006	Saipan	136/D 3
Northern Province, South Africa	46,168	119,606	5,120,600	Pietersburg	123/F 4
Northern Territory, Australia	519,784	1,346,241	175,876	Darwin	127/C 2
North Korea	46,540	120,539	22,224,195	P'yŏngyang	81/D 2
North-West, South Africa	45,347	117,450	3,506,800	Mmabatho	124/D 2
Northwest Territories, Canada	589,315	1,526,328	40,900	Yellowknife	140/E 2
Norway	125,181	324,220	4,546,123	Oslo	38/C 3
Nova Scotia, Canada	21,425	55,491	942,700	Halifax	158/E 3
Nunavut, Canada	733,590	1,900,000	28,200	Iqaluit	141/K 2
O					
Oceania	3,292,000	8,526,280	30,199,000	....	162
Ohio, U.S.	44,828	116,103	11,353,140	Columbus	143/K 3
Oklahoma, U.S.	69,903	181,048	3,450,654	Oklahoma City	153/E 3
Oman	82,031	212,460	2,807,125	Muscat	101/G 4
Ontario, Canada	412,580	1,068,582	11,874,400	Toronto	140/H 3
Oregon, U.S.	97,132	251,571	3,421,399	Salem	142/B 3
Orkney Islands, Scotland	376	974	19,480	Kirkwall	31/N13
P					
Pakistan	310,403	803,944	150,694,740	Islamabad	101/H 3
Palau	177	458	19,717	Koror	136/C 4
Panama	30,193	78,200	2,960,784	Panamá	177/F 4
Papua New Guinea	178,259	461,690	5,295,816	Port Moresby	136/D 5
Paraguay	157,047	406,752	6,036,900	Asunción	188/D 2
Pennsylvania, U.S.	46,058	119,291	12,281,054	Harrisburg	161/G 4
Peru	496,223	1,285,220	28,409,897	Lima	184/C 3
Philippines	115,830	300,000	84,619,974	Manila	114
Pitcairn Islands, U.K.	18	47	47	Adamstown	137/N 7
Poland	120,725	312,678	38,622,660	Warsaw	43/K 2
Portugal	35,552	92,080	10,102,022	Lisbon	46/A 3
Prince Edward Island, Canada	2,184	5,657	138,500	Charlottetown	158/F 2
Puerto Rico, U.S.	3,508	9,085	3,885,877	San Juan	173/M7
Q					
Qatar	4,247	11,000	817,052	Doha	100/F 3
Québec, Canada	594,857	1,540,680	7,410,500	Québec	141/J 3
Queensland, Australia	666,872	1,727,200	2,977,813	Brisbane	134/A 3
R					
Réunion, France	969	2,510	755,171	St-Denis	125/R15
Rhode Island, U.S.	1,231	3,189	1,048,319	Providence	161/L 4
Romania	91,699	237,500	22,271,839	Bucharest	51/F 3
Russia	6,592,735	17,075,200	144,526,278	Moscow	74/H 3
Rwanda	10,169	26,337	7,810,056	Kigali	121/G 3
S					
Sabah, Malaysia	28,460	73,711	2,449,389	Kota Kinabalu	91/E 2
Saint Helena & Dependencies, U.K.	158	410	7,367	Jamestown	26/J 6
Saint Kitts and Nevis	104	269	38,763	Basseterre	173/N 7
Saint Lucia	239	620	162,157	Castries	173/N 8
Saint Pierre & Miquelon, France	93.5	242	6,976	Saint-Pierre	159/J 2
Saint Vincent & the Grenadines	131	340	116,812	Kingstown	173/N 8
Sakhalin, Russia	29,500	76,405	632,000	Yuzhno-Sakhalinsk	75/Q 4
Samoa	1,104	2,860	178,173	Apia	137/R 9
San Marino	23.4	60.6	28,119	San Marino	63/F 5
São Tomé and Príncipe	371	960	175,883	São Tomé	120/A 2
Sarawak, Malaysia	48,050	124,449	2,012,616	Kuching	90/D 3
Sardinia, Italy	9,301	24,090	1,648,044	Cagliari	48/A 2
Saskatchewan, Canada	251,865	652,330	1,015,800	Regina	140/F 3
Saudi Arabia	756,981	1,960,582	24,293,844	Riyadh	100/D 4
Scotland, U.K.	30,414	78,772	5,128,000	Edinburgh	31/J 8
Senegal	75,749	196,190	10,580,307	Dakar	114/B 3
Serbia and Montenegro	39,517	102,350	10,655,774	Belgrade	50/D 3
Seychelles	176	455	80,469	Victoria	27/M6
Shetland Islands, Scotland	552	1,430	22,440	Lerwick	31/N12
Sicily, Italy	9,926	25,708	5,076,700	Palermo	48/C 3
Sierra Leone	27,699	71,740	5,732,681	Freetown	114/B 4
Singapore	244	632.6	4,608,595	Singapore	89/H 6
Slovakia	18,859	48,845	5,430,033	Bratislava	43/K 4
Slovenia	7,836	20,296	1,935,677	Ljubljana	50/B 3
Society Islands, French Polynesia	677	1,753	117,703	Papeete	137/K 6
Solomon Islands	10,985	28,450	509,190	Honiara	136/E 6
Somalia	246,200	637,658	8,025,190	Mogadishu	107/G 4
South Africa	471,008	1,219,912	42,768,678	Cape Town; Pretoria	107/E 7
South America	6,879,916	17,819,000	345,782,000	....	203
South Australia, Australia	379,922	984,000	1,400,630	Adelaide	127/C 3
South Carolina, U.S.	31,189	80,779	4,012,012	Columbia	163/G 3
South Dakota, U.S.	77,121	199,744	754,844	Pierre	154/D 1
South Korea	38,023	98,480	48,324,000	Seoul	81/D 4
Spain	194,884	504,750	40,217,413	Madrid	46/C 2
Sri Lanka	25,332	65,610	19,742,439	Colombo	92/D 6
Sudan	967,494	2,505,809	38,114,160	Khartoum	107/E 3
Sumatra, Indonesia	182,811	473,481	43,259,707	Medan	89/D 3
Suriname	63,039	163,270	435,449	Paramaribo	182/B 1
Svalbard, Norway	23,957	62,049	2,332	Longyearbyen	74/C 2
Swaziland	6,703	17,360	1,161,219	Mbabane; Lobamba	125/E 2
Sweden	173,731	449,964	8,878,085	Stockholm	38/E 3
Switzerland	15,943	41,292	7,318,638	Bern	60/D 4
Syria	71,498	185,180	17,585,540	Damascus	102/D 3
T					
Tahiti, French Polynesia	402	1,041	150,707	Papeete	137/X15
Taiwan	13,892	35,980	22,603,000	T'aipei	87/J 3
Tajikistan	55,251	143,100	6,863,752	Dushanbe	74/H 6
Tanzania	364,699	945,090	35,922,454	Dar es Salaam; Dodoma	107/F 5
Tasmania, Australia	26,178	67,800	452,851	Hobart	132/C 4
Tennessee, U.S.	42,146	109,158	5,689,283	Nashville	162/D 3
Texas, U.S.	267,277	692,248	20,851,820	Austin	142/G 5
Thailand	198,455	513,998	64,265,276	Bangkok	94/C 3
Tibet, China	471,428	1,221,000	2,560,000	Lhasa	99/D 5
Togo	21,927	56,790	5,429,299	Lomé	115/F 4
Tokelau, New Zealand	3.9	10	1,445	....	137/H 5
Tonga	289	748	108,141	Nuku'alofa	137/H 7
Trinidad and Tobago	1,980	5,128	1,104,209	Port-of-Spain	173/N 9
Tristan da Cunha, St. Helena	38	98	313	Edinburgh	26/J 7
Tuamotu Archipelago, French Polynesia	266	690	15,370	Apataki	137/L 6
Tunisia	63,170	163,610	9,924,742	Tunis	111/H 2
Turkey	301,382	780,580	68,109,469	Ankara	102/C 2
Turkmenistan	188,455	488,100	4,775,544	Ashgabat	74/F 6
Turks and Caicos Islands, U.K.	166	430	19,350	Grand Turk	177/H 1
Tuvalu	10	26	11,305	Funafuti	136/G 5
U					
Uganda	91,135	236,040	25,632,794	Kampala	107/F 4
Ukraine	233,089	603,700	48,055,439	Kiev	72/F 4
United Arab Emirates	29,182	75,581	2,484,818	Abu Dhabi	100/F 4
United Kingdom	94,525	244,820	60,094,648	London	31
United States	3,618,765	9,372,610	290,342,554	Washington, D.C.	142
Uruguay	68,039	176,220	3,413,329	Montevideo	179/D 6
Utah, U.S.	84,904	219,902	2,233,169	Salt Lake City	142/D 4
Uzbekistan	172,741	447,400	25,981,647	Tashkent	74/G 5
V					
Vanuatu	5,699	14,760	199,414	Port-Vila	136/F 6
Vatican City	0.17	0.44	890	....	65/F 7
Venezuela	352,143	912,050	24,654,694	Caracas	181/E 3
Vermont, U.S.	9,614	24,900	608,827	Montpelier	161/K 3
Victoria, Australia	87,876	227,600	4,244,282	Melbourne	132/C 3
Vietnam	127,243	329,560	81,624,716	Hanoi	94/D 2
Virginia, U.S.	42,326	109,625	7,078,515	Richmond	163/H 2
Virgin Islands, British	59	153	21,730	Road Town	173/M7
Virgin Islands, U.S.	136	352	124,778	Charlotte Amalie	173/M7
W					
Wake Island, U.S.	2.5	6.5	302	....	136/F 3
Wales, U.K.	8,017	20,764	2,921,100	Cardiff	31/J10
Wallis and Futuna, France	106	275	15,734	Mata Utu	136/G 6
Washington, U.S.	70,637	182,949	5,894,121	Olympia	144/D 4
West Bank	2,263	5,860	2,237,194	....	105/C 4
Western Australia, Australia	975,096	2,525,500	1,587,050	Perth	127/B 3
Western Cape, South Africa	49,943	129,386	3,620,200	Cape Town	124/C 4
Western Sahara	102,703	266,000	261,794	....	110/B 4
West Virginia, U.S.	24,231	62,758	1,808,344	Charleston	143/K 4
Wisconsin, U.S.	65,499	169,643	5,363,675	Madison	143/H 3
World	(land) 57,505,734	148,940,000	6,230,586,132	....	52
Wyoming, U.S.	97,818	253,349	493,782	Cheyenne	142/E 3
Y					
Yemen	203,849	527,970	19,349,881	Sanaa	100/E 5
Yugoslavia, see Serbia and Montenegro					
Yukon Territory, Canada	186,660	483,450	29,900	Whitehorse	140/C 2
Z					
Zambia	290,583	752,610	10,307,333	Lusaka	107/E 6
Zimbabwe	150,803	390,580	12,576,742	Harare	123/F 3

Map Projections

A Difficult Problem Solved by Computers Today

A map projection is an image of the Earth or parts of the Earth on a flat plane. Every point on Earth can be identified with the aid of geographic coordinates, within a global coordinate grid, and this grid can be projected onto a flat surface. Today, computer cartography plays an important role in calculating the projection most appropriate for a particular purpose.

Basic Principles and Terms

The Earth rotates around its axis once a day. Its end points are the North and South poles; the line circling the Earth midway between the poles is the Equator. The arc from the Equator to each pole is divided into 90 degrees of latitude. The Equator itself represents 0° latitude and is divided into 360 degrees of longitude. Lines circling the globe from pole to pole which intersect with the Equator at 90-degree angles are called meridians, or great circles. The meridian passing through the Greenwich Observatory near London was chosen by international agreement as to prime meridian or 0° longitude in 1884. Meridians and lines of latitude (parallels) form the global coordinate grid, or graticule. The distance from the prime meridian to a given point to the west or east, expressed in degrees

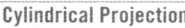

(coordinates) is its geographic longitude. Similarly, distances north or south of the Equator represent geographic latitude. Although all meridians are equal in length, parallels become shorter as they approach the poles. Thus, while the distance between two parallels (one degree of latitude) is approximately 112 km everywhere on Earth, the distance between two meridians (one degree of longitude) varies between 112 km at the Equator and zero at the poles where the meridians converge. Each degree of longitude and latitude is divided into 60 minutes. One minute of latitude equals one nautical mile (1.85 km).

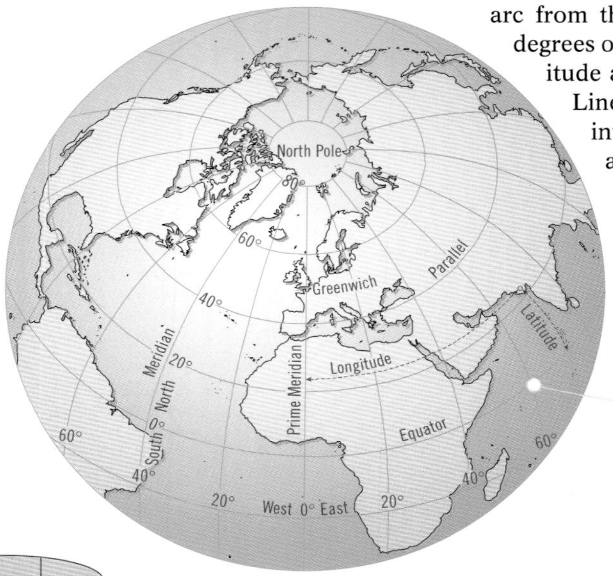

Distortion

There is only one way to represent the sphere of the Earth with absolute precision: as a globe. All attempts to project our planet's curved surface onto a plane create distortion. Depending upon the map projection selected, distortions appear in shapes and area sizes, angles or distances between points on the Earth. Only parallels or meridians (or some other set of lines) can be represented in accurate proportion. All other lines must be either

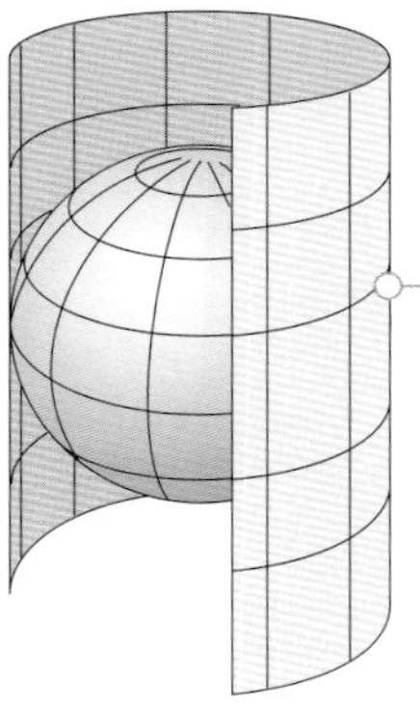

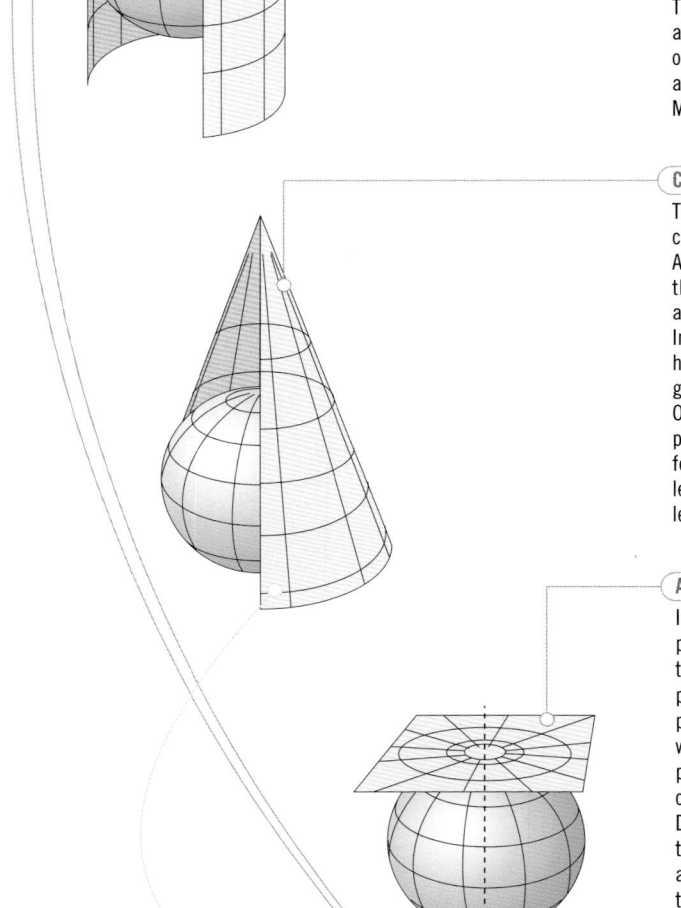

Cylindrical Projection

A cylinder of variable axis length is wrapped around the Earth. The cylinder can touch the Earth at the Equator, for example, or penetrate through the Earth, as is the case in the (conformal) Mercator projection.

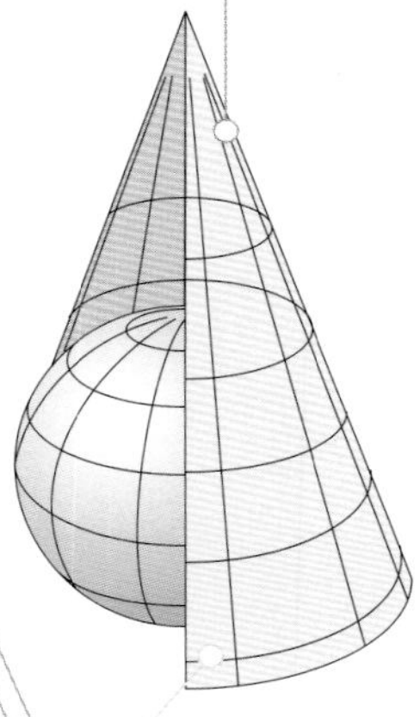

Conic Projection

This projection is produced by capping the Earth with a cone. Axis length is variable. Normally, the cone axis is aligned with an Earth axis or with the Equator. In the conic projection shown here, the cone can be made tangent to any desired parallel. One popular version of the conic projection is the Lambert Conformal Conic, in which two parallels are represented in conforming lengths.

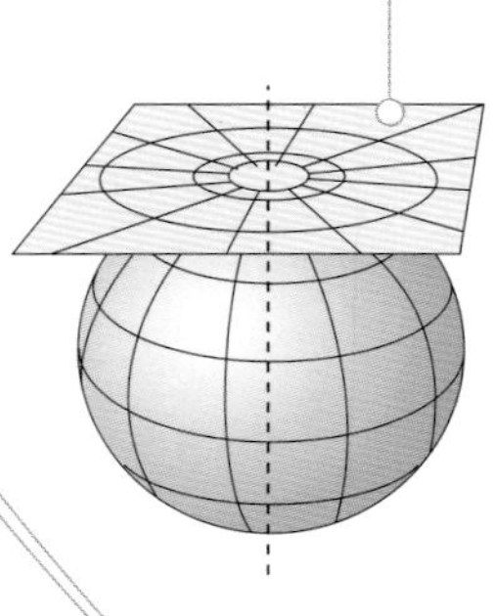

Azimuthal Projection

In azimuthal projections, the projection surface is a plane that touches the Earth at a single point. It is ordinarily used as a polar projection of the Earth — with a pole at the center of the projection. This type of projection can only show one hemisphere. Depending upon the distance from the projection axis to the Earth's axis, map projections are referred to as polar, equatorial or oblique-axis. A version frequently used for maps of continents is the Lambert Azimuthal Equal Area Projection, which shows areas with relatively little distortion of shapes.

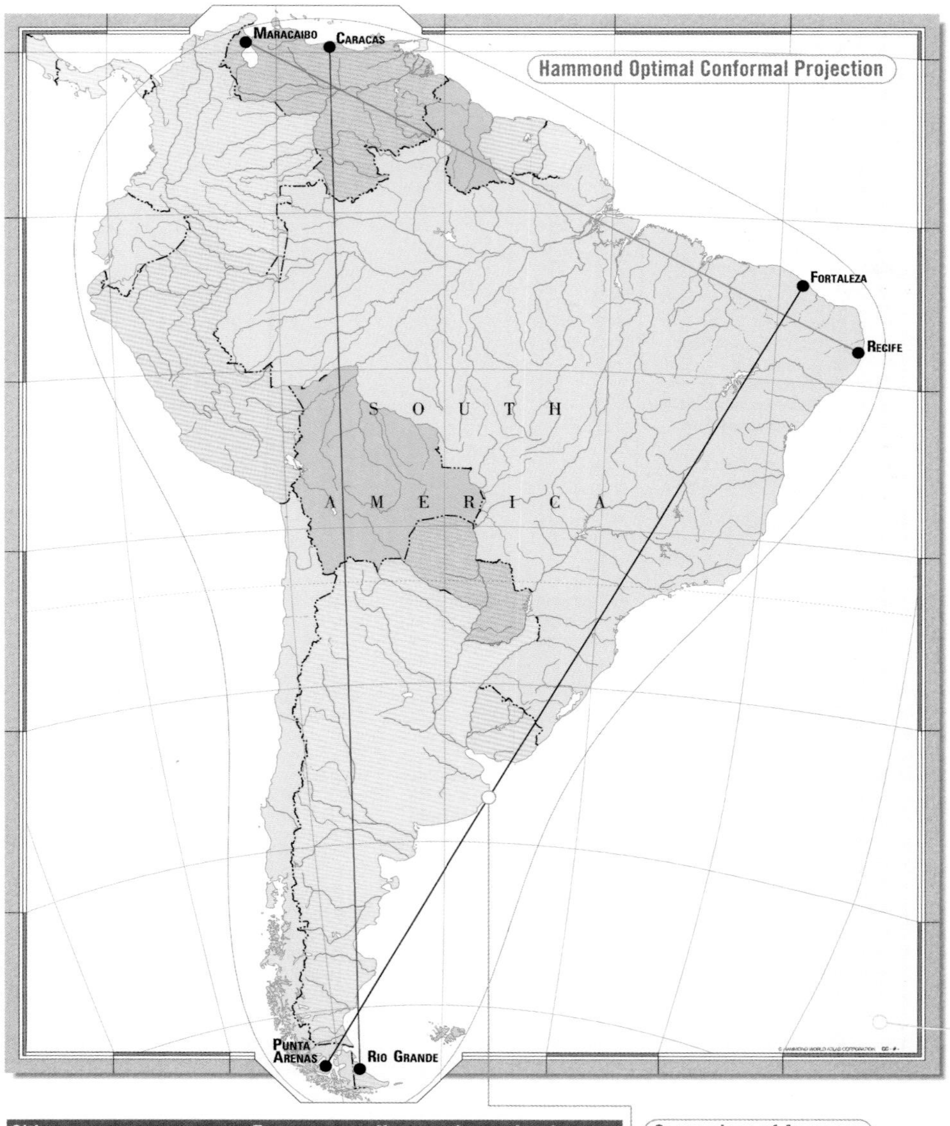

Cities	True distance	Hammond Projection	Lambert Projection
Caracas – Rio Grande	7 149 km	7 126 km	6 944 km
Maracaibo – Recife	4 560 km	4 578 km	4 533 km
Fortaleza – Punta Arenas	6 246 km	6 266 km	6 163 km

Comparison of Accuracy

The use of the Lambert Azimuthal Equal Area Projection for maps of continents produces distortions ranging from 2.3% (Europe) to 15% (Asia). The Hammond Optimal Conformal reduces these distortions by half and improves the reliability of distance measurements based on these maps.

Robinson Projection

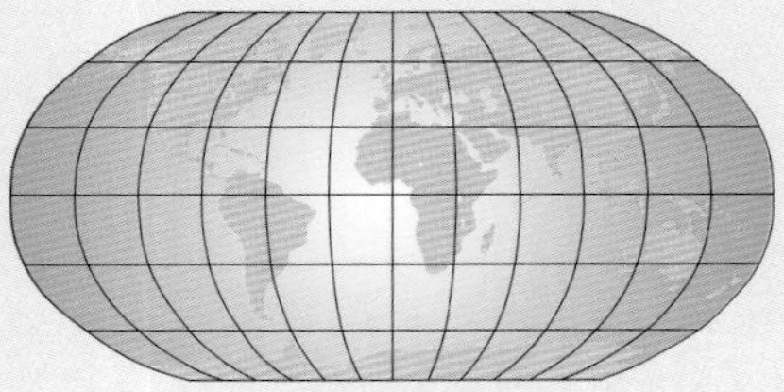

Mercator Projection

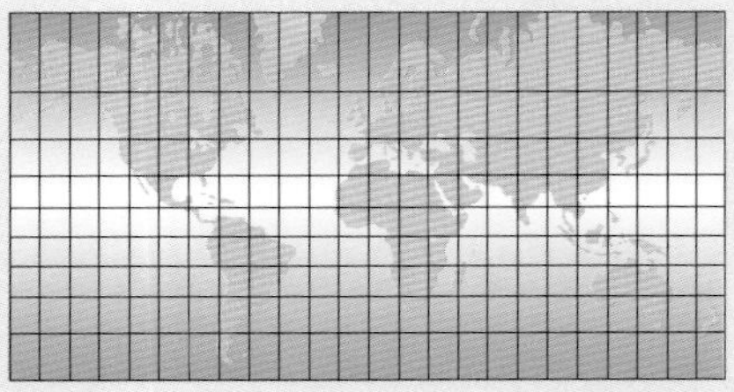

too long or too short. Accordingly, the scale on a flat map cannot be true everywhere. On world maps or very large areas, variations in scale may be extreme.

Projections: Selected Examples

The Mercator projection is a conformal, normal-axis cylindrical projection in which all meridians and parallels intersect at right angles. Because all compass directions appear as straight lines, the Mercator projection is still an important navigational tool. Moreover, every small region conforms to the shape on a globe – hence the name conformal. But because its meridians are evenly-spaced vertical lines that do not converge (unlike those on the globe), the horizontal parallels must be drawn farther apart as they approach the poles to maintain a correct relationship. Only the Equator is true to scale, and the size of areas in the higher latitudes is dramatically distorted.

The Robinson projection was used to create the two-page world map in the Map Section. It combines elements of both conformal and equal-area projections to show the whole earth with relatively true shapes and reasonably equal areas. This projection is a mediating pseudo-cylindrical representation.

The conic projection is used frequently for air navigation charts. It was used to create most of the national and regional maps in this atlas.

The Hammond Optimal Conformal projection presents an optimal view of an area by reducing shifts in scale over an entire region to the minimum degree possible. The concept underlying the Optimal Conformal projection is that, for any region on the globe, there is an ideal projection for which scale variations can be kept as small as possible. Consequently, unlike other projections, the Optimal Conformal does not use a standard formula to construct a map. Each map is a unique projection – the optimal projection for that specific area.

In practice, the cartographer first defines the map subject, then, working on a computer, draws a boundary around the region to be mapped. Next, a sophisticated software program evaluates the size and shape of the region to determine the most accurate way to project it. The result is a precise map with the minimum possible degree of distortion. All of the continent maps in this Atlas (with the exception of Antarctica) have been drawn using this projection.

Projections Compared

The following diagrams show the distortions produced by several commonly used projections. By using a simple face with familiar shapes (the Plan) as the starting point, it is easy to see the advantages and drawbacks of each. Areas or continents on a map change much like the shapes of the face in the diagram. The distortion appears not only in the features themselves, but also in the changing shapes, angles, and areas of the background grid, or graticule.

The Plan

The Plan shows the "continents" either as perfect circles or true straight lines on the Earth. They should appear that way on a "perfect" map.

Orthographic Projection (Parallel Projection)

This azimuthal view shows the "continents" on Earth as seen from space. The facial features occupy half of the Earth. Toward the edge, the eyes grow increasingly elliptical, the nose appears larger and less straight, and the mouth curves into a smile.

Mercator Projection

This cylindrical projection preserves angles exactly, but the mouth is now smiling broadly and shows extreme distortion at the map's outer edge. Typical of the rapid expansion of forms toward the outer edge is the extreme enlargement of Greenland on Mercator world maps.

Peters Projection

This equal-area cylindrical projection represents areas in their correct proportions, but it does not closely resemble the Plan. Angles, local shapes, and global relations are significantly distorted.

Gnomonic Projection

This strange-looking projection is neither conformal nor equal-area. It is a centrally positioned azimuthal projection, meaning that the center of projection lies in the center of the Earth. Although its outer regions are badly distorted, the straight mouth and precise triangle of the nose indicate a key advantage of this map: all great circles appear as straight lines. This enables the user to find the shortest path between any two points on the map simply by connecting them with a straight line.

Hammond Optimal Conformal Projection

As one can easily see, this projection minimizes inaccuracies between the angles and shapes of the Plan, yielding a near-perfect map of the given area, up to a complete hemisphere. Like all conformal maps, the Optimal projection preserves every angle exactly, but it is more successful than previous projections at spreading the inevitable curvature across the entire map. The sides of the triangle appear almost straight, although the sum of the angles is greater than 180°. Although the eyes are somewhat too large, this is the only map with eyes that appear concentric. Both mathematically and visually, it offers the best conformal map that can be made of the ideal Plan.

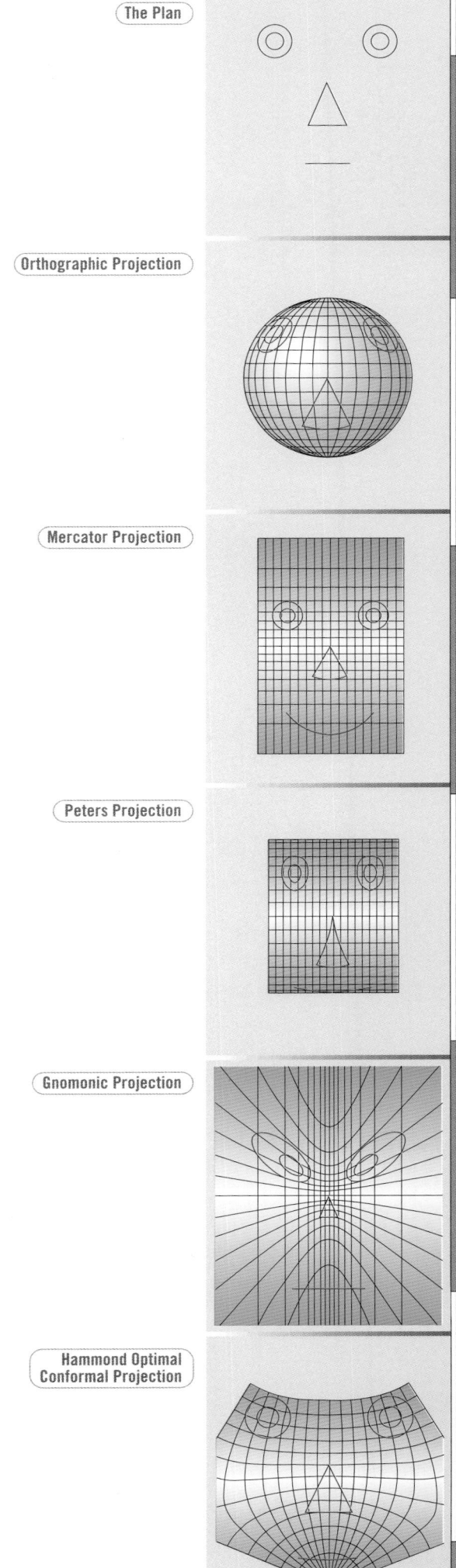

The Plan

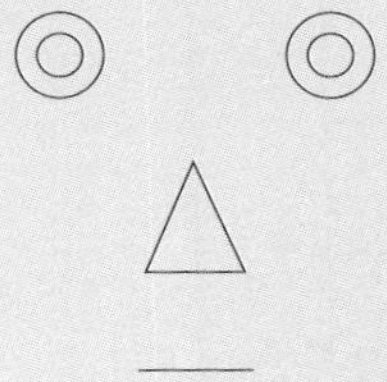

Orthographic Projection

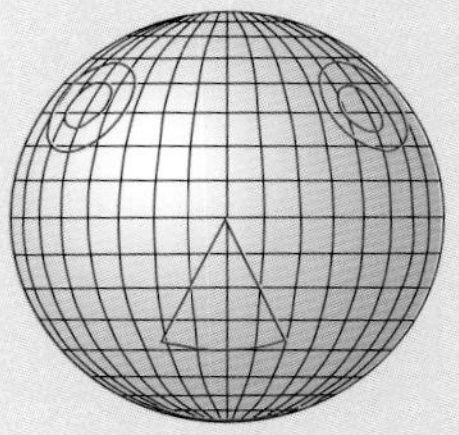

Mercator Projection

Peters Projection

Gnomonic Projection

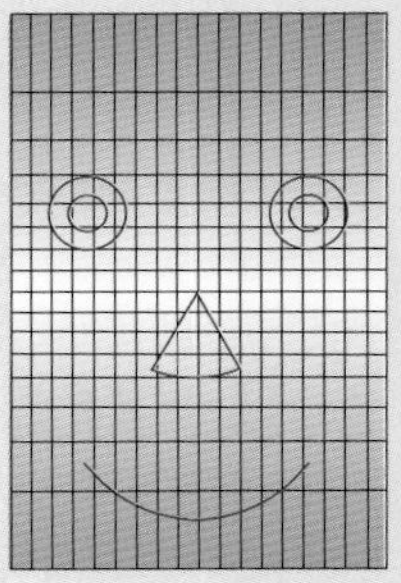

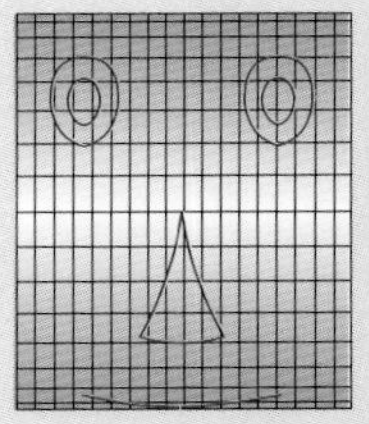

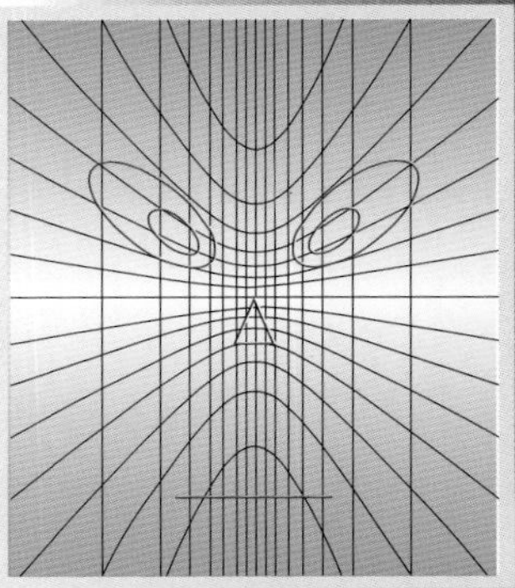

Hammond Optimal Conformal Projection

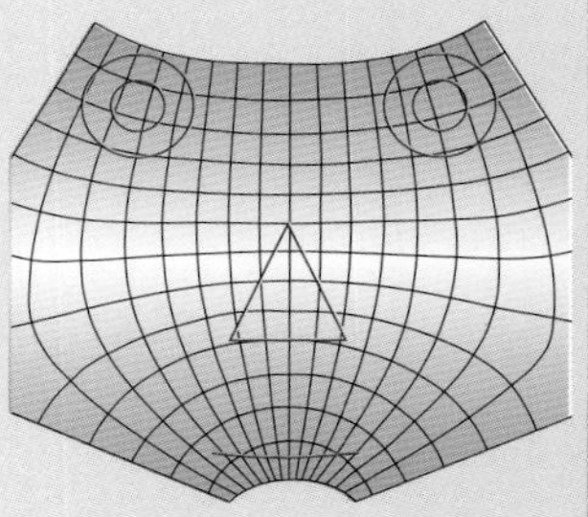

"Facts which at first seem improbable will...
stand forth in naked and simple beauty"

Galileo Galilei

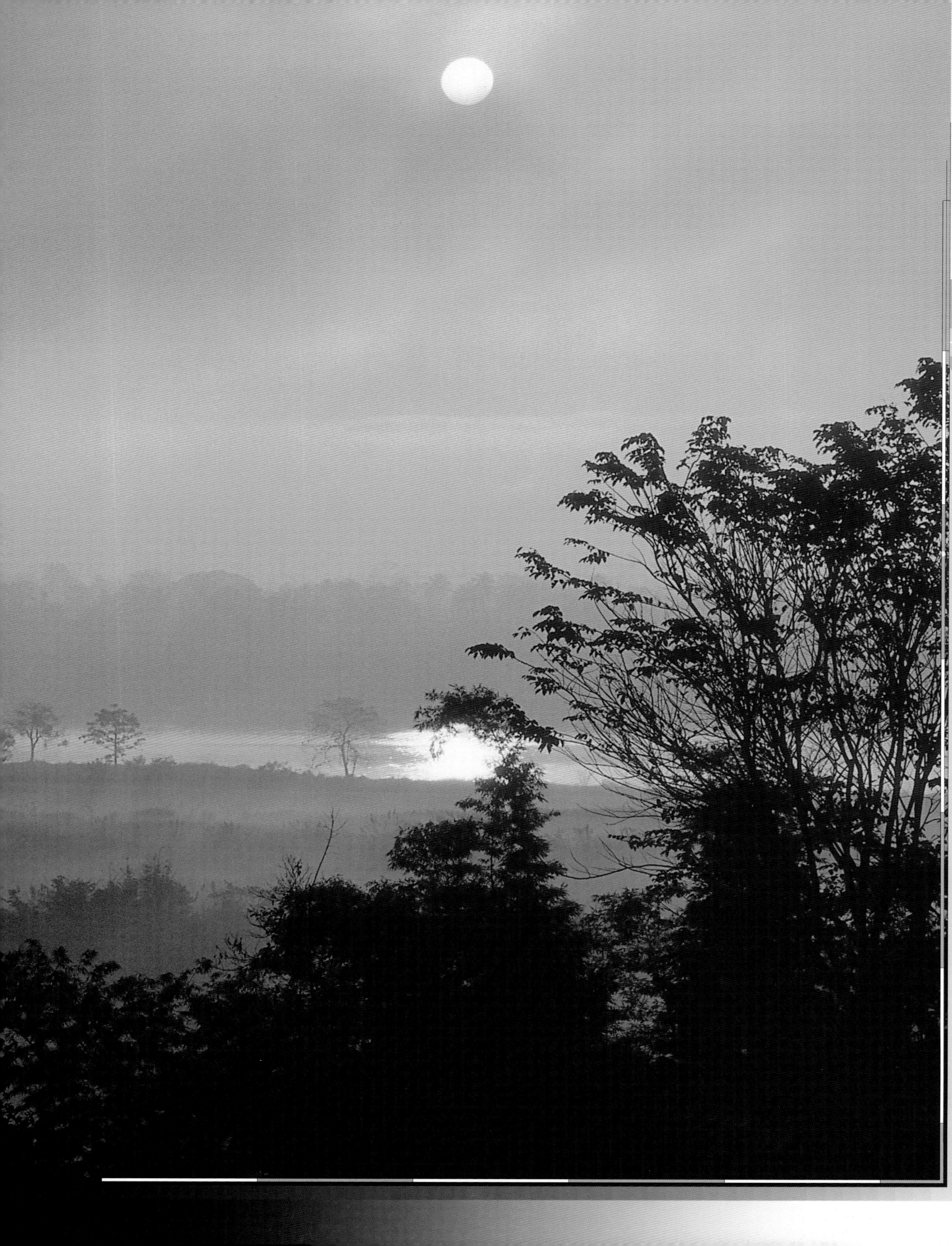

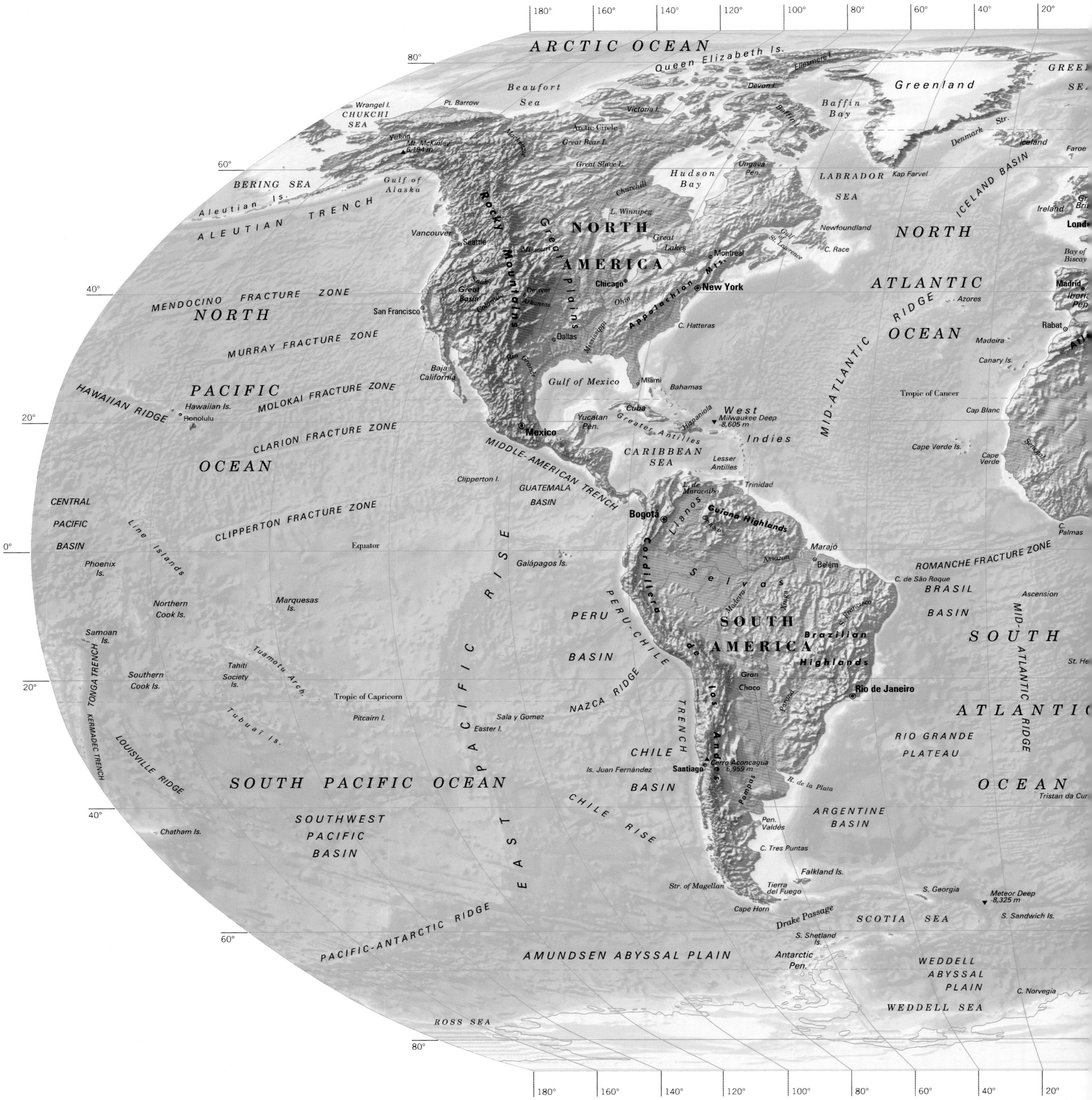

ARCTIC OCEAN

Beaufort
Sea

Queen Elizabeth Is.
Ellesmere I.
Devon I.

Greenland

GREEN...
SEA

Wrangel I.
Pt. Barrow
CHUKCHI
SEA

Victoria I.

Baffin
Bay

Baffin

Denmark Str.
Iceland
Faroe

Yukon
Mt. McKinley
6,194 m
Great Bear L.
Arctic Circle
Great Slave L.

Hudson
Bay

Ungava
Pen.

LABRADOR
SEA
Kap Farvel

ICELAND BASIN

Ireland
Gr...
Br...

BERING SEA
Gulf of
Alaska
Aleutian Is.
ALEUTIAN TRENCH

Rocky Mountains
Great Plains

NORTH
AMERICA

Churchill
L. Winnipeg

Great
Lakes
Montreal

Newfoundland
C. Race

NORTH

London

MENDOCINO FRACTURE ZONE
NORTH

San Francisco

Seattle
Vancouver

Snake
Great
Basin
Denver
Arkansas
Missouri
Chicago
Ohio

Mississippi
Appalachian Mts.
New York
C. Hatteras

ATLANTIC

OCEAN

MID-ATLANTIC
RIDGE
Azores

Madrid
Iberian
Pen.

Rabat

MURRAY FRACTURE ZONE

Baja
California
Rio Grande
Dallas
Miami

Gulf of Mexico
Bahamas

Cuba
Greater Antilles
Hispaniola
West
Milwaukee Deep
-8,605 m
Indies

Tropic of Cancer

Madeira
Canary Is.

Cap Blanc

HAWAIIAN RIDGE
PACIFIC
Hawaiian Is.
Honolulu
MOLOKAI FRACTURE ZONE

Yucatan
Pen.
Mexico

CARIBBEAN
SEA
Lesser
Antilles

Cape Verde Is.
Cape
Verde

S...

CLARION FRACTURE ZONE

Clipperton I.
GUATEMALA
BASIN

L. de
Maracaibo
Trinidad

OCEAN

MIDDLE-AMERICAN TRENCH

Bogotá
Llanos
Guiana Highlands

C.
Palmas

CENTRAL
PACIFIC
BASIN

CLIPPERTON FRACTURE ZONE

Equator
Galápagos Is.

Marajó

ROMANCHE FRACTURE ZONE
BRASIL
BASIN

Ascension

Cordillera
Amazon
Selvas
Madeira
Belém
C. de São Roque

Phoenix
Is.
Line Islands

Northern
Cook Is.
Marquesas
Is.

PERU
BASIN

PERU-CHILE
SOUTH
AMERICA
Brazilian
Highlands

MID-ATLANTIC RIDGE
SOUTH

St. He...

Samoan
Is.
Southern
Cook Is.
Tahiti
Society
Is.
Tropic of Capricorn
Pitcairn I.

NAZCA RIDGE

Gran
Choco

Paraná
Rio de Janeiro

ATLANTIC

Tuamotu Arch.
Sala y Gomez
Easter I.

CHILE
TRENCH
Los Andes

RIO GRANDE
PLATEAU

Tubuai Is.

EAST PACIFIC RISE

CHILE
BASIN
Is. Juan Fernández
Santiago
Cerro Aconcagua
6,959 m
R. de la Plata

OCEAN

Tristan da Cun...

SOUTH PACIFIC OCEAN
Chatham Is.
SOUTHWEST
PACIFIC
BASIN

Pampas
ARGENTINE
BASIN

Pen.
Valdés
C. Tres Puntas

TONGA TRENCH
KERMADEC TRENCH
LOUISVILLE RIDGE

CHILE RISE

Falkland Is.

S. Georgia

Meteor Deep
-8,325 m

Str. of Magellan
Tierra
del Fuego
Cape Horn

S. Sandwich Is.

PACIFIC-ANTARCTIC RIDGE
AMUNDSEN ABYSSAL PLAIN

Drake Passage
S. Shetland
Is.
Antarctic
Pen.

SCOTIA SEA

WEDDELL
ABYSSAL
PLAIN

C. Norvegia

ROSS SEA

WEDDELL SEA

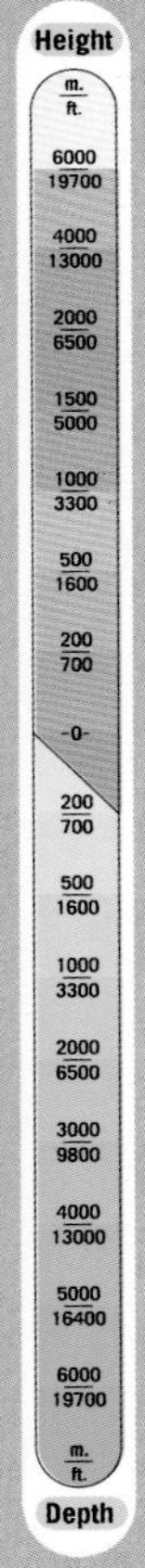

Height

m.   ft.
6000 19700
4000 13000
2000 6500
1500 5000
1000 3300
500   1600
200   700
- 0 -
200   700
500   1600
1000 3300
2000 6500
3000 9800
4000 13000
5000 16400
6000 19700
m.   ft.

Depth

Population

⊛ Over 5,000,000   ⊚ 500,000 - 1,999,999
⊛ 2,000,000 - 4,999,999   ○ Under 500,000

20° 40° 60° 80° 100° 120° 140° 160° 180°

ARCTIC OCEAN

Svalbard
Spitsbergen
Franz Josef Land
Severnaya Zemlya
New Siberian Is.
80°

Nordkapp
BARENTS SEA
Novaya Zemlya
Kara Sea
Yamal Pen.
Arctic Circle
Kolyma Ra.

NORWEGIAN SEA
Kiølen
Kola Pen.
White Sea
Ob'
Yenisey
West Siberian Plain
Central Siberian Plateau
Lena
Aldan
60°
BERING SEA
Kamchatka Pen.
SEA OF OKHOTSK

Stockholm
Baltic Sea
L. Ladoga
Moscow
Ural Mountains
Irtysh
L. Baykal
Amur
Sakhalin
Kuril Is.
NORTHWEST PACIFIC BASIN
EMPEROR SEAMOUNT CHAIN

NORTH
EUROPE
Carpathians
Dnieper
Kirgiz Steppe
A S I A
Altai Mts.
Gobi Desert
Hokkaidō
JAPAN TRENCH
40°

Paris
Alps
Danube
Don
Volga
Aral Sea
Balkhash
Tian Shan
Sea of Japan
NORTH PACIFIC

Rome
Black Sea
Istanbul
Caucasus
Elbrus 5,642 m
Caspian Sea
Amu Darya
Takla Makan
Kunlun Mts.
Beijing
Huang
Yellow Sea
Tōkyō
Honshū

MEDITERRANEAN SEA
Sicily
Aegean Sea
Taurus Mts.
Cyprus
Zagros Mts.
Tehran
Tigris
Euphrates
Hindu Kush
Indus
Himalaya
Salween
East China Sea
RYUKYU TRENCH
20°

Cairo
Nile
Hijaz
Red Sea
Persian Gulf
Karachi
Ganges
Mt. Everest 8,848 m
Mekong
Red
Taiwan
Hainan
PHILIPPINE SEA
Mariana Is.
Tropic of Cancer

Ahaggar
Sahara
Arabian Pen.
Rub' al Khali
Narmada
ARABIAN SEA
Mumbai (Bombay)
BAY OF BENGAL
SOUTH CHINA SEA
Luzon
Manila
Challenger Deep -11,033 m
MARIANA TRENCH
CENTRAL PACIFIC BASIN
0°

AFRICA
L. Chad
Sudan
White Nile
Blue Nile
Gulf of Aden
Socotra
Ethiopian Plateau
CARLSBERG RIDGE
C. Comorin
Maldive Is.
Sri Lanka
Andaman Is.
Isthmus of Kra
Palawan
Mindanao
Sulu Sea
Celebes Sea
Halmahera
Caroline Is.
MELANESIAN BASIN
Marshall Is.
CENTRAL PACIFIC BASIN

Lagos
Bioko
São Tomé
Congo Basin
Kinshasa
Kilimanjaro 5,895 m
Victoria
L. Tanganyika
SOMALI BASIN
Seychelles
Chagos Arch.
Cocos Is.
Equator
INDIAN OCEAN
NINETYEAST RIDGE
CENTRAL INDIAN RIDGE
JAVA TRENCH
Sumatra
Jakarta
Java
Java Sea
Borneo
Celebes
Banda Sea
New Guinea
Bismarck Arch.
Solomon Is.
New Britain

ANGOLA BASIN
L. Nyasa
Comoros Is.
Madagascar
Réunion
Mauritius
Mozambique Chan.
-7,450 m
Timor Sea
Arafura Sea
Gulf of Carpentaria
Cape York Pen.
Great Barrier Reef
CORAL SEA
New Hebrides
Fiji Is.
20°

WALVIS RIDGE
Lusaka
Zambezi
Johannesburg
Orange
Kalahari Desert
Drakensberg
Cape of Good Hope
SOUTHWEST INDIAN RIDGE
BROKEN PLATEAU
C. Leeuwin
Great Victoria Desert
AUSTRALIA
Great Australian Bight
Darling
Murray
Great Dividing Ra.
Sydney
Mt. Kosciusko 2,228 m
Melbourne
TASMAN SEA
New Caledonia
North C.
North I.
40°

Kerguélen
McDonald Is.
KERGUÉLEN PLATEAU
SOUTHEAST INDIAN RIDGE
AUSTRALIAN-ANTARCTIC BASIN
MID-INDIAN RIDGE
Tasmania
South I.

ENDERBY ABYSSAL PLAIN
60°

Antarctic Circle
C. Batterbee
ROSS SEA
C. Adare
80°

A N T A R C T I C A

20° 40° 60° 80° 100° 120° 140° 160° 180°

Scale 1:70,000,000   Robinson Projection

MI   600   1200   1800   2400
KM   600   1200   1800   2400   3000   3600

Europe

Height

m. / ft.
6000 / 19700
4000 / 13000
2000 / 6500
1500 / 5000
1000 / 3300
500 / 1600
200 / 700
0
200 / 700
500 / 1600
1000 / 3300
2000 / 6500
3000 / 9800
4000 / 13000
5000 / 16400
6000 / 19700

m. / ft.

Depth

NORWEGIAN BASIN

NORWEGIAN

BASIN

Vesterålen

Lofoten

VORING PLATEAU

Iceland

Reykjavik

Hekla 1,491 m

JAN MAYEN RIDGE

Arctic Circle

SEA

Trondheim

ICELAND BASIN

Faroe Is.

HEBRIDIAN SHELF

Shetland Is.

Slittertinden 2,470 m

Glomma

Bergen

ROCKALL

PLATEAU

Rockall

Hebrides

Orkney Is.

Moray Firth

NORTH

SEA

Skagerrak

Göteborg

Lindesnes

Vänern

Stockholm

Vättern

Gotland

ATLANTIC

OCEAN

ROCKALL TROUGH

Ben Nevis 1,343 m

Aberdeen

Glasgow

Belfast

Jutland

Kattegat

Öland

PORCUPINE BANK

Ireland

I. of Man

Dublin

Irish Sea

Pennine Chain

Liverpool

Great

Britain

Fyn

Copenhagen

Bornholm

BALTIC

PORCUPINE ABYSSAL PLAIN

C. Clear

St. George's Chan.

Birmingham

Thames

London

Frisian Islands

Weser

Hamburg

Elbe

Berlin

Oder

NORTH

CELTIC SHELF

AREA OF OPTIMIZATION

Land's End

English Channel

Channel Is.

Amsterdam

The Hague

Rhine

Brussels

Cologne

Bonn

Leipzig

Le Havre

Seine

Paris

BISCAY ABYSSAL PLAIN

Nantes

Loire

Stuttgart

Danube

Vienna

Bratislava

Munich

Cabo Finisterre

Bay of Biscay

Bordeaux

Central

Bern

Lyon

Mont Blanc 4,807 m

Turin

Milan

Po

Venice

IBERIAN

ABYSSAL

PLAIN

Miño

Cordillera Cantábrica

Bilbao

Garonne

Massif

Lot

Rhône

Genoa

A L P S

Dinaric Alps

Zagreb

Daero

Pyrenees

Ebro

Marseille

G. of Lion

Ligurian

Sea

Adriatic

Saragossa

Tagus

Madrid

Barcelona

Corsica

Apennines

Rome

Lisbon

Júcar

Valencia

Balearic Islands

Minorca

Sardinia

Tyrrhenian

Sea

Naples

Cabo de São Vicente

Sierra Morena

Ibiza

Mallorca

ALGERIAN PLAIN

Capo Teulada

–3,630m

Cádiz

Cerro de Mulhacén 3,478 m

Str. of Gibraltar

Málaga

M E D I T E R R A

Palermo

Mt. Etna 3,323 m

Tangier

Algiers

Sicily

Capo Passero

Rabat

Oran

A F R I C A

Tunis

Pantelleria

Malta

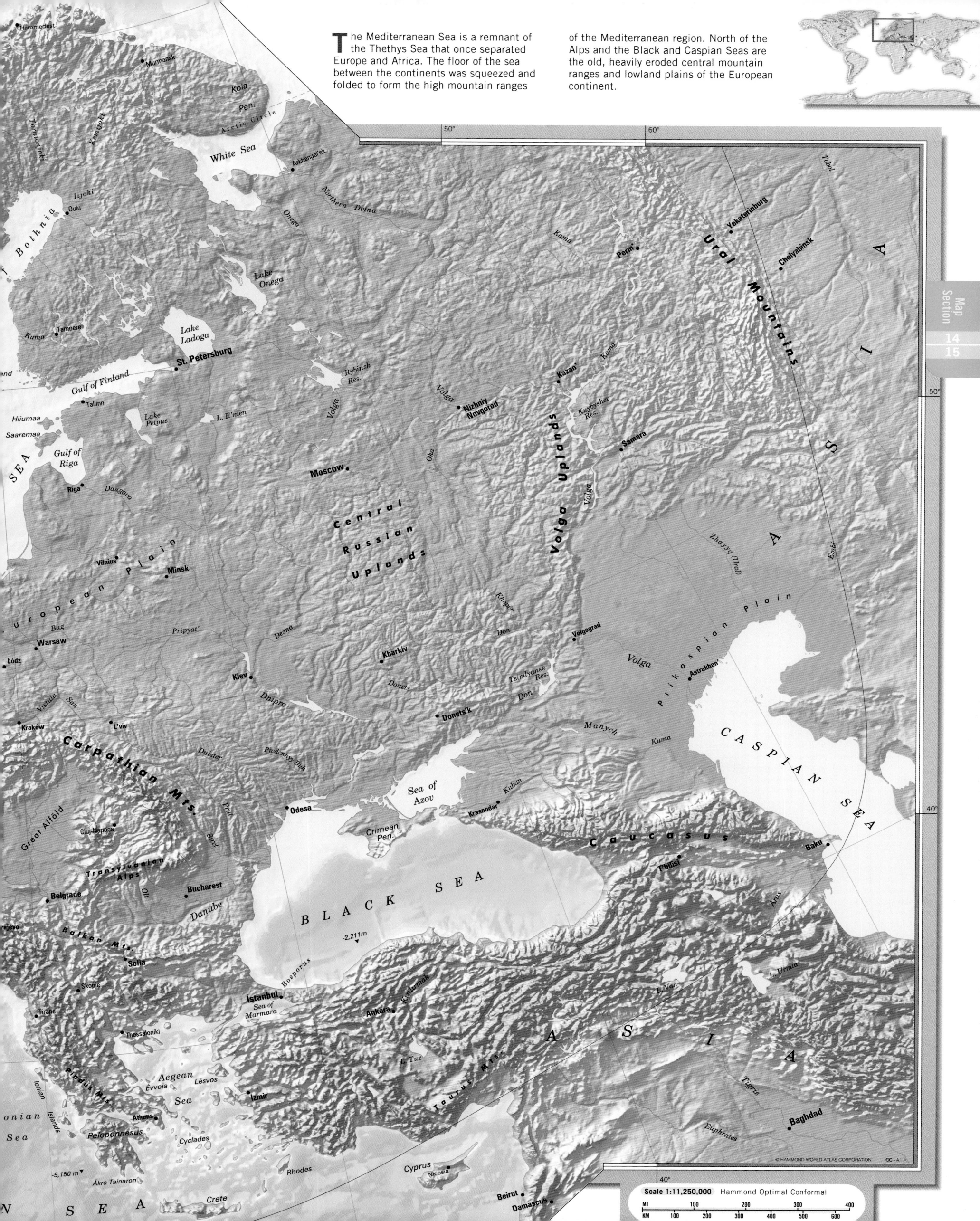

The Mediterranean Sea is a remnant of the Thethys Sea that once separated Europe and Africa. The floor of the sea between the continents was squeezed and folded to form the high mountain ranges of the Mediterranean region. North of the Alps and the Black and Caspian Seas are the old, heavily eroded central mountain ranges and lowland plains of the European continent.

50°
60°

Hammerfest
Murmansk
Kola
Pen.
Arctic Circle
White Sea
Arkhangel'sk
Teriberka
Yekaterinburg
Northern Dvina
Kamchatka
Kama
Perm'
Chelyabinsk
Ural Mountains
Onega
Iijoki
Oulu
Kazan'
Kama
A S I A
Lake
Onega
Kuma
Kuybyshev
Res.
Kumo
Tampere
Lake
Ladoga
Rybinsk
Res.
Volga
Nizhniy
Novgorod
St. Petersburg
Volga
Samara
Gulf of Finland
Hiiumaa
Tallinn
Lake
Peipus
L. Il'men
Oka
Volga
Volga Uplands
Saaremaa
SEA
Gulf of
Riga
Moscow
Volga
Zhayyq (Ural)
Emba
Riga
Daugava
Central
Russian
Uplands
Prikaspian Plain
Vilnius
Minsk
European Plain
Warsaw
Bug
Pripyat'
Desna
Khopër
Don
Volgograd
Volga
Astrakhan
CASPIAN SEA
Łódź
Vistula
San
Kiev
Dnipro
Kharkiv
Donets
Tsimlyansk
Res.
Don
Kraków
L'viv
Carpathian Mts.
Dnister
Pivdennyy Buh
Donets'k
Manych
Kuma
Great Alföld
Cluj-Napoca
Prut
Siret
Odesa
Sea of
Azov
Kuban
Krasnodar
Caucasus
Baku
Transylvanian
Alps
Olt
Crimean
Pen.
Tbilisi
Aras
Belgrade
Bucharest
BLACK SEA
L. Urmia
Sarajevo
Danube
-2,211m
Balkan Mts.
Bosporus
ASIA
Sofia
L. Van
Skopje
Istanbul
Sea of
Marmara
Ankara
Kızılırmak
Tiranë
Thessaloniki
L. Tuz
Tigris
Pindus Mts.
Evvoia
Lésvos
Taurus Mts.
Aegean
Sea
İzmir
Athens
Ionian
Islands
Peloponnesus
Cyclades
Euphrates
Baghdad
-5,150 m
Rhodes
Cyprus
Nicosia
Crete
Beirut
Ionian
Sea
EAN
SEA
Damascus

© HAMMOND WORLD ATLAS CORPORATION

40°

40°

50°

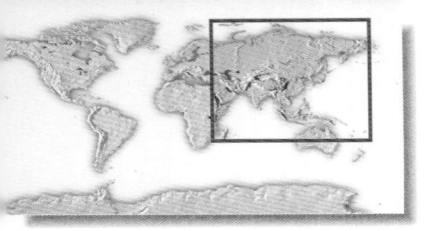

Asia

Although the Ural Mountains and the Caspian Sea form a boundary between Europe and Asia, geologists view both continents as part of the Eurasian Plate. The largest contiguous land mass on earth, this plate also comprises the Himalayas, the world's highest and most extensive mountain system. Deep ocean trenches sear the boundaries of the Pacific and Indo-Australian plates.

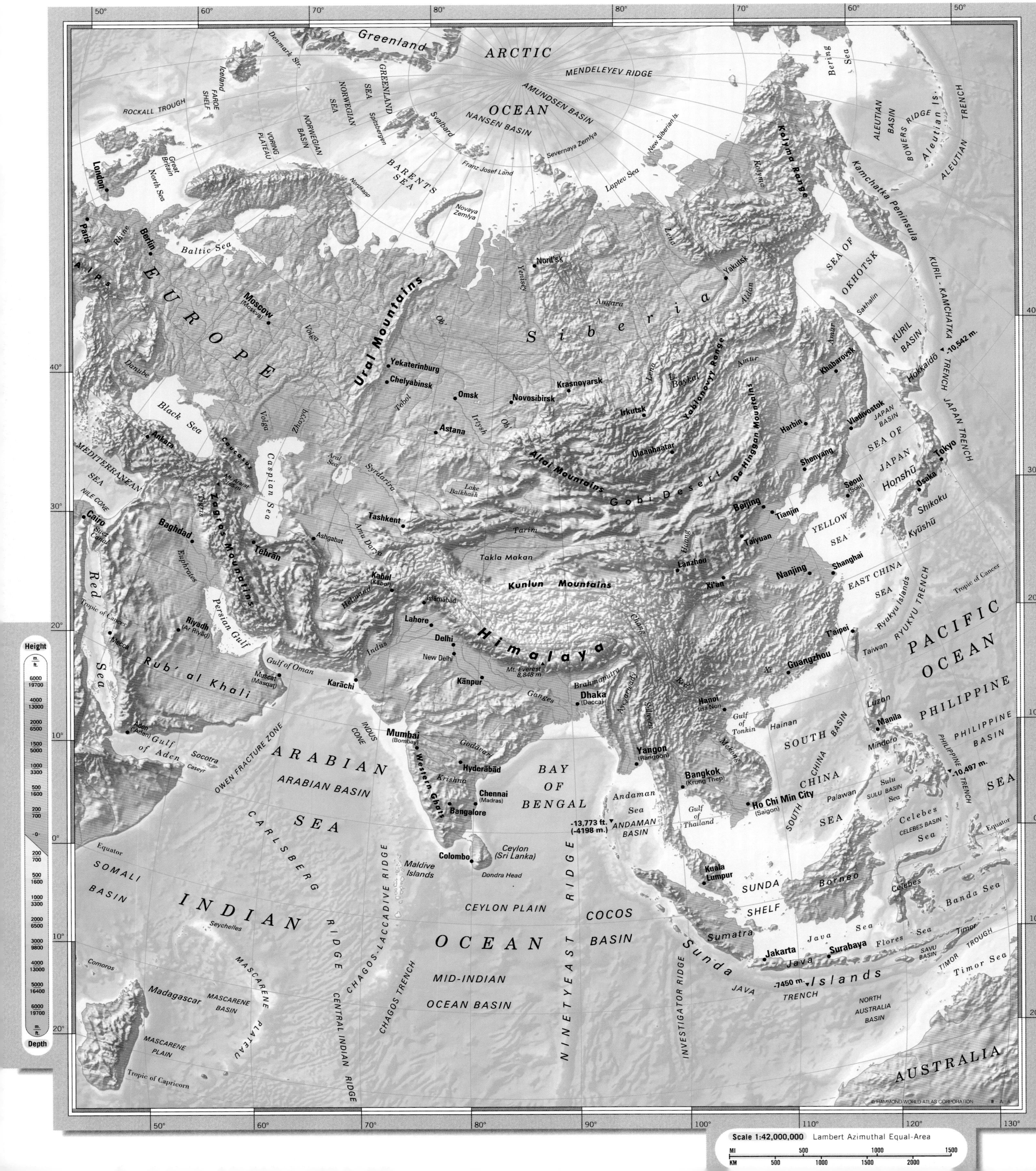

Height
m.
ft.
6000 19700
4000 13000
2000 6500
1500 5000
1000 3300
500 1600
200 700
-0-
200 700
500 1600
1000 3300
2000 6500
3000 9800
4000 13000
5000 16400
6000 19700
m.
ft.
Depth

ARCTIC OCEAN

MENDELEYEV RIDGE
AMUNDSEN BASIN
NANSEN BASIN

Greenland

GREENLAND SEA
NORWEGIAN SEA
NORWEGIAN BASIN
BARENTS SEA

ROCKALL TROUGH
Iceland
FAROE SHELF
VORING PLATEAU
Svalbard
Franz Josef Land
Severnaya Zemlya
New Siberian Is.

Bering Sea
BOWERS RIDGE
ALEUTIAN BASIN
Aleutian Is.
ALEUTIAN TRENCH

London
Great Britain
North Sea
Baltic Sea
Novaya Zemlya
Laptev Sea
Kolyma Range
Kamchatka Peninsula
KURIL-KAMCHATKA TRENCH

Paris
Berlin
Rhine
Moscow (Moskva)
Ural Mountains
Ob
Yenisey
Nor'ilsk
Yakutsk
Lena
Amur
Sakhalin
SEA OF OKHOTSK
KURIL BASIN
JAPAN TRENCH
-10,542 m.
Hokkaidō

ALPS
EUROPE
Danube
Volga
Yekaterinburg
Chelyabinsk
Omsk
Tobol
Irtysh
Ob
Krasnoyarsk
Novosibirsk
Siberia
Angara
L. Baykal
Lena
Yablonovyy Range
Irkutsk
Khabarovsk
Vladivostok
JAPAN BASIN
SEA OF JAPAN

Black Sea
Ankara
Caucasus
Caspian Sea
Aral Sea
Syrdarya
Astana
Ulaanbaatar
Da Hingan Mountains
Harbin
Shenyang
Seoul (Sŏul)
Honshū
Tokyo
Osaka

MEDITERRANEAN SEA
NILE CONE
Cairo
Suez Canal
Zagros Mountains
Tigris
Tashkent
Amu Darya
Lake Balkhash
Tarim
Altai Mountains
Gobi Desert
Beijing
Tianjin
Taiyuan
YELLOW SEA
Shikoku
Kyūshū

Red Sea
Baghdad
Euphrates
Tehrān
Ashgabat
Takla Makan
Lanzhou
Huang
Xi'an
Nanjing
Shanghai
EAST CHINA SEA
Tropic of Cancer
RYUKYU TRENCH

Tropic of Cancer
Mecca
Riyadh (Ar Riyāḍ)
Persian Gulf
Kabul (Kābol)
Helmand
Islāmābād
Kunlun Mountains
Chang
Ryukyu Islands

Rub' al Khali
Gulf of Oman
Muscat (Masqaṭ)
Lahore
Delhi
New Delhi
Himalaya
Mt. Everest 8,848 m.
Guangzhou
T'aipei
Taiwan
PACIFIC OCEAN

Aden ('Adan)
Gulf of Aden
Socotra
Karāchi
Indus
Kānpur
Brahmaputra
Dhaka (Dacca)
Xi
Hanoi (Ha Noi)
Luzon
PHILIPPINE BASIN

Mumbai (Bombay)
INDUS CONE
Godāvari
Hyderābād
Krishna
Ganges
BAY OF BENGAL
Ayeyarwady
Yangon (Rangoon)
Gulf of Tonkin
Hainan
Mindoro
Manila
PHILIPPINE SEA

OWEN FRACTURE ZONE
ARABIAN BASIN
Chennai (Madras)
Bangalore
Andaman Sea
Bangkok (Krung Thep)
Mekong
SOUTH CHINA BASIN
Palawan
SULU BASIN
Sulu Sea

ARABIAN SEA
Western Ghats
-13,773 ft. (-4198 m.)
ANDAMAN BASIN
Gulf of Thailand
Ho Chi Min City (Saigon)
SOUTH CHINA SEA
CELEBES BASIN
Celebes Sea
Equator

CARLSBERG RIDGE
Equator
Colombo
Ceylon (Sri Lanka)
Dondra Head
Maldive Islands
Celebes
Banda Sea

SOMALI BASIN
Seychelles
MASCARENE BASIN
CHAGOS-LACCADIVE RIDGE
CEYLON PLAIN
NINETYEAST RIDGE
COCOS BASIN
Kuala Lumpur
SUNDA SHELF
Borneo

INDIAN OCEAN
MASCARENE PLATEAU
CENTRAL INDIAN RIDGE
MID-INDIAN OCEAN BASIN
Sumatra
SUNDA
Jakarta
Java
Surabaya
Flores Sea
Timor
SAVU BASIN
TIMOR TROUGH
Timor Sea

Madagascar
Comoros
JAVA TRENCH
Java Islands
-7450 m.
NORTH AUSTRALIA BASIN

MASCARENE PLAIN
INVESTIGATOR RIDGE
Tropic of Capricorn
AUSTRALIA

Scale 1:42,000,000   Lambert Azimuthal Equal-Area
MI   500   1000   1500
KM   500   1000   1500   2000

© HAMMOND WORLD ATLAS CORPORATION

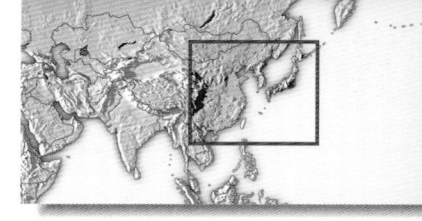
V ast highland basins and deserts stand in marked contrast to the fertile plains of the region. Deserts, such as the Gobi, dominate the northwestern part of this region, while the waters and floodplains of great Huang Ho (Yellow) and the Yangtze (Chang) Rivers in the east provide the basis for the cultivation of food crops that feed millions of people.

Height

MI.
FT.

6000
19700

4000
13000

2000
6500

1500
5000

1000
3300

500
1600

200
700

0

200
700

500
1600

1000
3300

2000
6500

3000
9800

4000
13000

5000
16400

6000
19700

MI.
FT.

Depth

KURIL BASIN

Etorofu

Kunashiri

Sakhalin

Hokkaidō

La Perouse Str.

Sapporo

Honshū

Tokyo

Osaka

Kyōto

Shikoku

Fukuoka

Kyūshū

PACIFIC OCEAN

Okino-Tori-Shima

RYUKYU TRENCH

Tropic of Cancer

Amami Is.

Ryukyu Islands

Okinawa

Sakishima Is.

Babuyan Is.

Babuyan Islands

Tatar Strait

Khabarovsk

Amur

Vladivostok

Ussuri (Wusuli)

SEA OF JAPAN

JAPAN BASIN

Lake Khanka

Pusan

Korea Strait

Cheju

EAST CHINA SEA

Taipei

Kaohsiung

Taiwan (Formosa)

Bashi Channel

Taiwan Strait

Blagoveshchensk

Harbin

Da Hinggan Mts.

Nen

Gan

Changchun

Shenyang

Anshan

Dalian

Korea Bay

Shandong Peninsula

Qingdao

YELLOW SEA

Shanghai

Hangzhou

Fuzhou

Xiamen

SOUTH CHINA SEA

Guangzhou

Xi

Hulun L.

Kerulen (Herlen)

Ulaanbaatar

Onon

Beijing

Tianjin

Bo Hai (Gulf of Chihli)

Jinan

Huang

Hongze Lake

Gaoyou L.

Nanjing

Huai

Chang (Yangtze)

Poyang L.

Nanchang

Chang

Hanoi (Ha Noi)

Hai Phong)

Gulf of Tonkin

Uvs L.

Hövsgöl L.

Selenge

Orhon

Gobi Desert

Ordos (Mu Us Shamo)

Huang

Wei

Xi'an

Taiyuan

Zhengzhou

Han

Wuhan

Chang

Changsha

Xiong

Xiang

Leizhou Peninsula

Hainan Str.

Hainan

Nanning

Uyuk L.

Har Us Nur

Hyargas Nur

Qilian Mts.

Yellow

Yumen

Lanzhou

Huang

Chengdu

Chongqing

Jialing (Jialing Jiang)

Wu

Gongga Shan 7556m

Min

Guiyang

Hongshui

Red

Kunming

Shan Plateau

Mekong (Lancang)

Yalong

Jinsha

Mekong

Salween

Irrawaddy 5881m

Changan

Scale 1:14,500,000   Lambert Conformal Conic Projection

MI   125   250   375   500

KM   125   250   375   500   625   750

Southeast Asia

Several tectonic plates converge in Southeast Asia to form an extended arc of islands adjacent to deep ocean trenches. Many of the islands are characterized by extreme volcanic activity.

Located on the continental shelf along the South China Sea is the vast delta (70,000 sq. km.) of the Mekong, the "Mother of Waters," whose course from the Tibetan Plateau to the sea measures 4,500 km.

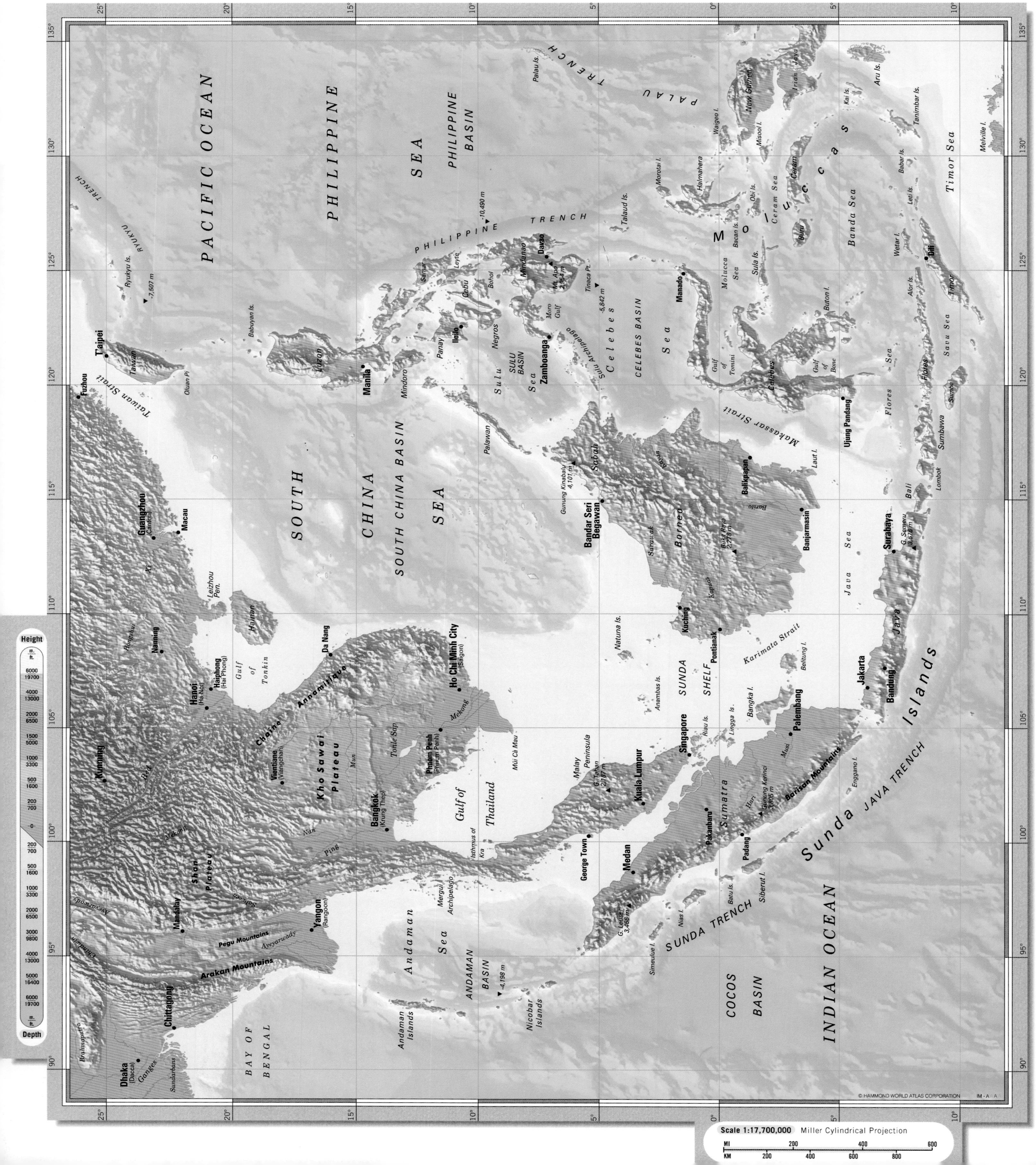

PACIFIC OCEAN

PHILIPPINE SEA

PHILIPPINE BASIN

PALAU TRENCH

RYUKYU TRENCH

Ryukyu Is.
▼ -7,507 m

Taipei
Fuzhou
Taiwan
Taiwan Strait
Oluan Pt.

Babuyan Is.
Luzon

Manila
Mindoro

Samar
Leyte
Cebu
Bohol
Panay
Iloilo
Negros
Sulu Sea
Sulu
Palawan

PHILIPPINE TRENCH
▼ -10,490 m

Mindanao
Davao
Mt. Apo 2,954 m
Moro Gulf
Tinaca Pt.
Zamboanga
▼ -5,842 m
Sulu Archipelago

Palau Is.

Talaud Is.
Manado

Morotai I.
Halmahera
Molucca Sea
Bacan Is.
Obi Is.
Sula Is.
Buru

MOLUCCAS

Ceram
Ceram Sea
Banda Sea

Waigeo I.
Misool I.
New Guinea
Irian Jaya
Kai Is.
Aru Is.

Obi I.

Buton I.
Celebes

Gulf of Tomini
Gulf of Bone

CELEBES BASIN

Celebes Sea

Wetar I.
Alor Is.
Leti Is.
Timor
Dili
Babar Is.
Tanimbar Is.

Timor Sea
Melville I.

Makassar Strait

Ujung Pandang
Flores Sea
Flores
Sumba
Savu Sea

Balikpapan

SOUTH CHINA BASIN

SOUTH CHINA SEA

Guangzhou (Canton)
Macau

Leizhou Pen.
Hainan

Gulf of Tonkin

Da Nang
Haiphong (Hai Phong)
Hanoi (Ha Noi)

Natuna Is.

Gunung Kinabalu 4,101 m
Sabah
Bandar Seri Begawan

Borneo
Sarawak

Kapuas
Barito
Bukit Raya 2,278 m

Banjarmasin

Surabaya
G. Semeru 3,676 m

Java Sea
Bali
Lombok
Sumbawa

JAVA

Kuching
Pontianak

SUNDA SHELF
Karimata Strait
Karimata I.
Belitung I.
Anambas Is.

Jakarta
Bandung

ISLANDS

Kunming

Nanning

Vientiane (Viangchan)

Chaine Annamitique

Ho Chi Minh City (Saigon)
Mekong

Phnom Penh (Phnum Penh)

Tonle Sap

Mekong

Mui Ca Mau

Malay Peninsula
G. Tahan 2,187 m

Singapore

Riau Is.
Lingga Is.
Bangka I.

Kuala Lumpur

Palembang

Sumatra

Barisan Mountains
Gunung Kerinci 3,805 m

Kho Sawai Plateau
Mun

Bangkok (Krung Thep)

Shan Plateau

Nan
Ping

Gulf of Thailand

Thailand

Isthmus of Kra

Mergui Archipelago

George Town

Medan
Pakanbaru

Padang

Enggano I.
Batu Is.
Nias I.
G. Leuser 3,466 m
Siberut

SUNDA TRENCH

SUNDA JAVA TRENCH

INDIAN OCEAN

COCOS BASIN

Kunming
Mandalay
Yangon (Rangoon)
Pegu Mountains
Ayeyarwady
Arakan Mountains

Salween

Sittang

Irrawaddy

Andaman Sea

Andaman Islands

ANDAMAN BASIN
▼ -4,198 m

Nicobar Islands

Dhaka (Dacca)
Ganges
Sundarbans
Chittagong
Brahmaputra

BAY OF BENGAL

Height	
m. / ft.	
6000	19700
4000	13000
2000	6500
1500	5000
1000	3300
500	1600
200	700
—	
200	700
500	1600
1000	3300
2000	6500
3000	9800
4000	13000
5000	16400
6000	19700
m. / ft.	
Depth	

Scale 1:17,700,000 Miller Cylindrical Projection

MI		200		400		600
KM	200	400	600	800		

The collision of the Indian subcontinent with Eurasia about 50 million years ago gave birth to the Himalayas. Since that time, the Indian subcontinent has penetrated some 2,000 km into Eurasia, thrusting rock upward to form the world's loftiest mountain range, with peaks as high as 9,000 meters. Today, such mighty rivers as the Ganges (2,700 km long) flow from sources in the Himalayas.

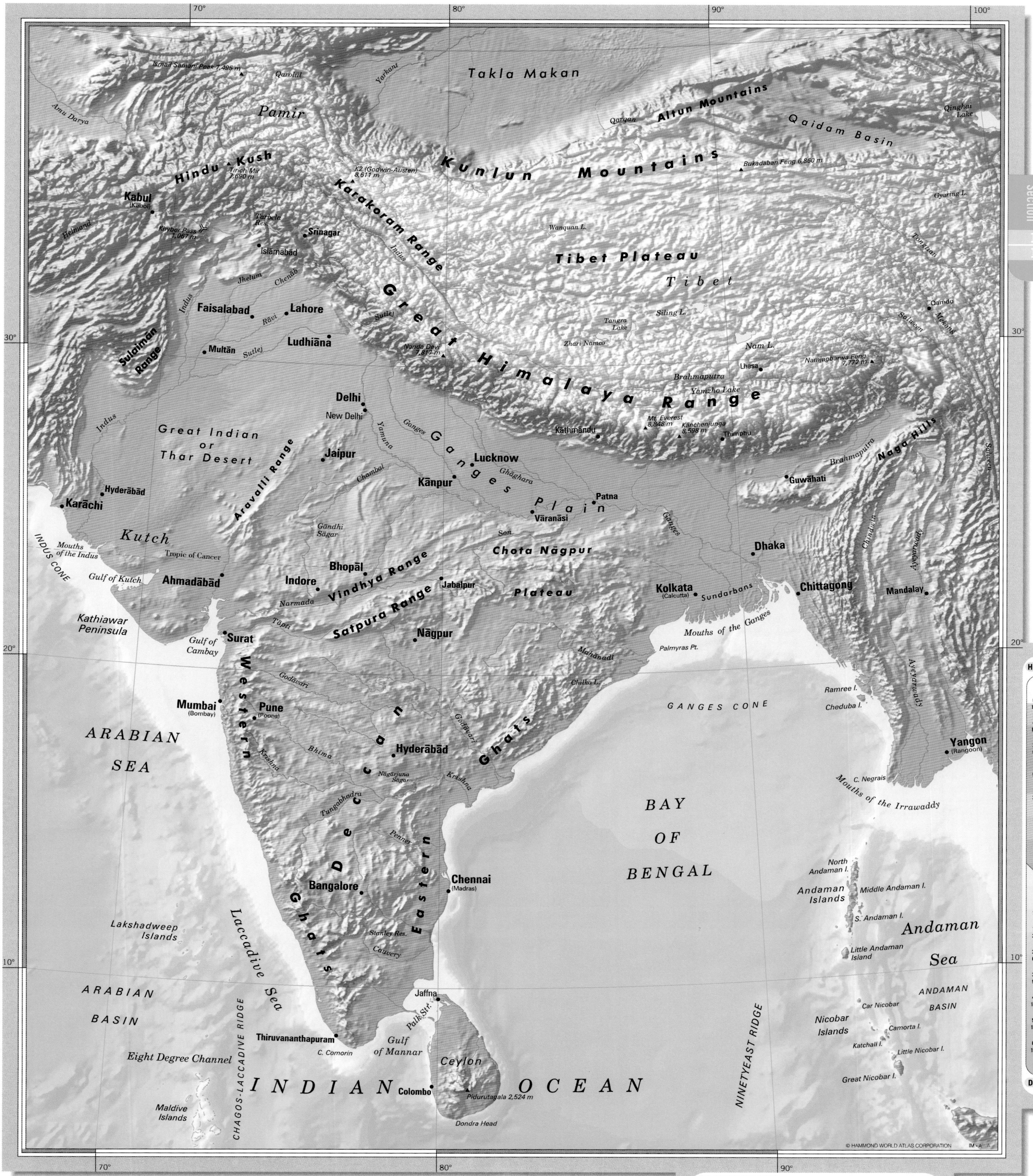

Southern Asia

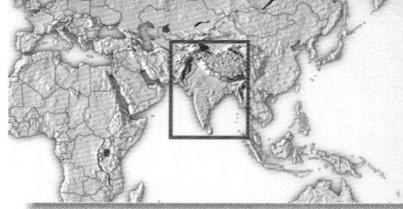

70°   80°   90°   100°

Ismail Samani Peak 7,495 m
Qarabul
Yarkant
Takla Makan

Pamir
Qarqan
Altun Mountains
Qaidam Basin
Qinghai Lake

Amu Darya
Hindu Kush
Tirich Mir 7,690 m
K2 (Godwin-Austen) 8,611 m

Kunlun   **Mountains**

Bukadaban Feng 6,860 m
Gyaring L.

Helmand
Kabul
(Kabol)
Khyber Pass 1,067 m
Tarbela Res.
Srinagar
Karakoram Range

Wanquan L.

Tibet Plateau

Tengri Nor

Islamabad
Jhelum
Indus
Chenab

T i b e t

Faisalabad   **Lahore**
Ravi
Sutlej
Great
Nanga Devi 7,812 m

Zhari Namco
Tangra Lake
Siling L.
Nam L.

Ludhiāna
Sutlej
Multān

Sulaimān Range

Indus

Himalaya
Brahmaputra
Lhasa
Yamzho Lake

Oaindo
Mekong
Salween

Delhi
New Delhi
Yamuna
Range
Mt. Everest 8,848 m
Kathmandu
Kānchenjunga 8,598 m
Thimphu

Naga Hills

Great Indian or Thar Desert
Aravalli Range
Jaipur
Chambal
Ganges
Lucknow
Ghāghara
Plain

Brahmaputra
Guwāhati

Hyderābād
Kānpur
Son
Patna
Vāranāsi
Ganges

Karāchi
Kutch
Indus
Mouths of the Indus
INDUS CONE
Tropic of Cancer
Gāndhi Sāgar

Chota Nāgpur

Dhaka
Chittagong
Chindwin
Mandalay

Gulf of Kutch
Ahmadābād
Indore
Bhopāl
Vindhya Range
Narmada
Jabalpur
Plateau
Kolkata
(Calcutta)
Sundarbans

Kathiawar Peninsula
Satpura Range
Tāpti
Nāgpur

Irrawaddy

Gulf of Cambay
Surat
Godavari

Mahānadi
Mouths of the Ganges
Palmyras Pt.
Chilka L.
Ramree I.
Cheduba I.

GANGES CONE

A R A B I A N   S E A

Mumbai
(Bombay)
Pune
(Poona)
Bhima
Hyderābād
Krishna
Nāgārjuna Sāgar
Godavari
Western

C. Negrais
Mouths of the Irrawaddy

Yangon
(Rangoon)

D e c c a n

Krishna
Ghats
Bangalore
Tungabhadra
Penner
Stanley Res.
Cauvery
Chennai
(Madras)

**B A Y
O F
B E N G A L**

North Andaman I.
Andaman Islands
Middle Andaman I.
S. Andaman I.

**Andaman
Sea**

Eastern

Lakshadweep Islands
Laccadive Sea
Chagos-Laccadive Ridge

Little Andaman Island

**ANDAMAN
BASIN**

**A R A B I A N
B A S I N**
Eight Degree Channel

Jaffna
Palk Str.
Thiruvananthapuram
C. Comorin
Gulf of Mannar
Ceylon
Pidurutagala 2,524 m

Car Nicobar
Nicobar Islands
Camorta I.
Katchall I.
Little Nicobar I.

I N D I A N   O C E A N
Colombo
Dondra Head
Maldive Islands

Great Nicobar I.

NINETYEAST RIDGE

© HAMMOND WORLD ATLAS CORPORATION
IM•A

Height
m.   ft.
6000 19700
4000 13000
2000 6500
1500 5000
1000 3300
500   1600
200   700
0
200   700
500   1600
1000 3300
2000 6500
3000 9800
4000 13000
5000 16400
6000 19700
m.   ft.
Depth

Scale 1:13,100,000   Lambert Conformal Conic Projection
MI   100   200   300   400
KM 100 200 300 400 500 600

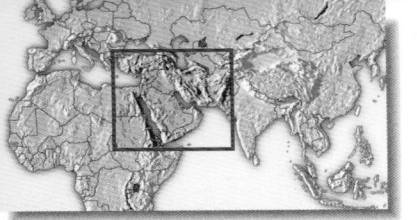

Near and Middle East

Some 25 million years ago, the Red Sea opened, separating the Arabian Peninsula from Africa. At some time in the distant future, a new arm of the sea may extend from the southern Red Sea through the Afar Depression into continental Africa. Today, the oil fields along the Persian Gulf and around the Caspian seaport of Baku hold about two-thirds of the world's known oil reserves.

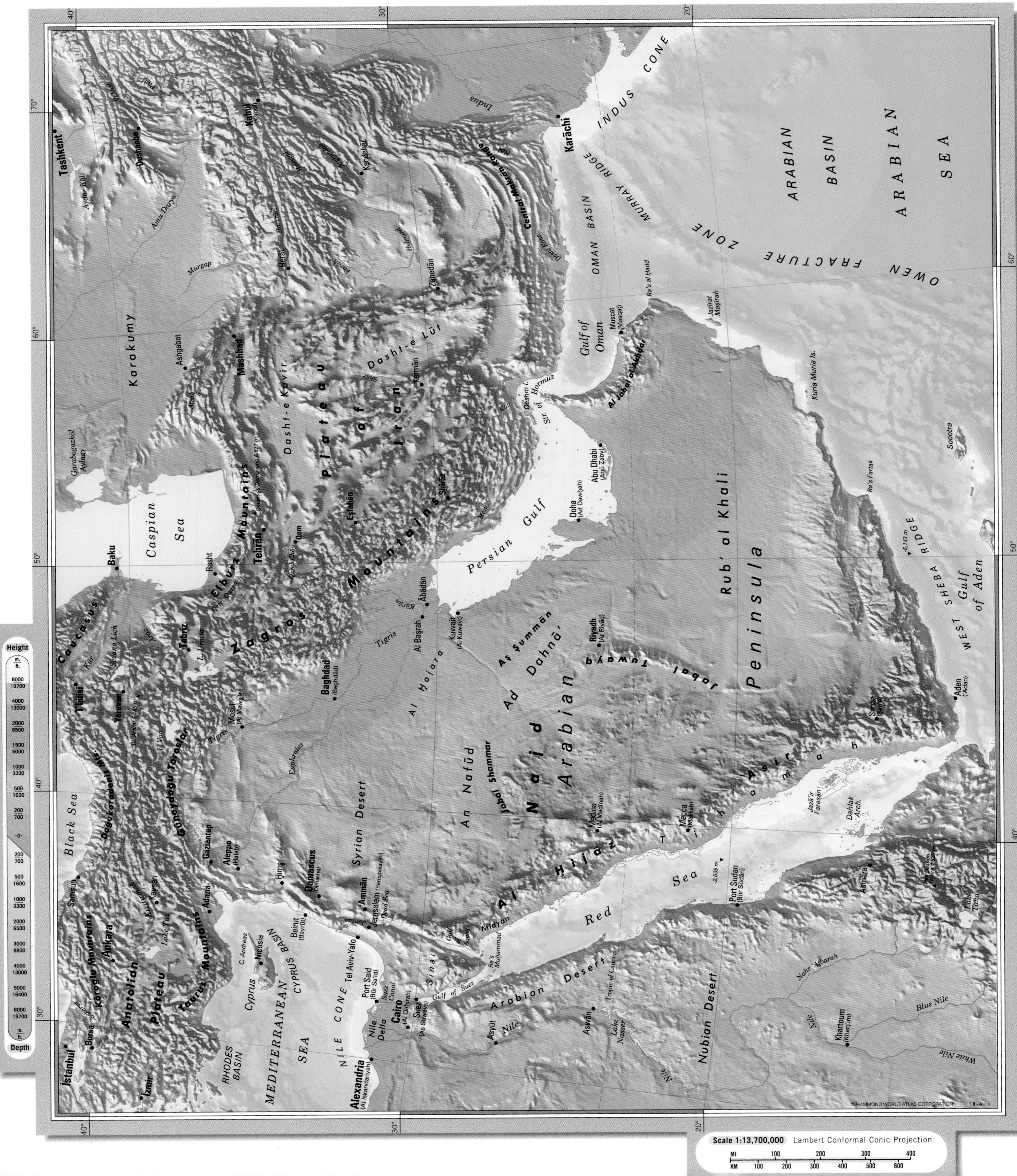

Height
m.
ft.
6000
19700
4000
13000
2000
6500
1500
5000
1000
3300
500
1600
200
700
0
200
700
500
1600
1000
3300
2000
6500
3000
9800
4000
13000
5000
16400
6000
19700
m.

Depth

INDUS CONE

ARABIAN

BASIN

ARABIAN

SEA

MURRAY RIDGE

Indus

Karāchi

OMAN BASIN

OWEN FRACTURE ZONE

Tashkent

Aydar-Köli

Kabul
(Kābol)

Dushanbe

Amu Darya

Herāt

Qandahār

Central Makran Range

Zāhedān

Gulf
of
Oman

Str. of Hormuz

Muscat
(Masqat)

Jazīrat
Masīrah

Ra's al Hadd

Kuria Muria Is.

Karakumy

Garabogazköl
Aylagy

Ashgabat

Murgap

Mashhad

Dasht-e Kavir

Dasht-e Lūt

Kermān

Al Jabal al Akhdar

Socotra

Caspian
Sea

Baku

Elburz Mountains

Tehrān

Rasht

Qom

Eşfahān

Shīrāz

Zagros Mountains

Plateau of Iran

Abu Dhabi
(Abū Zaby)

Doha
(Ad Dawḥah)

Persian
Gulf

Rub' al Khali

WEST SHEBA RIDGE

Gulf of Aden

Tbilisi

Yerevan

Tabriz

L. Urmia

Mosul
(Al Mawşil)

Baghdād
(Baghdād)

Abādān

Kuwait
(Al Kuwayt)

Al Başrah

Tigris

Riyadh
(Ar Riyāḍ)

Jabal Ṭuwayq

Arabian
Peninsula

Aden
('Adan)

Caucasus

Samsun

Kür

Sevana Lich

Nāvestī

Tigris

Euphrates

Al Ḥaṣa

Aş Şummān

Ad Dahnā'

Najd

Şaⁿ'ā'

Black Sea

Ankara

Taurus Mountains

Lake Tuz

Gaziantep

Aleppo
(Ḥalab)

Ḥimş

Damascus
(Dimashq)

Euphrates

Syrian Desert

An Nafūd

Jabal Shammar

Arabian

Jazā'ir Farasān

Dahlak Arch.

Asmara

Anatolian Plateau

Köroğlu Mountains

Güneydoğu Toroslar

Adana

C. Andreas

Nicosia

CYPRUS

Beirut
(Bayrūt)

Amman

Jerusalem
(Yerushalayim)

Dead Sea

Medina
(Al Madinah)

Mecca
(Makkah)

Al Ḥijāz

'Asīr

Tihāmah

Sirḍan
(Sirḍan)

-2,635 m.

Jazā'ir Farasān

Istanbul

Bursa

Izmir

CYPRUS BASIN

Tel Aviv-Yafo

Sinai

Gulf of Aqaba

Midyān

Ra's Muhammad

Red Sea

Port Sudan
(Bür Sūdān)

RHODES BASIN

MEDITERRANEAN SEA

NILE CONE

Port Said
(Būr Sa'īd)

Suez Canal

Suez
(As Suways)

Gulf of Suez

Arabian Desert

Tropic of Cancer

Nubian Desert

Nahr 'Aṭbarah

Blue Nile

Alexandria
(Al Iskandarīyah)

Nile
Delta

Cairo
(Al Qāhirah)

Nile

Asyūţ

Aswān

Lake Nasser

Nile

Khartoum
(Kharţūm)

White Nile

© HAMMOND WORLD ATLAS CORPORATION

Scale 1:13,700,000 Lambert Conformal Conic Projection

MI   100   200   300   400
KM   100 200 300 400 500 600

Africa comprises some 30 million square kilometers - one-fifth of the world's total land area. Except for the young Altas Mountains, the continent consists of an ancient shelf divided into basins by low rises.

The African Sahara is the largest desert in the world. The East African Rift System, marked by the volcano Kilimanjaro (5,892 m) and other major peaks, runs north to south through the eastern half of the continent.

Africa

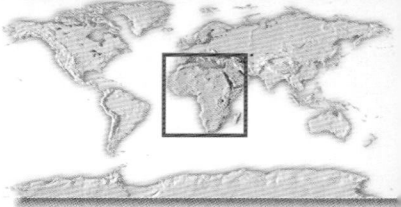

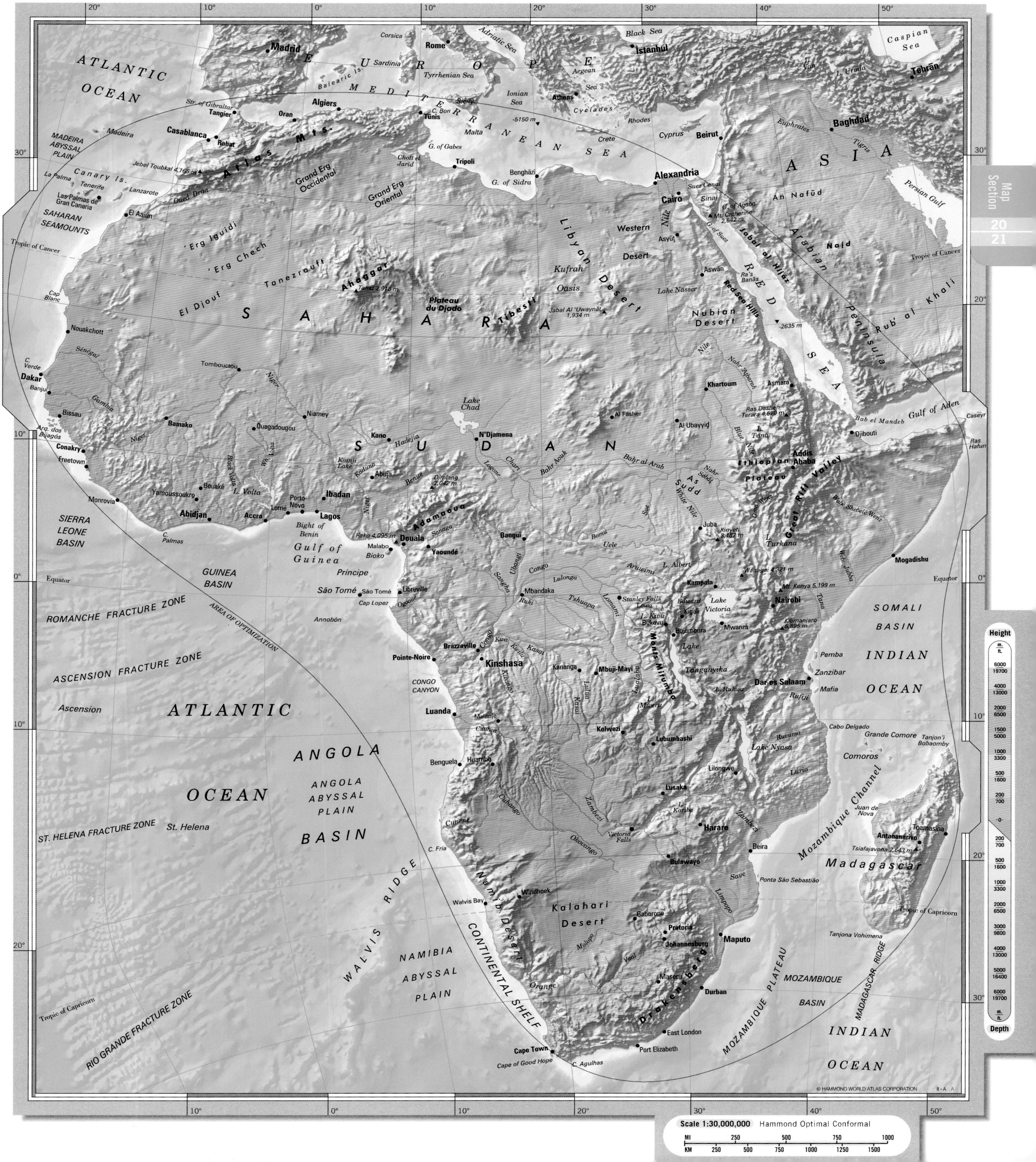

ATLANTIC OCEAN

EUROPE

Madrid · Rome · Istanbul · Caspian Sea

Corsica · Adriatic Sea · Black Sea

Sardinia · Tyrrhenian Sea · Aegean Sea · Van · L. Urmia · Tehrān

Balearic Is. · MEDITERRANEAN SEA · Ionian Sea · Cyclades · Rhodes · ASIA

Str. of Gibraltar · Tangier · Oran · Sicily · C. Bon · Athens · Baghdad

Algiers · Tunis · Malta · Cyprus · Beirut · Euphrates · Tigris

MADEIRA ABYSSAL PLAIN · Madeira · Casablanca · Rabat · Atlas Mts. · Grand Erg Occidental · Crete · Benghāzi · Alexandria · Persian Gulf

Jebel Toubkal 4,165 m · Chott el Jarid · Tripoli · G. of Gabes · Suez Canal · Sinai · Cairo · An Nafūd · Najd · Arabian Peninsula

Canary Is. · Tenerife · Lanzarote · La Palma · El Aaiún · Grand Erg Oriental · G. of Sidra · Gulf of Aqaba · Mt. Catherine 2,642 m · Western · Asyūţ · Gulf of Suez · Jabal al Hijāz

SAHARAN SEAMOUNTS · 'Erg Iguidi · 'Erg Chech · Ahaggar · Tamgak 2,918 m · Plateau du Djado · Tibesti · Libyan Desert · Kufrah Oasis · Desert · Aswān · Lake Nasser · Ra's Bānās · -2635 m · RED · Rub' al Khali

Tropic of Cancer · Cap Blanc · Tanezrouft · El Djouf · SAHARA · Jabal Al 'Uwaynāt 1,934 m · Nubian Desert · SEA · Tropic of Cancer

C. Verde · Dakar · Banjul · Sénégal · Tombouctou · Niger · Khartoum · Asmara · Ras Dashen Terara 4,620 m · Bab el Mandeb · Gulf of Aden · Caseyr

Bissau · Arq. dos Bijagos · Gambia · Bamako · Ouagadougou · Niamey · Kano · Hadejia · N'Djamena · Al Fāsher · Al Ubayyid · Blue Nile · Tana · Ras Hafun

Conakry · Freetown · SUDAN · Kainji Lake · Kaduna · Abuja · Benue · Logone · Chari · Bahr Aouk · Bahr al Arab · White Nile · As Sudd · Addis Ababa · Ethiopian Plateau

SIERRA LEONE BASIN · Monrovia · Yamoussoukro · Bouaké · L. Volta · Porto-Novo · Ibadan · Dimlang 2,042 m · Sangha · Bangui · Uele · Juba · Kinyeti 3,182 m · Great Rift Valley · Wabe Shebele Wenz

Abidjan · Accra · Lomé · Lagos · Bight of Benin · Adamaoua · Bomu · Webi Jubba

C. Palmas · Pako 4,095 m · Douala · Yaoundé · Ubangi · Congo · Lulonga · Turkana · Wabe

GUINEA BASIN · Gulf of Guinea · Malabo · Bioko · Príncipe · Mbandaka · Stanley Falls · L. Albert · Kampala · Mt. Kenya 5,199 m · SOMALI BASIN

Equator · São Tomé · São Tomé · Libreville · Cap Lopez · Ruki · Tshuapa · Lomami · Edward · Lake Victoria · Nairobi · Equator

ROMANCHE FRACTURE ZONE · Annobón · Ogooué · Sankuru · L. Kivu · Bukavu · Kigali · Kilimanjaro 5,895 m · INDIAN OCEAN

AREA OF OPTIMIZATION · Brazzaville · Congo · Kwa · Kasai · Bujumbura · Mwanza · Pemba

ASCENSION FRACTURE ZONE · Pointe-Noire · Kinshasa · Kananga · Mbuji-Mayi · Monts Mitumba · Lake · Zanzibar

Ascension · CONGO CANYON · Kwango · Kwilu · Lake Tanganyika · Dar es Salaam · Mafia

ATLANTIC · Luanda · Malanje · Lualaba · Maseru · L. Rukwa · Rufiji · Height

OCEAN · Kolwezi · Lubumbashi · Lake Nyasa · Ruvuma · Cabo Delgado · Grande Comore · Tanjon'i Bobaomby · m. · ft.

ANGOLA · Benguela · Huambo · Luena · Comoros · Lúrio · 6000 · 19700

ANGOLA ABYSSAL PLAIN · Lusaka · Lilongwe · 4000 · 13000

St. Helena · Cuanza · L. Kariba · Juan de Nova · 2000 · 6500

ST. HELENA FRACTURE ZONE · BASIN · Cunene · Harare · Zambezi · 1500 · 5000

C. Fria · Cubango · Victoria Falls · Beira · 1000 · 3300

WALVIS RIDGE · Okavango · Bulawayo · Save · Ponta São Sebastião · Madagascar · 500 · 1600

Windhoek · Kalahari Desert · Tsiafajavona 2,643 m · Mozambique Channel · 200 · 700

Walvis Bay · Namib Desert · CONTINENTAL SHELF · Gaborone · Limpopo · Tanjona Vohimena · -0-

NAMIBIA ABYSSAL PLAIN · Pretoria · Maputo · 200 · 700

Tropic of Capricorn · Orange · Molopo · Johannesburg · Vaal · MOZAMBIQUE PLATEAU · MOZAMBIQUE · 500 · 1600

RIO GRANDE FRACTURE ZONE · Maseru · Durban · BASIN · MADAGASCAR RIDGE · 1000 · 3300

Drakensberg · East London · INDIAN · 2000 · 6500

Cape Town · Port Elizabeth · OCEAN · 3000 · 9800

Cape of Good Hope · C. Agulhas · 4000 · 13000

© HAMMOND WORLD ATLAS CORPORATION · II-A · 5000 · 16400

6000 · 19700

m. · ft.

Depth

Scale 1:30,000,000   Hammond Optimal Conformal

MI   250   500   750   1000

KM   250   500   1000   1250   1500

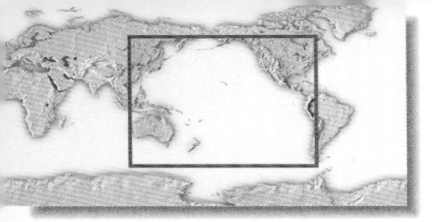

Australia and Pacific Ocean

Situated on the Indo-Australian Plate, the continent of Australia lies on a stable foundation. The earth is considerably more active off the coasts of New Zealand and Japan and around the Aleutians.

There the subduction of oceanic crust is accompanied by lively volcanic activity caused primarily by the breakup of the East Pacific Rise extending from the Baja Peninsula in California to the Antarctic.

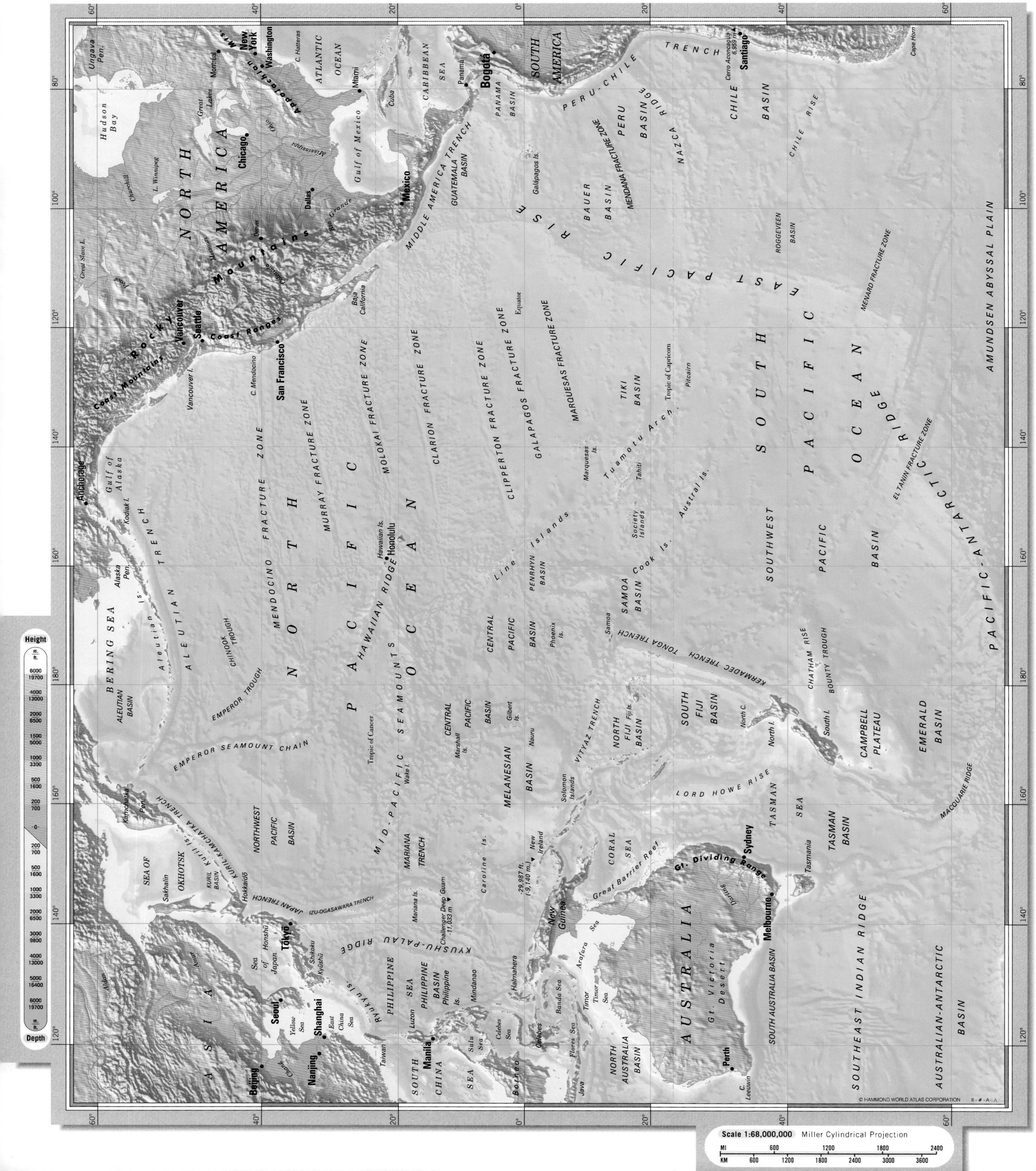

Height

m.	ft.
6000	19700
4000	13000
2000	6500
1500	5000
1000	3300
500	1600
200	700
0	-
200	700
500	1600
1000	3300
2000	6500
3000	9800
4000	13000
5000	16400
6000	19700

| m. | ft. |

Depth

© HAMMOND WORLD ATLAS CORPORATION   II – # – A – A

Scale 1:68,000,000   Miller Cylindrical Projection

MI		600		1200		1800		2400
KM	600		1200		2400		3000	3600

Map labels

Ungava Pen. · Hudson Bay · NORTH AMERICA · New York · Washington · Montreal · Chicago · Dallas · Mexico · Bogotá · SOUTH AMERICA · Santiago · Cerro Aconcagua 6,959 m · Cape Horn

ATLANTIC OCEAN · C. Hatteras · Miami · Cuba · CARIBBEAN SEA · Panama · PANAMA BASIN · Gulf of Mexico · Great Lakes · L. Winnipeg · Churchill · Great Slave L. · L. Athabasca · Mississippi · Ohio · Rio Grande · Missouri · Denver · Columbia · Yukon · Colorado

PERU-CHILE TRENCH · PERU-CHILE BASIN · PERU BASIN · MENDAÑA FRACTURE ZONE · NAZCA RIDGE · BAUER BASIN · CHILE BASIN · CHILE RISE · ROGGEVEEN BASIN · MENARD FRACTURE ZONE · Galápagos Is. · AMUNDSEN ABYSSAL PLAIN

Rocky Mountains · Coast Ranges · Coast Mountains · Vancouver · Seattle · San Francisco · Anchorage · Gulf of Alaska · Vancouver I. · C. Mendocino · Baja California · Kodiak I. · Alaska Pen.

MIDDLE AMERICA TRENCH · GUATEMALA TRENCH · GUATEMALA BASIN · Equator · EAST PACIFIC RISE · CLIPPERTON FRACTURE ZONE · GALAPAGOS FRACTURE ZONE · MARQUESAS FRACTURE ZONE · Tropic of Capricorn · Pitcairn · TIKI BASIN · Tahiti · Society Islands · Marquesas Is. · Tuamotu Arch. · Australis I.

CLARION FRACTURE ZONE · MOLOKAI FRACTURE ZONE · MURRAY FRACTURE ZONE · MENDOCINO FRACTURE ZONE · NORTH PACIFIC OCEAN · Line Islands · PENRHYN BASIN · Cook Is. · Samoa · SAMOA BASIN · SOUTHWEST PACIFIC BASIN · SOUTH PACIFIC OCEAN · PACIFIC-ANTARCTIC RIDGE · ELTANIN FRACTURE ZONE

ALEUTIAN TRENCH · BERING SEA · Aleutian Is. · ALEUTIAN BASIN · CHINOOK TROUGH · EMPEROR TROUGH · Hawaiian Is. · Honolulu · HAWAIIAN RIDGE · MID-PACIFIC SEAMOUNTS · EMPEROR SEAMOUNT CHAIN · Tropic of Cancer · Wake I. · Marshall Is. · CENTRAL PACIFIC BASIN · Gilbert Is. · Nauru · MELANESIAN BASIN · CENTRAL PACIFIC BASIN · Phoenix Is. · VITYAZ TRENCH · NORTH FIJI BASIN · Fiji Is. · SOUTH FIJI BASIN · TONGA TRENCH · KERMADEC TRENCH · BOUNTY TROUGH · CHATHAM RISE · North I. · South I. · North C. · CAMPBELL PLATEAU · EMERALD BASIN · MACQUARIE RIDGE

ASIA · Kamchatka · KURIL-KAMCHATKA TRENCH · SEA OF OKHOTSK · Sakhalin · Hokkaidō · KURIL BASIN · KURIL IS. · Sea of Japan · Honshū · Tōkyō · Shikoku · Kyūshū · RYUKYU IS. · JAPAN TRENCH · IZU-OGASAWARA TRENCH · KYUSHU-PALAU RIDGE · NORTHWEST PACIFIC BASIN · MARIANA TRENCH · Mariana Is. · Guam · Challenger Deep -11,033 m · -29,981 ft. (-9,140 m.) · New Ireland · Caroline Is. · PHILIPPINE SEA · PHILIPPINE BASIN · Luzon · Manila · Philippine Is. · Mindanao · Halmahera · New Guinea

Beijing · Seoul · Nanjing · Shanghai · Yellow Sea · East China Sea · Taiwan · Chang · SOUTH CHINA SEA · Borneo · Celebes · Celebes Sea · Sulu Sea · Banda Sea · Flores Sea · Java · Timor · Timor Sea · Arafura Sea · Coral Sea · Great Barrier Reef · Solomon Islands · LORD HOWE RISE · NORTH AUSTRALIA BASIN · AUSTRALIA · Gt. Victoria Desert · Darling · Gt. Dividing Range · Sydney · Melbourne · Perth · C. Leeuwin · TASMAN SEA · TASMAN BASIN · Tasmania · SOUTH AUSTRALIA BASIN · SOUTHEAST INDIAN RIDGE · AUSTRALIAN-ANTARCTIC BASIN

Two mountain ranges enclose the North American heartland: the old, heavily eroded Appalachian chain in the East and the Rocky Mountains of the Cordillera system in the West. The northernmost points of the continent are on Ellesmere Island and Greenland. Geographers place the southern continental boundary on the Isthmus of Tehuantepec in Mexico, although it is culturally a part of Central America.

North America

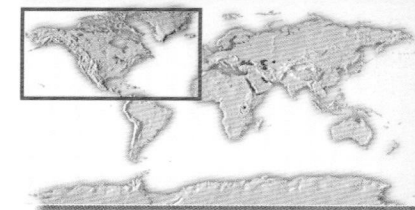

ASIA

BERING SEA · CHUKCHI SEA

Gulf of Anadyr'

St. Lawrence I.

Bering Strait

Aleutian Is.

ALEUTIAN TRENCH

ARCTIC OCEAN

CANADA BASIN

BEAUFORT SEA

BEAUFORT SHELF · AMUNDSEN GULF

Brooks Range

Alaska Range

Gulf of Alaska

Yukon

Fairbanks

Anchorage

Mt. McKinley 20,320 ft. (6,194 m)

Alaska Pen.

Nome

Seward Pen.

Norton Sd.

Kodiak I.

Coast Mountains

Queen Charlotte Islands

Vancouver I.

CASCADIA BASIN

Alexander Archipelago

Hecate Str.

Mackenzie Mts.

Great Bear Lake

Great Slave Lake

Yellowknife

L. Athabasca

Dease

Victoria Island

Banks I.

Prince of Wales I.

Melville I.

Parry Is.

Queen Elizabeth Islands

C. Kellett

NORTH MAGNETIC POLE

Sverdrup Is.

Bathurst

M'Clintock Chan.

Boothia Pen.

Gulf of Boothia

Somerset I.

Prince of Wales I.

Bradeur

Devon I.

Ellesmere Island

C. Columbia

Parry Channel

GREENLAND SEA

Jan Mayen

NORWEGIAN SEA

Faroe Is.

Iceland

Reykjavik

Arctic Circle

Denmark Strait

IRMINGER BASIN

REYKJANES RIDGE

Greenland

Baffin Bay

Baffin Island

Foxe Basin

Melville Pen.

Davis Strait

Cumberland Sd.

Kap Morris Jesup

Nuuk (Godthåb)

Kap Farvel

LABRADOR BASIN

LABRADOR SEA

−3,800 m

Hudson Strait

C. Chidley

Ungava Peninsula

Ungava Bay

Laurentian Plateau

Hudson Bay

James Bay

Southampton I.

Churchill

Nelson

Severn

Albany

Smallwood Res.

Labrador

Newfoundland

C. Race

St. John's

GRAND BANKS

Cabot Str.

Gulf of St. Lawrence

Cape Breton I.

Sable I.

C. Sable

Halifax

Saint John

Québec

Montreal

Ottawa

St. Lawrence

Lake Winnipeg

Winnipeg

Saskatchewan

Saskatoon

Regina

Calgary

Edmonton

Peace

Athabasca

North Saskatchewan

South Saskatchewan

ROCKY MOUNTAINS

Columbia

Fraser

Fr. Flattery

Seattle

Victoria

Vancouver

Portland

Cascade Range

Coast Ranges

C. Mendocino

San Francisco

Sierra Nevada

Great Basin

Salt Lake City

Great Salt Lake

Snake

Yellowstone

GREAT PLAINS

Missouri

Red

Thunder Bay

Lake Superior

Duluth

Minneapolis

Lake Michigan

Milwaukee

Chicago

Sudbury

L. Huron

Toronto

Detroit

L. Erie

Cleveland

L. Ontario

Buffalo

Pittsburgh

Boston

C. Cod

New York

Philadelphia

Washington

APPALACHIAN MTS.

Piedmont

Norfolk

C. Hatteras

CONTINENTAL SHELF

ATLANTIC OCEAN

Bermuda

BERMUDA RISE

HATTERAS ABYSSAL PLAIN

Mississippi

Missouri

Platte

Omaha

Des Moines

Kansas City

St. Louis

Indianapolis

Columbus

Cincinnati

Ohio

Mt. Mitchell 6,684 ft. (2,037 m)

Nashville

Charlotte

Tennessee

Memphis

Atlanta

Birmingham

Arkansas

Wichita

Tulsa

Ozark Plateau

North Canadian

Oklahoma City

Red

Fort Worth

Dallas

Denver

Mt. Elbert 14,433 ft. (4,399 m)

Colorado Plateau

Powell

Albuquerque

Rio Grande

Phoenix

Tucson

Los Angeles

San Diego

Channel Islands

I. Guadalupe

PACIFIC OCEAN

MENDOCINO FRACTURE ZONE

MURRAY FRACTURE ZONE

MOLOKAI FRACTURE ZONE

CLARION FRACTURE ZONE

CLIPPERTON FRACTURE ZONE

−6,225 m

Tropic of Cancer

Pt. Arguello

Is. Revillagigedo

Punta Eugenia

Baja California

Cabo San Lucas

Gulf of California

Sierra Madre Occidental

El Paso

Ciudad Juárez

Chihuahua

San Antonio

Houston

Corpus Christi

Monterrey

Culiacán

Tampico

Guadalajara

Mexico

Veracruz

Volcán Citlaltépetl 5,700 m

Acapulco

Sierra Madre del Sur

Sierra Madre Oriental

MEXICO BASIN

SIGSBEE ESCARPMENT

GULF OF MEXICO

New Orleans

Jacksonville

Tampa

Miami

C. Canaveral

Florida Pen.

Florida Keys

Straits of Florida

Grand Bahama

Nassau

Andros

Bahamas

Havana

Cuba

CAMPECHE BANK

Bahía de Campeche

YUCATAN BASIN

Yucatan Channel

Mérida

Yucatan Peninsula

WEST INDIES

NARES ABYSSAL PLAIN

Tropic of Cancer

Turks & Caicos Is.

PUERTO RICO TRENCH

Milwaukee Deep −8,605 m

Puerto Rico

San Juan

Virgin Is.

Anguilla

Barbuda

St. Kitts

Antigua

Montserrat

Guadeloupe

Dominica

Martinique

St. Lucia

St. Vincent

Barbados

LESSER ANTILLES

GREATER ANTILLES

Hispaniola

Santiago

Port-au-Prince

Santo Domingo

Jamaica

Kingston

Windward Passage

Mona Pass.

CAYMAN TRENCH

−7,680 m

NICARAGUA RISE

CARIBBEAN SEA

Guatemala

San Salvador

Tegucigalpa

Managua

San José

COCOS RIDGE

Panama Canal

Panamá

G. of Panama

Barranquilla

Caracas

Lago de Maracaibo

COLUMBIA BASIN

VENEZUELA BASIN

Aruba

Curaçao

Bonaire

Grenada

Trinidad

MIDDLE AMERICA TRENCH

AREA OF OPTIMIZATION

EAST PACIFIC RISE

TEHUANTEPEC FRACTURE ZONE

GUATEMALA BASIN

SOUTH AMERICA

Height	
m.	ft.
6000	19700
4000	13000
2000	6500
1500	5000
1000	3300
500	1600
200	700
0	0
200	700
500	1600
1000	3300
2000	6500
3000	9800
4000	13000
5000	16400
6000	19700
m.	ft.
Depth	

© Hammond World Atlas Corporation

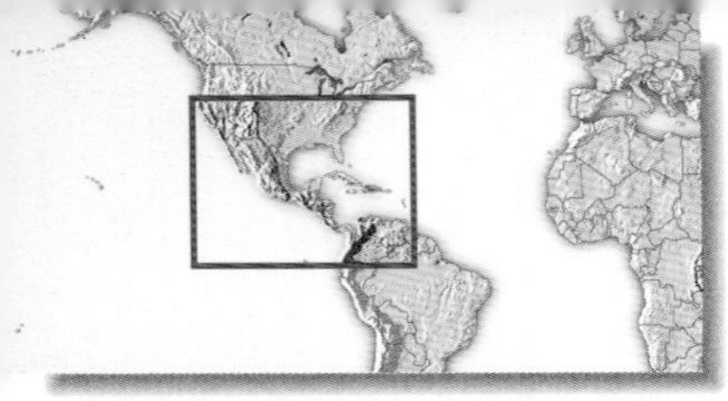

Middle America

North and South America are connected only by a narrow land bridge. Actually, the two land masses are separated by the relatively small Caribbean Plate, whose western boundary is defined by the East Middle America Trench, which reaches a depth of 6662 m off the coast of Chiapas in Mexico. There, the Cocos Plate is thrust under the Caribbean Plate, causing considerable earthquake and volcanic activity.

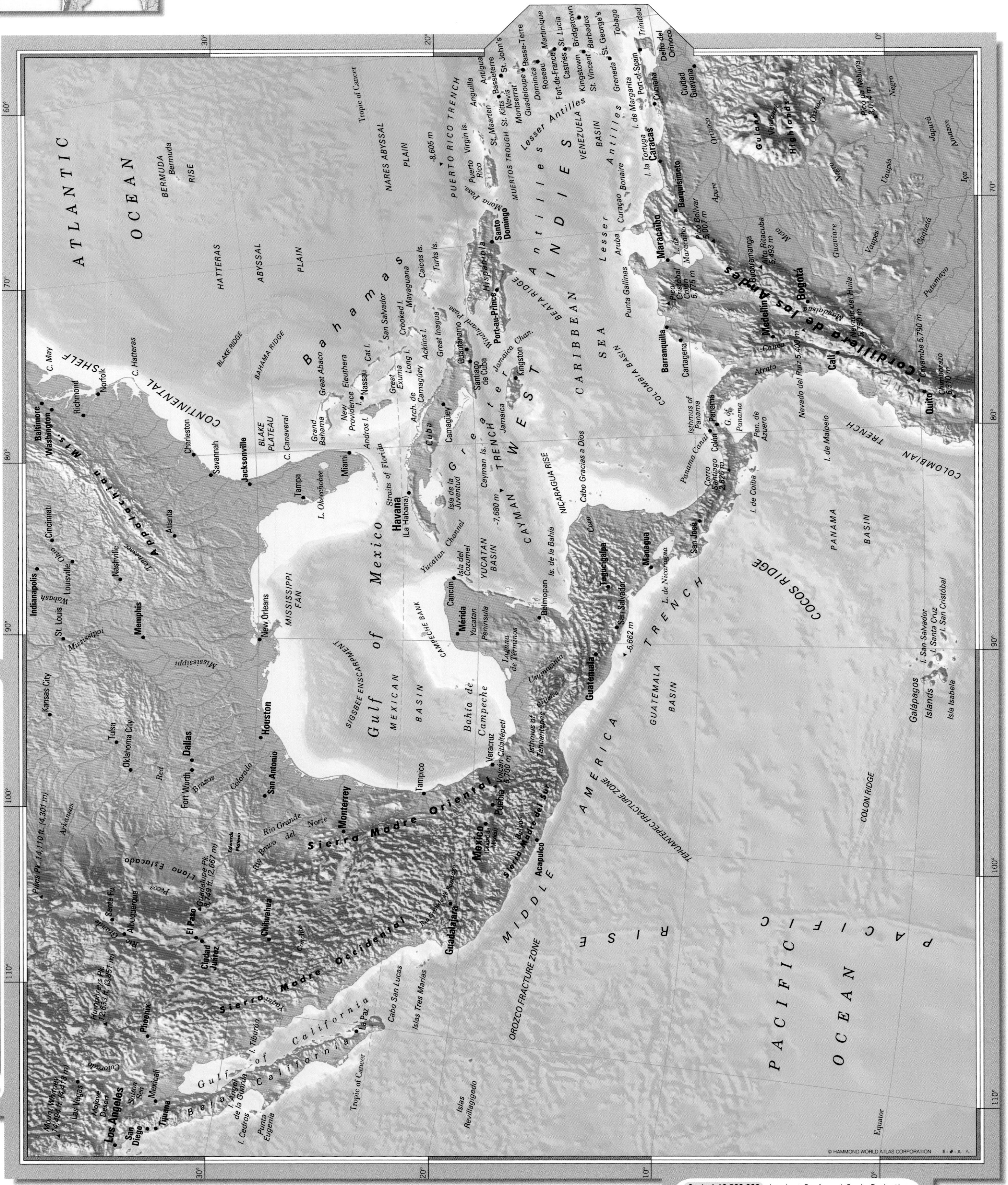

Scale 1:19,500,000 Lambert Conformal Conic Projection

© HAMMOND WORLD ATLAS CORPORATION

The Andes, extending 7200 km from north to south, are a product of the subduction of the Nazca Plate beneath the South American Plate. Some 130 million years ago, a 7000-km-wide strip of Pacific seafloor disappeared into the earth's crust. The rock melted, and the magma rising to the surface formed the Andes range, with snow-capped volcanoes rising to more than 6,000 meters above sea level.

South America

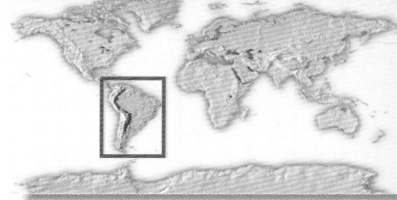

CARIBBEAN SEA

Punta Gallinas
Willemstad
Barranquilla
Maracaibo
Caracas
Port-of-Spain
Trinidad
G. of Paria

Panama Canal
San José
Gulf of Panama
Panama
PANAMA
Isla de Malpelo
Cabo Corrientes
Bucaramanga
Medellín
Alto Ritacuba, 5,493 m
Bogotá
Pico Bolívar 5,007 m
L. de Maracaibo
Delta del Orinoco
Ciudad Guayana
Salto del Angel
Georgetown
Paramaribo
Cayenne

Nevado del Tolima 5,215 m
Cali
Nevado del Huila 5,750 m
Cauca
Magdalena
Meta
Arauca
Orinoco
Mt. Roraima 2,772 m
Guiana Highlands

DEMERARA ABYSSAL PLAIN
ATLANTIC OCEAN
PARA ABYSSAL PLAIN
CEARA ABYSSAL PLAIN

Equator
Quito
Chimborazo 6,267 m
Guayaquil
G. de Guayaquil
Salto Grande
Caquetá
Salto Angostura
Vaupés
Guaviare
Napo
Pico de la Neblina 3,014 m
Negro
Rep. de Balbina
Ilha de Marajó
B. de Marajó
Pará
Belém
B. de São Marcos
São Luís
Rep. de Tucuruí

Cordillera de los Andes
LLANOS
Guaviare

Punta Galera
Iquitos
Amazon
Pulumayo
Içá
Japurá
Manaus
Amazon
Teresina
Fortaleza
I. Fernando de Noronha

Punta Aguja
Marañón
Ucayali
Yavari
Juruá
Purus
Madeira
Tapajós
Xingú
Tocantins
Parnaíba

Trujillo
La Montaña
Nevado Huascarán 6,768 m
Huallaga
Selvas
Teles Pires
Araguaia
Cabo de São Roque
Natal

PERU-CHILE TRENCH
Callao
Lima
Cusco
Madre de Diós
Mamoré
Guaporé
Iténes
Serra dos Parecis
Juruena
Caatingas
Rep. de Sobradinho
São Francisco
Recife
Maceió

PACIFIC OCEAN
NAZCA RIDGE
Lake Titicaca
Nevado Ancohuma 6,550 m
La Paz
Arequipa
Altiplano
Arica
Poopó
Planalto do Mato Grosso
Culuene
Brasília
Goiânia
Brazilian Highlands
Jequitinhonha
Salvador
Paraguaçu

Antofagasta
-8,064 m
Cordillera de los Andes
Desierto de Atacama
Volcán Llullaillaco 6,723 m
Gran Chaco
Pilcomayo
Campo Grande
Paraguai
Belo Horizonte
Pica da Bandeira 2,890 m
BRAZIL BASIN

Tropic of Capricorn
I. San Félix
I. San Ambrosio
San Miguel de Tucumán
Cerro Ojos del Salado 6,880 m
Bermejo
Paraná
Asunción
Represa de Itaipu
Cataratas del Iguaçu
Iguaçu
Curitiba
São Paulo
Río de Janeiro
Santos
Cabo de São Tomé
Cabo Frio
Tropic of Capricorn

CHALLENGER FRACTURE ZONE
I. Juan Fernández
I. Alejandro Selkirk
I. Robinson Crusoe
Salado del Norte
Uruguay
Serra do Mar
SANTOS PLATEAU

Cerro Aconcagua 6,959 m
L. Mar Chiquita
Córdoba
Santa Fe
Rosario
Pampas
Paraná
Porto Alegre
RIO GRANDE PLATEAU

Valparaíso
Santiago
Mendoza
Buenos Aires
Montevideo
La Plata
Río de la Plata
Cabo San Antonio

CHILE BASIN
Concepción
Salado
Colorado
Bahía Blanca
Bahía Blanca
CONTINENTAL SHELF
ATLANTIC OCEAN
ARGENTINE BASIN

PERU-CHILE TRENCH
Negro
Golfo San Matías
Pen. Valdés
-6,098 m

Puerto Montt
L. Nahuel Huapí
Limay
Chubut

CHILE RISE
Isla Chiloé
Arch. de Los Chonos
Pen. Taitao
Cabo Tres Montes
G. Corcovado
Lago Buenos Aires
Golfo San Jorge
Cabo Tres Puntas
Deseado
Patagonia
Chico
Santa Cruz
Bahía Grande
FALKLAND ESCARPMENT

Arch. Reina Adelaida
Isla Wellington
West Falkland
East Falkland
Falkland Is.
Strait of Magellan
Tierra del Fuego
Punta Arenas
Cape Horn
C. San Diego

© HAMMOND WORLD ATLAS CORPORATION
IM-A-A

Scale 1:24,000,000 Lambert Azimuthal Equal-Area

MI 200 400 600 800
KM 200 400 600 800 1000 1200

| Height |
| m. ft. |
| 6000 19700 |
| 4000 13000 |
| 2000 6500 |
| 1500 5000 |
| 1000 3300 |
| 500 1600 |
| 200 700 |
| -0- |
| 200 700 |
| 500 1600 |
| 1000 3300 |
| 2000 6500 |
| 3000 9800 |
| 4000 13000 |
| 5000 16400 |
| 6000 19700 |
| m. ft. |
| Depth |

According to an estimate published by the United Nations, roughly 8 billion people will be living on earth in the year 2025 - the majority of them in Asia and Africa. Their environment will have changed dramatically in the interim. The growing global population requires a constantly increasing supply of food, energy, and clean drinking water. Progressive land development threatens the survival of numerous animal and plant species. Even today, wars and migration can often be traced to deteriorating environmental conditions.

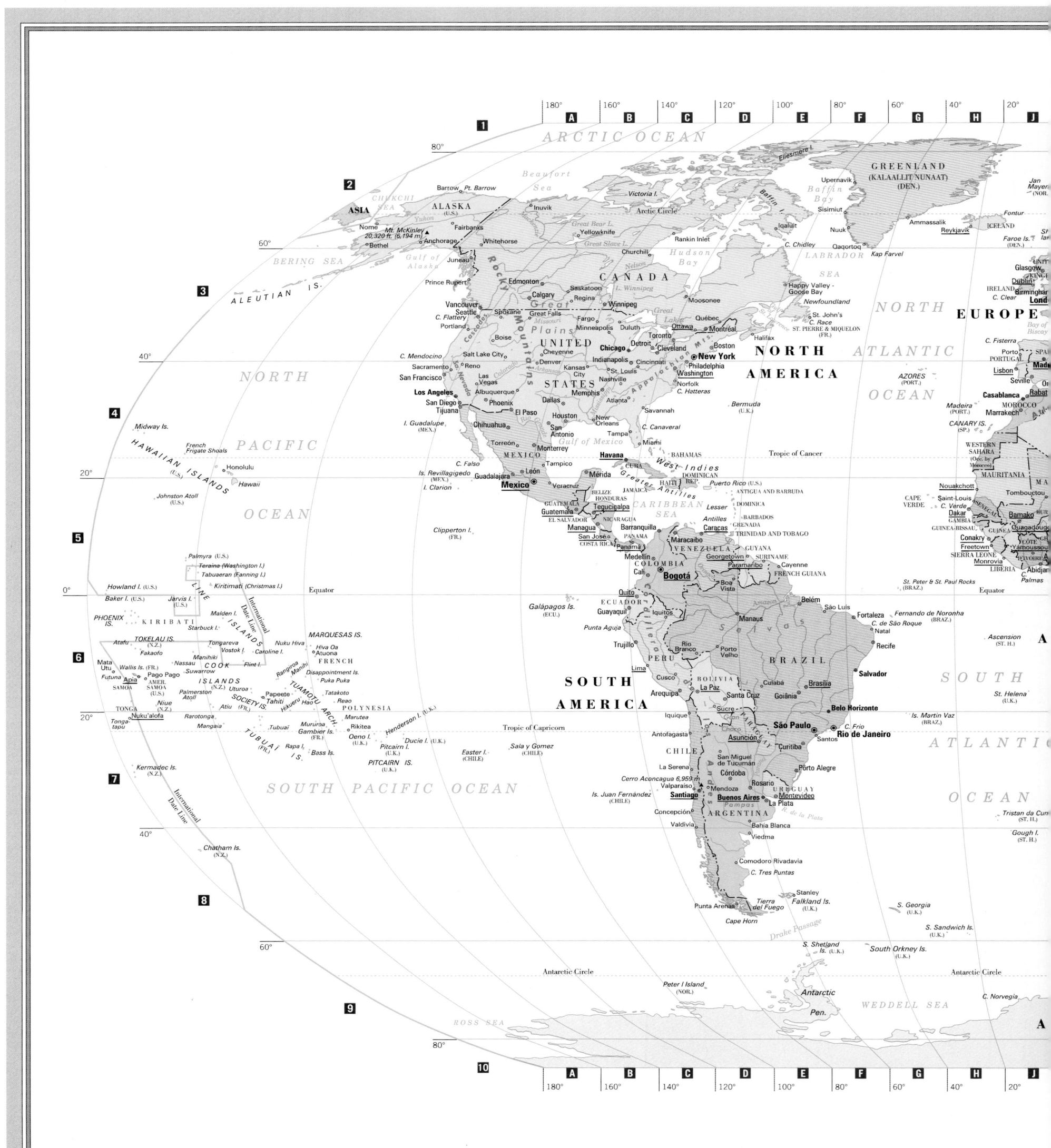

Population

◉ Over 5,000,000   ◎ 500,000 - 1,999,999

⊕ 2,000,000 - 4,999,999   ○ Under 500,000

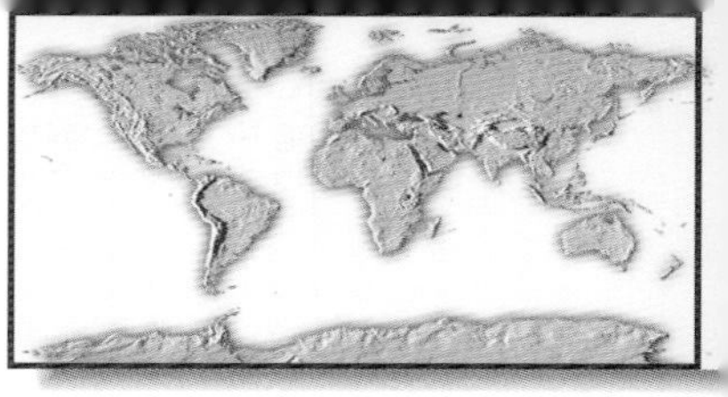

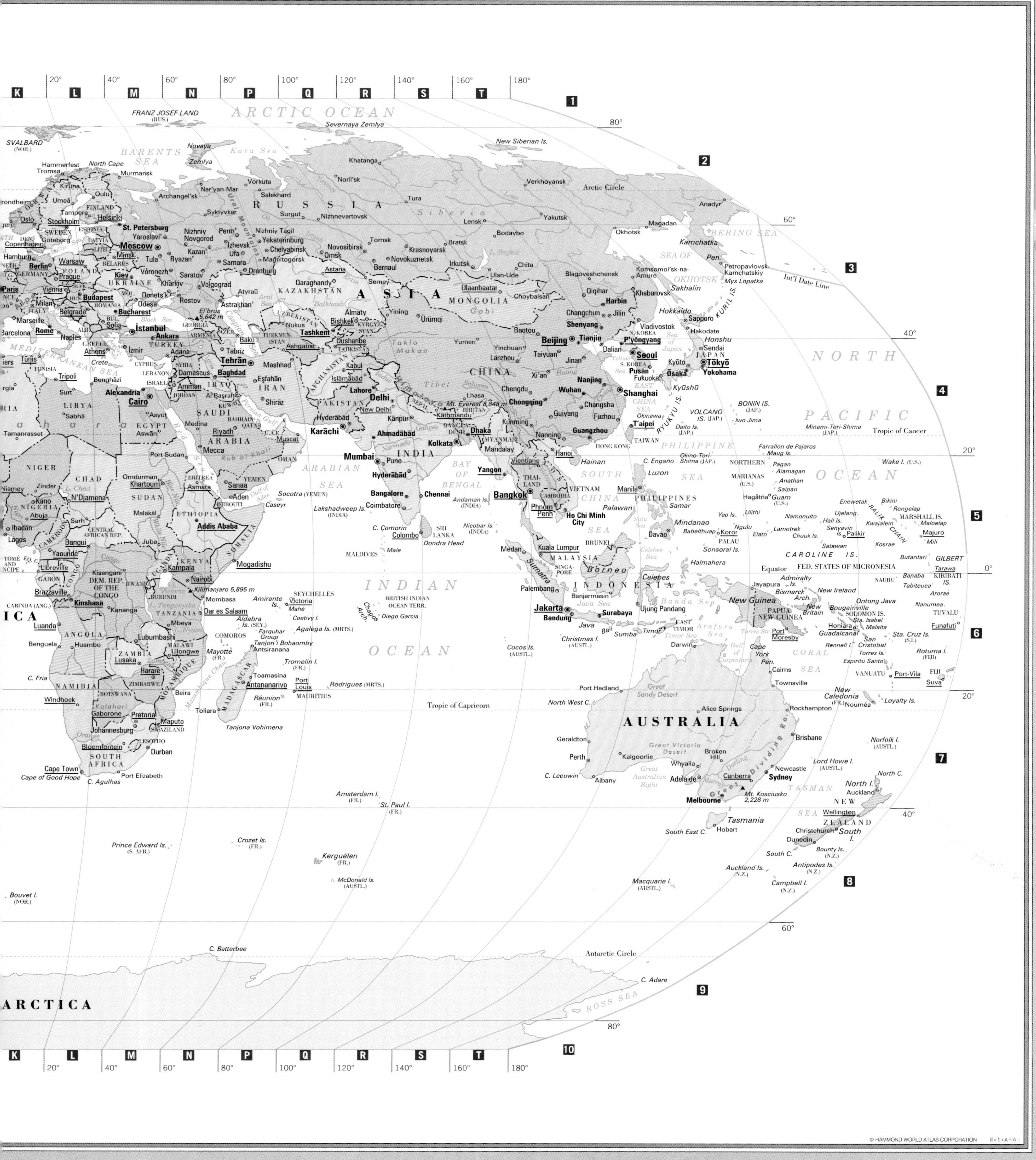

World

ARCTIC OCEAN

K | **L** | **M** | **N** | **P** | **Q** | **R** | **S** | **T**

20° · 40° · 60° · 80° · 100° · 120° · 140° · 160° · 180°

FRANZ JOSEF LAND (RUS.)

80°

1

SVALBARD (NOR.)

Severnaya Zemlya

BARENTS SEA · Novaya · Kara Sea · New Siberian Is.

2

North Cape · Zemlya

Hammerfest · Murmansk · Vorkuta · Khatanga · Arctic Circle

Tromsø · Kiruna · Nar'yan-Mar · Noril'sk · Verkhoyansk

Umeå · Oulu · Archangel'sk · Salekhard · Tura · Yakutsk · Anadyr'

80°

60°

Trondheim · FINLAND · Syktyvkar · Surgut · Nizhnevartovsk · Lensk · Bodaybo · Okhotsk · Magadan · BERING SEA

Oslo · Stockholm · Tampere · Helsinki · St. Petersburg · Perm' · Yekaterinburg · Tomsk · Krasnoyarsk · Bratsk · Chita · Blagoveshchensk · Komsomol'sk-na-Amure · Petropavlovsk-Kamchatskiy

3

SWEDEN · ESTONIA · Yaroslavl' · Nizhniy Novgorod · Nizhniy Tagil · Chelyabinsk · Omsk · Novokuznetsk · Irkutsk · Ulan-Ude · Khabarovsk · Sakhalin · Mys Lopatka · Int'l Date Line

Hamburg · DEN. · Minsk · Moscow · Tula · Izhevsk · Kazan' · Ufa · Magnitogorsk · Barnaul · Novosibirsk · L. Baykal · SEA OF OKHOTSK · Kamchatka

Copenhagen · Berlin · Warsaw · POLAND · BELARUS · Ryazan' · Saratov · Samara · Orenburg · Qaraghandy · Astana · RUSSIA · Siberia · Yenisey

Paris · Prague · Vienna · UKRAINE · Kiev · Voronezh · Volgograd · Atyraū · Semey · Harbin · Vladivostok · Hokkaido · Sapporo · Hakodate

Milan · Budapest · ROMANIA · Odesa · Rostov · Astrakhan' · Aral Sea · Balkhash · Almaty · Yining · Ürümqi · MONGOLIA · Ulaanbaatar · Choybalsan · Changchun · Jilin · Shenyang · N. KOREA · P'yŏngyang · Honshū · Sendai · 40°

Marseille · Belgrade · Bucharest · BUL. · GEORGIA · El'brus 5,642 m · UZBEKISTAN · Nukus · Bishkek · KYRGYZSTAN · Gobi · Baotou · Beijing · Tianjin · Dalian · Seoul · JAPAN · Tōkyō

Barcelona · Rome · Sofia · İstanbul · Ankara · ARMENIA · Baku · TURKMEN-ISTAN · Tashkent · Dushanbe · TAJIKISTAN · Yumen · Yinchuan · ASIA · Pusan · Kyōto · Ōsaka · Yokohama

MEDITERRANEAN SEA · Athens · GREECE · TURKEY · İzmir · Adana · SYRIA · Ashgabat · Mashhad · AFGHANISTAN · Kabul · Lanzhou · Taiyuan · Jinan · Yellow Sea · Fukuoka · Kyūshū

Tunis · Crete · CYPRUS · LEBANON · Damascus · Tehrān · Tabriz · Eşfahān · Islāmābād · Xi'an · CHINA · Nanjing · Shanghai · 40°

4

Tripoli · Benghāzī · ISRAEL · Amman · Baghdad · IRAQ · IRAN · Shiraz · PAKISTAN · New Delhi · Lhasa · Chengdu · Chongqing · Wuhan · Changsha · T'aipei · TAIWAN · PACIFIC

Alexandria · Cairo · JORDAN · Al Başrah · KUWAIT · Lahore · Delhi · NEPAL · Kāthmāndu · BHUTAN · Kunming · Guiyang · Fuzhou · BONIN IS. (JAP.) · OCEAN

LIBYA · EGYPT · Asyūţ · Medina · SAUDI · BAHRAIN · QATAR · U.A.E. · Muscat · Karāchi · Ahmadābād · Kānpur · BANGLA-DESH · Dhaka · MYANMAR · Mandalay · Nanning · Guangzhou · HONG KONG · VOLCANO IS. (JAP.) · Iwo Jima · Minami-Tori-Shima (JAP.) · Tropic of Cancer

Sabhā · Aswān · ARABIA · Riyadh · Mecca · Mumbai · INDIA · Kolkata · Yangon · THAI-LAND · South China Sea · RYUKYU IS. · Okinawa I. (JAP.) · Daito Is. (JAP.) · Wake I. (U.S.) · 20°

5

NIGER · CHAD · SUDAN · ERITREA · Sanaa · YEMEN · Socotra (YEMEN) · ARABIAN SEA · Hyderābād · BAY OF BENGAL · Bangalore · Coimbatore · Chennai · Andaman Is. (INDIA) · Bangkok · CAMBODIA · VIETNAM · Hanoi · Hainan · Manila · PHILIPPINES · NORTHERN MARIANAS (U.S.) · Pagan · Anathan · Saipan · Farallon de Pajaros · Maug Is. · Okino-Tori-Shima (JAP.) · C. Engaño · Luzon · Hagåtña · Guam · Enewetak · Bikini · Rongelap · MARSHALL IS. · Maloelap

N'Djamena · Khartoum · Omdurman · Sarh · ETHIOPIA · DJIBOUTI · Aden · Gulf of Aden · Lakshadweep Is. (INDIA) · C. Comorin · SRI LANKA · Nicobar Is. (INDIA) · Phnom Penh · Ho Chi Minh City · Palawan · Samar · Mindanao · Davao · Yap Is. · Ulithi · Namonuito · Hall Is. · Ngulu · Babelthuap · PALAU · Koror · Chuuk Is. · Lamotrek · Satawan · Palikir · Kwajalein · Majuro · Mili

NIGERIA · Kano · Abuja · CENTRAL AFRICAN REP. · Juba · Addis Ababa · SOMALIA · Colombo · Dondra Head · MALDIVES · Malé · Medan · BRUNEI · Celebes Sea · Sonsorol Is. · Elato · Satawal · KOSRAE · CAROLINE IS. · Butaritari · GILBERT IS. · KIRIBATI

6

TOGO · CAMEROON · Bangui · Yaoundé · Libreville · UGANDA · KENYA · Nairobi · INDIAN · Equator · MALAYSIA · SINGA-PORE · Kuala Lumpur · Borneo · Halmahera · INDONESIA · Equator · FED. STATES OF MICRONESIA · NAURU · Tarawa

SÃO TOMÉ AND PRÍNCIPE · GABON · CONGO · DEM. REP. OF THE CONGO · Kisangani · RWANDA · BURUNDI · L. Victoria · Kilimanjaro 5,895 m · SEYCHELLES · Victoria · Mahé · BRITISH INDIAN OCEAN TERR. · OCEAN · Palembang · Ujung Pandang · Celebes · Banda Sea · New Guinea · Admiralty Is. · Jayapura · Bismarck Arch. · New Ireland · Ontong Java · Banaba · Tabiteuea · Arorae · Nanumea · TUVALU

Brazzaville · Kinshasa · Luanda · Kananga · Lubumbashi · TANZANIA · Dar es Salaam · Mbeya · Amirante Is. · Coetivy I. · Agalega Is. (MRTS.) · Farquhar Group · Tanjon' Bobaomby · Java · Bali · Sumba · Timor · EAST TIMOR · Arafura Sea · Bougainville · SOLOMON IS. · Sta. Isabel · Malaita · Honiara · New Britain · PAPUA NEW GUINEA · Port Moresby · Guadalcanal · San Cristobal · Sta. Cruz Is. (S.I.) · Rotuma I. (FIJI) · Funafuti

7

ANGOLA · Huambo · MALAWI · Lilongwe · ZAMBIA · Lusaka · Harare · Antsiranana · Aldabra Is. (SEY.) · Chagos Arch. · Diego Garcia · COMOROS · Mayotte (FR.) · MADAGASCAR · Antananarivo · Cocos Is. (AUSTL.) · Christmas I. (AUSTL.) · Darwin · Gulf of Carpentaria · Cape York Pen. · Torres Str. · Rennell I. · Espíritu Santo · VANUATU · Port-Vila · FIJI · Suva

Benguela · NAMIBIA · BOTSWANA · ZIMBABWE · MOZAMBIQUE · Beira · Toamasina · Port Louis · MAURITIUS · Rodrigues (MRTS.) · Port Hedland · North West C. · Great Sandy Desert · Alice Springs · Rockhampton · New Caledonia (FR.) · Nouméa · Loyalty Is. · 20°

Windhoek · Kalahari · Gaborone · Pretoria · Maputo · SWAZILAND · Réunion (FR.) · Tromelin I. (FR.) · Tanjona Vohimena · Tropic of Capricorn · AUSTRALIA · Great Victoria Desert · Brisbane · Norfolk I. (AUSTL.)

Bloemfontein · Johannesburg · LESOTHO · SOUTH AFRICA · Durban · Geraldton · Perth · Kalgoorlie · Broken Hill · Whyalla · Newcastle · Lord Howe I. (AUSTL.) · North C.

7

Cape Town · Cape of Good Hope · C. Agulhas · Port Elizabeth · Amsterdam I. (FR.) · St. Paul I. (FR.) · C. Leeuwin · Albany · Great Australian Bight · Adelaide · Murray · Sydney · Canberra · Mt. Kosciusko 2,228 m · TASMAN SEA · North I. · Auckland · NEW ZEALAND · 40°

Melbourne · Wellington

8

Prince Edward Is. (S. AFR.) · Crozet Is. (FR.) · Kerguélen (FR.) · McDonald Is. (AUSTL.) · Macquarie I. (AUSTL.) · Auckland Is. (N.Z.) · Tasmania · Hobart · South East C. · Christchurch · Dunedin · South C. · South I. · Bounty Is. (N.Z.) · Antipodes Is. (N.Z.) · Campbell I. (N.Z.)

60°

Bouvet I. (NOR.)

C. Batterbee · Antarctic Circle · C. Adare · ROSS SEA

9

ANTARCTICA

80°

K | **L** | **M** | **N** | **P** | **Q** | **R** | **S** | **T**

20° · 40° · 60° · 80° · 100° · 120° · 140° · 160° · 180°

10

© HAMMOND WORLD ATLAS CORPORATION · II-1-A-A

Scale 1:70,000,000 Robinson Projection

MI · 600 · 1200 · 1800 · 2400

KM · 600 · 1200 · 1800 · 2400 · 3000 · 3600

The four large peninsulas of the Peloponnesus extend like fingers into the Mediterranean south of the Gulf of Corinth. The peninsula as a whole is bounded by the Ionian Sea to the west and the Mirtóōn Sea to the east. The ancient Greeks regarded Cape Taínaron, located at the tip of the central peninsula, as the end of the world. The Peloponnesus, the Gulf of Corinth, and the Pindus Mountains to the north are excellent examples of the effects of the upward and downward thrust of segments of the earth's crust caused by the collision of the African and Eurasian Plates.

(See Map Section 8-9 for additional information.)

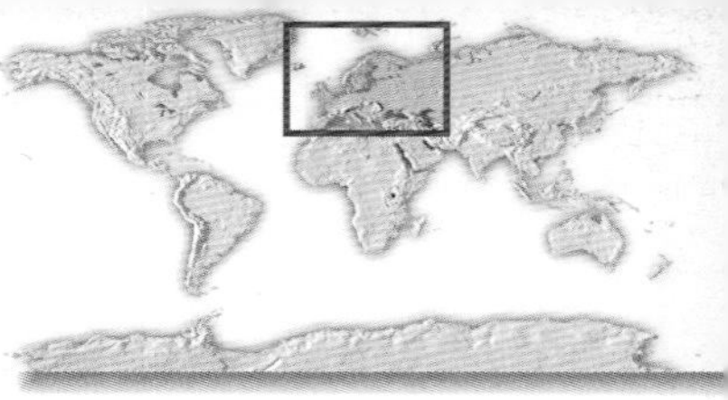

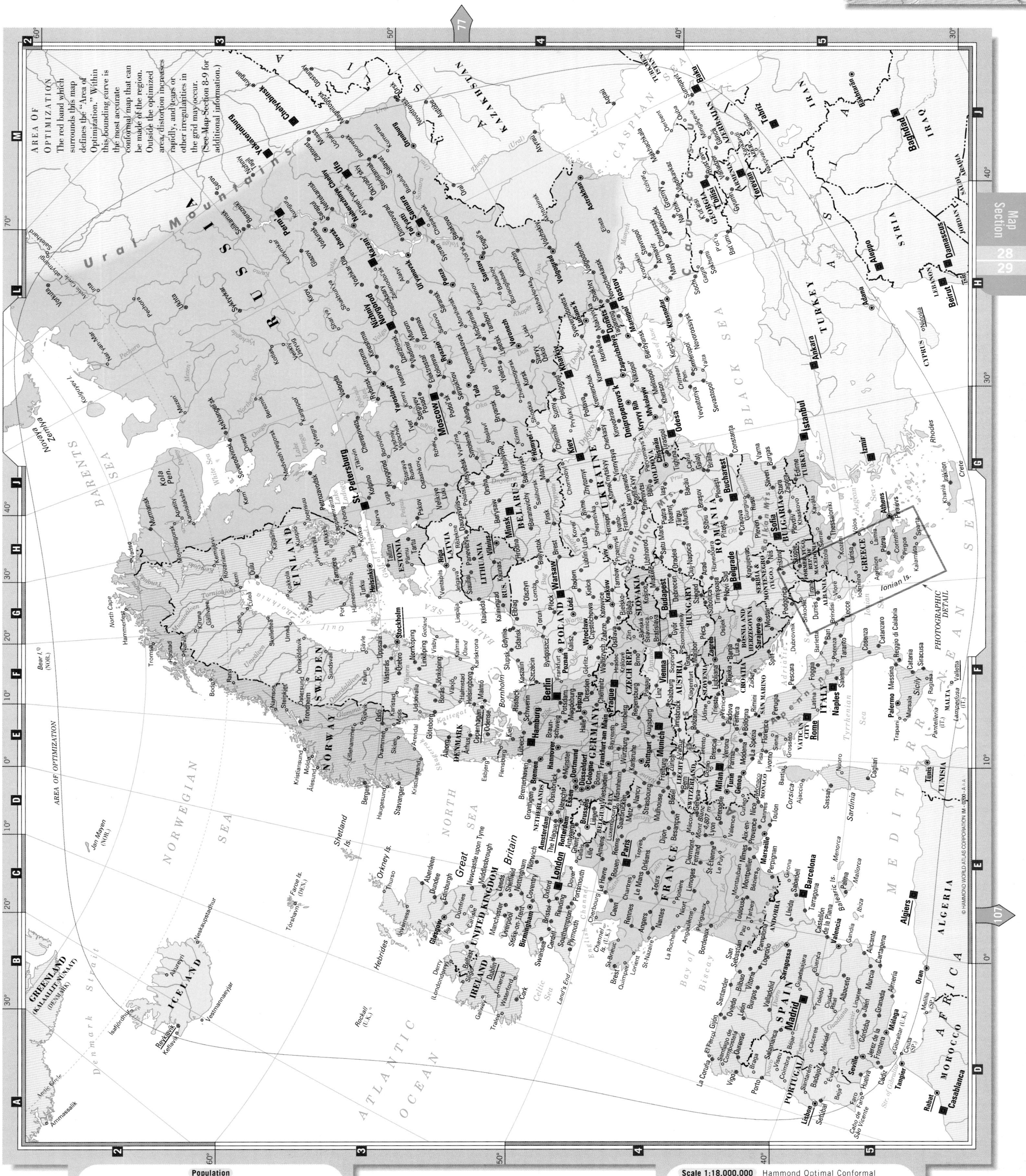

AREA OF OPTIMIZATION
The red band which surrounds this map defines the "Area of Optimization." Within this bounding curve is the most accurate conformal map that can be made of the region. Outside the optimized area, distortion increases rapidly, and leaps or other irregularities in the grid may occur.

Population

■ Over 3,000,000	● 500,000 - 999,999	○ Under 100,000
■ 1,000,000 - 2,999,999	● 100,000 - 499,999	

Scale 1:18,000,000   Hammond Optimal Conformal

MI   200   400   600

KM 200   400   600   800

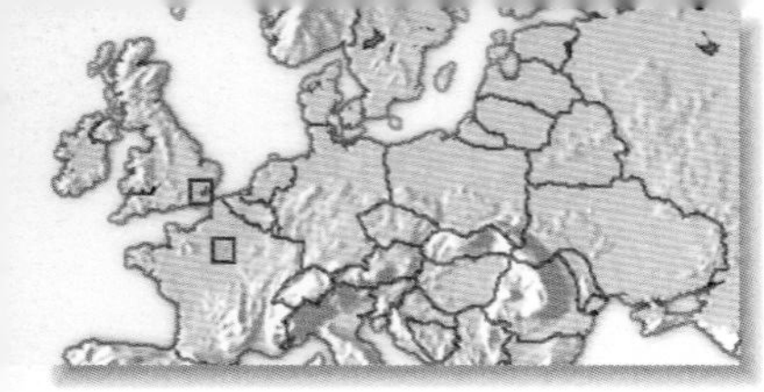

London, Paris

Both of these major commercial centers are situated on the banks of major rivers: the Thames and the Seine. With more than seven million inhabitants, Greater London is one of the largest cities on earth.

Though Paris itself has a population of only 2.5 million, its greater metropolitan area is home to some ten million people. The Channel Tunnel has reduced travel time from Paris to London to only a few hours.

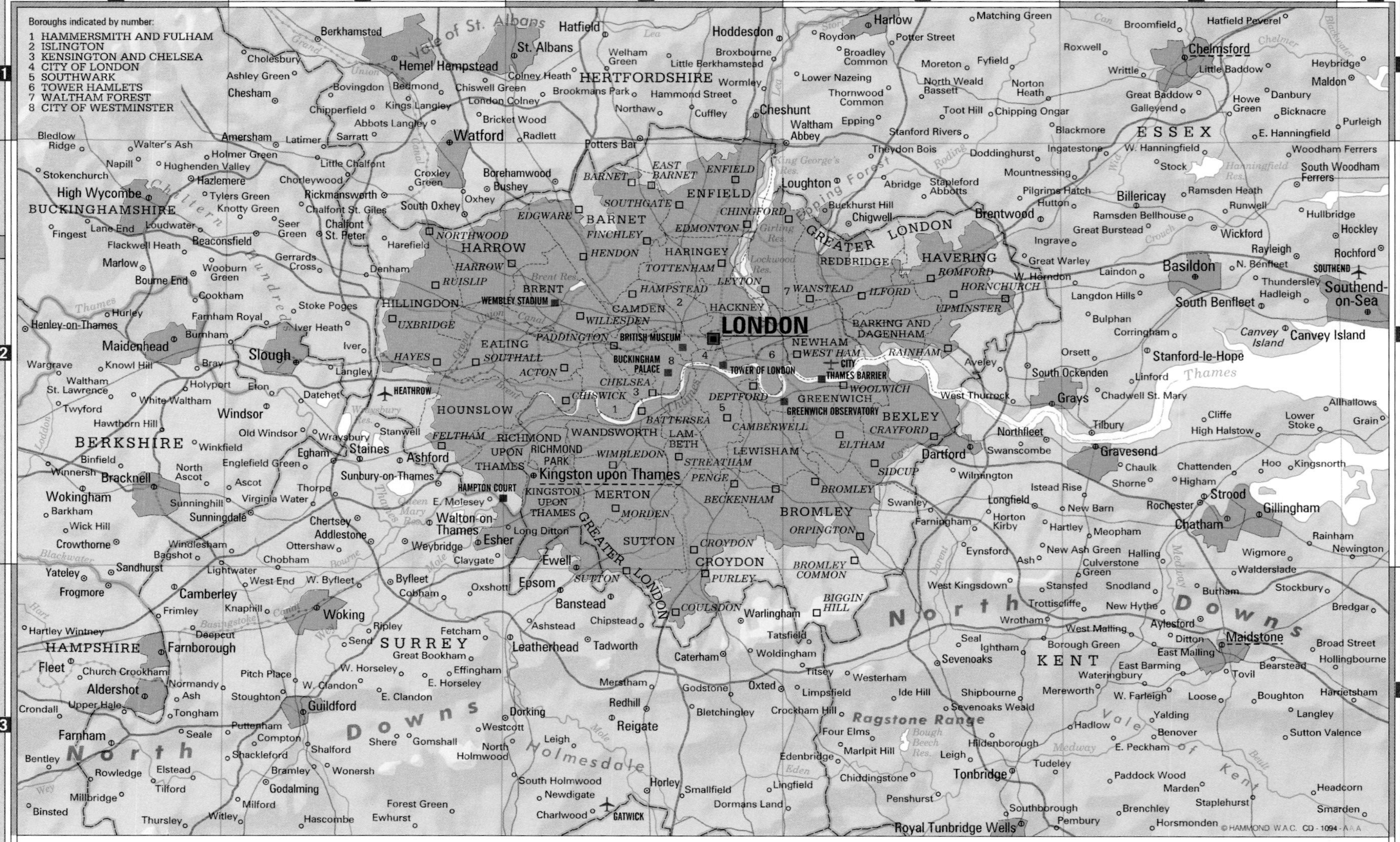

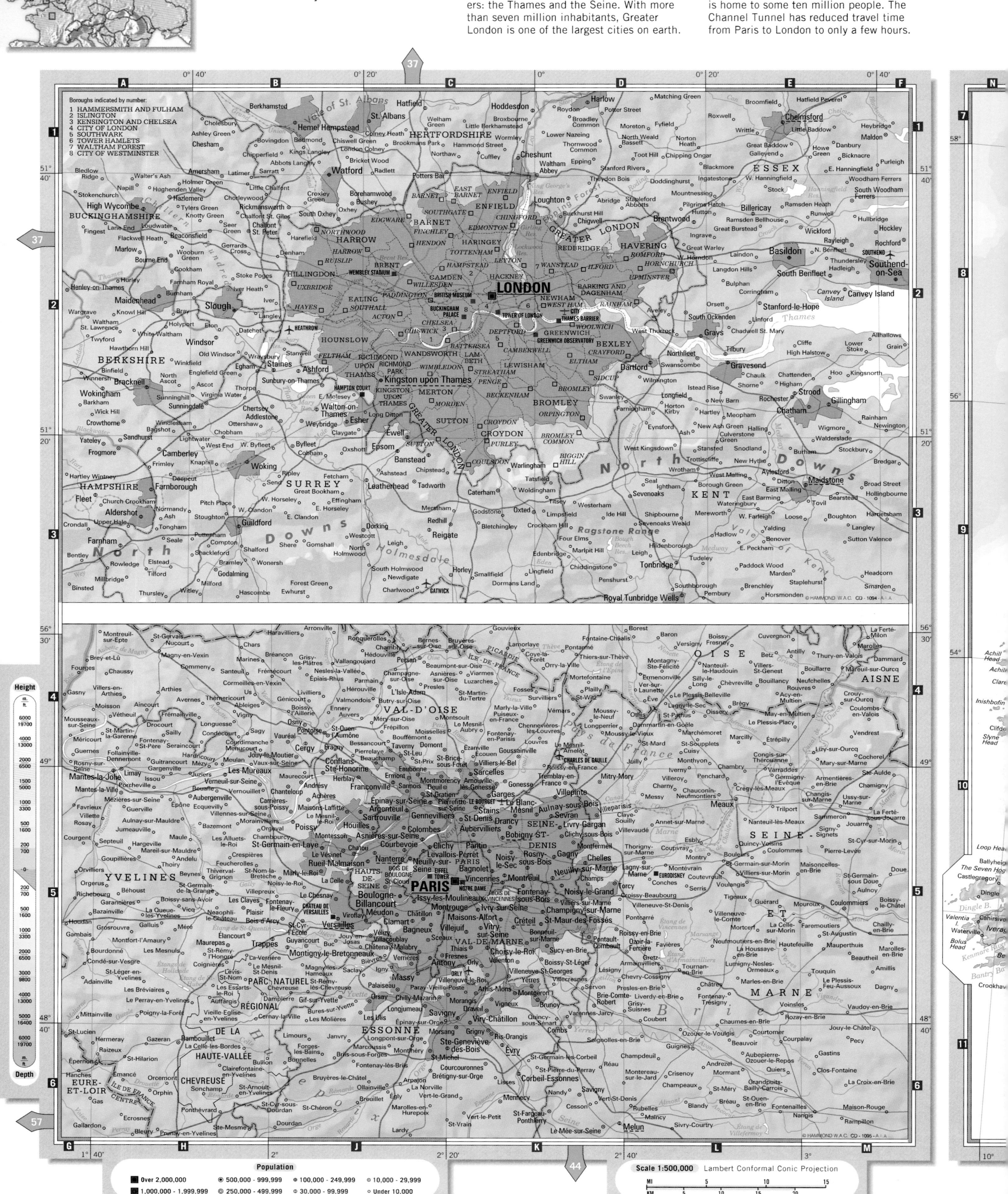

Boroughs indicated by number:
1 HAMMERSMITH AND FULHAM
2 ISLINGTON
3 KENSINGTON AND CHELSEA
4 CITY OF LONDON
5 SOUTHWARK
6 TOWER HAMLETS
7 WALTHAM FOREST
8 CITY OF WESTMINSTER

Population

■ Over 2,000,000
■ 1,000,000 - 1,999,999
⊛ 500,000 - 999,999
⊛ 250,000 - 499,999
⊙ 100,000 - 249,999
⊙ 30,000 - 99,999
○ 10,000 - 29,999
○ Under 10,000

Scale 1:500,000   Lambert Conformal Conic Projection

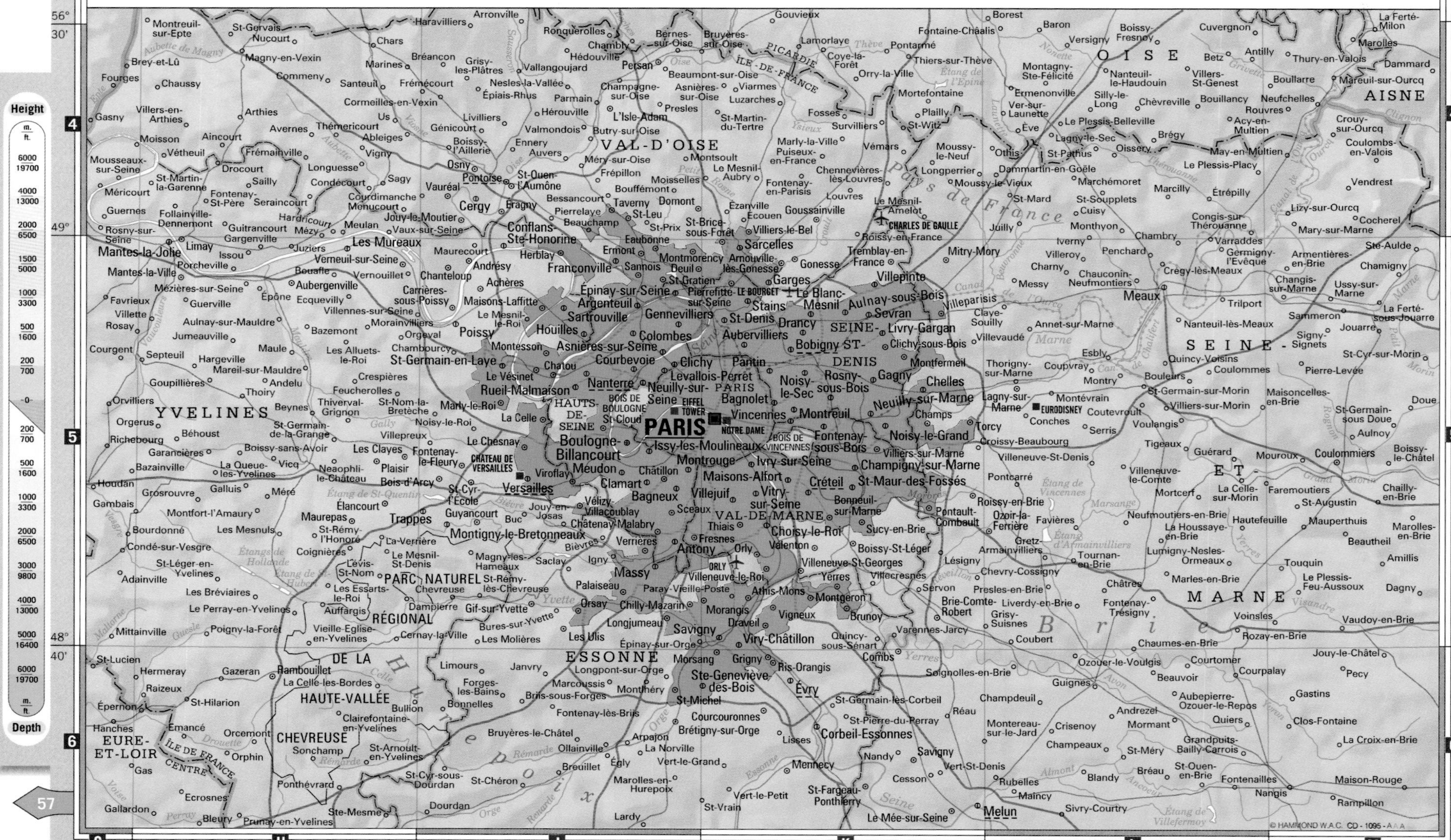

The British Isles are only 32 km from the European continent. Britain's isolated geographic position is due chiefly to its irregular coastline with its many steep, towering cliffs, which offers only very few points of access for ships. The most important commercial centers of the United Kingdom and Ireland developed where fjords and estuaries extend far into the island interior.

Scale 1:3,000,000 Lambert Conformal Conic Projection

MI 25 50 75 100
KM 25 50 75 100 150

© HAMMOND WORLD ATLAS CORPORATION CM - 1004 - A - A

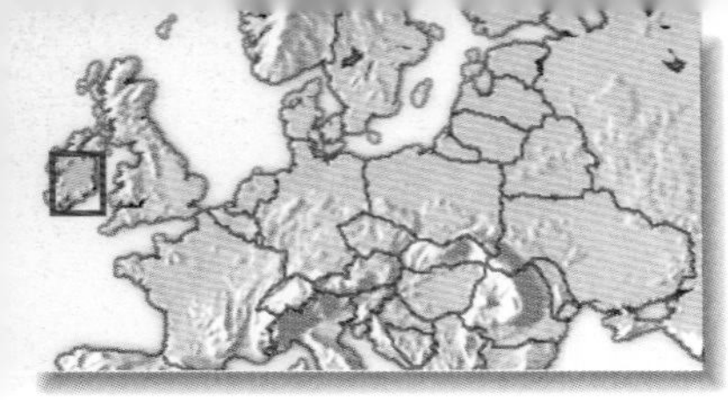

Central and Southern Ireland

The "Emerald Isle" of Ireland derives its name from the lush, evergreen vegetation that flourishes in Ireland's oceanic climate. Low-pressure centers passing over the island from the Atlantic bring substantial precipitation, which falls more frequently in the west than in the east. Moreover, the influence of the Gulf Stream keeps temperatures relatively mild even during the winter months.

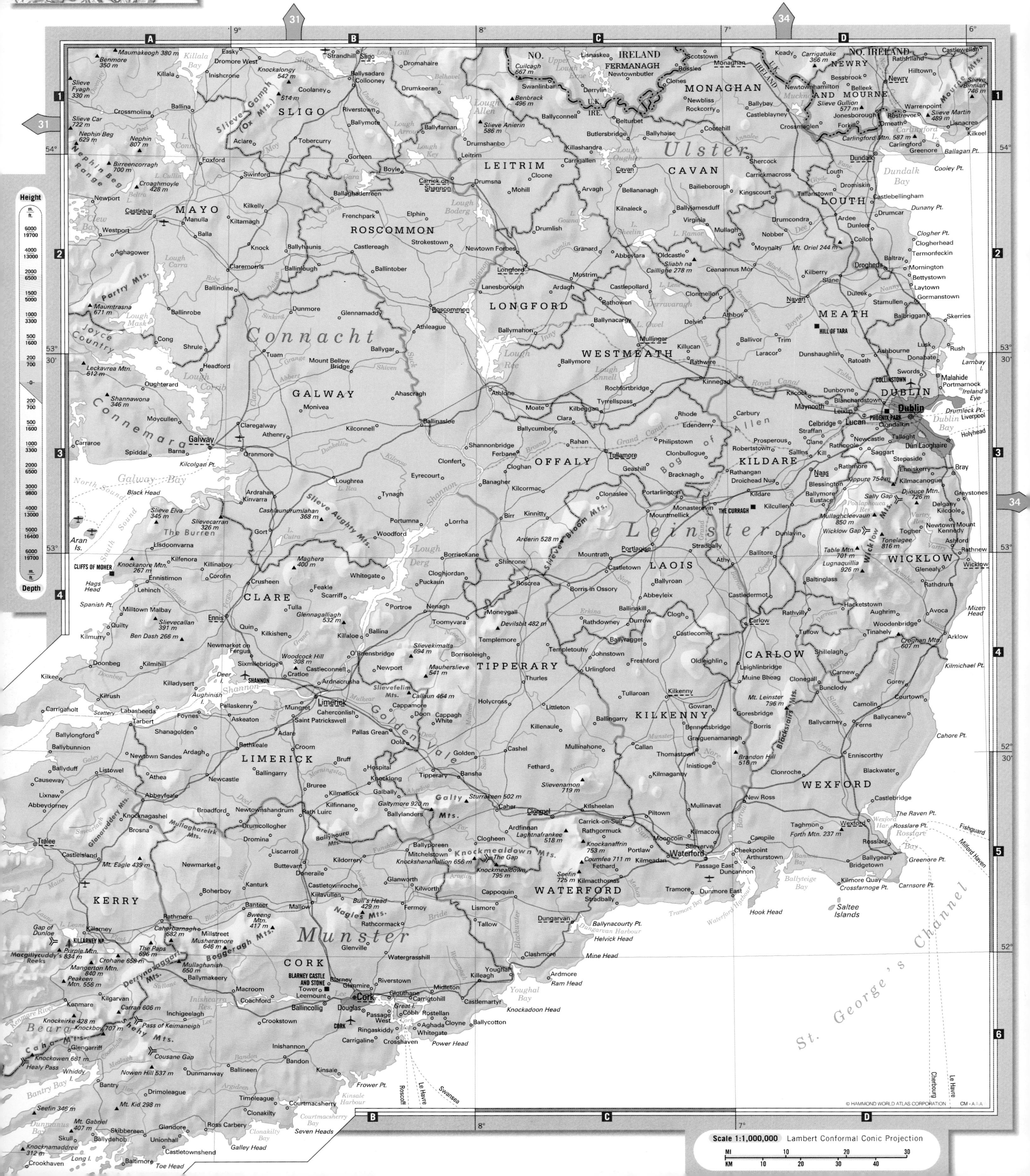

Scale 1:1,000,000   Lambert Conformal Conic Projection

Glen Mòr, the largest linear fault in northern Scotland, divides central Scotland into the Northern Highlands and the Grampian Mountains to the south. Ben Nevis (1,343 m) is the highest peak in the Grampian range. The sparsely forested highlands covered by broad moors and heaths provide ideal grazing areas for sheep. Farmland is found primarily in the lowlands and along the coast.

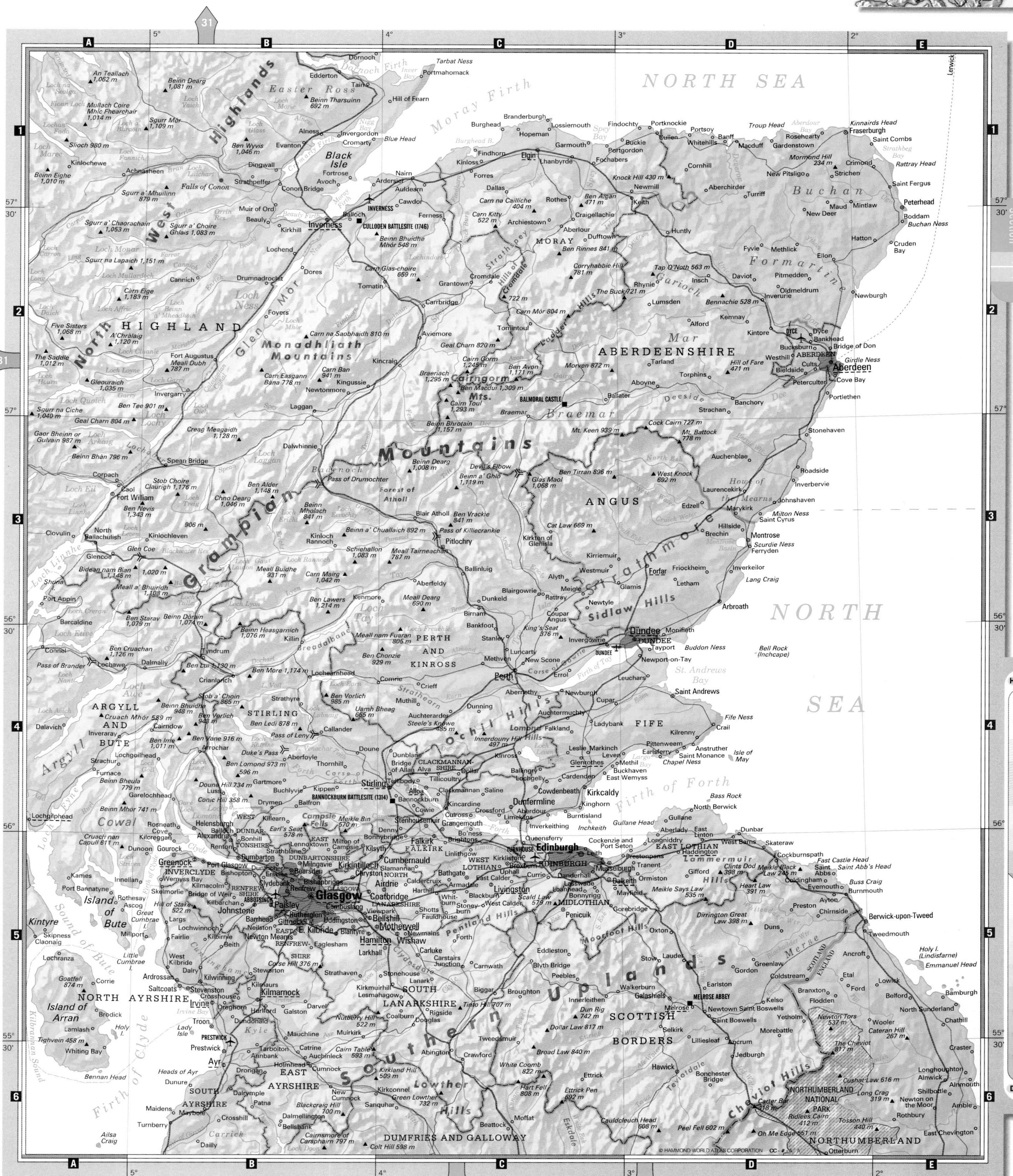

Central Scotland

Map Section 32 33

NORTH SEA

NORTH SEA

Population

| ■ Over 2,000,000 | ◉ 500,000 - 999,999 | ◉ 100,000 - 249,999 | ○ 10,000 - 29,999 |
| ■ 1,000,000 - 1,999,999 | ◉ 250,000 - 499,999 | ○ 30,000 - 99,999 | ○ Under 10,000 |

Scale 1:1,000,000   Lambert Conformal Conic Projection

Height

m. ft.
6000 19700
4000 13000
2000 6500
1500 5000
1000 3300
500 1600
200 700
0
200 700
500 1600
1000 3300
2000 6500
3000 9800
4000 13000
5000 16400
6000 19700
m. ft.

Depth

© HAMMOND WORLD ATLAS CORPORATION

Lake District National Park offers a striking display of the diversity of the landscape of the British Isles. The park contains not only England's largest lake, Lake Windermere, but also its highest peak, Seafell Pike (978 m). Sheep graze on the lush, green meadows of this area. Although the landscape seems almost alpine, many of the lakes here lie below sea level.

During the Ice Age, a land bridge connected Great Britain and Ireland. When the waters rose again, the Irish Sea formed and separated the two large islands.

Population

■ Over 2,000,000   ⬤ 500,000 - 999,999   ⬤ 100,000 - 249,999   ⊙ 10,000 - 29,999
■ 1,000,000 - 1,999,999   ⬤ 250,000 - 499,999   ⬤ 30,000 - 99,999   ⚬ Under 10,000

Northeastern Ireland, Northern England and Wales

Scale 1:1,000,000 Lambert Conformal Conic Projection

© HAMMOND WORLD ATLAS CORPORATION

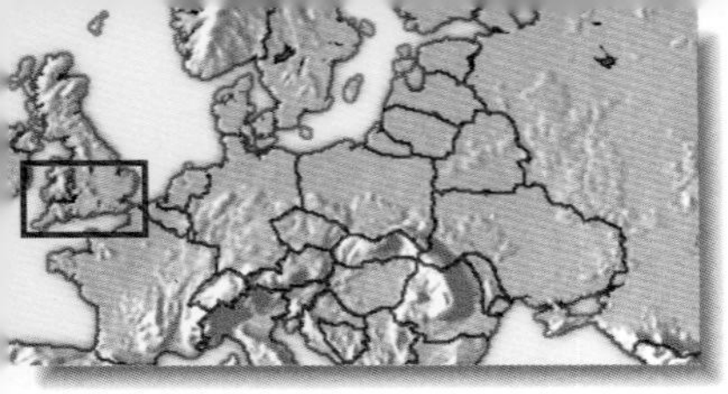

Southern Great Britain is traditionally divided into two regions characterized by yellow and green coloration. Yellow is the eastern region, where wheat is grown, and, as in Spain, annual precipitation

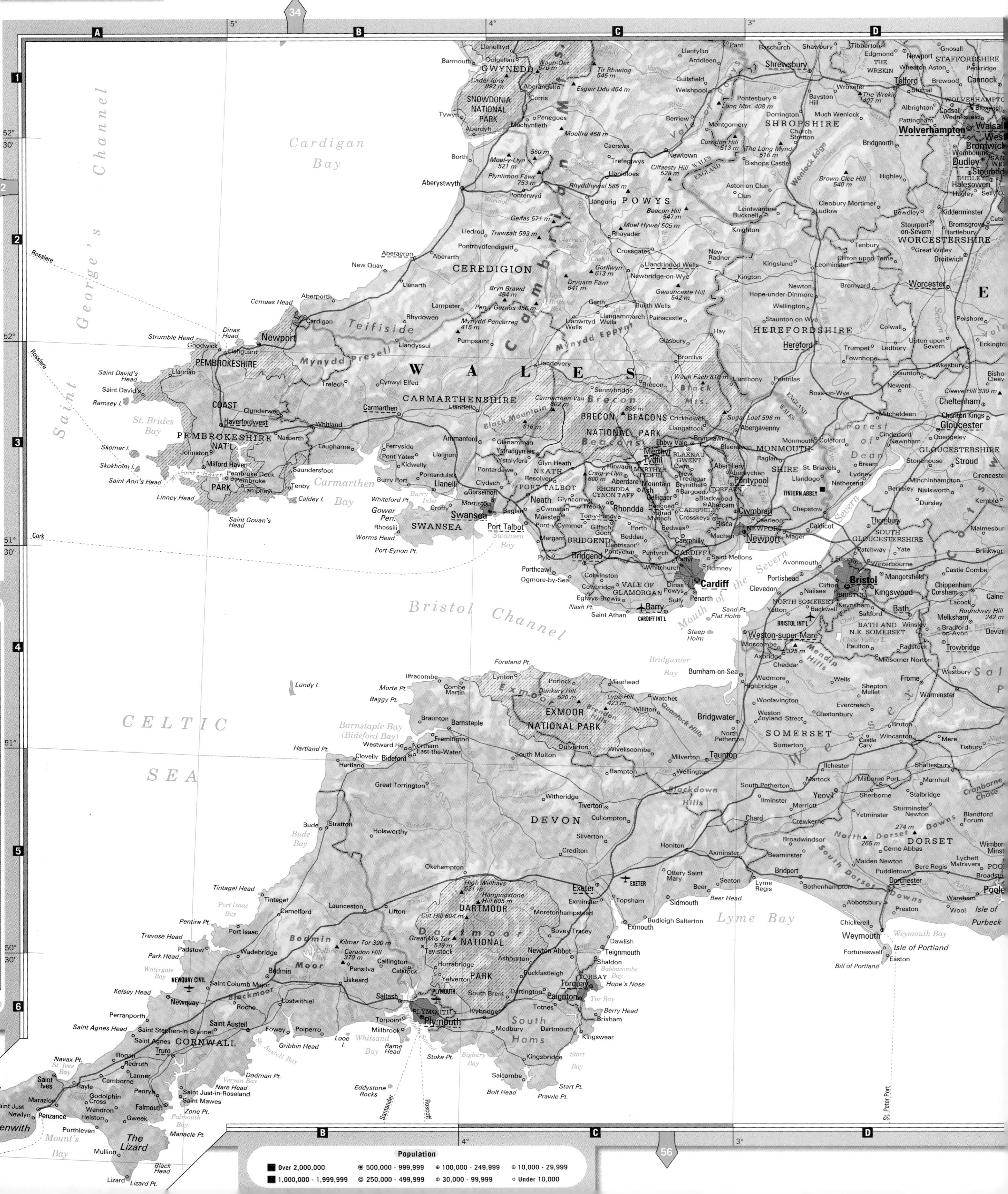

Population

■ Over 2,000,000	⊙ 500,000 - 999,999
■ 1,000,000 - 1,999,999	⊙ 250,000 - 499,999
⊙ 100,000 - 249,999	⊙ 10,000 - 29,999
⊙ 30,000 - 99,999	○ Under 10,000

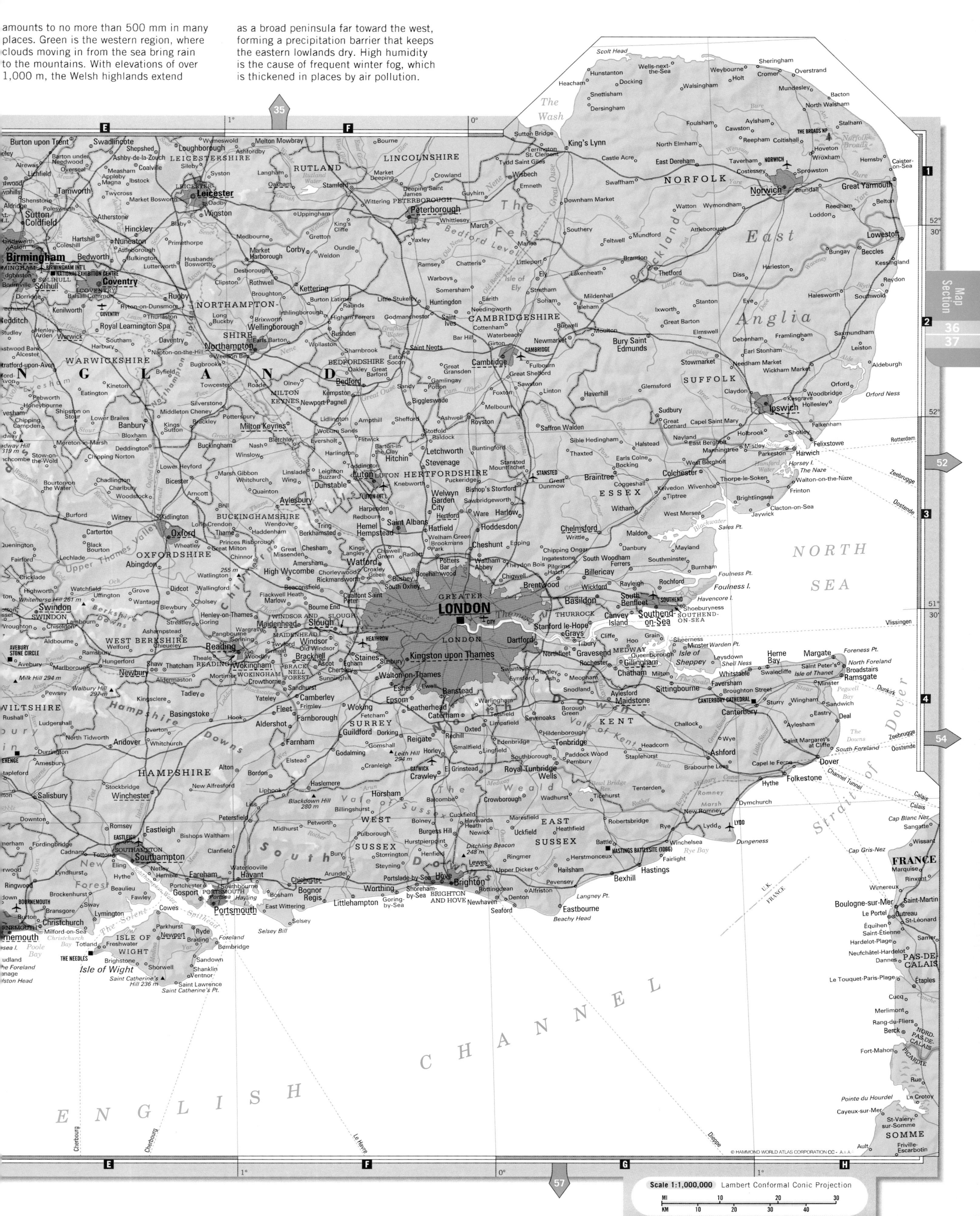

amounts to no more than 500 mm in many places. Green is the western region, where clouds moving in from the sea bring rain to the mountains. With elevations of over 1,000 m, the Welsh highlands extend as a broad peninsula far toward the west, forming a precipitation barrier that keeps the eastern lowlands dry. High humidity is the cause of frequent winter fog, which is thickened in places by air pollution.

Scale 1:1,000,000   Lambert Conformal Conic Projection

Scandinavia and Finland, Iceland

Marked by fjords, deep valleys, and lakes, the landscape of northern Europe was clearly shaped during the Ice Age. Although glaciers have long since receded in this region, the picture in Iceland is very different. The Vatnajökull Ice Cap covers an area of some 8,410 square kilometers, and melt caused by subglacial eruptions poses a significant danger to coastal settlements.

Scale 1:6,000,000   Lambert Conformal Conic Projection

Stockholm, Helsinki, Copenhagen

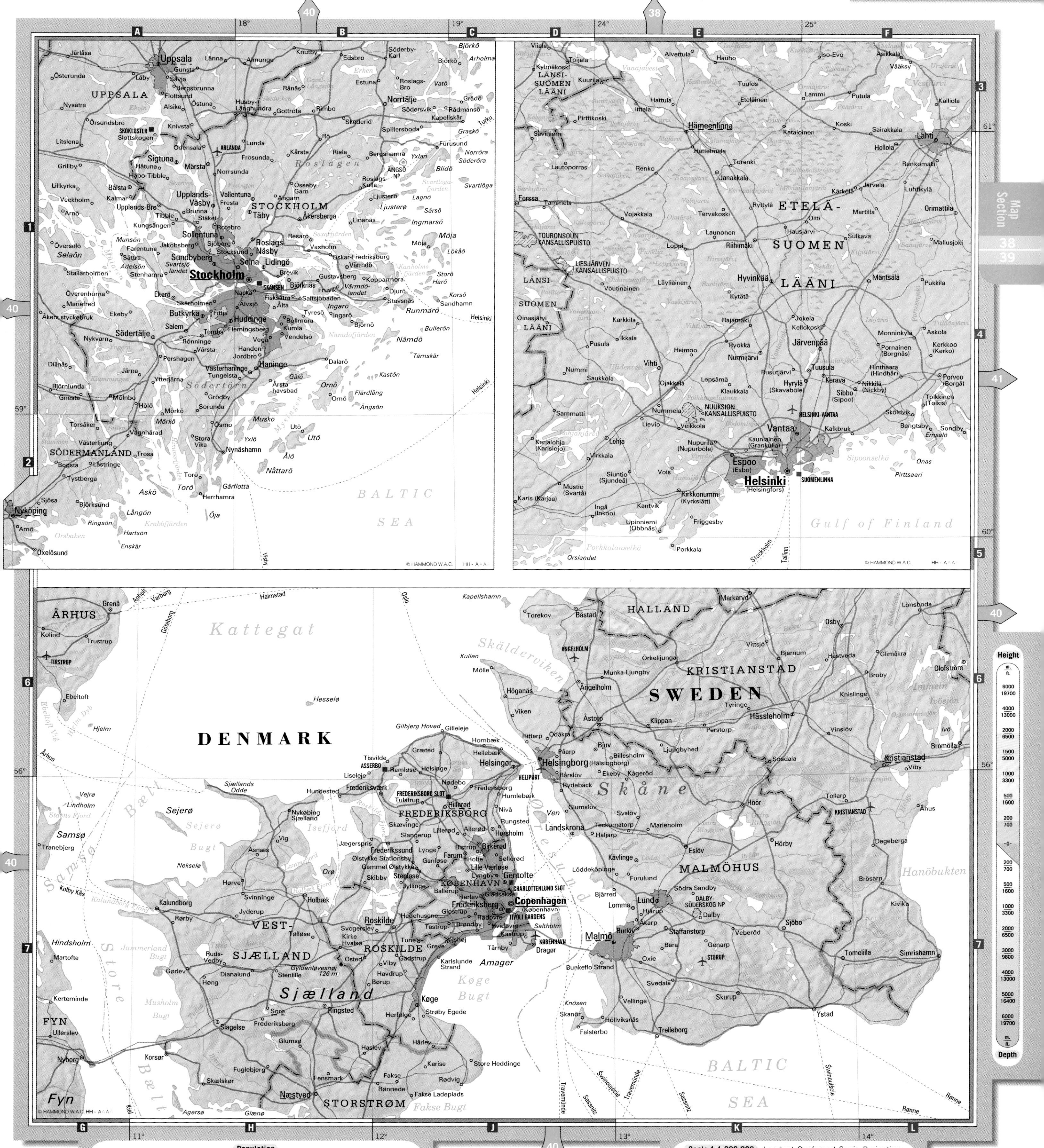

Helsinki, Copenhagen and Stockholm are situated at strategically favorable points on the Baltic Sea coast. With its many bays and rocky islands as well as Finland's largest harbor, Helsinki commands the entrance to the Gulf of Finland, Copenhagen the entrance to the Øresund. Stockholm, located where Lake Mälaren joins the Baltic Sea, is called the "Venice of the north" for its many waterways.

Population

■ Over 2,000,000	⊛ 500,000 - 999,999
■ 1,000,000 - 1,999,999	⊚ 250,000 - 499,999
● 100,000 - 249,999	○ 10,000 - 29,999
● 30,000 - 99,999	∘ Under 10,000

Scale 1:1,000,000 Lambert Conformal Conic Projection

Height	
m.	ft.
4000	13000
2000	6500
1500	5000
1000	3300
500	1600
200	700
-0-	
200	700
500	1600
1000	3300
2000	6500
3000	9800
4000	13000
5000	16400
6000	19700
m.	ft.

Depth

The Baltic Sea is connected to the North Sea by the Skagerrak and the Kattegat. Covering 390,000 square km (including the Kattegat), it has an average depth of 55 m and measures 459 m at its deepest point. Originally an inland lake, the Baltic is fed by the rivers of northern Europe and exchanges little water with the North Sea. Thus its salinity is low: 8 % at the surface. Tides play only a minor role in the region. At high tide, the water level rises no more than 40 cm in the Kattegat, between 20 and 30 cm in the Store Baelt, and only a few centimeters along the central coastlines.

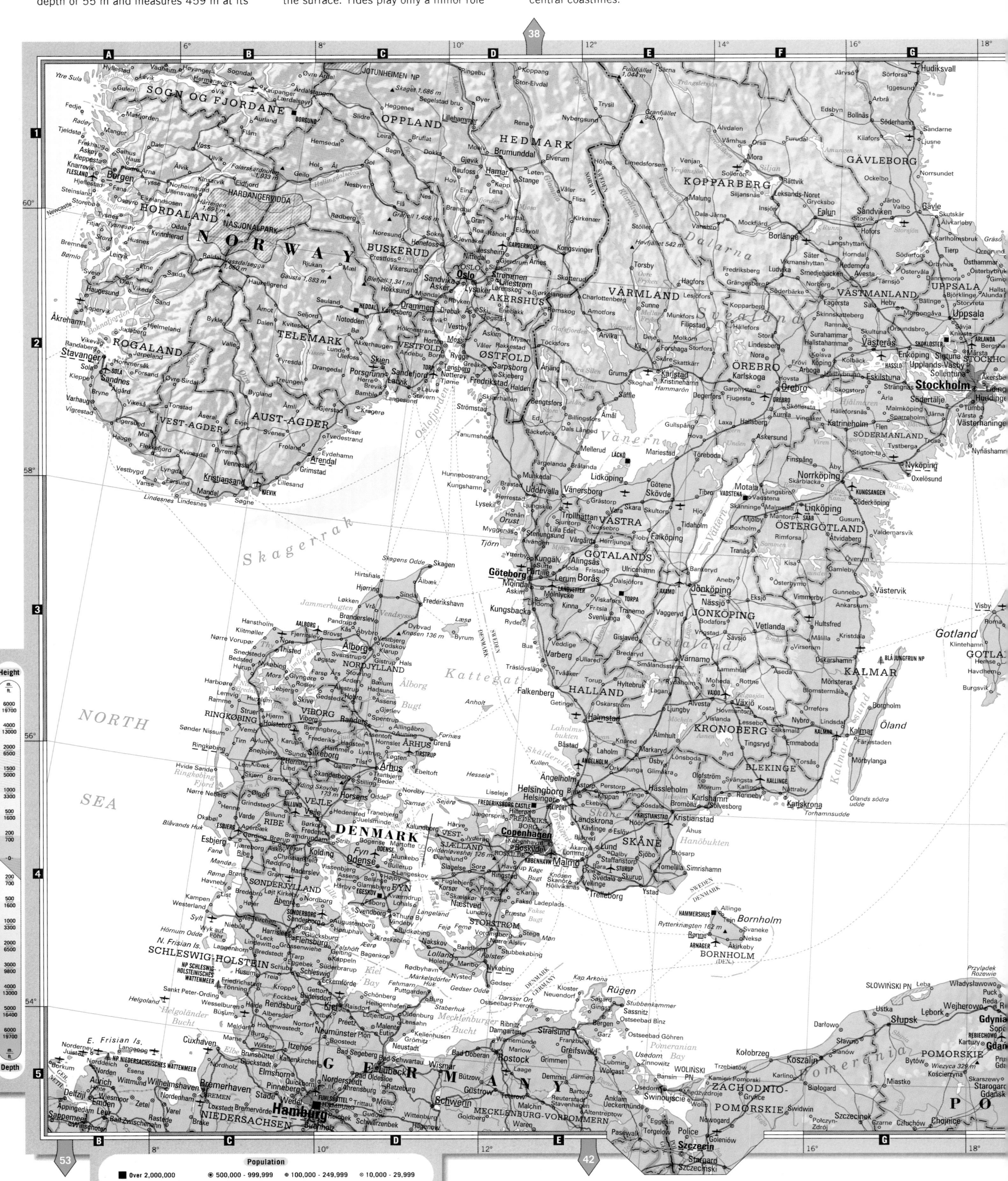

Population

- ■ Over 2,000,000
- ■ 1,000,000 - 1,999,999
- ● 500,000 - 999,999
- ● 250,000 - 499,999
- ● 100,000 - 249,999
- ● 30,000 - 99,999
- ○ 10,000 - 29,999
- ○ Under 10,000

Height

m. / ft.
6000 / 19700
4000 / 13000
2000 / 6500
1500 / 5000
1000 / 3300
500 / 1600
200 / 700
-0-
200 / 700
500 / 1600
1000 / 3300
2000 / 6500
3000 / 9800
4000 / 13000
5000 / 16400
6000 / 19700
m. / ft.

Depth

Countries & Regions

FINLAND — SUOMEN LÄÄNI — LÄNSI — ETELÄ-SUOMEN LÄÄNI — ITÄ-SUOMEN LÄÄNI
ESTONIA — LATVIA — LITHUANIA — RUSSIA — BELARUS — POLAND
LENINGRADSKAYA OBLAST' — NOVGORODSKAYA OBLAST' — PSKOVSKAYA OBLAST' — TVERSKAYA OBLAST'
RESPUBLIKA KARELIYA — KALININGRADSKAYA OBLAST'
VITSYEBSKAYA VOBLASTS' — MINSKAYA VOBLASTS' — MAHILYOWSKAYA VOBLASTS' — HRODZYENSKAYA VOBLASTS'
WARMIŃSKO-MAZURSKIE — PODLASKIE

Water bodies

Gulf of Bothnia — BALTIC SEA — Gulf of Finland — Gulf of Riga — Gulf of Gdansk
Lake Ladoga — Lake Peipus — Lake Pskov — Narva Bay — Pärnu Bay
Kurshskiy Zaliv — L. Il'men

Major cities

Helsinki (Helsingfors) — Tallinn — ST. PETERSBURG (Leningrad) — Riga — Vilnius — Kaunas
Minsk — Mahilyow — Novgorod — Pskov — Kaliningrad — Klaipėda — Tartu — Pärnu

Selected place names

Pori — Tampere — Turku — Espoo — Vantaa — Rauma — Lahti — Kouvola — Kotka — Lappeenranta — Imatra — Vyborg
Narva — Kohtla-Järve — Rakvere — Viljandi — Valga — Võru — Kuressaare — Haapsalu — Paide
Ventspils — Valmiera — Cēsis — Jūrmala — Jelgava — Daugavpils — Rēzekne — Liepāja — Saldus
Šiauliai — Panevėžys — Utena — Ukmergė — Marijampolė — Alytus — Tauragė — Telšiai
Velikiye Luki — Ostrov — Luga — Gatchina — Sestroretsk — Kronshtadt — Kolpino — Pushkin
Vitsyebsk — Orsha — Maladzyechna — Barysaw — Polatsk — Navapolatsk — Hrodna — Lida

Åland (Ahvenanmaa) — Hiiumaa — Saaremaa — Gotska Sandön — Muhu

Emumägi 166 m — Munamägi 318 m — Gaizina Kalns 311 m — Gora Lysaya 342 m

Scale 1:3,000,000 Lambert Conformal Conic Projection

MI 25 50 75 100
KM 25 50 75 100

© HAMMOND WORLD ATLAS CORPORATION

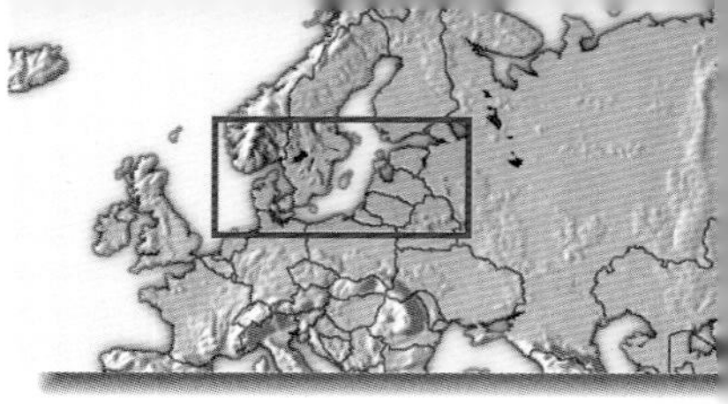

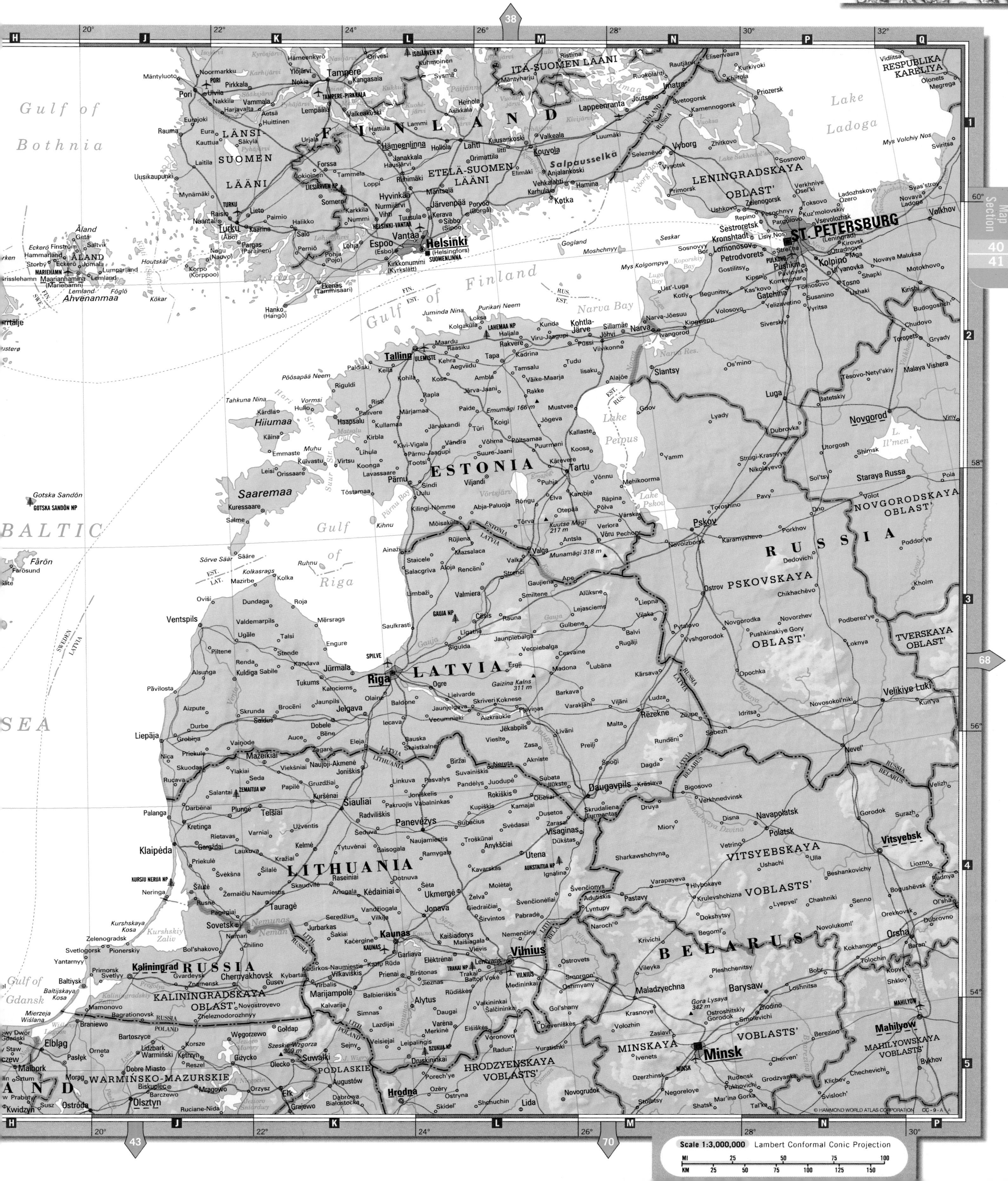

Next to the Rhine, the Elbe (1,165 km) is the longest and busiest river in North Central Europe. Its drainage basin encompasses some 144,000 square km. The Elbe flows from its source at 1,500 m above sea in the Riesengebirge Range in the Czech Republic to its mouth in the North Sea at Cuxhaven in Germany where it reaches a width of 15 km. Hamburg marks the beginning of the long (100 km) Elbe estuary, in which tidal activity is significant as far up-river as Geesthacht. Although international treaties have brought some improvement in water quality, the Elbe is still one of the most heavily polluted rivers in Europe.

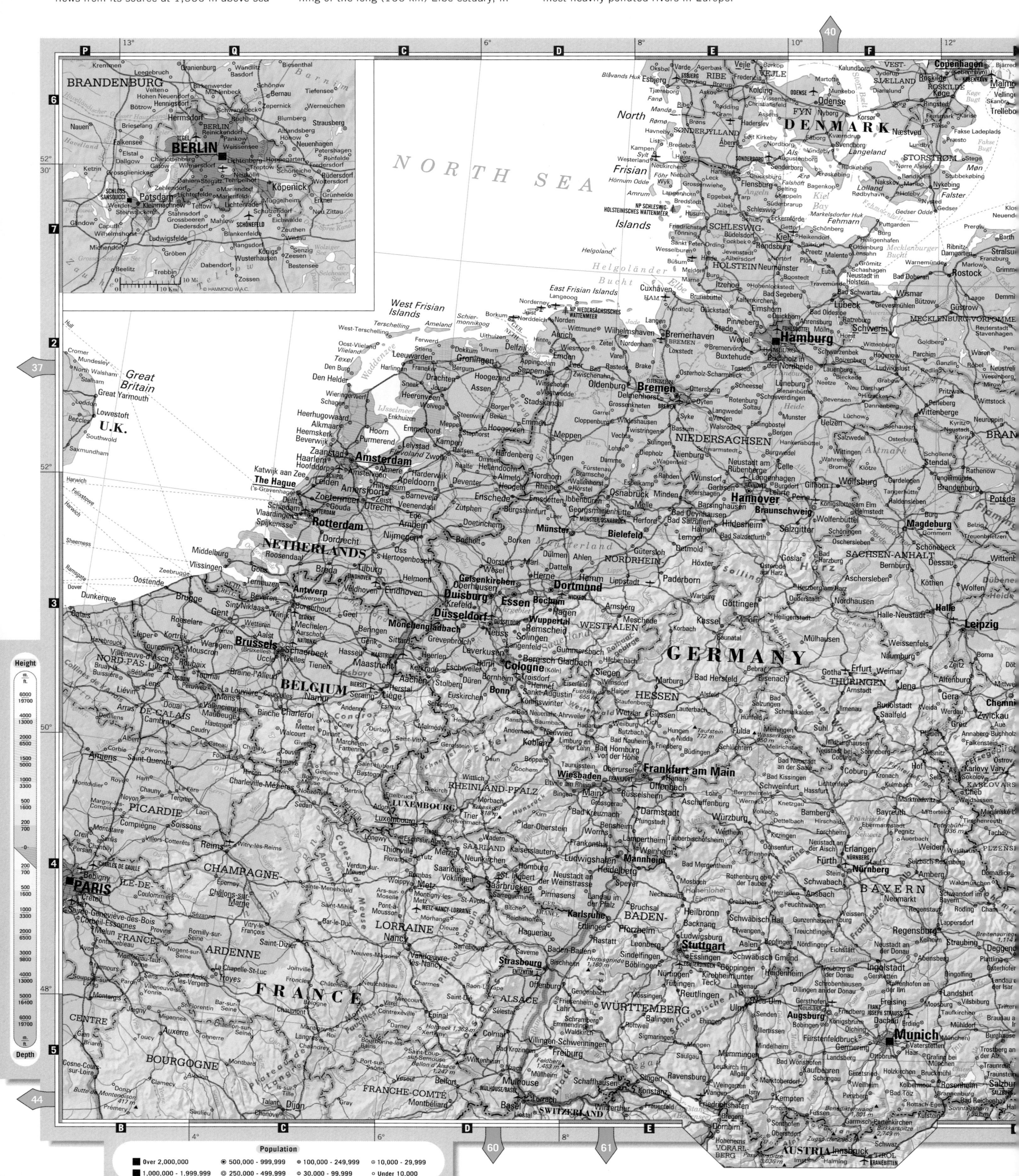

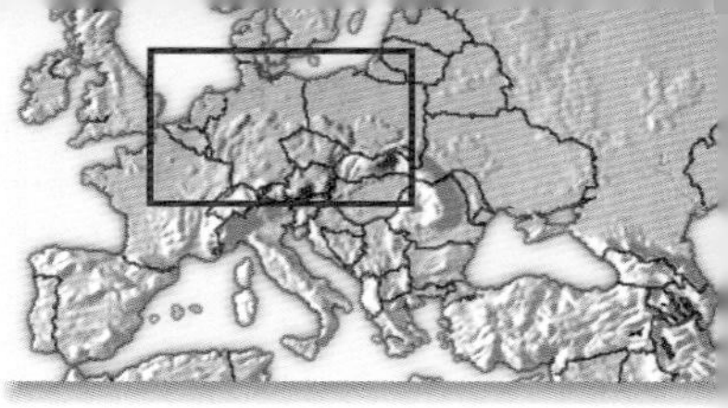

BALTIC SEA

SWEDEN

DENMARK

BORNHOLM

RUSSIA

KALININGRADSKAYA OBLAST

Kaliningrad

LITHUANIA

Vilnius

Kaunas

POLAND

Gdańsk
Gdynia
Sopot

Szczecin

POMORSKIE

WARMIŃSKO-MAZURSKIE

Olsztyn

Bydgoszcz

Toruń

KUJAWSKO-POMORSKIE

Białystok

PODLASKIE

MAZOWIECKIE

Warsaw
(Warszawa)

WIELKOPOLSKIE

Poznań

LUBUSKIE

Zielona Góra

Gorzów Wielkopolski

Łódź

ŁÓDZKIE

Lublin

LUBELSKIE

Lubelska Uplands

DOLNOŚLĄSKIE

Wrocław

Częstochowa

OPOLSKIE

Opole

ŚLĄSKIE

Katowice
Sosnowiec

Kraków

MAŁOPOLSKIE

ŚWIĘTOKRZYSKIE

Radom

PODKARPACKIE

Rzeszów

BELARUS

BRESTSKAYA VOBLASTS'

Brest

HRODZYENSKAYA VOBLASTS'

Hrodna

UKRAINE

L'viv

L'VIVS'KA OBLAST'

VOLYNS'KA OBLAST

ZAKARPATS'KA OBLAST

CZECH REPUBLIC

Prague
(Praha)

Brno

Dresden

Berlin

SACHSEN

Cottbus

SLOVAKIA

Košice

Carpathian Mountains

AUSTRIA

Vienna
(Wien)

Bratislava

HUNGARY

BUDAPEST

Miskolc

ROMANIA

© HAMMOND WORLD ATLAS CORPORATION

About 1,200 km long and up to 250 km wide, the Alps are the largest mountain system in Europe. Their highest peak is Mont Blanc (4,807 m). The Alps occupy an area of 220,000 square km and form the watershed between the North Sea and the Mediterranean Sea along the north-south axis and between the Black Sea and the Mediterranean Sea to the east. Geologically speaking, the Alps are a young mountain system and continue to rise at a rate of several millimeters per year due to continental drift, growing higher as the African Plate presses against the European.

Population

- ■ Over 2,000,000
- ■ 1,000,000 - 1,999,999
- ◆ 500,000 - 999,999
- ◆ 250,000 - 499,999
- ● 100,000 - 249,999
- ● 30,000 - 99,999
- ● 10,000 - 29,999
- ○ Under 10,000

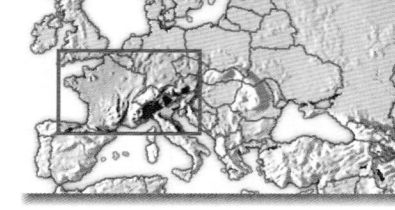

Scale 1:3,000,000   Lambert Conformal Conic Projection

MI 25 50 75 100
KM 25 50 75 100

©HAMMOND WORLD ATLAS CORPORATION   CM - 1015 - A - A

The central core of the Iberian Peninsula is the Meseta plateau, which is almost completely surrounded by mountain ranges. This ring of mountains is encircled by narrow bands of coastal lowlands.

The topographic pattern is reflected in the vegetation. Sheep graze in the grassy areas and juniper groves of the sparse highlands where vast fields of wheat and sunflowers yield modest harvests. Olive groves and

maquis-garrigue growth are the dominant features of lowland vegetation, which is interspersed with oaks. The valleys of rivers such as the Ebro and the Guadalquivir are intensely cultivated.

Main map

FRANCE

MIDI-PYRÉNÉES · Toulouse · Castres · Albi · Montauban · Carcassonne · Narbonne · Perpignan · LANGUEDOC-ROUSSILLON · Béziers · Sète · Montpellier · Nîmes · Arles · PROVENCE-ALPES-CÔTE D'AZUR · Aix-en-Provence · Marseille · Toulon · Hyères · Côte d'Azur · Cannes · Antibes · Nice · Monaco · Bastia

Gulf of Lion

AQUITAINE · Mont-de-Marsan · Pau · Tarbes · Lourdes · ANDORRA · Andorra la Vella · Figueres · Roses · Cap de Creus · Golf de Roses

Pyrénées · Pic Long 3,192 m · Pico de Aneto 3,404 m · Monte Perdido 3,355 m

SPAIN / ESPAÑA

Saragossa (Zaragoza) · ARAGÓN · Huesca · Lleida (Lérida) · CATALUNA · Manresa · Terrassa · Sabadell · Mataró · Badalona · **Barcelona** · L'Hospitalet de Llobregat · Girona (Gerona) · Costa Brava · Tarragona · Reus · Costa Dorada · Tortosa

Sierra de Gúdar · Peñarroya 2,019 m · Castellón de la Plana · Costa del Azahar · Sagunto · **Valencia** · VALENCIA · Costa de Valencia · Gandía · Dénia · Cabo de la Nao · Benidorm · **Alicante** · Costa Blanca · Elche · Torrevieja · Murcia · Cartagena · Cabo de Palos

MEDITERRANEAN SEA

Golfo de Valencia

ISLAS BALEARES / Balearic Islands (Islas Baleares)

Minorca (Menorca) · Mahón · Ciutadella · Cabo de Formentor · Pollença · Alcúdia · Sóller · Inca · **Mallorca** · **Palma de Mallorca** · Manacor · Cabo de ses Salines · Cabrera · Ibiza (Eivissa) · Sant Antoni de Portmany · Santa Eulalia del Río · Formentera

ALGERIA · Bou Kadir

Inset K–L (Barcelona region)

Manresa · Sant Vicenç de Castellet · PARQUE NATURAL DEL MONTSENY · La Garriga · Sant Celoni · Montserrat 1,236 m · CATALUNA · Granollers · Arenys de Mar · Terrassa · Sabadell · Mollet del Vallès · Mataró · Rubí · Barberá del Vallès · El Masnou · Sant Cugat del Vallès · Santa Coloma de Gramenet · Sant Adrià de Besòs · **Barcelona** · L'Hospitalet de Llobregat · CASTELL DE MONTJUIC · Viladecans · El Prat de Llobregat · Gavà · Castelldefels · Sitges · Vilanova i la Geltrú

MEDITERRANEAN SEA

Inset M–N (Madrid region)

Sierra de Guadarrama · Puerto de Navacerrada · Manzanares el Real · CASTILLA–LA MANCHA · Guadarrama · El Escorial · San Lorenzo de El Escorial · Galapagar · Torrelodones · Colmenar Viejo · Algete · El Pardo · Las Rozas de Madrid · Alcobendas · Alcalá de Henares · Majadahonda · Barajas · Torrejón de Ardoz · Pozuelo de Alarcón · HORTALEZA · San Fernando de Henares · Boadilla del Monte · Coslada · **MADRID** · VILLAVERDE · VALLECAS · Móstoles · Alcorcón · Leganés · Getafe · Fuenlabrada · Parla · Pinto

Inset (Azores)

ATLANTIC OCEAN · AZORES (PORTUGAL) · Corvo · Flores · Santa Cruz das Flores · Graciosa · Santa Cruz da Graciosa · São Jorge · Velas · Faial · Horta · Pico · Ponta do Pico 2,351 m · Lajes · Terceira · Angra do Heroísmo · Praia da Vitória · São Miguel · Ribeira Grande · Ponta Delgada · Vila Franca do Campo · Santa Maria · Vila do Porto

Inset P–Q (Lisbon region)

Ericeira · Mafra · Vila Franca de Xira · LISBOA · Sintra · Cabo da Roca · Cascais · Cabo Raso · Estoril · Oeiras · BELÉM TOWER · **Lisbon (Lisboa)** · Amadora · Odivelas · Loures · Alverca do Ribatejo · SANTARÉM · Almada · Barreiro · Moita · Montijo · Costa da Caparica · Seixal · SETÚBAL · Palmela · Setúbal · Cabo Espichel · Sesimbra

ATLANTIC OCEAN · Baía de Setúbal

Scale

Scale 1:3,000,000 · Lambert Conformal Conic Projection

MI 0 25 50 75 100
KM 0 25 50 75 100 150

© HAMMOND W.A.C.

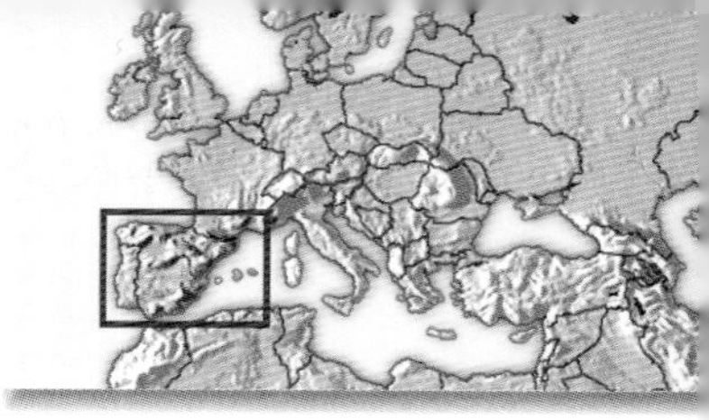

The once remarkably fertile and heavily forested Mediterranean region suffers today from soil erosion and a severe shortage of water. Deforestation began with the ancient Greeks and Romans, who needed huge quantities of wood for heating and ship-building. Forest fires are still a regular summer occurrence. The exposed soil is carried off by rain, thus depleting a valuable water storage medium.

Rivers often run dry during the summer months, particularly in the south, where rain does not fall for as much as six months at a time.

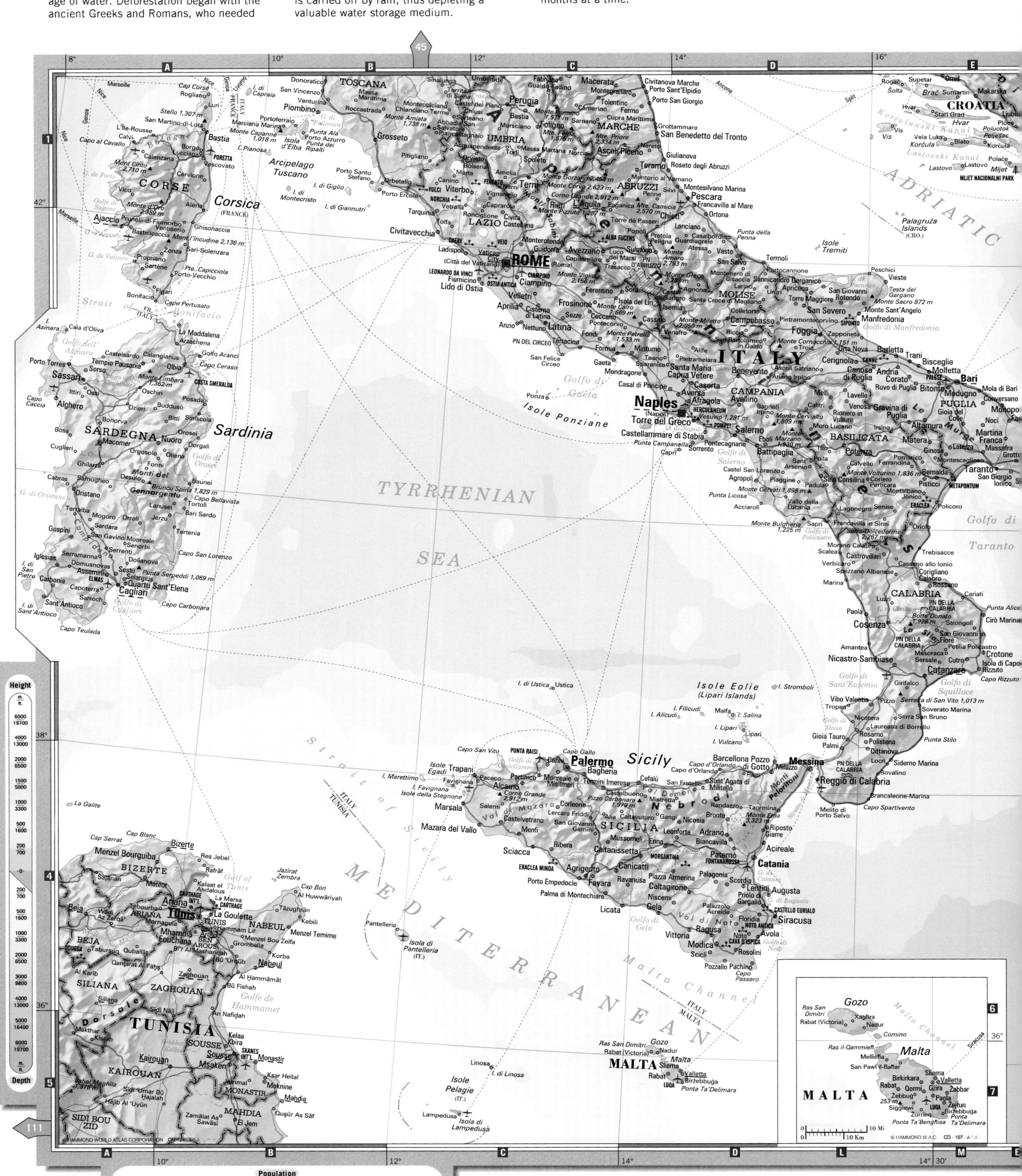

Southern Italy, Albania, Greece

BOSNIA AND HERZEGOVINA
SERBIA AND MONTENEGRO (YUGOSLAVIA)
MONTENEGRO
SERBIA
KOSOVO
BULGARIA
ALBANIA
FORMER YUGOSLAV REPUBLIC OF MACEDONIA
GREECE
TURKEY
Sofia
Skopje
Tiranë
Athens
Thessaloníki
IONIAN SEA
AEGEAN SEA
Ionian Islands
Thracian Sea
Northern Sporades
Cyclades
Mirtóön Sea
Sea of Crete
Crete
Évvoia
Pindus Mts
Gulf of Corinth
Strait of Otranto
Salentina Penisola
Scale 1:3,000,000 Lambert Conformal Conic Projection
Map Section 48 49
© HAMMOND W.A.C.

When the Alps and neighboring mountain ranges formed during the Tertiary some 65 million years ago, the folding process extended into the Mediterranean region, creating the Dinaric Alps on the western Balkan Peninsula. The ridges of these folds can be seen today along the Dalmatian coast, where they rise from the sea as elongated islands. The troughs of the folded range are covered by water.

The product of a similar upthrusting process, the Carpathians are cut by the Danube, which is 2,850 km long and second only to the Volga among the longest rivers of Europe.

Scale 1:3,000,000 Lambert Conformal Conic Projection

Netherlands,
Northwestern Germany

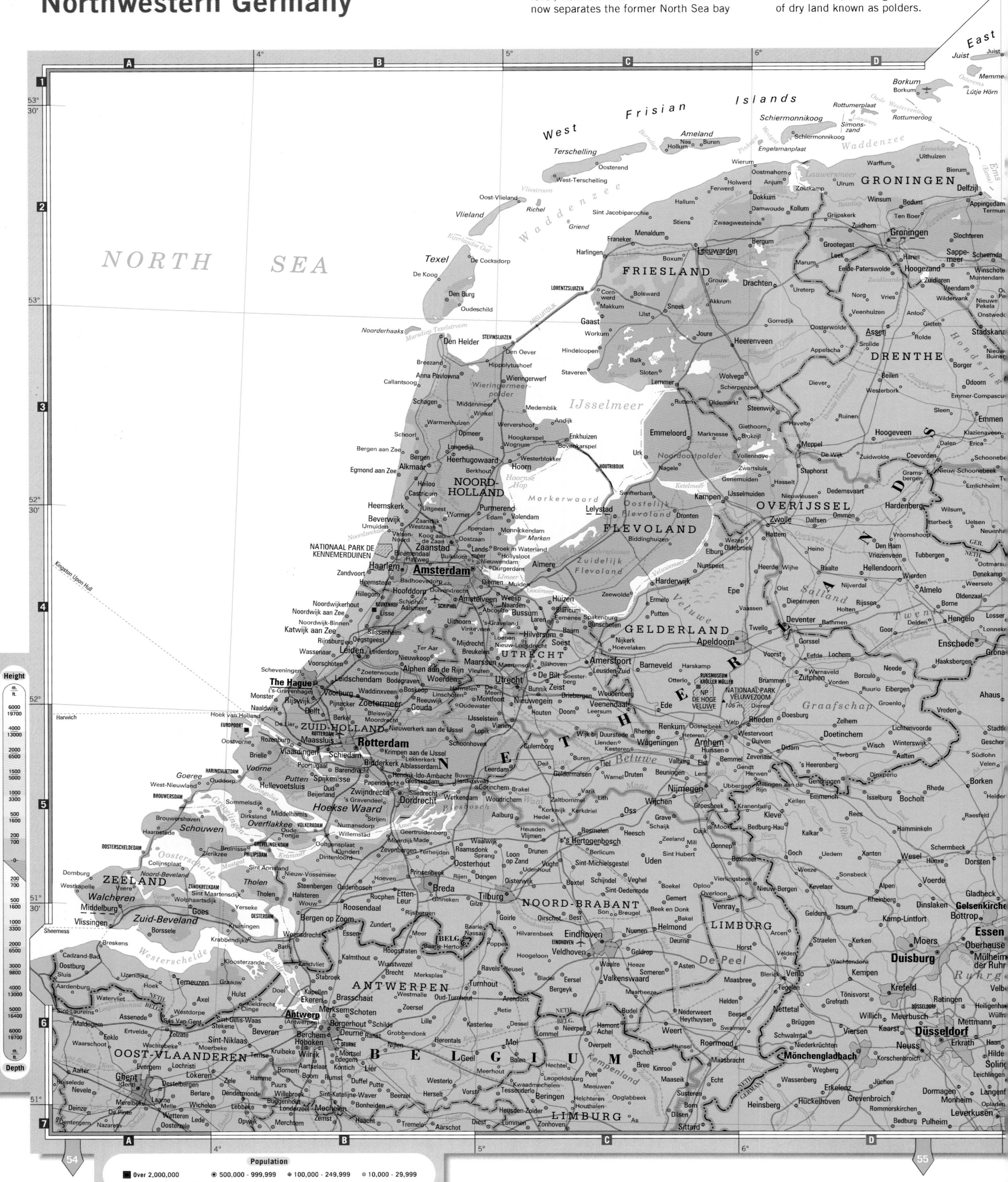

Population

| ■ Over 2,000,000 | ● 500,000-999,999 | ● 100,000-249,999 | ○ 10,000-29,999 |
| ■ 1,000,000-1,999,999 | ● 250,000-499,999 | ○ 30,000-99,999 | ○ Under 10,000 |

54

55

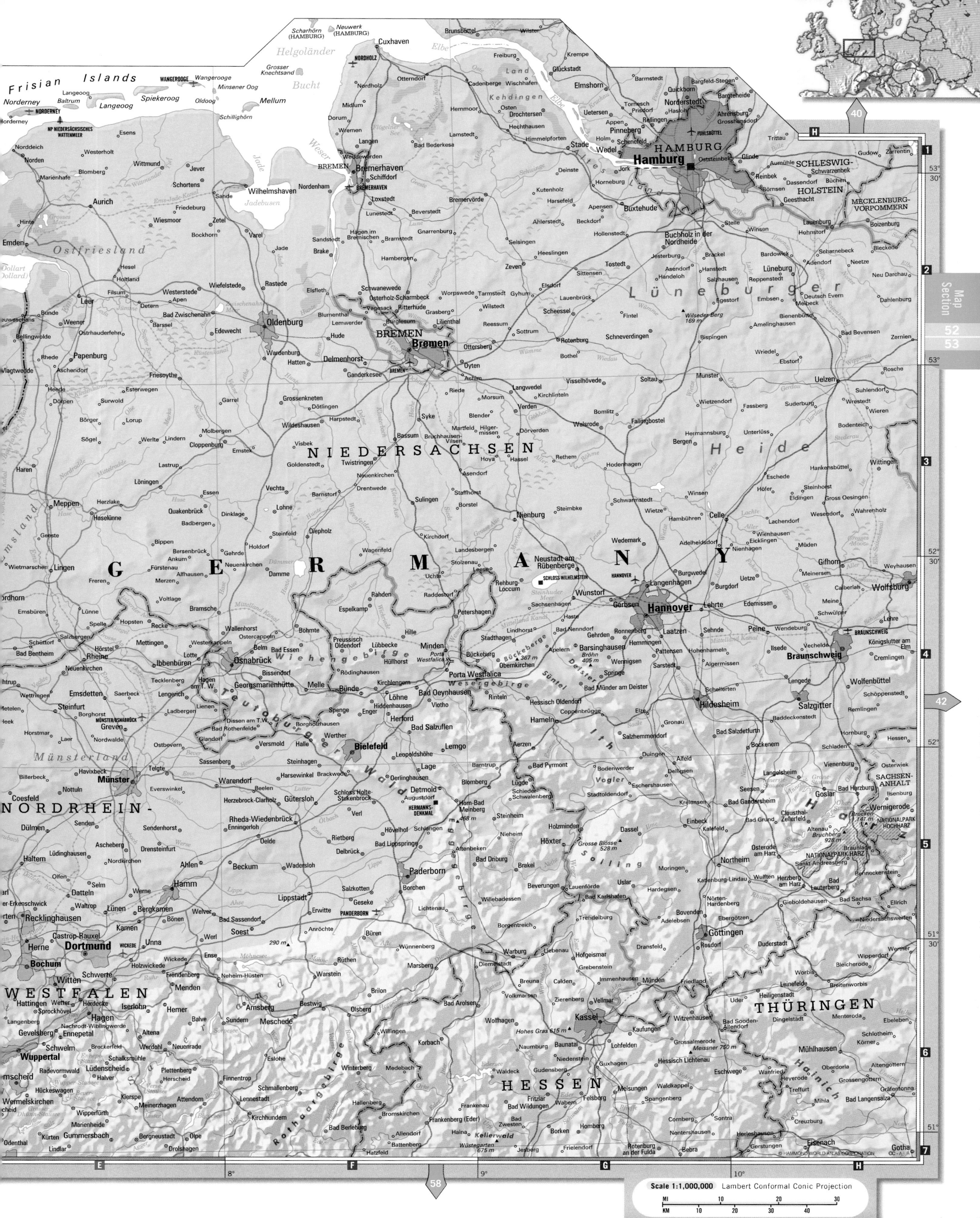

Frisian Islands
Norderney
Baltrum
Langeoog
Spiekeroog
Wangerooge
Minsener Oog
Mellum
Helgoländer Bucht
Scharhörn (HAMBURG)
Neuwerk (HAMBURG)
Cuxhaven
NP NIEDERSÄCHSISCHES WATTENMEER
Ostfriesland
Aurich
Emden
Leer
Wilhelmshaven
Jadebusen
Bremerhaven
BREMEN
Bremen
Oldenburg
Delmenhorst
Papenburg
Meppen
Lingen
Stade
Buxtehude
HAMBURG
Hamburg
Norderstedt
Elmshorn
Pinneberg
Wedel
SCHLESWIG-HOLSTEIN
MECKLENBURG-VORPOMMERN
Lauenburg
Lüneburg
Lüneburger Heide
Buchholz in der Nordheide
Uelzen
Celle
Soltau
Verden
Nienburg
Wolfsburg
Braunschweig
Salzgitter
Wolfenbüttel
Hildesheim
Hannover
Langenhagen
Garbsen
Neustadt am Rübenberge
Steinhuder Meer
SCHLOSS WILHELMSTEIN
Hameln
Minden
Porta Westfalica
Bad Oeynhausen
Herford
Bielefeld
Osnabrück
Ibbenbüren
Rheine
Münster
Münsterland
Teutoburger Wald
Wiehengebirge
Wesergebirge
Deister
Süntel
Ith
Solling
Vogler
Eggegebirge
Detmold
HERMANNSDENKMAL
Lemgo
Gütersloh
Rheda-Wiedenbrück
Paderborn
Lippstadt
Soest
Hamm
Dortmund
Bochum
Herne
Recklinghausen
Witten
Hagen
Wuppertal
Iserlohn
Arnsberg
Meschede
Rothaargebirge
Sauerland
Gummersbach
Winterberg
Göttingen
Northeim
Goslar
Harz
NATIONALPARK HARZ
NATIONALPARK HOCHHARZ
Brocken 1141 m
Wernigerode
SACHSEN-ANHALT
Kassel
Hohes Gras 615 m
Kellerwald
Wüstegarten 675 m
Meissner 750 m
Hainich
Mühlhausen
Eisenach
Gotha
THÜRINGEN
HESSEN
NIEDERSACHSEN
NORDRHEIN-WESTFALEN
GERMANY
Scale 1:1,000,000 Lambert Conformal Conic Projection
MI 10 20 30
KM 10 20 30 40
© HAMMOND WORLD ATLAS CORPORATION

Map Section 52 53
40
42
58

An extension of the Middle Rhine High-lands, the Ardennes form a high plateau that stretches across much of northeastern Central Europe. Its highest point (694 m) is in the Hautes Fagnes (Belgium).

Exposed to the west, the heavily wooded, sparsely settled uplands dotted with numerous moors have a rugged climate. Average annual precipitation is 1,400 mm, and heavy snowfalls are common.

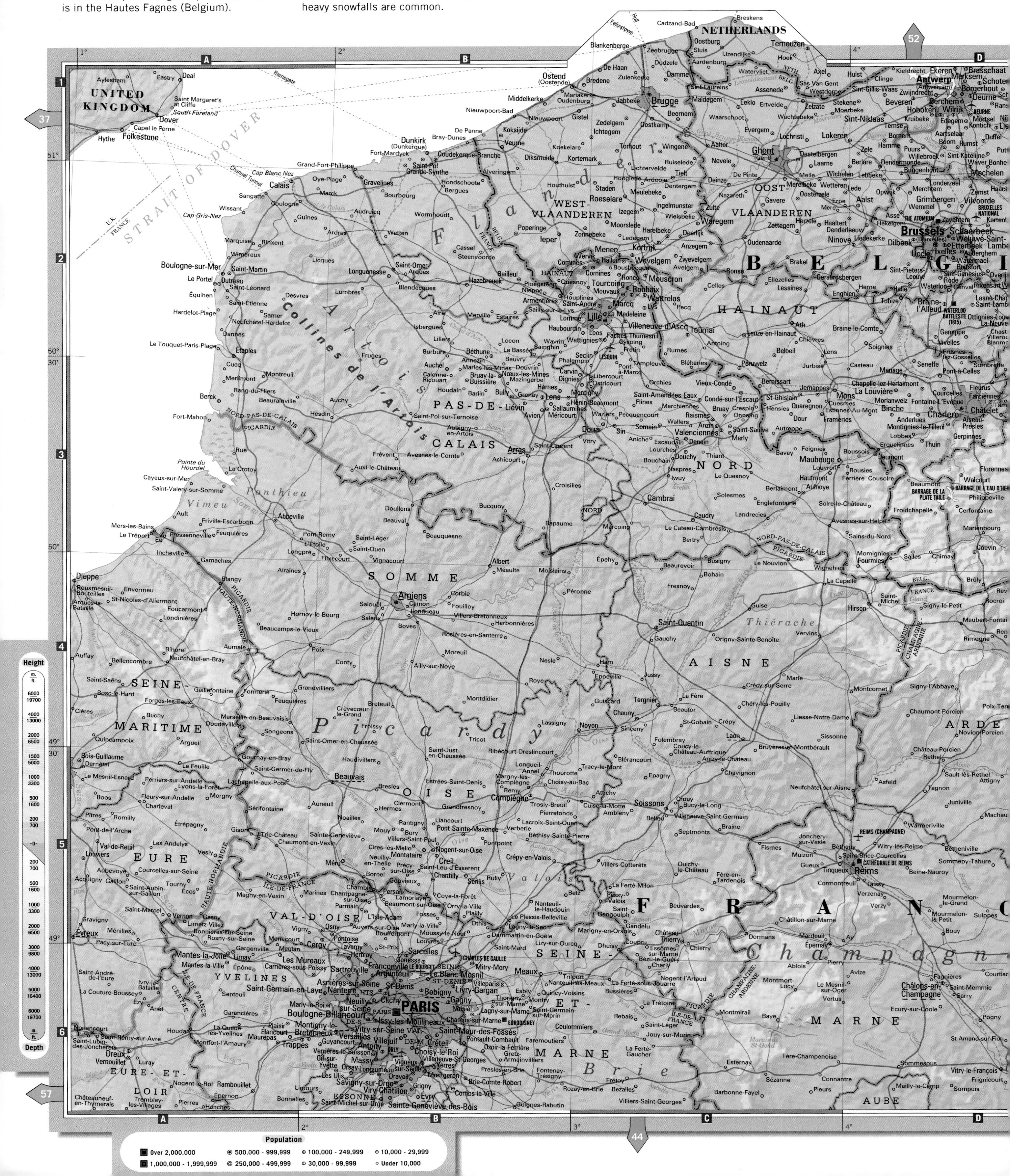

Map of northern France, Belgium, and the southern Netherlands, including Paris, Lille, Brussels, Antwerp, Ghent, Brugge, and Reims.

Height
m. / ft.
6000 / 19700
4000 / 13000
2000 / 6500
1500 / 5000
1000 / 3300
500 / 1600
200 / 700
-0-
200 / 700
500 / 1600
1000 / 3300
2000 / 6500
3000 / 9800
4000 / 13000
5000 / 16400
6000 / 19700
m. / ft.
Depth

Belgium, Northern France, Western Germany

Map Section 54 55 58

Scale 1:1,000,000   Lambert Conformal Conic Projection

MI   10   20   30
KM   10   20   30   40

Tidal activity along the Channel coast of Normandy is unusually vigorous. In the Bay of Mont-Saint-Michel, the sea recedes several kilometers at low tide and rises roughly 15 m when the tide is in.

Normandy's gentle climate is favorable to agriculture, and vast fields of grain line the banks of the Seine and the Loire. The region is known for its orchards, which supply apples used in the production of cider and Calvados (apple brandy). Heaths, moors, and woodlands are prevalent in the highlands of Brittany, where the climate is much less agreeable.

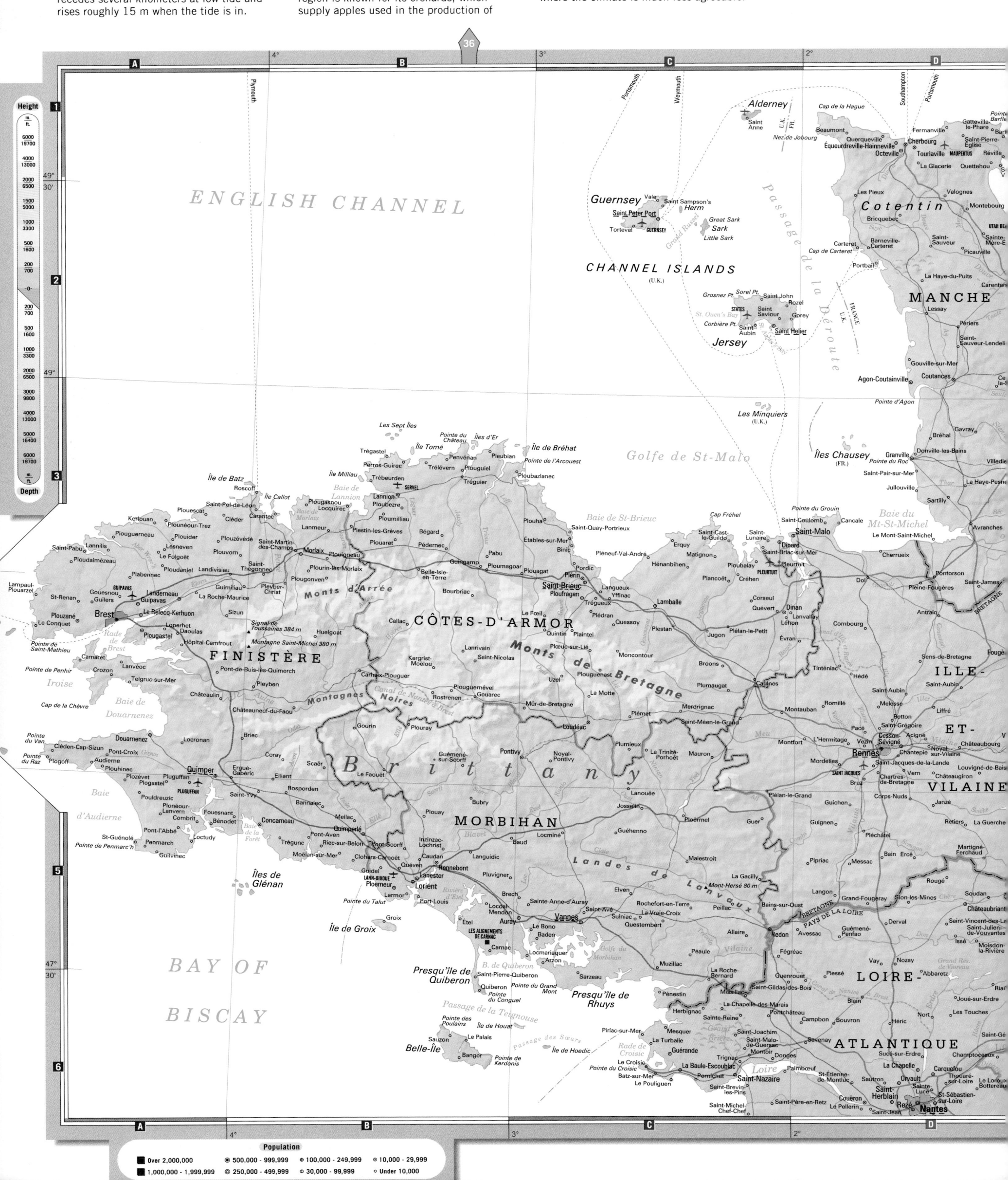

Population

■ Over 2,000,000	◉ 500,000 - 999,999	◉ 100,000 - 249,999	◎ 10,000 - 29,999
■ 1,000,000 - 1,999,999	◉ 250,000 - 499,999	◎ 30,000 - 99,999	○ Under 10,000

Northwestern France

SEINE-MARITIME
EURE
CALVADOS
ORNE
Normandy
SARTHE
MAYENNE
Maine
Anjou
MAINE-ET-LOIRE
INDRE-ET-LOIRE
LOIR-ET-CHER
EURE-ET-LOIR
YVELINES
VAL-D'OISE
OISE
SOMME
Picardy
ESSONNE
LOIRET
Orléanais
CHER
INDRE
Pays de Caux
Collines de Normandie
Collines du Maine
Baie de la Seine
PARIS
Rouen
Le Havre
Caen
Le Mans
Alençon
Chartres
Évreux
Orléans
Tours
Angers
Laval
Blois
Beauvais
Dieppe
Fécamp
Étretat
Cap d'Antifer
Honfleur
Deauville
Lisieux
Bayeux
Saint-Lô
Vire
Argentan
Falaise
Dreux
Rambouillet
Versailles
Nogent-le-Rotrou
Châteaudun
Vendôme
Saumur
Amboise
Vierzon
Romorantin-Lanthenay
La Flèche
Château-Gontier
Mantes-la-Jolie
Vernon
Louviers
Elbeuf
Bernay
L'Aigle
Mortagne-au-Perche
Sées
Flers
Mayenne
Sablé-sur-Sarthe
Cholet
OMAHA BEACH
GOLD BEACH
JUNO BEACH
SWORD BEACH
Cork
Portsmouth
Signal d'Écouves 417 m
Mont des Avaloirs 417 m
344 m
HAUTE-NORMANDIE
BASSE-NORMANDIE
PICARDIE
ÎLE-DE-FRANCE
CENTRE
PAYS DE LA LOIRE
E
F
G
H
1°
0°
1°
2°
49°
30'
48°
30'
48°
47°
30'
1
2
3
4
5
6
37
44
44
Map Section
56
57
Scale 1:1,000,000
Lambert Conformal Conic Projection
MI 10 20 30
KM 10 20 30 40
© HAMMOND WORLD ATLAS CORPORATION

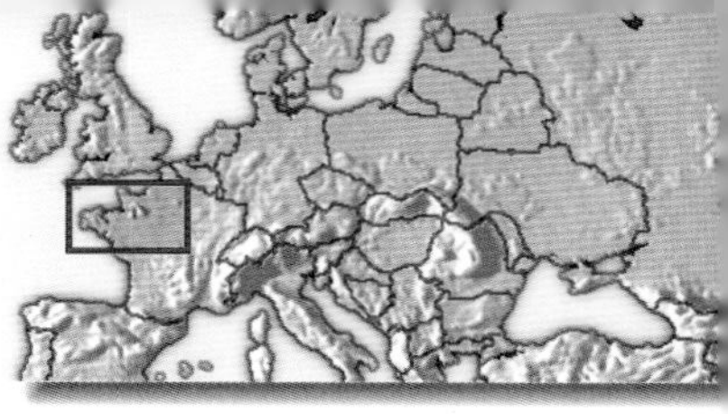

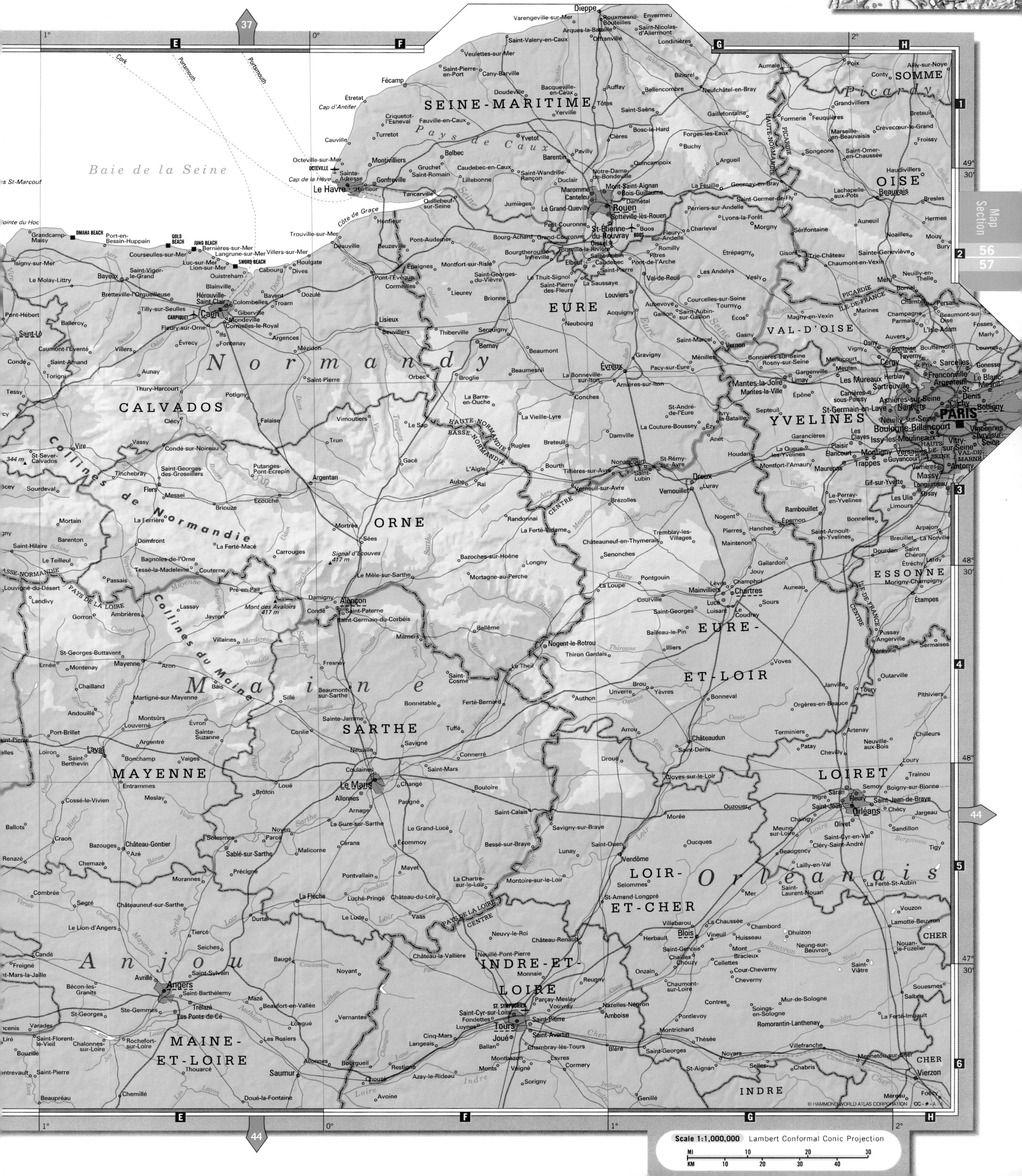

At first glance, the three neighboring central ranges of the Franconian-Thuringian uplands appear quite similar. The Fichtelgebirge, the Thüringer Wald and the Frankenwald are all covered by dense mountain forests. Yet each has its own unique features: the granite massifs of the Fichtelgebirge, the deep valleys that cut through the higher elevations of the Thüringer Wald, and the high plateaus of the Frankenwald. The central uplands extend eastward through the Erzgebirge, whose old mixed forests were largely destroyed by intensive mining and gave way to less robust coniferous growth.

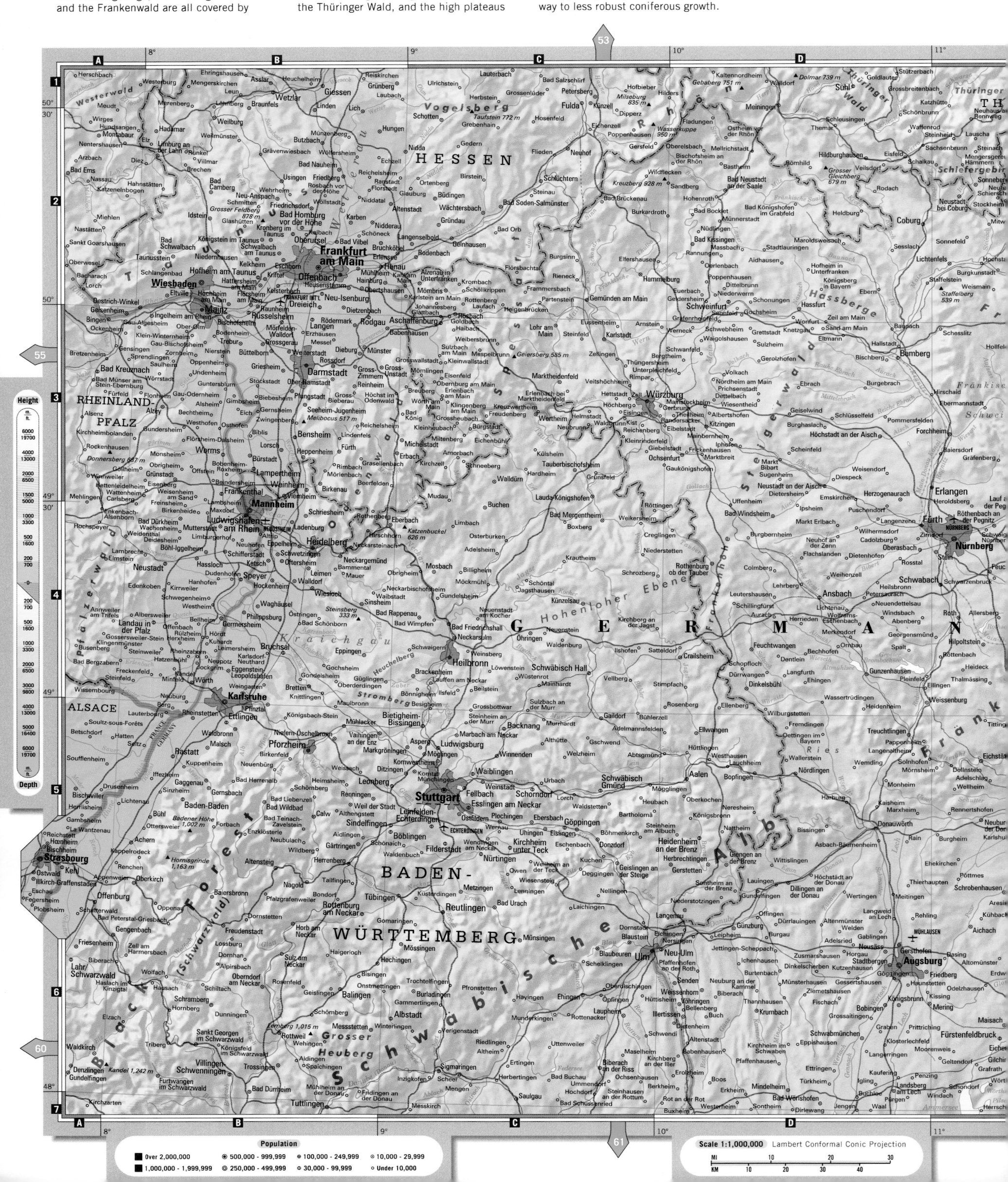

Scale 1:1,000,000   Lambert Conformal Conic Projection

Countries / Regions:
SACHSEN · BAYERN · THÜRINGEN · CZECH REPUBLIC · Bohemia · Mähren · OBERÖSTERREICH · AUSTRIA · ÚSTECKÝ KRAJ · KARLOVARSKÝ KRAJ · STŘEDOČESKÝ KRAJ · PLZEŇSKÝ KRAJ · BUDĚJOVICKÝ KRAJ · Středočeská Vrchovina

Major cities: Prague (Praha) · Plzeň · Regensburg · Munich (München) · Ingolstadt · Landshut · Passau · Linz · Bayreuth · České Budějovice · Český Krumlov

Selected place names:
Ziegenrück · Plauen · Hof · Münchberg · Kulmbach · Bad Berneck im Fichtelgebirge · Marktredwitz · Cheb · Karlovy Vary · Sokolov · Most · Litvínov · Chomutov · Kadaň · Žatec · Louny · Rakovník · Beroun · Kladno · Mělník · Mladá Boleslav · Roudnice nad Labem · Litoměřice · Ústí · Děčín

Selb · Aš · Bayreuth · Weiden in der Oberpfalz · Amberg · Schwandorf · Cham · Neumarkt in der Oberpfalz · Nabburg · Tirschenreuth · Waldsassen · Mariánské Lázně · Tachov · Planá · Stříbro · Nýřany · Rokycany · Zbiroh · Hořovice · Příbram · Benešov · Tábor · Sezimovo Ústí · Soběslav · Bechyně · Písek · Milevsko · Blatná · Strakonice · Klatovy · Sušice · Domažlice · Horažďovice · Vimperk · Prachatice · Netolice · Třeboň · Nové Hrady · Kaplice

Regenstauf · Straubing · Deggendorf · Plattling · Vilshofen · Freyung · Grafenau · Zwiesel · Bodenmais · Frauenau · Regen · Viechtach · Kötzting · Furth im Wald · Roding · Bogen · Osterhofen · Dingolfing · Eggenfelden · Pfarrkirchen · Simbach am Inn · Braunau am Inn · Ried im Innkreis · Schärding

Dachau · Freising · Erding · Moosburg · Mainburg · Pfaffenhofen an der Ilm · Schrobenhausen · Neuburg an der Donau · Kelheim · Abensberg · Rottenburg an der Laaber · Landau an der Isar · Wasserburg am Inn · Mühldorf · Altötting · Burghausen · Traunstein

Wels · Steyr · Enns · Mauthausen · Perg · Freistadt · Bad Leonfelden · Rohrbach · Aigen · Ulrichsberg

Mountains / peaks:
Fichtelberg 1,214 m · Klínovec 1,244 m · Spičák 991 m · Schneeberg 1,019 m · Auersberg 1,019 m · Haj 758 m · Lysina 982 m · Dyleň 940 m · Knížecí Stolec 1,226 m · Entenbühl 901 m · Čerchov 1,042 m · Velký Zvon 863 m · Koráb 773 m · Ostrý 1,293 m · Grosser Arber 1,456 m · Grosser Rachel 1,453 m · Lusen 1,370 m · Boubín 1,362 m · Plöckenstein 1,378 m · Smrčina 1,338 m · Dreisesselberg 1,302 m · Poppberg 657 m · Schwarzach 1,238 m · Praha 862 m · Radeč 721 m · Třemšín 827 m · Javorová Skála 723 m · Vrchy 533 m · Javorník 1,089 m · Černá Hora 1,315 m · Sokol 1,253 m · Chlum 1,191 m · Klet' 1,083 m · Kohout 870 m · Poluška 919 m · Vítkův Kámen 1,053 m · Vitkův Kamen · Myslivna 1,040 m · Vielberg 1,112 m · Sternstein 1,122 m · Viehberg 1,112 m · Sedlo 726 m · Bezděz 604 m · Milešovka 837 m

Rivers / features: Danube (Donau) · Vltava · Labe · Berounka · Regen · Isar · Inn · Naab · Ohře · Otava · Lužnice · Mže

Národní Park Šumava · Nationalpark Bayerischer Wald · Böhmerwald · Bayerischer Wald · Oberpfälzer Wald · Fichtelgebirge · Frankenwald · Franjkenwald · Mühlviertel · Hausruck · Erzgebirge / Krušné hory · Tepelská Plošina · Schloss Herrenchiemsee · Franz Joseph Strauss (airport) · Ruzyně

© HAMMOND WORLD ATLAS CORP.

Switzerland is the most important source and reservoir of drinking water in Central Europe. It borders on the two largest Alpine lakes - Lake Constance and Lake Geneva - and pre-Alpine central

Switzerland is dotted with many smaller lakes. Major rivers such as the Rhine and the Rhône flow from sources in Switzerland. Glaciers also provide huge storehouses of water. Covering some 125 square km,

the Aletsch Glacier, which descends from the Jungfraujoch, is the largest in the Alps. Its tongue has receded more than 1,000 m since the early 20th century.

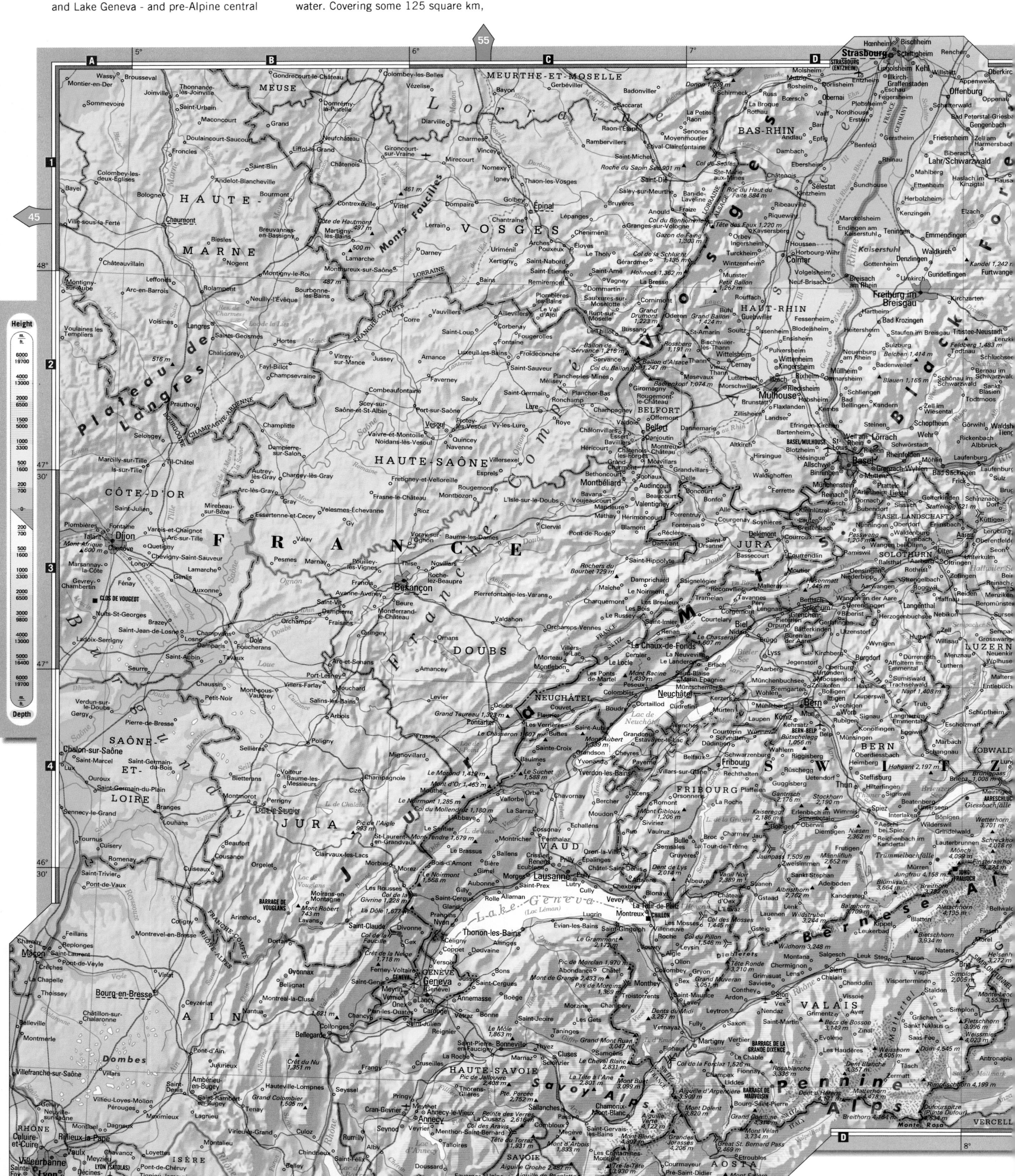

Population	
■ Over 2,000,000	◉ 500,000-999,999
■ 1,000,000 - 1,999,999	◎ 250,000-499,999
	● 100,000 - 249,999
	⊙ 30,000 - 99,999
	○ 10,000 - 29,999
	○ Under 10,000

Scale 1:1,000,000   Lambert Conformal Conic Projection

© HAMMOND WORLD ATLAS CORPORATION   CC - 1018 - A - 1

At the end of its course (652 km), the Po, the longest river on the Apennine Peninsula, empties into the Adriatic Sea south of Venice. Its drainage basin covers an area of about 75,000 square km. Fast-flowing tributaries descending from the Alps and the Apennines deposit heavy loads of sediment in the Po delta, which extends some 80 m farther into the sea every year. Numerous dams along the lower reaches of the river raise the riverbed above the level of the surrounding fertile plain. The Po often overflows its banks during periods of heavy rain in the spring and fall.

Population

■ Over 2,000,000 ● 500,000 - 999,999 ◉ 100,000 - 249,999 ○ 10,000 - 29,999
■ 1,000,000 - 1,999,999 ◎ 250,000 - 499,999 ◌ 30,000 - 99,999 ∘ Under 10,000

Northern Italy

ADRIATIC SEA
Golfo di Venezia
Golfo di Trieste
SLOVENIA
CROATIA
Istria
TRENTO
VICENZA
VERONA
TREVISO
BELLUNO
PORDENONE
UDINE
GORIZIA
VENEZIA
PADOVA
ROVIGO
FERRARA
BOLOGNA
MODENA
RAVENNA
FORLÌ-CESENA
RIMINI
SAN MARINO
PESARO E URBINO
ANCONA
MACERATA
PERUGIA
AREZZO
FIRENZE
PRATO
PISTOIA
SIENA
Polesine
Romagna
Montefeltro
Chianti
Mouths of the Po
Po
Adige
Appennino Tosco-Emiliano
Appennino Umbro-Marchigiano
Alpe di San Benedetto
Monti Pratomagno
Casentino
Colline Metallifere
Val Lagarina
Laguna Veneta
Valli di Comacchio
Verona
Vicenza
Padova
Venice (Venezia)
Mestre
Treviso
Udine
Trieste
Gorizia
Nova Gorica
Koper
Pula
Rovinj
Poreč
Ferrara
Bologna
Modena
Ravenna
Rimini
Forlì
Cesena
Pesaro
Fano
Ancona
Florence (Firenze)
Prato
Arezzo
Siena
Chioggia
Rovigo
Imola
Faenza
Carpi
Rt Kamenjak
Scale 1:1,000,000 Lambert Conformal Conic Projection
MI 10 20 30
KM 10 20 30 40
48
65
50
Map Section 62 63
© HAMMOND WORLD ATLAS CORPORATION

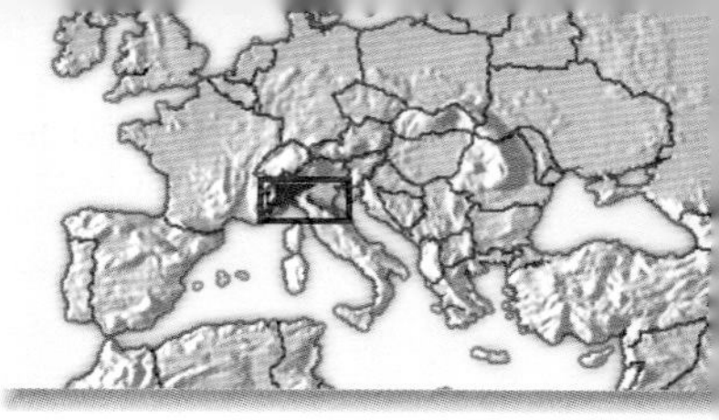

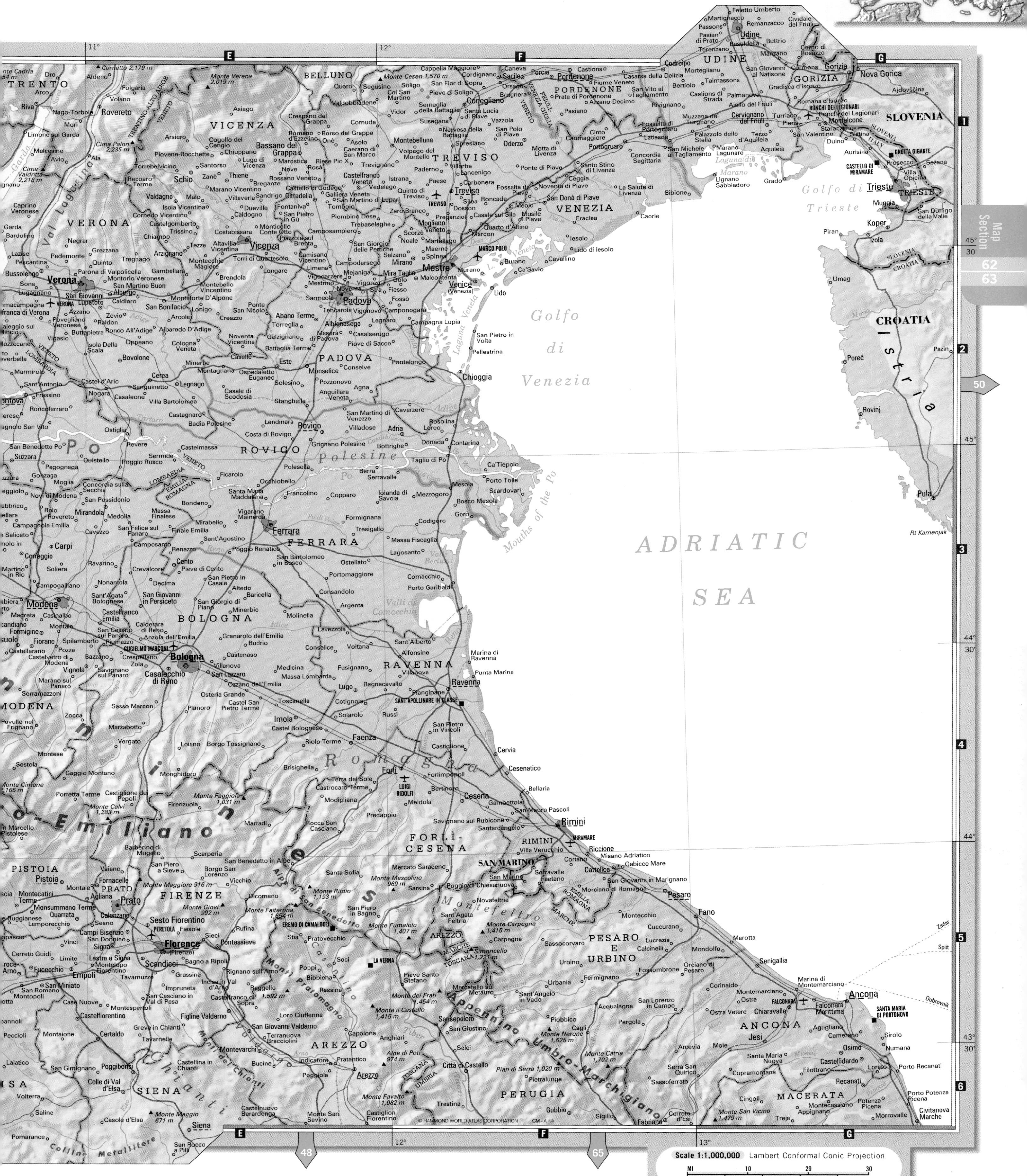

Southeastern France

The Alps dominate this region, with many peaks exceeding 3000 meters in height. Provence, to the south, features rugged terrain, fragrant lavender fields, and a spectacular coastline. The famed French Riviera (Côte d'Azur), which stretches from St-Tropez through Cannes and Nice to the Italian border, boasts some of the most fashionable resorts in the world.

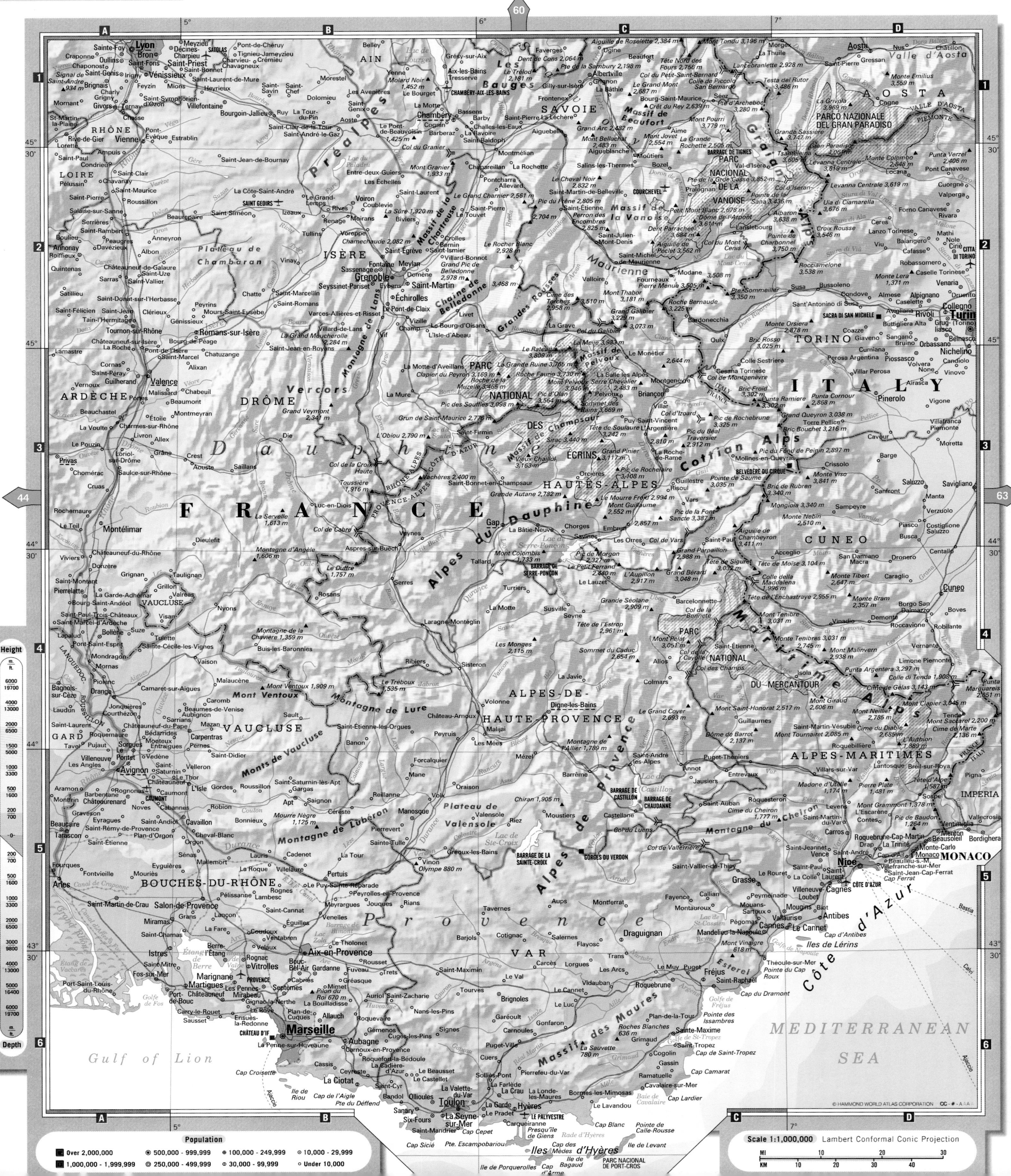

Scale 1:1,000,000 — Lambert Conformal Conic Projection

Population	
■ Over 2,000,000	⊛ 500,000 - 999,999
■ 1,000,000 - 1,999,999	⊙ 250,000 - 499,999
⊛ 100,000 - 249,999	○ 30,000 - 99,999
⊙ 10,000 - 29,999	○ Under 10,000

The Apennines, which cover an area roughly 1,500 km long and 150 km wide, have their own distinct climate. Average temperatures are lower while precipitation is heavier than elsewhere in the country.

In 1921, 292 square km in the southern reaches of this range of limestone formations were set aside as the Abbruzzi National Park, which remains a refuge for bears, wolves, and golden eagles.

Central Italy

Population

■ Over 2,000,000	● 500,000 - 999,999
■ 1,000,000 - 1,999,999	● 250,000 - 499,999
● 100,000 - 249,999	○ 10,000 - 29,999
◉ 30,000 - 99,999	○ Under 10,000

Scale 1:1,000,000   Lambert Conformal Conic Projection

© HAMMOND WORLD ATLAS CORPORATION

The Mediterranean Sea is connected to the Atlantic by the Straight of Gibraltar. It covers a total surface area of 3.02 million square km and reaches a maximum depth of 5,121 m west of the Peloponnesus.

Due to more rapid evaporation, salinity in the Mediterranean (39.1 % in the east) is higher than in the Atlantic. Consequently, a strong surface current carries low-saline water into the Mediterranean from the

Atlantic, while saltier water flows westward through the straight along the seafloor. The narrow passage between the two bodies of water also limits tidal activity in the Mediterranean.

Population

■ Over 2,000,000	⬤ 500,000 - 999,999	⬤ 100,000 - 249,999	⬤ 10,000 - 29,999
■ 1,000,000 - 1,999,999	⬤ 250,000 - 499,999	⬤ 30,000 - 99,999	⬤ Under 10,000

Mediterranean Region

AUSTRIA
HUNGARY
ROMANIA
SLOVENIA
CROATIA
BOSNIA AND HERZEGOVINA
SERBIA & MONTENEGRO (YUGOSLAVIA)
BULGARIA
MOLD.
UKRAINE
FORMER YUGOSLAV REP. OF MACEDONIA
ALBANIA
GREECE
TURKEY
ITALY
MALTA
LIBYA
EGYPT
BUDAPEST
Belgrade
Zagreb
Ljubljana
Sarajevo
BUCHAREST
Sofia
Skopje
Tiranë
Athens
ROME
Naples
ISTANBUL
Tripoli
Benghāzi
Valletta
BLACK SEA
ADRIATIC SEA
TYRRHENIAN SEA
IONIAN SEA
AEGEAN SEA
MEDITERRANEAN SEA
Sea of Crete
Gulf of Sidra
Sicily
Crete
Cyclades
Dodecanese
Malta Channel
Strait of Otranto
Delta of the Danube
Scale 1:6,000,000 Lambert Conformal Conic Projection
MI 50 100 150 200
KM 50 100 150 200 250 300
© HAMMOND WORLD ATLAS CORPORATION

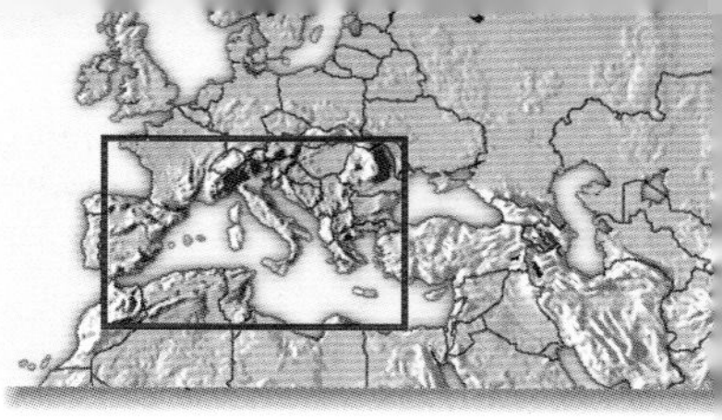

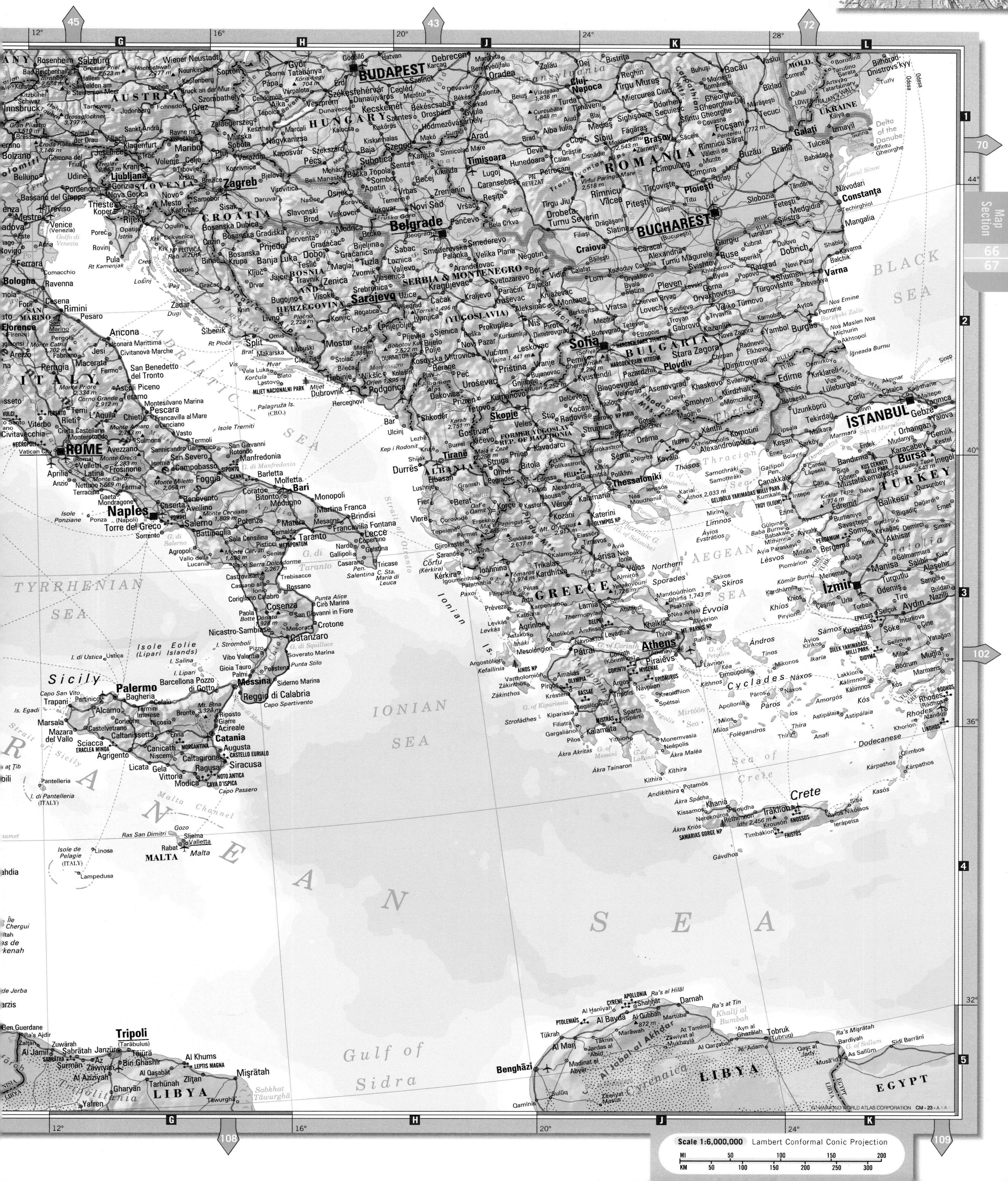

Receding ice left behind a landscape of lakes, morainic ridges, drumlins, and other glacial formations in northeastern Europe. The Finnish lake region alone comprises some 55,000 mostly shallow lakes.

Northeastern Europe is known for its vast woodlands. With 68 percent of its area covered by firs, pines, alders, and beeches, Finland is the most heavily forested country in Europe. The climate is continental for

the most part, becoming subpolar in the north. Coastal waters begin to freeze over toward the end of the year. Tundra vegetation is predominant in the north.

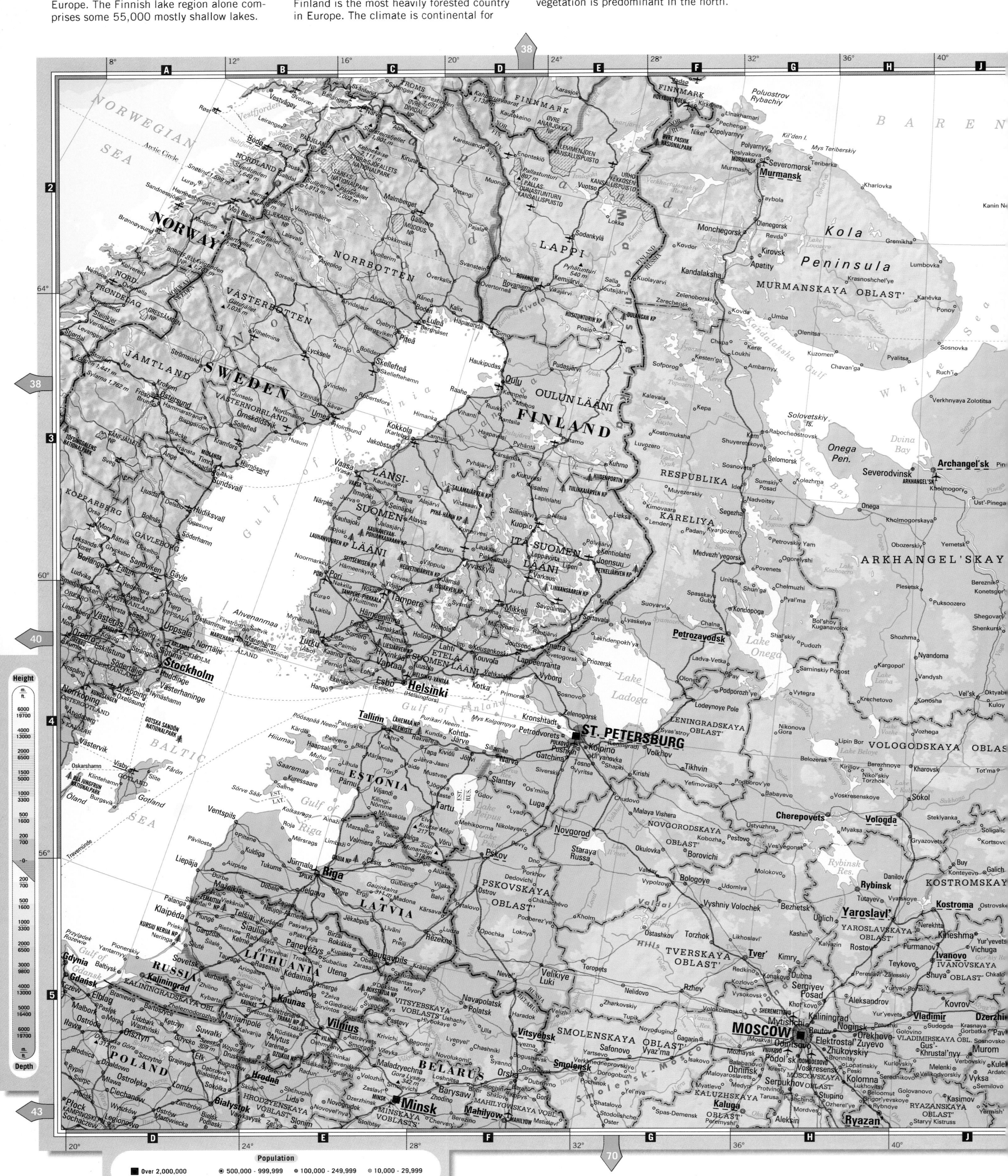

ST. PETERSBURG (Leningrad)

MOSCOW

Map Section
68
69

KARA SEA

Yugorskiy Peninsula

Pay-Khoy Mts.

Kolguyev Island

Kanin Pen.

Cheshskaya Bay

Pechora Bay

Molozemel'skaya Tundra

Bol'shezemel'skaya Tundra

NENETSKIY AVT. OKRUG

RESPUBLIKA KOMI

U S S I A

Northern Ural's

OBLAST'

Gora Narodnaya 1,894 m

Solikamsk
Berezniki
OBLAST'

KOMI-PERMYATSKIY AVTONOMNYY OKRUG

PERMSKAYA OBLAST'

SVERDLOVSKAYA OBLAST'

TYUMENSKAYA OBLAST'

Perm'

Yekaterinburg

Nizhniy Tagil

Tyumen'

KIROVSKAYA OBLAST'

Kirov

RESPUBLIKA UDMURTIYA

Izhevsk

NIZHEGORODSKAYA OBLAST'

RESPUBLIKA MARIY-EL

Yoshkar-Ola

RESPUBLIKA CHUVASHIYA

Nizhniy Novgorod (Gor'kiy)

Cheboksary

Kazan'

RESPUBLIKA TATARSTAN

Naberezhnye Chelny

Nizhnekamsk

RESPUBLIKA BASHKORTOSTAN

Ufa

Chelyabinsk
Kopeysk

CHELYABINSKAYA OBLAST'

Kurgan

KURGANSKAYA OBLAST'

Magnitogorsk

QAZAQSTAN

KAZAKHSTAN

Ul'yanovsk

QOSTANAY

Qostanay
Rüdnyy

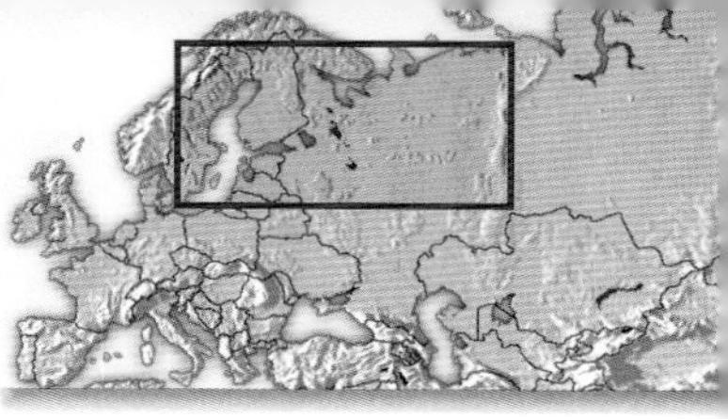

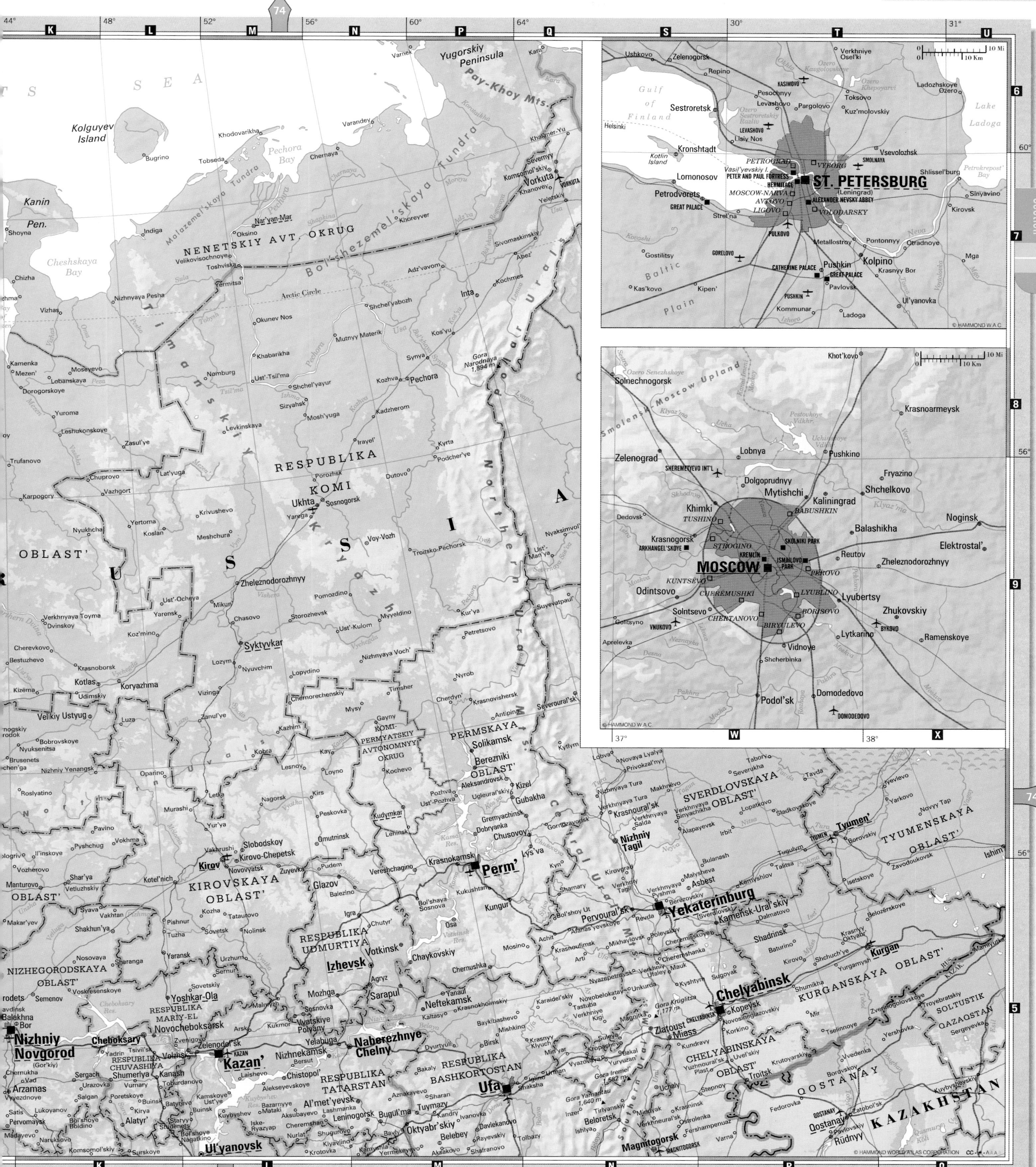

Scale 1:6,000,000 Lambert Conformal Conic Projection

MI 50 100 150 200
KM 50 100 150 200 250

© HAMMOND WORLD ATLAS CORPORATION

St. Petersburg inset:

Gulf of Finland
Helsinki
Kronshtadt
Kotlin Island
Sestroretsk
Lomonosov
Petrodvorets
GREAT PALACE
PETROGRAD
PETER AND PAUL FORTRESS
HERMITAGE
MOSCOW-NARVA
AVTOVO
LIGOVO
VOLODARSKY
VYBORG
ALEXANDER NEVSKY ABBEY
Pushkin
CATHERINE PALACE
GREAT PALACE
PAVLOVSK
Pavlovsk
Kolpino
Lake Ladoga
Shlissel'burg
Kirovsk
Baltic Plain

Moscow inset:

Solnechnogorsk
Zelenograd
SHEREMETYEVO INT'L
Khimki
TUSHINO
Krasnogorsk
ARKHANGEL'SKOYE
STROGINO
KREMLIN
MOSCOW
ISMAYLOVO PARK
KUNTSEVO
CHEREMUSHKI
LYUBLINO
Lyubertsy
BORISOVO
BIRYULEVO
CHERTANOVO
Vidnoye
Podol'sk
Domodedovo
DOMODEDOVO
Balashikha
Noginsk
Elektrostal'
Reutov
Zheleznodorozhnyy
Zhukovskiy
Ramenskoye
Lytkarino
BYKOVO
Mytishchi
Kaliningrad
BABUSHKIN
Shchelkovo
Fryazino
Krasnoarmeysk
Pushkino
Lobnya
Dolgoprudnyy
Moscow Upland

The Black Sea receives substantial flows of fresh water from such rivers as the Danube, the Don, and the Dnepr. Thus its salinity near the surface is only half that of the Atlantic. Salt-rich water also flows into this sea from the Mediterranean Sea along the floor of the Bosporus Strait. This stable, layered configuration produces an oxygen shortage at the bottom of the Black Sea that is hostile to living organisms.

By contrast, the Danube Delta teems with life. It is a paradise for birds - one of the last in Europe - and provides spawning grounds for over one hundred different species of fish.

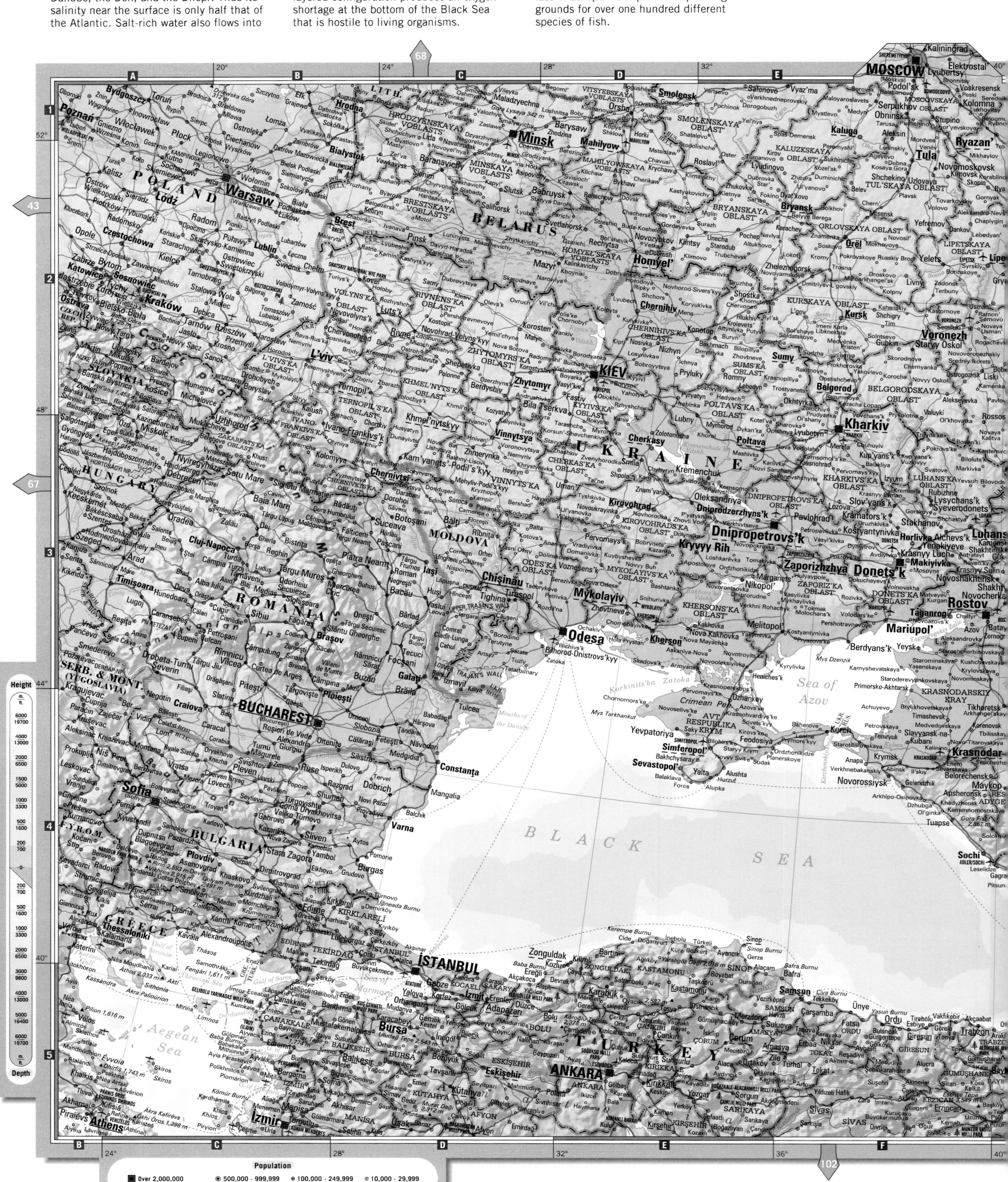

Population
- ■ Over 2,000,000
- ■ 1,000,000 - 1,999,999
- ⬤ 500,000 - 999,999
- ⬤ 250,000 - 499,999
- ⬤ 100,000 - 249,999
- ⬤ 30,000 - 99,999
- ⊙ 10,000 - 29,999
- ○ Under 10,000

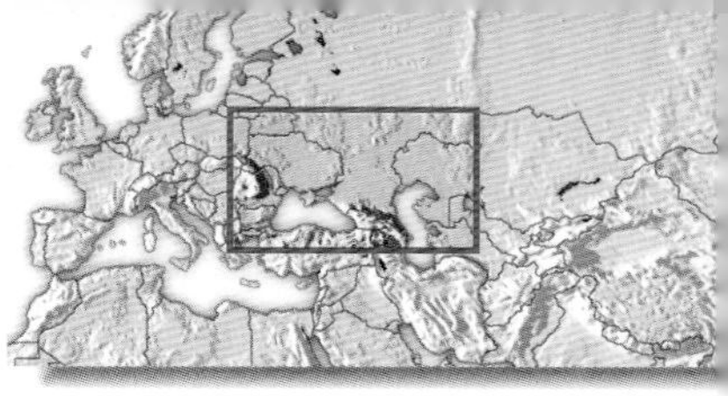

RUSSIA

KAZAKHSTAN

GEORGIA

AZERBAIJAN

ARMENIA

UZBEKISTAN

TURKMENISTAN

IRAN

CASPIAN SEA

Aral Sea

Major cities and labels:

Arzamas · Ul'yanovsk · Tol'yatti · Samara · Penza · Saratov · Volgograd · Volzhskiy · Astrakhan · Orenburg · Orsk · Magnitogorsk · Sterlitamak · Aqtöbe · Novotroitsk · Qostanay · Rudnyy

Elista · Stavropol' · Armavir · Nevinnomyssk · Cherkessk · Kislovodsk · Pyatigorsk · Nal'chik · Vladikavkaz · Groznyy · Makhachkala · Kaspiysk

T'bilisi · Bat'umi · Rust'avi · Vanadzor · Gyumri · Yerevan · Ganca · Sumqayit · Baku

Atyraū · Aqtaū · Oral · Balykshy

REPUBLIKA MORDOVIYA · REPUBLIKA CHUVASHIYA · REPUBLIKA TATARSTAN · REPUBLIKA BASHKORTOSTAN · PENZENSKAYA OBLAST' · SAMARSKAYA OBLAST' · SARATOVSKAYA OBLAST' · VOLGOGRADSKAYA OBLAST' · ASTRAKHANSKAYA OBLAST' · ROSTOVSKAYA OBLAST' · RESPUBLIKA KALMYKIYA · STAVROPOL'SKIY KRAY · ORENBURGSKAYA OBLAST' · CHELYABINSKAYA OBLAST' · QOSTANAY

BATYS QAZAQSTAN · ATYRAŪ · AQTÖBE · MANGGHYSTAŪ · QYZYLORDA · QORAQALPOGHISTON RESPUBLIKASI · DASHHOWUZ · AHAL · BALKAN

RESPUBLIKA KARACHAYEVO-CHERKESIYA · RESPUBLIKA KABARDINO-BALKARIYA · RESP. SEVER. OSETIYA-ALANIYA · RESPUBLIKA INGUSHETIYA · RESPUBLIKA CHECHNYA · RESPUBLIKA DAGESTAN

Ustyurt Plateau · Mughalzhar Taūy · Naryn Qum · Garabogazköl Aylagy

Scale 1:6,000,000 — Lambert Conformal Conic Projection

MI 50 100 150 200

KM 50 100 150 200 250 300

Northern Ukraine lies within a mixed-forest zone of oak, beech, and pine that gives way to a forest-steppe in the heartland, where the roots of trees reach groundwater at only a very few places.

The topography in the south is dominated by plains. The rich, black soil (chernozem) of the forest-steppes and plains yields bountiful harvests of wheat, barley, sugar beets, and sunflower seeds.

Ukraine holds the world's largest reserves of anthracite coal in the Donets River Basin, as well as rich deposits of iron and manganese ore.

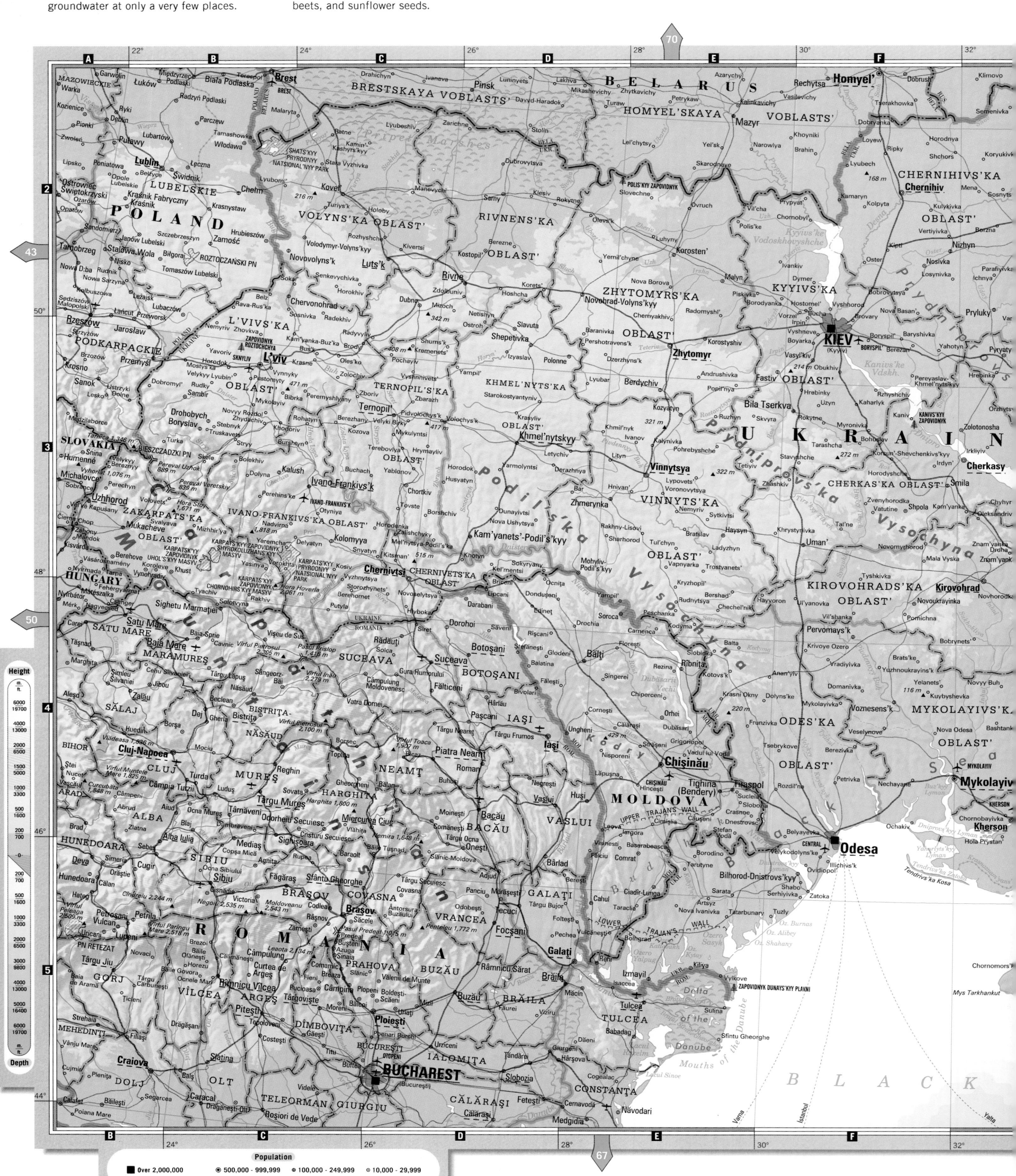

Scale 1:3,000,000   Lambert Conformal Conic Projection

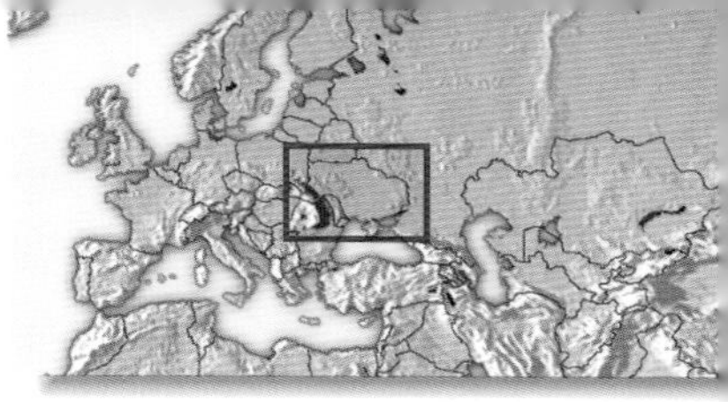

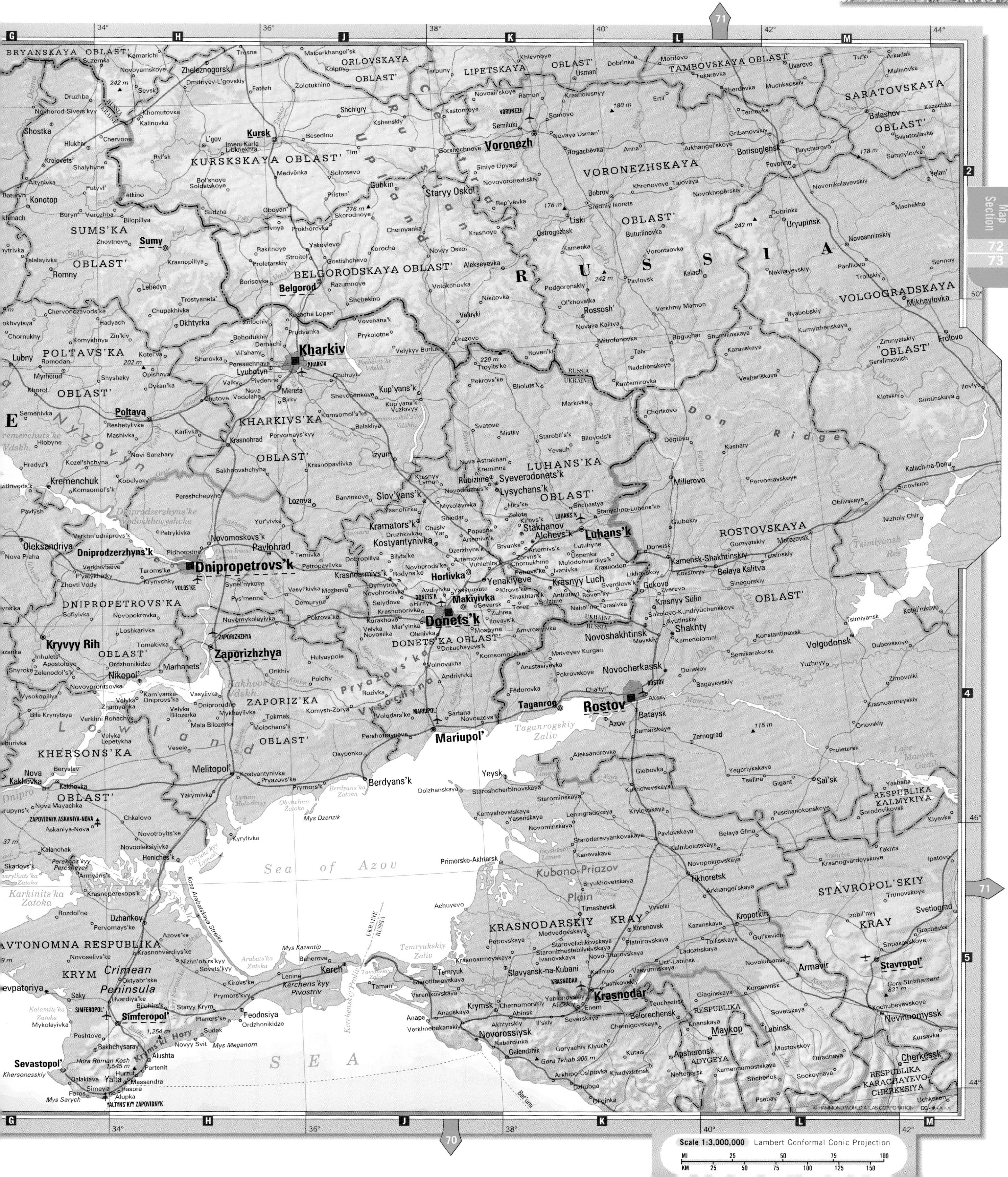

Russia measures more than 4,000 km from north to south and stretches across 9,600 km of territory from west to east - spanning nearly half the globe in the northern latitudes. The Russian landscape is dominated by vast plains west of the Yenisey River. The climate is predominantly continental and cool. The coldest temperatures in the northern hemisphere have been recorded near the villages of Oymyakon and Verkhoyansk in eastern Siberia. Long winters with little snow keep the ground frozen for much of the year in about two-thirds of the country, while the climate along the Black Sea coast is subtropical.

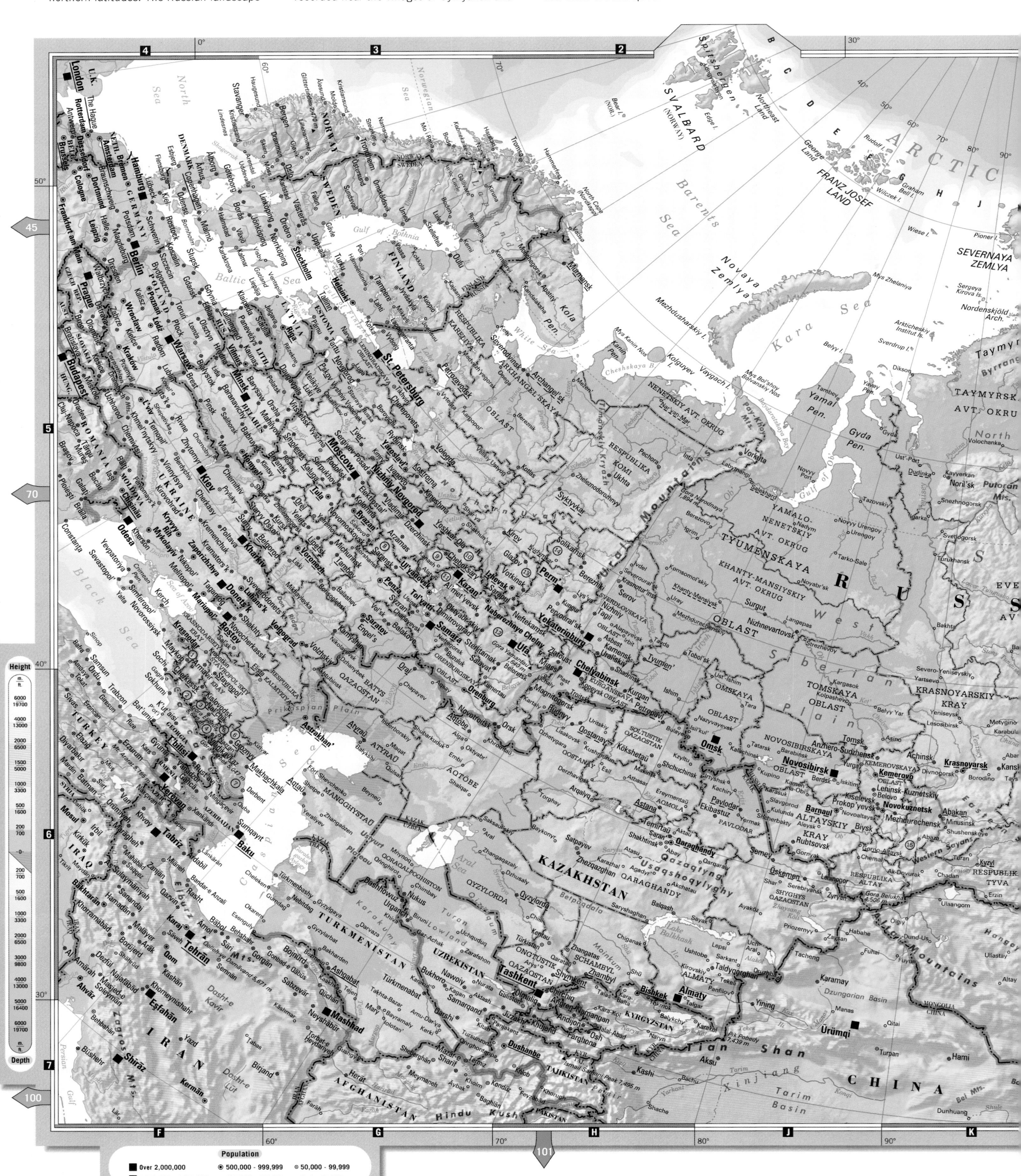

Population

■ Over 2,000,000
■ 1,000,000 - 1,999,999
● 500,000 - 999,999
● 100,000 - 499,999
◉ 50,000 - 99,999
○ Under 50,000

Russia and Neighboring Countries

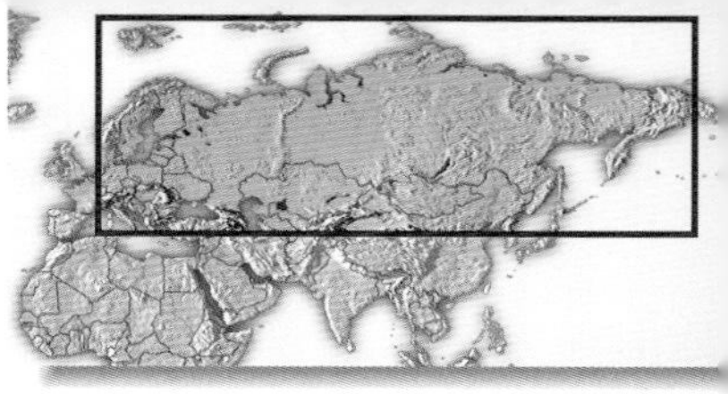

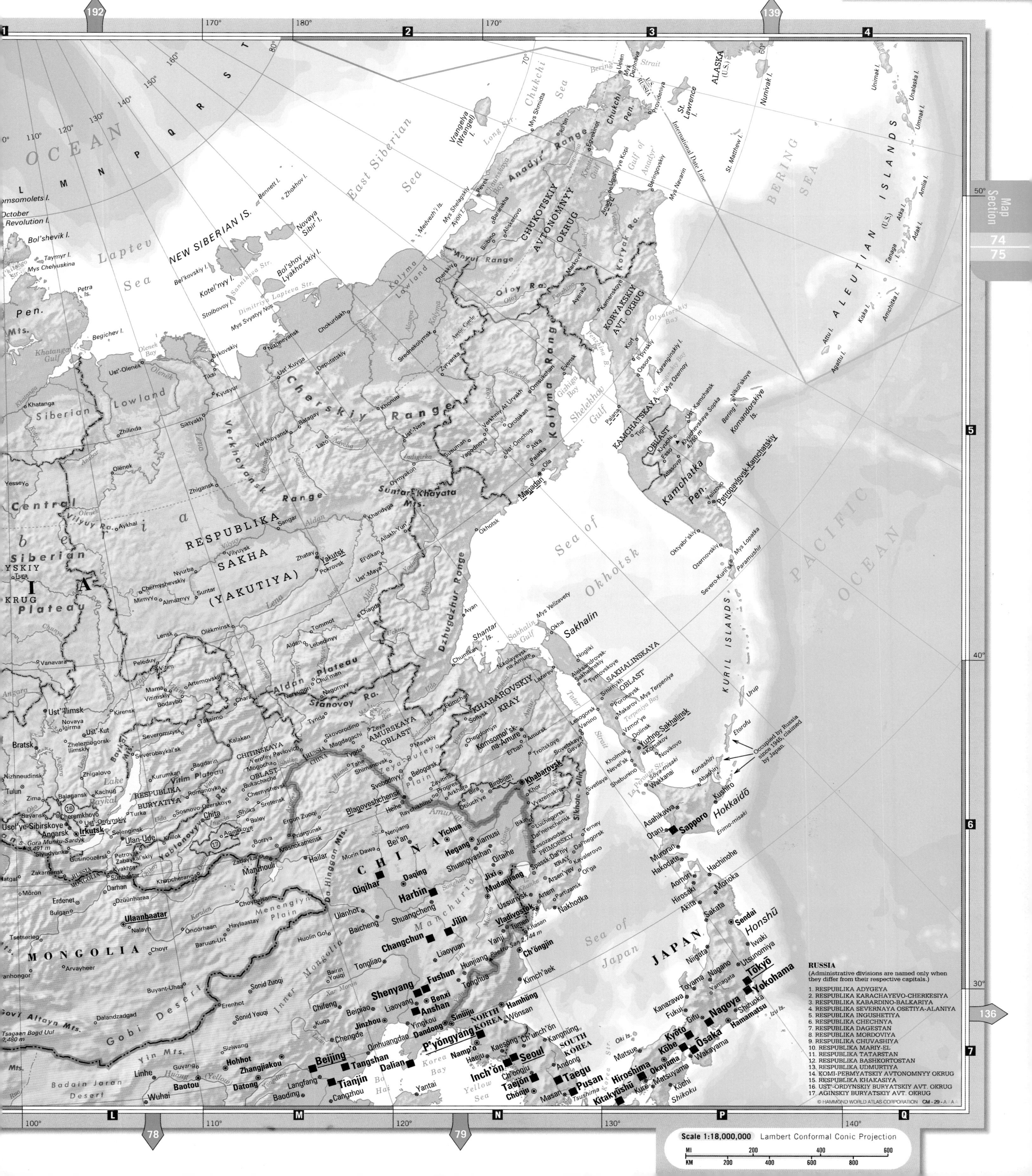

RUSSIA
(Administrative divisions are named only when
they differ from their respective capitals.)

1. RESPUBLIKA ADYGEYA
2. RESPUBLIKA KARACHAYEVO-CHERKESIYA
3. RESPUBLIKA KABARDINO-BALKARIYA
4. RESPUBLIKA SEVERNAYA OSETIYA-ALANIYA
5. RESPUBLIKA INGUSHETIYA
6. RESPUBLIKA CHECHNYA
7. RESPUBLIKA DAGESTAN
8. RESPUBLIKA MORDOVIYA
9. RESPUBLIKA CHUVASHIYA
10. RESPUBLIKA MARIY-EL
11. RESPUBLIKA TATARSTAN
12. RESPUBLIKA BASHKORTOSTAN
13. RESPUBLIKA UDMURTIYA
14. KOMI-PERMYATSKIY AVTONOMNYY OKRUG
15. RESPUBLIKA KHAKASIYA
16. UST'-ORDYNSKIY BURYATSKIY AVT. OKRUG
17. AGINSKIY BURYATSKIY AVT. OKRUG

© HAMMOND WORLD ATLAS CORPORATION   CM - 29 - A - A

Scale 1:18,000,000   Lambert Conformal Conic Projection

MI   200   400   600
KM   200   400   600   800

The Indus is the longest river in southwest Asia (3200 km), and its delta covers an area of 7,800 square km. The river flows from its source at an elevation of 5,182 meters in the Trans-Himalayas and is fed by snowmelt and glacial meltwater from the mountains of the Tibet Plateau. After leaving the Himalayas, it flows onto the Punjab Plain and through a vast alluvial lowland before emptying into the Arabian Sea south of Hyderabad. Water levels on the Indus fluctuate with the rhythm of the monsoon rains. Dams and canals ensure a reliable supply of water to the world's largest irrigation zone.

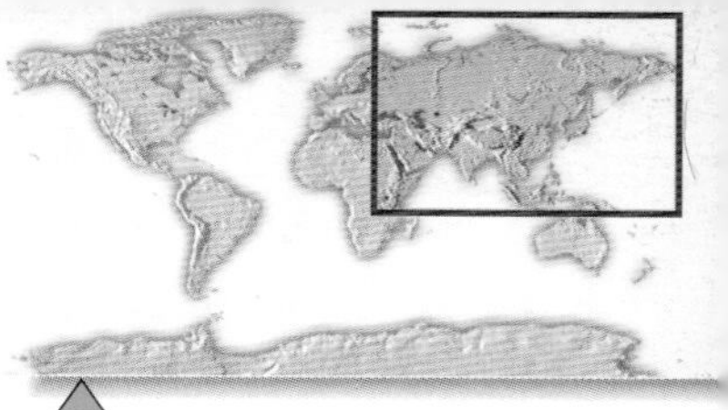

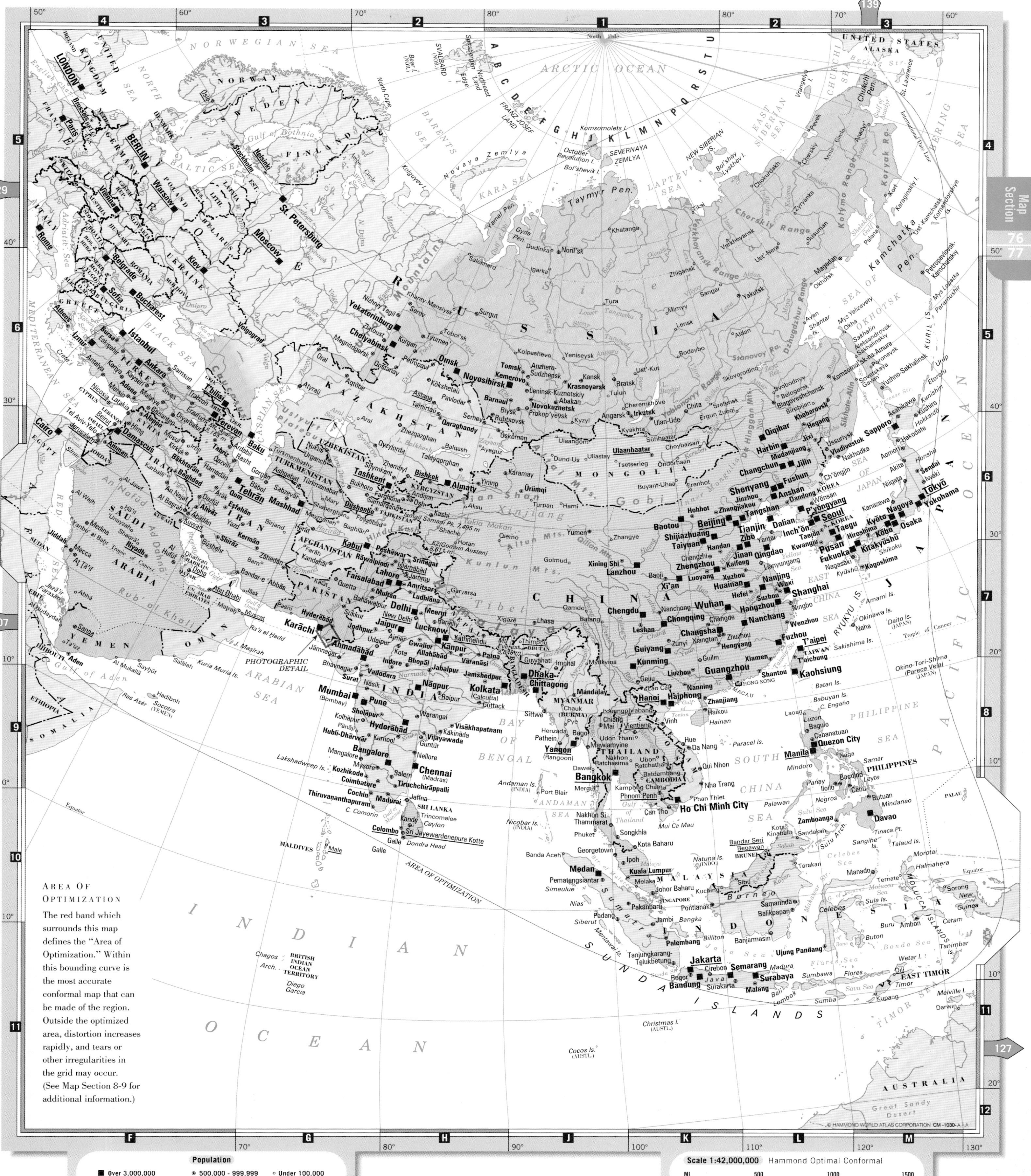

AREA OF OPTIMIZATION

The red band which surrounds this map defines the "Area of Optimization." Within this bounding curve is the most accurate conformal map that can be made of the region. Outside the optimized area, distortion increases rapidly, and tears or other irregularities in the grid may occur. (See Map Section 8-9 for additional information.)

Population

■ Over 3,000,000   ⊛ 500,000 - 999,999   ⊙ Under 100,000
■ 1,000,000 - 2,999,999   ● 100,000 - 499,999

Scale 1:42,000,000   Hammond Optimal Conformal

© HAMMOND WORLD ATLAS CORPORATION   CM -1030-A-L-A

E astern Asia is the most populous region on Earth. Its most prominent topographic features are the plains and deserts of the central highlands, and its broad, fertile loess plains. The climate is controlled by monsoon winds. In the winter, the East Asian monsoon carries dry, cold air - often accompanied by dust storms - from a cold high-pressure center in the Asian heartland to the Pacific. Temperatures in China drop to below freezing north of the Qilian Shan in the winter, while warm, moist air flows inland from the sea during the summer.

Height

m. ft.	
6000	19700
4000	13000
2000	6500
1500	5000
1000	3300
500	1600
200	700
- 0 -	
200	700
500	1600
1000	3300
2000	6500
3000	9800
4000	13000
5000	16400
6000	19700

Depth

Population

■ Over 2,000,000	● 500,000 - 999,999	● 100,000 - 249,999	◦ 10,000 - 29,999
■ 1,000,000 - 1,999,999	◉ 250,000 - 499,999	◦ 30,000 - 99,999	◦ Under 10,000

Eastern Asia

120° 125° 130° 135° 140° 145° 150°
H J K L M N P Q
75
87
2 3 4 5 6
45° 40° 35° 30°
AMURSKAYA OBLAST'
R U S S I A
KHABAROVSKIY KRAY
SAKHALINSKAYA OBLAST'
Sakhalin
SEA OF OKHOTSK
YEVREYSKAYA AVT. OBLAST'
PRIMORSKIY KRAY
HEILONGJIANG
JILIN
LIAONING
NEI MONGOL AUT. REG.
SHANDONG
JIANGSU
SHANGHAI
NORTH KOREA
SOUTH KOREA
J A P A N
SEA OF JAPAN
YELLOW SEA
EAST CHINA SEA
PACIFIC OCEAN
Bo Hai (Gulf of Chihli)
Korea Bay
Liaodong Bay
Tonghan Bay
Korea Strait
Cheju Str.
Tatar Strait
La Perouse Str.
Tsugaru Str.
Aniva Sea
Terpeniya Bay
Uchiura Bay
Toyama Bay
Amakusa Sea
Tosa Bay
Izu Islands
Ōsumi Is.
Ōsumi Str.
Gotō Is.
Oki Is.
Xiao Hinggan Mts.
Da Hinggan Mts.
Yilehuli Mts.
Sikhote-Alin
Zeya-Bureya Plain
Bureya Mts.
Turana Mts.
Wanda Mts.
Zhangguangcai Mts.
Changbai Mts.
Hamgyong Mts.
Zapadno-Sakhalinskie Mts.
Kitami Mts.
Hokkaidō
Honshū
Shikoku
Kyūshū
Occupied by Russia since 1945, claimed by Japan.
Blagoveshchensk
Khabarovsk
Komsomol'sk-na-Amure
Yuzhno-Sakhalinsk
Vladivostok
Nakhodka
Ussuriysk
Harbin
Qiqihar
Daqing
Changchun
Jilin
Shenyang
Fushun
Anshan
Benxi
Dalian
Dandong
Jinzhou
Yichun
Hegang
Jiamusi
Shuangyashan
Jixi
Mudanjiang
Tangshan
Tianjin
Qingdao
Yantai
Weihai
Nanjing
Shanghai
Suzhou
Wuxi
Changzhou
Hangzhou
Sinŭiju
P'yŏngyang
Namp'o
Hamhŭng
Wŏnsan
Ch'ŏngjin
Kimch'aek
Kaesŏng
Seoul
Inch'ŏn
Taejŏn
Taegu
Kwangju
Ulsan
Pusan
Cheju
Sapporo
Asahikawa
Hakodate
Aomori
Morioka
Akita
Sendai
Niigata
Tōkyō
Yokohama
Kawasaki
Chiba
Nagoya
Kyōto
Ōsaka
Kōbe
Sakai
Hiroshima
Okayama
Kitakyūshū
Fukuoka
Kumamoto
Kagoshima
Nagasaki
Hamamatsu
Shizuoka
Kanazawa
Toyama
Nagano
Utsunomiya
Maebashi
© HAMMOND WORLD ATLAS CORPORATION
Scale 1:9,000,000 Lambert Conformal Conic Projection
MI 100 200 300
KM 100 200 300 400

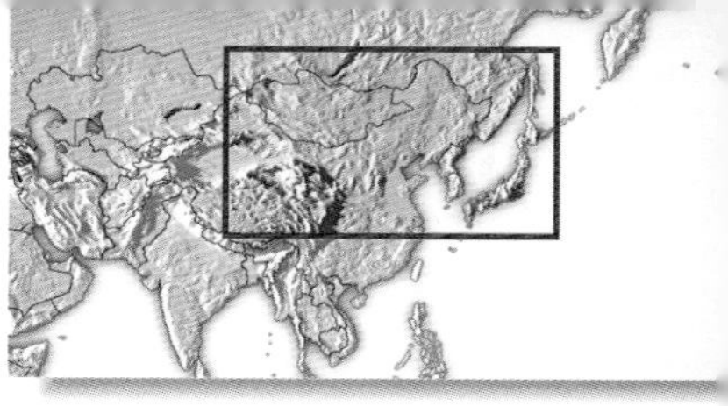

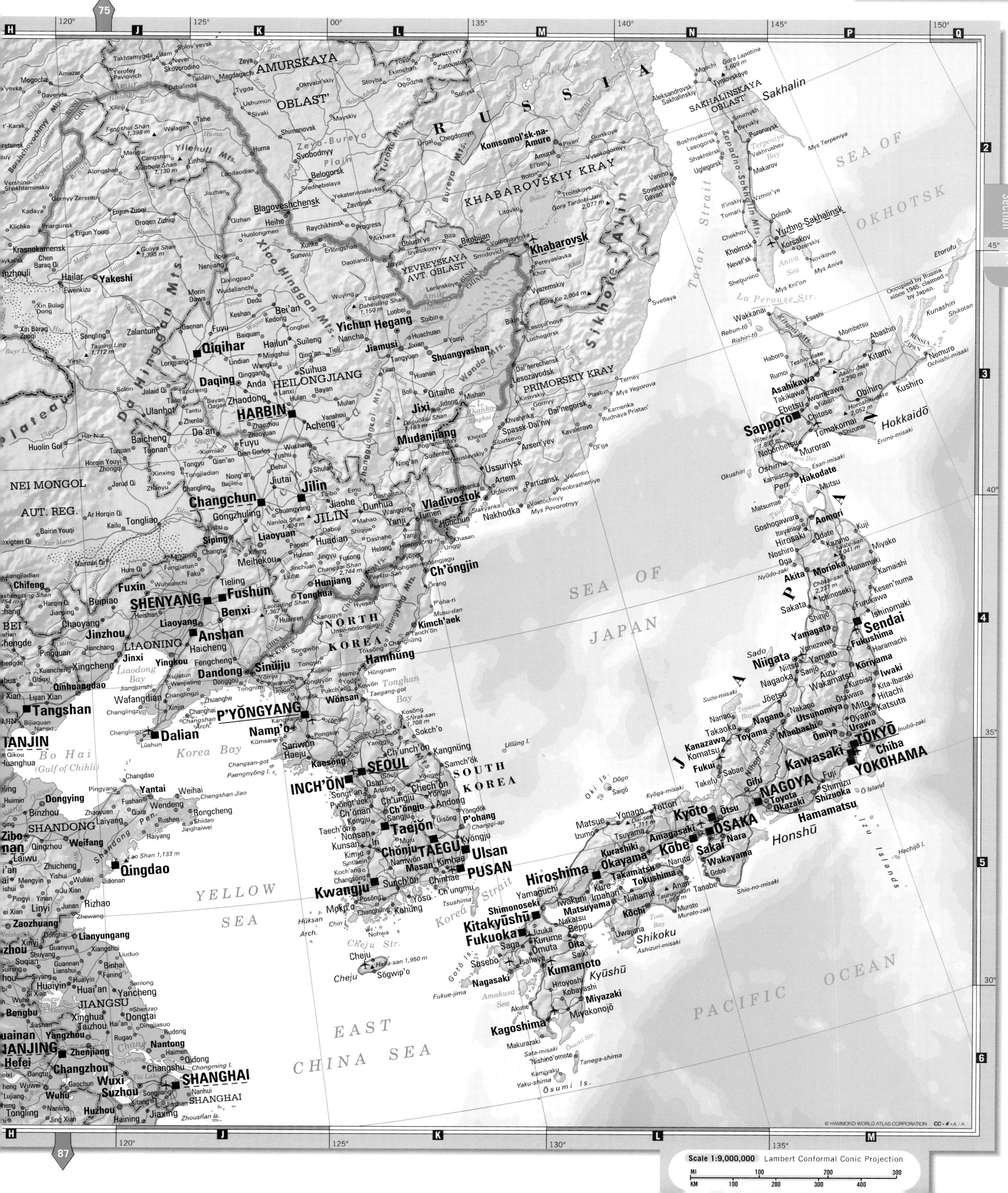

Map Section 78 79

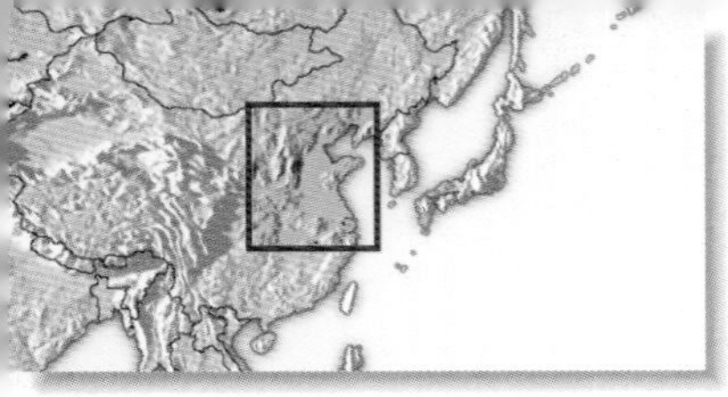

Northeastern China

The alluvial plain created by the Huang (Yellow) River is the cradle of Chinese civilization. Now lined by levees along its lower reaches, the river lies up to 10 m above the surrounding land.

The Huang has often overflowed its banks, causing devastating floods, and even changed its course, emptying into the sea at different points north and south of the Shandong Peninsula.

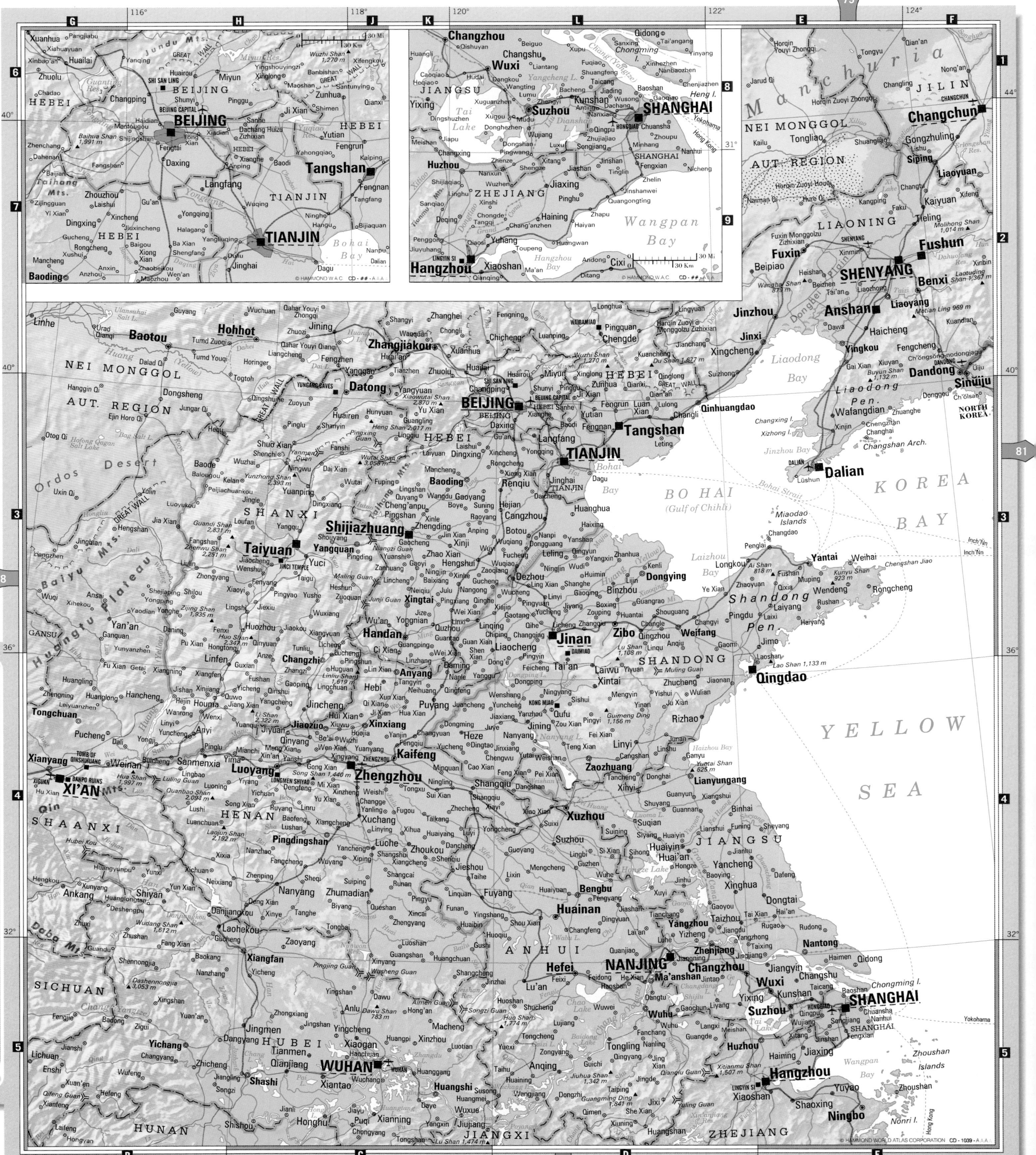

Population

■ Over 2,000,000	◉ 500,000 - 999,999
■ 1,000,000 - 1,999,999	◉ 250,000 - 499,999
● 100,000 - 249,999	○ 10,000 - 29,999
◉ 30,000 - 99,999	○ Under 10,000

Scale 1:6,000,000 Lambert Conformal Conic Projection

© HAMMOND WORLD ATLAS CORPORATION CD - 1039 - A.A.A

The Korean peninsula is the home of a distinct culture that was influenced early on by China and bears the indelible imprint of Buddhism. Korea was annexed by Japan in 1910 and divided into a communist north and a pro-western south in 1948. In the years since the end of the Korean War (1950-1953), South Korea has become a major industrial power.

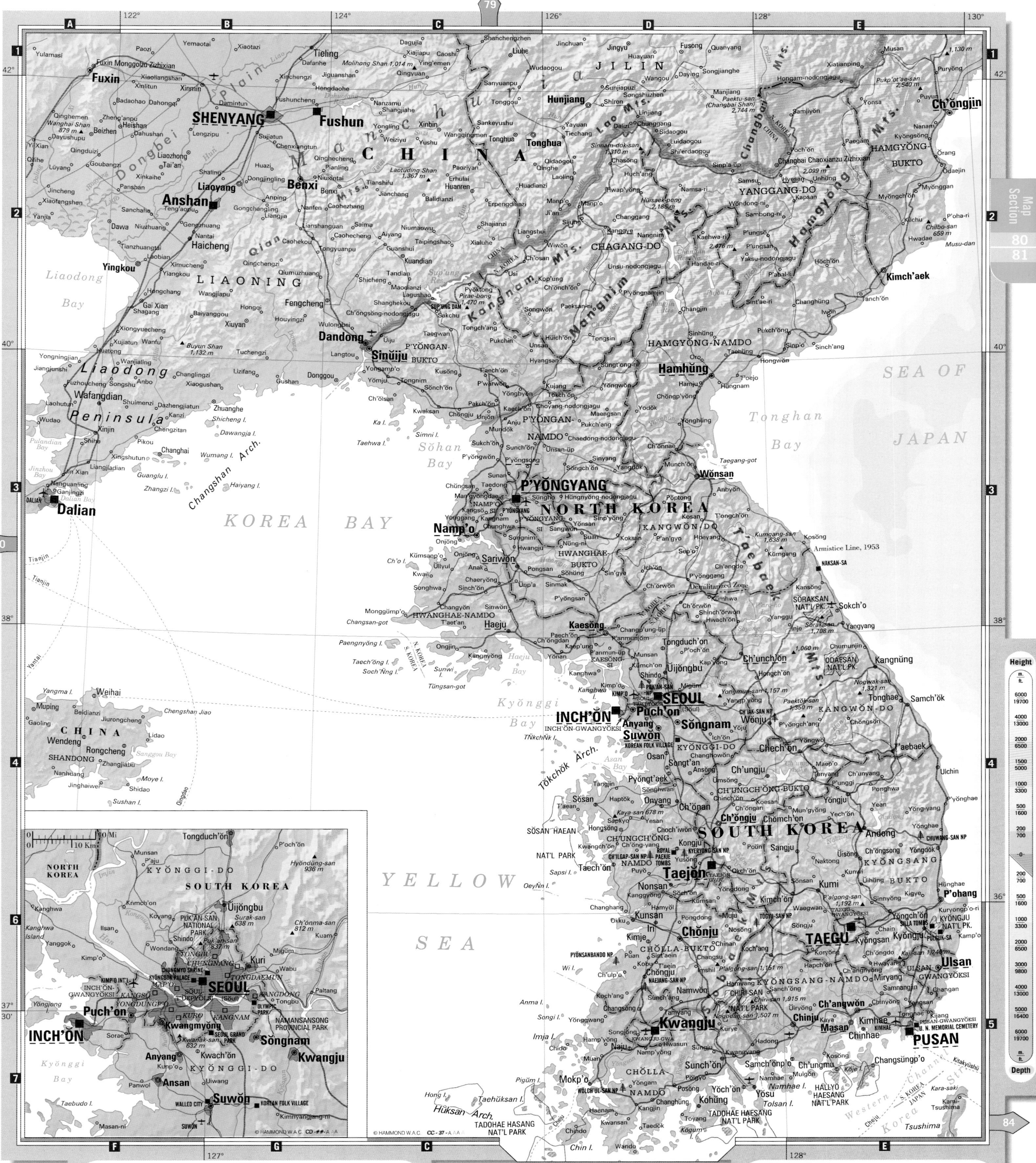

Korea

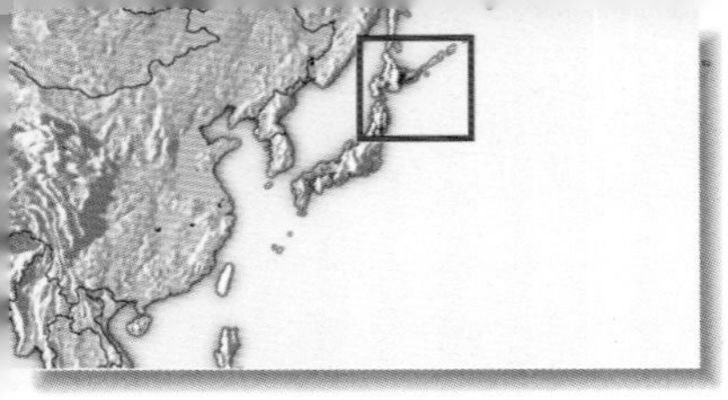

Northern Japan

Hokkaidō, Japan's northernmost major island, is home to the Ainu, a people unrelated to the Japanese who also settled on Sakhalin and the Kuril Islands. Their origin is unknown. Long ago, the Ainu retreated to the fertile inland valleys to farm, hunt, and fish. Today, only 14,000 Ainu live on the island. Hokkaido hosted the Winter Olympics in 1972.

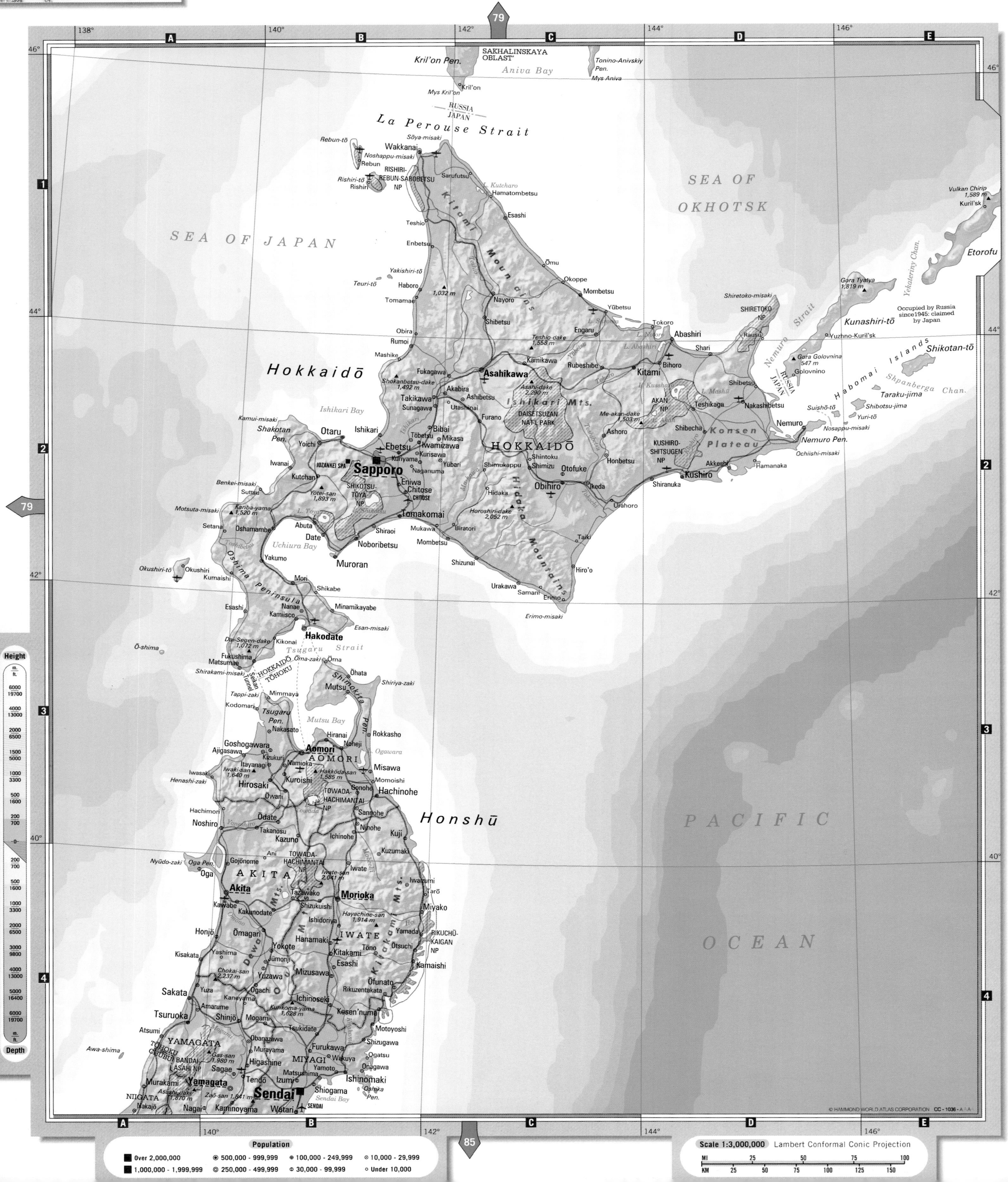

SEA OF OKHOTSK

SEA OF JAPAN

La Perouse Strait

RUSSIA
JAPAN

Hokkaidō

HOKKAIDŌ

Sapporo

Asahikawa

Honshū

PACIFIC

OCEAN

Height
m.	ft.
6000	19700
4000	13000
2000	6500
1500	5000
1000	3300
500	1600
200	700
0	0
200	700
500	1600
1000	3300
2000	6500
3000	9800
4000	13000
5000	16400
6000	19700

m.
ft.
Depth

Population
■ Over 2,000,000	● 500,000 - 999,999
■ 1,000,000 - 1,999,999	● 250,000 - 499,999
◉ 100,000 - 249,999	○ 10,000 - 29,999
○ 30,000 - 99,999	○ Under 10,000

Scale 1:3,000,000   Lambert Conformal Conic Projection

© HAMMOND WORLD ATLAS CORPORATION   CC - 1036 - A

Tokyo is one of the most densely populated cities on Earth. This modern metropolis is also a major Japanese commercial center, and its industrial region spreads far beyond the city boundaries.

Osaka is the second-largest commercial and industrial center in Japan. The former capital, with its roughly 1,500 temples, is regarded as the heart of the Japanese culture.

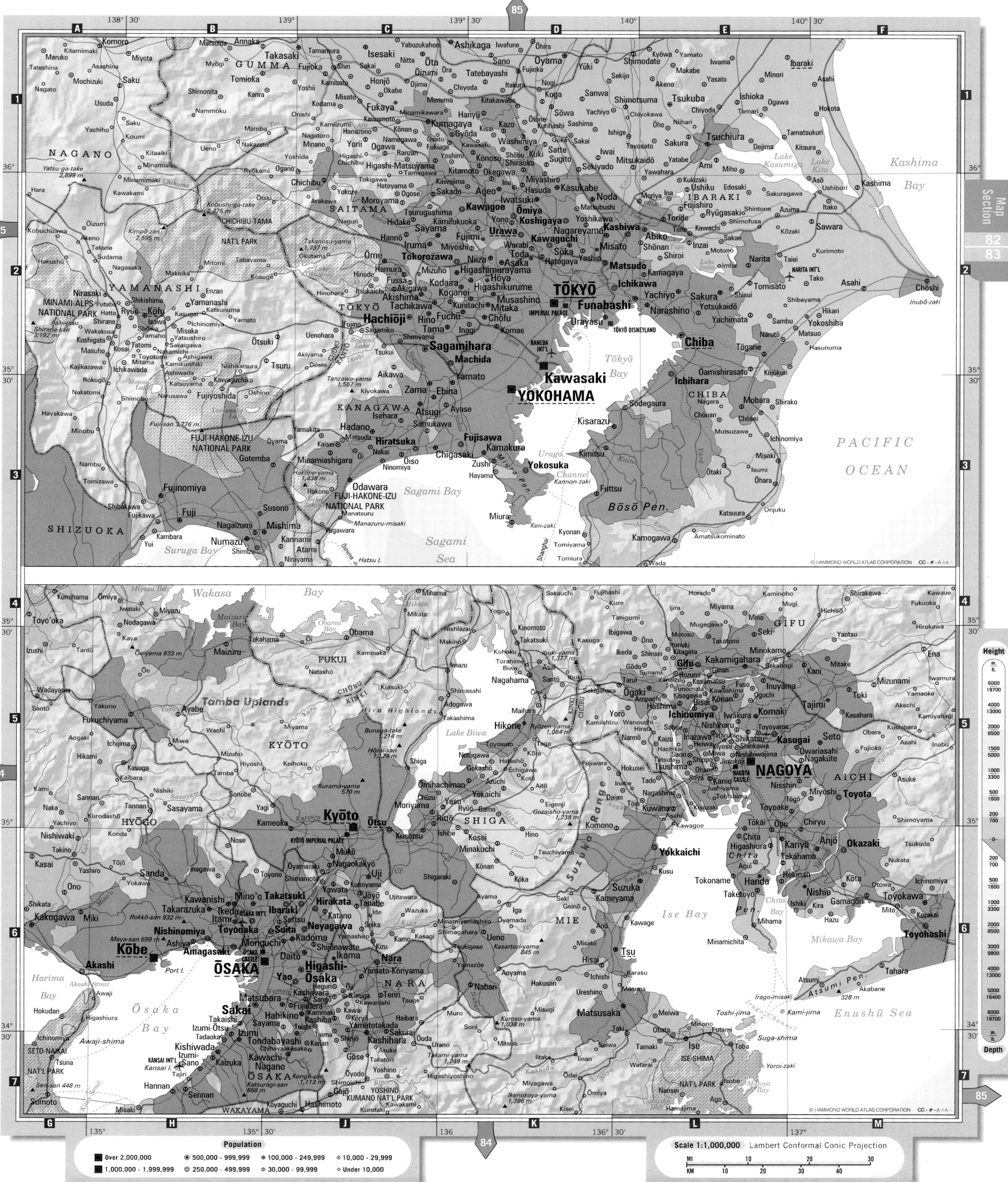

Tōkyō – Yokohama, Ōsaka – Nagoya

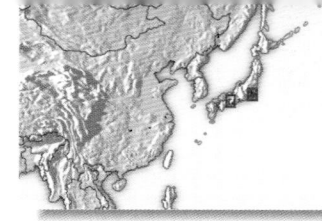

Height
m.
ft.
6000 / 19700
4000 / 13000
2000 / 6500
1500 / 5000
1000 / 3300
500 / 1600
200 / 700
0
200 / 700
500 / 1600
1000 / 3300
2000 / 6500
3000 / 9800
4000 / 13000
5000 / 16400
6000 / 19700
Depth

Population

■ Over 2,000,000	⊙ 500,000 – 999,999	⊙ 100,000 – 249,999	⊙ 10,000 – 29,999
■ 1,000,000 – 1,999,999	⊙ 250,000 – 499,999	⊙ 30,000 – 99,999	○ Under 10,000

Scale 1:1,000,000   Lambert Conformal Conic Projection

© HAMMOND WORLD ATLAS CORPORATION

The heart of Japan's industrial might lies in four highly urbanized clusters, three of which are located on the southern coast of Honshu (Tokyo/Yokohama, Nagoya, Kobe/Osaka). The fourth cluster is located in northern Kyushu. Despite its lack of iron ore, coal, and petroleum and its limited arable land, Japan has become a major economic power since the end of World War II.

Using imported raw materials, skilled Japanese work force produces cars, electronics, optical equipment, textiles, and other quality products for the global market.

Population

■ Over 2,000,000	⊛ 500,000 - 999,999 ⊚ 100,000 - 249,999 ○ 10,000 - 29,999
■ 1,000,000 - 1,999,999	⊜ 250,000 - 499,999 ⊙ 30,000 - 99,999 ○ Under 10,000

138° F 140° 142° H 144° J

E

38°

MIYAGI
Ishinomaki
Higashine Sendai Matsushima
Sagae YAMAGATA Yamoto Onagawa
Murakami Asahi-dake Tendo Shiogama
Awa-shima 1,870 m Zaō-san 1,841 m Sendai
Hajiki-zaki BANDAI-ASAHI Yamagata SENDAI Bay
Aikawa Nakajō NP Kaminoyama Iwanuma
Ryōtsu Nagai Takahata Shiroishi Watari
Shibata Yonezawa Kakuda
NIIGATA Niigata Iide-san BANDAI-ASAHI Sōma
Niitsu 2,105 m Fukushima NP Haramachi
Sado Gosen Azuma-san 2,035 m
Sawasaki-bana Shirone Kitakata Nihonmatsu Namie
Ogi Tsubame Yamato Motomiya
Suzu-misaki Kamo FUKUSHIMA Miharu
Sanjō Aizu- Kōriyama Ōtakine-yama
Mitsuke Wakamatsu 1,193 m Iwaki
Nagaoka Tajima Sukagawa
CHŪBU Tōkamachi Nasu-dake 1,917 m Yabuki Ishikawa
Kashiwazaki Ojiya Shirakawa Iwaki
TŌHOKU Kuroiso Tanagura
NIIGATA Arai Abukuma-Kōchi Shioya-saki
Itoigawa NIKKO NAT'L Ōtawara Kita-Ibaraki
Jōetsu Myōkō-san 2,446 m Shirane-san 2,578 m PARK Takahagi
Iiyama Nakano PARK Nikkō Daigo Hitachi
Nyūzen Nantai-san 2,484 m Imaichi Hitachi-ōta
Uozu Ōmachi JŌSHIN-ETSU Katsuta
Toyama Ueda GUMMA Numata Utsunomiya Nakaminato
Namerikawa KŌGEN Azumaya-san 2,333 m Kanuma Ishibashi Mōka Kasama
Ōyama Nagano Maebashi Kiryū Mito
Yatsuo Tate-yama NAT'L Tochigi TOCHIGI Hokota
3,015 m PARK Asama-yama 2,542 m Takasaki Oyama Shimodate Tsuchiura
Takayama Yari-ga-take Matsumoto Isesaki Ōta Yūki IBARAKI Ishioka
Norikura-dake 3,026 m 3,180 m, Hotaka Maruko Fujioka Yatabe Kashima
Hotaka 3,190 m JAPANESE Okaya SAITAMA Kumagaya Sakai Tsukuba
ALPS NAT'L Suwa Kuki Mitsukaidō
Ontake-san 3,063 m PARK Chino Kobushi-gatake 2,475 m Kasukabe Iwai
NAGANO Ina CHICHIBU-TAMA Kawagoe Ryūgasaki
Ina NAT'L PARK Sayama Koshigaya Sawara
Komagane Kawaguchi Narita Int'l Chōshi
GIFU MINAMI ALPS Tokorozawa Airport Inubō-zaki
Mino NAT'L PARK Tachikawa Urawa Kawaguchi
Seki Nirasaki Hachiōji TŌKYŌ Chōfu TŌKYŌ Chiba
Shirane-san 3,192 m PARK Sagamihara Kawasaki CHIBA
Kakamigahara Iida FUJI Fujisawa YOKOHAMA Bōsō
Inuyama Ena Akaishi-dake 3,120 m HAKONE- Chigasaki Yokosuka Kisarazu
Nakatsugawa Mizunami Fuji-Gotemba Hadano Yokosuka Kimitsu
Chinomiya Tajimi YAMANASHI Isehara Kyonan Futtsu Ōtaki
Nagoya Seto KANAGAWA Odawara Katsuura
AICHI Fuji Susono Mishima Kamogawa
Toyota Okazaki Mishima Tomiyama Tateyama
Toyokawa SHIZUOKA Numazu Izu Nojima-zaki
Nishio Hamakita Shimizu Atami Sagami
Iwata Fujieda Sea
Gamagōri Shizuoka Yaizu FUJI-HAKONE-
CHŪBU Toi IZU NAT'L Honshū
KINKI Toyohashi Yuizu PARK
Irago-misaki Hamamatsu Suruga Shimoda
SHIMA NAT'L PARK Kosai Bay Irō-zaki
Daiō-zaki Omae-zaki CHŪBU Ō Island
TŌKYŌ Ōshima

PACIFIC

OCEAN

2

36°

3

Izu

Islands

Kōzu-shima

TŌKYŌ

Miyake-jima
MIYAKEJIMA

Mikura-jima

FUJI-HAKONE-
IZU NAT'L
PARK

Hachijō-jima
Hachijō
HACHIJŌJIMA

(JAPAN)

Aoga-shima

Beyoneisu-retsugan

Koshiki Sendai Kokubu Miyakonojō
Kushikino Iijuin KAGOSHIMA Nichinan
Kaseda Kaneya Kōyama Kyūshū
Kagoshima Makurazaki Sata-misaki Tarumizu
Nishino'omote
Tanega-shima
Kamiyaku Nakatane
Yaku 1,935 m Ōsumi

Shanghai

Kuchino-shima

Suwanose-jima

KAGOSHIMA

EAST
CHINA
SEA

Naze Amami-ōshima
Setouchi Kikai
Tokara Islands Amami
Tokuno
Tokunoshima

Okinoerabu

Ryukyu Yoron
(Nansei-Shotō) Hedo-misaki
Okinawa Is. Iheya
Io Yonaha-dake
Motobu 498 m
Nago Okinawa
Ginowan Gushikawa
Kumé Naha Urasoe
Itoman Kyan-zaki
Keelung
Senkaku-Shotō OKINAWA

Kitadaitō
Minamidaitō

PACIFIC
OCEAN

Okidaitō

Sakishima Hirara
Islands Tamara Miyako
Yonaguni Ishigaki Miyako Is.
Iriomote Ishigaki
Yaeyama Is.

5

30°

6

28°

7

26°

8

24°

9

© HAMMOND WORLD ATLAS CORPORATION CD-1035-A·A·A   © HAMMOND W.A.C. CC-1116-A·A·A

E 138° F G 124° H 126° J 128° K 130° L

Scale 1:3,000,000 Lambert Conformal Conic Projection

MI   25   50   75   100
KM 25 50 75 100 125 150

0   60 Mi
0   60 Km

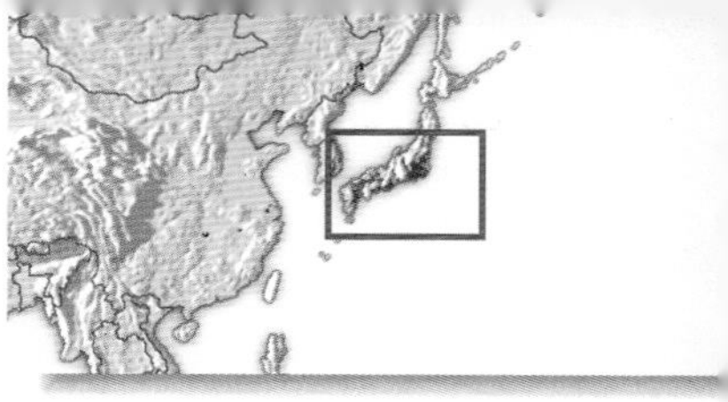

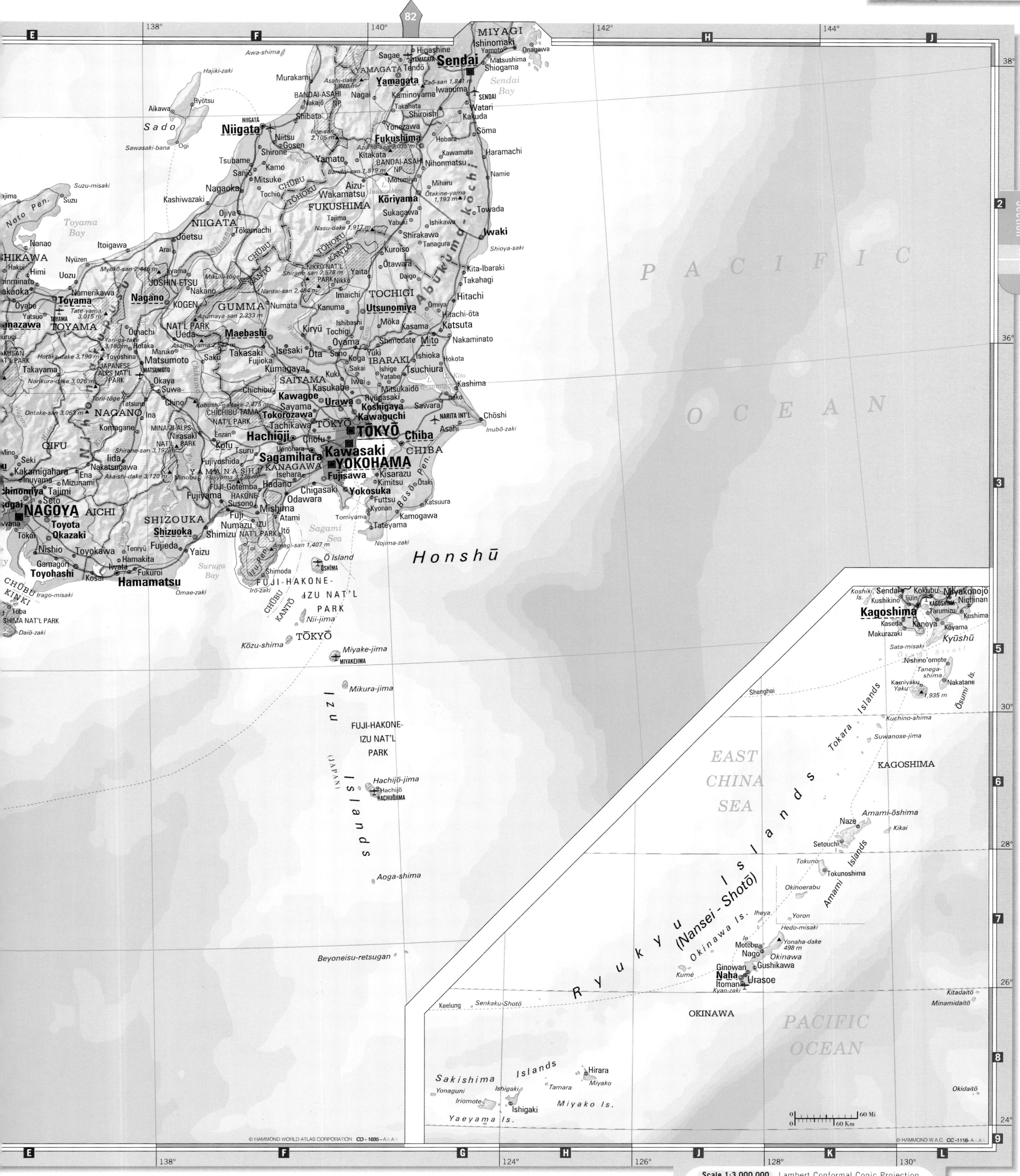

Southeastern China was once the most backward part of the country. Growth has accelerated in recent years, particularly in Guangzhou (Canton) - for many years the only city in China where foreign trade was possible - and Shenzhen, which benefits from its proximity to Hong Kong (a special administration of the People's Republic of China since 1997) and is now an autonomous economic district.

Taiwan, the island refuge of the Nationalist Chinese government since 1949, has developed into a major industrial power.

Population

■ Over 2,000,000	◉ 500,000 - 999,999	◉ 100,000 - 249,999	○ 10,000 - 29,999
■ 1,000,000 - 1,999,999	◉ 250,000 - 499,999	○ 30,000 - 99,999	○ Under 10,000

Major provinces/regions: SHAANXI, HENAN, ANHUI, JIANGSU, HUBEI, HUNAN, JIANGXI, ZHEJIANG, FUJIAN, GUANGDONG, GUANGXI ZHUANGZU AUTONOMOUS REGION, HAINAN, TAIWAN

Major cities: NANJING, SHANGHAI, WUHAN, Hefei, Hangzhou, Ningbo, Nanchang, Changsha, Fuzhou, T'AIPEI, GUANGZHOU, Nanning, Kaohsiung, Kowloon, Victoria, Macau, Haikou

Seas and waters: EAST CHINA SEA, SOUTH CHINA SEA, Gulf of Tonkin, Taiwan Strait, Bashi Channel, Pearl R. Est.

Other features: Three Gorges Dam (U.C.), Hainan Dao, Leizhou Peninsula, Paracel Islands (Sovereignty disputed), Dongsha I. (Pratas I.) Pratas Reef (CHINA), Tropic of Cancer, PHILIPPINES, Luzon

Hong Kong inset: HONG KONG, Shenzhen, Sheung Shui–Fanling, Yuen Long, Tai Po, Sha Tin, Tuen Mun, Tsuen Wan, Tin Shui Wai, New Kowloon, Kowloon, Victoria, Lantau Island, Lantau Peak 934 m, GUANGDONG, SOUTH CHINA SEA

Scale 1:6,000,000   Lambert Conformal Conic Projection

MI 50 100 150 200
KM 50 100 150 200 250 300

© HAMMOND WORLD ATLAS CORPORATION

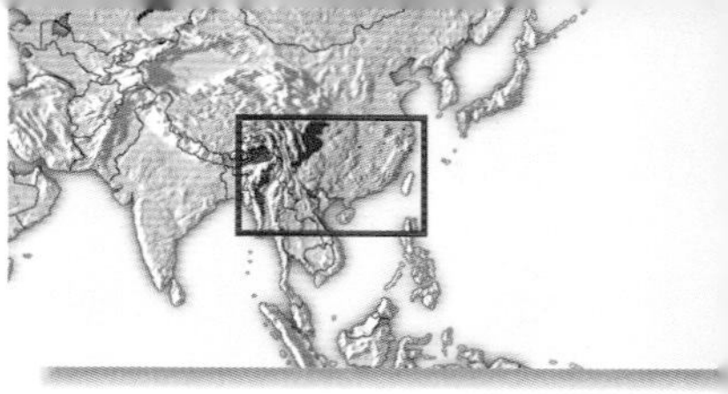

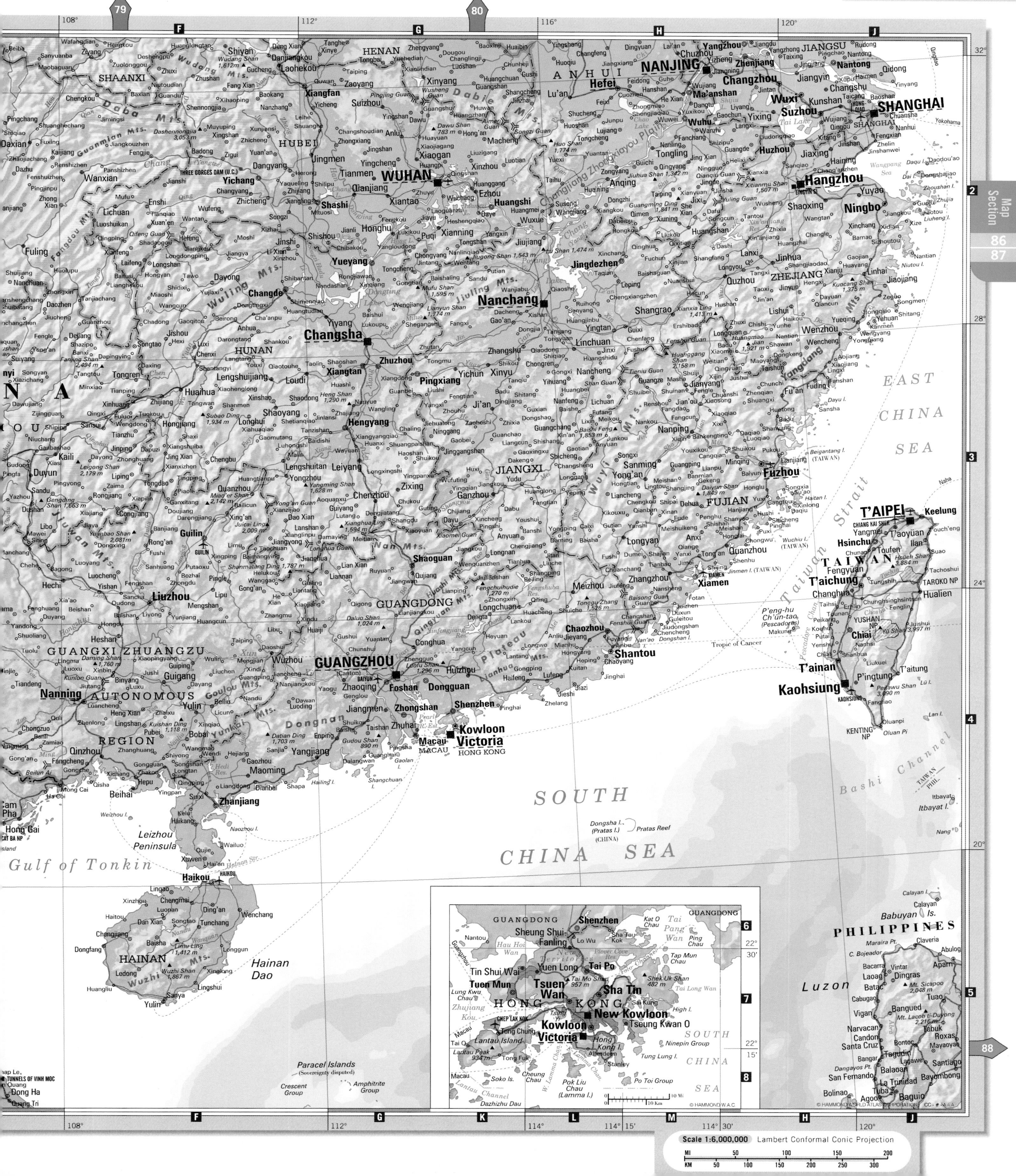

Philippines

Only ten percent of the 7,000 islands that comprise the Philippines are inhabited. The region was originally settled primarily by Malays. A Spanish dominion from 1565 until 1898, the islands became a bastion of Catholicism in Southeast Asia. The 48 years of U.S. rule that followed also left an indelible imprint on the island nation.

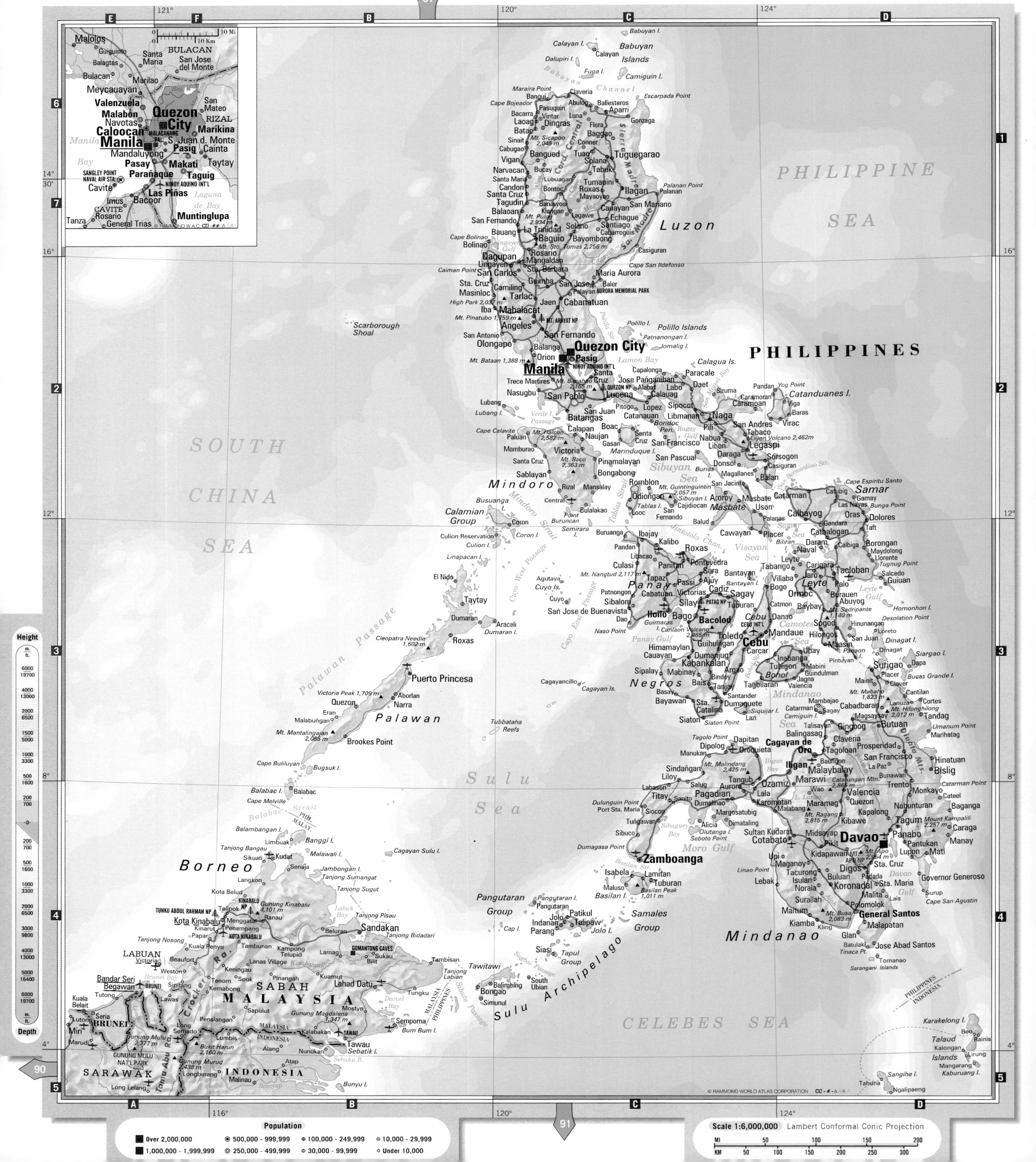

Luzon

PHILIPPINES

PHILIPPINE SEA

SOUTH CHINA SEA

Quezon City
Manila

Mindoro

Palawan

Puerto Princesa

Panay
Iloilo
Bacolod

Negros
Cebu
Leyte
Samar

Bohol

Sulu Sea

Mindanao

Cagayan de Oro

Zamboanga
Davao

General Santos

Borneo

SABAH
MALAYSIA

BRUNEI
Bandar Seri Begawan

Kota Kinabalu

Sulu Archipelago

CELEBES SEA

INDONESIA
SARAWAK

Inset (metro Manila)
BULACAN
Valenzuela
Malabon
Caloocan
Quezon City
Manila
Pasay
Parañaque
Las Piñas
Makati
Taguig
Muntinlupa
Manila Bay
Laguna de Bay
RIZAL
Marikina
Pasig

Height / Depth scale (metres / feet)
Height	m.	ft.
	6000	19700
	4000	13000
	2000	6500
	1500	5000
	1000	3300
	500	1600
	200	700
	0	0
	200	700
	500	1600
	1000	3300
	2000	6500
	3000	9800
	4000	13000
	5000	16400
	6000	19700
Depth	m.	ft.

Population
■ Over 2,000,000	◉ 500,000 - 999,999	● 100,000 - 249,999	○ 10,000 - 29,999
■ 1,000,000 - 1,999,999	◉ 250,000 - 499,999	◦ 30,000 - 99,999	· Under 10,000

Scale 1:6,000,000 Lambert Conformal Conic Projection

| MI | 50 | 100 | 150 | 200 |
| KM | 50 | 100 | 200 | 300 |

© HAMMOND WORLD ATLAS CORPORATION

Malaysia and Indonesia are the easternmost outposts of Islam. Indonesia is now the most populous Islamic nation in the world. Only the island of Bali has a predominantly Hindu population. A major producer of wood, tin, and rubber positioned along important international shipping routes, Malaysia has developed one of the most productive economies in the region.

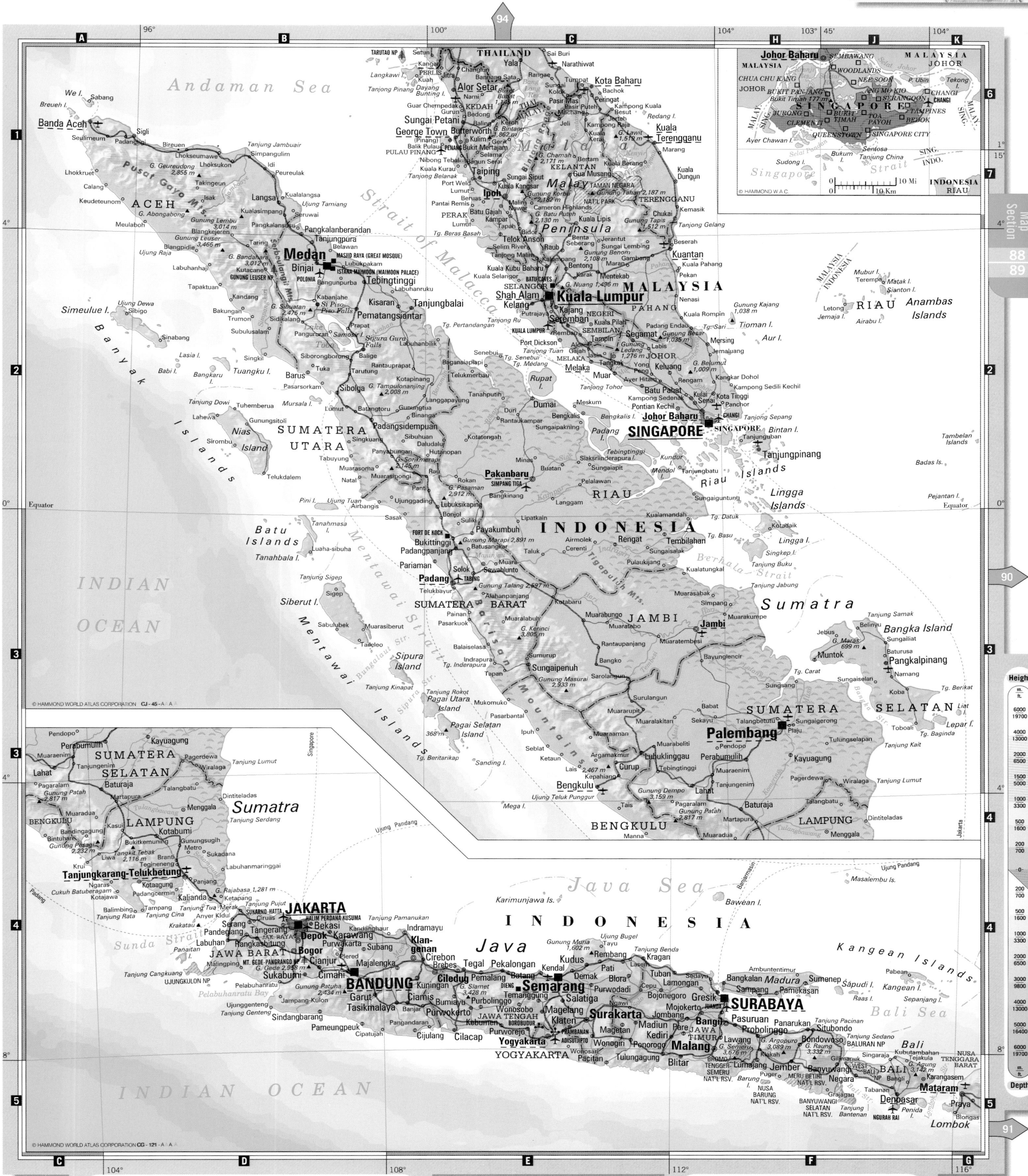

Population

- ■ Over 2,000,000
- ■ 1,000,000 - 1,999,999
- ● 500,000 - 999,999
- ● 250,000 - 499,999
- ◉ 100,000 - 249,999
- ⊙ 30,000 - 99,999
- ○ 10,000 - 29,999
- ○ Under 10,000

Scale 1:6,000,000   Lambert Conformal Conic Projection

© HAMMOND WORLD ATLAS CORPORATION

Indonesia covers most of the Malaysian archipelago. The Greater Sunda Islands of Sumatra and Java are characterized by "spines" of steep folded mountain ranges that tower above broad floodplains.

The hot, tropical climate, with annual rainfall of about 6,000 mm, supports flourishing rain-forest growth that once covered over 60 percent of the land surface. Today, the rain forest has given way to secondary forest,

alang-alang grass, and ferns - the result of extensive logging and burning. The best known of the roughly 200 active volcanoes in the region is Krakatoa, which last erupted in 1883, causing thousands of deaths.

Scale 1:9,000,000   Lambert Conformal Conic Projection

© HAMMOND WORLD ATLAS CORPORATION   CD - 1047 - A A A

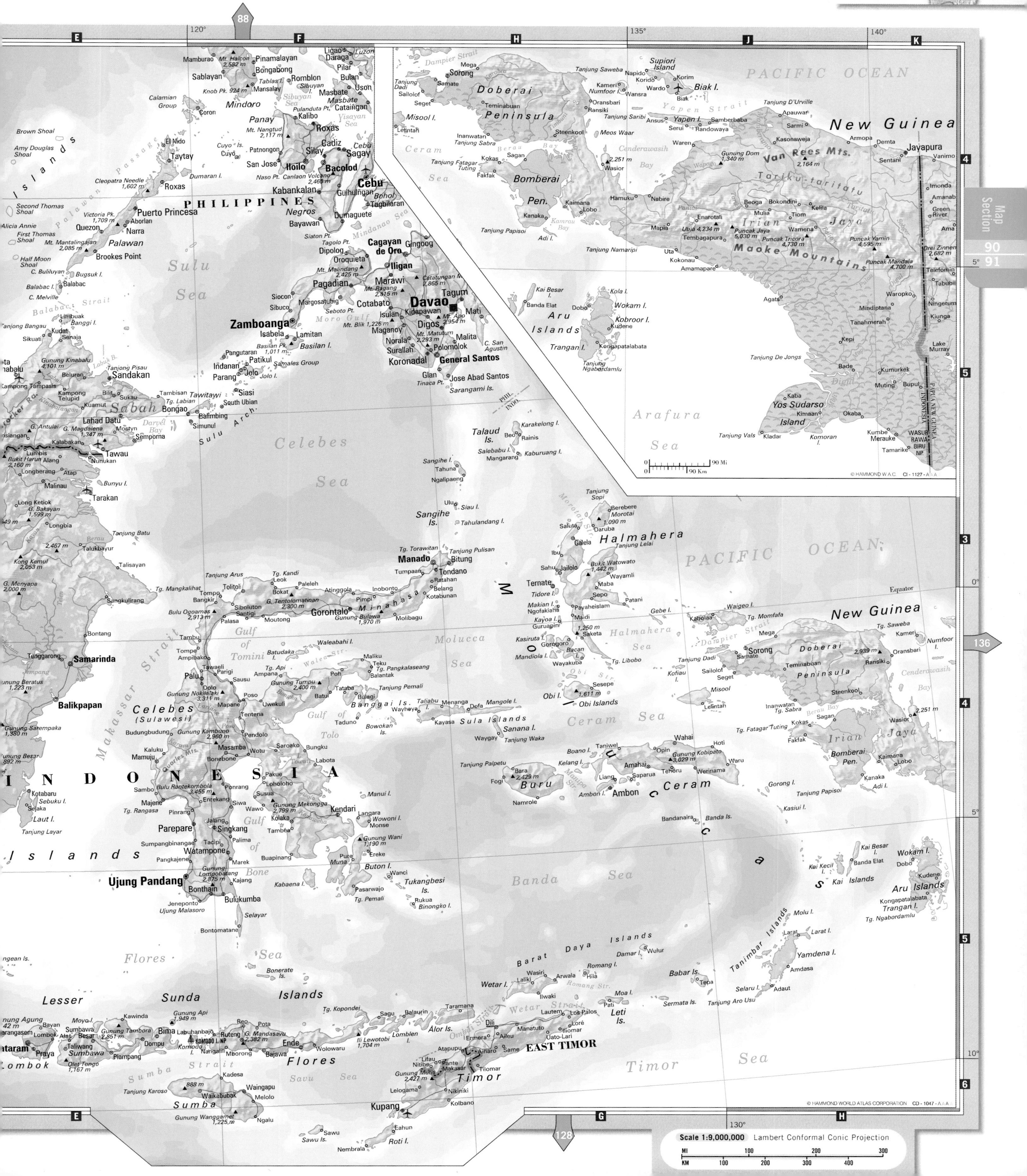

The map shows the Asian monsoon region, through which expansive air currents move in an alternating, semi-annual rhythm. ("Monsoon" comes from the Arabic "mausim," or "season [suitable for sea voyages].") The southwest monsoon that comes from the sea brings life-giving rains to this densely populated region during the summer. A rainless monsoon season causes severe famine, while extreme precipitation often results in flood disasters. Roughly half of the world's population lives in monsoon regions. Most working people in this part of the world are employed in subsistence agriculture, primarily in rice cultivation.

CHINA

SICHUAN · GUIZHOU · HUNAN · YUNNAN · GUANGXI ZHUANGZU AUT. REG. · GUANGDONG

Changsha · Xiangtan · Zhuzhou · Liling · Pingxiang · Hengyang · Chenzhou · Shaoguan · Guilin · Liuzhou · **Nanning** · **Guangzhou** (Canton) · Foshan · Dongguan · Zhongshan · Shenzhen · Macau · **Victoria** HONG KONG

Guiyang · Anshun · Lupanshui · Panzhihua · **Kunming** · Dali · Gejiu · Wenshan

ARUNACHAL PRADESH · ASSAM · NAGALAND · MANIPUR · MIZORAM · TRIPURA · MEGHALAYA

Chittagong · Sylhet · Aizawl · Imphal · Kohima · Dibrugarh

KACHIN · SAGAING · SHAN · CHIN · MANDALAY · MAGWAY · KAYAH · KAYIN · MON · BAGO · AYEYARWADY · RAKHINE · TANINTHARYI

MYANMAR (BURMA)

Mandalay · Myitkyinā · Lashio · Monywa · Meiktila · Myingyan · Taunggyi · Magway · Prome · Bago (Pegu) · **YANGON** (Rangoon) · Pathein (Bassein) · Mawlamyine (Moulmein) · Dawei (Tavoy) · Mergui (Myeik) · Sittwe (Akyab)

LAOS · Louangphrabang · **Vientiane** (Viangchan) · Savannakhet · Pakxe

THAILAND

Chiang Mai · Chiang Rai · Lampang · Phitsanulok · Khon Kaen · Nakhon Ratchasima · Ubon Ratchathani · Nakhon Sawan · **BANGKOK** (Krung Thep) · Chon Buri · Rayong · Hua Hin · Chumphon · Surat Thani · Nakhon Si Thammarat · Songkhla · Hat Yai · Phuket · Krabi · Trang · Yala · Pattani · Narathiwat

VIETNAM

Hanoi (Ha Noi) · Haiphong (Hai Phong) · Nam Dinh · Thanh Hoa · Vinh · Hue · Da Nang · Hoi An · Qui Nhon · Nha Trang · Da Lat · Cam Ranh · Phan Rang · Phan Thiet · **Bien Hoa** · **HO CHI MINH CITY** (Saigon) · Vung Tau · My Tho · Can Tho · Rach Gia · Ca Mau · Bac Lieu · Soc Trang

CAMBODIA

Phnom Penh (Phnum Pénh) · Battambang · Siemreap · Kampong Cham · Takev · Kampot · Sihanoukville

MALAYSIA

Kota Baharu · Kuala Terengganu · Alor Setar · Sungai Petani · Gunung Lawit 1,519 m

Bodies of water and features:

Gulf of Tonkin · SOUTH CHINA SEA · Hainan Dao · HAINAN · Haikou · Sanya · Paracel Islands (Sovereignty disputed)

Gulf of Thailand · Bight of Bangkok · Phu Quoc I. · Con Son · Mouths of the Mekong

Andaman Sea · Strait of Malacca · Mergui Archipelago · Isthmus of Kra · Mouths of the Ayeyarwady

ANDAMAN AND NICOBAR ISLANDS (INDIA)

North Andaman I. · Middle Andaman I. · S. Andaman I. · Port Blair · Little Andaman Island · Car Nicobar · Katchall I. · Little Nicobar I. · Great Nicobar I. · Nicobar Islands

Great Coco I. (MYANMAR) · Cheduba I. · Ramree I. · C. Negrais

Peaks:

Namjagbarwa Feng 7,772 m · Kangto 7,047 m · Hkakabo Razi 5,881 m · Gongga Shan 7,556 m · Mt. Victoria 3,200 m · Phu Luong 2,984 m · Phou Bia 2,818 m · Fan Si Pan 3,143 m · Doi Inthanon 2,600 m · Ngoc Linh 2,600 m · Ch'u Yang Sin 2,442 m · B'nom M'hai 1,642 m · Phnum Aôral 1,771 m · Bukit Bubat 1,145 m · Gunung Lawit 1,519 m

Indochina · Malay Peninsula · Shan Plateau · Khorat Plateau · Phanom Dongrak Mts. · Kravanh Mts. · Bilauktaung · Arakan Yoma · Tenasserim · Dawna Range

Scale 1:9,000,000   Lambert Conformal Conic Projection

MI   100   200   300
KM   100   200   300

© HAMMOND WORLD ATLAS CORPORATION

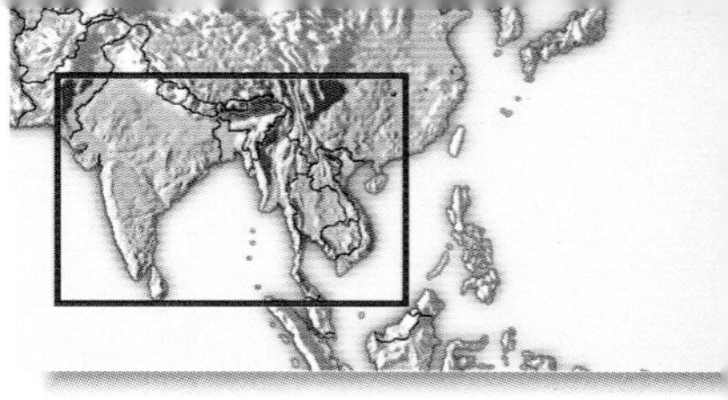

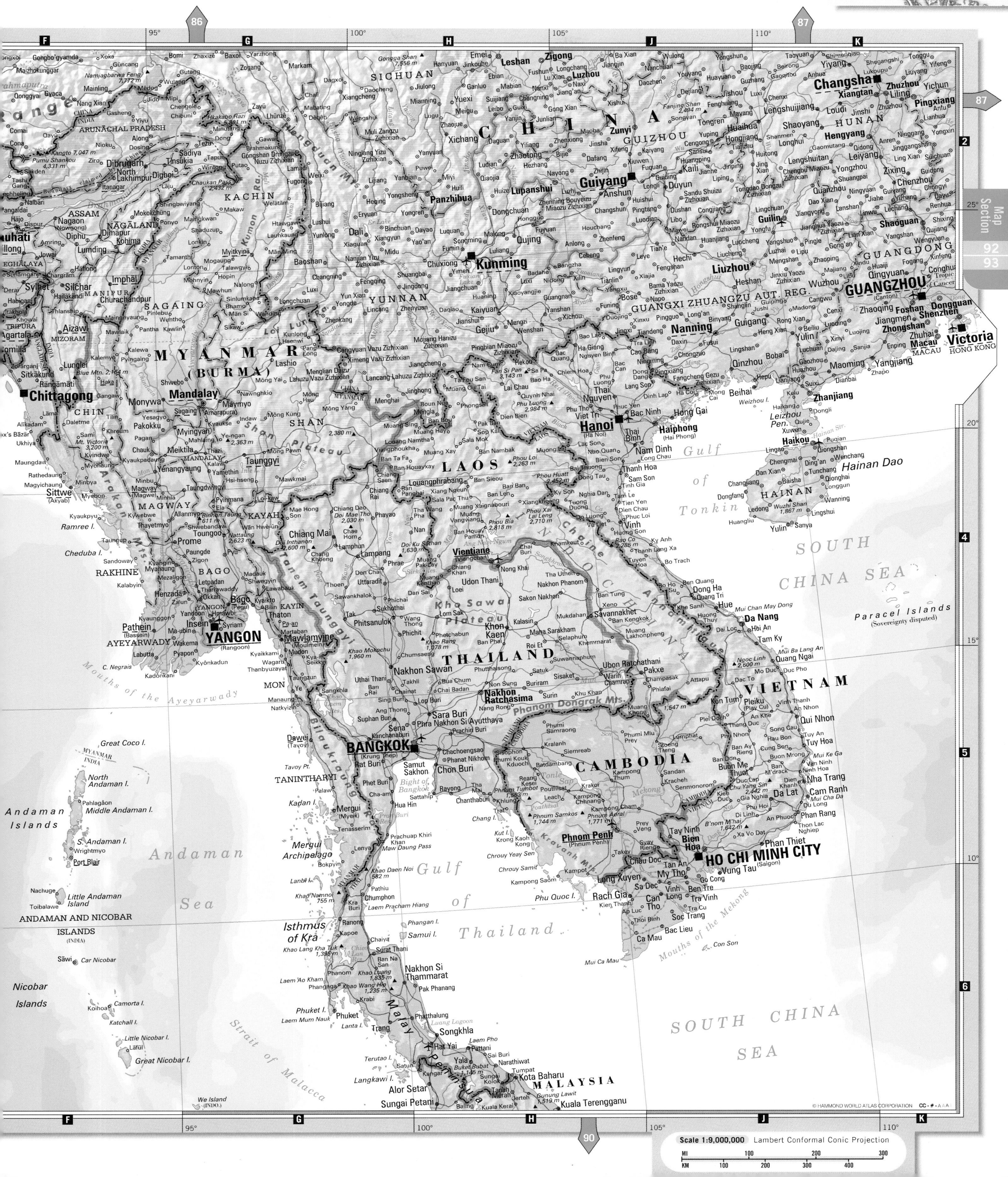

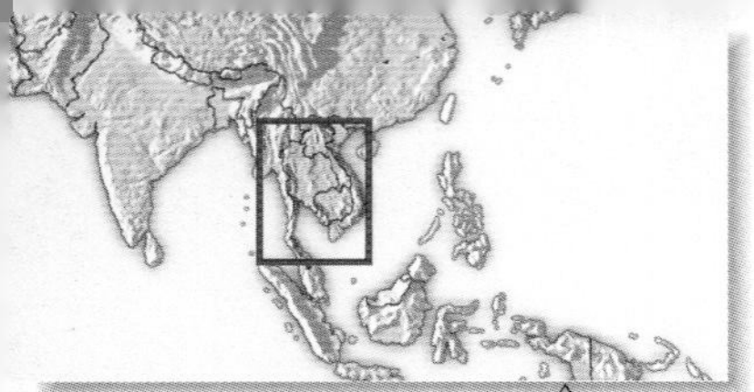

Indochina

The backbone of eastern India is formed by several mountain ranges to the southeast of the Himalayas that drain into the fertile plains of the Mekong, Salween, Irawadi, and Menam Chao Phraya rivers.

The region has a monsoon climate, with rainfall decreasing toward the interior. Vegetation ranges from dense tropical rain forest to moist and arid savannahs farther inland.

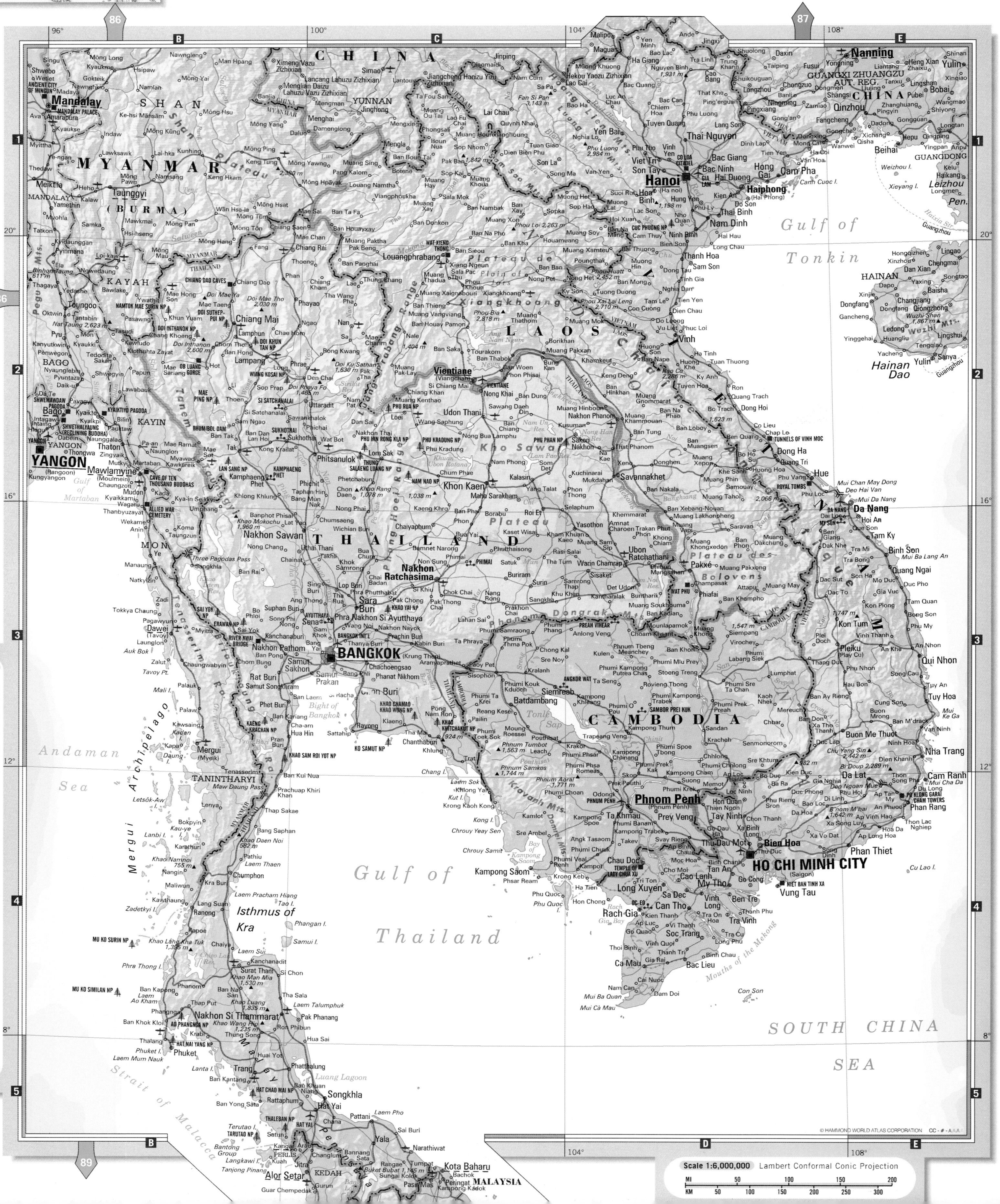

Scale 1:6,000,000   Lambert Conformal Conic Projection

© HAMMOND WORLD ATLAS CORPORATION   CC - # - A A A

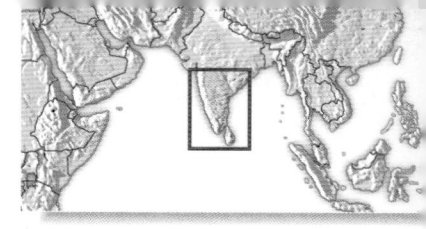

Virtually no other country is as dependent upon monsoons as India. Monsoon rains are essential to the rice harvests that feed nearly a billion people. The southwest monsoon provides 90 percent of the region's precipitation (Cherrapunji holds the record, with 10,870 mm of rainfall per year). It also replenishes groundwater reserves that supply millions of people in India's metropolitan centers with drinking water.

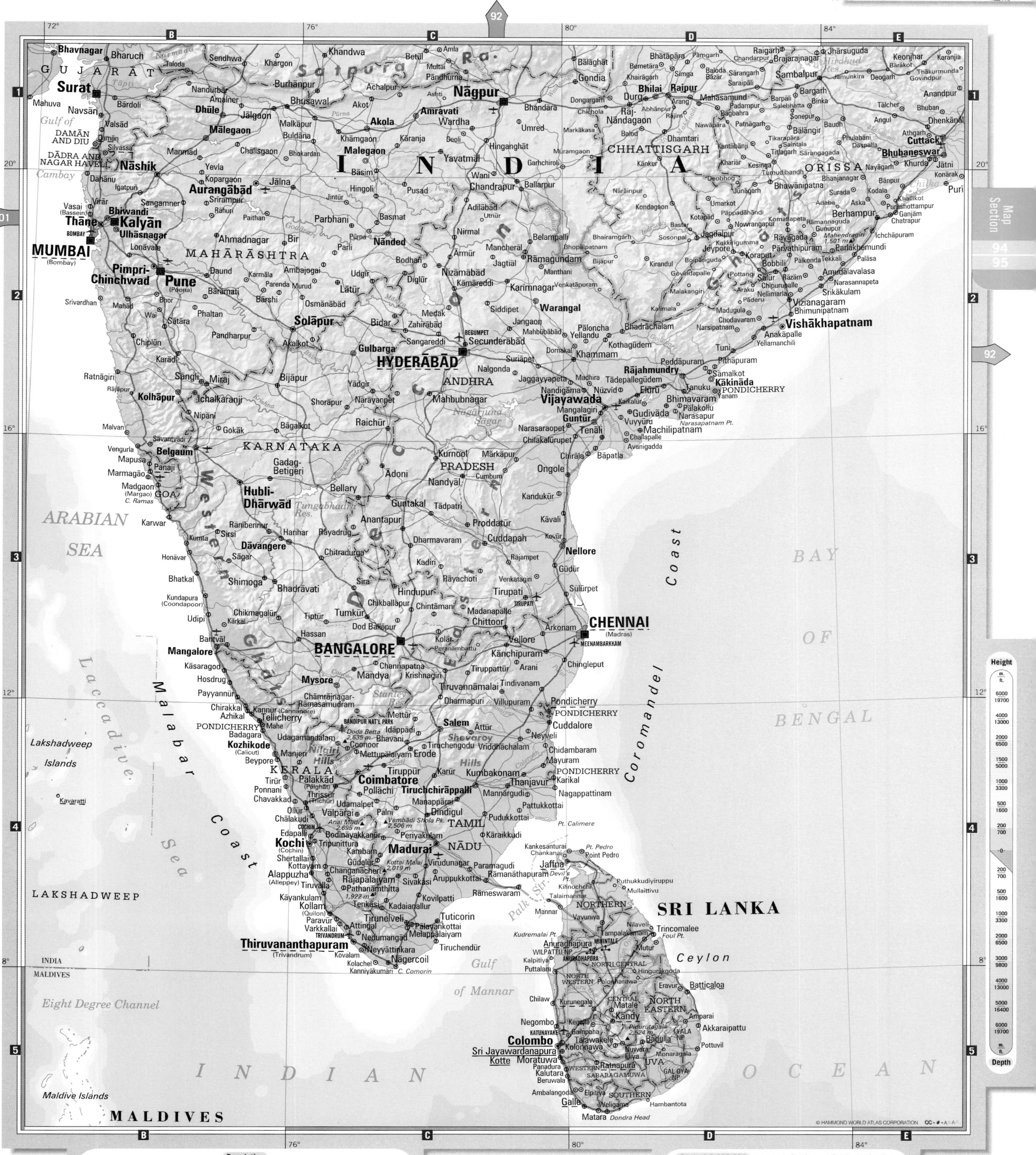

Population	
■ Over 2,000,000	◉ 500,000 - 999,999 · 100,000 - 249,999 ◦ 10,000 - 29,999
◼ 1,000,000 - 1,999,999	◉ 250,000 - 499,999 ◦ 30,000 - 99,999 · Under 10,000

Scale 1:6,000,000   Lambert Conformal Conic Projection

Height
m. / ft.
6000 / 19700
4000 / 13000
2000 / 6500
1500 / 5000
1000 / 3300
500 / 1600
200 / 700
0
200 / 700
500 / 1600
1000 / 3300
2000 / 6500
3000 / 9800
4000 / 13000
5000 / 16400
6000 / 19700
m. / ft.
Depth

© HAMMOND WORLD ATLAS CORPORATION

Over 2,700 km long, the Ganges flows from headwaters 4,000 meters above sea level in the Himalayas. It joins the Brahmaputra in Bengal, forming a fertile delta comprising some 56,000 square km.

Used intensively for irrigation, the river now carries much less water than in the past, especially during the dry months. The water shortage in the region is exacerbated by progressive deforestation in the

Himalayas, which has reduced the capacity to store monsoon rainwater. Water now runs off rapidly during the rainy season, causing frequent catastrophic flooding and taking thousands of lives.

101

Population

■ Over 2,000,000	● 500,000 - 999,999
■ 1,000,000 - 1,999,999	● 250,000 - 499,999
● 100,000 - 249,999	● 10,000 - 29,999
● 30,000 - 99,999	○ Under 10,000

Scale 1:3,000,000   Lambert Conformal Conic Projection

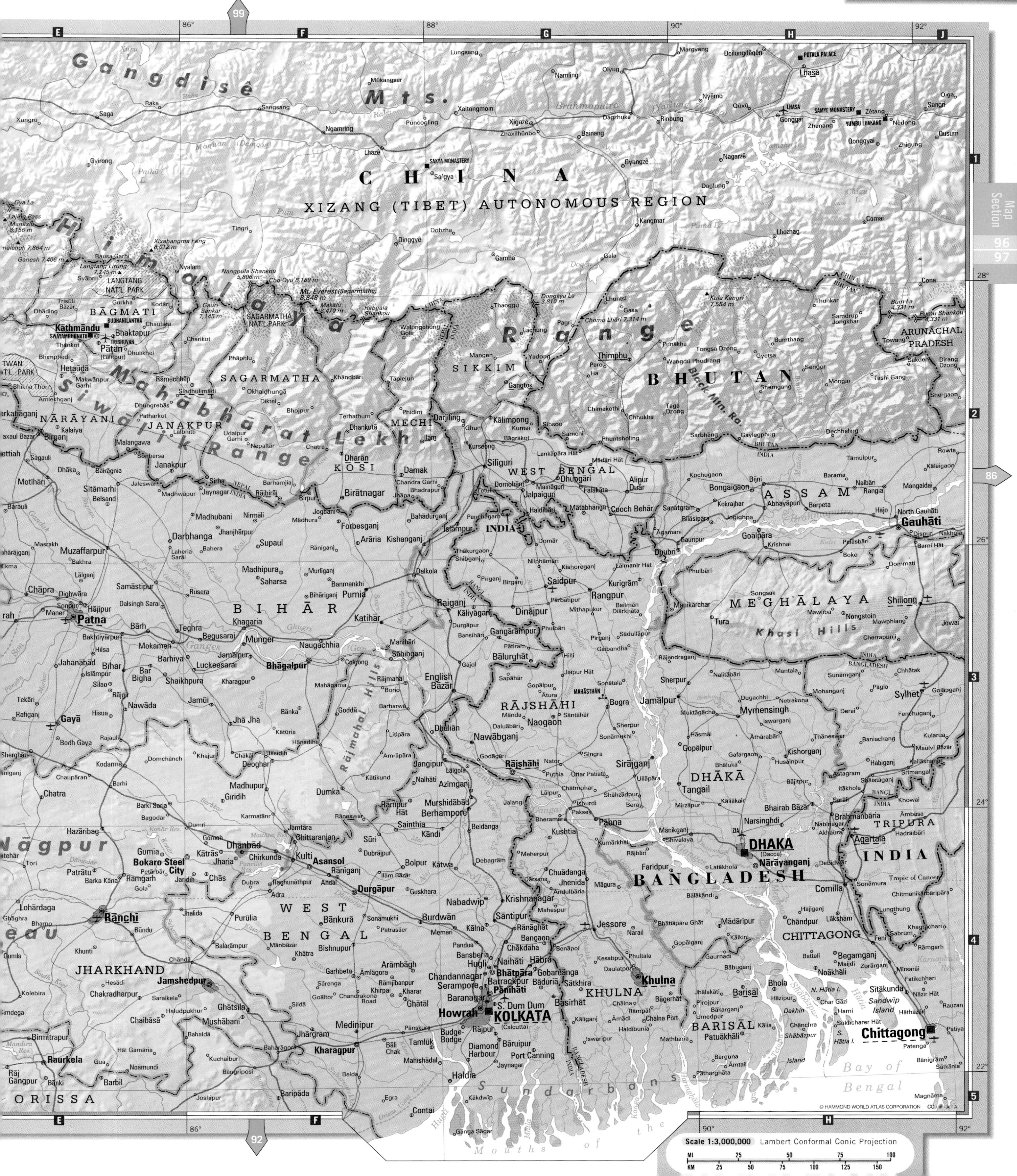

© HAMMOND WORLD ATLAS CORPORATION

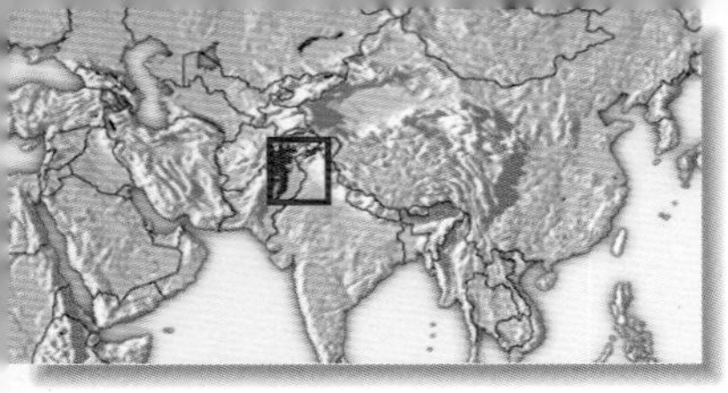

Punjab Plain

This plain, irrigated by a fan of eastern tributaries of the Indus, forms the granary of India and Pakistan. For thousands of years, a vast network of canals and dams has covered the plain. Thanks to this irrigation system, the Punjab is fertile agricultural land and the most productive wheat and cotton-growing region in western India. Most of the area is in Pakistan, which gained independence from India in 1947.

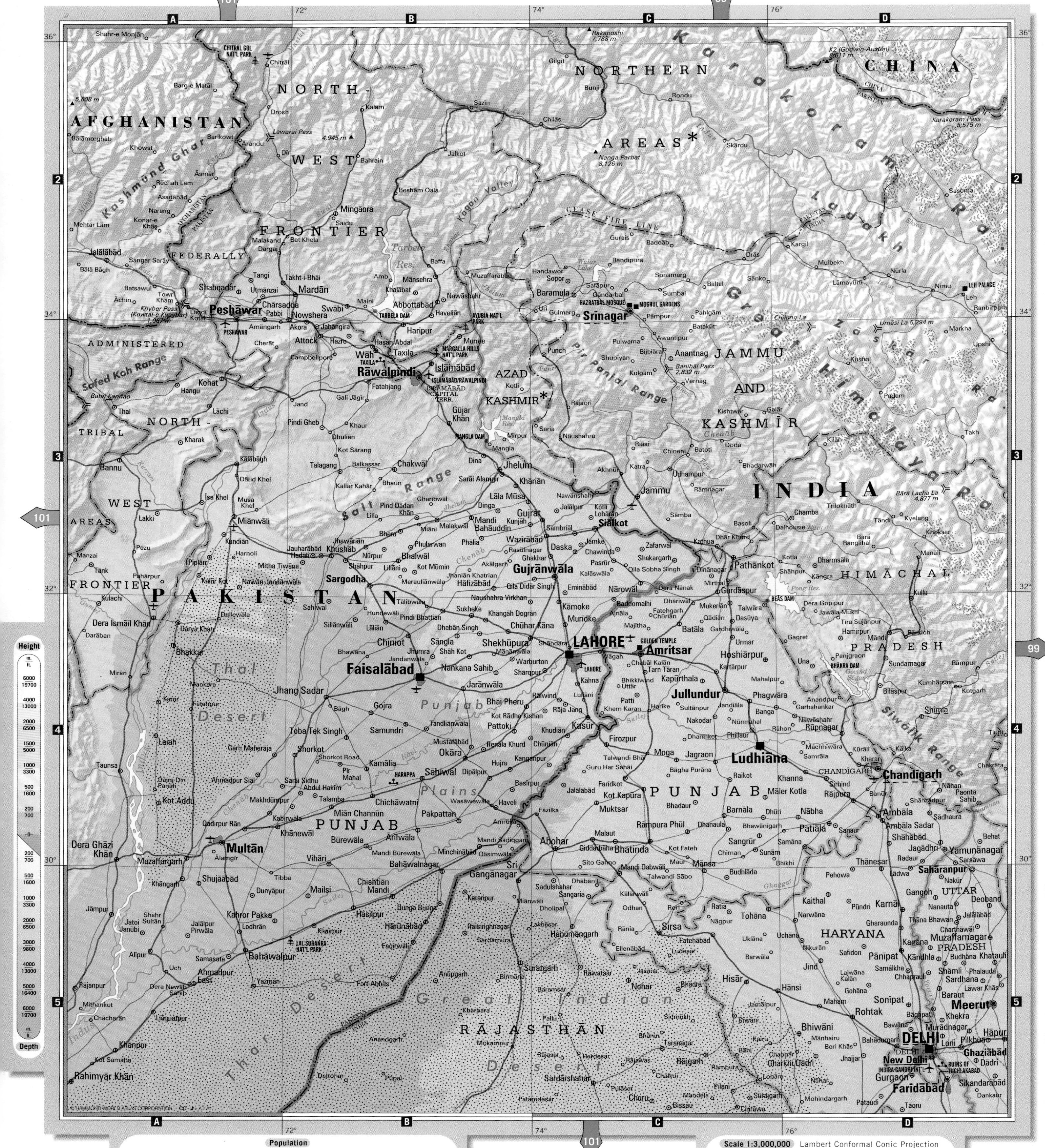

Population

Symbol	Range
■	Over 2,000,000
●	500,000 – 999,999
⊙	100,000 – 249,999
○	10,000 – 29,999
■	1,000,000 – 1,999,999
⊙	250,000 – 499,999
⊙	30,000 – 99,999
○	Under 10,000

Scale 1:3,000,000   Lambert Conformal Conic Projection

MI   25   50   75   100
KM   25   50   75   100

K nown as the "Roof of the World," central Asia is dominated by the vast mountain systems of the Hindu Kush, the Pamir, the Tian Shan and the Himalayas, extending over 2,400 km from Pakistan to Bhutan. Here, the Indian plate thrusts beneath the Asian continent, pushing Tibet upward. The young mountain range is still rising at a rate of about one centimeter per year.

Central Asia

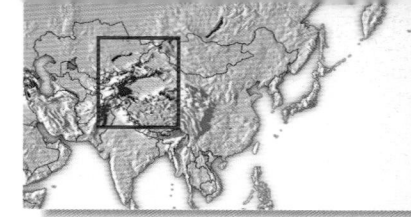

Map Section
98
99
74
78
101
86
92
97

Population

■ Over 2,000,000 ● 500,000 - 999,999 ● 100,000 - 249,999 ○ 10,000 - 29,999
■ 1,000,000 - 1,999,999 ● 250,000 - 499,999 ○ 30,000 - 99,999 ○ Under 10,000

*AZAD KASHMIR AND THE NORTHERN AREAS ARE ADMINISTERED BY PAKISTAN BUT DO NOT HAVE PROVINCIAL STATUS.

Scale 1:9,000,000   Lambert Conformal Conic Projection

Height

6000 / 19700
4000 / 13000
1500 / 6500
1000 / 3300
500 / 1600
200 / 700
0

Depth

200 / 700
1000 / 3300
2000 / 6500
3000 / 9800
4000 / 13000
5000 / 16400
6000 / 19700

Saudi Arabia occupies most of the Arabian Peninsula. Arid plains and deserts, such as the Rub' al Khali, cover ninety-nine percent of the country. Oases are found only at the foot of plateaus and near intermittently dry riverbeds known as wadis. A rift structure thrusts the southwestern edge of the peninsula abruptly upward from the Red Sea, forming an imposing escarpment, and then descends steeply toward the northeast. Water is extremely scarce. Sparse winter rains fall only in the north and in the Oman mountain region. The coastal areas, however, are very humid.

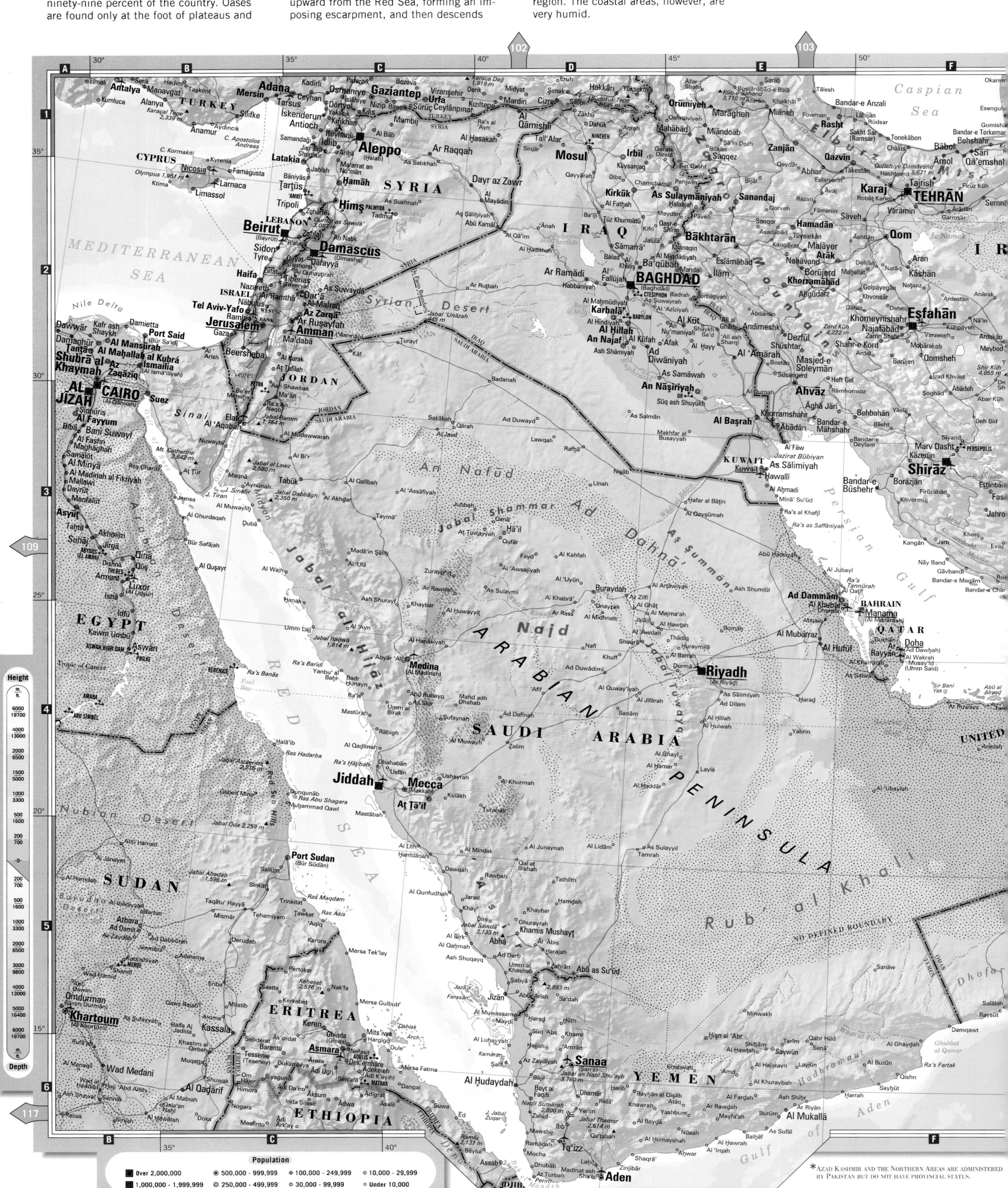

Population

Symbol	Range
■	Over 2,000,000
■	1,000,000 - 1,999,999
◉	500,000 - 999,999
◉	250,000 - 499,999
◎	100,000 - 249,999
◉	30,000 - 99,999
○	10,000 - 29,999
○	Under 10,000

Height
m. / ft.
6000 / 19700
4000 / 13000
2000 / 6500
1500 / 5000
1000 / 3300
500 / 1600
200 / 700
- 0 -
200 / 700
500 / 1600
1000 / 3300
2000 / 6500
3000 / 9800
4000 / 13000
5000 / 16400
6000 / 19700
Depth

TURKMENISTAN

UZBEKISTAN

TAJIKISTAN

TAJIKISTAN

CHINA

Ashgabat

Mashhad

AFGHANISTAN

Kabul

Herāt

Kandahār

Quetta

PAKISTAN

BALOCHISTĀN

Zāhedān

Kermān

OMAN

Muscat

ARAB EMIRATES

Bandar-e ʿAbbās

Gulf of Oman

Makran Coast

KARACHI

Hyderābād

SINDH

PUNJAB

Peshāwar

Islāmābād

Rāwalpindi

Srīnagar

KASHMIR

JAMMU AND KASHMIR

Faisalābad

LAHORE

Amritsar

Ludhiāna

Chandīgarh

Multan

DELHI

New Delhi

Meerut

Faridābād

Bīkaner

Jaipur

RĀJASTHĀN

INDIA

Jodhpur

Ajmer

Great Indian Desert (Thar)

AHMADĀBĀD

Gāndhīnagar

GUJARĀT

Vadodara (Baroda)

Rājkot

Jāmnagar

Bhāvnagar

Surat

Kathiāwar

Porbandar

Nāsik

MUMBAI (Bombay)

Thāna

Kalyān

Pimpri-Chinchwad

Pune (Poona)

MAHĀRĀSHTRA

Aurangābād

Sholāpur

Kolhāpur

Belgaum

KARNATAKA

Hubli-Dhārwār

Indore

MADHYA PRADESH

Ujjain

ARABIAN SEA

Gulf of Maşirah

Kuria Muria Is.

Tropic of Cancer

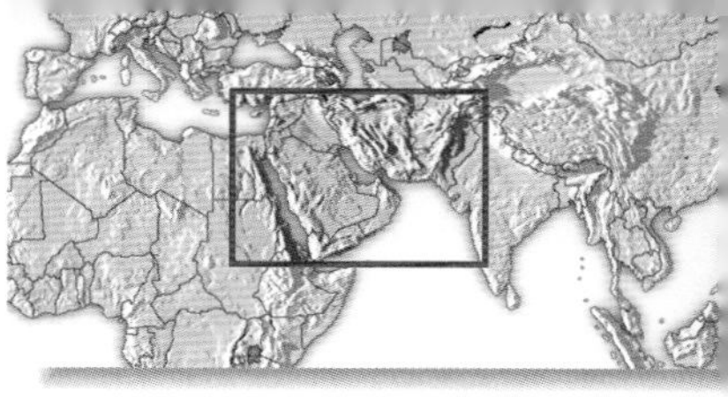

Both the Tigris and the Euphrates, the longest river in the Middle East (3,380 km), flow from sources in eastern Turkey and are of crucial geopolitical importance. Turkey uses the rivers for irrigation and hydroelectric power and can control the flow of water into neighboring countries with such large facilities as the Ataturk Dam. These two life-giving arteries of the Middle East converge to form the Shatt al Arab, which flows into the Persian Gulf. The world's largest oil reserves are located here in a total of 15 oil fields with known reserves of 1.5 billion tons each.

Northern Middle East

Map Section
102
103
71
101
RUSSIA
GEORGIA
T'bilisi
ARMENIA
Yerevan
AZERBAIJAN
Baku
Sumqayıt
CASPIAN SEA
TURKMENISTAN
Ashgabat
Türkmenbashy
Garabogazköl Aylagy
IRAN
TEHRĀN
Tabrīz
Ardabīl
Rasht
Qazvīn
Karaj
Qom
Kāshān
Eşfahān
Shīrāz
Yazd
Kermān
Mashhad
Hamadān
Bakhtarān
Sanandaj
Orūmīyeh
Ahvāz
Ābādān
Bandar-e Būshehr
Bandar-e 'Abbās
Sabzevār
Semnān
Dasht-e Kavīr
Dasht-e Lūt
KHORĀSĀN
EŞFAHĀN
FĀRS
KERMĀN
HORMOZGĀN
MĀZANDARĀN
GĪLĀN
ZANJĀN
SEMNĀN
Elburz Mountains
Zagros Mountains
BAGHDAD
Mosul
Irbil
Kirkūk
As Sulaymānīyah
Karbalā'
An Najaf
Al Başrah
An Nāşirīyah
Al 'Amārah
KUWAIT
Kuwait
Persian Gulf
SAUDI ARABIA
Ad Dammām
BAHRAIN
Manama
QATAR
Strait of Hormuz
OMAN
Musandam Pen.
Black Sea
Sea of Marmara
İSTANBUL
Scale 1:6,000,000 Lambert Conformal Conic Projection
MI 0 50 100 150 200
KM 0 50 100 150 200 250 300
© HAMMOND W.A.C.

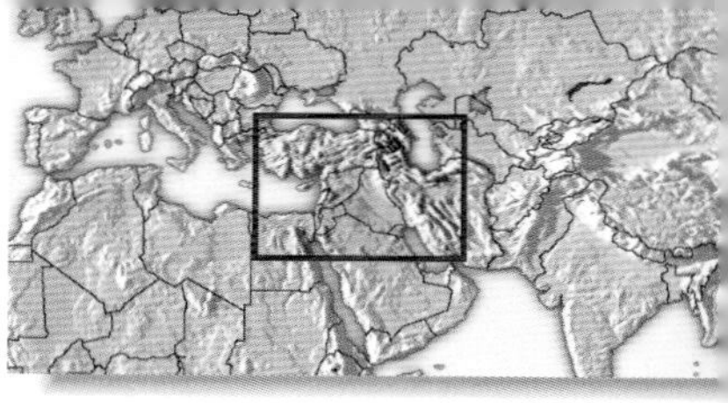

Eastern Mediterranean Region

The countries of the eastern Mediterranean region are faced with a constant shortage of water. Competition for water has always been a leading cause of conflicts in this part of the world. Citrus fruits are the most important products harvested in heavily irrigated strips of land along the coasts. Winter rains fall to the west of the uplands, while the higher plateaus and mountains offer only dry, sparse grazing.

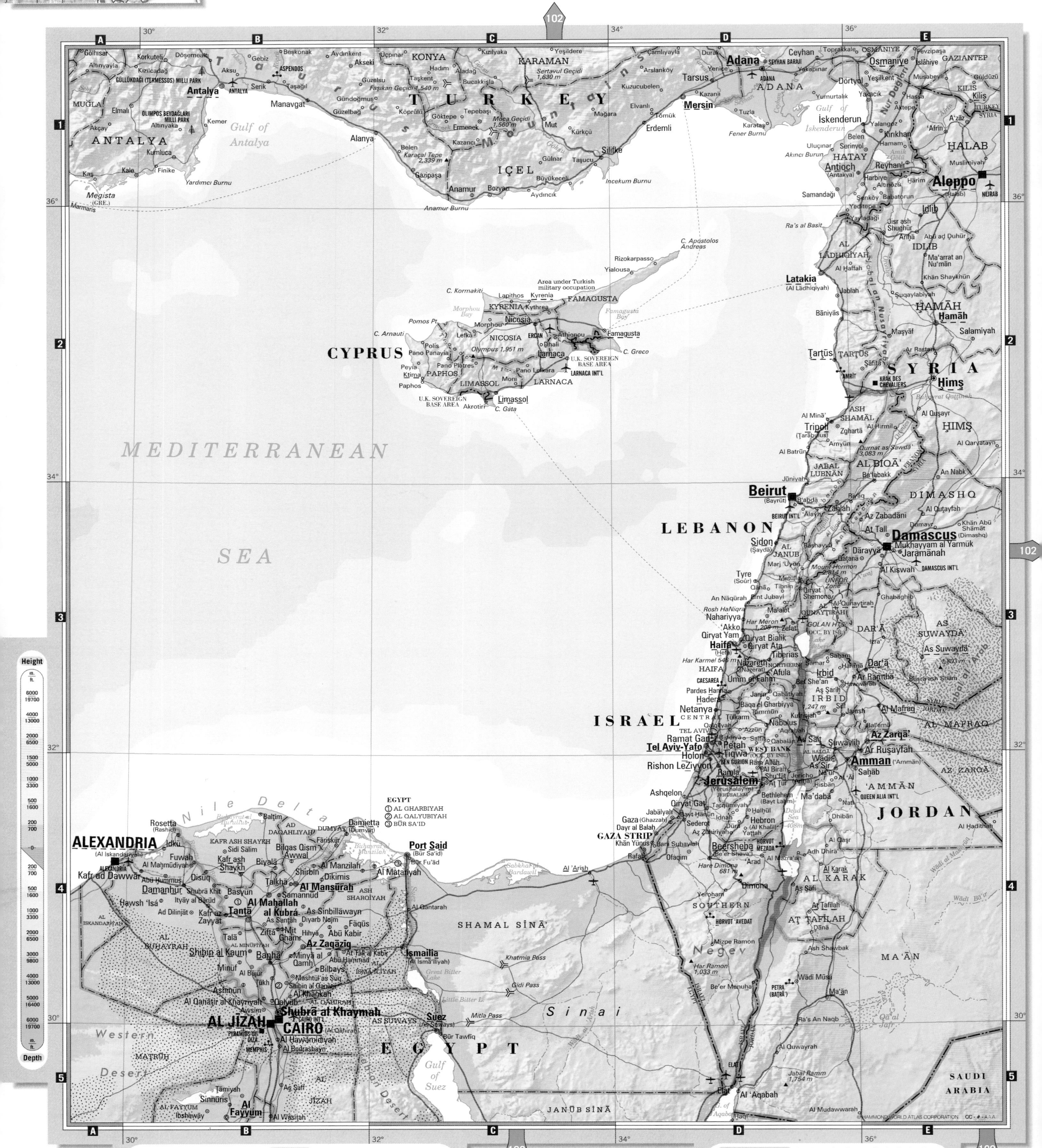

Population	
■ Over 2,000,000	◉ 500,000 - 999,999	⊙ 100,000 - 249,999	◦ 10,000 - 29,999
▣ 1,000,000 - 1,999,999	● 250,000 - 499,999	◌ 30,000 - 99,999	∘ Under 10,000

Scale 1:3,000,000 Lambert Conformal Conic Projection

Two tectonic plates glide past each other in the Jordan River Valley. The eastern plate drifts northward along the western plate, creating a dislocation of about 105 km in the south. The fault line shifts westward in several places. There, the Earth's crust expands and sinks, a process that has given birth to the Lake of Genezareth, and the Dead Sea, whose surface lies at 408 m below sea level - the lowest point on the surface of the Earth.

Jordan River Valley

MEDITERRANEAN SEA

Beirut (Bayrūt)
Damascus (Dimashq)
Jerusalem (Yerushalayim)
Tel Aviv-Yafo
Haifa (Hefa)
Amman ('Ammān)
Az Zarqā'

LEBANON
SYRIA
ISRAEL
JORDAN
WEST BANK*
GAZA STRIP*

GOLAN HEIGHTS (OCCUPIED BY ISRAEL)

Lake Tiberias (Yam Kinneret)

Dead Sea (-408m)

*WEST BANK AND GAZA STRIP ARE ISRAELI OCCUPIED WITH CURRENT STATUS SUBJECT TO THE ISRAELI-PALESTINIAN INTERIM AGREEMENT - PERMANENT STATUS TO BE DETERMINED

Scale 1:1,000,000   Lambert Conformal Conic Projection

MI   10   20   30
KM   10 20 30 40 50

Height	
m. / ft.	
6000 / 19700	
4000 / 13000	
2000 / 6500	
1500 / 5000	
1000 / 3300	
500 / 1600	
200 / 700	
0	
200 / 700	
500 / 1600	
1000 / 3300	
2000 / 6500	
3000 / 9800	
4000 / 13000	
5000 / 16400	
6000 / 19700	
Depth	

© HAMMOND WORLD ATLAS CORPORATION

Taken from the southeast, this photograph shows the Nile Delta as a dark area in the foreground. It extends from Cairo at the apex of the delta to the Suez Canal (lower left), which connects the Mediterranean Sea and the Red Sea (upper middle). Desert-like areas are seen southwest of the delta and on the Sinai Peninsula. The Gulf of Aqaba protrudes like a spur from the Red Sea into the Arabian Peninsula. This depression extends into the Jordan River Valley and the Dead Sea toward the north and widens beneath the Red Sea in the south.

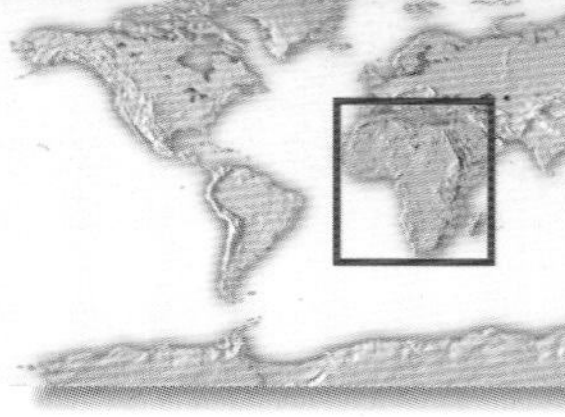

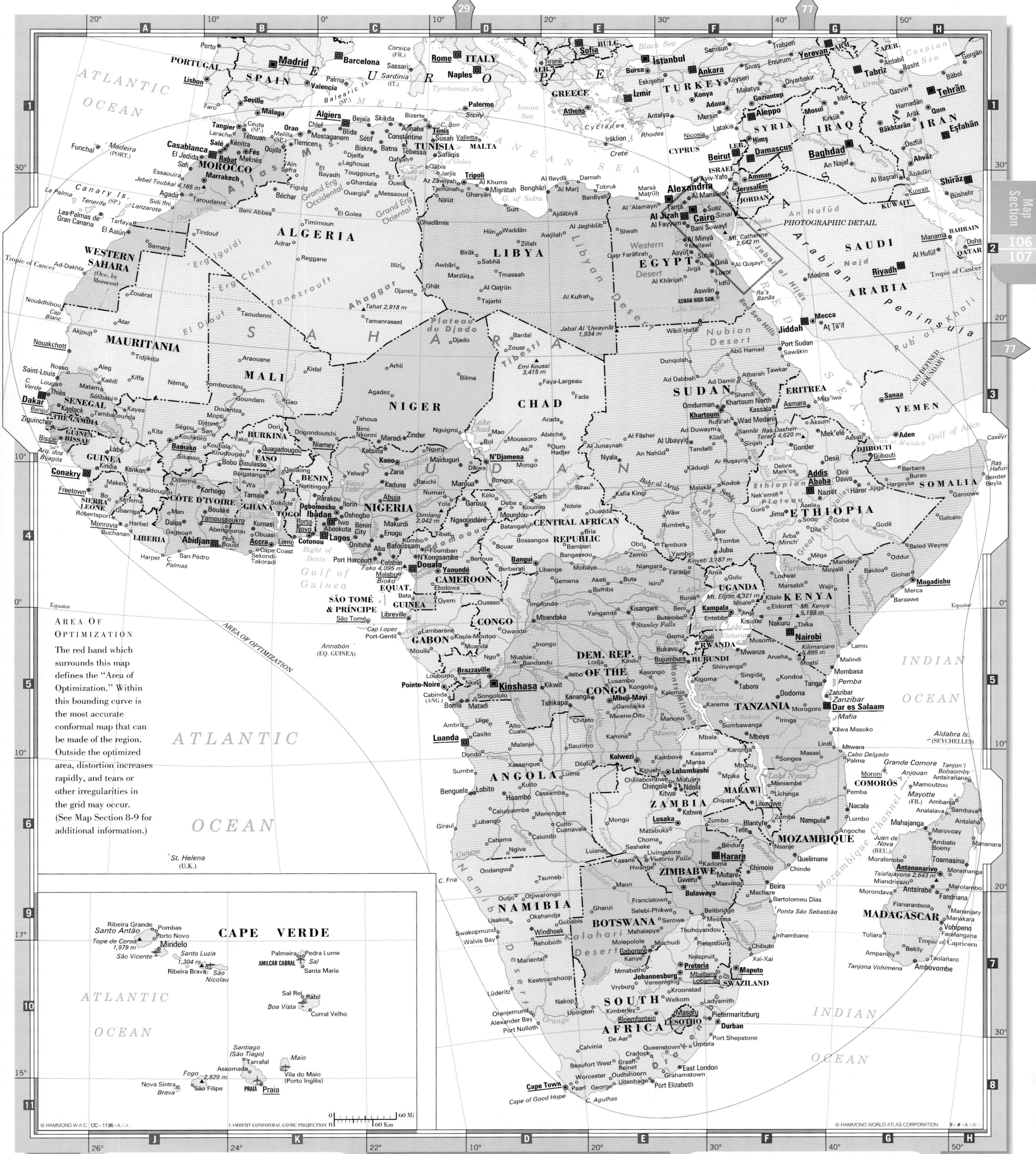

The Tibesti range covers 100,000 square km of territory between northern Chad and the Libyan border. The range is a volcanic mountain system that rises steeply from the Sahara. This volcanic activity deep within the African continent is the result of a thermal anomaly in the earth's interior known as a hot spot. Hot springs and mud pools offer striking evidence of persisting geological activity in the region. Due to its height, the Tibesti range draws more rain than the surrounding areas and is known as the "emerald isle" of the Sahara.

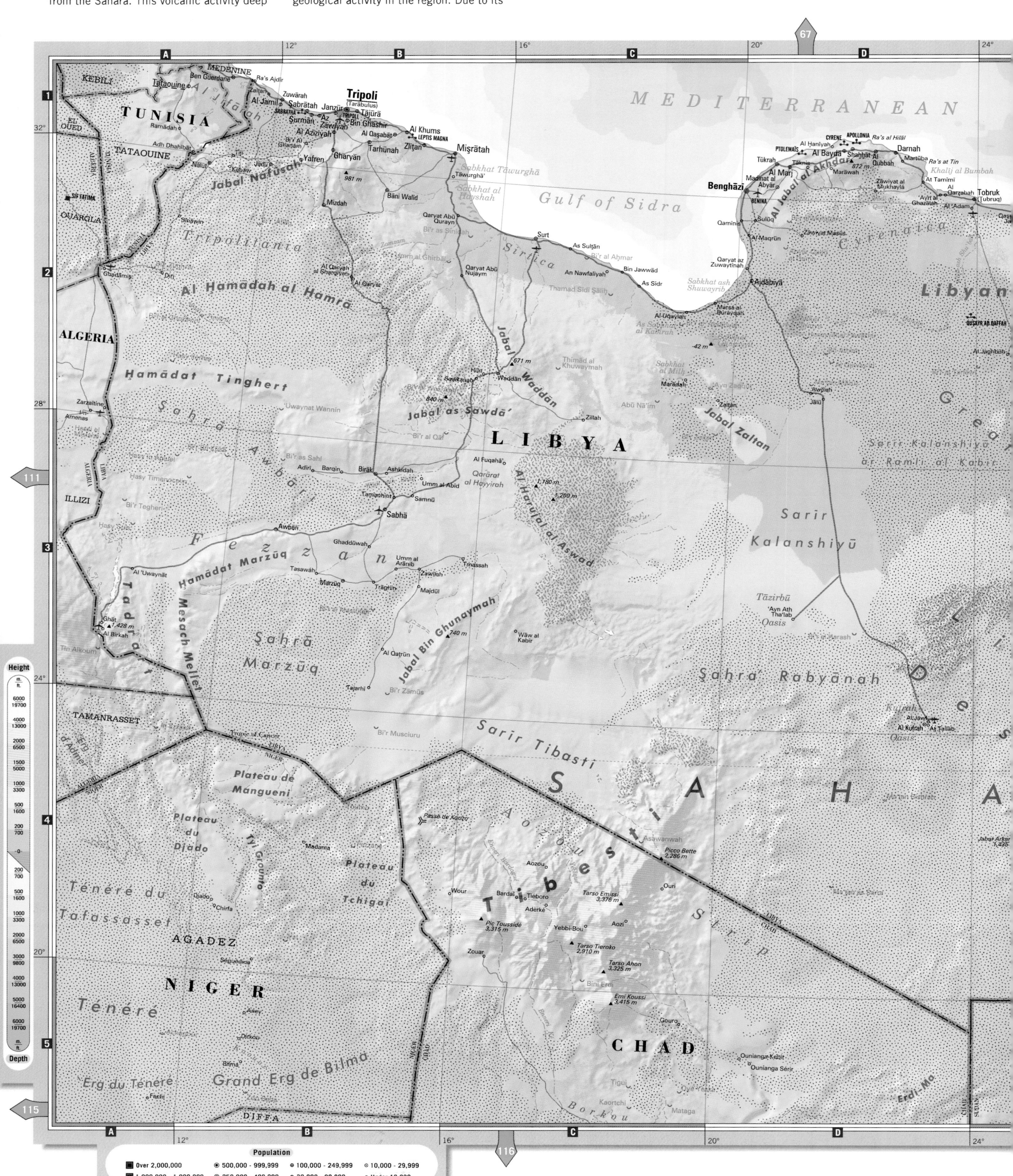

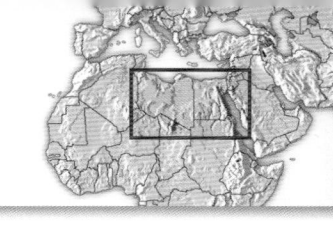

102
102
Map Section
108
109
100
117

Scale 1:6,000,000 Polyconic Projection

© HAMMOND WORLD ATLAS CORPORATION

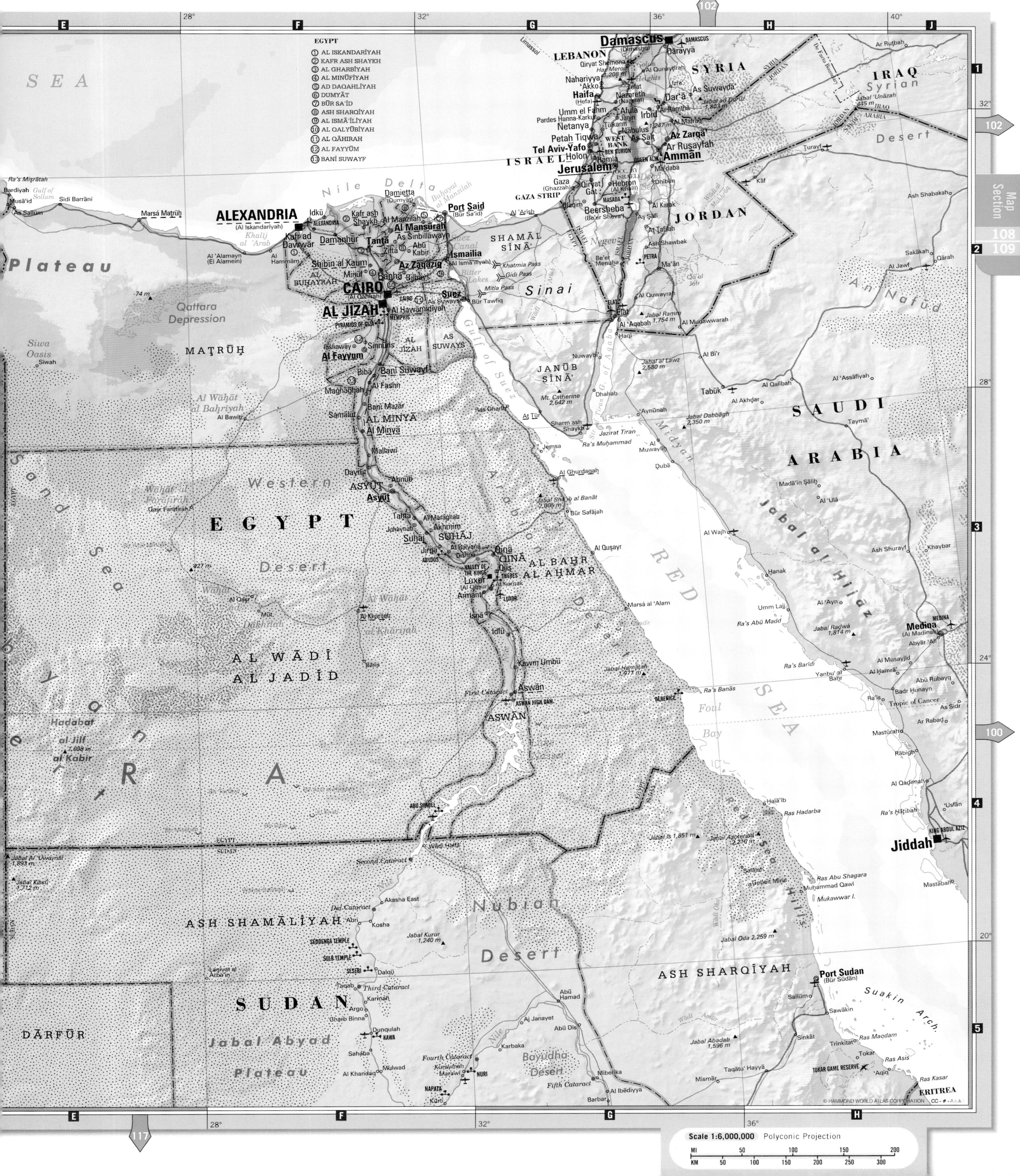

The Sahara, the world's largest desert, covers some 9.1 million square km. It is 4,670 km long and 1,760 km wide. Evidence found in the Tassili-n-Ajjer mountains in Algeria shows that the region was once covered by lush green vegetation. Prehistoric drawings feature images of elephants, buffalo, hippos, and crocodiles. The earliest of the more than 1,000 rock drawings are 8,000 years old. Fewer species are depicted as the drawings grow more recent. Thus the course of the Sahara's transformation into a desert can be traced from drawing to drawing.

MOROCCO is divided into 7 non-administrative regions shown here. Scale does not permit showing the boundaries and names of Morocco's provinces and prefectures.

Population

■ Over 2,000,000	◉ 500,000 - 999,999
■ 1,000,000 - 1,999,999	◉ 250,000 - 499,999
⦿ 100,000 - 249,999	○ 10,000 - 29,999
⦾ 30,000 - 99,999	○ Under 10,000

Height
m. / ft.
6000 / 19700
4000 / 13000
2000 / 6500
1500 / 5000
1000 / 3300
500 / 1600
200 / 700
-0-
200 / 700
500 / 1600
1000 / 3300
2000 / 6500
3000 / 9800
4000 / 13000
5000 / 16400
6000 / 19700
m. / ft.
Depth

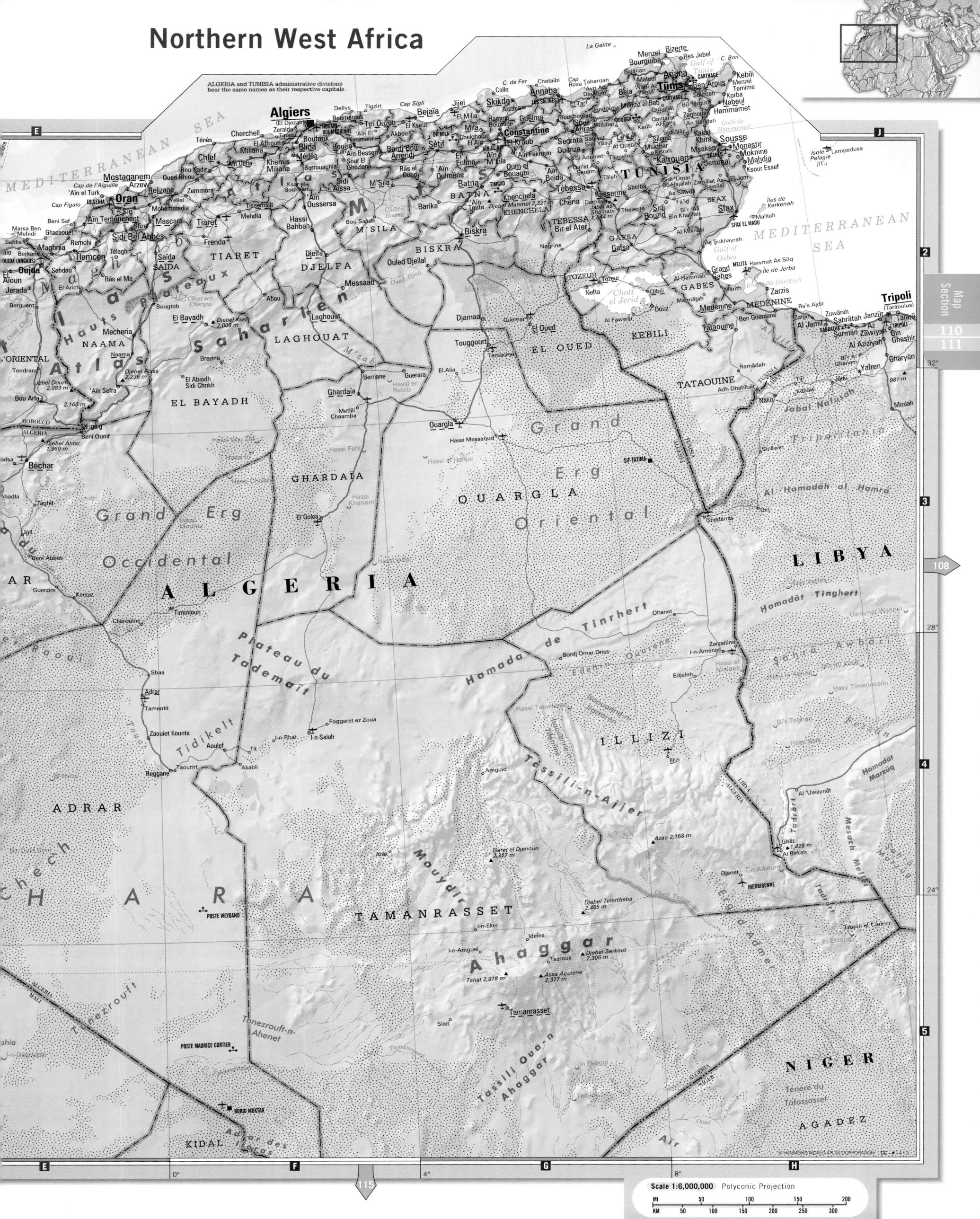

Northern West Africa

ALGERIA and TUNISIA administrative divisions
bear the same names as their respective capitals.

MEDITERRANEAN SEA

Algiers
(El Djezaïr)

La Galite

Menzel Bizerte
Bourguiba Res Jebel
C. Bon

Ariana **Tunis** Ben Arous
CARTHAGE
Kebili
Nabeul

TUNISIA

Sousse
Monastir
Moknine
Jemmal

Isole Lampedusa
Pelagie (IT.)

MEDITERRANEAN
SEA

Oran

Constantine

Annaba

Skikda

Jijel

Bejaïa

Sétif

Batna

Biskra

BISKRA

DJELFA

LAGHOUAT

Ghardaïa

GHARDAÏA

Chott
el Jerid

TOZEUR

GABES

MEDENINE

Tripoli
(Tarabulus)

KEBILI

TATAOUINE

EL OUED

Ouargla

QUARGLA

Grand
Erg
Oriental

LIBYA

A L G E R I A

Grand Erg
Occidental

Plateau du
Tademaït

Hamada de Tinrhert

Hamadát Tinghert

Hamada du
Tademaït

ILLIZI

Tidikelt

ADRAR

S A H A R A

TAMANRASSET

Ahaggar

Tahat 2,918 m
Assa Aguiene
2,377 m

N I G E R

AGADEZ

KIDAL

MOROCCO

Béchar

Scale 1:6,000,000 Polyconic Projection

MI   50   100   150   200

KM 50 100 150 200 250 300

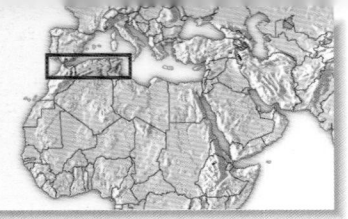

Northern Morocco, Algeria, Tunisia

The Atlas Mountains of northern Africa are a protective wall that shields northern Morocco, Algeria, and Tunisia against encroachment by the desert to the south. Moist air from the sea brings welcome rains. Many of the ports along the coast lie in the lee of capes formed by steeply sloping mountain ridges that jut sharply into the sea.

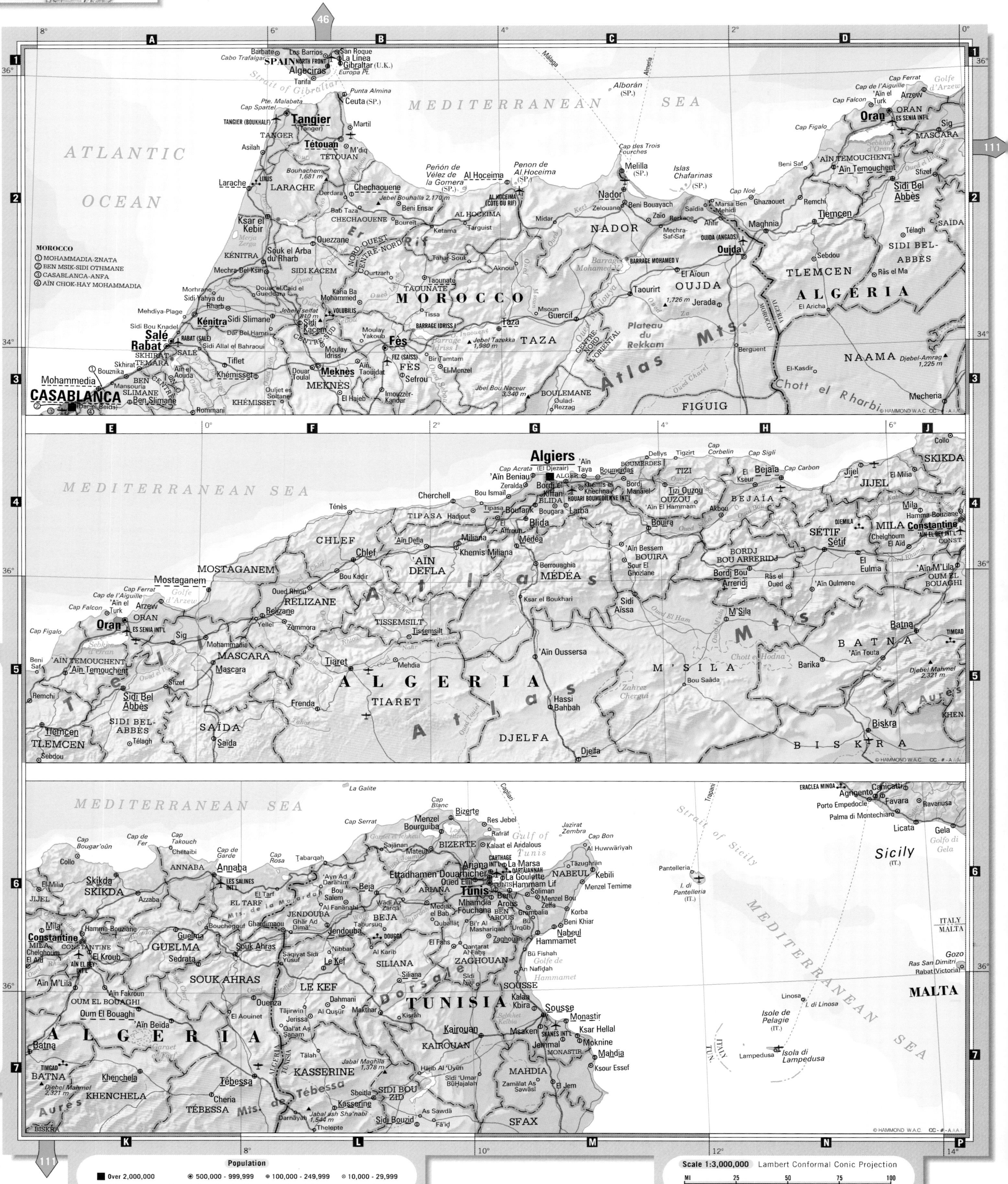

Height

m.	ft.
6000	19700
4000	13000
2000	6500
1500	5000
1000	3300
500	1600
200	700
	-0-

Depth

m.	ft.
200	700
500	1600
1000	3300
2000	6500
3000	9800
4000	13000
5000	16400
6000	19700

Population

■ Over 2,000,000
■ 1,000,000 - 1,999,999
⊛ 500,000 - 999,999
⊚ 250,000 - 499,999
⊙ 100,000 - 249,999
⊙ 30,000 - 99,999
○ 10,000 - 29,999
∘ Under 10,000

Scale 1:3,000,000 Lambert Conformal Conic Projection

MI 25 50 75 100
KM 25 50 75 100 125 150

© HAMMOND W.A.C.

Nile River Delta

Measuring 6,671 km from source to mouth, the Nile is the longest river on Earth. Alternating periods of flooding and low water have shaped the lives of people in the region for millennia.

A complex network of irrigation canals supplies the fertile Nile Delta with water. The Suez Canal in the northeast of the country serves as a vital link between the Mediterranean and Red seas.

Population

- ■ Over 2,000,000
- ■ 1,000,000 - 1,999,999
- ◉ 500,000 - 999,999
- ◉ 250,000 - 499,999
- ◉ 100,000 - 249,999
- ◉ 30,000 - 99,999
- ○ 10,000 - 29,999
- ○ Under 10,000

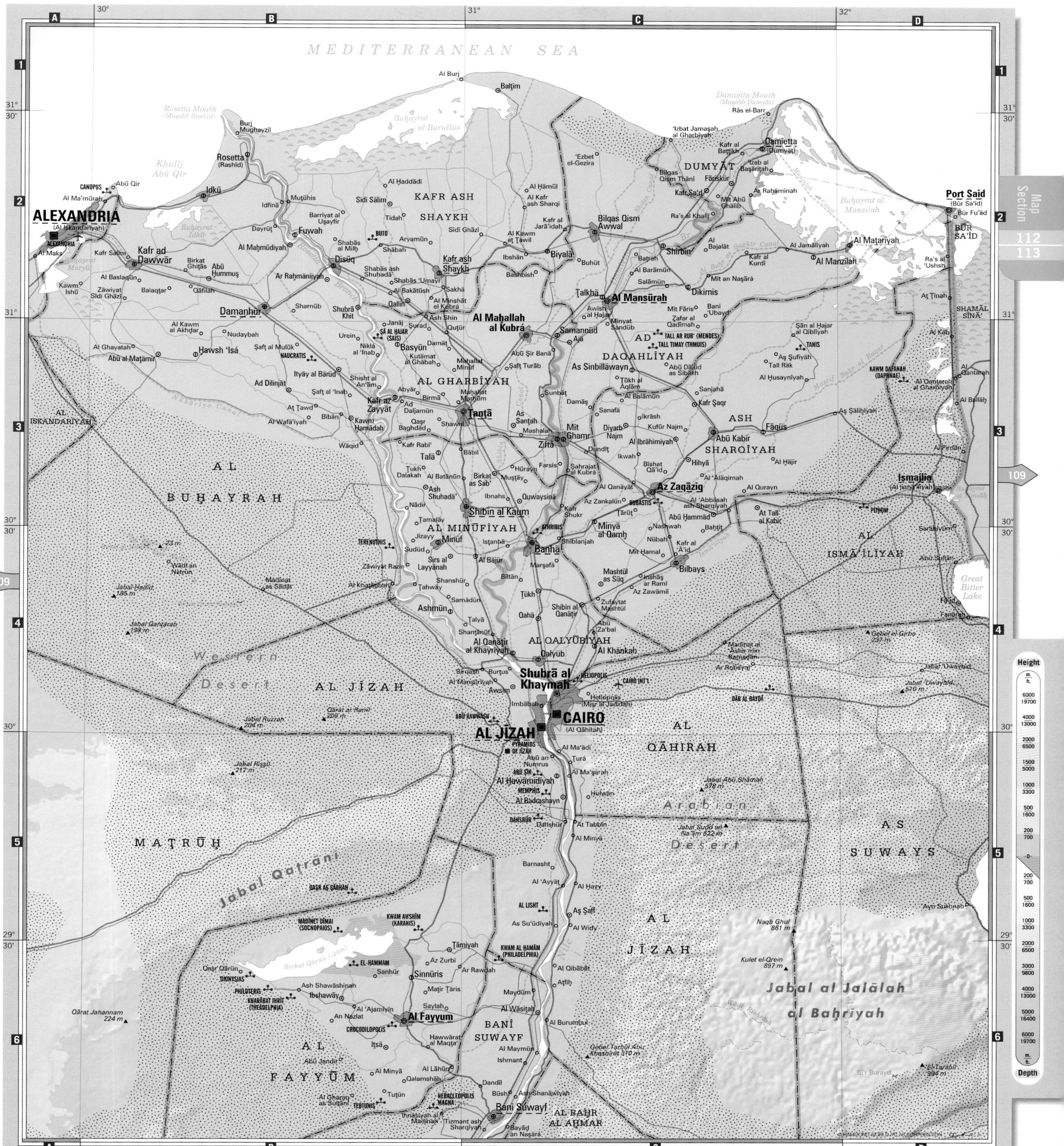

Scale 1:1,000,000 Lambert Conformal Conic Projection

MI   10   20   30
KM   10   20   30   40

Height

m.	ft.
6000	19700
4000	13000
2000	6500
1000	3300
500	1600
200	700
0	0
200	700
500	1600
1000	3300
2000	6500
3000	9800
4000	13000
5000	16400
6000	19700

m. / ft.

Depth

The course of the Niger could hardly be more unusual. The river descends from the Loma Mountains on the border between Sierra Leone and Guinea, but rather than flowing directly to the Atlantic, it pursues a circuitous route through Mali, Niger, and Nigeria before finally emptying into the Gulf of Guinea. With a length of 4,184 km, it is the third-longest river in Africa. The Niger deposits large quantities of sediment in its wide delta (20,000 square km), which lies above rich reserves of oil and natural gas. Nearly 90 percent of Nigeria's income comes from petroleum exports.

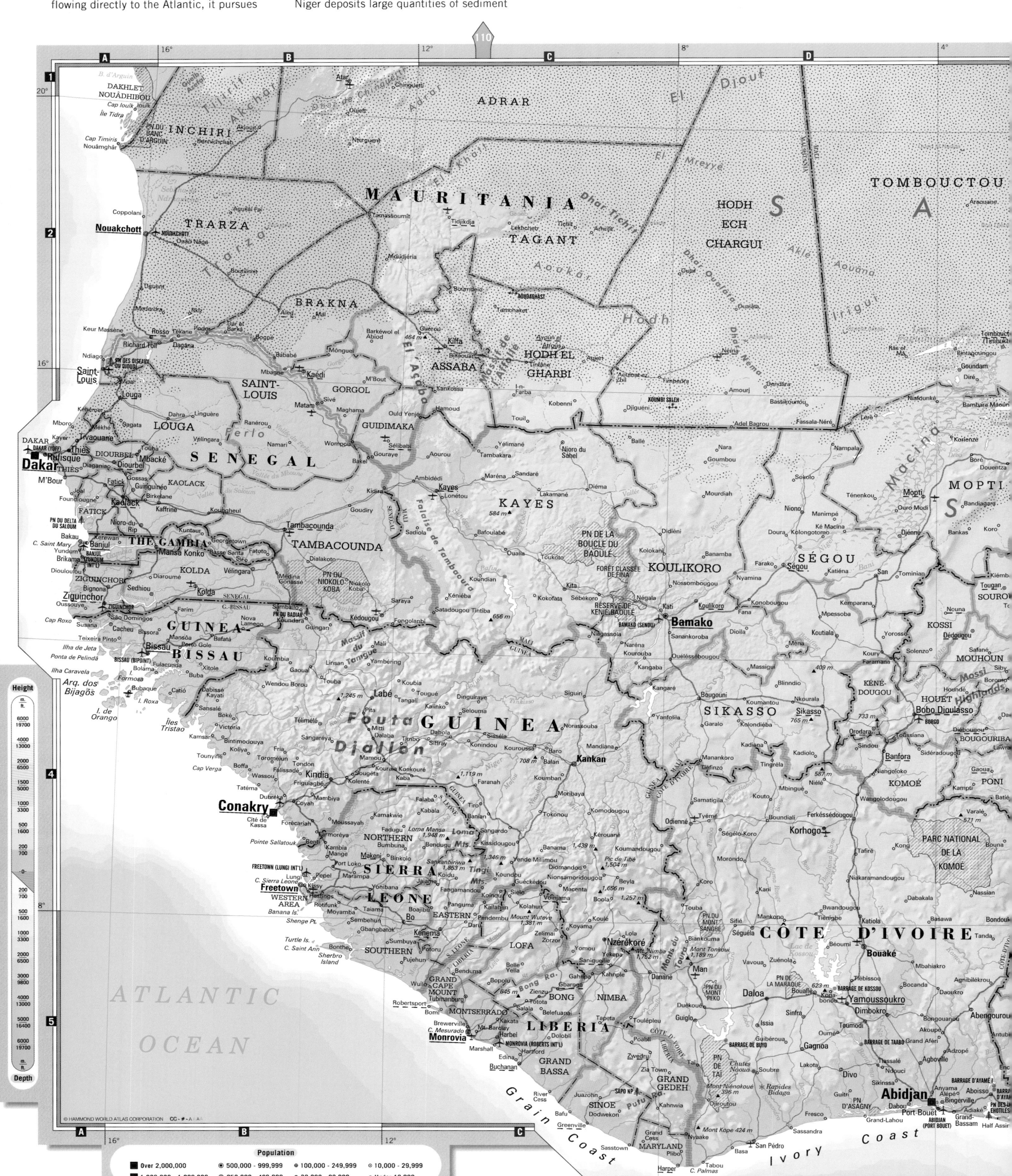

110

Population

■ Over 2,000,000
■ 1,000,000 - 1,999,999
● 500,000 - 999,999
◉ 250,000 - 499,999
⊙ 100,000 - 249,999
◎ 30,000 - 99,999
○ 10,000 - 29,999
○ Under 10,000

© HAMMOND WORLD ATLAS CORPORATION

Southern West Africa

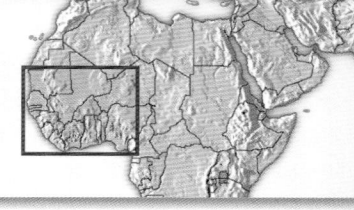

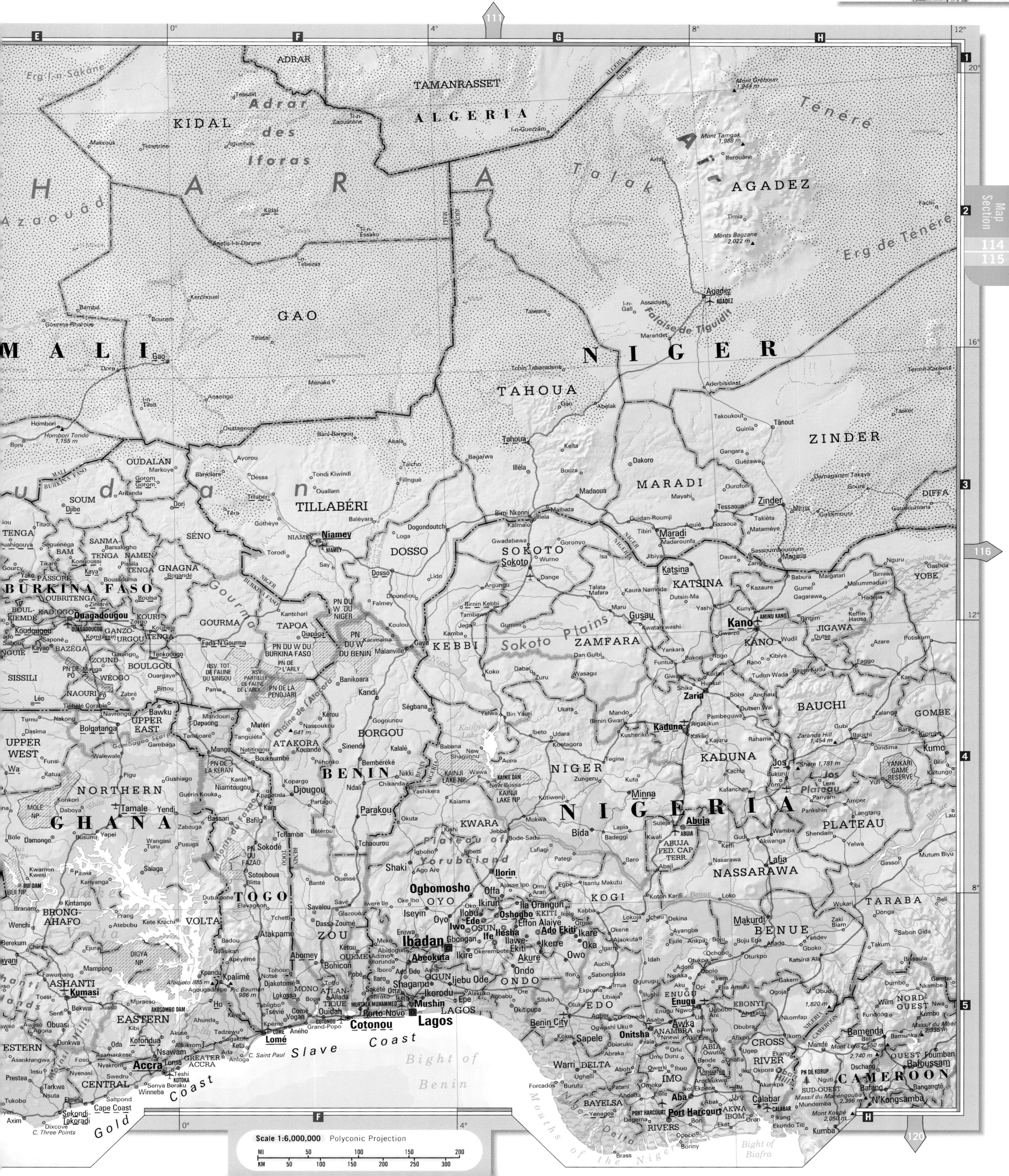
MALI
NIGER
ALGERIA
BURKINA FASO
GHANA
TOGO
BENIN
NIGERIA
CAMEROON
S A H A R A
Sudan
Adrar des Iforas
Erg I-n-Sakâne
Azaouâd
Ténéré
Aïr
Talak
Erg de Ténéré
Falaise de Tiguidit
KIDAL
GAO
TAMANRASSET
AGADEZ
TAHOUA
ZINDER
DIFFA
MARADI
TILLABÉRI
DOSSO
SOKOTO
KATSINA
KANO
JIGAWA
YOBE
BAUCHI
GOMBE
KEBBI
ZAMFARA
KADUNA
NIGER
KWARA
ABUJA FED. CAP. TERR.
PLATEAU
NASSARAWA
TARABA
BENUE
KOGI
OYO
OSUN
EKITI
ONDO
OGUN
LAGOS
EDO
DELTA
BAYELSA
RIVERS
IMO
ABIA
ANAMBRA
ENUGU
EBONYI
CROSS RIVER
AKWA IBOM
ATAKORA
BORGOU
ZOU
MONO
ATLANTIQUE
OUÉMÉ
VOLTA
EASTERN
GREATER ACCRA
CENTRAL
ASHANTI
BRONG-AHAFO
NORTHERN
UPPER EAST
UPPER WEST
OUDALAN
SOUM
GOURMA
TAPOA
Niamey
Ouagadougou
Agadez
Zinder
Maradi
Sokoto
Kano
Katsina
Kaduna
Zaria
Jos
Abuja
Minna
Ilorin
Ogbomosho
Ibadan
Abeokuta
Lagos
Porto-Novo
Cotonou
Lomé
Accra
Kumasi
Tamale
Enugu
Onitsha
Port Harcourt
Calabar
Makurdi
Bamenda
Sekondi-Takoradi
Cape Coast
Slave Coast
Gold Coast
Bight of Benin
Bight of Biafra
Mouths of the Niger
Niger Delta
Plateau of Yorubaland
Sokoto Plains
Jos Plateau
Chaîne de l'Atacora
Mont Gréboun 1,944 m
Mont Tamgak 1,988 m
Monts Bagzane 2,022 m
Hombori Tondo 1,155 m
Shere 1,781 m
Scale 1:6,000,000 Polyconic Projection
MI 0 50 100 150 200
KM 0 50 100 150 200 250 300

Like the bow of a ship, the Mandara Mountains of northern Cameroon extend into the arid plains of Nigeria and the swamplands of Chad. The wooded highland savannah is relatively fertile, as rainfall from May to November is sufficient to support agriculture. Some of this water flows into the riverless depression of the Chad Basin and Lake Chad, the large, shallow lake at its center. Lake Chad is one of the few fresh water reservoirs along the edge of the Sahel region, which encompasses substantial parts of Chad, Niger, and Sudan.

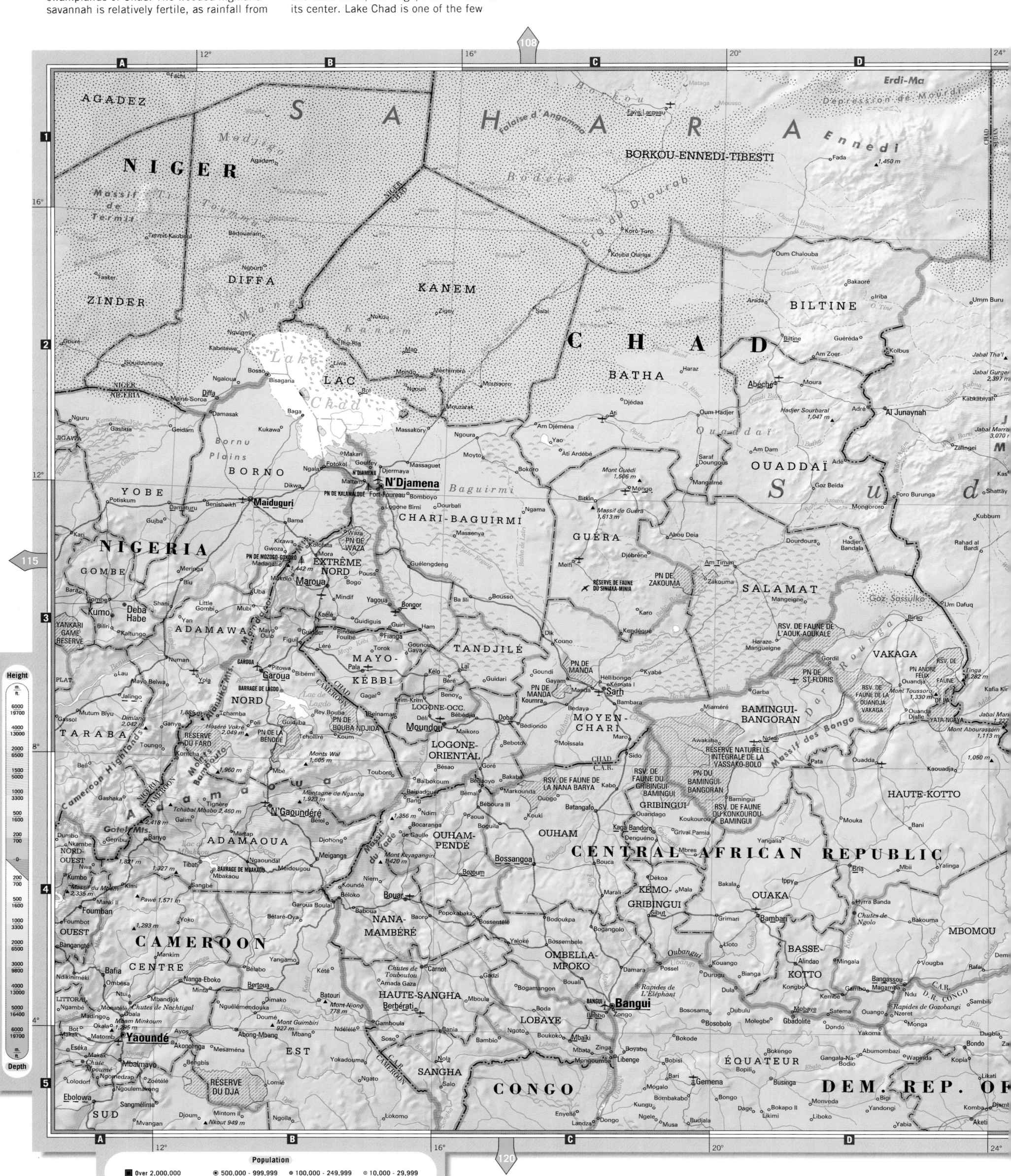

Population		
■ Over 2,000,000	⊚ 500,000 - 999,999	⊙ 100,000 - 249,999	○ 10,000 - 29,999
▣ 1,000,000 - 1,999,999	⊙ 250,000 - 499,999	⊙ 30,000 - 99,999	○ Under 10,000

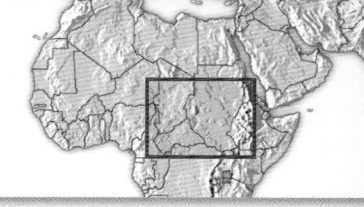

RED SEA

ERITREA

ASH SHAMĀLĪYAH

AL KHARTŪM

Khartoum (Al Khurtūm)
Omdurman (Umm Durmān)
Khartoum North (Al Khurtūm Bahrī)
KHAZZĀN JABAL AL AWLIYĀ

ASH SHARQĪYAH

Kassala

DĀRFŪR

SUDAN

KURDUFĀN

Kurdufān

Jibāl An Nūbah

Wad Medani

Al Qadārif

SENNAR DAM

DINDER NAT'L PARK

ROSEIRES DAM

AL WUSTA

Lake Tana

Bahir Dar

Blue Nile Falls

Gonder

ETHIOPIA

Ethiopian Plateau

CH'OK'E

Debre Mark'os

ADDIS ABABA (Ādīs Ābeba)
BOLE

DEBRE LIBANOS MONASTERY

A 'ĀLĪ AN NĪL

Malakāl

GAMBELA NAT'L PARK

BAHR AL GHAZĀL

Wāw

SOUTHERN NATIONAL PARK

HAUT-MBOMOU

RSV. DE FAUNE DE ZEMONGO

ROMA NP

OMO NAT'L PARK

MAGO NP

NECHISAR NP

ABIYATA-SHALLA LAKES NAT'L PARK

Jima

AL ISTIWĀ' ĪYAH

Juba

ORIENTALE

PN DE LA GARAMBA

NIMULE NP

THE CONGO

UGANDA

Gulu

KENYA

EASTERN

L. Turkana (L. Rudolf)

SIBILOI NAT'L PARK

CENTRAL ISLAND NP

RIFT VALLEY

MARSABIT NAT'L RSV.

MATHENIKO GAME RSV.

KIDEPO VALLEY NP

Chalbi Desert

Libyan Desert

Teiga Plateau

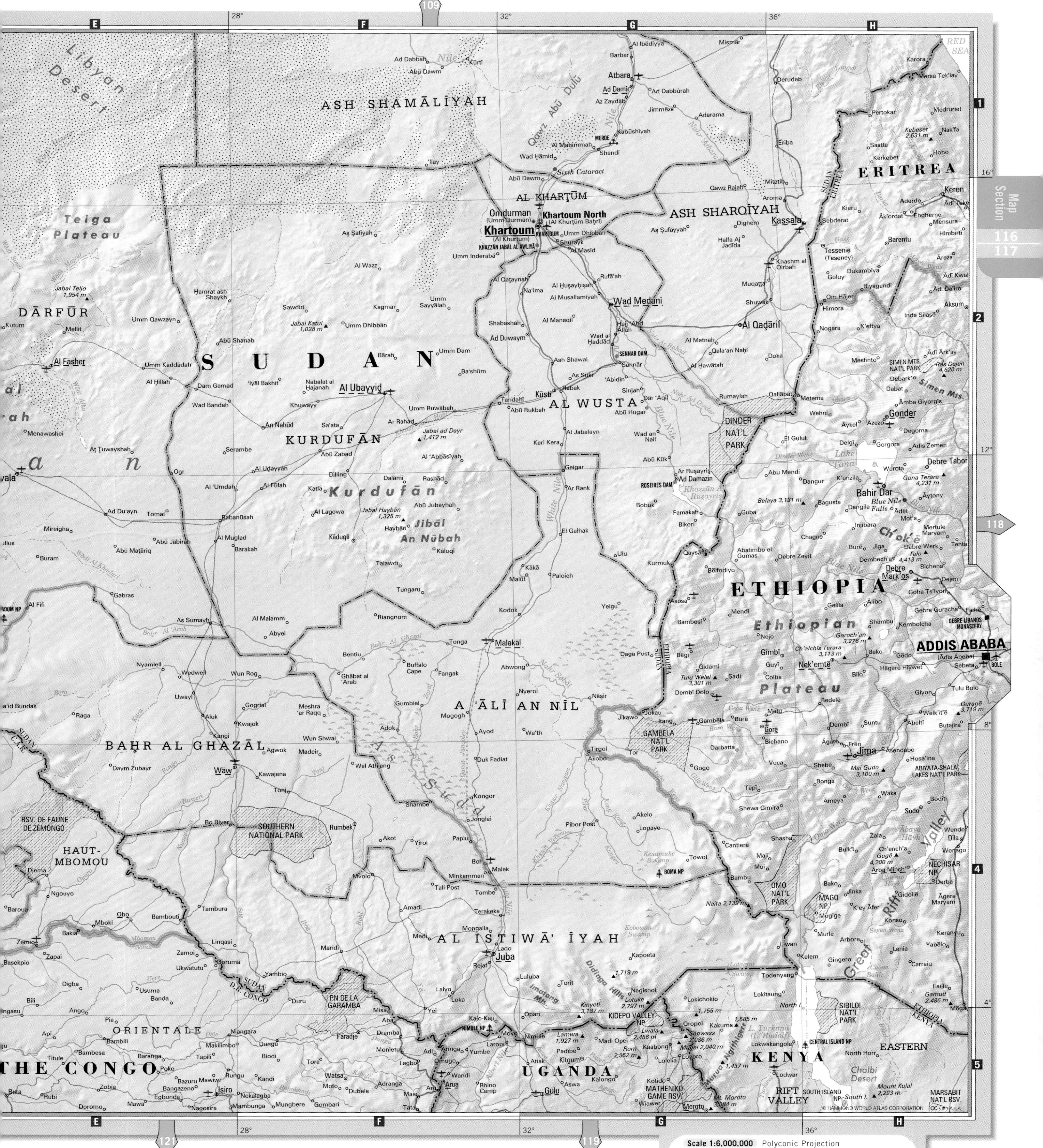

Scale 1:6,000,000   Polyconic Projection

MI   50   100   150   200

KM   50   100   150   200

© HAMMOND WORLD ATLAS CORPORATION

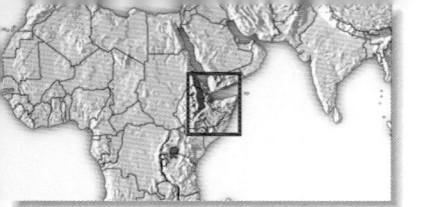

Ethiopia, Somalia

A hot spot beneath the Afar Depression in eastern Ethiopia gave birth to two young seas some 30 million years ago: the Gulf of Aden and the Red Sea. The volcanic islands in the Bab el Mandeb Strait bear witness to the geological forces that caused Africa and the Arabian Peninsula to drift apart. As they continue to diverge, the Red Sea is gradually becoming an ocean.

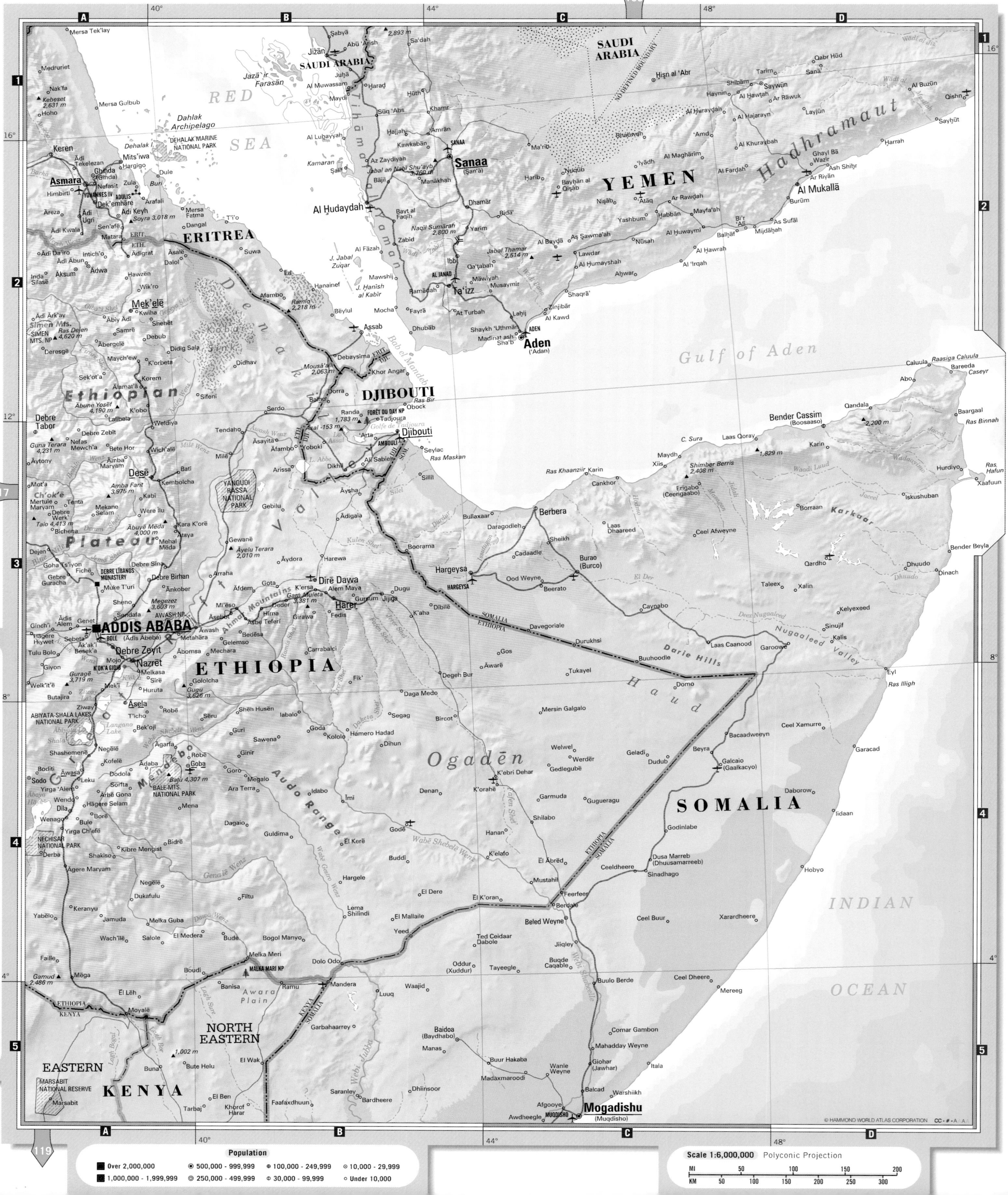

SAUDI ARABIA

YEMEN

Hadhramaut

Sanaa (San'a)

Al Hudaydah

Ta'izz

Aden ('Adan)

Gulf of Aden

RED SEA

Dahlak Archipelago

DEHALAK MARINE NATIONAL PARK

ERITREA

Asmara

DJIBOUTI

Djibouti

Ethiopian

Plateau

ETHIOPIA

ADDIS ABABA (Ādīs Ābeba)

Dirē Dawa

Harēr

Hargeysa

Berbera

Bender Cassim (Boosaaso)

Karkaar

Ogadēn

Haud

SOMALIA

INDIAN OCEAN

KENYA

NORTH EASTERN

EASTERN

MARSABIT NATIONAL RESERVE

Mogadishu (Muqdisho)

SIMEN MTS. NP — Ras Dejen 4,620 m

Batu 4,307 m

Gamud 2,486 m

Shimber Berris 2,408 m

Population

■ Over 2,000,000	⊛ 500,000 - 999,999	⊙ 100,000 - 249,999	○ 10,000 - 29,999
■ 1,000,000 - 1,999,999	⊛ 250,000 - 499,999	⊙ 30,000 - 99,999	○ Under 10,000

Height

m. / ft.
6000 / 19700
4000 / 13000
2000 / 6500
1500 / 5000
1000 / 3300
500 / 1600
200 / 700
-0-
200 / 700
500 / 1600
1000 / 3300
2000 / 6500
3000 / 9800
4000 / 13000
5000 / 16400
6000 / 19700
m. / ft.

Depth

Scale 1:6,000,000 Polyconic Projection

MI 50 100 150 200
KM 50 100 150 200 250 300

The East African Rift System runs from Ethiopia to Mozambique and splits into two branches at Lake Victoria. The many lakes in the region bear witness to the plate rift that began some 40 million years ago and is still in progress today. Its margin is lined by some of the highest mountains on the continent - most of them volcanoes like Kilimanjaro (5,895 m).

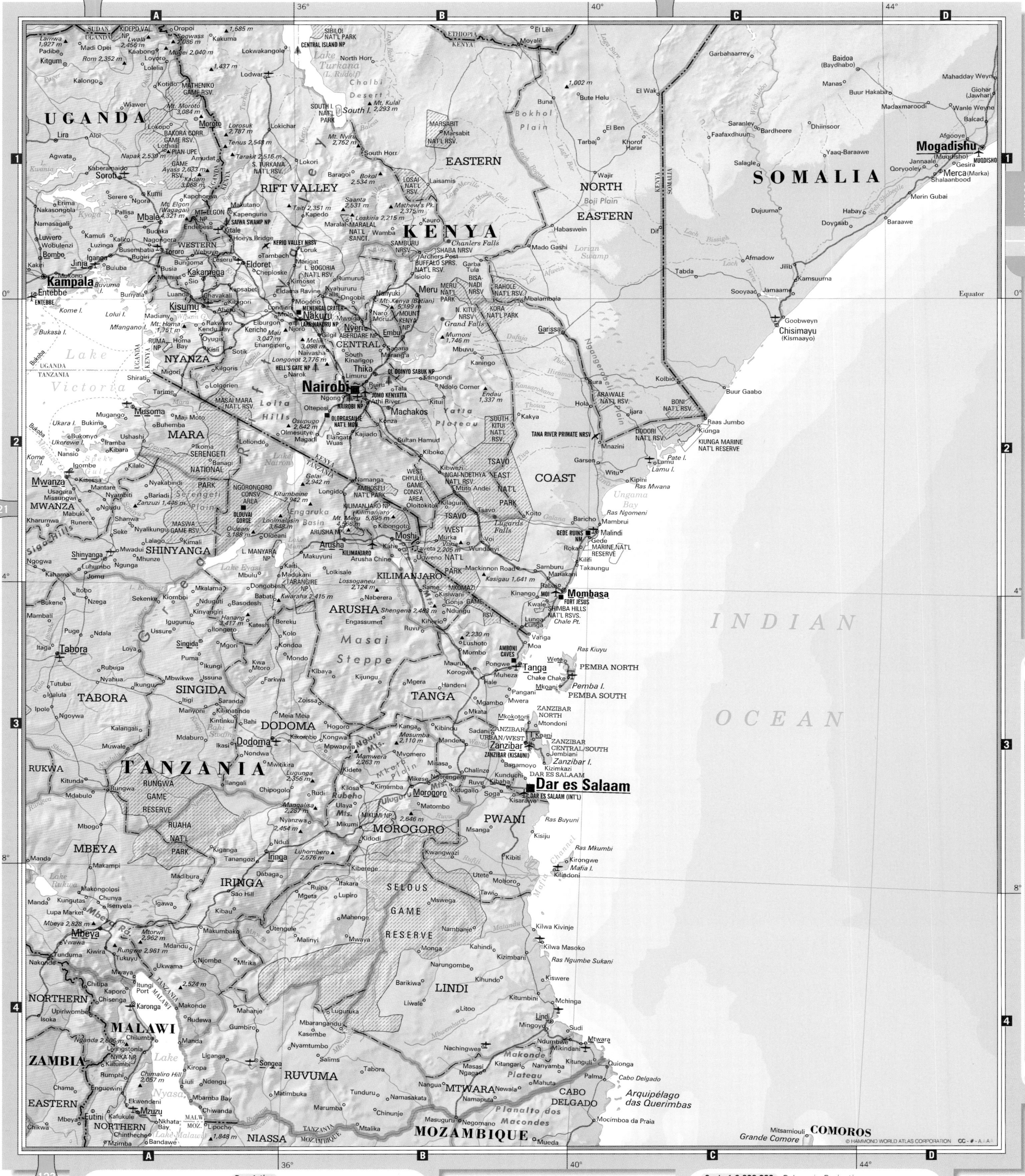

East Central Africa

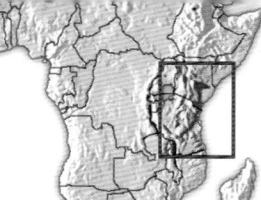

Map Section
118
119

Population

- ■ Over 2,000,000
- ■ 1,000,000 - 1,999,999
- ● 500,000 - 999,999
- ● 250,000 - 499,999
- ⦿ 100,000 - 249,999
- ○ 30,000 - 99,999
- ⊙ 10,000 - 29,999
- ○ Under 10,000

Scale 1:6,000,000 Polyconic Projection

MI   50   100   150   200
KM 50 100 150 200 250 300

Height

m.	ft.
6000	19700
4000	13000
2000	6500
1500	5000
1000	3300
500	1600
200	700
0	0
200	700
1000	3300
2000	6500
3000	9800
5000	16400
6000	19700

Depth

© HAMMOND WORLD ATLAS CORPORATION

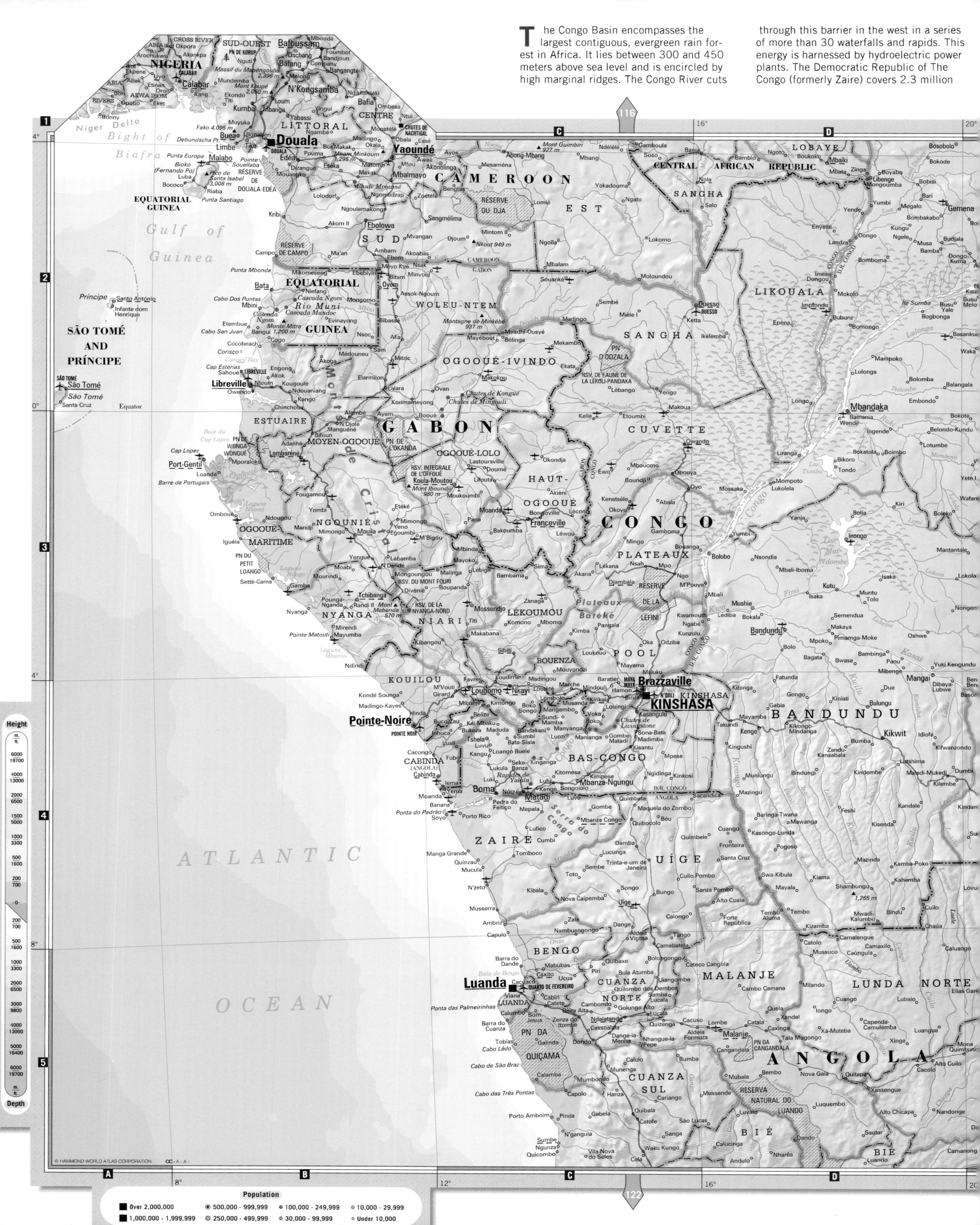

The Congo Basin encompasses the largest contiguous, evergreen rain forest in Africa. It lies between 300 and 450 meters above sea level and is encircled by high marginal ridges. The Congo River cuts through this barrier in the west in a series of more than 30 waterfalls and rapids. This energy is harnessed by hydroelectric power plants. The Democratic Republic of The Congo (formerly Zaire) covers 2.3 million

Population

■ Over 2,000,000	◉ 500,000-999,999	◉ 100,000-249,999	◉ 10,000-29,999
■ 1,000,000-1,999,999	◉ 250,000-499,999	◉ 30,000-99,999	◦ Under 10,000

Height
m. / ft.
6000 / 19700
4000 / 13000
2000 / 6500
1500 / 5000
1000 / 3300
500 / 1600
200 / 700
0
200 / 700
500 / 1600
1000 / 3300
2000 / 6500
3000 / 9800
4000 / 13000
5000 / 16400
6000 / 19700
m. / ft.
Depth

© HAMMOND WORLD ATLAS CORPORATION   CC-A-A

square km of territory and occupies most of the Congo Basin. An abundance of arable land and mineral resources make it potentially one of the richest countries of Africa. It is, however, one of the poorest.

West Central Africa

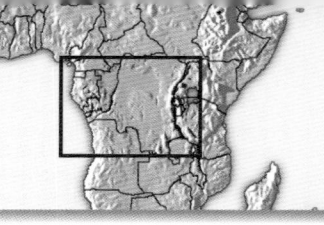

Scale 1:6,000,000   Polyconic Projection

One of the most arid regions of the world is the Namib, a desert that stretches for more than 2,000 km along the western coast of Africa from Angola to South Africa. Annual precipitation here rarely exceeds 50 mm. The desert owes its existence to the cold Benguela Current and cool prevailing winds that carry very little moisture. The Namib is a diverse desert landscape. A prominent topographic feature is the Namib-Naukluft Park south from Walvis Bay, which encompasses some 34,000 square km of sand dunes with an abundant array of forms. Some star dunes here rise to heights of 550 meters.

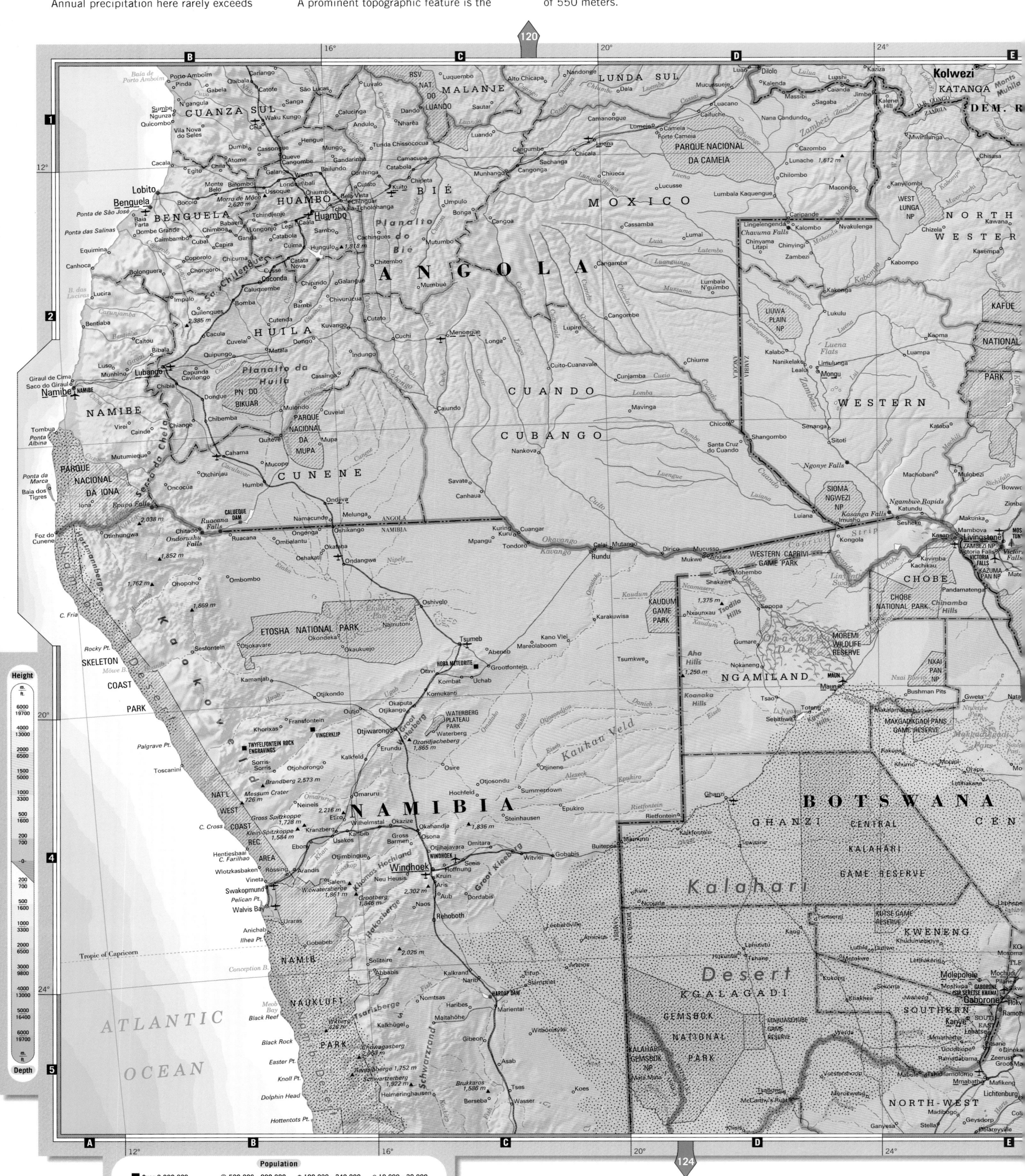

Population

- ■ Over 2,000,000
- ■ 1,000,000 - 1,999,999
- ● 500,000 - 999,999
- ● 250,000 - 499,999
- ● 100,000 - 249,999
- ● 30,000 - 99,999
- ○ 10,000 - 29,999
- ○ Under 10,000

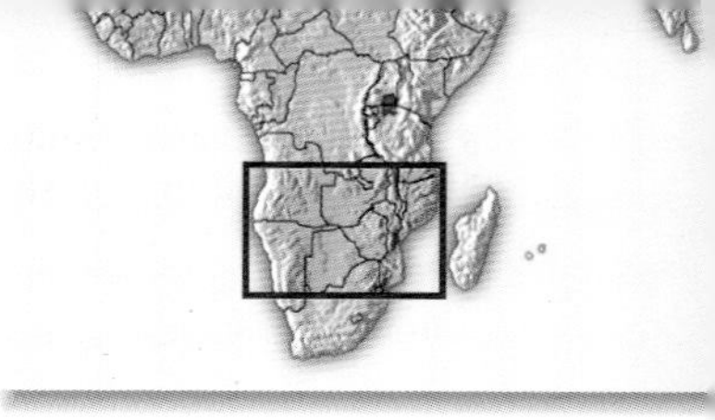

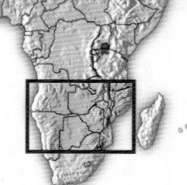

Scale 1:6,000,000   Polyconic Projection

© HAMMOND WORLD ATLAS CORPORATION

Extending from northern South Africa to the Cape Provinces, the Drakensberg mountains are among the most imposing and beautiful natural features of South Africa. Known as the Great Escarpment,

the range comprises rock of different hardness that has been selectively eroded into impressive landscape formations. Billions of years old, the continental plate holds rich ore and diamond deposits that are

intensively mined today. Madagascar - separated from the African continent - is the home of many plant and animal species that have developed in isolation and are found nowhere else in the world.

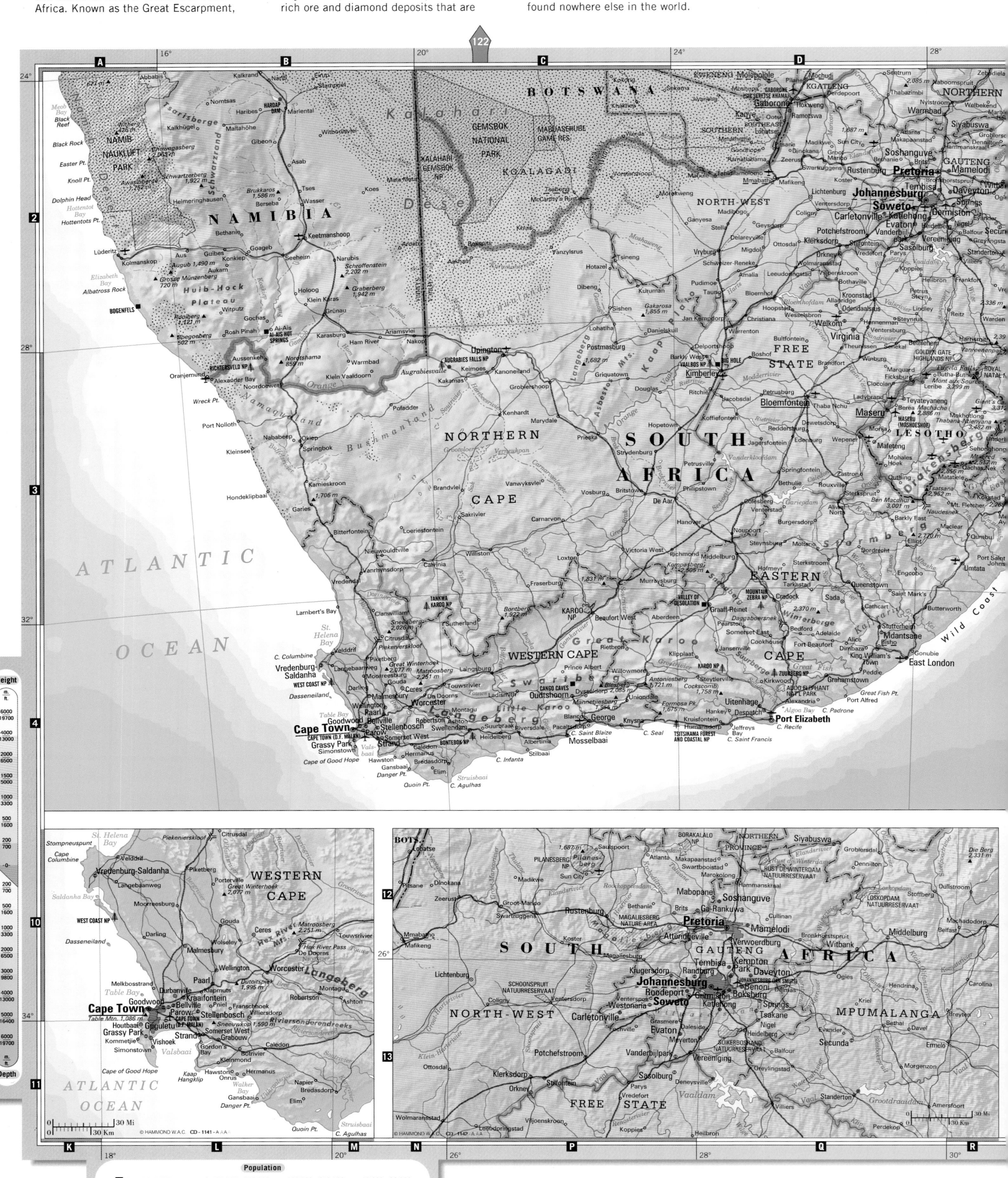

Height

6000 / 19700
4000 / 13000
2000 / 6500
1500 / 5000
1000 / 3300
500 / 1600
200 / 700
0
200 / 700
500 / 1600
1000 / 3300
2000 / 6500
3000 / 9800
4000 / 13000
5000 / 16400
6000 / 19700

Depth

Population

■ Over 2,000,000   ⊛ 500,000 - 999,999   ⊚ 100,000 - 249,999   ⊙ 10,000 - 29,999

■ 1,000,000 - 1,999,999   ⊜ 250,000 - 499,999   ⊚ 30,000 - 99,999   ∘ Under 10,000

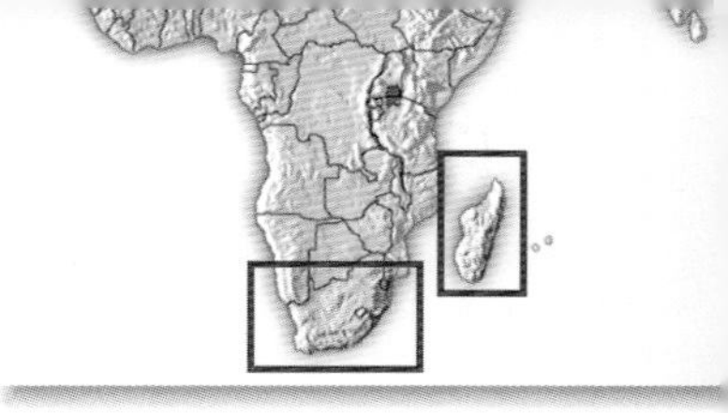

123

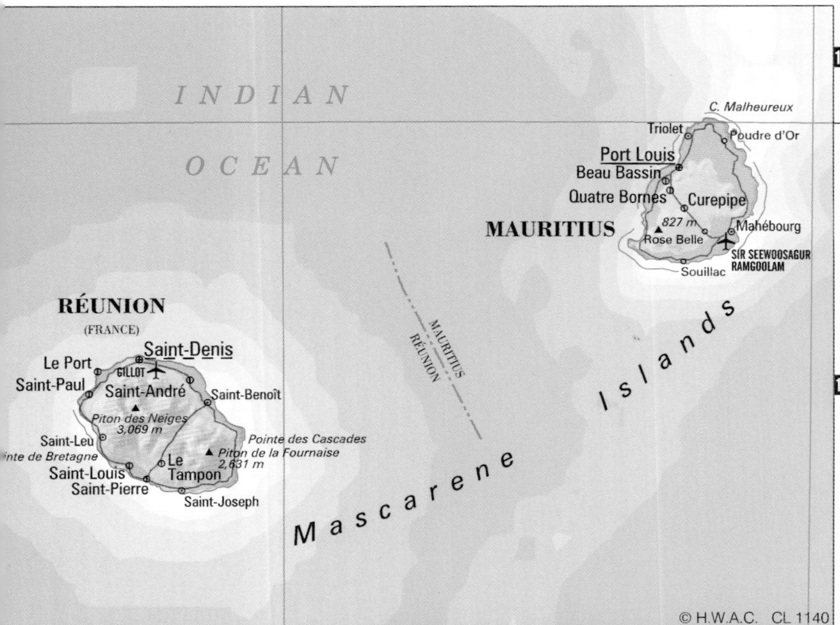

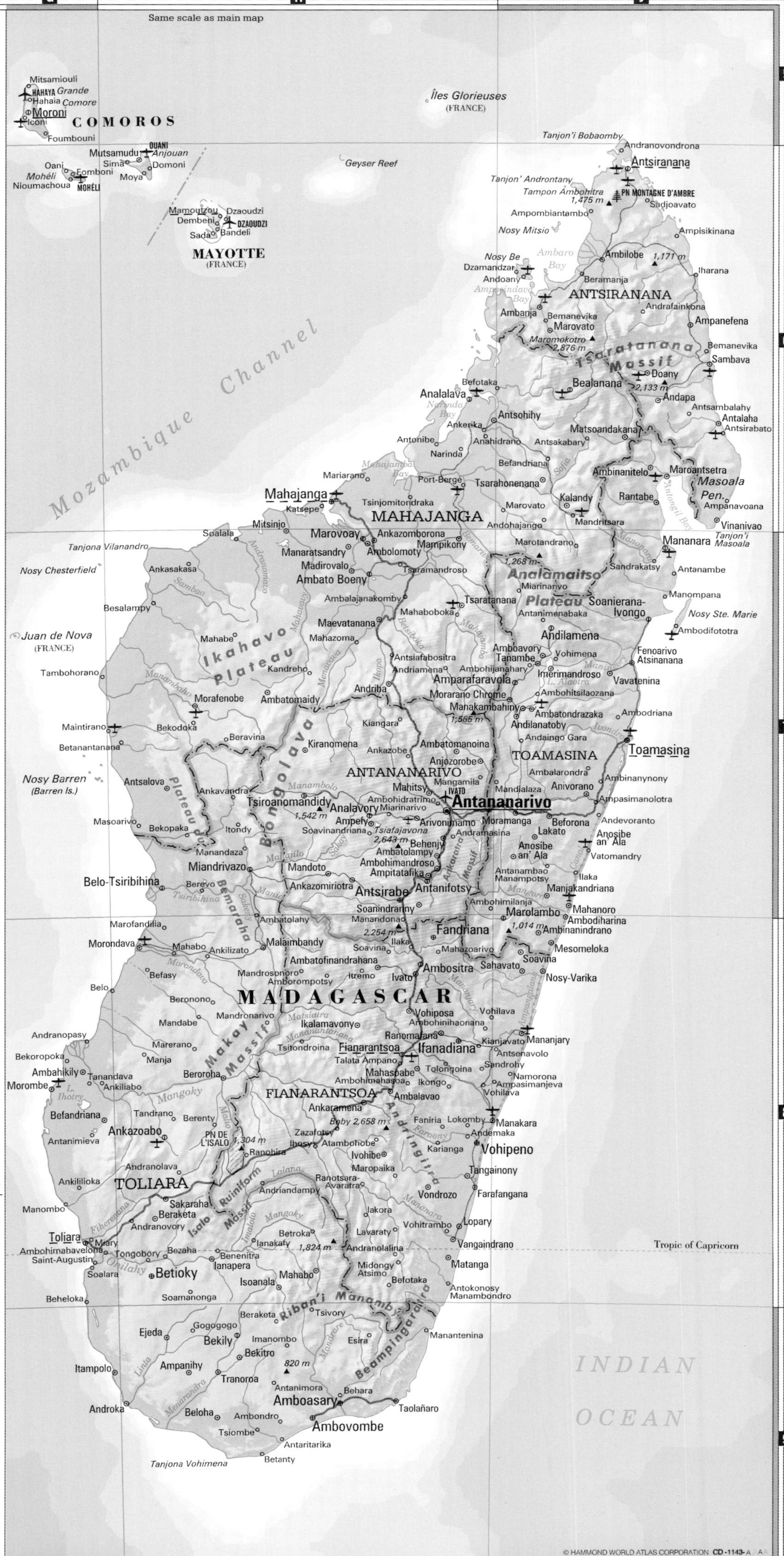

Map
Section

124
125

Same scale as main map

MOZAMBIQUE

GAZA

INHAMBANE

MAPUTO

SWAZILAND

MPUMALANGA

KWAZULU-NATAL

Matola
Maputo

Durban

COMOROS

Grande Comore
Moroni

Mohéli

MAYOTTE
(FRANCE)

Îles Glorieuses
(FRANCE)

Geyser Reef

ANTSIRANANA

Antsiranana

PN MONTAGNE D'AMBRE

Nosy Be

Tsaratanana Massif

Masoala Pen.

MAHAJANGA

Mahajanga

Analamaitso Plateau

Ikahavo Plateau

Juan de Nova
(FRANCE)

Nosy Chesterfield

Nosy Barren
(Barren Is.)

TOAMASINA

Toamasina

ANTANANARIVO

Antananarivo
IVATO

Bongolava Plateau

MADAGASCAR

Antsirabe

Fandriana

Makay Massif

FIANARANTSOA

Fianarantsoa

Ifanadiana

Andringitra

TOLIARA

Toliara

PN DE L'ISALO

Isalo Massif

Betioky

Tropic of Capricorn

Amboasary

Ambovombe

Tanjona Vohimena

INDIAN OCEAN

INDIAN OCEAN

Mozambique Channel

MAURITIUS

Port Louis
Beau Bassin
Quatre Bornes
Curepipe
Mahébourg
SIR SEEWOOSAGUR RAMGOOLAM

RÉUNION
(FRANCE)

Saint-Denis
GILLOT
Saint-André
Saint-Benoît
Le Port
Saint-Paul
Saint-Leu
Piton des Neiges
3,069 m
Piton de la Fournaise
2,631 m
Saint-Louis
Saint-Pierre
Saint-Joseph
Le Tampon

Mascarene Islands

© HAMMOND WORLD ATLAS CORPORATION   CC-65-A-A-A

© H.W.A.C. CL 1140

© HAMMOND WORLD ATLAS CORPORATION   CD-1143-A-A-A

Scale 1:6,000,000   Lambert Conformal Conic Projection

MI   50   100   150   200

KM   50   100   150   200   250   300

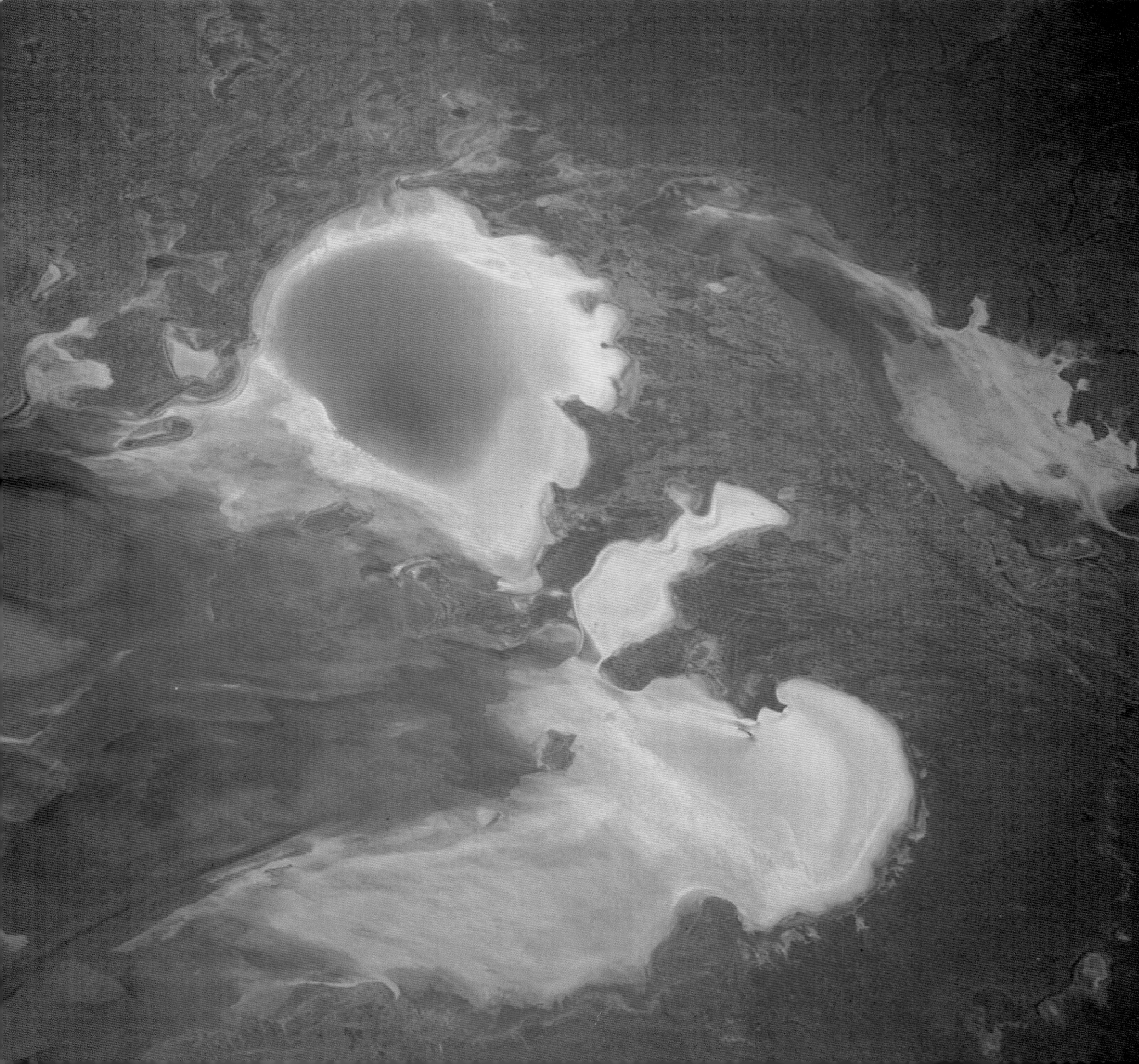

Lake Eyre, located at the edge of the Victoria Desert, is the largest lake basin on the continent (8,900 square km), although it fills with water only after heavy rains. For most of the year, the bed of this salt lake is dry. With depths of up to 16 m below sea level, it is the lowest point in Australia. The much larger northern basin shown on the left (the highly reflective areas) comprises two lakebeds. The western lobe is Belt Bay, and the eastern lobe is Madigan Bay. The coloration, especially of Madigan Bay, indicates that there was some water in this lobe at the time the image was taken.

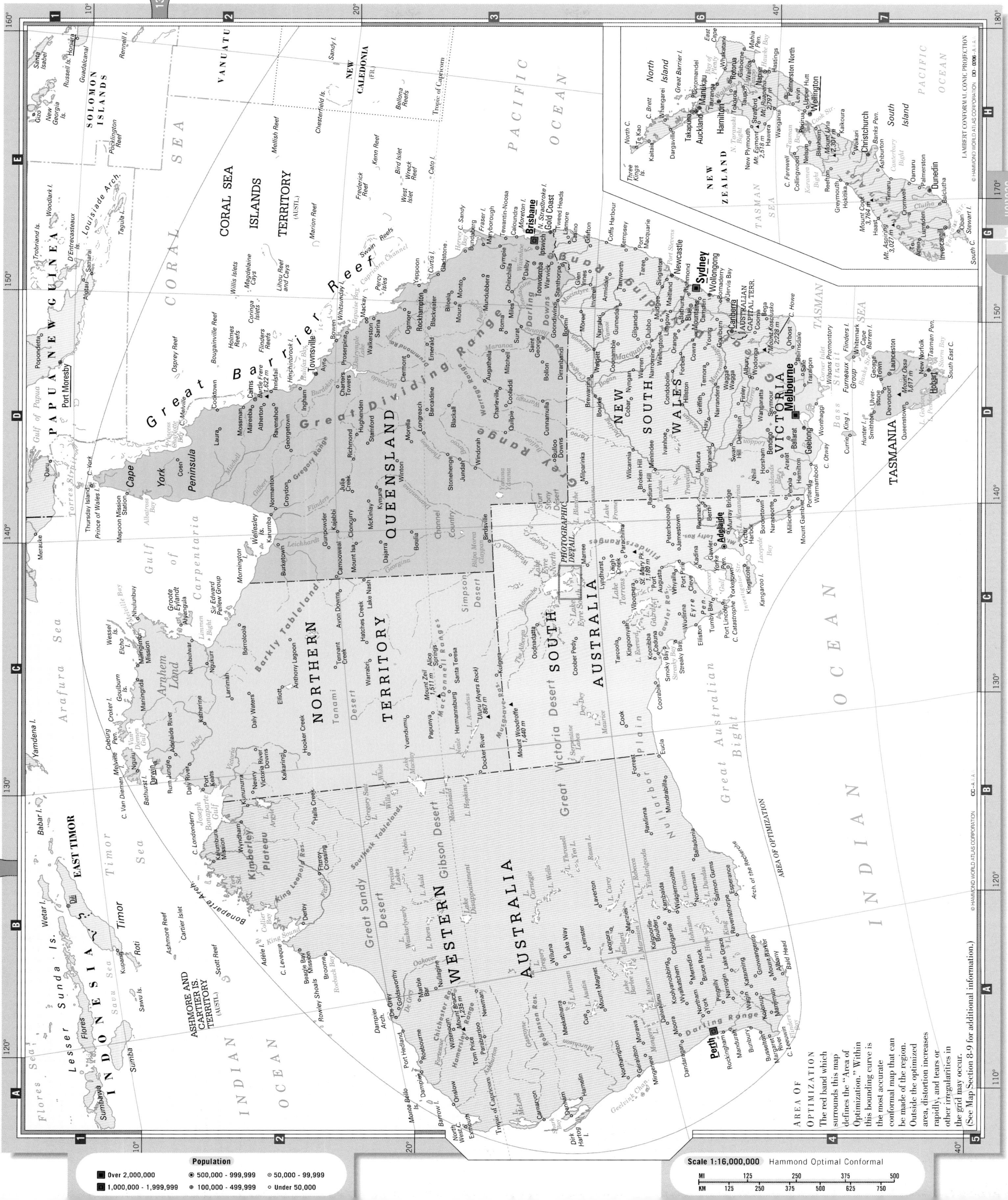

Map Section
126
127

PACIFIC OCEAN
CORAL SEA
SOLOMON ISLANDS
VANUATU
NEW CALEDONIA (FR.)
CORAL SEA ISLANDS TERRITORY (AUSTL.)
PAPUA NEW GUINEA
INDONESIA
EAST TIMOR
Arafura Sea
Timor Sea
Flores Sea
Savu Sea
Gulf of Carpentaria
Gulf of Papua
Torres Strait

NEW ZEALAND
North Island
South Island
TASMAN SEA
PACIFIC OCEAN
Wellington
Auckland
Christchurch
Dunedin

NORTHERN TERRITORY
QUEENSLAND
WESTERN AUSTRALIA
SOUTH AUSTRALIA
NEW SOUTH WALES
VICTORIA
TASMANIA
AUSTRALIAN CAPITAL TERR.

Great Dividing Range
Great Barrier Reef
Great Sandy Desert
Gibson Desert
Great Victoria Desert
Simpson Desert
Tanami Desert
Barkly Tableland
Kimberley Plateau
Arnhem Land
Nullarbor Plain
Great Australian Bight
Macdonnell Ranges
Flinders Ranges

INDIAN OCEAN
TASMAN SEA
PACIFIC OCEAN

Brisbane
Gold Coast
Sydney
Wollongong
Canberra
Melbourne
Geelong
Ballarat
Adelaide
Perth
Hobart
Launceston
Darwin
Townsville
Cairns
Alice Springs
Kalgoorlie

Cape York Peninsula
Uluru (Ayers Rock) 867 m
Mount Woodroffe 1,440 m
Mount Kosciusko 2,228 m
Lake Eyre −16 m

PHOTOGRAPHIC DETAIL

AREA OF OPTIMIZATION
The red band which surrounds this map defines the "Area of Optimization." Within this bounding curve is the most accurate conformal map that can be made of the region. Outside the optimized area, distortion increases rapidly, and tears or other irregularities in the grid may occur. (See Map Section 8-9 for additional information.)

Population
■ Over 2,000,000
■ 1,000,000 - 1,999,999
● 500,000 - 999,999
● 100,000 - 499,999
○ 50,000 - 99,999
○ Under 50,000

Scale 1:16,000,000 Hammond Optimal Conformal
MI   125   250   375   500
KM 125 250 375 500 625 750

LAMBERT CONFORMAL CONIC PROJECTION
© HAMMOND WORLD ATLAS CORPORATION

Papua New Guinea lies on the seam between the Indo-Australian and Pacific Plates. Consequently, it is a region of massive earthquakes, active volcanoes, and rugged mountain terrain that provides a unique natural refuge for plants and wildlife today. The tropical rain forest is home to rare birds of paradise and butterflies with wingspans of up to 25 cm. It is also the geographical boundary for many Australian species, including the duck-billed platypus of the order Monotremata. Most Papuans had no contact with modern civilization until 1933.

Population

■ Over 2,000,000   ◉ 500,000 - 999,999   ◉ 100,000 - 249,999   ○ 10,000 - 29,999
■ 1,000,000 - 1,999,999   ◉ 250,000 - 499,999   ◉ 30,000 - 99,999   ○ Under 10,000

136°   140°   144°   148°

New Guinea

Agats
Kopaigo
Mindiptana
Waropko
Ningerum
Muller Range
Korba
Kopaigo
Porgera
Lalabia
Wapenamanda
Mt. Herbert 4,267 m
ENGA
MADANG
Alexishafen
Madang
Long I.
Tolokiwa
Bok
Umboi
Sakar I.
Gloucester
C. Merkus
Bismarck Sea

Pirimapun
Tanahmerah
IRIAN JAYA
Klunga
Nomad
Tari
Komo
Mendi
Mt. Hagen 4,509 m
WESTERN
HIGHLANDS
Bundi
Simbai
Aiome
Tauta
Saidor
Siassi
Wasu
Sharnhorst Pt.
Sialum
WEST NEW BRITAIN
New Britain

Kepi
Kumurkek
Muting
Lake Murray
Daral Hills
Murray Range
SOUTHERN HIGHLANDS
Mt. Bosavi 2,397 m
Ialibu
Kagua
Erave
Pangia
Mendi
Kerowagi
Minj
Kundiawa
CHIMBU
Goroka
EASTERN HIGHLANDS
Okapa
Kainantu
Kaiapit
Boana
Mt. Bangeta 4,121 m
Kitumala Pt.
Huon Peninsula
Finschhafen
Cape Cretin

Bade
Bupul
WESTERN
Balimo
Karimui
Obura
Marawaka
Mt. Tabletop 3,686 m
Mumeng
Lae
Cape Gerhards
Huon Gulf
Solomon Sea

Yos Sudarso Island
Kaba
Kimaan
Okaba
PAPUA NEW GUINEA
GULF
Kikori
Akoma
Ihu
Kerema
Mutua
MOROBE
Menyamya
Aseki
Wau
Butolo
Baimuru
Garaina
Morobe

Tanjung De Jongs
Tanjung Vals
Kladar
Komoran I.
Kumbe
Merauke
Weam
Morehead
Sibidiri
Mari
Fly R. Delta
Kiwai I.
Parama I.
Daru
Bell Point
Cape Blackwood
Gulf of Papua
Malalaua
Kukipi
Guari
Mt. Albert Edward 3,990 m
Tapini
Ioma
Woitape
Manau
Efogi
Gona
Buna
Popondetta
Kokoda
Dyke Ackland Bay
C. Nelson

MALUKU / IRIAN JAYA
INDONESIA
PAPUA NEW GUINEA
Sogeri
Purutu
Wabuda I.
Umuda I.
Saibai I.
PAPUA NEW GUINEA / AUSTRALIA
Torres Strait
Warrior Reefs
Portlock Reefs
Pandora Passage
CENTRAL
Kairuku
Bereina
JACKSON
NATIONAL CAPITAL DISTRICT
Port Moresby
Hood Point
STANLEY RANGE
Mt. Suckling 3,676 m
Kwikila
Efogi
Abau
Magarida
NORTHERN
Afore
Tufi
Robinson River

Badu I.
Moa I.
Thursday Island
Prince of Wales I.
Sladt Point
Cape York
Cape York
CAPE YORK ABOR. RSV.
Cowal Creek
Abor. Community
JARDINE R. NAT'L PARK
False Orford Ness
Boot Reefs
Eastern Fields

Cape Wessel
Wessel Is-
Marchinbar I.
The English Companys Is.
Cape Wilberforce
Elcho I.
Pt. Napier
Galiwinku
Nhulunbuy
Yirrkala
Cape Arnhem
Arnhem Bay
MAPOON
Mapoon Mission Station
ABORIGINAL RESERVE
Shelburne Bay
Cape Grenville
Temple Bay
Cape York
GREAT

Point Alexander
Cape Grey
Bagbiringula Point
Point Arrowsmith
Cape Shield
Isle Woodah
Bickerton I.
WEIPA
ABOR.
WEIPA RSV.
Weipa South
Duifken Point
Albatross Bay
IRON RANGE NAT'L PARK
Mt. Tozer 525 m
Iron Range
Cape Weymouth
Cape Direction
LOCKHART R.
Mt. Carter 665 m
Lockhart River Abor. Community
GREAT BARRIER
CORAL SEA

Gulf of Carpentaria
Umbakumba
Alyangula
Groote Eylandt
Ungwariba Point
Illyungmadja Point
Tasman Pt.
Cape Beatrice
Thud Point
AURUKUN
ABOR.
ARCHER BEND NAT'L PARK
ROKEBY-CROLL CR. NAT'L PARK
Cape York
Peninsula
Coen
Claremont Pt.
Cape Melville
CAPE MELVILLE NAT'L PARK
Abbey Pk. 585 m
Barrow Point
Murdock Point
Osprey Reef
CORAL SEA ISLANDS

Warrakunta Point
Limmen Bight
Maria I.
Sir Edward Pellew Group
WEST I. ABOR. LAND
Vanderlin I.
VANDERLIN I. ABOR. LAND
Cape Keer-weer
LAND
PORMPURAAW ABOR.
LAND
Mt. Ryan 518 m
Musgrave
LAKEFIELD NAT'L PARK
Princess Charlotte Bay
Starcke NP
Lookout Point
Cape Flattery
MARINE
BARRIER
REEF
Bougainville Reef
TERRITORY

BORROLOOLA ABOR. LAND
Borroloola
ROBINSON RIVER ABOR. LAND
Robinson River
MORNINGTON I.
Mornington I.
MORNINGTON I. ABOR. LAND
Cape Van Diemen
Wellesley Islands
Pt. Parker
Point Burrowes
Sweers I.
Bentinck I.
Alligator Point
Karumba
Dunbar
Mitchell
Palmerville
KOWANYAMA ABOR. LAND
Kowanyama Abor. Community
MITCHELL AND ALICE RIVERS NAT'L PARK
Rutland Plains
Laura
Cooktown
Hope Vale Abor. Comm.
HOPE VALE
Cape Bedford
ENDEAVOUR RIVER NP
BLACK MOUNTAIN NP
Mt. Pinnigan
CEDAR BAY NP
Wujal Wujal Abor. Comm.
Cape Tribulation
DAINTREE NAT'L PARK
CAPE TRIBULATION NAT'L PARK
Cape Kimberley
DAGMAR RANGE NP
Mossman
Port Douglas
Holmes Reef

Calvert Hills
Wollogorang
Westmoreland
DOOMADGEE ABOR. LAND
Doomadgee Abor. Community
Corinda
Burketown
Normanton
Mount Molloy
Clifton Beach
CAIRNS
Cairns
BARRON GORGE NP
Mareeba
Edmonton
Kairi
Gordonvale
BELLENDEN KER NP
EUBENANGEE SWAMP NP
Innisfail
Flinders Reefs

Creswell Downs
Anthony Lagoon
WAANYI-GARAWA ABORIGINAL LAND
Chillagoe
Dimbulah
Herberton
Atherton
Babinda
Millaa Millaa
Ravenshoe
Kurrimine Beach
El Arish
Mission Beach
PALMERSTON NP
Tully
HERBERT RIVER FALLS NP
Cape Sandwich
HINCHINBROOK I. NP
Hinchinbrook I.
Halifax
Palm Is.
Palm Island Abor. Settlement

Allingham
Lawn Hill
LAWN HILL NP
Croydon
Georgetown
Forsayth
Vena Park
Abingdon Downs
Mount Surprise
QUEENSLAND
Gregory Range
FORTY MILE SCRUB NP
Mount Garnet
Herbert R. Falls
Yamanie Falls
YAMANIE FALLS NP
EDMUND KENNEDY NP
Ingham
Trebonne
Macknade
Cardwell

Alexandria
Mount Isa
Cloncurry
Julia Creek
Richmond
Maxwelton
Hughenden
Pentland
Homestead
Lynd
Greenvale
JOURAMA FALLS NP
MOUNT SPEC NP
Pallarenda
Picnic Bay
MAGNETIC I. NAT'L PARK
Magnetic I.
Townsville
MOUNT ELLIOT NP
Cape Cleveland
CAPE CLEVELAND NP
Giru
Ayr
Cape Bowling Green
BOWLING GREEN BAY NP

Soudan
Avon Downs
Camooweal
Mary Kathleen
McKinlay
Malbon
Duchess
Selwyn
Prairie
Stamford
Charters Towers
Home Hill
Cape Upstart
CAPE UPSTART NP
Abbot Point
Bowen
Mt. Abbot 1,056 m
MT. ABERDEEN NP
Collinsville
PORCUPINE GORGE NATIONAL PARK
Proserpine
Cannonvale
WHITSUNDAY IS. NAT'L PARK
CONWAY RANGE NP
Lindeman I.
Cape Conway
EUNGELLA NAT'L PARK
Seaforth

Scale 1:6,000,000   Lambert Conformal Conic Projection

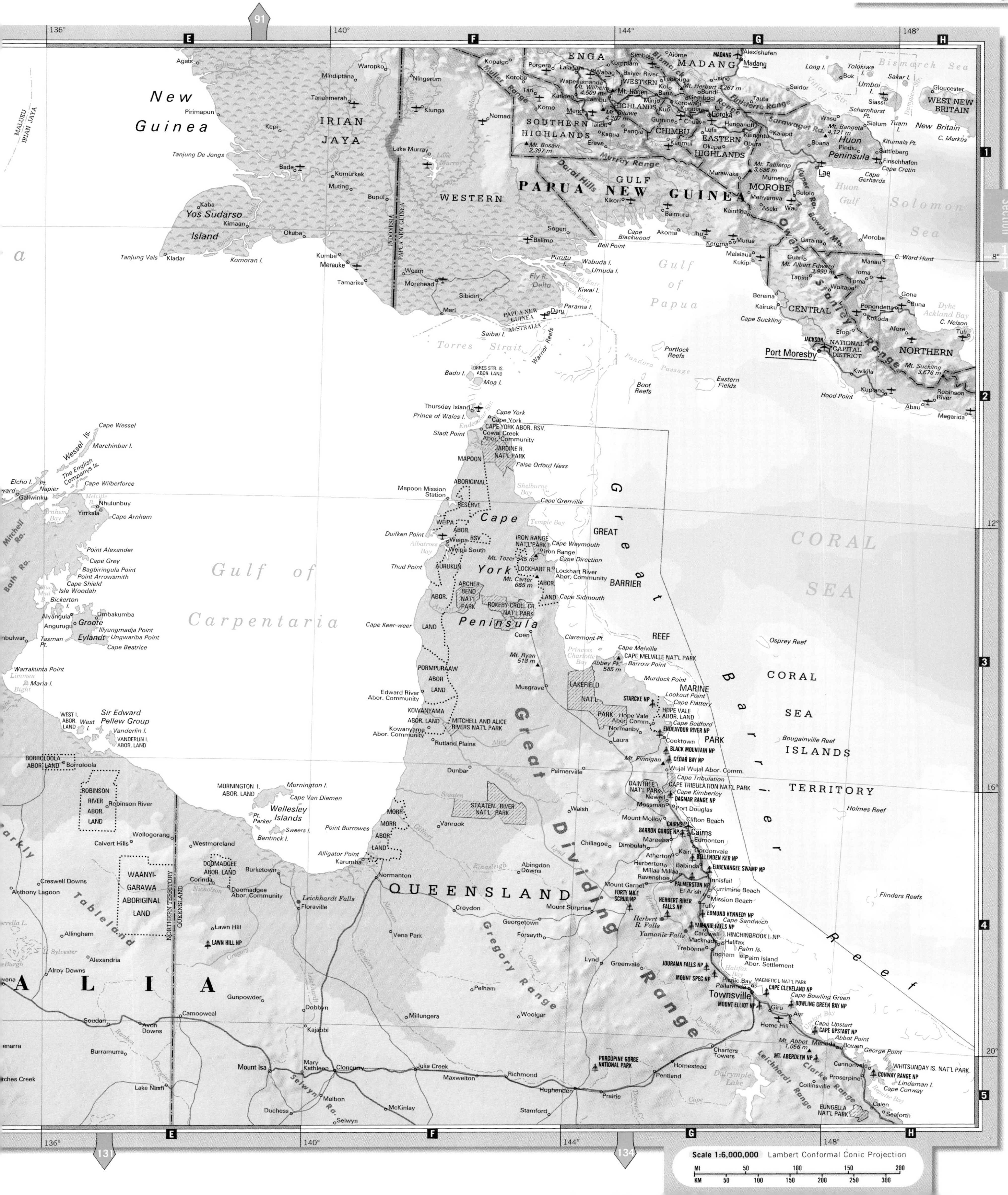

Australia is covered by more desert for its size than any other inhabited continent. Known collectively as the "outback," these desert regions are located primarily in the west and the interior. Many of the rivers that flow sporadically into the central basin seldom reach their terminal lakes, which are dry salt flats for most of the year. The basin has enormous groundwater reserves left over from the ice age, however. These are tapped from artesian wells to water grazing lands for sheep. Cultivation is possible only in a few coastal areas concentrated primarily around Perth and Adelaide. The isolated monolith of Ayers Rock rises from the plain in the Northern Territory. It is sacred to the Aborigines, who call it Uluru.

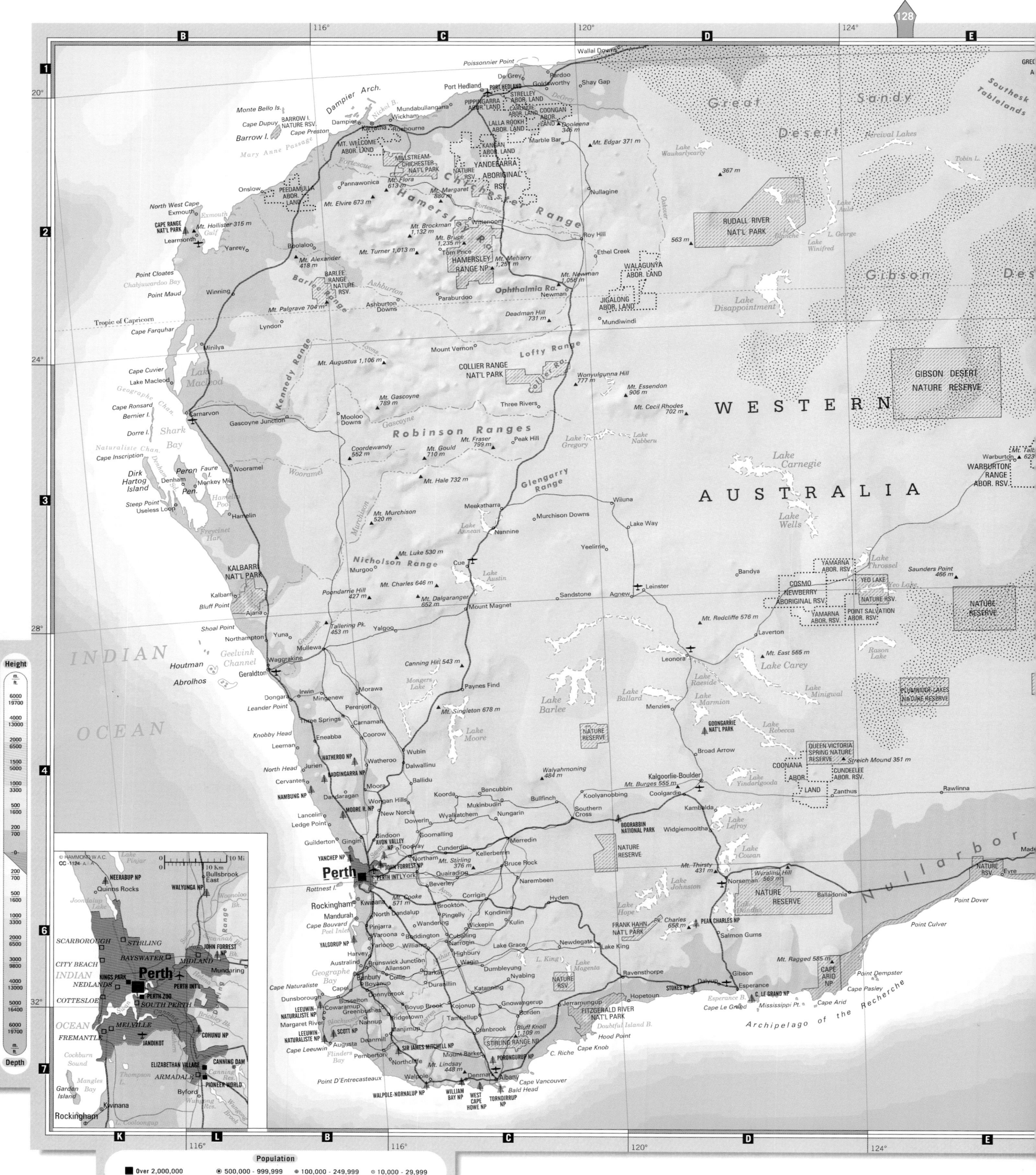

Height
m. / ft.
6000 / 19700
4000 / 13000
2000 / 6500
1500 / 5000
1000 / 3300
500 / 1600
200 / 700
0
200 / 700
500 / 1600
1000 / 3300
2000 / 6500
3000 / 9800
4000 / 13000
5000 / 16400
6000 / 19700
m. / ft.
Depth

Population

■ Over 2,000,000	◉ 500,000 - 999,999
■ 1,000,000 - 1,999,999	◎ 250,000 - 499,999
● 100,000 - 249,999	⊙ 30,000 - 99,999
⊚ 10,000 - 29,999	○ Under 10,000

Northern Territory

Queensland

South Australia

New South Wales

Victoria

Great Australian Bight

Great Victoria Desert

Simpson Desert

Tanami Desert

MacDonnell Ranges

Musgrave Range

Flinders Ranges

Gawler Ranges

Woomera Prohibited Area

Nullarbor Plain

Channel Country

Selected places and features

Tanami, Central Desert Abor. Land, Warlmanpa Abor. Land, Kaytej Aboriginal Land, Balwina Aboriginal Reserve, Ngarti Abor. Land, Chilla Well Abor. Land, Mount Allan Abor. Land, Yunkanjini Abor. Land, Haasts Bluff Aboriginal Land, Petermann Aboriginal Land, Lake Amadeus Abor. Land, Pitjantjatjara Aboriginal Lands, Maralinga Tjarutja Aboriginal Land, Yalata Abor. Land, Warrabri Abor. Land, Mt. Barkly Abor. Land, Utopia Abor. Land, Ti-Tree Abor. Land, Alyawarra Abor. Land, Hermannsburg Abor. Land, Santa Teresa Abor. Land, Yuendumu Abor. Land

Mount Isa, Leichhardt Dam, Camooweal, Gunpowder, Dobbyn, Millungera, Mary Kathleen, Cloncurry, Julia Creek, Malbon, McKinlay, Duchess, Selwyn, Kynuna, Dajarra, Carandotta, Noranside, Boulia, Glenormiston, Bedourie, Diamantina Lakes, Birdsville, Pandie Pandie, Cordillo Downs, Durham Downs, Nappa Merrie, Noccundra, Windorah, Betoota, Currawilla

Alice Springs, Tennant area, Tanami, Willowra, Willowra, Barrow Creek, Central Mt. Stuart, Stirling, Ti-Tree, Aileron, Napperby, Papunya, Haasts Bluff, Hermannsburg, Areyonga, Yuendumu, Docker River, Yulara, Kulgera, Mount Cavenagh, Umbeara, Abminga, Tieyon, Pedirka, Maria, Alberga, Oodnadatta, Coober Pedy, Marla, Mintabie, Emabella, Ernabella, Andado, Rumbalara, Erldunda, Henbury, Tempe Downs, Angas Downs

Mountains: Mt. Figg 521 m, Mt. Cairns 597 m, Mt. Theo 584 m, Mt. Patricia 578 m, Mt. Singleton 808 m, Mt. Doreen, Mt. Davenport 817 m, Mt. Stanley 887 m, Mt. Stuart 844 m, Mt. Top 708 m, Mt. Treachery 763 m, Mt. Freeling 1,006 m, Mt. Swan 640 m, Mt. Strangways 1,036 m, Mt. Brassey 1,203 m, Mt. Hogarth 338 m, Mt. Leisler 901 m, Mt. Liebig 1,525 m, Mt. Edward 1,423 m, Mt. Zeil 1,511 m, Mt. Lyell Brown 881 m, Mt. Laughlen 1,169 m, Mt. Kathleen 367 m, Mt. Harris 1,067 m, Mt. Rodinga 493 m, Mt. Rawlinson 689 m, Mt. Aloysius 1,085 m, Mt. Squires 705 m, Mt. Whinham 1,231 m, Mt. Morris 1,288 m, Mt. Everard 1,173 m, Mt. Davies 1,058 m, Mt. Woodroffe 1,440 m, Mt. Hakee 451 m, Mt. Crombie 835 m, Mt. Illbillee 917 m, Mt. Lindsay 819 m, Mt. Sir Thomas 773 m, Mt. Pooraninta 678 m, Mt. Olga 1,069 m, Uluru (Ayers Rock) 867 m, Mt. Illamurta

Parks: Simpsons Gap NP, Finke Gorge NP, Uluru NP, Witjira Nat'l Park, Simpson Desert National Park, Simpson Desert Consv. Park, Elliot Price Consv. Park, Lake Eyre Nat'l Park, Gammon Ranges NP, Flinders Ranges Nat'l Park, Nullarbor Nat'l Park, Yumbarra Consv. Park, Yalata, Sturt Nat'l Park, Kinchega Nat'l Park, Danggali Consv. Park, Mungo NP, Mallee Cliffs NP, Hattah-Kulkyne NP, Ngarkat Consv. Park, Billiat Consv. Park, Innes NP, Flinders Chase NP, Coffin Bay NP, Lincoln NP, Hincks Consv. Park, Pinkawillinie Consv. Park, Para Wirra Nat'l Park

Lake Eyre North, Lake Eyre South, Lake Torrens, Lake Gairdner, Lake Frome, Lake Blanche, Lake Callabonna, Lake Gregory, Lake Everard, Lake Harris, Lake Macfarlane, Lake Acraman, Lake Yamma Yamma, Lake Machattie, Lake Maurice, Lake Dey-Dey, Lake Amadeus, Lake Hopkins, Lake MacDonald, Lake Mackay, Lake White, Lake Hazlett, Lake Neale, Lake Warrandirinna

Woomera, Marree, Lyndhurst, Copley, Parachilna, Blinman, Hawker, Quorn, Port Augusta, Wilmington, Wilpena, Leigh Creek, Andamooka, Roxby Downs, Olympic Dam, Coward Springs, William Creek, Anna Creek, Mount Eba, Kingoonya, Glendambo, Tarcoola, Wirraminna, Pimba

Ceduna, Streaky Bay, Smoky Bay, Penong, Koonibba, Coorabie, Eucla Motel, Mundrabilla, Cook, Fisher, Hughes, Reid, Forrest, Wynbring, Ooldea, Wirrulla, Minnipa, Wudinna, Kimba, Iron Knob, Iron Baron, Whyalla, Cowell, Cleve, Lock, Elliston, Port Kenny, Streaky Bay, Port Lincoln, Tumby Bay, Cummins, Wasleys

Broken Hill, Silverton, Cockburn, Olary, Yunta, Burra, Peterborough, Orroroo, Jamestown, Gladstone, Crystal Brook, Port Pirie, Snowtown, Clare, Auburn, Balaklava, Kadina, Wallaroo, Moonta, Ardrossan, Maitland, Minlaton, Yorketown, Edithburgh

Adelaide, Gawler, Murray Bridge, Tailem Bend, Mannum, Morgan, Waikerie, Renmark, Berri, Loxton, Pinnaroo, Lameroo, Bordertown, Wentworth, Dareton, Wakerie, Barmera, Karadoc, Pooncarie, Menindee

Tropic of Capricorn

© HAMMOND W.A.C. / © HAMMOND WORLD ATLAS CORPORATION

Adelaide inset

Adelaide, Elizabeth, Salisbury, Parafield, Port Adelaide, Prospect, Grange, Henley Beach, Glenelg, Brighton, Unley, Mitcham, Stirling, Marineland, Festival Centre, Adelaide Zoo, Adelaide Int'l, Belair Rec. Pk., Cleland Rec. Area, Morialta Conservation Park, Para Wirra Nat'l Park, Millbrook Res., Mount Torrens, Birdwood, Gumeracha, Lobethal, Woodside, Balhannah, Hahndorf, Nairne, Mt. Barker, Echunga, Happy Valley, Mt. Bold Res., Mt. Lofty 727 m

Gulf St. Vincent

Mount Lofty Ranges

Scale 1:6,000,000 — Lambert Conformal Conic Projection

MI 50 100 150 200
KM 50 100 150 200

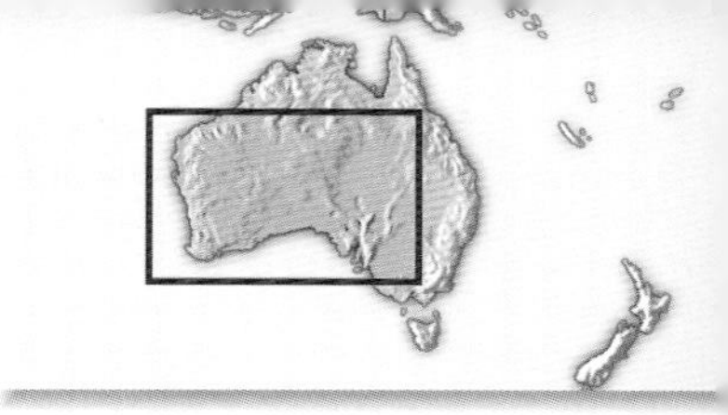

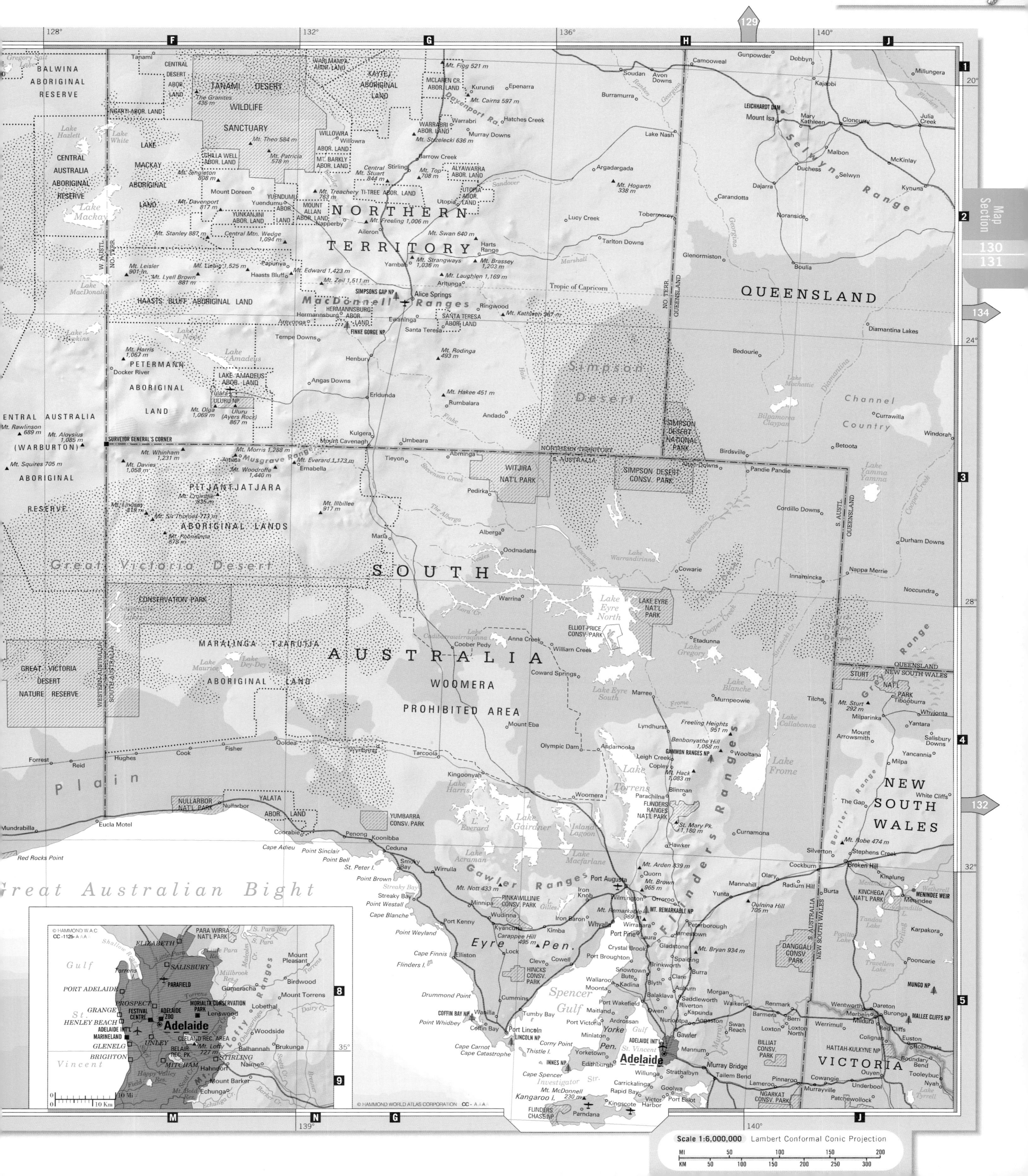

Southeastern Australia

Tasmania lies within the cool-temperate West Wind Drift of the southern hemisphere. The resulting climate provides abundant precipitation and ideal conditions for fruit and berry cultivation. The northern area of southeastern Australia, where New South Wales merges with the monsoon region of Queensland, is much warmer. Areas of subtropical rain forests are also found along the northern coast.

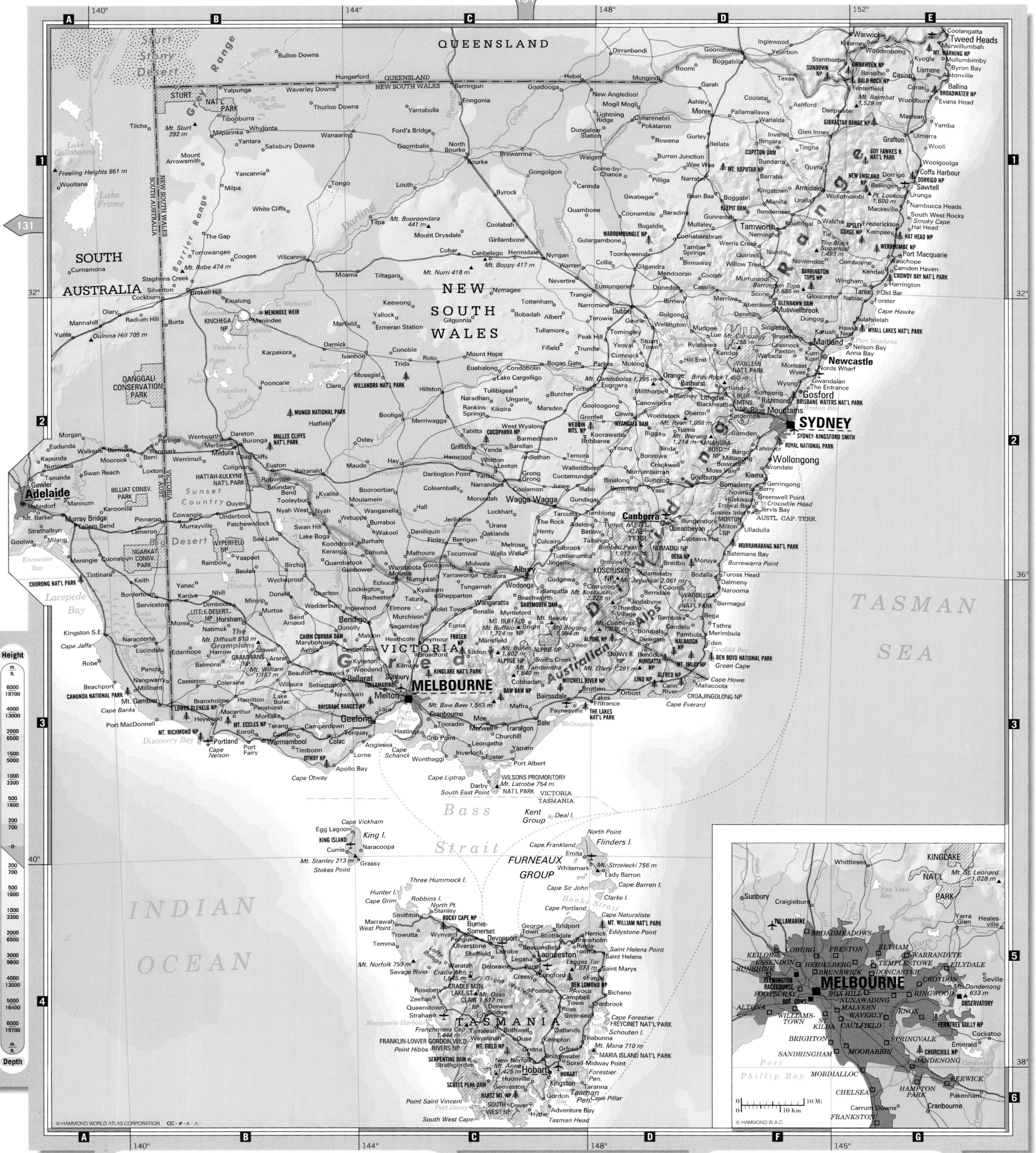

QUEENSLAND

NEW SOUTH WALES

SOUTH AUSTRALIA

VICTORIA

TASMANIA

TASMAN SEA

INDIAN OCEAN

Bass Strait

Adelaide

MELBOURNE

SYDNEY

Canberra

Newcastle

Wollongong

Hobart

Height
m. / ft.
6000 / 19700
4000 / 13000
2000 / 6500
1500 / 5000
1000 / 3300
500 / 1600
200 / 700
0
200 / 700
500 / 1600
1000 / 3300
2000 / 6500
3000 / 9800
4000 / 13000
5000 / 16400
6000 / 19700
m.
Depth

Population

■ Over 2,000,000	● 500,000 - 999,999
■ 1,000,000 - 1,999,999	● 250,000 - 499,999
● 100,000 - 249,999	○ 10,000 - 29,999
○ 30,000 - 99,999	○ Under 10,000

Scale 1:6,000,000 Lambert Conformal Conic Projection

MI 50 100 150 200
KM 50 100 150 200 300

© HAMMOND WORLD ATLAS CORPORATION

Melbourne inset

MELBOURNE
KINGLAKE NAT'L PARK
Tullamarine
BROADMEADOWS
KEILOR COBURG PRESTON ELTHAM
ESSENDON HEIDELBERG TEMPLESTOWE WARRANDYTE
SUNSHINE BRUNSWICK DONCASTER LILYDALE
FLEMINGTON RACECOURSE
FOOTSCRAY BOX HILL NUNAWADING CROYDON
ALTONA WILLIAMSTOWN ST KILDA MALVERN KNOX RINGWOOD
BRIGHTON CAULFIELD WAVERLEY FERNTREE GULLY NP
SANDRINGHAM MOORABBIN SPRINGVALE
MORDIALLOC DANDENONG
CHELSEA CHURCHILL PARK
HAMPTON PARK BERWICK
FRANKSTON CARRUM DOWNS CRANBOURNE

Port Phillip Bay

0 10 Mi
0 10 Km

Due to its relatively pleasant climate and reliable rainfall, the region between Sydney and Melbourne is home to most Australians. Lush forests of eucalyptus are found here, and the Blue Mountains west of Sydney are presumably named for the shimmering blue of indigenous eucalyptus trees. Mount Kosciusko, Australia's highest peak, rises to an elevation of 2,228 meters south of Canberra.

Sydney – Melbourne

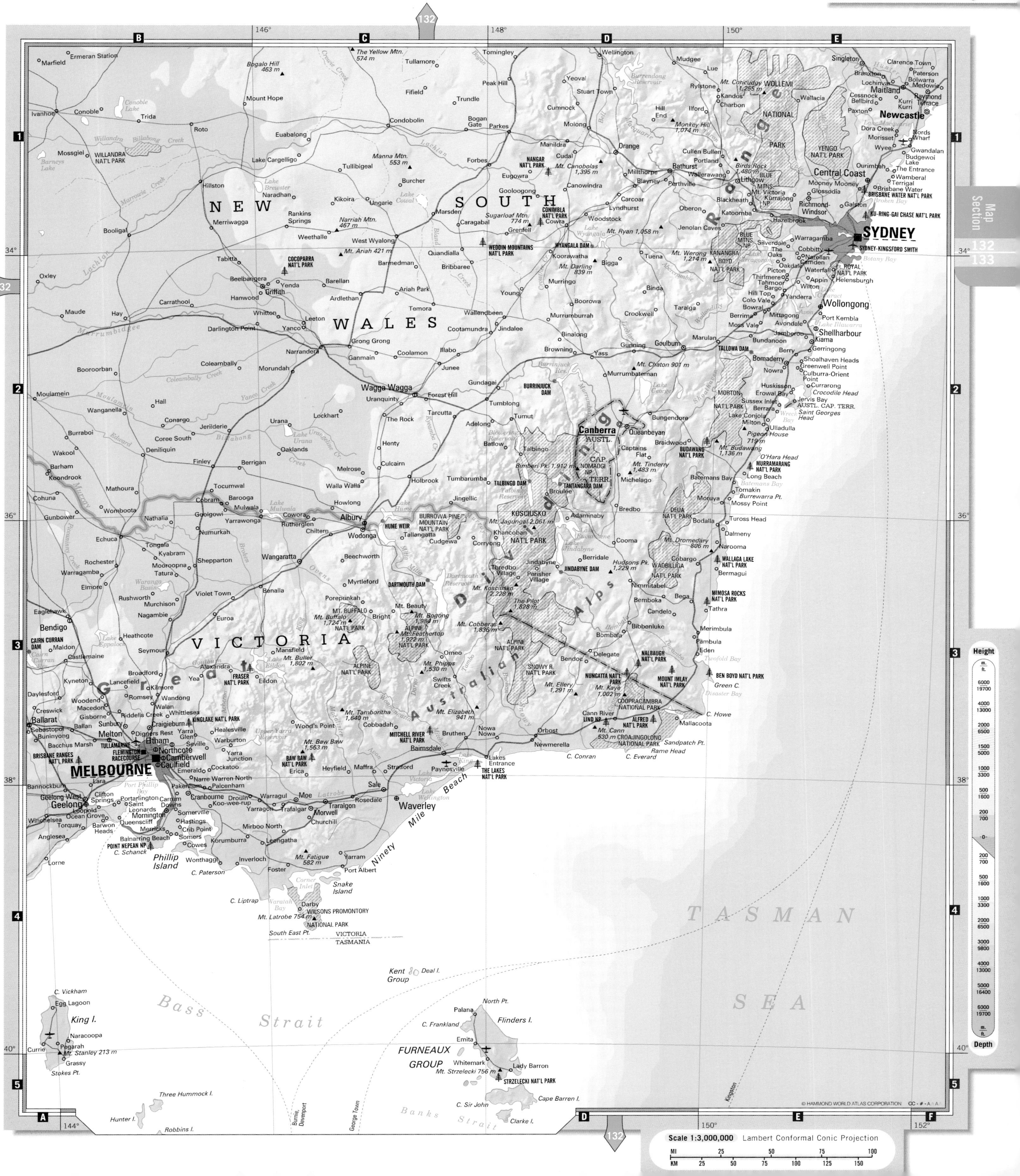

Scale 1:3,000,000   Lambert Conformal Conic Projection

© HAMMOND WORLD ATLAS CORPORATION

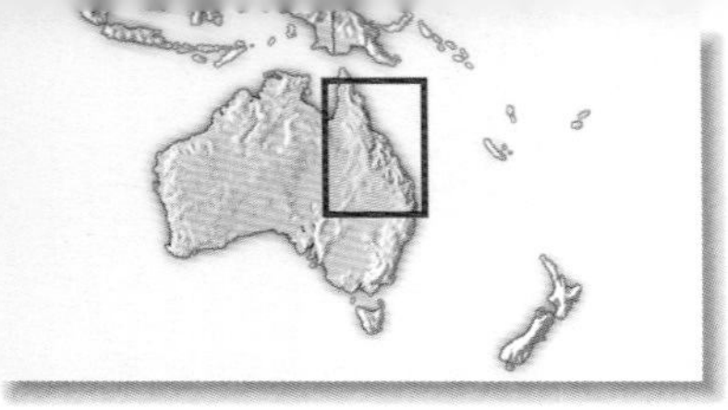

Northeastern Australia

The Great Barrier Reef is a complex of coral reefs, atolls, and shoals that runs along the northeastern coast of Australia for about 2,600 km. Its foundations lie on the shelf of the Coral Sea at depths of up to 180 m. Water levels and climatic conditions have a major impact on reef growth. A rapid rise in sea level endangers coral organisms, which cannot survive in depths below 55 m.

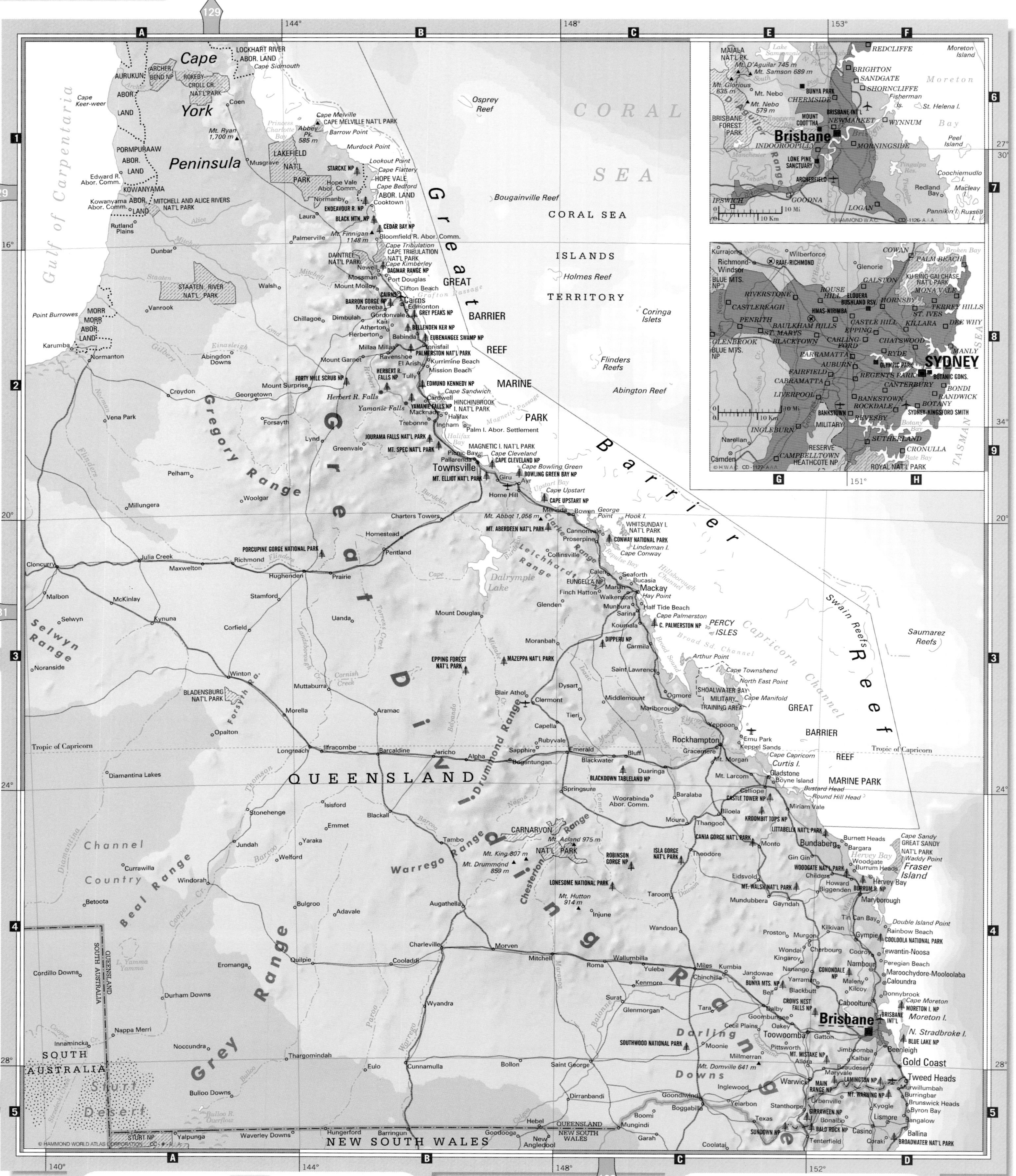

Height
m. ft.
6000 19700
4000 13000
2000 6500
1500 5000
1000 3300
500 1600
200 700
0
200 700
500 1600
1000 3300
2000 6500
3000 9800
4000 13000
5000 16400
6000 19700
m. ft.
Depth

Population

■ Over 2,000,000   ⊛ 500,000 - 999,999   ⊙ 100,000 - 249,999   ○ 10,000 - 29,999
■ 1,000,000 - 1,999,999   ⊛ 250,000 - 499,999   ⊙ 30,000 - 99,999   ○ Under 10,000

Scale 1:6,000,000 Lambert Conformal Conic Projection

MI   50   100   150   200
KM   50   100   150   200   250   300

New Zealand

Active volcanoes, geysers, glaciers, fjords, sandy beaches, evergreen beach forests, ferns the size of trees, parrots - the list of New Zealand's natural beauties goes on and on. The North Island lies along the Pacific "Ring of Fire" and is therefore subject to volcanic eruptions. The South Island, where glaciers descend far into forested areas, is much calmer.

Map Section 134 135

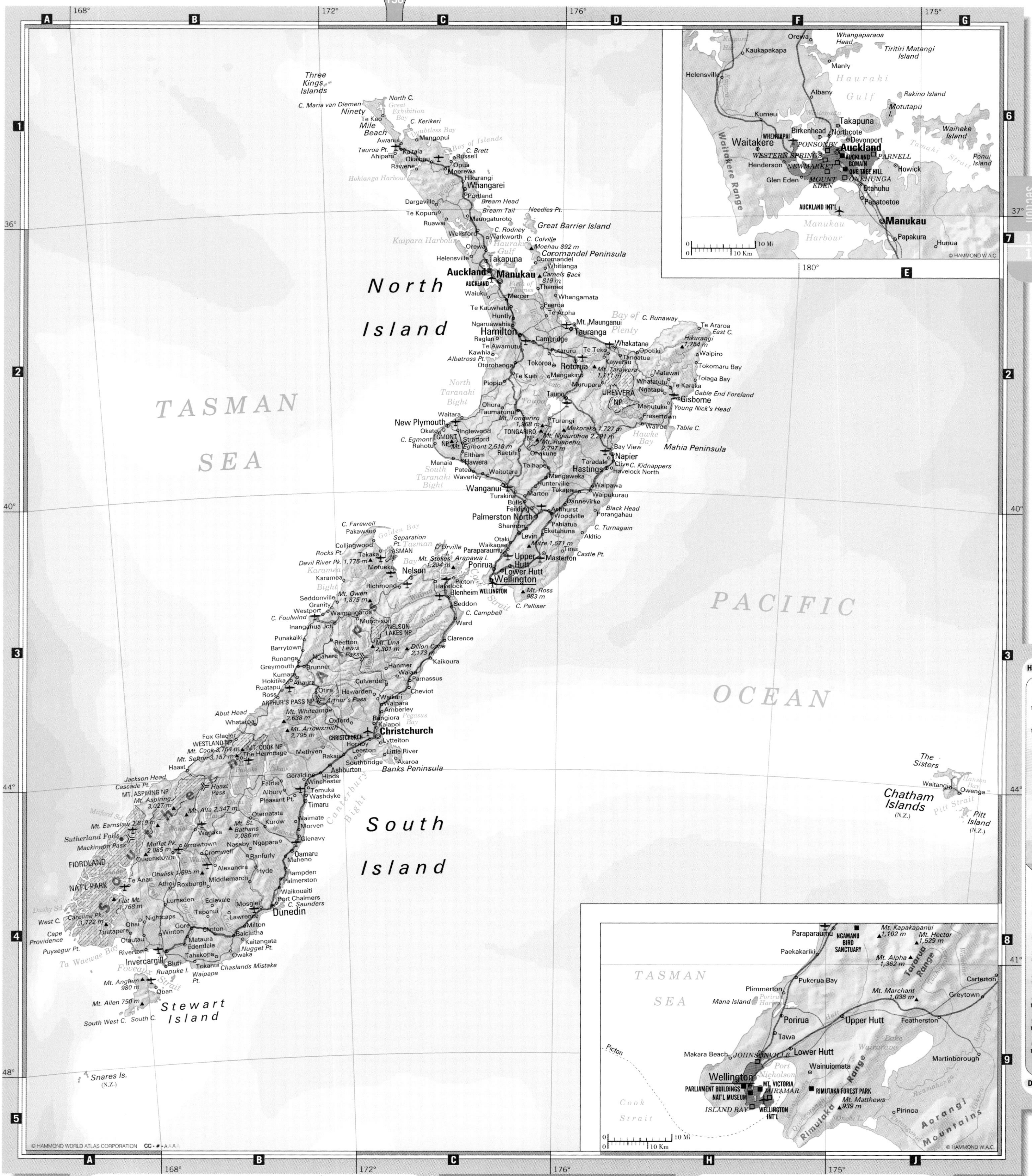

TASMAN SEA

PACIFIC OCEAN

North Island

Three Kings Islands
North C.
C. Maria van Diemen
Ninety Mile Beach
Te Kao
Awanui
Tauroa Pt.
Ahipara
Kaitaia
Mangonui
C. Brett
Russell
Opua
Moerewa
Hikurangi
Whangarei
Dargaville
Portland
Bream Head
Bream Tail
Te Kopuru
Maungaturoto
Needles Pt.
Ruawai
C. Rodney
Warkworth
C. Colville
Great Barrier Island
Wellsford
Moehau 892 m
Coromandel Peninsula
Helensville
Whitianga
Takapuna
Thames
Auckland
Manukau
Camels Back 819 m
Waikuku
Whangamata
Mercer
Te Kauwhata
Peeria
Bay of Plenty
Huntly
Whangarei
Ngaruawahia
Raglan
Hamilton
Cambridge
Mt. Maunganui
Tauranga
Te Puke
C. Runaway
Te Araroa
East C.
Awakino
Tokoroa
Rotorua
Te Teko
Whakatane
Opotiki
Waipiro
Kawhia
Te Awamutu
Mangakino
Mt. Tarawera 1,111 m
Matawai
Tolaga Bay
Albatross Pt.
Otorohanga
Te Kuiti
Taupo
UREWERA NP.
Ngatapa
Gisborne
Young Nick's Head
Gable End Foreland
Ohura
Taumarunui
Manutuke
Frasertown
New Plymouth
Waitara
Mt. Tongariro 1,968 m
Mokorako 1,727 m
Wairoa
Table C.
Okato
Inglewood
TONGARIRO
Mt. Ngauruhoe 2,291 m
Bay View
Mahia Peninsula
C. Egmont
Stratford
Mt. Ruapehu 2,797 m
Napier
Mt. Egmont 2,518 m
Eltham
Raetihi
Ohakune
Taradale
Hastings
Clive
C. Kidnappers
Manaia
Hawera
Taihape
Havelock North
Patea
Waverley
Waitotara
Mangaweka
Waipawa
Wanganui
Turakina
Hunterville
Waipukurau
Bulls
Dannevirke
Feilding
Ashhurst
Woodville
Porangahau
Palmerston North
Pahiatua
Black Head
Shannon
Otaki
Levin
Akitio
Te Turnagain
Waikanae
Eketahuna
Paraparaumu
Mt. Mitre 1,571 m
Castle Pt.
Upper Hutt
Masterton
Lower Hutt
Wellington
Mt. Ross 983 m
C. Palliser

South Island

C. Farewell
Golden Bay
Pakawau
Collingwood
Separation Pt.
D'Urville
Rocks Pt.
Takaka
TASMAN NP.
Arapawa I.
Devil River Pk. 1,775 m
Motueka
Mt. Stokes 1,204 m
Karamea
Nelson
Picton
Richmond
Havelock
Seddonville
Hira
Blenheim
WELLINGTON
Granity
Mt. Owen 1,875 m
Seddon
Westport
NELSON LAKES NP.
Ward
Punakaiki
Murchison
C. Campbell
Reefton
Mt. Una 2,301 m
Dillon Cone 2,173 m
Greymouth
Ngahere
Lewis Pass
Clarence
Runanga
Hanmer
Kumara
Brunner
Waiau
Parnassus
Hokitika
Otira
Hawarden
Cheviot
Ruatapu
ARTHUR'S PASS NP.
Arthur's Pass
Waikari
Ross
Culverden
Waipara
Mt. Whitcombe 2,638 m
Oxford
Amberley
Abut Head
Mt. Arrowsmith 2,795 m
Rangiora
Pegasus Bay
Whataroa
Kaiapoi
Fox Glacier
Mt. Cook 3,764 m
Christchurch
WESTLAND NP.
Mt. Sefton 3,157 m
Hornby
Lyttelton
MT. COOK NP.
The Hermitage
Methven
Leeston
Little River
Jackson Head
Rakaia
Southbridge
Akaroa
Cascade Pt.
Haast
Banks Peninsula
MT. ASPIRING NP.
Mt. Aspiring 3,027 m
Geraldine
Hinds
Mt. Alta 2,347 m
Fairlie
Ashburton
Albury
Winchester
Mt. Earnslaw 2,819 m
Moffat Pk. 2,085 m
Mt. St. Bathans 2,086 m
Temuka
Sutherland Falls
Pleasant Pt.
Timaru
Mackinnon Pass
Arrowtown
Milford Sound
Wanaka
Cromwell
Otematata
Waimate
Queenstown
Naseby
Ngapara
Kurow
Morven
FIORDLAND
Obelisk 1,695 m
Alexandra
Hyde
Oamaru
Glenavy
NAT'L PARK
Ranfurly
Maheno
Te Anau
Athol
Roxburgh
Middlemarch
Hampden
Dusky Sd.
Flat Mt. 1,768 m
Palmerston
West C.
Lumsden
Tapanui
Waikouaiti
Caroline Pk. 1,722 m
Ohai
Edendale
Mosgiel
Port Chalmers
Cape Providence
Nightcaps
Gore
Lawrence
C. Saunders
Puysegur Pt.
Winton
Mataura
Balclutha
Dunedin
Riverton
Tahakopa
Kaitangata
Invercargill
Edendale
Owaka
Nugget Pt.
Bluff
Tokanui
Waipapa Pt.
Chaslands Mistake
Mt. Anglem 980 m
Ruapuke I.
Oban
Mt. Allen 750 m

Stewart Island

Snares Is. (N.Z.)

The Sisters
Waitangi
Chatham Islands (N.Z.)
Pitt Island (N.Z.)
Pitt Strait
Owenga

Inset map (top right, Auckland)

Whangaparaoa Head
Kaukapakapa
Orewa
Tiritiri Matangi Island
Helensville
Manly
Kumeu
Albany
Rakino Island
Takapuna
Motutapu
Waitakere
WHENUAPAI
Birkenhead
Northcote
Devonport
Waiheke Island
Henderson
WESTERN SPRINGS
PONSONBY
AUCKLAND DOMAIN
PARNELL
Auckland
Howick
Glen Eden
NEWMARKET
ONE TREE HILL
Ponui Island
MOUNT EDEN
ONEHUNGA
Otahuhu
AUCKLAND INT'L
Papatoetoe
Manukau
Manukau Harbour
Papakura
Hunua

Inset map (bottom right, Wellington)

Paraparaumu
NGAMANU BIRD SANCTUARY
Mt. Kapakapanui 1,102 m
Mt. Hector 1,529 m
Paekakariki
Carterton
Mt. Alpha 1,362 m
Pukerua Bay
Greytown
Plimmerton
Mt. Marchant 1,038 m
Mana Island
Porirua
Tawa
Upper Hutt
Featherston
Makara Beach
JOHNSONVILLE
Lower Hutt
Picton
Wainuiomata
Wellington
PARLIAMENT BUILDINGS
NAT'L MUSEUM
Mt. Victoria
MIRAMAR
RIMUTAKA FOREST PARK
Mt. Matthews 939 m
ISLAND BAY
WELLINGTON INT'L
Martinborough
Pirinoa
Cook Strait
Aorangi Mountains

Population

Symbol	Population
■	Over 2,000,000
■	1,000,000 - 1,999,999
●	500,000 - 999,999
◉	250,000 - 499,999
⊙	100,000 - 249,999
●	30,000 - 99,999
⊙	10,000 - 29,999
○	Under 10,000

Height
m. / ft.
6000 / 19700
4000 / 13000
2000 / 6500
1500 / 5000
1000 / 3300
500 / 1600
200 / 700
0
200 / 700
500 / 1600
1000 / 3300
2000 / 6500
3000 / 9800
4000 / 13000
5000 / 16400
6000 / 19700
m. / ft.
Depth

Scale 1:6,000,000 Lambert Conformal Conic Projection

MI 50 100 150 200
KM 50 100 150 200 250 300

The Pacific Ocean is the largest body of water on Earth. It covers about 166 million square km, while the world's total land area amounts to only 150 million square km. It is more than twice the size of the Atlantic and Indian oceans and holds roughly 46% of the Earth's water. The ocean is by no means as peaceful as its name suggests. Tropical storms known as typhoons generate waves up to 34 m high. Evidently, Ferdinand Magellan, who gave the ocean its name in 1520, enjoyed calm seas on his voyage across the Pacific.

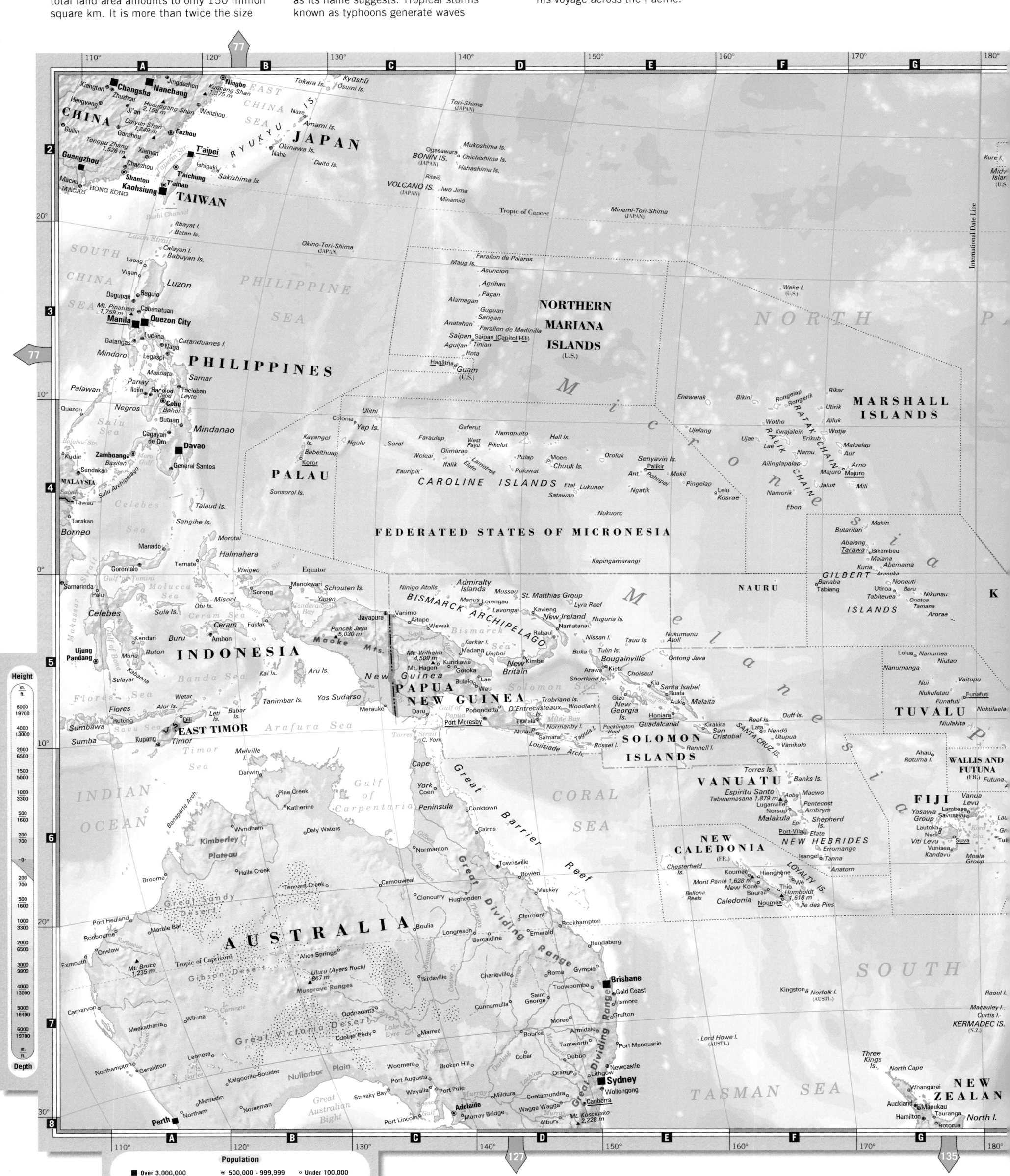

Population
- Over 3,000,000
- 1,000,000 - 2,999,999
- 500,000 - 999,999
- 100,000 - 499,999
- Under 100,000

Central Pacific Ocean

Main Map

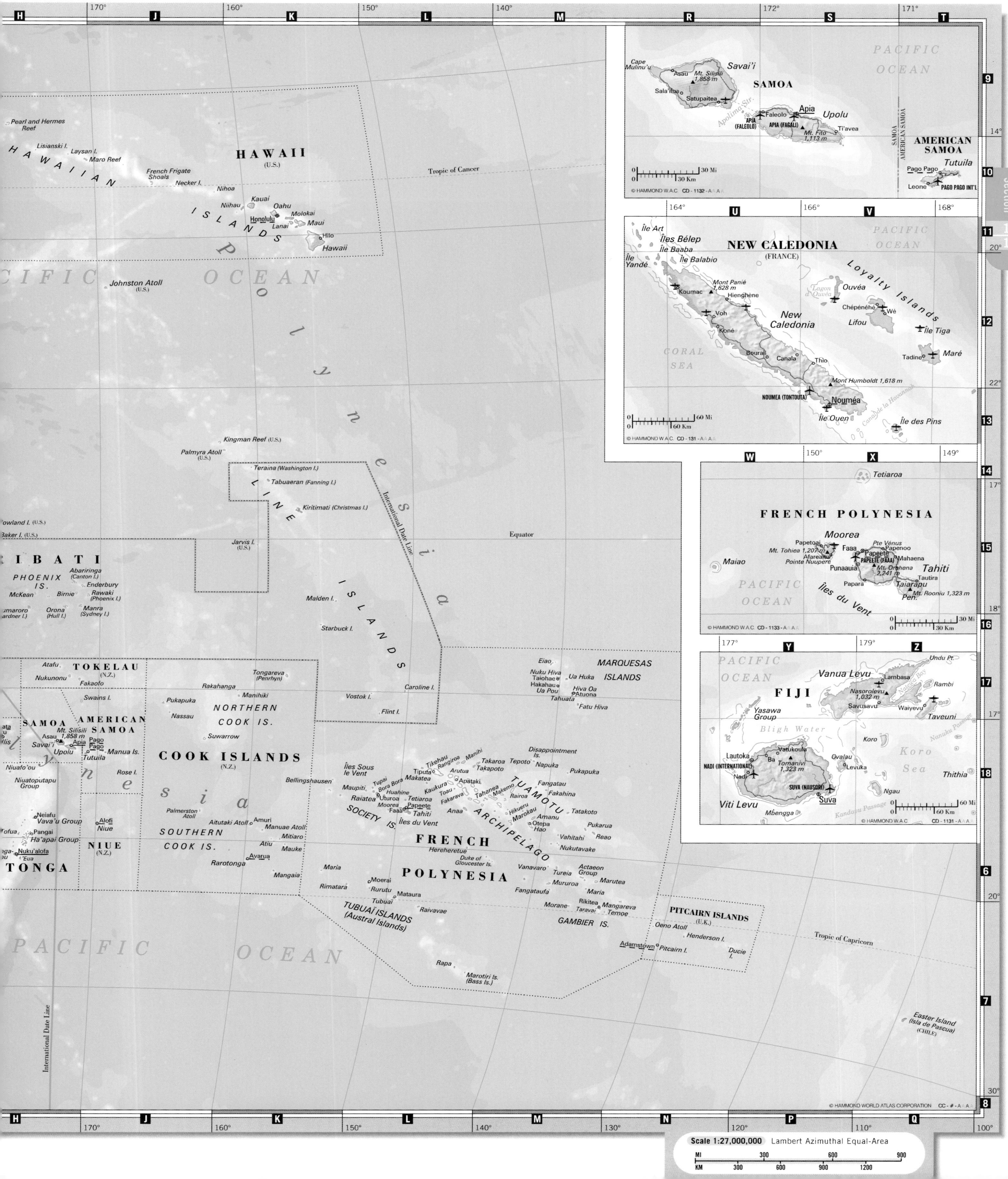

HAWAIIAN ISLANDS

Pearl and Hermes Reef
Lisianski I.
Laysan I.
Maro Reef
French Frigate Shoals
Necker I.
Nihoa
Niihau
Kauai
Oahu
Honolulu
Molokai
Lanai
Maui
Hilo
Hawaii

HAWAII (U.S.)

Tropic of Cancer

Johnston Atoll (U.S.)

PACIFIC OCEAN

Kingman Reef (U.S.)
Palmyra Atoll (U.S.)
Teraina (Washington I.)
Tabuaeran (Fanning I.)
Kiritimati (Christmas I.)

Jarvis I. (U.S.)

Equator

International Date Line

KIRIBATI
PHOENIX IS.
Abariringa (Canton I.)
McKean
Birnie
Enderbury
Rawaki (Phoenix I.)
Orona (Hull I.)
Manra (Sydney I.)
Gardner I.
Howland I. (U.S.)
Baker I. (U.S.)

Malden I.

Starbuck I.

Vostok I.
Caroline I.
Flint I.

LINE ISLANDS

P o l y n e s i a

M i c r o n e s i a

Eiao
Nuku Hiva
Taiohae
Ua Huka
Hakahau
Ua Pou
Tahuata
Hiva Oa
Atuona
Fatu Hiva

MARQUESAS ISLANDS

TOKELAU
Atafu
Nukunonu
Fakaofo
Swains I.

Rakahanga
Tongareva (Penrhyn)
Manihiki
Pukapuka
Nassau
Suwarrow

NORTHERN COOK IS.

SAMOA
AMERICAN SAMOA
Asau
Mt. Silisili 1,858 m
Apia
Pago Pago
Upolu
Tutuila
Manua Is.

Niuafo'ou
Niuatoputapu Group
Rose I.

COOK ISLANDS (N.Z.)

Bellingshausen
Palmerston Atoll
Aitutaki Atoll
Manuae Atoll
Amuri
Mitiaro
Atiu
Mauke

Neiafu
Vava'u Group
Alofi
Niue

SOUTHERN COOK IS.

NIUE (N.Z.)

Pangai
Ha'apai Group
Nuku'alofa
'Eua

TONGA

Rarotonga
Mangaia
Maria
Moerai
Rurutu
Rimatara
Mataura
Tubuai
Raivavae

TUBUAI ISLANDS (Austral Islands)

Rapa
Marotiri Is. (Bass Is.)

Tikehau
Rangiroa
Manihi
Mataiva
Tiputa
Arutua
Takaroa
Takapoto
Tepoto
Napuka
Disappointment Is.
Pukapuka

Îles Sous le Vent
Tupai
Bora Bora
Maupiti
Huahine
Raiatea
Tahaa
Uturoa
Moorea
Tetiaroa
Faaa
Tahiti
Papeete

SOCIETY IS.
Îles du Vent

Kaukura
Apataki
Toau
Fakarava
Anaa

Makatea

Fangatau
Fakahina
Katiu
Tahanea
Makemo
Raroia
Marokau
Hikueru
Amanu
Hao
Otepa
Vahitahi
Reao
Nukutavake

TUAMOTU ARCHIPELAGO

Hereheretue
Duke of Gloucester Is.
Vanavaro
Tureia
Marutea
Actaeon Group
Mururoa
Maria
Fangataufa
Morane
Rikitea
Mangareva
Temoe

GAMBIER IS.

FRENCH POLYNESIA

PITCAIRN ISLANDS (U.K.)
Oeno Atoll
Henderson I.
Adamstown
Pitcairn I.
Ducie I.

Tropic of Capricorn

PACIFIC OCEAN

Easter Island (Isla de Pascua) (CHILE)

Inset: Samoa

SAMOA

Cape Mulinu'u
Asau
Mt. Silisili 1,858 m
Savai'i
Sala'ilua
Satupaitea
Apolima Str.
Faleolo
APIA (FALEOLO)
Apia
APIA (FAGALI)
Upolu
Mt. Fito 1,113 m
Ti'avea

SAMOA
AMERICAN SAMOA

AMERICAN SAMOA
Pago Pago
Tutuila
Leone
PAGO PAGO INT'L

PACIFIC OCEAN

0   30 Mi
0   30 Km

© HAMMOND W.A.C. CD-1132-A-A-A

Inset: New Caledonia

NEW CALEDONIA (FRANCE)

Île Art
Îles Bélep
Île Baaba
Île Balabio
Île Yandé

Koumac
Mont Panié 1,628 m
Hienghène
Voh
Koné
Boura
Canala
Thio
Mont Humboldt 1,618 m

New Caledonia

Loyalty Islands
Lagon d'Ouvéa
Ouvéa
Chépénéhé
Wé
Lifou
Île Tiga
Tadine
Maré

CORAL SEA

NOUMEA (TONTOUTA)
Nouméa
Île Ouen
Île des Pins
Canal de la Havannah

PACIFIC OCEAN

0   60 Mi
0   60 Km

© HAMMOND W.A.C. CD-131-A-A-A

Inset: French Polynesia

FRENCH POLYNESIA

Tetiaroa

Moorea
Papetoai
Mt. Tohiea 1,207 m
Afareaitu
Pointe Nuupere
Pte Vénus
Papenoo
Faaa
Papeete
PAPEETE (FAAA)
Mahaena
Mahina
Punaauia
Mt. Orohena 2,241 m
Papara
Tahiti
Tautira
Taiarapu
Pen.
Mt. Rooniu 1,323 m

Maiao
Maiao

Îles du Vent

PACIFIC OCEAN

0   30 Mi
0   30 Km

© HAMMOND W.A.C. CD-1133-A-A-A

Inset: Fiji

FIJI

PACIFIC OCEAN

Undu Pt.
Vanua Levu
Nasorolevu 1,032 m
Lambasa
Rambi
Savusavu
Waiyevu
Taveuni

Yasawa Group

Bligh Water

Koro

Koro Sea

Lautoka
Vatukoula
Ba
Tavua
Vatukoula
Tomanivi 1,323 m
NADI (INTERNATIONAL)
Nadi
Ovalau
Levuka
Thithia
Ngau

Viti Levu
SUVA (NAUSORI)
Suva
Mbengga
Kandavu Passage

© HAMMOND W.A.C. CD-1131-A-A-A

Scale 1:27,000,000   Lambert Azimuthal Equal-Area

MI   300   600   900
KM   300   600   900   1200

© HAMMOND WORLD ATLAS CORPORATION   CC-#-A-A

With a depth of 1.6 km, the Grand Canyon is one of the deepest river gorges in the world. This image taken toward the west shows the Colorado River, which has cut through rock billions of years old to form the canyon. The Grand Canyon is 260 km long and averages about 16 km in width at the top but narrows to as few as 15 m in places along the valley floor. The river flows over 150 rapids on its course through the canyon. The valley itself is only a few million years old. Visible in the image are the snow-covered Kaibab Plateau north of the canyon and the Coconino Plateau to the south.

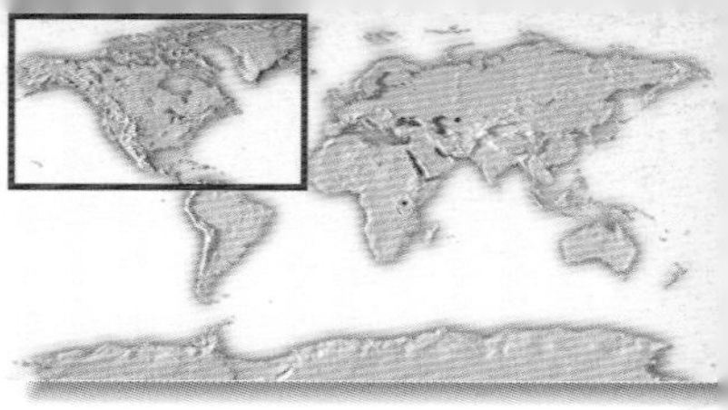

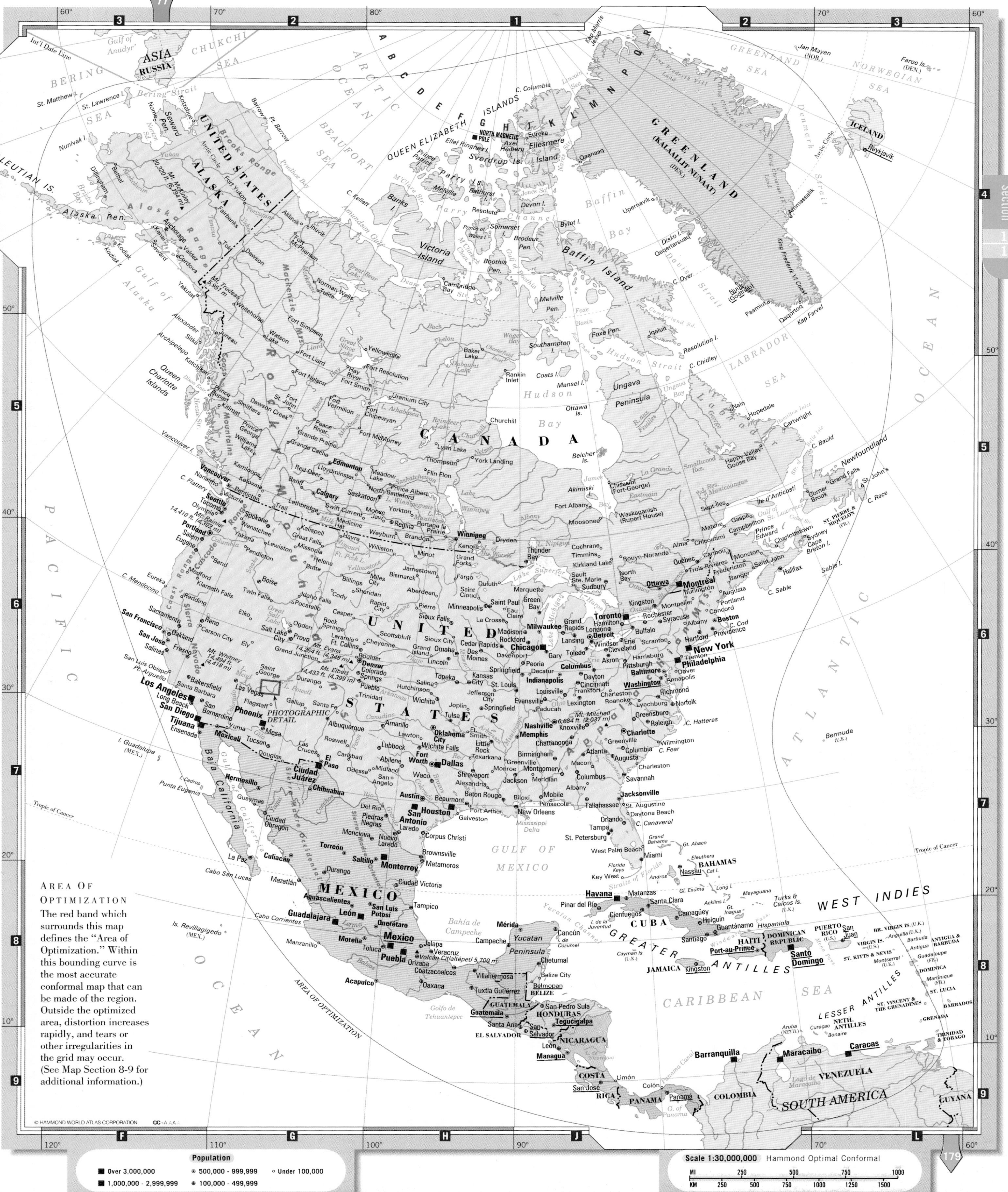

AREA OF OPTIMIZATION
The red band which surrounds this map defines the "Area of Optimization." Within this bounding curve is the most accurate conformal map that can be made of the region. Outside the optimized area, distortion increases rapidly, and tears or other irregularities in the grid may occur. (See Map Section 8-9 for additional information.)

© HAMMOND WORLD ATLAS CORPORATION   CC-A AA A

Population

■ Over 3,000,000	● 500,000 - 999,999	○ Under 100,000
■ 1,000,000 - 2,999,999	● 100,000 - 499,999	

Scale 1:30,000,000 Hammond Optimal Conformal

| MI | 250 | 500 | 750 | 1000 |
| KM | 250 | 500 | 750 | 1000 | 1250 |

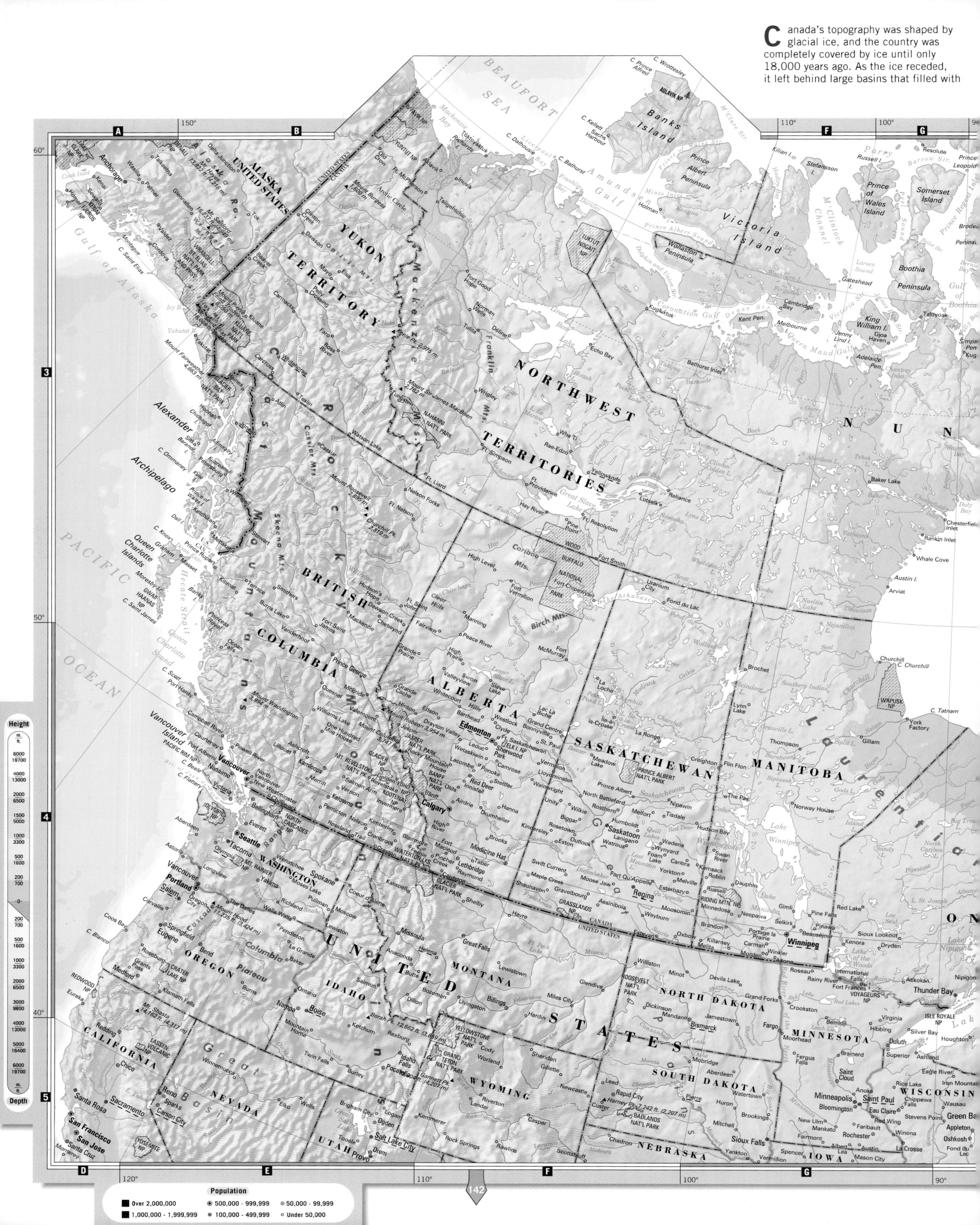

BEAUFORT SEA

Banks Island

AULAVIK NP

C. Wrottesley
C. M'Clure
C. Prince Alfred
Kellett
Sachs Harbour
Holman
C. Dalhousie

Prince of Wales Island

Somerset Island

Boothia Peninsula

Victoria Island

Prince Albert Peninsula

Wollaston Peninsula

NUNAVUT

NORTHWEST TERRITORIES

YUKON TERRITORY

ALASKA
UNITED STATES

BRITISH COLUMBIA

ALBERTA

SASKATCHEWAN

MANITOBA

LAURENTIA

ONTARIO

WASHINGTON

OREGON

CALIFORNIA

NEVADA

IDAHO

UTAH

MONTANA

WYOMING

NORTH DAKOTA

SOUTH DAKOTA

NEBRASKA

MINNESOTA

WISCONSIN

IOWA

UNITED STATES

CANADA
UNITED STATES

PACIFIC OCEAN

Gulf of Alaska

Alexander Archipelago

Queen Charlotte Islands

Vancouver Island

ROCKY MOUNTAINS

COAST MOUNTAINS

CASCADE RANGE

Great Basin

Columbia Plateau

Coronation Gulf

Great Bear Lake

Great Slave Lake

Lake Athabasca

Lake Winnipeg

Height
m. / ft.
6000 / 19700
4000 / 13000
2000 / 6500
1500 / 5000
1000 / 3300
500 / 1600
200 / 700
0
200 / 700
500 / 1600
1000 / 3300
2000 / 6500
3000 / 9800
5000 / 16400
6000 / 19700
m. / ft.
Depth

Population

■ Over 2,000,000	◉ 500,000 - 999,999	◦ 50,000 - 99,999
■ 1,000,000 - 1,999,999	◉ 100,000 - 499,999	◦ Under 50,000

melt water. Today, Canada has more than two million lakes. The country is larger than the United States but very thinly populated, as widespread settlement has been discouraged by the extremely short growing season north of the 55th parallel, the extremely poor, thin soils north of the St. Lawrence Valley, and low levels of precipitation in the northwestern coniferous forest and tundra region.

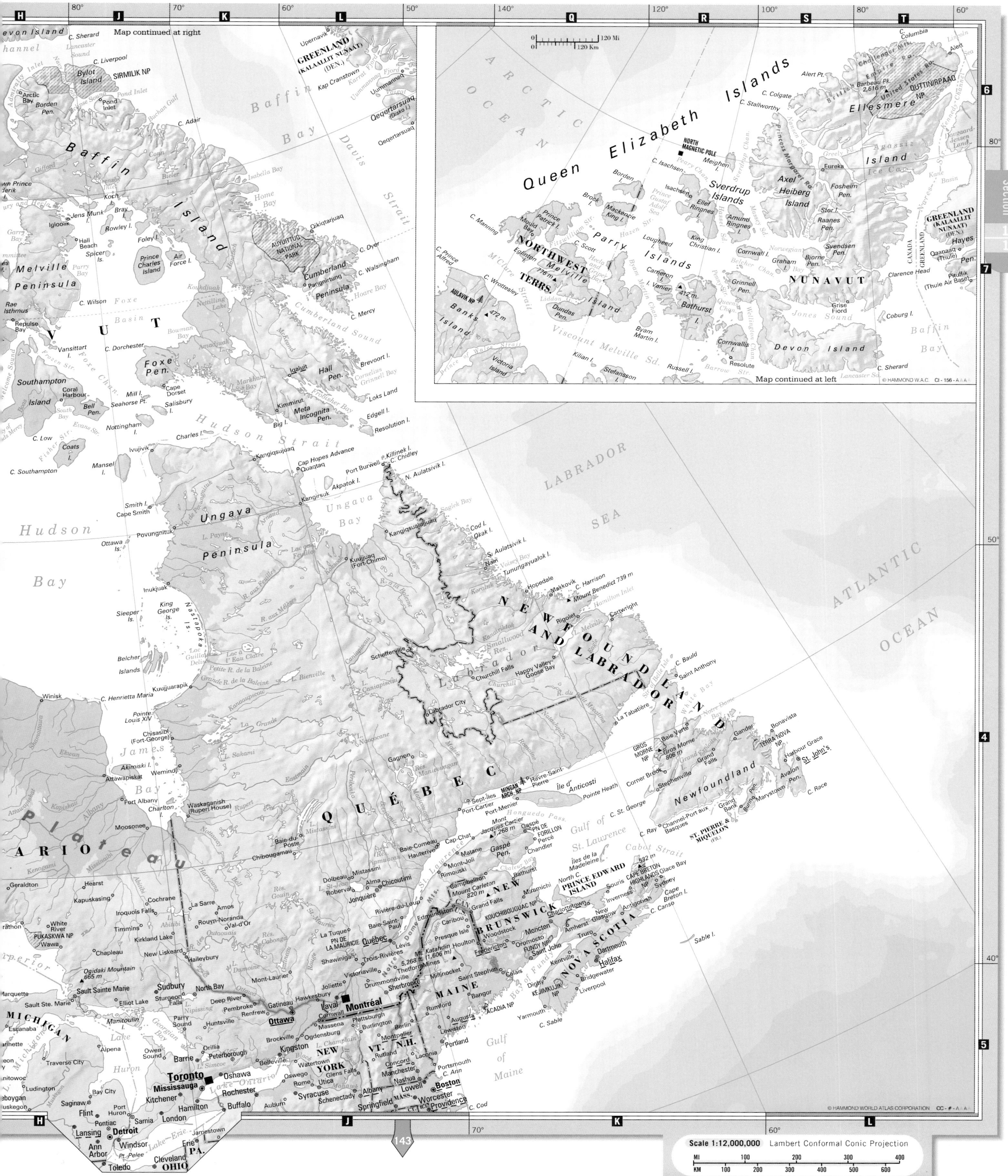

Scale 1:12,000,000   Lambert Conformal Conic Projection

© HAMMOND WORLD ATLAS CORPORATION

The Rocky Mountains, the Mississippi River system, which flows along a course of more than 6,400 km from the north to the Gulf of Mexico, and the Great Lakes along the border to Canada are the most striking major landscape features of the United States. The geologically young Rocky Mountains extend nearly 4,800 km from Alaska through Canada and into New Mexico. The five Great Lakes form the largest contiguous area of fresh water in the world, covering some 245,000 square km. Lake Ontario and Lake Erie are joined by the spectacular Niagara Falls.

United States

MANITOBA · ONTARIO · QUÉBEC

CANADA

Laurentian Plateau

Winnipeg · Kenora · Dryden · Thunder Bay · Sudbury · Ottawa · Montréal · Québec

NEW BRUNSWICK · NOVA SCOTIA · P.E.I. · NEWF. & LAB.

MINNESOTA · WISCONSIN · MICHIGAN · MAINE · VT. · N.H. · MASS. · CONN. · R.I.

Lake Superior · Lake Michigan · Lake Huron · Lake Erie · Lake Ontario

Minneapolis · St. Paul · Duluth · Milwaukee · Chicago · Detroit · Toronto · Buffalo · New York · Boston

IOWA · ILLINOIS · INDIANA · OHIO · PENNSYLVANIA · NEW YORK · N.J.

Des Moines · Kansas City · St. Louis · Indianapolis · Columbus · Pittsburgh · Philadelphia · Baltimore · Washington

KANSAS · MISSOURI · KENTUCKY · WEST VIRGINIA · VIRGINIA · MD. · DEL.

Wichita · Tulsa · Oklahoma City · Springfield · Memphis · Nashville · Knoxville · Charlotte · Richmond · Norfolk · Virginia Beach

OKLAHOMA · ARKANSAS · TENNESSEE · NORTH CAROLINA

Appalachian Mts. · Mt. Mitchell 6,684 ft. (2,037 m) · GREAT SMOKY MTNS. NP

Dallas · Fort Worth · Little Rock · Birmingham · Atlanta · Columbia · SOUTH CAROLINA

TEXAS · LOUISIANA · MISSISSIPPI · ALABAMA · GEORGIA

Houston · San Antonio · Austin · Baton Rouge · New Orleans · Jackson · Montgomery · Jacksonville · Savannah

ATLANTIC OCEAN

Bermuda (U.K.)

GULF OF MEXICO

FLORIDA · Tampa · St. Petersburg · Orlando · West Palm Beach · Ft. Lauderdale · Miami · EVERGLADES NAT'L PARK · Key West · Florida Keys

BAHAMAS · Grand Bahama · Great Abaco · Nassau · New Providence I. · Andros I. · Cat I. · San Salvador (Watling I.) · Long I. · Mayaguana · Acklins I. · Great Inagua · Turks and Caicos Is. (U.K.)

Tropic of Cancer

Havana · CUBA · Matanzas · Santa Clara · Cienfuegos · Camagüey · Holguín · Guantánamo · Santiago de Cuba · I. de la Juventud

Straits of Florida · Yucatán Channel

MÉRIDA · YUCATÁN · QUINTANA ROO · Cancún · Cozumel I. · Cabo Catoche · Valladolid

VERACRUZ · Tampico · Ciudad Madero

CARIBBEAN SEA · Cayman Is. (U.K.)

HAITI · DOMINICAN REPUBLIC · Port-au-Prince · Santo Domingo · Hispaniola · Golfe de la Gonâve · Windward Passage

Scale 1:12,000,000 Lambert Conformal Conic Projection

MI 100 200 300 400
KM 100 200 300 400 500 600

© HAMMOND WORLD ATLAS CORPORATION

The glacier-covered Rocky Mountains, with peaks over 4,000 m high, and the volcanic Cascade Range are both products of a collision between the Pacific and North American plates. Over the course of the past several billion years, microplates have been pulverized, folded, thrust upward, or pressed deep into the earth along the line of convergence. Several thousand kilometers of the oceanic plate have disappeared beneath the North American continent. This rock melts and returns to the surface as lava through volcanoes like Mount Saint Helens and Mount Rainier.

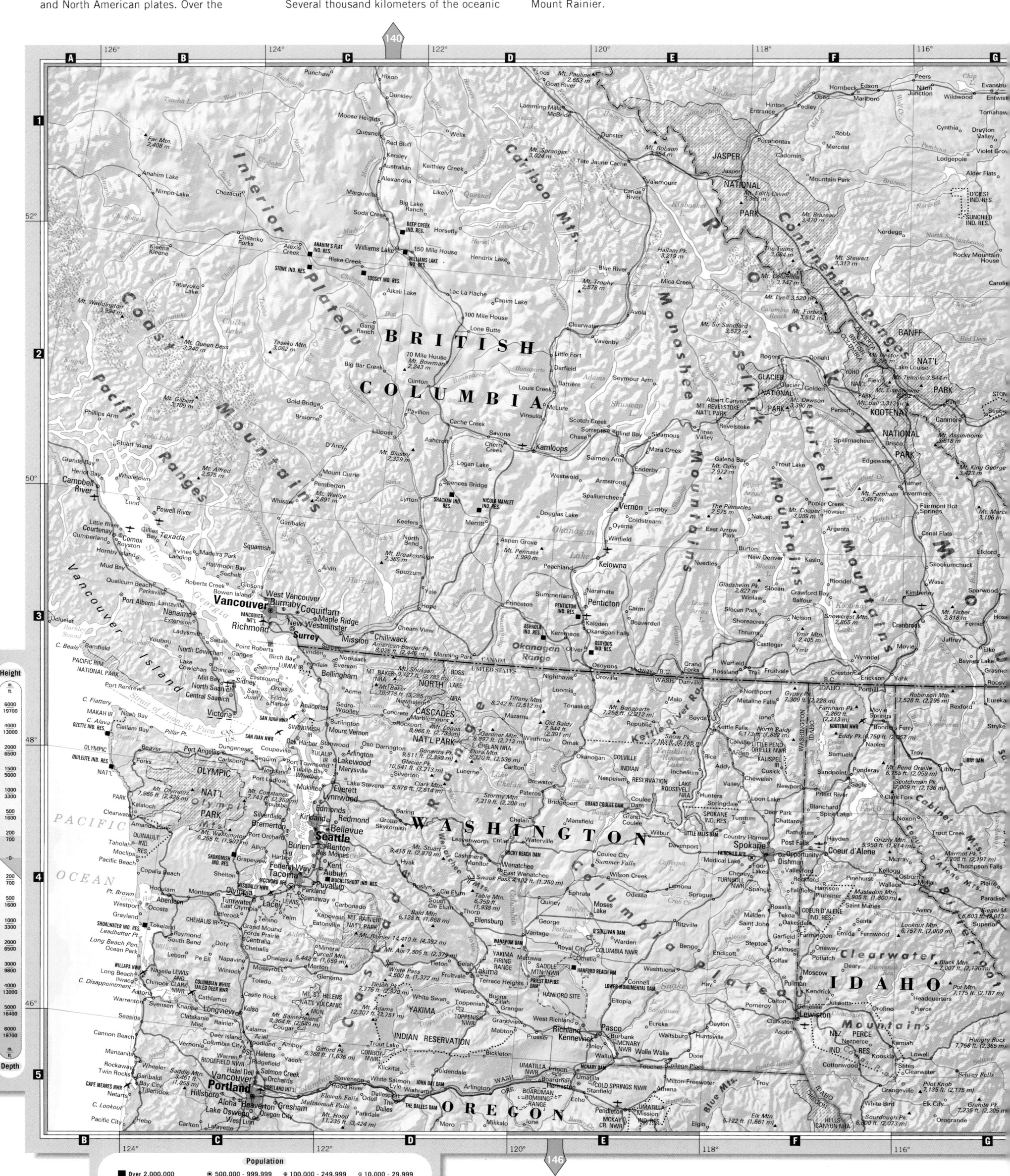

Population

■ Over 2,000,000	◉ 500,000–999,999	◉ 100,000–249,999	◉ 10,000–29,999
■ 1,000,000–1,999,999	◉ 250,000–499,999	◉ 30,000–99,999	○ Under 10,000

ALBERTA

SASKATCHEWAN

MONTANA

GREAT PLAINS

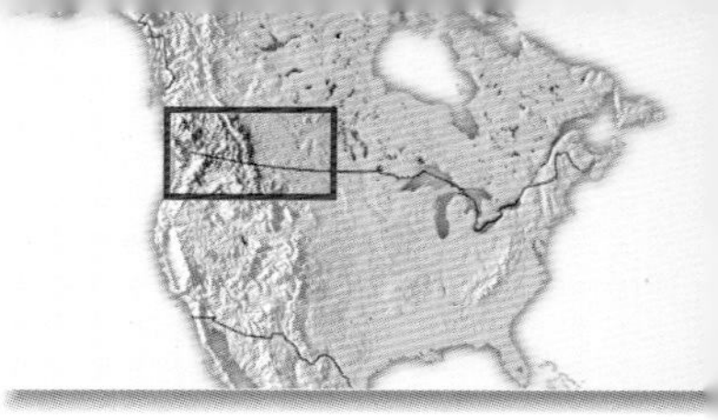

Scale 1:3,000,000   Lambert Conformal Conic Projection

© HAMMOND WORLD ATLAS CORPORATION

A rid areas of North America, like the Great Basin and the nearby salt lakes, are most prevalent in the central western states, where high mountain chains hold back moisture-bearing winds.

Thus annual precipitation west of the Sierra Nevada can be as high as 1,300 m, while Reno on the rim of the Great Basin receives only about 150 m of precipitation a year. The Great Salt Lake is a remnant of

Lake Bonneville, an ice-age lake with depths of up to 330 m and a surface area of over 50,000 square km. Depending upon drainage, today the Great Salt Lake covers some 5,000 square km with a mean depth of three meters.

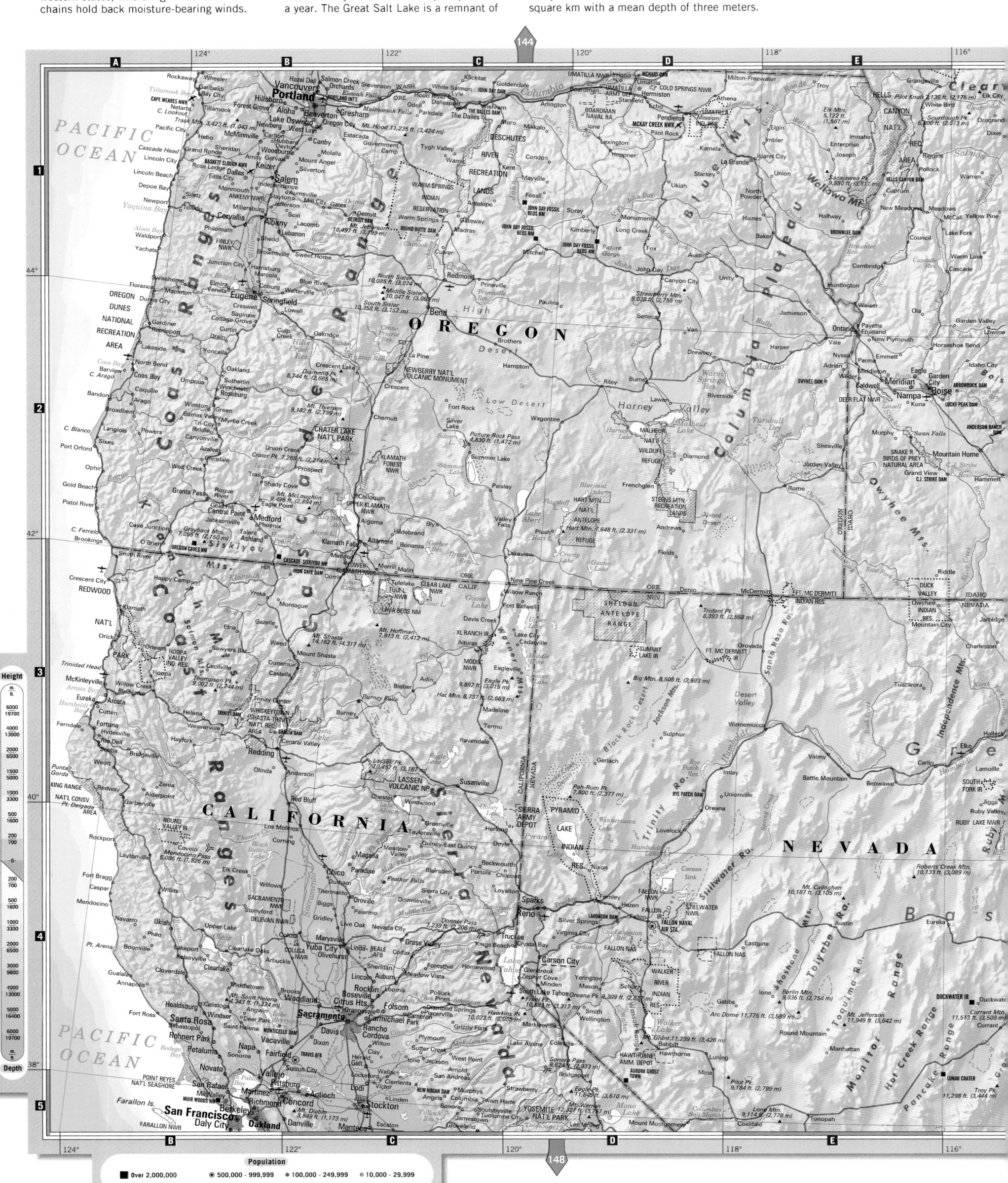

Population		
■ Over 2,000,000	◉ 500,000 - 999,999	◎ 100,000 - 249,999	⊙ 10,000 - 29,999
■ 1,000,000 - 1,999,999	◉ 250,000 - 499,999	⊙ 30,000 - 99,999	○ Under 10,000

MONTANA

WYOMING

IDAHO

UTAH

NEVADA

COLORADO

YELLOWSTONE NAT'L PARK

GRAND TETON N.P.

Great Salt Lake

Salt Lake City

West Valley City

Provo

Ogden

Twin Falls

Idaho Falls

Pocatello

Billings

Bozeman

Casper

Rock Springs

Green River

Grand Junction

ROCKY Mts.

WIND RIVER INDIAN RES.

Great Divide Basin

Great Salt Lake Desert

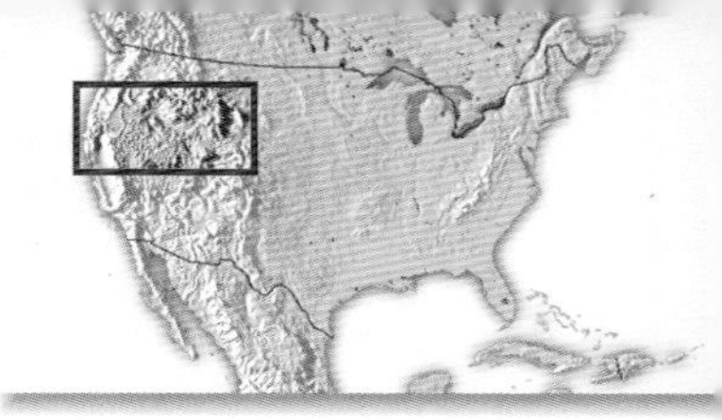

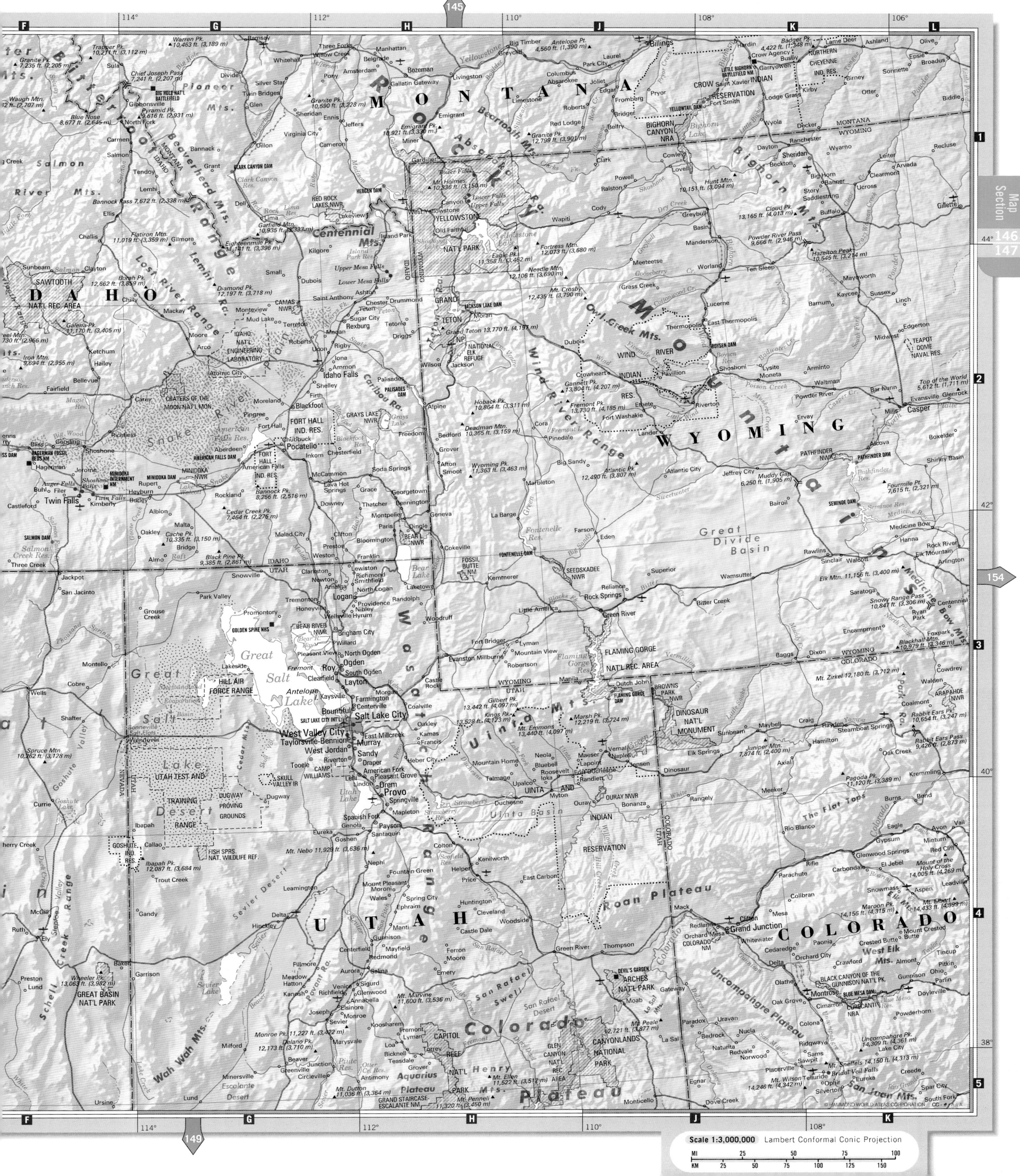

Sevier Desert

Wasatch Range

Uinta Mts.

Grand Teton 13,770 ft. (4,197 m)

Gannett Pk. 13,804 ft. (4,207 m)

Scale 1:3,000,000   Lambert Conformal Conic Projection

MI   25   50   75   100

KM   25   50   75   100   150

The world's most famous geologic fault runs straight through the state of California. The U.S. southwest is part of the Pacific Plate, which is drifting northwestward along the fault line at a rate of 5.6 cm per year. The San Andreas Fault is actually a bundle of parallel faults that extends north from the Gulf of Mexico to a point about 350 km north of San Francisco. The landscape bears the imprint of this plate movement: A number of valleys are sealed off; rainwater accumulates in the fracture zones and gives rise to characteristic bands of vegetation.

Height

m.
ft.

6000
19700

4000
13000

2000
6500

1500
5000

1000
3300

500
1600

200
700

- 0 -

200
700

500
1600

1000
3300

2000
6500

3000
9800

4000
13000

5000
16400

6000
19700

m.
ft.

Depth

Population
■ Over 2,000,000
■ 1,000,000 - 1,999,999
⊚ 500,000 - 999,999
⊚ 250,000 - 499,999
⊙ 100,000 - 249,999
⊙ 30,000 - 99,999
⊙ 10,000 - 29,999
○ Under 10,000

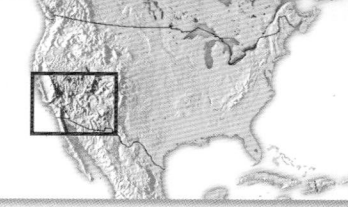

Southwestern United States

Map Section
148
149

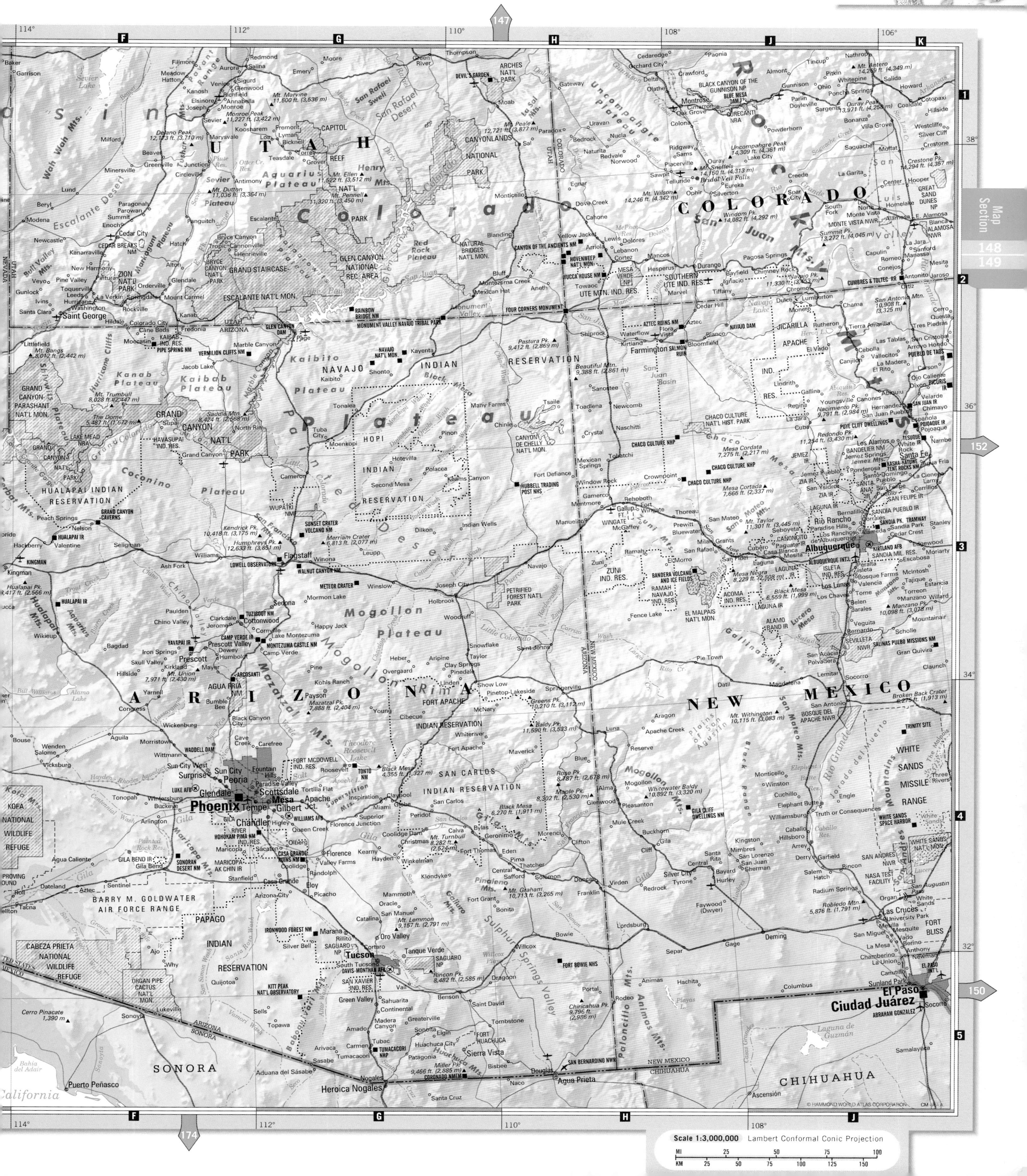
UTAH
ARIZONA
COLORADO
NEW MEXICO
SONORA
CHIHUAHUA
California
Colorado Plateau
Rocky Mts.
San Juan Mts.
Mogollon Plateau
Kaibito Plateau
Kaibab Plateau
Coconino Plateau
Painted Desert
Aquarius Plateau
Uncompahgre Plateau
Sevier Plateau
Escalante Desert
Wah Wah Mts.
Mogollon Rim
Mazatzal Mts.
San Mateo Mts.
White Sands Missile Range
GRAND CANYON NAT'L PARK
NAVAJO INDIAN RESERVATION
HOPI INDIAN RESERVATION
FORT APACHE INDIAN RESERVATION
SAN CARLOS INDIAN RESERVATION
PAPAGO INDIAN RESERVATION
HUALAPAI INDIAN RESERVATION
ZUNI IND. RES.
JICARILLA APACHE IND. RES.
BARRY M. GOLDWATER AIR FORCE RANGE
CABEZA PRIETA NATIONAL WILDLIFE REFUGE
KOFA NATIONAL WILDLIFE REFUGE
ORGAN PIPE CACTUS NAT'L MON.
CANYONLANDS NATIONAL PARK
ARCHES NAT'L PARK
CAPITOL REEF NAT'L PARK
BRYCE CANYON NAT'L PARK
ZION NAT'L PARK
GLEN CANYON NATIONAL REC. AREA
GRAND STAIRCASE-ESCALANTE NAT'L MON.
CANYON DE CHELLY NAT'L MON.
PETRIFIED FOREST NAT'L PARK
FOUR CORNERS MONUMENT
Phoenix
Tucson
Albuquerque
Santa Fe
El Paso
Ciudad Juárez
Flagstaff
Prescott
Farmington
Gallup
Las Cruces
Rio Rancho
Saint George
Heroica Nogales
Puerto Peñasco
Yuma
Scottsdale
Mesa
Tempe
Glendale
Chandler
Gilbert
Durango
Montrose
Kingman
Sierra Vista
Douglas
Agua Prieta
Deming
Silver City
Socorro
Grants
Lordsburg
Winslow
Holbrook
Show Low
Sedona
Page
Moab
114°
112°
110°
108°
106°
38°
36°
34°
32°
F
G
H
J
K
1
2
3
4
5
147
152
150
174
© HAMMOND WORLD ATLAS CORPORATION
Scale 1:3,000,000 Lambert Conformal Conic Projection
MI 0 25 50 75 100
KM 0 25 50 75 100 125 150

The sensational discovery of the Spindle-top Oil Field in 1901 made Texas the principal source of energy in the United States. The Mississippi, the Rio Grande, and other rivers that drain the continental interior have dumped vast quantities of sediment into a deep trough in the coastal plain and the Gulf of Mexico (with depths of up to 15 km). The rich deposits of oil and natural gas located there are the product of great deposits of ancient organic material and the sealing effect of the layers of sediment, which inhibited the natural process of decomposition.

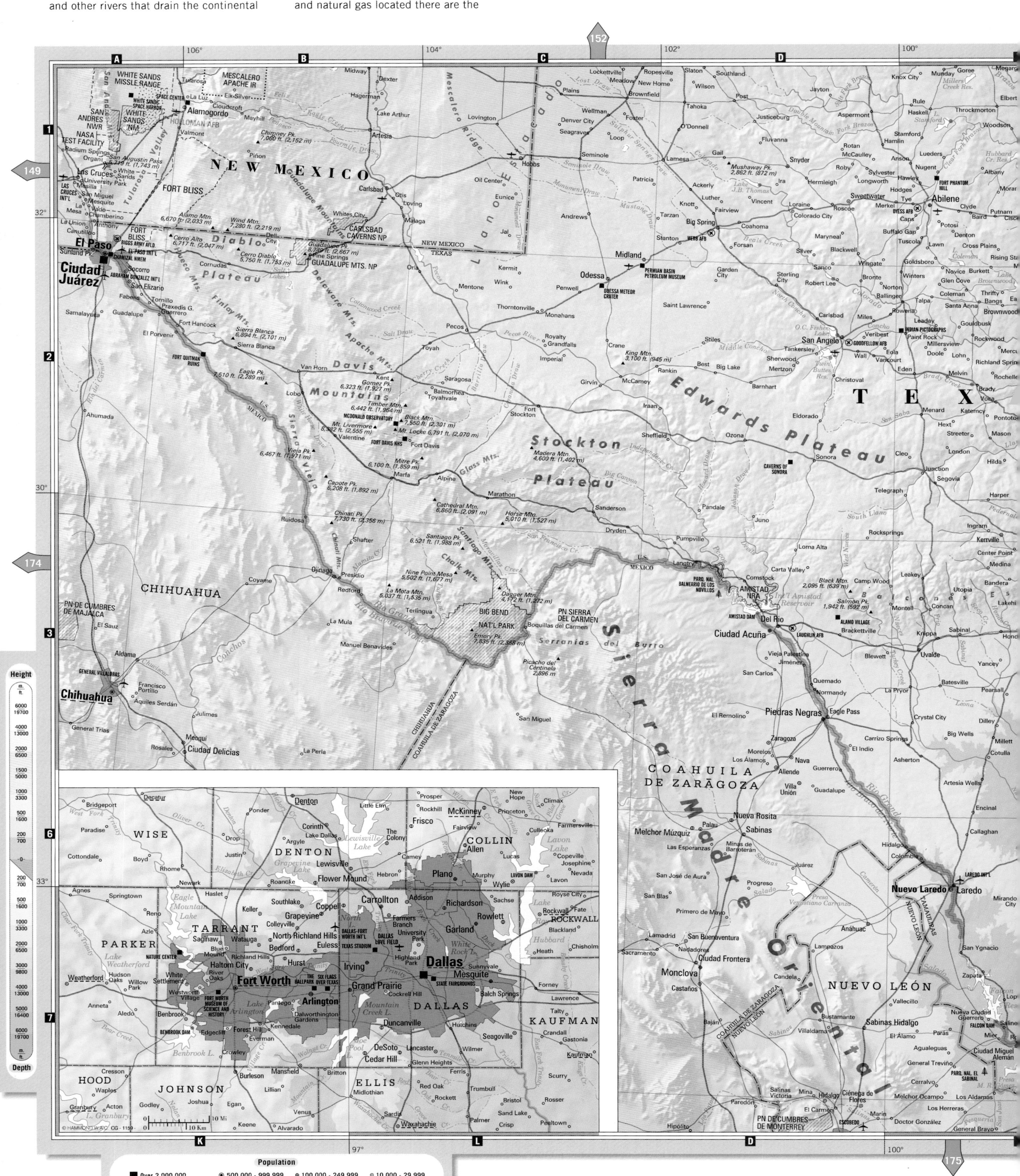

152
149
174
175

Height
m. ft.
6000 19700
4000 13000
2000 6500
1500 5000
1000 3300
500 1600
200 700
0
200 700
500 1600
1000 3300
2000 6500
3000 9800
4000 13000
5000 16400
6000 19700
m. ft.
Depth

Population
■ Over 2,000,000
■ 1,000,000 - 1,999,999
● 500,000 - 999,999
● 250,000 - 499,999
● 100,000 - 249,999
○ 30,000 - 99,999
○ 10,000 - 29,999
○ Under 10,000

Southern Texas

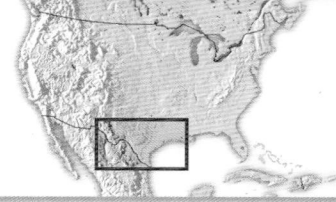

Scale 1:3,000,000 Lambert Conformal Conic Projection

Scarcity of water is the dominant characteristic of the Great Plains. So much water has been drawn from the Ogallala aquifer beneath the plateaus of Texas and New Mexico during the past few centuries that it would take several thousand years to restore the groundwater to its original level. Geologists estimate that available reserves will be exhausted within a few years. Without this essential water supply, some five million acres of irrigated land - on which 12 percent of all the cotton, corn, wheat and millet produced in the U.S. are grown - would no longer be arable.

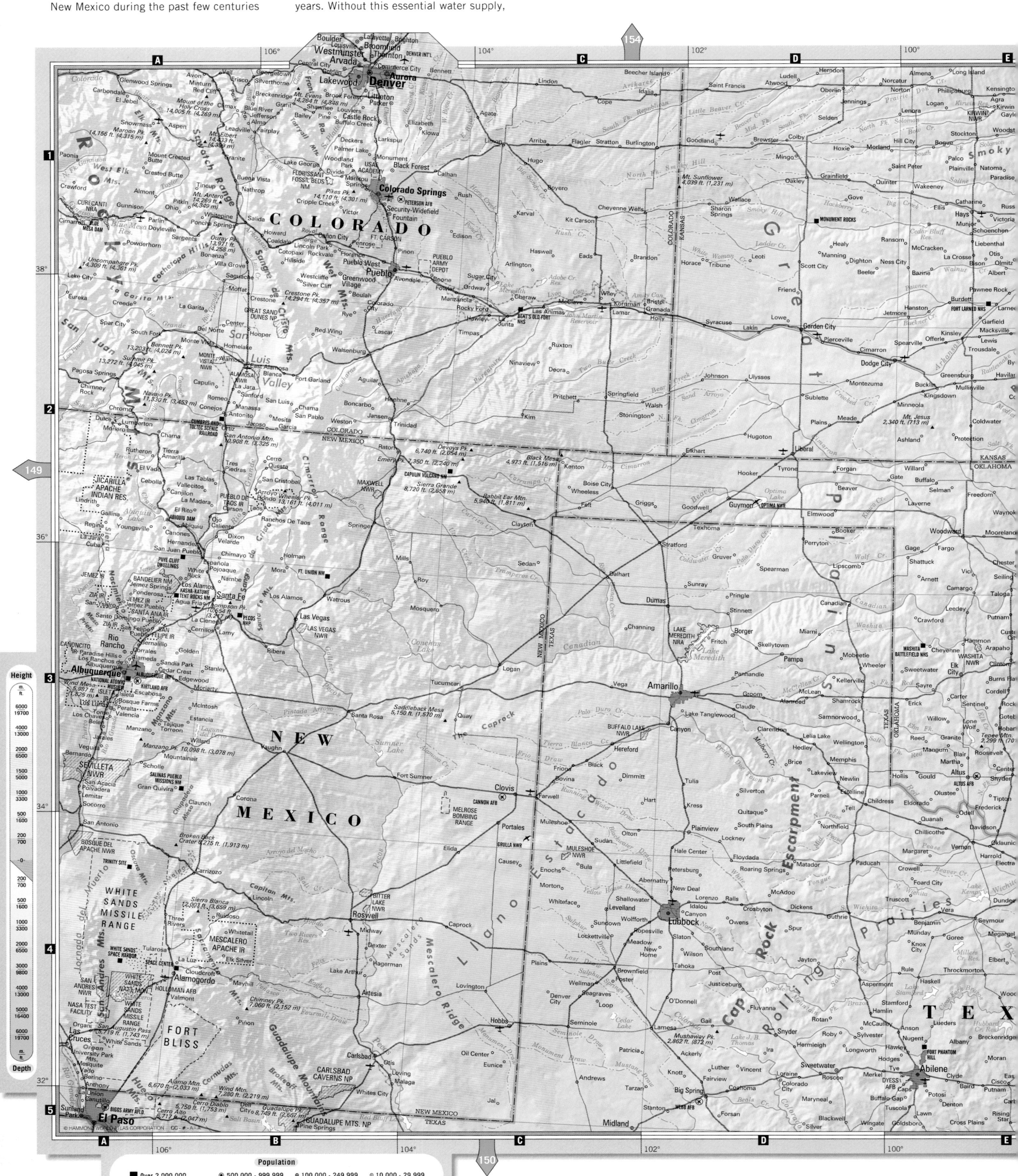

KANSAS

MISSOURI

ILLINOIS

OKLAHOMA

ARKANSAS

LOUISIANA

TEXAS

Kansas City
Independence
Overland Park
Olathe
Topeka
Lawrence
Wichita
Hutchinson
Salina
Jefferson City
Springfield
Joplin
Columbia
Saint Louis
East St. Louis
St. Charles
Tulsa
Broken Arrow
Oklahoma City
Norman
Midwest City
Edmond
Moore
Stillwater
Muskogee
Fort Smith
Little Rock
North Little Rock
Hot Springs
Hot Springs National Park
Pine Bluff
Wichita Falls
Fort Worth
Arlington
Dallas
Garland
Mesquite
Plano
Richardson
Irving
Carrollton
Denton
McKinney
Texarkana
Shreveport
Bossier City
Monroe
West Monroe

GEOGRAPHICAL CENTER OF THE 49 CONTIGUOUS STATES

BOSTON Mts.
OUACHITA Mts.
OZARK PLATEAU
FLINT HILLS

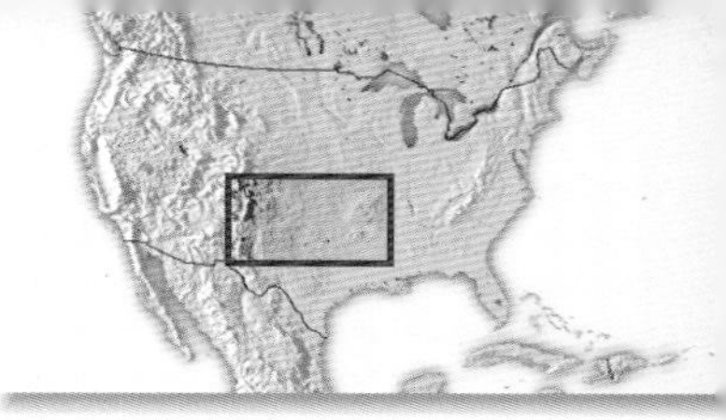

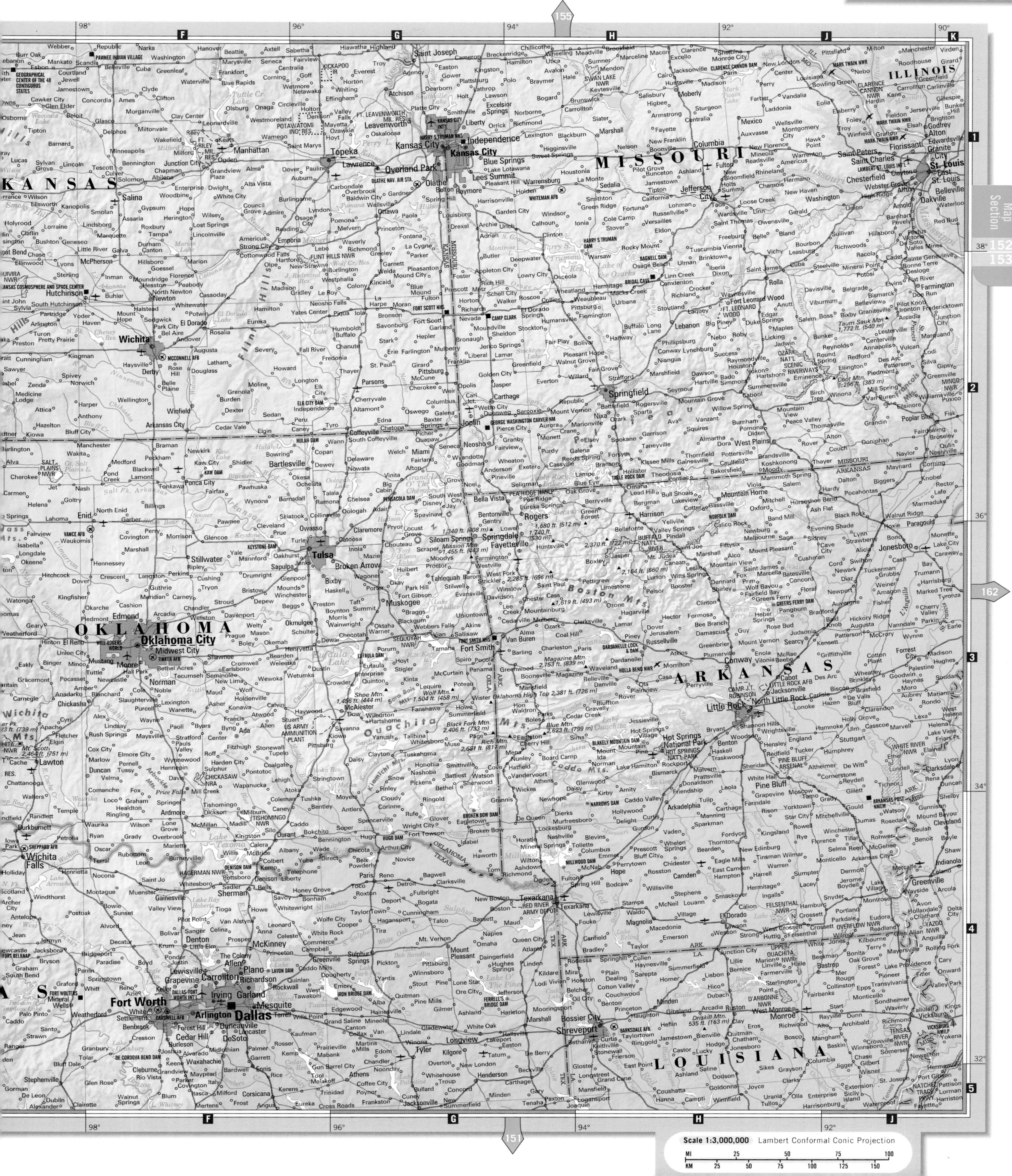

Map Section
152
153
162

The Great Plains comprise one of the largest agricultural regions on Earth. Often plagued throughout their history by catastrophic droughts and erosion, the dry grassland states of the "Dust Bowl" were hardest hit in 1935, the year in which 908 hours of dust storms - the infamous "Black Blizzards" - ravaged the region, carrying away much of the exposed topsoil and depositing it as far away as the Atlantic Ocean. Overcultivation and poor land management were to blame for this disaster, which took a heavy toll in soil and arable land.

Population
- ■ Over 2,000,000
- ■ 1,000,000 - 1,999,999
- ◉ 500,000 - 999,999
- ◉ 250,000 - 499,999
- ◉ 100,000 - 249,999
- ◉ 30,000 - 99,999
- ◉ 10,000 - 29,999
- ○ Under 10,000

WISCONSIN

MINNESOTA

IOWA

ILLINOIS

MISSOURI

Minneapolis · Saint Paul

Milwaukee

Madison

CHICAGO

Des Moines

Cedar Rapids

Davenport · Moline · Rock Island

Omaha · Council Bluffs

Lincoln

Sioux City · South Sioux City

Topeka · Lawrence

Kansas City · Overland Park · Independence · Lees Summit

Springfield

Peoria

Saint Louis · East St. Louis

Rockford

Scale 1:3,000,000 Lambert Conformal Conic Projection

MI 25 50 75 100

KM 25 50 75 100 150

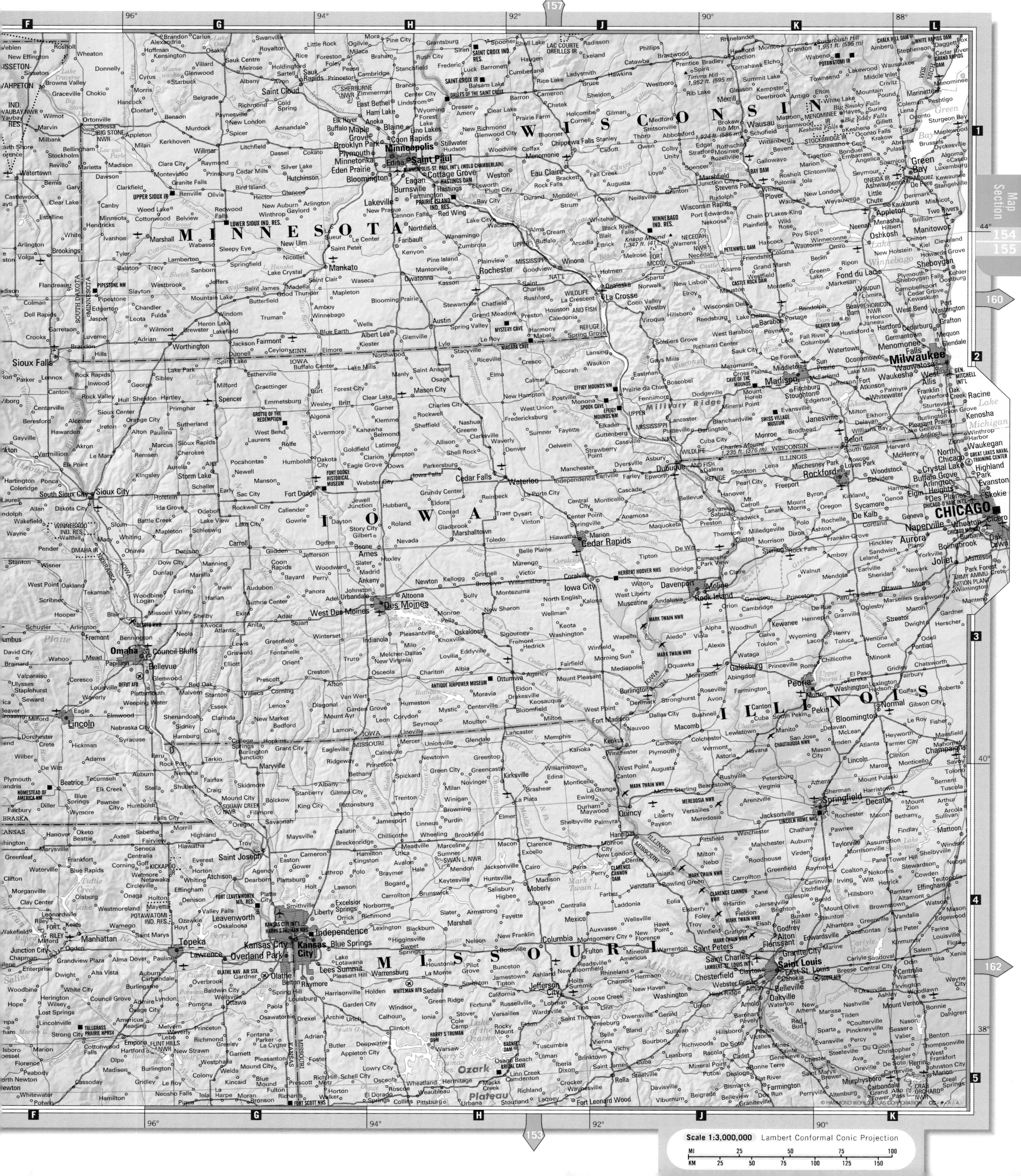

The drainage basins of the Hudson Bay, the Atlantic, and the Gulf of Mexico, to which the Mississippi flows, converge in Minnesota. The state's predominantly flat, rolling moraine topography and its continental climate are ideal for sheep and cattle grazing. The northern half of the state and much of the east are now densely forested again, the eastern region in particular having recovered from almost total deforestation in the early years of the 20th century. The fertile prairies of Manitoba and Saskatchewan to the north also offer prime land for wheat farming and cattle grazing.

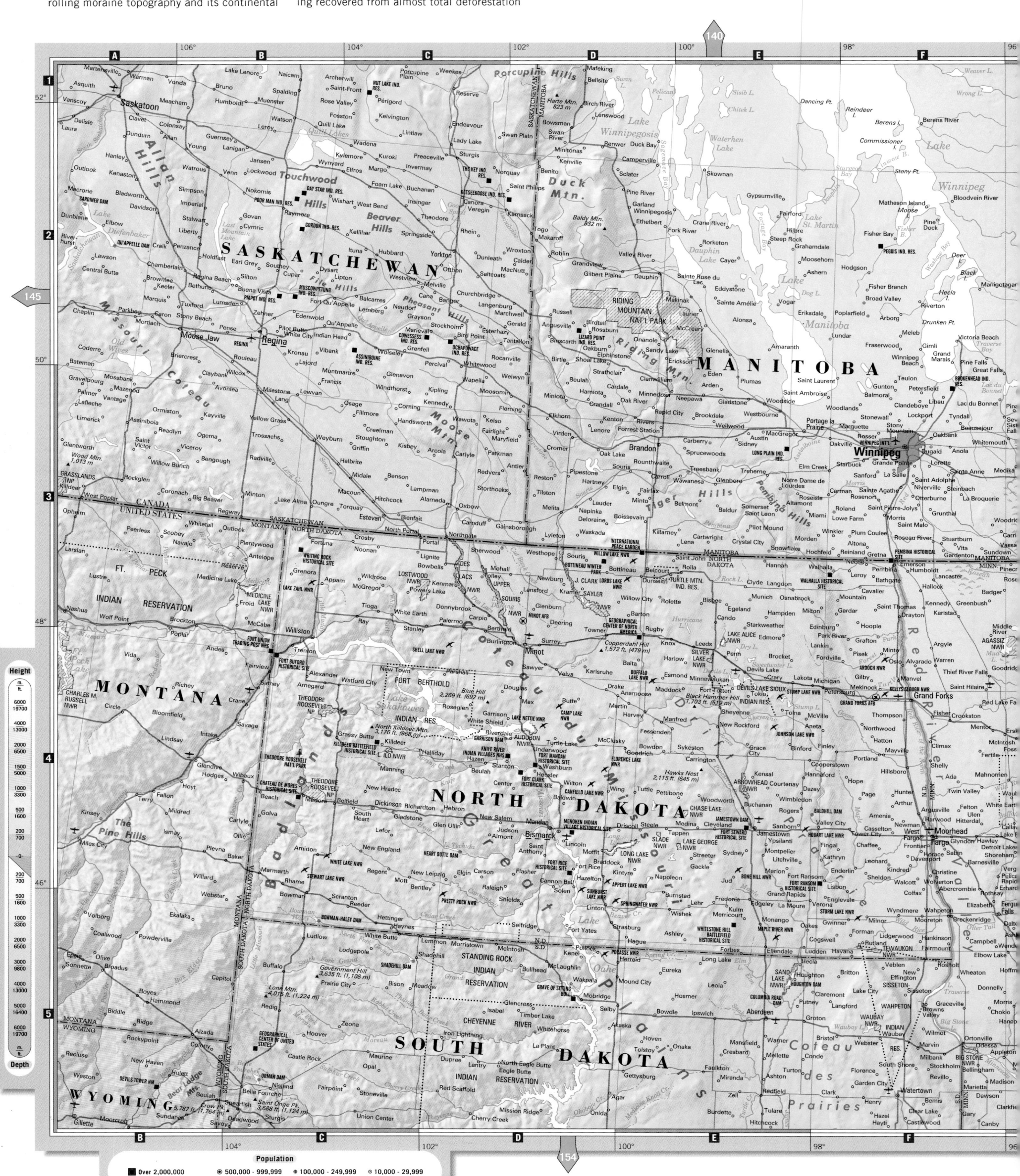

Population

Symbol	Population
■ Over 2,000,000	◉ 500,000-999,999	◎ 100,000-249,999	⊙ 10,000-29,999
■ 1,000,000-1,999,999	◉ 250,000-499,999	⊙ 30,000-99,999	○ Under 10,000

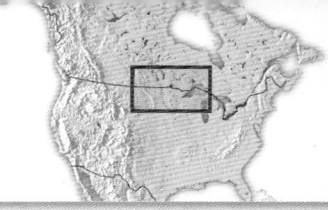

The low, undulating mountain chains of Newfoundland are part of the Appalachian system. Shaped by glacial action, the sparsely populated island highlands are covered by tundra and forest growth.

The waters around this island at the Gulf of St. Lawrence are rich in fish, as are those of Nova Scotia further south. The strongest tides in the world have been measured at the funnel-shaped mouth of

of the Bay of Fundy between Nova Scotia and Maine and New Brunswick to the east. The average difference between low and high tides here is 14.5 meters, with peaks of 16.3 meters.

Population			
■ Over 2,000,000	⊛ 500,000-999,999	⊚ 100,000-249,999	⊙ 10,000-29,999
■ 1,000,000-1,999,999	◉ 250,000-499,999	⊙ 30,000-99,999	∘ Under 10,000

Southeastern Canada, Northeastern U.S.

Scale 1:3,000,000 Lambert Conformal Conic Projection

| MI | 0 | 25 | 50 | 75 | 100 |
| KM | 0 | 25 | 50 | 75 | 100 | 125 | 150 |

Thanks to a relatively mild climate and an abundance of natural resources, the Great Lakes region is one of the most heavily populated areas of North America. Ontario is situated on the Canadian Shield -- a base of old ore-rich rock - and some of the world's largest deposits of nickel, copper, gold, silver, and platinum are located near Sudbury. The Appalachians farther south have large reserves of anthracite coal.

Raw materials from these locations can be shipped easily through the Great Lakes or by river to the major industrial centers on the Atlantic Coast.

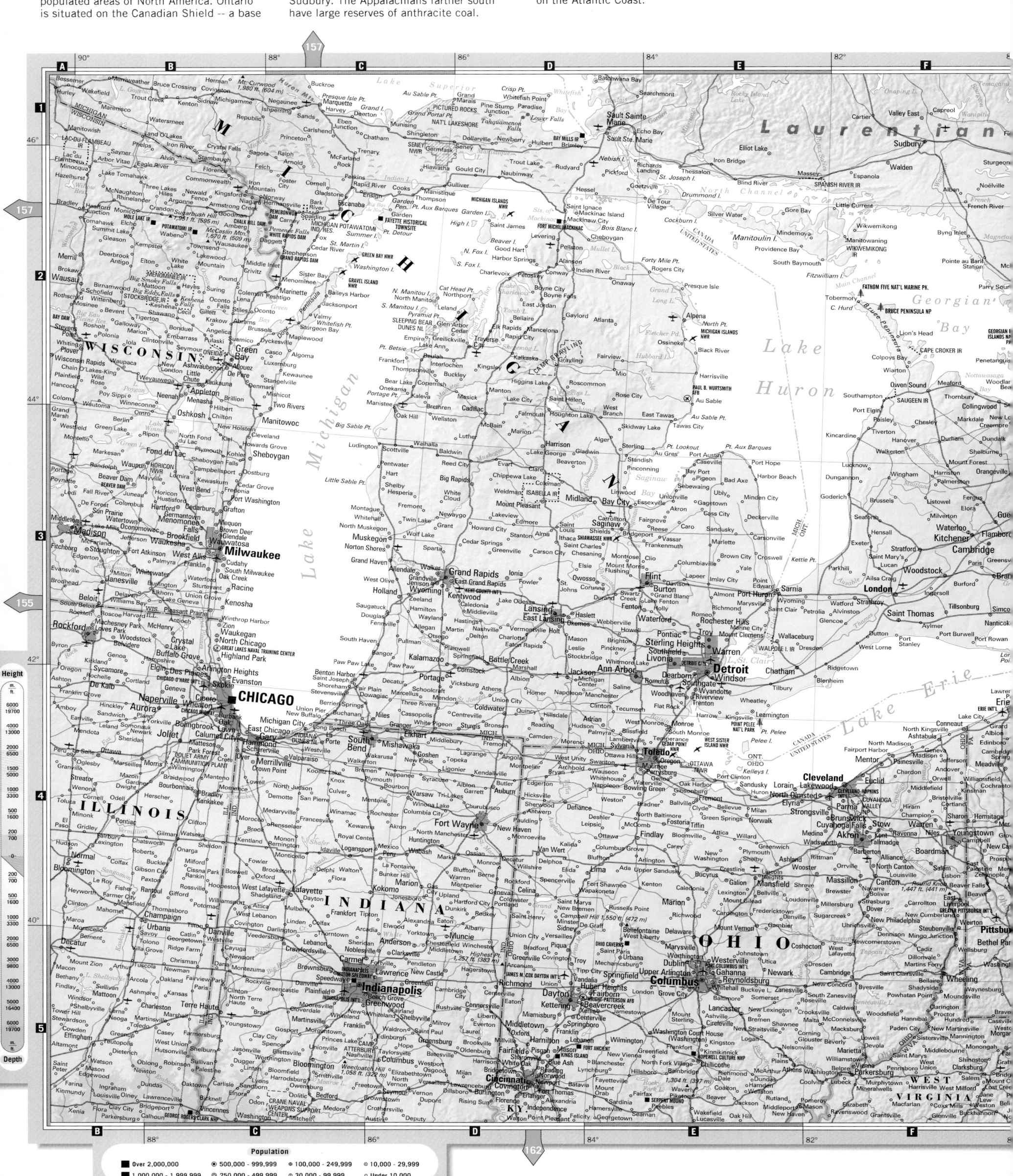

157

157

155

162

Population

■ Over 2,000,000	◉ 500,000 - 999,999	⊚ 100,000 - 249,999	○ 10,000 - 29,999
■ 1,000,000 - 1,999,999	◉ 250,000 - 499,999	⊙ 30,000 - 99,999	∘ Under 10,000

Height
m. ft.
6000 19700
4000 13000
2000 6500
1500 5000
1000 3300
500 1600
200 700
0
200 700
500 1600
1000 3300
2000 6500
3000 9800
4000 13000
5000 16400
6000 19700
m. ft.
Depth

QUÉBEC

ONTARIO

Ottawa · Gatineau · Nepean · Kanata

Montréal · Laval · LaSalle · Longueuil

TORONTO · Brampton · Mississauga · Oakville · Burlington · Hamilton · Saint Catharines · Niagara Falls · Welland · Port Colborne

Buffalo · Lackawanna · Cheektowaga · Tonawanda · North Tonawanda · Lockport · Niagara Falls · Hamburg

Lake Ontario

Rochester · Greece · Syracuse · Utica · Rome · Oswego · Auburn · Geneva · Ithaca · Binghamton · Elmira · Corning

NEW YORK

Adirondack Mountains · Mt. Marcy 5,344 ft. (1,629 m) · Lake Placid · Saranac Lake · Lake George

Albany · Schenectady · Troy · Saratoga Springs · Amsterdam · Gloversville · Cooperstown · BASEBALL HALL OF FAME

VERMONT · Burlington · Montpelier · Rutland · Bennington · Mt. Mansfield 4,393 ft. (1,339 m)

NEW HAMPSHIRE · Concord · Manchester · Nashua · Mt. Washington 6,288 ft. (1,917 m)

MAINE

MASSACHUSETTS · Boston · Worcester · Springfield · Cambridge · Quincy · Lowell · Lawrence · Fitchburg · Pittsfield

R.I. · Providence · Pawtucket · Cranston · Warwick · Newport

CONN. · Hartford · New Haven · Bridgeport · Waterbury · Stamford · New Britain · Norwalk · Danbury · New London · Meriden

Long Island Sound

Martha's Vineyard · Block Island · Montauk Pt.

NEW YORK · Yonkers · New Rochelle · White Plains · Mount Vernon

Long Island · Patchogue · Riverhead · Southampton · Hampton Bays

NEW JERSEY · Newark · Jersey City · Elizabeth · Paterson · Trenton · Camden · New Brunswick · Perth Amboy · Asbury Park · Long Branch · Toms River · Atlantic City · Ocean City

PENNSYLVANIA · Allegheny Mts. · Appalachian Mts. · Williamsport · Scranton · Wilkes-Barre · Altoona · State College · Harrisburg · Reading · Allentown · Bethlehem · Easton · Lancaster · York · Philadelphia · Upper Darby · Chester · Erie · DuBois · Bradford · Indiana · Johnstown

Philadelphia

MARYLAND · Baltimore · Dundalk · Towson · Columbia · Annapolis · Frederick · Hagerstown · Cumberland · Mt. Davis 3,213 ft. (979 m)

DEL. · Dover · Wilmington · Smyrna

Chesapeake Bay · Delaware Bay · C. May · C. Henlopen

VIRGINIA · Arlington · Washington · Front Royal

ATLANTIC OCEAN

Cape May

© HAMMOND WORLD ATLAS CORPORATION

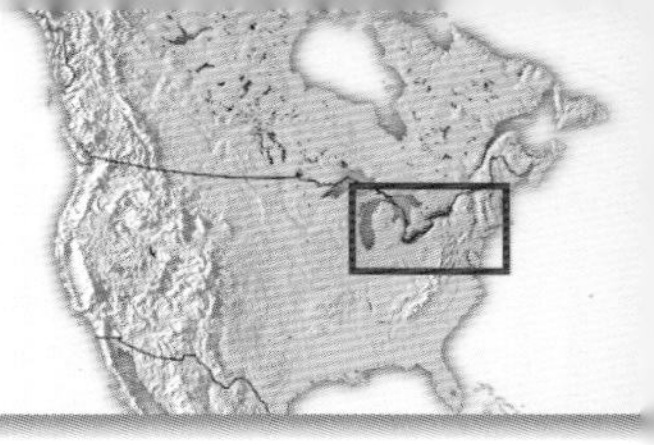

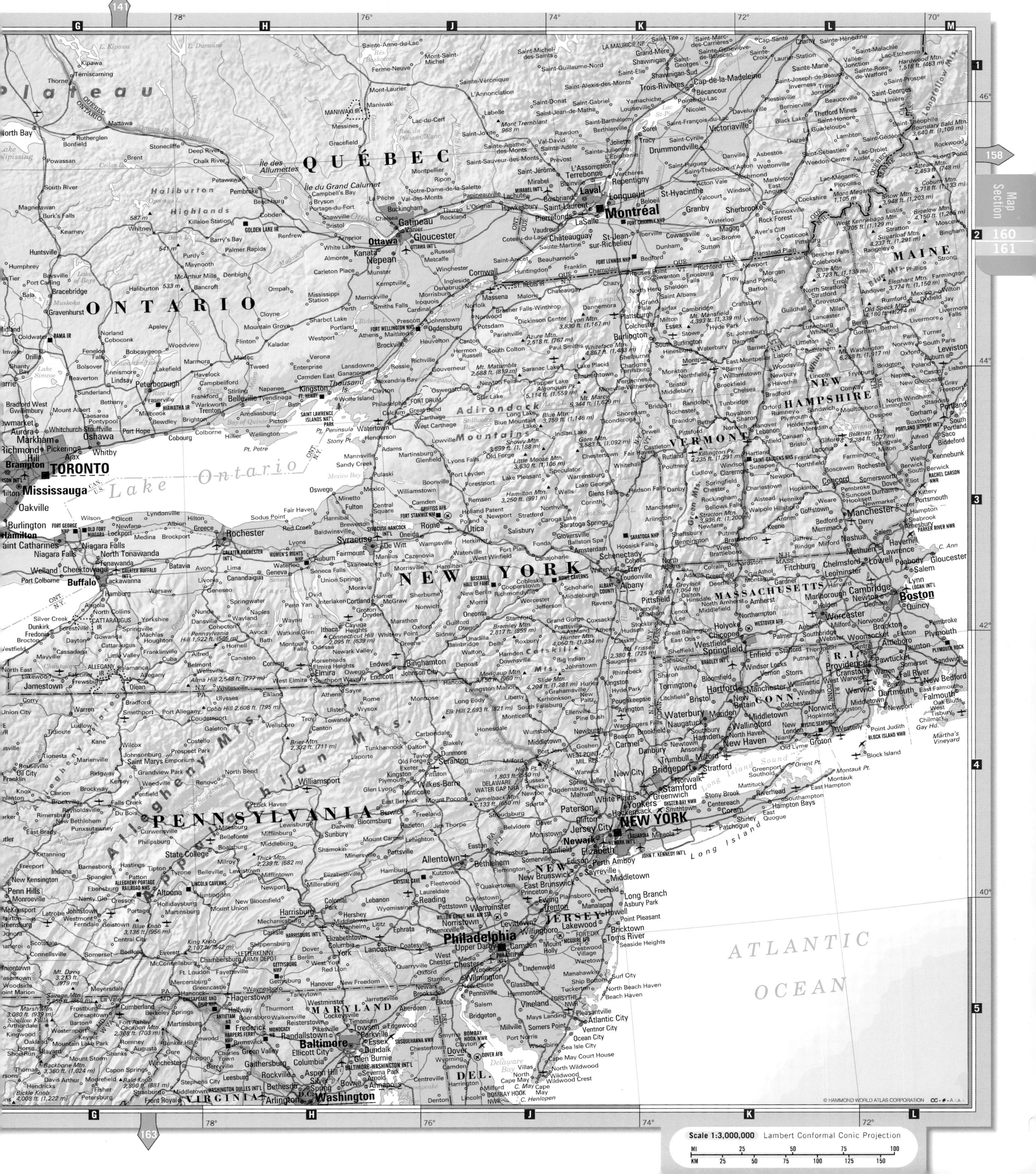

The mideastern region of the United States is dominated by the Appalachian Mountain system, a complex of low, rolling chains some 2,600 km long that separates the Atlantic coastal plain from the lowlands of the North American continent. They are broken by natural gaps in only a few places. Although the Appalachians bear a certain resemblance to the central mountain ranges of Europe, they are home to a much wider diversity of species - in part a consequence of the migration of animals toward the south along the northeast-southwest axis of the Appalachians during the last ice age.

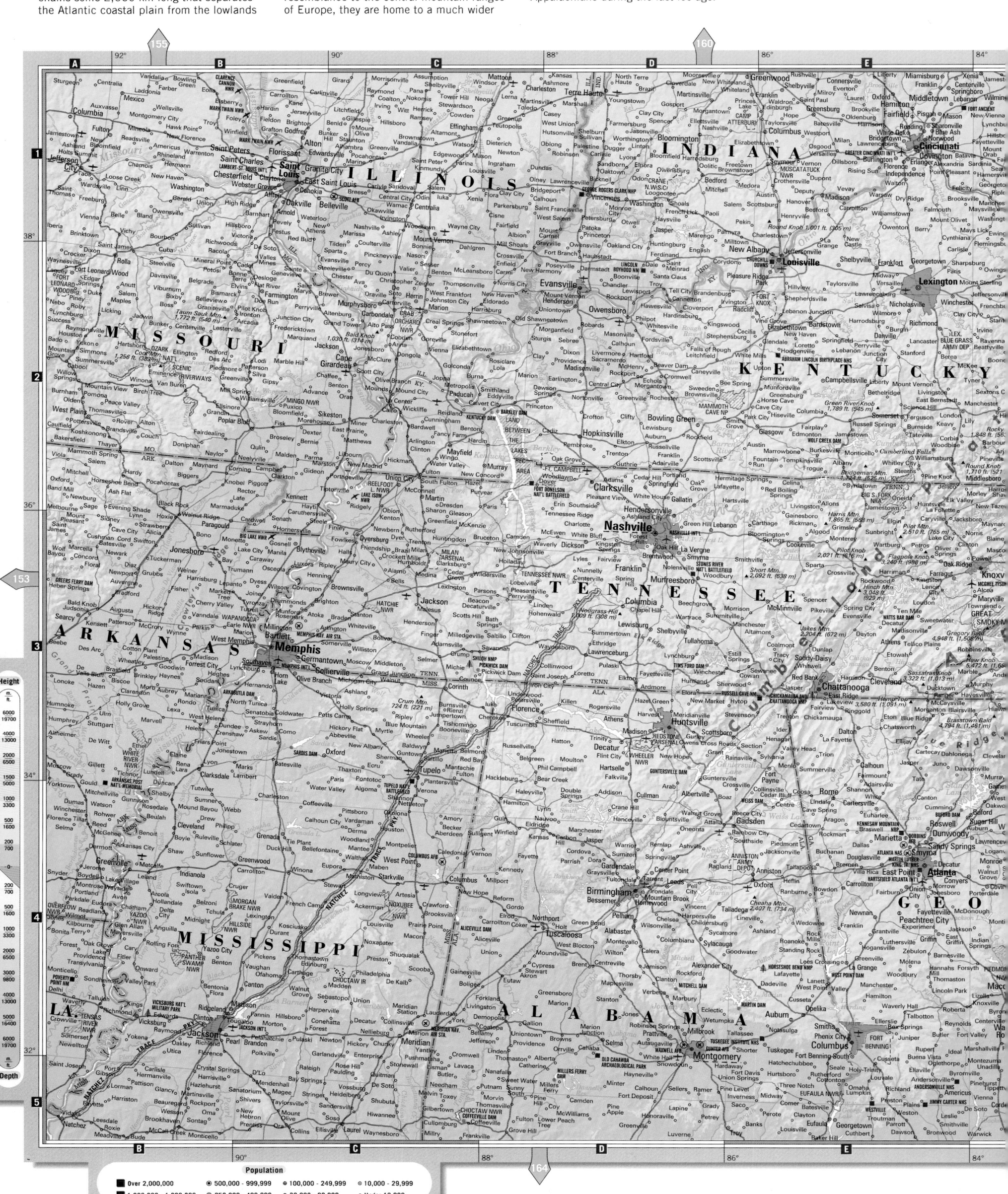

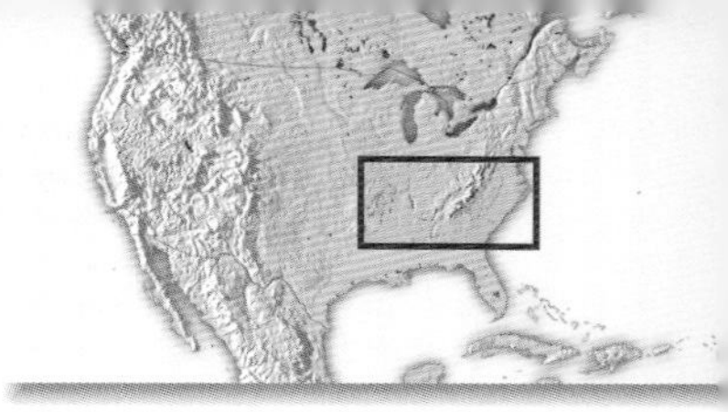

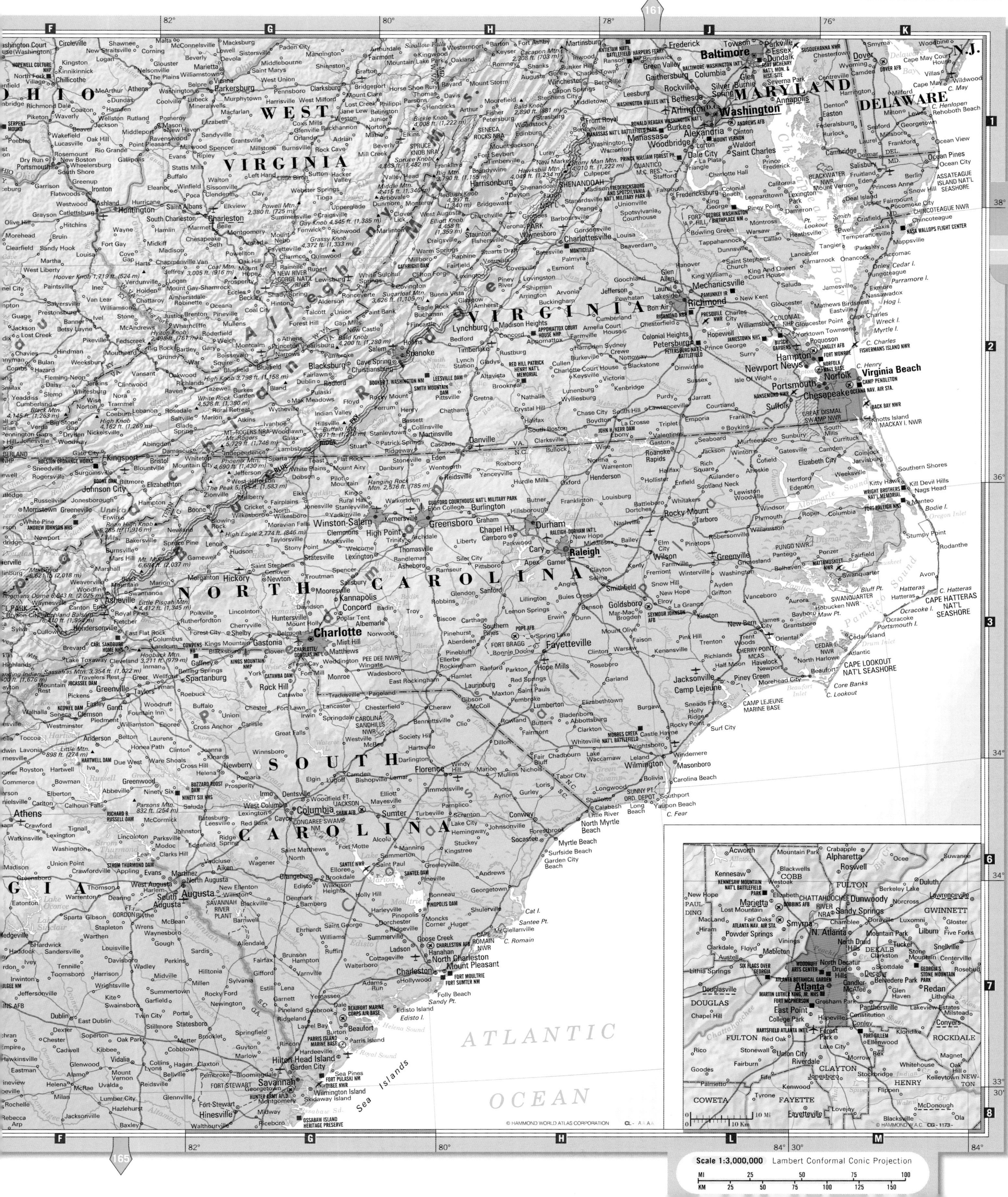

OHIO

WEST VIRGINIA

VIRGINIA

MARYLAND

DELAWARE

N.J.

NORTH CAROLINA

SOUTH CAROLINA

GEORGIA

ATLANTIC OCEAN

Baltimore
Washington, D.C.
Richmond
Raleigh
Charlotte
Columbia
Atlanta
Savannah
Charleston
Virginia Beach
Norfolk

© HAMMOND WORLD ATLAS CORPORATION

Scale 1:3,000,000   Lambert Conformal Conic Projection

MI   25   50   75   100

KM   25   50   75   100   125   150

The Mississippi is the mightiest river in North America and one of the longest in the world. Ordinarily, the river discharges more sediment into the Gulf of Mexico than waves, tides, and currents can carry away. Yet the "bird's-foot delta" and its vast wetlands are actually shrinking. Dredging and dams are partly responsible for this, but so is the river itself. The Mississippi has shifted its course back and forth several times during the last millennium and is now sending increasing amounts of sediment into an arm it abandoned some 3,800 years ago.

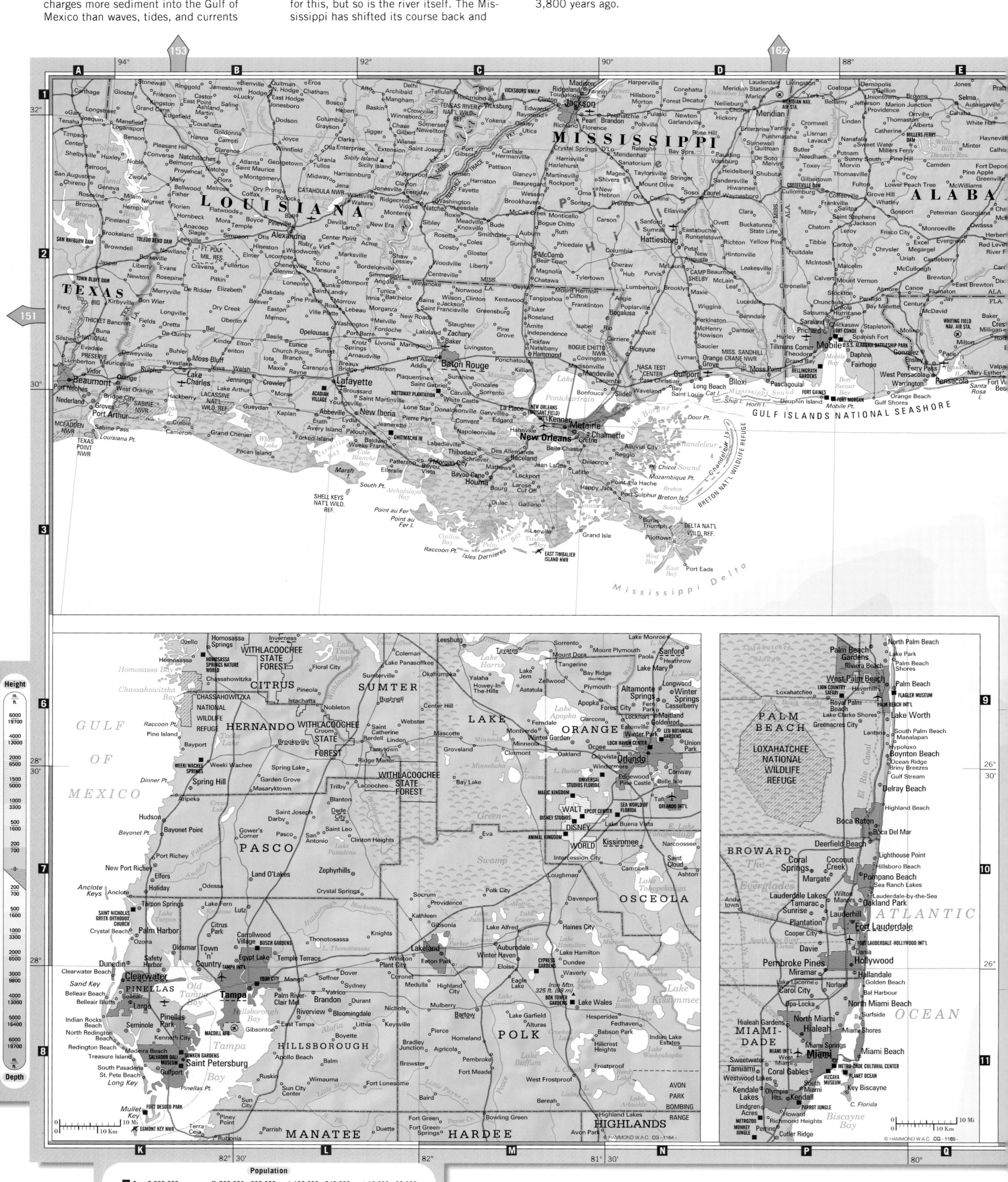

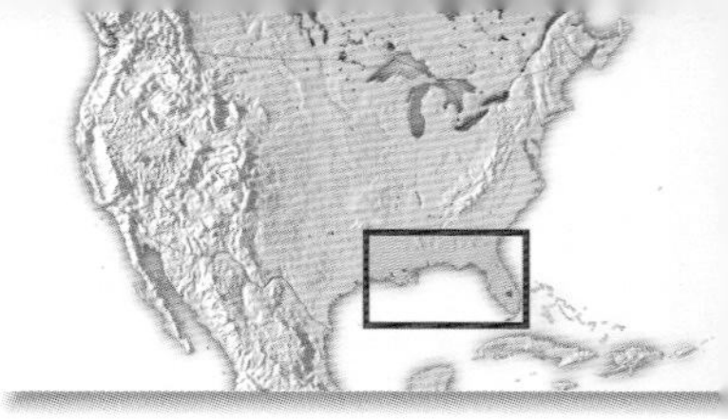

Map Section
164
165
173

ATLANTIC

OCEAN

GULF OF

MEXICO

GEORGIA

FLORIDA

ALA.

Sea Islands

Cities and places:

Montgomery, Maxwell AFB, Gunter AFB, Wetumpka, Millbrook, Notasulga, Tallassee, Smiths, Phenix City, Columbus, Fort Benning, Tuskegee, Tuskegee Institute NHS, Hurtsboro, Union Springs, Clayton, Eufaula, Georgetown, Cuthbert, Dothan, Ozark, Enterprise, Headland, Abbeville, Blakely, Bainbridge, Thomasville, Valdosta, Albany, Tifton, Fitzgerald, Douglas, Waycross, Savannah, Hilton Head Island, Parris Island Marine Base, Hinesville, Brunswick, Jesup, Jacksonville, Tallahassee, Panama City, Tyndall AFB, Lynn Haven, Springfield, Callaway, Apalachicola, Port Saint Joe, Perry, Live Oak, Lake City, Gainesville, Ocala, Jacksonville Beach, St. Augustine, Daytona Beach, Ormond Beach, Port Orange, New Smyrna Beach, Titusville, Cocoa, Merritt Island, Kennedy Space Ctr., Cape Canaveral, Orlando, Walt Disney World, Kissimmee, Sanford, Deltona, Melbourne, Palm Bay, Homosassa Springs, Spring Hill, New Port Richey, Tarpon Springs, Clearwater, Dunedin, Largo, Tampa, Saint Petersburg, MacDill AFB, Plant City, Lakeland, Winter Haven, Bartow, Sebring, Bradenton, Sarasota, Venice, Port Charlotte, Punta Gorda, North Fort Myers, Cape Coral, Fort Myers, Bonita Springs, Naples, Lehigh Acres, Sanibel I., Captiva I., Fort Pierce, Port Saint Lucie, Stuart, Jupiter, Palm Beach Gardens, West Palm Beach, Lake Worth, Boynton Beach, Delray Beach, Boca Raton, Deerfield Beach, Pompano Beach, Coral Springs, Fort Lauderdale, Hollywood, Pembroke Pines, Hialeah, Carol City, Miami, Miami Beach, Coral Gables, Kendall, Homestead, Florida City, Key Largo, Marathon, Key West

Lake Okeechobee

Everglades National Park

Big Cypress National Preserve

Florida Keys

Dry Tortugas Nat'l Pk.

Key West Nat'l Wildlife Refuge

Los Angeles – San Diego

The sprawling metropolis of Los Angeles on California's West Coast extends over a distance of 184 km from Ventura to San Bernardino. The region its plagued by an increasingly severe shortage of water, since groundwater reserves are nearly exhausted. Even the many reservoirs in the area are barely able to meet the needs of local farmers and a rapidly growing population.

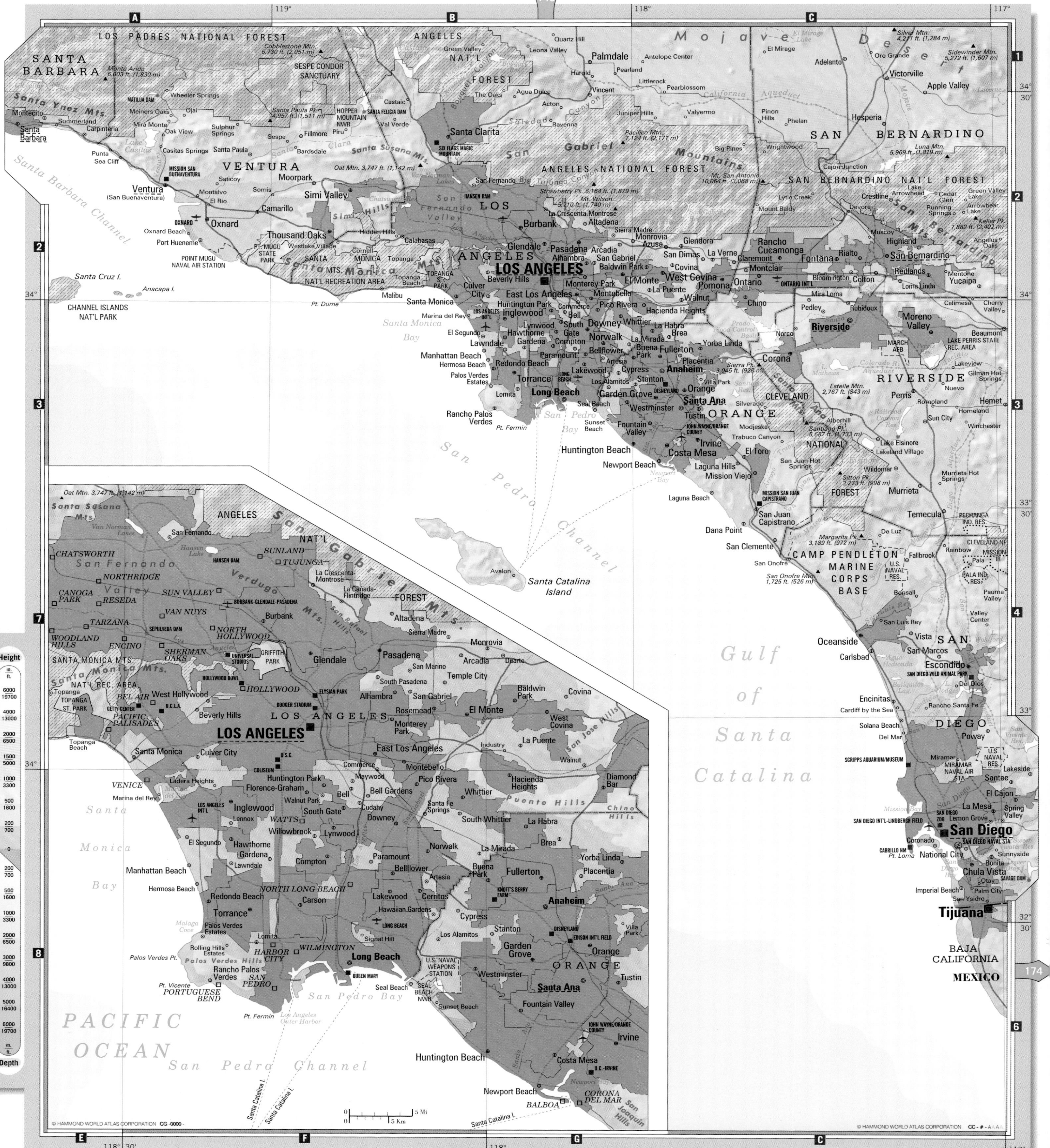

174

Height

m.	ft.
6000	19700
4000	13000
2000	6500
1500	5000
1000	3300
500	1600
200	700
0	0
200	700
500	1600
1000	3300
2000	6500
3000	9800
4000	13000
5000	16400
6000	19700
m.	ft.

Depth

Population
- Over 2,000,000
- 1,000,000 - 1,999,999
- 500,000 - 999,999
- 250,000 - 499,999
- 100,000 - 249,999
- 30,000 - 99,999
- 10,000 - 29,999
- Under 10,000

Scale 1:1,000,000 Lambert Conformal Conic Projection

MI 10 20 30
KM 10 20 30 40

© HAMMOND WORLD ATLAS CORPORATION

Four different roads to the future: Seattle has grown steadily in recent years through a steady influx of people into the less densely populated northwest. New technologies have created new jobs here and in Silicon Valley, the region between San Francisco and San Jose. Detroit relies on the automobile industry, and Chicago is already one of the world's leading commercial centers.

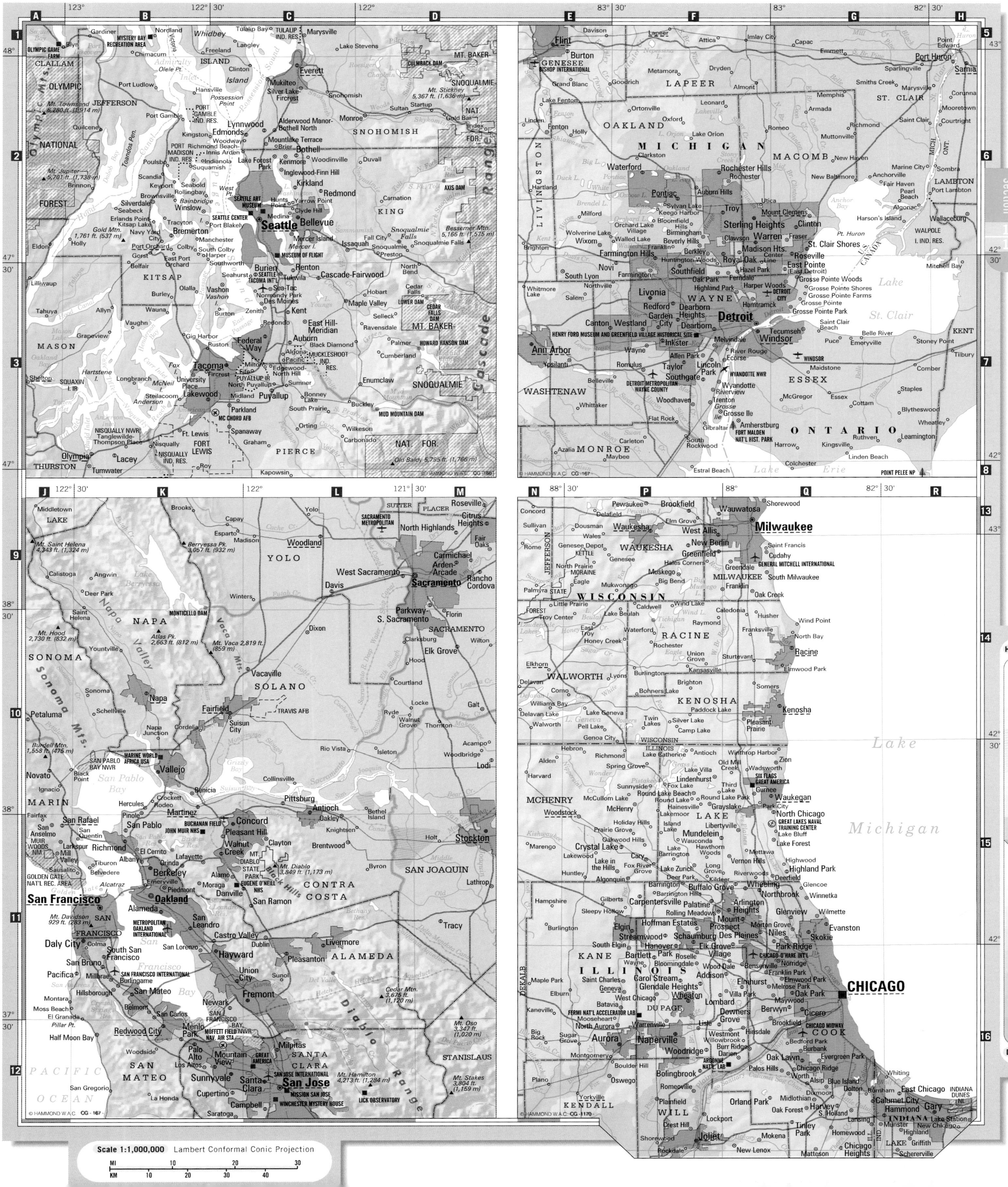

Seattle, San Francisco, Detroit, Chicago

Scale 1:1,000,000 Lambert Conformal Conic Projection

MI 10 20 30
KM 10 20 30 40

Roughly 18,000 years ago, the sea level along the East Coast of the United States was about 100 meters lower than it is today. The old valleys along the coast were "drowned" when the waters rose again and flooded the coastal plain. These sunken valleys are still recognizable today as long, funnel-shaped bays on the northern and middle Atlantic coasts. Raritan Bay at the mouth of the Hudson River and the Chesapeake and Delaware Bays are among the most prominent examples. They are actually estuaries with fluctuating salinity levels that provide a habitat for a unique range of fauna.

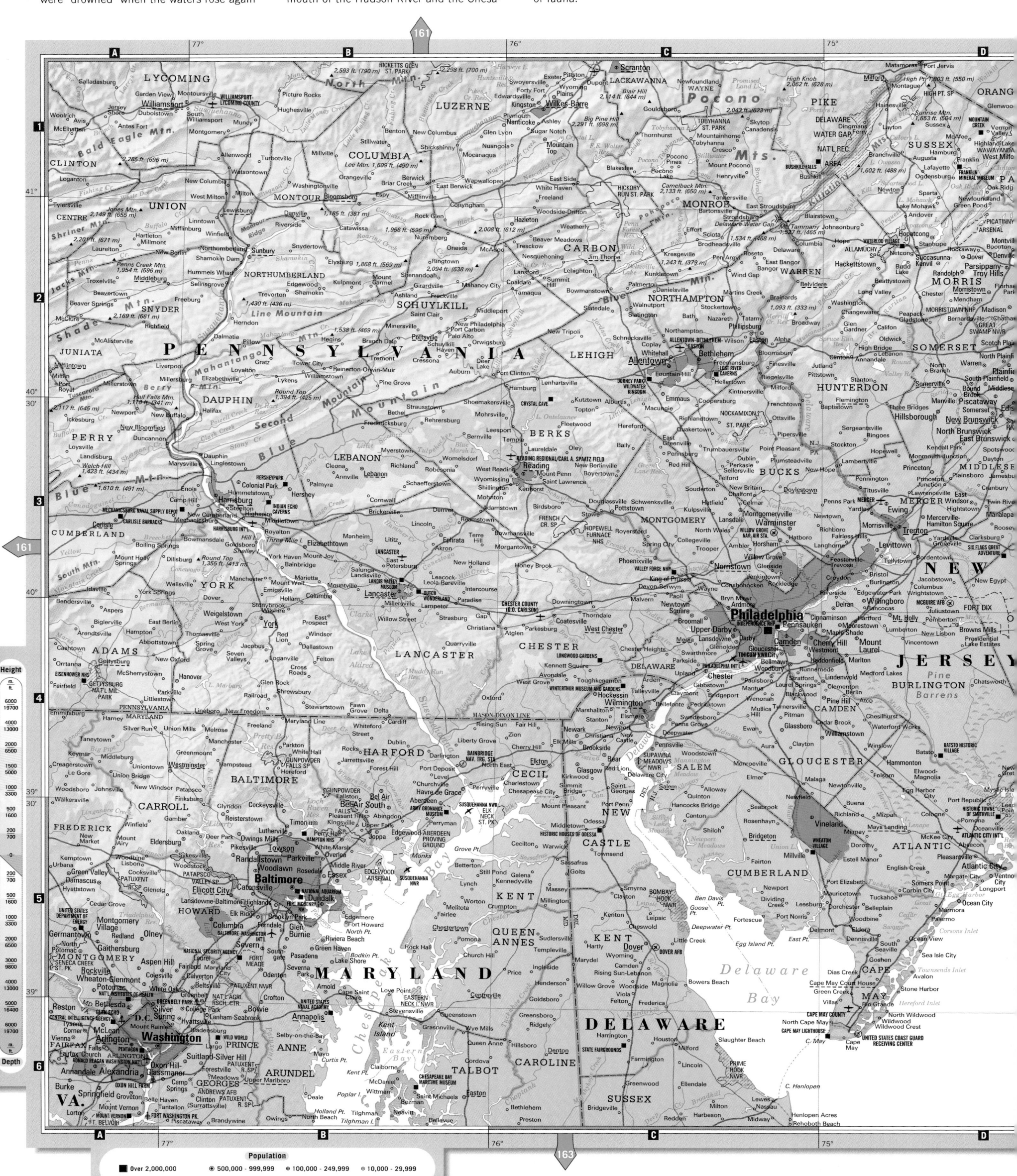

Population
Over 2,000,000 ● 500,000 - 999,999 ○ 100,000 - 249,999 ◦ 10,000 - 29,999
1,000,000 - 1,999,999 ● 250,000 - 499,999 ○ 30,000 - 99,999 ◦ Under 10,000

161

Scale 1:1,000,000   Lambert Conformal Conic Projection

© HAMMOND WORLD ATLAS CORPORATION   CC - # - A A A

© HAMMOND W.A.C.   CG - 1171

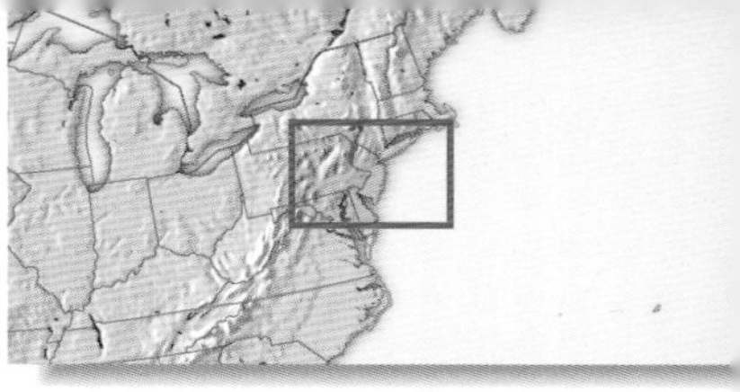

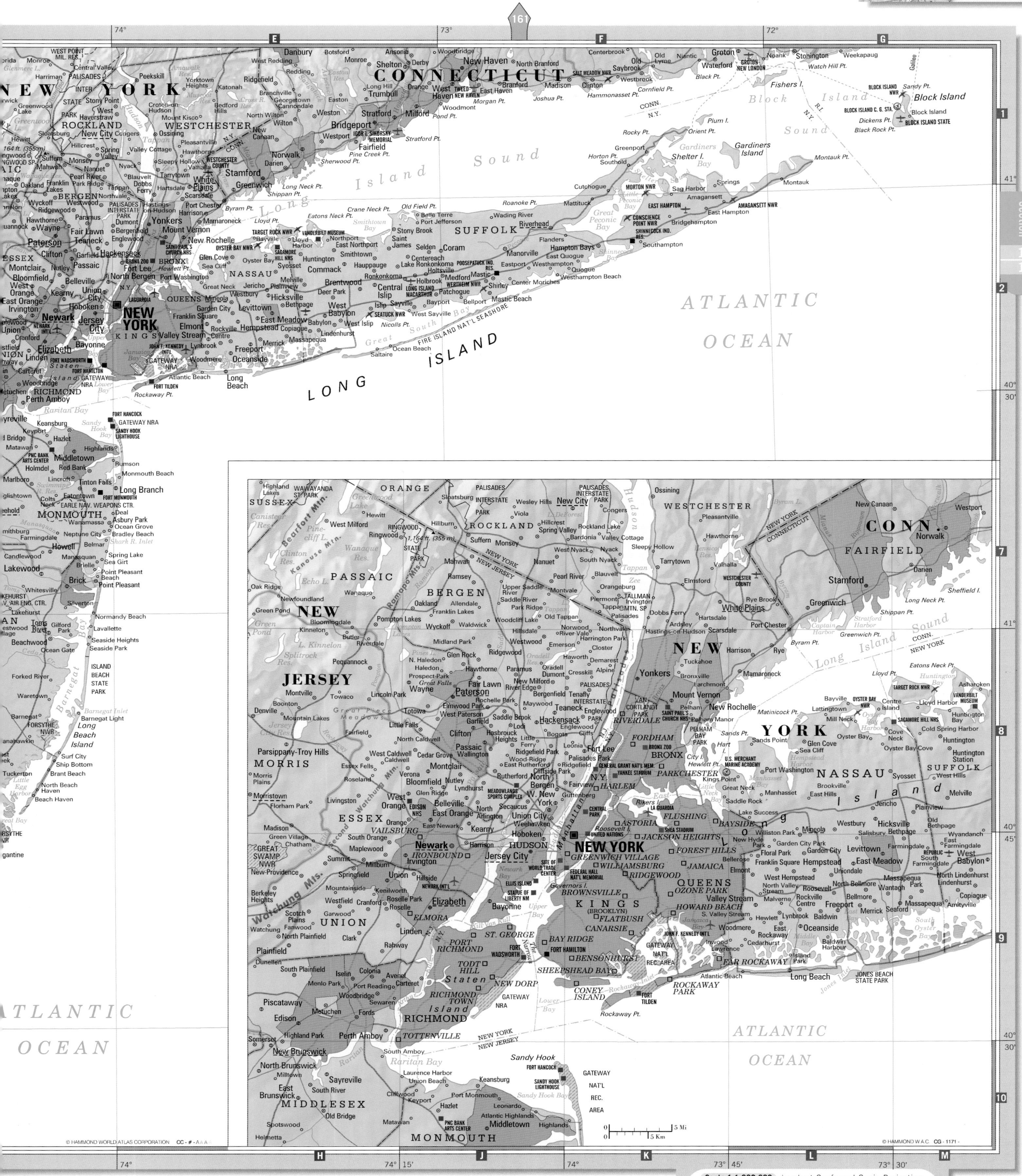

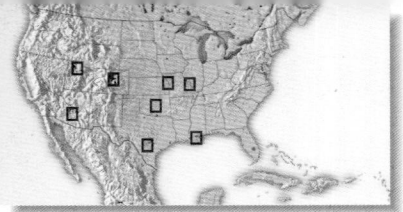

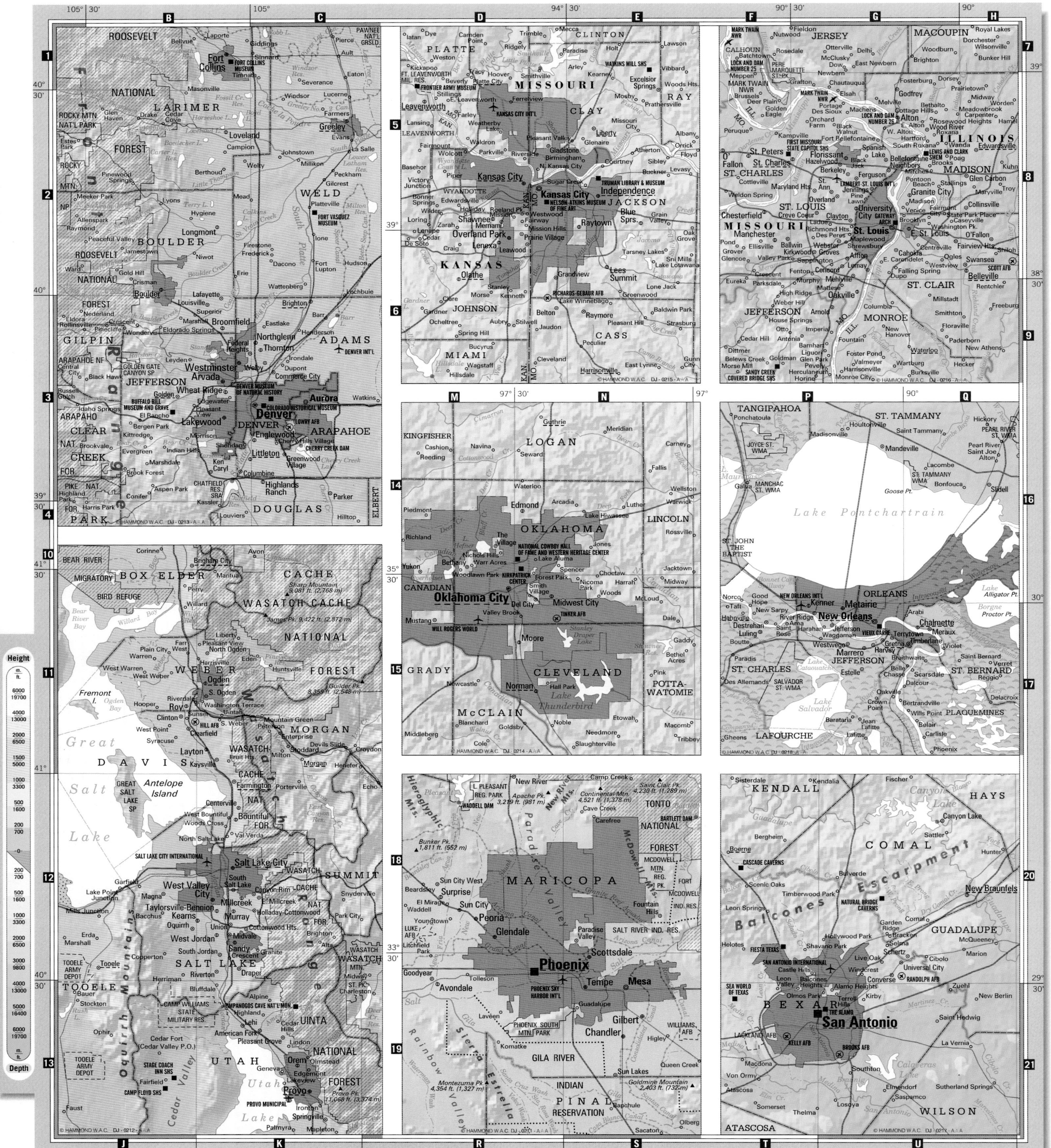

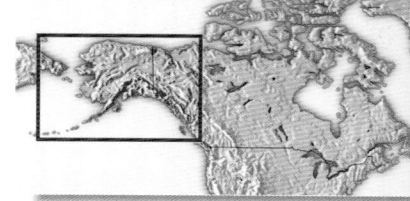

Alaska

Alaska, the forty-ninth state of the U.S., comprises four major geographic zones. In the south, the heavily glaciated Alaska Range extends along the Pacific coast, with its many fjords. Its highest peak is Mount McKinley, which at 6,194 meters is also the highest mountain in North America. The Brooks Range in the north extends eastward to the shores of the Beaufort Sea. The interior is dominated by the Yukon River system. The island chain of the Aleutians is the most geologically active area in the region. Here, the Pacific Plate submerges beneath the continental plate along the Aleutian Trench.

Population

■ Over 2,000,000	◉ 500,000 - 999,999
■ 1,000,000 - 1,999,999	◉ 250,000 - 499,999
◉ 100,000 - 249,999	○ 10,000 - 29,999
◉ 30,000 - 99,999	○ Under 10,000

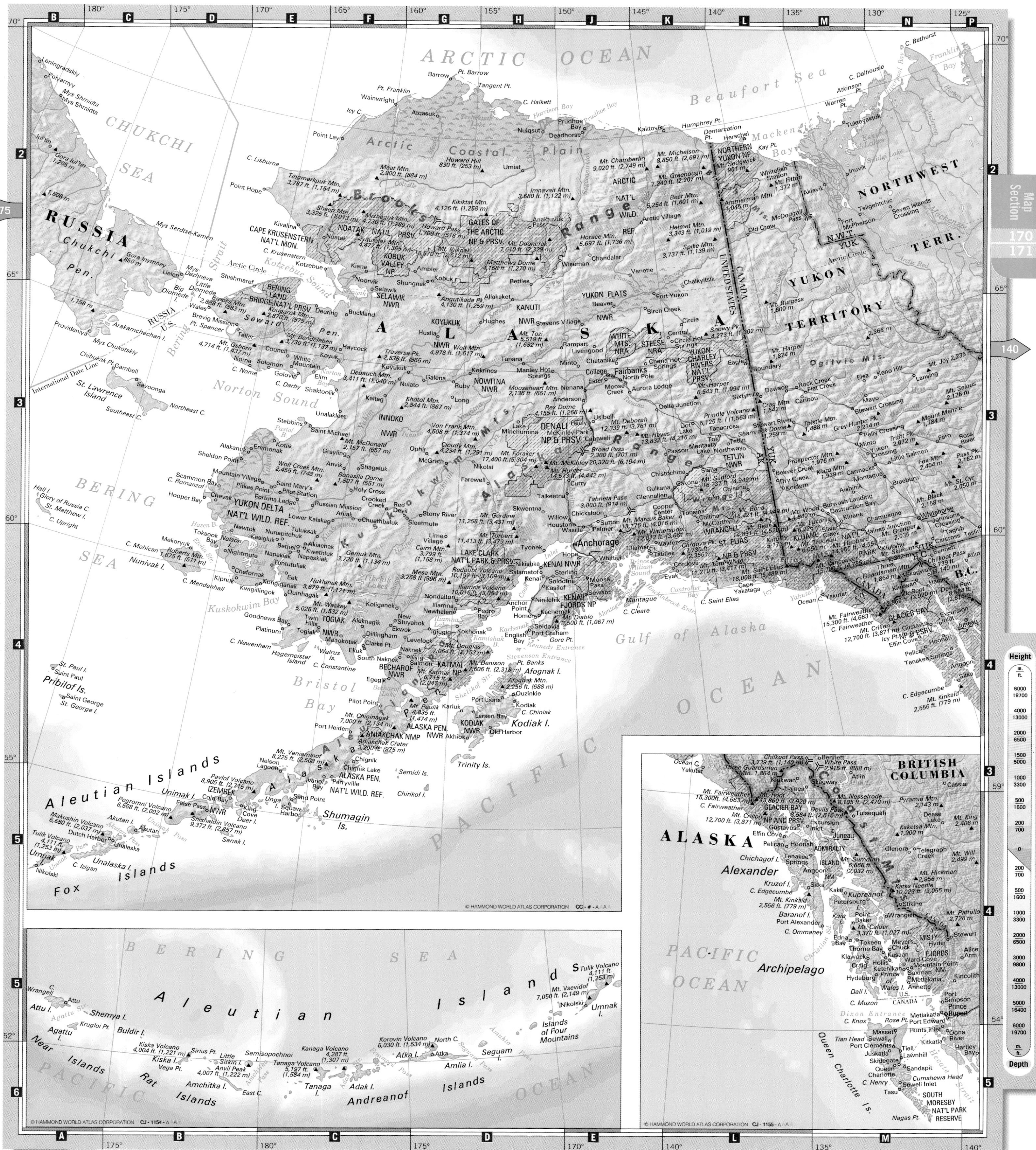

Scale 1:9,000,000   Lambert Conformal Conic Projection

Height

Depth

© HAMMOND WORLD ATLAS CORPORATION

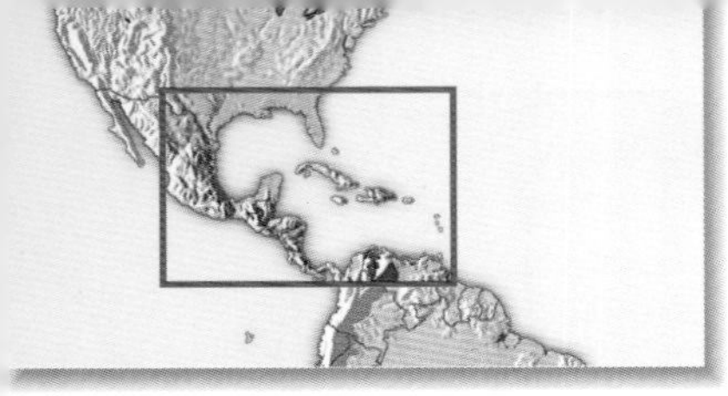

Middle America

MEXICO
① DISTRITO FEDERAL
② MÉXICO
③ MORELOS
④ TLAXCALA
⑤ QUERÉTARO DE ARTEAGA
⑥ AGUASCALIENTES

Height

m.	ft.
6000	19700
4000	13000
2000	6500
1500	5000
1000	3300
500	1600
200	700
0	
200	700
500	1600
1000	3300
2000	6500
3000	9800
4000	13000
5000	16400
6000	19700

Depth

Population
- ■ Over 2,000,000
- ■ 1,000,000 - 1,999,999
- ● 500,000 - 999,999
- ● 250,000 - 499,999
- ● 100,000 - 249,999
- ● 30,000 - 99,999
- ○ 10,000 - 29,999
- ○ Under 10,000

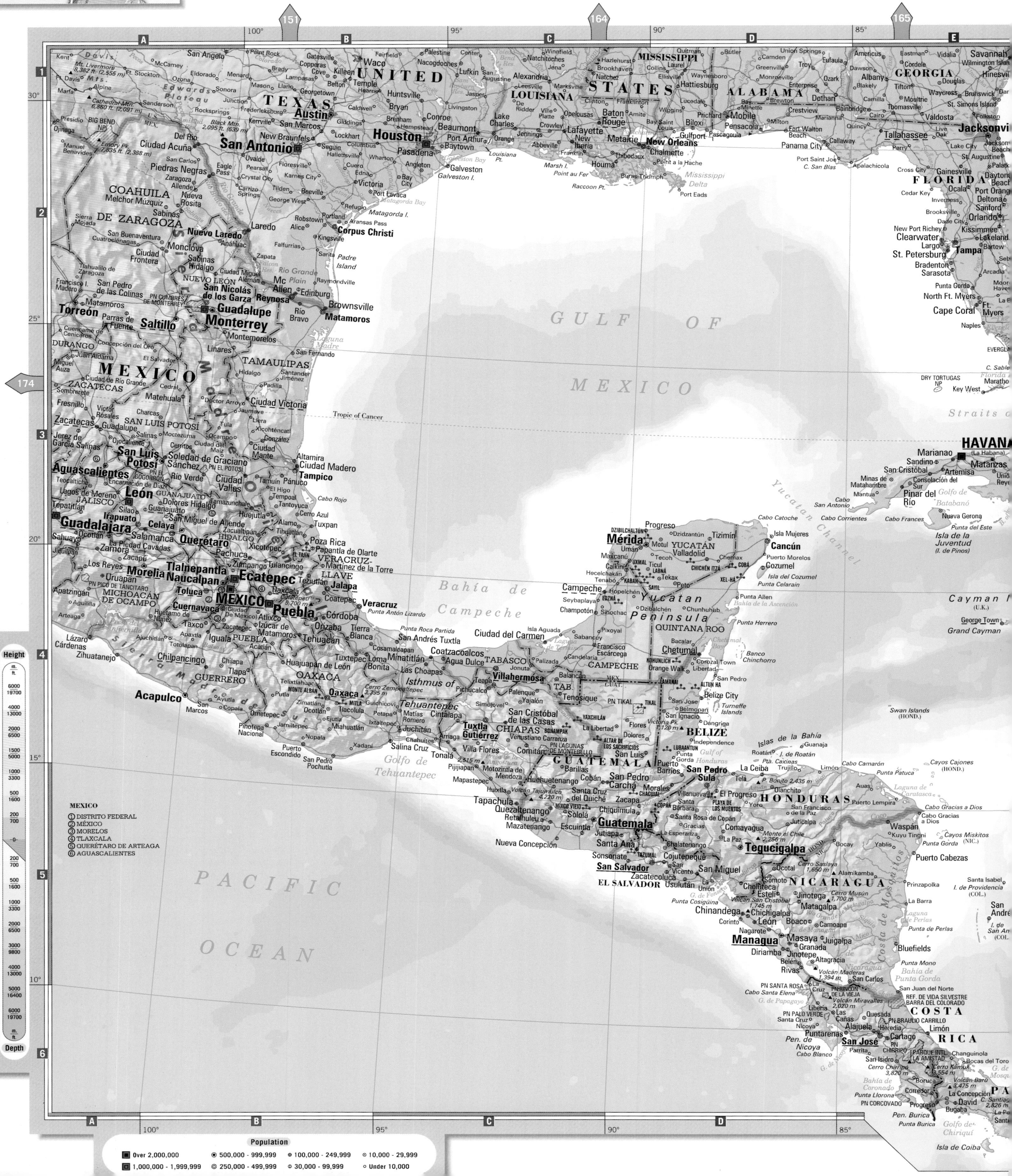

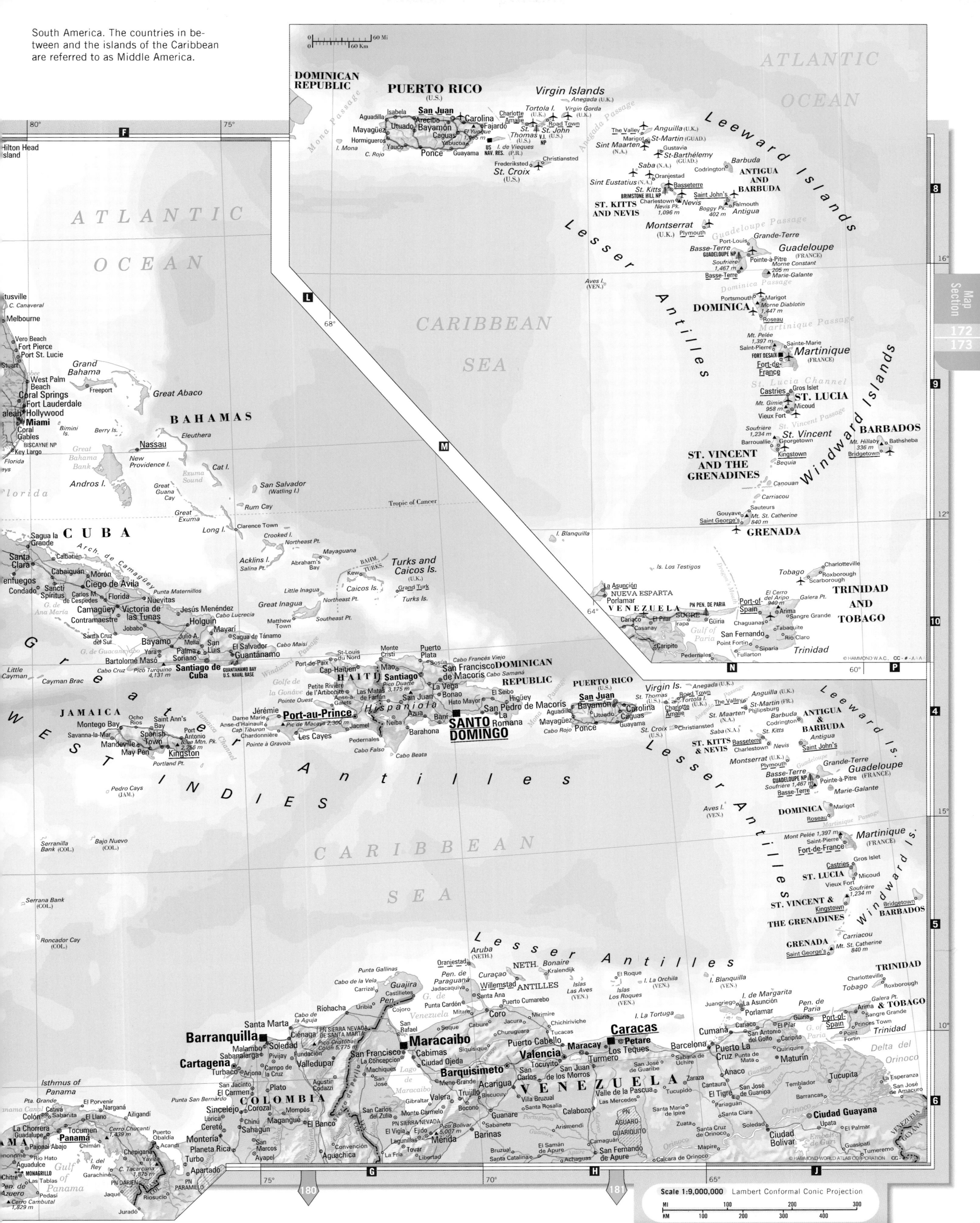

South America. The countries in between and the islands of the Caribbean are referred to as Middle America.

Scale 1:9,000,000 Lambert Conformal Conic Projection

Mexico has a unique blend of Native American and Spanish cultural heritages. Today, this Latin American culture is spreading north across the Rio Grande into the Anglo-American cultural region at an increasingly rapid pace. Bordered on the east and west by the parallel chains of the Sierra Madre Occidental and the Sierra Madre Oriental, Mexico's vast highlands are home to a large part of the Mexican population. The heavily urbanized area around Mexico City stretches from Guadalajara to Veracruz.

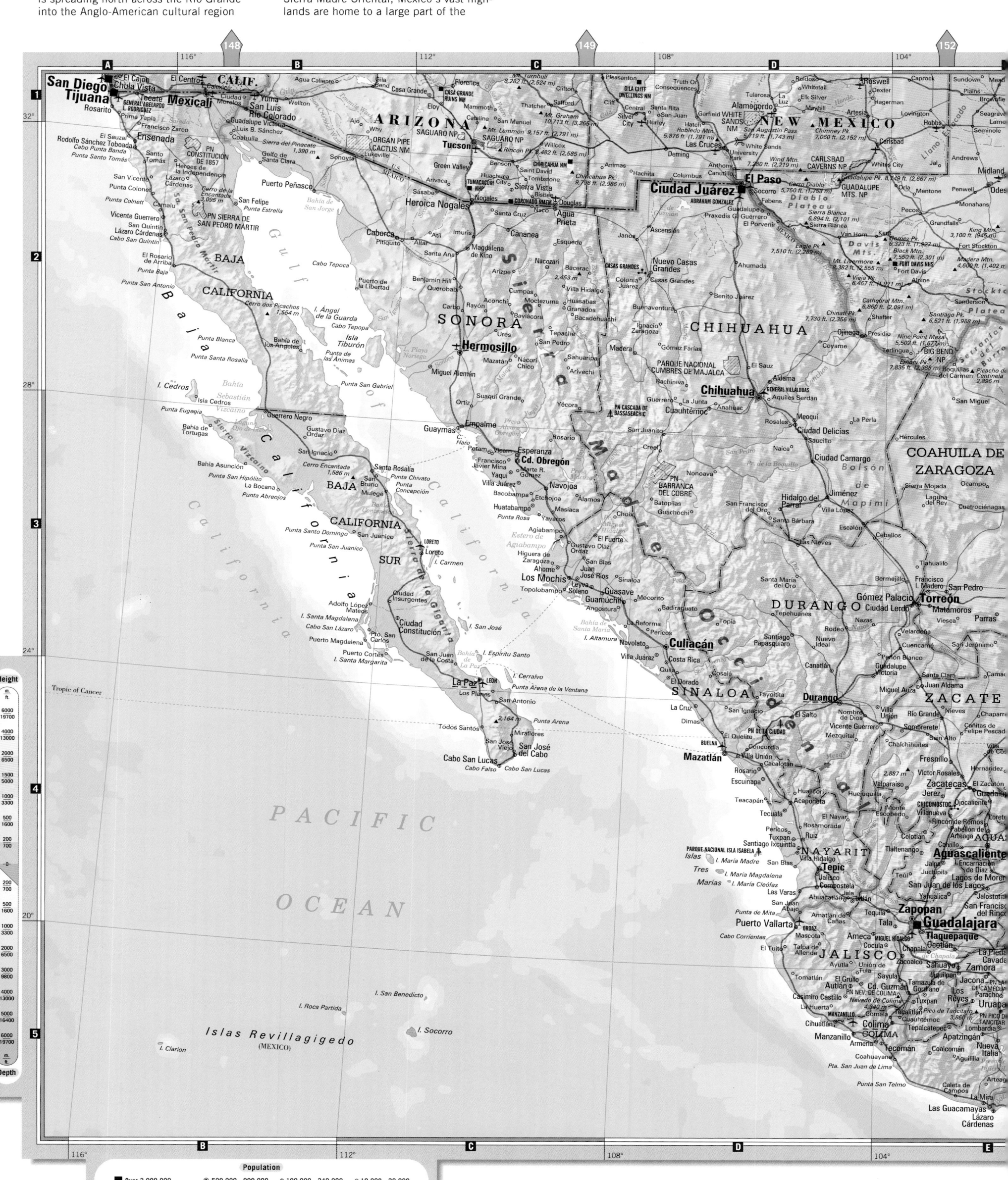

Northern and Central Mexico

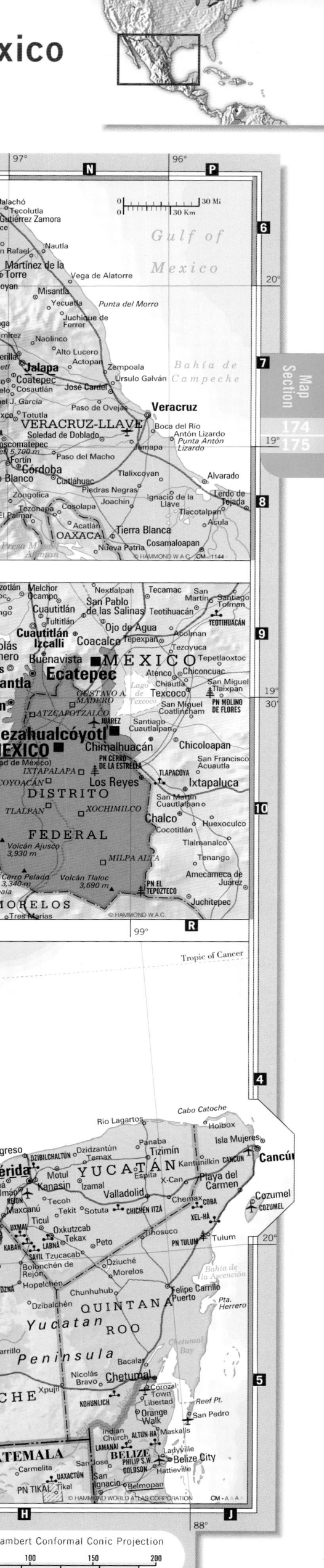

Scale 1:6,000,000   Lambert Conformal Conic Projection

© Hammond World Atlas Corporation

Costa Rica, the "Rich Coast," differs from its neighbors in many ways. Stable political relationships have enabled the country to preserve a large part of its tropical rain forest, which receives abundant precipitation from the northeast trade wind on the Caribbean side. Though much more dry in comparison, the Pacific coastal region is known around the world for its splendid orchids. The long (50 km) Valle Central in the interior highlands has a particularly mild climate and fertile volcanic soil. This is Costa Rica's traditional coffee-growing region.

Population

■ Over 2,000,000	⊛ 500,000 - 999,999
■ 1,000,000 - 1,999,999	⊙ 250,000 - 499,999

⊛ 100,000 - 249,999   ⊙ 10,000 - 29,999
⊙ 30,000 - 99,999   ○ Under 10,000

Southern Mexico, Central America, Western Caribbean

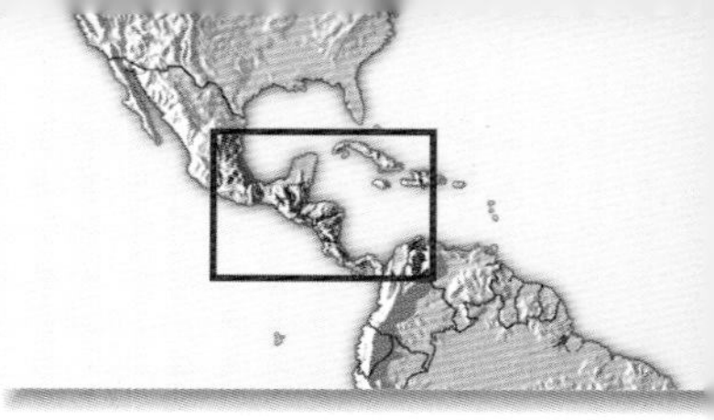

HAVANA
(La Habana)
Marianao
Guanabacoa
Matanzas
Cárdenas
Varadero
Sagua la Grande
Cifuentes
Santa Clara
Cienfuegos
Placetas
Sancti Spíritus
Ciego de Ávila
Camagüey
Nuevitas
Las Tunas
Holguín
Bayamo
Manzanillo
Santiago de Cuba
Guantánamo
GUANTANAMO BAY UNITED STATES NAVAL BASE
CUBA
Isla de la Juventud
(I. de Pinos)
Pinar del Río
San Cristóbal
Artemisa
Nicholas Channel
Old Bahama Channel
Golfo de Batabanó
Golfo de Guacanayabo
Jardines de la Reina
Cayman Islands
(U.K.)
Grand Cayman
George Town
Little Cayman
Cayman Brac
Greater Antilles
WEST INDIES
BAHAMAS
Great Inagua
Turks and Caicos Is.
(U.K.)
ATLANTIC OCEAN
Windward Passage
Hispaniola
HAITI
DOMINICAN REPUBLIC
Port-au-Prince
Cap-Haïtien
Gonaïves
Jérémie
Les Cayes
Jacmel
Navassa I.
(U.S.)
Jamaica Channel
JAMAICA
Montego Bay
Kingston
Spanish Town
Mandeville
May Pen
Blue Mtn. Pk. 2,256 m
Swan Islands
(HOND.)
Pedro Cays
(JAM.)
Serranilla Bank
(COL.)
Bajo Nuevo
(COL.)
CARIBBEAN SEA
Quita Sueño Bank
(COL.)
Serrana Bank
(COL.)
Roncador Cay
(COL.)
Isla de Providencia
(COL.)
San Andrés
Isla de San Andrés
(COL.)
NICARAGUA
Puerto Cabezas
Waspán
Bluefields
El Rama
Cayos Miskitos
COSTA RICA
San José
Limón
Puntarenas
Alajuela
Cartago
PANAMA
Panamá
Colón
Isthmus of Panama
Golfo de los Mosquitos
Gulf of Panama
Península de Azuero
Golfo de Chiriquí
David
Santiago
Chitré
COLOMBIA
Barranquilla
Cartagena
Santa Marta
Valledupar
Riohacha
Montería
Sincelejo
Cúcuta
LA GUAJIRA
MAGDALENA
CESAR
SUCRE
BOLÍVAR
CÓRDOBA
ANTIOQUIA
CHOCÓ
ATLÁNTICO
NORTE DE SANTANDER
SANTANDER
VENEZUELA
ZULIA
TACHIRA
Isla Beata
Scale 1:6,000,000 Lambert Conformal Conic Projection
MI 50 100 150 200
KM 50 100 150 200 250 300

The highest mountain peak in the Americas, with an elevation of 6,959 meters, is glacier-covered Mount Aconcagua. This northeastward-looking image shows the north-south axis of the Andes along the border between Chile and Argentina. The narrow valley running east to west immediately south of Mount Aconcagua contains a section of the American Highway that connects Mendoza, Argentina, with Santiago, Chile. Although composed of volcanic material, Mount Aconcagua - unlike many of its neighbors in the Andes - is not a volcano itself.

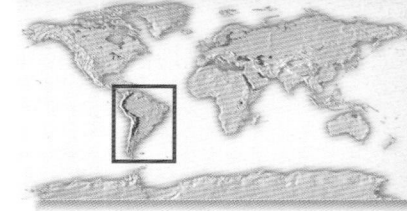

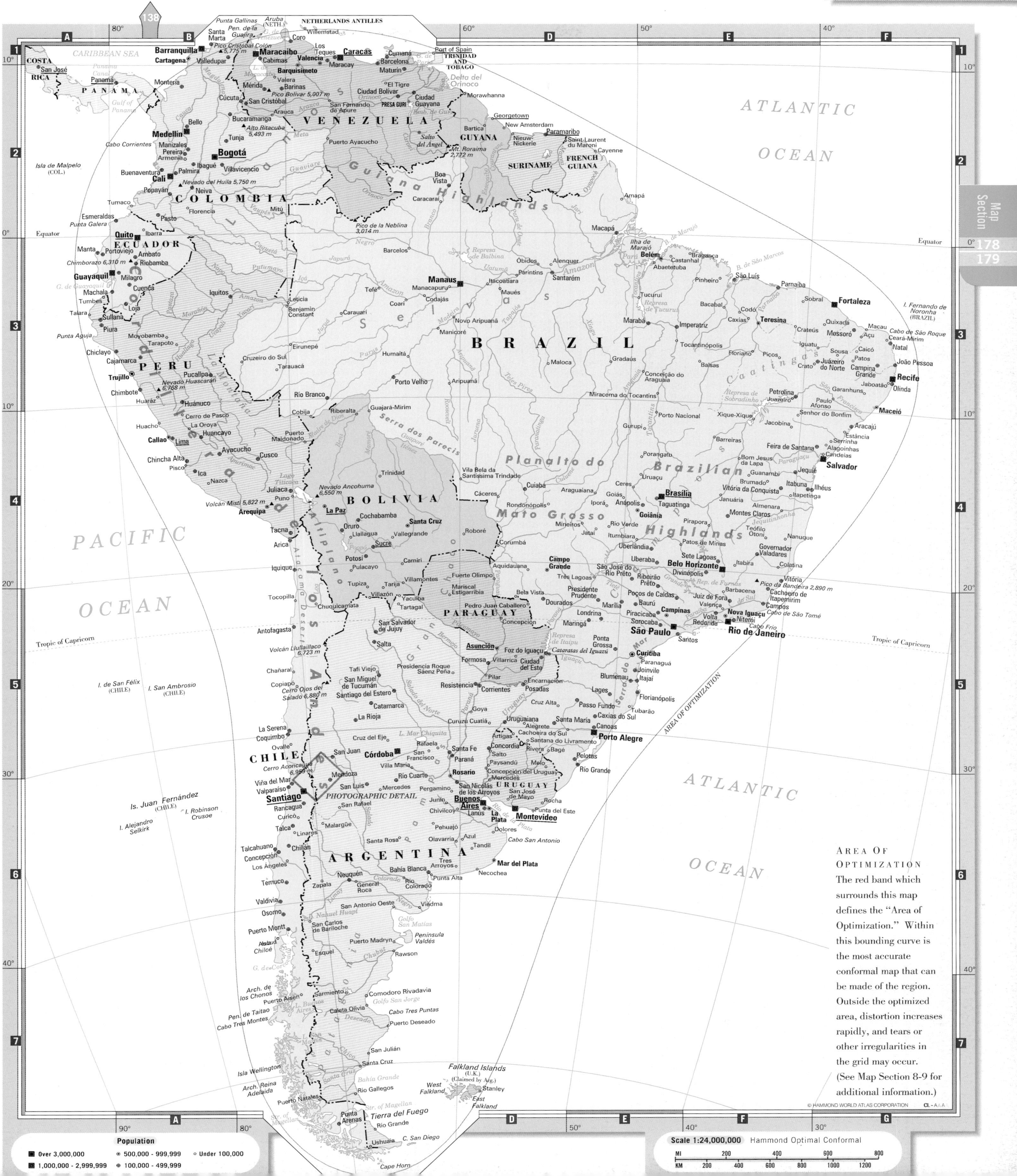

178
179

AREA OF OPTIMIZATION
The red band which surrounds this map defines the "Area of Optimization." Within this bounding curve is the most accurate conformal map that can be made of the region. Outside the optimized area, distortion increases rapidly, and tears or other irregularities in the grid may occur. (See Map Section 8-9 for additional information.)

Population

- ■ Over 3,000,000
- ● 500,000 - 999,999
- ○ Under 100,000
- ■ 1,000,000 - 2,999,999
- ● 100,000 - 499,999

Scale 1:24,000,000   Hammond Optimal Conformal

MI   200   400   600   800
KM   200   400   600   800   1000   1200

© HAMMOND WORLD ATLAS CORPORATION

The Orinoco is fed by the third-largest drainage basin in South America, a region that covers 70 percent of Venezuela and 25 percent of Colombia. Extreme topographic contrasts and a warm, humid climate make this one of the world's most diverse landscapes. Water flows from the heights of snow-covered Pico Bolívar (5,007 m) through tropical jungle, over virtually treeless plains known as Llanos, and on to the flood plain of the Orinoco. Here lie the oil reserves of Venezuela, which are among the largest in the world. Farther south, in the Guiana Highlands, water plunges 979 meters from the top of a flat-topped plateau at Angel Falls, the highest waterfall in the world.

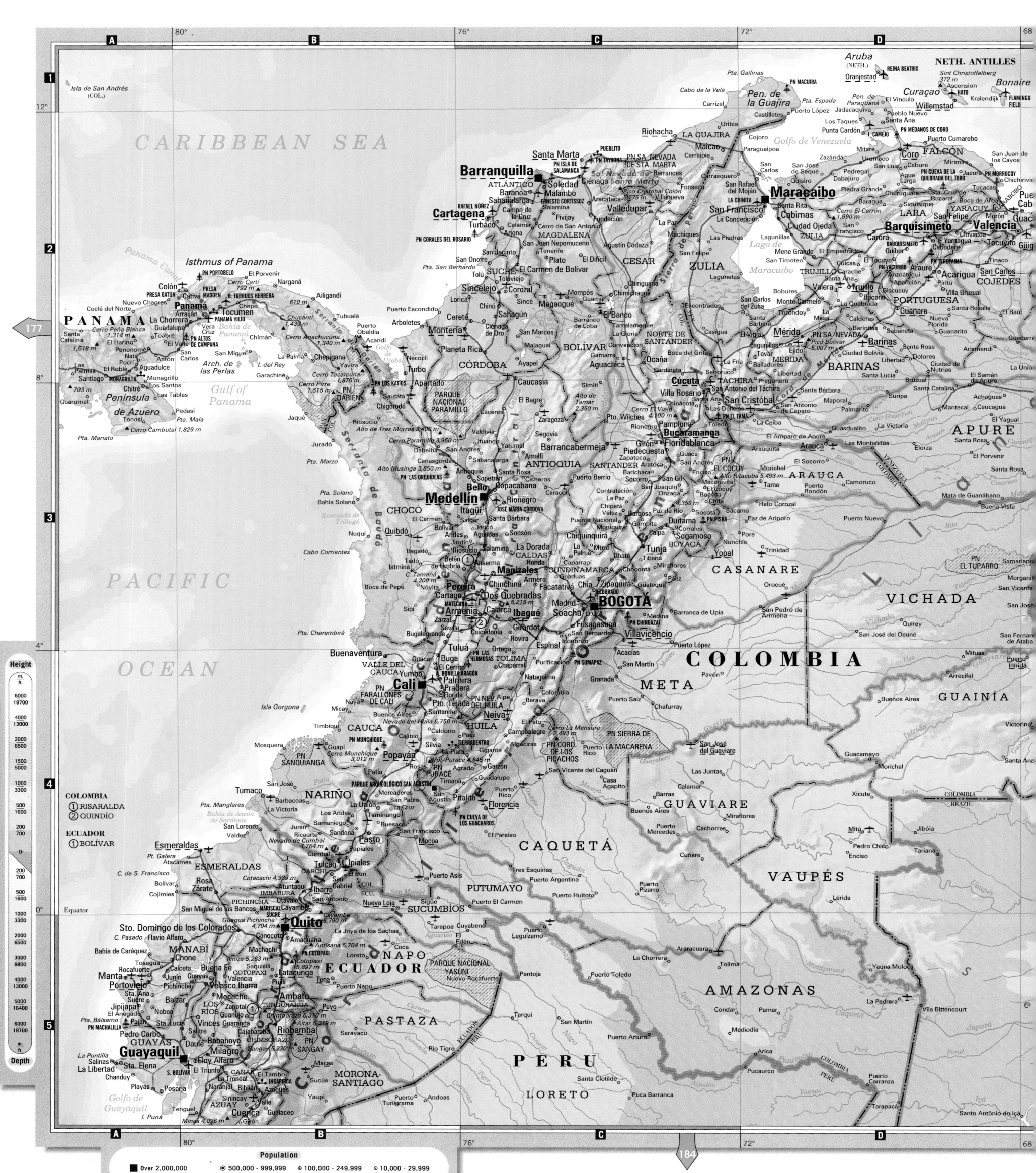

COLOMBIA
① RISARALDA
② QUINDÍO

ECUADOR
① BOLÍVAR

Population
■ Over 2,000,000
■ 1,000,000 - 1,999,999
● 500,000 - 999,999
● 250,000 - 499,999
◉ 100,000 - 249,999
◎ 30,000 - 99,999
○ 10,000 - 29,999
○ Under 10,000

Columbia, Venezuela, Ecuador

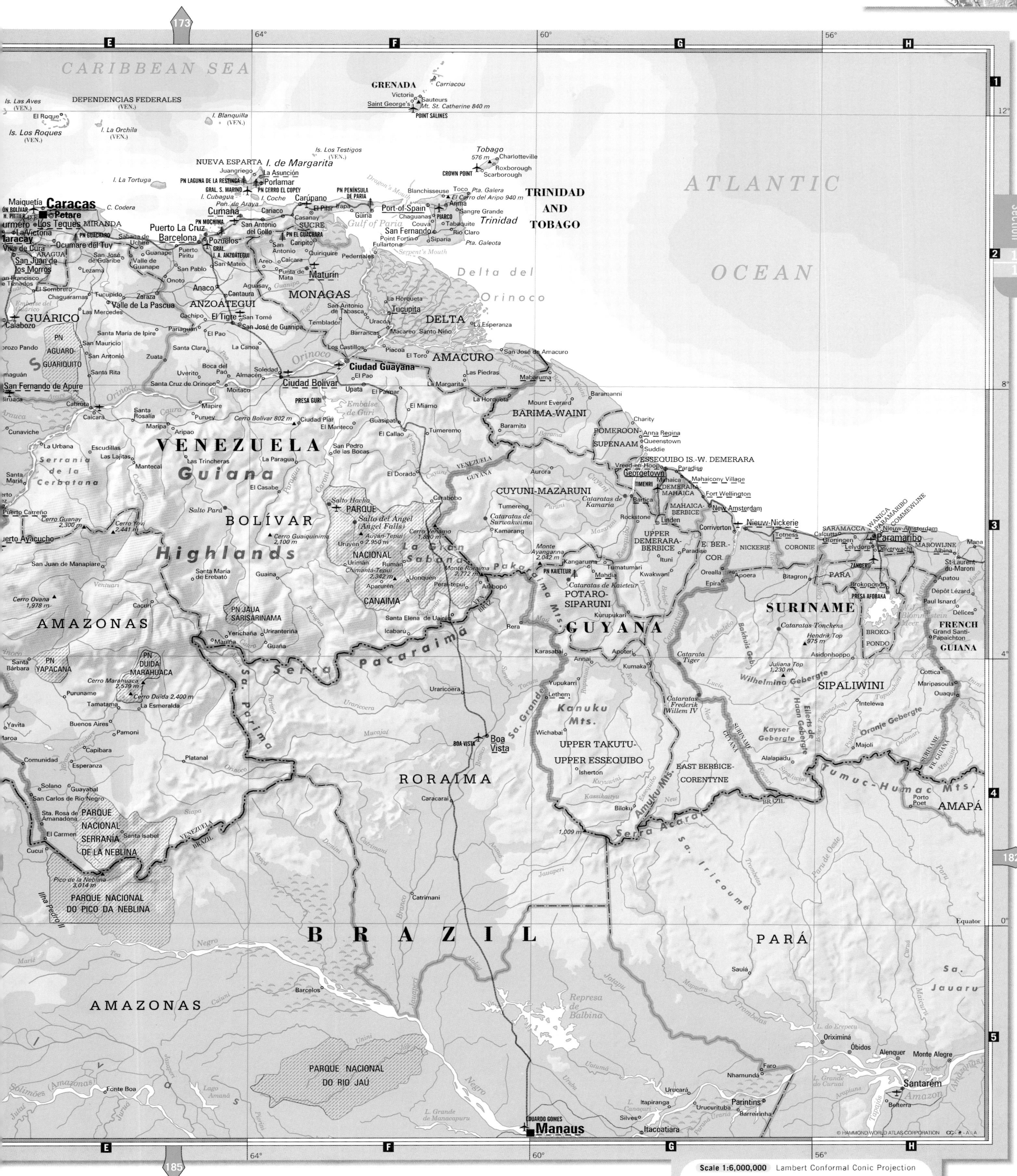

64° 60° 56°

E F G H

1

12°

CARIBBEAN SEA

Is. Las Aves (VEN.)
DEPENDENCIAS FEDERALES (VEN.)
El Roque
Is. Los Roques (VEN.)
I. Blanquilla (VEN.)
I. La Orchila (VEN.)
I. La Tortuga (VEN.)

GRENADA Carriacou
Victoria
Sauteurs
Saint George's Mt. St. Catherine 840 m
POINT SALINES

NUEVA ESPARTA I. de Margarita
Juangriego La Asunción
PN LAGUNA DE LA RESTINGA Porlamar
GRAL. S. MARINO PN CERRO EL COPEY
I. Cubagua I. Coche Carúpano
Peri. de Araya PN PENÍNSULA DE PARIA

Is. Los Testigos (VEN.)

Tobago 576 m
Charlotteville
Roxborough
Scarborough
CROWN POINT

TRINIDAD AND TOBAGO

Maiquetía **Caracas**
ÓN BOLÍVAR H. PITTIER Petare
Los Teques
urmero La Victoria MIRANDA
Maracay
Villa de Cura ARAGUA
Ocumare del Tuy
San Juan de los Morros
an Francisco de Tiznados
El Sombrero
GUÁRICO Calabozo
PN AGUARO-GUARIQUITO
orozo Pando
maguán
San Fernando de Apure
iruaca

Cumaná SUCRE
Puerto La Cruz
Barcelona
Pozuelos Puerto Piritu
Uchire
Sabana de Uchire
San José de Guaribe
Valle de Guanape
Onoto
Anaco ANZOÁTEGUI
Cantaura
El Tigre San Tomé
San José de Guanipa
Pariaguán
El Pao
La Canoa
Zuata
Santa Clara
Santa Rita

San Antonio del Golfo
PN MOCHIMA
Casanay
Cariaco
El Pilar
Güiria
Pedernales

Blanchisseuse Toco Pta. Galera
El Cerro del Aripo 940 m
Port-of-Spain Arima
Chaguanas Sangre Grande
San Fernando Couva
Point Fortin Tabaquite
Fullarton Rio Claro
Siparia Pta. Galeota

Trinidad

Gulf of Paria
Dragon's Mouth
Serpent's Mouth

ATLANTIC OCEAN

2

8°

Delta del Orinoco

La Horqueta
Tucupita
San Antonio de Tabasca
Uracoa
Macareo Santo Niño
DELTA AMACURO
San José de Amacuro

MONAGAS
Maturín
Aguasay
Temblador
Barrancas
Los Castillos
Piacoa
El Toro
Las Piedras
Maiuba
Baramanni

VENEZUELA
Guiana

Santa Rosalía
Caicara
Mapire
Purvey
El Casabe
San Pedro de las Bocas

Soledad Ciudad Guayana
El Pao
Ciudad Bolívar
PRESA GURI
Cerro Bolívar 802 m
Ciudad Piar
El Manteco
Guasipati
El Callao
Tumeremo
El Dorado

Mount Everard
Charity
BARIMA-WAINI
Baramita
POMEROON-SUPENAAM
Anna Regina
Queenstown
Suddie
ESSEQUIBO IS.-W. DEMERARA
Vreed-en-Hoop Paradise
Georgetown
TIMEHRI MAHAICA
DEMERARA-MAHAICA
Mahaicony Village
Fort Wellington
MAHAICA-BERBICE
New Amsterdam

BOLÍVAR
Highlands
Serrania de la Cerbatana

Santa
an
PuertoCarreño
Cerro Guanay 2,300 m
Cerro Yovi 2,441 m
San Juan de Manapiare
Cerro Ovana 1,978 m

Salto Pará
Salto Hacha PARQUE
Cerro Guaiquinima 2,100 m
Santa María de Erebató
Guaina

Salto del Angel (Angel Falls)
Auyán-Tepui 2,950 m
Uruyén
NACIONAL Urimán
Chimantá-Tepui 2,342 m
Apurarén
CANAIMA

Cerro Venamo 1,800 m
La Gran Sabana
Monte Roraima 2,772 m
Pera-tepui
Uonquen

CUYUNI-MAZARUNI
Tumereng
Cataratas de Kamaria
Aurora
Bartica
Rockstone
Linden
Corriverton
Nieuw-Nickerie

Cataratas de Surwakwima
Kamarang
Monte Ayanganna 2,042 m
Kangaruma
Tumatumari
Kwakwani
Ituni
Paradise
UPPER DEMERARA-BERBICE
E. BER.- COR.

3

4°

AMAZONAS

PN YAPACANA
PN DUIDA MARAHUACA
Cerro Marahuaca 2,579 m
Cerro Duida 2,400 m
La Esmeralda

Yerichana
Urirantería
Marina
Guaña

Icabarú
Santa Elena de Uairén

POTARO-SIPARUNI
PN KAIETEUR
Cataratas de Kaieteur
Mahdia
Kurupukari
Orealla
Apoera
Epira

GUYANA
SURINAME
SIPALIWINI

Santa Bárbara
Sa. Parima
Puruname
Tamatama
Yavita
Maroa
Solano
Guayabal
Comunidad
Esperanza
Capibara
San Carlos de Río Negro
Sta. Rosa de Amanadona
El Carmen
Cucui

Serra Pacaraimá
Uraricoera
Mucajaí

BOA VISTA Boa Vista

Kanuku Mts.
Wichabai
UPPER TAKUTU-UPPER ESSEQUIBO
Isherton

Karasabai
Annai
Kumaka
Apoteri
Rera

EAST BERBICE-CORENTYNE

Cataratas Tonckens
Hendrik Top 975 m
BROKO-PONDO

FRENCH GUIANA
Grand Santi-Papaichton

4

PARQUE NACIONAL SERRANÍA DE LA NEBLINA
Santa Isabel

Pico de la Neblina 3,014 m
PARQUE NACIONAL DO PICO DA NEBLINA

VENEZUELA BRAZIL

RORAIMA
Caracaraí

1,009 m
Serra Acaraí
Biloku
Serra Iricoumé

Tumuc-Humac Mts
Porto Poet
AMAPÁ

182

5

B R A Z I L

AMAZONAS
Barcelos

PARÁ

Sauiá

Parque Nacional do Rio Jaú

Represa de Balbina
Oriximiná
Óbidos Alenquer
Monte Alegre
Nhamundá
Urucará
Itapiranga
Urucurituba
Parintins
Barreirinha
Silves
Manaus
EDUARDO GOMES
Itacoatiara

Santarém

Equator 0°

E F G H
64° 60° 56°

Scale 1:6,000,000 Lambert Conformal Conic Projection

MI 50 100 150 200
KM 50 100 150 200 250 300

© HAMMOND WORLD ATLAS CORPORATION

The Amazon Basin of northern Brazil comprises the world's largest rain forest, an area covering some 4.5 million square km. The Amazon, its more than 200 tributaries, and the vast rain forest are home to over one million different species of plants and animals. Millions of acres of this vital ecosystem are destroyed every year. Without its protective cover of foliage, the exposed, sensitive soil hardens into unfertile laterite and is subject to heavy erosion. The Amazon Basin has an average relative humidity of 90 percent and receives up to 4,000 mm of precipitation per year.

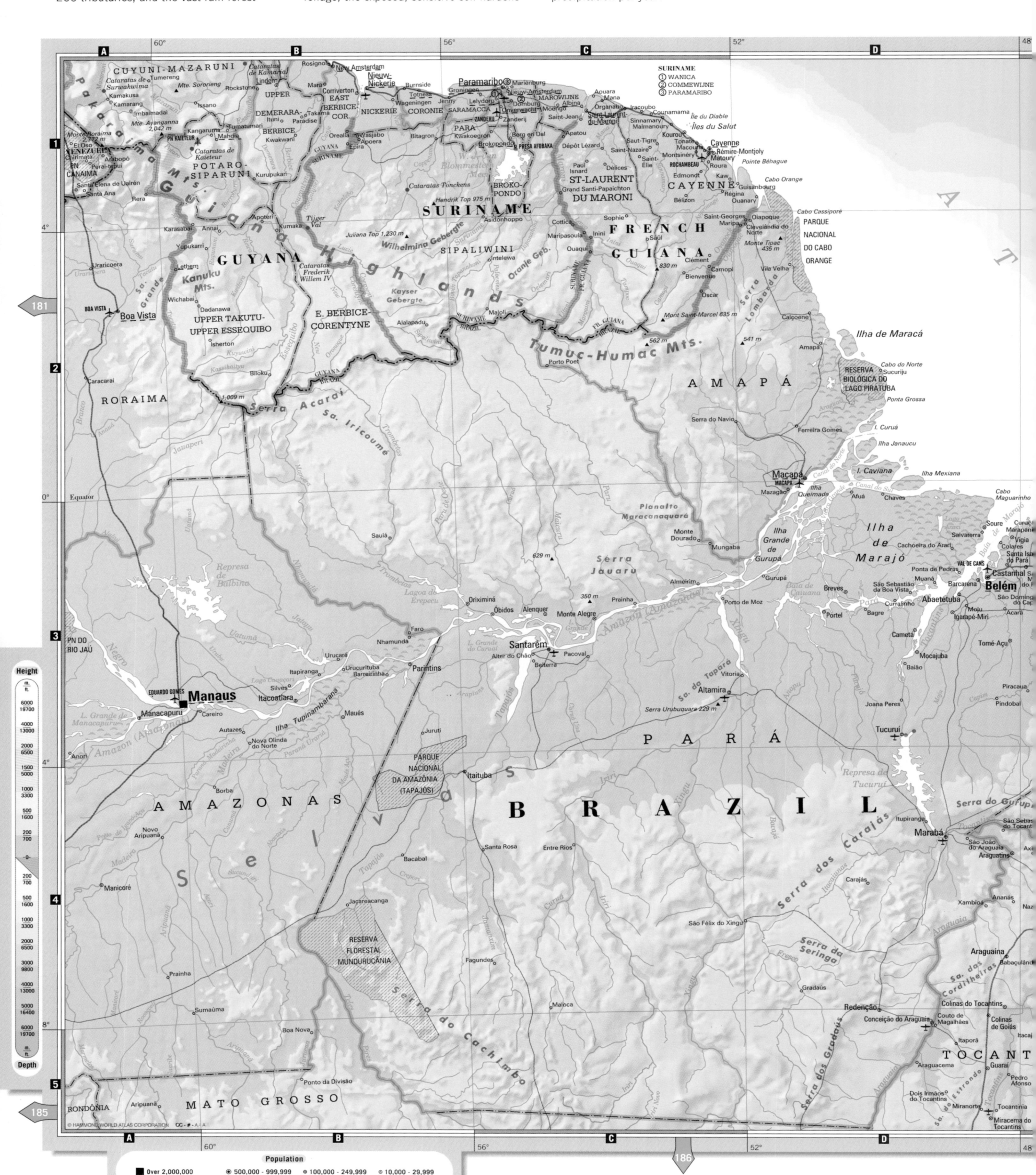

Height

m.	ft.
6000	19700
4000	13000
2000	6500
1500	5000
1000	3300
500	1600
200	700
0	
200	700
500	1600
1000	3300
2000	6500
3000	9800
4000	13000
5000	16400
6000	19700

Depth

Population

■ Over 2,000,000	◉ 500,000 - 999,999	◉ 100,000 - 249,999	◉ 10,000 - 29,999
■ 1,000,000 - 1,999,999	◉ 250,000 - 499,999	◉ 30,000 - 99,999	◦ Under 10,000

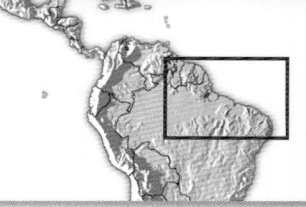

Scale 1:6,000,000   Lambert Conformal Conic Projection

A unique feature of the climate of the west coast of South America is the El Niño phenomenon, which occurs about every three to seven years. At these times, temperatures rise in the equatorial coastal waters, drastically reducing the amount of nutrient-rich cold water that ascends from the depths to the surface and thus decimating the fish population. Unusually heavy rainfall in Peru and Ecuador resulting from El Niño has been known to cause severe landslides on the steep mountain slopes. The Andes reach their widest point in Bolivia, where the Cordillera Occidental and the Cordillera Oriental frame the expansive Bolivian highland, the Altiplano, which grows progressively more arid south of Lake Titicaca and culminates in a high desert.

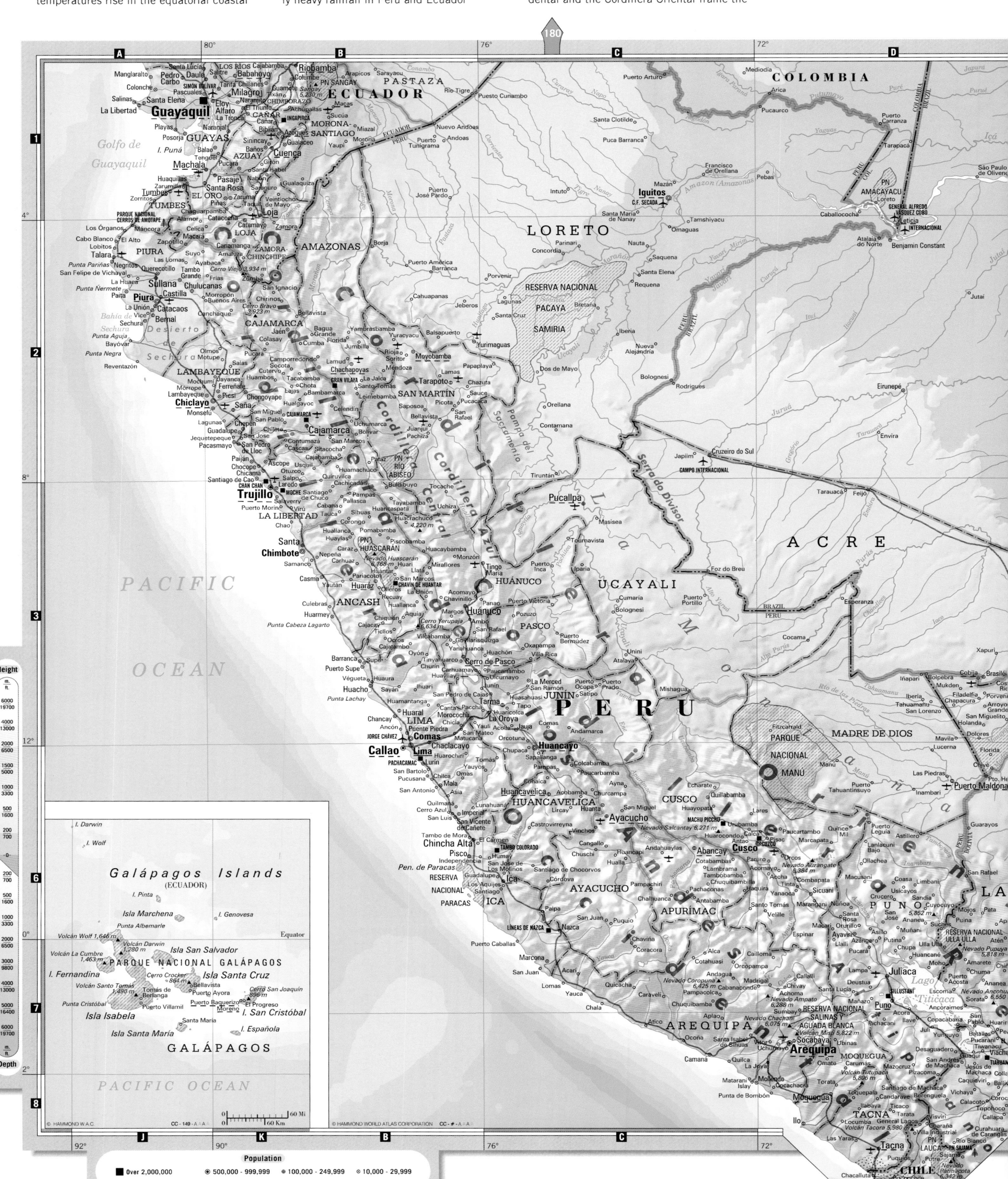

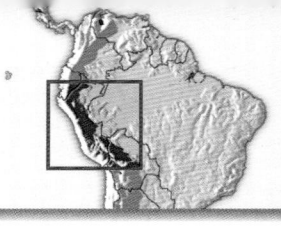

181
188
189
182
184 185
186

Map Section

AMAZONAS

BRAZIL

PARÁ

RONDÔNIA

MATO GROSSO

PANDO

BENI

BOLIVIA

SANTA CRUZ

COCHABAMBA

MATO GROSSO DO SUL

PARQUE NACIONAL DO RIO JAÚ

RESERVA FLORESTAL MUNDURUCÂNIA

PARQUE NACIONAL DE AMAZÔNIA (TAPAJÓS)

RESERVA FLORESTAL DO JURUENA

PARQUE NACIONAL DOS PACAÁS NOVOS

RESERVA NACIONAL MANURIPI HEATH AMAZÓNICA

PARQUE NACIONAL ISIBORO SÉCURE

Manaus · Manacapuru · Eduardo Gomes · Tefé · Coari · Carauari · Fonte Boa · Santo Antônio do Içá · Maraã · Codajás · Anori · Autazes · Careiro · Itacoatiara · Silves · Itapiranga · Urucurituba · Urucará · Parintins · Barreirinha · Nhamundá · Faro · Oriximiná · Óbidos · Alenquer · Santarém · Boferra · Juruti · Itaituba · Jacareacanga · Maués · Nova Olinda do Norte · Borba · Novo Aripuaná · Manicoré · Sumaúma · Humaitá · Calama · Porto Velho · Lábrea · Canutama · Tapauá · Bôca do Acre · Pauini · Ariquemes · Jaru · Ji-Paraná (Rondônia) · Presidente Médici · Cacoal · Espigão d'Oeste · Pimenta Bueno · Rolim de Moura · Vilhena · Colorado do Oeste · Aripuanã · Alta Floresta · Sinop · Entre Rios · Arenópolis · Diamantino · Nortelândia · Alto Paraguai · Nobres · Rosário Oeste · Tangará da Serra · Barra do Bugres · Cáceres · Cuiabá · Várzea Grande · Chapada dos Guimarães · Nova Brasilândia · Acorizal · Poconé · Barão de Melgaço · Santo Antônio do Leverger · Dom Aquino · Jaciara · Poxoréo · Rondonópolis · Itiquira

Rio Branco · Puerto Rapirrán · Nuevo Mundo · Santos Mercado · Manoa · Fortaleza · Abuná · Guajará-Mirim · Guayaramerín · Riberalta · Villa Bella · Triunfo · Santo Domingo · Loma Alta · Mapiri · San Pedro · Las Piedras · Ivón · Pollar · Concepción · Tres Mapajos · Santa Rosa · Sena · Maravillas · Asunción · San Lorenzo · El Perú · Alejandría · Costa Marques · Mayo Mayo · La Horquilla · Puerto Siles · Chalamama · Las Pampitas · Versalles · Remanso · Mateguá · Bella Vista · Piso Firme · Puerto Alegre · Puerto Saucedo · San Cristóbal · Porvenir · Puerto Frey · Monte Cristo · Vila Bela da Santíssima Trindade · Pontes e Lacerda · Planalto do Mato Grosso

Trinidad · San Borja · San Ignacio · Loreto · Yaguarú · Limoquije · Los Cusis · Santa María · San Pablo · Ascención · Yotaú · El Puente · Concepción · San Javier · San Ignacio · Santa Ana · San Rafael · San Miguel · San Diego · Santa Rosa de la Roca · Cuyuchi · Las Petas · San Matías · Cáceres · Montero · Warnes · Cochabamba · La Paz

Scale 1:6,000,000   Lambert Conformal Conic Projection

MI 50 100 150 200
KM 50 100 150 200 250 300

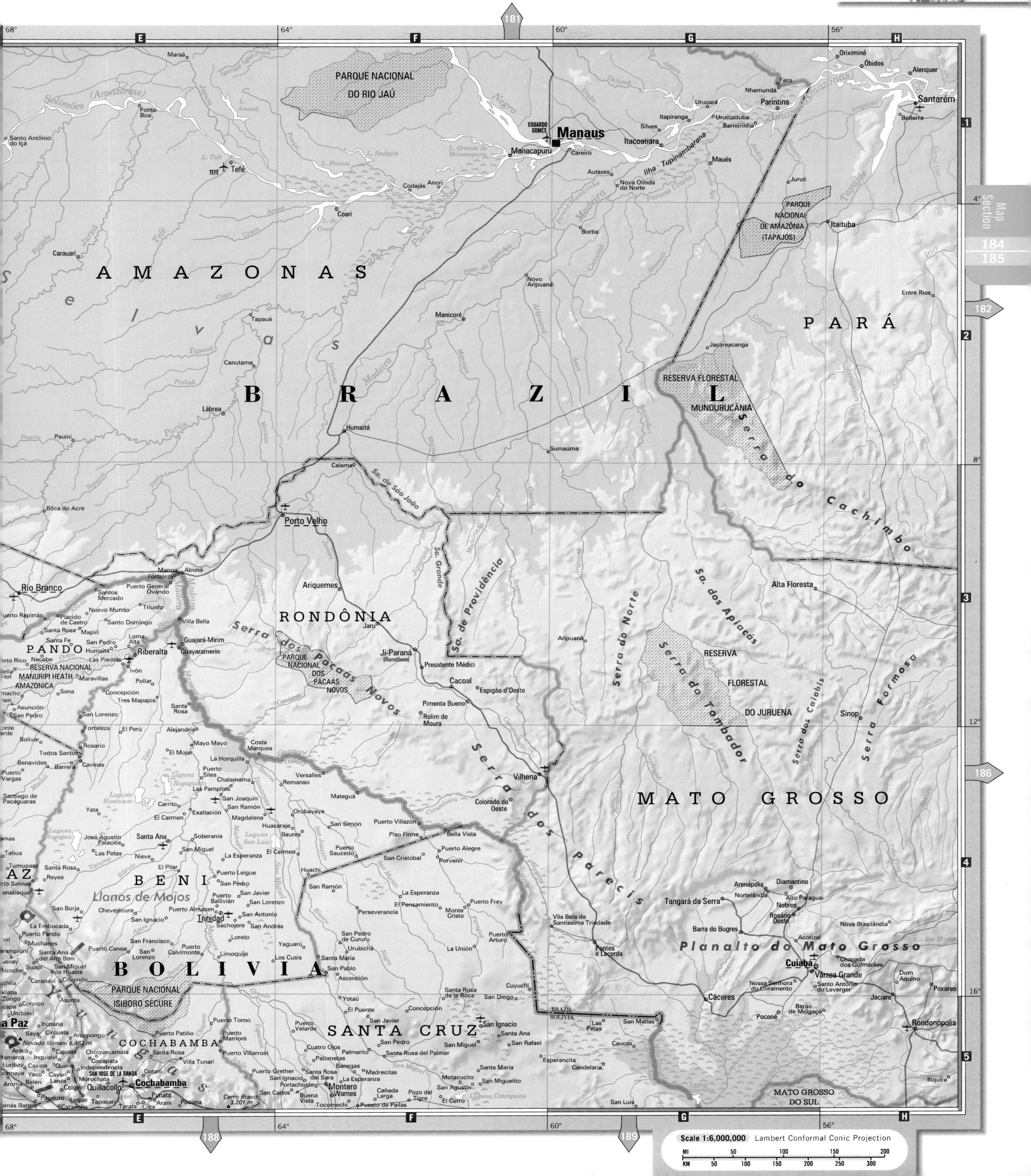

Brazil is the fifth largest country on earth and covers nearly half of the South American continent. Its tropical-subtropical climate and extensive highlands provide ideal conditions for the cultivation of coffee.

The very old underlying rock is also rich in iron ore, gold, and diamonds. The most important energy source - water - is harnessed effectively in the Paraná River system (Itaipú hydroelectric plant). Substantial

oil reserves have been discovered off the coast near Rio de Janeiro. Eighty percent of the population lives in the cities, the largest of which are Sao Paulo and Rio de Janeiro.

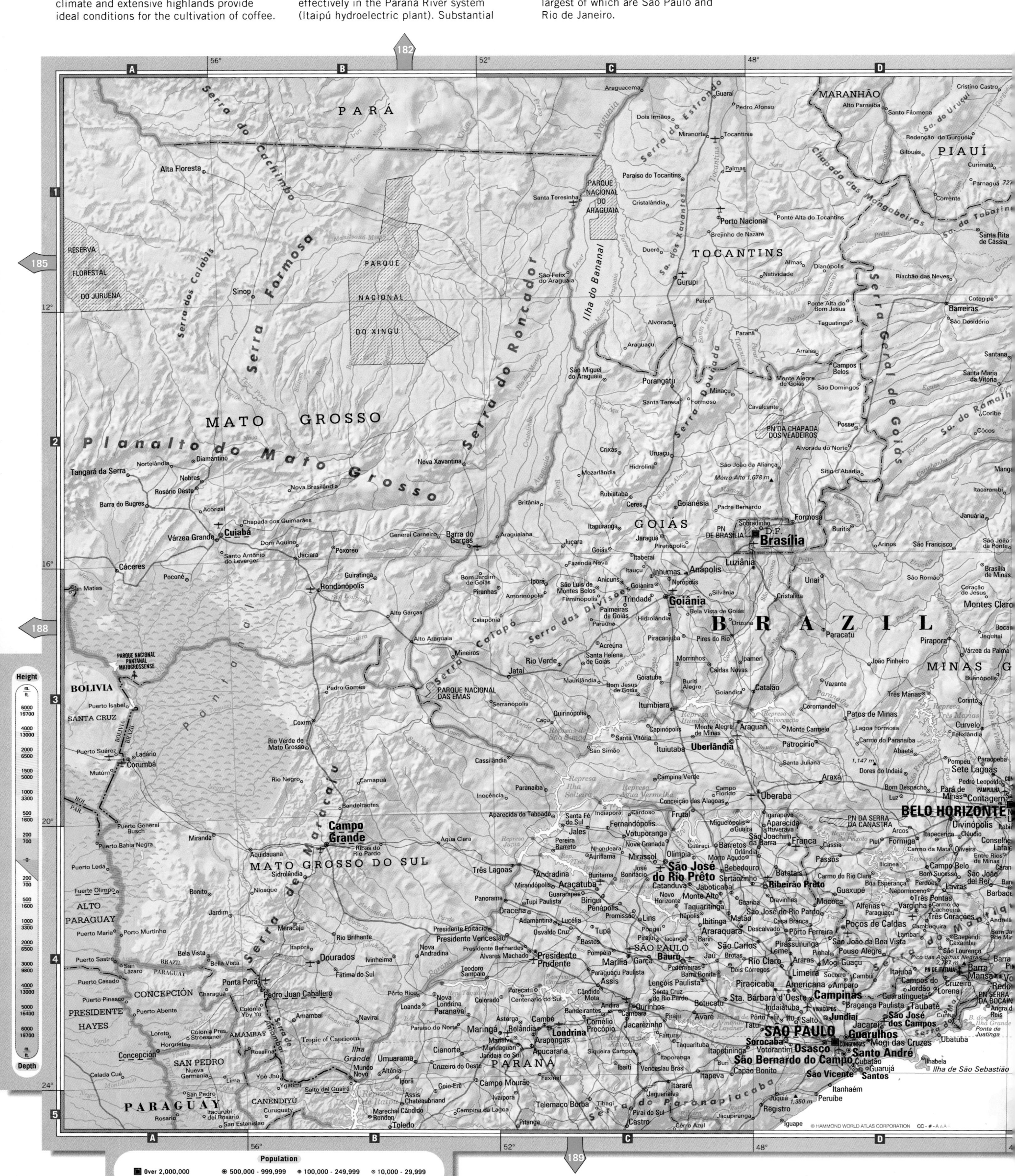

182
185
188
189

Population

■ Over 2,000,000	⊛ 500,000 - 999,999
■ 1,000,000 - 1,999,999	⊚ 250,000 - 499,999
⊛ 100,000 - 249,999	⊙ 10,000 - 29,999
⊚ 30,000 - 99,999	○ Under 10,000

© HAMMOND WORLD ATLAS CORPORATION

Height
m.
ft.
6000 19700
4000 13000
2000 6500
1500 5000
1000 3300
500 1600
200 700
0
200 700
500 1600
1000 3300
2000 6500
3000 9800
4000 13000
5000 16400
6000 19700
m.
ft.
Depth

183

Scale 1:6,000,000   Lambert Conformal Conic Projection

© HAMMOND WORLD ATLAS CORPORATION

The Gran Chaco, South America's vast heartland, through which the many tributaries of the Paraguay and the Paraná flow, has a hot, subtropical climate with heavy precipitation in the east and much drier conditions in the west. The winds blowing inland from the Pacific travel over cold ocean currents and thus carry little moisture. The prevailing climate has produced coastal deserts in Chile and Peru, where average precipitation often falls below 4 mm. One such desert is the Atacama, an arid region rich in ore deposits where the mean annual temperature is a moderate 66° F.

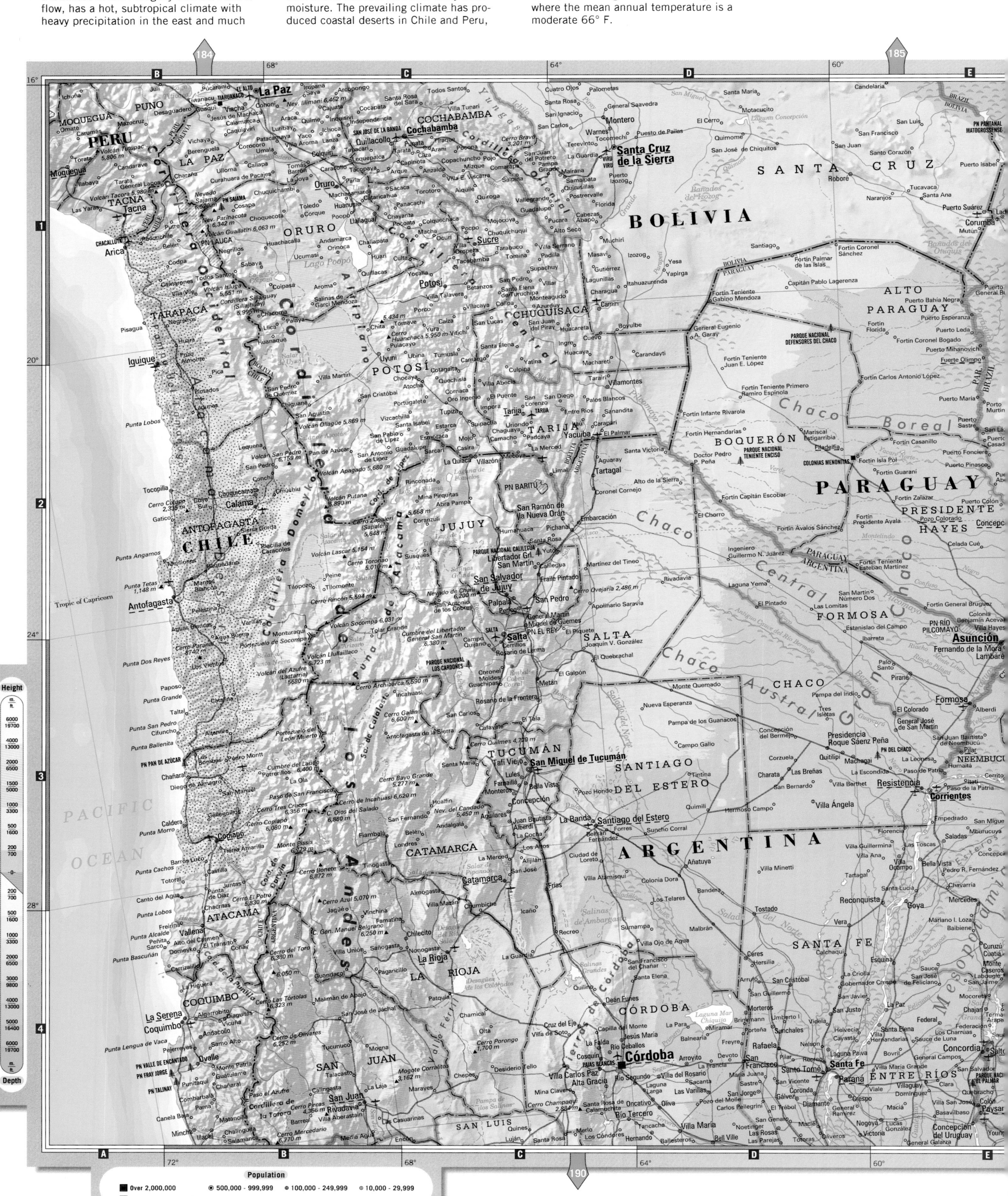

Scale 1:6,000,000 Lambert Conformal Conic Projection

© HAMMOND WORLD ATLAS CORPORATION

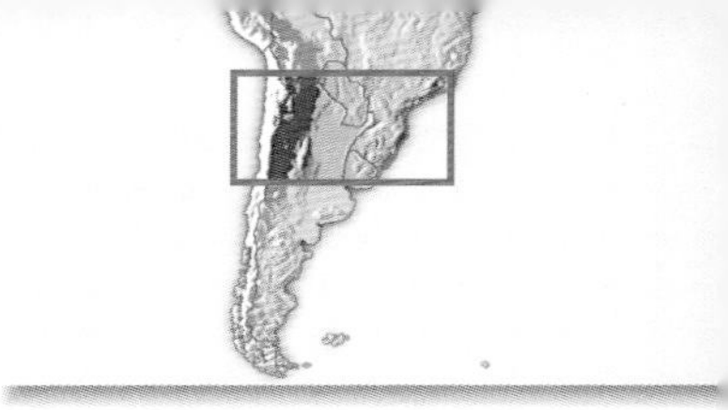

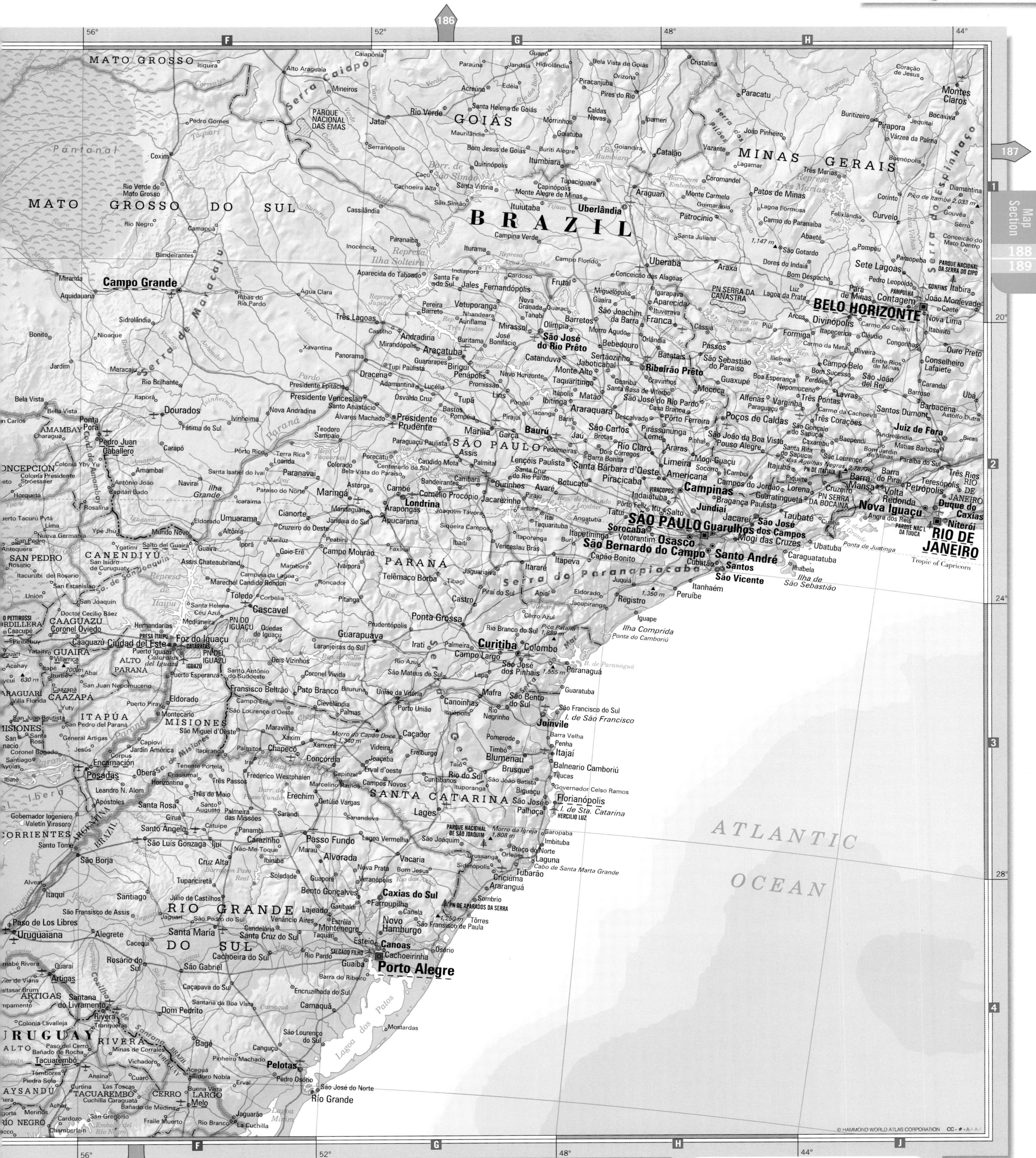

The expansive grasslands of Argentina, the Pampas, were probably covered with light forest growth before settlers began clearing the land for wheat farming and to provide grazing land for cattle. With good access to shipping routes, the area around the mouths of the Paraná and Uruguay rivers is one of South America's most important economic regions. Climatic conditions in the south are extreme, both in east Patagonia, with its salt swamps, and in Tierra del Fuego, where storms off Cape Horn have been the bane of seafarers for centuries.

Height

m. / ft.
6000 / 19700
4000 / 13000
2000 / 6500
1500 / 5000
1000 / 3300
500 / 1600
200 / 700
0
200 / 700
500 / 1600
1000 / 3300
2000 / 6500
3000 / 9800
4000 / 13000
5000 / 16400
6000 / 19700
m. / ft.

Depth

Population
■ Over 2,000,000
■ 1,000,000 - 1,999,999
⬤ 500,000 - 999,999
◉ 250,000 - 499,999
◉ 100,000 - 249,999
◎ 30,000 - 99,999
○ 10,000 - 29,999
○ Under 10,000

© HAMMOND WORLD ATLAS CORPORATION

Southern Chile and Argentina

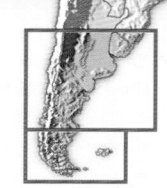

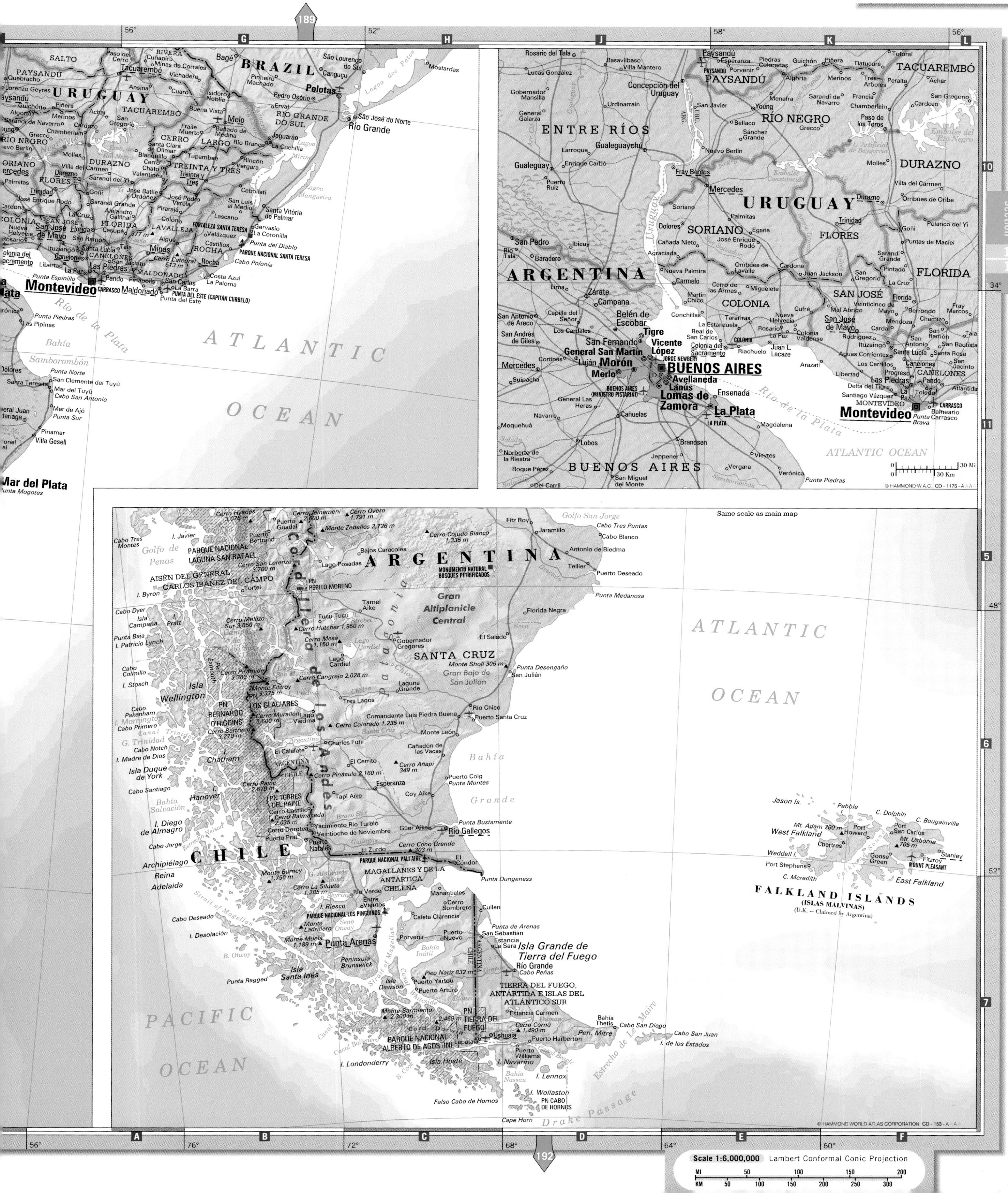

189
192
G H J K L
A B C D E F
56° 52° 58° 56° 76° 72° 68° 64° 60° 34° 48° 52°
10 11 5 6 7
BRAZIL
URUGUAY
ATLANTIC OCEAN
SALTO
PAYSANDÚ
TACUAREMBÓ
RIVERA
CERRO LARGO
RÍO NEGRO
DURAZNO
TREINTA Y TRES
FLORIDA
LAVALLEJA
ROCHA
CANELONES
MALDONADO
RIO GRANDE DO SUL
Montevideo
Pelotas
Rio Grande
Melo
Mar del Plata
Punta Mogotes
Villa Gesell
Pinamar
Bahía Samborombón
Río de la Plata
Lagoa dos Patos
Lagoa Mirim
Lagoa Mangueira
FORTALEZA SANTA TERESA
PARQUE NACIONAL SANTA TERESA
PUNTA DEL ESTE (CAPITÁN CURBELO)
CARRASCO
ENTRE RÍOS
BUENOS AIRES
SORIANO
COLONIA
SAN JOSÉ
FLORES
BUENOS AIRES
Tigre
Vicente López
JORGE NEWBERY
Avellaneda
Lanús
Lomas de Zamora
La Plata
LA PLATA
Morón
Merlo
General San Martín
San Fernando
Belén de Escobar
Zárate
Campana
BUENOS AIRES (MINISTRO PISTARINI)
Fray Bentos
Mercedes
Colonia del Sacramento
Gualeguaychú
Paraná
Uruguay
Río de la Plata
ATLANTIC OCEAN
0 30 Mi
0 30 Km
© HAMMOND W.A.C. CD - 1175 - A
Same scale as main map
ATLANTIC OCEAN
PACIFIC OCEAN
SANTA CRUZ
Gran Altiplanicie Central
Gran Bajo de San Julián
Cordillera de los Andes
Meseta
Golfo San Jorge
Golfo de Penas
Bahía Grande
MONUMENTO NATURAL BOSQUES PETRIFICADOS
PARQUE NACIONAL LAGUNA SAN RAFAEL
AISÉN DEL GENERAL CARLOS IBÁÑEZ DEL CAMPO
PN PERITO MORENO
PN LOS GLACIARES
PN BERNARDO O'HIGGINS
PN TORRES DEL PAINE
PARQUE NACIONAL PALI AIKE
PARQUE NACIONAL LOS PINGÜINOS
PARQUE NACIONAL ALBERTO DE AGOSTINI
PN TIERRA DEL FUEGO
PN CABO DE HORNOS
MAGALLANES Y DE LA ANTÁRTICA CHILENA
TIERRA DEL FUEGO, ANTÁRTIDA E ISLAS DEL ATLÁNTICO SUR
Isla Grande de Tierra del Fuego
Puerto Deseado
Río Gallegos
Puerto Santa Cruz
Punta Arenas
Puerto Natales
Ushuaia
Río Grande
El Calafate
Cerro San Lorenzo 3,700 m
Cerro Fitzroy 3,375 m
Monte San Valentín
Strait of Magellan
Estrecho de Le Maire
Drake Passage
Cape Horn
Isla Wellington
Isla Hoste
I. Navarino
I. de los Estados
Isla Santa Inés
Isla Dawson
FALKLAND ISLANDS (ISLAS MALVINAS)
(U.K. -- Claimed by Argentina)
West Falkland
East Falkland
Stanley
MOUNT PLEASANT
Jason Is.
© HAMMOND WORLD ATLAS CORPORATION CD - 153 - A
Scale 1:6,000,000 Lambert Conformal Conic Projection
MI 50 100 150 200
KM 50 100 150 200 250 300

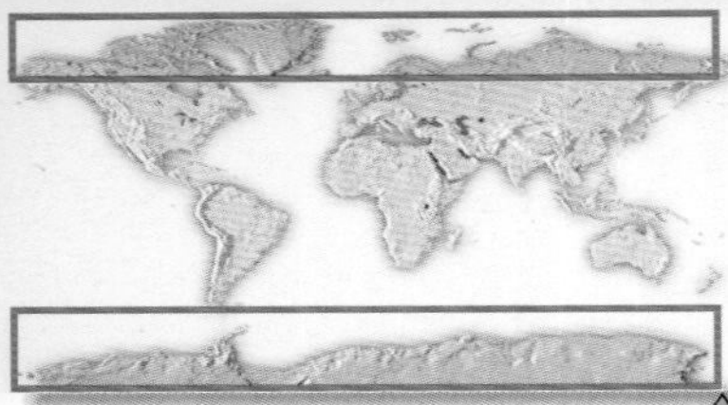

Arctic Regions, Antarctica

Polar climates extend from the poles in the direction of the equator up to a line along which average temperatures during the warmest month do not exceed 40° F. Except for Greenland, the Arctic is a landless region of sea and ice. Antarctica is the coldest, driest continent on earth and has the highest average elevation. A record low temperature of -129.8° F was recorded at the Vostok Research Station.

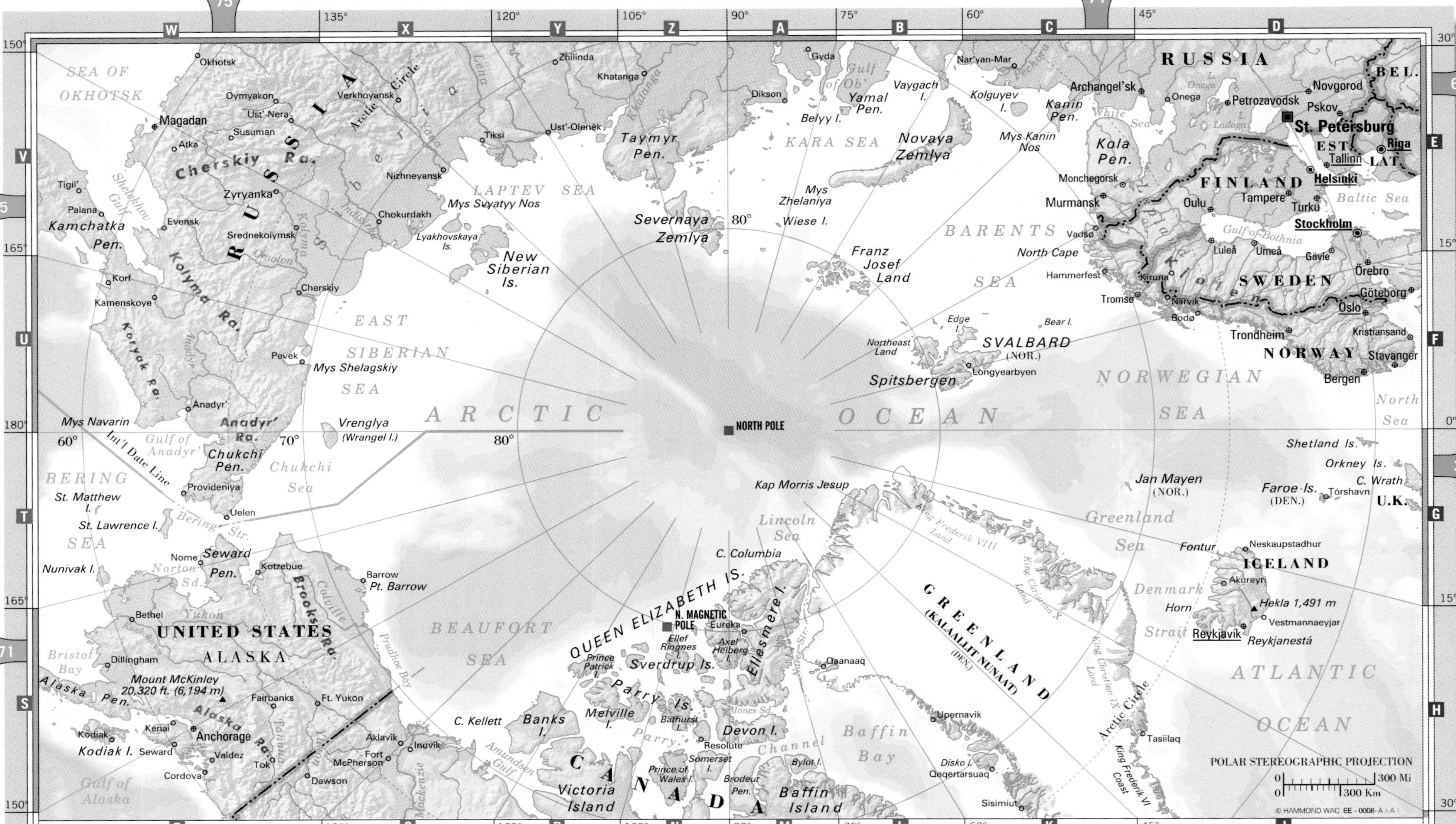

POLAR STEREOGRAPHIC PROJECTION

0 [ ] 300 Mi
0 [ ] 300 Km

© HAMMOND WAC EE-0008-A-A-A

POLAR STEREOGRAPHIC PROJECTION

0 [ ] 500 Mi
0 [ ] 500 Km

© HAMMOND WAC EE-0009-A-A-A

Height

m.
ft.

6000 / 19700
4000 / 13000
2000 / 6500
1500 / 5000
1000 / 3300
500 / 1600
200 / 700
–0–
200 / 700
500 / 1600
1000 / 3300
2000 / 6500
3000 / 9800
4000 / 13000
5000 / 16400
6000 / 19700

m.
ft.

Depth

Population

■ Over 2,000,000
■ 1,000,000 - 1,999,999
▪ 500,000 - 999,999
• 100,000 - 499,999
◦ 50,000 - 99,999
○ Under 50,000

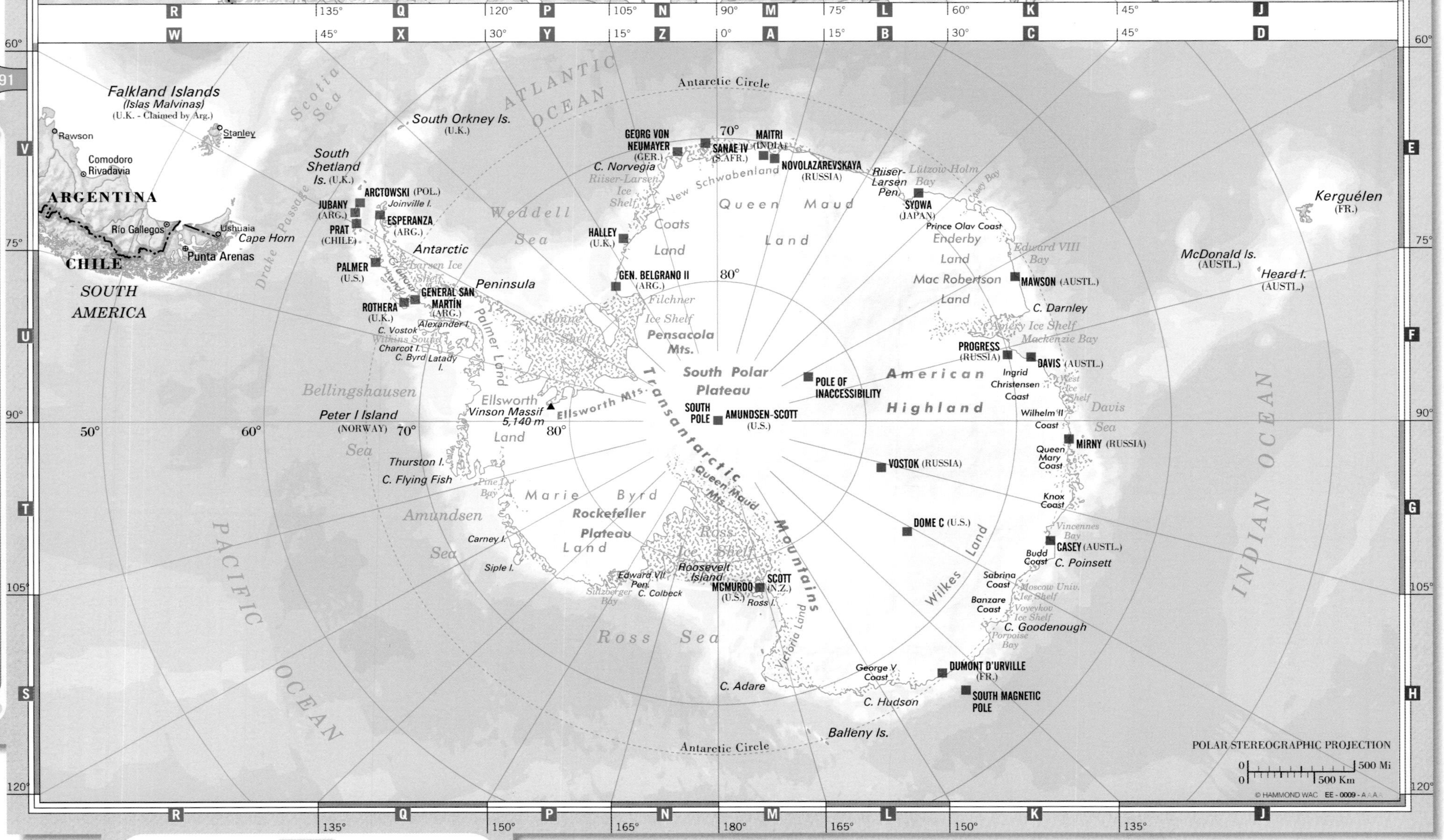

World Statistics

Elements of the Solar System

	Mean Distance from Sun: in Miles	in Kilometers	Period of Revolution around Sun	Period of Rotation on Axis	Equatorial Diameter in Miles	in Kilometers	Surface Gravity (Earth = 1)	Mass (Earth = 1)	Mean Density (Water = 1)	Number of Satellites
Mercury	35,990,000	57,900,000	87.97 days	58.7 days	3,032	4,880	0.38	0.055	5.4	0
Venus	67,240,000	108,200,000	224.70 days	243 days†	7,521	12,104	0.91	0.815	5.2	0
Earth	93,000,000	149,700,000	365.26 days	23h 56m	7,926	12,755	1.00	1.00	5.5	1
Mars	141,610,000	227,900,000	686.98 days	24h 37m	4,221	6,794	0.38	0.107	3.9	2
Jupiter	483,675,000	778,400,000	11.86 years	9h 55m	88,846	142,984	2.36	317.8	1.3	39
Saturn	890,800,000	1,433,500,000	29.46 years	10h 30m	74,898	120,536	0.92	95.2	0.7	30
Uranus	1,784,800,000	2,872,500,000	84.01 years	17h 14m†	31,763	51,118	0.89	14.5	1.3	21
Neptune	2,793,100,000	4,495,100,000	164.79 years	16h 6m	30,778	49,532	1.13	17.1	1.6	8
Pluto	3,647,000,000	5,870,000,000	247.70 years	6.4 days†	1,485	2,390	0.07	0.002	2.1	1

† Retrograde motion

Source: NASA, National Space Science Cen-

Dimensions of the Earth

	Area in: Sq. Miles	Sq. Kilometers
Superficial area	196,939,000	510,072,000
Land surface	57,506,000	148,940,000
Water surface	139,433,000	361,132,000

	Distance in: Miles	Kilometers
Equatorial circumference	24,902	40,075
Polar circumference	24,860	40,007
Equatorial diameter	7,926.4	12,756.4
Polar diameter	7,899.8	12,713.6
Equatorial radius	3,963.2	6,378.2
Polar radius	3,949.9	6,356.8

Volume of the Earth	2.6×10^{11} cubic miles	10.84×10^{11} cubic kilometers
Mass or weight	6.6×10^{21} short tons	6.0×10^{21} metric tons
Maximum distance from Sun	94,600,000 miles	152,000,000 kilometers
Minimum distance from Sun	91,300,000 miles	147,000,000 kilometers

Oceans and Major Seas

	Area in: Sq. Miles	Sq. Kms.	Greatest Depth in: Feet	Meters
Pacific Ocean	63,855,000	165,384,000	36,198	11,033
Atlantic Ocean	31,744,000	82,217,000	28,374	8,648
Indian Ocean	28,417,000	73,600,000	25,344	7,725
Arctic Ocean	5,427,000	14,056,000	17,880	5,450
Caribbean Sea	970,000	2,512,300	24,720	7,535
Mediterranean Sea	969,000	2,509,700	16,896	5,150
South China Sea	895,000	2,318,000	15,000	4,600
Bering Sea	875,000	2,266,250	15,800	4,800
Gulf of Mexico	600,000	1,554,000	12,300	3,750
Sea of Okhotsk	590,000	1,528,100	11,070	3,370
East China Sea	482,000	1,248,400	9,500	2,900
Yellow Sea	480,000	1,243,200	350	107
Sea of Japan	389,000	1,007,500	12,280	3,740
Hudson Bay	317,500	822,300	846	258
North Sea	222,000	575,000	2,200	670
Black Sea	185,000	479,150	7,365	2,245
Red Sea	169,000	437,700	7,200	2,195
Baltic Sea	163,000	422,170	1,506	459

The Continents

	Area in: Sq. Miles	Sq. Kms.	Percent of World's Land
Asia	17,159,867	44,444,100	29.8
Africa	11,701,147	30,306,000	20.3
North America	9,355,975	24,232,000	16.3
South America	6,879,916	17,819,000	12.0
Antarctica	5,500,000	14,245,000	9.6
Europe	4,066,019	10,531,000	7.1
Australia	2,967,893	7,686,850	5.1

Major Ship Canals

	Length in: Miles	Kms.	Minimum Depth in: Feet	Meters
Volga-Baltic, Russia	225	362	–	–
Baltic-White Sea, Russia	140	225	16	5
Suez, Egypt	100.76	162	42	13
Albert, Belgium	80	129	16.5	5
Moscow-Volga, Russia	80	129	18	6
Volga-Don, Russia	62	100	–	–
Göta, Sweden	54	87	10	3
Kiel (Nord-Ostsee), Germany	53.2	86	38	12
Panama Canal, Panama	50.72	82	41.6	13
Houston Ship, U.S.A.	50	81	36	11

Largest Islands

	Area in: Sq. Miles	Sq. Kms.
Greenland	840,000	2,175,600
New Guinea	305,000	789,950
Borneo	286,000	740,740
Madagascar	226,656	587,040
Baffin, Canada	195,928	507,454
Sumatra, Indonesia	164,000	424,760
Honshu, Japan	88,000	227,920
Great Britain	84,400	218,896
Victoria, Canada	83,896	217,290
Ellesmere, Canada	75,767	196,236
Celebes, Indonesia	72,986	189,034
South I., New Zealand	58,393	151,238
Java, Indonesia	48,842	126,501
North I., New Zealand	44,187	114,444
Cuba	42,803	110,860
Newfoundland, Canada	42,031	108,860
Luzon, Philippines	40,420	104,688
Iceland	39,768	103,000
Mindanao, Philippines	36,537	94,631
Ireland	32,589	84,406
Hokkaido, Japan	30,436	78,829
Sakhalin, Russia	29,500	76,405

	Area in: Sq. Miles	Sq. Kms.
Hispaniola, Haiti & Dom. Rep.	29,399	76,143
Banks, Canada	27,038	70,028
Tasmania, Australia	26,410	68,402
Ceylon, Sri Lanka	25,332	65,610
Svalbard, Norway	23,957	62,049
Devon, Canada	21,331	55,247
Novaya Zemlya (north isl.), Russia	18,600	48,200
Tierra del Fuego, Chile & Argentina	18,301	47,400
Marajó, Brazil	17,991	46,597
Alexander, Antarctica	16,700	43,250
Axel Heiberg, Canada	16,671	43,178
Melville, Canada	16,274	42,150
Southampton, Canada	15,913	41,215
New Britain, Papua New Guinea	14,100	36,519
Taiwan	13,836	35,835
Kyushu, Japan	13,770	35,664
Hainan, China	13,127	33,999
Prince of Wales, Canada	12,872	33,338
Spitsbergen, Norway	12,355	31,999
Vancouver, Canada	12,079	31,285
Timor, Indonesia	11,527	29,855
Sicily, Italy	9,926	25,708

	Area in: Sq. Miles	Sq. Kms.
Somerset, Canada	9,570	24,786
Sardinia, Italy	9,301	24,090
Shikoku, Japan	6,860	17,767
New Caledonia, France	6,530	16,913
Nordaustlandet, Norway	6,409	16,599
Samar, Philippines	5,050	13,080
Negros, Philippines	4,906	12,707
Palawan, Philippines	4,550	11,785
Panay, Philippines	4,446	11,515
Jamaica	4,232	10,961
Hawaii, United States	4,038	10,458
Viti Levu, Fiji	4,010	10,386
Cape Breton, Canada	3,981	10,311
Mindoro, Philippines	3,759	9,736
Kodiak, Alaska, U.S.A.	3,670	9,505
Cyprus	3,572	9,251
Puerto Rico, U.S.A.	3,435	8,897
Corsica, France	3,352	8,682
New Ireland, Papua New Guinea	3,340	8,651
Crete, Greece	3,218	8,335
Anticosti, Canada	3,066	7,941
Wrangel, Russia	2,819	7,301

Principal Mountains

	Height in : Feet	Meters
Everest, Nepal-China	29,028	8,848
K2 (Godwin Austen), Pakistan-China	28,250	8,611
Kanchenjunga, Nepal-India	28,208	8,598
Lhotse, Nepal-China	27,923	8,511
Makalu, Nepal-China	27,789	8,470
Dhaulagiri, Nepal	26,810	8,172
Nanga Parbat, Pakistan	26,660	8,126
Annapurna, Nepal	26,504	8,078
Nanda Devi, India	25,645	7,817
Rakaposhi, Pakistan	25,550	7,788
Kongur Shan, China	25,325	7,719
Tirich Mir, Pakistan	25,230	7,690
Gongga Shan, China	24,790	7,556
Ismail Samani Peak, Tajikistan	24,590	7,495
Pobedy Peak, Kyrgyzstan	24,406	7,439
Chomo Lhari, Bhutan-China	23,997	7,314
Muztag, China	23,891	7,282
Cerro Aconcagua, Argentina	22,831	6,959
Ojos del Salado, Chile-Argentina	22,572	6,880
Bonete, Chile-Argentina	22,546	6,872
Tupungato, Chile-Argentina	22,310	6,800
Pissis, Argentina	22,241	6,779
Mercedario, Argentina	22,211	6,770
Huascarán, Peru	22,205	6,768
Llullaillaco, Chile-Argentina	22,057	6,723
Nevada Ancohuma, Bolivia	21,489	6,550
Chimborazo, Ecuador	20,561	6,267
McKinley, Alaska	20,320	6,194
Logan, Yukon, Canada	19,524	5,951
Cotopaxi, Ecuador	19,347	5,897
Kilimanjaro, Tanzania	19,340	5,895
El Misti, Peru	19,101	5,822
Pico Cristóbal Colón, Colombia	18,947	5,775
Huila, Colombia	18,865	5,750
Citlaltépetl (Orizaba), Mexico	18,700	5,700
Damavand, Iran	18,605	5,671
El'brus, Russia	18,510	5,642
St. Elias, Alaska, U.S.A.-Yukon, Canada	18,008	5,489
Dykh-tau, Russia	17,070	5,203
Batian (Kenya), Kenya	17,058	5,199
Ararat, Turkey	16,946	5,165
Vinson Massif, Antarctica	16,864	5,140
Margherita (Ruwenzori), Africa	16,795	5,119
Kazbek, Georgia-Russia	16,558	5,047
Puncak Jaya, Indonesia	16,503	5,030
Blanc, France	15,771	4,807
Klyuchevskaya Sopka, Russia	15,584	4,750
Fairweather, Br. Col., Canada	15,300	4,663
Dufourspitze (Mte. Rosa), Italy-Switzerland	15,203	4,634
Ras Dashen, Ethiopia	15,157	4,620
Matterhorn, Switzerland	14,691	4,478
Whitney, California, U.S.A.	14,494	4,418
Elbert, Colorado, U.S.A.	14,433	4,399
Rainier, Washington, U.S.A.	14,410	4,392
Shasta, California, U.S.A.	14,162	4,317
Pikes Peak, Colorado, U.S.A.	14,110	4,301
Finsteraarhorn, Switzerland	14,022	4,274
Mauna Kea, Hawaii, U.S.A.	13,796	4,205
Mauna Loa, Hawaii, U.S.A.	13,677	4,169
Jungfrau, Switzerland	13,642	4,158
Grossglockner, Austria	12,457	3,797
Fujiyama, Japan	12,389	3,776
Cook, New Zealand	12,349	3,764

Longest Rivers

	Length in: Miles	Kms.
Nile, Africa	4,145	6,671
Amazon, S. America	4,007	6,448
Mississippi-Missouri-Red Rock, U.S.A.	3,710	5,971
Chang Jiang (Yangtze), China	3,500	5,633
Ob'-Irtysh, Russia-Kazakhstan	3,362	5,411
Yenisey-Angara, Russia	3,100	4,989
Huang He (Yellow), China	2,950	4,747
Congo, Africa	2,780	4,474
Amur-Shilka-Onon, Asia	2,744	4,416
Lena, Russia	2,734	4,400
Mackenzie-Peace-Finlay, Canada	2,635	4,241
Paraná-La Plata, S. America	2,630	4,232
Mekong, Asia	2,610	4,200
Niger, Africa	2,580	4,152
Missouri-Red Rock, U.S.A.	2,564	4,125
Yenisey, Russia	2,500	4,028
Mississippi, U.S.A.	2,348	3,778
Murray-Darling, Australia	2,310	3,718
Volga, Russia	2,290	3,685
Madeira, S. America	2,013	3,240
Purus, S. America	1,995	3,211
Yukon, Alaska-Canada	1,979	3,185
Zambezi, Africa	1,950	3,138
São Francisco, Brazil	1,930	3,106
St. Lawrence, Canada-U.S.A.	1,900	3,058
Rio Grande, Mexico-U.S.A.	1,885	3,034
Syrdarya-Naryn, Asia	1,859	2,992
Indus, Asia	1,800	2,897
Danube, Europe	1,775	2,857
Brahmaputra, Asia	1,700	2,736
Tocantins, Brazil	1,677	2,699
Salween, Asia	1,675	2,696
Euphrates, Asia	1,650	2,655
Xi (Si), China	1,650	2,655
Amu Darya, Asia	1,616	2,601
Nelson-Saskatchewan, Canada	1,600	2,575
Orinoco, S. America	1,600	2,575
Paraguay, S. America	1,584	2,549
Kolyma, Russia	1,562	2,514
Ganges, Asia	1,550	2,494
Zhayyq (Ural), Kazakhstan-Russia	1,509	2,428
Japurá, S. America	1,500	2,414
Arkansas, U.S.A.	1,450	2,334
Colorado, U.S.A.-Mexico	1,450	2,334
Negro, S. America	1,400	2,253
Dnepr (Dnyapro, Dnipro), Russia-Belarus-Ukraine	1,368	2,202
Orange, Africa	1,350	2,173
Ayeyarwady, Myanmar	1,325	2,132
Brazos, U.S.A.	1,309	2,107
Ohio-Allegheny, U.S.A.	1,306	2,102
Kama, Russia	1,252	2,031
Don, Russia	1,222	1,967
Red, U.S.A.	1,222	1,966
Columbia, U.S.A.-Canada	1,214	1,953
Tigris, Asia	1,181	1,901
Darling, Australia	1,160	1,867
Angara, Russia	1,135	1,827
Sungari, Asia	1,130	1,819
Pechora, Russia	1,124	1,809
Snake, U.S.A.	1,038	1,670
Churchill, Canada	1,000	1,609
Pilcomayo, S. America	1,000	1,609
Uruguay, S. America	994	1,600
Platte-N. Platte, U.S.A.	990	1,593
Ohio, U.S.A.	981	1,578
Magdalena, Colombia	956	1,538
Pecos, U.S.A.	926	1,490
Oka, Russia	918	1,477
Canadian, U.S.A.	906	1,458
Colorado, Texas, U.S.A.	894	1,439
Dnister (Nistru), Ukraine-Moldova	876	1,410
Fraser, Canada	850	1,369
Rhine, Europe	820	1,319
Northern Dvina, Russia	809	1,302
Ottawa, Canada	790	1,271

Principal Natural Lakes

	Area in: Sq. Miles	Sq. Kms.	Max. Depth in: Feet	Meters
Caspian Sea, Asia	143,243	370,999	3,264	995
Lake Superior, U.S.A.-Canada	31,820	82,414	1,329	405
Lake Victoria, Africa	26,628	69,215	270	82
Lake Huron, U.S.A.-Canada	23,010	59,596	748	228
Lake Michigan, U.S.A.	22,400	58,016	923	281
Aral Sea, Kazakhstan-Uzbekistan	15,830	41,000	213	65
Lake Tanganyika, Africa	12,650	32,764	4,700	1,433
Lake Baykal, Russia	12,162	31,500	5,316	1,620
Great Bear Lake, Canada	12,096	31,328	1,356	413
Lake Nyasa (Malawi), Africa	11,555	29,928	2,320	707
Great Slave Lake, Canada	11,031	28,570	2,015	614
Lake Erie, U.S.A.-Canada	9,940	25,745	210	64
Lake Winnipeg, Canada	9,417	24,390	60	18
Lake Ontario, U.S.A.-Canada	7,540	19,529	775	244
Lake Balkhash, Kazakhstan	7,081	18,340	87	27
Lake Chad, Africa*	7,000	18,130	25	8
Lake Ladoga, Russia	6,900	17,871	738	225
Lake Maracaibo, Venezuela	5,120	13,261	100	31
Lake Onega, Russia	3,761	9,741	377	115
Lake Eyre, Australia*	3,500-0	9,065-0	–	–
Lake Titicaca, Peru-Bolivia	3,200	8,288	1,000	305
Lake Nicaragua, Nicaragua	3,100	8,029	230	70
Lake Athabasca, Canada	3,064	7,936	400	122
Reindeer Lake, Canada*	2,568	6,651	–	–
Lake Turkana (Rudolf), Africa	2,463	6,379	240	73
Ysyk-Köl, Kyrgyzstan	2,425	6,281	2,303	702
Lake Torrens, Australia*	2,230	5,776	–	–
Vänern, Sweden	2,156	5,584	328	100
Nettilling Lake, Canada*	2,140	5,543	–	–
Lake Winnipegosis, Canada	2,075	5,374	38	12
Lake Albert, Africa	2,075	5,374	160	49
Kariba Lake, Zambia-Zimbabwe	2,050	5,310	295	90
Lake Nipigon, Canada	1,872	4,848	540	165
Lake Mweru, Africa	1,800	4,662	60	18
Lake Manitoba, Canada	1,799	4,659	12	4
Lake Taymyr, Russia	1,737	4,499	85	26
Lake Khanka, China-Russia	1,700	4,403	33	10
Lake Kioga, Uganda	1,700	4,403	25	8
Lake of the Woods, U.S.A.-Canada	1,679	4,349	70	21

* Figures subject to great seasonal variations.

Population of Countries and Major Cities

The following pages include population figures for all countries, and cities with more than 100,000 inhabitants. All national capitals, regardless of size are also listed. Countries are listed alphabetically, and cities are grouped alphabetically within each country. Capitals are indicated with an asterisk (*). The population figures, given in thousands, represent the most current information available.

Country / City	Population in thousands
A	
Afghanistan	**28,717**
Herāt	177
Kabul*	1,424
Mazār-e Sharīf	131
Qandahār	226
Albania	**3,582**
Tiranë*	244
Algeria	**32,818**
Algiers*	1,688
Annaba	228
Batna	185
Bechar	107
Bejaïa	118
Biskra	130
Blida	132
Chelif	130
Constantine	450
Mostaganem	115
Oran	599
Sétif	186
Sidi Bel-Abbes	155
Skikda	129
Tébessa	108
Tiaret	106
Tlemcen	108
Andorra	**69**
Andorra la Vella*	16
Angola	**10,766**
Luanda*	1,530
Antigua and Barbuda	**67**
Saint John's*	22
Argentina	**38,741**
Almirante Brown	449
Avellaneda	347
Bahía Blanca	240
Belén de Escobar	117
Berazateugi	245
Buenos Aires*	2,961
Catamaraca	110
Concordia	116
Córdoba	1,148
Corrientes	258
Florencio Varela	249
Formosa	154
General San Martín	408
General Sarmiento	647
Godoy Cruz	179
Guaymallén	201
Lanús	467
La Plata	520
La Rioja	104
Las Heras	146
Lomas de Zamora	573
Mar del Plata	512
Mariano Moreno	286
Mendoza	122
Merlo	386
Morón	642
Neuquén	167
Paraná	207
Pilar	113
Posadas	202
Quilmes	509
Resistencia	228
Río Cuarto	135
Rosario	895
Salta	367
San Fernando	141
San Isidro	249
San Juan	119
San Luis	110
San Miguel de Tucumán	471
San Nicolás de los Arroyes	115
San Salvador de Jujuy	181
Santa Fé	343
Santiago del Estero	189
Tigre	254
Vicente López	289
Villa Nueva	201
Armenia	**3,326**
Gyumri	120
Vanadzor	146
Yerevan*	1,199
Australia	**19,732**
Adelaide	957
Baulkham Hills	114
Brisbane	1146
Canberra*	276
Geelong	126
Gold Coast	226
Gosford	129
Hobart	127
Melbourne	2,762
Newcastle	262
Perth	1019
Salisbury	106
Stirling	173
Sydney	3,098
Townsville	101
Warringah	172
Waverley	118
Wollongong	211
Austria	**8,188**
Graz	238
Innsbruck	118
Linz	203
Salzburg	144
Vienna*	1,540
Azerbaijan	**7,831**
Baku*	1,149
Gäncä	281
Sumgayıt	235
B	
Bahamas, The	**297**
Nassau*	172
Bahrain	**667**
Manama*	140
Bangladesh	**138,448**
Barisāl	180
Chittagong	1,560
Comilla	184
Dhaka*	3,638
Dinājpur	137
Jamālpur	108
Jessore	176
Khulna	601
Mymensingh	189
Naogaon	105
Nārāyanganj	285
Nawābganj	130
Pābna	110
Rājshāhi	302
Rangpur	221
Saidpur	108
Sirājganj	100
Sylhet	110
Tangail	108
Barbados	**277**
Bridgetown*	7
Belarus	**10,322**
Babruysk	226
Baranavichy	170
Barysaw	152
Brest	287
Homyel'	503
Hrodna	295
Mahilyow	363
Mazyr	105
Minsk*	1,655
Orsha	125
Pinsk	128
Vitsyebsk	365
Belgium	**10,289**
Antwerp	468
Brugge	117
Brussels*	954
Charleroi	206
Ghent	230
Liège	195
Namur	103
Schaerbeek	103
Belize	**266**
Belmopan*	8
Benin	**7,041**
Cotonou	537
Djougou	134
Parakou	104
Porto-Novo*	179
Bhutan	**2,140**
Thimphu*	30
Bolivia	**8,586**
Cochabamba	404
El Alto	404
La Paz*	711
Oruro	183
Potosí	112
Santa Cruz de la Sierra	695
Sucre*	131
Bosnia & Herzegovina	**3,989**
Banja Luka	196
Doboj	103
Mostar	127
Prijedor	113
Sarajevo*	529
Tuzla	132
Zenica	146
Botswana	**1,573**
Gaborone*	175
Brazil	**182,033**
Alvorada	133
Americana	154
Anápolis	222
Aracaju	402
Araçatuba	146
Arapiraca	125
Araraquara	101
Barra Mansa	145
Baurú	254
Belém	765
Belo Horizonte	2,206
Betim	153
Blumenau	185
Boa Vista	119
Brasília*	1,493
Cachoeiro de Itapemirim	112
Campina Grande	298
Campinas	748
Campo Grande	516
Campos	276
Canoas	269
Carapicuíba	207
Caruaru	181
Cascavel	175
Caxias do Sul	263
Colombo	105
Contegem	196
Cuiabá	253
Curitiba	842
Diadema	305
Divinópolis	142
Dourados	117
Duque du Caxias	326
Embu	156
Feira de Santana	340
Florianópolis	192
Fortaleza	1,027
Foz do Iguaçu	186
Franca	228
Goiânia	912
Governador Valadares	210
Gravataí	167
Guarapuava	107
Guarulhos	545
Ilhéus	135
Imperatriz	210
Ipatinga	120
Itabuna	170
Itajaí	115
Itapevi	108
Itaquaquecetuba	165
Jacareí	143
Jequié	115
João Pessoa	497
Joinvile	326
Juazeiro do Norte	164
Juiz de Fora	378
Jundiaí	253
Lages	137
Limeira	177
Londrina	355
Luziânia	194
Macapá	147
Maceió	555
Manaus	1,006
Marabá	102
Maracanau	133
Marília	145
Maringá	226
Mauá	295
Mogi das Cruzes	126
Montes Claros	233
Mossoró	177
Muribeca dos Guararapes	201
Natal	460
Nilópolis	105
Niterói	401
Nova Friburgo	111
Nova Iguaçu	562
Novo Hamburgo	199
Olinda	341
Osasco	567
Passo Fundo	135
Parnaíba	105
Pelotas	261
Petrolina	124
Petrópolis	165
Piracicaba	223
Poços de Caldas	105
Ponta Grossa	220
Porto Alegre	1,237
Porto Velho	226
Presidente Prudente	158
Recife	1,297
Ribeirão Prêto	416
Rio Branco	167
Rio Claro	130
Rio de Janeiro	5,474
Rio Grande	158
Salvador	2,070
Santa Bárbara d'Oeste	140
Santa Maria	193
Santarém	168
Santo André	518
Santos	416
São Bernardo do Campo	550
São Caetano do Sul	149
São Carlos	101
São Gonçalo	296
São João de Meriti	221
São José do Rio Preto	263
São José dos Campos	386
São Luís	164
São Leopoldo	160
São Paulo	9,394
São Vicente	268
Sapucia do Sul	105
Sete Lagoas	138
Sorocaba	349
Suzano	110
Taboão da Serra	160
Taubaté	186
Teresina	556
Uberaba	199
Uberlândia	355
Uruguaiana	103
Vitória	184
Vila Velha Argolas	114
Vitória da Conquista	180
Volta Redonda	220
Brunei	**358**
Bandar Seri Begawan*	46
Bulgaria	**7,538**
Burgas	196
Dobrich	104
Pleven	131
Plovdiv	341
Ruse	170
Sliven	106
Sofia*	1,114
Stara Zagora	150
Varna	309
Burkina Faso	**13,228**
Bobo Dioulasso	229
Ouagadougou*	442
Burundi	**6,096**
Bujumbura*	235
C	
Cambodia	**13,125**
Phnom Penh*	620
Cameroon	**15,746**
Bafoussam	140
Bamenda	130
Douala	1,030
Garoua	170
Maroua	150
Ngaoundéré	100
N'Kongsamba	110
Yaoundé*	654
Canada	**32,207**
Abbotsford	105
Brampton	268
Burlington	137
Burnaby	179
Calgary	768
Cambridge	101
Coquitlam	102
Edmonton	616
Gatineau	101
Gloucester	104
Halifax	114
Hamilton	322
Kitchener	178
Laval	330
London	326
Longueuil	128
Markham	173
Mississauga	544
Montréal	1,016
Nepean	115
Oakville	128
Oshawa	134
Ottawa*	323
Québec	167
Regina	180
Richmond	149
Richmond Hill	102
Saint Catharines	131
Saint John's	102
Saskatoon	194
Surrey	304
Thunder Bay	114
Toronto	654
Vancouver	514
Vaughan	133
Windsor	198
Winnipeg	618
Cape Verde	**412**
Praia*	62
Central African Republic	**3,684**
Bangui*	597
Chad	**9,253**
Moundou	102
N'Djamena*	530
Sarh	113
Chile	**15,665**
Antofagasta	227
Arica	161
Barrancas	184
Calama	120
Chillán	146
Concepción	327
Coquimbo	115
Iquique	151
La Serena	109
Maipú	254
Osorno	114
Puente Alto	254
Puerto Montt	112
Punta Arenas	114
Quilpué	102
Rancagua	180
Renca	129
San Bernardo	191
Santiago*	4,298
Talca	161
Talcahuano	246
Temuco	211
Valdivia	114
Valparaíso	282
Viña del Mar	304
China	**1,286,975**
Acheng	193
Aksu	126
Anda	133
Ankang	129
Anqing	247
Anshan	1,215
Anshun	175
Anyang	395
Baicheng	214
Baiyin	199
Baoding	485
Baoji	325
Baotou	980
Bei'an	193
Beihai	116
Beijing*	5,715
Beipiao	190
Bengbu	441
Benxi	767
Binzhou	129
Cangzhou	222
Changchun	1,698
Changde	253
Changji	109
Changsha	1,077
Changshu	180
Changzhi	307
Changzhou	523
Chaoyang	218
Chaozhou	289
Chengde	243
Chengdu	1,719
Chenzhou	166
Chifeng	344
Chongqing	2,265
Chuzhou	120
Cixi	101
Da'an	124
Da Xian	185
Dali	134
Dalian	1,632
Dandong	525
Daqing	676
Datong	779
Deyang	171
Dezhou	183
Dongguan	271
Dongtai	131
Dongying	257
Dunhua	225
Duyun	130
Ezhou	137
Fengcheng	250
Foshan	291
Fuling	164
Fushun	1,210
Fuxin	623
Fuyang	161
Fuyu	174
Fuzhou	890
Ganzhou	219
Gejiu	212
Gongzhuling	228
Guangyuan	173
Guangzhou	2,892
Guigang	111
Guilin	371
Guiyang	1,009
Haicheng	196
Haikou	271
Hailar	176
Hailun	128
Hami	146
Handan	798
Hangzhou	1,119
Hanzhong	157
Harbin	2,468
Hebi	196
Hefei	733
Hegang	507
Hengyang	469
Heze	154
Hohhot	654
Honghu	130
Huadian	166
Huai'an	113
Huaibei	332
Huaihua	120
Huainan	674
Huaiyin	221
Huangshi	432
Huizhou	147
Hunjiang	475
Huzhou	398
Jiamusi	477
Ji'an	143
Jiangmen	219
Jiangyin	145
Jiaohe	172
Jiaozuo	386
Jiaxing	205
Jilin	1,038
Jinan	1,361
Jinchang	100
Jincheng	128
Jingdezhen	274
Jingmen	158
Jinhua	139
Jining (Nei Mong.)	248
Jining (Shandong)	190
Jinxi	349
Jinzhou	573
Jiujiang	284
Jiutai	173
Jixi	638
Kaifeng	503
Kaili	109
Kaiyuan	122
Karamay	194
Kashi	158
Korla	137
Kunming	1,108
Kunshan	100
Laiwu	186
Langfang	146
Lanzhou	1,205
Laohekou	108
Leiyang	129
Lengshuijiang	126
Leshan	333
Lianyuan	114
Lianyungang	352
Liaocheng	149
Liaoyang	485
Liaoyuan	341
Liling	107
Linchuan	161
Linfen	174
Linhe	131
Linyi	210
Liuzhou	602
Longyan	134
Loudi	121
Lu'an	137
Luohe	122
Luoyang	730
Lupanshui	342
Luzhou	262
Ma'anshan	297
Manzhouli	119
Maoming	162
Meihekou	205
Meizhou	120
Mianyang	250
Mudanjiang	562
Nanchang	1,026
Nanchong	179
Nanjing	2,114
Nanning	723
Nanping	188
Nantong	324
Nanyang	229
Neijiang	240
Ningbo	548
Panzhihua	407
Pingdingshan	442
Pingxiang	306
Puyang	120
Qingdao	1,317
Qingjiang	172
Qingyuan	134
Qinhuangdao	360
Qinzhou	105
Qiqihar	1,066
Qitaihe	218
Quanzhou	178
Qujing	163
Quzhou	105
Renqiu	128
Rizhao	109
Sanmenxia	114
Sanming	159
Shanghai	7,551
Shangqiu	159
Shangrao	127
Shangzhi	208
Shantou	558
Shaoguan	334
Shaoxing	180
Shaoyang	242
Shashi	277
Shenyang	3,588
Shenzhen	466
Sheung Shui-Fanling	201
Shihezi	160
Shijiazhuang	1,065
Shiyan	241
Shizuishan	245
Shuangyashan	392
Shuangcheng	131
Siping	310
Suihua	219
Suining	134
Suizhou	139
Suzhou (Anhui)	147
Suzhou (Jiangsu)	697
Tai'an	246
Taiyuan	1,514
Taizhou	151
Tangshan	1,042
Tianjin	4,521
Tianmen	138
Tianshui	238
Tieling	247
Tin Shui Wai	150
Tongchuan	259
Tonghua	321
Tongliao	247
Tongling	212
Tseung Kwan O	137
Ulanhot	152
Ürümqi	1071
Wafangdian	250
Wanxian	156
Weifang	359
Weinan	135
Wenzhou	204
Wuhai	261
Wuhan	3,177
Wuhu	419
Wuwei	125
Wuxi	806
Wuzhou	213
Xiamen	391
Xi'an	1,954
Xiangfan	390
Xiangtan	429
Xianning	110
Xiantao	124
Xianyang	328
Xiaogan	140
Xiaoshan	159
Xichang	133
Xingcheng	102
Xinghua	155
Xingtai	270
Xining	559
Xintai	209
Xinxiang	453
Xinyang	185
Xinyu	163
Xuchang	196
Xuzhou	795
Yan'an	106
Yancheng	239
Yangjiang	203
Yangquan	338
Yangzhou	306
Yanji	233

Country City	Population in thousands
Yantai	400
Yibin	241
Yichang	364
Yichun (Heilonjiang)	787
Yichun (Jiangxi)	134
Yinchuan	350
Yingkou	423
Yining	172
Yixing	186
Yiyang	180
Yong'an	109
Yuci	189
Yueyang	296
Yulin	130
Yumen	112
Yuyao	103
Zaozhuang	309
Zhangjiakou	525
Zhangzhou	178
Zhanjiang	384
Zhaodong	164
Zhaoqing	173
Zhengzhou	1,139
Zhenjiang	355
Zhongshan	256
Zhoukou	136
Zhuhai	162
Zhumadian	121
Zhuzhou	383
Zibo	864
Zigong	385
Zixing	107
Zunyi	269
Colombia	**41,662**
Armenia	211
Barrancabermeja	136
Barranquilla	1,000
Bello	260
Bogotá*	5,699
Bucaramanga	403
Buenaventura	187
Cali	1,625
Cartagena	576
Cúcuta	462
Dos Quebradas	115
Envigado	110
Floridablanca	177
Ibagué	336
Itagüí	168
Manizales	341
Medellín	1,485
Montería	182
Neiva	223
Palmira	189
Pasto	244
Pereira	329
Popayán	175
Santa Marta	211
Sincelejo	120
Soacha	181
Soledad	236
Tuluá	104
Tunjá	102
Valledupar	209
Villavicencio	190
Comoros	**633**
Moroni*	30
Congo, Dem. Rep. of the	**56,625**
Boma	264
Bukavu	210
Kananga	372
Kikwit	183
Kinshasa*	3,800
Kisangani	373
Kolwezi	545
Lubumbashi	739
Matadi	173
Mbandaka	166
Mbuji-Mayi	613
Panda-Likasi	146
Tshikapa	110
Congo, Rep. of the	**2,954**
Brazzaville*	938
Pointe-Noire	576
Costa Rica	**3,896**
San José*	279
Côte d'Ivoire	**16,962**
Abidjan	1,929
Bouaké	330
Daloa	122
Korhogo	109
Yamoussoukro*	107
Croatia	**4,422**
Rijeka	144
Split	175
Zagreb*	779
Cuba	**11,263**
Bayamo	138
Camagüey	249
Ciego de Ávila	101
Cienfuegos	130
Guantánamo	208
Havana*	2,176
Holguín	242
Las Tunas	127
Manzanillo	108
Marianao	128
Matanzas	123
Pinar del Río	129
Santa Clara	205
Santiago de Cuba	430
Victoria de las Tunas	115
Cyprus	**772**
Nicosia*	47
Czech Republic	**10,249**
Brno	379
Olomouc	103
Ostrava	319
Plzeň	166
Prague*	1,179
D	
Denmark	**5,384**
Ålborg	117
Århus	209
Copenhagen*	467
Odense	143
Djibouti	**457**
Djibouti*	200
Dominica	**70**
Roseau*	6
Dominican Republic	**8,716**
La Romana	140
San Francisco de Macorís	162
San Pedro de Macorís	125
Santiago de los Caballeros	365
Santo Domingo*	1.610
E	
East Timor	**998**
Dili*	13
Ecuador	**13,710**
Ambato	124
Cuenca	195
Esmeraldas	100
Guayaquil	1,513
Loja	111
Machala	146
Manta	130
Milagro	103
Portoviejo	153
Quito*	1,113
Riobamba	101
Santo Domingo de los Colorados	171
Egypt	**74,719**
Alexandria	3,380
Al Fayyum	250
Al Jīzah	2,144
Al Maḩallah al Kubrá	408
Al Mansūra	371
Al Minyā	208
Aswān	220
Asyūt	321
Az Zaqāzīq	287
Banhā	136
Banī Suwayf	179
Cairo*	6,663
Damanhūr	222
Ismailia	255
Kafr ad Dawwār	226
Luxor	146
Port Said	460
Qinā	141
Shibīn al Kaum	158
Shubrā al Khaymah	834
Suez	376
Suhāj	156
Tantā	380
El Salvador	**6,470**
Mejicanos	132
San Miguel	128
San Salvador*	415
Santa Ana	139
Soyapango	261
Equatorial Guinea	**510**
Malabo*	30
Eritrea	**4,362**
Asmara*	435
Estonia	**1,409**
Tallinn*	482
Tartu	114
Ethiopia	**66,558**
Addis Ababa*	2,316
Bahir Dar	116
Debrezit	117
Dessi	195
Dirē Dawa	195
Gonder	167
Hārer	123
Jimma	120
Mekele	120
Nazerit	147
F	
Fiji	**869**
Suva*	70
Finland	**5,191**
Esbo (Espoo)	191
Helsinki*	525
Oulu	109
Tampere	183
Turku	165
Vantaa	166
France	**60,181**
Aix-en-Provence	127
Amiens	136
Angers	146
Besançon	119
Bordeaux	213
Boulogne-Billancourt	102
Brest	153
Caen	116
Clermont-Ferrand	140
Dijon	152
Grenoble	154
Le Havre	197
Le Mans	148
Lille	178
Limoges	136
Lyon	422
Marseille	808
Metz	124
Montpellier	211
Mulhouse	110
Nancy	102
Nantes	252
Nice	346
Nîmes	134
Orléans	108
Paris*	2,175
Perpignan	108
Reims	185
Rennes	204
Rouen	105
Saint-Denis	122
Saint-Étienne	202
Strasbourg	256
Toulon	170
Toulouse	366
Tours	133
Villeurbanne	120
G	
Gabon	**1,322**
Libreville*	362
Gambia, The	**1,501**
Banjul*	42
Georgia	**4,934**
Bat'umi	136
K'ut'aisi	235
Rust'avi	159
Sokhumi	121
T'bilisi*	1,260
Germany	**82,398**
Aachen	242
Augsburg	257
Bergisch Gladbach	104
Berlin*	3,434
Bielefeld	319
Bochum	396
Bonn	292
Bottrop	119
Braunschweig	259
Bremen	551
Bremerhaven	130
Chemnitz	294
Cologne	954
Cottbus	126
Darmstadt	139
Dortmund	599
Dresden	491
Duisburg	535
Düsseldorf	576
Erfurt	209
Erlangen	102
Essen	627
Frankfurt am Main	645
Freiburg	191
Fürth	103
Gelsenkirchen	294
Gera	129
Göttingen	122
Hagen	214
Halle	310
Hamburg	1,652
Hamm	180
Hannover	513
Heidelberg	137
Heilbronn	116
Herne	178
Hildesheim	105
Ingolstadt	105
Jena	103
Karlsruhe	275
Kassel	194
Kiel	246
Koblenz	109
Köpenick	118
Krefeld	244
Leipzig	511
Leverkusen	161
Lübeck	215
Ludwigshafen	162
Magdeburg	279
Mainz	179
Mannheim	310
Moers	105
Mönchengladbach	259
Mülheim an der Ruhr	178
Munich	1,229
Münster	259
Neuss	147
Nürnberg	494
Oberhausen	224
Offenbach	115
Oldenburg	143
Osnabrück	163
Paderborn	121
Pforzheim	113
Potsdam	140
Recklinghausen	125
Regensburg	122
Remscheid	123
Reutlingen	104
Rostock	237
Saarbrücken	191
Salzgitter	118
Schwerin	122
Siegen	112
Solingen	166
Stuttgart	594
Ulm	115
Wiesbaden	271
Witten	106
Wolfsburg	128
Wuppertal	387
Würzburg	129
Zwickau	108
Ghana	**20,468**
Accra*	954
Kumasi	399
Tamale	136
Tema	100
Greece	**10,666**
Athens*	772
Iráklion	115
Kallithéa	114
Lárisa	113
Pátrai	153
Peristérion	137
Piraiévs	183
Thessaloníki	384
Grenada	**89**
Saint George's*	5
Guatemala	**13,909**
Guatemala*	823
Mixco	305
Quezaltenango	109
San Pedro Carchá	103
Villa Nueva	192
Guinea	**9,030**
Conakry*	950
Labē	110
Guinea-Bissau	**1,361**
Bissau*	109
Guyana	**702**
Georgetown*	72
Pickersgill	249
H	
Haiti	**7,528**
Port-au-Prince*	690
Honduras	**6,670**
San Pedro Sula	287
Tegucigalpa*	577
Hungary	**10,045**
Budapest*	2,017
Debrecen	212
Győr	129
Kecskemét	103
Miskolc	196
Nyíregyháza	114
Pécs	170
Szeged	175
Székesfehérvár	109
I	
Iceland	**281**
Reykjavík*	111
India	**1,049,700**
Abohar	107
Ādoni	136
Āgra	892
Agartala	157
Ahmadābād	2,877
Ahmadnagar	181
Aīzawl	155
Ajmer	403
Akola	328
Alīgarh	481
Allahābād	793
Alleppey	175
Alwar	205
Ambāla	119
Amravati	422
Amritsar	709
Amroha	137
Anand	110
Anantapur	175
Arrah	157
Asansol	262
Aurangābād	573
Bahraich	135
Bally	184
Bālurghāt	120
Bangalore	2,660
Bānkurā	115
Baranagar	225
Bārāsat	170
Bareilly	587
Barrackpur	133
Basīrhāt	101
Beāwar	105
Belgaum	326
Bellary	245
Berhampore	115
Berhampur	210
Bhadrāvati	130
Bhāgalpur	253
Bhārātpur	105
Bharuch	133
Bhatinda	159
Bhātpāra	305
Bhavnagar	402
Bhilai	386
Bhīlwāra	184
Bhīmavaram	121
Bhind	110
Bhiwandi	379
Bhiwāni	122
Bhopāl	1,063
Bhubaneswar	412
Bhūj	102
Bhusawal	145
Bīdar	108
Bīhar	201
Bijāpur	187
Bīkaner	416
Bilāspur	180
Bīr	112
Bokaro Steel City	334
Budaun	117
Bulandshahr	127
Burdwān	245
Burhānpur	173
Champdāni	101
Chandannagar	120
Chandigarh	504
Chandrapur	226
Chāpra	137
Chennai (Madras)	3,841
Chittoor	133
Cochin	565
Coimbatore	816
Cuddalore	145
Cuddapah	121
Cuttack	403
Darbhanga	218
Daryābād	270
Dāvangere	266
Dehra Dūn	270
Delhi	7,207
Dewās	164
Dhānbād	152
Dhūlia	278
Dibrugarh	120
Dindigul	182
Dombivli	103
Durg	151
Durgāpur	426
Elūrū	213
English Bāzār	139
Erode	160
Etāwah	124
Faizābād	124
Farīdābād	618
Farrukhābād	195
Fatehpur	118
Firozābād	215
Gadag-Betigeri	134
Gāndhīhām	105
Gandhinagar	123
Gayā	292
Ghaziābād	454
Gondia	109
Gorakhpur	506
Gudivāda	102
Gulbarga	304
Guna	100
Guntakal	108
Guntūr	471
Gurgaon	121
Guwāhati	584
Gwalior	691
Hābra	100
Haldīa	100
Hālisahar	114
Hāpur	146
Hardwār	147
Hāthras	113
Hindupur	105
Hisār	173
Hooghly-Chinsura	152
Hoshiārpur	123
Howrah	950
Hubli-Dhārwār	648
Hyderābād	3,044
Ichalkaranji	215
Imphāl	199
Indore	1,092
Jabalpur	742
Jaipur	1,458
Jālgaon	242
Jālna	175
Jammu	206
Jāmnagar	342
Jamshedpur	461
Jaunpur	136
Jhānsi	301
Jodhpur	666
Jullundur	510
Junāgadh	130
Kākināda	280
Kalyān	1,015
Kāmārhāti	267
Kānchīpuram	145
Kanchrāpārā	100
Kānpur	1,874
Karīmnagar	149
Karnāl	174
Kāthgodām	104
Katihār	135
Khammam	128
Khandwa	145
Kharagpur	262
Kolhāpur	406
Kolkata (Calcutta)	4,400
Korba	125
Kota	537
Kozhikode (Calicut)	420
Krishnanagar	121
Kulti	109
Kumbakonam	139
Kurnool	237
Lātūr	197
Lucknow	1,619
Ludhiāna	1,043
Machilipatnam	159
Madurai	941
Mahbubnagar	117
Mālegaon	343
Mandya	120
Mangalore	273
Mathurā	227
Maunath Bhanjan	137
Medinipur	125
Meerut	754
Mira-Bhayandar	176
Miraj	122
Mirzāpur	169
Morādābād	429
Morena	147
Mumbai (Bombay)	9,926
Munger	150
Murwāra	163
Muzaffarnagar	241
Muzaffarpur	241
Mysore	481
Nabadwīp	125
Nadiād	167
Nāgercoil	190
Nāgpur	1,625
Naihāti	133
Nānded	275
Nandyāl	120
Nāsik	657
Navsāri	126
Nellore	317
New Bombay	350
New Delhi*	301
Nizāmābād	241
North Barrackpore	101
Ongole	101
Pālghāt	123
Pāli	137
Pānīpat	191
Pānihāti	276
Parbhani	190
Pathānkot	124
Patiāla	238
Patna	917
Pīlībhīt	107
Pimpri-Chinchwad	517
Pollāchi	115
Pondicherry	203
Porbandar	117
Proddatūr	134
Pune (Poona)	1,567
Purī	125
Purnia	115
Quilon	140
Rāe Bareli	130
Raichūr	158
Raiganj	151
Raipur	439
Rājahmundry	325
Rājapālaiyam	114
Rāj-Nāndagaon	125
Rāmagundam	215
Rāmpur	244
Rānchī	599
Ratlām	183
Raurkela	356
Rewa	129
Rishra	103
Rohtak	216
Sāgar	195
Sahāranpur	375
Salem	367
Sambalpur	131
Sambhal	151
Sāngli	193
Sāntipur	107
Satna	157
Secunderābād	171
Serampore	137
Shāhjahānpur	238
Shillong	132
Shimoga	179
Shivpurī	108
Sholāpur	604
Sīkar	148
Silchar	115
Silīguri	217
Sirsa	113
Sītāpur	122
Sonīpat	144
South Dum Dum	233
Sri Gangānagar	161
Srīnagar	606
Surat	1,499
Surendranagar	106
Tellicherry	104
Tenāli	144
Thāna	803
Thanjavur	202
Thiruvananthapuram	524
Tiruchchirāppalli	387
Tirunelveli	136
Tirupati	174
Tiruppūr	236
Tiruvannāmalai	109
Titāgarh	114
Tonk	100
Tumkūr	139
Tuticorin	200
Udaipur	309
Ujjain	362
Ulbāria	155
Ulhāsnagar	369
Unnāo	107
Uttarpara-Kotrung	101
Vadodara (Baroda)	1,031
Vālpārai	106
Vārānāsi	929
Vellore	175
Vijayawada	702
Visākhapatnam	752
Vizianagaram	160
Warangal	448
Wardha	103
Yamunānagar	144
Yavatmāl	109

Country City	Population in thousands
Indonesia	**234,893**
Ambon	205
Balikpapan	309
Banda Aceh	143
Bandung	2,026
Bangil	386
Banjarmasin	443
Bekasi	146
Bengkulu	170
Binjai	127
Blitar	113
Bogor	271
Ciamis	105
Cianjur	109
Cibinong	264
Cilacap	142
Ciedug	293
Cimahi	197
Ciparay	135
Cirebon	225
Denpasar	210
Depok	382
Garut	146
Gorontalo	133
Gresik	102
Jakarta*	8,228
Jambi	301
Jayapura	101
Jember	115
Karawang	143
Kediri	235
Klangenan	291
Klaten	120
Kudus	183
Kupang	111
Madiun	166
Magelang	123
Majalaya	177
Malang	650
Manado	321
Mataram	276
Medan	1,685
Padang	477
Pakanbaru	341
Palangkaraya	113
Palembang	1,084
Pangkalpinang	108
Parepare	109
Pasuran	134
Pekalongan	227
Pematangsiantar	203
Pontianak	397
Probolinggo	131
Purwokerto	158
Salatiga	103
Samarinda	335
Semarang	1,004
Sukabumi	120
Surabaya	2,410
Surakarta	504
Tanjungbalai	108
Tanjungkarang-Telukbetung	458
Tanjungpinang	106
Tasikmalaya	194
Tebingtinggi	117
Tegal	226
Ujung Pandang	913
Yogyakarta	412
Iran	**68,279**
Āmol	155
Ahvāz	828
Arāk	379
Ardabīl	330
Bābol	153
Bākhtarān	666
Bandar-e `Abbās	384
Bandar-e Mushehr	141
Bīrjand	115
Bojnūrd	126
Borūjerd	212
Būshehr	141
Dezfūl	202
Eşfahān	1,221
Eslāmshahr	240
Gorgān	178
Hamadān	406
Īlām	137
Karaj	588
Kāshān	166
Kermān	350
Khomeynīshahr	127
Khorramābād	277
Khvoy	153
Malāyer	150
Marāgheh	129
Mashhad	1,964
Masjed-e Soleymān	109
Najafābād	182
Neyshābūr	155
Orūmīyeh	396
Qā'emshahr	133
Qazvīn	299
Qom	780
Rasht	374
Sabzevār	161
Sanandaj	271
Sārī	186
Shīrāz	1,043
Sīrjān	120
Tabrīz	1,166
Tajrīsh	157
Tehrān*	6,750
Yazd	306
Zāhedān	420
Zanjān	281
Iraq	**24,683**
Ad Dīwānīyah	196
Al `Amārah	209
Al Başrah	406
Al Ḩillah	269
Al Karrādah	236
Al Kūt	183
An Najaf	309
An Nāşirīyah	266
Ar Ramādī	193
As Sulaymānīyah	364
Baghdad*	3,841
Ba`qūbah	115
Dīwānīyah	196
Irbīl	486
Karbalā'	297
Kirkūk	419
Mosul	664
Ireland	**3,924**
Cork	123
Dublin*	495
Israel	**6,117**
Ashdod	128
Bat Yam	142
Beersheba	153
Bene Beraq	129
Haifa	252
Holon	164
Jerusalem*	591
Netanya	148
Petah Tiqwa	153
Ramat Gan	122
Rishon LeZiyyon	165
Tel Aviv-Yafo	356
Italy	**57,998**
Ancona	103
Bari	341
Bergamo	116
Bologna	412
Bolzano	100
Brescia	197
Cagliari	212
Catania	330
Catanzaro	104
Cosenza	104
Ferrara	111
Florence	402
Foggia	155
Genoa	676
La Spezia	102
Lecce	102
Livorno	171
Messina	272
Mestre	182
Milan	1,371
Modena	176
Monza	121
Naples	1,025
Novara	103
Padova	215
Palermo	697
Parma	174
Perugia	110
Pescara	129
Piacenza	102
Prato	167
Reggio di Calabria	178
Reggio nell'Emilia	109
Rimini	115
Rome*	2,693
Salerno	153
Sassari	120
Siracusa	125
Taranto	232
Torre del Greco	101
Trieste	231
Turin	962
Verona	253
Vicenza	109
J	
Jamaica	**2,696**
Kingston*	104
Japan	**127,214**
Abiko	1288
Ageo	213
Aizu-Wakamatsu	118
Akashi	293
Akishima	107
Akita	318
Amagasaki	466
Anjō	159
Aomori	298
Asahikawa	360
Asaka	120
Ashikaga	163
Atsugi	218
Beppu	127
Chiba	887
Chigasaki	221
Chofū	205
Daitō	129
Ebetsu	124
Ebina	118
Fuchū	227
Fuji	234
Fujieda	128
Fujimi	103
Fujinomiya	120
Fujisawa	379
Fukaya	104
Fukui	252
Fukuoka	1,341
Fukushima	291
Fukuyama	379
Funabashi	550
Gifu	403
Habikino	119
Hachiōji	536
Hachinohe	242
Hadano	168
Hakodate	288
Hamamatsu	582
Handa	111
Higashi-Hiroshima	123
Higashikurume	113
Higashimurayama	142
Higashi-Ōsaka	515
Hikone	108
Himeji	478
Hino	168
Hirakata	403
Hiratsuka	255
Hirosaki	177
Hiroshima	1,126
Hitachi	193
Hitachineka	152
Hōfu	118
Hōya	103
Ibaraki	261
Ichihara	278
Ichikawa	449
Ichinomiya	274
Iida	107
Ikeda	102
Ikoma	113
Imabari	118
Iruma	148
Ise	100
Isesaki	126
Ishinomaki	120
Itami	192
Iwaki	360
Iwakuni	106
Iwatsuki	109
Izumi	173
Jōetsu	135
Kadoma	136
Kagoshima	552
Kakamigahara	132
Kakogawa	266
Kamagaya	103
Kamakura	168
Kanazawa	456
Kariya	132
Kashihara	125
Kashiwa	328
Kasuga	105
Kasugai	288
Kasukabe	203
Katsuta	110
Kawachi-Nagano	121
Kawagoe	331
Kawaguchi	460
Kawanishi	154
Kawasaki	1,250
Kiryū	115
Kisarazu	123
Kishiwada	200
Kitakyūshū	1,011
Kitami	112
Kōbe	1,493
Kōchi	331
Kōfu	196
Kōriyama	335
Kodaira	179
Koganei	112
Kokubunji	111
Komaki	143
Komatsu	109
Koshigaya	308
Kumagaya	156
Kumamoto	662
Kurashiki	430
Kure	203
Kurume	237
Kushiro	192
Kyōto	1,468
Machida	377
Maebashi	284
Matsubara	133
Matsudo	465
Matsue	153
Matsumoto	209
Matsusaka	124
Matsuyama	473
Mino'o	125
Misato	131
Mishima	111
Mitaka	172
Mito	247
Miyakonojō	133
Miyazaki	306
Moriguchi	152
Morioka	289
Muroran	103
Musashino	136
Nagano	360
Nagaoka	193
Nagareyama	151
Nagasaki	423
Nagoya	2,172
Naha	301
Nara	366
Narashino	154
Neyagawa	251
Niigata	501
Niihama	126
Niiza	150
Nishinomiya	438
Nishio	101
Nobeoka	125
Noda	120
Numazu	208
Obihiro	173
Odawara	200
Ōgaki	150
Ōita	436
Okayama	627
Okazaki	337
Okinawa	120
Ōme	141
Ōmiya	456
Ōmuta	139
Ōsaka	2,599
Ota	148
Ōta	140
Otaru	151
Ōtsu	288
Oyama	155
Saga	168
Sagamihara	606
Sakai	792
Sakata	101
Sakura	171
Sanda	112
Sapporo	1,822
Sasebo	241
Sayama	161
Sendai	1,008
Seto	132
Shimizu	237
Shimonoseki	252
Shizuoka	470
Sōka	225
Suita	348
Suzuka	186
Tachikawa	165
Takamatsu	333
Takaoka	172
Takarazuka	213
Takasaki	240
Takatsuki	357
Tama	146
Toda	108
Tokorozawa	330
Tokushima	268
Tokuyama	105
Tōkyō*	8,135
Tomakomai	172
Tondabayashi	127
Tottori	150
Toyama	326
Toyohashi	365
Toyokawa	117
Toyonaka	392
Toyota	351
Tsu	163
Tsuchiura	135
Tsukuba	166
Tsuruoka	101
Ube	174
Ueda	125
Uji	189
Urawa	485
Urasoe	103
Urayasu	133
Utsunomiya	444
Wakayama	387
Yachiyo	169
Yaizu	118
Yamagata	255
Yamaguchi	140
Yamato	213
Yao	275
Yatsushiro	106
Yokkaichi	291
Yokohama	3,427
Yokosuka	429
Yonago	139
Zama	126
Jordan	**5,460**
Amman*	970
Ar Ruşayfah	137
Az Zarqā'	351
Irbid	208
K	
Kazakhstan	**16,764**
Aqtöbe	264
Almaty	1,176
Atyraū	149
Aqmola*	287
Aqtaū	174
Atyraū	151
Ekibastuz	141
Kökshetaū	144
Oral	220
Öskemen	334
Pavlodar	349
Petropavl	248
Qaraghandy	596
Qostanay	234
Qyzylorda	164
Rudnyy	130
Semey	342
Shymkent	404
Taldyqorghan	125
Temirtaū	213
Zhambyl	317
Zhezqazghan	108
Kenya	**31,639**
Kisumu	185
Mombasa	465
Nairobi*	1,346
Nakuru	163
Kiribati	**99**
Tarawa*	2
Korea, North	**22,466**
Ch'ŏngjin	754
Haeju	131
Hamhŭng	775
Kaesŏng	346
Kimch'aek	281
Namp'o	691
P'yŏngyang*	2,639
Sariwŏn	130
Sinŭiju	500
Wŏnsan	350
Korea, South	**48,289**
Andong	117
Ansan	252
Anyang	481
Ch'angwŏn	323
Ch'echŏn	102
Cheju	233
Chinhae	120
Chinju	256
Ch'ŏnan	211
Ch'ŏngju	478
Chŏnju	517
Ch'unch'ŏn	174
Ch'ungju	128
Inch'ŏn	2,203
Iri	203
Kangnŭng	153
Kimhae	106
Kohŭng	217
Kumi	206
Kunp'o	100
Kunsan	218
Kuri	109
Kwangju (Kwangju-Jikhalsi)	1,236
Kwangju (Kyŏnggi-Do)	906
Kwangmyŏng	329
Kyŏngju	142
Masan	494
Mokp'o	243
Nonsan	226
P'ohang	318
Puch'ŏn	668
Pusan	3,802
Seoul*	10,776
Sŏngnam	541
Sunch'ŏn	167
Suwŏn	665
Taegu	2,256
Taejŏn	1,183
Ŭijŏngbu	212
Ulsan	682
Wŏnju	173
Yŏsu	173
Kuwait	**2,183**
Al Jahrah	139
As Sālimīyah	116
Jalīb ash Shuyūkh	115
Kuwait*	31
Kyrgyzstan	**4,893**
Bishkek*	628
Osh	219
L	
Laos	**5,922**
Vientiane*	377
Latvia	**2,349**
Daugavpils	123
Liepāja	106
Riga*	865
Lebanon	**3,728**
Beirut*	1,000
Sidon	110
Tripoli	240
Lesotho	**1,862**
Maseru*	109
Liberia	**3,317**
Monrovia*	421
Libya	**5,499**
Benghāzī	446
Mişrātah	121
Tripoli*	590
Liechtenstein	**33**
Vaduz*	5
Lithuania	**3,593**
Kaunas	422
Klaipėda	204
Panevėžys	132
Šiauliai	148
Vilnius*	582
Luxembourg	**454**
Luxembourg*	75
M	
Macedonia, F.Y.R of	**2,063**
Gostivar	116
Skopje*	441
Madagascar	**16,980**
Amboasary	110
Ambovombe	144
Antananarivo*	676
Antsirabe	120
Betioky	140
Fandriana	135
Ifanadiana	102
Mahajanga	101
Toamasina	127
Vohipeno	106
Malawi	**11,651**
Blantyre	332
Lilongwe*	234
Malaysia	**23,093**
Alor Setar	125
George Town	219
Ipoh	383
Johor Baharu	329
Kelang	244
Kota Baharu	220
Kuala Lumpur*	1,145
Kuala Terengganu	229
Kuantan	198
Kuching	148
Petaling Jaya	255
Sandakan	126
Seremban	183
Shah Alam	102
Sibu	126
Sungai Petani	116
Taiping	183
Maldives	**330**
Male*	55
Mali	**11,626**
Bamako*	658
Malta	**400**
Valletta*	9
Marshall Islands	**56**
Majuro*	22
Mauritania	**2,913**
Nouakchott*	390
Mauritius	**1,210**
Port Louis*	144
Mexico	**104,907**
Acapulco de Juárez	621
Aguascalientes	594
Buenavista	194
Campeche	191
Cancún	397
Celaya	278
Chalco de Díaz Covarrubias	125
Chetumal	122
Chihuahua	658
Chilpancingo de los Bravos	143
Chimalhuacán	483
Ciudad Adolfo López Mateos	468
Ciudad Apodaca	270
Ciudad del Carmen	126
Ciudad General Escobedo	231
Ciudad Juárez	1,187
Ciudad Madero	182
Ciudad Obregón	251
Ciudad Valles	106
Ciudad Victoria	249
Coacalco de Berriozabal	252
Coatzacoalcos	226
Colima	120
Córdoba	134
Cuautitlán Izcalli	434
Cuautla Morelos	137
Cuernavaca	327
Culiacán Rosales	541
Durango de Victoria	427
Ecatepec de Morelos	1,622
Ensenada	223
Garza García	126
Gómez Palacio	210
Guadalajara	1,646
Guadalupe	670
Hermosillo	546
Heroica Matamoros	376
Heroica Nogales	157
Iguala de la Independencia	105
Irapuato	319
Ixtapaluca	236
Jalapa Enríquez	373
Jiutepec	142
La Paz	163
León	1,021
Los Mochis	201
Los Reyes Acaquilpan	211
Mazatlán	328
Mérida	663
Metepec	159
Mexicali	663
Mexico*	8,605
Minatitlán	109
Monclova	193
Monterrey	1,111
Morelia	550
Naucalpan de Juárez	835
Nezahualcóyotl	1,225
Nuevo Laredo	309
Oaxaca de Juárez	252
Orizaba	119
Pachuca de Soto	232
Piedras Negras	126
Poza Rica	151
Puebla de Zaragoza	1,272
Puerto Vallarta	151
Querétaro	536
Reynosa	404
Salamanca	137
Saltillo	563
San Cristóbal de las Casas	112
San Luis Potosí	629
San Luis Río Colorado	127
San Nicolás de los Garzas	497
San Pablo de las Salinas	147
Santa Catarina	226
Sánchez	170
Tampico	295
Tapachula	180
Tehuacán	205
Tepic	266
Texcoco de Mora	102
Tijuana	1,149
Tlalnepantla de Galeana	715
Tlaquepaque	459
Toluca de Lerdo	435

Country / City	Population in thousands
Tonalá	315
Torreón	503
Tuxtla Gutiérrez	425
Uruapan	226
Veracruz	412
Villahermosa	331
Villa Nicolás Romero	216
Zacatecas	114
Zamora de Hidalgo	123
Zapopan	911
Micronesia, Federated States of	**137**
Palikir*	6
Moldova	**4,440**
Bălţi	159
Chişinău*	665
Tighina (Bendery)	130
Tiraspol	182
Monaco	**32**
Monaco*	27
Mongolia	**2,712**
Ulaanbaatar*	575
Morocco	**31,689**
Agadir	261
Beni Mallal	140
Casablanca	2,541
El Aaiún	137
El Jadida	119
Fès	508
Kénitra	293
Khouribga	152
Ksar el Kebir	107
Marrakech	521
Meknès	378
Mohammedia	169
Nador	208
Oujda	362
Rabat*	917
Safi	262
Salé	579
Témara	126
Tangier	519
Taza	121
Tétouan	278
Mozambique	**17,479**
Beira	397
Chimoio	171
Maputo*	967
Matola	425
Nacala	158
Nampula	303
Quelimane	150
Myanmar (Burma)	**42,511**
Akyab	108
Bago (Pegu)	151
Insein	144
Mandalay	533
Mawlamyine (Moulmein)	220
Monywa	107
Pathein (Bassein)	144
Sittwe (Akyab)	108
Taunggyi	108
Yangon* (Rangoon)	2,513
N	
Namibia	**1,927**
Windhoek*	147
Nauru	**13**
Yaren (district)	0.4
Nepal	**26,470**
Birātnagar	129
Kāthmāndu*	421
Pāţan (Lalitpur)	116
Netherlands	**16,151**
Amersfoort	104
Amsterdam*	713
Apeldoorn	149
Arnhem	133
Breda	127
Dordrecht	112
Eindhoven	194
Enschede	147
Groningen	169
Haarlem	150
Leiden	113
Maastricht	118
Nijmegen	146
Rotterdam	590
The Hague*	445
Tilburg	161
Utrecht	232
Zaandam	130
Zaanstad	131
Zoetermeer	101
New Zealand	**3,951**
Auckland	346
Christchurch	309
Dunedin	118
Hamilton	108
Manukau	254
North Shore	172
Waitakere	156
Wellington*	158
Nicaragua	**5,129**
Chinandega	118
León	160
Managua*	883
Masaya	121
Niger	**11,059**
Maradi	109
Niamey*	392
Zinder	120
Nigeria	**133,882**
Aba	271
Abeokuta	387
Abuja*	306
Ado Ekiti	325
Akure	147
Awka	101
Benin City	207
Bida	114
Calabar	158
Deba Habe	125
Ede	278
Effon Alaiye	139
Enugu	286
Gusau	143
Ibadan	1,295
Ife	269
Ijebu Ode	142
Ikare	128
Ikerre	221
Ikire	112
Ikirun	164
Ikorodu	167
Ila Orangun	239
Ilawe - Ekiti	167
Ilesha	342
Ilobu	180
Ilorin	431
Inisa	108
Iseyin	197
Iwo	335
Jos	185
Kaduna	310
Kano	700
Katsina	187
Kuma	134
Lafia	111
Lagos	1,347
Maiduguri	289
Makurdi	111
Minna	126
Mushin	302
Offa	178
Ogbomosho	660
Oka	130
Ondo	154
Onitsha	337
Oshogbo	441
Owo	166
Oyo	237
Port Harcourt	371
Sapele	126
Shagamu	106
Shaki	161
Shomolu	134
Sokoto	186
Warri	114
Zaria	345
Norway	**4,546**
Bergen	203
Oslo*	508
Stavanger	108
Trondheim	143
O	
Oman	**2,807**
Muscat*	67
P	
Pakistan	**150,695**
Bahāwalpur	180
Chiniot	106
Dera Ghāzi Khān	102
Faisalābad	1,104
Gujrānwāla	659
Gujrāt	155
Hyderābād	752
Islāmābād*	204
Jhang Sadar	196
Jhelum	106
Karāchi	5,076
Kasūr	156
Lahore	2,953
Lārkāna	124
Mardān	148
Mīrpur Khās	124
Multān	732
Nawābshāh	102
Okāra	127
Peshāwar	566
Quetta	286
Rahīmyār Khān	119
Rāwalpindi	795
Sāhīwāl	151
Sargodha	291
Shekhūpura	141
Siālkot	302
Sukkur	191
Wāh	127
Palau	**20**
Koror*	9
Panama	**2,961**
Panamá*	456
San Miguelito	282
Papua New Guinea	**5,296**
Port Moresby*	193
Paraguay	**6,037**
Asunción*	547
Ciudad del Este	134
San Lorenzo	133
Peru	**28,410**
Arequipa	625
Ayacucho	106
Cajamarca	112
Callao	512
Chiclayo	412
Chimbote	269
Chincha Alta	110
Comas	287
Cusco	256
Huancayo	258
Huánuco	119
Ica	161
Iquitos	275
Juliaca	143
Lima*	376
Piura	278
Pucallpa	172
Santa	146
Sullana	147
Tacna	174
Trujillo	509
Philippines	**84,620**
Angeles	234
Antipolo	346
Bacolod	402
Bacoor	251
Bago	132
Baguio	227
Baliuag	103
Batangas	212
Biñan	160
Binangonan	141
Bislig	104
Butuan	247
Cabanatuan	201
Cadiz	126
Cagayan de Oro	428
Cainta	202
Calamba	219
Calbayog	129
Caloocan	1.023
Cebu	662
Concepcion	101
Cotabato	147
Dagupan	126
Dasmariñas	262
Davao	1.007
Digos	107
General Santos	327
Ilagan	107
Iligan	273
Iloilo	335
Imus	177
Kabankalan	139
Koranadal	118
Lapu-Lapu	174
Las Pinas	413
Legaspi	142
Lipa	178
Lubao	110
Lucena	178
Mabalacat	130
Makati	484
Malabon	347
Malasiqui	101
Malaybalay	112
Malolos	47
Mandaluyong	287
Mandaue	195
Manila*	1.655
Marawi	114
Marikina	357
Meycauayan	137
Muntinglupa	400
Naga	127
Navotas	229
Olongapo	180
Ormoc	144
Ozamiz	102
Pagadian	125
Panabo	131
Parañaque	391
Pasay	409
Pasig	471
Puerto Princesa	130
Quezon City	1.989
Roxas	119
Sagay	128
San Carlos (Negros Occ.)	101
San Carlos (Pangasinan)	134
San Fernando	193
San Jose	101
San Jose del Monte	201
San Juan del Monte	124
San Miguel	108
San Pablo	184
San Pedro	189
Santa Maria	161
Santa Rosa	138
Sariaya	101
Silang	124
Silay	123
Surigao	105
Tacloban	167
Taguig	381
Tagum	157
Talisay	120
Tanauan	104
Tarlac	230
Taytay	145
Toledo	121
Tuguegarai	107
Urdaneta	100
Valencia	129
Valenzuela	437
Zamboanga	511
Poland	**38,623**
Białystok	268
Bielsko-Biała	181
Bydgoszcz	380
Bytom	230
Chorzów	132
Częstochowa	257
Dąbrowa Górnicza	135
Elblag	126
Gdańsk	462
Gdynia	251
Gliwice	212
Gorzów Wielkopolski	123
Grudziądz	102
Jastrzębie Zdroj	102
Kalisz	106
Katowice	366
Kielce	213
Koszalin	108
Kraków	746
Legnica	104
Łódź	849
Lublin	349
Olsztyn	161
Opole	127
Płock	121
Poznań	587
Radom	226
Ruda Śląska	169
Rybnik	142
Rzeszów	151
Słupsk	100
Sosnowiec	259
Szczecin	411
Tarnów	121
Toruń	201
Tychy	190
Wałbrzych	142
Warsaw*	1,651
Włocławek	121
Wodzisław Śląski	111
Wrocław	641
Zabrze	203
Zielona Góra	113
Portugal	**10,102**
Lisbon*	818
Porto	330
Q	
Qatar	**817**
Doha*	217
R	
Romania	**22,272**
Arad	190
Bacău	205
Baia Mare	149
Botoşani	126
Brăila	234
Braşov	324
Bucharest*	2,068
Buzău	148
Cluj-Napoca	329
Constanţa	351
Craiova	304
Drobeta-Turnu Severin	115
Focşani	101
Galaţi	326
Iaşi	344
Oradea	223
Piatra Neamţ	123
Piteşti	179
Ploieşti	253
Reşiţa	106
Rîmnicu Vîlcea	114
Satu Mare	132
Sibiu	165
Suceava	114
Timisoara	334
Tîrgu Mures	164
Russia	**144,526**
Abakan	158
Achinsk	122
Al'met'yevsk	137
Angarsk	268
Anzhero-Sudzhensk	105
Arkhangel'sk	410
Armavir	161
Arzamas	111
Astrakhan'	508
Balakovo	207
Balashikha	136
Barnaul	595
Belgorod	314
Belovo	112
Berezniki	197
Biysk	233
Blagoveshchensk	212
Bratsk	260
Bryansk	456
Cheboksary	446
Chelyabinsk	1,130
Cherepovets	318
Cherkessk	118
Chita	365
Dimitrovgrad	131
Dzerzhinsk	286
Elektrostal'	152
Engel's	185
Glazov	107
Groznyy	354
Irkutsk	630
Ivanovo	474
Izhevsk	652
Kaliningrad (Kalin.)	413
Kaliningrad (Moscow)	136
Kaluga	344
Kamensk-Ural'skiy	206
Kamyshin	128
Kansk	111
Kazan'	1,086
Kemerovo	513
Khabarovsk	608
Khimki	136
Kineshma	103
Kirov	491
Kiselevsk	125
Kislovodsk	110
Kolomna	162
Kolpino	145
Komsomol'sk-na-Amure	314
Kostroma	281
Kovrov	162
Krasnodar	636
Krasnoyarsk	917
Kurgan	360
Kursk	434
Kuznetsk	102
Leninsk-Kuznetskiy	131
Lipetsk	466
Lyubertsy	164
Magadan	138
Magnitogorsk	439
Makhachkala	325
Maykop	162
Mezhdurechensk	108
Miass	170
Michurinsk	106
Moscow*	8,527
Murmansk	454
Murom	125
Mytishchi	153
Naberezhnye Chelny	527
Nakhodka	164
Nal'chik	236
Neftekamsk	117
Nevinnomyssk	127
Nizhnekamsk	206
Nizhnevartovsk	245
Nizhniy Novgorod	1,425
Nizhniy Tagil	431
Noginsk	121
Noril'sk	170
Novgorod	233
Novocheboksarsk	123
Novocherkassk	187
Novokuybyshevsk	113
Novokuznetsk	597
Novomoskovsk	144
Novorossiysk	193
Novoshakhtinsk	106
Novosibirsk	1,424
Novotroitsk	108
Obninsk	106
Odintsovo	131
Oktyabr'skiy	108
Omsk	1,164
Orekhovo-Zuyevo	135
Orël	343
Orenburg	554
Orsk	275
Penza	548
Perm'	1,091
Pervoural'sk	143
Petropavlovsk-Kamchatskiy	265
Petrozavodsk	279
Podol'sk	204
Prokop'yevsk	265
Pskov	207
Pyatigorsk	128
Rostov	1,013
Rubtsovsk	171
Ryazan'	524
Rybinsk	251
Saint Petersburg	4,329
Salavat	156
Samara	1,232
Saransk	321
Sarapul	110
Saratov	899
Sergiyev Posad	115
Serov	102
Serpukhov	140
Severodvinsk	249
Shakhty	227
Shchelkovo	108
Smolensk	349
Sochi	328
Solikamsk	109
Staryy Oskol'	190
Stavropol'	333
Sterlitamak	255
Surgut	261
Syktyvkar	226
Syzran'	175
Taganrog	290
Tambov	311
Tol'yatti	682
Tomsk	498
Tula	534
Tver'	449
Tyumen'	491
Ufa	1,092
Ukhta	112
Ulan-Ude	364
Ul'yanovsk	664
Usol'ye-Sibirskoye	107
Ussuriysk	161
Ust'-Ilimsk	113
Velikiye Luki	116
Vladikavkaz	308
Vladimir	335
Vladivostok	637
Volgodonsk	183
Volgograd	997
Vologda	290
Volzhskiy	282
Vorkuta	111
Voronezh	899
Votkinsk	105
Yakutsk	196
Yaroslavl'	628
Yekaterinburg	1,351
Yelets	118
Yoshkar-Ola	248
Yuzhno-Sakhalinsk	160
Zelenograd	179
Zhukovskiy	101
Zlatoust	207
Rwanda	**7,810**
Kigali*	233
S	
Saint Kitts and Nevis	**39**
Basseterre*	13
Saint Lucia	**162**
Castries*	13
Saint Vincent and the Grenadines	**117**
Kingstown*	15
Samoa	**178**
Apia*	32
San Marino	**28**
San Marino*	3
Sao Tome and Principe	**176**
São Tomé*	43
Saudi Arabia	**24,294**
Ad Dammām	350
Al Hufūf	101
Aţ Ţā'if	410
Jiddah	1,500
Mecca	630
Medina	400
Riyadh*	1,800
Senegal	**10,580**
Dakar*	1,641
Kaolack	193
Saint Louis	132
Thiès	216
Zinguinchor	162
Serbia & Montenegro (Yugoslavia)	**10,656**
Belgrade*	1,555
Kragujevac	147
Niš	176
Novi Sad	179
Podgorica	118
Priština	125
Subotica	100
Uroševac	114
Seychelles	**80**
Victoria*	24
Sierra Leone	**5,733**
Freetown*	470
Singapore	**4,609**
Singapore*	3,462
Slovakia	**5,430**
Bratislava*	442
Košice	235
Slovenia	**1,936**
Ljubljana*	287
Maribor	105
Solomon Islands	**509**
Honiara*	30
Somalia	**8,025**
Mogadishu*	600
South Africa	**42,769**
Alexandra	125
Benoni	114
Bloemfontein	127
Boksburg	120
Botshabelo	178
Cape Town*	855
Carletonville	119
Daveyton	152
Diepmeadow	241
Durban	716
East London	102
Evaton	201
Germiston	134
Johannesburg	714
Katlehong	202
Kempton Park	107
Khayelitsa	190
KwaMashu	157
Lekoa	218
Mamelodi	155
Ntuzuma	102
Pietermaritzburg	156
Port Elizabeth	303
Pretoria*	526
Roodeport	163
Sandton	101
Soshanguve	146
Soweto	597
Tembisa	209
Umlazi	299
Virginia	118
Spain	**40,217**
Albacete	141
Alcalá de Henares	166
Alcorcón	142
Algeciras	104
Alicante	275
Almería	167
Badajoz	130
Badalona	219
Baracaldo	104
Barcelona	1,631
Bilbao	372
Burgos	166
Cádiz	155
Cartagena	180
Castellón de la Plana	139
Córdoba	316
Elche	191
Fuenlabrada	158

Country / City	Population in thousands
Getafe	144
Gijón	270
Granada	271
Huelva	145
Jaén	113
Jerez de la Frontera	190
La Coruña	255
La Laguna	125
Las Palmas de Gran Canaria	372
Leganés	178
León	147
L'Hospitalet de Llobregat	266
Lleida	114
Logroño	125
Madrid*	3,041
Málaga	531
Mataró	102
Móstoles	199
Murcia	342
Orense	109
Oviedo	202
Palma	322
Pamplona	182
Sabadell	189
Salamanca	167
San Sebastián	178
Santa Coloma de Gramenet	132
Santa Cruz de Tenerife	204
Santander	195
Saragossa	607
Seville	714
Tarragona	115
Terrassa	161
Valencia	764
Valladolid	337
Vigo	289
Vitoria	214
Sri Lanka	**19,742**
Colombo*	615
Dehiwala-Mount Lavinia	196
Galle	109
Jaffna	129
Kandy	104
Moratuwa	170
Sri Jayawardanapura (Kotte)	109
Sudan	**38,114**
Al Qaḑārif	189
Al Ubayyiḑ	228
Juba	115
Kassala	234
Khartoum*	925
Khartoum North	341
Nyala	112
Omdurman	229
Port Sudan	305
Wad Medanī	219
Suriname	**435**
Paramaribo*	180
Swaziland	**1,161**
Mbabane*	38
Sweden	**8,878**
Borås	102
Göteborg	433
Helsingborg	109
Jönköping	114
Linköping	122
Malmö	234
Norrköping	120
Örebro	121
Stockholm*	675
Uppsala	167
Västerås	120
Switzerland	**7,319**
Basel	174
Bern*	127
Geneva	174
Lausanne	116
Zürich	344
Syria	**17,586**
Aleppo	1,542
Al Mamishlī	113
Ar Raqqah	138
Damascus*	1,549
Dar'ā	180
Dayr az Zawr	133
Dūmā	131
Ḩamāh	273
Ḩimş	558
Idlib	113
Jaramānah	138
Latakia	303
Ţarţūs	137
T	
Taiwan	**22,603**
Changhua	165
Chiai	262
Chungli	270
Chutung	105
Fengshan	291
Fengyüan	121
Hsinchu	340
Hsinchuang	299
Hsintien	226
Hualien	108
Kaohsiung	1,424
Keelung (Chilung)	368
P'ingchen	147
P'ingtung	172
Sanchung	376
Shulin	112
T'aichung	850
T'ainan	706
T'aipei*	2,639
T'aoyüan	241
Yungho	250
Tajikistan	**6,864**
Dushanbe*	602
Khujand	163
Tanzania	**35,922**
Dar es Salaam*	1,361
Dodoma*	204
Mbeya	194
Mwanza	223
Tabora	214
Tanga	188
Zanzibar	158
Thailand	**64,265**
Bangkok*	5,876
Chiang Mai	167
Chon Buri	187
Khon Kaen	206
Nakhon Ratchasima	278
Nakhon Sawan	152
Nakhon Si Thammarat	112
Nonthaburi	233
Sara Buri	107
Songkhla	243
Togo	**5,429**
Lomé*	450
Tonga	**108**
Nuku'alofa*	21
Trinidad and Tobago	**1,104**
Port-of-Spain*	51
Tunisia	**9,925**
Al Qayrawān	103
Aryānah	153
Ettadhamen Douarhicher	149
Sūsah	125
Safāqis	231
Tūnis*	674
Turkey	**68,109**
Adana	916
Adapazarı	171
Adıyaman	100
Ankara*	2,559
Antalya	378
Antioch	124
Aydın	107
Balıkesir	171
Batman	147
Bursa	835
Çorum	117
Denizli	204
Diyarbakır	381
Edirne	102
Elazığ	205
Erzurum	242
Eskişehir	413
Gaziantep	603
Gebze	159
Iskenderun	155
Isparta	112
İstanbul	6,620
İzmir	1,757
İzmit	257
Kağıthane	269
Kahramanmaraş	228
Karabük	105
Kayseri	421
Kırıkkale	185
Konya	513
Kütahya	131
Malatya	282
Manisa	159
Mersin	422
Ordu	102
Osmaniye	122
Samsun	304
Sivas	222
Tarsus	188
Trabzon	144
Urfa	277
Uşak	105
Van	153
Zonguldak	117
Turkmenistan	**4,776**
Ashgabat*	407
Chärjew	164
Dashhowuz	114
Tuvalu	**11**
Funafuti*	2
U	
Uganda	**24,699**
Kampala*	774
Ukraine	**48,055**
Alchevs'k	127
Bila Tserkva	209
Berdyans'k	137
Cherkasy	308
Chernihiv	311
Chernivtsi	261
Dniprodzerzhyns'k	287
Dnipropetrovs'k	1,190
Donets'k	1,121
Horlivka	336
Ivano-Frankivs'k	230
Kam'yanets'-Podol's'kyy	106
Kerch	181
Kharkiv	1,622
Kherson	368
Khmel'nytskyy	250
Kirovohrad	280
Kiev*	2,643
Kostyantynivka	107
Kramators'k	203
Krasnyy Luch	114
Kremenchuk	245
Kryvyy Rih	729
Luhans'k	505
Luts'k	215
L'viv	807
Lysychans'k	127
Makiyivka	426
Mariupol'	523
Melitopol'	178
Mykolayiv	515
Nikopol'	160
Odesa	1,096
Oleksandriya	106
Pavlohrad	136
Poltava	324
Rivne	244
Sevastopol'	371
Simferopol'	357
Slov'yans'k	138
Stakhanov	113
Sumy	305
Syeverodonets'k	134
Ternopil'	225
Uzhhorod	125
Vinnytsya	384
Yenakiyeve	120
Yevpatoriya	108
Zaporizhzhya	898
Zhytomyr	299
United Arab Emirates	**2,485**
Abu Dhabi*	243
Al 'Ayn	102
Ash Shāriqah	125
Dubayy	266
United Kingdom	**60,095**
Aberdeen	219
Basildon	101
Belfast	295
Birmingham	966
Blackburn	106
Blackpool	146
Bolton	139
Bournemouth	155
Bradford	289
Brighton	125
Bristol	408
Cardiff	272
Coventry	299
Derby	224
Dudley	192
Dundee	151
Edinburgh	448
Glasgow	618
Gloucester	114
Hillingdon	231
Huddersfield	144
Ipswich	130
Kingston upon Hull	311
Kingston upon Thames	132
Leeds	424
Leicester	319
Liverpool	482
London*	6,680
Luton	172
Manchester	403
Middlesbrough	147
Newcastle upon Tyne	189
Newport	116
Northampton	180
Norwich	171
Nottingham	270
Oldham	104
Oxford	119
Peterborough	135
Plymouth	245
Poole	138
Portsmouth	175
Preston	178
Reading	213
Rotherham	121
Saint Helens	106
Sheffield	432
Slough	111
Southampton	210
Southend-on-Sea	159
Stockport	133
Stoke-on-Trent	267
Sunderland	183
Sutton Coldfield	106
Swansea	171
Swindon	145
Thanet	117
Walsall	175
Watford	113
West Bromwich	146
Wolverhampton	258
York	125
United States	**290,343**
Abilene	116
Akron	217
Albuquerque	449
Alexandria	128
Allentown	107
Amarillo	174
Amherst	117
Anaheim	328
Anchorage	260
Ann Arbor	114
Arlington (Tex.)	333
Arlington (Va.)	189
Arvada	102
Athens	101
Atlanta	417
Augusta	200
Aurora (Colo.)	276
Aurora (Ill.)	142
Austin	657
Bakersfield	247
Baltimore	651
Baton Rouge	228
Beaumont	114
Bellevue	110
Berkeley	103
Birmingham	243
Boise	186
Boston	589
Bridgeport	140
Brownsville	140
Buffalo	293
Burbank	100
Cambridge	101
Cape Coral	102
Carrollton	110
Cedar Rapids	121
Chandler	177
Charlotte	541
Chattanooga	156
Chesapeake	199
Chicago	2,896
Chula Vista	174
Cincinnati	331
Citrus Heights	107
Clarksville	103
Clearwater	109
Cleveland	478
Colorado Springs	361
Columbia	116
Columbus (Ga.)	186
Columbus (Ohio)	711
Concord	122
Coral Springs	118
Corona	125
Corpus Christi	277
Costa Mesa	109
Dallas	1,189
Daly City	104
Dayton	166
Denver	555
Des Moines	199
Detroit	951
Downey	107
Durham	187
East Los Angeles	124
Elizabeth	121
El Monte	116
El Paso	564
Erie	104
Escondido	134
Eugene	138
Evansville	122
Fayetteville	121
Flint	125
Fontana	129
Fort Collins	119
Fort Lauderdale	152
Fort Wayne	206
Fort Worth	535
Fremont	203
Fresno	428
Fullerton	126
Garden Grove	165
Garland	216
Gary	103
Gilbert	110
Glendale (Ariz.)	219
Glendale (Calif.)	195
Grand Prairie	128
Grand Rapids	198
Green Bay	102
Greensboro	224
Hampton	146
Hartford	122
Hayward	140
Henderson	175
Hialeah	226
Hollywood	139
Honolulu	372
Houston	1,954
Huntington Beach	190
Huntsville	158
Independence	113
Indianapolis	792
Inglewood	113
Irvine	143
Irving	192
Jackson	184
Jacksonville	736
Jersey City	240
Joliet	106
Kansas City (Kans.)	147
Kansas City (Mo.)	442
Knoxville	174
Lafayette	110
Lakewood	144
Lancaster	119
Lansing	119
Laredo	177
Las Vegas	478
Lexington	261
Lincoln	226
Little Rock	183
Livonia	101
Long Beach	462
Los Angeles	3,695
Louisville	256
Lowell	105
Lubbock	200
Madison	208
Manchester	107
McAllen	106
Memphis	650
Mesa	396
Mesquite	125
Metairie	146
Miami	362
Milwaukee	597
Minneapolis	383
Mobile	199
Modesto	189
Montgomery	202
Moreno Valley	142
Naperville	128
Nashville	570
Newark	274
New Haven	124
New Orleans	485
Newport News	180
New York	8,008
Norfolk	234
North Las Vegas	115
Norwalk	103
Oakland	399
Oceanside	161
Oklahoma City	506
Omaha	390
Ontario	158
Orange	129
Orlando	186
Overland Park	149
Oxnard	170
Palmdale	117
Paradise	186
Pasadena (Calif.)	134
Pasadena (Tex.)	142
Paterson	149
Pembroke Pines	137
Peoria (Ariz.)	108
Peoria (Ill.)	113
Philadelphia	1,518
Phoenix	1,321
Pittsburgh	335
Plano	222
Pomona	149
Portland	529
Portsmouth	101
Providence	174
Provo	105
Pueblo	102
Raleigh	276
Rancho Cucamonga (Cucamonga)	128
Reno	180
Richmond	198
Riverside	255
Rochester	220
Rockford	150
Sacramento	407
Saint Louis	348
Saint Paul	287
Saint Petersburg	248
Salem	137
Salinas	151
Salt Lake City	182
San Antonio	1,145
San Bernardino	185
San Diego	1,223
San Francisco	777
San Jose	895
Santa Ana	338
Santa Clara	102
Santa Clarita	151
Santa Rosa	148
Savannah	132
Scottsdale	203
Seattle	563
Shreveport	200
Simi Valley	111
Sioux Falls	124
South Bend	108
Spokane	196
Springfield (Ill.)	111
Springfield (Mass.)	152
Springfield (Mo.)	152
Stamford	117
Sterling Heights	124
Stockton	244
Sunnyvale	132
Sunrise Manor	156
Syracuse	147
Tacoma	194
Tallahassee	151
Tampa	303
Tempe	159
Thousand Oaks	117
Toledo	314
Topeka	122
Torrance	138
Tucson	487
Tulsa	393
Vallejo	117
Vancouver	144
Ventura	101
Virginia Beach	425
Waco	114
Warren	138
Washington, D.C.*	572
Waterbury	107
West Covina	105
West Valley City	109
Westminster	101
Wichita	344
Wichita Falls	104
Winston-Salem	186
Worcester	173
Yonkers	196
Uruguay	**3,413**
Montevideo*	1,360
Uzbekistan	**25,982**
Andijon	297
Angren	133
Bukhoro	228
Chirchiq	159
Farghona	198
Jizzakh	108
Marghilon	125
Namangan	312
Nawoiy	110
Nukus	175
Olmaliq	116
Qarshi	163
Qŭqon	176
Samarqand	370
Tashkent*	2,094
Urganch	129
V	
Vanuatu	**199**
Port-Vila*	19
Vatican City	**1**
Vatican City*	1
Venezuela	**24,655**
Acarigua	117
Barcelona	222
Barinas	154
Barquisimeto	625
Baruta	183
Cabimas	166
Caracas*	1,822
Catia La Mar	100
Ciudad Bolívar	225
Ciudad Guayana	453
Coro	125
Cumaná	212
Guacara	101
Guarenas	134
Los Teques	141
Maracaibo	1,250
Maracay	354
Maturín	207
Mérida	171
Petare	338
Puerto Cabello	129
Puerto La Cruz	156
San Cristóbal	221
San Francisco	198
Turmero	174
Valencia	904
Vietnam	**81,625**
Bien Hoa	274
Cam Pha	105
Cam Ranh	118
Can Tho	208
Da Lat	103
Da Nang	370
Haiphong	450
Hanoi*	1,090
Ho Chi Minh City	2,900
Hong Gai	123
Hue	212
Long Xuyen	129
My Tho	105
Nam Dinh	166
Nha Trang	213
Phan Thiet	114
Qui Nhon	160
Rach Gia	138
Thai Nguyen	125
Vinh	111
Vung Tau	124
Y	
Yemen	**19,350**
Al Ḩudaydah	155
Al Mukallā	154
Aden	562
Sanaa*	972
Ta'izz	178
Z	
Zambia	**10,307**
Chingola	168
Kabwe	167
Kitwe	247
Lusaka*	982
Ndola	376
Zimbabwe	**12,577**
Bulawayo	622
Chitungwiza	275
Gweru	125
Harare*	1,189
Mutare	132
Uroševac	114
Areas of Special Sovereignty	
Hong Kong (China)	**7,303**
Kowloon	775
New Kowloon	1,527
Sha Tin	550
Tai Po	260
Tsuen Wan	700
Tuen Mun	432
Victoria*	1,251
Yuen Long	143
Macau (China)	**462**
Macau*	343
Puerto Rico (U.S.)	**3,958**
Bayamón	202
Carolina	162
Ponce	159
San Juan*	427

Foreign Geographic Terms

Foreign Term	Language	English Meaning
A		
Adrar	Berber	Mountains
Aiguille	French	Peak
Ákra	Greek	Cape
Altos	Spanish	Mountains
Älv, Älven	Swedish	River
Anse	French	Cove
Archipiélago	Spanish	Archipelago
Arcipelago	Italian	Archipelago
Arquipélago	Portuguese	Archipelago
Arrecife	Spanish	Reef
Arroyo	Spanish	Stream
'Ayn	Arabic	Spring
B		
Baai	Dutch	Bay
Bab	Arabic	Strait
Bach	German	Stream
Bælt	Danish	Strait
Bahía	Spanish	Bay
Baḥr	Arabic	River, Sea
Baia	Portuguese	Bay
Baie	French	Bay
Ballon	French	Dome
Bana	Japanese	Cape
Bañados	Spanish	Marsh
Bandar	Persian	Harbor
Barrage	French	Dam, Reservoir
Bassin	French	Basin
Bāčtlāq	Persian	Marsh
Be'er	Hebrew	Well
Belt	German	Strait
Ben, Beinn	Gaelic	Mountain
Berg	Afrikaans, German	Mountain
Bi'r	Arabic	Well
Birkat	Arabic	Lake
Boca	Spanish	River Mouth
Bogd	Mongolian	Range
Bolsón	Spanish	Depression
Botn	Norwegian	Bay
Brazo	Spanish	River Branch
Bucht	German	Bay
Bugt	Danish	Bay
Buhayrat	Arabic	Lake, Lagoon
Bukit	Malay	Mountain
Bukt, Bukten	Swedish	Bay
Bulu	Indonesian	Mountain
Burj	Arabic	Hill
Burnu, Burun	Turkish	Cape
Busen	German	Bay
C		
Cabo	Portuguese, Spanish	Cape
Cañada	Spanish	Stream
Canal	Portuguese, Spanish	Channel
Canale	Italian	Canal
Cap	French	Cape
Capo	Italian	Cape
Cataratas	Spanish	Waterfalls
Catena	Spanish	Range
Causse	French	Upland
Cayos	Spanish	Cays
Cerro(s)	Spanish	Hill(s)
Chaîne	French	Range
Chapada	Portuguese	Hills
Chott	Arabic	Intermittent Lakes, Marshes
Chroüy	Cambodian	Cape
Chute(s)	French	Waterfall(s)
Ciénaga	Spanish	Marsh
Cima	Italian, Spanish	Peak
Cime	French	Peak
Città	Italian	City
Ciudad	Spanish	City
Co	Tibetan	Lake
Col	French	Pass
Colina(s)	Spanish	Hill(s)
Colle	Italian	Pass
Colline	Italian	Hills
Collines	French	Hills
Cordillera	Spanish	Range
Corno	Italian	Peak
Costa	Portuguese, Spanish	Coast
Côte	French	Coast, Ridge
Coteau	French	Hills
Csatorna	Magyar	Canal
Cuchilla	Spanish	Hills
Cumbre	Spanish	Peak
D		
Dağ, Daği	Turkish	Mountain
Dake	Japanese	Mountain
Dal, Dalen	Swedish	Valley
Damágheh	Persian	Cape
Daryácheh	Persian	Lake
Dasht	Persian	Desert
Desierto	Spanish	Desert
Détroit	French	Strait
Dhar	Arabic	Escarpment
Diep	Dutch	Channel
Dijk	Dutch	Dike
Ding	Chinese	Hill
Djebel	Arabic	Mountain(s)
Doi	Thai	Mountain
Dyb	Danish	Strait
E		
Eiland	Dutch	Island
Elv	Norwegian	River
Embalse	Spanish	Reservoir
Emi	Berber	Mountain
Enseada	Portuguese	Cove
Ensenada	Spanish	Cove
Erg	Arabic	Desert
Estrecho	Spanish	Strait
Étang	French	Lagoon
F		
Falaise	French	Cliff
Feld	German	Plain
Feng	Chinese	Mountain
Firth	Gaelic	Estuary
Fjärden	Swedish	Bay, Sound
Fjord, Fjorden	Norwegian	Inlet
Fjördhur	Icelandic	Bay
Fljót	Icelandic	River
Flói	Icelandic	Bay
Foci	Italian	River Mouths
G		
Gat	Danish, Dutch	Marine Channel
Gebirge	German	Range
Geçidi	Turkish	Pass
Gobi	Mongolian	Desert
Göl	Turkish	Lake
Golfe	French	Gulf
Golfo	Italian, Spanish	Gulf
Gora	Russian	Mountain
Got	Korean	Cape
Graben	German	Ditch
Guan	Chinese	Pass
Guelb	Arabic	Mountain
Gunung	Indonesian	Mountain
H		
Hai	Chinese	Sea
Hamada	Arabic	Desert
Ḥammādat	Arabic	Plateau
Hāmūn	Persian	Intermittent Salt Lake
Har	Hebrew	Mountain
Havet	Norwegian	Bay
Ḥawḍ	Arabic	Oasis
Hāyk'	Amharic (Ethiopia)	Lake
Hegy	Magyar	Mountain
Heide	Arabic	Heath
Hoek	Dutch	Point
Höhe	German	Height
Holm	Danish, Swedish	Island
Horn	German	Point
Hornatina	Czech, Slovak	Plateau
Hory	Czech, Slovak	Range
Hügel	German	Hill
I		
Île(s)	French	Island(s)
Ilha(s)	Portuguese	Island(s)
Insel(n)	German	Island(s)
Irmak	Turkish	River
Isla(s)	Spanish	Island(s)
Isola, Isole	Italian	Island, Islands
J		
Jabal	Arabic	Mountains
Järvi	Finnish	Lake
Jazīrat, Jazā'ir	Arabic	Island, Islands
Jbel	Arabic	Mountain(s)
Jezero	Czech, Slovak	Lake
Jezioro	Polish	Lake
Jiao	Chinese	Cape
Jibāl	Arabic	Mountain(s)
Joki	Finnish	River
Jökull	Icelandic	Glacier
Jolgeh	Persian	Plain
K		
Kaap	Dutch	Cape
Kabīr	Persian	Mountains
Kanaal	Dutch	Canal
Kanal	German, Serbo-Croatian	Canal
Kangri	Tibetan	Peak
Kap	German	Cape
Kapp	Norwegian	Cape
Kavīr	Persian	Desert
Kawlat	Arabic	Mountain
Kawm	Arabic	Hill
Kep	Albanian	Cape
Khalīj	Arabic	Gulf
Khao	Thai	Mountain
Khatt	Arabic	Intermittent River
Khawr	Arabic	Intermittent River
Khazzān	Arabic	Dam
Khuan	Thai	Lake
Kloof	Dutch	Gap
Kogel	German	Mountain
Kop	Dutch	Peak
Kopf	German	Peak
Kreb	Arabic	Dune
Küh	Persian	Mountain
L		
La	Tibetan	Pass
Lac(s)	French	Lake(s)
Laem	Thai	Cape
Laga, Lagh	Swahili	Intermittent River
Lago(s)	Italian, Portuguese, Spanish	Lake(s)
Lagoa	Portuguese	Lake
Laguna	Spanish	Lagoon
Les	Czech	Mountains
Ling	Chinese	Mountain
Llano(s)	Spanish	Plain(s)
Loch, Lough	Gaelic	Inlet, Lake
M		
Mägi	Estonian	Mountain
Mare	Italian	Sea
Marsá	Arabic	Bay
Maṣabb	Arabic	River Mouth
Maṣrif	Arabic	Canal
Massif	French	Upland
Meer	Afrikaans, Dutch, German	Lake, Sea
Meseta	Spanish	Plateau
Mifraz	Hebrew	Bay
Misaki	Japanese	Cape
Mont(s)	French	Mountain(s)
Montagna	Italian	Mountain
Montagne(s)	French	Mountain(s)
Montaña(s)	Spanish	Mountain(s)
Monte	Italian, Portuguese, Spanish	Mountain
Montes	Portuguese, Spanish	Mountains
Monti	Italian	Mountains
Morne	French	Mountain
Morro	Portuguese, Spanish	Mountain
Mui	Vietnamese	Cape
Mys	Russian	Cape
N		
Nafūd	Arabic	Desert
Naḥal	Hebrew	River
Nahr	Arabic	River
Namakzār	Persian	Salt Flat
Neem	Estonian	Cape
Nek	Dutch	Pass
Nevado	Spanish	Snow-covered Peak
Nina	Estonian	Cape
Nos	Russian	Cape
Nosy	Malagasy	Island
O		
Ø, Øy	Norwegian	Island
Odde	Danish	Point
Óros	Greek	Mountain
Otok	Serbo-Croatian	Island
Ouadi, Oued	Arabic	Intermittent River
Ozero	Russian	Lake
P		
Pampa	Spanish	Plain
Pantanal	Portuguese, Spanish	Swamp
Pas	Dutch	Pass
Pas	French	Strait
Paso	Spanish	Pass
Passage	French	Marine Channel
Peña, Peñasco	Spanish	Peak
Pereval	Russian	Pass
Phnum	Cambodian	Mountain
Phou	Lao	Mountain
Pi	Chinese	Cape
Pic	French	Peak
Picacho	Spanish	Peak
Picco	Italian	Peak
Pico(s)	Portuguese, Spanish	Peak(s)
Pik	Russian	Peak
Pique	French	Peak
Piton	French	Mountain
Piz, Pizzo	Italian	Peak
Planalto	Portuguese	Plateau
Planina	Serbo-Croatian	Plain
Plato	Afrikaans	Plateau
Playa	Spanish	Beach
Plošina	Czech	Plateau
Pointe	French	Point
Ponta	Portuguese	Point
Presa	Spanish	Dam, Reservoir
Presqu'île	French	Peninsula
Prokhod	Bulgarian	Pass
Promontorio	Italian	Promontory
Puncak	Indonesian	Mountain
Punt	Dutch	Point
Punta	Italian, Spanish	Point
Q		
Qanāt	Arabic	Canal
Qiryat	Hebrew	City
Qolleh	Persian	Mountain
R		
Rada	Spanish	Anchorage
Rade	French	Anchorage
Rann	Hindi	Marsh
Rapides	French	Rapids
Ras, Ra's	Arabic	Cape
Recifes	Portuguese	Reefs
Represa	Portuguese	Dam, Reservoir
Retto	Japanese	Islands
Rio	Portuguese	River
Río	Spanish	River
Rivier	Dutch	River
Rivière	French	River
Rosh	Hebrew	Cape
Rt	Serbo-Croatian	Cape
S		
Sabana	Spanish	Savanna
Sabkhat	Arabic	Lagoon, Salt Marsh
Sāgar	Hindi	Lake
Saguia	Arabic	Intermittent River
Ṣaḥrā'	Arabic	Desert
Saki	Japanese	Cape
Salar	Spanish	Salt Flat
Salina(s)	Spanish	Salt Flat(s)
Salto(s)	Portuguese, Spanish	Waterfall(s)
San	Japanese	Mountain
Sarīr	Arabic	Desert
Sebjet	Arabic	Dry Lake
Sebkha	Arabic	Salt Flat
See	German	Lake
Selkä	Finnish	Bay
Serra	Portuguese	Range
Serranía(s)	Spanish	Ridge(s)
Seto	Japanese	Strait
Sgurr	Gaelic	Mountain
Shan	Chinese	Mountain
Shankou	Chinese	Pass
Shaṭṭ	Arabic	Intermittent Lake
Shet'	Amharic (Ethiopia)	River
Shima	Japanese	Island
Shotō	Japanese	Islands
Sierra	Spanish	Range
Sistema	Spanish	Range
Sjö, Sjön	Swedish	Lake
Slieve	Gaelic	Mountain
Sø	Danish	Lake
Sommet	French	Peak
Sopka	Russian	Volcano
Spitze	German	Peak
Stausee	German	Reservoir
Stretto	Italian	Strait
Sund	Danish, Swedish	Sound
T		
Tal	German	Valley
Tall	Arabic	Mountain
Tanjona	Malagasy	Cape
Tanjong	Malay	Cape
Tanjung	Indonesian	Cape
Tassili	Berber	Plateau
Ténéré	Berber	Desert
Tepe	Turkish	Peak
Terara	Amharic (Ethiopia)	Mountain
Tō	Japanese	Island
Tó	Magyar	Lake
Tōge	Japanese	Pass
Tunturi	Finnish	Mountain
U		
Udde	Swedish	Point
Udolni	Czech	Reservoir
Uul	Mongolian	Mountain
Úval	Czech	Valley
V		
Val	French, Italian	Valley
Valle	Italian, Spanish	Valley
Vallée	French	Valley
Vallen	Dutch	Waterfall
Valli	Italian	Lagoon
Vatn	Norwegian	Lake
Veld	Dutch	Plain
Vig	Danish	Bay
Vik, Viken	Swedish	Bay
Virful	Romanian	Mountain
Vliet	Dutch	Channel
Vodoskhovyshche	Ukrainian	Reservoir
Volcán	Spanish	Volcano
Vrch	Serbo-Croatian	Mountain
Vrchy	Czech, Slovak	Range
Vysočina	Czech, Slovak	Plateau
W		
Wabē	Amharic (Ethiopia)	River
Wādī	Arabic	Intermittent River
Wāḥat	Arabic	Oasis
Wald	German	Forest, Mountains
Webi	Somali	River
Wenz	Amharic (Ethiopia)	River
Y		
Yam	Hebrew	Lake, Sea
Yama	Japanese	Mountain
Z		
Zaki	Japanese	Point
Zatoka	Ukranian	Gulf
Zee	Dutch	Lake, Sea
Zemlya	Russian	Land

Index of the World

This index is a comprehensive listing of the places and geographic features found in the atlas. Names are arranged in strict alphabetical order, without regard to hyphens or spaces. Every name is followed by the country or area to which it belongs. Except for cities, towns and cultural areas, all entries include a reference to feature type, such as province, river, island, peak, and so on. The page number and alpha-numeric code appear in blue to the right of each listing. The page number directs you to the largest scale map on which the name can be found. The code refers to the grid squares formed by the horizontal and vertical lines of latitude and longitude on each map. Following the letters from left to right and the numbers from top to bottom helps you to quickly locate the square containing the place or feature. Inset maps have their own alpha-numeric codes. Names on the map that are accompanied by a point symbol are indexed to the symbol's grid location. Other names are indexed in the grid in which the initial letter of the name falls. When a map name contains a subordinate or alternate name, both names are listed in the index. To conserve space and provide room for more entries, many abbreviations are used in this index. The primary abbreviations are listed below.

Index Abbreviations

A
Ab,Can	Alberta
Abor.	Aboriginal
Acad.	Academy
ACT	Australian Capital Territory
A.F.B.	Air Force Base
Afld.	Airfield
Afg.	Afghanistan
Afr.	Africa
Ak,US	Alaska
Al,US	Alabama
Alb.	Albania
Alg.	Algeria
Amm. Dep.	Ammunition Depot
And.	Andorra
Ang.	Angola
Angu.	Anguilla
Ant.	Antarctica
Anti.	Antigua and Barbuda
Ar,US	Arkansas
Arch.	Archipelago
Arg.	Argentina
Arm.	Armenia
Arpt.	Airport
Aru.	Aruba
ASam.	American Samoa
Ash.	Ashmore and Cartier Islands
Aus.	Austria
Austl.	Australia
Aut.	Autonomous
Az,US	Arizona
Azer.	Azerbaijan
Azor.	Azores

B
Bahm.	Bahamas, The
Bahr.	Bahrain
Bang.	Bangladesh
Bar.	Barbados
BC,Can	British Columbia
Bela.	Belarus
Belg.	Belgium
Belz.	Belize
Ben.	Benin
Berm.	Bermuda
Bfld.	Battlefield
Bhu.	Bhutan
Bol.	Bolivia
Bor.	Borough
Bosn.	Bosnia and Herzegovina
Bots.	Botswana
Braz.	Brazil
BrIn.	British Indian Ocean Territory
Bru.	Brunei
Bul.	Bulgaria
Burk.	Burkina Faso
Buru.	Burundi
BVI	British Virgin Islands

C
Ca,US	California
CAfr.	Central African Republic
Camb.	Cambodia
Camr.	Cameroon
Can.	Canada
Can.	Canal
Canl.	Canary Islands
Cap.	Capital
Cap. Dist.	Capital District
Cap. Terr.	Capital Territory
Cay.	Cayman Islands
C.d'Iv.	Côte d'Ivoire
C.G.	Coast Guard
Chan.	Channel
Chl.	Channel Islands
Co.	County
Co,US	Colorado
Col.	Colombia
Com.	Comoros
Cont.	Continent
CpV.	Cape Verde Islands
CR	Costa Rica
Cr.	Creek
Cro.	Croatia
CSea.	Coral Sea Islands Territory
Ct,US	Connecticut
Ctr.	Center
Ctry.	Country
Cyp.	Cyprus
Czh.	Czech Republic

D
DC,US	District of Columbia
De,US	Delaware
Den.	Denmark
Depr.	Depression
Dept.	Department
Des.	Desert
DF	Distrito Federal
Dist.	District
Djib.	Djibouti
Dom.	Dominica
Dpcy.	Dependency
D.R.Congo	Democratic Republic of the Congo
DRep.	Dominican Republic

E
Ecu.	Ecuador
Emb.	Embankment
Eng.	Engineering
Eng,UK	England
EqG.	Equatorial Guinea
Erit..	Eritrea
ESal.	El Salvador
Est.	Estonia
Eth.	Ethiopia
ETim.	East Timor
Eur.	Europe

F
Falk.	Falkland Islands
Far.	Faroe Islands
Fed. Dist.	Federal District
Fin.	Finland
Fl,US	Florida
For.	Forest
Fr.	France
FrAnt.	French Southern and Antarctic Lands
FrG.	French Guiana
FrPol.	French Polynesia
FYROM	Former Yugoslav Rep. of Macedonia

G
Ga,US	Georgia
Galp.	Galapagos Islands
Gam.	Gambia, The
Gaza	Gaza Strip
GBis.	Guinea-Bissau
Geo.	Georgia
Ger.	Germany
Gha.	Ghana
Gib.	Gibraltar
Glac.	Glacier
Gov.	Governorate
Govt.	Government
Gre.	Greece
Grld.	Greenland
Gren.	Grenada
Grsld.	Grassland
Guad.	Guadeloupe
Guat.	Guatemala
Gui.	Guinea
Guy.	Guyana

H
Har.	Harbor
Hi,US	Hawaii
Hist.	Historic(al)
Hon.	Honduras
Hts.	Heights
Hun.	Hungary

I
Ia,US	Iowa
Ice.	Iceland
Id,US	Idaho
Il,US	Illinois
IM	Isle of Man
In,US	Indiana
Ind. Res.	Indian Reservation
Indo.	Indonesia
Int'l	International
Ire.	Ireland
Isl., Isls.	Island, Islands
Isr.	Israel
Isth.	Isthmus
It.	Italy

J
Jam.	Jamaica
Jor.	Jordan

K
Kaz.	Kazakhstan
Kiri.	Kiribati
Ks,US	Kansas
Kuw.	Kuwait
Ky,US	Kentucky
Kyr.	Kyrgyzstan

L
La,US	Louisiana
Lab.	Laboratory
Lag.	Lagoon
Lakesh.	Lakeshore
Lat.	Latvia
Lcht.	Liechtenstein
Ldg.	Landing
Leb.	Lebanon
Les.	Lesotho
Libr.	Liberia
Lith.	Lithuania
Lux.	Luxembourg

M
Ma,US	Massachusetts
Madg.	Madagascar
Madr.	Madeira
Malay.	Malaysia
Mald.	Maldives
Malw.	Malawi
Mart.	Martinique
May.	Mayotte
Mb,Can	Manitoba
Md,US	Maryland
Me,US	Maine
Mem.	Memorial
Mex.	Mexico
Mi,US	Michigan
Micr.	Micronesia, Federated States of
Mil.	Military
Mn,US	Minnesota
Mo,US	Missouri
Mol.	Moldova
Mon.	Monument
Mona.	Monaco
Mong.	Mongolia
Monts.	Montserrat
Mor.	Morocco
Moz.	Mozambique
Mrsh.	Marshall Islands
Mrta.	Mauritania
Mrts.	Mauritius
Ms,US	Mississippi
Mt.	Mount
Mt,US	Montana
Mtn., Mts.	Mountain, Mountains
Mun. Arpt.	Municipal Airport
Myan.	Myanmar

N
NAm.	North America
Namb.	Namibia
NAnt.	Netherlands Antilles
Nat'l	National
Nav.	Naval
NB,Can	New Brunswick
Nbrhd.	Neighborhood
NC,US	North Carolina
NCal.	New Caledonia
ND,US	North Dakota
Ne,US	Nebraska
Neth.	Netherlands
Nf,Can	Newfoundland and Labrador
Nga.	Nigeria
NH,US	New Hampshire
NI,UK	Northern Ireland
Nic.	Nicaragua
NJ,US	New Jersey
NKor.	North Korea
NM,US	New Mexico
NMar.	Northern Mariana Islands
Nor.	Norway
NS,Can	Nova Scotia
Nv,US	Nevada
Nun.,Can	Nunavut
NW,Can	Northwest Territories
NY,US	New York
NZ	New Zealand

O
Obl.	Oblast
Oh,US	Ohio
Ok,US	Oklahoma
On,Can	Ontario
Or,US	Oregon

P
Pa,US	Pennsylvania
PacUS	Pacific Islands, U.S.
Pak.	Pakistan
Pan.	Panama
Par.	Paraguay
Par.	Parish
PE,Can	Prince Edward Island
Pen.	Peninsula
Phil.	Philippines
Phys. Reg.	Physical Region
Pitc.	Pitcairn Islands
Plat.	Plateau
PNG	Papua New Guinea
Pol.	Poland
Port.	Portugal
Poss.	Possession
Pkwy.	Parkway
PR	Puerto Rico
Pref.	Prefecture
Prov.	Province
Prsv.	Preserve
Pt.	Point

Q
Qu,Can	Quebec

R
Rec.	Recreation(al)
Ref.	Refuge
Reg.	Region
Rep.	Republic
Res.	Reservoir, Reservation
Reun.	Réunion
RI,US	Rhode Island
Riv.	River
Rom.	Romania
Rsv.	Reserve
Rus.	Russia
Rvwy.	Riverway
Rwa.	Rwanda

S
SAfr.	South Africa
Sam.	Samoa
SAm.	South America
SaoT.	São Tomé and Príncipe
SAr.	Saudi Arabia
Sc,UK	Scotland
SC,US	South Carolina
SD,US	South Dakota
Seash.	Seashore
Sen.	Senegal
Serb.	Serbia & Montenegro (Yugoslavia)
Sey.	Seychelles
SGeo.	South Georgia and Sandwich Islands
Sing.	Singapore
Sk,Can	Saskatchewan
SKor.	South Korea
SLeo.	Sierra Leone
Slov.	Slovenia
Slvk.	Slovakia
SMar.	San Marino
Sol.	Solomon Islands
Som.	Somalia
Sp.	Spain
Spr., Sprs.	Spring, Springs
SrL.	Sri Lanka
Sta.	Station
StH.	Saint Helena
Str.	Strait
StK.	Saint Kitts and Nevis
StL.	Saint Lucia
StP.	Saint Pierre and Miquelon
StV.	Saint Vincent and the Grenadines
Sur.	Suriname
Sval.	Svalbard
Swaz.	Swaziland
Swe.	Sweden
Swi.	Switzerland

T
Tah.	Tahiti
Tai.	Taiwan
Taj.	Tajikistan
Tanz.	Tanzania
Ter.	Terrace
Terr.	Territory
Thai.	Thailand
Tn,US	Tennessee
Tok.	Tokelau
Trg.	Training
Trin.	Trinidad and Tobago
Trkm.	Turkmenistan
Trks.	Turks and Caicos Islands
Tun.	Tunisia
Tun.	Tunnel
Turk.	Turkey
Tuv.	Tuvalu
Twp.	Township
Tx,US	Texas

U
UAE	United Arab Emirates
Ugan.	Uganda
UK	United Kingdom
Ukr.	Ukraine
Uru.	Uruguay
US	United States
USVI	U.S. Virgin Islands
Ut,US	Utah
Uzb.	Uzbekistan

V
Va,US	Virginia
Val.	Valley
Van.	Vanuatu
VatC.	Vatican City
Ven.	Venezuela
Viet.	Vietnam
Vill.	Village
Vol.	Volcano
Vt,US	Vermont

W
Wa,US	Washington
Wal,UK	Wales
Wall.	Wallis and Futuna
WBnk.	West Bank
Wi,US	Wisconsin
Wild.	Wildlife, Wilderness
WSah.	Western Sahara
WV,US	West Virginia
Wy,US	Wyoming

Y
Yem.	Yemen
Yk,Can	Yukon Territory

Z
Zam.	Zambia
Zim.	Zimbabwe

A

A'alī an Nīl (pol. reg.), Sudan 117/F4
Aa (riv.), Fr. 54/B2
Aa (riv.), Ger. 52/D5
Aach (riv.), Ger. 61/F2
Aach, Ger. 61/E2
Aachen, Ger. 55/F2
Aalbach (riv.), Ger. 58/C3
Aalborg (int'l arpt.), Den. 40/C3
Aalburg, Neth. 52/C5
Aalen, Ger. 58/D5
Aalsmeer, Neth. 52/B4
Aalst, Belg. 54/D2
Aalten, Neth. 52/D5
Aalter, Belg. 54/C1
Aar (riv.), Ger. 55/H3
Aarau, Swi. 60/E3
Aarberg, Swi. 60/D3
Aarburg, Swi. 60/D3
Aardenburg, Neth. 54/C1
Aare (riv.), Swi. 66/E1
Aargau (canton), Swi. 61/E3
Aarred (lake), WSah. 110/B4
Aarschot, Belg. 55/D2
Aartselaar, Belg. 55/D1
Aarwangen, Swi. 60/D3
Aba, Nga. 115/G5
Aba, D.R. Congo 121/G2
Aba, China 78/E5
Abā as Su'ūd, SAr. 100/D5
Abadab (peak), Sudan 109/G5
Ābādān, Iran 103/G4
Ābādeh, Iran 103/H4
Abadla, Alg. 111/E3
Abádszalók, Hun. 50/E2
Abaeté, Braz. 186/D3
Abaetetuba, Braz. 182/D3
Abag Qi, China 78/G3
Abaí, Par. 189/F3
Abaiang (isl.), Kiri. 136/G4
Abaji, Nga. 115/G4
Abajo (mts.), Ut, US 142/D4
Abak, Nga. 115/G5
Abakaliki, Nga. 115/H5
Abakan, Rus. 74/K4
Abala, Niger 115/F3
Abala, Congo 120/C3
Abalak, Niger 115/G3
Aban, Rus. 74/K4
Abancay, Peru 184/C4
Abanga (riv.), Gabon 120/B2
Abano Terme, It. 63/E3
Abapó, Bol. 188/D1
Abar Kūh, Iran 103/H4
Abarán, Sp. 46/E3
Abariringa (Canton) (isl.), Kiri. 137/H5
'Abasān, Gaza 105/A6
Abashiri, Japan 82/D1
Abashiri (lake), Japan 82/C2
Abasolo, Mex. 175/F3
Abasolo, Mex. 175/E4
Abatimbo el Gumas, Eth. 117/G3
Abau, PNG 129/H2
Abay, Kaz. 74/H5
Abaya (well), Chad 116/C2
Abaza, Rus. 99/F1
Abbabis, Namb. 122/C5
Abbadia Lariana, It. 61/F6
Abbadia San Salvatore, It. 48/B1
Abbaretz, Fr. 56/D5
Abbazia di Casamari, It. 65/C4
Abbazia di Fossanova, It. 65/C5
Abbazia di Montecassino, It. 65/C5
Abbe (lake), Djib. 118/B3
Abbert (riv.), Ire. 32/B3
Abbeville, Fr. 54/A3
Abbeville, Al, US 165/F2
Abbeville, La, US 164/B3
Abbeville, Ga, US 165/G2
Abbeville, SC, US 163/F3
Abbeville, Ms, US 162/C3
Abbey (peak), Austl. 134/B1
Abbey, Sk, Can. 145/K2
Abbeydorney, Ire. 32/A5
Abbeyfeale, Ire. 32/A5
Abbeylara, Ire. 32/C2
Abbeyleix, Ire. 32/C4
Abbiategrasso, It. 62/B3
Abbot (mt.), Austl. 134/B3
Abbot (pt.), Austl. 129/H4
Abbots Bromley, Eng, UK 35/G6
Abbots Langley, Eng, UK 30/B1
Abbotsbury, Eng, UK 36/D5
Abbotsford, Wi, US 155/J1
Abbotsinch (int'l arpt.), Sc, UK 33/B5
Abbott, Tx, US 151/F2
Abbottābād, Pak. 98/B2
Abbottsburg, NC, US 163/H3
Abbottstown, Pa, US 168/B4
Abcoude, Neth. 52/B4
Ābdānān, Iran 100/E2
Abdul Hakīm, Pak. 98/B4
Abdulino, Rus. 71/K1
Abéché, Chad 116/D2
Abejorral, Col. 183/K7
Abel Erasmuspas (pass), SAfr. 123/F5
Ābeltī, Eth. 117/H3
Abemama (isl.), Kiri. 136/G4
Abenab, Namb. 122/C3
Abenberg, Ger. 58/D4
Abengourou, C.d'Iv. 114/E5
Åbenrå, Den. 40/C4
Abens (riv.), Ger. 42/F4
Abensberg, Ger. 59/E5
Abeokuta, Nga. 115/F5
Aber, Wal, UK 34/D5
Aber Wrac'h (riv.), Fr. 56/A3
Aberaeron, Wal, UK 36/B2
Aberangell, Wal, UK 36/C1
Aberarth, Wal, UK 36/B2
Abercarn, Wal, UK 36/C3
Aberchirder, Sc, UK 33/D1
Abercrombie, ND, US 156/F4
Abercrombie (riv.), Austl. 133/D2
Aberdare, Wal, UK 36/C3
Aberdare NP, Kenya 119/B2
Aberdaron, Wal, UK 34/D6
Aberdeen, Austl. 132/D2
Aberdeen, Sc, UK 33/D2
Aberdeen (co.), Sc, UK 33/D2
Aberdeen (lake), Nun, Can. 140/F2
Aberdeen, China 87/L8
Aberdeen, SAfr. 124/D4
Aberdeen, Id, US 147/G2
Aberdeen, Md, US 168/B5
Aberdeen, Ms, US 162/C4
Aberdeen, NC, US 163/H3
Aberdeen, SD, US 156/E5
Aberdeen, Wa, US 144/C4
Aberdeen Proving Ground, Md, US 168/B5
Aberdeenshire (co.), Sc, UK 33/D2
Aberdour, Sc, UK 33/C4
Aberdour (bay), Sc, UK 33/D1
Aberdyfi, Wal, UK 36/B1
Aberfeldy, Sc, UK 33/C3
Aberfoyle, Sc, UK 33/B4
Abergavenny, Wal, UK 36/C3
Abergele, Wal, UK 34/E5
Ābergelē, Eth. 118/A2
Aberlady, Sc, UK 33/D5
Aberlour, Sc, UK 33/C2
Abernathy, Tx, US 152/D4
Abernethy, Sc, UK 33/C4
Aberporth, Wal, UK 36/B2
Abersoch, Wal, UK 34/D6
Abersychan, Wal, UK 36/C3
Abert (lake), Or, US 146/C2
Abertillery, Wal, UK 36/C3
Aberystwyth, Wal, UK 36/B2
Abez', Rus. 69/P2
Abhá, SAr. 100/D5
Abhānpur, India 95/D1
Abhar, Iran 103/G2
Abhayāpuri, India 97/H2
Abia (prov.), Nga. 115/G5
'Ābidīn, Sudan 117/G2
Abidjan, C.d'Iv. 114/D5
Abidjan (Port Bouet) (int'l arpt.), C.d'Iv. 114/E5
Abidogun, Nga. 115/F5
Abiko, Japan 83/E2
Abilene, Ks, US 153/F1
Abilene, Tx, US 150/E1
Abingdon, Il, US 155/J3
Abingdon, Va, US 163/G2
Abingdon, Eng, UK 37/E3
Abingdon, Md, US 168/B5
Abingdon Downs, Austl. 134/A2
Abington, Sc, UK 33/C6
Abington (reef), Austl. 134/C2
Abino (pt.), On, Can. 160/U10
Abinsk, Rus. 73/K5
Abiquiu (lake), NM, US 152/A2
Abiquiu, NM, US 149/J2
Abiquiu (dam), NM, US 149/J2
Abisko, Swe. 38/F1
Abitibi (riv.), On, Can. 141/H4
Abitibi (lake), On,Qu, Can. 141/H4
Ābiy Ādī, Eth. 118/A2
Ābīyata (lake), Eth. 118/A4
Abiyata-Shala Lakes NP, Eth. 117/H4
Abja-Paluoja, Est. 41/L2
Abkhazia Aut. Rep., Geo. 71/G4
Ableiges, Fr. 30/H4
Abminga, Austl. 131/G3
Abnūb, Egypt 109/F3
Abo, Som. 118/D3
Åbo (Turku), Fin. 41/K1
Aboh, Nga. 115/G5
Abohar, India 98/C4
Aboisso, C.d'Iv. 114/E5
Abomey, Ben. 115/F5
Ābomsa, Eth. 118/A3
Abondance, Fr. 60/C5
Abong-Mbang, Camr. 120/C2
Abongabong (mtn.), Indo. 89/B1
Abony, Hun. 50/D2
Aborlan, Phil. 88/B3
Abou Deia, Chad 116/C3
Abourassein, Djebel (peak), CAfr. 116/E3
Aboyne, Sc, UK 33/D2
Abra Pampa, Arg. 188/C2
Abraham Gonzalez (int'l arpt.), Mex. 177/A2
Abraham Lincoln Birthplace Nat'l Hist. Site, Ky, US 162/E2
Abraham's Bay, Bahm. 177/H1
Abraka, Nga. 115/G5
Abrams, Wi, US 160/B2
Abrantes, Port. 46/A3
Abreojos (pt.), Mex. 174/B3
'Abrī, Sudan 109/F4
Abridge, Eng, UK 30/D2
Abrud, Rom. 51/F2
Abruzzi (pol. reg.), It. 65/C3
Abruzzi (prov.), It. 45/K5
Abruzzo, PN d', It. 48/C2
Absam, Aus. 61/H3
Absaroka (range), Mt,Wy, US 147/H1
Absarokee, Mt, US 147/J1
Absdorf, Aus. 51/N7
Absecon, NJ, US 168/D5
Abtsgmünd, Ger. 58/D5
Abū aḑ Ḑuhūr, Syria 104/E2
Abū al Maţāmīr, Egypt 113/B3
Abū 'Alī (isl.), SAr. 103/G5
Abū an Numrus, Egypt 113/C5
Abū 'Arīsh, SAr. 100/D5
Abū Dā'ūd as Sibākh, Egypt 113/C3
Abū Dawm, Sudan 117/F1
Abū Dawm, Sudan 117/G1
Abu Dhabi (int'l arpt.), UAE 101/F4
Abu Dhabi (Abū Z̧aby) (cap.), UAE 101/F4
Abū Dīs, Sudan 109/G5
Abū Ḩadrīyah, SAr. 103/G5
Abū Hamad, Sudan 109/G5
Abū Ḩammād, Egypt 113/C3
Abū Hugar, Sudan 117/G2
Abū Ḩummuş, Egypt 113/B2
Abū Jābirah, Sudan 117/E3
Abū Jandīr, Egypt 113/B6
Abū Jubayhah, Sudan 117/F3
Abū Kabīr, Egypt 113/C3
Abū Kamāl, Syria 102/E3
Abū Kūk, Sudan 117/G2
Abū Maţāriq, Sudan 117/E3
Abu Mendi, Eth. 117/G3
Abū Qashsh, WBnk. 105/C5
Abū Qīr, Egypt 113/B2
Abū Rawwāsh (ruin), Egypt 113/C4
Abū Rimth (wadi), Egypt 113/C4
Abu Road, India 101/K4
Abū Rubayq, SAr. 100/C4
Abū Rukbah, Sudan 117/G2
Abu Shagara (cape), Sudan 109/H4
Abū Shāmah (peak), Egypt 113/C5
Abū Shanab, Sudan 117/E2
Abu Simbel (ruin), Egypt 109/F4
Abū Şīr (ruin), Egypt 113/C5
Abū Şīr Banā, Egypt 113/C3
Abū Sulţān, Egypt 113/D4
Abū Zabad, Sudan 117/F2
Abū Za'bal, Egypt 113/C4
Abū Z̧aby (Abu Dhabi) (cap.), UAE 101/F4
Abuja (cap.), Nga. 115/G4
Abuja (int'l arpt.), Nga. 115/G4
Abuja Capital Terr., Nga. 115/G4
Abukuma (riv.), Japan 85/G2
Abukuma (plat.), Japan 85/G2
Abulog, Phil. 88/C1
Abumombazi, D.R. Congo 121/E2
Abuná (riv.), Bol. 185/E3
Abunã (riv.), Braz. 185/E3
Abunã, Braz. 185/E3
Ābune Yosēf (peak), Eth. 118/A2
Abut Head (pt.), NZ 135/B3
Abuta, Japan 82/B2
Ābuyē Mēda (peak), Eth. 118/A3
Abuyog, Phil. 88/D3
Abwong, Sudan 117/G3
Åby, Swe. 40/G2
Abyār, Egypt 113/B3
Abyār 'Alī, SAr. 100/C4
Åbybro, Den. 40/C3
Abydos (ruin), Egypt 109/F3
Abyei, Sudan 117/F3
Acacías, Col. 180/C4
Acacoyagua, Mex. 176/C3
Academy of Sciences, VatC. 65/G7
Acadia NP, Me, US 158/C4
Acadia Valley, Ab, Can. 145/J2
Acadian Village, La, US 164/B2
Acahay, Par. 189/E3
Acajutiba, Braz. 187/F1
Acámbaro, Mex. 175/E4
Acampo, Ca, US 167/M10
Acandí, Col. 180/B2
Acaponeta (riv.), Mex. 174/D4
Acaponeta, Mex. 174/D4
Acapulco de Juárez, Mex. 175/E5
Acará, Braz. 182/D3
Acarai (mts.), Guy. 181/G4
Acaraí, Serra (mts.), Braz. 182/B2
Acaraú, Braz. 183/F3
Acaraú (riv.), Braz. 183/F3
Acari, Braz. 183/G4
Acari (riv.), Braz. 182/B4
Acarí, Peru 184/C4
Acarigua, Ven. 180/D2
Acatlán de Osorio, Mex. 176/B2
Acatlán de Pérez Figueroa, Mex. 175/N8
Acatzingo, Mex. 175/M7
Acayucan, Mex. 176/C2
Acceglio, It. 64/C4
Accha, Peru 184/D4
Acciaroli, It. 48/D2
Accomac, Va, US 163/K2
Accra (cap.), Gha. 115/E5
Accrington, Eng, UK 35/F4
Aceguá, Uru. 189/F4
Aceh (prov.), Indo. 89/A1
Acerra, It. 65/D6
Aceuchal, Sp. 46/B3
Ach (riv.), Aus. 59/G6
Ach, Aus. 59/F6
Achaguas, Ven. 180/D3
Achalpur, India 95/C1
Achao, Chile 190/B4
Achar, Uru. 191/K10
Achegour (well), Niger 108/A5
Achen (pass), Ger. 61/H2
Acheng, China 79/K2
Achères, Fr. 30/J5
Acheron (riv.), Austl. 133/B3
Achhnera, India 96/A2
Achicourt, Fr. 54/B3
Achila, Bol. 184/D4
Achill (isl.), Ire. 30/N10
Achill Head (pt.), Ire. 30/N9
Achiltibuie, Sc, UK 31/R7
Achim, Ger. 53/G2
Achim, Ouadi (riv.), Chad 116/C1
Āchīn, Afg. 98/A2
Achinsk, Rus. 74/K4
Achit, Rus. 69/N4
Achmîm (well), Mrta. 114/D2
Achnasheen, Sc, UK 33/A1
Achoma, Peru 184/D4
A'chràlaig (peak), Sc, UK 33/A2
Achuapa, Nic. 176/E3
Achupallas, Ecu. 184/B1
Achuyevo, Rus. 73/J5
Achziv NP, Isr. 105/C2
Acigné, Fr. 56/D4
Acilia, It. 65/B4
Acireale, It. 48/D4
Ackerly, Tx, US 150/D1
Ackerman, Ms, US 162/C4
Acklins (isl.), Bahm. 173/G3
Ackworth Moor Top, Eng, UK 35/G4
Acland (mt.), Austl. 134/C4
Aclare, Ire. 32/B1
Acme, La, US 164/C2
Acme, Wa, US 144/C3
Acobamba, Peru 184/C4
Acolla, Peru 184/C3
Acolman, Mex. 175/R9
Acoma Ind. Res., NM, US 149/J3
Acomayo, Peru 184/D4
Acomayo, Peru 184/B3
Aconcagua (peak), Arg. 190/C2
Aconchi, Mex. 174/C2
Acopiara, Braz. 183/G4
Acora, Peru 184/D4
Acorizal, Braz. 185/G4
Acornhoek, SAfr. 123/F5
Acqualagna, It. 63/F6
Acquanegra sul Chiese, It. 62/D3
Acquapendente, It. 48/B1
Acquasanta Terme, It. 65/C2
Acquasparta, It. 65/B2
Acquaviva Piceno, It. 65/C2
Acqui Terme, It. 62/B4
Acquigny, Fr. 57/G2
Acraman (lake), Austl. 131/G5
Acrata (pt.), Alg. 112/G4
Acre (state), Braz. 184/D3
Acre (riv.), Braz. 184/D3
Acreúna, Braz. 186/C3
Acropolis, Gre. 49/N9
Actaeon Group (isls.), FrPol. 137/M7
Acton, Ca, US 166/B2
Acton (nbrhd.), Eng, UK 30/C2
Acton, On, Can. 160/S8
Acton, Tx, US 150/K7
Acton, Mt, US 145/K5
Acton Vale, Qu, Can. 161/K2
Actopan, Mex. 175/L6
Actopan, Mex. 175/N7
Açu, Braz. 183/G4
Açude Aratas (res.), Braz. 183/F4
Açude Banabuiu (res.), Braz. 183/G4
Açude Oros (res.), Braz. 183/G4
Acula, Mex. 175/P8
Aculeo (lag.), Chile 190/N8
Acworth, Ga, US 163/L6
Acy-en-Multien, Fr. 30/L4
Ad Dabbah, Sudan 117/F1
Ad Dabbūrah, Sudan 117/G1
Ad Dafīnah, SAr. 100/D4
Ad Dahnā' (des.), SAr. 100/D3
Ad Daljamūn, Egypt 113/B3
Ad Damazin, Sudan 117/G3
Ad Damīr, Sudan 117/G1
Ad Dammām, SAr. 100/F3
Ad Dāmūr, Leb. 105/C1
Ad Daqahliyah (gov.), Egypt 102/B3
Ad Darb, SAr. 100/D5
Ad Dawḩah (Doha) (cap.), Qatar 100/F3
Ad Dilam, SAr. 100/E4
Ad Dilinjāt, Egypt 113/B3
Ad Dīwānīyah, Iraq 103/F4
Ad Du'ayn, Sudan 117/E3
Ad Dujayl, Iraq 103/F3
Ad Duwādimī, SAr. 100/D4
Ad Duwayd, SAr. 102/E4
Ad Duwaym, Sudan 117/G2
Ad-Dakhla, WSah. 110/B5
Ada, Ok, US 153/F3
Ada, Mn, US 156/F4
Ada, Oh, US 160/E4
Ada, Gha. 115/F5
Ada, Serb. 50/E3
Ādaba, Eth. 118/A4
Adaba, India 95/E2
Adainville, Fr. 30/G5
Adair, Ok, US 153/G2
Adair (cape), Nun, Can. 141/J1
Adair, Ia, US 155/G3
Adair (bay), Mex. 175/F5
Adairsville, Ga, US 162/E3
Adairville, Ky, US 162/D2
Adaja (riv.), Sp. 46/C2
Adak (isl.), Ak, US 171/C6
Adak (str.), Ak, US 171/C6
Adam, Oman 101/G4
Adam (mt.), UK 191/E6
Adamantina, Braz. 189/G2
Adamaoua (prov.), Camr. 116/B4
Adamaoua (plat.), Camr., Nga. 107/D4
Adamawa (state), Nga. 116/B3
Adamello (peak), It. 61/G5
Adaminaby, Austl. 133/D3
Adamovka, Rus. 71/L2
Adams, Ma, US 161/K3
Adams, Ne, US 155/F3
Adams, NY, US 161/H3
Adams, Tn, US 162/D2
Adams, Wi, US 155/K2
Adams (mt.), Wa, US 144/D4
Adams (lake), BC, Can. 144/E2
Adams (riv.), BC, Can. 144/E2
Adams (co.), Pa, US 168/A4
Adams Run, SC, US 163/G4
Adamstown (cap.), Pitc. 137/M7
Adamstown, Pa, US 168/B3
Adamsville, Tn, US 162/C3
Adamsville, Tx, US 151/E2
Adamw (plat.), Nga. 115/H5
Aden ('Adan), Yem. 118/C2
'Adan (Aden), Yem. 118/C2
Adana (int'l arpt.), Turk. 102/C2
Adana, Turk. 102/C2
Adana (prov.), Turk. 102/C2
Adanhé, Gabon 120/B3
Adapazarı, Turk. 51/K5
Adarama, Sudan 117/G1
Adare, Ire. 32/B4
Adare (cape), Ant. 192/M
Adarza (peak), Fr. 46/E1
Adaut, Indo. 128/C2
Adavale, Austl. 134/B4
Add (riv.), Sc, UK 33/A4
Adda (riv.), Sudan 116/D3
Adda (riv.), It. 45/H4
Addicks (dam), Tx, US 151/M9
Addicks (res.), Tx, US 151/M9
Addis, La, US 164/C2
Addison, Il, US 167/P16
Addison, Al, US 162/D3
Addison, Tx, US 150/L7
Addison (Webster Springs), WV, US 163/G1
Addlestone, Eng, UK 30/B2
Addo Elephant NP, SAfr. 124/D4
Addy, Wa, US 144/F3
Adé, Chad 116/D2
Adekeieh (Ādī K'eyih), Erit. 118/A2
Adel, Ga, US 165/G2
Adel, Ia, US 155/G3
'Adel Bagrou, Mrta. 114/D3
Adelaide (pen.), Nun, Can. 140/G2
Adelaide (riv.), Austl. 128/C3
Adelaide, Austl. 131/M8
Adelaide (int'l arpt.), Austl. 131/M8
Adelaide, SAfr. 124/D4
Adelaide River, Austl. 128/C3
Adelaide Zoo, Austl. 131/M8
Adelanto, Ca, US 166/C1
Adèle (isl.), Austl. 128/A3
Adelebsen, Ger. 53/G5
Adelheidsdorf, Ger. 53/H3
Adelmannsfelden, Ger. 58/D5
Adelong, Austl. 133/D2
Adelschlag, Ger. 58/E5
Adelsheim, Ger. 58/C4
Adelsön (isl.), Swe. 39/A1
Adelsried, Ger. 58/D6
Aden (gulf), Afr.,Asia 77/D8
Aden (int'l arpt.), Yem. 118/C2
Aden, Ab, Can. 145/J3
Adenau, Ger. 55/F3
Adendorf, Ger. 53/H2
Aderbissinat, Niger 115/G3
Adèrké, Chad 108/C4
Ādēt, Eth. 117/H3
Adh Dhahībāt, Tun. 111/H2
Adh Dhirā', Jor. 104/D4
Adi, D.R. Congo 121/G2
Adi (isl.), Indo. 91/H4
Ādī Ābun, Eth. 118/A2
Ādī Ārk'ay, Eth. 117/H2
Ādī Da'iro, Eth. 100/C6
Ādīs Ābeba (Adekeieh), Erit. 118/A2
Ādī Kwala, Erit. 118/A2
Ādī Tekelezan, Erit. 118/A2
Ādī Ugrī, Erit. 118/A2
Adiaké, C.d'Iv. 114/E5
Adieu (cape), Austl. 131/G5
Ādīgala, Eth. 118/B3
Adige (riv.), It. 67/F1
Adige (Etsch) (riv.), It. 61/G4
Adigeni, Geo. 71/G4
Adigo (Etsch) (riv.), It. 61/G4
Ādīgrat, Eth. 118/A2
Adilcevaz, Turk. 103/E2
Adimo, Nga. 115/F5
Adin, Ca, US 146/C3
Adiora (well), Mali 115/E2
Adīrī, Libya 108/B3
Adirondack (mts.), NY, US 161/J2
Addis Ababa (Ādīs Ābeba) (cap.), Eth. 118/A3
Ādīs Ābeba (Addis Ababa) (cap.), Eth. 118/A3
Ādīs 'Alem, Eth. 118/A3
Ādīs Zemen, Eth. 117/H2
Adisutjipto (int'l arpt.), Indo. 89/E4
Adıyaman, Turk. 102/D2
Adiyaman (prov.), Turk. 102/D2
Adjud, Rom. 51/H2
Adjuntas, de la Presa (res.), Mex. 175/F4
Adler/Sochi (int'l arpt.), Rus. 70/F4
Adlington, Eng, UK 35/F4
Adliswil, Swi. 61/E3
Admiral, Sk, Can. 145/K3
Admirality (isl.), Ak, US 140/C3
Admirality (inlet), Nun, Can. 141/H1
Admirality Island Nat'l Mon., Ak, US 171/M4
Admiralty (inlet), Wa, US 167/B2
Admiralty (isls.), PNG 136/D5
Admiralty (gulf), Austl. 128/B3
Admiralty Gulf Abor. Rsv., Austl. 128/B3
Admire, Ks, US 153/F1
Adnan Menderes (int'l arpt.), Turk. 70/C5
Ado (riv.), Japan 83/J5
Ado Ekiti, Nga. 115/G5
Ado Odo, Nga. 115/F5
Adobe Creek (res.), Co, US 152/C1
Adogawa, Japan 83/K5
Adok, Sudan 117/F3
Adolfo López Mateos, Mex. 174/B3
Ādoni, India 95/C3
Adorf, Ger. 59/F2
Adoru, Nga. 115/G5
Adour (riv.), Fr. 66/D2
Adra, India 97/F4
Adra, Sp. 46/D4
Adranga, D.R. Congo 121/G2
Adrano, It. 48/D4
Adrar, Alg. 111/E4
Adrar (phys. reg.), Mrta. 114/B1
Adrar (pol. reg.), Mrta. 114/C1
Adrar (pol. reg.), Alg. 115/F1
Adrar (reg.), Mrta. 110/C5
Adrar (wilaya), Alg. 111/E4
Adrar bou Nasser (peak), Mor. 110/E2
Adrar Sotuf (mts.), WSah. 110/B5
Adré, Chad 116/D2
Adria, It. 63/F3
Adrian, Mo, US 153/G1
Adrian, Mi, US 160/D4
Adrian, Or, US 146/E2
Adrian, Mn, US 155/G2
Adrian, WV, US 163/G1
Adriatic (sea), Eur. 67/G2
Adro, It. 62/C2
Aduana del Sásabe, Mex. 175/G5
Adukrom, Gha. 115/E5
Adulis (ruin), Erit. 118/A2
Adur (riv.), Eng, UK 37/F5
Adutiškis, Lith. 41/M4
Advance, Mo, US 162/C2
Adventure Bay, Austl. 132/C4
Advocate Harbour, NS, Can. 158/E3
Ādwa, Eth. 118/A2
Adwick le Street, Eng, UK 35/G4
Adycha (riv.), Rus. 75/P3
Adygeya, Resp., Rus. 70/F3
Adzopé, C.d'Iv. 114/E5
Adz'va (riv.), Rus. 69/P2
Adz'vavom, Rus. 69/N2
Ae, Sc, UK 34/E1
Aegean (sea), Gre. 49/J3
Aegviidu, Est. 41/L2
Aerø (isl.), Den. 40/D4
Aeron (riv.), Wal, UK 36/B2
Aesch, Swi. 60/D3
Aeschi bei Spiez, Swi. 60/D4
Aetna, Ab, Can. 145/H3
Äetsä, Fin. 41/K1
Afadjoto (peak), Gha. 115/F5
'Afak, Iraq 103/F3
Āfambo, Eth. 118/B3
Āfambo, Erit. 118/B2
Afanas'yevskoye, Rus. 69/N4
Afándou, Gre. 102/B2
Afareaitu, FrPol. 137/X15
Āfdem, Eth. 118/B3
Afek NP, Isr. 105/B4
Aff (riv.), Fr. 44/B3
Affenrücken, Namb. 124/A3
Affoltern im Emmental, Swi. 60/D3
Affric (lake), Sc, UK 33/A2
Affton, Mo, US 155/J4
Afghanistan (ctry.) 101/H2
Afgooye, Som. 119/D1
Afia, Gabon 120/B2
'Afīf, SAr. 100/D4
Afikpo, Nga. 115/G5
Afipskiy, Rus. 73/K5
Afiqim, Isr. 105/D3
Aflou, Alg. 66/D4
Afmadow, Som. 119/C1
Afobaka (dam), Sur. 182/C1
Afogados da Ingàzeira, Braz. 183/G4
Afognak (isl.), Ak, US 171/H4
Afognak (peak), Ak, US 171/H4
Afollé (phys. reg.), Mrta. 114/C2
Afonso Bezerra, Braz. 183/G4
Afore, PNG 129/H2
Afragola, It. 65/D6
Afrânio, Braz. 183/F5
Africa (cont.) 107/*
Afrin (riv.), Turk. 104/E1
'Afrīn, Syria 104/E1
Afrique (peak), Fr. 60/A3
Afsluitdijk (dam), Neth. 52/C2
Afte (riv.), Ger. 53/F5
Afton, Ok, US 153/G2
Afton, Wy, US 147/H2
Afton, Ia, US 155/G3
Afton, Mn, US 157/Q7
Afuá, Braz. 182/D3
Afuidich (lake), WSah. 110/B5
'Afula, Isr. 105/C3
Afyon, Turk. 102/B2
Afyon (prov.), Turk. 102/B2
Afzalgarh, India 96/B1
Agadem, Niger 116/B1
Agades (int'l arpt.), Niger 115/G2
Agadez, Niger 115/G2
Agadez (dept.), Niger 111/H5
Agadir, Mor. 110/C3
Agadir (Inezgane) (int'l arpt.), Mor. 110/C3
Agadyr', Kaz. 99/B2
Agago (riv.), Ugan. 117/G5
Āgamani, India 97/G2
Agamor (well), Mali 115/F2
Agano (riv.), Japan 85/F2
Agar, SD, US 154/D1
Āgarfa, Eth. 118/A4
Āgaro, Eth. 117/H4
Agartala, India 97/H4
Agassiz Ice Cap (ice field), Nun, Can. 141/T6
Agassiz NWR, Mn, US 156/F3
Agate, Co, US 154/C4
Agate Fossil Beds Nat'l Mon., Ne, US 154/C2
Agats, Indo. 129/E1
Agattu (isl.), Ak, US 171/A5
Agattu (str.), Ak, US 171/A5
Agbabu, Nga. 115/G5
Agbor Bojiboji, Nga. 115/G5
Agboville, C.d'Iv. 114/D5
Ağcabädi, Azer. 103/F1
Ağdam, Azer. 103/F2
Ağdärä, Azer. 103/F1
Ağdaş, Azer. 71/H4
Agde, Fr. 44/E5
Agdz, Mor. 110/D3
Agen, Fr. 44/D4
Agency (lake), Or, US 146/B2
Agency, Mo, US 155/G4
Agency, Ia, US 155/H3
Ageo, Japan 83/D2
Ager (riv.), Aus. 59/G7
Ageræk, Den. 40/C4
Āgere Maryam, Eth. 118/A4
Agerisee (lake), Swi. 61/E3
Agersø (isl.), Den. 39/H7
Ageyevo, Rus. 70/F1
Agger (riv.), Ger. 55/G1
Aggteleki NP, Slvk. 50/E1
Āghā Jārī, Iran 103/G4
Aghada, Ire. 32/B6
Aghagallon, NI, UK 34/B3
Aghagower, Ire. 32/A2
Agiabampo, Mex. 174/C3
Ağın, Turk. 102/D2
Aginskiy Buryatskiy (aut. okrug), Rus. 78/G1
Aginskoye, Rus. 78/G1
Agivey, NI, UK 34/B1
Agjert, Mrta. 114/C2
Agliana, It. 63/D6
Ağlıköy, Turk. 70/E4
Agly (riv.), Fr. 44/E5
Agna, It. 63/E3
Agnanderón, Gre. 49/G3
Agnes, Tx, US 150/K7
Agnew, Austl. 130/D4
Agnibilékrou, C.d'Iv. 114/E5
Agnita, Rom. 51/G3
Agno (int'l arpt.), Swi. 61/E6
Agno (riv.), It. 63/E1
Agnone, It. 65/D4
Agny (riv.), Fr. 64/B1
Ago, Japan 83/L7
Ago Are, Nga. 115/F4
Agogna (riv.), It. 45/H4
Agon (pt.), Fr. 56/D3
Agon-Coutainville, Fr. 56/D2
Agona, Gha. 115/E5
Agoo, Phil. 87/J5
Agordo, It. 45/K3
Agougadzépe, Togo 115/F5
Agout (riv.), Fr. 44/D5
Āgra, India 96/B2
Agra, Ks, US 154/E4
Agraciada, Uru. 191/J10
Agrado, Col. 180/C4
Ágreda, Sp. 46/E2
Ağri (prov.), Turk. 71/G5
Ağrı (Mount Ararat) (peak), Turk. 103/F2
Agriá, Gre. 49/H3
Agricola, Fl, US 164/M8
Agrigento, It. 48/C4
Agrihan (isl.), NMar. 136/D3
Agrínion, Gre. 49/G3
Agrio (riv.), Arg. 190/C3
Agryz, Rus. 69/M4
Ağstafa, Azer. 71/H4
Ağsu, Azer. 71/J4
Agsumal (dry lake), WSah. 110/B4
Água Branca, Braz. 183/G4
Água Branca, Braz. 183/F4
Agua Buena, Chile 188/B3
Agua Caliente, Az, US 149/F4
Agua Caliente Ind. Res., Ca, US 148/D4
Água Clara, Braz. 189/F2
Agua de Dios, Col. 183/L8
Agua Dulce, Ca, US 166/B2
Agua Dulce, Mex. 176/C2
Agua Fria, NM, US 149/J3
Agua Fria NM, Az, US 149/F3
Agua Hedionda (lake), Ca, US 166/C4
Agua Larga, Ven. 180/D2
Agua Prieta, Mex. 175/H5
Agua Vermelha (res.), Braz. 186/C3
Aguachica, Col. 180/C2
Aguadas, Col. 183/K7
Aguadilla, PR 173/M8
Aguadulce, Pan. 180/A2
Aguaí, Braz. 187/K7
Agualeguas, Mex. 177/E4
Agualva-Cacém, Port. 47/P10
Aguan (riv.), Hon. 172/D4
Aguapeí (riv.), Braz. 186/C4
Aguapey (riv.), Arg. 189/E4
Aguaray, Arg. 188/D2
Aguarico (riv.), Peru 180/B5
Aguaro-Guariquito NP, Ven. 173/H6
Águas (hills), Braz. 187/L7
Águas Belas, Braz. 183/G5
Aguas Blancas, Chile 188/B3
Aguas Corrientes, Uru. 191/K11
Águas da Prata, Braz. 187/K6
Águas de Lindóia, Braz. 187/K7
Águas Formosas, Braz. 187/E3
Aguasay, Ven. 181/F2
Aguascalientes, Mex. 174/E4
Aguascalientes (state), Mex. 172/A3
Aguaytía (riv.), Peru 184/C3
Águeda, Port. 46/A2
Agueda (riv.), Sp. 46/B2
Aguelhok, Mali 115/F2
Agüenit, WSah. 110/B5
Aguêraktem (well), Mali 110/D5
Agugliano, It. 63/G6
Agui, Japan 83/L6
Aguié, Niger 115/G3
Aguijan (isl.), NMar. 136/D3
Aguila, Az, US 149/F4
Aguilâl Faï, Mrta. 114/B2
Aguilar, Co, US 152/B2
Aguilar, Sp. 46/C4
Aguilar de Campóo, Sp. 46/C1
Aguilares, Arg. 188/C3
Aguilas, Sp. 46/E4
Aguililla, Mex. 174/E5
Aguja (pt.), Peru 184/A2
Agulhas (cape), SAfr. 124/M11
Agulhas Negras, Pico das (peak), Braz. 187/M7
Agung (vol.), Indo. 89/F5
Agusan (riv.), Phil. 88/D3
Agustín Codazzi, Col. 180/C2
Agutaya, Phil. 88/C3
Agwata, Ugan. 119/A1
Agwok, Sudan 117/F4
Aha (hills), Bots. 122/D3
Ahaggar (mts.), Alg. 111/G5
Ahal (prov.), Trkm. 71/L5
Aham, Ger. 59/F5
Ahar, Iran 103/F2
Ahascragh, Ire. 32/B3
Ahau, Fiji 136/G6
Ahaura, NZ 135/B3
Ahaus, Ger. 52/E4
Aherlow (riv.), Ire. 32/B5
Ahero, Kenya 119/A2
Ahfir, Mor. 112/C2
Ahipara, NZ 135/C1
Ahırlı, Turk. 102/C2
Ahlat, Turk. 102/E2
Ahlen, Ger. 53/E5
Ahlerstedt, Ger. 53/G2
Ahmadābād, India 101/K4
Ahmadnagar, India 95/B2
Ahmadpur East, Pak. 98/A5
Ahmadpur Siāl, Pak. 98/A4
Ahmar (mts.), Eth. 118/B3
Ahmar, 'Erg el (des.), Mali 110/D4
Ahmed (well), WSah. 110/B5
Ahmeyine (well), Mrta. 110/B5
Ahoada, Nga. 115/G5
Ahoghill, NI, UK 34/B2
Ahome, Mex. 174/C3
Ahon (peak), Chad 108/C4
Ahoskie, NC, US 163/J2
Ahr (riv.), Ger. 42/D3
Ahram, Iran 103/G4
Ahraurā, India 96/D3
Ahrensburg, Ger. 53/H1
Ahse (riv.), Ger. 53/F5
Ahuacatitlán, Mex. 175/K8
Ahuacatlán, Mex. 174/D4
Ahuachapán, ESal. 176/D3
Ahualulco, Mex. 175/E4
Ahumada, Mex. 177/A2
Ahun, Fr. 44/E3
Ahunda, Gha. 115/F5
Åhus, Swe. 40/F4
Aḩuzzam, Isr. 105/B5
Ahvāz, Iran 103/G4
Ahvenanmaa (prov.), Fin. 38/F4
Ahwahnee, Ca, US 148/C2
Aḩwar, Yem. 118/C2
Ai (riv.), China 81/C2
Ai (mtn.), China 80/E3
Ai-Ais, Namb. 124/B2
Ai-Ais Hot Springs, Namb. 124/B2
Ai-shima (isl.), Japan 84/B3
Aibag Gol (riv.), China 80/B2
Aichach, Ger. 58/E6
Aichi (pref.), Japan 85/E3
Aidhausen, Ger. 58/D2
Aidlingen, Ger. 58/B5
Aiello del Friuli, It. 63/G2
Aiffres, Fr. 44/C3
Aigen im Mühlkreis, Aus. 59/G5
Aigle, Pic de l' (peak), Fr. 60/B4
Aiglemont, Fr. 55/D4
Aigoual (peak), Fr. 44/E4
Aiguá, Uru. 191/G2
Aiguebelle, Fr. 64/C1
Aigueblanche, Fr. 64/C1
Aigues (riv.), Fr. 44/F4
Aigües Tortes y Lago de San Mauricio, PN, Sp. 47/F1
Aiguillon, Fr. 44/D4
Aikawa, Japan 85/F1
Aikawa, Japan 83/C2
Aiken, SC, US 163/G4
Ailao (mtn.), China 86/D3
Ailao (mts.), China 86/D4
Aileron, Austl. 131/G2
Aileu, ETim. 128/B2
Ailigandí, Pan. 180/B2
Ailinglapalap (isl.), Mrsh. 136/F4
Aille (riv.), Fr. 64/C6
Aillevillers-et-Lyaumont, Fr. 60/C2
Aillon (riv.), Fr. 64/C1
Ailly-sur-Noye, Fr. 54/B4
Ailsa Craig (isl.), Sc, UK 33/A6
Ailsa Craig, On, Can. 160/F3
Ailuk (isl.), Mrsh. 136/G3
Aimäjärvi (lake), Fin. 39/E3
Aime, Fr. 64/C1
Aimen (pass), China 80/C5
Aimogasta, Arg. 188/C4
Aimorés, Braz. 187/E3
Aimorés, Serra dos (mts.), Braz. 187/E3
Ain (dept.), Fr. 64/B1
Ain (riv.), Fr. 44/F4
'Aïn Beïda, Alg. 112/K7
Aïn Ben Tili, Mrta. 110/C4
'Aïn Beniau, Alg. 112/G4
'Aïn Bessem, Alg. 112/G4
Aïn Chok-Hay Mohammadia (prov.), Mor. 112/A2
'Aïn Defla, Alg. 112/F4
'Aïn Defla (wilaya), Alg. 112/F4
Aïn el Aouda, Mor. 112/A3
'Aïn El Bey (int'l arpt.), Alg. 112/K6
'Aïn El Hammam, Alg. 112/H4
'Aïn el Turk, Alg. 112/D2
'Aïn Fakroun, Alg. 112/K6
'Aïn M'lila, Alg. 112/K6
'Aïn Oulmene, Alg. 112/H5
'Aïn Oussersa, Alg. 112/G5
'Aïn Sefra, Alg. 111/E2
Aïn Taoujdat, Mor. 112/B3
'Aïn Taya, Alg. 112/G4
'Aïn Temouchent, Alg. 112/D2
'Aïn Touta, Alg. 112/H5
Ainaro, ETim. 128/B2
Ainaži, Lat. 41/L3
Aincourt, Fr. 30/H4
Aínos (peak), Gre. 49/G3
Aínos Ethnikós Dhrimós, (nat'l. park), Gre. 49/G3
Ainsdale, Eng, UK 35/E4
Ainslie (lake), NS, Can. 159/G2
Ainsworth, Ne, US 154/E2
Aiome, PNG 129/G1
Aipe, Col. 180/C4
Aiquile, Bol. 188/C1
Aïr (plat.), Niger 111/G5
Air Force (isl.), Nun, Can. 141/J2
Airabu (isl.), Indo. 89/D2
Airaines, Fr. 54/A4
Airasca, It. 64/D3
Airbangis, Indo. 89/B2
Airdrie, Sc, UK 33/C5
Airdrie, Ab, Can. 145/G2
Aire (riv.), Eng, UK 35/G3
Aire, Canal d' (canal), Fr. 54/B2
Aire-sur-la-Lys, Fr. 54/B2
Aire-sur-l'Adour, Fr. 44/C5
Airgin Sum, China 78/G3
Airmolek, Indo. 89/C3
Airola, It. 65/D5
Airolo, Swi. 61/E4
Airton, Eng, UK 35/F3
Airuno, It. 62/C2
Airvault, Fr. 44/C3
Aisch (riv.), Ger. 45/J2
Aiseau-Presles, Belg. 55/D3
Aisén del General Carlos Ibáñez del Campo (pol. reg.), Chile 190/B5
Aishihik, Yk, Can. 171/L3
Aisne (riv.), Fr. 42/B4
Aïssa (peak), Alg. 111/E2
Aist (riv.), Aus. 59/H6
Aït Ben Haddou, Mor. 110/D3
Aït Ourir, Mor. 110/D3
Aitape, PNG 136/D5
Aith, Sc, UK 31/W13
Aitkin, Mn, US 157/H4
Aitō, Japan 83/K5
Aitolikón, Gre. 49/G3
Aitrach, Ger. 61/G2
Aitrang, Ger. 61/G2
Aitutaki Atoll (isl.), CookIs. 137/J6
Aiuaba, Braz. 183/F4
Aiud, Rom. 51/F2
Aiuruoca (riv.), Braz. 187/M7
Aiuruoca, Braz. 187/M6
Aix (mt.), Wa, US 144/D4
Aix-en-Provence, Fr. 64/B5
Aix-les-Bains, Fr. 64/B1
Aiyang, China 81/C2
Aíyina, Gre. 49/H4
Aiyínion, Gre. 49/H2
Aíyion, Gre. 49/H3
Aīzawl, India 86/B4
Aizkraukle, Lat. 41/L3
Aizpute, Lat. 41/J3
Aizu-Wakamatsu, Japan 85/F2
Aj Bogd (peak), Mong. 78/D3
Aj Janayet, Sudan 109/G5
Ajā, Egypt 113/C3
'Ajab Shīr, Iran 103/F2
Ajaccio, Fr. 48/A2
Ajaccio (gulf), Fr. 66/E2
Ajaigarh, India 96/C3
Ajalpan, Mex. 175/M8
Ajana, Austl. 130/B3
Ajaokuta, Nga. 115/G5
Ajaria Aut. Rep., Geo. 71/G4
Ajasse Ipo, Nga. 115/G4
Ajax, On, Can. 160/U8
Ajay (riv.), India 97/F3
Ajdābiyā, Libya 108/D2
Ajdovščina, Slov. 45/K4
Ajigasawa, Japan 82/B3
'Ajjah, WBnk. 105/C4
Ajka, Hun. 50/C2
'Ajlūn, Jor. 105/D4
Ajmer, India 92/B2
Ajnāla, India 98/C4
Ajo, Az, US 149/F4
Ajo, Cabo de (cape), Sp. 44/B5
Ajuchitlán del Progreso, Mex. 172/A4
Ajusco (vol.), Mex. 175/Q10
Ajuy, Phil. 88/C3
Ak-Dovurak, Rus. 99/F1
Aka (riv.), Japan 85/F1
Aka Eze, Nga. 115/G5
Akabane, Japan 83/M6
Akabira, Japan 82/C2
Akabli, Alg. 111/F4
Akademik Obruchev (mts.), Rus. 78/C1
Akagera, PN de l', Rwa. 121/G3
Akaishi-dake (peak), Japan 85/F3
Āk'ak'ī Besek'a, Eth. 118/A3
Akālgarh, Pak. 98/B3
Akalkot, India 95/C2
Akaltara, India 96/D4
Akan (lake), Japan 82/D2
Akan NP, Japan 82/D2
Akana, Congo 120/C3
Akankpa, Nga. 115/H5
Akaroa, NZ 135/C3
Åkarp, Swe. 40/E4
Akarsu, Turk. 102/D2
Akasha East, Sudan 109/F4
Akashi, Japan 83/G6
Akashi (str.), Japan 83/G6
Akaska, SD, US 156/D5
Akbarpur, India 96/D2
Akbarpur, India 96/B2
Akbaytal (pass), Taj. 99/B4
Akbou, Alg. 112/H4
Akçaabat, Turk. 70/F4
Akçakale, Turk. 102/D2
Akçakoca, Turk. 51/K5
Akçaova, Turk. 51/J5
Akçapınar, Turk. 102/D2
Akçay, Turk. 104/A1
Akchâr (phys. reg.), Mrta. 110/B5
Akchatau, Kaz. 74/H5
Akdağmadeni, Turk. 70/E5
Akdar, Al Jabal al (mts.), Libya 67/J4
Akechi, Japan 83/M5
Akeley, Mn, US 157/G4
Akelo, Sudan 117/G4
Akeno, Japan 83/A2
Akeno, Japan 83/E1
Åkers styckebruk, Swe. 39/A1
Åkersberga, Swe. 40/H2
Akershus (co.), Nor. 38/D3
Akershus Castle, Nor. 38/S8
Aketi, D.R. Congo 121/E2
Akhalk'alak'i, Geo. 71/G4
Akhalts'ikhe, Geo. 71/G4
Akharnaí, Gre. 49/N8
Akhaura, Bang. 97/H4
Akhelóos (riv.), Gre. 49/G3
Akhiok, Ak, US 171/H4
Akhisar, Turk. 70/C5
Akhmeta, Geo. 71/H4
Akhmīm, Egypt 109/F3
Akhnūr, India 98/C3
Akhtopol, Bul. 51/H4
Akhtuba (riv.), Rus. 71/H3
Akhtubinsk, Rus. 71/H2
Akhtyrskiy, Rus. 73/K5
Aki, Japan 84/C4
Aki (riv.), Japan 83/C2
Akiachak, Ak, US 171/F3
Akiéni, Gabon 120/C3
Akigawa, Japan 83/C2
Akimiski (isl.), On, Can. 141/H3
Akıncı (pt.), Turk. 104/D1
Akıncılar, Turk. 102/D1
Akins, Ok, US 153/G3
Åkirkeby, Den. 40/F4
Akishima, Japan 83/C2
Akita, Japan 82/B4
Akita (pref.), Japan 82/B4
Akitio, NZ 135/D3
Akiyama, Japan 83/C2
Akjoujt, Mrta. 114/B2
Akka, Mor. 110/C3
Akkerhaugen, Nor. 40/C2
Akkeshi, Japan 82/D2
Acre ('Akko), Isr. 105/C3
'Akko (Acre), Isr. 105/C3
Akkrum, Neth. 52/C2
Akkystau, Kaz. 71/K2
Aklavik, NW, Can. 171/L2
'Aklé 'Aouâna (dune), Mrta. 114/D2
Aknīste, Lat. 41/L3
Aknoul, Mor. 112/C2
Akō, Japan 84/D3
Akoabas, Camr. 120/C2
Akobo, Sudan 117/G4
Ākobo Wenz (riv.), Eth. 117/G4
Akoga, Gabon 120/B2

Akok – Alsike

Akok, Gabon 120/B2
Akom II, Camr. 120/B2
Akoma, PNG 129/G1
Akonolinga, Camr. 120/C2
Akora, Pak. 98/B2
Āk'ordat, Erit. 117/H2
Akören, Turk. 102/C2
Akosombo (dam), Gha. 115/F5
Akot, Sudan 117/F4
Akot, India 95/C1
Akoupé, C.d'Iv. 114/E5
Akpatok (isl.), Qu, Can. 141/K2
Akpınar, Turk. 103/M6
Akqi, China 99/C3
Akrab, Kaz. 71/K2
Akranes, Ice. 38/M7
Ákrathos (cape), Gre. 49/J2
Åkrehamn, Nor. 40/A2
Akrítas (cape), Gre. 49/G4
Akron, Al, US 162/D4
Akron, Co, US 154/C3
Akron, In, US 160/C4
Akron, Ia, US 155/F2
Akron, Mi, US 160/E3
Akron, NY, US 160/W9
Akron, Oh, US 160/F4
Akron, Pa, US 168/B3
Akrotiri, Cyp. 104/C2
Aksai Chin (reg.), India 99/C4
Aksakovo, Rus. 69/M5
Aksaray, Turk. 102/C2
Aksaray (prov.), Turk. 102/C2
Aksay, Rus. 73/K4
Aksay Kazakzu Zizhixian, China 78/C4
Akşehir, Turk. 102/B2
Akşehir (lake), Turk. 102/B2
Akseki, Turk. 102/B2
Aksoran (peak), Kaz. 99/C2
Aksu, Turk. 104/B1
Aksu (riv.), Turk. 104/B1
Aksu, China 99/D3
Aksu (riv.), Kaz. 99/C2
Aksubayevo, Rus. 69/L5
Āksum, Eth. 118/A2
Aktash, Uzb. 74/G6
Aktau, Kaz. 74/H4
Aktepe, Turk. 104/E1
Aktí (pen.), Gre. 70/C4
Aktogay, Kaz. 99/C2
Aktumsyk, Kaz. 71/L3
Aku, Nga. 115/G5
Akula, D.R. Congo 120/E2
Akune, Japan 84/B4
Akure, Nga. 115/G5
Akureyri, Ice. 38/N6
Akuse, Gha. 115/F5
Akutan (isl.), Ak, US 171/E5
Akutan, Ak, US 171/E5
Akutan Pass (str.), Ak, US 171/E5
Akwa Ibom (state), Nga. 115/G5
Akwanga, Nga. 115/H4
Akxokesay, China 78/C4
Akyab (Sittwe), Myan. 93/F3
Akyar, Rus. 71/L2
Akyazı, Turk. 51/K5
Akzhal, Kaz. 99/D2
Ål, Nor. 40/C1
Al 'Abbāsah ash Sharqīyah, Egypt 113/C3
Al 'Abbāsīyah, Sudan 117/F2
Āl 'Ābis, SAr. 100/D5
Al 'Adam, Libya 67/J5
Al Aḩmadī, Kuw. 103/G4
Al 'Ajamīyīn, Egypt 113/B6
Al Akhḑar, SAr. 109/H2
Al 'Āl, Jor. 105/D5
Al 'Alamayan (El Alamein), Egypt 109/F2
Al 'Alāqimah, Egypt 113/C3
Al 'Amārah, Iraq 103/F4
Al Anbār (gov.), Iraq 102/E3
Al 'Aqabah, Jor. 109/G2
Al 'Arīsh, Egypt 104/C4
Al Arţāwīyah, SAr. 100/E3
Al 'Assāfīyah, SAr. 109/H2
Al 'Awdah, SAr. 100/E3
Al 'Awsajīyah, SAr. 100/D3
Al 'Ayn, SAr. 109/H3
Al 'Ayn, UAE 101/G4
Al 'Ayyāţ, Egypt 113/C5
Al 'Azīzīyah, Iraq 103/F3
Al Azīzīyah, Libya 67/G4
Al Bāb, Syria 102/D2
Al Badrashayn, Egypt 113/C5
Al Baḩr Al Aḩmar (gov.), Egypt 109/G3
Al Bajalāt, Egypt 113/C2
Al Bājūr, Egypt 113/C4
Al Bakātūsh, Egypt 113/B2
Al Balāmūn, Egypt 113/C3
Al Ballāḩ, Egypt 113/D3
Al Balqā' (gov.), Jor. 104/D4
Al Balyanā, Egypt 109/G3
Al Bāqūrah, Jor. 105/D3
Al Barāmūn, Egypt 113/C2
Al Barrah, SAr. 100/E4
Al Baslaqūn, Egypt 113/B2
Al Başrah, Iraq 103/F4
Al Başrah (gov.), Iraq 103/F4
Al Batānūn, Egypt 113/C3
Al Batrūn, Leb. 104/D2
Al Bawīţi, Egypt 109/F2
Al Bayḑā, Libya 67/J4
Al Bayḑā, Yem. 118/C2
Al Biqā' (valley), Leb. 104/D3
Al Biqā (gov.), Leb. 105/D1
Al Bi'r, SAr. 109/H2
Al Bīrah, WBnk. 105/C5
Al Birk, SAr. 100/D5
Al Birkah, Libya 111/H4
Al Buḩayrah (gov.), Egypt 113/B3
Al Buraymī, Oman 101/G4
Al Burj, Egypt 113/B1
Al Burumbul, Egypt 113/C6
Al Buzūn, Yem. 118/D2
Al Fallūjah, Iraq 103/E3
Al Fanānahl, Tun. 112/L6
Al Farḑah, Yem. 118/D2
Al Fāsher, Sudan 117/E2
Al Fatḩah, Iraq 103/E3
Al Fāw, Iraq 103/G4
Al Fawwār, Tun. 111/H2
Al Fayyūm (gov.), Egypt 102/B3
Al Fayyum, Egypt 113/B6
Al Fāzah, Yem. 118/B2
Al Fifi, Sudan 117/E3
Al Firdān, Egypt 113/D3
Al Fuhūd, Iraq 103/F4
Al Fujayrah, UAE 101/G3
Al Fūlah, Sudan 117/F3
Al Fuqahā', Libya 108/C3
Al Gharaq as Sulţānī, Egypt 113/B6
Al Ghāriyah, Syria 105/F4
Al Ghāţ, SAr. 100/E3
Al Ghayatah, Egypt 113/B3
Al Ghayḑah, Yem. 100/F5
Al Ghayl, SAr. 100/E4
Al Ghurdaqah, Egypt 109/G3
Al Ḩaddādī, Egypt 113/B2
Al Ḩaddār, SAr. 100/E4
Al Ḩadīthah, SAr. 102/D4
Al Ḩadīthah, Iraq 102/E3
Al Ḩaḑr, Iraq 103/E3
Al Ḩaffah, Syria 104/E2
Al Ḩajar ash Sahrqī (mts.), Oman 101/G4
Al Ḩajarayn, Yem. 118/D2
Al Ḩājir, Egypt 113/C3
Al Ḩamādah al Ḩamrā (upland), Libya 108/A2
Al Ḩamar, SAr. 100/E4
Al Hamdab, Sudan 100/B5
Al Ḩammah, Tun. 66/F4
Al Ḩammām, Egypt 109/F2
Al Ḩammāmāt, Tun. 48/B4
Al Ḩamrā', SAr. 109/H4
Al Ḩāmūl, Egypt 113/C2
Al Hanākīyah, SAr. 100/D4
Al Ḩanīyah, Libya 67/J4
Al Ḩārithah, Iraq 103/F4
Al Ḩārrah, Syria 105/D2
Al Harūj al Aswad (hill), Libya 108/C3
Al Ḩasakah, Syria 102/E2
Al Ḩasakah (prov.), Syria 102/E2
Al Ḩawāmidīyah, Egypt 113/C5
Al Ḩawātah, Sudan 117/G2
Al Ḩawrah, Yem. 118/C2
Al Ḩawţah, SAr. 100/E3
Al Ḩawţah, Yem. 118/D2
Al Ḩayy, Iraq 103/F3
Al Ḩayy, Egypt 113/C5
Al Ḩayyānīyah, SAr. 102/E4
Al Ḩillah, Iraq 103/F3
Al Ḩillah, SAr. 100/E4
Al Ḩillah, Sudan 117/E2
Al Hindīyah, Iraq 103/F3
Al Hirmil, Leb. 104/E2
Al Ḩişn, Jor. 105/D4
Al Hoceima, Mor. 112/C2
Al Hoceima (prov.), Mor. 112/B2
Al Hoceima (Côte du Rif) (int'l arpt.), Mor. 112/C2
Al Ḩudaydah, Yem. 118/B2
Al Hufūf, SAr. 100/E3
Al Ḩulwah, SAr. 100/E4
Al Ḩumayshah, Yem. 118/C2
Al Ḩurayḑah, Yem. 118/D2
Al Ḩuşayḩişah, Sudan 117/G2
Al Ḩusaynīyah, Egypt 113/C3
Al Ḩuwaymī, Yem. 118/C2
Al Ḩuwayyiţ, SAr. 100/D3
Al Huwwārīyah, Tun. 48/B4
Al Ibēdiyya, Sudan 100/B5
Al Ibrāhīmīyah, Egypt 113/C3
Al 'Irqah, Yem. 118/C2
Al Iskandarīyah, Iraq 103/F3
Al Iskandarīyah (gov.), Egypt 102/B3
Al Iskandarīyah, Egypt 113/A2
Al Ismā'īlīyah (gov.), Egypt 104/C4
Al Ismā'īlīyah, Egypt 113/D3
Al Istiwā'īyah (pol. reg.), Sudan 117/F4
Al Jabal Akaur (mts.), Oman 101/G4
Al Jabal al Akhḑar (mts.), Libya 108/D2
Al Jabalayn, Sudan 117/G2
Al Jaghbūb, Libya 108/E2
Al Jamālīyah, Egypt 113/C2
Al Jamīl, Libya 67/G4
Al Jamm, Tun. 48/B5
Al Janad (int'l arpt.), Yem. 118/C2
Al Janūb (gov.), Leb. 105/C2
Al Jawārah, Oman 101/G5
Al Jawf, SAr. 102/D4
Al Jawf, Libya 108/D3
Al Jibāb, Syria 105/E2
Al Jifārah (plain), Libya 111/H2
Al Jifārah, SAr. 100/E4
Al Jifārah (plain), Tun. 66/F4
Al Jīzah, Egypt 113/C4
Al Jīzah, Jor. 105/D5
Al Jubayl, SAr. 103/G5
Al Judaydah, Leb. 105/D1
Al Judayyidah, Jor. 105/D5
Al Junaynah, Sudan 116/D2
Al Junaynah, SAr. 100/D4
Al Kāb, Egypt 113/D3
Al Kāf (gov.), Tun. 112/L6
Al Kāf, Tun. 112/L6
Al Kafr ash Sharqī, Egypt 113/C2
Al Kahfah, SAr. 103/E5
Al Kāmil, Oman 101/G4
Al Karak (gov.), Jor. 104/D4
Al Karak, Jor. 109/G2
Al Karāmah, Jor. 105/D5
Al Karīb, Tun. 112/L6
Al Karnak, Egypt 109/G3
Al Kawd, Yem. 118/C2
Al Kawm al Akhḑar, Egypt 113/B3
Al Kawm aţ Ţawīl, Egypt 113/C2
Al Khabrā', SAr. 100/D3
Al Khābūrah, Oman 101/G4
Al Khalīl (Hebron), WBnk. 105/C5
Al Khāliş, Iraq 103/F3
Al Khandaq, Sudan 109/F5
Al Khānkah, Egypt 113/C4
Al Khārijah, Egypt 109/F3
Al Kharrārah, Qatar 100/F4
Al Kharţūm (pol. reg.), Sudan 117/G2
Al Kharţūm Baḩrī (Khartoum North), Sudan 117/G2
Al Khaţāţibah, Egypt 113/B4
Al Khiḑr, Iraq 103/F4
Al Khiyām, Leb. 105/D2
Al Khubar, SAr. 100/F3
Al Khums, Libya 67/G4
Al Khuraybah, Yem. 118/D2
Al Khurmah, SAr. 100/D4
Al Khurtum (Khartoum) (cap.), Sudan 117/G2
Al Kiswah, Syria 105/E2
Al Kittah, Jor. 105/D4
Al Kūfah, Iraq 103/F3
Al Kufrah, Libya 108/D3
Al Kūt, Iraq 103/F3
Al Lādhiqīyah (Latakia), Syria 104/D2
Al Lādhiqīyah (prov.), Syria 104/D2
Al Lagowa, Sudan 117/F3
Al Lāhūn, Egypt 113/B6
Al Lidām, SAr. 100/D4
Al Lisht (ruin), Egypt 113/C5
Al Līth, SAr. 100/D4
Al Luḩayyah, Yem. 118/B2
Al Ma'ādī, Egypt 113/C5
Al Madīnah, SAr. 100/C4
Al Madīyah (prov.), Tun. 48/B5
Al Madīyah (gov.)., Alg. 112/M7
Al Madwar, Jor. 105/D4
Al Mafraq, Jor. 105/E4
Al Maghārīm, Yem. 118/C2
Al Maghrib (reg.), Alg. 110/E2
Al Maghrib (reg.), Alg.,Mor. 66/C4
Al Maḩallah al Kubrá, Egypt 113/C3
Al Mahdīyah, Tun. 48/B5
Al Maḩmūdīyah, Iraq 103/F3
Al Maḩmūdīyah, Egypt 113/B2
Al Majdal, Jor. 105/D4
Al Majma'ah, SAr. 100/E3
Al Maks, Egypt 113/A2
Al Malamm, Sudan 117/F3
Al Mālikīyah, Syria 102/E2
Al Ma'mūrah, Egypt 113/B2
Al Manāmah (Manama) (cap.), Bahr. 100/F3
Al Manaqīl, Sudan 117/G2
Al Mansūrah, Egypt 113/C2
Al Manşūrīyah, Egypt 113/C4
Al Manzilah, Egypt 113/C2
Al Maqrūn, Libya 108/D2
Al Marāghah, Egypt 109/F3
Al Marj, Libya 67/J4
Al Marsá, Tun. 48/B4
Al Ma'şarah, Egypt 113/C5
Al Masīd, Sudan 117/G2
Al Matammah, Sudan 117/G1
Al Maţarīyah, Egypt 113/D2
Al Matnah, Sudan 117/G2
Al Mawşil (Mosul), Iraq 103/E2
Al Mayādin, Syria 102/E3
Al Maymūn, Egypt 113/C6
Al Mazra'ah, Jor. 104/D4
Al Midhnab, SAr. 100/D3
Al Mīnā', Leb. 104/D2
Al Mindak, SAr. 100/D4
Al Minshāt el Kubrá, Egypt 113/B2
Al Minyā, Egypt 109/F2
Al Minyā, Egypt 113/C5
Al Minyā, Egypt 113/B6
Al Miqdādiyah, Iraq 103/F3
Al Mubarraz, SAr. 100/E4
Al Mudawwarah, Jor. 109/G2
Al Muglad, Sudan 117/E3
Al Mukallā, Yem. 118/D2
Al Muknīn, Tun. 48/B5
Al Munastīr, Tun. 48/B5
Al Munastīr (gov.), Alg. 112/M7
Al Murnāqīyah, Tun. 48/B4
Al Musallamīyah, Sudan 117/G2
Al Musayjīd, SAr. 109/H3
Al Musayyib, Iraq 103/F3
Al Muthanná (gov.), Iraq 103/F4
Al Muwaqqar, Jor. 105/E5
Al Muwassam, SAr. 118/B1
Al Muwayh, SAr. 100/D4
Al Muwayliḩ, SAr. 109/G3
Al Qābil, Oman 101/G4
Al Qaḑārif, Sudan 117/G2
Al Qaḑīmah, SAr. 100/C4
Al Qādisīyah (gov.), Iraq 103/F4
Al Qāhirah (Cairo) (cap.), Egypt 113/C4
Al Qāhirah (gov.), Egypt 102/B3
Al Qaḩmah, SAr. 100/D5
Al Qā'im, Iraq 102/E3
Al Qāmishlī, Syria 102/E2
Al Qanāţir al Khayrīyah, Egypt 113/C4
Al Qanāyāt, Egypt 113/C3
Al Qantarah, Egypt 113/D3
Al Qanţarah al Gharbīyah, Egypt 113/D3
Al Qaryah al Sharqīyah, Libya 108/B2
Al Qaryāt, Libya 108/B2
Al Qaryatayn, Syria 104/E2
Al Qarẕabah, Libya 67/J4
Al Qaşabāt, Libya 67/G4
Al Qaşr, Egypt 109/F3
Al Qaşr, Jor. 105/D6
Al Qaşrayn (gov.), Tun. 112/L7
Al Qaşrayn, Tun. 112/L7
Al Qaţaynah, Sudan 117/G2
Al Qaţīf, SAr. 100/F3
Al Qaţrūn, Libya 108/B3
Al Qayrawān, Tun. 48/B5
Al Qayrawān (gov.), Tun. 48/A5
Al Qayşūmah, SAr. 103/F4
Al Qibābāt, Egypt 113/C6
Al Qubbah, Libya 67/J4
Al Qunayţirah (prov.), Syria 105/D2
Al Qunayţirah, Jor. 105/E5
Al Qunayţirah, Syria 105/D2
Al Qunfudhah, SAr. 100/D5
Al Qurayn, Egypt 113/C3
Al Qurnah, Iraq 103/F4
Al Quşayr, Syria 104/E2
Al Quşayr, Egypt 109/G3
Al Quşūr, Tun. 112/L7
Al Quţayfah, Syria 105/F1
Al Quway'id (well), Libya 108/D2
Al Quway'īyah, SAr. 100/E4
Al Quwayrah, Jor. 104/D5
Al 'Ubaylah, SAr. 100/F4
Al Ubayyiḑ, Sudan 117/F2
Al Uḑayyah, Sudan 117/F2
Al 'Ulá, SAr. 109/H3
Al 'Umdah, Sudan 117/F3
Al Uqaylah, Libya 108/C2
Al Uqşur, Egypt 109/G3
Al 'Uwaynāt (peak), Sudan 108/E4
Al 'Uwaynāt, Libya 111/H4
Al 'Uyūn, SAr. 100/D3
Al 'Uzayr, Iraq 103/F4
Al Wādī al Jadīd (wadi), Egypt 102/B5
Al Wafā'īyah, Egypt 113/B3
Al Wāḩāt al Baḩrīyah (reg.), Egypt 109/F2
Al Wāḩāt al Khārijah (reg.), Egypt 109/F3
Al Wajh, SAr. 109/H3
Al Wakrah, Qatar 100/F3
Al Wāsiţah, Egypt 113/C6
Al Wazz, Sudan 117/F2
Al Widy, Egypt 113/C5
Al Wusta (pol. reg.), Sudan 117/G2
Al Yādūdah, Jor. 105/D5
Al Yāmūn, WBnk. 105/C4
Ala (pt.), It. 48/B1
Ala, It. 63/E2
Ala (riv.), China 78/B3
Alabama (state), US 143/J5
Alabama (riv.), Al,Ga, US 143/J5
Alabama and Coushatta Ind. Res., Tx, US 151/G2
Alabaster, Al, US 162/D4
Alabat, Phil. 88/C2
Alaca, Turk. 102/C1
Alacalı, Turk. 51/J5
Alaçam, Turk. 70/E4
Alaçatı, Turk. 49/K3
Alachua, Fl, US 165/G3
Alacrán (reef), Mex. 176/D1
Alacranes (res.), Cuba 177/F1
Aladağ, Turk. 104/C1
Alaejos, Sp. 46/C2
Alafia (riv.), Fl, US 164/L8
Alagir, Rus. 71/H4
Alagna Valsesia, It. 62/A1
Alagnon (riv.), Fr. 44/E4
Alagoa Grande, Braz. 183/H4
Alagoas (state), Braz. 183/G5
Alagoinhas, Braz. 187/F2
Alagón, Sp. 47/E2
Alagón (riv.), Sp. 46/C2
Alah (riv.), Phil. 88/D4
Alahanpanjang, Indo. 89/C3
Alajärvi, Fin. 68/D3
Alajärvi (lake), Fin. 39/E4
Alajõe, Est. 41/M2
Alajuela, CR 177/E4
Alakanuk, Ak, US 171/F3
Alakol (lake), Kaz. 74/J5
Alakuko, Nga. 115/G5
Alalapadu, Sur. 182/B2
Alalaú (riv.), Braz. 181/F5
Alamaån (riv.), Swe. 39/K6
Alamagan (isl.), NMar. 136/D3
'Alāmarvdasht (riv.), Iran 103/H5
Ālamat'ā, Eth. 118/A2
Alameda, Sk, Can. 156/C3
Alameda (co.), Ca, US 167/L11
Alameda, Ca, US 167/K11
Alameda, NM, US 149/J3
Alameda (cr.), Ca, US 167/L11
Ālamgīr, Pak. 98/A4
Alamikamba, Nic. 177/E3
Alamito (cr.), Tx, US 150/B3
Alamo, Mex. 176/B1
Alamo (lake), Az, US 149/F3
Alamo, Ca, US 167/K11
Alamo, Ga, US 163/F4
Alamo (mtn.), NM, US 150/B1
Alamo, Nv, US 148/E2
Alamo, Tn, US 162/C3
Alamo Band Ind. Res., NM, US 149/J3
Alamo Village, Tx, US 150/D3
Alamor, Ecu. 184/A2
Álamos, Mex. 174/C3
Alamosa, Co, US 152/B2
Alamosa (cr.), NM, US 152/B3
Alamosa Nat'l Wild.Ref., Co, US 149/K2
Åland (isl.), Fin. 38/G3
Aland (riv.), Ger. 42/F2
Alang, Indo. 88/B4
Alanreed, Tx, US 152/D3
Alanson, Mi, US 160/D2
Alantika, Monts (mts.), Camr.,Nga. 116/B3
Alanya, Turk. 104/C1
Alaotra (lake), Madg. 125/J7
Alapaha, Ga, US 165/G2
Alapaha (riv.), Ga, US 165/G2
Alapayevsk, Rus. 69/P4
Alaplı, Turk. 51/K5
Alarcón (res.), Sp. 46/D3
Alarka, NC, US 163/F3
Alas, Indo. 91/E5
Alaşehir, Turk. 102/B2
Alaserjärvi (lake), Fin. 39/F3
Alashtar, Iran 103/G3
Alaska (gulf), Ak, US 171/J4
Alaska (pen.), Ak, US 171/F4
Alaska (range), Ak, US 171/H3
Alaska (state), US 171/*
Alassio, It. 62/B6
Ālāt, Azer. 103/G2
Alataw (pass), China 99/D2
Alatri, It. 65/C4
Alatyr', Rus. 69/K5
Alaverdi, Arm. 71/H4
Alavus, Fin. 68/D3
Alaw (riv.), Wal, UK 34/D5
Alawa Ngandi Abor. Land, Austl. 128/D3
'Ālayh, Leb. 105/D1
Alayor, Sp. 46/C3
Alayskiy (mts.), Kyr. 99/B4
Alazeya (riv.), Rus. 75/R3
Alb (riv.), Ger. 58/B5
Alba, Tx, US 153/G4
Alba (prov.), Rom. 51/F2
Alba Adriatica, It. 65/C2
Alba de Tormes, Sp. 46/C2
Alba Fucens (ruin), It. 65/C3
Alba Iulia, Rom. 51/F2
Albacete, Sp. 46/E3
Albaida, Sp. 47/E3
Albairate, It. 62/B3
Ålbæk, Den. 40/D3
Albalate del Arzobispo, Sp. 47/E2
Alban, On, Can. 160/F1
Alban, Fr. 44/E5
Albán, Col. 183/L8
Albania, Col. 183/M7
Albania (ctry.) 49/F2
Albanian Alps, North (mts.), Serb. 49/F1
Albano (lake), It. 65/B4
Albano Laziale, It. 65/B4
Albany, Austl. 130/C5
Albany (riv.), On, Can. 141/H3
Albany, NZ 135/F6
Albany, Ca, US 167/K11
Albany, Ga, US 165/F2
Albany, In, US 160/D4
Albany, Ky, US 162/E2
Albany, Mn, US 157/G5
Albany, Mo, US 155/G3
Albany (cap.), NY, US 161/K3
Albany, Ok, US 153/F4
Albany, Or, US 146/B1
Albany, Tx, US 150/E1
Albaredo D'Adige, It. 63/E3
Albarine (riv.), Fr. 60/B5
Albarracín, Sp. 46/E2
Albatross (pt.), NZ 135/C2
Albatross (bay), Austl. 127/D2
Albatross Rock (pt.), Namb. 124/A2
Albbruck, Ger. 60/E2
Albemarle (pt.), Ecu. 184/J6
Albemarle, NC, US 163/G3
Albemarle (sound), NC, US 163/J3
Albenga, It. 62/B5
Alberche (riv.), Sp. 46/C2
Alberdi, Par. 188/E3
Alberga, Austl. 131/G3
Alberga (cr.), Austl. 127/C3
Alberhill, Ca, US 166/C3
Alberndorf in der Riedmark, Aus. 59/H6
Alberschwende, Aus. 61/F3
Albersdorf, Ger. 40/C4
Albersweiler, Ger. 58/B4
Albert, Austl. 132/C2
Albert (lake), Austl. 132/A2
Albert (lake), D.R.Congo, Ugan. 107/E4
Albert, Fr. 54/B3
Albert, Ks, US 152/E1
Albert Canyon, BC, Can. 144/F2
Albert Edward (mt.), PNG 129/G2
Albert Kanaal (riv.), Belg. 55/E2
Albert Lea, Mn, US 155/H2
Albert Nile (riv.), Ugan. 117/F5
Alberta (prov.), Can. 140/E3
Alberta, Al, US 162/D4
Alberta Beach, Ab, Can. 144/G1
Alberti, Arg. 190/E2
Albertinia, SAfr. 124/C4
Albertirsa, Hun. 50/D2
Alberto de Agostini, PN, Chile 191/B7
Alberton, PE, Can. 158/E2
Alberton, SAfr. 124/Q13
Alberton, Mt, US 144/G4
Albertshofen, Ger. 58/D3
Albertville, Sk, Can. 145/M1
Albertville, Fr. 64/C1
Albertville, Al, US 162/D3
Albertville, Mn, US 157/N6
Albestroff, Fr. 55/F6
Albeuve, Swi. 60/D4
Albi, Fr. 44/E5
Albia, Ia, US 155/H3
Albignasego, It. 63/E3
Albin, Wy, US 154/B3
Albina (pt.), Ang. 122/A2
Albina, Sur. 182/C1
Albinea, It. 62/D4
Albino, It. 62/C2
Albion, Id, US 147/G2
Albion, Il, US 162/C1
Albion, In, US 160/D4
Albion, Mi, US 160/D3
Albion, Ne, US 154/E3
Albion, NY, US 161/G3
Albion, Pa, US 160/F4
Albisola Marina, It. 62/B5
Albisola Superiore, It. 62/B5
Alblasserdam, Neth. 52/B5
Albocácer, Sp. 47/E2
Albon, Fr. 64/A2
Alborán (isl.), Mor. 110/E2
Alborán (isl.), Sp. 66/C4
Ålborg, Den. 40/C3
Ålborg (bay), Den. 40/D3
Albox, Sp. 46/D4
Albright Knox Art Gallery, NY, US 160/V10
Albrighton, Eng, UK 36/D1
Albristhorn (peak), Swi. 60/D5
Albufeira, Port. 46/A4
Albula (riv.), Swi. 45/H3
Albuñol, Sp. 46/D4
Albuquerque (int'l arpt.), NM, US 149/J3
Albuquerque, NM, US 149/J3
Alburquerque, Sp. 46/B3
Alburtis, Pa, US 168/C3
Albury, NZ 135/B4
Albury, Austl. 133/C3
Alby-sur-Chéran, Fr. 60/C6
Alca, Peru 184/C4
Alcabideche, Port. 47/P10
Alcácer do Sal, Port. 46/A3
Alcalá, Col. 183/K8
Alcalá de Chivert, Sp. 47/F2
Alcalá de Guadaira, Sp. 46/C4
Alcalá de Henares, Sp. 47/N9
Alcalá de los Gazules, Sp. 46/C4
Alcalá la Real, Sp. 46/D4
Alcalde (pt.), Chile 188/B4
Alcamo, It. 48/C4
Alcanadre (riv.), Sp. 47/E2
Alcanar, Sp. 47/E2
Alcañices, Sp. 46/B2
Alcañiz, Sp. 47/E2
Alcántara, Sp. 46/B3
Alcántara (res.), Sp. 46/B3
Alcântara, Braz. 183/E3
Alcântaras, Braz. 183/F3
Alcantarilla, Sp. 46/E4
Alcaraz, Sp. 46/D3
Alcaraz (range), Sp. 46/D3
Alcaraz, Sierra de (mts.), Sp. 66/C3
Alcatraz (isl.), Ca, US 167/K11
Alcatrazes (isl.), Braz. 187/L9
Alcaudete, Sp. 46/C4
Alcázar de San Juan, Sp. 46/D3
Alcester, SD, US 155/F2
Alcester, Eng, UK 37/E2
Alchevs'k, Ukr. 73/K3
Alcira, Sp. 47/E3
Alcira, Arg. 190/D2
Alçıtepe, Turk. 49/K2
Alco, Ar, US 153/H3
Alcoa, Tn, US 162/F3
Alcobaça, Braz. 187/F3
Alcobaça, Port. 46/A3
Alcobendas, Sp. 47/N8
Alcoche, Bol. 185/E4
Alcochete, Port. 47/Q10
Alcolu, SC, US 163/G4
Alcora, Sp. 47/E2
Alcorcón, Sp. 47/N9
Alcorisa, Sp. 47/E2
Alcoutim, Port. 46/B4
Alcova, Wy, US 147/K2
Alcoy, Sp. 47/E3
Alcúdia, Sp. 47/G3
Aldabra (isls.), Sey. 107/G5
Aldama, Mex. 177/B3
Aldama, Mex. 175/F4
Aldan (plat.), Rus. 75/N4
Aldan (riv.), Rus. 77/N3
Aldan, Rus. 75/N4
Aldar, Mong. 99/G2
Aldbourne, Eng, UK 37/E4
Aldbrough, Eng, UK 35/H4
Alde (riv.), Eng, UK 37/H2
Aldeburgh, Eng, UK 37/H2
Aldeia Formoza, Ang. 120/C5
Aldeia Nova de São Bento, Port. 46/B4
Aldeia Viçosa, Ang. 120/C5
Alden, Il, US 167/N15
Alden, NY, US 160/W10
Aldenhoven, Ger. 55/F2
Aldeno, It. 61/H6
Alder (lake), Wa, US 144/C4
Alder Flats, Ab, Can. 144/G1
Aldergrove, NI, UK 34/B2
Aldergrove (int'l arpt.), NI, UK 34/B2
Alderley Edge, Eng, UK 35/F5
Aldermaston, Eng, UK 37/E4
Alderney (isl.), Chl, UK 44/B2
Alderney (The Blaye) (arpt.), Chl, UK 56/C1
Alderpoint, Ca, US 146/B3
Aldershot, Eng, UK 37/F4
Aldershot, On, Can. 160/T9
Alderson, WV, US 163/G2
Aldersyde, Ab, Can. 145/H2
Alderwood Manor-Bothell North, Wa, US 167/C2
Aldine, Tx, US 151/M9
Aldingen, Ger. 61/E1
Aldred (lake), Pa, US 168/B4
Aldridge, Eng, UK 37/E1
Ale Water (riv.), Sc, UK 33/D6
Aledo, Il, US 155/J3
Aledo, Tx, US 150/K7
Aleg, Mrta. 114/B2
Alegre, Braz. 187/E4
Alegrete, Braz. 189/F4
Alejandría, Bol. 185/E4
Alejandro Gallinal, Uru. 191/G2
Alejandro Roca, Arg. 190/E2
Alejandro Selkirk (isl.), Chile 179/A6
Alejo Ledesma, Arg. 190/E2
Aleknagik, Ak, US 171/G4
Aleksandro-Nevskiy, Rus. 70/G1
Aleksandrov, Rus. 68/H4
Aleksandrov Gay, Rus. 71/J2
Aleksandrovac, Serb. 50/E4
Aleksandrovka, Rus. 73/K4
Aleksandrovsk, Rus. 69/N4
Aleksandrovsk-Sakhalinskiy, Rus. 79/N1
Aleksandrovskoye, Rus. 71/G3
Aleksandrów Kujawski, Pol. 43/K2
Aleksandrów Łódzki, Pol. 43/K3
Alekseyevka, Rus. 71/J1
Alekseyevka, Rus. 73/K2
Alekseyevka, Kaz. 99/B1
Alekseyevskoye, Rus. 69/L5
Aleksin, Rus. 68/H5
Aleksinac, Serb. 50/E4
Alem Maya, Eth. 118/B3
Além Paraíba, Braz. 187/P6
Alembé, Gabon 120/B3
Alemdar, Turk. 103/N6
Alençon, Fr. 57/F4
Alenquer, Braz. 182/C3
Alento (riv.), It. 65/D3
Alenuihaha (chan.), Hi, US 142/S9
Alépé, C.d'Iv. 114/E5
Aleppo (Ḩalab), Syria 104/E1
Alerce Andino, PN, Chile 190/B4
Aléria, Fr. 48/A1
Alert (pt.), Nun, Can. 141/S6
Alert, Nun, Can. 141/T6
Aleşd, Rom. 50/F2
Alessandria (prov.), It. 62/B3
Alessandria, It. 62/B4
Ålestrup, Den. 40/C3
Ålesund, Nor. 38/C3
Aletschhorn (peak), Swi. 60/D5
Aleutian (isls.), Ak, US 171/C5
Aleutian (range), Ak, US 171/G4
Alex, Ok, US 153/F3
Alexander (isl.), Ant. 192/V
Alexander (mt.), Austl. 130/B2
Alexander (pt.), Austl. 129/E3
Alexander, ND, US 156/C4
Alexander, Tx, US 151/E1
Alexander Archipelago (isls.), Ak, US 171/L4
Alexander Bay, SAfr. 124/B3
Alexander City, Al, US 162/E4
Alexander Graham Bell Nat'l Hist. Park, NS, Can. 159/G2
Alexander Hamilton (int'l arpt.), USVI 173/M8
Alexander Nevsky Abbey, Rus. 69/T7
Alexandra, NZ 135/B4
Alexandra, Austl. 133/B3
Alexándria, Gre. 49/H2
Alexandria, Austl. 129/E4
Alexandria, Braz. 183/G4
Alexandria (int'l arpt.), Egypt 113/A2
Alexandria, Rom. 51/G4
Alexandria, SAfr. 124/D4
Alexandria, BC, Can. 144/C1
Alexandria, In, US 160/D4
Alexandria, Ky, US 162/E1
Alexandria, La, US 164/B2
Alexandria, Mn, US 157/G5
Alexandria, Ne, US 155/F3
Alexandria, Sc, UK 33/B5
Alexandria, SD, US 154/F2
Alexandria, Va, US 168/A6
Alexandria Bay, NY, US 161/J2
Alexandrina (lake), Austl. 127/C4
Alexandroúpolis, Gre. 49/J2
Alexeck (riv.), Namb. 122/C4
Alexis, Il, US 155/J3
Alexis Creek, BC, Can. 144/C1
Alexishafen, PNG 129/G1
Aley (riv.), Rus. 99/D1
Aleysk, Rus. 99/D1
Alfama (nbrhd.), Port. 47/P10
Alfarim, Port. 47/P11
Alfaro, Sp. 46/E1
Alfatar, Bul. 51/H4
Alfbach (riv.), Ger. 55/F3
Alfeld, Ger. 53/G5
Alfenas, Braz. 187/L6
Alfhausen, Ger. 53/E3
Alfiós (riv.), Gre. 49/G4
Alfonsine, It. 63/F4
Alfonso Bonilla Aragón (int'l arpt.), Col. 180/B4
Alford, Eng, UK 35/J5
Alford, Sc, UK 33/D2
Alford, Fl, US 165/F2
Alfred, NY, US 161/H3
Alfred, Me, US 161/L3
Alfred (mt.), BC, Can. 144/B2
Alfred NP, Austl. 133/D3
Alfreton, Eng, UK 35/G5
Alfriston, Eng, UK 37/G5
Alfter, Ger. 55/G2
Alga, Kaz. 71/L2
Algabas, Kaz. 71/K2
Ålgård, Nor. 40/A2
Algarrobito, Chile 188/B4
Algarrobo, Chile 190/N8
Algarve (reg.), Port. 46/A4
Algeciras, Col. 180/C4
Algeciras, Sp. 46/C4
Algemesí, Sp. 47/E3
Alger, Mi, US 160/D2
Alger (wilaya), Alg. 112/G4
Algeria (ctry.) 111/F3
Algermissen, Ger. 53/G4
Algete, Sp. 47/N8
Alghero, It. 48/A2
Algiers (El Djezair) (cap.), Alg. 112/G4
Algoa, Tx, US 151/M9
Algoa (bay), SAfr. 124/D4
Algodonales, Sp. 46/C4
Algoma, Wi, US 160/C2
Algoma, Or, US 146/C2
Algoma, Ms, US 162/C3
Algona, Wa, US 167/C3
Algona, Ia, US 155/G2
Algonac, Mi, US 167/G6
Algonquin (peak), NY, US 161/K2
Algonquin, Il, US 167/P14
Algood, Tn, US 162/E2
Algorta, Uru. 191/K10
Algueirão, Port. 47/P10
Algund (Lagundo), It. 61/H4
Alhama de Granada, Sp. 46/D4
Alhama de Murcia, Sp. 46/E4
Alhambra, Ca, US 166/F7
Alhambra, Il, US 155/K4
Alhandra, Port. 47/P10
Alhandra, Braz. 183/H4
Alhaurín el Grande, Sp. 46/C4
'Alī al Gharbī, Iraq 103/F3
'Alī ash Sharqī, Iraq 103/F3
Āli Bayramlı, Azer. 103/G2
'Ali SabîehL, Djib. 118/B3
Alia, It. 48/C4
Alía, Sp. 46/C3
'Alīābād, Iran 103/H4
Aliade, Nga. 115/H5
Aliağa, Turk. 70/C5
Aliákmon (riv.), Gre. 49/G2
Aliákmonos (lake), Gre. 49/G2
Alíartos, Gre. 49/H3
Alibey (lake), Ukr. 72/F5
Alibey (riv.), Turk. 103/M6
Alibeyköy, Turk. 51/J5
Ālībo, Eth. 117/H3
Alicante (int'l arpt.), Sp. 47/E3
Alicante, Sp. 47/E3
Alice (pt.), It. 49/E3
Alice (riv.), Austl. 129/F3
Alice, SAfr. 124/D4
Alice, Tx, US 151/E4
Alice Springs, Austl. 131/G2
Aliceville, Al, US 162/C4
Aliceville (dam), Al, US 162/C4
Aliceville (lake), Al, US 162/C4
Alicia, Ar, US 162/B3
Alicia, Phil. 88/C4
Alicudi (isl.), It. 48/D3
Alicurá (res.), Arg. 190/C4
Alife, It. 65/D5
Alīganj, India 96/B2
Alīgarh, India 96/B2
Alijilán, Arg. 188/C4
Alijó, Port. 46/B2
Alīkadam, Bang. 93/F3
Alima (riv.), Congo 120/C3
Alindao, CAfr. 116/D4
Alingār (riv.), Afg. 98/A2
Alingsås, Swe. 40/E3
Alīpur, Pak. 98/A5
Alīpur Duār, India 97/G2
Alirājpur, India 101/K4
Aliskerovo, Rus. 75/S3
Alistráti, Gre. 49/H2
Alivérion, Gre. 49/J3
Aliwal North, SAfr. 124/D3
Alix, Ab, Can. 145/H1
Alixan, Fr. 64/B3
Aljezur, Port. 46/A4
Aljustrel, Port. 46/A4
Alkali Lake, BC, Can. 144/C2
Alken, Belg. 55/E2
Alkhan-Kala, Rus. 71/H4
Alkmaar, Neth. 52/B3
Alkoum (well), Alg. 111/H4
Alkoven, Aus. 59/H6
Alku (wadi), Sudan 117/E2
All American (canal), Ca, US 148/E4
Allada, Ben. 115/F5
Allagash (riv.), Me, US 158/C2
Allahābād, India 96/C3
Allaire, Fr. 56/C5
Allakaket, Ak, US 171/H2
Allakh-Yun', Rus. 75/P3
Allaman, Swi. 60/C5
Allan, Sk, Can. 145/L2
Allan (hills), Sk, Can. 145/L2
Alland, Aus. 51/N7
Allanmyo, Myan. 86/B5
Allanridge, SAfr. 124/D2
Allanson, Austl. 130/C5
'Allāq (well), Libya 108/A2
`Allāqt (wadi), Egypt 100/B4
Allariz, Sp. 46/B1
Allatoona (lake), Ga, US 162/E3
Allauch, Fr. 64/B6
Alldays, SAfr. 123/F4
Alle, Swi. 60/D3
Allegan, Mi, US 160/D3
Allegany, NY, US 161/G3
Allegheny (plat.), Pa, US 161/G4
Allegheny (riv.), Pa, US 161/G4
Allegheny (mts.), US 143/K4
Allegheny Portage Railroad Nat'l Hist. Site, Pa, US 161/G4
Allemands (lake), La, US 164/C3
Allen, Ok, US 153/F3
Allen (mt.), NZ 135/A4
Allen, Arg. 190/D3
Allen, Ne, US 155/F2
Allen, Tx, US 150/L6
Allen (riv.), Eng, UK 36/B5
Allen Park, Mi, US 167/F7
Allenby Bridge, Jor.,WBnk. 105/D5
Allendale, Eng, UK 35/F2
Allendale, Mi, US 160/D3
Allendale, NJ, US 169/J7
Allendale, SC, US 163/G4
Allende, Mex. 177/D3
Allende, Mex. 175/E3
Allendorf, Ger. 53/F6
Allensbach, Ger. 61/F2
Allentown, Pa, US 168/C2
Allentown-Bethlehem-Easton (arpt.), Pa, US 168/C2
Allentsteig, Aus. 43/H4
Allenwood, Pa, US 168/B1
Aller (riv.), Ger. 53/H3
Allerkanal (canal), Ger. 53/H4
Allerød, Den. 39/J7
Allersberg, Ger. 58/E4
Allershausen, Ger. 59/E6
Allevard, Fr. 64/C2
Allex, Fr. 64/A3
Allgäu Alps (range), Aus.,Ger. 42/F5
Allhallows, Eng, UK 30/F2
Alliance, Oh, US 160/F4
Alliance, Ne, US 154/C2
Alliance, Ab, Can. 145/J1
Allied War Cemetery, Myan. 94/B2
Allier (riv.), Fr. 66/D1
Allier, Montagne de l' (peak), Fr. 64/C4
Alligator (lake), Fl, US 165/H3
Alligator (pt.), Austl. 129/F4
Alligator (riv.), NC, US 163/J3
Allingåbro, Den. 40/D3
Allinge, Den. 40/F4
Allinges, Fr. 60/C5
Allingham, Austl. 129/E4
Allison, Ia, US 155/H2
Alliston, On, Can. 161/G2
Alloa, Sc, UK 33/C4
Allonnes, Fr. 57/F6
Allonnes, Fr. 57/F5
Allons, Tn, US 162/E2
Allora, Austl. 134/C5
Allos, Fr. 64/C4
Allouez, Wi, US 160/B2
Allow (riv.), Ire. 32/B5
Alloway, NJ, US 168/C4
Alloway (cr.), NJ, US 168/C4
Allschwil, Swi. 60/D2
Allumettes (isl.), Qu, Can. 161/H2
Alluvial City, La, US 164/D3
Allyn, Wa, US 144/C4
Alm (riv.), Aus. 59/G7
Alma, Ar, US 153/G3
Alma, Ga, US 165/G2
Alma, Ks, US 153/F1
Alma, Mi, US 160/D3
Alma, NS, Can. 158/E3
Alma, Ne, US 154/E3
Alma, NM, US 149/H4
Alma (hill), NY, US 161/G3
Alma, Qu, Can. 158/B1
Alma, Wi, US 155/J1
Almacelles, Sp. 47/F2
Almacén, Ven. 181/F2
Almada, Port. 47/P10
Almadén, Sp. 46/C3
Almafuerte, Arg. 190/D2
Almagro, Sp. 46/D3
Almanor (lake), Ca, US 146/C3
Almansa, Sp. 47/E3
Almanza, Sp. 46/C1
Almanzor, Pico de (peak), Sp. 46/C2
Almanzora (riv.), Sp. 46/D4
Almartha, Mo, US 153/H2
Almas, Braz. 186/D1
Almas, Pico das (peak), Braz. 187/E2
Almas, Rio das (riv.), Braz. 186/C2
Almaty Oblast, Kaz. 99/C3
Almaty (int'l arpt.), Kaz. 99/C3
Almazán, Sp. 46/D2
Almaznyy, Rus. 75/M3
Almazora, Sp. 47/E3
Almeida, Port. 46/B2
Almeirim, Port. 46/A3
Almeirim, Braz. 182/C3
Almelo, Neth. 52/D4
Almena, Ks, US 154/E4
Almenara (peak), Sp. 46/D3
Almenara, Sp. 47/E3
Almenara, Braz. 187/E3
Almendra (res.), Sp. 46/B2
Almendralejo, Sp. 46/B3
Almenno San Salvatore, It. 62/C2
Almere, Neth. 52/C4
Almería, Sp. 46/D4
Almería (gulf), Sp. 46/D4
Almese, It. 64/D2
Al'met'yevsk, Rus. 69/M5
Älmhult, Swe. 40/F3
Almina (pt.), Sp. 112/B2
Almirós, Gre. 49/H3
Almiroú (gulf), Gre. 49/J5
Almo, Id, US 147/G2
Almodôvar, Port. 46/A4
Almodóvar del Campo, Sp. 46/C3
Almodóvar del Río, Sp. 46/C4
Almoharín, Sp. 46/B3
Almond (riv.), Sc, UK 33/C4
Almont, ND, US 156/D4
Almont, Mi, US 160/E3
Almont (riv.), Fr. 30/L6
Almont, Co, US 149/J1
Almonte, On, Can. 161/H2
Almonte, Sp. 46/B4
Almora, India 96/B1
Almoradi, Sp. 47/E3
Almorox, Sp. 46/C2
Almte. Montt (gulf), Chile 191/B7
Almudévar, Sp. 47/E1
Almuñécar, Sp. 46/D4
Almunge, Swe. 39/B1
Almus, Turk. 102/D1
Alness, Sc, UK 33/B1
Alness (riv.), Sc, UK 33/B1
Alnmouth, Eng, UK 33/E6
Alnwick, Eng, UK 33/E6
Ålö (isl.), Swe. 39/B2
Alofi, NZ 137/J6
Alofi (isl.), Wall. 136/H6
Aloha, Or, US 146/B1
Aloi, Ugan. 119/A1
Aloja, Lat. 41/L3
Along, India 86/B2
Alongshan, China 79/J1
Alónnisos (isl.), Gre. 49/H3
Alonsa, Mb, Can. 156/E2
Alor (isl.), Indo. 128/B2
Alor (isls.), Indo. 128/B2
Alor Gajah, Malay. 89/C2
Alor Setar, Malay. 89/C1
Álora, Sp. 46/C4
Alotau, PNG 136/E6
Aloysius (mt.), Austl. 131/F3
Alpachiri, Arg. 190/E3
Alpaugh, Ca, US 148/C3
Alpe di Poti (peak), It. 63/E7
Alpe di Succiso (peak), It. 62/D5
Alpedrete, Sp. 47/M8
Alpen, Ger. 52/D5
Alpena, Mi, US 160/E2
Alpena, SD, US 154/E1
Alpercatas, Serra das (mts.), Braz. 183/E4
Alperschällihorn (peak), Swi. 61/F4
Alpes de Provence (range), Fr. 45/G5
Alpes-de-Haute-Provence (dept.), Fr. 64/C4
Alpes-Maritimes (dept.), Fr. 64/D5
Alpha, Austl. 134/B3
Alpha, Il, US 155/J3
Alpha (mt.), NZ 135/J8
Alpha, NJ, US 168/C2
Alpharetta, Ga, US 163/M6
Alphen aan de Rijn, Neth. 52/B4
Alpi Apuane (range), It. 45/J4
Alpi Dolomitiche (range), It. 45/J4
Alpi Orobie (range), It. 45/J3
Alpiarça, Port. 46/A3
Alpignano, It. 64/D2
Alpine, NJ, US 169/K8
Alpine, Wy, US 147/H2
Alpine, Tx, US 150/C2
Alpirsbach, Ger. 61/E1
Alpnach, Swi. 61/E4
Alps (mts.), Eur. 29/E4
Alqōsh, Iraq 103/E2
Alrewas, Eng, UK 37/E1
Alroy Downs, Austl. 129/E4
Als (isl.), Den. 42/F1
Alsace (dept.), Fr. 58/A5
Alsace (pol. reg.), Fr. 55/G6
Alsager, Eng, UK 35/F5
Alsask, Sk, Can. 145/K2
Alsasua, Sp. 44/B5
Alsdorf, Ger. 55/F2
Alsea (bay), Or, US 146/A1
Alsenz, Ger. 55/G4
Alsenz (riv.), Ger. 55/G4
Alsheim, Ger. 58/B3
Alsike, Swe. 39/A1

Alsip, Il, US 167/Q16
Alstahaug, Nor. 38/E2
Alstead, NH, US 161/K3
Alster (riv.), Ger. 53/H1
Alsting, Fr. 55/F5
Alston, Eng, UK 35/F2
Alstonville, Austl. 132/E1
Alsunga, Lat. 41/J3
Alt (riv.), Eng, UK 35/E4
Alta, Nor. 38/G1
Ålta, Swe. 39/B1
Alta (mt.), NZ 135/B4
Alta, Ia, US 155/G2
Alta Gracia, Arg. 188/C4
Alta Vista, Ks, US 153/F1
Altach, Aus. 61/F3
Altadena, Ca, US 166/F7
Altagracia, Nic. 176/E4
Altagracia de Orituco, Ven. 183/P8
Altai (mts.), Asia 77/H5
Altai (mts.), China 74/J5
Altamache (riv.), Ga, US 163/F5
Altamaha (riv.), Ga, US 165/H2
Altamira, Braz. 182/C3
Altamira, Chile 188/B3
Altamira, Mex. 176/B1
Altamira do Maranhão, Braz. 183/E4
Altamont, Il, US 162/C1
Altamont, Ks, US 153/G2
Altamont, Mb, Can. 156/E3
Altamont, Or, US 146/C2
Altamont, Tn, US 162/E3
Altamonte Springs, Fl, US 164/N6
Altamura, It. 48/E2
Altanteel, Mong. 78/C2
Altar (vol.), Ecu. 180/B5
Altar, Mex. 174/C2
Altar de los Sacrificios (ruin), Guat. 176/D2
Altar Wash (riv.), Az, US 149/G5
Altare, It. 62/B5
Altario, Ab, Can. 145/J2
Altavilla Irpina, It. 65/D6
Altavilla Vicentina, It. 63/E2
Altavista, Va, US 163/H2
Altay, China 99/E2
Altay, Mong. 78/D2
Altay, Mong. 78/B2
Altay Resp., Rus. 74/J4
Altayskiy Kray, Rus. 99/C1
Altdorf, Swi. 61/E4
Altdorf bei Nürnberg, Ger. 59/E4
Altea, Sp. 47/E3
Altedo, It. 63/E4
Altena, Ger. 53/E6
Altenahr, Ger. 55/G2
Altenau (riv.), Ger. 53/F5
Altenau, Ger. 53/H5
Altenbeken, Ger. 53/F5
Altenberg bei Linz, Aus. 59/H6
Altenburg, Ger. 42/G3
Altenburg, Mo, US 162/C2
Altenfelden, Aus. 59/G6
Altenglan, Ger. 55/G4
Altengottern, Ger. 53/H6
Altenkirchen, Ger. 55/G2
Altenmarkt an der Triesting, Aus. 51/N7
Altenmünster, Ger. 58/D6
Altenstadt, Ger. 61/G2
Altenstadt, Ger. 61/G1
Altenstadt, Ger. 58/B2
Altensteig, Ger. 58/B5
Altentreptow, Ger. 40/E5
Altepexi, Mex. 175/M8
Alter do Chão, Braz. 182/C3
Alter Rhein (riv.), Ger. 52/D5
Altes Land (phys. reg.), Ger. 53/G1
Altha, Fl, US 165/F2
Altheim, Aus. 59/G6
Altheim, Ger. 61/F1
Altheimer, Ar, US 153/J3
Althengstett, Ger. 58/B5
Althofen, Aus. 45/L3
Althorpe, Eng, UK 35/H4
Althütte, Ger. 58/C5
Alticane, Sk, Can. 145/L1
Altındere NP, Turk. 70/F4
Altınözü, Turk. 104/E1
Altıntaş, Turk. 102/B2
Altınyaka, Turk. 104/B1
Altınyayla, Turk. 102/B2
Altiplanicie del Payón (rocks), Arg. 190/C3
Altiplano (plat.), Bol.,Peru 179/C4
Altiplano (plat.), Peru 185/D4
Altkirch, Fr. 60/D2
Altlandsberg, Ger. 42/Q6
Altmark (phys. reg.), Ger. 42/F2
Altmühl (riv.), Ger. 45/J2
Altmünster, Aus. 59/G7
Altnaharra, Sc, UK 31/R7
Alto (peak), It. 61/G4
Alto, La, US 153/J4
Alto (peak), Braz. 186/D2
Alto, Tx, US 150/G2
Alto (mtn.), Tx, US 150/B2
Alto Araguaia, Braz. 186/B3
Alto Chicapa, Ang. 120/D5
Alto Cuale, Ang. 120/D4
Alto Cuilo, Ang. 120/D5
Alto de la Sierra, Arg. 188/D2
Alto de Tamar (peak), Col. 180/C3
Alto del Carmen, Chile 188/B4
Alto Garças, Braz. 186/B3
Alto Longá, Braz. 183/F4
Alto Lucero, Mex. 175/N7
Alto Molócuè, Moz. 123/H2
Alto Paraguai, Braz. 185/G4
Alto Paraguay (dept.), Par. 186/A4
Alto Paraná (dept.), Par. 189/F3
Alto Parnaíba, Braz. 183/E5
Alto Pass, Il, US 162/C2
Alto Pencoso, Arg. 190/D2
Alto Purús (riv.), Peru 184/D3
Alto Santo, Braz. 183/G4
Alto Seco, Bol. 188/C1
Alto Yuruá (riv.), Peru 184/C3
Altomünster, Ger. 58/E6
Alton, Eng, UK 37/F4
Alton, Il, US 155/J4
Alton, Ia, US 155/F2
Alton, Mo, US 153/J2
Alton, Ut, US 149/F2
Alton Downs, Austl. 131/H3
Altona, Mb, Can. 156/F3
Altona, Ger. 53/G1
Altona (nbrhd.), Austl. 132/F5
Altônia, Braz. 189/F2
Altoona, Ia, US 155/H3
Altoona, Pa, US 161/G4
Altopascio, It. 63/D6
Altos, Braz. 183/F4
Altos de Camapana NP, Pan. 180/B2
Altotonga, Mex. 175/M7
Altötting, Ger. 59/F6
Altrincham, Eng, UK 35/F5
Altrip, Ger. 58/B4
Altukhovo, Rus. 70/E1
Altun (mts.), China 77/H6
Altun Ha (ruin), Belz. 176/D2
Alturas, Ca, US 146/C3
Alturas, Fl, US 164/M8
Altus (A.F.B.), Ok, US 152/E3
Altus, Ok, US 152/E3
Altykarasu, Kaz. 71/K2
Altynivka, Ukr. 73/G2
Altynkul', Uzb. 71/L4
Altzayanca, Mex. 175/M7
Alucra, Turk. 102/D1
Aluk, Sudan 117/E3
Alūksne, Lat. 41/M3
Alum Fork (riv.), Ar, US 153/H3
Aluminé, Arg. 190/C3
Alunda, Swe. 40/H1
Alupka, Ukr. 70/E3
Ālūs, Iraq 102/E3
Alushta, Ukr. 73/H5
Aluta, D.R. Congo 121/F3
Alva, Ok, US 153/E2
Alva, Sc, UK 33/C4
Alva, Fl, US 165/H4
Alvalade, Port. 46/A4
Alvaneu-Bad, Swi. 61/F4
Älvängen, Swe. 40/E3
Alvarado, Mn, US 156/F3
Alvarado, Col. 183/L8
Alvarado, Mex. 175/P8
Alvarado, Tx, US 150/K7
Álvares Machado, Braz. 189/G2
Álvarez, Arg. 190/E2
Alvaro Obregón, Presa (dam), Mex. 174/C2
Alvdal, Nor. 38/D3
Älvdalen, Swe. 40/F1
Alvear, Arg. 189/E4
Alvechurch, Eng, UK 37/E2
Alverca, Port. 47/P10
Alveringem, Belg. 54/B1
Alvesta, Swe. 40/F3
Alviano (lake), It. 65/B2
Alvignano, It. 65/D5
Ålvik, Nor. 40/B1
Alvin, BC, Can. 144/C3
Alvin, Tx, US 151/M9
Alvin, Wi, US 157/K5
Alvinston, On, Can. 160/F3
Alvito, Port. 46/B3
Älvkarleby, Swe. 40/G1
Alvorada, Braz. 189/F4
Alvorada, Braz. 186/C2
Alvorada do Norte, Braz. 186/D2
Alvord, Tx, US 153/F4
Alvord (des.), Or, US 146/D2
Älvsborg (co.), Swe. 38/E4
Älvsbyn, Swe. 38/G2
Älvsjö, Swe. 39/B1
Alwen (riv.), Wal, UK 34/E5
Alxa Youqi, China 78/E4
Alxa Zuoqi, China 78/F4
Alyangula, Austl. 129/E3
Alyawarra Abor. Land, Austl. 131/G2
Alyth, Sc, UK 33/C3
Alytus, Lith. 41/L4
Alz (riv.), Aus. 50/A1
Alz (riv.), Ger. 42/G4
Alzada, Mt, US 154/B1
Alzano Lombardo, It. 62/C2
Alzenau in Unterfranken, Ger. 58/C2
Alzette (riv.), Lux. 55/F4
Alzey, Ger. 58/B3
Am Dam, Chad 116/D2
Am Djéména, Chad 116/C2
Am Timan, Chad 116/D3
Am Zoer, Chad 116/D2
Ama, PNG 91/K4
Amacayacú NP, Col. 184/D1
Amacuro (delta), Ven. 181/F2
Amacuro (riv.), Ven. 181/F2
Amacuzac (riv.), Mex. 175/K8
Amada Gaza, CAfr. 116/B4
Amadeus (lake), Austl. 127/C3
Āmādi, Bang. 97/G4
Amadi, Sudan 117/F4
Amadjuak (lake), Nun, Can. 141/J2
Amado, Az, US 149/G5
Amadora, Port. 47/P10
Amagá, Col. 183/K6
Amagansett, NY, US 169/F2
Amagansett Nat'l Wild. Ref., NY, US 169/F2
Amagasaki, Japan 83/H6
Amager (isl.), Den. 39/J7
Amagi, Japan 84/B4
Amagi-san (peak), Japan 85/F3
Amagon, Ar, US 153/J3
Amaguaña, Ecu. 180/B5
Amahai, Indo. 91/G4
Amajac (riv.), Mex. 175/N7
Amakusa (sea), Japan 79/K5
Åmål, Swe. 40/E2
Amala (riv.), Kenya 119/A2
Amalat (riv.), Rus. 78/G1
Amalfi, It. 65/D6
Amalfi, Col. 180/C3
Amalga, Ut, US 147/H3
Amalia, SAfr. 124/D2
Amaliás, Gre. 49/G4
Amalner, India 95/B1
Amaluza, Ecu. 184/B2
Amamapare, Indo. 91/J4
Amambaí, Braz. 189/F2
Amambaí (riv.), Braz. 186/B4
Amambay (dept.), Par. 186/A4
Amambay (dept.), Braz. 189/F2
Amambay, Serra (mts.), Braz.,Par. 189/F2
Amami (isls.), Japan 77/M7
Amami-O-Shima (isl.), Japan 85/K6
Amamula, D.R. Congo 121/F3
Amanã (lake), Braz. 181/E5
Amanab, PNG 91/K4
Amanbidji Abor. Land, Austl. 128/C4
Amance, Fr. 60/C2
Amanda Park, Wa, US 144/C4
Amandola, It. 65/C2
Amānganj, India 96/C3
Amāngarh, Pak. 98/A2
Amantea, It. 48/E3
Amanu (isl.), FrPol. 137/L6
Amanzimtoti, SAfr. 125/E3
Amapá, Braz. 182/D2
Amapá (state), Braz. 181/H4
Amarante, Braz. 183/F4
Amarante, Port. 46/A2
Amarante do Marahão, Braz. 183/E4
Amaranth, Mb, Can. 156/E2
Amarapura, Myan. 86/C4
Amareleja, Port. 46/B3
Amarete, Bol. 184/D4
Amargosa (range), Ca, US 148/D2
Amargosa (riv.), Ca,Nv, US 148/D2
Amargosa (des.), Nv, US 148/D2
Amargosa, Braz. 187/F2
Amarillo, Tx, US 152/D3
Amarkantak, India 96/C4
Amaro (peak), It. 65/D3
Amarpātan, India 96/C3
Amarume, Japan 82/A4
Amarwāra, India 96/B4
Amaseno (riv.), It. 65/C5
Amasra, Turk. 51/L5
Amasya, Turk. 70/E4
Amasya (prov.), Turk. 70/E4
Amata, Austl. 131/F3
Amatlán de Cañas, Mex. 174/D4
Amatrice, It. 65/C2
Amatsukominato, Japan 83/E3
Amawalk (res.), NY, US 169/E1
Amay, Belg. 55/E2
Amayuca, Mex. 175/L8
Amazar, Rus. 79/J1
Amazon (riv.), Braz. 179/C3
Amazon (Amazonas) (riv.), Braz. 179/C3
Amazonas, Cuba 177/G1
Amazonas (state), Braz. 180/C5
Amazonas (state), Ven. 181/E3
Amazonas (Amazon) (riv.), Braz. 179/C3
Amazônia (Tapajós), PN de, Braz. 185/G2
Amb, Pak. 98/B2
Āmba Gīyorgīs, Eth. 117/H2
Āmba Maryam, Eth. 118/A3
Ambāh, India 96/B2
Ambahikily, Madg. 125/G8
Ambajogai, India 95/C2
Ambāla, India 98/D4
Ambāla Sadar, India 98/D4
Ambalajanakomby, Madg. 125/H7
Ambalangoda, SrL. 95/D5
Ambalarondra, Madg. 125/J7
Ambalavao, Madg. 125/H8
Ambalema, Col. 183/L8
Ambam, Camr. 120/B2
Ambanja, Madg. 125/J6
Ambarnyy, Rus. 68/G2
Ambaro (bay), Madg. 125/J6
Āmbāsa, India 97/H4
Ambato, Ecu. 180/B5
Ambato Boeny, Madg. 125/H7
Ambatofinandrahana, Madg. 125/H8
Ambatolahy, Madg. 125/H8
Ambatolampy, Madg. 125/H7
Ambatomaidy, Madg. 125/H7
Ambatomanoina, Madg. 125/H7
Ambatondrazaka, Madg. 125/J7
Ambazac, Fr. 44/D4
Ámbelos (cape), Gre. 49/H3
Amber, Ok, US 153/F3
Amberg, Wi, US 157/L5
Amberg, Ger. 59/E4
Ambergate, Eng, UK 35/G5
Ambergris Cay (isl.), Belz. 176/E2
Ambérieu-en-Bugey, Fr. 60/B6
Amberley, NZ 135/C3
Amberloup, Belg. 55/E3
Ambidédi, Mali 114/C3
Ambikāpur, India 96/D4
Ambilobe, Madg. 125/J6
Ambinanindrano, Madg. 125/J8
Ambinanitelo, Madg. 125/J6
Ambinanynony, Madg. 125/J7
Ambla, Est. 41/L2
Amble, Eng, UK 33/E6
Ambler, Ak, US 171/G2
Ambler, Pa, US 168/C3
Ambleside, Eng, UK 35/F3
Amblève, Belg. 55/F3
Amblève (riv.), Belg. 42/C3
Ambo, Peru 184/B3
Amboasary, Madg. 125/H9
Amboavory, Madg. 125/J7
Ambodifototra, Madg. 125/J7
Ambodiharina, Madg. 125/J8
Ambodriana, Madg. 125/J7
Ambohidratrimo, Madg. 125/H7
Ambohijanahary, Madg. 125/J7
Ambohimahasoa, Madg. 125/H8
Ambohimahavelona, Madg. 125/G8
Ambohimandroso, Madg. 125/H7
Ambohimilanja, Madg. 125/H7
Ambohinihaonana, Madg. 125/H8
Ambohitsilaozana, Madg. 125/J7
Amboise, Fr. 57/F6
Ambolomoty, Madg. 125/H7
Ambon, Indo. 91/G4
Ambondro, Madg. 125/H9
Amboni Caves, Tanz. 119/B3
Amborompotsy, Madg. 125/H8
Amboseli NP, Kenya 119/B2
Ambositra, Madg. 125/H8
Ambouli (int'l arpt.), Djib. 118/B3
Ambovombe, Madg. 125/H9
Amboy, Ca, US 148/E3
Amboy, Mn, US 155/G2
Amboy, Il, US 155/K3
Amboy, Wa, US 144/C5
Ambrières-le-Grand, Fr. 57/E4
Ambriz, Ang. 120/C4
Ambrolauri, Geo. 71/G4
Ambrose, Ga, US 165/G2
Ambrym (isl.), Van. 136/F6
Ambuntentimur, Indo. 89/F4
Amchitka (isl.), Ak, US 75/T4
Amchitka Pass (str.), Ak, US 171/B6
'Amd, Yem. 118/C2
Amdasa, Indo. 128/C1
Amealco, Mex. 175/K6
Ameca, Mex. 174/D4
Amecameca de Juárez, Mex. 175/R10
Ameghino, Arg. 190/E2
Ameglia, It. 62/C5
Ameisberg (peak), Aus. 59/G5
Ameland (isl.), Neth. 52/C2
Amelia (isl.), Fl, US 165/H2
Amelia, It. 65/B2
Amelia City, Fl, US 165/H2
Amelia Court House, Va, US 163/J2
Ameliasburg, On, Can. 161/H2
Amelinghausen, Ger. 53/H2
Amenia, ND, US 156/F4
Amer (chan.), Neth. 52/B5
American (riv.), Ca, US 167/M9
American (lake), Wa, US 167/B3
American Bolder (peak), Wa, US 144/D3
American College, It. 65/G8
American Falls, Id, US 147/G2
American Falls (dam), Id, US 147/G2
American Falls (res.), Id, US 147/G2
American Fork, Ut, US 147/H3
American Highland (rocks), Ant. 192/F
American Samoa (terr.), US 137/T10
American, South Fork (riv.), Ca, US 146/C4
American, South Fork (riv.), Ca, US 149/J1
American, North Fork (riv.), Ca, US 146/C4
Americana, Braz. 189/H2
Americus, Ga, US 165/F1
Americus, Ks, US 153/F1
Americus, Mo, US 155/J4
Ameringkogel (peak), Aus. 45/L3
Amersfoort, Neth. 52/C4
Amersfoort, SAfr. 125/E2
Amersham, Eng, UK 37/F3
Amery, Wi, US 157/H5
Amery Ice Shelf, Ant. 192/E
Ames, Ks, US 154/F4
Ames, Ia, US 155/H2
Ames, Tx, US 151/N8
Amesbury, Eng, UK 37/E4
Amesbury, Ma, US 161/L3
Amet, India 92/B2
Amethi, India 96/C2
Āmeya, Eth. 117/H4
Amfíklia, Gre. 49/H3
Amfilokhía, Gre. 49/G3
Ámfissa, Gre. 49/H3
Amga (riv.), Rus. 75/N3
Amguema (riv.), Rus. 75/T3
Amguid, Alg. 111/G4
Amgun' (riv.), Rus. 75/P4
Amgun' (riv.), Rus. 79/M1
Amherst, NS, Can. 158/E3
Amherst, Wi, US 157/K5
Amherst (isl.), Qu, Can. 159/F2
Amherst, Ma, US 161/K3
Amherst, NY, US 160/V10
Amherst, Va, US 163/H2
Amherstburg, On, Can. 167/F7
Amherstdale-Robinette, WV, US 163/G2
Amhurst (mt.), Austl. 128/B4
Ami, Japan 83/E1
Amiata (peak), It. 48/B1
Amidon, ND, US 156/C4
Amiens, Fr. 54/B4
Amik (lake), Turk 104/E1
Amila (isl.), Ak, US 75/U4
Amilcar Cabral (int'l arpt.), CpV. 107/K10
Amillis, Fr. 30/M5
Amíndaion, Gre. 49/G2
Aminius, Namb. 122/C4
Aminu Kano (int'l arpt.), Nga. 115/H3
Amistad (dam), Tx, US 150/D3
Amistad (int'l. res), Mex.,US 150/D3
Amistad Nat'l Rec. Area, Tx, US 150/D3
Amite, La, US 164/C2
Amite (cr.), La, US 164/C2
Amity (canal), Co, US 152/C1
Amity, Ar, US 153/H3
Amity, Or, US 146/B1
Amityville, NY, US 169/M9
Amla, India 96/B5
Āmlāgora, India 97/F4
Amlash, Iran 103/G2
Amlekhganj, Nepal 97/E2
Åmli, Nor. 40/C2
Amlia (isl.), Ak, US 171/D6
Amlwch, Wal, UK 34/D5
'Ammān (gov.), Jor. 104/E4
Amman (riv.), Wal, UK 36/C3
'Ammān (Amman) (cap.), Jor. 100/C2
Amman ('Ammān) (cap.), Jor. 105/D5
Ammanford, Wal, UK 36/C3
Ammannsville, Tx, US 151/F3
Ammarfjället (peak), Swe. 38/E2
Ammassalik, Grld 192/J
Ammer (riv.), Ger. 58/B5
Ammersee (lake), Ger. 45/J3
Ammon, Id, US 147/H2
Amnat Charoen, Thai. 94/D3
Amnéville, Fr. 55/F5
Amo (riv.), China 86/D4
Āmol, Iran 103/H2
Amora, Port. 47/P10
Amorbach, Ger. 58/C3
Amorgós, Gre. 49/J4
Amorgós (isl.), Gre. 67/K3
Amorinópolis, Braz. 186/C3
Amory, Ms, US 162/C4
Amos, Qu, Can. 141/J4
Åmose (riv.), Den. 39/H7
Åmot, Nor. 40/B2
Amotfors, Swe. 40/E2
Amourj, Mrta. 114/D2
Amozoc, Mex. 175/L7
Ampachi, Japan 83/L5
Ampana, Indo. 91/F4
Ampanavoana, Madg. 125/J6
Ampanefena, Madg. 125/J6
Ampangalana (canal), Madg. 125/J8
Ampanihy, Madg. 125/H9
Amparafaravola, Madg. 125/J7
Amparai, SrL. 95/D5
Amparo, Braz. 187/K7
Ampasimanjeva, Madg. 125/J8
Ampasimanolotra, Madg. 125/J7
Ampasindava (bay), Madg. 125/H6
Ampato (peak), Peru 184/D4
Ampefy, Madg. 125/H7
Amper, Nga. 115/H4
Amper (riv.), Ger. 59/E6
Ampfing, Ger. 59/F6
Ampflwang im Hausruckwald, Aus. 59/G6
Amphitrite Group (isls.), Asia 87/G5
Ampibako, Indo. 91/F4
Ampisikinana, Madg. 125/J6
Ampitatafika, Madg. 125/H7
Ampombiantambo, Madg. 125/J6
Amposta, Sp. 47/F2
Ampthill, Eng, UK 37/F2
Ampuis, Fr. 64/A2
Amqui, Qu, Can. 158/D1
'Amrān, Yem. 118/B2
Amrāpāra, India 97/F3
Amreli, India 101/K4
Amring, India 86/B3
'Amrīt (ruin), Syria 104/D2
Amritsar, India 98/C4
Amroha, India 96/B1
Amrūka, Pak. 98/B4
Amstel (riv.), Neth. 52/B4
Amstelveen, Neth. 52/B4
Amsterdam (isl.), Fr. 27/N7
Amsterdam, Ga, US 165/F2
Amsterdam, NY, US 161/J3
Amsterdam (cap.), Neth. 52/B4
Amsterdam, SAfr. 125/E2
Amsterdam (Schipol) (int'l arpt.), Neth. 52/B4
Amsterdam Rijnkan. (riv.), Neth. 52/C4
Amstetten, Aus. 45/L2
Āmtali, Bang. 97/H4
Amtkel, Geo. 71/G4
Amu Darya (riv.), Asia 77/F8
Amu Darya (riv.), Uzb. 71/L4
Amu Darya (riv.), Trkm. 74/G5
Amu-Dar'ya, Trkm. 74/G6
Amudālavalasa, India 95/D2
Amudar'ya (riv.), Trkm. 101/J1
Amudat, Ugan. 119/A1
Amukta Pass (str.), Ak, US 171/D5
Amuku (mts.), Guy. 181/G4
Amund Ringnes (isl.), Nun, Can. 141/S7
Amundsen (sea), Ant. 192/S
Amundsen (bay), Ant. 192/D
Amundsen (gulf), NW, Can. 140/D1
Amundsen-Scott, US, Ant. 192/A
Amunge (lake), Swe. 40/F1
Amur (riv.), Asia 77/M4
`Amūr (wadi), Sudan 109/G5
`Amur (wadi), Sudan 100/B5
Amur (Heilong) (riv.), China, Rus. 75/N4
Amur (Heilong) (riv.), China,Rus 79/J1
Amuri, NZ 137/K6
Amurrio, Sp. 44/B5
Amursk, Rus. 79/M1
Amurskaya Oblast, Rus. 75/N4
Amvrosiyivka, Ukr. 73/K4
Amyūn, Leb. 104/D2
An Khe, Viet. 94/E3
An Nabaţīyah at Taḩtā, Leb. 105/C2
An Nabī Shīt, Leb. 105/E1
An Nafīḑah, Tun. 48/B4
An Nafūd (des.), SAr. 109/H2
An Nahūd, Sudan 117/F2
An Najaf, Iraq 103/F4
An Najaf (gov.), Iraq 103/E4
An Nāqūrah, Leb. 105/C2
An Nāşirīyah, Iraq 103/F4
An Nawfalīyah, Libya 108/C2
An Nazlat, Egypt 113/B6
An Nhon, Viet. 94/E3
An Nu'manīyah, Iraq 103/F3
An Phuoc, Viet. 94/E4
An Teallach (peak), Sc, UK 33/A1
An Uaimh, Ire. 32/D2
Ana María (gulf), Cuba 173/F3
Anaa (isl.), FrPol. 137/L6
Anabar (riv.), Rus. 75/L3
'Anabtā, WBnk. 105/C4
Anacapa (isl.), Ca, US 148/C4
Anacapri, It. 65/D6
Anachucuna (mtn.), Pan. 180/B2
Anaco, Ven. 181/E2
Anacoco, La, US 164/B2
Anaconda (range), Mt, US 145/H5
Anaconda-Deer Lodge County, Mt, US 145/H4
Anacortes, Wa, US 144/C3
Anadarko, Ok, US 153/E3
Anadia, Port. 46/A2
Anadyr', Rus. 75/T3
Anadyr' (riv.), Rus. 75/T3
Anadyr' (gulf), Rus. 75/U3
Anadyr' (range), Rus. 75/S3
Anáfi (isl.), Gre. 49/J4
Anafi (isl.), Gre. 67/K3
Anagni, It. 65/C4
'Ānah, Iraq 102/E3
Anaheim, Ca, US 166/G8
Anaheim Stadium, Ca, US 166/G8
Anahidrano, Madg. 125/H6
Anahim Lake, BC, Can. 144/B1
Anahim's Flat Ind. Res., BC, Can. 144/C1
Anáhuac, Mex. 177/D4
Anahuac, Tx, US 151/N9
Anahuac (lake), Tx, US 151/N9
Anahuac, Mex. 174/D2
Anahuac NWR, Tx, US 151/G3
Anai Mudi (peak), India 95/C4
Anajatuba, Braz. 183/E3
Anak, NKor. 81/C3
Anakāpalle, India 95/D2
Anaktuvuk Pass, Ak, US 171/H2
Analalava, Madg. 125/H6
Analamaitso (plat.), Madg. 125/J7
Analavory, Madg. 125/H7
Anambas (isls.), Indo. 90/C3
Anambra (state), Nga. 115/G5
Anamoose, ND, US 156/D4
Anamosa, Ia, US 155/J2
Anamur, Turk. 104/C1
Anamur (pt.), Turk. 104/C1
Anan, Japan 84/D4
Ananás, Braz. 182/D4
Anand, India 92/B3
Ananda Temple, Myan. 86/B4
Anandgarh, India 98/B5
Anandpur, India 98/D4
Anandpur, India 95/E1
Ananea, Bol. 184/D4
Ananea, Peru 184/D4
Anantapur, India 95/C3
Anantnag, India 98/C3
Anan'yevo, Kyr. 99/C3
Anan'yiv, Ukr. 72/E4
Anapa, Rus. 73/J5
Añapi (peak), Arg. 191/C6
Anápolis, Braz. 186/C3
Anapskaya, Rus. 73/J5
Anapu (riv.), Braz. 182/D3
Anār, Iran 103/H4
Anārak, Iran 103/H3
Anastasia (isl.), Fl, US 165/H3
Anastasiyevka, Rus. 73/K4
'Anātā, WBnk. 105/C5
Anathan (isl.), NMar. 136/D3
Anatolia (reg.), Turk. 70/D5
Añatuya, Arg. 188/D4
Anauá (riv.), Braz. 181/F4
Anbo, China 81/B3
Anbu, China 87/H4
Anbyŏn, NKor. 81/D3
Ancash (dept.), Peru 184/B3
Ancaster, On, Can. 160/T9
Ancenis, Fr. 57/D6
Anchangzhen, China 87/E2
Anchau, Nga. 115/H4
Anchieta, Braz. 187/E4
Anchor (bay), Mi, US 167/G6
Anchorage, Ak, US 171/J3
Anchorena, Arg. 190/D2
Anchor Point, Ak, US 171/H4
Anchorville, Mi, US 167/G6
Anchovy, Jam. 177/G2
Ancient Bristlecone Pine Forest, Ca, US 148/C2
Ancient City of Oc-Eo, Viet. 94/D4
Anclote (riv.), Fl, US 164/K7
Anclote, Fl, US 164/K7
Anclote Keys (isl.), Fl, US 164/K7
Ancoeur (riv.), Fr. 30/L6
Ancohuma (peak), Bol. 184/D4
Ancón, Peru 184/B3
Ancón de Sardinas (bay), Col. 180/B4
Ancona, It. 63/G6
Ancona (prov.), It. 63/G5
Ancoraimes, Bol. 184/D4
Ancre (riv.), Fr. 54/B3
Ancroft, Eng, UK 33/E5
Ancrum, Sc, UK 33/D5
Ancud, Chile 190/B4
Ancud (gulf), Chile 190/B4
Anda, China 79/K2
Andacollo, Arg. 190/C3
Andacollo, Chile 188/B4
Andado, Austl. 131/G3
Andagua, Peru 184/C4
Andahuaylas, Peru 184/C4
Andaingo Gara, Madg. 125/J7
Andāl, India 97/F4
Andalgalá, Arg. 188/C3
Åndalsnes, Nor. 38/C3
Andalusia, Al, US 165/E2
Andalusia (reg.), Sp. 66/B3
Andalusia, Il, US 155/J3
Andaman (sea), Asia 77/J8
Andaman (isls.), India 77/H8
Andaman and Nicobar (isls.), India 93/F5
Andaman, South (isl.), India 93/F5
Andamarca, Bol. 188/C1
Andamarca, Peru 184/C3
Andamooka, Austl. 131/H4
Andapa, Madg. 125/J6
Andara, Namb. 122/D3
Andaraí, Braz. 187/E2
Andau, Aus. 50/C2
Ande, China 94/D1
Andebu, Nor. 40/D2
Andechs, Ger. 61/H2
Andeer, Swi. 61/F4
Andelfingen, Swi. 61/E2
Andelle (riv.), Fr. 54/A5
Andelot-Blancheville, Fr. 60/B1
Andelsbach (riv.), Ger. 61/F2
Andelu, Fr. 30/H5
Andemaka, Madg. 125/H8
Andenne, Belg. 55/E3
Anderlues, Belg. 55/D3
Andermatt, Swi. 61/E4
Andernach, Ger. 55/G3
Anderson, Ak, US 171/J3
Anderson, Mo, US 153/G2
Anderson, In, US 160/D4
Anderson (isl.), Wa, US 167/B3
Anderson (inlet), Wa, US 167/B3
Anderson, Ca, US 146/B3
Anderson (riv.), NW, Can. 140/D2
Anderson, SC, US 163/F3
Anderson, Tx, US 151/G2
Anderson Ranch (res.), Id, US 147/F2
Anderson Ranch (dam), Id, US 146/F2
Andersonville, Ga, US 162/E4
Andersonville Nat'l Hist. Site, Ga, US 162/E4
Andes, Mt, US 156/B4
Andes (mts.), SAm. 179/C5
Andes, Col. 183/K7
Andevoranto, Madg. 125/J7
Andfjorden (chan.), Nor. 38/F1
Andhra Pradesh (state), India 92/C4
Andijk, Neth. 52/C3
Andijon, Uzb. 99/B3
Andikíthira (isl.), Gre. 67/J4
Andilamena, Madg. 125/J7
Andilanatoby, Madg. 125/J7
Andīmeshk, Iran 103/G3
Andíparos (isl.), Gre. 49/J4
Andira (riv.), Braz. 185/G1
Andira, Braz. 186/C4
Ándissa, Gre. 49/J3
Andoain, Sp. 44/B5
Andoany, Madg. 125/J6
Andoas, Peru 180/B5
Andohajango, Madg. 125/J6
Andong, SKor. 84/A2
Andong, China 80/L9
Andorf, Aus. 59/G6
Andorno Micca, It. 62/B2
Andorra, Sp. 47/E2
Andorra (ctry.) 47/F1
Andorra la Vella (cap.), And. 47/F1
Andover, Eng, UK 37/E4
Andover, Ks, US 153/F2
Andover, Me, US 161/L2
Andover, Mn, US 157/P6
Andover, NJ, US 168/D2
Andover, Oh, US 160/F4
Andøy, Nor. 38/F1
Andøya (isl.), Nor. 38/E1
Andradas, Braz. 187/K7
Andradina, Braz. 189/G2
Andrafainkona, Madg. 125/J6
Andraitx, Sp. 47/G3
Andramasina, Madg. 125/H7
Andranolalina, Madg. 125/H8
Andranolava, Madg. 125/H8
Andranomavo (riv.), Madg. 125/H7
Andranopasy, Madg. 125/G8
Andranovondrona, Madg. 125/J6
Andranovory, Madg. 125/H8
André Félix, PN, CAfr. 116/D3
Andreanof (isls.), Ak, US 171/C5
Andrelândia, Braz. 187/M6
Andrespol, Pol. 43/K3
Andrésy, Fr. 30/J5
Andrew Johnson Nat'l Hist. Site, Tn, US 163/F2
Andrews, NC, US 162/F3
Andrews, Or, US 146/D2
Andrews, Tx, US 150/C1
Andrews (A.F.B.), Md, US 168/B6
Andrews, SC, US 163/H4
Andreyevka, Rus. 71/K1
Andrezel, Fr. 30/L6
Andria, It. 48/E2
Andriamena, Madg. 125/H7
Andriandampy, Madg. 125/H8
Andriba, Madg. 125/H7
Andringitra (mts.), Madg. 125/H8
Andrítsaina, Gre. 49/G4
Andriyivka, Ukr. 73/J4
Androka, Madg. 125/H9
Androntany (cape), Madg. 125/J6
Ándros, Gre. 49/J4
Ándros (isl.), Gre. 67/K3
Andros (isl.), Bahm. 139/K7
Androscoggin (riv.), Me, US 158/B3
Androscoggin (riv.), NH, US 161/L2
Andrushivka, Ukr. 72/E2
Andújar, Sp. 46/C3
Āndulbāria, Bang. 97/G4
Andulo, Ang. 122/C1
Andytown, Fl, US 164/P10
Aneby, Swe. 40/F3
Anecón Grande (peak), Arg. 190/C4
Anefis I-n-Darane, Mali 115/F2
Anegada (isl.), UK 173/J4
Anegada (bay), Arg. 190/E4
Anegada Passage (chan), NAm. 173/J4
Aného, Togo 115/F5
Aneityum (isl.), Van. 136/F7
Añelo, Arg. 190/C3
Aneroid, Sk, Can. 145/L3
Anet, Fr. 57/G3
Aneta, ND, US 156/F4
Aneth, Ut, US 149/H2
Aneto, Pico de (peak), Sp. 47/F1
Aney, Niger 108/B5
Anfu, China 93/K2
Ang Mo Kio (nbrhd.), Sing. 89/J6
Ang Nam Ngum (lake), Laos 93/H4
Ang Thong, Thai. 94/C3
Angads (Oujda) (int'l arpt.), Mor. 112/D2
Angamma, Falaise d' (cliff), Chad 116/C1
Angamos (pt.), Chile 188/B2
Angara (riv.), Rus. 77/J4
Angarn, Swe. 39/B1
Angarsk, Rus. 78/E1
Angas Downs, Austl. 131/G3
Angaston, Austl. 131/H5
Angatuba, Braz. 189/G2
Angel (riv.), Ger. 53/E5
Ángel (falls), Ven. 181/F3
Ángel de la Guarda (isl.), Mex. 174/B2
Angela, Mt, US 145/L4
Angèle, Montagne d' (peak), Fr. 64/B4
Angeles, Phil. 88/C2
Angeles National Forest, Ca, US 166/B1
Angeles Nat'l Forest, Ca, US 166/F7
Ängelholm, Swe. 40/E3
Angelholm (int'l arpt.), Swe. 40/E3
Ängelholm, Den. 39/J6
Angelica, Wi, US 160/B2
Angelim, Braz. 183/G5
Angelina (riv.), Tx, US 151/G2
Angeln (reg.), Ger. 42/E1
Angelus (lake), Mi, US 167/F6
Angelus Oaks (Camp Angelus), Ca, US 166/D2
Angera, It. 62/B2
Ångermanalven (riv.), Swe. 38/E2
Angermünde, Ger. 43/H2
Angers, Fr. 57/E6
Angerville, Fr. 57/H4
Anghiari, It. 63/F6
Angical do Piauí, Braz. 183/F4
Angicos, Braz. 183/G4
Angie, La, US 164/D2
Angier, NC, US 163/H3
Angk Tasaom, Camb. 94/D4
Angkor (ruin), Camb. 94/C3
Anglais (bay), Qu, Can. 158/C1
Angle Inlet, Mn, US 157/G3
Angleine (riv.), Fr. 57/E4
Anglem (mt.), NZ 135/A4
Anglès, Sp. 47/G2
Anglesea, Austl. 133/B4
Anglesey (isl.), Wal, UK 34/D5
Anglet, Fr. 44/C5
Angleton, Tx, US 150/G3
Anglin (riv.), Fr. 44/D3
Ango, D.R. Congo 121/F1
Angoche, Moz. 123/H3
Angohrān, Iran 101/G3
Angol, Chile 190/B3
Angola, In, US 160/D4
Angola, NY, US 161/G3
Angola, La, US 164/C2
Angola (ctry.) 107/D6
Angoon, Ak, US 171/M4
Angostura (res.), Mex. 172/C4
Angostura (res.), SD, US 154/C2
Angostura (dam), SD, US 154/C2
Angostura, Mex. 174/C3
Angoulême, Fr. 44/D4
Angra do Heroísmo, Azor., Port. 47/S12
Angra dos Reis, Braz. 187/M7
Angren, Uzb. 99/B3
Angri, It. 65/D6
Ängsö NP, Swe. 39/B1
Ängsön (isl.), Swe. 39/B1
Angu, D.R. Congo 121/F2
Anguilla, Ms, US 162/B4
Anguilla (isl.), UK 173/N8
Anguillara Sabazia, It. 65/B3
Anguillara Veneta, It. 63/E3
Anguille (mts.), Nf, Can. 159/H2
Angul, India 95/E1
Angumu, D.R. Congo 121/F3
Angurugu, Austl. 129/E3
Angus (co.), Sc, UK 33/C3
Angus, Tx, US 151/F1
Angusville, Mb, Can. 156/D2
Angutikada Peak (mt.), Ak, US 171/G2
Angwa (riv.), Zim. 123/F3
Angwin, Ca, US 146/B4
Anhanduí (riv.), Braz. 186/B4
Anhée, Belg. 55/D3
Anholt (isl.), Den. 40/D3
Anhua, China 87/F2
Anhui (prov.), China 78/H5
Ani, Japan 82/B4
Aniak, Ak, US 171/G3
Aniakchak, Ak, US 171/G4
Aniakchak Nat'l Mon. and Preserve, Ak, US 171/G4
Anichab, Namb. 122/B4
Aniche, Fr. 54/C3
Anicuns, Braz. 186/C3
Aniene (riv.), It. 65/B4
Anikhovka, Rus. 71/M2
Anille (riv.), Fr. 57/F5
Animas, NM, US 149/H5
Animas (riv.), Co,NM, US 149/J2
Animas (mts.), NM, US 149/H5
Anin, Myan. 94/B3
Ānīn, WBnk. 105/C3
Anina, Rom. 50/E3
Anita, Ia, US 155/G3
Aniva (bay), Rus. 82/C1
Aniva (sea), Rus. 79/N2
Anivorano, Madg. 125/J7
Anizy-le-Château, Fr. 54/C4
Anjalankoski, Fin. 41/M1
Anjār, India 101/K4
'Anjar, Leb. 105/D1
'Anjarah, Jor. 105/D4
Anjō, Japan 83/M6
Anjou (reg.), Fr. 66/C1
Anjou, Qu, Can. 159/N6
Anjouan (isl.), Com. 125/H6
Anjozorobe, Madg. 125/H7
Anju, NKor. 81/C3
Anju, China 86/E2
Anjum, Neth. 52/D2
Ankang, China 78/F5
Ankara (prov.), Turk. 102/C1
Ankara (cap.), Turk. 102/C2
Ankaramena, Madg. 125/H8
Ankaratra (mass.), Madg. 125/H7
Ankarsrum, Swe. 40/G3
Ankasakasa, Madg. 125/H7
Ankavandra, Madg. 125/H7
Ankazoabo, Madg. 125/H8
Ankazobe, Madg. 125/H7
Ankazomborona, Madg. 125/H7
Ankazomiriotra, Madg. 125/H7
Ankeny, Ia, US 155/H3
Ankeny NWR, Or, US 146/B1
Ankerika, Madg. 125/H6
Ankiliabo, Madg. 125/G8
Ankililioka, Madg. 125/G8
Ankilizato, Madg. 125/H8
Anklam, Ger. 40/E5
Ānkober, Eth. 118/A3
Ankoro, D.R. Congo 121/F4
Ankpa, Nga. 115/G5
Ankum, Ger. 53/E3
Anliu, China 87/G4
Anloga, Gha. 115/F5
Anlong, China 93/J2
Anlong Bouyeizu Miaozu Zizhixian, China 86/E3
Anlong Veng, Camb. 94/D3
Anloo, Neth. 52/D2
Anlu, China 80/C5
Anma (isl.), SKor. 81/D5
Ann Arbor, Mi, US 160/E3
Anna, Tx, US 153/F4
Anna, Rus. 73/L2
Anna, Il, US 162/C2
Anna (lake), Va, US 163/J1
Anna Bay, Austl. 132/E2
Anna Creek, Austl. 131/H4
Anna Maria, Fl, US 165/G4
Anna Pavlowna, Neth. 52/B3
Anna Pink (bay), Chile 190/B5
Anna Plains, Austl. 128/A4
Anna Regina, Guy. 181/G3
Annaba, Alg. 112/K6
Annaba (wilaya), Alg. 112/K6
Annabella, Ut, US 149/F1
Annaberg-Buchholz, Ger. 59/G1
Annaclone, NI, UK 34/B3
Annai, Guy. 181/G4
Annaka, Japan 83/B1
Annalong, NI, UK 34/C3
Annan, Sc, UK 35/E2
Annan (riv.), Sc, UK 33/C6
Annandale, Mn, US 155/G1
Annandale, NJ, US 168/D2
Annandale, Va, US 168/A6
Annapolis, Ca, US 146/B4
Annapolis, Mo, US 153/J2
Annapolis (riv.), NS, Can. 158/E3
Annapolis (cap.), Md, US 168/B6
Annapolis Royal, NS, Can. 158/E3
Annapurna (peak), Nepal 96/D1
Annbank Station, Sc, UK 33/B6
Anne (mt.), Austl. 132/C4
Anne Arundel (co.), Md, US 168/B6
Annean (lake), Austl. 127/A3
Annecy (lake), Fr. 60/C6
Annecy, Fr. 60/C6
Annecy (Meythet) (arpt.), Fr. 60/C6
Annecy-le-Vieux, Fr. 60/C6
Annemasse, Fr. 60/C5
Anner (riv.), Ire. 32/C5
Annet-sur-Marne, Fr. 30/L5
Anneta, Tx, US 150/K7
Annette, Ak, US 171/M4
Anneyron, Fr. 64/A2
Annezin, Fr. 54/B2
Annieopsquatch (mts.), Nf, Can. 159/J1
Anning (riv.), China 86/D3
Anning, China 86/D3
Anniston, Al, US 162/E4
Anniston Army Depot, Al, US 162/D4
Annobón (isl.), EqG. 107/C5
Annonay, Fr. 64/A2
Annot, Fr. 64/C5
Annunziata, It. 65/D5
Annville, Pa, US 168/B3
Annweiler, Ger. 55/G5
Anō, Japan 83/K6
Año Nuevo (pt.), Ca, US 148/A2
Áno Viánnos, Gre. 49/J5
Anoia (riv.), Sp. 47/K7
Anoka, Mn, US 157/P6
Anoka (co.), Mn, US 157/P6
Anola, Mb, Can. 156/F3
Anolaima, Col. 183/L8
Anori, Braz. 185/F1
Anosibe An' Ala, Madg. 125/J7
Ânou-Zeggarene (riv.), Niger 115/G2
Anould, Fr. 60/C1
Anóyia, Gre. 49/J5
Anping, China 81/B2
Anping, China 80/C3
Anping, China 80/H7
Anpu, China 94/E1
Anqing, China 87/H2
Anqiu, China 80/D3
Anren, China 93/K2
Anrhomer (peak), Mor. 110/D3
Anröchte, Ger. 53/F5
Ans, Belg. 55/E2
Ansai, China 80/B3
Ansan, SKor. 81/F7
Anşār, Leb. 105/C2
Ansbach, Ger. 58/D4
Anse Rouge, Haiti 177/H2
Anse-à-Galets, Haiti 177/H2
Anse-d'Hainault, Haiti 177/H2
Anserma, Col. 183/K7
Ansfelden, Aus. 59/H6
Anshan, China 81/B2
Anshun, China 86/E3
Anshunchang, China 86/D2
Ansina, Uru. 189/F4
Ansley, Ne, US 154/E3
Anson (bay), Austl. 128/C3
Anson, Tx, US 150/E1
Ansŏng, SKor. 81/D4
Ansongo, Mali 115/F3
Ansonia, Ct, US 161/K4
Ansted, WV, US 163/G1
Anstruther, Sc, UK 33/D4
Ansus, Indo. 91/J4
Ant (isl.), Micr. 136/E4
Ant (riv.), Eng, UK 37/H1
Anta, Peru 184/C4
Antabamba, Peru 184/C4
Antakya, Turk. 104/E1
Antalaha, Madg. 125/J6
Antalya (gulf), Turk. 104/B1
Antalya (int'l arpt.), Turk. 104/B1
Antalya, Turk. 104/B1
Antalya (prov.), Turk. 102/B2
Antanambao Manampotsy, Madg. 125/J7
Antanambe, Madg. 125/J7
Antananarivo (cap.), Madg. 125/H7
Antananarivo (prov.), Madg. 125/H7
Antanifotsy, Madg. 125/H7
Antanimenabaka, Madg. 125/J7
Antanimieva, Madg. 125/G8

Antani – As Suma

Antanimora, Madg. 125/H9
Antar (peak), Alg. 111/E3
Antarctic (pen.), Ant. 192/W
Antarctic Circle 192/Z
Antarctica (cont.) 192/*
Antaritarika, Madg. 125/H9
Antas, Rio das (riv.), Braz. 189/G4
Antella, It. 63/E6
Antelope, Tx, US 153/E4
Antelope, Mt, US 156/B3
Antelope, Or, US 146/C1
Antelope (isl.), Ut, US 147/G3
Antelope (peak), Mt, US 145/K5
Antelope Center, Ca, US 166/C1
Antelope Mine, Zim. 123/F4
Antenor Navarro, Braz. 183/G4
Antequera, Sp. 46/C4
Antequera, Par. 189/E3
Antero (mt.), Co, US 149/J1
Antes Fort, Pa, US 168/A1
Anthering, Aus. 59/G7
Anthony, Ks, US 153/E2
Anthony, Fl, US 165/G3
Anthony, NM, US 150/A1
Anthony Lagoon, Austl. 129/D4
Anti-Atlas (mts.), Mor. 110/C3
Anti-Lebanon (mts.), Leb. 104/D3
Antibes, Fr. 64/D5
Anticosti, Ile d' (isl.), Qu, Can. 141/K4
Antiesen (riv.), Aus. 59/G6
Antietam Nat'l Bfld., Md, US 161/H5
Antifer (cape), Fr. 57/F1
Antigo, Wi, US 157/K5
Antigonish, NS, Can. 159/G3
Antigua, Sp. 110/B3
Antigua (isl.), Anti. 173/N8
Antigua and Barbuda (ctry.) 173/N8
Antigua Guatemala, Guat. 176/D3
Antiguo Cauce del Río Bermejo (riv.), Arg. 188/D3
Antiguo Morelos, Mex. 175/F4
Antilly, Fr. 30/L4
Anţilyās, Leb. 105/D1
Antimony, Ut, US 149/G1
Anting, China 80/L8
Antioch, Ca, US 146/C4
Antioch, Il, US 160/B3
Antioquia, Col. 180/C3
Antioquia (dept.), Col. 177/H5
Antipina, Rus. 69/N3
Antipodes (isls.), NZ 27/T8
Antique Airpower Museum, Ia, US 155/H3
Antisana (vol.), Ecu. 180/B5
Antler, Sk, Can. 156/D3
Antlers, Ok, US 153/G3
Antofagasta, Chile 188/B2
Antofagasta (pol. reg.), Chile 188/B2
Antofagasta de la Sierra, Arg. 188/C3
Antoing, Belg. 54/C2
Antokonosy Manambondro, Madg. 125/H8
Antón, Pan. 180/A2
Anton Lizardo (pt.), Mex. 175/P7
Antón Lizardo, Mex. 175/P7
Antongil (bay), Madg. 125/J6
Antonibe, Madg. 125/H6
Antoniesberg (peak), SAfr. 124/C4
Antonina do Norte, Braz. 183/G4
Antônio Carlos, Braz. 187/N6
Antonio de Biedma, Arg. 191/D5
Antônio João, Braz. 189/F2
Antonito, Co, US 149/J2
Antonovo, Bul. 51/H4
Antony, Fr. 30/J5
Antrain, Fr. 56/D4
Antratsyt, Ukr. 73/K3
Antrim (dist.), NI, UK 34/B2
Antrim (mts.), NI, UK 34/B1
Antrim, NI, UK 34/B2
Antrim, NH, US 161/L3
Antrodoco, It. 65/C3
Antronapiana, It. 60/E5
Antsakabary, Madg. 125/J6
Antsalova, Madg. 125/H7
Antsambalahy, Madg. 125/J6
Antsenavolo, Madg. 125/J8
Antsiafabositra, Madg. 125/H7
Antsirabato, Madg. 125/J6
Antsirabe, Madg. 125/H7
Antsirañana (prov.), Madg. 125/J6
Antsirañana, Madg. 125/J6
Antsla, Est. 41/M3
Antsohihy, Madg. 125/H6
Antubia, Gha. 114/E5
Antuco (vol.), Chile 190/C3
Antulai (mtn.), Malay. 91/E3
Antwerp, Oh, US 160/D4
Antwerp (Deurne) (int'l arpt.), Belg. 52/B6
Antwerpen, Belg. 52/B6
Anūpgarh, India 98/B5
Anūpshahr, India 96/B1
Anuradhapura, SrL. 95/D4
Anuradhapura (ruin), SrL. 95/D4
Anutt, Mo, US 153/J2
Anvik, Ak, US 171/F3
Anvil Peak (mt.), Ak, US 171/B6
Anxi, China 78/D3
Anxi, China 87/H3
Anxin, China 80/G7
Anyama, C.d'Iv. 114/D5
Anyang, SKor. 81/F7
Anyang (riv.), SKor. 81/F7
Anyang, China 80/C3
A'nyêmaqên (mts.), China 78/D4
Anyer Kidul, Indo. 89/D4
Anyi, China 80/B4
Anykščiai, Lith. 41/L4
Anyuan, China 87/H3
Anyuan, China 87/G3
Anyuy (riv.), Rus. 79/M2
Anza (riv.), It. 60/E6
Anzá, Col. 183/K6
'Anzah, WBnk. 105/C4
Anzaldo, Bol. 188/C1
Anze, China 80/C3
Anzegem, Belg. 54/C2
Anzhero-Sudzhensk, Rus. 74/J4
Anzhou, China 80/G7
Anzin, Fr. 54/C3
Anzing, Ger. 59/E6
Anzio, It. 65/B5
Anzoátegui (state), Ven. 181/E2
Anzoátegui, Ven. 180/D2
Anzoátegui (int'l arpt.), Ven. 181/E2
Anzoátegui, Col. 183/K8
Anzola dell'Emilia, It. 63/E4
Ao Kham (pt.), Thai. 94/B4
Ao Phangnga NP, Thai. 94/B4
Aoba (isl.), Van. 136/F6
Aoga (isl.), Japan 85/F4
Aogaki, Japan 83/H5
Aoiz, Sp. 44/C5
Aojiang, China 87/J3
Aomori, Japan 82/B3
Aomori (pref.), Japan 82/B3
Aonla, India 96/B1
Aoquanxu, China 87/G3
Aoral (peak), Camb. 94/D3
Aorangi (mts.), NZ 135/J9
Áos, Gre. 49/J4
Aosta, It. 64/D1
Aoste, Fr. 64/B1
Aouara, FrG. 182/C1
Aoudaghast (ruin), Mrta. 114/C2
'Aouînat ez Zbil, Mrta. 114/C2
Aouk-Aoukale, Rsv. de Faune de l', Chad 116/D3
Aoukar (phys. reg.), Mrta. 114/C2
Aoulef, Alg. 111/F4
Aourou, Mali 114/C3
Aouste-sur-Sye, Fr. 64/B3
Aoyama, Japan 83/K6
Aozi, Chad 108/C4
Aozou, Chad 108/C4
Aozou Strip (reg.), Chad 108/C4
Ap Binh Chau, Viet. 94/D4
Ap Loc Thanh, Viet. 94/D4
Ap Long Hoa, Viet. 94/E4
Ap Luc, Viet. 94/D4
Ap Tan My, Viet. 94/E4
Ap Vinh Hao, Viet. 94/E4
Apa (riv.), Braz.,Par. 186/A4
Apache, Ok, US 153/E3
Apache (mts.), Tx, US 150/B2
Apache (lake), Az, US 149/G4
Apache Creek, NM, US 149/H4
Apache Junction, Az, US 149/G4
Apagado (vol.), Bol.,Chile 188/C2
Apalachee (bay), Fl, US 165/F3
Apalachee (riv.), Ga, US 163/F4
Apalachicola, Fl, US 165/F3
Apalachicola (riv.), Fl, US 165/F2
Apan, Mex. 175/L7
Apanovka, Kaz. 71/M1
Apaporis (riv.), Col. 180/D5
Aparados da Serra, PN de, Braz. 189/G4
Aparecida, Braz. 189/H2
Aparecida do Taboado, Braz. 189/G2
Aparición, Ven. 180/D2
Aparri, Phil. 88/C1
Apartadó, Col. 180/B3
Aparurén, Ven. 181/F3
Apataki, FrPol. 137/L6
Apátfalva, Hun. 50/E2
Apatin, Serb. 50/D3
Apatity, Rus. 68/G2
Apatou, FrG. 182/C1
Apatzingán de la Constitución, Mex. 174/E5
Apauwar, Indo. 91/J4
Apaxco, Mex. 175/K7
Apaxtla de Castrejon, Mex. 175/F5
Ape, Lat. 41/M3
Apeldoorn, Neth. 52/C4
Apelern, Ger. 53/G4
Apen, Ger. 53/E2
Apennines (mts.), It. 29/F4
Apensen, Ger. 53/G2
Apere (riv.), Bol. 185/E4
Apex, NC, US 163/H3
Apéyémé, Togo 115/F5
Aphrodisias (ruin), Turk. 102/B2
Api, D.R. Congo 121/F2
Api (riv.), D.R. Congo 121/F2
Api (cape), Indo. 91/F4
Api (cape), Indo. 90/C3
Api (peak), Indo. 91/E5
Api (peak), Nepal 99/D5
Apia (cap.), Sam. 137/S9
Apía, Col. 183/K7
Apia (Fagali) (int'l arpt.), Sam. 137/S9
Apia (Faleolo) (int'l arpt.), Sam. 137/S9
Apiacá (riv.), Braz. 185/G3
Apiacás, Serra dos (mts.), Braz. 185/G3
Apiaí, Braz. 189/G3
Apishapa (riv.), Co, US 154/B5
Apizaco, Mex. 175/L7
Aplao, Peru 184/C5
Apo (mt.), Phil. 88/D4
Apodi, Braz. 183/G4
Apoera, Sur. 181/G3
Apolima (str.), Sam. 137/R9
Apolinario Saravia, Arg. 188/C3
Apollo Bay, Austl. 132/B3
Apollo Beach, Fl, US 164/L8
Apollonía, Gre. 49/J4
Apollonia (ruin), Libya 67/J4
Apolo, Bol. 184/D4
Apopka (lake), Fl, US 165/H3
Apopka, Fl, US 164/M6
Aporé (riv.), Braz. 189/G1
Apore (riv.), Braz. 186/B3
Apostle (isls.), Wi, US 157/J4
Apostle Islands Nat'l Lakeshore, Wi, US 157/J4
Apóstoles, Arg. 189/F3
Apostolic Palace, VatC. 65/G7
Apostolos Andreas (cape), Cyp. 104/D2
Apostolove, Ukr. 73/G4
Apoteri, Guy. 181/G3
Appalachian (mts.), US 143/K4
Appam, ND, US 156/C3
Appelscha, Neth. 52/D3
Appen, Ger. 53/G1
Appennino Abruzzese (mts.), It. 65/C3
Appennino Ligure (mts.), It. 45/H4
Appennino Napoletano (mts.), It. 65/D4
Appennino Tosco-Emiliano (mts.), It. 45/J4
Appennino Umbro-Marchigiano (mts.), It. 45/K5
Appenweier, Ger. 60/D1
Appenzell, Swi. 61/F3
Appenzell (canton), Swi. 61/F3
Appert Lake Nat'l Wild. Ref., ND, US 156/D4
Appignano, It. 63/G7
Appin, Austl. 133/E2
Appingedam, Neth. 52/D2
Apple (riv.), Wi, US 157/Q6
Apple Valley, Ca, US 166/C1
Apple Valley, Mn, US 157/P7
Appleby, Eng, UK 35/F2
Appleby, Tx, US 151/G2
Appleby Magna, Eng, UK 37/E1
Appleton, Mn, US 155/F1
Appleton, NY, US 160/V9
Appleton, Wi, US 160/B2
Appleton City, Mo, US 153/G1
Appling, Ga, US 163/F4
Appomattox, Va, US 163/H2
Appomattox Court House Nat'l Hist. Park, Va, US 163/H2
Approuage (riv.), FrG. 182/C2
Aprelevka, Rus. 69/W9
Aprica, It. 61/G5
Aprica, Passo dell' (pass), It. 61/G5
Apricena, It. 48/D2
Aprilia, It. 65/B4
Apriltsi, Bul. 51/G4
Apsheronsk, Rus. 73/K5
Apsley, On, Can. 161/G2
Apsley (str.), Austl. 128/C2
Apsley Gorge NP, Austl. 132/E1
Apt, Fr. 64/B5
Apucarana, Braz. 189/G2
Apuiarés, Braz. 183/G3
Apulia (reg.), It. 67/H2
Apulo, Col. 183/L8
Apure (riv.), Ven. 173/H6
Apure (prov.), Ven. 180/D3
Apurímac (riv.), Peru 179/B4
Apurímac (dept.), Peru 184/C4
Āq Qal'eh, Iran 103/H2
Aqaba (gulf), Asia 77/B7
'Aqdā, Iran 103/H3
'Aqīq, Sudan 100/C5
Aqmola Oblast, Kaz. 99/A1
'Aqqābah, WBnk. 105/C4
Aqqikkol (lake), China 99/E4
'Aqrabah, WBnk. 105/C4
'Aqrah, Iraq 103/E2
Aqsay, Kaz. 71/K2
Aqtaū, Kaz. 71/J4
Aqtöbe, Kaz. 71/L2
Aqtöbe (int'l arpt.), Kaz. 71/L2
Aqtöbe Oblast, Kaz. 71/L3
Aqua Fria (riv.), Az, US 149/F4
Aquanaval (riv.), Mex. 174/E3
Aquapei (riv.), Braz. 189/G2
Aquarius (plat.), Ut, US 147/H4
Aquarius (mts.), Az, US 149/F3
Aquia, Peru 184/B3
Aquidabán (riv.), Par. 186/A4
Aquidauana, Braz. 189/F2
Aquidauana (riv.), Braz. 186/B3
Aquila, Swi. 61/E5
Aquileia, It. 63/G2
Aquiles Serdán, Mex. 177/B3
Aquilla, Tx, US 151/F2
Aquin, Haiti 177/H2
Aquino, It. 65/C5
Aquiraz, Braz. 183/G3
Aquitaine (pol. reg.), Fr. 44/C4
Ar (riv.), China 78/D4
Ar Horqin Qi, China 80/E2
Ar Rabaḑ, SAr. 109/H4
Ar Rafīd, Jor. 105/D3
Ar Rafīd, Syria 105/D3
Ar Rahad, Sudan 117/F2
Ar Raḩāminah, Egypt 113/C2
Ar Raḩmānīyah, Egypt 113/B2
Ar Ramādī, Iraq 103/E3
Ar Ramthā, Jor. 105/D3
Ar Rank, Sudan 117/G3
Ar Raqqah, Syria 102/D3
Ar Raqqah (prov.), Syria 102/D2
Ar Rashīdīyah, Leb. 105/C2
Ar Rass, SAr. 100/D3
Ar Rastan, Syria 104/E2
Ar Rawḑah, SAr. 100/D3
Ar Rawḑah, Yem. 118/C2
Ar Rawḑah, Egypt 113/B6
Ar Rāwuk, Yem. 118/D2
Ar Rayyān, Qatar 100/F3
Ar Rifā'ī, Iraq 103/F4
Ar Rīḩīyah, WBnk. 105/C6
Ar Riyāḑ (Riyadh) (cap.), SAr. 100/E4
Ar Riyān, Yem. 118/D2
Ar Rubayqī, Egypt 113/C4
Ar Rumaythah, Iraq 103/F4
Ar Rummān, Jor. 105/D4
Ar Ruşayfah, Jor. 105/E4
Ar Ruşayriş, Sudan 117/G3
Ar Ruţbah, Iraq 102/E3
Ar Ruways, Qatar 100/F3
Ar-Asgat, Mong. 78/F2
Ara (riv.), Ire. 32/B5
Ara (riv.), Japan 85/F2
Ara Terra, Eth. 118/B4
'Arab (gulf), Egypt 109/F2
Arab, Al, US 162/D3
'Arab (wadi), Jor. 105/D3
'Arabah (wadi), Egypt 109/G2
Araban, Turk. 102/D2
Arabatsk (bay), Ukr. 73/H5
Arabatsk Spit (pen.), Ukr. 73/H4
Arabi, Ga, US 165/G2
Arabian (sea), Asia 77/F8
Arabian (des.), Egypt 109/G3
Arabian (pen.), Asia 100/D3
Arabopó, Ven. 181/F3
Araç (riv.), Turk. 70/E4
Araç, Turk. 70/E4
Araça (riv.), Braz. 181/F4
Araca, Bol. 188/C1
Aracaju, Braz. 187/F1
Aracataca, Col. 180/C2
Aracati, Braz. 183/G4
Araçatuba, Braz. 189/G2
Araceli, Phil. 88/B3
Aracena, Sp. 46/B4
Aračinovo, FYROM 49/G1
Aracoiaba, Braz. 183/G4
Aracruz, Braz. 187/E3
Araçuaí, Braz. 187/E3
Araçuaí (riv.), Braz. 187/E3
Arad (prov.), Rom. 50/E2
Arad, Rom. 50/E2
Arada, Chad 116/D2
'Arādah, UAE 100/F4
Ārādān, Iran 103/H3
Arafali, Erit. 118/A2
Arafura (sea), Austl.,Indo. 128/D2
Aragats (peak), Arm. 71/H4
Araglin (riv.), Ire. 32/B5
Arago, Or, US 146/A2
Arago (cape), Or, US 146/A2
Aragón (reg.), Sp. 66/C2
Aragón (riv.), Sp. 66/C2
Aragon, NM, US 149/H4
Aragon, Ga, US 162/E3
Aragua (state), Ven. 181/E2
Araguacema, Braz. 182/D5
Araguaçu, Braz. 186/C2
Araguaia (riv.), Braz. 179/D3
Araguaia, PN do, Braz. 186/C1
Araguaiana, Braz. 186/C2
Araguaína, Braz. 182/D4
Araguari, Braz. 186/C3
Araguari (riv.), Braz. 182/D2
Araguari (riv.), Braz. 189/H1
Araguatins, Braz. 182/D4
Arai, Japan 85/F2
Araioses, Braz. 183/F3
Arāk, Iran 103/G3
Arak, Alg. 111/F4
Arakan (mts.), Myan. 93/F3
Arakawa, Japan 83/C2
Árakhthos (riv.), Gre. 49/G3
Araklı, Turk. 70/G4
Araku, India 95/D2
Aral, Kaz. 74/G5
Aral (sea), Kaz. 77/E5
Aralık, Turk. 103/F2
Aralsor (lake), Kaz. 71/H2
Aramac, Austl. 134/B3
Arāmbāgh, India 97/F4
Aramon, Fr. 64/A5
Ārān, Iran 103/G3
Aran (isls.), Ire. 31/P10
Aran Fawddwy (peak), Wal, UK 34/E6
Aranda de Duero, Sp. 46/D2
Arandelovac, Serb. 50/E3
Arandis, Namb. 122/B4
Arandu, Pak. 98/A2
Arang, India 95/D1
Arani, Bol. 188/C1
Arani, India 95/C3
Aranjuez, Sp. 46/D2
Aranos, Namb. 122/C5
Aransas (riv.), Tx, US 151/F3
Aransas NWR, Tx, US 151/F3
Aransas Pass, Tx, US 151/F4
Arantina, Braz. 187/M6
Aranuka (isl.), Kiri. 136/G5
Aranyaprathet, Thai. 94/C3
Araouane, Mali 114/E2
Arapaho, Ok, US 152/E3
Arapahoe, Ne, US 154/E3
Arapahoe Nat'l Rec. Area, Co, US 154/A3
Arapahoe NWR, Co, US 147/K3
Arapawa (isl.), NZ 135/C3
Arapicos, Ecu. 184/B1
Arapiraca, Braz. 187/F1
Arapiuns (riv.), Braz. 181/H5
Arapongas, Braz. 189/G2
'Ar'ara, WBnk. 105/C4
Araracuara, Col. 180/C5
Araranguá, Braz. 189/G4
Araraquara, Braz. 189/G2
Araras, Braz. 189/H2
Ararat, Austl. 132/B3
Ararat, Mount (Ağrı) (peak), Turk. 103/F2
Arari, Braz. 183/E3
Arari (lake), Braz. 182/D3
Arāria, India 97/F2
Araripe, Chapada do (uplands), Braz. 183/F4
Araripina, Braz. 183/F4
Araruna, Braz. 183/H4
Aras (riv.), Iran 74/E6
Aras (riv.), Turk. 102/E2
Aratane (well), Mrta. 114/C2
Aratoca, Col. 180/C3
Aratuba, Braz. 183/G4
Arau, Malay. 94/C5
Arauá (riv.), Braz. 185/E2
Arauca (riv.), Col. 180/D3
Arauca (riv.), Col.,Ven. 181/E3
Arauca (dept.), Col. 180/D3
Arauca, Col. 180/D3
Arauco, Chile 190/B3
Arauquita, Col. 180/D3
Araure, Ven. 180/D2
Aravaca, Sp. 47/N9
Arawa, PNG 136/E5
Arawale Nat'l Reserve, Kenya 119/C2
Araxá, Braz. 186/D3
Araya (pen.), Ven. 181/E2
Arazatí, Uru. 191/K11
Ārba Minch', Eth. 117/H4
Ārbē Gona, Eth. 118/A4
Arbeca, Sp. 47/F2
Arbedo, Swi. 61/F5
Arbeláez, Col. 183/L8
Arbīl (gov.), Iraq 103/E3
Arboga, Swe. 40/F2
Arbois, Fr. 60/B4
Arbois, Mont d' (peak), Fr. 60/C6
Arboletes, Col. 180/B2
Arbon, Swi. 61/F2
Arbor Vitae, Wi, US 157/K5
Arbore, Eth. 117/H4
Arborfield, Sk, Can. 145/N1
Arborg, Mb, Can. 156/F2
Arbovale, WV, US 163/H1
Arbrå, Swe. 40/G1
Arbroath, Sc, UK 33/D3
Arbuckle (mts.), Ok, US 153/F3
Arbuckle (lake), Fl, US 165/H4
Arbuckle, Ca, US 146/B4
Arc (riv.), Fr. 44/F5
Arc (mtn.), Nv, US 146/E4
Arc-en-Barrois, Fr. 60/B2
Arc-et-Senans, Fr. 60/B3
Arc-lès-Gray, Fr. 60/B3
Arc-sur-Tille, Fr. 60/B3
Arcachon, Fr. 44/C4
Arcadia, Ca, US 166/F7
Arcadia, Fl, US 165/H4
Arcadia, In, US 160/C4
Arcadia, La, US 153/H4
Arcadia, Mo, US 162/B2
Arcadia, Ne, US 154/E3
Arcadia, NS, Can. 158/D4
Arcadia, Ok, US 153/F3
Arcadia, Wi, US 155/J1
Arcanum, Oh, US 160/D5
Arcata, Ca, US 146/A3
Arcata (bay), Ca, US 146/A3
Arce, It. 65/C4
Arceburgo, Braz. 187/K6
Arcelia, Mex. 175/E5
Arcen, Neth. 52/D6
Arcene, It. 62/C2
Arceto, It. 63/D4
Arcevia, It. 63/F7
Archangel (Arkhangel'sk), Rus. 68/J2
Archbold, Oh, US 160/D4
Archdale, NC, US 163/H3
Archena, Sp. 46/E3
Archer, Fl, US 165/G3
Archer (riv.), Austl. 129/F3
Archer Bend NP, Austl. 129/F3
Archer City, Tx, US 153/E4
Archerfield (arpt.), Austl. 134/E7
Archers Post, Kenya 119/B1
Arches, Fr. 60/C1
Arches NP, Ut, US 147/J4
Archibald, La, US 153/J4
Archibarca (peak), Arg. 188/C3
Archidona, Sp. 46/C4
Archie, Mo, US 153/G1
Archiestown, Sc, UK 33/C2
Archman, Trkm. 71/L5
Archman, Trkm. 71/L5
Arcipelago Toscano (isl.), It. 45/H5
Arcisate, It. 61/E6
Arco, It. 61/G6
Arco, Id, US 147/G2
Arco, Paso del (pass), Arg. 190/C3
Arcola, Sk, Can. 156/C3
Arcola, It. 62/C5
Arcola, Ms, US 162/B4
Arcole, It. 63/E3
Arcopongo, Bol. 188/C1
Arcos, Braz. 186/D4
Arcos de Jalón, Sp. 46/D2
Arcos de la Frontera, Sp. 46/C4
Arcos de Valdevez, Port. 46/A2
Arcosanti, Az, US 149/F3
Arcoverde, Braz. 183/G5
Arctic (ocean) 26/A1
Arctic Bay, Nun, Can. 141/H1
Arctic Circle 26/C2
Arctic Coastal (plain), Ak, US 171/F2
Arctic Red (riv.), NW, Can. 171/M2
Arctic Village, Ak, US 171/J2
Arctowski, Pol., Ant. 192/W
Arda (riv.), Bul. 70/C4
Arda (riv.), It. 63/C3
Ardabīl, Iran 103/G2
Ardabīl (gov.), Iran 103/G2
Ardagh, Ire. 32/A4
Ardagh, Ire. 32/C2
Ardahan, Turk. 71/G4
Ardakān, Iran 103/H3
Ardal, Iran 103/G4
Årdalstangen, Nor. 40/B1
Ardanuç, Turk. 71/G4
Ardatov, Rus. 68/J5
Arddleen, Wal, UK 36/C1
Ardea, It. 65/B4
Ardèche (dept.), Fr. 64/A3
Ardèche (riv.), Fr. 44/F4
Ardee, Ire. 34/B4
Arden, Mb, Can. 156/E2
Arden, Den. 40/C3
Arden (mt.), Austl. 131/H5
Arden, De, US 168/C4
Arden, Wa, US 144/F3
Arden-Arcade, Ca, US 167/M9
Ardennes (for.), Fr. 42/C4
Ardennes (dept.), Fr. 55/D4
Ardennes (for.), Belg. 44/F1
Ardennes, Canal des (canal), Fr. 55/D4
Ardenno, It. 61/F5
Arderin (peak), Ire. 32/C3
Ardersier, Sc, UK 33/B1
Ardeşen, Turk. 71/G4
Ardesio, It. 61/F6
Ardestān, Iran 103/H3
Ardez, Swi. 61/G4
Ardfinnan, Ire. 32/C5
Ardglass, NI, UK 34/C3
Ardila (riv.), Sp. 46/B3
Ardino, Bul. 51/G5
Ardivachar (pt.), Sc, UK 31/Q8
Ardle (riv.), Sc, UK 33/C3
Ardlethan, Austl. 133/C2
Ardmore, Ire. 32/C6
Ardmore, Ok, US 153/F3
Ardmore, Pa, US 168/C4
Ardmore, SD, US 154/C2
Ardmore, Tn, US 162/D3
Ardnacrusha, Ire. 32/B4
Ardnamurchan (pt.), Sc, UK 31/Q8
Ardoch Nat'l Wild. Ref., ND, US 156/F3
Ardon, Swi. 60/D5
Ardooie, Belg. 54/C2
Ardrahan, Ire. 32/B3
Ardres, Fr. 54/A2
Ardrossan, Sc, UK 33/B5
Ardrossan, Austl. 131/H5
Ards (pen.), Sc, UK 34/C3
Ards (dist.), NI, UK 34/C2
Ardsley, NY, US 169/K7
Åre, Swe. 38/E3
Areado, Braz. 187/K6
Arecibo, PR 173/M8
Areia Branca, Braz. 183/G4
Arena (pt.), Ca, US 146/B4
Arena de la Ventana Punta (pt.), Mex. 174/C3
Arenal (vol.), CR 177/E4
Arenápolis, Braz. 185/G4
Arenas de San Pedro, Sp. 46/C2
Arenas, Punta de (pt.), Arg. 191/C7
Arendal, Nor. 40/C2
Arendonk, Belg. 52/C6
Arendtsville, Pa, US 168/A4
Arenig Fawr (peak), Wal, UK 34/E6
Arenys de Mar, Sp. 47/L6
Arenzano, It. 62/B5
Arenzville, Il, US 155/J4
Areo, Ven. 181/F2
Areópolis, Gre. 49/H4
Arequipa, Peru 184/D5
Arequipa (dept.), Peru 184/C5
Arequito, Arg. 190/E2
Aresing, Ger. 58/E5
Arévalo, Sp. 46/C2
Areyonga, Austl. 131/G3
Āreza, Erit. 118/A2
Arezzo, It. 63/E7
Arezzo (prov.), It. 63/E5
Arfa' Deh, Iran 103/H3
Arga (riv.), Sp. 44/C5
Argadargada, Austl. 131/H2
Argalastí, Gre. 49/H3
Argamakmur, Indo. 89/C3
Argamasilla de Alba, Sp. 46/D3
Argamasilla de Calatrava, Sp. 46/C3
Argan, China 99/E3
Arganda, Sp. 47/N9
Argao, Phil. 88/C3
Argatone (peak), It. 65/C4
Argegno, It. 61/F6
Argelès-Gazost, Fr. 44/C5
Argelès-sur-Mer, Fr. 44/E5
Argelia, Col. 183/K7
Argen (riv.), Ger. 61/F2
Argenbühl, Ger. 61/F2
Argences, Fr. 57/E2
Argens (riv.), Fr. 45/G5
Argenta, It. 63/E4
Argenta, BC, Can. 144/F2
Argentan, Fr. 57/E3
Argentat, Fr. 44/D4
Argentera (peak), It. 64/D4
Argenteuil, Fr. 30/J5
Argentina (riv.), It. 62/A5
Argentina (ctry.) 179/C6
Argentino (lake), Arg. 191/B6
Argenton-sur-Creuse, Fr. 44/D3
Argentona, Sp. 47/L6
Argentré, Fr. 57/E4
Argeş (riv.), Rom. 70/C3
Argeş (prov.), Rom. 51/G3
Arghandab (riv.), Afg. 101/J2
Argideen (riv.), Ire. 32/B6
Argıthanı, Turk. 102/B2
Argo, Sudan 109/F5
Argolis (gulf), Gre. 67/J3
Argonne, Wi, US 157/K5
Argonne (for.), Fr. 42/C4
Argonne Nat'l Lab., Il, US 167/P16
Argopuro (peak), Indo. 89/F4
Árgos, Gre. 49/H4
Árgos Orestikón, Gre. 49/G2
Argostólion, Gre. 49/G3
Argueil, Fr. 57/G1
Arguello (pt.), Ca, US 142/B5
Arguenon (riv.), Fr. 56/C4
Argun (riv.), China,Rus 79/J1
Argungu, Nga. 115/G3
Argusville, ND, US 156/F4
Argut (riv.), Rus. 78/B2
Arguut, Mong. 78/E2
Argyle, Mn, US 156/F3
Argyle (lake), Austl. 128/C4
Argyle, Tx, US 150/K6
Argyll (reg.), Sc, UK 33/A4
Argyll and Bute (co.), Sc, UK 33/A4
Arhangay (prov.), Mong. 78/D2
Arhli, Niger 115/G2
Arholma (isl.), Swe. 39/C1
Arhreijît (well), Mrta. 110/B5
Arhrîjît, Mrta. 114/C2
Århus, Den. 40/D3
Århus (co.), Den. 40/D3
Ariah (mtn.), Austl. 133/C2
Ariah Park, Austl. 133/C2
Ariamsvlei, Namb. 124/B3
Ariari (riv.), Col. 180/C4
Arias, Arg. 190/E2
Aribinda, Burk. 115/E3
Arica, Col. 180/D5
Arica, Chile 188/B1
Arica (Chacalluta) (int'l arpt.), Chile 188/B1
Arıcak, Turk. 102/E2
Ariccia, It. 65/B4
Arichat, NS, Can. 159/G3
Arid (cape), Austl. 130/D5
Arida, Japan 84/D3
Aridhaía, Gre. 49/H2
Arido (peak), Ca, US 166/A1
Aridol (lake), WSah. 110/B4
Ariège (riv.), Fr. 44/D5
Ariel, Wa, US 144/C5
Arienzo, It. 65/D5
Arifiye, Turk. 51/K5
Ārifwāla, Pak. 98/B4
Arīḩā, Syria 104/E2
Arīḩā (Jericho), WBnk. 105/C5
Arikaree (riv.), Co, US 154/C4
Arilje, Serb. 50/E4
Arima, Trin. 181/F2
Aringa, Ugan. 121/G2
Arinos (riv.), Braz. 185/G3
Arinos, Braz. 186/D2
Arinthod, Fr. 60/B5
Ario de Rosales, Mex. 175/E5
Ariogala, Lith. 41/K4
Aripao, Ven. 181/E3
Aripeka, Fl, US 164/K7
Aripine, Az, US 149/G3
Aripuanã, Braz. 185/G3
Aripuanã (riv.), Braz. 179/C3
Ariquemes, Braz. 185/F3
Aris, Namb. 122/C4
Arish, Austl. 134/B2
`Arīsh (wadi), Egypt 109/G2
Arismendi, Ven. 180/D2
Arissa, Eth. 118/B3
Ariton, Al, US 165/F2
Arivaca, Az, US 149/G5
Arivechi, Mex. 174/C2
Arivonimamo, Madg. 125/H7
Ariza, Sp. 46/D2
Arize (riv.), Fr. 47/F1
Arizona (state), US 149/F3
Arizona, Arg. 190/D2
Arizona City, Az, US 149/G4
Arizpe, Mex. 174/C2
Årjäng, Swe. 40/E2
Arjay, Ky, US 162/F2
Arjeplog, Swe. 38/F2
Arjona, Col. 180/C2
Arjona, Sp. 46/C4
Arkabutla (dam), Ms, US 162/B3
Arkadak, Rus. 71/G2
Arkadelphia, Ar, US 153/H3
Arkaig (lake), Sc, UK 33/A3
Arkalokhórion, Gre. 49/J5
Arkansas (riv.), US 143/K4
Arkansas (state), US 143/H4
Arkansas City, Ks, US 153/F2
Arkansas Post Nat'l Mem., Ar, US 153/J3
Arkansas, Salt Fork (riv.), Ok, US 153/F2
Arkanū (peak), Libya 108/E4
Arkhángelos, Gre. 102/B2
Arkhangel'sk (int'l arpt.), Rus. 68/J2
Arkhangel'skaya Oblast, Rus. 68/H3
Arkhangel'sk (Archangel), Rus. 68/J2
Arkhangel'skaya, Rus. 73/L5
Arkhangel'skoye, Rus. 69/W9
Arkhangel'skoye, Rus. 73/L2
Arkhara, Rus. 79/L2
Arkhipo-Osipovka, Rus. 70/F3
Arkhyz, Rus. 71/G4
Arklow, Ire. 34/B6
Arkona (cape), Ger. 40/E4
Arksey, Eng, UK 35/G4
Arkticheskiy Institut (isls.), Rus. 74/H2
Ärla, Swe. 40/G2
Arlanda (int'l arpt.), Swe. 40/G2
Arlanza (riv.), Sp. 46/C1
Arlazón (riv.), Sp. 46/D1
Arlbergpass (pass), Aus. 61/G3
Arles, Fr. 64/A5
Arlesheim, Swi. 60/D3
Arlington, Az, US 149/F4
Arlington, Co, US 152/C1
Arlington, Ga, US 165/F2
Arlington, Ks, US 153/E2
Arlington, Ky, US 162/C2
Arlington, Mn, US 155/G1
Arlington, Ne, US 155/F3
Arlington, NY, US 161/K4
Arlington, Oh, US 160/E4
Arlington, Or, US 144/D5
Arlington, SD, US 155/F1
Arlington, Tn, US 162/C3
Arlington, Tx, US 150/K7
Arlington (lake), Tx, US 150/K7
Arlington, Va, US 168/A6
Arlington, Vt, US 161/K3
Arlington, Wa, US 144/C3
Arlington Heights, Il, US 160/C3
Arló, Hun. 43/L4
Arlon, Belg. 55/E4
Arltunga, Austl. 131/G2
Arluno, It. 62/B2
Arly (riv.), Fr. 60/C6
Arm (riv.), Sk, Can. 145/M2
Armada, Mi, US 167/G6
Armadale (nbrhd.), Austl. 130/L7
Armadale, Sc, UK 33/C5
Armagh, NI, UK 34/B3
Armagh (dist.), NI, UK 34/B3
Armançon (riv.), Fr. 44/F3
Armando Laydner (res.), Braz. 186/C4
Armant, Egypt 109/G3
Armavir, Arm. 71/H4
Armavir, Rus. 73/L5
Armenia (ctry.) 71/H5
Armenia, Col. 183/K8
Armentières, Fr. 54/B2
Armentières-en-Brie, Fr. 30/M5
Armería, Mex. 174/E5
Armero, Col. 183/L8
Armidabán (riv.), Par. 189/E2
Armidale, Austl. 132/D1
Armilla, Sp. 46/D4
Arminto, Wy, US 147/K2
Armona, Ca, US 148/C2
Armopa, Indo. 91/J4
Armour, SD, US 154/E2
Armoy, NI, UK 34/B1
Armstrong, Arg. 190/E2
Armstrong, BC, Can. 144/E2
Armstrong, On, Can. 157/K2
Armstrong, Mo, US 155/H4
Armstrong, Tx, US 151/F4
Armstrong Creek, Wi, US 157/K5
Armthorpe, Eng, UK 35/G4
Ārmūr, India 95/C2
Armutlu, Turk. 51/J5
Army Ammunition Plant, Il, US 155/K3
Army Dep., Or, US 146/D1
Army Ordnance Museum, Md, US 168/B5
Armyans'k, Ukr. 73/G4
Arnage, Fr. 57/F5
Arnager (int'l arpt.), Den. 40/F4
Arnaía, Gre. 49/H2
Arnaud (riv.), Qu, Can. 141/J3
Arnaudville, La, US 164/C2
Arnauti (cape), Cyp. 104/C2
Arnavutköy, Turk. 103/M6
Arncott, Eng, UK 37/E3
Arnedo, Sp. 46/D1
Arnegard, ND, US 156/C4
Arneiroz, Braz. 183/F4
Arnett, Ok, US 152/E2
Arnheim, Mi, US 157/K4
Arnhem, Neth. 52/C5
Arnhem (cape), Austl. 129/E3
Arnhem (bay), Austl. 129/E3
Arnhem Land (reg.), Austl. 128/D3
Arnhem Land Abor. Land, Austl. 128/D3
Arnières-sur-Iton, Fr. 57/G3
Arno (riv.), It. 66/F2
Arnö, Swe. 39/A2
Arnö, Swe. 39/A1
Arno (isl.), Mrsh. 136/G4
Arnold (riv.), Austl. 128/D3
Arnold, Eng, UK 35/G6
Arnold, Ca, US 146/C4
Arnold, Md, US 168/B5
Arnold, Mi, US 157/L4
Arnold, Mo, US 162/B1
Arnold, Ne, US 154/D3
Arnoldstein, Aus. 45/K3
Arnon (riv.), Fr. 44/E3
Arnouville-lès-Gonesse, Fr. 30/K5
Arnprior, On, Can. 161/H2
Arnsberg, Ger. 53/F6
Arnside, Eng, UK 35/F3
Arnstein, Ger. 58/C3
Arnstorf, Ger. 59/F5
Aro Usu (cape), Indo. 128/C2
Aroab, Namb. 124/B2
Aroases, Braz. 183/F4
Aroche, Sp. 46/B4
Arochukwu, Nga. 115/G5
Aroland, On, Can. 157/L2
Arolsen, Ger. 53/G6
Aroma, Sudan 117/H2
Aroma, Bol. 188/C1
Aron, Fr. 57/E4
Aron (riv.), Fr. 44/E3
Arona, It. 62/B2
Aronde (riv.), Fr. 54/B5
Aroostook, NB, Can. 158/D2
Arorae (isl.), Kiri. 136/G5
Aroroy, Phil. 88/C2
Åros, Nor. 38/S8
Arosa, Swi. 61/F4
Aroser Rothern (peak), Swi. 61/F4
Ærøskøbing, Den. 40/D4
Arp, Ga, US 165/G2
Arpaçay, Turk. 71/G4
Arpajon, Fr. 30/J6
Arpajon-sur-Cère, Fr. 44/E4
Arqalyq, Kaz. 99/A1
Arquata Scrivia, It. 62/B4
Arque, Bol. 188/C1
Arques, Fr. 54/B2
Arques-la-Bataille, Fr. 57/G1
'Arrāba, Isr. 105/C3
'Arrābah, WBnk. 105/C4
Arrah, India 97/E3
Arraha, Eth. 118/B3
Arraias (riv.), Braz. 185/H3
Arraias, Braz. 186/D2
Arraiján, Pan. 180/B2
Arrais (riv.), Fr. 47/F1
Arram, Eng, UK 35/H4
Arran (isl.), Sc, UK 31/R8
Arrancabarba (peak), Nic. 177/E4
Arras, Fr. 54/B3
Arreau, Fr. 44/D5
Arrecifal, Col. 180/D4
Arrecife, Sp. 110/B3
Arrecifes, Arg. 190/E2
Arrée, Monts d' (mts.), Fr. 44/B2
Arresø (lake), Den. 39/J7
Arrey, NM, US 149/J4
Arriaga, Mex. 176/C2
Arriba, Co, US 154/C4
Arrington, Va, US 163/H2
Arriola, Co, US 149/H2
Arriondas, Sp. 46/C1
Arrochar, Sc, UK 33/B4
Arrone, It. 65/B2
Arrone (riv.), It. 65/B3
Arronville, Fr. 30/J4
Arroscia (riv.), It. 62/B4
Arrou, Fr. 57/G4
Arroux (riv.), Fr. 44/F3
Arrow (riv.), Eng, UK 36/C2
Arrowbear Lake, Ca, US 166/C2
Arrowhead (lake), Tx, US 153/E4
Arrowhead NWR, ND, US 156/E4
Arrowrock (res.), Id, US 146/F2
Arrowrock (dam), Id, US 146/F2
Arrowsmith (mt.), NZ 135/B3
Arrowsmith (pt.), Austl. 129/E3
Arrowtown, NZ 135/B4
Arrowwood, Ab, Can. 145/H2
Arroyito, Arg. 188/D4
Arroyo de la Luz, Sp. 46/B3
Arroyo del Macho (riv.), NM, US 152/B4
Arroyo Grande, Bol. 184/D3
Arroyo Grande, Ca, US 148/B3
Arroyo Hondo, NM, US 152/B2
Arroyo Hondo (riv.), Ca, US 167/L12
Arroyo Trabuco (riv.), Ca, US 166/C3
Arroyo Valle (brook), Ca, US 167/L11
Arrufó, Arg. 188/D4
Års, Den. 40/C3
Ars-sur-Moselle, Fr. 55/F5
Arsanjān, Iran 103/H4
Arsen'yev, Rus. 79/L3
Ársí (prov.), Eth. 118/A4
Arsiero, It. 63/E2
Arsk, Rus. 69/L4
Arslanköy, Turk. 104/D1
Årsta havsbad, Swe. 39/B1
Árta, Gre. 49/G3
Arta (gulf), Gre. 49/G3
'Arta, Djib. 118/B3
Artá, Sp. 47/G3
Arteaga, Mex. 174/E5
Arteixo, Sp. 46/A1
Artem, Rus. 79/L3
Artemisa, Cuba 177/F1
Artemivs'k, Ukr. 73/K3
Artemove, Ukr. 73/J3
Artemovskiy, Rus. 75/M4
Artena, It. 65/B4
Artenay, Fr. 57/G4
Artesia, Ca, US 166/F8
Artesia, Ms, US 162/C4
Artesia, NM, US 152/B4
Artesia Wells, Tx, US 150/E3
Arth, Swi. 61/E3
Arthies, Fr. 30/H4
Arthur (riv.), Austl. 130/C5
Arthur (pt.), Austl. 134/C3
Arthur, ND, US 156/F4
Arthur, Ne, US 154/D3
Arthur, WV, US 163/H1
Arthur City, Tx, US 153/G4
Arthur Kill (riv.), US 169/J9
Arthur's Pass NP, NZ 135/B3
Arthurdale, WV, US 161/G5
Arthur's (pass), NZ 135/B3
Arthurstown, Ire. 32/D5
Arti, Rus. 69/N4
Artigas (dept.), Uru. 189/E4
Artigas, Uru. 189/E4
Art'ik, Arm. 103/E1
Artogne, It. 62/D2
Artois (reg.), Fr. 42/A3
Artova, Turk. 102/D1
Artsyz, Ukr. 51/J3
Artuby (riv.), Fr. 64/C5
Artur Nogueira, Braz. 187/J7
Arturo Merino Benitez (int'l arpt.), Chile 190/N8
Artux, China 99/C4
Artvin (prov.), Turk. 71/G4
Artvin, Turk. 71/G4
Artyom, Azer. 71/J4
Aru, D.R. Congo 121/G2
Aru (isls.), Indo. 128/D1
Arua, Ugan. 121/G2
Aruba (isl.), Aru., Neth. 179/B1
Arucas, Sp. 110/B3
Arudy, Fr. 44/C5
Arujá, Braz. 187/K8
Arun (riv.), China 97/F2
Arun (riv.), Eng, UK 37/F5
Arunāchal Pradesh (state), India 93/F2
Arundel, Eng, UK 37/F5
Aruppukkottai, India 95/C4
'Ārūrah, WBnk. 105/C4
Arus (cape), Indo. 91/F3
Arusha (prov.), Tanz. 119/B3
Arusha, Tanz. 119/B2
Arusha Chine, Tanz. 119/B2
Arusha NP, Tanz. 119/B2
Arutua (isl.), FrPol. 137/L6
Aruwimi (riv.), D.R. Congo 107/E4
Arvada, Co, US 154/B4
Arvada, Wy, US 154/A1
Arvagh, Ire. 32/C2
Arvan (riv.), Fr. 64/C2
Arvayheer, Mong. 78/E2
Arve (riv.), Fr. 60/C6
Arvidsjaur, Swe. 38/F2
Arviat, Nun, Can. 140/G2
Arvika, Swe. 40/E2
Arvin, Ca, US 148/C3
Arvon (mt.), Mi, US 157/K4
Arvonia, Va, US 163/H2
Arwala, Indo. 128/B1
Aryamūn, Egypt 113/B2
Aryānah, Tun. 48/B4
Aryānah (gov.), Tun. 48/A4
Arys', Kaz. 99/A3
Arz (riv.), Fr. 44/B3
Arzachena, It. 48/A2
Arzamas, Rus. 69/K5
Arzano, It. 65/D6
Arzbach, Ger. 55/G3
Arzberg, Ger. 59/F2
Ärzen, Ger. 53/G4
Arzew, Alg. 112/E5
Arzgir, Rus. 71/H3
Arzignano, It. 63/E2
Arzl im Pitztal, Aus. 61/G3
Arzúa, Sp. 46/A1
As, Belg. 55/E1
Aš, Czh. 59/F2
Ås, Nor. 40/D2
As Sabkhah, Syria 102/D3
As Sabkhat al Kabīrah (swamp), Libya 108/C2
Aş Şaff, Egypt 113/C5
Aş Şāfī, Jor. 104/D4
Aş Şāfiyah, Sudan 117/F2
Aş Şāliḩīyah, Syria 102/E3
Aş Şāliḩīyah, Egypt 113/C3
As Sālimīyah, Kuw. 103/G4
As Sallūm, Egypt 108/E2
As Salmān, Iraq 103/F4
As Salţ, Jor. 105/D4
As Salwá, SAr. 100/F4
As Samāwah, Iraq 103/F4
Aş Şanamayn, Syria 105/E2
As Sanţah, Egypt 113/C3
Aş Şarafand, Leb. 105/C2
Aş Şarīḩ, Jor. 105/D3
Aş Şawma'ah, Yem. 118/C2
As Sīb, Oman 101/G4
As Sidr, Libya 108/C2
As Sidr, SAr. 100/C4
As Sinbillāwayn, Egypt 113/C3
Aş Şubayḩī, Jor. 105/D4
As Sudd (reg.), Sudan 107/F4
As Sufāl, Yem. 118/D2
Aş Şufayyah, Sudan 117/G2
Aş Şufīyāh, Egypt 113/C3
As Sukhnah, Syria 102/D3
As Sukhnah, Jor. 105/E4
As Suki, Sudan 117/G2
As Sulaymānīyah, Iraq 103/F3
As Sulaymānīyah (gov.), Iraq 103/F3
As Sulaymī, SAr. 100/D3
As Sulayyil, SAr. 100/E4
As Sulţān, Libya 108/C2
As Sumayḩ, Sudan 117/E3

Aş Şumm – Baba Bu

Aş Şummān (range), SAr. 103/F5
As Su'ūdīyah, Egypt 113/C5
As Suwāqah, Jor. 105/E6
Aş Şuwār, Syria 102/E3
As Suwaydā', Syria 105/F3
As Suwaydā' (gov.), Syria 105/E3
As Suwayq, Oman 101/G4
Aş Şuwayrah, Iraq 103/F3
As Suways (gov.), Egypt 109/G2
Asab, Namb. 122/C5
Asaba, Nga. 115/G5
Asad (lake), Syria 102/D2
Asadābād, Afg. 98/A2
Asadābād, Iran 103/G3
Asagny, PN d', C.d'Iv. 114/D5
Asahan (riv.), Indo. 90/A3
Asahi (riv.), Japan 84/C3
Asahi, Japan 85/G3
Asahi, Japan 83/M5
Asahi, Japan 83/L5
Asahi, Japan 83/F1
Asahi-dake (peak), Japan 82/C2
Asahikawa, Japan 82/C2
Asai, Japan 83/K5
Asaka, Japan 83/D2
Asake (riv.), Japan 83/K5
'Asal (depr.), Djib. 118/B3
Āsalē, Eth. 118/B2
'Asalūyeh, Iran 103/H5
Asama-yama (peak), Japan 85/F2
Asamankese, Gha. 115/E5
Asan (bay), SKor. 81/D4
Asankrangwa, Gha. 115/E5
Asansol, India 97/F4
Asashi-dake (peak), Japan 85/F1
Asashina, Japan 83/A1
Asau, Sam. 137/R9
Asawanwah (well), Libya 108/C4
Āsayita, Eth. 118/B3
Asbach, Ger. 55/G2
Asbach-Bäumenheim, Ger. 58/D5
Āsbe Teferī, Eth. 118/B3
Asbest, Rus. 69/P4
Asbestos, Qu, Can. 161/L2
Asbestos. (mts.), SAfr. 124/C3
Asbury, Ia, US 155/J2
Asbury Park, NJ, US 168/D3
Ascención (bay), Mex. 172/D4
Ascensión, Arg. 190/E2
Ascención, Bol. 185/F4
Ascensión, Mex. 175/J5
Ascension, NAnt. 180/D1
Ascensione, Monte dell (peak), It. 65/C2
Aschach (riv.), Aus. 59/G6
Aschach an der Donau, Aus. 59/H6
Aschaffenburg, Ger. 58/C3
Aschau am Inn, Ger. 59/F6
Ascheberg, Ger. 53/E5
Aschendorf, Ger. 53/E2
Aschersleben, Ger. 42/F3
Ascog, Sc, UK 33/A5
Ascoli Piceno (prov.), It. 65/C1
Ascoli Piceno, It. 65/C2
Ascoli Satriano, It. 48/D2
Ascona, Swi. 61/E5
Ascope, Peru 184/B2
Ascot, Eng, UK 30/B2
Āsebot, Eth. 118/B3
Åseda, Swe. 40/F3
Aseki, PNG 129/G1
Āsela, Eth. 118/A4
Åsele, Swe. 38/F2
Āsendabo, Eth. 117/H4
Asendorf, Ger. 53/G2
Asendorf, Ger. 53/F3
Asenovgrad, Bul. 51/G4
Åseral, Nor. 40/B2
Aserei (peak), It. 62/C4
Asfeld, Fr. 55/D5
Ash, Eng, UK 30/A3
Ash, Eng, UK 30/D3
Ash Flat, Ar, US 153/J2
Ash Fork, Az, US 149/F3
Ash Shabakah, Iraq 102/E4
Ash Shāghūr, Jor. 105/D5
Ash Shamal (gov.), Leb. 104/E2
Ash Shamālīyah (pol. reg.), Sudan 109/E4
Ash Shāmīyah, Iraq 103/F4
Ash Shanāwīyah, Egypt 113/C6
Ash Shāriqah, UAE 101/G3
Ash Sharqāt, Iraq 103/E3
Ash Sharqīyah (prov.), Sudan 109/G5
Ash Shaţrah, Iraq 103/F4
Ash Shawal, Sudan 117/G2
Ash Shawāshinah, Egypt 113/B6
Ash Shawbak, Jor. 104/D4
Ash Shaykh Sa'd, Syria 105/E3
Ash Shiḩr, Yem. 118/D2
Ash Shīn, Egypt 113/B2
Ash Shuhadā', Egypt 113/B3
Ash Shumlūl, SAr. 100/E3
Ash Shuqayq, SAr. 100/D5
Ash Shurayf, SAr. 100/C3
Asha, Nga. 115/F5
Ashampstead, Eng, UK 37/E4
Ashanti (pol. reg.), Gha. 115/E5
Ashanti (uplands), Gha. 114/E5
Asharoken, NY, US 169/M8
Ashbourne, Ire. 34/B4
Ashbourne, Eng, UK 35/G5
Ashburn, Ga, US 165/G2
Ashburton, NZ 135/B3
Ashburton, Eng, UK 36/C5
Ashburton (riv.), Austl. 127/A3
Ashburton Downs, Austl. 130/C2
Ashby, Mn, US 156/G4
Ashby (canal), Eng, UK 37/E1
Ashby-de-la-Zouch, Eng, UK 37/E1
Ashcroft, BC, Can. 144/D2
Ashdod, Isr. 105/B5
Ashdot Ya'aqov, Isr. 105/D3
Ashdown, Ar, US 153/G4
Asheboro, NC, US 163/H3
Asher, Ok, US 153/F3
Ashern, Mb, Can. 156/E2
Asherton, Tx, US 150/E3
Asheville, NC, US 163/F3
Ashfield, Austl. 133/E1
Ashford, Austl. 132/D1
Ashford, Ire. 34/B5
Ashford, Eng, UK 30/B2
Ashford, Eng, UK 37/G4
Ashford, Al, US 165/F2
Ashfordby, Eng, UK 37/F1
Ashgabat (cap.), Trkm. 101/G1
Ashgrove, On, Can. 160/T8
Ashhurst, NZ 135/C3
Ashibetsu, Japan 82/C2
Ashigawa, Japan 83/B2
Ashikaga, Japan 83/C1
Ashington, Eng, UK 35/G1
Ashino (lake), Japan 83/C3
Ashiwada, Japan 83/B3
Ashiya, Japan 83/H6
Ashiyasu, Japan 83/A2
Ashizuri-Misaki (cape), Japan 84/C4
Ashkal (lake), Tun. 112/L6
Ashkelon NP, Isr. 105/B5
Ashkhabad (int'l arpt.), Trkm. 101/G1
Ashkīdah, Libya 108/B3
Ashland, Al, US 162/E4
Ashland, Ks, US 152/E2
Ashland, Ky, US 163/F1
Ashland, La, US 153/H4
Ashland, Mo, US 153/H1
Ashland, Ms, US 162/C3
Ashland, Mt, US 145/L5
Ashland, NY, US 161/J3
Ashland, Oh, US 160/E4
Ashland, Or, US 146/B2
Ashland, Pa, US 168/B2
Ashland, Tx, US 151/G1
Ashland, Wi, US 157/J4
Ashland City, Tn, US 162/D2
Ashley, ND, US 156/E4
Ashley, Austl. 132/D1
Ashley, Il, US 162/C1
Ashley, Pa, US 168/C1
Ashley Green, Eng, UK 30/B1
Ashmore, Il, US 160/B5
Ashmore and Cartier Islands (terr.), Austl. 127/B2
Ashmore (reef), Austl. 128/A3
Ashmūn, Egypt 113/B4
Ashnola Ind. Res., BC, Can. 144/D3
Ashoknagar, India 96/A3
Ashoro, Japan 82/C2
Ashqelon, Isr. 105/B5
Ashstead, Eng, UK 30/C3
Ashta, India 92/C3
Ashtabula, Oh, US 160/F4
Ashtarak, Arm. 71/H4
Ashti, India 95/C1
Āshtīān, Iran 103/G3
Ashton, SAfr. 124/M10
Ashton, Fl, US 164/N7
Ashton, Id, US 147/H1
Ashton, Il, US 155/K3
Ashton, SD, US 154/E1
Ashton-In-Makerfield, Eng, UK 35/F5
Ashton-under-Lyne, Eng, UK 35/F5
Ashuapmushuan (riv.), Qu, Can. 158/A1
Ashville, Oh, US 160/E5
Ashville, Al, US 162/D4
Ashwabay (mt.), Wi, US 157/J4
Ashwaubenon, Wi, US 160/B2
Ashwell, Eng, UK 37/F2
Asia (cont.) 77/*
Asia, Peru 184/B4
Asiago, It. 61/H6
Asidonhoppo, Sur. 182/C2
Asikkala, Fin. 41/L1
Asikkalanselkä (lake), Fin. 39/F3
Asilah, Mor. 112/A2
Asillo, Peru 184/D4
Asina, It. 65/C4
Asinara (gulf), It. 48/A2
Asinara (isl.), It. 48/A2
Asino, Rus. 74/J4
Asipovichy, Bela. 70/D1
`Asīr (mts.), SAr. 100/D5
Asis (cape), Sudan 109/H5
Aska, India 95/E2
Aşkale, Turk. 102/E2
Askam in Furness, Eng, UK 35/E3
Askaniya-Nova, Ukr. 73/G4
Askeaton, Ire. 32/B4
Asker, Nor. 40/D2
Askern, Eng, UK 35/G4
Askersund, Swe. 40/F2
Askew, Ms, US 162/B3
Askham, SAfr. 124/C2
Askim, Nor. 40/D2
Askim, Swe. 40/D3
Áskion (peak), Gre. 49/G2
Askiz, Rus. 99/F1
Askja (crater), Ice. 38/P6
Askö (isl.), Swe. 39/A2
Askola, Fin. 39/F4
Askot, India 96/C1
Askov, Mn, US 157/H4
Askov, Den. 40/C4
Askøy, Nor. 40/A1
Askvoll, Nor. 38/C3
Āsmār, Afg. 98/A2
Asmara (cap.), Erit. 118/A2
Asnæs, Den. 39/H7
Asnen (lake), Swe. 40/F3
Asnières-sur-Oise, Fr. 30/K4
Asnières-sur-Seine, Fr. 30/J5
Aso (riv.), It. 65/C1
Asō, Japan 83/E2
Aso NP, Japan 84/B4
Aso-san (peak), Japan 84/B4
Asola, It. 62/D3
Asolo, It. 63/E2
Āsosa, Eth. 117/G3
Asoteriba (peak), Sudan 109/H4
Asotin, Wa, US 144/F4
Aspach, Aus. 59/G6
Asparn, Aus. 51/N7
Aspatria, Eng, UK 35/E2
Aspe, Sp. 47/E3
Aspen (lake), Or, US 146/B2
Aspen Grove, BC, Can. 144/D3
Aspen Hill, Md, US 168/A5
Aspendos (ruin), Turk. 104/B1
Asperg, Ger. 58/C5
Aspermont, Tx, US 152/D4
Aspers, Pa, US 168/A4
Aspetuck (riv.), Ct, US 169/E1
Aspiring (mt.), NZ 135/B4
Aspres-sur-Buëch, Fr. 64/B3
Aspy (bay), NS, Can. 159/G2
Asquith, Sk, Can. 145/L1
Assa, Mor. 110/C3
Assa Aguiene (peak), Alg. 111/G5
Assab, Erit. 118/B2
Assam (state), India 93/F2
Assaouas, Niger 115/G2
Assaré, Braz. 183/G4
Assaria, Ks, US 153/F1
Assateague Island Nat'l Seashore, Md, US 163/K1
Asse, Belg. 55/D2
Assegairivier (riv.), SAfr. 123/F5
Assemini, It. 48/A3
Assen, Neth. 52/D3
Assenede, Belg. 54/C1
Assens, Den. 40/C4
Assens, Den. 40/D3
Assentoft, Den. 40/D3
Assesse, Belg. 55/E3
Assiniboia, Sk, Can. 145/M3
Assiniboine (riv.), Sk, Can. 156/D2
Assiniboine (riv.), Mb, Can. 140/F4
Assiniboine (mt.), Ab, Can. 144/G2
Assiniboine Ind. Res., Sk, Can. 156/C2
Assis, Braz. 189/G2
Assis Chateaubriand, Braz. 189/F3
Assisi, It. 65/B1
Assling, Ger. 59/F6
Asso, It. 62/C2
Assok-Ngoum, Gabon 120/B2
Assomada, CpV. 107/K10
Assou (riv.), Fr. 47/G1
Assumption, Il, US 155/K4
Astagram, Bang. 97/H3
Astakós, Gre. 49/G3
Astana (cap.), Kaz. 99/B1
Astara, Iran 103/G2
Astara, Azer. 71/J5
Astatula, Fl, US 164/M6
Asten, Aus. 59/H6
Asten, Neth. 52/C6
Asti (prov.), It. 62/B3
Astico (riv.), It. 63/E1
Astillero, Peru 184/D4
Astipálaia (isl.), Gre. 67/K3
Astipálaia, Gre. 67/K3
Astle, NB, Can. 158/D2
Aston, Eng, UK 37/E2
Aston on Clun, Eng, UK 36/D2
Astorga, Braz. 189/G2
Astoria (nbrhd.), NY, US 169/K8
Astoria, Il, US 155/J3
Astoria, Or, US 144/C4
Åstorp, Swe. 40/E3
Astra, Arg. 190/D5
Astrakhan', Rus. 71/J3
Astrakhanskaya Oblast, Rus. 71/H3
Astrodome, Tx, US 151/M9
Ástros, Gre. 49/H4
Astroworld, Tx, US 151/M9
Astudillo, Sp. 46/C1
Asturias (dist.), Sp. 46/B1
Astwood Bank, Eng, UK 37/E2
Asuka, Japan 83/J7
Asuke, Japan 83/M5
Asuncion (isl.), NMar. 136/D3
Asunción, Bol. 184/E3
Asunción (cap.), Par. 188/E3
Asunción (Silvio Pettirossi) (int'l arpt.), Par. 188/E3
Asunción Ixtaltepec, Mex. 172/B4
Asunden (lake), Swe. 40/F3
Asunta, Bol. 185/E5
Aswa (riv.), Ugan. 117/G5
Aswa, Ugan. 117/G5
Aswān (gov.), Egypt 109/G4
Aswān, Egypt 109/G3
Aswan High (dam), Egypt 109/G4
Asyūţ (gov.), Egypt 109/F3
Asyūţ, Egypt 109/F3
Asyūţī (wadi), Egypt 109/F3
Aszód, Hun. 51/R9
At Ta'mīn (gov.), Iraq 103/E3
At Tabbīn, Egypt 113/C5
Aţ Ţafīlah (gov.), Jor. 104/D4
Aţ Ţafīlah, Jor. 104/D4
Aţ Ţā'if, SAr. 100/D4
At Tall, Syria 105/E1
At Tall al Kabīr, Egypt 113/C3
Aţ Ţallāb, Libya 108/D3
At Tamīmī, Libya 67/J4
Aţ Ţawd, Egypt 113/B3
Aţ Ţayyibah, Leb. 105/D2
Aţ Ţayyibah, Jor. 105/D3
Aţ Ţīnah, Egypt 113/D2
Aţ Ţunayb, Jor. 105/D5
Aţ Ţūr, Egypt 109/G2
Aţ Ţūr, WBnk. 105/C5
At Turbah, Yem. 118/C2
Aţ Ţuwayshah, Sudan 117/E2
Aţ Ţuwayyah, SAr. 102/E5
Atabapo (riv.), Ven. 181/E4
Atacama (des.), Chile 179/B4
Atacama (pol. reg.), Chile 188/B4
Atacames, Ecu. 180/B4
Atafu (isl.), Tok. 137/H5
Atakpamé, Togo 115/F5
Atalaia do Norte, Braz. 184/D2
Atalándi, Gre. 49/H3
Atalaya, Peru 184/C3
Atamanovka, Kaz. 78/G1
Atambohobe, Madg. 125/H8
Atambua, Indo. 128/B2
Atami, Japan 85/F3
Atap, Indo. 91/E3
Atapupu, Indo. 128/B2
'Atāq, Yem. 118/C2
Atarfe, Sp. 46/D4
Atarra, India 96/C3
Atas Bogd (peak), Mong. 78/D3
Atascadero, Ca, US 148/B3
Atascosa (riv.), Tx, US 151/E3
Atascosa, Tx, US 150/E3
Atasu, Kaz. 99/B2
Atatürk (dam), Turk. 102/D2
Ataturk (int'l arpt.), Turk. 103/M7
Atatürk (res.), Turk 102/D2
Atauro (isl.), ETim. 128/B2
Ātaya, Eth. 118/A3
Atbara, Sudan 117/G1
Atbara (riv.), Eth. 117/H2
Atbara (riv.), Sudan 107/F3
'Atbarah, Nahr (riv.), Sudan 100/B5
Atbasar, Kaz. 99/A1
Atchafalaya (riv.), La, US 151/J2
Atchafalaya (bay), La, US 151/J3
Atchison, Ks, US 155/G4
Atco, NJ, US 168/D4
Atebubu, Gha. 115/E5
Ateca, Sp. 46/E2
Ateelva (riv.), Nor. 38/G1
Atén, Bol. 184/D4
Atencingo, Mex. 175/L8
Atenco, Mex. 175/Q10
Atenco, Mex. 175/R9
Atengo (riv.), Mex. 174/D4
Aterno (riv.), It. 65/C3
Atessa, It. 65/D3
Aţfīḩ, Egypt 113/C6
Atglen, Pa, US 168/C4
Ath, Belg. 54/C2
Athabasca (riv.), Ab, Can. 140/E3
Athabasca (lake), Ab,Sk, Can. 140/E3
Āthārabāri, Bang. 97/H3
Athboy, Ire. 32/D2
Athea, Ire. 32/A5
Athena, Or, US 144/E5
Athenry, Ire. 32/B3
Athens, On, Can. 161/J2
Athens (Athínai) (cap.), Gre. 49/N9
Athens, Al, US 162/D3
Athens, Ar, US 153/H3
Athens, NY, US 161/K3
Athens, Oh, US 160/E5
Athens, Pa, US 161/H4
Athens, Mi, US 160/D3
Athens, WV, US 163/G2
Athens, Tn, US 162/E3
Athens, Ga, US 163/F4
Athens, Il, US 155/K4
Athens, Tx, US 151/G1
Atherstone, Eng, UK 37/E1
Atherton, Eng, UK 35/F4
Atherton, Austl. 134/B2
Athgarh, India 95/E1
Athi (riv.), Kenya 119/B2
Athi River, Kenya 119/B2
Athienou, Cyp. 104/C2
Athínai (Athens) (cap.), Gre. 49/N9
Athis-Mons, Fr. 30/K5
Athleague, Ire. 32/B2
Athlone, Ire. 32/C3
Athok, Myan. 86/B5
Athol, Ma, US 161/K3
Athol, NZ 135/B4
Atholl (for.), Sc, UK 33/B3
Áthos (peak), Gre. 49/J2
Athribis (ruin), Egypt 113/C4
Athy, Ire. 32/D4
Ati, Chad 116/C2
Ati Ardébé, Chad 116/C2
Atiak, Ugan. 121/H2
Atibaia (riv.), Braz. 187/K7
Atibaia, Braz. 187/K8
Atico, Peru 184/C5
Atienza, Sp. 46/D2
Atikokan, On, Can. 157/J3
Atil, Mex. 174/C2
Atinggola, Indo. 91/F3
Atitlán (lake), Guat. 176/D3
Atiu (isl.), CookIs. 137/K7
Atizapan, Mex. 175/Q10
Atka, Rus. 75/R3
Atka (isl.), Ak, US 171/D5
Atka, Ak, US 171/D5
Atkarsk, Rus. 71/H2
Atkins, Ar, US 153/H3
Atkins, Va, US 163/G2
Atkinson (isl.), Tx, US 151/N9
Atlacomulco de Fabela, Mex. 175/K7
Atlanta, SAfr. 123/E5
Atlanta (cap.), Ga, US 163/M7
Atlanta, Il, US 155/K3
Atlanta, La, US 164/B2
Atlanta, Mi, US 160/D2
Atlanta, Tx, US 153/G4
Atlanta Botanical Garden, Ga, US 163/M7
Atlanta Nav. Air Sta., Ga, US 163/L7
Atlantic, NC, US 163/J3
Atlantic (ocean) 26/G3
Atlantic (peak), Wy, US 147/J2
Atlantic, Ia, US 155/G3
Atlantic (co.), NJ, US 168/D4
Atlantic Beach, Fl, US 165/H2
Atlantic Beach, NY, US 169/L9
Atlantic City, Wy, US 147/J2
Atlantic City, NJ, US 168/D5
Atlantic City International (arpt.), NJ, US 168/D5
Atlantic Highlands, NJ, US 169/J10
Atlantico (dept.), Col. 177/H4
Atlántida, Uru. 191/L11
Atlantique (prov.), Ben. 115/F5
Atlas (mts.), Afr. 66/C4
Atlas (peak), Ca, US 167/K10
Atlasovo, Rus. 75/R4
Atlatlahuaca, Mex. 175/Q10
Atlin, BC, Can. 171/M3
Atlin (lake), BC, Can. 171/M3
'Atlit, Isr. 105/B3
Atlixco, Mex. 175/L8
Atmore, Al, US 164/E2
Atnarko (riv.), BC, Can. 144/B1
Atocha, Bol. 188/C2
Atoka, Ok, US 153/F3
Atoka (res.), Ok, US 153/F3
Atoka, Tn, US 162/C3
Atome, Ang. 122/B1
Atomic City, Id, US 147/G2
Atondo, D.R. Congo 121/F3
Atotonilco, Mex. 175/L6
Atouila, 'Erg (des.), Mali 110/D5
Atoyac (riv.), Mex. 176/B2
Atoyac, Mex. 175/E5
Atqasuk, Ak, US 171/G1
Atrai (riv.), Bang. 97/G3
Atrak (riv.), Iran 74/F6
Ätran (riv.), Swe. 40/E3
Atrato (riv.), Col. 173/F6
Atrauli, India 96/B1
Atri, It. 65/C2
Atripalda, It. 65/D6
Atsugi, Japan 83/C3
Atsumi, Japan 83/M6
Atsumi (pen.), Japan 83/M6
Attalens, Swi. 60/C4
Attalla, Al, US 162/D3
Attapu, Laos 94/D3
Attapulgus, Ga, US 165/F2
Attawapiskat, On, Can. 141/H3
Attawapiskat (riv.), On, Can. 141/H3
Attean (mtn.), Me, US 161/L2
Attel (riv.), Ger. 59/F7
Attendorn, Ger. 53/E6
Atteridgeville, SAfr. 124/Q12
Attersee (lake), Aus. 45/K3
Attert, Belg. 55/E4
Attica, Ks, US 153/E2
Attica, Oh, US 160/E4
Attica, In, US 160/C4
Attica, Mi, US 167/F5
Attigliano, It. 65/B2
Attigny, Fr. 55/D5
'Attīl, WBnk. 105/C4
Attingal, India 95/C4
Attleboro, Ma, US 161/L4
Attleborough, Eng, UK 37/E1
Attnang-Puchheim, Aus. 59/G6
Attock, Pak. 98/B3
Attoyac (riv.), Tx, US 151/G2
Attu (isl.), Ak, US 171/A5
Āttūr, India 95/C4
Atuel (riv.), Arg. 190/D2
Atuntaqui, Ecu. 180/B4
Atuona, FrPol. 137/M5
Ātura, Bang. 97/G3
Atura, Ugan. 121/H2
Åtvidaberg, Swe. 40/G2
Atwater, Ca, US 148/B2
Atwood, Ok, US 153/F3
Atwood, Ks, US 154/D4
Atwood, Co, US 154/C3
Atyraū (int'l arpt.), Kaz. 71/J3
Atyraū, Kaz. 71/J3
Atyraū Oblast, Kaz. 71/J3
Atzcapotzalco (nbrhd.), Mex. 175/Q10
Au, Swi. 61/F3
Au, Aus. 61/F3
Au Gres, Mi, US 160/E2
Au in der Hallertau, Ger. 59/E5
Au Sable (riv.), Mi, US 160/E2
Au Sable (pt.), Mi, US 160/E2
Au Sable, Mi, US 160/E2
Auari (riv.), Braz. 181/E3
Auas, Hon. 177/E3
Auasbila, Hon. 177/E3
Aub, Namb. 122/C4
Aubá, ETim. 128/B2
Aubagne, Fr. 64/B6
Aubange, Belg. 55/E4
Aube, Fr. 57/F3
Aube (riv.), Fr. 42/C4
Aube (dept.), Fr. 55/D6
Aubepierre-Ozouer-le-Repos, Fr. 30/L6
Aubergenville, Fr. 30/H5
Auberry, Ca, US 148/C2
Aubert (peak), Swi. 60/C4
Aubervilliers, Fr. 30/K5
Aubetin (riv.), Fr. 54/C6
Aubette (riv.), Fr. 54/A5
Aubette de Magny (riv.), Fr. 30/H4
Aubevoye, Fr. 57/G2
Aubignon, Fr. 64/B4
Aubigny-en-Artois, Fr. 54/B3
Aubigny-sur-Nère, Fr. 44/E3
Aubin, Fr. 44/E4
Aubonne, Swi. 60/C5
Auboué, Fr. 55/E5
Aubrac (mts.), Fr. 44/E4
Aubrey, Ar, US 162/B3
Aubrives, Fr. 55/D3
Auburn, Austl. 131/H5
Auburn (nbrhd.), Austl. 134/H8
Auburn, Al, US 162/E4
Auburn, Ca, US 146/C4
Auburn, Ga, US 162/F3
Auburn, Il, US 155/K4
Auburn, In, US 160/D4
Auburn, Ks, US 153/G1
Auburn, Ky, US 162/D2
Auburn, Ma, US 161/L3
Auburn, Me, US 161/L2
Auburn, Ms, US 164/C2
Auburn, Ne, US 155/G3
Auburn, NY, US 161/H3
Auburn, Pa, US 168/B2
Auburn, Wa, US 144/C4
Auburn Hills, Mi, US 167/F6
Auburndale, Fl, US 164/M7
Aubusson, Fr. 44/E4
Aucá Mahuida (peak), Arg. 190/C3
Auce, Lat. 41/K3
Auch, Fr. 44/D5
Auchel, Fr. 54/B3
Auchenblae, Sc, UK 33/D3
Auchencairn, Sc, UK 34/E2
Auchi, Nga. 115/G5
Auchinleck, Sc, UK 33/B6
Auchterarder, Sc, UK 33/C4
Auchtermuchty, Sc, UK 33/C4
Auchy-lès-Hesdin, Fr. 54/B3
Aucilla (riv.), Fl, US 165/G2
Auckland (isls.), NZ 27/T8
Auckland (int'l arpt.), NZ 135/F6
Auckland, NZ 135/F6
Auckland Domain, NZ 135/F6
Aude (riv.), Fr. 66/D2
Auden, On, Can. 157/L2
Auderghem, Belg. 55/D2
Audet, Qu, Can. 158/B3
Audeux (riv.), Fr. 60/C3
Audience Hall, VatC. 65/G7
Audierne (bay), Fr. 44/A3
Audincourt, Fr. 60/C3
Audlem, Eng, UK 35/F6
Audley, Eng, UK 35/F5
Audo (range), Eth. 118/B4
Audruicq, Fr. 54/B2
Audubon, Ia, US 155/G3
Audubon NWR, ND, US 156/D4
Audun-le-Roman, Fr. 55/E5
Audun-le-Tiche, Fr. 55/E5
Aue (riv.), Ger. 53/E2
Aue, Ger. 59/F1
Auer (Ora), It. 61/H5
Auerbach, Ger. 59/F1
Auerbach in der Oberpfalz, Ger. 59/E3
Auersberg (peak), Ger. 59/F2
Aufess (riv.), Ger. 58/E3
Auffargis, Fr. 30/H5
Auffay, Fr. 57/G1
Augathella, Austl. 134/B4
Auger (falls), Id, US 147/F2
Augher, NI, UK 34/A3
Aughinish (isl.), Ire. 32/A4
Aughnacloy, NI, UK 34/B3
Aughrim, Ire. 34/B6
Auglaize (riv.), Oh, US 160/D4
Augrabies Falls NP, SAfr. 124/C3
Augrabiesvalle (falls), SAfr. 124/C3
Augsburg, Ger. 58/D6
Augsburg (Mühlhausen) (arpt.), Ger. 58/D6
Augub (peak), Namb. 124/A2
Augusta, Austl. 130/B5
Augusta, It. 48/D4
Augusta (gulf), It. 48/D4
Augusta, Ar, US 153/J3
Augusta, Ga, US 163/G4
Augusta, Il, US 155/J3
Augusta, Ks, US 153/F2
Augusta (cap.), Me, US 158/C3
Augusta, Mt, US 145/H4
Augusta, NJ, US 168/D1
Augusta, Wi, US 155/J1
Augusta, WV, US 161/G5
Augustdorf, Ger. 53/F5
Augustenborg, Den. 40/C4
Augustine Ind. Res., Ca, US 148/D4
Augusto César Sandino (int'l arpt.), Nic. 176/E3
Augustów, Pol. 41/K5
Augustus (mt.), Austl. 130/C3
Auk Bok (isl.), Myan. 94/B3
Aukam, Namb. 124/B2
Auki, Sol. 136/F5
Aukstatija NP, Lith. 41/M4
Aulander, NC, US 163/J2
Aulatsivik, North (isl.), Nf, Can. 141/K3
Aulatsivik, South (isl.), Nf, Can. 141/K3
Auld (lake), Austl. 127/B3
Auldearn, Sc, UK 33/C1
Aulencia (riv.), Sp. 47/M9
Aulendorf, Ger. 61/F2
Aulla, It. 62/C5
Aulnay-sous-Bois, Fr. 30/K5
Aulnay-sur-Mauldre, Fr. 30/H5
Aulne (riv.), Fr. 44/A2
Aulneau (pen.), On, Can. 157/G3
Aulnoy, Fr. 30/M5
Aulnoye-Aymeries, Fr. 54/C3
Aulnut (int'l arpt.), Fr. 44/E4
Ault (peak), Swi. 61/F4
Ault, Fr. 54/A3
Ault, Co, US 154/B3
Aumale, Fr. 54/A4
Aumetz, Fr. 55/E5
Aumsville, Or, US 146/B1
Aumühle, Ger. 53/H1
Auna, Nga. 115/G4
Aunay-sur-Odon, Fr. 57/E2
Aune (riv.), Fr. 57/F5
Auneau, Fr. 57/G4
Aunette (riv.), Fr. 54/B5
Auneuil, Fr. 54/B5
Auning, Den. 40/D3
Auob (riv.), Namb. 122/C5
Auobrivier (riv.), SAfr. 122/D5
Aups, Fr. 64/C5
Aur (isl.), Mrsh. 136/G4
Aur (isl.), Malay. 89/D2
Aura, NJ, US 168/C4
Aurach (riv.), Ger. 58/D3
Aurach, Ger. 58/D4
Auraiya, India 96/B2
Aurangābād, India 97/E3
Aurangābād, India 95/B2
Auray, Fr. 56/C5
Aureilhan, Fr. 44/D5
Aurelia, Ia, US 155/G2
Aurelian (wall), It. 65/G8
Aurès (mts.), Alg. 66/E4
Aurich, Ger. 53/E2
Auriflama, Braz. 189/G2
Aurillac, Fr. 44/E4
Auriol, Fr. 64/B6
Aurisina, It. 63/G2
Aurland, Nor. 40/B1
Aurolzmünster, Aus. 59/G6
Aurora, Braz. 183/G4
Aurora, On, Can. 161/G3
Aurora, Guy. 181/G3
Aurora, Phil. 88/C4
Aurora, Co, US 154/B4
Aurora, Il, US 160/B4
Aurora, Mo, US 153/H2
Aurora, NC, US 163/J3
Aurora, Ne, US 154/E3
Aurora, Ut, US 149/G1
Aurora Ghost Town, Nv, US 146/D4
Aurora Lodge, Ak, US 171/J3
Aurunci (mts.), It. 65/C5
Aus, Namb. 124/B2
Ausa (riv.), It. 63/G1
Ausable (riv.), On, Can. 160/F3
Auschwitz (Oświęcim), Pol. 43/K3
Ausert, WSah. 110/B5
Ausoni (mts.), It. 65/C5
Aussenkehr, Namb. 124/B3
Aussillon, Fr. 44/E5
Aust-Agder (co.), Nor. 38/C4
Austell, Ga, US 163/L7
Austin (lake), Austl. 127/A3
Austin, Mb, Can. 156/E3
Austin (isl.), Nun, Can. 140/G2
Austin, In, US 162/E1
Austin, Ky, US 162/D2
Austin, Mn, US 155/H2
Austin, Nv, US 146/E4
Austin, Or, US 146/D1
Austin (cap.), Tx, US 151/F2
Austin Bayou (riv.), Tx, US 151/M9
Austonio, Tx, US 151/G2
Austral (Tubuaï Islands) (isls.), FrPol. 137/K7
Australia (ctry.) 127/*
Australia (cont.) 127/*
Australian, BC, Can. 144/C1
Australian Capital Terr., Austl. 127/D4
Australind, Austl. 130/B5
Austria (ctry.) 45/L3
Austurhorn (pt.), Ice. 38/P7
Autaugaville, Al, US 162/D4
Autazes, Braz. 182/B3
Auterive, Fr. 44/D5
Authie (riv.), Fr. 42/B3
Authion (riv.), Fr. 57/E6
Authon-du-Perche, Fr. 57/F4
Autlán de Navarro, Mex. 174/D5
Automne (riv.), Fr. 54/B5
Autore (peak), It. 65/C4
Autreppe, Belg. 54/C3
Autun, Fr. 44/F3
Auvergne, Ar, US 153/J3
Auvergne (pol. reg.), Fr. 44/E4
Auvergne, Austl. 128/C3
Auvers-sur-Oise, Fr. 30/J4
Auvézère (riv.), Fr. 44/D4
Aux Barques (pt.), Mi, US 160/E2
Aux Barques (pt.), Mi, US 160/C2
Auxerre, Fr. 44/E3
Auxi-le-Château, Fr. 54/B3
Auxonne, Fr. 60/B3
Auxvasse, Mo, US 155/J4
Auyán-Tepuí (peak), Ven. 181/F3
Auyuittuq NP, Nun, Can. 141/K2
Auzangate (peak), Peru 184/D4
Ava, Mo, US 153/H2
Ava, Il, US 162/C2
Ava, Myan. 94/A1
Āvaj, Iran 103/G3
Avallon, Fr. 44/E3
Avaloirs (peak), Fr. 57/E4
Avalon, Ca, US 166/B4
Avalon (pen.), Nf, Can. 141/L4
Avalon, Mo, US 155/H4
Avalon, NJ, US 168/D5
Avanigadda, India 95/D2
Avanne-Aveney, Fr. 60/B3
Avaré, Braz. 189/G2
Avarua, NZ 137/K7
Avcilar, Turk. 103/M7
Avdiyivka, Ukr. 73/J3
Avebury, Eng, UK 37/E4
Avebury Stone Circle, Eng, UK 37/E4
Aveiro, Port. 46/A2
Aveiro (dist.), Port. 46/A2
Aveley, Eng, UK 30/D2
Avelgem, Belg. 54/C2
Avellaneda, Arg. 191/J11
Avellino, It. 65/D6
Avellino (prov.), It. 65/D6
Avelon (riv.), Fr. 54/A5
Aven (riv.), Fr. 56/B4
Avenal, Ca, US 148/B2
Avenches, Swi. 60/D4
Avenel, NJ, US 169/H9
Avernes, Fr. 30/H4
Aversa, It. 65/D6
Avery, Id, US 144/G4
Avery Island, La, US 164/C3
Aves (isl.), Ven. 173/J4
Avesnes-le-Comte, Fr. 54/B3
Avesnes-sur-Helpe, Fr. 54/C3
Avessac, Fr. 56/D5
Avesta, Swe. 40/G1
Aveyron (riv.), Fr. 44/D4
Avezzano, It. 65/C3
Avich (lake), Sc, UK 33/A4
Aviemore, Sc, UK 33/C2
Avigliana, It. 64/D2
Avignon, Fr. 64/A5
Aviḩayil, Isr. 105/B4
Ávila de los Caballeros, Sp. 46/C2
Avilés, Sp. 46/C1
Avio, It. 63/D2
Avion, Fr. 54/B3
Aviron (pt.), Nf, Can. 159/J2
Avis, Pa, US 168/A1
Avisio (riv.), It. 61/H5
Avize, Fr. 54/D6
Avlum, Den. 40/C3
Avoca (riv.), Ire. 34/B6
Avoca, Austl. 132/C4
Avoca, Austl. 132/B3
Avoca, Ia, US 155/G3
Avoca, NY, US 161/H3
Avoch, Sc, UK 33/B1
Avoine, Fr. 57/F6
Avola, It. 48/D4
Avola, BC, Can. 144/E2
Avon (lake), Austl. 133/E2
Avon (riv.), Fr. 30/L6
Avon (riv.), Eng, UK 36/C6
Avon (riv.), Sc, UK 33/C1
Avon, Al, US 165/F2
Avon, Il, US 155/J3
Avon, Mn, US 157/G5
Avon, Ms, US 162/B4
Avon, NC, US 163/K3
Avon, NY, US 161/H3
Avon Downs, Austl. 129/E5
Avon Park, Fl, US 164/M8
Avon Park Bombing Range, Fl, US 165/H4
Avon Valley NP, Austl. 130/C4
Avon Water (riv.), Sc, UK 33/B5
Avonbeg (riv.), Ire. 34/B6
Avondale, Co, US 152/B1
Avondale, Pa, US 168/C4
Avondale, Austl. 133/E2
Avonlea, Sk, Can. 156/B2
Avonmore (riv.), Ire. 34/B5
Avonmouth, Eng, UK 36/D3
Avraga, Mong. 78/F2
Avranches, Fr. 56/D3
Avre (riv.), Fr. 42/B4
Avrillé, Fr. 57/E5
Avrora, Azer. 103/G2
Avtovo (nbrhd.), Rus. 69/T7
Āvupalli, India 92/D4
Awa-shima (isl.), Japan 82/A4
Awaé, Camr. 120/B2
A'waj (riv.), Syria 104/E3
Awaji, Japan 83/H6
Awakaba, CAfr. 116/D3
Awans, Belg. 55/E2
Awantīpur, India 98/C3
Awanui, NZ 135/C1
Awara (plain), Kenya 118/B5
Āwarē, Eth. 118/C3
Āwasa, Eth. 118/A4
Āwash, Eth. 118/B3
Awash NP, Eth. 118/A3
Āwash Wenz (riv.), Eth. 117/H3
Awasibberge (peak), Namb. 122/B5
Awaso, Gha. 115/E5
Awat, China 99/D3
Awatere (riv.), NZ 135/C3
Awbārī (des.), Libya 111/H4
Awbārī, Libya 108/B3
Awbeg (riv.), Ire. 32/B5
Awdheegle, Som. 118/C5
Awe (lake), Sc, UK 33/A4
Awgu, Nga. 115/G5
Āwira Wenz (riv.), Eth. 118/A2
Awīsh al Ḩajar, Egypt 113/C2
Awjilah, Libya 108/D2
Awka, Nga. 115/G5
Awsīm, Egypt 113/C4
Ax-les-Thermes, Fr. 44/D5
Axamo (int'l arpt.), Swe. 40/F3
Axams, Aus. 61/H3
Axarfjördhur (inlet), Ice. 38/N6
Axbridge, Eng, UK 36/D4
Axel, Neth. 52/A6
Axel Heiberg (isl.), Nun, Can. 141/S7
Axial, Co, US 147/K3
Axim, Gha. 115/E5
Axios (riv.), Gre. 49/H2
Axis (dam), Wa, US 167/D2
Axixá do Tocantins, Braz. 182/E4
Axminster, Eng, UK 36/D5
Axochiapan, Mex. 175/L8
Axson, Ga, US 165/G2
Axtell, Ks, US 155/F4
Axtell, Ne, US 154/E3
Ay (riv.), Fr. 56/D2
Ay (riv.), Rus. 69/N5
Ay, Fr. 54/C5
Ayabaca, Peru 184/B2
Ayabe, Japan 83/H5
Ayacucho, Arg. 190/F3
Ayacucho, Peru 184/C4
Ayacucho (dept.), Peru 184/C4
Ayagöz, Kaz. 99/D2
Ayaguz (riv.), Kaz. 99/D2
Ayakkum (lake), China 99/E4
Ayama, Japan 83/K6
Ayamonte, Sp. 46/B4
Ayan, Rus. 75/P4
Ayancık, Turk. 70/E4
Ayanganna (mtn.), Guy. 181/G3
Ayangba, Nga. 115/G5
Ayanka, Rus. 75/S3
Ayapel, Col. 180/C2
Ayaş, Turk. 102/C1
Ayase, Japan 83/C3
Ayass (peak), Ugan. 119/A1
Ayaviri, Peru 184/D4
Āybak, Afg. 74/G6
Aybas, Kaz. 71/J3
Aybastı, Turk. 70/F4
Aydabul, Kaz. 99/A1
Ayden, NC, US 163/J3
Aydın, Turk. 102/A2
Aydin (prov.), Turk. 102/B2
Aydıncık, Turk. 102/C1
Aydıncık, Turk. 104/C1
Aydınkent, Turk. 104/B1
Aydinli, Turk. 103/N7
Āydora, Eth. 118/B3
Aydyrlinskiy, Rus. 71/L1
Āyelu (peak), Eth. 118/B3
Ayem, Gabon 120/B3
Ayer, Swi. 60/D5
Ayer Hitam, Malay. 89/C2
Ayer's Cliff, Qu, Can. 161/K2
Ayers Rock (Uluru) (peak), Austl. 131/F3
Ayeyarwady (state), Myan. 93/F4
Ayiá, Gre. 49/H3
Ayía Paraskeví, Gre. 49/K3
Ayiásos, Gre. 49/K3
Ayina (riv.), Congo 120/C2
Áyios Athanásios, Gre. 49/J2
Áyios Evstrátios (isl.), Gre. 67/K3
Áyios Ioánnis (cape), Gre. 49/J5
Áyios Kírikos, Gre. 49/K4
Áyios Konstandínos, Gre. 49/H3
Áyios Matthaíos, Gre. 49/F3
Áyios Nikólaos, Gre. 49/J5
Āykel, Eth. 117/H2
Aykhal, Rus. 75/M3
Aylesbury, Eng, UK 37/F3
Aylesford, NS, Can. 158/E3
Aylesford, Eng, UK 37/G4
Aylesham, Eng, UK 37/H4
Ayllón, Sp. 46/D2
Aylmer, On, Can. 160/F3
Aylmer (lake), NW, Can. 140/F2
Aylsham, Eng, UK 37/H1
Aylsham, Sk, Can. 145/N1
'Ayn Ad Darāhim, Tun. 112/L6
'Ayn al 'Arab, Syria 102/D2
'Ayn al Ghazālah, Libya 67/J4
'Ayn Ath Tha'lab, Libya 108/D3
'Ayn Sukhnah, Egypt 113/D5
Ayna, Peru 184/C4
Aynor, SC, US 163/H4
'Aynūnah, SAr. 109/G2
Ayod, Sudan 117/F3
Ayolas, Par. 189/E3
Ayon (isl.), Rus. 75/S3
Ayora, Sp. 47/E3
Ayorou, Niger 115/F3
Ayos, Camr. 120/C2
Ayotzintepec, Mex. 176/B2
'Ayoûn 'Abd el Mâlek (well), Mrta. 110/D4
'Ayoûn el 'Atroûs, Mrta. 114/C2
Ayr (riv.), Sc, UK 33/B5
Ayr, Sc, UK 33/B6
Ayr, Austl. 134/B2
Āysha, Eth. 118/B3
Ayton, Sc, UK 33/D5
Ayton, Eng, UK 35/H3
Āytony, Eth. 117/H3
Aytos, Bul. 51/H4
Aytré, Fr. 44/C3
Ayubia NP, Pak. 98/B3
Ayutinskiy, Rus. 73/L4
Ayutla, Mex. 174/D4
Ayutla de los Libres, Mex. 172/B4
Ayutthaya (ruin), Thai. 94/C3
Ayvacık, Turk. 49/K3
Aywaille, Belg. 55/E3
Az Zabābidah, WBnk. 105/C4
Az Zabadānī, Syria 105/E1
Az Ẓāhirīyah, WBnk. 105/B6
Az Zankalūn, Egypt 113/C3
Az Zaqāzīq, Egypt 113/C3
Az Zarqā' (gov.), Jor. 104/E3
Az Zarqā', Jor. 105/E4
Az Zawāmil, Egypt 113/C4
Az Zāwiyah, Libya 67/G4
Az Zaydāb, Sudan 117/G1
Az Zaydīyah, Yem. 118/B2
Az Zilfī, SAr. 100/D3
Az Zrārīyah, Leb. 105/C2
Az Zubayr, Iraq 103/F4
Az Zurbī, Egypt 113/B6
Azad Kashmir (terr.), Pak. 98/B3
Āzādshahr, Iran 103/G3
Azahar (coast), Sp. 47/F3
Azalea, Or, US 146/B2
Azalia, Mi, US 167/E7
Azamgarh, India 96/D2
Azángaro (riv.), Peru 184/D4
Azángaro, Peru 184/D4
Azao (peak), Alg. 111/H4
Azaouâd (phys. reg.), Mali 115/E2
Azapa, Chile 184/D5
Āzar Shahr, Iran 103/F2
Āzarān, Iran 103/F2
Āzarbāyjān-e Gharbī (gov.), Iran 103/F2
Āzarbāyjān-e Sharqī (gov.), Iran 103/F2
Azare, Nga. 115/H4
Azay-le-Rideau, Fr. 57/F6
A'zāz, Syria 104/E1
Azemmour, Mor. 110/C2
Azerbaijan (ctry.) 71/H4
Āzezo, Eth. 117/H2
Azhikal, India 95/B4
Azhu-Tayga (peak), Rus. 99/E1
Azilal, Mor. 110/D3
Azīmganj, India 97/G3
Azizbekov, Arm. 103/F2
Azle, Tx, US 150/K7
Aznā, Iran 103/G3
Aznakayevo, Rus. 69/M5
Azogues, Ecu. 180/B5
Azores (dpcy.), Port. 47/R12
Azourki (peak), Mor. 110/D3
Azov (sea), Ukr.,Rus. 74/D5
Azov, Rus. 73/K4
Azovs'ke, Ukr. 73/H5
Azoyú, Mex. 176/B2
Azpeitia, Sp. 44/B5
Azrou, Mor. 110/D2
Aztec, NM, US 149/J2
Aztec, Az, US 149/F4
Aztec Ruins Nat'l Mon., NM, US 149/H2
Azua de Compostela, DRep. 173/G4
Azuaga, Sp. 46/C3
Azuara, Sp. 47/E2
Azuay (dept.), Ecu. 180/B5
Azuchi, Japan 83/K5
Azuero (pen.), Pan. 173/E6
Azufre (vol.), Chile 188/B3
Azufre, Paso el (pass), Chile 188/B4
Azuga, Rom. 51/G3
Azul (mtn.), CR 176/E4
Azul (riv.), Guat. 176/D2
Azul, Arg. 190/F3
Azul (peak), Arg. 188/B4
Azul (riv.), Mex. 175/H5
Azul, Cordillera (mts.), Peru 184/B2
'Aẓūm (wadi), Sudan 116/D2
Azuma, Japan 83/E2
Azuma-san (peak), Japan 85/G2
Azumaya-san (peak), Japan 85/F2
Azurduy, Bol. 188/C1
Azure (mtn.), NY, US 161/J2
Azusa, Ca, US 166/C2
Azzaba, Alg. 112/K6
Azzano, It. 63/D3
Azzano Decimo, It. 63/F2
Azzano San Paolo, It. 62/C2
Azzate, It. 62/B2
'Azzūn, WBnk. 105/C4

B

Bà (riv.), Sc, UK 33/B3
Ba, Fiji 137/Y18
Bà (riv.), China 78/F5
Ba Illi, Chad 116/C3
Ba Lang An (cape), Viet. 94/E3
Ba Quan (cape), Viet. 94/D4
Ba Ra, Viet. 94/D4
Ba Xian, China 80/H7
Baa, Indo. 128/A2
Baan Baa, Austl. 132/D1
Baar, Swi. 61/E3
Baargaal, Som. 118/D3
Baarle-Hertog, Belg. 52/B6
Baarle-Nassau, Neth. 52/B6
Baarn, Neth. 52/C4
Bab Taza, Mor. 112/B2
Baba (pt.), Turk. 51/K5
Baba (peak), Bul. 51/F4
Baba (mts.), Afg. 101/J2
Baba Burnu (pt.), Turk. 49/K3

Map Section
206
207

Bangalow, Austl. 134/D5
Bangaon, India 97/G4
Bangar, Phil. 87/J5
Bāngarmau, India 96/C2
Bangassou, CAfr. 116/D4
Bangau (cape), Malay. 88/B4
Bangazeno, D.R. Congo 121/F2
Bangeta (mt.), PNG 129/G1
Banggai (isls.), Indo. 91/F4
Banggong (lake), China 99/C5
Banghiang (riv.), Laos 94/D2
Bangil, Indo. 89/F4
Bangka (isl.), Indo. 77/K10
Bangka (str.), Indo. 90/B4
Bangkalan, Indo. 89/F4
Bangkaru (isl.), Indo. 89/B2
Bangkinang, Indo. 89/C2
Bangkir, Indo. 91/F3
Bangko, Indo. 89/C3
Bangkok (int'l arpt.), Thai. 94/C3
Bangkok (Krung Thep) (cap.), Thai. 94/C3
Bangkok, Bight of (bay), Thai. 93/H5
Bangladesh (ctry.) 97/G4
Bangli, Indo. 89/F5
Bangma (mts.), China 86/C4
Bangor, Sk, Can. 156/C2
Bangor, NI, UK 34/C2
Bangor, Wal, UK 34/D5
Bangor, Mi, US 160/C3
Bangor, Fr. 56/B6
Bangor, Me, US 141/K4
Bangor, Pa, US 168/C2
Bangor-is-y-Coed, Wal, UK 35/F6
Bangoran (riv.), CAfr. 116/C3
Bāngriposi, India 97/F4
Bangs (mt.), Az, US 149/F2
Bangs, Tx, US 150/E2
Bangu, D.R. Congo 121/E5
Bangued, Phil. 88/C1
Bangui (cap.), CAfr. 116/C4
Bangui (int'l arpt.), CAfr. 116/C4
Bangui, EqG. 120/B2
Bangui, Phil. 88/C1
Bangunpurba, Indo. 89/B2
Bangzha, China 86/E3
Banhā, Egypt 113/C4
Banhine, PN de, Moz. 123/G4
Baní, DRep. 173/G4
Bani, CAfr. 116/D4
Bani (riv.), Mali 114/D3
Banī Mazār, Egypt 109/F2
Banī Suhaylah, Gaza 105/A6
Banī Suwayf (gov.), Egypt 102/B3
Banī Suwayf, Egypt 113/C6
Banī 'Ubayd, Egypt 113/C2
Bāni Walīd, Libya 108/B2
Bani-Bangou, Niger 115/F3
Bania, CAfr. 120/D2
Baniachang, Bang. 97/H3
Banian, Gui. 114/C4
Bánica, DRep. 177/J2
Banifing (riv.), Mali 114/D3
Banihāl (pass), India 98/C3
Banikoara, Ben. 115/F4
Banisa, Kenya 118/B5
Banister (riv.), Va, US 163/H2
Bāniyās, Syria 104/D2
Banja Koviljača, Serb. 50/D3
Banja Luka, Bosn. 50/C3
Banjar, Indo. 89/E4
Banjarmasin, Indo. 90/D4
Banjia, China 94/B1
Banjiang, China 87/F3
Banjul (cap.), Gam. 114/A3
Banjul (Yundum) (int'l arpt.), Gam. 114/A3
Bankä, Azer. 103/G2
Bānka, India 97/F3
Banka Banka, Austl. 128/D4
Bankas, Mali 114/E3
Bankengting, China 87/H3
Bankeryd, Swe. 40/F3
Bankfoot, Sc, UK 33/C3
Bankhead, Sc, UK 33/D2
Bankhead (lake), Al, US 162/D4
Bānki, India 97/E4
Bankilare, Niger 115/F3
Banks, Al, US 165/F2
Banks (pen.), NZ 127/H7
Banks (cape), Austl. 132/B3
Banks (isl.), Austl. 129/F2
Banks (str.), Austl. 127/D5
Banks (isl.), NW, Can. 139/E2
Banks (cape), Ak, US 171/H4
Banks (lake), Wa, US 144/E4
Banks (isls.), Van. 136/F6
Bankstown (arpt.), Austl. 134/G8
Bankstown (nbrhd.), Austl. 134/H8
Bānkurā, India 97/F4
Bankya, Bul. 49/H1
Banmankhi, India 97/F3
Banmauk, Myan. 86/B3
Banmian, China 87/H3
Bann (riv.), NI, UK 34/B3
Bann (riv.), Ire. 32/D4
Banna (riv.), It. 62/A3
Bannack, Mt, US 147/G1
Bannalec, Fr. 56/B5
Bannang Sata, Thai. 89/C1
Banner, Wy, US 147/K1
Banner, Ky, US 163/F2
Banning, Ca, US 148/D4
Bannock (pass), Id, US 147/G1
Bannockburn, Sc, UK 33/C4
Bannockburn, Austl. 133/B4
Bannockburn Battlesite, Sc, UK 33/C4
Bannow (bay), Ire. 32/D5
Bannu, Pak. 98/A3
Banon, Fr. 64/B4
Baños, Ecu. 184/B1
Banphot Phisai, Thai. 94/B3
Banpo Ruins, China 80/B4
Bānpur, India 95/E2
Bansberia, India 97/G4
Bānsdīh, India 97/E3
Bansha, Ire. 32/B5
Banshi, China 87/G3
Bānsi, India 96/B3
Bānsi, India 96/D2
Bansihāri, India 97/G3
Bansin, Ger. 40/F5
Bansko, Bul. 49/H2
Banskobystrický (pol. reg.), Slvk. 43/K4
Banstead, Eng, UK 30/C3
Bānswāra, India 92/B3
Bantayan (isl.), Phil. 88/C3
Bantayan, Phil. 88/C3
Banté, Ben. 115/F4
Banteer, Ire. 32/B5
Bantenan (cape), Indo. 89/F5
Bantong Group (isls.), Thai. 94/B5
Bantry, Ire. 32/A6
Bantry (bay), Ire. 32/A6
Bantvāl, India 95/B3
Bañuelo (peak), Sp. 46/C3
Banūr, India 98/D4
Banxi, China 87/F2
Banyak (isls.), Indo. 90/A3
Banyo, Camr. 116/A4
Banyoles, Sp. 47/G1
Banyuwangi, Indo. 89/F5
Banz, PNG 129/G1
Banzare (coast), Ant. 192/J
Banzart (lake), Tun. 48/A4
Banzart (Bizerte), Tun. 48/A4
Bao Ha, Viet. 86/E4
Bao Lac, Viet. 86/E4
Bao Loc, Viet. 94/D4
Baode, China 80/B3
Baodi, China 80/H7
Baoding, China 80/G7
Baofeng, China 80/C4
Baoguangsi, China 86/E2
Baoji, China 78/F5
Baojing, China 93/J2
Baokang, China 80/B5
Baoro, CAfr. 116/B4
Baoruco (mts.), DRep. 177/J2
Baoshan, China 86/C3
Baoshan, China 80/L8
Baotian, China 86/E3
Baotou, China 80/B2
Baoulé (riv.), Mali 114/C3
Baoxing, China 86/D2
Baoxinji, China 87/G1
Baoying, China 80/D4
Bāpatla, India 95/D3
Bapaume, Fr. 54/B3
Baptistown, NJ, US 168/C2
Bāqa el Gharbiyya, Isr. 105/C4
Baqên, China 78/C5
Ba'qūbah, Iraq 103/F3
Baquedano, Chile 188/B2
Bar (riv.), Fr. 42/C4
Bar, Serb. 49/F1
Bar, Ukr. 72/D3
Bar Bigha, India 97/E3
Bar el Ksaïb (well), Mali 110/D5
Bar Harbor, Me, US 158/C3
Bar Hill, Eng, UK 37/G2
Bar-le-Duc, Fr. 55/E6
Bar-sur-Aube, Fr. 44/F2
Bar-sur-Seine, Fr. 44/F2
Bara, Swe. 40/E4
Bara, Indo. 91/G4
Barā Bangāhal, India 98/D3
Bāra Banki, India 96/C2
Bārā Lācha La (pass), India 98/D3
Baraawe, Som. 119/D1
Barabai, Indo. 90/E4
Barabinsk, Rus. 74/H4
Baraboo, Wi, US 155/K2
Baracaldo, Sp. 44/B5
Barachois, NB, Can. 158/E2
Barachois, Qu, Can. 158/E1
Barachois (pt.), NS, Can. 159/G3
Baracoa, Cuba 177/H1
Barada (riv.), Syria 104/E3
Baradero, Arg. 191/J10
Baradine, Austl. 132/D1
Barāgaon, India 97/E3
Baragoi, Kenya 119/B1
Baragua, Ven. 180/D2
Baraguá, Cuba 177/G1
Bārah, Sudan 117/F2
Barajas (int'l arpt.), Sp. 47/N9
Barajas, Sp. 47/N9
Barajevo, Serb. 50/E3
Barāk (riv.), India 86/B3
Baraka, D.R. Congo 121/G4
Baraka (riv.), Sudan 117/H1
Barakah, Sudan 117/E3
Barākar (riv.), India 97/F3
Barakī Barak, Afg. 101/J2
Bārākot, India 95/E1
Baralaba, Austl. 134/C4
Baram (cape), Malay. 90/D3
Baram (riv.), Malay. 90/D3
Bar'am NP, Isr. 105/C2
Barama, India 97/H2
Barama (riv.), Guy. 181/G3
Baramanni, Guy. 181/G3
Baramita, Guy. 181/F3
Baramsar, India 98/C5
Baramula, India 98/C2
Baran', Bela. 41/P4
Bāran, India 92/C2
Baranagar, India 97/G4
Baranga, D.R. Congo 121/F2
Barani (well), Alg. 110/E4
Baranikha, Rus. 75/S3
Baranivka, Ukr. 72/D2
Barano d'Ischia, It. 65/C6
Baranoa, Col. 180/C2
Baranof (isl.), Ak, US 140/C3
Baranya (prov.), Hun. 50/C3
Barão de Cocais, Braz. 187/E3
Barão de Grajaú, Braz. 183/F4
Barão de Melgaço, Braz. 185/H5
Baraolt, Rom. 51/G2
Baraque de Fraiture (hill), Belg. 55/E3
Baras, Phil. 88/D2
Barat Daya (isls.), Indo. 91/G5
Barate, Indo. 128/A2
Baratier, Congo 120/C4
Barato, India 86/B3
Barauli, India 97/E2
Baraut, India 98/D5
Baraya, Col. 180/C4
Barbacena, Braz. 186/E4
Barbacoas, Col. 180/B4
Barbacoas, Ven. 183/P8
Barbados (ctry.) 173/P8
Barbalha, Braz. 183/G4
Barbaros, Turk. 51/H5
Barbas (cape), Mor. 110/A5
Barbastro, Sp. 47/F1
Barbate de Franco, Sp. 46/C4
Barbeau (peak), Nun, Can. 141/T6
Barbentane, Fr. 64/A5
Barberà del Vallès, Sp. 47/L6
Barberaz, Fr. 64/B1
Barberino di Mugello, It. 63/E6
Barberton, Oh, US 160/F4
Barberton, SAfr. 125/E2
Barbil, India 97/E4
Barbon, Eng, UK 35/F3
Barbona (peak), It. 62/D6
Barbosa, Col. 180/C3
Barbosa, Col. 183/K6
Barboursville, Va, US 163/H1
Barbourville, Ky, US 162/F2
Barbuda (isl.), Anti. 173/N8
Barby, Fr. 64/B1
Barcaldine, Sc, UK 33/A3
Barcaldine, Austl. 134/B3
Barcarena, Braz. 182/D3
Barcarrota, Sp. 46/B3
Barcău (riv.), Rom. 67/J1
Barcellona Pozzo di Gotto, It. 48/D3
Barcelona, Ven. 181/E2
Barcelona (int'l arpt.), Sp. 47/L7
Barcelona, Sp. 47/L7
Barcelonnette, Fr. 64/C4
Barcelos, Braz. 181/F5
Barcelos, Port. 46/A2
Barcin, Pol. 43/J2
Barclay, Tx, US 151/F2
Barcoo (riv.), Austl. 127/D3
Barcs, Hun. 50/C3
Barczewo, Pol. 41/J5
Bard, Ca, US 148/E4
Bärdä, Azer. 103/F1
Bardaï, Chad 108/C4
Bardas Blancas, Arg. 190/C2
Bardejov, Slvk. 43/L4
Bardeskan, Iran 101/G1
Bardheere, Som. 119/C1
Bardi, It. 62/C4
Bardīyah, Libya 108/E2
Bardney, Eng, UK 35/H5
Bārdoli, India 95/B1
Bardolino, It. 63/D2
Bardonecchia, It. 64/C2
Bardonia, NY, US 169/K7
Bardsdale, Ca, US 166/B2
Bardsey (isl.), Wal, UK 34/D6
Bardstown, Ky, US 162/E2
Bardwell, Ky, US 162/C2
Bardwell, Tx, US 151/F1
Bareeda, Som. 118/D3
Bareggio, It. 62/B3
Barei (wadi), Sudan 116/D2
Bareilly, India 96/B1
Bareli, India 96/B4
Barellan, Austl. 133/C2
Barendrecht, Neth. 52/B5
Barentin, Fr. 57/F1
Barenton, Fr. 57/E3
Barents (sea), Eur. 29/H1
Barentu, Erit. 117/H2
Bäretswil, Swi. 61/E3
Barfleur, Fr. 56/D1
Barfleur (pt.), Fr. 56/D1
Barg-e Maṯāl, Afg. 98/A2
Barga, It. 62/D5
Barga, China 99/D5
Bargara, Austl. 134/D4
Bargarh, India 95/D1
Barge, It. 64/D3
Bargfeld-Stegen, Ger. 53/H1
Bargi, India 96/B4
Bargo, Austl. 133/E2
Bargoed, Wal, UK 36/C3
Bargteheide, Ger. 53/H1
Bārguna, Bang. 97/H4
Barguzin (riv.), Rus. 78/G1
Bārh, India 97/E3
Barhaj, India 96/D2
Barhalganj, India 96/D2
Barham, Austl. 133/B2
Barhamjia, Nepal 97/F2
Barharwā, India 97/F3
Barhi, India 97/E3
Barhiya, India 97/F3
Bari, It. 48/E2
Bāri, India 96/A2
Bari, D.R. Congo 120/D2
Bari Sardo, It. 48/A3
Bariadi, Tanz. 119/A2
Bariano, It. 62/C2
Baricella, It. 63/E4
Barichara, Col. 180/C3
Baricho, Kenya 119/B2
Barigazzo (peak), It. 62/C4
Barika, Alg. 112/H5
Barikiwa, Tanz. 119/B4
Barīkowṯ, Afg. 98/A2
Barillas, Guat. 176/D3
Barima (riv.), Guy. 181/G2
Barima-Waini (pol. reg.), Guy. 181/F3
Barinas (state), Ven. 180/D2
Barinas, Ven. 180/D2
Baring, Wa, US 144/D4
Baringa, D.R. Congo 121/E3
Baringa I, D.R. Congo 121/E2
Baringa-Twana, D.R. Congo 120/D4
Barinitas, Ven. 180/D2
Baripāda, India 97/F5
Bariri, Braz. 189/G2
Bārīs, Egypt 109/F3
Barisakho, Geo. 71/H4
Barisāl, Bang. 97/H4
Barisāl (pol. reg.), Bang. 97/H4
Barisan (mts.), Indo. 90/B4
Barisciano, It. 65/C3
Barito (riv.), Indo. 90/D4
Baritu, PN, Arg. 188/C2
Barjols, Fr. 64/C5
Bark (pt.), Wi, US 157/J4
Bark (lake), On, Can. 161/G2
Bark (riv.), Wi, US 167/N13
Bark River, Mi, US 160/C2
Barka Kāna, India 97/E4
Barkam, China 86/D2
Barkava, Lat. 41/M3
Barker (cr.), Austl. 131/M9
Barker (dam), Tx, US 151/M9
Barker, NY, US 160/V9
Barkéwol el Abiod, Mrta. 114/B2
Barkham, Eng, UK 30/A2
Barki Saria, India 97/E3
Barking and Dagenham (bor.), Eng, UK 30/D2
Barkley (dam), Ky, US 162/C2
Barkley (sound), BC, Can. 144/B3
Barkley (lake), Ky, US 162/D2
Barkly East, SAfr. 124/D3
Barkly Tableland (plat.), Austl. 127/C2
Barkly West, SAfr. 124/D3
Barkol (Barkol Kazak Zizhixian), China 78/C3
Barkol Kazak Zizhixian (Barkol), China 78/C3
Barksdale (A.F.B.), La, US 153/H4
Barlaston, Eng, UK 35/F6
Barlby, Eng, UK 35/G4
Barlee (range), Austl. 130/B2
Barlee (lake), Austl. 127/A3
Barlee Range Nature Reserve, Austl. 130/B2
Barletta, It. 48/E2
Barlin, Fr. 54/B3
Barlinek, Pol. 43/H2
Barling, Ar, US 153/G3
Barmedman, Austl. 133/C2
Bārmer, India 101/K3
Barmera, Austl. 131/J5
Barmouth, Wal, UK 36/B1
Barmstedt, Ger. 53/G1
Barna, Ire. 32/A3
Barnāla, India 98/C4
Barnard, Ks, US 154/E4
Barnard Castle, Eng, UK 35/G2
Barnasht, Egypt 113/C5
Barnaul, Rus. 99/D1
Bärnbach, Aus. 45/L3
Barnegat (bay), NJ, US 168/D4
Barnegat, NJ, US 168/D4
Barnegat (inlet), NJ, US 168/D4
Barnegat Light, NJ, US 168/D4
Barnes, Wi, US 157/J4
Barnesboro, Pa, US 161/G4
Barnesville, Mn, US 156/F4
Barnesville, Ga, US 162/E4
Barnet, Vt, US 161/K2
Barnet (nbrhd.), Eng, UK 30/C2
Barneveld, Neth. 52/C4
Barneville-Carteret, Fr. 56/D2
Barney, Ga, US 165/G2
Barneys (lake), Austl. 133/B1
Barnhart, Mo, US 162/B1
Barnhart, Tx, US 150/D2
Barni Hāt, India 97/H2
Barnoldswick, Eng, UK 35/F4
Barnsdall, Ok, US 153/F2
Barnsley, Eng, UK 35/G4
Barnsley (co.), Eng, UK 35/G4
Barnstaple, Eng, UK 36/B4
Barnstaple (Bideford) (bay), Eng, UK 36/B4
Barnstorf, Ger. 53/F3
Barntrup, Ger. 53/G5
Barnum, Wy, US 147/K2
Barnwell, Ab, Can. 145/H3
Barnwell, SC, US 163/G4
Baro, Gui. 114/C4
Baro, Nga. 115/G4
Baro Wenz (riv.), Eth. 117/G3
Baroda (Vadodara), India 92/B3
Barodia Kalān, India 96/B3
Baron, Ok, US 153/G3
Baron, Fr. 30/L4
Barona Ranch Ind. Res., Ca, US 148/D4
Barone (peak), It. 62/B2
Barong, China 78/D5
Barons, Ab, Can. 145/H2
Barooga, Austl. 133/B2
Baroua, CAfr. 117/E4
Barow (riv.), Ire. 34/A5
Barowghīl (pass), Afg. 101/K1
Barpāli, India 95/D1
Barpeta, India 97/H2
Barqin, Libya 108/B3
Barquisimeto, Ven. 180/D2
Barquisimeto (int'l arpt.), Ven. 180/D2
Barr, Fr. 60/D1
Barr, Sc, UK 34/D1
Barra (isl.), Sc, UK 31/Q8
Barra, Braz. 187/E1
Barra Bonita, Braz. 189/G2
Barra del Colorado, PN, CR 172/E5
Barra do Bugres, Braz. 185/G4
Barra do Corda, Braz. 183/E4
Barra do Cuanza, Ang. 120/C5
Barra do Dande, Ang. 120/C5
Barra do Garças, Braz. 186/B2
Barra do Piraí, Braz. 187/N7
Barra do Ribeiro, Braz. 189/G4
Barra Head (pt.), Sc, UK 31/Q8
Barra Mansa, Braz. 187/M7
Barra Patuca, Hon. 177/E3
Barra Punta Gorda, Nic. 177/F4
Barra Velha, Braz. 189/G3
Barraba, Austl. 132/D1
Barrackpur, India 97/G4
Barrage d'Ayamé I (dam), C.d'Iv. 114/E5
Barrage d'Ayamé Li (dam), C.d'Iv. 114/E5
Barrage de Bimont (res.), Fr. 64/B5
Barrage de Buyo (dam), C.d'Iv. 114/D5
Barrage de Castillon (dam), Fr. 64/C5
Barrage de Chaudanne (dam), Fr. 64/C5
Barrage de Kossou (dam), C.d'Iv. 114/D5
Barrage de la Grande Dixence (dam), Swi. 60/D5
Barrage de la Plate Taile (dam), Belg. 55/D3
Barrage de la Sainte-Croix (dam), Fr. 64/C5
Barrage de Lagdo (dam), Camr. 116/B3
Barrage de l'Eau d'Heure (dam), Belg. 55/D3
Barrage de Mauvoisin (dam), Swi. 60/D6
Barrage de Mbakaou (dam), Camr. 116/B4
Barrage de Serre-Ponçon (dam), Fr. 64/C4
Barrage de Taabo (dam), C.d'Iv. 114/D5
Barrage de Tignes (dam), Fr. 64/C1
Barrage de Vouglans (dam), Fr. 60/B5
Barrage Idriss I (res.), Mor. 112/B2
Barrage Mohamed V (res.), Mor. 112/C2
Barragem da Chicamba Real (dam), Moz. 123/G3
Barragem de Cabora Bassa (dam), Moz. 123/G2
Barragem Paso Real (res.), Braz. 189/F4
Barranca, Peru 184/B2
Barranca, Peru 184/B3
Barranca de Upía, Col. 180/C3
Barranca del Cobre PN, Mex. 174/D3
Barrancabermeja, Col. 180/C3
Barrancas, Col. 180/C2
Barrancas, Ven. 181/F2
Barrancas, Arg. 190/C3
Barrancas, Chile 190/N8
Barrancas, Arroyo (cr.), Arg. 188/E4
Barranco de Loba, Col. 180/C2
Barrancos, Port. 46/B3
Barranquilla, Col. 180/C2
Barras, Col. 180/C4
Barras, Braz. 183/F4
Barre, Vt, US 161/K2
Barre de Portugais (pt.), Gabon 120/B3
Barreal, Arg. 188/B4
Barreiras, Braz. 186/D2
Barreirinha, Braz. 182/B3
Barreirinhas, Braz. 183/F3
Barreiro, Port. 47/P10
Barreiros, Braz. 183/H5
Barrême, Fr. 64/C5
Barren (isl.), Madg. 125/G7
Barren (riv.), Ky, US 162/D2
Barren (Nosy Barren) (isls.), Madg. 125/G7
Barren River (lake), Ky, US 162/D2
Barrera, Bol. 185/E4
Barretal, Mex. 175/F3
Barretos, Braz. 189/G2
Barrett, Tx, US 151/M9
Barrhead, Sc, UK 33/B5
Barrhead, Ab, Can. 140/E3
Barrhill, Sc, UK 34/D1
Barrie, On, Can. 161/G2
Barrier (range), Austl. 131/J4
Barrière, BC, Can. 144/D2
Barrilla Draw (riv.), Tx, US 150/C2
Barrington, Il, US 167/P15
Barrington Hills, Il, US 167/P15
Barrington Tops (peak), Austl. 132/D1
Barrington Tops NP, Austl. 132/D1
Barringun, Austl. 132/C1
Barrīyat al Uşayfir, Egypt 113/B2
Barro Duro, Braz. 183/F4
Barron, Wi, US 157/J5
Barron Gorge NP, Austl. 134/B2
Barronett, Wi, US 157/J5
Barros Luco, Chile 188/B3
Barroso, Braz. 186/E4
Barrouallie, StV. 173/N9
Barrow (isl.), Austl. 127/A3
Barrow (pt.), Austl. 134/B1
Barrow (str.), Nun, Can. 140/G1
Barrow (riv.), Ire. 32/D4
Barrow, Ak, US 171/G1
Barrow (pt.), Ak, US 171/G1
Barrow Creek, Austl. 131/G2
Barrow Island, Austl. 130/B2
Barrow-in-Furness, Eng, UK 35/E3
Barrowby, Eng, UK 35/H6
Barrowford, Eng, UK 35/F4
Barruelo de Santullán, Sp. 46/C1
Barry, Wal, UK 36/C4
Barry M. Goldwater Air Force Range, Az, US 149/F4
Barry's Bay, On, Can. 161/H2
Barrytown, NZ 135/B3
Barsakel'mes (lake), Uzb. 71/L4
Barsalogho, Burk. 115/E3
Bārshi, India 95/B2
Barsinghausen, Ger. 53/G4
Bårslöv, Swe. 39/J6
Barssel, Ger. 53/E2
Barstow, Ca, US 148/D3
Bartang (riv.), Taj. 99/B4
Bartenheim, Fr. 60/D2
Barth, Ger. 40/E4
Bartholomä, Ger. 58/C5
Bartholomäberg, Aus. 61/F3
Bartica, Guy. 181/G3
Bartın, Turk. 70/E4
Bartle Frere (peak), Austl. 127/D2
Bartlesville, Ok, US 153/G2
Bartlett, Il, US 167/P16
Bartlett, Tn, US 162/C3
Bartlett, Ne, US 154/E3
Bartlett, Tx, US 151/F2
Bartley, WV, US 163/G2
Bartolomé Masó, Cuba 177/G1
Bartolomeu Dias, Moz. 123/G4
Barton, ND, US 156/D3
Barton, Vt, US 161/K2
Barton, Md, US 161/G5
Barton under Needwood, Eng, UK 37/E1
Barton-in-the-Clay, Eng, UK 37/F3
Barton-upon-Humber, Eng, UK 35/H4
Bartonsville, Pa, US 168/C2
Bartoszyce, Pol. 41/J4
Bartow, Ger. 40/E5
Bartow, Fl, US 164/M8
Barú (vol.), Pan. 177/F4
Bāruipur, India 97/G4
Baruman (riv.), Indo. 89/C2
Barumun (riv.), Indo. 90/B3
Barus, Indo. 89/B2
Baruta, Ven. 183/P7
Baruth, Ger. 43/G2
Baruun Huuray (phys. reg.), Mong. 78/C2
Baruun-Urt, Mong. 78/G2
Baruunsuu, Mong. 78/F3
Barview, Or, US 146/A2
Barvinkove, Ukr. 73/J3
Barwa Sāgar, India 96/B3
Barwāha, India 92/C3
Barwāla, India 98/C5
Barwāni, India 92/B3
Barwick, Ga, US 165/G2
Barwon (riv.), Austl. 127/D3
Barwon Heads, Austl. 133/B4
Barycz (riv.), Pol. 43/J3
Barysaw, Bela. 41/N4
Barysh, Rus. 71/H1
Baryshivka, Ukr. 72/F2
Barzanò, It. 62/C2
Bas-Caraquet, NB, Can. 158/E2
Bas-Congo (pol. reg.), D.R. Congo 120/A4
Bas-Rhin (dept.), Fr. 60/D1
Basa, C.d'Iv. 114/D5
Basaldella, It. 63/G1
Basankusu, D.R. Congo 120/D2
Basarabeasca, Mol. 72/E4
Basauri, Sp. 44/B5
Basavilbaso, Arg. 191/J10
Basawa, C.d'Iv. 114/D4
Basay, Phil. 88/C3
Bascharage, Lux. 55/E4
Baschurch, Eng, UK 36/D1
Bascom, Fl, US 165/F2
Bascuñán (pt.), Chile 188/B4
Basdorf, Ger. 42/Q6
Baseball Hall of Fame, NY, US 161/J3
Basekpio, D.R. Congo 117/E4
Basel, Swi. 60/D2
Basel/Mulhouse (int'l arpt.), Fr. 60/D2
Baselga di Pinè, It. 61/H5
Baselice, It. 65/D5
Baselland (canton), Swi. 60/D3
Bashaw, Ab, Can. 145/H1
Bashbîsh, Egypt 113/C2
Bashee (riv.), SAfr. 124/E3
Bashi (chan.), Phil.,Tai. 87/J4
Bashkaus (riv.), Rus. 78/B1
Bashkortostan Resp., Rus. 74/F4
Bashmakovo, Rus. 71/G1
Bāsht, Iran 103/G4
Bashtanka, Ukr. 72/G4
Ba'shūm, Sudan 117/F2
Basilan (isl.), Phil. 88/C4
Basilan (str.), Phil. 88/C4
Basilan (peak), Phil. 88/C4
Basildon, Eng, UK 37/G3
Basile, La, US 164/B2
Basilica di Fieschi, It. 62/C5
Basilicata (reg.), It. 48/D2
Bāsim, India 95/C1
Basin, Wy, US 147/J1
Basin, Mt, US 145/H4
Basingstoke (canal), Eng, UK 30/A3
Basingstoke, Eng, UK 37/E4
Basīrhāt, India 97/G4
Basīrpur, Pak. 98/B4
Baška, Cro. 45/L4
Baskahegan (lake), Me, US 158/C3
Başkale, Turk. 103/F2
Baskatong (res.), Qu, Can. 161/J1
Baskerville (cape), Austl. 128/A4
Baskett Slough Nat'l Wild. Ref., Or, US 146/B1
Baskil, Turk. 102/D2
Baskin, La, US 153/J4
Başkomutan NP, Turk. 102/B2
Başköy, Turk. 102/D2
Basmat, India 95/C2
Bāsmenj, Iran 103/F2
Bāsoda, India 96/A4
Basodesh, Tanz. 119/A3
Basodino (peak), It. 61/E5
Basoko, D.R. Congo 121/E2
Basoli, India 98/C3
Basongo, D.R. Congo 121/E4
Basque Provinces (prov.), Sp. 44/B5
Bass (str.), Austl. 127/D4
Bass Is. (Marotiri) (isl.), FrPol. 137/L7
Bass River, NS, Can. 158/F3
Bass Rock (isl.), Sc, UK 33/D4
Bassae (Vassés) (ruin), Gre. 49/G4
Bassano, Ab, Can. 145/H2
Bassano del Grappa, It. 63/E2
Bassano Romano, It. 65/B3
Bassari, Togo 115/F4
Bassas da India (isl.), Reun., Fr. 123/H4
Basse Santa Su, Gam. 114/B3
Basse-Kotto (pref.), CAfr. 116/D4
Basse-Normandie (pol. reg.), Fr. 57/D3
Basse-Terre (isl.), Guad. 173/J4
Basse-Terre, Fr. 173/N8
Bassecourt, Swi. 60/D3
Bassein (riv.), Myan. 93/F4
Bassein (Pathein), Myan. 86/B5
Bassein (Vasai), India 101/K5
Bassenge, Belg. 55/E2
Bassenheim, Ger. 55/G3
Bassens, Fr. 64/B1
Bassenthwaite (lake), Eng, UK 35/E2
Basseterre (cap.), StK. 173/N8
Bassett, Tx, US 153/G4
Bassett, Ne, US 154/E2
Bassett, Va, US 163/H2
Bassikounou, Mrta. 114/D3
Bassum, Ger. 53/F3
Basswood (lake), Can.,US 157/J3
Båstad, Swe. 40/E3
Bastak, Iran 103/H5
Basţām, Iran 103/H2
Bastar, India 95/D2
Bastelicaccia, Fr. 48/A2
Bastheim, Ger. 58/D2
Bastī, India 96/D2
Bastia, Fr. 48/A1
Bastia, It. 65/B1
Bastogne, Belg. 55/E4
Bastos, Braz. 189/G2
Bastrop, La, US 153/J4
Bastrop, Tx, US 150/F2
Basu (cape), Indo. 89/C3
Basyūn, Egypt 113/B3
Bat Khela, Pak. 98/A2
Bat Shelomo, Isr. 105/B3
Bat Yam, Isr. 105/B4
Bata, EqG. 120/B2
Bata-Siala, D.R. Congo 120/C4
Bataan (mt.), Phil. 88/C2
Batabanó (gulf), Cuba 172/E3
Batac, Phil. 88/C1
Batagay, Rus. 75/P3
Batai (pass), Pak. 98/A3
Batak, Bul. 49/J2
Batakan, Indo. 90/D4
Batakūt, India 98/C3
Batāla, India 98/C4
Batalha, Port. 46/A3
Batalha, Braz. 183/F4
Batallas, Bol. 184/D5
Bataly, Kaz. 71/M1
Batama, D.R. Congo 121/F2
Batamshinskiy, Kaz. 71/L2
Batan (isls.), Phil. 77/M7
Batang, China 86/C2
Batang, Indo. 89/E4
Batangafo, CAfr. 116/C4
Batangas, Phil. 88/C2
Batangtoru, Indo. 89/B2
Bātāru, India 92/B2
Batatais, Braz. 189/H2
Batataria (bay), La, US 164/C3
Batavia, NY, US 161/G3
Batavia, Il, US 167/P16
Batavia, Oh, US 162/E1
Bataysk, Rus. 73/K4
Batchelor, La, US 164/C2
Batchelor, Austl. 128/C3
Batchwana Bay, On, Can. 160/D1
Bătdambang, Camb. 94/C3
Bate (bay), Austl. 134/H9
Bateman, Sk, Can. 145/L2
Batemans (bay), Austl. 133/E2
Batemans Bay, Austl. 133/E2
Batesburg-Leesville, SC, US 163/G4
Batesville, Al, US 165/F1
Batesville, Ar, US 153/J3
Batesville, In, US 160/D5
Batesville, Ms, US 162/C3
Batesville, Tx, US 150/E3
Batesville, Va, US 163/H2
Batetskiy, Rus. 41/P2
Bath (range), Austl. 129/D3
Bath, NS, Can. 158/D2
Bath, On, Can. 161/H2
Bath, Eng, UK 36/D4
Bath, Neth. 52/B6
Bath, NY, US 161/H3
Bath, Pa, US 168/C2
Bath (Berkeley Springs), WV, US 161/G5
Bath and Northeast Somerset, (co.), Eng, UK 36/D4
Bath Springs, Tn, US 162/C3
Batha (pref.), Chad 116/C2
Batha (riv.), Chad 116/C2
Batha de Laïri (riv.), Chad 116/C3
Bathgate, ND, US 156/F3
Bathgate, Sc, UK 33/C5
Bathmen, Neth. 52/D4
Bathsheba, Bar. 173/P9
Bathurst, NB, Can. 158/E2
Bathurst (inlet), Nun, Can. 140/F2
Bathurst (isl.), Nun, Can. 139/G2
Bathurst (cape), NW, Can. 171/N1
Bathurst, Austl. 133/D1
Bathurst (isl.), Austl. 128/C2
Bathurst Abor. Land, Austl. 128/C2
Bathurst Inlet, Nun, Can. 140/F2
Batī, Eth. 118/B3
Batian (peak), Kenya 119/B2
Bāţiāq-e Gāv Khūnī (lake), Iran 103/H3
Batié, Burk. 114/E4
Batik (mts.), China 78/C2
Bāţin (wadi), SAr. 100/E3
Batiquitos (lag.), Ca, US 166/C4
Batiscan (riv.), Qu, Can. 158/A2
Batley, Eng, UK 35/G4
Batlow, Austl. 133/D2
Batman, Turk. 102/E2
Batman (dam), Turk. 102/E2
Batna (wilaya), Alg. 111/G2
Batna, Alg. 112/J5
Batoche Nat'l Hist. Site, Sk, Can. 145/L1
Batoka, Zam. 123/E3
Baton Rouge (cap.), La, US 164/C2
Batopilas, Mex. 174/D3
Batoti, India 98/C3
Batouri, Camr. 116/B4
Batovi (riv.), Braz. 186/B2
Baţrā' (ruin), Jor. 104/D4
Baţrah, Egypt 113/C2
Batsawul, Afg. 98/A2
Båtsfjord, Nor. 38/J1
Batsto, NJ, US 168/D4
Batsto (riv.), NJ, US 168/D4
Batsto Historic Village, NJ, US 168/D4
Battaglia Terme, It. 63/E3
Battali, Bang. 97/H4
Battenberg, Ger. 53/F6
Bätterkinden, Swi. 60/D3
Battersby, Eng, UK 35/G3
Battersea (nbrhd.), Eng, UK 30/C2
Battiest, Ok, US 153/G3
Battipaglia, It. 65/D6
Battle (riv.), Ab,Sk, Can. 140/E3
Battle, Eng, UK 37/G5
Battle (riv.), Ab, Can. 145/J1
Battle Creek, Mi, US 160/D3
Battle Creek, Ne, US 154/F3
Battle Creek, Ia, US 155/G2
Battle Lake, Mn, US 157/G4
Battle Mountain, Nv, US 146/E3
Battleboro, NC, US 163/J2
Battlefield, Mo, US 153/H2
Battleford, Sk, Can. 145/K1
Battock (mt.), Sc, UK 33/D3
Batu (peak), Eth. 118/A4
Batu (isls.), Indo. 90/A4
Batu (peak), Malay. 90/D3
Batu (bay), Malay. 90/D3
Batu (cape), Indo. 91/E3
Batu Caves, Malay. 89/C2
Batu Gajah, Malay. 89/C1
Batu Pahat, Malay. 89/C2
Batu Puteh (peak), Malay. 89/C1
Batuco, Chile 190/N8
Batudaka (isl.), Indo. 91/F4
Batuensambang (peak), Indo. 90/D3
Batui, Indo. 91/F4
Batulaki, Phil. 88/D4
Batumi (int'l arpt.), Geo. 71/G4
Bat'umi, Geo. 71/G4
Baturaja, Indo. 89/D4
Baturino, Rus. 69/P5
Baturité, Braz. 183/G4
Baturusa, Indo. 89/D3
Baturyn, Ukr. 73/G2
Batusangkar, Indo. 89/C3
Batyrevo, Rus. 69/K5
Batys Qazaqstan, Kaz. 74/E5
Batys Qazaqstan Oblast, Kaz. 74/E5
Batz-sur-Mer, Fr. 56/C6
Bauang, Phil. 88/C1
Baubau, Indo. 128/A1
Bauchi (state), Nga. 115/H4
Bauchi, Nga. 115/H4
Baud, Fr. 56/B5
Baudette, Mn, US 157/G3
Baudh, India 95/E1
Baudó (riv.), Col. 180/B3
Baudó (mts.), Col. 177/G5
Baudon, Pic de (peak), Fr. 64/D5
Baugé, Fr. 57/E5
Baukau, ETim. 128/B2
Bauld (cape), Nf, Can. 141/L3
Baulkham Hills, Austl. 133/E1
Baulmes, Swi. 60/C4
Bauman (peak), Togo 115/F5
Baume-les-Dames, Fr. 60/C3
Baumholder, Ger. 55/G4
Baunach, Ger. 58/D3
Baunach (riv.), Ger. 58/D2
Baunatal, Ger. 53/G6
Baunei, It. 48/A2
Baungon, Phil. 88/D3
Baures, Bol. 185/F4
Baures (riv.), Bol. 185/E4
Baurú, Braz. 189/G2
Bauska, Lat. 41/L3
Bautino, Kaz. 71/J3
Bautzen, Ger. 43/H3
Bavans, Fr. 60/C3
Bavarian Alps (mts.), Aus., Ger. 67/F1
Bavay, Fr. 54/C3
Båven (lake), Swe. 40/G2
Baveno, It. 61/E6
Bavent, Fr. 57/E2
Baviácora, Mex. 174/C2
Bavilliers, Fr. 60/C2
Bavly, Rus. 69/M5
Baw Baw (mt.), Austl. 133/C3
Baw Baw NP, Austl. 133/C3
Bawan, Indo. 90/D4
Bawāna, India 98/D5
Bawang (cape), Indo. 90/C4
Bawean (isl.), Indo. 90/D5
Bawku, Gha. 115/E4
Bawlake, Myan. 94/B2
Bawlf, Ab, Can. 145/H1
Baxian, China 87/F1
Baxkorgan, China 99/F4
Baxley, Ga, US 165/G2
Baxoi, China 86/C2
Baxter, Mn, US 157/G4
Baxter Springs, Ks, US 153/G2
Bay (dam), Wi, US 155/K1
Bay, Ar, US 162/B3
Bay Bulls, Nf, Can. 159/L2
Bay City, Tx, US 151/G3
Bay City, Mi, US 160/E3
Bay City, Wi, US 155/H1
Bay City, Or, US 144/C5
Bay de Verde, Nf, Can. 159/L1
Bay Lake, Mn, US 157/H4
Bay Lake, Fl, US 164/M7
Bay L'Argent, Nf, Can. 159/K2
Bay Mills Ind. Res., Mi, US 160/D1
Bay Minette, Al, US 164/E2
Bay Port, Mi, US 160/E3
Bay Ridge (nbrhd.), NY, US 169/J9
Bay Ridge (Bayridge), Fl, US 164/M6
Bay Roberts, Nf, Can. 159/L2
Bay Saint Lawrence, NS, Can. 159/G2
Bay Saint Louis, Ms, US 164/D2
Bay Springs, Ms, US 164/D2
Bay Springs (lake), Ms, US 162/C3
Bay View, NZ 135/D2
Bayāḑ an Naşārá, Egypt 113/C6
Bayamo, Cuba 177/G1
Bayamón, PR 173/M8
Bayan, Indo. 91/E5
Bayan, Mong. 78/D2
Bayan, China 79/K2
Bayan Har (mts.), China 78/D5
Bayan Mod, China 78/E3
Bayan Obo, China 78/F3
Bayan Qagan, China 79/J2
Bayan-Ölgiy (prov.), Mong. 78/B2
Bayan-Ovoo, Mong. 78/C3
Bayan-Ulaan, Mong. 78/E2
Bayanaul, Kaz. 99/C1
Bayanbulag, Mong. 78/F2
Bayangol, Rus. 78/E1
Bayanhongor, Mong. 78/E2
Bayanhongor (prov.), Mong. 78/D3
Bayanhushuu, Mong. 78/C2
Bayanhushuu, Mong. 78/E2
Bayannuur, Mong. 99/F2
Bayano (lake), Pan. 177/G4
Bayansayr, Mong. 78/D2
Bayanterem, Mong. 78/G2
Bayantsagaan, Mong. 78/E2
Bayard, WV, US 161/G5
Bayard, NM, US 149/H4
Bayard, Ne, US 154/C3
Bayard, Ia, US 155/G3
Bayat, Turk. 70/E4
Bayawan, Phil. 88/C3
Baybach (riv.), Ger. 55/G3
Baybay, Phil. 88/D3
Bayboro, NC, US 163/J3
Bayburt (prov.), Turk. 70/F4
Bayburt, Turk. 102/E1
Baychunas, Kaz. 71/K3
Baychurovo, Rus. 73/M2
Baydaratskaya (bay), Rus. 74/G2
Baydhabo (Baidoa), Som. 118/B5
Baydrog (riv.), Mong. 78/D2
Bayel, Fr. 60/A1
Bayelsa (state), Nga. 115/G5
Bayerischer Wald (hills), Ger. 59/F4
Bayerischer Wald NP, Ger. 59/G5
Bayern (state), Ger. 42/F4
Bayeux, Fr. 57/E2
Bayeux, Braz. 183/H4
Bayfield, Co, US 149/J2
Baygorria (res.), Uru. 191/K10
Bayḩān al Qişāb, Yem. 118/C2
Baykal (mts.), Rus. 75/L4
Baykal (lake), Rus. 77/L4
Baykal, Rus. 78/E1
Baykal'sk, Rus. 78/E1
Baykan, Turk. 102/E2
Baykibashevo, Rus. 69/N5
Baykit, Rus. 74/K3
Baykonyr, Kaz. 74/G5
Baymak, Rus. 71/L1
Baynes Lake, BC, Can. 144/G3
Bayo Grande (peak), Arg. 188/C3
Bayombong, Phil. 88/C1
Bayon, Fr. 60/C1
Bayona, Sp. 46/A1
Bayonet (pt.), Fl, US 164/K7
Bayonet Point, Fl, US 164/K7
Bayonne, NJ, US 169/J9
Bayonne, Fr. 44/C5
Bayonne-Anglet (Biarritz) (arpt.), Fr. 44/C5
Bayou Bartholomew (riv.), Ar, US 162/B4
Bayou Cane, La, US 164/C3
Bayou D'Arbonne (lake), La, US 151/H1
Bayou de View (riv.), Ar, US 162/B3
Bayou Lafourche (riv.), La, US 164/C3
Bayou Macon (riv.), La, US 162/B4
Bayou Meto (riv.), Ar, US 162/B3
Bayou Nezpique (bayou), La, US 151/H2
Bayou Phalia (riv.), Ms, US 162/B4
Bayou Pierre (riv.), La, US 151/H1
Bayou Pierre (riv.), Ms, US 162/A4
Bayou Queue de Tortue (riv.), La, US 164/B2
Bayou Teche (riv.), La, US 151/H2
Bayou Vista, La, US 164/C3
Bayóvar, Peru 184/A2
Bayport, Mn, US 157/Q6
Bayport, Fl, US 164/K6
Bayport, NY, US 169/E2
Bayramaly, Trkm. 101/H1
Bayramıç, Turk. 49/K3
Bayreuth, Ger. 59/E3
Bayridge (Bay Ridge), Fl, US 164/M6
Bayrūt (gov.), Leb. 105/C1
Bayrūt (Beirut) (cap.), Leb. 105/C1
Bays (lake), On, Can. 161/G2
Bayse (riv.), Fr. 47/E1
Bayşehir (lake), Turk. 102/B2
Bayside (nbrhd.), NY, US 169/K8
Bayston Hill, Eng, UK 36/D1
Baysville, On, Can. 161/G2
Bayswater (nbrhd.), Austl. 130/K6
Bayt al Faqīh, Yem. 118/B2
Bayt Fajjār, WBnk. 105/C5
Bayt Ḩanīnā, WBnk. 105/C5
Bayt Ḩānūn, Gaza 105/B5
Bayt Jālā, WBnk. 105/C5
Bayt Lāhiyah, Gaza 105/B5
Bayt Laḩm (Bethlehem), WBnk. 105/C5
Bayt Sāḩūr, WBnk. 105/C5
Baytown, Tx, US 151/N9
Bayudha (des.), Sudan 109/G5
Bayunglencir, Indo. 89/C3
Bayville, NY, US 169/L8
Baywood-Los Osos, Ca, US 148/B3
Bayy al Kabīr (wadi), Libya 108/B2
Bayzhansay, Kaz. 99/A3
Baza, Sp. 46/D4
Bazainville, Fr. 30/G5
Bazardüzü (peak), Azer. 71/H4

Bāzarg – Bern-Be

Bāzargān, Iran 103/F2
Bazarnyye Mataki, Rus. 69/L5
Bazarshulan, Kaz. 71/J2
Bazèga (prov.), Burk. 115/E4
Bazemont, Fr. 30/H5
Bazet, Fr. 44/D5
Bazhong, China 87/E2
Bazine, Ks, US 152/E1
Bazoches-sur-Hoëne, Fr. 57/F3
Bazouges, Fr. 57/E5
Bāzpur, India 96/B1
Bazuru, D.R. Congo 121/F2
Bazzano, It. 63/E4
Beach, ND, US 156/B4
Beach Haven, NJ, US 168/D4
Beach Meadows, NS, Can. 158/E3
Beachburg, On, Can. 161/H2
Beachport, Austl. 132/B3
Beachton, Ga, US 165/F2
Beachwood, NJ, US 168/D4
Beachy (pt.), Eng, UK 44/D1
Beachy (head), Eng, UK 37/G5
Beacon, NY, US 161/K4
Beacon, Tn, US 162/C3
Beacon (peak), Wal, UK 36/C2
Beacon Hill, Fl, US 165/F3
Beaconsfield, Austl. 132/C4
Beaconsfield, Qu, Can. 159/N7
Beaconsfield, Eng, UK 37/F3
Beagle (gulf), Austl. 128/C3
Beagle Bay Abor. Rsv., Austl. 128/A4
Beagle Bay Mission, Austl. 128/A4
Beal (range), Austl. 134/A4
Béal Traversier, Pic du (peak), Fr. 64/C3
Bealanana, Madg. 125/J6
Beale AFB, Ca, US 146/C4
Beals (cr.), Tx, US 150/D1
Beaminster, Eng, UK 36/D5
Beampingaratra (ridge), Madg. 125/H9
Beamsville, On, Can. 160/U9
Bear (hills), Sk, Can. 145/K1
Bear (isl.), Nor. 74/B2
Bear (mt.), Ak, US 171/K3
Bear (mt.), Ak, US 171/K2
Bear (riv.), Ca, US 146/C4
Bear, De, US 168/C4
Bear (hill), Ne, US 154/D3
Bear (mtn.), SD, US 154/C2
Bear (lake), Ut, US 142/D3
Bear (cr.), Wy, US 154/B3
Bear Creek, Al, US 162/D3
Bear Lake, Mi, US 160/C2
Bear Lake NWR, Id, US 147/H2
Bear Lodge (mts.), Wy, US 154/B1
Bear River, NS, Can. 158/E3
Bear River (bay), Ut, US 147/G3
Bear River NWR, Ut, US 147/G3
Bear Town, Ms, US 164/C2
Beara (reg.), Ire. 32/A6
Bearden, Ar, US 153/H4
Bearden, Ok, US 153/F3
Beardmore, On, Can. 157/L3
Beardstown, Il, US 155/J3
Bearfort (mtn.), NJ, US 169/H7
Bearma (riv.), India 96/B4
Bearpaw (mts.), Mt, US 145/J3
Bearsden, Sc, UK 33/B5
Bearstead, Eng, UK 30/E3
Beartooth (mts.), Mt, US 147/H1
Beās (riv.), India 96/B3
Beas de Segura, Sp. 46/D3
Beasain, Sp. 44/B5
Beata (cape), DRep. 173/G4
Beata (pt.), DRep. 177/J2
Beata (isl.), Thai. 177/J2
Beatenberg, Swi. 60/D4
Beatrice, Zim. 123/F3
Beatrice, Ne, US 155/F3
Beatrice (cape), Austl. 129/E3
Beattie, Ks, US 155/F4
Beattock, Sc, UK 33/C6
Beatty, Nv, US 148/D2
Beattystown, NJ, US 168/D2
Beattyville, Ky, US 162/F2
Beau Bassin-Rose Hill, Mrts. 125/T15
Beaucaire, Fr. 64/A5
Beaucamps-le-Vieux, Fr. 54/A4
Beauceville, Qu, Can. 158/B2
Beauchamp, Fr. 30/J4
Beauchastel, Fr. 64/A3
Beaucourt, Fr. 60/C3
Beaudesert, Austl. 134/D4
Beaufort, Fr. 60/B4
Beaufort, Lux. 55/F4
Beaufort, Fr. 64/C1
Beaufort, Austl. 132/B3
Beaufort (sea), Can.,US 139/C2
Beaufort, Malay. 88/A4
Beaufort, SC, US 163/G4
Beaufort, NC, US 163/J3
Beaufort (inlet), NC, US 163/J3
Beaufort Castle (ruins), Leb. 105/D2
Beaufort Marine Corps Air Base, SC, US 163/G4
Beaufort West, SAfr. 124/C4
Beaufort-en-Vallée, Fr. 57/E6
Beaugency, Fr. 57/G5
Beauharnois, Qu, Can. 161/K2
Beauharnois (co.), Qu, Can. 159/M7
Beaujolais (mts.), Fr. 44/F4
Beaulieu, Eng, UK 37/E5
Beaulieu-sur-Mer, Fr. 64/D5
Beauly, Sc, UK 33/B2
Beauly (riv.), Sc, UK 33/B2
Beauly Firth (lake), Sc, UK 33/B2
Beaumaris, Wal, UK 34/D5
Beaumes-de-Venise, Fr. 64/B4
Beaumesnil, Fr. 57/F2
Beaumont, Fr. 56/D1
Beaumont, Belg. 55/D3
Beaumont, Ms, US 164/D2
Beaumont, Ca, US 166/D3
Beaumont, Fr. 44/E4
Beaumont, Ab, Can. 145/H1
Beaumont, Tx, US 151/G2
Beaumont-de-Lomagne, Fr. 44/D5
Beaumont-le-Roger, Fr. 57/F2
Beaumont-lès-Valence, Fr. 64/A3
Beaumont-sur-Oise, Fr. 30/J4
Beaumont-sur-Sarthe, Fr. 57/F4
Beaupréau, Fr. 57/E6
Beauquesne, Fr. 54/B3
Beauraing, Belg. 55/D3
Beaurainville, Fr. 54/A3
Beauregard, Ms, US 164/C2
Beaurepaire, Fr. 64/B2
Beaurevoir, Fr. 54/C4
Beausejour, Mb, Can. 156/F2
Beausoleil, Fr. 64/D5
Beautheil, Fr. 30/M5
Beautiful (mtn.), NM, US 149/H2
Beautor, Fr. 54/C4
Beauvais, Fr. 54/B5
Beauval, Fr. 54/B3
Beauvoir, Fr. 30/L6
Beaver (hills), Sk, Can. 156/C2
Beaver (riv.), Yk, Can. 140/D2
Beaver, Ak, US 171/J2
Beaver (lake), Ar, US 153/H2
Beaver (cr.), Co, US 154/C4
Beaver (cr.), Co,Ks, US 154/D4
Beaver, La, US 164/B2
Beaver (isl.), Mi, US 160/D2
Beaver (cr.), Ne, US 154/E3
Beaver, Oh, US 163/F1
Beaver, Ok, US 152/D2
Beaver, Pa, US 160/F4
Beaver, Ut, US 149/F1
Beaver (riv.), Ut, US 147/J4
Beaver, Wa, US 144/B3
Beaver (dam), Wi, US 155/K2
Beaver Bay, Mn, US 157/J4
Beaver City, Ne, US 154/E3
Beaver Creek, Yk, Can. 171/K3
Beaver Crossing, Ne, US 155/F3
Beaver Dam, Ky, US 162/D2
Beaver Dam, Wi, US 155/K2
Beaver Dam (lake), Wi, US 155/K2
Beaver Falls, Pa, US 160/F4
Beaver Meadows, Pa, US 168/C2
Beaver Springs, Pa, US 168/A2
Beaverbank, NS, Can. 158/F3
Beavercreek, Oh, US 160/D5
Beaverdam, Va, US 163/J2
Beaverdell, BC, Can. 144/E3
Beaverhead (mts.), Mt, US 147/G1
Beaverhead (riv.), Mt, US 147/G1
Beaverhill (lake), Ab, Can. 145/H1
Beaverton, On, Can. 161/G2
Beaverton, Mi, US 160/D3
Beaverton, Or, US 146/B1
Beavertown, Pa, US 168/A2
Beāwar, India 92/B2
Bebe, Tx, US 151/F3
Bébédjia, Chad 116/C3
Bebedouro, Braz. 189/G2
Beberibe, Braz. 183/G4
Bebington, Eng, UK 35/E5
Beboto, Chad 116/C3
Béboura Iii, CAfr. 116/C4
Bebra, Ger. 53/G7
Becal, Mex. 176/D1
Bécancour, Qu, Can. 161/K1
Beccles, Eng, UK 37/H2
Bečej, Serb. 50/E3
Becerreá, Sp. 46/B1
Bechar, Alg. 111/E3
Bechar (wilaya), Alg. 110/E3
Becharof (lake), Ak, US 171/G4
Bechhofen, Ger. 55/G5
Bechhofen, Ger. 58/D4
Bechtheim, Ger. 58/B3
Bechyně, Czh. 59/H4
Becida, Mn, US 157/G4
Beckdorf, Ger. 53/G2
Beckenham (nbrhd.), Eng, UK 30/D2
Beckenried, Swi. 61/E4
Becker, Ms, US 162/C4
Beckingen, Ger. 55/F5
Beckingham, Eng, UK 35/H5
Beckley, WV, US 163/G2
Beckton, Wy, US 147/K1
Beckum, Ger. 53/F5
Beckville, Tx, US 151/G1
Beckwourth, Ca, US 146/C4
Beclean, Rom. 51/G2
Bécon-les-Granits, Fr. 57/E5
Becs de Bosson (peak), Swi. 60/D5
Bedale, Eng, UK 35/G3
Bédaoyo, Chad 116/C4
Bédarieux, Fr. 44/E5
Bédarrides, Fr. 64/A4
Bedaya, Chad 116/C3
Bedburg, Ger. 55/F2
Bedburg-Hau, Ger. 52/D5
Beddau, Wal, UK 36/C3
Beddgelert, Wal, UK 34/D5
Bedelē, Eth. 117/H3
Beder, Den. 40/D3
Bederkesa, Ger. 53/G1
Bederkesa, Ger. 53/F1
Bedēsa, Eth. 118/B3
Bedford (cape), Austl. 134/B1
Bedford, Qu, Can. 161/K2
Bedford, SAfr. 124/D4
Bedford, Eng, UK 37/F2
Bedford, Ia, US 155/G3
Bedford, In, US 162/D1
Bedford, Ky, US 162/E1
Bedford, NH, US 161/L3
Bedford, Pa, US 161/G4
Bedford, Tx, US 150/K7
Bedford, Va, US 163/H2
Bedford, Wy, US 147/H2
Bedford Hills, NY, US 169/E1
Bedford Level (phys. reg.), Eng, UK 37/F2
Bedford Park, Il, US 167/Q16
Bedfordshire (co.), Eng, UK 37/F2
Bedias, Tx, US 151/G2
Bédiondo, Chad 116/C3
Bedlington, Eng, UK 35/G1
Bedmond, Eng, UK 30/B1
Bedok (nbrhd.), Sing. 89/J6
Bedong, Malay. 89/C1
Bedonia, It. 62/C4
Bédouaram, Niger 116/B2
Bedourie, Austl. 131/H3
Bedretto, Swi. 61/E5
Bedrock, Co, US 149/H1
Bedsted, Den. 40/C3
Bedum, Neth. 52/D2
Bedwas, Wal, UK 36/C3
Bedworth, Eng, UK 37/E2
Bee (cr.), Eng, UK 107/F6
Bee Branch, Ar, US 153/H3
Bee Spring, Ky, US 162/D2
Beebe, Ar, US 153/J3
Beech Grove, In, US 160/C5
Beecher Falls, Vt, US 161/L2
Beecher Island, Co, US 154/C4
Beechgrove, Tn, US 162/D3
Beechworth, Austl. 133/C3
Beechy, Sk, Can. 145/L2
Beef Island (int'l arpt.), UK 173/M8
Beek, Neth. 55/E2
Beek, Neth. 52/C5
Beekman, La, US 153/J4
Beelbangera, Austl. 133/C2
Beelen, Ger. 53/F5
Beeler, Ks, US 152/D1
Beelitz, Ger. 42/P7
Beenleigh, Austl. 134/D4
Beer, Eng, UK 36/C5
Beer (pt.), Eng, UK 36/C5
Be'er Menuḥa, Isr. 104/D4
Be'er Sheva' (Beersheba), Isr. 105/B6
Beerato, Som. 118/C3
Beerfelden, Ger. 58/B3
Be'eri, Isr. 105/A6
Beernem, Belg. 54/C1
Beersheba (Be'er Sheva'), Isr. 105/B6
Beerzel, Belg. 55/D1
Beesel, Neth. 52/D6
Beeville, Tx, US 150/F3
Befale, D.R. Congo 121/E2
Befandriana, Madg. 125/G8
Befandriana, Madg. 125/J6
Befasy, Madg. 125/H8
Befori, D.R. Congo 121/E2
Beforona, Madg. 125/J7
Befotaka, Madg. 125/H8
Befotaka, Madg. 125/J6
Beg (lake), NI, UK 34/B2
Bega (riv.), Ger. 53/F5
Bega, Austl. 133/D3
Bega Veche (riv.), Cro. 50/E3
Begamganj, India 96/B4
Begamganj, Bang. 97/H4
Bégard, Fr. 56/B3
Begarslan (peak), Trkm. 71/K4
Begejci, Serb. 50/E3
Beggs, Ok, US 153/F3
Begī, Eth. 117/G3
Begichev (isl.), Rus. 75/M2
Begna (riv.), Nor. 38/D3
Begoml', Bela. 41/N4
Begumpet (int'l arpt.), India 95/C2
Begunitsy, Rus. 41/N2
Begusarai, India 97/F3
Béhague (pt.), FrG. 182/D1
Behāla, India 92/E3
Behala (str.), Indo. 90/B4
Behamberg, Aus. 59/H6
Behara, Madg. 125/H9
Behat, India 98/D4
Behbahān, Iran 103/G4
Beheloka, Madg. 125/G8
Behenjy-Afovany, Madg. 125/H7
Behleg, China 78/C4
Béhoust, Fr. 30/H5
Behren-lès-Forbach, Fr. 55/F5
Behri (riv.), Nepal 96/C1
Behshahr, Iran 103/H2
Bei (mts.), China 74/K5
Bei'an, China 79/K2
Beiba, China 78/F5
Beibei, China 87/E2
Beida (riv.), China 78/D4
Beidianzi, China 81/A4
Beierfeld, Ger. 59/F1
Beigantang (isl.), Tai. 87/J3
Beigua (peak), It. 62/B5
Beiguo, China 80/L8
Beihai, China 87/F4
Beijing (prov.), China 78/H3
Beijing (cap.), China 80/H7
Beijing Capital (int'l arpt.), China 80/H6
Beilen, Neth. 52/D3
Beiling, China 87/G3
Beiliu, China 87/F4
Beilngries, Ger. 59/E4
Beilstein, Ger. 58/C4
Beilu (riv.), China 78/C5
Beilun (pass), China 87/E4
Bein Tharsuinn (peak), Sc, UK 33/B1
Beinamar, Chad 116/B3
Beinasco, It. 64/D2
Beindersheim, Ger. 58/B3
Beinn a' Chuallaich (peak), Sc, UK 33/B3
Beinn a' Ghlò (peak), Sc, UK 33/C3
Beinn a' Mheadhoin (lake), Sc, UK 33/B2
Beinn Bhàn (peak), Sc, UK 33/A3
Beinn Bheula (peak), Sc, UK 33/B4
Beinn Bhrotain (peak), Sc, UK 33/C2
Beinn Bhuidhe (peak), Sc, UK 33/B4
Beinn Bhuidhe Mhór (peak), Sc, UK 33/B2
Beinn Dearg (peak), Sc, UK 33/B1
Beinn Dearg (peak), Sc, UK 33/C3
Beinn Dòrain (peak), Sc, UK 33/B4
Beinn Eighe (peak), Sc, UK 33/A1
Beinn Heasgarnich (peak), Sc, UK 33/B3
Beinn Mholach (peak), Sc, UK 33/B3
Beinn Mhór (peak), Sc, UK 33/A4
Beinwil am See, Swi. 60/E3
Beipiao, China 80/E2
Beira (int'l arpt.), Moz. 123/G3
Beira, Moz. 123/G3
Beira Alta, Ang. 120/C5
Beirong, China 87/F2
Beiru (riv.), China 80/C4
Beirut (int'l arpt.), Leb. 105/C1
Beirut (Bayrūt) (cap.), Leb. 105/C1
Beiseker, Ab, Can. 145/H2
Beishan, China 78/D3
Beishan, China 87/F3
Beit Jann, Isr. 105/C3
Beitbridge, Zim. 123/F4
Beith, Sc, UK 33/B5
Beiuş, Rom. 50/F2
Beizhen, China 81/A2
Beja, Port. 46/B3
Beja (dist.), Port. 46/A4
Bejaïa, Alg. 112/H4
Bejaïa (wilaya), Alg. 112/H4
Béjar, Sp. 46/C2
Bejhi (riv.), Pak. 101/J3
Bekasi, Indo. 89/D4
Bekdash, Trkm. 71/K4
Békés (prov.), Hun. 50/E2
Békés, Hun. 50/E2
Békéscsaba, Hun. 50/E2
Bekilli, Turk. 102/B2
Bekily, Madg. 125/H9
Bekitro, Madg. 125/H9
Bekodoka, Madg. 125/H7
Bek'ojī, Eth. 118/A4
Bekopaka, Madg. 125/H7
Bekoropoka, Madg. 125/G8
Bekwai, Gha. 115/E5
Bel, La, US 164/B2
Bel Air, Md, US 168/B4
Bel Air South, Md, US 168/B5
Bel Aire, Ks, US 153/F2
Belá, Slvk. 43/K4
Bela, Pak. 101/J3
Bela, D.R. Congo 121/G2
Belā, India 92/D2
Bela Crkva, Serb. 50/E3
Bela Cruz, Braz. 183/F3
Bela Palanka, Serb. 50/F4
Bělá pod Bezdězem, Czh. 59/H1
Belā Pratāpgarh, India 96/C3
Bela Vista, Ang. 122/C2
Bela Vista, Braz. 189/E2
Bela Vista, Moz. 125/F2
Bela Vista de Goiás, Braz. 186/C3
Bela Vista do Paraíso, Braz. 189/G2
Belabérim (well), Niger 116/B2
Bélabo, Camr. 116/B4
Belair Rec. Pk., Austl. 131/M9
Belampalli, India 95/C2
Belan (riv.), India 96/D3
Belanak (cape), Malay. 89/C1
Belang, Indo. 91/F3
Belarus (ctry.) 29/G3
Belas, Port. 47/P10
Belawan, Indo. 89/B2
Belaya (riv.), Rus. 74/F4
Belaya (peak), Eth. 117/H3
Belaya Glina, Rus. 73/L4
Belaya Kalitva, Rus. 73/L3
Belbo (riv.), It. 62/B3
Bełchatów, Pol. 43/K3
Belchen (peak), Ger. 60/D2
Belcher, La, US 153/H4
Belcher (isls.), Can. 139/J4
Belcher (isls.), On, Can. 141/H3
Belcher (chan.), Nun, Can. 141/S7
Belchite, Sp. 47/E2
Belcourt, ND, US 156/E3
Belda, India 97/F4
Beldānga, India 97/G4
Belebey, Rus. 69/M5
Beled Weyne, Som. 118/C4
Belefuanai, Libr. 114/C5
Bélel, Camr. 116/B4
Belém, Braz. 183/H4
Belém, Braz. 182/D3
Belém de São Francisco, Braz. 183/G5
Belem Tower, Port. 47/P10
Belen, Turk. 104/E1
Belen, Turk. 104/C1
Belén, Nic. 172/D5
Belen, NM, US 149/J3
Belén, Uru. 188/E4
Belén, Chile 188/B1
Belén, Arg. 188/C3
Belén, Bol. 185/E5
Belén de Escobar, Arg. 191/J11
Belén de Umbría, Col. 183/K7
Belene, Bul. 51/G4
Bélep (isls.), NCal. 137/T11
Beles Wenz (riv.), Eth. 117/G3
Belesar (res.), Sp. 46/B1
Belev, Rus. 70/F1
Belfair, Wa, US 167/B3
Belfast (dist.), NI, UK 34/B2
Belfast (cap.), NI, UK 34/C2
Belfast, SAfr. 125/E2
Belfast Lough (bay), NI, UK 34/C2
Belfaux, Swi. 60/D4
Belfield, ND, US 156/C4
Bēlfodiyo, Eth. 117/G3
Belford, Eng, UK 33/E5
Belfort (dept.), Fr. 60/C2
Belfort, Fr. 60/C2
Belfountain, On, Can. 160/S8
Belfry, Mt, US 147/J1
Belgioioso, It. 62/C3
Belgium (ctry.) 42/C3
Belgorod, Rus. 73/J2
Belgorodskaya Oblast, Rus. 70/F2
Belgrade, Mn, US 157/G5
Belgrade, Mo, US 162/B2
Belgrade (Beograd) (cap.), Serb. 50/E3
Belgreen, Al, US 162/D3
Belhavel (lake), Ire. 32/B1
Belhaven, NC, US 163/J3
Beli Drim (riv.), Serb. 49/G1
Beli Drim (riv.), Alb. 50/E4
Beli Manastir, Cro. 50/D3
Beli Timok (riv.), Serb. 50/F4
Belidzhi, Rus. 71/J4
Bélinga, Gabon 120/C2
Belington, WV, US 163/H1
Belinskiy, Rus. 71/G1
Belinyu, Indo. 89/D3
Belitsa, Bul. 49/H2
Belitung (isl.), Indo. 90/C4
Belize, Ang. 120/C4
Belize (riv.), Belz. 176/D2
Belize (ctry.) 176/D2
Belize City, Belz. 176/D2
Bélizon, FrG. 182/C1
Beljanica (peak), Serb. 50/E3
Belk, Tx, US 153/G4
Belknap (mtn.), NH, US 161/L3
Bel'kovskiy (isl.), Rus. 75/N2
Bell, Ger. 55/G3
Bell (isl.), Nf, Can. 159/L2
Bell, Fl, US 165/G3
Bell, Ca, US 166/F8
Bell, Austl. 134/C4
Bell (pt.), Austl. 131/G5
Bell (riv.), Austl. 133/D1
Bell (riv.), Qu, Can. 141/J4
Bell (pen.), Nun, Can. 141/H2
Bell (pt.), PNG 129/F2
Bell Gardens, Ca, US 166/F8
Bell Rock (Inchcape) (isl.), Sc, UK 33/D4
Bell Ville, Arg. 188/D5
Bella Flor, Bol. 184/E3
Bella Vista, Arg. 188/E4
Bella Vista, Arg. 188/C3
Bella Vista, Bol. 185/F4
Bella Vista, Par. 189/E2
Bella Vista, Ar, US 153/G2
Bellac, Fr. 44/D3
Bellachat (peak), Fr. 64/C1
Bellaco, Uru. 191/K10
Bellaghy, NI, UK 34/B2
Bellagio, It. 61/F6
Bellaire, Oh, US 160/F4
Bellaire, Mi, US 160/D2
Bellaire, Tx, US 151/M9
Bellamy, Al, US 162/C4
Bellananagh, Ire. 32/C2
Bellano, It. 61/F5
Bellaria, It. 63/F5
Bellary, India 95/C3
Bellata, Austl. 132/D1
Bellavista (cape), It. 48/A3
Bellavista, Ecu. 184/J7
Bellavista, Peru 184/B2
Bellavista, Peru 184/B2
Bellbird, Austl. 133/E1
Belle, Mo, US 153/J1
Belle (riv.), On, Can. 167/G7
Belle, WV, US 163/G1
Belle Chasse, La, US 164/D3
Belle Fourche (res.), SD, US 156/C5
Belle Fourche, SD, US 154/C1
Belle Fourche (riv.), Wy,SD, US 154/"B2
Belle Glade, Fl, US 165/H4
Belle Haven, Va, US 168/A6
Belle Isle, Fl, US 164/N7
Belle Isle (str.), NF, Can. 139/M4
Belle Plaine, Ks, US 153/F2
Belle Plaine, Ia, US 155/H3
Belle River, On, Can. 167/G7
Belle Terre, NY, US 169/E2
Belle Yella, Libr. 114/C5
Belle-Anse, Haiti 177/H2
Belle-Ile (isl.), Fr. 44/B3
Belle-Isle-en-Terre, Fr. 56/B3
Belleair, Fl, US 164/K8
Belleair Beach, Fl, US 164/K8
Belleair Bluffs, Fl, US 164/K8
Belleek, NI, UK 34/B3
Bellefontaine, Oh, US 160/E4
Bellefontaine, Ms, US 162/C4
Bellefonte, Ar, US 153/H2
Bellefonte, Pa, US 161/H4
Bellefonte, De, US 168/C4
Bellegarde-sur-Valserine, Fr. 60/B5
Bellême, Fr. 57/F4
Bellenberg, Ger. 61/G1
Bellencombre, Fr. 57/G1
Bellenden Ker NP, Austl. 134/B2
Belleoram, Nf, Can. 159/K2
Belleplain, NJ, US 168/D5
Bellerive-sur-Allier, Fr. 44/E3
Bellerose, NY, US 169/L9
Belleu, Fr. 54/C5
Belleview, Fl, US 165/G3
Belleview, Mo, US 162/B2
Belleville, On, Can. 161/H2
Belleville, Fr. 60/A5
Belleville, Ar, US 153/H3
Belleville, Il, US 162/C1
Belleville, Ks, US 154/F4
Belleville, Mi, US 167/E7
Belleville, NJ, US 169/J8
Belleville, Pa, US 161/H4
Belleville-sur-Meuse, Fr. 55/E5
Bellevue, Id, US 147/F2
Bellevue, Ia, US 155/J2
Bellevue, Md, US 168/B6
Bellevue, Ne, US 155/G3
Bellevue, Oh, US 160/E4
Bellevue, Wa, US 144/C4
Belley, Fr. 60/B6
Bellflower, Ca, US 166/F8
Bellheim, Ger. 58/B4
Bellignat, Fr. 60/B5
Bellinge, Den. 40/D4
Bellingen, Austl. 132/E1
Bellingham, Eng, UK 35/F1
Bellingham, Mn, US 155/F1
Bellingham, Wa, US 144/C3
Bellingrath Gardens and Home, Al, US 164/D2
Bellingshausen (sea), Ant. 192/U
Bellingshausen (isl.), FrPol. 137/K6
Bellingwolde, Neth. 53/E2
Bellinzago Novarese, It. 62/B2
Bellinzona, Swi. 61/F5
Belliveau Cove, NS, Can. 158/D3
Bellizzi, It. 65/D6
Bellmawr, NJ, US 168/C4
Bellmead, Tx, US 151/F2
Bellmore, NY, US 169/L9
Bello, Col. 183/K6
Bellona, It. 65/D5
Bellona Reefs (reef), NCal. 136/E7
Bellot (str.), Nun, Can. 140/G1
Bellows Falls, Vt, US 161/K3
Bellport, NY, US 169/F2
Bells, Tn, US 162/C3
Bells, Tx, US 153/F4
Bellsbank, Sc, UK 33/B6
Bellshill, Sc, UK 33/B5
Bellsite, Mb, Can. 156/D1
Belluno (prov.), It. 63/E1
Belluno, It. 45/K3
Bellville, SAfr. 124/L10
Bellville, Ga, US 163/G4
Bellville, Oh, US 160/E4
Bellville, Tx, US 150/F3
Bellwald, Swi. 60/E5
Bellwood, La, US 164/B2
Belly (riv.), Ab, Can. 145/H3
Belm, Ger. 53/F4
Belmar, NJ, US 168/D3
Bélmez, Sp. 46/C3
Belmond, Ia, US 155/H2
Belmont, Mb, Can. 156/E3
Belmont, NS, Can. 158/F3
Belmont, Ca, US 167/K11
Belmont, La, US 164/B2
Belmont, Ms, US 162/C3
Belmont, Mt, US 145/K4
Belmont, NC, US 163/G3
Belmont, Ne, US 154/C2
Belmont, NY, US 161/G3
Belmonte, Port. 46/B2
Belmonte, Sp. 46/D3
Belmonte, Braz. 187/F2
Belmopan (cap.), Belz. 176/D2
Belmullet, Ire. 31/P9
Belo, Madg. 125/G8
Belo Campo, Braz. 187/E2
Belo Horizonte, Braz. 186/E3
Belo Jardim, Braz. 183/G5
Belo-Tsiribihina, Madg. 125/H7
Beloeil, Belg. 54/C2
Beloeil, Qu, Can. 159/P6
Belogorsk, Rus. 79/K1
Beloha, Madg. 125/H9
Beloit, Ks, US 154/E4
Beloit, Wi, US 155/K2
Belokany, Azer. 71/H4
Béloko, CAfr. 116/B4
Belomorsk, Rus. 68/G2
Belondo-Kundu, D.R. Congo 120/D3
Beloomut, Rus. 68/H5
Beloozërsk, Bela. 70/C1
Belorado, Sp. 44/B5
Belorechensk, Rus. 73/K5
Belören, Turk. 102/C2
Beloretsk, Rus. 69/N5
Beloslav, Bul. 51/H4
Belovo, Bul. 49/J1
Belovo, Rus. 74/J4
Beloye (lake), Rus. 74/D3
Belozersk, Rus. 68/H3
Belozërskoye, Rus. 69/Q5
Belper, Eng, UK 35/G5
Belpre, Oh, US 160/F5
Belsand, India 97/E2
Belsay, Eng, UK 35/G1
Belt, Mt, US 145/J4
Belterra, Braz. 182/C3
Belterwijde (lake), Neth. 52/D3
Beltheim, Ger. 55/G3
Belton (lake), Tx, US 151/F2
Belton, Mo, US 153/G1
Belton, SC, US 163/F3
Belton, Eng, UK 37/H1
Belton, Tx, US 150/F2
Beltra (lake), Ire. 32/A2
Beltrán, Arg. 188/C3
Beltsville, Md, US 168/B5
Belturbet, Ire. 32/C1
Beltzville (lake), Pa, US 168/C2
Belukha (peak), Rus. 99/E2
Belumut (peak), Malay. 89/C2
Beluran, Malay. 88/B4
Belvedere, Ca, US 167/K11
Belvédère du Cirque, Fr. 64/D3
Belvedere Park, Ga, US 163/M7
Belvidere, SD, US 154/D2
Belvidere, Il, US 155/K2
Belvidere, NJ, US 168/C2
Belview, Mn, US 155/G1
Belvoir NP, Isr. 105/D3
Belwood, On, Can. 160/S8
Belyando (riv.), Austl. 127/D3
Belyayevka, Rus. 71/L2
Belynkovichi, Bela. 70/E1
Belyy (isl.), Rus. 74/G2
Belyy Yar, Rus. 74/J4
Belyye Berega, Rus. 70/E1
Belz, Ukr. 72/C2
Belzig, Ger. 42/G2
Belzoni, Ms, US 162/B4
Bełżyce, Pol. 43/M3
Bémal, CAfr. 116/C4
Bemanevika, Madg. 125/J6
Bemanevika, Madg. 125/J6
Bemaraha (plat.), Madg. 125/H7
Bemarivo (riv.), Madg. 125/H7
Bembe, Ang. 120/C4
Bembéréké, Ben. 115/F4
Bembezi (riv.), Zim. 123/F3
Bembibre, Sp. 46/B1
Bembo, Ang. 120/D5
Bemboka, Austl. 133/D3
Bembridge, Eng, UK 37/E5
Bemebesi, Zim. 123/F4
Bemetāra, India 95/D1
Bemidji, Mn, US 157/G4
Bemis, SD, US 155/F1
Bemmel, Neth. 52/C5
Bempton, Eng, UK 35/H3
Ben Aigan (hill), Sc, UK 33/C1
Ben Alder (peak), Sc, UK 33/B3
Ben Améra (well), Mrta. 110/B5
Ben Avon (peak), Sc, UK 33/C2
Ben Boyd NP, Austl. 133/E3
Ben Chonzie (peak), Sc, UK 33/C4
Ben Cleuch (peak), Sc, UK 33/C4
Ben Cruachan (peak), Sc, UK 33/A4
Ben Dash (peak), Ire. 32/A4
Ben Davis (pt.), NJ, US 168/C5
Ben Giang, Viet. 94/D3
Ben Gurion (int'l arpt.), Isr. 105/B4
Ben Hope (peak), Sc, UK 31/R7
Ben Ime (peak), Sc, UK 33/B4
Ben Lawers (peak), Sc, UK 33/B3
Ben Ledi (peak), Sc, UK 33/B4
Ben Lomond (peak), Sc, UK 33/B4
Ben Lomond, Ca, US 148/A2
Ben Lomond NP, Austl. 132/C4
Ben Lui (peak), Sc, UK 33/B4
Ben Macdui (peak), Sc, UK 33/C2
Ben More (peak), Sc, UK 31/Q8
Ben More (peak), Sc, UK 33/B4
Ben More Assynt (peak), Sc, UK 31/R7
Ben Msik-Sidi Othmane (prov.), Mor. 112/A2
Ben Nevis (peak), Sc, UK 33/B3
Ben Quang, Viet. 94/D2
Ben Rinnes (peak), Sc, UK 33/C2
Ben Slimane, Mor. 110/D2
Ben Slimane (prov.), Mor. 112/A3
Ben Starav (peak), Sc, UK 33/A3
Ben Tee (peak), Sc, UK 33/B2
Ben Thuy, Viet. 86/E5
Ben Tirran (peak), Sc, UK 33/C3
Ben Tre, Viet. 94/D4
Ben Vane (peak), Sc, UK 33/B4
Ben Vorlich (peak), Sc, UK 33/B4
Ben Vrackie (peak), Sc, UK 33/C3
Ben Wyvis (peak), Sc, UK 33/B1
Ben Zohra (well), Alg. 110/E3
Bena, Mn, US 157/G4
Bena-Bendi, D.R. Congo 120/E4
Bena-Dibele, D.R. Congo 121/E4
Bena-Makima, D.R. Congo 121/E4
Benabarre, Sp. 47/F1
Benahmed, Mor. 110/D2
Benalla, Austl. 133/B3
Benalmádena, Sp. 46/C4
Benalto, Ab, Can. 144/G1
Benāpol, Bang. 97/G4
Benavente, Sp. 46/C1
Benavides, Bol. 185/E4
Benavides, Tx, US 151/E4
Benbane (pt.), NI, UK 34/B1
Benbecula (isl.), Sc, UK 31/Q8
Benbonyathe (peak), Austl. 131/H4
Benbrack (peak), Ire. 32/C1
Benbrook (lake), Tx, US 150/K7
Benbrook (dam), Tx, US 150/K7
Benbrook, Tx, US 150/K7
Benburb, NI, UK 34/B3
Benchley, Tx, US 151/F2
Bencubbin, Austl. 130/C4
Bend, Or, US 146/C1
Bend, Tx, US 151/E2
Benda (cape), Indo. 89/E4
Bende, Nga. 115/G5
Bendeleben (mt.), Ak, US 171/F2
Bendemeer, Austl. 132/D1
Bender Beyla, Som. 118/D3
Bender Cassim (Bosaaso), Som. 118/D3
Bendersville, Pa, US 168/A4
Bendery (Tighina), Mol. 72/E4
Bendigo, Austl. 133/B3
Bendoc, Austl. 133/D3
Bendorf, Ger. 40/C4
Bendugu, SLeo. 114/C4
Benduma, Libr. 114/C5
Bēne, Lat. 41/K3
Bene Beraq, Isr. 105/B4
Benedict (mt.), Nf, Can. 141/L3
Benediktbeuern, Ger. 61/H2
Benediktenwand (peak), Ger. 61/H2
Beneditinos, Braz. 183/F4
Benenitra, Madg. 125/H8
Benešov, Czh. 59/H3
Benevento (prov.), It. 65/D5
Benevento, It. 65/D5
Benfeld, Fr. 60/D1
Benga, Moz. 123/G3
Bengal (bay), Asia 77/H8
Bengal, Bay of (gulf), Asia 92/E4
Bengbis, Camr. 120/C2
Bengbu, China 80/D4
Benge, Wa, US 144/E4
Benghāzī, Libya 67/J4
Bengkalis, Indo. 89/C2
Bengkalis (isl.), Indo. 90/B3
Bengkayang, Indo. 90/C3
Bengkulu, Indo. 89/C3
Bengkulu (prov.), Indo. 89/C4
Bengo (riv.), Ang. 120/C5
Bengo (prov.), Ang. 120/C5
Bengo (bay), Ang. 120/C5
Bengough, Sk, Can. 156/B3
Bengtsby, Fin. 39/F4
Bengtsfors, Swe. 40/E2
Benguela, Ang. 122/B2
Benguela (prov.), Ang. 122/B2
Benguerir, Mor. 110/D2
Benguerua (isl.), Moz. 123/G4
Bengweulu (lake), Zam. 121/G5
Bengweulu (swamp), Zam. 121/G5
Beni, Nepal 96/D1
Beni, D.R. Congo 121/G2
Beni (riv.), Bol. 179/C4
Beni (dept.), Bol. 185/E4
Beni Abbes, Alg. 111/E3
Beni Bouayach, Mor. 112/C2
Beni Ensar, Mor. 112/B2
Beni Khiar, Tun. 112/M6
Beni Mellal, Mor. 110/D2
Beni Ounif, Alg. 111/E2
Beni Saf, Alg. 112/D2
Beni Tajit, Mor. 110/E2
Benicarló, Sp. 47/F2
Benicia, Ca, US 167/K10
Benidorm, Sp. 47/E3
Benifayó, Sp. 47/E3
Benin (ctry.) 115/F4
Benin City, Nga. 115/G5
Benina (int'l arpt.), Libya 67/J4
Benisa, Sp. 47/F3
Benisheikh, Nga. 116/B3
Benito, Mb, Can. 156/D2
Benito Juárez, Mex. 174/D2
Benjamin, Tx, US 152/E4
Benjamin Constant, Braz. 184/D2
Benjamin Hill, Mex. 174/C2
Benjamin, Isla (isl.), Chile 190/B5
Benkei-misaki (cape), Japan 82/B2
Benkelman, Ne, US 154/D3
Benld, Il, US 155/K4
Benllech, Wal, UK 34/D5
Benmore (peak), Ire. 32/A1
Bennachie (hill), Sc, UK 33/D2
Bennan (pt.), Sc, UK 33/A6
Benndale, Ms, US 164/D2
Benneckenstein, Ger. 53/H5
Bennett, BC, Can. 171/M3
Bennett (isl.), Rus. 75/Q2
Bennett, Co, US 154/B4
Bennett (peak), Co, US 152/A2
Bennett, Wi, US 157/J4
Bennettsbridge, Ire. 32/C4
Bennettsville, SC, US 163/H3
Bennichchab, Mrta. 114/B2
Bennington, Id, US 147/H2
Bennington, Ks, US 153/F1
Bennington, Ne, US 155/F3
Bennington, Ok, US 153/F3
Bennington, Vt, US 161/K3
Bénodet, Fr. 56/A5
Benoit, Ms, US 162/B4
Benom (peak), Malay. 89/C2
Bénoué (riv.), Camr. 116/B3
Bénoue, PN de la, Camr. 116/B3
Benover, Eng, UK 30/E3
Benoy, Chad 116/C3
Bensenville, Il, US 167/Q16
Bensheim, Ger. 58/B3
Benson, Mn, US 157/G5
Benson, La, US 150/H2
Benson, Sk, Can. 156/C3
Benson, Az, US 149/G5
Benson, NC, US 163/H3
Bensonhurst (nbrhd.), NY, US 169/K9
Benta (riv.), Hun. 51/Q10
Benta Seberang, Malay. 89/C1
Bentham, Eng, UK 35/F3
Bentheim, Ger. 53/E4
Benti, Gui. 114/B4
Bentiaba, Ang. 122/B2
Bentiaba (riv.), Ang. 122/B2
Bentinck (isl.), Austl. 129/E4
Bentiu, Sudan 117/F3
Bentley, ND, US 156/C4
Bentley, Ok, US 153/F3
Bentley, Eng, UK 35/G4
Bentley, Eng, UK 30/A3
Bento Gonçalves, Braz. 189/G4
Benton, Ar, US 153/H3
Benton, La, US 153/H4
Benton, Il, US 162/C2
Benton, Ms, US 162/B4
Benton, Ky, US 162/C2
Benton, Mo, US 162/C2
Benton, Tn, US 162/E3
Benton, Pa, US 168/B1
Benton Harbor, Mi, US 160/C3
Benton Lake NWR, Mt, US 145/J4
Bentong, Malay. 89/C2
Bentonia, Ms, US 162/B4
Bentonville, Ar, US 153/G2
Bentonville, Va, US 163/H1
Bent's Old Fort Nat'l Hist. Site, Co, US 152/C1
Benua Martinus, Indo. 90/D3
Benue (state), Nga. 115/H5
Benue (riv.), Nga. 107/C4
Benxi, China 81/B2
Benxi, China 81/C2
Beo, Indo. 91/G3
Beočin, Serb. 50/D3
Beoga, Indo. 91/J4
Beograd (int'l arpt.), Serb. 50/E3
Beograd (Belgrade) (cap.), Serb. 50/E3
Beohāri, India 96/C3
Béoumi, C.d'Iv. 114/D5
Béoux (riv.), Fr. 64/B3
Beowawe, Nv, US 146/E3
Beppu (bay), Japan 84/B4
Beppu, Japan 84/B4
Bequia (isl.), StV. 173/N9
Bequimão, Braz. 183/E3
Bera, Bang. 97/G3
Beragh, NI, UK 34/A2
Beraketa, Madg. 125/H8
Beraketa, Madg. 125/H9
Beramanja, Madg. 125/J6
Beras Basah (cape), Malay. 89/C2
Berasia, India 96/A4
Berat, Alb. 49/F2
Beratus (peak), Indo. 91/E4
Beratzhausen, Ger. 59/E4
Berau (bay), Indo. 91/H4
Berau (riv.), Indo. 91/E3
Beravina, Madg. 125/H7
Berbenno di Valtellina, It. 61/F5
Berbera, Som. 118/C3
Berbérati, CAfr. 116/B4
Berbice (riv.), Guy. 181/G3
Berceto, It. 62/C4
Berchem, Belg. 52/B6
Bercher, Swi. 60/C4
Berching, Ger. 59/E4
Berchogur, Kaz. 71/L2
Berchtesgaden, Ger. 45/K3
Berchtesgaden, NP Ger. 45/K3
Berck, Fr. 54/A3
Berclair, Tx, US 151/F3
Berdale, Som. 118/C4
Berdorf, Lux. 55/F4
Berdsk, Rus. 74/J4
Berdyans'k, Ukr. 73/J4
Berdyansk (bay), Ukr. 73/J4
Berdychiv, Ukr. 72/E3
Béré, Chad 116/C3
Bere Regis, Eng, UK 36/D5
Berea, Ky, US 162/E2
Berea, Les. 124/D3
Bereah, Fl, US 164/M8
Berebere, Indo. 91/G3
Bereguardo, It. 62/C3
Berehomet, Ukr. 72/C3
Berehove, Ukr. 43/M4
Bereina, PNG 129/G2
Bereku, Tanz. 119/A3
Berekum, Gha. 115/E5
Berenguela, Bol. 188/B1
Berenice (ruin), Egypt 109/G4
Berens (isl.), Mb, Can. 156/F1
Berens River, Mb, Can. 156/F1
Berenty, Madg. 125/H8
Beresford, NB, Can. 158/E2
Beresford, SD, US 155/F2
Bereşti, Rom. 51/H2
Berettyóújfalu, Hun. 50/E2
Berevo, Madg. 125/H7
Berezan', Ukr. 72/F2
Berezhany, Ukr. 72/C3
Berezhnoye, Rus. 68/H4
Berezino, Bela. 41/N5
Berezivka, Ukr. 72/F4
Bereznik, Rus. 68/J3
Berezniki, Rus. 69/N4
Berezovo, Rus. 74/G3
Berëzovskiy, Rus. 69/P4
Berezovyy, Rus. 79/L1
Berg, Ger. 61/H2
Berg, Swi. 61/F2
Berg, Lux. 55/F4
Berg, Ger. 58/B5
Berg (riv.), SAfr. 124/B4
Berg bei Rohrbach, Aus. 59/G5
Berg en Dal, Sur. 182/C1
Berga, Sp. 47/F1
Bergama, Turk. 70/C5
Bergamo (prov.), It. 61/F6
Bergamo, It. 62/C2
Bergara, Sp. 46/D1
Bergatruete, Ger. 61/F2
Bergedorf, Ger. 53/H2
Bergen, Nor. 40/A1
Bergen, Ger. 40/E4
Bergen, Ger. 53/G3
Bergen, Neth. 52/B3
Bergen (co.), NJ, US 168/D2
Bergen aan Zee, Neth. 52/B3
Bergen op Zoom, Neth. 52/B5
Bergenfield, NJ, US 169/K8
Berger, Nor. 38/S9
Bergerac, Fr. 44/D4
Bergeresse (riv.), Fr. 57/H5
Bergeyk, Neth. 52/C6
Bergheim, Aus. 59/G7
Bergheim, Ger. 55/F2
Bergheim, Tx, US 151/E3
Bergisch Gladbach, Ger. 55/G2
Bergkamen, Ger. 53/E5
Bergman, Ar, US 153/H2
Bergnäset, Swe. 68/D2
Bergneustadt, Ger. 55/G1
Bergrheinfeld, Ger. 42/F4
Bergsbrunna, Swe. 39/A1
Bergse Maas (riv.), Neth. 52/B5
Bergshamra, Swe. 40/H2
Bergsvatnet (lake), Nor. 38/R9
Bergsviken, Swe. 38/G2
Bergtheim, Ger. 58/D3
Berguent, Mor. 112/C2
Bergues, Fr. 54/B2
Bergum, Neth. 52/D2
Bergumermeer (lake), Neth. 52/D2
Bergün-Bravuogn, Swi. 61/F4
Bergviken (lake), Swe. 40/G1
Berh, Mong. 78/G2
Berhala (str.), Indo. 89/C3
Berhampore, India 97/G3
Berhampur, India 95/E2
Beri Khās, India 98/D5
Berikat (cape), Indo. 89/D3
Bering (str.), Rus.,US 171/E3
Bering (isl.), Rus. 75/S4
Bering (sea), Asia,NAm. 171/D3
Beringen, Belg. 55/E1
Beringovskiy, Rus. 75/T3
Beritarikap (cape), Indo. 89/C3
Berja, Sp. 46/D4
Berkane, Mor. 112/C2
Berkel (riv.), Ger. 42/D2
Berkel, Neth. 52/B5
Berkeley, Eng, UK 36/D3
Berkeley Heights, NJ, US 169/H9
Berkeley Lake, Ga, US 163/M7
Berkeley Springs (Bath), WV, US 161/G5
Berkhamsted, Eng, UK 30/B1
Berkheim, Ger. 61/G1
Berkhout, Neth. 52/B3
Berkley, Mi, US 167/F6
Berkovitsa, Bul. 51/F4
Berks (co.), Pa, US 168/C3
Berkshire (co.), Eng, UK 37/E3
Berkshire Downs (hills), Eng, UK 37/E3
Berlaimont, Fr. 54/C3
Berlanga de Duero, Sp. 46/D2
Berlare, Belg. 54/D1
Berleburg, Ger. 53/F6
Berlicum, Neth. 52/C5
Berlin (cap.), Ger. 42/Q6
Berlin (state), Ger. 42/Q6
Berlin, Ga, US 165/G2
Berlin, NJ, US 168/D4
Berlin, Md, US 163/K1
Berlin (mtn.), Nv, US 146/E4
Berlin, Wi, US 155/K2
Bermagui, Austl. 133/E3
Bermejillo, Mex. 174/E3
Bermejo (riv.), Arg. 179/D5
Bermejo, Arg. 190/D1
Bermeo, Sp. 44/B5
Bermillo de Sayago, Sp. 46/B2
Bermuda (isl.), UK 139/L6
Bermudian (cr.), Pa, US 168/A4
Bern (canton), Swi. 60/D4
Bern (cap.), Swi. 60/D4
Bern-Belp (int'l arpt.), Swi. 60/D4

Bernabé Rivera, Uru. 189/E4
Bernal, Peru 184/A2
Bernalda, It. 48/E2
Bernalillo, NM, US 149/J3
Bernard (riv.), NW, Can. 140/D1
Bernardo, NM, US 149/J3
Bernardo O'Higgins, PN, Chile 191/B6
Bernardston, Ma, US 161/K3
Bernardsville, NJ, US 168/D2
Bernau, Ger. 60/E2
Bernau, Ger. 42/Q6
Bernay, Fr. 57/F2
Bernbeuren, Ger. 61/G2
Bernburg, Ger. 42/F3
Berne, In, US 160/D4
Berne (riv.), Ger. 53/F2
Bernes-sur-Oise, Fr. 30/J4
Bernese Alps (mtn.), Swi. 45/G3
Bernhardswald, Ger. 59/F4
Bernice, La, US 153/H4
Bernie, Mo, US 162/C2
Bernier (isl.), Austl. 130/B3
Bernier (bay), Nun, Can. 140/G1
Bernières-sur-Mer, Fr. 57/E2
Bernierville, Qu, Can. 158/B2
Bernin, Fr. 64/B2
Bernina (mtn.), Swi. 61/F5
Bernina (peak), Swi. 61/F5
Bernina, Passo del (pass), Swi. 61/G5
Bernissart, Belg. 54/C3
Bernkastel-Kues, Ger. 55/G4
Bernsbach, Ger. 59/F1
Bernville, Pa, US 168/B3
Beromünster, Swi. 60/E3
Béron (riv.), Fr. 57/E5
Beronono, Madg. 125/H8
Beroroha, Madg. 125/H8
Beroun, Czh. 59/H3
Berounka (riv.), Czh. 43/G4
Berovo, FYROM 49/H2
Berra, It. 63/E4
Berrara, Austl. 133/E2
Berre (lake), Fr. 44/F5
Berre-l'Étang, Fr. 64/B6
Berrechid, Mor. 110/D2
Berri, Austl. 131/J5
Berriane, Alg. 111/F2
Berridale, Austl. 133/D3
Berriedale, Sc, UK 31/S7
Berrien Springs, Mi, US 160/C4
Berriew, Wal, UK 36/C1
Berrigan, Austl. 133/B2
Berrima, Austl. 133/E2
Berriozábal, Mex. 176/C2
Berrondo, Uru. 191/K11
Berrotarán, Arg. 190/D2
Berrouaghia, Alg. 112/G4
Berry (canal), Fr. 57/G6
Berry (pt.), NS, Can. 159/G3
Berry (isls.), Bahm. 173/F2
Berry (reg.), Fr. 66/D1
Berry, Ky, US 162/E1
Berry (pt.), Eng, UK 36/C6
Berry (cr.), Ab, Can. 145/J2
Berry, Austl. 133/E2
Berry (mtn.), Pa, US 168/A2
Berryessa (peak), Ca, US 167/K9
Berryessa (lake), Ca, US 146/B4
Berryville, Ar, US 153/H2
Berryville, Va, US 163/J1
Berseba, Namb. 124/B2
Bersenbrück, Ger. 53/E3
Bershad', Ukr. 72/E3
Bersut, Rus. 69/L5
Bertam, Malay. 89/C1
Bertha, Mn, US 157/G4
Berthierville, Qu, Can. 161/K1
Berthold, ND, US 156/D3
Berthoud, Co, US 154/B3
Bertinoro, It. 63/F5
Bertiolo, It. 63/G2
Bertogne, Belg. 55/E3
Bertolínia, Braz. 183/F4
Bertoua, Camr. 116/B4
Bertram (mt.), Austl. 128/B4
Bertram, Tx, US 151/E2
Bertrand, NB, Can. 158/E2
Bertrand (peak), Arg. 191/B6
Bertrix, Belg. 55/E4
Bertry, Fr. 54/C3
Beru (isl.), Kiri. 136/G5
Beruas, Malay. 89/C1
Beruit (isl.), Malay. 90/D3
Beruwala, SrL. 95/C5
Bervie Water. (riv.), Sc, UK 33/D3
Berwa, India 92/B2
Berwick, Me, US 161/L3
Berwick, NS, Can. 158/E3
Berwick (nbrhd.), Austl. 132/G6
Berwick, Pa, US 168/B1
Berwick-Upon-Tweed, Eng, UK 33/D5
Berwyn (mts.), Wal, UK 34/E6
Berwyn, Il, US 167/Q16
Beryl, Ut, US 149/F2
Beryslav, Ukr. 73/G4
Berzence, Hun. 50/C2
Bès (riv.), Fr. 44/E2
Besalampy, Madg. 125/H7
Besançon, Fr. 60/C3
Bésao, Chad 116/B4
Besar (isl.), Indo. 128/A2
Besar (peak), Malay. 89/C2
Besar (peak), Indo. 91/E4
Besbre (riv.), Fr. 44/E3
Besedino, Rus. 73/J2
Beserah, Malay. 89/C2
Beshām Qala, Pak. 98/B2
Beshenkovichi, Bela. 41/N4
Beshlo Wenz (riv.), Eth. 118/A3
Beshneh, Iran 103/H4
Besikama, Indo. 128/B2
Beşiri, Turk. 102/E2
Beška, Serb. 50/E3
Beskids (mts.), Pol. 43/L4
Beskol', Kaz. 99/D2
Beşkonak, Turk. 104/B1
Beslan, Rus. 71/H4
Besna Kobila (peak), Serb. 50/F4
Besozzo, It. 62/B2
Bessacarr, Eng, UK 35/G5
Bessancourt, Fr. 30/J4
Bessarabia (reg.), Mol. 51/J2
Bessbrook, NI, UK 34/B3
Bessé-sur-Braye, Fr. 57/F5
Bessemer, Al, US 162/D4
Bessemer, Mi, US 157/J4
Bessemer (mtn.), Wa, US 167/D2
Bessines-sur-Gartempe, Fr. 44/D3
Best, Neth. 52/C5
Best, Tx, US 150/D2
Bestensee, Ger. 42/Q7
Bestobe, Kaz. 99/B1
Bestuzhevo, Rus. 69/K3
Bestwig, Ger. 53/F6
Beswick, Austl. 128/D3
Beswick Abor. Res., Austl. 128/D3
Bet Guvrin, Isr. 105/B5
Bet Qama, Isr. 105/B6
Bet She'an, Isr. 105/D3
Bet Shemesh, Isr. 105/B5
Betaghstown, Ire. 34/B4
Betanantanana, Madg. 125/H7
Betania, Col. 183/K7
Betanty, Madg. 125/H9
Betanzos, Sp. 46/A1
Betanzos, Bol. 188/C1
Bétaré-Oya, Camr. 116/B4
Bete Hor, Eth. 118/A3
Bétérou, Ben. 115/F4
Beth Alpha Synagogue (ruin), Isr. 105/C3
Beth She'an NP, Isr. 105/D3
Beth She'arim NP, Isr. 105/C3
Bethal, SAfr. 124/E2
Bethanie, SAfr. 123/E5
Bethanie, Namb. 124/B2
Bethany, On, Can. 161/G2
Bethany (res.), Ca, US 167/L11
Bethany, Mo, US 155/G3
Bethany, Il, US 155/K4
Bethany, La, US 150/G1
Bethel, Ak, US 171/F3
Bethel, Me, US 161/L2
Bethel, Ok, US 153/G3
Bethel, Pa, US 168/B3
Bethel, Vt, US 161/K3
Bethel Acres, Ok, US 153/F3
Bethel Island, Ca, US 167/L10
Bethel Park, Pa, US 160/F4
Bethelridge, Ky, US 162/E2
Bétheniville, Fr. 55/D5
Bétheny, Fr. 54/D5
Bethesda, Wal, UK 34/D5
Bethesda, Md, US 168/A6
Béthisy-Sainte-Pierre, Fr. 54/B5
Bethlehem, NH, US 161/L2
Bethlehem, SAfr. 124/E3
Bethlehem, Pa, US 168/C2
Bethlehem, Md, US 168/C6
Bethlehem (Bayt Laḩm), WBnk. 105/C5
Bethoncourt, Fr. 60/C2
Bethpage, NY, US 169/M9
Bethulie, SAfr. 124/D3
Béthune, Fr. 54/B2
Béthune (riv.), Fr. 44/D2
Bethune, Sk, Can. 145/M2
Betioky, Madg. 125/H8
Betoota, Austl. 134/A4
Betpaqdala (des.), Kaz. 74/G5
Betroka, Madg. 125/H8
Betschdorf, Fr. 58/A5
Betsiamites, Qu, Can. 158/C1
Betsiamites (riv.), Qu, Can. 158/C1
Betsiamites (riv.), Qu, Can. 141/J3
Betsiamites Ind. Res., Qu, Can. 158/C1
Betsiboka (riv.), Madg. 125/H7
Betsie (pt.), Mi, US 160/C2
Betsy Layne, Ky, US 163/F2
Bettancourt-la-Ferrée, Fr. 55/D6
Bette (peak), Libya 108/C4
Bettembourg, Lux. 55/F4
Betteravia, Ca, US 148/B3
Betterton, Md, US 168/B5
Bettiah, India 97/E2
Bettlach, Swi. 60/D3
Bettles, Ak, US 171/H2
Betton, Fr. 56/D4
Betūl, India 96/A5
Betulia, Col. 183/K6
Betuwe (phys. reg.), Neth. 52/C5
Betwa (riv.), India 96/B3
Betws-y-Coed, Wal, UK 34/E5
Betz, Fr. 30/L4
Betzdorf, Ger. 55/G2
Betzenstein, Ger. 59/E3
Béu, Ang. 120/C4
Beulah, ND, US 156/D4
Beulah, Mb, Can. 156/D2
Beulah, Co, US 152/B1
Beulah, Mi, US 160/C2
Beulah (lake), Wi, US 167/P14
Beulah, Austl. 132/B2
Beulah, Ms, US 162/B4
Beulah, Wy, US 154/B1
Beulakerwijde (lake), Neth. 52/C3
Beuningen, Neth. 52/C5
Beure, Fr. 60/C3
Beuvillers, Fr. 57/F2
Beuvray (peak), Fr. 44/F3
Beuvron (riv.), Fr. 44/D3
Beuvronne (riv.), Fr. 30/L5
Beuvry, Fr. 54/B2
Beuzeville, Fr. 57/F2
Bevagna, It. 65/B2
Bevensen, Ger. 53/H2
Bevent, Wi, US 155/K1
Bever (riv.), Ger. 53/E4
Bévera (riv.), Fr. 64/D5
Beveren, Belg. 52/B6
Beverin (peak), Swi. 61/F4
Beverley, Eng, UK 35/H4
Beverley, Austl. 130/C5
Beverly, Oh, US 160/F5
Beverly, WV, US 163/H1
Beverly Hills, Ca, US 166/F7
Beverly Hills, Mi, US 167/F6
Beverstedt, Ger. 53/F2
Beverungen, Ger. 53/G5
Beverwijk, Neth. 52/B4
Bevil Oaks, Tx, US 151/G2
Bewār, India 96/B3
Bewcastle, Eng, UK 35/F1
Bewdley, On, Can. 161/G2
Bewdley, Eng, UK 36/D2
Bewl Bridge (res.), Eng, UK 37/G4
Bex, Swi. 60/D5
Bexbach, Ger. 55/G5
Bexhill, Eng, UK 37/G5
Bexley (bor.), Eng, UK 30/D2
Bextograk, China 99/E4
Beyçayırı, Turk. 51/H5
Beycuma, Turk. 51/K5
Beykoz (nbrhd.), Turk. 103/N6
Beyla, Gui. 114/C4
Beylerbeyi Palace, Turk. 103/N6
Bēylul, Erit. 118/B2
Beyne-Heusay, Belg. 55/E2
Beynes, Fr. 30/H5
Beyneū, Kaz. 71/K3
Beyoglu (nbrhd.), Turk. 103/M6
Beyoneisu-Retsugan (isl.), Japan 85/F5
Beypazarı, Turk. 102/B1
Beypore, India 95/B4
Beyra, Som. 118/C4
Beyşehir, Turk. 104/E1
Beysug (bay), Rus. 73/K4
Bezaha, Madg. 125/H8
Bezau, Aus. 61/F3
Bezdan, Serb. 50/D3
Bezděz (peak), Czh. 59/H1
Bezdrev (lake), Czh. 59/H4
Bezhetsk, Rus. 68/H4
Bezhta, Rus. 71/H4
Béziers, Fr. 44/E5
Bhabua, India 96/D3
Bhadarwāh, India 98/C3
Bhadaur, India 98/C4
Bhadohī, India 96/D3
Bhādra, India 98/C5
Bhadrāchalam, India 95/D2
Bhadrak, India 92/E3
Bhadrapur, Nepal 97/G2
Bhadreswar, India 92/A3
Bhāgalpur, India 97/F3
Bhāi Pheru, Pak. 98/B4
Bhairab (riv.), Bang. 97/G4
Bhairab Bāzār, Bang. 97/H3
Bhairahawa, Nepal 96/D2
Bhairamgarh, India 95/D2
Bhakkar, Pak. 98/A4
Bhākra (dam), India 98/D4
Bhaktapur, Nepal 97/E2
Bhāluka, Bang. 97/H3
Bhalwāl, Pak. 98/B3
Bḩamdūn, Leb. 105/D1
Bhamo, Myan. 86/C3
Bhandāra, India 95/C1
Bhandāri, India 86/B3
Bhānder, India 96/B3
Bhānin, India 98/C5
Bhanjanagar, India 95/E2
Bhānrer (range), India 96/B4
Bhānwad, India 92/A3
Bharatpur, Nepal 97/E2
Bhārātpur, India 96/A2
Bhareli (riv.), India 86/B3
Bharno, India 97/E4
Bharthana, India 96/B2
Bhasāwar, India 96/A2
Bhātiāpāra Ghāt, Bang. 97/G4
Bhatinda, India 98/C4
Bhatkal, India 95/B3
Bhātpāra, India 97/G4
Bhaun, Pak. 98/B3
Bhavāni (riv.), India 95/C4
Bhavāni, India 95/C4
Bhavnagar, India 95/B1
Bhawāna, Pak. 98/B4
Bhawāni Mandi, India 92/C3
Bhawānīgarh, India 98/D4
Bhera, Pak. 98/B3
Bheramara, Bang. 97/G3
Bheri (zone), Nepal 96/C1
Bhīkhi, India 98/C4
Bhikkīwind Uttār, India 98/C4
Bhikna Thorī, Nepal 97/E2
Bhīlwāra, India 92/B2
Bhīma (riv.), India 101/L5
Bhima (riv.), India 92/C4
Bhīmavaram, India 95/D2
Bhīmmāl, India 101/K4
Bhīmphedi, Nepal 97/E2
Bhind, India 96/B2
Bhinga, India 96/C2
Bhiwandi, India 95/B2
Bhiwāni, India 98/D5
Bhojpur, Nepal 97/F2
Bhokardan, India 95/B1
Bhola, Bang. 97/H4
Bhongaon, India 96/B2
Bhopāl, India 92/C3
Bhopālpatnam, India 95/D2
Bhor, India 95/B2
Bhraoin (lake), Sc, UK 33/A1
Bhuban, India 95/E1
Bhūj, India 101/J4
Bhumibol (dam), Thai. 94/B2
Bhutan (ctry.) 97/G2
Bi (riv.), China 78/C5
Bi Doup (peak), Viet. 94/E3
Bia (riv.), C.d'Iv. 114/E5
Biá (riv.), Braz. 184/E2
Biaboye, D.R. Congo 121/G2
Biak (isl.), Indo. 91/J4
Biak (int'l arpt.), Indo. 91/J4
Biak, Indo. 91/J4
Biakowieski NP, Pol. 43/M2
Biała Podlaska, Pol. 43/M2
Białobrzegi, Pol. 43/L3
Białogard, Pol. 40/G4
Białowieski NP, Pol. 70/B1
Białowieski NP, Pol. 43/K4
Białystok, Pol. 43/M2
Bianca (peak), It. 61/G4
Biancavilla, It. 48/D4
Bianco, (peak), It. 65/C4
Biandrate, It. 62/B3
Biandronno, It. 62/B2
Bianga, CAfr. 116/D4
Biankouma, C.d'Iv. 114/D5
Bianya, China 86/E3
Bianyang, China 87/E3
Bianze, It. 62/B3
Biaro, D.R. Congo 121/F2
Biarritz, Fr. 44/C5
Biarvitz (Bayonne-Anglet) (arpt.), Fr. 44/C5
Biasca, Swi. 61/E5
Bibai, Japan 82/B2
Bibala, Ang. 122/B2
Bībān, Egypt 113/B3
Bibassé, Gabon 120/B2
Bibbenluke, Austl. 133/D3
Bibbiano, It. 62/D4
Bibbiena, It. 63/E6
Bibémi, Camr. 116/B3
Biberach, Ger. 60/E1
Biberach, Ger. 61/G1
Biberach an der Riss, Ger. 61/F1
Biberist, Swi. 60/D3
Bibione, It. 63/G2
Biblián, Ecu. 180/B5
Biblis, Ger. 58/B3
Bibrka, Ukr. 72/C3
Bicas, Braz. 187/N6
Bicas, Braz. 187/E3
Bicaz, Rom. 72/D4
Bicester, Eng, UK 37/E3
Bichano, Eth. 117/G4
Bicheno, Austl. 132/D4
Bichhia, India 96/C4
Bickerton (isl.), Austl. 129/E3
Bickle (peak), WV, US 163/H1
Bickleigh, Sk, Can. 145/K2
Bickleton, Wa, US 144/D5
Bicknacre, Eng, UK 30/E1
Bicknell, Ut, US 149/G1
Bicknell, In, US 162/D1
Bicske, Hun. 50/D2
Bīd Boland, Iran 103/G4
Bida, Nga. 115/G4
Bidadari (cape), Malay. 88/B4
Bidaga (rapids), C.d'Iv. 114/D5
Bīdar, India 95/C2
Biddeford, Me, US 161/L3
Biddinghuizen, Neth. 52/C4
Biddiyā, WBnk. 105/C4
Biddle, Mt, US 154/B1
Biddū, WBnk. 105/C5
Biddulph, Eng, UK 35/F5
Bidean nam Bian (peak), Sc, UK 33/A3
Bideford, Eng, UK 36/B4
Bideford (Barnstaple) (bay), Eng, UK 36/B4
Bidente (riv.), It. 63/F4
Bidford-on-Avon, Eng, UK 37/E2
Bidhūna, India 96/B2
Bīdokht, Iran 101/G2
Bidor, Malay. 89/C1
Bidouze (riv.), Fr. 47/E1
Bidrē, Eth. 118/A4
Bieber, Ca, US 146/C3
Biebesheim am Rhein, Ger. 58/B3
Biebzra (riv.), Pol. 43/M2
Biel, Swi. 60/D3
Bielawa, Pol. 43/J3
Bieldside, Sc, UK 33/D2
Bielefeld, Ger. 53/F4
Bieler (lake), Swi. 60/D3
Bieler (lake), Nun, Can. 141/J1
Biella, It. 62/B2
Bielsk Podlaski, Pol. 43/M2
Bielsko-Biała, Pol. 43/K4
Bien Hoa, Viet. 94/D4
Bien Son, Viet. 94/D1
Bienenbüttel, Ger. 53/H2
Bienfait, Sk, Can. 156/C3
Bienne (riv.), Fr. 60/B5
Bienno, It. 61/G6
Bientina, It. 62/D6
Bienvenue, FrG. 182/C2
Bienville, La, US 153/H4
Bienville (lake), Qu, Can. 141/J3
Bière, Swi. 60/C4
Bierset (int'l arpt.), Belg. 55/E2
Bierum, Neth. 52/D2
Bierutów, Pol. 43/J3
Biesbosch (reg.), Neth. 52/B5
Biesenthal, Ger. 42/Q6
Biesles, Fr. 60/B1
Biesme (riv.), Fr. 55/D5
Bieszczadzki NP, Pol. 70/B2
Bieszczadzkii NP, Pol. 43/M4
Bietigheim, Ger. 58/C5
Bietschhorn (peak), Swi. 60/D5
Bièvre, Belg. 55/E4
Bièvre (riv.), Fr. 30/J5
Bièvres, Fr. 30/J5
Biferno (riv.), It. 65/D4
Bifoun, Gabon 120/B3
Big (des.), Austl. 132/B2
Big (cr.), BC, Can. 144/C2
Big (riv.), NW, Can. 140/D1
Big (isl.), On, Can. 140/G4
Big (cr.), Ga, US 163/M6
Big (cr.), Ks, US 154/D4
Big (lake), Mi, US 167/E6
Big (riv.), Mo, US 154/J5
Big (mtn.), Nv, US 146/D3
Big (mtn.), WV, US 163/H1
Big Arm, Mt, US 144/G4
Big Bald (mtn.), NB, Can. 158/D2
Big Baldy (mtn.), Mt, US 145/J4
Big Bar Creek, BC, Can. 144/C2
Big Bear City, Ca, US 148/D3
Big Bear Lake, Ca, US 148/D3
Big Beaver, Sk, Can. 156/B3
Big Belt (mts.), Mt, US 145/J4
Big Bend, Wi, US 167/P14
Big Bend (dam), SD, US 154/E1
Big Bend, Swaz. 125/E2
Big Bend NP, Tx, US 150/C3
Big Black (riv.), Ms, US 162/B4
Big Blue (riv.), Ne, US 155/F3
Big Blue, West Fork (riv.), Ne, US 154/E3
Big Boggy NWR, Tx, US 151/G3
Big Cabin, Ok, US 153/G2
Big Canyon (riv.), Tx, US 150/C2
Big Creek, Ca, US 148/C2
Big Creek, Id, US 147/F1
Big Cypress (swamp), Fl, US 165/H4
Big Cypress National Preserve, Fl, US 165/H4
Big de Noc (bay), Mi, US 157/L5
Big Eau Plaine (res.), Wi, US 155/J1
Big Eddy (falls), Wi, US 155/K1
Big Falls, Mn, US 157/H3
Big Flat (brook), NJ, US 168/D1
Big Foot (pass), SD, US 154/C2
Big Fork (riv.), Mn, US 157/H4
Big Hole, SAfr. 124/D3
Big Hole (riv.), Mt, US 147/G1
Big Hole Nat'l Bfld., Mt, US 147/G1
Big Horn, Wy, US 147/K1
Big Indian, NY, US 161/J3
Big Lake, Tx, US 150/D2
Big Lake Nat'l Wild. Ref., Ar, US 162/B3
Big Lake Ranch, BC, Can. 144/D1
Big Lost (riv.), Id, US 147/G2
Big Marine (lake), Mn, US 157/Q6
Big Muddy (cr.), Mt, US 156/B3
Big Muddy (lake), Sk, Can. 145/M3
Big Muskego (lake), Wi, US 167/P14
Big Nemaha, North Fork (riv.), Ne, US 155/F3
Big Pine, Ca, US 148/C2
Big Pine (hill), Pa, US 168/C1
Big Pine Key, Fl, US 165/H5
Big Pines, Ca, US 166/C2
Big Piney, Mo, US 153/H2
Big Piney (riv.), Mo, US 162/B2
Big Pipe (cr.), Md, US 168/A4
Big Raccoon (riv.), In, US 160/C5
Big Rapids, Mi, US 160/D3
Big Rock (cr.), Il, US 167/N16
Big Rock, Il, US 167/N16
Big Rock, Va, US 163/F2
Big Sable (pt.), Mi, US 160/C2
Big Sandy (riv.), Wy, US 147/J3
Big Sandy, Wy, US 147/J2
Big Sandy (cr.), Co, US 154/C4
Big Sandy, Mt, US 145/J3
Big Satilla (cr.), Ga, US 165/G2
Big Sioux (riv.), Ia,SD, US 155/F2
Big Smoky (falls), Wi, US 157/K5
Big South Fork National River and Recreation Area, Tn, US 162/E2
Big Spring, Tx, US 150/D1
Big Stone (lake), Mn,SD, US 155/F1
Big Stone Gap, Va, US 163/F2
Big Stone NWR, Mn, US 155/F1
Big Sunflower (riv.), Ms, US 162/B4
Big Sur, Ca, US 148/B2
Big Thicket National Preserve, Tx, US 151/G2
Big Thompson (riv.), Co, US 154/B3
Big Timber, Mt, US 145/K5
Big Trout (lake), On, Can. 140/H3
Big Tujunga Canyon (canyon), Ca, US 166/B2
Big Valley, Ab, Can. 145/H1
Big Wells, Tx, US 150/E3
Big Wood (riv.), Id, US 147/F2
Biga, Turk. 51/H5
Bigadiç, Turk. 70/D5
Bigbury (bay), Eng, UK 36/C6
Bigelow (mtn.), Me, US 161/L2
Bigfoot, Tx, US 151/E3
Bigfork, Mn, US 157/H4
Bigfork, Mt, US 145/G3
Bigga, Austl. 133/D2
Biggar, Sk, Can. 145/L1
Biggar, Sc, UK 33/C5
Bigge (isl.), Austl. 128/B3
Bigge (riv.), Ger. 55/G1
Biggenden, Austl. 134/D4
Biggers, Ar, US 162/B2
Biggin Hill (nbrhd.), Eng, UK 30/D3
Biggleswade, Eng, UK 37/F2
Biggs, Ca, US 146/C4
Biggs Army Airfield, Tx, US 150/A2
Bighorn, Mt, US 145/L4
Bighorn (lake), Mt, US 147/J1
Bighorn (mts.), Wy, US 142/E3
Bighorn (riv.), Wy, US 142/E2
Bighorn (riv.), Wy, US 140/F4
Bighorn Canyon NRA, Mt, US 147/J1
Bight of Benin (bay), Afr. 107/C4
Bight of Biafra (bay), Afr. 120/A1
Bigi, D.R. Congo 121/E2
Biglerville, Pa, US 168/A4
Bignona, Sen. 114/A3
Bigosovo, Bela. 41/M4
Bigsby (isl.), On, Can. 157/G3
Biguaçu, Braz. 189/G3
Bihać, Bosn. 50/B3
Bīhar, India 97/E3
Bihār (state), India 92/D3
Biharamulo, Tanz. 121/G3
Biharamulo Game Rsv., Tanz. 121/G3
Bihārīganj, India 97/F3
Biharkeresztes, Hun. 50/E2
Bihor (co.), Rom. 43/M5
Bihorel, Fr. 57/G1
Bihoro, Japan 82/D2
Bijagós (arch.), GBis. 107/A3
Bijāpur, India 95/D2
Bījār, Iran 103/F3
Bijāwar, India 96/B3
Bijbiāra, India 98/C3
Bijeljina, Bosn. 50/D3
Bijelo Polje, Serb. 50/D4
Bijiang, China 86/C3
Bijiaquan, China 80/J7
Bijie, China 86/E3
Bijni, India 97/H2
Bijnor, India 96/B1
Bikar (isl.), Mrsh. 136/G3
Bikenibeu, Kiri. 136/G4
Bikfayyā, Leb. 105/D1
Bikin (riv.), Rus. 79/M2
Bikin, Rus. 79/L2
Bikini (isl.), Mrsh. 136/F3
Bikita, Zim. 123/F4
Bikori, Sudan 117/G3
Bikoro, D.R. Congo 120/D3
Bikramganj, India 97/E3
Bikuar, PN do, Ang. 122/B2
Bila Krynytsya, Ukr. 73/G4
Bila Tserkva, Ukr. 72/F3
Bilād Manaḩ, Oman 101/G4
Bilāra, India 92/B2
Bilāri, India 96/B1
Bilāsipāra, India 97/H2
Bilāspur, India 98/D4
Bilāspur, India 96/B1
Bilāspur, India 96/D4
Biläsuvar, Azer. 103/G2
Bilauktaung (range), Myan.,Thai. 94/B3
Bilauri, Nepal 96/C1
Bilbao, Sp. 44/B5
Bilbays, Egypt 113/C4
Bileća, Bosn. 50/D4
Bilecik (prov.), Turk. 102/B1
Bīleh Savār, Iran 103/G2
Biłgoraj, Pol. 43/M3
Bilgrām, India 96/C2
Bilhaur, India 96/C2
Bilhorod-Dnistrovs'kyy, Ukr. 72/F4
Bili (riv.), D.R. Congo 116/D4
Bili, D.R. Congo 121/F1
Bilibino, Rus. 75/S3
Bilila, Malw. 123/G2
Bilin (riv.), Myan. 94/B2
Bilin, Myan. 86/C5
Bílina (riv.), Czh. 59/G2
Bílina, Czh. 59/G1
Biliran (isl.), Phil. 88/D3
Bilisht, Alb. 49/G2
Bilit, Malay. 88/B4
Biliu (riv.), China 81/B3
Bill, Wy, US 154/B2
Bill of Portland (pt.), Eng, UK 36/D5
Bill Williams (riv.), Az, US 149/F3
Billaouâr, Mrta. 114/C2
Bille (riv.), Ger. 53/H1
Billerbeck, Ger. 53/E5
Billère, Fr. 44/C5
Billericay, Eng, UK 30/E2
Billesholm, Swe. 39/K6
Billiat Consv. Park, Austl. 131/J5
Billiat Consv. Park, Austl. 132/B2
Billigheim, Ger. 58/C4
Billiluna Abor. Land, Austl. 128/B4
Billinge, Eng, UK 35/F4
Billingham, Eng, UK 35/G2
Billings, Ok, US 153/F2
Billings, Mt, US 145/K5
Billingsfors, Swe. 40/E2
Billingshurst, Eng, UK 37/F4
Billiton (isl.), Indo. 77/K10
Billund, Den. 40/C4
Billund (int'l arpt.), Den. 40/C4
Bilma, Niger 108/B5
Bīlo, Eth. 117/H3
Biloela, Austl. 134/C4
Bilohirs'k, Ukr. 73/H5
Biloku, Guy. 181/G4
Biloluts'k, Ukr. 73/K3
Bilopillya, Ukr. 73/H2
Bilovods'k, Ukr. 73/K3
Biloxi, Ms, US 164/D2
Bilpa Morea Claypan (lake), Austl. 131/H3
Bilqas Qism Awwal, Egypt 113/C2
Bilqas Qism Thânî, Egypt 113/C2
Bilsi, India 96/B1
Biltān, Egypt 113/C4
Bilthar, India 96/D2
Bilthoven, Neth. 52/C4
Biltine, Chad 116/D2
Biltine (pref.), Chad 116/D2
Biltmore, Tn, US 163/F2
Bilüü, Mong. 99/E2
Bilyayivka, Ukr. 72/F4
Bilyts'ke, Ukr. 73/J3
Bilzen, Belg. 55/E2
Bima, Indo. 91/E5
Bimberi (peak), Austl. 133/D2
Bimbo, CAfr. 116/C4
Bimini (isls.), Bahm. 173/F2
Bin 'Arūs, Tun. 48/B4
Bin 'Arus (gov.), Tun. 48/B4
Bin Ghashīr, Libya 67/G4
Bin Jawwād, Libya 108/C2
Bin Qirdān, Tun. 67/F4
Bin Yauri, Nga. 115/G4
Bina (riv.), Ger. 59/F6
Bina-Etāwa, India 96/B3
Binalong, Austl. 133/D2
Binanga, Indo. 89/B2
Binasco, It. 62/C3
Binatang, Malay. 90/D3
Binbrook, Eng, UK 35/H5
Binbrook, On, Can. 160/T9
Binche, Belg. 55/D3
Binchuan, China 86/D3
Binda, Austl. 133/D2
Binder Foulbé, Chad 116/B3
Bindki, India 96/C2
Bindoon, Austl. 130/C4
Bindoy, Phil. 88/C3
Bindu, D.R. Congo 120/D4
Bindungi, D.R. Congo 120/D4
Bindura, Zim. 123/F3
Binéfar, Sp. 47/F2
Binfield, Eng, UK 37/F4
Binford, ND, US 156/E4
Binga (mtn.), Moz. 123/G3
Binga, Zim. 123/E3
Bingara, Austl. 132/D1
Bingcaowan, China 78/E4
Bingen, Ger. 55/G4
Binger, Ok, US 153/E3
Bingerville, C.d'Iv. 114/E5
Bingham, Eng, UK 35/H6
Bingham, Me, US 161/M2
Binghamton, NY, US 161/J3
Bingley, Eng, UK 35/G4
Bingöl, Turk. 102/E2
Bingol (prov.), Turk. 102/E2
Binh Chanh, Viet. 94/D4
Binh Chau, Viet. 94/D4
Binh Son, Viet. 94/E3
Binhai, China 80/D4
Binhon (peak), Myan. 86/B5
Binic, Fr. 56/C3
Binisalem, Sp. 47/G3
Binjai, Indo. 89/B2
Binka, India 95/D1
Binkılıç, Turk. 51/J5
Binkolo, SLeo. 114/C4
Binnah (cape), Som. 118/D3
Binnaway, Austl. 132/D1
Binningen, Swi. 60/D2
Binongko (isl.), Indo. 91/F5
Binscarth, Mb, Can. 156/D2
Binsted, Eng, UK 30/A3
Bint Jubayl, Leb. 105/C2
Bintagoungou, Mali 114/E2
Bintan (isl.), Indo. 89/D2
Bintang (peak), Malay. 89/C1
Bintang (range), Malay. 89/C1
Bintimodouya, Gui. 114/B4
Bintuhan, Indo. 89/C3
Binyamina, Isr. 105/B3
Binyang, China 87/F4
Binza, D.R. Congo 120/C4
Binzhou, China 80/D3
Bío-Bío (riv.), Chile 190/B3
Bío-Bío (pol. reg.), Chile 190/B3
Biodi, D.R. Congo 121/G2
Biograd, Cro. 50/B4
Biogradska Gora NP, Serb. 49/F1
Biogradska NP, Serb. 50/D4
Bioko (pol. reg.), EqG. 120/B2
Bioko (isl.), EqG. 107/C4
Bioko (Fernando Po) (isl.), EqG. 120/B2
Biola, Ca, US 148/B2
Biot, Fr. 64/D5
Biougra, Mor. 110/C3
Bipoint (Bissau) (int'l arpt.), GBis. 114/B4
Bippen, Ger. 53/E3
Bir (cape), Djib. 118/B3
Bīr, India 95/B2
Bîr Abu el-Husein (well), Egypt 109/F4
Bi'r Abu Hashim (well), Egypt 109/G4
Bîr Abu Minqâr (well), Egypt 109/E3
Bir Aïdiat (well), Mrta. 110/C4
Bi'r al Aḩmar (well), Libya 108/C2
Bi'r al 'Akkārīyah (well), Libya 108/C2
Bi'r Al Ghanam, Libya 108/B1
Bi'r al Ghuzayyil (well), Libya 108/A2
Bi'r al Ḩarash (well), Libya 108/D3
Bi'r Al Mashariqah, Tun. 112/L6
Bi'r al Mastūtah (well), Libya 108/B3
Bi'r al Mufaţţam (well), Libya 108/D2
Bi'r al Qāf (well), Libya 108/B2
Bi'r al Washkah (well), Libya 108/B2
Bi'r 'Alī, Yem. 118/D2
Bi'r as Sahl (well), Libya 108/B3
Bi'r as Sinidah (well), Libya 108/B2
Bi'r aţ Ţarfāwī (well), Libya 108/E2
Bir Bel Guerdâne (well), Mrta. 110/C4
Bi'r Burayd (well), Egypt 113/D6
Bîr Dibis (well), Egypt 109/F4
Bir el Ater, Alg. 66/F4
Bi'r Ghadir (well), Egypt 109/G3
Bîr Misâha (well), Egypt 109/E4
Bir Moghreïn, Mrta. 110/C4
Bîr Ounâne (well), Mali 110/E5
Bîr Safājah (well), Egypt 109/G3
Bir Tamtam, Mor. 112/B3
Bîr Tarfâwi (well), Egypt 109/F4
Bi'r Umm Hibal (well), Egypt 109/G4
Bi'r Zayt, WBnk. 105/C5
Bira, Rus. 79/L2
Birāk, Libya 108/B3
Birao, CAfr. 116/D3
Birātnagar, Nepal 97/F2
Biratori, Japan 82/C2
Birch (mts.), Ab, Can. 140/E3
Birch (cr.), Mt, US 145/H3
Birch Bay, Wa, US 144/C3
Birch Creek, Ak, US 171/J2
Birch Hills, Sk, Can. 145/M1
Birch River, Mb, Can. 156/D1
Birch Tree, Mo, US 153/J2
Birchenough Bridge, Zim. 123/G3
Birchip, Austl. 132/B2
Bircot, Eth. 118/B4
Bird (cr.), Ok, US 153/F2
Bird Island, Mn, US 155/G1
Bird Islet (isl.), Austl. 127/E3
Bird Point, Sk, Can. 156/C2
Birds Rock (peak), Austl. 133/E1
Birdsboro, Pa, US 168/C3
Birdsnest, Va, US 163/K2
Birdsville, Austl. 131/H3
Birdtail, Mb, Can. 156/D2
Birdum, Austl. 128/D3
Birdwood, Austl. 131/M8
Birecik, Turk. 102/D2
Bireuen, Indo. 89/B1
Bīrganj, Nepal 97/E2
Birganj, Bang. 97/G3
Birigui, Braz. 189/G2
Biritiba-Mirim, Braz. 187/K8
Bīrjand, Iran 101/G2
Birkat al Ja'ār (well), Egypt 113/B4
Birkat as Sab', Egypt 113/C3
Birkat Ghiţās, Egypt 113/B2
Birkat Umm Rīshah (well), Egypt 113/B4
Birkelane, Sen. 114/B3
Birken-Honigsessen, Ger. 55/G2
Birkenau, Ger. 58/B3
Birkenfeld, Ger. 55/G4
Birkenfeld, Ger. 58/B5
Birkenhead, Eng, UK 35/E5
Birkenhead, NZ 135/F6
Birkenheide, Ger. 58/B4
Birkenwerder, Ger. 42/Q6
Birkerød, Den. 39/J7
Birkirkara, Malta 48/L7
Birkkarspitze (peak), Aus. 61/H3
Birky, Ukr. 73/J3
Bîrlad (riv.), Rom. 70/C3
Bîrlad, Rom. 51/H2
Birmā, Egypt 113/B3
Birmāna, India 98/B5
Birmingham, Eng, UK 37/E2
Birmingham (co.), Eng, UK 37/E2
Birmingham (int'l arpt.), Eng, UK 37/E2
Birmingham, Al, US 162/D4
Birmingham, Mi, US 167/F6
Birmitrapur, India 97/E4
Birnam, Sc, UK 33/C3
Birnamwood, Wi, US 155/K1
Birney, Mt, US 147/K1
Birnhorn (peak), Aus. 45/K3
Birni Nkonni, Niger 115/G3
Birnie (isl.), Kiri. 137/H5
Birnin Gwari, Nga. 115/G4
Birnin Kebbi, Nga. 115/G3
Birnin Kudu, Nga. 115/H4
Birniwa, Nga. 115/H3
Birobjian, Rus. 79/L2
Bīrpur, India 97/F2
Birqash, Egypt 113/C4
Birr, Ire. 32/C3
Birreencorragh (peak), Ire. 32/A2
Birrimbah, Austl. 128/D4
Birrindudu, Austl. 128/C4
Birriwa, Austl. 132/D2
Birs (riv.), Swi. 45/G3
Birsk, Rus. 69/M5
Birstein, Ger. 58/C2
Birštonas, Lith. 41/L4
Birtle, Mb, Can. 156/D2
Biru, China 78/C5
Biruaca, Ven. 181/E3
Biruni, Uzb. 74/G5
Biryulevo (nbrhd.), Rus. 69/W9
Biržai, Lith. 41/L3
Birżebbuġa, Malta 48/M7
Bis (lake), Hun. 51/F4
Bisa-Nadi Nat'l Rsv., Kenya 119/B1
Bisagana, Nga. 116/B2
Bisai, Japan 83/L5
Bīsalpur, India 96/B1
Bisamberg, Aus. 51/N7
Bisauli, India 96/B1
Bisbee, ND, US 156/E3
Bisbee, Az, US 149/H5
Biscarrosse (lake), Fr. 44/C4
Biscarrosse, Fr. 44/C4
Biscay (bay), Fr.,Sp. 29/D4
Biscayne (bay), Fl, US 164/P11
Biscayne NP, Fl, US 173/E2
Bisceglie, It. 48/E2
Bischberg, Ger. 58/D3
Bischheim, Fr. 55/G6
Bischofsgrün, Ger. 59/E2
Bischofsheim, Ger. 58/B3
Bischofsheim an der Rhön, Ger. 58/D2
Bischofshofen, Aus. 45/K3
Bischofszell, Swi. 61/F3
Bischwiller, Fr. 60/D2
Biscoe, NC, US 163/H3
Biscoe (Fredonia), Ar, US 153/J3
Biscubio (riv.), It. 63/F5
Biscucuy, Ven. 180/D2
Bisenge, D.R. Congo 121/E2
Bīshah (riv.), SAr. 100/D4
Bīshat Qā'id, Egypt 113/C3
Bishkek (cap.), Kyr. 99/B3
Bishnupur, India 97/F4
Bisho, SAfr. 124/D4
Bishop, Ca, US 148/C2
Bishop, Tx, US 151/F4
Bishop Auckland, Eng, UK 35/G2
Bishop Ind. Res., Ca, US 148/C2
Bishop International (arpt.), Mi, US 167/E6
Bishop Wilton, Eng, UK 35/H4
Bishopbriggs, Sc, UK 33/B5
Bishops Castle, Eng, UK 36/D1
Bishops Cleeve, Eng, UK 36/D3
Bishop's Falls, Nf, Can. 159/K1
Bishop's Stortford, Eng, UK 37/G3
Bishops Waltham, Eng, UK 37/E5
Bishopton, Sc, UK 33/B5
Bishopville, SC, US 163/G3
Bishrah (well), Libya 108/D4
Bisingen, Ger. 58/B6
Biskra, Alg. 112/H5
Biskupiec, Pol. 41/J5
Bislig, Phil. 88/D3
Bismarck, On, Can. 160/U9
Bismarck (sea), PNG 136/D5
Bismarck (arch.), PNG 136/D5
Bismarck (range), PNG 129/G1
Bismarck, Ar, US 153/H3
Bismarck, Mo, US 162/B2
Bismarck (cap.), ND, US 156/D4
Bismil, Turk. 102/E2
Bismuna (lag.), Nic. 177/F3
Biso, Ugan. 121/G2
Bison, Ks, US 152/E1
Bison, SD, US 156/C5
Bispgarden, Swe. 38/F3
Bispingen, Ger. 53/G2
Bissau, India 98/C5
Bissau (cap.), GBis. 114/B4
Bissau (Bipoint) (int'l arpt.), GBis. 114/B4
Bissaula, Nga. 115/H5
Bissendorf, Ger. 53/F4
Bissett, Mb, Can. 157/G2
Bissingen, Ger. 58/D5
Bissingen an der Enz, Ger. 58/C5
Bissora, GBis. 114/B3
Bistagno, It. 62/B4
Bistriţa, Rom. 51/G2
Bistriţa (riv.), Rom. 51/G2
Bistriţa-Našăud (prov.), Rom. 51/G2
Bistrup, Den. 39/J7
Biswān, India 96/C2
Bita (riv.), Col. 180/D3
Bitagron, Sur. 182/B1
Bitale, Tanz. 121/G4
Bitam, Gabon 120/B2
Bitburg, Ger. 55/F4
Bitche, Fr. 55/G5
Bitéa, Ouadi (riv.), Chad 116/D2
Bithnok, India 92/B2
Bitkin, Chad 116/C3
Bitlis, Turk. 102/E2
Bitlis (prov.), Turk. 102/E2
Bitola, FYROM 49/G2
Bitonto, It. 48/E2
Bitter (lake), Egypt 109/G2
Bitter (cr.), Wy, US 147/J3
Bitter Creek, Wy, US 147/J3
Bitter Lake Nat'l Wildlife Reserve, NM, US 152/B4
Bitterfontein, SAfr. 124/B3
Bittern Lake, Ab, Can. 145/H1
Bitterroot (range), Id, US 147/F1
Bitterroot (riv.), Mt, US 145/G4
Bitti, It. 48/A2
Bittou, Burk. 115/E4
Bitung, Indo. 91/G3
Bituruna, Braz. 189/G3
Biu, Nga. 116/B3
Biviers, Fr. 64/B2
Bivolari, Rom. 72/D4
Biwa, Japan 83/K5
Bixby, Ok, US 153/G3
Bixby, Mo, US 162/B2
Biyagundi, Erit. 117/H2
Biyalā, Egypt 113/C2
Biyang, China 80/C4
Biysk, Rus. 99/E1
Bizard (isl.), Qu, Can. 159/M7
Bizerte (Banzart), Tun. 48/A4
Bjärnum, Swe. 39/K6
Bjärred, Swe. 40/E4
Bjelovar, Cro. 50/C3
Bjerge (riv.), Den. 39/H7
Bjerkvik, Nor. 38/F1
Bjerringbro, Den. 40/C3
Bjorkdale, Sk, Can. 145/N1
Bjørkelangen, Nor. 40/D2
Björklinge, Swe. 40/G1
Björknäs, Swe. 39/B1
Björkö, Swe. 39/C1
Björkö (isl.), Swe. 39/C1
Björksund, Swe. 39/A2
Bjørnafjorden (estu.), Nor. 40/A1
Bjorne (pen.), Nun, Can. 141/S7
Björnlunda, Swe. 39/A1
Björnö, Swe. 39/B1
Bjugn, Nor. 38/D3
Bjuv, Swe. 40/E3
Blå Jungfrun NP, Swe. 40/G3
Blaby, Eng, UK 37/E1
Blace, Serb. 50/E4
Blachownia, Pol. 43/K3
Black (sea), Asia,Eur. 77/C5
Black (mts.), Bhu. 97/H2
Black (isl.), Mb, Can. 156/F2
Black (bay), On, Can. 157/K3
Black (riv.), On, Can. 157/M3
Black (mt.), Yk, Can. 171/M3
Black (riv.), China,Vie 94/C1
Black (for.), Ger. 42/D5
Black (pt.), Namb. 122/B5
Black (pt.), NZ 135/D3
Black (pt.), Eng, UK 36/A6
Black (pt.), NI, UK 34/C2
Black (isl.), Sc, UK 33/B1
Black (mts.), Wal, UK 36/C3
Black (mtn.), Wal, UK 36/C3
Black (mts.), Az, US 148/E3
Black (pt.), Ct, US 169/F1
Black (mtn.), Id, US 144/G4
Black (mtn.), Ky, US 163/F2
Black (lake), Mi, US 160/D2
Black (cr.), Ms, US 164/D2
Black (mesa), NM, US 149/J3
Black (range), NM, US 149/J4
Black (mesa), Ok, US 152/C2
Black (cr.), Pa, US 168/B2
Black (hills), SD, US 142/F3
Black, Tx, US 152/C3
Black (mtn.), Tx, US 150/D3
Black (mtn.), Tx, US 150/C2
Black (riv.), Viet. 93/H3
Black (Da) (riv.), Viet. 86/E4
Black Bear (cr.), Ok, US 153/F2
Black Bourton, Eng, UK 37/E3
Black Butte (lake), Ca, US 146/B4
Black Canyon City, Az, US 149/F3
Black Canyon Of The Gunnison Nat'l Mon., Co, US 147/K4
Black Coulee Nat'l Wild. Ref., Mt, US 145/K3
Black Creek, Wi, US 157/K5
Black Diamond, Wa, US 167/C3
Black Diamond, Ab, Can. 145/G2
Black Eagle, Mt, US 145/J4
Black Forest, Co, US 152/B1
Black Forest (Schwarzwald) (for.), Ger. 58/B6
Black Fork (mtn.), Ok, US 153/G3
Black Hammer (hill), ND, US 156/E4
Black Head (pt.), Ire. 32/A3
Black Hills Caverns, SD, US 154/C1
Black Lake, Qu, Can. 158/B2
Black Lake Bayou (riv.), La, US 153/H4
Black Mesa (int), Az, US 149/G4
Black Mesa (int.), Az, US 149/H4
Black Mesa (mesa), Az, US 149/G2
Black Mountain, NC, US 163/F3
Black Mountain NP, Austl. 134/B1

Black P – Borgo S

Black Pine (peak), Id, US 147/G2
Black Point, Ca, US 167/K10
Black Reef (pt.), Namb. 122/B5
Black River, Mi, US 160/E2
Black River, Jam. 177/G2
Black River Falls, Wi, US 155/J1
Black Rock (des.), Nv, US 146/D3
Black Rock, Ar, US 162/B2
Black Rock (pt.), RI, US 169/G1
Black Sea Lowland (lowland), Ukr. 72/E4
Black Sea Lowlands (reg.), Ukr. 51/J3
Black Sturgeon (riv.), On, Can. 157/K3
Black Sugarloaf (peak), Austl. 132/D1
Black Volta (riv.), Burk. 107/B4
Black Warrior (riv.), Al, US 162/D4
Black Warrior, Locust Fk. (riv.), Al, US 162/D4
Blackadder Water. (riv.), Sc, UK 33/D5
Blackall, Austl. 134/B4
Blackbeard Island NWR, Ga, US 165/H2
Blackberry (cr.), Il, US 167/P16
Blackburn, Eng, UK 35/F4
Blackburn, Sc, UK 33/C5
Blackburn, Mo, US 155/H4
Blackburne (int'l arpt.), UK 173/N8
Blackburn with Darwen (co.), Eng, UK 35/F4
Blackbutt, Austl. 134/D4
Blackcraig (peak), Sc, UK 33/B6
Blackdown (hills), Eng, UK 36/C5
Blackdown (hill), Eng, UK 37/F4
Blackdown Tableland NP, Austl. 134/C3
Blackduck, Mn, US 157/G4
Blackfalds, Ab, Can. 145/H1
Blackfoot (res.), Id, US 147/H2
Blackfoot, Id, US 147/G2
Blackfoot (riv.), Id, US 147/H2
Blackfoot, Mt, US 145/H3
Blackfoot Ind. Res., Mt, US 145/H3
Blackfoot Ind. Res., Ab, Can. 145/H2
Blackgum, Ok, US 153/G3
Blackhall Rocks, Eng, UK 35/G2
Blackheath, Austl. 133/E1
Blackie, Ab, Can. 145/H2
Blackland, Tx, US 150/L7
Blackmoor (upland), Eng, UK 36/B5
Blackmore, Eng, UK 30/D1
Blackpool, Eng, UK 35/E4
Blackpool (co.), Eng, UK 35/E4
Blackpool (arpt.), Eng, UK 35/E4
Blackrod, Eng, UK 35/F4
Blacks Fk. (riv.), Wy, US 147/J3
Blacks Harbour, NB, Can. 158/D3
Blacksburg, Va, US 163/G2
Blacksburg, SC, US 163/G3
Blackshear, Ga, US 165/G2
Blackshear (lake), Ga, US 162/F5
Blackstairs (mts.), Ire. 32/D5
Blackstone, Va, US 163/H2
Blacksville, Ga, US 163/M8
Blacktown (nbrhd.), Austl. 134/G8
Blackville, NB, Can. 158/E2
Blackville, SC, US 163/G4
Blackwater (riv.), Mo, Ire. 153/H1
Blackwater (riv.), Ire. 34/B4
Blackwater (res.), Sc, UK 33/B3
Blackwater, Ire. 32/D5
Blackwater (cr.), Fl, US 164/L7
Blackwater (riv.), Eng, UK 30/A2
Blackwater, Austl. 134/C3
Blackwater (riv.), Mo, US 155/H4
Blackwater (inlet), Eng, UK 37/G3
Blackwater Draw (riv.), Tx, US 152/C3
Blackwater NWR, Md, US 163/J1
Blackwell, Ok, US 153/F2
Blackwell, Tx, US 150/D1
Blackwells, Ga, US 163/L6
Blackwood (riv.), Austl. 130/B5
Blackwood (cape), PNG 129/G1
Blackwood, Wal, UK 36/C3
Blackwood, NJ, US 168/C4
Bladel, Neth. 52/C6
Bladenboro, NC, US 163/H3
Bladensburg, Md, US 168/B6
Bladensburg NP, Austl. 134/A3
Bladnoch (riv.), Sc, UK 34/D2
Bladworth, Sk, Can. 145/L2
Blaenau-Ffestiniog, Wal, UK 34/E6
Blaenau Gwent (co.), Wal, UK 36/C3
Blaenavon, Wal, UK 36/C3
Blagnac (int'l arpt.), Fr. 44/D5
Blagnac, Fr. 44/D5
Blagny, Fr. 55/E4
Blagodarniy, Rus. 71/G3
Blagoevgrad, Bul. 49/H1
Blagoveshchensk, Rus. 79/K1
Blain, Fr. 56/D6
Blaine, Tn, US 162/F2
Blaine, Mn, US 157/P6
Blaine Lake, Sk, Can. 145/L1
Blainville, Qu, Can. 159/N6
Blainville-sur-Orne, Fr. 57/E2
Blair, Ok, US 152/E3
Blair, Ne, US 155/F3
Blair, Wi, US 155/J1
Blair (hill), Pa, US 168/C1
Blair Athol, Austl. 134/B3
Blair Atholl, Sc, UK 33/C3
Blairgowrie, Sc, UK 33/C3
Blairmore, Ab, Can. 144/G3
Blairsden, Ca, US 146/C4
Blairstown, NJ, US 168/D2
Blairsville, Ga, US 162/F3
Blaise (riv.), Fr. 44/F2
Blaj, Rom. 51/F2
Blake (pt.), Mi, US 157/K3
Blakely, Pa, US 161/J4
Blakely, Ga, US 165/F2
Blakely Mountain (dam), Ar, US 153/H3
Blakeslee, Pa, US 168/C1
Blamont, Fr. 60/C3
Blanc (peak), Fr. 60/C6
Blanc (cape), Fr. 64/C6
Blanc Nez (cape), Fr. 54/A2
Blanca (peak), NM, US 152/B4
Blanca, Co, US 152/B2
Blanca (bay), Arg. 179/C6
Blanca (coast), Sp. 47/E4
Blanca (peak), Tx, US 150/B2
Blanca (pt.), Mex. 174/B2
Blanchard, Ok, US 153/F3
Blanchard, Id, US 144/F3
Blanchardstown, Ire. 34/B5
Blanchardville, Wi, US 155/K2
Blanche (peak), Swi. 60/D5
Blanche (riv.), Fr. 64/C4
Blanche (lake), Austl. 130/D2
Blanche (cape), Austl. 131/G5
Blanchester, Oh, US 160/E5
Blanchisseuse, Trin. 181/F2
Blanco (riv.), Arg. 188/B4
Blanco (riv.), Bol. 185/F4
Blanco (lake), Chile 191/C7
Blanco (cape), CR 176/E4
Blanco (cape), Mor. 110/A5
Blanco, SAfr. 124/C4
Blanco, NM, US 149/J2
Blanco (cape), Or, US 142/A3
Blanco, Tx, US 150/E2
Blanco (cr.), Tx, US 151/F3
Blanco (riv.), Tx, US 151/E2
Bland (cr.), Austl. 133/C1
Bland, Mo, US 153/J1
Bland, Va, US 163/G2
Blandford Forum, Eng, UK 36/D5
Blanding, Ut, US 149/H2
Blandy, Fr. 30/L6
Blanes, Sp. 47/G2
Blangkejeren, Indo. 89/B2
Blangpidie, Indo. 89/B2
Blangy-sur-Bresle, Fr. 54/A4
Blankenberge, Belg. 54/C1
Blankenese, Ger. 53/G1
Blankenfelde, Ger. 42/Q7
Blankenheim, Ger. 55/F3
Blanket, Tx, US 150/E2
Blanquilla (isl.), Ven. 173/J5
Blanquillo, Uru. 191/G2
Blansko, Czh. 43/J4
Blanton, Fl, US 164/L7
Blantyre, Sc, UK 33/B5
Blantyre, Malw. 123/G2
Blanzy, Fr. 44/F3
Blaricum, Neth. 52/C4
Blarney, Ire. 32/B6
Blarney Castle and Stone, Ire. 32/B6
Blas (peak), Swi. 61/E4
Blatná, Czh. 59/G4
Blato, Cro. 50/C4
Blatten, Swi. 60/D5
Blau (riv.), Ger. 58/C6
Blaubeuren, Ger. 58/C6
Blauen (peak), Ger. 60/D2
Blaustein, Ger. 58/C6
Blauvelt, NY, US 169/K7
Blåvands (pt.), Den. 40/C4
Blavet (riv.), Fr. 44/B3
Blaye, Fr. 44/C4
Blaye, The (Alderney) (arpt.), Chl, UK 56/C1
Blayney, Austl. 133/D1
Blaze (pt.), Austl. 128/C3
Bleckede, Ger. 53/H2
Bled, Slov. 45/L3
Bledlow Ridge, Eng, UK 30/A2
Blefjell (peak), Nor. 40/C2
Blégny, Belg. 55/E2
Bléharies, Belg. 54/C2
Bleiburg, Aus. 50/B2
Bleicherode, Ger. 53/H6
Bleik (peak), Ger. 61/G2
Bleiswijk, Neth. 52/B4
Blekinge (co.), Swe. 38/E4
Blendecques, Fr. 54/B2
Blender, Ger. 53/G3
Blenheim, On, Can. 160/F3
Blenheim, NZ 135/C3
Blénod-lès-Pont-à-Mousson, Fr. 55/F6
Bléone (riv.), Fr. 45/G4
Blera, It. 65/B3
Bléré, Fr. 57/G6
Blerick, Neth. 52/D6
Blesberg (peak), SAfr. 124/C4
Blessing, Tx, US 151/F3
Blessington, Ire. 34/B5
Bletchingley, Eng, UK 30/C3
Bletchley, Eng, UK 37/F3
Bletterans, Fr. 60/B4
Bleury, Fr. 30/H6
Bleus, Monts (mts.), D.R. Congo 121/G2
Blevins, Ar, US 153/H4
Blewbury, Eng, UK 37/E3
Blewett, Tx, US 150/D3
Blewett Falls (lake), NC, US 163/H3
Blida (wilaya), Alg. 112/G4
Blida, Alg. 112/G4
Blidö (isl.), Swe. 39/B1
Blidworth, Eng, UK 35/G5
Blies (riv.), Ger. 55/G5
Blieskastel, Ger. 55/G5
Bligh Water (bay), Fiji 137/Y18
Blik (mt.), Phil. 91/F2
Blind Bay, BC, Can. 144/E2
Blind River, On, Can. 160/E1
Blinman, Austl. 131/H4
Blinndio, Mali 114/D4
Blinnenhorn (peak), Swi. 61/E5
Bliss, Id, US 147/F2
Bliss (dam), Id, US 147/F2
Blissfield, NB, Can. 158/D2
Blissfield, Mi, US 160/E4
Blitar, Indo. 89/F5
Blithe (riv.), Eng, UK 35/F6
Blithfield (res.), Eng, UK 35/G6
Blitta, Togo 115/F4
Block (isl.), RI, US 169/F1
Block House, NS, Can. 158/E3
Block Island (sound), Ma, US 158/B5
Block Island (New Shoreham), RI, US 169/G1
Block Island Coast Guard Station, RI, US 169/G1
Block Island Nat'l Wild. Ref., RI, US 169/G1
Block Island State (arpt.), RI, US 169/G1
Blodelsheim, Fr. 60/D2
Bloemendaal, Neth. 52/B4
Bloemfontein (cap.), SAfr. 124/D3
Bloemhof, SAfr. 124/D2
Bloemhofdam (res.), SAfr. 124/D2
Blois, Fr. 57/G5
Blokzijl, Neth. 52/C3
Blomberg, Ger. 53/G5
Blomberg, Ger. 53/E1
Blommestein (lake), Sur. 181/H3
Blomstermåla, Swe. 40/G3
Blonay, Swi. 60/C5
Blönduós, Ice. 38/N6
Blongas, Indo. 89/G5
Blood Indian Res., Ab, Can. 145/H2
Bloodvein (riv.), Mb,On, Can. 140/G3
Bloodvein River, Mb, Can. 156/F2
Bloody Foreland (pt.), Ire. 31/P9
Bloomer, Wi, US 155/J1
Bloomfield, Nf, Can. 159/L1
Bloomfield, Ct, US 161/K4
Bloomfield, Ia, US 155/H3
Bloomfield, In, US 162/D1
Bloomfield, Mo, US 162/C2
Bloomfield, Mt, US 156/B4
Bloomfield, NJ, US 169/J8
Bloomfield, NM, US 149/J2
Bloomfield Hills, Mi, US 167/F6
Blooming Grove, Tx, US 151/F1
Blooming Prairie, Mn, US 155/H2
Bloomingdale, Fl, US 164/L8
Bloomingdale, Ga, US 163/G4
Bloomingdale, Il, US 167/P16
Bloomingdale, NJ, US 169/H7
Bloomington, Ca, US 166/C2
Bloomington, Id, US 147/H2
Bloomington, Il, US 155/K3
Bloomington, In, US 160/C5
Bloomington, Mn, US 157/P7
Bloomington, Tx, US 151/F3
Bloomington Springs, Tn, US 162/E2
Bloomsburg, Pa, US 168/B2
Bloomsbury, NJ, US 168/C2
Bloomville, Oh, US 160/E4
Blora, Indo. 89/E4
Blotzheim, Fr. 60/D2
Blouberg (peak), SAfr. 123/F4
Blountstown, Fl, US 165/F2
Blountsville, Al, US 162/D3
Blountville, Tn, US 163/F2
Blovice, Czh. 59/G3
Blowering (res.), Austl. 133/D2
Blowing Rock, NC, US 163/G2
Bloxham, Eng, UK 37/E2
Bloxwich, Eng, UK 36/E1
Blšanka (riv.), Czh. 45/K1
Blūdān, Syria 105/E1
Bludenz, Aus. 61/F3
Blue (mtn.), Ar, US 153/G3
Blue (hills), Wi, US 157/J5
Blue (mtn.), NB, Can. 158/D2
Blue (hill), ND, US 156/D4
Blue (hill), Pa, US 161/G4
Blue (mtn.), NH, US 161/L2
Blue (mtn.), NY, US 161/J3
Blue, Az, US 149/H4
Blue (mts.), Or,Wa, US 142/C2
Blue (riv.), Co, US 154/A4
Blue (mtn.), India 86/B4
Blue and Gray Museum, Ga, US 165/G2
Blue Ash, Oh, US 162/E1
Blue Cypress (lake), Fl, US 165/H4
Blue Earth, Mn, US 155/G2
Blue Earth (riv.), Mn, US 155/G2
Blue Eye, Mo, US 153/H2
Blue Head (pt.), Sc, UK 33/C1
Blue Hill, Ne, US 154/E3
Blue Island, Il, US 167/Q16
Blue Lagoon NP, Zam. 123/E2
Blue Lake, Ca, US 146/B3
Blue Lake NP, Austl. 134/D4
Blue Marsh Lake (res.), Pa, US 168/B3
Blue Mesa (res.), Co, US 147/K4
Blue Mesa (dam), Co, US 149/J1
Blue Mound, Ks, US 153/G1
Blue Mound, Tx, US 150/K7
Blue Mountain (peak), Jam. 177/G2
Blue Mountain, Ms, US 162/C3
Blue Mountain (ridge), Pa, US 168/A3
Blue Mountain Lake, NY, US 161/J3
Blue Mountains, Austl. 133/E1
Blue Mud (bay), Austl. 129/D3
Blue Nile (riv.), Eth. 118/B3
Blue Nile (riv.), Eth.,Sudan 117/G2
Blue Nile (falls), Eth. 117/H3
Blue Nile (riv.), Sudan 107/F3
Blue Nose (peak), Mt, US 147/F1
Blue Rapids, Ks, US 155/F4
Blue Ridge, Ga, US 162/E3
Blue Ridge (mts.), Ga, US 162/G3
Blue Ridge Pky., US 163/G2
Blue River, Or, US 146/B1
Blue River, BC, Can. 144/E1
Blue Springs, Mo, US 155/G4
Blue Springs, Ne, US 155/F3
Bluebell, Ut, US 147/H3
Bluefield, WV, US 163/G2
Bluefield, Va, US 163/G2
Bluefields (bay), Nic. 177/F4
Bluefields, Nic. 177/F4
Bluejoint (lake), Or, US 146/D2
Bluenose (lake), Nun, Can. 140/E2
Bluestem (lake), Ok, US 153/F2
Bluestone (lake), WV, US 163/G2
Bluewater, NM, US 149/J3
Bluff (cr.), Ks,Ok, US 153/F2
Bluff, Austl. 134/C3
Bluff (peak), Austl. 130/C5
Bluff (pt.), Austl. 130/B3
Bluff, NZ 135/B4
Bluff, Ut, US 149/H2
Bluff (pt.), NC, US 163/J3
Bluff City, Ar, US 153/H4
Bluff City, Ks, US 153/F2
Bluff Dale, Tx, US 151/E1
Bluff Face (range), Austl. 128/B4
Bluffton, Ar, US 153/H3
Bluffton, In, US 160/D4
Bluffton, Oh, US 160/E4
Blum, Tx, US 151/F1
Blumberg, Ger. 61/E2
Blumberg, Ger. 42/Q6
Blumenau, Braz. 189/G3
Blumenthal, Ger. 53/G2
Blumenthal, Ger. 53/F2
Blümlisalp (peak), Swi. 60/D5
Blunt, SD, US 154/E1
Blustry (mt.), BC, Can. 144/D2
Bly, Or, US 146/C2
Blyn, Wa, US 167/B1
Blyth, Austl. 131/H5
Blyth, Eng, UK 35/G5
Blyth, Eng, UK 35/G1
Blyth Bridge, Sc, UK 33/C5
Blythe, Ca, US 148/E4
Blythe, Ga, US 163/F4
Blythe Bridge, Eng, UK 35/F6
Blytheswood, On, Can. 167/G7
Blytheville, Ar, US 162/C3
Bnom Mhai (peak), Viet. 94/D4
Bø, Nor. 40/C2
Bo, SLeo. 114/C5
Bo Duc, Viet. 94/D4
Bo Hai (Chihli) (gulf), China 75/M6
Bo Ho Su, Viet. 94/D2
Bo Phloi, Thai. 94/B3
Bo River, Sudan 117/E4
Bo Trach, Viet. 94/D2
Boa Esperança, Braz. 186/D4
Boa Esperança (res.), Braz. 183/E4
Boa Nova, Braz. 182/B5
Boa Viagem, Braz. 183/G4
Boa Vista (int'l arpt.), Braz. 181/F4
Boa Vista, Braz. 181/F4
Boa Vista (isl.), CpV. 107/K10
Boac, Phil. 88/C2
Boaco, Nic. 176/E3
Boadilla del Monte, Sp. 47/N9
Bo'ai, China 80/C4
Boajibu, SLeo. 114/C4
Boalsburg, Pa, US 161/H4
Boana, PNG 129/G1
Boano (isl.), Indo. 91/G4
Board Camp, Ar, US 153/G3
Boardman, Oh, US 160/F4
Boardman, Or, US 144/E5
Boardman Bombing Range, Or, US 144/E5
Boardman Naval Ra., Or, US 146/D1
Boas (riv.), Nun, Can. 141/H2
Boavita, Col. 180/C3
Boaz, Al, US 162/D3
Bob Sandlin (lake), Tx, US 153/G4
Boba, Hun. 50/C2
Bobadah, Austl. 132/C2
Bobai, China 87/F4
Bobaomby (cape), Madg. 125/J5
Bobbili, India 95/D2
Bobbio, It. 62/C4
Bobcaygeon, On, Can. 161/G2
Bobenge, D.R. Congo 121/F2
Bobenheim-Roxheim, Ger. 58/B3
Bobigny, Fr. 30/K5
Bobila, D.R. Congo 121/E2
Bobingen, Ger. 61/G1
Bobisi, D.R. Congo 120/D2
Böblingen, Ger. 58/C5
Bobo Dioulasso, Burk. 114/D4
Bobonong, Bots. 123/F4
Boboshevo, Bul. 49/H1
Bobotov Kuk (peak), Serb. 50/D4
Bobovdol, Bul. 50/F4
Bobr, Bela. 41/N4
Bóbr (riv.), Pol. 43/H3
Bobrov, Rus. 73/L2
Bobrovskoye, Rus. 69/K3
Bobrovytsya, Ukr. 72/F2
Bobrynets', Ukr. 73/G3
Bobuk, Sudan 117/G3
Bobures, Ven. 180/D2
Boby (peak), Madg. 125/H8
Boca de Aroa, Ven. 180/D2
Boca de Pepé, Col. 180/B3
Boca del Grita, Ven. 180/C2
Boca del Guafo (chan.), Chile 190/B4
Boca del Mar, Fl, US 164/P10
Boca del Pao, Ven. 181/E2
Boca del Río, Mex. 175/N7
Bôca do Acre, Braz. 185/E3
Boca Grande, Fl, US 165/G4
Boca Raton, Fl, US 164/P10
Bocaina (mts.), Braz. 187/M7
Bocaina, Braz. 183/F4
Bocairente, Sp. 47/E3
Bocaiúva, Braz. 186/E3
Bocanda, C.d'Iv. 114/D5
Bocaranga, CAfr. 116/B4
Bocas del Toro, Pan. 177/F4
Bocay, Nic. 176/E3
Bocay (riv.), Nic. 176/E3
Bochil, Mex. 176/C2
Bochnia, Pol. 43/L4
Bocholt, Belg. 55/E1
Bocholt, Ger. 52/D5
Bochov, Czh. 59/G2
Bochum, SAfr. 123/F4
Bochum, Ger. 53/E6
Bockau, Ger. 59/F1
Bockenem, Ger. 53/H4
Bockenheim an der Weinstrasse, Ger. 55/H4
Bockhorn, Ger. 59/E6
Bockhorn, Ger. 53/F2
Bocking, Eng, UK 37/G3
Bococo, EqG. 120/B2
Bocoio, Ang. 122/B2
Boconó, Ven. 180/D2
Bocq (riv.), Belg. 55/D3
Boda, CAfr. 116/C4
Bodafors, Swe. 40/F3
Bodalla, Austl. 133/E3
Bodaybo, Rus. 75/M4
Bodcau (cr.), Ar, US 153/H4
Bodcaw, Ar, US 153/H4
Boddam, Sc, UK 33/E2
Boddington, Austl. 130/C5
Bode (riv.), Ger. 42/F3
Bode-Sadu, Nga. 115/G4
Bodega (bay), Ca, US 146/B4
Bodegraven, Neth. 52/B4
Bodélé (reg.), Chad 116/C1
Bodenheim, Ger. 58/B3
Bodenkirchen, Ger. 59/F6
Bodenmais, Ger. 59/G4
Bodensee (Constance) (lake), Swi.,Ger. 61/F2
Bodenteich, Ger. 53/H3
Bodfish, Ca, US 148/C3
Bodh Gaya, India 97/E3
Bodhan, India 95/C2
Bodie (isl.), NC, US 163/K3
Bodio, Swi. 61/E5
Bodkin (pt.), Md, US 168/B5
Bodmin, Eng, UK 36/B6
Bodmin Moor (upland), Eng, UK 36/B6
Bodø, Nor. 38/E2
Bodomijärvi (lake), Fin. 39/E4
Bodonchiyn (riv.), Mong. 78/C2
Bodoukpa, CAfr. 116/C4
Bodrog (riv.), Slvk.,Hun. 43/L4
Bodrum, Turk. 102/A2
Bódvaszilas, Hun. 43/L4
Boëge, Fr. 60/C5
Boegoeberg (peak), Namb. 124/A2
Boekel, Neth. 52/C5
Boende, D.R. Congo 121/E3
Boerne, Tx, US 151/E3
Boeuf (riv.), La, US 162/B4
Boffa, Gui. 114/B4
Bog of Allen (swamp), Ire. 34/A5
Boga, D.R. Congo 121/G2
Bogalo (mtn.), Austl. 133/C1
Bogalusa, La, US 164/D2
Bogamangon, CAfr. 116/C4
Bogan (riv.), Austl. 127/D4
Bogan Gate, Austl. 133/C1
Bogandé, Burk. 115/E3
Bogangolo, CAfr. 116/C4
Bogantungan, Austl. 134/B3
Bogard, Mo, US 155/H4
Bogata, Tx, US 153/G4
Bogatić, Serb. 50/D3
Bogatoye, Rus. 71/J1
Bogatynia, Pol. 43/H3
Bogatyrëvo, Kaz. 71/J2
Boğazkale-Alacahöyük NP, Turk. 102/C1
Boğazlıyan, Turk. 102/C2
Bogbonga, D.R. Congo 120/D2
Bogcang (riv.), China 99/E5
Bogda (peak), China 99/E3
Bogda (mts.), China 78/B3
Bogdanci, FYROM 49/H2
Bogdanovka, Geo. 71/G4
Bogen, Nor. 38/F1
Bogen, Ger. 59/F5
Bogenfels, Namb. 124/A2
Bogenli, China 79/K2
Bogense, Den. 40/D4
Boggabilla, Austl. 134/C5
Boggabri, Austl. 132/D1
Boggeragh (mts.), Ire. 32/A5
Boggy (peak), Anti. 173/N8
Boglárlelle, Hun. 50/C2
Bogliasco, It. 62/C5
Bognor Regis, Eng, UK 37/F5
Bogny-sur-Meuse, Fr. 55/D4
Bogo, Camr. 116/B3
Bogo, Phil. 88/C3
Bogol Manyo, Eth. 118/B4
Bogong (mt.), Austl. 133/C3
Bogor, Indo. 89/D4
Bogoria Nat'l Rsv., Kenya 119/B1
Bogoro, D.R. Congo 121/G2
Bogoroud (well), Chad 116/B2
Bogotá (cap.), Col. 183/L8
Bogotá (riv.), Col. 183/L8
Bogota, NJ, US 169/J8
Bogovino, FYROM 49/G2
Bogra, Bang. 97/G3
Bogra (pol. reg.), Bang. 97/G3
Bogsta, Swe. 39/A2
Boguchar, Rus. 73/L3
Bogué, Mrta. 114/B2
Bogue, Ks, US 154/E4
Bogue Chitto (riv.), La, US 164/C2
Bogue Chitto, Ms, US 164/C2
Bogue Chitto NWR, La, US 164/C2
Bogue Homo (cr.), Ms, US 164/D2
Boguila Kota, CAfr. 116/C4
Bogushëvsk, Bela. 41/P4
Bohai (bay), China 80/D3
Bohain-en-Vermandois, Fr. 54/C4
Bohemia (reg.), Czh. 43/G4
Bohemian (for.), Czh.,Ger. 42/G4
Bohemian (for.), Ger.,Czh. 45/K2
Boherboy, Ire. 32/A5
Bohicon, Ben. 115/F5
Böhl-Iggelheim, Ger. 58/B4
Böhme (riv.), Ger. 53/G3
Böhmenkirch, Ger. 58/C5
Bohmte, Ger. 53/F4
Bohners Lake, Wi, US 167/P14
Bohodukhiv, Ukr. 73/H2
Bohol (isl.), Phil. 88/C3
Bohol (str.), Phil. 88/C3
Böhönye, Hun. 50/C2
Bohu, China 99/E3
Bohuslav, Ukr. 72/F3
Boiestown, NB, Can. 158/D2
Boigny-sur-Bionne, Fr. 57/H5
Boiling Springs, Pa, US 168/A3
Boiling Springs, SC, US 163/G3
Boimbo, D.R. Congo 120/D3
Boinu (riv.), Myan. 86/B4
Boipāriguda, India 95/D2
Boipeba (isl.), Braz. 187/F2
Boiro, Sp. 46/A1
Bois (isl.), Nf, Can. 159/K2
Bois Blanc (isl.), Mi, US 160/D2
Bois de Boulogne (dept.), Fr. 30/J5
Bois de Vincennes (dept.), Fr. 30/K5
Bois, Rio dos (riv.), Braz. 186/C3
Bois-d'Amont, Fr. 60/C4
Bois-d'Arcy, Fr. 30/J5
Bois-des-Filion, Qu, Can. 159/N6
Bois-Guillaume, Fr. 57/G2
Boisbriand, Qu, Can. 159/N6
Boise (riv.), Fr. 47/F1
Boise (mts.), Id, US 146/F2
Boise (riv.), Id, US 146/A3
Boise (cap.), Id, US 146/E2
Boise City, Ok, US 152/C2
Boissevain, Mb, Can. 156/D3
Boissevain, Va, US 163/G2
Boissy-Fresnoy, Fr. 30/L4
Boissy-L'Aillerie, Fr. 30/J4
Boissy-le-Châtel, Fr. 30/M5
Boissy-Saint-Léger, Fr. 30/K5
Boissy-Sans-Avoir, Fr. 30/H5
Boizenburg, Ger. 53/H2
Bojano, It. 65/D5
Bojeador (cape), Phil. 88/C1
Boji (plain), Kenya 119/B1
Bojkovice, Czh. 43/J4
Bojnūrd, Iran 103/J2
Bojonegoro, Indo. 89/E4
Boju, Nga. 115/G5
Boju Ega, Nga. 115/H5
Bok, PNG 129/G1
Bok Tower Gardens, Fl, US 164/M8
Bokala, D.R. Congo 120/D3
Bokapo Li, D.R. Congo 121/E2
Bokaro Steel City, India 97/F4
Bokat, Indo. 91/F3
Bokata, D.R. Congo 121/E2
Bokatola, D.R. Congo 120/D3
Bokchito, Ok, US 153/F3
Boké, Gui. 114/B4
Boké (pol. reg.), Gui. 114/B4
Bokele, D.R. Congo 121/E3
Bokengo, D.R. Congo 121/E2
Bokhan, Rus. 78/E1
Bokhol (plain), Kenya 119/B1
Boknafjorden (estu.), Nor. 38/C4
Boko, India 97/H3
Boko, Congo 120/C4
Boko, Kaz. 99/D2
Boko Songo, Congo 120/C4
Bokode, D.R. Congo 120/D2
Bokol (peak), Kenya 119/B1
Bokondini, Indo. 91/J4
Bokoro, Chad 116/C2
Bokote, D.R. Congo 120/E3
Bokpyin, Myan. 94/B4
Boksburg, SAfr. 124/Q13
Bokspits, Bots. 124/C2
Bokungu, D.R. Congo 121/E3
Bol, Chad 116/B2
Bol'shaya Khobda (riv.), Kaz. 71/K2
Bol'shaya Kinel' (riv.), Rus. 71/K1
Bol'shaya Ussurka (riv.), Rus. 79/L2
Bol'shoy Irgiz (riv.), Rus. 71/J1
Bol'shoy Uzen' (riv.), Rus. 71/J2
Bol'shoy Yenisey (riv.), Rus. 78/D1
Bolama, GBis. 114/B4
Bolama, D.R. Congo 121/E2
Bolān (pass), Pak. 101/J3
Bolaños de Calatrava, Sp. 46/D3
Bolayır, Turk. 51/H5
Bolbec, Fr. 57/F1
Bolckow, Mo, US 155/G3
Boldeşti-Scăeni, Rom. 51/H3
Boldon, Eng, UK 35/G2
Bole, Gha. 115/E4
Bole (int'l arpt.), Eth. 118/A3
Bole, China 99/D3
Bolekhiv, Ukr. 72/B3
Boleko, D.R. Congo 120/D3
Boleng (peak), Indo. 128/A2
Boles, Ar, US 153/G3
Bolesławiec, Pol. 43/H3
Boley, Ok, US 153/F3
Bolgatanga, Gha. 115/E4
Bolhrad, Ukr. 51/J3
Boli, China 79/L2
Bolia, D.R. Congo 120/D3
Boliden, Swe. 38/G2
Boligee, Al, US 162/C4
Bolinao (cape), Phil. 88/B1
Bolinao, Phil. 88/B1
Boling, Tx, US 151/G3
Bolingbrook, Il, US 160/B4
Bolivar (pen.), Tx, US 151/G3
Bolivar, Tx, US 153/F4
Bolivar, Mo, US 153/H2
Bolivar, Oh, US 160/F4
Bolívar (peak), Ven. 181/F3
Bolívar (state), Ven. 181/E3
Bolívar, Ecu. 180/A4
Bolívar, Col. 180/B3
Bolívar (dept.), Col. 180/C2
Bolívar (peak), Ven. 180/D2
Bolívar, Arg. 190/E3
Bolivar, Tn, US 162/C3
Bolívar, Bol. 185/E4
Bolívar, Peru 184/B2
Bolivia (ctry.) 179/C4
Bolivia, NC, US 163/H3
Böljane (riv.), Swe. 39/K6
Bolkhov, Rus. 70/F1
Bollate, It. 62/C2
Bollène, Fr. 64/A4
Bolligen, Swi. 60/D4
Bollin (riv.), Eng, UK 35/F5
Bollington, Eng, UK 35/F5
Bollmora, Swe. 39/B1
Bollnäs, Swe. 40/G1
Bollon, Austl. 134/B5
Bollullos Par del Condado, Sp. 46/B4
Bolmen (lake), Swe. 40/E3
Bolney, Eng, UK 37/F5
Bolnisi, Geo. 71/H4
Bolo, D.R. Congo 120/D3
Bolobo, D.R. Congo 120/D3
Bologna, It. 63/E5
Bologna (prov.), It. 63/E3
Bologne, Fr. 60/B1
Bolognesi, Peru 184/C3
Bolognesi, Peru 184/C2
Bologoye, Rus. 68/G4
Bolomba, D.R. Congo 120/D2
Bolombo (riv.), D.R. Congo 121/E2
Bolombo, D.R. Congo 121/E3
Bolon', Rus. 79/M2
Bolon' (lake), Rus. 79/M2
Bolonchén de Rejón, Mex. 176/D2
Bolongongo, Ang. 120/C5
Bolonguera, Ang. 122/B2
Bolpebra, Bol. 184/D3
Bolpur, India 97/F4
Bolsena (lake), It. 48/B1
Bolsena, It. 65/A2
Bol'shakovo, Rus. 41/J4
Bol'shaya Belozërka, Ukr. 73/H4
Bol'shaya Breëstovitsa, Bela. 43/N2
Bol'shaya Chernigovka, Rus. 71/J1
Bol'shaya Damba, Kaz. 71/J3
Bol'shaya Rogovaya (riv.), Rus. 69/P2
Bol'shaya Sosnova, Rus. 69/M4
Bol'shaya Synya (riv.), Rus. 69/N2
Bol'shaya Znamenka, Ukr. 73/H4
Bol'shevik (isl.), Rus. 77/H2
Bol'shevik, Bela. 70/D1
Bol'shezemel'skaya (tundra), Rus. 69/M2
Bol'shoy Bolvanskiy Nos (pt.), Rus. 74/F2
Bol'shoy Kuganavolok, Rus. 68/H3
Bol'shoy Lyakhov (isl.), Rus. 77/P2
Bol'shoy Lyakhovskiy (isl.), Rus. 75/Q2
Bol'shoy Ut, Rus. 69/N4
Bol'shoy Yenisey (riv.), Rus. 99/G1
Bol'shoye Boldino, Rus. 69/K5
Bol'shoye Nagatkino, Rus. 69/K5
Bol'shoye Soldatskoye, Rus. 73/H2
Bolsover, Eng, UK 35/G5
Bolsover, On, Can. 161/G2
Bolsward, Neth. 52/C2
Bolt (pt.), Eng, UK 36/C6
Boltaña, Sp. 47/F1
Boltigen, Swi. 60/D4
Bolton, Eng, UK 35/F4
Bolton (co.), Eng, UK 35/F4
Bolton, On, Can. 160/T8
Bolton Abbey, Eng, UK 35/G4
Bolu, Turk. 70/D4
Bolu (prov.), Turk. 70/D4
Bolungavík, Ice. 38/M6
Bolus Head (pt.), Ire. 30/N11
Bolvadin, Turk. 104/E1
Bolwarra, Austl. 133/E1
Bóly, Hun. 50/D3
Bolyarovo, Bul. 51/H4
Bolzano, It. 61/H5
Bolzano-Bozen (prov.), It. 61/H4
Bom Conselho, Braz. 183/G5
Bom Despacho, Braz. 186/D3
Bom Jardim de Goiás, Braz. 186/B3
Bom Jardin de Minas, Braz. 187/M6
Bom Jesus, Ang. 120/C5
Bom Jesus, Braz. 189/G4
Bom Jesus, Braz. 183/E5
Bom Jesus, Braz. 183/H4
Bom Jesus da Gurguéia, Serra (mts.), Braz. 187/E1
Bom Jesus da Lapa, Braz. 187/E2
Bom Jesus de Goiás, Braz. 186/C3
Bom Jesus do Gurgueia, Serra do (mts.), Braz. 183/F5
Bom Jesus do Itabapoana, Braz. 187/E4
Bom Jesus dos Perdões, Braz. 187/K8
Bom Sucesso, Braz. 186/D4
Boma, D.R. Congo 120/C4
Boma NP, Sudan 117/G4
Bomaderry, Austl. 133/E2
Bomaneh, D.R. Congo 121/E2
Bomba, Ang. 122/B2
Bombakabo, D.R. Congo 120/D2
Bombala, Austl. 133/D3
Bombala (riv.), Austl. 133/D3
Bombay (Mumbai), India 101/K5
Bombay Hook NWR, De, US 168/C5
Bomberai (pen.), Indo. 91/H4
Bombo, Ugan. 121/H2
Bomboma, D.R. Congo 120/D2
Bombombi, D.R. Congo 121/F2
Bomboyo, Chad 116/B2
Bomerano, It. 65/D6
Bomi, Libr. 114/C5
Bomi, China 86/B2
Bomili, D.R. Congo 121/F2
Bomlitz, Ger. 53/G3
Bømlo (isl.), Nor. 40/A2
Bomokandi (riv.), D.R. Congo 121/F2
Bomongo, D.R. Congo 120/D2
Bomu (riv.), D.R. Congo 107/E4
Bon Air, Va, US 163/J2
Bon Secour (bay), Al, US 164/E2
Bon Wier, Tx, US 151/H2
Bon, Cap (Ra's aţ Ţīb) (cape), Tun. 48/B4
Bon-Encontre, Fr. 44/D4
Bona (mt.), Ak, US 171/K3
Bonāb, Iran 103/J4
Bonabéri, Camr. 120/B1
Bonaduz, Swi. 61/F4
Bonaire (isl.), NAnt. 173/H5
Bonalbo, Austl. 132/E1
Bonampak (ruin), Mex. 176/D2
Bonanza, Ut, US 147/J3
Bonanza, Or, US 146/C2
Bonanza, Co, US 149/J1
Bonanza (peak), Wa, US 144/D3
Bonao, DRep. 173/G4
Bonaparte (arch.), Austl. 128/B3
Bonaparte (riv.), BC, Can. 144/D2
Bonaparte (lake), BC, Can. 144/D2
Bonaparte (mt.), Wa, US 144/E3
Bonaparte (isls.), Austl. 127/B2
Bonasila Dome (mt.), Ak, US 171/F3
Bonaventure, Qu, Can. 158/E1
Bonaventure (riv.), Qu, Can. 158/E1
Bonavista, Nf, Can. 159/L1
Bonavista (cape), Nf, Can. 159/L1
Bonavista (bay), Nf, Can. 159/L1
Boncarbo, Co, US 152/B2
Bonchamp-lès-Laval, Fr. 57/E4
Bonchester Bridge, Sc, UK 33/D6
Boncourt, Swi. 60/D3
Bond, Co, US 147/K4
Bondari, Rus. 71/G1
Bondeno, It. 63/E4
Bondi (nbrhd.), Austl. 134/H8
Bondo, D.R. Congo 121/E2
Bondoc (pen.), Phil. 88/C2
Bondoukou, C.d'Iv. 114/E4
Bondowoso, Indo. 89/F4
Bonduel, Wi, US 155/K1
Bone (gulf), Indo. 77/M10
Bone (cape), Tun. 112/M6
Bone Hill Nat'l Wild. Ref., ND, US 156/E4
Bonebone, Indo. 91/F4
Bonefro, It. 65/D4
Bönen, Ger. 53/E5
Bonerate (isls.), Indo. 91/F5
Bo'ness, Sc, UK 33/C4
Bonesteel, SD, US 154/E2
Bonete (peak), Arg. 188/B3
Bonfield, On, Can. 161/G1
Bonfol, Swi. 60/D3
Bonfouca, La, US 164/D2
Bong (co.), Libr. 114/C5
Bong (range), Libr. 114/C5
Bong (lake), China 99/F5
Bong Son, Viet. 94/E3
Bonga, Ang. 122/C2
Bonga, Eth. 117/H4
Bongabong, Phil. 88/C2
Bongaigaon, India 97/H2
Bongandanga, D.R. Congo 121/E2
Bongao, Phil. 88/B4
Bonggi (isl.), Malay. 91/E2
Bongka (riv.), Indo. 91/F4
Bongo, D.R. Congo 121/E4
Bongo, D.R. Congo 120/E2
Bongolava (uplands), Madg. 125/H7
Bongor, Chad 116/B3
Bongou (riv.), CAfr. 116/D4
Bongouanou, C.d'Iv. 114/D5
Bongoville, Gabon 120/C3
Bonham, Tx, US 153/F4
Bonheiden, Belg. 55/D1
Bonhill, Sc, UK 33/B5
Boni, Mali 115/E3
Boni Nat'l Rsv., Kenya 119/C2
Bonifacio, Fr. 48/A2
Bonifacio (str.), Fr.,It. 66/F2
Bonifay, Fl, US 165/F2
Bönigen, Swi. 60/D4
Bonin (isls.), Japan 136/C2
Bonita, Az, US 149/H4
Bonita, Ca, US 166/C5
Bonita, La, US 153/J4
Bonita Springs, Fl, US 165/H4
Bonito (peak), Hon. 176/E3
Bonito, Braz. 183/H5
Bonito, Braz. 189/E2
Bonito de Santa Fé, Braz. 183/G4
Bonjol, Indo. 89/C3
Bonn, Ger. 55/G2
Bonndorf im Schwarzwald, Ger. 61/E2
Bonne, Fr. 60/C5
Bonne (riv.), Fr. 64/B3
Bonne Terre, Mo, US 162/B2
Bonneau, SC, US 163/H4
Bonnefjorden (fd.), Nor. 38/S8
Bonnelles, Fr. 30/J6
Bonner-West Riverside, Mt, US 145/H4
Bonners Ferry, Id, US 144/F3
Bonnet (lake), Mb, Can. 156/F2
Bonnétable, Fr. 57/F4
Bonneuil-sur-Marne, Fr. 30/K5
Bonneval, Fr. 57/G4
Bonneville, Fr. 60/C5
Bonney Lake, Wa, US 167/C3
Bonnie, Il, US 162/C1
Bonnie Doone, NC, US 163/H3
Bonnières-sur-Seine, Fr. 57/G2
Bonnieux, Fr. 64/B5
Bönnigheim, Ger. 58/C4
Bonnybridge, Sc, UK 33/C5
Bonnyman, Ky, US 163/F2
Bonnyrigg, Sc, UK 33/C5
Bonnyville, Ab, Can. 140/E3
Bono, Ar, US 162/B3
Bonorva, It. 48/A2
Bons-en-Chablais, Fr. 60/C5
Bonsall, Ca, US 166/C4
Bontang, Indo. 91/E3
Bontberg (peak), SAfr. 124/C4
Bontebok NP, SAfr. 124/C4
Bonthain, Indo. 91/E5
Bonthe, SLeo. 114/B5
Bontoc, Phil. 88/C1
Bontomatane, Indo. 91/F5
Bonyeri, Gha. 114/E5
Bonyhád, Hun. 50/D2
Bonzart (lake), Tun. 112/L6
Booker, Tx, US 152/D2
Booker T. Washington Nat'l Mon., Va, US 163/H2
Boola, Gui. 114/C4
Boolaloo, Austl. 130/B2
Booligal, Austl. 133/B1
Boom, Belg. 55/D1
Boomi, Austl. 134/C5
Boone, Co, US 152/B1
Boone (riv.), Ia, US 155/H2
Boone, Ia, US 155/H2
Boone, NC, US 163/G2
Boone (dam), Tn, US 163/F2
Booneville, Ar, US 153/H3
Booneville, Ky, US 162/F2
Booneville, Ms, US 162/C3
Boonsboro, Md, US 161/H5
Boonton, NJ, US 169/H8
Bööntsagaan (lake), Mong. 78/D2
Boonville, Ca, US 146/B4
Boonville, In, US 162/D1
Boonville, Mo, US 155/H4
Boonville, NY, US 161/J3
Boopi (riv.), Bol. 185/E5
Boorabbin NP, Austl. 130/D4
Boorama, Som. 118/B3
Booroondara (mt.), Austl. 132/C1
Booroorban, Austl. 133/B2
Boorowa, Austl. 133/D2
Boos, Fr. 57/G2
Boos (int'l arpt.), Fr. 57/G2
Boos, Ger. 61/G1
Boostedt, Ger. 40/D4
Booster, Ar, US 153/H3
Boot Reefs (reef), PNG 129/G2
Boothia (pen.), Nun, Can. 140/G1
Boothia (gulf), Can. 139/H2
Bootjack, Ca, US 148/C2
Bootle, Eng, UK 35/E5
Booué, Gabon 120/B3
Bopa, Ben. 115/F5
Bopfingen, Ger. 58/D5
Bopili, D.R. Congo 121/E2
Bopolu, Libr. 114/C5
Boppard, Ger. 55/G3
Boppy (mt.), Austl. 132/C1
Boqueirão, Serra do (mts.), Braz. 187/E1
Boqueron (dept.), Par. 188/D2
Boquete (peak), Arg. 190/C4
Boquilla (res.), Mex. 174/D3
Boquillas del Carmen, Mex. 150/C3
Bor, Czh. 59/F3
Bor, Rus. 69/K4
Bor, Serb. 50/F3
Bor, Sudan 117/F4
Bor, Turk. 102/C2
Bor Ul (mts.), China 74/K5
Bora Bora (isl.), FrPol. 137/K6
Borabu, Thai. 94/C2
Borah (peak), Id, US 147/G1
Borås, Swe. 40/E3
Borāzjān, Iran 103/G4
Borba, Braz. 182/B4
Borba, Port. 46/B3
Borbera (riv.), It. 62/B3
Borbona, It. 65/C2
Borbonnais (reg.), Fr. 44/D3
Borbore (riv.), It. 62/B3
Borča, Serb. 50/E3
Borcea Branch (riv.), Rom. 51/H3
Borchen, Ger. 53/F5
Borçka, Turk. 71/G4
Borculo, Neth. 52/D4
Borda da Mata, Braz. 187/K7
Bordeaux, Fr. 44/C4
Bordelonville, La, US 164/C2
Borden, PE, Can. 158/F2
Borden (pen.), Nun, Can. 141/H1
Borden, Austl. 130/C5
Borden (isl.), NW, Can. 141/R7
Bordentown, NJ, US 168/D3
Bordertown, Austl. 132/B3
Bordighera, It. 64/D5
Bordj Bou Arreridj, Alg. 112/H4
Bordj Bou Arreridj (wilaya), Alg. 112/H4
Bordj el Kiffan, Alg. 112/G4
Bordj Manaïel, Alg. 112/G4
Bordj Moktar, Alg. 111/F5
Bordj Omar Driss, Alg. 111/G3
Bordj Sainte-Marie, Alg. 110/E4
Bordon, Eng, UK 37/F4
Boré, Mali 114/E3
Borē, Eth. 118/A4
Borehamwood, Eng, UK 30/C2
Borest, Fr. 30/L4
Boretto, It. 62/D4
Borgå (Porvoo), Fin. 41/L1
Borgaretto, It. 62/A2
Borgarnes, Ice. 38/N7
Borgaro Torinese, It. 62/A2
Børgefjell NP, Nor. 38/E2
Borgentreich, Ger. 53/G5
Borger, Tx, US 152/D3
Börger, Ger. 53/E3
Borger, Neth. 52/D3
Borgerhout, Belg. 52/B6
Borges Blanques, Sp. 47/F2
Borghetto Lodigiano, It. 62/C3
Borghetto Santo Spirito, It. 62/B5
Borgholm, Swe. 40/G3
Borgholzhausen, Ger. 53/F4
Borghorst, Ger. 53/E4
Borgloon, Belg. 55/E2
Borgnäs (Pornainen), Fin. 39/F4
Borgne (riv.), Swi. 60/D5
Borgne (lake), La, US 164/D3
Borgo, It. 61/H5
Borgo, Fr. 48/A1
Borgo (int'l arpt.), Burk. 114/D4
Borgo a Mozzano, It. 62/D6
Borgo Maggiore, SMar. 63/F6
Borgo Sabotino, It. 65/B5
Borgo San Dalmazzo, It. 64/D4
Borgo San Giacomo, It. 62/C3

Borgo San Lorenzo, It. 63/E6
Borgo Tossignano, It. 63/E5
Borgo Val di Taro, It. 62/C5
Borgo Vercelli, It. 62/B3
Borgofranco d'Ivrea, It. 62/A1
Borgomanero, It. 62/B2
Borgonovo Val Tidone, It. 62/C3
Borgosatollo, It. 62/D3
Borgosesia, It. 62/B2
Borgou (prov.), Ben. 115/F4
Borgund, Nor. 40/B1
Bori, Nga. 115/G5
Borikhan, Laos 94/C2
Borinskoye, Rus. 70/F1
Borio, India 97/F3
Borisoglebsk, Rus. 73/M2
Borisovka, Rus. 73/J2
Borisovo (nbrhd.), Rus. 69/W9
Borispol (int'l arpt.), Ukr. 72/F2
Borja, Sp. 46/E2
Borja, Peru 184/B2
Borken, Ger. 53/G6
Borken, Ger. 52/D5
Børkop, Den. 40/C4
Borkou (reg.), Chad 108/C5
Borkou-Ennedi-Tibesti (pref.), Chad 116/C1
Borkum (isl.), Ger. 52/D1
Borkum, Ger. 52/D1
Borkum (arpt.), Ger. 52/D1
Borlänge, Swe. 40/F1
Bormes-les-Mimosas, Fr. 64/C6
Bormida, It. 62/B5
Bormida (riv.), It. 45/H4
Bormida di Millesimo (riv.), It. 62/B4
Bormio, It. 61/G5
Born, Neth. 55/E1
Borna, Ger. 42/G3
Borndiep (chan.), Neth. 52/C2
Borne (riv.), Fr. 60/C6
Borne, Neth. 52/D4
Bornel, Fr. 54/B5
Bornem, Belg. 55/D1
Borneo (isl.), Indo.,Malay. 77/L9
Borneo (isl.), Indo. 91/E3
Bornheim, Ger. 55/G2
Bornholm (co.), Den. 40/F4
Bornholm (isl.), Den. 40/F4
Bornholmsgat (chan.), Den.,Swi. 43/H1
Borno, It. 61/G6
Borno (state), Nga. 116/B2
Bornos, Sp. 46/C4
Börnsen, Ger. 53/H2
Bornus (plain), Nga. 116/B2
Boro (riv.), Sudan 117/E3
Borobudur (ruin), Indo. 89/E4
Borodino, Rus. 74/K4
Borodino, Ukr. 51/J2
Borodyanka, Ukr. 72/E2
Borohoro (mts.), China 99/D3
Boromo, Burk. 114/E4
Boron, Ca, US 148/D3
Borongan, Phil. 88/D3
Borough Green, Eng, UK 30/D3
Boroughbridge, Eng, UK 35/G3
Borovany, Czh. 59/H5
Borovichi, Rus. 68/G4
Borovlyanka, Rus. 99/D1
Borovo, Cro. 50/D3
Borovo, Bul. 51/G4
Borovsk, Rus. 70/F1
Borovskiy, Rus. 69/Q4
Borovskoy, Kaz. 69/Q5
Borraan, Som. 118/D3
Borre, Nor. 40/D2
Borrego Springs, Ca, US 148/D4
Borris, Ire. 32/D4
Borris in Ossory, Ire. 32/C4
Borrisokane, Ire. 32/B4
Borrisoleigh, Ire. 32/C4
Bornida (riv.), It. 62/B3
Borroloola, Austl. 129/E4
Borroloola Abor. Land, Austl. 129/D4
Borşa, Rom. 51/F2
Borsec, Rom. 72/C4
Borshchiv, Ukr. 72/D3
Borshchovochnyy (mts.), Rus. 79/H1
Borso del Grappa, It. 63/E2
Borsod-Abaúj-Zemplén (co.), Hun. 43/L4
Borssele, Neth. 52/A6
Borstel, Ger. 53/F3
Bort-les-Orgues, Fr. 44/E4
Bortala (riv.), China 99/D3
Borth, Wal, UK 36/B2
Boruca, CR 177/F4
Borūjen, Iran 103/G4
Borūjerd, Iran 103/G3
Børup, Den. 39/H7
Boryslav, Ukr. 43/M4
Boryspil', Ukr. 72/F2
Borzna, Ukr. 72/G2
Borzonasca, It. 62/C5
Borzya, Rus. 78/H1
Bosa, It. 48/A2
Bosaaso (Bender Cassim), Som. 118/D3
Bosanska Dubica, Bosn. 50/C3
Bosanska Gradiška, Bosn. 50/C3
Bosanska Kostajnica, Bosn. 50/C3
Bosanska Krupa, Bosn. 50/C3
Bosanski Brod, Bosn. 50/D3
Bosanski Petrovac, Bosn. 50/C3
Bosanski Šamac, Bosn. 50/D3
Bošany, Slvk. 43/K4
Bosavi (mt.), PNG 129/F1
Bosc-le-Hard, Fr. 57/G1
Boscawen, NH, US 161/L3
Bosco, La, US 153/H4
Bosco, It. 65/B1
Bosco Mesola, It. 63/F4
Boscobel, Wi, US 155/J2
Bosconero, It. 62/A2
Boscoreale, It. 65/D6
Bose, China 87/E4
Bosham, Eng, UK 37/F5
Boshnyakovo, Rus. 79/N2
Boshof, SAfr. 124/D3
Boshrūyeh, Iran 103/J3
Boskoop, Neth. 52/B4
Boskovice, Czh. 43/J4
Bosler, Wy, US 154/B3
Bosna (riv.), Bosn. 50/D3
Bosnia and Herzegovina (ctry.) 50/C3
Bošnjaci, Cro. 50/D3
Bōsō (pen.), Japan 85/G3
Bosobolo, D.R. Congo 116/C4
Bososama, D.R. Congo 116/D4
Bosporus (str.), Turk. 70/D4
Bosporus (riv.), Turk. 103/N6
Bosque del Apache Nat'l Wild Ref., NM, US 149/J4
Bosque Farms, NM, US 149/J3
Bosques Petrificados, Mon. Natural, Arg. 191/C5
Boss, Mo, US 162/B2
Bossangoa, CAfr. 116/C4
Bossembele, CAfr. 116/C4
Bossentélé, CAfr. 116/C4
Bossier City, La, US 153/H4
Bosso, Niger 116/B2
Bossut (cape), Austl. 128/A4
Bostān, Iran 103/G4
Bostan, China 99/D4
Bostānābād-e Bālā, Iran 103/F2
Bosten (lake), China 99/E3
Boston (mts.), Ar, US 153/H3
Boston, Tx, US 153/G4
Boston, Eng, UK 35/H6
Boston, Ga, US 165/G2
Boston (cap.), Ma, US 158/B4
Bostwick, Fl, US 165/H3
Bosut (riv.), Cro. 50/D3
Boswell, In, US 160/C4
Boswil, Swi. 61/E3
Bot Makak, Camr. 120/B2
Botād, India 101/K4
Botany, Austl. 133/E1
Botelerpunt (pt.), SAfr. 125/F2
Botelhos, Braz. 187/K6
Botene, Laos 94/C1
Botev (peak), Bul. 51/G4
Botevgrad, Bul. 51/F4
Bothaspas (pass), SAfr. 125/E2
Bothaville, SAfr. 124/D2
Bothel, Eng, UK 35/E2
Bothel, Ger. 53/G2
Bothell, Wa, US 167/C2
Bothenhampton, Eng, UK 36/D5
Bothnia (gulf), Swe.,Fin. 38/G2
Bothwell, Austl. 132/C4
Botkyrka, Swe. 39/A1
Botletle (riv.), Bots. 122/D4
Botlikh, Rus. 71/H4
Botoşani, Rom. 72/D4
Botoşani (prov.), Rom. 51/H2
Botou, China 80/D3
Botrange (peak), Belg. 55/F3
Botrivier, SAfr. 124/L11
Botsford, Ct, US 169/E1
Botswana (ctry.) 107/E7
Bottanuco, It. 62/C2
Botte Donato (peak), It. 48/E3
Bottesford, Eng, UK 35/H6
Bottesford, Eng, UK 35/H4
Botticino, It. 62/D2
Bottineau, ND, US 156/D3
Bottineau Winter Park, ND, US 156/D3
Bottrighe, It. 63/F3
Bottrop, Ger. 52/D5
Botucatu, Braz. 189/G2
Botwood, Nf, Can. 159/K1
Bötzow, Ger. 42/Q6
Bou (riv.), C.d'Iv. 114/D4
Bou Arfa, Mor. 111/E2
Boû Djébéha (well), Mali 114/E2
Bou Hamdane, Oued (riv.), Alg. 112/K6
Bou Ismaïl, Alg. 112/G4
Bou Izakarn, Mor. 110/C3
Bou Kadir, Alg. 112/F4
Bou Laber (well), Alg. 110/D4
Boû Lanouâr, Mrta. 110/A5
Bou Naceur (peak), Mor. 112/C3
Bou Regreg (riv.), Mor. 112/A3
Bou Saâda, Alg. 112/H5
Bou Salem, Tun. 112/L6
Bou Sellam, Oued (riv.), Alg. 112/H4
Bouaflé, C.d'Iv. 114/D5
Bouafle, Fr. 30/H5
Bouaké, C.d'Iv. 114/D5
Bouali, CAfr. 116/C4
Bouanga, Congo 120/D3
Bouar, CAfr. 116/B4
Bouba Ndjida, PN de, Camr. 116/B3
Boubín (peak), Czh. 59/G5
Bouc-Bel-Air, Fr. 64/B6
Bouca, CAfr. 116/C4
Bouchain, Fr. 54/C3
Bouchegouf, Alg. 112/K6
Boucherville, Qu, Can. 159/P6
Bouches-du-Rhône (dept.), Fr. 64/A5
Bouchet (mtn.), Fr. 64/D3
Boucle Du Baoulé, PN de la, Mali 114/C3
Boudenib, Mor. 110/E3
Boudi, Eth. 118/B4
Boudreaux (lake), La, US 164/C3
Boudry, Swi. 60/C4
Bouenza (riv.), Congo 120/C3
Bouenza (pol. reg.), Congo 120/C3
Boufarik, Alg. 112/G4
Bouffémont, Fr. 30/J4
Bougainville (cape), Austl. 128/B3
Bougainville (reef), Austl. 127/D2
Bougainville (isl.), PNG 136/E5
Bougainville (reef), PNG 129/G3
Bougainville (cape), UK 191/F6
Bougara, Alg. 112/G4
Bougar'oûn (cape), Alg. 112/K6
Bough Beech (res.), Eng, UK 30/D3
Boughton, Eng, UK 30/E3
Bougouni, Mali 114/D4
Bougouriba (prov.), Burk. 114/E4
Bougtob, Alg. 66/D4
Bouguenais, Fr. 44/C3
Bouhachem (peak), Mor. 112/B2
Bouhalla (peak), Mor. 112/B2
Bouillancy, Fr. 30/L4
Bouillon, Belg. 55/E4
Bouira, Alg. 112/G4
Bouira (wilaya), Alg. 112/G4
Boujad, Mor. 110/D2
Boukhalf (Tangier) (int'l arpt.), Mor. 112/B2
Boukoko, CAfr. 120/D2
Boukoumbé, Ben. 115/F4
Boulaide, Lux. 55/E4
Boulaouane, Mor. 110/C2
Boulay-Moselle, Fr. 55/F5
Boulazac, Fr. 44/D4
Boulder (riv.), Mt, US 147/H1
Boulder, Co, US 154/B3
Boulder, Mt, US 145/H4
Boulder City, Nv, US 148/E3
Boulder Creek, Ca, US 148/A2
Boulder Hill, Il, US 167/P16
Boulemane, Mor. 110/D2
Boulemane (prov.), Mor. 112/C3
Bouleurs, Fr. 30/L5
Boulgo (prov.), Burk. 115/E4
Boulia, Austl. 131/H2
Boulieu-lès-Annonay, Fr. 64/A2
Bouligny, Fr. 55/E5
Boulkiemde (prov.), Burk. 115/E3
Boullarre, Fr. 30/M4
Boulogne (riv.), Fr. 44/C3
Boulogne-Billancourt, Fr. 30/J5
Boulogne-sur-Mer, Fr. 54/A2
Bouloire, Fr. 57/F5
Boulsa, Burk. 115/E3
Boulsworth (hill), Eng, UK 35/F4
Boumalne, Mor. 110/D3
Boumba (riv.), Camr. 120/C2
Boûmdeïd, Mrta. 114/C2
Boumerdas (wilaya), Alg. 112/G4
Boumerdes, Alg. 112/G4
Boun Nua, Laos 86/D4
Bouna, C.d'Iv. 114/E4
Bound Brook, NJ, US 168/D2
Boundary, Yk, Can. 171/K3
Boundary (peak), Nv, US 142/C4
Boundary Bald (mtn.), Me, US 161/L2
Boundary Bend, Austl. 132/B2
Boundiali, C.d'Iv. 114/D4
Boundji, Congo 120/C3
Bountiful, Ut, US 147/H3
Boupanda, Congo 120/C3
Bouquet (res.), Ca, US 166/B1
Bouquet (canyon), Ca, US 166/B2
Bourail, NCal. 137/U12
Bourbeuse (riv.), Mo, US 155/J4
Bourbon, In, US 160/C4
Bourbon, Mo, US 153/J1
Bourbon l'Archambault, Fr. 44/E3
Bourbonnais, Il, US 160/C4
Bourbonnais (reg.), Fr. 66/D1
Bourbonne-les-Bains, Fr. 60/B2
Bourbourg, Fr. 54/B2
Bourbre (riv.), Fr. 64/B1
Bourbriac, Fr. 56/B4
Bourdonné, Fr. 30/G5
Boureït, Mor. 112/B2
Bourem, Mali 115/E2
Bouressa (riv.), Mali 115/F2
Bourg, La, US 164/C3
Bourg-Achard, Fr. 57/F2
Bourg-de-Péage, Fr. 64/B2
Bourg-en-Bresse, Fr. 60/B5
Bourg-lès-Valence, Fr. 64/A3
Bourg-Saint-Andéol, Fr. 64/A4
Bourg-Saint-Maurice, Fr. 64/C1
Bourg-Saint-Pierre, Swi. 60/D6
Bourganeuf, Fr. 44/D4
Bourges, Fr. 44/E3
Bourget (lake), Fr. 60/B6
Bourgneuf (bay), Fr. 44/B3
Bourgogne (canal), Fr. 60/B3
Bourgogne (pol. reg.), Fr. 44/F3
Bourgoin-Jallieu, Fr. 64/B1
Bourgtheroulde-Infreville, Fr. 57/F2
Bourgueil, Fr. 57/F6
Bourke, Austl. 132/C1
Bourmont, Fr. 60/B1
Bourne (riv.), Fr. 64/B2
Bourne, Eng, UK 37/F1
Bourne (riv.), Eng, UK 37/E4
Bourne End, Eng, UK 37/F3
Bournemouth, Eng, UK 37/E5
Bournemouth (co.), Eng, UK 37/E5
Bournemouth (arpt.), Eng, UK 37/E5
Bournville, Eng, UK 37/E2
Bourquin (hill), Ne, US 154/D3
Bourscheid, Lux. 55/F4
Bourtanger Moor (reg.), Ger. 53/E3
Bourth, Fr. 57/F3
Bourton on the Water, Eng, UK 37/E3
Bousbecque, Fr. 54/C2
Bouse, Az, US 149/E4
Bousso, Chad 116/C3
Boussois, Fr. 54/D3
Boussouma, Burk. 115/E3
Boutilimit, Mrta. 114/B2
Bouvard (cape), Austl. 130/B5
Bouvet (isl.), Nor. 27/K8
Bouvron, Fr. 56/D6
Bouxières-aux-Dames, Fr. 55/F6
Bouxwiller, Fr. 55/G6
Bouza, Niger 115/G3
Bouzillé, Fr. 57/D6
Bouznika, Mor. 112/A3
Bouzonville, Fr. 55/F5
Bovalino, It. 48/E3
Bovegno, It. 62/D2
Boven Tapanahoni (riv.), Sur. 181/H4
Boven Tappanahoni (riv.), Sur. 182/C2
Boven-Hardinxveld, Neth. 52/B5
Bovenden, Ger. 53/G5
Bovenkarspel, Neth. 52/C3
Bovenwijde (lake), Neth. 52/D3
Boves, Fr. 54/B4
Boves, It. 64/D4
Bovey, Mn, US 157/H4
Bovey Tracey, Eng, UK 36/C5
Bovezzo, It. 62/D2
Bovina, Tx, US 152/C3
Bovingdon, Eng, UK 30/B1
Bovino, It. 50/B5
Bovolone, It. 63/E3
Bovril, Arg. 188/E4
Bow (riv.), Ab, Can. 140/E3
Bow (cr.), Ks, US 154/E4
Bow (riv.), Ab, Can. 145/H2
Bow City, Ab, Can. 145/H2
Bow Island, Ab, Can. 145/J3
Bow River Abor. Land, Austl. 128/B4
Bowbells, ND, US 156/C3
Bowdle, SD, US 156/E5
Bowdoin NWR, Mt, US 145/L3
Bowdon, ND, US 156/E4
Bowdon, Eng, UK 35/F5
Bowdon, Ga, US 162/E4
Bowen, Austl. 134/C3
Bowen, Arg. 190/D2
Bowen Island, BC, Can. 144/C3
Bowers Beach, De, US 168/C5
Bowes, Eng, UK 35/G3
Bowie, Tx, US 153/F4
Bowie, Az, US 149/H4
Bowie, Md, US 168/B6
Bowling Green, Oh, US 160/E4
Bowling Green, Fl, US 164/M8
Bowling Green (cape), Austl. 134/B2
Bowling Green, Ky, US 162/D2
Bowling Green, Mo, US 155/J4
Bowling Green, Va, US 163/J1
Bowling Green Bay NP, Austl. 134/B2
Bowman, ND, US 156/C4
Bowman (bay), Nun, Can. 141/J2
Bowman, Ga, US 163/F3
Bowman (mt.), BC, Can. 144/D2
Bowman-Haley (dam), ND, US 156/C5
Bowman-Haley (lake), ND, US 156/C4
Bowmansdale, Pa, US 168/B3
Bowmanstown, Pa, US 168/C2
Bowmansville, Pa, US 168/B3
Bowmanville, On, Can. 160/V8
Bowmore, Sc, UK 31/Q9
Bowness-on-Solway, Eng, UK 35/E2
Bowokan (isls.), Indo. 91/F4
Bowral, Austl. 133/E2
Bowring, Ok, US 153/F2
Bowron (riv.), BC, Can. 144/D1
Bowsman, Mb, Can. 156/D1
Bowutu (mts.), PNG 129/G1
Bowwood, Zam. 122/E3
Box Elder (riv.), Mt, US 156/B5
Box Elder (cr.), SD, US 154/C3
Box Elder (cr.), Co, US 154/B3
Box Elder, SD, US 154/C1
Box Elder, Mt, US 145/J3
Box Hill (nbrhd.), Austl. 132/G5
Box Springs, Ga, US 162/E4
Boxberg, Ger. 58/C4
Boxelder, Wy, US 154/B2
Boxholm, Swe. 40/F2
Boxing, China 80/D3
Boxley, Ar, US 153/H3
Boxmeer, Neth. 52/C5
Boxodoi, China 78/H3
Boxtel, Neth. 52/C5
Boxum, Neth. 52/C2
Boyabat, Turk. 70/E4
Boyabo, D.R. Congo 120/D2
Boyabo, D.R. Congo 116/C5
Boyaca (dept.), Col. 180/C3
Boyalık, Turk. 103/M6
Boyanup, Austl. 130/B5
Boyarka, Ukr. 72/F2
Boyce, La, US 164/B2
Boychinovtsi, Bul. 51/F4
Boyd, Tx, US 150/K6
Boydell, Ar, US 153/J4
Boyds, Wa, US 144/E3
Boydton, Va, US 163/H2
Boye, China 80/C3
Boyer (riv.), Ia, US 155/G2
Boyero, Co, US 154/C4
Boyertown, Pa, US 168/C3
Boyes, Mt, US 154/B1
Boyette, Fl, US 164/L8
Boykins, Va, US 163/J2
Boyle, Ire. 32/B2
Boyle, Ms, US 162/B4
Boyne (riv.), Ire. 34/B4
Boyne City, Mi, US 160/D2
Boyne Falls, Mi, US 160/D2
Boyne Island, Austl. 134/C3
Boynton, Ok, US 153/G3
Boynton Beach, Fl, US 164/P9
Boysen (res.), Wy, US 147/J2
Boysen (dam), Wy, US 147/J2
Boyuibe, Bol. 188/D2
Boyup Brook, Austl. 130/C5
Boz (pt.), Turk. 51/J5
Bozcaada, Turk. 49/K3
Bozcaada (isl.), Gre. 49/J3
Bozel, Fr. 64/C2
Bozeman, Mt, US 147/H1
Bozhai, China 87/F3
Bozkir, Turk. 102/C2
Bozkurt, Turk. 70/E4
Bozman, Md, US 168/B6
Bozoum, CAfr. 116/C4
Bozova, Turk. 102/D2
Bozüyük, Turk. 104/E1
Bozyazı, Turk. 104/C1
Bozzolo, It. 62/D3
Bra, It. 62/A3
Braan (riv.), Sc, UK 33/C3
Bråån (riv.), Swe. 39/K7
Brabourne Lees, Eng, UK 37/G4
Brač (isl.), Cro. 48/E1
Bracciano (lake), It. 48/B1
Bracciano, It. 65/B3
Bracebridge, On, Can. 161/G2
Bracieux, Fr. 57/G5
Bracigliano, It. 65/D6
Brackel, Ger. 53/H2
Bracken, Sk, Can. 145/K3
Brackenheim, Ger. 58/C4
Brackett, Wi, US 155/J1
Brackettville, Tx, US 150/D3
Brackley, Eng, UK 37/E2
Bracknagh, Ire. 32/C3
Bracknell, Eng, UK 37/F4
Bracknell Forest (co.), Eng, UK 37/F4
Brackwede, Ger. 53/F5
Braço do Norte, Braz. 189/G4
Braço Menor do Araguaia (riv.), Braz. 186/C2
Brad, Rom. 51/F2
Bradano (riv.), It. 50/B5
Bradda (pt.), IM, UK 34/D3
Braddock, ND, US 156/D4
Braden, Tn, US 162/C3
Bradenton, Fl, US 165/G4
Bradford, Eng, UK 35/G4
Bradford (co.), Eng, UK 35/G4
Bradford, Ar, US 153/J3
Bradford, Oh, US 160/D4
Bradford, Pa, US 161/G4
Bradford, Vt, US 161/K3
Bradford West Gwillimbury, On, Can. 161/G2
Bradford-on-Avon, Eng, UK 36/D4
Brading, Eng, UK 37/E5
Bradley, Wi, US 157/K5
Bradley, Ar, US 153/H4
Bradley (int'l arpt.), Ct, US 161/K4
Bradley, Il, US 160/C4
Bradley, Ca, US 148/B3
Bradley Beach, NJ, US 168/D3
Bradley Junction, Fl, US 164/M8
Bradner, Oh, US 160/E4
Brady, Mt, US 145/J3
Brady, Ne, US 154/D3
Brady, Tx, US 150/E2
Brady (cr.), Tx, US 150/E2
Braeburn, Yk, Can. 171/L3
Braemar (reg.), Sc, UK 33/C2
Braemar, Sc, UK 33/C2
Braeriach (peak), Sc, UK 33/C2
Braga, Port. 46/A2
Braga (dist.), Port. 46/A2
Bragado, Arg. 190/E2
Bragança, Port. 46/B2
Bragança (dist.), Port. 46/B2
Bragança, Braz. 183/E3
Bragança Paulista, Braz. 187/K7
Bragg Creek, Ab, Can. 144/G2
Braggs, Ok, US 153/G3
Bragin, Bela. 72/F2
Braham, Mn, US 157/H5
Brahmakund, India 86/C3
Brāhmanbāria, Bang. 97/H4
Brahmaputra (riv.), Asia 77/J7
Braich-y-Pwll (pt.), Wal, UK 34/D6
Braid (riv.), NI, UK 34/B2
Braidwood, Il, US 160/B4
Braidwood, Austl. 133/D2
Brăila, Rom. 51/H3
Brăila (prov.), Rom. 51/H3
Brainard, Ne, US 155/F3
Brainards, NJ, US 168/C2
Braine, Fr. 54/C5
Braine-l'Alleud, Belg. 55/D2
Braine-le-Comte, Belg. 55/D2
Brainerd, Mn, US 157/G4
Braintree, Eng, UK 37/G3
Braithwaithe (pt.), Austl. 128/D2
Brajarajnagar, India 95/D1
Brak (riv.), SAfr. 124/C3
Brak (riv.), SAfr. 124/D3
Brake, Ger. 53/F2
Brakel, Belg. 54/C2
Brakel, Ger. 53/G5
Brakel, Neth. 52/C5
Brakna (pol. reg.), Mrta. 114/B2
Brålanda, Swe. 40/E2
Bralorne, BC, Can. 144/C2
Bram (peak), It. 64/D4
Bram, Fr. 44/E5
Bramalea, On, Can. 160/T8
Braman, Ok, US 153/F2
Bramdrupdam, Den. 40/C4
Bramhope, Eng, UK 35/G4
Bramley, Eng, UK 30/B3
Bramley (mtn.), NY, US 161/J3
Brampton, Eng, UK 35/F2
Brampton, On, Can. 160/T8
Bramsche, Ger. 53/F4
Bramstedt, Ger. 53/F2
Bran (riv.), Sc, UK 33/A1
Branam, Gha. 115/E5
Brancaleone-Marina, It. 48/E4
Brancepeth, Sk, Can. 145/M1
Branch, Mn, US 157/H5
Branch, Nf, Can. 159/L2
Branch, La, US 164/B2
Branch Dale, Pa, US 168/B2
Branch, North (riv.), Md, US 168/B5
Branch, South (riv.), WV, US 163/H1
Branchville, NJ, US 168/D1
Branchville, Ct, US 169/E1
Branco (riv.), Braz. 179/C2
Brand, Aus. 61/F3
Brandberg (peak), Namb. 122/B4
Brandbu, Nor. 40/D1
Brande, Den. 40/C4
Brandenburg, Ger. 42/G2
Brandenburg (state), Ger. 42/P6
Brandenburg, Ky, US 162/D2
Brander, Pass of (pass), Sc, UK 33/A4
Branderburgh, Sc, UK 33/C1
Brandesburton, Eng, UK 35/H4
Brandfort, SAfr. 124/D3
Brandizzo, It. 62/A2
Brandon, Mb, Can. 156/E3
Brandon (peak), Ire. 32/D5
Brandon, Eng, UK 35/G2
Brandon, Eng, UK 37/G2
Brandon, Co, US 152/C1
Brandon, Fl, US 164/L8
Brandon, Mn, US 157/G5
Brandon, Ms, US 162/C4
Brandon, SD, US 155/F2
Brandon, Vt, US 161/K3
Brandsen, Arg. 191/J11
Brandsville, Mo, US 153/J2
Brandvlei, SAfr. 124/C3
Brandýs nad Labem, Czh. 59/H2
Brandywine, Md, US 168/B6
Brandywine (riv.), Pa, US 168/C4
Brandywine, WV, US 163/H1
Branford, Ct, US 169/F1
Branford, Fl, US 165/G3
Branges, Fr. 60/B4
Braniewo, Pol. 41/H4
Brannenburg, Ger. 45/K3
Bransgore, Eng, UK 37/E5
Branson, Mo, US 153/H2
Brant (co.), On, Can. 160/S9
Brant Beach, NJ, US 168/D4
Brantford, On, Can. 160/S9
Branti, Indo. 89/D4
Brantley, Al, US 165/E2
Brantwood, Wi, US 157/J5
Branxholm, Austl. 132/C4
Branxholme, Austl. 132/B3
Branxton, Austl. 133/E1
Branxton, Eng, UK 33/D5
Branzoll (Bronzolo), It. 61/H4
Brasfield, Ar, US 153/J3
Brashear, Mo, US 155/H3
Brasher Falls-Winthrop, NY, US 161/J2
Brasiléia, Braz. 184/D3
Brasília (cap.), Braz. 186/D2
Brasília de Minas, Braz. 186/D3
Brasilia, PN de, Braz. 186/C2
Braşov, Rom. 51/G3
Braşov (prov.), Rom. 51/G3
Brass, Nga. 115/G5
Brasschaat, Belg. 52/B6
Brassey (mt.), Austl. 131/G2
Brasstown Bald (peak), Ga, US 162/F3
Brastad, Swe. 40/D2
Braswell, Ga, US 162/E4
Brat (isl.), Cro. 67/H2
Bratislava (cap.), Slvk. 50/C1
Bratislava (Ivanka) (int'l arpt.), Slvk. 50/C1
Bratislavský (pol. reg.), Slvk. 43/J4
Bratsigovo, Bul. 49/J1
Bratsk, Rus. 75/L4
Brats'ke, Ukr. 72/F4
Bratslav, Ukr. 72/E3
Brattleboro, Vt, US 161/K3
Bratunac, Bosn. 50/D3
Braubach, Ger. 55/G3
Braulio Carrillo, PN, CR 172/E5
Braunau am Inn, Aus. 59/G6
Braunfels, Ger. 58/B1
Braunlage, Ger. 53/H5
Bräunlingen, Ger. 61/E2
Braunschweig, Ger. 53/H4
Braunschweig (arpt.), Ger. 53/H4
Braunton, Eng, UK 36/B4
Brava (coast), Sp. 47/G2
Brava (pt.), Chile 191/C7
Brava (isl.), CpV. 107/J11
Brava (pt.), Uru. 191/K11
Brave, Pa, US 160/F5
Bråviken (inlet), Swe. 40/G2
Bravo (peak), Bol. 188/C1
Bravo (peak), Peru 184/B2
Bravo del Norte (riv.), Mex. 172/A2
Brawley, Ca, US 148/E4
Bray (pt.), Ire. 34/B5
Bray, Ire. 34/B5
Bray, Eng, UK 30/A2
Bray (isl.), Nun, Can. 141/J2
Bray-Dunes, Fr. 54/B1
Braye (riv.), Fr. 44/D3
Braymer, Mo, US 155/H4
Brazeau (riv.), Ab, Can. 144/F1
Brazeau (mt.), Ab, Can. 144/F1
Brazey-en-Plaine, Fr. 60/B3
Brazil, In, US 160/C5
Brazil (ctry.) 179/D3
Brazil, Tn, US 162/C3
Brazilian Highlands (uplands), Braz. 179/E4
Brazo Casiquiare (riv.), Ven. 181/E4
Brazo Sur (riv.), Arg. 191/C6
Brazópolis, Braz. 187/L7
Brazoria (co.), Tx, US 151/M9
Brazoria NWR, Tx, US 151/G3
Brazos (riv.), US 139/H6
Brazos, Double Mountain Fork (riv.), Tx, US 152/D4
Brazos, Salt Fork (riv.), Tx, US 152/D4
Brazzaville (cap.), Congo 120/C4
Brčko, Bosn. 50/D3
Brda (riv.), Pol. 40/G5
Brdy (mts.), Czh. 43/G4
Brea, Ca, US 166/G8
Breadalbane (dist.), Sc, UK 33/B4
Breakenridge (mt.), BC, Can. 144/D3
Bream (pt.), NZ 135/C1
Bream, Eng, UK 36/D3
Bream Tail (pt.), NZ 135/C2
Breamish (riv.), Eng, UK 33/D6
Bréancon, Fr. 30/J4
Bréau, Fr. 30/L6
Breaux Bridge, La, US 164/C2
Breaza, Rom. 51/G3
Brebbia, It. 62/B2
Brebes, Indo. 89/E4
Brécey, Fr. 57/D3
Brech, Fr. 56/C5
Brêche (riv.), Fr. 54/B5
Brechen, Ger. 58/B2
Brechin, Sc, UK 33/D3
Brecht, Belg. 52/B6
Breckenridge, Mn, US 156/F4
Breckenridge, Mo, US 155/H4
Breckenridge, Tx, US 151/E1
Breckerfeld, Ger. 53/E6
Breckland (phys. reg.), Eng, UK 37/G2
Brecknock (pen.), Chile 191/C7
Brecon, Wal, UK 36/C3
Brecon Beacons (mts.), Wal, UK 36/C3
Bréda (riv.), Fr. 64/C2
Breda, Neth. 52/B5
Bredaryd, Swe. 40/E3
Bredasdorp, SAfr. 124/M11
Bredbo, Austl. 133/D2
Bredebro, Den. 40/C4
Bredene, Belg. 54/B1
Bredgar, Eng, UK 30/F3
Bredstedt, Ger. 40/C4
Bree, Belg. 55/E1
Breë (riv.), SAfr. 124/B4
Breeches (cr.), Pa, US 168/A3
Breed, Wi, US 157/K5
Breese, Il, US 162/C1
Breezand, Neth. 52/B3
Breezy Point, Mn, US 157/G4
Breg (riv.), Ger. 42/E5
Bregagno (peak), It. 61/F5
Bregalinca (riv.), FYROM 49/H2
Breganze, It. 63/E2
Bregenz, Aus. 61/F3
Bregenzer Ache (riv.), Aus. 61/F3
Bregovo, Bul. 50/F3
Brégy, Fr. 30/L4
Bréhal, Fr. 56/D3
Breidhafjördhur (bay), Ice. 38/M6
Breil-Brigels, Swi. 61/F4
Breil-sur-Roya, Fr. 64/D5
Breisach, Ger. 60/D1
Breitbrunn am Chiemsee, Ger. 59/F7
Breitenauriegel (peak), Ger. 59/G5
Breitenbach, Swi. 60/D3
Breitenbach, Ger. 55/G5
Breitenbrunn, Ger. 59/E4
Breitenbrunn, Ger. 59/F2
Breitenfurt bei Wien, Aus. 51/N7
Breitenworbis, Ger. 53/H6
Breithorn (peak), Swi. 60/D5
Breithorn (peak), Swi. 60/D6
Brejinho de Nazaré, Braz. 186/C1
Brejo, Braz. 183/F3
Brejo do Cruz, Braz. 183/G4
Brejo Santo, Braz. 183/G4
Brembate di Sopra, It. 62/C2
Brembilla, It. 62/C2
Brembio, It. 62/C3
Brembo (riv.), It. 61/F6
Bremen, Ger. 53/F2
Bremen (int'l arpt.), Ger. 53/F2
Bremen (state), Ger. 40/C5
Bremen, Ga, US 162/E4
Bremen, In, US 160/C4
Bremen, Oh, US 160/E5
Bremer (riv.), Austl. 134/E7
Bremerhaven, Ger. 53/F1
Bremerhaven (arpt.), Ger. 53/F1
Bremerton, Wa, US 144/C4
Bremervörde, Ger. 53/G2
Bremgarten, Swi. 61/E3
Bremgarten bei Bern, Swi. 60/D4
Bremnes, Nor. 40/A2
Bremond, Tx, US 151/F2
Bremsa (riv.), Nor. 38/R8
Brenchley, Eng, UK 30/E3
Brend (riv.), Ger. 58/D2
Brendel (lake), Mi, US 167/E7
Brendola, It. 63/E3
Brendon (hills), Eng, UK 36/C4
Brenham, Tx, US 151/F2
Brenne (riv.), Fr. 42/C5
Brenner (pass), Aus. 61/H4
Brenner (riv.), Austl. 131/N9
Brenno (riv.), Swi. 61/E5
Breno, It. 61/G6
Brent, On, Can. 161/G1
Brent (riv.), Eng, UK 30/B2
Brent (bor.), Eng, UK 30/C2
Brent (res.), Eng, UK 30/C2
Brent, Al, US 162/D4
Brenta (peak), It. 61/G5
Brenta (riv.), It. 45/J4
Brenton, WV, US 163/G2
Brentwood, Eng, UK 30/D2
Brentwood, Ca, US 167/L11
Brentwood, Tn, US 162/D2
Brentwood, NY, US 169/E2
Brenz (riv.), Ger. 58/D5
Brescello, It. 62/D4
Brescia (prov.), It. 61/G6
Brescia, It. 62/D2
Breskens, Neth. 54/C1
Breslau, Tx, US 151/F3
Bresle (riv.), Fr. 44/D1
Bresles, Fr. 54/B5
Bresque (riv.), Fr. 64/C5
Bressana, It. 62/C3
Bressanone, It. 45/J3
Bressay (isl.), Sc, UK 31/W13
Bressuire, Fr. 44/C3
Brest, Bela. 43/M2
Brest (int'l arpt.), Bela. 43/M2
Brest, Fr. 56/A4
Brestskaya Voblasts, Bela. 70/C1
Bretagne (pt.), Fr. 125/T15
Bretagne (pol. reg.), Fr. 44/B2
Bretagne, Monts de (mts.), Fr. 44/B2
Bretaña, Peru 184/C2
Breteuil, Fr. 57/F3
Breteuil, Fr. 54/B4
Brethren, Mi, US 160/C2
Brétigny-sur-Orge, Fr. 30/J6
Breton, Ab, Can. 144/G1
Breton (cape), NS, Can. 159/H3
Breton (isls.), La, US 164/D3
Breton (sound), La, US 164/D3
Breton Cove, NS, Can. 159/G2
Breton Nat'l Wild. Ref., La, US 164/D3
Brett (cape), NZ 135/C1
Brett (riv.), Eng, UK 37/G2
Brettach (riv.), Ger. 58/C4
Bretten, Ger. 58/B4
Bretteville-L'Orgueilleuse, Fr. 57/E2
Bretzenheim, Ger. 55/G4
Breuberg, Ger. 58/C3
Breueh (isl.), Indo. 89/A1
Breugel, Neth. 52/C5
Breuillet, Fr. 30/J6
Breukelen, Neth. 52/B4
Breuna, Ger. 53/G6
Breuvannes-en-Bassigny, Fr. 60/B1
Brevard, NC, US 163/F3
Breves, Braz. 182/D3
Brevig Mission, Ak, US 171/E2
Brevik, Nor. 40/C2
Brevik, Swe. 39/B1
Brevoort (isl.), Nun, Can. 141/K2
Brewarrina, Austl. 132/C1
Brewer, Mo, US 162/C2
Brewerton, NY, US 161/H3
Brewerville, Libr. 114/C5
Brewood, Eng, UK 36/D1
Brewster (cape), Austl. 128/B3
Brewster (lake), Austl. 133/C1
Brewster, Fl, US 164/M8
Brewster, Ks, US 154/D4
Brewster, Mn, US 155/G2
Brewster, Ne, US 154/E3
Brewster, Oh, US 160/F4
Brewster, Wa, US 144/E3
Brewton, Al, US 164/E2
Brey-et-Lû, Fr. 30/G4
Breyten, SAfr. 125/E2
Brežice, Slov. 50/B3
Brezina, Alg. 111/F2
Březnice, Czh. 59/G3
Breznik, Bul. 50/F4
Brezoi, Rom. 51/G3
Brézolles, Fr. 57/G3
Brezovo, Bul. 51/G4
Bria, CAfr. 116/D4
Briançon, Fr. 64/C3
Briar Creek, Pa, US 168/B1
Briare, Fr. 44/E3
Bribbaree, Austl. 133/C2
Bric de Rubren (peak), Fr. 64/C3
Bric Rosso (peak), It. 64/D3
Brice, Tx, US 152/D3
Briceni, Mol. 72/D3
Brickerville, Pa, US 168/B3
Bricket Wood, Eng, UK 30/B1
Brickley (brook), Austl. 130/L7
Bricktown, NJ, US 168/D3
Bricquebec, Fr. 56/D2
Bridal Cave, Mo, US 153/H1
Bridal Veil (falls), Co, US 149/J2
Bride, IM, UK 34/D3
Bride (riv.), Ire. 32/B5
Bridge, Id, US 147/G2
Bridge (riv.), BC, Can. 144/C2
Bridge City, Tx, US 151/H2
Bridge of Allan, Sc, UK 33/C4
Bridge of Don, Sc, UK 33/D2
Bridge of Weir, Sc, UK 33/B5
Bridgehampton, NY, US 169/F2
Bridgeman (mtn.), Ky, US 162/E2
Bridgend, Wal, UK 36/C3
Bridgend (co.), Wal, UK 36/C3
Bridgeport, Ca, US 146/D4
Bridgeport, Ct, US 169/E1
Bridgeport, Il, US 162/D1
Bridgeport, Mi, US 160/E3
Bridgeport, Ne, US 154/C3
Bridgeport, NJ, US 168/C4
Bridgeport, Tx, US 150/K6
Bridgeport (lake), Tx, US 151/F1
Bridgeport, Wa, US 144/E3
Bridgeport, WV, US 160/F5
Bridger, Mt, US 147/J1
Bridgeton, NJ, US 168/C5
Bridgetown, Ire. 32/D5
Bridgetown, NS, Can. 158/E3
Bridgetown, Oh, US 162/E1
Bridgetown, Austl. 130/C5
Bridgetown (cap.), Bar. 173/P9
Bridgeville, Qu, Can. 158/E1
Bridgeville, Ca, US 146/B3
Bridgeville, De, US 168/C6
Bridgewater, Austl. 132/C4
Bridgewater, NS, Can. 158/E3
Bridgewater, Va, US 163/H1
Bridgnorth, Eng, UK 36/D1
Bridgton, Me, US 161/L2
Bridgwater, Eng, UK 36/D4
Bridgwater (bay), Eng, UK 36/C4
Bridlington (bay), Eng, UK 35/H3
Bridlington, Eng, UK 35/H3
Bridport, Austl. 132/C4
Bridport, Eng, UK 36/D5
Bridport, Vt, US 161/K3
Brie (reg.), Fr. 42/B4
Brie-Comte-Robert, Fr. 30/K5
Briec, Fr. 56/A4
Brieg Brzeg, Pol. 43/J3
Brielle, Neth. 52/B5
Brielle, NJ, US 168/D3
Brienz, Swi. 60/E4
Brier (isl.), Ns., Can. 158/D3
Brier (cr.), Ga, US 163/G4
Brier (mtn.), Pa, US 161/H4
Brier, Wa, US 167/C2
Briercrest, Sk, Can. 145/M2
Brierfield, Eng, UK 35/F4
Brieselang, Ger. 42/Q6
Brig, Swi. 60/D5
Brigach (riv.), Ger. 58/B7
Brigantine, NJ, US 168/D5
Brigg, Eng, UK 35/H4
Briggs, Tx, US 150/F2
Briggs Corner, NB, Can. 158/E2
Brigham City, Ut, US 147/G3
Brighouse, Eng, UK 35/G4
Brighstone, Eng, UK 37/E5
Bright, Austl. 133/C3
Brightlingsea, Eng, UK 37/H3
Brighton (nbrhd.), Austl. 131/M9
Brighton (nbrhd.), Austl. 132/G5
Brighton (nbrhd.), Austl. 134/F6
Brighton, On, Can. 161/H2
Brighton, Eng, UK 37/F5
Brighton, Co, US 154/B4
Brighton, Il, US 155/J4
Brighton, Mi, US 160/E3
Brighton, Tn, US 162/C3
Brighton, Wi, US 167/P14
Brighton and Hove (co.), Eng, UK 37/F5
Brightons, Sc, UK 33/C5
Brignais, Fr. 64/A1
Brignoles, Fr. 64/C6
Brihante (riv.), Braz. 189/F2
Brihuega, Sp. 46/D2
Briis-sous-Forges, Fr. 30/J6
Brikama, Gam. 114/A3
Brilhante (riv.), Braz. 186/B4
Brill, Eng, UK 37/E3
Brillion, Wi, US 160/B2
Brilon, Ger. 53/F6
Brimington, Eng, UK 35/G5
Brimley, Mi, US 160/D1
Brimstone Hill NP, StK. 173/N8
Brindisi, It. 49/E2
Brinkley, Ar, US 153/J3
Brinkmann, Arg. 188/D4
Brinktown, Mo, US 153/H1
Brinkworth, Austl. 131/H5
Brinkworth, Eng, UK 36/E3
Brinnon, Wa, US 167/B2
Brinson, Ga, US 165/F2
Briny Breezes, Fl, US 164/P9
Brion (isl.), Qu, Can. 159/G2
Brión, Sp. 46/A1
Brione, Swi. 61/E5
Briones (res.), Ca, US 167/K11
Brionne, Fr. 57/F2
Briouze, Fr. 57/E3
Brisbane, Austl. 134/F6
Brisbane (int'l arpt.), Austl. 134/F6
Brisbane (riv.), Austl. 134/E7
Brisbane Forest Park, Austl. 134/E6
Brisbane Ranges NP, Austl. 133/B3
Brisbane Water, Austl. 133/E1
Brisbane Water NP, Austl. 133/E1
Brisco, BC, Can. 144/F2
Brisighella, It. 63/E5
Brissago, Swi. 61/E5
Bristol, NB, Can. 158/D2
Bristol, Qu, Can. 161/H2
Bristol, Eng, UK 36/D4
Bristol (co.), Eng, UK 36/D4
Bristol (chan.), Eng, Wal, UK 36/B4
Bristol (bay), Ak, US 171/F4
Bristol (lake), Ca, US 148/E3
Bristol, Co, US 152/C1
Bristol, Ct, US 161/K4
Bristol, Fl, US 165/F2
Bristol, Ga, US 165/G2
Bristol, NH, US 161/L3
Bristol, Pa, US 168/D3
Bristol, RI, US 161/L4
Bristol, SD, US 156/F5
Bristol, Tn, US 163/F2
Bristol, Tx, US 150/L7
Bristol, Vt, US 161/K2
Bristolville, Oh, US 160/F4
Bristow, Ok, US 153/F3
Britânia, Braz. 186/C2
British (mts.), Ak, US 171/K2
British Columbia (prov.), Can. 140/D3
British Empire (range), Nun, Can. 141/S6
British Indian Ocean Terr. (terr.), UK 77/G10
British Mountains (range), Can.,Ak, US 171/K2
British Museum, Eng, UK 30/C2
Brits, SAfr. 123/E5
Britstown, SAfr. 124/C3
Britt, Ia, US 155/H2
Brittany (reg.), Fr. 44/B3
Britton, SD, US 156/F5
Britton, Tx, US 150/K7
Brive-la-Gaillarde, Fr. 44/D4
Brives-Charensac, Fr. 44/E4
Briviesca, Sp. 44/B5
Brivio, It. 62/C2
Brixham, Eng, UK 36/C6
Brixworth, Eng, UK 37/F2
Brlik, Kaz. 99/B3
Brněnský (pol. reg.), Czh. 43/J4
Beneěov, Czh. 59/H3
Brnik (int'l arpt.), Slov. 45/L3
Brno, Czh. 43/J4
Broa (bay), Cuba 177/F1
Broad (riv.), Ga, US 163/F4
Broad Arrow, Austl. 130/D4
Broad Law (peak), Sc, UK 33/C6
Broad Sound (isls.), Austl. 134/C2
Broad Street, Eng, UK 30/E3
Broad Valley, Mb, Can. 156/F2
Broadacres, Sk, Can. 145/K1
Broadbent, Or, US 146/A2
Broaddus, Tx, US 151/G2
Broadford, Ire. 32/B5
Broadford, Austl. 133/B3
Broadkill (riv.), De, US 168/C6
Broadley Common, Eng, UK 30/D1
Broadmeadows (nbrhd.), Austl. 132/F5
Broadstairs, Eng, UK 37/H4
Broadstone, Eng, UK 36/E5
Broadus, Mt, US 154/B1
Broadview, Mt, US 145/K4
Broadwater, Ne, US 154/C3
Broadwater NP, Austl. 132/E1
Broadway (hill), Eng, UK 37/E3
Broadway, NJ, US 168/C2
Broadwindsor, Eng, UK 36/D5
Broby, Swe. 39/L6
Broc, Swi. 60/D4
Brocēni, Lat. 41/K3
Brochet, Mb, Can. 140/F3
Brock (isl.), NW, Can. 141/R7
Brock, Sk, Can. 145/K2
Brocken (peak), Ger. 53/H5
Brockenhurst, Eng, UK 37/E5
Brocket, ND, US 156/E3
Brocket, Ab, Can. 145/H3
Brockman (mt.), Austl. 130/C2
Brockport, NY, US 161/H3
Brockton, Mt, US 156/B3
Brockton, Ma, US 161/L3
Brockville, On, Can. 161/J2
Brockway, Pa, US 161/G4
Brocton, NY, US 161/G3
Brodeur (pen.), Nun, Can. 140/G1
Brodhead, Wi, US 155/K2
Brodhead (cr.), Pa, US 168/C1
Brodheadsville, Pa, US 168/C2
Brodick, Sc, UK 33/A5

Byala, Bul. 51/G4
Byala, Bul. 51/H4
Byala Slatina, Bul. 51/F4
Byam Martin (isl.), Nun, Can. 141/R7
Byam Martin (chan.), Nun, Can. 141/R7
Byarezina (riv.), Bela. 68/E5
Byaroza, Bela. 70/C1
Byars, Ok, US 153/F3
Bydgoszcz, Pol. 43/J2
Byemoor, Ab, Can. 145/H2
Byers, Ks, US 152/E2
Byesville, Oh, US 160/F5
Byfield, Eng, UK 37/E2
Byfleet, Eng, UK 30/B3
Byford, Austl. 130/L7
Bygland, Nor. 40/B2
Bykhov, Bela. 41/P5
Bykle, Nor. 40/B2
Bykovo, Rus. 71/H2
Bykovo (int'l arpt.), Rus. 69/X9
Bykovskiy, Rus. 75/N2
Bylas, Az, US 149/G4
Bylchau, Wal, UK 34/E5
Bylot (isl.), Can. 139/K2
Bylot (isl.), Nun, Can. 141/J1
Byng, Ok, US 153/F3
Byng Inlet, On, Can. 160/F2
Bynum, Tx, US 151/F2
Bynum, Mt, US 145/H4
Bynum Run (riv.), Md, US 168/B4
Byram (lake), NY, US 169/L7
Byram (pt.), Ct, US 169/L8
Byram (riv.), Ct, US 169/E1
Byrd (cape), Ant. 192/U
Byrd, US, Ant. 192/S
Byrdstown, Tn, US 162/E2
Byremo, Nor. 40/B2
Byrock, Austl. 132/C1
Byromville, Ga, US 162/F4
Byron, Ca, US 167/L11
Byron, Il, US 155/K2
Byron, Ga, US 162/F4
Byron (isl.), Chile 191/B5
Byron Bay, Austl. 134/D5
Byrranga (mts.), Rus. 74/K2
Byrum, Den. 40/D3
Bystice (riv.), Czh. 59/F2
Bystrá (peak), Slvk. 43/K4
Bystřice, Czh. 59/H3
Bytantay (riv.), Rus. 75/N3
Bytom, Pol. 43/K3
Bytów, Pol. 40/G4
Byumba, Rwa. 121/G3

C

C (canal), Co, US 149/H1
C.F. Secada (int'l arpt.), Peru 184/C1
C.J. Strike (res.), Id, US 146/E2
C.J. Strike (dam), Id, US 146/E2
C.W. McConaughy (lake), Ne, US 154/C3
Ca (riv.), Viet. 93/J4
Ca Mau (cape), Viet. 94/D4
Ca Mau, Viet. 94/D4
Caacupé, Par. 189/E3
Caaguazú (dept.), Par. 189/E3
Caaguazú, Par. 189/E3
Caála, Ang. 122/B2
Caatingas (phys. reg.), Braz. 179/E3
Caazapá, Par. 189/E3
Caazapá (dept.), Par. 189/E3
Cabadbaran, Phil. 88/D3
Cabaiguán, Cuba 177/G1
Caballo, NM, US 149/J4
Caballo (res.), NM, US 149/J4
Caballococha, Peru 184/D1
Caban-Coch (res.), Wal, UK 36/C2
Cabana, Peru 184/B3
Cabanaconde, Peru 184/D4
Cabañaquinta, Sp. 46/C1
Cabanatuan, Phil. 88/C2
Cabanes, Sp. 47/F2
Cabannes, Fr. 64/A5
Cabano, Qu, Can. 158/C2
Cabarroguis, Phil. 88/C1
Cabatuan, Phil. 88/C3
Cabedelo, Braz. 183/H4
Cabella Ligure, It. 62/C4
Cabestany, Fr. 44/E5
Cabeza del Buey, Sp. 46/C3
Cabeza Lagarto (pt.), Peru 184/B3
Cabeza Prieta Nat'l. Wild. Ref., Az, US 149/F4
Cabezas, Bol. 188/D1
Cabezón de la Sal, Sp. 46/C1
Cabildo, Arg. 190/E3
Cabimas, Ven. 180/D2
Cabinda, Ang. 120/C4
Cabinda (prov.), Ang. 120/B4
Cabinet (mts.), Mt, US 144/G3
Cabiri, Ang. 120/C5
Cabo, Braz. 183/H5
Cabo Blanco, Arg. 191/D5
Cabo Blanco, Peru 184/A2
Cabo Bojador, WSah. 110/B4
Cabo Corrientes, Cabo (cape), Mex. 174/D4
Cabo de Hornos, PN, Chile 191/D7
Cabo Delgado (prov), Moz. 123/H2
Cabo do Norte (cape), Braz. 182/D2
Cabo Falso (bank), Hon. 177/F3
Cabo Frio, Braz. 187/E4
Cabo Gracias a Dios, Nic. 177/F3
Cabo Orange, PN do, Braz. 182/D2
Cabo San Lucas, Mex. 174/C4
Cabo Verde, Braz. 187/K6
Cabonga (res.), Qu, Can. 141/J4
Cabool, Mo, US 153/H2
Caboolture, Austl. 134/D4
Cabora Bassa (lake), Moz. 123/F2
Cabot, Ar, US 153/H3
Cabot (str.), NS,NF, Can. 141/K4
Cabourg, Fr. 57/E2
Cabra, Sp. 46/C4
Cabra Corral (res.), Arg. 188/C3
Cabra de Santo Cristo, Sp. 46/D4
Cabramatta (nbrhd.), Austl. 134/G8
Cabras, It. 48/A3
Cabrera, Isla de (isl.), Sp. 66/D3
Cabri, Sk, Can. 145/K2
Cabriel (riv.), Sp. 46/E3
Cabriès, Fr. 64/B6
Cabrillo Nat'l Mon., Ca, US 166/C5
Cabrobó, Braz. 183/G5
Cabruta, Ven. 181/E3
Cabudare, Ven. 180/D2
Cabugao, Phil. 88/C1
Cabure, Ven. 180/D2
Caçador, Braz. 189/G3
Čačak, Serb. 50/E4
Cacala, Ang. 122/B1
Cacalotán, Mex. 174/D4
Caçapava, Braz. 187/L8
Caçapava do Sul, Braz. 189/F4
Cacapon (mtn.), WV, US 161/G5
Cacapon (riv.), WV, US 163/H1
Caccia (cape), It. 48/A2
Cacequi, Braz. 189/F4
Cáceres, Col. 180/C3
Cáceres, Sp. 46/B3
Cáceres, Braz. 185/G5
Cachapoal (riv.), Chile 190/N9
Cacharí, Arg. 191/J12
Cache, Ok, US 153/E3
Cache (cr.), Ca, US 146/B4
Cache (peak), Id, US 147/G2
Cache Creek, BC, Can. 144/D2
Cache la Poudre (riv.), Co, US 154/B3
Cache Slough (riv.), Ca, US 167/L10
Cacheu, GBis. 114/A3
Cachicadán, Peru 184/B3
Cachimbo, Serra do (mts.), Braz. 182/B4
Cachingues, Ang. 122/C2
Cachipo, Ven. 181/E2
Cachoeira Alta, Braz. 189/G1
Cachoeira de Minas, Braz. 187/L7
Cachoeira do Arari, Braz. 182/D3
Cachoeira do Sul, Braz. 189/F4
Cachoeira Paulista, Braz. 187/L7
Cachoeiras de Macacu, Braz. 187/P7
Cachoeirinha, Braz. 189/G4
Cachoeiro de Itapemirim, Braz. 187/E4
Cachorras, Col. 180/C4
Cachos (pt.), Chile 188/B3
Cacoal, Braz. 185/F3
Cacolo, Ang. 120/D5
Caconda, Ang. 122/B2
Caconde, Braz. 187/K6
Cacongo, Ang. 120/C4
Caçu, Braz. 186/C3
Cacuaco, Ang. 120/C5
Cacula, Ang. 122/B2
Caculuvar (riv.), Ang. 122/B3
Cacuri, Ven. 181/E3
Cacuso, Ang. 120/C5
Cadaadle, Som. 118/C3
Čadca, Slvk. 43/K4
Caddo (mts.), Ar, US 153/H3
Caddo (riv.), Ar, US 153/H3
Caddo, Ok, US 153/F3
Caddo, Tx, US 151/E1
Caddo Mills, Tx, US 153/F4
Caddo Valley, Ar, US 153/H3
Cadelbosco di Sopra, It. 62/D4
Cadelle (peak), It. 61/F5
Cadenberge, Ger. 53/G1
Cadenet, Fr. 64/B5
Cader Idris (peak), Wal, UK 36/C1
Cadet, Mo, US 162/B2
Cadibarrawirracanna (lake), Austl. 131/G4
Cadillac, Mi, US 160/D2
Cadillac, Sk, Can. 145/L3
Cadiz, Oh, US 160/F4
Cádiz, Sp. 46/B4
Cádiz (gulf), Port.,Sp. 46/B4
Cadiz, Ca, US 148/E3
Cadiz, Ky, US 162/D2
Cadiz (lake), Ca, US 148/E3
Cadiz, Phil. 88/C3
Cadnam, Eng, UK 37/E5
Cadogan, Ab, Can. 145/J1
Cadolzburg, Ger. 58/D4
Cadomin, Ab, Can. 144/F1
Cadott, Wi, US 155/J1
Cadria (peak), It. 61/G6
Cadwell, Ga, US 163/F4
Cadzand-Bad, Neth. 54/C1
Caen, Fr. 57/E2
Caen (bay), Fr. 44/C2
Caerano di San Marco, It. 63/F2
Caerleon, Wal, UK 36/D3
Caernarfon, Wal, UK 34/D5
Caernarfon (bay), Wal, UK 34/D5
Caernarfon Castle, Wal, UK 34/D5
Caerphilly, Wal, UK 36/C3
Caerphilly (co.), Wal, UK 36/C3
Caersws, Wal, UK 36/C1
Caesarea, On, Can. 161/G2
Caesarea NP, Isr. 105/B3
Caeté, Braz. 187/E3
Cafarnaum, Braz. 187/E1
Cafasse, It. 64/D2
Cafayate, Arg. 188/C3
Cagayan (isls.), Phil. 88/C3
Cagayan de Oro, Phil. 88/D3
Cagayan Sulu (isl.), Phil. 88/B4
Cagayancillo, Phil. 88/C3
Cagli, It. 63/F6
Cagliari, It. 48/A3
Cagliari (gulf), It. 66/F3
Cagne (riv.), Fr. 64/D5
Cagnes-sur-Mer, Fr. 64/D5
Cagoyan (riv.), Phil. 88/C1
Cagua, Ven. 183/N7
Caguán (riv.), Col. 180/C4
Caguas, PR 173/M8
Caha (mts.), Ire. 32/A6
Cahaba, Al, US 162/D4
Cahaba (riv.), Al, US 162/D4
Cahama, Ang. 122/B3
Caher, Ire. 32/C5
Caherbarnagh (peak), Ire. 32/A5
Caherconlish, Ire. 32/B4
Cahirsiveen, Ire. 30/N11
Cahokia, Il, US 155/J4
Cahone, Co, US 149/H2
Cahore (pt.), Ire. 32/D4
Cahors, Fr. 44/D4
Cahuacan, Mex. 175/Q9
Cahuapanas, Peru 184/B2
Cahuilla Ind. Res., Ca, US 148/D4
Cahuinari (riv.), Col. 180/D5
Cahuita, PN, CR 177/F4
Cahul, Mol. 51/J3
Cai (riv.), Braz. 189/G4
Cai Nuoc, Viet. 94/D4
Caia, Moz. 123/G3
Caiabis, Serra dos (mts.), Braz. 185/G4
Caianda, Ang. 121/E5
Caiapó (riv.), Braz. 186/C3
Caiapó, Serra (mts.), Braz. 186/B3
Caiapônia, Braz. 186/C3
Caiazzo, It. 65/D5
Caibarién, Cuba 177/G1
Caicara, Ven. 181/F2
Caicara, Ven. 181/E3
Caiçara, Braz. 183/H4
Caicedo, Col. 183/K6
Caicedonia, Col. 183/K8
Caicó, Braz. 183/G4
Caicos (isls.), Uk 173/G3
Caicos Passage (chan.), Bahm. 177/H1
Caieiras, Braz. 187/K8
Caifuche, Ang. 122/D1
Cailloma, Peru 184/D4
Caillou (bay), La, US 164/C3
Caillou (lake), La, US 164/C3
Cailly (riv.), Fr. 54/A4
Caiman (pt.), Phil. 88/B2
Caimbambo, Ang. 122/B2
Cainde, Ang. 122/B2
Caine (riv.), Bol. 188/C1
Cainnyigoin, China 78/E5
Cainsville, Mo, US 155/H3
Cainta, Phil. 88/F6
Caio (peak), It. 62/D5
Caiongo, Ang. 120/C4
Cairate, It. 62/B2
Cairn (mt.), Ak, US 171/G3
Cairn Curran (res.), Austl. 133/A3
Cairn Curran (dam), Austl. 133/A3
Cairn Gorm (peak), Sc, UK 33/C2
Cairn Table (peak), Sc, UK 33/B6
Cairn Toul (peak), Sc, UK 33/C2
Cairndow, Sc, UK 33/B4
Cairngorm (mts.), Sc, UK 33/B2
Cairnryan, Sc, UK 34/C2
Cairns (int'l arpt.), Austl. 134/B2
Cairns, Austl. 134/B2
Cairns (mt.), Austl. 131/G2
Cairnsmore of Carsphairn (peak), Sc, UK 33/B6
Cairo (Al Qāhirah) (cap.), Egypt 113/C4
Cairo (int'l arpt.), Egypt 113/C4
Cairo (peak), It. 65/C4
Cairo, Ga, US 165/F2
Cairo, Il, US 162/C2
Cairo, Mo, US 155/H4
Cairo, Ne, US 154/E3
Cairo Montenotte, It. 62/B5
Caister-on-Sea, Eng, UK 37/H1
Caistor, Eng, UK 35/H5
Caistor Centre, On, Can. 160/T9
Caistorville, On, Can. 160/T9
Caitou, Ang. 122/B2
Caiuana (bay), Braz. 182/D3
Caiundo, Ang. 122/C2
Caixi, China 87/H3
Caiza, Bol. 188/C2
Caizi (lake), China 80/D5
Cajabamba, Ecu. 180/B5
Cajabamba, Peru 184/B2
Cajacay, Peru 184/B3
Cajamarca (ruin), Peru 184/B2
Cajamarca (dept.), Peru 184/B2
Cajamarca, Peru 184/B2
Cajapió, Braz. 183/E3
Cajari, Braz. 183/E3
Cajatambo, Peru 184/B3
Cajazeiras, Braz. 183/G4
Cajibío, Col. 180/B4
Cajidiocan, Phil. 88/C2
Cajón (pt.), Cuba 177/E1
Cajon Junction, Ca, US 166/C2
Cajones (isl.), Nic. 177/F2
Caju (isl.), Braz. 183/F3
Cajuapara (riv.), Braz. 183/E4
Cajuata, Bol. 188/C1
Çal, Turk. 102/B2
Cala d'Oliva, It. 48/A2
Cala, Piombo, Punta di (pt.), It. 66/F3
Calabar (int'l arpt.), Nga. 115/H5
Calabar, Nga. 115/H5
Calabasas, Ca, US 166/B2
Calabash, NC, US 163/H4
Calabozo, Ven. 181/E2
Calabria (pol. reg.), It. 67/H3
Calabria, Parco Nazionale della, It. 48/D3
Calaburras (pt.), Sp. 46/C4
Calaceite, Sp. 47/F2
Calacoto, Bol. 184/D5
Calafat, Rom. 50/F4
Calagua (isls.), Phil. 88/C2
Calahorra, Sp. 46/E1
Calaí, Ang. 122/C3
Calais, Fr. 54/A2
Calais, Me, US 141/K4
Calais, Canal de (canal), Fr. 54/A2
Calama, Braz. 185/F3
Calama, Chile 188/B2
Calamar, Col. 180/C4
Calamar, Col. 180/C2
Calamarca, Bol. 188/B1
Calamba, Ang. 120/C5
Calambrone, It. 62/D6
Calamian Gr. (isls.), Phil. 91/E1
Calamian Group (isls.), Phil. 88/B2
Calamocha, Sp. 46/E2
Calamonte, Sp. 46/B3
Calamus (riv.), Ne, US 154/E2
Călan, Rom. 50/F3
Calañas, Sp. 46/B4
Calanda, Sp. 47/E2
Calang, Indo. 89/A1
Calangianus, It. 48/A2
Calapan, Phil. 88/C2
Calapooia (riv.), Or, US 146/B1
Călărași (prov.), Rom. 51/H3
Călărași, Rom. 51/H3
Călărași, Mol. 72/E4
Calarcá, Col. 183/K8
Calasparra, Sp. 46/E3
Calatayud, Sp. 46/E2
Calatorao, Sp. 46/E2
Calauag, Phil. 88/C2
Calaveras (res.), Ca, US 167/L12
Calaveras (riv.), Ca, US 146/C4
Calavite (cape), Phil. 88/C2
Calavon (riv.), Fr. 64/B5
Calayan (isl.), Phil. 88/C1
Calbayog, Phil. 88/D2
Calberlah, Ger. 53/H4
Calbiga, Phil. 88/D3
Calbuco, Chile 190/B4
Calca, Peru 184/D4
Calcasieu (lake), La, US 151/H3
Calcasieu (riv.), La, US 151/H2
Calceta, Ecu. 180/A5
Calchaquí, Arg. 188/D4
Calchaquí (riv.), Arg. 188/C3
Calci, It. 62/D6
Calcinate, It. 62/C2
Calcinato, It. 62/D3
Calcinelli, It. 63/F6
Calcio, It. 62/C3
Calcium, NY, US 161/J2
Calçoene, Braz. 182/D2
Calcutta, India 97/G4
Calcutta (int'l arpt.), India 97/G4
Calcutta, Sur. 181/H3
Caldaro (Kaltern), It. 45/J3
Caldas (dept.), Col. 180/C3
Caldas, Col. 183/K6
Caldas, Braz. 187/K6
Caldas da Rainha, Port. 46/A3
Caldas Novas, Braz. 186/C3
Caldbeck, Eng, UK 35/E2
Calden, Ger. 53/G6
Calder, Sk, Can. 156/D2
Calder (riv.), Eng, UK 35/F4
Calder (mt.), Ak, US 171/M4
Caldera, Chile 188/B3
Calderara di Reno, It. 63/E4
Calderas, Ven. 180/D2
Caldercruix, Sc, UK 33/C5
Calderdale (co.), Eng, UK 35/F4
Caldes de Montbui, Sp. 47/L6
Caldew (riv.), Eng, UK 35/F2
Caldicot, Wal, UK 36/D3
Caldiero, It. 63/E3
Çaldıran, Turk. 103/E2
Caldogno, It. 63/E2
Caldonazzo, It. 61/H6
Caldono, Col. 180/B4
Caldwell, Id, US 146/E2
Caldwell, NJ, US 169/H8
Caldwell, Oh, US 160/F5
Caldwell, Tx, US 150/F2
Caldwell, Wi, US 167/P14
Caldy (isl.), Eng, UK 36/B3
Caledon, NI, UK 34/B3
Caledon, SAfr. 124/L11
Caledon, On, Can. 160/T8
Caledon (riv.), SAfr. 124/D3
Caledon East, On, Can. 160/T8
Caledonia (hills), NB, Can. 158/E3
Caledonia, Mi, US 160/D3
Caledonia, Mn, US 155/J2
Caledonia, Ms, US 162/C4
Caledonia, NS, Can. 158/E3
Caledonia, Oh, US 160/E4
Caledonia, Wi, US 167/P14
Caledonian (canal), Sc, UK 33/B2
Calella, Sp. 47/G2
Calen, Austl. 134/C3
Calenzana, Fr. 48/A1
Calenzano, It. 63/E6
Calera, Ok, US 153/F4
Calera, Al, US 162/D4
Calera de Tango, Chile 190/N8
Calestano, It. 62/D4
Caleta Clarencia, Chile 191/C7
Caleta de Campos, Mex. 174/E5
Caleta Olivia, Arg. 190/D5
Caletones, Chile 190/N9
Calf of Man (isl.), IM, UK 34/C3
Calgary (int'l arpt.), Ab, Can. 145/G2
Calgary, Ab, Can. 145/G2
Calhan, Co, US 154/B4
Calheta, Port. 110/A2
Calheta, Azor., Port. 47/S12
Calhoun, Al, US 164/E1
Calhoun, Ga, US 162/E3
Calhoun, Il, US 162/C1
Calhoun, Ky, US 162/D2
Calhoun, Mo, US 153/H1
Calhoun City, Ms, US 162/C4
Calhoun Falls, SC, US 163/F3
Cali, Col. 180/B4
Calico Ghost Town, Ca, US 148/D3
Calico Rock, Ar, US 153/H2
Calicut (Kozhikode), India 95/B4
Calida (coast), Sp. 46/E4
Caliente, Nv, US 148/E2
Califon, NJ, US 168/D2
California (state), US 142/C4
California (gulf), Mex. 139/F6
California (aqueduct), Ca, US 148/B2
California, Md, US 163/J1
California, Mo, US 153/H1
California City, Ca, US 148/D3
Calilegua, Arg. 188/C2
Calilegua, PN, Arg. 188/C2
Călimănești, Rom. 51/G3
Calimaya, Mex. 175/Q10
Calimere (pt.), India 95/C4
Calimesa, Ca, US 166/C2
Calingasta, Arg. 188/B4
Calion, Ar, US 153/H4
Calipatria, Ca, US 148/E4
Calistoga, Ca, US 146/B4
Calitri, It. 48/D2
Calixa-Lavallée, Qu, Can. 159/P6
Calizzano, It. 62/B5
Calkiní, Mex. 176/D1
Çalköy, Turk. 102/B2
Callac, Fr. 56/B4
Callaghan (mt.), Nv, US 146/E4
Callaghan, Tx, US 150/E4
Callahan, Fl, US 165/H2
Callahonna (lake), Austl. 127/D3
Callalli, Peru 184/D4
Callan, Ire. 32/C4
Callander, Sc, UK 33/B4
Callantsoog, Neth. 52/B3
Callao, Peru 184/B4
Callao, Ut, US 147/G4
Callao, Va, US 163/J2
Callapa, Bol. 188/B1
Callaun (peak), Ire. 32/B4
Callaway, Mn, US 156/G4
Callaway, Fl, US 165/F2
Calle Larga, Chile 190/N8
Callender, Ia, US 155/G2
Callian, Fr. 64/C5
Calliham, Tx, US 151/E3
Callington, Eng, UK 36/B5
Calliope, Austl. 134/C4
Callosa de Segura, Sp. 47/E3
Calmar, Ia, US 155/J2
Calmar, Ab, Can. 145/H1
Calne, Eng, UK 36/E4
Calolziocorte, It. 62/C2
Calonga (riv.), Ang. 122/B2
Calonne (riv.), Fr. 57/F2
Calonne-Ricouart, Fr. 54/B3
Caloocan, Phil. 88/E6
Caloosahatchee (riv.), Fl, US 165/H4
Caloosahatchee Nat'l Wild. Ref., Fl, US 165/H4
Calore (riv.), It. 67/G2
Caloundra, Austl. 134/D4
Calpe, Sp. 47/F3
Calpulálpan, Mex. 175/L7
Calstock, Eng, UK 36/B6
Caltagirone, It. 48/D4
Caltanissetta, It. 48/D4
Caltavuturo, It. 48/C4
Caluango, Ang. 120/D5
Calucinga, Ang. 122/C1
Calueque (dam), Ang. 122/B3
Calulo, Ang. 120/C5
Calumbo, Ang. 120/C5
Calumet, Mi, US 157/K4
Calumet (riv.), Il, US 167/Q16
Calumet City, Il, US 160/C4
Calumet Sag (chan.), Il, US 167/Q16
Caluquembe, Ang. 122/B2
Caluso, It. 62/A2
Caluula (pt.), Som. 118/D3
Caluula, Som. 118/D3
Calva, Az, US 149/G4
Calvados (dept.), Fr. 57/E3
Calvary, Ga, US 165/F2
Calvello, It. 48/D2
Calvenzano, It. 62/C3
Calvert, Nf, Can. 159/L2
Calvert, Al, US 164/D2
Calvert, Tx, US 151/F2
Calvert City, Ky, US 162/C2
Calvert Hills, Austl. 129/E4
Calverton, Eng, UK 35/G5
Calverton, Md, US 168/B5
Calvi, Fr. 48/A1
Calvi (peak), It. 63/E5
Calvi Risorta, It. 65/D5
Calviá, Sp. 47/G3
Calvilli (peak), It. 65/C5
Calvillo, Mex. 174/E4
Calvin, Ok, US 153/F3
Calvinia, SAfr. 124/B3
Calvisano, It. 62/D3
Calvitero (peak), Sp. 46/C2
Calw, Ger. 58/B5
Calzada de Calatrava, Sp. 46/D3
Cam or Rhee (riv.), Eng, UK 37/F2
Cam Pha, Viet. 87/E4
Cam Ranh, Viet. 94/E4
Cam Thuy, Viet. 94/D1
Camabatela, Ang. 120/C5
Camaçari, Braz. 187/F2
Camacho, Bol. 188/C2
Camacho, Bol. 185/E3
Camacho, Mex. 174/E3
Camacupa, Ang. 122/C2
Camaguán, Ven. 181/E2
Camagüey (arch.), Cuba 173/F3
Camagüey, Cuba 177/G1
Camaiore, It. 62/D6
Camajuaní, Cuba 177/G1
Camalengue, Ang. 120/D5
Camalu, Mex. 174/A2
Camamu, Braz. 187/F2
Camaná, Peru 184/C5
Camanche (res.), Ca, US 146/C4
Camanche, Ia, US 155/J3
Camanducaia, Braz. 187/K7
Camanongue, Ang. 122/D1
Camapuã, Braz. 189/F1
Camaquã, Braz. 189/G4
Camaquã (riv.), Braz. 189/F4
Camarat (cape), Fr. 64/C6
Camaret-sur-Aigues, Fr. 64/A4
Camaret-sur-Mer, Fr. 56/A4
Camargo, Ok, US 152/E2
Camargo, Sp. 46/D1
Camargo, Bol. 188/C2
Camarillo, Ca, US 166/A2
Camariñas, Sp. 46/A1
Camarón (cape), Hon. 177/E3
Camarones (bay), Arg. 190/D5
Camarones, Arg. 190/D5
Camarones, Chile 188/B1
Camas, Sp. 46/B4
Camas NWR, Id, US 147/G2
Camas Prairie (grsld.), Id, US 144/F4
Camas Valley, Or, US 146/B2
Camatagua, Ven. 183/P8
Camaxilo, Ang. 120/D5
Cambados, Sp. 46/A1
Cambará, Braz. 189/G2
Cambay (gulf), India 92/B3
Cambé, Braz. 189/G2
Camberley, Eng, UK 30/A3
Camberwell (nbrhd.), Eng, UK 30/C2
Camberwell, Austl. 133/B3
Cambiano, It. 62/A3
Cambo (riv.), Ang. 120/D5
Cambo Camana, Ang. 120/D5
Cambodia (ctry.) 94/D3
Cambondo, Ang. 120/C5
Camborne, Eng, UK 36/A6
Cambrai, Fr. 54/C3
Cambria, Ca, US 148/B3
Cambrian (mts.), Wal, UK 34/E5
Cambridge (gulf), Austl. 128/C3
Cambridge, On, Can. 160/F3
Cambridge (int'l arpt.), Eng, UK 37/G2
Cambridge, Eng, UK 37/G2
Cambridge, NZ 135/C2
Cambridge, Id, US 146/E1
Cambridge, Il, US 155/J3
Cambridge, Ma, US 161/L3
Cambridge, Md, US 163/J1
Cambridge, Mn, US 157/H5
Cambridge, Ne, US 154/D3
Cambridge, Oh, US 160/F4
Cambridge, Vt, US 161/K2
Cambridge Bay, Nun, Can. 140/F2
Cambridge City, In, US 160/D5
Cambridge Springs, Pa, US 160/F4
Cambridge-Narrows, NB, Can. 158/E3
Cambridgeshire (co.), Eng, UK 37/F2
Cambrils, Sp. 47/F2
Cambuí, Braz. 187/K7
Cambulo, Ang. 121/E4
Cambuquira, Braz. 187/L6
Cambuslang, Sc, UK 33/B5
Cambutal (mtn.), Pan. 180/A3
Camden, Austl. 134/G9
Camden (sound), Austl. 128/A3
Camden (co.), Eng, UK 30/C2
Camden, Al, US 164/E2
Camden, Ar, US 153/H4
Camden, De, US 168/C5
Camden, Mi, US 160/D4
Camden, NC, US 163/J2
Camden, NJ, US 168/C4
Camden (co.), NJ, US 168/C4
Camden, NY, US 161/J3
Camden, SC, US 163/G3
Camden, Tn, US 162/C2
Camden, Tx, US 151/G2
Camden East, On, Can. 161/H2
Camden Haven, Austl. 132/E1
Camdenton, Mo, US 153/H1
Cameia, Ang. 122/D1
Cameia, PN da, Ang. 121/E5
Cameia, PN da, Ang. 122/D1
Camel (riv.), Eng, UK 36/B6
Camelback (mtn.), Pa, US 168/C1
Camelford, Eng, UK 36/B5
Camels Back (peak), NZ 135/C2
Camenca, Mol. 72/E3
Camerano, It. 63/G6
Cameri, It. 62/B3
Camerino, It. 65/C1
Camerón (riv.), Mex. 150/D4
Cameron (isl.), Nun, Can. 141/R7
Cameron, Az, US 149/G3
Cameron (peak), Co, US 154/B3
Cameron, La, US 164/B3
Cameron, Mo, US 155/G4
Cameron, Mt, US 147/H1
Cameron, Tx, US 151/F2
Cameron, Wi, US 157/J5
Cameron Highlands, Malay. 89/C1
Cameron Park, Ca, US 146/C4
Cameroon (ctry.) 107/D4
Cameroon Highlands (uplands), Nga. 116/A4
Cametá, Braz. 182/D3
Camey, Tx, US 150/L6
Camfield, Austl. 128/C4
Camicia (peak), It. 65/C3
Camiguin (isl.), Phil. 88/C1
Camiling, Phil. 88/C2
Camilla, Ga, US 165/F2
Camilo Aldao, Arg. 190/E2
Caminha, Port. 46/A2
Camiranga, Braz. 183/E3
Camiri, Bol. 188/D2
Camisano Vicentino, It. 63/E2
Camissombo, Ang. 121/E5
Çamlıdere, Turk. 70/E4
Çamlık NP, Turk. 102/C2
Camlin (riv.), Ire. 32/C2
Çamlıyayla, Turk. 104/D1
Camo-Camo, Moz. 123/G4
Camoapa, Nic. 176/E3
Camocim, Braz. 183/F3
Camogli, It. 62/C5
Camolin, Ire. 32/D4
Camon, Fr. 54/B4
Camooweal, Austl. 129/E4
Camopi, FrG. 182/C2
Camopi (riv.), FrG. 182/C2
Camorta (isl.), India 93/F6
Camoruco, Col. 180/D3
Camotes (sea), Phil. 88/D3
Camp Angelus (Angelus Oaks), Ca, US 166/D2
Camp Atterbury, In, US 162/D1
Camp Blanding Mil. Res., Fl, US 165/G3
Camp Grayling, Mi, US 160/D2
Camp Hill, Pa, US 168/B3
Camp J.T. Robinson, Ar, US 153/H3
Camp Lake, Wi, US 167/P14
Camp Lake Nat'l Wild. Ref., ND, US 156/D4
Camp Lejeune, NC, US 163/J3
Camp Lejeune Marine Base, NC, US 163/J3
Camp Pendleton, Ca, US 148/D4
Camp Ripley Mil. Res., Mn, US 157/G4
Camp Roberts, Ca, US 148/B3
Camp Shelby, Ms, US 164/D2
Camp Springs, Md, US 168/B6
Camp Verde, Az, US 149/G3
Camp Verde Ind. Res., Az, US 149/G3
Camp Williams, Ut, US 147/G3
Camp Wood, Tx, US 150/D3
Campagna di Roma (reg.), It. 65/B4
Campagna Lupia, It. 63/F3
Campagnano di Roma, It. 65/B3
Campagnola Emilia, It. 63/D4
Campamento, Uru. 189/E4
Campana (isl.), Chile 191/B6
Campana, Arg. 191/J11
Campanario, Sp. 46/C3
Campanario (peak), Arg. 190/C2
Campanella (cape), It. 65/D6
Campanha, Braz. 187/L6
Campania (prov.), It. 48/D2
Campbell (cape), NZ 135/C3
Campbell (isl.), NZ 27/T8
Campbell, Ca, US 167/L12
Campbell, Fl, US 164/N7
Campbell, Mn, US 156/F4
Campbell, Mo, US 162/B2
Campbell (hill), Oh, US 160/E4
Campbell, Oh, US 160/F4
Campbell, Ne, US 154/E3
Campbell, Tx, US 153/G4
Campbell Town, Austl. 132/C4
Campbellford, On, Can. 161/H2
Campbellpore, Pak. 98/B3
Campbell's Bay, Qu, Can. 161/H2
Campbellsport, Wi, US 160/B3
Campbellsville, Ky, US 162/E2
Campbellton, NB, Can. 158/D1
Campbellton, Fl, US 165/F2
Campbelltown (nbrhd.), Austl. 134/G9
Campbellville, On, Can. 160/T9
Campbeltown, Sc, UK 31/R9
Campbon, Fr. 56/D6
Campden, On, Can. 160/U9
Campeche (state), Mex. 172/C4
Campeche, Mex. 176/D2
Campeche (bay), Mex. 139/H7
Campello sul Clitunno, It. 65/B2
Camperdown, Austl. 132/B3
Camperville, Mb, Can. 156/D2
Campestre, Braz. 187/K6
Campi Bisenzio, It. 63/E6
Campidano (range), It. 48/A3
Campile, Ire. 32/D5
Campillo de Altobuey, Sp. 46/E3
Campillos, Sp. 46/C4
Campina da Lagoa, Braz. 189/F3
Campina Grande, Braz. 183/H4
Campina Verde, Braz. 186/C3
Campinas, Braz. 187/J7
Campione d'Italia, It. 61/E6
Campli, It. 65/C2
Camplong, Indo. 128/A2
Campo, Camr. 120/B2
Campo, Ca, US 148/D4
Campo (int'l arpt.), Braz. 184/C2
Campo Belo, Braz. 186/D4
Campo de Criptana, Sp. 46/D3
Campo de la Cruz, Col. 180/C2
Campo dei Fiori (peak), It. 62/B2
Campo Erê, Braz. 189/F3
Campo Florido, Braz. 189/G1
Campo Formoso, Braz. 187/E1
Campo Gallo, Arg. 188/D3
Campo Grande, Braz. 189/F2
Campo Ind. Res., Ca, US 148/D4
Campo Largo, Braz. 189/G3
Campo Ligure, It. 62/B4
Campo Limpo Paulista, Braz. 187/K8
Campo Maior, Port. 46/B3
Campo Maior, Braz. 183/F4
Campo Mourão, Braz. 189/F3
Campo Quijano, Arg. 188/C3
Campo Redondo, Braz. 183/G4
Campo Tencia (peak), Swi. 61/E5
Campo Tizzoro, It. 63/D5
Campoalegre, Col. 180/C4
Campobasso (prov.), It. 65/D4
Campobasso, It. 65/D4
Campobello (isl.), Ns., Can. 158/D3
Campodarsego, It. 63/E3
Campodolcino, It. 61/F5
Campogalliano, It. 63/D4
Campomorone, It. 62/B4
Camponogara, It. 63/F3
Camporosso, It. 62/A5
Camporredondo (res.), Sp. 46/C1
Camporredondo, Peru 184/B2
Campos (phys. reg.), Braz. 179/D5
Campos Belos, Braz. 186/D2
Campos de Hielo Norte (glacier), Chile 191/B5
Campos de Hielo Sur (glacier), Chile 191/B6
Campos del Puerto, Sp. 47/G3
Campos do Jordão, Braz. 187/L7
Campos dos Goytacazes, Braz. 187/E4
Campos Novos, Braz. 189/G3
Campos Sales, Braz. 183/F4
Camposampiero, It. 63/E2
Camposanto, It. 63/E4
Camposauro (peak), It. 65/D5
Campotosto (lake), It. 65/C3
Campsie Fells (hills), Sc, UK 33/B4
Campti, La, US 164/B2
Campton, Ky, US 163/F2
Camrose, Ab, Can. 145/H1
Çan, Turk. 70/C4
Can (riv.), Eng, UK 30/E1
Can Tho, Viet. 94/D4
Cana, Sk, Can. 156/C2
Canaan, Ar, US 153/H3
Canaan, Vt, US 161/L2
Canaan (riv.), NB, Can. 158/E2
Canaan, NH, US 161/K3
Canaan Game Ref., NB, Can. 158/E2
Canaçari (lake), Braz. 182/B3
Canada (ctry.) 140/*
Cañada de Gómez, Arg. 190/E2
Cañada Larga, Bol. 185/F5
Cañada Nieto, Uru. 191/J10
Cañada Rosquín, Arg. 190/E2
Canadensis, Pa, US 168/C1
Canadian, Tx, US 152/D3
Canadian (riv.), US 139/G6
Canadian, North (riv.), Ok, US 142/F4
Cañadón de las Vacas, Arg. 191/C6
Cañadon Grande (mts.), Arg. 190/C5
Cañadón Seco, Arg. 190/D5
Canaima, PN, Ven. 181/F3
Canajoharie, NY, US 161/J3
Çanakkale, Turk. 49/K2
Çanakkale (prov.), Turk. 70/C5
Canal Flats, BC, Can. 144/G2
Canal Point, Fl, US 165/H4
Canala, NCal. 137/U12
Canalbianco (riv.), It. 63/E2
Canale, It. 62/A3
Canale Cavour (canal), It. 62/B2
Canals, Sp. 47/E3
Canals, Arg. 190/E2
Canandaigua, NY, US 161/H3
Cananea, Mex. 174/C2
Canaos (riv.), Braz. 189/G3
Cañar (dept.), Ecu. 180/B5
Cañar, Ecu. 184/B1
Canard (riv.), On, Can. 167/G7
Canarsie (nbrhd.), NY, US 169/K9
Canary (isls.), Sp. 110/A3
Cañas, CR 176/E4
Cañasgordas, Col. 180/B3
Canatlán de las Manzanas, Mex. 174/D3
Canaveral (pen.), Fl, US 165/H3
Canaveral (cape), Fl, US 165/H3
Canaveral Nat'l Seashore, Fl., US 165/H3
Canavieiras, Braz. 187/F2
Canbelego, Austl. 132/C1
Canberra (cap.), Austl. 133/D2
Canby, Or, US 146/B1
Canby, Mn, US 155/F1
Cancale, Fr. 56/D3
Cance (riv.), Fr. 64/A2
Cancello-Arnone, It. 65/D5
Canchaque, Peru 184/B2
Canche (riv.), Fr. 44/E1
Cancun (int'l arpt.), Mex. 176/E1
Cancún, Mex. 176/E1
Candarave, Peru 188/B1
Çandarli (gulf), Gre. 102/A2
Candás, Sp. 46/C1
Candás, Sp. 46/B1
Candé, Fr. 57/D5
Candeias, Braz. 187/F2
Candela, Mex. 150/D4
Candelaria (riv.), Mex. 176/D2
Candelaria, Mex. 176/D2
Candelaria, Arg. 190/D2
Candelária, Braz. 189/F4
Candelaria, Bol. 188/E1
Candeleda, Sp. 46/C2
Candelo, It. 62/B2
Candelo, Austl. 133/D3
Candia Lomellina, It. 62/B3
Candiac, Qu, Can. 159/N7
Cândido Mendes, Braz. 183/E3
Cândido Mota, Braz. 189/G2
Canding (cape), Indo. 90/D5
Candiolo, It. 64/D3
Çandır, Turk. 102/C2
Candler-McAfee, Ga, US 163/M7
Candlewood, NJ, US 168/D3
Cando, ND, US 156/E3
Cando, Sk, Can. 145/K1
Candon, Phil. 88/C1
Cane (cr.), Ga, US 165/G2
Cane Beds, Az, US 149/F2
Cane Field (int'l arpt.), Dom. 173/N9
Canegrate, It. 62/B2
Canela, Braz. 189/G4
Canela Baja, Chile 188/B4
Canelli, It. 62/B4
Canelones (dept.), Uru. 191/F2
Canelones, Uru. 191/K11
Canepina, It. 65/B3
Cañete, Sp. 46/E2
Canete, Río de (riv.), Peru 184/B4
Caneva, It. 63/F2
Caney (cr.), Tx, US 151/G3
Caney, Ok, US 153/F3
Caney, Ks, US 153/G2
Caney (riv.), Ks,Ok, US 175/F2
Caneyville, Ky, US 162/D2
Canfield, Ar, US 153/H4
Canfield Lake Nat'l Wild. Ref., ND, US 156/D4
Cangallo, Peru 184/C4
Cangamba, Ang. 122/C2
Cangandala, Ang. 120/D5
Cangas, Sp. 46/A1
Cangas de Narcea, Sp. 46/B1
Cangas de Onís, Sp. 46/C1
Cangkuang (cape), Indo. 89/D4
Cango Caves, SAfr. 124/C4
Cangoa, Ang. 122/C2
Cangombe, Ang. 122/D2
Cangonga, Ang. 122/C2
Cangqian, China 87/H3
Cangrejo (peak), Arg. 191/B6
Cangshan, China 80/D4
Cangshan, China 79/J1
Canguaretama, Braz. 183/H4
Canguçu, Braz. 189/F4
Cangumbe, Ang. 122/C1
Cangwu, China 93/K3
Cangyuan (Cangyuan Vazu Zizhixian), China 86/C4
Cangzhou, China 80/D3
Canh Cuoc (isl.), Viet. 94/D1
Canhaua, Ang. 122/C3
Canhoca, Ang. 122/B2
Canhotinho, Braz. 183/G5
Cania Gorge NP, Austl. 134/C4
Caniapiscau (lake), Qu, Can. 141/K3
Caniapiskau (riv.), Qu, Can. 141/J3
Canicatti, It. 48/C4
Canigou, Pic du (peak), Fr. 44/E5
Canik (mts.), Turk. 102/C1
Caniles, Sp. 46/D4
Canim Lake, BC, Can. 144/D2
Canindé, Braz. 183/G4
Canindé (riv.), Braz. 183/F4
Canindeyú (dept.), Par. 186/B5
Canino, It. 48/B1
Canistear (res.), NJ, US 169/H7
Canisteo, NY, US 161/H3
Cañitas de Felipe Pescador, Mex. 174/E4
Canjáyar, Sp. 46/D4
Canje (riv.), Guy. 182/B1
Canjilon, NM, US 149/J2
Cankhor, Som. 118/C3
Çankırı, Turk. 70/E4
Çankırı (prov.), Turk. 70/E4
Canlaon (vol.), Phil. 88/C3
Canmore, Ab, Can. 144/G2
Cann (mtn.), Austl. 133/D3
Cann (riv.), Austl. 133/D3
Cann River, Austl. 133/D3
Canna (isl.), Sc, UK 31/Q8
Cannara, It. 65/B2
Canne (ruin), It. 48/E2
Cannel City, Ky, US 163/F2
Cannelton, In, US 162/D2
Canner (riv.), Fr. 55/F5
Cannero Riviera, It. 61/E5
Cannes, Fr. 64/D5
Canneto sull'Oglio, It. 62/D3
Cannich, Sc, UK 33/B2
Canning (peak), Austl. 130/C4
Canning (riv.), Austl. 130/K7
Canning (dam), Austl. 130/L7
Cannobio, It. 61/E5
Cannock, Eng, UK 36/D1
Cannon (A.F.B.), NM, US 152/C3
Cannon Ball, ND, US 156/D4
Cannon Beach, Or, US 144/C5
Cannon Falls, Mn, US 155/H1
Cannonball (riv.), ND, US 156/D4
Cannondale, Ct, US 169/E1
Cannonvale, Austl. 134/C3
Cannonville, Ut, US 149/F2
Caño Guaritico (riv.), Ven. 180/D3
Caño Negro Nat'l Wild. Ref., CR 177/E4
Canoas, Braz. 189/G4
Canobolas (mt.), Austl. 133/D1
Canoe, Al, US 164/E2
Canoe River, BC, Can. 144/E1
Canoga Park (nbrhd.), Ca, US 166/E7
Canoinhas, Braz. 189/G3
Canon City, Co, US 152/B1
Cañón de Río Blanco, PN, Mex. 175/M8
Cañón del Sumidero, PN, Mex. 176/C2
Cañon Largo (riv.), NM, US 149/J2
Canonbie, Sc, UK 35/F1
Cañoncito Ind. Res., NM, US 149/J3
Canones, NM, US 149/J2
Canoochee (riv.), Ga, US 165/G1
Canopus (ruin), Egypt 113/B2
Canora, Sk, Can. 156/C2
Canosa di Puglia, It. 48/E2
Canouan (isl.), StV. 173/N9
Canowindra, Austl. 133/D1
Cansado, Mrta. 110/A5
Canso, NS, Can. 159/G3
Canso (cape), NS, Can. 159/G3
Canta, Peru 184/B3
Cantabria (prov.), Sp. 44/B5
Cantabria (dist.), Sp. 46/C1
Cantal (mass.), Fr. 44/E4
Cantalejo, Sp. 46/D2
Cantanhede, Port. 46/A2
Cantanhede, Braz. 183/E3
Cantaura, Ven. 181/E2
Canteleu, Fr. 57/G2
Canterbury (nbrhd.), Austl. 134/H8
Canterbury, Eng, UK 37/H4
Canterbury Bight (bay), NZ 127/H7
Canterbury Cathedral, Eng, UK 37/H4
Cantiere, Eth. 117/G4
Cantil, Ca, US 148/D3
Cantilan, Phil. 88/D3
Cantillana, Sp. 46/C4
Canto del Agua, Chile 188/B4
Canto do Buriti, Braz. 183/F5
Canton, Ga, US 162/E3
Canton, Il, US 155/J3
Canton, Ks, US 153/F1
Canton, Mi, US 167/E7
Canton, Mo, US 155/J3
Canton, Ms, US 162/B4
Canton, NC, US 163/F3
Canton, NJ, US 168/C5
Canton, NY, US 161/J2
Canton, Oh, US 160/F4
Canton, Ok, US 153/E2
Canton (lake), Ok, US 153/E2
Canton, Pa, US 161/H4
Canton, SD, US 155/F2
Canton, Tx, US 151/G1
Canton (Abariringa) (isl.), Kiri. 137/H5
Cantoria, Sp. 46/D4
Cantù, It. 62/C2
Cantwell, Ak, US 171/J3
Cañuelas, Arg. 191/J11
Canumã (riv.), Braz. 182/B4
Canunda NP, Austl. 132/B3
Canutama, Braz. 185/E2
Canutillo, Tx, US 150/A2
Canvey (isl.), Eng, UK 30/E2
Canvey Island, Eng, UK 37/G3
Canwood, Sk, Can. 145/L1
Cany-Barville, Fr. 57/F1

Catema – Chartre

Catemaco (lake), Mex. 176/C2
Catemaco, Mex. 176/C2
Catende, Braz. 183/H5
Cateran (hill), Eng, UK 33/E5
Caterham, Eng, UK 30/C3
Caterham and Warlingham, Eng, UK 37/F4
Catete, Ang. 120/C5
Catfish (cr.), Fl, US 164/N8
Catharine, Ks, US 152/E1
Cathcart, SAfr. 124/D4
Cathedral (mtn.), Tx, US 150/C2
Cathedral City, Ca, US 148/D4
Cathédrale de Reims, Fr. 54/D5
Catherine (peak), Egypt 109/G2
Catherine, Al, US 162/D4
Catherine Palace, Rus. 69/T7
Cathlamet, Wa, US 144/C4
Ca'Tiepolo, It. 63/F4
Catierick, Eng, UK 35/G3
Catingueira, Braz. 183/G4
Catió, GBis. 114/B4
Cativá, Pan. 177/G4
Catlettsburg, Ky, US 163/F1
Catlin, Il, US 160/C4
Catmon, Phil. 88/D3
Cato (isl.), Aus. 127/E3
Catoche, Cabo (cape), Mex. 176/E1
Catofe, Ang. 120/C5
Catolé do Rocha, Braz. 183/G4
Catolo, Ang. 120/D5
Catonsville, Md, US 168/B5
Catoosa, Ok, US 153/G2
Catria (peak), It. 63/F7
Catriló, Arg. 190/E3
Catrimani, Braz. 181/F4
Catrimani (riv.), Braz. 181/F4
Catrine, Sc, UK 33/B6
Catshill, Eng, UK 36/D2
Catskill, NY, US 161/K3
Catskill (mts.), NY, US 161/J3
Cattaraugus, NY, US 161/G3
Cattaraugus Ind. Res., NY, US 161/G3
Cattawissa (cr.), Pa, US 168/B2
Cattolica, It. 63/F6
Catu, Braz. 187/F2
Catubig, Phil. 88/D2
Catuipe, Braz. 189/F4
Catur (riv.), Ang. 120/D4
Cauayan, Phil. 88/C3
Cauayan, Phil. 88/C1
Cauca (riv.), Col. 180/C3
Cauca (riv.), Col. 179/B2
Cauca (dept.), Col. 180/B4
Caucagua, Ven. 180/D3
Caucagua, Ven. 183/P7
Caucaia, Braz. 183/G3
Caucas, Bol. 185/G5
Caucasia, Col. 180/C3
Caucasus (mts.), Geo.,Rus. 71/G4
Caucasus (mts.), Geo. 74/F6
Caucasus (mts.), Asia 102/E1
Caudan, Fr. 56/B5
Caudebec-en-Caux, Fr. 57/F1
Caudebec-lès-Elbeuf, Fr. 57/G2
Caudete, Sp. 47/E3
Caudry, Fr. 54/C3
Cauese, Montes (mts.), Moz. 123/F2
Cauldcleuch Head (peak), Sc, UK 33/D6
Caulfield, Mo, US 153/H2
Caulfield, Austl. 133/B3
Caulnes, Fr. 56/C4
Caumont (arpt.), Fr. 64/A5
Caumont-L'Éventé, Fr. 57/E2
Caumont-sur-Durance, Fr. 64/A5
Caúngula, Ang. 120/D5
Cauquenes, Chile 190/B2
Caura (riv.), Ven. 181/E3
Cauresi (riv.), Moz. 123/G3
Cauron (riv.), Fr. 64/B6
Causapscal, Qu, Can. 158/D1
Căușeni, Mol. 72/E4
Causeway, Ire. 32/A5
Causey, NM, US 152/C4
Caussade, Fr. 44/D4
Cautário (riv.), Braz. 185/F3
Cauterets, Fr. 44/C5
Cauto (riv.), Cuba 177/G1
Cauvery (riv.), India 92/C5
Cauville, Fr. 57/F1
Cava de'Tirreni, It. 65/D6
Cava d'Ispica (ruin), It. 48/D4
Cávado (riv.), Port. 46/A2
Cavaglià, It. 62/B3
Cavaillon, Fr. 64/B5
Cavalaire-sur-Mer, Fr. 64/C6
Cavalcante, Braz. 186/D2
Cavalese, It. 61/H5
Cavalier, ND, US 156/F3
Cavalla (Cavally) (riv.), Libr. 114/D5
Cavallermaggiore, It. 62/A3
Cavallino, It. 63/F3
Cavallo, Capo al (cape), Fr. 48/A1
Cavally (riv.), C.d'Iv. 114/C5
Cavally (Cavalla) (riv.), Libr. 114/D5
Cavan, Ire. 32/C2
Cavari, Bol. 185/E5
Cavarzere, It. 63/F3
Cave, It. 65/B4
Cave City, Ar, US 153/J3
Cave City, Ky, US 162/E2
Cave Creek, Az, US 149/G4
Cave Junction, Or, US 146/B2
Cave of Ten Thousand Buddhas, Myan. 94/B2
Cave Of The Mounds, Wi, US 155/K2
Cave Run (lake), Ky, US 163/F1
Cave Spring, Va, US 163/G2
Cave Spring, Ga, US 162/E3
Caverns of Sonora, Tx, US 150/D2
Cavezzo, It. 63/E4
Caviana (isl.), Braz. 182/D2
Cavinas, Bol. 185/E4
Cavite (co.), Phil. 88/E7
Cavite, Phil. 88/E7
Cavnic, Rom. 51/F2
Cavour, It. 64/D3
Cavriana, It. 62/D3
Cawayan, Phil. 88/C3
Cawdor, Sc, UK 33/C1
Cawker City, Ks, US 154/E4
Cawood, Eng, UK 35/G4
Cawston, Eng, UK 37/H1
Caxambu, Braz. 187/M6
Caxata, Bol. 185/E5
Caxias, Braz. 183/F4
Caxias do Sul, Braz. 189/G4
Caxinas (pt.), Hon. 176/E2
Caxinga, Ang. 120/D5
Caxito, Ang. 120/B5
Çay, Turk. 102/B2
Çayağzı, Turk. 103/N6
Çayağzı (riv.), Turk. 103/N6
Cayambe, Ecu. 180/B4
Cayambe (vol.), Ecu. 180/B4
Cayastá, Arg. 188/D4
Cayce, SC, US 163/G4
Çaycuma, Turk. 70/E4
Çayeli, Turk. 71/G4
Cayenne (cap.), FrG. 182/C1
Cayenne (dist.), FrG. 182/C1
Cayer, Mb, Can. 156/E2
Cayeux-sur-Mer, Fr. 54/A3
Çayırhan, Turk. 51/K5
Çaylar, Turk. 102/E2
Cayley, Ab, Can. 145/H2
Cayman (isls.), UK 139/J8
Cayman Brac (isl.), UK 173/F4
Caynabo, Som. 118/C3
Cayo Coco (isl.), Cuba 177/G1
Cayo Cocorocuma (isl.), Hon. 177/F3
Cayo Fragosa (isl.), Cuba 177/G1
Cayo Guayabo (isl.), Cuba 177/G1
Cayo Largo (isl.), Cuba 177/F1
Cayo Romano (isl.), Cuba 177/G1
Cayo Sabinal (isl.), Cuba 177/G1
Cayos Arcas (isl.), Mex. 176/D1
Cayos Cajones (isl.), Hon. 172/E4
Cayos de Albuquerque (isl.), Col. 177/F3
Cayos del Este Sudeste (isl.), Col. 177/F3
Cayos Miskitos (isl.), Nic. 172/E5
Cayucos, Ca, US 148/B3
Cayuga, In, US 160/C5
Cayuga (lake), NY, US 161/H3
Cayuga (cr.), NY, US 160/V10
Cayuga, Tx, US 150/G2
Cayuga Heights, NY, US 161/H3
Cazalla de la Sierra, Sp. 46/C4
Cazenovia, NY, US 161/J3
Cazères, Fr. 44/D5
Cazin, Bosn. 50/B3
Cazis, Swi. 61/F4
Cazombo, Ang. 122/D1
Cazones (riv.), Mex. 176/B1
Cazorla, Sp. 46/D4
Cazula, Moz. 123/G2
Cazzago San Martino, It. 62/D2
Cea (riv.), Sp. 46/C1
Ceanannus Mór (Kells), Ire. 32/D2
Ceará (state), Braz. 183/F4
Ceará-Mirim, Braz. 183/H4
Cébaco (isl.), Pan. 177/F5
Ceballos, Mex. 174/D3
Cebolla, NM, US 149/J2
Cebollati, Uru. 191/G2
Cebollati (riv.), Uru. 191/G2
Cebreros, Sp. 46/C2
Cebu, Phil. 88/C3
Cebu (isl.), Phil. 88/C3
Cebu (int'l arpt.), Phil. 88/C3
Ceccano, It. 65/C4
Cecil, Wi, US 155/K1
Cecil (co.), Md, US 168/C4
Cecil Macks (pass), Swaz. 125/E2
Cecil Plains, Austl. 134/C4
Cecil Rhodes (mt.), Austl. 130/D3
Cecilia, Ky, US 162/E2
Cecilton, Md, US 168/C5
Cecilville, Ca, US 146/B3
Cecina (riv.), It. 63/D6
Cecina, It. 45/J5
Cecita (lake), It. 48/E3
Ceclavín, Sp. 46/B3
Cedar (lake), Tx, US 152/C4
Cedar, Mi, US 160/D2
Cedar (lake), On, Can. 161/G1
Cedar (mtn.), Ca, US 167/L11
Cedar (lake), Sk,Mb, Can. 140/F3
Cedar (mts.), Ut, US 147/G3
Cedar (riv.), Ne, US 154/E3
Cedar (cr.), Ia, US 155/H3
Cedar (riv.), Mn, US 155/G1
Cedar (cr.), Ia, US 155/H2
Cedar (isl.), Md, US 163/K2
Cedar Bay NP, Austl. 134/B1
Cedar Bayou (riv.), Tx, US 151/M8
Cedar Bluff, Al, US 162/E3
Cedar Bluff (res.), Ks, US 154/E4
Cedar Breaks Nat'l Mon., Ut, US 149/F2
Cedar Brook, NJ, US 168/D4
Cedar City, Ut, US 149/F2
Cedar Creek, Ar, US 153/H3
Cedar Creek (peak), Id, US 147/G2
Cedar Creek (res.), Tx, US 175/F1
Cedar Crest, NM, US 149/J3
Cedar Falls, Ia, US 155/H2
Cedar Falls (dam), Wa, US 167/D3
Cedar Falls, Wa, US 167/D3
Cedar Glen, Ca, US 166/C2
Cedar Grove, Md, US 168/A5
Cedar Grove, NJ, US 169/J8
Cedar Grove, Tn, US 162/C3
Cedar Grove, Wi, US 160/C3
Cedar Hill, NM, US 149/J2
Cedar Hill, Tn, US 162/D2
Cedar Hill, Tx, US 150/L7
Cedar Island, NC, US 163/J3
Cedar Island NWR, NC, US 163/J3
Cedar Key, Fl, US 165/G3
Cedar Mills, Mn, US 155/G1
Cedar Park, Tx, US 151/F2
Cedar Point Nat'l Wild. Ref., Oh, US 160/E4
Cedar Rapids, Ia, US 155/J3
Cedar River, Mi, US 160/C2
Cedar Springs, Mi, US 160/D3
Cedar Springs, Tx, US 151/F2
Cedar Vale, Ks, US 153/F2
Cedarburg, Wi, US 160/C3
Cedaredge, Co, US 149/J1
Cedarhurst, NY, US 169/L9
Cedartown, Ga, US 162/E3
Cedarville, Ar, US 153/G3
Cedarville, Ca, US 146/C3
Cedegolo, It. 61/G5
Cedeira, Sp. 46/A1
Cedral, Mex. 175/E4
Cedro, Braz. 183/G4
Cedros (isl.), Mex. 139/F7
Ceduna, Austl. 131/G5
Cee, Sp. 46/A1
Ceel Afweyne, Som. 118/C3
Ceel Buur, Som. 118/C4
Ceel Dheere, Som. 118/C5
Ceel Xamurre, Som. 118/D4
Ceeldheere, Som. 118/C4
Ceerigaabo (Erigabo), Som. 118/C3
Cefalù, It. 48/D3
Cefn-Mawr, Wal, UK 35/E6
Cefni (riv.), Wal, UK 34/D5
Cega (riv.), Sp. 46/C2
Ceggia, It. 63/F2
Cegléd, Hun. 50/D2
Čegrane, FYROM 49/G2
Cehegin, Sp. 46/E3
Ceheng Bouyeizu Zizhixian, China 86/E3
Cehu Silvaniei, Rom. 51/F2
Ceiriog (riv.), Wal, UK 35/E6
Çekerek (riv.), Turk. 70/F4
Çekerek, Turk. 102/C1
Cela, Ang. 122/B1
Celada Cué, Par. 188/E2
Celákovice, Czh. 59/H2
Celano, It. 65/C3
Celanova, Sp. 46/B1
Celaya, Mex. 175/E4
Celbridge, Ire. 32/D3
Celebes (isl.), Indo. 77/L10
Celebes (sea), Asia 77/M9
Celebes (Sulawesi) (isl.), Indo. 91/E4
Celendín, Peru 184/B2
Celenza Valfortore, It. 65/D4
Celeste, Tx, US 153/F4
Celestún, Mex. 176/D1
Celica, Ecu. 184/B2
Céligny, Swi. 60/C5
Celina, Tx, US 153/F4
Celina, Oh, US 160/D4
Celina, Tn, US 162/E2
Celje, Slov. 50/B2
Cella, Sp. 46/E2
Celldömölk, Hun. 50/C2
Celle (riv.), Fr. 42/B4
Celle, Ger. 53/H3
Celle Ligure, It. 62/B5
Celles, Belg. 54/C2
Cellettes, Fr. 57/G5
Cellole, It. 65/C5
Čelopek, FYROM 50/E5
Celorico da Beira, Port. 46/B2
Celtic (sea), Eur. 31/P11
Cemaes (pt.), Wal, UK 36/B2
Cemaru (peak), Indo. 90/D3
Cembra, It. 61/H5
Cenajo (res.), Sp. 46/E3
Cenderawasih (bay), Indo. 91/H4
Cene, It. 62/C2
Cenepa (riv.), Peru 184/B1
Çengerli, Turk. 102/D2
Cengong, China 93/J2
Cenia, Sp. 47/F2
Ceno (riv.), It. 62/C3
Centallo, It. 64/D3
Centenario do Sul, Braz. 189/G2
Centennial (mts.), Id, US 147/G1
Centennial Wash (riv.), Az, US 149/F4
Center, Co, US 149/J2
Center, Mo, US 155/J4
Center, ND, US 156/D4
Center, Ne, US 154/F2
Center, Ok, US 153/F3
Center, Tx, US 151/G2
Center City, Mn, US 157/H5
Center Hill, Fl, US 164/M6
Center Hill (lake), Tn, US 162/E2
Center Moriches, NY, US 169/F2
Center Point, Al, US 162/D4
Center Point, Ia, US 155/J2
Center Point, La, US 164/B2
Center Point, Tx, US 150/E3
Centerbrook, Ct, US 169/F1
Centereach, NY, US 169/E2
Centerfield, Ut, US 147/H4
Centerville, Ga, US 162/F4
Centerville, Ga, US 163/M7
Centerville, In, US 160/D5
Centerville, Ia, US 155/H3
Centerville, Mo, US 162/B2
Centerville, Oh, US 160/D5
Centerville, Ok, US 152/E3
Centerville, SD, US 155/F2
Centerville, Tn, US 162/D3
Centerville, Tx, US 151/G2
Centerville, Ut, US 147/H3
Cento, It. 63/E4
Cento Croci, Passo di (pass), It. 62/C5
Central (peak), Arg. 190/C4
Central (dist.), Bots. 122/E4
Central, Braz. 187/E1
Central (pol. reg.), Gha. 115/E5
Central (dist.), Isr. 105/B4
Central (prov.), Kenya 119/B2
Central (dept.), Par. 188/E3
Central, Phil. 88/C2
Central (prov.), PNG 129/G2
Central (prov.), SrL. 95/D5
Central (int'l arpt.), Ukr. 72/F4
Central, Ak, US 171/K2
Central, Az, US 149/H4
Central, NM, US 149/H4
Central African Republic (ctry.) 116/C4
Central Australia (Warburton) Abor. Rsv., Austl. 131/E3
Central Australia Abor. Land, Austl. 131/F2
Central Butte, Sk, Can. 145/L2
Central City, Co, US 154/B4
Central City, Il, US 162/C1
Central City, Ky, US 162/D2
Central City, Ia, US 155/J2
Central City, Ne, US 154/F3
Central City, Pa, US 161/G4
Central Desert Abor. Rsv., Austl. 131/F2
Central Desert Aboriginal Land, Austl. 128/C4
Central Falls, RI, US 161/L4
Central Intelligence Agency Fed. Govt. Res., Va, US 168/A6
Central Island NP, Kenya 117/H5
Central Islip, NY, US 169/E2
Central Kalahari Game Reserve, Bots. 122/D4
Central Makrān (range), Pak. 101/H3
Central Mount Stuart (peak), Austl. 131/G2
Central Mount Wedge (peak), Austl. 131/F2
Central Park, NY, US 169/K8
Central Patricia, On, Can. 157/J2
Central Point, Or, US 146/B2
Central Russian Uplands (uplands), Rus. 73/J1
Central Saanich, BC, Can. 144/C3
Central Siberian (plat.), Rus. 75/L3
Central Square, NY, US 161/H3
Central Ural (mts.), Rus. 69/N4
Central Valley, Ca, US 146/B3
Central Valley, NY, US 168/D1
Centralia, Il, US 162/C1
Centralia, Ks, US 155/F4
Centralia, Mo, US 155/H4
Centralia, Wa, US 144/C4
Centre (prov.), Camr. 116/A4
Centre (pol. reg.), Fr. 44/D3
Centre (pol. reg.), Mor. 110/D2
Centre, Al, US 162/E3
Centre (co.), Pa, US 168/A2
Centre Island, NY, US 169/L8
Centre Nord (pol. reg.), Mor. 110/D2
Centre Sud (pol. reg.), Mor. 110/D3
Centre-Nord (pol. reg.), Mor. 112/B2
Centre-Sud (pol. reg.), Mor. 112/B2
Centreville, Al, US 162/D4
Centreville, Md, US 168/B5
Centreville, Mi, US 160/D4
Centreville, Ms, US 164/C2
Centreville, NS, Can. 158/E3
Century, Fl, US 164/E2
Cenxi, China 93/K3
Cepagatti, It. 65/D3
Ceparana, It. 62/C5
Cepet (cape), Fr. 64/B6
Čepin, Cro. 50/D3
Ceprano, It. 65/C4
Cepu, Indo. 89/E3
Ceram (isl.), Indo. 91/G4
Ceram (sea), Indo. 91/G4
Cerano, It. 62/B3
Cérans-Foulletourte, Fr. 57/F5
Ceraso (cape), It. 48/A2
Cerbat (mts.), Az, US 149/E3
Cerbère, Fr. 44/E5
Cercal, Port. 46/A4
Cercedilla, Sp. 47/M8
Cerchio, It. 65/C3
Čerchov (peak), Czh. 59/F4
Cerdanyola del Vallès, Sp. 47/L7
Cère (riv.), Fr. 44/E4
Cereal, Ab, Can. 145/J2
Ceredigion (co.), Wal, UK 36/B3
Cerenti, Indo. 89/C3
Ceres, Arg. 188/D4
Ceres, Braz. 186/C2
Ceres, It. 64/D2
Ceres, SAfr. 124/L10
Ceres, Ca, US 148/B2
Ceresco, Ne, US 155/F3
Cerese, It. 63/D3
Céreste, Fr. 64/B5
Céret, Fr. 44/E5
Cereté, Col. 180/C2
Cerfone (riv.), It. 63/E6
Cerfontaine, Belg. 55/D3
Cergy, Fr. 30/J4
Ceriale, It. 62/B5
Cerignola, It. 48/D2
Cerisy-la-Salle, Fr. 56/D2
Çerkeş, Turk. 70/E4
Çerkezköy, Turk. 51/J5
Çermik, Turk. 102/D2
Černá (riv.), Czh. 59/H5
Černá (peak), Czh. 59/G5
Cernavodă, Rom. 51/J3
Cernay, Fr. 60/D2
Cernay-la-Ville, Fr. 30/H5
Cerne Abbas, Eng, UK 36/D5
Cernier, Swi. 60/C3
Cérou (riv.), Fr. 44/D4
Cerralvo, Mex. 150/E4
Cerralvo (isl.), Mex. 174/C3
Cerreto di Spoleto, It. 65/B2
Cerreto Guidi, It. 63/D6
Cerreto Sannita, It. 65/D5
Cerreto, Passo del (pass), It. 62/D5
Cerrig-y-Druidion, Wal, UK 34/E5
Çërrik, Alb. 49/F2
Cerrillos, NM, US 149/J3
Cerrillos, Arg. 188/C3
Cerrito, Par. 188/E3
Cerritos, Ca, US 166/F8
Cerritos, Mex. 175/E4
Cerro, NM, US 152/B2
Cerro Azul, Mex. 176/B1
Cêrro Azul, Braz. 189/G3
Cerro Azul, Peru 184/B4
Cerro Castillo, Chile 191/B6
Cerro Chato, Uru. 191/G2
Cerro Colorados (res.), Arg. 190/C3
Cêrro Corá, Braz. 183/G4
Cerro de la Estrella, PN, Mex. 175/Q10
Cerro de las Armas, Uru. 191/K11
Cerro de las Campanas, PN, Mex. 175/E4
Cerro de Pasco, Peru 184/B3
Cerro de San Antonio, Col. 180/C2
Cerro Dorotea, Chile 191/B6
Cerro El Copey, PN, Ven. 181/F2
Cerro Largo (dept.), Uru. 189/F5
Cerro Maggiore, It. 62/B2
Cerro Nanchital, Mex. 176/C2
Cerro Sombrero, Chile 191/C7
Cerros de Amotape, PN, Peru 184/A2
Certaldo, It. 63/E6
Certosa di Pavia, It. 62/C3
Certosa di Pisa, It. 62/D6
Cervantes, Austl. 130/B4
Cervaro, It. 65/C5
Cervaro (riv.), It. 50/B5
Cervati (peak), It. 48/D2
Cervellino (peak), It. 62/D4
Cervera, Sp. 47/F2
Cervera de Pisuerga, Sp. 46/C1
Cervera del Río Alhama, Sp. 46/E1
Cerveteri, It. 65/B4
Cerveyrette (riv.), Fr. 64/C3
Cervia, It. 63/F5
Cervignano del Friuli, It. 63/G2
Cervina (peak), It. 61/H4
Cervinara, It. 65/D5
Cervione, Fr. 48/A1
Cervo (riv.), It. 62/B1
Cervo, It. 62/B6
Cervo, Sp. 66/B2
Cervo (hills), Braz. 187/K7
Cesana Torinese, It. 64/C3
Cesano, It. 65/B3
Cesano (riv.), It. 63/F6
Cesano Boscone, It. 62/C3
Cesano Maderno, It. 62/C2
César (riv.), Col. 173/G5
César (dept.), Col. 180/C2
Cesar (prov.), Col. 177/H4
Cesen (peak), It. 63/F2
Cesena, It. 63/F5
Cesenatico, It. 63/F5
Cēsis, Lat. 41/L3
České Budějovice, Czh. 59/H5
České Středohoří (mts.), Czh. 59/G2
Českomoravská Vysočina (mts.), Czh. 43/H4
Český Brod, Czh. 59/H2
Český Krumlov, Czh. 59/H5
Český Les Sumava (mts.), Czh. 59/F3
Česma (riv.), Cro. 50/C3
Çeşme, Turk. 49/K3
Cessford, Ab, Can. 145/J2
Cessnock, Austl. 133/E1
Cesson, Fr. 30/K6
Cesson-Sévigné, Fr. 56/D4
Cestohowa, Tx, US 151/F3
Cestos (riv.), Libr. 114/C5
Cesvaine, Lat. 41/M3
Cetara, It. 65/D6
Cetina (riv.), Cro. 50/C4
Cetinje, Serb. 50/D4
Çetinkaya, Turk. 102/D2
Çetmi, Turk. 102/B2
Céu Azul, Braz. 189/F3
Ceurda del Pozo (res.), Sp. 46/D2
Ceuta, Sp. 112/B2
Ceva, It. 62/B5
Cevedale (peak), It. 61/G5
Cévennes (mts.), Fr. 44/E4
Cevio, Swi. 61/E5
Ceyhan, Turk. 104/C2
Ceylânpınar, Turk. 102/E2
Ceylon (isl.), SrL. 77/H9
Ceylon, Mn, US 155/G2
Ceyreste, Fr. 64/B6
Ceyzériat, Fr. 60/B5
Cèze (riv.), Fr. 44/F4
Ch'o (isl.), NKor. 81/C3
Ch'ok'ē (mts.), Eth. 118/A3
Ch'ungman (riv.), NKor. 81/C2
Cha Da (cape), Viet. 94/E4
Cha-am, Thai. 94/B3
Cha'anpu, China 87/F2
Chabāl Kalān, India 98/C4
Chabás, Arg. 190/E2
Chabeuil, Fr. 64/B3
Chābi, India 96/C4
Chabjuwardoo (bay), Austl. 130/B2
Chablé, Mex. 176/D2
Chabris, Fr. 57/G6
Chacabuco, Arg. 190/E2
Chacalluta, Chile 184/D5
Chacalluta (Arica) (int'l arpt.), Chile 188/B1
Chacao, Chile 190/B4
Chachani (peak), Peru 184/D5
Chachapoyas, Peru 184/B2
Chācharān, Pak. 98/A5
Chachoengsao, Thai. 94/C3
Chaclacayo, Peru 184/B3
Chaco (dept.), Arg. 188/D3
Chaco (riv.), NM, US 149/H2
Chaco (mesa), NM, US 149/J3
Chaco Austral (plain), Arg. 188/D3
Chaco Boreal (plain), Par. 188/D2
Chaco Central (plain), Arg. 188/D2
Chaco Culture Nat'l Hist. Park, NM, US 149/J2
Chaco Culture Nat'l Hist. Park, NM, US 149/H3
Chaco Culture Nat'l Hist. Park, NM, US 149/J3
Chaco, PN del, Arg. 188/E3
Chacoma, Bol. 188/B1
Chacritas, Chile 188/B4
Chacujal (ruin), Guat. 176/D3
Chad (ctry.) 107/D3
Chad (lake), Afr. 116/B2
Chadan, Rus. 99/F1
Chadao, China 80/G6
Chadbourn, NC, US 163/H3
Chadiza, Zam. 123/G2
Chadlington, Eng, UK 37/E3
Chadong, China 87/F2
Chadron, Ne, US 154/C2
Chadwell Saint Mary, Eng, UK 30/E2
Chadwick, Il, US 155/K2
Chae Hom, Thai. 94/B2
Chaedong-nodongjagu, NKor. 81/D3
Chaeryŏng, NKor. 81/C3
Chafarinas (isl.), Sp. 112/C2
Chaffee, ND, US 156/F4
Chaffee, Mo, US 162/C2
Chafurray, Col. 180/C4
Chāgai, Pak. 101/H3
Chagan, Kaz. 99/C1
Chagang-do (prov.), NKor. 81/D2
Chagda, Rus. 75/P4
Chagdo Kangri (mtn.), China 99/D5
Chagne, Eth. 117/H3
Chagny, Fr. 44/F3
Chagos (arch.), BIOT, UK 77/G10
Chaguanas, Trin. 181/F2
Chaguaramas, Ven. 183/P8
Chaguarpamba, Ecu. 184/B1
Chaguaya, Bol. 188/C2
Chagyl, Trkm. 71/K4
Cha'gyüngoinba, China 99/F5
Chahuites, Mex. 176/C2
Chai Badan, Thai. 94/C3
Chaibāsā, India 97/E4
Chailland, Fr. 57/E4
Chailles, Fr. 57/G5
Chailly-en-Brie, Fr. 30/M5
Chain, SKor. 81/E5
Chain O'Lakes-King, Wi, US 155/K1
Chainat, Thai. 94/C3
Chaîne Annamitique (mts.), Laos 93/H4
Chaîne Annamitique (mts.), Laos,Viet. 94/D2
Chaîne de Belledonne (range), Fr. 64/B2
Chaîne de l'Atacora (mts.), Ben. 115/F4
Chaine de la Selle (peak), Haiti 177/J2
Chaingy, Fr. 57/G5
Chainpur, Nepal 96/C1
Chaiya, Thai. 94/B4
Chaiyaphum, Thai. 94/C3
Chajarí, Arg. 188/E4
Chākāi, India 97/F3
Chakari, Zim. 123/F3
Chākdaha, India 97/G4
Chake Chake, Tanz. 119/B3
Chākia, India 96/D3
Chakradharpur, India 97/E4
Chakrāta, India 98/D4
Chakwāl, Pak. 98/B3
Chala, Peru 184/C4
Chalain (lake), Fr. 60/B4
Chalais, Swi. 60/D5
Chālakudi, India 95/C4
Chalamama, Bol. 185/E4
Chalaronne (riv.), Fr. 60/A5
Chalatenango, ESal. 176/D3
Chalbi (des.), Kenya 119/B1
Chalchihuites, Mex. 174/E4
Ch'alchīs (peak), Eth. 117/H3
Chalchyn (riv.), Mong. 79/H2
Chalco, Mex. 175/R10
Chale (pt.), Kenya 119/B3
Chaleur (bay), NB,,Qu, Can. 158/D2
Chalfont, Pa, US 168/C3
Chalfont Saint Giles, Eng, UK 30/B2
Chalfont Saint Peter, Eng, UK 30/B2
Chalhuanca, Peru 184/C4
Chali, China 86/C2
Chalifert (canal), Fr. 30/L5
Chalindrey, Fr. 60/B2
Chaling, China 87/G3
Chalinguita, Chile 188/B4
Chalinze, Tanz. 119/B3
Chālisgaon, India 95/B1
Chalk (mts.), Tx, US 150/C3
Chalk Hill (dam), Mi, US 157/L5
Chalk River, On, Can. 161/H1
Chalkar, Kaz. 71/J2
Chalkoi, India 98/C5
Chalkyitsik, Ak, US 171/K2
Challana, Bol. 184/D4
Challans, Fr. 44/C3
Challapalle, India 95/D2
Challapata, Bol. 188/C1
Challenger (mts.), Nun, Can. 141/T6
Challes-les-Eaux, Fr. 64/B1
Challis, Id, US 147/F1
Challock, Eng, UK 37/G4
Chalmette, La, US 164/D3
Chalna, Rus. 68/G3
Chālna, Bang. 97/G4
Chālna Port, Bang. 97/G4
Chalon-sur-Saône, Fr. 60/A4
Chalonnes-sur-Loire, Fr. 57/E6
Châlons-sur-Marne, Fr. 55/D6
Châlonvillars, Fr. 60/C2
Chaltyr', Rus. 73/K4
Chālūs, Iran 103/G2
Cham, Swi. 61/E3
Cham, Ger. 59/F4
Cham (riv.), Ger. 59/F4
Chama, Co, US 152/B2
Chama, Zam. 119/A4
Chama, NM, US 149/J2
Chama (riv.), NM, US 149/J2
Chamah (peak), Malay. 89/C1
Chaman, Pak. 101/J2
Chaman Bīd, Iran 103/J2
Chamba, India 98/D3
Chambal (riv.), India 92/C2
Chambaran (plat.), Fr. 44/F4
Chambas, Cuba 177/G1
Chamberino, NM, US 150/A1
Chamberlain (lake), Me, US 158/C2
Chamberlain, SD, US 154/E2
Chamberlain, Uru. 191/K10
Chamberlain, Sk, Can. 145/M2
Chamberlin (mt.), Ak, US 171/K2
Chambers (bay), Austl. 128/C3
Chambers (isl.), Mi, US 157/L5
Chambers, Ne, US 154/E2
Chambers (cr.), Tx, US 151/F1
Chambers (co.), Tx, US 151/N9
Chambersburg, Pa, US 161/H5
Chambéry, Fr. 64/B1
Chambéry-Aix-les-Bains (arpt.), Fr. 64/B1
Chambeshi, Zam. 121/G5
Chambeshi (riv.), Zam. 121/G5
Chambeyron, Aiguille de (peak), Fr. 64/C3
Chambishi, Zam. 123/F2
Chamblee, Ga, US 163/M7
Chambly, Fr. 30/J4
Chambly, Qu, Can. 159/P7
Chambord, Fr. 57/G5
Chambourcy, Fr. 30/J5
Chambray-lès-Tours, Fr. 57/F6
Chambry, Fr. 30/L5
Chamchamāl, Iraq 103/F3
Chamechaude (peak), Fr. 64/B2
Chameis, Namb. 124/A2
Chamical, Arg. 188/C4
Chamigny, Fr. 30/M5
Chamizal Nat'l Mem., Tx, US 150/A2
Chamizo, Uru. 191/L11
Cha'mo Hāyk' (lake), Eth. 117/H4
Chamois, Mo, US 153/J1
Chamonix-Mont-Blanc, Fr. 60/C6
Champ-sur-Drac, Fr. 64/B2
Champagne, Yk, Can. 171/L3
Champagne (reg.), Fr. 42/C4
Champagne (Reims) (arpt.), Fr. 54/D5
Champagne-Ardenne (pol.reg), Fr. 44/F2
Champagne-sur-Oise, Fr. 30/J4
Champagney, Fr. 60/C2
Champagnole, Fr. 60/B4
Champaign, Il, US 160/B4
Champaquí (peak), Arg. 188/C4
Champasak, Laos 94/D3
Champawat, India 96/C1
Champdeuil, Fr. 30/L6
Champeaux, Fr. 30/L6
Champéry, Swi. 60/C5
Champex, Swi. 60/D5
Champhol, Fr. 57/G4
Champigneulles, Fr. 55/F6
Champigny-sur-Marne, Fr. 30/K5
Champion, Oh, US 160/F4
Champion, Ab, Can. 145/H2
Champlain, NY, US 161/K2
Champlain (lake), NY,Vt, US 143/M3
Champlin, Mn, US 157/P6
Champlitte, Fr. 60/B2
Champotón, Mex. 176/D2
Champotón (riv.), Mex. 176/D2
Champs-sur-Marne, Fr. 30/K5
Champsevraine, Fr. 60/B2
Champtoceaux, Fr. 56/D6
Champvans, Fr. 60/B3
Chāmrājnagar-Rāmasamudram, India 95/C4
Chamusca, Port. 46/A3
Chan Chan (ruin), Peru 184/B3
Chan May Dong (cape), Viet. 94/E2
Chana, Thai. 94/C5
Chañaral, Chile 188/B4
Chañaral, Chile 188/B3
Chança (riv.), Port. 46/B4
Chancay, Peru 184/B3
Chance Cove (pt.), Nf, Can. 159/L2
Chance Harbour, NB, Can. 158/D3
Chānchra, Bang. 97/H4
Chanco, Chile 190/B2
Chancy, Swi. 60/B5
Chandalar, Ak, US 171/J2
Chandalar (riv.), Ak, US 171/J2
Chandannagar, India 97/G4
Chandarpur, India 95/D1
Chandausi, India 96/B1
Chandeleur (isls.), La, US 164/D3
Chandeleur (sound), La, US 164/D3
Chanderi, India 96/B3
Chandīgarh (state), India 98/D4
Chandīgarh, India 98/D4
Chāndil, India 97/F4
Chandlees (riv.), Braz. 184/D3
Chandler, Qu, Can. 158/E1
Chandler (lake), Ak, US 171/H2
Chandler, Az, US 149/G4
Chandler, In, US 162/D1
Chandler, Mn, US 155/G2
Chandler, Ok, US 153/F3
Chandler, Tx, US 151/G1
Chandolin, Swi. 60/D5
Chāndpur, India 96/B1
Chāndpur, Bang. 97/H4
Chandra Garhi, Nepal 97/G2
Chandrakona Road, India 97/F4
Chanduy, Ecu. 180/A5
Chang (riv.), China 77/L6
Chang (isl.), Camb. 93/H5
Chang (lake), China 80/C5
Chang (Yangtze) (riv.), China 80/D5
Chang Khoeng, Thai. 86/C5
Changan, SKor. 81/E5
Changanācheri, India 95/C4
Changane (riv.), Moz. 123/G4
Chang'anzhen, China 80/L9
Changara, Moz. 123/G3
Changbai (peak), China 81/E2
Changbai (mts.), NKor. 79/K3
Changbai Chaoxianzu Zizhixian, China 81/E2
Changchun, China 79/K3
Changdang (lake), China 80/D5
Changdao, China 80/E3
Changde, China 87/F2
Ch'angdo, NKor. 81/D3
Changé, Fr. 57/F5
Changeon (riv.), Fr. 57/F6
Changewater, NJ, US 168/D2
Changfeng, China 80/D4
Changgang, NKor. 81/D2
Changge, China 80/C4
Changgi-ap (cape), SKor. 84/A2
Changhai, China 81/B3
Changhang, SKor. 81/D4
Changhowŏn, SKor. 81/D4
Changhua, Tai. 87/J3
Changhŭng, SKor. 81/D5
Changhŭng, NKor. 81/E2
Changi (nbrhd.), Sing. 89/J6
Changi (int'l arpt.), Sing. 89/J6
Changis-sur-Marne, Fr. 30/M5
Changjiang, China 87/F5
Changjiang Zhongxiayou (plain), China 87/G2
Changjin (lake), NKor. 81/D2
Changjin (res.), NKor. 81/D2
Changjin, NKor. 81/D2
Changle, China 87/J2
Changle, China 80/D3
Changle, China 87/E2
Changli, China 80/D3
Changling, China 80/E1
Changlingji, China 87/G1
Changlingzi, China 81/B3
Changlingzi, China 79/J4
Changlingzi, China 79/J4
Changliushui, China 78/F4
Changlun, Malay. 94/C5
Changmar, China 99/C5
Changning, China 93/G3
Changning, China 86/E2
Ch'angnyŏng, SKor. 81/E5
Changping, China 80/H6
Changp'ung-ŭp, NKor. 81/D3
Changqing, China 80/D3
Changsan-got (cape), NKor. 81/C3
Changsha, China 87/G2
Changshan, China 87/H4
Changshan (arch.), China 79/J4
Changsheng, China 87/G3
Changshoudian, China 87/G2
Changshu, China 80/L8
Changshun, China 87/E3
Changsŏng, SKor. 81/D5
Changsu, SKor. 81/D5
Changsŭngp'o, SKor. 81/E5
Changtu, China 80/F2
Changuinola, Pan. 177/F4
Changweiliang, China 78/C4
Ch'angwŏn, SKor. 81/E5
Changwu, China 78/F4
Changxing, China 80/K8
Changyang, China 87/F2
Changyi, China 80/D3
Changyŏn, NKor. 81/C3
Changyuan, China 80/C4
Changzhi, China 80/C3
Changzhou, China 80/K8
Chanhassen, Mn, US 157/N7
Chankanai, SrL. 95/C4
Chanlers (falls), Kenya 119/B1
Channapatna, India 95/C3
Channel (isls.), UK 29/D4
Channel Country (phys. reg.), Austl. 127/C3
Channel Islands NP, Ca, US 166/A3
Channel Islands NP, Ca, US 148/C3
Channel Tunnel (tun.), Eng, UK,Fr. 37/H5
Channel-Port aux Basques, Nf, Can. 159/H2
Channelview, Tx, US 151/M9
Channing, Tx, US 152/C3
Chantada, Sp. 46/B1
Chanteloup-les-Vignes, Fr. 30/J5
Chantepie, Fr. 56/D4
Chanthaburi, Thai. 94/C3
Chantilly, Fr. 54/B5
Chantraine, Fr. 60/C1
Chantrey (inlet), Nun, Can. 140/G2
Chanute, Ks, US 153/G2
Chao (riv.), China 78/H3
Chao (lake), China 80/D5
Chao, Peru 184/B3
Chao Phraya (riv.), Thai. 94/C3
Chaobai (riv.), China 79/H4
Chaor (riv.), China 79/J2
Chaoyang, China 87/H4
Chaoyang, China 80/E2
Chaozhou, China 87/H4
Chap Le, Viet. 94/D2
Chapacura, Bol. 184/D3
Chapada Diamantina, PN, Braz. 187/E2
Chapada dos Guimarães, Braz. 186/B2
Chapada dos Veadeiros, PN da, Braz. 186/D2
Chapadinha, Braz. 183/F3
Chapala (lake), Mex. 174/E4
Chapala, Mex. 174/E4
Chapará (riv.), Bol. 188/C1
Chaparé (riv.), Bol. 185/E5
Chapareillan, Fr. 64/B2
Chaparral, Col. 180/C4
Chaparrosa, Mex. 174/E4
Chapayev, Kaz. 71/J2
Chapayevsk, Rus. 71/J1
Chapecó, Braz. 189/F3
Chapecó (riv.), Braz. 189/F3
Chapel en le Frith, Eng, UK 35/G5
Chapel Hill, Tn, US 162/D3
Chapel Hill, Ga, US 163/L7
Chapel Hill, NC, US 163/H3
Chapel Ness (pt.), Sc, UK 33/D4
Chapel Saint Leonards, Eng, UK 35/J5
Chapelfell Top (peak), Eng, UK 35/F2
Chapelle-lez-Herlaimont, Belg. 55/D3
Chapeltown, Eng, UK 35/G5
Chaplain (lake), Wa, US 167/D2
Chapleau, On, Can. 141/H4
Chaplin, Sk, Can. 145/L2
Chaplin (riv.), Ky, US 162/E2
Chaplygin, Rus. 70/F1
Chapman, Ks, US 153/F1
Chapman, Al, US 164/E2
Chapmanville, WV, US 163/F2
Chaponost, Fr. 64/A1
Chappār, India 98/D5
Chappell, Ne, US 154/C3
Chāpra, India 97/E3
Char (well), Mrta. 110/B5
Char Gāzi, Bang. 97/H4
Chara, Rus. 75/M4
Chara (riv.), Rus. 75/M4
Charagua, Bol. 188/D1
Charagua, Par. 189/E2
Charambirá (pt.), Col. 180/B3
Charaña, Bol. 188/B1
Charandra (riv.), Gre. 49/N8
Ch'arants'avan, Arm. 103/F1
Charata, Arg. 188/D3
Charbon, Austl. 133/D1
Charcas, Mex. 175/E4
Charcot (isl.), Ant. 192/U
Chard, Eng, UK 36/D5
Chardon, Oh, US 160/F4
Chardonnière, Haiti 177/H2
Charente (riv.), Fr. 66/C1
Chargrām, Bang. 93/F3
Chari (riv.), Chad 107/D3
Chari-Baguirmi (pref.), Chad 116/B3
Chārīkār, Afg. 101/J1
Charikot, Nepal 97/F2
Chariton (riv.), Mo,Ia, US 155/H3
Chariton, Ia, US 155/H3
Charity, Guy. 181/G3
Charkhāri, India 96/B3
Charkhi Dādri, India 98/D5
Charlbury, Eng, UK 37/E3
Charlemagne, Qu, Can. 159/P6
Charlemont, NI, UK 34/B3
Charleroi, Belg. 55/D3
Charleroi, Pa, US 161/G4
Charleroi à Bruxelles, Canal de (canal), Belg. 55/D2
Charles (isl.), Qu, Can. 141/J2
Charles (hill), Il, US 155/J2
Charles (pt.), Austl. 128/C3
Charles (peak), Austl. 130/D5
Charles (mt.), Austl. 130/C3
Charles (cape), Va, US 163/K2
Charles City, Ia, US 155/H2
Charles City, Va, US 163/J2
Charles de Gaulle (int'l arpt.), Fr. 30/K4
Charles Fuhr, Arg. 191/C6
Charles H. Russell NWR, Mt, US 156/A4
Charles M. Russell Nat'l Wild Ref., Mt, US 145/L4
Charles Town, WV, US 161/H5
Charleston, Ar, US 153/G3
Charleston, Il, US 160/B5
Charleston, Mo, US 162/C2
Charleston, Ms, US 162/B3
Charleston, Nv, US 146/F3
Charleston (peak), Nv, US 148/E2
Charleston, SC, US 163/H4
Charleston (A.F.B.), SC, US 163/G4
Charleston (cap.), WV, US 163/G1
Charlestown, StK. 173/N8
Charlestown, NH, US 161/K3
Charlestown, In, US 162/E1
Charlestown, Md, US 168/C4
Charleval, Fr. 57/G2
Charleville, Austl. 134/B4
Charleville-Mézières, Fr. 55/D4
Charlevoix, Mi, US 160/D2
Charlevoix (lake), Mi, US 160/D2
Charlotte (lake), BC, Can. 144/B1
Charlotte (har.), Fl, US 165/G4
Charlotte, Mi, US 160/D3
Charlotte, Tn, US 162/D2
Charlotte, Vt, US 161/K2
Charlotte, NC, US 163/G3
Charlotte, Tx, US 150/E3
Charlotte Amalie, USVI 173/M8
Charlotte Court House, Va, US 163/H2
Charlotte Hall, Md, US 163/J1
Charlotte/Douglas (int'l arpt.), NC, US 163/G3
Charlottenberg, Swe. 40/E2
Charlottenburg, Ger. 42/Q6
Charlottesville, Va, US 163/H1
Charlottetown (cap.), PE, Can. 158/F2
Charlotteville, Trin. 181/F2
Charlton, Austl. 132/B3
Charlton (isl.), On, Can. 141/H3
Charlton Kings, Eng, UK 36/D3
Charlwood, Eng, UK 30/C3
Charly, Fr. 54/C6
Charly, Fr. 64/A1
Charmco, WV, US 163/G1
Charmes (res.), Fr. 60/B2
Charmes, Fr. 60/C1
Charmes-sur-Rhône, Fr. 64/A3
Charmey, Swi. 60/D4
Charnay-lès-Mâcon, Fr. 44/F3
Charny, Qu, Can. 158/B2
Charny, Fr. 30/L5
Charny-sur-Meuse, Fr. 55/E5
Charolais, Monts du (mts.), Fr. 44/F3
Charouine, Alg. 111/E3
Charquemont, Fr. 60/C3
Chars, Fr. 30/H4
Chārsadda, Pak. 98/A2
Charsk, Kaz. 99/D2
Charters Towers, Austl. 134/B3
Charthāwāl, India 98/D5
Chartres, Fr. 57/G4
Chartres, UK 191/E6
Chartres-de-Bretagne, Fr. 56/D4

Map Section
216
217

Courcelles-sur-Seine, Fr. 57/G2
Courchevel (arpt.), Fr. 64/C2
Courcouronnes, Fr. 30/K6
Courdimanche, Fr. 30/H4
Courgenay, Swi. 60/D3
Courgent, Fr. 30/G5
Courmayeur, It. 60/C6
Cournon-d'Auvergne, Fr. 44/E4
Courpalay, Fr. 30/L6
Courrendlin, Swi. 60/D3
Courroux, Swi. 60/D3
Coursan, Fr. 44/E5
Courseulles-sur-Mer, Fr. 57/E2
Courtelary, Swi. 60/D3
Courtenay, ND, US 156/E4
Courtepin, Swi. 60/D4
Courthézon, Fr. 64/A4
Courtice, On, Can. 160/V8
Courtisols, Fr. 55/D6
Courtland, Ca, US 167/L10
Courtland, Ks, US 154/F4
Courtland, Va, US 163/J2
Courtmacsherry, Ire. 32/B6
Courtmacsherry (bay), Ire. 32/B6
Courtney, Tx, US 151/F2
Courtomer, Fr. 30/L6
Courtown, Ire. 32/D4
Courtright, On, Can. 167/H6
Courville-sur-Eure, Fr. 57/G4
Cousance, Fr. 60/B4
Cousane (pass), Ire. 32/A6
Coushatta, La, US 164/B1
Cousolre, Fr. 55/D3
Coutances, Fr. 56/D2
Couteau (hills), Sk, Can. 145/L2
Couterne, Fr. 57/E3
Coutevroult, Fr. 30/L5
Couto de Magalhães, Braz. 182/D5
Coutras, Fr. 44/C4
Coutts, Ab, Can. 145/J3
Couva, Trin. 181/F2
Couvet, Swi. 60/C4
Couvin, Belg. 55/D3
Couzeix, Fr. 44/D4
Covadonga, PN, Sp. 46/C1
Covasna (prov.), Rom. 51/G3
Covasna, Rom. 51/H3
Cove, Ar, US 153/G3
Cove, Sc, UK 33/B5
Cove, Tx, US 151/N9
Cove Bay, Sc, UK 33/D2
Cove Gap, WV, US 163/F1
Cove Neck, NY, US 169/L8
Covelo, Ca, US 146/B4
Covendo, Bol. 185/E4
Coventry, Eng, UK 37/E2
Coventry (co.), Eng, UK 37/E2
Coventry (canal), Eng, UK 37/E1
Covered, Turk. 103/M6
Covesville, Va, US 163/H2
Covilhã, Port. 46/B2
Covina, Ca, US 166/G7
Covington, Ga, US 162/F4
Covington, In, US 160/C4
Covington, Ky, US 162/E1
Covington, La, US 164/C2
Covington, Mi, US 157/K4
Covington, Ok, US 153/F2
Covington, Oh, US 160/D4
Covington, Tn, US 162/C3
Covington, Tx, US 151/F1
Covington, Va, US 163/H2
Covo, It. 62/C3
Cow (cr.), Or, US 146/B2
Cow Creek, Wy, US 154/B2
Cow Green (res.), Eng, UK 35/F2
Cowal (reg.), Sc, UK 33/A4
Cowal (lake), Austl. 133/C1
Cowal Creek Aboriginal Community, Austl. 129/F2
Cowan, Tn, US 162/D3
Cowan (nbrhd.), Austl. 134/H8
Cowan (lake), Austl. 127/B4
Cowangie, Austl. 132/B2
Cowansville, Qu, Can. 161/K2
Cowaramup, Austl. 130/B5
Coward Springs, Austl. 131/H4
Cowarie, Austl. 131/H3
Cowboy (hill), Ne, US 154/C3
Cowbridge, Wal, UK 36/C4
Cowden, Il, US 155/K4
Cowdenbeath, Sc, UK 33/C4
Cowee (mts.), NC, US 163/F3
Cowell, Austl. 131/H5
Cowes, Eng, UK 37/E5
Cowes, Austl. 133/B4
Cowessess Ind. Res., Sk, Can. 156/C2
Coweta (co.), Ga, US 163/L8
Cowhouse (cr.), Tx, US 151/E2
Cowichan (lake), BC, Can. 144/B3
Cowie, Sc, UK 33/C4
Cowlesville, NY, US 160/W10
Cowley, Ab, Can. 145/G3
Cowley, Wy, US 147/J1
Cowlitz (riv.), Wa, US 144/D4
Cowora, Austl. 133/C3
Cowpens Nat'l Bfld., SC, US 163/G3
Cowra, Austl. 133/D1
Cox City, Ok, US 153/F3
Coxhoe, Eng, UK 35/G2
Coxilha de Santana (hills), Braz. 189/F4
Coxim, Braz. 189/F1
Coxim (riv.), Braz. 186/B3
Cox's Bāzār, Bang. 93/F3
Cox's Cove, Nf, Can. 159/H1
Coxs Mills, WV, US 163/G1
Coxsackie, NY, US 161/K3
Coy, Al, US 164/E2
Coy Aike, Arg. 191/C6
Coya, Chile 190/N9
Coya Sur, Chile 188/B2
Coyah, Gui. 114/B4
Coyame, Mex. 150/B3
Coyanosa Draw (riv.), Tx, US 150/C2
Coye-la-Forêt, Fr. 30/K4
Coyoacán (nbrhd.), Mex. 175/R10
Coyote (cr.), Ca, US 167/L12
Coyotepec, Mex. 175/K7
Coyuca de Benítez, Mex. 175/E5
Coyutla, Mex. 175/M6
Cozad, Ne, US 154/E3
Cozhê, China 99/E5
Cozumel, Mex. 176/E1
Cozumel (int'l arpt.), Mex. 176/E1
Cozumel (isl.), Mex. 139/J7
Crab (cr.), Wa, US 144/E4
Crab Orchard Nat'l Wild. Ref., Il, US 155/K5
Crab Orchard NWR, Il, US 162/C2
Crabapple, Ga, US 163/M6
Cradle (mtn.), Austl. 132/C4
Cradock, SAfr. 124/D4
Craftsbury, Vt, US 161/K2
Crag (mt.), Yk, Can. 171/K3
Crag (peak), Eng, UK 35/F3
Craig, Ak, US 171/M4
Craig, Co, US 147/K3
Craig (mt.), Co, US 154/B3
Craig, Mo, US 155/G3
Craig, Mt, US 145/J4
Craig (cr.), Va, US 163/G2
Craigavad, NI, UK 34/C2
Craigavon (dist.), NI, UK 34/B3
Craigavon, NI, UK 34/B3
Craigellachie, Sc, UK 33/C2
Craigieburn, Austl. 132/F5
Craigsville, WV, US 163/G1
Craigsville, Va, US 163/H1
Craik, Sk, Can. 145/M2
Crail, Sc, UK 33/D4
Crailsheim, Ger. 58/D4
Craiova, Rom. 51/F3
Cramalina (peak), Swi. 61/E5
Cramlington, Eng, UK 35/G1
Cran-Gevrier, Fr. 60/C6
Crana (riv.), Ire. 34/A1
Cranborne Chase (for.), Eng, UK 36/D5
Cranbourne, Austl. 132/G6
Cranbrook, Austl. 132/D4
Cranbrook, Austl. 130/C5
Cranbrook, BC, Can. 144/G3
Cranbury, NJ, US 168/D3
Crandall, Mb, Can. 156/D2
Crandall, Tx, US 150/L7
Crandon, Wi, US 157/K5
Crane (lake), Il, US 155/J3
Crane, Mt, US 156/B4
Crane, Mo, US 153/H2
Crane, Tx, US 150/C2
Crane Hill, Al, US 162/D3
Crane Lake, Mn, US 157/H3
Crane Naval Weapons Support Center, In, US 160/C5
Crane Neck (pt.), NY, US 169/E2
Crane NWSC, In, US 162/D1
Crane Prairie (res.), Or, US 146/C2
Crane River, Mb, Can. 156/E2
Cranfills Gap, Tx, US 150/F2
Cranford, NJ, US 169/H9
Cranleigh, Eng, UK 37/F4
Cranston, RI, US 161/L4
Craon, Fr. 57/E5
Craponne (canal), Fr. 64/A5
Craponne, Fr. 64/A1
Crary, ND, US 156/E3
Crasna (riv.), Rom. 50/F2
Crasnoe, Mol. 72/E4
Craster, Eng, UK 33/E6
Crater (peak), Or, US 146/B2
Crater (lake), Or, US 146/B2
Crater Lake NP, Or, US 146/B2
Craters Of The Moon Nat'l Mon., Id, US 147/G2
Crateús, Braz. 183/F4
Crati (riv.), It. 48/E3
Cratloe, Ire. 32/B4
Crato, Port. 46/B3
Crato, Braz. 183/G4
Cravens, La, US 164/B2
Cravinhos, Braz. 189/H2
Crawford, Co, US 149/J1
Crawford, Ga, US 163/F4
Crawford, Ms, US 162/C4
Crawford, Ok, US 152/E3
Crawford, Sc, UK 33/C6
Crawford, Tx, US 151/F2
Crawford Bay, BC, Can. 144/F3
Crawfordsville, In, US 160/C4
Crawfordville, Fl, US 165/F2
Crawfordville, Ga, US 163/F4
Crawley, Eng, UK 37/F4
Cray (riv.), Eng, UK 30/D2
Crayford (nbrhd.), Eng, UK 30/D2
Crazy (mts.), Mt, US 145/J4
Crazy Horse Monument, SD, US 154/C2
Crazy Woman (cr.), Wy, US 147/K1
Creag Meagaidh (peak), Sc, UK 33/B3
Creagerstown, Md, US 168/A4
Creal Springs, Il, US 162/C2
Cream, Wi, US 155/J1
Creasy (Mifflinville), Pa, US 168/B1
Creazzo, It. 63/E3
Crêches-sur-Saône, Fr. 60/A5
Crécy-sur-Serre, Fr. 54/C4
Credit (riv.), On, Can. 160/T8
Crediton, Eng, UK 36/C5
Cree (riv.), Sc, UK 34/D2
Cree (lake), Sk, Can. 140/F3
Cree (riv.), Sk, Can. 140/F3
Creede, Co, US 149/J2
Creedman Coulee Nat'l Wild. Ref., Mt, US 145/K3
Creedmoor, Tx, US 151/F2
Creek (Pryor), Ok, US 153/G2
Creel, Mex. 174/D3
Creelman, Sk, Can. 156/C3
Creemore, On, Can. 160/F2
Creetown, Sc, UK 34/D2
Creglingen, Ger. 58/D4
Crégy-lès-Meaux, Fr. 30/L5
Créhange, Fr. 55/F5
Créhen, Fr. 56/C3
Creighton, Sk, Can. 140/F3
Creighton, Ne, US 154/F2
Creighton, SD, US 154/C1
Creignish, NS, Can. 159/G3
Creil, Fr. 54/B5
Crema, It. 62/C3
Crémieu, Fr. 60/B6
Cremlingen, Ger. 53/H4
Cremona, Ab, Can. 144/G2
Cremona, It. 62/D3
Cremona (prov.), It. 62/C2
Crenshaw, Ms, US 162/B3
Creola, Al, US 164/D2
Creole, La, US 164/B3
Crepaja, Serb. 50/E3
Crepori (riv.), Braz. 182/B4
Crépy, Fr. 54/C4
Creran (lake), Sc, UK 33/A3
Cres (isl.), Cro. 67/G1
Cres, Cro. 45/L4
Cresaptown, Md, US 161/G5
Cresbard, SD, US 154/E1
Crescent (lake), Fl, US 165/H3
Crescent, Ok, US 153/F3
Crescent, Or, US 146/C2
Crescent City, Ca, US 146/A3
Crescent City, Fl, US 165/H3
Crescent Group (isls.), Asia 87/F5
Crescent Lake, Or, US 146/C2
Crescent Lake Nat'l. Wild. Ref., Ne, US 154/C3
Crescentino, It. 62/B3
Cresco, Ia, US 155/H2
Cresco, Pa, US 168/C1
Crespano del Grappa, It. 63/E2
Crespellano, It. 63/E4
Crespières, Fr. 30/H5
Crespin, Fr. 54/C3
Crespo, Arg. 188/D5
Cresskill, NJ, US 169/K8
Cresson, Pa, US 161/G4
Cresson, Tx, US 150/K7
Cressona, Pa, US 168/B2
Cressy, Austl. 132/C4
Crest, Fr. 64/B3
Crest Hill, Il, US 167/P16
Crestline, Ca, US 166/C2
Crestline, Oh, US 160/E4
Creston, Nf, Can. 159/K2
Creston, Ca, US 148/B3
Creston, Ia, US 155/G3
Creston, BC, Can. 144/F3
Crestone, Co, US 152/B2
Crestone (peak), Co, US 152/B2
Crestview, Fl, US 164/E2
Crestwood Village, NJ, US 168/D4
Creswell, Eng, UK 35/G5
Creswell, Or, US 146/B2
Creswell Downs, Austl. 129/D4
Creswick, Austl. 133/A3
Crêt de la Neige (peak), Fr. 60/B5
Crêt du Nu (peak), Fr. 60/B5
Crêt du Rey (peak), Fr. 64/C1
Crete, Il, US 160/C4
Crete (sea), Gre. 67/K3
Crete, Ne, US 155/F3
Crete (isl.), Gre. 29/G5
Créteil, Fr. 30/K5
Cretin (cape), PNG 129/G1
Creuch (hill), Sc, UK 33/B5
Creus (cape), Sp. 47/G1
Creuse (riv.), Fr. 66/D1
Creussen (riv.), Ger. 59/E3
Creussen, Ger. 59/E3
Creutzwald-la-Croix, Fr. 55/F5
Creuzburg, Ger. 53/H6
Crevacuore, It. 62/B2
Crevalcore, It. 63/E4
Crèvecœur-le-Grand, Fr. 54/B4
Crevillente, Sp. 47/E3
Crevoladossola, It. 61/E5
Crewe, Eng, UK 35/F5
Crewe, Va, US 163/H2
Crewkerne, Eng, UK 36/D5
Crews (lake), Fl, US 164/K7
Crianlarich, Sc, UK 33/B4
Crib Point, Austl. 133/B4
Criccieth, Wal, UK 34/D6
Crichton, Sk, Can. 145/L3
Criciúma, Braz. 189/G4
Cricket, NC, US 163/G2
Crickhowell, Wal, UK 36/C3
Cricklade, Eng, UK 37/E3
Crieff, Sc, UK 33/C4
Criffell (hill), Sc, UK 34/E2
Crikvenica, Cro. 45/L4
Crillon (mt.), Ak, US 171/L4
Crimean (pen.), Rom. 51/L3
Crimean (mts.), Ukr. 73/H5
Crimond, Sc, UK 33/E1
Cripple Creek, Co, US 152/B1
Criquetot-L'Esneval, Fr. 57/F1
Crisenoy, Fr. 30/L6
Crisfield, Md, US 163/K2
Crisp (pt.), Mi, US 160/D1
Crisp, Tx, US 150/L7
Crissier, Swi. 60/C4
Crissiumal, Braz. 189/F3
Crissolo, It. 64/D3
Cristal, Monts de (mts.), Gabon 120/B2
Cristalândia, Braz. 186/C1
Cristalina, Braz. 186/D3
Cristalinho (riv.), Braz. 186/C2
Cristina, Braz. 187/L7
Cristino Castro, Braz. 183/E5
Cristóbal (pt.), Ecu. 184/J7
Cristóbal Colón (peak), Col. 180/C2
Cristoforo Colombo (int'l arpt.), It. 62/B5
Cristuru Secuiesc, Rom. 51/G2
Crişul Negru (riv.), Rom. 50/E2
Crişul Repede (riv.), Rom. 72/B4
Crivitz, Wi, US 160/B2
Crixás, Braz. 186/C2
Crixás-Açu (riv.), Braz. 186/C2
Crna Reka (riv.), FYROM 49/G2
Črnomelj, Slov. 50/B3
Croaghmoyle (peak), Ire. 32/A2
Croatia (ctry.) 50/C3
Croce (peak), It. 61/H5
Croce, Pico di (peak), It. 61/H4
Croche (peak), Fr. 60/C6
Croche (riv.), Qu, Can. 158/A1
Crocker, Mo, US 153/H2
Crocker (range), Malay. 91/E3
Crocker (peak), Ecu. 184/J7
Crocketford, Sc, UK 34/E1
Crockett, Ca, US 167/K10
Crockett, Tx, US 151/G2
Crockett Mills, Tn, US 162/C3
Crockham Hill, Eng, UK 30/D3
Crocodile (pt.), Austl. 133/E2
Crocodilopolis (ruin), Egypt 113/B6
Crodo, It. 61/E5
Crofton, Ky, US 162/D2
Crofton, Md, US 168/B6
Crofty, Wal, UK 36/B3
Croghan (mtn.), Ire. 34/B6
Crohane (peak), Ire. 32/A6
Croisette (cape), Fr. 64/B6
Croisic (bay), Fr. 56/C6
Croisic (pt.), Fr. 56/C6
Croisilles, Fr. 54/B3
Croissy-Beaubourg, Fr. 30/K5
Croix (lake), On, Can. 157/J3
Croix Rousse (peak), Fr. 64/D2
Croker (cape), Austl. 128/D2
Croker (isl.), Austl. 127/C2
Crolles, Fr. 64/B2
Cromarty, Sc, UK 33/B1
Cromarty Firth (bay), Sc, UK 33/B1
Crombie (mt.), Austl. 131/F3
Cromdale, Sc, UK 33/C2
Cromdale (hills), Sc, UK 33/C2
Cromer, Mb, Can. 156/D3
Cromer, Eng, UK 37/H1
Cromwell, NZ 135/B4
Cromwell, Al, US 162/C4
Cromwell, Ky, US 162/D2
Cromwell, Ok, US 153/F3
Crondall, Eng, UK 30/A3
Crong A Na (riv.), Viet. 94/D3
Cronulla (nbrhd.), Austl. 134/H9
Crook, Eng, UK 35/G2
Crooked (isl.), Bahm. 173/G3
Crooked (isl.), Fl, US 165/F3
Crooked (lake), Fl, US 165/H4
Crooked (cr.), Ks, US 152/D2
Crooked (riv.), Or, US 146/C1
Crooked Creek, Ak, US 171/G3
Crooked Island Passage (chan.), Bahm. 177/H1
Crookhaven, Ire. 32/A7
Crooks, SD, US 155/F2
Crooks Tower (peak), SD, US 154/C1
Crookston, Mn, US 156/F4
Crookstown, Ire. 32/B6
Crooksville, Oh, US 160/E5
Crookwell, Austl. 133/D2
Croom, Ire. 32/B4
Croom, Fl, US 164/L6
Crosby, Mn, US 157/H4
Crosby, ND, US 156/C3
Crosby, Eng, UK 35/E5
Crosby, Ms, US 164/C2
Crosby (mt.), Wy, US 147/J2
Crosby, Tx, US 151/M9
Crosbyton, Tx, US 152/D4
Cross (cape), Namb. 122/B4
Cross, Tx, US 151/F2
Cross Anchor, SC, US 163/G3
Cross City, Fl, US 165/G3
Cross Fell (peak), Eng, UK 35/F2
Cross Hill, SC, US 163/G3
Cross Plains, Tx, US 150/E1
Cross Plains, Wi, US 155/K2
Cross River (state), Nga. 115/H5
Cross River (res.), NY, US 169/E1
Cross Roads, Tx, US 151/G1
Cross Roads, Pa, US 168/B4
Crossett, Ar, US 153/J4
Crossfarnoge (pt.), Ire. 32/D5
Crossfield, Ab, Can. 145/G2
Crossford, Sc, UK 33/C4
Crossgar, NI, UK 34/C3
Crossgates, Wal, UK 36/C2
Crosshaven, Ire. 32/B6
Crosshill, Sc, UK 33/B6
Crosshouse, Sc, UK 33/B5
Crosskeys, Wal, UK 36/C3
Crosslake, Mn, US 157/G4
Crossmaglen, NI, UK 32/D1
Crossmichael, Sc, UK 34/E2
Crossmolina, Ire. 32/A1
Crossroads, Ire. 31/P9
Crossville, Il, US 162/C1
Crossville, Al, US 162/E3
Crossville, Tn, US 162/E3
Crosswicks (cr.), NJ, US 168/D3
Crostolo (riv.), It. 62/D3
Croston, Eng, UK 35/F4
Croswell, Mi, US 160/E3
Crothersville, In, US 162/E1
Croton-Harmon (Croton-On-Hudson), NY, US 169/E1
Croton-On-Hudson (Croton-Harmon), NY, US 169/E1
Crotone, It. 49/E3
Crottendorf, Ger. 59/F1
Croult (riv.), Fr. 30/K5
Crouy, Fr. 54/C5
Crouy-sur-Ourcq, Fr. 30/M4
Crow (cr.), Co, US 154/B3
Crow (riv.), Mn, US 157/N6
Crow (peak), SD, US 154/C1
Crow Creek Ind. Res., SD, US 154/E1
Crow Ind. Res., Mt, US 147/J1
Crow Ind. Res., Mt, US 145/K5
Crow Wing (riv.), Mn, US 157/G4
Crow, North Fork (riv.), Mn, US 157/G5
Crow, North Fork (riv.), Mn, US 155/G1
Crow, South Fork (riv.), Mn, US 157/G5
Crow, South Fork (riv.), Mn, US 155/G1
Crowborough, Eng, UK 37/G4
Crowder, Ok, US 153/G3
Crowdy Bay NP, Austl. 132/E1
Crowe (riv.), On, Can. 161/H2
Crowell, Tx, US 152/E4
Crowheart, Wy, US 147/J2
Crowie (cr.), Austl. 133/C1
Crowland, Eng, UK 37/F1
Crowle, Eng, UK 35/H4
Crowley (lake), Ca, US 148/C2
Crowley, La, US 164/B2
Crowley, Tx, US 150/K7
Crowley's (ridge), Ar, US 162/B3
Crown Point, In, US 160/C4
Crown Point (int'l arpt.), Trin. 181/F2
Crown Prince Frederik (isl.), Nun, Can. 141/H1
Crownpoint, NM, US 149/H3
Crows Nest (peak), SD, US 154/C1
Crows Nest Falls NP, Austl. 134/D4
Crowther (cr.), Austl. 133/D2
Crowthorne, Eng, UK 37/F4
Crowville, La, US 153/J4
Croxley Green, Eng, UK 30/B2
Croydon (bor.), Eng, UK 30/C2
Croydon (nbrhd.), Eng, UK 30/C2
Croydon, Austl. 134/A2
Croydon (nbrhd.), Austl. 132/G5
Croydon, Pa, US 168/D3
Crozet (isls.), Fr. 27/M8
Crozon, Fr. 56/A4
Cruach Mhór (peak), Sc, UK 33/A4
Cruach nan Capull (peak), Sc, UK 33/A5
Cruas, Fr. 64/A3
Crucero, Peru 184/D4
Cruden Bay, Sc, UK 33/E2
Cruger, Ms, US 162/B4
Cruick Water (riv.), Sc, UK 33/D3
Crum (mtn.), Ms, US 162/C3
Crumlin, NI, UK 34/B2
Crummock Water (lake), Eng, UK 35/E2
Crump (lake), Or, US 146/D2
Crump, Tn, US 162/C3
Crumpton, Md, US 168/C5
Cruseilles, Fr. 60/C5
Crusheen, Ire. 32/B4
Crusnes (riv.), Fr. 55/E5
Cruz (cape), Cuba 177/G2
Cruz Alta, Arg. 190/E2
Cruz Alta (peak), Port. 47/P10
Cruz Alta, Braz. 189/F4
Cruz del Eje, Arg. 188/C4
Cruz Grande, Mex. 176/B2
Cruzeiro, Braz. 187/M7
Cruzeiro do Oeste, Braz. 189/F2
Cruzeiro do Sul, Braz. 184/C2
Cruzeta, Braz. 183/G4
Cruzília, Braz. 187/M6
Crvenka, Serb. 50/D3
Cryn-y-Brain (peak), Wal, UK 35/E5
Crystal, Mn, US 157/P6
Crystal, NM, US 149/H2
Crystal (lake), Pa, US 168/C1
Crystal Bay, Nv, US 146/D4
Crystal Beach, Fl, US 164/K7
Crystal Brook, Austl. 131/H5
Crystal Cave, Pa, US 168/C2
Crystal City, Mb, Can. 156/E3
Crystal City, Tx, US 150/E3
Crystal Falls, Mi, US 157/K4
Crystal Hill, Va, US 163/H2
Crystal Lake, Fl, US 165/F2
Crystal Lake, Il, US 160/B3
Crystal River, Fl, US 165/G3
Crystal Springs, Ms, US 164/C2
Crystal Springs, Fl, US 164/L7
Crystal Springs (res.), Ca, US 167/K11
Csenger, Hun. 43/M5
Csepreg, Hun. 50/C2
Csongrád, Hun. 50/E2
Csorna, Hun. 50/C2
Csorvás, Hun. 50/E2
Csóványos (peak), Hun. 50/D2
Csurgó, Hun. 50/C2
Ctesiphon (ruin), Iraq 103/F3
Cu Lao (isl.), Viet. 94/E4
Cuajinicuilapa, Mex. 176/B2
Cualedro, Sp. 46/B2
Cuamba, Moz. 123/H2
Cuanavale (riv.), Ang. 122/C2
Cuando (riv.), Ang. 122/D3
Cuangar, Ang. 122/C3
Cuango, Ang. 120/D5
Cuango, Ang. 120/D4
Cuango (riv.), Ang. 120/D5
Cuanza (riv.), Ang. 107/D6
Cuanza Norte (prov.), Ang. 120/C5
Cuanza Sul (prov.), Ang. 120/C5
Cuareim (riv.), Braz. 189/E4
Cuaró, Uru. 189/F4
Cuart de Poblet, Sp. 47/E3
Cuarto (riv.), Arg. 190/D2
Cuatir (riv.), Ang. 122/C2
Cuatro Ojos, Bol. 188/D1
Cuauhtémoc, Mex. 174/E5
Cuauhtémoc, Mex. 174/D2
Cuautepec, Mex. 175/L6
Cuautitlán, Mex. 175/Q9
Cuautitlán Izcalli, Mex. 175/Q9
Cuautla, Mex. 175/L8
Cuba (ctry.) 177/F1
Cuba, Il, US 155/J3
Cuba, Ks, US 154/F4
Cuba, Mo, US 153/J1
Cuba, NM, US 149/J2
Cuba, NY, US 161/G3
Cuba, Port. 46/B3
Cuba City, Wi, US 155/J2
Cubagua (isl.), Ven. 181/E2
Cubal, Ang. 122/B2
Cubal (riv.), Ang. 122/B2
Cuballing, Austl. 130/C5
Cubango (riv.), Ang. 107/D6
Cubatão, Braz. 187/K8
Cubati, Braz. 183/G4
Cubero, NM, US 149/J3
Çubuk, Turk. 102/C1
Cuc Phuong NP, Viet. 86/E4
Cucamonga (Rancho Cucamonga), Ca, US 166/C2
Cuccurano, It. 63/F6
Cucharas (riv.), Co, US 152/B2
Cuchi, Ang. 122/C2
Cuchi (riv.), Ang. 122/C2
Cuchilla Caraguatá, Uru. 189/F5
Cuchillo, NM, US 149/J4
Cuchillo-Có, Arg. 190/D3
Cuchivero (riv.), Ven. 181/E3
Cuchumatanes (mts.), Guat. 176/D3
Cuckfield, Eng, UK 37/F4
Cuckmere (riv.), Eng, UK 37/G5
Cucuí, Braz. 181/E4
Cúcuta, Col. 180/C3
Cucuyagua, Hon. 176/D3
Cudahy, Wi, US 160/C3
Cudahy, Ca, US 166/F8
Cudal, Austl. 133/D1
Cuddalore, India 95/C4
Cuddington, Eng, UK 35/F5
Cudgewa, Austl. 133/C3
Cudillero, Sp. 46/B1
Cudrefin, Swi. 60/D4
Cudworth, Eng, UK 35/G4
Cudworth, Sk, Can. 145/M1
Cue, Austl. 130/C3
Cuebe (riv.), Ang. 122/C2
Cueio (riv.), Ang. 122/D2
Cueli (riv.), Ang. 122/C2
Cuéllar, Sp. 46/C2
Cuéllar-Baza, Sp. 46/D4
Cuenca, Ecu. 180/B5
Cuenca, Sp. 46/D2
Cuencamé de Ceniceros, Mex. 174/E3
Cuengo (riv.), Ang. 120/D5
Cuernavaca, Mex. 175/K8
Cuero, Tx, US 151/F3
Cuers, Fr. 64/C6
Cuesmes, Belg. 54/C3
Cueto, Cuba 177/H1
Cuetzalán, Mex. 175/M6
Cueva de la Quebrada del Toro, PN, Ven. 180/D2
Cuevas de Vinromá, Sp. 47/F2
Cuevas del Almanzora, Sp. 46/E4
Cuevo, Bol. 188/D2
Cuffley, Eng, UK 30/C1
Cufré, Uru. 191/K11
Cuges-les-Pins, Fr. 64/B6
Cugir, Rom. 51/F3
Cuglieri, It. 48/A2
Cugnaux, Fr. 44/D5
Cugo (riv.), Ang. 120/D4
Cuiabá, Braz. 186/A2
Cuiabá (riv.), Braz. 185/G5
Cuicas, Ven. 180/D2
Cuijk, Neth. 52/C5
Cuilapa, Guat. 176/D3
Cuilcagh (peak), NI, UK 32/C1
Cuilco (riv.), Guat. 176/C3
Cuillin (sound), Sc, UK 31/Q8
Cuilo, Ang. 120/D4
Cuilo (riv.), Ang. 120/C4
Cuilo Pombo, Ang. 120/C4
Cuima, Ang. 122/B2
Cuisance (riv.), Fr. 60/B4
Cuise-la-Motte, Fr. 54/C5
Cuiseaux, Fr. 60/B5
Cuisery, Fr. 60/A4
Cuisy, Fr. 30/L4
Cuité, Braz. 183/G4
Cuitláhuac, Mex. 175/N8
Cuito (riv.), Ang. 122/C2
Cuito-Cuanavale, Ang. 122/C2
Cuiuni (riv.), Braz. 181/E5
Cujmir, Rom. 50/F3
Cukuh Batuberagam (cape), Indo. 89/C4
Culasi, Phil. 88/C3
Culbertson (dam), Ne, US 154/D3
Culburra-Orient Point, Austl. 133/E2
Culcairn, Austl. 133/C2
Culdaff (riv.), Ire. 34/A1
Culdaff, Ire. 34/A1
Culebras, Peru 184/B3
Culemborg, Neth. 52/C5
Culfa, Azer. 103/F2
Culgoa (riv.), Austl. 127/D3
Culiacán Rosales, Mex. 174/D3
Culion (isl.), Phil. 88/B3
Culion Reservation, Phil. 88/C3
Culiseu (riv.), Braz. 186/B2
Cullen, Arg. 191/C7
Cullen, La, US 153/H4
Cullen, Sc, UK 33/D1
Cullen, Va, US 163/H2
Cullen Bullen, Austl. 133/E1
Cullenagh (riv.), Ire. 32/A4
Culleoka, Tx, US 150/L6
Cullera, Sp. 47/E3
Culleredo, Sp. 46/A1
Cullin (lake), Ire. 32/A2
Cullinan, SAfr. 123/F5
Cullman, Al, US 162/D3
Culloden Battlesite, Sc, UK 33/B2
Cullomburg, Al, US 164/D2
Cullompton, Eng, UK 36/C5
Cullowhee, NC, US 163/F3
Cully, Swi. 60/C5
Cullybackey, NI, UK 34/B2
Culmback (dam), Wa, US 167/D2
Culmore, NI, UK 34/A1
Culoz, Fr. 60/B6
Culp Creek, Or, US 146/B2
Culpeper, Va, US 163/J1
Culpina, Bol. 188/C2
Culross, Sc, UK 33/C4
Culta, Bol. 188/C1
Cultra (lake), Ire. 32/B3
Cults, Sc, UK 33/D2
Culuene (riv.), Braz. 185/H4
Culver (pt.), Austl. 130/E5
Culver, Ks, US 153/F1
Culver, In, US 160/C4
Culver, Mn, US 157/H4
Culver, Or, US 146/C1
Culver City, Ca, US 166/F7
Culverden, NZ 135/C3
Culvers (lake), NJ, US 168/D1
Culverstone Green, Eng, UK 30/E3
Cumã (bay), Braz. 183/E3
Cumaná, Ven. 181/E2
Cumane (riv.), Fr. 64/B2
Cumaría, Peru 184/C3
Cumba, Peru 184/B2
Cumbal, Col. 180/B4
Cumberland (isl.), Ga, US 165/H2
Cumberland, Md, US 161/G5
Cumberland, Wa, US 167/D3
Cumberland, Wi, US 157/H5
Cumberland (riv.), Ky,Tn, US 143/J4
Cumberland (pen.), Nun, Can. 141/K2
Cumberland (sound), Nun, Can. 141/K2
Cumberland (falls), Ky, US 162/E2
Cumberland, Ky, US 163/F2
Cumberland, BC, Can. 144/B3
Cumberland (co.), NJ, US 168/A3
Cumberland (plat.), US 162/D3
Cumberland (lake), Ky, US 162/E2
Cumberland, Va, US 163/H2
Cumberland Gap NHP, NC,Va, US 163/F2
Cumberland Island Nat'l Seashore, Ga, US 165/H2
Cumbernauld, Sc, UK 33/C5
Cumbi, Ang. 120/C4
Cumbre del Laudo (peak), Arg. 188/B3
Cumbre del Libertador General San Martín (peak), Arg. 188/C3
Cumbres and Toltec Railroad, Co, US 149/J2
Cumbres Bastonal, Cerro (peak), Mex. 176/C2
Cumbres de Majalca, PN, Mex. 174/D2
Cumbres de Monterrey, PN, Mex. 172/A2
Cumbres de Monterrey, PN, Mex. 174/E3
Cumbria (co.), Eng, UK 35/E2
Cumbrian (mts.), Eng, UK 35/E2
Cumbum, India 95/C3
Cumiana, It. 64/D3
Cumming, Ga, US 162/E3
Cummins, Austl. 131/G5
Cumnock, Sc, UK 33/B6
Cumnock, Austl. 133/D1
Cumpas, Mex. 174/C2
Çumra, Turk. 102/C2
Cuñapirú, Uru. 191/G1
Cuñaré, Col. 180/C4
Cunaviche, Ven. 181/E3
Cunco, Chile 190/B3
Cunde (riv.), Ang. 122/C2
Cundeelee Abor. Rsv., Austl. 130/D4
Cunderdin, Austl. 130/C4
Cundinamarca (dept.), Col. 180/C3
Cunduacán, Mex. 176/C2
Cunene (prov.), Ang. 122/B3
Cunene (riv.), Ang. 107/D6
Cuneo (prov.), It. 62/A3
Cuneo, It. 64/D4
Cuneo (prov.), Fr. 64/D3
Cuney, Tx, US 150/G1
Cung Son, Viet. 94/E3
Cunha, Braz. 187/M8
Cunhinga, Ang. 122/C2
Cunhinga (riv.), Ang. 122/C1
Cunjamba, Ang. 122/D2
Cunnamulla, Austl. 134/B5
Cunningham, Ks, US 153/E2
Cunningham, Ky, US 162/C2
Cunningham, Tx, US 153/G4
Cunninghame (reg.), Sc, UK 33/B5
Čuokkaraš'ša (peak), Nor. 38/H1
Cuorgnè, It. 64/D2
Cuozhen, China 87/H2
Cupar, Sk, Can. 156/B2
Cupar, Sc, UK 33/C4
Cupello, It. 65/D3
Cupertino, Ca, US 167/K12
Cupra Marittima, It. 65/C1
Cupramontana, It. 63/G7
Ćuprija, Serb. 50/E4
Cuprum, Id, US 146/E1
Cuquenán (riv.), Ven. 181/F3
Curaçá, Braz. 183/G5
Curaçao (isl.), Neth. 173/H5
Curacautín, Chile 190/C3
Curacaví, Chile 190/N8
Curahuara de Carangas, Bol. 184/D5
Curahuara de Pacajes, Bol. 188/B1
Curanilahue, Chile 190/B3
Curaray (riv.), Peru 180/C5
Curaray (riv.), Peru 180/B5
Curaray (riv.), Ecu.,Peru 184/C1
Curarén, Hon. 176/E3
Curaumilla (pt.), Chile 190/N8
Curcubăta (peak), Rom. 51/F2
Cure (riv.), Fr. 42/B5
Curecanti National Recreation Area, Co, US 147/K4
Curecanti Natl'l Rec. Area, Co, US 152/A1
Curepipe, Mrts. 125/T15
Curepto, Chile 190/B2
Curiche Grande (riv.), Bol. 185/G5
Curicó, Chile 190/C2
Curimatá, Braz. 186/D1
Curitiba, Braz. 189/G3
Curitibanos, Braz. 189/G3
Curnamona, Austl. 131/H4
Curno, It. 62/C2
Curoca (riv.), Ang. 122/B3
Curone (riv.), It. 62/C3
Currais Novos, Braz. 183/G4
Curral Velho, CpV. 107/K10
Curralinho, Braz. 182/D3
Currant (mtn.), Nv, US 146/F4
Currant, Nv, US 146/F4
Currarong, Austl. 133/E2
Currawilla, Austl. 134/A4
Current (riv.), Mo, US 162/B2
Currie, Austl. 133/A4
Currie, Sc, UK 33/C5
Currie, Nv, US 147/F3
Currituck, NC, US 163/J2
Currituck (sound), NC, US 163/K2
Curry, Ak, US 171/H3
Curtea de Argeş, Rom. 51/G3
Curtici, Rom. 50/E2
Curtin, Or, US 146/B2
Curtina, Uru. 189/E5
Curtis (riv.), Austl. 134/D4
Curtis (isl.), NZ 136/G8
Curtis, Sp. 46/A1
Curtis, Ar, US 153/H4
Curtis, La, US 153/H4
Curtis (pt.), Md, US 168/B6
Curú Nat'l Wild. Ref., CR 177/E4
Curuá (riv.), Braz. 182/C4
Curuá (isl.), Braz. 182/D2
Curuá (riv.), Braz. 181/H5
Curuá Una (riv.), Braz. 181/H5
Curuçá, Braz. 182/E3
Curuçú (riv.), Braz. 184/D2
Curup, Indo. 89/C3
Cururupu, Braz. 183/E3
Curuzú Cuatiá, Arg. 188/E4
Curvelo, Braz. 186/D3
Curwensville, Pa, US 161/G4
Curwood (mt.), Mi, US 157/K4
Cusco, Peru 184/D4
Cusco (dept.), Peru 184/C4
Cushendall, NI, UK 34/B1
Cusher (riv.), NI, UK 34/B3
Cushet Law (peak), Eng, UK 33/D6
Cushing, Ok, US 153/F3
Cushing, Tx, US 151/G2
Cushman, Ar, US 153/J3
Cusick, Wa, US 144/F3
Cusna (peak), It. 62/D5
Cussava (riv.), Ang. 122/B2
Cusse, Ang. 122/B2
Cusset, Fr. 44/E3
Cusseta, Ga, US 162/E4
Cusseta, Al, US 162/E4
Custer (peak), SD, US 154/C1
Custer, SD, US 154/C2
Custer, Mt, US 145/L4
Custer City, Ok, US 152/E3
Custines, Fr. 55/F6
Custódia, Braz. 183/G5
Cut (hill), Eng, UK 36/C5
Cut and Shoot, Tx, US 151/G2
Cut Bank, Mt, US 145/H3
Cut Bank (cr.), Mt, US 145/H3
Cut Knife, Sk, Can. 145/K1
Cut Off, La, US 164/C3
Cutato, Ang. 122/C2
Cutato, Ang. 122/C2
Cutato (riv.), Ang. 120/D5
Cutchogue, NY, US 169/F2
Cutenda, Ang. 122/B2
Cutervo, Peru 184/B2
Cuthbert, Ga, US 165/F2
Cutler Ridge, Fl, US 165/H5
Cutral-Có, Arg. 190/C3
Cutro, It. 49/E3
Cuttack, India 95/E1
Cutten, Ca, US 146/A3
Cuvelai, Ang. 122/B2
Cuvergnon, Fr. 30/L4
Cuvette (pol. reg.), Congo 120/C3
Cuvier (cape), Austl. 130/B3
Cuvo (riv.), Ang. 122/B1
Cuxac, Fr. 47/G1
Cuxhaven, Ger. 53/F1
Cuyabeno, Ecu. 180/C5
Cuyahoga (riv.), Oh, US 160/F4
Cuyahoga Falls, Oh, US 160/F4
Cuyahoga Valley Nat'l Park, Oh, US 160/F4
Cuyama (riv.), Ca, US 148/B3
Cuyapaipe Ind. Res., Ca, US 148/D4
Cuyo (isls.), Phil. 91/F1
Cuyo, Phil. 88/C3
Cuyo East Passage (chan.), Phil. 88/C3
Cuyo West Passage (chan.), Phil. 88/C3
Cuyocuyo, Peru 184/D4
Cuyuchi, Bol. 185/F4
Cuyuni (riv.), Guy. 181/G3
Cuyuni (riv.), Ven. 181/F3
Cuyuni-Mazaruni (pol. reg.), Guy. 181/F3
Cuzco (ruin), Peru 184/D4
Cwm, Wal, UK 36/C3
Cwmafan, Wal, UK 36/C3
Cwmbran, Wal, UK 36/C3
Cyangugu, Rwa. 121/G3
Cyclades (isls.), Gre. 67/K3
Cymric, Sk, Can. 156/B2
Cynthia, Ab, Can. 144/G1
Cynthiana, Ky, US 162/E1
Cynwyl Elfed, Wal, UK 36/B3
Cypress (hills), Ab, Can. 145/J3
Cypress, Al, US 162/D4
Cypress, Ca, US 166/F8
Cypress (lake), Fl, US 164/N7
Cypress, Tx, US 151/M9
Cypress (cr.), Tx, US 151/M8
Cypress Gardens, Fl, US 164/M8
Cyprus (ctry.) 104/C2
Cyrenaica (reg.), Libya 67/J5
Cyrene (ruin), Libya 67/J4
Cyril, Ok, US 153/E3
Cyril E. King (int'l arpt.), USVI 173/M8
Cyrus, Mn, US 157/G5
Cysoing, Fr. 54/C2
Cywyn (riv.), Wal, UK 36/B3
Czaplinek, Pol. 43/J2
Czarna Białostocka, Pol. 43/M2
Czarnków, Pol. 43/J2
Czech Republic (ctry.) 43/H4
Częstochowa, Pol. 43/K3
Człuchów, Pol. 40/G5

D

D'Aguilar (range), Austl. 134/E6
D'Arcachon,Bassin di (lag.), Fr. 44/C4
D'Arcy, BC, Can. 144/C2
D' Ouvéa (lag.), NCal. 137/V12
D'Urville (isl.), NZ 135/C3
D. F. Malan (Cape Town) (int'l arpt.), SAfr. 124/L10
D.C. (fed. dist.), US 163/J1
Da (riv.), China 78/D5
Da (Black) (riv.), Viet. 86/E4
Da Hinggan (mts.), China 77/M5
Da Hoa, Viet. 94/D4
Da Juh, China 78/C4
Da Lat, Viet. 94/E4
Da Nang, Viet. 94/E2
Da Nang (cape), Viet. 94/E2
Da Qaidam, China 78/D4
Da Te, Myan. 94/B2
Da Xian, China 87/E2
Daaden, Ger. 55/G2
Da'an, China 79/J2
Daba (mts.), China 78/F5
Dabaga, Tanz. 119/A4
Dabai, Nga. 115/G4
Dabajuro, Ven. 180/D2
Dabakala, C.d'Iv. 114/D4
Dabas, Hun. 50/D2
Dabat, Eth. 117/H2
Dabeiba, Col. 180/B3
Dabeibu, China 87/H2
Dabein, Myan. 94/B2
Dabendorf, Ger. 42/Q7
Dabhoi, India 92/B3
Dabie (mts.), China 87/G2
Dabissé Kayati, Gui. 114/B4
Dabo, Fr. 55/G6
Dabob (bay), Wa, US 167/B2
Daboji, China 79/K3
Dabola, Gui. 114/C4
Daborow, Som. 118/D4
Dabou, C.d'Iv. 114/D5
Daboya, Gha. 115/E4
Dabra, India 96/B3
Dąbrowa Białostocka, Pol. 41/K5
Dąbrowa Górnicza, Pol. 43/K3
Dabu, China 87/G3
Dăbuleni, Rom. 51/G4
Dac Sut, Viet. 94/D3
Dac To, Viet. 94/D3
Dacca (Dhaka) (cap.), Bang. 97/H4
Dachang, China 80/L8
Dachang Huizu Zizhixian, China 80/H7
Dachau, Ger. 59/E6
Dacheng, China 87/G2
Dacono, Co, US 154/B3
Dadanawa, Guy. 182/B2
Dade (co.), Fl, US 164/P11
Dade City, Fl, US 164/L7
Dades, Oued (riv.), Mor. 110/D3
Dadeville, Al, US 162/E4
Dadi (cape), Indo. 91/H4
Ḑadnah, UAE 101/G3
Dadong, China 94/E1
Dādra and Nagar Haveli (state), India 92/B4
Dādri, India 98/D5
Dādu, Pak. 101/J3
Dadu (riv.), China 78/E5
Daduru (riv.), SrL. 92/C6
Daen Noi (peak), Thai. 94/B4
Dăeni, Rom. 51/J3
Daet, Phil. 88/C2
Dafang, China 86/E3
Dafanhe, China 81/B1
Dafeng, China 80/E4
Dafna, Isr. 105/D2
Dafu, China 86/D2
Dafu, China 87/H2
Dag, India 92/C3
Daga Medo, Eth. 118/B4
Daga Post, Sudan 117/G3
Dagaio, Eth. 118/B4
Dagana, Sen. 114/B2
Dağardı, Turk. 102/B2
Dağbaşı, Turk. 102/D2
Dagda, Lat. 41/M3
Dage, D.R. Congo 121/E2
Dagestan, Resp., Rus. 71/H4
Dagestanskiye Ogni, Rus. 71/J4
Daggaboersnek (pass), SAfr. 124/D4
Dagger (mtn.), Tx, US 150/C3
Daggett, Mi, US 160/C2
Daglung, China 97/H1
Dagmar Range NP, Austl. 134/B2
Dagneux, Fr. 60/B6
Dagny, Fr. 30/M5
Dagongcha, China 78/D4
Dagu, China 80/H7
Daguan, China 87/E3
Daguan, China 86/D3
D'Aguilar (mt.), Austl. 134/E6
Dagujia, China 81/C1
Daguokui (peak), China 79/K2
Dagupan, Phil. 88/C1
Daguragu Abor. Land, Austl. 128/C4
Dagxoi, China 93/G2
Dagzê (lake), China 99/E5
Dagzhuka, China 97/G1
Dahana (des.), SAr. 77/D7
Dāhānu, India 95/B2
Daharki, Pak. 92/A2
Dahei (riv.), China 80/B2
Daheiding (peak), China 79/K2
Dahekou, China 78/F5
Dahenan, China 80/G7
Dahlak (arch.), Erit. 118/B1
Dahlem, Ger. 55/F3
Dahlem, Ger. 42/Q7
Dahlenburg, Ger. 53/H2
Dahlgren, Il, US 162/C1
Dahlonega, Ga, US 162/F3
Dahmani, Tun. 112/L7
Dahme (riv.), Ger. 43/G3
Dahn, Ger. 55/G5
Dahongliutan, China 99/C4
Dahongqi, China 81/B2
Dahra, Sen. 114/B3
Dahshūr, Egypt 113/C5
Dahshūr (ruin), Egypt 113/C5
Dahūk, Iraq 103/E2
Dahūk (gov.), Iraq 103/E2
Dahuofang (res.), China 80/D2
Dahushan, China 81/B2
Dai (isl.), Indo. 128/C1
Dai (isl.), China 87/J2
Dai (lake), China 80/C2
Dai Loc, Viet. 94/E3
Dai Xian, China 80/C3
Dai-Segen-dake (peak), Japan 82/B3
Dai-sen (peak), Japan 84/C3
Daian, Japan 83/L5
Daicheng, China 80/D3
Daigo, Japan 85/G2
Daik-u, Myan. 94/B2
Dā'il, Syria 105/E3

Dailekh, Nepal 96/C1
Dailly, Sc, UK 33/B6
Daimiao, China 80/D3
Daimiel, Sp. 46/D3
Daingerfield, Tx, US 153/G4
Dainkognubma, China 78/D5
Daintree NP, Austl. 129/G4
Daiō-zaki (pt.), Japan 85/E3
Dāira Dīn Panāh, Pak. 98/A4
Daireaux, Arg. 190/E3
Dairy (cr.), Austl. 131/N8
Dairyland, Wi, US 157/H4
Daisen-Oki NP, Japan 84/C3
Daisetsuzan NP, Japan 82/C2
Daisy, Ok, US 153/G3
Daisy, Ar, US 153/H3
Daisy, Ky, US 163/F2
Daito (isl.), Japan 77/N7
Daitō, Japan 83/J6
Daiyun (peak), China 87/G3
Dajabón, DRep. 177/J2
Dajarra, Austl. 131/H2
Dajing, China 93/K3
Dak Nhe, Viet. 94/D3
Dakar (cap.), Sen. 114/A3
Dakar (pol. reg.), Sen. 114/A3
Dakar (Yoff) (int'l arpt.), Sen. 114/A3
Dakeng, China 87/G3
Daketa Shet' (riv.), Eth. 118/B2
Dakhin Shābāzpur (isl.), Bang. 97/H4
Dakhlet Nouadhibou (pol. reg.), Mrta. 114/A1
Dakoro, Niger 115/G3
Dakota (co.), Mn, US 157/P7
Dakota City, Ia, US 155/G2
Dakota City, Ne, US 155/F2
Dakovica, Serb. 50/E4
Dakovo, Cro. 50/D3
Dal (riv.), Swe. 74/B3
Dal Cataract (falls), Sudan 109/F4
Dala, Ang. 120/E5
Dala-Järna, Swe. 40/F1
Dalaas, Aus. 61/F3
Dalaba, Gui. 114/B4
Dalad Qi, China 80/B2
Dalai (lake), China 78/H3
Dalaman, Turk. 102/B2
Dalaman (int'l arpt.), Turk. 102/B2
Dalaman (cap.), Syria 105/E4
Dalāmī, Sudan 117/F3
Dalandzadgad, Mong. 78/E3
Dalangwan, China 87/G4
Dalaoba, China 99/D3
Dalarna (riv.), Swe. 38/E3
Dalarö, Swe. 39/B1
Dalatangi (pt.), Ice. 38/Q6
Dalavich, Sc, UK 33/B3
Dalbeattie, Sc, UK 34/E2
Dalby, Austl. 134/C4
Dalby, Swe. 40/E4
Dalby, Swe. 39/K7
Dalby-Söderskog NP, Swe. 39/K7
Dalcross (int'l arpt.), Sc, UK 33/B1
Dale, Nor. 40/A1
Dale, In, US 162/D1
Dale, Tx, US 153/G5
Dale, SC, US 163/G4
Dale City, Va, US 163/J1
Dale Hollow (lake), Tn, US 162/E2
Dalen, Nor. 40/C2
Dalen, Neth. 52/D3
Daleside, SAfr. 124/O13
Daletme, Myan. 93/F3
Daleville, Al, US 165/F2
Dalfsen, Neth. 52/D3
Dalgan (riv.), Ire. 32/B2
Dalgaranger (mt.), Austl. 130/C3
Dalhart, Tx, US 152/C2
Dalhousie, NB, Can. 158/D1
Dalhousie, India 98/C3
Dalhousie (cape), NW, Can. 140/D1
Dali, China 80/B4
Dali (riv.), China 78/F4
Dali, China 86/D3
Dalian (bay), China 81/A3
Dalian, China 81/A3
Dalian (int'l arpt.), China 80/C3
Daliang, China 78/H5
Dalias, Sp. 46/D4
Daliburgh, Sc, UK 31/Q8 Fr.
Dalidag (peak), Azer. 103/F2
Daling (riv.), China 79/H3
Dāliyat el Karmil, Isr. 105/C3
Dalizi, China 81/D2
Dalj, Cro. 50/D3
Dalkeith, Sc, UK 33/C5
Dalkola, India 97/F3
Dall (isl.), Ak, US 140/C3
Dall (lake), Ak, US 171/F3
Dallas, Sc, UK 33/C1
Dallas, Ga, US 162/E4
Dallas, Or, US 146/B1
Dallas (co.), Tx, US 150/L7
Dallas, Tx, US 150/L7
Dallas City, Il, US 155/J3
Dallas Love Field (arpt.), Tx, US 150/L7
Dallas-Fort Worth (int'l arpt.), Tx, US 150/K7
Dallastown, Pa, US 168/B4
Dalles of the Saint Croix, Mn, US 157/H5
Dallesport, Wa, US 144/C2
Dallgow, Ger. 42/Q6
Dallol Bosso (riv.), Niger,Mali 115/F3
Dalmally, Sc, UK 33/B3
Dalmatia (reg.), Cro. 67/G1
Dalmatia, Pa, US 168/B2
Dalmatovo, Rus. 69/P4
Dalmellington, Sc, UK 33/B6
Dalmeny, Austl. 133/E3
Dalmine, It. 62/C2
Dal'negorsk, Rus. 79/M3
Dal'nerechensk, Rus. 79/L2
Dalol, It. 118/B2
Dalqū, Sudan 109/F4
Dalroy, Ab, Can. 145/H2
Dalry, Sc, UK 33/B5

Dalrymple, Sc, UK 33/B6
Dalrymple (lake), Austl. 127/D3
Dals Långed, Swe. 40/D3
Dalsjöfors, Swe. 40/E3
Dalton, Ar, US 162/E2
Dalton, Ga, US 162/E3
Dalton, Ma, US 161/K3
Dalton, Mn, US 156/F4
Dalton, Pa, US 161/H2
Dalton-in-Furness, Eng, UK 35/E3
Daltonganj, India 97/E3
Dalu, China 78/B5
Dalugha, Sp. 117/H3
Dalupiri (isl.), Phil. 88/C1
Dalvík, Ice. 38/N6
Dalwallinu, Austl. 130/K8
Dalwhinnie, Sc, UK 33/B3
Dalworthington Gardens, Tx, US 150/K7
Daly (bay), Nun, Can. 141/J2
Daly (riv.), Austl. 128/C3
Daly City, China 164/P10
Daly River Wild. Sanct., Austl. 128/C3
Daly River Aboriginal Land, Austl. 128/C3
Daly Waters, Austl. 128/C3
Dalyup, Austl. 130/D5
Dam (riv.), China 99/F5
Dam Doi, Viet. 94/D4
Dam Gamad, Sudan 117/F2
Damagaram Takaya, Niger 115/H3
Damāgheh-ye Kūh (pt.), Iran 103/J5
Damak, Nepal 97/F2
Damaleng, China 99/C3
Damal, Hon. 176/E3
Damanhūr, Egypt 113/B2
Damanzhir, CAfr. 116/C4
Damar (isl.), Indo. 92/B3
Damasak, Nga. 116/B2
Damascus, Ar, US 153/H3
Damascus, In, US 161/F3
Damascus, Va, US 163/G2
Damascus (Dimashq) (cap.), Syria 105/E4
Damascus, Md, US 168/A5
Damāt, Egypt 113/B3
Damaturu, Nga. 116/B3
Damāvand (mtn.), Iran 103/H3
Damāvand, Iran 103/H3
Damaying, China 87/G3
Damba, Ang. 120/C4
Dambam, Turk. 51/H5
Dāmbuk, India 86/B2
Dame Marie, Haiti 177/H2
Dame Marie (cape), Haiti 177/H2
Damenglong, China 94/C1
Dameron, Md, US 163/J1
Damerham, Eng, UK 37/E5
Dāmghān, Iran 103/H2
Damietta (Dumyāṭ), Egypt 113/C2
Damietta Branch (riv.), Egypt 113/C2
Damigny, Fr. 57/F4
Daming (mtn.), China 87/F4
Daming, China 87/G3
Damintun, China 81/B2
Damion (peak), Fr. 55/G4
Dāmiyā, Jor. 105/D4
Dammard, Fr. 30/M4
Dammarie-en-Goële, Fr. 30/L4
Dammastock (peak), Swi. 61/E4
Damme, Belg. 54/C1
Damme, Ger. 53/F2
Damo, China 87/F2
Damodar (riv.), India 97/F3
Damoh, India 96/C4
Damongo, Gha. 115/F4
Damoura (Oued ed Dartuch (cape), Sp. 47/G3
Damparis, Fr. 60/D3
Dampier, Austl. 130/C3
Dampier (str.), Indo. 87/H1
Dampier (arch.), Austl. 127/A2
Dampier Downs, Austl. 126/C3
Dampierre, Fr. 60/B3
Dampierre-sur-Salon, Fr. 60/B3
Damprichard, Fr. 60/C3
Damqawt, Yem. 114/B2
Damqog (Maquan) (riv.), China 96/E1
Damsterdiep (riv.), Neth. 52/D2
Damvant, Swi. 60/C3
Damville, Fr. 57/G3
Damvix, Fr. 54/C4
Damxung, China 99/F5
Damzhung, China 99/F5
Dan-e-Rūd, Iran 103/J4
Dan, Isr. 105/D2
Dan (riv.), NC, US 163/G2
Dan Sai, Thai. 94/C2
Dānā, Jor. 105/D4
Dana, Nepal 96/D1
Dana Point, Ca, US 166/C4
Danakil (reg.), Djib. 118/B3
Dānān, Iran 103/G4
Dānān, Iran 103/H4
Danao, Phil. 88/C3
Danba, China 86/D2
Dāravyya, Syria 105/E4
Danbari (riv.), Serb. 50/E4
Danbury, Eng, UK 37/G3
Danbury, NC, US 163/G2
Danby, Austl. 133/C4
Danby (cape), Ak, US 148/G3
Date, Japan 82/C2
Dateland, Az, US 149/F4
Datia, India 96/B3
Datian, China 87/F3
Datian (peak), China 87/F3
Datil, NM, US 149/J3
Datong, China 80/C2
Datong, China 80/D4
Datong (riv.), China 78/D4
Datong, China 80/D4
Datong (mts.), China 78/H4

Danderhall, Sc, UK 33/C5
Dandīl, Egypt 113/C6
Dando, Ang. 120/C4
Dandong, China 81/C2
Dandridge, Tn, US 163/F2
Dane (riv.), Eng, UK 35/F5
Dang (riv.), China 78/D4
Dangal, Erit. 118/B2
Dangayos (pt.), Phil. 87/J5
Dange, Nga. 115/G3
Dangé-ia-Menha, Ang. 120/C4
Dangchang, China 87/F2
Danger (isl.), SAfr. 124/L11
Dangila, SAfr. 117/H3
Dangkou, China 80/L8
Dangme (riv.), Bhu. 165/H2
Dangriga, Belz. 176/D2
Dangshan, China 80/D4
Dangtu, China 81/B4
Dangur, Eth. 117/H3
Dangyang, China 87/E2
Dani, China 87/G2
Dania, Fl, US 164/P10
Daniel (riv.), Namb. 122/D4
Danieb (riv.), Namb. 122/D4
Danielskuil, SAfr. 124/C3
Danielsville, Ga, US 163/F3
Danielsville, Pa, US 168/C2
Danilov, Rus. 68/J4
Daning, China 80/B3
Danjiangkou (res.), China 78/G5
Danjiangkou, China 87/E2
Danjoutin, Fr. 60/C2
Dank, Oman 101/G4
Dankaur, India 98/D5
Dankheh Gompa, India 101/L2
Dankov, Rus. 70/L1
Dankova (peak), Kyr. 99/C3
Danleng, China 86/D2
Danli, Hon. 176/E3
Dannelly (res.), Al, US 162/D4
Dannemora, NY, US 161/K2
Dannenberg, Ger. 42/F2
D'Armanvilliers, Fr. 30/L5
Dannes, Fr. 54/A2
Dannevirke, NZ 135/D3
Dannhauser, SAfr. 125/E3
Dano, Burk. 114/E4
Dansalan, Phil. 89/D3
Dansville, NY, US 161/H3
Dantzler, Ms, US 164/D2
Danube (Donau) (riv.), Eur. 29/G4
Danube (riv.), Aus. 61/E1
Danube (cape), Ant. 192/E
Danube, Delta of the (delta), Rom. 27/H3
Danube, Mouths of the (mouth), Rom.,Ukr. 73/K4
Danumarrka Hall, Eng, UK 35/G1
Danville, Qu, Can. 161/K2
Danville, Ar, US 153/H3
Danville, Il, US 160/D3
Danville, Oh, US 161/G3
Danville, Pa, US 168/B2
Danville, Va, US 163/H2
Danville, Vt, US 161/K2
Danville, Wa, US 144/E3
Dao, Phil. 88/C3
Dao Xian, China 87/F3
Daocheng, China 86/D2
Daodou'ao, China 87/J2
Daora, It. 87/B4
Daoshui, China 87/E2
Daotiandi, China 79/L2
Daoukro, C.d'Iv. 114/E5
Daoulas, Fr. 56/A4
Daowo, Pol. 40/G4
Daozhen, China 87/E2
Dapa, Phil. 88/D3
Dapaong, Togo 115/F3
Daphne, Al, US 164/E2
Dapingying, China 87/F2
Dapitan, Phil. 88/C3
Dapo, China 94/E2
Dapozi, China 87/F3
Daqiao, China 86/D3
Daqiao, China 87/H3
Daqing, China 79/K2
Daqing (China) (peak), China 80/H7
Daqo (isl.), China 87/J3
Daqu (riv.), China 87/J3
Daquanwan, China 78/C3
Dar-e Rūd, Iran 103/J4
Daryābād, India 98/D3
Dārzīn, Iran 101/G3
Dar 'Aqīl, Sudan 79/K3
Dar Bel Hamri, Mor. 112/B2
Dar el Barka, Mrta. 114/B2
Dar es Salaam (prov.), Tanz. 119/B3
Dar es Salaam (peak), Fr. 79/K4
Dar es Salaam (int'l arpt.), Tanz. 119/B3
Dar es Salaam (cap.), Tanz. 119/B3
Dar Rounga (reg.), CAfr. 116/D3
Dar'ā, Syria 105/E3
Dar'ā (prov.), Syria 105/E3
Darāb, Iran 101/G3
Darabani, Rom. 41/H4
Daraga, Phil. 88/C2
Daragodleh, Som. 118/C3
Daram, Phil. 88/D3
Dārān, Iran 103/G3
Darasun, Rus. 78/G1
Dāraya, Syria 105/C4
Dat Do, Viet. 94/D4
Datadian, Indo. 90/E3
Dātāganj, India 98/D3
Datchet, Eng, UK 37/F4
Dateia, India 96/B3
Datong, China 87/F3
Daxin, China 94/D1
Dazhu, China 87/E2
Dazhou, China 87/E2
Dayr al Balah, Gaza 105/A4

Derā N – Dornha

Derā Nānak, India 98/C3
Dera Nawāb Sāhib, Pak. 98/A5
Derai, Bang. 97/H3
Deram Shet' (riv), Eth. 118/A3
Derazhnya, Ukr. 72/D3
Derbent, Rus. 71/J4
Derby, Austl. 128/A4
Derby, Eng, UK 35/G6
Derby (co.), Eng, UK 35/G6
Derby, Ct, US 169/E1
Derby, Ks, US 153/F2
Derbyshire (co.), Eng, UK 35/G6
Derdap NP, Serb. 50/F3
Derdara, Mor. 112/B2
Derdepoort, SAfr. 123/E5
Derecske, Hun. 50/E2
Dereköy, Turk. 51/H5
Dereköy (riv.), Turk. 103/M6
Derendingen, Swi. 60/D3
Deresgē, Eth. 118/A2
Dergachi, Rus. 71/J2
Derhachi, Ukr. 73/J2
Derik, Turk. 102/E2
Derinkuyu, Turk. 102/C2
Derkul, Kaz. 71/J2
Derma, Ms, US 162/C4
Dermott, Ar, US 153/J4
Dernau, Ger. 55/G2
Déroute, Passage de la (Chan), Fr., UK 44/B2
Derravaragh (lake), Ire. 32/C2
Derreen (riv.), Ire. 32/D4
Derrevaragh (lake), Ire. 34/A4
Derry, NH, US 161/L3
Derry, NM, US 149/J4
Derryboy, NI, UK 34/C3
Derrylin, NI, UK 32/C1
Derrynasaggart (mts.), Ire. 32/A6
Dersingham, Eng, UK 37/G1
Derudeb, Sudan 117/H1
Deruta, It. 65/B2
Dervaig, Sc, UK 31/Q8
Derval, Fr. 56/D5
Derventa, Bosn. 50/C3
Dervio, It. 61/F5
Dervock, NI, UK 34/B1
Derwent (riv.), Austl. 132/C4
Derwent, Ab, Can. 145/J1
Derwent (res.), Eng, UK 35/F2
Derwent (riv.), Eng, UK 35/E2
Derwent Bridge, Austl. 132/C4
Derwent Water (lake), Eng, UK 35/E2
Derzhavīnsk, Kaz. 99/A1
Des Allemands, La, US 164/C3
Des Arc, Ar, US 153/J3
Des Arc, Mo, US 162/B2
Des Lacs NWR, ND, US 156/C3
Des Moines (riv.), Ia, Mn, US 143/H3
Des Moines (int'l arpt.), Ia, US 155/H3
Des Moines (cap.), Ia, US 155/H3
Des Moines, Wa, US 144/C4
Des Moines, East Fork (riv.), Ia, US 155/G2
Des Plaines, Il, US 160/C3
Desaguadero, Peru 188/B1
Desaguadero (riv.), Bol. 185/E9
Desagües de los Colorados, Arg. 188/C4
Desagües del Río Salvage, Arg. 188/C4
Desana, It. 62/B3
Desborough, Eng, UK 37/F2
Descabezado Grande (vol.), Chile 190/C2
Descalvado, Braz. 189/H2
Descartes, Fr. 44/D3
Deschutes (riv.), Or, US 146/C1
Deschutes River Recreation Lands, Or, US 146/C1
Desdunes, Haiti 177/H2
Dese (riv.), It. 63/F2
Desē, Eth. 118/A3
Deseado (riv.), Arg. 179/C7
Deseado (cape), Chile 191/B7
Desengaño (pt.), Arg. 191/D6
Desenzano del Garda, It. 62/D3
Deseret Depot, Ut, US 147/G3
Désert (riv.), Qu, Can. 161/H1
Desert (valley), Nv, US 146/D3
Desert (lake), Nv, US 148/E2
Desert Center, Ca, US 148/E4
Desert Hot Springs, Ca, US 148/D4
Désertines, Fr. 44/E3
Deshengpu, China 80/B4
Deshler, Oh, US 160/E4
Desiderio Tello, Arg. 188/C4
Desio, It. 62/C2
Desloge, Mo, US 162/B2
Desna (riv.), Rus. 69/W9
Desolación (isl.), Chile 191/B7
Desolation (pt.), Phil. 88/D3
Desoto, Tx, US 150/L7
Desoto Nat'l Wild.Ref., Ne, US 155/F3
Despatch, SAfr. 124/D4
Déssa, Niger 115/F3
Dessau, Ger. 42/G3
Dessel, Belg. 52/C6
Dessoubre (riv.), Fr. 60/C3
Destelbergen, Belg. 54/C1
Destêrro, Braz. 183/G4
Destin, Fl, US 164/E2
Destruction Bay, Can. 171/L3
Desulo, It. 48/A2
Desvres, Fr. 54/A2
Det Udom, Thai. 94/D3
Deta, Rom. 50/E3
Dete, Zim. 123/E3
Detern, Ger. 53/E2
Detmold, Ger. 53/F5
Detour (pt.), Mi, US 160/C2
Detrital Wash (riv.), Az, US 148/E3
Detroit (riv.), Can.,US 167/F7
Detroit, Mi, US 160/E3
Detroit, Or, US 146/B1
Detroit (dam), Or, US 146/B1
Detroit (lake), Or, US 146/B1
Detroit, Tx, US 153/G4
Detroit City (arpt.), Mi, US 167/G7
Detroit Lakes, Mn, US 156/G4
Detroit Metropolitan Wayne County (int'l arpt.), Mi, US 160/E3
Dettelbach, Ger. 58/D3
Dettifoss (falls), Ice. 38/P6
Dettwiller, Fr. 55/G6
Deua NP, Austl. 133/D2
Deuil-la-Barre, Fr. 30/J5
Deûle (riv.), Fr. 54/B2
Deurne, Belg. 52/B6
Deurne, Neth. 52/C6
Deurne (Antwerp) (int'l arpt.), Belg. 52/B6
Deustua, Peru 184/D4
Deutsch Evern, Ger. 53/H2
Deutsch Wagram, Aus. 51/P7
Deutschkreutz, Aus. 50/C2
Deutschlandsberg, Aus. 50/B2
Deux-Montagnes, Qu, Can. 159/N6
Deux-Montagnes (lake), Qu, Can. 159/M7
Deux-Montagnes (co.), Qu, Can. 159/M6
Deva, Rom. 50/F3
Dévaványa, Hun. 50/E2
Develi, Turk. 102/C2
Deventer, Neth. 52/D4
Deveron (riv.), Sc, UK 33/D2
Devil River (peak), NZ 135/C3
Devil's Playground (des.), Ca, US 148/E3
Deville, Fr. 55/D4
Deville, La, US 164/B2
Devil's (isl.), FrG. 182/C1
Devils (riv.), Mex. 175/E2
Devil's (pt.), SrL. 95/D4
Devils (lake), ND, US 156/E3
Devils (riv.), Tx, US 150/D3
Devil's Elbow (pass), Sc, UK 33/C3
Devil's Garden, Ut, US 149/H1
Devils Lake, ND, US 156/E3
Devils Paw (mt.), Ak, US 171/M4
Devils Postpile Nat'l Mon., Ca, US 148/C2
Devils Tower Nat'l Mon., Wy, US 154/B1
Devilsbit (peak), Ire. 32/C4
Devin, Bul. 49/J2
Devine, Tx, US 151/E3
Devizes, Eng, UK 36/E4
Devnya, Bul. 51/H4
Devola, Oh, US 160/F5
Devoll (riv.), Alb. 67/J2
Devoll (riv.), Alb.,Gre. 50/E5
Devon, Ab, Can. 145/H1
Devon (isl.), Nun, Can. 141/H1
Devon (riv.), Sc, UK 33/C4
Devon (co.), Eng, UK 36/C5
Devon-Berwyn, Pa, US 168/C3
Devonport, Austl. 132/C4
Devonport, NZ 135/F6
Devore, Ca, US 166/C2
Devoto, Arg. 188/D4
Devoys (peak), NM, US 152/C2
Devrek (riv.), Turk. 70/D4
Devrek, Turk. 70/D4
Devrez (riv.), Turk. 70/E4
Devure (riv.), Zim. 123/F3
Dewa (pt.), Indo. 89/A2
Dewa (mts.), Japan 82/B4
Dewar, Ok, US 153/G3
Dewās, India 92/C3
Dewberry, Ab, Can. 145/J1
Dewetsdorp, SAfr. 124/D3
Dewey, Ok, US 153/G2
Dewey, Az, US 149/F3
Deweyville, Tx, US 151/H2
Dewsbury, Eng, UK 35/G4
Dexter, Ga, US 163/F4
Dexter, Ks, US 153/F2
Dexter, Mo, US 162/C2
Dexter, NM, US 152/B4
Dey-Dey (lake), Austl. 127/C3
Deyang, China 86/E2
Deyhūk, Iran 103/J3
Deyyer, Iran 103/G5
Dez (riv.), Iran 74/E6
Dezfūl, Iran 103/G3
Dezhneva (cape), Rus. 142/W12
Dezhou, China 80/D3
Dhābān, India 98/C5
Dhabān Singh, Pak. 98/B4
Dhāding, Nepal 97/E2
Dhahab, Egypt 109/G2
Dhahabān, SAr. 100/C4
Dhahran (int'l arpt.), SAr. 100/F3
Dhahran, SAr. 100/D5
Dhākā (pol. div.), Bang. 97/G4
Dhāka, India 97/E2
Dhākā (pol. reg.), Bang. 97/H4
Dhākā (Dacca) (cap.), Bang. 97/H4
Dhaleswari (riv.), Bang. 97/H4
Dhali, Cyp. 104/C2
Dhamār, Yem. 118/C2
Dhāmpur, India 96/B1
Dhamtari, India 95/D1
Dhanaula, India 98/C4
Dhanaura, India 96/B1
Dhānbād, India 97/F4
Dhangadhī, Nepal 96/C1
Dhankutā, Nepal 97/F2
Dhār, India 92/C3
Dhar de Chinguetti (cliff), Mrta. 110/B5
Dhār Khurd, India 98/C3
Dhar Néma (cliff), Mrta. 114/D2
Dhar Oualâta (cliff), Mrta. 114/D2
Dhar Tîchît (cliff), Mrta. 114/C2
Dharampur, India 92/B3
Dharān, Nepal 97/F2
Dharchula, Nepal 96/C1
Dhāri, India 101/K4
Dhāriwāl, India 98/C4
Dharmapuri, India 95/C3
Dharmavaram, India 95/C3
Dharmjaygarh, India 96/D4
Dharmkot, India 98/C4
Dharmsāla, India 98/D3
Dhasan (riv.), India 96/B3
Dhaulāgiri (zone), Nepal 96/D1
Dhaulāgiri (peak), Nepal 96/D1
Dhaura, India 96/B3
Dhaurahra, India 96/C1
Dhekialjuli, India 86/B3
Dhelfoí, Gre. 49/H3
Dhelfoí (Delphi) (ruin), Gre. 49/H3
Dhelvinákion, Gre. 49/G3
Dheskáti, Gre. 49/G3
Dheune (riv.), Fr. 60/A4
Dhī Qār (gov.), Iraq 103/F4
Dhībān, Jor. 105/D5
Dhidhimótikhon, Gre. 51/H5
Dhiinsoor, Som. 119/C1
Dhíkaia, Gre. 51/H5
Dhílos (ruin), Gre. 49/J4
Dhimitsána, Gre. 49/H4
Dhírfis (peak), Gre. 49/H3
Dhístomon, Gre. 49/H3
Dhlo Dhlo (ruin), Zim. 123/F3
Dhofar (reg.), Oman 100/F5
Dhokímion, Gre. 49/G3
Dholipal, India 98/C5
Dholka, India 101/K4
Dholpur, India 96/A2
Dhomokós, Gre. 49/H3
Dhonoúsa (isl.), Gre. 49/J4
Dhorāji, India 101/K4
Dhorpātan, Nepal 96/D1
Dhoxáton, Gre. 49/J2
Dhronbach (riv.), Ger. 55/F4
Dhubāb, Yem. 118/B2
Dhubri, India 97/G2
Dhuizon, Fr. 57/G5
Dhūlia, India 95/B1
Dhuliān, Pak. 98/B3
Dhuliān, India 97/F3
Dhulikhel, Nepal 97/E2
Dhungrebās, Nepal 97/E2
Dhupgāri, India 97/G2
Dhūri, India 98/C4
Dhuudo, Som. 118/D3
Dhuudo (riv.), Som. 118/D3
Dhuusamarreeb (Dusa Marreb), Som. 118/C4
Di Linh, Viet. 94/E4
Dia (isl.), Gre. 49/J5
Diablo (mt.), Ak, US 171/H4
Diablo (range), Ca, US 148/B2
Diablo (mtn.), Tx, US 150/B2
Diablo (plat.), Tx, US 150/B2
Diablo, Punta del (pt.), Uru. 191/G2
Diablotin (peak), Dom. 173/N9
Diadema, Braz. 187/K8
Diadema Argentina, Arg. 190/D5
Diaganiao, Sen. 114/A3
Diagonal, Ia, US 155/G3
Diaguitas, Chile 188/B4
Dialakoto, Sen. 114/B3
Diamante (riv.), Arg. 190/D2
Diamante, Arg. 188/D5
Diamantina, Braz. 187/E3
Diamantina (riv.), Austl. 127/D3
Diamantina Lakes, Austl. 134/A3
Diamantina, Chapada (hills), Braz. 187/E1
Diamantino, Braz. 185/G4
Diamond (cr.), Austl. 132/G5
Diamond (peak), Id, US 147/G1
Diamond, Or, US 146/D2
Diamond (peak), Or, US 146/B2
Diamond Bar, Ca, US 166/G8
Diamond Harbour, India 97/G4
Diamond Springs, Ca, US 146/C4
Dian (lake), China 86/D3
Dianalund, Den. 40/D4
Dianbai, China 87/F4
Diancang (mtn.), China 86/D3
Dianjiang, China 87/E2
Diano Marina, It. 62/B6
Dianópolis, Braz. 186/D1
Dianshan (lake), China 80/L8
Diapaga, Burk. 115/F3
Diaroumé, Sen. 114/B3
Dias Creek, NJ, US 168/D5
Diavolezza (peak), Swi. 61/F5
Diaz, Ar, US 153/J3
Dibai, India 96/B1
Dibaya, D.R. Congo 121/E4
Dibaya-Lubwe, D.R. Congo 120/D4
Dibbin NP, Jor. 105/D4
Dibella (well), Niger 116/B1
Dibeng, SAfr. 124/C2
Dibiāpur, India 96/B2
Dībīlē, Eth. 118/B3
Diboll, Tx, US 150/G2
Dibrugarh, India 86/B3
Dibs, Iraq 103/F3
Dickens, Tx, US 152/D4
Dickens (pt.), RI, US 169/G1
Dickinson, ND, US 156/C4
Dickinson, Tx, US 151/M9
Dickinson Bayou (riv.), Tx, US 151/M9
Dickinson Center, NY, US 161/J2
Dickson, Ab, Can. 144/G1
Dickson, Ok, US 153/F3
Dickson, Tn, US 162/D2
Dicle (dam), Turk. 102/E2
Dicomano, It. 63/E6
Didam, Neth. 52/D5
Didcot, Eng, UK 37/E3
Didhav, Eth. 118/B2
Didiéni, Mali 114/C3
Didig Sala, Eth. 118/A2
Didinga (hills), Sudan 117/G4
Didsbury, Ab, Can. 145/G2
Dīdwāna, India 101/K3
Didyma (ruin), Turk. 102/A2
Die, Fr. 64/B3
Die Berg (peak), SAfr. 123/F5
Dieblich, Ger. 55/G3
Diébougou, Burk. 114/E4
Dieburg, Ger. 58/B3
Diedersdorf, Ger. 42/Q7
Diefenbaker (lake), Sk, Can. 140/F3
Diefenbaker (lake), Sk, Can. 145/L2
Diego de Almagro (isl.), Chile 191/B6
Diego de Almagro, Chile 188/B3
Diego Garcia (isl.), UK 77/G10
Diekirch, Lux. 55/F4
Diekirch (dist.), Lux. 55/E4
Diéma, Mali 114/C3
Diemen, Neth. 52/B4
Diemtigen, Swi. 60/D4
Dien Bien, Viet. 86/D4
Dien Chau, Viet. 94/D2
Dien Khanh, Viet. 94/E3
Dieng (ruin), Indo. 89/E4
Diepenbeek, Belg. 55/E2
Diepenveen, Neth. 52/D4
Diepholz, Ger. 53/F3
Diepoldsau, Swi. 61/F3
Dieppe, Fr. 57/G1
Dieppe, NB, Can. 158/E2
Dierdorf, Ger. 55/G2
Dieren, Neth. 52/D4
Dierks, Ar, US 153/G3
Diespeck, Ger. 58/D3
Diessen am Ammersee, Ger. 61/H2
Diest, Belg. 55/E2
Dietenheim, Ger. 61/G1
Dietenhofen, Ger. 58/D4
Dieterich, Il, US 162/C1
Dietersheim, Ger. 58/D3
Dietfurt an der Altmühl, Ger. 59/E4
Dietikon, Swi. 61/E3
Dietmannsried, Ger. 61/G2
Dietzenbach, Ger. 58/B2
Dieue-sur-Meuse, Fr. 55/E5
Dieulefit, Fr. 64/B3
Dieulouard, Fr. 55/F6
Dieuze, Fr. 55/F6
Dieveniškės, Lith. 41/L4
Diever, Neth. 52/D3
Diez, Ger. 58/B2
Dif, Kenya 119/C1
Diffa, Niger 116/B2
Diffa (dept.), Niger 116/B2
Differdange, Lux. 55/E4
Difficult (mt.), Austl. 132/B3
Dīg, India 96/A2
Digba, D.R. Congo 117/E4
Digboi, India 86/B3
Digby, NS, Can. 158/E3
Digby Neck (pen), Ns, Can. 158/D3
Diggers Rest, Austl. 133/B3
Dighem, Sudan 117/G2
Dighton, Ks, US 152/D1
Dighwāra, India 97/E3
Dīglūr, India 95/C2
Digne-les-Bains, Fr. 64/C4
Digoin, Fr. 44/E3
Digor, Turk. 103/E1
Digos, Phil. 88/D4
Digul (riv.), Indo. 91/K4
Digya NP, Gha. 115/E5
Dihang (riv.), India 86/B2
Dihun, Eth. 118/B4
Dijon, Fr. 60/A3
Dik, Chad 116/C3
Dikhil, Djib. 118/B3
Dikirnis, Egypt 113/C2
Diklosmta (peak), Geo. 71/H4
Diksmuide, Belg. 54/B1
Dikson, Rus. 74/J2
Diktel, Nepal 97/F2
Dikwa, Nga. 116/B2
Dīla, Eth. 118/A4
Dilbeek, Belg. 55/D2
Dilek Yarımadası NP, Turk. 102/A2
Dili (cap.), ETim. 128/B2
Dilijan, Arm. 71/H4
Dilkon, Az, US 149/G3
Dillenburg, Ger. 55/H2
Diller, Ne, US 155/F3
Dilley, Tx, US 150/E3
Dillia (riv.), Niger 116/A2
Dillikot, Nepal 96/C1
Dilling, Sudan 117/F2
Dillingen, Ger. 55/F5
Dillingen an der Donau, Ger. 58/D5
Dillingham, Ak, US 171/G4
Dillnås, Swe. 39/A1
Dillon, Mt, US 147/G1
Dillon, SC, US 163/H3
Dillon Cone (peak), NZ 135/C3
Dillonvale, Oh, US 160/F4
Dillsboro, In, US 162/E1
Dillsburg, Pa, US 168/A3
Dilolo, D.R. Congo 121/E5
Dilsen, Belg. 55/E1
Dimako, Camr. 116/B4
Dimāpur, India 86/B3
Dimaro, It. 61/G5
Dimas, Mex. 174/D4
Dimashq (prov.), Syria 105/E1
Dimashq (Damascus) (cap.), Syria 105/E1
Dimataling, Phil. 88/C4
Dimbaza, SAfr. 124/D4
Dimbelenge, D.R. Congo 121/E4
Dimbokro, C.d'Iv. 114/D5
Dimboola, Austl. 132/B3
Dîmbovita (prov.), Rom. 51/G3
Dîmbovita (riv.), Rom. 72/C5
Dimbulah, Austl. 134/B2
Dime Box, Tx, US 151/F2
Dimitriya Lapteva (str.), Rus. 75/P2
Dimitrovgrad, Bul. 51/G4
Dimitrovgrad, Rus. 71/J1
Dimitrovgrad, Serb. 51/F4
Dimlang (peak), Nga. 116/A3
Dimmitt, Tx, US 152/C3
Dimock, SD, US 154/F2
Dimovo, Bul. 51/F4
Dina, Pak. 98/B3
Dinach, Som. 118/D3
Dinagat, Phil. 88/D3
Dinagat (isl.), Phil. 91/G1
Dinājpur (pol. reg.), Bang. 97/G3
Dinājpur, Bang. 97/G3
Dinan, Fr. 56/C4
Dīnānagar, India 98/C3
Dinant, Belg. 55/D3
Dinar, Turk. 102/B2
Dinard, Fr. 56/C3
Dinaric Alps (mts.), Cro. 50/C3
Dinas (pt.), Wal, UK 36/B2
Dinas Powys, Wal, UK 36/C4
Dinder NP, Sudan 117/G2
Dinder Wenz (riv.), Eth. 117/G2
Dindima, Nga. 115/H4
Dindori, India 96/C4
Dinga, Pak. 98/B3
Ding'an, China 87/F5
Dingbian, China 78/F4
Dingelstädt, Ger. 53/H6
Dinggyê, China 97/F1
Dingjiang, China 87/G3
Dingjiasuo, China 79/J5
Dingle, Ire. 30/F10
Dingle (bay), Ire. 30/N10
Dingle, Id, US 147/H2
Dingmans Ferry, Pa, US 168/D1
Dingolfing, Ger. 59/F5
Dingras, Phil. 88/C1
Dingshuzhen, China 80/K8
Dingtao, China 80/C4
Dinguiraye, Gui. 114/C4
Dingwall, Sc, UK 33/B1
Dingwall, NS, Can. 159/G2
Dingxi, China 78/E4
Dingxiang, China 80/C3
Dingxing, China 80/G7
Dingyuan, China 80/D4
Dinh Lap, Viet. 94/D1
Dinkel (riv.), Ger. 53/E4
Dinkelsbühl, Ger. 58/D4
Dinkelscherben, Ger. 58/D6
Dinklage, Ger. 53/F3
Dinnebito Wash (riv.), Az, US 149/G2
Dinner (pt.), Fl, US 164/K7
Dinnington, Eng, UK 35/G1
Dinokana, SAfr. 122/E5
Dinosaur, Co, US 147/J3
Dinosaur Nat'l Monument, Co, US 147/J3
Dinslaken, Ger. 52/D5
Dinsmore, Sk, Can. 145/L2
Dintel Mark (riv.), Neth. 52/B5
Dintenloord, Neth. 52/B5
Dintiteladas, Indo. 89/D4
Dinuba, Ca, US 148/C2
Dinwiddie, Va, US 163/J2
Dinxperlo, Neth. 52/D5
Dioïla, Mali 114/D3
Diomandou, Gui. 114/C4
Dion (riv.), Gui. 114/C4
Dionysias (ruin), Egypt 113/B6
Diósd, Hun. 51/Q10
Diouloulou, Sen. 114/A3
Dioundiou, Niger 115/F3
Diourbel (pol. reg.), Sen. 114/A3
Diourbel, Sen. 114/A3
Dīpālpur, Pak. 98/B4
Diphu, India 86/B3
Diphu (pass), India 86/C2
Diplo, Pak. 101/J4
Dipni (dam), Turk. 102/E2
Dipolog, Phil. 88/C3
Dipperu NP, Austl. 134/C3
Dipperz, Ger. 58/C1
Dique (canal), Col. 177/H4
Dīr, Pak. 98/A2
Dira (well), Chad 116/B2
Dirang Dzong, India 97/J2
Diré, Mali 114/E2
Dirē Dawa, Eth. 118/B3
Direct, Tx, US 153/G4
Direction (cape), Austl. 129/F3
Diriamba, Nic. 176/E4
Dirico, Ang. 122/D3
Dirj, Libya 111/H3
Dirk Hartog (isl.), Austl. 127/A3
Dirkou, Niger 108/B5
Dirksland, Neth. 52/B5
Dirlewang, Ger. 61/G2
Dirranbandi, Austl. 134/C5
Dirrington Great Law (hill), Sc, UK 33/D5
Dirs, SAr. 100/D5
Dirty Devil (riv.), Ut, US 147/H4
Disappointment (lake), Austl. 127/B3
Disappointment (isls.), FrPol. 137/L6
Disappointment (cape), Wa, US 144/B4
Disaster (bay), Austl. 133/D3
Discovery (bay), Austl. 132/B3
Discovery Bay, Jam. 177/G2
Disentis-Mustér, Swi. 61/E4
Disgrazi (peak), It. 61/F5
Dishman, Wa, US 144/F4
Dishnā, Egypt 109/G3
Disko (isl.), Grld. 139/M3
Disko (Qeqertarsuaq) (isl.), Grld. 141/L2
Disley, Eng, UK 35/F5
Dismal (riv.), Ne, US 154/D3
Disna, Bela. 41/N4
Disney, Ok, US 153/G2
Disney Studios, Fl, US 164/M7
Disneyland, Ca, US 166/G8
Dison, Belg. 55/E2
Dispur, India 93/F2
Disraëli, Qu, Can. 158/B3
Diss, Eng, UK 37/H2
Dissen am Teutoburger Wald, Ger. 53/F4
Distington, Eng, UK 34/E2
Distrito Especial (cap. dist.), Col. 183/L8
Distrito Federal (fed. dist.), Braz. 186/D2
Distrito Federal (fed. dist.), Col. 180/C3
Distrito Federal (fed. dist.), Mex. 172/A5
Distrito Federal (fed. dist.), Ven. 181/E2
Disūq, Egypt 113/B2
Ditang, China 80/L9
Ditchling Beacon (hill), Eng, UK 37/F5
Dittaino (riv.), It. 48/D4
Dittelbrunn, Ger. 58/D2
Ditton, Eng, UK 30/E3
Ditzingen, Ger. 58/C5
Diu, India 92/B3
Diuata (mts.), Phil. 88/D3
Diva (riv.), Serb. 50/D4
Dīvān Darreh, Iran 103/F3
Divatte (riv.), Fr. 56/D6
Dive (riv.), Fr. 44/D3
Divénié, Congo 120/C3
Dives (riv.), Fr. 57/E2
Dives-sur-Mer, Fr. 57/E2
Divette (riv.), Fr. 56/D1
Divide, Co, US 152/B1
Divide, Mt, US 147/G1
Dividing Creek, NJ, US 168/C5
Divinolândia, Braz. 187/K6
Divinópolis, Braz. 186/D4
Divisa Nova, Braz. 187/K6
Divisões, Serra das (mts.), Braz. 186/C3
Divisor, Serra do (mts.), Braz.,Peru 184/C2
Divnogorsk, Rus. 74/K4
Divnoye, Rus. 71/G3
Divo, C.d'Iv. 114/D5
Divonne-les-Bains, Fr. 60/C5
Divriği, Turk. 102/D2
Divuma, D.R. Congo 121/E5
Dix (lake), Swi. 60/D5
Dixcove, Gha. 115/E5
Dixfield, Me, US 161/L2
Dixie, Ga, US 165/G2
Dixie, Al, US 164/E2
Dixie, Id, US 146/F1
Dixie, Wa, US 144/E4
Dixmoor, Il, US 167/Q16
Dixon, Ca, US 146/C4
Dixon, Ky, US 162/D2
Dixon, Il, US 155/K3
Dixon, Mt, US 144/G4
Dixon, NM, US 152/B2
Dixon, Mo, US 153/H2
Dixon, Wy, US 147/K3
Dixon Entrance (chan.), Can.,US 139/D4
Diyadin, Turk. 103/E2
Diyāla (gov.), Iraq 103/F3
Diyarb Najm, Egypt 113/C3
Diyarbakır, Turk. 102/E2
Diyarbakir (prov.), Turk. 102/E2
Dizangué, Camr. 120/B2
Dja (riv.), Camr. 116/B5
Djado, Niger 108/B4
Djado (plat.), Niger 107/D2
Djakotomé, Ben. 115/F5
Djamaa, Alg. 111/G2
Djamba, D.R. Congo 121/F2
Djambala, Congo 120/C3
Djamu, D.R. Congo 121/G2
Djanet, Alg. 111/H4
Djebel Tichka (peak), Mor. 110/C3
Djebel-Amrag (mtn.), Alg. 112/D3
Djébrène, Chad 116/C3
Djédaa, Chad 116/C2
Djedi, Oued (riv.), Alg. 111/G2
Djelfa, Alg. 66/D4
Djema, CAfr. 117/E4
Djemila (ruin), Alg. 112/H4
Djénné, Mali 114/D3
Djerem (riv.), Camr. 116/B4
Djermaya, Chad 116/B2
Djibo, Burk. 115/E3
Djibouti (cap.), Djib. 118/B3
Djibouti (ctry.) 118/B2
Djiguéni, Mrta. 114/C3
Djiouce (mtn.), Ire. 32/D3
Djiroutou, C.d'Iv. 114/D5
Djohong, Camr. 116/B4
Djouab (riv.), Congo 120/C2
Djoué (riv.), Congo 120/C3
Djougou, Ben. 115/F4
Djoum, Camr. 120/C2
Djugu, D.R. Congo 121/G2
Djúpivogur, Ice. 38/P7
Djurö, Swe. 39/B1
D'Lo, Ms, US 164/D2
Dmanisi, Geo. 71/H4
Dmitriyev-L'govskiy, Rus. 73/H1
Dmitriyevskiy, Kaz. 71/L2
Dmytrivka, Ukr. 73/G2
Dnepr (riv.), Rus. 74/D4
Dnestrovsc, Mol. 72/E4
Dnieper (lowland), Ukr. 72/F2
Dnieper (upland), Ukr. 72/E3
Dnipro (riv.), Ukr. 29/H3
Dniprodzerzhyns'ke Vodoskhovyshche (res.), Ukr. 73/H3
Dniprodzerzhyns'k, Ukr. 73/H3
Dnipropetrovs'k, Ukr. 73/H3
Dnipropetrovs'ka Oblast (Ukr. 70/E2
Dniprorudne, Ukr. 73/H4
Dniprovs'kyy Lyman (estu.), Ukr. 51/K2
Dnister (riv.), Eur. 74/C5
Dnister (riv.), Ukr. 42/M4
Dnistrovs'kyy Lyman (estu.), Ukr. 51/K2
Dno, Rus. 41/N3
Dnyapro (riv.), Bela. 41/P4
Do (lake), Mali 115/E3
Do (riv.), China 78/D5
Do Gonbadān, Iran 103/G4
Do Luong, Viet. 94/D2
Do Rāh (pass), Afg. 101/K1
Do Son, Viet. 94/D1
Doa, Moz. 123/G3
Doaktown, NB, Can. 158/D2
Doany, Madg. 125/J6
Doba, Chad 116/C3
Dobbins (A.F.B.), Ga, US 163/L7
Dobbs Ferry, NY, US 169/K7
Dobbyn, Austl. 129/F4
Dobele, Lat. 41/K3
Döbeln, Ger. 42/G3
Doberai (pen.), Indo. 91/H4
Dobiegniew, Pol. 43/H2
Dobo, Indo. 128/D1
Dobogo-kó (peak), Hun. 51/Q9
Doboj, Bosn. 50/D3
Dobřany, Czh. 59/G3
Dobre Miasto, Pol. 41/J5
Dobrich, Bul. 51/H4
Dobrinka, Rus. 71/G1
Dobrinka, Rus. 73/L1
Dobříš, Czh. 59/H3
Dobromyl', Ukr. 43/M4
Dobropillya, Ukr. 73/J3
Dobrovnik, Slov. 50/C2
Dobruja (reg.), Bul.,Rom. 67/K2
Dobrush, Bela. 70/D1
Dobryanka, Rus. 69/N4
Dobryanka, Ukr. 72/F1
Dobson, NC, US 163/G2
Dobzha, China 97/G1
Doce (riv.), Braz. 187/E3
Dochart (riv.), Sc, UK 33/B4
Dock Junction, Ga, US 165/H2
Docker River, Austl. 131/F3
Docking, Eng, UK 37/G1
Doctor Arroyo, Mex. 175/E4
Doctor Cecilio Báez, Par. 189/E3
Doctor Coss, Mex. 150/E5
Doctor González, Mex. 150/E5
Doctor Pedro P. Peña, Par. 188/D2
Doctor Petru Groza, Rom. 50/F2
Dod Ballāpur, India 95/C3
Doda (riv.), India 98/D3
Doda, India 98/C3
Doda Betta (peak), India 95/C4
Dodder (riv.), Ire. 34/B5
Doddinghurst, Eng, UK 30/D2
Dodge, Tx, US 151/G2
Dodge City, Ks, US 152/D2
Dodger Stadium, Ca, US 166/F7
Dodgeville, Wi, US 155/J2
Dodman (pt.), Eng, UK 36/B6
Dodola, Eth. 118/A4
Dodoma (prov.), Tanz. 119/A3
Dodoma, Tanz. 119/A3
Dodori Nat'l Rsv., Kenya 119/C2
Dodsland, Sk, Can. 145/K2
Dodson, La, US 164/B1
Dodson, Mt, US 145/K3
Dodwekon, Libr. 114/C5
Dodworth, Eng, UK 35/G4
Doe Run, Mo, US 162/B2
Doel, Belg. 52/B6
Doerun, Ga, US 165/G2
Doesburg, Neth. 52/D4
Doetinchem, Neth. 52/D5
Dofa, Indo. 91/G4
Dog (lake), Mb, Can. 156/E2
Dog (isl.), Fl, US 165/F3
Dog (riv.), BC, Can. 144/C2
Dogai Coring (lake), China 99/E5
Dogana, SMar. 63/F6
Doğanhisar, Turk. 102/B2
Doğankent (riv.), Turk. 70/F4
Doğanşar, Turk. 102/D1
Doğanşehir, Turk. 102/D2
Doğanyurt, Turk. 70/E4
Döğer, Turk. 102/B2
Dogliani, It. 62/A3
Dōgo (isl.), Japan 79/L4
Dogondoutchi, Niger 115/G3
Doğubayazıt, Turk. 103/F2
Doğukaradeniz (mts.), Turk. 102/D1
Doha (int'l arpt.), Qatar 100/F3
Doha (Ad Dawḩah) (cap.), Qatar 100/F3
Dohad, India 92/B3
Dohrīghāt, India 96/D2
Doi Inthanon NP, Thai. 86/C5
Doi Khun Tan NP, Thai. 94/B2
Doi Suthep-Pui NP, Thai. 86/C5
Doimara, India 86/B3
Doiras (res.), Sp. 46/B1
Dois Córregos, Braz. 189/G2
Dois de Julho (int'l arpt.), Braz. 187/F2
Dois Irmãos do Tocantins, Braz. 182/D5
Dois Irmãos, Serra (mts.), Braz. 183/F5
Dois Vizinhos, Braz. 189/F3
Doische, Belg. 55/D3
Doka, Sudan 117/G2
Dokka, Nor. 40/D1
Dokkum, Neth. 52/D2
Dokkumer Ee (riv.), Neth. 52/C2
Dokshitsy, Bela. 41/M4
Doksy, Czh. 59/H1
Dokuchayevs'k, Ukr. 73/J4
Dol-de-Bretagne, Fr. 56/D3
Dolan Springs, Az, US 148/E3
Dolbeau, Qu, Can. 158/A1
Dolcedorme (peak), It. 48/E3
Dole, Fr. 60/B3
Dolent (peak), Swi. 60/D6
Dolgellau, Wal, UK 36/C1
Dolgoprudnyy, Rus. 69/W9
Doli, India 92/B2
Dolianova, It. 48/A3
Dolinsk, Rus. 79/N2
Dolinskoye, Ukr. 72/E4
Dolj (prov.), Rom. 51/F3
Dollar, Sc, UK 33/C4
Dollar Bay, Mi, US 157/K4
Dollar Law (peak), Sc, UK 33/C5
Dollard, Sk, Can. 145/K3
Dollard (Dollart) (bay), Neth.,Ger. 53/E2
Dollard-des-Ormeaux, Qu, Can. 159/N7
Dollart (Dollard) (bay), Neth.,Ger. 53/E2
Dollarville, Mi, US 160/D1
Doller (riv.), Fr. 42/D5
Dollnstein, Ger. 58/E5
Dolmance Palace, Turk. 103/M6
Dolmar (peak), Ger. 58/D1
Dolmen (ruin), It. 48/E2
Dolna Banya, Bul. 51/F4
Dolni Dŭbnik, Bul. 51/G4
Dolní Kounice, Czh. 45/M2
Dolnośląskie (prov.), Pol. 43/J3
Dolo (riv.), It. 62/D4
Dolo, It. 63/F3
Dolo, Eth. 118/B4
Dolo, Indo. 91/E4
Dolo Odo, Eth. 118/B4
Dolobli, Libr. 114/C5
Dolomieu, Fr. 64/B1
Dolomite Alps (mts.), It. 67/F1
Dolon (riv.), Fr. 64/A2
Doloon, Mong. 78/F3
Dolores, Arg. 190/F3
Dolores, Bol. 184/D3
Dolores, Guat. 176/D2
Dolores, Phil. 88/D2
Dolores, Uru. 191/J10
Dolores, Co, US 149/H2
Dolores (riv.), Co, US 147/J4
Dolores, Ven. 180/D2
Dolphin (pt.), Namb. 122/B5
Dolphin (cape), UK 191/F6
Dolphin and Union (str.), Nun, Can. 140/E2
Dolphinholme, Eng, UK 35/F4
Dölsach, Aus. 45/K3
Dolton, Il, US 167/Q16
Dolyna, Ukr. 72/C3
Dolyns'ka, Ukr. 73/G3
Dolzhanskaya, Rus. 73/J4
Dom (peak), Indo. 91/J4
Dom (peak), Swi. 60/D5
Dom Aquino, Braz. 186/B2
Dom Carlos (pt.), Moz. 123/G4
Dom Noi (res.), Thai. 94/D3
Dom Pedrito, Braz. 189/F4
Doma, Zim. 123/F3
Domanivka, Ukr. 72/F4
Domār, Bang. 97/G2
Domariāganj, India 96/D2
Domasi, Malw. 123/G2
Domat-Ems, Swi. 61/F4
Domažlice, Czh. 59/F4
Dombarovskiy, Rus. 71/L2
Dombasle-sur-Meurthe, Fr. 55/F6
Dombay-Ul'gen (peak), Geo. 71/G4
Dombe Grande, Ang. 122/B2
Dombes (lake), Fr. 60/B5
Dombey (cape), Austl. 128/C3
Domboshawa, Zim. 123/F3
Dombóvár, Hun. 50/D2
Dombrád, Hun. 50/E1
Domburg, Sur. 182/C1
Domburg, Neth. 52/A5
Domchānch, India 97/E3
Dome, Az, US 148/E4
Dome (peak), Az, US 149/F2
Dome C, US, Ant. 192/J
Dôme de Barrot (peak), Fr. 64/C4
Dôme de l'Arpont (peak), Fr. 64/C2
Domène, Fr. 64/B2
Domérat, Fr. 44/E3
Domeyko, Chile 188/B4
Domfront, Fr. 57/E3
Domínguez, Arg. 188/E4
Dominica (ctry.) 173/N8
Dominica Passage (chan.), Dom.,Guad. 173/N9
Dominican Republic (ctry.) 173/H4
Dominion, NS, Can. 159/G2
Domiongo, D.R. Congo 121/E4
Dommartin-lès-Remiremont, Fr. 60/C2
Dommartin-lès-Toul, Fr. 55/E6
Dommati, India 97/H3
Dommel (riv.), Belg. 55/E1
Domo, Eth. 118/C4
Domodedovo, Rus. 69/W9
Domodedovo (int'l arpt.), Rus. 69/W9
Domodossola, It. 61/E5
Domohāni, India 97/G2
Domoni, Com. 125/H6
Domont, Fr. 30/J4
Dompu, Indo. 91/E5
Domremy, Sk, Can. 145/M1
Domrémy-la-Pucelle, Fr. 60/B1
Dömsöd, Hun. 50/D2
Domusnovas, It. 48/A3
Domuyo (vol.), Arg. 190/C3
Domvilk (mt.), Austl. 134/C5
Domžale, Slov. 45/L3
Don (cape), Austl. 128/C2
Don (riv.), Eng, UK 35/G5
Don (riv.), Sc, UK 33/D2
Don (ridge), Rus. 74/E5
Don (riv.), Rus. 29/J4
Don Benito, Sp. 46/C3
Don Pedro (res.), Ca, US 148/B2
Dona Ana, Moz. 123/G3
Donabate, Ire. 34/B5
Donada, It. 63/F3
Donaghadee, NI, UK 34/C2
Donaghmore, NI, UK 34/B2
Donald, Austl. 132/B3
Donald, BC, Can. 144/F2
Donaldson, Ar, US 153/H3
Donaldsonville, La, US 164/C2
Donalsonville, Ga, US 165/F2
Doñana, PN, Sp. 46/B4
Donath, Swi. 61/F4
Donau (Danube) (riv.), Aus.,Ger. 45/H2
Donaueschingen, Ger. 61/E2
Donauwörth, Ger. 58/D5
Doncaster (nbrhd.), Austl. 132/G5
Doncaster, Eng, UK 35/G4
Doncaster (co.), Eng, UK 35/G4
Donchery, Fr. 55/D4
Dondo, D.R. Congo 116/D4
Dondo, Moz. 123/G3
Dondo, Ang. 120/C5
Dondra Head (pt.), SrL. 95/D5
Donduseni, Mol. 72/D3
Donegal (bay), Ire. 31/P9
Donegal, Ire. 31/P9
Donegal (dist.), Ire. 34/A1
Doneraile, Ire. 32/B5
Donets (riv.), Rus. 71/G2
Donets' (riv.), Ukr. 73/J3
Donetsk (int'l arpt.), Ukr. 73/J3
Donets'ka Oblast, Ukr. 70/F3
Donetsk, Rus. 73/L3
Donets'k, Ukr. 73/J3
Dong (riv.), China 78/E3
Dong, India 93/G2
Dong (riv.), Viet. 93/J5
Dong Dang, Viet. 93/J3
Dong Ha, Viet. 94/D2
Dong Hoi, Viet. 94/D2
Dong Noi (riv.), Viet. 94/D4
Dong Tau, Viet. 94/D2
Dong Ujimqin Qi, China 78/H2
Donga (riv.), Nga. 115/H4
Donga, Nga. 115/H5
Dongai (riv.), Camr. 116/A4
Dongar Parāsia, India 96/B4
Dongara, Austl. 130/B4
Dongargarh, India 95/D1
Dongbei (plain), China 80/E2
Dongchuan, China 86/D3
Dong'e, China 80/D3
Dongen, Neth. 52/B5
Donges, Fr. 56/C6
Dongfang, China 94/E2
Dongfang, China 87/F5
Donggou, China 81/C3
Dongguan, China 87/G4
Dongguang, China 80/D3
Donghai, China 80/D4
Donghen, Laos 94/D2
Donghezhen, China 80/L8
Dongio, Swi. 61/E5
Dongjia, China 87/G2
Dongjing (riv.), China 87/G2
Dongjingling, China 81/B2
Dongkeng, China 87/H3
Dongkya (pass), China 97/G2
Dongli, China 93/K3
Dongliao (riv.), China 80/F2
Donglük, China 99/E4
Dongmen, China 94/D1
Dongming, China 80/C4
Dongnan (plat.), China 87/F4
Dongo, It. 61/F5
Dongo, D.R. Congo 120/D2
Dongo, D.R. Congo 121/E2
Dongo, Ang. 122/B2
Dongo-Kuma, D.R. Congo 120/E2
Dongobesh, Tanz. 119/A3
Dongola, Il, US 162/C2
Dongou, Congo 120/D2
Dongping, China 80/D4
Dongqiao, China 99/F5
Dongsha (isl.), China 87/H4
Dongsha (Pratas) (isl.), China 87/H4
Dongshajiao, China 87/J2
Dongshan (isl.), China 87/H4
Dongshan, China 80/L8
Dongshao, China 87/G3
Dongsheng, China 80/B3
Dongtai, China 80/E4
Dongtiao (riv.), China 80/L9
Dongting (lake), China 87/G2
Dongtingxi, China 87/F2
Dongue, Ang. 122/B2
Dongxing, China 94/D1
Dongxing, China 87/F3
Dongying, China 80/D3
Dongzhen, China 78/E4
Dongzhi, China 87/H2
Donie, Tx, US 151/F2
Donihue, Chile 190/N9
Donington, Eng, UK 35/H6
Doniphan, Mo, US 162/B2
Donjek (riv.), Yk, Can. 140/C2
Donji Komren, Serb. 50/E4
Donji Vakuf, Bosn. 50/C3
Donk, Neth. 52/C5
Donna, Tx, US 151/E4
Donnas, It. 62/A1
Donnelly, Mn, US 156/F5
Donner (pass), Ca, US 146/C4
Donner und Blitzen (riv.), Or, US 146/D2
Donnersberg (peak), Ger. 55/G4
Donnybrook, Austl. 134/D4
Donnybrook, Austl. 130/B5
Donnybrook, ND, US 156/D3
Donon (peak), Fr. 60/D1
Donora, Pa, US 161/G4
Donoratico, It. 45/J5
Donskoy, Rus. 73/L4
Donsol, Phil. 88/C2
Donville-les-Bains, Fr. 56/D3
Donyan (riv.), Myan. 86/B5
Donzdorf, Ger. 58/C5
Donzère, Fr. 64/A4
Donzy, Fr. 44/E3
Doole, Tx, US 150/E2
Dooleena (peak), Austl. 130/C2
Doomadgee Abor. Land, Austl. 129/E4
Doomadgee Aboriginal Community, Austl. 129/E4
Doon, Ire. 32/B4
Doon (lake), Sc, UK 33/B6
Doon (riv.), Sc, UK 33/B6
Doon Doon Abor. Land, Austl. 128/C4
Doonbeg (riv.), Ire. 32/A4
Doonbeg, Ire. 32/A4
Doonerak (mt.), Ak, US 171/H2
Door (pen.), Wi, US 157/L5
Door (pt.), La, US 164/D2
Doorn, Neth. 52/C4
Doorn (riv.), SAfr. 124/B3
Doppo (peak), It. 62/D2
Doqên (lake), China 97/G1
Dora, Mo, US 153/H2
Dora (lake), Fl, US 164/M6
Dora, Al, US 162/D4
Dora (lake), Austl. 127/B3
Dora Baltea (riv.), It. 64/D1
Dora Creek, Austl. 133/E1
Dora di Rhêmes (riv.), It. 64/D1
Dora Riparia (riv.), It. 45/G4
Dorada (coast), Sp. 47/F2
Dorāh Ān (pass), Pak. 99/B4
Doraville, Ga, US 163/M7
Dorchester, NB, Can. 158/E3
Dorchester (cape), Nun, Can. 141/J2
Dorchester, Eng, UK 36/D5
Dorchester, Ne, US 155/F3
Dorchester, NJ, US 168/D5
Dorchester, SC, US 163/G4
Dordabis, Namb. 122/C4
Dordogne (riv.), Fr. 66/D1
Dordrecht, Neth. 52/B5
Dordrecht, SAfr. 124/D3
Dore (mts.), Fr. 44/E4
Dore (riv.), Fr. 44/E4
Dores, Sc, UK 33/B2
Dores do Indaiá, Braz. 186/D3
Dorfen (riv.), Ger. 59/E6
Dorfen, Ger. 59/F6
Dorgali, It. 48/A2
Dörgön (lake), Mong. 78/C2
Dori, Burk. 115/E3
Doria, It. 62/B5
Dorion, On, Can. 157/K3
Dorion, Qu, Can. 159/M7
Dorking, Eng, UK 30/C3
Dorlisheim, Fr. 60/D1
Dormagen, Ger. 55/F1
Dormans, Fr. 54/C5
Dormans Land, Eng, UK 30/D3
Dornach, Swi. 60/D3
Dornakal, India 95/D2
Dornbirn, Aus. 61/F3
Dorney Park/ Wildwater Kingdom, Pa, US 168/C2
Dornhan, Ger. 61/E1

Map Section

222

223

Dorno – Eastma

Dorno, It. 62/B3
Dornoch, Sc, UK 33/B1
Dornoch Firth (inlet), Sc, UK 33/B1
Dornod (prov.), Mong. 78/G2
Dornogovĭ (prov.), Mong. 78/F3
Dornstadt, Ger. 58/C6
Dornstetten, Ger. 58/B6
Doro, Mali 115/E2
Dorog, Hun. 51/Q9
Dorogobuzh, Rus. 68/G5
Dorogorskoye, Rus. 69/K2
Dorohoi, Rom. 72/D4
Doromo, D.R. Congo 121/F2
Doron de Chavière (riv.), Fr. 64/C2
Dorothy, NJ, US 168/D5
Dorowa Mining Lease, Zim. 123/F3
Dörpen, Ger. 53/E3
Dorra, Djib. 118/B2
Dorrance, Ks, US 153/E1
Dorre (isl.), Austl. 130/B3
Dorridge, Eng, UK 37/E2
Dorrigo, Austl. 132/E1
Dorrigo NP, Austl. 132/E1
Dorrington, Eng, UK 36/D1
Dorris, Ca, US 146/C3
Dorsale (mts.), Tun. 66/F4
Dorsbach (riv.), Ger. 58/B2
Dorset (co.), Eng, UK 36/D5
Dorsten, Ger. 52/D5
Dortan, Fr. 60/B5
Dortches, NC, US 163/J2
Dortmund, Ger. 53/E5
Dortmund (Wickede) (int'l arpt.), Ger. 53/E5
Dortmund-Ems (canal), Ger. 53/E4
Dörtyol, Turk. 104/E1
Dorum, Ger. 53/F1
Doruma, D.R. Congo 117/E4
Dorval, Qu, Can. 159/N7
Dörverden, Ger. 53/G3
Dos Bahias (cape), Arg. 190/D5
Dos de Mayo, Peru 184/C2
Dos Hermanas, Sp. 46/C4
Dos Palos, Ca, US 148/B2
Dos Pozos, Arg. 190/D4
Dos Puntas (cape), EqG. 120/B2
Dos Quebradas, Col. 183/K8
Dos Reyes (pt.), Chile 188/B3
Döşemealtı, Turk. 104/B1
Dosewallips (riv.), Wa, US 167/A2
Dōshi (riv.), Japan 83/C2
Dōshi, Japan 83/C2
Dosing, India 86/B3
Dospat, Bul. 49/J2
Dosse (riv.), Ger. 42/G2
Dosso (dept.), Niger 115/F3
Dosso, Niger 115/F3
Dosson, It. 63/F2
Dossor, Kaz. 71/K3
Dothan, Al, US 165/F2
Dot Lake, Ak, US 171/K3
Dötlingen, Ger. 53/F3
Dotnuva, Lith. 41/K4
Döttingen, Swi. 61/E2
Doty, Wa, US 144/C4
Douai, Fr. 54/C3
Douala, Camr. 120/B1
Douala (int'l arpt.), Camr. 120/B1
Douar el Cäid el Gueddara, Mor. 112/A2
Douar Toulal, Mor. 112/B3
Douarnenez (bay), Fr. 44/A2
Douarnenez, Fr. 56/A4
Double Island (pt.), Austl. 134/D4
Double Mtn. Fork (riv.), Tx, US 175/E1
Double Springs, Al, US 162/D3
Doubs, Fr. 60/C4
Doubs (dept.), Fr. 60/C3
Doubs (riv.), Fr. 66/E1
Doubtful (bay), Austl. 128/B3
Doubtful Island (bay), Austl. 130/C5
Doubtless (bay), NZ 135/C1
Doucette, Tx, US 151/G2
Douchy-les-Mines, Fr. 54/C3
Doudeville, Fr. 57/F1
Doue, Fr. 30/M5
Doué-la-Fontaine, Fr. 57/E6
Douentza, Mali 114/E3
Dougga (ruin), Tun. 112/L6
Dougherty, Tx, US 153/G4
Douglas, Austl. 128/C3
Douglas (lake), BC, Can. 144/D2
Douglas, Ire. 32/B6
Douglas, SAfr. 124/C3
Douglas (cap.), IM, UK 34/D3
Douglas, Sc, UK 33/C5
Douglas (mt.), Ak, US 171/H4
Douglas, Az, US 149/H5
Douglas (co.), Ga, US 163/L7
Douglas, Ga, US 165/G2
Douglas, Mi, US 160/C3
Douglas, ND, US 156/D4
Douglas (lake), Tn, US 163/F3
Douglas, Wy, US 154/B2
Douglass, Ks, US 153/F2
Douglass, Tx, US 151/G2
Douglassville, Pa, US 168/C3
Douglastown, NB, Can. 158/E2
Douglasville, Ga, US 163/L7
Dougou, China 87/G1
Doujiang, China 87/F3
Doulaincourt-Saucourt, Fr. 60/B1
Doullens, Fr. 54/B3
Doumé, Camr. 116/B4
Doumé, Gabon 120/C3
Doumé (riv.), Camr. 116/B4
Dounby, Sc, UK 31/V14
Doune (peak), Sc, UK 33/B4
Doune, Sc, UK 33/B4
Doupovské Hory (mts.), Czh. 45/K1
Dour, Belg. 54/C3
Doura, Mali 114/D3
Dourada, Serra (mts.), Braz. 186/C2
Dourados, Braz. 189/F2
Dourados (riv.), Braz. 186/B4
Dourbali, Chad 116/B3
Dourdan, Fr. 30/J6
Dourdou (riv.), Fr. 44/E4
Dourdoura, Chad 116/D3
Dourh (peak), Mor. 111/E2
Douro (riv.), Port. 66/B2
Douron (riv.), Fr. 56/B3
Dousman, Wi, US 167/P13
Doussard, Fr. 60/C6
Douvaine, Fr. 60/C5
Douve (riv.), Fr. 56/D2
Douvrin, Fr. 54/B2
Doux (riv.), Fr. 44/F4
Douze (riv.), Fr. 44/C4
Dove Creek, Co, US 149/H2
Dover, Austl. 132/C4
Dover (pt.), Austl. 130/E5
Dover, Eng, UK 37/H4
Dover (str.), UK,Fr. 44/D1
Dover, Ar, US 153/H3
Dover (A.F.B.), De, US 168/C5
Dover (cap.), De, US 168/C5
Dover, Fl, US 164/L8
Dover, Ks, US 153/G1
Dover, NH, US 161/L3
Dover, NJ, US 168/D2
Dover, Oh, US 160/F4
Dover, Ok, US 153/F3
Dover, Pa, US 168/B4
Dover, Tn, US 162/D2
Dover Bluff, Ga, US 165/H2
Doveridge, Eng, UK 35/G6
Dovrefjell NP, Nor. 38/D3
Dovsk, Bela. 70/D1
Dow, Ok, US 153/G3
Dow City, Ia, US 155/G3
Dowagiac, Mi, US 160/C4
Dowerin, Austl. 130/C4
Dowghā'ī, Iran 101/G1
Dowi (cape), Indo. 89/B2
Dowlatābād, Iran 103/J4
Dowling, Ab, Can. 145/H2
Down (dist.), NI, UK 34/C3
Downers Grove, Il, US 167/P16
Downey, Ca, US 166/F8
Downey, Id, US 147/G2
Downham Market, Eng, UK 37/G1
Downieville, Ca, US 146/C4
Downingtown, Pa, US 168/C4
Downpatrick, NI, UK 34/C3
Downs, Ks, US 154/E4
Downsville, NY, US 161/J3
Downton, Eng, UK 37/E4
Dows, Ia, US 155/H2
Dowshī, Afg. 101/J1
Doygaab, Som. 119/C1
Doyle, Ca, US 146/C3
Doylestown, Pa, US 168/C3
Doyleville, Co, US 149/J1
Dōzen (isl.), Japan 84/C3
Dozier, Al, US 165/E2
Dozulé, Fr. 57/E2
Drâa (cape), Mor. 110/C3
Drâa, Oued (riv.), Mor. 107/B2
Drac (riv.), Fr. 44/F4
Dracena, Braz. 189/G2
Drachten, Neth. 52/D2
Drăgăneşti-Olt, Rom. 51/G3
Drăgăşani, Rom. 51/G3
Dragoman, Bul. 51/F4
Dragon's Mouth (str.), Trin.,Ven. 181/F2
Dragoon, Az, US 149/G4
Dragør, Den. 39/J7
Draguignan, Fr. 64/C5
Drain, Or, US 146/B2
Drake, ND, US 156/D4
Drake (passg.), SAm. 191/D8
Drakensberg (mts.), SAfr. 107/E8
Drakesville, Ia, US 155/H3
Dráma, Gre. 49/J2
Dramba, D.R. Congo 121/G2
Drammen, Nor. 40/D2
Drammensfjorden (fd.), Nor. 38/R8
Dramselva (riv.), Nor. 38/R8
Drance (riv.), Swi. 60/D5
Drancy, Fr. 30/K5
Drangedal, Nor. 40/C2
Dranse (riv.), Fr. 60/C5
Dransfeld, Ger. 53/G5
Drap, Fr. 64/D5
Draper, Ut, US 147/H3
Draperstown, NI, UK 34/B2
Drās, India 98/C2
Drau (riv.), Aus. 45/K3
Drava (riv.), Cro. 50/C2
Dráva (riv.), Hun. 50/C3
Drava (riv.), Slov. 45/L3
Draveil, Fr. 30/K5
Drawa (riv.), Pol. 43/H2
Drawienski NP, Pol. 43/H2
Drawsko Pomorskie, Pol. 43/H2
Drayton, ND, US 156/F3
Drayton Valley, Ab, Can. 144/G1
Dreghorn, Sc, UK 33/B5
Drei Zinnen (peak), PNG 91/K4
Dreiesselberg (peak), Ger. 59/G5
Dreisam (riv.), Ger. 60/D2
Drensteinfurt, Ger. 53/E5
Drenthe (prov.), Neth. 52/D3
Drentse Hoofdvaart (riv.), Neth. 52/D3
Drentwede, Ger. 53/F3
Dresano, It. 62/C3
Dresden, Ger. 74/B4
Dresden, Oh, US 160/E4
Dresden, On, Can. 160/E3
Dresden, Tn, US 162/C2
Dresser, Wi, US 155/H1
Dreux, Fr. 57/G3
Drew, Ms, US 162/B4
Drews (res.), Or, US 146/C2
Drewsey, Or, US 146/D2
Drexel, Mo, US 153/G1
Dreyer, Tx, US 151/F3
Drezdenko, Pol. 43/H2
Driebergen, Neth. 52/C4
Driedorf, Ger. 55/H2
Driffield, Eng, UK 35/H4
Drift Prairie (grsld.), ND, US 156/E4
Driggs, Id, US 147/H2
Drigh Road, Pak. 101/J4
Drimoleague, Ire. 32/A6
Drin (gulf), Alb. 49/F2
Drin (riv.), Alb. 67/H2
Drina (riv.), Bosn.,Serb. 67/H2
Dripping Springs, Tx, US 151/E2
Driscoll, ND, US 156/D4
Driscoll, Tx, US 151/F4
Driskill (mtn.), La, US 153/H4
Drniš, Cro. 50/C4
Dro, It. 61/G6
Drøbak, Nor. 40/D2
Drobeta-Turnu Severin, Rom. 50/F3
Drochia, Mol. 72/D3
Drochtersen, Ger. 53/G1
Drocourt, Fr. 30/H4
Drogheda, Ire. 34/B4
Drogichin, Bela. 72/C1
Drohobych, Ukr. 72/B3
Droichead Nuadh, Ire. 32/D3
Droitwich, Eng, UK 36/D2
Drolshagen, Ger. 55/G1
Dromahaire, Ire. 32/B1
Drôme (riv.), Fr. 57/E2
Drôme (dept.), Fr. 64/B3
Dromedary (mt.), Austl. 133/E3
Dromina, Ire. 32/B5
Dromiskin, Ire. 34/B4
Dromore (riv.), Ire. 34/A3
Dromore, NI, UK 34/B3
Dromore West, Ire. 32/B1
Dronero, It. 64/D4
Dronfield, Eng, UK 35/G5
Drongan, Sc, UK 33/B6
Dronne (riv.), Fr. 44/D4
Dronten, Neth. 52/C3
Drop, Tx, US 150/K6
Dropt (riv.), Fr. 44/D4
Drosh, Pak. 98/A2
Droskovo, Rus. 70/F1
Drottningholm Palace, Swe. 39/A1
Droué, Fr. 57/G4
Drouette (riv.), Fr. 54/A6
Drouin, Austl. 133/B4
Druento, It. 64/D2
Druid Hills, Ga, US 163/M7
Drum (inlet), NC, US 163/J3
Drumaness, NI, UK 34/C3
Drumbeg, NI, UK 34/C2
Drumcar, Ire. 34/B4
Drumcollogher, Ire. 32/B5
Drumcondra, Ire. 32/D2
Drumheller, Ab, Can. 145/H2
Drumkeeran, Ire. 32/B1
Drumleck (pt.), Ire. 34/B5
Drumlish, Ire. 32/C2
Drummond (mt.), Austl. 134/B4
Drummond (pt.), Austl. 131/G5
Drummond (range), Austl. 127/D3
Drummond, NB, Can. 158/D2
Drummond, Id, US 147/H2
Drummond (isl.), MI, US 160/E1
Drummond, Mt, US 145/H4
Drummond, Wi, US 157/J4
Drummonds, Tn, US 162/C3
Drummondville, Qu, Can. 161/K2
Drummore, Sc, UK 34/D2
Drumnadrochit, Sc, UK 33/B2
Drumnakilly, NI, UK 34/A2
Drumochter, Pass of (pass), Sc, UK 33/B3
Drumright, Ok, US 153/F3
Drumshanbo, Ire. 32/B1
Drumsna, Ire. 32/B2
Drunen, Neth. 52/C5
Drunken (pt.), Mb, Can. 156/F2
Druridge (bay), Eng, UK 35/G1
Drusenheim, Fr. 55/G6
Druskininkai, Lith. 41/K4
Druten, Neth. 52/C5
Druya, Bela. 41/M4
Druzhba, Kaz. 99/D2
Druzhba, Ukr. 73/G1
Druzhkivka, Ukr. 73/J3
Drvar, Bosn. 50/C3
Drwęca (riv.), Pol. 43/K2
Dry (lake), ND, US 156/E3
Dry (cr.), Ca, US 146/C4
Dry Cimarron (riv.), Ok, US 152/C2
Dry Creek, Yk, Can. 171/K3
Dry Creek, La, US 164/B2
Dry Fork (riv.), Wy, US 154/B1
Dry Fork Marias (riv.), Mt, US 145/H3
Dry Prong, La, US 164/B2
Dry Ridge, Ky, US 162/E1
Dry Run, Oh, US 163/F1
Dry Tortugas (isl.), Fl, US 165/G5
Dry Tortugas Nat'l Pk., Fl, US 165/G5
Dryanovo, Bul. 51/G4
Dryden, On, Can. 157/H3
Dryden, Mi, US 167/F6
Dryden, NY, US 161/H3
Dryden, Tx, US 150/C2
Dryden, Va, US 163/F2
Drygarn Fawr (peak), Wal, UK 36/C2
Drymen, Sc, UK 33/B4
Drysdale (riv.), Austl. 128/B3
Drysdale River NP, Austl. 128/B3
Du (riv.), China 78/G5
Du Bois, Pa, US 161/G4
Du Dja, Réserve, Camr. 116/B5
Du Long, Viet. 94/E4
Du Page (co.), Il, US 167/P16
Du Page (riv.), Il, US 167/P16
Du Page, East Branch (riv.), Il, US 167/P16
Du Quoin, Il, US 162/C1
Duaringa, Austl. 134/C3
Duarte (peak), DRep. 173/G4
Duarte, Ca, US 166/G7
Ḑubā, SAr. 109/G3
Dubach, La, US 153/H4
Dubai (int'l arpt.), UAE 101/G3
Dubăsari, Mol. 72/E4
Dubawnt (riv.), NW, Can. 140/F2
Dubawnt (lake), Nun, Can. 140/F2
Dubawnt (lake), Can. 139/G3
Dubayy, UAE 101/G3
Dubele, D.R. Congo 121/G2
Dübendorf, Swi. 61/E3
Dübener Heide (phys. reg.), Ger. 42/G3
Dubino, It. 61/F5
Dublin (cap.), Ire. 34/B5
Dublin (co.), Ire. 34/B5
Dublin, Ca, US 167/L11
Dublin, Ga, US 163/F4
Dublin, Md, US 168/B4
Dublin, Oh, US 160/E4
Dublin, Pa, US 168/C3
Dublin, Tx, US 151/E1
Dublin, Va, US 163/G2
Dubna, Rus. 70/F1
Dubna, Rus. 68/H4
Dubnica nad Váhom, Slvk. 43/K4
Dubno, Ukr. 72/C2
Dubois, Wy, US 147/J2
Dubois, Id, US 147/G1
Duboistown, Pa, US 168/A1
Dubossary (res.), Mol. 51/J2
Dubovskiy, Rus. 71/G2
Dubovskoye, Rus. 73/M4
Dubovyy Umët, Rus. 71/J1
Dubra, India 97/F4
Dubrājpur, India 97/F4
Dubréka, Gui. 114/B4
Dubrovka, Rus. 70/E1
Dubrovka, Rus. 41/P2
Dubrovnik (int'l arpt.), Serb. 50/D4
Dubrovnik, Cro. 50/D4
Dubrovno, Bela. 41/P4
Dubrovytsya, Ukr. 72/D2
Dubulu, D.R. Congo 116/D4
Dubuque, Ia, US 155/J2
Duc Lap, Viet. 94/D3
Duc Pho, Viet. 94/E3
Duc Phong, Viet. 94/D4
Duchcov, Czh. 59/G1
Duchesne, Ut, US 147/H3
Duchesne (riv.), Ut, US 147/H3
Duchess, Austl. 131/H2
Duchess, Ab, Can. 145/J2
Ducie (isl.), Pitc. 137/N7
Duck (lake), Mi, US 167/E7
Duck (cr.), Nv, US 147/F4
Duck (riv.), Tn, US 162/D3
Duck Bay, Mb, Can. 156/D1
Duck Hill, Ms, US 162/C4
Duck Lake, Sk, Can. 145/L1
Duck (mtn.), Mb, Can. 156/D2
Duck Valley Ind. Res., Id, US 146/E2
Duckabush (riv.), Wa, US 167/A2
Ducktown, Tn, US 162/E3
Duckwater, Nv, US 146/F4
Duckwater Ind. Res., Nv, US 148/E1
Duclair, Fr. 57/F2
Duda (riv.), Col. 180/C4
Duddon (riv.), Eng, UK 35/E3
Dudelange, Lux. 55/F5
Dudenhofen, Ger. 58/B4
Duderstadt, Ger. 53/H5
Dudh Kosi (riv.), Nepal 97/F2
Dūdhi, India 96/D3
Dudhwa NP, India 96/C1
Dudignac, Arg. 190/E2
Düdingen, Swi. 60/D4
Dudinka, Rus. 74/J3
Dudley, Eng, UK 36/D1
Dudley (co.), Eng, UK 36/D1
Dudub, Eth. 118/C4
Dudzele, Belg. 54/C1
Due, D.R. Congo 120/D4
Due West, SC, US 163/F3
Duékoué, C.d'Iv. 114/D5
Dueñas, Sp. 46/C2
Duenweg, Mo, US 153/G2
Dueré, Braz. 186/C1
Duette, Fl, US 164/L8
Dueville, It. 63/E2
Dufaja (riv.), Kenya 119/B2
Duff (isls.), Sol. 136/F5
Duffel, Belg. 55/D1
Dufferin (co.), On, Can. 160/S8
Duffield, Eng, UK 35/G6
Duff's Corners, On, Can. 160/S9
Dufftown, Sc, UK 33/C2
Dufour (Dufourspitze) (peak), Swi. 62/A1
Dufourspitze (Dufour) (peak), Swi. 62/A1
Dugachhi, Bang. 97/H3
Dugald, Mb, Can. 156/F3
Dugbia, D.R. Congo 121/F2
Dugdemona (riv.), La, US 151/H1
Dugger, In, US 162/D1
Dugi (isl.), Cro. 45/L4
Dugi Otok (isl.), Cro. 67/G2
Dugny-sur-Meuse, Fr. 55/E5
Dugo Selo, Cro. 50/C3
Dugu, Eth. 118/B3
Dugway, Ut, US 147/G3
Dugway Proving Grounds, Ut, US 147/G3
Duich (lake), Sc, UK 33/A2
Duida (peak), Ven. 181/E4
Duida Marahuaca, PN, Ven. 181/E4
Duifken (pt.), Austl. 129/F3
Duingen, Ger. 53/G4
Duino, It. 63/G2
Duisburg, Ger. 52/D6
Duitama, Col. 180/C3
Duiven, Neth. 52/D5
Duivendrecht, Neth. 52/B4
Dujuuma, Som. 119/C1
Duk Fadiat, Sudan 117/F4
Dukafulu, Eth. 118/A4
Dukambīya, Erit. 117/H2
Duke, Mo, US 153/H2
Duke of Gloucester (isls.), FrPol. 137/L7
Duke's (pass), Sc, UK 33/B4
Dukhān, Qatar 100/F3
Dukla Pass (Dukielska) (pass), Pol. 43/L4
Dūkštas, Lith. 41/M4
Dula, D.R. Congo 116/D4
Dulac, La, US 164/C3
Dulan, China 78/D4
Dulce (riv.), Arg. 188/D4
Dulce, NM, US 149/J2
Dulce (gulf), Pan. 177/F4
Dulce Nombre de Culmí, Hon. 176/E3
Dule, Erit. 118/A2
Duleek, Ire. 34/B4
Dŭlgopol, Bul. 51/H4
Duliu (riv.), China 93/J2
Duliu, China 80/H7
Dullewāla, Pak. 98/A4
Dullstroom, SAfr. 123/F5
Dülmen, Ger. 53/E5
Dulnain (riv.), Sc, UK 33/C2
Dulong (pass), China 86/B3
Dulovo, Bul. 51/H4
Dulunguin (pt.), Phil. 88/C4
Duluth, Mn, US 157/H4
Duluth, Ga, US 163/M6
Dulverton, Eng, UK 36/C4
Dūmā, Syria 105/E1
Dūmā, WBnk. 105/C4
Dumagasa (pt.), Phil. 88/C4
Dumaguete, Phil. 88/C3
Dumai, Indo. 89/C2
Dumalinao, Phil. 88/C4
Dumanjug, Phil. 88/C3
Dumaran, Phil. 88/B3
Dumaran (isl.), Phil. 91/E1
Dumas, Tx, US 152/D3
Dumas, Ar, US 153/J4
Ḑumayr, Syria 104/E3
Ḑumayr, Syria 105/F1
Dumbarton, Sc, UK 33/B5
Dumbi, D.R. Congo 120/D4
Dumbi, Ang. 122/B1
Ďumbier (peak), Slvk. 43/K4
Dumbleyung, Austl. 130/C5
Dumbrăveni, Rom. 51/G2
Dume (pt.), Ca, US 166/B2
Dumei, China 87/H3
Dumfries, Sc, UK 34/E1
Dumfries and Galloway (co.), Sc, UK 33/C6
Duminichi, Rus. 70/E1
Dumka, India 97/F3
Dumlu, Turk. 71/G4
Dummar, Syria 105/E1
Dümmer (lake), Ger. 53/F3
Dumoine (riv.), Qu, Can. 161/H1
Dumoine (lake), Qu, Can. 141/J4
Dumont, NJ, US 169/K8
Dumont d'Urville, Fr., Ant. 192/K
Dumraon, India 97/E3
Dumri, India 97/F4
Dumyat (gov.), Egypt 102/B3
Dumyāţ (Damietta), Egypt 113/C2
Dumyāţ, Massabb (Damietta) (mouth), Egypt 113/C1
Dún Laoghaire, Ire. 34/B5
Dun Rig (peak), Sc, UK 33/C5
Dunaföldvár, Hun. 50/D2
Dunaharaszti, Hun. 51/R10
Dunajec (riv.), Pol. 43/L4
Dunakeszi, Hun. 51/R9
Dunany (pt.), Ire. 34/B4
Dunaszekcso, Hun. 50/D2
Dunaújváros, Hun. 50/D2
Dunavecse, Hun. 50/D2
Dunavtsi, Bul. 50/F4
Dunayivtsi, Ukr. 72/D3
Dunbar, Sc, UK 33/D5
Dunbar, Austl. 134/A2
Dunblane, Sk, Can. 145/L2
Dunblane, Sc, UK 33/C4
Dunboyne, Ire. 34/B5
Duncan, Ok, US 153/F3
Duncan, Az, US 149/H4
Duncan, Ms, US 162/B3
Duncan, BC, Can. 144/C3
Duncannon, Ire. 32/D5
Duncannon, Pa, US 168/A3
Duncansby Head (pt.), Sc, UK 31/V14
Duncanville, Tx, US 150/L7
Dund-Us, Mong. 78/C2
Dundaga, Lat. 41/K3
Dundalk (bay), Ire. 34/B4
Dundalk, Ire. 34/B4
Dundalk, On, Can. 160/F2
Dundalk, Md, US 168/B5
Dundas (lake), Austl. 130/D5
Dundas (str.), Austl. 128/C2
Dundas (pen.), NW, Can. 141/R7
Dundas, On, Can. 160/T9
Dundas, Oh, US 163/F1
Dundas, Il, US 162/C1
Dundee, SAfr. 125/E3
Dundee, Sc, UK 33/D4
Dundee (co.), Sc, UK 33/D4
Dundee (arpt.), Sc, UK 33/C4
Dundee, Fl, US 164/M7
Dundee, Ms, US 162/B3
Dundee, Tx, US 152/E4
Dundgovi (prov.), Mong. 78/F2
Dundīţ, Egypt 113/C3
Dundonald, Sc, UK 33/B5
Dundrum (bay), NI, UK 34/C3
Dundrum, NI, UK 34/C3
Dundurn, Sk, Can. 145/L2
Dundwa (range), Nepal 96/D2
Dundwārāganj, India 96/B2
Dunedin, NZ 135/B4
Dunedin, Fl, US 164/K7
Dunedoo, Austl. 132/D2
Dunellen, NJ, US 169/H9
Dunes City, Or, US 146/A2
Dunfanaghy, Ire. 31/Q9
Dunfermline, Sc, UK 33/C4
Dunga Bunga, Pak. 98/B5
Dungalear Station, Austl. 132/D1
Dungannon, NI, UK 34/B3
Dungannon (co.), NI, UK 34/B3
Dungannon, On, Can. 160/F3
Dungarpur, India 92/B3
Dungarvan, Ire. 32/C5
Dungarvan (har.), Ire. 32/C5
Dungau (reg.), Ger. 59/F5
Dungeness (pt.), Arg. 191/C7
Dungeness (pt.), Eng, UK 37/G5
Dungeness, Wa, US 144/C3
Dungiven, NI, UK 34/B2
Dunglow, Ire. 31/P9
Dungog, Austl. 132/D2
Dungu, D.R. Congo 121/G2
Dungu (riv.), D.R. Congo 117/F5
Dunham, Qu, Can. 161/K2
Dunhua, China 79/K3
Dunhuang, China 78/C3
Dunkeld, Sc, UK 33/C3
Dunkellin (riv.), Ire. 32/B3
Dunkerque (Dunkirk), Fr. 44/E1
Dunkery (hill), Eng, UK 36/C4
Dunkirk (Dunkerque), Fr. 44/E1
Dunkirk, In, US 160/D4
Dunkirk, NY, US 161/G3
Dunkley, BC, Can. 144/C1
Dunkwa, Gha. 115/E5
Dunlap, Tn, US 162/E3
Dunlap, Ia, US 155/G3
Dunlavin, Ire. 32/D3
Dunleath, Sk, Can. 156/C2
Dunleer, Ire. 34/B4
Dunloe, Gap of (pass), Ire. 32/A5
Dunloy, NI, UK 34/B2
Dunmanus (bay), Ire. 32/A6
Dunmanway, Ire. 32/A6
Dunmore, Ire. 32/B2
Dunmore, Pa, US 161/J4
Dunmore, WV, US 163/H1
Dunmore East, Ire. 32/C5
Dunmurry, NI, UK 34/B2
Dunn, La, US 153/J4
Dunn, NC, US 163/H3
Dunnamanagh, NI, UK 34/A2
Dunnamore, NI, UK 34/B2
Dunnell, Mn, US 155/G2
Dunnellon, Fl, US 165/G3
Dünnern (riv.), Swi. 60/D3
Dunnet Head (pt.), Sc, UK 31/V14
Dunning, Sc, UK 33/C4
Dunningen, Ger. 61/E1
Dunnington, Eng, UK 35/H4
Dunnsville, Va, US 163/J2
Dunnville, On, Can. 160/T10
Dunolly, Austl. 132/B3
Dunoon, Sc, UK 33/B5
Dunqulah, Sudan 109/F5
Dunqunāb, Sudan 100/C4
Dunragit, Sc, UK 34/D2
Duns, Sc, UK 33/D5
Dunsborough, Austl. 130/B5
Dunscore, Sc, UK 34/E1
Dunseith, ND, US 156/D3
Dunseverick, NI, UK 34/B1
Dunshaughlin, Ire. 34/B4
Dunsmuir, Ca, US 146/B3
Dunstable, Eng, UK 37/F3
Dunster, BC, Can. 144/E1
Duntocher, Sc, UK 33/B5
Dunure, Sc, UK 33/B6
Dunville, Nf, Can. 159/L2
Dunwoody, Ga, US 163/M7
Dunyāpur, Pak. 98/A5
Duobukur (riv.), China 79/J1
Duojing, China 87/E4
Duolun, China 78/H3
Dupont, In, US 162/E1
Dupont, Pa, US 168/C1
Dupree, SD, US 154/D1
Dupuy (cape), Austl. 130/B2
Duque Bacelar, Braz. 183/F4
Duque de Caxias, Braz. 187/N7
Duque de York (isl.), Chile 191/A6
Duquette, Mn, US 157/H4
Dūrā, WBnk. 105/C5
Durack (range), Austl. 128/B4
Durack (riv.), Austl. 128/B4
Durağan, Turk. 70/E4
Durak, Turk. 104/D1
Durand, Mi, US 160/E3
Durand, Wi, US 155/J1
Durango (state), Mex. 172/A3
Durango, Sp. 44/B5
Durango, Co, US 149/J2
Durango de Victoria, Mex. 174/D3
Duranillin, Austl. 130/C5
Durant, Ok, US 153/F4
Durant, Fl, US 164/L8
Durant, Ms, US 162/C4
Durazno (dept.), Uru. 191/F2
Durazno, Uru. 191/K10
Durban, SAfr. 125/E3
Durban (Louis Botha) (int'l arpt.), SAfr. 125/E3
Durbanville, SAfr. 124/L10
Durbe, Lat. 41/J3
Durbion (riv.), Fr. 60/C1
Durbuy, Belg. 55/E3
Dúrcal, Sp. 46/D4
Durdevac, Cro. 50/C2
Durdevo, Serb. 50/E3
Durdur (riv.), Som. 118/B3
Düre, China 99/E2
Dureji, Pak. 101/J3
Düren, Ger. 55/F2
Durg, India 95/D1
Durgāpur, India 97/G3
Durgāpur, India 97/F4
Durgerdam, Neth. 52/B4
Durham, On, Can. 160/F2
Durham (co.), On, Can. 160/V8
Durham (co.), Eng, UK 35/F2
Durham, Eng, UK 35/G2
Durham, Ca, US 146/C4
Durham, Ks, US 153/F1
Durham, Mo, US 155/J4
Durham, NC, US 163/H3
Durham, NH, US 161/L3
Durham Bridge, NB, Can. 158/D2
Durham Downs, Austl. 134/A4
Duri, Indo. 89/C2
Durlston (pt.), Eng, UK 36/E5
Ḑurmā, SAr. 100/E4
Durmitor NP, Serb. 49/F1
Durnford (pt.), WSah. 110/B5
Duror, Sc, UK 33/A5
Dürrenroth, Swi. 60/D3
Durrës, Alb. 49/F2
Durrington, Eng, UK 37/E4
Dürrlauingen, Ger. 58/D6
Durrow, Ire. 32/C4
Dürrwangen, Ger. 58/D4
Dursley, Eng, UK 36/D3
Dursunbey, Turk. 70/D5
Durtal, Fr. 57/E5
Duru, D.R. Congo 117/F4
Durugu, D.R. Congo 116/C4
Durukhsi, Eth. 118/C3
Durusu (lake), Turk. 103/M6
Durusu, Turk. 103/M6
Durūz (peak), Syria 109/H1
D'Urville (cape), Indo. 91/J4
Dusa Marreb (Dhuusamarreeb), Som. 118/C4
Dusanovo, Serb. 49/G1
Dusetos, Lith. 41/L4
Dushak, Trkm. 101/H1
Dushan, China 87/E3
Dushanbe (cap.), Taj. 74/G6
Dusheti, Geo. 71/H4
Dushui (riv.), China 87/E3
Dusky (sound), NZ 135/A4
Düsseldorf (int'l arpt.), Ger. 52/D6
Düsseldorf, Ger. 52/D6
Dusti, Taj. 101/J1
Dustin, Ok, US 153/F3
Duszniki-Zdrój, Pol. 43/J3
Dutch (riv.), Eng, UK 35/H4
Dutch (cr.), BC, Can. 144/F2
Dutch Harbor, Ak, US 171/E5
Dutch John, Ut, US 147/J3
Dutch Wonderland, Pa, US 168/B3
Dutlwe, Bots. 122/D4
Dutoitspiek (peak), SAfr. 124/L10
Dutovo, Rus. 69/N3
Dutse, Nga. 115/H4
Dutsen Wai, Nga. 115/H4
Dutsin-Ma, Nga. 115/G3
Dutton, On, Can. 160/F3
Dutton (mt.), Ut, US 149/F1
Dutton, Mt, US 145/J4
Dutukpene, Gha. 115/F4
Duvall, Wa, US 167/D2
Duvno, Bosn. 50/C4
Düxanbibazar, China 99/D4
Duxun, China 87/H4
Duyang, China 87/E3
Duyun, China 87/E3
Dūz, Tun. 66/F4
Düzce, Turk. 51/K5
Düzici, Turk. 102/D2
Dve Mogili, Bul. 51/G4
Dvina (bay), Rus. 68/H2
Dvinskoy, Rus. 69/K3
Dvořiště (lake), Czh. 59/H4
Dvorníky, Slvk. 50/C1
Dwārka, India 101/J4
Dwārkeswar (riv.), India 97/F4
Dwight, Ks, US 153/F1
Dwight, Il, US 160/B4
Dworshak (res.), Id, US 144/F4
Dwyer (Faywood), NM, US 149/H4
Dwyfor (riv.), Wal, UK 34/D6
Dwyka (riv.), SAfr. 124/C4
Dyat'kovo, Rus. 70/E1
Dybvad, Den. 40/D3
Dyce, Sc, UK 33/D2
Dyce (int'l arpt.), Sc, UK 33/D2
Dyckesville, Wi, US 160/C2
Dyer, In, US 160/C4
Dyer (cape), Nun, Can. 141/K2
Dyer, Nv, US 148/C2
Dyer, Tn, US 162/C2
Dyer (cape), Chile 191/B6
Dyersburg, Tn, US 162/C2
Dyersville, Ia, US 155/J2
Dyess, Ar, US 162/B3
Dyess (A.F.B.), Tx, US 150/E1
Dyfed (co.), Wal, UK 36/B2
Dyffryn, Wal, UK 34/D6
Dyfi (riv.), Wal, UK 36/C1
Dyje (riv.), Czh. 43/J4
Dykan'ka, Ukr. 73/H3
Dyke Ackland (bay), PNG 129/H2
Dykh-tau (peak), Rus. 71/G4
Dyle (riv.), Belg. 42/C3
Dyleň (peak), Czh. 59/F3
Dylewska (peak), Pol. 43/K2
Dymchurch, Eng, UK 37/G4
Dymer, Ukr. 72/F2
Dymytrov, Ukr. 73/J3
Dysart, Sk, Can. 156/B2
Dysart, Austl. 134/C3
Dysart, Ia, US 155/H2
Dysseldorp, SAfr. 124/C4
Dyul'tydag (peak), Rus. 71/H4
Dyurtyuli, Rus. 69/M5
Dzalanyama (range), Moz. 123/G2
Dzamandzar, Madg. 125/J6
Dzaoudzi (cap.), May. 125/H6
Dzaoudzi (int'l arpt.), May. 125/H6
Dzavhan (riv.), Mong. 78/C2
Dzavhan (prov.), Mong. 78/D2
Dzel, Mong. 99/F2
Dzenzik (pt.), Ukr. 73/J4
Dzerzhinsk, Rus. 68/J4
Dzerzhinsk, Bela. 41/M5
Dzerzhyns'k, Ukr. 73/J3
Dzerzhyns'k, Ukr. 72/D2
Dzhalinda, Rus. 79/J1
Dzhambeyty, Kaz. 71/K2
Dzhanga, Trkm. 103/H1
Dzhankoy, Ukr. 73/H5
Dzhanybek, Kaz. 71/H2
Dzharylgach (gulf), Ukr. 51/L2
Dzhebel, Bul. 49/J2
Dzhebrail, Azer. 103/F2
Dzhirgatal', Taj. 99/B4
Dzhubga, Rus. 70/F3
Dzhugdzhur (range), Rus. 77/N4
Dzhusaly, Kaz. 74/G5
Działdowo, Pol. 43/L2
Dzibalchén, Mex. 176/D2
Dzibilchaltún (ruin), Mex. 176/D1
Dzidzantún, Mex. 176/D1
Dzierżoniów, Pol. 43/J3
Dzitbalché, Mex. 176/D1
Dziuché, Mex. 176/D2
Dzöölön, Mong. 78/D1
Dzukija NP, Lith. 41/L4
Dzungarian (basin), China 74/J5
Dzur, Mong. 78/D2
Dzüünbayan, Mong. 78/G3
Dzüünbulag, Mong. 78/G2
Dzüünharaa, Mong. 78/F2
Dzüünhövöö, Mong. 99/F1
Dzuunmod, Mong. 78/F2

E

E.D.F. (canal), Fr. 64/B5
E.T. Joshua (int'l arpt.), StV. 173/N9
Eads, Co, US 152/C1
Eagan, Mn, US 157/P7
Eagle (riv.), Nf, Can. 141/L3
Eagle (cr.), Sk, Can. 145/K2
Eagle (hills), Sk, Can. 145/K1
Eagle (mt.), Ire. 32/A5
Eagle, Ak, US 171/K3
Eagle (lake), Ca, US 146/C3
Eagle (mts.), Ca, US 148/E4
Eagle (peak), Ca, US 146/C3
Eagle (peak), Ca, US 146/D4
Eagle, Co, US 147/K4
Eagle (riv.), Co, US 147/K4
Eagle, Id, US 146/E2
Eagle (cr.), Ky, US 162/E1
Eagle (mtn.), Mn, US 157/J4
Eagle, Ne, US 155/F3
Eagle (peak), Tx, US 150/B2
Eagle (pt.), Tx, US 150/N9
Eagle, Wi, US 167/P14
Eagle (peak), Wy, US 147/H1
Eagle Bend, Mn, US 157/G4
Eagle Butte, SD, US 154/D1
Eagle Crags (peak), Ca, US 148/D3
Eagle Grove, Ia, US 155/H2
Eagle Lake, Fl, US 164/M8
Eagle Lake, Tx, US 150/F3
Eagle Mills, Ar, US 153/H4
Eagle Mountain (lake), Tx, US 153/F4
Eagle Pass, Tx, US 150/D3
Eagle Point, Or, US 146/B2
Eagle River, Mi, US 157/K4
Eagle River, Wi, US 157/K5
Eagle Rock, Va, US 163/H2
Eaglehawk, Austl. 133/B3
Eaglesfield, Sc, UK 35/E1
Eaglesham, Sc, UK 33/B5
Eagleton, Ar, US 153/G3
Eagletown, Ok, US 153/G3
Eagleville, Ca, US 146/C3
Eagleville, Mo, US 155/H3
Eahun, Indo. 128/A2
Eakly, Ok, US 153/E3
Ealing (bor.), Eng, UK 30/B2
Ear Falls, On, Can. 157/H2
Earby, Eng, UK 35/F4
Earith, Eng, UK 37/G2
Earl Grey, Sk, Can. 156/B2
Earl Stonham, Eng, UK 37/H2
Earle, Ar, US 162/B3
Earle Nav. Weapons Ctr., NJ, US 168/D3
Earlimart, Ca, US 148/C3
Earling, Ia, US 155/G3
Earlington, Ky, US 162/D2
Earls Barton, Eng, UK 37/F2
Earls Colne, Eng, UK 37/G3
Earl's Seat (peak), Sc, UK 33/B4
Earlsboro, Ok, US 153/F3
Earlsferry, Sc, UK 33/D4
Earlston, Sc, UK 33/D5
Earltown, NS, Can. 158/F3
Earlville, Ia, US 155/J2
Earlville, Il, US 155/K3
Early, Ia, US 155/G2
Early, Tx, US 150/E2
Earn (riv.), Sc, UK 33/C4
Earn (lake), Sc, UK 33/B4
Earnslaw (mt.), NZ 135/B4
Earp, Ca, US 148/E3
Easington, Eng, UK 35/G2
Easingwold, Eng, UK 35/G3
Easky, Ire. 32/B1
Easley, SC, US 163/F3
East (mt.), Austl. 130/D4
East (cape), NZ 135/D2
East (cape), Ak, US 171/B6
East (mesa), Ca, US 148/E4
East (cape), Fl, US 165/H5
East (pt.), NJ, US 168/C5
East (riv.), NY, US 169/K8
East (bay), Tx, US 151/G3
East (passg.), Wa, US 167/C3
East Alamosa, Co, US 152/B2
East Alligator (riv.), Austl. 128/D3
East Anglia (reg.), Eng, UK 37/H2
East Angus, Qu, Can. 161/L2
East Arrow Park, BC, Can. 144/F2
East Ayrshire (co.), Sc, UK 33/B6
East Baines (riv.), Austl. 128/C3
East Bangor, Pa, US 168/C2
East Barming, Eng, UK 30/E3
East Barnet (nbrhd.), Eng, UK 30/C2
East Berbice-Corentyne (pol. reg.), Guy. 181/G3
East Bergholt, Eng, UK 37/H3
East Berlin, Pa, US 168/B4
East Bernstadt, Ky, US 162/E2
East Berwick, Pa, US 168/B1
East Bethel, Mn, US 157/H5
East Bijou (cr.), Co, US 154/B4
East Brady, Pa, US 161/G4
East Brewton, Al, US 164/E2
East Brunswick, NJ, US 169/H10
East Cache (cr.), Ok, US 153/E3
East Caicos (isl.), UK 177/J1
East Calder, Sc, UK 33/C5
East Camden, Ar, US 153/H4
East Carbon, Ut, US 147/H4
East Chevington, Eng, UK 33/E6
East Chicago, In, US 160/C4
East China (sea), Asia 77/M6
East Clandon, Eng, UK 30/B3
East Coulee, Ab, Can. 145/H2
East Dart (riv.), Eng, UK 36/C5
East Dereham, Eng, UK 37/G1
East Detroit (East Pointe), Mi, US 167/G7
East Dismal (swamp), NC, US 163/J3
East Dublin, Ga, US 163/F4
East Dumbartonshire (co.), Sc, UK 33/B5
East Falkland (isl.), UK 179/D8
East Falmouth, Ma, US 161/L4
East Farmingdale, NY, US 169/M9
East Flat Rock, NC, US 163/F3
East Fork (riv.), Tx, US 153/F4
East Fork Chandalar (riv.), Ak, US 171/J2
East Fork Trinity (riv.), Tx, US 150/L6
East Frisian (isls.), Neth. 42/D2
East Frisian (isls.), Ger. 40/B5
East Ghor (canal), Jor. 105/D4
East Glacier Park, Mt, US 145/H3
East Glen (riv.), Eng, UK 35/H6
East Grand Rapids, Mi, US 160/D3
East Greenville, Pa, US 168/C3
East Griffin, Ga, US 162/E4
East Grinstead, Eng, UK 37/F4
East Gull Lake, Mn, US 157/G4
East Hampton, NY, US 169/F2
East Hampton (arpt.), NY, US 169/F2
East Hanningfield, Eng, UK 30/E2
East Haven, Ct, US 169/F1
East Helena, Mt, US 145/J4
East Hill-Meridian, Wa, US 167/C3
East Hills, NY, US 169/L8
East Hodge, La, US 164/B1
East Horseley, Eng, UK 30/B3
East Jordan, Mi, US 160/D2
East Kilbride, Sc, UK 33/B5
East Korea (bay), NKor. 79/K4
East Lamma (chan.), China 87/L8
East Lansing, Mi, US 160/D3
East Las Vegas, Nv, US 148/E2
East Leake, Eng, UK 35/G6
East Linton, Sc, UK 33/D5
East Liverpool, Oh, US 160/F4
East London, SAfr. 124/D4
East Los Angeles, Ca, US 166/F7
East Lothian (co.), Sc, UK 33/D5
East Malling, Eng, UK 30/E3
East Meadow, NY, US 169/L9
East Midlands (int'l arpt.), Eng, UK 35/G6
East Millcreek, Ut, US 147/H3
East Mojave Nat'l Scenic Area, Ca, US 148/E3
East Molesey, Eng, UK 30/B2
East Montpelier, Vt, US 161/K2
East Naples, Fl, US 165/H4
East Newark, NJ, US 169/J9
East Nishnabotna (riv.), Ia, US 155/G3
East Nodaway (riv.), Ia, US 155/G3
East Northport, NY, US 169/E2
East Olympia, Wa, US 144/C4
East Orange, NJ, US 169/J8
East Otis, Ma, US 161/K3
East Palatka, Fl, US 165/H3
East Palestine, Oh, US 160/F4
East Peckham, Eng, UK 30/E3
East Petersburg, Pa, US 168/B3
East Point, La, US 150/H1
East Point, Ga, US 163/M7
East Pointe (East Detroit), Mi, US 167/G7
East Port Orchard, Wa, US 167/B2
East Prairie, Mo, US 162/C2
East Prospect, Pa, US 168/B4
East Quogue, NY, US 169/F2
East Riding of Yorkshire (co.), Eng, UK 35/H4
East Renfrewshire (co.), Sc, UK 33/B5
East Retford, Eng, UK 35/H5
East Ridge, Tn, US 162/E3
East Rockaway, NY, US 169/L9
East Rockingham, NC, US 163/H3
East Rutherford, NJ, US 169/J8
East Saint Louis, Il, US 155/J4
East Siberian (sea), Rus. 75/S2
East Side, Pa, US 168/C1
East Stroudsburg, Pa, US 168/C2
East Sussex (co.), Eng, UK 37/G5
East Tampa, Fl, US 164/L8
East Tawas, Mi, US 160/E2
East Thermopolis, Wy, US 147/J2
East Timbalier Island Nat'l Wild. Ref., La, US 164/C3
East Timor (ctry.) 128/B2
East Troy, Wi, US 167/P14
East Walker (riv.), Ca, Nv, US 146/D4
East Wemyss, Sc, UK 33/C4
East Wenatchee, Wa, US 144/D4
East Windsor, NJ, US 168/D3
East Wittering, Eng, UK 37/F5
East York (city), On, Can. 160/U8
East-the-Water, Eng, UK 36/B4
Eastabuchie, Ms, US 164/D2
Eastbourne, Eng, UK 37/G5
Eastend, Sk, Can. 145/K3
Easter (pt.), Namb. 122/B5
Easter (Isla de Pascua) (isl.), Chile 137/Q7
Eastern (pt.), Nf, Can. 159/H2
Eastern (pol. reg.), Gha. 115/E5
Eastern (chan.), Japan 84/A4
Eastern (prov.), Kenya 119/B1
Eastern (prov.), SLeo. 114/C4
Eastern (prov.), SrL. 95/D5
Eastern (plain), Eng, UK 35/H4
Eastern (bay), Md, US 168/B6
Eastern Fields (reef), PNG 129/G2
Eastern Ghats (mts.), India 92/C5
Eastern Highlands (prov.), PNG 129/G1
Eastern Neck Island NWR, Md, US 168/B5
Eastern Sayans (mts.), Rus. 74/K4
Eastfield, Eng, UK 35/H3
Eastgate, Nv, US 146/E4
Eastland, Tx, US 151/E1
Eastleigh, Eng, UK 37/E5
Eastleigh (int'l arpt.), Eng, UK 37/E5
Eastmain (riv.), Can. 139/K4

Eastma – Emināb

Eastmain (riv.), Qu, Can. 141/J3
Eastman, Ga, US 163/F4
Eastman, Wi, US 155/J2
Easton, Eng, UK 36/D5
Easton, Ca, US 148/C2
Easton, Ct, US 169/E1
Easton (res.), Ct, US 169/E1
Easton, Ma, US 161/L3
Easton, La, US 164/B2
Easton, Md, US 163/J1
Easton, Mo, US 155/G4
Easton, Pa, US 168/C2
Easton, Tx, US 151/G1
Eastport, NY, US 169/F2
Eastriggs, Sc, UK 35/E2
Eastry, Eng, UK 37/H4
Eastsound, Wa, US 144/C3
Eastville, Va, US 163/K2
Eastwood, Eng, UK 35/G6
Eatington, Eng, UK 37/E2
Eaton, Co, US 154/B3
Eaton, In, US 160/D4
Eaton, Oh, US 160/D5
Eaton Park, Fl, US 164/M7
Eaton Rapids, Mi, US 160/D3
Eaton Socon, Eng, UK 37/F2
Eatonia, Sk, Can. 145/K2
Eatons Neck (pt.), NY, US 169/M8
Eatonton, Ga, US 163/F4
Eatontown, NJ, US 168/D3
Eatonville, Fl, US 164/N6
Eatonville, Wa, US 144/C4
Eau (riv.), Eng, UK 35/H5
Eau Claire (lake), Qu, Can. 141/J3
Eau Claire (riv.), Wi, US 155/J1
Eau Claire, Wi, US 155/J1
Eau d'Heure (riv.), Belg. 55/D3
Eaubonne, Fr. 30/J5
Eaulne (riv.), Fr. 54/A4
Eauripik (isl.), Micr. 136/D4
Eauze, Fr. 44/D5
Ebalo (riv.), D.R. Congo 116/D5
Ebano, Mex. 176/B1
Ebble (riv.), Eng, UK 37/E4
Ebbw Vale, Wal, UK 36/C3
Ebebiyín, EqG. 120/B2
Ebeggi (well), Alg. 111/G5
Ebéjico, Col. 183/K6
Ebeleben, Ger. 53/H6
Ebeltoft, Den. 40/D3
Ebeltoft Vig (bay), Swe. 39/G6
Eben Junction, Mi, US 157/L4
Ebensburg, Pa, US 161/G4
Ebensee, Aus. 50/A2
Eberbach, Ger. 58/B4
Ebergassing, Aus. 51/P7
Ebergötzen, Ger. 53/H5
Ebermannstadt, Ger. 58/E3
Ebern, Ger. 58/D2
Ebernburg, Ger. 55/G4
Ebersbach an der Fils, Ger. 58/C5
Ebersberg, Ger. 59/E6
Eberschwang, Aus. 59/G6
Ebersheim, Fr. 60/D1
Eberswalde-Finow, Ger. 43/G2
Ebetsu, Japan 82/B2
Ebian, China 93/H2
Ebina, Japan 83/C3
Ebingen, Ger. 61/F1
Ebinur (lake), China 99/D3
Ebnat-Kappel, Swi. 61/F3
Ebo (lake), Mali 114/E3
Ebola (riv.), D.R. Congo 121/E2
Ebolowa, Camr. 120/B2
Ebon (isl.), Mrsh. 136/F4
Ebony, Namb. 122/B4
Ebony, Va, US 163/J2
Ebonyi (state), Nga. 141/H5
Eboro, Gabon 120/B2
Ebrach, Ger. 58/D3
Ebreichsdorf, Aus. 51/N8
Ebro, Mn, US 157/G4
Ebro (riv.), Sp. 29/D4
Ebron (riv.), Fr. 64/B3
Ebstorf, Ger. 53/H2
Ecatepec, Mex. 175/Q9
Ecclefechan, Sc, UK 35/E1
Eccles, Eng, UK 35/F5
Eccles, WV, US 163/G2
Eccleshall, Eng, UK 35/F6
Echague, Phil. 88/C1
Echallens, Swi. 60/C4
Echarate, Peru 184/C4
Echaz (riv.), Ger. 58/C6
Éché Fadadinga (riv.), Niger 115/H3
Éché Téfidinga (riv.), Niger 116/B2
Echigawa, Japan 83/K5
Eching, Ger. 59/E6
Échirolles, Fr. 64/B2
Echo, La, US 164/B2
Echo (lake), NJ, US 168/D1
Echo Bay, On, Can. 160/D1
Echo Bay, NW, Can. 140/E2
Echols, Ky, US 162/D2
Echt, Neth. 55/E1
Echterdingen (int'l arpt.), Ger. 58/C5
Echternach, Lux. 55/F4
Echuca, Austl. 133/B3
Echunga, Austl. 131/M9
Echunga (cr.), Austl. 131/M9
Echzell, Ger. 58/B2
Écija, Sp. 46/C4
Ečka, Serb. 50/E3
Eckernförde, Ger. 40/C4
Eckerö, Fin. 41/H1
Eckerö (isl.), Fin. 41/H1
Eckington, Eng, UK 35/G5
Eckington, Eng, UK 36/D2
Eckville, Ab, Can. 144/G1
Eclectic, Al, US 162/D4
Eclipse Sound (bay), Nun, Can. 141/H1
Écommoy, Fr. 57/F5
Ecorse, Mi, US 167/F7
Ecorse (riv.), Mi, US 167/F7
Écos, Fr. 57/G2
Écouché, Fr. 57/E3
Écouen, Fr. 30/K4
Ecquevilly, Fr. 30/H5
Ecrins, PN, Fr. 45/G4
Ecrosnes, Fr. 30/H6
Écrouves, Fr. 55/E6
Ecru, Ms, US 162/C3
Ecuador (ctry.) 179/B3
Ecublens, Swi. 60/C4
Ed, Swe. 40/D2
Ēd, Erit. 118/B2
Edam, Neth. 52/C3
Edam, Sk, Can. 145/K1
Edapalli, India 95/C4
Eday (isl.), Sc, UK 31/V14
Edchera, Mor. 110/B4
Edderton, Sc, UK 33/B1
Eddleston, Sc, UK 33/C5
Eddy (peak), Id, US 144/F3
Eddystone, Mb, Can. 156/E2
Eddystone (pt.), Austl. 132/D4
Eddystone Rocks (isls.), Eng, UK 36/B6
Eddyville, Ia, US 155/H3
Eddyville, Ky, US 162/C2
Ede, Nga. 115/G5
Ede, Neth. 52/C4
Edéa, Camr. 120/B2
Edegem, Belg. 55/D1
Edehin Ouarene (des.), Alg. 111/G4
Edéia, Braz. 189/G1
Edelény, Hun. 43/L4
Edemissen, Ger. 53/H4
Eden, Austl. 133/D3
Eden, Mb, Can. 156/E2
Eden (riv.), Sc, UK 33/D4
Eden, Az, US 149/H4
Eden, Md, US 163/K1
Eden, NC, US 163/H2
Eden, Tx, US 150/E2
Eden, Wy, US 147/J2
Eden Mills, On, Can. 160/S8
Eden Prairie, Mn, US 157/P7
Edenbridge, Eng, UK 30/D3
Edenburg, SAfr. 124/D3
Edendale, NZ 135/B4
Edendale, SAfr. 125/E3
Edenderry, Ire. 32/C3
Edenhope, Austl. 132/B3
Edenkoben, Ger. 58/B4
Edenside (valley), Eng, UK 35/F2
Edenton, NC, US 163/J2
Edenwold, Sk, Can. 156/B2
Eder (riv.), Ger. 42/E3
Eder-Stausee (lake), Ger. 53/F6
Edewecht, Ger. 53/E2
Edgar (mt.), Austl. 130/D2
Edgar, Mt, US 147/J1
Edgar, Ne, US 154/F3
Edgar, Wi, US 155/K1
Edgar Springs, Mo, US 153/J2
Edgard, La, US 164/C2
Edgartown, Ma, US 158/B5
Edgbaston, Eng, UK 37/E2
Edge (isl.), Sval. 74/C2
Edgecliff, Tx, US 150/K7
Edgecumbe (cape), Ak, US 171/L4
Edgefield, La, US 164/B1
Edgefield, SC, US 163/G4
Edgeley, ND, US 156/E4
Edgell (isl.), Nun, Can. 141/K2
Edgemere, Md, US 168/B5
Edgemont, SD, US 154/C2
Edgerton, Ab, Can. 145/J1
Edgerton, Mn, US 155/F2
Edgerton, Oh, US 160/D4
Edgerton, Wi, US 155/K2
Edgerton, Wy, US 154/A2
Edgewater, BC, Can. 144/F2
Edgewater, Fl, US 165/H3
Edgewater Park, NJ, US 168/D3
Edgewood, Fl, US 164/N7
Edgewood, Il, US 162/C1
Edgewood, Md, US 168/B5
Edgewood, NM, US 149/J3
Edgewood, Pa, US 168/B2
Edgewood, Tx, US 151/G1
Edgewood Arsenal, Md, US 168/B5
Edgewood-North Hill, Wa, US 167/C3
Edgmond, Eng, UK 36/D1
Edgware (nbrhd.), Eng, UK 30/C2
Édhessa, Gre. 49/H2
Edievale, NZ 135/B4
Edina, Libr. 114/C5
Edina, Mo, US 155/H3
Edina, Mn, US 157/P7
Edinboro, Pa, US 160/F4
Edinburg, ND, US 156/F3
Edinburg, Ms, US 162/C4
Edinburg, Tx, US 151/E4
Edinburg, Va, US 163/H1
Edinburgh (cap.), Sc, UK 33/C5
Edinburgh (co.), Sc, UK 33/C5
Edinburgh, In, US 160/D5
Edinet, Mol. 72/D3
Edingeni, Malw. 123/G2
Edirne (prov.), Turk. 70/C4
Edirne, Turk. 51/H5
Edison, Ca, US 148/C3
Edison, Co, US 152/B1
Edison, Ga, US 165/F2
Edison, NJ, US 169/H9
Edison Nat'l Hist. Site, NJ, US 169/J8
Edisto, SC, US 163/G4
Edisto (isl.), SC, US 163/G4
Edisto (riv.), SC, US 163/G4
Edisto Island, SC, US 163/G4
Edisto, South Fork (riv.), SC, US 163/G4
Edith Cavell (mt.), BC, Can. 144/E1
Edithburgh, Austl. 131/H5
Edjeleh, Alg. 111/H4
Édjérir (riv.), Mali 115/F2
Edmond, Ok, US 153/F3
Edmonds, Wa, US 144/C4
Edmondt, FrG. 182/C1
Edmonton (nbrhd.), Eng, UK 30/C2
Edmonton, Austl. 134/B2
Edmonton (cap.), Ab, Can. 145/H1
Edmonton, Ky, US 162/E2
Edmonton (int'l arpt.), Ab, Can. 145/H1
Edmore, Mi, US 160/D3
Edmore, ND, US 156/E3
Edmund Kennedy NP, Austl. 134/B2
Edmundston, NB, Can. 158/C2
Edna, Ks, US 153/G2
Edna, Tx, US 151/F3
Edna Bay, Ak, US 171/M4
Edo (state), Nga. 115/G5
Edo (riv.), Japan 83/D2
Edolo, It. 61/G5
Edom, Tx, US 151/G1
Edosaki, Japan 83/E2
Edremit (gulf), Gre.,Turk. 70/C5
Edsbro, Swe. 39/B1
Edsbyn, Swe. 40/F1
Eduardo Castex, Arg. 190/D2
Eduardo Gomes (int'l arpt.), Braz. 182/A3
Edward (isl.), On, Can. 157/K3
Edward (mt.), Austl. 131/F2
Edward (riv.), Austl. 133/B2
Edward (lake), D.R. Congo, Ugan. 107/E5
Edward River Abor. Community, Austl. 134/A1
Edward VII (pen.), Ant. 192/P
Edward VIII (bay), Ant. 192/D
Edwards (plat.), Tx, US 142/F5
Edwards, Ms, US 162/B4
Edwards (riv.), Il, US 155/J3
Edwards (A.F.B.), Ca, US 148/C3
Edwardsville, Il, US 155/K4
Edwardsville, Pa, US 168/C1
Edwin, Al, US 165/F2
Edzell, Sc, UK 33/D3
Edzná (ruin), Mex. 176/D2
Eefde, Neth. 52/D4
Eek, Ak, US 171/F3
Eeklo, Belg. 54/C1
Eel (riv.), Ca, US 146/B4
Eel, South Fork (riv.), Ca, US 146/B3
Eelde-Paterswolde, Neth. 52/D2
Eem (riv.), Neth. 52/C4
Eemenes, Neth. 52/C4
Eems (Ems) (riv.), Ger., Neth. 52/D2
Eemshaven (har.), Neth. 52/D2
Eemskanaal (riv.), Neth. 52/D2
Eersel, Neth. 52/C6
Efate (isl.), Van. 136/F6
Eferding, Aus. 59/H6
Effie, Mn, US 157/H4
Effigy Mounds Nat'l Mon., Ia, US 155/J2
Effingham, Eng, UK 30/B3
Effingham, Il, US 162/C1
Effingham, Ks, US 155/G4
Effingham, On, Can. 160/U9
Effon Alaiye, Nga. 115/G5
Effort, Pa, US 168/C2
Efogi, PNG 129/G2
Eforie, Rom. 51/J3
Efringen-Kirchen, Ger. 60/D2
Egadi (isls.), It. 67/G3
Egan (riv.), Ger. 58/D5
Egan, Tx, US 150/K7
Egaña, Uru. 191/K10
Egbe, Nga. 115/G4
Egbunda, D.R. Congo 121/F2
Egegik, Ak, US 171/G4
Egeland, ND, US 156/E3
Eger (riv.), Ger. 42/G3
Eger, Hun. 43/L5
Egeskov, Den. 40/D4
Egestorf, Ger. 53/H2
Egg, Aus. 61/F3
Egg, Swi. 61/E3
Egg Harbor City, NJ, US 168/D4
Egg Island (pt.), NJ, US 168/C5
Egg Lagoon, Austl. 133/A4
Eggebek, Ger. 40/C4
Eggegebirge (ridge), Ger. 53/F5
Eggelsberg, Aus. 59/F6
Eggenburg, Aus. 45/L2
Eggenfelden, Ger. 59/F6
Eggenstein-Leopoldshafen, Ger. 58/B4
Eggesin, Ger. 40/F5
Eggiwil, Swi. 60/D4
Egglescliffe, Eng, UK 35/G3
Eggleston, Eng, UK 35/G2
Eggstätt, Ger. 59/F7
Egham, Eng, UK 30/B2
Éghezée, Belg. 55/D2
Egilsstadhir, Ice. 38/P6
Egito, Ang. 122/B2
Egiyn (riv.), Mong. 78/E1
Égletons, Fr. 44/E4
Eglinton, NI, UK 34/A1
Eglinton (isl.), NW, Can. 141/Q7
Eglinton (Londonderry) (arpt.), UK 34/A1
Eglisau, Swi. 61/E2
Eglwys-Brewis, Wal, UK 36/C4
Égly, Fr. 30/J6
Egmond aan Zee, Neth. 52/B3
Egmont (bay), PE, Can. 158/E2
Egmont (mt.), NZ 135/C2
Egmont (cape), NZ 135/C2
Egmont Key Nat'l Wild. Ref., Fl, US 164/K8
Egmont NP, NZ 135/C2
Egna (Neumarkt), It. 61/H5
Egnach, Swi. 61/F2
Egnar, Co, US 149/H2
Egoumbi, Gabon 120/B3
Egra, India 97/F5
Egremont, Eng, UK 34/E3
Eğridir, Turk. 102/B2
Eğridir (lake), Turk. 102/B2
Éguas, Rio das (riv.), Braz. 186/D2
Éguilles, Fr. 64/B5
Egvekinot, Rus. 75/U3
Egypt (ctry.) 109/F3
Egypt Lake, Fl, US 164/L7
Eha Amufu, Nga. 115/G5
Ehebach (riv.), Ger. 58/D3
Ehekirchen, Ger. 58/D5
Ehime (pref.), Japan 84/C4
Ehingen, Ger. 61/F1
Ehingen, Ger. 58/D4
Ehrenberg, Az, US 148/E4
Ehrhardt, SC, US 163/G4
Ehringshausen, Ger. 58/B1
Ehrwald, Aus. 61/G3
Eiao (isl.), FrPol. 137/L5
Eibar, Sp. 44/B5
Eibelstadt, Ger. 58/C3
Eibenstock, Ger. 59/F1
Eibergen, Neth. 52/D4
Eich, Ger. 58/B3
Eichel (riv.), Fr. 55/G6
Eichenau, Ger. 58/E6
Eichenbühl, Ger. 58/C3
Eichendorf, Ger. 59/F5
Eichenzell, Ger. 58/C2
Eichstätt, Ger. 58/E5
Eichwalde, Ger. 42/Q7
Eicklingen, Ger. 53/H3
Eid, Nor. 38/C3
Eidelstedt, Ger. 53/G1
Eidfjord, Nor. 40/B1
Eidsfoss, Nor. 38/R9
Eidsvold, Austl. 134/C4
Eidsvoll, Nor. 40/D1
Eifel (plat.), Ger. 42/D3
Eiffel Flats, Zim. 123/F3
Eiffel Tower, Fr. 30/J5
Eigenji, Japan 83/K5
Eiger (peak), Swi. 60/D4
Eigersund, Nor. 40/A2
Eigg (isl.), Sc, UK 31/Q8
Eight Degree (chan.), India,Mald. 95/B5
Eighteenmile (peak), Id, US 147/G1
Eighty Mile Beach (beach), Austl. 128/A4
Eijerlandse Gat (chan.), Neth. 52/B2
Eijsden, Neth. 55/E2
Eikelandsosen, Nor. 40/A1
Eikeren (lake), Nor. 38/R9
Eil, Loch (inlet), Sc, UK 33/A3
Eildon, Austl. 133/B3
Eilerts de Haan (mts.), Sur. 181/G4
'Ein Māhil, Isr. 105/C3
Eina, Nor. 40/D1
Einbeck, Ger. 53/G5
Eindhoven (int'l arpt.), Neth. 52/C6
Eindhoven, Neth. 52/C6
Einsiedeln, Swi. 61/E3
Einville-au-Jard, Fr. 55/F6
Eirunepé, Braz. 184/D2
Eirup, Namb. 122/C5
Eisack (Isarco) (riv.), It. 61/H4
Eisch (riv.), Lux. 55/E4
Eiseb (riv.), Namb. 122/C4
Eisenach, Ger. 53/H7
Eisenberg, Ger. 58/B3
Eisenerz, Aus. 45/L3
Eisenhower (mt.), Ab, Can. 144/G2
Eisenhower Nat'l Hist. Site, Pa, US 168/A4
Eisenhüttenstadt, Ger. 43/H2
Eisenstadt, Aus. 50/C2
Eiserfeld, Ger. 55/G2
Eisfeld, Ger. 58/D2
Eisingen, Ger. 58/C3
Eišiškės, Lith. 41/L4
Eislingen, Ger. 58/C5
Eitelborn, Ger. 55/G3
Eiter (riv.), Ger. 53/F3
Eitorf, Ger. 55/G2
Eitting, Ger. 59/E6
Ejea de los Caballeros, Sp. 47/E1
Ejeda, Madg. 125/H9
Ejido, Ven. 180/D2
Ejin Horo Qi, China 80/B3
Ejin Qi, China 78/E3
Ejule, Nga. 115/G5
Ejura, Gha. 115/E5
Ejutla de Crespo, Mex. 176/B2
Ekalaka, Mt, US 156/B5
Ekang, Nga. 115/H5
Ekata, Gabon 120/C2
Ekeby, Swe. 40/E3
Ekeby, Swe. 39/A1
Ekenäs (Tammisaari), Fin. 41/K2
Ekeren, Belg. 52/B6
Ekerö, Swe. 39/A1
Eket, Nga. 120/A1
Eketahuna, NZ 135/C3
Ekhínos, Gre. 49/J2
Ekibastuz, Kaz. 99/C1
Ekimchan, Rus. 79/L1
Ekma, India 97/E3
Ekoko, D.R. Congo 121/E2
Ekoli, D.R. Congo 121/F3
Ekoln (lake), Swe. 39/A1
Ekondo Titi, Camr. 120/B1
Ekpoma, Nga. 115/G5
Eksjö, Swe. 40/F3
Ekuk, Ak, US 171/G4
Ekuku, D.R. Congo 121/E3
Ekukula, D.R. Congo 121/E2
Ekwan (riv.), On, Can. 141/H3
Ekwendeni, Malw. 123/G1
Ekwok, Ak, US 171/G4
El Aaiún, WSah. 110/B4
El Aaiún (Hassan) (int'l arpt.), WSah. 110/B4
El Aargub, WSah. 110/B5
El Aatf (reg.), WSah. 110/B5
El Abanico, Chile 190/C3
El Abiodh Sidi Chrikh, Alg. 111/F2
Ēl Ābrēd, Eth. 118/C4
El Affroun, Alg. 112/G4
El Aïoun, Mor. 112/C2
El Alamein (Al 'Alamayan), Egypt 109/F2
El Álamo, Mex. 150/E4
El Alia, Alg. 111/G2
El Alto, Peru 184/A2
El Alto (int'l arpt.), Bol. 188/B1
El Amparo de Apure, Ven. 180/D3
El Anegado, Ecu. 180/A5
El Aouinet, Alg. 112/K7
El Arahal, Sp. 46/C4
El Arhlaf (well), Mrta. 114/D2
El Aricha, Alg. 112/D2
El Arrayán, Chile 190/N8
El Astillero, Sp. 46/D1
El Avila, PN, Ven. 183/P7
El Bagre, Col. 180/C3
El Banco, Col. 180/C2
El Barco, Sp. 46/B1
El Barco de Ávila, Sp. 46/C2
El Baúl, Ven. 180/D2
El Bayadh (wilaya), Alg. 111/F2
El Bayadh, Alg. 111/F2
El Ben, Kenya 119/C1
El Bolsón, Arg. 190/C4
El Bonillo, Sp. 46/D3
El Borouj, Mor. 110/D2
El Burgo de Osma, Sp. 46/D2
El Caín, Arg. 190/C4
El Cajon, Ca, US 166/D5
El Cajón (res.), Hon. 176/E3
El Calafate, Arg. 191/B6
El Callao, Ven. 181/F3
El Campo, Tx, US 151/F3
El Capitan (peak), Mt, US 144/G4
El Carmen, Bol. 185/F4
El Carmen, Bol. 185/E4
El Carmen, Chile 190/B3
El Carmen, Col. 180/B3
El Carmen, Mex. 150/D5
El Carmen, Peru 184/B4
El Carmen, Ven. 181/E4
El Carmen de Bolívar, Col. 180/C2
El Casabe, Ven. 181/F3
El Casar de Talamanca, Sp. 47/N8
El Centro Nav. Air Facility, Ca, US 148/D4
El Cerrito, Ca, US 167/K11
El Cerrito, Col. 180/B4
El Cerrito, Arg. 191/C6
El Cerro, Bol. 188/D1
El Cerro del Aripo (peak), Trin. 181/F2
El Cerrón (peak), Ven. 180/D2
El Chico, PN, Mex. 175/L6
El Chorro, Arg. 188/D2
El Cocuy, Col. 180/C3
El Cocuy (dept.), Col. 180/C3
El Colegio, Col. 183/L8
El Colorado, Arg. 188/E3
El Cóndor, Arg. 191/C7
El Cuy, Arg. 190/C3
El Der (riv.), Som. 118/C3
El Dere, Eth. 118/B4
El Descanso, Mex. 148/D4
El Difícil, Col. 180/C2
El Djezair (Algiers) (cap.), Alg. 112/G4
El Djouf (des.), Alg. 110/D5
El Dorado, Ks, US 153/F2
El Dorado, Ar, US 153/H4
El Dorado (lake), Ks, US 153/F2
El Dorado, Ven. 181/F3
El Dorado, Mex. 174/D3
El Dorado Springs, Mo, US 153/G2
El Edén, Ecu. 180/B5
El Eglab (plat.), Alg. 110/D4
El Empedrado, Ven. 180/D2
El Escorial, Sp. 47/M8
El Espinar, Sp. 46/C2
El Eulma, Alg. 112/H4
El Fahs, Tun. 112/L6
El Ferrol, Sp. 46/A1
El Fuerte, Mex. 174/C3
El Fureidīs, Isr. 105/B3
El Galhak, Sudan 117/G3
El Galpón, Arg. 188/C3
El Gogorrón, PN, Mex. 172/A3
El Golea, Alg. 111/F3
El Golfete (lake), Guat. 176/D3
El Granada, Ca, US 167/K11
El Grullo, Mex. 174/D5
El Guachara, PN, Ven. 181/F2
El Guapo, Ven. 183/P7
El Gulut, Eth. 117/G2
El Had Harrara, Mor. 110/C2
El Hajeb, Mor. 112/B3
El Hank (cliff), Mali, 110/D4
El Harino, Pan. 180/A2
El Harta (well), Alg. 111/E4
El Higo, Mex. 176/B1
El Indio, Tx, US 150/D3
El Jadida, Mor. 110/C2
El Kbab, Mor. 110/D2
El Kelaâ des Srarhna, Mor. 110/D2
Ēl Kerē, Eth. 118/B4
El Khatt (depr.), Mrta. 114/C2
El Khnâchîch (cliff), Mali 110/E5
Ēl K'oran, Eth. 118/C4
El Kroub, Alg. 112/K6
El Kseur, Alg. 112/H4
Ēl Lēh, Eth. 118/A5
El Libertador General Bernardo O'Higgins (pol. reg.), Chile 190/N8
El Limón, Mex. 175/F4
El Mahia (phys. reg.), Mali 111/E5
El Maitén, Arg. 190/C4
El Mallaile, Eth. 118/B4
El Malpais Nat'l Mon., NM, US 149/H3
El Manteco, Ven. 181/F3
El Manzanito, Chile 190/N8
El Manzano, Chile 190/N9
El Medera, Eth. 118/B4
El Messir (well), Chad 116/C2
El Miamo, Ven. 181/F3
El Milia, Alg. 112/J4
El Mirage, Ca, US 166/C1
El Mirage (lake), Ca, US 148/D3
El Mojar, Bol. 185/E4
El Montcau (peak), Sp. 47/K6
El Monte, Ca, US 166/F7
El Morrito (pt.), Chile 190/C1
El Morro, NM, US 149/H3
El Mrâyer (well), Mrta. 110/C5
El Mreyyé (phys. reg.), Mrta. 114/C2
El Mzereb (well), Mali 110/D4
El Naranjo de Carlos Sarabia, Mex. 175/F4
El Nayar, Mex. 174/D4
El Nevado (peak), Arg. 190/C2
El Nido, Ca, US 148/B2
El Nido, Phil. 88/B3
El Olivar Alto, Chile 190/N9
El Oro (dept.), Ecu. 184/A1
El Oso, Ven. 182/A1
El Oued (wilaya), Alg. 111/G2
El Oued, Alg. 111/G2
El Palmar, Ven. 181/F3
El Palmar, Bol. 188/D2
El Palmar, Mex. 175/N8
El Palmar, PN, Arg. 188/E4
El Pao, Ven. 181/F2
El Pao, Ven. 181/E2
El Pao, Ven. 183/M8
El Paraíso, Hon. 176/E3
El Paraíso, Col. 180/C4
El Paraíso, Mex. 175/E5
El Pardo, Sp. 47/N8
El Paso, Il, US 155/K3
El Paso, Tx, US 150/A2
El Paso de Robles (Paso Robles), Ca, US 148/B3
El Paso International (int'l arpt.), Tx, US 150/A2
El Pato, Col. 180/C4
El Pensamiento, Bol. 185/F4
El Perú, Bol. 185/E4
El Pilar, Ven. 181/F2
El Pilar, Bol. 185/E4
El Pintado, Arg. 188/D3
El Piquete, Arg. 188/C3
El Plumerillo (Mendoza) (int'l arpt.), Arg. 190/C2
El Portal, Ca, US 148/C2
El Porvenir, Mex. 148/D4
El Porvenir, Mex. 150/B2
El Porvenir, Pan. 180/B2
El Porvenir, Ven. 180/D3
El Potosí, Mex. 175/E3
El Potosí, PN, Mex. 172/B3
El Prat de Llobregat, Sp. 47/L7
El Progreso, Ecu. 184/K7
El Progreso, Guat. 176/D3
El Progreso, Hon. 176/E3
El Progreso Industrial, Mex. 175/Q9
El Puente, Bol. 185/F5
El Puente, Bol. 188/C2
El Puerto de Santa María, Sp. 46/B4
El Pun, Ecu. 180/B4
El Quebrachal, Arg. 188/C3
El Quelite, Mex. 174/D4
El Quisco, Chile 190/N8
El Rama, Nic. 177/E3
El Rastro, Ven. 183/N8
El Remolino, Mex. 150/D3
El Reno, Ok, US 153/F3
El Rey, PN, Arg. 188/C3
El Rio, Ca, US 166/A2
El Rio (canal), Fl, US 164/P10
El Rito, NM, US 149/J2
El Roble, Pan. 180/A2
El Roque, Ven. 181/E2
El Rosario de Arriba, Mex. 174/B2
El Sabinal, PN, Mex. 150/E4
El Sacromonte, PN, Mex. 175/L7
El Salado, Col. 183/K8
El Salado, Arg. 191/D6
El Salto, Mex. 174/D4
El Salvador, Cuba 177/H1
El Salvador (ctry.) 176/D3
El Salvador (int'l arpt.), ESal. 176/D3
El Salvador, Mex. 175/E3
El Samán de Apure, Ven. 180/D3
El Sauz, Mex. 150/A3
El Sauzal, Mex. 174/A2
El Segundo, Ca, US 166/F8
El Shab (well), Egypt 109/F4
El Socorro, Col. 180/D3
El Sombrero, Arg. 190/C5
El Sombrero, Ven. 183/N8
El Sosneado, Arg. 190/C2
El Tabo, Chile 190/N8
El Tajín (ruin), Mex. 175/M6
El Tala, Arg. 188/C3
El Tama, PN, Ven. 180/C3
El Tambo, Ecu. 180/B5
El Tarf (wilaya), Alg. 112/K6
El Tarf, Alg. 112/L6
El Teleno (peak), Sp. 46/B1
El Tepozteco, PN, Mex. 175/R10
El Tiemblo, Sp. 46/C2
El Tigre, Ven. 181/E2
El Tocuyo, Ven. 180/D2
El Toro, Ca, US 166/C3
El Toro, Ven. 181/F2
El Toro, Tx, US 151/F3
El Tránsito, Chile 188/B4
El Trébol, Arg. 188/D5
El Triunfo, Mex. 176/D2
El Triunfo, Ecu. 180/B5
El Tucuche (peak), Trin. 181/F2
El Tuito, Mex. 174/D4
El Tuparro, PN, Col. 180/D3
El Vado, NM, US 149/J2
El Valle, Pan. 180/A2
El Venado (isl.), Nic. 177/F4
El Viejo, Nic. 176/E3
El Viejo (peak), Col. 180/C3
El Vigía, Ven. 180/D2
El Vínculo, Ven. 180/D1
El Volcán, Chile 190/N8
El Wak, Kenya 119/C1
El Yagual, Ven. 180/D3
El Yunque (peak), PR 173/M8
El Zacatón, Mex. 174/E4
El Zurdo, Arg. 191/C6
El'ton (lake), Rus. 71/H2
El-Gezira, 'Erg, Egypt 113/C2
El-Girba (peak), Egypt 113/D4
El-Hammam (ruin), Egypt 113/B6
El-Kasdir, Alg. 112/D3
El-Menzel, Mor. 112/B3
El-Tarâbîl (peak), Egypt 113/D6
Ela, Myan. 86/C5
El'Acâba (pol. reg.), Mrta. 114/C2
Elaho (riv.), BC, Can. 144/C2
Elaine, Ar, US 162/B3
Elan (riv.), Wal, UK 36/C2
Élancourt, Fr. 30/H5
Elands (riv.), SAfr. 123/E5
Elandsrivier (riv.), SAfr. 124/Q12
Elangata Wuas, Kenya 119/B2
Elarmilon, Gabon 120/B2
Elassón, Gre. 49/H3
Elat (int'l arpt.), Isr. 104/D5
Elat, Isr. 109/G2
Elátia, Gre. 49/H3
Elato (isl.), Micr. 136/D4
Elavagnon, Togo 115/F5
Elazığ, Turk. 102/D2
Elazığ (prov.), Turk. 102/D2
Elba, Al, US 165/E2
Elba (isl.), It. 48/B1
El'ban, Rus. 79/M1
Elbasan, Alb. 49/G2
Elbbach (riv.), Ger. 55/G2
Elbe (riv.), Ger. 29/F3
Elbe (Labe) (riv.), Czh.,Ger. 43/H2
Elbe-Seitenkanaal (canal), Ger. 53/H2
Elbert, Tx, US 152/E4
Elberton, Ga, US 163/F3
Elbeuf, Fr. 57/G2
Elbigenalp, Aus. 61/G3
Elbląg, Pol. 41/H4
Elbow (riv.), Ab, Can. 144/G2
Elbow, Sk, Can. 145/L2
Elbow Lake, Mn, US 156/G5
El'brus (peak), Rus. 71/G4
Elburg, Neth. 52/C4
Elburgon, Kenya 119/A2
Elburn, Il, US 167/N16
Elburz (mts.), Iran 74/E6
Elche, Sp. 47/E3
Elche de la Sierra, Sp. 46/D3
Elchingen, Ger. 58/D6
Elcho (isl.), Austl. 129/D2
Elcho, Wi, US 157/K5
Eld (inlet), Wa, US 167/A3
Elda, Sp. 47/E3
Eldama Ravine, Kenya 119/A1
Elde (riv.), Ger. 42/G2
Eldersburg, Md, US 168/B5
El'dikan, Rus. 75/P3
Eldivan, Turk. 70/E4
Eldon, Ia, US 155/H3
Eldon, Mo, US 153/H1
Eldon, Wa, US 167/A2
Eldora, Ia, US 155/H2
Eldora, NJ, US 168/D5
Eldorado, Arg. 189/F3
Eldorado, Braz. 189/G3
Eldorado, Braz. 189/F2
Eldorado (int'l arpt.), Col. 183/L8
Eldorado, Il, US 162/C2
Eldorado, Ok, US 152/E3
Eldorado, Tx, US 150/D2
Eldoret, Kenya 119/A1
Eldridge, Al, US 162/D4
Eldridge, Ia, US 155/J3
Eleanor, WV, US 163/G1
Electra, Tx, US 152/E3
Elefsís, Gre. 49/N8
Elefsís (arpt.), Gre. 49/N8
Elefsís (ruin), Gre. 49/N8
Eleja, Lat. 41/K3
Elek, Hun. 50/E2
Eléktrėnai, Lith. 41/L4
Elektrostal', Rus. 69/X9
Elele, Nga. 115/G5
Elena, Arg. 190/D2
Elena, Bul. 51/G4
Elephant (mtn.), Me, US 161/L2
Elephant Butte, NM, US 149/J4
Elephant Butte (res.), NM, US 149/J4
Elesbão Veloso, Braz. 183/F4
Eleşkirt, Turk. 103/E2
Eleuthera (isl.), Bahm. 139/K7
Eleven Point (riv.), Mo,Ar, US 153/J2
Elevtheroúpolis, Gre. 49/J2
Elfers, Fl, US 164/K7
Elfershausen, Ger. 58/C2
Elfin Cove, Ak, US 171/L4
Elfrida, On, Can. 160/T9
Elfros, Sk, Can. 156/C2
Elgg, Swi. 61/E3
Elgin, Mb, Can. 156/D3
Elgin, Sc, UK 33/C1
Elgin, Az, US 149/G5
Elgin, Il, US 160/B3
Elgin, Ks, US 153/F2
Elgin, ND, US 156/D4
Elgin, Nv, US 148/E2
Elgin, Ok, US 153/E3
Elgin, Or, US 146/E1
Elgin, SC, US 163/G3
Elgin, Tn, US 162/E2
Elgin, Tx, US 150/F2
Elgin Mills, On, Can. 160/U8
Elgóibar, Sp. 44/B5
Elgon (Wagagai) (peak), Ugan. 119/A1
Elias Garcia, Ang. 120/E5
Elida, NM, US 152/C4
Elida, Oh, US 160/D4
Elie, Sc, UK 33/D4
Elila (riv.), D.R. Congo 121/F3
Elila, D.R. Congo 121/F3
Elim, Ak, US 171/F3
Elim, SAfr. 124/L11
Elimäki, Fin. 41/M1
Eling, Eng, UK 37/E5
Eliot, Me, US 161/L3
Elipa, D.R. Congo 121/E3
Elisenvaara, Rus. 41/N1
Eliseu Martins, Braz. 183/F5
Elista, Rus. 71/H3
Elixhausen, Aus. 59/G7
Elizabeth (mtn.), Austl. 133/C3
Elizabeth (nbrhd.), Austl. 131/M8
Elizabeth (bay), Namb. 124/A2
Elizabeth, Co, US 154/B4
Elizabeth, Ga, US 163/L7
Elizabeth, La, US 164/B2
Elizabeth (isls.), Ma, US 158/B5
Elizabeth, Mn, US 156/F4
Elizabeth, NJ, US 169/J9
Elizabeth (cr.), Tx, US 150/K6
Elizabeth, WV, US 163/G1
Elizabeth City, NC, US 163/J2
Elizabethan Village Hist. Site, Austl. 130/L7
Elizabethton, Tn, US 163/F2
Elizabethtown, Il, US 162/C2
Elizabethtown, In, US 162/E1
Elizabethtown, Ky, US 162/E2
Elizabethtown, NC, US 163/H3
Elizabethtown, Pa, US 168/B3
Elizabethtown, NY, US 161/K2
Elizabethville, Pa, US 168/B2
Elizondo, Sp. 44/C5
Ełk, Pol. 41/K5
Elk (riv.), BC, Can. 144/G2
Elk (riv.), Al,Tn, US 162/D3
Elk (mts.), Co, US 147/K4
Elk (mtn.), Or, US 146/E1
Elk (hill), Pa, US 161/J4
Elk (riv.), WV, US 163/G1
Elk City, Ks, US 153/G2
Elk City (dam), Ks, US 153/G2
Elk City, Ok, US 152/E3
Elk Creek, Ca, US 146/B4
Elk Creek, Ne, US 155/F3
Elk Grove, Ca, US 167/M10
Elk Grove Village, Il, US 167/P16
Elk Mills, Md, US 168/C4
Elk NP, Ab, Can. 145/H1
Elk Point, SD, US 155/F2
Elk Rapids, Mi, US 160/D2
Elk Ridge, Md, US 168/B5
Elk Ridge (ridge), Tn, US 162/D3
Elk River, Mn, US 157/H5
Elk Silver, NM, US 152/B4
Elk Slough (riv.), Ca, US 167/L10
Elk Springs, Co, US 147/J3
Elk Valley, Tn, US 162/E2
Elkader, Ia, US 155/J2
Elkenroth, Ger. 55/G2
Elkford, BC, Can. 144/G2
Elkhart, Ks, US 152/D2
Elkhart, In, US 160/D4
Elkhart, Tx, US 150/G2
Elkhorn, Mb, Can. 156/D3
Elkhorn (riv.), Ne, US 143/G3
Elkhorn, Wi, US 155/K2
Elkhovo, Bul. 51/H4
Elkin, NC, US 163/G2
Elkins, WV, US 163/H1
Elkland, Pa, US 161/H4
Elko, Nv, US 146/F3
Elko, BC, Can. 144/G3
Elkton, Ky, US 162/D2
Elkton, Md, US 168/C4
Elkton, Tn, US 162/D3
Elkton, Va, US 163/H1
Elkview, WV, US 163/G1
Elkwater, Ab, Can. 145/J3
Ellamar, Ak, US 171/J3
Elland, Eng, UK 35/G4
Ellaville, Ga, US 162/E4
Ellé (riv.), Fr. 56/B5
Elle (riv.), Ger. 55/F2
Ellef Ringnes (isl.), Nun., Can. 141/R7
Ellefeld, Ger. 59/F2
Ellen (riv.), Eng, UK 35/E2
Ellen (mt.), Ut, US 149/G1
Ellenābād, India 98/C5
Ellenberg, Ger. 58/D4
Ellendale, Austl. 128/B4
Ellendale, De, US 168/C6
Ellendale, ND, US 156/E4
Ellensburg, Wa, US 144/D4
Ellenton, Ga, US 165/G2
Ellenville, NY, US 161/J4
Ellenwood, Ga, US 163/M7
Eller (riv.), Ger. 53/H5
Ellerbach (riv.), Ger. 55/G4
Ellerbe, NC, US 163/H3
Ellero (riv.), It. 62/A4
Ellerslie, Ga, US 162/E4
Ellerslie, La, US 164/C3
Ellerslie, PE, Can. 158/F2
Ellery (mt.), Austl. 133/D3
Ellesmere (isl.), Can. 139/J2
Ellesmere Port, Eng, UK 35/F5
Ellettsville, In, US 160/C5
Ellezelles, Belg. 54/C2
Elliant, Fr. 56/B4
Ellice (riv.), Nun, Can. 140/F2
Ellicott City, Md, US 168/B5
Ellijay, Ga, US 162/E3
Ellington, Mo, US 162/B2
Ellinikón (int'l arpt.), Gre. 49/N9
Ellinwood, Ks, US 153/E1
Elliot, SAfr. 124/D3
Elliot Key (isl.), Fl, US 165/H5
Elliot Lake, On, Can. 160/E1
Elliot Price Consv. Park, Austl. 131/H4
Elliott, Ia, US 155/G3
Elliott, Austl. 128/D4
Elliott, SC, US 163/G3
Elliott (peak), Va, US 163/H1
Ellis, Id, US 147/F1
Ellis, Ks, US 152/E1
Ellis (co.), Tx, US 150/L7
Ellis Island, NJ,NY, US 169/J9
Ellisras, SAfr. 123/E4
Elliston, Austl. 131/G5
Elliston, Mt, US 145/H4
Ellisville, Ms, US 164/D2
Ellon, Sc, UK 33/D2
Elloree, SC, US 163/G4
Elloughton, Eng, UK 35/H4
Ellrich, Ger. 53/H5
Ellsinore, Mo, US 162/B2
Ellsworth, Ks, US 153/E1
Ellsworth (mts.), Ant. 192/U
Ellsworth (A.F.B.), SD, US 154/C1
Ellsworth, Wi, US 155/H1
Ellsworth Land (phys. reg.), Ant. 192/U
Ellwangen, Ger. 58/D5
Elm, Swi. 61/F4
Elm (lake), SD, US 156/E5
Elm (riv.), SD, US 154/E1
Elm City, NC, US 163/J3
Elm Creek, Mb, Can. 156/F3
Elm Fork (riv.), Ok, US 152/E3
Elm Fork (riv.), Tx, US 150/L6
Elm Grove, Wi, US 167/P13
Elma, Ia, US 155/H2
Elma, NY, US 160/V10
Elmadağ, Turk. 70/E5
Elmalı, Turk. 104/A1
Elmas (int'l arpt.), It. 48/A3
Elmer, La, US 164/B2
Elmer, Mo, US 155/H4
Elmer, NJ, US 168/C4
Elmgrove (pt.), Tx, US 151/N9
Elmhurst, Il, US 167/Q16
Elmina, Gha. 115/E5
Elmira, NY, US 161/H3
Elmira, Or, US 146/B1
Elmira Heights, NY, US 161/H3
Elmo, Mt, US 144/G4
Elmont, NY, US 169/L9
Elmora (nbrhd.), NJ, US 169/J9
Elmore, Mn, US 155/G2
Elmore, Austl. 133/B3
Elmore City, Ok, US 153/F3
Elmsdale, PE, Can. 158/E2
Elmsdale, NS, Can. 158/F3
Elmsford, NY, US 169/K7
Elmshorn, Ger. 53/G1
Elmstein, Ger. 55/G5
Elmswell, Eng, UK 37/G2
Elmvale, On, Can. 161/G2
Elmwood, Ok, US 152/D2
Elmwood, Ne, US 155/F3
Elmwood Park, Il, US 167/Q16
Elmwood Park, NJ, US 169/J8
Elmwood Park, Wi, US 167/Q14
Elne, Fr. 44/E5
Elnora, In, US 162/D1
Elói Mendes, Braz. 187/L6
Eloise, Fl, US 164/M8
Elon College, NC, US 163/H2
Elora, On, Can. 160/F3
Elora, Tn, US 162/D3
Élorn (riv.), Fr. 44/A2
Elortondo, Arg. 190/E2
Elorza, Ven. 180/D3
Elouera Nat'l Rsv., Austl. 134/H8
Elowah (falls), Or, US 144/D5
Eloy, Az, US 149/G4
Eloy Alfaro, Ecu. 180/B5
Éloyes, Fr. 60/C1
Elphin, Ire. 32/B2
Elphinstone, Mb, Can. 156/D2
Elqui (riv.), Chile 188/B4
Elrod, Al, US 162/D4
Elrose, Sk, Can. 145/K2
Elroy, Wi, US 155/J2
Elroy, NC, US 163/J3
Elsa (riv.), Sp. 67/B2
Elsa (res.), Sp. 46/B2
Elsa, Yk, Can. 171/L3
Elsa, Tx, US 151/F4
Elsah, Il, US 155/J4
Elsberry, Mo, US 155/J4
Elsdorf, Ger. 55/F2
Elsdorf, Ger. 53/G2
Else (riv.), Ger. 53/F4
Elsen (lake), China 99/F4
Elsenfeld, Ger. 58/C3
Elsenz (riv.), Ger. 58/B4
Elsey, Mo, US 153/H2
Elsfleth, Ger. 53/F2
Elsie, Mi, US 160/D3
Elsinore (lake), Ca, US 166/C3
Elsinore, Ut, US 149/F1
Elsloo, Neth. 55/E2
Elsmere, De, US 168/C4
Elst, Neth. 52/C5
Elstal, Ger. 42/Q6
Elstead, Eng, UK 37/F4
Elsterberg, Ger. 59/F1
Eltari (int'l arpt.), Indo. 128/A2
Eltham (nbrhd.), Eng, UK 30/D2
Eltham, NZ 135/C2
Eltham, Austl. 133/B3
Eltmann, Ger. 58/D3
Elton, Wi, US 157/K5
Elton, La, US 164/B2
Eltopia, Wa, US 144/E4
Eltville am Rhein, Ger. 58/B2
Elva, Est. 41/M2
Elvanlı, Turk. 104/D1
Elvas, Port. 46/B3
Elven, Fr. 56/C5
Elverum, Nor. 40/D1
Elvins, Mo, US 162/B2
Elvire (mt.), Austl. 130/C2
Elvo (riv.), It. 62/B2
Elwell (lake), Mt, US 145/J3
Elwood, In, US 160/D4
Elwood, Ne, US 154/E3
Elwood-Magnolia, NJ, US 168/D4
Elwy (riv.), Wal, UK 34/E5
Ely, Eng, UK 37/G2
Ely, Mn, US 157/J4
Ely, Nv, US 147/F4
Elyaqim, Isr. 105/C3
Elyashiv, Isr. 105/B4
Elyria, Oh, US 160/E4
Elysburg, Pa, US 168/B2
Elysian Park, Ca, US 166/F7
Elz, Ger. 58/B2
Elz (riv.), Ger. 58/B6
Elzach, Ger. 60/E1
Elzbach (riv.), Ger. 55/G3
Elze, Ger. 53/G4
Emajõgi (riv.), Est. 41/M2
Emām Taqī, Iran 101/G1
Emāmshahr, Iran 103/H2
Emån (riv.), Swe. 40/F3
Emancé, Fr. 30/H6
Emas, PN das, Braz. 186/B3
Emba (riv.), Kaz. 70/K3
Embarcación, Arg. 188/C2
Embarras (riv.), Il, US 162/C1
Embarrass, Mn, US 157/H4
Embarrass, Wi, US 155/K1
Embi, Kaz. 71/L2
Embi (riv.), Kaz. 74/F5
Embira (riv.), Braz. 184/D3
Embondo, D.R. Congo 120/D2
Emborcação (res.), Braz. 186/D3
Embrach, Swi. 61/E3
Embrun, Fr. 64/C3
Embsen, Ger. 53/H2
Embu, Kenya 119/B2
Emden, Il, US 155/K3
Emden, Ger. 53/E2
Emei (peak), China 86/D2
Emeishan, China 86/D2
Emerald, Austl. 134/C3
Emerald, Austl. 132/G5
Emeriau (pt.), Austl. 128/A4
Emerson, Mb, Can. 156/F3
Emerson, Ar, US 153/H4
Emerson, NJ, US 169/J8
Emery (peak), NM, US 152/C2
Emery, SD, US 154/F2
Emery, Ut, US 149/G1
Emeryville, On, Can. 167/G7
Emeryville, Ca, US 167/K11
Emet, Turk. 102/B2
Emida, Id, US 144/F4
Emigrant (peak), Mt, US 147/H1
Emigrant, Mt, US 147/H1
Emigsville, Pa, US 168/B3
Emilia-Romagna (pol. reg.), It. 45/J4
Emiliano Zapata, Mex. 176/D2
Emilius (peak), It. 64/D1
Emin, China 99/D2
Emin (riv.), China 99/D2
Eminābād, Pak. 98/C3

Map Section
224
225

Eminen – Fairfi

Eminence, Mo, US 153/J2
Emir Pasha (gulf), Tanz. 121/G3
Emirdağ, Turk. 102/B2
Emirgazi, Turk. 102/C2
Emissi, Tarso (peak), Chad 108/C4
Emita, Austl. 133/C4
Emlembe (peak), Swaz. 125/E2
Emlenton, Pa, US 161/G4
Emlichheim, Ger. 52/D3
Emma (riv.), Sur. 181/H4
Emmaboda, Swe. 40/F3
Emmanuel Head (pt.), Eng, UK 33/E5
Emmaste, Est. 41/K2
Emmaus, Pa, US 168/C2
Emme (riv.), Swi. 60/D4
Emmeloord, Neth. 52/C3
Emmen, Neth. 52/D3
Emmendingen, Ger. 60/D1
Emmental (valley), Swi. 60/D3
Emmer (riv.), Ger. 53/G4
Emmer-Compascuum, Neth. 52/E3
Emmerbach (riv.), Ger. 53/E5
Emmerich, Ger. 52/D5
Emmet, Ar, US 153/H4
Emmet, Austl. 134/B4
Emmetsburg, Ia, US 155/G2
Emmett, Mi, US 167/G6
Emmett, Id, US 146/E2
Emmingen-Liptingen, Ger. 61/E2
Emmitsburg, Md, US 168/A4
Emmonak, Ak, US 171/F3
Emmons (mt.), Ut, US 147/H3
Emneth, Eng, UK 37/G1
Emód, Hun. 50/E2
Emory, Tx, US 153/G4
Emory (peak), Tx, US 150/C3
Emosson (lake), Swi. 60/C5
Empalme, Mex. 174/C3
Empangeni, SAfr. 125/E3
Empedrado, Chile 190/B2
Empedrado, Arg. 188/E3
Empire, Mi, US 160/C2
Empire, Ga, US 163/F4
Empoli, It. 63/D6
Emporia, Ks, US 153/F1
Emporia, Va, US 163/J2
Emporium, Pa, US 161/G4
'Emrānī, Iran 101/G2
Ems (riv.), Ger. 42/D2
Ems (Eems) (riv.), Ger.,Neth. 52/D2
Ems-Jade (canal), Ger. 53/E2
Emsbüren, Ger. 53/E4
Emsdetten, Ger. 53/E4
Emskirchen, Ger. 58/D3
Emsland (reg.), Ger. 42/D2
Emstek, Ger. 53/F3
Emu, China 79/K3
Emu Park, Austl. 134/C3
Emumägi (hill), Est. 41/M2
Emur (riv.), China 79/J1
Emyvale, Ire. 34/B3
'En Gedi, Isr. 105/C6
'En Harod, Isr. 105/C3
Ena, Japan 85/E3
Enangiperi, Kenya 119/A2
Enarotali, Indo. 91/J4
Enbetsu, Japan 82/B1
Encampment, Wy, US 147/K3
Encantada, Cerro (peak), Mex. 174/B3
Encantada, Cerro de la (peak), Mex. 174/B2
Encarnación, Par. 189/F3
Encarnación de Díaz, Mex. 174/E4
Enchi, Gha. 114/E5
Encinal, Tx, US 150/E3
Encinitas, Ca, US 166/C4
Encino (nbrhd.), Ca, US 166/E7
Encino, Tx, US 150/E4
Enciso, Col. 180/C3
Enciso, Col. 180/D4
Encón, Arg. 188/C5
Encontrados, Ven. 180/C2
Encounter (bay), Austl. 132/A2
Encruzilhada do Sul, Braz. 189/F4
Encs, Hun. 43/L4
Endau (peak), Kenya 119/B2
Ende (isl.), Indo. 128/A2
Ende, Indo. 128/A2
Endeavour, Sk, Can. 156/C1
Endeavour (str.), Austl. 129/F2
Endeavour River NP, Austl. 134/B1
Endebess, Kenya 119/A1
Enderbury (isl.), Kiri. 137/H5
Enderby, BC, Can. 144/E2
Enderby Land (phys. reg.), Ant. 192/D
Enderlin, ND, US 156/F4
Endicott, NY, US 161/H3
Endicott, Wa, US 144/F4
Endingen, Ger. 60/D1
Endwell (Hooper), NY, US 161/H3
Endyalgourt (isl.), Austl. 128/C2
Ene (riv.), Peru 184/C3
Eneabba, Austl. 130/B4
Enebakk, Nor. 40/D2
Enem, Rus. 73/K5
Energeticheskiy, Kaz. 99/C3
Energetik, Rus. 71/L2
Enewetak (isl.), Mrsh. 136/F3
Enez, Turk. 49/K2
Enfield, NS, Can. 158/F3
Enfield (nbrhd.), Eng, UK 30/C2
Enfield (bor.), Eng, UK 30/C2
Enfield, Ct, US 161/K4
Enfield, Il, US 162/C1
Enfield, NC, US 163/J2
Enfield, NH, US 161/K3
Enga (prov.), PNG 129/F1
Engaño (cape), Phil. 77/M8
Engaru, Japan 82/C1
Engaruka (basin), Tanz. 119/A2
Engassumet, Tanz. 119/B3
Engcobo, SAfr. 124/E3
Engelberg, Swi. 61/E4
Engelhartszell, Aus. 59/G5
Engel's, Rus. 71/H2
Engelskirchen, Ger. 55/G2
Engelsmanplaat (isl.), Neth. 52/D2
Engen, Ger. 61/E2
Engenheiro Paulo de Frontin, Braz. 187/N7
Enger, Ger. 53/F4
Engerwitzdorf, Aus. 59/H6
Enggano (isl.), Indo. 90/B5
Enghershatu (peak), Erit. 100/C5
Enghien, Belg. 54/D2
Engi, Swi. 61/F4
England, Ar, US 153/J3
England, Eng, UK 35/F4
England, UK 36/D2
Engle, NM, US 149/J4
Englefield Green, Eng, UK 30/B2
Englefontaine, Fr. 54/C3
Englevale, ND, US 156/F4
Englewood, Fl, US 165/G4
Englewood, NJ, US 169/K8
Englewood Cliffs, NJ, US 169/K8
English (riv.), On, Can. 157/H2
English, In, US 162/D1
English (chan.), UK,Fr. 29/D4
English Bay, Ak, US 171/H4
English Bāzār, India 97/G3
English Creek, NJ, US 168/D5
English Harbour West, Nf, Can. 159/K2
English River, On, Can. 157/J3
Englishtown, NJ, US 168/D3
Engong, Gabon 120/B2
Engucwini, Malw. 119/A4
Énguera, Sp. 47/E3
Engure, Lat. 41/K3
Enguri (riv.), Geo. 71/G4
Enhtal, Mong. 78/F2
Enid, Ok, US 153/F2
Enid (lake), Ms, US 162/C3
Enigma, Ga, US 165/G2
Eniwa, Japan 82/B2
Enka, NC, US 163/F3
Enkenbach-Alsenborn, Ger. 55/G5
Enkhuizen, Neth. 52/C3
Enkirch, Ger. 55/G4
Enköping, Swe. 40/G2
Enna, It. 48/D4
Enné, Ouadi (riv.), Chad 116/C2
Ennedi (plat.), Chad 116/D1
Ennell, Lough (lake), Ire. 32/C3
Ennepe (riv.), Ger. 53/E6
Ennepetal, Ger. 53/E6
Enneri Bardagué (riv.), Chad 108/C4
Enneri Blaka (riv.), Niger 108/B4
Enneri Ké (riv.), Chad 108/C5
Enneri Maro (riv.), Chad 108/C5
Enneri Yébiqué (riv.), Chad 108/C4
Enneri Zergamouchi (riv.), Niger 108/B4
Ennery, Fr. 30/J4
Enngonia, Austl. 132/C1
Enningerloh, Ger. 53/F5
Ennis, Ire. 32/B4
Ennis, Mt, US 147/H1
Ennis, Tx, US 151/F1
Enniscorthy, Ire. 32/D5
Enniskerry, Ire. 34/B5
Enniskillen, NI, UK 31/Q9
Ennismore, On, Can. 161/G2
Ennistimon, Ire. 32/A4
Enns (riv.), Aus. 43/H5
Enns, Aus. 59/H6
Ennuye (riv.), Fr. 64/B4
Enoch, Ut, US 149/F2
Enochs, Tx, US 152/C4
Enogger (res.), Austl. 134/E6
Enola, Ar, US 153/H3
Enola, Pa, US 168/B3
Enontekiö, Fin. 38/G1
Enoree, SC, US 163/G3
Enoree (riv.), SC, US 163/G3
Enosburg Falls, Vt, US 161/K2
Enping, China 87/G4
Enrekang, Indo. 91/E4
Enrick (riv.), Sc, UK 33/B2
Enrique Carbó, Arg. 191/J10
Enriquillo, DRep. 177/J2
Enschede, Neth. 52/D4
Ensdorf, Ger. 59/E4
Ense, Ger. 53/E5
Enseleni, SAfr. 125/F3
Ensenada, Arg. 191/K11
Ensenada, Mex. 174/A2
Ensheim (arpt.), Ger. 55/G5
Ensheim (Saarbrücken) (arpt.), Ger. 55/G5
Enshi, China 87/F2
Ensign, Mi, US 160/C2
Ensisheim, Fr. 60/D2
Enskär (isl.), Swe. 39/A2
Ensley, Fl, US 164/E2
Ensuès-la-Redonne, Fr. 64/B6
Entebbe, Ugan. 121/H2
Entebbe (int'l arpt.), Ugan. 121/H2
Entenbühl (peak), Ger. 59/F3
Enterprise, On, Can. 161/H2
Enterprise, Al, US 165/F2
Enterprise, Ks, US 153/F1
Enterprise, La, US 164/C2
Enterprise, Ms, US 162/C4
Enterprise, Ok, US 153/G3
Enterprise, Or, US 146/E1
Entiat, Wa, US 144/D4
Entlebuch, Swi. 60/E4
Entraigues-sur-Sorgue, Fr. 64/A5
Entrance, Ab, Can. 144/F1
Entre Lagos, Chile 190/B4
Entre Ríos (prov.), Arg. 188/E4
Entre Ríos, Bol. 188/C2
Entre Rios, Braz. 182/C4
Entre Rios, Braz. 187/F1
Entre Ríos (mts.), Hon. 176/E3
Entre Rios de Minas, Braz. 186/D4
Entre Vientos, Chile 191/C7
Entre-Deux-Guiers, Fr. 64/B2
Entre-Rios, Moz. 123/H2
Entrevaux, Fr. 64/C5
Entroncamento, Port. 46/A3
Entry (isl.), Qu, Can. 159/G2
Entwistle, Ab, Can. 144/G1
Entzheim, Fr. 60/D1
Entzheim (Strasbourg) (int'l arpt.), Fr. 60/D1
Enu (isl.), Indo. 128/D1
Enugu, Nga. 115/G5
Enugu Ngwo, Nga. 115/G5
Enumclaw, Wa, US 167/D3
Enushū (sea), Japan 83/M6
Envermeu, Fr. 57/G1
Envigado, Col. 183/K6
Envira, Braz. 184/D2
Enyamba, D.R. Congo 121/F3
Enyang, China 87/E2
Enyellé, Congo 120/D2
Enz (riv.), Ger. 42/E4
Enza (riv.), It. 62/D4
Enzan, Japan 85/F3
Enzbach (riv.), Ger. 55/F4
Enzersdorf an der Fischa, Aus. 51/P7
Enzklösterle, Ger. 58/B5
Eola, Tx, US 150/D2
Eolia, Mo, US 155/J4
Épaignes, Fr. 57/F2
Epalinges, Swi. 60/C4
Epáno Arkhánai, Gre. 49/J5
Epanomí, Gre. 49/H2
Epcot Center, Fl, US 164/M7
Epe, Nga. 115/F5
Epe, Neth. 52/C4
Épehy, Fr. 54/C3
Epéna, Congo 120/D2
Epenarra, Austl. 129/D5
Épernay, Fr. 54/C5
Épernon, Fr. 57/G3
Epfig, Fr. 60/D1
Ephesus (ruin), Turk. 67/K3
Ephraim, Wi, US 157/L5
Ephraim, Ut, US 147/H4
Ephrata, Pa, US 168/B3
Ephrata, Wa, US 144/E4
Epi (isl.), Van. 136/F6
Épiais-Rhus, Fr. 30/J4
Epídhavros (Epidaurus) (ruin), Gre. 49/H4
Épinal, Fr. 60/C1
Épinal (Mirecourt) (arpt.), Fr. 60/C1
Épinay-sur-Orge, Fr. 30/J6
Épinay-sur-Seine, Fr. 30/J5
Epira, Guy. 181/G3
Epirus (reg.), Gre. 67/J3
Epomeo (vol.), It. 65/C6
Épône, Fr. 54/A6
Eppalock (lake), Austl. 133/B3
Eppelborn, Ger. 55/F5
Eppelheim, Ger. 58/B4
Eppenbrunn, Ger. 55/G5
Eppeville, Fr. 54/C4
Epping, Eng, UK 30/D1
Epping (for.), Eng, UK 30/D2
Epping (nbrhd.), Austl. 134/H8
Epping Forest NP, Austl. 134/B3
Eppingen, Ger. 58/B4
Eppishausen, Ger. 61/G1
Epps, La, US 153/J4
Epsie, Mt, US 145/M5
Epsom, Eng, UK 30/C3
Epsom and Ewell, Eng, UK 37/F4
Epte (riv.), Fr. 54/A4
Epukiro, Namb. 122/C4
Epukiro (riv.), Namb. 122/D4
Epulu (riv.), D.R. Congo 121/G2
Epupa (falls), Ang. 122/B3
Epworth, Eng, UK 35/H4
Epworth, Ia, US 155/J2
Eqlīd, Iran 103/H4
Equateur (pol. reg.), D.R. Congo 116/D5
Equator (fall), Ecu. 180/A4
Equatorial Guinea (ctry.) 120/B2
Équeurdreville-Hainneville, Fr. 56/D1
Équihen-Plage, Fr. 54/A2
Equimina, Ang. 122/B2
Er (lake), China 93/H2
Er (isl.), Fr. 56/B3
Er Rachidia, Mor. 110/D3
Er Reina, Isr. 105/C3
Er Rif (mts.), Mor. 66/B4
Era (riv.), It. 63/A5
Era (riv.), PNG 129/G1
Eraclea (ruin), It. 48/E2
Eraclea, It. 63/F2
Eraclea Minoa (ruin), It. 48/C4
Éragny, Fr. 30/J4
Eran, Phil. 88/B3
Erandique, Hon. 176/D3
Erath, La, US 164/B3
Erave (riv.), PNG 129/G1
Erave, PNG 129/F1
Erawan NP, Thai. 94/B3
Erba, It. 62/C2
Erbaa, Turk. 70/F4
Erbach, Ger. 58/B3
Erbendorf, Ger. 59/F3
Erbeskopf (peak), Ger. 55/G4
Ercan (int'l arpt.), Cyp. 104/C2
Ercé-en-Lamée, Fr. 56/D5
Erçek, Turk. 103/E2
Erçek (lake), Turk. 103/E2
Ercilla, Chile 190/B3
Erciş, Turk. 103/E2
Erciyes (peak), Turk. 102/C2
Erclin (riv.), Fr. 54/C3
Ercolano, It. 65/D6
Érd, Hun. 51/Q10
Erdao (riv.), China 79/K3
Erdek (gulf), Turk. 51/H5
Erdek, Turk. 51/H5
Erdemli, Turk. 104/D1
Erdenet, Mong. 78/E2
Erdenetsogt, Mong. 78/F3
Erdi (well), Chad 108/C4
Erdi-Ma (upland), Chad 108/D5
Erding, Ger. 59/E6
Erdre (riv.), Fr. 44/C3
Erdweg, Ger. 58/E6
Erechim, Braz. 189/F3
Ereen Davaanï (mts.), Mong. 78/G2
Ereğli, Turk. 102/C2
Ereğli, Turk. 51/K5
Ereke, Indo. 91/F4
Eremo delle Carceri, It. 65/B1
Eremo di Camaldoli, It. 63/E6
Erenhaberga (mts.), China 99/D3
Erenler, Turk. 51/K5
Erentepe, Turk. 102/E2
Erepecu (lake), Braz. 181/H5
Ērer Shet' (riv.), Eth. 118/B3
Eresma (riv.), Sp. 46/C2
Erétria, Gre. 49/H3
Erevan (int'l arpt.), Arm. 103/F1
Ereymentaū, Kaz. 74/H4
Érezée, Belg. 55/E3
Erfa (riv.), Ger. 58/C3
Erfoud, Mor. 110/D3
Erft (riv.), Ger. 42/D3
Erftstadt, Ger. 55/F2
Erfurt, Ger. 42/F3
`Erg Chech (des.), Mali,Alg. 107/B2
Erg du Djourab (des.), Chad 116/C2
`Erg Iguidi (des.), Alg.,Mrta. 110/D4
Ergene Nehri (riv.), Turk. 51/H5
Ērgli, Lat. 41/L3
Ergué-Gabéric, Fr. 56/A4
Ergun (riv.), China,Rus 79/J1
Ergun Youqi, China 79/J1
Ergun Zuoqi, China 79/J1
Erhard, Mn, US 156/F4
Erhlin, Tai. 87/J4
Erhulai, China 81/C2
Eriba, Sudan 117/H1
Erica, Neth. 52/D3
Erica, Austl. 133/C3
Ericeira, Port. 47/P10
Ericht (lake), Sc, UK 33/B3
Ericht (riv.), Sc, UK 33/B3
Erick, Ok, US 152/E3
Erickson, Mb, Can. 156/E2
Erickson, BC, Can. 144/F3
Ericsburg, Mn, US 157/H3
Erie, Ks, US 153/G2
Erie (int'l arpt.), Pa, US 160/F3
Erie, Pa, US 160/F3
Erie (lake), Can.,US 139/J5
Erie (canal), NY, US 160/V9
Erie (co.), NY, US 160/V10
Erie NWR, Pa, US 161/G4
Erigabo (Ceerigaabo), Som. 118/C3
Eriksdale, Mb, Can. 156/E2
Eriksmalå, Swe. 40/F3
Erikub (isl.), Mrsh. 136/F4
Erima, Ugan. 121/H2
Erímanthos (peak), Gre. 49/G4
Erimo, Japan 82/C2
Erimo-misaki (cape), Japan 82/C3
Erin, Tn, US 162/D2
Erin, On, Can. 160/S8
Erithraí, Gre. 49/H3
Eritrea (ctry.) 107/F3
Erkelenz, Ger. 55/F1
Erken (isl.), Swe. 41/H1
Erken (lake), Swe. 39/B1
Erkheim, Ger. 61/G1
Erkina (riv.), Ire. 32/C4
Erkner, Ger. 42/Q7
Erkrath, Ger. 52/D6
Erlach, Swi. 60/D3
Erlands Point-Kitsap Lake, Wa, US 167/B2
Erlang (peak), China 86/D2
Erlangen, Ger. 58/E3
Erlanger, Ky, US 162/E1
Erlau (riv.), Ger. 59/G5
Erldunda, Austl. 131/G3
Erlenbach (riv.), Ger. 58/B4
Erlenbach am Main, Ger. 58/C3
Erlenbach bei Marktheidenfeld, Ger. 58/C3
Erlenbach im Simmental, Swi. 60/D4
Erlinsbach, Swi. 60/E3
Erlongshan, China 79/K2
Erlongshan (res.), China 80/F2
Erme (riv.), Eng, UK 36/C6
Ermelo, Neth. 52/C4
Ermelo, SAfr. 125/E2
Ermenek (riv.), Turk. 104/C1
Ermenek, Turk. 104/C1
Ermenonville, Fr. 30/L4
Ermera, ETim. 128/B2
Ermeran Station, Austl. 133/B1
Ermineskin Ind. Res., Ab, Can. 145/H1
Ermióni, Gre. 49/H4
Ermont, Fr. 30/J5
Ermoúpolis, Gre. 49/J4
Erms (riv.), Ger. 58/C6
Ernabella, Austl. 131/G3
Erndtebrück, Ger. 55/H2
Ernée, Fr. 57/E4
Ernée (riv.), Fr. 44/C2
Ernesto Cortissoz (int'l arpt.), Col. 180/C2
Ernsthofen, Aus. 59/H6
Erode, India 95/C4
Erolzheim, Ger. 61/G1
Eromanga, Austl. 134/A4
Eros, La, US 153/H4
Erowal Bay, Austl. 133/E2
Erpe, Belg. 54/C2
Erpel, Ger. 55/G2
Erpengdianzi, China 81/C2
Erpu, China 78/C3
Erquelinnes, Belg. 55/D3
Erquy, Fr. 56/C3
Errego, Moz. 123/H3
Errigal (mtn.), Ire. 31/P9
Erris Head (pt.), Ire. 31/P9
Erro (riv.), It. 62/B4
Errochty (lake), Sc, UK 33/B3
Errol, Sc, UK 33/C4
Errol, NH, US 161/L2
Erromango (isl.), Van. 136/F6
Erse (riv.), Ger. 53/H4
Ersekë, Alb. 49/G2
Ershibadu, China 87/H2
Erskine, Mn, US 156/F4
Erskine, Ab, Can. 145/H1
Erstein, Fr. 60/D1
Erstfeld, Swi. 61/E4
Ertai, China 99/D3
Ertai, China 78/B2
Ertil', Rus. 73/L2
Ertingen, Ger. 61/F1
Ertis (riv.), Kaz. 74/H4
Ertix (riv.), China 78/B2
Ertvelde, Belg. 54/C1
Eruh, Turk. 102/E2
Erundu, Namb. 122/C4
Eruwa, Nga. 115/F5
Erval, Braz. 189/F5
Erval d'Oeste, Braz. 189/G3
Ervália, Braz. 187/E4
Ervay, Wy, US 147/K2
Erve (riv.), Fr. 57/E4
Ervia (riv.), It. 64/D5
Erwin, Tn, US 163/F2
Erwin, NC, US 163/H3
Erwitte, Ger. 53/F5
Eryuan, China 86/C3
Erzen (riv.), Alb. 49/F2
Erzgebirge (Krušné Hory) (mts.), Czh.,Ger. 45/K1
Erzhausen, Ger. 58/B3
Erzin, Rus. 78/D1
Erzincan, Turk. 102/D2
Erzincan (prov.), Turk. 102/D2
Erzurum, Turk. 102/E2
Erzurum (prov.), Turk. 102/E1
Es Senia (int'l arpt.), Alg. 112/E5
Esa'ala, PNG 136/E5
Esambo, D.R. Congo 121/E3
Esan-misaki (cape), Japan 82/B3
Esashi, Japan 82/B3
Esashi, Japan 82/C1
Esashi, Japan 82/B4
Esbiye, Turk. 70/F4
Esbjerg, Den. 40/C4
Esbjerg (int'l arpt.), Den. 40/C4
Esbly, Fr. 30/L5
Esbo (Espoo), Fin. 41/L1
Esbon, Ks, US 154/E4
Escabosa, NM, US 149/J3
Escada, Braz. 183/H5
Escalante, Ut, US 149/G2
Escalante (des.), Ut, US 147/G4
Escalante (riv.), Ut, US 149/G2
Escalón, Mex. 174/D3
Escalona, Sp. 46/C2
Escambia (riv.), Fl, US 164/E2
Escampobariou (pt.), Fr. 64/C6
Escanaba, Mi, US 160/C2
Escanaba (riv.), Mi, US 157/L4
Escarpada (pt.), Phil. 88/C1
Escatawpa (riv.), Ms, US 164/D2
Escaudain, Fr. 54/C3
Escaut (riv.), Fr. 42/B3
Esch (riv.), Fr. 55/E6
Esch-sur-Alzette, Lux. 55/E4
Esch-sur-Sure, Lux. 55/E4
Eschach (riv.), Ger. 61/E1
Eschau, Fr. 60/D1
Eschborn, Ger. 58/B2
Eschede, Ger. 53/H3
Eschen, Lcht. 61/F3
Eschenbach, Ger. 58/C5
Eschenbach in der Oberpfalz, Ger. 59/E3
Eschershausen, Ger. 53/G5
Esches (riv.), Fr. 54/B5
Escholzmatt, Swi. 60/D4
Eschwege, Ger. 53/H6
Eschweiler, Ger. 55/F2
Escobedo (int'l arpt.), Mex. 150/D5
Escoma, Bol. 184/D4
Escondido, Ca, US 166/C4
Escondido (cr.), Ca, US 166/C4
Escoutay (riv.), Fr. 64/A3
Escudillas, Ven. 181/E3
Escuinapa de Hidalgo, Mex. 174/D4
Escuintla, Guat. 176/D3
Esdraelon (plain), Isr. 105/C3
Eséka, Camr. 120/B2
Esenboga (int'l arpt.), Turk. 102/C1
Esence (peak), Turk. 102/D2
Esenguly, Trkm. 103/H2
Esens, Ger. 53/E1
Esera (riv.), Sp. 47/F1
Eşfahān, Iran 103/G3
Eşfahān (gov.), Iran 103/H3
Esfandak, Iran 101/H3
Esfarāyen, Iran 103/J2
Esfarvarīn, Iran 103/G3
Esgair Ddu (peak), Wal, UK 36/C1
Esh, Eng, UK 35/G2
Esh Winning, Eng, UK 35/G2
Esha Ness (cape), Sc, UK 31/W13
Eshan Yizu Zizhixian, China 86/D3
Esher, Eng, UK 30/B2
Eshimba, D.R. Congo 121/F4
Eshkol NP, Isr. 105/A6
Eshowe, SAfr. 125/E3
Eshtehārd, Iran 103/G3
Esil (riv.), Kaz. 77/F4
Esil, Kaz. 99/A1
Esine, It. 61/G6
Esino (riv.), It. 63/G6
Esira, Madg. 125/H9
Esk (riv.), Eng, UK 35/E2
Esk, North (riv.), Sc, UK 33/C5
Esk, South (riv.), Sc, UK 33/C5
Esk, South (riv.), Austl. 132/C4
Eskdale (valley), Sc, UK 33/C6
Eskifjördhur, Ice. 38/Q6
Eskil, Turk. 102/C2
Eskilstuna, Swe. 40/G2
Eskimalatya, Turk. 102/D2
Eskimo (lakes), NW, Can. 140/C2
Eskipazar, Turk. 70/E4
Eskişehir, Turk. 102/B2
Eskişehir (prov.), Turk. 102/B2
Esko, Mn, US 157/H4
Esla (riv.), Sp. 46/C1
Eslāmābād, Iran 103/F3
Eslāmābād, Iran 103/G2
Eslohe, Ger. 53/F6
Eslöv, Swe. 40/E4
Eslöv, Swe. 39/K7
Eşme, Turk. 102/B2
Esmeralda, Cuba 177/G1
Esmeraldas (dept.), Ecu. 180/B4
Esmeraldas, Ecu. 180/B4
Esmond, ND, US 156/E3
Esmont, Va, US 163/H2
Esmoraca, Bol. 188/C2
Esnagami (lake), On, US 157/L2
Esneux, Belg. 55/E2
Espada (pt.), Col. 180/D1
Espakeh, Iran 101/H3
Espalion, Fr. 44/E4
Espanola, On, Can. 160/F1
Española (isl.), Ecu. 184/K7
Española, NM, US 149/J3
Esparraguera, Sp. 47/K6
Esparta, Hon. 176/E3
Esparto, Ca, US 167/K9
Espejo, Sp. 46/C4
Espelkamp, Ger. 53/F4
Esperança, Braz. 183/H4
Esperance (bay), Austl. 130/D5
Esperance, Austl. 130/D5
Esperance (bay), Den. 40/E4
Esperance (int'l arpt.), Neth. 173/N8
Esperancita, Bol. 185/F5
Esperantina, Braz. 183/F3
Esperantinópolis, Braz. 183/E4
Esperanza, Arg. 191/C6
Esperanza, Arg., Ant. 192/W
Esperanza (mts.), Hon. 176/E3
Esperanza, Mex. 175/M8
Esperanza, Mex. 174/C3
Esperanza, Peru 184/D3
Esperanza, Uru. 191/K10
Esperanza, Ven. 181/E4
Esperia, It. 65/C5
Espichel (cape), Port. 47/P11
Espigão d'Oeste, Braz. 185/F3
Espinal, Col. 180/C3
Espinal, Mex. 175/M6
Espinar, Peru 184/D4
Espinhaço, Serra do (mts.), Braz. 187/E4
Espinho, Port. 46/A2
Espinillo (pt.), Uru. 191/F2
Espinosa, Braz. 187/E2
Espírito Santo (state), Braz. 187/E3
Espíritu Santo (bay), Cuba 176/E2
Espiritu Santo (isl.), Mex. 174/C3
Espiritu Santo (cape), Phil. 88/D2
Espiritu Santo (isl.), Van. 136/F6
Espita, Mex. 176/D1
Esplanada, Braz. 187/F1
Espluga de Francolí, Sp. 47/E2
Espluges, Sp. 47/L7
Espoo (Esbo), Fin. 41/L1
Esposende, Port. 46/A2
Esprit-Saint, Qu, Can. 158/C1
Espungabera, Moz. 123/G4
Espy, Pa, US 168/B1
Esqueda, Mex. 174/C2
Esquel, Arg. 190/C4
Esquina, Arg. 188/E4
Esrum Sø (lake), Den. 39/J6
Essaouira, Mor. 110/C3
Esse (riv.), Ger. 53/G5
Essé, Camr. 120/B1
Essen, Belg. 52/B6
Essen, Ger. 53/E3
Essen, Ger. 52/E6
Essenbach, Ger. 59/F5
Essendon (mt.), Austl. 130/D3
Essendon (nbrhd.), Austl. 132/F5
Essenheim, Ger. 55/H4
Essequibo (riv.), Guy. 179/D2
Essequibo Island-West Demerara (pol. reg.), Guy. 181/G3
Essex, On, Can. 167/G7
Essex (co.), On, Can. 167/G7
Essex (co.), Eng, UK 30/E1
Essex, Ca, US 148/E3
Essex, Ia, US 155/G3
Essex, Md, US 168/B5
Essex, Mt, US 145/H3
Essex (co.), NJ, US 168/D2
Essex, Vt, US 161/K2
Essex Fells, NJ, US 169/H8
Essexville, Mi, US 160/E3
Essie, Ky, US 163/F2
Esslingen, Ger. 58/C5
Esso, Rus. 75/R4
Essômes-sur-Marne, Fr. 54/C5
Essonne (riv.), Fr. 44/E2
Est (prov.), Camr. 116/B5
Est, Canal de l' (canal), Fr. 55/E5
Estaca de Bares, Punta de la (cape), Sp. 66/B2
Estacada, Or, US 146/B1
Estación Santa Engracia, Mex. 175/F3
Eşţahbān, Iran 103/H4
Estaires, Fr. 54/B2
Estancia, NM, US 149/J3
Estância, Braz. 187/F1
Estancia Carmen, Arg. 191/D7
Estanislao del Campo, Arg. 188/D3
Estarca, Bol. 188/C2
Estats, Pico de (peak), Sp. 44/D5
Estavayer-le-Lac, Swi. 60/C4
Estcourt, SAfr. 125/E3
Este, It. 63/E3
Este, Punta del (pt.), Cuba 172/E3
Esteio, Braz. 189/G4
Estelí, Nic. 176/E3
Estell Manor (Risley), NJ, US 168/D5
Estella, Sp. 44/B5
Estelle (mtn.), Ca, US 166/C3
Estelline, Tx, US 152/D3
Estelline, SD, US 155/F1
Estepa, Sp. 46/C4
Estepona, Sp. 46/C4
Ester, Ak, US 171/J3
Esterel (upland), Fr. 64/C6
Esterhazy, Sk, Can. 156/C2
Esterias (cape), Gabon 120/B2
Esternay, Fr. 54/C6
Estero (pt.), Ca, US 148/B3
Estero de Agiabampo (lag.), Mex. 174/C3
Estéron (riv.), Fr. 45/G5
Esteros de Iberá (swamp), Arg. 188/E4
Esterwegen, Ger. 53/E3
Estes Park, Co, US 154/B3
Estevan, Sk, Can. 156/C3
Estherville, Ia, US 155/G2
Estill, SC, US 163/G4
Estill Springs, Tn, US 162/D3
Estinnes-au-Mont, Belg. 55/D3
Esto, Fl, US 165/F2
Eston, Sk, Can. 145/K2
Eston and South Bank, Eng, UK 35/G2
Estonia (ctry.) 41/L2
Estoril, Port. 47/P10
Estrablin, Fr. 64/A1
Estral Beach, Mi, US 167/F8
Estrées-Saint-Denis, Fr. 54/B5
Estrêla, Braz. 189/G4
Estrella (pt.), Mex. 174/B2
Estremadura (reg.), Sp. 66/B3
Estremoz, Port. 46/B3
Estrondo, Serra do (mts.), Braz. 182/D5
Estuna, Swe. 39/B1
Esturaire (prov.), Gabon 120/B3
Esvres, Fr. 57/F6
Esztergom, Hun. 50/D2
Et Ţaiyiba, Isr. 105/C4
Et Ţīra, Isr. 105/B4
Étables-sur-Mer, Fr. 56/C3
Etadunna, Austl. 131/H4
Etah, India 96/B2
Étain, Fr. 55/E5
Etaka (riv.), Namb. 122/B3
Etal, Eng, UK 33/D5
Etal (isl.), Micr. 136/E4
Étalle, Belg. 55/E4
Étampes, Fr. 57/H4
Étaples, Fr. 54/A2
Etāwah, India 96/B2
Etāwah Branch (riv.), India 96/B2
Etchojoa, Mex. 174/C3
Etéké, Gabon 120/B3
Etel (riv.), Fr. 56/B5
Étel, Fr. 56/B5
Etelïnen, Fin. 39/E4
Etembue, EqG. 120/B2
Ethe, Belg. 55/E4
Ethel, Ar, US 162/B3
Ethel Creek, Austl. 130/D2
Ethelbert, Mb, Can. 156/D2
Ethete, Wy, US 147/J2
Ethiopia (ctry.) 107/F4
Ethiopian (plat.), Eth. 107/F4
Ethiopian Seminary, VatC. 65/F7
Ethridge, Tn, US 162/D3
Eti (riv.), Japan 83/K5
Etili, Turk. 51/H6
Etinan, Nga. 120/A1
Etiro, Namb. 122/B4
Étival-Clairefontaine, Fr. 60/C1
Etive, Loch (inlet), Sc, UK 33/A4
Etna (peak), It. 48/D4
Etna, Ca, US 146/B3
Etne, Nor. 40/A2
Etobicoke (co), On, Can. 160/T8
Étoile, D.R. Congo 123/E1
Étoile-sur-Rhône, Fr. 64/A3
Etolin (str.), Ak, US 171/E3
Eton, Eng, UK 30/B2
Eton, Ga, US 162/E3
Etorofu (isl.), Rus. 77/P5
Etosha NP, Namb. 122/B3
Etosha Pan (salt pan), Namb. 122/C3
Etoumbi, Congo 120/C3
Etowah, Tn, US 162/E3
Etowah (riv.), Ga, US 162/E3
Étréchy, Fr. 57/H3
Etrek (riv.), Trkm. 103/H2
Étrelles, Fr. 57/D4
Étrépagny, Fr. 57/G2
Étrépilly, Fr. 30/L4
Étretat, Fr. 57/F1
Etropole, Bul. 51/G4
Etroubles, It. 60/D6
Etsch (Adigo) (riv.), It. 61/G4
Ettadhamen Douarhicher, Tun. 112/M6
Ettelbruck, Lux. 55/F4
Etten-Leur, Neth. 52/B5
Ettenheim, Ger. 60/D1
Etterbeek, Belg. 55/D2
Etters (Goldsboro), Pa, US 168/B3
Ettlingen, Ger. 58/B5
Ettrick, Sc, UK 33/C6
Ettrick, Wi, US 155/J1
Ettrick Pen (peak), Sc, UK 33/C6
Ettrick Water (riv.), Sc, UK 33/C5
Ettringen, Ger. 61/G1
Etzikom Coulee (riv.), Ab, Can. 145/J3
Eu, Fr. 54/A3
'Eua (isl.), Tonga 137/H7
Euabalong, Austl. 133/C1
Eubenangee Swamp NP, Austl. 134/B2
Euchiniko (riv.), BC, Can. 144/C1
Eucla, Austl. 131/F4
Euclid, Oh, US 160/F4
Euclides da Cuhna, Braz. 187/F1
Eucumbene (lake), Austl. 133/D3
Eudunda, Austl. 132/A2
Euerbach, Ger. 58/D2
Eufaula, Al, US 165/F2
Eufaula (dam), Ok, US 153/G3
Eufaula, Ok, US 153/G3
Eufaula (lake), Ok, US 143/G4
Eugendorf, Aus. 59/G7
Eugene, Or, US 146/B1
Eugene O'Neill NHS, Ca, US 167/L11
Eugenia (pt.), Mex. 174/B3
Eugowra, Austl. 133/D1
Euharlee, Ga, US 162/E3
Euless, Tx, US 150/K7
Eulo, Austl. 134/B5
Eulonia, Ga, US 165/H2
Eume (res.), Sp. 46/B1
Eumungerie, Austl. 132/D1
Eungella NP, Austl. 134/C3
Eunice, La, US 164/B2
Eunice, NM, US 150/C1
Eupen, Belg. 55/F2
Euphrates (riv.), Iraq,Syria 77/D6
Euphrates (riv.), Syria,Iraq 100/C1
Eupora, Ms, US 162/C4
Eura, Fin. 41/K1
Eurajoki, Fin. 41/J1
Eure (dept.), Fr. 54/A5
Eure (riv.), Fr. 44/D2
Eure-et-Loir (dept.), Fr. 54/A6
Eureka (sound), Nun, Can. 141/S7
Eureka, Co, US 149/J2
Eureka, Il, US 155/K3
Eureka, Ks, US 153/F2
Eureka, Mt, US 144/G3
Eureka, Nv, US 146/F4
Eureka, SD, US 156/E5
Eureka, Tx, US 151/F1
Eureka, Ut, US 147/G4
Eureka, Wa, US 144/E4
Eureka Springs, Ar, US 153/H2
Euroa, Austl. 133/B3
Eurodisney, Fr. 30/L5
Euron (riv.), Fr. 60/C1
Europa (pt.), EqG. 120/B2
Europa (isl.), Fr. 123/J4
Europa (pt.), Gib. 46/C4
Europabrücke, Aus. 61/H3
Europe (cont.) 29/*
Europoort, Neth. 52/B5
Euskirchen, Ger. 55/F2
Eussenheim, Ger. 58/C3
Eustis, Fl, US 165/H3
Eustis, Me, US 161/L2
Euston, Austl. 132/B2
Eutaw, Al, US 162/D4
Eutin, Ger. 40/D4
Eutini, Malw. 123/G1
Euville, Fr. 55/E6
Euxton, Eng, UK 35/F4
Eva, Fl, US 164/M7
Eva Downs, Austl. 129/D4
Evadale, Tx, US 151/G2
Evander, SAfr. 124/E2
Evans (mt.), Co, US 152/B1
Evans, La, US 164/B2
Evans (str.), Nun, Can. 141/H2
Evans, Co, US 154/B3
Evans, WV, US 163/G1
Evans, Ga, US 163/F4
Evans Head, Austl. 132/E1
Evansburg, Ab, Can. 144/G1
Evanston, Il, US 160/C3
Evanston, Wy, US 147/H3
Evansville, Ar, US 153/G3
Evansville, Il, US 162/C1
Evansville, In, US 162/D2
Evansville, Mn, US 157/G4
Evansville, Wi, US 155/K2
Evant, Tx, US 150/E2
Evanton, Sc, UK 33/B1
Evart, Mi, US 160/D3
Evaton, SAfr. 124/D2
Evaz, Iran 103/H5
Ève, Fr. 30/L4
Evel (riv.), Fr. 56/C5
Eveleth, Mn, US 157/H4
Even Yehuda, Isr. 105/B4
Evening Shade, Ar, US 153/J2
Evenlode (riv.), Eng, UK 37/E3
Evensk, Rus. 75/R3
Evenkiyskiy Aut. Okrug, Rus. 75/R3
Evensville, Tn, US 162/E3
Everard (lake), Austl. 131/G4
Everard (mt.), Austl. 131/G3
Everard (cape), Austl. 133/D3
Evercreech, Eng, UK 36/D4
Everest, Ks, US 155/G4
Everest (Sagarmatha) (mtn.), China,Nepal 97/F2
Everett, Ga, US 165/H2
Everett, Pa, US 161/G4
Everett, Wa, US 144/C4
Evergem, Belg. 54/C1
Everglades City, Fl, US 165/H5
Everglades NP, Fl, US 165/H5
Evergreen, Al, US 164/E2
Evergreen Park, Il, US 167/Q16
Everman, Tx, US 150/K7
Eversholt, Eng, UK 37/F3
Everson, Wa, US 144/C3
Everswinkel, Ger. 53/E5
Everton, Mo, US 153/H2
Everton, In, US 160/D5
Evesham, Eng, UK 37/E2
Évian-les-Bains, Fr. 60/C5
Evinayong, EqG. 120/B2
Évinos (riv.), Gre. 49/G3
Evje, Nor. 40/B2
Evolène, Swi. 60/D5
Évora (dist.), Port. 46/A3
Évora, Port. 46/B3
Évran, Fr. 56/D4
Evre (riv.), Fr. 57/D6
Évrecy, Fr. 57/E2
Évreux, Fr. 57/G2
Évron, Fr. 57/E4
Evrótas (riv.), Gre. 49/H4
Évry, Fr. 30/K6
Evvoia (gulf), Gre. 70/B5
Evvoia (isl.), Gre. 70/B5
Évvoia (gulf), Gre. 49/H3
Evxinoúpolis, Gre. 49/H3
Ewan, NJ, US 168/C4
Ewaninga, Austl. 131/G2
Ewarton, Jam. 177/G2
Ewaso Ng'iro (riv.), Kenya 119/B1
Ewaso Ngiro (riv.), Kenya 119/A2
Ewell, Eng, UK 30/C3
Ewell, Md, US 163/J2
Ewenkizu Zizhiqi, China 79/H2
Ewhurst, Eng, UK 30/B3
Ewing, Mo, US 155/J3
Ewing, Ky, US 162/F1
Ewing, Ne, US 154/E2
Ewing, NJ, US 168/D3
Ewo, Congo 120/C3
Exaltación, Bol. 185/E4
Exaplátanos, Gre. 49/H2
Excel, Al, US 164/E2
Excello, Mo, US 155/H4
Excelsior Springs, Mo, US 155/G4
Excursion Inlet, Ak, US 171/L4
Exe (riv.), Eng, UK 36/C4
Exeland, Wi, US 157/J5
Exeter, On, Can. 160/F3
Exeter, Eng, UK 36/C5
Exeter (arpt.), Eng, UK 36/C5
Exeter, Ca, US 148/C2
Exeter, Mo, US 153/H2
Exeter, Ne, US 154/F3
Exeter, NH, US 161/L3
Exeter, Pa, US 161/J4
Exira, Ia, US 155/G3
Exminster, Eng, UK 36/C5
Exmoor (upland), Eng, UK 36/C4
Exmoor NP, Eng, UK 36/C4
Exmore, Va, US 163/K2
Exmouth (gulf), Austl. 130/B2
Exmouth, Austl. 130/B2
Exmouth (pen.), Chile 191/B6
Exmouth, Eng, UK 36/C5
Experiment, Ga, US 162/E4
Exploits (riv.), Nf, Can. 159/J1
Extension, La, US 164/C2
Extension, BC, Can. 144/C3
Extrema, Braz. 187/K7
Extrême Nord (prov.), Camr. 116/B3
Exu, Braz. 183/G4
Exuma (sound), Bahm. 173/F3
Eyach (riv.), Ger. 58/B6
Eyak, Ak, US 171/J3
Eyam, Eng, UK 35/G5
Eyangu, D.R. Congo 121/E3
Eyasi (lake), Tanz. 119/A2
Eyb (riv.), Ger. 58/C5
Eybens, Fr. 64/B2
Eydehamn, Nor. 40/C2
Eye, Eng, UK 37/H2
Eye (brook), Eng, UK 37/F1
Eyemouth, Sc, UK 33/D5
Eyguières, Fr. 64/B5
Eyl, Som. 118/D4
Eyn Hemed (ruin), Isr. 105/C5
Eyn Hemeo NP, Isr. 105/C5
Eynsford, Eng, UK 30/D2
Eyragues, Fr. 64/A5
Eyre, Austl. 130/E5
Eyre (pen.), Austl. 131/G5
Eyre, North (lake), Austl. 131/H4
Eyre, South (lake), Austl. 131/H4
Eyrecourt, Ire. 32/B3
Eyrieux (riv.), Fr. 64/A3
Eyüp (nbrhd.), Turk. 103/M6
Eyüp, Turk. 103/M6
Ézanville, Fr. 30/K4
Ezequiel Ramos Mexía (res.), Arg. 190/C3
Ezhou, China 87/G2
Ezine, Turk. 49/K3
Ézy-sur-Eure, Fr. 57/G3
Ezzane (well), Alg. 108/A4
Ezzell, Tx, US 151/F3

F

F.D. Roosevelt (int'l arpt.), NAnt. 173/N8
F.E. Walter (res.), Pa, US 168/C1
F.E. Warren (A.F.B.), Wy, US 154/B3
Faaa, FrPol. 137/X15
Faaa (Papeete) (int'l arpt.), FrPol. 137/X15
Faafaxdhuun, Som. 119/C1
Fabbrico, It. 63/D4
Fabens, Tx, US 150/A2
Fabero, Sp. 46/B1
Fåborg, Den. 40/D4
Fabrica di Roma, It. 65/B3
Fabrichnyy, Kaz. 99/C3
Fabyan, Ab, Can. 145/J1
Facatativá, Col. 183/L8
Faches-Thumesnil, Fr. 54/C2
Facundo, Arg. 190/C5
Fada (lake), Sc, UK 33/A1
Fada, Chad 116/D1
Fada-N'Gourma, Burk. 115/F3
Fadghamī, Syria 102/E3
Fadugu, SLeo. 114/C4
Faenza, It. 63/E5
Faetano, SMar. 63/F6
Fafa (riv.), CAfr. 116/C4
Fafe, Port. 46/A2
Fafen Shet' (riv.), Eth. 118/C4
Fagali (Apia) (int'l arpt.), Sam. 137/S9
Făgăraş, Rom. 51/G3
Fagersta, Swe. 40/F2
Fagerstrand, Nor. 38/S8
Faggiola (peak), It. 63/E5
Faggo, Nga. 115/H4
Fagnano (lake), Arg. 191/D7
Fagnano Olona-Bergoro, It. 62/B2
Fagnières, Fr. 55/D6
Faguibine (lake), Mali 114/D2
Fagundes, Braz. 182/C4
Fahl (well), Alg. 111/F3
Fahrenzhausen, Ger. 59/E6
Faial (isl.), Azor., Port. 47/S12
Faiano, It. 65/D6
Fā'id, Egypt 113/D4
Faido, Swi. 61/E5
Faille, Eth. 118/A4
Failsworth, Eng, UK 35/F4
Fains-Véel, Fr. 55/E6
Fair Bluff, NC, US 163/H3
Fair Grove, Mo, US 153/H2
Fair Haven, Mi, US 167/G6
Fair Haven, NY, US 161/H3
Fair Haven, Vt, US 161/K3
Fair Hill, Md, US 168/C4
Fair Isle (isl.), Sc, UK 31/W14
Fair Lawn, NJ, US 169/J8
Fair Oaks, Ca, US 167/M9
Fair Oaks, Ga, US 163/L7
Fair Plain, Mi, US 160/C3
Fair Play, Mo, US 153/H2
Fairbanks, Ak, US 171/J3
Fairbanks, La, US 153/H4
Fairborn, Oh, US 160/D5
Fairburn, Ga, US 163/L7
Fairburn, SD, US 154/C2
Fairbury, Il, US 155/K3
Fairbury, Ne, US 155/F3
Fairchild (A.F.B.), Wa, US 144/F4
Fairdealing, Mo, US 162/B2
Fairfax, Ca, US 167/J11
Fairfax, Mb, Can. 156/D3
Fairfax, Mo, US 155/G3
Fairfax, Oh, US 162/F1
Fairfax, Ok, US 153/F2
Fairfax, SC, US 163/G4
Fairfax, SD, US 154/E2
Fairfax, Va, US 168/A6
Fairfax (co.), Va, US 168/A6
Fairfax, Vt, US 161/K2
Fairfield (nbrhd.), Austl. 134/G8
Fairfield, Ca, US 146/B4
Fairfield, Ct, US 169/E1

Fairfield (co.), Ct, US 169/L7
Fairfield, Ia, US 155/J3
Fairfield, Id, US 147/F2
Fairfield, Il, US 162/C1
Fairfield, Mt, US 145/J4
Fairfield, NC, US 163/J3
Fairfield, Ne, US 154/E3
Fairfield, NJ, US 169/H8
Fairfield, Oh, US 160/D5
Fairfield, Pa, US 168/A4
Fairfield, Tx, US 151/F2
Fairfield, Va, US 163/H2
Fairfield, Wa, US 144/F4
Fairfield Bay, Ar, US 153/H3
Fairford, Mb, Can. 156/E2
Fairford, Eng, UK 37/E3
Fairgrove, Mi, US 160/E3
Fairhope, Al, US 164/E2
Fairland, In, US 160/D5
Fairland, Md, US 168/B5
Fairland, Ok, US 153/G2
Fairlawn, Va, US 163/G2
Fairlee, Md, US 168/B5
Fairless Hills, Pa, US 168/D3
Fairlie, Sc, UK 33/B5
Fairlie, NZ 135/B4
Fairlight, Sk, Can. 156/D3
Fairlight, Eng, UK 37/G5
Fairmead, Ca, US 148/B2
Fairmont, Mn, US 155/G2
Fairmont, NC, US 163/H3
Fairmont, WV, US 160/F5
Fairmont Hot Springs, BC, Can. 144/G2
Fairmount, ND, US 156/F4
Fairmount, NY, US 161/H3
Fairmount, Ga, US 162/E3
Fairplains, NC, US 163/G2
Fairplay, Ky, US 162/E2
Fairpoint, SD, US 154/C1
Fairport Harbor, Oh, US 160/F4
Fairton, NJ, US 168/C5
Fairvale, NB, Can. 158/E3
Fairview, Ab, Can. 140/E3
Fairview, Ga, US 162/E3
Fairview, Ks, US 155/G4
Fairview, Mt, US 156/B4
Fairview, Mo, US 153/G2
Fairview, Mi, US 160/D2
Fairview, NJ, US 169/K8
Fairview, Ok, US 153/E2
Fairview, Tn, US 162/D3
Fairview, Tx, US 150/L6
Fairview, Tx, US 150/D1
Fairview (peak), Zim. 123/G3
Fairview Park, In, US 160/C5
Fairweather (mt.), Can.,US 171/L4
Fairweather (cape), Ak, US 171/L4
Faisalābad, Pak. 98/B4
Faison, NC, US 163/H3
Faistós (ruin), Gre. 49/J5
Faizābād, India 96/D2
Fajardo, PR 173/M8
Fak Tha, Thai. 94/C2
Fakahina (isl.), FrPol. 137/M6
Fakaofo (isl.), Tok. 137/H5
Fakarava (isl.), FrPol. 137/L6
Fakfak, Indo. 91/H4
Fako (peak), Camr. 120/B1
Fakse, Den. 40/E4
Fakse Ladeplads, Den. 40/E4
Faku, China 80/E2
Fal (riv.), Eng, UK 36/B6
Falaba, SLeo. 114/C4
Falaise, Fr. 57/E3
Fālākāta, India 97/G2
Falam, Myan. 86/B4
Falāmah, WBnk. 105/C4
Falán, Col. 183/L7
Fálanna, Gre. 49/H3
Falciano del Massico, It. 65/C5
Fălciu, Rom. 51/J2
Falcon (cape), Alg. 112/D2
Falcon (res.), Mex., US 150/E4
Falcon (dam), Tx, US 150/E4
Falcón (state), Ven. 180/D2
Falcon Lake, Mb, Can. 157/G3
Falconara (arpt.), It. 63/G6
Falconara Marittima, It. 63/G6
Falconer, NY, US 161/G3
Falémé (riv.), Mali 114/C3
Faleolo, Sam. 137/S9
Faleolo (Apia) (int'l arpt.), Sam. 137/S9
Faleşti, Mol. 72/D4
Falfurrias, Tx, US 150/E4
Falissadé, Gui. 114/B4
Falkenberg, Swe. 40/E3
Falkensee, Ger. 42/Q6
Falkenstein, Ger. 59/F2
Falkenstein, Ger. 59/F4
Falkirk, Sc, UK 33/C5
Falkirk (co.), Sc, UK 33/C5
Falkland, Sc, UK 33/C4
Falkland (isls.), UK 179/C8
Falkland Sound (str.), UK 191/E7
Falköping, Swe. 40/E2
Falkville, Al, US 162/D3
Fall (riv.), Ks, US 153/F2
Fall City, Wa, US 167/D2
Fall Creek, Wi, US 155/J1
Fall River, Ks, US 153/F2
Fall River, Ma, US 161/L4
Fall River, Wi, US 155/K2
Fallbrook, Ca, US 166/C4
Fallere (peak), It. 60/D6
Fallingbostel, Ger. 53/G3
Fallon, Mt, US 156/B4
Fallon, Nv, US 146/D4
Fallon Ind. Res., Nv, US 146/D4
Fallon Naval Air Station, Nv, US 146/D4
Falls Church, Va, US 168/A6
Falls City, Ne, US 155/G3
Falls City, Or, US 146/B1
Falls City, Tx, US 151/E3
Falls Creek, Pa, US 161/G4
Falls Lake (res.), NC, US 163/H2
Falls of Rough, Ky, US 162/D2
Fallston, Md, US 168/B4
Falmey, Niger 115/F3
Falmouth, Anti. 173/N8
Falmouth, Eng, UK 36/A6
Falmouth (bay), Eng, UK 36/A6
Falmouth, Ky, US 162/E1
Falmouth, Ma, US 161/L4
Falmouth, Mi, US 160/D2
Falmouth, NS, Can. 158/E3
Falmouth, Va, US 163/J1
False Cape Bossut (cape), Austl. 128/A4
False Orford Ness (cape), Austl. 129/F2
False Pass, Ak, US 171/F5
Falshöft (pt.), Ger. 40/C4
Falso (cape), Hon. 177/F3
Falso Cabo de Hornos (cape), Chile 191/C7
Falso, Cabo (cape), Mex. 174/C4
Falster (isl.), Den. 38/E5
Falsterbo, Den. 39/J7
Falterona (peak), It. 63/E6
Fălticeni, Rom. 72/D4
Falun, Swe. 40/F1
Famagusta (dist.), Cyp. 104/C2
Famagusta, Cyp. 104/C2
Famagusta (bay), Cyp. 104/C2
Famaillá, Arg. 188/C3
Famakah, Sudan 117/G3
Fāmanīn, Iran 100/E1
Famatina, Arg. 188/C4
Fameck, Fr. 55/F5
Famenne (reg.), Belg. 55/E3
Family (lake), Mb, Can. 157/G2
Famoso, Ca, US 148/C3
Fan Si Pan (peak), Viet. 86/D4
Fana, Nor. 40/A1
Fana, Mali 114/D3
Fanārah, Egypt 113/D4
Fanchang, China 80/D5
Fancy Farm, Ky, US 162/C2
Fandriana, Madg. 125/H8
Fane (riv.), Ire. 32/D2
Fang, Thai. 94/B2
Fang Xian, China 80/B4
Fangak, Sudan 117/F3
Fangamandou, Gui. 114/C4
Fangatau (isl.), FrPol. 137/L6
Fangataufa (isl.), FrPol. 137/L7
Fangcheng, China 80/C4
Fangcheng Gezu Zizhixian, China 87/F4
Fangcun, China 87/H3
Fangdao, China 87/H3
Fangdou (mts.), China 87/E2
Fangjiatun, China 79/J3
Fangliao, Tai. 87/J4
Fangshan, China 80/B3
Fangshan, China 80/G7
Fangxi, China 87/G2
Faniria, Madg. 125/H8
Fanjing (peak), China 87/F3
Fannich (lake), Sc, UK 33/A1
Fannie (lake), Fl, US 164/M7
Fannin, Ms, US 162/C4
Fannin, Tx, US 151/F3
Fanning (Tabuaeran) (isl.), Kiri. 137/K4
Fanø (isl.), Den. 40/C4
Fano, It. 63/G6
Fanshan, China 87/J3
Fanshawe, Ok, US 153/G3
Fanshi, China 80/C3
Fanwood, NJ, US 169/H9
Faqīrwāli, Pak. 98/B5
Faqqū'ah, WBnk. 105/C3
Fāqūs, Egypt 113/C3
Far (mtn.), BC, Can. 144/B1
Far Rockaway (nbrhd.), NY, US 169/K9
Fara in Sabina, It. 65/B3
Fara Novarese, It. 62/B2
Faradje, D.R. Congo 121/G2
Farafangana, Madg. 125/H8
Farāh, Afg. 74/G6
Farāh (riv.), Afg. 74/G6
Fa'rah (wadi), WBnk. 105/C4
Farako, Mali 114/D3
Farallon (isls.), Ca, US 146/B5
Farallón Centinela (isl.), Ven. 183/P7
Farallon de Medinilla (isl.), NMar. 136/D3
Farallon de Pajaros (isl.), NMar. 136/D2
Farallon NWR, Ca, US 146/B5
Farallones de Cali, PN, Col. 180/B4
Faramana, Burk. 114/D3
Faranah, Gui. 114/C4
Faranah (pol. reg.), Gui. 114/C4
Farángi Samariás NP, Gre. 49/H5
Faraony (riv.), Madg. 125/H8
Farasan (isls.), Sudan 118/B1
Faraulep (isl.), Micr. 136/D4
Farber, Mo, US 155/J4
Farciennes, Belg. 55/D3
Fare (riv.), Fr. 57/F5
Fareham, Eng, UK 37/E5
Farellones, Chile 190/N8
Faremoutiers, Fr. 54/C6
Farentuna, Swe. 39/A1
Farewell (cape), NZ 135/C3
Farewell, Ak, US 171/H3
Farfa (riv.), It. 65/B3
Färgelanda, Swe. 40/D2
Farghona, Uzb. 99/B3
Fargo, Ga, US 165/G2
Fargo, ND, US 156/F4
Fargo, Ok, US 152/E2
Faribault, Mn, US 155/H1
Farīdābād, India 98/D5
Farīdkot, India 98/C4
Farīdpur, India 96/B1
Farīdpur (pol. reg.), Bang. 97/G4
Farīdpur, Bang. 97/G4
Farilhao (cape), Namb. 122/B4
Farim, GBis. 114/B3
Farina, Il, US 162/C1
Farindale, Ar, US 153/H3
Färingsö (isl.), Swe. 39/A1
Fāriskūr, Egypt 113/C2
Farit (peak), Eth. 118/A3
Färjestaden, Swe. 40/G3
Farkadhón, Gre. 49/H3
Farkasgyepú, Hun. 50/C2
Farkwa, Tanz. 119/A3
Farley, Ia, US 155/J2
Farlington, Ks, US 153/G2
Farmer City, Il, US 155/K3
Farmers Branch, Tx, US 150/L7
Farmersburg, In, US 160/C5
Farmersville, Tx, US 150/L6
Farmerville, La, US 153/H4
Farmingdale, NJ, US 168/D3
Farmingdale, NY, US 169/M9
Farmington, Ar, US 153/G2
Farmington, De, US 168/C6
Farmington, Il, US 155/J3
Farmington, Me, US 161/L2
Farmington, Mi, US 167/F7
Farmington, Mn, US 155/H1
Farmington, Mo, US 162/B2
Farmington, NH, US 161/L3
Farmington, NM, US 149/H2
Farmington, Ut, US 147/H3
Farmington, Wa, US 144/F4
Farmington Hills, Mi, US 167/E6
Farmoréya, Gui. 114/B4
Farmville, NC, US 163/J3
Farmville, Va, US 163/H2
Farnborough, Eng, UK 37/F4
Farnham (mt.), BC, Can. 144/F2
Farnham, Eng, UK 37/F4
Farnham (peak), Id, US 144/F3
Farnham Royal, Eng, UK 30/B2
Farningham, Eng, UK 30/D2
Farnworth, Eng, UK 35/F4
Faro, Braz. 182/B3
Faro (riv.), Camr. 116/B4
Faro, Yk, Can. 171/M3
Faro (int'l arpt.), Port. 46/B4
Faro, Port. 46/B4
Faro (dist.), Port. 46/A4
Faro, PN de, Camr. 116/B3
Faroe (isls.), Den. 29/D2
Fåron (isl.), Swe. 41/H3
Farösund, Swe. 41/H3
Farquhar (cape), Austl. 130/B2
Farragut, Tn, US 162/E3
Farranfore (arpt.), Ire. 32/A5
Farrāshband, Iran 103/H4
Farrokh Shahr, Iran 103/G3
Farroupilha, Braz. 189/G4
Farrukhābād, India 96/B2
Farrukhnagar, India 96/A1
Fārs (gov.), Iran 103/H4
Fársala, Gre. 49/H3
Fārsān, Iran 103/G3
Farsīs, Egypt 113/C3
Farsø, Den. 40/C3
Farson, Wy, US 147/J2
Farsund, Nor. 40/B2
Fartura, Braz. 189/G2
Farum, Swe. 39/J7
Farwell, Tx, US 152/C3
Fasā, Iran 103/H4
Fasano, It. 49/E2
Faşıkan (pass), Turk. 104/C1
Fassala-Néré, Mrta. 114/D3
Fassberg, Ger. 53/H3
Fast Castle (pt.), Sc, UK 33/D5
Fastiv, Ukr. 72/E2
Fatagar Tuting (cape), Indo. 91/H4
Fatahjang, Pak. 98/B3
Fate, Tx, US 150/L7
Fate, Monte delle (peak), It. 65/C5
Fatehābād, India 98/C5
Fatehgarh Chūriān, India 98/C4
Fatehpur, Pak. 98/A4
Fatehpur, India 96/C3
Fatehpur, India 96/C2
Fatëzh, Rus. 73/H1
Fathom Five NP, On, Can. 161/F2
Fatick (pol. reg.), Sen. 114/A3
Fatick, Sen. 114/A3
Fatigue (mt.), Austl. 133/C4
Fátima, Port. 46/A3
Fátima do Sul, Braz. 189/F2
Fātir (wadi), Leb. 105/D1
Fatoto, Gam. 114/B3
Fatsa, Turk. 70/F4
Fatu Hiva (isl.), FrPol. 137/M6
Fatunda, D.R. Congo 120/D4
Faucilles (mts.), Fr. 42/C4
Faughan (riv.), NI, UK 34/A2
Fauglia, It. 62/D6
Fauldhouse, Sc, UK 33/C5
Faulkton, SD, US 154/E1
Faulquemont, Fr. 55/F5
Faure (isl.), Austl. 130/B3
Făurei, Rom. 51/H3
Fauske, Nor. 38/E2
Fauville-en-Caux, Fr. 57/F1
Fauvillers, Belg. 55/E4
Favalto (peak), It. 63/F7
Favara, It. 48/C4
Fave (riv.), Fr. 60/C1
Faverges, Fr. 60/C6
Faverney, Fr. 60/C2
Faversham, Eng, UK 37/G4
Favières, Fr. 30/L5
Favignana, It. 48/C4
Favria, It. 62/A2
Favrieux, Fr. 30/G5
Fawley, Eng, UK 37/E5
Fawn (riv.), On, Can. 140/H3
Fawn Grove, Pa, US 168/B4
Fawumang, Gha. 115/E5
Faxaflói (bay), Ice. 38/M7
Faxinal, Braz. 189/G2
Faya-Largeau, Chad 116/C1
Fayd, SAr. 102/E5
Fayence, Fr. 64/C5
Fayette, Al, US 162/D4
Fayette (co.), Ga, US 163/M8
Fayette, Ia, US 155/J2
Fayette, Mo, US 155/H4
Fayette, Ms, US 164/C2
Fayette Historical Townsite, Mi, US 160/C2
Fayetteville, Ar, US 153/G2
Fayetteville, Ga, US 163/M8
Fayetteville, NC, US 163/H3
Fayetteville, Oh, US 162/F1
Fayetteville, Pa, US 161/H5
Fayetteville, Tn, US 162/D3
Fayetteville, Tx, US 151/F3
Fayetteville, WV, US 163/G1
Fayl-la-Forêt, Fr. 60/B2
Fayrā, Yem. 118/B2
Faywood (Dwyer), NM, US 149/H4
Fazao, Monts du (mts.), Togo 115/F4
Fazao, PN du, Togo 115/F4
Fazenda Nova, Braz. 186/C3
Fāzilka, India 98/C4
Fdérik, Mrta. 110/B5
Feakle, Ire. 32/B4
Feale (riv.), Ire. 32/A5
Fear (cape), NC, US 163/J4
Feasterville-Trevose, Pa, US 168/D3
Feather (riv.), Ca, US 146/C4
Feather (falls), Ca, US 146/C4
Feather, Mid. Fk. (riv.), Ca, US 146/C4
Featherston, NZ 135/J9
Featherstone, Eng, UK 35/G4
Featherstone, Zim. 123/F3
Feathertop (mt.), Austl. 133/C3
Fécamp, Fr. 57/F1
Fecht (riv.), Fr. 60/D1
Federación, Arg. 188/E4
Federal, Arg. 188/E4
Federal Dam, Mn, US 157/G4
Federal Hall Nat'l Mem., NY, US 169/K9
Federal Way, Wa, US 144/C4
Federally Admin. Tribal Areas, Pak. 98/A2
Federalsburg, Md, US 163/K1
Federsee (lake), Ger. 58/C6
Fedhaven, Fl, US 164/N8
Fedīs, Eth. 118/B3
Fedje, Nor. 40/A1
Fedorovka, Kaz. 69/P5
Fëdorovka, Kaz. 71/J2
Fedorovka, Rus. 71/J1
Fëdorovka, Rus. 73/K4
Fedscreek, Ky, US 163/F2
Feeny, NI, UK 34/A2
Feerfeer, Som. 118/C4
Fegersheim, Fr. 58/A6
Fégréac, Fr. 56/C5
Fehérgyarmat, Hun. 50/F2
Fehmarn (isl.), Den. 40/D4
Fehmarn Belt (str.), Den. 42/F1
Fei Huang (riv.), China 80/D4
Fei Xian, China 80/D4
Feia (lake), Braz. 187/E4
Feicheng, China 80/D3
Feidong, China 80/D5
Feignies, Fr. 54/C3
Feijó, Braz. 184/D3
Feilding, NZ 135/C3
Feillans, Fr. 60/A5
Feira, Port. 46/A2
Feira de Santana, Braz. 187/F2
Feistritz (riv.), Aus. 45/L3
Feixi, China 80/D5
Fejér (co.), Hun. 50/D2
Fejø (isl.), Ger. 40/D4
Feke, Turk. 102/C2
Feketić, Serb. 50/D3
Felanitx, Sp. 47/G3
Felch, Mi, US 157/L5
Feldafing, Ger. 61/H2
Feldaist (riv.), Aus. 59/H6
Feldberg (peak), Ger. 60/E2
Feldkirch, Aus. 61/F3
Feldkirchen an der Donau, Aus. 59/H6
Feldkirchen bei Graz, Aus. 50/B2
Feldkirchen in Kärnten, Aus. 45/L3
Feletto, It. 62/A2
Feletto Umberto, It. 63/G1
Feliciano, Arroyo (brook), Arg. 188/E4
Felicity, Oh, US 162/E1
Felino, It. 62/D4
Felipe Carrillo Puerto, Mex. 176/D2
Felix (riv.), NM, US 150/B1
Felixburg, Zim. 123/F3
Felixdorf, Aus. 50/C2
Felixlândia, Braz. 186/D3
Felixstowe, Eng, UK 37/H3
Felizzano, It. 62/B4
Fell, Ger. 55/F4
Fellbach, Ger. 58/C5
Felling, Eng, UK 35/G2
Fellows, Ca, US 148/C3
Fellsmere, Fl, US 165/H4
Felsberg, Ger. 53/G6
Felsberg, Swi. 61/F4
Felsenthal, Ar, US 153/H4
Felt, Ok, US 152/C2
Feltham (nbrhd.), Eng, UK 30/B2
Felton, Ca, US 148/A2
Felton, Ca, US 148/A2
Felton, De, US 168/C5
Felton, Mn, US 156/F4
Felton, Pa, US 168/B4
Feltwell, Eng, UK 37/G2
Fema (peak), It. 65/C2
Femø (isl.), Den. 40/D4
Femundsmarka NP, Nor. 38/D3
Fen (riv.), China 78/G5
Fénay, Fr. 60/B3
Fence, Wi, US 157/K5
Fence Lake, NM, US 149/H3
Fenchuganj, Bang. 97/H3
Fene, Sp. 46/A1
Fenelon Falls, On, Can. 161/G2
Fener (pt.), Turk. 104/D1
Feng Xian, China 80/D4
Feng Xian, China 78/F5
Fengári (peak), Gre. 49/J2
Fengcheng, China 81/C2
Fengchuihudie (peak), China 87/G3
Fenggeling, China 78/F5
Fenghuang, China 93/J2
Fenghuang, China 87/E3
Fengjie, China 87/F2
Fengkou, China 87/G2
Fengle (riv.), China 80/D5
Fengle, China 87/E2
Fengle, China 87/H3
Fenglin, Tai. 87/J4
Fenglingdu, China 78/G5
Fengnan, China 80/J7
Fengning, China 80/D2
Fengqing, China 86/C3
Fengqiu, China 80/C4
Fengrun, China 80/J7
Fengshan, China 93/J3
Fengshan, China 79/H3
Fengshan, China 87/F3
Fengshuba (res.), China 87/G3
Fengshui (peak), China 79/J1
Fengtai, China 80/H7
Fengtian, China 87/G3
Fengtian, China 87/G3
Fengxian, China 80/L9
Fengxiang, China 78/F5
Fengyang, China 80/D4
Fengyüan, Tai. 87/J3
Fengzhen, China 80/C2
Fengzhou, China 78/F5
Feni, Bang. 97/H4
Fenimore Pass (str.), Ak, US 171/C5
Fenner, Ca, US 148/E3
Fennimore, Wi, US 155/J2
Fennville, Mi, US 160/C3
Fenoarivo Atsinanana, Madg. 125/J7
Fenshui (pass), China 87/H3
Fenshui Guan (pass), China 87/H4
Fenshuizhen, China 87/F2
Fensmark, Den. 40/D4
Fensterbach (riv.), Ger. 59/F4
Fenton, La, US 164/B2
Fenton, Mi, US 160/E3
Fenton (lake), Mi, US 167/E7
Fenwick, WV, US 163/G1
Fenxi, China 80/B3
Fenyang, China 80/B3
Feodosiya, Ukr. 73/H5
Férai, Gre. 51/H5
Ferbane, Ire. 32/C3
Ferdinand, In, US 162/D1
Ferdinandshof, Ger. 43/G2
Ferdows, Iran 101/G2
Fère-Champenoise, Fr. 54/C6
Fère-en-Tardenois, Fr. 54/C5
Ferentillo, It. 65/B2
Ferentino, It. 65/C4
Ferento (ruin), It. 65/B3
Fereydūn Shahr, Iran 103/G3
Fergus (riv.), Ire. 32/B4
Fergus, On, Can. 160/F3
Fergus Falls, Mn, US 156/F4
Ferguson (lake), Nun, Can. 140/F2
Ferguson, Ky, US 162/E2
Ferihegy (int'l arpt.), Hun. 50/D2
Ferkéssédougou, C.d'Iv. 114/D4
Ferlach, Aus. 45/L3
Ferland, On, Can. 157/K2
Ferland, Sk, Can. 145/L3
Ferland-et-Boilleau, Qu, Can. 158/B1
Ferlo (valley), Sen. 114/B3
Fermanagh (dist.), NI, UK 34/A3
Fermanville, Fr. 56/D1
Ferme-Neuve, Qu, Can. 161/J1
Fermeuse, Nf, Can. 159/L2
Fermi Nat'l Accelerator Lab., Il, US 167/P16
Fermignano, It. 63/F6
Fermin (pt.), Ca, US 166/F8
Fermo, It. 65/C1
Fermoselle, Sp. 46/B2
Fermoy, Ire. 32/B5
Fern Park, Fl, US 164/N6
Fern Ridge (lake), Or, US 146/B1
Fernán-Núñez, Sp. 46/C4
Fernández, Arg. 188/D3
Fernandina (isl.), Ecu. 184/J7
Fernandina Beach, Fl, US 165/H2
Fernando de la Mora, Par. 188/E3
Fernando de Noronha (isl.), Braz. 179/F3
Fernando Po (Bioko) (isl.), EqG. 120/B2
Fernandópolis, Braz. 189/G2
Ferndale, Ca, US 146/A3
Ferndale, Fl, US 164/M6
Ferndale, Md, US 168/B5
Ferndale, Mi, US 167/F7
Ferndale, Pa, US 161/G4
Ferndale, Wa, US 144/C3
Ferndown, Eng, UK 37/E5
Ferness, Sc, UK 33/C2
Ferney-Voltaire, Fr. 60/C5
Fernie, BC, Can. 144/G3
Fernley, Nv, US 146/D4
Fernpass (pass), Aus. 61/G3
Ferns, Ire. 32/D4
Ferntree Gully NP, Austl. 132/G5
Fernwood, Id, US 144/F4
Ferrandina, It. 48/E2
Ferrara, It. 63/E4
Ferrara (prov.), It. 63/E3
Ferrat (cape), Fr. 64/D5
Ferrat (cape), Alg. 112/E5
Ferreira do Alentejo, Port. 46/A3
Ferreira Gomes, Braz. 182/D2
Ferrell's Bridge (dam), Tx, US 153/G4
Ferrelo (cape), Or, US 146/A2
Ferreñafe, Peru 184/B2
Ferret (cape), Fr. 44/C4
Ferrette, Fr. 60/D3
Ferriday, La, US 164/C2
Ferriere, It. 62/C4
Ferrière-la-Grande, Fr. 54/D3
Ferrières, Belg. 55/E3
Ferris, Tx, US 150/L7
Ferrisburg, Vt, US 161/K2
Ferron, Ut, US 147/H4
Ferrum, Va, US 163/G2
Ferry Pass, Fl, US 164/E2
Ferryden, Sc, UK 33/D3
Ferryfield (int'l arpt.), Eng, UK 37/G5
Ferryhill, Eng, UK 35/G2
Ferryland, Nf, Can. 159/L2
Ferryside, Wal, UK 36/B3
Fershampenuaz, Rus. 69/N5
Ferté-Bernard, Fr. 57/F4
Fertile, Mn, US 156/F4
Fertő (Neusiedler) (lake), Aus. 45/M3
Ferwerd, Neth. 52/C2
Fès (prov.), Mor. 112/B3
Fès, Mor. 112/B2
Fesches-le-Châtel, Fr. 60/C2
Feshi, D.R. Congo 120/D4
Feshie (riv.), Sc, UK 33/C2
Fessenden, ND, US 156/E4
Fessenheim, Fr. 60/D2
Festival Centre, Austl. 131/M8
Festus, Mo, US 162/B1
Fet, Nor. 38/T8
Fetcham, Eng, UK 30/B3
Feteşti, Rom. 51/H3
Fethaland (pt.), Sc, UK 31/W13
Fethard, Ire. 32/C5
Fethard, Ire. 32/C5
Fethiye, Turk. 102/B2
Fetsund, Nor. 38/T8
Feucherolles, Fr. 30/H5
Feucht, Ger. 58/E4
Feuchtwangen, Ger. 58/D4
Feuilles (lake), Qu, Can. 141/J3
Feuilles, Rivière aux (riv.), Qu., Can. 139/K4
Feuquières, Fr. 54/A4
Feuquières-en-Vimeu, Fr. 54/A3
Feurs, Fr. 44/F4
Fevzipaşa, Turk. 104/E1
Feyẕābād, Afg. 99/B4
Feyzin, Fr. 64/A1
Fez (Saiss) (int'l arpt.), Mor. 112/B3
Fezzane (well), Niger 108/B4
Ffestiniog, Wal, UK 34/E6
Fiambalá, Arg. 188/C3
Fianarantsoa, Madg. 125/H8
Fianarantsoa (prov.), Madg. 125/H8
Fianga, Chad 116/B3
Fiano Romano, It. 65/B3
Fiastrone (riv.), It. 65/C1
Ficarolo, It. 63/E4
Fichē, Eth. 118/A3
Fichtelberg (peak), Ger. 59/F2
Fichtelgebirge (mts.), Ger. 42/F3
Fichtelnaab (riv.), Ger. 59/E3
Ficksburg, SAfr. 124/D3
Ficulle, It. 65/B2
Fidenza, It. 62/D4
Fié (riv.), Gui. 114/C4
Field (isl.), Austl. 128/D3
Field (riv.), Austl. 131/M9
Field, Ab, Can. 144/F2
Field, On, Can. 160/F1
Fieldon, Il, US 155/J4
Fields, La, US 164/B2
Fields, Or, US 146/D2
Fieni, Rom. 51/G3
Fier, Alb. 49/F2
Fier (riv.), Fr. 60/B6
Fierzë (lake), Alb. 49/G1
Fiesch, Swi. 60/E5
Fiesole, It. 63/E6
Fiesso, It. 63/F3
Fiesso Umbertiano, It. 63/E4
Fife (co.), Sc, UK 33/D4
Fife, Wa, US 167/C3
Fife, Ga, US 163/L7
Fife Ness (pt.), Sc, UK 33/D4
Fifield, Austl. 133/C1
Fifth Cataract (falls), Sudan 109/G5
Fiftysix, Ar, US 153/H3
Figalo (cape), Alg. 112/D2
Figari, Fr. 48/A2
Figeac, Fr. 44/E4
Figg (mt.), Austl. 128/D5
Figline Valdarno, It. 63/E6
Figtree, Zim. 123/F4
Figueira da Foz, Port. 46/A2
Figueres, Sp. 47/G1
Figuig, Mor. 111/E2
Figuig (prov.), Mor. 112/C3
Figuil, Camr. 116/B3
Fiherenana (riv.), Madg. 125/G8
Fijāj (lake), Tun. 66/F4
Fiji (ctry.) 137/Y17
Fik', Eth. 118/B3
Filabusi, Zim. 123/F4
Filadelfia, Col. 183/K7
Filadélfia, Braz. 183/E4
Filadelfia, Par. 188/D2
Filadelfia, Bol. 184/D3
Filandia, Col. 183/K8
Filattiera, It. 62/C5
Filchner Ice Shelf, Ant. 192/Y
File (hills), Sk, Can. 145/M2
Filer, Id, US 147/F2
Filey (bay), Eng, UK 35/H3
Filey, Eng, UK 35/H3
Filí, Gre. 49/N8
Filiaşi, Rom. 51/F3
Filiatái, Gre. 49/G3
Filiatrá, Gre. 49/G4
Filicudi (isl.), It. 48/D3
Filingué, Niger 115/F3
Filippiás, Gre. 49/G3
Fílippoi (ruin), Gre. 49/J2
Filipstad, Swe. 40/F2
Filisur, Swi. 61/F4
Fillière (riv.), Fr. 60/C6
Fillmore, Sk, Can. 156/C3
Fillmore, Ca, US 166/B2
Fillmore, Ut, US 149/F1
Fillmore, Mo, US 155/G3
Filo (mt.), Sam. 137/S9
Filomeno Mata, Mex. 175/M6
Filótion, Gre. 49/J4
Filottrano, It. 63/G7
Fils (riv.), Ger. 58/C5
Filsum, Ger. 53/E2
Filton, Eng, UK 36/D3
Fīltu, Eth. 118/B4
Fimi (riv.), D.R. Congo 120/D3
Fina, Rsv. de, Mali 114/C3
Finale Emilia, It. 63/E4
Finale Ligure, It. 62/B5
Fiñana, Sp. 46/D4
Fincastle, Va, US 163/H2
Finch, Mt, US 145/L4
Finch Hatton, Austl. 134/C3
Finchley (nbrhd.), Eng, UK 30/C2
Findel (int'l arpt.), Lux. 55/F4
Findhorn, Sc, UK 33/C1
Findhorn (riv.), Sc, UK 33/B2
Findlay, Oh, US 160/E4
Findlay, Il, US 155/K4
Findochty, Sc, UK 33/D1
Finesville, NJ, US 168/C2
Fingal, ND, US 156/F4
Fingal, Austl. 132/C4
Finger, Tn, US 162/C3
Finger Lakes, NY, US 161/H3
Fingest, Eng, UK 30/A2
Fíngoè, Moz. 123/F2
Finhaut, Swi. 60/C5
Finike, Turk. 104/B1
Finistère (dept.), Fr. 56/A4
Finisterre, Sp. 46/A1
Finisterre (cape), Sp. 46/A1
Finisterre (range), PNG 129/G1
Finjasjön (lake), Swe. 39/K6
Finke (riv.), Austl. 131/G3
Finke Gorge NP, Austl. 131/G3
Finkenwerder, Ger. 53/G1
Finksburg, Md, US 168/B5
Finland (ctry.) 38/H2
Finland (gulf), Eur. 74/C4
Finland, Mn, US 157/J4
Finlay (riv.), BC, Can. 140/D3
Finlay (mts.), Tx, US 150/B2
Finlayson, Mn, US 157/H4
Finley, Austl. 133/B2
Finley, ND, US 156/F4
Finley, Ok, US 153/G3
Finley, Tn, US 162/C2
Finley, Wa, US 144/E4
Finley NWR, Or, US 146/B1
Finn (riv.), Ire. 31/Q9
Finnegan, Ab, Can. 145/H2
Finnentrop, Ger. 53/E6
Finnigan (mt.), Austl. 134/B1
Finnis (cape), Austl. 131/G5
Finnmark (co.), Nor. 38/G1
Fino (riv.), It. 65/C2
Fino Mornasco, It. 62/C2
Fins, Oman 101/G4
Finschhafen, PNG 129/G1
Finsing, Ger. 59/E6
Finspång, Swe. 40/F2
Finsteraarhorn (peak), Swi. 60/E4
Finstown, Sc, UK 31/V14
Finström, Fin. 41/H1
Fintel, Ger. 53/G2
Fintona, NI, UK 34/A3
Fioio (riv.), It. 65/C4
Fionn Loch (lake), Sc, UK 33/A1
Fionnay, Swi. 60/D5
Fiora (riv.), It. 45/J5
Fiorano, It. 63/D4
Fiordland NP, NZ 135/A4
Fiorenzuola d'Arda, It. 62/C4
Fiori, Monte de (peak), It. 65/C2
Fīq, Syria 105/D3
Fircrest, Wa, US 167/C3
Fire Island Nat'l Seashore, NY, US 169/E2
Firebaugh, Ca, US 148/B2
Firebrand (pass), Mt, US 145/H3
Firenze (prov.), It. 63/E5
Firenze (Florence), It. 63/E6
Firenzuola, It. 63/E5
Firesteel (cr.), SD, US 154/E1
Firestone, Co, US 154/B3
Firmat, Arg. 190/E2
Firmi, Fr. 44/E4
Firminópolis, Braz. 186/C3
Firminy, Fr. 44/F4
Firozābād, India 96/B2
Firozpur, India 98/C4
First Cataract (falls), Egypt 109/G3
Firth, Id, US 147/G2
Firth of Forth (inlet), Sc, UK 33/C4
Firth of Lorn (inlet), Sc, UK 31/Q8
Firth of Tay (inlet), Sc, UK 33/C4
Firth of Thames (inlet), NZ 135/C2
Fīrūz Kūh, Iran 103/H3
Fīrūzābād, Iran 103/H4
Firyuza, Trkm. 101/G1
Fischa (riv.), Aus. 51/P7
Fischach, Ger. 61/G1
Fischamend Markt, Aus. 51/P7
Fischbacher Alpen (mts.), Aus. 45/L3
Fischbek, Ger. 53/G2
Fischen im Allgäu, Ger. 61/G3
Fisenge, Zam. 123/F2
Fish (riv.), Namb. 122/C5
Fish Camp, Ca, US 148/C2
Fishburn, Eng, UK 35/G2
Fisher, Austl. 131/F4
Fisher (bay), Mb, Austl. 156/F2
Fisher (mt.), BC, Can. 144/G3
Fisher (str.), Nun, Can. 141/H2
Fisher, Ar, US 162/B3
Fisher, Il, US 160/B4
Fisher, La, US 164/B2
Fisher, Mn, US 156/F4
Fisher, WV, US 163/H1
Fisher Bay, Mb, Can. 156/F2
Fisher Branch, Mb, Can. 156/F2
Fisherman (isl.), Austl. 134/F6
Fishermans Island Nat'l Wild. Ref., Va, US 163/K2
Fishers (isl.), NY, US 169/G1
Fishersville, Va, US 163/H1
Fishguard, Wal, UK 36/B3
Fishing (lake), Mb, Can. 157/G1
Fishing (cr.), NC, US 163/J2
Fisht (peak), Rus. 70/F4
Fishtoft, Eng, UK 35/J6
Fisk, Mo, US 162/B2
Fiske, Sk, Can. 145/K2
Fisksätra, Swe. 39/B1
Fismes, Fr. 54/C5
Fitchburg, Ma, US 161/L3
Fitchburg, Wi, US 155/K2
Fitful Head (pt.), Sc, UK 31/W14
Fitjar, Nor. 40/A2
Fittja, Swe. 39/A1
Fitton (mt.), Yk, Can. 171/L2
Fitz Roy, Arg. 190/D5
Fitzcarrald, Peru 184/D3
Fitzgerald, Ga, US 165/G2
Fitzgerald River NP, Austl. 130/C5
Fitzhugh, Ok, US 153/F3
Fitzroy (peak), Arg. 191/B6
Fitzroy, UK 191/F6
Fitzroy (riv.), Austl. 127/B2
Fitzroy Crossing, Austl. 128/B4
Fitzwilliam (isl.), On, Can. 160/E2
Fitzwilliam (str.), NW, Can. 141/R7
Fiuggi, It. 65/C4
Fiume Veneto, It. 63/F2
Fiumicino, It. 65/B4
Five Forks, Ga, US 163/M7
Five Islands, NS, Can. 158/E3
Five Sisters (peak), Sc, UK 33/A2
Fivemile (cr.), Wy, US 147/J2
Fivemiletown, NI, UK 34/A3
Fivizzano, It. 62/D5
Fizi, D.R. Congo 121/G4
Fizuli, Azer. 71/H5
Fjell, Nor. 40/A1
Fjellstrand, Nor. 38/S8
Fjerritslev, Den. 40/C3
Fjugesta, Swe. 40/F2
Flå, Nor. 40/C1
Flachslanden, Ger. 58/D4
Flackwell Heath, Eng, UK 30/A2
Fladungen, Ger. 58/D1
Flagler, Co, US 154/C4
Flagler Beach, Fl, US 165/H3
Flagler Museum, Fl, US 164/P9
Flagpole (peak), Tn, US 162/E2
Flagstaff, Az, US 149/G3
Flagstaff (lake), Or, US 146/D2
Flåm, Nor. 40/B1
Flambeau (riv.), Wi, US 157/J5
Flamborough Head (pt.), Eng, UK 35/H3
Flamborough, Eng, UK 35/H3
Flamborough, On, Can. 160/T9
Fläming (hills), Ger. 42/G2
Flaming Gorge (dam), Ut, US 147/J3
Flaming Gorge (res.), Ut.,Wy, US 147/J3
Flaming Gorge NRA, Wy, US 147/J3
Flamingo, Fl, US 165/H5
Flamingo Field (int'l arpt.), NAnt. 180/D1
Flanagan (riv.), On, Can. 157/H1
Flanders (reg.), Belg.,Fr. 54/B2
Flanders, NY, US 169/F2
Flandes, Col. 183/L8
Flandreau, SD, US 155/F1
Flärdlång (isl.), Swe. 39/B1
Flasher, ND, US 156/D4
Flat (mt.), NZ 135/A4
Flat Bay, Nf, Can. 159/H1
Flat Creek, Yk, Can. 171/L3
Flat Holm (isl.), Eng, UK 36/C4
Flat River, Mo, US 162/B2
Flat Rock, Mi, US 160/E3
Flat Rock, NC, US 163/G2
Flatbush (nbrhd.), NY, US 169/K9
Flateby, Nor. 38/T8
Flathead (lake), Mt, US 145/H4
Flathead (range), Mt, US 145/H3
Flathead (riv.), Mt, US 144/G4
Flathead Indian Res., Mt, US 144/G4
Flathead, South Fork (riv.), Mt, US 145/H4
Flatiron (mtn.), Id, US 147/G1
Flatonia, Tx, US 151/F3
Flattery (cape), Austl. 134/B1
Flattery (cape), Wa, US 142/A2
Flatwillow (cr.), Mt, US 145/K4
Flatwoods, La, US 164/B2
Flatwoods, Ky, US 163/F1
Flavio Alfaro, Ecu. 180/B5
Flawil, Swi. 61/F3
Flaxcombe, Sk, Can. 145/K2
Flaxlanden, Fr. 60/D2
Flayosc, Fr. 64/C5
Fleet, Eng, UK 37/F4
Fleet, Ab, Can. 145/J1
Fleetwood, Eng, UK 35/E4
Fleetwood, Pa, US 168/C3
Flekkefjord, Nor. 40/B2
Fleming, Sk, Can. 156/D2
Fleming, Co, US 154/C3
Fleming-Neon, Ky, US 163/F2
Flemingsberg, Swe. 39/A1
Flemingsburg, Ky, US 162/F1
Flemington, Mo, US 153/H2
Flemington, NJ, US 168/D2
Flemington Racecourse, Austl. 132/F5
Flemish Brabant (prov.), Belg. 55/D2
Flen, Swe. 40/G2
Flensburg, Ger. 40/C4
Flero, It. 62/D3
Fleron, Belg. 55/E2
Flers, Fr. 57/E3
Flesher (pass), Mt, US 145/H4
Flesk (riv.), Ire. 32/A5
Flesland (int'l arpt.), Nor. 40/A1
Fletcher, Ok, US 153/E3
Fletcher (pond), Mi, US 160/E2
Fletcher, NC, US 163/F3
Fletschhorn (peak), Swi. 60/D5
Fleurance, Fr. 44/D5
Fleurier, Swi. 60/C4
Fleurus, Belg. 55/D3
Fleury-les-Aubrais, Fr. 57/G5
Fleury-sur-Andelle, Fr. 57/G2
Fleury-sur-Orne, Fr. 57/E2
Flevoland (isl.), Neth. 42/C2
Flevoland (prov.), Neth. 52/C4
Flexenpass (pass), Aus. 61/G3
Flieden, Ger. 58/C2
Flieden (riv.), Ger. 58/C2
Fliess, Aus. 61/G3
Flimby, Eng, UK 34/E2
Flims, Swi. 61/F4
Flin Flon, Mb, Can. 140/F3
Flinders (range), Austl. 131/H5
Flinders (bay), Austl. 130/B5
Flinders (isl.), Austl. 127/D4
Flinders (riv.), Austl. 127/D2
Flinders Chase NP, Austl. 131/H5
Flinders Ranges (mts.), Austl. 127/C4
Flinders Ranges NP, Austl. 131/H4
Flinders Reefs (isls.), Austl. 134/C2
Flinders Reefs (reef), Austl. 129/H4
Flines-lez-Raches, Fr. 54/C3
Flint (lake), Nun, Can. 141/J2
Flint (isl.), Kiri. 137/K6
Flint, Wal, UK 35/E5
Flint (riv.), Ga, US 163/M8
Flint (hills), Ks, US 153/F2
Flint, Mi, US 160/E3
Flint City, Al, US 162/D3
Flint Hills Nat'l Wild. Ref., Ks, US 155/G4
Flint, South Branch (riv.), Mi, US 167/F5
Flintbek, Ger. 40/D4
Flinton, On, Can. 161/H2
Flintshire (co.), Wal, UK 35/E5
Flippen, Ga, US 163/M8
Flisa, Nor. 40/E1
Flitwick, Eng, UK 37/F2
Flix, Sp. 47/F2
Flixecourt, Fr. 54/B3
Flize, Fr. 55/D4
Flo, Tx, US 151/G2
Floby, Swe. 40/E2
Floda, Swe. 40/E3
Flodden, Eng, UK 33/D5
Flögelner See (riv.), Ger. 53/F1
Flöha (riv.), Ger. 43/G3
Floing, Fr. 55/D4
Flomaton, Al, US 164/E2
Flonheim, Ger. 58/B3
Flora (mt.), Austl. 130/C2
Flora, Nor. 38/C3
Flora, Il, US 162/C1
Flora, In, US 160/C4
Flora, La, US 164/B2
Flora, Ms, US 162/B4
Flora, Phil. 88/C1
Flora (mtn.), Wa, US 144/D3
Flora Vista, NM, US 149/H2
Floral, Ar, US 153/J3
Floral City, Fl, US 164/L6
Floral Park, NY, US 169/L9
Florala, Al, US 165/E2
Florange, Fr. 55/F5
Florânia, Braz. 183/G4
Floraville, Austl. 129/E4
Floreffe, Belg. 55/D3
Florence (Firenze), It. 63/E6
Florence, Al, US 162/D3
Florence, Ar, US 153/J4
Florence, Az, US 149/G4
Florence, Co, US 152/B1
Florence, Ks, US 153/F1
Florence, Ky, US 162/E1
Florence, Ms, US 162/B4
Florence, Mt, US 145/G4
Florence, Or, US 146/A2
Florence, SC, US 163/H3
Florence, SD, US 155/F1
Florence, Tx, US 151/F2
Florence, Wi, US 157/K5
Florence Junction, Az, US 149/G4
Florence Lake Nat'l Wild. Ref., ND, US 156/D4
Florence-Graham, Ca, US 166/F8
Florenceville, NB, Can. 158/D2
Florencia, Col. 180/C4
Florencia, Arg. 188/E4
Florennes, Belg. 55/D3
Florentino Ameghino, Arg. 190/D4
Florenton, Mn, US 157/H4
Florenville, Belg. 55/E4
Flores (isl.), Azor., Port. 47/R12
Flores, Braz. 183/G4
Flores, Guat. 176/D2
Flores (isl.), Indo. 77/M10
Flores (sea), Indo. 77/L10
Flores (dept.), Uru. 191/F2
Flores do Piauí, Braz. 183/F4
Flores, Arroyo de los (cr.), Arg. 190/E3
Floresta, Braz. 183/G5
Floreşti, Mol. 72/E4
Floresville, Tx, US 151/E3
Florham Park, NJ, US 169/H8
Floriano, Braz. 183/F4
Florianópolis, Braz. 189/G3
Florida, Bol. 184/D4
Florida, Bol. 188/D1
Florida, Col. 180/B4
Florida, Cuba 177/G1
Florida (str.), Cuba,US 143/K7
Florida, Hon. 176/D3
Florida, Peru 184/B2
Florida, Uru. 191/K11
Florida (dept.), Uru. 191/F2
Florida (state), US 165/F2
Florida (cape), Fl, US 164/P11
Florida, NY, US 168/D1
Florida City, Fl, US 165/H5
Florida Keys (isl.), Fl, US 165/H5
Florida Keys (isls.), Fl, US 139/J7
Florida Negra, Arg. 191/D6
Floridablanca, Col. 180/C3
Florida's Silver Springs, Fl, US 165/G3
Floridia, It. 48/D4
Florien, La, US 164/B2
Florin, Ca, US 167/M10
Flórina, Gre. 49/G2
Florissant, Mo, US 155/J4
Florissant Fossil Beds Nat'l Monument, Co, US 152/B1
Florissant Fossil Beds Nat'l Mon., Co, US 154/B4
Flörsbachtal, Ger. 58/C2
Flörsheim am Main, Ger. 58/B2
Flörsheim-Dalsheim, Ger. 58/B3
Florstadt, Ger. 58/B2
Flossenbürg, Ger. 59/F3
Flottsund, Swe. 39/A1
Flower Mound, Tx, US 150/K6
Floyd (riv.), Ia, US 155/F2
Floyd, Va, US 163/G2
Floyd, Ga, US 163/L7
Floydada, Tx, US 152/D4
Fluchthorn (peak), Aus. 61/G4
Flüelapass (pass), Swi. 61/F4
Flüelen, Swi. 61/E4
Fluessen (lake), Neth. 52/C3
Fluker, La, US 164/C2
Flume (riv.), Fr. 56/D4
Flums, Swi. 61/F3
Flushing, Mi, US 160/E3
Flushing (nbrhd.), NY, US 169/K8
Fluvanna, Tx, US 152/D4
Fly (riv.), PNG 129/F2
Fly River (delta), PNG 129/F2
Flying Fish (cape), Ant. 192/T
Fnjóská (riv.), Ice. 38/P6
Foam Lake, Sk, Can. 156/C2
Foard City, Tx, US 152/E4
Foča, Bosn. 50/D4
Fochabers, Sc, UK 33/C1
Fochville, SAfr. 124/P13
Fockbek, Ger. 40/C4
Focşani, Rom. 51/H3

Fuente – George
Map Section
228
229

Fuentes de Oñoro, Sp. 46/B2
Fuentesaúco, Sp. 46/C2
Fuerte (riv.), Mex. 174/C3
Fuerte Olimpo, Par. 188/E2
Fuerteventura (isl.), Canl., Sp. 110/B3
Fufang, China 87/H3
Fuga (isl.), Phil. 88/C1
Fuglebjerg, Den. 40/D4
Fugong, China 93/G2
Fugou, China 80/C4
Fuhai, China 99/E2
Fuhlsbüttel (Hamburg) (int'l arpt.), Ger. 53/G1
Fuhne (riv.), Ger. 42/F3
Fuhse (riv.), Ger. 53/H4
Fuji, Japan 85/F3
Fuji (riv.), Japan 85/F3
Fuji-Hakone-Izu NP, Japan 85/F3
Fuji-san (peak), Japan 85/F3
Fujian (prov.), China 87/H3
Fujieda, Japan 85/F3
Fujihashi, Japan 83/K4
Fujiidera, Japan 83/J6
Fujikawa, Japan 83/B3
Fujimi, Japan 83/D2
Fujino, Japan 83/C2
Fujinomiya, Japan 83/B3
Fujioka, Japan 85/F2
Fujioka, Japan 83/M5
Fujioka, Japan 83/D1
Fujisawa, Japan 85/F3
Fujishiro, Japan 83/E2
Fujiwara, Japan 83/K5
Fujiyoshida, Japan 85/F3
Fukagawa, Japan 82/C2
Fukang, China 99/E3
Fukaya, Japan 83/C1
Fukiage, Japan 83/C1
Fukuchiyama, Japan 83/H5
Fukue, Japan 84/A4
Fukue (isl.), Japan 79/K5
Fukui, Japan 84/E2
Fukui (pref.), Japan 84/E3
Fukuoka (pref.), Japan 84/B4
Fukuoka, Japan 84/B4
Fukuoka (int'l arpt.), Japan 84/B4
Fukuoka, Japan 83/M4
Fukuroi, Japan 85/E3
Fukushima, Japan 85/G2
Fukushima (pref.), Japan 85/F2
Fukushima, Japan 82/B3
Fukuyama, Japan 84/C3
Fulacunda, GBis. 114/B4
Fūlādī (mtn.), Afg. 101/J2
Fulbourn, Eng, UK 37/G2
Fulbright, Tx, US 153/G4
Fulda (riv.), Ger. 42/E3
Fulda, Ger. 58/C1
Fulda, Mn, US 155/G2
Fulford, Eng, UK 35/G4
Fuling, China 87/E2
Fullarton, Trin. 181/F2
Fullerton, La, US 164/B2
Fullerton, Ca, US 166/G8
Fullerton, Ne, US 154/F3
Fullerton (Whitehall), Pa, US 168/C2
Fully, Swi. 60/D5
Fulpmes, Aus. 61/H3
Fulton, Al, US 164/E2
Fulton, Ar, US 153/H4
Fulton (co.), Ga, US 163/M7
Fulton, Ky, US 162/C2
Fulton, Ks, US 153/G1
Fulton, Mo, US 153/J1
Fulton, Ms, US 162/C3
Fulton, NY, US 161/H3
Fulton, On, Can. 160/T9
Fulton, Tx, US 150/F3
Fultondale, Al, US 162/D4
Fulufjället (peak), Swe. 40/E1
Fuluo, China 87/F3
Fulwood, Eng, UK 35/F4
Fumaiolo (peak), It. 63/F6
Fumay, Fr. 55/D4
Fumel, Fr. 44/D4
Fumin, China 86/D3
Funabashi, Japan 83/D2
Funafuti (cap.), Tuv. 136/G5
Funafuti (isl.), Tuv. 136/G5
Funan, China 80/C4
Funchal (int'l arpt.), Port. 110/A2
Funchal, Port. 110/A2
Fundación, Col. 180/C2
Fundão, Port. 46/B2
Fundong, Camr. 115/H5
Fundy (bay), NB,NS, Can. 141/K4
Fundy NP, NB, Can. 158/E3
Funhalouro, Moz. 123/G4
Funing, China 80/D4
Funing, China 86/E4
Funshion (riv.), Ire. 32/B5
Funsi, Gha. 115/E4
Funston, Ga, US 165/G2
Funtua, Nga. 115/G4
Funza, Col. 183/L8
Fuorn, Pass dal (Ofenpass) (pass), Swi. 61/G4
Fuping, China 80/C3
Fuqiao, China 80/L8
Fuqū', Jor. 105/D6
Fuquan, China 93/J2
Fur (riv.), China 81/C2
Furan (riv.), Fr. 60/B6
Furancungo, Moz. 123/G2
Furano, Japan 82/C2
Fure (riv.), Fr. 64/B2
Fürfeld, Ger. 55/G4
Furmanov, Rus. 68/J4
Furmanovo, Kaz. 71/J2
Furnace, Sc, UK 33/A4
Furnas (res.), Braz. 179/E5
Furneaux Group (isls.), Austl. 127/D4
Fürstenau, Ger. 53/E3
Fürstenfeld, Aus. 50/C2
Fürstenfeldbruck, Ger. 58/E6
Fürstenwalde, Ger. 43/H2
Fürth, Ger. 58/B3
Furth, Ger. 59/F5
Fürth, Ger. 58/D4
Furth im Wald, Ger. 59/F4
Furtwangen im Schwarzwald, Ger. 60/E1
Furudal, Swe. 40/F1
Furukawa, Japan 82/B4
Furulund, Swe. 39/K7
Furusund, Swe. 39/B1
Fury and Hecla (str.), Nun, Can. 141/H2
Fusagasugá, Col. 183/L8
Fushan, China 80/B4
Fushan, China 80/E3
Fushi, China 87/H3
Fushi, China 87/F3
Fushu, China 87/H3
Fushun, China 81/B2
Fushun, China 86/E2
Fushuncheng, China 81/B2
Fusignano, It. 63/E5
Fusio, Swi. 61/E5
Fuso, Japan 83/L5
Fusong, China 79/K3
Fussa, Japan 83/C2
Füssen, Ger. 61/G2
Fusui, China 94/D1
Futaba, Japan 83/A2
Futaleufú, Chile 190/C4
Futami, Japan 83/L7
Futog, Serb. 50/D3
Futrono, Chile 190/B4
Futtsu, Japan 85/F3
Futuna (isl.), Wall. 136/H6
Fuveau, Fr. 64/B6
Fuwah, Egypt 113/B2
Fuxian (lake), China 93/H3
Fuxin, China 80/E2
Fuxin Monggolzu Zizhixian, China 80/E2
Fuxing, China 87/E2
Fuyang, China 80/C4
Fuyang, China 87/H4
Fuyi (riv.), China 87/F3
Fuyu, China 79/J2
Fuyu, China 79/J2
Fuyuan, China 86/E3
Fuyun, China 78/B2
Fuzhou, China 87/H3
Fuzhoucheng, China 81/A3
Fwamba, D.R. Congo 121/E4
Fyfield, Eng, UK 30/D1
Fyn (co.), Den. 40/D4
Fyn (isl.), Den. 40/D4
Fyne, Loch (inlet), Sc, UK 33/A5
Fyresdal, Nor. 40/C2
Fysingen (lake), Swe. 39/A1
Fyvie, Sc, UK 33/D2

G

Ga, Gha. 115/E4
Ga Vache (isl.), Haiti 177/H2
Gaalkacyo (Galcaio), Som. 118/C4
Gaast, Neth. 52/C2
Gabarus, NS, Can. 159/G3
Gabas (riv.), Fr. 44/C5
Gabbs, Nv, US 146/E4
Gabčíkovo, Slvk. 50/C2
Gabela, Ang. 120/C5
Gabes (gulf), Tun. 107/D1
Gabia, D.R. Congo 120/D4
Gabicce Mare, It. 63/F6
Gable End (pt.), NZ 135/D2
Gablingen, Ger. 58/D6
Gablitz, Aus. 51/N7
Gabon (riv.), Gabon 120/B2
Gabon (ctry.) 120/B3
Gaborone (cap.), Bots. 122/E5
Gaborone (Sir Seretse Khama) (int'l arpt.), Bots. 122/E5
Gabras, Sudan 117/E3
Gabriel (mt.), Ire. 32/A6
Gabriel Leyva Solano, Mex. 174/C3
Gabrovo, Bul. 51/G4
Gaby, It. 62/A1
Gacé, Fr. 57/F3
Gachsārān, Iran 103/G4
Gackle, ND, US 156/E4
Gacko, Bosn. 50/D4
Gădăbäy, Azer. 103/F1
Gādarwāra, India 96/B4
Gadmen, Swi. 61/E4
Gadrut, Azer. 71/H5
Gadsden, Az, US 148/E4
Gadsden, Al, US 162/D3
Gadstrup, Den. 39/J7
Gadzema, Zim. 123/F3
Gadzi, CAfr. 116/C4
Găeşti, Rom. 51/G3
Gaeta, It. 65/C5
Gaeta (gulf), It. 48/C2
Gafargaon, Bang. 97/H3
Gaferut (isl.), Micr. 136/D4
Gaffney, SC, US 163/G3
Gagal, Chad 116/B3
Gagarawa, Nga. 115/H3
Gagarin, Rus. 68/G5
Gage, Ok, US 152/E2
Gage, NM, US 149/H4
Gagetown, NB, Can. 158/D3
Gagetown, Mi, US 160/E3
Gaggenau, Ger. 58/B5
Gaggio Montano, It. 63/D5
Gaglianico, It. 62/B2
Gagnoa, C.d'Iv. 114/D5
Gagny, Fr. 30/K5
Gagra, Geo. 70/G4
Gagret, India 98/D4
Gahanna, Oh, US 160/E4
Gahnpa, Libr. 114/C5
Gai Xian, China 81/B2
Gaibandha, Bang. 97/G3
Gaichtpass (pass), Aus. 61/G3
Gaidain'goinba, China 78/D4
Gail (riv.), Aus. 45/K3
Gail (riv.), It. 50/A2
Gail, Tx, US 150/D1
Gaildorf, Ger. 58/C5
Gaillac, Fr. 44/D5
Gaillefontaine, Fr. 57/G1
Gaillon, Fr. 57/G2
Gailtaler (mts.), Aus. 45/K3
Gaiman, Arg. 190/D4
Gaimersheim, Ger. 59/E5
Gainesboro, Tn, US 162/E2
Gainesville, Al, US 162/C4
Gainesville, Fl, US 165/G3
Gainesville, Ga, US 162/F3
Gainesville, Mo, US 153/H2
Gainesville, Tx, US 153/F4
Gainford, Eng, UK 35/G2
Gainsborough, Sk, Can. 156/D3
Gainsborough, Eng, UK 35/H5
Gairdner (lake), Austl. 127/C4
Gairezi (riv.), Zim. 123/G3
Gairn (riv.), Sc, UK 33/C2
Gais, Swi. 61/F3
Gaiserwald, Swi. 61/F3
Gaithersburg, Md, US 163/J1
Gaizina (peak), Lat. 41/L3
Gājol, India 97/G3
Gakarosa (peak), SAfr. 124/C2
Gakem, Nga. 115/H5
Gakona, Ak, US 171/J3
Gal Oya NP, SrL. 95/D5
Gala, China 97/G1
Galan (peak), Arg. 188/C3
Galana (riv.), Kenya 119/B2
Galand, Iran 103/H2
Galanga, Ang. 122/B2
Galangue, Ang. 122/C2
Galapagar, Sp. 47/M8
Galápagos (isls.), Ecu. 184/J6
Galápagos (dept.), Ecu. 184/J7
Galápagos, PN, Ecu. 184/J7
Galār, India 98/C3
Galashiels, Sc, UK 33/D5
Galaţi (prov.), Rom. 51/H3
Galaţi, Rom. 51/J3
Galatina, It. 49/F2
Galatiní, Gre. 49/G2
Galátista, Gre. 49/H2
Galatone, It. 49/F2
Galaure (riv.), Fr. 64/A2
Galax, Va, US 163/G2
Galb Azefal (hill), WSah. 110/B5
Galbally, Ire. 32/B5
Galbiate, It. 62/C2
Galcaio (Gaalkacyo), Som. 118/C4
Galdácano, Sp. 46/D1
Gáldar, Sp. 110/B3
Galeana, Mex. 175/E3
Galela, Indo. 91/G3
Galena, Ak, US 171/G3
Galena (peak), Id, US 147/F2
Galena, Il, US 155/J2
Galena, Ks, US 153/G2
Galena, Md, US 168/C5
Galena, Mo, US 153/H2
Galena Bay, BC, Can. 144/F2
Galena Park, Tx, US 151/M9
Galeota (pt.), Trin. 181/F2
Galera (pt.), Trin. 181/F2
Galera (pt.), Ecu. 180/A4
Galera (pt.), Chile 190/B3
Galesburg, Il, US 155/J3
Galeton, Pa, US 161/H4
Galey (riv.), Ire. 32/A5
Galga (riv.), Hun. 51/R9
Galgamácsa, Hun. 51/R9
Galgorm, NI, UK 34/B2
Gali, Geo. 71/G4
Gali Jāgīr, Pak. 98/B3
Galich, Rus. 68/J4
Galicia (reg.), Sp. 66/A2
Galičica NP, FYROM 49/G2
Galičica NP, Alb. 50/E5
Gālīkash, Iran 103/H2
Galilee (reg.), Isr. 105/C3
Galileo Galilei (int'l arpt.), It. 62/D6
Galim, Camr. 116/B4
Galinakopf (peak), Aus. 61/F3
Galinda, Ang. 120/C5
Galion, Oh, US 160/E4
Galiuro (mts.), Az, US 149/G4
Galiwinku, Austl. 129/D3
Gallan Head (pt.), Sc, UK 31/Q7
Gallarate, It. 62/B2
Gallardon, Fr. 57/G3
Gallatin (riv.), Mt, US 147/H1
Gallatin, Mo, US 155/H4
Gallatin, Tn, US 162/D2
Gallatin Gateway, Mt, US 147/H1
Gallegos (riv.), Arg. 191/C6
Galleguillos, Chile 188/B3
Galley Head (pt.), Ire. 32/B6
Galleyend, Eng, UK 30/E1
Galliano, La, US 164/C3
Galliate, It. 62/B3
Gallicano, It. 62/D5
Galliera Veneta, It. 63/E2
Gallina, NM, US 149/J2
Gallinas (pt.), Col. 180/D1
Gallinas (riv.), NM, US 152/B3
Gallinas (mts.), NM, US 149/J3
Gallion, Al, US 162/D4
Gallipoli, It. 49/E2
Gallipoli (pen.), Turk. 67/K2
Gallipolis, Oh, US 163/F1
Gällivare, Swe. 38/G2
Gallneukirchen, Aus. 59/H6
Gallo (lake), It. 61/G4
Gallo (cape), It. 48/C3
Galloway, Wi, US 155/K1
Gallspach, Aus. 59/G6
Galluis, Fr. 30/H5
Gallup, NM, US 149/H3
Gallur, Sp. 46/E2
Gally (riv.), Fr. 30/H5
Gålö (isl.), Swe. 39/B1
Gal'on, Isr. 105/B5
Galston, Sc, UK 33/B5
Galston (nbrhd.), Austl. 134/H8
Galston, Austl. 133/E1
Galt, Ca, US 146/C4
Galten, Den. 40/C3
Galty (mts.), Ire. 32/B5
Galtymore (peak), Ire. 32/B5
Galva, Ks, US 153/F1
Galva, Il, US 155/J3
Galvarino, Chile 190/B3
Galveston, Tx, US 151/N9
Galveston (bay), Tx, US 151/N9
Galveston (co.), Tx, US 151/M9
Galveston (isl.), Tx, US 151/G3
Gálvez, Sp. 46/C3
Gálvez, Arg. 188/D5
Galway, Ire. 32/A3
Galway (bay), Ire. 31/P10
Galway (co.), Ire. 32/B3
Galway (Carnmore) (arpt.), Ire. 32/B3
Galzignano, It. 63/E3
Gam (riv.), Viet. 93/J3
Gamaches, Fr. 54/A4
Gamagara (riv.), SAfr. 124/C2
Gamagōri, Japan 83/M6
Gamarra, Col. 180/C2
Gamay, Phil. 88/D2
Gamba, China 97/G1
Gamba, D.R. Congo 121/F4
Gamba, Gabon 120/B3
Gambaga, Gha. 115/E4
Gambaga Scarp (cliff), Gha. 115/E4
Gambais, Fr. 30/H5
Gambang, Malay. 89/C2
Gambara, It. 62/D3
Gambat, Pak. 92/A2
Gambatesa, It. 65/D5
Gambēla, Eth. 117/G3
Gambell, Ak, US 171/D3
Gambella NP, Eth. 117/G3
Gambellara, It. 63/E3
Gamber, Md, US 168/B5
Gambettola, It. 63/F5
Gambia (riv.), Afr. 114/A3
Gambia (ctry.) 114/B3
Gambier (cape), Austl. 128/C2
Gambier (isls.), FrPol. 137/M7
Gambier, Oh, US 160/E4
Gámbita, Col. 180/C3
Gambo, Nf, Can. 159/K1
Gambolò, It. 62/B3
Gamboma, Congo 120/C3
Gamboula, CAfr. 116/B4
Gambsheim, Fr. 58/A5
Gameleira, Braz. 183/H5
Gamerco, NM, US 149/H3
Gamewell, NC, US 163/G3
Gaming, Aus. 45/L3
Gamka (riv.), SAfr. 124/C4
Gamkab (riv.), Namb. 124/B3
Gamleby, Swe. 40/G3
Gamlingay, Eng, UK 37/F2
Gammel Ølstykke, Den. 39/J7
Gammelstad, Swe. 68/D2
Gammertingen, Ger. 61/F1
Gammon Ranges NP, Austl. 131/H4
Gamo, Japan 83/K5
Gamo Gofa (pol. reg.), Eth. 117/H4
Gampaha, SrL. 95/C5
Gampern, Aus. 59/G7
Gamtog, China 86/C2
Gamud (peak), Eth. 118/A4
Gan, Fr. 44/C5
Gan (riv.), China 79/J1
Gan Gan, Arg. 190/C4
Gan Hashlosha NP, Isr. 105/C4
Ganado, Tx, US 151/F3
Gananoque, On, Can. 161/H2
Ganāveh, Iran 103/G4
Ganbashao, China 87/E3
Găncă, Azer. 71/H4
Gancheng, China 94/E2
Ganda, Ang. 122/B2
Gandajika, D.R. Congo 121/E4
Gandak (riv.), India 97/E2
Gandaki (zone), Nepal 96/D1
Gandara, Phil. 88/D2
Gāndarbal, India 98/C2
Gandarinha, Ang. 122/C1
Gandelin (riv.), Fr. 57/F5
Gander (lake), Nf, Can. 159/K1
Gander, Nf, Can. 159/K1
Ganderkesee, Ger. 53/F2
Gandesa, Sp. 47/F2
Gāndhi Sāgar (res.), India 92/B3
Gāndhīdhām, India 101/K4
Gāndhinagar, India 101/K4
Gandía, Sp. 47/E3
Gandino, It. 62/C2
Gandisê (mts.), China 97/E1
Gandjo, D.R. Congo 121/G3
Gandoca-Manzanillo Nat'l Wild. Ref., CR 177/F4
Gandy, Ut, US 147/G4
Ganeb (well), Mrta. 114/C2
Ganesh (mtn.), China 97/E1
Ganeshganj, India 92/C2
Gang, China 99/F4
Gang Ranch, BC, Can. 144/C2
Ganga (Ganges) (riv.), India 96/B1
Gānga Sāgar, India 97/G5
Gangala-Na-Bodio, D.R. Congo 116/D5
Gangāpur, India 92/C2
Gangara, Niger 115/H3
Gangārāmpur, India 97/G3
Gangaw, Myan. 86/B4
Gangca, China 78/E4
Gangdisê (mts.), China 99/D5
Gangelt, Ger. 55/F2
Ganges (riv.), Asia 77/A5
Ganges, BC, Can. 144/C3
Ganges, Fr. 44/E5
Ganges (Ganga) (riv.), India 96/B1
Ganges, Mouths of the (delta), India,Bang. 92/E3
Gangi, It. 48/D4
Gangkofen, Ger. 59/F6
Gango (riv.), Ang. 120/C5
Gangoh, India 98/D5
Gangtok, India 97/G2
Gangtou, China 87/H3
Ganjām, India 95/E2
Ganjingzi, China 81/A3
Ganløse, Den. 39/J7
Ganluo, China 93/H2
Ganmain, Austl. 133/C2
Gann Valley, SD, US 154/E1
Gannan, China 79/J2
Gannat, Fr. 44/E3
Gannett (peak), Wy, US 147/J2
Ganquan, China 80/B3
Gansbaai, SAfr. 124/L11
Gänserndorf, Aus. 51/P7
Gansu (prov.), China 78/D4
Gantheaume (pt.), Austl. 128/A4
Gantrisch (peak), Swi. 60/D4
Gantsevichi, Bela. 70/C1
Gantt, Al, US 165/E2
Gantt, SC, US 163/F3
Ganxitang, China 87/F3
Ganye, Nga. 116/A3
Ganyesa, SAfr. 124/D2
Ganyu, China 80/D4
Ganyushkino, Kaz. 71/J3
Ganzhou, China 87/G3
Ganzlin, Ger. 42/G2
Ganzourgou (prov.), Burk. 115/E3
Gao, Niger 115/G3
Gao, Mali 115/E2
Gao (pol. reg.), Mali 115/F2
Gao, D.R. Congo 121/G2
Gao Xian, China 86/E2
Gao'an, China 87/G2
Gaobei, China 87/G3
Gaocheng, China 80/C3
Gaochun, China 80/D5
Gaojian, China 87/J2
Gaolan (isl.), China 87/G4
Gaolan, China 78/E4
Gaoligong (mts.), Myan. 86/C3
Gaoling, China 81/A4
Gaomi, China 80/D3
Gaomutang, China 87/F3
Gaoping, China 80/C4
Gaoqiao, China 80/L8
Gaoqing, China 80/D3
Gaoqitou, China 87/F2
Gaor Bheinn (Gulvain) (peak), Sc, UK 33/A3
Gaotai, China 78/D4
Gaotang, China 80/D3
Gaotian, China 87/H3
Gaoua, Burk. 114/E4
Gaoual, Gui. 114/B4
Gaoxingxu, China 87/G3
Gaoyang, China 80/C3
Gaoyi, China 80/C3
Gaoyou (lake), China 79/H5
Gaoyou, China 80/D4
Gaozhou, China 87/F4
Gap, Fr. 64/C3
Gap, Pa, US 168/B4
Gap Mills, WV, US 163/G2
Gapeau (riv.), Fr. 64/B6
Gar, China 99/C5
Gar (riv.), China 78/C5
Gara (lake), Ire. 32/B2
Garabogazköl, Trkm. 71/K4
Garabogazköl (gulf), Trkm. 74/F5
Garacad, Som. 118/D4
Garachiné, Pan. 180/B2
Garachiné (pt.), Pan. 177/G4
Garah, Austl. 132/D1
Garai (riv.), Bang. 92/E3
Garaina, PNG 129/G1
Garajonay, PN de, Sp. 110/A3
Garalo, Mali 114/D4
Garamba, PN de la, D.R. Congo 117/F4
Garancières, Fr. 54/A6
Garango, Burk. 115/E4
Garanhuns, Braz. 183/G5
Garba, CAfr. 116/D3
Garba Tula, Kenya 119/B1
Garbahaarrey, Som. 118/B5
Garber, Ok, US 153/F2
Garberville, Ca, US 146/B3
Garbsen, Ger. 53/G4
Garça, Braz. 189/G2
Garças, Rio das (riv.), Braz. 186/B3
Garching an der Alz, Ger. 59/F6
Garcia, Co, US 152/B2
Garcia de Sota (res.), Sp. 46/C3
Gard (dept.), Fr. 64/A4
Gard (riv.), Fr. 66/E1
Garda, It. 63/D2
Garda (lake), It. 65/F1
Gardabani, Geo. 71/H4
Gardanne, Fr. 64/B6
Gardar, ND, US 156/F3
Gardelegen, Ger. 42/F2
Garden (isl.), Austl. 130/K7
Garden (pen.), Mi, US 157/L5
Garden (isl.), Mi, US 160/D2
Garden, Mi, US 160/C2
Garden (riv.), On, Can. 160/E1
Garden City, Ga, US 163/G4
Garden City, Id, US 146/E2
Garden City, Ks, US 152/D2
Garden City, Mi, US 167/F7
Garden City, Mo, US 153/G1
Garden City, NY, US 169/L9
Garden City, SD, US 154/F1
Garden City, Tx, US 150/D2
Garden City Beach, SC, US 163/H4
Garden City Park, NY, US 169/L9
Garden Grove, Ca, US 166/G8
Garden Grove, Fl, US 164/L7
Garden Grove, Ia, US 155/H3
Garden Valley, Id, US 146/F1
Garden View, Pa, US 168/A1
Gardena, Ca, US 166/F8
Gardendale, Al, US 162/D4
Gardenstown, Sc, UK 33/D1
Gardenton, Mb, Can. 156/F3
Gardēz, Afg. 101/J2
Gardhīwāla, India 98/C4
Gardi, Ga, US 165/H2
Gardiner (dam), Sk, Can. 145/L2
Gardiner, Mt, US 147/H1
Gardiner, Or, US 146/A2
Gardiner, Wa, US 167/B1
Gardiners (isl.), NY, US 169/F1
Gardiners (bay), NY, US 169/F1
Gardner, Ks, US 153/G1
Gardner, Il, US 160/B4
Gardner (lake), Me, US 158/D3
Gardner, Ma, US 161/L3
Gardner, Fl, US 165/H4
Gardner (mtn.), Wa, US 144/D3
Gardner (Nikumaroro) (isl.), Kiri. 137/H5
Gardone val Trompia, It. 62/D2
Gare Favre, Congo 120/C4
Gare Girard, Congo 120/C4
Gare Loch (inlet), Sc, UK 33/B4
Gareat el Tarf (salt pan), Alg. 112/K7
Garelochhead, Sc, UK 33/B4
Garéoult, Fr. 64/C6
Garessio, It. 62/B5
Garet el Djenoun (peak), Alg. 111/G4
Garfield, Ks, US 152/E1
Garfield, NJ, US 169/J8
Garfield (lake), Fl, US 164/M8
Garfield (mtn.), Mt, US 147/G1
Garfield, NM, US 149/J4
Garfield, Ga, US 163/F4
Garfield, Tx, US 151/F2
Garfield, Wa, US 144/F4
Gärflotta (isl.), Swe. 39/A2
Garforth, Eng, UK 35/G4
Gargaliánoi, Gre. 49/G4
Gargan (peak), Fr. 44/D4
Gargas, Fr. 64/B5
Gargenville, Fr. 54/A6
Garges-lès-Gonesse, Fr. 30/K5
Gargnano, It. 63/D2
Gargrave, Eng, UK 35/F4
Gargždai, Lith. 41/J4
Garh Mahārāja, Pak. 98/A4
Garhākotā, India 96/B4
Garhbeta, India 97/F4
Garhchiroli, India 95/C1
Garhi, India 96/C4
Garhmuktesar, India 96/B1
Garhshankar, India 98/D4
Garibaldi, Braz. 189/G4
Garibaldi, Or, US 144/C5
Garibaldi, BC, Can. 144/C3
Garies, SAfr. 124/B3
Garigliano (riv.), It. 65/C5
Garioch (reg.), Sc, UK 33/D2
Garissa, Kenya 119/B2
Garland, Mb, Can. 156/D2
Garland, Ks, US 153/G2
Garland, Tx, US 150/L7
Garland, NC, US 163/H3
Garlandville, Ms, US 162/C4
Garlasco, It. 62/B3
Garliava, Lith. 41/K4
Garlieston, Sc, UK 34/D2
Garmeh, Iran 103/J2
Garmisch-Partenkirchen, Ger. 61/H3
Garmouth, Sc, UK 33/C1
Garmsār, Iran 103/H3
Garmuda, Eth. 118/C4
Garneill, Mt, US 145/K4
Garner, Ia, US 155/H2
Garner, NC, US 163/H3
Garneton, Zam. 123/F2
Garnett, Ks, US 153/G1
Garnett, SC, US 163/G4
Garnish, Nf, Can. 159/K2
Garnpung (lake), Austl. 132/B2
Garonne (riv.), Fr. 66/D1
Garoowe, Som. 118/D3
Garopaba, Braz. 189/G4
Garou (lake), Mali 115/E2
Garoua, Camr. 116/B3
Garoua (int'l arpt.), Camr. 116/B3
Garoua Boulaï, Camr. 116/B4
Garphyttan, Swe. 40/F2
Garraf (mts.), Sp. 47/K7
Garreg, Wal, UK 34/D6
Garrel, Ger. 53/F3
Garretson, SD, US 155/F2
Garrett, In, US 160/D4
Garrett, Tx, US 151/F1
Garrett, Wy, US 154/B2
Garrison, Mo, US 153/H2
Garrison, Mn, US 157/H4
Garrison, ND, US 156/D4
Garrison (dam), ND, US 156/D4
Garrison, Ky, US 163/F1
Garrison, Mt, US 145/H4
Garrison, Tx, US 151/G2
Garrison, Ut, US 147/F4
Garron (pt.), NI, UK 34/C1
Garrovillas, Sp. 46/B3
Garry (lake), Sc, UK 33/B2
Garry (riv.), Sc, UK 33/A2
Garry (bay), Nun, Can. 141/H2
Garry (lake), Nun, Can. 140/F2
Gars am Inn, Ger. 59/F6
Gars am Kamp, Aus. 43/H4
Garsen, Kenya 119/C2
Garstang, Eng, UK 35/F4
Garsten, Aus. 59/H6
Garte (riv.), Ger. 53/H6
Gartempe (riv.), Fr. 44/D3
Garth, Wal, UK 36/C2
Gartmore, Sc, UK 33/B4
Gärtringen, Ger. 58/B5
Garut, Indo. 89/D4
Garvagh, NI, UK 34/B2
Garwa, India 96/D3
Garwolin, Pol. 43/L3
Garwood, NJ, US 169/H9
Garwood, Tx, US 150/F3
Gary, In, US 160/C4
Gary, SD, US 155/F1
Gary, Tx, US 151/G1
Gary, WV, US 163/G2
Garyarsa, China 99/D5
Garyi, China 86/C2
Garyville, La, US 164/C2
Garz, Ger. 40/E4
Garza García, Mex. 175/E3
Garzê, China 86/D2
Garzón, Col. 180/C4
Gas, Fr. 30/G6
Gas (lake), China 99/F4
Gas City, In, US 160/D4
Gas-san (peak), Japan 82/B4
Gasa, Bhu. 97/G2
Gæsafjöll (peak), Ice. 38/P6
Gasan, Phil. 88/C2
Gaschurn, Aus. 61/G4
Gasconade (riv.), Mo, US 155/J4
Gasconde (riv.), Mo, US 153/H2
Gascony (reg.), Fr. 66/D2
Gascoyne (mt.), Austl. 130/C3
Gascoyne (riv.), Austl. 127/A3
Gascoyne Junction, Austl. 130/B3
Gash (riv.), Erit. 117/H2
Gashaka, Nga. 116/A4
Gasheng, India 86/B2
Gasny, Fr. 57/G2
Gaspar (str.), Indo. 90/C4
Gaspard (riv.), BC, Can. 144/C2
Gasparilla (isl.), Fl, US 165/G4
Gaspé, Qu, Can. 158/E1
Gaspé (bay), Qu, Can. 158/E1
Gaspé (pen.), Qu, Can. 141/K4
Gaspoltshofen, Aus. 59/G6
Gasport, NY, US 160/V9
Gassin, Fr. 64/C6
Gassino Torinese, It. 62/A2
Gassville, Ar, US 153/H2
Gastins, Fr. 30/M6
Gaston, NC, US 163/J2
Gaston (lake), NC, US 163/H2
Gastonia, Tx, US 150/L7
Gastonia, NC, US 163/G3
Gastoúni, Gre. 49/G4
Gat, Isr. 105/B5
Gata (cape), Cyp. 104/C2
Gata (cape), Sp. 46/D4
Gata (mts.), Sp. 46/B2
Gata de Gorgos, Sp. 47/F3
Gatchina, Rus. 41/P2
Gate, Ok, US 152/D2
Gate City, Va, US 163/F2
Gatehouse-Of-Fleet, Sc, UK 34/D2
Gates, Or, US 146/B1
Gates of The Arctic NP and Prsv., Ak, US 171/G2
Gateshead (isl.), Nun, Can. 140/F1
Gateshead, Eng, UK 35/G2
Gateshead (co.), Eng, UK 35/G2
Gatesville, Tx, US 150/F2
Gatesville, NC, US 163/J2
Gateway, Co, US 149/H1
Gateway, Or, US 146/C1
Gateway NRA, NJ, US 169/K9
Gateway NRA, NJ, US 168/D2
Gathright (dam), Va, US 163/H2
Gaths Mine, Zim. 123/F4
Gatico, Chile 188/B2
Gatineau, Qu, Can. 161/J2
Gatineau (riv.), Qu, Can. 161/J1
Gatlinburg, Tn, US 163/F3
Gatow, Ger. 42/Q7
Gattendorf, Aus. 45/M2
Gatteville-le-Phare, Fr. 56/D1
Gattianara, It. 62/B2
Gatton, Austl. 134/D4
Gatún (lake), Pan. 177/G4
Gatún (dam), Pan. 177/G4
Gatvand, Iran 103/G3
Gatwick (int'l arpt.), Eng, UK 30/C3
Gau Algesheim, Ger. 58/B3
Gau Bischofsheim, Ger. 58/B3
Gau Odernheim, Ger. 58/B3
Gaubickelheim, Ger. 55/H4
Gauchy, Fr. 54/C4
Gaucín, Sp. 46/C4
Gauja (riv.), Est.,Lat. 41/L3
Gauja NP, Lat. 41/L3
Gaujiena, Lat. 41/M3
Gaukönigshofen, Ger. 58/C3
Gauley (riv.), WV, US 163/G1
Gaunless (riv.), Eng, UK 35/G2
Gaupne, Nor. 38/C3
Gaur (riv.), Sc, UK 33/B3
Gauri Sankar (peak), Nepal 97/F2
Gauripur, India 97/G2
Gaurnadi, Bang. 97/H4
Gause, Tx, US 151/F2
Gausta (peak), Nor. 40/C2
Gauteng (prov.), SAfr. 123/F5
Gauting, Ger. 59/E6
Gavà, Sp. 47/L7
Gavardo, It. 62/D2
Gavāter, Iran 101/H3
Gāvbandī, Iran 103/H5
Gávdhos (isl.), Gre. 67/K4
Gave de Pau (riv.), Fr. 47/E1
Gavel-Långsjön (lake), Swe. 39/B1
Gavere, Belg. 54/C2
Gāvgān, Iran 103/F2
Gavi, It. 62/B4
Gavião, Port. 46/B3
Gavins Point (dam), SD, US 154/F2
Gaviota, Ca, US 148/B3
Gavirate, It. 62/B2
Gävle, Swe. 40/G1
Gävleborg (co.), Swe. 38/E3
Gavray, Fr. 56/D3
Gawai, Myan. 86/C3
Gawler, Austl. 131/H5
Gawler Ranges (mts.), Austl. 127/C4
Gawso, Gha. 115/E5
Gaxun (lake), China 78/D3
Gay, Rus. 71/L2
Gay (peak), WV, US 163/G1
Gaya, Niger 115/F4
Gayā, India 97/E3
Gaya (riv.), China 79/K3
Gayam, Chad 116/C3
Gayaza, Ugan. 121/G3
Gaylegphug, Bhu. 97/H2
Gaylord, Ks, US 154/E4
Gaylord, Mi, US 160/D2
Gaylord, Mn, US 155/G1
Gayndah, Austl. 134/C4
Gayny, Rus. 69/M3
Gays Mills, Wi, US 155/J2
Gayville, SD, US 155/F2
Gaz, Iran 103/G3
Gaz-Achak, Trkm. 74/G5
Gaza (prov.), Moz. 123/G4
Gaza (Ghazzah), Gaza 105/A5
Gaza Strip, Gaza 105/A6
Gazanjyk, Trkm. 71/K5
Gazanjyk, Trkm. 103/H2
Gazaoua, Niger 115/G3
Gazelle, Ca, US 146/B3
Gazeran, Fr. 30/H6
Gaziantep, Turk. 102/D2
Gaziantep (prov.), Turk. 102/D2
Gaziköy, Turk. 51/H5
Gazimur (riv.), Rus. 79/H1
Gazipaşa, Turk. 104/C1
Gazon de Faing (peak), Fr. 60/D1
Gazzaniga, It. 62/C2
Gbadolite, D.R. Congo 116/D4
Gbangbatok, SLeo. 114/B5
Gbarnga, Libr. 114/C5
Gboko, Nga. 115/H5
Gbongan, Nga. 115/G5
Gd Res de Vioreau (res.), Fr. 56/D5
Gdansk (gulf), Pol. 68/C5
Gdańsk, Pol. 40/H4
Gdov, Rus. 41/M2
Gdynia, Pol. 40/H4
Ge (lake), China 80/D5
Geal Charn (peak), Sc, UK 33/C2
Geal Charn (peak), Sc, UK 33/A3
Geary, NB, Can. 158/D3
Geary, Ok, US 153/E3
Geashill, Ire. 32/C3
Geba Wenz (riv.), Eth. 117/G3
Gebaberg (peak), Ger. 58/D1
Gebe (isl.), Indo. 91/G3
Gebeit Mine, Sudan 109/H4
Gebhardshain, Ger. 55/G2
Gebilu, Eth. 118/B3
Gebiz, Turk. 104/B1
Gebra-Hainleite, Ger. 53/H6
Gebre Guracha, Eth. 118/A3
Gedara (Umm Qays) (ruin), Jor. 105/D3
Gede (peak), Indo. 89/D4
Gede, Kenya 119/C2
Gedera, Isr. 105/B5
Gedern, Ger. 58/C2
Gedi (riv.), Turk. 67/K3
Gedi Ruins Nat'l Mon., Kenya 119/B2
Gedikbulak, Turk. 103/E2
Gedinne, Belg. 55/D4
Gediz, Turk. 102/B2
Gediz (riv.), Turk. 102/A2
Gedlegubē, Eth. 118/C4
Gēdo, Eth. 117/H3
Gedser, Den. 40/D4
Gedser (cape), Den. 40/D4
Gedsted, Den. 40/C3
Geel, Belg. 55/E1
Geelong, Austl. 133/B4
Geelong West, Austl. 133/B4
Geelvink (chan.), Austl. 127/A3
Geertruidenberg, Neth. 52/B5
Geeste (riv.), Ger. 53/F1
Geeste, Ger. 53/E3
Geestemünde, Ger. 53/F1
Geesthacht, Ger. 53/H2
Geeveston, Austl. 132/C4
Gefrees, Ger. 59/E2
Gegeya Shet' (riv.), Eth. 118/A2
Gē'gyai, China 99/D5
Gehrde, Ger. 53/F3
Gehrden, Ger. 53/G4
Geidam, Nga. 116/A2
Geifas (peak), Wal, UK 36/C2
Geigar, Sudan 117/G3
Geikie (isl.), On, Can. 157/K2
Geikie (riv.), Sk, Can. 140/F3
Geikie Gorge NP, Austl. 128/B4
Geilenkirchen, Ger. 55/F2
Geilo, Nor. 40/C1
Geinō, Japan 83/K6
Geiselhöring, Ger. 59/F5
Geiselwind, Ger. 58/D3
Geisenfeld, Ger. 59/E5
Geisenhausen, Ger. 59/F6
Geisenheim, Ger. 55/G4
Geislingen, Ger. 61/E1
Geislingen an der Steige, Ger. 58/C5
Geistown, Pa, US 161/G4
Geita, Tanz. 121/H3
Gejiu, China 86/D4
Gekeng, China 87/H3
Gel (riv.), Sudan 117/F4
Gela, It. 48/D4
Gela (gulf), It. 48/D4
Geladī, Eth. 118/C4
Gelai (peak), Tanz. 119/B2
Gelang (cape), Malay. 89/C1
Gelderland (prov.), Neth. 52/C4
Geldermalsen, Neth. 52/C5
Geldern, Ger. 52/D5
Geldersheim, Ger. 58/D2
Geldrop, Neth. 52/C6
Geleen, Neth. 55/E2
Gelemso, Eth. 118/B3
Gelendost, Turk. 102/B2
Gelendzhik, Rus. 73/K5
Gelibolu, Turk. 51/H5
Gelibolu Yarımadas NP, Turk. 49/K2
Gelīla, Eth. 117/H3
Gelincik (peak), Turk. 103/E2
Gelinggang, Indo. 90/D4
Gelligaer, Wal, UK 36/C3
Gelnhausen, Ger. 58/C2
Gelsenkirchen, Ger. 52/E5
Geltendorf, Ger. 61/H1
Gelterkinden, Swi. 60/D3
Gelting, Ger. 40/C4
Gemas, Malay. 90/B3
Gembloux, Belg. 55/D2
Gembogl, PNG 129/G1
Gemena, D.R. Congo 120/D2
Gémenos, Fr. 64/B6
Gemert, Neth. 52/C5
Gemlik (gulf), Turk. 51/J5
Gemlik, Turk. 51/J5
Gemona del Friuli, It. 45/K3
Gemsbok NP, Bots. 122/D5
Gemuk (mt.), Ak, US 171/G3
Gemünden am Main, Ger. 58/C2
Gen (riv.), China 78/J1
Genalē Wenz (riv.), Eth. 118/B4
Genappe, Belg. 55/D2
Genargentu (mts.), It. 48/A2
Genarp, Swe. 39/K7
Genay, Fr. 60/A6
Genazzano, It. 65/B4
Genç, Turk. 102/E2
Gendringen, Neth. 52/D5
Gendt, Neth. 52/C5
Genemuiden, Neth. 52/D3
General Acha, Arg. 190/D3
General Alfredo Vasquez Cobo (int'l arpt.), Col. 184/D2
General Alvear, Arg. 190/D2
General Alvear, Arg. 190/E3
General Arenales, Arg. 190/E2
General Artigas, Par. 189/E3
General Belgrano, Arg. 190/F2
General Belgrano II, Arg., Ant. 192/X
General Bravo, Mex. 150/E5
General Cabrera, Arg. 190/E2
General Campos, Arg. 188/E4
General Carneiro, Braz. 186/B2
General Carrera (lake), Chile 190/B5
General Cepeda, Mex. 175/E3
General Conesa, Arg. 190/D4
General Deheza, Arg. 190/E2
General Edward Lawrence Logan (Logan Int'l) (int'l arpt.), Ma, US 161/L3
General Enrique Godoy, Arg. 190/D3
General Eugenio A. Garay, Par. 188/D2
General Francisco Villa, Mex. 175/F3
General Galarza, Arg. 191/J10
General Grant Grove, Ca, US 148/C2
General Grant Nat'l Mem., NY, US 169/K8
General José de San Martín, Arg. 188/E3
General Juan Álvarez, PN, Mex. 175/F5
General Juan José Rios, Mex. 174/C3
General Juan Madariaga, Arg. 191/F3
General La Madrid, Arg. 190/E3
General Lagos, Chile 188/B1
General Las Heras, Arg. 191/J11
General Lavalle, Arg. 191/K12
General Manuel Belgrano (peak), Arg. 188/C4
General Martín Miguel de Güemes, Arg. 188/C3
General Mitchell (int'l arpt.), Wi, US 160/C3
General Pico, Arg. 190/E2
General Pinto, Arg. 190/E2
General Ramírez, Arg. 188/D5
General Roca, Arg. 190/D3
General Saavedra, Bol. 188/D1
General Sampaio, Braz. 183/G4
General San Martín, Arg., Ant. 192/V
General San Martín, Arg. 190/E3
General San Martín, Arg. 191/J11
General Santiago Marino (int'l arpt.), Ven. 181/F2
General Santos, Phil. 88/D4
General Sherman Tree, Ca, US 148/C2
General Terán, Mex. 175/F3
General Treviño, Mex. 150/E4
General Trías, Mex. 150/A3
General Trias, Phil. 88/E7
General Viamonte, Arg. 190/E2
General Villalobas (int'l arpt.), Mex. 150/A3
General Villegas, Arg. 190/E2
General Zaragoza, Mex. 175/F4
General-Toshevo, Bul. 51/J4
Generoso (peak), Swi. 61/F6
Genesee, Id, US 144/F4
Genesee (co.), Mi, US 167/E6
Genesee (riv.), NY, US 161/G3
Genesee, Wi, US 167/P14
Genesee Depot, Wi, US 167/P14
Geneseo, Il, US 155/J3
Geneseo, Ks, US 153/E1
Geneseo, NY, US 161/H3
Genet, Eth. 118/A3
Geneva (Léman) (lake), Fr. 45/G3
Geneva (lake), Fr.,Swi. 66/E1
Geneva (Genève), Swi. 45/G3
Geneva (int'l arpt.), Swi. 60/C5
Geneva, Al, US 165/F2
Geneva, Id, US 147/H2
Geneva, Il, US 160/B4
Geneva, In, US 160/D4
Geneva, Ne, US 154/F3
Geneva, NY, US 161/H3
Geneva, Oh, US 160/F4
Geneva, Tx, US 151/H2
Genève, Swi. 60/C5
Genève (canton), Swi. 60/C5
Gengding (mtn.), China 87/E3
Gengenbach, Ger. 60/E1
Genglou, China 87/G4
Gengma Daizu Vazu Zizhixian, China 86/C4
Gengzhuang, China 81/B2
Génicourt, Fr. 30/J4
Genil (riv.), Sp. 66/B3
Genillé, Fr. 57/G6
Génissieux, Fr. 64/B2
Genk, Belg. 55/E2
Genlis, Fr. 60/B3
Gennach (riv.), Ger. 61/G2
Gennep, Neth. 52/C5
Gennevilliers, Fr. 30/J5
Genoa (riv.), Austl. 133/D3
Genoa (Genova), It. 62/B5
Genoa, Il, US 155/K2
Genoa, Ne, US 154/F3
Genoa, Oh, US 160/E4
Genoa City, Wi, US 167/P14
Genola, Ut, US 147/H4
Génova, Col. 183/K8
Genova (Genoa), It. 62/B5
Genova (prov.), It. 62/C4
Genova (gulf), It. 66/F1
Genovesa (isl.), Ecu. 184/K6
Gensingen, Ger. 55/G4
Gent (Ghent), Belg. 54/C1
Gent-Brugge Kanaal (canal), Belg. 54/C1
Genteng, Indo. 90/D5
Genteng (cape), Indo. 89/D4
Gentofte, Den. 39/J7
Gentry, Ar, US 153/G2
Genval, Belg. 55/D2
Genzano di Roma, It. 65/B4
Geographe (bay), Austl. 130/B5
Geographe (chan.), Austl. 130/B3
Geographical Center of North America, ND, US 156/D3
Geographical Center of the 48 Contiguous States, Ks, US 154/E4
Geographical Center of United States, SD, US 154/C1
Geok-Tepe, Trkm. 103/J2
Georg von Neumayer, Ger., Ant. 192/Z
George (pt.), Austl. 134/C3
George (lake), Austl. 131/D2
George (riv.), Can. 139/L4
George (riv.), Qu, Can. 141/K3
George, SAfr. 124/C4
George (lake), Ugan. 121/G3
George, Ia, US 155/F2
George, Wa, US 144/E4
George Land (isl.), Rus. 74/E2
George Rogers Clark Nat'l Hist. Park, In, US 162/D1
George Town, Austl. 132/C4
George Town (cap.), Cay. 177/F2
George Town, Malay. 89/C1
George V (coast), Ant. 192/L
George Washington Birthplace Nat'l Mon., Va, US 163/J1
George Washington Carver Nat'l Mon., Mo, US 153/G2

George West, Tx, US 151/E3
Georgensmünd, Ger. 58/E4
Georges (riv.), Austl. 134/G9
Georgetown, Austl. 134/A2
Georgetown, On, Can. 160/T8
Georgetown, PE, Can. 159/F2
Georgetown, Gam. 114/B3
Georgetown (cap.), Guy. 181/G3
Georgetown, StV. 173/N9
Georgetown, Co, US 154/B4
Georgetown, Ct, US 169/E1
Georgetown, De, US 163/K1
Georgetown, Fl, US 165/H3
Georgetown, Ga, US 165/F2
Georgetown, Ga, US 165/H2
Georgetown, Id, US 147/H2
Georgetown, Il, US 160/C5
Georgetown, Ky, US 162/E1
Georgetown, La, US 164/B2
Georgetown, Oh, US 162/F1
Georgetown, SC, US 163/H4
Georgetown, Tx, US 151/F2
Georgi Traykov, Bul. 51/H4
Georgia (ctry.) 71/G4
Georgia (str.), BC, Can. 144/B3
Georgia (state), US 143/K5
Georgia Agrirama, Ga, US 165/G2
Georgian (bay), On, Can. 141/H4
Georgian Bay Islands NP, On, Can. 160/F2
Georgiana, Al, US 164/E2
Georgina (riv.), Austl. 127/C3
Georgsmarienhütte, Ger. 53/F4
Gepatsch (lake), Aus. 61/G4
Gera, Ger. 42/G3
Geraardsbergen, Belg. 54/C2
Geral de Goiás, Serra (mts.), Braz. 186/D1
Geral, Serra (mts.), Braz. 189/G3
Gerald, Sk, Can. 156/D2
Gerald, Mo, US 153/J1
Geraldine, NZ 135/B4
Geraldine, Mt, US 145/J4
Geraldton, Austl. 130/B4
Geraldton, On, Can. 157/L3
Gérardmer, Fr. 60/C1
Gerasdorf bei Wien, Aus. 51/N7
Gerāsh, Iran 103/H5
Gerber (res.), Or, US 146/C2
Gerbéviller, Fr. 60/C1
Gerbier de Jonc (peak), Fr. 44/F4
Gerbrunn, Ger. 58/C3
Gerdau (riv.), Ger. 53/H3
Gerdine (mt.), Ak, US 171/H3
Gère (riv.), Fr. 64/B2
Gerede, Turk. 70/E4
Geres, Iles D' (isls.), Fr. 66/E2
Geretsried, Ger. 61/H2
Gérgal, Sp. 46/D4
Gerger, Turk. 102/D2
Gerhards (cape), PNG 129/G1
Gerik, Malay. 89/C1
Gering, Ne, US 154/C3
Gerlach, Nv, US 146/D3
Gerlachovský Štít (peak), Slvk. 43/L4
Gerlafingen, Swi. 60/D3
Germantown, Md, US 168/A5
Germantown, Tn, US 162/C3
Germantown, Wi, US 160/B3
Germany (ctry.) 42/E3
Germering, Ger. 59/E6
Germersheim, Ger. 58/B4
Germfask, Mi, US 160/D1
Germigny-L'Evêque, Fr. 30/L5
Germinaga, It. 61/E6
Germiston, SAfr. 124/E2
Gernsbach, Ger. 58/B5
Geroldsgrün, Ger. 59/E2
Gerolsbach, Ger. 59/E5
Gerolstein, Ger. 55/F3
Gerolzhofen, Ger. 58/D3
Geronimo, Az, US 149/G4
Gerpinnes, Belg. 55/D3
Gerra (Verzasca), Swi. 61/E5
Gerrards Cross, Eng, UK 30/B2
Gerringong, Austl. 133/E2
Gers (riv.), Fr. 44/D5
Gersau, Swi. 61/E4
Gersfeld, Ger. 58/C2
Gersheim, Ger. 55/G5
Gerspenz (riv.), Ger. 58/B3
Gerstetten, Ger. 58/E5
Gerstheim, Fr. 60/D1
Gersthofen, Ger. 58/D6
Gerstungen, Ger. 53/H7
Gervais, Or, US 146/B1
Gervanne (riv.), Fr. 64/B3
Gervasio, Uru. 191/G2
Gerze, Turk. 70/E4
Gërzë, China 99/D5
Gescher, Ger. 52/E5
Geseke, Ger. 53/F5
Gesher, Isr. 105/D3
Gesher Ha Ziw, Isr. 105/C2
Gesira, Som. 119/D1
Gespunsart, Fr. 55/D4
Gessertshausen, Ger. 58/D6
Gesso (riv.), It. 62/A4
Gesso (riv.), Fr. 64/D4
Gesves, Belg. 55/E3
Geta, Fin. 41/H1
Getafe, Sp. 47/N9
Getai, China 80/B4
Gete (riv.), Belg. 55/E2
Getinge, Swe. 40/E3
Gettorf, Ger. 40/C4
Gettysburg, Pa, US 161/H5
Gettysburg, SD, US 154/E1
Gettysburg Nat'l Mil. Park, Pa, US 168/A4
Getúlio Vargas, Braz. 189/F3
Geul (riv.), Neth. 55/E2
Geureudong (peak), Indo. 89/B1
Geurie, Austl. 132/D2
Gevar'am, Isr. 105/B5
Gevaş, Turk. 103/E2
Gevelsberg, Ger. 53/E6
Gevgelija, FYROM 49/H2
Gewanē, Eth. 118/B3
Gex, Fr. 60/C5
Geyer, Ger. 59/F1
Geyersberg (peak), Ger. 58/C3
Geyikli, Turk. 49/K3
Geysdorp, SAfr. 124/D2
Geyser (reef), Madg. 125/H6
Geyve, Turk. 51/K5
Gez (riv.), China 99/B4
Ghabāghib, Syria 105/E2
Ghābat al 'Arab, Sudan 117/F3
Ghadāmis, Libya 111/H3
Ghaddūwah, Libya 108/B3
Ghaggar (riv.), India 98/C5
Ghaghara (riv.), India 96/C2
Ghāghra, India 97/E4
Ghakhar, Pak. 98/C3
Ghana (ctry.) 115/E4
Ghantiāli, India 101/K3
Ghanzi, Bots. 122/D4
Ghanzi (dist.), Bots. 122/D4
Ghār Ad Dimā', Tun. 112/L6
Gharaunda, India 98/D5
Gharb Binna, Sudan 109/F5
Gharbah (wadi), Egypt 113/C5
Gharbī, Jazīrat al (isl.), Tun. 66/F4
Ghardaïa, Alg. 111/F2
Ghardaïa (wilaya), Alg. 111/F3
Ghardimaou, Tun. 112/L6
Gharghoda, India 96/D4
Gharībwāl, Pak. 98/B3
Gharm, Taj. 99/B4
Gharqābād, Iran 103/G3
Gharyān, Libya 67/G4
Ghāt, Libya 111/H4
Ghātāl, India 97/F4
Ghātampur, India 96/C2
Ghātsīla, India 97/F4
Ghayl Bā Wazīr, Yem. 118/D2
Ghazaouet, Alg. 112/D2
Ghaziābād, India 98/D5
Ghāzīpur, India 96/D3
Ghāzīpur, India 96/C3
Ghaznī, Afg. 101/J2
Ghazzah (Gaza), Gaza 105/A5
Ghedi, It. 62/D3
Gheen, Mn, US 157/H4
Ghemme, It. 62/B2
Ghent (Gent), Belg. 54/C1
Gheorghe Gheorghiu-Dej, Rom. 51/H2
Gheorgheni, Rom. 72/C4
Gherla, Rom. 51/F2
Gheura, India 101/K3
Ghilarza, It. 48/A2
Ghinda (Gīnda), Erit. 118/A2
Ghio (lake), Arg. 190/C5
Ghirārah (gulf), Gabon 111/H2
Ghisalba, It. 62/C2
Ghisonaccia, Fr. 48/A1
Gholson, Tx, US 151/F2
Ghora Bāri, Pak. 101/J4
Ghorāi, Nepal 96/D1
Ghost Town, Nv, US 148/D2
Ghotki, Pak. 92/A2
Ghugri (riv.), India 97/F3
Ghum, India 97/G2
Ghurayrah, SAfr. 100/D5
Ghūriān, Afg. 101/H2
Ghuwaybah (wadi), Egypt 113/D5
Gia Lam (int'l arpt.), Viet. 86/E4
Gia Nghia, Viet. 94/D4
Gia Rai, Viet. 94/D4
Gia Vuc, Viet. 94/E3
Giaginskaya, Rus. 73/L5
Gianicolo (hill), It. 65/G8
Giannutri (isl.), It. 48/B1
Giant Sequoia Nat'l Mon., Ca, US 148/C2
Giant's Castle (peak), SAfr. 124/E3
Giant's Causeway, NI, UK 34/B1
Giarre, It. 48/D4
Giaveno, It. 64/D2
Giba`i Shet' (riv.), Eth. 118/A2
Gibb River, Austl. 128/B4
Gibbon, Ne, US 154/E3
Gibbonsville, Id, US 147/G1
Gibbstown, NJ, US 168/C4
Gībē Shet' (riv.), Eth. 117/H4
Gībē Wenz (riv.), Eth. 117/H3
Gibeon, Namb. 122/C5
Giberville, Fr. 57/E2
Gibloux (peak), Swi. 60/D4
Gibraleón, Sp. 46/B4
Gibraltar (pt.), Eng, UK 35/J5
Gibraltar (res.), Ca, US 166/A1
Gibraltar (cap.), Gib. 46/C4
Gibraltar (str.), Mor.,Sp. 29/D5
Gibraltar, Mi, US 167/F7
Gibraltar, Ven. 173/G6
Gibraltar Range NP, Austl. 132/E1
Gibsland, La, US 153/H4
Gibson, Austl. 130/D5
Gibson (des.), Austl. 127/B3
Gibson, Ga, US 163/F4
Gibson, NC, US 163/H3
Gibson City, Il, US 160/B4
Gibson Desert Nature Reserve, Austl. 130/E3
Gibsonburg, Oh, US 160/E4
Gibsonia, Fl, US 164/M7
Gibsons, BC, Can. 144/C3
Gibsonton, Fl, US 164/L8
Gīdamī, Eth. 117/G3
Giddarbāha, India 98/C4
Gidden (lake), Fl, US 164/L6
Giddings, Tx, US 151/F2
Gideon, Mo, US 162/C2
Gidollē, Eth. 117/H4
Giebelstadt, Ger. 58/C3
Gieboldehausen, Ger. 53/H5
Giedraičiai, Lith. 41/L4
Gien, Fr. 44/E3
Giengen an der Brenz, Ger. 58/D5
Gier (riv.), Fr. 44/F4
Giessbachfälle (falls), Swi. 60/E4
Giessen (riv.), Fr.,Ger. 60/D1
Giessen, Ger. 58/B1
Giessendam, Neth. 52/B5
Gieten, Neth. 52/D2
Giethoorn, Neth. 52/D3
Gif-sur-Yvette, Fr. 30/J5
Gīfān, Iran 103/J2
Gifford, Sc, UK 33/D5
Gifford, Fl, US 165/H4
Gifford, Il, US 160/B4
Gifford (riv.), Nun, Can. 141/H1
Gifford (peak), Wa, US 144/D5
Gifford, SC, US 163/G4
Giffre (riv.), Fr. 60/C5
Gifhorn, Ger. 53/H4
Gifu, Japan 83/L5
Gig Harbor, Wa, US 144/C4
Gigant, Rus. 73/L4
Gigante, Col. 180/C4
Giggleswick, Eng, UK 35/F3
Giglio (isl.), It. 67/F2
Gignac, Fr. 47/G1
Gignac-la-Nerthe, Fr. 64/B6
Gijón, Sp. 46/C1
Gikongoro, Rwa. 121/G3
Gil de Vilches, PN, Chile 190/C2
Gila (riv.), Az, NM, US 149/G4
Gila, NM, US 149/H4
Gila (mts.), Az, US 149/G4
Gila Bend, Az, US 149/F4
Gila Bend Ind. Res., Az, US 149/F4
Gila Cliff Dwellings Nat'l Mon., NM, US 149/H4
Gīlān (gov.), Iran 103/G2
Gīlān-e Gharb, Iran 103/F3
Gilat, Isr. 105/B6
Gilberdyke Newport, Eng, UK 35/H4
Gilbert (riv.), Austl. 127/D2
Gilbert (mt.), BC, Can. 144/B2
Gilbert (isls.), Kiri. 136/G5
Gilbert, Az, US 149/G4
Gilbert, Ia, US 155/H2
Gilbert, La, US 166/C1
Gilbert, Mn, US 157/H4
Gilbert (peak), Ut, US 147/H3
Gilbert Plains, Mb, Can. 156/D2
Gilbertown, Al, US 164/D2
Gilberts, Il, US 167/P15
Gilbjerg (pt.), Den. 39/J6
Gilbués, Braz. 183/E5
Gilby, ND, US 157/F3
Gilching, Ger. 58/E6
Gilchrist, Tx, US 151/G3
Gilé, Moz. 123/H3
Gilfach Goch, Wal, UK 36/C3
Gilford, NI, UK 34/B3
Gilford, NH, US 161/L3
Gilford Park, NJ, US 168/D4
Gilgandra, Austl. 132/D1
Gilgil, Kenya 119/B2
Gilgit (riv.), Pak. 98/C1
Gilgit, Pak. 98/C2
Gilgit (riv.), India 99/B4
Gilgunnia, Austl. 132/C2
Gilimanuk, Indo. 89/F5
Gill, Ma, US 161/K3
Gill, Lough (lake), Ire. 32/B1
Gillam, Mb, Can. 140/G3
Gilleleje, Den. 39/J6
Gillespie, Il, US 155/K4
Gillett, Ar, US 153/J3
Gillett, Wi, US 160/B2
Gillett, Tx, US 151/F3
Gillette, Wy, US 154/B1
Gillies Bay, BC, Can. 144/B3
Gillingham, Eng, UK 37/G4
Gillot (int'l arpt.), Fr. 125/S15
Gilly, Swi. 60/C5
Gilly-sur-Isère, Fr. 64/C1
Gilman, Wi, US 157/J5
Gilman, Il, US 160/C4
Gilman City, Mo, US 155/H3
Gilman Hot Springs, Ca, US 166/D3
Gilmer, Tx, US 151/G1
Gilmore, Id, US 147/G1
Gīlo Wenz (riv.), Eth. 117/G4
Gilqit (riv.), Pak. 101/K1
Gilroy, Ca, US 148/B2
Giluwe (mt.), PNG 129/F1
Gilyuy (riv.), Rus. 79/K1
Gilze, Neth. 52/B5
Gīmbī, Eth. 117/G3
Gimbsheim, Ger. 58/B3
Gimel, Swi. 60/C4
Gimie (mt.), StL. 173/N9
Gimli, Mb, Can. 156/F2
Gimo, Swe. 40/H1
Gimone (riv.), Fr. 47/F1
Gin Gin, Austl. 134/C4
Ginan, Japan 83/L5
Gīnch'ī, Eth. 118/A3
Gīnda (Ghinda), Erit. 118/A2
Gingelom, Belg. 55/E2
Gingero, Eth. 117/H4
Gingin, Austl. 130/B4
Gingindlovu, SAfr. 125/E3
Gingoog, Phil. 88/D3
Gingst, Ger. 40/E4
Gīnīr, Eth. 118/B4
Ginneken, Neth. 52/B5
Ginnosar, Isr. 105/D3
Ginosa, It. 48/E2
Ginowan, Japan 85/J7
Gioia (gulf), It. 48/D3
Gioia dei Marsi, It. 65/C4
Gioia del Colle, It. 48/E2
Gioia Tauro, It. 48/D3
Giornico, Swi. 61/E5
Gioüra (isl.), Gre. 49/J3
Gioveretto (peak), It. 61/G5
Giovi (peak), It. 63/E6
Gipping (riv.), Eng, UK 37/G2
Gipsy, Mo, US 162/B2
Girard, Ks, US 153/G2
Girard, Pa, US 160/F3
Girard, Il, US 155/K4
Girardot, Col. 183/L8
Girardota, Col. 183/K6
Girardville, Qu, Can. 158/A1
Girardville, Pa, US 168/B2
Giraud (peak), Fr. 64/D4
Giraul, Ang. 122/B2
Giraul (riv.), Ang. 122/B2
Giraumont, Fr. 55/E5
Girawa, Eth. 118/B3
Girdle Ness (pt.), Sc, UK 33/D2
Giresun (prov.), Turk. 70/F4
Giresun, Turk. 70/F4
Girgnasco, It. 62/B2
Giri (riv.), D.R. Congo 120/D2
Gīrīdīh, India 97/F3
Girifalco, It. 48/E3
Girilambone, Austl. 132/C1
Girling (res.), Eng, UK 30/C2
Giromagny, Fr. 60/C2
Girón, Ecu. 180/B5
Girón, Col. 180/C3
Girona, Sp. 47/G2
Gironcourt-sur-Vraine, Fr. 60/B1
Gironde (riv.), Fr. 66/C1
Gironella, Sp. 47/F1
Girraween NP, Austl. 132/D1
Giru, Austl. 134/B2
Giruá, Braz. 189/F4
Girvan, Sc, UK 34/D1
Girvin, Tx, US 150/C2
Gisborne, NZ 135/D2
Gisborne, Austl. 133/B3
Gisenyi, Rwa. 121/G3
Gislaved, Swe. 40/E3
Gisors, Fr. 54/A5
Gissi, It. 65/D3
Gistel, Belg. 54/B1
Gistrup, Den. 40/D3
Gitarama, Rwa. 121/G3
Gitega, Buru. 121/G3
Gittsfjället (peak), Swe. 38/E2
Giubiasco, Swi. 61/F5
Giugliano in Campania, It. 65/D6
Giulianello, It. 65/B4
Giulianova, It. 65/C2
Giurgeni, Rom. 51/H3
Giurgiu, Rom. 51/G4
Giurgiu (prov.), Rom. 51/G3
Giussano, It. 62/C2
Giv'at Brenner, Isr. 105/B5
Giv'at Hayyim, Isr. 105/B4
Giv'atayim, Isr. 105/B4
Give, Den. 40/C4
Givet, Fr. 55/D3
Givors, Fr. 64/A1
Giwa, Nga. 115/G4
Giyani, SAfr. 123/F4
Gizhiga (bay), Rus. 75/R3
Gizo, Sol. 136/E5
Giżycko, Pol. 41/J4
Gjerdrum, Nor. 40/D1
Gjerlev, Den. 40/D3
Gjerstad, Nor. 40/C2
Gjirokastër, Alb. 49/G2
Gjoa Haven, Nun, Can. 140/G2
Gjøvik, Nor. 40/D1
Glabbeek, Belg. 55/E2
Glace Bay, NS, Can. 159/H2
Glacier, BC, Can. 144/F2
Glacier (peak), Wa, US 144/D3
Glacier Bay NP, Ak, US 171/L4
Glacier NP, BC, Can. 144/F2
Glacier NP, Mt, US 145/H3
Gladbeck, Ger. 52/D5
Gladbrook, Ia, US 155/H2
Glade Spring, Va, US 163/G2
Gladewater, Tx, US 151/G1
Gladsakse, Den. 39/J7
Gladsheim (peak), BC, Can. 144/F3
Gladstone, Austl. 134/C3
Gladstone, Austl. 131/H5
Gladstone, Mb, Can. 156/E2
Gladstone, Mi, US 160/C2
Gladstone, ND, US 156/C4
Gladwin, Mi, US 160/D3
Gladys, Va, US 163/H2
Glafsfjorden (lake), Swe. 40/D2
Glaisdale, Eng, UK 35/H3
Glamis, Sk, Can. 145/L2
Glamis, Sc, UK 33/D3
Glamis, Ca, US 148/E4
Glamsbjerg, Den. 40/D4
Glan (riv.), Ger. 42/D4
Glan, Phil. 88/D4
Glanamman, Wal, UK 36/C3
Glanaruddery (mts.), Ire. 32/A5
Glancy, Ms, US 164/C2
Gland, Swi. 60/C5
Gland (riv.), Fr. 55/D4
Glandon (riv.), Fr. 64/C2
Glandore, Ire. 32/A6
Glandorf, Ger. 53/F4
Glanmire, Ire. 32/B6
Glænø (isl.), Den. 39/H7
Glanworth, Ire. 32/B5
Glärnisch (range), Swi. 61/E3
Glarus, Swi. 61/F3
Glarus (canton), Swi. 61/E4
Glarus Alps (range), Swi. 45/H3
Glas Maol (peak), Sc, UK 33/C3
Glasbury, Wal, UK 36/C2
Glasco, Ks, US 154/F4
Glasgow, Sc, UK 33/B5
Glasgow (co.), Sc, UK 33/B5
Glasgow, De, US 168/C4
Glasgow, Ky, US 162/E2
Glasgow, Mt, US 145/L3
Glasgow, Va, US 163/H2
Glashütten, Ger. 58/B2
Glaslyn (riv.), Wal, UK 34/D6
Glaslyn, Sk, Can. 145/K1
Glass (lake), Sc, UK 33/B1
Glass (riv.), Sc, UK 33/B2
Glass (mts.), Tx, US 150/C2
Glassboro, NJ, US 168/C4
Glastonbury, Eng, UK 36/D4
Glatt (riv.), Swi. 61/E1
Glatt (riv.), Ger. 58/B6
Glattbach, Ger. 58/C3
Glattfelden, Swi. 61/E2
Glavinitsa, Bul. 51/H4
Glazoué, Ben. 115/F5
Glazov, Rus. 69/M4
Gleason, Wi, US 157/K5
Gleason, Tn, US 162/C2
Glebovka, Rus. 73/K4
Gleichen, Ab, Can. 145/H2
Gleisdorf, Aus. 50/B2
Glems (riv.), Ger. 58/C5
Glemsford, Eng, UK 37/G2
Glen, Mn, US 157/H4
Glen (riv.), Eng, UK 35/H6
Glen, Mt, US 147/G1
Glen (canyon), Ut, US 149/G2
Glen Allan, Ms, US 162/B4
Glen Allen, Va, US 163/J2
Glen Arbor, Mi, US 160/D2
Glen Burnie, Md, US 168/B5
Glen Canyon (dam), Az, US 149/G2
Glen Canyon Nat'l Rec. Area, Az,Ut, US 147/H4
Glen Coe (pass), Sc, UK 33/B3
Glen Cove, NY, US 169/L8
Glen Cove, Tx, US 150/E2
Glen Echo (park), Md, US 168/A6
Glen Eden, NZ 135/F6
Glen Elder, Ks, US 154/E4
Glen Flora, Tx, US 151/F3
Glen Gardner, NJ, US 168/D2
Glen Haven, Ga, US 163/M7
Glen Innes, Austl. 132/D1
Glen Lyon, Pa, US 168/B1
Glen Mòr (valley), Sc, UK 33/B2
Glen Ridge, NJ, US 169/J8
Glen Rock, NJ, US 169/J8
Glen Rock, Pa, US 168/B4
Glen Rose, Tx, US 151/F1
Glen Ullin, ND, US 156/D4
Glen Williams, On, Can. 160/T8
Glenan (isl.), Fr. 44/A3
Glenarm (riv.), NI, UK 34/C2
Glenarm, NI, UK 34/C2
Glenavon, Sk, Can. 156/C2
Glenavy, NI, UK 34/B2
Glenavy, NZ 135/B4
Glenbawn (dam), Austl. 132/D2
Glenboro, Mb, Can. 156/E3
Glenbrook, Nv, US 146/D4
Glenbrook (nbrhd.), Austl. 134/G8
Glenburn, ND, US 156/D3
Glenbush, Sk, Can. 145/L1
Glencaple, Sc, UK 34/E2
Glenclova, Zim. 123/F3
Glencoe, Ok, US 153/F2
Glencoe, Sc, UK 33/A3
Glencoe, On, Can. 160/F3
Glencoe, Il, US 167/Q15
Glencoe, Mn, US 155/G1
Glencoe, SAfr. 125/E3
Glencross, SD, US 156/D5
Glendale, Wi, US 160/C3
Glendale, Ca, US 166/F7
Glendale, Zim. 123/F3
Glendale, Az, US 149/F4
Glendale, Or, US 146/B2
Glendale, Ut, US 149/F2
Glendale, Ky, US 162/E2
Glendale, Mo, US 155/H3
Glendale, Tx, US 151/G2
Glendale Heights, Il, US 167/P16
Glenden, Austl. 134/C3
Glendive, Mt, US 156/B4
Glendo (dam), Wy, US 154/B2
Glendo (res.), Wy, US 154/B2
Glendo, Wy, US 154/B2
Glendon, NC, US 163/H3
Glendora, Ca, US 166/C2
Glendun (riv.), NI, UK 34/B1
Glenealy, Ire. 34/B6
Glenelg, Sc, UK 31/R8
Glenelg (riv.), Austl. 132/B3
Glenelg (nbrhd.), Austl. 131/M8
Glenelg, Md, US 168/B5
Glenella, Mb, Can. 156/E2
Glenelly (riv.), NI, UK 34/A2
Glenfield, NY, US 161/J3
Glengarriff, Ire. 32/A6
Glengarry (range), Austl. 130/C3
Glenluce, Sc, UK 34/D2
Glenmere (lake), NY, US 168/D1
Glenmora, La, US 164/B2
Glenmorgan, Austl. 134/C4
Glenn Heights, Tx, US 150/L7
Glennallen, Ak, US 171/J3
Glennamaddy, Ire. 32/B2
Glenns Ferry, Id, US 147/F2
Glennville, Ga, US 165/H2
Glennville, Ca, US 148/C3
Glenolden, Pa, US 168/C4
Glenoma, Wa, US 144/C4
Glenora, BC, Can. 171/M4
Glenorie, Austl. 134/H8
Glenormiston, Austl. 131/H2
Glenpool, Ok, US 153/F3
Glenrock, Wy, US 154/B2
Glenrothes, Sc, UK 33/C4
Glens Falls, NY, US 161/K3
Glenshane (pass), NI, UK 34/B2
Glenside, Pa, US 168/C3
Glenties, Ire. 31/P9
Glentrool, Sc, UK 34/D1
Glentworth, Sk, Can. 145/L3
Glenveagh NP, Ire. 31/Q9
Glenview, Il, US 167/Q15
Glenville, Ire. 32/B5
Glenville, WV, US 163/G1
Glenville, Mn, US 155/H2
Glenwood, Ab, Can. 145/H3
Glenwood, Al, US 165/E2
Glenwood, Ar, US 153/H3
Glenwood, Ga, US 163/F4
Glenwood, Ia, US 155/G3
Glenwood, Mn, US 157/G5
Glenwood, NM, US 149/H4
Glenwood, NJ, US 168/D1
Glenwood, Ut, US 149/G1
Glenwood City, Wi, US 155/H1
Gleouraich (peak), Sc, UK 33/A2
Glidden, Ia, US 155/G2
Glidden, Sk, Can. 145/K2
Glifádha, Gre. 49/N9
Glimåkra, Swe. 40/F3
Glina, Cro. 50/C3
Glinde, Ger. 53/H1
Glindow, Ger. 42/P7
Glitra (riv.), Nor. 38/R8
Glitrevatn (lake), Nor. 38/R8
Gliwice, Pol. 43/K3
Globe, Az, US 149/G4
Glockturm (peak), Aus. 61/G4
Glodeni, Mol. 72/D4
Gloggnitz, Aus. 43/H5
Głogów, Pol. 43/J3
Głogówek, Pol. 43/J3
Glomma (riv.), Nor. 38/D3
Glonn (riv.), Ger. 58/E6
Gloria (bay), Cuba 177/G1
Glorious (mt.), Austl. 134/E6
Glory of Russia (cape), Ak, US 171/D3
Glossodia, Austl. 133/E1
Glossop, Eng, UK 35/G5
Gloster, La, US 150/H1
Gloster, Ms, US 164/C2
Gloster, Ga, US 163/M7
Glostrup, Den. 39/J7
Glotovka, Rus. 71/H1
Gloucester, Ma, US 161/L3
Gloucester, On, Can. 161/J2
Gloucester, Austl. 132/D1
Gloucester, PNG 129/H1
Gloucester, Eng, UK 36/D3
Gloucester (co.), NJ, US 168/C4
Gloucester (Gloucester Court House), Va, US 163/J2
Gloucester City, NJ, US 168/C4
Gloucester Court House (Gloucester), Va, US 163/J2
Gloucester Point, Va, US 163/J2
Gloucestershire (co.), Eng, UK 36/D3
Glouster, Oh, US 160/E5
Glouthane, Ire. 32/B6
Glover, Ok, US 153/G3
Glover (isl.), Nf, Can. 159/J1
Glovers Reef (reef), Belz. 176/E2
Gloversville, NY, US 161/J3
Glovertown, Nf, Can. 159/K1
Głowno, Pol. 43/K3
Głubczyce, Pol. 43/J3
Glubokiy, Rus. 73/L3
Glubokoye, Kaz. 99/D1
Głuchołazy, Pol. 43/J3
Glücksburg, Ger. 40/C4
Glückstadt, Ger. 53/G1
Glumslöv, Swe. 39/J7
Glumsø, Den. 39/H7
Glyde (riv.), Ire. 32/D2
Glyn Heath, Wal, UK 36/C3
Glyncorrwg, Wal, UK 36/C3
Glyndon, Mn, US 156/F4
Glyndon, Md, US 168/B5
Glyngøre, Den. 40/C3
Glynn, NI, UK 34/C2
Gmünd, Aus. 43/H4
Gmunden, Aus. 59/G7
Gnagna (prov.), Burk. 115/E3
Gnarrenburg, Ger. 53/G2
Gnesta, Swe. 39/A1
Gnezdovo, Rus. 70/D1
Gniew, Pol. 41/H5
Gniezno, Pol. 43/J2
Gnjilane, Serb. 50/E4
Gnosall, Eng, UK 36/D1
Gnowangerup, Austl. 130/C5
Gō (riv.), Japan 84/C3
Go Cong, Viet. 94/D4
Go Dau Ha, Viet. 94/D4
Go Quao, Viet. 94/D4
Goa (state), India 92/B4
Goageb, Namb. 124/B2
Goālpāra, India 97/H2
Goāltor, India 97/F4
Goat Fell (peak), Sc, UK 33/A5
Goat River, BC, Can. 144/D1
Goathland, Eng, UK 35/H3
Goba, Eth. 118/A4
Goba, Moz. 125/F2
Gobabeb, Namb. 122/B4
Gobabis, Namb. 122/C4
Gobardānga, India 97/G4
Gobernador Castro, Arg. 190/F2
Gobernador Costa, Arg. 190/C5
Gobernador Crespo, Arg. 188/D4
Gobernador Duval, Arg. 190/D3
Gobernador Gregores, Arg. 191/C6
Gobernador Ingeniero Valetín Virasoro, Arg. 189/E4
Gobernador Mansilla, Arg. 191/J10
Gobi (des.), China,Mon 77/K5
Gobindpur, India 97/E5
Göblberg (peak), Aus. 59/G6
Gobō, Japan 84/D4
Gobowen, Eng, UK 35/E6
Goch, Ger. 52/D5
Gochas, Namb. 124/B2
Gochsheim, Ger. 58/D2
Goda, Eth. 118/B4
Godāgāri, Bang. 97/G3
Godalming, Eng, UK 37/F4
Godāvari (riv.), India 77/G8
Godbout, Qu, Can. 158/D1
Goddā, India 97/F3
Godē, Eth. 118/B4
Godeanu (peak), Rom. 50/F3
Godech, Bul. 50/F4
Goderich, On, Can. 160/F3
Godfrey, Il, US 155/J4
Godhra, India 92/B3
Godinlabe, Som. 118/C4
Godinne, Belg. 55/D3
Godley, Tx, US 150/K7
Godmanchester, Eng, UK 37/F2
Gōdo, Japan 83/L5
Gödölló, Hun. 43/K5
Godolphin Cross, Eng, UK 36/A6
Godoy Cruz, Arg. 190/C2
Gods (lake), Mb, Can. 140/G3
Gods (riv.), Mb, Can. 140/G3
Gods Mercy (bay), Nun, Can. 141/H2
Godstone, Eng, UK 30/C3
Godthåb (Nuuk), Grld. 139/M3
Godwin Austen (K2) (peak), Pak. 98/D2
Goeree (isl.), Neth. 52/A5
Goes, Neth. 52/A5
Goessel, Ks, US 153/F1
Goetzville, Mi, US 160/D1
Goff, Ks, US 155/G4
Goffstown, NH, US 161/L3
Gofitskoye, Rus. 71/G3
Gogebic (range), Mi, US 157/J4
Gogebic (lake), Mi, US 157/K4
Göggingen, Ger. 58/D6
Gogland (isl.), Rus. 41/M1
Gogo, Eth. 117/G4
Gogo, Austl. 128/B4
Gogogogo, Madg. 125/H9
Gogōme, Japan 82/B4
Gogounou, Ben. 115/F4
Gogra (riv.), India 92/D2
Gogrial, Sudan 117/F3
Goha Ts'iyon, Eth. 118/A3
Gohad, India 96/B2
Gohāna, India 98/D5
Goharganj, India 96/A4
Gohbach (riv.), Ger. 53/G3
Goiana, Braz. 183/H4
Goiandira, Braz. 186/C3
Goianésia, Braz. 186/C2
Goiânia, Braz. 186/C3
Goianinha, Braz. 183/H4
Goianira, Braz. 186/C3
Goiás, Braz. 186/C2
Goiás (state), Braz. 186/C2
Goiatuba, Braz. 186/C3
Goil (lake), Sc, UK 33/B4
Goinsargoin, China 86/C2
Goio-Erê, Braz. 189/F3
Goirle, Neth. 52/C5
Góis, Port. 46/A2
Goito, It. 63/D3
Gojam (prov.), Eth. 117/H3
Gojeb Wenz (riv.), Eth. 117/H4
Gojō, Japan 84/D3
Gojra, Pak. 98/B4
Gok (riv.), Turk. 70/E4
Goka, Japan 83/D1
Gokāk, India 95/B2
Gokase (riv.), Japan 84/B4
Gokashō, Japan 83/K5
Gokasho (bay), Japan 83/L7
Gökçeada (isl.), Turk. 102/A1
Gökçebey, Turk. 51/L5
Gökçekaya (dam), Turk. 102/B1
Göksu (riv.), Turk 102/D2
Göksun, Turk. 102/D2
Gokteik, Myan. 94/B1
Göktepe, Turk. 104/C1
Gokwe, Zim. 123/F3
Gol, Nor. 40/C1
Gola, India 97/E4
Gola Gokarannāth, India 96/C1
Golan Hts. (reg.), Syria 104/D3
Golasecca, It. 62/B2
Gölbaşı, Turk. 102/D2
Gölbaşı, Turk. 102/C2
Golbey, Fr. 60/C1
Golborne, Eng, UK 35/F5
Golconda, Il, US 162/C2
Gölcük, Turk. 51/J5
Gold (coast), Gha. 115/E5
Gold (mtn.), Wa, US 167/B2
Gold (cr.), BC, Can. 144/G3
Gold Bar, Wa, US 167/D2
Gold Beach, Fr. 57/E2
Gold Beach, Or, US 146/A2
Gold Bridge, BC, Can. 144/C2
Gold Coast, Austl. 134/D5
Gold Hill, Or, US 146/B2
Gold Point, Nv, US 148/D2
Goldach, Swi. 61/F3
Gołdap, Pol. 41/K4
Goldbach, Ger. 58/C3
Goldberg, Ger. 40/E5
Golden, NM, US 152/A3
Golden, Ire. 32/B4
Golden (bay), NZ 135/C3
Golden, Co, US 154/B4
Golden, BC, Can. 144/F2
Golden Beach, Fl, US 164/P11
Golden City, Mo, US 153/G2
Golden Gate, Fl, US 165/H4
Golden Gate (chan.), Ca, US 167/J11
Golden Gate Highlands NP, SAfr. 124/D3
Golden Gate Nat'l Recreation Area, Ca., US 148/A2
Golden Lake Ind. Res., On, Can. 161/H2
Golden Prairie, Sk, Can. 145/K2
Golden Rock (int'l arpt.), StK. 173/N8
Golden Spike Nat'l Hist. Site, Ut, US 147/G3
Golden Temple, India 98/C4
Golden Vale (plain), Ire. 32/B4
Golden Valley, Zim. 123/F3
Golden Valley, Mn, US 157/P6
Goldendale, Wa, US 144/D5
Goldene Aue (reg.), Ger. 42/F3
Goldenrod, Fl, US 164/N6
Goldenstedt, Ger. 53/F3
Goldfield, Nv, US 148/D2
Goldfield, Ia, US 155/H2
Goldkronach, Ger. 59/E2
Goldlauter, Ger. 58/D1
Goldonna, La, US 164/B1
Goldsboro, Md, US 168/C5
Goldsboro, NC, US 163/J3
Goldsboro, Tx, US 150/E1
Goldsboro (Etters), Pa, US 168/B3
Goldsworthy, Austl. 130/C2
Goldthwaite, Tx, US 151/E2
Göle, Turk. 71/G4
Goleniów, Pol. 40/F5
Golfito Nat'l Wild. Ref., CR 177/F4
Golfo Aranci, It. 48/A2
Golfo de Santa Clara, Mex. 174/B2
Gölhısar, Turk. 102/B2
Goliad, Tx, US 151/F3
Golinda, Tx, US 151/F2
Golitsyno, Rus. 69/W9
Gölköy, Turk. 70/F4
Gollach (riv.), Ger. 58/D3
Göllheim, Ger. 58/B3
Gölmarmara, Turk. 102/A2
Golmud, China 78/C4
Gololcha, Eth. 118/B3
Golomoti Station, Malw. 123/G2
Golovanovo, Rus. 68/J5
Golovin, Ak, US 171/F3
Golovino, Rus. 68/J5
Golovnina (peak), Rus. 82/D2
Golovnino, Rus. 82/D2
Golpāyegān, Iran 103/G3
Gölpazarı, Turk. 51/K5
Gols, Aus. 45/M3
Gol'shany, Bela. 41/M4
Goltry, Ok, US 153/E2
Golts, Md, US 168/C5
Golub-Dobrzyń, Pol. 43/K2
Golubovci (int'l arpt.), Serb. 50/D4
Golungo Alto, Ang. 120/C5
Golva, ND, US 156/C4
Golyam Perelik (peak), Bul. 49/J2
Golyama Kamchiya (riv.), Bul. 51/H4
Golyama Syutkya (peak), Bul. 49/J2
Goma (int'l arpt.), D.R. Congo 121/G3
Goma, D.R. Congo 121/G3
Gomantong Caves, Malay. 88/B4
Gomaringen, Ger. 58/C6
Gomati (riv.), India 96/C2
Gombari, D.R. Congo 121/G2
Gombe (riv.), Tanz. 121/G4
Gombe, Ang. 120/C4
Gombe NP, Tanz. 121/G4
Gombe-Matadi, D.R. Congo 120/C4
Gomera (isl.), Sp. 110/A4
Gomez (peak), Tx, US 150/B2
Gómez Farías, Mex. 174/D2
Gómez Palacio, Mex. 174/E3
Gomīshān, Iran 100/F1
Gommern, Ger. 42/F2
Gomo, China 99/E5
Gomoh, India 97/F4
Goms (valley), Swi. 60/E5
Gomshall, Eng, UK 30/B3
Gomshall, Eng, UK 37/F4
Gona, PNG 129/H2
Gonābād, Iran 101/G2
Gonaïves, Haiti 177/H2
Gonarezhou NP, Zim. 123/F4
Gonâve (gulf), Haiti 173/G4
Gonâve (isl.), Haiti 177/H2
Gonbad-e Qābūs, Iran 103/H2
Gönc, Hun. 43/L4
Gonçalves Dias, Braz. 183/E4
Gondā, India 96/C2
Gondal, India 101/K4
Gondelsheim, Ger. 58/B4
Gonder, Eth. 117/H2
Gonder (pol. reg.), Eth. 117/H2
Gondola Point, NB, Can. 158/E3
Gondomar, Port. 46/A2
Gondomar, Sp. 46/A1
Gondrecourt-le-Château, Fr. 60/B1
Gondreville, Fr. 55/E6
Gondrexange (lake), Fr. 55/F6
Gönen, Turk. 70/C4
Gonesse, Fr. 30/K5
Gonfaron, Fr. 64/C6
Gonfreville-L'Orcher, Fr. 57/F1
Gong Xian, China 93/H2
Gong Xian, China 80/C4
Gong'an, China 87/F3
Gongbo'gyamda, China 93/F2
Gongchangling, China 81/B2
Gongche, China 87/F4
Gongga (peak), China 86/D2
Gonggar, China 97/H1
Gongguan, China 87/F4
Gonghe, China 78/E4
Gongliu, China 99/D3
Gongo, D.R. Congo 120/D4
Gongola (riv.), Nga. 115/H4
Gongolgon, Austl. 132/C1
Gongping, China 87/G4
Gongshan Drungzu Nuzu Zizhixian, China 93/G2
Gongtian, China 87/G2
Gongwan (mts.), China 86/D3
Gongxi, China 87/G3
Gongzhuling, China 80/F2
Goñi, Uru. 191/K10
Gonja, Tanz. 119/B3
Gonjo, China 86/C2
Gónnoi, Gre. 49/H3
Gonohe, Japan 82/B3
Gonubie, SAfr. 124/D4
Gonvick, Mn, US 157/G4
Gonyú, Hun. 50/C2
Gonzaga, It. 63/D4
Gonzaga, Phil. 88/C1
Gonzales, La, US 164/C2
Gonzales, Ca, US 148/B2
Gonzales, Tx, US 151/F3
Gonzalez, Fl, US 164/E2
González, Mex. 175/F4
Goobweyn, Som. 119/C2
Goochland, Va, US 163/J2
Good Hart, Mi, US 160/D2
Good Hope, Cape of (cape), SAfr. 124/L11
Good Spirit (lake), Sk, Can. 156/C2
Goodenough (cape), Ant. 192/J
Goodes, Ga, US 163/L7
Goodfellow (A.F.B.), Tx, US 150/D2
Goodhope, Bots. 122/E5
Gooding, Id, US 147/F2
Goodland, Fl, US 165/H5
Goodland, Ks, US 154/D4
Goodman, Mo, US 153/G2
Goodman, Wi, US 157/K5
Goodna (nbrhd.), Austl. 134/E7
Goodnews Bay, Ak, US 171/F4
Goodooga, Austl. 132/C1
Goodrich, Mi, US 167/F6
Goodrich, ND, US 156/D4
Goodrich, Tx, US 151/G2
Goodridge, Mn, US 156/G3
Goodview, Mn, US 155/J1
Goodwater, Al, US 162/D4
Goodwell, Ok, US 152/D2
Goodwick, Wal, UK 36/B2
Goodwin, Ar, US 162/B3
Goodwood, SAfr. 124/L10
Gooimeer (lake), Neth. 52/C4
Goole, Eng, UK 35/H4
Goolgowi, Austl. 133/B2
Gooloogong, Austl. 133/D1
Goolwa, Austl. 131/H5
Goomalling, Austl. 130/C4
Goombalie, Austl. 132/C1
Goombungee, Austl. 134/C4
Goondiwindi, Austl. 134/C5
Goongarrie NP, Austl. 130/D4
Goor, Neth. 52/D4
Goose (riv.), ND, US 156/F4
Goose (lake), Ca, US 142/B3
Goose (cr.), Id, US 147/G2
Goose (pt.), De, US 168/C5
Goose Creek, SC, US 163/G4
Goose Green, UK 191/F6
Gooseberry (cr.), Wy, US 147/J1
Goostrey, Eng, UK 35/F5
Gopālganj, India 97/E2
Gopālganj, Bang. 97/G4
Gopālpur, Bang. 97/G3
Gopat (riv.), India 96/D3
Göppingen, Ger. 58/C5
Góra, Pol. 43/J3
Góra Kalwaria, Pol. 43/L3
Gorakhpur, India 96/D2
Gorakhpur, India 96/C4
Goras, India 96/A3
Goražde, Bosn. 50/D4
Gorchs, Arg. 191/J11
Gorczański NP, Pol. 43/L4
Gorda (pt.), Cuba 177/F1
Gorda (pt.), Nic. 177/F3
Gorda (pt.), Nic. 177/F4
Gorda (pt.), Ca, US 146/A3
Gordes, Fr. 64/B5
Gordevio, Swi. 61/E5
Gordeyevka, Rus. 70/D1
Gordil, CAfr. 116/D3
Gørding, Den. 40/C4
Gordo, Al, US 162/D4
Gordola, Swi. 61/E5
Gordon, Austl. 132/C4
Gordon (lake), Austl. 127/D5
Gordon, Sc, UK 33/D5
Gordon, Al, US 165/F2
Gordon, Ga, US 163/F4
Gordon (cr.), Ne, US 154/D2
Gordon Downs, Austl. 128/C4
Gordon Ind. Res., Sk, Can. 156/B2
Gordonsbaai, SAfr. 124/L11
Gordonsville, Va, US 163/H1
Gordonvale, Austl. 134/B2
Gore, Va, US 161/G5
Gore (mtn.), NY, US 161/J3
Goré, Chad 116/C4
Gorē, Eth. 117/G3
Gore, NZ 135/B4
Gore Bay, On, Can. 160/E2
Gore Point (cape), Ak, US 171/H4
Gorebridge, Sc, UK 33/C5
Goree, Tx, US 152/E4
Görele, Turk. 70/F4
Gorelovo (arpt.), Rus. 69/T7
Goresbridge, Ire. 32/D4
Goreville, Il, US 162/C2
Gorey, Ire. 32/D4
Gorey, Chl, UK 56/C2
Gorgān, Iran 103/H2
Gorgān (riv.), Iran 103/H2
Gorge du Loup, Lux. 55/F4
Gorges du Verdon, Fr. 64/C5
Gorges du Ziz, Mor. 110/D2
Gorgol (riv.), Mrta. 114/B2
Gorgol (pol. reg.), Mrta. 114/B3
Gorgona, Isola di (isl.), It. 62/C6
Gorgonzola, It. 62/C2
Gorgora, Eth. 117/H2
Gorham, Me, US 161/L3
Gorham, NH, US 161/L2
Gori, Geo. 71/H4
Gorinchem, Neth. 52/B5
Goring, Eng, UK 37/E3
Goring-by-Sea, Eng, UK 37/F5
Goris, Arm. 103/F2
Gorizia, It. 63/G2
Gorizia (prov.), It. 63/G1
Gorj (prov.), Rom. 51/F3
Gor'kiy (res.), Rus. 68/J4
Gørlev, Den. 39/H7
Gorlice, Pol. 43/L4
Görlitz, Ger. 43/H3
Gorllwyn (peak), Wal, UK 36/C2
Gorman, Ca, US 148/C3
Gorman, Tx, US 151/E1
Gormanstown, Ire. 34/B4
Gormī, India 96/B2
Gormley, On, Can. 160/U8
Gorna Oryakhovitsa, Bul. 51/G4
Gorner (glacier), Swi. 60/D6
Gornji Milanovac, Serb. 50/E3
Gornji Vakuf, Bosn. 50/C4
Gorno-Altaysk, Rus. 99/E1
Gornozavodsk, Rus. 69/N4
Gornyak, Rus. 70/F1
Gornyak, Rus. 99/D1
Gornyatskiy, Rus. 73/L3
Gornyy, Rus. 79/L3
Gornyy Balykley, Rus. 71/H2
Gornyy Zerentuy, Rus. 79/H1
Goro, It. 63/F4
Goro, Eth. 118/B4
Goroch'an (peak), Eth. 117/H3
Gorodets, Rus. 69/J4
Gorodok, Bela. 41/N4
Gorodovikovsk, Rus. 73/L4
Gorogoro, Indo. 91/G4
Goroka, PNG 129/G1
Gorom Gorom, Burk. 115/E3
Goromonzi, Zim. 123/F3
Gorong (isl.), Indo. 91/H4
Gorongoza, Moz. 123/G3
Gorongoza, PN da, Moz. 123/G3
Gorontalo, Indo. 91/F3
Goronyo, Nga. 115/G3
Gorredijk, Neth. 52/D3
Gorreh, Iran 103/G4
Gorron, Fr. 57/E4
Gorseinon, Wal, UK 36/B3
Gorshechnoye, Rus. 73/K2
Gorskoye, Ukr. 73/K3
Gorssel, Neth. 52/D4
Gorst, Wa, US 167/B2
Gort, Ire. 32/B3
Gorteen, Ire. 32/B2
Gortin, NI, UK 34/A2
Görwihl, Ger. 60/E2
Goryachiy Klyuch, Rus. 73/K5
Goryn' (riv.), Ukr. 70/C2
Gorzano (peak), It. 65/C2
Gorzów Wielkopolski, Pol. 43/H2
Gos, Eth. 118/C3
Gosainganj, India 96/D2
Göschenen, Swi. 61/E4
Gōse, Japan 83/J7
Gosen, Japan 85/F2
Gosford, Austl. 133/E1
Gosforth, Eng, UK 35/G2
Goshen, NS, Can. 159/G3
Goshen, In, US 160/D4

Goshen – Gros-Mo
Map Section 230 231
Goshen, NJ, US 168/D5
Goshen, NY, US 161/J4
Goshen, Ut, US 147/H4
Goshen Hole (lowland), Ne, Wy, US 154/B4
Goshogawara, Japan 82/B3
Goshute (lake), Nv, US 147/F3
Goshute (valley), Nv, US 147/F3
Goshute Ind. Res., Nv,Ut, US 147/F4
Goslar, Ger. 53/H5
Gosnell, Ar, US 162/C3
Gospić, Cro. 50/B3
Gosport, Eng, UK 37/E5
Gosport, Al, US 164/E2
Gosport, In, US 160/C5
Gossas, Sen. 114/A3
Gossau, Swi. 61/F3
Gossensass (Colle Isarco), It. 61/H4
Gossersweiler-Stein, Ger. 55/G5
Gostepriimnyy, Rus. 71/M2
Gostilitsy, Rus. 69/S7
Gostishchevo, Rus. 73/J2
Gostivar, FYROM 49/G2
Gostyń, Pol. 43/J3
Gostynin, Pol. 43/K2
Göta (riv.), Swe. 40/G2
Gota, Eth. 118/B3
Götaland (reg.), Swe. 40/E3
Gotebo, Ok, US 152/E3
Göteborg, Swe. 40/D3
Göteborg Och Bohus (co.), Swe. 38/D4
Gotel (mts.), Nga.,Cam. 116/A4
Gotemba, Japan 85/F3
Götene, Swe. 40/E2
Gotha, Ger. 53/H7
Gothenburg, Ne, US 154/D3
Gothèye, Niger 115/F3
Gotland (isl.), Swe. 74/B4
Gotland (co.), Swe. 38/F4
Gotō (isls.), Japan 79/K5
Gotse Delchev, Bul. 49/H2
Gotska Sandön (isl.), Swe. 41/H2
Gotska Sandön NP, Swe. 41/H2
Gōtsu, Japan 84/C3
Gottenheim, Ger. 60/D1
Göttingen, Ger. 53/G5
Gottmadingen, Ger. 61/E2
Gottolengo, It. 62/D3
Gottröta, Swe. 39/B1
Götzis, Aus. 61/F3
Gouarec, Fr. 56/B4
Goubangzi, China 81/A2
Gouda, SAfr. 124/L10
Gouda, Neth. 52/B4
Goudiry, Sen. 114/B3
Gouesnou, Fr. 56/A4
Gouessant (riv.), Fr. 56/C4
Gouet (riv.), Fr. 56/C4
Gough (isl.), StH 26/J7
Gough, Ga, US 163/F4
Gouin (res.), Qu, Can. 141/J4
Goulais (riv.), On, Can. 160/D1
Goulburn, Austl. 133/D2
Goulburn (isls.), Austl. 127/C2
Goulburn, North (isl.), Austl. 128/D2
Goulburn, South (isl.), Austl. 128/D2
Gould (mt.), Austl. 130/C3
Gould, Ar, US 153/J4
Gould, Ok, US 152/E3
Gould City, Mi, US 160/D1
Gouldbusk, Tx, US 150/E2
Goulds, Nf, Can. 159/L2
Gouldsboro, Pa, US 168/C1
Gouldtown, Sk, Can. 145/L2
Goulfey, Camr. 116/B2
Goulimine, Mor. 110/C3
Goulmima, Mor. 110/D3
Goulou (peak), China 87/E3
Goulou (mts.), China 87/F4
Goumbou, Mali 114/D3
Gouménissa, Gre. 49/H2
Goundam, Mali 114/E2
Goundi, Chad 116/C3
Gounou Gaya, Chad 116/B3
Goupillières, Fr. 30/H5
Gouraye, Mrta. 114/B3
Gourcy, Burk. 115/E3
Gourdon, Fr. 44/D4
Gouré, Niger 115/H3
Gourin, Fr. 56/B4
Gourits (riv.), SAfr. 124/C4
Gourma (prov.), Burk. 115/F3
Gourma (phys. reg.), Burk. 115/F3
Gourma Rharous, Mali 115/E2
Gournay-en-Bray, Fr. 54/A5
Gouro, Chad 108/C5
Gourock, Sc, UK 33/B5
Goussainville, Fr. 30/K4
Gouvêa, Braz. 187/E3
Gouveia, Port. 46/B2
Gouverneur, NY, US 161/J2
Gouvieux, Fr. 30/K4
Gouville-sur-Mer, Fr. 56/D2
Gouvy, Belg. 55/E3
Gouyave, Gren. 173/N9
Govan, Sk, Can. 156/B2
Govardhan, India 96/A2
Gove (Gove City), Ks, US 152/D1
Goverla (peak), Ukr. 72/C3
Governador Archer, Braz. 183/E4
Governador Celso Ramos, Braz. 189/G3
Governador Dix-Sept Rosado, Braz. 183/G4
Governador Eugênio Barros, Braz. 183/E4
Governador Valadares, Braz. 187/E3
Government (hill), SD, US 156/C5
Government (peak), Mi, US 157/K4
Government (peak), Wy, US 154/B3
Government Camp, Or, US 146/C1
Government Palace, VatC. 65/G7
Governor Generoso, Phil. 88/D4
Governors (isl.), NY, US 169/J9
Govĭ Altayn (mts.), Mong. 75/K5
Govi-Altay (prov.), Mong. 78/D2
Govind Sāgar (res.), India 98/D4
Govindapalle, India 95/D2
Govindgarh, India 96/C3
Govindpur, India 95/E1
Gowanda, NY, US 161/G3
Gower (pen.), Wal, UK 36/B3
Gower, Mo, US 155/G4
Gower's Corner, Fl, US 164/L7
Gowk, Iran 101/G3
Gowna (lake), Ire. 32/C2
Gowran, Ire. 32/C4
Gowrie, Ia, US 155/G2
Goxhill, Eng, UK 35/H4
Goya, Arg. 188/E4
Göyçay, Azer. 71/H4
Goyen (riv.), Fr. 56/A4
Goyllarisquizga, Peru 184/B3
Göynük, Turk. 51/K5
Goyt (riv.), Eng, UK 35/F5
Göytäpä, Azer. 103/G2
Goz Beïda, Chad 116/D2
Goz Sassulko (dune), CAfr. 116/D3
Gozaisho-yama (peak), Japan 83/K5
Gözeli, Turk. 102/D2
Gozha (lake), China 99/D5
Gozo (isl.), Malta 67/G3
Gozzano, It. 62/B2
Graaff-Reinet, SAfr. 124/D4
Graafschap (phys. reg.), Neth. 52/D4
Graæted, Den. 39/J6
Graauw, Neth. 52/B6
Graben, Ger. 61/G1
Graberberg (peak), Namb. 124/B2
Grabouw, SAfr. 124/L11
Grabow, Ger. 42/F2
Graça Aranha, Braz. 183/E4
Gračac, Cro. 50/B3
Gračanica, Bosn. 50/D3
Grace, Id, US 147/H2
Grace City, ND, US 156/E4
Gracefield, Qu, Can. 161/H1
Gracemere, Austl. 134/C3
Gracemont, Ok, US 153/E3
Graceville, Fl, US 165/F2
Graceville, Mn, US 156/F5
Grächen, Swi. 60/D5
Grachev Kust, Rus. 71/J2
Grachëvka, Rus. 73/M5
Gracias, Hon. 176/D3
Gracias a Dios (cape), Hon. 177/F3
Graciosa (isl.), Azor., Port. 47/S12
Gradačac, Bosn. 50/D3
Gradaús, Braz. 182/D4
Gradaús, Serra dos (mts.), Braz. 182/D5
Gradisca d'Isonzo, It. 63/G2
Grado, It. 63/G2
Grädö, Swe. 39/C1
Grado, Sp. 46/B1
Grady, Al, US 165/E2
Grady, Ar, US 153/J3
Grady, Ok, US 153/F3
Graettinger, Ia, US 155/G2
Gräfelfing, Ger. 59/E6
Grafenau, Ger. 59/G5
Gräfenberg, Ger. 58/E3
Grafenrheinfeld, Ger. 58/D3
Gräfentonna, Ger. 53/H6
Grafenwöhr, Ger. 59/E3
Graffignana, It. 62/C3
Grafing bei München, Ger. 59/E6
Gråfjell (peak), Nor. 40/C1
Graford, Tx, US 153/E4
Grafrath, Ger. 61/H1
Grafton, Austl. 132/E1
Grafton, NB, Can. 158/D2
Grafton, Il, US 155/J4
Grafton, ND, US 156/F3
Grafton, Wi, US 160/C3
Grafton, WV, US 160/F5
Grafton Passage, Austl. 134/B2
Gragnano, It. 65/D6
Graham (isl.), BC, Can. 140/C3
Graham (isl.), Nun, Can. 141/S7
Graham, On, Can. 157/J3
Graham (mt.), Az, US 149/H4
Graham, Fl, US 165/G3
Graham (lake), Me, US 158/C3
Graham, NC, US 163/H2
Graham, Ok, US 153/F3
Graham, Tx, US 153/E4
Graham Bell (isl.), Rus. 74/G1
Graham Land (phys. reg.), Ant. 192/V
Grahamdale, Mb, Can. 156/E2
Grahamstown, SAfr. 124/D4
Grahamsville, NY, US 161/J4
Graian Alps (range), Fr. 66/E1
Graiguenamanagh, Ire. 32/D4
Grain (coast), Libr. 114/C5
Grain, Eng, UK 37/G4
Grainau, Ger. 61/H3
Grainfield, Ks, US 154/D4
Grajagan, Indo. 89/F5
Grajaú, Braz. 183/E4
Grajaú (riv.), Braz. 183/E4
Grajewo, Pol. 41/K5
Gram, Den. 40/C4
Gramada, Bul. 50/F4
Gramastetten, Aus. 59/H6
Gramat (plat.), Fr. 44/D4
Gramat, Fr. 44/D4
Gramatneusiedl, Aus. 51/N7
Grammont (peak), Fr. 64/D5
Grampian (mts.), Sc, UK 33/B3
Grampians NP, Austl. 132/B3
Gramsbergen, Neth. 52/D3
Gramsh, Alb. 49/G2
Gran, Nor. 40/D1
Gran (des.), Mex. 148/E4
Gran Altiplanicie Central (plat.), Arg. 191/C6
Gran Bajo de San Julián (plain), Arg. 191/C6
Gran Bajo Oriental (plain), Arg. 190/C5
Gran Canaria (int'l arpt.), Sp. 110/B4
Gran Canaria (isl.), Sp. 110/B4
Gran Chaco (plain), SAm. 179/C5
Gran Isla del Maíz (isl.), Nic. 177/F3
Gran Laguna Salada (lag.), Arg. 190/D5
Gran Paradiso (peak), It. 64/D1
Gran Paradiso, PN (Nat'l Parc), It. 45/G4
Gran Piedra (hill), Cuba 177/H2
Gran Pilastro (peak), It. 45/J3
Gran Quivira, NM, US 149/J3
Gran Sasso d'Italia (mts.), It. 65/C3
Gran Vilaya (ruin), Peru 184/B2
Grana (riv.), It. 64/D4
Granada, Co, US 152/C1
Granada, Col. 180/C4
Granada, Nic. 176/E4
Granada, Sp. 46/D4
Granadilla de Abona, Sp. 110/A3
Granados, Mex. 174/C2
Granard, Ire. 32/C2
Granarolo dell'Emilia, It. 63/E4
Granbury (lake), Tx, US 151/F1
Granbury, Tx, US 151/F1
Granby (riv.), BC, Can. 144/E3
Granby, Qu, Can. 161/K2
Granby, Co, US 154/B3
Granby, Mo, US 153/G2
Grand (lake), Nb, Can. 158/E2
Grand (canal), China 80/D4
Grand (lake), Nf, Can. 141/L4
Grand (falls), Kenya 119/B2
Grand (riv.), Ia,Mo, US 155/G3
Grand (isl.), Mi, US 157/L4
Grand Aféri, C.d'Iv. 114/E5
Grand Arc (peak), Fr. 64/C1
Grand Bahama (isl.), Bahm. 139/K7
Grand Bank, Nf, Can. 159/K2
Grand Bassa (co.), Libr. 114/C5
Grand-Bassam, C.d'Iv. 114/E5
Grand Bay, NB, Can. 158/D3
Grand Bay, Al, US 164/D2
Grand Bérard (peak), Fr. 64/C4
Grand Blanc, Mi, US 160/E3
Grand Brière (swamp), Fr. 56/C6
Grand Calumet (isl.), Qu, Can. 161/H2
Grand Canal d'Alsace (canal), Fr. 60/D2
Grand Cane, La, US 150/H1
Grand Canyon, Az, US 149/F2
Grand Canyon (canyon), Az, US 149/F2
Grand Canyon Caverns, Az, US 149/F3
Grand Canyon Nat'l Park, Az, US 149/F2
Grand Canyon-Parashant Nat'l Mon., Ut, US 149/F2
Grand Cape Mount (co.), Libr. 114/C5
Grand Cayman (isl.), Cay. 172/E4
Grand Centre, Ab, Can. 140/E3
Grand Cess, Libr. 114/C5
Grand-Charmont, Fr. 60/C2
Grand Chenier, La, US 164/B3
Grand Colombier (peak), Fr. 60/B6
Grand Combine (peak), Swi. 60/D6
Grand Coulee (dam), Wa, US 144/E4
Grand Coulee, Wa, US 144/E4
Grand-Couronne, Fr. 57/G2
Grand Drumont (peak), Fr. 60/C2
Grand Erg de Bilma (des.), Niger 108/B5
Grand Erg Occidental (des.), Alg. 107/C1
Grand Erg Oriental (des.), Alg. 107/C1
Grand Eyvia (riv.), It. 64/D1
Grand Falls, NB, Can. 158/D2
Grand Falls, Nf, Can. 159/K1
Grand Forks, BC, Can. 144/E3
Grand Forks (A.F.B.), ND, US 156/F4
Grand Forks, ND, US 156/F4
Grand-Fort-Philippe, Fr. 54/B2
Grand-Fougeray, Fr. 56/D5
Grand Galibier (peak), Fr. 64/C2
Grand Goâve, Haiti 177/H2
Grand Gorge, NY, US 161/J3
Grand Harbour, NB, Can. 158/D3
Grand Haven, Mi, US 160/C3
Grand Island, Ne, US 154/E3
Grand Isle, La, US 164/D3
Grand Isle, Vt, US 161/K2
Grand Jide (co.), Libr. 114/D5
Grand Junction, Co, US 147/J4
Grand Junction, Tn, US 162/C3
Grand-Lahou, C.d'Iv. 114/D5
Grand Manan (isl.), NB, Can. 158/D3
Grand Marais, Mn, US 157/J4
Grand Marais, Mb, Can. 156/F2
Grand Marsh, Wi, US 155/K2
Grand Meadow, Mn, US 155/H2
Grand Mont (pt.), Fr. 56/C5
Grand Mont Ruan (peak), Fr. 60/C5
Grand Mound, Wa, US 144/C4
Grand Muveran (peak), Swi. 60/D5
Grand North Fork (riv.), SD, US 156/C5
Grand Parpaillon (peak), Fr. 64/C4
Grand Pic de Belledonne (peak), Fr. 64/B2
Grand Pinier (peak), Fr. 64/C3
Grand-Popo, Ben. 115/F5
Grand Portage, Mn, US 157/K4
Grand Portage Ind. Res., Mn, US 157/J4
Grand Portage Nat'l Mon., Mn, US 157/K4
Grand Portal (pt.), Mi, US 160/C1
Grand Prairie, Tx, US 150/L7
Grand Prairie (plain), Ar, US 162/B3
Grand Pré Nat'l Hist. Park, NS, Can. 158/E3
Grand Queyron (peak), Fr. 64/D3
Grand Rapids, Mn, US 157/H4
Grand Rapids, ND, US 156/E4
Grand Rapids (dam), Mi, US 160/C2
Grand Rapids, Mi, US 160/D3
Grand Rhône (riv.), Fr. 44/F5
Grand Ronde, Or, US 146/B1
Grand Ronde (riv.), Wa, US 144/F4
Grand Russel (chan.), UK 56/C2
Grand Saline, Tx, US 151/G1
Grand Santi, FrG. 182/C1
Grand South Fork (riv.), SD, US 156/C5
Grand Staircase-Escalante Nat'l Mon., Ut, US 149/F2
Grand Taureau (peak), Fr. 60/C4
Grand Teton (peak), Wy, US 147/H2
Grand Teton NP, Wy, US 147/H2
Grand Tower, Il, US 162/C2
Grand Traverse (bay), Mi, US 160/D2
Grand Valley, On, Can. 160/S8
Grand Veymont (peak), Fr. 64/B3
Grand View, Id, US 146/E2
Grand, East Fork (riv.), Ia, Mo, US 155/G3
Grand, South Fork (riv.), SD, US 154/C1
Grandcamp-Maisy, Fr. 57/D2
Grandcour, Swi. 60/C4
Grande (bay), Arg. 179/C8
Grande (isl.), Braz. 186/B4
Grande (lake), Braz. 181/H5
Grande (pt.), Chile 188/B3
Grande (peak), It. 48/C4
Grande (peak), It. 65/C3
Grande (pt.), Pan. 177/G4
Grande (riv.), Uru. 191/K10
Grande (peak), NM, US 152/C2
Grande Autane (peak), Fr. 64/C3
Grande Cache, Ab, Can. 140/E3
Grande Comore (isl.), Com. 125/G5
Grande de Curuaí (lake), Braz. 182/C3
Grande de Gurupá (isl.), Braz. 182/D3
Grande de Manacapuru (lake), Braz. 182/A3
Grande de Tierra del Fuego (isl.), Chile,Arg. 191/D7
Grande do Curuaí (lake), Braz. 181/H5
Grande Pointe, Mb, Can. 156/F3
Grande Prairie, Ab, Can. 140/E3
Grande Ronde (riv.), Or, US 146/E1
Grande Saline, Haiti 177/H2
Grande Sassière (peak), Fr. 64/D1
Grande Séolane (peak), Fr. 64/C4
Grande, Serra (mts.), Braz. 181/F4
Grande-Anse, Qu, Can. 158/A2
Grande-Cascapédia, Qu, Can. 158/E1
Grande-Entrée, Qu, Can. 159/G2
Grande-Rivière, Qu, Can. 158/E1
Grande-Synthe, Fr. 54/B1
Grande-Terre (isl.), Guad. 173/J4
Grande-Vallée, Qu, Can. 158/E1
Grandes Jorasses (peak), It. 60/D6
Grandes Rousses (range), Fr. 64/C2
Grandfalls, Tx, US 150/C2
Grandfield, Ok, US 153/E3
Grandfresnoy, Fr. 54/B5
Grandin, Mo, US 162/B2
Grândola, Port. 46/A3
Grandpuits-Bailly-Carrois, Fr. 30/L6
Grandson, Swi. 60/C4
Grandview, Mb, Can. 156/D2
Grandview, Tx, US 151/F1
Grandview, Wa, US 144/E4
Grandview Park, Pa, US 161/G4
Grandview Plaza, Ks, US 153/F1
Grandvillars, Fr. 60/C2
Grandville, Mi, US 160/D3
Grandvilliers, Fr. 54/A4
Grâne, Fr. 64/A3
Graneros, Chile 190/N9
Graney (riv.), Ire. 32/B4
Granfjället (peak), Swe. 40/E1
Grange (nbrhd.), Austl. 131/M8
Grange (riv.), Ire. 32/B3
Grange, Eng, UK 35/F3
Grange, Mont de (peak), Fr. 60/C5
Grangemouth, Sc, UK 33/C4
Granger (mt.), Yk, Can. 171/L3
Granger, In, US 160/C4
Granger, Tx, US 151/F2
Granger, Wa, US 144/D4
Granges-sur-Vologne, Fr. 60/C1
Grängesberg, Swe. 40/F1
Grangeville, Id, US 144/F5
Granier (peak), Fr. 64/B2
Granite, Ok, US 152/E3
Granite (peak), Mt, US 147/J1
Granite (peak), Mt, US 147/G1
Granite (mtn.), Mt, US 145/J4
Granite Bay, BC, Can. 144/B2
Granite Canon, Wy, US 154/B3
Granite City, Il, US 155/J4
Granite Falls, Mn, US 155/G1
Granite Shoals, Tx, US 151/E2
Graniteville, Mo, US 162/B2
Granity, NZ 135/B3
Granja, Braz. 183/F3
Grankulla (Kauniainen), Fin. 39/E4
Grannis, Ar, US 153/G3
Granollers, Sp. 47/L6
Grans, Fr. 64/B5
Grant, Al, US 162/D3
Grant, Co, US 152/B1
Grant, Mi, US 160/D3
Grant, Mt, US 147/G1
Grant, Ne, US 154/D3
Grant (range), Nv, US 146/F4
Grant (mt.), Nv, US 146/D4
Grant City, Mo, US 155/G3
Grant-Kohrs Ranch Nat'l Hist. Site, Mt, US 145/H4
Grantham, Eng, UK 35/H6
Grantley Adams (int'l arpt.), Bar. 173/P9
Granton, Wi, US 155/J1
Grantown-on-Spey, Sc, UK 33/C2
Grants, NM, US 149/J3
Grants Pass, Or, US 146/B2
Grantsboro, NC, US 163/J3
Grantsburg, Wi, US 157/H5
Grantsdale, Mt, US 145/G4
Grantsville, WV, US 163/G1
Grantville, Ga, US 162/E4
Granville, Fr. 56/D3
Granville (lake), Mb, Can. 140/F3
Granville, Il, US 155/K3
Granville Ferry, NS, Can. 158/E3
Grapeland, Tx, US 151/G2
Grapeview, Wa, US 167/B3
Grapeview, Wa, US 144/C4
Grapevine, Ar, US 153/H3
Grapevine (lake), Tx, US 150/K6
Grapevine, Tx, US 150/K7
Gras-Ellenbach, Ger. 58/B3
Grasberg, Ger. 53/F2
Grasbrunn, Ger. 59/E6
Graskö (isl.), Swe. 39/C1
Graskop, SAfr. 123/F5
Grasmere, BC, Can. 144/G3
Grasmere, Eng, UK 35/E3
Grasmere, SAfr. 124/P13
Grasø (isl.), Swe. 40/H1
Grasonville, Md, US 168/B6
Grass (lake), Il, US 167/P15
Grass Creek, Wy, US 147/J2
Grass Range, Mt, US 145/K4
Grass Valley, Ca, US 146/C4
Grasse, Fr. 64/C5
Grassie, On, Can. 160/T9
Grassina, It. 63/E6
Grassington, Eng, UK 35/G3
Grasslands NP, Sk, Can. 145/L3
Grassy (peak), WV, US 163/G1
Grassy, Austl. 133/B5
Grassy Butte, ND, US 156/C4
Grassy Key (isl.), Fl, US 165/H5
Grassy Lake, Ab, Can. 145/J3
Grassy Park, SAfr. 124/L11
Grästorp, Swe. 40/E2
Grates Cove, Nf, Can. 159/L1
Gratkorn, Aus. 50/B2
Gratz, Pa, US 168/B2
Graubünden (canton), Swi. 61/F4
Graulhet, Fr. 44/E5
Graus, Sp. 47/F1
Gravatá, Braz. 183/H5
Grave, Neth. 52/C5
Grave of Sitting Bull, SD, US 156/D5
Gravedona, It. 61/F5
Gravel Island Nat'l Wild. Ref., Wi, US 160/C2
Gravelbourg, Sk, Can. 145/L3
Gravelines, Fr. 54/B2
Gravellona Toce, It. 61/E6
Gravelly, Ar, US 153/H3
Gravelotte, SAfr. 123/F4
Gravenhurst, On, Can. 161/G2
Grävenwiesbach, Ger. 58/B2
Gravesend, Eng, UK 30/E2
Graveson, Fr. 64/A5
Gravigny, Fr. 57/G2
Gravina di Puglia, It. 48/E2
Gray, Fr. 60/B3
Gray, Me, US 161/L3
Gray, Ga, US 163/F4
Grayback (mtn.), Or, US 146/B2
Grayland, Wa, US 144/B4
Grayling, Ak, US 171/F3
Grayling, Mi, US 160/D2
Grays, Eng, UK 30/E2
Grays (lake), Id, US 147/H2
Grays (har.), Wa, US 144/B4
Grays Lake NWR, Id, US 147/H2
Grayslake, Il, US 167/P15
Grayson, Sk, Can. 156/C2
Grayson, La, US 164/B1
Grayson, Ky, US 163/F1
Graysville, Al, US 162/D4
Grayville, Il, US 162/D1
Graz, Aus. 50/B2
Grazalema, Sp. 46/C4
Grazzanise, It. 65/D5
Greåker, Nor. 40/D2
Gréasque, Fr. 64/B6
Great (lake), Austl. 132/C4
Great (plain), US 152/D1
Great (isl.), Ire. 32/B6
Great (falls), Mt, US 145/J4
Great (bay), NH, US 158/B4
Great (falls), NJ, US 169/J8
Great (basin), Nv, US 142/C4
Great (basin), Nv, US 140/E4
Great Abaco (isl.), Bahm. 139/K7
Great Alföld (plain), Hun., Serb. 50/D2
Great America, Ca, US 167/L12
Great Australian Bight (bay), Austl. 127/B4
Great Baddow, Eng, UK 30/E1
Great Bahama (bank), Bahm. 173/F2
Great Barford, Eng, UK 37/F2
Great Barrier (isl.), NZ 127/H6
Great Barrier (reef), Austl. 127/D2
Great Barrier Reef Marine Park, Austl. 129/G3
Great Barrington, Ma, US 161/K3
Great Barton, Eng, UK 37/G2
Great Basin NP, Nv, US 147/F4
Great Bear (lake), NW, Can. 140/D2
Great Bend, Ks, US 153/E1
Great Bend, NY, US 161/J2
Great Bitter (lake), Egypt 104/C4
Great Bookham, Eng, UK 30/B3
Great Brak (riv.), SAfr. 124/C3
Great Britain (isl.), UK 29/D3
Great Burstead, Eng, UK 30/E2
Great Cedar (swamp), NJ, US 168/D5
Great Coco (isl.), Myan. 93/F5
Great Cornard, Eng, UK 37/G2
Great Cumbrae (isl.), Sc, UK 33/B5
Great Dismal Swamp NWR, Va, US 163/J2
Great Divide (basin), Wy, US 147/J2
Great Dividing (range), Austl. 127/D2
Great Dunmow, Eng, UK 37/G3
Great Egg (har.), NJ, US 168/D5
Great Egg Harbor (riv.), NJ, US 168/D4
Great Exhibition (bay), NZ 135/C1
Great Exuma (isl.), Bahm. 139/K7
Great Falls, Mb, Can. 156/F2
Great Falls, Mt, US 145/J4
Great Falls, SC, US 163/G3
Great Fish (riv.), SAfr. 124/D4
Great Fish (pt.), SAfr. 124/D4
Great Gransden, Eng, UK 37/F2
Great Guana Cay (isl.), Bahm. 173/F3
Great Harwood, Eng, UK 35/F4
Great Himalaya (range), Asia 92/D2
Great Inagua (isl.), Bahm. 139/K7
Great Indian (des.), India,Pak. 92/B2
Great Karoo (plat.), SAfr. 124/C4
Great Kei (riv.), SAfr. 124/D4
Great Lakes Nav. Trg. Sta., Il, US 160/C3
Great Miami (riv.), Oh, US 160/D4
Great Milton, Eng, UK 37/E3
Great Mis Tor (hill), Eng, UK 36/B5
Great Missenden, Eng, UK 37/F3
Great Moose (lake), Me, US 158/C3
Great Mosque (Masjid Raya), Indo. 89/B2
Great Neck, NY, US 169/L8
Great Nicobar (isl.), India 93/F6
Great Ouse (riv.), Eng, UK 37/E2
Great Palace, Rus. 69/S7
Great Palace, Rus. 69/T7
Great Peconic (bay), NY, US 169/F2
Great Pee Dee (riv.), SC, US 163/H3
Great Piece Meadows (swamp), NJ, US 169/H8
Great Rift (valley), Afr. 121/G4
Great Ruaha (riv.), Tanz. 119/A3
Great Sacandara (lake), NY, US 161/J3
Great Salt (lake), Ut, US 139/F5
Great Salt Lake (des.), Ut, US 142/D3
Great Salt Plains (lake), Ok, US 153/E2
Great Sand (hills), Sk, Can. 145/K2
Great Sand Dunes Nat'l Park, Co, US 149/K2
Great Sand Sea (des.), Egypt,Libya 108/D2
Great Sandy (des.), Austl. 127/B2
Great Scarcies (riv.), SLeo. 114/B4
Great Shelford, Eng, UK 37/G2
Great Shunner Fell (peak), Eng, UK 35/F3
Great Slave (lake), NW, Can. 139/F3
Great Smoky Mountains NP, Tn, US 162/F3
Great South (bay), US 169/E2
Great Stour (riv.), Eng, UK 37/G4
Great Torrington, Eng, UK 36/B5
Great Victoria (des.), Austl. 127/B3
Great Victoria Desert Nature Reserve, Austl. 131/E4
Great Village, NS, Can. 158/F3
Great Wall (wall), China 78/F4
Great Warley, Eng, UK 30/D2
Great Wass (isl.), Me, US 158/D3
Great Western Tiers (mts.), Austl. 132/C4
Great White Heron Nat'l Wildlife Refuge, Fl, US 165/H5
Great Winterhoek (peak), SAfr. 124/L10
Great Witley, Eng, UK 36/D2
Great Yarmouth, Eng, UK 37/H1
Great Zab (riv.), Iraq 103/E2
Great Zimbabwe (ruin), Zim. 123/F4
Greater Accra (pol. reg.), Gha. 115/F5
Greater Antilles (isls.), NAm. 139/J7
Greater Barsuki (des.), Kaz. 71/L3
Greater Buffalo (int'l arpt.), NY, US 160/V10
Greater Cincinnati (int'l arpt.), Oh, US 162/E1
Greater London (co.), Eng, UK 30/D2
Greater Manchester (co.), Eng, UK 35/F4
Greater Pittsburgh (int'l arpt.), Pa, US 160/F4
Greater Rochester (int'l arpt.), NY, US 161/H3
Greater Sunda (isls.), Indo. 90/C4
Greaterville, Az, US 149/G5
Greatham, Eng, UK 35/G2
Grebenhain, Ger. 58/C2
Grebenstein, Ger. 53/G6
Grébon (peak), Niger 115/H2
Grecco, Uru. 191/K10
Greco (cape), Cyp. 104/D2
Greco (peak), It. 65/C4
Greding, Ger. 59/E4
Gredos (mts.), Sp. 46/C2
Grée (riv.), Fr. 57/D6
Greece (ctry.) 49/G3
Greece, NY, US 161/H3
Greeley, Ks, US 153/G1
Greeley, Co, US 154/B3
Greeley (Greeley Center), Ne, US 154/E3
Greeleyville, SC, US 163/H4
Greely Ford (ford), Nun, Can. 141/S6
Green, Mi, US 157/K4
Green (lake), Wi, US 160/B3
Green (mts.), Vt, US 161/K3
Green (pond), NJ, US 169/H7
Green (riv.), Ut,Wy, US 142/E4
Green, Or, US 146/B2
Green (bay), Wi, US 155/L1
Green, Tx, US 151/F3
Green (swamp), NC, US 163/H3
Green (cape), Austl. 133/E3
Green Bay, Wi, US 160/B2
Green Bay Nat'l Wild. Ref., Wi, US 160/C2
Green City, Mo, US 155/H3
Green Cove Springs, Fl, US 165/H3
Green Creek, NJ, US 168/D5
Green Forest, Ar, US 153/H2
Green Haven, Md, US 168/B5
Green Hill, Tn, US 162/D2
Green Lake, Tx, US 150/F3
Green Lake, Wi, US 155/K2
Green Lane (res.), Pa, US 168/C3
Green Lowther (peak), Sc, UK 33/C6
Green Peter (lake), Or, US 146/B1
Green Pond, Al, US 162/D4
Green Pond, NJ, US 168/D1
Green Ridge, Mo, US 153/H1
Green River, On, Can. 160/U8
Green River, PNG 91/K4
Green River (hill), Ky, US 162/E2
Green River (lake), Ky, US 162/E2
Green River, Ut, US 149/G1
Green River, Wy, US 147/J3
Green Springs, Oh, US 160/E4
Green Valley, Az, US 149/G5
Green Valley, Ca, US 166/B1
Green Valley, Md, US 161/H5
Green Valley Lake, Ca, US 166/C2
Green Village, NJ, US 169/H9
Greenacres, Ca, US 148/C3
Greenacres City, Fl, US 164/P9
Greenbelt (park), Md, US 168/B6
Greenbelt, Md, US 168/B6
Greenbrier, Ar, US 153/H3
Greenbrier (riv.), WV, US 163/G2
Greenbush, Mn, US 156/F3
Greenbushes, Austl. 130/C5
Greencastle, Ire. 34/B1
Greencastle, In, US 160/C5
Greencastle, Pa, US 161/H5
Greencastle, Mo, US 155/H3
Greendale, Wi, US 167/Q14
Greene, NY, US 161/J3
Greene, Ia, US 155/H2
Greeneville, Tn, US 163/F2
Greenfield, Ca, US 148/B2
Greenfield, Ia, US 155/G3
Greenfield, Il, US 155/J4
Greenfield, In, US 160/D5
Greenfield, Mo, US 153/H2
Greenfield, Ma, US 161/K3
Greenfield, Nf, Can. 158/E3
Greenfield, Oh, US 160/E5
Greenfield, Tn, US 162/C2
Greenfield, Wi, US 167/P14
Greenfield Park, Qu, Can. 159/P7
Greenisland, NI, UK 34/C2
Greenland, Mi, US 157/K4
Greenland (sea) 139/R2
Greenland (Kalaallit Nunaat) (dpcy.), Den. 139/N2
Greenlaw, Sc, UK 33/D5
Greenleaf, Ks, US 155/F4
Greenmount, Md, US 168/B4
Greenock, Sc, UK 33/B5
Greenore (pt.), Ire. 32/D5
Greenore, Ire. 34/B3
Greenough (riv.), Austl. 130/B4
Greenough (mt.), Ak, US 171/K2
Greenport, NY, US 169/F1
Greens (peak), Az, US 149/H3
Greens Bayou (riv.), Tx, US 151/M9
Greensboro, Al, US 162/D4
Greensboro, Fl, US 165/F2
Greensboro, Ga, US 163/F4
Greensboro, Md, US 168/C6
Greensboro, NC, US 163/H2
Greensburg, In, US 160/D5
Greensburg, Ks, US 152/E2
Greensburg, Ky, US 162/E2
Greensburg, La, US 164/C2
Greensburg, Pa, US 161/G4
Greenspond, Nf, Can. 159/L1
Greenstreet, Sk, Can. 145/K1
Greensville, On, Can. 160/T9
Greentop, Mo, US 155/H3
Greenup, Ky, US 163/F1
Greenup, Il, US 162/C1
Greenvale, Austl. 134/B2
Greenville, Libr. 114/C5
Greenville, Al, US 164/E2
Greenville, Ca, US 146/C3
Greenville, Fl, US 165/G2
Greenville, Ga, US 162/E4
Greenville, Ky, US 162/D2
Greenville, Il, US 155/K4
Greenville, Mi, US 160/D3
Greenville, Mo, US 162/B2
Greenville, Ms, US 162/B4
Greenville, NC, US 163/J3
Greenville, Oh, US 160/D4
Greenville, SC, US 163/F3
Greenville, Tx, US 153/F4
Greenville, Ut, US 149/F1
Greenwater (riv.), Wa, US 167/D3
Greenwell Point, Austl. 133/E2
Greenwich, Oh, US 160/E4
Greenwich (pt.), Ct, US 169/L8
Greenwich (bor.), Eng, UK 30/D2
Greenwich, Ct, US 169/L7
Greenwich Observatory, Eng, UK 30/D2
Greenwich Village (nbrhd.), NY, US 169/K9
Greenwood, On, Can. 160/U8
Greenwood, Ar, US 153/G3
Greenwood, De, US 168/C6
Greenwood, Fl, US 165/F2
Greenwood, In, US 160/C5
Greenwood, Ms, US 162/B4
Greenwood, SC, US 163/F3
Greenwood (lake), SC, US 163/F3
Greenwood Lake, NY, US 168/D1
Greenwood Village, Co, US 152/B1
Greer, SC, US 163/F3
Greers Ferry (dam), Ar, US 153/J3
Greers Ferry, Ar, US 153/H3
Greers Ferry (lake), Ar, US 162/A3
Greeson (lake), Ar, US 153/H3
Grefrath, Ger. 52/D6
Gregoire Kayibanda (Kigali) (int'l arpt.), Rwa. 121/G3
Gregório (riv.), Braz. 184/D2
Gregory (peak), NC, US 162/F3
Gregory, SD, US 154/E2
Gregory (riv.), Austl. 129/E4
Gregory (range), Austl. 127/D2
Gregory (lake), Austl. 127/B3
Gregory Lake Abor. Land, Austl. 128/B5
Greifswald, Ger. 40/E4
Greifwalder Bodden (bay), Ger. 43/G1
Greilickville, Mi, US 160/D2
Greimberg (peak), Aus. 45/L3
Gremikha, Rus. 68/H1
Gremyachinsk, Rus. 69/N4
Grenå, Den. 40/D3
Grenada (ctry.) 173/N9
Grenada, Ms, US 162/C4
Grenada (lake), Ms, US 162/C4
Grenade, Fr. 44/D5
Grenay, Fr. 54/B3
Grenchen, Swi. 60/D3
Grenfell, Sk, Can. 156/C2
Grenfell, Austl. 133/D1
Grennach (riv.), Ger. 58/D6
Grenoble, Fr. 64/B2
Grenola, Ks, US 153/F2
Grenora, ND, US 156/C3
Grenville (cape), Austl. 129/F2
Grenzach-Wyhlen, Ger. 60/D2
Gréoux-les-Bains, Fr. 64/B5
Gresham, Or, US 146/B1
Gresham Park, Ga, US 163/M7
Gresik, Indo. 89/F4
Gressåmoen NP (nat'l park), Nor. 68/B2
Gressåmoen NP, Nor. 38/E2
Gressan, It. 64/D1
Gresse (riv.), Fr. 64/B3
Gresston, Ga, US 165/G1
Grésy-sur-Aix, Fr. 64/B1
Greta (riv.), Eng, UK 35/E2
Gretna, Austl. 132/C4
Gretna, Mb, Can. 156/F3
Gretna, Sc, UK 35/E2
Gretna, Fl, US 165/F2
Gretna, La, US 164/C3
Gretna, Va, US 163/H2
Gretton, Eng, UK 37/F1
Grettstadt, Ger. 58/D3
Gretz-Armainvilliers, Fr. 30/L5
Greve (riv.), It. 63/E5
Greve, Den. 39/J7
Greve in Chianti, It. 63/E6
Grevelingendam (dam), Neth. 52/B5
Greven, Ger. 53/E4
Grevená, Gre. 49/G2
Grevenbroich, Ger. 55/F1
Grevenmacher (dist.), Lux. 55/F4
Grevenmacher, Lux. 55/F4
Grevesmühlen, Ger. 42/F2
Grevlingen (chan.), Neth. 52/A5
Grey (cape), Austl. 129/E3
Grey (range), Austl. 127/D3
Grey (riv.), Nf, Can. 159/J2
Grey (pt.), NI, UK 34/C2
Grey Abbey, NI, UK 34/C2
Grey Peaks NP, Austl. 134/B2
Grey River, Nf, Can. 159/J2
Greybull (riv.), Wy, US 147/J1
Greybull, Wy, US 147/J1
Greycliff, Mt, US 145/K5
Greylingstad, SAfr. 124/E2
Greylock (mt.), Ma, US 161/K3
Greymouth, NZ 135/B3
Greystoke, Eng, UK 35/F2
Greystones, Ire. 34/B5
Greytown, NZ 135/J9
Greytown, SAfr. 125/E3
Grez-Doiceau, Belg. 55/D2
Grezzana, It. 63/E2
Gribanovskiy, Rus. 73/L2
Gribbin (pt.), Eng, UK 36/B6
Gribingui (riv.), CAfr. 116/C4
Gribingui (pref.), CAfr. 116/C4
Gribingui-Bamingui, Rsv. de Faune du, CAfr. 116/C4
Gridley, Ca, US 146/C4
Gridley, Il, US 155/K3
Gridley, Ks, US 153/G1
Griefensee (lake), Swi. 61/E3
Griekwastad, SAfr. 124/C3
Griend (isl.), Neth. 52/C2
Gries am Brenner, Aus. 61/H3
Griesheim, Ger. 58/B3
Grieskirchen, Aus. 59/G6
Griesskogel (peak), Aus. 61/H3
Griesstätt, Ger. 59/F7
Griffin, Sk, Can. 156/C3
Griffin (lake), Fl, US 164/M6
Griffin, Ga, US 162/E4
Griffiss (A.F.B.), NY, US 161/J3
Griffith, In, US 167/R16
Griffith, Austl. 133/C2
Griffith Park, Ca, US 166/F7
Griffithville, Ar, US 153/J3
Grifton, NC, US 163/J3
Griggs, Ok, US 152/C2
Grigna (peak), It. 61/F6
Grignan, Fr. 64/A4
Grignano Polesine, It. 63/E3
Grignon, Fr. 64/C1
Grigny, Fr. 64/A1
Grigny, Fr. 30/K6
Grigoriopol, Mol. 72/E4
Grigor'yevskoye, Rus. 68/H5
Grijalva (riv.), Mex. 176/C2
Grijpskerk, Neth. 52/D2
Grillby, Swe. 39/A1
Grillon, Fr. 64/A4
Grim (cape), Austl. 132/C4
Grimari, CAfr. 116/D4
Grimaud (riv.), Fr. 64/C6
Grimaud, Fr. 64/C6
Grimbergen, Belg. 55/D2
Grimesland, NC, US 163/J3
Grimethorpe, Eng, UK 35/G4
Grimisuat, Swi. 60/D5
Grimmen, Ger. 40/E4
Grimsby, Eng, UK 35/H4
Grimsby, On, Can. 160/T9
Grimselpass (pass), Swi. 61/E4
Grimsey (isl.), Ice. 38/N6
Grimsley, Tn, US 162/E2
Grimstad, Nor. 40/C2
Grindavík, Ice. 38/M7
Grindelwald, Swi. 60/E4
Grindsted, Den. 40/C4
Grinnel (pen.), Nun, Can. 141/S7
Grinnell, Ia, US 155/H3
Grintavec (peak), Slov. 45/L3
Griqualand East (reg.), SAfr. 124/E3
Griqualand West (reg.), SAfr. 124/C2
Gris-Nez (cape), Fr. 54/A2
Grise Fiord, Nun, Can. 141/S7
Grisslehamn, Swe. 41/H1
Griswold, Ia, US 155/G3
Grisy-les-Plâtres, Fr. 30/J4
Grisy-Suisnes, Fr. 30/L5
Grivaï Pamia, CAfr. 116/C4
Grivette (riv.), Fr. 30/L4
Grizzly (bay), Ca, US 167/K10
Grizzly (mtn.), Id, US 144/F4
Grizzly Flats, Ca, US 146/C4
Grmeč (mts.), Bosn. 50/C3
Groaíras, Braz. 183/F3
Grobbendonk, Belg. 52/B6
Gröben, Ger. 42/Q7
Gröbenzell, Ger. 59/E6
Grobiņa, Lat. 41/J3
Groblersdal, SAfr. 123/F5
Groblershoop, SAfr. 124/C3
Grödby, Swe. 39/A1
Grodków, Pol. 43/J3
Grodzisk Wielkopolski, Pol. 43/J2
Grodzyanka, Bela. 41/N5
Groenlo, Neth. 52/D4
Groesbeck, Tx, US 151/F2
Groesbeek, Neth. 52/C5
Groix, Fr. 56/B5
Groix (isl.), Fr. 44/B3
Grójec, Pol. 43/L3
Grömitz, Ger. 40/D4
Gromo, It. 61/F6
Gronau, Ger. 53/G4
Gronau, Ger. 52/E4
Grong Grong, Austl. 133/C2
Groningen (prov.), Neth. 52/D2
Groningen, Sur. 182/C1
Groningen, Neth. 52/D2
Gronlait (peak), It. 61/H5
Gronlid, Sk, Can. 145/M1
Grono, Swi. 61/F5
Groom, Tx, US 152/D3
Groot Kleeberg (mts.), Namb. 122/C4
Groot Marico (riv.), SAfr. 123/E5
Groot Waterberg (mts.), Namb. 122/C4
Groot-Letabarivier (riv.), SAfr. 123/F4
Groot-Marico, SAfr. 122/E5
Groot-Marico (riv.), SAfr. 124/D2
Grootberg (peak), Namb. 122/B4
Grootdraaidam (res.), SAfr. 124/Q13
Groote Eylandt (isl.), Austl. 127/C2
Grootegast, Neth. 52/D2
Grootfontein, Namb. 122/C3
Grootgeluk, SAfr. 123/E4
Grootvloer (salt pan), SAfr. 124/C3
Gropello Cairoli, It. 62/B3
Gros Islet, StL. 173/N9
Gros Morne (peak), Nf, Can. 141/L4
Gros Morne NP, Nf, Can. 159/J1
Gros Ventre (riv.), Wy, US 147/H2
Gros-Morne, Qu, Can. 158/E1

Grosbliederstroff, Fr. 55/G5
Grosio, It. 61/G5
Grosne (riv.), Fr. 44/F3
Grosnez (pt.), Chl, UK 56/C2
Grosrouvre, Fr. 30/H5
Gross Barmen, Namb. 122/C4
Gross Bieberau, Ger. 58/B3
Gross Oesingen, Ger. 53/H3
Gross Spitzkoppe (peak), Namb. 122/B4
Gross Unstadt, Ger. 58/B3
Gross-Enzersdorf, Aus. 51/P7
Gross-Gerungs, Aus. 43/H4
Gross-Zimmern, Ger. 58/B3
Grossa (pt.), Braz. 182/D2
Grossaitingen, Ger. 61/G1
Grossalmerode, Ger. 53/G6
Grossbeeren, Ger. 42/Q7
Grossbottwar, Ger. 58/C5
Grossbreitenbach, Ger. 58/D1
Grosse (isl.), Mi, US 167/F7
Grosse Aue (riv.), Ger. 53/F4
Grosse Ile, Mi, US 167/F7
Grosse Laber (riv.), Ger. 59/F5
Grosse Mühl (riv.), Aus. 59/G6
Grosse Münzenberg (peak), Namb. 124/A2
Grosse Nister (riv.), Ger. 55/G2
Grosse Pointe, Mi, US 167/G7
Grosse Pointe Farms, Mi, US 167/G7
Grosse Pointe Park, Mi, US 167/G7
Grosse Pointe Shores, Mi, US 167/G7
Grosse Pointe Woods, Mi, US 167/G7
Grosse Rodl (riv.), Aus. 59/H6
Grossengottern, Ger. 53/H6
Grossenkneten, Ger. 53/F3
Grossenlüder, Ger. 58/C1
Grossenwiehe, Ger. 40/C4
Grosser Ahrensberg (peak), Ger. 53/G5
Grosser Aletsch (glacier), Swi. 60/D5
Grosser Arber (peak), Ger. 59/G4
Grosser Bösenstein (peak), Aus. 45/L3
Grosser Daumen (peak), Ger. 61/G3
Grosser Feldberg (peak), Ger. 58/B2
Grosser Gleichberg (peak), Ger. 58/D2
Grosser Heuberg (mts.), Ger. 58/B6
Grosser Knechtsand (isl.), Ger. 53/F1
Grosser Peilstein (peak), Aus. 43/H4
Grosser Plessower (lake), Ger. 42/P7
Grosser Priel (peak), Aus. 45/L3
Grosser Rachel (peak), Ger. 59/G5
Grosser Seddiner (lake), Ger. 42/P7
Grosser Selchower (lake), Ger. 42/Q7
Grosses Coques, NS, Can. 158/D3
Grosses Meer (lake), Ger. 53/E2
Grosses Moor (swamp), Ger. 53/H3
Grosseto, It. 48/B1
Grossgerau, Ger. 58/B3
Grossglienicke, Ger. 42/Q7
Grossglockner (peak), Aus. 45/K3
Grosshansdorf, Ger. 53/H1
Grossheubach, Ger. 58/C3
Grosskrotzenburg, Ger. 58/B2
Grossmaischeid, Ger. 55/G3
Grosso (cape), Fr. 45/H5
Grossos, Braz. 183/G4
Grossrosseln, Ger. 55/F5
Grosssiegharts, Aus. 43/H4
Grosswallstadt, Ger. 58/C3
Grosswangen, Swi. 60/E3
Grosuplje, Slov. 45/L4
Grote Gete (riv.), Belg. 55/D2
Groton, SD, US 156/E5
Groton, NY, US 161/H3
Groton, Ct, US 161/K4
Groton-New London (arpt.), Ct, US 169/F1
Grotta Gigante, It. 63/G2
Grottaferrata, It. 65/B4
Grottaglie, It. 49/E2
Grottammare, It. 65/C2
Grotte de Han, Belg. 55/E3
Grotte Santo Stefano, It. 65/B2
Grotto, Wa, US 144/D4
Grotto of the Redemption, Ia, US 155/G2
Grottoes, Va, US 163/H1
Grouin (pt.), Fr. 56/D3
Grouse Creek, Ut, US 147/G3
Grouw, Neth. 52/C2
Grovdageaidnu-Kautokeino, Nor. 38/G1
Grove, Ok, US 153/G2
Grove (cr.), Tx, US 150/L7
Grove, Eng, UK 37/E3
Grove (pt.), Md, US 168/B5
Grove City, Oh, US 160/E5
Grove City, Pa, US 160/F4
Grove Hill, Al, US 164/E2
Groveland, Fl, US 164/M6
Grover, Wy, US 147/H2
Grover, Ut, US 149/G1
Grover, Co, US 154/B3
Grover City, Ca, US 148/B3
Groves, Tx, US 151/H3
Groveton, NH, US 161/L2
Groveton, Tx, US 151/G2
Groveton, Va, US 168/A6
Growler Wash (riv.), Az, US 149/F4
Groznyy, Rus. 71/H4
Grubbs, Ar, US 162/B3
Gruchet-le-Valasse, Fr. 57/F1
Grudovo, Bul. 51/H4
Grudziądz, Pol. 43/K2
Grugliasco, It. 64/D2
Grulla Nat'l Wild. Ref., NM, US 152/C3
Grumeti (riv.), Tanz. 119/A2
Grumo Nevano, It. 65/D6
Grums, Swe. 40/E2
Grun de Saint-Maurice (peak), Fr. 64/C3
Grünau, Namb. 124/B2
Grünau im Almtal, Aus. 59/G7
Grünburg, Aus. 59/H7
Gründau, Ger. 58/C2
Grundy, Va, US 163/F2
Grundy Center, Ia, US 155/H2
Grune (pt.), Eng, UK 35/E2
Grünheide, Ger. 42/Q7
Grünsfeld, Ger. 58/C3
Grünstadt, Ger. 58/B3
Grunthal, Mb, Can. 156/F3
Grünwald, Ger. 59/E6
Gruver, Tx, US 152/D2
Gruyères, Swi. 60/D4
Gruzdžiai, Lith. 41/K3
Gryady, Rus. 41/P2
Gryazi, Rus. 70/F1
Gryazovets, Rus. 68/J4
Grycksbo, Swe. 40/F1
Gryfice, Pol. 40/F5
Gryfino, Pol. 43/H2
Grygla, Mn, US 157/G3
Gryon, Swi. 60/D5
Gschwandt, Aus. 59/G7
Gschwend, Ger. 58/C5
Gstaad, Swi. 60/D5
Gsteig, Swi. 60/D5
Great Sand Dunes Nat'l Monument, Co, US 152/B2
Great Tenasserim (riv.), Myan. 94/B3
Gua, India 97/E4
Gua Musang, Malay. 89/C1
Guabún (pt.), Chile 190/B4
Guaca, Col. 180/C3
Guacamayo, Col. 180/D4
Guacanayabo (gulf), Cuba 173/F3
Guacara, Ven. 183/N7
Guacarí, Col. 180/B4
Guacharo, PN, Ven. 183/P7
Guachipas, Arg. 188/C3
Guachochi, Mex. 174/D3
Guácimo, CR 177/F4
Guaçuí, Braz. 187/E4
Guadalajara, Sp. 46/D2
Guadalajara, Mex. 174/E4
Guadalcanal (isl.), Sol. 136/E6
Guadalcanal, Sp. 46/C3
Guadalentín (riv.), Sp. 46/D4
Guadalimar (riv.), Sp. 46/D3
Guadalix (riv.), Sp. 47/N8
Guadalope (riv.), Sp. 47/E2
Guadalquivir (riv.), Sp. 66/B3
Guadalupe, Bol. 188/C1
Guadalupe, Bol. 188/C2
Guadalupe, Braz. 183/F4
Guadalupe, Col. 180/C4
Guadalupe, Mex. 150/D3
Guadalupe, Mex. 150/A2
Guadalupe, Mex. 174/E4
Guadalupe, Mex. 175/E3
Guadalupe (isl.), Mex. 139/E7
Guadalupe, Pan. 180/B2
Guadalupe, Peru 184/B2
Guadalupe, Peru 184/C4
Guadalupe, Sp. 46/C3
Guadalupe (mts.), Sp. 46/C3
Guadalupe, Ca, US 148/B3
Guadalupe (mts.), NM, US 150/B1
Guadalupe (peak), Tx, US 150/B2
Guadalupe (riv.), Tx, US 151/F3
Guadalupe Mountains NP, Tx, US 150/B2
Guadalupe Victoria, Mex. 175/M7
Guadalupe Victoria, Mex. 174/D3
Guadalupe Victoria, Mex. 174/B1
Guadarrama, Ven. 180/D2
Guadarrama (riv.), Sp. 46/C3
Guadarrama, Sp. 47/M8
Guadarrama, Sierra de (mts.), Sp. 66/B2
Guadeloupe (isl.), Fr. 173/N8
Guadeloupe NP, Fr. 173/N8
Guadeloupe Passage (chan), Fr. 173/J4
Guadiana (riv.), Sp. 66/B3
Guadiana (riv.), Port.,Sp. 46/B3
Guadiana Menor (riv.), Sp. 46/D4
Guadix, Sp. 46/D4
Guadolquivir (riv.), Sp. 46/D4
Guaduas, Col. 183/L7
Guafo (isl.), Chile 190/B4
Guage, Ky, US 163/F2
Guagua Pichincha (peak), Ecu. 180/B5
Guaíba, Braz. 189/G4
Guáimaro, Cuba 177/G1
Guaina, Ven. 181/F3
Guainía (riv.), Col. 180/D4
Guainía (dept.), Col. 180/D4
Guaiquinima (peak), Ven. 181/F3
Guaira, Braz. 189/F3
Guairá (dept.), Par. 189/E3
Guaíra, Braz. 189/G2
Guaiteca (isl.), Chile 190/B4
Guajará-Mirim, Braz. 185/E3
Guajira (pen.), Col. 179/B1
Gualaceo, Ecu. 180/B5
Gualaco, Hon. 176/E3
Gualala, Ca, US 146/B4
Gualán, Guat. 176/D3
Gualaquiza, Ecu. 184/B1
Gualdo Tadino, It. 65/B1
Gualeguay, Arg. 191/J10
Gualeguay (riv.), Arg. 188/E5
Gualeguaychú, Arg. 191/J10
Gualey (riv.), WV, US 163/G1
Guallatiri (vol.), Chile 188/B1
Gualtieri, It. 62/D4
Guam (isl.), Pac., US 136/D3
Guamá (riv.), Braz. 183/E3
Guamal, Col. 180/C2
Guamblin, Isla (isl.), Chile 190/A5
Guamote, Ecu. 184/B1
Guamúchil, Mex. 174/C3
Gu'an, China 80/H7
Guan Xian, China 86/D2
Guan Xian, China 80/C3
Guaña, Ven. 181/F3
Guanabacoa, Cuba 177/F1
Guanabara (bay), Braz. 187/N7
Guanahacabibes (pen.), Cuba 177/E1
Guanahacabibes (gulf), Cuba 176/E1
Guanaja (isl.), Hon. 176/E2
Guanaja, Hon. 176/E2
Guanajay, Cuba 177/F1
Guanajuato (state), Mex. 172/A3
Guanajuato, Mex. 175/E4
Guanambi, Braz. 187/E2
Guanape, Ven. 181/E2
Guanare (riv.), Ven. 173/H6
Guanare, Ven. 180/D2
Guanarito, Ven. 180/D2
Guanay (peak), Ven. 181/E3
Guanay, Bol. 184/E4
Guanbei, China 87/H3
Guanbei, China 87/G3
Guanchao, China 87/G3
Guandacol, Arg. 188/B4
Guandi (mtn.), China 80/B3
Guandu, China 80/B5
Guane, Cuba 177/E1
Guanfangpu, China 78/F5
Guangchang, China 87/H3
Guangde, China 80/D5
Guangdong (prov.), China 87/K6
Guangfu, China 86/E2
Guanghai, China 87/G4
Guangling, China 80/C3
Guanglu (isl.), China 81/B3
Guangmao (mtn.), China 86/D3
Guangming (peak), China 87/H2
Guangnan, China 86/E3
Guangping, China 80/C3
Guangping, China 87/F4
Guangping, China 87/H3
Guangrao, China 80/D3
Guangshan, China 80/C4
Guangxi (aut. reg.), China 93/J3
Guangyuan, China 78/F5
Guangze, China 87/H3
Guangzhou, China 87/G4
Guanhães, Braz. 187/E3
Guanipa (riv.), Ven. 173/J6
Guanmian (mts.), China 87/F2
Guannan, China 80/D4
Guano (lake), Or, US 146/D2
Guanshui, China 81/C2
Guantánamo, Cuba 177/H1
Guantánamo Bay U.S. Naval Base, Cuba 177/H2
Guantao, China 80/C3
Guanting (res.), China 80/G6
Guanujo, Ecu. 180/B5
Guanyinqiao, China 78/E5
Guanyun, China 80/D4
Guanzhou, China 87/F2
Guapí, Col. 180/B4
Guapó, Braz. 189/G1
Guaporé (riv.), Braz. 179/C4
Guaporé, Braz. 189/G4
Guaqui, Bol. 188/B1
Guar Chempedak, Malay. 89/C1
Guarabira, Braz. 183/H4
Guaraci, Braz. 189/G2
Guaraciaba do Norte, Braz. 183/F4
Guaraí, Braz. 182/D5
Guaranda, Ecu. 180/B5
Guarani, Braz. 187/N6
Guarapari, Braz. 187/E4
Guarapuava, Braz. 189/G3
Guarará, Braz. 187/N6
Guararapes, Braz. 189/G2
Guararapes (int'l arpt.), Braz. 183/H5
Guararema, Braz. 187/K8
Guaratinga, Braz. 187/F3
Guaratinguetá, Braz. 187/L7
Guaratuba, Braz. 189/G3
Guarayos, Bol. 184/D4
Guarcino, It. 65/C4
Guarda (dist.), Port. 46/B2
Guarda, Port. 46/B2
Guardamar, Sp. 47/E3
Guardamiglio, It. 62/C3
Guardarrama (riv.), Sp. 47/N8
Guardatinajas, Ven. 183/N8
Guardea, It. 65/B2
Guardia Alta (peak), It. 61/H4
Guardia Mitre, Arg. 190/E4
Guardia Sanframondi, It. 65/D5
Guardiagrele, It. 65/D3
Guardialfiera (lake), It. 65/D4
Guareña, Sp. 46/B3
Guarenas, Ven. 183/P7
Guari, PNG 129/G2
Guariba, Braz. 189/G2
Guaribe (riv.), Braz. 182/A5
Guárico (riv.), Ven. 173/H6
Guárico (res.), Ven. 181/E2
Guárico (state), Ven. 181/E2
Guarico (pt.), Cuba 177/H1
Guarinó (riv.), Col. 183/K7
Guarne, Col. 183/K6
Guarujá, Braz. 187/K9
Guarulhos (int'l arpt.), Braz. 187/K8
Guarulhos, Braz. 187/K8
Guarumal, Pan. 180/A3
Guasave, Mex. 174/C3
Guasca, Col. 183/M8
Guasdualito, Ven. 180/D3
Guasimal, Cuba 177/G1
Guasipati, Ven. 181/F3
Guastalla, It. 62/D4
Guatapé, Col. 183/K6
Guatemala (cap.), Guat. 176/D3
Guatemala (ctry.) 176/D3
Guateque, Col. 180/C3
Guatire, Ven. 183/P7
Guatulame, Chile 188/B4
Guaviare (dept.), Col. 180/C4
Guaviare (riv.), Col. 179/C2
Guaxupé, Braz. 189/H2
Guayabal, Ven. 181/E4
Guayabal de Síquima, Col. 183/L8
Guayabero (riv.), Col. 180/C4
Guayalejo (riv.), Mex. 175/F4
Guayama, PR 173/M8
Guayape (riv.), Hon. 176/E3
Guayaquil (gulf), Ecu.,Peru 179/A3
Guayaquil, Ecu. 180/B5
Guayaquil (gulf), Ecu. 180/A5
Guayaramerín, Bol. 185/E3
Guayas (riv.), Col. 180/C4
Guayas, Ecu. 180/B5
Guayas (prov.), Ecu. 180/A5
Guayatayoc (lake), Arg. 188/C2
Guaycurú (riv.), Arg. 188/E3
Guaymas, Mex. 174/C3
Guba, Eth. 117/G3
Gubakha, Rus. 69/N4
Gubbio, It. 63/F7
Guben, Ger. 43/H3
Gubi, Nga. 115/H4
Gubin, Pol. 43/H3
Gubkin, Rus. 73/J2
Gucheng, China 86/E1
Gucheng, China 80/B4
Gucheng, China 80/C3
Gucheng, China 80/G7
Gūdalūr, India 95/C4
Gúdar (range), Sp. 47/E2
Gudaut'a, Geo. 71/G4
Gudenå (riv.), Den. 40/D3
Gudensberg, Ger. 53/G6
Gudermes, Rus. 71/H4
Gudi, Nga. 115/H4
Gudivāda, India 95/D2
Gudo (peak), Eth. 117/H4
Gudong, China 87/E3
Gudou (peak), China 87/G4
Gudow, Ger. 53/H1
Güdül, Turk. 51/L5
Guebli (lake), Mrta. 110/B5
Guebwiller, Fr. 60/D2
Guecho, Sp. 44/B5
Guéckédou, Gui. 114/C4
Guédi (peak), Chad 116/C2
Guelb Azefal (hill), Mrta. 110/B5
Guelb er Rîchât (peak), Mrta. 110/C5
Guélengdeng, Chad 116/B3
Guelma (wilaya), Alg. 112/K6
Guelma, Alg. 112/K6
Guelph, On, Can. 160/S8
Guelta Zemmur, WSah. 110/B4
Guemar, Alg. 111/G2
Guémené-Penfao, Fr. 56/D5
Guémené-sur-Scorff, Fr. 56/B4
Guénange, Fr. 55/F5
Guenrouet, Fr. 56/D5
Guer, Fr. 56/C5
Güer Aike, Arg. 191/C6
Güera, Mor. 110/A5
Guéra (pref.), Chad 116/C3
Guérande, Fr. 56/C6
Guerara, Alg. 111/G2
Guérard, Fr. 30/L5
Guercif, Mor. 112/C2
Guéréda, Chad 116/D2
Guéret, Fr. 44/D3
Guerguerat, Mor. 110/A5
Guérin Kouka, Togo 115/F4
Guernes, Fr. 30/G4
Guernsey (int'l arpt.), Chl, UK 56/C2
Guernsey (isl.), Chl, UK 44/B2
Guernsey, Wy, US 154/B2
Guernsey, Sk, Can. 145/M2
Guérou, Mrta. 114/C2
Guerra, Tx, US 151/E4
Guerrero, Mex. 150/D3
Guerrero (state), Mex. 175/E5
Guerrero Negro, Mex. 174/B3
Guerville, Fr. 30/H5
Guerzim, Alg. 111/E3
Guesle (riv.), Fr. 30/H6
Gueugnon, Fr. 44/F3
Gueux, Fr. 54/C5
Gueydan, La, US 164/B2
Guézawa, Niger 115/H3
Gugē (peak), Eth. 117/H4
Gūged, Iran 103/G3
Guggisberg, Swi. 60/D4
Gugielmo Marconi (int'l arpt.), It. 63/E4
Güglingen, Ger. 58/B4
Guglionesi, It. 65/D4
Gugu (peak), Eth. 118/A3
Guguan (isl.), NMar. 136/D3
Gugueragu, Eth. 118/C4
Guguletu, SAfr. 124/L10
Guhe, China 87/H2
Gui (riv.), China 87/F4
Guiana Highlands (uplands), Ven. 181/E3
Guiana Highlands (uplands), SAm. 179/C2
Guiana Highlands (uplands), Guy.,Sur. 182/A1
Guibéroua, C.d'Iv. 114/D5
Guibes, Namb. 124/B2
Guichen, Fr. 56/D5
Guichi, China 87/H2
Guichón, Uru. 191/K10
Guidan-Roumji, Niger 115/G3
Guidari, Chad 116/C3
Guidder, Camr. 116/B3
Guidel, Fr. 56/B5
Guidiguis, Camr. 116/B3
Guidimouni, Niger 115/H3
Guiding, China 93/J2
Guidizzolo, It. 62/D3
Guidjiba, Camr. 116/B3
Guidong, China 93/K2
Guidonia, It. 65/B4
Guiers (riv.), Fr. 64/B2
Guigang, China 87/F4
Guiglo, C.d'Iv. 114/D5
Guignen, Fr. 56/D5
Guignes-Rabutin, Fr. 30/L6
Güigüe, Ven. 183/N7
Guiguinto, Phil. 88/E6
Guihulngan, Phil. 88/C3
Guija, Moz. 123/G5
Guijuelo, Sp. 46/C2
Guil (riv.), Fr. 64/C3
Guilderton, Austl. 130/B4
Guildford, Eng, UK 30/B3
Guildhall, Vt, US 161/L2
Guilers, Fr. 56/A4
Guilford, NY, US 161/J3
Guilford Courthouse Nat'l Mil. Park, NC, US 163/H2
Guilherand, Fr. 64/A3
Guilin (int'l arpt.), China 87/F3
Guilin, China 87/F3
Guiling, China 87/F3
Guillaume (peak), Fr. 64/C3
Guillaume-Delisle (lake), Qu, Can. 141/J3
Guillaumes, Fr. 64/C4
Guillena, Sp. 46/B4
Guillestre, Fr. 64/C3
Guilsfield, Wal, UK 36/C1
Guilvinec, Fr. 56/A5
Guimarães, Port. 46/A2
Guimarães, Braz. 183/E3
Guimarânia, Braz. 189/H1
Guimaras (isl.), Phil. 88/C3
Guimba, Phil. 88/C2
Guimbiri (peak), Camr. 120/C1
Guimeng (mtn.), China 80/D4
Guin, Al, US 162/D4
Guinan, China 78/E4
Guinard (riv.), Sc, UK 33/A1
Guindulman, Phil. 88/D3
Guinea (ctry.) 114/C4
Guinea (gulf), Afr. 107/C4
Guinea-Bissau (ctry.) 114/B3
Guînes, Fr. 54/A2
Guingamp, Fr. 56/B3
Guingan, Gui. 114/B3
Guinguinéo, Sen. 114/B3
Guinia, Niger 115/H3
Guintinguintin (mt.), Phil. 88/C2
Guiones (pt.), CR 176/E4
Guipavas, Fr. 56/A4
Guipavas (int'l arpt.), Fr. 56/A4
Guiping, China 87/F4
Guir, Hamada du (plat.), Alg. 66/C5
Guir, Oued (riv.), Alg. 110/E2
Guiratinga, Braz. 186/B3
Guiri, Camr. 116/B3
Güiria, Ven. 181/F2
Guisanbourg, FrG. 182/D1
Guisborough, Eng, UK 35/G2
Guiscard, Fr. 54/C4
Guise, Fr. 54/C4
Guiseley, Eng, UK 35/G4
Guitiriz, Sp. 46/B1
Guitrancourt, Fr. 30/H4
Guitri, C.d'Iv. 114/D5
Guiuan, Phil. 88/D3
Guixi, China 86/D2
Guixi, China 87/H2
Guiyang, China 87/E3
Guiyang, China 87/G3
Güiza (riv.), Col. 180/B4
Guizhou (prov.), China 93/J2
Gujan-Mestras, Fr. 44/C4
Gūjar Khān, Pak. 98/B3
Gujarāt (state), India 92/B3
Gujba, Nga. 116/A3
Gujrānwāla, Pak. 98/C3
Gujrāt, Pak. 98/C3
Gukovo, Rus. 73/K3
Gulang, China 78/E4
Gulaothi, India 96/A1
Gulargambone, Austl. 132/D1
Gularia, Nepal 96/C1
Gulbene, Lat. 41/M3
Guldenbach (riv.), Ger. 55/G3
Guldima, Eth. 118/B4
Güldüzü, Turk. 104/E1
Guleitou, China 87/H4
Gulen, Nor. 40/A1
Gulf (prov.), PNG 129/G1
Gulf (coast. pl.), Tx, US 175/F2
Gulf Coastal (plain), Tx, US 175/F2
Gulf Hammock (swamp), Fl, US 165/G3
Gulf Islands National Seashore, Ms, US 164/D2
Gulf Shores, Al, US 164/E2
Gulf Stream, Fl, US 164/P10
Gulfport, Ms, US 164/D2
Gulfport, Fl, US 164/K8
Gulganj, India 96/B3
Gulgong, Austl. 132/D2
Gulidlimaka (pol. reg.), Mrta. 114/B3
Guliston, Uzb. 74/G5
Guliya (peak), China 79/J2
Gulkana, Ak, US 171/J3
Gul'kevichi, Rus. 73/L5
Gull (riv.), On, Can. 157/K3
Gull (lake), Ab, Can. 145/H1
Gull Bay, On, Can. 157/K3
Gull Bay Ind. Res., On, Can. 157/K3
Gull Lake, Sk, Can. 145/K2
Gulladuff, NI, UK 34/B2
Gullane, Sc, UK 33/D4
Gullane (pt.), Sc, UK 33/D4
Gullhaug, Nor. 38/R9
Gulliver, Mi, US 160/C2
Gullspång, Swe. 40/F2
Güllükdağı (Termessos) NP, Turk. 104/A1
Gulmarg, India 98/C2
Gülnar, Turk. 104/C1
Gulpen, Neth. 55/E2
Gülpınar, Turk. 49/K3
Gulu, Ugan. 121/H2
Gŭlŭbovo, Bul. 51/G4
Guluy, Erit. 117/H2
Gulyantsi, Bul. 51/G4
Gum, Nepal 92/D2
Gumal (riv.), Pak. 98/A4
Gumare, Bots. 122/D3
Gumbiel, Sudan 117/F3
Gumbiro, Tanz. 119/A4
Gumbrechtshoffen, Fr. 55/G6
Gumdag, Trkm. 103/H2
Gumel, Nga. 115/H3
Gumeracha, Austl. 131/M8
Gumia, India 97/E4
Gumine, PNG 129/G1
Gumla, India 97/E4
Gumma (pref.), Japan 85/F2
Gummersbach, Ger. 55/G1
Gummi, Nga. 115/G3
Gumpoldskirchen, Aus. 51/N7
Gumti (riv.), India 97/H4
Gümüşhacıköy, Turk. 70/E4
Gümüşhane (prov.), Turk. 70/F4
Gümüşhane, Turk. 102/D1
Gümüşova, Turk. 51/K5
Gun Barrel City, Tx, US 151/F1
Guna, India 92/C3
Gunbower, Austl. 133/B2
Güncang, China 86/B2
Gundagai, Austl. 133/D2
Gundelfingen, Ger. 60/D1
Gundelfingen an der Donau, Ger. 58/D5
Gundelsheim, Ger. 58/C4
Gundersheim, Ger. 58/B3
Gundershoffen, Fr. 55/G6
Gundji, D.R. Congo 121/E2
Gündoğmuş, Turk. 104/C1
Güneydogu Toroslar (mts.), Turk. 102/D2
Gunib, Rus. 71/H4
Gunib (riv.), Namb. 122/C4
Gunja, Cro. 50/D3
Gunlock, Ut, US 149/F2
Gunnaur, India 96/B1
Gunnebo, Swe. 40/G3
Gunnedah, Austl. 132/D1
Gunning, Austl. 133/D2
Gunnison (riv.), Co, US 147/J4
Gunnison, Co, US 149/J1
Gunnison, Ut, US 147/H4
Gunnison, Ms, US 162/B4
Gunnison, North Fork (riv.), Co, US 152/A1
Gunpowder, Austl. 129/E4
Gunpowder (riv.), Md, US 168/B5
Gunpowder Falls State Park, Md, US 168/B4
Gunskirchen, Aus. 59/G6
Gunsta, Swe. 39/A1
Gunt (riv.), Taj. 99/B4
Guntakal, India 95/C3
Gunter (A.F.B.), Al, US 162/D4
Guntersblum, Ger. 58/B3
Guntersville (dam), Al, US 162/D3
Guntersville, Al, US 162/D3
Guntersville (lake), Al, US 162/D3
Gunton, Mb, Can. 156/F2
Guntown, Ms, US 162/C3
Guntramsdorf, Aus. 51/N7
Gunung Leuser NP, Indo. 89/B2
Gunung Mulu NP, Malay. 88/A4
Gunungsitoli, Indo. 89/B2
Gunungsugih, Indo. 89/D4
Gunungtua, Indo. 89/B2
Gunupur, India 95/D2
Günz (riv.), Ger. 42/F4
Günzburg, Ger. 58/D6
Gunzenhausen, Ger. 58/D4
Guo (riv.), China 78/H5
Guoju, China 87/J2
Guoyang, China 80/D4
Gura Humorului, Rom. 72/C4
Guragē (peak), Eth. 118/A3
Gurais, India 98/C2
Gurbantünggut (des.), China 78/B2
Gurdāspur, India 98/C3
Gurdon, Ar, US 153/H4
Gurgaon, India 98/D5
Gurgei (peak), Sudan 116/E2
Gürgentepe, Turk. 70/F4
Gurguéia (riv.), Braz. 183/E5
Gurī, Eth. 118/B4
Guri (dam), Ven. 181/F3
Guri (res.), Ven. 179/C2
Gurig NP, Austl. 128/D2
Gurjaani, Geo. 71/H4
Gurk (riv.), Aus. 45/L3
Gurkha, Nepal 97/E1
Gurkovo, Bul. 51/G4
Gurkthaler Alpen (mts.), Aus. 45/K3
Gurley, Austl. 132/D1
Gurley, Al, US 162/D3
Gurley, SC, US 163/H3
Gurnee, Il, US 167/Q15
Guro, Moz. 123/G3
Gürpınar, Turk. 103/E2
Gürpinar, Turk. 103/M7
Gursarai, India 96/B3
Gurskoye, Rus. 79/M1
Gursum, Eth. 118/B3
Guru Har Sahāi, India 98/C4
Guru Sikhar (peak), India 101/K4
Guruapin, Indo. 91/G3
Gürün, Turk. 102/D2
Gurun, Malay. 89/C1
Gurupá, Braz. 182/D3
Gurupi (riv.), Braz. 183/E3
Gurupi (cape), Braz. 183/E3
Gurupi, Braz. 186/C1
Gurupi, Serra do (mts.), Braz. 182/D4
Guruve, Zim. 123/F3
Gus'-Khrustal'nyy, Rus. 68/J5
Gusau, Nga. 115/G3
Gusev, Rus. 41/K4
Gushan, China 81/B3
Gushgy, Trkm. 101/H1
Gushi, China 80/C4
Gushiago, Gha. 115/E4
Gushikawa, Japan 85/J7
Gushui, China 87/G4
Gusinje, Serb. 50/D4
Gusinoozërsk, Rus. 75/L4
Guskhara, India 97/F4
Guspini, It. 48/A3
Gussola, It. 62/D4
Gustavia, Fr. 173/N8
Gustavo A. Madero (nbrhd.), Mex. 175/Q10
Gustavo Díaz Ordaz, Mex. 174/B3
Gustavo Díaz Ordaz, Mex. 174/C3
Gustavsberg, Swe. 39/B1
Gustavus, Ak, US 171/L4
Gusterath, Ger. 55/F4
Gustine, Ca, US 148/B2
Gustine, Tx, US 150/E2
Güstrow, Ger. 40/E5
Gusum, Swe. 40/G2
Gutang, China 86/B2
Gutau, Aus. 59/H6
Gütersloh, Ger. 53/F5
Guthrie, Tx, US 152/D4
Guthrie, Ok, US 153/F3
Guthrie, Ky, US 162/D2
Guthrie Center, Ia, US 155/G3
Gutian, China 87/H3
Gutiérrez, Bol. 188/D1
Gutiérrez Zamora, Mex. 175/M6
Guting, China 87/G3
Guttannen, Swi. 61/E4
Guttenberg, NJ, US 169/K8
Guttenberg, Ia, US 155/J2
Guttingen, Swi. 61/F2
Gutulia NP, Nor. 38/E3
Guwāhati, India 93/F2
Guxhagen, Ger. 53/G6
Guxian, China 80/B3
Guxian, China 87/G3
Guy, Ar, US 153/H3
Guy, Tx, US 151/M9
Guy Fawkes River NP, Austl. 132/E1
Guyana (ctry.) 181/G3
Guyancourt, Fr. 30/J5
Guyandotte (riv.), WV, US 163/F1
Guyang, China 80/B2
Guyhirn, Eng, UK 37/G1
Guyī, Eth. 117/G3
Guymon, Ok, US 152/D2
Guyong, China 86/C3
Guyot (mt.), NC, US 163/F3
Guyoult (riv.), Fr. 56/D3
Guyra, Austl. 132/D1
Guysborough, NS, Can. 159/G3
Guyton, Ga, US 163/G4
Guyuan, China 78/H3
Guyuan, China 78/F4
Güzelbağ, Turk. 104/B1
Güzelsu, Turk. 104/B1
Guzhang, China 93/J2
Guzhen, China 80/D4
Guzmán (lake), Mex. 174/D2
Gvardeysk, Rus. 41/J4
Gwa, Myan. 86/B5
Gwaai, Zim. 123/E3
Gwabegar, Austl. 132/D1
Gwadabawa, Nga. 115/G3
Gwādar, Pak. 101/H3
Gwai (riv.), Zim. 123/E3
Gwaii Haanas NP, BC, Can. 140/C3
Gwalior, India 96/B2
Gwanda, Zim. 123/F4
Gwandalan, Austl. 133/E1
Gwarzo, Nga. 115/G4
Gwash (riv.), Eng, UK 37/F1
Gwaunceste (peak), Wal, UK 36/C2
Gwda (riv.), Pol. 43/J2
Gweek, Eng, UK 36/A6
Gwembe, Zam. 123/E3
Gwersyllt, Wal, UK 35/E5
Gweru, Zim. 123/F3
Gweta, Bots. 122/E4
Gwinner, ND, US 156/F4
Gwinnett (co.), Ga, US 163/M7
Gwoza, Nga. 116/B3
Gwydir (riv.), Austl. 132/D1
Gwynedd (co.), Wal, UK 34/D5
Gwyrfai (riv.), Wal, UK 34/D5
Gy, Fr. 60/B3
Gya (pass), China 97/E1
Gyaca, China 93/F2
Gyál, Hun. 51/R10
Gyangrang, China 99/E5
Gyangzê, China 97/G1
Gyaring (lake), China 78/D5
Gyaring, China 78/D4
Gyasikan, Gha. 115/F5
Gyda, Rus. 74/H2
Gyda (pen.), Rus. 77/G2
Gyêmdong, China 86/B2
Gyetsa, Bhu. 97/H2
Gyhum, Ger. 53/G2
Gyirong, China 97/E1
Gyldenløveshøj (peak), Den. 40/D4
Gympie, Austl. 134/D4
Gyobingauk, Myan. 86/B5
Gyōda, Japan 83/C1
Gyoma, Hun. 50/E2
Gyömrő, Hun. 51/R10
Gyór, Hun. 50/C2
Gyór-Moson-Sopron (co.), Hun. 43/J5
Gyórújbarát, Hun. 50/C2
Gypsum, Ks, US 153/F1
Gypsum, Co, US 147/K4
Gypsumville, Mb, Can. 156/E2
Gypsy (peak), Wa, US 144/F3
Gyula, Hun. 50/E2
Gyumri, Arm. 71/G4
Gżira, Malta 48/L7

H

Hå, Nor. 40/A2
Ha, Bhu. 97/G2
Ha Bonim, Isr. 105/B3
Ha Coi, Viet. 87/E4
Ha Giang, Viet. 86/E4
Ha Noi (Hanoi) (cap.), Viet. 86/E4
Ha Tien, Viet. 94/D4
Ha Tinh, Viet. 94/D2
Haacht, Belg. 55/D2
Haag, Aus. 59/H6
Haag am Hausruck, Aus. 59/G6
Haag an der Amper, Ger. 59/E6
Haag in Oberbayern, Ger. 59/F6
Haaksbergen, Neth. 52/D4
Haaltert, Belg. 54/D2
Haamstede, Neth. 52/A5
Haan, Ger. 52/E6
Ha'apai Group (isl.), Tonga 137/H7
Haapajärvi (lake), Fin. 39/E4
Haapavesi, Fin. 68/E2
Haapsalu, Est. 41/K2
Haar, Ger. 59/E6
Haardt (mts.), Ger. 45/G2
Haarlem, Neth. 52/B4
Haast (pass), NZ 135/B4
Haast, NZ 135/B3
Haasts Bluff, Austl. 131/F2
Haasts Bluff Aboriginal Land, Austl. 131/F2
Hab (riv.), Pak. 101/J3
Habahe, China 99/E2
Habartov, Czh. 59/F2
Habaswein, Kenya 119/B1
Habay, Som. 119/C1
Ḩabbān, Yem. 118/C2
Ḩabbānīyah, Iraq 103/E3
Habicht (peak), Aus. 61/H3
Habiganj, Bang. 97/H3
Habikino, Japan 83/J6
Håbo-Tibble, Swe. 39/A1
Habomai (isls.), Rus. 82/D2
Haboro, Japan 82/B1
Hābra, India 97/G4
Habsheim, Fr. 60/D2
Hacha (falls), Ven. 181/F3
Hache (riv.), Ger. 53/F3
Hachenburg, Ger. 55/G2
Hachijō, Japan 85/F4
Hachijō (isl.), Japan 79/M5
Hachikai, Japan 83/L5
Hachimori, Japan 82/B3
Hachinohe, Japan 82/B3
Hachiōji, Japan 85/F3
Hachita, NM, US 149/H5
Hacıbektaş, Turk. 102/C2
Hacienda Heights, Ca, US 166/G8
Hacılar, Turk. 102/C2
Hack (mt.), Austl. 131/H4
Hackberry, La, US 164/B3
Hackberry, Az, US 149/F3
Hackberry (cr.), Ks, US 154/D4
Hackensack, Mn, US 157/G4
Hackensack, NJ, US 169/J8
Hackensack (riv.), NJ, US 169/J9
Hacker Valley, WV, US 163/G1
Hacketstown, Ire. 32/D4
Hackettstown, NJ, US 168/D2
Hackleburg, Al, US 162/D3
Hackney (bor.), Eng, UK 30/C2
Haḑabat al Jilf al Kabīr (plat.), Egypt 109/E4
Hadadong, China 99/D3
Hadāli, Pak. 98/B3
Hadamar, Ger. 58/B2
Hadano, Japan 85/F3
Hadarba (cape), Sudan 109/H4
Haddad, Ouadi (riv.), Chad 116/C2
Haddenham, Eng, UK 37/F3
Haddington, Sc, UK 33/D5
Haddix, Ky, US 163/F2
Haddock, Ga, US 163/F4
Haddon (Westmont), NJ, US 168/C4
Haddonfield, NJ, US 168/C4
Hadejia, Nga. 115/H3
Hadejia (riv.), Nga. 107/C3
Hadelner (canal), Ger. 53/F1
Ḩadera, Isr. 105/B4
Haderslev, Den. 40/C4
Hadhramaut (reg.), Yem. 100/E6
Ḩadīd (peak), Egypt 113/B4
Hadım, Turk. 102/C2
Hadjer Bandala, Chad 116/D3
Hadjout, Alg. 112/G4
Hadleigh, Eng, UK 30/E2
Hadley (bay), Nun, Can. 140/E1
Hadlow, Eng, UK 30/E3
Hadong, SKor. 81/D5
Hadrāībāri, India 97/H4
Hadrian's Wall (wall), Eng, UK 35/F1
Hadrian's Mausoleum, It. 65/G7
Hadselfjorden (inlet), Nor. 38/E1
Hadsten, Den. 40/D3
Hadsund, Den. 40/D3
Hadyach, Ukr. 73/H2
Haeju (bay), NKor. 81/C4
Haeju, NKor. 81/C3
Haena (pt.), Hi, US 142/S9
Haenam, SKor. 81/D5
Haenertsburg, SAfr. 123/F4
Haengyŏng-ni, NKor. 79/K3
Ḩafar al Bāţin, SAr. 103/F4
Hafford, Sk, Can. 145/L1
Hafik, Turk. 102/D2
Hāfizābād, Pak. 98/B3
Hāflong, India 86/B3
Hafnarfjördhur, Ice. 38/N7
Hafnarhreppur, Ice. 38/P7
Haft Gel, Iran 103/G4
Hafun (pt.), Som. 118/D3
Hagan, Ga, US 163/G4
Hagansport, Tx, US 153/G4
Hagarville, Ar, US 153/H3
Hagåtña (cap.), Guam 136/D3
Hagelstadt, Ger. 59/F5
Hagemeister (isl.), Ak, US 171/F4
Hagen, Ger. 53/E6
Hagen am Teutoburger Wald, Ger. 53/E4
Hagen im Bremischen, Ger. 53/F2
Hagenow, Ger. 40/D5
Hāgere Hiywet, Eth. 117/H3
Hāgere Selam, Eth. 118/A4
Hagerman, NM, US 152/B4
Hagerman, Id, US 147/F2
Hagerman Fossil Beds Nat'l Mon., Id, US 147/F2
Hagerstown, In, US 160/D5
Hagerstown, Md, US 161/H5
Hagetmau, Fr. 44/C5
Hagfors, Swe. 40/E1
Haggin (mt.), Mt, US 145/H4
Hagi, Japan 84/B3
Hagley, Eng, UK 36/D2
Hagnau am Bodensee, Ger. 61/F2
Hags (pt.), Ire. 32/A4
Hague (cape), Fr. 56/D1
Hague, ND, US 156/E4
Hague, Sk, Can. 145/L1
Haguenau, Fr. 55/G6
Hagunía, WSah. 110/B4
Hahaia, Com. 125/G5
Hahashima (isls.), Japan 136/D2
Hahaya (int'l arpt.), Com. 125/G5
Hahira, Ga, US 165/G2
Hahle (riv.), Ger. 53/H5
Hahndorf, Austl. 131/M9
Hahnenbach (riv.), Ger. 55/G4
Hahnstätten, Ger. 58/B2
Hahnville, La, US 164/C3
Hai (riv.), China 80/D3
Hai Duong, Viet. 94/D1
Hai Hau, Viet. 87/E4
Hai Phong, Viet. 87/E4
Hai Van (pass), Viet. 94/E2
Hai'an, China 87/F4
Hai'an, China 80/E4
Haibach, Ger. 58/C3
Haibara, Japan 83/J6
Haicheng, China 81/B2
Haidenaab (riv.), Ger. 59/E3
Haidershofen, Aus. 59/H6
Haidian, China 80/H7
Haifa (dist.), Isr. 104/D3
Haifa (arpt.), Isr. 105/C3
Haifa (Ḩefa), Isr. 105/B3
Haifeng, China 87/G4
Haigerloch, Ger. 58/B6
Haigler, Ne, US 154/D3
Haikang, China 87/F4
Haikou, China 87/F4
Haikou, China 87/J2
Haikou (int'l arpt.), China 87/F4
Ḩā'il, SAr. 102/E5
Hailākāndi, India 93/F3
Hailar (riv.), China 79/J2
Hailar, China 79/H2
Haile, La, US 153/H4
Hailey, Id, US 147/F2
Haileybury, On, Can. 141/J4
Hailing (isl.), China 87/F4
Hailsham, Eng, UK 37/G5
Hailstone Nat'l Wild. Ref., Mt, US 145/K4
Hailun, China 79/K2
Haimen, China 80/E5
Haimhausen, Ger. 59/E6
Haiming, Aus. 61/G3
Haiming, Ger. 59/F6
Haimoo, Fin. 39/E4
Haina, Ger. 53/F6
Hainan (isl.), China 77/L8
Hainan (prov.), China 93/J4
Hainan (str.), China 93/K3
Hainaut (prov.), Belg. 54/B2
Hainburg, Ger. 58/C1
Haines, Or, US 146/E1
Haines, Ak, US 171/L3
Haines City, Fl, US 164/M7
Haines Junction, Yk, Can. 171/L3
Hainesville, Il, US 167/P15
Hainesville, Tx, US 151/G1
Hainesville, NJ, US 168/D1
Hainich (mts.), Ger. 42/F3
Haining, China 80/L9
Haitan (isl.), China 87/H3
Haiti (ctry.) 177/H2
Haitou, China 87/F5
Haixing, China 80/D3
Haiyan, China 78/E4
Haiyan, China 80/L9
Haiyang (isl.), China 81/B3
Haiyang, China 80/E3
Haiyuan, China 78/F4
Haizhou (bay), China 80/D4
Háj (peak), Czh. 59/F2
Hajdń Bihar (co.), Hun. 43/L5
Hajdú-Bihar (prov.), Hun. 50/E2
Hajdúboszormény, Hun. 43/L5
Hajdúdorog, Hun. 43/L5
Hajdúhadház, Hun. 50/E2
Hajdúnánás, Hun. 43/L5
Hajdúszoboszló, Hun. 43/L5
Hājib Al 'Uyūn, Tun. 48/A5
Hājīganj, Bang. 97/H4
Hajiki-zaki (pt.), Japan 85/F1
Hājīpur, India 97/E3
Ḩajj 'Abd Allāh, Sudan 117/G2
Ḩajjah, Yem. 118/B2
Ḩājjīābād, Iran 103/H4
Hajnówka, Pol. 43/M2
Hājo, India 97/H2
Hajós, Hun. 50/D2
Haka, Myan. 86/B4
Hakahau, FrPol. 137/L5
Hakee (mt.), Austl. 131/G3
Hakkari (prov.), Turk. 103/E2
Hakken-san (peak), Japan 84/D3
Hakkōda-san (peak), Japan 82/B3
Hakodate, Japan 82/B3
Hakone, Japan 83/C3
Hakone-yama (peak), Japan 83/C3
Hakosberge (mts.), Namb. 122/C4
Haku-san (peak), Japan 85/E2
Hakui, Japan 85/E2
Hakusan, Japan 83/K6
Hakusan NP, Japan 85/E2
Hakushū, Japan 83/A2
Hāla, Pak. 101/J3
Ḩalab (Aleppo), Syria 104/E1
Ḩalab (prov.), Syria 102/D2
Ḩalabjah, Iraq 103/F3
Halachó, Mex. 175/M6
Halagang, China 80/H7
Ḩalā'ib, Sudan 109/H4
Halbrite, Sk, Can. 156/C3
Halcon (mt.), Phil. 88/C2
Halden, Nor. 40/D2
Haldensleben, Ger. 42/F2
Haldenwang, Ger. 61/G2
Haldīa, India 97/G4
Haldībāri, India 97/G2
Haldībunia, Bang. 97/G4
Haldimand, On, Can. 160/T10
Haldimand-Norfolk (co.), On, Can. 160/S10
Hale, Eng, UK 35/F5
Hale, Tanz. 119/B3
Hale (riv.), Austl. 131/G3
Hale, Arg. 190/E2
Hale, Mo, US 155/H4
Hale (mt.), Austl. 130/C3
Hale Center, Tx, US 152/D3
Haleakala NP, Hi, US 142/T10
Haledon, NJ, US 169/J8
Halen, Belg. 55/E2
Hales Corners, Wi, US 167/P14
Halesowen, Eng, UK 36/D2
Halesworth, Eng, UK 37/H2
Haleyville, Al, US 162/D3
Half Assini, Gha. 114/E5
Half Falls (mtn.), Pa, US 168/A3
Half Moon, NC, US 163/J3
Half Moon Bay, Ca, US 167/J12
Half Tide Beach, Austl. 134/C3
Halfa Aj Jadīda, Sudan 117/G2
Halfbreed Nat'l Wild. Ref., Mt, US 145/K5
Halfing, Ger. 59/F7
Halfmoon Bay, BC, Can. 144/C3
Halfway, Mo, US 153/H2
Halfway, Md, US 161/H5
Halfway, Or, US 146/E1
Halfweg, Neth. 52/B4
Ḩalḩūl, WBnk. 105/C5

Halibu – Hedmar
Map Section 232 233

Haliburton, On, Can. 161/G2
Haliburton Highlands (uplands), On, Can. 161/G2
Halifax, Austl. 134/B2
Halifax (bay), Austl. 127/D2
Halifax, Eng, UK 35/G4
Halifax, NC, US 163/J2
Halifax (cap.), NS, Can. 158/F3
Halifax (int'l arpt.), NS, Can. 158/F3
Halifax, Pa, US 168/B3
Halifax, Va, US 163/H2
Halikko, Fin. 41/K1
Ḩalīl (riv.), Iran 101/G3
Halim Perdana Kusuma (int'l arpt.), Indo. 89/D4
Haliun, Mong. 78/D2
Haljala, Est. 41/M2
Häljarp, Swe. 39/J7
Halkett (cape), Ak, US 171/H1
Hall, Austl. 133/B2
Hall (pt.), Austl. 128/B3
Hall (isls.), Micr. 136/E4
Hall (pen.), Nun, Can. 141/K2
Hall (isl.), Ak, US 171/D3
Hall, Mt, US 145/H4
Hall Beach, Nun, Can. 141/H2
Hall Park, Ok, US 153/F3
Halla-san (peak), SKor. 79/K5
Halladale (riv.), Sc, UK 31/S7
Hallam (peak), BC, Can. 144/E1
Hallam (Hellam), Pa, US 168/B4
Halland (co.), Swe. 38/E4
Hallandale, Fl, US 164/P11
Hällbybrunn, Swe. 40/G2
Halle, Ger. 74/B4
Halle, Belg. 55/D2
Halle, Ger. 53/F4
Halle-Neustadt, Ger. 42/F3
Halleck, Nv, US 146/F3
Hällefors, Swe. 40/F2
Hälleforsnäs, Swe. 40/G2
Hallein, Aus. 45/K3
Hallenberg, Ger. 53/F6
Hallertau (reg.), Ger. 59/E5
Hallettsville, Tx, US 151/F3
Halley, UK, Ant. 192/Y
Halliday, ND, US 156/C4
Halling, Eng, UK 30/E3
Hallingdalselvi (riv.), Nor. 40/C1
Hallock, Mn, US 156/F3
Halls, Tn, US 162/C3
Halls Creek, Austl. 128/B4
Hallsberg, Swe. 40/F2
Hallstahammar, Swe. 40/G2
Hallstavik, Swe. 40/H1
Hallsville, Tx, US 151/G1
Hallu (riv.), Fr. 42/B4
Halluin, Fr. 54/C2
Hallum, Neth. 52/C2
Hallwang, Aus. 59/G7
Hallwilersee (lake), Swi. 60/E3
Hallyŏ Haesang NP, SKor. 84/A3
Halmahera (isl.), Indo. 77/M9
Halmahera (sea), Indo. 91/G4
Halmstad, Swe. 40/E3
Ḩalq al Wādī, Tun. 48/B4
Ḩalq al Wādī, Tun. 67/F4
Hals, Den. 40/D3
Hälsingborg (Helsingborg), Swe. 40/E3
Halstead, Ks, US 153/F1
Halstead, Eng, UK 37/G3
Halsteren, Neth. 52/B5
Haltang (riv.), China 78/C4
Haltemprice, Eng, UK 35/H4
Haltern, Ger. 53/E5
Haltom City, Tx, US 150/K7
Halton (co.), On, Can. 160/T8
Halton (co.), Eng, UK 35/F5
Halton Hills, On, Can. 160/T8
Haltwhistle, Eng, UK 35/F2
Haludpukhur, India 97/F4
Halver, Ger. 53/E6
Halverder Aa (riv.), Ger. 53/E4
Ham, Fr. 54/C4
Ham, Chad 116/B3
Ham Lake, Mn, US 157/H5
Ham River, Namb. 124/B3
Ham, Oued El (riv.), Alg. 112/G5
Ham-sous-Varsberg, Fr. 55/F5
Hamada, Japan 84/C3
Hamada de Tinrhert (plat.), Alg. 111/G4
Hamada du Drâa (plat.), Alg. 110/D3
Hamada Safia (plat.), Mali 110/D5
Hamadān, Iran 103/G3
Hamadān (gov.), Iran 103/G3
Hamādat Marzūq (plat.), Libya 111/H4
Ḩamādat Tinghert (uplands), Libya 111/H3
Ḩamāh, Syria 104/E2
Ḩamāh (prov.), Syria 104/E2
Hamajima, Japan 83/L7
Hamakita, Japan 85/E3
Hamam, Turk. 104/E1
Hamamatsu, Japan 85/E3
Hamami (reg.), Mrta. 110/C5
Hamanaka, Japan 82/D2
Hamar, Nor. 40/D1
Ḩamāţah (peak), Egypt 109/G3
Hamath Tiberias NP, Isr. 105/D3
Hamatombetsu, Japan 82/C1
Hambergen, Ger. 53/F2
Hamble, Eng, UK 37/E5
Hambleton (hills), Eng, UK 35/G3
Hambühren, Ger. 53/G3
Hamburg, Ar, US 153/J4
Hamburg, Ger. 53/G1
Hamburg (state), Ger. 40/D5
Hamburg, Ia, US 155/G3
Hamburg, NJ, US 168/D1
Hamburg, NY, US 161/G3
Hamburg, Pa, US 168/C2
Hamburg (Fuhlsbüttel) (int'l arpt.), Ger. 53/G1
Ḩamḑ (wadi), SAr. 100/C3
Ḩamḑah, SAr. 100/D5
Ḩamdānah, SAr. 100/D5
Hamden, Ct, US 161/K4
Hamden, NY, US 161/J3
Hamden, Oh, US 163/F1
Häme (prov.), Fin. 38/G3
Hämeenkyrö, Fin. 41/K1
Hämeenlinna, Fin. 41/L1
Hamelin, Austl. 130/B3
Hamelin Pool (bay), Austl. 130/B3
Hameln, Ger. 53/G4
Hamero Hadad, Eth. 118/B4
Hamersley (range), Austl. 127/A3
Hamersley Range NP, Austl. 130/C2
Hamersville, Oh, US 162/F1
Hamford Water (inlet), Eng, UK 37/H3
Hamgyŏng (mts.), NKor. 79/K3
Hamgyŏng-bukto (prov.), NKor. 81/E2
Hamgyŏng-namdo (prov.), NKor. 81/D2
Hamhŭ-si (prov.), NKor. 81/D3
Hamhŭng, NKor. 81/D3
Hami, China 78/C3
Ḩamīdīyeh, Iran 103/G4
Hamill, SD, US 154/E2
Hamilton, Austl. 132/B3
Hamilton, On, Can. 160/T9
Hamilton (har.), On, Can. 160/T9
Hamilton (inlet), Nf, Can. 139/M4
Hamilton, NZ 135/C2
Hamilton, Sc, UK 33/B5
Hamilton, Al, US 162/D3
Hamilton (mt.), Ca, US 167/L12
Hamilton, Co, US 147/K3
Hamilton (lake), Fl, US 164/M7
Hamilton, Ga, US 162/E4
Hamilton, Ks, US 153/F2
Hamilton, Mi, US 160/C3
Hamilton, Mo, US 155/H4
Hamilton, Mt, US 145/G4
Hamilton, NY, US 161/J3
Hamilton (mtn.), NY, US 161/J3
Hamilton, Oh, US 160/D5
Hamilton, Tx, US 151/E2
Hamilton Mil. Res., NY, US 169/J9
Hamilton-Wentworth (co.), On, Can. 160/S9
Ḩamīm (wadi), Libya 108/D2
Hamina, Fin. 41/M1
Hamiota, Mb, Can. 156/D2
Hamīrpur, India 98/D4
Hamīrpur, India 96/C3
Hamju, NKor. 81/D3
Hamlet, NC, US 163/H3
Hamlin, Tx, US 152/D4
Hamlin, WV, US 163/F1
Hamm, Ger. 55/G2
Hamm, Ger. 58/B3
Hamm, Ger. 53/E5
Hamma-Bouziane, Alg. 112/K6
Ḩammām Al Anf, Tun. 48/B4
Ḩammāmāt (gulf), Gabon 111/H1
Hammāmāt (gulf), Tun. 66/F3
Hammanskraal, SAfr. 123/F5
Hammarland, Fin. 41/H1
Hammarön (isl.), Swe. 40/E2
Hammarsjön (lake), Swe. 39/L7
Hammarstrand, Swe. 38/F3
Hamme, Belg. 55/D1
Hamme (riv.), Ger. 53/F2
Hammel, Den. 40/C3
Hammelburg, Ger. 58/C2
Hammer (cr.), Pa, US 168/B3
Hammerfest, Nor. 38/G1
Hammershus, Den. 40/F4
Hammersmith and Fulham (bor.), Eng, UK 30/A1
Hammett, Id, US 146/F2
Hamminkeln, Ger. 52/D5
Hammon, Ok, US 152/E3
Hammonasset (pt.), Ct, US 169/F1
Hammond, In, US 160/C4
Hammond, La, US 164/C2
Hammond, Mt, US 154/B1
Hammond Street, Eng, UK 30/C1
Hammonton, NJ, US 168/D4
Hamnvik, Nor. 38/F1
Hamois, Belg. 55/E3
Hamon, Congo 120/C4
Hamont-Achel, Belg. 52/C6
Hamoud, Mrta. 114/C3
Hampden, ND, US 156/E3
Hampden, NZ 135/B4
Hampden Sydney, Va, US 163/H2
Hampshire, Il, US 155/K2
Hampshire Downs (hills), Eng, UK 37/E4
Hampstead (nbrhd.), Eng, UK 30/C2
Hampstead, Md, US 168/B4
Hampton, Ar, US 153/H4
Hampton, Fl, US 165/G3
Hampton, Ia, US 155/H2
Hampton, NB, Can. 158/E3
Hampton, NH, US 161/L3
Hampton, Or, US 146/C2
Hampton, Pa, US 168/A4
Hampton, SC, US 163/G4
Hampton, Tn, US 163/F2
Hampton, Va, US 163/J2
Hampton Bays, NY, US 169/F2
Hampton Court, Eng, UK 30/C2
Hampton Nat'l Hist. Site, Md, US 168/B5
Hampton Park (nbrhd.), Austl. 132/G6
Hampton Roads (est.), Va, US 163/J2
Hamp'yŏng, SKor. 81/D5
Ḩamrat ash Shaykh, Sudan 117/E2
Hamtramck, Mi, US 167/F7
Hamuku, Indo. 91/J4
Hamura, Japan 83/C2
Hamyang, SKor. 81/D5
Hamyŏl, SKor. 81/D4
Han (riv.), China 77/M6
Hana (riv.), India 96/C5
Hanahan, SC, US 163/G4
Hanainef, Erit. 118/B2
Hanak, Turk. 71/G4
Ḩanak, SAr. 109/H3
Hanamaki, Japan 82/B4
Hanan, Eth. 118/C4
Hanang (peak), Tanz. 119/A3
Hanau, Ger. 58/B2
Hanazono, Japan 83/C1
Hanceville, Al, US 162/D3
Hancheng, China 80/B4
Hanches, Fr. 57/G3
Hancock (lake), Fl, US 164/M8
Hancock, Md, US 161/G5
Hancock, Mi, US 157/K4
Hancock, Mn, US 156/G5
Hancock, NY, US 161/J4
Hancock, Wi, US 155/K1
Hancocks Bridge, NJ, US 168/C5
Handa, Japan 83/L6
Handae-ri, NKor. 81/D2
Handan, China 80/C3
Handawor, India 98/C2
Handel, Sk, Can. 145/K1
Handeloh, Ger. 53/G2
Handen, Swe. 39/B1
Handeni, Tanz. 119/B3
Handiā, India 96/D3
Handsworth, Sk, Can. 156/C3
Handsworth, Eng, UK 37/E1
Hanford, Ca, US 148/C2
Hanford Reach Nat'l Mon., Wa, US 144/E4
Hanford Site, Wa, US 144/E4
Hangayn (mts.), Mong. 74/K5
Hanggin Qi, China 80/B3
Hanging Rock (mtn.), NC, US 163/G2
Hangingstone (hill), Eng, UK 36/C5
Hangklip (cape), SAfr. 124/L11
Hangman (cr.), Wa, US 144/F4
Hangö (Hanko), Fin. 41/K2
Hangu, Pak. 98/A3
Hangu, China 80/H7
Hangzhou, China 80/L9
Hangzhou (bay), China 80/L9
Hanhofen, Ger. 58/B4
Hanhöhiy (mts.), Mong. 78/C2
Hani, Turk. 102/E2
Haninge, Swe. 40/H2
Hanja (riv.), Ang. 122/B2
Hanjalipan, Indo. 90/D4
Hanjiang, China 87/H3
Hankensbüttel, Ger. 53/H3
Hankey, SAfr. 124/D4
Hankinson, ND, US 156/F4
Hanko (Hangö), Fin. 41/K2
Hanle, India 99/C5
Hanley, Sk, Can. 145/L2
Hanmer, NZ 135/C3
Hann (mt.), Austl. 128/B3
Hanna, La, US 164/B2
Hanna, Ab, Can. 145/J2
Hannaford, ND, US 156/E4
Hannah, ND, US 156/E3
Hannahs Mill, Ga, US 162/E4
Hannan, Japan 83/H7
Hannibal, Mo, US 155/J4
Hannibal, NY, US 161/H3
Hannibal, Oh, US 160/F5
Hanningfield (res.), Eng, UK 30/E2
Hannō, Japan 83/C2
Hannover, Ger. 53/G4
Hannover (int'l arpt.), Ger. 53/G4
Hannut, Belg. 55/E2
Hanöbukten (bay), Swe. 38/E5
Hanoi (Ha Noi) (cap.), Viet. 86/E4
Hanover, On, Can. 160/F2
Hanover (isl.), Chile 191/B6
Hanover, SAfr. 124/D3
Hanover, Il, US 155/J2
Hanover, In, US 162/E1
Hanover, Ks, US 155/F4
Hanover, Mn, US 157/N6
Hanover, NH, US 161/K3
Hanover, Pa, US 168/B4
Hanover, Va, US 163/J2
Hanover Park, Il, US 167/P16
Hānsdiha, India 97/F3
Hansen (dam), Ca, US 166/F7
Hanshan, China 80/D5
Hānsi, India 98/C5
Hanska (lake), Mn, US 155/G1
Hanson (bay), NZ 135/E3
Hanstedt, Ger. 53/H2
Hanstholm, Den. 40/C3
Hanston, Ks, US 152/E1
Hansville, Wa, US 167/B2
Hantengri Feng (peak), China 99/D3
Hantsport, NS, Can. 158/E3
Hantzsch (riv.), Nun, Can. 141/J2
Hanumāngarh, India 98/C5
Hanuy (riv.), Mong. 78/E2
Hanwood, Austl. 133/C2
Hanyū, Japan 83/D1
Hanyuan, China 86/D2
Hanza, Ang. 120/C5
Hanzhong, China 78/F5
Hao (isl.), FrPol. 137/L6
Haoshan, China 87/G3
Haouach, Ouadi (riv.), Chad 116/D1
Håøya (isl.), Nor. 38/S8
Haparanda, Swe. 68/E2
Hapch'ŏn, SKor. 81/E5
Hapeville, Ga, US 163/M7
Happy Camp, Ca, US 146/B3
Happy Jack, Az, US 149/G3
Happy Jack, La, US 164/D3
Happy Valley (res.), Austl. 131/M9
Happy Valley-Goose Bay, Nf, Can. 141/K3
Haptŏk, SKor. 81/D4
Hāpur, India 96/A1
Ḩaql, SAr. 109/G2
Haquira, Peru 184/C4
Har (lake), Mong. 78/C2
Har Karmel (peak), Isr. 105/C3
Har Meron (peak), Isr. 105/C3
Har Nur, China 79/J2
Har Ramon (peak), Isr. 104/D4
Har Tavor (peak), Isr. 105/C3
Har Us (lake), Mong. 78/C2
Har-Ayrag, Mong. 78/F2
Har-Us (riv.), Mong. 78/D2
Hara, Japan 83/A2
Haraa (riv.), Mong. 78/F2
Ḩaraḑ, SAr. 100/E4
Ḩaraḑ, Yem. 118/B1
Ḩarajah, SAr. 100/D5
Haramachi, Japan 85/G2
Harappa (ruin), Pak. 98/B4
Harare (cap.), Zim. 123/F3
Harare (int'l arpt.), Zim. 123/F3
Haravilliers, Fr. 30/J4
Haraz, Chad 116/C2
Haraze-Mangueigne, Chad 116/D3
Harbel, Libr. 114/C5
Harbeson, De, US 168/C6
Harbin, China 79/K2
Harbiye, Turk. 104/E1
Harbonnières, Fr. 54/B4
Harboøre, Den. 40/C3
Harbor Beach, Mi, US 160/E3
Harbor City (nbrhd.), Ca, US 166/F8
Harbor Springs, Mi, US 160/D2
Harbour Breton, Nf, Can. 159/K2
Harbour Grace, Nf, Can. 159/L2
Harbour Main, Nf, Can. 159/L2
Harburg, Ger. 53/G2
Harburg, Ger. 58/D5
Harbury, Eng, UK 37/E2
Hårby, Den. 40/D4
Hard, Aus. 61/F3
Hardā, India 92/C3
Hardangervidda NP, Nor. 40/B1
Hardap (dam), Namb. 122/C5
Hardau (riv.), Ger. 53/H3
Hardaway, Al, US 162/E4
Hardee (co.), Fl, US 164/M8
Hardeeville, SC, US 163/G4
Hardegsen, Ger. 53/G5
Hardelot-Plage, Fr. 54/A2
Harden City, Ok, US 153/F3
Hardenberg, Neth. 52/D3
Harderwijk, Neth. 52/C4
Hardesar, India 98/C5
Hardheim, Ger. 58/C3
Hardin, Ky, US 162/C2
Hardin, Il, US 155/J4
Hardin, Mt, US 145/L5
Hardin, Tx, US 151/G2
Harding, SAfr. 125/E3
Harding (res.), Ga, US 162/E4
Hardinsburg, Ky, US 162/D2
Hardisty, Ab, Can. 145/J1
Hardoi, India 96/C2
Hardoi Branch (riv.), India 96/C2
Hardricourt, Fr. 30/H4
Hardscrabble Wash (riv.), Az, US 149/H3
Hardtner, Ks, US 153/E2
Hardwār, India 101/L3
Hardwick, Ga, US 163/F4
Hardwood (mtn.), Me, US 161/L1
Hardy, Ar, US 153/J2
Hardy, Ne, US 154/F3
Hardy (pen.), Chile 191/C7
Hare Bay, Nf, Can. 159/K1
Hare Dimona (peak), Isr. 104/D4
Harefield, Eng, UK 30/B2
Harelbeke, Belg. 54/C2
Haren, Ger. 53/E3
Haren, Neth. 52/D2
Hārer, Eth. 118/B3
Harerge (prov.), Eth. 118/B3
Harewa, Eth. 118/B3
Harfleur, Fr. 57/F1
Harford (co.), Md, US 168/B4
Hargele, Eth. 118/B4
Hargesheim, Ger. 55/G4
Hargeville, Fr. 30/H5
Hargeysa, Som. 118/C3
Hargeysa (int'l arpt.), Som. 118/C3
Harghita (prov.), Rom. 51/G2
Harghita (peak), Rom. 51/G2
Hargīgo, Erit. 118/A2
Harhorin, Mong. 78/E2
Hari (str.), Est. 41/K2
Hari (river), Indo. 89/C3
Hari (riv.), Indo. 90/B4
Ḩarīb, Yem. 118/C2
Haribes, Namb. 122/C5
Harihar, India 95/B3
Hariharganj, India 97/E3
Harīke, India 98/C4
Ḩārim, Syria 104/E1
Harima (sea), Japan 84/D3
Harima (bay), Japan 83/G6
Harima, Japan 83/G6
Ḩarīmā, Jor. 105/D3
Haringey (bor.), Eng, UK 30/C2
Haringhāta (riv.), Bang. 97/G4
Haringvliet (chan.), Neth. 52/B5
Haringvlietdam (dam), Neth. 52/B5
Harīpur, Pak. 98/B3
Harīrūd (riv.), Afg. 77/F6
Ḩāris, WBnk. 105/C4
Harisal, India 92/C3
Harjavalta, Fin. 41/K1
Harker Heights, Tx, US 151/F2
Harlan, Ky, US 163/F2
Harlan, Ia, US 155/G3
Harlan Co. (lake), Ne, US 154/E3
Harlan County (dam), Ne, US 154/E3
Harlech, Wal, UK 34/D6
Harlem, Ga, US 163/F4
Harlem, Mt, US 145/K3
Harlem (nbrhd.), NY, US 169/K8
Harleston, Eng, UK 37/H2
Harleton, Tx, US 151/G1
Hårlev, Den. 39/J7
Harleyville, SC, US 163/G4
Harlingen, Neth. 52/C2
Harlingen, Tx, US 150/F4
Harlington, Eng, UK 37/F3
Harlow, ND, US 156/E3
Harlow, Eng, UK 30/D1
Harlowton, Mt, US 145/K4
Harmannsdorf, Aus. 51/N7
Harmelen, Neth. 52/B4
Harmony, Mn, US 155/H2
Harnātānr, India 97/E2
Harnes, Fr. 54/B3
Harney (valley), Or, US 146/D2
Harney (lake), Or, US 146/D2
Harney (peak), SD, US 154/C2
Harney, Md, US 168/A4
Harni, Bang. 97/H4
Harnoli, Pak. 98/A3
Harö (isl.), Swe. 39/B1
Haro, Sp. 44/B5
Haro (cape), Mex. 174/C3
Harold, Ca, US 166/B1
Harpenden, Eng, UK 37/F3
Harper, Libr. 114/D5
Harper (mt.), Yk, Can. 171/L3
Harper (mt.), Ak, US 171/K3
Harper (lake), Ca, US 148/D3
Harper, Ks, US 153/E2
Harper, Or, US 146/E2
Harper, Tx, US 150/E2
Harper, Wa, US 167/B2
Harper Woods, Mi, US 167/F7
Harpers Ferry Nat'l Hist. Park, WV, US 161/H5
Harpersville, Al, US 162/D4
Harperville, Ms, US 162/C4
Harpeth (riv.), Tn, US 162/D2
Harpstedt, Ger. 53/F3
Harqin Qi, China 79/H3
Harqin Zuoyi Monggolzu Zizhixian, China 80/D2
Ḩarrah, Yem. 118/D2
Harrai, India 96/B4
Harran, Turk. 102/D2
Ḩarrān al 'Awāmīd, Syria 105/F2
Harrell, Ar, US 153/H4
Harricana (riv.), Qu, Can. 141/J4
Harrietsham, Eng, UK 30/F3
Harrietts Bluff, Ga, US 165/H2
Harriman, Tn, US 162/E3
Harriman, NY, US 168/D1
Harrington, Austl. 132/E1
Harrington, De, US 168/C6
Harrington Park, NJ, US 169/K8
Harris (isl.), Sc, UK 31/Q8
Harris (lake), Austl. 131/G4
Harris (mtn.), Tn, US 162/E2
Harris (mt.), Austl. 131/F3
Harris (co.), Tx, US 151/M9
Harrisburg, Ar, US 162/B3
Harrisburg, Il, US 162/C2
Harrisburg, Ne, US 154/C3
Harrisburg, Or, US 146/B1
Harrisburg (cap.), Pa, US 168/B3
Harrisburg (arpt.), Pa, US 168/B3
Harrislee, Ger. 40/C4
Harrismith, SAfr. 124/E3
Harrison (cape), Nf, Can. 141/L3
Harrison (lake), BC, Can. 144/C3
Harrison (bay), Ak, US 171/H1
Harrison, Ar, US 153/H2
Harrison, Ga, US 163/F4
Harrison, Id, US 144/F4
Harrison, Mi, US 160/D2
Harrison, Ne, US 154/C2
Harrison, NJ, US 169/J9
Harrison, NY, US 169/L8
Harrison, Oh, US 160/D5
Harrison, Tn, US 162/E3
Harrisonburg, La, US 164/C2
Harrisonburg, Va, US 163/H1
Harrisonville, Mo, US 153/G1
Harriston, On, Can. 160/F3
Harriston, Ms, US 164/C2
Harristown, Il, US 155/K4
Harrisville, Ms, US 164/C2
Harrisville, Mi, US 160/E2
Harrisville, WV, US 163/G1
Harrodsburg, In, US 162/D1
Harrodsburg, Ky, US 162/E2
Harrogate, Eng, UK 35/G4
Harrogate-Shawnee, Tn, US 162/F2
Harrold, Tx, US 152/E3
Harrow, On, Can. 160/E3
Harrow (bor.), Eng, UK 30/B2
Harrow (nbrhd.), Eng, UK 30/C2
Harrow, Austl. 132/B3
Harry S Truman (dam), Mo, US 153/H1
Harry S Truman (res.), Mo, US 155/H4
Harry S Truman Nat'l Hist. Site, Mo, US 155/G4
Harsefeld, Ger. 53/G2
Harsewinkel, Ger. 53/F5
Harskamp, Neth. 52/C4
Harson's Island, Mi, US 167/G6
Hart, Tx, US 152/C3
Hart, Mi, US 160/C3
Hart (riv.), Eng, UK 30/A3
Hart (isl.), NY, US 169/K8
Hart (lake), Or, US 146/C2
Hart (riv.), Yk, Can. 140/C2
Hart (mtn.), Or, US 146/D2
Hart (mt.), Austl. 128/B4
Hart Fell (peak), Sc, UK 33/C6
Hart Mtn. Nat'l Antelope Refuge, Or, US 146/D2
Ḩartā, Jor. 105/D3
Hartbeesrivier (riv.), SAfr. 124/C3
Harte (mtn.), Can. 156/D1
Hårteigen (peak), Nor. 40/B1
Hartelkanaal (riv.), Neth. 52/B5
Hartford, Libr. 114/C5
Hartford, Al, US 165/F2
Hartford (cap.), Ct, US 161/K4
Hartford, Ks, US 153/G1
Hartford, Ky, US 162/D2
Hartford, NJ, US 168/D4
Hartford, Wi, US 160/B3
Hartford City, In, US 160/D4
Hartheim, Ger. 60/D2
Harthill, Sc, UK 33/C5
Hartington, Ne, US 155/F2
Hartkirchen, Aus. 59/H6
Hartland, NB, Can. 158/D2
Hartland, Eng, UK 36/B4
Hartland (pt.), Eng, UK 36/B4
Hartland, Mi, US 167/E6
Hartland, Vt, US 161/K3
Hartlebury, Eng, UK 36/D2
Hartlepool, Eng, UK 35/G2
Hartlepool (co.), Eng, UK 35/G2
Hartleton, Pa, US 168/A2
Hartley, Eng, UK 30/D2
Hartley, Ia, US 155/G2
Hartley Bay, BC, Can. 171/N5
Hartley Wintney, Eng, UK 30/A3
Hartly, De, US 168/C5
Hartmannberge (mts.), Namb. 122/B3
Hartney, Mb, Can. 156/D3
Harts, WV, US 163/F1
Harts (riv.), SAfr. 122/E5
Harts Range, Austl. 131/G2
Hartsdale, NY, US 169/K7
Hartselle, Al, US 162/D3
Hartsfield Atlanta Int'l (int'l arpt.), Ga, US 163/M7
Hartshill, Eng, UK 37/E1
Hartshorn, Mo, US 153/J2
Hartshorne, Ok, US 153/G3
Hartsön (isl.), Swe. 39/A2
Hartstene (isl.), Wa, US 167/B3
Hartsville, SC, US 163/G3
Hartsville, Tn, US 162/D2
Hartville, Mo, US 153/H2
Hartwell (dam), Ga, US 163/F3
Hartwell, Ga, US 163/F3
Hartwell (res.), SC, US 163/F3
Hartz Mountain NP, Austl. 132/C4
Haruhi, Japan 83/L5
Harun (peak), Indo. 88/A4
Hārūnābād, Pak. 98/B5
Hārūt (riv.), Afg. 101/H2
Harvard, Ma, US 161/L3
Harvard, Il, US 155/K2
Harvard, Ne, US 154/E3
Harvest, Al, US 162/D3
Harvey, ND, US 156/E4
Harvey, Mi, US 157/L4
Harvey, NB, Can. 158/E3
Harvey, Il, US 167/Q16
Harvey, Austl. 130/B5
Harveys (lake), Pa, US 168/B1
Harwich, Eng, UK 37/H3
Harwood, ND, US 156/F4
Harworth, Eng, UK 35/G5
Haryana (state), India 99/C6
Harz (mts.), Ger. 42/F3
Hasan (peak), Turk. 102/C2
Hasan Abdāl, Pak. 98/B3
Hasanpur, India 96/B1
Ḩāşbayyā, Leb. 105/D2
Hasbrouck Heights, NJ, US 169/J8
Hascombe, Eng, UK 30/B3
Hasdo (riv.), India 96/D4
Hase (riv.), Ger. 42/D2
Hasel (riv.), Ger. 58/D1
Haselünne, Ger. 53/E3
Hasenmatt (peak), Swi. 60/D3
Hashaat, Mong. 78/E2
Hashima, Japan 83/L5
Hashimoto, Japan 84/D3
Hashtgerd, Iran 103/G3
Hasi el Farsía (well), WSah. 110/C4
Hāsilpur, Pak. 98/B5
Haskell, Ok, US 153/G3
Haskell, Tx, US 152/E4
Haskell, Ar, US 153/H3
Haslach an der Mühl, Aus. 59/H5
Haslach im Kinzigtal, Ger. 60/E1
Hasle bei Burgdorf, Swi. 60/D3
Haslemere, Eng, UK 37/F4
Hasler (cr.), Mi, US 167/F6
Haslet, Tx, US 150/K7
Haslett, Mi, US 160/D3
Haslev, Den. 39/H7
Haslingden, Eng, UK 35/F4
Haslington, Eng, UK 35/F5
Hasloh, Ger. 53/G1
Hāsmāi, Bang. 97/G3
Haspra, Ukr. 73/H5
Haspres, Fr. 54/C3
Hassa, Turk. 104/E1
Hassan (El Aaiún) (int'l arpt.), WSah. 110/B4
Hassayampa (riv.), Az, US 149/F3
Hassberge (hills), Ger. 58/D2
Hasse, Tx, US 150/E2
Hassel, Ger. 53/G3
Hassel Sound (str.), Nun, Can. 141/S7
Hasselt, Belg. 55/E2
Hasselt, Neth. 52/D3
Hassfurt, Ger. 58/D2
Hassi Bahbah, Alg. 112/G5
Hassi bou Zid (well), Alg. 111/F3
Hassi el Hadjar (well), Alg. 111/G3
Hassi el Mislane (well), Alg. 111/H4
Hassi er Rebib (well), Alg. 111/G2
Hassi Messaoud, Alg. 111/G3
Hässleholm, Swe. 40/E3
Hasslo (int'l arpt.), Swe. 40/G2
Hassloch, Ger. 58/B4
Haste, Ger. 53/G4
Hastings, Fl, US 165/H3
Hastings, Mi, US 160/D3
Hastings, Pa, US 161/G4
Hastings, SLeo. 114/B4
Hastings, NZ 135/D2
Hastings, Ne, US 154/E3
Hastings, Mn, US 157/Q7
Hastings (dam), Mn, US 157/Q7
Hastings, Eng, UK 37/G5
Hastings, Austl. 133/B4
Hastings Battlesite, Eng, UK 37/G5
Hastings-On-Hudson, NY, US 169/K7
Hästveda, Swe. 39/K6
Hasuda, Japan 83/D2
Hasunuma, Japan 83/E2
Hasvik, Nor. 38/G1
Haswell, Co, US 152/C1
Hat (mtn.), Ca, US 146/C3
Hat Chao Mai NP, Thai. 94/B5
Hāt Gāmāria, India 97/E4
Hat Head, Austl. 132/E1
Hat Head NP, Austl. 132/E1
Hat Nai Yang NP, Thai. 94/B5
Hat Yai, Thai. 94/C5
Hat Yai (int'l arpt.), Thai. 94/C5
Hatansuudal, Mong. 78/E3
Hatashō, Japan 83/K5
Hatavch, Mong. 78/G2
Hatay (prov.), Turk. 104/D1
Hatboro, Pa, US 168/C3
Hatch, Ut, US 149/F2
Hatch, NM, US 149/J4
Hatchechubbee, Al, US 162/E4
Hatcher (peak), Arg. 191/B6
Hatches Creek, Austl. 131/G2
Hatchie (riv.), Tn, US 162/C3
Hatchie NWR, Tn, US 162/C3
Hatchineha (lake), Fl, US 165/H3
Haţeg, Rom. 50/F3
Hatfield, Austl. 132/B2
Hatfield, Eng, UK 30/C1
Hatfield, Ar, US 153/G3
Hatfield, Pa, US 168/C3
Hatfield Peverel, Eng, UK 30/E1
Hatgal, Mong. 78/E1
Hāthazāri, Bang. 97/H4
Hathersage, Eng, UK 35/G5
Hāthras, India 96/B2
Hātia (riv.), Bang. 97/H4
Hātia, North (isl.), Bang. 97/H4
Hātia, South (isl.), Bang. 97/H4
Hato (int'l arpt.), NAnt. 180/D1
Hato Corozal, Col. 180/D3
Hato Mayor, DRep. 173/H4
Hatogaya, Japan 83/D2
Hatoyama, Japan 83/C2
Hatsu (isl.), Japan 83/C3
Hatta, India 96/B3
Hatta, Japan 83/A2
Hattah-Kulkyne NP, Austl. 131/J5
Hattelmala, Fin. 39/E4
Hattem, Neth. 52/D4
Hatten, Fr. 55/G6
Hatten, Ger. 53/F2
Hatteras, NC, US 163/K3
Hatteras (isl.), NC, US 163/K3
Hattersheim am Mein, Ger. 58/B2
Hattiesburg, Ms, US 164/D2
Hattieville, Belz. 176/D2
Hattingen, Ger. 53/E6
Hatton, ND, US 156/F4
Hatton, Sc, UK 33/E2
Hatton, Eng, UK 35/G6
Hatton, Ut, US 149/F1
Hatton, Al, US 162/D3
Hatton, Sk, Can. 145/K2
Hattula, Fin. 41/L1
Håtuna, Swe. 39/A1
Hatvan, Hun. 50/D2
Hatzenbühl, Ger. 58/B4
Hatzfeld, Ger. 53/F6
Hau Bon, Viet. 94/E3
Hau Giang (riv.), Viet. 94/D4
Haubourdin, Fr. 54/B2
Haubstadt, In, US 162/D1
Haud (reg.), Eth. 118/C4
Hauge, Nor. 40/B2
Haugen, Wi, US 157/J5
Haugesund, Nor. 40/A2
Haughton, La, US 153/H4
Hauho, Fin. 39/E3
Haukeligrend, Nor. 40/B2
Haukipudas, Fin. 68/E2
Haune (riv.), Ger. 42/E3
Haunsberg (peak), Aus. 59/F7
Haunstetten, Ger. 58/D6
Hauonselkä (lake), Fin. 39/E3
Hauppauge, NY, US 169/E2
Hauraki (gulf), NZ 135/C2
Haus, Nor. 40/A1
Hausach, Ger. 60/E1
Hausjärvi, Fin. 41/L1
Hausleiten, Aus. 51/N7
Hausstock (peak), Swi. 61/F4
Haut Atlas (mts.), Mor. 110/D3
Haut-Ogooue (prov.), Gabon 120/C3
Haut-Rhin (dept.), Fr. 60/D2
Haut-Zaïre, D.R. Congo 121/F2
Haute-Kotto (pref.), CAfr. 116/D4
Haute-Normandie (pol. reg.), Fr. 44/D2
Haute-Sangha (pref.), CAfr. 116/B4
Haute-Saône (dept.), Fr. 60/B2
Haute-Savoie (dept.), Fr. 60/C5
Hautefeuille, Fr. 30/L5
Hautes Fagnes (uplands), Belg. 55/E3
Hautes-Alpes (dept.), Fr. 64/C3
Hauteurs de Gâtine (uplands), Fr. 44/C3
Hauteville-Lompnes, Fr. 60/B6
Hautmont, Fr. 54/C3
Hautsx (plat.), Alg. 111/E2
Hautsx (plat.), Alg.,Mor. 66/C4
Havana, ND, US 156/F5
Havana, Fl, US 165/F2
Havana, Il, US 155/J3
Havannah, Canal de la (chan.), NCal. 137/V13
Havant, Eng, UK 37/F5
Havasu (lake), Az, Ca, US 148/E3
Havasu Nat'l Wild Ref., Az, US 148/E3
Havasupai Ind. Res., Az, US 149/F2
Havdhem, Swe. 40/H3
Havdrup, Den. 40/E4
Havel (riv.), Ger. 43/G2
Havel (canal), Ger. 42/P6
Havelange, Belg. 55/E3
Haveli, Pak. 98/B4
Haveliān, Pak. 98/B2
Havelländischer Grosser Hauptkanal (canal), Ger. 42/P6
Havelock, NB, Can. 158/E2
Havelock, On, Can. 161/H2
Havelock, NZ 135/C3
Havelock, NC, US 163/J3
Havelock North, NZ 135/D2
Havelte, Neth. 52/D3
Haven, Ks, US 153/F2
Havencore (isl.), Eng, UK 37/G3
Haverfordwest, Wal, UK 36/B3
Haverhill, Eng, UK 37/G2
Haverhill, Fl, US 164/P9
Haverhill, Ma, US 161/L3
Haverhill, NH, US 161/K2
Havering (bor.), Eng, UK 30/D2
Haviland, Ks, US 152/E2
Ḩavīq, Iran 103/G2
Havířov, Czh. 43/K4
Havixbeck, Ger. 53/E5
Havlíčkuv Brod, Czh. 43/H4
Havneby, Den. 40/C4
Havnehage (isl.), Den. 39/G7
Hâvre (riv.), Fr. 56/D6
Havre, Mt, US 145/K3
Havre de Grace, Md, US 168/B4
Havre North, Mt, US 145/K3
Havre-Aubert, Qu, Can. 159/G2
Havre-Saint-Pierre, Qu, Can. 141/K3
Havsa, Turk. 51/H5
Havza, Turk. 70/E4
Haw (peak), NC, US 162/E3
Haw (riv.), NC, US 163/H2
Hawaii (state), US 142/S10
Hawaii (isl.), Hi, US 142/U11
Hawaii Volcanoes Nat'l Pk., Hi, US 142/U11
Hawaiian (isls.), US 137/H2
Hawaiian Gardens, Ca, US 166/F8
Ḩawallī, Kuw. 103/G4
Hawarden, Wal, UK 35/E5
Hawarden, NZ 135/C3
Hawarden, Ia, US 155/F2
Hawea (lake), NZ 135/B4
Hawera, NZ 135/C2
Hawes, Eng, UK 35/F3
Hawesville, Ky, US 162/D2
Haweswater (res.), Eng, UK 35/F2
Hawick, Sc, UK 33/D6
Hawk Point, Mo, US 155/J4
Hawke (bay), NZ 127/H6
Hawke (cape), Austl. 132/E2
Hawker, Austl. 131/H4
Hawkesbury, On, Can. 161/J2
Hawkesbury (pt.), Austl. 128/D2
Hawkesbury (riv.), Austl. 134/G8
Hawkins, Wi, US 157/J5
Hawkins (peak), Ca, US 146/D4
Hawkinsville, Ga, US 163/F4
Hawks Nest (peak), ND, US 156/E4
Hawks Nest, Austl. 132/E2
Hawksbill (mtn.), Va, US 163/H1
Hawley, Mn, US 156/F4
Hawley, Co, US 152/C2
Hawley, Tx, US 150/E1
Haworth, Ok, US 153/G4
Haworth, NJ, US 169/K8
Hawr al Ḩammār (lake), Iraq 103/F4
Ḩawsh 'Isá, Egypt 113/B3
Hawston, SAfr. 124/L11
Hawthorn Hill, Eng, UK 30/A2
Hawthorn Woods, Il, US 167/P15
Hawthorne, Ca, US 166/F8
Hawthorne, Fl, US 165/G3
Hawthorne, NJ, US 169/J8
Hawthorne, NY, US 169/K8
Hawthorne, Nv, US 146/D4
Hawthorne, Tx, US 151/G2
Hawthorne Ammunition Depot, Nv, US 146/D4
Ḩawwārah, Jor. 105/D3
Ḩawwārat al Maqţa', Egypt 113/B6
Hawzēn, Eth. 118/A2
Haxby, Eng, UK 35/G3
Haxtun, Co, US 154/C3
Hay, Austl. 133/B2
Hay (cape), Austl. 128/C3
Hay (pt.), Austl. 134/C3
Hay (riv.), Austl. 131/A1
Hay (riv.), Can. 139/F4
Hay (riv.), Ab, BC, Can. 140/E3
Hay, Wal, UK 36/C2
Hay, Wa, US 144/F4
Hay River, NW, Can. 140/E2
Hay Springs, Ne, US 154/C2
Hayachine-san (peak), Japan 82/B4
Hayakawa, Japan 83/A3
Hayama, Japan 83/D3
Hayange, Fr. 55/F5
Haybān (peak), Sudan 117/F3
Haybān, Sudan 117/F3
Haybes, Fr. 55/D4
Haycock, Ak, US 171/F2
Haydān (wadi), Jor. 105/D5
Hayden, Az, US 149/G4
Hayden, Co, US 147/K3
Hayden, Id, US 144/F4
Hayden-Rhodes (aqueduct), Az, US 149/F4
Haydock, Eng, UK 35/F5
Haydon Bridge, Eng, UK 35/F2
Hayes (riv.), Mb, Can. 140/G3
Hayes (nbrhd.), Eng, UK 30/B2
Hayes (pen.), Grld. 141/T7
Hayes (mt.), Ak, US 171/J3
Hayes, SD, US 154/D1
Hayes, Wi, US 160/B2
Hayes Center, Ne, US 154/D3
Hayesville, NC, US 162/F3
Hayfork, Ca, US 146/B3
Hayingen, Ger. 61/F1
Hāyk' (lake), Eth. 117/H4
Haylaastay, Mong. 75/M5
Hayle (riv.), Eng, UK 36/A6
Hayle, Eng, UK 36/A6
Hayling (isl.), Eng, UK 37/F5
Haylow, Ga, US 165/G2
Haymana, Turk. 102/C2
Haynes, ND, US 156/C5
Haynes, Ar, US 162/B3
Haynesville, La, US 153/H4
Hayneville, Al, US 162/D4
Haynin, Yem. 118/D2
Hayrabolu, Turk. 51/H5
Hays, Ks, US 152/E1
Hays, Ab, Can. 145/J2
Hays, Mt, US 145/K4
Haystack (peak), On, Can. 157/K2
Haysville, Ks, US 153/F2
Haysville, In, US 162/D1
Haysyn, Ukr. 72/E3
Hayti, Mo, US 162/C2
Hayti, SD, US 155/F1
Hayvoron, Ukr. 72/E3
Hayward, Wi, US 157/J4
Haywards Heath, Eng, UK 37/F5
Haywood, Ok, US 153/G3
Hazār (mtn.), Iran 103/J4
Hazard, Ky, US 163/F2
Hazāribag, India 97/E4
Hazebrouck, Fr. 54/B2
Hazel, SD, US 154/F1
Hazel, Ky, US 162/C2
Hazel Dell, Wa, US 144/C5
Hazel Green, Al, US 162/D3
Hazel Grove, Eng, UK 35/F5
Hazel Hill, NS, Can. 159/G3
Hazel Park, Mi, US 167/F7
Hazelbrook, Austl. 133/E1
Hazeldean, NB, Can. 158/D2
Hazelhurst, Wi, US 157/K5
Hazelton, ND, US 156/D4
Hazelton, Ks, US 153/E2
Hazelton (peak), Wy, US 147/K1
Hazen (str.), NW,Nun, Can. 141/R7
Hazen (bay), Ak, US 171/E3
Hazen, Ar, US 153/J3
Hazen, ND, US 156/D4
Hazen, Nv, US 146/D4
Hazenmore, Sk, Can. 145/L3
Hāzipur, Bang. 97/H4
Hazlehurst, Ga, US 165/G2
Hazlehurst, Ms, US 164/C2
Hazlemere, Eng, UK 30/A2
Hazlet, NJ, US 169/J10
Hazlet, Sk, Can. 145/K2
Hazleton, Pa, US 168/C2
Hazlett (lake), Austl. 131/F2
H̱azor, Isr. 105/D3
Hazratbal Mosque, India 98/C2
Hazro, Pak. 98/B3
Hazu, Japan 83/M6
He (riv.), China 93/K2
He Xian, China 87/F3
He Xian, China 80/D5
Heacham, Eng, UK 37/G1
Head of Bay d'Espoir, Nf, Can. 159/K2
Head of Saint Margarets Bay, NS, Can. 158/F3
Headcorn, Eng, UK 37/G4
Headford, Ire. 32/A3
Headingley, Eng, UK 35/G4
Headland, Al, US 165/F2
Headlands, Zim. 123/G3
Headquarters, Id, US 144/G4
Heads of Ayr (pt.), Sc, UK 33/B6
Heafford Junction, Wi, US 157/K5
Healdsburg, Ca, US 146/B4
Healdton, Ok, US 153/F3
Healesville, Austl. 132/G5
Healy (pass), Ire. 32/A6
Healy, Ak, US 171/J3
Healy, Ks, US 152/D1
Heanor, Eng, UK 35/G6
Heany Junction, Zim. 123/F4
Heard (isl.), Austl. 192/E
Hearne, Tx, US 151/F2
Hearst, On, Can. 141/H4
Heart (riv.), ND, US 156/C4
Heart Butte (dam), ND, US 156/D4
Heart Law (hill), Sc, UK 33/D5
Hearts Hill, Sk, Can. 145/K1
Heath (pt.), QU, Can. 159/G1
Heath, Tx, US 150/L7
Heathcote, Austl. 133/B3
Heathcote NP, Austl. 134/G9
Heatherton, Nf, Can. 159/H1
Heathfield, Eng, UK 37/G5
Heathrow, Fl, US 164/N6
Heathrow (int'l arpt.), Eng, UK 30/B2
Heathsville, Va, US 163/J2
Hebbronville, Tx, US 151/E4
Hebbs Cross, NS, Can. 158/E3
Hebden Bridge, Eng, UK 35/F4
Hebei (prov.), China 78/G4
Hebel, Austl. 132/C1
Heber, Az, US 149/G3
Heber, Ca, US 148/E4
Heber City, Ut, US 147/H3
Heber Springs, Ar, US 153/H3
Hebert, La, US 164/C1
Hebertshausen, Ger. 59/E6
Hebgen (lake), Mt, US 147/H1
Hebgen (dam), Mt, US 147/H1
Hebi, China 80/C4
Hebo, Or, US 146/B1
Hebrides (sea), Sc, UK 31/Q8
Hebrides (isls.), UK 29/D3
Hebron, NS, Can. 158/D4
Hebron, Il, US 167/P15
Hebron, ND, US 156/C4
Hebron, Ne, US 154/F3
Hebron, Tx, US 150/L6
Hebron (Al Khalīl), WBnk. 105/C5
Heby, Swe. 40/G2
Hecate (str.), BC, Can. 139/D4
Hecelchakán, Mex. 176/D1
Hechi, China 87/F3
Hechingen, Ger. 58/B6
Hechtel, Belg. 55/E1
Hechthausen, Ger. 53/G1
Hechuan, China 87/E2
Heckington, Eng, UK 35/H6
Hecla, SD, US 156/E5
Hecla (isl.), Mb, Can. 156/F2
Hecla and Griper (bay), NW, Can. 141/R7
Hector (mt.), Ab, Can. 144/F2
Hector (mt.), NZ 135/J8
Hector, Ar, US 153/H3
Hector, Mn, US 155/G1
Hecun, China 87/H2
Heddal, Nor. 40/C2
Hédé, Fr. 56/D4
Hedehusene, Den. 39/J7
Hedel, Neth. 52/C5
Hedemora, Swe. 40/F1
Hedensted, Den. 40/C4
Hedi (res.), China 87/F4
Hedley, Tx, US 152/D3
Hedmark (co.), Nor. 38/D3

Hollis – Hutchi
Map Section 234 235

Hollis, Ak, US 171/M4
Hollis, Ok, US 152/E3
Hollister (mt.), Austl. 130/B2
Hollister, Ca, US 148/B2
Hollister, Mo, US 153/H2
Hollister, NC, US 163/J2
Hollogne-aux-Pierres, Belg. 55/E2
Hollola, Fin. 41/L1
Holloman (A.F.B.), NM, US 152/A4
Hollum, Neth. 52/C2
Höllviksnäs, Swe. 40/E4
Holly, Co, US 152/C1
Holly, Mi, US 160/E3
Holly, Wa, US 167/B2
Holly Grove, Ar, US 153/J3
Holly Hill, Fl, US 165/H3
Holly Hill, SC, US 163/G4
Holly Ridge, NC, US 163/J3
Holly Springs, Ms, US 162/C3
Hollysloot, Neth. 52/C4
Hollywood, Ar, US 153/H3
Hollywood (nbrhd.), Ca, US 166/F7
Hollywood, Fl, US 164/P10
Hollywood, SC, US 163/G4
Hollywood Bowl, Ca, US 166/F7
Hollywood Park, Tx, US 150/E3
Holm, Ger. 53/G1
Holman, NM, US 152/B2
Holman, NW, Can. 140/E1
Hólmavík, Ice. 38/N6
Holmdel, NJ, US 168/D3
Holme upon Spalding Moor, Eng, UK 35/H4
Holmen, Wi, US 155/J2
Holmenkollen, Nor. 38/S8
Holmer Green, Eng, UK 30/A2
Holmes (mt.), Wy, US 147/H1
Holmes (riv.), BC, Can. 144/E1
Holmes Chapel, Eng, UK 35/F5
Holmes Reef (reef), Austl. 129/H4
Holmes Reefs (isl.), Austl. 127/D2
Holmesdale (valley), Eng, UK 30/C3
Holmestrand, Nor. 40/D2
Holmfirth, Eng, UK 35/G4
Holmhead, Sc, UK 33/B6
Holmsbu, Nor. 38/S9
Holmsjön (lake), Swe. 38/F3
Holmsund, Swe. 38/G3
Holmsvatnet (lake), Nor. 38/R9
Hölö, Swe. 39/A1
Holoby, Ukr. 72/C2
Holon, Isr. 105/B4
Holoog, Namb. 124/B2
Holroyd, Austl. 133/E1
Holsfjorden (lake), Nor. 38/R8
Holstebro, Den. 40/C3
Holstein, Ia, US 155/G2
Holston (riv.), Tn, US 162/F3
Holston Ordnance Works Fed. Govt. Res., Tn, US 163/F2
Holston, North Fork (riv.), Va, US 163/F2
Holsworthy, Eng, UK 36/B5
Holt, Fl, US 164/E2
Holt, Mi, US 160/D3
Holt, Ca, US 167/M11
Holt, Al, US 162/D4
Holt, Mo, US 155/G4
Holt, Eng, UK 37/H1
Holtålen, Nor. 38/D3
Holte, Den. 39/J7
Holten, Neth. 52/D4
Holtland, Ger. 53/E2
Holton, Ks, US 155/G4
Holts Summit, Mo, US 153/H1
Holtsville, NY, US 169/E2
Holtville, NB, Can. 158/D2
Holtville, Ca, US 148/E4
Holwerd, Neth. 52/C2
Holy (isl.), Sc, UK 34/A5
Holy Cross, Ak, US 171/G3
Holy Trinity, Al, US 162/E4
Holycross, Ire. 32/C4
Holyhead, Wal, UK 34/D5
Holyoke, Ma, US 161/K3
Holyoke, Co, US 154/C3
Holyport, Eng, UK 30/A2
Holyrood, Ks, US 153/E1
Holyrood, Nf, Can. 159/L2
Holywell, Wal, UK 35/E5
Holywood, NI, UK 34/C2
Holzminden, Ger. 53/G5
Holzwickede, Ger. 53/E5
Hom (riv.), Namb. 124/B3
Homa (mt.), Kenya 119/A2
Homa Bay, Kenya 119/A2
Homathko (riv.), BC, Can. 144/B2
Homberg, Ger. 53/G6
Homberg, Ger. 52/D6
Hombori, Mali 115/E3
Hombori Tondo (peak), Mali 115/E3
Hombourg-Haut, Fr. 55/F5
Homburg, Ger. 55/G5
Home (bay), Nun, Can. 141/K2
Home Hill, Austl. 134/B2
Homécourt, Fr. 55/E5
Homelake, Co, US 149/J2
Homeland, Ga, US 165/G2
Homeland, Ca, US 166/C3
Homeland, Fl, US 164/M8
Homer, La, US 153/H4
Homer, Mi, US 160/D3
Homer, NY, US 161/H3
Homer, Ga, US 163/F3
Homer, Ak, US 171/H4
Homerville, Ga, US 165/G2
Homestead, Fl, US 165/H5
Homestead, Austl. 134/B3
Homestead of America Nat'l Mon., Ne, US 155/F3
Homewood, Il, US 167/Q16
Homewood, Ca, US 146/C4
Homewood, Al, US 162/D4
Homib (riv.), Erit. 100/C5
Hommersåk, Nor. 40/A2
Homochitto (riv.), Ms, US 162/B5
Homoine, Moz. 123/G4
Homonhon (isl.), Phil. 88/D3
Homosassa (bay), Fl, US 164/K6
Homosassa, Fl, US 164/K6
Homosassa Springs, Fl, US 164/K6
Homosassa Springs Nature World, Fl, US 164/K6
Homyel', Bela. 70/D1
Homyel'skaya Voblasts, Bela. 70/D1
Hon, Ar, US 153/G3
Hon Chong, Viet. 94/D4
Hon Quan, Viet. 94/D4
Honbetsu, Japan 82/C2
Honda, Col. 183/L7
Honddu (riv.), Wal, UK 36/C2
Hondeklipbaai, SAfr. 124/B3
Hondo, Japan 84/B4
Hondo (riv.), Belz. 176/D2
Hondo, Tx, US 150/E3
Hondo (cr.), Tx, US 150/E3
Hondschoote, Fr. 54/B2
Hondsrug (hills), Neth. 42/D2
Hondsrug (reg.), Neth. 52/D3
Honduras (gulf), NAm. 172/D4
Honduras (ctry.) 176/E3
Honea Path, SC, US 163/F3
Hønefoss, Nor. 40/D1
Honesdale, Pa, US 161/J4
Honey (cr.), Wi, US 167/N14
Honey (lake), Ca, US 146/C3
Honey Brook, Pa, US 168/C3
Honey Creek, Wi, US 167/P14
Honey Grove, Tx, US 153/G4
Honeybourne, Eng, UK 37/E2
Honeyville, Ut, US 147/G3
Honfleur, Fr. 57/F2
Hong (isl.), SKor. 81/C5
Hong, Den. 39/H7
Hong (lake), China 80/C5
Hong (riv.), China 80/C4
Hong (Red) (riv.), Viet. 86/E4
Hong Gai, Viet. 87/E4
Hong Kong (dpcy.), China 87/K7
Hong Kong (see Chep Lak Kok) (int'l. arpt.), China */*
Hong Kong (isl.), China 87/L7
Hongam-nodongjagu, NKor. 81/E1
Hong'an, China 80/C5
Hongchang, China 81/B2
Hongch'ŏn, SKor. 81/D4
Hongdu (riv.), China 93/J2
Hongdu, China 87/F4
Honggouzi, China 78/C4
Hongguo, China 86/E3
Honghu, China 87/G2
Hongjiang, China 87/F3
Honglai, China 87/H3
Hongliu (riv.), China 78/F4
Hongliuhe, China 78/C3
Hongliuquan, China 78/D3
Honglu, China 87/H3
Hongqi, China 81/B2
Hongqiao, China 87/J2
Hongqiao (int'l arpt.), China 80/L8
Hongqizhen, China 94/E2
Hongshui (riv.), China 93/J3
Hongsŏng, SKor. 81/D4
Hongtian, China 87/H3
Hongtong, China 80/B3
Honguedo Passage, (chan.), Qu, Can. 141/K4
Honguedo Passage, Qu, Can. 158/E1
Hongwŏn, NKor. 81/D2
Hongya, China 86/D2
Hongyan, China 87/F2
Hongyang, China 87/H4
Hongyuan, China 78/E5
Hongze (lake), China 79/H5
Hongze, China 80/D4
Hœnheim, Fr. 55/G6
Honiara (cap.), Sol. 136/E5
Honiton, Eng, UK 36/C5
Honjō, Japan 82/B4
Honjō, Japan 83/C1
Honobia, Ok, US 153/G3
Honolulu (cap.), Hi, US 142/W13
Honoraville, Al, US 165/E2
Hönow, Ger. 42/O6
Honshu (isl.), Japan 75/O6
Honshū (isl.), Japan 77/P6
Hontianske Nemce, Slvk. 50/D1
Hoo, Eng, UK 30/E2
Hood (mt.), Ca, US 167/J10
Hood (canal), Wa, US 167/B2
Hood, Ca, US 167/L10
Hood (mt.), Or, US 146/C1
Hood (pt.), Austl. 130/C5
Hood (pt.), PNG 129/G2
Hood (co.), Tx, US 150/K7
Hood River, Or, US 144/D5
Hoofddorp, Neth. 52/B4
Hoogeloon, Neth. 52/C6
Hoogeveen, Neth. 52/D3
Hoogeveense Vaart (canal), Neth. 52/D3
Hoogezand, Neth. 52/D2
Hooghly (riv.), India 97/F5
Hooghly-Chinsura, India 97/G4
Hoogkarspel, Neth. 52/C3
Hooglede, Belg. 54/C2
Hoogstraten, Belg. 52/B6
Hook (sound), Austl. 134/C3
Hook, Eng, UK 37/F4
Hook Head (pt.), Ire. 32/D5
Hooker, Ok, US 152/D2
Hooker Creek, Austl. 128/C4
Hooker Creek Abor. Land, Austl. 128/C4
Hooksett, NH, US 161/L3
Hoonah, Ak, US 171/L4
Hoopa, Ca, US 146/B3
Hoopa Valley Ind. Res., Ca, US 146/B3
Hooper, Co, US 152/B2
Hooper, Ne, US 155/F3
Hooper (Endwell), NY, US 161/H3
Hooper Bay, Ak, US 171/E3
Hoopeston, Il, US 160/C4
Hoople, ND, US 156/F3
Hoopstad, SAfr. 124/D2
Höör, Swe. 40/E4
Hoorn, Neth. 52/C3
Hoornse Hop (bay), Neth. 52/C3
Hoosick Falls, NY, US 161/K3
Hoover (dam), Az, US 142/D4
Hoover (peak), WV, US 163/F2
Hoover, SD, US 154/C1
Höövör, Mong. 78/G2
Hopa, Turk. 71/G4
Hopatcong, NJ, US 168/D2
Hopatcong (lake), NJ, US 168/D2
Hope (lake), Austl. 127/A4
Hope, BC, Can. 144/D3
Hope, Wal, UK 35/E5
Hope, Ak, US 171/J3
Hope, Ar, US 153/H4
Hope, In, US 160/D5
Hope, Ks, US 153/F1
Hope, ND, US 156/F4
Hope, NJ, US 168/D2
Hope, Tx, US 151/F3
Hope Mills, NC, US 163/H3
Hope Vale Abor. Land, Austl. 129/G3
Hope Vale Aboriginal Community, Austl. 134/B1
Hope-under-Dinmore, Eng, UK 36/D2
Hopedale, Nf, Can. 141/K3
Hopelchén, Mex. 176/D2
Hopeman, Sc, UK 33/C1
Hopes Advance (cape), Qu, Can. 141/K2
Hope's Nose (pt.), Eng, UK 36/C6
Hopetoun, Austl. 130/D5
Hopetown, SAfr. 124/D3
Hopewell, NS, Can. 159/F3
Hopewell, NJ, US 168/D3
Hopewell, Va, US 163/J2
Hopewell Cape, NB, Can. 158/E3
Hopewell Culture Nat'l Mon., Oh, US 160/E5
Hopewell Furnace NHS, Pa, US 168/C3
Hopi Ind. Res., Az, US 149/G2
Hopin, Myan. 86/C3
Hôpital-Camfrout, Fr. 56/A4
Hopkins (lake), Austl. 131/F3
Hopkins (riv.), Austl. 132/B3
Hopkins, Mo, US 155/G3
Hopkins, Mn, US 157/P7
Hopkinsville, Ky, US 162/D2
Hopkinton, RI, US 161/L4
Hopkinton, NH, US 161/L3
Hoppecke (riv.), Ger. 53/F6
Hoppegarten, Ger. 42/O6
Hopper Mtn. NWR, Ca, US 166/B2
Hoppstädten-Weiersbach, Ger. 55/G4
Hopsten, Ger. 53/E4
Hoquiam, Wa, US 144/C4
Hor, China 78/E4
Horace (mt.), Ak, US 171/J2
Horace, ND, US 156/F4
Horadiz, Azer. 103/F2
Horado, Japan 83/L4
Hōrai-san (peak), Japan 83/J5
Horasan, Turk. 102/E1
Horatio, Ar, US 153/G4
Horažďovice, Czh. 59/G4
Horb am Neckar, Ger. 58/B6
Horbat Qesari (ruin), Isr. 104/D3
Hörbranz, Aus. 61/F2
Horbury, Eng, UK 35/G4
Hörby, Swe. 39/K7
Horche, Sp. 46/D2
Horconcitos, Pan. 177/F4
Horcones (riv.), Arg. 188/C3
Hordaland (co.), Nor. 38/C3
Horden, Eng, UK 35/G3
Hœrdt, Fr. 55/G6
Hördt, Ger. 58/B4
Horezu, Rom. 51/G3
Horgau, Ger. 58/D6
Horgen, Swi. 61/E3
Horh (peak), Mong. 78/F3
Horicon, Wi, US 155/K2
Horicon NWR, Wi, US 155/K2
Horinger, China 80/B2
Horiult, Mong. 78/E2
Horizontina, Braz. 189/F3
Horley, Eng, UK 30/C3
Horlivka, Ukr. 73/K3
Hormigüeros, PR 173/M8
Hormozgān (gov.), Iran 103/J5
Hormūd-e Mīr Khūnd, Iran 103/H5
Hormuz (str.), Oman 101/G3
Horn (cape), Arg. 191/D8
Horn (pt.), Ice. 38/M6
Horn (isl.), Ms, US 164/D2
Horn Lake, Ms, US 162/B3
Horn-Bad Meinberg, Ger. 53/F5
Hornachuelos, Sp. 46/C4
Hornád (riv.), Slvk. 43/L4
Hornavan (lake), Swe. 38/F2
Hornbach, Ger. 55/G5
Hornbæk, Den. 39/J6
Hornbeck, La, US 164/B2
Hornbeck, Ab, Can. 144/F1
Hornberg, Ger. 61/E1
Hornburg, Ger. 53/H4
Hornby, NZ 135/C3
Hornby, On, Can. 160/T8
Hornby Island, BC, Can. 144/B3
Horncastle, Eng, UK 35/H5
Hornchurch (nbrhd.), Eng, UK 30/D2
Horndal, Swe. 40/G1
Horné Saliby, Slvk. 50/C1
Horneburg, Ger. 53/G1
Hornell, NY, US 161/H3
Hornersville, Mo, US 162/B2
Horní Bříza, Czh. 59/G3
Horní Slavkov, Czh. 59/F2
Hornisgrinde (peak), Ger. 58/B5
Hornitos, Ca, US 148/B2
Hornos, (cape), Chile 191/D7
Hornoy-le-Bourg, Fr. 54/A4
Hornsby (nbrhd.), Austl. 134/H8
Hornsea, Eng, UK 35/H4
Hornslet, Den. 40/D3
Hörnum (cape), Ger. 40/C4
Horodenka, Ukr. 72/C3
Horodnya, Ukr. 72/F2
Horodok, Ukr. 72/D3
Horodok, Ukr. 72/B3
Horodyshche, Ukr. 72/F3
Horokhiv, Ukr. 72/C2
Horoshiri-dake (peak), Japan 82/C2
Hořovice, Czh. 59/G3
Horqin Youyi Zhongqi, China 79/J2
Horqin Zuoyi Houqi, China 80/E2
Horqin Zuoyi Zhongqi, China 80/E1
Horqueta, Par. 189/E2
Horrabridge, Eng, UK 36/B5
Hörsching, Aus. 59/H6
Horse (cr.), Co, US 154/B4
Horse (mtn.), Tx, US 150/C2
Horse Cave, Ky, US 162/E2
Horse Creek, Wy, US 154/B3
Horse Shoe Run, WV, US 161/G5
Horsefly, BC, Can. 144/D1
Horsefly (riv.), BC, Can. 144/D1
Horsefly (lake), BC, Can. 144/D1
Horseheads, NY, US 161/H3
Horseshoe Beach, Fl, US 165/G3
Horseshoe Bend, Ar, US 153/J2
Horseshoe Bend, Id, US 146/E2
Horseshoe Bend Nat'l Mil. Park, Al, US 162/E4
Horsethief (cr.), BC, Can. 144/F2
Horsey (isl.), Eng, UK 37/J3
Horsforth, Eng, UK 35/G4
Horsham, Austl. 132/B3
Horsham, Eng, UK 37/F4
Horsham, Pa, US 168/C3
Hørsholm, Den. 39/J7
Horsmonden, Eng, UK 30/E3
Horšovský Týn, Czh. 59/F3
Horst, Ger. 53/H2
Horst, Neth. 52/D6
Hörstel, Ger. 53/E4
Horstmar, Ger. 53/E4
Horta, Azor., Port. 47/S12
Hortaleza (nbrhd.), Sp. 47/N9
Horten, Nor. 40/D2
Hortense, Ga, US 165/H2
Hortes, Fr. 60/B2
Hortobágyi NP, Hun. 70/B3
Horton (riv.), NW, Can. 140/D2
Horton, Ks, US 155/G4
Horton (pt.), NY, US 169/F1
Horton Kirby, Eng, UK 30/D2
Høruphav, Den. 40/C4
Horusický Rybník (lake), Czh. 59/H4
Horvot 'Avedat (ruin), Isr. 104/D4
Horvot Dor, Isr. 105/B3
Horw, Swi. 61/E3
Horwich, Eng, UK 35/F4
Hosa'ina, Eth. 117/H4
Hösbach, Ger. 58/C2
Hosdrug, India 95/B3
Hosenfeld, Ger. 58/C1
Hosenofu (well), Libya 108/D4
Hoséré Vokré (peak), Camr. 116/B3
Hosford, Fl, US 165/F2
Hoshāb, Pak. 101/H3
Hoshangābād, India 96/A4
Hoshcha, Ukr. 72/D2
Hoshiārpur, India 98/C4
Hosingen, Lux. 55/F3
Hosmer, SD, US 156/E5
Hosmer, BC, Can. 144/G3
Hospental, Swi. 61/E4
Hospital, Ire. 32/B5
Hospital, Chile 190/N8
Hosston, La, US 153/G4
Hosszúpereszteg, Hun. 50/C2
Hoste (isl.), Chile 191/C7
Hostomel', Ukr. 72/F2
Hoswick, Sc, UK 31/W13
Hot, Thai. 94/B2
Hot Creek (range), Nv, US 146/E4
Hot Springs, SD, US 154/C2
Hot Springs NP, Ar, US 153/H3
Hot Springs Village, Ar, US 153/H3
Hot Sulphur Springs, Co, US 154/A3
Hotaka, Japan 85/E2
Hotaka-dake (peak), Japan 85/E2
Hotan (riv.), China 99/D4
Hotan, China 99/C4
Hotazel, SAfr. 124/C2
Hotevilla, Az, US 149/G3
Hotham (cape), Austl. 128/C3
Hoti, Indo. 91/H4
Hot'kovo, Rus. 69/W8
Hotont, Mong. 78/E2
Hottah (lake), NW, Can. 140/E2
Hottentot (bay), Namb. 124/A2
Hottentots (pt.), Namb. 122/B5
Hotton, Belg. 55/E3
Hou (riv.), China 78/F5
Houamuang, Laos 86/D4
Houari Boumedienne (int'l arpt.), Alg. 112/G4
Houat (isl.), Fr. 56/C6
Houchang, China 87/E3
Houdain, Fr. 54/B3
Houdan, Fr. 57/G3
Houdan, Fr. 30/G5
Houet (prov.), Burk. 114/D4
Houffalize, Belg. 55/E3
Houghton, SD, US 156/E5
Houghton (pt.), Mi, US 157/K4
Houghton (dam), SD, US 156/E5
Houghton, Mi, US 157/K4
Houghton, NY, US 161/G3
Houghton (lake), Mi, US 160/D2
Houghton Lake, Mi, US 160/D2
Houghton-le-Spring, Eng, UK 35/G2
Houilles, Fr. 30/J5
Houlgate, Fr. 57/E2
Houlton, Me, US 141/K4
Houlton, Wi, US 157/Q6
Houma, La, US 164/C3
Houma, China 80/B4
Houndé, Burk. 114/E4
Houplines, Fr. 54/B2
Hourn, Loch (inlet), Sc, UK 33/A2
Hourtin, Fr. 44/C4
Housatonic (riv.), Ct, US 169/E1
House (range), Ut, US 149/F1
Housesteads Roman Fort, Eng, UK 35/F1
Houssen, Fr. 60/D1
Houston, De, US 168/C6
Houston, Fl, US 165/G2
Houston, Mn, US 155/J2
Houston, Mo, US 153/J2
Houston, Ms, US 162/C4
Houston, Tx, US 151/M9
Houston (lake), Tx, US 151/G2
Houston Intercontinental (int'l arpt.), Tx, US 151/M9
Houston Ship (chan.), Tx, US 151/M9
Houstonia, Mo, US 153/H1
Houtbaai, SAfr. 124/L11
Houten, Neth. 52/C4
Houthalen, Belg. 55/E1
Houthulst, Belg. 54/B2
Houtman Abrolhos (isl.), Austl. 130/B4
Houtribdijk (dam), Neth. 52/C3
Houtskär (isl.), Fin. 41/J1
Houyet, Belg. 55/E3
Houyingzi, China 81/B2
Houzhenzi, China 78/F5
Hov, Nor. 40/D1
Hova, Swe. 40/F2
Hovd (prov.), Mong. 78/C2
Hove, Eng, UK 37/F5
Hövelhof, Ger. 53/F5
Hoven, SD, US 154/E1
Hovenweep Nat'l Mon., Co, US 149/H2
Hoveton, Eng, UK 37/H1
Hovfjället (peak), Swe. 40/E1
Hovingham, Eng, UK 35/H3
Hovland, Mn, US 157/K4
Hovmantorp, Swe. 40/F3
Hövsgöl (prov.), Mong. 99/G2
Hövsgöl (lake), Mong. 78/E1
Hovsta, Swe. 40/F2
Howa, Oued (riv.), Chad 116/D2
Howar (wadi), Sudan 117/E1
Howard, Austl. 134/D4
Howard (isl.), Austl. 129/D2
Howard, NB, Can. 158/E2
Howard, Co, US 152/B1
Howard, Fl, US 164/P11
Howard, Ks, US 153/F2
Howard (co.), Md, US 168/B5
Howard, SD, US 154/F1
Howard Beach (nbrhd.), NY, US 169/K9
Howard City, Mi, US 160/D3
Howard Draw (riv.), Tx, US 150/D2
Howard Hanson (res.), Wa, US 167/D3
Howard Hanson (dam), Wa, US 167/D3
Howard Prairie (lake), Or, US 146/B2
Howards Grove, Wi, US 160/C3
Howden, Eng, UK 35/H4
Howe, Ok, US 153/G3
Howe, Tx, US 153/F4
Howe (sound), BC, Can. 144/C3
Howe (cape), Austl. 133/D3
Howe Caverns, NY, US 161/J3
Howe Green, Eng, UK 30/E1
Howe of the Mearns (reg.), Sc, UK 33/D3
Howell, Mi, US 160/E3
Howell, NJ, US 168/D3
Howey-in-the-Hills, Fl, US 164/M6
Howick, NZ 135/F6
Howick, SAfr. 125/E3
Howison, Ms, US 164/D2
Howland (isl.), Pac., US 137/H4
Howley, Nf, Can. 159/J1
Howlong, Austl. 133/C2
Howrah, India 97/G4
Howser, BC, Can. 144/F2
Hoxie, Ks, US 154/D4
Hoxie, Ar, US 162/B2
Höxter, Ger. 53/G5
Hoxud, China 99/E3
Hoy (isl.), Sc, UK 31/V14
Hoya, Ger. 53/G3
Hōya, Japan 83/D2
Høyanger, Nor. 40/B1
Hoyerswerda, Ger. 43/H3
Hoylake, Eng, UK 35/E5
Hoyland Nether, Eng, UK 35/G4
Hoyo de Manzanares, Sp. 47/N8
Hoyos, Sp. 46/B2
Hoyoux (riv.), Belg. 55/E3
Hoyt, NB, Can. 158/D3
Hoyt, Mt, US 156/B4
Hoyt, Ok, US 153/G3
Hoyt, Ks, US 155/G4
Hoyt Tamir (riv.), Mong. 78/E2
Hozumi, Japan 83/L5
Hracholusky (res.), Czh. 59/F3
Hradec Králové, Czh. 43/H3
Hradište (peak), Czh. 59/G2
Hradyz'k, Ukr. 73/G3
Hranice, Czh. 59/F2
Hrasnica, Bosn. 50/D4
Hrastnik, Slov. 50/B2
Hrazdan, Arm. 103/F1
Hrebinka, Ukr. 73/G1
Hrebinky, Ukr. 72/F3
Hřivice, Czh. 59/G2
Hrodna, Bela. 41/K5
Hrodzyenskaya Voblasts, Bela. 68/E5
Hrolleifsborg (peak), Ice. 38/M6
Hron (riv.), Slvk. 70/A2
Hronov, Czh. 43/J3
Hrubieszów, Pol. 72/B2
Hrubý Jeseník (mts.), Czh.,Pol. 43/J3
Hrútafjöll (peak), Ice. 38/P6
Hrymayliv, Ukr. 72/D3
Hsenwi, Myan. 93/G3
Hsi-hseng, Myan. 86/C4
Hsinchu, Tai. 87/J3
Hsipaw, Myan. 94/B1
Hsüeh (peak), Tai. 87/J3
Hts-de-Seine (dept.), Fr. 57/H3
Hu Xian, China 78/F5
Hua (peak), China 80/B4
Hua Hin, Thai. 94/B3
Hua Sai, Thai. 94/C4
Hua Xian, China 80/C4
Huab (riv.), Namb. 122/B3
Huacaraje, Bol. 185/F4
Huacareta, Bol. 188/D2
Huacaya, Bol. 188/D2
Huacaybamba, Peru 184/B3
Huachacalla, Bol. 188/B1
Huacheng, China 87/G3
Huachi, China 78/F4
Huachi, Bol. 185/F4
Huacho, Peru 184/B3
Huachón, Peru 184/C3
Huachuan, China 79/L2
Huachuca (mts.), Az, US 149/G5
Huachuca City, Az, US 149/G5
Huacrachuco, Peru 184/B3
Huade, China 78/G3
Huadian, China 79/K3
Huadianzi, China 81/C2
Huahine (isl.), FrPol. 137/K6
Huai (riv.), China 80/C4
Huai Yot, Thai. 94/B5
Huai'an, China 80/C2
Huai'an, China 80/D4
Huaibei, China 78/H5
Huaibin, China 78/F5
Huaihua, China 87/F3
Huaiji, China 87/G4
Huailai, China 80/G6
Huainan, China 80/D4
Huaining, China 87/H2
Huairen, China 80/C3
Huairou, China 80/H6
Huaiyang, China 80/C4
Huaiyin, China 80/D4
Huaiyin, China 80/D4
Huaiyuan, China 80/D4
Huajicori, Mex. 174/D4
Huajuapan de León, Mex. 176/B2
Hualahuises, Mex. 175/F3
Hualañé, Chile 190/C2
Hualapai (peak), Az, US 149/F3
Hualapai (mts.), Az, US 149/F3
Hualapai Ind. Res., Az, US 149/F3
Hualfín, Arg. 188/C3
Hualgayoc, Peru 184/B2
Hualien, Tai. 87/J4
Hualla, Peru 184/C4
Huallaga (riv.), Peru 179/B3
Huallanca, Peru 184/B3
Huamachuco, Peru 184/B2
Huamantanga, Peru 184/B3
Huamantla, Mex. 175/M7
Huambo, Ang. 122/B2
Huambo (dist.), Ang. 122/B2
Huambos, Peru 184/B2
Huan (riv.), China 80/C5
Huan Xian, China 78/F4
Huanan, China 79/L2
Huanaque, Bol. 188/B2
Huancané, Peru 184/D4
Huancapi, Peru 184/C4
Huancaspata, Peru 184/B3
Huancavelica, Peru 184/C4
Huancavelica (dept.), Peru 184/C4
Huancayo, Peru 184/C4
Huanchaca (peak), Bol. 188/C2
Huang (riv.), China 77/L6
Huang (Yellow) (riv.), China 78/G4
Huangbayi, China 78/F5
Huangbei, China 87/H3
Huangchuan, China 80/C4
Huangcun, China 87/F3
Huanggang (peak), China 87/H3
Huanggang, China 87/G3
Huanghua, China 80/D3
Huangjinbu, China 87/H2
Huangjinggou, China 86/E2
Huangli, China 80/K8
Huangling, China 80/B4
Huangliu, China 87/F5
Huanglong, China 80/B4
Huanglong, China 87/G3
Huanglongtan, China 80/B4
Huangmao (peak), China 87/H3
Huangmei, China 87/G2
Huangniupu, China 78/F5
Huangpi, China 80/C5
Huangping, China 93/J2
Huangqi (lake), China 80/C2
Huangshan, China 87/H2
Huangshi, China 87/G2
Huangshidu, China 87/F4
Huangtang (lake), China 80/C5
Huangtianpu, China 87/F3
Huangtu (plat.), China 80/B4
Huangtudian, China 87/F2
Huangueléń, Arg. 190/E3
Huangwan, China 80/L9
Huangyunpu, China 80/B4
Huangzhai, China 87/H2
Huangzhan, China 87/G2
Huangzhong, China 78/E4
Huaning, China 86/D3
Huanjiang, China 93/J3
Huanren, China 81/C2
Huanta, Peru 184/C4
Huantai, China 80/D3
Huántar, Peru 184/B3
Huantunas (lake), Bol. 185/E4
Huánuco, Peru 184/B3
Huánuco (dept.), Peru 184/C3
Huanuni, Bol. 188/C1
Huanxi, China 87/G3
Huapi (mts.), Nic. 176/E3
Huaping, China 86/D3
Huaqiaozhen, China 87/F5
Huaquechula, Mex. 175/L8
Huaquillas, Ecu. 184/A1
Huara, Chile 188/B1
Huaral, Peru 184/B3
Huaraz, Peru 184/B3
Huari, Bol. 188/C1
Huari, Peru 184/B3
Huaricolca, Peru 184/C3
Huarina, Bol. 184/D5
Huarmey, Peru 184/B3
Huarochirí, Peru 184/B4
Huarocondo, Peru 184/C4
Huásabas, Mex. 174/C2
Huasahuasi, Peru 184/C3
Huascarán (peak), Peru 184/B3
Huascarán, PN, Peru 184/B3
Huasco (riv.), Chile 188/B4
Huashi (mts.), China 87/G3
Huashi, China 87/G3
Huatabampo, Mex. 174/C3
Huatong, China 81/A2
Huatusco, Mex. 175/N7
Huauchinango, Mex. 175/L6
Huaura, Peru 184/B3
Huautla de Jiménez, Mex. 176/B2
Huayacocotla, Mex. 175/L6
Huayang, China 87/J2
Huayangzhen, China 78/F5
Huaying, China 87/E2
Huaylas, Peru 184/B3
Huayllay, Peru 184/B3
Huayopata, Peru 184/C4
Huayuan, China 81/D1
Huayuan, China 93/J2
Huayuan, China 87/G2
Huazhaizi, China 78/E4
Huazhou, China 93/K3
Huazi, China 81/B2
Hub, Ms, US 164/D2
Hubbard, Sk, Can. 156/C2
Hubbard (mt.), Ak, US 171/L3
Hubbard, Ia, US 155/H2
Hubbard (lake), Mi, US 160/E2
Hubbard, Or, US 146/B1
Hubbard, Tx, US 151/F2
Hubbard Creek (res.), Tx, US 150/E1
Hubbards, NS, Can. 158/E3
Hubbell Trading Post Nat'l Hist. Site, Az, US 149/H3
Hubei (pass), China 80/B4
Huber Heights, Oh, US 160/D5
Hubli-Dhārwār, India 95/B3
Huch'ang, NKor. 81/D2
Hückelhoven, Ger. 55/F1
Hückeswagen, Ger. 55/G1
Hucknall, Eng, UK 35/G5
Hudai, China 80/L8
Huddersfield, Eng, UK 35/G4
Huddinge, Swe. 40/G2
Hude, Ger. 53/F2
Hudiksvall, Swe. 40/G1
Hudson (cape), Ant. 192/L
Hudson (bay), Can. 139/J3
Hudson, On, Can. 157/H2
Hudson, Qu, Can. 159/M7
Hudson (str.), Nun,Qu, Can. 141/J2
Hudson, Fl, US 164/K7
Hudson, Il, US 155/K3
Hudson, Mi, US 160/D4
Hudson, NC, US 163/G3
Hudson (co.), NJ, US 169/J9
Hudson, NY, US 161/K3
Hudson (riv.), NJ, NY, US 161/K3
Hudson (lake), Ok, US 153/G2
Hudson, Tx, US 151/G2
Hudson, Wi, US 157/Q7
Hudson Bay, Sk, Can. 140/F3
Hudson Falls, NY, US 161/K3
Hudson Oaks, Tx, US 150/K7
Hudsons (peak), Austl. 133/D3
Hudson's Hope, BC, Can. 140/D3
Hue, Viet. 94/D2
Hueco (mts.), Tx, US 150/B2
Huedin, Rom. 51/F2
Huehuetenango, Guat. 176/D3
Huehuetla, Mex. 175/L6
Huehuetlán, Mex. 175/L8
Huejotzingo, Mex. 175/L7
Huejuquilla el Alto, Mex. 174/E4
Huejutla de Reyes, Mex. 176/B1
Huelgoat, Fr. 56/B4
Huelma, Sp. 46/D4
Huelva (riv.), Sp. 46/B4
Huelva, Sp. 46/B4
Huequi (vol.), Chile 190/B4
Huercal-Overa, Sp. 46/E4
Huerfano (riv.), Co, US 154/B5
Huesca, Sp. 47/E1
Huéscar, Sp. 46/D4
Huesos (stream), Arg. 190/F3
Huetamo de Nuñez, Mex. 175/E5
Huete, Sp. 46/D2
Huexoculco, Mex. 175/R10
Hüfingen, Ger. 61/E2
Huger, SC, US 163/H4
Hugh Town, Eng, UK 31/Q12
Hughenden, Austl. 134/B3
Hughenden, Ab, Can. 145/J1
Hughenden Valley, Eng, UK 30/A2
Hughes, Arg. 190/E2
Hughes, Austl. 131/F4
Hughes, Ak, US 171/H2
Hughes, Ar, US 162/B3
Hughes Springs, Tx, US 153/G4
Hughesville, Pa, US 168/B1
Hughson, Ca, US 148/B2
Huglfing, Ger. 61/H2
Hugli (riv.), India 92/E3
Hugo, Co, US 154/C4
Hugo, Mn, US 157/Q6
Hugo, Ok, US 153/G3
Hugo (lake), Ok, US 153/G3
Hugo (dam), Ok, US 153/G3
Hugoton, Ks, US 152/D2
Huguan, China 80/C3
Huguo, China 79/H2
Hui (riv.), China 79/H2
Hui Xian, China 80/C4
Huib-Hock (plat.), Namb. 124/B2
Huichapan, Mex. 175/K6
Hŭich'ŏn, NKor. 81/D2
Huila (dept.), Col. 180/C4
Huila (dept.), Ang. 122/B2
Huilango, Mex. 175/Q9
Huili, China 93/H2
Huimanguillo, Mex. 176/C2
Huimin, China 80/D3
Huinan, China 79/K3
Huinca Renancó, Arg. 190/D2
Huining, China 78/F4
Hŭisaek-pong (peak), NKor. 81/D2
Huishui, China 93/J2
Huisne (riv.), Fr. 44/D2
Huisseau-sur-Cosson, Fr. 57/G5
Huissen, Neth. 52/C5
Huitong, China 93/J2
Huittinen, Fin. 41/K1
Huitzilan, Mex. 175/M7
Huitzuco, Mex. 175/K8
Huixcolotla, Mex. 175/M8
Huixquilucan, Mex. 175/Q10
Huixtla, Mex. 176/C3
Huize, China 86/D3
Huizen, Neth. 52/C4
Huizhou, China 87/G4
Hujirt, Mong. 78/E2
Hujra, Pak. 98/B4
Hŭksan (arch.), SKor. 79/J5
Hukuntsi, Bots. 122/D4
Hulah (dam), Ok, US 153/F2
Hulah (lake), Ok, US 153/F2
Hulan, China 79/K2
Hulan (riv.), China 79/K2
Hulbert, Ok, US 153/G3
Hulbert, Mi, US 160/D1
Hulett, Wy, US 154/B1
Hull (riv.), Eng, UK 35/H4
Hull, Ia, US 155/F2
Hull (Orona) (isl.), Kiri. 137/H5
Hullbridge, Eng, UK 30/E2
Hüllhorst, Ger. 53/F4
Hullo, Est. 41/K2
Hulst, Neth. 52/B6
Hultsfred, Swe. 40/F3
Hulu (riv.), China 78/F4
Hulun (lake), China 78/H2
Ḩulwān, Egypt 113/C5
Hulyaypole, Ukr. 73/J4
Huma (riv.), China 75/N4
Huma, China 79/K1
Humahuaca, Arg. 188/C2
Humaitá, Par. 188/E3
Humaitá, Braz. 185/F2
Humaitá, Bol. 185/E3
Humaljärvi (lake), Fin. 39/E4
Humansdorp, SAfr. 124/D4
Humansville, Mo, US 153/H2
Humay, Peru 184/C4
Humbe, Ang. 122/B3
Humber (riv.), Eng, UK 35/H4
Humber (riv.), Nf, Can. 158/J1
Humber (bay), On, Can. 160/U8
Humber, West (riv.), On, Can. 160/T8
Humberside (arpt.), Eng, UK 35/H4
Humberston, Eng, UK 35/H4
Humberto de Campos, Braz. 183/F3
Humble, Tx, US 151/M9
Humboldt, Sk, Can. 145/M1
Humboldt (bay), Col. 177/G5
Humboldt (peak), NCal. 137/V12
Humboldt, Az, US 149/F3
Humboldt (bay), Ca, US 146/A3
Humboldt, Ks, US 153/G2
Humboldt, Ia, US 155/G2
Humboldt, Mn, US 155/G3
Humboldt, Ne, US 155/G3
Humboldt (lake), Nv, US 146/D3
Humboldt (riv.), Nv, US 146/D3
Humboldt, Tn, US 162/C3
Humboldt, North Fork (riv.), Nv, US 146/F3
Hume (dam), Austl. 133/C3
Humedān, Iran 101/G3
Humenné, Slvk. 43/L4
Humeston, Ia, US 155/H3
Humlebæk, Den. 39/J7
Humlum, Den. 40/C3
Hummels Wharf, Pa, US 168/B2
Hummelstown, Pa, US 168/B3
Humnoke, Ar, US 153/J3
Humphrey, Ar, US 153/J3
Humphrey, Ne, US 153/F3
Humphrey, On, Can. 161/G2
Humphrey Point (cape), Ak, US 171/K2
Humphreys (peak), Az, US 149/G3
Humphreys (mt.), Ca, US 148/C2
Humpty Doo, Austl. 128/C3
Humshaugh, Eng, UK 35/F1
Hūn, Libya 108/B2
Hun (riv.), China 79/J3
Hunan (prov.), China 93/K2
Hunchun, China 79/L3
Hundested, Den. 39/H7
Hundewāli, Pak. 98/B4
Hundred, WV, US 160/F5
Hundred Fifty Mile House, BC, Can. 144/D1
Hundred Mile House, BC, Can. 144/D2
Hundsangen, Ger. 55/G3
Hunedoara (prov.), Rom. 50/F3
Hunedoara, Rom. 50/F3
Hünenberg, Swi. 61/E3
Hung Yen, Viet. 94/D1
Hungaroring, Hun. 51/R9
Hungary (ctry.) 50/D2
Hungen, Ger. 58/B2
Hungerford, Austl. 132/C1
Hungerford, Eng, UK 37/E4
Hŭnghae, SKor. 81/E4
Hŭngnam, NKor. 81/D3
Hŭngnyŏng-nodongjagu, NKor. 81/D3
Hungry (peak), Id, US 144/G4
Hungry Horse (dam), Mt, US 145/G3
Hungulo, Ang. 122/C2
Hüngüy (riv.), Mong. 78/C2
Hunjiang, China 81/D2
Hunkui, Nga. 115/G4
Hunmanby, Eng, UK 35/H3
Hunnebostrand, Swe. 40/D2
Hunsel, Neth. 52/C6
Hunsrück (mts.), Ger. 42/D4
Hunstanton, Eng, UK 37/G1
Hunt (mtn.), Wy, US 147/K1
Hunte (riv.), Ger. 42/E2
Hunter (mt.), Ak, US 171/H3
Hunter, ND, US 156/F4
Hunter (mtn.), NY, US 161/J3
Hunter (riv.), Austl. 132/D2
Hunter, Tx, US 150/E3
Hunter (isl.), Austl. 127/D5
Hunter Army Afld., Ga, US 165/H1
Hunterdon (co.), NJ, US 168/C2
Hunters, Wa, US 144/E3
Hunters Creek Village, Tx, US 151/M9
Huntersville, NC, US 163/G3
Hunterville, NZ 135/C2
Huntingburg, In, US 162/D1
Huntingdon, Qu, Can. 161/J2
Huntingdon, Eng, UK 37/F2
Huntingdon, Tn, US 162/C2
Huntingdon, Pa, US 161/G4
Huntingdon, Eng, UK 35/G4
Huntington, In, US 160/D4
Huntington, NY, US 169/M8
Huntington (bay), NY, US 169/M8
Huntington, Or, US 146/E1
Huntington (cr.), Pa, US 168/B1
Huntington, Tx, US 150/G2
Huntington, Ut, US 147/H4
Huntington, WV, US 163/F1
Huntington Bay, NY, US 169/M8
Huntington Beach, Ca, US 166/G8
Huntington Park, Ca, US 166/F8
Huntington Station, NY, US 169/M8
Huntington Woods, Mi, US 167/F7
Huntland, Tn, US 162/D3
Huntley, Il, US 167/P15
Huntly, Sc, UK 33/D2
Huntly, NZ 135/C2
Hunts Inlet, BC, Can. 171/M4
Hunts Point, Wa, US 167/C2
Huntsville, On, Can. 161/G2
Huntsville, Al, US 162/D3
Huntsville, Ar, US 153/H2
Huntsville, Mo, US 155/H4
Huntsville (res.), Pa, US 168/B1
Huntsville, Tn, US 162/E2
Huntsville, Tx, US 151/G2
Huntsville, Wa, US 144/E4
Hunua, NZ 135/G7
Hunucmá, Mex. 176/D1
Hünxe, Ger. 52/D5
Hunyuan, China 80/C3
Huo (mtn.), China 80/B3
Huo Xian, China 80/B3
Huocheng, China 99/D3
Huojia, China 80/C4
Huolin Gol, China 79/H2
Huolongmen, China 79/K2
Huolupu, China 87/E2
Huon (gulf), PNG 129/G1
Huon (pen.), PNG 129/G1
Huong Hoa, Viet. 94/D2
Huong Khe, Viet. 94/D2
Huong Son, Viet. 94/D2
Huong Thuy, Viet. 93/J4
Huonville, Austl. 132/C4
Huoqiu, China 80/D4
Huoshan, China 80/D5
Huotong, China 87/H3
Huozhou, China 80/B3
Ḩuraymilā, SAr. 100/E3
Hūrayn, Egypt 113/B3
Hurd (cape), On, Can. 160/F2
Hurdal, Nor. 40/D1
Hurdiyo, Som. 118/D3
Hurdle Mills, NC, US 163/H2
Hure Qi, China 80/E2
Hurepoix (reg.), Fr. 30/H6
Hurley, Wi, US 157/J4
Hurley (riv.), Ire. 34/B4
Hurley, Ms, US 164/D2
Hurley, NY, US 161/J4
Hurley, Eng, UK 30/A2
Hurley, NM, US 149/H4
Hurlford, Sc, UK 33/B5
Hurlock, Md, US 163/K1
Huron (bay), Mi, US 157/K4
Huron (mts.), Mi, US 157/K4
Huron, Oh, US 160/E4
Huron (pt.), Mi, US 167/G6
Huron (riv.), Mi, US 167/E7
Huron, Ca, US 148/B2
Huron (lake), Can.,US 139/J5
Huron, SD, US 154/E1
Huron Islands Nat'l Wild. Ref., Mi, US 157/K4
Huron Mountain, Mi, US 157/L4
Hurricane (lake), ND, US 156/E3
Hurricane, Al, US 164/E2
Hurricane, Ut, US 149/F2
Hurricane, WV, US 163/F1
Hurricane (cliffs), Az, US 149/F2
Hurshat Tal NP, Isr. 105/D2
Hurst, Tx, US 150/K7
Hurstville, Austl. 133/E1
Hurtaut (riv.), Fr. 54/D4
Hürtgenwald (reg.), Ger. 55/F2
Hürth, Ger. 55/F2
Hurtsboro, Al, US 162/E4
Hurum, Nor. 38/S9
Hurup, Den. 40/C3
Huruta, Eth. 118/A3
Hurworth, Eng, UK 35/G3
Hurzuf, Ukr. 70/E3
Husainābād, India 97/E3
Husainpur, Bang. 97/H3
Huslia, Ak, US 171/G2
Húsavík, Ice. 38/P6
Ḩusayyāt al Fawākhir (well), Libya 108/D2
Husbands Bosworth, Eng, UK 37/E2
Husby-Långhundra, Swe. 39/B1
Hushan, China 87/H2
Husher, Wi, US 167/Q14
Hushi, China 78/E3
Huşi, Rom. 72/E4
Huskisson, Austl. 133/E2
Husnes, Nor. 40/A2
Hussar, Ab, Can. 145/H2
Hussigny-Godbrange, Fr. 55/E5
Hustisford, Wi, US 155/K2
Husum, Ger. 40/C4
Husum, Swe. 38/F3
Husyatyn, Ukr. 72/D3
Hutag, Mong. 78/E2
Hutanopan, Indo. 89/C2
Hutchins, Tx, US 150/L7
Hutchinson, Ks, US 153/F1

Ireton – Jaunpa
Map Section 236 237

Ireton, Ia, US 155/F2
Irfon (riv.), Wal, UK 36/C2
Irgiz, Kaz. 71/M2
Irharhar, Oued (riv.), Alg. 111/G4
Irhazer Oua-n-Agadez (riv.), Niger 115/G2
Irherm, Mor. 110/C3
Irherm n'Ougdal, Mor. 110/D3
Iri, SKor. 81/D5
Irian Jaya (reg.), Indo. 91/H4
Irian Jaya (prov.), Indo. 129/E1
Iriba, Chad 116/D2
Iricoume (mts.), Braz. 181/G4
Irig, Serb. 50/D3
Irigny, Fr. 64/A1
Irîgui (phys. reg.), Mali 114/D2
Iriklinskiy, Rus. 71/L2
Iriklinskiy (res.), Rus. 71/L2
Iringa (prov.), Tanz. 119/A4
Iringa, Tanz. 119/A3
Iriomote (isl.), Japan 85/G8
Iriri (riv.), Braz. 182/C4
Iriri Novo (riv.), Braz. 186/B1
Iriri-Novo (riv.), Braz. 182/C5
Irish (sea), Ire.,UK 34/C4
Irish Vale, NS, Can. 159/G3
Irituía, Braz. 183/E3
Irkliyiv, Ukr. 73/G3
Irkut (riv.), Rus. 78/E1
Irkutsk, Rus. 78/E1
Irkutsk (int'l arpt.), Rus. 78/E1
Irkutskaya Oblast, Rus. 78/E1
Irlam, Eng, UK 35/F5
Irma, Ab, Can. 145/J1
Irmo, SC, US 163/G3
Irō-zaki (pt.), Japan 85/F3
Iroise (bay), Fr. 44/A2
Iron (mtn.), Fl, US 164/M8
Iron (mtn.), Id, US 147/F2
Iron Baron, Austl. 131/H5
Iron Bridge (dam), Tx, US 153/G4
Iron Bridge, On, Can. 160/E1
Iron City, Ga, US 165/F2
Iron City, Tn, US 162/D3
Iron Gate (dam), Ca, US 146/B3
Iron Knob, Austl. 131/H5
Iron Lightning, SD, US 154/D1
Iron Mountain, Mi, US 157/K5
Iron Range, Austl. 129/F3
Iron Range NP, Austl. 129/F3
Iron River, Mi, US 157/K4
Iron Springs, Az, US 149/F3
Ironbound (nbrhd.), NJ, US 169/J9
Irondale, Al, US 162/D4
Ironton, Mn, US 157/H4
Ironton, Oh, US 163/F1
Ironton, Mo, US 162/B2
Ironwood, Mi, US 157/J4
Ironwood Forest Nat'l Mon., Az, US 149/G4
Iroquois, On, Can. 161/J2
Iroquois Falls, On, Can. 141/H4
Irpin', Ukr. 72/F2
Irput' (riv.), Rus. 70/E1
Irrawaddy (riv.), Myan. 77/J7
Irricana, Ab, Can. 145/H2
Irrigon, Or, US 144/E5
Irrua, Nga. 115/G5
Irsch, Ger. 55/F4
Irsen (riv.), Ger. 55/F3
Irsina, It. 48/E2
Irt (riv.), Eng, UK 35/E3
Irthing (riv.), Eng, UK 35/F1
Irthlingborough, Eng, UK 37/F2
Irtysh (riv.), Rus. 77/G4
Irtyshsk, Kaz. 99/C1
Iruma, Japan 83/C2
Irumu, D.R. Congo 121/G2
Irún, Sp. 44/C5
Irupana, Bol. 188/C1
Irvine, Sc, UK 33/B5
Irvine (bay), Sc, UK 33/B5
Irvine (riv.), Sc, UK 33/B5
Irvine, Ca, US 166/G8
Irvine, Ky, US 162/F2
Irvine, Ab, Can. 145/J3
Irvines Landing, BC, Can. 144/B3
Irving, Il, US 155/K4
Irving, Tx, US 150/L7
Irvington, NJ, US 169/J9
Irvington, NY, US 169/K7
Irvington, Ky, US 162/D2
Irvington, Il, US 162/C1
Irwin, Ia, US 155/G3
Irwin, Austl. 130/B4
Irwin, SC, US 163/G3
Irwinton, Ga, US 163/F4
Is (peak), Sudan 109/G4
Is-sur-Tille, Fr. 60/B2
Isa, Nga. 115/G3
Īsa Khel, Pak. 98/A3
Isabel, SD, US 156/D5
Isabel, Ks, US 153/E2
Isabel, La, US 164/D2
Isabela, Phil. 88/C4
Isabela (isl.), Ecu. 184/J7
Isabela, PR 173/M8
Isabelia (mts.), Nic. 176/E3
Isabella, Ok, US 153/E2
Isabella, Mn, US 157/J4
Isabella (bay), Nun, Can. 141/K2
Isabella (lake), Ca, US 148/C3
Isabella Ind. Res., Mi, US 160/D3
Isabelle (pt.), Mi, US 157/L4
Isaccea, Rom. 51/J3
Isachsen (cape), Nun, Can. 141/R7
Isachsen, Nun, Can. 141/R7
Ísafjardhardjúp (inlet), Ice. 38/M6
Ísafjördhur, Ice. 38/M6
Isahaya, Japan 84/B4
Isak, Indo. 89/B1
Isaka, D.R. Congo 120/D3
Isaka, D.R. Congo 120/D3
Isakovo, Rus. 68/G5
Isalo Ruiniform (mass.), Madg. 125/H8
Isalo, PN de l', Madg. 125/H8
Isana (riv.), Col. 180/D4
Isandhlwana Battlesite, SAfr. 125/E3
Isangano NP, Zam. 121/G5
Isangel, Van. 136/F6
Isangi, D.R. Congo 121/F2
Isango-Isoro, D.R. Congo 121/G3
Isanlu Makutu, Nga. 115/G4
Isaouanne-n-Irarraren (des.), Alg. 111/G4
Isaouanne-n-Tifernine (des.), Alg. 111/G4
Isar (riv.), Aus. 61/H3
Isarco (riv.), It. 45/J3
Isarco (Eisack) (riv.), It. 61/H4
Isaszeg, Hun. 51/R9
Isawa, Japan 83/B2
Isbergues, Fr. 54/B2
Iscar, Sp. 46/C2
Ischgl, Aus. 61/G3
Ischia, It. 65/C6
Ischia (isl.), It. 65/C6
Isclero (riv.), It. 65/D5
Ise (riv.), Ger. 53/H3
Ise (bay), Japan 85/E3
Ise, Japan 83/L7
Ise (riv.), Eng, UK 37/F2
Ise-Shima NP, Japan 85/E3
Isehara, Japan 85/F3
Isel (riv.), Aus. 67/G1
Iselin, NJ, US 169/H9
Isen (riv.), Ger. 42/G4
Isen, Ger. 59/F6
Isenthal, Swi. 61/E4
Isenyela, Tanz. 119/A4
'Iseo (lake), It. 62/C1
Iseo, It. 62/D2
Iseo (lake), It. 45/J4
Iseramagazi, Tanz. 121/H4
Isère (dept.), Fr. 60/B6
Isère (riv.), Fr. 44/F4
Iserlohn, Ger. 53/E6
Isernia, It. 65/D4
Isernia (prov.), It. 65/D4
Isesaki, Japan 85/F2
Iset' (riv.), Rus. 69/Q4
Isetskoye, Rus. 69/Q4
Iseyin, Nga. 115/F5
Isfahan (int'l arpt.), Iran 103/G3
'Isfiyā, Isr. 105/C3
Ishenga Oswe, D.R. Congo 121/E3
Isherton, Guy. 181/G4
Ishi (riv.), Japan 83/J7
Ishibashi, Japan 85/F2
Ishibe, Japan 83/K5
Ishidoriya, Japan 82/B4
Ishigaki (isl.), Japan 85/G8
Ishige, Japan 85/F2
Ishikari, Japan 82/B2
Ishikari (riv.), Japan 82/B2
Ishikari (bay), Japan 82/B2
Ishikari (mts.), Japan 82/C2
Ishikawa, Japan 85/G2
Ishikawa (pref.), Japan 85/E2
Ishiki, Japan 83/M6
Ishim, Rus. 69/R4
Ishim (riv.), Rus. 74/H4
Ishimbay, Rus. 71/L1
Ishinomaki, Japan 82/B4
Ishioka, Japan 85/G2
Ishizuchi-san (peak), Japan 84/C4
Ishlya, Rus. 69/N5
Ishmant, Egypt 113/C6
Ishøj, Den. 39/J7
Ishpeming, Mi, US 157/L4
Ishurdi, Bang. 97/G3
Isiboro Secure, PN (riv.), Bol. 185/E4
Isidoro Noblía, Uru. 189/F4
Isigny-le-Buat, Fr. 57/D3
Isigny-sur-Mer, Fr. 57/D2
Isil'kul', Rus. 74/H4
Isiolo, Kenya 119/B1
Isiro, D.R. Congo 121/F2
Isisford, Austl. 134/B4
Iskandarūnah, Leb. 105/C2
Iske-Ryazyap, Rus. 69/L5
İskenderun (gulf), Turk. 104/D1
İskenderun, Turk. 104/E1
İskilip, Turk. 70/E4
Iskininskiy, Kaz. 71/K3
Iskitim, Rus. 74/J4
Iskŭr (res.), Bul. 49/H1
Iskŭr (riv.), Bul. 49/H1
Iskŭr (riv.), Aus. 51/G4
Iskŭr (riv.), Bul. 67/K2
Iskur (lake), Hun. 51/F4
Iskushuban, Som. 118/D3
Isla (riv.), Sc, UK 33/C3
Isla, Mex. 176/C2
Isla Aguada, Mex. 176/D2
Isla Cabritos, PN, DRep. 177/J2
Isla Cedros, Mex. 174/B2
Isla Cristina, Sp. 46/B4
Isla de Maipo, Chile 190/N8
Isla de Salamanca, PN, Col. 180/C2
Isla de San Andrés (int'l arpt.), Col. 177/F3
Isla Gorge NP, Austl. 134/C4
Isla Guamblin, PN, Chile 190/B5
Isla Isabela, PN, Mex. 174/D4
Isla Magdalena, PN, Chile 190/B5
Isla Mujeres, Mex. 176/E1
Islām Kot, Pak. 101/K4
Islāmābād (cap.), Pak. 98/B3
Islāmābād (cap. terr.), Pak. 98/B3
Islāmābād/Rāwalpindi (int'l arpt.), Pak. 98/B3
Islāmnagar, India 96/B1
Islamorada, Fl, US 165/H5
Islāmpur, India 97/G2
Islāmpur, India 97/E3
Island (lake), Mn, US 157/H4
Island (co.), Wa, US 167/B2
Island (lake), Mb, Can. 140/G3
Island Bay (nbrhd.), NZ 135/H9
Island Bay Nat'l Wild. Ref., Fl, US 165/G4
Island Beach State Park, NJ, US 168/D4
Island City, Or, US 146/D1
Island Lagoon (lake), Austl. 131/H4
Island Lake, Il, US 167/P15
Island Park, NY, US 169/L9
Island Park, Id, US 147/H1
Island Park (res.), Id, US 147/H1
Island Pond, Vt, US 161/L2
Islands (bay), NF, Can. 158/H1
Islands (bay), NZ 135/C1
Islay (isl.), Sc, UK 31/Q9
Islay, Peru 184/C5
Islay, Ab, Can. 145/J1
Isle, Mn, US 157/H4
Isle au Haut (isl.), Me, US 158/C3
Isle aux Morts, Nf, Can. 159/H2
Isle Madame (isl.), Ns., Can. 159/G3
Isle of Anglesey (co.), Wal, UK 34/D5
Isle of Ely (phys. reg.), Eng, UK 37/G2
Isle of Man (Ronaldsway) (arpt.), IM, UK 34/D3
Isle of Portland (pen.), Eng, UK 36/D5
Isle of Thanet (phys. reg.), Eng, UK 37/H4
Isle of Whithorn, Sc, UK 34/D2
Isle of Wight (co.), Eng, UK 37/E5
Isle of Wight, Va, US 163/J2
Isle Royale (isl.), Mi, US 157/K3
Isle Royale NP, Mi, US 157/K3
Isle Wooden (isl.), Austl. 129/E3
Isleham, Eng, UK 37/G2
Isles Dernieres (isls.), La, US 164/C3
Isleta, NM, US 149/J3
Isleta Ind. Res., NM, US 149/J3
Isleten, Swi. 61/E4
Isleton, Ca, US 167/L10
Islington (bor.), Eng, UK 30/A1
Islip, NY, US 169/E2
Isluga (vol.), Chile 188/B1
Ismā'īlīyah (canal), Egypt 113/C4
Ismailovo Park, Rus. 69/W9
Ismail Samani (peak), Taj. 99/B4
Ismaning, Ger. 59/E6
İsmayıllı, Azer. 71/J4
Isnā, Egypt 109/G3
Isny, Ger. 61/G2
Iso-Evo, Fin. 39/F3
Iso-Roine (lake), Fin. 39/E3
Isoanala, Madg. 125/H8
Isobe, Japan 83/L7
Isojärven NP, Fin. 41/L1
Isojärvi (lake), Fin. 41/J1
Isoka, Zam. 121/H5
Isola, Fr. 64/D4
Isola, Ms, US 162/B4
Isola del Gran Sasso d'Italia, It. 65/C3
Isola del Liri, It. 65/C4
Isola della Scala, It. 63/D3
Isola di Capo Rizzuto, It. 49/E3
Isola Vicentina, It. 63/E2
Isole (riv.), Fr. 56/B5
Isonzo (riv.), It. 63/G1
Isorella, It. 62/D3
İsparta, Turk. 102/B2
İsparta (prov.), Turk. 102/B2
Isperikh, Bul. 51/H4
İspir, Turk. 71/G4
Israel (ctry.) 104/C3
Issac (lake), BC, Can. 144/D1
Issac (riv.), Austl. 127/D3
Issano, Guy. 182/B1
Issaquah, Wa, US 167/C2
Issaquah (cr.), Wa, US 167/C2
Issé, Fr. 56/D5
Issel (riv.), Ger. 52/D5
Isselburg, Ger. 52/D5
Issenheim, Fr. 60/D2
Issia, C.d'Iv. 114/D5
Issoire, Fr. 44/E4
Issou, Fr. 30/H5
Issum, Ger. 52/D5
Issuna, Tanz. 119/A3
Issutugan (riv.), Som. 118/C3
Issy-les-Moulineaux, Fr. 30/J5
Istachatta, Fl, US 164/L6
Istállós-Kő (peak), Hun. 50/E1
Istana Maimoon (Maimoon Palace), Indo. 89/B2
İstanbul (prov.), Turk. 70/D4
İstanbul, Turk. 103/M6
Işţanhā, Egypt 113/C4
Istead Rise, Eng, UK 30/E2
Istiaía, Gre. 49/H3
Istmina, Col. 180/B3
Istok, Serb. 50/E4
Istokpaga (lake), Fl, US 165/H4
Istra (riv.), Rus. 69/W9
Istrana, It. 63/F2
Istranca (mts.), Turk. 67/K2
Istres, Fr. 64/A5
Istria (reg.), Cro. 67/G1
Istria (pen.), Cro. 45/K4
Isulan, Phil. 88/D4
Isumi, Japan 83/E3
Iswarganj, Bang. 97/H3
Iswarīpur, Bang. 97/G4
Isyangulovo, Rus. 71/L1
Itá Ibaté, Arg. 189/E3
Itabaiana, Braz. 187/F1
Itabaiana, Braz. 183/H4
Itabaianinha, Braz. 187/F1
Itaberaba, Braz. 187/E2
Itaberaí, Braz. 186/C3
Itabira, Braz. 187/E3
Itabirito, Braz. 186/E4
Itaboraí, Braz. 187/P7
Itabuna, Braz. 187/F2
Itacaiunas (riv.), Braz. 182/D4
Itacajá, Braz. 182/E5
Itacarambi, Braz. 186/D2
Itacoatiara, Braz. 182/B3
Itacuaí (riv.), Braz. 184/D2
Itacuruba, Braz. 183/G5
Itacurubí del Rosario, Par. 189/E3
Itaga, Tanz. 121/H4
Itagibá, Braz. 187/F2
Itaguaí, Braz. 187/N7
Itaguatins, Braz. 183/E4
Itagüí, Col. 183/K6
Itahuazurenda, Bol. 188/D1
Itaí, Braz. 189/G2
Itaíba, Braz. 183/G5
Itaiçaba, Braz. 183/G4
Itainópolis, Braz. 183/F4
Itaiópolis, Braz. 189/G3
Itaipu (res.), Braz.,Par. 179/D5
Itaipú (dam), Par. 189/F3
Itaituba, Braz. 182/C4
Itajaí, Braz. 189/G3
Itajaí (riv.), Braz. 189/G3
Itajubá, Braz. 187/L7
Itākhola, Bang. 97/H3
Itako, Japan 85/G3
Itakura, Japan 83/D1
Itala, Som. 118/C5
Italy (ctry.) 67/F2
Italy, Tx, US 151/F1
Itamaraju, Braz. 187/F3
Itambacuri, Braz. 187/E3
Itambé, Braz. 183/H4
Itambé, Braz. 187/E2
Itambé, Pico de (peak), Braz. 187/E3
Itami, Japan 83/H6
Itamonte, Braz. 187/M7
Itampolo, Madg. 125/G9
Itanagar, India 86/B3
Itang, Eth. 117/G3
Itanhaém, Braz. 187/K9
Itanhomi, Braz. 187/E3
Itapagé, Braz. 183/G3
Itaparica (isl.), Braz. 187/F2
Itapé, Braz. 187/F2
Itapé, Par. 189/E3
Itapecerica, Braz. 186/D4
Itapecuru-Mirim, Braz. 183/E3
Itapemirim, Braz. 187/E4
Itaperuna, Braz. 187/E4
Itapetim, Braz. 183/G4
Itapetinga, Braz. 187/E2
Itapetininga, Braz. 189/G2
Itapeva, Braz. 189/G2
Itapevi, Braz. 187/K8
Itapicuru (riv.), Braz. 183/F4
Itapipoca, Braz. 183/G3
Itapira, Braz. 187/K7
Itapiranga, Braz. 182/B3
Itapiranga, Braz. 189/F3
Itapitanga, Braz. 187/F2
Itapiúna, Braz. 183/G4
Itápolis, Braz. 189/G2
Itaporã, Braz. 189/F2
Itaporã do Tocantins, Braz. 182/D5
Itaporanga, Braz. 189/G2
Itapúa (dept.), Par. 189/F3
Itapuranga, Braz. 186/C2
Itaquaquecetuba, Braz. 187/K8
Itaqui, Braz. 189/E4
Itarantim, Braz. 187/E2
Itararé, Braz. 189/G3
Itariri, Braz. 187/J9
Itārsi, India 96/A4
Itasca (lake), Mn, US 157/G4
Itasca, Tx, US 151/F1
Itatí, Arg. 188/E3
Itatiaia, PN de, Braz. 187/M7
Itatiba, Braz. 187/K7
Itaú, Bol. 188/D2
Itauçu, Braz. 186/C3
Itaueira, Braz. 183/F4
Itaueira (riv.), Braz. 183/F5
Itayanagi, Japan 82/B3
Itbayat, Phil. 87/J4
Itbayat (isl.), Phil. 87/J4
Itchen (riv.), Eng, UK 37/E4
Itéa, Gre. 49/H3
Itembiri (riv.), D.R. Congo 121/E2
Iténez (riv.), Bol. 179/C4
Ith (hills), Ger. 53/G4
Ithaca, Mi, US 160/D3
Ithaca, NY, US 161/H3
Ithaca (Itháki) (isl.), Gre. 49/G3
Itháki, Gre. 49/G3
Ithon (riv.), Wal, UK 36/C2
Itigi, Tanz. 119/A3
Itiquira (riv.), Braz. 185/H5
Itiruçu, Braz. 187/E2
Itō, Japan 85/F3
Itobo, Tanz. 119/A3
Itoigawa, Japan 85/E2
Itoko, D.R. Congo 121/E3
Itoman, Japan 85/J7
Iton (riv.), Fr. 44/D2
Itonamas (riv.), Bol. 185/E4
Itondy, Madg. 125/H7
Itonuki, Japan 83/L5
Itororó, Braz. 187/E2
Itremo, Madg. 125/H8
Itri, It. 65/C5
Iţsā, Egypt 113/B6
Itsukaichi, Japan 83/C2
Itter (riv.), Ger. 53/F6
Itterbeck, Ger. 52/D3
Ittiri, It. 48/A2
Itu, Nga. 115/G5
Itu, Braz. 189/H2
Ituango, Col. 180/C3
Ituberá, Braz. 187/F2
Ituí (riv.), Braz. 184/D2
Ituiutaba, Braz. 186/C3
Itumbiara (res.), Braz. 186/C3
Itumbiara, Braz. 186/C3
Itumirim, Braz. 187/M6
Ituna, Sk, Can. 156/C2
Itungi Port, Tanz. 119/A4
Ituni, Guy. 181/G3
Itupiranga, Braz. 182/D4
Ituporanga, Braz. 189/G3
Iturama, Braz. 189/G1
Iturbe, Par. 189/E3
Ituri (riv.), D.R. Congo 121/F2
Ituri Forest (for.), D.R. Congo 121/F2
Itutinga (res.), Braz. 187/M6
Ituverava, Braz. 189/H2
Ituxi (riv.), Braz. 185/E3
Ituzaingó, Uru. 191/K11
Ityāy al Bārūd, Egypt 113/B3
Itz (riv.), Ger. 42/F3
Iuka, Il, US 162/C1
Iuka, Ks, US 153/E2
Iuka, Ms, US 162/C3
Iul'tin, Rus. 171/C2
Iva, SC, US 163/F3
Ivaí (riv.), Braz. 186/B4
Ivaiporã, Braz. 189/G3
Ivalojoki (riv.), Fin. 38/H1
Ivančice, Czh. 45/M2
Ivanec, Cro. 50/C2
Ivangorod, Rus. 41/N2
Ivangrad, Serb. 50/D4
Ivanhoe, Austl. 128/C3
Ivanhoe, Austl. 133/B1
Ivanhoe, Mn, US 155/F1
Ivanhoe, Va, US 163/G2
Ivanivka, Ukr. 73/K3
Ivanjica, Serb. 50/E4
Ivanjska, Bosn. 50/C3
Ivanka (Bratislava) (int'l arpt.), Slvk. 50/C1
Ivankiv, Ukr. 72/E2
Ivankovo, Cro. 50/D3
Ivano-Frankivs'k, Ukr. 72/C3
Ivano-Frankivs'k (int'l arpt.), Ukr. 72/C3
Ivano-Frankivs'ka Oblast, Ukr. 70/C2
Ivanov, Ukr. 72/E3
Ivanof Bay, Ak, US 171/G4
Ivanovka, Rus. 69/M5
Ivanovo, Bela. 70/C1
Ivanovo, Rus. 68/J4
Ivanovskaya, Rus. 73/K5
Ivanovskaya Oblast, Rus. 68/J4
Ivanpah (lake), Nv, US 148/E3
Ivato (int'l arpt.), Madg. 125/H7
Ivato, Madg. 125/H8
Ivatsevichi, Bela. 70/C1
Ivaylovgrad (res.), Bul. 49/J2
Ivaylovgrad, Bul. 51/H5
Ivdel, Rus. 74/G3
Ivel, Ky, US 163/F2
Ivenets, Bela. 41/M5
Iver, Eng, UK 30/B2
Iver Heath, Eng, UK 30/B2
Iveragh (pen.), Ire. 30/P11
Iverny, Fr. 30/L5
Ivey, Ga, US 163/F4
Ivindo (riv.), Gabon 120/C2
Ivinheima (riv.), Braz. 186/B4
Ivinheima, Braz. 189/F2
Ivins, Ut, US 149/F2
Ivnya, Rus. 73/J2
Ivö (isl.), Swe. 39/L6
Ivohibe, Madg. 125/H8
Ivón, Bol. 185/E3
Ivondro (riv.), Madg. 125/J7
Ivösjön (lake), Swe. 40/F3
Ivrea, It. 62/A2
İvrindi, Turk. 70/C5
Ivry-la-Bataille, Fr. 57/G3
Ivry-sur-Seine, Fr. 30/K5
Ivujivik, Qu, Can. 141/J2
Ivvavik NP, Yk, Can. 171/K2
Ivybridge, Eng, UK 36/C6
Iwafune, Japan 83/D1
Iwai, Japan 85/F2
Iwaizumi, Japan 82/B4
Iwaki, Japan 85/G2
Iwaki-san (peak), Japan 82/B3
Iwakuni, Japan 84/C3
Iwakura, Japan 83/L5
Iwama, Japan 83/E1
Iwami, Japan 84/D3
Iwamizawa, Japan 82/B2
Iwamura, Japan 83/M5
Iwanai, Japan 82/B2
Iwanuma, Japan 85/G1
Iwasaki, Japan 82/A3
Iwata, Japan 85/E3
Iwataki, Japan 83/H4
Iwate, Japan 82/B4
Iwate (pref.), Japan 82/B4
Iwate-san (peak), Japan 82/B4
Iwatsuki, Japan 83/D2
Iwere Ile, Nga. 115/F5
Iwo, Nga. 115/G5
Iwo Jima (isl.), Japan 136/D2
Iwŏn, NKor. 81/E2
Iwuy, Fr. 54/C3
Ixcán (riv.), Guat. 176/D3
Ixelles, Belg. 55/D2
Ixiamas, Bol. 184/D4
Ixmiquilpan, Mex. 175/K6
Ixopo, SAfr. 125/E3
Ixtapalapa (nbrhd.), Mex. 175/Q10
Ixtapaluca, Mex. 175/L7
Ixtapan de la Sal, Mex. 175/K8
Ixtlán del Río, Mex. 174/D4
Ixworth, Eng, UK 37/G2
Iya (riv.), Rus. 78/D1
'Iyādh, Yem. 118/C2
'Iyāl Bakhīt, Sudan 117/F2
Iyevlevo, Rus. 69/Q4
Iyo, Japan 84/C4
Iyo (sea), Japan 84/B4
'Izab al Başāriţah, Egypt 113/C2
Izabal (lake), Guat. 172/D4
Īzad Khvāst, Iran 103/H4
Izamal, Mex. 176/D1
'Izbat Jamaşah al Gharbīyah, Egypt 113/C2
Izberbash, Rus. 71/H4
Izeaux, Fr. 64/B2
Izegem, Belg. 54/C2
Izhevsk, Rus. 69/M4
Izhma (riv.), Rus. 69/M2
Izhora (riv.), Rus. 69/T7
Izi (well), Alg. 111/F3
Izigan (cape), Ak, US 171/E5
Izkī, Oman 101/G4
Izmayil, Ukr. 51/J3
Izmir (prov.), Turk. 70/C5
İzmit, Turk. 51/J5
İzmit (gulf), Turk. 51/J5
Iznájar, Sp. 46/C4
İznik, Turk. 51/J5
İznik (lake), Turk. 51/J5
Izobil'noye, Rus. 71/K2
Izobil'nyy, Rus. 73/L5
Izola, Slov. 63/G2
Izozog, Bol. 188/D1
Izra', Syria 105/E3
Izsák, Hun. 50/D2
Iztaccíhuatl-Popocatépetl, PN, Mex. 175/L7
Izu (isls.), Japan 75/P6
Izu (pen.), Japan 85/F3
Izúcar de Matamoros, Mex. 175/L8
Izuhara, Japan 84/A3
Izumi, Japan 84/B4
Izumi, Japan 82/B4
Izumi, Japan 83/H7
Izumi-Ōtsu, Japan 83/H7
Izumi-Sano, Japan 83/H7
Izumo, Japan 84/C3
Izunagaoka, Japan 83/B3
Izushi, Japan 83/G5
Izvestkovyy, Rus. 79/L2
Izyaslav, Ukr. 72/D2
Izyum, Ukr. 73/J3

J

J.B. Thomas (lake), Tx, US 152/D4
J. Clark Sayler NWR, ND, US 156/D3
J. Ḩanīsh al Kabīr (isl.), Yem. 118/B2
J. Jabal Zuqar (isl.), Yem. 118/B2
J. Lee (lake), Ar, US 153/H4
J.P. Priest (lake), Tn, US 162/D2
J. Paul Getty Museum, Ca, US 166/E7
Jääsjärvi (lake), Fin. 41/M1
Jaba', WBnk. 105/C4
Jabal Abu Rujmayn (mts.), Syria 102/D3
Jabal Abyad (plat.), Sudan 109/F5
Jabal ad-Dayr (peak), Sudan 117/F2
Jabal Ajlūn (mts.), Jor. 105/D4
Jabal al 'Arab (mts.), Syria 104/E3
Jabal al Bārūk (peak), Leb. 105/D1
Jabal al Jaw'alīyāt (peak), Jor. 105/E6
Jabal al Lawz (peak), SAr. 109/G2
Jabal al Mudaysīsāt (peak), Jor. 105/E5
Jabal an Nabī Shu'ayb (peak), Yem. 118/B2
Jabal an Nusayriyab (mts.), Syria 104/E2
Jabal ar Ruwaq (mts.), Syria 102/D3
Jabal as Sawdā' (mts.), Libya 108/B2
Jabal ash Shām (peak), Oman 101/G4
Jabal ash Sha'nabī (peak), Tun. 112/L7
Jabal ash Shaykh (peak), Leb. 105/D2
Jabal 'Aybāl (peak), WBnk. 105/C4
Jabal Bin Ghunaymah (mts.), Libya 108/B3
Jabal Dabbāgh (peak), SAr. 109/G3
Jabāl Lubnan (gov.), Leb. 105/D1
Jabal Marrah (mts.), Sudan 116/E2
Jabal Nafūsah (mts.), Libya 111/H3
Jabal Qaţrānī (mts.), Egypt 113/B5
Jabal Raḑwá (peak), SAr. 109/H3
Jabal Ramm (peak), Jor. 104/D5
Jabal Thamar (peak), Yem. 118/C2
Jabal 'Unāzah (peak), SAr. 102/D3
Jabal 'Uwaybid, Egypt 113/D4
Jabal Waddān (mts.), Libya 108/C2
Jabal Zaltan (mts.), Libya 108/C2
Jabal'āmil (peak), Leb. 105/C2
Jabalí (pt.), Pan. 177/F5
Jabalón (riv.), Sp. 66/C3
Jabalpur, India 96/B4
Jabalyāh, Gaza 105/B5
Jabālyah, Gaza 105/A5
Jabbeke, Belg. 54/C1
Jabbūl (lake), Syria 102/D3
Jabiru, Austl. 128/D3
Jabjabah (wadi), Sudan 100/B4
Jablah, Syria 104/D2
Jablanica (mts.), Alb. 49/G2
Jablanica, Bosn. 50/C4
Jablonec nad Nisou, Czh. 43/H3
Jaboatão dos Guararapes, Braz. 183/H5
Jaboticabal, Braz. 189/G2
Jabron (riv.), Fr. 64/B4
Jabsar Gaxun, China 78/D4
Jabuka, Serb. 50/E3
Jabung (cape), Indo. 89/D3
Jaca, Sp. 47/E1
Jacaré (riv.), Braz. 187/E1
Jacareacanga, Braz. 182/B4
Jacareí, Braz. 187/L8
Jacarèzinho, Braz. 189/G2
Jaceel (riv.), Som. 118/D3
Jáchal (riv.), Arg. 188/B4
Jáchymov, Czh. 59/F2
Jaciara, Braz. 186/B2
Jacinto Arauz, Arg. 190/E3
Jacinto City, Tx, US 151/M9
Jaciparaná (riv.), Braz. 185/E3
Jack, Al, US 165/E2
Jack Lee (lake), Ar, US 151/H1
Jack Pine (mtn.), Mn, US 157/J4
Jackfish (lake), Sk, Can. 145/K1
Jackfish Lake, Sk, Can. 145/K1
Jackman, Me, US 161/L2
Jackpot, Nv, US 147/F3
Jacks Fork (riv.), Mo, US 162/B2
Jacks Mtn. (range), Pa, US 168/A2
Jacksboro, Tx, US 153/E4
Jacksboro, Tn, US 162/E2
Jackson (int'l arpt.), PNG 129/G2
Jackson, Al, US 164/E2
Jackson, Ca, US 146/C4
Jackson, Ga, US 162/F4
Jackson (lake), Ga, US 162/E4
Jackson, Ky, US 163/F2
Jackson, La, US 164/C2
Jackson, Mi, US 160/D3
Jackson, Mn, US 155/G2
Jackson, Mo, US 162/C2
Jackson (cap.), Ms, US 162/B4
Jackson, NC, US 163/J2
Jackson (mts.), Nv, US 146/D3
Jackson, Oh, US 163/F1
Jackson, Tn, US 162/C3
Jackson, Wy, US 147/H2
Jackson Head (pt.), NZ 135/B3
Jackson Heights (nbrhd.), NY, US 169/K9
Jackson Lake (dam), Wy, US 147/H2
Jacksonport, Wi, US 160/C2
Jacksonville, Al, US 162/E4
Jacksonville, Ar, US 153/H3
Jacksonville, Fl, US 165/H2
Jacksonville (int'l arpt.), Fl, US 165/H2
Jacksonville, Ga, US 165/G2
Jacksonville, Il, US 155/J4
Jacksonville, Or, US 146/B2
Jacksonville, Mo, US 155/H4
Jacksonville, NC, US 163/J3
Jacksonville, Tx, US 150/G2
Jacksonville Beach, Fl, US 165/H2
Jacksonville Nav. Air Sta., Fl, US 165/H2
Jacmel, Haiti 177/H2
Jacob Lake, Az, US 149/F2
Jacobābād, Pak. 101/J3
Jacobina, Braz. 187/E1
Jacobsdal, SAfr. 124/D3
Jacobson, Mn, US 157/H4
Jacobstown, NJ, US 168/D3
Jacobus, Pa, US 168/B4
Jácome, Ven. 183/P8
Jacona de Plancarte, Mex. 174/E5
Jacques Cartier (peak), Qu, Can. 158/E1
Jacques-Cartier (riv.), Qu, Can. 158/B2
Jacquet River, NB, Can. 158/D2
Jacuí (riv.), Braz. 189/F4
Jacuípe (riv.), Braz. 187/F1
Jacupiranga, Braz. 189/H3
Jacura, Ven. 180/D2
Jadacaquiva, Ven. 180/D2
Jaddi (pt.), Pak. 101/H3
Jade (bay), Ger. 42/E2
Jade (riv.), Ger. 53/F1
Jade, Ger. 53/F2
Jadebusen (bay), Ger. 53/F2
Jadito Wash (riv.), Az, US 149/G3
Jādū, Libya 108/B2
Jadwin, Mo, US 153/J2
Jaén, Sp. 46/D4
Jaen, Phil. 88/C2
Jaén, Peru 184/B2
Jaffa (cape), Austl. 132/A3
Jaffna, SrL. 95/C4
Jaffray, BC, Can. 144/G3
Jaffrey, NH, US 161/K3
Jagādhri, India 98/D4
Jagdīspur, India 96/C2
Jagdīspur, India 97/E3
Jagersfontein, SAfr. 124/D3
Jægerspris, Den. 40/D4
Jægerspris, Den. 39/H7
Jaggayyapeta, India 95/D2
Jagna, Phil. 88/D3
Jagraon, India 98/C4
Jagst (riv.), Ger. 45/J2
Jaguaquara, Braz. 187/F2
Jaguarão (riv.), Braz. 191/G2
Jaguarão, Braz. 189/F5
Jaguaretama, Braz. 183/G4
Jaguari, Braz. 189/F4
Jaguari (riv.), Braz. 189/F4
Jaguariaíva, Braz. 189/G3
Jaguaribara, Braz. 183/G4
Jaguaribe, Braz. 183/G4
Jaguaribe (riv.), Braz. 183/G4
Jaguariúna, Braz. 187/K7
Jaguaruana, Braz. 183/G4
Jagüé, Arg. 188/B4
Jagungal (mt.), Austl. 133/D3
Jahānābād, India 96/D3
Jahānābād, India 97/E3
Jahāngīra, Pak. 98/B3
Jahāngīrābād, India 96/B1
Jahleel (pt.), Austl. 128/C2
Jahrom, Iran 103/H4
Jai (brook), Sur. 181/H4
Jaiama, SLeo. 114/C4
Jaicós, Braz. 183/F4
Jailolo, Indo. 91/G3
Jailu (riv.), China 80/C4
Jaimalsar, India 92/B2
Jainca, China 78/E4
Jaipur, India 92/C2
Jaipur Hāt, Bang. 97/G3
Jāis, India 96/C2
Jaisalmer, India 101/K3
Jaisinghnagar, India 96/C4
Jaithāri, India 96/B4
Jājapur, India 92/E3
Jājarkot, Nepal 96/D1
Jājarm, Iran 103/J2
Jajce, Bosn. 50/C3
Jakarta (cap.), Indo. 89/D4
Jakes (mtn.), Tn, US 162/E3
Jakin, Ga, US 165/F2
Jakobsberg, Swe. 39/A1
Jakobstad (Pietarsaari), Fin. 68/D3
Jal, NM, US 150/C1
Jala, Mex. 174/D4
Jalacingo, Mex. 175/M7
Jalaid Qi, China 79/J2
Jalājil, SAr. 100/E3
Jalal-Abad, Kyr. 99/B3
Jalālābād, Afg. 98/A2
Jalālābād, India 98/C4
Jalālābād, India 98/D5
Jalālābād, India 96/B2
Jalāli, India 96/B2
Jalālpur, Pak. 98/C3
Jalālpur, India 96/D2
Jalālpur Pīrwāla, Pak. 98/A5
Jalamah, Isr. 105/C3
Jalang, Indo. 91/F4
Jalangi (riv.), India 97/G3
Jalangi, India 97/G3
Jålanti (lake), Fin. 39/D3
Jalapa, Mex. 176/C2
Jalapa, Guat. 176/D3
Jalapa, Mex. 175/N7
Jalatlaco, Mex. 175/Q10
Jālaun, India 96/B2
Jalbūn, WBnk. 105/C4
Jaldhāka (riv.), India 97/G2
Jales, Braz. 189/G2
Jalesar, India 96/B2
Jaleswar, Nepal 97/E2
Jalīb ash Shuyūkh, Kuw. 103/F4
Jalingo, Nga. 116/A3
Jalisco, Mex. 174/D4
Jāliţah, Jazīrat (isl.), Tun. 66/F3
Jalkot, Pak. 98/B2
Jallouvre, Pic de (peak), Fr. 60/C6
Jalon (riv.), Sp. 46/E2
Jālor, India 101/K3
Jalostotitlán, Mex. 174/E4
Jalpa, Mex. 174/E4
Jalpa de Méndez, Mex. 176/C2
Jalpaiguri, India 97/G2
Jalpan de Serra, Mex. 175/F4
Jaltenango de la Paz, Mex. 176/C3
Jaltepec (riv.), Mex. 176/C2
Jáltipan de Morelos, Mex. 176/C2
Jālū, Libya 108/D2
Jālūd, WBnk. 105/C4
Jaluit (isl.), Mrsh. 136/F4
Jalūlā', Iraq 103/F3
Jam, Iran 103/H5
Jamaame, Som. 119/C1
Jamaare (riv.), Nga. 115/H3
Jamaica (ctry.) 177/G2
Jamaica (chan.), Jam. 173/F4
Jamaica (bay), NY, US 168/K9
Jamaica (nbrhd.), NY, US 169/K9
Jamālpur, Bang. 97/G3
Jamālpur, India 98/C5
Jamālpur, India 97/F3
Jamanxim (riv.), Braz. 182/C4
Jamapa, Mex. 175/N7
Jamari (riv.), Braz. 185/F3
Jamberoo, Austl. 133/E2
Jambi (prov.), Indo. 89/C3
Jambi, Indo. 89/C3
Jāmbo, India 92/B2
Jamboaye (riv.), Indo. 89/B1
Jambongan (isl.), Malay. 88/B4
Jambuair (cape), Indo. 89/B1
James (bay), Qu, Can. 139/J4
James (pt.), Chile 190/B5
James (riv.), SD, US 154/E1
James (lake), NC, US 163/F3
James City, NC, US 163/J3
James M. Cox Dayton (int'l arpt.), Oh, US 160/D5
James Ross (str.), Nun, Can. 140/G1
Jamesburg, NJ, US 168/D3
Jamesport, Mo, US 155/H4
Jamestown, Austl. 131/H5
Jamestown, Ks, US 154/F4
Jamestown, Ky, US 162/E2
Jamestown, La, US 153/H4
Jamestown, Mo, US 153/H1
Jamestown (dam), ND, US 156/E4
Jamestown, ND, US 156/E4
Jamestown, NY, US 161/G3
Jamestown, Oh, US 160/E5
Jamestown, Tn, US 162/E2
Jamestown Nat'l Hist. Site, Va, US 163/J2
Jamesville, Va, US 163/K2
Jamieson, Or, US 146/E1
Jamīrāpāt (range), India 96/D4
Jāmke, Pak. 98/C3
Jammāl, Tun. 48/B5
Jammerbugt (bay), Den. 40/C3
Jammerland (bay), Den. 39/G7
Jammu, India 98/C3
Jammu and Kashmīr (state), India 99/C5
Jāmnagar, India 101/K4
Jampang-Kulon, Indo. 89/D4
Jāmpur, Pak. 98/A5
Jamshedpur, India 97/F4
Jāmtāra, India 97/F4
Jämtland (co.), Swe. 38/E3
Jamuda, Eth. 118/A4
Jamūi, India 97/F3
Jamuna (riv.), Bang. 97/G3
Jāmunkira, India 95/E1
Jan Kempdorp, SAfr. 124/D2
Jan Mayen (isl.), Nor. 192/G
Jan Smuts (Johannesburg) (int'l arpt.), SAfr. 124/E2
Janāj, Egypt 113/B3
Janakkala, Fin. 41/L1
Janakpur, India 96/C4
Janakpur (zone), Nepal 97/E2
Janakpur, Nepal 97/E2
Janaúba, Braz. 187/E2
Janaucu (isl.), Braz. 182/D2
Jand, Pak. 98/B3
Jandaia, Braz. 189/G1
Jandaia do Sul, Braz. 189/G2
Jandanwāla, Pak. 98/B4
Jandaq, Iran 103/H3
Jandiāla, India 98/C4
Jandikot (arpt.), Austl. 130/K7
Jandowae, Austl. 134/C4
Jándula (riv.), Sp. 46/C4
Jane (brook), Austl. 130/L6
Jane Lew, WV, US 163/G1
Janesville, Wi, US 155/K2
Jangamo, Moz. 123/G5
Jangaon, India 95/C2
Jangipur, India 97/G3
Janikowo, Pol. 43/K2
Janīn, WBnk. 105/C4
Janja, Bosn. 50/D3
Janjevo, Serb. 50/E4
Jannaale, Som. 119/D1
Janos, Mex. 174/C2
Jánoshalma, Hun. 50/D2
Jánosháza, Hun. 50/C2
Janów Lubelski, Pol. 43/M3
Jānsath, India 96/A1
Jansen, Sk, Can. 156/B2
Jansen, Co, US 152/B2
Jansenville, SAfr. 124/D4
Januária, Braz. 186/D2
Janville, Fr. 57/G4
Janvry, Fr. 30/J6
Janzé, Fr. 56/D5
Janzūr, Libya 67/G4
Jaora, India 92/C3
Japan (ctry.) 79/M4
Japan (sea), Asia 79/L3
Japanese Alps NP, Japan 85/E2
Japiim, Braz. 184/C2
Japurá (riv.), Braz. 179/C3
Jaqué, Pan. 180/B3
Jarābulus, Syria 102/D2
Jarad, SAr. 100/D5
Jaraguá, Braz. 186/C2
Jaraíz de la Vera, Sp. 46/C2
Jarales, NM, US 149/J3
Jarama (riv.), Sp. 46/D2
Jaramānah, Syria 105/E2
Jaramillo, Arg. 191/D5
Jarandilla de la Vera, Sp. 46/C2
Jarānwāla, Pak. 98/B4
Jarash, Jor. 105/D4
Jarbah, Jazīrat (isl.), Tun. 67/F4
Jarbidge, Nv, US 146/F3
Järbo, Swe. 40/G1
Jarby (pt.), IM, UK 34/D3
Jardas al 'Abīd, Libya 67/J4
Jardim, Braz. 189/E2
Jardim, Braz. 183/G4
Jardim do Seridó, Braz. 183/G4
Jardín, Col. 183/K7
Jardín América, Arg. 189/F3
Jardine (riv.), Austl. 129/F2
Jardine R. Nat'l Park, Austl. 129/F2
Jardines de la Reina (arch.), Cuba 177/G1
Jargalant, Mong. 78/E2
Jargalant, Mong. 99/F2
Jargalant, Mong. 78/D2
Jargeau, Fr. 57/H5
Jari (riv.), Braz. 179/D2
Jaridih, India 97/F4
Jarjīs, Tun. 67/F4
Järlåsa, Swe. 39/A1
Jarmen, Ger. 40/E5
Järna, Swe. 40/G2
Jarny, Fr. 55/E5
Jaro, Phil. 88/D3
Jarocin, Pol. 43/J3
Jarod, India 96/A4
Jaroměř, Czh. 43/H3
Jarosław, Pol. 43/M3
Jaroso, Co, US 152/B2
Jarratt, Va, US 163/J2
Jarrettsville, Md, US 168/B4
Jarrow, Eng, UK 35/G2
Jars (plain), Laos 94/C2
Jartai, China 78/F4
Jaru, Braz. 185/F3
Jarud Qi, China 80/E1
Järva-Jaani, Est. 41/L2
Järvakandi, Est. 41/L2
Järvelä, Fin. 39/F4
Järvenpää, Fin. 41/L1
Jarville-la-Malgrange, Fr. 55/F6
Jarvis (isl.), Pac., US 137/J5
Jarvisburg, NC, US 163/K2
Järvsö, Swe. 40/G1
Jás-Nagykun-Szonok (co.), Hun. 43/L5
Jasāna, India 98/C5
Jasenagykun-Seolnok (prov.), Hun. 50/E2
Jashpurnagar, India 97/E4
Jasidih, India 97/F3
Jasin, Malay. 89/C2
Jāsk, Iran 101/G3
Jasło, Pol. 43/L4
Jason (isl.), Mald. 191/E6
Jasonville, In, US 160/C5
Jasper, Ab, Can. 144/E1
Jasper, Al, US 162/D4
Jasper, Ar, US 153/H2
Jasper, Fl, US 165/G2
Jasper, Ga, US 162/E3
Jasper, In, US 162/D1
Jasper, Mn, US 155/F2
Jasper, Mo, US 153/G2
Jasper, Tn, US 162/E3
Jasper, Tx, US 151/H2
Jasper NP, Ab, Can. 144/E1
Jaspur, India 96/B1
Jastrebarsko, Cro. 50/B3
Jastrowie, Pol. 43/J2
Jastrzębie Zdroj, Pol. 43/K4
Jaswantnagar, India 96/B2
Jászapáti, Hun. 43/L5
Jászárokszállás, Hun. 50/D2
Jászberény, Hun. 43/K5
Jataí, Braz. 186/C3
Jatapu (riv.), Braz. 181/G5
Jatāra, India 96/B3
Jatate (riv.), Mex. 176/D2
Jāti, Pak. 101/J4
Jati, Braz. 183/G4
Jatibonico, Cuba 177/G1
Játiva, Sp. 47/E3
Jātni, India 95/E1
Jatoi Janūbi, Pak. 98/A5
Jaú (riv.), Braz. 181/F5
Jaú, Braz. 189/G2
Jaua Sarisarinama, PN, Ven. 181/E3
Jauaperi (riv.), Braz. 181/F5
Jauaperi (riv.), Braz. 181/E5
Jauaru (mts.), Braz. 181/H5
Jaubert (cape), Austl. 128/A4
Jaudy (riv.), Fr. 56/B3
Jauharābād, Pak. 98/B3
Jauja, Peru 184/C3
Jaumave, Mex. 175/F4
Jaun, Swi. 60/D4
Jaunay-Clan, Fr. 44/D3
Jaunjelgava, Lat. 41/L3
Jaunpass (pass), Swi. 60/D4

Jaunpi – Kailu

Jaunpiebalga, Lat. 41/M3
Jaunpils, Lat. 41/K3
Jaunpur, India 96/D3
Jauru (riv.), Braz. 186/A3
Jausiers, Fr. 64/C5
Java (isl.), Indo. 89/E4
Java (sea), Indo. 90/D5
Javari (riv.), Braz. 184/C2
Jávea, Sp. 47/F3
Javier (isl.), Chile 191/B5
Javier de Viana, Uru. 189/E4
Javorie (peak), Slvk. 50/D1
Javornice (riv.), Czh. 59/G2
Javorník (peak), Czh. 59/G4
Javorová Skála (peak), Czh. 59/H3
Javron-les-Chapelles, Fr. 57/E4
Jawāla Mukhi, India 98/D4
Jawhar, Som. 118/C5
Jawi, Indo. 90/C4
Jawor, Pol. 43/J3
Jay, Ok, US 153/G2
Jay, Me, US 161/L2
Jay, Fl, US 164/E2
Jayanca, Peru 184/B2
Jayapura, Indo. 91/K4
Jaynagar, India 97/G4
Jaynagar, India 97/F2
Jayton, Tx, US 152/D4
Jaywick, Eng, UK 37/H3
Jazīrat Būbiyan (isl.), Kuw. 103/G4
Jazīrat Maşirah (isl.), Oman 77/F5
Jazzīn, Leb. 105/D1
J.B. Thomas (lake), Tx, US 150/D1
Jbel Bani (mts.), Mor. 110/D3
Jean, Tx, US 153/E4
Jean Lafitte, La, US 164/C3
Jeanerette, La, US 164/C3
Jebba, Nga. 115/G4
Jeberos, Peru 184/B2
Jebjerg, Den. 40/C3
Jebus, Indo. 89/D3
Jed Water (riv.), Sc, UK 33/D6
Jedburgh, Sc, UK 33/D6
Jedlicze, Pol. 43/L4
Jędrzejów, Pol. 43/L3
Jeetze (riv.), Ger. 42/F2
Jeffers, Mn, US 155/G1
Jeffers, Mt, US 147/H1
Jefferson, Al, US 162/D4
Jefferson, Ga, US 163/F3
Jefferson, Oh, US 160/F4
Jefferson, Ia, US 155/G2
Jefferson (riv.), Mt, US 147/H1
Jefferson, NC, US 163/G2
Jefferson (mt.), Nv, US 146/E4
Jefferson, NY, US 161/J3
Jefferson, Or, US 146/B1
Jefferson (mt.), Or, US 146/C1
Jefferson, Tx, US 153/G4
Jefferson (co.), Wi, US 167/N14
Jefferson, Wi, US 155/K2
Jefferson, Va, US 163/J2
Jefferson City (cap.), Mo, US 153/H1
Jefferson City, Tn, US 163/F2
Jeffersonville, In, US 162/E1
Jeffersonville, Ky, US 162/F2
Jeffersonville, Ga, US 163/F4
Jeffrey, WV, US 163/G2
Jeffrey City, Wy, US 147/K2
Jeffrey's, Nf, Can. 159/H1
Jeffreys Bay, SAfr. 124/D4
Jega, Nga. 115/G3
Jegenstorf, Swi. 60/D3
Jeinemeni (peak), Chile 190/B5
Jejui Guazú (riv.), Par. 186/A5
Jēkabpils, Lat. 41/L3
Jekyll (isl.), Ga, US 165/H2
Jelcz-Laskowice, Pol. 43/J3
Jelence, Slvk. 50/D1
Jelenia Gora (prov.), Czh.,Ger. 43/E2
Jelenia Góra, Pol. 43/H3
Jelep (pass), China 92/E2
Jelgava, Lat. 41/K3
Jeli, Malay. 89/C1
Jelka, Slvk. 50/C1
Jellico, Tn, US 162/E2
Jellicoe, On, Can. 157/L3
Jelm, Wy, US 154/A3
Jelow Gīr, Iran 103/F3
Jeløya (isl.), Nor. 38/S9
Jelsi, It. 65/D4
Jema Shet' (riv.), Eth. 117/H3
Jemaa Sahim, Mor. 110/C2
Jemaja (isl.), Indo. 89/D2
Jemaluang, Malay. 89/C2
Jemappes, Belg. 54/C3
Jember, Indo. 89/F5
Jembiani, Tanz. 119/B3
Jemez (mts.), NM, US 149/J3
Jemez (riv.), NM, US 149/J3
Jemez Ind. Res., NM, US 149/J3
Jemez Pueblo, NM, US 149/J3
Jemez Springs, NM, US 149/J3
Jeminay, China 99/E2
Jemison, Al, US 162/D4
Jempang (lake), Indo. 91/E4
Jemsa, Egypt 109/G3
Jena, Ger. 42/F3
Jena, La, US 164/B2
Jenaz, Swi. 61/F4
Jenbach, Aus. 45/J3
Jendouba, Tun. 112/L6
Jendouba (gov.), Tun. 112/L6
Jeneponto, Indo. 91/E5
Jengen, Ger. 61/G2
Jenison, Mi, US 160/D3
Jenkins, Ky, US 163/F2
Jenkintown, Pa, US 168/C3
Jenks, Ok, US 153/G2
Jennersdorf, Aus. 50/C2
Jennings, La, US 164/B2
Jennings, Fl, US 165/G2
Jennings, Ks, US 154/D4
Jenny, Sur. 182/C1
Jenny Lind (isl.), Nun, Can. 140/F2
Jenolan Caves, Austl. 133/E1
Jens Muck (isl.), Nun, Can. 141/H2
Jensen, Ut, US 147/J3
Jensen Beach, Fl, US 165/H4
Jeppener, Arg. 191/J11
Jequetepeque, Peru 184/B2
Jequié, Braz. 187/E2
Jequitaí, Braz. 186/D3
Jequitinhonha (riv.), Braz. 179/E4
Jequitinhonha, Braz. 187/E3
Jerada, Mor. 112/C2
Jerantut, Malay. 89/C2
Jerdera, Indo. 128/D1
Jérémie, Haiti 177/H2
Jeremoabo, Braz. 187/F1
Jerer Shet' (riv.), Eth. 118/B3
Jerez de García Salinas, Mex. 174/E4
Jerez de la Frontera, Sp. 46/B4
Jerez de los Caballeros, Sp. 46/B3
Jericho, NY, US 169/L8
Jericho, Austl. 134/B3
Jericho (Arīḩā), WBnk. 105/C5
Jericó, Col. 183/K7
Jericó, Braz. 183/G4
Jerico Springs, Mo, US 153/G2
Jerilderie, Austl. 133/B2
Jerissa, Tun. 112/L7
Jermyn, Tx, US 153/E4
Jerome, Ar, US 153/J4
Jerome, Id, US 147/F2
Jerome, Az, US 149/F3
Jerramungup, Austl. 130/C5
Jersey (isl.), Chl, UK 44/B2
Jersey City, NJ, US 169/J9
Jersey City (res.), NJ, US 169/H8
Jersey Shore, Pa, US 168/A1
Jersey Village, Tx, US 151/M9
Jerseyville, Il, US 155/J4
Jerteh, Malay. 89/C1
Jerumenha, Braz. 183/F4
Jerusalem (dist.), Isr. 104/D4
Jerusalem, Ar, US 153/H3
Jerusalem (arpt.), WBnk. 105/C5
Jerusalem (Yerushalayim) (cap.), Isr. 105/C5
Jervis (inlet), BC, Can. 144/C2
Jervis Bay, Austl. 133/E2
Jerzu, It. 48/A3
Jesberg, Ger. 53/G6
Jesenice (res.), Czh. 59/F2
Jesenice, Slov. 45/L3
Jesi, It. 63/G6
Jessheim, Nor. 40/D1
Jessieville, Ar, US 153/H3
Jessore, Bang. 97/G4
Jessore (pol. reg.), Bang. 97/G4
Jessup (lake), Fl, US 165/H3
Jesuânia, Braz. 187/L6
Jesup, Ga, US 165/H2
Jesus (mt.), Ks, US 152/E2
Jésus (isl.), Qu, Can. 159/N6
Jesús, Par. 189/F3
Jesús Carranza, Mex. 176/C2
Jesús de Machaca, Bol. 188/B1
Jesús María, Col. 183/M7
Jesús María, Arg. 188/C4
Jesús Menéndez, Cuba 177/G1
Jet, Ok, US 153/E2
Jetmore, Ks, US 152/E1
Jetpur, India 101/K4
Jettingen-Scheppach, Ger. 58/D6
Jetzendorf, Ger. 59/E6
Jeu (riv.), Fr. 57/E6
Jeumont, Fr. 55/D3
Jevenstedt, Ger. 42/E1
Jever, Ger. 53/E1
Jevnaker, Nor. 40/D1
Jewar, India 96/A1
Jewel Cave Nat'l Mon., SD, US 154/C2
Jewell, Ks, US 154/E4
Jewell Junction, Ia, US 155/H2
Jewett, Tx, US 151/F2
Jezerce (peak), Alb. 50/D4
Jezerní Stěna (peak), Czh. 59/G4
Jeziorak (lake), Pol. 43/K2
Jhā Jhā, India 97/F3
Jhajjar, India 98/D5
Jhal Jhao, Pak. 101/J3
Jhālakāti, Bang. 97/H4
Jhālawār, India 92/C3
Jhalida, India 97/E4
Jhālū, India 96/B1
Jhang Sadar, Pak. 98/B4
Jhaniān Khatrian, Pak. 98/B3
Jhanjhārpur, India 97/F2
Jhānsi, India 96/B3
Jhāpa, Nepal 97/F2
Jhārgrām, India 97/F4
Jharia, India 97/F4
Jharkhand (state), India 92/D3
Jhārsuguda, India 97/E5
Jhawāriān, Pak. 98/B3
Jhelum, Pak. 98/B3
Jhelum (riv.), Pak. 98/B3
Jhelum (riv.), India 99/B5
Jhenida, Bang. 97/G4
Jhumra, Pak. 98/B4
Ji (riv.), China 78/D5
Ji Xian, China 80/C4
Ji Xian, China 80/H6
Ji-Paraná, Braz. 185/F3
Jia Xian, China 80/B3
Jiading, China 80/L8
Jiahe, China 93/K2
Jialing (riv.), China 77/K6
Jialu (riv.), China 78/G5
Jiamusi, China 79/L2
Ji'an, China 81/D2
Ji'an, China 87/G3
Jian (riv.), China 87/H3
Jianchang, China 81/C2
Jianchang, China 80/D2
Jiancheng, China 87/F4
Jiang (riv.), China 94/E1
Jiang Xian, China 80/B4
Jiang'an, China 93/J2
Jiangcheng Hanizu Yizu Zizhixian, China 86/D4
Jiangchuan, China 86/D3
Jiangdu, China 80/D4
Jianghua Yaozu Zizhixian, China 87/F3
Jiangjiadian, China 79/H3
Jiangjin, China 87/E2
Jiangjunhe, China 78/G5
Jiangjunshi, China 81/A3
Jiangjuntai, China 78/D3
Jiangkou, China 87/J2
Jiangkou, China 87/F2
Jiangkou, China 87/G3
Jiangkouzhen, China 87/F2
Jiangling, China 87/G2
Jiangmen, China 87/G4
Jiangmenchang, China 86/E2
Jiangning, China 80/D5
Jiangsu (prov.), China 79/H5
Jiangwan, China 87/G3
Jiangxi (prov.), China 80/C5
Jiangxiang, China 87/H1
Jiangya, China 87/F2
Jiangyin, China 80/E5
Jiangyong, China 87/F3
Jiangyou, China 86/E2
Jianhe, China 93/J2
Jianhu, China 80/D4
Jianli, China 87/G2
Jian'ou, China 87/H3
Jianping, China 79/H3
Jianshi, China 87/F2
Jianshui, China 86/D4
Jianyang, China 86/E2
Jianyang, China 87/H3
Jiaochangba, China 86/D1
Jiaocheng, China 80/C3
Jiaohe, China 79/K3
Jiaojiang, China 87/J2
Jiaokou, China 80/C3
Jiaolai (riv.), China 79/J3
Jiaonan, China 80/D4
Jiaotou, China 87/J2
Jiaozuo, China 80/C4
Jiapu, China 80/K8
Jiashan, China 80/D4
Jiashan, China 80/L9
Jiashi, China 99/C4
Jiaxiang, China 80/D4
Jiaxing, China 80/L9
Jiaya, China 87/F3
Jiayin, China 79/L2
Jiayou, China 87/E3
Jiayu, China 87/G2
Jiayuguan, China 78/D4
Jiazi, China 87/H4
Jibāl An Nūbah (mts.), Sudan 117/F3
Jibāl Múāb (mts.), Jor. 105/D5
Jibiya, Nga. 115/G3
Jibóia, Braz. 180/D4
Jibou, Rom. 51/F2
Jicarilla Apache Ind. Res., NM, US 149/J2
Jicarón (isl.), Pan. 177/F5
Jičín, Czh. 43/H3
Jidali (riv.), Som. 118/C3
Jiddah, SAr. 100/C4
Jidong, China 79/L2
Jiehualong, China 87/G3
Jieshi, China 87/G4
Jieshipu, China 78/F4
Jieshou, China 80/C4
Jiexiu, China 80/B3
Jieyang, China 87/H4
Jieznas, Lith. 41/L4
Jifnā, WBnk. 105/C5
Jiga, Eth. 117/H3
Jigalong Abor. Land, Austl. 130/D2
Jigawa (prov.), Nga. 115/H4
Jigger, La, US 164/C1
Jiggs, Nv, US 146/F3
Jiguaní, Cuba 177/G1
Jiguanshan, China 81/C1
Jigzhi, China 78/E5
Jihlava, Czh. 43/H4
Jihlava (riv.), Czh. 45/L2
Jihlavský (pol. reg.), Czh. 43/H4
Jiiqley, Som. 118/C4
Jijel (wilaya), Alg. 112/H4
Jijel, Alg. 112/H4
Jijia (riv.), Rom. 70/C3
Jijiga, Eth. 118/B3
Jijona, Sp. 47/E3
Jikawo, Eth. 117/G3
Jilhava (riv.), Czh. 43/H4
Jili (lake), China 78/B2
Jilib, Som. 119/C1
Jilin (prov.), China 79/K3
Jilin, China 79/K3
Jiliu (riv.), China 79/J1
Jiloca (riv.), Sp. 46/E2
Jilotepec, Mex. 175/K7
Jílové u Prahy, Czh. 59/H3
Jim Thorpe, Pa, US 168/C2
Jim Woodruff (dam), Fl, US 165/F2
Jīma, Eth. 117/H4
Jimaní, DRep. 177/J2
Jimbe, Ang. 121/E5
Jimbolia, Rom. 50/E3
Jimboomba, Austl. 134/D4
Jimei, China 87/H3
Jimena de la Frontera, Sp. 46/C4
Jiménez, Mex. 150/D3
Jiménez, Mex. 174/D3
Jimingsi, China 87/F2
Jimmēza, Sudan 117/G1
Jimmy Carter Nat'l Hist. Site, Ga, US 165/F1
Jimo, China 80/E3
Jimokuji, Japan 83/L5
Jimsar, China 99/E3
Jin (riv.), China 93/K2
Jin Xian, China 81/A3
Jin Xian, China 80/C3
Jinan, China 80/D3
Jin'an, China 87/H2
Jinchang, China 78/E4
Jincheng, China 81/A2
Jincheng, China 80/C4
Jinchuan, China 86/D2
Jinchuan, China 79/K3
Jinci Temple, China 80/C3
Jīnd, India 98/D5
Jindabyne (lake), Austl. 133/D3
Jindabyne (dam), Austl. 133/D3
Jindabyne, Austl. 133/D3
Jindalee, Austl. 133/D2
Jindřichuv Hradec, Czh. 43/H4
Jinfosi, China 78/D4
Jing (riv.), China 78/F5
Jing Xian, China 87/H2
Jing Xian, China 87/F3
Jingbian, China 80/B3
Jingde, China 87/H2
Jingdezhen, China 87/H2
Jingdong, China 93/H3
Jingellic, Austl. 133/C2
Jinggangshan, China 87/G3
Jinggu, China 86/D4
Jinghai, China 87/H4
Jinghai, China 80/H7
Jinghaiwei, China 81/B4
Jinghe, China 99/D3
Jinghong, China 86/D4
Jingjiang, China 80/E4
Jingle, China 80/B3
Jingmen, China 80/C5
Jingning, China 78/F4
Jingping (mts.), China 86/D3
Jingshan, China 80/C5
Jingtai, China 78/E4
Jingxi, China 87/E4
Jingyou, China 78/G4
Jingyu, China 79/K3
Jingyuan, China 78/E4
Jinhu, China 80/D4
Jinhua, China 87/H2
Jining, China 80/D4
Jining, China 80/C2
Jinja, Ugan. 119/A1
Jinjie, China 87/E4
Jinka, Eth. 117/H4
Jinkouhe, China 93/H2
Jinlansi, China 87/G3
Jinmen (isl.), Tai. 87/H3
Jinotega, Nic. 176/E3
Jinotepe, Nic. 176/E4
Jinping, China 86/D4
Jinping, China 87/F3
Jinqian (riv.), China 78/F5
Jinsha (riv.), China 77/J7
Jinsha, China 93/J2
Jinsha, China 87/H2
Jinshan, China 80/L9
Jinshanwei, China 80/L9
Jinshi, China 87/F2
Jinshui, China 78/F5
Jintan, China 80/D5
Jintang, China 87/G2
Jintotolo (chan.), Phil. 88/C3
Jintūr, India 95/C2
Jinxi, China 87/H3
Jinxi, China 80/E2
Jinxiang, China 80/D4
Jinxiu Yaozu Zizhixian, China 93/K3
Jinyun, China 87/J2
Jinzhai, China 80/C5
Jinzhou (bay), China 81/A3
Jinzhou, China 80/E2
Jiparana (riv.), Braz. 185/F3
Jipijapa, Ecu. 180/A5
Jiquilpan de Juárez, Mex. 174/E5
Jiquipilco, Mex. 175/Q9
Jīrēn, Eth. 117/H4
Jirgā, Egypt 109/F3
Jirin Gol, China 79/H3
Jiřkov, Czh. 59/G1
Jīroft, Iran 101/G3
Jīsh, Isr. 105/C2
Jishan, China 80/B4
Jishou, China 87/F2
Jisr ash Shughūr, Syria 104/E2
Jitan, China 87/G3
Jitra, Malay. 89/C1
Jiu (riv.), Rom. 70/B3
Jiucheng, China 87/E2
Jiudongshan, China 87/H4
Jiufeng, China 87/H3
Jiugong (mtn.), China 87/G2
Jiuhua (mtn.), China 87/H2
Jiujiang, China 87/G2
Jiulianshan, China 87/G3
Jiuling (mts.), China 87/G2
Jiulong, China 86/D2
Jiun (riv.), China 87/F4
Jiurongcheng, China 81/B4
Jiutai, China 79/K3
Jiutang, China 87/F4
Jiutepec, Mex. 175/K8
Jiuwan (mts.), China 87/E3
Jiuxincheng, China 80/G7
Jiuyongshou, China 78/F5
Jiuyuhang, China 80/K9
Jiuzhan, China 79/K1
Jīwani, Pak. 101/H3
Jixi, China 79/L2
Jixi, China 87/H2
Jixian, China 79/L2
Jiyang, China 80/D3
Jiyuan, China 80/C4
Jiz` (wadi), Yem. 100/F5
Jīzān, SAr. 100/D5
Jizayy, Egypt 113/B4
Jize, China 80/C3
Jizera (riv.), Czh. 43/H3
Jizl (wadi), SAr. 100/C3
Jizō-zaki (pt.), Japan 84/C3
Jizzakh, Uzb. 74/G5
Jmijin (riv.), SKor. 81/F6
Joaçaba, Braz. 189/G3
Joachín, Mex. 175/N8
Joaíma, Braz. 187/E3
Joal, Sen. 114/A3
Joana Peres, Braz. 182/D3
Joanna, SC, US 163/G3
João Câmara, Braz. 183/H4
João Lisboa, Braz. 183/E4
João Monlevade, Braz. 187/E3
João Pessoa, Braz. 183/H4
João Pinheiro, Braz. 186/D3
Joaquim Távora, Braz. 189/G2
Joaquin, Tx, US 151/G2
Joaquín V. González, Arg. 188/C3
Jobabo, Cuba 177/G1
Jocassee (dam), SC, US 163/F3
Jockgrim, Ger. 58/B4
Jocón, Hon. 176/E3
Jódar, Sp. 46/D4
Jodhpur, India 92/B2
Jodoigne, Belg. 55/D2
Joe, Mt, US 156/B4
Joe Pool (lake), Tx, US 150/L7
Joensuu, Fin. 68/F3
Jōetsu, Japan 85/F2
Jogbani, India 97/F2
Jōgeva, Est. 41/M2
Joggins, NS, Can. 158/E3
Joghdān, Iran 101/G3
Jogighpa, India 97/H2
Johannesberg, Ger. 58/C2
Johannesburg, Ca, US 148/D3
Johannesburg, SAfr. 124/E2
Johannesburg (Jan Smuts) (int'l arpt.), SAfr. 124/E2
Johanngeorgenstadt, Ger. 59/F2
Johilla (riv.), India 96/C4
John Day (riv.), Or, US 142/B2
John Day, Or, US 146/D1
John Day (dam), Or, US 144/D5
John Day Fossil Beds Nat'l Mon., Or, US 146/C1
John Day Fossil Beds Nat'l Mon., Or, US 146/D1
John Day,North Fork (riv.), Or, US 146/D1
John F. Kennedy (int'l arpt.), NY, US 169/K9
John Forrest NP, Austl. 130/L6
John H. Kerr (dam), Va, US 163/H2
John Martin (res.), Co, US 154/C4
John O'Groats, Sc, UK 31/S7
John Wayne/Orange County (int'l arpt.), Ca, US 166/G8
Johnshaven, Sc, UK 33/D3
Johnson (mtn.), Wy, US 154/B2
Johnson (co.), Tx, US 150/K7
Johnson (cr.), NY, US 160/V9
Johnson (Johnson City), Ks, US 152/D2
Johnson City, NY, US 161/J3
Johnson City, Tn, US 163/F2
Johnson City, Tx, US 150/E2
Johnson Draw (riv.), Tx, US 150/D2
Johnson Lake Nat'l Wild. Ref., ND, US 156/E4
Johnsonburg, NJ, US 168/D2
Johnsonburg, Pa, US 161/G4
Johnsons Crossing, Yk, Can. 171/M3
Johnsonville (nbrhd.), NZ 135/H9
Johnsonville, SC, US 163/H4
Johnston (falls), Zam. 121/G5
Johnston, Ia, US 155/H3
Johnston, Wal, UK 36/B3
Johnston (lake), Austl. 127/B4
Johnston, SC, US 163/G4
Johnston Atoll (isl.), Pac., US 137/J3
Johnston City, Il, US 162/C2
Johnstone, Sc, UK 33/B5
Johnstown, Ire. 32/C4
Johnstown, Oh, US 160/E4
Johnstown, NY, US 161/J3
Johnstown, On, Can. 161/J2
Johnstown, Pa, US 161/G4
Johnsville, Md, US 168/A4
Johor (state), Malay. 89/C2
Johor (river), Malay. 89/C2
Johor (str.), Malay.,Sing. 89/J6
Johor Baharu, Malay. 89/J6
Jöhstadt, Ger. 59/G1
Joigny, Fr. 44/E3
Joiner, Ar, US 162/B3
Joinvile, Braz. 189/G3
Joinville, Fr. 60/B1
Joinville (isl.), Ant. 192/W
Jojutla, Mex. 175/K8
Jokau, Sudan 117/G3
Jokela, Fin. 39/E4
Jokioinen, Fin. 41/K1
Jokkmokk, Swe. 38/F2
Jökulsargljufur NP, Ice. 38/P6
Jolanda di Savoia, It. 63/E4
Jolfā, Iran 103/F2
Jolgeh-ye Khūzestan (plain), Iran 103/G4
Joliet, Il, US 160/B4
Joliet, Mt, US 147/J1
Joliet Army Ammo. Plant, Il, US 160/B4
Joliette, Qu, Can. 161/K1
Jollyville, Tx, US 151/F2
Jolo (isl.), Phil. 91/F2
Jolo, Phil. 88/C4
Jomala, Fin. 41/H1
Jomalig (isl.), Phil. 88/C2
Jombang, Indo. 89/F4
Jombo (riv.), Ang. 120/D5
Jomda, China 86/C2
Jomo Kenyatta (int'l arpt.), Kenya 119/B2
Jomsom, Nepal 96/D1
Jomu, Tanz. 119/A2
Jona, Swi. 61/E3
Jonacatepec, Mex. 175/L8
Jonava, Lith. 41/L4
Jonchery-sur-Vesle, Fr. 54/C5
Jones, La, US 153/J4
Jones (inlet), NY, US 169/L9
Jones (sound), Can. 139/J2
Jones, Al, US 162/D4
Jones (mtn.), Pa, US 168/A2
Jones Beach State Park, NY, US 169/L9
Jonesboro, La, US 153/H4
Jonesboro, In, US 160/D4
Jonesboro, Il, US 162/C2
Jonesboro, Ar, US 162/B3
Jonesboro, Ga, US 163/M7
Jonesborough, NI, UK 34/B3
Jonesborough, Tn, US 163/F2
Jonestown, Ms, US 162/B3
Jonesville, La, US 164/C2
Jonesville, Va, US 163/F2
Jonesville, NC, US 163/G2
Jonglei, Sudan 117/F4
Joniškelis, Lith. 41/L3
Joniškis, Lith. 41/K3
Jönköping (co.), Swe. 38/E4
Jönköping, Swe. 40/F3
Jonquière, Qu, Can. 158/B1
Jonquières, Fr. 64/A4
Jonuta, Mex. 172/C4
Joondalup (lake), Austl. 130/K6
Joplin, Mo, US 153/G2
Joplin, Mt, US 145/J3
Joppa, Il, US 162/C2
Joppa (Joppatowne), Md, US 168/B5
Joppatowne (Joppa), Md, US 168/B5
Jora, India 96/A2
Jordan (ctry.) 104/D4
Jordan, On, Can. 160/U9
Jordan (riv.), Isr.,Jor. 105/D4
Jordan (lake), Al, US 162/D4
Jordan, Mt, US 145/L4
Jordan (riv.), Or, US 147/E2
Jordan (cr.), Pa, US 168/C2
Jordan Station, On, Can. 160/U9
Jordan Valley, Or, US 146/E2
Jordbro, Swe. 39/B1
Jorge (cape), Chile 191/B6
Jorge Chavez (int'l arpt.), Peru 184/B4
Jorge Newbury (Buenos Aires) (int'l arpt.), Arg. 191/J11
Jorhāt, India 86/B3
Joriāpāni, Nepal 96/C1
Jork, Ger. 53/G1
Jornada del Muerto (val.), NM, US 152/A4
Jørpeland, Nor. 40/B2
Jos, Nga. 115/H4
Jos (plat.), Nga. 115/H4
Jose Abad Santos, Phil. 88/D4
José Agustín Palacios, Bol. 185/E4
José Batlle y Ordóñez, Uru. 191/G2
José Bonifácio, Braz. 189/G2
José Cardel, Mex. 175/N7
José de Freitas, Braz. 183/F4
José Enrique Rodó, Uru. 191/K10
José María Córdova (int'l arpt.), Col. 183/K6
José María Morelos, Mex. 176/D2
Jose Marti (int'l arpt.), Cuba 177/F1
Jose Panganiban, Phil. 88/C2
José Pedro Varela, Uru. 191/G2
José, South (dept.), Uru. 191/F2
Josefa Camejo (int'l arpt.), Ven. 180/D2
Joseph, Or, US 146/E1
Joseph, Ut, US 149/F1
Joseph Bonaparte (gulf), Austl. 127/B2
Joseph City, Az, US 149/G3
Josephine, Tx, US 150/L6
Joshin-Etsu Kogen NP, Japan 85/F2
Joshipur, India 97/F5
Joshua, Tx, US 150/K7
Joshua (pt.), Ct, US 169/F1
Joshua Tree, Ca, US 148/D3
Joshua Tree NP, Ca, US 148/D4
Jossa (riv.), Ger. 58/C2
Josselin, Fr. 56/C5
Jotunheimen NP, Nor. 40/C1
Jouanne (riv.), Fr. 44/C2
Jouarre, Fr. 30/M5
Joué-lès-Tours, Fr. 57/F6
Joué-sur-Erdre, Fr. 56/D6
Jœuf, Fr. 55/F5
Jouques, Fr. 64/B5
Jourama Falls NP, Austl. 134/B2
Jourdanton, Tx, US 150/E3
Joure, Neth. 52/C3
Joutseno, Fin. 41/N1
Joutsijärvi, Fin. 68/E2
Joux (lake), Swi. 60/C4
Jouy, Fr. 57/G3
Jouy-en-Josas, Fr. 30/J5
Jouy-le-Châtel, Fr. 30/M6
Jouy-le-Moutier, Fr. 30/J4
Jouy-sur-Morin, Fr. 54/C6
Jovellanos, Cuba 177/F1
Jovet (peak), Fr. 64/C2
Joveyn (riv.), Iran 101/G1
Jow Khvāh, Iran 103/J3
Jowai, India 93/F2
Jowsheqān-e Qālī, Iran 103/G3
Joy (mt.), Yk, Can. 171/M3
Joyce, La, US 164/B2
Joyce's Country (dist.), Ire. 32/A2
Jōyō, Japan 83/J6
Jozankei Spa, Japan 82/B2
Ju (riv.), China 78/G5
Ju Xian, China 80/D4
Juan Aldama, Mex. 174/E3
Juan Bautista Alberdi, Arg. 188/C3
Juan de Fuca (str.), BC, Can.,US 140/D4
Juan de Nova (isl.), Fr. 107/G6
Juan Fernández (isls.), Chile 179/A6
Juan Fernández, Arg. 190/F3
Juan Jackson, Uru. 191/K10
Juan José Paso, Arg. 190/E2
Juan L. Lacaze, Uru. 191/K11
Juan Santamaria (int'l arpt.), CR 177/E4
Juancheng, China 80/C4
Juancho Yrausquin (int'l arpt.), Neth. 173/N8
Juanda (int'l arpt.), Indo. 89/F4
Juangriego, Ven. 181/F2
Juanjuí, Peru 184/B2
Juárez, Arg. 190/F3
Juárez, Mex. 150/D4
Juarez (arpt.), Mex. 175/Q10
Juaso, Gha. 115/E5
Juazeirinho, Braz. 183/G4
Juazeiro, Braz. 183/F5
Juazeiro do Norte, Braz. 183/G4
Juazohn, Libr. 114/C5
Juba, Sudan 117/F4
Jubany, Arg., Ant. 192/W
Jubbah, SAr. 102/E4
Jübek, Ger. 42/E1
Jubones (riv.), Ecu. 184/B1
Juby (cape), Mor. 110/B4
Júcar (riv.), Sp. 66/C3
Juçara, Braz. 186/C2
Jucás, Braz. 183/G4
Jüchen, Ger. 55/F1
Juchipila, Mex. 174/E4
Juchique de Ferrer, Mex. 175/N7
Juchitán de Zaragoza, Mex. 176/C2
Juchitepec, Mex. 175/R10
Jucurutu, Braz. 183/G4
Jud, ND, US 156/E4
Judaberg, Nor. 40/A2
Judenburg, Aus. 45/L3
Judian, China 86/C3
Judith (mts.), Mt, US 145/K4
Judith Gap, Mt, US 145/K4
Judson, ND, US 156/D4
Judsonia, Ar, US 153/J3
Juelsminde, Den. 40/D4
Jufrah (wadi), Egypt 113/C4
Jugon-les-Lacs, Fr. 56/C4
Juḩā, SAr. 118/B1
Juhaynah, Egypt 109/F3
Juicai (mtn.), China 87/F3
Juigalpa, Nic. 176/E3
Juilly, Fr. 30/L4
Juine (riv.), Fr. 44/E2
Juishui, Tai. 87/J4
Juist, Ger. 52/E1
Juist (arpt.), Ger. 52/E1
Juist (isl.), Ger. 52/D1
Juiz de Fora, Braz. 187/N6
Juizhen, China 87/H3
Jujurieux, Fr. 60/B5
Jujuy (prov.), Arg. 188/C2
Julbach, Ger. 59/F6
Julesburg, Co, US 154/C3
Juli, Peru 184/D5
Julia Creek, Austl. 134/A3
Juliaca, Peru 184/D4
Juliaetta, Id, US 144/F4
Julian, Ca, US 148/D4
Julian Alps (mts.), It. 45/K3
Juliana (lake), Fl, US 164/M7
Juliana Top (peak), Sur. 182/B2
Jülich, Ger. 55/F2
Juliff, Tx, US 151/M9
Julimes, Mex. 150/B3
Julio A. Mella, Cuba 177/H1
Júlio de Castilhos, Braz. 189/F4
Juliustown, NJ, US 168/D3
Jullouville, Fr. 56/D3
Jullundur, India 98/C4
Julu, China 80/C3
Juma (riv.), China 78/H4
Jumanggoin, China 86/C1
Jumbilla, Peru 184/B2
Jumbo, Zim. 123/F3
Jumeauville, Fr. 30/H5
Jumièges, Fr. 57/F2
Jumilla, Sp. 46/E3
Jūmīn (wadi), Tun. 112/L6
Juminda (pt.), Est. 41/L2
Jumla, Nepal 96/D1
Jümme (riv.), Ger. 53/E2
Jūmonji, Japan 82/B4
Jump (riv.), Wi, US 155/J1
Jumpertown, Ms, US 162/C3
Jūn, Leb. 105/C1
Junāgadh, India 101/K4
Jūnāgarh, India 95/D2
Junan, China 80/D4
Juncal (peak), Chile 190/N8
Junction (mtn.), Mt, US 145/H4
Junction, Tx, US 150/E2
Junction, Ut, US 149/F1
Junction City, Ar, US 153/H4
Junction City, Ks, US 153/F1
Junction City, Ky, US 162/E2
Junction City, La, US 150/H1
Junction City, Mo, US 162/B2
Junction City, Or, US 146/B1
Junction City, Wi, US 155/K1
Jundah, Austl. 134/A4
Jundiaí, Braz. 187/K8
Jundu (mts.), China 80/H6
June Lake, Ca, US 148/C2
Juneau, Wi, US 155/K2
Juneau (cap.), Ak, US 171/M4
Juneda, Sp. 47/F2
Junee, Austl. 133/C2
Jungar Qi, China 80/B3
Jungfrau (peak), Swi. 60/D4
Jungfraujoch, Swi. 60/D4
Jungkat, Indo. 90/C3
Junglinster, Lux. 55/F4
Juniata (riv.), Pa, US 161/H4
Juniata, Ne, US 154/E3
Juniata (co.), Pa, US 168/A2
Junik, Serb. 50/E4
Junín, Arg. 190/E2
Junín, Arg. 190/C2
Junín, Col. 180/B4
Junín, Ecu. 180/A5
Junín, Peru 184/B3
Junín (dept.), Peru 184/C3
Junín de los Andes, Arg. 190/C3
Junior, WV, US 163/H1
Juniper, NB, Can. 158/D2
Juniper (mtn.), Co, US 147/J3
Juniper, Ga, US 162/E4
Juniper Hills, Ca, US 166/C2
Junipero Serra (peak), Ca, US 148/B2
Jūniyah, Leb. 104/D3
Junji (pass), China 80/C3
Junkou, China 87/H3
Junlian, China 86/E2
Juno, Ga, US 162/E3
Juno, Tx, US 150/D2
Juno Beach, Fr. 57/E2
Juno Beach, Fl, US 165/H4
Junpu, China 87/H2
Junsele, Swe. 38/F3
Juntas, Chile 188/B4
Ju'nyunggoin, China 78/D5
Juodupė, Lith. 41/L3
Juparanã (lake), Braz. 187/E3
Jupiá (res.), Braz. 186/C4
Jupiter, Fl, US 165/H4
Jupiter (riv.), Qu, Can. 158/F1
Jupiter (mt.), Wa, US 167/A2
Juquiá, Braz. 189/H3
Juquitiba, Braz. 187/J8
Jur (riv.), Sudan 117/F3
Jur pri Bratislave, Slvk. 50/C1
Jura (dept.), Fr. 60/B4
Jura (canton), Swi. 60/D3
Jura (isl.), Sc, UK 31/Q9
Jura (pen.), Sc, UK 31/R8
Jura (mts.), Fr. 66/E1
Juradó, Col. 180/B3
Jurançon, Fr. 44/C5
Jurbarkas, Lith. 41/K4
Jurbise, Belg. 54/C2
Jurien, Austl. 130/B4
Jūrmala, Lat. 41/K3
Jurong (nbrhd.), Sing. 89/H6
Juruá (riv.), Braz. 179/C3
Juruena (riv.), Braz. 179/D4
Juruena, Res. Florestal do, Braz. 185/G3
Juruti, Braz. 182/B3
Jushi, China 87/F4
Jushiyama, Japan 83/L5
Jushui, China 87/H3
Juskatla, BC, Can. 171/M5
Jussey, Fr. 60/B2
Jussy, Swi. 60/C5
Jussy, Fr. 54/C4
Justice, WV, US 163/G2
Justiceburg, Tx, US 152/D4
Justin, Tx, US 150/K6
Justo Daract, Arg. 190/D2
Jutaí (riv.), Braz. 181/E5
Jutaí, Braz. 184/D2
Jutiapa, Guat. 176/D3
Juticalpa, Hon. 176/E3
Jutland (pen.), Den. 38/D4
Jutland, NJ, US 168/D2
Juventud, Isla de la (Isla de Pinos) (isl.), Cuba 172/E3
Juye, China 80/D4
Jūyom, Iran 103/H4
Juzhang (riv.), China 80/C5
Juziers, Fr. 30/H4
Južna Morava (riv.), Serb. 50/E4
Juzur Qarqannah (isl.), Congo 111/H2
Jwaneng, Bots. 122/E5
Jwayyā, Leb. 105/C2
Jyderup, Den. 40/D4
Jylisjärvi (lake), Fin. 39/E3
Jyllinge, Den. 39/J7

K

K'ok'a (lake), Eth. 118/A3
K2 (Godwin Austen) (peak), Pak. 98/D2
Ka (isl.), NKor. 81/C3
Ka Lae (cape), Hi, US 142/U11
Kaabong, Ugan. 117/G5
Kaakhka, Trkm. 101/G1
Kaap Plato (plat.), SAfr. 124/C3
Kaapmuiden, SAfr. 123/F5
Kaarina, Fin. 41/K1
Kaarst, Ger. 52/D6
Kaartjärvi (lake), Fin. 39/E4
Kaba, Gui. 114/C4
Kaba, Hun. 50/E2
Kaba, Indo. 129/E1
Kaba (riv.), China 99/E2
Kabadak (riv.), Bang. 97/G4
Kabaena (isl.), Indo. 91/F5
Kabah (ruin), Mex. 176/D1
Kabala, SLeo. 114/C4
Kabale, Ugan. 121/G3
Kabalega (falls), Ugan. 121/G2
Kabalega NP, Ugan. 121/G2
Kabalo, D.R. Congo 121/F4
Kabamba (lake), D.R. Congo 121/F5
Kabambare, D.R. Congo 121/F4
Kabango, D.R. Congo 121/F4
Kabanjahe, Indo. 89/B2
Kabankalan, Phil. 88/C3
Kabardinka, Rus. 73/J5
Kabardino-Balkariya, Resp., Rus. 75/Q6
Kabare, D.R. Congo 121/G3
Kābāw, Libya 108/A2
Kabba, Nga. 115/G5
Kabeke, D.R. Congo 121/G4
Kabelekese, D.R. Congo 121/E4
Kaberamaido, Ugan. 119/A1
Kabeta, D.R. Congo 121/F3
Kabetawa, Niger 116/B2
Kabetogama (lake), Mn, US 157/H3
Kabeya Maji, D.R. Congo 121/F4
Kabī, Eth. 118/A3
Kabin Buri, Thai. 94/C3
Kabinda, D.R. Congo 121/F4
Kabīr Kūh (mts.), Iran 103/F3
Kabîr, Oued el (riv.), Alg. 112/H4
Kabīrwāla, Pak. 98/A4
Kabkābīyah, Sudan 116/E2
Kableshkovo, Bul. 51/H4
Kabo, CAfr. 116/C4
Kabobo, D.R. Congo 121/G4
Kābol (Kābul) (cap.), Afg. 101/J2
Kabolaa, Indo. 91/H4
Kabompo, Zam. 122/E2
Kabompo (riv.), Zam. 122/D2
Kabong, Malay. 90/D3
Kabongo, D.R. Congo 121/F4
Kabrai, India 96/C3
Kābul (riv.), Afg. 101/J2
Kābul (Kābol) (cap.), Afg. 101/J2
Kabunda, D.R. Congo 123/F2
Kaburuang (isl.), Indo. 91/G3
Kabūshīyah, Sudan 117/G1
Kabwe, Zam. 123/F2
Kačanik, Serb. 49/G1
Kačėrgine, Lith. 41/K4
Kachalola, Zam. 123/F2
Kachemak, Ak, US 171/H4
Kachemak (bay), Ak, US 171/H4
Kachia, Nga. 115/G4
Kachikau, Bots. 122/E3
Kachin (state), Myan. 93/G2
Kachiry, Kaz. 99/C1
Kachug, Rus. 78/F1
Kaçkar Daği (peak), Turk. 71/G4
Kada, Myan. 94/B2
Kadam (peak), Ugan. 119/A1
Kadam (isl.), Myan. 93/G5
Kadăn, Czh. 59/G2
Kadan (isl.), Myan. 94/B3
Kadavu (isl.), Fiji 136/G6
Kadaya, Rus. 79/H1
Kadéï (riv.), CAfr. 116/B4
Kadesa, Indo. 91/F5
Kadiana, Mali 114/D4
Kadiköy (nbrhd.), Turk. 103/N7
Kadina, Austl. 131/H5
Kadınhanı, Turk. 102/C2
Kadiogo (prov.), Burk. 115/E3
Kadiolo, Mali 114/D4
Kadirli, Turk. 102/D2
Kadışehri, Turk. 102/C1
Kadoka, SD, US 154/D2
Kadoma, Zim. 123/F3
Kadoma, Japan 83/J6
Kadônkani, Myan. 93/G4
Kadoshkino, Rus. 71/H1
Kadrina, Est. 41/M2
Kaduna (state), Nga. 115/G4
Kaduna, Nga. 115/G4
Kaduna (riv.), Nga. 107/C4
Kāduqli, Sudan 117/F3
Kadzharan, Arm. 71/H5
Kadzherom, Rus. 69/M2
Kaech'ŏn, NKor. 81/C3
Kaédi, Mrta. 114/B2
Kaehwa-ri, NKor. 81/D2
Kaélé, Camr. 116/B3
Kaeng Khro, Thai. 94/C2
Kaeng Krachan NP, Thai. 94/B3
Kaep'ung, NKor. 81/D4
Kaesŏng, NKor. 81/D3
Kaesŏng-si (prov.), NKor. 81/D4
Kafakumba, D.R. Congo 121/E5
Kafanchan, Nga. 115/H4
Kafar Jar Ghar (mts.), Afg. 101/J2
Kaffraria (reg.), SAfr. 124/D4
Kaffrine, Sen. 114/B3
Kafia Kingi, Sudan 116/E3
Kafirévs (cape), Gre. 49/J3
Kafr ad Dawwār, Egypt 113/B2
Kafr al 'Ā'id, Egypt 113/C4
Kafr al Baţţīkh, Egypt 113/C2
Kafr al Jarā'idah, Egypt 113/C2
Kafr al Kurdī, Egypt 113/C2
Kafr Ash Shaykh (gov.), Egypt 109/F1
Kafr ash Shaykh, Egypt 113/B2
Kafr az Zayyāt, Egypt 113/B3
Kafr Kannā, Isr. 105/C3
Kafr Mandā, Isr. 105/C3
Kafr Qari', Isr. 105/C3
Kafr Qāsim, Isr. 105/B4
Kafr Rabī', Egypt 113/B3
Kafr Sa'd, Egypt 113/C2
Kafr Salīm, Egypt 113/B2
Kafr Şaqr, Egypt 113/C3
Kafr Shukr, Egypt 113/C3
Kafr Yāsīf, Isr. 105/C3
Kafu (riv.), Ugan. 121/G2
Kafubu (riv.), D.R. Congo 123/E1
Kafue (dam), Zam. 123/F2
Kafue, Zam. 123/F2
Kafue (riv.), Zam. 122/E2
Kafue Flats (swamp), Zam. 123/E2
Kafue Gorge (res.), Zam. 123/E2
Kafue NP, Zam. 122/E2
Kafukule, Malw. 123/G1
Kafulwe, Zam. 121/G5
Kaga, Japan 84/E2
Kaga Bandoro, CAfr. 116/C4
Kagan, Uzb. 74/G6
Kāgān (valley), Pak. 98/B2
Kagang, China 78/E4
Kagawa (pref.), Japan 84/D3
Kagera (riv.), Tanz. 121/G3
Kågeröd, Swe. 39/K7
Kağıthane, Turk. 103/M6
Kâğithane (riv.), Turk. 103/M6
Kağızman, Turk. 103/E1
Kagmar, Sudan 117/F2
Kagoshima (int'l arpt.), Japan 84/B5
Kagoshima (bay), Japan 84/B5
Kagoshima, Japan 84/B5
Kagoshima (dept.), Japan 85/L5
Kagua, PNG 129/F1
K'aha, Eth. 118/B3
Kahama, Tanz. 121/H3
Kaharlyk, Ukr. 72/F3
Kahayan (riv.), Indo. 90/D4
Kahe, Tanz. 119/B2
Kahemba, D.R. Congo 120/D4
Kahindi, Tanz. 119/B4
Kahl am Main, Ger. 58/C2
Kahmsara (riv.), Rus. 78/D1
Kāhna, Pak. 98/C4
Kahnple, Libr. 114/C5
Kahnūj, Iran 101/G3
Kahnwia, Libr. 114/C5
Kahoka, Mo, US 155/J3
Kahoolawe (isl.), Hi, US 142/T10
Kahperusvaara (peak), Fin. 38/G1
Kahramanmaraş, Turk. 102/D2
Kahramanmaraş (prov.), Turk. 102/D2
Kahror Pakka, Pak. 98/A5
Kâhta, Turk. 102/D2
Kahuku (pt.), Hi, US 142/T10
Kahului, Hi, US 142/T10
Kahuzi-Biega, PN de, D.R. Congo 121/F3
Kai (isls.), Indo. 91/H5
Kai Besar (isl.), Indo. 91/H5
Kai Kecil (isl.), Indo. 91/H5
Kai Mbaku, D.R. Congo 120/C4
Kaiama, Nga. 115/F4
Kaiapit, PNG 129/G1
Kaiapoi, NZ 135/C3
Kaibab (plat.), Az, US 149/F2
Kaibab Ind. Res., Az, US 149/F2
Kaibara, Japan 83/H5
Kaibito, Az, US 149/G2
Kaibito (plat.), Az, US 149/G2
Kaidu (riv.), China 99/D3
Kaieteur (falls), Guy. 181/G3
Kaieteur NP, Guy. 181/G3
Kaifeng, China 80/C4
Kāigaon, Nepal 96/D1
Kaijiang, China 87/E2
Kaikalūr, India 95/D2
Kaikoura, NZ 135/C3
Kailahun, SLeo. 114/C4
Kaili, China 87/E3
Kailu, China 80/E2

Kailua, Hi, US 142/T11
Kaimar, China 78/D5
Kaimganj, India 96/B2
Kaimur (range), India 96/C3
Käina, Est. 41/K2
Kainab (riv.), Namb. 124/B2
Kainach (riv.), Aus. 50/B2
Kainan, Japan 84/D3
Kainantu, PNG 129/G1
Kaindu, Zam. 123/E2
Kainji (dam), Nga. 115/G4
Kainji (lake), Nga. 107/C3
Kainji Lake NP, Nga. 115/F4
Kainoúryion, Gre. 49/G3
Kaintiba, PNG 129/G1
Kaipara (riv.), NZ 135/F6
Kaiparowits (plat.), Ut, US 149/G2
Kaiping, China 80/J7
Kairāna, India 98/D5
Kairi, Austl. 134/B2
Kairu, India 98/C5
Kairuku, PNG 129/G2
Kaisei, Japan 83/C3
Kaiseregg (peak), Swi. 60/D4
Kaisersesch, Ger. 55/G3
Kaiserslautern, Ger. 55/G5
Kaisheim, Ger. 58/D5
Kaišiadorys, Lith. 41/L4
Kait (cape), Indo. 89/D3
Kaitaia, NZ 135/C1
Kaitangata, NZ 135/B4
Kaithal, India 98/D5
Kaiti, Tanz. 119/A2
Kaiwi (chan.), Hi, US 142/T10
Kaiyang, China 93/J2
Kaiyuan, China 80/F2
Kaiyuan, China 86/D4
Kaizu, Japan 83/L5
Kaizuka, Japan 83/H7
Kajaani, Fin. 74/C3
Kajabbi, Austl. 129/F5
Kajang (peak), Malay. 89/D2
Kajang, Malay. 89/C2
Kajang, Indo. 91/F5
Kaji-san (peak), SKor. 84/A3
Kajiado, Kenya 119/B2
Kajikazawa, Japan 83/A2
Kajo-Kaji, Sudan 121/G2
Kajuru, Nga. 115/G4
Kākā, Sudan 117/G3
Kakabeka Falls, On, Can. 157/K3
Kakada (well), Chad 116/B1
Kakadu NP, Austl. 128/D3
Kakagi (lake), On, Can. 157/H3
Kakamas, SAfr. 124/C3
Kakamega, Kenya 119/A1
Kakamigahara, Japan 83/L5
Kakanj, Bosn. 50/D3
Kakata, Libr. 114/C5
Kākdwīp, India 97/G5
Kake, Ak, US 171/M4
Kaketsa (mt.), BC, Can. 171/M4
Kākhk, Iran 101/G2
Kakhovka, Ukr. 72/G4
Kakhovs'ke Vodoskhovyshche (res.), Ukr. 70/E3
Kakielo, D.R. Congo 123/F2
Kākināda, India 95/D2
Kakiri, Ugan. 121/H2
Kakkirigumma, India 95/D2
Kako (riv.), Japan 83/G6
Kakogawa, Japan 83/G6
Kakonga, Zam. 122/D2
Kakonko, Tanz. 121/G3
Kākori, India 96/C2
Kakrāla, India 96/B2
Kakrima (riv.), Gui. 114/B4
Kaktovik, Ak, US 171/K1
Kaku, India 92/B2
Kakuda, Japan 85/G2
Kakuma, Kenya 117/G5
Kakumbi, Zam. 123/F2
Kakuna, D.R. Congo 121/E4
Kakunodate, Japan 82/B4
Kakuri, Nga. 115/G4
Kakuto, Ugan. 121/G3
Kakya, Kenya 119/B2
Kāl-e Shūr (riv.), Iran 103/J2
Kalā Chāy, Iran 103/G2
Kala-i-Mor, Trkm. 101/H1
Kalaa Kebira, Tun. 48/B5
Kalaallit Nunaat (Greenland) (dpcy.), Den. 139/N2
Kālābāgh, Pak. 98/A3
Kalabahi, Indo. 128/B2
Kalabakan, Malay. 88/B4
Kalabo, Zam. 122/D2
Kalabyin, Myan. 86/B5
Kalach, Rus. 73/L2
Kalach-na-Donu, Rus. 71/G2
Kalachinsk, Rus. 74/H4
Kaladan (riv.), Myan. 93/F3
Kaladar, On, Can. 161/H2
Kālāgarh, India 96/B1
Kalahari (des.), Namb. 107/D7
Kalahari-Gemsbok NP, SAfr. 124/C2
Kalaiya, Nepal 97/E2
Kalakan, Rus. 75/M4
Kalalé, Ben. 115/F4
Kalāleh, Iran 103/H2
Kalaloch, Wa, US 144/B4
Kalām, Pak. 98/B2
Kalama, Wa, US 144/C4
Kalamákion, Gre. 49/N8
Kalamaloué, PN de, Camr. 116/B2
Kalamare, Bots. 123/E4
Kalamariá, Gre. 49/H2
Kalamáta, Gre. 49/H4
Kalamazoo, Mi, US 160/D3
Kalamazoo (riv.), Mi, US 160/D3
Kalamitsk (bay), Ukr. 73/G5
Kalampáka, Gre. 49/G3
Kalanchak, Ukr. 73/G4
Kalandy, Madg. 125/J6
Kalangali, Tanz. 119/A3
Kalanguy, Rus. 78/H1
Kālānwāli, India 98/C5
Kalaotoa (isl.), Indo. 128/A1
Kalasin, Thai. 94/C2
Kalāswāla, Pak. 98/C3
Kalāt, Pak. 101/J3
Kalaupapa, Hi, US 142/T10
Kalávrita, Gre. 49/H3
Kalaw, Myan. 86/C4
Kalbā, UAE 101/G3
Kälbäcär, Azer. 103/F1
Kalbach, Ger. 58/B2
Kalbar, Austl. 134/D4
Kalbarri, Austl. 130/B3
Kalbarri NP, Austl. 130/B3
Kaldakvísl (riv.), Ice. 38/N7
Kale, Turk. 104/A1
Kale, Turk. 102/D1
Kalecik, Turk. 102/C1
Kaleden, BC, Can. 144/E3
Kaledupa (isl.), Indo. 128/A1
Kalefeld, Ger. 53/H5
Kalehe, D.R. Congo 121/G3
Kalema, D.R. Congo 121/F4
Kalemie (int'l arpt.), D.R. Congo 121/G4
Kalemie, D.R. Congo 121/G4
Kalemyo, Myan. 86/B4
Kalenda, D.R. Congo 121/E5
Kalety, Pol. 43/K3
Kaleva, Mi, US 160/C2
Kalevala, Rus. 68/F2
Kalewa, Myan. 86/B4
Kaleya, Zam. 123/E2
Kalgoorlie-Boulder, Austl. 130/D4
Kāli (riv.), India 96/B1
Kali (riv.), India 96/B2
Kāli (riv.), Nepal 96/D2
Kālia, Bang. 97/H4
Kāliākair, Bang. 97/H3
Kalianda, Indo. 89/D4
Kalibo, Phil. 88/C3
Kalida, Oh, US 160/D4
Kālīganj, Bang. 97/G4
Kālikot, Nepal 96/C1
Kalima, D.R. Congo 121/F3
Kalimala, India 95/D2
Kalimantan (reg.), Indo. 90/D4
Kálimnos, Gre. 67/K3
Kālimpong, India 97/G2
Kaliningrad, Rus. 69/W9
Kaliningrad, Rus. 41/J4
Kaliningradskaya Oblast, Rus. 68/D5
Kalinino, Rus. 73/K5
Kalininsk, Rus. 71/H2
Kalinkavichy, Bela. 72/E1
Kalinko, Gui. 114/C4
Kalinovka, Rus. 73/H2
Kaliro, Ugan. 119/A1
Kalis, Som. 118/D3
Kalisizo, Ugan. 121/G3
Kalispel Ind. Res., Wa, US 144/F3
Kalispell, Mt, US 144/G3
Kalisz, Pol. 43/K3
Kaliua, Tanz. 121/G4
Kalix, Swe. 68/D2
Kalixälven (riv.), Swe. 38/G2
Kāliyāganj, India 97/G3
Kālka, India 98/D4
Kalkaringi, Austl. 128/C4
Kalkaska, Mi, US 160/D2
Kalkbruk, Fin. 39/F4
Kalkfeld, Namb. 122/C4
Kalkfontein, Bots. 122/D4
Kalkhügel, Namb. 122/C5
Kālkini, Bang. 97/H4
Kalkrand, Namb. 122/C5
Kallar Kahār, Pak. 98/B3
Kallaste, Est. 41/M2
Kallham, Aus. 59/G6
Kallinge, Swe. 40/F3
Kallinge (int'l arpt.), Swe. 40/F3
Kalliola, Fin. 39/F4
Kallithéa, Gre. 49/N9
Kallsjön (lake), Swe. 38/E3
Kalmalo, Nga. 115/G3
Kalmar (co.), Swe. 38/F4
Kalmar (int'l arpt.), Swe. 40/G3
Kalmar, Swe. 40/G3
Kalmar, Swe. 39/A1
Kalmarsund (sound), Swe. 40/G3
Kalmthout, Belg. 52/B6
Kalmykia, Resp., Rus. 74/E5
Kalmykovo, Kaz. 71/J2
Kālna, India 97/G4
Kalnai, India 96/D4
Kalnciems, Lat. 41/K3
Kalni (riv.), Bang. 97/H3
Kalnibolotskaya, Rus. 73/L4
Kalocsa, Hun. 50/D2
Kalofer, Bul. 49/J1
Kalokhórion, Gre. 49/H2
Kaloko, D.R. Congo 121/F4
Kālol, India 101/K4
Kalole, D.R. Congo 121/F3
Kalombo, Zam. 122/D2
Kalomo, Zam. 123/E3
Kalona, Ia, US 155/J3
Kalongan, Indo. 88/D4
Kalongo, Ugan. 119/A1
Kaloqi, Sudan 117/F3
Kālpi, India 96/B2
Kalpin, China 99/C3
Kalpitiya, SrL. 95/C4
Kalsdorf bei Graz, Aus. 50/B2
Kaltag, Ak, US 171/G3
Kaltasy, Rus. 69/M5
Kaltbrunn, Swi. 61/F3
Kaltenleutgeben, Aus. 51/N7
Kaltennordheim, Ger. 58/D1
Kaltern (Caldaro), It. 45/J3
Kalu (riv.), SrL. 92/D6
Kaluga, Rus. 68/H5
Kaluku, Indo. 91/E4
Kalulushi, Zam. 123/F2
Kalumburu Abor. Rsv., Austl. 128/B3
Kalumburu Mission, Austl. 128/B3
Kalumpang, Malay. 89/C2
Kalundborg, Den. 40/D4
Kalundborg (inlet), Den. 39/G7
Kalungu, Ugan. 121/G3
Kalungwishi (riv.), Zam. 121/G5
Kalūr Kot, Pak. 98/A3
Kalush, Ukr. 72/C3
Kaluzhkaya Oblast, Rus. 68/G5
Kalvarija, Lith. 41/K4
Kalwelwe, Zam. 123/F2
Kalyān, India 92/B4
Kalyazin, Rus. 68/H4
Kalynivka, Ukr. 72/E3
Kama (res.), Rus. 69/M4
Kama, D.R. Congo 121/F3
Kama, Myan. 86/B5
Kama (riv.), Rus. 29/K3
Kamachumu, Tanz. 121/G3
Kamagaya, Japan 83/E2
Kamaishi, Japan 82/B4
Kamajai, Lith. 41/L4
Kamakura, Japan 83/D3
Kamakusa, Guy. 182/A1
Kamakwie, SLeo. 114/B4
Kamalampaka, Tanz. 121/G4
Kamālia, Pak. 98/B4
Kaman, Turk. 102/C2
Kāman, India 96/A2
Kamande, D.R. Congo 121/G3
Kamango (lake), Mali 114/E2
Kamango, D.R. Congo 121/G2
Kamanjab, Namb. 122/B3
Kamanyola, D.R. Congo 121/G3
Kamaran (isl.), Yem. 118/B2
Kamarang, Guy. 181/F3
Kāmāreddi, India 95/C2
Kāmārhāti, India 92/E3
Kamaria (falls), Guy. 181/G3
Kamas, Ut, US 147/H3
Kamāsin, India 96/C3
Kamativi, Zim. 123/E3
Kamba, Nga. 115/G3
Kamba-Poko, D.R. Congo 120/D4
Kambalda, Austl. 130/D4
Kambam, India 95/C4
Kambar, Pak. 92/A2
Kambara, Japan 83/B3
Kambaswana, D.R. Congo 121/E4
Kambia, SLeo. 114/B4
Kambja, Est. 41/M2
Kambove, D.R. Congo 121/F5
Kambuno (peak), Indo. 91/F4
Kamchatka (pen.), Rus. 77/Q4
Kamchatskaya Oblast, Rus. 75/R4
Kamchiya (riv.), Bul. 70/C4
Kamela, Or, US 146/D1
Kamen, Ger. 53/E5
Kamen'-na-Obi, Rus. 99/D1
Kamena, D.R. Congo 121/F4
Kamende, D.R. Congo 121/F4
Kamenets, Bela. 43/M2
Kameničná, Slvk. 50/D2
Kamenjak, Rt (cape), Cro. 45/K4
Kamenka, Kaz. 71/J2
Kamenka, Rus. 71/H1
Kamenka, Rus. 69/K2
Kamenka, Rus. 73/K2
Kamenka, Rus. 79/M3
Kamennogorsk, Rus. 41/N1
Kamennomostskaya, Rus. 73/L5
Kameno, Bul. 51/H4
Kamenolomni, Rus. 73/L4
Kamensk-Shakhtinskiy, Rus. 73/L3
Kamensk-Ural'skiy, Rus. 69/P4
Kamenskoye, Rus. 75/S3
Kameoka, Japan 83/J5
Kameri, Indo. 91/H4
Kames, Sc, UK 33/A5
Kameyama, Japan 83/K6
Kami, Japan 83/G5
Kami (isl.), Japan 83/M6
Kami-koshiki (isl.), Japan 84/A5
Kamiah, Id, US 144/F4
Kamień Pomorski, Pol. 40/F5
Kamieskroon, SAfr. 124/B3
Kamifukuoka, Japan 83/D2
Kamiisco, Japan 82/B3
Kamiishizu, Japan 83/K5
Kamiizumi, Japan 83/C1
Kamiji, D.R. Congo 121/E4
Kamikawa, Japan 82/C2
Kamikuishiki, Japan 83/B2
Kamin'-Kashyrs'kyy, Ukr. 72/C2
Kamina, D.R. Congo 121/F5
Kaminaka, Japan 83/J5
Kaminoho, Japan 83/M4
Kaminoyama, Japan 85/G1
Kamisato, Japan 83/C1
Kamishak (bay), Ak, US 171/H4
Kamiyahagi, Japan 83/M5
Kamiyaku, Japan 85/L5
Kamla (riv.), India 97/F3
Kamloops, BC, Can. 144/D2
Kamlot, Camb. 94/C4
Kammaki, Japan 83/J6
Kamnik, Slov. 45/L3
Kamo, Arm. 103/F1
Kamo, Japan 85/F2
Kamo (riv.), Japan 83/E3
Kamo, Japan 83/J6
Kamogawa, Japan 85/G3
Kamojima, Japan 84/D3
Kāmoke, Pak. 98/C4
Kamonia, D.R. Congo 121/E4
Kamp (riv.), Aus. 43/H4
Kamp-Bornhofen, Ger. 55/G3
Kamp-Lintfort, Ger. 52/D5
Kampala (cap.), Ugan. 121/H2
Kampalili (mt.), Phil. 88/D4
Kampar, Malay. 89/C1
Kampar (riv.), Indo. 90/B3
Kampar (river), Indo. 89/C2
Kampen, Ger. 40/C4
Kampen, Neth. 52/C3
Kampene, D.R. Congo 121/F3
Kamphaeng Phet, Thai. 94/C5
Kamphaeng Phet (ruin), Thai. 94/B2
Kamp'o, SKor. 81/E5
Kampong Cham, Camb. 94/D4
Kampong Chhnang, Camb. 94/D3
Kampong Kadok, Malay. 94/C5
Kampong Khleang, Camb. 94/D3
Kampong Kuala Besut, Malay. 89/C1
Kampong Raja, Malay. 89/C1
Kampong Saom (bay), Camb. 90/B1
Kampóng Saom, Camb. 94/C4
Kampong Sedenak, Malay. 89/C2
Kampong Sedili Kechil, Malay. 89/D2
Kampong Spoe, Camb. 94/D4
Kampong Tampasis, Malay. 91/E2
Kampong Telupid, Malay. 88/B4
Kampong Thum, Camb. 94/D3
Kampong Trabek, Camb. 94/D4
Kampot, Camb. 94/D4
Kampti, Burk. 114/E4
Kamrau (bay), Indo. 91/H4
Kamsack, Sk, Can. 156/D2
Kamsar, Gui. 114/B4
Kamsdorf, Ger. 59/E1
Kamskoye Ust'ye, Rus. 69/L5
Kamsuuma, Som. 119/C1
Kamtsha (riv.), D.R. Congo 120/D4
Kamui-misaki (cape), Japan 82/B2
Kámuk (mtn.), CR 177/F4
Kamuli, Ugan. 119/A1
Kamuzu (Lilongwe) (int'l arpt.), Malw. 123/G2
Kamwandu, D.R. Congo 121/E4
Kam'yanets'-Podil's'kyy, Ukr. 72/D3
Kam'yanka, Ukr. 73/G3
Kam'yanka-Buz'ka, Ukr. 72/C2
Kam'yanka-Dniprovs'ka, Ukr. 73/H4
Kāmyārān, Iran 103/F3
Kamyshevatskaya, Rus. 73/J4
Kamyshin, Rus. 71/H2
Kamyshla, Rus. 69/M5
Kamyshlov, Rus. 69/P4
Kamyzyak, Rus. 71/J3
Kanaaupscow (riv.), Qu, Can. 141/J3
Kanab, Ut, US 149/F2
Kanab (plat.), Az, US 149/F2
Kanab (cr.), Az, US 149/F2
Kanaga (mt.), Ak, US 171/C6
Kanairiktok (riv.), Nf, Can. 141/K3
Kanākir, Syria 105/E2
Kanan, Japan 83/J7
Kananga, D.R. Congo 121/E4
Kanaoudi, India 96/C4
Kanarraville, Ut, US 149/F2
Kanash, Rus. 69/K5
Kanasin, Mex. 176/D1
Kanata, On, Can. 161/J2
Kanawake Ind. Res., Qu, Can. 159/N7
Kanawha, Ia, US 155/H2
Kanawha (riv.), WV, US 163/F1
Kanazawa, Japan 85/E2
Kanazi, Tanz. 121/G3
Kanchanaburi, Thai. 94/B3
Kanchanadit, Thai. 94/B4
Kānchenjunga (peak), Nepal 92/E2
Kānchīpuram, India 95/C3
Kandahār, Afg. 101/J2
Kanda-Kanda, D.R. Congo 121/E4
Kandalaksha, Rus. 68/G2
Kandalaksha (gulf), Rus. 38/K2
Kandale, D.R. Congo 120/D4
Kandang, Indo. 89/B2
Kandanghaur, Indo. 89/D4
Kándanos, Gre. 49/H5
Kandava, Lat. 41/K3
Kandavu Passage, Fiji 137/Y18
Kandé, Togo 115/F4
Kandel (peak), Ger. 60/E1
Kandel, Ger. 58/B4
Kandep, PNG 129/F1
Kander (riv.), Swi. 60/D4
Kandern, Ger. 60/D2
Kandersteg, Swi. 60/D5
Kandhkot, Pak. 101/J3
Kāndhla, India 98/D5
Kandi, Ben. 115/F4
Kāndi, India 97/G4
Kandi, D.R. Congo 121/G2
Kandi (cape), Indo. 91/F3
Kandıra, Turk. 51/K5
Kandos, Austl. 133/D1
Kandrāch, Pak. 101/J3
Kandreho, Madg. 125/H7
Kandry, Rus. 69/M5
Kandukūr, India 95/C3
Kandy, SrL. 95/D5
Kane, Pa, US 161/G4
Kane (co.), Il, US 167/P16
Kane, Il, US 155/J4
Kane (basin), Grld. 141/T7
Kanem (reg.), Chad 116/B2
Kanem (pref.), Chad 116/B2
Kaneohe, Hi, US 142/W13
Kaneville, Il, US 167/N16
Kanëvka, Rus. 68/H2
Kanevskaya, Rus. 73/K4
Kaneyama, Japan 82/B4
Kang, Bots. 122/D4
Kanga (riv.), Bang. 97/G5
Kanga, D.R. Congo 121/G2
Kanga, Tanz. 119/B3
Kangaba, Mali 114/C4
Kangal, Turk. 102/D2
Kangān, Iran 103/H5
Kangān, Iran 101/G3
Kangan Abor. Land, Austl. 130/C2
Kanganpur, Pak. 98/C4
Kangar, Malay. 94/C5
Kangaré, Mali 114/C4
Kangaroo (isl.), Austl. 127/C4
Kangaruma, Guy. 181/G3
Kangasala, Fin. 41/L1
Kangāvar, Iran 103/F3
Kangbao, China 78/G3
Kangding, China 86/D2
Kangdong (nbrhd.), SKor. 81/G6
Kangean (isl.), Indo. 89/F4
Kangean (isls.), Indo. 89/F4
Kangen (riv.), Sudan 117/G4
Kangendala, PN da, Ang. 120/D5
Kanggye, NKor. 81/D2
Kanggyŏng, SKor. 81/D4
Kanghwa, SKor. 81/F6
Kangi, Sudan 117/E3
Kangiqcliniq (Rankin Inlet), Nun, Can. 140/G2
Kangiqsualujjuaq, Qu, Can. 141/K3
Kangiqsujuaq, Qu, Can. 141/J2
Kangirsuk, Qu, Can. 141/J2
Kangjin, SKor. 81/D5
Kangkar Dohol, Malay. 89/C2
Kangmar, China 97/G1
Kangnam (mts.), NKor. 81/C2
Kangnam, NKor. 81/C3
Kangnam (nbrhd.), SKor. 81/G6
Kangnŭng, SKor. 84/A2
Kangnyŏng, NKor. 81/C4
Kango, Gabon 120/B2
Kangondi, Kenya 119/B2
Kangping, China 80/E2
Kāngra, India 98/D3
Kangrinboqê (peak), China 99/D5
Kangsŏ, NKor. 81/C3
Kangsŏ (nbrhd.), SKor. 81/F6
Kangto (peak), China 86/B3
Kangu, D.R. Congo 120/C4
Kangwŏn-do (prov.), NKor. 81/D3
Kangwŏn-do (prov.), SKor. 84/A2
Kangxiwar, China 99/C4
Kanha NP, India 96/C4
Kanhān (riv.), India 92/C3
Kanholmsfjärden (sound), Swe. 39/B1
Kani, C.d'Iv. 114/D4
Kani, Myan. 86/B4
Kani, Japan 83/M5
Kaniama, D.R. Congo 121/F4
Kanie, Japan 83/L5
Kanin (pen.), Rus. 69/K1
Kanin Nos, Rus. 68/J1
Kanin Nos (pt.), Rus. 74/E3
Kaningo, Kenya 119/B2
Kaniv, Ukr. 72/F3
Kaniva, Austl. 132/B3
Kanivs'ke Vodoskhovyshche (res.), Ukr. 72/F2
Kanjiža, Serb. 50/E2
Kankakee, Il, US 160/C4
Kankakee (riv.), Il, US 160/C4
Kankan (pol. reg.), Gui. 114/C4
Kankan, Gui. 114/C4
Kānker, India 95/D1
Kankesanturai, SrL. 95/D4
Kankossa, Mrta. 114/C3
Kanmen, China 87/J2
Kanmuri-yama (peak), Japan 84/C3
Kannami, Japan 83/B3
Kannapolis, NC, US 163/G3
Kannauj, India 96/B2
Kannon-zaki (pt.), Japan 83/D3
Kannus, Fin. 68/D3
Kano (state), Nga. 115/H4
Kano, Nga. 115/H4
Kano Vlei, Namb. 122/C3
Kanona, Zam. 123/F2
Kanoneiland, SAfr. 124/C3
Kan'onji, Japan 84/C3
Kanopolis, Ks, US 153/E1
Kanopolis (lake), Ks, US 154/E4
Kanosh, Ut, US 149/F1
Kanouse (mtn.), NJ, US 169/H7
Kanowit, Malay. 90/D3
Kanoya, Japan 84/B5
Kānpur, India 96/C2
Kanra, Japan 83/B1
Kansai (int'l arpt.), Japan 83/H7
Kansai (isl.), Japan 83/H7
Kansarokana (riv.), Kenya 119/B2
Kansas, Il, US 160/C5
Kansas (state), US 143/G4
Kansas (riv.), US 143/G4
Kansas, Al, US 162/D4
Kansas City, Ks, US 155/G4
Kansas City (int'l arpt.), Mo, US 155/G4
Kansas City, Mo, US 155/G4
Kansas Cosmosphere and Space Center, Ks, US 153/F1
Kansasville, Wi, US 167/P14
Kansenia, D.R. Congo 121/F5
Kansk, Rus. 74/K4
Kansŏng, SKor. 81/E3
Kantābānji, India 95/D1
Kantchari, Burk. 115/F3
Kantemirovka, Rus. 73/K3
Kānth, India 96/B1
Kantharalak, Thai. 94/D3
Kantō (prov.), Japan 85/F2
Kantunilkin, Mex. 176/E1
Kanturk, Ire. 32/B5
Kantvik, Fin. 39/E4
Kanuku (mts.), Guy. 181/G4
Kanuma, Japan 85/F2
Kanyanga, Gha. 115/E4
Kanye, Bots. 122/E5
Kanyilombi, Zam. 122/E2
Kanyutkwin, Myan. 94/B2
Kanzenze, D.R. Congo 121/F5
Kanzi, China 81/B3
Kaoh Nhek, Camb. 94/D3
Kaohsiung (int'l arpt.), Tai. 87/J4
Kaohsiung, Tai. 87/J4
Kaolack (pol. reg.), Sen. 114/B3
Kaolack, Sen. 114/A3
Kaolinovo, Bul. 51/H4
Kaoma, Zam. 122/E2
Kaongweshi (riv.), D.R. Congo 121/E5
Kaortchi (well), Chad 108/C5
Kaouadja, CAfr. 116/D4
Kaouar (reg.), Niger 108/B5
Kapa, Myan. 94/B3
Kapakapanui (mt.), NZ 135/J8
Kapalala, Zam. 123/F2
Kapalong, Phil. 88/D4
Kapambwe, D.R. Congo 121/E4
Kapan, Arm. 103/F2
Kapanga, D.R. Congo 121/E5
Kapaonik (mts.), Serb. 49/G1
Kapchorwa, Ugan. 119/A1
Kapedo, Kenya 119/B1
Kapellen, Belg. 52/B6
Kapellshamn (isl.), Swe. 39/J6
Kapellskär, Swe. 39/C1
Kapenguria, Kenya 119/A1
Kapengwe, Zam. 123/F2
Kapfenberg, Aus. 45/L3
Kapidaği (pen.), Turk. 51/H5
Kapingamarangi (isl.), Micr. 136/E4
Kapiri Mposhi, Zam. 123/F2
Kapiskau (riv.), On, Can. 141/H3
Kaplan, La, US 164/B3
Kaplice, Czh. 59/H5
Kapoe, Thai. 94/B4
Kapoeta, Sudan 117/G4
Kapona, D.R. Congo 121/G4
Kaporo, Malw. 119/A4
Kapos (riv.), Hun. 50/C2
Kaposvár, Hun. 50/C2
Kapowsin, Wa, US 144/C4
Kapp, Nor. 40/D1
Kappeln, Ger. 40/C4
Kappl, Aus. 61/G3
Kapsabet, Kenya 119/A1
Kapsan, NKor. 81/E2
Kapuas (riv.), Indo. 90/C4
Kapuas Hulu (mts.), Indo.,Malay. 90/D3
Kapunda, Austl. 131/H5
Kapūrthala, India 98/C4
Kapuskasing, On, Can. 141/H4
Kaputa, Zam. 121/G5
Kapuvár, Hun. 50/C2
Kapydzhik (peak), Azer. 103/F2
Kap'yŏng, SKor. 81/D4
Kara (riv.), Rus. 69/Q1
Kara, Rus. 69/Q1
Kara, Togo 115/F4
Kara (sea), Rus. 74/G2
Kara K'orē, Eth. 118/A3
Kara-Balta, Kyr. 99/B3
Kara-Kala, Trkm. 103/J2
Kara-Köl, Kyr. 99/B3
Kara-Saki (pt.), Japan 84/A3
Karaali, Turk. 102/C2
Karaart, Taj. 99/B4
Karabau, Kaz. 71/K2
Karabiğa, Turk. 51/H5
Karabra (riv.), Indo. 91/H4
Karabudakhkent, Rus. 71/H4
Karabük, Turk. 70/E4
Karabula, Rus. 74/K4
Karabulak, Rus. 71/H4
Karaburun, Turk. 51/J5
Karaca (peak), Turk. 102/D2
Karacadağ, Turk. 51/H5
Karacaköy, Turk. 51/J5
Karaçal (peak), Turk. 104/C1
Karacaoğlan, Turk. 51/H5
Karachala, Azer. 71/J5
Karachayevo-Cherkesiya, Resp., Rus. 75/Q6
Karachev, Rus. 70/E1
Karachi (int'l arpt.), Pak. 101/J4
Karāchi, Pak. 101/J4
Karād, India 95/B2
Karadere, Turk. 51/K5
Karagayly, Kaz. 99/C2
Karaginskiy (isl.), Rus. 77/R4
Karagoš (peak), Rus. 99/E1
Karaidel'skiy, Rus. 69/N5
Kāraikkudi, India 95/C4
Karaj, Iran 103/G3
Karak, Malay. 89/C2
Karakax (riv.), China 99/C4
Karakelong (isl.), Indo. 91/G3
Karakhoto (ruin), China 78/E3
Karakol, Kyr. 99/C3
Karakoram (pass), India 98/D2
Karakoram (range), India 99/C4
Karakoro (riv.), Mali 114/C3
Karakorum (pass), China 101/L1
Karakorum (ruin), Mong. 78/E2
Karaköse, Turk. 103/E2
Karaköy, Turk. 102/E2
Karakul', Uzb. 74/G6
Karakul' (lake), Taj. 99/B4
Karakumy (des.), Trkm. 74/F5
Karakuwisa, Namb. 122/C3
Karakyon (peak), Trkm. 103/H1
Karakyr (peak), Trkm. 101/H1
Karam (riv.), Indo. 91/E4
Karamagay, China 78/B2
Karaman, Turk. 102/C2
Karaman (prov.), Turk. 102/C2
Karamay, China 99/D2
Karambi, Tanz. 121/G3
Karamea, NZ 135/C3
Karamea Bight (bay), NZ 127/H7
Karamet-Niyaz, Trkm. 101/H1
Karamiran, China 99/E4
Karamiran (pass), China 99/E4
Karamiran (riv.), China 99/D4
Karamürsel, Turk. 51/J5
Karamyshevo, Rus. 41/N3
Karangasem, Indo. 89/F5
Karanginskiy (isl.), Rus. 75/S4
Karanginskiy (bay), Rus. 75/S4
Karanjia, India 95/E1
Karanpur, India 98/B5
Karapelit, Bul. 51/H4
Karapınar, Turk. 102/C2
Karasabai, Guy. 181/G3
Karaşar, Turk. 70/E4
Karasburg, Namb. 124/B3
Karasjohka-Karasjok, Nor. 38/H1
Karasu, Turk. 51/K5
Karasu, Japan 83/L6
Karasuk, Rus. 99/C1
Karatá (lag.), Nic. 177/F3
Karatal (riv.), Kaz. 99/C2
Karataş, Turk. 104/D1
Karatau (mts.), Kaz. 99/A3
Karathuri, Myan. 94/B4
Karatobe, Kaz. 71/K2
Karaton, Kaz. 71/K3
Karatoya (riv.), Bang. 97/G3
Karatsu, Japan 84/A4
Karauli, India 96/A2
Karaurgan, Turk. 102/E1
Karáva (peak), Gre. 49/G3
Karavan, Kyr. 99/B3
Karawang, Indo. 89/D4
Karayaka, Turk. 70/F4
Karayazı, Turk. 102/E2
Karazhal, Kaz. 99/B2
Karbaka, Sudan 109/G5
Karbalā', Iraq 103/F3
Karbalā (gov.), Iraq 103/E3
Karben, Ger. 58/B2
Karcag, Hun. 50/E2
Kardhámila, Gre. 49/K3
Kardhítsa, Gre. 49/G3
Kardhitsomagoúla, Gre. 49/G3
Kärdla, Est. 41/K2
Kareha (riv.), India 97/E3
Karelī, India 96/B4
Karelia (reg.), Rus. 38/J2
Kareliya, Resp., Rus. 74/D3
Karema, Tanz. 121/G4
Karenga (riv.), Rus. 78/H1
Karera, India 96/B3
Karesuando, Swe. 38/G1
Karêt (reg.), Mrta. 110/D4
Kärevere, Est. 41/M2
Kargala, Rus. 71/K2
Kargasok, Rus. 74/J4
Kargı, Turk. 70/E4
Kargil, India 98/D2
Kargopol', Rus. 68/H3
Karhal, India 96/B2
Karhijärvi (lake), Fin. 41/K1
Karhula, Fin. 41/M1
Kariá, Gre. 49/G3
Karia Ba Mohammed, Mor. 112/B2
Kariaí, Gre. 49/J2
Karianga, Madg. 125/H8
Kariba, Zam.,Zim. 123/F3
Kariba (dam), Zim. 123/F3
Kariba (lake), Zim. 107/E6
Kariba-yama (peak), Japan 82/A2
Karibib, Namb. 122/B4
Karibumba, D.R. Congo 121/G2
Karikal, India 95/C4
Karimama, Ben. 115/F3
Karimata (str.), Indo. 90/C4
Karimata (isl.), Indo. 90/D4
Karīmnagar, India 95/C2
Karimui, PNG 129/G1
Karimunjawa (isls.), Indo. 89/E4
Karin, Som. 118/C3
Karin, Som. 118/D3
Kariótissa, Gre. 49/H2
Karis (Karjaa), Fin. 39/D4
Karise, Den. 40/E4
Karisimbi (vol.), D.R. Congo 121/G3
Karislojo (Karjalohja), Fin. 39/D4
Káristos, Gre. 49/J3
Kariya, Japan 83/L6
Karjaa (Karis), Fin. 39/D4
Karjalohja (Karislojo), Fin. 39/D4
Karkaar (mts.), Som. 118/D3
Karkar (isl.), PNG 136/D5
Karkinits'ka Zatoka (gulf), Ukr. 70/D3
Karkkila, Fin. 41/L1
Kärkölä, Fin. 39/F4
Karkonski NP, Pol. 43/H3
Karkur, Isr. 105/B4
Karl E. Mundt NWR, SD, US 154/E2
Karla Marksa (peak), Taj. 99/B4
Karleby (Kokkola), Fin. 68/D3
Karlholmsbruk, Swe. 40/G1
Karlino, Pol. 40/F4
Karlivka, Ukr. 73/H3
Karlo-Libknekhtovsk, Ukr. 73/K3
Karlovac, Cro. 50/B3
Karlovo, Bul. 51/G4
Karlovy Vary, Czh. 59/F2
Karlovy Vary (arpt.), Czh. 59/F2
Karlovarský (pol. reg.), Czh. 42/G3
Karlsdorf-Neuthard, Ger. 58/B4
Karlsfeld, Ger. 59/E6
Karlshamn, Swe. 40/F3
Karlshuld, Ger. 58/E5
Karlskoga, Swe. 40/F2
Karlskron, Ger. 59/E5
Karlskrona, Swe. 40/F3
Karlslunde Strand, Den. 39/J7
Karlsruhe, ND, US 156/D3
Karlsruhe, Ger. 58/B4
Karlstad, Mn, US 156/F3
Karlstad, Swe. 40/E2
Karlstadt, Ger. 58/C3
Karlstein am Main, Ger. 58/C2
Karluk, Ak, US 171/H4
Karmah, Sudan 109/F5
Karmāla, India 95/B2
Karmatānr, India 97/F3
Karmi'el, Isr. 105/C3
Karnāl, India 98/D5
Karnali (zone), Nepal 96/C1
Karnali (riv.), Nepal 96/C1
Karnaphuli (res.), Bang. 97/H4
Karnataka (state), India 92/C4
Karnes City, Tx, US 151/F3
Karnobat, Bul. 51/H4
Kärnten (prov.), Aus. 45/K3
Karo, Chad 116/C3
Karoi, Zim. 123/F3
Karomatan, Phil. 88/C4
Karonga, Malw. 119/A4
Karoo NP, SAfr. 124/D4
Karoo NP, SAfr. 124/C4
Karoonda, Austl. 132/A2
Karor, Pak. 98/A4
Karora, Sudan 100/C5
Karoso (cape), Indo. 91/E5
Karpakora, Austl. 132/B2
Kárpathos, Gre. 67/K4
Kárpathos (isl.), Gre. 102/A3
Karpatskiy NP, Ukr. 72/C3
Karpenísion, Gre. 49/G3
Karpogory, Rus. 69/K3
Karratha, Austl. 130/C2
Kars (riv.), Turk. 71/G4
Kars, Turk. 103/E1
Kars (prov.), Turk. 71/G4
Kars (riv.), SAfr. 124/M11
Kars (prov.), Geo. 103/E1
Kärsämäki, Fin. 68/E3
Karsantı, Turk. 102/C2
Kārsava, Lat. 41/M3
Kårsta, Swe. 39/B1
Kartaly, Rus. 71/M1
Kartārpur, India 98/C4
Kartushi, D.R. Congo 121/F4
Kartuzy, Pol. 40/H4
Karuah, Austl. 132/D2
Karuma (falls), Ugan. 121/H2
Karumba, Austl. 134/A2
Karūn (riv.), Iran 74/E6
Karunjie, Austl. 128/B4
Karup, Den. 40/C3
Karūr, India 95/C4
Karushe, D.R. Congo 121/F3
Karval, Co, US 152/C1
Karviná, Czh. 43/K4
Karwar, India 95/B3
Karymskoye, Rus. 78/G1
Kaş, Turk. 104/A1
Kås, Den. 40/C3
Kas, Sudan 116/E2
Kasaan, Ak, US 171/M4
Kasagi, Japan 83/J6
Kasahara, Japan 83/M5
Kāsai (riv.), India 97/F4
Kasai, Japan 84/D3
Kasai (riv.), D.R. Congo 107/D5
Kasai Occidental (pol. reg.), D.R. Congo 121/E4
Kasai Oriental (pol. reg.), D.R. Congo 121/E3
Kasaji, D.R. Congo 121/E5
Kasakalawe, Zam. 121/G5
Kasalu, Zam. 123/E2
Kasama, Japan 85/G2
Kasama, Zam. 121/G5
Kasamatsu, Japan 83/L5
Kasane, Bots. 122/E3
Kasanga (falls), Zam. 122/E3
Kasanga, Tanz. 121/G5
Kasangulu, D.R. Congo 120/C4
Kasanka NP, Zam. 123/F2
Kasaoka, Japan 84/C3
Kasar (cape), Sudan 109/H5
Kasartori-yama (peak), Japan 83/K6
Kasba (lake), NW,Nun, Can. 140/F2
Kasba Tadla, Mor. 110/D2
Kaseda, Japan 84/B5
Kaseke, D.R. Congo 123/E1
Kasembe, Tanz. 119/B4
Kasempa, Zam. 122/E2
Kasenga, D.R. Congo 121/G5
Kasenyi, D.R. Congo 121/G2
Kasese, Ugan. 121/G2
Kasese, D.R. Congo 121/F3
Kaset Wisai, Thai. 94/C3
Kāsganj, India 96/B2
Kashabowie, On, Can. 157/J3
Kashaf (riv.), Iran 101/H1
Kasha-Katuwe Tent Rocks Nat'l Mon., NM, US 149/J3
Kāshān, Iran 103/G3
Kashary, Rus. 73/L3
Kashi, China 99/C4
Kashiba, Zam. 121/G5
Kashiba, Japan 83/J6
Kashihara, Japan 83/J6
Kashima, Japan 85/G3
Kashima, Japan 84/B4
Kashima (bay), Japan 83/F1
Kashin, Rus. 68/H4
Kāshīpur, India 96/B1
Kashiwa, Japan 83/D2
Kashiwara, Japan 83/J6
Kashiwazaki, Japan 85/F2
Kāshmar, Iran 101/G1
Kashmūnd Ghar (range), Afg. 98/A2
Kashof (riv.), Iran 103/J2
Kashofu, D.R. Congo 121/G3
Kasia, India 96/D2
Kasidiji (riv.), D.R. Congo 121/E5
Kasigau (peak), Kenya 119/B2
Kasigluk, Ak, US 171/F3
Kasilof, Ak, US 171/H3
Kasimov, Rus. 68/J5
Kasimovo (arpt.), Rus. 69/T6
Kasindi, D.R. Congo 121/G2
Kasinge, D.R. Congo 121/F4
Kasiruta (isl.), Indo. 91/G4
Kasiui (isl.), Indo. 91/H4
Kasiya, Malw. 123/G2
Kaskaskia (riv.), Il, US 155/K4
Kas'kovo, Rus. 41/N2
Kaslo, BC, Can. 144/F3
Kasonaweja, Indo. 91/J4
Kasongan, Indo. 90/D4
Kasongo, D.R. Congo 121/F4
Kasongo-Lunda, D.R. Congo 120/D4
Kasonguele, D.R. Congo 121/F4
Kásos (isl.), Gre. 102/A3
Kaspi, Geo. 71/H4
Kaspichan, Bul. 51/H4
Kaspiysk, Rus. 71/H4
Kaspiyskiy, Rus. 71/H3
Kassala, Sudan 117/H2
Kassándra (pen.), Gre. 70/B5
Kassándria, Gre. 49/H2
Kassel, Ger. 53/G6
Kassikaityu (riv.), Guy. 181/G4
Kasson, Mn, US 155/H1
Kastamonu (prov.), Turk. 70/E4
Kastamonu, Turk. 70/E4
Kastanéai, Gre. 51/H5
Kaštel Stari, Cro. 50/C4
Kaštel Sućurac, Cro. 50/C4
Kastellaun, Ger. 55/G3
Kastéllion, Gre. 49/J5
Kasterlee, Belg. 52/B6
Kastl, Ger. 59/E4
Kastön (isl.), Swe. 39/B1
Kastoría, Gre. 49/G2
Kastornoye, Rus. 73/K2
Kastrakíou (lake), Gre. 49/G3
Kastrup, Den. 39/J7
Kasuga, Japan 83/K5
Kasuga, Japan 83/H5
Kasugai, Japan 83/B2
Kasugai, Japan 83/L5
Kasui, Indo. 89/D4
Kasukabe, Japan 85/F3
Kasuku (riv.), D.R. Congo 121/F3
Kasulu, Tanz. 121/G4
Kasumiga (lake), Japan 85/G2
Kasungu, Malw. 123/G2
Kasungu NP, Malw. 123/G2
Kasupe, Malw. 123/G2
Kasūr, Pak. 98/C4
Kat O Chau (isl.), China 87/M6
Kataba, Zam. 122/E3
Katagum (riv.), Nga. 116/A2
Katako-Kombe, D.R. Congo 121/F3
Katákolon, Gre. 49/G4
Katale, D.R. Congo 121/G3
Kataloinen, Fin. 39/E4
Katana, D.R. Congo 121/G3
Katanda, D.R. Congo 121/E4
Katanda, D.R. Congo 121/G3
Katanga, (pol. reg.), D.R. Congo 121/F5
Katangi, India 96/B4
Katanning, Austl. 130/C5
Katano, Japan 83/J6
Katanti, D.R. Congo 121/F3
Katarniān Ghāt, India 96/C1
Katastárion, Gre. 49/G4
Katavi NP, Tanz. 121/G4
Katchall (isl.), India 93/F6
Katea, D.R. Congo 121/F4
Katea, D.R. Congo 121/E4
Katebo, Ugan. 121/H3
Katemcy, Tx, US 150/E2
Katenga, D.R. Congo 121/G4
Kateríni, Gre. 49/H2
Kates Needle (mt.), Ak, US 171/M4
Katesh, Tanz. 119/A3
Katete, Malw. 123/G2
Katete, Zam. 123/G2
Katghora, India 96/D4
Katha, Myan. 86/C3
Katherine, Az, US 148/E3
Katherine, Austl. 128/D3
Katherine (riv.), Austl. 128/D3
Katherine Gorge NP, Austl. 128/D3
Kāthgodām, India 96/B1
Kathiawar (pen.), India 101/K4
Kathleen, Ga, US 165/G1
Kathleen, Fl, US 164/L7
Kathleen (mt.), Austl. 131/G2
Kāthmāndu (cap.), Nepal 97/E2
Kathryn, ND, US 156/F4
Kathua, India 98/C3
Kati, Mali 114/C3
Katiéna, Mali 114/D3
Katihār, India 97/F3
Kātikund, India 97/F3
Katiola, C.d'Iv. 114/D4
Katla, Sudan 117/F3
Katlehong, SAfr. 124/E2
Katlenburg-Lindau, Ger. 53/H5
Katma, China 99/E4
Katmai (mt.), Ak, US 171/H4
Katmai NP, Ak, US 171/G4
Káto Akhaía, Gre. 49/G3
Káto Nevrokópion, Gre. 49/H2
Katoba, Tanz. 121/G4
Katokhí, Gre. 49/G3
Katombe, D.R. Congo 121/E4
Katonah, NY, US 169/E1
Katonga (riv.), Ugan. 121/G2
Katoomba, Austl. 133/E1
Katoúna, Gre. 49/G3
Katowice, Pol. 43/K3
Katra, India 98/C3
Katra, India 96/C3
Kātrās, India 97/F4
Katrichev, Rus. 71/H2
Katrine (lake), Sc, UK 33/B4
Katrineholm, Swe. 40/G2
Katsepe, Madg. 125/H6
Katshi, D.R. Congo 121/F4
Katsikás, Gre. 49/G3
Katsina (state), Nga. 115/G3
Katsina, Nga. 115/G3
Katsina Ala (riv.), Nga. 115/H5
Katsina Ala, Nga. 115/H5
Katsunuma, Japan 83/B2
Katsura (riv.), Japan 83/J5
Katsuragi, Japan 84/D3
Katsuragi-san (peak), Japan 83/H7
Katsuta, Japan 85/G2
Katsuura, Japan 85/G3
Katsuyama, Japan 84/E2
Katsuyama, Japan 83/B3
Kattegat (str.), Den. 40/D3
Katua, Gha. 115/E4
Katul (mtn.), Sudan 117/F2
Katumajävi (lake), Fin. 39/E4
Katumbi, Malw. 119/A4
Katun' (riv.), Rus. 78/B1
Katunayake (int'l arpt.), SrL. 95/C5
Katun'chuya (riv.), Rus. 99/E1
Katundu, Zam. 122/E3
Kātūria, India 97/F3
Katuta Kampemba, Zam. 121/G5
Kātwa, India 97/G4
Katwa, D.R. Congo 121/G2
Katwe-Kabatooro, Ugan. 121/G3
Katwijk aan Zee, Neth. 52/B4
Katy, Tx, US 151/G3
Katzenbach (riv.), Ger. 58/B4
Katzenbuckel (peak), Ger. 58/C4
Katzenelnbogen, Ger. 55/G3
Katzhütte, Ger. 58/D1
Katzwinkel, Ger. 55/F3
Kau-ye (isl.), Myan. 94/B4
Kauai (isl.), Hi, US 142/S9
Kauai (chan.), Hi, US 142/S10
Kaudum (riv.), Namb. 122/D3
Kaudum Game Park, Namb. 122/D3
Kaufbeuren, Ger. 61/G2
Kaufering, Ger. 61/G1
Kaufman (co.), Tx, US 150/L7
Kaufman, Tx, US 151/F1
Kaufungen, Ger. 53/G6
Kauhava, Fin. 68/D3
Kauiki (pt.), Hi, US 142/U10
Kaukapakapa, NZ 135/F6
Kaukauna, Wi, US 160/B2
Kaukaveld (uplands), Namb. 122/B3
Kaukura (isl.), FrPol. 137/L6
Kaulashishi (hill), Zam. 123/F2
Kaulsdorf, Ger. 59/E1
Kaumba, D.R. Congo 121/F5
Kaunas (res.), Lith. 41/L4
Kaunas, Lith. 41/K4
Kaunas (int'l arpt.), Lith. 41/K4
Kauniainen (Grankulla), Fin. 39/E4
Kaupanger, Nor. 40/B1
Kaura Namoda, Nga. 115/G3
Kauro, Kenya 119/B1
Kauttua, Fin. 41/K1
Kavadarci, FYROM 49/H2
Kavajë, Alb. 49/F2
Kavála, Gre. 49/J2
Kavalerovo, Rus. 79/M3
Kāvali, India 95/C3
Kavango (riv.), Namb. 122/C3
Kavār, Iran 103/H4
Kavarna, Bul. 51/J4
Kavarskas, Lith. 41/L4
Kavgolovskoye (lake), Rus. 69/T6
Kavieng, PNG 136/E5
Kavimba, Bots. 122/E3
Kavīr-e Bāfq (Salt pan), Iran 103/H4

Map Section

Kimhae – Koppie
Map Section
240
241

Kimhae, SKor. 84/A3
Kimhae (int'l arpt.), SKor. 84/A3
Kími, Gre. 49/J3
Kimi, Camr. 116/A4
Kímina, Gre. 49/H2
Kimitsu, Japan 85/F3
Kimje, SKor. 81/D5
Kimméria, Gre. 49/J2
Kimmirut, Nun, Can. 141/K2
Kimnyangjang-ni, SKor. 81/G7
Kímolos (isl.), Gre. 49/J4
Kimongo, Congo 120/C4
Kimoset, Kenya 119/A1
Kimovaara, Rus. 68/F3
Kimovsk, Rus. 70/F1
Kimpanga, D.R. Congo 121/F4
Kimpese, D.R. Congo 120/C4
Kimp'o, SKor. 81/F6
Kimp'o (int'l arpt.), SKor. 81/F6
Kimpō-zan (peak), Japan 83/B2
Kimry, Rus. 68/H4
Kinabalu (peak), Malay. 88/B4
Kinabalu NP, Malay. 88/B4
Kinabatangan (riv.), Malay. 91/E2
Kinaliada (isl.), Turk. 103/M7
Kinalung, Austl. 132/B2
Kinango, Kenya 119/B3
Kinapat (cape), Indo. 89/B3
Kinard, Fl, US 165/F2
Kinards, SC, US 163/G3
Kinarut, Malay. 88/B4
Kinbasket (lake), BC, Can. 144/E1
Kinbrace, Sc, UK 31/S7
Kincaid, Sk, Can. 145/L3
Kincaid, Ks, US 153/G1
Kincardine, Sc, UK 33/C4
Kincardine, On, Can. 160/F2
Kinchafoonee (cr.), Ga, US 165/F1
Kincolith, BC, Can. 171/N4
Kincraig, Sc, UK 33/C2
Kinda, D.R. Congo 121/F5
Kindambi, D.R. Congo 120/E4
Kindberg, Aus. 45/L3
Kindembe, D.R. Congo 120/D4
Kinder, La, US 164/B2
Kinder Scout (peak), Eng, UK 35/G5
Kindersley, Sk, Can. 145/K2
Kindia (pol. reg.), Gui. 114/B4
Kindia, Gui. 114/B4
Kinding, Ger. 59/E5
Kindred, ND, US 156/F4
Kindsbach, Ger. 55/G5
Kindu, D.R. Congo 121/F3
Kinel', Rus. 71/J1
Kineshma, Rus. 68/J4
Kineton, Eng, UK 37/E2
King (isl.), Austl. 127/D4
King (lake), Austl. 130/C5
King (mt.), Austl. 134/B4
King (riv.), Austl. 133/C3
King (sound), Austl. 127/B2
King (mt.), BC, Can. 171/N4
King (isl.), NZ 127/H6
King, NC, US 163/G2
King (hill), Pa, US 161/G4
King (mtn.), Tx, US 150/C2
King (co.), Wa, US 167/D2
King Abdul Aziz (int'l arpt.), SAr. 109/H4
King And Queen Court House, Va, US 163/J2
King Christian (isl.), Nun, Can. 141/R7
King Christian IX Land (reg.), Grld. 139/P3
King Christian X Land (reg.), Grld. 139/Q2
King City, Ca, US 148/B2
King City, Mo, US 155/G3
King City, On, Can. 160/T8
King Cove, Ak, US 171/F4
King Frederik VI Coast (reg.), Grld. 139/N3
King Frederik VIII Land (reg.), Grld. 139/Q2
King George (isls.), FrPol. 137/L6
King George (mt.), BC, Can. 144/G2
King George, Va, US 163/J1
King George Is. (isls.), Qu, Can. 141/J3
King George's (res.), Eng, UK 30/C2
King Hussein (arpt.), Jor. 105/E4
King Khaled (int'l arpt.), SAr. 100/E4
King Leopold (range), Austl. 128/B4
King of Prussia, Pa, US 168/C3
King Peak (mt.), Yk, Can. 171/K3
King Salmon, Ak, US 171/G4
King William (isl.), Nun, Can. 140/G2
King William, Va, US 163/J2
King William's Town, SAfr. 124/D4
Kinganga, D.R. Congo 120/C4
Kingaroy, Austl. 134/C4
Kingfisher, Ok, US 153/F3
Kinghorn, Sc, UK 33/C4
Kingisepp, Rus. 41/N2
Kinglake NP, Austl. 132/G5
Kingman, Ks, US 153/E2
Kingman, Az, US 149/E3
Kingman (reef), Pac., US 137/J4
Kingombe, D.R. Congo 121/F3
Kingoonyah, Austl. 131/G4
Kings (peak), Ut, US 147/H3
Kings, Ms, US 162/B4
Kings (riv.), Ca, US 148/C2
Kings (cr.), Tx, US 150/L7
Kings Beach, Ca, US 146/C4
Kings Canyon NP, Ca, US 148/C2
Kings Island, Oh, US 160/D5
Kings Langley, Eng, UK 30/B1
King's Lynn, Eng, UK 37/G1
Kings Mountain, NC, US 163/G3
Kings Mountain Nat'l Mil. Park, SC, US 163/G3
Kings Park, Austl. 130/K6
Kings Point, NY, US 169/L8
King's Seat (hill), Sc, UK 33/C4
Kings Sutton, Eng, UK 37/E2
Kingsbridge, Eng, UK 36/C6
Kingsburg, Ca, US 148/C2
Kingsbury, Tx, US 151/F3
Kingsclere, Eng, UK 37/E4
Kingscote, Austl. 131/H5
Kingscourt, Ire. 32/D2
Kingsdown, Ks, US 152/E2
Kingsford, Mi, US 157/K5
Kingsland, Eng, UK 36/D2
Kingsland, Ar, US 153/H4
Kingsland, Ga, US 165/H2
Kingsland, Tx, US 151/E2
Kingsley, Ia, US 155/G2
Kingsley, Mi, US 160/D2
Kingsley (dam), Ne, US 154/D3
Kingsnorth, Eng, UK 30/E2
Kingsport, Tn, US 163/F2
Kingston, Austl. 132/C4
Kingston, Austl. 136/F7
Kingston, On, Can. 161/H2
Kingston (cap.), Jam. 177/G2
Kingston, La, US 164/B1
Kingston, Mo, US 155/G4
Kingston, NM, US 149/J4
Kingston, NY, US 161/K4
Kingston, Oh, US 160/E5
Kingston, Ok, US 153/F4
Kingston, Pa, US 168/C1
Kingston, RI, US 161/L4
Kingston, Tn, US 162/E3
Kingston, Wa, US 167/B2
Kingston S.E., Austl. 132/A3
Kingston Springs, Tn, US 162/D2
Kingston upon Hull, Eng, UK 35/H4
Kingston upon Hull (co.), Eng, UK 35/H4
Kingston upon Thames, Eng, UK 30/C2
Kingston Upon Thames (bor.), Eng, UK 30/C2
Kingstown, Austl. 132/D1
Kingstown (cap.), StV. 173/N9
Kingstree, SC, US 163/H4
Kingsville, On, Can. 160/E3
Kingsville, Tx, US 151/F4
Kingsville, Md, US 168/B5
Kingsville Nav. Air Sta., Tx, US 151/F4
Kingswear, Eng, UK 36/C6
Kingswood, Ky, US 162/D2
Kingswood, Eng, UK 36/D4
Kington, Eng, UK 36/D2
Kingushi, D.R. Congo 120/D4
Kingussie, Sc, UK 33/B2
Kingwood, WV, US 161/G5
Kingwood, Tx, US 151/M8
Kiniama, D.R. Congo 123/F1
Kiniati, D.R. Congo 120/D4
Kınık, Turk. 70/C5
Kinistino Ind. Res., Sk, Can. 145/M1
Kinkaid (mt.), Ak, US 171/L4
Kinkaid (lake), Il, US 162/C2
Kinkala, Congo 120/C4
Kinki (prov.), Japan 84/D3
Kinkosi, D.R. Congo 120/C4
Kinloch Rannoch, Sc, UK 33/B3
Kinlochewe, Sc, UK 33/A1
Kinlochleven, Sc, UK 33/B3
Kinloss, Sc, UK 33/C1
Kinmel, Wal, UK 34/E5
Kinmundy, Il, US 162/C1
Kinna, Swe. 40/E3
Kinnairds (pt.), Sc, UK 33/D1
Kinnegad, Ire. 32/C3
Kinnelon, NJ, US 169/H8
Kinnelon (lake), NJ, US 169/H8
Kinneret, Isr. 105/D3
Kinnikinnick, Oh, US 160/E5
Kinnitty, Ire. 32/C3
Kino (riv.), Japan 84/D3
Kinomoto, Japan 83/K5
Kinrooi, Belg. 55/E1
Kinross, Sc, UK 33/C4
Kinsach (riv.), Ger. 59/F4
Kinsale (har.), Ire. 32/B6
Kinsale, Ire. 32/B6
Kinsale, On, Can. 160/U8
Kinsarvik, Nor. 40/B1
Kinsey, Mt, US 145/M4
Kinshasa (pol. reg), D.R. Congo 120/C4
Kinshasa (cap.), D.R. Congo 120/C4
Kinsley, Ks, US 152/E2
Kinsman, Oh, US 160/F4
Kinston, Al, US 165/E2
Kinston, NC, US 163/J3
Kinta, Ok, US 153/G3
Kintampo, Gha. 115/E4
Kintinku, Tanz. 119/A3
Kintnersville, Pa, US 168/C2
Kintore, Sc, UK 33/D2
Kintyre, ND, US 156/E4
Kintyre (isl.), Sc, UK 31/R8
Kintzheim, Fr. 60/D1
Kinu (riv.), Japan 85/F2
Kinvarra, Ire. 32/B3
Kinwow (bay), Mb, Can. 156/F2
Kinyangiri, Tanz. 119/A3
Kinyeti (peak), Sudan 117/G5
Kinzig (riv.), Ger. 42/E4
Kiomboi, Tanz. 119/A3
Kiowa, Ok, US 153/G3
Kiowa, Ks, US 153/E2
Kiowa (cr.), Co, US 154/B4
Kiowa, Co, US 154/B4
Kipange, D.R. Congo 121/F4
Kiparissía, Gre. 49/G4
Kiparissía (gulf), Gre. 67/J3
Kipawa (lake), Qu, Can. 161/G1
Kipawa, Qu, Can. 161/G1
Kipen', Rus. 69/S7
Kipili, Tanz. 121/G4
Kipilingu, D.R. Congo 123/F2
Kipini, Kenya 119/C2
Kipkarren (riv.), Kenya 119/A1
Kipling, Sk, Can. 156/C2
Kipnuk, Ak, US 171/F4
Kippel, Swi. 60/D5
Kippen, Sc, UK 33/B4
Kippens, Nf, Can. 159/H1
Kippure (peak), Ire. 34/B5
Kipti, Ukr. 72/F2
Kipushi, D.R. Congo 123/E1
Kira, Japan 83/M6
Kira Panayía (isl.), Gre. 49/H3
Kirakira, Sol. 136/F6
Kirandul, India 95/D2
Kiranomena, Madg. 125/H7
Kīratpur, India 96/B1
Kirawa, Nga. 116/B3
Kirazlı, Turk. 49/K2
Kirbla, Est. 41/K2
Kirby, Ar, US 153/H3
Kirby, Mt, US 147/K1
Kirbyville, Tx, US 151/H2
Kırcasalih, Turk. 51/H5
Kirchberg, Swi. 60/D3
Kirchberg, Swi. 61/F3
Kirchberg, Ger. 55/G4
Kirchberg, Ger. 59/F1
Kirchberg an der Iller, Ger. 61/G1
Kirchberg an der Jagst, Ger. 58/C4
Kirchdorf, Ger. 53/F3
Kirchdorf an der Krems, Aus. 59/H7
Kirchen, Ger. 55/G2
Kirchenlamitz, Ger. 59/E2
Kirchenthumbach, Ger. 59/E3
Kirchheim, Ger. 61/G1
Kirchheim bei München, Ger. 59/E6
Kirchheim unter Teck, Ger. 58/C5
Kirchheimbolanden, Ger. 58/B3
Kirchhundem, Ger. 53/F6
Kirchlengern, Ger. 53/F4
Kirchlinteln, Ger. 53/G3
Kirchsee (lake), Ger. 61/H2
Kirchseeon, Ger. 59/E6
Kirchweidach, Ger. 59/F6
Kirchzarten, Ger. 60/D2
Kirchzell, Ger. 58/C3
Kircubbin, NI, UK 34/C3
Kircudbright (bay), Sc, UK 34/D2
Kirensk, Rus. 75/L4
Kirgiz Steppe (upland), Kaz. 74/F5
Kirgizskiy (mts.), Kyr. 99/B3
Kiri, D.R. Congo 120/D3
Kiriákion, Gre. 49/H3
Kiribati (ctry.) 136/H5
Kırık, Turk. 102/E1
Kırıkhan, Turk. 104/E1
Kırıkkale, Turk. 102/C2
Kırıkkale (prov.), Turk. 102/C2
Kirikkuduk, China 78/C3
Kirillov, Rus. 68/H4
Kirishi, Rus. 41/Q2
Kirishima-Yaku NP, Japan 84/B5
Kirishima-yama (peak), Japan 84/B5
Kiritimati (Christmas) (isl.), Kiri. 137/K4
Kırkağaç, Turk. 70/C5
Kirkburton, Eng, UK 35/G4
Kirkby, Eng, UK 35/F5
Kirkby in Ashfield, Eng, UK 35/G5
Kirkby Lonsdale, Eng, UK 35/F3
Kirkby Stephen, Eng, UK 35/F3
Kirkbymoorside, Eng, UK 35/H3
Kirkcaldy, Sc, UK 33/C4
Kirkcolm, Sc, UK 34/C2
Kirkconnel, Sc, UK 33/C6
Kirkcowan, Sc, UK 34/D2
Kirkcudbright, Sc, UK 34/D2
Kirke Hvalsø, Den. 39/H7
Kirkee, India 92/B4
Kirkenær, Nor. 40/E1
Kirkham, Eng, UK 35/F4
Kirkhill, Sc, UK 33/B2
Kirkinner, Sc, UK 34/D2
Kirkintilloch, Sc, UK 33/B5
Kirkkonummi (Kyrkslätt), Fin. 41/L1
Kirkland, Qu, Can. 159/N7
Kirkland (hill), Sc, UK 33/C6
Kirkland, Az, US 149/F3
Kirkland, Il, US 155/K2
Kirkland, Wa, US 144/C4
Kirkland Lake, On, Can. 141/H4
Kırklar (peak), Turk. 70/C5
Kırklareli, Turk. 51/H5
Kırklareli (prov.), Turk. 51/H5
Kirklees (co.), Eng, UK 35/G4
Kirkliston, Sc, UK 33/C5
Kirkmichael, IM, UK 34/D3
Kirkmuirhill, Sc, UK 33/C5
Kirkstone (pass), Eng, UK 35/F3
Kirksville, Mo, US 155/H3
Kirkton of Glenisla, Sc, UK 33/C3
Kirkūk, Iraq 103/F3
Kirkwall, Sc, UK 31/V14
Kirkwood, SAfr. 124/D4
Kirkwood, De, US 168/C4
Kirn, Ger. 55/G4
Kirongwe, Tanz. 119/B3
Kiropa, Tanz. 119/A4
Kirov, Rus. 69/L4
Kirov, Rus. 70/E1
Kirovo-Chepetsk, Rus. 69/L4
Kirovohrad, Ukr. 73/G3
Kirovohrads'ka Oblast, Ukr. 70/D2
Kirovsk, Bela. 70/D1
Kirovsk, Rus. 68/G2
Kirovsk, Rus. 69/U7
Kirovs'k, Ukr. 73/K3
Kirovskaya Oblast, Rus. 69/P5
Kirovs'ke, Ukr. 73/H5
Kirovs'ke, Ukr. 73/K3
Kirovskiy, Rus. 71/J3
Kirovskiy, Kaz. 74/H5
Kirovskiy, Rus. 79/L2
Kirriemuir, Sc, UK 33/D3
Kirriemuir, Ab, Can. 145/J2
Kirrweiler, Ger. 58/B4
Kirs, Rus. 69/M4
Kirsanov, Rus. 71/G1
Kırşehir, Turk. 102/C2
Kırşehir (prov.), Turk. 102/C2
Kirtland, NM, US 149/H2
Kirtland (A.F.B.), NM, US 149/J3
Kirtley, Wy, US 154/B2
Kirton, Eng, UK 35/H6
Kirton in Lindsey, Eng, UK 35/H5
Kiruna, Swe. 38/G2
Kirundu, D.R. Congo 121/F3
Kirwin (res.), Ks, US 154/E4
Kirwin, Ks, US 154/E4
Kirwin Nat'l Wildlife Res., Ks, US 152/E1
Kirya, Rus. 69/K5
Kiryū, Japan 85/F2
Kisa, Swe. 40/F3
Kisai, Japan 83/D1
Kisakata, Japan 82/A4
Kisangani, D.R. Congo 121/F2
Kisangani (int'l arpt.), D.R. Congo 121/F2
Kisantu, D.R. Congo 120/C4
Kisar (isl.), Indo. 128/B1
Kisaran, Indo. 89/B2
Kisarawe, Tanz. 119/B3
Kisarazu, Japan 85/F3
Kisauni (Zanzibar) (int'l arpt.), Tanz. 119/B3
Kisber, Hun. 43/K5
Kisbey, Sk, Can. 156/C3
Kisei, Japan 83/K7
Kiselevsk, Rus. 74/J4
Kisenda, D.R. Congo 120/D4
Kisenge, D.R. Congo 121/E5
Kisessa, Tanz. 119/A2
Kīsh, Iran 103/H5
Kīsh (isl.), Iran 103/H5
Kishanda, Tanz. 121/G3
Kishanganj, India 97/F2
Kishangarh, India 96/A2
Kishangarh, India 92/B2
Kishi, Nga. 115/F4
Kishiwada, Japan 83/H7
Kishoreganj, Bang. 97/G3
Kishorganj, Bang. 97/H3
Kishtwar, India 98/C3
Kishwaukee (riv.), Il, US 167/N15
Kisi, D.R. Congo 121/G3
Kisigo (riv.), Tanz. 119/A3
Kisii, Kenya 119/A2
Kisiju, Tanz. 119/B3
Kisiwani, Tanz. 119/B3
Kiska (isl.), Ak, US 75/T4
Kiska (mt.), Ak, US 171/B5
Kiskissink, Qu, Can. 158/A2
Kiskőrös, Hun. 50/D2
Kiskunfélegyháza, Hun. 50/D2
Kiskunhalas, Hun. 50/D2
Kiskunmajsa, Hun. 50/D2
Kiskunsági Nemzeti NP, Hun. 50/D2
Kislovodsk, Rus. 71/G4
Kismaayo, Som. 119/C2
Kismaayo (Chisimayu), Som. 119/C2
Kiso (riv.), Japan 85/E3
Kisogawa, Japan 83/L5
Kisoro, Ugan. 121/G3
Kisozaki, Japan 83/L5
Kisrah, Tun. 112/L7
Kíssamos, Gre. 49/H5
Kissee Mills, Mo, US 153/H2
Kissidougou, Gui. 114/C4
Kissimmee, Fl, US 164/N7
Kissimmee (lake), Fl, US 165/H4
Kissimmee (riv.), Fl, US 165/H4
Kissing, Ger. 58/D6
Kisslegg, Ger. 61/F2
Kissū (peak), Sudan 108/E4
Kissy, SLeo. 114/B4
Kist, Ger. 58/C3
Kisújszállás, Hun. 50/E2
Kisumu, Kenya 119/A2
Kisvárda, Hun. 43/M4
Kiswere, Tanz. 119/B4
Kit Carson, Co, US 152/C1
Kita, Mali 114/C3
Kita (lake), Japan 85/G2
Kita-Ibaraki, Japan 85/G2
Kitaaiki, Japan 83/B1
Kitab, Uzb. 74/G6
Kitadaitō (isl.), Japan 85/L8
Kitagata, Japan 83/L5
Kitakami, Japan 82/B4
Kitakami (mts.), Japan 82/B4
Kitakami (riv.), Japan 82/B4
Kitakata, Japan 85/F2
Kitakawabe, Japan 83/D1
Kitakyūshū, Japan 84/B4
Kitale, Kenya 119/A1
Kitami, Japan 82/C2
Kitami (mts.), Japan 79/N2
Kitamimaki, Japan 83/A1
Kitamoto, Japan 83/D1
Kitan (str.), Japan 83/G7
Kitangari, Tanz. 119/B4
Kitangiri (lake), Tanz. 119/A3
Kitaura, Japan 83/F1
Kitchener, On, Can. 160/F3
Kite, Ga, US 163/F4
Kitendwe, D.R. Congo 121/G4
Kitengo, D.R. Congo 121/F4
Kitgum, Ugan. 121/H2
Kíthira, Gre. 49/H4
Kíthira (isl.), Gre. 67/J3
Kíthnos, Gre. 49/J4
Kíthnos (isl.), Gre. 67/K3
Kithor, India 96/A1
Kitim, Jor. 105/D4
Kitimat, BC, Can. 140/D3
Kitkatla, BC, Can. 171/M5
Kitomesa, D.R. Congo 120/C4
Kitsap (co.), Wa, US 167/B3
Kitscoty, Ab, Can. 145/J1
Kitsman', Ukr. 72/C3
Kitt Peak National Observatory, Az, US 149/G5
Kittanning, Pa, US 161/G4
Kittatinny (mts.), NJ, US 168/C1
Kittery, Me, US 161/L3
Kitty Hawk, NC, US 163/K2
Kitu, D.R. Congo 121/F4
Kitui, Kenya 119/B2
Kitui Nat'l Rsv., Kenya 119/B2
Kitumala (pt.), PNG 129/G1
Kitumbeine (peak), Tanz. 119/B2
Kitumbini, Tanz. 119/B4
Kitunda, Tanz. 119/A3
Kitunguli, Tanz. 119/C4
Kitwe, Zam. 123/F2
Kitzbühel, Aus. 45/K3
Kitzingen, Ger. 58/D3
Kiunga, Kenya 119/C2
Kiunga, PNG 129/F1
Kiunga Marine Nat'l Res., Kenya 119/C2
Kiuruvesi, Fin. 68/E3
Kiuyu (pt.), Tanz. 119/B3
Kivalina, Ak, US 171/F2
Kivalo (mts.), Fin. 38/H2
Kivertsi, Ukr. 72/C2
Kivi-Vigala, Est. 41/L2
Kivijärvi (lake), Fin. 41/M1
Kivik, Swe. 39/L7
Kiviõli, Est. 41/M2
Kivu (lake), D.R. Congo 107/E5
Kiwai (isl.), PNG 129/F2
Kiwela, D.R. Congo 121/F4
Kiwira, Tanz. 119/A4
Kiyevka, Rus. 71/G3
Kiyevka, Kaz. 99/B1
Kıyıköy, Turk. 51/J5
Kiyokawa, Japan 83/C3
Kiyosu, Japan 83/L5
Kizamba, D.R. Congo 120/D5
Kizel, Rus. 69/N4
Kizëma, Rus. 69/K3
Kizhaba, Azer. 103/G2
Kizil (riv.), China 74/H6
Kızılcadağ, Turk. 104/A1
Kızılcahamam, Turk. 70/E4
Kızıldag NP, Turk. 102/B2
Kızılhisar, Turk. 102/B2
Kızılırmak (riv.), Turk. 70/E4
Kizil'skoye, Rus. 71/L1
Kızıltepe, Turk. 102/E2
Kızılyaka, Turk. 102/C2
Kizimbani, Tanz. 119/B4
Kizimkazi, Tanz. 119/B3
Kizlyar, Rus. 71/H4
Kizu (riv.), Japan 84/E3
Kizu, Japan 83/J6
Kizukuri, Japan 82/B3
Kizyl-Aatrek, Trkm. 103/H2
Kizyl-Su, Trkm. 103/H2
Kjeller, Nor. 38/T8
Kjerkestinden (peak), Nor. 38/F1
Kjevik (int'l arpt.), Nor. 40/C2
Kjølen (mts.), Nor. 38/E2
Klabava (riv.), Czh. 59/G3
Kladanj, Bosn. 50/D3
Kladar, Indo. 129/E2
Kladno, Czh. 59/H2
Kladovo, Serb. 50/F3
Klaeng, Thai. 94/C3
Klagenfurt, Aus. 45/L3
Klaipėda, Lith. 41/J4
Klakah, Indo. 89/F5
Klamath (riv.), Ca, US 142/B3
Klamath, Ca, US 146/A3
Klamath (mts.), Ca,Or, US 146/B2
Klamath Falls, Or, US 146/C2
Klamath Forest NWR, Or, US 146/C2
Klåmmingen (lake), Swe. 39/A1
Klangenan, Indo. 89/E4
Klapmuts, SAfr. 124/L10
Klar (riv.), Swe. 74/B4
Klarälven (riv.), Swe. 38/E3
Klarup, Den. 40/D3
Klaserie, SAfr. 123/F5
Klášterec nad Ohří, Czh. 59/G2
Klaten, Indo. 89/E4
Klatovy, Czh. 59/G4
Klaukkala, Fin. 39/E4
Klaus, Aus. 61/F3
Klausen (Chiusa), It. 61/H4
Klausenpass (pass), Swi. 61/E4
Klawock, Ak, US 171/M4
Klaza (mt.), Yk, Can. 171/L3
Klazienaveen, Neth. 52/E3
Kleena Kleene, BC, Can. 144/B2
Klein Karas, Namb. 124/B2
Klein Spitzkoppe (peak), Namb. 122/B4
Klein Vaaldoorn, Namb. 124/B3
Klein-Letabarivier (riv.), SAfr. 123/F4
Kleinblittersdorf, Ger. 55/G5
Kleinburg, On, Can. 160/T8
Kleine Elster (riv.), Ger. 43/G3
Kleine Emme (riv.), Swi. 60/E4
Kleine Gete (riv.), Belg. 55/D2
Kleine Laber (riv.), Ger. 59/F5
Kleine Nete (riv.), Belg. 55/D1
Kleinheubach, Ger. 58/C3
Kleinlützel, Swi. 60/D3
Kleinmachnow, Ger. 42/Q7
Kleinmond, SAfr. 124/L11
Kleinolifants (riv.), SAfr. 124/Q12
Kleinrinderfeld, Ger. 58/C3
Kleinsee, SAfr. 124/B3
Kleinwallstadt, Ger. 58/C3
Kleinwinternheim, Ger. 58/B3
Klemme, Ia, US 155/H2
Kleppe, Nor. 40/A2
Kleppestø, Nor. 40/A1
Klerksdorp, SAfr. 124/D2
Klesiv, Ukr. 72/D2
Klet' (peak), Czh. 59/H5
Kletnya, Rus. 70/E1
Kletskiy, Rus. 73/M3
Kleve, Ger. 52/D5
Klichev, Bela. 41/N5
Klichka, Rus. 79/H1
Klickitat, Wa, US 144/D5
Klickitat (riv.), Wa, US 144/D4
Klimovichi, Bela. 70/D1
Klimovo, Rus. 70/E1
Klina, Serb. 50/E4
Klinaklini (riv.), BC, Can. 144/B2
Kling, Phil. 88/D4
Klingenberg am Main, Ger. 58/C3
Klingenmünster, Ger. 58/B4
Klingenthal, Ger. 59/F2
Klínovec (peak), Czh. 59/F2
Klintehamn, Swe. 40/H3
Klintsy, Rus. 70/E1
Klip (riv.), SAfr. 124/E2
Klippan, Swe. 40/E3
Klipplaat, SAfr. 124/D4
Klisura, Bul. 51/G4
Klitmøller, Den. 40/C3
Kljajićevo, Serb. 50/D3
Ključ, Bosn. 50/C3
Kłodawa, Pol. 43/K2
Kłodzko, Pol. 43/J3
Klondike, Ga, US 163/M7
Klondyke, Az, US 149/G4
Klöntaler-See (lake), Swi. 61/E3
Kloosterzande, Neth. 52/B6
Kloster, Ger. 40/E4
Klosterbach (riv.), Ger. 53/F3
Klosterlechfeld, Ger. 61/G1
Klosterneuburg, Aus. 51/N7
Klosters, Swi. 61/F4
Klosterwappen (peak), Aus. 43/H5
Kloten, Swi. 61/E3
Klothuhta Zayat, Myan. 86/C5
Klötze, Ger. 42/F2
Kluane, Yk, Can. 171/L3
Kluane NP, Yk, Can. 171/K3
Kluczbork, Pol. 43/K3
Klundert, Neth. 52/B5
Klukshu, Yk, Can. 171/L3
Klukwan, Ak, US 171/L3
Klyavlino, Rus. 69/M5
Klyaz'ma (riv.), Rus. 68/J4
Klyuchevskaya (peak), Rus. 75/S4
Klyuchi, Rus. 75/R4
Knaphill, Eng, UK 30/B3
Knapp (hill), Wi, US 155/J1
Knappa, Or, US 144/C4
Knapstad, Nor. 38/T9
Knäred, Swe. 40/E3
Knaresborough, Eng, UK 35/G3
Knebworth, Eng, UK 37/F3
Kneehills (cr.), Ab, Can. 145/H2
Knetzgau, Ger. 58/D3
Knezha, Bul. 51/G4
Knife (riv.), ND, US 156/C4
Knife River Indian Villages Nat'l Hist. Site, ND, US 156/D4
Knight (inlet), BC, Can. 144/B2
Knighton, Wal, UK 36/C2
Knights, Fl, US 164/L7
Knightsen, Ca, US 167/L11
Knin, Cro. 50/C3
Knippa, Tx, US 150/E3
Knislinge, Swe. 39/L6
Knittelfeld, Aus. 45/L3
Knittlingen, Ger. 58/B4
Knivsta, Swe. 40/G2
Knížecí Stolec (peak), Czh. 59/H5
Knížecí Strom (peak), Czh. 59/F3
Knjaževac, Serb. 50/F4
Knob (cape), Austl. 130/C5
Knob (peak), Phil. 91/F1
Knobby (pt.), Austl. 130/B4
Knobel, Ar, US 162/B2
Knoch (hill), Sc, UK 33/D1
Knock, Ire. 32/B2
Knockadoon Head (pt.), Ire. 32/C6
Knockalongy (peak), Ire. 32/B1
Knockanaffrin (peak), Ire. 32/C5
Knockanore (mtn.), Ire. 32/A4
Knockboy (peak), Ire. 32/A6
Knockcloghrim, NI, UK 34/B2
Knockeirke (peak), Ire. 32/A6
Knocklong, Ire. 32/B5
Knockmealdown (peak), Ire. 32/C5
Knockmealdown (mts.), Ire. 32/B5
Knocknagashel, Ire. 32/A5
Knocknamaddree (peak), Ire. 32/A7
Knockowen (peak), Ire. 32/A6
Knockshanahullion (peak), Ire. 32/B5
Knoll (pt.), Namb. 122/B5
Knøsen (peak), Den. 40/D3
Knösen (pt.), Swe. 40/E4
Knosós (Knossos) (ruin), Gre. 49/J5
Knossos (Knosós) (ruin), Gre. 49/J5
Knott, Tx, US 150/D1
Knott End, Eng, UK 35/F4
Knottingley, Eng, UK 35/G4
Knott's Berry Farm, Ca, US 166/G8
Knotts Island, NC, US 163/K2
Knotty Green, Eng, UK 30/B2
Knowl Hill, Eng, UK 30/A2
Knowsley (co.), Eng, UK 35/F5
Knox, ND, US 156/E3
Knox, Pa, US 161/G4
Knox, In, US 160/C4
Knox (coast), Ant. 192/G
Knox (cape), BC, Can. 140/C3
Knox (nbrhd.), Austl. 132/G5
Knox City, Tx, US 152/E4
Knoxville, Ms, US 164/C2
Knoxville, Ia, US 155/H3
Knoxville, Tn, US 162/F3
Knoxville, Ga, US 162/F4
Knutby, Swe. 39/B1
Knutsford, Eng, UK 35/F5
Knysna, SAfr. 124/C4
Ko (riv.), Sen. 114/B3
Ko (peak), Rus. 79/M2
Ko Samut NP, Thai. 94/C3
Ko-saki (pt.), Japan 84/A3
Koanaka (hills), Bots. 122/D4
Koani, Tanz. 119/B3
Koāth, India 97/E3
Koba, Indo. 89/D3
Kobar Sink (depr.), Eth. 118/B2
Kobayashi, Japan 84/B5
Kōbe, Japan 83/H6
Kobelyaky, Ukr. 73/H3
København (int'l arpt.), Den. 40/E4
København (co.), Den. 39/J7
København (Copenhagen) (cap.), Den. 39/J7
Kobenni, Mrta. 114/C3
Kobern-Gondorf, Ger. 55/G3
Kobipato (peak), Indo. 91/G4
Koblach, Aus. 61/F3
Koblenz, Swi. 61/E2
Koblenz, Ger. 55/G3
K'obo, Eth. 118/A2
Kobowan (swamp), Sudan 117/G4
Kobozha, Rus. 68/G4
Kobra, Rus. 69/L3
Kobroor (isl.), Indo. 91/H5
Kobryn, Bela. 70/C1
Kobu, SKor. 81/D5
Kobuchizawa, Japan 83/A2
Kobuk, Ak, US 171/G2
Kobuk (riv.), Ak, US 171/G2
Kobuk Valley NP, Ak, US 171/G2
K'obulet'i, Geo. 71/G4
Kobushi-ga-take (peak), Japan 85/F3
Kocába (riv.), Czh. 59/H3
Kocaeli (prov.), Turk. 70/D4
Koçalı, Turk. 102/D2
Kočani, FYROM 49/H2
Kocapınar, Turk. 103/E2
Kočevje, Slov. 45/L4
Koch (isl.), Nun, Can. 141/J2
Koch'ang, SKor. 81/D5
Koch'ang, SKor. 81/D5
Kochel am See, Ger. 61/H2
Kochelsee (lake), Ger. 61/H2
Kochen'ga, Rus. 69/J3
Kocher (riv.), Ger. 45/H2
Kocherinovo, Bul. 49/H1
Kochetovka, Rus. 71/G1
Kochevo, Rus. 69/M4
Kōchi (pref.), Japan 84/C4
Kōchi, Japan 84/C4
Kochmes, Rus. 69/P2
Kochubey, Rus. 71/H3
Kochubeyevskoye, Rus. 73/L5
Kochugaon, India 97/H2
Kodaira, Japan 83/C2
Kodala, India 95/E2
Kodama, Japan 83/C1
Kodāri, Nepal 97/E2
Kodarmā, India 97/E3
Kodiak, Ak, US 171/H4
Kodiak (isl.), Ak, US 171/H4
Kodinār, India 101/K4
Kodomari, Japan 82/B3
Kodry (hills), Mol. 51/H2
Kodyma, Ukr. 72/E3
Koekelare, Belg. 54/B1
Koel (riv.), India 92/D3
Koes, Namb. 124/B2
Koesan, SKor. 81/D4
Koetari (riv.), Sur. 181/G4
Kofa (mts.), Az, US 149/E4
Kofa NWR, Az, US 149/E4
Kofçaz, Turk. 51/H5
Kofelē, Eth. 118/A4
Koffiefontein, SAfr. 124/D3
Kofiau (isl.), Indo. 91/G4
Koforidua, Gha. 115/E5
Kōfu, Japan 85/F3
Koga, Japan 85/F2
Koga, Tanz. 121/H4
Koganei, Japan 83/D2
Kogarah, Austl. 133/E1
Køge (bay), Den. 40/E4
Kogi, Nga. 115/G4
Kogon (riv.), Gui. 114/B4
Kŏgum (isl.), SKor. 81/D5
Kohāt, Pak. 98/A3
Kohila, Est. 41/L2
Kohīma, India 86/B3
Kohkīlūyeh and Bovīr Aḩmadi (gov.), Iran 103/G4
Kohler, Wi, US 160/C3
Kohls Ranch, Az, US 149/G3
Kohoku, Japan 83/K5
Kohout (peak), Czh. 59/H5
Kohtla-Järve, Est. 41/M2
Kohŭng, SKor. 81/D5
Kohunlich (ruin), Mex. 176/D2
Koichab (riv.), Namb. 122/B5
Koidern, Yk, Can. 171/K3
Koidu, SLeo. 114/C4
Koigi, Est. 41/L2
Koihoa, India 93/F6
Koilābās, Nepal 96/D2
Koímisis, Gre. 49/H2
Koindu, SLeo. 114/C4
Koito, Kenya 119/B2
Koito (riv.), Japan 83/D3
Koiva (riv.), Lat. 41/M3
Kŏje (isl.), SKor. 84/A3
Kojonup, Austl. 130/C5
Kojšovská (peak), Slvk. 43/L4
Kok (riv.), Myan. 94/B1
Kōka, Japan 83/K6
K'ok'a Gidib (dam), Eth. 118/A3
Kokai (riv.), Japan 83/E2
Kökar (isl.), Fin. 41/J3
Kokas, Indo. 91/H4
Kokemäenjoki (riv.), Fin. 41/J1
Kokhonak, Ak, US 171/H4
Kokhanovo, Bela. 41/N4
Kokkola (Karleby), Fin. 68/D3
Koknese, Lat. 41/L3
Koko, Nga. 115/G5
Koko, Nga. 115/G4
Kokoda, PNG 129/G2
Kokofata, Mali 114/C3
Kokola, D.R. Congo 121/G2
Kokomo, In, US 160/C4
Kokonau, Indo. 91/J4
Kokong, Bots. 122/D5
Kokonjärvi (lake), Fin. 39/D3
Kokrajhar, India 97/H2
Koksan, NKor. 81/D3
Kokshaal-Tau (mts.), Kyr. 99/C3
Kökshetaū, Kaz. 99/A1
Koksijde, Belg. 54/B1
Koksoak (riv.), Qu, Can. 141/K3
Koksovyy, Rus. 73/L3
Kokstad, SAfr. 124/E3
Kokubu, Japan 84/B5
Kokuy, Rus. 79/H1
Kol, PNG 129/G1
Kola (isl.), Indo. 91/H5
Kola (riv.), Rus. 68/G1
Kola (pen.), Rus. 68/H1
Kolachel, India 95/C4
Kolahun, Libr. 114/C4
Kolaka, Indo. 91/F4
Kolāras, India 96/A3
Kolašin, Serb. 50/D4
Kolbäck, Swe. 40/G2
Kolbano, Indo. 128/B2
Kolbio, Kenya 119/C2
Kolbotn, Nor. 38/S8
Kolbus, Sudan 116/D2
Kolbuszowa, Pol. 43/L3
Kolda, Sen. 114/B3
Kolda (pol. reg.), Sen. 114/B3
Kolding, Den. 40/C4
Kole, D.R. Congo 121/F2
Kolebira, India 97/E4
Kölen (mts.), Swe. 38/E2
Kolenté, Gui. 114/B4
Kolepom (Yos Sudarso) (isl.), Indo. 136/C5
Kolezhma, Rus. 68/G2
Kolgaküla, Est. 41/L2
Kolgompya (cape), Rus. 41/N2
Kolguyev (isl.), Rus. 69/K1
Koliba (riv.), Gui. 114/B3
Koliganek, Ak, US 171/G4
Kolín, Czh. 43/H3
Kolind, Den. 39/G6
Koliya, Gui. 114/B4
Kolka, Lat. 41/K3
Kolkasrags (pt.), Lat. 41/K3
Kolkhozabad, Taj. 101/J1
Kollbach (riv.), Ger. 59/F5
Kollnburg, Ger. 59/F4
Kollum, Neth. 52/D2
Kolmanskop, Namb. 124/A2
Köln (Cologne), Ger. 55/F2
Kolno, Pol. 43/L2
Koło, Pol. 70/A1
Kolo, Tanz. 119/A3
Kołobrzeg, Pol. 40/F4
Kolofata, Camr. 116/B3
Kologriv, Rus. 69/K4
Kolokani, Mali 114/C3
Kololo, Eth. 118/B4
Kolomna, Rus. 68/H5
Kolomyya, Ukr. 72/C3
Kolondiéba, Mali 114/D4
Kolongotomo, Mali 114/D3
Kolonnawa, SrL. 95/C5
Kolosib, India 86/B3
Kolossa (riv.), Mali 114/D3
Kolpashevo, Rus. 74/J4
Kolpino, Rus. 69/T7
Kolpny, Rus. 70/F1
Kolpyta, Ukr. 72/F2
Kolsva, Swe. 40/F2
Kolubara (riv.), Serb. 50/D3
Koluszki, Pol. 43/K3
Koluton (riv.), Kaz. 99/A1
Kolva (riv.), Rus. 69/N2
Kolwezi, D.R. Congo 121/F5
Kolyma (riv.), Rus. 77/Q3
Kolyma (range), Rus. 77/Q3
Kolyma Lowland (plain), Rus. 75/R2
Kolyshley, Rus. 71/H1
Kom (peak), Bul. 51/F4
Kom (riv.), Gabon 120/C2
Koma, Myan. 94/B3
Koma (riv.), Japan 83/C2
Komádi, Hun. 50/E2
Komadugu Gana (riv.), Nga. 115/H4
Komadugu Yobe (riv.), Nga. 115/H3
Komae, Japan 83/D2
Komagane, Japan 85/E3
Komaki, Japan 83/L5
Komaki (arpt.), Japan 83/L5
Komanda, D.R. Congo 121/G2
Komandorskiye (isls.), Rus. 77/R4
Komarichi, Rus. 73/H1
Komarin, Bela. 72/F2
Komárno, Slvk. 50/D2
Komárom, Hun. 50/D2
Komárom-Esztergom (prov.), Hun. 50/D2
Komatipoort, SAfr. 123/F5
Komatirivier (riv.), SAfr. 124/Q13
Komatlapeta, India 95/D2
Komatsu, Japan 84/E2
Komatsu (int'l arpt.), Japan 84/E2
Komatsushima, Japan 84/D3
Komba, D.R. Congo 121/E2
Kombat, Namb. 122/C3
Kombe, D.R. Congo 121/F4
Kombissiri, Burk. 115/E3
Kome (isl.), Ugan. 119/A2
Komering (riv.), Indo. 89/D4
Komi-Permyatskiy Aut. Okrug, Rus. 69/M2
Komjatice, Slvk. 43/K4
Komló, Hun. 50/D2
Kommetjie, SAfr. 124/L11
Kommunar, Rus. 41/P2
Komo, PNG 129/F1
Komodo (isl.), Indo. 91/E5
Komodo Island NP, Indo. 91/E5
Komodougou, Gui. 114/C4
Komoé (riv.), C.d'Iv. 114/E5
Komono, Congo 120/C3
Komono, Japan 83/L5
Komoran (isl.), Indo. 91/J5
Komoro, Japan 83/A1
Komotiní, Gre. 49/J2
Kompasberg (peak), SAfr. 124/D3
Kompiam, PNG 129/F1
Komsomolets (isl.), Rus. 77/J1
Komsomol's'k, Ukr. 73/G3
Komsomol'sk-na-Amure, Rus. 79/M1
Komsomol's'ke, Ukr. 73/J3
Komsomol's'ke, Ukr. 73/K4
Komsomol'skiy, Rus. 69/P2
Komsomol'skiy, Rus. 69/K5
Komsomol'skiy, Kaz. 71/K3
Komsomol'skiy, Rus. 74/G3
Komsomol'skiy, Rus. 71/H3
Komsomol'skoye, Rus. 71/H2
Komukanti, Namb. 122/C3
Kömür (pt.), Turk. 49/K3
Komysh-Zorya, Ukr. 73/J4
Komyshnya, Ukr. 73/G2
Kon (riv.), Kaz. 99/A2
Kon Plong, Viet. 94/E3
Kon Tum, Viet. 94/D3
Konabonou, C.d'Iv. 114/D5
Konakovo, Rus. 68/H4
Kōnan, Japan 83/K6
Kōnan, Japan 83/L5
Kōnan, Japan 83/C1
Konar (riv.), Afg. 98/A2
Konār (riv.), India 97/E4
Konār (res.), India 97/E4
Konar-e Khāş, Afg. 98/A2
Konārak, Iran 101/H3
Konārak, India 95/E2
Konawa, Ok, US 153/F3
Konaweha (riv.), Indo. 91/F4
Konda (riv.), Rus. 78/G1
Konda, Japan 83/H6
Kondagaon, India 95/D2
Kondé Sounga, Congo 120/B4
Kondinin, Austl. 130/C5
Kondoa, Tanz. 119/A3
Kondopoga, Rus. 68/G3
Kondūz, Afg. 74/G6
Koné, NCal. 137/U12
Konetsgor'ye, Rus. 68/J3
Kong, C.d'Iv. 114/D4
Kong (isl.), Camb. 94/C4
Kong (riv.), Laos 94/D3
Kong Kong (riv.), Sudan 117/G4
Kong Krailat, Thai. 94/B2
Kong Miao, China 80/D4
Kongapatalabata, Indo. 128/D1
Kongbo, CAfr. 116/D4
Kongiganak, Ak, US 171/F4
Kongju, SKor. 81/D4
Kongnŭng (riv.), SKor. 81/F6
Kongō-zan (peak), Japan 83/J7
Kongola, Namb. 122/D3
Kongolo, D.R. Congo 121/F4
Kongor, Sudan 117/F4
Kongoussi, Burk. 115/E3
Kongsberg, Nor. 40/C2
Kongsvinger, Nor. 40/E1
Kongtan, China 86/E2
Kongué, Chutes de (falls), Gabon 120/C2
Kongur (peak), China 99/C4
Kongwa, Tanz. 119/B3
Koniecpol, Pol. 43/K3
Königs Wusterhausen, Ger. 42/Q7
Königsberg in Bayern, Ger. 58/D2
Königsberg-Stein, Ger. 58/B5
Königsbronn, Ger. 58/D5
Königsbrunn, Ger. 61/G1
Königsdorf, Ger. 61/H2
Königsfeld im Schwarzwald, Ger. 61/E1
Königslutter am Elm, Ger. 53/H4
Königstein im Taunus, Ger. 58/B2
Königswinter, Ger. 55/G2
Konin, Pol. 43/K2
Konindou, Gui. 114/C4
Konispol, Alb. 49/G3
Kónitsa, Gre. 49/G2
Köniz, Swi. 60/D4
Konjic, Bosn. 50/C4
Könkämäeno (riv.), Fin. 68/D1
Konkiep (riv.), Namb. 122/C5
Konkiep, Namb. 124/B2
Konkola, Zam. 123/E2
Konkori, Gha. 115/E4
Konkouré (riv.), Gui. 114/B4
Konkourou-Bamingui, Rsv. de Faune du, CAfr. 116/D4
Konnevesi, Fin. 68/E3
Konobougou, Mali 114/D3
Konolfingen, Swi. 60/D4
Konosha, Rus. 68/J3
Kōnosu, Japan 83/D1
Konotop, Ukr. 73/G2
Konqi (riv.), China 74/J5
Konsen (plat.), Japan 82/D2
Końskie, Pol. 43/L3
Konso, Eth. 117/H4
Konstancin-Jeziorna, Pol. 43/L2
Konstantinovka, Ukr. 73/H3
Konstantinovsk, Rus. 73/L4
Konstantynów Łódzki, Pol. 43/K3
Konstanz, Ger. 61/F2
Kontagora, Nga. 115/G4
Kontcha, Camr. 116/B4
Konteyevo, Rus. 68/J4
Kontich, Belg. 55/D1
Kontiolahti, Fin. 68/F3
Konuralp, Turk. 51/K5
Kóny, Hun. 50/C2
Konya, Turk. 102/C2
Konya (prov.), Turk. 102/C2
Konz, Ger. 55/F4
Konza, Kenya 119/B2
Koo-wee-rup, Austl. 133/B4
Koocenusa (lake), Mt, US 144/G3
Koog aan de Zaan, Neth. 52/B4
Koolpinyah, Austl. 128/C3
Koolyanobbing, Austl. 130/C4
Koondrook, Austl. 133/B2
Koonga, Est. 41/L2
Koonibba, Austl. 131/G4
Koontz Lake, In, US 160/C4
Kooparmora, Swe. 39/B1
Koorawatha, Austl. 133/D2
Koorda, Austl. 130/C4
Koosa, Est. 41/M2
Koosharem, Ut, US 149/G1
Kooskia, Id, US 144/G4
Kootenai Nat'l Wild. Ref., Id, US 144/F3
Kootenay (lake), BC, Can. 140/E3
Kootenay (riv.), BC, Can. 144/G2
Kootenay NP, BC, Can. 144/F2
Kootingal, Austl. 132/D1
Kop (pass), Turk. 102/E1
Kopāganj, India 96/D2
Kopaigo, PNG 129/F1
Kopargaon, India 95/B2
Kopargo, Ben. 115/F4
Kópavogur, Ice. 38/N7
Kope (peak), C.d'Iv. 114/D5
Köpenick, Ger. 42/Q7
Koper, Slov. 45/K4
Kopervik, Nor. 40/A2
Kopeysk, Rus. 69/P5
Kopfing im Innkreis, Aus. 59/G6
Kopia, D.R. Congo 121/E2
Kopili (riv.), India 86/B3
Köping, Swe. 40/G2
Koplik, Alb. 49/F1
Kopondei (cape), Indo. 128/A2
Koporskiy (bay), Rus. 41/N2
Koppang, Nor. 40/D1
Kopparberg (co.), Swe. 38/E3
Kopparberg, Swe. 40/F2
Koppi (riv.), Rus. 79/M2
Koppies, SAfr. 124/D2

Kopriv – Kyonan

Koprivnica, Cro. 50/C2
Koprivshtitsa, Bul. 51/G4
Kopru (riv.), Turk. 104/B1
Köprülü, Turk. 104/C1
Köprülü Kanyon NP, Turk. 102/B2
Kop'ung, NKor. 81/C2
Kopyl', Bela. 70/C1
Kopys', Bela. 41/P4
Kor (riv.), Iran 100/F2
Kora, India 96/C2
Kōra, Japan 83/K5
Kora NP, Kenya 119/B2
Korab (peak), Alb. 49/G2
Koráb (peak), Czh. 59/G4
Korablino, Rus. 70/G1
K'orahē, Eth. 118/C4
Korakuen Garden, Japan 84/C3
Koraluk (riv.), Nf, Can. 141/K3
Koramlik, China 99/E4
Korana (riv.), Cro. 45/L4
Korazim NP, Isr. 105/D3
Korba, India 96/D4
Korbach, Ger. 53/F6
K'orbeta, Eth. 118/A2
Korbu (peak), Malay. 89/C1
Korçë, Alb. 49/G2
Korčula (isl.), Cro. 67/H2
Korčula, Cro. 50/C4
Korčulanski Kanal (chan.), It. 48/E1
Korčulanski Kanal (chan.), Cro. 50/C4
Kord Kūy, Iran 103/H2
Kordel, Ger. 55/F4
Kordestān (gov.), Iran 103/F3
Korea (bay), China,NKor. 75/N6
Korea (str.), Japan,Skor. 75/P6
Korean Folk Village, SKor. 81/G7
Korem, Eth. 118/A2
Korenovsk, Rus. 73/K5
Korets', Ukr. 72/D2
Korf, Rus. 75/S3
Korgas, China 99/D3
Korhogo, C.d'Iv. 114/D4
Korido, Indo. 91/J4
Korienzé, Mali 114/E3
Korim, Indo. 91/J4
Korinós, Gre. 49/H2
Kórinthos (Corinth), Gre. 49/H4
Kórinthos (Corinth) (ruin), Gre. 49/H4
Kóris-Hegy (peak), Hun. 50/C2
Köritz, Ger. 42/G2
Kōriyama, Japan 85/G2
Korizo, Passe de (pass), Chad 108/B4
Korkino, Rus. 69/P5
Korkodon (riv.), Rus. 75/R3
Korkuteli, Turk. 104/B1
Korla, China 99/E3
Kormakiti (cape), Cyp. 104/C2
Körmend, Hun. 50/C2
Kornat (isl.), Cro. 45/L5
Körner, Ger. 53/H6
Korneuburg, Aus. 51/N7
Kornman, Co, US 152/C1
Korntal-Münchingen, Ger. 58/C5
Kornwestheim, Ger. 58/C5
Koro, C.d'Iv. 114/D4
Koro, Mali 114/E3
Koro (sea), Fiji 137/Z18
Koro Toro, Chad 116/C1
Koroba, PNG 129/F1
Korocha, Rus. 73/J2
Köroğlu (peak), Turk. 70/D4
Korogwe, Tanz. 119/B3
Koroit, Austl. 132/B3
Koronadal, Phil. 88/D4
Korónia (lake), Gre. 49/H2
Koronowo, Pol. 43/J2
Koropíon, Gre. 49/N9
Koror (cap.), Palau 136/C4
Körös (riv.), Hun. 50/E2
Korosten', Ukr. 72/E2
Korostyshiv, Ukr. 72/E2
Korotaikha (riv.), Rus. 69/P1
Korovin (mt.), Ak, US 171/D5
Korovino, Rus. 71/K1
Korpo (Korppoo), Fin. 41/J1
Korppoo (Korpo), Fin. 41/J1
Korsakov, Rus. 79/N2
Korschenbroich, Ger. 52/D6
Korsö (isl.), Swe. 39/B1
Korsør, Den. 40/D4
Korsun'-Shevchenkivs'kyy, Ukr. 72/F3
Korsze, Pol. 41/J4
Kortemark, Belg. 54/C1
Kortenaken, Belg. 55/E2
Kortenberg, Belg. 55/D2
Kortessem, Belg. 55/E2
Korti Linchang, China 99/E2
Kortrijk, Belg. 54/C2
Kortsevo, Rus. 68/J4
Korumburra, Austl. 133/B4
Korup, PN de, Camr. 115/H5
Koryak (range), Rus. 77/R3
Koryakskiy Aut. Okrug, Rus. 75/S3
Koryazhma, Rus. 69/K3
Kōryō, Japan 83/J6
Koryŏng, SKor. 81/E5
Koryukivka, Ukr. 72/G2
Kós, Gre. 102/A2
Kós (isl.), Gre. 102/A2
Kosai, Japan 85/E3
Kosai, Japan 83/A2
Kosan, NKor. 81/D3
Kosaya Gora, Rus. 70/F1
Koschagyl, Kaz. 71/K3
Kösching, Ger. 59/E5
Kościan, Pol. 43/J2
Kościerzyna, Pol. 40/G4
Kosciusko, Ms, US 162/C4
Kosciusko (mt.), Austl. 133/D3
Köse, Turk. 102/D1
Kose, Est. 41/L2
Kosei, Japan 83/K6
Kosha, Sudan 109/F4
Koshigaya, Japan 85/F3
Koshiki (isls.), Japan 85/K5
Koshkar, Kaz. 71/K3
Koshkonong, Mo, US 153/J2
Koshkonong (lake), Wi, US 155/K2
Kosi (zone), Nepal 97/F2
Kosi, India 96/A2
Kosi (riv.), India 92/E2
Košice, Slvk. 43/L4
Košický (pol. reg.), Slvk. 43/L4
Kosiv, Ukr. 72/C3
Koski, Fin. 39/F3
Koskinoú, Gre. 102/B2
Koslan, Rus. 69/L3
Kosoba (peak), Kaz. 99/C2
Kosŏng, SKor. 81/E5
Kosŏng, NKor. 81/E3
Kosovo (prov.), Serb. 50/E4
Kosovo (reg.), Serb. 49/G1
Kosovo Polje, Serb. 50/E4
Kosovska Kamenica, Serb. 50/E4
Kosovska Mitrovica, Serb. 50/E4
Kosový (riv.), Czh. 59/F3
Kosrae (isl.), Micr. 136/F4
Kosse, Tx, US 151/F2
Kossi (prov.), Burk. 114/D3
Kossou (lake), C.d'Iv. 114/D5
Kosta, Swe. 40/F3
Kostelec nad Černými Lesy, Czh. 59/H3
Koster, SAfr. 124/D2
Kostinbrod, Bul. 51/F4
Kostomuksha, Rus. 68/F2
Kostopil', Ukr. 72/D2
Kostromskaya Oblast, Rus. 68/J4
Kostroma (riv.), Rus. 68/J4
Kostroma, Rus. 68/J4
Kostrzyn, Pol. 43/H2
Kostrzyn, Pol. 43/J2
Kostyantynivka, Ukr. 73/J3
Kostyantynivka, Ukr. 73/H4
Kostyukovichi, Bela. 70/E1
Kosuge, Japan 83/B2
Kos'va (riv.), Rus. 69/N4
Kos'yu (riv.), Rus. 69/N2
Kos'yu, Rus. 69/N2
Koszalin, Pol. 40/G4
Kőszeg, Hun. 50/C2
Kot Addu, Pak. 98/A4
Kot Fateh, India 98/C4
Kot Kapūra, India 98/C4
Kot Mūmin, Pak. 98/B3
Kot Rādha Kishan, Pak. 98/C4
Kot Samāba, Pak. 98/A5
Kot Sārang, Pak. 98/B3
Kota, India 96/D4
Kota, India 92/C2
Kōta, Japan 83/M6
Kota Baharu, Malay. 89/C1
Kota Belud, Malay. 88/B4
Kota Kinabalu (int'l arpt.), Malay. 88/B4
Kota Kinabalu, Malay. 88/B4
Kota Tinggi, Malay. 89/C2
Kotaagung, Indo. 89/D4
Kotabaru, Indo. 91/E4
Kotabaru, Indo. 89/C3
Kotabesi, Indo. 90/D4
Kotabumi, Indo. 89/D4
Kotabunan, Indo. 91/F3
Kotadaik, Indo. 89/D3
Kotajawa, Indo. 89/D4
Kotapād, India 95/D2
Kotapinang, Indo. 89/C2
Kotatengah, Indo. 89/C2
Kotdwāra, India 96/B1
Kotel, Bul. 51/H4
Kotel'nich, Rus. 69/L4
Kotel'nikovo, Rus. 71/G3
Kotel'nyy (isl.), Rus. 75/P2
Kotel'va, Ukr. 73/H2
Kotgarh, India 98/D4
Kothagūdem, India 95/D2
Köthen, Ger. 42/F3
Kotido, Ugan. 119/A1
Kotka, Fin. 41/M1
Kotla, India 98/D3
Kotlas, Rus. 69/K3
Kotli, Pak. 98/B3
Kotli Lohārān, Pak. 98/C3
Kotlik, Ak, US 171/F3
Kotlin (isl.), Rus. 69/S7
Kotly, Rus. 41/N2
Kotō, Japan 83/K5
Kotoka (int'l arpt.), Gha. 115/E5
Koton Karifi, Nga. 115/G4
Kotor, Serb. 50/D4
Kotor Varoš, Bosn. 50/C3
Kotovo, Rus. 71/H2
Kotovsk, Rus. 71/G1
Kotovs'k, Ukr. 72/E4
Kotri, Pak. 101/J3
Kottai Malai (peak), India 95/C4
Kottayam, India 95/C4
Kotte (Sri Jayawardanapura), SrL. 95/C5
Kotto (riv.), CAfr. 116/D4
Kotuy (riv.), Rus. 77/K3
Kotzebue, Ak, US 171/F2
Kotzebue (sound), Ak, US 171/E2
Kötzting, Ger. 59/F4
Kouandé, Ben. 115/F4
Kouango, CAfr. 116/C4
Kouba Olanga, Chad 116/C2
Koubia, Gui. 114/C4
Kouchibouguac (bay), Nb, Can. 158/E2
Kouchibouguac NP, NB, Can. 158/E2
Koudougou, Burk. 115/E3
Koufonísion (isl.), Gre. 49/J5
Kougarok (mt.), Ak, US 171/E2
Kougoulé, Gabon 120/B2
Kouhu, Tai. 87/J4
Kouilou, Congo 120/B4
Kouilou (riv.), Congo 120/C3
Koukdjuak (riv.), Nun, Can. 141/J2
Kouki, CAfr. 116/C4
Koukourou, CAfr. 116/D4
Koula-Moutou, Gabon 120/C3
Koulé, Gui. 114/C4
Koulikoro (pol. reg.), Mali 114/C3
Koulikoro, Mali 114/D3
Koulou, Niger 115/F3
Koulountou (riv.), Sen. 114/B3
Koum, Camr. 116/B3
Koumac, NCal. 137/U12
Koumala, Austl. 134/C3
Koumameyong, Gabon 120/B2
Koumandougou, Gui. 114/D4
Koumantou, Mali 114/D4
Koumban, Gui. 114/C4
Koumbi Saleh (ruin), Mrta. 114/D3
Koumbia, Gui. 114/B4
Koumi, Japan 83/A1
Koumra, Chad 116/C3
Koundara, Gui. 114/B3
Koundé, CAfr. 116/B4
Koundian, Mali 114/C3
Koundou, Gui. 114/C4
Koungheul, Sen. 114/B3
Kouno, Chad 116/C3
Kounradskiy, Kaz. 99/C2
Kountze, Tx, US 151/G2
Koupé (peak), Camr. 120/B1
Koupela, Burk. 115/E3
Kouraïa Konkouré, Gui. 114/B4
Kouritenga (prov.), Burk. 115/E3
Kourou, FrG. 182/C1
Kourouba, Mali 114/C3
Kouroussa, Gui. 114/C4
Koury, Mali 114/D3
Koussi (peak), Chad 108/C5
Koutiala, Mali 114/D3
Kouto, C.d'Iv. 114/D4
Kouvola, Fin. 41/M1
Kouyou (riv.), Congo 120/C3
Kovačica, Serb. 50/E3
Kovada Gölü NP, Turk. 102/B2
Kovalam, India 95/C4
Kovashi (riv.), Rus. 69/S7
Kovda, Rus. 68/G2
Kovdor, Rus. 68/F2
Kovdozero (lake), Rus. 38/J2
Kovel', Ukr. 72/C2
Kovilj, Serb. 50/E3
Kovilpatti, India 95/C4
Kovrov, Rus. 68/J4
Kovūr, India 95/C3
Kovylkino, Rus. 71/G1
Kowanyama Abor. Land, Austl. 129/F3
Kowanyama Aboriginal Community, Austl. 134/A1
Kowe, D.R. Congo 121/F3
Kowkcheh (riv.), Afg. 99/A4
Kowloon, China 87/L7
Kowŏn, NKor. 79/K4
Kowt-e 'Ashrow, Afg. 101/J2
Koxlax, China 99/D4
Kōyaguchi, Japan 83/J7
Koyama, Gui. 114/C5
Kōyama, Japan 84/B5
Koyang, SKor. 81/F6
Koynare, Bul. 51/G4
Koyuk, Ak, US 171/F3
Koyukuk (riv.), Ak, US 171/H2
Kozacha Lopan', Ukr. 73/J2
Kozakai, Japan 83/M6
Kōzaki, Japan 83/E2
Kozaklı, Turk. 102/C2
Kozan, Turk. 102/C2
Kozáni, Gre. 49/G2
Kozara NP, Aus. 50/C3
Kozel'shchyna, Ukr. 73/G3
Kozel'sk, Rus. 70/E1
Kozha, Rus. 69/L4
Kozhikode (Calicut), India 95/B4
Kozhozero (lake), Rus. 68/H3
Kozhva, Rus. 69/N2
Kozhva (riv.), Rus. 69/M2
Kozienice, Pol. 43/L3
Kozloduy, Bul. 51/F4
Kozlovo, Rus. 68/H4
Kozlu, Turk. 70/D4
Kozluk, Turk. 102/E2
Koźmin, Pol. 43/J3
Koz'mino, Rus. 69/L3
Koznitsa (peak), Bul. 51/F4
Kozova, Ukr. 72/C3
Kōzu (isl.), Japan 85/F3
Kożuchów, Pol. 43/H3
Kozyatyn, Ukr. 72/E3
Kpagouda, Togo 115/F4
Kpalimé, Togo 115/F5
Kpandu, Gha. 115/F5
Kpémé, Togo 115/F5
Kra (isth.), Myan. 93/G6
Kra Buri, Thai. 94/B4
Kraai (riv.), SAfr. 124/D3
Kraaifontein, SAfr. 124/L10
Krabbendijke, Neth. 52/B6
Krabbfjärden (sound), Swe. 39/A2
Krabi, Thai. 94/B4
Kracheh, Camb. 94/D3
Kragan, Indo. 89/E4
Kragerø, Nor. 40/C2
Kragujevac, Serb. 50/E3
Kraiburg am Inn, Ger. 59/F6
Kraichbach (riv.), Ger. 58/B4
Kraichgau (reg.), Ger. 45/H2
Krailling, Ger. 59/E6
Krakatau (vol.), Indo. 89/D4
Krakor, Camb. 94/D3
Kraków, Pol. 43/K3
Krakow, Wi, US 160/B2
Kråkstad, Nor. 38/S8
Kralanh, Camb. 94/C3
Kralendijk, NAnt. 180/D1
Kraljevo, Serb. 50/E4
Kralkızı (dam), Turk. 102/E2
Královéhradecký (pol. reg.), Czh. 43/H3
Kralovice, Czh. 59/G3
Kralupy nad Vltavou, Czh. 59/H2
Kramators'k, Ukr. 73/J3
Kramer, ND, US 156/D3
Kramfors, Swe. 38/F3
Krammer (chan.), Neth. 52/B5
Kranéa Elassónos, Gre. 49/G3
Kranebitten (int'l arpt.), Aus. 61/H3
Kranenburg, Ger. 52/D5
Kranídhion, Gre. 49/H4
Kranj, Slov. 45/L3
Kranji (res.), Sing. 89/H6
Kranskop, SAfr. 125/E3
Kranzberg, Namb. 122/B4
Krapkowice, Pol. 43/J3
Krāslava, Lat. 41/M4
Kraslice, Czh. 59/F2
Krasnaya Gorbatka, Rus. 68/J5
Krasnaya Sloboda, Bela. 70/C1
Krasne, Ukr. 72/C3
Krasni Okny, Ukr. 72/E4
Kraśnik, Pol. 43/M3
Kraśnik Fabryczny, Pol. 43/M3
Krasninsk, Rus. 69/N5
Krasnoarmeysk, Rus. 71/H2
Krasnoarmeysk, Rus. 69/W9
Krasnoarmeyskaya, Rus. 73/K5
Krasnoarmeyskiy, Rus. 73/M4
Krasnoarmiys'k, Ukr. 73/J3
Krasnoborsk, Rus. 69/K3
Krasnodar (int'l arpt.), Rus. 73/K5
Krasnodar, Rus. 73/K5
Krasnodarskiy Kray, Rus. 74/D5
Krasnodon, Ukr. 73/K3
Krasnogorsk, Rus. 69/W9
Krasnogvardeyskoye, Rus. 73/L5
Krasnohorivka, Ukr. 73/J3
Krasnohrad, Ukr. 73/H3
Krasnohvardiys'ke, Ukr. 73/H5
Krasnokamensk, Rus. 79/H1
Krasnokamsk, Rus. 69/M4
Krasnokholmskiy, Rus. 69/M5
Krasnolesnyy, Rus. 73/K2
Krasnooskol'skoye (res.), Ukr. 73/J3
Krasnopavlivka, Ukr. 73/J3
Krasnoperekops'k, Ukr. 73/G5
Krasnopillya, Ukr. 73/H2
Krasnoshchel'ye, Rus. 68/H2
Krasnoslobodsk, Rus. 71/G1
Krasnoslobodsk, Rus. 71/H2
Krasnotur'insk, Rus. 74/G4
Krasnoufimsk, Rus. 69/N4
Krasnoural'sk, Rus. 69/P4
Krasnovishersk, Rus. 69/N3
Krasnowodsk (int'l arpt.), Trkm. 103/H1
Krasnowodsk (Türkmenbashi), Trkm. 103/H2
Krasnoyarsk, Rus. 74/K4
Krasnoyarskiy, Rus. 71/L2
Krasnoyarskiy Kray, Rus. 74/K4
Krasnoye, Bela. 41/M4
Krasnoye, Rus. 73/K2
Krasnyy Bor, Rus. 69/T7
Krasnyy Chikoy, Rus. 78/F1
Krasnyy Gulyay, Rus. 71/J1
Krasnyy Kholm, Rus. 71/K2
Krasnyy Klyuch, Rus. 69/N5
Krasnyy Kut, Rus. 71/H2
Krasnyy Luch, Ukr. 73/K3
Krasnyy Lyman, Ukr. 70/F2
Krasnyy Oktyabr', Rus. 69/Q5
Krasnyy Sulin, Rus. 73/L4
Krasnyy Yar, Rus. 71/J3
Krasnyy Yar, Rus. 71/J1
Krasnyy Yar, Rus. 71/H2
Krasyliv, Ukr. 72/D3
Kratovo, FYROM 49/H1
Krautheim, Ger. 58/C4
Kravanh (mts.), Camb. 93/H5
Kraynovka, Rus. 71/H4
Kražiai, Lith. 41/K4
Kreb en Nâga (cliff), Mali 110/D5
Krechetovo, Rus. 68/H3
Kreck (riv.), Ger. 58/D2
Krefeld, Ger. 52/D6
Kreiensen, Ger. 53/G5
Kremastón (lake), Gre. 49/G3
Křemelna (riv.), Czh. 59/G4
Kremenchuk, Ukr. 73/G3
Kremenchuts'ke Vdskl. (res.), Ukr. 70/E2
Kremenets', Ukr. 72/C2
Kreminna, Ukr. 73/K3
Kremlin, Rus. 69/W9
Kremlin, Mt, US 145/J3
Kremmen, Ger. 42/Q6
Kremmling, Co, US 147/K3
Krempe, Ger. 53/G1
Krems an der Donau, Aus. 43/H4
Kremsmünster, Aus. 59/H6
Krenglbach, Aus. 59/G6
Kresgeville, Pa, US 168/C2
Kresna, Bul. 49/H2
Kress, Tx, US 152/D3
Kressbronn am Bodensee, Ger. 61/F2
Kresta (gulf), Rus. 75/T3
Kréstena, Gre. 49/G4
Kresty, Rus. 68/H5
Kretinga, Lith. 41/J4
Kreuzau, Ger. 55/F2
Kreuzberg (peak), Ger. 58/C2
Kreuzlingen, Swi. 61/F2
Kreuztal, Ger. 55/G2
Kreuzwertheim, Ger. 58/C3
Kría Vrísi, Gre. 49/H2
Kribi, Camr. 120/B2
Krieglach, Aus. 45/L3
Kriens, Swi. 61/E3
Kriftel, Ger. 58/B2
Kril'on (pen.), Rus. 82/B1
Kril'on (cape), Rus. 82/C1
Kril'on, Rus. 82/C1
Krim-Krim, Chad 116/B3
Krimpen aan de Ijssel, Neth. 52/B5
Krinídhes, Gre. 49/J2
Kriós (cape), Gre. 49/H5
Krishna (riv.), India 77/G8
Krishnagiri, India 95/C3
Krishnai, India 97/H2
Krishnanagar, India 97/G4
Kristdala, Swe. 40/G3
Kristiansand, Nor. 40/B2
Kristianstad (co.), Swe. 38/E4
Kristianstad (int'l arpt.), Swe. 40/F4
Kristianstad, Swe. 40/F3
Kristiansund, Nor. 38/C3
Kristinehamn, Swe. 40/F2
Kriva Palanka, FYROM 49/H1
Krivichi, Bela. 41/M4
Krivushevo, Rus. 69/L3
Krk (isl.), Cro. 67/G1
Krk, Cro. 45/L4
Krnov, Czh. 43/J3
Krokodil (riv.), SAfr. 123/F5
Krokodilrivier (riv.), SAfr. 123/E5
Krokom, Swe. 38/E3
Krókos, Gre. 49/G2
Krokstadelva, Nor. 38/R8
Krolevets', Ukr. 73/G2
Krombach, Ger. 58/C2
Kroměříž, Czh. 43/J4
Kromy, Rus. 70/E1
Kronach, Ger. 59/E2
Kronau, Sk, Can. 156/B2
Kronberg im Taunus, Ger. 58/B2
Krong Kaoh Kong, Camb. 94/C4
Krong Keb, Camb. 94/D4
Kronoberg (co.), Swe. 38/E4
Kronshtadt, Rus. 69/S6
Kronstorf, Aus. 59/H6
Kroombit Tops NP, Austl. 134/C4
Kroonstad, SAfr. 124/D2
Kropachevo, Rus. 69/N5
Kropotkin, Rus. 73/L5
Kropp, Ger. 40/C4
Krosno, Pol. 43/L4
Krosno Odrzańskie, Pol. 43/H2
Krotoszyn, Pol. 43/J3
Krotovka, Rus. 69/L5
Krottenkopf (peak), Aus. 61/G3
Krotz Springs, La, US 164/C2
Krousón, Gre. 49/J5
Kröv, Ger. 55/G4
Krško, Slov. 50/B3
Kruckau (riv.), Ger. 53/G1
Kruger NP, SAfr. 123/F4
Krugersdorp, SAfr. 124/P13
Kruglitsa (peak), Rus. 69/N5
Krugloi (cape), Ak, US 171/A5
Krui, Indo. 89/C3
Kruibeke, Belg. 52/B6
Kruin, Namb. 122/C4
Kruiningen, Neth. 52/B6
Kruisfontein, SAfr. 124/D4
Krujë, Alb. 49/F2
Krulevshchina, Bela. 41/M4
Krum, Tx, US 153/F4
Krumbach, Ger. 61/G1
Krummenau, Swi. 61/F3
Krumovgrad, Bul. 51/G5
Krün, Ger. 61/H3
Krung Thep (Bangkok) (cap.), Thai. 94/C3
Kruså, Den. 40/C4
Krusenstern (cape), Ak, US 171/F2
Kruševac, Serb. 50/E4
Kruševo, FYROM 49/G2
Krušné Hory (Erzgebirge) (mts.), Czh.,Ger. 45/K1
Kruszwica, Pol. 43/K2
Krutoyarskiy, Rus. 69/P5
Kruzof (isl.), Ak, US 171/L4
Krychaw, Bela. 70/D1
Krylovskaya, Rus. 73/K4
Krym, Aut. Rep., Ukr. 73/G5
Krymsk, Rus. 73/K5
Krynica, Pol. 43/L4
Krynychky, Ukr. 73/H3
Kryve Ozero, Ukr. 72/F4
Kryvyy Rih, Ukr. 73/G4
Kryzhopil', Ukr. 72/E3
Krzna (riv.), Pol. 43/M3
Krzyż, Pol. 43/J2
Ksar el Boukhari, Alg. 112/G5
Ksar el Kebir, Mor. 112/B2
Ksel (peak), Alg. 111/F2
Ksen'yevka, Rus. 79/H1
Kshenskiy, Rus. 73/J2
Ktima, Cyp. 104/C2
Ku Sathan (peak), Thai. 94/C2
Ku-Ring-Gai Chase NP, Austl. 133/E1
Ku-Ring-Gai NP, Austl. 134/H8
Kuah, Malay. 94/B5
Kuai (riv.), China 78/H5
Kuala Belait, Bru. 90/D3
Kuala Berang, Malay. 89/C1
Kuala Dungun, Malay. 89/C1
Kuala Kangsar, Malay. 89/C1
Kuala Kelawang, Malay. 89/C2
Kuala Kerai, Malay. 89/C1
Kuala Kubu Baharu, Malay. 89/C2
Kuala Kurau, Malay. 89/C1
Kuala Lipis, Malay. 89/C1
Kuala Lumpur (int'l arpt.), Malay. 89/C2
Kuala Lumpur (cap.), Malay. 89/C2
Kuala Pahang, Malay. 89/C2
Kuala Penyu, Malay. 88/A4
Kuala Pilah, Malay. 89/C2
Kuala Rompin, Malay. 89/C2
Kuala Selangor, Malay. 89/C2
Kuala Terengganu, Malay. 89/C1
Kualalangsa, Indo. 89/B1
Kualamandah, Indo. 89/C3
Kualasimpang, Indo. 89/B1
Kualatungkal, Indo. 89/C3
Kuam, SKor. 81/G6
Kuamut, Malay. 88/B4
Kuancheng, China 80/D2
Kuandian, China 81/C2
Kuantan, Malay. 89/C2
Kuban' (riv.), Rus. 74/D5
Kubano-Priazov (plain), Rus. 73/K5
Kubaysah, Iraq 102/E3
Kubbum, Sudan 116/D3
Kubenskoye (lake), Rus. 68/H4
Kubokawa, Japan 84/C4
Kubrat, Bul. 51/H4
Kubumesaai, Indo. 90/E3
Kubutambahan, Indo. 89/F5
Kučevo, Serb. 50/E3
Kuchaiburi, India 97/F4
Kuchen (peak), Aus. 61/G3
Kuchen, Ger. 58/C5
Kuchinarai, Thai. 94/D2
Kuching, Malay. 90/D3
Kuchino (isl.), Japan 85/K6
Kuchinoerabu (isl.), Japan 84/A5
Kuchl, Aus. 45/K3
Kūchnay Darvīshān, Afg. 101/H2
Kuçovë, Alb. 49/F2
Küçükbahçe, Turk. 49/K3
Küçükcekmece (lake), Turk. 103/M6
Küçükkuyu, Turk. 49/K3
Kuda, Indo. 90/D3
Kudamatsu, Japan 84/B3
Kudan, Nga. 115/G4
Kudara, Taj. 99/B4
Kudat, Malay. 88/B4
Kudene, Indo. 128/D1
Kudirkos-Naumiestis, Lith. 41/K4
Kudremalai (pt.), SrL. 95/C4
Kudus, Indo. 89/E4
Kudymkar, Rus. 69/M4
Kufrah (oasis), Libya 108/D3
Kufrinjah, Jor. 105/D4
Kufstein, Aus. 45/K3
Kufūr Najm, Egypt 113/C3
Kugaaruk, Nun, Can. 141/H2
Kugarchi, Rus. 71/L1
Kugluktuk, Nun, Can. 140/E2
Kuhardt, Ger. 58/B4
Kühbach, Ger. 58/E6
Kūhdasht, Iran 103/F3
Kūhestak, Iran 103/J5
Kuhmo, Fin. 68/F2
Kuhmoinen, Fin. 41/L1
Kūhpāyeh, Iran 103/H3
Kuikuina, Nic. 177/E3
Kuinder of Tjonger (riv.), Neth. 52/C3
Kuiseb (riv.), NAmb. 122/B4
Kuishan (mtn.), China 87/F4
Kuitan, China 87/G4
Kuito, Ang. 122/C2
Kuiu (isl.), Ak, US 140/C3
Kuivajärvi (lake), Fin. 39/D4
Kuivastu, Est. 41/K2
Kujang, NKor. 81/D3
Kujawsko Pomorskie (prov.), Pol. 43/K2
Kujawy (reg.), Pol. 43/K2
Kuji, Japan 82/B3
Kujū-san (peak), Japan 84/B4
Kujūkuri, Japan 83/E2
Kukalaya (riv.), Nic. 177/E3
Kukawa, Nga. 116/B2
Kuke (riv.), China 86/C3
Kukës, Alb. 49/G1
Kuki, Japan 85/F2
Kukipi, PNG 129/G2
Kukizaki, Japan 83/E2
Kukkia (lake), Fin. 41/L1
Kukmor, Rus. 69/L4
Kukushtan, Rus. 69/N4
Kūl (riv.), Iran 100/C3
Kula, Bul. 50/F4
Kula, Serb. 50/D3
Kula, Turk. 102/B2
Kula Kangri (peak), Bhu. 97/H1
Kulachi, Pak. 98/A4
Kulagino, Kaz. 71/J2
Kulai, Malay. 89/C2
Kulākh, SAr. 100/D4
Kulal (mt.), Kenya 119/B1
Kulaly (isl.), Kaz. 71/J3
Kulandag (mts.), Trkm. 71/K4
Kularua, Bang. 97/J3
Kulashi, Geo. 71/G4
Kuldīga, Lat. 41/J3
Kule, Bots. 122/D4
Kulebaki, Rus. 68/J5
Kulen, Camb. 94/D3
Kulen Shet' (riv.), Eth. 118/B3
Kulet el-Qrein (peak), Egypt 113/C6
Kulgām, India 98/C3
Kulgera, Austl. 131/G3
Kulgunino, Rus. 71/L1
Kulim, Malay. 89/C1
Kulin, Austl. 130/C5
Kullamaa, Est. 41/L2
Kullen (cape), Swe. 40/E3
Kullu, India 98/D4
Kulm, ND, US 156/E4
Kulma (wadi), Sudan 116/D2
Kulmbach, Ger. 59/E2
Kŭlob, Taj. 99/A4
Kuloy (riv.), Rus. 69/J2
Kuloy, Rus. 68/J3
Kuloy, Rus. 69/J2
Kulpahār, India 96/B3
Kulpmont, Pa, US 168/B2
Kulpsville, Pa, US 168/C3
Kul'sary, Kaz. 71/K3
Külsheim, Ger. 58/C3
Kulsi (riv.), India 97/H2
Kulti, India 97/F4
Kulu, Turk. 102/C2
Kulunda, Rus. 74/H4
Kulunda (lake), Rus. 99/C1
Kulunda (riv.), Rus. 99/D1
Kulunda Steppe (plain), Kaz. 99/C1
Kulykivka, Ukr. 72/F2
Kŭm (riv.), SKor. 81/D4
Kuma (riv.), Rus. 74/E5
Kumagaya, Japan 85/F2
Kumai, India 97/G2
Kumaishi, Japan 82/A2
Kumak, Rus. 71/M2
Kumaka, Guy. 181/G4
Kumamoto (int'l arpt.), Japan 84/B4
Kumamoto (pref.), Japan 84/B4
Kumamoto, Japan 84/B4
Kumano (riv.), Japan 84/D4
Kumano, Japan 84/E4
Kumanovo, FYROM 49/G1
Kumār (riv.), Bang. 97/G4
Kumara, NZ 135/B3
Kumārkhāli, Bang. 97/G4
Kumasi, Gha. 115/E5
Kumatori, Japan 83/H7
Kumba, Camr. 120/B1
Kumbakonam, India 95/C4
Kumbe, Indo. 129/F2
Kumbia, Austl. 134/C4
Kŭmch'ŏn, SKor. 81/F6
Kumé (isl.), Japan 85/J7
Kumertau, Rus. 71/K1
Kumeu, NZ 135/F6
Kŭmgang, NKor. 81/D3
Kumgang-san (peak), NKor. 81/E3
Kumhārsain, India 98/D4
Kŭmho (riv.), SKor. 81/E5
Kŭmhwa, SKor. 81/D3
Kumi, SKor. 81/E4
Kumi, Ugan. 119/A1
Kumihama, Japan 83/G4
Kumiyama, Japan 83/J6
Kumjawng (pass), India 86/C3
Kumköy, Turk. 103/N6
Kumla, Swe. 40/F2
Kumla, Swe. 39/B1
Kumluca, Turk. 104/B1
Kümmersbruck, Ger. 59/E4
Kumon (range), Myan. 93/G2
Kŭmsan, SKor. 81/D4
Kŭmsanp'o, NKor. 81/C3
Kumsenga, Tanz. 121/G3
Kumta, India 95/B3
Kumurkek, Indo. 129/F1
Kumylzhenskaya, Rus. 73/M3
Kuna, Id, US 146/E2
Kunashiri (isl.), Rus. 75/Q5
Kūnch, India 96/B3
Kunchha, Nepal 97/E1
Kunda, Est. 41/M2
Kunda, India 96/C3
Kundapura (Coondapoor), India 101/K6
Kundarkhi, India 96/B1
Kundauli, India 96/D2
Kundelungu, Monts (mts.), D.R. Congo 121/F5
Kundelungu, PN de, D.R. Congo 121/F5
Kundiān, Pak. 98/A3
Kundiawa, PNG 129/G1
Kundla, India 101/K4
Kundravy, Rus. 69/P5
Kunduchi, Tanz. 119/B3
Kundur (isl.), Indo. 89/C2
Kunene (riv.), Namb. 122/B3
Kungälv, Swe. 40/D3
Kungsangen (int'l arpt.), Swe. 40/G2
Kungsängen, Swe. 39/A1
Kungsbacka, Swe. 40/E3
Kungshamn, Swe. 40/D2
Kungu, D.R. Congo 120/D2
Kungu, Zam. 121/G5
Kungur, Rus. 69/N4
Kungutas, Tanz. 119/A4
Kungyangon, Myan. 94/B2
Kunhegyes, Hun. 50/E2
Kunhing, Myan. 86/C4
Kunimi-dake (peak), Japan 84/B4
Kuningan, Indo. 89/E4
Kunishiri (isl.), Rus. 77/P5
Kunitachi, Japan 83/C2
Kunjāh, Pak. 98/B3
Kunjirap (pass), China 101/L1
Kunkletown, Pa, US 168/C2
Kunlong, Myan. 93/G3
Kunlun (mts.), China 77/H6
Kunlun (pass), China 99/C4
Kunmadaras, Hun. 43/L5
Kunming (int'l arpt.), China 86/D3
Kunming, China 86/D3
Kunmunya Abor. Rsv., Austl. 128/B3
Kunp'o, SKor. 81/F7
Kunsan, SKor. 81/D5
Kunshan, China 80/L8
Kunszentmárton, Hun. 50/E2
Kuntaur, Gam. 114/B3
Kuntsëvo (nbrhd.), Rus. 69/W9
Kuntshankoie, D.R. Congo 121/E3
Kunu (riv.), India 101/L3
Kununurra, Austl. 128/C3
Kunwāri (riv.), India 96/A2
Kunwi, SKor. 81/E4
Kun'ya, Rus. 41/P3
Kunya, Nga. 115/H3
Kunyu (mtn.), China 80/E3
Künzell, Ger. 58/C1
K'unzila, Eth. 117/H3
Kunzulu, D.R. Congo 120/D3
Kunžvartské (pass), Czh. 59/G5
Kuocang (peak), China 87/J2
Kuohijärvi (lake), Fin. 41/L1
Kuolayarvi, Rus. 68/F2
Kuolimo (lake), Fin. 41/M1
Kuopio, Fin. 68/E3
Kuopio (prov.), Fin. 38/H3
Kup, PNG 129/G1
Kupa (riv.), Cro. 45/L4
Kupang, Indo. 128/A2
Kuper (range), PNG 129/G1
Kupiano, PNG 129/H2
Kupino, Rus. 74/H4
Kupiškis, Lith. 41/L4
Kuppenheim, Ger. 58/B5
Kupreanof (isl.), Ak, US 140/C3
Kup'yans'k, Ukr. 73/J3
Kup'yans'k-Vuzlovyy, Ukr. 73/J3
Kuqa, China 75/M5
Kür (riv.), Azer. 74/E6
Kur (riv.), Rus. 79/M1
Kurakh, Rus. 71/H4
Kurakhove, Ukr. 73/J4
Kurakino, Rus. 71/H1
Kūrālī, India 98/D4
Kurama-yama (peak), Japan 83/J5
Kurashiki, Japan 84/C3
Kuraymah, Sudan 109/F5
Kurayoshi, Japan 84/C3
Kurayyimah, Jor. 105/D4
Kurchum, Kaz. 99/D2
Kürdämir, Azer. 103/G1
Kurdistan (reg.), Asia 74/E6
Kurdufān (pol. reg.), Sudan 117/F2
Kŭrdzhali (res.), Bul. 49/J2
Kŭrdzhali, Bul. 51/G5
Küre, Turk. 70/E4
Kure, Japan 84/C3
Kure (isl.), Hi, US 136/H2
Küre (mts.), Turk 102/C1
Kūrebhār, India 96/D2
Kuressaare, Est. 41/K2
Kureyka (riv.), Rus. 74/K3
Kurgan, Rus. 69/Q5
Kurganskaya Oblast, Rus. 69/P5
Kurganinsk, Rus. 73/L5
Kurgaon, India 96/A2
Kuri, SKor. 81/G6
Kuria (isl.), Kiri. 136/G4
Kuria Muria (isls.), Oman 77/F5
Kurīgrām, Bang. 97/G3
Kurihashi, Japan 83/D1
Kurikoma-yama (peak), Japan 82/B4
Kuril (isls.), Rus. 77/Q5
Kurilovka, Rus. 71/J2
Kuril'sk, Rus. 82/E1
Kurimoto, Japan 83/F2
Kuring Kuru, Namb. 122/C3
Kurinwas (riv.), Nic. 177/E3
Kurisawa, Japan 82/B2
Kuriyama, Japan 82/B2
Kürkçü, Turk. 104/C1
Kurkiyoki, Rus. 41/N1
Kurlovskiy, Rus. 68/J5
Kurmuk, Eth. 117/G3
Kurnool, India 95/C3
Kuro (nbrhd.), SKor. 81/F7
Kuro-shima (isl.), Japan 84/A5
Kurodashō, Japan 83/G5
Kuroishi, Japan 82/B3
Kuroiso, Japan 85/G2
Kuroki, Sk, Can. 156/C2
Kurort-Darasun, Rus. 78/G1
Kuroso-yama (peak), Japan 83/K6
Kurotaki, Japan 83/J7
Kurow, NZ 135/B4
Kurrajong, Austl. 134/G8
Kurram (riv.), Pak. 101/K2
Kurri Kurri, Austl. 133/E1
Kurrimine Beach, Austl. 134/B2
Kursavka, Rus. 73/M5
Kuršėnai, Lith. 41/K3
Kurseong, India 97/G2
Kursiu Nerija NP, Lith. 41/J4
Kursk, Rus. 73/J2
Kurskaya Spit (bar), Lith.,Rus. 41/J4
Kurskiy (lag.), Lith.,Rus. 43/L1
Kurskiy (lag.), Lith. 41/J4
Kurskskaya Oblast, Rus. 70/E2
Kuršumlija, Serb. 50/E4
Kurşunlu, Turk. 70/E4
Kurtalan, Turk. 102/E2
Kürten, Ger. 55/G1
Kurtköy, Turk. 103/N7
Kuru (riv.), Bhu. 97/H2
Kuru (riv.), Sudan 117/E3
Kuruca (pass), Turk. 102/E2
Kuruçay, Turk. 102/D2
Kuruçay (riv.), Turk. 71/G4
Kuruktag (mts.), China 78/B3
Kuruman, SAfr. 124/C2
Kurumansrivier (riv.), SAfr. 124/C2
Kurume, Japan 84/B4
Kurumkan, Rus. 78/G1
Kurundi, Austl. 131/G2
Kurupukari, Guy. 181/G3
Kurur (peak), Sudan 109/F4
Kurwongbah (lake), Austl. 134/E6
Kur'ya, Rus. 69/N3
Kurye, SKor. 81/D5
Kuryong (riv.), NKor. 81/C3
Kuryongp'o-ri, SKor. 81/E5
Kuşadası, Turk. 102/A2
Kusakan, Kaz. 71/M1
Kusatsu, Japan 83/J5
Kusel, Ger. 55/G4
Kushālgarh, India 101/K4
Kushchevskaya, Rus. 73/K4
Kusheriki, Nga. 115/G4
Kushida (riv.), Japan 83/K7
Kushigata, Japan 83/A2
Kushihara, Japan 83/M5
Kushikino, Japan 84/B5
Kushima, Japan 84/B5
Kushimoto, Japan 84/D4
Kushiro (riv.), Japan 82/D2
Kushiro, Japan 82/D2
Kushiro-Shitsugen NP, Japan 82/D2
Kushmurun (lake), Kaz. 69/Q5
Kushol, India 98/D3
Kushtia, Bang. 97/G4
Kushtia (pol. reg.), Bang. 97/G4
Kushui (riv.), China 78/F4
Kushum (riv.), Kaz. 71/J2
Kusiyana (riv.), Bang. 97/H3
Kuskokwim (bay), Ak, US 171/F4
Kuskokwim (mts.), Ak, US 171/G3
Kuskokwim (riv.), Ak, US 171/F3
Kusma, Nepal 96/D1
Küsnacht, Swi. 61/E3
Kusŏng, NKor. 81/C3
Kussharo (lake), Japan 82/C2
Küssnacht am Rigi, Swi. 61/E3
Kustarevka, Rus. 71/G1
Küstenkanal (canal), Ger. 53/E3
Kusterdingen, Ger. 58/C5
Kūstī, Sudan 117/G2
Kusu, Japan 83/L6
Kusuman, Thai. 94/D2
Kut (isl.), Camb. 93/H5
Kuta, Nga. 115/G4
Kutacane, Indo. 89/B2
Kütahya, Turk. 102/B2
Kütahya (prov.), Turk. 102/B2
Kutais, Rus. 73/K5
K'ut'aisi (int'l arpt.), Geo. 71/G4
K'ut'aisi, Geo. 71/G4
Kutāmat al Ghābah, Egypt 113/B3
Kutch (gulf), India 92/A3
Kutch (reg.), India 92/A3
Kutchan, Japan 82/B1
Kutcharo (lake), Japan 82/C1
Kutenholz, Ger. 53/G2
Kutiwenji, Nga. 115/G4
Kutná Hora, Czh. 43/H4
Kutno, Pol. 43/K2
Kutse Game Reserve, Bots. 122/D4
Kutsuki, Japan 83/J5
Küttigen, Swi. 60/E3
Kutu, D.R. Congo 120/D3
Kutu-Owanga, D.R. Congo 121/E3
Kutulik, Rus. 78/E1
Kutum, Sudan 117/E2
Kutzenhausen, Ger. 58/D6
Kutztown, Pa, US 168/C2
Kuujjua (riv.), NW, Can. 140/E1
Kuujjuaq, Qu, Can. 141/K3
Kuujjuarapik, Qu, Can. 141/J3
Kuuli-Mayak, Trkm. 103/H1
Kuurila, Fin. 39/E3
Kuusamo, Fin. 38/J2
Kuusankoski, Fin. 41/M1
Kuutse (hill), Est. 41/M2
Kuvandyk, Rus. 71/L2
Kuvango, Ang. 122/C2
Kuwait (ctry.) 103/F4
Kuwait (cap.), Kuw. 103/F4
Kuwait (int'l arpt.), Kuw. 103/F4
Kuwānā (riv.), India 92/D2
Kuwana, Japan 83/L5
Kuybyshev, Rus. 69/L5
Kuybyshev (res.), Rus. 74/E4
Kuybyshevka, Ukr. 72/F4
Kuybyshevskiy, Kaz. 69/Q5
Kuye (riv.), China 78/G4
Kūysanjaq, Iraq 103/F2
Küysu, China 78/C3
Kuyto (lake), Rus. 38/J2
Kuytun, China 99/E3
Kuytun (riv.), China 99/D3
Kuyu Tingni, Nic. 177/F3
Kuyuwini (riv.), Guy. 181/G4
Kuze, Japan 83/K4
Kuzitrin (riv.), Ak, US 171/E2
Kuz'molovskiy, Rus. 69/T6
Kuznetsk, Rus. 71/H1
Kuzomen', Rus. 68/H2
Kuzovatovo, Rus. 71/H1
Kuzucubelen, Turk. 104/D1
Kuzumaki, Japan 82/B3
Kvaløy (isl.), Nor. 38/F1
Kværndrup, Den. 40/D4
Kvarner (gulf), Cro. 67/G1
Kvarneric (chan.), Cro. 50/B3
Kvigtinden (peak), Nor. 38/E2
Kvinesdal, Nor. 40/B2
Kvinnherad, Nor. 40/B2
Kviteseid, Nor. 40/C2
Kwa (riv.), D.R. Congo 107/D5
Kwa Mtoro, Tanz. 119/A3
Kwaadmechelen, Belg. 55/E1
Kwach'ŏn, SKor. 81/F7
Kwail, NKor. 81/C3
Kwajalein (isl.), Mrsh. 136/F4
Kwajok, Sudan 117/F3
Kwakoegron, Sur. 182/C1
Kwaksan, NKor. 81/C3
Kwakwani, Guy. 181/G3
Kwale, Kenya 119/B3
Kwali, Nga. 115/G4
Kwam al Ḩamām (ruin), Egypt 113/C6
Kwam Awshīm (ruin), Egypt 113/B5
Kwamashu, SAfr. 125/E3
Kwamen Kwesi, Gha. 115/E4
Kwamouth, D.R. Congo 120/D3
Kwanak-san (peak), SKor. 81/F7
Kwando (riv.), Namb. 122/D3
Kwangch'ŏn, SKor. 81/D4
Kwangju, SKor. 81/D5
Kwangju, SKor. 81/G7
Kwangju-jikhalsi (prov.), SKor. 81/D5
Kwangmyŏng, SKor. 81/F7
Kwango (riv.), D.R. Congo 107/D5
Kwangwazi, Tanz. 119/B3
Kwangyang, SKor. 81/D5
Kwania (lake), Ugan. 119/A1
Kwansan, SKor. 81/D5
Kwara (state), Nga. 115/G4
Kwaraha (peak), Tanz. 119/A3
Kwatarkwashi, Nga. 115/G3
Kwazulu Natal (prov.), SAfr. 125/E3
Kwekwe, Zim. 123/F3
Kweneng (dist.), Bots. 122/E4
Kwenge (riv.), D.R. Congo 120/D4
Kwethluk, Ak, US 171/F3
Kwidzyn, Pol. 41/H5
Kwigillingok, Ak, US 171/F4
Kwīha, Eth. 118/A2
Kwikila, PNG 129/G2
Kwilu (riv.), D.R. Congo 107/D5
Kwinana, Austl. 130/K7
Kwitara (riv.), Guy. 182/B2
Ky Anh, Viet. 94/D2
Ky Son, Viet. 94/D2
Kya-in Seikkyi, Myan. 94/B2
Kyabé, Chad 116/C3
Kyabram, Austl. 133/B3
Kyaikkami, Myan. 94/B2
Kyaikpi, Myan. 94/B2
Kyaiktiyo Pagoda, Myan. 94/B2
Kyaikto, Myan. 86/C5
Kyaka, Tanz. 121/G3
Kyakhta, Rus. 78/F1
Kyalite, Austl. 132/B2
Kyan-zaki (cape), Japan 85/J7
Kyancutta, Austl. 131/G5
Kyangin, Myan. 86/B5
Kyargozero, Rus. 68/G3
Kyaukki, Myan. 94/B2
Kyaukme, Myan. 86/C4
Kyaukpadaung, Myan. 86/B4
Kyaukpyu, Myan. 86/B5
Kyaukse, Myan. 86/C4
Kyaunggon, Myan. 86/B5
Kybartai, Lith. 41/K4
Kyeamba (cr.), Austl. 133/C2
Kyegegwa, Ugan. 121/G2
Kyelang, India 98/D3
Kyenjojo, Ugan. 121/G2
Kyeryong-san NP, SKor. 81/D4
Kyidaunggan, Myan. 86/C5
Kyikug, China 78/E4
Kyindwe, Myan. 86/B4
Kyjov, Czh. 43/J4
Kyle (reg.), Sc, UK 33/B5
Kyle, SD, US 154/C2
Kyle, Sk, Can. 145/K2
Kyle, Tx, US 151/F3
Kylemore, Sk, Can. 156/C2
Kyll (riv.), Ger. 42/D3
Kylmäkoski, Fin. 39/D3
Kym (riv.), Eng, UK 37/F2
Kymi (prov.), Fin. 38/H3
Kymijärvi (lake), Fin. 39/F4
Kymijoki (riv.), Fin. 41/M1
Kymore, India 96/B4
Kyn, Rus. 69/N4
Kyneton, Austl. 133/B3
Kynšperk nad Ohří, Czh. 59/F2
Kynuna, Austl. 134/A3
Kyoga (lake), Ugan. 119/A1
Kyōga-misaki (cape), Japan 84/D3
Kyogle, Austl. 134/D5
Kyonan, Japan 85/F3

Kyŏnga – Lancas
Map Section
242
243

Kyŏngan (riv.), SKor. 81/G7
Kyŏngbok Palace, SKor. 81/F6
Kyŏnggi (bay), SKor. 81/C4
Kyŏnggi-Do (prov.), SKor. 81/D4
Kyŏngju, SKor. 84/A3
Kyŏngju NP, SKor. 81/E5
Kyŏngju NP, SKor. 84/A3
Kyŏngsan, SKor. 84/A3
Kyŏngsang-bukto (prov.), SKor. 81/E4
Kyŏngsang-namdo (prov.), SKor. 81/E5
Kyŏngsŏng, NKor. 81/E2
Kyônkadun, Myan. 86/B5
Kyōto (pref.), Japan 84/D3
Kyōto, Japan 83/J5
Kyōtō Imperial Palace, Japan 83/J6
Kyōwa, Japan 83/E1
Kyrenia, Cyp. 104/C2
Kyrenia (dist.), Cyp. 104/C2
Kyrgyzstan (ctry.) 99/B3
Kyritz, Ger. 42/G2
Kyrkslätt (Kirkkonummi), Fin. 41/L1
Kyrösjärvi (lake), Fin. 41/K1
Kyrta, Rus. 69/N2
Kyrykuduk, Kaz. 71/J2
Kyrylivka, Ukr. 73/H4
Kyshtym, Rus. 69/P5
Kythrea, Cyp. 104/C2
Kytlym, Rus. 69/N4
Kytätä, Fin. 39/E4
Kyunhla, Myan. 86/B4
Kyūshū (isl.), Japan 77/M6
Kyūshū Highlands (uplands), Japan 84/B4
Kyustendil, Bul. 49/H1
Kyusyur, Rus. 75/N2
Kywebwe, Myan. 86/B5
Kyyiv (Kiev) (cap.), Ukr. 72/F2
Kyyivs'ka Oblast, Ukr. 70/D2
Kyyivs'ke Vodoskhovyshche (res.), Ukr. 70/D2
Kyzyl, Rus. 78/C1
Kzyltu, Kaz. 74/H4

L

L'Achigan (riv.), Qu, Can. 159/N6
L'Anguille (riv.), Ar, US 162/B3
L'Anse, Mi, US 157/K4
L'Aquila (prov.), It. 65/C3
L'Aquila, It. 65/C3
L' Ariana (lake), Fl, US 164/M7
L'Artois, Collines de (hills), Fr. 42/A3
L'Assomption (riv.), Qu, Can. 159/P6
L'Assomption (co.), Qu, Can. 159/N6
L'Hongrin (lake), Swi. 60/D5
L'Oriental (pol. reg.), Mor. 111/E2
La Algaba, Sp. 46/B4
La Almunia de Doña Godina, Sp. 46/E2
La Amistad Int'l Park, CR 172/E6
La Araucanía (pol. reg.), Chile 190/B3
La Ascensión, Mex. 175/F3
La Asturiana, Arg. 190/D3
La Asunción, Ven. 181/F2
La Aurora (int'l arpt.), Guat. 176/D3
La Baie, Qu, Can. 158/B1
La Banda, Arg. 188/C3
La Bañeza, Sp. 46/C1
La Barge, Wy, US 147/H2
La Barra, Nic. 177/F3
La Barra, Uru. 191/G2
La Barre-en-Ouche, Fr. 57/F3
La Bassée, Fr. 54/B2
La Bâthie, Fr. 64/C1
La Bâtie-Neuve, Fr. 64/C3
La Baule-Escoublac, Fr. 56/C6
La Belle, Fl, US 165/H4
La Birse (riv.), Swi. 60/D3
La Blanquilla (isl.), Ven. 181/E2
La Bocana, Mex. 174/B3
La Bonneville-sur-Iton, Fr. 57/G3
La Bouilladisse, Fr. 64/B6
La Bresse, Fr. 60/C2
La Broque, Fr. 60/D1
La Broquerie, Mb, Can. 156/F3
La Cadière-d'Azur, Fr. 64/B6
La Caldera de Taburiente, PN, Sp. 110/A3
La Calera, Col. 183/M8
La Calera, Chile 190/N8
La Campana, Sp. 46/C4
La Campana, PN, Chile 190/N8
La Cañada (peak), Cuba 177/F1
La Canada-Flintridge, Ca, US 166/F7
La Canoa, Ven. 181/F2
La Capelle, Fr. 54/C4
La Carlota, Sp. 46/C4
La Carlota, Arg. 190/E2
La Carolina, Sp. 46/D3
La Catedral (peak), Mex. 175/Q9
La Ceiba, Ven. 180/D3
La Ceiba (int'l arpt.), Hon. 176/E3
La Ceiba, Hon. 176/E3
La Ceja, Col. 183/K6
La Celle-les-Bordes, Fr. 30/H6
La Celle-Saint-Cloud, Fr. 30/J5
La Celle-sur-Morin, Fr. 30/L5
La Center, Ky, US 162/C2
La Chapelle-de-Guinchay, Fr. 60/A5
La Chapelle-des-Marais, Fr. 56/C6
La Chapelle-Saint-Luc, Fr. 44/F2
La Chapelle-sur-Erdre, Fr. 56/D6
La Chartre-sur-le-Loir, Fr. 57/F5
La Chaussée-Saint-Victor, Fr. 57/G5
La Chaux-de-Bonds, Swi. 60/C3
La Chinita (int'l arpt.), Ven. 180/D2
La Chorrera, Col. 180/C5
La Cienega, NM, US 149/J3
La Ciotat, Fr. 64/B6
La Ciudad, PN, Mex. 174/D4
La Clusaz, Fr. 60/C6
La Cocha, Arg. 188/C3
La Colle-sur-Loup, Fr. 64/D5
La Concepción, Pan. 177/F4
La Concepción, Nic. 176/E4
La Concepcíon, Ven. 180/D2
La Condamine (nbrhd.), Mona. 62/J8
La Coronilla, Uru. 191/G2
La Coruña, Sp. 46/A1
La Côte-Saint-André, Fr. 64/B2
La Couronne, Fr. 44/D4
La Couture-Boussey, Fr. 57/G3
La Crau, Fr. 64/C6
La Crèche, Fr. 44/C3
La Crescent, Mn, US 155/J2
La Crescenta-Montrose, Ca, US 166/F7
La Criolla, Arg. 188/D4
La Croche, Qu, Can. 158/A2
La Croix-en-Brie, Fr. 30/M6
La Crosse, Ks, US 152/E1
La Crosse, Wi, US 155/J2
La Crosse, Va, US 163/H2
La Cruz, Col. 180/B4
La Cruz, CR 176/E4
La Cruz, Uru. 191/K10
La Cruz, Chile 190/N8
La Cruz, Mex. 174/D4
La Cuchilla, Uru. 189/F5
La Cumbre (vol.), Ecu. 184/J7
La Cygne, Ks, US 153/G1
La Dôle (peak), Swi. 60/C5
La Dorada, Col. 183/L7
La Doré, Qu, Can. 158/A1
La Dormida, Arg. 190/D2
La Durande (peak), Fr. 66/D1
La Embocada, Bol. 185/E4
La Escondida, Arg. 190/C3
La Escondida, Arg. 188/E3
La Esmeralda, Ven. 181/E4
La Esperanza, Arg. 190/C4
La Esperanza, Bol. 185/F4
La Esperanza, Bol. 185/F5
La Esperanza, Bol. 185/E4
La Esperanza, Hon. 176/D3
La Esperanza, Ven. 181/F2
La Estanzuela, Uru. 191/K11
La Estrada, Sp. 46/A1
La Estrella, Chile 190/N9
La Falda, Arg. 188/C4
La Fare-les-Oliviers, Fr. 64/B5
La Farlède, Fr. 64/C6
La Fayette, Ga, US 162/E3
La Fère, Fr. 54/C4
La Ferrière-aux-Étangs, Fr. 57/E3
La Ferté-Gaucher, Fr. 54/C6
La Ferté-Imbault, Fr. 57/G6
La Ferté-Macé, Fr. 57/E3
La Ferté-Milon, Fr. 30/M7
La Ferté-Sous-Jouarre, Fr. 54/C6
La Ferté-St-Aubin, Fr. 57/G5
La Ferté-Vidame, Fr. 57/F3
La Flèche, Fr. 57/E5
La Follette, Tn, US 162/E2
La Fontaine, In, US 160/D4
La Francia, Arg. 188/D4
La Fría, Ven. 180/C2
La Gacilly, Fr. 56/C5
La Garde, Fr. 64/C6
La Garde-Adhémar, Fr. 64/A4
La Garita (mts.), Co, US 152/A2
La Garita, Co, US 149/J2
La Garriga, Sp. 47/L6
La Gineta, Sp. 46/E3
La Glacerie, Fr. 56/D1
La Gloria, Col. 180/C2
La Gloria, Tx, US 151/E4
La Gran Sabana (plain), Ven. 181/F3
La Grand Moucherolle (peak), Fr. 64/B2
La Grande (riv.), Qu, Can. 141/J3
La Grande (riv.), Can. 139/K4
La Grande, Or, US 146/D1
La Grande Rochette (peak), Fr. 64/C2
La Grande Ruine (peak), Fr. 64/C3
La Grange, Austl. 128/A4
La Grange, Ga, US 162/E4
La Grange, Ky, US 162/E1
La Grange, Mo, US 155/J3
La Grange, NC, US 163/J3
La Grange, Tx, US 151/F3
La Grange, Wy, US 154/B3
La Grave, Fr. 64/C2
La Grita, Ven. 177/J4
La Grivola (peak), It. 64/D1
La Grue Bayou (riv.), Ar, US 162/B3
La Gruyère (lake), Swi. 60/D4
La Guadeloupe, Qu, Can. 158/B3
La Guaira, Ven. 183/P7
La Guajira (pen.), Col. 177/H4
La Guajira (dept.), Col. 177/H4
La Guardia, Sp. 46/A2
La Guardia, Arg. 188/C4
La Guardia, Bol. 188/D1
La Guardia (int'l arpt.), NY, US 169/K8
La Guerche-de-Bretagne, Fr. 56/D5
La Habana (Havana) (cap.), Cuba 172/E3
La Habra, Ca, US 166/G8
La Harpe, Ks, US 153/G2
La Have (riv.), NS, Can. 158/E3
La Haye-du-Puits, Fr. 56/D2
La Haye-Pesnel, Fr. 56/D3
La Higuera, Chile 188/B4
La Honda, Ca, US 167/K12
La Horqueta, Ven. 181/F3
La Horqueta, Ven. 181/F2
La Horquilla, Bol. 185/E4
La Houssaye-en-Brie, Fr. 30/L5
La Huaca, Peru 184/A2
La Huacana, Mex. 175/E5
La Huerta, Mex. 174/D5
La Isla, Mex. 175/Q10
La Jalca, Peru 184/B2
La Jara, NM, US 149/J2
La Jara, Co, US 149/K2
La Javie, Fr. 64/C4
La Jolla Ind. Res., Ca, US 148/D4
La Joya, Bol. 188/C1
La Joya, Peru 184/D5
La Joya de los Sachas, Ecu. 180/B5
La Junta, Co, US 152/C2
La Junta, Mex. 174/D2
La Juventud (isl.), Cuba 139/J7
La Laguna, Sp. 110/A3
La Laja, Arg. 188/B4
La Léchère, Fr. 64/C1
La Leonesa, Arg. 188/E3
La Libertad, Guat. 176/D2
La Libertad, Hon. 176/E3
La Libertad, Ecu. 180/A5
La Libertad (dept.), Peru 184/B3
La Ligua, Chile 190/C2
La Línea de la Concepción, Sp. 46/C4
La Llagosta, Sp. 47/L6
La Lobería, Arg. 190/E4
La Loche, Sk, Can. 140/F3
La Loggia, It. 62/A3
La Londe-les-Maures, Fr. 64/C6
La Loupe, Fr. 57/G4
La Louvière, Belg. 55/D3
La Luisiana, Sp. 46/C4
La Machine, Fr. 44/E3
La Maddalena, It. 48/A2
La Madeleine, Fr. 54/C2
La Madera, NM, US 149/J2
La Magdalena, Col. 183/L6
La Malbaie, Qu, Can. 158/B2
La Mancha (reg.), Sp. 66/C3
La Margarita, Ven. 181/F2
La Marque, Tx, US 151/N9
La Martre (lake), NW, Can. 140/E2
La Masica, Hon. 176/E3
La Mauricie NP, Qu, Can. 158/A2
La Media Luna (isls.), Hon. 177/F3
La Meije (peak), Fr. 64/C2
La Mensura (peak), Col. 180/C4
La Merca, Sp. 46/B1
La Merced, Bol. 188/C2
La Merced, Peru 184/C3
La Merced, Arg. 188/C4
La Mesa, Ca, US 166/C5
La Mesa (int'l arpt.), Hon. 176/E3
La Mesa, Ven. 180/D2
La Mesa, Col. 183/L8
La Mesa, NM, US 150/A1
La Mira, Mex. 174/E5
La Mirada, Ca, US 166/F8
La Moine (riv.), Il, US 155/J3
La Monna (peak), It. 65/C4
La Montaña (phys. reg.), Peru 179/B3
La Monte, Mo, US 153/H1
La Mota (mtn.), Tx, US 150/C3
La Motte, Fr. 56/C4
La Motte-d'Aveillans, Fr. 64/B3
La Motte-du-Caire, Fr. 64/C4
La Motte-Servolex, Fr. 64/B1
La Moure, ND, US 156/E4
La Mula, Mex. 150/B3
La Mure, Fr. 64/B3
La Negra, Arg. 190/C3
La Neuveville, Swi. 60/D3
La Norville, Fr. 30/J6
La Ola, Chile 188/B3
La Orchila (isl.), Ven. 173/H5
La Orotava, Sp. 110/A3
La Oroya, Peru 184/C3
La Palma, Pan. 177/G4
La Palma, Col. 183/L7
La Palma (isl.), Sp. 107/A2
La Paloma, Uru. 191/G2
La Pampa (prov.), Arg. 190/D3
La Para, Arg. 188/D4
La Paragua, Ven. 181/F3
La Paz, Arg. 190/D2
La Paz, Arg. 188/E4
La Paz (cap.), Bol. 188/B1
La Paz (dept.), Bol. 184/D4
La Paz, Col. 180/C3
La Paz, Col. 180/C2
La Paz, Hon. 176/E3
La Paz, Mex. 174/C3
La Paz (bay), Mex. 174/C3
La Paz, Phil. 88/D3
La Paz, Uru. 191/K11
La Paz, Uru. 191/K11
La Pêche, Qu, Can. 161/H2
La Pedrera, Col. 180/D5
La Peña, Pan. 172/E6
La Peña, Col. 183/L7
La Penne-sur-Huveaune, Fr. 64/B6
La Perla, Mex. 150/B3
La Perouse (str.), Japan,Rus. 77/P5
La Petite-Raon, Fr. 60/C1
La Piedad Cavadas, Mex. 174/E4
La Pine, Or, US 146/C2
La Place, La, US 164/C2
La Plant, SD, US 154/D1
La Plata, Arg. 191/K11
La Plata, Col. 180/C4
La Plata (riv.), Co, US 149/H2
La Plata, Md, US 163/J1
La Plata, Mo, US 155/H3
La Pobla de Lillet, Sp. 47/F1
La Pocatière, Qu, Can. 158/B2
La Poile, Nf, Can. 159/H2
La Pola de Gordón, Sp. 46/C1
La Porte, In, US 160/C4
La Porte, Tx, US 151/M9
La Porte City, Ia, US 155/H2
La Posta Ind. Res., Ca, US 148/D4
La Prairie (co.), Qu, Can. 159/N7
La Prairie, Qu, Can. 159/P7
La Pryor, Tx, US 150/E3
La Puebla, Sp. 47/G3
La Puebla de Almoradiel, Sp. 46/D3
La Puebla de Cazalla, Sp. 46/C4
La Puebla de Montalbán, Sp. 46/C3
La Puente, Ca, US 166/G7
La Puntilla (pt.), Ecu. 180/A5
La Quebrada, Ven. 180/D2
La Queue-les-Yvelines, Fr. 54/A6
La Quiaca, Arg. 188/C2
La Rambla, Sp. 46/C4
La Ravoire, Fr. 64/B1
La Reforma, Arg. 190/D3
La Reforma, Mex. 174/C3
La Rinconada, Sp. 46/C4
La Rioja (dist.), Sp. 46/C3
La Rioja (prov.), Arg. 188/C4
La Rioja, Arg. 188/C4
La Robla, Sp. 46/C1
La Roche, Swi. 60/D4
La Roche-Bernard, Fr. 56/C5
La Roche-de-Glun, Fr. 64/A3
La Roche-de-Rame, Fr. 64/C3
La Roche-en-Ardenne, Belg. 55/E3
La Roche-Maurice, Fr. 56/A4
La Roche-sur-Foron, Fr. 60/C5
La Roche-sur-Yon, Fr. 44/C3
La Rochelle, Fr. 44/C3
La Rochette, Fr. 64/C2
La Roda, Sp. 46/D3
La Romana, DRep. 173/H4
La Ronge, Sk, Can. 140/F3
La Roque-d'Anthéron, Fr. 64/B5
La Rotta, It. 63/D6
La Rúa, Sp. 46/B1
La Rumorosa, Mex. 148/D4
La Sabana, Ven. 183/P7
La Sal, Ut, US 149/H1
La Sal (mts.), Ut, US 147/J4
La Salle, Mb, Can. 156/F3
La Salle, Co, US 154/B3
La Salle, Il, US 155/K3
La Salle les Alpes, Fr. 64/C3
La Salute di Livenza, It. 63/F2
La Sara, Arg. 191/C7
La Sarraz, Swi. 60/C4
La Sarre, Qu, Can. 141/J4
La Saussaye, Fr. 57/F2
La Sauvette (peak), Fr. 64/C6
La Serena, Chile 188/B4
La Servelle (peak), Fr. 64/B3
La Seu d'Urgell, Sp. 47/F1
La Seyne-sur-Mer, Fr. 64/B6
La Sierpe, Cuba 177/G1
La Sila (mts.), It. 48/E3
La Silueta (peak), Chile 191/B7
La Solana, Sp. 46/D3
La Souterraine, Fr. 44/D3
La Spezia, It. 62/C5
La Spezia (prov.), It. 62/C4
La Sûre (peak), Fr. 64/B2
La Suze-sur-Sarthe, Fr. 57/F5
La Tabatière, Qu, Can. 141/L3
La Tebaida, Col. 183/K8
La Teste, Fr. 44/C4
La Tête à l'Ane (peak), Fr. 60/C6
La Thuile, It. 64/C1
La Tigra, PN, Hon. 176/E3
La Toma, Arg. 190/D2
La Tortue (isl.), Haiti 177/H1
La Tortuga (isl.), Ven. 181/E2
La Tour-d'Aigues, Fr. 64/B5
La Tour-de-Peilz, Swi. 60/C5
La Tour-de-Trême, Swi. 60/D4
La Tour-du-Pin, Fr. 64/B1
La Tranca, Arg. 190/D2
La Tremblade, Fr. 44/C4
La Trinidad, Phil. 88/C1
La Trinitaria, Mex. 176/C2
La Trinité, Fr. 64/D5
La Trinité-des-Monts, Qu, Can. 158/C1
La Trinité-Porhoët, Fr. 56/C4
La Troncal, Ecu. 180/B5
La Troya (riv.), Arg. 188/B4
La Turballe, Fr. 56/C6
La Turbie, Fr. 62/H8
La Uníon, Ven. 180/E2
La Unión, ESal. 176/E3
La Unión, Col. 180/B4
La Unión, Sp. 47/E4
La Unión, Chile 190/B4
La Unión, Col. 183/K7
La Unión, Bol. 185/F4
La Unión, Peru 184/A2
La Unión, Peru 184/B3
La Union, NM, US 150/A2
La Unión, Mex. 175/E5
La Urbana, Ven. 181/E3
La Vale, Md, US 161/G5
La Valette-du-Var, Fr. 64/B6
La Vecilla, Sp. 46/C1
La Vega, Col. 183/L8
La Vergne, Tn, US 162/D2
La Verkin, Ut, US 149/F2
La Verna, It. 63/E6
La Verne, Ca, US 166/C2
La Vernia, Tx, US 151/E3
La Verrière, Fr. 30/H5
La Victoria, Col. 180/B4
La Victoria, Col. 183/J8
La Victoria, Ven. 180/D3
La Victoria, Ven. 183/N7
La Vieille-Lyre, Fr. 57/F3
La Vieja (riv.), Col. 183/K8
La Virginia, Col. 183/K8
La Voulte-sur-Rhône, Fr. 64/A3
La Vraie-Croix, Fr. 56/C5
La Wantzenau, Fr. 55/G6
Laa an der Thaya, Aus. 45/M2
Laaber, Ger. 59/E4
Laage, Ger. 40/E5
Laakirchen, Aus. 59/G7
Laarne, Belg. 54/C1
Laas (Lasa), It. 61/G4
Laas Caanood, Som. 118/C3
Laas Dhaareed, Som. 118/C3
Laas Qoray, Som. 118/D3
Laatzen, Ger. 53/G4
Laax, Swi. 61/F4
Labadieville, La, US 164/C3
Labang, Malay. 90/D3
Labasheeda, Ire. 32/A4
Labason, Phil. 88/C3
L'Abbaye, Swi. 60/C4
Labdah (Leptis Magna) (ruin), Libya 45/G3
Labé (pol. reg.), Gui. 114/B4
Labé, Gui. 114/B4
Labe (Elbe) (riv.), Czh.,Ger. 43/H2
Labelle, Qu, Can. 161/J1
Laberweinting, Ger. 59/F5
Labian (cape), Malay. 88/B4
Labin, Cro. 45/L4
Labinsk, Rus. 73/L5
Labis, Malay. 89/C2
Labná (ruin), Mex. 176/D1
Labo, Phil. 88/C2
Laborde, Arg. 190/E2
Laborec (riv.), Slvk. 43/L4
Labota, Indo. 91/F4
Labouglé, Arg. 188/E4
Laboulaye, Arg. 190/E2
Labrador (reg.), Can. 139/L4
Labrador (sea), Can., NAm 139/M4
Labrador City, Nf, Can. 141/K3
Lábrea, Braz. 185/E2
Labrieville, Qu, Can. 158/C1
Labruguière, Fr. 44/E5
Labry, Fr. 55/E5
Labuan (terr.), Bru. 88/A4
Labuhan, Indo. 89/D4
Labuhanbajo, Indo. 91/E5
Labuhanbilik, Indo. 89/C2
Labuhanhaji, Indo. 89/B2
Labuhanmaringgai, Indo. 89/D4
Labuhanruku, Indo. 89/B2
Labuk (riv.), Malay. 91/E2
Labuk (bay), Malay. 91/E2
Labuništa, FYROM 49/G2
Labutta, Myan. 86/B5
Läby, Swe. 39/A1
Labytnangi, Rus. 74/G3
Laç, Alb. 49/F2
Lac (pref.), Chad 116/B2
Lac Afwein (riv.), Kenya 119/B1
Lac Court Oreilles Ind. Res., Wi, US 157/J5
Lac du Bonnet, Mb, Can. 156/F2
Lac du Flambeau, Wi, US 157/K5
Lac du Flambeau Ind. Res., Wi, US 157/K4
Lac La Biche, Ab, Can. 140/E3
Lac La Hache, BC, Can. 144/D2
Lac la Martre, NW, Can. 140/E2
Lac Pelletier, Sk, Can. 145/L3
Lac Seul, On, Can. 157/H2
Lac Son, Viet. 94/D1
Lac Thien, Viet. 90/C1
Lac-Alouette, Qu, Can. 159/N6
Lac-au-Saumon, Qu, Can. 158/D1
Lac-aux-Sables, Qu, Can. 158/A2
Lac-Beauport, Qu, Can. 158/B2
Lac-Bouchette, Qu, Can. 158/A1
Lac-Brome, Qu, Can. 161/K2
Lac-des-Aigles, Qu, Can. 158/C2
Lac-Drolet, Qu, Can. 158/B3
Lac-du-Cerf, Qu, Can. 161/J1
Lac-Édouard, Qu, Can. 158/A2
Lac-Etchemin, Qu, Can. 158/B2
Lac-Mégantic, Qu, Can. 158/B3
Lacadena, Sk, Can. 145/K2
L'Acadie, Qu, Can. 159/P7
Lacantum (riv.), Mex. 176/D2
Lacassine Nat'l Wild. Ref., La, US 151/H2
Lacaune, Fr. 44/E5
Laccadive (sea), Asia 92/B5
Lacchiarella, It. 62/C3
Lacco Ameno, It. 65/C6
Lacepede (bay), Austl. 127/C4
Lacerdónia, Moz. 123/G3
Laces (Latsch), It. 61/G4
Lacey, Ar, US 153/J4
Lacey, Wa, US 144/C4
Lach Bissigh (riv.), Som. 119/C1
Lach Dera (riv.), Som. 119/C1
Lacha (lake), Rus. 68/H3
Lachapelle-aux-Pots, Fr. 54/A5
Lachay (pt.), Peru 184/B3
Lachen, Swi. 61/E3
Lachenaie, Qu, Can. 159/N6
Lachendorf, Ger. 53/H3
Lachhmangarh, India 96/A2
Lāchi, Pak. 98/A3
Lachine, Qu, Can. 159/N7
Lachlan (riv.), Austl. 127/D4
Lachte (riv.), Ger. 53/H3
Lachung, India 97/G2
Lachute, Qu, Can. 161/J2
Laçin, Azer. 103/F2
Lackawanna, NY, US 160/V10
Lackawanna (co.), Pa, US 168/C1
Lackland (A.F.B.), Tx, US 151/E3
Läckö, Swe. 40/E2
Laclubar, ETim. 128/B2
Lacob ti-Duyong (mt.), Phil. 87/J5
Lacock, Eng, UK 36/D4
Lacomb, Or, US 146/B1
Lacombe, La, US 164/D2
Lacombe, Ab, Can. 145/H1
Lacon, Il, US 155/K3
Laconia, NH, US 161/L3
Lacoochee, Fl, US 164/L7
Lacreek Nat'l Wild. Ref., SD, US 154/D2
Lacroix-Saint-Ouen, Fr. 54/B5
Lacross (isl.), Austl. 128/C3
Lacy-Lakeview, Tx, US 151/F2
Ladakh (mts.), India 101/L2
Ladário, Braz. 188/E1
Ladbergen, Ger. 53/E4
Ladder (hills), Sc, UK 33/C2
Ladder (cr.), Ks, Co, US 154/D4
Laddonia, Mo, US 155/J4
Lądek-Zdrój, Pol. 43/J3
Ladenburg, Ger. 58/B4
Ladera Heights, Ca, US 166/F8
Ladismith, SAfr. 124/C4
Ladispoli, It. 65/B4
Lado, Sudan 117/F4
Ladoga, Rus. 69/T7
Ladoga (lake), Rus. 68/F3
Ladoix-Serrigny, Fr. 60/A3
Ladozhskaya, Rus. 73/K5
Ladozhskoye Ozero, Rus. 69/U6
Ladrillero (mtn.), Chile 191/B7
Ladson, SC, US 163/G4
Ladva-Vetka, Rus. 68/G3
Lādwa, India 98/D5
Lady Barron, Austl. 133/D5
Lady Isle (isl.), Sc, UK 33/B5
Lady Lake, Sk, Can. 156/C1
Lady Lake, Fl, US 165/H3
Ladybank, Sc, UK 33/C4
Ladybower (res.), Eng, UK 35/G5
Ladybrand, SAfr. 124/D3
Ladysmith, Wi, US 157/J5
Ladysmith, BC, Can. 144/C3
Ladysmith, SAfr. 125/E3
Ladyville, Belz. 175/H5
Ladyzhyn, Ukr. 72/E3
Lae (isl.), Mrsh. 136/F4
Lae, Thai. 94/C2
Laer, Ger. 53/E4
Lafayette, Al, US 162/E4
Lafayette, Ca, US 167/K11
Lafayette, Co, US 154/B4
Lafayette, In, US 160/C4
Lafayette, La, US 164/B2
Lafayette, NJ, US 168/D1
Lafayette, Or, US 144/C5
Lafayette, Tn, US 162/D2
Lafe, Ar, US 162/B2
Lafia, Nga. 115/H4
Lafiagi, Nga. 115/G4
Lafitte, La, US 164/C3
Lafleche, Sk, Can. 145/L3
Lafnitz (riv.), Aus. 45/L3
Lafontaine, Qu, Can. 159/M6
Lāfūl, India 93/F6
Laga (mts.), It. 65/C2
Laga Balal (riv.), Kenya 117/H5
Laga Mado Gali (riv.), Kenya 119/B1
Laga Merille (riv.), Kenya 119/B1
Lagacéville, NB, Can. 158/E2
Lagamar, Braz. 189/H1
Lagan, Swe. 40/E3
Lagan (riv.), NI, UK 34/B3
Lagan (riv.), Swe. 40/E3
Lagarto, Braz. 187/F1
Lagawe, Phil. 88/C1
Lagbo, D.R. Congo 121/G2
Lagdo (lake), Camr. 116/B3
Lage, Ger. 53/F5
Lage Vaart (canal), Neth. 52/C4
Lågen (riv.), Nor. 40/C1
Lages, Braz. 189/G3
Laggan, Sc, UK 33/B2
Laggan (lake), Sc, UK 33/B3
Lagh Bogal (riv.), Kenya 118/A5
Lagh Bor (riv.), Kenya 118/A5
Lagh Kutulo (riv.), Kenya 119/C1
Laghouat (wilaya), Alg. 111/F2
Laghouat, Alg. 111/F2
Laghtnafrankee (peak), Ire. 32/C5
Lagnieu, Fr. 60/B6
Lagnö (isl.), Swe. 39/B1
Lagny-le-Sec, Fr. 30/L4
Lagny-sur-Marne, Fr. 30/L5
Lago Cardiel, Arg. 191/C6
Lago da Pedra, Braz. 183/E4
Lago de Atitlán, PN, Guat. 176/D3
Lago Piratuba, Reserva Biológica do, Bol. 182/B4
Lago Posadas, Arg. 191/C5
Lago Puelo, PN, Arg. 190/C4
Lago Verde, Chile 190/C5
Lago Viedma, Arg. 191/B6
Lagoa, Port. 46/A4
Lagoa da Prata, Braz. 189/H2
Lagoa Formosa, Braz. 186/D3
Lagoa Vermelha, Braz. 189/G4
Lagoda (lake), Rus. 38/J3
Lagodekhi, Geo. 71/H4
Lagonegro, It. 48/D2
Lagord, Fr. 44/C3
Lagos, Nga. 115/F5
Lagos (state), Nga. 115/F5
Lagos, Port. 46/A4
Lagos de Moreno, Mex. 174/E4
Lagosanto, It. 63/F4
Lagrange, In, US 160/D4
Laguardia, Sp. 44/B5
Laguna (cr.), Ca, US 167/M10
Laguna, NM, US 149/J3
Laguna (dam), Az, US 148/E4
Laguna (mts.), Ca, US 148/D4
Laguna (bay), Phil. 88/F7
Laguna, Braz. 189/G4
Laguna Atascosa NWR, Tx, US 151/F4
Laguna Beach, Fl, US 165/F2
Laguna Beach, Ca, US 166/C3
Laguna Blanca, PN, Arg. 190/C3
Laguna de Duero, Sp. 46/C2
Laguna de la Restinga, PN, Ven. 181/E2
Laguna del Laja, PN, Chile 190/C3
Laguna del Rey, Mex. 174/E3
Laguna Grande, Arg. 190/D4
Laguna Grande, Arg. 191/C6
Laguna Hills, Ca, US 166/C3
Laguna Ind. Res., NM, US 149/J3
Laguna Larga, Arg. 188/D4
Laguna Paiva, Arg. 188/D4
Laguna San Rafael, PN, Chile 190/B5
Laguna Verde, Chile 190/N8
Laguna Yema, Arg. 188/D3
Lagunas, Chile 188/B2
Lagunas, Peru 184/B2
Lagunas, Peru 184/C2
Lagunas de Chacahua, PN, Mex. 176/B2
Lagunas de Montebello, Mex. 172/C4
Lagunas de Zempoala, PN, Mex. 175/Q10
Lagundo (Algund), It. 61/H4
Lagunetas, Ven. 180/D2
Lagunillas, Ven. 180/D2
Lagunillas, Chile 190/N8
Lagunillas, Bol. 188/D1
Laguntara (lag.), Hon. 177/E3
Lagushao, China 81/C2
Lahad Datu, Malay. 88/B4
Lahan Sai, Thai. 94/C3
Lahār, India 96/B2
Lāharpur, India 96/C2
Lahat, Indo. 89/C3
Laheria Sarāi, India 97/E2
Lahewa, Indo. 89/B2
Laḩij, Yem. 118/C2
Lāhījān, Iran 103/G2
Lahn (riv.), Ger. 42/E3
Lahnstein, Ger. 55/G3
Laholm, Swe. 40/E3
Laholms (bay), Den. 40/F3
Lahoma, Ok, US 153/E2
Lahontan (res.), Nv, US 146/D4
Lahontan (dam), Nv, US 146/D4
Lahore, Pak. 98/C4
Lahore (int'l arpt.), Pak. 98/C4
Lahr, Ger. 60/D1
Lāhrūd, Iran 103/F2
Lahti, Fin. 41/L1
Laï, Chad 116/C3
Lai Chau, Viet. 94/C1
Lai-hka, Myan. 94/B1
Laiagam, PNG 129/F1
Lai'an, China 80/D4
Laichingen, Ger. 58/C5
Laidon (lake), Sc, UK 33/B3
Laifeng Tujiazu Zizhixian, China 87/F2
L'Aigle, Fr. 57/F3
Laigueglia, It. 62/B6
Laihia, Fin. 38/G3
Lailly-en-Val, Fr. 57/G5
Lainate, It. 62/C2
Laindon, Eng, UK 30/E2
Laingsburg, SAfr. 124/C4
Lainioälven (riv.), Swe. 38/G1
Laird, Sk, Can. 145/L1
Lais, Indo. 89/C3
Lais, Phil. 88/D4
Laisamis, Kenya 119/B1
Laishevo, Rus. 69/L5
Laishui, China 80/G7
Laisvall, Swe. 38/F2
Laitila, Fin. 41/J1
Laives (Leifers), It. 61/H5
Laiwu, China 80/D3
Laixi, China 80/E3
Laiyang, China 80/E3
Laiyuan, China 80/C3
Laizhou (bay), China 80/D3
Laja (lake), Chile 190/C3
Lajas, Peru 184/B2
Lajatico, It. 63/D7
Laje, Braz. 187/E1
Lajeado, Braz. 189/G4
Lajedo, Braz. 183/G5
Lajes, Azor., Port. 47/S12
Lajes (int'l arpt.), Azor., Port. 47/S12
Lajes, Braz. 183/G4
Lajing (pass), Nepal 97/E1
Lajord, Sk, Can. 156/B2
Lajosmizse, Hun. 50/D2
Lāju, India 86/B3
Lajwāna Kalān, India 98/D5
Lakamané, Mali 114/C3
Lakato, Madg. 125/J7
Lake (co.), Fl, US 164/M6
Lake (co.), Il, US 167/P15
Lake Mason NWR, Mt, US 145/K4
Lake Minchumina, Ak, US 171/H3
Lake Woodruff Nat'l Wild. Ref., Fl, US 165/H3
Lake Alfred, Fl, US 164/M7
Lake Alice NWR, ND, US 156/E3
Lake Alma, Sk, Can. 156/B3
Lake Alpine, Ca, US 146/C4
Lake Amadeus Abor. Land, Austl. 131/F3
Lake Andes, SD, US 154/E2
Lake Andes Nat'l Wild. Ref., SD, US 154/E2
Lake Ann, Mi, US 160/D2
Lake Arrowhead, Ca, US 166/C2
Lake Arthur, NM, US 152/B4
Lake Arthur, La, US 164/B2
Lake Barrington, Il, US 167/P15
Lake Beulah, Wi, US 167/P14
Lake Bluff, Il, US 167/Q15
Lake Boga, Austl. 132/B2
Lake Bolac, Austl. 132/B3
Lake Buena Vista, Fl, US 164/M7
Lake Butler, Fl, US 165/G2
Lake Cargelligo, Austl. 133/C1
Lake Catherine, Il, US 167/P15
Lake Charles, La, US 164/B2
Lake City, Ar, US 162/B3
Lake City, Ca, US 146/C3
Lake City, Co, US 149/J1
Lake City, Fl, US 165/G2
Lake City, Ga, US 163/M7
Lake City, Ia, US 155/G2
Lake City, Mi, US 160/D2
Lake City, Mn, US 155/H1
Lake City, Pa, US 160/F3
Lake City, SC, US 163/H4
Lake City, SD, US 156/F5
Lake City, Tn, US 162/E2
Lake Clark NP, Ak, US 171/H3
Lake Clarke Shores, Fl, US 164/P9
Lake Conjola, Austl. 133/E2
Lake Cowichan, BC, Can. 144/B3
Lake Creek (riv.), Ut, US 147/G4
Lake Crystal, Mn, US 155/G1
Lake Dallas, Tx, US 150/K6
Lake Delton, Wi, US 155/K2
Lake District NP, Eng, UK 35/E2
Lake Elmo, Mn, US 157/Q7
Lake Elsinore, Ca, US 166/C3
Lake Fenton, Mi, US 160/E3
Lake Fern, Fl, US 164/K7
Lake Forest, Il, US 167/Q15
Lake Forest Park, Wa, US 167/C2
Lake Fork (riv.), Ut, US 147/H3
Lake Fork, Id, US 146/E1
Lake Garfield, Fl, US 164/M8
Lake Geneva, Wi, US 160/B3
Lake George, Co, US 152/B1
Lake George, NY, US 161/K3
Lake George, Mi, US 160/D3
Lake George NWR, ND, US 156/E4
Lake Grace, Austl. 130/C5
Lake Hamilton, Ar, US 153/H3
Lake Hamilton, Fl, US 164/M7
Lake Havasu City, Az, US 148/E3
Lake Helen, Fl, US 165/H3
Lake Hughes, Ca, US 148/C3
Lake Ilo NWR, ND, US 156/C4
Lake in the Hills, Il, US 167/P15
Lake Isom Nat'l Wild. Ref., Tn, US 162/C2
Lake Jackson, Tx, US 150/G3
Lake Jem, Fl, US 164/M6
Lake King, Austl. 130/C5
Lake Lenore, Sk, Can. 145/M1
Lake Linden, Mi, US 157/K4
Lake Lotawana, Mo, US 153/G1
Lake Louise, Ab, Can. 144/F2
Lake Lucerne, Fl, US 164/P11
Lake Macleod, Austl. 130/B3
Lake Malawi NP, Malw. 123/G2
Lake Mary, Fl, US 164/N6
Lake Mburo NP, Ugan. 121/G3
Lake McDonald, Mt, US 145/H3
Lake Mead Nat'l Rec. Area, Az, Nv, US 148/E2
Lake Meredith Nat'l Rec. Area, Tx, US 152/D3
Lake Mills, Ia, US 155/H2
Lake Mills, Wi, US 155/K2
Lake Mohawk, NJ, US 168/D1
Lake Monroe, Fl, US 164/N6
Lake Montezuma, Az, US 149/G3
Lake Murray, PNG 129/F1
Lake Nakuru NP, Kenya 119/B2
Lake Nash, Austl. 131/H2
Lake Nettie Nat'l Wild. Ref., ND, US 156/D4
Lake Odessa, Mi, US 160/D3
Lake Orion, Mi, US 167/F6
Lake Oswego, Or, US 146/B1
Lake Panasoffkee, Fl, US 164/L6
Lake Park, Mn, US 156/F4
Lake Park, Ga, US 165/G2
Lake Park, Ia, US 155/G2
Lake Park, Fl, US 164/P9
Lake Placid, NY, US 161/K2
Lake Placid, Fl, US 165/H4
Lake Pleasant, NY, US 161/J3
Lake Preston, SD, US 155/F1
Lake Ronkonkoma, NY, US 169/E2
Lake Saint Croix Beach, Mn, US 157/Q7
Lake Shore, Mn, US 157/G4
Lake Shore, Md, US 168/B5
Lake Station, In, US 167/R16
Lake Stevens, Wa, US 144/C3
Lake Success, NY, US 169/L8
Lake Tanglewood, Tx, US 152/D3
Lake Thibadeau Nat'l Wild. Ref., Mt, US 145/K3
Lake Tomahawk, Wi, US 157/K5
Lake Toxaway, NC, US 163/F3
Lake View, Ar, US 153/J3
Lake View, Ia, US 155/G2
Lake Villa, Il, US 167/P15
Lake Waccamaw, NC, US 163/H3
Lake Wales, Fl, US 164/M8
Lake Way, Austl. 130/D3
Lake Worth, Fl, US 164/P9
Lake Zahl Nat'l Wild. Ref., ND, US 156/C3
Lake Zurich, Il, US 167/P15
Lakefield, On, Can. 161/G2
Lakefield, Mn, US 155/G2
Lakefield NP, Austl. 129/F3
Lakehills, Tx, US 150/E3
Lakehurst, NJ, US 168/D3
Lakehurst Nav. Air Eng. Ctr., NJ, US 168/D3
Lakeland, Ga, US 165/G2
Lakeland, La, US 164/C2
Lakeland, Fl, US 164/M7
Lakeland, Mn, US 157/Q7
Lakeland Village, Ca, US 166/C3
Lakemoor, Il, US 167/P15
Lakenheath, Eng, UK 37/G2
Lakeport, Ca, US 146/B4
Lakeport, Tx, US 151/G1
Lakes Entrance, Austl. 133/D3
Lakesfjorden (inlet), Nor. 38/H1
Lakeside, Ca, US 166/D5
Lakeside, Mt, US 144/G3
Lakeside, Ne, US 154/C2
Lakeside, Or, US 146/A2
Lakeside, Ut, US 147/G3
Lakeside, Va, US 163/J2
Laketown, Ut, US 147/H3
Lakeview, Ar, US 153/H2
Lakeview, Ca, US 166/C3
Lakeview, Ga, US 162/E3
Lakeview, Mi, US 160/D3
Lakeview, Mt, US 147/H1
Lakeview, Or, US 146/C2
Lakeview, Tx, US 152/D3
Lakeview Estates, Ga, US 163/M7
Lakeville (lake), Mi, US 167/F6
Lakeville, Mn, US 155/H1
Lakeway, Tx, US 151/F2
Lakewood, Ca, US 166/F8
Lakewood, Co, US 154/B4
Lakewood, Il, US 167/P15
Lakewood, NJ, US 168/D3
Lakewood, NY, US 161/G3
Lakewood, Oh, US 160/F4
Lakewood, Wa, US 144/C3
Lakewood, Wi, US 157/K5
Lakhāsar, India 98/B5
Lakhemaa NP, Est. 41/L2
Lakhīmpur, India 96/C2
Lakhnādon, India 96/B4
Lakhpat, India 101/J4
Lakhva, Bela. 72/D1
Laki (vol.), Ice. 38/N7
Lakin, Ks, US 152/D2
Lakki, Pak. 98/A3
Lakkíon, Gre. 67/K3
Lakonía (gulf), Gre. 67/J3
Lakor (isl.), Indo. 128/C2
Lakota, ND, US 156/E3
Lakota, C.d'Iv. 114/D5
Lakshadweep (isls.), India 77/F8
Lakshadweep (terr.), India 92/B6
Lākshām, Bang. 97/H4
Lal Suhanra NP, Pak. 98/B5
Lala, Phil. 88/C4
Lāla Mūsa, Pak. 98/B3
Lalago, Tanz. 119/A2
Lālajīn, Iran 103/G3
Lalana (riv.), Madg. 125/H8
Lalang (riv.), Indo. 90/B4
Lâlapaşa, Turk. 51/H5
Lalara, Gabon 120/B2
Lalauli, India 96/C3
L'Albaron (peak), Fr. 64/D2
Lālbhitti, Nepal 97/E2
Lālganj, India 97/E3
Lālgola, India 97/G3
Lālī, Iran 103/G3
Lāliān, Pak. 98/B4
Lalībela, Eth. 118/A2
Laliki, Indo. 128/B1
Lalín, Sp. 46/A1
Lalin (riv.), China 79/K3
Lalinde, Fr. 44/D4
Lalitpur, India 96/B3
Lalitpur (Pāţan), Nepal 97/E2
Lalla Rookh Abor. Land, Austl. 130/C2
Lālmanir Hāt, Bang. 97/G3
Lālpur, Bang. 97/G3
Lalyo, Sudan 117/F4
Lam Pao (res.), Thai. 86/D5
Lāma, Bang. 93/F3
Lamachan (peak), Sc, UK 34/D1
Lamadi, China 93/G2
Lamadrid, Mex. 150/D4
Lamag, Malay. 88/B4
Lamakera, Indo. 128/A2
Lamaline, Nf, Can. 159/K2
Lamanai (ruin), Belz. 176/D2
Lamandau (riv.), Indo. 90/D4
Lamar, Ar, US 153/H3
Lamar, Mo, US 153/G2
Lamar, Co, US 152/C1
Lamar, SC, US 163/G3
Lamarche, Fr. 60/B1
Lamarche-sur-Saône, Fr. 60/B3
Lamarque, Arg. 190/D3
Lamas, Peru 184/B2
Lamastre, Fr. 64/A3
Lāmayūrū, India 98/D2
Lambach, Aus. 59/G6
Lamballe, Fr. 56/C4
Lambaré, Par. 188/E3
Lambaréné, Gabon 120/B3
Lambari, Braz. 187/L6
Lambasa, Fiji 137/Z17
Lambay (isl.), Ire. 34/B5
Lambayeque (dept.), Peru 184/A2
Lambayeque, Peru 184/B2
Lambé Coba (riv.), Mali 114/C3
Lambeg, NI, UK 34/B3
Lambert, Ms, US 162/B3
Lambert-St. Louis (int'l arpt.), Mo, US 155/J4
Lamberton, Mn, US 155/G1
Lambert's Bay, SAfr. 124/B4
Lambertville, Mi, US 160/E4
Lambertville, NJ, US 168/D3
Lambesc, Fr. 64/B5
Lambeth (bor.), Eng, UK 30/C2
Lambourn, Eng, UK 37/E3
Lambrama, Peru 184/C4
Lambrecht, Ger. 58/B4
Lambro (riv.), It. 62/C2
Lambsburg, Va, US 163/G2
Lambsheim, Ger. 58/B3
Lambton, Qu, Can. 158/B3
Lambton (co.), On, Can. 167/H6
Lame Deer, Mt, US 145/L5
Lamego, Port. 46/B2
Lamentin (int'l arpt.), Fr. 173/N9
Lamèque, NB, Can. 158/E2
Lameroo, Austl. 131/J5
Lamesa, Tx, US 150/D1
Lamía, Gre. 49/H3
Lamine (riv.), Mo, US 153/H1
Lamington (riv.), NJ, US 168/D2
Lamington NP, Austl. 134/D5
Lamitan, Phil. 88/C4
Lamlash, Sc, UK 33/A5
Lamma (isl.), China 87/L8
Lammefjord (inlet), Den. 39/H7
Lammermuir (hills), Sc, UK 33/D5
Lammhult, Swe. 40/F3
Lammi, Fin. 41/L1
Lamming Mills, BC, Can. 144/D1
Lamoille, Nv, US 146/F3
Lamon (bay), Phil. 88/C2
Lamona, Wa, US 144/E4
Lamone (riv.), It. 45/J4
Lamongan, Indo. 89/F4
Lamoni, Ia, US 155/H3
Lamont, Ok, US 153/F2
Lamont, Fl, US 165/G2
Lamont, Ca, US 148/C3
Lamorlaye, Fr. 30/K4
Lamotrek (isl.), Micr. 136/D4
Lamotte-Beuvron, Fr. 57/H5
Lampa, Chile 190/N8
Lampa, Peru 184/D4
Lampang, Thai. 94/B2
Lampasas, Tx, US 151/E2
Lampasas (riv.), Tx, US 175/F2
Lampaul-Plouarzel, Fr. 56/A4
Lampazos de Naranjo, Mex. 150/D4
Lampe, Mo, US 153/H2
Lampedusa, It. 48/C5
Lampedusa (isl.), It. 29/F5
Lampertheim, Ger. 58/B3
Lampeter, Wal, UK 36/B2
Lampeter, Pa, US 168/B4
Lamphey, Wal, UK 36/B3
Lamphun, Thai. 94/B2
Lampman, Sk, Can. 156/C3
Lamporecchio, It. 63/D6
Lampson, Wi, US 157/J5
Lampung (prov.), Indo. 89/D4
Lamstedt, Ger. 53/G1
Lamu, Kenya 119/C2
Lamu (isl.), Kenya 119/C2
Lamud, Peru 184/B2
Lamwa (peak), Ugan. 117/G5
Lamy, NM, US 152/B3
Lan (isl.), Tai. 87/J4
Lan Sang NP, Thai. 94/B2
Lana, It. 61/H4
Lana, Río de la (riv.), Mex. 176/C2
Lanai (isl.), Hi, US 142/T10
Lanaken, Belg. 55/E2
Lanao (lake), Phil. 88/D4
Lanark, Sc, UK 33/C5
Lanark, Il, US 155/K2
Lanas Village, Malay. 88/B4
Lanba, China 86/E3
Lanbi (isl.), Myan. 93/G5
Lancang (riv.), China 86/C2
Lancang (Mekong) (riv.), China 78/D5
Lancashire (plain), Eng, UK 35/E4
Lancashire (co.), Eng, UK 35/F4
Lancaster (sound), Nun, Can. 141/H1
Lancaster, Eng, UK 35/F3
Lancaster, Ca, US 148/C3
Lancaster, Ky, US 162/E2
Lancaster, Mn, US 156/F3
Lancaster, Mo, US 155/H3
Lancaster, NH, US 161/L2
Lancaster, NY, US 160/V10
Lancaster, Oh, US 160/E5
Lancaster (arpt.), Pa, US 168/B3

Lancas – Lenora

Lancaster (co.), Pa, US 168/B4
Lancaster, Pa, US 168/B3
Lancaster, SC, US 163/G3
Lancaster, Tx, US 150/L7
Lancaster, Va, US 163/J2
Lancaster, Wi, US 155/J2
Lance (cr.), Wy, US 154/B2
Lance Creek, Wy, US 154/B2
Lancebranlette (peak), Fr. 64/C1
Lancefield, Austl. 133/B3
Lancelin, Austl. 130/B4
Lancenigo, It. 63/F2
Lancer, Sk, Can. 145/K2
Lanchester, Eng, UK 35/G2
Lanch'khut'i, Geo. 71/G4
Lanciano, It. 65/D3
L'Ancienne-Lorette, Qu, Can. 158/B2
Lanco, Chile 190/B3
Lançon-Provence, Fr. 64/B5
Łańcut, Pol. 43/M3
Lancy, Swi. 60/C5
Land Between The Lakes Recreation Area, Ky, US 162/C2
Land Kehdingen (reg.), Ger. 53/G1
Land O'Lakes, Fl, US 164/L7
Land O'Lakes, Wi, US 157/K4
Landau an der Isar, Ger. 59/F5
Landau in der Pfalz, Ger. 58/B4
Landeck, Aus. 61/G3
Landen, Belg. 55/E2
Lander, Wy, US 147/J2
Landerneau, Fr. 56/A4
Landes (reg.), Fr. 44/C4
Landes de Lanvaux (mts.), Fr. 44/B3
Landesbergen, Ger. 53/G3
Landi Kotal, Pak. 98/A2
Landis, Sk, Can. 145/K1
Landis Valley Museum, Pa, US 168/B3
Landisburg, Pa, US 168/A3
Landivisiau, Fr. 56/A3
Landivy, Fr. 57/D4
Landrecies, Fr. 54/C3
Landri Sales, Braz. 183/F4
Landriano, It. 62/C3
Landrum, SC, US 163/F3
Land's End (pt.), Eng, UK 36/A6
Landsberg, Ger. 61/G1
Landsborough (cr.), Austl. 134/B3
Landser, Fr. 60/D2
Landshut, Ger. 59/F5
Landskrona, Swe. 40/E4
Landsmeer, Neth. 52/B4
Landstuhl, Ger. 55/G5
Landvetter (int'l arpt.), Swe. 40/E3
Landza, Congo 120/D2
Lane (riv.), Fr. 57/F6
Lane End, Eng, UK 30/A2
Lanercost, Eng, UK 35/F2
Lanesborough, Ire. 32/C2
Lanester, Fr. 56/B5
Lanett, Al, US 162/E4
Lang, Sk, Can. 156/B3
Lang Craig (pt.), Sc, UK 33/D3
Lang Kha Tuk (peak), Thai. 94/B4
Lang Son, Viet. 87/E4
Lang Suan, Thai. 94/B4
Langadhás, Gre. 49/H2
Langádhia, Gre. 49/H4
Langano (lake), Eth. 118/A4
Langara, Indo. 91/F4
Langdon, ND, US 156/E3
Langdon, Ab, Can. 145/H2
Langdon Hills, Eng, UK 30/E2
Langeac, Fr. 44/E4
Langeais, Fr. 57/F6
Langebaanweg, SAfr. 124/L10
Langeberg (mts.), SAfr. 124/L10
Langeland (isl.), Ger. 40/D4
Langelsheim, Ger. 53/H5
Langen (lake), Nor. 38/S8
Langen, Ger. 58/B3
Langen, Ger. 53/F1
Langenaltheim, Ger. 58/D5
Langenargen, Ger. 61/F2
Langenau, Ger. 58/D5
Langenbach, Ger. 59/E6
Langenberg, Ger. 53/E6
Langenburg, Sk, Can. 156/D2
Längenfeld, Aus. 61/G3
Langenfeld, Ger. 55/F1
Langenhagen, Ger. 53/G4
Langenhorn, Ger. 40/C4
Langenlois, Aus. 43/H4
Langenpreising, Ger. 59/E6
Langenselbold, Ger. 58/C2
Langenstein, Aus. 59/H6
Langenthal, Swi. 60/D3
Langenwang, Aus. 45/L3
Langenzenn, Ger. 58/D3
Langenzersdorf, Aus. 51/N7
Langeoog (isl.), Ger. 53/E1
Langeoog, Ger. 53/E1
Langepas, Rus. 74/H3
Langerringen, Ger. 61/G1
Langeskov, Den. 40/D4
Langesund, Nor. 40/C2
Langeten (riv.), Swi. 60/D3
Langfang, China 80/H7
Langford, SD, US 156/F5
Langfurth, Ger. 58/D4
Langgam, Indo. 89/C2
Langgapayung, Indo. 89/B2
Langgar, China 78/C6
Langham, Eng, UK 37/F1
Langham, Sk, Can. 145/L1
Langhirano, It. 62/D4
Langholm, Sc, UK 35/F1
Langhorne, Pa, US 168/D3
Langjökull (glacier), Ice. 38/N7
Langkawi (isl.), Thai. 93/G6
Langkon, Malay. 88/B4
Langley, Eng, UK 30/E3
Langley, Eng, UK 30/B2
Langley, Wa, US 167/C1
Langley (A.F.B.), Va, US 163/J2
Langlois, Or, US 146/A2
Langnau im Emmental, Swi. 60/D4
Langney (pt.), Eng, UK 37/G5
Langogne, Fr. 44/E4
Langon, Fr. 56/D5
Långön (isl.), Swe. 39/A2
Langon, Fr. 44/C4
Langøya (isl.), Nor. 38/E1
Langqên (riv.), China 99/C5
Langquaid, Ger. 59/F5
Langres, Fr. 60/B2
Langres, de (plat.), Fr. 66/E1
Langru, China 99/C4
Langrune-sur-Mer, Fr. 57/E2
Langsa, Indo. 89/B1
Langshyttan, Swe. 40/G1
Langstaff, On, Can. 160/U8
Langston, Ok, US 153/F3
Langtang, Nga. 115/H4
Langtang, China 87/F2
Langtang Lirung (peak), Nepal 97/E1
Langtang NP, Nepal 97/E1
Langtou, China 81/C2
Langtry, Tx, US 150/D3
Languedoc (reg.), Fr. 66/D2
Languedoc-Roussillon (pol. reg.), Fr. 44/E5
Langueux, Fr. 56/C3
Languidic, Fr. 56/B5
Langwedel, Ger. 53/G3
Langweid an Lech, Ger. 58/E6
Langwies, Swi. 61/F4
Langxi, China 80/D5
Lanham-Seabrook, Md, US 168/B6
Lanigan (riv.), Sk, Can. 145/M2
Lanigan, Sk, Can. 145/M2
Lanin (vol.), Arg. 190/C3
Lanin, PN, Arg. 190/C3
Lankāpāra Hāt, India 97/G2
Länkärän, Azer. 103/G2
Lankin, ND, US 156/F3
Lankou, China 87/G4
Lanlacuni Bajo, Peru 184/D4
Lanmeur, Fr. 56/B3
Länna, Swe. 39/A1
Lannemezan (plat.), Fr. 44/D5
Lannemezan, Fr. 47/F1
Lanner, Eng, UK 36/A6
Lannilis, Fr. 56/A3
Lannion, Fr. 56/B3
Lannion (bay), Fr. 44/B2
Lannion (Servel) (arpt.), Fr. 56/B3
L'Annonciation, Qu, Can. 161/J1
Lanouée, Fr. 56/C4
Lans, Montagne de (mts.), Fr. 64/B3
Lansdale, Pa, US 168/C3
Lansdowne, On, Can. 161/H2
Lansdowne, India 96/B1
Lansdowne, Pa, US 168/C4
Lansdowne-Baltimore Highlands, Md, US 168/B5
L'Anse Ind. Res., Mi, US 157/K4
Lansford, ND, US 156/D3
Lansford, Pa, US 168/C2
Lanshan, China 87/G3
Lansing, Yk, Can. 171/M3
Lansing, Il, US 167/Q16
Lansing, Ia, US 155/J2
Lansing (cap.), Mi, US 160/D3
Lanslebourg-Mont-Cenis, Fr. 64/C2
Lanta (isl.), Thai. 93/G6
Lantana, Fl, US 164/P9
Lantang, China 87/G4
Lantau (isl.), China 87/K7
Lantau (peak), China 87/K8
Lantau (chan.), China 87/K8
Lanterne (riv.), Fr. 60/C2
Lantosque, Fr. 64/D5
Lantouy, Laos 86/D4
Lantry, SD, US 154/D1
Lantz, NS, Can. 158/F3
Lantzville, BC, Can. 144/B3
Lanús, Arg. 191/J11
Lanusei, It. 48/A3
Lanuvio, It. 65/B4
Lanuza, Phil. 88/D3
Lanvallay, Fr. 56/C4
Lanvéoc, Fr. 56/A4
Lanxi, China 79/K2
Lanxi, China 87/H2
Lanza, Bol. 188/C1
Lanzara, It. 65/D6
Lanzarote (int'l arpt.), Sp. 110/B3
Lanzarote (isl.), Canl., Sp. 107/A2
Lanžhot, Czh. 43/J4
Lanzhou, China 78/E4
Lanzo d'Intelvi, It. 61/F6
Lanzo Torinese, It. 64/D2
Lao (mts.), China 81/D2
Lao (riv.), China 87/G2
Lao (peak), China 80/E3
Lao Cai, Viet. 86/D4
Lao Fu Chai, Laos 94/C1
Laoag, Phil. 88/C1
Laobian, China 81/B2
Laocheng, China 78/F5
Laodao (riv.), China 87/G2
Laodaodian, China 79/K1
Laoguanzui, China 87/G2
Laoha (riv.), China 79/H3
Laohekou, China 80/B4
Laohutun, China 81/A3
Laojun (mtn.), China 80/B4
Laoling, China 81/D2
Laon, Fr. 54/C4
Laos (ctry.) 94/C2
Laoshan, China 80/E3
Laotuding (peak), China 81/C2
Laou (riv.), Mor. 112/B2
Lapa, Braz. 189/G3
Lapalud, Fr. 64/A4
Lapataia, Arg. 191/C7
Lapeer, Mi, US 160/E3
Lapeer (co.), Mi, US 167/F6
Lapia, Nga. 115/G4
Lapine, Al, US 165/E2
Lapinlahti, Fin. 68/E3
Lapithos, Cyp. 104/C2
Lapland (reg.), Eur. 38/F1
Lapoint, Ut, US 147/J3
Laporte, Pa, US 161/H4
Laporte, Co, US 154/B3
Lapotina (mtn.), Rus. 79/N1
Lappeenranta, Fin. 41/N1
Lappersdorf, Ger. 59/F4
Lappi (prov.), Fin. 38/H2
Lâpseki, Turk. 49/K2
Laptev (sea), Rus. 77/M2
Lapua, Fin. 68/D3
Lapundra, India 101/K3
Lăpuşna, Mol. 72/E4
Łapy, Pol. 43/M2
Laqīyat al Arba'īn, Sudan 135/F4
Laquey, Mo, US 153/H2
Lār, Iran 103/H5
Lara (state), Ven. 180/D2
Lara, Austl. 133/B4
Laracha, Sp. 46/A1
Larache (prov.), Mor. 112/B2
Larache, Mor. 112/A2
Laracor, Ire. 32/D2
Laragne-Montéglin, Fr. 64/B4
Lārak (isl.), Iran 103/J5
Laramie (mts.), Wy, US 154/B2
Laramie, Wy, US 154/B3
Laramie (riv.), Wy, US 154/B3
Laramie (peak), Wy, US 154/B2
Laranjeiras do Sul, Braz. 189/F3
Larantuka, Indo. 128/A2
Larat (isl.), Indo. 91/H5
Larat, Indo. 128/C1
Larba, Alg. 112/G4
Larchmont, NY, US 169/K8
L'Arcouest (pt.), Fr. 56/B3
Lærdalsøyri, Nor. 40/B1
Lardier (cape), Fr. 64/C6
Laredo, Sp. 44/B5
Laredo, Mo, US 155/H3
Laredo, Peru 184/B3
Laredo, Mt, US 145/K3
Laredo, Tx, US 150/E4
Laredo (int'l arpt.), Tx, US 150/E4
Laren, Neth. 52/C4
Lares, Peru 184/C4
Larga (lag.), Tx, US 151/F4
L'Argentière-la-Bessée, Fr. 64/C3
Largo (bay), Sc, UK 33/D4
Largo, Fl, US 164/K8
Largo (cr.), NM, US 149/H3
Largo, Md, US 168/B6
Largs, Sc, UK 33/B5
Largue (riv.), Fr. 60/D2
Lariang (riv.), Indo. 91/E4
Lariano, It. 65/B4
Larino, It. 65/D4
Lárisa, Gre. 49/H3
Lark (riv.), Eng, UK 37/G2
Lark Harbour, Nf, Can. 159/H1
Lārkāna, Pak. 101/J3
Larkhall, Sc, UK 33/C5
Larkspur, Ca, US 167/J11
Larkspur, Co, US 154/B4
L'Arly, PN de, Burk. 115/F4
Larmor-Plage, Fr. 56/B5
Larnaca, Cyp. 104/C2
Larnaca (int'l arpt.), Cyp. 104/C2
Larnaca (dist.), Cyp. 104/C2
Larne, NI, UK 34/C2
Larne (dist.), NI, UK 34/C2
Larne Lough (inlet), NI, UK 34/C2
Larned, Ks, US 152/E1
Larochette, Lux. 55/F4
Laropi, Ugan. 121/G2
Laroque-d'Olmes, Fr. 44/D5
Larose, La, US 164/C3
Larreynaga, Nic. 176/E3
Larrimah, Austl. 128/D3
Larroque, Arg. 191/J10
Larrys (cr.), Pa, US 168/A1
Larry's River, NS, Can. 159/G3
Larsen Bay, Ak, US 171/H4
Larsen Ice Shelf, Ant. 192/V
Larsen Sound (bay), Nun, Can. 140/G1
Larslan, Mt, US 145/L3
Larto, La, US 164/C2
Laruns, Fr. 44/C5
Larvik, Nor. 40/D2
Las Animas, Co, US 152/C1
Las Aves (isls.), Ven. 173/H5
Las Bayas, Arg. 190/C4
Las Bombas, Chile 188/B3
Las Breñas, Arg. 188/D3
Las Cabezas de San Juan, Sp. 46/C4
Las Cabras, Chile 190/N9
Las Casuarinas, Arg. 188/B4
Las Cruces, NM, US 149/J4
Las Delicias, Ven. 180/C3
Las Esperanzas, Mex. 150/D4
Las Flores, Arg. 190/F3
Las Guacamayas, Mex. 174/E5
Las Hermosas, PN, Col. 180/C4
Las Higueras, Arg. 190/D2
Las Juntas, Col. 180/C4
Las Lajas (peak), Arg. 190/C3
Las Lajas, Arg. 190/C3
Las Lajitas, Ven. 181/E3
Las Lomas, Peru 184/A2
Las Lomitas, Arg. 188/D3
Las Margaritas, Mex. 176/D2
Las Martinas, Cuba 177/E1
Las Mercedes, Ven. 181/E2
Las Minas (peak), Hon. 176/D3
Las Montañitas, Ven. 180/D3
Las Navas, Phil. 88/D2
Las Nieves, Mex. 174/D3
Las Orquídeas, PN, Col. 180/B3
Las Palmas, Pan. 177/F4
Las Palmas (riv.), Mex. 148/D4
Las Palmas de Cocalán, PN, Chile 190/N9
Las Palmas de Gran Canaria, Sp. 110/B3
Las Pampitas, Bol. 185/E4
Las Parejas, Arg. 188/D5
Las Pedroñeras, Sp. 46/D3
Las Perdices, Arg. 190/E2
Las Perlas (arch.), Pan. 177/G4
Las Petas, Bol. 185/E4
Las Petas, Bol. 185/G5
Las Piedras, Ven. 180/C2
Las Piedras, Ven. 181/F2
Las Piedras, Uru. 191/K11
Las Piedras, Peru 184/D4
Las Piedras, Bol. 185/E3
Las Pinas, Phil. 88/E7
Las Pipinas, Arg. 191/F2
Las Plumas, Arg. 190/D4
Las Rosas, Mex. 176/C2
Las Rosas, Arg. 188/D5
Las Rozas de Madrid, Sp. 47/N9
Las Tablas, Pan. 180/A3
Las Tablas, NM, US 149/J2
Las Tórtolas (peak), Chile 188/B4
Las Toscas, Uru. 189/F5
Las Toscas, Arg. 188/E4
Las Trincheras, Ven. 181/E3
Las Varas, Mex. 174/D4
Las Varillas, Arg. 188/D4
Las Vegas, NM, US 152/B3
Las Vegas, Nv, US 148/E2
Las Vegas Nat'l Wildlife Reserve, NM, US 152/B3
Las Yaras, Peru 188/B1
Lasa (Laas), It. 61/G4
Lasahau, Indo. 128/A1
Lasalle, Qu, Can. 159/N7
Lasan, Indo. 90/E3
Lasanbāri, India 86/B3
Lasberg, Aus. 59/H6
Lascano, Uru. 191/G2
Lascar (vol.), Chile 188/C2
Lascar, Co, US 152/B2
Lasem, Indo. 89/E4
Lashburn, Sk, Can. 145/K1
Lashio, Myan. 86/C4
Lashkar Gāh, Afg. 101/H2
Lashmanka, Rus. 69/L5
Lasia (isl.), Indo. 89/B2
Lasne-Chapelle-Saint-Lambert, Belg. 55/D2
Læsø (isl.), Den. 40/D3
Lasolo (riv.), Indo. 91/F4
Lassay-les-Châteaux, Fr. 57/E4
Lassen (peak), Ca, US 146/C3
Lassen Volcanic NP, Ca, US 146/C3
L'Assomption, Qu, Can. 159/P6
Lasswade, Sc, UK 33/C5
Last Mtn. (lake), Sk, Can. 145/M2
Lastoursville, Gabon 120/C3
Lastovo (isl.), Cro. 48/E1
Lastovo, Cro. 50/C4
Lastovski Kanal (canal), Cro. 48/E1
Lastra a Signa, It. 63/E6
Lästringe, Swe. 39/A2
Lastrup, Ger. 53/E3
Lat Yao, Thai. 94/B3
Lata, Sol. 136/F6
Latacunga, Ecu. 180/B5
Latady (isl.), Ant. 192/U
Latākhola, Bang. 97/H4
Latakia (Al Lādhiqīyah), Syria 104/D2
L'Atakora (prov.), Ben. 115/F4
Lātehār, India 97/E4
Latemar (peak), It. 61/H5
Laterrière, Qu, Can. 158/B1
Laterza, It. 48/E2
Latexo, Tx, US 151/G2
Latham, Ks, US 153/F2
Lathan (riv.), Fr. 44/C3
Lathrop, Ca, US 167/M11
Lathrop, Mo, US 155/G4
Latimer, Eng, UK 30/B2
Latimer, Ia, US 155/H2
Latina, It. 65/B5
Latina (prov.), It. 65/C5
Latina Scalo, It. 65/B4
Latisana, It. 63/G2
Latium (reg.), It. 67/G2
Laton, Ca, US 148/C2
Latorica (riv.), Slvk.,Ukr. 43/M4
Latouche Treville (cape), Austl. 128/A4
Latrobe, Pa, US 161/G4
Latrobe, Austl. 132/C4
Latrobe (mt.), Austl. 133/C4
Latsch (Laces), It. 61/G4
Lattes, Fr. 44/E5
Lattingtown, NY, US 169/L8
Lātūr, India 95/C2
Latvia (ctry.) 41/L3
Lat'yuga, Rus. 69/L2
Lau Group (isl.), Fiji 136/H6
Laubach, Ger. 58/B1
Lauca, PN, Chile 184/D5
Lauca, PN, Chile 188/B1
Lauch (riv.), Fr. 45/G3
Lauchert (riv.), Ger. 58/C6
Lauchheim, Ger. 58/D5
Lauda-Königshofen, Ger. 58/C3
Lauder, Mb, Can. 156/D3
Lauder, Sc, UK 33/D5
Lauderdale (lakes), Wi, US 167/N14
Lauderdale, Ms, US 162/C4
Lauderdale Lakes, Fl, US 164/P10
Lauderdale-by-the-Sea, Fl, US 164/P10
Lauderhill, Fl, US 164/P10
Laudun, Fr. 64/A4
Lauenbrück, Ger. 53/G2
Lauenburg, Ger. 53/H2
Lauenen, Swi. 60/D5
Lauenförde, Ger. 53/H5
Lauer (riv.), Ger. 58/D2
Lauf, Ger. 58/E3
Laufach, Ger. 58/C2
Laufen, Swi. 60/D3
Laufen, Ger. 59/F7
Laufenburg, Swi. 60/E2
Lauffen am Neckar, Ger. 58/C4
Laugharne, Wal, UK 36/B3
Laughlen (mt.), Austl. 131/G2
Laughlin (A.F.B.), Tx, US 150/D3
Lauhanvuoren NP, Fin. 68/D3
Lauhkaung, Myan. 86/C3
Lauingen, Ger. 58/D5
Laukuva, Lith. 41/K4
Launceston, Austl. 132/C4
Launceston, Eng, UK 36/B5
Laune (riv.), Ire. 32/A5
Launette (riv.), Fr. 30/L4
Launglon, Myan. 94/B3
Launonen, Fin. 39/E4
Laupen, Swi. 60/D4
Lauperswil, Swi. 60/D4
Laupheim, Ger. 61/F1
L'Aupillon (peak), Fr. 64/C4
Laura, Austl. 134/B1
Laura, Austl. 131/H5
Laura, Sk, Can. 145/L2
Laureana di Borrello, It. 48/E3
Laurel, De, US 163/K1
Laurel, Fl, US 165/G4
Laurel, In, US 160/D5
Laurel, Md, US 168/B5
Laurel, Ms, US 164/D2
Laurel, Ne, US 155/F2
Laurel, Va, US 163/J2
Laurel Bay, SC, US 163/G4
Laurel Hill, Fl, US 165/E2
Laurel Springs, NJ, US 168/C4
Laureldale, Pa, US 168/C3
Laurelton, Pa, US 168/A2
Laurelvale, NI, UK 34/B3
Laurence Harbor, NJ, US 169/J10
Laurencekirk, Sc, UK 33/D3
Laurens, Ia, US 155/G2
Laurens, SC, US 163/F3
Laurentian (plat.), On, Can. 140/G3
Laurentides, Qu, Can. 159/N6
Laurier, Mb, Can. 156/E2
Laurier-Station, Qu, Can. 158/B2
Laurieston, Sc, UK 34/D2
Laurinburg, NC, US 163/H3
Lauris, Fr. 64/B5
Laurium, Mi, US 157/K4
Lauriya Nandangarh, India 97/E2
Lauro, It. 65/D6
Lausanne, Swi. 60/C4
Lauscha, Ger. 58/E2
Laut (isl.), Indo. 91/E4
Lautaro, Chile 190/B3
Lautem, ETim. 128/B2
Lauter (riv.), Ger. 42/E3
Lauter (riv.), Fr.,Ger. 58/B4
Lauter, Ger. 59/F1
Lauterach (riv.), Ger. 59/E4
Lauterbach (riv.), Ger. 58/E2
Lauterbach, Ger. 58/C1
Lauterbourg, Fr. 58/B5
Lauterbrunnen, Swi. 60/D4
Lauterecken, Ger. 55/G4
L'Authion (peak), Fr. 64/D4
Lautoka, Fiji 137/Y18
Lautoporras, Fin. 39/E4
Lauve, Nor. 40/D2
Lauwers (chan.), Neth. 52/D1
Lauwersmeer (lake), Neth. 52/D2
Lava Beds Nat'l Mon., Ca, US 146/C3
Lava Hot Springs, Id, US 147/G2
Lavaca (riv.), Tx, US 151/F3
Lavaca (bay), Tx, US 151/F3
Lavaca, Al, US 162/C4
Lavagna, It. 62/C5
Lavagna (riv.), It. 62/C4
Laval, Fr. 57/E4
Laval, Qu, Can. 159/N6
Lavalleja (dept.), Uru. 191/G2
Lavallette, NJ, US 168/D4
Lāvān (isl.), Iran 103/H5
Lavans-lès-Saint-Claude, Fr. 60/B5
Lavant (riv.), Aus. 45/L3
Lavapié (pt.), Chile 190/B3
Lavaraty, Madg. 125/H8
Lavassaare, Est. 41/L2
Lavaur, Fr. 44/D5
Lavelanet, Fr. 44/D5
Lavello, It. 48/D2
Lavena, It. 61/E6
Laveno, It. 61/E6
Laverne, Ok, US 152/E2
Laverton, Austl. 130/D4
Lavey, Swi. 60/D5
Lavezzola, It. 63/E4
Lavik, Nor. 40/A1
Lavillette, NB, Can. 158/E2
Lavina, Mt, US 145/K4
Lavino (riv.), It. 63/E4
Lavis, It. 61/H5
Lavon (dam), Tx, US 150/L6
Lavon, Tx, US 150/L6
Lavonia, Ga, US 163/F3
Lavos, Port. 46/A2
Lavras, Braz. 186/D4
Lavras da Mangabeira, Braz. 183/G4
Lávrion, Gre. 49/J4
Lavushi Manda NP, Zam. 123/F2
Lawa (riv.), FrG.,Sur. 182/C2
Lawa (riv.), FrG. 181/H4
Lawabauk, Myan. 86/C5
Lawang, Indo. 89/F4
Lāwar Khās, India 96/A1
Lawarai (pass), Pak. 98/A2
Lawas, Malay. 88/A4
Lawdar, Yem. 118/C2
Lawen, Or, US 146/D2
Lawit (peak), Malay. 89/C1
Lawit (mtn.), Indo. 90/D3
Lawksawk, Myan. 94/B1
Lawn, Nf, Can. 159/K2
Lawn, Tx, US 150/E1
Lawn Hill, Austl. 129/E4
Lawn Hill NP, Austl. 129/E4
Lawndale, Ca, US 166/F8
Lawnhill, BC, Can. 171/M5
Lawqah, SAr. 103/E4
Lawra, Gha. 114/E4
Lawrence, NZ 135/B4
Lawrence, In, US 160/C5
Lawrence, Ks, US 153/G1
Lawrence, Ma, US 161/L3
Lawrence, NY, US 169/L9
Lawrence, Ne, US 154/E3
Lawrence, Tx, US 150/L7
Lawrence Park, Pa, US 160/F3
Lawrence Station, NB, Can. 158/D3
Lawrenceburg, In, US 162/E1
Lawrenceburg, Ky, US 162/E1
Lawrenceburg, Tn, US 162/D3
Lawrencetown, NI, UK 34/B3
Lawrenceville, Ga, US 163/N7
Lawrenceville, Il, US 162/D1
Lawrenceville, NJ, US 168/D3
Lawrenceville, Va, US 163/J2
Lawson, Sk, Can. 145/L2
Lawson, Ar, US 153/H4
Lawson, Mo, US 155/G4
Lawtey, Fl, US 165/G2
Lawton, Ok, US 153/E3
Lawu (peak), Indo. 90/D5
Lax, Ga, US 165/G2
Laxå, Swe. 40/F2
Laxey, IM, UK 34/D3
Laxou, Fr. 55/F6
Lay (riv.), Fr. 44/C3
Lay-Saint-Christophe, Fr. 55/F6
Laya (riv.), Rus. 69/N2
Layar (cape), Indo. 91/E4
Laye (riv.), Fr. 64/B4
Layjūn, Yem. 118/D2
Laylān, Iraq 103/F3
Läyliäinen, Fin. 39/E4
Layon (riv.), Fr. 44/C3
Laysan (isl.), Hi, US 137/H2
Layton, Fl, US 165/H5
Layton, Ut, US 147/H3
Layton, NJ, US 168/D1
Laytonville, Ca, US 146/B4
Laytown, Ire. 34/B4
Lazarev, Rus. 75/Q4
Lazarevac, Serb. 50/E3
Lázaro Cárdenas, Mex. 148/E5
Lázaro Cárdenas, Mex. 174/B2
Lázaro Cárdenas, Mex. 174/E5
Lazdijai, Lith. 41/K4
Lazi, Phil. 88/C3
Lazio (prov.), It. 45/J5
Lazise, It. 63/D3
Lazo, Rus. 75/P3
Lazonby, Eng, UK 35/F2
Le Ban-Saint-Martin, Fr. 55/F5
Le Beausset, Fr. 64/B6
Le Bic, Qu, Can. 158/C1
Le Blanc, Fr. 44/D3
Le Blanc-Mesnil, Fr. 30/K5
Le Bono, Fr. 56/C5
Le Bourg-d'Oisans, Fr. 64/C2
Le Bourget (Paris) (Arpt.), Fr. 30/K5
Le Bourget-du-Lac, Fr. 64/B1
Le Breuil, Fr. 44/F3
Le Cannet, Fr. 64/D5
Le Cannet-des-Maures, Fr. 64/C6
Le Castellet, Fr. 64/B6
Le Cateau-Cambrésis, Fr. 54/C3
Le Center, Mn, US 155/H1
Le Chasseral (peak), Swi. 60/D3
Le Chasseron (peak), Swi. 60/C4
Le Chesnay, Fr. 30/J5
Le Chesne, Fr. 55/D4
Le Cheval Blanc (peak), Fr. 60/C5
Le Cheval Noir (peak), Fr. 64/C2
Le Cheylard, Fr. 44/F4
Le Claire, Ia, US 155/J3
Le Conquet, Fr. 56/A4
Le Cornate (peak), It. 45/J5
Le Coudray, Fr. 57/G4
Le Crès, Fr. 47/G1
Le Creusot, Fr. 44/F3
Le Croisic, Fr. 56/C6
Le Crotoy, Fr. 54/A3
Le Duffre (peak), Fr. 64/B4
Le Faouët, Fr. 56/B4
Le Fœil, Fr. 56/C4
Le Folgoët, Fr. 56/A3
Le Gore, Md, US 168/A4
Le Goulet, NB, Can. 158/E2
Le Grammont (peak), Swi. 60/C5
Le Grand (peak), Fr. 64/C1
Le Grand, Ca, US 148/B2
Le Grand (cape), Austl. 130/D5
Le Grand Ballon (peak), Fr. 60/D2
Le Grand Charnier (peak), Fr. 64/C2
Le Grand Coyer (peak), Fr. 64/C4
Le Grand-Lemps, Fr. 64/B2
Le Grand-Lucé, Fr. 57/F5
Le Grand-Quevilly, Fr. 57/G2
Le Grau-du-Roi, Fr. 44/F5
Le Grazie, It. 62/C5
Le Harve-Octeville (arpt.), Fr. 57/F1
Le Havre, Fr. 57/F1
Le Landeron, Swi. 60/D3
Le Lauzet-Ubaye, Fr. 64/C4
Le Lavandou, Fr. 64/C6
Le Lion-D'Angers, Fr. 57/E5
Le Locle, Swi. 60/C3
Le Loroux-Bottereau, Fr. 56/D6
Le Luc, Fr. 64/C6
Le Lude, Fr. 57/F5
Le Mans, Fr. 57/F4
Le Mars, Ia, US 155/F2
Le Mée-sur-Seine, Fr. 30/K6
Le Mêle-sur-Sarthe, Fr. 57/F3
Le Mesnil-Amelot, Fr. 30/K4
Le Mesnil-Aubry, Fr. 30/K4
Le Mesnil-Esnard, Fr. 54/A5
Le Mesnil-le-Roi, Fr. 30/J5
Le Mesnil-Saint-Denis, Fr. 30/H5
Le Mesnil-sur-Oger, Fr. 54/D6
Le Molay-Littry, Fr. 57/E2
Le Môle (peak), Fr. 60/C5
Le Monêtier-les-Bains, Fr. 64/C3
Le Mont-Saint-Michel, Fr. 56/D3
Le Morond (peak), Fr. 60/C4
Le Moure de la Gardille (peak), Fr. 44/E4
Le Mourre Froid (peak), Fr. 64/C3
Le Murge (mts.), It. 48/E2
Le Muy, Fr. 64/C6
Le Noirmont (peak), Fr. 60/C4
Le Noirmont, Swi. 60/C3
Le Noirmont (peak), Swi. 60/C5
Le Nouvion-en-Thiérache, Fr. 54/C3
Le Palais, Fr. 56/B6
Le Palais-sur-Vienne, Fr. 44/D4
Le Palyvestre (arpt.), Fr. 64/C6
Le Passage, Fr. 44/D4
Le Pellerin, Fr. 56/D6
Le Perray-en-Yvelines, Fr. 30/H5
Le Petit Ballon (peak), Fr. 60/D2
Le Petit Ferrand (peak), Fr. 64/C4
Le Plessis-Belleville, Fr. 30/L4
Le Plessis-Feu-Aussoux, Fr. 30/M5
Le Plessis-Placy, Fr. 30/L4
Le Pont-de-Beauvoisin, Fr. 64/B1
Le Pont-de-Claix, Fr. 64/B2
Le Pontet, Fr. 64/A5
Le Port, Fr. 125/S15
Le Portel, Fr. 54/A2
Le Pouliguen, Fr. 56/C6
Le Pouzin, Fr. 64/A3
Le Pradet, Fr. 64/C6
Le Puy-en-Velay, Fr. 44/E4
Le Puy-Sainte-Réparade, Fr. 64/B5
Le Quesnoy, Fr. 54/C3
Le Raizet (int'l arpt.), Fr. 173/N8
Le Rateau (peak), Fr. 64/C2
Le Relecq-Kerhuon, Fr. 56/A4
Le Rocher Blanc (peak), Fr. 64/C2
Le Rouret, Fr. 64/D5
Le Rove, Fr. 64/B6
Le Roy, Ks, US 153/G1
Le Roy, Mn, US 155/H2
Le Roy, Il, US 155/K3
Le Russey, Fr. 60/C3
Le Sap, Fr. 57/F3
Le Suchet (peak), Swi. 60/C4
Le Sueur, Mn, US 155/H1
Le Tampon, Fr. 125/S15
Le Teil, Fr. 64/A3
Le Teilleul, Fr. 57/E3
Le Theil, Fr. 57/F4
Le Tholonet, Fr. 64/B5
Le Tholy, Fr. 60/C1
Le Thor, Fr. 64/A5
Le Thuit-Signol, Fr. 57/F2
Le Touquet-Paris-Plage, Fr. 54/A2
Le Touvet, Fr. 64/B2
Le Tréboux (peak), Fr. 64/B4
Le Trélod (peak), Fr. 64/C1
Le Tréport, Fr. 54/A3
Le Val, Fr. 64/C6
Le Val-d'Ajol, Fr. 60/C2
Le Vésinet, Fr. 30/J5
Le Vigan, Fr. 44/E5
Le'an (riv.), China 87/H2
Lea (riv.), Eng, UK 37/F3
Lea (Lee) (riv.), Eng, UK 30/C1
Leach, Camb. 94/C3
Leach (riv.), Eng, UK 37/E3
Leacock-Leola-Bareville, Pa, US 168/B3
Lead, SD, US 140/F4
Lead Hill, Ar, US 153/H2
Leaday, Tx, US 150/E2
Leadbetter (pt.), Wa, US 144/B4
Leadenham, Eng, UK 35/H5
Leader, Sk, Can. 145/K2
Leader Water (riv.), Sc, UK 33/D5
Leadon (riv.), Eng, UK 36/D3
Leaf, Ms, US 164/D2
Leaf (riv.), Ms, US 162/C5
Leaghur (lake), Austl. 132/B2
League City, Tx, US 151/M9
Leah, Ga, US 163/F4
Leakesville, Ms, US 164/D2
Leakey, Tx, US 150/E3
Lealui, Zam. 122/D2
Leam (riv.), Eng, UK 37/E2
Leamington, On, Can. 160/E3
Leamington, Ut, US 147/G4
Leander (pt.), Austl. 130/B4
Leander, Tx, US 151/F2
Leandro N. Alem, Arg. 189/F3
Leane (lake), Ire. 32/A5
Leaota (peak), Rom. 51/G3
Learmonth, Austl. 130/B2
Leary, Ga, US 165/F2
Leasburg, Mo, US 153/J1
Leask, Sk, Can. 145/L1
Leatherhead, Eng, UK 30/C3
Leavenworth, Ks, US 155/G4
Leavenworth, Wa, US 144/D4
Łeba, Pol. 40/G4
Lebach, Ger. 55/F5
Lebak, Phil. 88/D4
Lebam, Wa, US 144/C4
Lébamba, Gabon 120/B3
Lebane, Serb. 50/E4
Lébango, Congo 120/C2
Lebanon (ctry.) 104/D3
Lebanon (mts.), Leb. 104/D3
Lebanon (co.), US 169/B2
Lebanon, Co, US 149/H2
Lebanon, In, US 160/C4
Lebanon, Ks, US 154/E4
Lebanon, Ky, US 162/E2
Lebanon, Mo, US 153/H2
Lebanon, NH, US 161/K3
Lebanon, NJ, US 168/D2
Lebanon, Oh, US 160/D5
Lebanon, Or, US 146/B1
Lebanon, Pa, US 168/B3
Lebanon, Tn, US 162/D2
Lebanon, Va, US 163/F2
Lebanon Junction, Ky, US 162/E2
Lebbeke, Belg. 55/D2
Lebeau, La, US 164/C2
Lebec, Ca, US 148/C3
Lebedinyy, Rus. 75/N4
Lebedyan', Rus. 70/F1
Lebedyn, Ukr. 73/H2
Lebene (riv.), Mor. 112/B2
Lébény, Hun. 50/C2
Lébiga, Congo 120/C3
Lebo, Ks, US 153/G1
Lebombo (mts.), SAfr. 123/F5
Lębork, Pol. 40/G4
Lebowakgomo, SAfr. 123/F5
Lebrija, Sp. 46/B4
Lebu, Chile 190/B3
Leça da Palmeira, Port. 46/A2
Lecce, It. 49/F2
Lecce nei Marsi, It. 65/C4
Lecco (lake), It. 62/C1
Lech, Aus. 61/G3
Lech (riv.), Ger. 67/F1
Lechang, China 93/K2
Lechbruck, Ger. 61/G2
Leche (lake), Cuba 177/G1
Lechlade, Eng, UK 37/E3
Lechtaler Alps (mts.), Aus. 61/G3
Leck, Ger. 40/C4
Leckavrea (mtn.), Ire. 32/A3
Lecompte, La, US 164/B2
Léconi, Gabon 120/C3
Lectoure, Fr. 44/D5
Łęczna, Pol. 43/M3
Leda (riv.), Ger. 53/E2
Ledang (peak), Malay. 89/C2
Ledbury, Eng, UK 36/D2
Lede, Belg. 54/C2
Ledegem, Belg. 54/C2
Ledesma, Sp. 46/B2
Ledge Point, Austl. 130/B4
Ledger, Mt, US 145/J3
Lediba, D.R. Congo 120/D3
Lêdo (cape), Ang. 120/C5
Ledong, China 87/F5
Ledro (lake), It. 61/G6
Ledu (peak), It. 61/F5
Leduc, Ab, Can. 145/H1
Lee (riv.), Ire. 32/A6
Lee (Lea) (riv.), Eng, UK 30/C1
Lee, Fl, US 165/G2
Lee, Ma, US 161/K3
Lee (mtn.), Pa, US 168/B1
Lee Creek, Ar, US 153/G3
Leech (lake), Mn, US 143/H2
Leedale, Ab, Can. 144/G1
Leedey, Ok, US 152/E3
Leeds, Eng, UK 35/G4
Leeds (co.), Eng, UK 35/G4
Leeds, Al, US 162/D4
Leeds, ND, US 156/E3
Leeds, Ut, US 149/F2
Leeds and Bradford (int'l arpt.), Eng, UK 35/G4
Leeds and Liverpool (canal), Eng, UK 35/G4
Leeds Point, NJ, US 168/D5
Leegebruch, Ger. 42/Q6
Leek, Eng, UK 35/F5
Leek, Neth. 52/D2
Leeman, Austl. 130/B4
Leemount, Ire. 32/B6
Leer, Ger. 53/E2
Leerdam, Neth. 52/C5
Leersum, Neth. 52/C4
Lees Crossing, Ga, US 162/E4
Lees Summit, Mo, US 153/G1
Leesburg, Fl, US 164/M6
Leesburg, Ga, US 165/F2
Leesburg, NJ, US 168/D5
Leesburg, Va, US 163/J1
Leesdale, Ms, US 164/C2
Leese, Ger. 53/G3
Leesport, Pa, US 168/C3
Leeston, NZ 135/C3
Leesville, La, US 164/B2
Leesville (lake), Va, US 163/H2
Leesville (dam), Va, US 163/H2
Leeton, Austl. 133/C2
Leeu (riv.), SAfr. 124/L10
Leeudoringstad, SAfr. 124/D2
Leeuwarden, Neth. 52/C2
Leeuwin (cape), Austl. 130/B5
Leeuwin-Naturaliste NP, Austl. 130/B5
Leeville, La, US 164/C3
Leeward (isls.), NAm. 173/J4
Leff (riv.), Fr. 44/B2
Leffe, It. 62/C2
Léfini (riv.), Congo 120/C3
Lefka, Cyp. 104/C2
Lefo (peak), Camr. 115/H5
Lefor, ND, US 156/C4
Lefroy (lake), Austl. 130/D4
Left Hand, WV, US 163/G1
Legana, Austl. 132/C4
Leganés, Sp. 47/N9
Legaspi, Phil. 88/C2
Legau, Ger. 61/G2
Legazpia, Sp. 44/B5
Legges Tor (peak), Austl. 132/C4
Legionowo, Pol. 43/L2
Léglise, Belg. 55/E4
Legnago, It. 63/E3
Legnaro, It. 63/E3
Legnica, Pol. 43/J3
Legnone (peak), It. 61/F5
Léguer (riv.), Fr. 56/B3
Leh, India 98/D2
Leh Palace, India 98/D2
Lehi, Ut, US 147/H3
Lehigh, Ok, US 153/F3
Lehigh (riv.), Pa, US 161/J4
Lehigh (co.), Pa, US 168/C2
Lehigh Acres, Fl, US 165/H4
Lehighton, Pa, US 168/C2
Lehijärvi (lake), Fin. 39/E3
Lehinch, Ire. 32/A4
Léhon, Fr. 56/C4
Lehr, ND, US 156/E4
Lehrberg, Ger. 58/D4
Lehrte, Ger. 53/G4
Lehututu, Bots. 122/D4
Lei (riv.), China 93/K2
Leia (riv.), It. 65/A3
Leiah, Pak. 98/A4
Leiblfing, Ger. 59/F5
Leibnitz, Aus. 50/B2
Leibo, China 93/H2
Leicester, Eng, UK 37/E1
Leicester (co.), Eng, UK 37/E1
Leicestershire (co.), Eng, UK 35/H6
Leichhardt (dam), Austl. 131/H2
Leichhardt (falls), Austl. 129/E4
Leichhardt (riv.), Austl. 129/F4
Leichlingen, Ger. 55/G1
Leiden, Neth. 52/B4
Leiderdorp, Neth. 52/B4
Leidschendam, Neth. 52/B4
Leigh, Eng, UK 35/F5
Leigh, Eng, UK 30/D3
Leigh, Eng, UK 30/C3
Leigh Creek, Austl. 131/H4
Leighlinbridge, Ire. 32/D4
Leighton Buzzard, Eng, UK 37/F3
Leigong (mtn.), China 87/F3
Leimebamba, Peru 184/B2
Leimen, Ger. 58/B4
Leimersheim, Ger. 58/B4
Leinan, Sk, Can. 145/L2
Leine (riv.), Ger. 42/D3
Leinefelde, Ger. 53/H6
Leinfelden-Echterdingen, Ger. 58/C5
Leinster (reg.), Ire. 34/A5
Leinster (mt.), Ire. 32/D4
Leinster, Austl. 130/D3
Leintwardine, Eng, UK 36/D2
Leipheim, Ger. 58/D6
Leipsic, Oh, US 160/E4
Leipsic (riv.), De, US 168/C5
Leipsic, De, US 168/C5
Leipzig, Ger. 74/B4
Leira, Nor. 40/C1
Leiranger, Nor. 38/E2
Leiria, Port. 46/A3
Leiria (dist.), Port. 46/A3
Leirsund, Nor. 38/T8
Leirvik, Nor. 40/A2
Leisi, Est. 41/K2
Leisler (mt.), Austl. 131/F2
Leiston-cum-Sizewell, Eng, UK 37/H2
Leisure City, Fl, US 165/H5
Leitchfield, Ky, US 162/D2
Leiter, Wy, US 154/A1
Leith, Sc, UK 33/C5
Leith (hill), Eng, UK 30/B3
Leitha (riv.), Aus. 43/J5
Leitrim (co.), Ire. 32/C2
Leitrim, Ire. 32/B2
Leixlip, Ire. 34/B5
Leiyang, China 87/G3
Leiyuanzhen, China 80/B4
Leizhou (pen.), China 93/J3
Lejasciems, Lat. 41/M3
Lejpalingis, Lith. 41/K4
Lek (riv.), Neth. 42/C3
Lékana, Congo 120/C3
Lekhainá, Gre. 49/G4
Lekhcheb, Mrta. 114/C2
Lekkerkerk, Neth. 52/B5
Lekki (lag.), Nga. 115/G5
Lékoli-Pandaka, Rsv. de Faune de la, Congo 120/C2
Lekoni, Gabon 120/C3
Lekóti (riv.), Congo 120/C3
Lekoumou (pol. reg.), Congo 120/C3
Leksands-Noret, Swe. 40/F1
Leksozero (lake), Rus. 38/J3
Leku, Eth. 118/A4
Lelai (cape), Indo. 91/G3
Leland, Il, US 155/K3
Leland, Mi, US 160/D2
Leland, Ms, US 162/B4
Leland, NC, US 163/H3
Lelång (lake), Swe. 40/E2
Lel'chitsy, Bela. 72/E2
Leleque, Arg. 190/C4
Lelia Lake, Tx, US 152/D3
Leling, China 80/D3
Lelintah, Indo. 91/H4
Lelogama, Indo. 128/A2
Lelu, Micr. 136/F4
Lelydorp, Sur. 182/C1
Lelystad, Neth. 52/C3
Lem, Den. 40/C3
Lema (peak), It. 61/E5
Lema Shilindi, Eth. 118/B4
Léman (Geneva) (lake), Fr. 60/C5
Lemberg (peak), Ger. 61/E1
Lemberg, Sk, Can. 156/C2
Lemberg, Ger. 55/G5
Lembu (peak), Indo. 89/B1
Leme, Braz. 189/H2
Lemenjoen NP, Fin. 38/H1
Lemeshkino, Rus. 71/H2
Lemgo, Ger. 53/F4
Lemhi, Id, US 147/G1
Lemhi (range), Id, US 147/G1
Lemitar, NM, US 149/J3
Lemland (isl.), Fin. 41/H2
Lemland, Fin. 41/J1
Lemmer, Neth. 52/C3
Lemmon, SD, US 156/C5
Lemmon (mt.), Az, US 149/G4
Lemon Grove, Ca, US 166/C5
Lemon Springs, NC, US 163/H3
Lemoore, Ca, US 148/C2
Lemoore Nav. Air Sta., Ca, US 148/B2
Lemoyne, Ne, US 154/D3
Lempa (riv.), ESal. 176/D3
Lempäälä, Fin. 41/K1
Lempdes, Fr. 44/E4
Lemro (riv.), Myan. 86/B4
Lemsid, WSah. 110/B4
Lemva (riv.), Rus. 69/P2
Lemvig, Den. 40/C3
Lemwerder, Ger. 53/F2
Lemyethna, Myan. 86/B5
Lena, Mb, Can. 156/E3
Lena, Nor. 40/D1
Lena (riv.), Rus. 77/M3
Lena, Il, US 155/K2
Lena, Ne, US 154/D3
Lena, SC, US 163/G4
Lena, Wi, US 160/B2
Lenape (lake), NJ, US 168/D5
Lençóis Maranhenses, PN dos, Braz. 183/F3
Lençóis Paulista, Braz. 189/G2
Lendery, Rus. 68/F3
Lendinara, It. 63/E3
Lene (lake), Ire. 32/C2
Lengau, Aus. 59/G6
Lengdorf, Ger. 59/F6
Lenge, D.R. Congo 121/F4
Lengede, Ger. 53/H4
Lengenfeld, Ger. 59/F1
Lengerich, Ger. 53/E4
Lenggries, Ger. 61/H2
Lenghu, China 78/C4
Lengnau, Swi. 60/D3
Lengshuijiang, China 87/F3
Lengshuitan, China 87/F3
Lengua de Vaca (pt.), Chile 188/B4
Lengué Namobessie (riv.), Camr. 120/C2
Lengwe NP, Malw. 123/G3
Lengzipu, China 81/B2
Lenhartsville, Pa, US 168/C2
Lenia, Eth. 117/H4
Lenina (lake), Ukr. 73/H3
Lenina (peak), Taj. 99/B4
Leninabad (int'l arpt.), Taj. 99/A3
Lenine, Ukr. 73/H5
Leningradskaya, Rus. 73/K4
Leningradskaya Oblast, Rus. 68/G3
Leningradskiy, Rus. 142/U12
Leninogor, Kaz. 99/D1
Leninogorsk, Rus. 69/M5
Leninsk, Rus. 69/M4
Leninsk-Kuznetskiy, Rus. 74/J4
Leninskiy, Rus. 70/F1
Leninskoye, Kaz. 71/L2
Leninskoye, Rus. 79/L2
Leninváros, Hun. 43/L5
Lenk, Swi. 60/D5
Lenne (riv.), Ger. 55/G1
Lennestadt, Ger. 53/F6
Lenningen, Ger. 58/C5
Lennox (hills), Sc, UK 33/B5
Lennox, Ca, US 166/F8
Lennox, SD, US 155/F2
Lennox (isl.), Chile 191/D7
Lennoxtown, Sc, UK 33/B5
Lennoxville, Qu, Can. 161/L2
Leno, It. 62/D3
Lenoir, NC, US 163/G3
Lenoir City, Tn, US 162/E3
Lenola, It. 65/C5
Lenora, Ks, US 154/D4

Lenore, Mb, Can. 156/D3
Lenore (lake), Sk, Can. 145/M1
Lenox, Ma, US 161/K3
Lenox, Ga, US 165/G2
Lenox, Ia, US 155/G3
Lens, Swi. 60/D5
Lens, Fr. 54/B3
Lens, Belg. 54/C2
Lensahn, Ger. 40/D4
Lensk, Rus. 75/M3
Lenswood, Mb, Can. 156/D1
Lenswood, Austl. 131/M8
Lent, Neth. 52/C5
Lentekhi, Geo. 71/G4
Lenting, Ger. 59/E5
Lentini, It. 48/D4
Lentvaris, Lith. 41/L4
Lenvik, Nor. 38/F1
Lenwood, Ca, US 148/D3
Leny, Pass of (pass), Sc, UK 33/B4
Lenya, Myan. 94/B4
Lenzburg, Swi. 60/E3
Lenzing, Aus. 59/G7
Lenzkirch, Ger. 61/E2
Léo, Burk. 115/E4
Leoben, Aus. 45/L3
Leográ (riv.), It. 63/E1
Leok, Indo. 91/F3
Leola, SD, US 156/E5
Leola, Ar, US 153/H3
Leominster, Ma, US 161/L3
Leominster, Eng, UK 36/D2
Leon (int'l arpt.), Mex. 174/C3
León, Mex. 175/E4
León, Nic. 176/E3
León, Sp. 46/C1
Leon, Ia, US 155/H3
Leon, Ok, US 153/F4
Leon (riv.), Tx, US 151/E2
León Muerto (pass), Chile 188/B3
Leon Valley, Tx, US 151/E3
Leon-Guanajuato (int'l arpt.), Mex. 175/E4
Leona, Tx, US 151/G2
Leona (riv.), Tx, US 150/E3
Leona Valley, Ca, US 165/B1
Leonard, Mi, US 167/F6
Leonard, ND, US 156/F4
Leonard, Tx, US 153/F4
Leonardo, NJ, US 169/J10
Leonardo da Vinci (int'l arpt.), It. 65/B4
Leonardtown, Md, US 163/J1
Leonardville, Namb. 122/C4
Leonardville, Ks, US 155/F4
Leonberg, Ger. 58/C5
Leonding, Aus. 59/H6
Leone (peak), It. 60/E5
Leone, ASam. 137/T10
Leones, Arg. 190/E2
Leonessa, It. 65/B2
Leonforte, It. 48/D4
Leongatha, Austl. 133/B4
Leonia, NJ, US 169/K8
Leonídhion, Gre. 49/H4
Leonora, Austl. 130/D4
Leopold, Austl. 133/B4
Leopoldina, Braz. 187/P6
Leopoldkanaal (riv.), Belg. 54/C1
Leopoldsburg, Belg. 55/E1
Leopoldsdorf, Aus. 51/N7
Leopoldsdorf im Marchfelde, Aus. 51/P7
Leopoldshöhe, Ger. 53/F4
Leota, Mn, US 155/F2
Leoti, Ks, US 152/D1
Leova, Mol. 72/E4
Lepaera, Hon. 176/D3
Lépanges-sur-Vologne, Fr. 60/C1
Lepanto, Ar, US 162/B3
Lepar (isl.), Indo. 89/D3
Lepe, Sp. 46/B4
Lepenoú, Gre. 49/G3
Lephepe, Bots. 122/E4
Lepi, Ang. 122/B2
L'Epine (pond), Fr. 30/K4
Leping, China 87/H2
L'Épiphanie, Qu, Can. 159/P6
Lepontine Alps (mts.), Swi. 66/F1
Lepreau Game Ref., NB, Can. 158/D3
Lepsämä, Fin. 39/E4
Lepsi, Kaz. 99/C2
Lepsy (riv.), Kaz. 99/C2
Leptis Magna (Labdah) (ruin), Libya 45/G3
Leptokariá, Gre. 49/H2
Leque, Bol. 185/E5
Lequena, Chile 188/B2
Lequepalca, Bol. 188/C1
Lequire, Ok, US 153/G3
Lera (peak), It. 64/D2
Léraba (riv.), Burk. 114/D4
Lercara Friddi, It. 48/C4
Lerdo de Tejada, Mex. 176/C2
Léré, Chad 116/B3
Lere, Nga. 115/H4
Léré, Mali 114/D3
Leribe, Les. 124/E3
Lerici, It. 62/C5
Lérida, Col. 180/D4
Lérida, Col. 183/L8
Lerik, Azer. 103/G2
Lerín, Sp. 46/E1
Lerma, Sp. 46/D1
Lerma (riv.), Mex. 139/G7
Lerma, Mex. 175/Q10
Lermoos, Aus. 61/G3
Lérouville, Fr. 55/E6
Leroux Wash (riv.), Az, US 149/G3
Leroy, ND, US 156/F3
Leroy, Al, US 162/E4
Leroy, Sk, Can. 145/M1
Leroy, Tx, US 151/F2
Lerum, Swe. 40/E3
Lerwick, Sc, UK 31/W13
Léry, Qu, Can. 159/N7
Les Alignements de Carnac, Fr. 56/B5
Les Allues-le-Roi, Fr. 30/H5
Les Andelys, Fr. 57/G2
Les Angles, Fr. 64/A5
Les Arcs, Fr. 64/C6
Les Avenières, Fr. 64/B1
Les Bauges (upland), Fr. 64/C1
Les Bois, Swi. 60/C3
Les Breuleux, Swi. 60/D3
Les Bréviaires, Fr. 30/H5
Les Cayes, Haiti 177/H2
Les Cèdres, Qu, Can. 159/M7
Les Clayes-sous-Bois, Fr. 30/H5
Les Contamines-Montjoie, Fr. 60/C6
Les Diablerets (range), Swi. 60/D5
Les Échelles, Fr. 64/B2
Les Escoumins, Qu, Can. 158/C1
Les Essarts-le-Roi, Fr. 30/H5
Les Gets, Fr. 60/C5
Les Haudères, Swi. 60/D5
Les Hautes-Rivières, Fr. 55/D4
Les Herbiers, Fr. 44/C3
Les Islettes, Fr. 55/E5
Les Mées, Fr. 64/B4
Les Mesnuls, Fr. 30/H5
Les Minquier (isl.), UK 56/C3
Les Molières, Fr. 30/J6
Les Monges (peak), Fr. 64/C4
Les Mosses, Swi. 60/D5
Les Mureaux, Fr. 54/A6
Les Orres, Fr. 64/C3
Les Pennes-Mirabeau, Fr. 64/B6
Les Pieux, Fr. 56/D2
Les Ponts-de-Cé, Fr. 57/E6
Les Ponts-de-Martel, Swi. 60/C4
Les Rosiers, Fr. 57/E6
Les Rousses, Fr. 60/C5
Les Sables-d'Olonne, Fr. 44/C3
Les Salines (int'l arpt.), Alg. 112/K6
Les Sept Iles (isl.), Fr. 56/B3
Les Touches, Fr. 56/D6
Les Ulis, Fr. 30/J5
Les Verrières, Swi. 60/C4
Lesa, It. 62/B2
L'Escarène, Fr. 64/D5
Leselidze, Geo. 70/G4
Leseru, Kenya 119/A1
Leshan, China 86/D2
Leshukonskoye, Rus. 69/K2
Lésigny, Fr. 30/K5
Lesima (peak), It. 62/C4
Lesja, Nor. 38/D3
Lesjöfors, Swe. 40/F2
Lesko, Pol. 43/M4
Leskovac, Serb. 50/E4
Leskovik, Alb. 49/G2
Leslie, Ar, US 153/H3
Leslie, Sc, UK 33/C4
Leslie, Ga, US 165/F2
Leslie, Mi, US 160/D3
Lesmahagow, Sc, UK 33/C5
Lesneven, Fr. 56/A3
Lešnica, Serb. 50/D3
Lesnoy, Rus. 69/M4
Lesogorsk, Rus. 79/N2
Lesopil'noye, Rus. 79/L2
Lesosibirsk, Rus. 74/K4
Lesotho (ctry.) 124/D3
Lesozavodsk, Rus. 79/L2
Lesparre-Médoc, Fr. 44/C4
Lesquin (int'l arpt.), Fr. 54/C2
Lessay, Fr. 56/D2
Lesse (riv.), Belg. 42/C3
Lessebo, Swe. 40/F3
Lesser Antilles (isls.), NAm. 173/H5
Lesser Caucasus (mts.), Asia 71/G4
Lesser Slave (lake), Ab, Can. 140/E3
Lesser Sunda (isls.), Indo. 91/E5
Lessines, Belg. 54/C2
Lessley, Ms, US 164/C2
Lesterville, Mo, US 162/B2
Lesung (peak), Indo. 90/D5
Lésvos (isl.), Gre. 70/C5
Leswalt, Sc, UK 34/C2
Leszno, Pol. 43/J3
Letaba, SAfr. 123/F4
L'Étang-du-Nord, Qu, Can. 159/G2
Létavértes, Hun. 50/E2
Letcher, SD, US 154/E2
Letchworth, Eng, UK 37/F3
Lete (riv.), It. 65/C5
Letegge (peak), It. 65/C1
Letham, Sc, UK 33/D3
Lethbridge, Ab, Can. 145/H3
Lethe (riv.), Ger. 53/F2
Lethem, Guy. 181/G4
Leti (isls.), Indo. 128/B2
Leti (isl.), Indo. 128/B2
Leticia, Col. 184/D2
Leting, China 80/D3
L'Etivaz, Swi. 60/D5
Letka, Rus. 69/L4
Letlhakane, Bots. 122/E4
Letlhakeng, Bots. 122/E5
Letnitsa, Bul. 51/G4
L'Étoile, Fr. 54/B3
Letong, Indo. 89/D2
Letpadan, Myan. 86/B5
Letschin, Ger. 43/H2
Letsôk-Aw (isl.), Myan. 90/A1
Letterkenny, Ire. 31/Q9
Letterkenny Army Depot, Pa, US 161/H4
Lettomanoppello, It. 65/D5
Letychiv, Ukr. 72/D3
Leu Botanical Gardens, Fl, US 164/N6
Leuca, It. 49/F3
Leucate, Fr. 44/E5
Leuchars, Sc, UK 33/D4
Leuk, Swi. 60/D5
Leukerbad, Swi. 60/D5
Leun, Ger. 58/B1
Leupp, Az, US 149/G3
Leurbost, Sc, UK 31/Q7
Leusden-Zuid, Neth. 52/C4
Leuser (peak), Indo. 89/B2
Leutershausen, Ger. 58/D4
Leutkirch im Allgäu, Ger. 61/G2
Leuven (Louvain), Belg. 55/D2
Leuze-en-Hainaut, Belg. 54/C2
Levádhia, Gre. 49/H3
Levallois-Perret, Fr. 30/J5
Levanger, Nor. 38/D3
Levanna Centrale (peak), Fr. 64/D2
Levante, Riviera di (coast), Fr. 62/C4
Levanto, It. 62/C5
Levashovo, Rus. 69/T6
Levashovo (arpt.), Rus. 69/T6
Levee No. 33 (canal), Fl, US 164/P10
Level (isl.), Chile 190/B5
Level, Md, US 168/B4
Levelland, Tx, US 152/C4
Levelock, Ak, US 171/G4
Leven, Sc, UK 33/D4
Leven, Eng, UK 35/H4
Leven (lake), Sc, UK 33/A3
Leven (riv.), Sc, UK 33/C4
Leven (lake), Sc, UK 33/C4
Leven (pt.), SAfr. 125/F2
Levens, Fr. 64/D5
Leventina (Prato), Swi. 61/E5
Leveque (cape), Austl. 128/A4
Lever (riv.), Braz. 186/C1
Leverburgh, Sc, UK 31/Q8
Levering, Mi, US 160/D2
Leverkusen, Ger. 55/F1
Lèves, Fr. 57/G4
Levice, Slvk. 50/D1
Levico Terme, It. 61/H5
Levier, Fr. 60/C4
Levin, NZ 135/C3
Lévis, Qu, Can. 158/B2
Lévis-Saint-Nom, Fr. 30/H5
Levittown, NY, US 169/L9
Levittown, Pa, US 168/D3
Levkás, Gre. 49/G3
Levkás (isl.), Gre. 67/J3
Levkímmi, Gre. 49/G3
Levkinskaya, Rus. 69/L2
Levoča, Slvk. 43/L4
Levrier (bay), Mrta. 110/A5
Levski, Bul. 51/G4
Levuka, Fiji 137/Y18
Levy (lake), Fl, US 165/G3
Lewellen, Ne, US 154/C3
Lewes, Eng, UK 37/G5
Lewin Brzeski, Pol. 43/J3
Lewis (hill), Nf, Can. 159/H1
Lewis (hills), Nf, Can. 159/H1
Lewis (isl.), Sc, UK 31/Q7
Lewis, Ks, US 152/E2
Lewis (pass), NZ 135/C3
Lewis, Co, US 149/H2
Lewis, Ia, US 155/G3
Lewis (riv.), Wa, US 144/D4
Lewis and Clark (lake), SD,Ne, US 154/E2
Lewis and Clark NWR, Wa, US 144/C4
Lewis Smith (lake), Al, US 162/D3
Lewisburg, Ky, US 162/D2
Lewisburg, Pa, US 168/B2
Lewisburg, Tn, US 162/D3
Lewisburg, Wv, US 162/F2
Lewisham (bor.), Eng, UK 30/C2
Lewisport, Ky, US 162/D2
Lewisporte, Nf, Can. 159/K1
Lewiston, Id, US 144/F4
Lewiston, Me, US 158/B3
Lewiston, NY, US 160/J9
Lewiston, Ut, US 147/J3
Lewiston Woodville, NC, US 163/J2
Lewistown, Il, US 155/J3
Lewistown, Mt, US 145/K4
Lewistown, Pa, US 161/H4
Lewisville, Ar, US 153/H4
Lewisville (lake), Tx, US 151/F1
Lewisville, Tx, US 150/L6
Lewotobi (peak), Indo. 128/A2
Léwou, Gabon 120/C3
Lewvan, Sk, Can. 156/B2
Lexa, Ar, US 162/B3
Lexington, Ga, US 163/F4
Lexington, Il, US 155/K3
Lexington, Ky, US 162/E1
Lexington, Mo, US 155/H4
Lexington, Ms, US 162/B4
Lexington, Ne, US 154/E3
Lexington, NC, US 163/G3
Lexington, Oh, US 160/E4
Lexington, Ok, US 153/F3
Lexington, Or, US 146/D1
Lexington, SC, US 163/G4
Lexington, Tn, US 162/C3
Lexington, Tx, US 151/F2
Lexington, Va, US 163/H2
Lexington Blue Grass Army Depot, Ky, US 162/E2
Lexington Park, Md, US 163/J1
Leyburn, Eng, UK 35/G3
Leye, China 87/E3
Leyland, Eng, UK 35/F4
Leysdown, Eng, UK 37/G4
Leysin, Swi. 60/D5
Leyte (isl.), Phil. 77/M8
Leyte (gulf), Phil. 88/D3
Leyte, Phil. 88/D3
Leyton (nbrhd.), Eng, UK 30/C2
Leytron, Swi. 60/D5
Lez (riv.), Fr. 44/F4
Ležajsk, Pol. 43/M3
Lezama, Ven. 183/P8
Lèze (riv.), Fr. 64/B5
Lezhë, Alb. 49/F2
Lezhi, China 86/E2
Lézignan-Corbières, Fr. 44/E5
Lezuza, Sp. 46/D3
L'gov, Rus. 73/H2
Lhanbyrd, Sc, UK 33/C1
Lhari, China 86/B2
Lhasa (riv.), China 99/F6
Lhasa (int'l arpt.), China 99/F5
Lhatog, China 86/C2
Lhazê, China 97/F1
L'Hermitage, Fr. 56/D4
Lhokkruet, Indo. 89/A1
Lhokseumawe, Indo. 89/B1
Lhoksukon, Indo. 89/B1
Lhorong, China 86/C2
L'Hospitalet de Llobregat, Sp. 47/L7
Lhozhag, China 97/H1
Lhuntsi, Bhu. 97/G2
Lhünzê, China 97/G2
Li, Thai. 94/B2
Li (riv.), China 93/K2
Li (mtn.), China 80/B4
Li anni (riv.), Leb. 105/C2
Li Xian, China 87/F2
Lian (riv.), China 87/E3
Lian Xian, China 87/G3
Liancheng, China 87/H3
Liancourt, Fr. 54/B5
Liancourt Rocks (isl.), Asia 84/B2
Liang, Indo. 91/G4
Liangcheng, China 80/C2
Liangcun, China 87/F3
Liangdong, China 87/F4
Lianghekou, China 87/F2
Liangjia, China 81/B2
Liangjiadian, China 81/A3
Liangpran (peak), Indo. 90/D3
Liangshui, China 87/G4
Liangting, China 78/F5
Liangwan (mts.), China 86/D3
Liangzhen, China 78/F4
Liangzi (lake), China 80/C5
Lianhua (mts.), China 87/G4
Lianhua, China 93/K2
Lianjiang, China 93/K3
Lianjiang, China 87/H3
Lianjiangkou, China 87/G3
Liannan Yaozu Zizhixian, China 87/G3
Lianping, China 87/G3
Lianpu, China 87/H3
Lianshanguan, China 81/B2
Lianshui, China 80/D4
Liantang, China 94/E1
Liantang, China 87/F3
Liantang, China 80/L8
Lianyuan (peak), China 87/F2
Lianyungang, China 80/D4
Liao (riv.), China 77/M5
Liaocheng, China 80/C3
Liaodong (pen.), China 81/A3
Liaodong (isls.), China 80/E3
Liaodong (gulf), China 79/J3
Liaodun, China 78/C3
Liaoning (prov.), China 79/J3
Liaoyang, China 81/B2
Liaoyuan, China 79/K3
Liaozhong, China 81/B2
Liāquatpur, Pak. 98/A5
Liard (riv.), Can. 139/E3
Liat (isl.), Indo. 89/D3
Libacao, Phil. 88/C3
Líbano, Col. 183/K8
Libby, Mt, US 144/F3
Libby (dam), Mt, US 144/G3
Libby, Mt, US 144/G3
Libčhovka (riv.), Czh. 59/H2
Libenge, D.R. Congo 120/D2
Liberal, Ks, US 152/D2
Liberal, Mo, US 153/G2
Libercourt, Fr. 54/C3
Liberdade, Braz. 187/M7
Liberdade (riv.), Braz. 186/B1
Liberec, Czh. 42/H3
Liberecký (pol. reg.), Czh. 43/H3
Liberi (arpt.), It. 65/D3
Liberia, CR 176/E4
Liberia (ctry.) 114/C5
Libertad, Belz. 176/D2
Libertad, Uru. 191/K11
Libertad, Ven. 180/D2
Libertad de Orituco, Ven. 183/P8
Libertador General San Martín, Arg. 188/C2
Liberty, Il, US 155/J4
Liberty, In, US 160/D5
Liberty, Ky, US 162/E2
Liberty (res.), Md, US 168/B5
Liberty, Mo, US 155/G4
Liberty, Ms, US 164/C2
Liberty, NC, US 163/H3
Liberty, NY, US 161/J4
Liberty, Ok, US 153/F4
Liberty, Sk, Can. 145/M2
Liberty, Tx, US 151/H2
Liberty, Tx, US 151/N8
Liberty (co.), Tx, US 151/N9
Liberty Grove, Md, US 168/B4
Libertyville, Al, US 165/E2
Libertyville, Il, US 167/P15
Libin, Belg. 55/E4
Libmanan, Phil. 88/C2
Libo, China 87/E3
Libobo (cape), Indo. 91/G4
Liboc (riv.), Czh. 43/G3
Libochovice, Czh. 59/H2
Liboko, D.R. Congo 121/E2
Libon, Phil. 88/C2
Librazhd, Alb. 49/G2
Libres, Mex. 175/M7
Libreville (cap.), Gabon 120/B2
Libreville (int'l arpt.), Gabon 120/B2
Libu, China 87/F4
Libya (ctry.) 108/C2
Libyan (plat.), Egypt,Libya 108/D2
Libyan (des.), Egypt,Libya 108/D2
Licantén, Chile 190/B2
Licata, It. 48/C4
Licciana Nardi, It. 62/D5
Lice, Turk. 102/E2
Lich, Ger. 58/B1
Licheng, China 80/D3
Licheng, China 80/C3
Lichfield, Eng, UK 37/E1
Lichinga, Moz. 123/G2
Lichtenau, Ger. 53/F5
Lichtenau, Ger. 58/B5
Lichtenau, Ger. 58/D4
Lichtenberg, Ger. 42/G6
Lichtenburg, SAfr. 124/D2
Lichtenfels, Ger. 58/D2
Lichtenrade, Ger. 42/G7
Lichtensteig, Swi. 61/F3
Lichtenvoorde, Neth. 52/D5
Lichtervelde, Belg. 54/C1
Lichuan, China 89/A1
Lichuan, China 87/H3
Lick Observatory, Ca, US 167/L12
Licking, Mo, US 153/J2
Licking (riv.), Ky, US 162/E1
Licques, Fr. 54/A2
Licun, China 87/F4
Licungo (riv.), Moz. 123/H2
Lida, Bela. 41/L5
Liddell Water (riv.), Sc, UK 35/F1
Liddes, Swi. 60/D6
Liddon (gulf), NW, Can. 141/R7
Lidgerwood, ND, US 156/F4
Lidhorikíon, Gre. 49/H3
Lidice, Czh. 59/H2
Lidingö, Swe. 40/H2
Lidköping, Swe. 40/E2
Lidlington, Eng, UK 37/F2
Lido, Niger 115/F3
Lido, It. 63/F1
Lido di Iesolo, It. 63/F3
Lido di Ostia, It. 65/B4
Lidzbark, Pol. 43/K2
Lidzbark Warmiński, Pol. 41/J4
Lié (riv.), Fr. 56/C4
Liebenau, Ger. 53/G6
Liebenau, Aus. 59/H5
Liebenbergsvlei (riv.), SAfr. 124/E2
Liebenthal, Ks, US 152/E1
Liebig (mt.), Austl. 131/F2
Liechtenstein (ctry.) 61/F3
Liedekerke, Belg. 55/D2
Liège, Belg. 55/E2
Liège (prov.), Belg. 55/E3
Lieksa, Fin. 68/F3
Lielvarde, Lat. 41/L3
Lienden, Neth. 52/C5
Lienen, Ger. 53/E4
Lienz, Aus. 45/K3
Liepāja, Lat. 41/J3
Liepna, Lat. 41/M3
Lier, Belg. 55/D1
Lierbyen, Nor. 38/R8
Lierneux, Belg. 55/E3
Lies (riv.), Belg. 44/E1
Lieser (riv.), Ger. 55/F3
Liesjärven NP, Fin. 41/K1
Liesjärven NP, Fin. 39/D4
Liesse-Notre-Dame, Fr. 54/C4
Liestal, Swi. 60/D3
Lieto, Fin. 41/K1
Lieurey, Fr. 57/F2
Liévin, Fr. 54/B3
Lievio, Fin. 39/E4
Lièvre (riv.), Qu, Can. 161/J1
Liez (lake), Fr. 60/B2
Liezen, Aus. 45/L3
Lifake, D.R. Congo 121/E2
Lifau, ETim. 128/B2
Liffey (riv.), Ire. 34/B5
Liffol-le-Grand, Fr. 60/B1
Lifford, Ire. 31/Q9
Liffré, Fr. 56/D4
Lifou (isl.), NCal. 137/V12
Lifouta, Gabon 120/C3
Lifton, Eng, UK 36/B5
Liganga, Tanz. 119/A4
Ligao, Phil. 91/F1
Līgatne, Lat. 41/L3
Lighthouse (pt.), Fl, US 165/F3
Lighthouse Point, Fl, US 164/P10
Lightning Ridge, Austl. 132/C1
Lightwater, Eng, UK 30/B3
Lignano Sabbiadoro, It. 63/G2
Lignite, ND, US 156/C3
Ligny-en-Barrois, Fr. 55/E6
Ligoncio (peak), It. 61/F5
Ligonha (riv.), Moz. 123/H2
Ligonier, In, US 160/D4
Ligoúrion, Gre. 49/H4
Ligovo (nbrhd.), Rus. 69/T7
Liguria (pol. reg.), It. 62/B4
Ligurian (sea), Eur. 66/F2
Lihou Reef and Kays (isl.), Austl. 127/E2
Lihue, Hi, US 142/S10
Lihula, Est. 41/K2
Lijiang Naxizu Zizhixian, China 86/D3
Lijin, China 80/D3
Likasi, D.R. Congo 121/F5
Likati, D.R. Congo 121/E2
Likely, BC, Can. 144/D1
Likhoslavl', Rus. 68/G4
Likhovskoy, Rus. 73/L3
Likimi, D.R. Congo 121/E2
Likoma (isl.), Malw. 123/G2
Likoto, D.R. Congo 121/E3
Likouala (pol. reg.), Congo 120/D2
Likouala (riv.), Congo 120/D2
Likouala aux Herbes (riv.), Congo 120/D2
Likouala Mossaka (riv.), Congo 120/D3
Likova (riv.), Rus. 69/W9
Likstammen (lake), Swe. 39/A2
Liku, Indo. 90/C3
Lilanga, D.R. Congo 121/E3
Lilbourn, Mo, US 162/C2
Lilburn, Ga, US 163/M7
L'Île-Perrot, Qu, Can. 159/N7
L'Île-Rousse, Fr. 48/A1
Lilian, Pak. 98/B3
Lilienthal, Ger. 53/F2
Liling, China 93/K2
Lilla, Pak. 98/B3
Lilla Edet, Swe. 40/E2
Lille, Fr. 54/C2
Lille, Belg. 52/B6
Lille Bælt (chan.), Ger. 40/C4
Lille Værløse, Den. 39/J7
Lillebonne, Fr. 57/F1
Lillehammer, Nor. 40/D1
Lillerød, Den. 39/J7
Lillers, Fr. 54/B2
Lillesand, Nor. 40/C2
Lillestrøm, Nor. 40/D2
Lillian, Tx, US 150/K7
Lillie, La, US 153/H4
Lilliesleaf, Sc, UK 33/D5
Lillington, NC, US 163/H3
Lilliwaup, Wa, US 167/A3
Lillkyrka, Swe. 39/A1
Lillo, Sp. 46/D3
Lillooet (riv.), BC, Can. 144/C2
Lillooet, BC, Can. 144/D2
Lilongwe (cap.), Malw. 123/G2
Lilongwe (Kamuzu) (int'l arpt.), Malw. 123/G2
Liloy, Phil. 88/C3
Lily, Ky, US 162/E2
Lily, Wi, US 157/K5
Lilydale (nbrhd.), Austl. 132/G5
Lim (riv.), Serb. 49/F1
Lima, Arg. 191/J11
Lima (riv.), It. 63/D4
Lima, Par. 189/E2
Lima (dept.), Peru 184/B3
Lima (riv.), Port. 47/A2
Lima (mtn.), Mn, US 157/J3
Lima, Mt, US 147/G1
Lima (res.), Mt, US 147/G1
Lima, NY, US 161/H3
Lima, Oh, US 160/D4
Lima Duarte, Braz. 187/N6
Limache, Chile 190/N8
Limal, Bol. 188/C2
Liman, Az, US 149/G3
Liman, Rus. 71/H3
Limanowa, Pol. 43/L4
Limassol (dist.), Cyp. 104/C2
Limassol, Cyp. 104/C2
Limavady (dist.), NI, UK 34/A2
Limavady, NI, UK 34/B1
Limay, Fr. 57/G3
Limay (riv.), Arg. 179/C7
Limay Mahuida, Arg. 190/D3
Limbach, Ger. 58/C4
Limbang (riv.), Malay. 88/A4
Limbani, Peru 184/D4
Limbara (peak), It. 48/A2
Limbaži, Lat. 41/L3
Limbdi, India 101/K4
Limbe, Camr. 120/B1
Limbe, Malw. 123/G2
Limbé, Haiti 177/H2
Limbiate, It. 62/C2
Limbourg, Belg. 55/E2
Limbuak, Malay. 88/B4
Limbunya, Austl. 128/C4
Limburg (prov.), Belg. 55/E1
Limburg an der Lahn, Ger. 58/B2
Limburgerhof, Ger. 58/B4
Limedsforsen, Swe. 40/E1
Limehouse, On, Can. 160/T8
Limeira, Braz. 189/H2
Limekilns, Sc, UK 33/C4
Limena, It. 63/E3
Limenária, Gre. 49/J2
Limerick (co.), Ire. 32/B5
Limerick, Ire. 32/B4
Limerick, Sk, Can. 145/L3
Limestone, Me, US 153/H3
Limestone (lake), Tx, US 151/F2
Limestone, Mt, US 147/J1
Limfjorden (chan.), Den. 40/C3
Limidario (peak), It. 61/E5
Limington, Me, US 161/L3
Limite, It. 63/D6
Limmat (riv.), Swi. 61/E3
Limmen Bight (bay), Austl. 127/C2
Limni, Gre. 49/H3
Limnos (isl.), Gre. 70/C5
Limoeiro, Braz. 183/H4
Limoeiro do Norte, Braz. 183/G4
Limoges, Fr. 44/D4
Limogne (plat.), Fr. 44/D4
Limón, Hon. 176/E3
Limón, CR 177/F4
Limon, Co, US 154/C4
Limone Piemonte, It. 64/D4
Limone sul Garda, It. 63/D2
Limoquije, Bol. 185/E4
Limours, Fr. 30/J6
Limousin (mts.), Fr. 44/D4
Limousin (pol. reg.), Fr. 44/D4
Limoux, Fr. 44/E5
Limpopo (riv.), Afr. 123/G5
Limpopo (riv.), Moz. 107/F7
Limpsfield, Eng, UK 30/D3
Limu (mtn.), China 87/F5
Limu, China 87/F3
Limulunga, Zam. 122/D2
Limuru, Kenya 119/B2
Lin Xian, China 80/C3
Līnah, SAfr. 103/E4
Linakhamari, Rus. 68/F1
Linanäs, Swe. 39/B1
Linao (pt.), Phil. 88/C4
Linapacan (isl.), Phil. 88/B3
Linard (peak), Swi. 61/G4
Linares, Sp. 46/D3
Linares, Chile 190/C2
Linares, Mex. 175/F3
Linariá, Gre. 49/J3
Linate (int'l arpt.), It. 62/C3
Lincang, China 86/D4
Linch, Wy, US 154/A2
Lincheng, China 80/C3
Linchuan, China 87/H3
Lincoln, Arg. 190/E2
Lincoln (sea), Can. 139/R1
Lincoln, On, Can. 160/U9
Lincoln, Eng, UK 35/H5
Lincoln, Ca, US 146/C4
Lincoln, De, US 168/C6
Lincoln, Il, US 155/K3
Lincoln, ND, US 156/D4
Lincoln (cap.), Ne, US 155/F3
Lincoln, NH, US 161/L2
Lincoln, NM, US 152/B4
Lincoln, Pa, US 168/B3
Lincoln (Lincoln Center), Ks, US 153/E1
Lincoln Boyhood Nat'l Mem., In, US 162/D1
Lincoln Caverns, Pa, US 161/G4
Lincoln Center (Lincoln), Ks, US 153/E1
Lincoln City, Or, US 146/A1
Lincoln Heath (woodld.), Eng, UK 35/H5
Lincoln Heights, Oh, US 160/E4
Lincoln Home Nat'l Hist. Site, Il, US 155/K4
Lincoln NP, Austl. 131/G5
Lincoln Park, Co, US 152/B1
Lincoln Park, Ga, US 162/E4
Lincoln Park, Mi, US 167/F7
Lincoln Park, NJ, US 169/H8
Lincolnshire (co.), Eng, UK 35/H5
Lincolnshire Wolds (grsld.), Eng, UK 35/H4
Lincolnton, Ga, US 163/F4
Lincolnton, NC, US 163/G3
Lincolnville, Ks, US 153/F1
Lincroft, NJ, US 168/D3
Lind, Den. 40/C3
Lind NP, Austl. 133/D3
Linda, Ca, US 146/C4
Lindale, Ga, US 162/E3
Lindale, Tx, US 151/G1
Lindau, Swi. 61/E3
Lindau, Ger. 61/F2
Linde (riv.), Neth. 52/D3
Lindeman (chan.), Austl. 134/C3
Lindeman (isl.), Austl. 129/H5
Linden, Ger. 58/B1
Linden, Guy. 181/G3
Linden, Al, US 162/D4
Linden, Az, US 149/G3
Linden, Fl, US 164/L6
Linden, In, US 160/C4
Linden, Mi, US 167/E6
Linden, NJ, US 169/J9
Linden, Tn, US 162/D3
Linden, Tx, US 153/G4
Linden Beach, On, Can. 167/G7
Lindenberg im Allgäu, Ger. 61/F2
Lindenfels, Ger. 58/B3
Lindenhurst, Il, US 167/P15
Lindenhurst, NY, US 169/E2
Lindenwold, NJ, US 168/D4
Lindern, Ger. 53/E3
Lindesberg, Swe. 40/F2
Lindesnes (cape), Nor. 40/B3
Lindesnes, Nor. 40/B2
Lindewitt, Ger. 40/C4
Lindgren Acres, Fl, US 164/P11
Lindhorst, Ger. 53/E5
Lindhos (ruin), Gre. 102/B2
Lindi (riv.), D.R. Congo 121/F2
Lindi (prov.), Tanz. 119/B4
Lindi, Tanz. 119/B4
Lindian, China 79/J2
Lindlar, Ger. 55/G1
Lindley, SAfr. 124/D2
Lindome, Swe. 40/E3
Lindon, Ut, US 147/H3
Lindon, Co, US 154/C4
Lindos, Gre. 49/J2
Lindre (lake), Fr. 55/F6
Lindrith, NM, US 149/J2
Lindsay (mt.), Austl. 130/C5
Lindsay (mt.), Austl. 131/F3
Lindsay, On, Can. 161/G2
Lindsay, Ca, US 148/C2
Lindsay, Mt, US 156/B4
Lindsay, Ok, US 153/F3
Lindsborg, Ks, US 153/F1
Lindsdal, Swe. 40/G3
Lindstrom, Mn, US 157/H5
Line (isls.), Kiri. 137/J4
Line Mountain (mtn.), Pa, US 168/B2
Lineas de Nazca, Peru 184/C4
Lineboro, Md, US 168/B4
Lineville, Al, US 162/E4
Lineville, Ia, US 155/H3
Linfen, China 80/B3
Linford, Eng, UK 30/E2
Ling (riv.), Sc, UK 33/A2
Ling Xian, China 93/K2
Ling Xian, China 80/D3
Linganore (cr.), Md, US 168/A5
Lingao, China 87/F5
Lingayen, Phil. 88/C1
Lingayen (gulf), Phil. 88/B1
Lingbao, China 80/B4
Lingbi, China 80/D4
Lingchuan, China 93/K2
Lingchuan, China 80/C4
Linge (riv.), Neth. 52/C5
Lingelengenda, Zam. 122/D2
Lingen, Ger. 53/E3
Lingfield, Eng, UK 30/C3
Lingga (isl.), Indo. 90/B3
Lingga (isls.), Indo. 89/D3
Linghu, China 80/L9
Lingle, Wy, US 154/B2
Linglestown, Pa, US 168/B3
Lingma, China 87/E4
Lingolsheim, Fr. 60/D1
Lingomo, D.R. Congo 121/E2
Lingqiu, China 80/C3
Lingshan, China 80/C3
Lingshan, China 87/F4
Lingshi, China 80/B3
Lingshui, China 87/F5
Lingtou, China 87/H3
Linguère, Sen. 114/B3
Lingunda, D.R. Congo 121/E3
Lingwu, China 78/F4
Lingxi, China 87/J3
Lingyin Si, China 80/L9
Lingyuan, China 87/H3
Lingyun, China 93/J3
Linhai, China 79/J1
Linhai, China 87/J2
Linhares, Braz. 187/E3
Linhe, China 78/F3
Linière, Qu, Can. 158/C1
Linjiang, China 81/D2
Linköping, Swe. 40/F2
Linkuva, Lith. 41/K3
Linlithgow, Sc, UK 33/C5
Linliu (mtn.), China 80/C3
Linn, Mo, US 153/J1
Linn, Tx, US 151/E4
Linn Creek, Mo, US 153/H1
Linneus, Mo, US 155/H4
Linney (pt.), Wal, UK 36/A3
Linnhe (lake), Sc, UK 33/A3
Linnich, Ger. 55/F2
Linntown, Pa, US 168/B2
Lino Lakes, Mn, US 157/P6
Linosa, It. 48/C5
Linosa (isl.), It. 48/C5
Linosa (isl.), It. 112/N7
Linqasi, Sudan 117/E4
Linqing, China 80/C3
Linqu, China 80/D3
Linquan, China 80/C4
Linru, China 80/C4
Lins, Braz. 189/G2
Linsan, Gui. 114/B4
Linschoten, Neth. 52/B4
Linshu, China 80/D4
Linshui, China 78/D4
Linta (riv.), Madg. 125/H9
Linthal (riv.), Swi. 61/F4
Linthal, Swi. 61/F4
Lintlaw, Sk, Can. 156/C1
Linton, In, US 156/D4
Linton, ND, US 156/D4
Linton, Eng, UK 37/G2
Linton, Ga, US 163/F4
Linville, La, US 153/H4
Linwood, Eng, UK 35/H5
Linwood, Mi, US 160/E3
Linwu, China 93/K2
Linxi, China 80/D2
Linxia, China 78/E4
Linyanti (swamp), Bots. 122/D3
Linyi, China 80/D4
Linyi, China 80/D3
Linyi, China 80/B4
Linying, China 80/C4
Linz (int'l arpt.), Aus. 59/H6
Linz, Aus. 59/H6
Linz am Rhein, Ger. 55/G2
Linze, China 78/E4
Linzhang, China 80/C3
Lioma, Moz. 123/H2
Lion (gulf), Fr.,Sp. 66/E2
Lion Country Safari, Fl, US 164/P9
Lion-sur-Mer, Fr. 57/E2
Lions Den, Zim. 123/F3
Lion's Head, On, Can. 160/F2
Liopa, Indo. 128/B1
Lioto, CAfr. 116/D4
Liozno, Bela. 41/P4
Lipari, It. 48/D3
Lipari (isl.), It. 67/G3
Lipari (isls.), It. 67/G3
Lipatkain, Indo. 89/C3
Lipcani, Mol. 72/D3
Liperi, Fin. 68/F3
Lipetsk (int'l arpt.), Rus. 70/F1
Lipetsk, Rus. 70/F1
Lipetskaya Oblast, Rus. 70/F1
Lipez (riv.), Bol. 188/C2
Liphook, Eng, UK 37/F4
Lipin Bor, Rus. 68/H3
Liping, China 87/F3
Lipljan, Serb. 50/E4
Lipno, Pol. 43/K2
Lipno (res.), Czh. 59/H5
Lipno, UN (lake), Czh. 45/L2
Lipobane (pt.), Moz. 123/H3
Lipomo, It. 62/C2
Lipova, Rom. 50/E2
Lippe (riv.), Ger. 42/D3
Lippstadt, Ger. 53/F5
Lipscomb, Tx, US 152/D2
Lipsko, Pol. 72/A2
Lipton, Sk, Can. 156/B1
Liptovská Lužna, Slvk. 43/K4
Liptovský Svätý Mikuláš, Slvk. 43/K4
Liptrap (cape), Austl. 133/B4
Lipu, China 87/F3
Lipu Lipu La (pass), India 99/D5
Lira, Ugan. 121/H2
Liranga, Congo 120/D3
Lirangwe, Malw. 123/G2
Lircay, Peru 184/C4
Liré, Fr. 57/D6
Liri (riv.), It. 48/C2
Liria, Sp. 47/E3
Liro (riv.), It. 61/F5
Lirung, Indo. 88/D5
Lisala, D.R. Congo 121/E2
Lisboa (dist.), Port. 46/A3
Lisboa (int'l arpt.), Port. 47/P10
Lisboa (Lisbon) (cap.), Port. 47/P10
Lisbon, La, US 153/H4
Lisbon, Md, US 168/A5
Lisbon, Me, US 161/L2
Lisbon, ND, US 156/F4
Lisbon, NH, US 161/L2
Lisbon, Oh, US 160/F4
Lisbon (Lisboa) (cap.), Port. 47/P10
Lisburn (dist.), NI, UK 34/B3
Lisburn, NI, UK 34/B2
Lisburne (cape), Ak, US 171/E2
Liscarroll, Ire. 32/B5
Liscomb Game Sanctuary, NS, Can. 159/F3
Lisdoonvarna, Ire. 32/A3
Lisieleje, Den. 40/D3
Lisha (riv.), China 93/H2
Lishe (riv.), China 86/D3
Lishi, China 80/F2
Lishu, China 87/H2
Lisianski (isl.), Hi, US 137/H2
Lisieux, Fr. 57/F2
Lisiy Nos, Rus. 69/T6
Liskeard, Eng, UK 36/B6
Liski, Rus. 70/F2
L'Isle, Il, US 167/P16
L'Isle-Adam, Fr. 30/J4
L'Isle-d'Abeau, Fr. 64/B2
L'Isle-en-Dodon, Fr. 44/D5
L'Isle-sur-la-Sorgue, Fr. 64/B5
L'Isle-sur-le-Doubs, Fr. 60/C3
L'Isle-sur-Tarn, Fr. 44/D5
L'Isle-Verte, Qu, Can. 158/C1
L'Islet, Qu, Can. 158/B2
Lismore, Ire. 32/C4
Lisman, Al, US 162/C4
Lismore, Austl. 132/E1
Lismore, Ire. 32/C5
Lisnacree, NI, UK 34/B3
Lisnaskea, NI, UK 32/C1
Lišov, Czh. 59/H4
Lispeszentadorján, Hun. 50/C2
Liss, Eng, UK 37/F4
Lisse, Neth. 52/B4
Lisses, Fr. 30/K6
List, Ger. 40/C4
Lister (riv.), Ger. 53/E6
Listowel, Ire. 32/A5
Listowel, On, Can. 160/F3
Listvyanka, Rus. 78/E1
Lit, Swe. 38/E3
Lit. Scarcies (riv.), SLeo. 114/B4
Litang (riv.), China 93/H2
Litang, China 86/D2
Līṭānī (riv.), Leb. 104/D3
Litani (riv.), Sur.,FrG. 182/C2
Litavka (riv.), Czh. 59/G3
Litchfield, Austl. 128/C3
Litchfield, Ct, US 161/K4
Litchfield, Il, US 155/K4
Litchfield, Mn, US 155/G1
Litchfield, Ne, US 154/E3
Litchville, ND, US 156/E4
Liteta, Zam. 123/E2
Litherland, Eng, UK 35/F5
Lith, Neth. 52/C5
Litherland, Eng, UK 35/F5
Lithgow, Austl. 133/E1
Lithia, Fl, US 164/L6
Lithia Springs, Ga, US 163/L7
Lithonia, Ga, US 163/M7
Lithuania (ctry.) 41/K4
Litija, Slov. 45/L3
Litipāra, India 97/F3
Lititz, Pa, US 168/B3
Litókhoron, Gre. 49/H2
Litoměřice, Czh. 59/H1
Litoo, Tanz. 119/B4
Litovko, Rus. 79/M2
Litslena, Swe. 39/A1
Littabella NP, Austl. 134/D4
Little (lake), La, US 164/C3
Little (mtn.), SC, US 163/F3
Little (riv.), Ga, US 162/B5
Little America, Wy, US 147/J3
Little Andaman (isl.), India 93/F5
Little Arkansas (riv.), Ks, US 153/F1
Little Arkansas (riv.), Ks, US 154/E4
Little Baddow, Eng, UK 30/E1
Little Beaver (cr.), Co, US 154/D4
Little Berkhamstead, Eng, UK 30/C1
Little Bighorn (riv.), Mt, Wy, US 147/K1
Little Birch, WV, US 163/G1
Little Bitter (lake), Egypt 104/C4
Little Blue (riv.), Ne, US 154/F3
Little Bow (riv.), Ab, Can. 145/H2
Little Calumet (riv.), Il, US 167/Q16
Little Catalina, Nf, Can. 159/L1
Little Cayman (isl.), Cay. 173/E4
Little Chalfont, Eng, UK 30/B2
Little Chute, Wi, US 160/B2
Little Colorado (riv.), Az, US 149/H3
Little Creek, De, US 168/C5
Little Cumbrae (isl.), Sc, UK 33/A5
Little Current, On, Can. 160/F2
Little Cypress (cr.), Tx, US 151/M8
Little Deschutes (riv.), Or, US 146/C2
Little Desert NP, Austl. 132/B3
Little Diomede (isl.), Ak, US 171/E2
Little Egg (har.), NJ, US 168/D4
Little Elm, Tx, US 150/L6
Little Falls, Mn, US 157/G5
Little Falls, NJ, US 169/J8
Little Falls (dam), Wa, US 144/F4
Little Ferry, NJ, US 169/J8
Little Fishing (cr.), Pa, US 168/B1
Little Fork (riv.), Mn, US 157/H3
Little Fort, BC, Can. 144/D2
Little Gombi, Nga. 116/B3
Little Grand Rapids, Mb, Can. 157/G1
Little Heart's Ease, Nf, Can. 159/L1
Little Inagua (isl.), Bahm. 173/G3
Little Kanawha (riv.), WV, US 163/G1
Little Karoo (valley), SAfr. 124/C4
Little Lake, Ca, US 148/D3
Little Lehigh (riv.), Pa, US 168/C3
Little Manatee (riv.), Fl, US 164/L8
Little Manatee, South Fork (riv.), Fl, US 164/L8
Little Marais, Mn, US 157/J4
Little Minch (str.), Sc, UK 31/Q8
Little Missouri (riv.), Mt,Wy, US 154/B1
Little Moose (mtn.), NY, US 161/J3
Little Muddy (riv.), ND, US 156/C3
Little Muncy (cr.), Pa, US 168/B1
Little Neck (bay), NY, US 169/K8
Little Nemaha (riv.), Ne, US 155/F3
Little Nicobar (isl.), India 93/F6
Little Ocmulgee (riv.), Ga, US 163/F4
Little Para (res.), Austl. 131/M8
Little Para (riv.), Austl. 131/M8
Little Patuxent (riv.), Md, US 168/B5
Little Payne (cr.), Fl, US 164/M8
Little Peconic (bay), NY, US 169/F2
Little Pee Dee (riv.), SC, US 163/H3
Little Pend Orielle NWR, Wa, US 144/F3
Little Pic (riv.), On, Can. 157/L3
Little Pine and Lucky Man Ind. Res., Sk, Can. 145/K1
Little Pisgah (mtn.), NC, US 163/F3
Little Powder (riv.), Mt, US 147/L1
Little Prairie, Wi, US 167/N14
Little Red (riv.), Ar, US 153/J3
Little River, BC, Can. 144/B3
Little River, NZ 135/C3
Little River, Ks, US 153/E1
Little River, SC, US 163/H4
Little Rock, Mn, US 157/G5
Little Rock (cap.), Ar, US 153/H3
Little Rock (A.F.B.), Ar, US 153/H3
Little Rock (cr.), Il, US 167/N16
Little Sable (pt.), Mi, US 160/C3
Little Salmon, Yk, Can. 171/L3
Little Sark (isl.), UK 56/C2
Little Schuylkill (riv.), Pa, US 168/B2
Little Sioux (riv.), Ia, US 143/G3
Little Sioux, West Fork (riv.), Ia, US 155/F2
Little Sitkin (isl.), Ak, US 171/B5
Little Snake (riv.), Co, US 147/J3
Little St. George (isl.), Fl, US 165/F3
Little Stour (riv.), Eng, UK 37/H4
Little Stukeley, Eng, UK 37/F2
Little Swatara (cr.), Pa, US 168/B3
Little Tallapoosa (riv.), Al, US 162/E4
Little Valley, NY, US 161/G3

Little – Loznic

Little Wabash (riv.), Il, US 162/C1
Little White (riv.), SD, US 154/D2
Little Wichita (riv.), Tx,Ok, US 153/E4
Little Wind (riv.), Wy, US 147/J2
Little Wood (riv.), Id, US 147/F2
Little Zab (riv.), Iraq 103/E3
Littleborough, Eng, UK 35/F4
Littlefield, Tx, US 152/C4
Littlefield, Az, US 149/F2
Littlefork, Mn, US 157/H3
Littlehampton, Eng, UK 37/F5
Littleport, Eng, UK 37/G2
Littlerock, Ca, US 166/C1
Littlerock, Wa, US 144/C4
Littlestown, Pa, US 168/A4
Littleton, Ire. 32/C4
Littleton, NH, US 161/L2
Littleton, Co, US 154/B4
Littoral (prov.), Camr. 116/A4
Litvínov, Czh. 59/G1
Lityn, Ukr. 72/E3
Liu (riv.), China 75/N6
Liuba, China 78/F5
Liuche, China 87/G3
Liuchen, China 87/F4
Liucheng, China 93/J3
Liudongqiao, China 87/H2
Liuduo, China 79/J5
Liuhe, China 79/K3
Liuheng (isl.), China 87/J2
Liujing, China 94/E1
Liukou, China 87/H2
Liukuei, Tai. 87/J4
Liuli, Tanz. 119/A4
Liulin, China 80/B3
Liushi, China 87/G3
Liushuquan, China 99/F3
Liuwa Plain NP, Zam. 122/D2
Liuxi (riv.), China 87/G4
Liuyang, China 93/K2
Liuyang (riv.), China 87/G2
Liuzhou, China 87/F3
Liuzigang, China 87/G2
Livádhion, Gre. 49/H2
Livanátai, Gre. 49/H3
Līvāni, Lat. 41/M3
Live Oak, Fl, US 165/G2
Live Oak, Ca, US 146/C4
Livengood, Ak, US 171/J2
Livenza (riv.), It. 63/F2
Liverdun, Fr. 55/F6
Liverdy-en-Brie, Fr. 30/L5
Livermore, Co, US 154/B3
Livermore, Me, US 161/L2
Livermore, Ky, US 162/D2
Livermore, Ia, US 155/G2
Livermore (mt.), Tx, US 150/B2
Livermore Falls, Me, US 161/L2
Liverpool (nbrhd.), Austl. 134/G8
Liverpool, NS, Can. 158/E3
Liverpool (bay), NW, Can. 140/C1
Liverpool (cape), Nun, Can. 141/J1
Liverpool, Eng, UK 35/F5
Liverpool (co.), Eng, UK 35/F5
Liverpool (bay), Wal, UK 35/E5
Liverpool, Pa, US 168/B2
Liverpool, Tx, US 151/M9
Liverton, Eng, UK 35/H2
Livet-et-Gavet, Fr. 64/B2
Livigno, It. 61/G4
Livilliers, Fr. 30/J4
Lívingston, Guat. 176/D3
Livingston, Sc, UK 33/C5
Livingston, Al, US 162/C4
Livingston, Ca, US 148/B2
Livingston (lake), Fl, US 164/M8
Livingston, Ky, US 162/E2
Livingston, La, US 164/C2
Livingston (co.), Mi, US 167/E6
Livingston, Mt, US 147/H1
Livingston, NJ, US 169/H8
Livingston, Tn, US 162/E2
Livingston, Tx, US 151/G2
Livingston (lake), Tx, US 151/G2
Livingston Manor, NY, US 161/J4
Livingstone, Zam. 122/E3
Livingstone (range), Ab, Can. 144/G2
Livingstone Memorial, Zam. 123/F2
Livingstone, Chutes de (falls), Congo 120/C4
Livingstonia, Malw. 119/A4
Livno, Bosn. 50/C4
Livny, Rus. 70/F1
Livojoki (riv.), Fin. 38/H2
Livonia, Mi, US 160/E3
Livonia, La, US 164/C2
Livonia, NY, US 161/H3
Livorno, It. 62/D6
Livorno (prov.), It. 62/D6
Livorno Ferraris, It. 62/B3
Livramento do Brumado, Braz. 187/E2
Livron-sur-Drôme, Fr. 64/A3
Livry-Gargan, Fr. 30/K5
L'ivs'ka (prov.), Ukr. 43/M4
Liwa, Chad 116/B2
Liwa, Indo. 89/D4
Liwale, Tanz. 119/B4
Liwan, Sudan 117/G4
Liwonde, Malw. 123/G2
Liwonde NP, Malw. 123/G2
Lixin, China 87/H3
Lixin, China 80/D4
Lixnaw, Ire. 32/A5
Lixoúrion, Gre. 49/G3
Lixus (ruin), Mor. 112/A2
Liyang, China 80/D5
Liyong, China 87/F3
Lizard, Eng, UK 36/A7
Lizard (pt.), Eng, UK 36/A7
Lizard Point Ind. Res., Sk, Can. 156/D2
Lizella, Ga, US 162/F4
Lizifang, China 81/B3
Liziping, China 86/D2
Lizy-sur-Ourcq, Fr. 54/C5
Ljubic, Serb. 50/E4
Ljubija, Bosn. 50/C3
Ljubinje, Bosn. 50/D4
Ljubljana (cap.), Slov. 45/L3
Ljubuški, Bosn. 50/C4
Ljungan (riv.), Swe. 38/F3
Ljungby, Swe. 40/E3
Ljungbyhed, Swe. 39/K6
Ljungsbro, Swe. 40/F2
Ljungskile, Swe. 40/D2
Ljusnan (riv.), Swe. 38/E3
Ljusne, Swe. 40/G1
Ljusterø (isl.), Swe. 41/H2
Ljusterö, Swe. 39/B1
Lkst (peak), Mor. 110/C3
Llabanere (int'l arpt.), Fr. 44/E5
Llaillay, Chile 190/N8
Llaima (vol.), Chile 190/C3
Llallagua, Bol. 188/C1
Llalli, Peru 184/D4
Llanberis, Wal, UK 34/D5
Llanberis, Pass of (pass), Wal, UK 34/D5
Llancañelo (lake), Arg. 190/C2
Llandeilo, Wal, UK 36/C3
Llandogo, Wal, UK 36/D3
Llandovery, Wal, UK 36/C3
Llandrillo, Wal, UK 34/E6
Llandrindod Wells, Wal, UK 36/C2
Llandudno, Wal, UK 34/E5
Llandyssul, Wal, UK 36/B2
Llanelltyd, Wal, UK 36/C1
Llanenddwyn, Wal, UK 34/D6
Llanerchymedd, Wal, UK 34/D5
Llanes, Sp. 46/C1
Llanfair-Pwllgwyngyll, Wal, UK 34/D5
Llanfairfechan, Wal, UK 34/E5
Llanfyllin, Wal, UK 36/C1
Llangammarch Wells, Wal, UK 36/C2
Llangattock, Wal, UK 36/C3
Llangollen, Wal, UK 35/E6
Llangurig, Wal, UK 36/C2
Llanidloes, Wal, UK 36/C2
Llanllyfni, Wal, UK 34/D5
Llano, Tx, US 151/E2
Llano (riv.), Tx, US 150/E2
Llano Estacado (plain), US 142/F5
Llanos (plain), Col.,Ven. 179/B2
Llanquihue (lake), Chile 190/B4
Llanrhaeadr, Wal, UK 35/E5
Llanrian, Wal, UK 36/A3
Llanrwst, Wal, UK 34/E5
Llanthony, Wal, UK 36/C3
Llanuwchllyn, Wal, UK 34/E6
Llata, Peru 184/B3
Llay, Wal, UK 35/F5
Lledrod, Wal, UK 36/C2
Lleida, Sp. 47/F2
Llera de Canales, Mex. 175/F4
Llerena, Sp. 46/B3
Lleyn (pen.), Wal, UK 34/D6
Llica, Bol. 188/B1
Llico, Chile 190/B3
Llívia, Sp. 44/D5
Llobregat (riv.), Sp. 47/F1
Llodio, Sp. 44/B5
Llorente, Phil. 88/D3
Lloret de Mar, Sp. 47/G2
Llorona (pt.), CR 172/E6
Lloyd (pt.), NY, US 169/M8
Lloyd Harbor, NY, US 169/M8
Lloydminster, Sk, Can. 145/K1
Lloyds (riv.), Nf, Can. 159/J1
Lluchmayor, Sp. 47/G3
Llullaillaco (vol.), Arg.,Chile 188/B3
Llwchwr (riv.), Wal, UK 36/B3
Llyn Alaw (lake), Wal, UK 34/D5
Llyn Brenig (lake), Wal, UK 34/E5
Llyn Brianne (res.), Wal, UK 36/C2
Llyn Efyrnwy (lake), Wal, UK 34/E6
Llyn Tegid (lake), Wal, UK 34/E6
Llyn Trawsfynydd (lake), Wal, UK 34/D6
Llynfi (riv.), Wal, UK 36/C3
Lo Wu, China 87/L6
Loa (riv.), Chile 179/C5
Loa, Ut, US 149/G1
Loanda, Gabon 120/B3
Loanda, Braz. 189/F2
Loange (riv.), D.R. Congo 120/D4
Loango Buele, D.R. Congo 120/C4
Loanhead, Sc, UK 33/C5
Loano, It. 62/B5
Loaoya (canal), Sp. 47/N8
Loashi, D.R. Congo 121/G3
Lobanskaya, Rus. 69/K2
Lobatse, Bots. 122/E5
Lobbes, Belg. 55/D3
Lobelville, Tn, US 162/D3
Lobenstein, Ger. 59/E2
Lobería, Arg. 190/F3
Lobethal, Austl. 131/M8
Łobez, Pol. 43/H2
L'Obiou (peak), Fr. 64/B3
Lobito, Ang. 122/B2
Lobitos, Peru 184/A2
Lobnya, Rus. 69/W8
Lobo (riv.), C.d'Iv. 114/D5
Lobo, Tx, US 150/B2
Lobos, Arg. 191/J11
Lobos (pt.), Chile 188/B2
Lobos (pt.), Chile 188/B4
Lobos, Punta de (pt.), Chile 190/M9
Lobva, Rus. 69/P4
Loc (riv.), Fr. 56/C5
Loc Ninh, Viet. 94/D4
Locana, It. 64/D2
Locarno, Swi. 61/E5
Loch Haven Center, Fl, US 164/N6
Loch na Sealga (sea), Sc, UK 33/A1
Loch Raven (res.), Md, US 168/B5
Lochaber (reg.), Sc, UK 33/A3
Lochans, Sc, UK 34/D2
Locharbriggs, Sc, UK 34/E1
Lochau, Aus. 61/F2
Lochawe, Sc, UK 33/A4
Lochboisdale, Sc, UK 31/Q8
Lochearnhead, Sc, UK 33/B4
Lochem, Neth. 52/D4
Lochend, Sc, UK 33/B2
Loches, Fr. 44/D3
Lochgelly, Sc, UK 33/C4
Lochgilphead, Sc, UK 33/A4
Lochgoilhead, Sc, UK 33/B4
Lochiel, SAfr. 125/E2
Lochindorb (lake), Sc, UK 33/C2
Lochinvar, Austl. 133/E1
Lochinvar NP, Zam. 123/E2
Lochmaben, Sc, UK 34/E1
Lochmaddy, Sc, UK 31/Q8
Łochów, Pol. 43/L2
Lochranza, Sc, UK 33/A5
Lochristi, Belg. 54/C1
Lochsa (riv.), Id, US 144/G4
Lochwinnoch, Sc, UK 33/B5
Lochy (lake), Sc, UK 33/B3
Lochy (riv.), Sc, UK 33/B3
Lock, Austl. 131/G5
Lock Haven, Pa, US 161/H4
Locke, Ca, US 167/L10
Locke (mt.), Tx, US 150/B2
Lockeford, Ca, US 146/C4
Lockeport, NS, Can. 158/E4
Lockerbie, Sc, UK 35/E1
Lockesburg, Ar, US 153/G4
Lockettville, Tx, US 152/C4
Lockhart, Austl. 133/C2
Lockhart, Fl, US 164/N6
Lockhart, Tx, US 150/F3
Lockhart Abor. Land, Austl. 129/F3
Lockhart Abor. Rsv., Austl. 134/A1
Lockhart River Aboriginal Community, Austl. 129/F3
Lockington, Austl. 132/C3
Lockney, Tx, US 152/D3
Locknitz (riv.), Ger. 42/F2
Lockport, Mb, Can. 156/F2
Lockport, La, US 164/C3
Lockport, Il, US 167/P16
Lockport, NY, US 160/V9
Lockwood, Sk, Can. 156/B2
Lockwood (res.), Eng, UK 30/C2
Locmariaquer, Fr. 56/C5
Locminé, Fr. 56/C5
Loco, Ok, US 153/F3
Locoal-Mendon, Fr. 56/B5
Locon, Fr. 54/B2
Locquirec, Fr. 56/B3
Locri, It. 48/E3
Locronan, Fr. 56/A4
Loctudy, Fr. 56/A5
Locumba, Peru 184/D5
Locust (cr.), Mo, Ia, US 155/H3
Locust Grove, Ok, US 153/G2
Lod, Isr. 105/B5
Lodan (cr.), Ne, US 155/F2
Lodde (riv.), Swe. 39/K7
Löddeköpinge, Swe. 39/K7
Loddon (riv.), Austl. 132/B3
Loddon (riv.), Eng, UK 37/E4
Loddon, Eng, UK 37/H1
Lodenice (riv.), Czh. 59/H2
Lodève, Fr. 44/E5
Lodeynoye Pole, Rus. 68/G3
Lodge (cr.), Ab, Can. 145/J3
Lodge Grass, Mt, US 147/K1
Lodge Pole, Mt, US 145/K3
Lodgepole, SD, US 156/C5
Lodgepole (cr.), Wy, Ne, US 154/B3
Lodgepole, Ab, Can. 144/G1
Lodhrān, Pak. 98/A5
Lodi, D.R. Congo 121/E4
Lodi, It. 62/C3
Lodi, Ca, US 146/C4
Lodi, Mo, US 162/B2
Lodi, NJ, US 169/J8
Lodi, Tx, US 153/G4
Lodi, Wi, US 155/K2
Lodi Vecchio, It. 62/C3
Lodja, D.R. Congo 121/E3
Lodosa, Sp. 46/D1
Lodrino, Swi. 61/E5
Lodwar, Kenya 119/A1
Łódź, Pol. 43/K3
Łódźkie, (prov.), Pol. 43/K3
Loei, Thai. 94/C2
Loenen, Neth. 52/C4
Loengo, D.R. Congo 121/F4
Loeriesfontein, SAfr. 124/B3
Lofa (riv.), Libr. 114/C5
Lofa (co.), Libr. 114/C5
Löffingen, Ger. 61/E2
Lofonda, D.R. Congo 121/E2
Lofoten (isle.), Nor. 38/D2
Loftus, Eng, UK 35/H2
Lofty (range), Austl. 130/C3
Lofty (mt.), Austl. 131/M8
Loga, Niger 115/F3
Logan (nbrhd.), Austl. 134/F7
Logan (Trudeau) (mt.), Yk., Can. 171/K3
Logan, Ia, US 155/G3
Logan, Ks, US 154/E4
Logan (pass), Mt, US 145/H3
Logan, NM, US 152/C3
Logan, Oh, US 160/E5
Logan, Ut, US 147/H3
Logan (mt.), Wa, US 144/D3
Logan, WV, US 163/G2
Logan Int'l (General Edward Lawrence Logan) (int'l arpt.), Ma, US 161/L3
Logan Lake, BC, Can. 144/D2
Logan Martin (lake), Al, US 162/D4
Logansport, La, US 150/H2
Logansport, In, US 160/C4
Loganton, Pa, US 168/A1
Loganville, Ga, US 162/F4
Loganville, Pa, US 168/B4
Logatec, Slov. 45/L4
Loge (riv.), Ang. 120/C4
Loggieville, NB, Can. 158/E2
Logone (riv.), Chad 107/D3
Logone Birni, Camr. 116/B3
Logone Occ. (riv.), Chad 116/B4
Logone Oriental (riv.), Chad 116/C3
Logone-Occidental (pref.), Chad 116/B3
Logone-Oriental (pref.), Chad 116/B3
Lograto, It. 62/D3
Logroño, Sp. 44/B5
Logrosán, Sp. 46/C3
Løgstør, Den. 40/C3
Løgten, Den. 40/D3
Lohals, Den. 40/D4
Lohārdaga, India 97/E4
Lohāru, India 98/C5
Lohatlha, SAfr. 124/C3
Lohāwat, India 92/B2
Lohfelden, Ger. 53/G6
Lohja, Fin. 41/L1
Lohjanjärvi (lake), Fin. 41/K1
Lohman, Mo, US 153/H1
Lohmar, Ger. 55/G2
Lohn, Tx, US 150/E2
Löhnberg, Ger. 58/B1
Löhne, Ger. 53/F4
Lohne, Ger. 53/F3
Loholoho, Indo. 91/F4
Lohr, Ger. 58/C3
Loi-kaw, Myan. 86/C5
Loiano, It. 63/E5
Loica, Chile 190/N9
Loile (riv.), D.R. Congo 121/E3
Loing (riv.), Fr. 42/B5
Loir (riv.), Fr. 44/D3
Loir-et-Cher (dept.), Fr. 57/G5
Loire (dept.), Fr. 64/A2
Loire (riv.), Fr. 29/E4
Loire-Atlantique (dept.), Fr. 56/D6
Loiret (dept.), Fr. 57/G5
Loiron, Fr. 57/E4
Loisin (riv.), Fr. 55/E5
Loita (hills), Kenya 119/A2
Loja, Sp. 46/C4
Loja, Ecu. 184/B2
Loja (prov.), Ecu. 184/B2
Løjt Kirkeby, Den. 40/C4
Loka, Sudan 117/F4
Lokandu, D.R. Congo 121/F3
Lökåö (isl.), Swe. 39/B1
Lökbatan, Azer. 103/G1
Lokeren, Belg. 54/D1
Lokhvytsya, Ukr. 73/G2
Lokichar, Kenya 119/A1
Lokichokio, Kenya 117/G4
Lokitaung, Kenya 117/G4
Lokka, Fin. 68/E2
Løkken, Den. 40/C3
Loknya, Rus. 41/P3
Loko, Nga. 115/G5
Lokofe, D.R. Congo 121/E3
Lokoja, Nga. 115/G5
Lokolama, D.R. Congo 120/D3
Lokolia, D.R. Congo 121/E3
Lokolo (riv.), D.R. Congo 120/D3
Lokomby, Madg. 125/H8
Lokomo, Camr. 120/C2
Lokopo, Ugan. 119/A1
Lokori, Kenya 119/B1
Lokoro (riv.), D.R. Congo 120/D3
Lökösháza, Hun. 50/E2
Lokossa, Ben. 115/F5
Lokot', Rus. 70/E1
Loks (isl.), Nun, Can. 141/K2
Loksa, Est. 41/L2
Lokwakangole, Kenya 117/G5
Lola, Gui. 114/C5
Lola, Ky, US 162/C2
Lolelia, Ugan. 117/G5
Lolgorien, Kenya 119/A2
Lolingo, D.R. Congo 121/E2
Loliondo, Tanz. 119/A2
Lolita, Tx, US 151/F3
Lolkisale, Tanz. 119/B2
Lolland (isl.), Den. 40/D4
Lollar, Ger. 58/B3
Lolo, D.R. Congo 121/E2
Lolo (riv.), Gabon 120/C3
Lolo, D.R. Congo 121/F3
Lolo, Mt, US 145/G4
Lolo (peak), Mt, US 144/G4
Lolodorf, Camr. 120/B2
Lolua, Tuv. 136/G5
Lolui (isl.), Ugan. 119/A2
Lom, Nor. 38/D3
Lom, Bul. 51/F4
Lom (riv.), Camr. 116/B4
Lom Sak, Thai. 94/C2
Loma (pt.), Ca, US 166/C5
Loma (mts.), SLeo. 114/C4
Loma, Mt, US 145/J4
Loma Alta, Bol. 185/E3
Loma Alta, Tx, US 150/D3
Loma Bonita, Mex. 176/C2
Loma Linda, Ca, US 166/C2
Loma Mansa (peak), SLeo. 114/C4
Loma Negra, Arg. 190/E3
Lomami (riv.), D.R. Congo 107/E5
Lomas, Peru 184/C4
Lomas de Zamora, Arg. 191/J11
Lomazzo, It. 62/C2
Lomba (riv.), Ang. 122/D2
Lombard, Il, US 167/P16
Lombarda, Serra (mts.), Braz. 182/D2
Lombardia (pol.reg.), It. 61/E6
Lombardia (pol. reg.), It. 45/H4
Lombardia, Mex. 174/E5
Lombe, Ang. 120/D5
Lombe, Indo. 128/A1
Lomblen (isl.), Indo. 91/F5
Lombok, Indo. 91/E5
Lombok (isl.), Indo. 91/E5
Lombok (str.), Indo. 89/F5
Lombolo, Congo 120/C4
Lomé (cap.), Togo 115/F5
Lomé (int'l arpt.), Togo 115/F5
Lomela (riv.), D.R. Congo 121/E3
Lomela, D.R. Congo 121/E3
Lomello, It. 62/B3
Lometa, Tx, US 151/E2
Lomié, Camr. 120/C2
Lomira, Wi, US 160/B3
Lomita, Ca, US 166/F8
Lomma (riv.), Nor. 38/S8
Lomma, Swe. 40/E4
Lomme, Fr. 54/B2
Lommel, Belg. 52/C6
Lomnice (riv.), Czh. 59/G4
Lomnice nad Lužnicí, Czh. 59/H4
Lomond (lake), Sc, UK 33/B4
Lomond (hills), Sc, UK 33/C4
Lomond, Ab, Can. 145/H2
Lomone (riv.), It. 63/E4
Lomonosov, Rus. 69/S7
Lompobatang (peak), Indo. 91/E5
Lompoc, Ca, US 148/B3
Łomża, Pol. 43/M2
Lonato, It. 62/D3
Lonāvale, India 95/B2
Loncoche, Chile 190/B3
Loncopué, Arg. 190/C3
Londerzeel, Belg. 55/D2
Londiani, Kenya 119/A2
Londinières, Fr. 57/G1
London, On, Can. 160/F3
London (cap.), UK 30/C2
London, Ky, US 162/E2
London, Oh, US 160/E5
London, Tx, US 150/E2
London Bridge, Az, US 148/E3
London Colney, Eng, UK 30/C1
London (reef), Nic. 177/F3
London, City of (bor.), Eng, UK 30/A1
Londonderry (dist.), NI, UK 34/A2
Londonderry, NI, UK 34/A2
Londonderry (cape), Austl. 128/B3
Londonderry (isl.), Chile 191/C7
Londonderry (Eglinton) (arpt.), UK 34/A1
Londres, Arg. 188/C3
Londrina, Braz. 189/G2
Londuimbali, Ang. 122/B2
Lone (mtn.), SD, US 156/C5
Lone (riv.), Ger. 58/C5
Lone Butte, BC, Can. 144/D2
Lone Grove, Ok, US 153/F3
Lone Pine, Ca, US 148/C2
Lone Pine Ind. Res., Ca, US 148/C2
Lone Pine Sanct., Austl. 134/E7
Lone Rock, Sk, Can. 145/K1
Lone Star, Tx, US 153/G4
Lone Star, La, US 164/C2
Lone Wolf, Ok, US 152/E3
Lonepine, La, US 164/B2
Lonesome NP, Austl. 134/C4
Lonétou, Mali 114/C3
Long (isl.), Bahm. 139/K7
Long (isl.), Nf., Can. 158/K2
Long (pt.), On, Can. 160/F3
Long (cr.), Sk, Can. 145/M3
Long (riv.), China 87/F3
Long (peak), Fr. 47/F1
Long (isl.), Ire. 32/A7
Long (isl.), PNG 129/G1
Long (str.), Rus. 75/T2
Long, Thai. 94/B2
Long (lake), Sc, UK 33/A2
Long (mtn.), Wal, UK 36/C1
Long, Ak, US 171/G3
Long (pt.), Mi, US 157/K4
Long (lake), ND, US 156/D4
Long (isl.), NY, US 169/K9
Long Beach, In, US 160/C4
Long Beach, Ms, US 164/D2
Long Beach, Ca, US 166/F8
Long Beach, NY, US 169/L9
Long Beach, On, Can. 160/U10
Long Beach (pen.), Wa, US 144/B4
Long Beach, Wa, US 144/B4
Long Beach (isl.), NJ, US 168/D4
Long Beach, Austl. 133/E2
Long Beach, NC, US 163/H4
Long Beach (Daugherty Field) (arpt.), Ca, US 166/F8
Long Branch, NJ, US 168/E3
Long Buckby, Eng, UK 37/E2
Long Cay (isl.), India 177/H1
Long Chau, Viet. 87/E4
Long Crag (hill), Eng, UK 33/E6
Long Creek, Or, US 146/D1
Long Crendon, Eng, UK 37/F3
Long Ditton, Eng, UK 30/C2
Long Eaton, Eng, UK 35/G6
Long Eddy, NY, US 161/J4
Long Grove, Il, US 167/P15
Long Hill, Ct, US 169/E1
Long Island, Ks, US 154/E4
Long Island MacArthur (arpt.), NY, US 169/E2
Long Ketiok, Indo. 91/E3
Long Key (isl.), Fl, US 165/H5
Long Lake, SD, US 156/E5
Long Lake, NY, US 161/J3
Long Lake Ind. Res., On, Can. 157/L3
Long Lake NWR, ND, US 156/D4
Long Lane, Mo, US 153/H2
Long Lelang, Malay. 88/A5
Long Mynd, The (hill), Eng, UK 36/D1
Long Neck (pt.), Ct, US 169/M7
Long Phu, Viet. 94/D4
Long Plain Ind. Res., Mb, Can. 156/E3
Long Pond, Me, US 161/L2
Long Prairie, Mn, US 157/G5
Long Range (mts.), Nf, Can. 159/H2
Long Semado, Malay. 88/A4
Long Sutton, Eng, UK 35/J6
Long Valley, NJ, US 168/D2
Long Xian, China 78/F5
Long Xuyen, Viet. 94/D4
Long, Loch (inlet), Sc, UK 33/B4
Longa, Ang. 122/C2
Longa (riv.), Ang. 120/C5
Longá (riv.), Braz. 183/F3
Long'an, China 93/J3
Longare, It. 63/E3
Longaví, Chile 190/C2
Longberang, Indo. 91/E3
Longbia, Indo. 91/E3
Longboat Key, Fl, US 165/G4
Longboh, Indo. 90/E3
Longbranch, Wa, US 167/B3
Longchamps, Belg. 55/E3
Longchang, China 86/E2
Longchuan, China 93/G3
Longchuan (riv.), China 86/C3
Longchuan, China 87/G3
Longdale, Ok, US 153/E2
Longde, China 78/F4
Longdongping, China 87/F2
Longeau (riv.), Fr. 55/E5
Longeuve (riv.), Fr. 57/E4
Longeville-en-Barrois, Fr. 55/E6
Longeville-lès-Metz, Fr. 55/F5
Longeville-lès-Saint-Avold, Fr. 55/F5
Longfellow (mts.), Me, US 158/B3
Longfield, Eng, UK 30/D2
Longford (co.), Ire. 32/C2
Longford, Ire. 32/C2
Longford, Austl. 132/C4
Longgang, China 87/H3
Longguang, China 87/E4
Longgun, China 87/F5
Longhoughton, Eng, UK 33/E6
Longhua (pass), China 87/F3
Longhua, China 80/D2
Longhui, China 87/F3
Longido, Tanz. 119/B2
Longjiang, China 79/J2
Longjie, China 86/E3
Longjumeau, Fr. 30/J5
Longkou, China 80/E3
Longlac, On, Can. 157/L3
Longli, China 93/J2
Longmen, China 94/E1
Longmen, China 86/D3
Longmen Shiyao, China 80/C4
Longmont, Co, US 154/B3
Longnan, China 87/G3
Longniddry, Sc, UK 33/D5
Longnor, Eng, UK 35/G5
Longny-au-Perche, Fr. 57/F3
Longo, Congo 120/D2
Longonjo, Ang. 122/B2
Longonot (peak), Kenya 119/B2
Longperrier, Fr. 30/K4
Longpont-sur-Orge, Fr. 30/J6
Longport, NJ, US 168/D5
Longpré-les-Corps-Saints, Fr. 54/A3
Longquan, China 87/H2
Longreach, Austl. 134/B3
Longriba, China 78/E5
Longridge, Eng, UK 35/F4
Longs (peak), Co, US 154/B3
Longshan, China 87/F2
Longshou (mts.), China 78/E4
Longstreet, La, US 150/H1
Longtan, China 87/F4
Longton, Ks, US 153/F2
Longtown, Eng, UK 35/F2
Longué-Jumelles, Fr. 57/E6
Longueau, Fr. 54/B4
Longueil-Annel, Fr. 54/B5
Longuenesse, Fr. 54/B2
Longuesse, Fr. 30/H4
Longueuil, Qu, Can. 159/P6
Longuyon, Fr. 55/E5
Longvic, Fr. 60/B3
Longview, Ms, US 162/C4
Longview, Tx, US 151/G1
Longview, Wa, US 144/C4
Longview, Ab, Can. 145/G2
Longville, La, US 164/B2
Longwo, China 87/G4
Longwood, Fl, US 164/N6
Longwood, NC, US 163/H3
Longwood Gardens, Pa, US 168/C4
Longworth, Tx, US 150/D1
Longwy, Fr. 55/E4
Longxi, China 78/E4
Longxingshi, China 87/G3
Longyan, China 87/H3
Longyearbyen, Nor. 74/B2
Longyou, China 87/H2
Longzhou, China 94/D1
Loni, India 98/D5
Lonigo, It. 63/E3
Löningen, Ger. 53/E3
Lonkin, Myan. 86/C3
Lonneker, Neth. 52/D4
Lonoke, Ar, US 153/J3
Lonquimay, Arg. 190/E3
Lons, Fr. 44/C5
Lons-le-Saunier, Fr. 60/B4
Lönsboda, Swe. 40/F3
Lonton, Myan. 86/C3
Lontzen, Belg. 55/F2
Lonza (riv.), Swi. 60/D5
Looc, Phil. 88/C2
Looe (isl.), Eng, UK 36/B6
Loogootee, In, US 162/D1
Lookout (pt.), Mi, US 160/E2
Lookout (pt.), Austl. 134/B1
Lookout (cape), Or, US 146/B1
Lookout (mtn.), Id, US 144/G4
Lookout (pt.), Md, US 163/J1
Lookout (cape), NC, US 163/J3
Loolmalasin (peak), Tanz. 119/A2
Looma, Austl. 128/B4
Loomis, Ca, US 146/C4
Loomis, Wa, US 144/E3
Loon Lake, Wa, US 144/F3
Loon op Zand, Neth. 52/C5
Loop, Tx, US 152/C4
Loop Head (pt.), Ire. 30/P10
Loos, Fr. 54/C2
Loos, BC, Can. 144/D1
Loose, Eng, UK 30/E3
Loose Creek, Mo, US 153/J1
Lop (lake), China 78/C3
Lop Buri, Thai. 94/C3
Lopary, Madg. 125/H8
Lopatin, Rus. 71/H4
Lopatinskiy, Rus. 68/H5
Lopatkovo, Rus. 69/P4
Lopaye, Sudan 117/G4
Lopeno, Tx, US 150/E4
Loperhet, Fr. 56/A4
Lopez (cape), Gabon 120/B3
Lopez (pt.), Ca, US 148/B2
Lopez, Phil. 88/C2
López Mateos, Mex. 175/Q9
Lopik, Neth. 52/B5
Lopori (riv.), D.R. Congo 121/E2
Lopphavet (bay), Nor. 38/G1
Loppi, Fin. 41/L1
Loppijärvi (lake), Fin. 39/E4
Lopukhovka, Rus. 71/H2
Lopydino, Rus. 69/M3
Lora (cr.), Austl. 131/G4
Lora del Río, Sp. 46/C4
Lorain, Oh, US 160/E4
Loraine, Tx, US 150/D1
Loralai, Pak. 101/J2
Lorca, Sp. 46/E4
Lorch, Ger. 55/G3
Lorch, Ger. 58/C5
Lord Howe (isl.), Austl. 136/E8
Lordegān, Iran 103/G4
Lords Lake Nat'l Wild. Ref., ND, US 156/D3
Lordsburg, NM, US 149/H4
Loré, ETim. 128/B2
Lorelei, Ger. 55/G3
Lorena, Braz. 187/L7
Lorengau, PNG 136/D5
Lørenskog, Nor. 40/D2
Lorentz (riv.), Indo. 91/J5
Lorentzsluizen (dam), Neth. 52/C2
Lorenzo, Tx, US 152/D4
Lorenzo Geyres, Uru. 190/F2
Loreo, It. 63/F3
Lorestān (gov.), Iran 103/G3
Loreto, It. 63/G7
Loreto, Ecu. 180/B5
Loreto (state), Peru 180/C5
Loreto, Phil. 88/D3
Loreto, Braz. 183/E4
Loreto, Col. 184/D1
Loreto, Bol. 185/E4
Loreto, Par. 189/E2
Loreto, Mex. 174/C3
Loreto (int'l arpt.), Mex. 174/C3
Loreto, Mex. 174/E4
Loreto Aprutino, It. 65/C3
Lorette, Mb, Can. 156/F3
Lorette, Fr. 64/A1
Loretteville, Qu, Can. 158/B2
Loretto, Tn, US 162/D3
Loretto, Ky, US 162/E2
Lorgues, Fr. 64/C6
Lorian (swamp), Kenya 119/B1
Lorica, Col. 180/C2
Lorient, Fr. 56/B5
Lorient (Lann-Bihoue) (arpt.), Fr. 56/B5
L'Oriental (pol. reg.), Mor. 112/C3
L'Orignal, On, Can. 161/J2
Lorillard (riv.), Nun, Can. 140/G2
Lorinci, Hun. 43/K5
Loring, Mt, US 145/L3
Loriol-sur-Drôme, Fr. 64/A3
Loris, SC, US 163/H3
Lorman, Ms, US 164/C2
Lorne, Austl. 133/A4
Lorne Park, On, Can. 160/T8
Loro Ciuffenna, It. 63/E6
Lorosuk (peak), Kenya 119/A1
Lorquin, Fr. 55/G6
Lörrach, Ger. 60/D2
Lorrain (plat.), Fr. 42/D4
Lorraine (pol. reg.), Fr. 60/C1
Lorraine, Ks, US 153/E1
Lorraine (reg.), Fr. 55/E5
Lorraine (pol.reg.), Fr. 44/G2
Lorraine, Qu, Can. 159/N6
Lorrha, Ire. 32/B3
Lorsch, Ger. 58/B3
Lorton, Eng, UK 35/E2
Lorton, Va, US 163/J1
Loruk, Kenya 119/B1
Lorup, Ger. 53/E3
Los Alamitos, Ca, US 166/F8
Los Álamos, Mex. 150/D3
Los Alamos, Ca, US 148/B3
Los Alamos, NM, US 149/J3
Los Alamos, NM, US 152/B3
Los Aldamas, Mex. 150/E4
Los Alerces, PN, Arg. 190/C4
Los Altos, Arg. 188/C4
Los Altos, Ca, US 167/K12
Los Amates, Guat. 176/D3
Los Andes, Col. 180/B4
Los Andes, Chile 190/N8
Los Angeles (co.), Ca, US 166/B2
Los Angeles (riv.), Ca, US 166/B2
Los Angeles (int'l arpt.), Ca, US 166/F8
Los Angeles, Ca, US 166/F7
Los Ángeles, Chile 190/B3
Los Angeles (aqueduct), Ca, US 148/C3
Los Angeles Outer (har.), Ca, US 166/F8
Los Aquijes, Peru 184/C4
Los Aztecas, Mex. 175/F4
Los Banos, Ca, US 148/B2
Los Barrios, Sp. 46/C4
Los Canarreos (arch.), Cuba 177/F1
Los Cardales, Arg. 191/J11
Los Cardoñes, PN, Arg. 188/C3
Los Castillos, Ven. 181/F2
Los Cerrillos, Uru. 191/K11
Los Charrúas, Arg. 188/E4
Los Chaves, NM, US 149/J3
Los Chonos (arch.), Chile 179/B7
Los Cóndores, Arg. 188/C5
Los Corrales de Buelna, Sp. 46/C1
Los Coyotes Ind. Res., Ca, US 148/D4
Los Cusis, Bol. 185/E4
Los Estados (isl.), Arg. 191/D7
Los Fresnos, Tx, US 150/F4
Los Glaciares, PN, Arg. 191/B6
Los Herreras, Mex. 150/E5
Los Katios, PN, Col. 180/B3
Los Lagos, Chile 190/B3
Los Lagos (pol. reg.), Chile 190/B4
Los Llanos de Aridane, Sp. 110/A3
Los Lunas, NM, US 149/J3
Los Mármoles, PN, Mex. 176/B1
Los Menucos, Arg. 190/C4
Los Mochis, Mex. 174/C3
Los Molinos, Ca, US 146/B3
Los Monos, Arg. 190/C5
Los Mosquitos (gulf), Pan. 177/F4
Los Muermos, Chile 190/B4
Los Navalmorales, Sp. 46/C3
Los Navalucillos, Sp. 46/C3
Los Nevados, PN, Col. 183/K8
Los Olmos (cr.), Tx, US 151/E4
Los Órganos, Peru 184/A2
Los Padres National Forest, Ca, US 166/A1
Los Palacios y Villafranca, Sp. 46/C4
Los Palos, ETim. 128/B2
Los Pingüinos, PN, Chile 191/C7
Los Pinos (riv.), Co, US 152/A2
Los Planes, Mex. 174/C3
Los Ranchos de Albuquerque, NM, US 149/J3
Los Reyes, Mex. 175/R10
Los Reyes de Salgado, Mex. 174/E5
Los Riecillos, Chile 190/N8
Los Ríos (prov.), Ecu. 184/B1
Los Roques (isls.), Ven. 173/H5
Los Santos, Pan. 180/A3
Los Santos de Maimona, Sp. 46/B3
Los Sauces, Chile 190/B3
Los Tamariscos, Arg. 190/C5
Los Taques, Ven. 180/D2
Los Telares, Arg. 188/D4
Los Teques, Ven. 183/N7
Los Testigos (isls.), Ven. 181/F2
Los Vientos, Chile 188/B3
Los Vilos, Chile 190/C1
Los Yébenes, Sp. 46/D3
Losai Nat'l Rsv., Kenya 119/B1
Losheim, Ger. 55/F4
Loshkarëvka, Ukr. 73/H4
Loshnitsa, Bela. 41/N4
Łosice, Pol. 43/M2
Losinj (isl.), Cro. 67/G1
Lošinj (isl.), Cro. 45/L4
Loskiria (peak), Kenya 119/B1
Losne, Fr. 60/B3
Losone, Swi. 61/E5
Lossburg, Ger. 61/E1
Losser, Neth. 52/E4
Lossie (riv.), Sc, UK 33/C1
Lossiemouth, Sc, UK 33/C1
Lössnitz, Ger. 59/F1
Lossoganeu (hill), Tanz. 119/B3
Lost (lake), La, US 164/C3
Lost (riv.), Or, US 146/C2
Lost Creek (res.), Or, US 146/B2
Lost Creek, WV, US 163/G1
Lost Creek, Ky, US 163/F2
Lost Draw (riv.), Tx, US 150/C1
Lost Hills, Ca, US 148/C3
Lost Mountain, Ga, US 163/L7
Lost River (range), Id, US 147/G1
Lost River Caverns, Pa, US 168/C2
Lost Springs, Ks, US 153/F1
Lostallo, Swi. 61/F5
Lostwithiel, Eng, UK 36/B6
Lostwood NWR, ND, US 156/C3
Losynivka, Ukr. 72/F2
Lot (riv.), Fr. 66/D1
Lota, Chile 190/B3
Løten, Nor. 40/D1
Lotfābād, Iran 101/G1
Lothaa, Ugan. 119/A1
Lotikipi (plain), Kenya 117/G4
Loto, D.R. Congo 121/E3
Lotogipi (swamp), Kenya 117/G4
Lotoi (riv.), D.R. Congo 120/D3
Lotsane (riv.), Bots. 123/E4
Lott, Tx, US 151/F2
Lotte, Ger. 53/E4
Lotuke (peak), Sudan 117/G4
Lotumbe, D.R. Congo 120/D3
Lou (riv.), China 80/B5
Louang Namtha, Laos 86/D4
Louangphrabang, Laos 86/D5
Louann, Ar, US 153/H4
Loubomo, Congo 120/C4
Loudéac, Fr. 56/C4
Loudi, China 87/F3
Loudima, Congo 120/C4
Loudon, Tn, US 162/E3
Loudonville, NY, US 161/K3
Loudonville, Oh, US 160/E4
Loudun, Fr. 44/D3
Loudwater, Eng, UK 30/A2
Loué, Fr. 57/E4
Loue (riv.), Fr. 44/F3
Louessé (riv.), Congo 120/C3
Louet (riv.), Fr. 57/E6
Loufan, China 80/B3
Louga, Sen. 114/A3
Louga (pol.reg.), Sen. 114/B3
Lough Foyle (lake), UK 34/A1
Loughborough, Eng, UK 37/E1
Loughbrickland, NI, UK 34/B3
Lougheed (isl.), Nun, Can. 141/R7
Loughgall, NI, UK 34/B3
Loughman, Fl, US 164/M7
Loughrea, Ire. 32/B3
Loughton, Eng, UK 30/D2
Louhans, Fr. 60/B4
Louingi, Congo 120/C4
Louis Botha (Durban) (int'l arpt.), SAfr. 125/E3
Louis Creek, BC, Can. 144/D2
Louis Trichardt, SAfr. 123/F4
Louisa (lake), Fl, US 164/M7
Louisa, Ky, US 163/F1
Louisa, Va, US 163/H1
Louisbourg, NS, Can. 159/H3
Louisburg, Ks, US 153/G1
Louisburg, NC, US 163/H2
Louisdale, NS, Can. 159/G3
Louise, Tx, US 151/F3
Louiseville, Qu, Can. 161/K1
Louisiade (arch.), PNG 136/E6
Louisiana (pt.), La, US 151/H3
Louisiana (state), US 143/H5
Louisiana, Mo, US 155/J4
Louisville, Al, US 165/F2
Louisville, Co, US 154/B4
Louisville, Ga, US 163/F4
Louisville, Il, US 162/C1
Louisville, Ky, US 162/E1
Louisville, Ms, US 162/C4
Louisville, Ne, US 155/F3
Louisville, Oh, US 160/F4
Loukhi, Rus. 68/G2
Loukkos (riv.), Mor. 112/A2
Loukouo, Congo 120/C3
Loulé, Port. 46/A4
Loum, Camr. 120/B1
Louny, Czh. 59/G2
Loup (riv.), Fr. 64/C5
Loup (riv.), Ne, US 154/E3
Loup City, Ne, US 154/E3
Lourches, Fr. 54/C3
Lourdes, Nf, Can. 159/H1
Lourdes, Fr. 44/C5
Lourdes/Tarbes (int'l arpt.), Fr. 44/D5
Loures, Port. 47/P10
Louriçal, Port. 46/A2
Lourinhã, Port. 46/A3
Loury, Fr. 57/H4
Lousã, Port. 46/A2
Lousa, Port. 47/Q10
Loushan (pass), China 87/E2
Loutété, Congo 120/C4
Louth, Ire. 34/B4
Louth, Eng, UK 35/H5
Louth (co.), Ire. 34/B4
Louth, Austl. 132/C1
Loutrá Aidhipsoú, Gre. 49/H3
Loutrákion, Gre. 49/H4
Louts (riv.), Fr. 47/E1
Loútsa, Gre. 49/P9
Louvain (Leuven), Belg. 55/D2
Louvale, Ga, US 162/E4
Louveira, Braz. 187/K8
Louverné, Fr. 57/E4
Louviers, Fr. 57/G2
Louviers, Co, US 154/B4
Louvigné-de-Bais, Fr. 56/D4
Louvigné-du-Désert, Fr. 57/D4
Louvres, Fr. 30/K4
Louvroil, Fr. 54/C3
Lovaart (riv.), Belg. 54/B1
Lovat' (riv.), Rus. 68/F4
Lovat' (riv.), Bela.,Rus. 41/P3
Lovćen NP, Serb. 49/F1
Lovćenac, Serb. 50/D3
Love Point, Md, US 168/B5
Lovech (prov.), Bul. 49/J1
Lovech, Bul. 51/G4
Lovejoy, Ga, US 163/M8
Lovelady, Tx, US 151/G2
Loveland, Co, US 154/B3
Lovell, Wy, US 147/J1
Lovelock, Nv, US 146/D3
Lovere, It. 62/D2
Loverna, Sk, Can. 145/K2
Loves Park, Il, US 155/K2
Lovilia, Ia, US 155/H3
Loving, NM, US 150/B1
Lovingston, Va, US 163/H2
Lovington, NM, US 152/C4
Lovios, Sp. 46/A2
Lövö, Hun. 50/C2
Lovosice, Czh. 59/H1
Lovozero (lake), Rus. 68/G2
Lóvua, Ang. 120/E4
Low (des.), Or, US 146/C2
Low (cape), Nun, Can. 141/H2
Lowa (riv.), D.R. Congo 107/E5
Lowdham, Eng, UK 35/H6
Lowe, Ks, US 152/D1
Lowe Farm, Mb, Can. 156/F3
Lowell, Ar, US 153/G2
Lowell, In, US 160/C4
Lowell, Oh, US 160/F5
Lowell (lake), Id, US 146/E2
Lowell, Or, US 146/B2
Lowell, Id, US 144/G4
Lowell Observatory, Az, US 149/G3
Löwen (riv.), Namb. 124/B2
Löwenstein, Ger. 58/C4
Lower (falls), Mi, US 160/D1
Lower (dam), Wa, US 167/D3
Lower (lake), Ca, US 146/C3
Lower (falls), Wy, US 147/H1
Lower (bay), NJ, US 168/D2
Lower Arrow (lake), BC, Can. 144/E3
Lower Brailes, Eng, UK 37/E2
Lower Brule Ind. Res., SD, US 154/D1
Lower Engadine (valley), Swi. 61/G4
Lower Ganges (canal), India 96/B2
Lower Glenelg NP, Austl. 132/B3
Lower Granite (gorge), Az, US 149/E2
Lower Heyford, Eng, UK 37/E3
Lower Hutt, NZ 135/H9
Lower Kalskag, Ak, US 171/F3
Lower Klamath (lake), Ca, US 146/C3
Lower Klamath NWR, Or, US 146/C2
Lower Mesa (falls), Id, US 147/H1
Lower Monumental (dam), Wa, US 144/E4
Lower Nazeing, Eng, UK 30/D1
Lower Otay (lake), Ca, US 166/D5
Lower Peach Tree, Al, US 164/E2
Lower Red (lake), Mn, US 157/G4
Lower Rhine (riv.), Neth. 52/C5
Lower Rouge (riv.), Mi, US 167/E7
Lower Sioux Ind. Res., Mn, US 155/G1
Lower Stoke, Eng, UK 30/E2
Lower Suwannee Nat'l Wild. Ref., Fl, US 165/G3
Lower Trajan's Wall (wall), Mol.,Ukr. 51/J3
Lower Tunguska (riv.), Rus. 77/J3
Lower Wedgeport, NS, Can. 158/E4
Lower West Pubnico, NS, Can. 158/E4
Lower Zambezi NP, Zam. 123/F2
Lowery (lake), Fl, US 164/M7
Lowestoft, Eng, UK 37/H2
Lowick, Eng, UK 33/E5
Łowicz, Pol. 43/K2
Lowman, Id, US 146/F1
Lowry City, Mo, US 153/H1
Lowther (hills), Sc, UK 33/C6
Lowville, NY, US 161/J3
Lowville, On, Can. 160/T9
Loxahatchee, Fl, US 164/P9
Loxahatchee National Wildlife Refuge, Fl, US 165/H4
Loxahatchee Slough (swamp), Fl, US 164/P9
Loxstedt, Ger. 53/F2
Loxton, Austl. 131/J5
Loxton, SAfr. 124/C3
Loxton North, Austl. 131/J5
Loya, Tanz. 119/A3
Loyal, Wi, US 155/J1
Loyall, Ky, US 163/F2
Loyalton, Ca, US 146/C4
Loyalton, Pa, US 168/B2
Loyalty (isls.), NCal. 136/F7
Loyettes, Fr. 60/B6
Loyev, Bela. 72/F2
Loyne (lake), Sc, UK 33/A2
Loyno, Rus. 69/M4
Loyoro, Ugan. 117/G5
Loysville, Pa, US 168/A3
Loznica, Serb. 50/D3

Loznit – Magee

Loznitsa, Bul. 51/H4
Lozova, Ukr. 73/J3
Lozovik, Serb. 50/E3
Lozym, Rus. 69/L3
Lü (isl.), Tai. 87/J4
Lu (riv.), China 80/C5
Lu (mtn.), China 80/D3
Lu (peak), China 87/G2
Lu Xian, China 93/J2
Lua (riv.), Congo 116/C5
Lua (riv.), D.R. Congo 120/D2
Lua Dekere (riv.), D.R. Congo 120/D2
Luabo, Moz. 123/H3
Luacano, Ang. 122/D1
Luachimo, Ang. 121/E4
Luachimo (riv.), Ang. 121/E5
Luaco, Ang. 121/E4
Luaha-Sibuha, Indo. 89/B3
Luala (riv.), Moz. 123/H3
Lualaba (riv.), D.R. Congo 107/E5
Luale, D.R. Congo 121/E2
Luali, D.R. Congo 120/C4
Luama (riv.), D.R. Congo 121/F4
Luambe NP, Zam. 123/G2
Luampa, Zam. 122/E2
Luampa (riv.), Zam. 122/E2
Luan (riv.), China 75/M5
Lu'an, China 80/D5
Luan Xian, China 80/D3
Luancheng, China 87/F4
Luanchuan, China 80/B4
Luanco, Sp. 46/C1
Luanda (prov.), Ang. 120/C5
Luanda, Kenya 119/A1
Luanda (cap.), Ang. 120/C5
Luando (riv.), Ang. 120/D5
Luando, Ang. 122/C1
Luando, Rsv. Nat. do, Ang. 120/D5
Luang (peak), Thai. 94/B4
Luang (lag.), Malay. 93/H6
Luangue (riv.), Ang. 120/D4
Luangue, Ang. 120/D5
Luanguinga (riv.), Ang. 122/D2
Luangwa (riv.), Zam. 121/G5
Luanhaizi, China 78/C5
Luano (int'l arpt.), D.R. Congo 123/E1
Luanping, China 80/D2
Luanshya, Zam. 123/F2
Luao (riv.), D.R. Congo 121/E5
Luao, Ang. 121/E5
Luapula (riv.), Zam. 121/G5
Luapula (prov.), Zam. 121/G5
Luarca, Sp. 46/B1
Luashi, D.R. Congo 121/E5
Luatize (riv.), Moz. 123/F2
Luau (riv.), Ang. 121/E5
Luba, EqG. 120/B2
Lubaantun (ruin), Belz. 176/D2
Lubaczów, Pol. 43/M3
Lubalo, Ang. 120/D5
Lubań, Pol. 43/H3
Lubāna, Lat. 41/M3
Lubang (isl.), Phil. 88/B2
Lubang, Phil. 88/C2
Lubango, D.R. Congo 121/F3
Lubango, Ang. 122/B2
Lubansenshi (riv.), Zam. 121/G5
Lubao, D.R. Congo 121/F4
Lubartów, Pol. 43/M3
Lubawa, Pol. 43/K2
Lübbecke, Ger. 53/F4
Lubbeek, Belg. 55/D2
Lubbock, Tx, US 152/D4
Lubeck, WV, US 163/G1
Lubefu (riv.), D.R. Congo 121/E4
Lubefu, D.R. Congo 121/F4
Lubelska (uplands), Pol. 43/M3
Lubelskie (prov.), Pol. 43/M3
Lubenka, Kaz. 71/K2
Lubero, D.R. Congo 121/G3
Lubero (riv.), D.R. Congo 121/G3
Lubéron, Montagne de (mts.), Fr. 64/B5
Lubi (riv.), D.R. Congo 121/E4
Lubień Kujawski, Pol. 43/K2
Lubika, D.R. Congo 121/G4
Lubilash (riv.), D.R. Congo 121/E5
Lubin, Pol. 43/J3
Lublin, Pol. 43/M3
Lubliniec, Pol. 43/K3
Lubmin, Ger. 40/E4
Lubnaig (lake), Sc, UK 33/B4
Lubny, Ukr. 73/G2
Luboń, Pol. 43/J2
Lubongola, D.R. Congo 121/F3
Lubrín, Sp. 46/D4
Lubsko, Pol. 43/H3
Lubuagan, Phil. 88/C1
Lububu, D.R. Congo 121/F4
Lubudi, D.R. Congo 121/F5
Lubudi (riv.), D.R. Congo 121/E4
Lubue (riv.), D.R. Congo 120/D4
Lubuklinggau, Indo. 89/C3
Lubukpakam, Indo. 89/B2
Lubuksikaping, Indo. 89/C2
Lubumbashi, D.R. Congo 123/E1
Lubunda, D.R. Congo 121/F4
Lubunza, D.R. Congo 121/E4
Lubuskie (prov.), Pol. 43/H2
Lubutu, D.R. Congo 121/F3
Lubwe, Zam. 121/G5
Luc An Chau, Viet. 94/D1
Luc-en-Diois, Fr. 64/B3
Luc-sur-Mer, Fr. 57/E2
Lucala, Ang. 120/C5
Lucala (riv.), Ang. 120/C5
Lucan, Ire. 34/B5
Lucan, On, Can. 160/F3
Lucania (mt.), Yk, Can. 171/K3
Lücaoshan, China 78/D4
Lucapa, Ang. 121/E5
Lucas, Ks, US 153/E1
Lucas, Tx, US 150/L6
Lucas González, Arg. 191/J10
Lucasville, Oh, US 163/F1
Lucca (prov.), It. 62/D5
Lucca, It. 62/D6
Lucciana, Fr. 48/A1
Lucé, Fr. 57/G4
Luce (bay), Sc, UK 34/D2
Luce Bayou (riv.), Tx, US 151/M8
Lucedale, Ms, US 164/D2
Lucélia, Braz. 189/G2
Lucena, Sp. 46/C4
Lucena, Phil. 88/C2
Lucena del Cid, Sp. 47/E2
Lučenec, Slvk. 43/K4
Lucens, Swi. 60/C4
Lucerna, Peru 184/D4
Lucerne (lake), Ca, US 166/C1
Lucerne, Wy, US 147/J2
Lucerne, Wa, US 144/D3
Lucerne (Luzern), Swi. 45/H3
Lucerne (Vierwaldstättersee) (lake), Swi. 61/E3
Lucero (lake), NM, US 152/A4
Lucero (mesa), NM, US 149/J3
Luchang, China 86/D3
Luché-Pringé, Fr. 57/F3
Luchegorsk, Rus. 79/L2
Lucheng, China 80/C3
Lucheng, China 87/E3
Lucheringo (riv.), Moz. 123/G2
Lüchow, Ger. 42/F2
Luchuan, China 93/K3
Lüchun, China 86/D4
Lucia, Ca, US 148/B2
Lucie (riv.), Sur. 182/B2
Lucile, Ga, US 165/F2
Lucindale, Austl. 132/B3
Lucira, Ang. 122/B2
Luciras (bay), Ang. 122/B2
Lucito, It. 65/D4
Luck, Wi, US 157/H5
Luckeesarai, India 97/F3
Luckenwalde, Ger. 43/G2
Lucknow, On, Can. 160/F3
Lucknow, India 96/C2
Lucky, La, US 153/H4
Lucky Lake, Sk, Can. 145/L2
Lucky Peak (dam), Id, US 146/E2
Luco dei Marsi, It. 65/C4
Lucomagno, Passo del (pass), Swi. 61/E4
Lücongpo, China 78/G5
Lucrecia (cape), Cuba 177/H1
Lucrezia, It. 63/F6
Lucunga, Ang. 120/C4
Lucusse, Ang. 122/D2
Lucy Creek, Austl. 131/H2
Ludden, ND, US 156/E4
Ludell, Ks, US 154/D4
Lüdenscheid, Ger. 53/E6
Lüderitz, Namb. 124/A2
Ludesar, India 98/C5
Ludesch, Aus. 61/F3
Ludgershall, Eng, UK 37/E4
Ludhiāna, India 98/C4
Ludian, China 93/H2
Luding, China 86/D2
Ludinghausen, Ger. 53/E5
Ludington, Mi, US 160/C3
Ludlow, SD, US 156/C5
Ludlow, Pa, US 161/G4
Ludlow, Vt, US 161/K3
Ludlow, Ca, US 148/D3
Ludlow, Eng, UK 36/D2
Ludogorie (reg.), Bul. 51/H4
Ludowici, Ga, US 165/H2
Luduş, Rom. 51/G2
Ludvika, Swe. 40/F1
Ludwigs (canal), Ger. 59/E4
Ludwigsburg, Ger. 58/C5
Ludwigsfelde, Ger. 42/Q7
Ludwigshafen, Ger. 61/F2
Ludwigshafen, Ger. 58/B4
Ludwigslust, Ger. 42/F2
Ludwigsstadt, Ger. 59/E2
Ludza, Lat. 41/M3
Lue, Austl. 133/D1
Luebo, D.R. Congo 121/E4
Lueders, Tx, US 150/E1
Lueki, D.R. Congo 121/F3
Luemba (riv.), Ang. 121/E5
Luemba, D.R. Congo 121/G3
Luembe (riv.), Ang. 122/D1
Luembi (riv.), D.R. Congo 121/F4
Luena, D.R. Congo 121/F5
Luena, Ang. 122/C1
Luena (riv.), Zam. 122/D2
Luena (flats), Zam. 122/D2
Luengue (riv.), Ang. 122/D3
Luenha (riv.), Moz. 123/G3
Lueta (riv.), D.R. Congo 121/E4
Lüeyang, China 78/F5
Lufa, PNG 129/G1
Lufeng, China 87/G4
Lufico, Ang. 120/C4
Lufira (riv.), D.R. Congo 121/F5
Lufkin, Tx, US 150/G2
Lufu, D.R. Congo 120/C4
Lufupa (riv.), Zam. 122/E2
Luga, D.R. Congo 121/G2
Luga, Rus. 41/N2
Luga (bay), Rus. 41/N2
Luga (riv.), Rus. 41/N2
Lugagnano, It. 63/D3
Lugagnano Val d'Arda, It. 62/C4
Lugano (lake), It. 61/E6
Lugano, Swi. 61/E6
Luganville, Van. 136/F6
Lugards (falls), Kenya 119/B2
Lugavčina, Serb. 50/E3
Lugazi, Ugan. 121/H2
Lügde, Ger. 53/G5
Lugela, Moz. 123/H3
Lugenda (riv.), Moz. 123/H2
Lugg (riv.), Eng, UK 36/D2
Lugg (riv.), Wal, UK 36/C2
Lugnaquillia (peak), Ire. 34/B6
Lugo, It. 63/E5
Lugo, Sp. 46/B1
Lugo di Vicenza, It. 63/E2
Lugoff, SC, US 163/G3
Lugogo (riv.), Ugan. 121/H2
Lugoj, Rom. 50/E3
Lugovoy, Kaz. 99/B3
Lugovskoye, Rus. 71/H2
Lugrin, Fr. 60/C5
Lugu, China 86/D2
Lugulu (riv.), D.R. Congo 121/F3
Lugunga (peak), Tanz. 119/B3
Luguruka, Tanz. 119/B4
Luhans'k (int'l arpt.), Ukr. 73/K3
Luhans'k, Ukr. 73/K3
Luhans'ka Oblast, Ukr. 70/F2
Lühe (riv.), Ger. 53/H2
Luhe (riv.), Ger. 59/F3
Luhe, China 80/D4
Luhe-Wildenau, Ger. 59/F3
Luhit (riv.), India 86/C3
Luhombero (peak), Tanz. 119/B3
Luhongshi, China 87/F3
Luhtikylä, Fin. 39/F4
Luhumbo, Tanz. 119/A2
Luhuo, China 86/D2
Luhyny, Ukr. 72/E2
Lui (riv.), Zam. 122/D2
Luia, Ang. 121/E5
Luia (riv.), Moz. 123/G2
Luia (riv.), Moz. 122/D2
Luiana, Ang. 122/D3
Luiana (riv.), Ang. 122/D3
Luichart (lake), Sc, UK 33/B1
Luidaogou, China 81/D2
Luie (riv.), D.R. Congo 120/D4
Luigi Ridolfi (arpt.), It. 63/F5
Luilaka (riv.), D.R. Congo 121/E3
Luilu (riv.), D.R. Congo 121/E4
Luino, It. 61/E6
Luis B. Sánchez, Mex. 174/B1
Luís Correia, Braz. 183/F3
Luís Domingues, Braz. 183/E3
Luis Munoz (int'l arpt.), PR 173/M8
Luisant, Fr. 57/G4
Luiza, D.R. Congo 121/E4
Luján, Arg. 191/J11
Luján, Arg. 188/C5
Lujiang, China 80/D5
Lukácsháza, Hun. 50/C2
Lukala (riv.), D.R. Congo 120/D4
Lukanga (swamp), Zam. 123/E2
Lukavac, Bosn. 50/D3
Luke (A.F.B.), Az, US 149/F4
Luke (mt.), Austl. 130/C3
Lukenie (riv.), D.R. Congo 120/D3
Lukeville, Az, US 149/F5
Lukhovitsy, Rus. 68/H5
Lŭki, Bul. 49/J2
Luki, D.R. Congo 120/C4
Lukolela, D.R. Congo 120/D3
Lukolela, D.R. Congo 121/F4
Lukoupu, China 87/G2
Lukovit, Bul. 51/G4
Łuków, Pol. 43/M3
Lukoyanov, Rus. 69/K5
Lukuga (riv.), D.R. Congo 121/F4
Lukula, D.R. Congo 120/C4
Lukula (riv.), D.R. Congo 120/C4
Lukulu, Zam. 122/D2
Lukulu (riv.), Zam. 121/G5
Lukunor (isl.), Micr. 136/E4
Lukusashi (riv.), Zam. 123/F2
Lukusuzi NP, Zam. 123/G2
Lukwasa, India 96/A3
Lukwesa, Zam. 121/G5
Luleå, Swe. 68/D2
Luleälven (riv.), Swe. 38/G2
Lüleburgaz, Turk. 51/H5
Lules, Arg. 188/C3
Luliang, China 93/H2
Luliāni, Pak. 98/C4
Lulimba, D.R. Congo 121/G4
Luling (pass), China 80/B4
Luling, Tx, US 150/F3
Lulong, China 80/D3
Lulonga, D.R. Congo 120/D2
Lulonga (riv.), D.R. Congo 107/E4
Lulsgate (int'l arpt.), Eng, UK 36/D4
Lulua (riv.), D.R. Congo 107/E5
Luluba, Sudan 117/F4
Lumai, Ang. 122/D2
Lumajang, Indo. 89/F5
Lumajangdong (lake), China 99/D5
Lumangwe (falls), Zam. 121/G5
Lumbala Kaquengue, Ang. 122/D2
Lumbala N'guimbo, Ang. 122/D2
Lumbe (riv.), Zam. 122/E3
Lumber (riv.), SC, US 163/H3
Lumber City, Ga, US 165/G2
Lumberton, Ms, US 164/D2
Lumberton, NC, US 163/H3
Lumberton, NJ, US 168/D4
Lumberton, NM, US 149/J2
Lumberton, Tx, US 151/G2
Lumbini (zone), Nepal 96/D2
Lumbis, Indo. 88/B4
Lumbo, Moz. 123/J2
Lumbovka, Rus. 68/J2
Lumbrales, Sp. 46/B2
Lumbrein, Swi. 61/F4
Lumbres, Fr. 54/B2
Lumby, BC, Can. 144/E2
Lumding, India 86/B3
Lumeje, Ang. 122/D1
Lumigny-Nesles-Ormeaux, Fr. 30/L5
Luminárias, Braz. 187/M6
Lummen, Belg. 55/E2
Lummi Ind. Res., Wa, US 144/C3
Lumparland, Fin. 41/J1
Lumphat, Camb. 94/D3
Lumpkin, Ga, US 165/F1
Lumsden, Sk, Can. 156/B2
Lumsden, Sc, UK 33/D2
Lumsden, NZ 135/B4
Lumu, China 80/L8
Lumut, Malay. 89/C1
Lumut, Indo. 89/B2
Lumut (cape), Indo. 89/D3
Lumut, Malay. 89/C1
Luna (mtn.), Ca, US 166/C2
Luna, NM, US 149/H4
Luna, Phil. 88/C1
Lunache, Ang. 122/D2
Lunahuaná, Peru 184/B4
Lunan (mts.), China 86/D3
Lunar Crater, Nv, US 146/F4
Lunay, Fr. 57/F5
Luncarty, Sc, UK 33/C4
Lund, Swe. 40/E4
Lund, Nv, US 147/F4
Lund, Ut, US 149/F1
Lund, BC, Can. 144/B3
Lunda, Swe. 39/B1
Lunda Norte (prov.), Ang. 120/D5
Lunda Sul (prov.), Ang. 121/E5
Lundar, Mb, Can. 156/E2
Lundazi, Zam. 123/G2
Lundbreck, Ab, Can. 145/G3
Lundby, Den. 40/D4
Lunde, Nor. 40/C2
Lundell, Ar, US 162/B3
Lundi (riv.), Zim. 123/F3
Lundu, Zam. 121/H5
Lundy (isl.), Eng, UK 36/B4
Lune (riv.), Eng, UK 35/F2
Lune (riv.), Eng, UK 35/F2
Lune (riv.), Ger. 53/F2
Lüneburg, Ger. 53/H2
Lüneburger Heide (reg.), Ger. 42/F2
Lunel, Fr. 44/F5
Lünen, Ger. 53/E5
Lunenburg, NS, Can. 158/E3
Lunenburg, Vt, US 161/L2
Lunenburg, Va, US 163/H2
Lunestedt, Ger. 53/F2
Lunéville, Fr. 45/G2
Lung (riv.), Ire. 32/B2
Lung Kwu Chau (isl.), China 87/K7
Lunga (riv.), Zam. 123/E2
Lunga, West (riv.), Zam. 121/F5
Lunga-Lunga, Kenya 119/B3
Lungdo, China 99/D5
Lungern, Swi. 60/E4
Lungi, SLeo. 114/B4
Lungi (Freetown) (int'l arpt.), SLeo. 114/B4
Lunglei, India 93/F3
Lungsang, China 99/E6
Lungtian, India 86/B4
Lungue-Bungo (riv.), Ang. 122/C2
Lungwebungu (riv.), Zam. 122/D2
Luni (riv.), India 92/B3
Luning, Nv, US 146/D4
Lunino, Rus. 71/H1
Luninyets, Bela. 70/C1
Lunita, La, US 150/H2
Lunkinjärvi (lake), Fin. 39/D4
Lünne, Ger. 53/E4
Luntai, China 99/D3
Lunzu, Malw. 123/G2
Luo (riv.), China 78/F4
Luobei, China 79/L2
Luobuzhuang, China 99/E4
Luocheng, China 87/F3
Luodian, China 87/E3
Luoding, China 87/F4
Luofu (peak), China 87/G4
Luohe, China 80/C4
Luojing, China 93/K3
Luoma (lake), China 80/D4
Luonan, China 87/F5
Luongo (riv.), Zam. 121/G5
Luoning, China 80/B4
Luoping, China 86/E3
Luoqiao, China 87/H3
Luoqing (riv.), China 87/F3
Luoshan, China 80/C4
Luoshuikan, China 87/F2
Luotian, China 87/G2
Luoxu, China 87/F4
Luoyang, China 87/F3
Luoyang, China 80/C4
Luoyukou, China 80/B3
Luozi, D.R. Congo 120/C4
Lupa Market, Tanz. 119/A4
Lupane, Zim. 123/E3
Lupanshui, China 86/E3
Lupeni, Rom. 51/F3
Lupire, Ang. 122/C2
Lupiro, Tanz. 119/B4
Lupon, Phil. 88/D4
Luputa, D.R. Congo 121/E4
Luqa (int'l arpt.), Malta 48/L7
Luqu, China 78/E5
Luquan, China 86/D3
Luquembo, Ang. 120/D5
Lūrah (riv.), Afg. 101/J2
Luraville, Fl, US 165/G2
Luray, Fr. 57/G3
Luray, Ks, US 154/E4
Luray, Va, US 163/H1
Lure, Fr. 60/C2
Lure, Montagne de (mts.), Fr. 64/B4
Lurgan, NI, UK 34/B3
Luri, Fr. 48/A1
Luribay, Bol. 188/C1
Lurín, Peru 184/B4
Lúrio, Moz. 123/J2
Lúrio (riv.), Moz. 107/F6
Lurnfeld, Aus. 45/K3
Lurøy, Nor. 38/E2
Lurton, Ar, US 153/H3
Lusahunga, Tanz. 121/G3
Lusaka (cap.), Zam. 123/F2
Lusaka (int'l arpt.), Zam. 123/F2
Lusaka (prov.), Zam. 123/F2
Lusamba, D.R. Congo 121/F4
Lusambo, D.R. Congo 121/E4
Lusangi, D.R. Congo 121/F4
Luseland, Sk, Can. 145/K1
Lusemfwa (riv.), Zam. 123/F2
Lusen (peak), Ger. 59/G5
Lusenga NP, Zam. 121/G5
Lush (mt.), Austl. 128/B4
Lushan, China 80/C4
Lushi, China 80/B4
Lushiko (riv.), D.R. Congo 120/D4
Lushnjë, Alb. 49/F2
Lushoto, Tanz. 119/B3
Lushui, China 86/C3
Lüshun, China 80/E3
Lusignan, Fr. 44/D3
Lusk, Ire. 34/B4
Lusk, Wy, US 154/B2
Luso, Ang. 122/B2
Luss, Sc, UK 33/B4
Lustenau, Aus. 61/F3
Lustre, Mt, US 145/M3
Lutang, China 87/G3
Lutembo (riv.), Ang. 122/D2
Luther (pass), Ca, US 148/B1
Luther, Mi, US 160/D2
Luther, Tx, US 150/D1
Luthern, Swi. 60/D3
Luthersville, Ga, US 162/E4
Lutherville, Md, US 168/B5
Luthle, Bots. 122/D4
Lütjehorn (isl.), Ger. 52/D1
Lütjenburg, Ger. 40/D4
Luton, Eng, UK 37/F3
Luton (co.), Eng, UK 37/F3
Luton (int'l arpt.), Eng, UK 37/F3
Lutong, Malay. 90/D3
Lutry, Swi. 60/C5
Łutselk'e, NW, Can. 140/E2
Lutsen, Mn, US 157/J4
Lutshi, D.R. Congo 121/F4
Lutshima, D.R. Congo 120/D4
Lutshima (riv.), D.R. Congo 120/D4
Luts'k, Ukr. 72/C2
Lutter (riv.), Ger. 53/F5
Lutterbach, Fr. 60/D2
Lutterworth, Eng, UK 35/G6
Lutuhyne, Ukr. 73/K3
Lutz (riv.), Aus. 61/F3
Lutz, Fl, US 164/L7
Lützow-Holm (bay), Ant. 192/C
Luumäki, Fin. 41/M1
Luuq, Som. 118/B5
Luvalo, Ang. 120/D5
Luverne, Al, US 165/E2
Luverne, Mn, US 155/F2
Luvo, Ang. 120/C4
Luvozero, Rus. 68/F2
Luvu, D.R. Congo 120/C4
Luvua (riv.), D.R. Congo 121/G4
Luwegu (riv.), Tanz. 119/B4
Luwembe, Zam. 123/F2
Luwero, Ugan. 121/H2
Luwingu, Zam. 121/G5
Lux, Fr. 60/A4
Luxapallila (cr.), Al, US 162/C4
Luxembourg (ctry.) 55/E4
Luxembourg (cap.), Lux. 55/F4
Luxembourg (prov.), Belg 55/E4
Luxemburg, Wi, US 160/C2
Luxeuil-les-Bains, Fr. 60/C2
Luxi, China 87/F2
Luxi, China 86/C3
Luxi, China 86/D3
Luxico (riv.), Ang. 120/D4
Luxikou, China 87/G2
Luxomni, Ga, US 163/M7
Luxor (int'l arpt.), Egypt 135/G3
Luxora, Ar, US 162/C3
Luxu, China 87/F4
Luxu, China 80/L8
Luy (riv.), Fr. 47/E1
Lüyang, China 81/A2
Luye (riv.), Fr. 64/C3
Luyi, China 80/C4
Luynes, Fr. 57/F6
Luz (coast), Port.,Sp. 46/B4
Luz, Braz. 186/D3
Luza (riv.), Rus. 69/L3
Luza, Rus. 69/K3
Luzarches, Fr. 30/K4
Luzein, Swi. 61/F4
Luzern, Swi. 61/E3
Luzern (canton), Swi. 60/E3
Luzern (Lucerne), Swi. 45/H3
Luzerne (co.), Pa, US 168/B1
Luzhai, China 93/J3
Luzhi, China 86/E3
Lüzhi (riv.), China 86/D3
Luzhou, China 86/E2
Luziânia, Braz. 186/D3
Luzilândia, Braz. 183/F3
Luzinga, Ugan. 119/A1
Lužnice (riv.), Czh. 43/H4
Luzon (isl.), Phil. 114/C1
Luzon (str.), Phil. 136/A3
Lužuice (riv.), Czh. 45/L2
Luzzara, It. 63/D4
Luzzi, It. 48/E3
L'viv, Ukr. 72/C3
L'vivs'ka Oblast, Ukr. 72/B2
Lwala (peak), Ugan. 117/G5
Lwena Mission, Zam. 121/G5
Lwi (riv.), Myan. 94/C1
Lyady, Rus. 41/N2
Lyakhovichi, Bela. 70/C1
Lyantonde, Ugan. 121/G3
Lyapin (riv.), Rus. 69/P2
Lychett Matravers, Eng, UK 36/D5
Lycksele, Swe. 38/F2
Lycoming (co.), Pa, US 168/A1
Lydd, Eng, UK 37/G5
Lydenburg, SAfr. 123/F5
Lydia, La, US 164/C3
Lydney, Eng, UK 36/D3
Lyell (mt.), BC, Can. 144/F2
Lyell Brown (mt.), Austl. 131/F2
Lyepel', Bela. 41/N4
Lyford, Tx, US 151/F4
Lykens, Pa, US 168/B2
Lyle, Mn, US 155/H2
Lyle, Wa, US 144/D5
Lyles, Tn, US 162/D3
Lyleton, Mb, Can. 156/D3
Lyman, Ms, US 164/D2
Lyman, Wy, US 147/H3
Lyman, Ut, US 149/G1
Lyman, SC, US 163/F3
Lyme (bay), Eng, UK 44/B1
Lyme Regis, Eng, UK 36/D5
Lymington, Eng, UK 37/E5
Lymm, Eng, UK 35/F5
Łyna (riv.), Pol. 43/L1
Lynas (pt.), Wal, UK 34/D5
Lynbrook, NY, US 169/L9
Lynch, Ne, US 154/E2
Lynch, Md, US 168/B5
Lynch Station, Va, US 163/H2
Lynchburg, Mo, US 153/H2
Lynchburg, Ms, US 162/B3
Lynchburg, Oh, US 162/F1
Lynchburg, Tn, US 162/D3
Lynchburg, Va, US 163/H2
Lynches (riv.), SC, US 163/G3
Lynd, Austl. 134/B2
Lynden, Wa, US 144/C3
Lyndhurst, NJ, US 169/J8
Lyndhurst, Austl. 131/H4
Lyndhurst, Eng, UK 37/E5
Lyndhurst, Austl. 133/D1
Lyndon, Austl. 130/B2
Lyndon, Ks, US 153/G1
Lyndon, Vt, US 161/K2
Lyndon B. Johnson (lake), Tx, US 151/E2
Lyndon B. Johnson Nat'l Hist. Park, Tx, US 151/E2
Lyndon B. Johnson Space Center, Tx, US 151/M9
Lyndonville, NY, US 161/G3
Lyne (riv.), Eng, UK 35/F1
Lyness, Sc, UK 31/V14
Lyngby, Den. 39/J7
Lyngdal, Nor. 40/B2
Lynge, Den. 39/J7
Lyngen (inlet), Nor. 38/G1
Lynn, Ar, US 153/J2
Lynn, Ma, US 161/L3
Lynn, Al, US 162/D3
Lynn Haven, Fl, US 165/F2
Lynn Lake, Mb, Can. 140/F3
Lynnwood, Wa, US 144/C4
Lynton, Eng, UK 36/C4
Lyntupy, Bela. 41/M4
Lynwood, Ca, US 166/F8
Lynx (lake), NW, Can. 140/F2
Lyon, Fr. 64/A1
Lyon (Satolas) (int'l arpt.), Fr. 60/B6
Lyon (riv.), Sc, UK 33/B3
Lyon (lake), Sc, UK 33/B3
Lyon (canal), Co, US 152/C1
Lyon, Ms, US 162/B3
Lyon (mtn.), NY, US 161/K2
Lyonne (riv.), Fr. 64/B2
Lyons (riv.), Austl. 130/C3
Lyons, Ga, US 163/F4
Lyons, In, US 162/D1
Lyons, Ks, US 153/E1
Lyons, NY, US 161/H3
Lyons, Wi, US 167/P14
Lyons Falls, NY, US 161/J3
Lyons-la-Forêt, Fr. 57/G2
Lype (hill), Eng, UK 36/C4
Lypovets', Ukr. 72/E3
Lyra (reef), PNG 136/E5
Lys (riv.), It. 62/A1
Lys (riv.), Fr. 44/E1
Lys-lez-Lannoy, Fr. 54/C2
Lysá (peak), Czh. 43/K4
Lysá nad Labem, Czh. 59/H2
Lysaker, Nor. 40/D2
Lysaya (hill), Bela. 41/M4
Lysekil, Swe. 40/D2
Lyseren (lake), Nor. 38/T8
Łysica (peak), Pol. 43/L3
Lysina (peak), Czh. 59/F2
Lysite, Wy, US 147/K2
Lyss, Swi. 60/D3
Lystrup, Den. 40/D3
Lys'va, Rus. 69/N4
Lysychans'k, Ukr. 73/K3
Lysyye Gory, Rus. 71/H2
Lytham Saint Anne's, Eng, UK 35/E4
Lytkarino, Rus. 69/W9
Lytle (cr.), Ca, US 166/C2
Lytle, Tx, US 150/E3
Lytle Creek, Ca, US 166/C2
Lyttelton, NZ 135/C3
Lytton, BC, Can. 144/D2
Lyuban', Bela. 70/D1
Lyubar, Ukr. 72/D3
Lyubech, Ukr. 72/F2
Lyubertsy, Rus. 69/W9
Lyubeshiv, Ukr. 72/C2
Lyubimets, Bul. 51/H5
Lyublino (nbrhd.), Rus. 69/W9
Lyuboml', Ukr. 72/C2
Lyubotyn, Ukr. 73/H3
Lyudinovo, Rus. 70/E1
Lywd (riv.), Wal, UK 36/C3

M

M'Clintock (chan.), Can. 139/G2
M'Sila (wilaya), Alg. 111/F2
M. Aleman (res.), Mex. 172/B4
M.R. Gómez, Presa (dam), Mex. 150/E4
Ma (riv.), Viet. 86/E4
Ma-ubin, Myan. 86/B5
Ma'ād, Jor. 105/D3
Ma'alot-Tarshiha, Isr. 105/C2
Ma'ān (gov.), Jor. 104/E4
Ma'ān, Jor. 104/D4
Maan, Camr. 120/B2
Ma'an, China 80/L9
Maanĭt, Mong. 78/E2
Maanĭt, Mong. 78/F2
Maanselkä (mts.), Fin. 38/H1
Ma'anshan, China 80/D5
Maardu, Est. 41/L2
Maarheeze, Neth. 52/C6
Maarianhamina (Mariehamn), Fin. 41/H1
Ma'arrat an Nu'mān, Syria 104/E2
Maarssen, Neth. 52/C4
Maartensdijk, Neth. 52/C4
Maas (riv.), Belg. 42/C4
Maas (riv.), Neth. 52/C5
Maasbracht, Neth. 55/E1
Maasbree, Neth. 52/D6
Maaseik, Belg. 55/E1
Maasin, Phil. 88/D3
Maassluis, Neth. 52/B5
Maasstroom, SAfr. 123/F4
Maastricht, Neth. 55/E2
Maastricht (int'l arpt.), Neth. 55/E2
Maave, Moz. 123/G4
Ma'ayan Harod NP, Isr. 105/C3
Maba, Indo. 91/G3
Mababe (depr.), Bots. 122/D3
Mabaho (mt.), Phil. 88/D3
Mabalacat, Phil. 88/C2
Mabalane, Moz. 123/G4
Mabank, Tx, US 151/F1
Mabaruma, Guy. 181/G2
Mabating, China 93/G2
Mabechi (riv.), Japan 82/B3
Mabel, Mn, US 155/J2
Maben, Ms, US 162/C4
Mabian, China 93/H2
Mabie, WV, US 163/H1
Mabili (riv.), Congo 120/C2
Mabinay, Phil. 88/C3
Mabini, Phil. 88/D3
Mablethorpe, Eng, UK 35/J5
Mableton, Ga, US 163/L7
Mabopane, SAfr. 124/Q12
Mabote, Moz. 123/G4
Mabou, NS, Can. 159/G2
Mabroûk, Mali 115/E2
Mabton, Wa, US 144/E4
Mabu (peak), Moz. 123/H3
Mabuasehube Game Reserve, Bots. 122/D5
Mabubas, Ang. 120/C5
Mabuki, Tanz. 119/A2
Mabule, Bots. 124/D2
Mac. Robertson Land (phys. reg.), Ant. 192/D
Macá (peak), Chile 190/B5
Macachín, Arg. 190/E3
Macaé, Braz. 187/E4
Macael, Sp. 46/D4
Macaíba, Braz. 183/H4
Macalister (riv.), Austl. 133/C3
Macaloge, Moz. 123/G2
Mação, Port. 46/A3
Macapá, Braz. 182/D2
Macapá (int'l arpt.), Braz. 182/D3
Macará, Ecu. 184/B2
Macaravita, Col. 180/C3
Macareo Santo Niño, Ven. 181/F2
Macari, Peru 184/D4
Macarthur, Austl. 132/B3
Macas, Ecu. 180/B5
Macau, Braz. 183/G4
Macau (dpcy.), China 77/L7
Macau (cap.), Macau 87/G4
Macauley (isl.), NZ 136/G7
Macaya (riv.), Col. 180/C4
Macaya, Pic de (peak), Haiti 177/H2
MacBride (lake), Ia, US 155/J3
Maccagno, It. 61/E5
Maccan, NS, Can. 158/E3
Maccarese, It. 65/B4
Macclenny, Fl, US 165/G2
Macclesfield (canal), Eng, UK 35/F5
Macclesfield, Eng, UK 35/F5
Macdhui (peak), SAfr. 124/D3
Macdiarmid, On, Can. 157/K3
MacDill (A.F.B.), Fl, US 164/K8
MacDonald (lake), Austl. 131/F2
Macdonald (peak), Mt, US 145/H4
Macdonald (lake), Austl. 127/B3
MacDonald (riv.), Austl. 133/E1
MacDonnell Ranges (mts.), Austl. 127/C3
MacDowell (lake), On, Can. 157/H1
MacDowell (riv.), On, Can. 157/H1
Macduff, Sc, UK 33/D1
Maceda, Sp. 46/B1
Macedon, Austl. 133/B3
Macedonía (int'l arpt.), Gre. 49/H2
Macedonia, Ar, US 153/H4
Macedonia (reg.), Gre.,FYROM 67/J2
Maceió, Braz. 187/G1
Maceió (pt.), Braz. 183/G4
Macenta, Gui. 114/C4
Macerata (prov.), It. 65/C1
Maces Bay, NB, Can. 158/D3
Macfarlan, WV, US 163/G1
Macfarlane (lake), Austl. 131/H5
Macgillycuddy's Reeks (mts.), Ire. 32/A6
MacGregor, Mb, Can. 156/E3
Macha, Bol. 188/C1
Machacamarca, Bol. 188/C1
Machache (peak), Les. 124/D3
Machachi, Ecu. 180/B5
Machado (swamp), Col. 177/H4
Machado, Braz. 187/L6
Machadodorp, SAfr. 125/E2
Machaerus (Mukāwir) (ruin), Jor. 105/D5
Machagai, Arg. 188/D3
Machaíla, Moz. 123/G4
Machakos, Kenya 119/B2
Machala, Ecu. 184/B1
Machalí, Chile 190/N9
Machalilla, PN, Ecu. 180/A5
Machang, Malay. 89/C1
Machanga, Moz. 123/G4
Machaquilá (riv.), Guat. 176/D2
Macharetí, Bol. 188/D2
Machattie (lake), Austl. 131/H3
Machaze, Moz. 123/G4
Machecoul, Fr. 44/C3
Macheke, Zim. 123/F3
Machekha, Rus. 73/M2
Machemma (ruin), SAfr. 123/F4
Machen, Wal, UK 36/C3
Macheng, China 80/C5
Machesney Park, Il, US 155/K2
Māchhīwāra, India 98/D4
Machhlīshahr, India 96/D3
Machi, China 78/F5
Machias, NY, US 161/G3
Machichaco (cape), Sp. 44/B5
Machico, Port. 110/A2
Machida, Japan 83/C2
Machili (riv.), Zam. 122/E3
Machilipatnam, India 95/D2
Machiques, Ven. 180/C2
Machobani, Zam. 122/E3
Machovo Jezero (lake), Czh. 59/H1
Machu Picchu (ruin), Peru 184/C4
Machupo (riv.), Bol. 185/E4
Machynlleth, Wal, UK 36/C1
Maciá, Arg. 188/E5
Macia, Moz. 123/G5
Maciel, Arg. 188/D5
Măcin, Rom. 51/J3
Macina (phys. reg.), Mali 114/D3
Macintyre (riv.), Austl. 127/E3
Mack, Co, US 147/J4
Mackay, Austl. 134/C3
Mackay, Id, US 147/G2
Mackay (lake), Austl. 127/B3
MacKenzie (bay), Ant. 192/E
Mackenzie, Austl. 134/C3
Mackenzie (riv.), Can. 139/E3
Mackenzie, BC, Can. 140/D3
Mackenzie (bay), NW,Yk, Can. 171/L2
Mackenzie (riv.), NW, Can. 140/D2
Mackenzie (mts.), Can. 139/D3
Mackenzie King (isl.), NW, Can. 141/R7
Mackin (riv.), BC, Can. 144/C1
Mackinac (str.), Mi, US 160/D2
Mackinac Island, Mi, US 160/D2
Mackinaw (riv.), Il, US 155/K3
Mackinaw City, Mi, US 160/D2
Mackinnon (pass), NZ 135/A4
Mackinnon Road, Kenya 119/B2
Macklin, Sk, Can. 145/K1
Macmillan (riv.), Yk, Can. 171/L3
Macknade, Austl. 134/B2
Macks Creek, Mo, US 153/H2
Macksburg, Oh, US 160/F5
Macksville, Ks, US 152/E2
Macksville, Austl. 132/E1
Macland, Ga, US 163/L7
Maclean, Austl. 132/E1
Maclear, SAfr. 124/E3
Macleay (isl.), Austl. 134/F7
Macleod (lake), Austl. 130/B3
MacNutt, Sk, Can. 156/D2
Macomb (co.), Mi, US 167/G6
Macomb, Il, US 155/J3
Macomer, It. 48/A2
Macomia, Moz. 123/J2
Mâcon, Fr. 44/F3
Macon, Ga, US 162/F4
Macon, Il, US 155/K4
Macon (cr.), Mi, US 167/E7
Macon, Mo, US 155/H4
Macon, Ms, US 162/C4
Macon, North Branch (cr.), Mi, US 167/E7
Maconcourt, Fr. 60/B1
Macondo, Ang. 122/D2
Macondo (riv.), Ang. 122/D2
Macosquin, NI, UK 34/B1
Macotera, Sp. 46/C2
Macoun, Sk, Can. 156/C3
Macoupin (cr.), Il, US 155/J4
Macouria, FrG. 182/C1
Macovane (pt.), Moz. 123/G4
Macquarie (isl.), Austl. 27/S8
Macquarie (lake), Austl. 133/E1
Macquarie (riv.), Austl. 127/D5
Macroom, Ire. 32/B6
Macrorie, Sk, Can. 145/L2
MacTier, On, Can. 161/G2
Macuelizo, Hon. 176/D3
Macuim (riv.), Braz. 185/E2
Macuira, PN, Col. 180/D1
Macuma (riv.), Ecu. 184/B1
Macumba (riv.), Austl. 127/C3
Macungie, Pa, US 168/C2
Macusani, Peru 184/D4
Macuspana, Mex. 176/C2
Macuzari, Presa (dam), Mex. 174/C3
Macy, Ne, US 155/F2
Mad (riv.), Ca, US 146/B3
Mādabā, Jor. 105/D5
Madagali, Nga. 116/B3
Madagascar (ctry.) 125/H8
Madā'in Şālih, SAr. 135/H3
Madama, Niger 108/B4
Madan, Bul. 49/J2
Madanapalle, India 95/C3
Madang (int'l arpt.), PNG 129/G1
Madang (prov.), PNG 129/G1
Madanīyīn (gov.), Tun. 111/H2
Madanīyīn, Tun. 66/F4
Madao, China 78/F5
Madaoua, Niger 115/G3
Madaras, Hun. 50/D2
Mādāri Hāt, India 97/G2
Mādārīpur, Bang. 97/H4
Madarounfa, Niger 115/G3
Madauk, Myan. 86/C5
Madawaska (riv.), On, Can. 161/H2
Madaxmaroodi, Som. 119/D1
Madaya, Myan. 94/B1
Madayevo, Rus. 69/K5
Maddaket, Ma, US 158/B5
Maddaloni, It. 65/D5
Madden (dam), Pan. 180/B2
Madden, Ms, US 162/C4
Maddock, ND, US 156/E4
Made, Neth. 52/B5
Madeir, Sudan 117/F4
Madeira (isl.), Port. 110/A2
Madeira (riv.), Braz. 179/C3
Madeira (isl.), Madr., Port. 107/A1
Madeira Beach, Fl, US 164/K8
Madeira Park, BC, Can. 144/B3
Madeirinha (riv.), Braz. 185/F3
Mädelegabel (peak), Ger. 61/G3
Madeleine (riv.), Qu, Can. 158/E1
Madeleine, Iles de la (isl.), Qu, Can. 141/K4
Madelia, Mn, US 155/G1
Madeline (isl.), Wi, US 157/J4
Madeline, Ca, US 146/C3
Maden, Turk. 102/D2
Mäder, Aus. 61/F3
Madera, Ca, US 148/B2
Madera (riv.), Bol. 185/E3
Madera, Mex. 174/C2
Madera (mtn.), Tx, US 150/C2
Madera Canyon, Az, US 149/G5
Maderas (vol.), Nic. 176/E4
Madgaon (Margao), India 95/B3
Madhipura, India 97/F3
Madhira, India 95/D2
Madhubani, India 97/F2
Madhumati (riv.), Bang. 97/G4
Madhupur, India 97/F3
Mādhura, India 97/F2
Madhwāpur, India 97/E2
Madhya Pradesh (state), India 92/C3
Madi Opei, Ugan. 117/G5
Madiany, Kenya 119/A2
Madibogo, SAfr. 124/D2
Madibura, Tanz. 119/A4
Madidi (riv.), Bol. 185/E4
Madihui, China 78/G4
Madikwe, SAfr. 123/E5
Madill, Ok, US 153/F3
Madimba, D.R. Congo 120/C4
Madīnat al Abyār, Libya 67/J4
Madīnat al 'Āshir min Ramaḑān, Egypt 113/C4
Madīnat as Sādāt, Egypt 113/B4
Madīnat ash Sha'b, Yem. 118/C2
Madīnat ath Thawrah, Syria 102/D3
Madīnet Dīmai (ruin), Egypt 113/B5
Madingo, Congo 120/B1
Madingo-Kayes, Congo 120/C4
Madingou, Congo 120/C4
Madirovalo, Madg. 125/H7
Madison, Sk, Can. 145/K2
Madison, Al, US 162/D3
Madison, Ar, US 162/B3
Madison, Ca, US 167/K9
Madison, Ct, US 169/F1
Madison, Fl, US 165/G2
Madison, Ga, US 163/F4
Madison, In, US 162/E1
Madison, Ks, US 153/F1
Madison, Mn, US 155/F1
Madison, Mo, US 155/H4
Madison, Ms, US 162/B4
Madison (riv.), Mt, US 142/D2
Madison, Ne, US 154/F3
Madison, NJ, US 169/H9
Madison, Oh, US 160/F4
Madison, SD, US 155/F1
Madison, Va, US 163/H1
Madison (cap.), Wi, US 155/K2
Madison, WV, US 163/G1
Madison Heights, Mi, US 167/F6
Madison Heights, Va, US 163/H2
Madisonville, Ky, US 162/D2
Madisonville, La, US 164/C2
Madisonville, Tn, US 162/E3
Madisonville, Tx, US 151/G2
Madiun, Indo. 89/E4
Madjngo, Gabon 120/C2
Mado Gashi, Kenya 119/B1
Madoc, On, Can. 161/H2
Madoi, China 78/D5
Madon (riv.), Fr. 42/D4
Madona, Lat. 41/M3
Madone d'Utelle (peak), Fr. 64/D5
Madong, China 93/K3
Madongchuan, China 78/F4
Madras, Or, US 146/C1
Madras (Chennai), India 95/D3
Madre (lag.), Mex. 175/F3
Madre de Deus de Minas, Braz. 187/M6
Madre de Dios (riv.), Bol.,Peru 179/C4
Madre de Dios (isl.), Chile 191/A6
Madre de Dios (dept.), Peru 184/D3
Madrecitas, Bol. 185/F5
Madrid, Col. 183/L8
Madrid (dist.), Sp. 46/C2
Madrid (cap.), Sp. 47/N9
Madrid, Ia, US 155/H3
Madridejos, Sp. 46/D3
Madrigal, Peru 184/D4
Madrigal de las Altas Torres, Sp. 46/C2
Madrigalejo, Sp. 46/C3
Madrisahorn (peak), Swi. 61/F4
Madroñera, Sp. 46/C3
Madsen, On, Can. 157/H2
Maduda, D.R. Congo 120/C4
Madugula, India 95/D2
Madukani, Tanz. 119/A2
Madura (isl.), Indo. 77/L10
Madura, Austl. 130/E4
Madurai, India 95/C4
Madzharovo, Bul. 51/G5
Mae Chan, Thai. 94/B1
Mae Charim, Thai. 94/C2
Mae Hong Son, Thai. 86/C5
Mae Ping NP, Thai. 94/B2
Mae Ramat, Thai. 94/B2
Mae Sai, Thai. 94/B1
Mae Sariang, Thai. 94/B2
Mae Sot, Thai. 94/B2
Mae Taeng, Thai. 94/B2
Mae Tho (peak), Thai. 94/B2
Mae Ya (mtn.), Thai. 94/B2
Maebashi, Japan 85/F2
Maella, Sp. 47/F2
Maengsan, NKor. 81/D3
Maenza, It. 65/C4
Maep'o, SKor. 81/E4
Maerne, It. 63/F2
Maeser, Ut, US 147/J3
Maevatanana-Ambanivohitra, Madg. 125/H7
Maewo (isl.), Van. 136/F6
Mafeking, Mb, Can. 156/D1
Mafeteng, Les. 124/D3
Maffe, Belg. 55/E3
Maffra, Austl. 133/C3
Mafia (isl.), Tanz. 119/C3
Mafia (chan.), Tanz. 119/B4
Mafikeng, SAfr. 124/D2
Máfil, Chile 190/B3
Mafou (riv.), Gui. 114/C4
Mafra, Port. 47/P10
Mafra, Braz. 189/G3
Mafungabusi (plat.), Zim. 123/F3
Magadan, Rus. 75/R4
Magadanskaya Oblast, Rus. 75/R4
Magadi, Kenya 119/B2
Magadino, Swi. 61/E5
Magalhães de Almeida, Braz. 183/F3
Magalia, Ca, US 146/C4
Magalies Berg (mts.), SAfr. 124/P12
Magaliesburg, SAfr. 124/P12
Magallanes, Phil. 88/C2
Magallanes y Antártica Chilena (prov.), Chile 191/C7
Magamba, CAfr. 116/D4
Magangué, Col. 180/C2
Maganoy, Phil. 88/D4
Mağara, Turk. 104/C1
Magaria, Niger 115/H3
Magarida, PNG 129/H2
Magat (riv.), Phil. 88/C1
Magazine, Ar, US 153/H3
Magazine (mtn.), Ar, US 153/H3
Magdagachi, Rus. 79/K1
Magdalena, Arg. 191/K11
Magdalena, Bol. 185/E4
Magdalena (dept.), Col. 177/H4
Magdalena (riv.), Col. 179/B2
Magdalena (peak), Malay. 88/B4
Magdalena, NM, US 149/J3
Magdalena de Kino, Mex. 174/C2
Magdeburg, Ger. 74/B4
Magdeburger Börde (ledge), Ger. 42/F2
Magdelaine Cays (isl.), Austl. 127/E2
Magé, Braz. 187/N7
Mage-shima (isl.), Japan 84/B5
Magee (isl.), NI, UK 34/C2
Magee, Ms, US 164/D2

Map Section

246

247

Manzan – Maubou
Map Section
248
249

Manzanita Ind. Res., Ca, US 148/D4
Manzano, It. 63/G2
Manzano (peak), NM, US 149/J3
Manzano, NM, US 149/J3
Manzano (mts.), NM, US 149/J3
Manzanola, Co, US 152/C1
Manzanza, D.R. Congo 121/G4
Manzhouli, China 79/H2
Manziana, It. 65/B3
Manzil Bū Zalafah, Tun. 48/B4
Manzil Tamīn, Tun. 48/B4
Manzilah (lake), Egypt 104/B4
Manzilah (canal), Egypt 113/C2
Manzini, Swaz. 125/E2
Manzini (Matsapa) (int'l arpt.), Swaz. 125/E2
Mao, Chad 116/B2
Mao Songsang, India 86/B3
Maoba, China 93/J2
Maobaguan, China 78/F5
Maodianzi, China 81/C2
Mao'ergai, China 78/E5
Maojing, China 78/F4
Maoke (mts.), Indo. 91/J4
Maoming, China 87/F4
Maoniushan, China 78/D4
Maoshan, China 80/H6
Maotian, China 78/F5
Maotou (peak), China 86/D3
Maowen Qiangzu Zizhixian, China 86/D2
Maoyang, China 87/H3
Maozhou, China 80/H7
Mapai, Moz. 123/F4
Mapam (lake), China 99/D5
Mapane, Indo. 91/F4
Mapastepec, Mex. 176/C3
Mapi (riv.), Indo. 91/J5
Mapia, Indo. 91/J4
Mapimí, Bolsón de (depr.), Mex. 174/D3
Mapire, Ven. 181/E3
Mapiri, Bol. 185/E3
Mapiri, Bol. 184/D4
Maple (peak), Az, US 149/H4
Maple (riv.), Ia, US 155/G2
Maple, On, Can. 160/T8
Maple Creek, Sk, Can. 145/K3
Maple Grove, Qu, Can. 159/N7
Maple Grove, Mn, US 157/P6
Maple Park, Il, US 167/N16
Maple Ridge, BC, Can. 144/C3
Maple River Nat'l Wild. Ref., ND, US 156/E4
Maple Shade, NJ, US 168/D4
Maple Valley, Wa, US 167/C3
Maples, Mo, US 153/J2
Maplesville, Al, US 162/D4
Mapleton, Ut, US 147/H3
Mapleton, Or, US 146/B1
Mapleton, Ia, US 155/G2
Mapleton, Mn, US 155/H2
Maplewood, Wi, US 160/C2
Maplewood, NJ, US 169/H9
Maplewood, Mn, US 157/P6
Map'o (nbrhd.), SKor. 81/F6
Mapoon Aboriginal Reserve, Austl. 129/F2
Mapoon Mission Station, Austl. 129/F2
Maporal, Ven. 180/D3
Mappsville, Va, US 163/K2
Mapuera (riv.), Braz. 181/G5
Mapumolo, SAfr. 125/E3
Maputa, SAfr. 125/F2
Maputo (int'l arpt.), Moz. 125/F2
Maputo (riv.), Moz. 123/G5
Maputo (prov.), Moz. 123/G5
Maputo (cap.), Moz. 125/F2
Maqat, Kaz. 71/K3
Maqdam (cape), Sudan 135/H5
Maqên, China 78/D5
Maquan (riv.), China 99/D6
Maquan (Damqog) (riv.), China 96/E1
Maquela do Zombo, Ang. 120/C4
Maquinchao, Arg. 190/C4
Maquoketa, Ia, US 155/J2
Maquoketa (riv.), Ia, US 155/J2
Maquoketa, North Fork (riv.), Ia, US 155/J2
Mar (reg.), Sc, UK 33/D2
Mar (mts.), Braz. 179/E5
Mar Chiquita (lag.), Arg. 188/D4
Mar de Ajó, Arg. 191/F3
Mar del Plata, Arg. 190/F3
Mar del Tuyú, Arg. 191/F3
Mar-Mac, NC, US 163/H3
Mara (riv.), Tanz. 119/A2
Mara (prov.), Tanz. 119/A2
Mara, Guy. 182/B1
Mara Creek, BC, Can. 144/E2
Maraã, Braz. 185/E1
Marabá, Braz. 182/D4
Maracá (isl.), Braz. 182/D2
Maracaibo (lake), Ven. 179/B2
Maracaibo, Ven. 180/D2
Maracaju, Braz. 189/F2
Maracaju, Serra de (mts.), Braz. 186/B4
Maracanã, Braz. 183/E3
Maracanaquará (plat.), Braz. 182/C3
Maracás, Braz. 187/E2
Maracay, Ven. 183/N7
Maracena, Sp. 46/D4
Marādah, Libya 108/C2
Maradi (dept.), Afr. 115/G2
Maradi, Niger 115/G3
Marāgheh, Iran 103/F2
Mārahra, India 96/B2
Marahuaca (peak), Ven. 181/E4
Maraira (pt.), Phil. 88/C1
Marais de St-Gond (swamp), Fr. 54/C6
Marais des Cygnes (riv.), Ks, Mo, US 153/G1
Marajó (bay), Braz. 179/E3
Maralal, Kenya 119/B1
Maralal Nat'l Sanct., Kenya 119/B1
Marali, CAfr. 116/C4
Maralik, Arm. 103/E1
Maralinga-Tjarutja Aboriginal Land, Austl. 131/F4
Maramag, Phil. 88/D4
Marambaia (isl.), Braz. 187/N8
Marampa, SLeo. 114/B4
Maramureş (co.), Rom. 43/M5
Maran, Malay. 89/C2
Marana (lag.), Cro. 63/G1
Marana, Az, US 149/G4
Marand, Iran 103/F2
Marandet, Niger 115/G2
Marang, Malay. 89/C1
Marangani, Peru 184/D4
Maranguape, Braz. 183/G3
Maranhão (riv.), Braz. 186/C2
Maranhão (state), Braz. 183/E5
Marano di Napoli, It. 65/D6
Marano Lagunare, It. 63/G2
Marano sul Panaro, It. 63/D5
Marano Vicentino, It. 63/E2
Maranoa (riv.), Austl. 127/D3
Marañón (riv.), Peru 179/B3
Marans, Fr. 44/C3
Maraoue, PN de la, C.d'Iv. 114/D5
Marapanim, Braz. 182/E3
Marapi (peak), Indo. 89/C3
Maras (peak), Indo. 89/D3
Mărăşeşti, Rom. 51/H3
Marathón, Gre. 49/N8
Marathón (arpt.), Gre. 49/N8
Marathon, Fl, US 165/H5
Marathon, On, Can. 157/L3
Marathon, NY, US 161/H3
Marathon, Tx, US 150/C2
Marau, Braz. 189/F4
Maraulīānwāla, Pak. 98/B3
Maravatío de Ocampo, Mex. 175/E5
Maravilha, Braz. 189/F3
Maravillas, Bol. 185/E3
Maravillas (cr.), Tx, US 150/C3
Marāwah, Libya 67/J4
Marawaka, PNG 129/G1
Marawī, Sudan 135/F5
Marawi, Phil. 88/D3
Marayes, Arg. 188/C4
Marazion, Eng, UK 36/A6
Marbach, Swi. 60/D4
Marbach am Neckar, Ger. 58/C5
Marbache, Fr. 55/F6
Marbella, Sp. 46/C4
Marble (canyon), Az, US 149/G2
Marble, NC, US 162/F3
Marble Bar, Austl. 130/C2
Marble Canyon, Az, US 149/G2
Marble Falls, Tx, US 150/E2
Marble Hall, SAfr. 123/F5
Marble Hill, Mo, US 162/C2
Marblemount, Wa, US 144/D3
Marbleton, Qu, Can. 161/L2
Marbleton, Wy, US 147/H2
Marburg (lake), Pa, US 168/B4
Marbury, Al, US 162/D4
Marcali, Hun. 50/C2
Marcallo, It. 62/B3
Marcapata, Peru 184/D4
Marcelin, Sk, Can. 145/L1
Marceline, Mo, US 155/H4
Marcelino Ramos, Braz. 189/G3
Marcella, Ar, US 153/J3
Marcellina, It. 65/B3
Marcellus, Mi, US 160/D3
March (A.F.B.), Ca, US 166/C3
March, Eng, UK 37/G1
Marchant (mt.), NZ 135/J9
Marche (pol. reg.), It. 65/C2
Marche, Congo 120/C4
Marche (mts.), Fr. 44/d3
Marche-en-Famenne, Belg. 55/E3
Marchémoret, Fr. 30/L4
Marchena, Sp. 46/C4
Marchena (isl.), Ecu. 184/J6
Marcheno, It. 62/D2
Marches (reg.), It. 67/G2
Marchiennes, Fr. 54/C3
Marchin, Belg. 55/E3
Marchinbar (isl.), Austl. 129/E2
Marchtrenk, Aus. 59/H6
Marchwell, Sk, Can. 156/D2
Marciana Marina, It. 48/B1
Marcianise, It. 65/D5
Marcilly, Fr. 30/L4
Marcilly-sur-Tille, Fr. 60/B2
Marck, Fr. 54/A2
Marckolsheim, Fr. 60/D1
Marco, Fl, US 165/H5
Marco (isl.), Fl, US 165/H5
Marco, Braz. 183/F3
Marco Polo (int'l arpt.), It. 63/F3
Marcoing, Fr. 54/C3
Marcola, Or, US 146/B1
Marcon, It. 63/F2
Marcona, Peru 184/C4
Marconi (mt.), BC, Can. 144/G2
Marcos Juárez, Arg. 190/E2
Marcosli (riv.), BC, Can. 144/C1
Marcoussis, Fr. 30/J6
Marcovia, Hon. 176/E3
Marcq-en-Barœul, Fr. 54/C2
Marcus, Ia, US 155/G2
Marcus Baker (mt.), Ak, US 171/J3
Marcy (mt.), NY, US 161/K2
Mardān, Pak. 98/B2
Marden, Eng, UK 30/E3
Mardeuil, Fr. 54/C5
Mardin, Turk. 102/E2
Mardin (prov.), Turk. 102/E2
Maré (isl.), NCal. 137/W12
Marecchia (riv.), It. 63/F5
Marechal Cândido Rondon, Braz. 189/F3
Marechal Deodoro, Braz. 187/G1
Maree (lake), Sc, UK 31/R8
Mareeba, Austl. 134/B2
Mareham le Fen, Eng, UK 35/H5
Mareil-sur-Mauldre, Fr. 30/H5
Marek, Indo. 91/F4
Maréna, Mali 114/C3
Marengo, Wi, US 157/J4
Marengo, Il, US 167/N15
Marengo, Ia, US 155/H3
Marengo, In, US 162/D1
Marengo, Sk, Can. 145/K2
Marenisco, Mi, US 157/K4
Marennes, Fr. 44/C4
Mareolaboom, Namb. 122/C3
Marerano, Madg. 125/H8
Maresfield, Eng, UK 37/G5
Mareuil-sur-Ourcq, Fr. 30/M4
Marfa, Tx, US 150/B2
Marfield, Austl. 133/B1
Marfino, Rus. 71/J3
Margalla Hills NP, Pak. 98/B3
Margam, Wal, UK 36/C3
Marganets', Ukr. 73/H4
Margao (Madgaon), India 95/B3
Margaree, NS, Can. 159/G2
Margaree Valley, NS, Can. 159/G2
Margaret, Tx, US 152/E3
Margaret (riv.), Austl. 128/B4
Margaret (mt.), Austl. 130/C2
Margaret River, Austl. 130/B5
Margarita (peak), Ca, US 166/C4
Margarita (isl.), Ven. 181/F2
Margarita, Isla de (isl.), Trin. 173/J5
Margarítion, Gre. 49/G3
Margate, Eng, UK 37/H4
Margate, Fl, US 164/P10
Margate, SAfr. 125/E3
Margate City, NJ, US 168/D5
Margeride (mts.), Fr. 44/E4
Margeta (cape), Indo. 128/B2
Margherita (peak), Ugan. 121/G2
Marghilon, Uzb. 99/B3
Marghita, Rom. 50/F2
Margny-lès-Compiègne, Fr. 54/B5
Margo, Sk, Can. 156/C2
Margog Caka (lake), China 99/E5
Margos, Peru 184/B3
Margosatubig, Phil. 88/C4
Margraten, Neth. 55/E2
Marguareis (peak), It. 64/D4
Marguerite, BC, Can. 144/C1
Margyang, China 97/H1
Mari, PNG 129/F2
Mari, Braz. 183/H4
Maria, Qu, Can. 158/E1
Maria (mt.), Austl. 132/D4
Maria (isl.), Austl. 129/D3
Maria Aurora, Phil. 88/C2
María Cleófas (isl.), Mex. 174/D4
Maria da Fé, Braz. 187/L7
Maria Island NP, Austl. 132/D4
Maria Juana, Arg. 188/D4
María Madre (isl.), Mex. 174/D4
María Magdalena (isl.), Mex. 174/D4
Maria van Diemen (cape), NZ 135/C1
Mariāhū, India 96/D3
Mariakani, Kenya 119/B2
Mariakerke, Belg. 54/B1
Marialva, Braz. 186/C4
Marian, Austl. 134/C3
Marianao, Cuba 177/F1
Marianna, Fl, US 165/F2
Marianna, Ar, US 162/B3
Mariano Comense, It. 62/C2
Mariano I. Loza, Arg. 188/E4
Mariánské Lázně, Czh. 59/F3
Mariarano, Madg. 125/H6
Marias (riv.), Mt, US 145/H3
Mariato (pt.), Pan. 180/A3
Ma'rib, Yem. 118/C2
Maribo, Den. 40/D4
Maribor, Slov. 50/B2
Maricá, Braz. 187/P7
Maricopa, Ca, US 148/C3
Maricopa, Az, US 149/F4
Maricopa (mts.), Az, US 149/F4
Maricopa Ak Chin Ind. Res., Az, US 149/F4
Maridalsvatn (lake), Nor. 38/S8
Marīdī, Sudan 117/F4
Marié (riv.), Braz. 181/E5
Marie Byrd Land (phys. reg.), Ant. 192/S
Marie-Galante (isl.), Dom. 173/J4
Mariefred, Swe. 39/A1
Mariehamn (int'l arpt.), Fin. 41/H1
Mariehamn (Maarianhamina), Fin. 41/H1
Marieholm, Swe. 39/K7
Mariel, Cuba 177/F1
Marienbourg, Belg. 55/D3
Mariënburg, Sur. 182/C1
Mariendorf, Ger. 42/Q7
Marienfelde, Ger. 42/Q7
Marienhafe, Ger. 53/E1
Marienheide, Ger. 55/G1
Mariental, Namb. 122/C5
Marienville, Pa, US 161/G4
Mariestad, Swe. 40/E2
Marietta, Ga, US 163/L7
Marietta, Mn, US 155/F1
Marietta, Ms, US 162/C3
Marietta, Oh, US 160/F5
Marietta, Ok, US 153/F4
Marietta, Pa, US 168/B3
Marieval, Sk, Can. 156/C2
Marigat, Kenya 119/A1
Marigliano, It. 65/D6
Marignane, Fr. 64/B6
Marigot, Fr. 173/N8
Marigot, Dom. 173/N9
Marihatag, Phil. 88/D3
Marijampolė, Lith. 41/K4
Marikina, Phil. 88/F6
Marikina (riv.), Phil. 88/F6
Marilao, Phil. 88/E6
Marília, Braz. 189/G2
Mariluz, Braz. 189/F3
Marín, Mex. 150/D5
Marín, Sp. 46/A1
Marin (co.), Ca, US 167/J10
Marin-Epagnier, Swi. 60/D3
Marina, It. 48/D3
Marina, Ca, US 148/B2
Marina del Rey (harbor), Ca, US 166/F8
Marina del Rey, Ca, US 166/F8
Marina di Andora, It. 62/B6
Marina di Carrara, It. 62/D5
Marina di Massa, It. 62/D5
Marina di Montemarciano, It. 63/G6
Marina di Pisa, It. 62/D6
Marina di Ravenna, It. 63/F5
Marina di Vasto, It. 65/D3
Mar'ina Gorka, Bela. 41/N5
Marinduque (isl.), Phil. 88/C2
Marine, Il, US 155/K4
Marine City, Mi, US 160/E3
Marine Nat'l Res., Kenya 119/C2
Marine World Africa USA, Ca, US 167/K10
Marineland, Austl. 131/M8
Marineland of Florida, Fl, US 165/H3
Marines, Fr. 30/H4
Marinette, Wi, US 160/C2
Maringa (riv.), D.R. Congo 121/E2
Maringá, Braz. 189/G2
Maringouin, La, US 164/C2
Maringuè, Moz. 123/G3
Marinha Grande, Port. 46/A3
Marinhas, Port. 46/A2
Marino, It. 65/B4
Marion (reef), Austl. 127/E2
Marion, Al, US 162/D4
Marion, Ar, US 162/B3
Marion (cr.), Fl, US 164/M7
Marion (lake), Fl, US 164/M7
Marion, Ia, US 155/J2
Marion, Il, US 162/C2
Marion, In, US 160/D4
Marion, Ks, US 153/F1
Marion, Ky, US 162/C2
Marion, La, US 153/H4
Marion, Mi, US 160/D2
Marion, Ms, US 162/C4
Marion, NC, US 163/F3
Marion, ND, US 156/E4
Marion, Oh, US 160/E4
Marion, SC, US 163/H3
Marion (lake), SC, US 143/K5
Marion, SD, US 155/F2
Marion, Va, US 163/G2
Marion, Wi, US 155/K1
Marion Bridge, NS, Can. 159/G3
Marion Junction, Al, US 162/D4
Marionville, Mo, US 153/H2
Maripa, Ven. 181/E3
Maripa, FrG. 182/D2
Maripasoula, FrG. 182/C2
Mariposa, Ca, US 148/C2
Mariposa Grove, Ca, US 148/C2
Mariquita, Col. 183/L7
Mariscal Estigarribia, Par. 188/D2
Mariscal Sucre (int'l arpt.), Ecu. 180/B5
Marissa, Il, US 162/C1
Mārith, Tun. 66/F4
Maritime Alps (mts.), Fr. 66/E1
Maritsa (riv.), Bul. 70/C4
Maritsa (riv.), Turk. 51/H5
Mariupol', Ukr. 73/J4
Mariupol (int'l arpt.), Ukr. 73/J4
Mariy-El, Resp., Rus. 74/E4
Marj 'Uyūn, Leb. 105/D2
Märjamaa, Est. 41/L2
Mark (riv.), Belg. 52/B6
Mark Twain (lake), Mo, US 155/H4
Mark Twain Nat'l Wild. Ref., Il, Ia, US 155/J3
Mark Twain Nat'l Wild. Ref., Il, Mo, US 155/J4
Marka (riv.), Ger. 53/E3
Marka, Som. 119/D1
Mārkā, Jor. 105/D5
Markagunt (plat.), Ut, US 149/F2
Markākasa, India 95/D1
Markakol (lake), Kaz. 78/D4
Markam, China 86/C2
Mārkāpur, India 95/C3
Markaryd, Swe. 40/E3
Markazī (gov.), Iran 103/G3
Markdale, On, Can. 160/F2
Markdorf, Ger. 61/F2
Marked Tree, Ar, US 162/B3
Markelsdorfer (pt.), Ger. 40/D4
Marken (isl.), Neth. 52/C4
Markerwaard (polder), Neth. 52/C3
Markesan, Wi, US 155/K2
Market Bosworth, Eng, UK 37/E1
Market Deeping, Eng, UK 37/F1
Market Drayton, Eng, UK 35/F6
Market Harborough, Eng, UK 37/F2
Market Rasen, Eng, UK 35/H5
Market Weighton, Eng, UK 35/H4
Markethill, NI, UK 34/B3
Markgroningen, Ger. 58/C5
Markha, India 98/D3
Markham, On, Can. 159/S8
Markham (bay), Nun, Can. 141/J2
Markham (riv.), PNG 129/G1
Markham, Tx, US 151/F3
Marki, Pol. 43/L2
Markinch, Sc, UK 33/C4
Markit, China 99/C4
Markivka, Ukr. 73/K3
Markle, In, US 160/D4
Markleeville, Ca, US 146/D4
Marknesse, Neth. 52/C3
Markneukirchen, Ger. 59/F2
Markópoulon, Gre. 49/N9
Markounda, CAfr. 116/C4
Markova, Rus. 78/E1
Markovac, Serb. 50/E3
Markovo, Rus. 75/S3
Markoye, Burk. 115/F3
Marks, Rus. 71/H2
Marks, Ms, US 162/B3
Marksville, La, US 164/B2
Markt Bibart, Ger. 58/D3
Markt Erlbach, Ger. 58/D4
Markt Indersdorf, Ger. 59/E6
Markt Rettenbach, Ger. 61/G2
Markt Sankt Florian, Aus. 59/H6
Markt Schwaben, Ger. 59/E6
Marktbreit, Ger. 58/D3
Marktheidenfeld, Ger. 58/C3
Marktl, Ger. 59/F6
Marktoberdorf, Ger. 61/G2
Marktredwitz, Ger. 59/F3
Marl, Ger. 53/E5
Marla, Austl. 131/G3
Marlboro, Ab, Can. 144/F1
Marlboro, NJ, US 168/D3
Marlboro (Upper Marlboro), Md, US 168/B6
Marlborough, Ma, US 161/L3
Marlborough, Austl. 134/C3
Marlborough, Eng, UK 37/E4
Marle, Fr. 54/C4
Marlengo (Marling), It. 61/H4
Marlenheim, Fr. 55/G6
Marles-en-Brie, Fr. 30/L5
Marles-les-Mines, Fr. 54/B3
Marlette, Mi, US 160/E3
Marlin, Tx, US 151/F2
Marling (Marlengo), It. 61/H4
Marlinton, WV, US 163/G1
Marlow, Ok, US 153/F3
Marlow, Ger. 40/E4
Marlow, Eng, UK 37/F3
Marlow, Ga, US 163/G4
Marlpit Hill, Eng, UK 30/D3
Marlton, NJ, US 168/D4
Marly, Fr. 54/C3
Marly, Fr. 55/F5
Marly-la-Ville, Fr. 30/K4
Marly-le-Roi, Fr. 30/J5
Marmaduke, Ar, US 162/B2
Marmagão, India 95/B3
Marmande, Fr. 44/D4
Marmara (sea), Turk. 70/D4
Marmara (isl.), Turk. 67/K2
Marmara, Turk. 51/H5
Marmaraereğlisi, Turk. 51/H5
Marmaris, Turk. 102/B2
Marmarth, ND, US 156/C4
Marmelos, Rio dos (riv.), Braz. 182/A4
Marmet, WV, US 163/G1
Marmion (lake), On, Can. 157/J3
Marmion (lake), Austl. 130/D4
Marmirolo, It. 63/D3
Marmolada (peak), It. 45/J3
Marmolejo, Sp. 46/C3
Marmontana (peak), It. 61/F5
Marmora, On, Can. 161/H2
Marmora, NJ, US 168/D5
Marmot (peak), Mt, US 144/G4
Marmoutier, Fr. 55/G6
Marnay, Fr. 60/B3
Marnaz, Fr. 60/C5
Marne, Ger. 40/C5
Marne (dept.), Fr. 54/C6
Marne (riv.), Fr. 42/C4
Marne au Rhin, Canal de la (canal), Fr. 55/D6
Marneuli, Geo. 71/H4
Marnhull, Eng, UK 36/D5
Maro, Chad 116/C3
Maro (reef), Hi, US 137/H2
Maroa, Ven. 181/E4
Maroa, Il, US 155/K3
Maroantsetra, Madg. 125/J6
Marofandilia, Madg. 125/H8
Marokau (isl.), FrPol. 137/L6
Marolambo, Madg. 125/J8
Maroldsweisach, Ger. 58/D2
Marolles, Fr. 30/M4
Marolles-en-Brie, Fr. 30/M5
Marolles-en-Hurepoix, Fr. 30/J6
Maromme, Fr. 57/G2
Maromokotro (peak), Madg. 125/J6
Marondera, Zim. 123/F3
Marone, It. 62/D2
Maroni (riv.), FrG.,Sur. 179/D2
Maroni (riv.), Sur.,FrG. 182/C1
Maroni (riv.), Sur. 181/H3
Maroochydore-Mooloolaba, Austl. 134/D4
Maroon Town, Jam. 177/G2
Maropaika, Madg. 125/H8
Marostica, It. 63/E2
Marotandrano, Madg. 125/J7
Marotiri (Bass Is.) (isl.), FrPol. 137/L7
Marotta, It. 63/G6
Maroua, Camr. 116/B3
Marouini (riv.), FrG. 181/H4
Marovato, Madg. 125/J6
Marovato, Madg. 125/J6
Marovoay, Madg. 125/H7
Marowijne (dist.), Sur. 181/H3
Marpingen, Ger. 55/G5
Marple, Eng, UK 35/F5
Marqên Gangri (peak), China 78/D5
Marquan (riv.), China 92/E2
Marquand, Mo, US 162/B2
Marquard, SAfr. 124/D3
Marquarie (riv.), Austl. 132/C1
Marquesas (isls.), FrPol. 137/M5
Marquesas Keys (isls.), Fl, US 165/G5
Marquetalia, Col. 183/K7
Marquette, Ks, US 153/F1
Marquette, Mb, Can. 156/F2
Marquette, Mi, US 157/L4
Marquez, Tx, US 151/F2
Marquis, Sk, Can. 145/M2
Marquise, Fr. 54/A2
Marracuene, Moz. 125/F2
Marradi, It. 63/E5
Marrah (peak), Sudan 116/E2
Marrakech, Mor. 110/D3
Marrakech (Menara) (int'l arpt.), Mor. 110/C3
Marrawah, Austl. 132/C4
Marree, Austl. 131/H4
Marromeu, Moz. 123/G3
Marrowbone, Ky, US 162/E2
Marrowie (cr.), Austl. 133/B1
Marrupa, Moz. 123/H2
Mars, Pa, US 160/F4
Mars (peak), It. 62/A1
Mars Hill, NC, US 163/F3
Marsá al 'Alam, Egypt 135/G3
Marsá al Burayqah, Libya 108/C2
Marsa Ben Mehidi, Alg. 112/C2
Marsá Matrūh, Egypt 135/E2
Marsabit, Kenya 119/B1
Marsabit Nat'l Rsv., Kenya 117/H5
Marsabit National Reserve, Kenya 118/A5
Marşafā, Egypt 113/C4
Marsala, It. 48/C4
Marsange (riv.), Fr. 30/L5
Marsannay, Fr. 60/A3
Marsberg, Ger. 53/F6
Marsciano, It. 65/B2
Marsden, Eng, UK 35/G4
Marsden, Sk, Can. 145/K1
Marsden, Austl. 133/C1
Marsdiep Texelstroom (chan.), Neth. 52/B3
Marseille, Fr. 64/B6
Marseille au Rhône (canal), Fr. 64/A5
Marseille-en-Beauvaisis, Fr. 54/A4
Marseilles, Il, US 155/K3
Marsella, Col. 183/K8
Marsh (mtn.), Md, US 161/G5
Marsh (isl.), La, US 151/J3
Marsh (cr.), Pa, US 168/F1
Marsh (peak), Ut, US 147/J3
Marsh Gibbon, Eng, UK 37/E3
Marshall (riv.), Austl. 131/H2
Marshall, Sk, Can. 145/K1
Marshall, Libr. 114/C5
Marshall, Ar, US 153/H3
Marshall, Il, US 160/C5
Marshall, Mi, US 160/D3
Marshall, Mn, US 155/G1
Marshall, Mo, US 155/H4
Marshall, NC, US 163/F3
Marshall, Ok, US 153/F2
Marshall, Tx, US 151/G1
Marshall Islands (ctry.) 136/G3
Marshallton, De, US 168/C4
Marshalltown, Ia, US 155/H2
Marshallville, Ga, US 162/F4
Marshfield, Mo, US 153/H2
Marshfield, Wi, US 155/J1
Marshyhope (cr.), Md, US 168/C6
Marske-by-the-Sea, Eng, UK 35/G2
Marsland, Ne, US 154/C2
Märsta, Swe. 40/G2
Marston, Mo, US 162/C2
Marsyandi (riv.), Nepal 97/E1
Marta, It. 48/B1
Marta (mts.), Col. 177/H4
Martaban, Myan. 94/B2
Martaban (gulf), Myan. 94/B2
Martano (peak), It. 65/B2
Martap, Camr. 116/B4
Martapura, Indo. 89/D4
Martapura, Indo. 90/D4
Marte R. Gomez, Mex. 174/C3
Martelange, Belg. 55/E4
Martellago, It. 63/F2
Martensville, Sk, Can. 145/L1
Martfeld, Ger. 53/G3
Martha, Ok, US 152/E3
Martha, Ky, US 163/F1
Martha's Vineyard (isl.), Ma, US 158/B5
Martignacco, It. 63/G1
Martigné-Ferchaud, Fr. 56/D5
Martigné-sur-Mayenne, Fr. 57/E4
Martigny, Swi. 60/D5
Martigny-les-Bains, Fr. 60/B1
Martigues, Fr. 64/B6
Martil, Mor. 112/B2
Martilla, Fin. 39/F4
Martin, ND, US 156/D4
Martin, La, US 164/B1
Martin, Mi, US 160/D3
Martin, SD, US 154/D2
Martin (dam), Al, US 162/E4
Martin, Tn, US 162/C2
Martin (lake), Al, US 162/E4
Martín Chico, Uru. 191/J11
Martin Luther King, Jr. Nat'l Hist. Site, Ga, US 163/M7
Martina Franca, It. 49/E2
Martinborough, NZ 135/J9
Martindale, Tx, US 150/F3
Martinengo, It. 62/C2
Martinez, Ca, US 146/B4
Martinez, Ga, US 163/F4
Martínez de la Torre, Mex. 175/M6
Martínez del Tineo, Arg. 188/C2
Martinique (isl.), Fr. 173/N9
Martinique Passage (chan.), Dom.,Mart. 173/N9
Martínon, Gre. 49/H3
Martinópole, Braz. 183/F3
Martins, Braz. 183/G4
Martins Creek, Pa, US 168/C2
Martins Ferry, Oh, US 160/F4
Martins Mills, Tx, US 151/G1
Martinsburg, WV, US 161/H5
Martinsburg, Pa, US 161/G4
Martinsburg, NY, US 161/J3
Martinsicuro, It. 65/C2
Martinsville, Il, US 160/C5
Martinsville, In, US 160/C5
Martinsville, Ms, US 164/C2
Martinsville, Va, US 163/H2
Martock, Eng, UK 36/D5
Martofte, Den. 40/D4
Marton, NZ 135/C3
Martorell, Sp. 47/K7
Martos, Sp. 46/D4
Martovce, Slvk. 50/D2
Martres-Tolosane, Fr. 44/D5
Martūba, Libya 67/J4
Martuk, Kaz. 71/L2
Martuni, Arm. 71/H4
Marty, SD, US 154/E2
Martynovo, Kaz. 71/J2
Maru, Nga. 115/G3
Marudi, Malay. 88/A4
Marugame, Japan 84/C3
Maruim, Braz. 187/F1
Maruko, Japan 85/F2
Marulan, Austl. 133/E2
Marulanda, Col. 183/K7
Marum, Neth. 52/D2
Marumba, Tanz. 123/H1
Marungu (mts.), D.R. Congo 121/G5
Maruoka, Japan 84/E2
Marutea (isl.), FrPol. 137/M7
Marv Dasht, Iran 103/H4
Marvel, Co, US 149/H2
Marvell, Ar, US 162/B3
Marvin, SD, US 155/F1
Marvine (mt.), Ut, US 149/G1
Marwayne, Ab, Can. 145/J1
Marxheim, Ger. 58/D5
Mary (lake), Ms, US 164/C2
Mary, Trkm. 101/H1
Mary Anne Passage, Austl. 130/B2
Mary Esther, Fl, US 164/E2
Mary Kathleen, Austl. 131/H2
Mary-sur-Marne, Fr. 30/M4
Maryānaj, Iran 103/G3
Maryang, China 99/C4
Maryborough, Austl. 134/D4
Maryborough, Austl. 132/B3
Marydale, SAfr. 124/C3
Marydel, Md, US 168/C5
Maryfield, Sk, Can. 156/D3
Mar'yinka, Ukr. 73/J4
Marykirk, Sc, UK 33/D3
Maryland (co.), Libr. 114/C5
Maryland (state), US 143/L4
Maryland City, Md, US 168/B5
Maryland Junction, Zim. 123/F3
Maryland Line, Md, US 168/B4
Maryneal, Tx, US 150/D1
Maryport, Eng, UK 34/E2
Marystown, Nf, Can. 159/K2
Marysvale, Ut, US 149/F1
Marysville, Ca, US 146/C4
Marysville, Ks, US 155/F4
Marysville, Mi, US 160/E3
Marysville, Mt, US 145/H4
Marysville, Oh, US 160/E4
Marysville, Pa, US 168/B3
Marysville, Wa, US 144/C3
Maryūt (lake), Egypt 113/A2
Maryvale, Austl. 134/D5
Maryville, Mo, US 155/G3
Maryville, Tn, US 162/F3
Marzabotto, It. 63/E5
Marzano (peak), It. 48/D2
Marzo (pt.), Col. 180/B3
Marzūq, Libya 108/B3
Marzūq (des.), Libya 108/B3
Masabit Nat'l Rsv., Kenya 119/B1
Masada (ruin), Isr. 135/G2
Masada NP, Isr. 105/C6
Masagan (riv.), Som. 118/C3
Masai Mara Nat'l Rsv., Kenya 119/A2
Masai Steppe (grsld.), Tanz. 119/B3
Masaka, Ugan. 121/G3
Masākin, Tun. 48/B5
Masalembu Besar (isl.), Indo. 89/F4
Masallı, Azer. 103/G2
Masamagrell, Sp. 47/E3
Masamba, Indo. 91/F4
Masan, SKor. 81/E5
Masan-ni, SKor. 81/F7
Masanga, D.R. Congo 121/E3
Masangwe (hill), Tanz. 121/G4
Masaryktown, Fl, US 164/L7
Masasi, Tanz. 119/B4
Masavi, Bol. 188/D1
Masaya, Nic. 176/E4
Masbate, Phil. 88/C2
Masbate (isl.), Phil. 88/C2
Mascara, Alg. 112/F5
Mascarene (isls.), Mrts 125/T15
Mascot, Tn, US 162/F2
Mascota, Mex. 174/D4
Mascotte, Fl, US 164/M6
Mascouche, Qu, Can. 159/N6
Mase, D.R. Congo 121/F4
Masela (isl.), Indo. 128/C2
Maselheim, Ger. 61/F1
Maserà di Padova, It. 63/E3
Masereka, D.R. Congo 121/G3
Maseru (cap.), Les. 124/D3
Maseru (Moshoeshoe) (int'l arpt.), Les. 124/D3
Masevaux, Fr. 60/D2
Masfjorden, Nor. 40/A1
Masha, China 87/H3
Mashaba, Zim. 123/F4
Mashad (int'l arpt.), Iran 101/G1
Mashala, D.R. Congo 121/E4
Mashalah, Egypt 113/C3
Masham, Eng, UK 35/G3
Mashhad, Iran 101/G1
Mashike, Japan 82/B2
Mashivka, Ukr. 73/H3
Mashīz, Iran 103/J4
Māshkīd (riv.), Iran 101/H3
Mashonaland Central (prov.), Zim. 123/F3
Mashonaland East (prov.), Zim. 123/F3
Mashonaland West (prov.), Zim. 123/F3
Mashqharah, Leb. 105/D1
Mashtūl as Sūq, Egypt 113/C4
Mashū (lake), Japan 82/D2
Masiaca, Mex. 174/C3
Maside, Sp. 46/A1
Masīlah (wadi), Yem. 118/D2
Masim (peak), Rus. 71/L1
Masindi, Ugan. 121/G2
Masindi Port, Ugan. 121/H2
Masinloc, Phil. 88/B2
Masis, Arm. 103/F1
Masisea, Peru 184/C3
Masisi, D.R. Congo 121/G3
Masjed-e Soleymān, Iran 103/G4
Masjid Raya (Great Mosque), Indo. 89/B2
Mask (lake), Ire. 32/A2
Maskall, Belz. 176/D2
Maskan (cape), Som. 118/B3
Masker (peak), Mor. 110/D2
Maskin, Oman 101/G4
Maskūtān, Iran 101/G3
Masnou, Sp. 47/L7
Masoala (pen.), Madg. 125/J6
Masoala (cape), Madg. 125/J6
Masoarivo, Madg. 125/H7
Mason, Il, US 162/C1
Mason, Mi, US 160/D3
Mason, Nv, US 146/D4
Mason, Oh, US 160/D5
Mason, Ok, US 153/F3
Mason, Tx, US 150/E2
Mason (co.), Wa, US 167/A3
Mason (lake), Wa, US 167/B3
Mason, WV, US 163/F1
Mason and Dixon Line, Pa, US 168/B4
Mason City, Il, US 155/K3
Mason City, Ia, US 155/H2
Masonboro, NC, US 163/J3
Masone, It. 62/B5
Masontown, Pa, US 161/G5
Masonville, Ky, US 162/D2
Masquefa, Sp. 47/K6
Masrakh, India 97/E2
Maşrif Baḩr al Baqar (canal), Egypt 113/C3
Massa, It. 62/D5
Massa Finalese, It. 63/E4
Massa Fiscaglia, It. 63/F4
Massa Lombarda, It. 63/E5
Massa Lubrense, It. 65/D6
Massa Marittima, It. 48/B1
Massa Martana, It. 65/B2
Massa-Carrara (prov.), It. 62/C4
Massachusetts (bay), Ma, US 158/B4
Massachusetts (state), US 143/M3
Massaciuccoli (lake), It. 62/D5
Massafra, It. 49/E2
Massaguet, Chad 116/B2
Massakory, Chad 116/B2
Massandra, Ukr. 73/H5
Massangena, Moz. 123/G4
Massapê, Braz. 183/F3
Massapequa, NY, US 169/M9
Massapequa Park, NY, US 169/M9
Massarosa, It. 62/D6
Massbach, Ger. 58/D2
Massena, NY, US 161/J2
Massenya, Chad 116/C3
Masset, BC, Can. 171/M4
Massey, On, Can. 160/E1
Massey (sound), Nun, Can. 141/S7
Massey, Md, US 168/C5
Massibi, Ang. 121/E5
Massif Central (upland), Fr. 66/D1
Massif de Beaufort (mass.), Fr. 64/C1
Massif de Champsaur (mass.), Fr. 64/C3
Massif de Guéra (peak), Chad 116/C3
Massif de la Chartreuse (mass.), Fr. 64/B2
Massif de la Vanoise (mass.), Fr. 64/C2
Massif de l''Assâba (mass.), Mrta. 114/C2
Massif de Pelvoux (mass.), Fr. 64/C3
Massif de Termit (mass.), Niger 116/A1
Massif des Bongos (uplands), CAfr. 116/D3
Massif des Maures (mass.), Fr. 64/C6
Massif du Manéngouba (peak), Camr. 115/H5
Massif du Tamgue (mass.), Gui. 114/B3
Massigui, Mali 114/D4
Massillon, Oh, US 160/F4
Massinga, Moz. 123/G4
Massingir, Moz. 123/G4
Massy, Fr. 30/J5
Mastābah, SAr. 100/C4
Mastadon (mtn.), Id, US 144/G4
Maştağa, Azer. 71/J4
Masterton, NZ 135/C3
Mastgat (chan.), Neth. 52/B5
Mastic, NY, US 169/F2
Mastic Beach, NY, US 169/F2
Mastník (riv.), Czh. 59/H3
Mastūj (riv.), Pak. 98/A2
Mastung, Pak. 101/J3
Mastūrah, SAr. 100/C4
Masuda, Japan 84/B3
Masuguru, Tanz. 123/H1
Masuho, Japan 83/A2
Masurai (peak), Indo. 89/C3
Masvingo, Zim. 123/F4
Masvingo (prov.), Zim. 123/F4
Maswa Game Rsv., Tanz. 119/A2
Maşyāf, Syria 104/E2
Mat (riv.), Alb. 49/F2
Mata, D.R. Congo 121/E4
Mata Bia (peak), ETim. 128/B2
Mata de Guanábano, Ven. 180/D3
Mata Grande, Braz. 183/G5
Mata Mata, SAfr. 124/C2
Mata Utu, Wall. 137/H6
Matabeleland North (prov.), Zim. 123/E3
Matabeleland South (prov.), Zim. 123/F4
Mātābhānga, India 97/G2
Matadi, D.R. Congo 120/C4
Matador, Tx, US 152/D3
Matagalpa, Nic. 176/E3
Matagorda, Tx, US 151/G3
Matagorda (pen.), Tx, US 151/G3
Matagorda (bay), Tx, US 151/F3
Matagorda (isl.), Tx, US 151/F3
Matak (isl.), Indo. 89/D2
Matala, Ang. 122/B2
Matam, Sen. 114/B3
Matamba, D.R. Congo 121/E4
Mataméye, Niger 115/H3
Matamoras, Pa, US 168/D1
Matamoros, Mex. 174/E3
Ma'ţan as Sarra (well), Libya 108/D4
Matancilla, Chile 188/B4
Matanda, Zam. 123/F1
Matandu (riv.), Tanz. 119/B4
Matane, Qu, Can. 158/D1
Matane (riv.), Qu, Can. 158/D1
Matanga, Madg. 125/H8
Matanzas, Cuba 172/E3
Matão, Braz. 189/G2
Matape (riv.), Mex. 174/C2
Matapédia, Qu, Can. 158/D2
Mataquito (riv.), Chile 190/C2
Matara (ruin), Erit. 100/C6
Matara, Erit. 118/A2
Mataram, Indo. 91/E5
Matarânga, Gre. 49/G3
Matarani, Peru 184/C5
Mataranka, Austl. 128/D3
Mataró, Sp. 47/L6
Matatiele, SAfr. 124/E3
Mataura, FrPol. 137/L7
Mataura, NZ 135/B4
Mataura (riv.), NZ 135/B4
Matawai, NZ 135/D2
Matawan, NJ, US 169/J10
Matawin (riv.), Qu, Can. 158/A2
Matay, Kaz. 71/L3
Matay, Kaz. 99/C2
Matching Green, Eng, UK 30/D1
Matecaña (int'l arpt.), Col. 183/K8
Mateguá, Bol. 185/F4
Matehuala, Mex. 175/E4
Mateke (hills), Zim. 123/F4
Matera, It. 48/E2
Matéri, Ben. 115/F4
Maternillos (pt.), Cuba 173/F3
Matese (lake), It. 65/D5
Matese (mts.), It. 65/D5
Mátészalka, Hun. 43/M5
Matetsi, Zim. 122/E3
Mathay, Fr. 60/C3
Mathbaria, Bang. 97/G4
Matheniko Game Rsv., Ugan. 117/G5
Matheson Island, Mb, Can. 156/F2
Mathews, La, US 164/C3
Mathews (lake), Ca, US 166/C3
Mathew's (peak), Kenya 119/B1
Mathews, Va, US 163/J2
Mathi, It. 64/D2
Mathis, Tx, US 151/F3
Mathiston, Ms, US 162/C4
Mathoura, Austl. 133/B2
Mathurā, India 96/A2
Mati, Phil. 88/D4
Matias Barbosa, Braz. 187/N6
Matias Olímpio, Braz. 183/F3
Matías Romero, Mex. 176/C2
Matignon, Fr. 56/C3
Matíguas, Nic. 176/E3
Matilija (dam), Ca, US 166/A2
Matimbuka, Tanz. 119/A4
Matinha, Braz. 183/E4
Matinicock (pt.), NY, US 169/L8
Mātir, Tun. 48/A4
Maţir Ţāris, Egypt 113/B6
Matiyuri (riv.), Ven. 180/D3
Matkuli, India 96/B4
Mātla (riv.), India 97/G5
Matlock, Eng, UK 35/G5
Maţmāţah, Tun. 66/F4
Matn (riv.), Leb. 105/D1
Mato Grosso (plat.), Braz. 179/D4
Mato Grosso (state), Braz. 182/A5
Mato Grosso do Sul (state), Braz. 185/G5
Mato Grosso, Meseta do (plat.), Braz. 185/G4
Mato Verde, Braz. 187/E2
Matobo (Matopos) NP, Zim. 123/F4
Matões, Braz. 183/F4
Matolo-Rio, Moz. 125/F2
Matomb, Camr. 120/B2
Matombo, Tanz. 119/B3
Matopos, Zim. 123/F4
Matopos (Matobo) NP, Zim. 123/F4
Matosinhos, Port. 46/A2
Matoury, FrG. 182/C1
Matouti (pt.), Gabon 120/B3
Matoya (bay), Japan 83/L7
Maţraḩ, Oman 101/G4
Matrei am Brenner, Aus. 61/H3
Matrei in Osttirol, Aus. 45/K3
Matriz de Camaragibe, Braz. 183/H5
Matroosberg (peak), SAfr. 124/L10
Matsalu (gulf), Est. 41/K2
Matsapa (Manzini) (int'l arpt.), Swaz. 125/E2
Matsiatra (riv.), Madg. 125/H8
Matsoandakana, Madg. 125/J6
Matsubara, Japan 83/J6
Matsubushi, Japan 83/D2
Matsuda, Japan 83/C3
Matsudo, Japan 83/D2
Matsue, Japan 84/C3
Matsuida, Japan 83/B1
Matsumae, Japan 82/B3
Matsumoto, Japan 85/E2
Matsuo, Japan 83/E2
Matsusaka, Japan 83/L6
Matsushima, Japan 82/B4
Matsutō, Japan 84/E2
Matsuyama, Japan 84/C4
Matt, Swi. 61/F4
Mattamuskeet (lake), NC, US 163/J3
Mattamuskeet Nat'l Wild. Ref., NC, US 163/J3
Mattaponi (riv.), Va, US 163/J2
Mattarello, It. 61/H6
Mattawa, On, Can. 161/G1
Mattawa, Wa, US 144/E4
Matterhorn (peak), It.,Swi. 60/D6
Mattertal (valley), Swi. 60/D5
Matteson, Il, US 160/C4
Matthew Town, Bahm. 177/H1
Matthews, Mo, US 162/C2
Matthews (mt.), NZ 135/J9
Matthews, NC, US 163/G3
Matthews Dome (mt.), Ak, US 171/H2
Mattie (lake), Fl, US 164/M7
Mattig (riv.), Aus. 59/G6
Mattighofen, Aus. 59/G6
Mattituck, NY, US 169/F2
Mattmarksee (lake), Swi. 60/D5
Mattō, Japan 84/E2
Mattock (riv.), Ire. 34/B4
Mattoon, Wi, US 155/K1
Mattsee, Aus. 59/G7
Matucana, Peru 184/B3
Matumbla (mt.), NY, US 161/J2
Matundwe (range), Malw.,Moz. 123/G3
Maturín, Ven. 181/F2
Matusadona NP, Zim. 123/F3
Matutum (mt.), Phil. 91/G2
Matveyev Kurgan, Rus. 73/K4
Matzen, Aus. 51/P7
Mau, India 96/C3
Mau, India 96/C4
Mau (peak), Kenya 119/A2
Maú (riv.), Guy. 181/G3
Maú (riv.), Guy.,Ven. 182/B1
Mau Aimma, India 96/C3
Mau Rānīpur, India 96/B3
Mau-é-Ele, Moz. 123/G5
Maúa, Moz. 123/H2
Maubert-Fontaine, Fr. 55/D4
Maubeuge, Fr. 54/C3
Maubourguet, Fr. 44/D5

Mauchline, Sc, UK 33/B5
Maud, Ok, US 153/F3
Maud, Tx, US 153/G4
Maud, Sc, UK 33/D1
Maud (pt.), Austl. 130/B2
Maudaha, India 96/C3
Maude, Austl. 133/B2
Maudlow, Mt, US 145/J4
Mauerbach, Aus. 51/N7
Mauerkirchen, Aus. 59/G6
Maués, Braz. 182/B3
Maués Açu (riv.), Braz. 182/B4
Maug (isls.), NMar. 136/D2
Mauganj, India 96/C3
Maughold, IM, UK 34/D3
Maughold (pt.), IM, UK 34/D3
Mauguio, Fr. 44/F5
Mauherslieve (peak), Ire. 32/B4
Maui (isl.), Hi, US 142/T10
Mauk, Rus. 69/P5
Mauke (isl.), CookIs. 137/K7
Maukkadaw, Myan. 86/B4
Maulbronn, Ger. 58/B5
Mauldre (riv.), Fr. 54/A6
Maule, Fr. 30/H5
Maule (riv.), Chile 190/C2
Maule (pol. reg.), Chile 190/B2
Mauléon, Fr. 44/C3
Maullín, Chile 190/B4
Maulvi Bāzār, Bang. 97/H3
Maumakeogh (peak), Ire. 32/A1
Maumee, Oh, US 160/E4
Maumere, Indo. 128/A2
Maumtrasna (peak), Ire. 32/A2
Maun, Bots. 122/D3
Maun (int'l arpt.), Bots. 122/D3
Mauna Kea (peak), Hi, US 142/U11
Mauna Loa (peak), Hi, US 142/U11
Maunath Bhanjan, India 96/D3
Maunatlala, Bots. 123/E4
Maungaturoto, NZ 135/C2
Maungdaw, Myan. 93/F3
Mauperthuis, Fr. 30/M5
Maupertus (int'l arpt.), Fr. 56/D1
Maupiti (isl.), FrPol. 137/K6
Maur, Swi. 61/E3
Maur, India 98/C4
Maurāwān, India 96/C2
Maurecourt, Fr. 30/J5
Maurepas, Fr. 54/A6
Maurepas (lake), La, US 164/C2
Mauriac, Fr. 44/E4
Maurice (riv.), NJ, US 168/C5
Maurice (lake), Austl. 127/C3
Mauricetown, NJ, US 168/D5
Mauriceville, Tx, US 151/H2
Mauricie, PN de la, Qu, Can. 161/K1
Maurienne (valley), Fr. 45/G4
Maurilândia, Braz. 186/C3
Maurine, SD, US 154/C1
Mauritania (ctry.) 107/A3
Mauriti, Braz. 183/G4
Mauritius (ctry.) 125/T15
Mauro (peak), It. 65/D4
Mauron, Fr. 56/C4
Maurui, Tanz. 119/B3
Maury City, Tn, US 162/C3
Mauston, Wi, US 155/J2
Mauthausen, Aus. 59/H6
Maverick, Az, US 149/H4
Mavila, Peru 184/D3
Mavinga, Ang. 122/D2
Mavis (reef), Austl. 128/A3
Mavqi'im, Isr. 105/B5
Mavrommátion, Gre. 49/H3
Mavrovo NP, FYROM 49/G2
Mavuradonha (mts.), Zim. 123/F3
Maw (pt.), NC, US 163/J3
Maw Daung (pass), Thai. 94/B4
Mawa, D.R. Congo 121/F2
Mawāna, India 96/A1
Mawanga, D.R. Congo 120/D4
Mawasangka, Indo. 128/A1
Mawei, China 87/E3
Mawhun, Myan. 86/C3
Mawiwi, D.R. Congo 121/F2
Māwiyah, Yem. 118/C2
Mawjib (wadi), Jor. 105/D6
Mawkmai, Myan. 86/C4
Mawlaik, Myan. 86/B4
Mawlamyine (Moulmein), Myan. 94/B2
Mawliba, India 97/H3
Mawshij, Yem. 118/B2
Mawson, Austl., Ant. 192/E
Max, ND, US 156/D4
Max Meadows, Va, US 163/G2
Maxah Ind. Res., Wa, US 144/B3
Maxaranguape, Braz. 183/H4
Maxcanú, Mex. 176/D1
Maxdorf, Ger. 58/B4
Maxéville, Fr. 55/F6
Maxhütte-Haidhof, Ger. 59/F4
Maxie, Ms, US 164/D2
Maxie, La, US 164/B2
Maxixe, Moz. 123/G4
Maxton, NC, US 163/H3
Maxville, Mt, US 145/H4
Maxwell (A.F.B.), Al, US 162/D4
Maxwell Nat'l Wildlife Reserve, NM, US 152/B2
Maxwelton, Austl. 134/A3
May, Tx, US 150/E2
May (cape), NJ, US 168/D5
May Pen, Jam. 177/G2
May, Isle of (isl.), Sc, UK 33/D4
May-en-Multien, Fr. 30/M4
Maya (riv.), Rus. 77/N4
Maya (mts.), Guat. 176/D2
Maya (isl.), Indo. 90/C4
Maya Beach, Belz. 176/D2
Maya Maya (int'l arpt.), Congo 120/C4
Maya-san (peak), Japan 83/H6
Mayaguana (isl.), Bahm. 139/K7
Mayaguana Passage (chan.), Bahm. 177/H1
Mayagüez, PR 173/M8
Mayahi, Niger 115/G3
Mayakovskogo (peak), Taj. 99/B4
Mayala, D.R. Congo 120/D4
Mayama, Congo 120/C3
Mayamba, D.R. Congo 120/D4
Mayāmey, Iran 103/H2
Mayan, China 78/F5
Mayang, China 93/J2
Mayāng Imphāl, India 86/B3
Mayaoyao, Phil. 88/C1
Mayarí, Cuba 177/H1
Maybee, Mi, US 167/E8
Maybell, Co, US 147/J3
Maybole, Sc, UK 33/B6
Maych'ew, Eth. 118/A2
Maydān, Iraq 103/F3
Maydh, Som. 118/C3
Maydī, Yem. 118/B1
Maydolong, Phil. 88/D3
Maydūm, Egypt 113/C6
Mayébout, Gabon 120/C2
Mayen, Ger. 55/G3
Mayenne (dept.), Fr. 57/E4
Mayenne, Fr. 57/E4
Mayenne (riv.), Fr. 44/C3
Mayer, Az, US 149/F3
Mayer, Mn, US 157/N7
Mayesville, SC, US 163/G4
Mayet, Fr. 57/F5
Mayetta, Ks, US 155/G4
Mayfa'ah, Yem. 118/C2
Mayfair, Sk, Can. 145/L1
Mayfield, Sc, UK 33/C5
Mayfield, Ut, US 147/H4
Mayfield, Ky, US 162/C2
Mayhill, NM, US 152/B4
Maykain, Kaz. 99/C1
Maykop, Rus. 73/L5
Mayland, Eng, UK 37/G3
Maymont, Sk, Can. 145/L1
Maymyo, Myan. 86/C4
Mayna, Rus. 71/H1
Maynard, Ar, US 162/B2
Maynardville, Tn, US 162/F2
Maynooth, Ire. 32/D3
Maynooth, On, Can. 161/H2
Mayo (riv.), Arg. 190/C5
Mayo (co.), Ire. 32/A2
Mayo, Yk, Can. 171/L3
Mayo (riv.), Mex. 174/C3
Mayo, Fl, US 165/G2
Mayo, Md, US 168/B6
Mayo (res.), NC, US 163/H2
Mayo Belwa, Nga. 116/B3
Mayo Kébi (riv.), Chad 116/B3
Mayo Mayo, Bol. 185/E4
Mayo Oulo, Camr. 116/B3
Mayo-Kébbi (pref.), Chad 116/B3
Mayoko, Congo 120/C3
Mayon (vol.), Phil. 88/C2
Mayotte (dpcy.), Fr. 125/H6
Mayotte (isl.), Fr. 107/G6
Mayoworth, Wy, US 147/K2
Maypearl, Tx, US 151/F1
Mayport Nav. Air Sta., Fl, US 165/H2
Mays Landing, NJ, US 168/D5
Mays Lick, Ky, US 162/F1
Maysān (gov.), Iraq 103/F4
Mayskiy, Rus. 71/H4
Mayskiy, Rus. 73/L4
Mayskiy, Rus. 79/K1
Maysville, Ky, US 162/F1
Maysville, Mo, US 155/G4
Maysville, Ok, US 153/F3
Maythalūn, WBnk. 105/C4
Mayuka, Zam. 123/F1
Mayumba, Gabon 120/B3
Mayuram, India 95/C4
Mayville, ND, US 156/F4
Mayville, NY, US 161/G3
Mayville, Wi, US 160/B3
Mayville, Or, US 146/C1
Maywood, Ca, US 166/F8
Maywood, Il, US 167/Q16
Maywood, Mo, US 155/J4
Maywood, Ne, US 154/D3
Maywood, NJ, US 169/J8
Mazabuka, Zam. 123/E2
Mazagão, Braz. 182/D3
Mazama, Wa, US 144/D3
Mazamet, Fr. 44/E5
Mazan, Fr. 64/B4
Mazán, Peru 184/C1
Mazandaran (gov.), Iran 103/H2
Mazār-e Sharīf, Afg. 101/J1
Mazara del Vallo, It. 48/C4
Mazarrón, Sp. 46/E4
Mazartag, China 99/D4
Mazaruni (riv.), Guy. 181/G3
Mazatán, Mex. 174/C2
Mazatenango, Guat. 176/D3
Mazatlán, Mex. 174/D4
Mazatzal (peak), Az, US 149/G3
Mazatzal (mts.), Az, US 149/G3
Mazé, Fr. 57/E6
Mažeikiai, Lith. 41/K3
Mazenod, Sk, Can. 145/L3
Mazeppa NP, Austl. 134/B3
Mazetown, NI, UK 34/B3
Mazgirt, Turk. 102/D2
Mazie, Ok, US 153/G2
Mazıkıran (pass), Turk. 102/D2
Mazinda, D.R. Congo 120/D4
Mazingarbe, Fr. 54/B3
Mazingu, D.R. Congo 120/D4
Mazirbe, Lat. 41/K3
Mazocruz, Peru 188/B1
Mazoe, Zim. 123/F3
Mazoe (riv.), Moz. 123/G3
Mazomanie, Wi, US 155/K2
Mazomeno, D.R. Congo 121/F4
Mazon, Il, US 160/B4
Mazong (peak), China 78/D3
Mazowe (riv.), Zim. 123/F3
Mazowieckie (prov.), Pol. 43/L2
Mazsalaca, Lat. 41/L3
Mazunga, Zim. 123/F4
Mazury (reg.), Pol. 43/L2
Māzūz (well), Libya 108/D2
Mazyr, Bela. 72/E1
Mbabala (isl.), Zam. 121/G5
Mbabala, Zam. 123/E3
Mbabane (cap.), Swaz. 125/E2
Mbabo (peak), Camr. 116/B4
Mbacké, Sen. 114/B3
Mbagne, Mrta. 114/B2
Mbahiakro, C.d'Iv. 114/D5
Mbaïki, CAfr. 120/D2
Mbakaou, Camr. 116/B4
Mbakaou (lake), Camr. 116/B4
Mbala, Zam. 121/G5
Mbalabala, Zim. 123/F4
Mbalam, Camr. 120/C2
Mbalambala, Kenya 119/B2
Mbale, Ugan. 119/A1
Mbali, D.R. Congo 120/D3
Mbali-Iboma, D.R. Congo 120/D3
Mbalmayo, Camr. 120/B2
Mbam (riv.), Camr. 116/A4
Mbam Minkoum (peak), Camr. 120/B2
Mbamba Bay, Tanz. 123/G1
Mban (riv.), Camr. 120/B1
Mbandaka, D.R. Congo 120/D2
Mbandjok, Camr. 116/A4
Mbang, Camr. 120/C2
Mbanga, Camr. 120/B1
Mbanio (lag.), Gabon 120/B3
Mbanza Congo, Ang. 120/C4
Mbanza-Ngungu, D.R. Congo 120/D2
Mbaranganda (riv.), Tanz. 119/B4
Mbarangandu, Tanz. 119/B4
Mbarara, Ugan. 121/G3
Mbari (riv.), CAfr. 116/D4
Mbata, CAfr. 120/D2
Mbé, Camr. 116/B4
Mbengga (isl.), Fiji 137/Y18
Mberengwa, Zim. 123/F4
Mbereshi Mission, Zam. 121/G5
Mbeya, Tanz. 119/A4
Mbeya, Zam. 123/G1
Mbeya (prov.), Tanz. 119/A3
Mbeya (range), Tanz. 119/A4
Mbeya (peak), Tanz. 119/A4
M'Bigou, Gabon 120/B3
Mbii, CAfr. 116/D4
Mbinda, Congo 120/C3
Mbingué, C.d'Iv. 114/D4
Mbini (riv.), EqG. 120/B2
Mbini, EqG. 120/B2
Mbirira, Tanz. 121/G4
Mbirizi, Ugan. 121/G3
Mbizi, Zim. 123/F4
Mbogo, Tanz. 119/A3
Mboki, CAfr. 117/E4
Mboko, D.R. Congo 121/G3
Mboloma, Zam. 123/F2
Mbomo, Congo 120/C3
Mbomou (pref.), CAfr. 116/D4
Mbomou (riv.), CAfr. 117/E4
Mbonda (pt.), EqG. 120/B2
Mboro, Sen. 114/A3
Mborong, Indo. 91/F5
Mbouda, Camr. 120/B1
Mboula, CAfr. 116/C4
Mbouomo, Congo 120/C3
M'Bour, Sen. 114/A3
M'Bout, Mrta. 114/B2
Mbres, CAfr. 116/C4
Mbuji-Mayi, D.R. Congo 121/E4
Mbulu, Tanz. 119/A2
Mburucuya, Arg. 188/E4
Mbuvu, Kenya 119/B2
Mbuzi, Zam. 123/G2
Mbwemburu (riv.), Tanz. 119/B4
Mbwikwe, Tanz. 119/A3
McAdam, NB, Can. 158/D3
McAdoo, Pa, US 168/C2
McAdoo, Tx, US 152/D4
McAfee, NJ, US 168/D1
McAlester, Ok, US 153/G3
McAlisterville, Pa, US 168/A2
McAllen, Tx, US 151/E4
McAndrews, Ky, US 163/F2
McArthur, Oh, US 163/F1
McArthur Mills, On, Can. 161/H2
McBain, Mi, US 160/D2
McBean, Ga, US 163/G4
McBee, SC, US 163/G3
McBride, BC, Can. 144/D1
McBride, Ok, US 153/F4
McCabe, Mt, US 156/B3
McCall, Id, US 146/E1
McCall Creek, Ms, US 164/C2
McCamey, Tx, US 150/C2
McCammon, Id, US 147/G2
McCarran (int'l arpt.), Nv, US 148/E2
McCarthy, Ak, US 171/K3
McCarthy's Rust, Bots. 124/C2
McCaslin (mtn.), Wi, US 160/B2
McCaulley, Tx, US 150/D1
McCaysville, Ga, US 162/E3
McChord (A.F.B.), Wa, US 144/C4
McClanahan, Tx, US 151/F2
McClave, Co, US 152/C1
McClellan (cr.), Tx, US 152/D3
McClellanville, SC, US 163/H4
McCloud (riv.), Ca, US 146/B3
McClure, Il, US 162/C2
McClure, Pa, US 168/A2
McClusky, ND, US 156/D4
McColl, SC, US 163/H3
McComb, Ms, US 164/C2
McComb, Oh, US 160/E4
McConnell (A.F.B.), Ks, US 153/F2
McConnell, Tn, US 162/C2
McConnellsburg, Pa, US 161/H5
McConnelsville, Oh, US 160/F5
McCook, Ne, US 154/D3
McCook, Tx, US 151/E4
McCord, Sk, Can. 145/L3
McCormick, SC, US 163/F4
McCracken, Ks, US 152/E1
McCreary, Mb, Can. 156/E2
McCrory, Ar, US 153/J3
McCullom Lake, Il, US 167/P15
McCullough, Al, US 164/E2
McCune, Ks, US 153/G2
McCurtain, Ok, US 153/G3
McDade, Tx, US 150/F2
McDaniel, Md, US 168/B6
McDavid, Fl, US 164/E2
McDermitt, Nv, US 146/E3
McDonald (isls.), Austl. 192/E
McDonald (mt.), Ak, US 171/F3
McDonald Observatory, Tx, US 150/B2
McDonnell (mt.), Austl. 131/H5
McDonough, Ga, US 163/M8
McDougall (pass), NW, Yk., Can. 171/L2
McElhattan, Pa, US 168/A1
McEwen, Tn, US 162/D2
McFadden NWR, Tx, US 151/G3
McFarland, Ca, US 148/C3
McFarland, Mi, US 157/L4
McFarland, Wi, US 155/K2
McGaffey, NM, US 149/H3
McGee, Sk, Can. 145/K2
McGee Creek (lake), Ok, US 153/G3
McGehee, Ar, US 153/J4
McGhee Tyson (int'l arpt.), Tn, US 162/F3
McGill, Nv, US 147/F4
McGrath, Ak, US 171/G3
McGrath, Mn, US 157/H4
McGraw, NY, US 161/H3
McGraw Brook, NB, Can. 158/D2
McGregor, On, Can. 167/G7
McGregor, Mn, US 157/H4
McGregor, ND, US 156/C3
McGregor, Tx, US 151/F2
McGuire (A.F.B.), NJ, US 168/D3
McHenry, Il, US 160/B3
McHenry (co.), Il, US 167/N15
McHenry, Ky, US 162/D2
McHenry, Ms, US 164/D2
McHinga, Tanz. 119/B4
McHinji, Malw. 123/G2
McInnis (lake), On, Can. 157/H1
McIntosh, Mn, US 156/G4
McIntosh, SD, US 156/D5
McIntosh, Al, US 164/D2
McIntosh, NM, US 149/J3
McKay Creek Nat'l Wild. Ref., Or, US 146/D1
McKay Creek NWR, Or, US 144/E5
McKean (isl.), Kiri. 137/H5
McKeand (riv.), Nun, Can. 141/K2
McKee, Ky, US 162/F2
McKee City, NJ, US 168/D5
McKeesport, Pa, US 161/G4
McKellar, On, Can. 160/G2
McKenzie, Al, US 164/E2
McKenzie (riv.), Or, US 146/B1
McKenzie, Tn, US 162/C2
McKinlay, Austl. 134/A3
McKinley (mt.), Ak, US 171/H3
McKinley Park (Denali National Park), Ak, US 171/J3
McKinleyville, Ca, US 146/A3
McKinney, Tx, US 150/L6
McKinney Bayou (riv.), Tx,Ar, US 153/G4
McKittrick, Ca, US 148/C3
McLain, Ms, US 164/D2
McLaren Creek Abor. Land, Austl. 128/D5
McLaughlin, SD, US 156/D5
McLaurin, Ms, US 164/D2
McLean, Tx, US 152/D3
McLean, Il, US 155/K3
McLean, Va, US 168/A6
McLeansboro, Il, US 162/C1
McLeod (bay), NW, Can. 140/E2
McLeod (riv.), Ab, Can. 144/F1
McLeod (lake), Austl. 130/B3
McLoughlin (mt.), Or, US 146/B2
M'Clure (str.), NW, Can. 140/E2
McLure, BC, Can. 144/D2
McMillan, Ok, US 153/F3
McMinnville, Or, US 146/B1
McMinnville, Tn, US 162/E3
McMunn, Mb, Can. 157/G3
McMurdo, US, Ant. 192/M
McNab, Ar, US 153/H4
McNamee, NB, Can. 158/D2
McNary, Az, US 149/H3
McNary (dam), Or, US 144/E5
McNary NWR, Wa, US 144/E4
McNaughton, Wi, US 157/K5
McNeil, Ar, US 153/H4
McNeil (isl.), Wa, US 167/B3
McNeill, Ms, US 164/D2
McOcha, Malw. 123/G2
McPhee (res.), Co, US 149/H2
McPherson, Ks, US 153/F1
McQueeney, Tx, US 151/E3
McRae, Ar, US 153/J3
McRae, Ga, US 165/G1
McVille, ND, US 156/E4
McWilliams, Al, US 164/E2
Mdabulo, Tanz. 119/A3
Mdaburo, Tanz. 119/A3
Mdandu, Tanz. 119/A4
Mdantsane, SAfr. 124/D4
M'diq, Mor. 112/B2
Mê (riv.), China 78/E5
Me-akan-dake (peak), Japan 82/C2
Meacham, Sk, Can. 145/M1
Mead (lake), Az,Nv, US 139/F6
Mead, Ne, US 155/F3
Meade (riv.), Ak, US 171/G2
Meade, Ks, US 152/D2
Meadow, Tx, US 152/C4
Meadow, SD, US 156/C5
Meadow, Ut, US 149/F1
Meadow Lake, Sk, Can. 140/F3
Meadow Valley, Ca, US 146/C4
Meadow Valley Wash (riv.), Nv, US 148/E2
Meadow Vista, Ca, US 146/C4
Meadowlands, Mn, US 157/H4
Meadowlands Sports Complex, NJ, US 169/J8
Meadows, Id, US 146/E1
Meadows, Md, US 168/B6
Meadowvale, On, Can. 160/T8
Meadville, Ms, US 164/C2
Meadville, Pa, US 160/F4
Meadville, Mo, US 155/H4
Meaford, On, Can. 160/F2
Mealhada, Port. 46/A2
Meall a' Bhuiridh (peak), Sc, UK 33/B3
Meall Buidhe (peak), Sc, UK 33/B3
Meall Dearg (peak), Sc, UK 33/C3
Meall Dubh (peak), Sc, UK 33/B2
Meall nam Fuaran (peak), Sc, UK 33/C4
Meall Tairneachan (peak), Sc, UK 33/C3
Mearim (riv.), Braz. 183/E4
Measham, Eng, UK 37/E1
Meat (mt.), Ak, US 171/F2
Meath (co.), Ire. 34/B4
Meath Park, Sk, Can. 145/M1
Méaulte, Fr. 54/B4
Meaux, Fr. 30/L5
Mebenda (peak), Gabon 120/B3
Mebridege (riv.), Ang. 120/C4
Mecapalapa, Mex. 175/M6
Mècatina,Rivière du Petit (riv.), Nf,Qu, Can. 141/K3
Mecca (Makkah), SAr. 100/C4
Mecca, Ca, US 148/D4
Mechanicsburg, Oh, US 160/E4
Mechanicsburg, Pa, US 168/A3
Mechanicsburg Nav. Res., Pa, US 168/B3
Mechanicsville, Va, US 163/J2
Mechant (lake), La, US 164/C3
Mechara, Eth. 118/B3
Mechelen, Belg. 55/D1
Mecheria, Alg. 111/E2
Mechi (zone), Nepal 97/F2
Méchiméré, Chad 116/B2
Mechra-Bel-Ksiri, Mor. 112/B2
Mechrâ-Saf-Saf, Mor. 112/C2
Mecidiye, Turk. 51/H5
Mecitözü, Turk. 102/C1
Meckenbeuren, Ger. 61/F2
Meckenheim, Ger. 55/G2
Mecklenburg-Vorpommern (state), Ger. 40/E5
Mecklenburger (bay), Ger. 42/F1
Meconta, Moz. 123/H2
Mecoya, Bol. 188/C2
Mecsek (mts.), Hun. 67/H1
Mecuburi (riv.), Moz. 123/H2
Mecúfi, Moz. 123/J2
Mecuia (peak), Moz. 123/G2
Mecula, Moz. 123/H2
Meda, It. 62/C2
Medak, India 95/C2
Medan, Indo. 89/B2
Medang (cape), Indo. 89/C2
Médanos, Arg. 190/E3
Medanos de Coro, PN, Ven. 180/D2
Medanosa (pt.), Arg. 191/D6
Medaryville, In, US 160/C4
Medbourne, Eng, UK 37/F1
Mede Lomellina, It. 62/B3
Médéa (wilaya), Alg. 112/G4
Médéa, Alg. 112/G4
Medebach, Ger. 53/F6
Medeiros Neto, Braz. 187/E3
Medel (peak), Swi. 61/E4
Medellín, Col. 183/K6
Medemblik, Neth. 52/C3
Meden (riv.), Eng, UK 35/G5
Mederdra, Mrta. 114/B2
Medesano, It. 62/D4
Medetsiz (peak), Turk. 102/C2
Medford, NY, US 169/E2
Medford, Ok, US 153/F2
Medford, Or, US 146/B2
Medford, Wi, US 157/J5
Medford Lakes, NJ, US 168/D4
Medgidia, Rom. 51/J3
Medi, Sudan 117/F4
Media, Pa, US 168/C4
Media Agua, Arg. 188/B4
Medianeira, Braz. 189/F3
Mediapolis, Ia, US 155/J3
Mediaş, Rom. 51/G2
Medical Lake, Wa, US 144/F4
Medicina, It. 63/E5
Medicine (cr.), Mo, US 155/H3
Medicine (cr.), Ne, US 154/D3
Medicine (lake), Mt, US 145/M3
Medicine (riv.), Ab, Can. 144/G1
Medicine Bow (mts.), Wy, US 142/E3
Medicine Bow (riv.), Wy, US 147/K2
Medicine Bow (peak), Wy, US 154/A3
Medicine Hat, Ab, Can. 145/J2
Medicine Knoll (cr.), SD, US 156/E5
Medicine Lake, Mt, US 156/B3
Medicine Lake NWR, Mt, US 156/B3
Medicine Lodge, Ks, US 153/E2
Medicine Lodge (riv.), Ks,Ok, US 152/E2
Medika, Mb, Can. 156/G3
Medina, Col. 180/C3
Medina (int'l arpt.), SAr. 135/H3
Medina (riv.), Eng, UK 37/E5
Medina, ND, US 156/E4
Medina, NY, US 161/G3
Medina, Oh, US 160/F4
Medina, Tn, US 162/C3
Medina, Tx, US 150/E3
Medina (riv.), Tx, US 151/E3
Medina, Wa, US 167/C2
Medina de Pomar, Sp. 44/B5
Medina de Rioseco, Sp. 46/C2
Medina del Campo, Sp. 46/C2
Médina Gonassé, Sen. 114/B3
Medina-Sidonia, Sp. 46/C4
Medinaceli, Sp. 46/D2
Medininkai, Lith. 41/L4
Medinipur, India 97/F4
Medio (cr.), Tx, US 151/F3
Mediodía, Col. 180/C5
Mediouna, Mor. 110/D2
Mediterranean (sea) 29/E5
Medje, D.R. Congo 121/F2
Mednogorsk, Rus. 71/L2
Mêdog, China 86/B2
Medole, It. 62/D3
Medolla, It. 63/E4
Medora, In, US 162/D1
Medora, ND, US 156/C4
Médouneu, Gabon 120/B2
Medowie, Austl. 133/E1
Medstead, Sk, Can. 145/K1
Medulla, Fl, US 164/M8
Medveditsa (riv.), Rus. 74/E5
Medvedovskaya, Rus. 73/K5
Medvënka, Rus. 73/J2
Medvezh'i (isls.), Rus. 75/S2
Medvezh'yegorsk, Rus. 68/G3
Medvode, Slov. 45/L3
Medway (co.), Eng, UK 37/G4
Medyn', Rus. 68/G5
Medzilaborce, Slvk. 72/A3
Meekatharra, Austl. 130/C3
Meeker, Co, US 147/K3
Meelpaeg (lake), Nf, Can. 159/J1
Meenambarkkam (int'l arpt.), India 95/D3
Meer, Belg. 52/B6
Meerbusch, Ger. 52/D6
Meerhout, Belg. 55/E1
Meersburg, Ger. 61/F2
Meerssen, Neth. 55/E2
Meerut, India 96/A1
Meeteetse, Wy, US 147/J1
Meeuwen, Belg. 55/E1
Mēga, Eth. 118/A4
Mega (isl.), Indo. 89/C4
Mega, Indo. 91/H4
Megála Kalívia, Gre. 49/G3
Megáli Panayía, Gre. 49/H2
Megalo, Eth. 118/B4
Megálon Khoríon, Gre. 102/A2
Megalópolis, Gre. 49/H4
Meganom (cape), Ukr. 73/H5
Megantic (peak), Qu, Can. 158/B3
Mégara, Gre. 49/H3
Megargel, Tx, US 152/E4
Megargel, Al, US 164/E2
Megève, Fr. 60/C6
Megezez (peak), Eth. 118/A3
Meghalaya (state), India 93/F2
Meghna (riv.), Bang. 97/H4
Megiddo, Isr. 105/C3
Megista (isl.), Gre. 104/A1
Megrega, Rus. 41/Q1
Megri, Arm. 103/F2
Meguzalala, Moz. 123/F4
Mehaigne (riv.), Belg. 55/E2
Mehal Mēda, Eth. 118/A3
Mehamn, Nor. 38/H1
Meharry (mt.), Austl. 130/C2
Mehdia, Alg. 112/F5
Mehdīshahr, Iran 103/H3
Mehdiya-Plage, Mor. 112/A2
Mehe (riv.), Ger. 53/G1
Mehedinti (co.), Rom. 72/B5
Meherpur, Bang. 97/G4
Meherrin (riv.), Va, US 163/H2
Mehikoorma, Est. 41/M2
Mehlingen, Ger. 55/G4
Mehndāwal, India 96/D2
Mehrabad (int'l arpt.), Iran 103/G3
Mehrabān, Iran 103/F2
Mehrān (riv.), Iran 101/F3
Mehring, Ger. 55/F4
Mehrīz, Iran 103/H4
Mehrnbach, Aus. 59/G6
Mehtar Lām, Afg. 98/A2
Mei (riv.), China 87/G3
Meia Meia, Tanz. 119/A3
Meia Ponte (riv.), Braz. 186/C3
Meidougou, Camr. 116/B4
Meiganga, Camr. 116/B4
Meighen (isl.), Nun, Can. 141/R7
Meigle, Sc, UK 33/C3
Meigs, Ga, US 165/F2
Meigu, China 93/H2
Meihekou, China 79/K3
Meikle Bin (peak), Sc, UK 33/B4
Meikle Black Law (hill), Sc, UK 33/D5
Meikle Says Law (peak), Sc, UK 33/D5
Meikou, China 87/H3
Meiktila, Myan. 86/B4
Meilen, Swi. 61/E3
Meine, Ger. 53/H4
Meiners Oaks, Ca, US 166/A2
Meinersen, Ger. 53/H4
Meinerzhagen, Ger. 55/G1
Meiningen, Ger. 58/D1
Meiringen, Swi. 60/E4
Meisenheim, Ger. 55/G4
Meishan, China 86/D2
Meishan, China 87/H3
Meishan (res.), China 80/C5
Meishan, China 87/H3
Meishan, China 80/K8
Meishuikeng, China 87/H3
Meissen, Ger. 43/G3
Meissner (peak), Ger. 53/G6
Meitian, China 87/G3
Meitingen, Ger. 58/D5
Meiwa, Japan 83/L6
Meix-Devant-Virton, Belg. 55/E4
Meizhou, China 87/H3
Mejaniga, It. 63/E3
Mejaouda (well), Mrta. 110/D5
Mejillones, Chile 188/B2
Mejorada del Campo, Sp. 47/N9
Mekambo, Gabon 120/C2
Mekane Selam, Eth. 118/A3
Mek'elē, Eth. 118/A2
Mékhé, Sen. 114/A3
Mek'ī, Eth. 118/A3
Mekinock, ND, US 156/F3
Meknès, Mor. 112/B3
Meknès (prov.), Mor. 112/B3
Meko, Nga. 115/F5
Mekong (riv.), Asia 94/C1
Mekongga (peak), Indo. 91/F4
Mekoryuk, Ak, US 171/E3
Melaka, Malay. 89/C2
Melaka (state), Malay. 89/C2
Melanesia (reg.) 136/E5
Melappālaiyam, India 95/C4
Melawi (riv.), Indo. 90/D4
Melbeck, Ger. 53/H2
Melbourn, Eng, UK 37/G2
Melbourne, Austl. 132/G5
Melbourne (isl.), Nun, Can. 140/F2
Melbourne, Eng, UK 35/G6
Melbourne, Ar, US 153/J2
Melbourne, Fl, US 165/H3
Melbu, Nor. 38/E1
Melcher-Dallas, Ia, US 155/H3
Melchor (isl.), Chile 190/B5
Melchor Múzquiz, Mex. 150/D4
Melchor Ocampo, Mex. 150/E4
Melchor Ocampo, Mex. 175/Q9
Melcombe Regis, Eng, UK 36/D5
Meldola, It. 63/F5
Meldorf, Ger. 40/C4
Mele (cape), It. 62/B6
Meleb, Mb, Can. 156/F2
Melegnano, It. 62/C3
Melenci, Serb. 50/E3
Melenki, Rus. 68/J5
Melesse, Fr. 56/D4
Meleuz, Rus. 71/K1
Mélèzes (riv.), Qu, Can. 141/J3
Melezza (riv.), It. 61/E5
Melfa (riv.), It. 65/C4
Melfi, Chad 116/C3
Melfi, It. 48/D2
Melfort, Sk, Can. 145/M1
Melgaço, Port. 46/A1
Melgar, Col. 183/L8
Melgar de Fernamental, Sp. 46/C1
Melhus, Nor. 38/D3
Melibocus (peak), Ger. 58/B3
Melide, Swi. 61/E6
Meligalás, Gre. 49/G4
Melíki, Gre. 49/H2
Melili (peak), Kenya 119/B2
Melilla, Sp. 112/C2
Melimoyu (peak), Chile 190/B5
Melinca, Chile 190/B4
Melipilla, Chile 190/N8
Mélisey, Fr. 60/C2
Melissano, It. 49/F3
Melita, Mb, Can. 156/D3
Melita (int'l arpt.), Tun. 67/F4
Melito di Porto Salvo, It. 48/D4
Melitopol', Ukr. 73/H4
Melitota, Md, US 168/B5
Melka Guba, Eth. 118/A4
Melka Meri, Eth. 118/B4
Melkasa, Eth. 118/A3
Melkbosstrand, SAfr. 124/L10
Melksham, Eng, UK 36/D4
Mella (riv.), It. 62/D2
Mellac, Fr. 56/B5
Mellan Fryken (lake), Swe. 40/E2
Melle, Belg. 54/C2
Melle, Ger. 53/F4
Mellea (riv.), It. 62/A3
Mellègue, Oued (riv.), Alg. 112/K7
Mellerud, Swe. 40/E2
Mellette, SD, US 154/E1
Mellid, Sp. 46/A1
Mellieħa, Malta 48/L7
Melling, Eng, UK 35/F3
Mellingen, Swi. 61/E3
Mellit, Sudan 117/E2
Mellizo Sur (peak), Chile 191/B6
Mellrichstadt, Ger. 58/D2
Mellum (isl.), Ger. 53/F1
Melmoth, SAfr. 125/E3
Melnik, Bul. 49/H2
Mělník, Czh. 59/H2
Mel'nytsya-Podil's'ka, Ukr. 72/D3
Melo, Uru. 189/F5
Melocheville, Qu, Can. 159/N7
Melolo, Indo. 91/F5
Mélong, Camr. 120/B1
Melrose, Austl. 133/C2
Melrose, Sc, UK 33/D5
Melrose, La, US 164/B2
Melrose, Mn, US 157/G5
Melrose, Md, US 168/B4
Melrose, Wi, US 155/J1
Melrose Abbey, Sc, UK 33/D5
Melrose Bombing Range, NM, US 152/C3
Melrose Park, Il, US 167/Q16
Mels, Swi. 61/F3
Melstone, Mt, US 145/L4
Melsungen, Ger. 53/G6
Meltham, Eng, UK 35/G4
Melton, Austl. 133/B3
Melton Mowbray, Eng, UK 37/F1
Melúli (riv.), Moz. 123/H2
Melun, Fr. 30/K6
Melunga, Ang. 122/C3
Melvern, Ks, US 153/G1
Melvern (lake), Ks, US 155/G4
Melville (bay), Austl. 127/C2
Melville (cape), Austl. 134/B1
Melville (nbrhd.), Austl. 130/K7
Melville (lake), Nf, Can. 141/L3
Melville (pen.), Can. 139/J3
Melville (isl.), Can. 127/C2
Melville (cape), Phil. 88/B4
Melville, Sk, Can. 156/C2
Melville, La, US 164/C2
Melville, NY, US 169/M8
Melville, Mt, US 145/K4
Melville Abor. Land, Austl. 128/C2
Melville Hall (int'l arpt.), Dom. 173/N9
Melvin, Al, US 164/D2
Melvin, Tx, US 150/E2
Melvindale, Mi, US 167/F7
Mélykút, Hun. 50/D2
Melzo, It. 62/C3
Memaliaj, Alb. 49/F2
Memar (lake), China 99/D5
Memāri, India 97/G4
Memba, Moz. 123/J2
Membalong, Indo. 90/C4
Même (riv.), Fr. 57/F4
Memmert (isl.), Ger. 52/D1
Memmingen, Ger. 61/G2
Memot, Camb. 94/D4
Memphis, Tx, US 152/D3
Memphis, Mi, US 167/G6
Memphis, Mo, US 155/H3
Memphis, Tn, US 162/B3
Memphis (int'l arpt.), Tn, US 162/C3
Memphis (ruin), Egypt 113/C5
Memphis Nav. Air Sta., Tn, US 162/C3
Memphrémagog (lake), Qu, Can. 158/A3
Mena, Ar, US 153/G3
Mèna, Mali 114/D3
Mena, Ukr. 72/G2
Mena, Eth. 118/A4
Mena, Indo. 128/B2
Menafra, Uru. 191/K10
Menaggio, It. 61/F5
Menahga, Mn, US 157/G4
Menai (str.), Wal, UK 34/D5
Menai Bridge, Wal, UK 34/D5
Ménaka, Mali 115/F3
Menaldum, Neth. 52/C2
Menan, Id, US 147/H2
Menanga, Indo. 91/F4
Menara (Marrakech) (int'l arpt.), Mor. 110/C3
Menarandra (riv.), Madg. 125/H9
Menard, Tx, US 150/E2
Menasalbas, Sp. 46/C3
Menasha, Wi, US 155/K1
Menavava (riv.), Madg. 125/H7
Menawashei, Sudan 117/E2
Mencué, Arg. 190/C4
Mendawai (riv.), Indo. 90/D4
Mende, Fr. 44/E4
Mendebo (mts.), Eth. 118/A4
Menden, Ger. 53/E6
Mendenhall (cape), Ak, US 171/E4
Mendenhall, Ms, US 164/D2
Mendes, Braz. 187/N7
Méndez, Mex. 175/F3
Mendham, Sk, Can. 145/K2
Mendham, NJ, US 168/D2
Mendī, Eth. 117/G3
Mendi, PNG 129/F1
Mendig, Ger. 55/G3
Mendip (hills), Eng, UK 36/D4
Mendocino, Ca, US 146/B4
Mendocino (pass), Ca, US 146/B4
Mendocino (cape), Ca, US 142/A3
Mendol (isl.), Indo. 89/C2
Mendon, Mi, US 160/D3
Mendon, Mo, US 155/H4
Mendooran, Austl. 132/D1
Mendota, Ca, US 148/B2
Mendota, Il, US 155/K3
Mendota, Mn, US 157/P7
Mendoza, Cuba 177/E1
Mendoza (prov.), Arg. 190/C2
Mendoza, Arg. 190/C2
Mendoza, Uru. 191/K11
Mendoza, Peru 184/B2
Mendoza (El Plumerillo) (int'l arpt.), Arg. 190/C2
Mendrisio, Swi. 61/E6
Mene Grande, Ven. 180/D2
Menegosa (peak), It. 62/C4
Menemen, Turk. 70/C5
Menen, Belg. 54/C2
Menengai Crater, Kenya 119/B2
Menengiyn (plain), Mong. 75/M5
Menfi, It. 48/C4
Meng Xian, China 80/C4
Mengcheng, China 80/D4
Mengen, Ger. 61/F1
Mengen, Turk. 70/E4
Mengersgereuth-Hämmern, Ger. 58/D2
Mengerskirchen, Ger. 58/B1
Mengeš, Slov. 45/L3
Menggala, Indo. 89/D4
Menggatal, Malay. 88/B4
Menghai, China 94/C1
Mengibar, Sp. 46/D4
Mengjian, China 87/F4
Mengkofen, Ger. 59/F5
Mengla, China 94/C1
Menglian Daizu Lahuzu Vazu Zizhixian, China 86/C4
Mengman, China 94/C1
Mengshan, China 87/F3
Mengxing, China 94/C1
Mengyin, China 80/D4
Mengzi, China 86/D4
Ménilles, Fr. 57/G2
Menindee (dam), Austl. 132/B2
Menindee, Austl. 132/B2
Menindee (lake), Austl. 131/J5
Meningie, Austl. 132/A2
Menlo, Ga, US 162/E3
Menlo Park, Ca, US 167/K12
Menlo Park, NJ, US 169/H9
Menlolat (peak), Chile 190/B5
Mennecy, Fr. 30/K6
Mennetou-sur-Cher, Fr. 57/G6
Menoken Indian Village Historical Site, ND, US 156/D4
Menominee (riv.), Mi, Wi, US 157/L5
Menominee, Mi, US 160/C2
Menominee Ind. Res., Wi, US 155/K1
Menomonee Falls, Wi, US 160/B3
Menomonie, Wi, US 155/J1
Menongue, Ang. 122/C2
Menonitas Colonias, Par. 188/E2
Menorca (int'l arpt.), Sp. 47/H3
Menorca (Minorca) (isl.), Sp. 47/H2
Mentana, It. 65/B3
Mentasta Lake, Ak, US 171/K3
Mentawai (isls.), Indo. 77/J10
Mentawai (str.), Indo. 90/A4
Mentekab, Malay. 89/C2
Menteroda, Ger. 53/H6
Menthon-Saint-Bernard, Fr. 60/C6
Mentmore, NM, US 149/H3
Menton, Fr. 64/D5
Mentone, Ca, US 166/C2
Mentone, In, US 160/C4
Mentone, Tx, US 150/C2
Mentor, Mn, US 156/F4
Mentor, Oh, US 160/F4
Mentougou, China 80/H7
Mentue (riv.), Swi. 60/C4
Menucourt, Fr. 30/H4
Menuma, Japan 83/C1
Menyamya, PNG 129/G1
Menyapa (peak), Indo. 91/E3
Menyuan Huizu Zizhixian, China 78/E4
Menzel Bourquiba, Tun. 48/A4
Menzie (mt.), Yk, Can. 171/M3
Menzies, Austl. 130/D4
Menziken, Swi. 60/E3
Menzingen, Swi. 61/E3
Menznau, Swi. 60/E3
Meolo, It. 63/F2
Meon (riv.), Eng, UK 37/E5
Meopham, Eng, UK 30/E2
Meoquí, Mex. 150/B3
Meos Waar (isl.), Indo. 91/H4
Meota, Sk, Can. 145/K1
Méouge (riv.), Fr. 64/B4
Mepala, Ang. 120/C4
Mepistskaro (peak), Geo. 71/G4
Meppel, Neth. 52/D3
Meppen, Ger. 53/E3
Mequinenzo (res.), Sp. 47/E2
Mequon, Wi, US 160/C3
Mer, Fr. 57/G5
Mer Rouge, La, US 153/J4
Mera (riv.), It. 61/F5
Merak, Indo. 89/D4
Meramec (riv.), Mo, US 155/J5
Merano, It. 61/H4
Merasheen (isl.), Nf, Can. 159/K2
Merate, It. 62/C2
Meratus (mts.), Indo. 90/D4
Merauke, Indo. 129/F2
Merauke (riv.), Indo. 129/F2
Merbein, Austl. 132/B2
Mercaderes, Col. 180/B4
Mercantour, PN, Fr. 45/G4
Mercatello sul Metauro, It. 63/F6
Mercato, It. 65/D6
Mercato San Severino, It. 65/D6
Mercato Saraceno, It. 63/F6
Merced, Ca, US 148/B2
Merced (peak), Ca, US 148/C2
Merced (riv.), Ca, US 148/B2
Merced Grove, Ca, US 148/C2
Mercedario (peak), Arg. 188/B4
Mercedes, Arg. 190/D2
Mercedes, Arg. 191/J11
Mercedes, Arg. 188/E4
Mercedes, Uru. 191/J10
Mercedes, Tx, US 151/F4
Mercer, NZ 135/C2
Mercer, Mo, US 155/H3
Mercer (co.), NJ, US 168/D3
Mercer, Pa, US 160/F4
Mercer (isl.), Wa, US 167/C2
Mercer County (arpt.), NJ, US 168/D3
Mercer Island, Wa, US 167/C2
Mercersburg, Pa, US 161/H5
Mercerville-Hamilton Square, NJ, US 168/D3
Merchtem, Belg. 55/D2
Mercier, Qu, Can. 159/N7
Mercoal, Ab, Can. 144/F1
Mercogliano, It. 65/D6
Mercury, Nv, US 148/E2
Mercury, Tx, US 150/E2
Mercy (cape), Nun, Can. 141/K2
Mercy-le-Bas, Fr. 55/E5
Merdereau (riv.), Fr. 57/E4
Merderet (riv.), Fr. 56/D2
Merdrignac, Fr. 56/C4
Mere, Belg. 54/C2
Méré, Fr. 30/H5
Mere, Eng, UK 36/D4
Méreau, Fr. 57/H6
Mereb Wenz (riv.), Erit. 117/H2
Meredith (lake), Co, US 152/C1
Meredith, NH, US 161/L3
Meredith (cape), UK 191/E7
Meredosia, Il, US 155/J4
Meredosia Nat'l Wild. Ref., Il, US 155/J4
Mereeg, Som. 118/C5
Merefa, Ukr. 73/J3
Merelbeke, Belg. 54/C2
Merenberg, Ger. 58/B1
Mereuch, Camb. 94/D3
Méréville, Fr. 57/H4
Mereworth, Eng, UK 30/E3
Mergel (riv.), China 79/J2
Mergozzo, It. 61/E6
Mergui (arch.), Myan. 93/G5
Mergui (Myeik), Myan. 94/B3
Meriç, Turk. 51/H5
Meriç (riv.), Turk. 67/K2
Merichleri, Bul. 51/G4
Méricourt, Fr. 54/B3
Méricourt, Fr. 30/G4
Mérida, Mex. 176/D1
Mérida, Ven. 180/D2
Mérida (state), Ven. 180/D2
Mérida, Sp. 46/B3
Mérida, Cordillera de (mts.), Ven. 180/D3
Meriden, Ct, US 161/K4
Meriden, Wy, US 154/B3
Meridian, Ok, US 153/F3
Meridian, Pa, US 160/G4
Meridian, Ga, US 165/H2
Meridian, Id, US 146/E2
Meridian, Ms, US 162/C4
Meridian, Tx, US 150/F2
Meridian Nav. Air Sta., Ms, US 162/C4
Meridian Station, Ms, US 162/C4
Meridianville, Al, US 162/D3
Mérignac, Fr. 44/C4
Merignac (int'l arpt.), Fr. 44/C4
Merimbula, Austl. 133/D3
Merin Gubai, Som. 119/D1
Merinda, Austl. 134/C3
Mering, Ger. 58/D6
Meringa, Nga. 116/B3
Merino, Co, US 154/C3
Merinos, Uru. 191/K10
Merja Zerga (lake), Mor. 112/A2
Mérk, Hun. 50/F2
Merkel, Tx, US 150/D1
Merkendorf, Ger. 58/D4
Merkinė, Lith. 41/L4
Merksem, Belg. 52/B6
Merksplas, Belg. 52/B6
Merkus (cape), PNG 129/H1
Merlimont, Fr. 54/A3
Merlo, Arg. 191/J11
Merlo, Arg. 188/C5
Meroe (ruin), Sudan 117/G1
Merone, It. 62/C2
Merouane, Chott (lake), Alg. 66/E4
Merredin, Austl. 130/C4
Merri (cr.), Austl. 132/F5
Merriam (crater), Az, US 149/G3
Merrick (peak), Sc, UK 34/D1
Merrick, NY, US 169/L9
Merricks, Austl. 133/B4
Merrickville, On, Can. 161/J2
Merricourt, ND, US 156/E4
Merrill, Or, US 146/C2
Merrill, Wi, US 157/K5
Merrill Creek (res.), NJ, US 168/C2
Merrillville, In, US 160/C4
Merrimack, NH, US 161/L3
Merrimack (riv.), NH, US 158/B4

Merriman, Ne, US 154/D2
Merriott, Eng, UK 36/D5
Merritt, BC, Can. 144/D2
Merritt (isl.), Fl, US 165/H3
Merritt (dam), Ne, US 154/D2
Merritt (res.), Ne, US 154/D2
Merritt Island, Fl, US 165/H3
Merritt Island Nat'l Wild. Ref., Fl, US 165/H3
Merriwa, Austl. 132/D2
Merriwagga, Austl. 133/B1
Merriweather, Mi, US 157/K4
Merryville, La, US 164/B2
Mers-les-Bains, Fr. 54/A3
Mersa Fatma, Erit. 118/B2
Mersa Gulbub, Erit. 118/A1
Mersa Tek'lay, Erit. 100/C5
Mersch, Lux. 55/F4
Merse (reg.), Sc, UK 33/D5
Mersey (riv.), Eng, UK 35/F5
Merseyside (co.), Eng, UK 35/F5
Mershon, Ga, US 165/G2
Mersin, Turk. 104/D1
Mersin Galgalo, Eth. 118/C4
Mersing, Malay. 89/C2
Mērsrags, Lat. 41/K3
Merstham, Eng, UK 30/C3
Mertens, Tx, US 151/F1
Mertert, Lux. 55/F4
Mertesdorf, Ger. 55/F4
Merthyr Tydfil, Wal, UK 36/C3
Merthyr Tydfil (co.), Wal, UK 36/C3
Mértola, Port. 46/B4
Merton (bor.), Eng, UK 30/C2
Mertzon, Tx, US 150/D2
Mertzwiller, Fr. 55/G6
Méru, Fr. 54/B5
Meru, Kenya 119/B1
Meru (mt.), Tanz. 119/B2
Meru NP, Kenya 119/B1
Meruoca, Braz. 183/F3
Merville, Fr. 54/B2
Mervin, Sk, Can. 145/K1
Merwedekanaal (riv.), Neth. 52/C5
Méry-sur-Oise, Fr. 30/J4
Merzen, Ger. 53/E4
Merzenich, Ger. 55/F2
Merzifon, Turk. 70/E4
Merzig, Ger. 55/F5
Mesa (peak), Arg. 191/C6
Mesa (mt.), Ak, US 171/G3
Mesa, Az, US 149/G4
Mesa, Co, US 147/J4
Mesa Prieta (mesa), NM, US 152/A3
Mesa Verde NP, Co, US 149/H2
Mesabi (range), Mn, US 157/H4
Mesach Mellet (hills), Libya 111/H4
Mesagne, It. 49/E2
Mesaména, Camr. 120/C2
Mesarás (gulf), Gre. 49/J5
Mescalero (ridge), NM, US 152/C4
Mescalero Sands (des.), NM, US 152/B4
Meschede, Ger. 53/F6
Mesco, Punta di (pt.), It. 62/C5
Mescolino (peak), It. 63/F6
Meseta de Montemayor (plat.), Arg. 190/D5
Mesfinto, Eth. 117/H2
Meshchura, Rus. 69/L3
Meshgīn Shahr, Iran 103/F2
Meshra'ar Raqq, Sudan 117/F3
Mesick, Mi, US 160/D2
Mesilla, NM, US 149/J4
Mesita, Co, US 152/B2
Mesita, NM, US 149/J3
Meskum, Indo. 89/C2
Meslay-du-Maine, Fr. 57/E5
Mesola, It. 63/F4
Mesolóngion, Gre. 49/G3
Mesomeloka, Madg. 125/J8
Mesopotamia (reg.), Iraq 100/D2
Mesopotamia (reg.), Arg 188/E4
Mesoraca, It. 48/E3
Mespelbrunn, Ger. 58/C3
Mesquer, Fr. 56/C6
Mesquite, NM, US 149/J4
Mesquite, Tx, US 150/L7
Mesrouh (peak), Mor. 110/E2
Messaad, Alg. 66/D4
Messac, Fr. 56/D5
Messalo (riv.), Moz. 123/H2
Messancy, Belg. 55/E4
Messei, Fr. 57/E3
Messel, Ger. 58/B3
Messina, It. 48/D3
Messina (str.), It. 67/G3
Messina, SAfr. 123/F4
Messines, Qu, Can. 161/H1
Messinge (riv.), Moz. 123/G2
Messíni, Gre. 49/H4
Messini (gulf), Gre. 67/J3
Messkirch, Ger. 61/F2
Messstetten, Ger. 61/E1
Messum Crater (peak), Namb. 122/B4
Messy, Fr. 30/L5
Mesta (riv.), Bul. 51/F5
Mestia, Geo. 71/G4
Město, Czh. 59/F3
Mestre, It. 63/F3
Mestrino, It. 63/E3
Mesudiye, Turk. 70/F4
Mesumba (peak), Tanz. 119/B3
Mesurado (cape), Libr. 114/C5
Meta (dept.), Col. 180/C4
Meta (riv.), Col.,Ven. 179/C2
Meta, It. 65/D6
Meta Incognita (pen.), Nun, Can. 141/K2
Metabetchouan, Qu, Can. 158/B1
Métabetchouane (riv.), Qu, Can. 158/B2
Metacáua (pt.), Moz. 123/J2
Metahāra, Eth. 118/A3
Metairie, La, US 164/C3
Metaline Falls, Wa, US 144/F3
Metallifere, Colline (mts.), It. 63/D6
Metallostroy, Rus. 69/T7
Metamora, Mi, US 167/F6
Metán, Arg. 188/C3
Metangula, Moz. 123/G2
Metapontum (ruin), It. 48/E2
Metauro (riv.), It. 45/K5
Metcalfe, On, Can. 161/J2
Metcalfe, Ms, US 162/B4
Meteghan, NS, Can. 158/D3
Meteghan River, NS, Can. 158/D3
Metelen, Ger. 53/E4
Metema, Eth. 117/H2
Meteor Crater, Az, US 149/G3
Metéora, Gre. 49/G3
Metepec, Mex. 175/Q10
Metheringham, Eng, UK 35/H5
Methil, Sc, UK 33/C4
Methlick, Sc, UK 33/D2
Methow (riv.), Wa, US 144/D3
Methuen, Ma, US 161/L3
Methuen (mt.), Austl. 128/B3
Methven, Sc, UK 33/C4
Methven, NZ 135/B3
Metica (riv.), Col. 180/C4
Metiskow, Ab, Can. 145/J1
Metković, Cro. 50/C4
Metlakatla, BC, Can. 171/M4
Metlakatla, Ak, US 171/M4
Metlatonoc, Mex. 176/B2
Metlili Chaamba, Alg. 111/F2
Metoro, Moz. 123/H2
Metro, Indo. 89/D4
Metro Toronto Zoo, On, Can. 160/U8
Metro-Dade Cultural Center, Fl, US 164/P11
Metropolis, Il, US 162/C2
Metropolitana de Santiago (pol. reg.), Chile 190/N8
Metrozoo, Fl, US 164/P11
Métsovon, Gre. 49/G3
Mettawa, Il, US 167/Q15
Mettenheim, Ger. 59/F6
Metter, Ga, US 163/F4
Mettet, Belg. 55/D3
Mettingen, Ger. 53/E4
Mettlach, Ger. 55/F4
Mettler, Ca, US 148/C3
Mettmach, Aus. 59/G6
Mettmann, Ger. 52/D6
Mettūr, India 95/C4
Metu, Eth. 117/G3
Metuchen, NJ, US 169/H9
Metulla, Isr. 105/D2
Metz, Mo, US 153/G2
Metz, Fr. 55/F5
Metz-Nancy-Lorraine (int'l arpt.), Fr. 55/F6
Metzingen, Ger. 58/C5
Metztitlán, Mex. 175/L6
Meu (riv.), Fr. 56/C4
Meudon, Fr. 30/J5
Meudt, Ger. 55/G3
Meulaboh, Indo. 89/B1
Meulan, Fr. 30/H4
Meulebeke, Belg. 54/C2
Meung-sur-Loire, Fr. 57/G5
Meurthe (riv.), Fr. 60/C1
Meurthe-et-Moselle (dept.), Fr. 55/E6
Meuse (riv.), Fr. 42/C4
Meuse (dept.), Fr. 55/E6
Meuvette (riv.), Fr. 57/F3
Meuzin (riv.), Fr. 60/A3
Mevasseret Ẕiyyon, Isr. 105/C5
Mexborough, Eng, UK 35/G5
Mexia, Tx, US 151/F2
Mexiana (isl.), Braz. 182/D2
Mexicalcingo, Mex. 175/Q10
Mexican Hat, Ut, US 149/H2
Mexican Springs, NM, US 149/H3
Mexico (ctry.) 139/G7
México (state), Mex. 172/A5
Mexico (Ciudad de México) (cap.), Mex. 175/Q10
Mexico (gulf), NAm. 139/H7
Mexico, In, US 160/C4
Mexico, Me, US 161/L2
Mexico, Mo, US 155/J4
Mexico, NY, US 161/H3
Mexico (bay), NY, US 161/H3
Mexico Beach, Fl, US 165/F3
Meximieux, Fr. 60/B6
Meybod, Iran 103/H3
Meycauayan, Phil. 88/E6
Meydān-e Gel (lake), Iran 103/H4
Meyers Chuck, Ak, US 171/M4
Meyersdale, Pa, US 161/G5
Meyerton, SAfr. 124/Q13
Meylan, Fr. 64/B2
Meymaneh, Afg. 101/H1
Méyo Kyé, Gabon 120/B2
Meyrargues, Fr. 64/B5
Meyrin, Swi. 60/C5
Meythet, Fr. 60/C6
Meythet (Annecy) (arpt.), Fr. 60/C6
Meyzieu, Fr. 60/A6
Mezaligon, Myan. 86/B5
Mezdra, Bul. 51/F4
Mèze, Fr. 44/E5
Mézel, Fr. 64/C5
Mezen', Rus. 69/K2
Mezen' (bay), Rus. 69/J2
Mezen' (riv.), Rus. 74/E3
Mezha (riv.), Bela. 41/P4
Mezhdurechensk, Rus. 74/J4
Mezhdurechenskiy, Rus. 74/G4
Mezhdusharskiy (isl.), Rus. 74/E2
Mezhova, Ukr. 73/J3
Mézidon-Canon, Fr. 57/E2
Mézières-sur-Seine, Fr. 30/H5
Mezoberény, Hun. 50/E2
Mezokovácsháza, Hun. 50/E2
Mezőkövesd, Hun. 43/L5
Mezőtúr, Hun. 50/E2
Mezquital (riv.), Mex. 174/D4
Mézy, Fr. 30/H5
Mezzana (peak), It. 61/G5
Mezzocorona, It. 61/H5
Mezzogoro, It. 63/F4
Mezzolombardo, It. 61/H5
Mfangano (isl.), Kenya 119/A2
Mfou, Camr. 120/B2
Mfrika, Tanz. 119/A4
Mga, Rus. 69/U7
Mga (riv.), Rus. 69/U7
Mgachi, Rus. 79/N1
Mgambo, Tanz. 119/B3
Mgera, Tanz. 119/B3
Mgeta, Tanz. 119/B4
Mglin, Rus. 70/E1
Mgori, Tanz. 119/A3
M'goun (peak), Mor. 110/D3
Mhamdia Fūshānah, Tun. 48/B4
Mhòr (lake), Sc, UK 33/B2
Mhow, India 92/C3
Mhunze, Tanz. 119/A2
Mi (riv.), China 80/D3
Mi Xian, China 80/C4
Mi-shima (isl.), Japan 84/B3
Miahuatlán de Porfirio Díaz, Mex. 176/B2
Miajadas, Sp. 46/C3
Miaméré, CAfr. 116/C3
Miami, Tx, US 152/D3
Miami, Mb, Can. 156/E3
Miami, Ok, US 153/G2
Miami (canal), Fl, US 165/H4
Miami, Az, US 149/G4
Miami, Fl, US 164/P11
Miami (int'l arpt.), Fl, US 164/P11
Miami (riv.), Oh, US 162/E1
Miami Beach, Fl, US 164/P11
Miami Shores, Fl, US 164/P11
Miami Springs, Fl, US 164/P11
Miamisburg, Oh, US 160/D5
Miān Channūn, Pak. 98/B4
Miāna, India 96/A3
Miancaowan, China 78/D4
Mianchi, China 80/B4
Mīāndasht, Iran 103/J2
Mīāndoāb, Iran 103/F2
Miandrivazo, Madg. 125/H7
Mīāneh, Iran 103/F2
Mianhu, China 87/H4
Miāni, Pak. 98/B3
Mianmian (mts.), China 86/D2
Mianning, China 86/D2
Mianus (riv.), Ct, US 169/E1
Miānwāli, India 98/B5
Miānwāli, Pak. 98/A3
Mianyang, China 86/E2
Mianzhu, China 86/E2
Miāo, India 86/C3
Miao'er (peak), China 87/F3
Miaoshi, China 87/F2
Miarinarivo, Madg. 125/H7
Miarinarivo, Madg. 125/J7
Miary, Madg. 125/G8
Miass, Rus. 69/P5
Miass (riv.), Rus. 69/P5
Miastko, Pol. 40/G4
Miazal, Ecu. 184/B1
Mibenge, D.R. Congo 120/D3
Miberika, Sudan 135/G5
Mica Creek, BC, Can. 144/E1
Micanopy, Fl, US 165/G3
Micay, Col. 180/B4
Micco, Fl, US 165/H4
Miccosukee, Fl, US 165/F2
Miccosukee Ind. Res., Fl, US 165/H4
Michalovce, Slvk. 43/L4
Michaud (pt.), NS, Can. 159/G3
Michel (bay), Fr. 44/C2
Michelago, Austl. 133/D2
Michelfeld, Ger. 59/E3
Michelson (mt.), Ak, US 171/K2
Michelstadt, Ger. 58/C3
Michendorf, Ger. 42/Q7
Michie, Tn, US 162/C3
Michigamme (lake), Mi, US 157/K4
Michigamme, Mi, US 157/K4
Michigan, ND, US 156/E3
Michigan (lake), US 139/J5
Michigan (state), US 143/J2
Michigan Center, Mi, US 160/D3
Michigan City, In, US 160/C4
Michigan City, Ms, US 162/C3
Michigan Islands Nat'l Wild. Ref., Mi, US 160/D2
Michipicoten (isl.), On, Can. 157/M4
Michoacán de Ocampo (state), Mex. 172/A4
Michurin, Bul. 51/H4
Michurinsk, Rus. 71/G1
Mickle Fell (peak), Eng, UK 35/F2
Mickleton, Eng, UK 35/F2
Mico (riv.), Nic. 172/E5
Miconje, Ang. 120/C4
Micoud, StL. 173/N9
Micronesia (ctry.) 136/D4
Micronesia (reg.) 136/E3
Mid Yell, Sc, UK 31/W13
Midal (well), Niger 115/G2
Midale, Sk, Can. 156/C3
Midar, Mor. 112/C2
Middelburg, Neth. 52/A5
Middelburg, SAfr. 124/D3
Middelburg, SAfr. 125/E2
Middelharnis, Neth. 52/B5
Middelkerke, Belg. 54/B1
Middenmeer, Neth. 52/B3
Middle (ridge), Nf, Can. 159/K1
Middle (lake), Ca, US 146/C3
Middle (bay), NY, US 169/L9
Middle (mtn.), WV, US 163/G1
Middle Andaman (isl.), India 93/F5
Middle Caicos (isl.), UK 177/J1
Middle Concho (riv.), Tx, US 150/D2
Middle Fabius (riv.), Mo, US 155/H3
Middle Inlet, Wi, US 160/C2
Middle Lake, Sk, Can. 145/M1
Middle Loup (riv.), Ne, US 154/D3
Middle Pease (riv.), Tx, US 152/D3
Middle Raccoon (riv.), Ia, US 155/G3
Middle River, Mn, US 156/F3
Middle River, Md, US 168/B5
Middle Sister (peak), Or, US 146/C1
Middle Stewiacke, NS, Can. 158/F3
Middle Yuba (riv.), Ca, US 146/C4
Middlebourne, WV, US 160/F5
Middlebro, Mb, Can. 157/G3
Middleburg, Fl, US 165/H2
Middleburg, Pa, US 168/A2
Middleburg, Md, US 168/A4
Middleburgh, NY, US 161/J3
Middlebury, Vt, US 161/K2
Middlebury, In, US 160/D4
Middlefield, Oh, US 160/F4
Middlefield, Ma, US 161/K3
Middleham, Eng, UK 35/G3
Middlemarch, NZ 135/B4
Middlemount, Austl. 134/C3
Middleport, Oh, US 163/F1
Middleport, NY, US 160/W9
Middleport, Pa, US 168/B2
Middlesboro, Ky, US 162/F2
Middlesbrough, Eng, UK 35/G2
Middlesex (reg.), Eng, UK 37/F4
Middlesex, NJ, US 168/D2
Middlesex, NC, US 163/H3
Middleton, Eng, UK 35/F4
Middleton, NS, Can. 158/E3
Middleton, Id, US 146/E2
Middleton, Wi, US 155/K2
Middleton, Tn, US 162/C3
Middleton Cheney, Eng, UK 37/E2
Middleton-in-Teesdale, Eng, UK 35/F2
Middletown, NI, UK 34/B3
Middletown, NY, US 161/J4
Middletown, In, US 160/D4
Middletown, Ct, US 161/K4
Middletown, Oh, US 160/D5
Middletown, RI, US 161/L4
Middletown, NJ, US 169/J10
Middletown, Ca, US 146/B4
Middletown, Pa, US 168/B3
Middletown, Va, US 163/H1
Middletown, De, US 168/C5
Middleville, Mi, US 160/D3
Middlewich, Eng, UK 35/F5
Middlewood, NS, Can. 158/E3
Midelt, Mor. 110/D2
Midhurst, Eng, UK 37/F5
Midi (canal), Fr. 44/D5
Midi-Pyrénées (pol.reg.), Fr. 44/D4
Midkiff, WV, US 163/F1
Midland (nbrhd.), Austl. 130/L6
Midland, Mi, US 160/D3
Midland, On, Can. 161/G2
Midland, Or, US 146/C2
Midland, SD, US 154/D1
Midland, Tx, US 150/C2
Midland, Wa, US 167/C3
Midland City, Al, US 165/F2
Midland Park, NJ, US 169/J8
Midlands (prov.), Zim. 123/F3
Midleton, Ire. 32/B6
Midlothian (co.), Sc, UK 33/C5
Midlothian, Il, US 167/Q16
Midlothian, Tx, US 150/L7
Midlum, Ger. 53/F1
Midnight, Ms, US 162/B4
Midongy Atsimo, Madg. 125/H8
Midou (riv.), Fr. 44/C5
Midsayap, Phil. 88/D4
Midsomer Norton, Eng, UK 36/D4
Midu, China 93/H2
Midville, Ga, US 163/F4
Midway (isls.), Pac., US 136/H2
Midway, BC, Can. 144/E3
Midway, Al, US 165/F1
Midway, De, US 168/C6
Midway, Fl, US 165/F2
Midway, Ga, US 165/H2
Midway, Ky, US 162/E1
Midway, La, US 164/B2
Midway, Ne, US 154/E2
Midway, NM, US 152/B4
Midway, Tx, US 151/G2
Midwest, Wy, US 154/A2
Midwest City, Ok, US 153/F3
Midyan (reg.), SAr. 100/C3
Midyat, Turk. 102/E2
Midžor (peak), Serb. 51/F4
Mie (pref.), Japan 84/E3
Mie, Japan 84/B4
Miechów, Pol. 70/B2
Międzychód, Pol. 43/H2
Międzylesie, Pol. 43/J3
Międzyrzec Podlaski, Pol. 43/M3
Międzyrzecz, Pol. 43/H2
Międzyzdroje, Pol. 40/F5
Miehlen, Ger. 55/G3
Miéle I, Congo 120/C2
Mielec, Pol. 43/L3
Mier, Mex. 150/E4
Miercurea Cluc, Rom. 51/G2
Mieres, Sp. 46/C1
Miesbach, Ger. 45/J3
Mī'ēso, Eth. 118/B3
Mifflin, Pa, US 168/A2
Mifflinburg, Pa, US 168/A2
Mifflintown, Pa, US 161/H4
Mifflinville (Creasy), Pa, US 168/B1
Mifraẕ Ḥefa (bay), Isr. 105/B3
Migdal, Isr. 105/D3
Migdal Ha'emeq, Isr. 105/C3
Migdol, SAfr. 124/D2
Migennes, Fr. 44/E3
Migliarino, It. 62/D6
Mignanego, It. 62/B4
Mignano Monte Lungo, It. 65/C5
Mignovillard, Fr. 60/C4
Migori (riv.), Kenya 119/A2
Migori, Kenya 119/A2
Miguel Alemán, Mex. 174/C2
Miguel Aleman, Presa (dam), Mex. 175/M8
Miguel Alves, Braz. 183/F4
Miguel Auza, Mex. 174/E3
Miguel Calmon, Braz. 187/E1
Miguel Hidalgo (int'l arpt.), Mex. 174/E4
Miguel Hidalgo (res.), Mex. 174/C3
Miguel Pereira, Braz. 187/N7
Miguel Riglos, Arg. 190/E3
Miguelete, Uru. 191/K11
Miguelópolis, Braz. 189/G2
Miguelturra, Sp. 46/D3
Migŭm, SKor. 81/G6
Mihama, Japan 84/D3
Mihama, Japan 83/L6
Mihara, Japan 84/C3
Mihara, Japan 83/J6
Miharu, Japan 85/G2
Mihintale (ruin), SrL. 95/D4
Mihla, Ger. 53/H6
Miho, Japan 83/E2
Mihrābpur, Pak. 101/J3
Mijares (riv.), Sp. 47/E2
Mijas, Sp. 46/C4
Mijdāḥah, Yem. 118/D2
Mijdrecht, Neth. 52/B4
Mikasa, Japan 82/B2
Mikashevichi, Bela. 70/C1
Mikata, Japan 83/J4
Mikata (lake), Japan 83/J4
Mikawa (bay), Japan 83/M6
Mikengere, D.R. Congo 121/F5
Mikese, Tanz. 119/B3
Mikhaylov, Rus. 70/F1
Mikhaylovka, Rus. 73/M2
Mikhaylovsk, Rus. 69/N4
Mikhmoret, Isr. 105/B4
Miki, Japan 83/G6
Mikínai, Gre. 49/H4
Mikínai (Mycenae) (ruin), Gre. 49/H4
Mikindani, Tanz. 119/C4
Mikkalo, Or, US 146/C1
Mikkeli (prov.), Fin. 38/H3
Mikomeseng, EqG. 120/B2
Míkonos, Gre. 49/J4
Míkonos (isl.), Gre. 49/J4
Mikope, D.R. Congo 121/E4
Mikri Prespa NP, Gre. 49/G2
Mikuma, Japan 83/L6
Mikumi, Tanz. 119/B3
Mikumi NP, Tanz. 119/B3
Mikun', Rus. 69/L3
Mikuni, Japan 84/E2
Mikuni-tōge (pass), Japan 85/F2
Mikura (isl.), Japan 85/F4
Mila, Alg. 66/E3
Mila (wilaya), Alg. 112/H4
Milaca, Mn, US 157/H5
Milagres, Braz. 183/G4
Milagro, Ecu. 180/B5
Milak, India 96/B1
Milakpur, India 96/A2
Milam, Tx, US 151/H2
Milan (Milano), It. 45/H4
Milan, Ga, US 165/G1
Milan, In, US 162/E1
Milan, Mn, US 155/G1
Milan, Mo, US 155/H3
Milan, NH, US 161/L2
Milan, NM, US 149/J3
Milan, Oh, US 160/E4
Milan, Tn, US 162/C3
Milando, Ang. 120/D5
Milang, Austl. 132/A2
Milange, Moz. 123/G3
Milano (Milan), It. 45/H4
Milano (prov.), It. 62/C2
Milano, Tx, US 151/F2
Milas, Turk. 102/A2
Milazzo, It. 48/D3
Milbank, SD, US 155/F1
Milborne Port, Eng, UK 36/D5
Milburn, Ne, US 154/E3
Milburn, Ok, US 153/F3
Milden, Sk, Can. 145/L2
Mildenhall, Eng, UK 37/G2
Mildred, Mt, US 156/B4
Mildura, Austl. 132/B2
Mīlē, Eth. 118/B3
Mile, China 86/D3
Mīlē Wenz (riv.), Eth. 118/B3
Milepa, Tanz. 121/G5
Miles, Austl. 134/C4
Miles, Tx, US 150/D2
Miles City, Mt, US 145/M4
Milesburg, Pa, US 161/H4
Milešovka (peak), Czh. 59/G1
Milestone, Sk, Can. 156/B3
Miletto (peak), It. 65/D5
Milevsko, Czh. 59/H4
Milford, Ire. 32/B4
Milford (sound), NZ 135/A4
Milford, NI, UK 34/B3
Milford, Ct, US 169/E1
Milford, De, US 168/C6
Milford, Ga, US 165/F2
Milford, Ia, US 155/G2
Milford, Il, US 160/C4
Milford, Ks, US 155/F4
Milford (lake), Ks, US 155/F4
Milford, Ma, US 161/L3
Milford, Mi, US 167/E6
Milford, Ne, US 155/F3
Milford, NH, US 161/L3
Milford, NJ, US 168/C2
Milford, Pa, US 161/J4
Milford, Tx, US 151/F1
Milford, Ut, US 149/F1
Milford Haven (inlet), Wal., UK 36/A3
Milford Haven, Wal, UK 36/A3
Milford Station, NS, Can. 158/F3
Milford-on-Sea, Eng, UK 37/E5
Mili (isl.), Mrsh. 136/G4
Miliana, Alg. 112/G4
Milicz, Pol. 43/J3
Milikapiti, Austl. 128/C2
Milingimbi Mission, Austl. 129/D3
Military (ridge), Wi, US 155/J2
Milk (riv.), Mt, Can., US 140/F4
Milk (hill), Eng, UK 37/E4
Milk River, Ab, Can. 145/H3
Mill (isl.), Nun, Can. 141/J2
Mill, Neth. 52/C5
Mill (riv.), Ct, US 169/E1
Mill (cr.), Ct, US 168/E1
Mill Bay, BC, Can. 144/C3
Mill City, Or, US 146/B1
Mill Creek, Ok, US 153/F3
Mill Creek, WV, US 163/H1
Mill Neck, NY, US 169/L8
Mill Shoals, Il, US 162/C1
Mill Spring, Mo, US 162/B2
Mill Village, NS, Can. 158/E3
Millaa Millaa, Austl. 134/B2
Millau, Fr. 44/E4
Millboro, SD, US 154/E2
Millboro, Va, US 163/H2
Millbrae, Ca, US 167/K11
Millbridge, Eng, UK 30/A3
Millbrook, On, Can. 161/G2
Millbrook, Al, US 162/D4
Millbrook (res.), Austl. 131/M8
Millbrook, Eng, UK 36/B6
Millburn, NJ, US 169/H9
Millburne, Wy, US 147/H3
Mille Îles (riv.), Qu, Can. 159/N6
Mille Lacs (lake), Mn, US 143/H2
Mille Lacs Ind. Res., Mn, US 157/H4
Milledgeville, Ga, US 163/F4
Milledgeville, Il, US 155/K3
Milledgeville, Tn, US 162/C3
Millen, Ga, US 163/G4
Miller (peak), Az, US 149/G5
Miller, SD, US 154/E1
Miller (pt.), Tx, US 151/N9
Miller (int'l arpt.), Tx, US 175/F3
Millerovo, Rus. 73/L3
Millers Creek (res.), Tx, US 150/E1
Millers Ferry, Al, US 164/E1
Millers Ferry (dam), Al, US 164/E1
Millersburg, Oh, US 160/F4
Millersburg, Or, US 146/B1
Millersburg, Pa, US 168/B2
Millerstown, Pa, US 168/A2
Millersview, Tx, US 150/E2
Millersville, Pa, US 168/B4
Millerton (lake), Ca, US 148/C2
Millertown, Nf, Can. 159/J1
Millerville, Mn, US 157/G4
Millesimo, It. 62/B5
Millet, Ab, Can. 145/H1
Millett, Tx, US 150/E3
Milleur (pt.), Sc, UK 34/C1
Millevaches (plat.), Fr. 44/D4
Millgrove, On, Can. 160/T9
Millicent, Austl. 132/B3
Milligan, Fl, US 164/E2
Milliken, Co, US 154/B3
Millingen aan de Rijn, Neth. 52/D5
Millington, Md, US 168/C5
Millington, Tn, US 162/C3
Millinocket, Me, US 141/K4
Millisle, NI, UK 34/C2
Millmerran, Austl. 134/C4
Millmont, Pa, US 168/A2
Millom, Eng, UK 35/E3
Millport, Sc, UK 33/B5
Millport, Al, US 162/C4
Millry, Al, US 164/D2
Mills, NM, US 152/B2
Millsboro, De, US 163/K1
Millstone, WV, US 163/G1
Millstone (riv.), NJ, US 168/D3
Millstream-Chichester NP, Austl. 130/C2
Millstreet, Ire. 32/A5
Millthorpe, Austl. 133/D1
Millthrop, Eng, UK 35/F3
Milltown, In, US 162/D1
Milltown, NJ, US 169/H10
Milltown Malbay, Ire. 32/A4
Milltown-Head of Bay d'Espoir, Nf, Can. 159/K2
Millungera, Austl. 134/A2
Millville, Oh, US 160/D5
Millville, NJ, US 168/C5
Millville, Pa, US 168/B1
Millwood (dam), Ar, US 153/H4
Millwood (lake), Ar, US 153/G4
Millwood, Ga, US 165/G2
Millwood, WV, US 163/G1
Milmay, NJ, US 168/D5
Milnathort, Wal, UK 35/E5
Milne (bay), PNG 136/E5
Milngavie, Sc, UK 33/B5
Milnor, ND, US 156/F4
Milnrow, Eng, UK 35/F4
Milo (riv.), Gui. 114/C4
Milo, Ia, US 155/H3
Mílos, Gre. 49/J4
Mílos (isl.), Gre. 67/K3
Milpa, Austl. 132/B1
Milpa Alta (nbrhd.), Mex. 175/Q10
Milparinka, Austl. 131/J4
Milroy, In, US 160/D5
Milroy, Pa, US 161/H4
Milseburg (peak), Ger. 58/C1
Milstead, Ga, US 163/N7
Miltenberg, Ger. 58/C3
Milton, Austl. 133/E2
Milton, On, Can. 160/T8
Milton, Eng, UK 35/F2
Milton, Eng, UK 37/G4
Milton, NZ 135/B4
Milton, Fl, US 164/E2
Milton, Ia, US 155/H3
Milton, Il, US 155/J4
Milton, ND, US 156/E3
Milton, NH, US 161/L3
Milton, Pa, US 168/B1
Milton, Vt, US 161/K2
Milton, Wa, US 167/C3
Milton, Wi, US 155/K2
Milton Heights, On, Can. 160/T8
Milton Keynes, Eng, UK 37/F2
Milton Keynes (co.), Eng, UK 37/F2
Milton Ness (pt.), Sc, UK 33/D3
Milton of Campsie, Sc, UK 33/B5
Milton-Freewater, Or, US 144/E5
Miltona, Mn, US 157/G4
Miltonvale, Ks, US 154/F4
Miluo (riv.), China 87/G2
Milverton, On, Can. 160/F3
Milverton, Eng, UK 36/C4
Milwaukee, Wi, US 160/C3
Milwaukee (co.), Wi, US 167/P14
Milz (riv.), Ger. 58/D2
Mimbres, NM, US 149/J4
Mimbres (riv.), NM, US 149/J4
Mimet, Fr. 64/B6
Mimi (riv.), Japan 84/B4
Mimizan, Fr. 44/C4
Mimmaya, Japan 82/B3
Mimongo, Gabon 120/B3
Mimongo, Gabon 120/B3
Mimosa Rocks NP, Austl. 133/D3
Min (riv.), China 78/E5
Min Xian, China 78/E5
Min-Kush, Kyr. 99/B3
Mîna (riv.), Alg. 112/F5
Mina, Mex. 150/D4
Mina, Nv, US 146/D4
Mina Clavero, Arg. 188/C4
Mina Pirquitas, Arg. 188/C2
Mīnā' Su'ūd, Kuw. 103/G4
Mīnāb, Iran 103/J5
Minaçu, Braz. 186/C2
Minahasa (isl.), Indo. 91/F3
Minaki, On, Can. 157/G3
Minakuchi, Japan 83/K6
Minamata, Japan 84/B4
Minami Alps NP, Japan 85/F3
Minami-tori-shima (isl.), Japan 136/E2
Minamiaiki, Japan 83/B1
Minamiashigara, Japan 83/C3
Minamichita, Japan 83/L6
Minamidaitō (isl.), Japan 85/L8
Minamiiō (isl.), Japan 136/D2
Minamikawara, Japan 83/C1
Minamimaki, Japan 83/A2
Minamiyamashiro, Japan 83/J6
Minano, Japan 83/C1
Minas, Cuba 177/G1
Minas (peak), Ecu. 180/B5
Minas, Uru. 191/G2
Minas, Indo. 89/C2
Minas de Barroterán, Mex. 150/D4
Minas de Corrales, Uru. 189/F4
Minas de Matahambre, Cuba 177/F1
Minas de Ríotinto, Sp. 46/B4
Minas Gerais (state), Braz. 186/D3
Minatitlán, Mex. 176/C2
Minbu, Myan. 86/B4
Minbya, Myan. 86/B4
Minch, The (North Minch) (str.), Sc, UK 31/Q8
Mincha, Chile 188/B4
Minchinābād, Pak. 98/B4
Minchinhampton, Eng, UK 36/D3
Minchinmávida (vol.), Chile 190/B4
Mincio (riv.), It. 63/D2
Minco, Ok, US 153/F3
Mindanao (isl.), Phil. 77/M9
Mindanao (sea), Phil. 91/F2
Mindel (riv.), Ger. 42/F4
Mindelheim, Ger. 61/G1
Mindelo, CpV. 107/J10
Mindemoya, On, Can. 160/E2
Minden, Ger. 53/F4
Minden, La, US 153/H4
Minden, Ne, US 154/E3
Minden, Nv, US 146/D4
Minden, Tx, US 151/G1
Minden City, Mi, US 160/E3
Mindif, Camr. 116/B3
Mindiptana, Indo. 129/F1
Mindoro (isl.), Phil. 77/L8
Mindoro (str.), Phil. 88/C2
Mindouli, Congo 120/C4
Mindyak, Rus. 69/N5
Mine Centre, On, Can. 157/H3
Mine Head (pt.), Ire. 32/C6
Minehead, Eng, UK 36/C4
Mineiros, Braz. 186/B3
Mineola, NY, US 169/L8
Mineola, Mo, US 155/J4
Mineola, Tx, US 151/G1
Miner, Mt, US 147/H1
Miner, Mo, US 162/C2
Mineral, Tx, US 150/F3
Mineral, Wa, US 144/C4
Mineral del Monte, Mex. 175/L6
Mineral Point, Mo, US 162/B2
Mineral Point, Wi, US 155/J2
Mineral Springs, Ar, US 153/H4
Mineral Wells, Tx, US 151/E1
Mineral'nye Vody, Rus. 71/G3
Mineralnyye Vody (int'l arpt.), Rus. 71/G3
Mineralwells, WV, US 163/G1
Minerbe, It. 63/E3
Minerbio, It. 63/E4
Minerbio (pt.), Fr. 45/H5
Minersville, Ut, US 149/F1
Minersville, Pa, US 168/B2
Minetto, NY, US 161/H3
Mineville-Witherbee, NY, US 161/K2
Minfeld, Ger. 58/B4
Minfeng, China 99/D4
Ming (riv.), China 93/J3
Mingäçevir, Azer. 71/H4
Mingäçevir Su Anbari (res.), Azer. 71/H4
Mingala, CAfr. 116/D4
Mingāora, Pak. 98/B2
Mingenew, Austl. 130/B4
Mingin, Myan. 86/B4
Minglanilla, Sp. 46/E3
Mingo, Congo 120/C3
Mingo, Ks, US 154/D4
Mingo Junction, Oh, US 160/F4
Mingo NWR, Mo, US 162/B2
Mingouli, Chutes de (falls), Gabon 120/C2
Mingoyo, Tanz. 119/B4
Mingshan, China 86/D2
Mingshui, China 78/D3
Mingshui, China 79/K2
Mingun, Ancient City of, Myan. 86/B4
Minhang, China 80/L8
Minhe, China 78/E4
Minhla, Myan. 86/B5
Minhla, Myan. 86/B5
Minho (riv.), Port. 46/A1
Miniāri, India 92/B2
Minidoka (dam), Id, US 147/G2
Minidoka Internment Nat'l Mon., Id, US 147/F2
Minigwal (lake), Austl. 130/D4
Minilya, Austl. 130/B2
Minīn, Syria 105/E1
Miniota, Mb, Can. 156/D2
Ministro Pistarini (Buenos Aires) (int'l arpt.), Arg. 191/J11
Minitonas, Mb, Can. 156/D1
Minj, PNG 129/G1
Minkamman, Sudan 117/F4
Minkébé, Montagne de (peak), Gabon 120/C2
Minlaton, Austl. 131/H5
Minle, China 78/E4
Minna, Nga. 115/G4
Minneapolis, Ks, US 154/F4
Minneapolis, Mn, US 157/P7
Minneapolis-St.Paul (Wold-Chamberlain) (int'l arpt.), Mn, US 157/P7
Minnedosa, Mb, Can. 156/E2
Minnehaha (lake), Fl, US 164/M6
Minnehaha (falls), Mn, US 157/P7
Minneola, Ks, US 152/D2
Minneola, Fl, US 164/M6
Minneola (lake), Fl, US 164/M6
Minneota, Mn, US 155/G1
Minnequa (canal), Co, US 154/B4
Minnesota (state), US 143/G2
Minnesota (riv.), Mn, US 155/G1
Minnesota Zoo and Gardens, Mn, US 157/P7
Minnetonka, Mn, US 157/P7
Minnetonka (lake), Mn, US 157/N7
Minnewaska (lake), Mn, US 155/G1
Minnewaukan, ND, US 156/E3
Minnigaff, Sc, UK 34/D2
Minnipa, Austl. 131/G5
Minnis (lake), On, Can. 157/J2
Minnitaki (lake), On, Can. 157/H3
Miño (riv.), Sp. 46/A1
Mino, Japan 83/L4
Mino'o (riv.), Japan 83/H6
Minobu, Japan 85/F3
Minocqua, Wi, US 157/K5
Minokamo, Japan 83/M5
Minonk, Il, US 155/K3
Mino'o, Japan 83/H6
Minorca (Menorca) (isl.), Sp. 47/H2
Minori, It. 65/D6
Minori, Japan 83/E1
Minot, ND, US 156/D3
Minot (A.F.B.), ND, US 156/D3
Minqin, China 78/E4
Minqing, China 87/H3
Minquan, China 80/C4
Minsener Oog (isl.), Ger. 53/F1
Minsk (cap.), Bela. 41/M5
Minsk (int'l arpt.), Bela. 41/M5
Minskaya Voblasts, Bela. 41/M5
Mińsk Mazowiecki, Pol. 43/L2
Minster, Eng, UK 37/H4
Minster, Oh, US 160/D4
Mint Hill, NC, US 163/G3
Minta, Camr. 116/B4
Minter, Al, US 164/E1
Mintlaw, Sc, UK 33/E1
Minto, Mb, Can. 156/D3
Minto, NB, Can. 158/D2
Minto (inlet), NW, Can. 140/E1
Minto, Yk, Can. 171/L3
Minto, Ak, US 171/J2
Minto, ND, US 156/F3
Mintom Li, Camr. 120/C2
Minton, Sk, Can. 156/B3
Minturnae (ruin), It. 65/C5
Minturno, It. 65/C5
Mīnūdasht, Iran 103/H2
Minūf, Egypt 113/B4
Minusinsk, Rus. 74/K4
Minusio, Swi. 61/E5
Minutang, India 86/C2
Minvoul, Gabon 120/C2
Minwakh, Yem. 100/E5
Minxiao, China 87/F3
Minyā al Qamḥ, Egypt 113/C3
Min'yar, Rus. 69/N5
Minyat Sandūb, Egypt 113/C3
Minyip, Austl. 132/B3
Mio, Mi, US 160/D2
Mions, Fr. 64/A1
Miory, Bela. 41/M4
Mipi, India 86/B2
Miquan, China 99/E3
Miquelon, Nf, Fr. 159/J2
Mir, Rus. 69/P5
Mira, La, US 153/H4
Mira (riv.), NS, Can. 158/G3
Mira (riv.), Col. 180/B4
Mira (riv.), Port. 46/A4
Mira, Port. 46/A2
Mira Loma, Ca, US 166/C2
Mira Monte, Ca, US 166/A2
Mira Taglio, It. 63/F3
Mirabel (int'l arpt.), Can. 159/M6
Mirabel, Qu, Can. 159/M6
Mirabella Eclano, It. 65/D5
Mirabello, It. 63/E4
Miracema, Braz. 187/E4
Miradolo Terme, It. 62/C3
Mirador (pass), Chile 190/C4
Mirador, Braz. 183/E4
Miraflores, Col. 180/C4
Miraflores, Col. 180/C3
Miraflores, Peru 184/B3
Miraflores, Mex. 174/C4
Miragoâne, Haiti 177/H2
Miraj, India 95/B2
Miramar, Ca, US 166/C5
Miramar, Arg. 190/F3
Miramar (nbrhd.), NZ 135/H9
Miramar, Arg. 188/D4
Miramar, Fl, US 164/P11
Miramar Naval Air Station, Ca, US 166/C5
Miramare (arpt.), It. 63/F5
Miramas, Fr. 64/A5
Mirambéllou (gulf), Gre. 49/J5
Miramichi (bay), NB, Can. 158/E2
Miramichi, South West (riv.), NB, Can. 158/D2
Miramont-de-Guyenne, Fr. 44/D4
Mīrān, Pak. 98/A4
Miranda, It. 65/D4
Miranda, SD, US 154/E1
Miranda, Braz. 189/E2
Miranda (riv.), Braz. 186/A3
Miranda de Ebro, Sp. 44/B5
Miranda do Corvo, Port. 46/A2
Miranda do Douro, Port. 46/B2
Mirande, Fr. 44/D5
Mirandela, Port. 46/B2
Mirandiba, Braz. 183/G5
Mirando City, Tx, US 150/E4
Mirandópolis, Braz. 189/G2
Mirano, It. 63/F3
Miranorte, Braz. 182/D5
Mīrānpur, India 96/A1
Mirassol, Braz. 189/G2
Miravalles (vol.), CR 176/E4
Miravalles (peak), Sp. 46/B1
Mirbāţ, Oman 101/F5
Mirboo North, Austl. 133/C4
Mirebalais, Haiti 177/H2
Mirebeau, Fr. 60/B3
Mirecourt, Fr. 60/C1
Mirecourt (Épinal) (arpt.), Fr. 60/C1
Mireigha, Sudan 117/E3
Mirendi, Gabon 120/B3
Mirfield, Eng, UK 35/G4
Miri, Malay. 90/D3
Miriam Vale, Austl. 134/C4
Mirim (lake), Braz. 189/F5
Mirimire, Ven. 180/D2
Mírina, Gre. 49/J3
Miriñay (riv.), Arg. 188/E4
Mirinzal, Braz. 183/E3
Miritiparaná (riv.), Col. 180/D5
Mirna (riv.), Cro. 63/G5
Mirnyy, Rus. 75/M3
Mirnyy, Rus., Ant. 192/G
Mirow, Ger. 42/G2
Mīrpur, Pak. 98/B3
Mirria, Niger 115/H3
Mirror, Ab, Can. 145/H1
Mirror (lake), NJ, US 168/D4
Mirsali, China 99/E3
Mirthal, India 98/C3
Mirtóön (sea), Gre. 49/H4
Miryang, SKor. 84/A3
Mirzaani, Geo. 71/H4
Mirzāpur, Bang. 97/H3
Mirzāpur, India 96/D3
Misa (riv.), It. 63/G5
Misa, D.R. Congo 121/G1
Misaka, Japan 83/B2
Misaki, Japan 84/D3
Misaki, Japan 83/E3
Misano Adriatico, It. 63/F6
Misantla, Mex. 175/N7
Misasa, Tanz. 119/B3
Misato, Japan 83/D2
Misato, Japan 83/C1
Misato, Japan 83/K6
Misawa, Japan 82/B3
Miscano (riv.), It. 65/D5
Miscou (pt.), Qu, Can. 158/E1
Miscou (isl.), NB, Can. 158/E2
Miscou Centre, NB, Can. 158/E2
Misere (lake), La, US 164/B3
Misgār, Pak. 101/K1
Mishagua, Peru 184/C3
Mishan, China 79/L2
Mishawaka, In, US 160/C4
Misheguk (mt.), Ak, US 171/F2
Mishicot, Wi, US 160/C2
Mishima, Japan 85/F3
Mishkino, Rus. 69/M5
Mishmar Hanegev, Isr. 105/B6
Mishmar Hayarden, Isr. 105/D3
Misilmeri, It. 48/C3
Misiones (dept.), Arg. 189/E3
Miskolc, Hun. 43/L4
Mismār, Sudan 100/C5
Misono, Japan 83/L6
Misool (isl.), Indo. 91/H4
Misquah (hills), Mn, US 157/J4
Mişr al Jadīdah, Egypt 113/C4
Mişrātah, Libya 67/G4
Mişrātah (pt.), Libya 67/K5
Missão Velha, Braz. 183/G4
Missillac, Fr. 56/C6
Missinaibi (riv.), On, Can. 141/H3
Mission, BC, Can. 144/C3
Mission (bay), Ca, US 166/C5
Mission (mtn.), Ok, US 153/G2
Mission, Or, US 146/D1
Mission, Tx, US 151/E4
Mission Beach, Austl. 134/B2
Mission Bend, Tx, US 151/M9
Mission Ind. Res., Ca, US 166/C4
Mission Ridge, SD, US 154/D1
Mission San Buenaventura, Ca, US 166/A2
Mission San Jose, Ca, US 167/L12
Mission San Juan Capistrano, Ca, US 166/C3
Mission San Luis Obispo de Tolosa, Ca, US 148/B3
Mission San Miguel Arcangel, Ca, US 148/B3
Mission Viejo, Ca, US 166/C3
Mississagi (riv.), On, Can. 160/E1
Mississauga, On, Can. 160/T8
Mississippi (pt.), Austl. 130/D5
Mississippi (delta), US 139/J7
Mississippi (riv.), US 139/H6
Mississippi (state), US 143/H5
Mississippi (sound), Al,Ms, US 164/D2
Mississippi Sandhill Crane NWR, Ms, US 164/D2
Mississippi Station, On, Can. 161/H2
Missoula, Mt, US 145/H4
Missouri (riv.), US 139/F5
Missouri (state), US 143/H4
Missouri City, Tx, US 151/M9
Missouri Valley, Ia, US 155/G3
Missungwi, Tanz. 119/A2
Mist, Or, US 144/C5
Mistake (cr.), Austl. 134/B3
Mistake Creek, Austl. 128/C4
Mistaken (pt.), Nf, Can. 159/L2
Mistassini, Qu, Can. 158/A1
Mistassini (lake), Qu, Can. 141/J3
Mistatim, Sk, Can. 145/N1
Misti (vol.), Peru 184/D5
Mistissini, Qu, Can. 141/J3
Mistley, Eng, UK 37/H3
Mistrás (ruin), Gre. 49/H4
Mistretta, It. 48/D4
Misty Fjords Nat'l Mon., Ak, US 171/M4
Misugi, Japan 83/K6
Miswa, Zam. 123/F2
Mīt Abū Ghālib, Egypt 113/C2
Mīt an Naşārá, Egypt 113/C2

Mīt Fāris, Egypt	113/C2	Mkorn (peak), Mor.	110/D3	Moghul Gardens, India	98/C3	Molde, Nor. 38/C3
Mīt Ghamr, Egypt	113/C2	Mkumbi (pt.), Tanz.	119/B3	Mogi das Cruzes, Braz.	187/K8	Moldova (ctry.) 72/E4
Mīt Ḥamal, Egypt	113/C4	Mkushi, Zam.	123/F2	Mogi-Guaçu (riv.), Braz.	187/K7	Moldova, Rus. 51/G2
Mita, Punta de (pt.), Mex.	174/D4	Mkushi (riv.), Zam.	123/F2	Mogi-Guaçu, Braz.	187/K7	Moldova Nouǎ, Rom. 57/E2
Mitaka, Japan	83/K7	Mkuze (riv.), SAfr.	125/F2	Mogi-Mirim, Braz.	187/K7	Moldoveanu (peak), Rom. 51/G3
Mitake, Japan	83/M5	Mkuze, SAfr.	125/F2	Mogige, Eth.	117/H4	Mole (riv.), Eng, UK 64/C6
Mitama, Japan	83/K7	Mladá Boleslav, Czh.	59/H2	Mogil Mogil, Austl.	132/D1	Mole (riv.), Eng, UK 64/C6
Mitare, Ven.	180/D2	Mladá Vožice, Czh.	59/H3	Mogilno, Pol.	43/J2	Mole, D.R. Congo 121/D3
Mitatib, Sudan		Mladenovac, Serb.	50/E3	Mogincual, Moz.	123/H3	Mole Lake Ind. Res.,

Mun'gyŏ – Nat

Mun'gyŏng, SKor. 81/E4
Munhango, Ang. 122/C2
Munhino, Ang. 122/B2
Munich, ND, US 156/E3
Munich (München), Ger. 59/E6
Munising, Mi, US 157/L4
Muniungu, D.R. Congo 120/D4
Munjor, Ks, US 152/E1
Munka-Ljungby, Swe. 39/J6
Munkebo, Den. 40/D4
Munkedal, Swe. 40/D2
Munkfors, Swe. 40/E2
Munku-Sardyk (peak), Rus. 75/L4
Munku-Sasan (peak), Rus. 78/D1
Münnerstadt, Ger. 58/D2
Muñoz Gamero (pen.), Chile 191/B7
Munsan, SKor. 81/F6
Münsingen, Swi. 60/D4
Münsingen, Ger. 58/C6
Munsön (isl.), Swe. 39/A1
Munster, Fr. 60/D1
Münster, Swi. 61/E5
Munster (riv.), Ire. 32/C4
Munster (reg.), Ire. 32/B5
Münster, Ger. 58/B3
Munster, On, Can. 161/J2
Munster, Ger. 53/H3
Munster, In, US 167/R16
Münster, Ger. 53/E5
Münster/Osnabrück (int'l arpt.), Ger. 53/E4
Münstereifel, Ger. 55/F2
Münsterhausen, Ger. 58/D6
Münsterland (reg.), Ger. 42/D2
Münstermaifeld, Ger. 55/G3
Muntele Mare (peak), Rom. 51/F2
Muntendam, Neth. 52/D2
Muntinglupa, Phil. 88/F7
Muntok, Indo. 89/D3
Müntschemier, Swi. 60/D4
Muntu, D.R. Congo 120/D3
Münzenberg, Ger. 58/B2
Münzkirchen, Aus. 59/G6
Munzur Vadisi NP, Turk. 102/D2
Muong Het, Laos 94/D1
Muong Hin, Viet. 86/E5
Muong Khuong, Viet. 94/D1
Muong Lat, Viet. 86/E4
Muonio, Fin. 38/G2
Muonioälven (riv.), Swe. 38/G1
Muotathal, Swi. 61/E4
Mupa, Ang. 122/B3
Mupa, PN da, Ang. 122/B2
Muping, China 80/E3
Muqaddan (wadi), Sudan 117/F1
Muqaṭṭa', Sudan 117/G2
Muqeibila, Isr. 105/C3
Müqtädir, Azer. 71/J4
Mur (riv.), Aus. 67/G1
Mûr-de-Bretagne, Fr. 56/C4
Mur-de-Sologne, Fr. 57/G6
Mura (riv.), Slov.,Hun. 50/C2
Muradiye, Turk. 103/E2
Murādnagar, India 98/D5
Murakami, Japan 85/F1
Murallón (peak), Chile 191/B6
Muramgaon, India 95/D1
Muramvya, Buru. 121/G3
Murang'a, Kenya 119/B2
Murano, It. 63/F3
Murashi, Rus. 69/L4
Murat (peak), Turk. 102/B2
Muratlı, Turk. 102/E2
Muratlı, Turk. 51/H5
Murayama, Japan 82/B4
Mūrcheh Khvort, Iran 103/G3
Murchison (isl.), On, Can. 157/K3
Murchison, NZ 135/C3
Murchison, Austl. 133/B3
Murchison (mt.), Austl. 130/C3
Murchison (riv.), Austl. 127/A3
Murchison Downs, Austl. 130/C3
Murcia (pol. reg.), Sp. 46/E4
Murcia, Sp. 47/E4
Murderkill (riv.), De, US 168/C6
Murdo, SD, US 154/D2
Murdochville, Qu, Can. 158/E1
Murdock (pt.), Austl. 134/B1
Murdock, Mn, US 155/G1
Mürefte, Turk. 51/H5
Mureş (riv.), Rom. 70/B3
Mureş (prov.), Rom. 51/G2
Muret, Fr. 44/D5
Murewa, Zim. 123/F3
Murfreesboro, Ar, US 153/H3
Murfreesboro, Tn, US 162/D3
Murfreesboro, NC, US 163/J2
Murg (riv.), Ger. 55/H6
Murgap (riv.), Trkm. 74/G6
Murgenella Wildllife Sanctuary, Austl. 128/D2
Murghob, Taj. 99/B4
Murgon, Austl. 134/C4
Murgoo, Austl. 130/C3
Muri, Swi. 61/E3
Muri, China 78/D4
Muri bei Bern, Swi. 60/D4
Muria (peak), Indo. 89/E4
Muriaé, Braz. 187/E4
Murias de Paredes, Sp. 46/B1
Murici, Braz. 183/H5
Murīdke, Pak. 98/C4
Muriege, Ang. 121/E5
Müritz (lake), Ger. 42/G2
Murka, Kenya 119/B2
Murle, Eth. 117/H4
Murlīganj, India 97/F3
Murmansk (int'l arpt.), Rus. 68/G1
Murmansk, Rus. 68/G1
Murmanskaya Oblast Rus. 38/J1
Murmashi, Rus. 68/G1
Murnau, Ger. 61/H2
Murnpeowie, Austl. 131/H4
Muro, Sp. 47/G3
Muro, Japan 83/K6
Muro Lucano, It. 48/D2
Murom, Rus. 68/J5
Murongo, Tanz. 121/G3
Muroran, Japan 82/B2
Muros, Sp. 46/A1
Muroto, Japan 84/D4
Muroto-zaki (pt.), Japan 84/D4
Murowana Goślina, Pol. 43/J2
Murphy, Id, US 146/E2
Murphy, NC, US 162/E3
Murphy, Tx, US 150/L6
Murphys, Ca, US 146/C4
Murphysboro, Il, US 162/C2
Murphytown, WV, US 163/G1
Murr (riv.), Ger. 58/C5
Murra, Nic. 176/E3
Murramarang NP, Austl. 133/E2
Murray, Ut, US 147/H3
Murray, Ky, US 162/C2
Murray (lake), PNG 129/F1
Murray (range), PNG 129/F1
Murray, Id, US 144/G4
Murray (riv.), Austl. 127/D4
Murray Bridge, Austl. 131/H5
Murray Downs, Austl. 131/G2
Murray River, PE, Can. 159/F2
Murraysburg, SAfr. 124/C3
Murrayville, Austl. 132/B2
Murrayville, Ga, US 162/F3
Murree, Pak. 98/B3
Mürren, Swi. 60/D4
Murrhardt, Ger. 58/C5
Murrieta, Ca, US 166/C3
Murrieta Hot Springs, Ca, US 166/C3
Murringo, Austl. 133/D2
Murrumbateman, Austl. 133/D2
Murrumbidgee (riv.), Austl. 127/D4
Murrumburrah, Austl. 133/D2
Murrupula, Moz. 123/H2
Murrurundi, Austl. 132/D1
Mursala (isl.), Indo. 89/B2
Murshidābād, India 97/G3
Murska Sobota, Slov. 50/C2
Murtala Muhammed (int'l arpt.), Nga. 115/F5
Murtaröl (peak), Swi. 61/G4
Murten, Swi. 60/D4
Murtle (riv.), BC, Can. 144/D1
Murtoa, Austl. 132/B3
Murton, Eng, UK 35/G2
Murua, PNG 129/G1
Murua Ngithigerr (mts.), Kenya 117/G5
Murud (peak), Malay. 88/A5
Murud, India 95/C2
Murupara, NZ 135/D2
Mururoa (isl.), FrPol. 137/M7
Murwāra, India 96/C4
Murwillumbah, Austl. 134/D5
Mürz (riv.), Aus. 43/H5
Mürzzuschlag, Aus. 43/H5
Muş, Turk. 102/E2
Muş (prov.), Turk. 102/E2
Musa, D.R. Congo 120/D2
Musa Khel, Pak. 98/A3
Musabeyli, Turk. 104/E1
Musāfirkhāna, India 96/C2
Musā'id, Libya 108/E2
Musala (peak), Bul. 49/H1
Musan, NKor. 81/E1
Musanda, D.R. Congo 120/C4
Musandam (pen.), Oman 103/H5
Musasa, Tanz. 121/G3
Musashino, Japan 83/D2
Musay'īd, Qatar 100/F4
Musaymir, Yem. 118/C2
Muscat (cap.), Oman 101/G4
Muscatatuck NWR, In, US 162/E1
Muscatine, Ia, US 155/J3
Musciuru (well), Libya 108/B4
Musconetcong (riv.), NJ, US 168/C2
Muscoot (res.), NY, US 169/E1
Muscowpetung Ind. Res., Sk, Can. 156/B2
Muscoy, Ca, US 166/C2
Muse, Ok, US 153/G3
Muse, Tanz. 121/G4
Museum of Flight, Wa, US 167/C2
Musgrave (range), Austl. 127/C3
Musgrave, Austl. 134/A1
Musgravetown, Nf, Can. 159/L1
Mushābani, India 97/F4
Mushāsh (wadi), Isr. 105/C5
Mushaway (peak), Tx, US 150/D1
Musheramore (peak), Ire. 32/B5
Mushie, D.R. Congo 120/D3
Mushin, Nga. 115/F5
Musholm (bay), Den. 39/H7
Musi (riv.), Indo. 89/C3
Musile di Piave, It. 63/F2
Musinga (peak), Col. 180/B3
Muskego, Wi, US 167/P14
Muskegon, Mi, US 160/C3
Muskegon (riv.), Mi, US 160/D3
Muskingum (riv.), Oh, US 160/E4
Muskirā, India 96/B3
Muskö (isl.), Swe. 39/B1
Muskoday Ind. Res., Sk, Can. 145/M1
Muskogee, Ok, US 153/G3
Muskrat (cr.), Wy, US 147/K2
Muslimīyah, Syria 104/E1
Musofu, Zam. 123/F2
Musoka (lake), On, Can. 161/G2
Musoma, Tanz. 119/A2
Musone (riv.), It. 63/G6
Musquodoboit Harbour, NS, Can. 158/F3
Mussau (isl.), PNG 136/D5
Mussel Fk. (riv.), Mo, US 155/H3
Musselburgh, Sc, UK 33/C5
Musselshell (riv.), Mt, US 142/E2
Musselshell, Mt, US 145/K4
Mussende, Ang. 120/D5
Musserra, Ang. 120/C4
Mussomeli, It. 48/C4
Musson, Belg. 55/E4
Mussuco, Ang. 120/D5
Mussuma (riv.), Ang. 122/D2
Mustafābād, Pak. 98/B4
Mustafābad, India 96/C3
Mustafakemalpaşa, Turk. 70/D4
Mustahīl, Eth. 118/C4
Müstair, Swi. 61/G4
Mustān, Nepal 96/D1
Mustang, Ok, US 153/F3
Mustang (isl.), Tx, US 151/F4
Muşţāy, Egypt 113/C3
Mustayevo, Rus. 71/K2
Musters (lake), Arg. 190/C5
Mustio (Svartå), Fin. 39/D4
Mustvee, Est. 41/M2
Musu-dan (pt.), NKor. 81/E2
Musún (mtn.), Nic. 176/E3
Müsüslü, Azer. 103/F1
Mušutište, Serb. 49/G1
Muswellbrook, Austl. 132/D2
Mut, Turk. 104/C1
Mūt, Egypt 135/F3
Mutá, Ponta do (pt.), Braz. 187/F2
Mutambara, Zim. 123/G3
Mutango, Ang. 122/D3
Mutare, Zim. 123/G3
Mutenge, Zam. 123/F2
Mutepatepa, Zim. 123/F3
Muthill, Sc, UK 33/C4
Muting, Indo. 129/F1
Mutis (peak), Indo. 128/B2
Mutkyi, Myan. 94/B2
Mutnyy Materik, Rus. 69/M2
Mutoko, Zim. 123/G3
Mutombo, D.R. Congo 121/E4
Mutombo-Dibwe, D.R. Congo 121/E4
Mutombo-Mukulu, D.R. Congo 121/F4
Mutria (peak), It. 65/D5
Mutsamudu, Com. 125/H6
Mutshatsha, D.R. Congo 121/F5
Mutsu, Japan 82/B3
Mutsu (bay), Japan 82/B3
Mutsuzawa, Japan 83/E3
Muttaburra, Austl. 134/B3
Muttekopf (peak), Aus. 61/G3
Muttenz, Swi. 60/D2
Mutters, Aus. 61/H3
Mutterstadt, Ger. 58/B4
Muttler (peak), Swi. 61/G4
Muttonville, Mi, US 167/G6
Mutu (mtn.), Indo. 128/A2
Muţūhis, Egypt 113/B2
Mutum, Braz. 187/E3
Mutumbo, Ang. 122/C2
Mutumieque, Ang. 122/B3
Mutún, Bol. 188/E1
Mutur, SrL. 95/D4
Mutwanga, D.R. Congo 121/G2
Mutzig, Fr. 60/D1
Muwale, Tanz. 119/A3
Muyezerskiy, Rus. 68/F3
Muyinga, Buru. 121/G3
Mŭynoq, Uzb. 74/F5
Muyuka, Camr. 120/B1
Muyumba, D.R. Congo 121/F4
Muyuya, D.R. Congo 121/F5
Muzaffarābād, Pak. 98/B2
Muzaffargarh, Pak. 98/A4
Muzaffarnagar, India 98/D5
Muzaffarpur, India 97/E2
Muzambinho, Braz. 187/K6
Muzat (riv.), China 99/D3
Muzillac, Fr. 56/C5
Muzo, Col. 183/L7
Muzoka, Zam. 123/E3
Muzon (cape), Ak, US 171/M4
Muztag (peak), China 99/D4
Muztagata (peak), China 99/C4
Muzzana del Turgnano, It. 63/G2
Mvadhi-Ousyé, Gabon 120/C2
Mvangane, Camr. 120/B2
Mvolo, Sudan 117/F4
Mvomero, Tanz. 119/B3
Mvoung (riv.), Gabon 120/C2
M'vouti, Congo 120/C4
Mvuma, Zim. 123/F3
Mwadi-Kalumbu, D.R. Congo 120/D4
Mwadingusha, D.R. Congo 121/F5
Mwadui, Tanz. 119/A2
Mwami, Zim. 123/F3
Mwana (cape), Kenya 119/C2
Mwana-Ndeke, D.R. Congo 121/F4
Mwanza (gulf), Tanz. 119/A2
Mwanza, Malw. 123/G2
Mwanza (prov.), Tanz. 121/H3
Mwanza, Tanz. 121/H3
Mwanza, D.R. Congo 121/F4
Mwase Lundaz, Zam. 123/G2
Mwaya, Tanz. 119/B4
Mwaya, Tanz. 119/A4
Mweelrea (peak), Ire. 31/P10
Mweiga, Kenya 119/B2
Mweka, D.R. Congo 121/E4
Mwenda, Zam. 121/G5
Mwene-Ditu, D.R. Congo 121/E4
Mwenezi, Zim. 123/F4
Mwenezi (riv.), Zim. 123/F4
Mwenga, D.R. Congo 121/G3
Mwense, Zam. 121/G5
Mwenzo Mission, Zam. 121/H5
Mwera, Tanz. 119/B3
Mweru (lake), D.R. Congo 107/E5
Mweru-Wantipa (lake), D.R. Congo 121/G5
Mweru-Wantipa NP, Zam. 121/G5
Mwesi (mtn.), Tanz. 121/G4
Mwesi, Tanz. 121/G4
Mwimba, Tanz. 121/G5
Mwimba, D.R. Congo 121/E5
Mwinilunga, Zam. 122/E1
Mwitikira, Tanz. 119/A3
Mwombezhi (riv.), Zam. 122/E2
My Son Temples (ruin), Viet. 94/E3
My Tho, Viet. 94/D4
Myaksa, Rus. 68/H4
Myall Lakes NP, Austl. 132/E2
Myanaung, Myan. 86/B5
Myanmar (Burma) (ctry.) 93/G2
Myatlevo, Rus. 68/G5
Myaungmya, Myan. 86/B5
Myawadi, Myan. 94/B2
Mycenae (Mikínai) (ruin), Gre. 49/H4
Myebon, Myan. 93/F3
Myeik (Mergui), Myan. 94/B3
Myers, Mt, US 145/L4
Myerstown, Pa, US 168/B3
Myggenäs, Swe. 40/D2
Myingyan, Myan. 86/B4
Myintha, Myan. 86/B3
Myitinge (riv.), Myan. 86/C4
Myitkyinā, Myan. 86/C3
Myitta, Myan. 94/B3
Myittha, Myan. 94/B1
Myittha (riv.), Myan. 86/B4
Myjava, Slvk. 43/J4
Mykhaylivka, Ukr. 73/H4
Mykolayiv, Ukr. 72/B3
Mykolayiv, Ukr. 73/G4
Mykolayiv (int'l arpt.), Ukr. 72/G4
Mykolayivka, Ukr. 73/G5
Mykolayivs'ka Oblast, Ukr. 70/D3
Mykulyntsi, Ukr. 72/C3
Mylau, Ger. 59/F1
Mymensingh, Bang. 97/H3
Mymensingh (pol. reg.), Bang. 97/H3
Mynämäki, Fin. 41/J1
Mynaral, Kaz. 99/B2
Mynydd Eppynt (mts.), Wal, UK 36/C2
Mynydd Pencarreg (peak), Wal, UK 36/B2
Mynydd Preseli (mtn.), Wal, UK 36/B3
Myōgi, Japan 83/B1
Myohaung, Myan. 86/B4
Myohla, Myan. 86/C4
Myōkō-san (peak), Japan 85/F2
Myŏngch'ŏn, NKor. 81/E2
Myŏnggan, NKor. 81/E2
Myrhorod, Ukr. 73/G3
Myrnam, Ab, Can. 145/J1
Myronivka, Ukr. 72/F3
Myrtle, Ms, US 162/C3
Myrtle (isl.), Md, US 163/K2
Myrtle Beach, SC, US 163/H4
Myrtle Creek, Or, US 146/B2
Myrtleford, Austl. 133/C3
Mysen, Nor. 40/D2
Mysingen (bay), Swe. 39/B2
Myślenice, Pol. 43/K4
Myślibórz, Pol. 43/H2
Myslivna (peak), Czh. 59/H5
Mysore, India 95/C3
Mystery Bay Rec. Area, Wa, US 167/B1
Mystery Cave, Mn, US 155/H2
Mystic, Ga, US 165/G2
Mystic, Ia, US 155/H3
Mystic Island, NJ, US 168/D4
Mystic Seaport, Ct, US 161/L4
Mysy, Rus. 69/M3
Myszków, Pol. 43/K3
Mytishchi, Rus. 69/W9
Mýto, Czh. 59/G3
Myton, Ut, US 147/H3
Myyeldino, Rus. 69/M3
M'zab (reg.), Alg. 66/D4
Mže (riv.), Czh. 42/G4
Mzimba, Malw. 123/G1
Mzuzu, Malw. 123/G1

N

N'Djamena (cap.), Chad 116/B2
Na (riv.), Viet. 94/C1
Na Kae, Thai. 94/D2
Naaldwijk, Neth. 52/B4
Naama, Alg. 111/E2
Naantali, Fin. 41/K1
Naarden, Neth. 52/C4
Naarn im Machlande, Aus. 59/H6
Naas, Ire. 32/D3
Nabā (peak), Jor. 105/D5
Nababeep, SAfr. 124/B3
Nabadwīp, India 97/G4
Nabalat al Ḩajanah, Sudan 117/F2
Nabari, Japan 83/K6
Nabari (riv.), Japan 83/K6
Nabberu (lake), Austl. 130/D3
Nabburg, Ger. 59/F4
Naberera, Tanz. 119/B3
Naberezhnye Chelny, Rus. 69/M5
Nābha, India 98/D4
Nabiac, Austl. 132/E2
Nabīnagar, Bang. 97/H4
Nabire, Indo. 91/J4
Nabón, Ecu. 184/B1
Naboomspruit, SAfr. 123/F5
Nabua, Phil. 88/C2
Nābul, Tun. 48/B4
Nābul (gov.), Tun. 48/B4
Nābulus, WBnk. 105/C4
Nabunturan, Phil. 88/D4
Nacala, Moz. 123/J2
Nacaome, Hon. 176/E3
Nacebe, Bol. 185/E3
Nachi-Katsuura, Japan 84/D4
Nachingwea, Tanz. 119/B4
Náchod, Czh. 43/J3
Nachrodt-Wiblingwerde, Ger. 53/E6
Nachtigal, Chutes de (falls), Camr. 120/B1
Nachuge, India 93/F5
Nacimiento, Chile 190/B3
Nacimiento (peak), NM, US 149/J2
Nacimiento (res.), Ca, US 148/B3
Nacka, Swe. 39/B1
Nackawic, NB, Can. 158/D2
Nacmine, Ab, Can. 145/H2
Naco, Mex. 149/H5
Nacogdoches, Tx, US 151/G2
Nácori Chico, Mex. 174/C2
Nacozari de García, Mex. 174/C2
Nadadores, Mex. 150/D4
Nādbai, India 96/A2
Nadder (riv.), Eng, UK 36/D4
Nadi, Fiji 137/Y18
Nadi (int'l arpt.), Fiji 137/Y18
Nadiād, India 92/B3
Nādir, Egypt 113/B3
Nădlac, Rom. 50/E2
Nador, Mor. 112/C2
Nador (prov.), Mor. 112/C2
Nadur, Malta 48/L6
Nadvirna, Ukr. 72/C3
Nadvoitsy, Rus. 68/G3
Nadym, Rus. 74/H3
Naejang-san NP, SKor. 81/D5
Näfels, Swi. 61/F3
Nafferton, Eng, UK 35/H4
Nafī, SAr. 100/D3
Naftalan, Azer. 103/F1
Naga, Phil. 88/C2
Naga (hills), India 86/B3
Nagagami (riv.), On, Can. 157/M3
Nagahama, Japan 84/C4
Nagahama, Japan 83/K5
Nagai, Japan 85/G1
Nagaizumi, Japan 83/B3
Nagakute, Japan 83/M5
Nāgāland (state), India 93/F2
Nagambie, Austl. 133/B3
Nagano, Japan 85/F2
Nagano (pref.), Japan 85/E3
Naganuma, Japan 82/B2
Nagaoka, Japan 85/F2
Nagaokakyō, Japan 83/J6
Nagaon (Nowgong), India 86/B3
Nagappattinam, India 95/C4
Nagar, India 96/A2
Nagar Pārkar, Pak. 101/K4
Nagar Untāri, India 96/D3
Nagara (riv.), Japan 85/E3
Nagara, Japan 83/E3
Nagareyama, Japan 83/D2
Nāgārjuna Sāgar (res.), India 92/C4
Nagarote, Nic. 172/D5
Nagarzê, China 97/H1
Nagasaka, Japan 83/A2
Nagasaki, Japan 84/A4
Nagasaki (int'l arpt.), Japan 84/A4
Nagasaki (pref.), Japan 84/A4
Nagasaki Peace, Japan 84/A4
Nagashima, Japan 83/L5
Nagato, Japan 84/B3
Nagato, Japan 83/A1
Nagatoro, Japan 83/C1
Nāgaur, India 92/B2
Nāgda, India 92/C3
Nagele, Neth. 52/C3
Nāgercoil, India 95/C4
Nagīna, India 96/B1
Nagir, Pak. 101/K1
Nagishot, Sudan 117/G4
Nagles (mts.), Ire. 32/B5
Nago, Japan 85/J7
Nago-Torbole, It. 61/G6
Nāgod, India 96/C3
Nagold, Ger. 58/B5
Nagold (riv.), Ger. 58/B5
Nagongera, Ugan. 119/A1
Nagorno-Karabakh (prov.), Arm. 71/H5
Nagornyy, Rus. 75/N4
Nagorsk, Rus. 69/L4
Nagosira, D.R. Congo 121/F2
Nagoya, Japan 83/L5
Nagoya Castle, Japan 83/L5
Nagpula (pass), China 97/F1
Nāgpur, India 98/C5
Nāgpur, India 95/C1
Nagqu (riv.), China 78/C5
Nagqu, China 86/B2
Nags Head, NC, US 163/K3
Nagu (Nauvo), Fin. 41/J1
Naguri, Japan 83/C2
Nagy-Milic (peak), Hun. 43/L4
Nagyatád, Hun. 50/C2
Nagybatony, Hun. 50/D2
Nagyecsed, Hun. 43/M5
Nagyhalász, Hun. 50/E1
Nagykanizsa, Hun. 50/C2
Nagykáta, Hun. 50/D2
Nagykőrös, Hun. 50/D2
Naha, Japan 85/J7
Nahabuan, Indo. 90/D3
Naẖal Shillo (wadi), Isr. 105/C4
Nāhan, India 98/D4
Nahanni NP, NW, Can. 140/D2
Nāhar, India 98/D5
Nahariyya, Isr. 105/C3
Nahatlatch (riv.), BC, Can. 144/C3
Nahāvand, Iran 103/G3
Naẖel Soreq (riv.), Isr. 105/B5
Naḩḩālīn, WBnk. 105/C5
Nahol'no-Tarasivka, Ukr. 73/K3
Nahouri (prov.), Burk. 115/E4
Nahr Ad Dindar (riv.), Sudan 117/G2
Nahr Ar Rahad (riv.), Sudan 117/G2
Nahr aş Şafā (riv.), Leb. 105/C1
Nahr Ouassel (riv.), Alg. 112/F5
Nahuel Huapi (lake), Arg. 179/B7
Nahuel Huapí, PN, Arg. 190/C4
Nahuelbuta, PN, Chile 190/B3
Nahuentúe, Chile 190/B3
Nahunta, Ga, US 165/H2
Naica, Mex. 174/D3
Naicam, Sk, Can. 145/M1
Naiguatá, Ven. 183/P7
Naihāti, India 97/G4
Naij Gol (riv.), China 78/C4
Naij Tal, China 78/C4
Naikliu, Indo. 128/A2
Naila, Ger. 59/E2
Nailsea, Eng, UK 36/D4
Nailsworth, Eng, UK 36/D3
Nā'im (well), Libya 108/C2
Na'ima, Sudan 117/G2
Naiman Qi, China 80/E2
Nā'īn, Iran 103/H3
Nain, Nf, Can. 141/K3
Nainital, India 96/B1
Nainpur, India 96/C4
Naintré, Fr. 44/D3
Nairn (riv.), Sc, UK 33/B2
Nairn, Sc, UK 33/C1
Nairne, Austl. 131/M9
Nairobi (cap.), Kenya 119/B2
Nairobi NP, Kenya 119/B2
Naita (peak), Eth. 117/G4
Naivasha, Kenya 119/B2
Naives-Rosières, Fr. 55/E6
Najafābād, Iran 103/G3
Najd (des.), SAr. 102/E5
Nájera, Sp. 46/D1
Naju, SKor. 81/D5
Naka (riv.), Japan 84/D4
Naka, Japan 83/G5
Nakadōri (isl.), Japan 84/A4
Nakai, Japan 83/C3
Nakajō, Japan 85/F1
Nakamichi, Japan 83/B2
Nakaminato, Japan 85/G2
Nakamura, Japan 84/C4
Nakano, Japan 85/F2
Nakano (lag.), Japan 84/C3
Nakasato, Japan 82/B3
Nakashibetsu, Japan 82/D2
Nakasongola, Ugan. 121/H2
Nakatane, Japan 85/L5
Nakatomi, Japan 83/A3
Nakatsu, Japan 84/B4
Nakatsugawa, Japan 85/E3
Nakazato, Japan 83/B1
Nak'fa, Erit. 100/C5
Nakhodka, Rus. 79/L3
Nakhola, India 97/J2
Nakhon Nayok, Thai. 94/C3
Nakhon Pathom, Thai. 94/C3
Nakhon Phanom, Thai. 94/D2
Nakhon Ratchasima, Thai. 94/C3
Nakhon Sawan, Thai. 94/C3
Nakhon Si Thammarat, Thai. 94/B4
Nakhon Thai, Thai. 94/C2
Nakhtarāna, India 101/J4
Nakifuma, Ugan. 121/H2
Nakina, On, Can. 157/L2
Nakkila, Fin. 41/J1
Nakło nad Notecią, Pol. 43/J2
Naknek, Ak, US 171/G4
Nakodar, India 98/C4
Nakonde, Zam. 121/H5
Nakong, Gha. 115/E4
Nakop, Namb. 124/B3
Naksan-sa, SKor. 81/E3
Nakskov, Den. 40/D4
Naktong, SKor. 81/E4
Naktong (riv.), SKor. 84/A3
Nakūr, India 98/D5
Nakuru, Kenya 119/B2
Nakusp, BC, Can. 144/F2
Nāl (riv.), Pak. 101/J3
Nalao, China 86/E3
Nalayh, Mong. 78/F2
Nalázi, Moz. 123/G5
Nalbach, Ger. 55/F5
Nalbāri, India 97/H2
Nalbaugh NP, Austl. 133/D3
Nal'chik, Rus. 71/G4
Nalchik (int'l arpt.), Rus. 71/G4
Nale, Laos 94/C2
Nalgonda, India 95/C2
Nalhāti, India 97/F3
Nalitābāri, Bang. 97/H3
Naliya, India 101/J4
Nallıhan, Turk. 51/K5
Nalón (riv.), Sp. 46/B1
Nalong, Myan. 86/C3
Nālūt, Libya 111/H3
Nam (riv.), SKor. 81/D5
Nam (riv.), NKor. 81/D3
Nam (lake), China 99/E5
Nam Can, Viet. 94/D4
Nam Cum, Viet. 86/D4
Nam Dinh, Viet. 87/E4
Nam Nao NP, Thai. 94/C2
Nam Pat, Thai. 94/C2
Nam Phong, Thai. 94/C2
Nam Un (res.), Thai. 94/C2
Namacunde, Ang. 122/B3
Namacurra, Moz. 123/H3
Namadzi, Malw. 123/G2
Namāi, Nepal 96/D2
Namak (lake), Iran 103/G3
Namakzār-e Shahdād (salt pan), Iran 103/J4
Namang, Indo. 89/D3
Namanga, Kenya 119/B2
Namangan, Uzb. 99/B3
Namansansong Provicial Park, SKor. 81/G7
Namanyere, Tanz. 121/G4
Namapa, Moz. 123/H2
Namaputa, Tanz. 119/B4
Namaqualand (reg.), SAfr. 124/B3
Namari, Sen. 114/B3
Namaripi (cape), Indo. 91/J4
Namarrói, Moz. 123/H2
Namasagali, Ugan. 119/A1
Namasakata, Tanz. 123/H1
Namatanai, PNG 136/E5
Nambanje, Tanz. 119/B4
Nambe, NM, US 149/K3
Namborn, Ger. 55/G4
Nambour, Austl. 134/D4
Nambu, Japan 83/A3
Nambuangongo, Ang. 120/C5
Nambucca Heads, Austl. 132/E1
Nambung NP, Austl. 130/B4
Namco, China 99/F5
Namdae (riv.), NKor. 81/E2
Namdalseid, Nor. 38/D2
Nämdö (isl.), Swe. 39/B1
Nämdöfjärden (sound), Swe. 39/B1
Namegawa, Japan 83/C1
Namekagon (riv.), Wi, US 157/J4
Namentenga (prov.), Burk. 115/E3
Namerikawa, Japan 85/E2
Nametil, Moz. 123/H2
Namewaminikan (riv.), On, Can. 157/L3
Namhae (isl.), SKor. 81/D5
Namhae, SKor. 81/D5
Nami, Malay. 89/C1
Namib (des.), Namb. 107/D6
Namib-Naukluft Park, Namb. 122/B4
Namibe (int'l arpt.), Ang. 122/B2
Namibe, Ang. 122/B2
Namibe (dist.), Ang. 122/B2
Namibia (ctry.) 107/D7
Namie, Japan 85/G2
Namioka, Japan 82/B3
Namir, Mong. 78/C2
Namitete, Malw. 123/G2
Namja (pass), Nepal 99/D6
Namjagbarwa (peak), China 86/B2
Namlan, Myan. 94/B1
Namling, China 99/E6
Namloser Wetterspitze (peak), Aus. 61/G3
Nammoku, Japan 83/B1
Namnoi (peak), Myan. 94/B4
Namoi (riv.), Austl. 127/D4
Namonuito (isl.), Micr. 136/D4
Namorik (isl.), Mrsh. 136/F4
Namorona, Madg. 125/J8
Nampa, Id, US 146/E2
Nampala, Mali 114/D3
Namp'o, NKor. 81/C3
Nampula, Moz. 123/H2
Nampula (prov.), Moz. 123/H2
Namp'yŏng, SKor. 81/D5
Namrole, Indo. 91/G4
Nāmrup, India 86/B3
Namsa-ri, NKor. 81/D2
Namsang, Myan. 94/B1
Namsê (pass), China 99/D6
Namsos, Nor. 38/D2
Namtok Mae Surin NP, Thai. 86/C5
Namu (isl.), Mrsh. 136/F4
Namúli (mts.), Moz. 123/H2
Namuno, Moz. 123/H2
Namur (prov.), Belg. 55/D3
Namur, Belg. 55/D3
Namutoni, Namb. 122/C3
Namwala, Zam. 123/E2
Namwŏn, SKor. 81/D5
Namysłów, Pol. 43/J3
Nan, Thai. 94/C2
Nan (mts.), China 87/G3
Nan (riv.), China 78/F5
Nan (riv.), Thai. 87/F4
Nan'ao (isl.), China 87/H4
Nana Barya (riv.), Chad 116/C4
Nana Barya, Rsv. de Faune, CAfr. 116/C4
Nana Candundo, Ang. 122/D1
Nana-Mambéré (pref.), CAfr. 116/B4
Nanae, Japan 82/B3
Nanafalia, Al, US 162/D4
Nanaimo, BC, Can. 144/C3
Nanam, NKor. 81/E2
Nanango, Austl. 134/D4
Nanao, Japan 85/E2
Nanauta, India 98/D5
Nanay (riv.), Peru 184/C1
Nanbaozhen, China 80/L8
Nancagua, Chile 190/C2
Nancha, China 79/K2
Nanchang, China 87/G2
Nancheng, China 87/H3
Nanchong, China 86/E2
Nanchong, China 87/E2
Nanchuan, China 87/E2
Nancy, Fr. 55/F6
Nanda Devi (peak), India 99/C5
Nandan, China 93/J3
Nandashan, China 87/G2
Nānded, India 95/C2
Nandi Mill, Zim. 123/F4
Nandigāma, India 95/D2
Nanding (riv.), China 93/G3
Nandonge, Ang. 120/D5
Nandrin, Belg. 55/E3
Nandu, China 87/F4
Nandu (riv.), China 87/F5
Nandy, Fr. 30/K6
Nandyāl, India 95/C3
Nanfen, China 81/B2
Nanfeng, China 87/H3
Nang (isl.), Phil. 87/J4
Nang Rong, Thai. 94/C3
Nang Xian, China 86/B2
Nanga Parbat (peak), Pak. 98/C2
Nanga-Eboko, Camr. 116/B4
Nangalili, Indo. 91/F5
Nangamahap, Indo. 90/D4
Nangamentebah, Indo. 90/D3
Nangapinoh, Indo. 90/D4
Nangar NP, Austl. 133/D1
Nangata (pt.), Moz. 123/J2
Nangin, Myan. 94/B4
Nangis, Fr. 30/M6
Nangnim (mts.), NKor. 81/D2
Nangnim, NKor. 81/D2
Nangong, China 80/C3
Nangqên, China 78/D5
Nangtud (mt.), Phil. 88/C3
Nangua, Tanz. 119/B4
Nanguanling, China 81/A3
Nangwarry, Austl. 132/B3
Nanhsi, Tai. 87/J4
Nanhuang, China 81/A4
Nanhui, China 80/L8
Nanikelako, Zam. 122/D2
Nanjian Yizu Zizhixian, China 86/D3
Nanjiangkou, China 87/F4
Nanjing, China 80/D4
Nanka (riv.), Myan. 86/C4
Nankāna Sāhib, Pak. 98/B4
Nankoku, Japan 84/C4
Nankou, China 87/H3
Nankova, Ang. 122/C3
Nanlan (riv.), China 86/D4
Nanle, China 80/C3
Nanling, China 87/H2
Nanlinqiao, China 87/G2
Nanliu (riv.), China 93/J3
Nanlou (peak), China 79/K3
Nannestad, Nor. 40/D1
Nannine, Austl. 130/C3
Nanning, China 87/F4
Nannō, Japan 83/L5
Nannup, Austl. 130/B5
Nanny (riv.), Ire. 34/B4
Nanpan (riv.), China 86/E3
Nānpāra, India 96/C2
Nanpi, China 80/D3
Nanping, China 87/H3
Nanpu, China 80/J7
Nans-les-Pins, Fr. 64/B6
Nansei, Japan 83/L7
Nansemond Nat'l Wild. Ref., Va, US 163/J2
Nansen (sound), Nun, Can. 141/S6
Nansheng, China 87/H3
Nansio, Tanz. 119/A2
Nant (riv.), Fr. 57/G5
Nant (lake), Sc, UK 33/A4
Nantai, China 81/B2
Nantai-san (peak), Japan 85/F2
Nanterre, Fr. 30/J5
Nantes, Fr. 56/D6
Nantes à Brest (canal), Fr. 56/B4
Nanteuil-le-Haudouin, Fr. 30/L4
Nanteuil-lès-Meaux, Fr. 54/B6
Nantian, China 87/H3
Nantian, China 87/J2
Nanticoke, On, Can. 160/F3
Nanticoke, Pa, US 168/B1
Nanton, Ab, Can. 145/H2
Nantong, China 80/E4
Nantong, China 87/J1
Nantou, China 87/K6
Nantua, Fr. 60/B5
Nantucket, Ma, US 158/B5
Nantucket (isl.), Ma, US 158/C5
Nantucket (sound), Ma, US 158/B5
Nantucket Nat'l Wild. Ref., Ma, US 158/B5
Nantúpi, Moz. 123/H2
Nantwich, Eng, UK 35/F5
Nanty-Glo, Pa, US 161/G4
Nanuet, NY, US 169/J7
Nanuku Passage (chan.), Fiji 137/Y18
Nanumanga (isl.), Tuv. 136/G5
Nanumea (isl.), Tuv. 136/G5
Nanuque, Braz. 187/E3
Nanwon (res.), China 80/C4
Nanxi, China 86/E2
Nanxiang, China 80/L8
Nanxing, China 78/F5
Nanxun, China 80/L9
Nanyamba, Tanz. 119/B4
Nanyang, China 80/D4
Nanyang (lake), China 78/H4
Nanyang, China 80/C4
Nanyue, China 87/G3
Nanyuki, Kenya 119/B1
Nanzamu, China 81/C2
Nanzhang, China 80/B5
Nanzhao, China 80/C4
Nao, Cabo de la (cape), Sp. 47/F3
Não-Me-Toque, Braz. 189/F4
Naococane (lake), Qu, Can. 141/J3
Naogaon, Bang. 97/G3
Naokot, Pak. 92/A3
Naoli (riv.), China 79/L2
Naolinco, Mex. 175/N7
Naos, Namb. 122/C4
Naoua (falls), C.d'Iv. 114/D5
Náousa, Gre. 49/J4
Náousa, Gre. 49/H2
Naozhou (isl.), China 87/F4
Napa (riv.), Ca, US 167/K10
Napa (valley), Ca, US 167/K9
Napa (co.), Ca, US 167/K10
Napa, Ca, US 146/B4
Napa Junction, Ca, US 167/K10
Napak (peak), Ugan. 119/A1
Napakiak, Ak, US 171/F3
Napanee, On, Can. 161/H2
Napata (ruin), Sudan 135/F5
Napavine, Wa, US 144/C4
Nape, Laos 94/D2
Naperville, Il, US 160/B4
Napf (peak), Swi. 60/D4
Napido, Indo. 91/J4
Napier, SAfr. 124/L11
Napier, NZ 135/D2
Napier (pt.), Austl. 129/D2
Napier (mt.), Austl. 128/C4
Napier Broome (bay), Austl. 128/B3
Napierville (co.), Qu, Can. 159/N7
Napill, Eng, UK 30/A2
Napinka, Mb, Can. 156/D3
Naples (Napoli), It. 65/D6
Naples, Fl, US 165/H4
Naples, Id, US 144/F3
Naples, Me, US 161/L3
Naples, NY, US 161/H3
Naples, Tx, US 153/G4
Naples, Ut, US 147/J3
Naples Park, Fl, US 165/H4
Napo (prov.), Ecu. 180/B5
Napo (riv.), Ecu. 180/B5
Napo (riv.), Ecu.,Peru 179/B3
Napo (riv.), Peru 180/C5
Napo, China 93/J3
Napoleon, ND, US 156/E4
Napoleon, Oh, US 160/D4
Napoleon, Mi, US 160/D3
Napoleonville, La, US 164/C3
Napoli (gulf), It. 48/C2
Napoli (prov.), It. 65/D6
Napoli (Naples), It. 65/D6
Napoule (gulf), Fr. 64/C5
Nappa Merrie, Austl. 134/A4
Nappanee, In, US 160/C4
Napperby, Austl. 131/G2
Napton-on-the-Hill, Eng, UK 37/E2
Napuka (isl.), FrPol. 137/L6
Naqb Ghul (peak), Egypt 113/C5
Naqīl Sumārah (pass), Yem. 118/C2
Nara, Mali 114/D3
Nāra (riv.), Pak. 101/J4
Nara, Japan 83/J6
Nara Logna (pass), Nepal 99/D5
Naracoopa, Austl. 133/B4
Naracoorte, Austl. 132/B3
Naradhan, Austl. 133/C1
Narail, Bang. 97/G4
Naraini, India 96/C3
Nārāinpur, India 95/D2
Naramata, BC, Can. 144/E3
Naranbulag, Mong. 99/F2
Narang, Afg. 98/A2
Naranjal, Ecu. 180/B5
Naranjito, Ecu. 184/B1
Naranjos, Mex. 176/B1
Naranjos, Bol. 188/E1
Narāq, Iran 103/G3
Narasannapeta, India 95/E2
Narasapatnam (pt.), India 95/D2
Narasapur, India 95/D2
Narasaraopet, India 95/D2
Narashino, Japan 83/E2
Narat, China 99/D3
Narathiwat, Thai. 94/C5
Nārāyanganj, India 96/C4
Nārāyanganj, Bang. 97/H4
Nārāyani (zone), Nepal 97/E2
Narayani (riv.), Nepal 97/E2
Narbonne, Fr. 44/E5
Narceo (riv.), Sp. 46/B1
Narcoossee, Fl, US 164/N7
Nardò, It. 49/F2
Nare (pt.), Eng, UK 36/B6
Narellan, Austl. 134/G9
Narembeen, Austl. 130/C5
Naréna, Mali 114/C3
Nares (str.), Can.,Grld. 139/K2
Narew (riv.), Pol. 68/D5
Narganá, Pan. 180/B2
Narib, Namb. 122/C5
Narinda, Madg. 125/H6
Narinda (bay), Madg. 125/H6
Nariño (dept.), Col. 180/B4
Nariño, Col. 183/K7
Narita (int'l arpt.), Japan 85/G3
Narita, Japan 83/E2
Nariz (peak), Chile 191/C7
Narka, Ks, US 154/F4
Narkatiāganj, India 97/E2
Narmada (riv.), India 77/G7
Narman, Turk. 71/G4
Nærnes, Nor. 38/S8
Narni, It. 65/B2
Naro Moru, Kenya 119/B2
Naroch', Bela. 41/M4
Narodnaya (peak), Rus. 69/P2
Narok, Kenya 119/A2
Narón, Sp. 46/A1
Narooma, Austl. 133/E3
Narovlya, Bela. 72/E2
Nārowāl, Pak. 98/C3
Nærøy, Nor. 38/D2
Närpes (Närpiö), Fin. 68/D3
Närpiö (Närpes), Fin. 68/D3
Narra, Phil. 88/B3
Narrabri, Austl. 132/D1
Narrandera, Austl. 133/C2
Narre Warren North, Austl. 133/B3
Narriah (mtn.), Austl. 133/C1
Narrogin, Austl. 130/C5
Narromine, Austl. 132/D2
Narrows (dam), Ar, US 153/H3
Narrows (riv.), NY, US 169/J9
Narrows, Va, US 163/G2
Narsimhapur, India 96/B4
Narsingarh, India 92/C3
Narsinghdi, Bang. 97/H4
Narsī Patnam, India 95/D2
Nartuby (riv.), Fr. 64/C5
Narubis, Namb. 124/B2
Naruksovo, Rus. 69/K5
Narungombe, Tanz. 119/B4
Narusawa, Japan 83/B3
Naruto, Japan 84/D3
Narutō, Japan 83/E2
Narva (riv.), Est.,Rus. 68/E4
Narva (res.), Rus. 68/F4
Narva (bay), Rus.,Est. 41/M2
Narva, Est. 41/N2
Narva (riv.), Rus. 41/M2
Narva-Jõesuu, Est. 41/N2
Narvacan, Phil. 88/C1
Narvik, Nor. 38/F1
Narwāna, India 98/D5
Nar'yan-Mar, Rus. 69/M2
Naryn (riv.), Kyr. 74/H5
Naryn, Kyr. 99/C3
Naryn Khuduk, Rus. 71/H3
Narzole, It. 62/A3
NASA Test Center, Ms, US 164/D2
NASA Test Facility, NM, US 152/A4
NASA Wallops Space Ctr., Va, US 163/K2
Nasarawa, Nga. 115/G4
Năsăud, Rom. 51/G2
Naschel, Arg. 190/D2
Naschitti, NM, US 149/H2
Naseby, NZ 135/B4
Naselle, Wa, US 144/C4
Nash, Ok, US 153/E2
Nash, Eng, UK 37/F3
Nash (pt.), Wal, UK 36/C4
Nashoba, Ok, US 153/G3
Nashua, NH, US 161/L3
Nashua, Ia, US 155/H2
Nashua, Mt, US 145/L3
Nashville, Ar, US 153/H4
Nashville, Ga, US 165/G2
Nashville, In, US 160/C5
Nashville, Mi, US 160/D3
Nashville (int'l arpt.), Tn, US 162/D2
Nashville (cap.), Tn, US 162/D2
Nashville, Il, US 162/C1
Nashville, NC, US 163/J3
Nashwah, Egypt 113/C3
Našice, Cro. 50/D3
Nasielsk, Pol. 43/L2
Nasijärvi (lake), Fin. 41/K1
Nasikonis (cape), Indo. 128/A2
Nāşir, Sudan 117/G3
Nasīrābād, India 92/B2
Naso (pt.), Phil. 88/C3
Nason, Il, US 162/C1
Nasori (Suva) (int'l arpt.), Fiji 137/Y18
Nasorolevu (peak), Fiji 137/Z17
Nasosnyy, Azer. 71/J4
Nāsriganj, India 97/E3
Nass (riv.), BC, Can. 171/N4
Nassach (riv.), Ger. 58/D2
Nassau, Ger. 55/G3
Nassau (sound), Fl, US 165/H2
Nassau (cap.), Bahm. 173/F2
Nassau (isl.), CookIs. 137/J6
Nassau (bay), Chile 191/D7
Nassau, De, US 168/C6
Nassau (co.), NY, US 169/E2
Nassau Bay, Tx, US 151/M9
Nassawadox, Va, US 163/K2
Nasser (lake), Egypt 107/E2
Nassereith, Aus. 61/G3
Nassian, C.d'Iv. 114/E4
Nässjö, Swe. 40/F3
Nassogne, Belg. 55/E3
Nassoukou, Ben. 115/F4
Nastapoka (isls.), Qu, Can. 141/J3
Nastätten, Ger. 55/G3
Næstved, Den. 40/D4
Nasu-dake (peak), Japan 85/F2
Nasugbu, Phil. 88/C2
Nat (peak), Myan. 86/C5

Northern (dist.), Isr. 105/C3
Northern (pol. reg.), Gha. 115/E4
Northern (reg.), Malw. 119/A4
Northern (prov.), PNG 129/H2
Northern (prov.), SLeo. 114/B4
Northern (prov.), SrL. 95/D4
Northern Areas (terr.), Pak. 99/B4
Northern Cape (prov.), SAfr. 124/C3
Northern Cheyenne Ind. Res., Mt, US 147/K1
Northern Cook (isls.), CookIs. 137/J6
Northern Dvina (riv.), Rus. 29/J2
Northern Ireland, NI, UK 32/D1
Northern Light (lake), On, Can. 157/J3
Northern Marianas (dpcy.), US 136/D3
Northern Peninsula. Abor. Rsv., Austl. 129/F2
Northern Province (prov.), SAfr. 124/E2
Northern Sporades (isls.), Gre. 67/K3
Northern Territory (terr.), Austl. 127/C2
Northern Ural (hills), Rus. 69/K4
Northern Ural (mts.), Rus. 69/N3
Northern Urals (hills), Rus. 74/E4
Northfield, Tx, US 152/D3
Northfield, Vt, US 161/K2
Northfield, NH, US 161/L3
Northfield, Mn, US 155/H1
Northfleet, Eng, UK 30/D2
Northgate, Sk, Can. 156/C3
Northport, Al, US 162/D4
Northport, Mi, US 160/D2
Northport, Wa, US 144/F3
Northport (Old Northport), NY, US 169/E2
Northridge (nbrhd.), Ca, US 166/E7
Northrup, Tx, US 151/F2
Northumberland (co.), Eng, UK 33/D6
Northumberland (str.), NB,PE, Can. 158/E2
Northumberland, Pa, US 168/B2
Northumberland (co.), Pa, US 168/B2
Northumberland NP, Eng, UK 33/D6
Northvale, NJ, US 169/K7
Northville, NY, US 161/J3
Northville, Mi, US 167/E7
Northway, Ak, US 171/K3
Northwest (cape), Fl, US 165/H5
Northwest Gander (riv.), Nf, Can. 159/K1
Northwest Territories (terr.), Can. 140/E2
Northwestern (prov.), Zam. 122/E2
Northwich, Eng, UK 35/F5
Northwood, ND, US 156/F4
Northwood (nbrhd.), Eng, UK 30/B2
Northwood, Ia, US 155/H2
Norton, NB, Can. 158/E3
Norton (bay), Ak, US 171/F3
Norton (sound), Ak, US 171/E3
Norton, Ks, US 154/E4
Norton, Tx, US 150/D2
Norton, Va, US 163/F2
Norton, WV, US 163/H1
Norton, Zim. 123/F3
Norton Bridge, Eng, UK 35/F6
Norton Heath, Eng, UK 30/D1
Norton Shores, Mi, US 160/C3
Nortonville, Ky, US 162/D2
Nortorf, Ger. 40/C4
Norval, On, Can. 160/T8
Norvegia (cape), Ant. 192/Y
Nörvenich, Ger. 55/F2
Norwalk (riv.), Ct, US 169/M7
Norwalk, Ca, US 166/F8
Norwalk, Ct, US 169/M7
Norwalk, Oh, US 160/E4
Norwalk, Wi, US 155/J2
Norway (ctry.) 38/C3
Norway, Mi, US 157/L5
Norway, Me, US 161/L2
Norway House, Mb, Can. 140/G3
Norwegian (bay), Nun, Can. 141/S7
Norwegian (sea), Eur. 29/D2
Norwich (int'l arpt.), Eng, UK 37/H1
Norwich, Eng, UK 37/H1
Norwich, Ct, US 161/K4
Norwich, Ks, US 153/F2
Norwich, NY, US 161/J3
Norwich, Vt, US 161/K3
Norwood, Co, US 149/H1
Norwood, La, US 164/C2
Norwood, Ma, US 161/L3
Norwood, Mn, US 157/N7
Norwood, NC, US 163/G3
Norwood, NY, US 161/J2
Norwood, NJ, US 169/K8
Norwood, Oh, US 162/E1
Nos Emine (cape), Bul. 51/H4
Nos Kaliakra (pt.), Bul. 51/J4
Nos Maslen Nos (pt.), Bul. 51/H4
Nosappu-misaki (cape), Japan 82/D2
Nose, Japan 83/H6
Nose (hill), Ab, Can. 145/J1
Noshappu-misaki (cape), Japan 82/B1
Noshiro, Japan 82/B3
Nosivka, Ukr. 72/F2
Nosŏng, SKor. 81/D5
Nosong (cape), Malay. 88/A4
Nosop (riv.), Bots. 122/D5
Nosovaya, Rus. 69/K4
Noşratābād, Iran 101/G3
Noss Head (pt.), Sc, UK 31/S7
Nossa Senhora da Glória, Braz. 187/F1
Nossa Senhora do Livramento, Braz. 185/G4
Nossebro, Swe. 40/E2
Nossob (riv.), Namb. 122/C4
Nossobrivier (riv.), SAfr. 122/D5
Nossombougou, Mali 114/D3
Nosy Barren (Barren Islands) (isls.), Madg. 125/G7
Nosy Be (isl.), Madg. 125/H6
Nosy Chesterfield (isl.), Madg. 125/G7
Nosy Mitsio (isl.), Madg. 125/J6
Nosy Saint. Marie (isl.), Madg. 125/J7
Nosy-Varika, Madg. 125/J8
Notaresco, It. 65/C2
Notasulga, Al, US 162/E4
Notch (cape), Chile 191/B6
Notec (riv.), Pol. 43/J2
Noto, It. 48/D4
Noto (valley), It. 48/D4
Noto (gulf), It. 48/D4
Noto (pen.), Japan 85/E2
Noto Antica (ruin), It. 48/D4
Notodden, Nor. 40/C2
Notogawa, Japan 83/K5
Notoro (lake), Japan 82/C1
Notre Dame (mts.), Qu, Can. 158/B3
Notre Dame, Fr. 30/K5
Notre Dame (mts.), On, Can. 141/J4
Notre Dame (bay), Nf, Can. 141/L4
Notre Dame de Lourdes, Mb, Can. 156/E3
Notre-Dame-de-Bondeville, Fr. 57/G1
Notre-Dame-de-Île-Perrot, Qu, Can. 159/N7
Notre-Dame-de-la-Salette, Qu, Can. 161/J2
Notre-Dame-des-Monts, Qu, Can. 158/B2
Notre-Dame-du-Lac, Qu, Can. 158/C2
Notsé, Togo 115/F5
Nott (mt.), Austl. 131/G5
Nottawasaga (bay), On, Can. 160/F2
Nottaway (riv.), Qu, Can. 141/J3
Nøtterøy, Nor. 40/D2
Nottingham, Eng, UK 35/G6
Nottingham (isl.), Nun, Can. 141/H2
Nottingham (co.), Eng, UK 35/G6
Nottinghamshire (co.), Eng, UK 35/G5
Nottoway, Va, US 163/H2
Nottoway (riv.), Va, US 163/J2
Nottoway Plantation, La, US 164/C2
Nottuln, Ger. 53/E5
Notukeu (riv.), Sk, Can. 145/L3
Nouabalé (riv.), Congo 120/D2
Nouâdhibou, Mrta. 110/A5
Nouadhibou (int'l arpt.), Mrta. 110/A5
Nouakchott (cap.), Mrta. 114/B2
Nouakchott (int'l arpt.), Mrta. 114/B2
Nouâmghâr, Mrta. 114/A2
Nouan-le-Fuzelier, Fr. 57/H5
Noue (riv.), Fr. 47/F1
Nouméa (cap.), NCal. 137/V13
Noumea (Tontouta) (int'l arpt.), NCal. 137/V13
Nouna, Burk. 114/E3
Noupoort, SAfr. 124/D3
Nouvelle, Qu, Can. 158/D1
Nouvion-sur-Meuse, Fr. 55/D4
Nœux-les-Mines, Fr. 54/B3
Nouzonville, Fr. 55/D4
Nova Andradina, Braz. 189/F2
Nova Astrakhan', Ukr. 73/K3
Nova Basan', Ukr. 72/F2
Nova Borova, Ukr. 72/E2
Nova Brasilândia, Braz. 186/B2
Nova Caipemba, Ang. 120/C4
Nova Cruz, Braz. 183/H4
Nová Dubnica, Slvk. 43/K4
Nova Friburgo, Braz. 187/E4
Nova Gaia, Ang. 120/D5
Nova Gorica, Slov. 63/G2
Nova Gradiška, Cro. 50/C3
Nova Granada, Braz. 189/G2
Nova Iguaçu, Braz. 187/N7
Nova Kakhovka, Ukr. 72/G4
Nova Lamego, GBis. 114/B3
Nova Levante (Welshnofen), It. 61/H5
Nova Lima, Braz. 186/E3
Nova Londrina, Braz. 186/B4
Nova Lusitânia, Moz. 123/G3
Nova Mambone, Moz. 123/G4
Nova Mayachka, Ukr. 73/G4
Nova Odesa, Ukr. 72/F4
Nova Olinda, Braz. 183/G4
Nova Olinda do Norte, Braz. 182/B3
Nova Pazova, Serb. 50/E3
Nova Praha, Ukr. 73/G3
Nova Prata, Braz. 189/G4
Nova Russas, Braz. 183/F4
Nova Scotia (prov.), Can. 158/E3
Nova Sintra, CpV. 107/J11
Nova Sofala, Moz. 123/G4
Nova Timboteua, Braz. 183/E3
Nova Ushytsya, Ukr. 72/D3
Nova Varoš, Serb. 50/D4
Nova Vodolaha, Ukr. 73/H3
Nova Xavantina, Braz. 186/B2
Nova Zagora, Bul. 51/H4
Novaci, Rom. 51/F3
Novafeltria, It. 63/F6
Novaliches (res.), Phil. 88/F6
Novara, It. 62/B3
Novate Mezzola, It. 61/F5
Novato, Ca, US 146/B4
Novaya Igirma, Rus. 75/L4
Novaya Ivanovka, Ukr. 51/J3
Novaya Kalitva, Rus. 73/L2
Novaya Kazanka, Kaz. 71/J2
Novaya Ladoga, Rus. 41/Q1
Novaya Lyalya, Rus. 69/P4
Novaya Maluksa, Rus. 41/P2
Novaya Sibir' (isl.), Rus. 75/R2
Novaya Usman', Rus. 73/K2
Novaya Zemlya (isl.), Rus. 74/E2
Nove, It. 63/E2
Nové Hrady, Czh. 59/H5
Nové Město nad Váhom, Slvk. 43/J4
Nové Sedlo, Czh. 59/F2
Nové Strašecí, Czh. 59/G2
Nové Zámky, Slvk. 50/D2
Novelda, Sp. 47/E3
Novellara, It. 63/D4
Noventa, It. 63/E3
Noventa di Piave, It. 63/F2
Noventa Vicentina, It. 63/E3
Noves, Fr. 64/A5
Novgorod, Rus. 68/F4
Novgorodka, Rus. 41/N3
Novgorodskaya Oblast, Rus. 68/G4
Novgorodskoye, Ukr. 73/J3
Novhorod-Sivers'kyy, Ukr. 73/G2
Novhorodka, Ukr. 72/G3
Novi, Mi, US 167/E7
Novi Bečej, Serb. 50/E3
Novi di Modena, It. 63/D4
Novi Iskŭr, Bul. 51/F4
Novi Pazar, Bul. 51/H4
Novi Pazar, Serb. 50/E4
Novi Sad, Serb. 50/D3
Novi Sanzhary, Ukr. 73/H3
Novi Vinodolski, Cro. 45/L4
Novice, Tx, US 153/G4
Novice, Tx, US 150/E2
Novikovo, Rus. 79/N2
Novillars, Fr. 60/C3
Novinger, Mo, US 155/H3
Nóvita, Col. 180/B3
Novo (riv.), Braz. 187/N6
Novo Alexeyevka (int'l arpt.), Geo. 71/H4
Novo Aripuanã, Braz. 185/F2
Novo Hamburgo, Braz. 189/G4
Novo Horizonte, Braz. 189/G2
Novo Mesto, Slov. 50/B3
Novo Miloševo, Serb. 50/E3
Novo Oriente, Braz. 183/F4
Novo-Titarovskaya, Rus. 73/K5
Novoalekseyevka, Kaz. 71/K2
Novoaltaysk, Rus. 74/J4
Novoanninskiy, Rus. 73/M2
Novoazovs'k, Ukr. 73/K4
Novobelokatay, Rus. 69/N5
Novobogatinskoye, Kaz. 71/J3
Novocheboksarsk, Rus. 69/K4
Novocherkassk, Rus. 73/L4
Novodevich'ye, Rus. 71/J1
Novodruzhes'k, Ukr. 73/K3
Novodugino, Rus. 68/G5
Novogrudok, Bela. 41/L5
Novohrad-Volyns'kyy, Ukr. 72/D2
Novohradské Hory (mts.), Czh. 59/H5
Novohrodivka, Ukr. 73/J3
Novoizborsk, Rus. 41/M3
Novokhopërskiy, Rus. 73/L2
Novokubansk, Rus. 73/L5
Novokuybyshevsk, Rus. 71/J1
Novokuznetsk, Rus. 74/J4
Novolazarevskaya, Rus., Ant. 192/A
Novolukoml', Bela. 41/N4
Novominskaya, Rus. 73/K4
Novomoskovsk, Rus. 70/F1
Novomoskovs'k, Ukr. 73/H3
Novomykolayivka, Ukr. 73/H4
Novomyrhorod, Ukr. 72/F3
Novonikolayevskiy, Rus. 73/M2
Novonukutskiy, Rus. 78/E1
Novooleksiyivka, Ukr. 73/H4
Novopokrovka, Ukr. 73/H3
Novopokrovskaya, Rus. 73/L5
Novorontsovka, Ukr. 73/G4
Novorossiysk, Rus. 73/J5
Novorossiyskoye, Kaz. 71/L2
Novorzhev, Rus. 41/N3
Novoselivs'ke, Ukr. 73/G5
Novoselytsya, Ukr. 72/D3
Novosergiyevka, Rus. 71/K1
Novoshakhtinsk, Rus. 73/K4
Novosibirsk, Rus. 74/J4
Novosibirskaya Oblast, Rus. 74/J4
Novosil', Rus. 70/F1
Novosil'skoye, Rus. 73/K2
Novosineglazovskiy, Rus. 69/P5
Novosokol'niki, Rus. 41/P3
Novostroyevo, Rus. 41/J4
Novotroitsk, Rus. 71/L2
Novotroyits'ke, Ukr. 73/H4
Novoukrayinka, Ukr. 72/F3
Novoul'yanovsk, Rus. 71/J1
Novouzensk, Rus. 71/J2
Novovolyns'k, Ukr. 72/C2
Novovoronezhskiy, Rus. 73/K2
Novovyatsk, Rus. 69/L4
Novoyamskoye, Rus. 70/E1
Novozybkov, Rus. 70/D1
Novska, Cro. 50/C3
Novy (int'l arpt.), Rus. 79/M2
Nový Jičín, Czh. 43/K4
Novyy Buh, Ukr. 73/G4
Novyy Oskol, Rus. 73/J2
Novyy Port, Rus. 74/H3
Novyy Rozdol, Ukr. 72/C3
Novyy Svit, Ukr. 73/H5
Novyy Urengoy, Rus. 74/H3
Nowa Dęba, Pol. 43/L3
Nowa Nowa, Austl. 133/D3
Nowa Ruda, Pol. 43/J3
Nowa Sarzyna, Pol. 43/M3
Nowa Sól, Pol. 43/H3
Nowata, Ok, US 153/G2
Nowe, Pol. 43/K2
Nowe Miasto Lubawskie, Pol. 43/K2
Nowen (peak), Ire. 32/A6
Nowendoc, Austl. 132/D1
Nowgong, India 96/B3
Nowgong (Nagaon), India 86/B3
Nowitna (riv.), Ak, US 171/G3
Nowogard, Pol. 40/F5
Nowood (riv.), Wy, US 147/K2
Nowra, Austl. 133/E2
Nowrangapur, India 95/D2
Nowshera, Pak. 98/A2
Nowy Dwór Gdański, Pol. 41/H4
Nowy Sącz, Pol. 43/L4
Nowy Staw, Pol. 41/H4
Nowy Targ, Pol. 43/L4
Nowy Tomyśl, Pol. 43/J2
Noxapater, Ms, US 162/C4
Noxon, Mt, US 144/G4
Noxubee NWR, Ms, US 162/C4
Noya, Sp. 46/A1
Noyabr'sk, Rus. 74/H3
Noyal-Pontivy, Fr. 56/C4
Noyal-sur-Vilaine, Fr. 56/D4
Noyant, Fr. 57/F5
Noye (riv.), Fr. 54/B4
Noyen-sur-Sarthe, Fr. 57/E5
Noyers-sur-Cher, Fr. 57/G6
Noyil (riv.), India 95/C4
Noyon, Fr. 54/C4
Nozay, Fr. 56/D5
Nsah, Congo 120/C3
Nsak, Gabon 120/C2
Nsanje, Malw. 123/G3
Nsawam, Gha. 115/E5
Nsoc, EqG. 120/B2
Nsondia, D.R. Congo 120/D3
Nsopzup, Myan. 86/C3
Nsukka, Nga. 115/G5
Nsumbu NP, Zam. 121/G5
Nsuta, Gha. 115/E5
Ntem (riv.), Camr. 120/B2
Nterguent, Mrta. 114/B2
Ntoroko, Ugan. 121/G2
Ntoum, Gabon 120/B2
Ntui, Camr. 120/B1
Ntulume, D.R. Congo 121/E4
Ntungamo, Ugan. 121/G3
Ntusi, Ugan. 121/G2
Ntwetwe Pan (salt pan), Bots. 122/E4
Nu (riv.), China 93/G2
Nu (mts.), China 86/C3
Nu (Salween) (riv.), China 78/D5
Nuang (peak), Malay. 89/C2
Nuangola, Pa, US 168/C1
Nuanshui, China 87/H2
Nūbah, Egypt 113/C4
Nūbāriya (canal), Egypt 113/B3
Nubian (des.), Sudan 107/F2
Nucet, Rom. 50/F2
Nucla, Co, US 149/H1
Nucourt, Fr. 30/H4
Nudaybah, Egypt 113/B3
Nüdlingen, Ger. 58/D2
Nueces (riv.), Tx, US 150/E3
Nueltin (lake), Nun, Can. 140/G2
Nuenen, Neth. 52/C6
Nueva Alejandría, Peru 184/C2
Nueva Asunción (dept.), Par. 188/D2
Nueva Ciudad Guerrero, Mex. 150/E4
Nueva Concepción, Guat. 176/D3
Nueva Constitución, Arg. 190/D2
Nueva Esparta (state), Ven. 181/E2
Nueva Esperanza, Arg. 188/D3
Nueva Florida, Ven. 180/D2
Nueva Germania, Par. 189/E2
Nueva Gerona, Cuba 177/F1
Nueva Helvecia, Uru. 191/K11
Nueva Imperial, Chile 190/B3
Nueva Italia de Ruiz, Mex. 174/E5
Nueva Loja, Ecu. 180/B4
Nueva Lubecka, Arg. 190/C5
Nueva Ocotepéque, Hon. 176/D3
Nueva Palmira, Uru. 191/J10
Nueva Patria, Mex. 175/N8
Nueva Rosita, Mex. 150/D4
Nueva Villa de Padilla, Mex. 175/F3
Nueve de Julio, Arg. 190/E2
Nuevitas, Cuba 177/G1
Nuevo (gulf), Arg. 190/D4
Nuevo, Ca, US 166/C3
Nuevo Andoas, Peru 184/B1
Nuevo Balsas, Mex. 175/F5
Nuevo Berlín, Uru. 191/J10
Nuevo Casas Grandes, Mex. 174/D2
Nuevo Chagres, Pan. 177/F4
Nuevo Ideal, Mex. 174/D3
Nuevo Ixcatlán, Mex. 176/C2
Nuevo Laredo, Mex. 150/E4
Nuevo Leon (state), Mex. 172/A2
Nuevo León, Mex. 148/E4
Nuevo Mundo, Bol. 185/E3
Nuevo Progreso, Mex. 151/F4
Nuevo Rocafuerte, Ecu. 180/C5
Nufenen, Swi. 61/F4
Nufenenpass (pass), Swi. 61/E5
Nugaaleed (valley), Som. 118/D3
Nugent, Tx, US 150/E1
Nugget (pt.), NZ 135/B4
Nuguria (isls.), PNG 136/E5
Nuhne (riv.), Ger. 53/F6
Nui (isl.), Tuv. 136/G5
Nuiqsut, Ak, US 171/H1
Nuits-Saint-Georges, Fr. 60/A3
Nukata, Japan 83/M6
Nuklunek (mt.), Ak, US 171/F4
Nuku Hiva (isl.), FrPol. 137/L5
Nuku'alofa (cap.), Tonga 137/H7
Nukufetau (isl.), Tuv. 136/G5
Nukulaelae (isl.), Tuv. 136/H5
Nukumanu Atoll (atoll), PNG 136/E5
Nukunonu (isl.), Tok. 137/H5
Nukuoro (isl.), Micr. 136/E4
Nukus, Uzb. 74/F5
Nukutavake (isl.), FrPol. 137/M6
Nulato, Ak, US 171/G3
Nules, Sp. 47/E3
Nullagine, Austl. 130/D2
Nullarbor, Austl. 131/F4
Nullarbor (plain), Austl. 127/B4
Nullarbor NP, Austl. 131/F4
Numan, Nga. 116/B3
Numana, It. 63/G6
Numansdorp, Neth. 52/B5
Numata, Japan 85/F2
Numatinna (riv.), Sudan 117/E4
Numazu, Japan 85/F3
Numbi, D.R. Congo 121/G3
Nümbrecht, Ger. 55/G2
Numbulwar, Austl. 129/D3
Numfoor (isl.), Indo. 91/H4
Nummela, Fin. 39/E4
Nummi, Fin. 41/K1
Numurkah, Austl. 133/B3
Nunapitchuk, Ak, US 171/F3
Nunavut (terr.), Can. 141/K2
Nunawading (nbrhd.), Austl. 132/G5
Nunchía, Col. 180/C3
Nunda, NY, US 161/H3
Nundle, Austl. 132/D1
Nuneaton, Eng, UK 37/E1
Nŭng-ni, NKor. 81/D3
Nungarin, Austl. 130/C4
Nungatta NP, Austl. 133/D3
Nungo, Moz. 123/H2
Nungwe, Tanz. 121/H3
Nunivak (isl.), Ak, US 171/E4
Nunley, Ar, US 153/G3
Nunnelly, Tn, US 162/D3
Nunningen, Swi. 60/D3
Nuñoa, Peru 184/D4
Nunspeet, Neth. 52/C4
Nunthorpe, Eng, UK 35/G2
Nunukan, Indo. 88/B4
Nuomin (riv.), China 79/J1
Nuon (riv.), Libr. 114/C5
Nuoro, It. 48/A2
Nupurböle (Nupurila), Fin. 39/E4
Nupurila (Nupurböle), Fin. 39/E4
Nuqūb, Yem. 118/C2
Nuquí, Col. 180/B3
Nur (mts.), Turk. 104/E1
Nur, China 99/D4
Nura (riv.), Kaz. 99/B2
Nūrābād, Iran 103/G4
Nurata, Uzb. 74/G5
Nürburgring, Ger. 55/F3
Nure (riv.), It. 62/C3
Nuremberg, Pa, US 168/B2
Nurhak, Turk. 102/D2
Nuri (ruin), Sudan 109/F5
Nuria (peak), It. 65/C3
Nuriootpa, Austl. 131/H5
Nūrla, India 98/D2
Nurlat, Rus. 69/L5
Nūrmahal, India 98/C4
Nurmijärvi, Fin. 41/L1
Nürnberg (int'l arpt.), Ger. 58/E3
Nürnberg, Ger. 58/E4
Nūrpur, Pak. 98/B3
Nurri (mt.), Austl. 132/C1
Nursery, Tx, US 151/F3
Nürtingen, Ger. 58/C5
Nus, It. 64/D1
Nusa Tenggara Timur (prov.), Indo. 128/A2
Nūsah, Yem. 118/C2
Nūshābād, Iran 103/G3
Nushagak (riv.), Ak, US 171/G4
Nushki, Pak. 101/J3
Nutberry (hill), Sc, UK 33/C5
Nuth, Neth. 55/E2
Nuthe-Graben (riv.), Ger. 42/Q7
Nutley, NJ, US 169/J8
Nuttby (mtn.), NS, Can. 158/F3
Nutwood Downs, Austl. 128/D3
Nuuk (Godthåb), Grld. 139/M3
Nuuksion NP, Fin. 39/E4
Nuupere (pt.), FrPol. 137/X15
Nuvolento, It. 62/D2
Nuwākot, Nepal 96/D1
Nuwara Eliya, SrL. 95/D5
Nuwaybi', Egypt 109/G2
Nuy (riv.), SAfr. 124/L10
Nuza (mt.), Zim. 123/G3
Nüziders, Aus. 61/F3
Nūzvīd, India 95/D2
Nxai Pan (salt pan), Bots. 122/E3
Nxai Pan NP, Bots. 122/E3
Nxaunxau, Bots. 122/D3
Nya-Ghezi, D.R. Congo 121/G3
Nyaake, Libr. 114/D5
Nyabing, Austl. 130/C5
Nyabisindu, Rwa. 121/G3
Nyack, NY, US 169/K7
Nyah, Austl. 132/B2
Nyah West, Austl. 132/B2
Nyahua, Tanz. 119/A3
Nyahururu Falls, Kenya 119/B1
Nyainqêntanglha (peak), China 99/F5
Nyainqêntanglha (mts.), China 86/B2
Nyainrong, China 86/B1
Nyakabindi, Tanz. 119/A2
Nyakanyasi, Tanz. 121/G3
Nyaki NP, Malw. 119/A4
Nyaki NPP, Malw. 123/G1
Nyakrom, Gha. 115/E5
Nyaksimvol', Rus. 69/P3
Nyakulenga, Zam. 122/D2
Nyala, Sudan 117/E2
Nyalam, China 97/E1
Nyalikungu, Tanz. 119/A2
Nyamandhlovu, Zim. 123/F3
Nyamapande, Zim. 123/G3
Nyambiti, Tanz. 119/A2
Nyamina, Mali 114/D3
Nyamlell, Sudan 117/E3
Nyamtumbo, Tanz. 119/B4
Nyandoma, Rus. 68/J3
Nyanga (riv.), Gabon 120/B3
Nyanga (prov.), Gabon 120/B3
Nyanga, Gabon 120/B3
Nyanga NP, Zim. 123/G3
Nyanga-Nord, Rsv. de la, Gabon,Congo 120/B3
Nyangui (peak), Zim. 123/G3
Nyanyadzi, Zim. 123/G3
Nyanza (prov.), Kenya 119/A2
Nyanza-Lac, Buru. 121/G4
Nyanzwa, Tanz. 119/B3
Nyaruonga, Tanz. 121/G3
Nyasa (lake), Malw. 107/F6
Nyaunglebin, Myan. 94/B2
Nyazepetrovsk, Rus. 69/N4
Nyazura, Zim. 123/G3
Nybergsund, Nor. 40/E1
Nybro, Swe. 40/F3
Nyêmo, China 97/H1
Nyenasi, Gha. 115/E5
Nyeri, Kenya 119/B2
Nyerol, Sudan 117/G3
Nyikog (riv.), China 78/E5
Nyima, China 99/E5
Nyimba, Zam. 123/F2
Nyírábrány, Hun. 50/F2
Nyíradony, Hun. 43/L5
Nyírbátor, Hun. 43/M5
Nyíregyháza, Hun. 43/L5
Nyírmada, Hun. 43/M4
Nyiru (mt.), Kenya 119/B1
Nykirke, Nor. 38/S9
Nykøbing, Den. 40/D4
Nykøbing, Den. 40/C3
Nykøbing S, Den. 39/H7
Nyköping, Swe. 40/G2
Nykvarn, Swe. 39/A1
Nylrivier (riv.), SAfr. 123/F5
Nylstroom, SAfr. 123/F5
Nymagee, Austl. 132/C2
Nynäshamn, Swe. 40/G2
Nyngan, Austl. 132/C1
Nyoman (riv.), Bela. 68/E5
Nyon, Swi. 60/C5
Nyong (riv.), Camr. 116/A5
Nyons, Fr. 64/B4
Nýřany, Czh. 59/G3
Nyrob, Rus. 69/N3
Nýrsko (res.), Czh. 59/G4
Nýrsko, Czh. 59/G4
Nysa, Pol. 43/J3
Nysätra, Swe. 39/A1
Nyssa, Or, US 146/E2
Nysted, Den. 40/D4
Nyūdo-zaki (pt.), Japan 82/A4
Nyuk (lake), Rus. 68/F2
Nyukhcha, Rus. 69/K3
Nyuksenitsa, Rus. 69/K3
Nyúl, Hun. 50/C2
Nyunzu, D.R. Congo 121/G4
Nyurba, Rus. 75/M3
Nyuvchim, Rus. 69/L3
Nyūzen, Japan 85/E2
Nzega, Tanz. 119/A3
Nzérékoré (pol. reg.), Gui. 114/C4
Nzérékoré, Gui. 114/C5
Nzeret, D.R. Congo 116/D4
N'Zeto, Ang. 120/C4
Nzi (riv.), C.d'Iv. 114/D5

O

O'Ciese Ind. Res., Ab, Can. 144/G1
O' The Pines (lake), Tx, US 153/G4
O'Fallon (cr.), Mt, US 156/B4
O'Hares (cr.), Austl. 134/G8
O'Higgins (lake), Chile 191/B6
O'Sullivan (lake), On, Can. 157/L2
Ō-shima (isl.), Japan 82/A3
O.T. Downs, Austl. 129/D4
O.C. Fisher (lake), Tx, US 150/D2
Oa, Mull of (pt.), Sc, UK 31/Q9
Oadby, Eng, UK 37/E1
Oahe (lake), ND,SD, US 142/F2
Oahe (dam), SD, US 154/D1
Oahu (isl.), Hi, US 142/V13
Oak Bluffs, Ma, US 158/B5
Oak Creek, Co, US 147/K3
Oak Creek, Wi, US 160/C3
Oak Forest, Il, US 167/Q16
Oak Grove, La, US 153/J4
Oak Grove, Ar, US 153/H2
Oak Grove, Co, US 149/J1
Oak Grove, Tn, US 162/D2
Oak Grove, Ky, US 162/D2
Oak Harbor, Oh, US 160/E4
Oak Harbor, Wa, US 144/C3
Oak Hill, Mi, US 160/C2
Oak Hill, Fl, US 165/H3
Oak Hill, Tn, US 162/D2
Oak Hill, Oh, US 163/F1
Oak Hill, WV, US 163/G2
Oak Hill, Ga, US 163/M7
Oak Lake, Mb, Can. 156/D3
Oak Lawn, Il, US 160/C4
Oak Park, Il, US 167/Q16
Oak Park, Mi, US 167/F7
Oak Park, Ga, US 163/F4
Oak Ridge, Tn, US 162/E2
Oak Ridge, NJ, US 168/D1
Oak Ridges, On, Can. 160/U8
Oak River, Mb, Can. 156/D2
Oak View, Ca, US 166/A2
Oakbank, Mb, Can. 156/F3
Oakburn, Mb, Can. 156/D2
Oakdale, La, US 164/B2
Oakdale, Ca, US 148/B2
Oakdale, Austl. 133/E2
Oakes, ND, US 156/E4
Oakesdale, Wa, US 144/F4
Oakey, Austl. 134/C4
Oakham, Eng, UK 37/F1
Oakhurst, Ok, US 153/F2
Oakhurst, Ca, US 148/C2
Oakland, Fl, US 164/M6
Oakland, Il, US 160/B5
Oakland, Md, US 161/G5
Oakland, NJ, US 169/J7
Oakland (lake), Mi, US 167/F6
Oakland (co.), Mi, US 167/E6
Oakland, Or, US 146/B2
Oakland, Ne, US 155/F3
Oakland, Md, US 168/B5
Oakland (bay), Wa, US 167/A3
Oakland City, In, US 162/D1
Oakland Park, Fl, US 164/P10
Oaklands, Austl. 133/C2
Oakley, Ca, US 167/L10
Oakley, Ut, US 147/H3
Oakley, Id, US 147/G2
Oakley, Ks, US 154/D4
Oakley, Ms, US 162/B4
Oakley, Eng, UK 37/F2
Oakover (riv.), Austl. 127/B3
Oakridge, Or, US 146/B2
Oaktown, In, US 162/D1
Oakville, Mb, Can. 156/F3
Oakville, Mo, US 162/B1
Oakville, On, Can. 159/R9
Oakwood, Ga, US 162/F3
Oakwood, Va, US 163/F2
Oakwood, Tx, US 151/G2
Oakwood Hills, Il, US 167/P15
Oamaru, NZ 135/B4
Ōamishirasato, Japan 83/E2
Oani, Com. 125/G6
Oat (mtn.), Ca, US 166/B2
Oatlands, Austl. 132/C4
Oatman, Az, US 148/E3
Oaxaca (state), Mex. 172/B4
Oaxaca de Juárez, Mex. 176/B2
Ob' (riv.), Rus. 77/F3
Ob' (gulf), Rus. 77/G3
Ob Luang Gorge, Thai. 94/B2
Obala, Camr. 120/B1
Obama (bay), Japan 83/J4
Obama, Japan 83/J5
Oban, Sc, UK 31/R8
Oban (hills), Nga. 115/H5
Oban, NZ 135/B4
Obanazawa, Japan 82/B4
Obando, Col. 183/K8
Obara, Japan 83/M5
Obata, Japan 83/L7
Obaya, D.R. Congo 121/F3
Obbnäs (Upinniemi), Fin. 39/E4
Obed, Ab, Can. 144/F1
Obeliai, Lith. 41/L4
Obelisk (peak), NZ 135/B4
Ober Ramstadt, Ger. 58/B3
Ober-Olm, Ger. 58/B3
Oberá, Arg. 189/F3
Oberalppass (pass), Swi. 61/E4
Oberalpstock (peak), Swi. 61/E4
Oberammergau, Ger. 61/H2
Oberasbach, Ger. 58/D4
Oberau, Ger. 61/H2
Oberburg, Swi. 60/D3
Oberderdingen, Ger. 58/B4
Oberdiessbach, Swi. 60/D4
Oberding, Ger. 59/E6
Oberdorf, Swi. 60/D3
Oberdorla, Ger. 53/H6
Oberelsbach, Ger. 58/D2
Oberentfelden, Swi. 60/E3
Oberglatt, Swi. 61/E3
Obergünzburg, Ger. 61/G2
Oberhaching, Ger. 59/E6
Oberhausen, Ger. 52/D6
Oberkirch, Ger. 60/E1
Oberkochen, Ger. 58/D5
Oberkotzau, Ger. 59/E2
Oberlausitz (reg.), Ger. 43/H3
Oberlin, La, US 164/B2
Oberlin, Ks, US 154/D4
Obernai, Fr. 60/D1
Obernburg am Main, Ger. 58/C3
Oberndorf am Neckar, Ger. 61/E1
Oberndorf bei Salzburg, Aus. 59/F7
Oberneukirchen, Aus. 59/H6
Obernkirchen, Ger. 53/G4
Oberon, Austl. 133/D1
Oberösterreich (prov.), Aus. 43/G4
Oberpfälzer Wald (for.), Ger. 59/F3
Oberrieden, Swi. 61/E3
Oberriet, Swi. 61/F3
Obersaxen, Swi. 61/F4
Oberschleissheim, Ger. 59/E6
Oberschneiding, Ger. 59/F5
Obersiggenthal, Swi. 61/E3
Oberstammheim, Swi. 61/E2
Oberstaufen, Ger. 61/G2
Oberstdorf, Ger. 61/G3
Oberthal, Ger. 55/G4
Obertrum am See, Aus. 59/G7
Obertshausen, Ger. 58/B2
Oberursel, Ger. 58/B2
Oberuzwil, Swi. 61/F3
Oberviechtach, Ger. 59/F4
Oberwald, Swi. 61/E4
Oberwart, Aus. 50/C2
Oberwesel, Ger. 55/G3
Oberwiessenthal, Ger. 59/F2
Oberwil, Swi. 60/D4
Oberwölz, Aus. 45/L3
Obfelden, Swi. 61/E3
Obi (isl.), Indo. 91/G4
Obi (isls.), Indo. 91/G4
Obi (str.), Indo. 91/G4
Obiaruku, Nga. 115/G5
Óbidos, Port. 46/A3
Óbidos, Braz. 182/C3
Obihiro, Japan 82/C2
Obilić, Serb. 50/E4
Obing, Ger. 59/F6
Obion, Tn, US 162/C2
Obion (riv.), Tn, US 162/C2
Obion, North Fork (riv.), Tn, US 162/C2
Obion, South Fork (riv.), Tn, US 162/C2
Obira, Japan 82/B1
Obitochnaya (bay), Ukr. 73/H4
Obitsu (riv.), Japan 83/D3
Oblivskaya, Rus. 73/M3
Oblong, Il, US 162/D1
Obluch'ye, Rus. 79/L2
Obninsk, Rus. 68/H5
Obo, CAfr. 117/E4
Obo, China 78/E4
Obo Liang, China 99/F4
Obock, Djib. 118/B3
Obokote, D.R. Congo 121/F3
Obolo, Nga. 115/G5
Oborniki, Pol. 43/J2
Oborniki Śląskie, Pol. 43/J3
Obouya, Congo 120/C3
Oboyan', Rus. 73/J2
Obozerskiy, Rus. 68/J3
Obra (riv.), Pol. 43/J2
Obrenovac, Serb. 50/E3
Obrež, Serb. 50/E4
O'Brien, Or, US 146/B2
O'Briensbridge, Ire. 32/B4
Obrigheim, Ger. 58/B3
Obrigheim, Ger. 58/C4
Observatory, Austl. 132/G5
Obsharovka, Rus. 71/J1
Obtrumer (lake), Aus. 59/F7
Ōbu, Japan 83/L6
Obuasi, Gha. 115/E5
Obubra, Nga. 115/H5
Obudu, Nga. 115/H5
Obukhiv, Ukr. 72/F2
Obura, PNG 129/G1
Obw. (canton), Swi. 61/E4
Obzor, Bul. 51/H4
Ocala, Fl, US 165/G3
Ocampo, Mex. 174/E3
Ocaña, Col. 180/C2
Ocaña, Sp. 46/D3
Occhieppo Inferiore, It. 62/B2
Occhieppo Superiore, It. 62/A1
Occhiobello, It. 63/E4
Occhito (lake), It. 65/D4
Occidental, Cordillera (mts.), SAm. 184/B2
Occimiano, It. 62/B3
Ocean (cape), Ak, US 171/L3
Ocean (co.), NJ, US 168/D4
Ocean Beach, NY, US 169/E2
Ocean City, Md, US 163/K1
Ocean City, NJ, US 168/D5
Ocean Falls, BC, Can. 140/D3
Ocean Gate, NJ, US 168/D4
Ocean Grove, NJ, US 168/D3
Ocean Grove, Austl. 133/B4
Ocean Park, Wa, US 144/B4
Ocean Pines, Md, US 163/K1
Ocean Ridge, Fl, US 164/P9
Ocean View, De, US 163/K1
Ocean View, NJ, US 168/D5
Oceana, WV, US 163/G2
Oceana Nav. Air Sta., Va, US 163/J2
Oceano, Ca, US 148/B3
Oceanographic Museum, Mona. 62/J8
Oceanside, Ca, US 166/C4
Oceanside, NY, US 169/L9
Oceanville, NJ, US 168/D5
Ocee, Ga, US 163/M6
Ochakiv, Ukr. 72/F4
Och'amch'ire, Geo. 71/G4
Ochapowace Ind. Res., Sk, Can. 156/C2
Ochelata, Ok, US 153/G2
Ochiishi-misaki (cape), Japan 82/D2
Ochil (hills), Sc, UK 33/C4
Ochlocknee, Ga, US 165/F2
Ochlockonee (riv.), Fl, US 165/F2
Ocho Rios, Jam. 177/G2
Ochobo, Nga. 115/G5
Ochopee, Fl, US 165/H5
Ochsenfurt, Ger. 58/D3
Ochsenhausen, Ger. 61/F1
Ochsenkopf (peak), Aus. 61/F3
Ochtendung, Ger. 55/G3
Ochtrup, Ger. 53/E4
Ochtum (riv.), Ger. 53/F2
Ocilla, Ga, US 165/G2
Ockelbo, Swe. 40/G1
Ockenheim, Ger. 55/G4
Ocklawaha, Fl, US 165/H3
Ocmulgee (riv.), Ga, US 162/F4
Ocmulgee Nat'l Mon., Ga, US 162/F4
Ocna Mureş, Rom. 51/F2
Ocna Sibiului, Rom. 51/G3
Ocnele Mari, Rom. 72/C5
Ocnita, Mol. 72/D3
Ocoee, Fl, US 164/M6
Ocoña, Peru 184/C5
Ocoña (riv.), Peru 184/C4
Oconee (res.), Ga, US 163/F4
Oconee (riv.), Ga, US 163/F4
Oconomowoc, Wi, US 155/K2
Oconto, Wi, US 160/C2
Oconto (riv.), Wi, US 157/K5
Oconto Falls, Wi, US 160/B2
Ocosingo, Mex. 176/C2
Ocosta, Wa, US 144/B4
Ocotal, Nic. 176/E3
Ocotlán, Mex. 174/E4
Ocotlán de Morelos, Mex. 176/B2
Ocoyoacac, Mex. 175/Q10
Ocozocoautla de Espinosa, Mex. 176/C2
Ocracoke (isl.), NC, US 163/K3
Ocracoke, NC, US 163/K3
Ocros, Peru 184/B3
Octararo (cr.), Pa, US 168/B4
Octeville, Fr. 56/D1
Octeville-sur-Mer, Fr. 57/F1
October Revolution (isl.), Rus. 77/H2
Ocumare de la Costa, Ven. 183/N7
Ocumare del Tuy, Ven. 183/P7
Ocurí, Bol. 188/C1
Oda, Gha. 115/E5
Oda (peak), Sudan 109/H4
Oda, Japan 84/C3
Ódádhahraun (lava flow), Ice. 38/P7
Ŏdaejin, NKor. 81/E2
Odaesan NP, SKor. 84/A2
Ōdai, Japan 83/K7
Ōdaigahara-san (peak), Japan 84/E3
Ödåkra, Swe. 39/J6
Odanah, Wi, US 157/J4
Ōdate, Japan 82/B3
Odawara, Japan 85/F3
Odda, Nor. 40/B1
Odder, Den. 40/D4
Oddur (Xuddur), Som. 118/B4
Odebolt, Ia, US 155/G2
Odeborn (riv.), Ger. 53/F6
Odell, Tx, US 152/E3
Odell, Il, US 155/K3
Odell, Or, US 144/D5
Odelzhausen, Ger. 58/E6
Odem, Tx, US 151/F4
Odemira, Port. 46/A4
Ödemiş, Turk. 102/A2
Odendaalsrus, SAfr. 124/D2
Odensala, Swe. 39/A1
Odense, Den. 40/D4
Odense (int'l arpt.), Den. 40/D4
Odenthal, Ger. 55/G1
Odenton, Md, US 168/B5
Odenwald (reg.), Ger. 58/B3
Oder (Odra) (riv.), Ger.,Pol. 43/H2
Oder-Spree Kanal (canal), Ger. 42/Q7
Oderen, Fr. 60/C2
Oderhaff (lag.), Ger. 43/H2
Oderzo, It. 63/F2
Odesa, Ukr. 72/F4
Odes'ka Oblast, Ukr. 70/D3
Odessa, De, US 168/C5
Odessa, Fl, US 164/K7
Odessa, Mn, US 155/F1
Odessa, NY, US 161/H3
Odessa, Tx, US 150/C2
Odessa, Wa, US 144/E4
Odessa Meteor Crater, Tx, US 150/C2
Odet (riv.), Fr. 44/B2
Odhan, India 98/C5
Odienné, C.d'Iv. 114/D4
Odin, Ks, US 153/E1
Odin, Il, US 162/C1
Odin (mt.), BC, Can. 144/E2
Odintsovo, Rus. 69/W9
Odiongan, Phil. 88/C2
Odivelas, Port. 47/P10
Odobeşti, Rom. 51/H3
Odon (riv.), Fr. 44/C2
Odon, In, US 162/D1
Odongk, Camb. 94/D4
O'Donnell, Tx, US 152/D4
O'Donnells, Nf, Can. 159/L2
Odoorn, Neth. 52/D3
Odorheiu Secuiesc, Rom. 51/G2
Odra (Oder) (riv.), Ger.,Pol. 43/H2
Odum, Ga, US 165/G2
Odžaci, Serb. 50/D3
Odzala, PN d', Congo 120/C2
Odzi, Zim. 123/G3
Odzi (riv.), Zim. 123/G3
Odziba, Congo 120/C3
Ōe, Japan 83/H5
Ōe-yama (peak), Japan 83/H5
Oegstgeest, Neth. 52/B4
Oeiras, Braz. 183/F4
Oelde, Ger. 53/F5
Oelemari (riv.), Sur. 182/C2
Oelrichs, SD, US 154/C2
Oelsnitz, Ger. 59/F2
Oelwein, Ia, US 155/J2
Oeno (isl.), Pitc. 137/M7
Oenpelli, Austl. 128/D3
Oensingen, Swi. 60/D3
Oer-Erkenschwick, Ger. 53/E5
Oesling (mts.), Lux. 55/E4
Oesterdam (dam), Neth. 52/B6
Oestrich-Winkel, Ger. 58/B3
Oeta NP, Gre. 49/H3
Oetz, Aus. 61/G3
Oey'ŏn (isl.), SKor. 81/D3
Of, Turk. 70/G4
Ofahoma, Ms, US 162/C4
Ofaqim, Isr. 105/B6
Ofenhorn (peak), Swi. 61/E5
Ofenpass (Pass dal Fuorn) (pass), Swi. 61/G4
Offa, Nga. 115/G4
Offaly (co.), Ire. 34/A5
Offanengo, It. 62/C3
Offement, Fr. 60/C2
Offenbach, Ger. 58/B2
Offenbach an der Queich, Ger. 58/B4
Offenburg, Ger. 60/D1
Offerle, Ks, US 152/E2
Offerman, Ga, US 165/G2
Offida, It. 65/C2
Offingen, Ger. 58/D6
Offoué (riv.), Gabon 120/B3
Offoué, Rsv. Integrale de l', Gabon 120/B3
Offranville, Fr. 57/G1
Offstein, Ger. 58/B3
Offut (A.F.B.), Ne, US 155/G3
Oftersheim, Ger. 58/B4
Oftringen, Swi. 60/D3
Ōfunato, Japan 82/B4
Oga (pen.), Japan 82/A4
Oga, Japan 82/A4
Ogachi, Japan 82/B4
Ogadēn (reg.), Eth. 118/B4
Ōgaki, Japan 83/L5
Ogallala, Ne, US 154/D3
Ogano, Japan 83/C2
Ogasawara, Japan 136/D2
Ogatsu, Japan 82/B4
Ogawa, Japan 83/E1
Ogawa, Japan 83/C1
Ogawara (lake), Japan 82/B3
Ogbomosho, Nga. 115/G4
Ogden, Ar, US 153/G4
Ogden, Ut, US 147/H3
Ogden, Ks, US 155/F4
Ogden, Ia, US 155/G2
Ogdensburg, NY, US 161/J2
Ogdensburg, NJ, US 168/D1
Ogeechee (riv.), Ga, US 163/G4
Ogema, Sk, Can. 156/B3
Oggiono, It. 62/C2
Ogi, Japan 85/F2
Ogidaki (mtn.), On, Can. 141/H4
Ogies, SAfr. 124/E2
Ogilvie, Mn, US 157/H5
Ogilvie (riv.), Yk, Can. 140/C2
Ogilvie (mts.), Yk, Can. 140/C2
Oglala, SD, US 154/C2
Oglanly, Trkm. 71/K5
Oglanly, Trkm. 103/H2
Oglesby, Il, US 155/K3
Oglesby, Tx, US 175/F2
Oglethorpe, Ga, US 162/E4
Oglio (riv.), It. 45/J4
Ogmore, Austl. 134/C3
Ogmore-by-Sea, Wal, UK 36/C4
Ognon (riv.), Fr. 42/C5
Ogoamas (peak), Indo. 91/F3
Ogodzha, Rus. 79/L1
Ogoja, Nga. 115/H5
Ogooué (riv.), Gabon 107/C5
Ogooué-Ivindo (prov.), Gabon 120/C2
Ogooué-Lolo (prov.), Gabon 120/C3
Ogooue-Maritime (prov.), Gabon 120/B3
Ogorelyshi, Rus. 68/G3
Ogose, Japan 83/C2
Ogosta (riv.), Bul. 51/F4
Ogr, Sudan 117/E2
Ogre, Lat. 41/L3
Oguchi, Japan 83/L5
Ogulin, Cro. 50/B3
Ogun (riv.), Nga. 115/F5
Ogun (state), Nga. 115/F5
Ogurchinskiy (isl.), Trkm. 71/K5
Ogurugu, Nga. 115/G5
Oğuz, Turk. 102/D2
Ogwashi Uku, Nga. 115/G5
Oh Me Edge (hill), Eng, UK 33/D6
Ohafia, Nga. 115/G5
Ohai, NZ 135/A4
Ohakune, NZ 135/C2
Ohanet, Alg. 111/H3
Ōhara, Japan 83/E3
O'Hara Head (cape), Austl. 133/E2
Oharu, Japan 83/L5
Ōhata, Japan 82/B3
Ohau (lake), NZ 135/B4
Ohey, Belg. 55/E3

Oster, Ukr. 72/F2
Öster Ringsjön (lake), Swe. 39/K7
Osterburg, Ger. 42/F2
Osterburken, Ger. 58/C4
Österbybruk, Swe. 40/G1
Österbymo, Swe. 40/F3
Ostercappeln, Ger. 53/F4
Osterdalälven (riv.), Swe. 40/F1
Osterems (chan.), Ger. 52/D1
Östergötland (co.), Swe. 38/E4
Osterhofen, Ger. 59/G5
Osterholz-Scharmbeck, Ger. 53/F2
Osteria Grande, It. 63/E5
Ostermiething, Aus. 59/F6
Osterode am Harz, Ger. 53/H5
Östersund, Swe. 38/E3
Österunda, Swe. 39/A1
Östervåla, Swe. 40/G1
Osterwiek, Ger. 53/H5
Ostfildern, Ger. 58/C5
Østfold (co.), Nor. 38/D4
Ostfriesland (reg.), Ger. 53/E2
Östhammar, Swe. 40/H1
Ostheim vor der Rhön, Ger. 58/D2
Osthofen, Ger. 58/B3
Ostia Antica, It. 65/B4
Ostia Antica (ruin), It. 65/B4
Ostiano, It. 62/D3
Ostiglia, It. 63/E3
Ostional Nat'l Wild. Ref., CR 176/E4
Østmarka (reg.), Nor. 38/S8
Ostøya (isl.), Nor. 38/S8
Ostra, It. 63/G6
Östra Silen (lake), Swe. 40/E2
Ostra Vetere, It. 63/G6
Ostrach (riv.), Ger. 58/C6
Ostrava, Czh. 43/K4
Ostravský (pol. reg.), Slvk. 43/J4
Ostrhauderfehn, Ger. 53/E2
Oštri Rt (cape), Serb. 50/D4
Ostricourt, Fr. 54/C3
Ostróda, Pol. 41/H5
Ostrogozhsk, Rus. 73/K2
Ostroh, Ukr. 72/D2
Ostrołęka, Pol. 43/L2
Ostrolenka, Rus. 69/N5
Ostroshitskiy Gorodok, Bela. 41/M4
Ostrov, Rus. 41/N3
Ostrov, Czh. 59/F2
Ostrovets, Bela. 41/L4
Ostrovskoye, Rus. 68/J4
Ostrów Mazowiecka, Pol. 43/L2
Ostrów Wielkopolski, Pol. 43/J3
Ostrowiec Świętokrzyski, Pol. 43/L3
Ostryna, Bela. 41/L5
Ostrzeszów, Pol. 43/J3
Ostseebad Binz, Ger. 40/E4
Ostseebad Göhren, Ger. 40/E4
Ostseebad Prerow, Ger. 40/E4
Oststeinbek, Ger. 53/H1
Östuna, Swe. 39/A1
Ostuni, It. 49/E2
Ostwald, Fr. 58/A5
O'Sullivan (dam), Wa, US 144/E4
Osŭm (riv.), Bul. 49/J1
Osŭm (riv.), Slvk. 51/G4
Ōsumi (pen.), Japan 84/B5
Ōsumi (isls.), Japan 136/C1
Ōsumi (str.), Japan 79/L5
Osun (state), Nga. 115/G5
Osuna, Sp. 46/C4
Osupugo (peak), Kenya 119/A2
Osvaldo Cruz, Braz. 189/G2
Oswaldkirk, Eng, UK 35/G3
Oswaldtwistle, Eng, UK 35/F4
Oswegatchie, NY, US 161/J2
Oswegatchie (riv.), NY, US 161/J2
Oswego, Ks, US 153/G2
Oswego, NY, US 161/H3
Oswego (riv.), NY, US 161/H3
Oswego, Il, US 167/P16
Oswestry, Eng, UK 35/E6
Oświęcim (Auschwitz), Pol. 43/K3
Osyka, Ms, US 164/C2
Osypenko, Ukr. 73/J4
Ōta, Japan 85/F2
Ōta (riv.), Japan 84/C3
Otahuhu, NZ 135/F6
Ōtake, Japan 84/C3
Ōtaki, Japan 85/G3
Otaki, NZ 135/C3
Ōtaki, Japan 83/B2
Ōtakine-yama (peak), Japan 85/G2
Otanche, Col. 183/L7
Otaru, Japan 82/B2
Otasawiam (riv.), On, Can. 157/M3
Otautau, NZ 135/B4
Otavalo, Ecu. 180/B4
Otavi, Namb. 122/C3
Ōtawara, Japan 85/G2
Otay, Ca, US 166/C5
Otchinjau, Ang. 122/B3
Otego, NY, US 161/J3
Oțelu Roșu, Rom. 50/F3
Otematata, NZ 135/B4
Otepa, FrPol. 137/L6
Otepää, Est. 41/M2
Otero de Rey, Sp. 46/B1
Oteros (riv.), Mex. 174/C3
Otgon Tenger (peak), Mong. 78/D2
Othello, Wa, US 144/E4
Othis, Fr. 30/L4
Othonoí (isl.), Gre. 49/F3
Oti (riv.), Gha. 115/F4
Otinhungwa, Namb. 122/B3
Otira, NZ 135/B3
Otis, Ks, US 152/E1
Otis, La, US 164/B2
Otis, NM, US 150/B1
Otis Air National Guard Base, Ma, US 158/B5
Otjihajavara, Namb. 122/C4
Otjikango, Namb. 122/C4
Otjikondo, Namb. 122/B3
Otjimbingue, Namb. 122/C4
Otjinene, Namb. 122/C4
Otjiwarongo, Namb. 122/C4
Otjohorongo, Namb. 122/B4
Otjokavare, Namb. 122/B3
Otjosondjou (riv.), Namb. 122/C4
Otjosondu, Namb. 122/C4
Otley, Eng, UK 35/G4
Otočac, Cro. 50/B3
Otofuke, Japan 82/C2
Otog Qi, China 78/F4
Otog Qianqi, China 78/F4
Otok, Cro. 50/D3
Ōtone, Japan 83/D1
Otopeni (int'l arpt.), Rom. 51/H3
Otorohanga, NZ 135/C2
Otoskwin (riv.), On, Can. 157/J2
Otowa, Japan 83/M6
Otra (riv.), Nor. 74/A4
Otradnaya, Rus. 73/L5
Otradnoye, Rus. 69/T7
Otradnyy, Rus. 71/J1
Otranto (str.), Eur. 67/H2
Otrokovice, Czh. 43/J4
Otse, Bots. 124/D2
Otsego, Mi, US 160/D3
Ōtsu, Japan 83/J5
Ōtsuchi, Japan 82/B4
Ōtsuki, Japan 83/B2
Otta, Nga. 115/F5
Ottaviano, It. 65/D6
Ottawa, Ks, US 153/G1
Ottawa (cap.), Can. 161/J2
Ottawa (int'l arpt.), On, Can. 161/J2
Ottawa, Oh, US 160/D4
Ottawa (riv.), Can. 139/K5
Ottawa (isls.), Can. 139/J4
Ottawa, Il, US 155/K3
Ottawa (Outaouais) (riv.), Can. 161/G1
Ottawa Hills, Oh, US 160/E4
Ottawa NWR, Oh, US 160/E4
Ottensheim, Aus. 59/H6
Otter (riv.), Eng, UK 36/C5
Otter (cr.), Vt, US 161/K3
Otter, Mt, US 154/A1
Otter Creek (res.), Ut, US 147/H4
Otter Tail (lake), Mn, US 157/G4
Otter Tail (riv.), Mn, US 156/F4
Otterbach, Ger. 55/G5
Otterberg, Ger. 55/G4
Otterburn, Eng, UK 33/D6
Otterburne, Mb, Can. 156/F3
Otterlo, Neth. 52/C4
Otterndorf, Ger. 53/F1
Ottersberg, Ger. 53/G2
Ottershaw, Eng, UK 30/B2
Ottertail, Mn, US 157/G4
Ottery Saint Mary, Eng, UK 36/C5
Otthon, Sk, Can. 156/C2
Ottignies-Louvain-la-Neuve, Belg. 55/D2
Öttingen im Bayern, Ger. 58/D5
Ottmarsheim, Fr. 60/D2
Ottnang am Hausruck, Aus. 59/G6
Ottobeuren, Ger. 61/G2
Ottobrunn, Ger. 59/E6
Ottone, It. 62/C4
Ottosdal, SAfr. 124/D2
Ottsville, Pa, US 168/C3
Ottumwa, Ia, US 155/H3
Ottweiler, Ger. 55/G5
Otukpa, Nga. 115/G5
Otumba de Gómez Farías, Mex. 175/L7
Oturkpo, Nga. 115/H5
Otuzco, Peru 184/B2
Otway (rocks), Chile 191/B7
Otway (bay), Chile 191/C7
Otway NP, Austl. 132/B3
Otwell, In, US 162/D1
Otwock, Pol. 43/L2
Otyniya, Ukr. 72/C3
Ötztal Alps (mts.), Aus. 45/J3
Ötztaler Ache (riv.), Aus. 61/G3
Ou (mts.), Japan 82/B4
Ou (riv.), Laos 86/D4
Ouachita (lake), Ar, US 153/H3
Ouachita (riv.), Ar,La, US 143/H5
Ouachita (mts.), Ok, US 143/G5
Ouâd Nâga, Mrta. 114/B2
Ouadane, Mrta. 110/C5
Ouadda, CAfr. 116/D3
Ouaddaï (reg.), Chad 116/C2
Ouaddaï (pref.), Chad 116/D2
Ouagadougou (int'l arpt.), Burk. 115/E3
Ouagadougou (cap.), Burk. 115/E3
Ouahazeïne (well), Chad 116/C1
Ouahigouya, Burk. 115/E3
Ouaka (riv.), CAfr. 116/D4
Ouaka (pref.), CAfr. 116/D4
Oualâta, Mrta. 114/D2
Oualia, Mali 114/C3
Oualidia, Mor. 110/C2
Ouallam, Niger 115/F3
Ouanary, FrG. 182/D1
Ouanda Djalle, CAfr. 116/D3
Ouandago, CAfr. 116/C4
Ouandja, CAfr. 116/D3
Ouandja-Vakaga, Rsv. de Faune de la, CAfr. 116/D3
Ouango, CAfr. 116/D4
Ouanne (riv.), Fr. 44/E3
Ouaqui (riv.), FrG. 182/C2
Ouaqui, FrG. 182/C2
Ouara (riv.), CAfr. 117/E4
Ouarane (reg.), Mrta. 110/C5
Ouareau (riv.), Qu, Can. 161/H1
Ouargaye, Burk. 115/F4
Ouargla, Alg. 111/G3
Ouargla (wilaya), Alg. 111/G3
Ouarkziz, Jebel (mts.), Mor. 110/C3
Ouarzazate (int'l arpt.), Mor. 110/D3
Ouarzazate, Mor. 110/D3
Ouatagouna, Mali 115/F3
Oubangui (riv.), Congo 116/C5
Oubritenga (prov.), Burk. 115/E3
Ouche (riv.), Fr. 60/B3
Oucques, Fr. 57/G5
Oud-Beijerland, Neth. 52/B5
Oud-Turnhout, Belg. 52/B6
Ōuda, Japan 83/J7
Oudalan (prov.), Burk. 115/E3
Ouddorp, Neth. 52/A5
Oude Ijssel (riv.), Neth. 52/D5
Oude Pekela, Neth. 52/E2
Oude Westereems (chan.), Neth. 52/D1
Oude-Tonge, Neth. 52/B5
Oudenaarde, Belg. 54/C2
Oudenbosch, Neth. 52/B5
Oudenburg, Belg. 54/C1
Oudeschild, Neth. 52/B2
Oudewater, Neth. 52/B4
Oudon (riv.), Fr. 44/C3
Oudong, China 87/F3
Oudtshoorn, SAfr. 124/C4
Oued el Hadjar (well), Mali 114/E2
Oued Zem, Mor. 110/D2
Ouéléssébougou, Mali 114/D4
Ouémé (riv.), Ben. 115/F4
Ouéme (prov.), Ben. 115/F5
Ouen (isl.), NCal. 137/V13
Ouenza, Alg. 112/L7
Ouerrha (riv.), Mor. 112/B2
Ouessé, Ben. 115/F4
Ouesso, Congo 120/D2
Ouesso (int'l arpt.), Congo 120/D2
Ouest (prov.), Camr. 115/H5
Ouest (pt.), Haiti 177/H1
Ouest (pt.), Haiti 177/H2
Ouezzane, Mor. 112/B2
Oughterard, Ire. 32/A3
Ouham (riv.), CAfr. 116/C4
Ouham (pref.), CAfr. 116/C4
Ouham-Pendé (pref.), CAfr. 116/C4
Ouidah, Ben. 115/F5
Ouistreham, Fr. 57/E2
Oujaf, Mrta. 114/D2
Oujda, Mor. 112/D2
Oujda (prov.), Mor. 112/C2
Oujda (Angads) (int'l arpt.), Mor. 112/D2
Oujeft, Mrta. 114/B1
Oulad Teïma, Mor. 110/C3
Oulad-Rezzag, Mor. 112/C3
Oulangan NP, Fin. 68/F2
Ould Birni (well), Alg. 111/E4
Ould Yenjé, Mrta. 114/C3
Oule (riv.), Fr. 64/B4
Ouled Djellal, Alg. 66/E4
Ouljet es Soltane, Mor. 112/B3
Oullins, Fr. 64/A1
Oulnina (peak), Austl. 131/H5
Oulu, Fin. 68/E2
Oulu (prov.), Fin. 38/H2
Oulujärvi (lake), Fin. 38/H2
Oulx, It. 64/C2
Oum Chalouba, Chad 116/D2
Oum El Bouaghi, Alg. 112/K7
Oum er Rbia, Oued (riv.), Mor. 110/D2
Oum Hadjer, Chad 116/C2
Oumé, C.d'Iv. 114/D5
Ounara, Mor. 110/C3
Ounasjoki (riv.), Fin. 38/H2
Oundle, Eng, UK 37/F2
Oungre, Sk, Can. 156/C3
Ounianga Sérir, Chad 108/D5
Ounianga-Kébir, Chad 108/D5
Ouogo, CAfr. 116/C4
Oupeye, Belg. 55/E2
Our (riv.), Eur. 55/E4
Ouray, Co, US 149/J1
Ouray (peak), Co, US 149/J1
Ouray, Ut, US 147/J3
Ouray NWR, Ut, US 147/J3
Ource (riv.), Fr. 42/C5
Ourcq (riv.), Fr. 42/B4
Ourcq, Canal de l' (canal), Fr. 30/K5
Øure Anarjokka NP Nor. 38/H1
Øure Dividal NP, Nor. 38/F1
Ourém, Braz. 183/E3
Ouri, Chad 108/C4
Ouricuri, Braz. 183/F4
Ourimbah, Austl. 133/E1
Ourinhos, Braz. 189/G2
Ourique, Port. 46/A4
Ouro Branco, Braz. 183/G5
Ouro Fino, Braz. 187/K7
Ouro Modi, Mali 114/D3
Ouro Preto, Braz. 187/E4
Ourofon, Niger 115/H3
Ouroux-sur-Saône, Fr. 60/A4
Ourthe Occidentale (riv.), Belg. 55/E3
Ourthe Orientale (riv.), Belg. 55/E3
Ourtzarh, Mor. 112/B2
Ouse (riv.), Eng, UK 35/H4
Ouse, Austl. 132/C4
Ousley, Ga, US 165/G2
Oussouye, Sen. 114/A3
Oust (riv.), Fr. 44/B3
Outão, Port. 47/Q11
Outaouais (Ottawa) (riv.), Qu, Can. 161/G1
Outarville, Fr. 57/H4
Outeïd Arkas (well), Mali 114/D2
Outer Hebrides (isls.), Sc, UK 31/P8
Outer Santa Barbara Passage (chan.), Ca, US 148/C4
Outes, Sp. 46/A1
Outjo, Namb. 122/C4
Outlook, Mt, US 156/B3
Outlook, Sk, Can. 145/L2
Outreau, Fr. 54/A2
Outremont, Qu, Can. 159/N6
Ouvéa (isl.), NCal. 137/V12
Ouvèze (riv.), Fr. 44/F4
Ouyen, Austl. 132/B2
Ouyou Bézédinga (well), Niger 116/B1
Ouzinkie, Ak, US 171/H4
Ouzouer-le-Marché, Fr. 57/G5
Ovacık, Turk. 102/D2
Ovacık, Turk. 70/E4
Ovada, It. 62/B4
Ovalau (isl.), Fiji 137/Y18
Ovalle, Chile 188/B4
Ovan, Gabon 120/C2
Ovana (peak), Ven. 181/E3
Ovando, Mt, US 145/H4
Ovar, Port. 46/A2
Ovejaria (peak), Arg. 188/C3
Ovens (riv.), Austl. 133/C3
Overath, Ger. 55/G2
Overbrook, Ks, US 153/G1
Overbrook, Ok, US 153/F3
Överenhörna, Swe. 39/A1
Overflakkee (isl.), Neth. 52/B5
Overflow NWR, Ar, US 162/B4
Overgaard, Az, US 149/G3
Overhalla, Nor. 38/D2
Overijse, Belg. 55/D2
Overijssel (prov.), Neth. 52/D3
Overijssels (riv.), Neth. 52/D4
Överkalix, Swe. 38/G2
Overland Park, Ks, US 153/G1
Overlea, Md, US 168/B5
Overloon, Neth. 52/C5
Overo (peak), Arg. 190/C5
Overpelt, Belg. 52/C6
Overseal, Eng, UK 37/E1
Överselö, Swe. 39/A1
Overstrand, Eng, UK 37/H1
Overton, Eng, UK 37/E4
Overton, Wal, UK 35/F6
Overton, Nv, US 148/E2
Overton, Tx, US 151/G1
Övertorneå, Swe. 68/D2
Överum, Swe. 40/G3
Ovett, Ms, US 164/D2
Ovid, NY, US 161/H3
Ovidiopol', Ukr. 72/F4
Oviedo, Sp. 46/C1
Oviši, Lat. 41/J3
Ovoca, Ire. 34/B6
Ovoot, Mong. 78/G2
Övörhangay (prov.), Mong. 78/E2
Øvre Årdal, Nor. 40/B1
Övre Fryken (lake), Swe. 40/E1
Øvre Pasvik NP, Nor. 38/J1
Øvre Sirdal, Nor. 40/B2
Ovriá, Gre. 49/G3
Ovruch, Ukr. 72/E2
Owaka, NZ 135/B4
Owama, D.R. Congo 121/E3
Owando, Congo 120/C3
Ōwani, Japan 82/B3
Owariasahi, Japan 83/M5
Owase, Japan 84/E3
Owassa, Al, US 164/E2
Owassa (lake), NJ, US 168/D1
Owasso, Ok, US 153/G2
Owatonna, Mn, US 155/H1
Owego, NY, US 161/H3
Owel (lake), Ire. 32/C2
Owen (mt.), NZ 135/C3
Owen, Ger. 58/C5
Owen, Wi, US 155/J1
Owen, Austl. 131/H5
Owen Falls (dam), Ugan. 121/H2
Owen Roberts (int'l arpt.), UK 177/F2
Owen Sound, On, Can. 160/F2
Owen Stanley (range), PNG 129/G1
Owendo, Gabon 120/B2
Owenga, NZ 135/E4
Oweniny (riv.), Ire. 32/A1
Owenkillew (riv.), NI, UK 34/A2
Owens (lake), Ca, US 148/D2
Owens (peak), Ca, US 148/D3
Owens (riv.), Ca, US 148/C2
Owens, Tx, US 152/D4
Owens Cross Roads, Al, US 162/D3
Owensboro, Ky, US 162/D2
Owensburg, In, US 162/D1
Owensville, Mo, US 153/J1
Owensville, In, US 162/D1
Owenton, Ky, US 162/E1
Owerri, Nga. 115/G5
Owingen, Ger. 61/F2
Owings, Md, US 168/B6
Owings Mills, Md, US 168/B5
Owingsville, Ky, US 162/F1
Owl Creek (mts.), Wy, US 147/J2
Owo, Nga. 115/G5
Owosso, Mi, US 160/D3
Owrāmān, Iran 103/F3
Owutu, Nga. 115/G5
Owyhee (mts.), Id, US 146/E2
Owyhee, Nv, US 146/E3
Owyhee (riv.), Id, US 142/C3
Owyhee (dam), Or, US 146/E2
Owyhee, South Fork (riv.), Id,Nv, US 146/E2
Ox (Slieve Gamph) (mts.), Ire. 32/A1
Oxapampa, Peru 184/C3
Oxbow, Sk, Can. 156/C3
Oxbow (lake), Mi, US 167/F6
Oxelösund, Swe. 40/G2
Oxford, NS, Can. 158/F3
Oxford (canal), Eng, UK 37/E3
Oxford, Eng, UK 37/E3
Oxford, NZ 135/C3
Oxford, Al, US 162/E4
Oxford, Ar, US 153/J2
Oxford, In, US 160/C4
Oxford, Me, US 161/L2
Oxford, Mi, US 167/F6
Oxford, Ms, US 162/C3
Oxford, NC, US 163/H2
Oxford, Ne, US 154/E3
Oxford, NY, US 161/J3
Oxford, Oh, US 160/D5
Oxford, Pa, US 168/C4
Oxfordshire (co.), Eng, UK 37/E3
Oxhey, Eng, UK 30/B2
Oxie, Swe. 40/E4
Oxkutzcab, Mex. 176/D1
Oxley (cr.), Austl. 134/E7
Oxley, Austl. 133/B2
Oxnard (arpt.), Ca, US 166/A2
Oxnard, Ca, US 166/A2
Oxnard Beach, Ca, US 166/A2
Oxon Hill (farm), Md, US 168/A6
Oxon Hill-Glassmanor, Md, US 168/B6
Oxshott, Eng, UK 30/B3
Oxted, Eng, UK 30/D3
Oxton, Sc, UK 33/D5
Oy-Tal, Kyr. 99/B3
Oya, Malay. 90/D3
Oyabe, Japan 85/E2
Oyama, Japan 85/F2
Oyama, Japan 83/B3
Oyama, BC, Can. 144/E2
Ōyamada, Japan 83/K6
Ōyamazaki, Japan 83/J6
Oyapock (riv.), FrG.,Braz 179/D2
Oyé Yeska (well), Chad 108/C5
Oye-Plage, Fr. 54/B2
Oyem, Gabon 120/B2
Oyen, Ab, Can. 145/J2
Øyer, Nor. 40/D1
Øyeren (lake), Nor. 38/T8
Oykell (riv.), Sc, UK 31/R8
Oylen, Mn, US 157/G4
Oymyakon, Rus. 75/Q3
Oyo, Nga. 115/F5
Oyo (state), Nga. 115/F4
Oyo, Congo 120/C3
Ōyodo (riv.), Japan 84/B5
Ōyodo, Japan 83/J7
Oyón, Peru 184/B3
Oyonnax, Fr. 60/B5
Oyster (cr.), Tx, US 151/G3
Oyster Bay, NY, US 169/L8
Oyster Bay (har.), NY, US 169/L8
Oyster Bay Cove, NY, US 169/L8
Oyster Bay Nat'l Wild. Ref., NY, US 169/L8
Oyten, Ger. 53/G2
Oyugis, Kenya 119/A2
Ozamiz, Phil. 88/C3
Ozanne (riv.), Fr. 44/D2
Ozarichi, Bela. 70/D1
Ozark, Al, US 165/F2
Ozark (mts.), Ar,Mo, US 143/H4
Ozark, Ar, US 153/H3
Ozark, Mo, US 153/H2
Ozark (plat.), Mo, US 155/H4
Ozark Nat'l Scenic Riverways, Mo, US 162/B2
Ozarks (lake), Mo, US 143/H4
Ożarów, Pol. 72/A2
Ozawkie, Ks, US 155/G4
Ózd, Hun. 43/L4
Ozello, Fl, US 164/K6
Ozernovskiy, Rus. 75/R4
Ozernoy (cape), Rus. 75/S4
Ozernoye, Rus. 71/J2
Ozërnyy, Rus. 71/M2
Ozero Sasyk (lake), Ukr. 51/J3
Ozero Yalpuh (lake), Urk. 72/E5
Ozerskiy, Rus. 79/N2
Ozëry, Bela. 41/L5
Ozette (lake), Wa, US 144/B3
Ozette Ind. Res., Wa, US 144/B3
Ozherel'ye, Rus. 68/H5
Ozieri, It. 48/A2
Ozimek, Pol. 43/K3
Özkonak, Turk. 102/C2
Ozoir-la-Ferrière, Fr. 30/L5
Ozona, Fl, US 164/K7
Ozona, Tx, US 150/D2
Ozondjacheberg (peak), Namb. 122/C4
Ozone, Ar, US 153/H3
Ozone Park (nbrhd.), NY, US 169/K9
Ozora, Hun. 50/D2
Ozorków, Pol. 43/K3
Ozouer-le-Voulgis, Fr. 30/L6
Ōzu, Japan 84/C4
Ozuluama de Mascareñas, Mex. 176/B1
Ozurget'i, Geo. 71/G4
Ozzano dell'Emilia, It. 63/E5

P

P'abal-li, NKor. 81/E2
P'aju, SKor. 81/F6
P'aro-ho (lake), SKor. 81/D3
P'yŏngan-bukto (prov.), NKor. 81/C2
P. K. Le Rouxdam (res.), SAfr. 124/D3
Pa Sak (riv.), Thai. 93/H4
Pääjärvi (lake), Fin. 39/F3
Pa-an, Myan. 94/B2
Paar (riv.), Ger. 42/F4
Paarl, SAfr. 124/L10
Påarp, Swe. 39/J6
Pabbi, Pak. 98/A2
Pabean, Indo. 89/F4
Pabellón de Arteaga, Mex. 174/E4
Pabianice, Pol. 43/K3
Pablo Nat'l Wild. Ref., Mt, US 145/G4
Pābna (pol. reg.), Bang. 97/G3
Pābna, Bang. 97/G3
Pabradė, Lith. 41/L4
Pabu, Fr. 56/B3
Pacaás Novos, PN dos, Braz. 185/F3
Pacaás Novos, Serra dos (mts.), Braz. 185/E3
Pacajá (riv.), Braz. 182/D3
Pacajus, Braz. 183/G4
Pacaltsdorp, SAfr. 124/C4
Pacaraimã, Sierra (mts.), SAm. 182/A2
Pacasmayo, Peru 184/B2
Pacatuba, Braz. 183/G3
Pacaya Samiria, Res. Nacional, Peru 184/C2
Paccha, Peru 184/C3
Pacé, Fr. 56/D4
Pace, Fl, US 164/E2
Paceco, It. 48/C4
Pachacamac (ruin), Peru 184/B4
Pachaconas, Peru 184/C4
Pachamarca (riv.), Peru 184/C4
Pacheco (pass), Ca, US 148/B2
Pachelma, Rus. 71/G1
Pachino, It. 48/D4
Pachitea (riv.), Peru 184/C3
Pachiza, Peru 184/B2
Pachmarhī, India 96/B4
Pacho, Col. 183/L7
Pachuca, Mex. 175/L6
Pachwa, Ugan. 121/G2
Pacific (range), BC, Can. 144/B2
Pacific, Wa, US 167/C3
Pacific Beach, Wa, US 144/B4
Pacific City, Or, US 146/B1
Pacific Palisades (nbrhd.), Ca, US 166/E7
Pacific Rim NP, BC, Can. 144/B3
Pacifico (mtn.), Ca, US 166/B2
Pacinan (cape), Indo. 89/F4
Pacitan, Indo. 89/E5
Paço de Arcos, Port. 47/P10
Pacolet (riv.), SC, US 163/G3
Pácora, Col. 183/K7
Pacoval, Braz. 182/C3
Pacy-sur-Eure, Fr. 57/G2
Pad Īdan, Pak. 101/J3
Padada, Phil. 88/D4
Padam, India 98/D3
Padampur, India 95/D1
Padang (isl.), Indo. 89/C2
Padang, Indo. 89/C3
Padang Endau, Malay. 89/C2
Padangcermin, Indo. 89/D4
Padangpanjang, Indo. 89/C3
Padangsidempuan, Indo. 89/B2
Padangtigi, Indo. 89/A1
Padany, Rus. 68/G3
Padas (riv.), Malay. 88/A4
Padaung, Myan. 86/B5
Padcaya, Bol. 188/C2
Paddington (nbrhd.), Eng, UK 30/C2
Paddock Lake, Wi, US 167/P14
Paddock Wood, Eng, UK 30/E3
Paden City, WV, US 160/F5
Paderborn (arpt.), Ger. 53/F5
Paderborn, Ger. 53/F5
Paderno, It. 63/F2
Pāderu, India 95/D2
Padibe, Ugan. 117/G5
Padiham, Eng, UK 35/F4
Padilla, Bol. 188/C1
Padina, Serb. 50/E3
Padjelanta NP (nat'l park), Nor. 68/B2
Padova, It. 63/E3
Padova (prov.), It. 63/E2
Padrauna, India 96/D2
Padre (isl.), Tx, US 143/G6
Padre Bernardo, Braz. 186/C2
Padre Island National Seashore, Tx, US 175/F3
Padrón, Sp. 46/A1
Pādru, India 92/B2
Padstow, Eng, UK 36/B5
Paducah, Tx, US 152/D3
Paducah, Ky, US 162/C2
Padul, Sp. 46/D4
Padula, It. 48/D2
Paduli, It. 65/D5
Paech'ŏn, NKor. 81/D4
Paegam, NKor. 81/E2
Paekakariki, NZ 135/H8
Paeksan-ni, NKor. 81/D2
Paektŏk-san (peak), SKor. 81/E4
Paektu-san (peak), NKor. 81/E2
Paengnyŏng (isl.), NKor. 79/J4
Paeroa, NZ 135/C2
Paese, It. 63/F2
Páez, Col. 180/C3
Páez, Col. 180/C4
Pafúri, Moz. 123/F4
Pag, Cro. 50/B3
Pag (isl.), Cro. 67/G1
Pagadian, Phil. 88/C4
Pagai Selatan (isl.), Indo. 90/B4
Pagai Utara (isl.), Indo. 90/B4
Pagan (isl.), NMar. 136/D3
Pagan, Myan. 86/B4
Pagancillo, Arg. 188/B4
Pagani, It. 65/D6
Paganica, It. 65/C3
Pagaralam, Indo. 89/C4
Pagatan, Indo. 90/D4
Pagawyun, Myan. 94/B3
Page, ND, US 156/F4
Page, Ok, US 153/G3
Page, Az, US 149/G2
Pagėgiai, Lith. 41/J4
Pageland, SC, US 163/G3
Pager (riv.), Ugan. 117/G5
Pagerdewa, Indo. 89/D3
Pāgla, Bang. 97/H3
Paglieta, It. 65/D3
Pagny-sur-Moselle, Fr. 55/F6
Pago Pago (cap.), ASam. 137/T10
Pago Pago (int'l arpt.), ASam. 137/T10
Pagoda (peak), Co, US 147/K3
Pagosa Springs, Co, US 149/J2
Pagri, China 97/G2
Paguate, NM, US 149/J3
Pagwa River, On, Can. 157/M2
Pagwachuan (riv.), On, Can. 157/M3
Pah-Rum (peak), Nv, US 146/D3
Pahala, Hi, US 142/U11
Pahang (state), Malay. 89/C2
Pahang (riv.), Malay. 90/B3
Páhara (lag.), Nic. 177/F3
Pahāri Buzurg, India 96/C3
Pahārpur, Pak. 98/A3
Pahāsu, India 96/B1
Pahiatua, NZ 135/C3
Pahlgām, India 98/C2
Pahokee, Fl, US 165/H4
Pahranagat Nat'l Wild. Ref., Nv, US 148/E2
Pahrump, Nv, US 148/E2
Pahuatlán, Mex. 175/L6
Pahute (mesa), Nv, US 148/D2
Pai (lake), China 80/C5
Paiania (arpt.), Gre. 49/N9
Paicines, Ca, US 148/B2
Paide, Est. 41/L2
Paignton, Eng, UK 36/C6
Paiján, Peru 184/B2
Päijänne (lake), Fin. 38/H3
Paikü (lake), China 97/E1
Pailemán, Arg. 190/D4
Pailin, Camb. 94/C3
Paimbœuf, Fr. 56/C6
Paime, Col. 183/L7
Paimio, Fin. 41/K1
Painan, Indo. 89/C3
Paine (peak), Chile 191/B6
Paine, Chile 190/N8
Painesville, Oh, US 160/F4
Painio (lake), Fin. 39/D4
Painscastle, Wal, UK 36/C2
Paint (riv.), Mi, US 157/K4
Paint Bank, Va, US 163/G2
Paint Rock, Tx, US 150/E2
Painted (des.), Az, US 142/D4
Painted Rock (res.), Az, US 149/F4
Painted Rocks (dam), Az, US 149/F4
Paintsville, Ky, US 163/F2
Paipa, Col. 180/C3
Paisley, Sc, UK 33/B5
Paisley, On, Can. 160/F2
Paisley, Or, US 146/C2
Paita, Peru 184/A2
Paithan, India 95/B2
Pajala, Swe. 38/G2
Paján, Ecu. 180/A5
Pajas Blancas (Córdoba) (int'l arpt.), Arg. 188/C4
Pajęczno, Pol. 43/K3
Pak Ban, Laos 94/C1
Pak Beng, Laos 94/C2
Pak Chong, Thai. 94/C3
Pak Thong Chai, Thai. 94/C3
Pakanbaru, Indo. 89/C2
Pakawau, NZ 135/C3
Pakch'ŏn, NKor. 81/C3
Pakenham (cape), Chile 191/B6
Pakenham, Austl. 132/G6
Pákhnes (peak), Gre. 49/J5
Pakhra (riv.), Rus. 69/W9
Pakistan (ctry.) 101/H3
Paklenica NP (nat'l park), Cro. 45/L4
Pakokku, Myan. 86/B4
Pakowki (lake), Ab, Can. 145/J3
Pākpattan, Pak. 98/B4
Pakrac, Cro. 50/C3
Pakruojis, Lith. 41/K4
Paks, Hun. 50/D2
Paksey, Bang. 97/G3
Pakue, Indo. 91/F4
Pakwach, Ugan. 121/G2
Pakxe, Laos 94/D3
Pala, Ca, US 166/C4
Pala, Chad 116/B3
Pala Ind. Res., Ca, US 166/C4
Palace, Mona. 62/J8
Palacios, Tx, US 151/F3
Paladru (lake), Fr. 64/B2
Palafrugell, Sp. 47/G2
Palagonia, It. 48/D4
Palagruža (isls.), Cro. 67/H2
Pálairos, Gre. 49/G3
Palais (riv.), Fr. 57/E4
Palaiseau, Fr. 30/J5
Pālakollu, India 95/D2
Palalarivier (riv.), SAfr. 123/F4
Palamás, Gre. 49/H3
Palamós, Sp. 47/G2
Palana, Rus. 75/R4
Palana, Austl. 133/C4
Palanan, Phil. 88/C1
Palanan (pt.), Phil. 88/C1
Palanas, Phil. 88/C2
Palanga, Lith. 41/J4
Palangkaraya, Indo. 90/D4
Pālanpur, India 101/K4
Palapye, Bots. 123/E4
Palar (riv.), India 92/C5
Palas de Rey, Sp. 46/B1
Palasa, Indo. 91/F3
Palāsa, India 95/E2
Palāsbāri, India 97/H2
Palata, It. 65/D4
Palatine, Il, US 167/P15
Palatka, Rus. 75/R3
Palatka, Fl, US 165/H3
Palattsy, Kaz. 99/D2
Palau (ctry.) 136/C4
Palau, Mex. 150/D4
Palau We (isl.), Indo. 93/G6
Palauk, Myan. 94/B3
Palaw, Myan. 94/B3
Palawan (isl.), Phil. 77/L9
Palawan Passage (chan.), Phil. 91/E2
Palaya, Bol. 188/B1
Palayan, Phil. 88/C2
Palazzo dei Penitenzieri, It. 65/G7
Palazzo del Sant'Uffizio, VatC. 65/G7
Palazzo Salviati, It. 65/G8
Palazzo Torlonia, It. 65/G7
Palazzolo Acreide, It. 48/D4
Palazzolo dello Stella, It. 63/G2
Palazzolo sull'Oglio, It. 62/C2
Palca, Bol. 184/E5
Palcenham, Austl. 133/B4
Palco, Ks, US 154/E4
Paldiski, Est. 41/L2
Pale, Bosn. 50/D4
Paleleh, Indo. 91/F3
Palembang, Indo. 89/D3
Palen (lake), Ca, US 148/E4
Palena, It. 65/D4
Palena, Chile 190/C4
Palena (riv.), Chile 190/B4
Palencia, Sp. 46/C1
Palenque, Mex. 176/D2
Palenque, PN, Mex. 176/C2
Palermo, It. 48/C3
Palermo, Ca, US 146/C4
Palermo, ND, US 156/C3
Palermo, On, Can. 160/T9
Palermo, NJ, US 168/D5
Palese (int'l arpt.), It. 48/E2
Palestina, Col. 183/K7
Palestina, Chile 188/B2
Palestine, Ar, US 162/B3
Palestine, Il, US 162/D1
Palestine, Tx, US 150/G2
Palestine (lake), Tx, US 151/G1
Palestrina, It. 65/B4
Palestro, It. 62/B3
Pālghar, India 101/K5
Pālghāt, India 95/C4
P'algong-san (peak), SKor. 81/D5
P'algong-san (peak), SKor. 84/A2
Palgrave (pt.), Namb. 122/B4
Palgrave (mt.), Austl. 130/B2
Palhāna, India 96/C3
Palhano, Braz. 183/G4
Palhoça, Braz. 189/G3
Pāli, India 96/D4
Pāli, India 92/B2
Pali-Aike, PN, Chile 191/C7
Paliā Kalān, India 96/C1
Paliano, It. 65/C4
Palić, Serb. 50/D2
Palidoro, It. 65/B4
Palikir (cap.), Micr. 136/E4
Palima, Indo. 91/F4
Palioúrion (cape), Gre. 49/H3
Palisade, Mn, US 157/H4
Palisades, NY, US 169/K8
Palisades (cliff), NJ,NY 169/K8
Palisades, Id, US 147/H2
Palisades (dam), Id, US 147/H2
Palisades Interstate Park, NJ, US 168/D1
Palisades Park, NJ, US 169/K8
Paliseul, Belg. 55/E4
Pālitāna, India 101/K4
Palivere, Est. 41/K2
Palizada, Mex. 172/C4
Paljenik (peak), Bosn. 50/C3
Palk (str.), India, SrL. 92/C6
Pālkonda, India 95/D2
Pallamallawa, Austl. 132/D1
Pallano (peak), It. 65/D3
Pallarenda, Austl. 134/B2
Pallas Grean, Ire. 32/B4
Pallas-Ounastunturin NP, Fin. 38/H1
Pallasca, Peru 184/B3
Pallaskenry, Ire. 32/B4
Pallasovka, Rus. 71/H2
Pallastunturi (peak), Fin. 38/H1
Pallisa, Ugan. 119/A1
Palliser (cape), NZ 135/C3
Pallu, India 98/C5
Palm (isls.), Austl. 129/G4
Palm Bay, Fl, US 165/H3
Palm Beach (nbrhd.), Austl. 134/H8
Palm Beach, Fl, US 164/P9
Palm Beach (int'l arpt.), Fl, US 164/P9
Palm Beach (co.), Fl, US 164/P9
Palm Beach Gardens, Fl, US 164/P9
Palm Beach Shores, Fl, US 164/P9
Palm City, Ca, US 166/C5
Palm City, Fl, US 165/H4
Palm Desert, Ca, US 148/D4
Palm Harbor, Fl, US 164/K7
Palm Island Aboriginal Settlement, Austl. 134/B2
Palm River-Clair Mel, Fl, US 164/L8
Palm Springs, Ca, US 148/D4
Palma, Moz. 119/C4
Palma, Sp. 47/G3
Palma (riv.), Braz. 186/D2
Palma Campania, It. 65/D6
Palma del Río, Sp. 46/C4
Palma di Montechiaro, It. 48/C4
Palma Mallorca (int'l arpt.), Sp. 47/G3
Palma Soriano, Cuba 177/H1
Palmácia, Braz. 183/G4
Palmanova, It. 63/G2
Palmar (riv.), Ven. 177/H4
Palmares, Braz. 183/H5
Palmarito, Ven. 180/D3
Palmarito, Bol. 185/F5
Palmas (cape), Libr. 114/D5
Palmas, Braz. 189/G3
Palmas, Braz. 186/C1
Palmdale, Ca, US 166/B1
Palmeira, CpV. 107/K10
Palmeira, Braz. 189/G3
Palmeira das Missões, Braz. 189/F3
Palmeira dos Índios, Braz. 183/G5
Palmeirais, Braz. 183/F4
Palmeiras (riv.), Braz. 186/D2
Palmeiras de Goiás, Braz. 186/C3
Palmeirina, Braz. 183/G5
Palmela, Port. 47/Q10
Palmer, Sk, Can. 145/L3
Palmer, US, Ant. 192/V
Palmer, Ak, US 171/J3
Palmer, Ma, US 161/K3
Palmer, Tx, US 150/L7
Palmer, Wa, US 167/D3
Palmer Lake, Co, US 152/B1
Palmer Land (phys. reg.), Ant. 192/V
Palmer Rapids, On, Can. 161/H2
Palmerston, On, Can. 160/F3
Palmerston, NZ 135/B4
Palmerston (cape), Austl. 134/C3
Palmerston Atoll (atoll), CookIs. 137/J6
Palmerston North, NZ 135/C3
Palmerston NP, Austl. 134/B2
Palmerton, Pa, US 168/C2
Palmerville, Austl. 134/B1
Palmetto, Fl, US 165/G4
Palmetto, Ga, US 163/L7
Palmetto Bend (dam), Tx, US 151/F3
Palmi, It. 48/D3
Palmilla, Chile 190/C2
Palmillas (pt.), Cuba 177/F1
Palmira, Col. 180/B4
Palmital, Braz. 189/G2
Palmitas, Uru. 191/K10
Palmitos, Braz. 189/F3
Palmyra, Mi, US 160/E4
Palmyra (isl.), PacUS 137/J4
Palmyra, In, US 162/D1
Palmyra, Mo, US 155/J4
Palmyra, Pa, US 168/B3
Palmyra, Va, US 163/H2
Palmyra, Wi, US 155/K2
Palmyra (Tadmur) (ruin), Syria 102/D3
Palmyras (pt.), India 92/E3
Palnackie, Sc, UK 34/E2
Palo, Phil. 88/D3
Palo Alto, Pa, US 168/B2
Palo Alto Battlefield Nat'l Hist. Site, Tx, US 151/F4
Palo Duro (cr.), Tx, US 152/C3
Palo Pinto, Tx, US 151/E1
Palo Santo, Arg. 188/E3
Palo Verde, Ca, US 148/E4
Palo Verde, PN, CR 172/D5
Paloemeu (riv.), Sur. 182/C2
Paloh, Indo. 90/C3
Paloich, Sudan 117/G3
Palombara Sabina, It. 65/B3
Palometas, Bol. 188/D1
Palomeu (riv.), Sur. 181/H4
Palon (peak), It. 63/E2
Pāloncha, India 95/D2
Paloncillo (mts.), NM, US 149/H5
Palos (cape), Sp. 47/E4
Palos Blancos, Bol. 188/D2
Palos de la Frontera, Sp. 46/B4
Palos Hills, Il, US 167/Q16
Palos Verdes (pt.), Ca, US 166/F8
Palos Verdes (hills), Ca, US 166/F8
Palos Verdes Estates, Ca, US 166/F8
Palosco, It. 62/C2
Palouse (riv.), Wa, US 144/F4
Palouse, Wa, US 144/F4
Palpa, Peru 184/C4
Palpalá, Arg. 188/C3
Palpetu (cape), Indo. 91/G4
Paltamo, Fin. 68/E2
Paltang, SKor. 81/G6
Palu, Indo. 91/E4
Palu (isl.), Indo. 128/A2
Palu, Turk. 102/D2
Paluan, Phil. 88/C2
Palwal, India 96/A1
Pama, Burk. 115/F4
Pama, Chile 188/B4
Pamangkat, Indo. 90/C3
Pamanukan (cape), Indo. 89/D4
Pamar, Col. 180/D5
Pambeguwa, Nga. 115/H4
Pambula, Austl. 133/D3
Pamekasan, Indo. 89/F4
Pameungpeuk, Indo. 89/D4
Pāmgarh, India 96/D5
Pamiers, Fr. 44/D5
Pamir (reg.), Taj.,China 74/H6
Pamir (riv.), Afg.,Taj. 74/H6
Pamlico (riv.), NC, US 163/J3
Pamlico (sound), NC, US 163/J3
Pamoni, Ven. 181/E4
Pampa, Tx, US 152/D3
Pampa de Agnia, Arg. 190/C4
Pampa de los Guanacos, Arg. 188/D3
Pampa de los Salinas, Arg. 188/C4
Pampa del Indio, Arg. 188/E3
Pampa del Sacramento (plain), Peru 184/C2
Pampa del Tamarugal (plain), Chile 188/B1
Pampa Grande, Bol. 188/C1
Pampa Húmeda (plain), Arg. 190/E2
Pampa Pelada (plain), Arg. 190/C5
Pampa Seca (plain), Arg. 190/D3
Pampachiri, Peru 184/C4
Pampacolca, Peru 184/C4
Pampas (plain), Arg. 179/C6
Pampas (riv.), Peru 184/C4
Pampas, Peru 184/C4
Pampas, Peru 184/B3
Pampilhosa da Serra, Port. 46/B2
Pamplico, SC, US 163/H4
Pamplona, Col. 180/C3
Pamplona, Sp. 44/C5
Pampulha (int'l arpt.), Braz. 186/E3
Pāmpur, India 98/C2
Pamukova, Turk. 51/K5
Pamunkey Ind. Res., Va, US 163/J2
Pan de Azúcar, Bol. 188/C2
Pan de Azúcar, PN, Chile 188/B3
Pana, Gabon 120/C3
Pana, Il, US 155/K4
Panaba, Mex. 176/D1
Panabo, Phil. 88/D4
Panaca, Nv, US 148/E2
Panacachi, Bol. 188/C1
Panacea, Fl, US 165/F2
Panadura, SrL. 95/C5
Pānāgar, India 96/B4
Panagyurishte, Bul. 51/G4
Panaitan (isl.), Indo. 90/B5
Panaji, India 95/B3
Panama (ctry.) 177/F4
Panamá (bay), Pan. 177/G4
Panama (canal), Pan. 177/F4
Panamá (cap.), Pan. 177/G4
Panama (isth.), Pan. 177/F4
Panama (gulf), Pan. 177/G4
Panama, Ok, US 153/G3
Panama City, Fl, US 165/F2
Panamá Viejo (ruin), Pan. 180/B2
Panambi, Braz. 189/F4
Panamint (range), Ca, US 148/D2
Panao, Peru 184/B3
Panaon (isl.), Phil. 88/D3
Panaro (riv.), It. 45/J4
Panarukan, Indo. 89/F4
Panasoffkee (lake), Fl, US 164/L6
Panay (isl.), Phil. 77/M8
Panay (gulf), Phil. 88/C3
Pancake (range), Nv, US 146/E4
Pančevo, Serb. 50/E3
Panchagarh, Bang. 97/G2
Panchor, Malay. 89/D2
Pančicev vrh (peak), Serb. 50/E4
Pancilet (res.), India 97/F4
Panciu, Rom. 51/H3
Panda, D.R. Congo 121/F5
Panda, Moz. 123/G5
Pandale, Tx, US 150/D2
Pandamatenga, Bots. 122/E3
Pandan, Phil. 88/D2
Pandan, Phil. 88/C3
Pandan (str.), Sing. 89/H7
Pandaria, India 96/C4
Pandeglang, Indo. 89/D4
Pandėlys, Lith. 41/L3
Pāndhurna, India 95/C1
Pandie Pandie, Austl. 131/H3
Pandino, It. 62/C3
Pando, Uru. 191/L11
Pando (state), Bol. 185/E3
Pāndoh, India 98/D4
Pandora (passage), PNG 129/G2
Pandrup, Den. 40/C3
Pandua, India 97/G4
Panduro, Bol. 185/E5

Panela – Penge

Panelas, Braz. 183/G5
Panevėžys, Lith. 41/L4
Panfilov, Kaz. 99/D3
Panfilovo, Rus. 73/M2
Pang (riv.), Myan. 86/C4
Pang Kalom, Laos 86/D4
Pang Long, Myan. 86/C4
Pangai, Tonga 137/H6
Pangaíon (peak), Gre. 49/J2
Pangala, Congo 120/C3
Pangandaran, Indo. 89/E4
Pangani (riv.), Tanz. 119/B2
Pangani, Tanz. 119/B3
Pangbourne, Eng, UK 37/E4
Pangburn, Ar, US 153/J3
Pangi, D.R. Congo 121/F3
Pangia, PNG 129/G1
Pangjiabu, China 80/G6
Pangkajene, Indo. 91/E4
Pangkalanberandan, Indo. 89/B1
Pangkalanpembuang, Indo. 90/D4
Pangkalansusu, Indo. 89/B1
Pangkalaseang (cape), Indo. 91/F4
Pangkalpinang, Indo. 89/D3
Pangnirtung, Nun, Can. 141/K2
Pangsau (pass), India 86/C3
Panguipulli, Chile 190/B3
Panguitch, Ut, US 149/F2
Panguma, SLeo. 114/C4
Pangururan, Indo. 89/B2
Pangutaran, Phil. 88/C4
Pangutaran (isl.), Phil. 88/C4
Pangutaran Group (isls.), Malay. 88/B4
P'an'gyo, NKor. 81/D3
Panhandle, Tx, US 152/D3
Pania-Mutombo, D.R. Congo 121/E4
Paniai (lake), Indo. 91/J4
Panicale, It. 65/B1
Panié (peak), NCal. 137/U12
Pānihāti, India 97/G4
Pānīpat, India 98/D5
Panitan, Phil. 88/C3
Panj (riv.), Afg.,Taj. 74/G6
Panj (riv.), Afg. 101/K1
Panj (Pyandzh) (riv.), Afg.,Taj. 99/B4
Panjakent, Taj. 74/G6
Panjang, Indo. 89/D4
Panjgraon, India 98/D4
Panjgūr, Pak. 101/H3
Panjwīn, Iraq 103/F3
Panke (riv.), Ger. 42/Q6
Pankow, Ger. 42/Q6
Pankshin, Nga. 115/H4
P'anmun-ŭp, NKor. 81/D4
P'anmunjŏm, NKor. 81/D4
Panna, India 96/C3
Pannawonica, Austl. 130/C2
Pannikin (isl.), Austl. 134/F7
Pano Lefkara, Cyp. 104/C2
Pano Panayia, Cyp. 104/C2
Pano Platres, Cyp. 104/C2
Panora, Ia, US 155/G3
Panorama, Braz. 189/G2
Panshan, China 81/B2
Panshi, China 79/K3
Panshizhen, China 87/F2
Pānskura, India 97/F4
Pant, Eng, UK 36/C1
Pantai Remis, Malay. 89/C1
Pantanal (reg.), Braz. 189/E1
Pantanal (reg.), Braz. 186/A3
Pantanal Matogrossense PN, Braz. 188/E1
Pantano Wash (riv.), Az, US 149/G4
Pantar (isl.), Indo. 128/A2
Pante Makasar, ETim. 128/B2
Pantego, NC, US 163/J3
Pantego, Tx, US 150/K7
Pantelleria, It. 48/B4
Pantelleria (isl.), It. 29/F5
Pantha, Myan. 93/F3
Panther Swamp NWR, Ms, US 162/B4
Panthersville, Ga, US 163/M7
Panti, Indo. 89/C2
Pantigliate, It. 62/C3
Pantijan Abor. Land, Austl. 128/B4
Pantin, Fr. 30/K5
Pantoja, Peru 180/C5
Pantón, Sp. 46/B1
Pantukan, Phil. 88/D4
Panu, D.R. Congo 120/D3
Pánuco (riv.), Mex. 172/B3
Pánuco, Mex. 176/B1
Panwol, SKor. 81/F7
Panyabungan, Indo. 89/B2
Panyam, Nga. 115/H4
Panzhihua, China 86/D3
Panzós, Guat. 176/D3
Pao (riv.), Ven. 183/M8
Pão de Açúcar, Braz. 187/F1
Paola, It. 48/E3
Paola, Ks, US 153/G1
Paola, Fl, US 164/N6
Paola, Malta 48/M7
Paoli, In, US 162/D1
Paoli, Ok, US 153/F3
Paoli, Pa, US 168/C3
Paonia, Co, US 149/J1
Paonta Sahib, India 98/D4
Paoua, CAfr. 116/C4
Paoy Pet, Camb. 94/C3
Paozi, China 81/B1
Paoziyan, China 81/C2
Pap, Uzb. 99/B3
Pápa, Hun. 50/C2
Papa Westray (isl.), Sc, UK 31/V14
Papagayo (gulf), CR 172/D5
Papago Ind. Res., Az, US 149/F4
Papakura, NZ 135/F7
Papantla, Mex. 175/M6
Papaplaya, Peru 184/C2
Papar, Malay. 88/A4
Papara, FrPol. 137/X15
Papatoetoe, NZ 135/F6
Papeete (cap.), FrPol. 137/X15
Papeete (Faaa) (int'l arpt.), FrPol. 137/X15
Papenburg, Ger. 53/E2
Papendrecht, Neth. 52/B5
Papenoo, FrPol. 137/X15
Papetoai, FrPol. 137/X15
Paphos, Cyp. 104/C2
Paphos (dist.), Cyp. 104/C2
Papilė, Lith. 41/K3
Papillion, Ne, US 155/F3
Papineauville, Qu, Can. 161/J2
Papingut (peak), Alb. 49/G2
Papiu, Sudan 117/F4
Paposo, Chile 188/B3
Pāppadāhāndi, India 95/D2
Pappenheim, Ger. 58/D5
Papua (gulf), PNG 129/G2
Papua New Guinea (ctry.) 136/D5
Papudo, Chile 190/C2
Papun, Myan. 94/B2
Papunya, Austl. 131/F2
Paquera, CR 177/E4
Pará (state), Braz. 181/G5
Pará (riv.), Braz. 186/D3
Para (riv.), Braz. 182/D3
Pará (falls), Ven. 181/E3
Para (dist.), Sur. 181/H3
Pará de Minas, Braz. 186/D3
Para de Oeste (riv.), Braz. 181/H4
Para Wirra NP, Austl. 131/M8
Para, South (riv.), Austl. 131/M8
Paraburdoo, Austl. 130/C2
Paracale, Phil. 88/C2
Paracambi, Braz. 187/N7
Paracas (pen.), Peru 184/B4
Paracas, Res. Nacional, Peru 184/B4
Paracatu, Braz. 186/D3
Paracatu (riv.), Braz. 186/D3
Paracel (isls.), Asia 86/F5
Parachilna, Austl. 131/H4
Paracho de Verduzco, Mex. 174/E5
Parachute, Co, US 147/J4
Paraćin, Serb. 50/E4
Paracuru, Braz. 183/G3
Paradhísion (int'l arpt.), Gre. 102/B2
Paradip, India 92/E3
Paradise, Nf, Can. 159/L2
Paradise, Guy. 182/B1
Paradise, Ca, US 146/C4
Paradise, Ks, US 154/E4
Paradise, Mi, US 160/D1
Paradise, Mt, US 144/G4
Paradise, Nv, US 148/E2
Paradise, Pa, US 168/B4
Paradise, Tx, US 150/K6
Paradise Hills, NM, US 149/J3
Paradise Valley, Az, US 149/G4
Paradise Valley, Ab, Can. 145/J1
Paradox, Co, US 149/H1
Parafield (arpt.), Austl. 131/M8
Parafiyivka, Ukr. 73/G1
Paragominas, Braz. 183/E3
Paragonah, Ut, US 149/F2
Paragould, Ar, US 162/B2
Paragua (riv.), Ven. 181/F3
Paraguá (riv.), Bol. 185/F4
Paraguaçu (riv.), Braz. 179/E4
Paraguaçu, Braz. 187/L6
Paraguaçu Paulista, Braz. 189/G2
Paraguai (riv.), SAm. 179/D5
Paraguaipoa, Ven. 180/D2
Paraguaná (pen.), Ven. 173/G5
Paraguarí (dept.), Par. 189/E3
Paraguarí, Par. 189/E3
Paraguay (ctry.) 188/D2
Paraguay (riv.), Par. 186/A4
Paraiba (riv.), Braz. 189/J2
Paraiba (state), Braz. 183/G4
Paraíba do Sul (riv.), Braz. 179/E5
Paraíba do Sul, Braz. 187/N7
Paraibano, Braz. 183/F4
Paraibuna (riv.), Braz. 187/L8
Paraim (riv.), Braz. 186/D1
Parainen (Pargas), Fin. 41/K1
Paraíso, CR 177/F4
Paraíso, Mex. 176/C2
Paraíso do Norte, Braz. 189/F2
Paraíso do Tocantins, Braz. 186/C1
Paraisópolis, Braz. 187/L7
Parakou, Ben. 115/F4
Parama (isl.), PNG 129/F2
Paramakkudi, India 95/C4
Paramaribo (dist.), Sur. 181/H3
Paramaribo (cap.), Sur. 182/C1
Parambu, Braz. 183/F4
Paramillo (peak), Col. 180/C3
Paramillo, PN, Col. 173/F6
Paramirim (riv.), Braz. 187/E2
Paramirim, Braz. 187/E2
Paramithía, Gre. 49/G3
Paramoti, Braz. 183/G4
Paramount, Ca, US 166/F8
Paramus, NJ, US 169/J8
Paramushir (isl.), Rus. 77/Q5
Paraná (riv.), SAm. 179/D5
Paranã (riv.), Braz. 186/D2
Paraná (state), Braz. 186/C4
Paraná, Arg. 188/D4
Paranã, Braz. 186/D2
Paraná Ibicuy (riv.), Arg. 191/J10
Paraná Madeirinha (riv.), Braz. 182/B4
Paraná Urariá (riv.), Braz. 181/G5
Paranaguá (bay), Braz. 189/G3
Paranaguá, Braz. 189/G3
Paranaíba, Braz. 189/G1
Paranaíba (riv.), Braz. 186/D3
Paranapanema (riv.), Braz. 189/G2
Paranapiacaba, Serra do (mts.), Braz. 186/C5
Parañaque, Phil. 88/E6
Paranatinga (riv.), Braz. 179/D4
Paranavaí, Braz. 189/F2
Parang, Phil. 88/C4
Paraopeba, Braz. 186/D3
Paraopeba (riv.), Braz. 186/D3
Parapara, Ven. 183/N8
Paraparaumu (arpt.), NZ 135/H8
Paraparaumu, NZ 135/J8
Parapetí (riv.), Bol. 188/D1
Parás, Mex. 150/E4
Parāsi, Nepal 96/D2
Parati, Braz. 187/M8
Paratico, It. 62/C2
Paratinga (riv.), Braz. 187/L8
Paratinga, Braz. 187/E2
Paraúna, Braz. 186/C3
Paravūr, India 95/C4
Paray-Vieille-Poste, Fr. 30/K5
Paràzinho, Braz. 183/H4
Pārbati (riv.), India 101/L4
Pārbatipur, Bang. 97/G3
Parçay-Meslay, Fr. 57/F6
Parcé-sur-Sarthe, Fr. 57/E5
Parchim, Ger. 42/F2
Parczew, Pol. 43/M3
Pardes Hanna-Karkur, Isr. 105/B4
Pārdi, India 101/K4
Parding, China 99/E5
Pardo (riv.), Braz. 189/H2
Pardo (riv.), Braz. 186/B4
Pardone (cape), SAfr. 124/D4
Pardoo, Austl. 130/C2
Pardubice, Czh. 43/H3
Pardubický (pol. reg.), Czh. 43/J4
Pare, Indo. 89/F4
Pare (mts.), Tanz. 119/B2
Parece Vela (Okino-Tori-Shima) (isl.), Japan 77/N7
Parecis (mts.), Braz. 179/C4
Parede, Port. 47/P10
Paredes de Nava, Sp. 46/C1
Paredón, Mex. 150/D5
Paredón, Mex. 176/C2
Paredones, Chile 190/C2
Parelhas, Braz. 183/G4
Parempuyre, Fr. 44/C4
Parenda, India 95/B2
Parentis-en-Born, Fr. 44/C4
Parepare, Indo. 91/E4
Parera, Arg. 190/D2
Parets del Valles, Sp. 47/L6
Pargas (Parainen), Fin. 41/K1
Pargny-sur-Saulx, Fr. 55/D6
Pargolovo, Rus. 69/T6
Paria, Bol. 188/C1
Paria (riv.), Ut, US 149/G2
Paria (gulf), Ven. 181/F2
Paria (pen.), Ven. 173/J5
Pariacoto, Peru 184/B3
Pariaguán, Ven. 181/E2
Pariaman, Indo. 89/C3
Parichi, Bela. 70/D1
Parigi, Indo. 91/F4
Parigné-L'Évêque, Fr. 57/F5
Parikkala, Fin. 38/J3
Parima (mts.), Braz. 181/E4
Parima (riv.), Braz. 181/F4
Parinacota (peak), Bol. 184/D5
Parinacota (peak), Bol.,Chile 188/B1
Parinari, Peru 184/C2
Pariñas (pt.), Peru 184/A2
Paringa, Austl. 132/B2
Parîngu Mare (peak), Rom. 51/F3
Parintins, Braz. 182/B3
Paris, Tx, US 153/G4
Paris, Ar, US 153/H3
Paris (dept.), Fr. 54/B6
Paris, On, Can. 160/F3
Paris, Me, US 161/L2
Paris, Il, US 160/C5
Paris (cap.), Fr. 30/K5
Paris, Id, US 147/H2
Paris, Tn, US 162/C2
Paris, Ky, US 162/E1
Paris, Ms, US 162/C3
Paris, Mo, US 155/H4
Paris (Le Bourget) (arpt.), Fr. 30/K5
Parishville, NY, US 161/J2
Parita (bay), Pan. 177/F4
Park (riv.), ND, US 156/F3
Park (range), Co, US 147/K3
Park (pt.), Eng, UK 36/A5
Park City, Ks, US 153/F2
Park City, Il, US 167/Q15
Park City, Ky, US 162/D2
Park Falls, Wi, US 157/J5
Park Forest, Il, US 160/C4
Park Hill, Ok, US 153/G3
Park Rapids, Mn, US 157/G4
Park Ridge, Il, US 167/Q16
Park Ridge, NJ, US 169/J7
Park River, ND, US 156/F3
Park Valley, Ut, US 147/G3
Park View, Ia, US 155/J3
Parkano, Fin. 38/G3
Parkbeg, Sk, Can. 145/L2
Parkchester (nbrhd.), NY, US 169/K8
Parkdale, Ar, US 153/J4
Parkdale, Or, US 146/C1
Parker, Ks, US 153/G1
Parker, Pa, US 161/G4
Parker (lake), Fl, US 164/M7
Parker, Az, US 148/E3
Parker, SD, US 155/F2
Parker, Co, US 154/B4
Parker (peak), SD, US 154/C2
Parker (pt.), Austl. 129/E4
Parker (co.), Tx, US 150/K7
Parker, Tx, US 151/F1
Parker Dam, Az, Ca, US 149/E3
Parker River Nat'l Wild. Ref., Ma, US 161/L3
Parker's Cove, Nf, Can. 159/K2
Parkers Prairie, Mn, US 157/G4
Parkersburg, Ia, US 155/H2
Parkersburg, WV, US 163/G1
Parkersburg, Il, US 162/C1
Parkes, Austl. 133/D1
Parkesburg, Pa, US 168/C4
Parkeston, Eng, UK 37/H3
Parkgate, NI, UK 34/B2
Parkhill, On, Can. 160/F3
Parkhurst, Eng, UK 37/E5
Parkin, Ar, US 162/B3
Parkland, Wa, US 144/C4
Parkman, Sk, Can. 156/D3
Parks, Ar, US 153/H3
Parkside, Sk, Can. 145/L1
Parkside, Pa, US 168/C4
Parksley, Va, US 163/K2
Parkstetten, Ger. 59/F5
Parkston, SD, US 154/F2
Parksville, SC, US 163/F4
Parksville, BC, Can. 144/B3
Parkton, Md, US 168/B4
Parkton, NC, US 163/H3
Parkville, Md, US 168/B5
Parkville, Pa, US 168/B4
Parkway-Sacramento, Ca, US 167/L9
Parkwood, NC, US 163/H3
Parla, Sp. 47/N9
Parliament Buildings, NZ 135/H9
Parlier, Ca, US 148/C2
Parlin, Co, US 149/J1
Parma, Oh, US 160/F4
Parma (prov.), It. 62/C3
Parma, It. 62/D4
Parma (riv.), It. 62/D3
Parma, Id, US 146/E2
Parma, Mo, US 162/C2
Parmain, Fr. 30/J4
Parmelee, SD, US 154/D2
Parnaguá, Braz. 186/D1
Parnaíba (riv.), Braz. 179/E3
Parnaíba, Braz. 183/F3
Parnamirim, Braz. 183/G5
Parnarama, Braz. 183/F4
Parnassós (peak), Gre. 49/H3
Parnassós NP, Gre. 49/H3
Parnassus, NZ 135/C3
Parndana, Austl. 131/H5
Parnell, Tx, US 152/D3
Parnell (nbrhd.), NZ 135/F6
Párnis (peak), Gre. 49/N8
Párnis Óros NP, Gre. 49/N8
Párnon (mts.), Gre. 49/H4
Pärnu, Est. 41/L2
Pärnu (bay), Est. 41/L2
Pärnu-Jaagupi, Est. 41/L2
Paro, Bhu. 97/G2
Paron, Fr. 44/E2
Parona di Valpolicella, It. 63/D3
Paroo (riv.), Austl. 127/D3
Páros, Gre. 49/J4
Páros (isl.), Gre. 67/K3
Parow, SAfr. 124/L10
Parowan, Ut, US 149/F2
Parpan, Swi. 61/F4
Parrachée (mtn.), Fr. 64/C2
Parral, Chile 190/C3
Parramatta (nbrhd.), Austl. 134/H8
Parramore (isl.), Md, US 163/K2
Parras de la Fuente, Mex. 174/E3
Parrett (riv.), Eng, UK 36/D4
Parris Island, SC, US 163/G4
Parris Island Marine Base, SC, US 163/G4
Parrish, Fl, US 164/L8
Parrish, Al, US 162/D4
Parrita, CR 177/E4
Parrot Jungle, Fl, US 164/P11
Parrott, Ga, US 165/F2
Parr's Halt, Bots. 123/E4
Parrsboro, NS, Can. 158/E3
Parry (chan.), Can. 139/F2
Parry (isls.), Can. 139/F2
Parry (bay), Nun, Can. 141/H2
Parry Sound, On, Can. 160/F2
Parsberg, Ger. 59/E4
Parseierspitze (peak), Aus. 61/G3
Parshall, ND, US 156/C4
Parsippany-Troy Hills, NJ, US 169/H8
Parson, BC, Can. 144/F2
Parsons, Ks, US 153/G2
Parsons (mtn.), SC, US 163/F3
Parsons, Tn, US 162/C3
Parsons (mt.), Austl. 129/D3
Parsons (range), Austl. 129/D3
Parsons, WV, US 163/H1
Partago, Ben. 115/F4
Pårtefjället (peak), Swe. 38/F2
Partenstein, Ger. 58/C2
Parthenay, Fr. 44/C3
Partille, Swe. 40/E3
Partinico, It. 48/C3
Partizansk, Rus. 79/L3
Partizánske, Slvk. 43/K4
Partridge, Ks, US 153/E2
Partry (mts.), Ire. 32/A2
Partūr, India 92/C4
Paru (riv.), Braz. 181/H4
Paru de Oeste (riv.), Braz. 179/D2
Paruro, Peru 184/D4
Pārvathīpuram, India 95/D2
Parwich, Eng, UK 35/G5
Paryang, China 99/D5
Parys, SAfr. 124/D2
Pas de Morgins (pass), Fr. 60/C5
Pas-de-Calais (dept.), Fr. 54/A3
Pasadena, Nf, Can. 159/J1
Pasadena (lake), Fl, US 164/L7
Pasadena, Ca, US 166/F7
Pasadena, Tx, US 151/M9
Pasadena, Md, US 168/B5
Pasado (cape), Ecu. 180/A5
Pasaje, Ecu. 184/B1
Pasaman (peak), Indo. 89/C2
Pasān, India 96/D4
Pasanauri, Geo. 71/H4
Pasarbantal, Indo. 89/C3
Pasarkuok, Indo. 89/C3
Pasarsorkam, Indo. 89/B2
Pasarwajo, Indo. 128/A1
Pasawng, Myan. 94/B2
Pasay, Phil. 88/F6
Pascagoula (riv.), Ms, US 164/D2
Pascagoula, Ms, US 164/D2
Paşcani, Rom. 72/D4
Pasching, Aus. 59/H6
Pasco (co.), Fl, US 164/L7
Pasco, Fl, US 164/L7
Pasco (dept.), Peru 184/C3
Pasco, Wa, US 144/E4
Pascua (riv.), Chile 191/B6
Pascua, Isla de (Easter) (isl.), Chile 137/Q7
Pascuales, Ecu. 184/B1
Pasewalk, Ger. 40/E5
Pashkovo, Rus. 71/G1
Pashkovskiy, Rus. 73/K5
Pasian di Prato, It. 63/G1
Pasiano, It. 63/F2
Pasig, Phil. 88/F6
Pāsighāt, India 86/B2
Pasinler, Turk. 102/E2
Pasión, Río de la (riv.), Guat. 176/D2
Pasir Mas, Malay. 89/C1
Pasir Puteh, Malay. 89/C1
Pasłęk, Pol. 41/H4
Pasłęka (riv.), Pol. 43/L2
Pasley (cape), Austl. 130/D5
Pašman (isl.), Cro. 45/L5
Pasni, Pak. 101/H3
Paso de Indios, Arg. 190/C4
Paso de la Patria, Arg. 188/E3
Paso de los Libres, Arg. 189/E4
Paso de los Toros, Uru. 191/K10
Paso de Ovejas, Mex. 175/N7
Paso de Patria, Par. 188/E3
Paso del Cerro, Uru. 189/F4
Paso del Macho, Mex. 175/N8
Paso del Planchón (peak), Chile 190/C2
Paso Flores, Arg. 190/C4
Paso Real, Ven. 183/P8
Paso Robles (El Paso de Robles), Ca, US 148/B3
Paspébiac, Qu, Can. 158/E1
Pasrūr, Pak. 98/C3
Pass Christian, Ms, US 164/D2
Pass Peak (mt.), Yk, Can. 171/M3
Passa Quatro, Braz. 187/M7
Passage East, Ire. 32/D5
Passage Key Nat'l Wild. Ref., Fl, US 165/G4
Passage West, Ire. 32/B6
Passagem Franca, Braz. 183/F4
Passaic, NJ, US 169/J8
Passaic (riv.), NJ, US 168/D2
Passais, Fr. 57/E3
Passau, Ger. 59/G5
Passero (pt.), It. 48/D4
Passi, Phil. 88/C3
Passignano sul Trasimeno, It. 65/B1
Passo Corese, It. 65/B3
Passo Fundo, Braz. 189/F4
Passo Fundo, Barragem do (res.), Braz. 189/F3
Passons, It. 63/G1
Passoré (prov.), Burk. 115/E3
Passos, Braz. 189/H2
Passwang (peak), Swi. 60/D3
Passy, Fr. 60/C6
Pastavy, Bela. 41/M4
Pastaza (riv.), Peru 180/B5
Pastaza (dept.), Ecu. 180/B5
Pastaza (riv.), Ecu.,Peru 179/B3
Pastek (riv.), Pol. 41/J5
Pasto, Col. 180/B4
Pastol (bay), Ak, US 171/F3
Pastoriza, Sp. 46/B1
Pastos Bons, Braz. 183/E4
Pastura (peak), Az, US 149/H2
Pasuquin, Phil. 88/C1
Pasuruan, Indo. 89/F4
Pasvalys, Lith. 41/L3
Pásztó, Hun. 43/K5
Pata, CAfr. 116/D3
Pata, Bol. 184/D4
Patacamaya, Bol. 188/C1
Patag NP, Phil. 88/C3
Patagonia (phys. reg.), Arg. 179/B8
Patagonia, Az, US 149/G5
Patah (peak), Indo. 90/B4
Patamdesar, India 98/C5
Pātan, India 96/B4
Pātan, India 101/K4
Pāţan (Lalitpur), Nepal 97/E2
Pataná (peak), Braz. 189/G3
Patani, Nga. 115/G5
Patani, Indo. 91/G3
Patapédia (riv.), Qu, Can. 158/D1
Patapsco, Md, US 168/B4
Patapsco (riv.), Md, US 168/A5
Pataudi, India 98/D5
Patay, Fr. 57/G4
Pataz, Peru 184/B2
Patchewollock, Austl. 132/B2
Patchogue, NY, US 169/E2
Patchway, Eng, UK 36/D3
Pate (isl.), Kenya 119/C2
Patea, NZ 135/C2
Pategi, Nga. 115/G4
Pateley Bridge, Eng, UK 35/G3
Patenga, Bang. 97/H4
Paterna, Sp. 47/E3
Paternion, Aus. 45/K3
Paternò, It. 48/D4
Paterno, It. 65/C3
Pateros, Wa, US 144/E3
Paterson, NJ, US 169/J8
Paterson, Austl. 133/E1
Paterson (cape), Austl. 133/B4
Pathalgaon, India 96/D4
Pathanāmthitta, India 95/C4
Pathānkot, India 98/C3
Pātharghāta, Bang. 97/G4
Patharkot, Nepal 97/E2
Pathein (Bassein), Myan. 86/B5
Pathfinder (dam), Wy, US 147/K2
Pathfinder (res.), Wy, US 147/K2
Pathfinder NWR, Wy, US 147/K2
Pathiu, Thai. 94/B4
Pathlow, Sk, Can. 145/M1
Pati, Indo. 89/E4
Pati, Indo. 128/B2
Patía (riv.), Col. 180/B4
Patía, Col. 180/B4
Patiāla, India 98/D4
Patikul, Phil. 88/C4
Pātiram, India 97/G3
Patiya, Bang. 97/H4
Patkaglik, China 99/E4
Patna, Sc, UK 33/B6
Patna, India 97/E3
Patnāgarh, India 95/D1
Patnanongan (isl.), Phil. 88/C2
Patnongon, Phil. 88/C3
Patnos, Turk. 103/E2
Pato Branco, Braz. 189/F3
Patoka, In, US 162/D1
Patoka (riv.), In, US 162/D1
Patoka (lake), In, US 162/D1
Patos, Alb. 49/F2
Patos, Braz. 183/G4
Patos de Minas, Braz. 186/D3
Patos, dos (lake), Braz. 189/G4
Patoutville, La, US 164/C3
Patquía, Arg. 188/C4
Pátrai, Gre. 49/G3
Patrai (gulf), Gre. 49/G3
Pātrasāer, India 97/F4
Patrātu, India 97/E4
Patricia (mt.), Austl. 131/F2
Patricia, Ab, Can. 145/J2
Patricia, Tx, US 150/C1
Patricio Lynch (isl.), Chile 191/A6
Patrick (A.F.B.), Fl, US 165/H3
Patrick Springs, Va, US 163/G2
Patrington, Eng, UK 35/H4
Patrocínio, Braz. 186/D3
Patroon, Tx, US 151/H2
Patsaliga (cr.), Al, US 165/E2
Patscherkofel (peak), Aus. 61/H3
Pattani, Thai. 94/C5
Pattensen, Ger. 53/G4
Patterson, Ar, US 153/J3
Patterson, Ga, US 165/G2
Patterson, La, US 164/C3
Patterson, Mo, US 162/B2
Patti, It. 48/D3
Patti, India 98/C4
Pattingham, Eng, UK 36/D1
Pattison, Ms, US 164/C2
Pattoki, Pak. 98/B4
Patton, Pa, US 161/G4
Pattonsburg, Mo, US 155/G3
Pattukkottai, India 95/C4
Pattullo (mt.), BC, Can. 171/N4
Patu, Braz. 183/G4
Patuākhāli, Bang. 97/H4
Patuākhāli (pol. reg.), Bang. 97/G4
Patuca (riv.), Hon. 172/D5
Patuca (pt.), Hon. 177/E3
Patuca (mts.), Hon. 176/E3
Patuha (peak), Indo. 89/D4
Pătulele, Rom. 50/F3
Patuxent (riv.), Md, US 168/B5
Patuxent NWR, Md, US 168/B5
Patuxent River State Park, Md, US 168/B5
Páty, Hun. 51/Q9
Pátzcuaro, Mex. 175/E5
Pau, Fr. 44/C5
Pau dos Ferros, Braz. 183/G4
Paucarbamba, Peru 184/C4
Paucartambo, Peru 184/D4
Paucartambo, Peru 184/C3
Pauillac, Fr. 44/C4
Pauini (riv.), Braz. 185/E2
Pauini, Braz. 185/E2
Pauksa (peak), Myan. 86/B5
Pauktaw, Myan. 94/B2
Paul B. Wurtsmith (A.F.B.), Mi, US 160/E2
Paul Isnard, FrG. 182/C1
Paul Smiths, NY, US 161/J2
Paulaya (riv.), Hon. 176/E3
Paulden, Az, US 149/F3
Paulding, Oh, US 160/D4
Paulding, Ms, US 164/D1
Paulding (co.), Ga, US 163/L7
Paulina, Or, US 146/D1
Pauline, Ks, US 153/G1
Pauline (mt.), BC, Can. 144/E1
Paulínia, Braz. 187/J7
Paulins Kill (riv.), NJ, US 168/D2
Paulista, Braz. 183/H4
Paulistana, Braz. 183/F5
Paullina, Ia, US 155/G2
Paullo, It. 62/C3
Paulo Afonso, Braz. 183/G5
Paulo Afonso, PN de, Braz. 183/G5
Paulo Ramos, Braz. 183/E4
Paulpietersburg, SAfr. 125/E2
Pauls Valley, Ok, US 153/F3
Paulsboro, NJ, US 168/C4
Paulton, Eng, UK 36/D4
Pauma Valley, Ca, US 166/D4
Pauna, Col. 183/M7
Paungde, Myan. 86/B5
Pauri, India 99/C5
Pausa, Ger. 59/E1
Pavant (range), Ut, US 147/G4
Pavão, Braz. 187/E3
Pāveh, Iran 103/F3
Pavel Banya, Bul. 49/J1
Pavia, It. 62/C3
Pavia (prov.), It. 62/C2
Pavie, Fr. 44/D5
Pavilion, BC, Can. 144/D2
Pavillion, Wy, US 147/J2
Pavilly, Fr. 57/F1
Pāvilosta, Lat. 41/J3
Pavino, Rus. 69/K4
Pavlikeni, Bul. 51/G4
Pavlodar, Kaz. 99/C1
Pavlodar Oblast, Kaz. 99/B1
Pavlof (vol.), Ak, US 171/F4
Pavlohrad, Ukr. 73/H3
Pavlovo, Rus. 68/J5
Pavlovsk, Rus. 69/T7
Pavlovsk, Rus. 73/L2
Pavlovskaya, Rus. 73/K4
Pavlovskiy, Kaz. 69/P5
Pavlysh, Ukr. 73/G3
Pavo, Ga, US 165/G2
Pavón, Col. 180/C4
Pavone Canavese, It. 62/A2
Pavone del Mella, It. 62/D3
Pavullo nel Frignano, It. 63/D5
Pavy, Rus. 41/N2
Paw Paw, Mi, US 160/D3
Paw Paw Lake, Mi, US 160/C3
Pawa, D.R. Congo 121/F2
Pawan (riv.), Indo. 90/D4
Pawāyan, India 96/C1
Pawé (peak), Camr. 116/A4
Pawhuska, Ok, US 153/F2
Pawia, Gha. 115/E4
Pawn (riv.), Myan. 86/C4
Pawnee, Ok, US 153/F2
Pawnee (riv.), Ks, US 154/E4
Pawnee, Il, US 155/K4
Pawnee Buttes (butte), Co, US 154/C3
Pawnee City, Ne, US 155/F3
Pawnee Indian Village, Ks, US 154/F4
Pawnee Rock, Ks, US 152/E1
Pawtucket, RI, US 161/L4
Paxoí (isl.), Gre. 67/H3
Paxoí (Yáios), Gre. 49/G3
Paxson, Ak, US 171/J3
Paxton, Austl. 133/E1
Paxton, Il, US 160/B4
Paxton, Tx, US 151/G2
Pay, Rus. 68/G3
Pay-Khoy (mts.), Rus. 74/G3
Payagyi, Myan. 94/B2
Payaheislam, Indo. 91/G3
Payakumbuh, Indo. 89/C3
Payerne, Swi. 60/C4
Payette, Id, US 146/E1
Payette (riv.), Id, US 146/E2
Payette, North Fork (riv.), Id, US 146/E1
Payette, South Fork (riv.), Id, US 146/E1
Payne (cr.), Fl, US 164/M8
Payne (lake), Qu, Can. 141/J3
Paynes Find, Austl. 130/C4
Paynesville, Mn, US 157/G5
Paynesville, Austl. 133/C3
Paynton, Sk, Can. 145/K1
Pays de Caux (reg.), Fr. 44/D2
Pays de France (reg.), Fr. 30/K4
Pays de la Loire (pol. reg.), Fr. 56/D5
Pays de la Loire (reg.), Fr. 44/C3
Paysandú, Uru. 191/J10
Paysandú (dept.), Uru. 189/E5
Payson, Ut, US 147/H3
Payson, Az, US 149/G3
Payson, Il, US 155/J4
Payún (peak), Arg. 190/C3
Payyannūr, India 95/B3
Paz (riv.), Guat. 176/D3
Paz de Ariporo, Col. 180/D3
Paz de Río, Col. 180/C3
Pāzanān, Iran 103/G4
Pazar, Turk. 102/D1
Pazar, Turk. 71/G4
Pazarcık, Turk. 102/D2
Pazardzhik, Bul. 49/J1
Pazaryeri, Turk. 70/D5
Pazin, Cro. 45/K4
Pe Ell, Wa, US 144/C4
Pea (riv.), Al, US 165/F2
Pea Ridge, Ar, US 153/G2
Peabiru, Braz. 189/F2
Peabody, Ks, US 153/F1
Peabody, Ma, US 161/L3
Peace (riv.), BC, Can. 140/D3
Peace (riv.), Can. 139/F4
Peace Memorial Park, Japan 84/C3
Peace River, Ab, Can. 140/E3
Peace Valley, Mo, US 153/J2
Peach Springs, Az, US 149/F3
Peachland, BC, Can. 144/E3
Peachtree (cr.), Ga, US 163/M7
Peachtree City, Ga, US 162/E4
Peak Charles NP, Austl. 130/D5
Peak District NP, Eng, UK 35/G5
Peak Hill, Austl. 130/C3
Peak Hill, Austl. 133/D1
Peakeen (mtn.), Ire. 32/A6
Peal de Becerro, Sp. 46/D4
Peale (mt.), Ut, US 149/H1
Peapack-Gladstone, NJ, US 168/D2
Pearblossom, Ca, US 166/C1
Pearce (pt.), Austl. 128/C3
Pearisburg, Va, US 163/G2
Pearl (riv.), La,Ms, US 143/J5
Pearl, Ms, US 162/B4
Pearl, Tx, US 150/E2
Pearl and Hermes (reef), Hi, US 137/H2
Pearl Beach, Mi, US 167/G6
Pearl City, Il, US 155/K2
Pearl River (est.), China 87/G4
Pearl River, NY, US 169/J7
Pearland, Ca, US 166/B1
Pearland, Tx, US 151/M9
Pearsall, Tx, US 150/E3
Pearson, Ga, US 165/G2
Pearson (int'l arpt.), On, Can. 160/T8
Pearston, SAfr. 124/D4
Peary (chan.), Nun, Can. 141/R7
Pease, Mn, US 157/H5
Pease (riv.), Tx, US 152/E3
Peaugres, Fr. 64/A2
Péaule, Fr. 56/C5
Pebane, Moz. 123/H3
Pebas, Peru 184/D1
Pebble (isl.), Mald. 191/E6
Pebworth, Eng, UK 37/E2
Peć, Serb. 50/E4
Pecan (bayou), Tx, US 151/E2
Pecan Island, La, US 164/B3
Peccia, Swi. 61/E5
Peccioli, It. 63/D6
Pécel, Hun. 51/R10
Pech de Guillaument (peak), Fr. 44/E5
Pechanga Ind. Res., Ca, US 166/C4
Pechanga Ind. Res., Ca, US 148/D4
Pechea, Rom. 51/H3
Pechenga, Rus. 68/F1
Pechengi (res.), Ukr. 73/J3
Pechora, Rus. 69/N2
Pechora (bay), Rus. 69/M1
Pechora (riv.), Rus. 77/C3
Pechory, Rus. 41/M3
Pecica, Rom. 50/E2
Peckham, Ok, US 153/F2
Pecks Pond (pond), Pa, US 168/C1
Peclet, Aiguille de (peak), Fr. 64/C2
Peconic (riv.), NY, US 169/F2
Pecos (riv.), NM,Tx, US 150/D3
Pecos, Tx, US 150/C2
Pecos Nat'l Hist. Park, NM, US 152/B3
Pecq, Belg. 54/C2
Pecquencourt, Fr. 54/C3
Pécs, Hun. 50/D2
Pecy, Fr. 30/M6
Pedasí, Pan. 180/A3
Pedaso, It. 65/C1
Peddāpuram, India 95/D2
Pedder (lake), Austl. 127/D5
Peddie, SAfr. 124/D4
Pedemonte, It. 63/D3
Pedernales, Ven. 181/F2
Pedernales (riv.), Tx, US 175/F2
Pédernec, Fr. 56/B3
Pederneiras, Braz. 189/G2
Pedirka, Austl. 131/G3
Pedley, Ca, US 166/C3
Pedley, Ab, Can. 144/F1
Pedra Azul, Braz. 187/E3
Pedra do Feitiço, Ang. 120/C4
Pedra Lume, CpV. 107/K10
Pedralva, Braz. 187/L7
Pedregal, Ven. 180/D2
Pedreguer, Sp. 47/F3
Pedreira, Braz. 187/K7
Pedreiras, Braz. 183/E4
Pedricktown, NJ, US 168/C4
Pedro (pt.), SrL. 95/D4
Pedro, SD, US 154/C1
Pedro Afonso, Braz. 182/D5
Pedro Avelino, Braz. 183/G4
Pedro Bay, Ak, US 171/H4
Pedro Betancourt, Cuba 177/F1
Pedro Carbo, Ecu. 180/A5
Pedro Cays (isl.), Jam. 173/F4
Pedro Chico, Col. 180/D4
Pedro Gomes, Braz. 189/F1
Pedro II Braz. 183/F4
Pedro IV (isl.), Braz. 181/E4
Pedro Juan Caballero, Par. 189/F2
Pedro Leopoldo, Braz. 186/D3
Pedro Luro, Arg. 190/E3
Pedro Montt, Chile 188/B3
Pedro Osório, Braz. 189/F4
Pedro R. Fernández, Arg. 188/E4
Peduyim, Isr. 105/B6
Pee Dee (riv.), NC, US 163/G3
Pee Dee NWR, NC, US 163/G3
Peebles, Sc, UK 33/C5
Peebles, Oh, US 163/F1
Peedamulla Abor. Land, Austl. 130/B2
Peekskill, NY, US 168/E1
Peel (isl.), Austl. 134/F6
Peel (inlet), Austl. 130/B5
Peel (sound), Nun, Can. 140/G1
Peel (co.), On, Can. 160/T8
Peel (riv.), Yk, Can. 140/C2
Peel, IM, UK 34/D3
Peel Fell (peak), Eng, UK 33/D6
Peeltown, Tx, US 150/L7
Peene (riv.), Ger. 40/E5
Peer, Belg. 55/E1
Peerless, Mt, US 145/M3
Peers, Ab, Can. 144/F1
Peetz, Co, US 154/C3
Pegarah, Austl. 133/B4
Pegasus (bay), NZ 135/C3
Pegli, It. 62/B5
Peglia (peak), It. 65/B2
Pegnitz (riv.), Ger. 42/F4
Pegnitz, Ger. 59/E3
Pego, Sp. 47/E3
Pego do Altar (res.), Port. 46/A3
Pegognaga, It. 63/D4
Pégomas, Fr. 64/C5
Pegswood, Eng, UK 35/G1
Pegu (Bago), Myan. 86/C5
Peguis Ind. Res., Mb, Can. 156/F2
Pegwell (bay), Eng, UK 37/H4
Pehlivanköy, Turk. 51/H5
Péhonko, Ben. 115/F4
Pehowa, India 98/D5
Pehuajó, Arg. 190/E2
Pehuenche (pass), Chile 190/C2
Pei Xian, China 80/D4
Peigan Ind. Res., Ab, Can. 145/H3
Peijiachuankou, China 80/B3
Peikang, Tai. 87/J4
Peillac, Fr. 56/C5
Peine, Chile 188/B2
Peine, Ger. 53/H4
Peipus (lake), Est.,Rus. 74/C4
Peitawu (peak), Tai. 87/J4
Peiting, Ger. 61/G2
Peixe, Braz. 186/C2
Peixe, Rio do (riv.), Braz. 186/C2
Peixoto (res.), Braz. 186/D4
Pejantan (isl.), Indo. 89/D2
Pejerreyes, Chile 188/B4
Pekalongan, Indo. 89/E4
Pekan, Malay. 89/C2
Pekan Nanas, Malay. 90/B3
Pekhora (riv.), Rus. 69/W9
Pekin, Il, US 155/K3
Pekin (New Pekin), In, US 162/D1
Pelabuhanratu, Indo. 89/D4
Pelabuhanratu (bay), Indo. 89/D4
Pelado (vol.), Mex. 175/Q10
Pelagie (isls.), It. 67/G4
Pelahatchie, Ms, US 162/C4
Pelaihari, Indo. 90/D4
Pelalawan, Indo. 89/C2
Pelat (peak), Fr. 64/C4
Peleaga (peak), Rom. 50/F3
Peleduy, Rus. 75/M4
Pelee (pt.), On, Can. 160/E4
Pelee (isl.), On, Can. 160/E4
Pelée (peak), Fr. 173/N9
Pelequén, Chile 190/N9
Pelham, Austl. 134/A2
Pelham, Al, US 162/D4
Pelham, Ga, US 165/F2
Pelham, NY, US 169/K8
Pelham, On, Can. 160/U9
Pelham Bay Park, NY, US 169/K8
Pelham Manor, NY, US 169/K8
Pelhřimov, Czh. 43/H4
Pelican (pt.), Namb. 122/B4
Pelican, Ak, US 171/L4
Pelican (lake), Mn, US 157/N6
Pelican (isl.), Tx, US 151/N9
Pelican Island Nat'l Wild. Ref., Fl, US 165/H4
Pelican Rapids, Mn, US 156/F4
Pélissanne, Fr. 64/B5
Pelister (peak), FYROM 49/G2
Pelister NP, FYROM 49/G2
Peljekaise NP, Swe. 38/F2
Pelješac (pen.), Cro. 49/E1
Pelkie, Mi, US 157/K4
Pell City, Al, US 162/D4
Pell Lake, Wi, US 167/P14
Pélla, Gre. 49/H2
Pélla (ruin), Gre. 49/H2
Pella, Ia, US 155/H3
Pellegrini, Arg. 190/E3
Pellestrina, It. 63/F3
Péllice (riv.), It. 64/D3
Pello, Fin. 68/E2
Pellston, Mi, US 160/D2
Pelly (bay), Nun, Can. 140/H2
Pelly (riv.), Yk, Can. 140/C2
Pelly Crossing, Yk, Can. 171/L3
Peloponnesus (reg.), Gre. 67/J3
Peloritani (mts.), It. 48/D4
Pelotas (riv.), Braz. 189/G3
Pelotas, Braz. 189/F4
Pelplin, Pol. 41/H5
Pelsor, Ar, US 153/H3
Pelto (lake), La, US 164/C3
Pélussin, Fr. 64/A2
Pelvoux (peak), Fr. 64/C3
Pelvoux, Fr. 64/C3
Pemalang, Indo. 89/E4
Pemali (cape), Indo. 91/F4
Pematangsiantar, Indo. 89/B2
Pemba, Moz. 123/J2
Pemba (prov.), Tanz. 119/B3
Pemba (isl.), Tanz. 119/B3
Pemba, Zam. 123/E3
Pemba (isl.), Afr. 107/G5
Pemberton, Austl. 130/C5
Pemberton, BC, Can. 144/C2
Pemberton, NJ, US 168/D4
Pembina, ND, US 156/F3
Pembina (hills), Mb, Can. 156/E3
Pembina (riv.), Can.,US 156/E3
Pembina Historical Site, ND, US 156/F3
Pembine, Wi, US 157/L5
Pembroke, Wal, UK 36/B3
Pembroke, Fl, US 164/M8
Pembroke, Ga, US 163/G4
Pembroke, Ky, US 162/D2
Pembroke, Ma, US 161/L3
Pembroke, NC, US 163/H3
Pembroke, NH, US 161/L3
Pembroke, On, Can. 161/H2
Pembroke, Va, US 163/G2
Pembroke Dock, Wal, UK 36/B3
Pembroke Pines, Fl, US 164/P11
Pembrokeshire (co.), Wal, UK 36/A3
Pembrokeshire Coast NP, Wal, UK 36/A3
Pembury, Eng, UK 37/G4
Pemebonwon (dam), Mi, US 157/L5
Pemenee (falls), Wi, US 157/L5
Pemuco, Chile 190/B3
Pen Argyl, Pa, US 168/C2
Pen y Gurnos (peak), Wal, UK 36/C2
Pen-y-Cae, Wal, UK 35/E6
Pen-y-Ghent (peak), Eng, UK 35/F3
Pen-y-Gogarth (pt.), Wal, UK 34/E5
Peña Blanca (mtn.), Pan. 177/F4
Peña de Cerredo (mtn.), Sp. 46/C1
Pena Forte, Braz. 183/G4
Penafiel, Port. 46/A2
Peñafiel, Sp. 46/C2
Peñaflor, Chile 190/N8
Peñalara (peak), Sp. 66/C2
Penalva, Braz. 183/E3
Penamacor, Port. 46/B2
Penambulai (isl.), Indo. 129/D1
Penampang, Malay. 88/B4
Penang (int'l arpt.), Malay. 89/C1
Penápolis, Braz. 189/G2
Peñaranda de Bracamonte, Sp. 46/C2
Peñarroya (peak), Sp. 47/E2
Peñarroya-Pueblonuevo, Sp. 46/C3
Penarth, Wal, UK 36/C4
Penas (gulf), Arg. 190/B5
Peñas (cape), Arg. 191/D7
Peñas, Bol. 184/D5
Peñas (cape), Sp. 46/C1
Peñasco (riv.), NM, US 150/B1
Pencahue, Chile 190/C2
Pench (riv.), India 96/B5
Penchard, Fr. 30/L5
Penco, Chile 190/B3
Peñd (res.), Col. 183/K6
Pend Oreille (mt.), Id, US 144/F3
Pend Oreille (lake), Id, US 144/F3
Pend Orielle (riv.), Wa, US 144/F3
Pendé (riv.), CAfr. 116/C4
Pendelikón (peak), Gre. 49/N8
Pendembu, SLeo. 114/C4
Pendências, Braz. 183/G4
Pender, Ne, US 155/F2
Pender (bay), Austl. 128/A4
Pender Bay Abor. Land, Austl. 128/A4
Pendik (nbrhd.), Turk. 103/N7
Pendjar (riv.), Burk. 115/F4
Pendjari, PN de la, Ben. 115/F4
Pendle (hill), Eng, UK 35/F4
Pendleton, In, US 160/D5
Pendleton, Or, US 146/D1
Pendleton Mil. Res., Va, US 163/K2
Pendolo, Indo. 91/F4
Pendopo, Indo. 89/C3
Pendroy, Mt, US 145/H3
Pene-Mende, D.R. Congo 121/G4
Peneda-Gerês, PN, Port. 46/A2
Penedo, Braz. 187/F1
Penegoes, Wal, UK 36/C1
Penetanguishene, On, Can. 160/G2
Penfield, Pa, US 161/G4
Peng Xian, China 86/D2
Penganga (riv.), India 92/C4
Penge (nbrhd.), Eng, UK 30/C2
Penge, SAfr. 123/F5
Penge, D.R. Congo 121/F4

Penggong, China 80/K9
Penghu (isls.), Tai. 87/H4
Penghu, China 87/H3
Penghu (Pescadores) (isls.), China 87/H4
Penglai, China 80/E3
Penglaizhen, China 86/E2
Penguin, Austl. 132/C4
Penha, Braz. 189/G3
Penhalonga, Zim. 123/G3
Penhir (pt.), Fr. 56/A4
Penhold, Ab, Can. 145/H1
Penibético (mts.), Sp. 46/D4
Penice (peak), It. 62/C4
Peniche, Port. 46/A3
Penicuik, Sc, UK 33/C5
Peninsula (pt.), NY, US 161/H3
Península de Paria, PN, Ven. 181/F2
Peñíscola, Sp. 47/F2
Peñita, Chile 188/B4
Penitente, Serra do (mts.), Braz. 183/E5
Penkridge, Eng, UK 36/D1
Penmaenmawr, Wal, UK 34/E5
Penmarc'h (pt.), Fr. 56/A5
Penmarch, Fr. 56/A5
Penn, ND, US 156/E3
Penn Forest (res.), Pa, US 168/C2
Penn Hills, Pa, US 161/G4
Penn Yan, NY, US 161/H3
Penna (peak), It. 65/B1
Penna, Punta della (cape), It. 65/D3
Pennant (pt.), NS, Can. 158/F3
Pennant, Sk, Can. 145/K2
Pennask (mt.), BC, Can. 144/D3
Penne (pt.), It. 49/E2
Penne, It. 65/C3
Pennell (mt.), Ut, US 149/G2
Penner (riv.), India 92/C5
Penney Farms, Fl, US 165/H3
Penniac, NB, Can. 158/D2
Pennine Alps (mts.), Swi. 45/G4
Pennine Chain (mts.), Eng, UK 35/F2
Pennington, NJ, US 168/D3
Pennington Gap, Va, US 163/F2
Pennino (peak), It. 65/B1
Penns (cr.), Pa, US 168/A2
Penns Creek (mtn.), Pa, US 168/A2
Penns Grove, NJ, US 168/C4
Penns Park, Pa, US 168/D3
Pennsauken, NJ, US 168/C4
Pennsboro, WV, US 160/F5
Pennsburg, Pa, US 168/C3
Pennsville, NJ, US 168/C4
Pennsylvania (hill), NY, US 161/H3
Pennsylvania (state), US 161/G4
Penny (str.), Nun, Can. 141/S7
Pennypack (cr.), Pa, US 168/C3
Penobscot (bay), Me, US 158/C3
Penobscot (riv.), Me, US 158/C3
Peñol, Col. 183/K6
Penola, Austl. 132/B3
Peñón Blanco, Mex. 174/D3
Penon de Al Hoceima (isl.), Sp. 112/C2
Penong, Austl. 131/G4
Penonomé, Pan. 180/A2
Penpont, Sc, UK 34/E1
Penrhyn (Tongareva) (isl.), Cookls. 137/J5
Penrhyn Mawr (pt.), IM, UK 34/D5
Penrhyn Mawr (pt.), Wal, UK 34/D6
Penrith, Eng, UK 35/F2
Penrith (nbrhd.), Austl. 134/G8
Penrose, Co, US 152/B1
Penryn, Eng, UK 36/A6
Pensacola (mts.), Ant. 192/X
Pensacola, Fl, US 164/E2
Pensacola (bay), Fl, US 164/E2
Pensacola (dam), Ok, US 153/G2
Pense, Sk, Can. 156/B2
Penshurst, Eng, UK 30/D3
Penshurst, Austl. 132/B3
Pensiangan, Malay. 88/B4
Pensilva, Eng, UK 36/B5
Pensilvania, Col. 183/K7
Pentagon Fed. Govt. Res., Va, US 168/A6
Pentecost (isl.), Van. 136/F6
Pentecoste, Braz. 183/G3
Penteleu (peak), Rom. 51/H3
Penthalaz, Swi. 60/C4
Penticton, BC, Can. 144/E3
Penticton Ind. Res., BC, Can. 144/E3
Pentire (pt.), Eng, UK 36/B5
Pentland (hills), Sc, UK 33/C5
Pentland, Austl. 134/B3
Pentland Firth (inlet), Sc, UK 31/V14
Pentwater, Mi, US 160/C3
Pentyrch, Wal, UK 36/C3
Peñuelas, PN, Chile 190/N8
Penvénan, Fr. 56/B3
Pènwègon, Myan. 94/B2
Penwell, Tx, US 150/C2
Penwith (pen.), Eng, UK 36/A6
Penza, Rus. 71/H1
Penzenskaya Oblast, Rus. 71/G1
Penzance, Eng, UK 36/A6
Penzance, Sk, Can. 145/M2
Penzberg, Ger. 61/H2
Penzé (riv.), Fr. 56/B3
Penzhina (riv.), Rus. 75/S3
Penzhina (bay), Rus. 75/S3
Penzing, Ger. 61/G1
Penzlin, Ger. 42/G2
Peoria, Az, US 149/F4
Peoria, Il, US 155/K3
Pepe (cape), Cuba 177/F1
Pepel, SLeo. 114/B4
Pepin (lake), Mn,Wi, US 155/H1
Pepinster, Belg. 55/E2
Peqin, Alb. 49/F2
Pequaming, Mi, US 157/K4
Pequannock, NJ, US 169/H8
Pequea (cr.), Pa, US 168/B4
Pequeña Isla del Maíz (isl.), Nic. 177/F3
Pequest (riv.), NJ, US 168/D2
Pequot Lakes, Mn, US 157/G4
Perabumulih, Indo. 89/D3
Perai-Tepuí, Ven. 181/F3
Perak (riv.), Malay. 89/C1
Perak (state), Malay. 89/C1
Perales (riv.), Sp. 47/M9
Peralta, Sp. 46/E1
Peralta, Uru. 191/K10
Peralta, NM, US 149/J3
Pérama, Gre. 49/J5
Pérama, Gre. 49/N9
Peranāmbattu, India 95/C3
Percé, Qu, Can. 158/E1
Percée (peak), Fr. 60/C6
Percha (dam), NM, US 149/J4
Perche, Collines du (hills), Fr. 44/D2
Perchtoldsdorf, Aus. 51/N7
Percilla, Tx, US 151/G2
Percival, Sk, Can. 156/C2
Percival (lakes), Austl. 130/E2
Percy, Fr. 57/D3
Percy, Il, US 162/C1
Percy (isls.), Austl. 127/E3
Percy Isles (chan.), Austl. 134/C3
Perdekop, SAfr. 125/E2
Pérdhika, Gre. 49/G3
Perdido, Al, US 164/E2
Perdido (mtn.), Sp. 44/D5
Perdões, Braz. 186/D4
Perdue, Sk, Can. 145/L1
Perechyn, Ukr. 43/M4
Peregian Beach, Austl. 134/D4
Perehins'ke, Ukr. 72/C3
Pereira, Col. 183/K8
Pereira Barreto, Braz. 189/G2
Pereiro, Braz. 183/G4
Perelló, Sp. 47/F2
Peremëtnoye, Kaz. 71/J2
Peremyshl', Rus. 68/H5
Peremyshlyany, Ukr. 72/C3
Perenjori, Austl. 130/C4
Peresechnaya, Ukr. 73/H2
Pereshchepyne, Ukr. 73/H3
Pereslavl'-Zalesskiy, Rus. 68/H4
Peretola (int'l arpt.), It. 63/E6
Perevolotskiy, Rus. 71/K2
Pereyaslav-Khmel'nyts'kyy, Ukr. 72/F2
Pereyaslavka, Rus. 79/M2
Perg, Aus. 59/H6
Pergamino, Arg. 190/E2
Pergamum (ruin), Turk. 70/C5
Pergine Valsugana, It. 61/H5
Perham, Mn, US 157/G4
Peri-Mirim, Braz. 183/E3
Periam, Rom. 50/E2
Péribonca (riv.), Qu, Can. 158/B1
Perico, Cuba 177/F1
Perico, Arg. 188/C3
Pericos, Mex. 174/D3
Pericos, Mex. 174/D4
Peridot, Az, US 149/G4
Périers, Fr. 56/D2
Périgueux, Fr. 44/D4
Perijá (mts.), Ven. 177/H4
Peringat, Malay. 89/C1
Perisher Village, Austl. 133/D3
Peristéra (isl.), Gre. 49/H3
Peristéri, Gre. 49/N8
Perito Moreno, Arg. 190/C5
Perito Moreno, PN, Arg. 191/B5
Periyakulam, India 95/C4
Perkasie, Pa, US 168/C3
Perkins, Ok, US 153/F3
Perkins, Mi, US 160/C2
Perkins, Ga, US 163/G4
Perkinston, Ms, US 164/D2
Perkiomen (cr.), Pa, US 168/C3
Perl, Ger. 55/F5
Perlas (lag.), Nic. 172/E5
Perlas, (pt.), Nic. 177/F3
Perleberg, Ger. 42/F2
Perlez, Serb. 50/E3
Perlis (state), Malay. 94/B5
Perm', Rus. 69/N4
Përmet, Alb. 49/G2
Permian Basin Petroleum Museum, Tx, US 150/C2
Permskaya Oblast, Rus. 69/N4
Pernambuco (state), Braz. 183/G5
Pernate, It. 62/B3
Pernell, Ok, US 153/F3
Pernes-les-Fontaines, Fr. 64/B4
Pernik, Bul. 50/F4
Perniö, Fin. 41/K1
Peron (pen.), Austl. 130/B3
Peron, North (isl.), Austl. 128/C3
Péronne, Fr. 54/B4
Perosa Argentina, It. 64/D3
Perote, Al, US 165/F2
Perote, Mex. 175/M7
Pérouges, Fr. 60/B6
Perovo (nbrhd.), Rus. 69/W9
Perranporth, Eng, UK 36/A6
Perray (riv.), Fr. 30/H6
Perriers-sur-Andelle, Fr. 57/G2
Perrigny, Fr. 60/B4
Perrin, Tx, US 153/E4
Perrine, Fl, US 164/P11
Perris, Ca, US 166/C3
Perris (res.), Ca, US 166/C3
Perris St. Rec. Area, Ca, US 166/C3
Perro (lag.), NM, US 152/B3
Perron des Encombres (peak), Fr. 64/C2
Perros-Guirec, Fr. 56/B3
Perry (riv.), Nun, Can. 140/F2
Perry, Fl, US 165/G2
Perry (lake), Ks, US 155/G4
Perry, Ga, US 162/F4
Perry, Ia, US 155/G3
Perry, Mo, US 155/J4
Perry, Ok, US 153/F2
Perry (co.), Pa, US 168/A3
Perry Hall, Md, US 168/B5
Perryman, Md, US 168/B5
Perrysburg, Oh, US 160/E4
Perryton, Tx, US 152/D2
Perrytown, Ar, US 153/H4
Perryville, Ak, US 171/G4
Perryville, Ar, US 153/H3
Perryville, Ky, US 162/E2
Perryville, Md, US 168/B4
Perryville, Mo, US 162/C2
Perryville, Tn, US 162/C3
Persan, Fr. 30/J4
Persepolis (ruin), Iran 103/H4
Perseverancia, Bol. 185/F4
Pershagen, Swe. 39/A1
Pershore, Eng, UK 36/D2
Pershotravens'k, Ukr. 72/D2
Pershotravnevoye, Ukr. 73/J4
Pershotravnevoye, Ukr. 72/D2
Persian (gulf), Asia 77/D7
Perstorp, Swe. 40/E3
Pertandangan (cape), Indo. 89/C2
Perth, Austl. 132/C4
Perth, Austl. 130/K6
Perth (int'l arpt.), Austl. 130/K6
Perth, On, Can. 161/H2
Perth, Sc, UK 33/C4
Perth Amboy, NJ, US 169/H9
Perth and Kinross (co.), Sc, UK 33/C4
Perth Zoo, Austl. 130/K6
Perth-Andover, NB, Can. 158/D2
Perthville, Austl. 133/D1
Pertokar, Erit. 117/H1
Pertuis, Fr. 64/B5
Pertuis Breton (inlet), Fr. 44/C3
Pertusato (cape), Fr. 48/A2
Peru (ctry.) 184/C3
Peru, Ks, US 153/F2
Peru, Il, US 155/K3
Peru, In, US 160/C4
Peru, Ne, US 155/G3
Perućačko (lake), Bosn. 50/D4
Perugia, It. 65/B1
Perugia (prov.), It. 65/B1
Peruíbe, Braz. 187/K9
Perushtitsa, Bul. 49/J1
Péruwelz, Belg. 54/C2
Pervari, Turk. 102/E2
Pervomaysk, Rus. 69/J5
Pervomays'k, Ukr. 72/F3
Pervomays'ke, Ukr. 73/G5
Pervomayskiy, Rus. 71/G1
Pervomayskiy, Rus. 71/J2
Pervomayskiy, Rus. 78/H1
Pervomayskoye, Rus. 71/H2
Pervomayskoye, Rus. 73/L3
Pervomays'kyy, Ukr. 73/J3
Pervoural'sk, Rus. 69/N4
Perwez, Belg. 55/D2
Péry, Swi. 60/D3
Pesa (riv.), It. 63/E5
Pesagi (peak), Indo. 89/D4
Pesaro, It. 63/F6
Pesaro E Urbino (prov.), It. 63/F5
Pescadero (pt.), Ca, US 148/A2
Pescadero, Ca, US 148/A2
Pescadore (chan.), Tai. 87/H4
Pescadores (Penghu) (isls.), China 87/H4
Pescantina, It. 63/D3
Pescara (riv.), It. 65/D3
Pescara (prov.), It. 65/C3
Pescara, It. 65/D3
Pescasseroli, It. 65/C4
Peschanokopskoye, Rus. 73/L4
Peschanyy (cape), Kaz. 71/J4
Peschici, It. 48/E2
Pescia, It. 63/D6
Pescina, It. 65/C3
Pescocostanzo, It. 65/D4
Peseux, Swi. 60/C4
Pesha (riv.), Rus. 69/L2
Peshawar (int'l arpt.), Pak. 98/A2
Peshāwar, Pak. 98/A2
Peshkopi, Alb. 49/G2
Peshtera, Bul. 49/J1
Peshtigo (riv.), Wi, US 157/L5
Peshtigo, Wi, US 160/C2
Peski, Rus. 68/H5
Peskovka, Rus. 69/M4
Pesmes, Fr. 60/B3
Peso da Régua, Port. 46/B2
Pesochnyy, Rus. 69/T6
Pesqueira, Braz. 183/G5
Pesquería (riv.), Mex. 150/D5
Pessac, Fr. 44/C4
Pest (co.), Hun. 43/K5
Pest (prov.), Hun. 50/D2
Pestovkoye (lake), Rus. 69/W8
Pestovo, Rus. 68/G4
Petacciato, It. 65/D4
Petah Tiqwa, Isr. 105/B4
Petal, Ms, US 164/D2
Petalión (gulf), Gre. 67/K3
Petaluma (riv.), Ca, US 167/J10
Petaluma, Ca, US 146/B4
Pétange, Lux. 55/E4
Petārbār, India 97/E4
Petare, Ven. 183/P7
Pétas, Gre. 49/G3
Petatlán, Mex. 175/E5
Petatlán (riv.), Mex. 174/D3
Petauke, Zam. 123/F2
Petawawa, On, Can. 161/H2
Petawawa (riv.), On, Can. 161/G2
Peten Itzá (lake), Guat. 176/D2
Petenwell (dam), Wi, US 155/J1
Peter (pond), Sk, Can. 140/F3
Peter (isl.), Nor., Ant. 192/U
Peterborough, Austl. 131/H5
Peterborough, On, Can. 161/G2
Peterborough, Eng, UK 37/F1
Peterborough (co.), Eng, UK 37/F1
Peterculter, Sc, UK 33/D2
Peterhead, Sc, UK 33/E1
Peterlee, Eng, UK 35/G2
Peterman, Al, US 164/E2
Petermann Aboriginal Land, Austl. 131/F3
Peteroa (vol.), Chile 190/C2
Petersaurach, Ger. 58/D4
Petersberg, Ger. 58/C1
Petersburg, Ak, US 171/M4
Petersburg, In, US 162/D1
Petersburg, Il, US 155/K3
Petersburg, ND, US 156/E3
Petersburg, Tx, US 152/D4
Petersburg, Va, US 163/J2
Petersburg, WV, US 163/H1
Petersburg Nat'l Bfld., Va, US 163/J2
Petersfield, Mb, Can. 156/F2
Petersfield, Eng, UK 37/F4
Petershagen, Ger. 53/F4
Petershagen, Ger. 42/Q6
Petershausen, Ger. 59/E6
Peterson (A.F.B.), Co, US 152/B1
Pétervására, Hun. 43/L4
Peterview, Nf, Can. 159/K1
Petilia Policastro, It. 48/E3
Pétionville, Haiti 177/H2
Petit Buëch (riv.), Fr. 64/B4
Petit Goâve, Haiti 177/H2
Petit Loango, PN du, Gabon 120/B3
Petit Mont Blanc (peak), Fr. 64/C2
Petit Rosne (riv.), Fr. 30/J4
Petit-Cap, Qu, Can. 158/E1
Petit-Couronne, Fr. 57/G2
Petit-de-Grat, NS, Can. 159/G3
Petit-Matane, Qu, Can. 158/D1
Petit-Noir, Fr. 60/B4
Petit-Saguenay, Qu, Can. 158/B1
Petitcodiac, NB, Can. 158/E3
Petite Miquelon (isl.), Nf, Can. 159/J2
Petite Nation (riv.), Qu, Can. 161/J1
Petite Rivière de l'Artibonite, Haiti 177/H2
Petite Rivière Noire (peak), Mrts. 125/T15
Petite-Rosselle, Fr. 55/F5
Petkeljärven NP, Fin. 68/F3
Petlād, India 101/K4
Petlalcingo, Mex. 176/B2
Peto, Mex. 176/D1
Petorca, Chile 190/C2
Petoskey, Mi, US 160/D2
Petra (isls.), Rus. 75/M2
Petre (pt.), On, Can. 161/H3
Petrel, Sp. 47/E3
Petrella (peak), It. 65/C5
Petrella Tifernina, It. 65/D4
Petretsovo, Rus. 69/N3
Petrey, Al, US 165/E2
Petrich, Bul. 49/H2
Petrified Forest NP, Az, US 149/H3
Petrikov, Bela. 70/D1
Petrila, Rom. 51/F3
Petritoli, It. 65/C1
Petrivka, Ukr. 72/F4
Petrodvorets, Rus. 69/S7
Petrograd (nbrhd.), Rus. 69/T7
Petrokhanski Prokhod (pass), Bul. 51/F4
Petrokrepost' (bay), Rus. 69/U7
Petrokrepost', Rus. 69/U7
Petrolândia, Braz. 183/G5
Petrolia, Tx, US 153/E3
Petrolia, On, Can. 160/E3
Petrolina, Braz. 183/F5
Petropavl, Kaz. 74/G4
Petropavlivka, Ukr. 73/J3
Petropavlovsk-Kamchatskiy, Rus. 75/R4
Petropavlovskoye, Rus. 71/H3
Petrópolis, Braz. 187/N7
Petros, Tn, US 162/E2
Petroşani, Rom. 51/F3
Petroso (peak), It. 65/C4
Petrovaradin, Serb. 50/D3
Petrovsk, Rus. 71/H1
Petrovsk-Zabaykal'skiy, Rus. 78/F1
Petrovskaya, Rus. 73/J5
Petrovs'ke, Ukr. 73/K3
Petrovskiy Yam, Rus. 68/G3
Petrovskoye, Rus. 71/L1
Petrozavodsk, Rus. 68/G3
Petrus Steyn, SAfr. 124/E2
Petrusburg, SAfr. 124/D3
Petrusville, SAfr. 124/D3
Petrykivka, Ukr. 73/H3
Pettenbach, Aus. 59/H7
Petteril (riv.), Eng, UK 35/F2
Pettibone, ND, US 156/E4
Pettigrew, Ar, US 153/H3
Pettus, Tx, US 150/F3
Petushki, Rus. 68/H5
Petworth, Eng, UK 37/F5
Petzeck (peak), Aus. 45/K3
Peuerbach, Aus. 59/G6
Peulik (mt.), Ak, US 171/G4
Peumo, Chile 190/N9
Peureulak, Indo. 89/B1
Pevek, Rus. 75/T3
Pevely, Mo, US 162/B1
Pevensey, Eng, UK 37/G5
Pewaukee, Wi, US 167/P13
Pewaukee (lake), Wi, US 167/X13
Pewsey, Eng, UK 37/E4
Peyia, Cyp. 104/C2
Peyk, Iran 103/G3
Peymeinade, Fr. 64/C5
Peyrehorade, Fr. 44/C5
Peyrins, Fr. 64/B2
Peyrolles-en-Provence, Fr. 64/B5
Peyruis, Fr. 64/B4
Peza (riv.), Rus. 69/K2
Pézenas, Fr. 44/E5
Pezu, Pak. 98/A3
Pfaffenhausen, Ger. 61/G1
Pfaffenhofen an der Ilm, Ger. 58/D6
Pfaffenhofen an der Ilm, Ger. 59/E5
Pfaffenhoffen, Fr. 55/G6
Pfäffikon, Swi. 61/E3
Pfaffing, Ger. 59/F6
Pfaffnau, Swi. 60/D3
Pfahl (ridge), Ger. 59/F4
Pfälzer Wald (mts.), Ger. 55/G5
Pfälzerwald (mts.), Ger. 58/A4
Pfalzgrafenweiler, Ger. 58/B5
Pfarrhof Esternberg, Aus. 59/G5
Pfarrkirchen, Ger. 59/F6
Pfatter, Ger. 59/F5
Pfeffenhausen, Ger. 59/E5
Pfettrach (riv.), Ger. 59/E5
Pfieffe (riv.), Ger. 53/G6
Pfinztal, Ger. 58/B5
Pflugerville, Tx, US 151/F2
Pforzheim, Ger. 58/B5
Pfreimd (riv.), Ger. 59/F3
Pfreimd, Ger. 59/F3
Pfronstetten, Ger. 61/F1
Pfronten, Ger. 61/G2
Pfroslkopf (peak), Aus. 61/G4
Pfullendorf, Ger. 61/F2
Pfunds, Aus. 61/G4
Pfungstadt, Ger. 58/B3
Phagwāra, India 98/C4
Phalaborwa, SAfr. 123/F4
Phalauda, India 98/D5
Phalempin, Fr. 54/C2
Phālia, Pak. 98/B3
Phalodi, India 101/K3
Phalombe, Malw. 123/G2
Phalsbourg, Fr. 55/G6
Phaltan, India 95/B2
Phan, Thai. 94/B2
Phan Rang Viet. 94/E4
Phan Thiet, Viet. 94/E4
Phanat Nikhom, Thai. 94/C3
Phang Hoei (range), Thai. 94/C3
Phangan (isl.), Thai. 93/H6
Phangnga, Thai. 94/B4
Phanom, Thai. 94/B4
Phanom Dongrak (mts.), Thai. 93/H5
Phāphlu, Nepal 97/F2
Pharr, Tx, US 151/E4
Phat Diem, Viet. 87/E4
Phatthalung, Thai. 94/C5
Phaya Fo (peak), Thai. 94/C2
Phayao, Thai. 94/B2
Pheasant (hills), Sk, Can. 156/C2
Phelan, Ca, US 166/C2
Phelps, Wi, US 157/K4
Phelps (lake), NC, US 163/J3
Phenix City, Al, US 162/E4
Phepane (riv.), SAfr. 122/D5
Phet Buri, Thai. 94/B3
Phetchabun, Thai. 94/C2
Phiafai, Laos 94/D3
Phibun Mangsahan, Thai. 94/D3
Phichai, Thai. 94/C2
Phichit, Thai. 94/C2
Phidim, Nepal 97/F2
Phil Campbell, Al, US 162/D3
Philadelphia, NY, US 161/J2
Philadelphia, Ms, US 162/C4
Philadelphia (int'l arpt.), Pa, US 168/C4
Philadelphia, Pa, US 168/C4
Philip, SD, US 154/D1
Philip S.W. Goldson (int'l arpt.), Belz. 176/D2
Philipp, Ms, US 162/B4
Philippeville, Belg. 55/D3
Philippi, WV, US 163/G1
Philippine (sea), Asia 77/M8
Philippines (ctry.) 114/*
Philippsburg, Ger. 58/B4
Philipsburg, Pa, US 161/G4
Philipsburg, Neth. 173/J4
Philipsburg, Mt, US 145/H4
Philipsdam (dam), Neth. 52/B5
Philipstown, Ire. 32/C3
Philipstown, SAfr. 124/D3
Phillaur, India 98/C4
Phillip (isl.), Austl. 133/B4
Phillips, Me, US 161/L2
Phillips, Wi, US 157/J5
Phillips Arm, BC, Can. 144/B2
Phillipsburg, Ga, US 165/G2
Phillipsburg, Ks, US 154/E4
Phillipsburg, Mo, US 153/H2
Phillipsburg, NJ, US 168/C2
Philo, Ca, US 146/B4
Philomath, Or, US 146/B1
Philoteris (ruin), Egypt 113/B6
Philpot, Ky, US 162/D2
Phimai, Thai. 94/C3
Phimai (ruin), Thai. 94/C3
Phipps (mtn.), Austl. 133/C3
Phitsanulok, Thai. 94/C2
Phnom Penh (Phnum Pénh) (cap.), Camb. 94/D4
Phnum Penh (int'l arpt.), Camb. 94/D4
Phnum Pénh (Phnom Penh) (cap.), Camb. 94/D4
Phnum Tbeng Meanchey, Camb. 94/D3
Pho (pt.), Thai. 94/C5
Phoenix (isls.), Kiri. 137/H5
Phoenix (cap.), Az, US 149/F4
Phoenix (mtn.), NC, US 163/G2
Phoenix, Or, US 146/B2
Phoenix (Rawaki) (isl.), Kiri. 137/H5
Phoenix Park, Ire. 34/B5
Phoenix Sky Harbor (int'l arpt.), Az, US 149/F4
Phoenixville, Pa, US 168/C3
Phon, Thai. 94/C3
Phon Phisai, Thai. 94/C2
Phon Thong, Thai. 94/C2
Phongsali, Laos 86/D4
Phou Bia (peak), Laos 94/C2
Phou Huatt (peak), Viet. 86/E5
Phou Khoun, Laos 94/C2
Phou Loi (peak), Laos 86/D4
Phou Xai Lai Leng (peak), Laos 94/D2
Phra Nakhon Si Ayutthaya, Thai. 94/C3
Phra Phutthabat, Thai. 94/C3
Phra Thong (isl.), Thai. 94/B4
Phrae, Thai. 94/C2
Phsar Ream, Camb. 94/C4
Phu Hin Rong Kla NP, Thai. 94/C2
Phu Hoi, Viet. 94/E4
Phu Kradung, Thai. 94/C2
Phu Kradung NP, Thai. 94/C2
Phu Loc, Viet. 94/D2
Phu Luong, Viet. 94/D1
Phu Luong (peak), Viet. 86/E4
Phu Ly, Viet. 94/D1
Phu My, Viet. 94/E3
Phu Nhon, Viet. 94/E3
Phu Phan NP, Thai. 94/D2
Phu Quoc (isl.), Camb. 93/H5
Phu Quoc (isl.), Viet. 94/C4
Phu Quoc, Viet. 94/C4
Phu Rieng Sron, Viet. 94/D4
Phu Rua NP, Thai. 94/C2
Phu Tho, Viet. 86/E4
Phu Vang, Viet. 94/D2
Phuc Loi, Viet. 94/D2
Phuc Yen, Viet. 86/E4
Phuket (isl.), Thai. 93/G6
Phuket, Thai. 94/B5
Phulabāni, India 95/E1
Phularwan, Pak. 98/B3
Phulbāri, Bang. 97/G3
Phulbāri, India 97/H3
Phuldungsei, India 86/B4
Phūlpur, India 96/D3
Phultala, Bang. 97/G4
Phumi Banam, Camb. 94/D4
Phumi Chhlong, Camb. 94/D3
Phumi Choan, Camb. 94/C4
Phumi Chuuk, Camb. 94/D4
Phumi Kampong Putrea Chas, Camb. 94/D3
Phumi Kampong Trabek, Camb. 94/D3
Phumi Kouk Kduoch, Camb. 94/C3
Phumi Krek, Camb. 94/D4
Phumi Labang Siek, Camb. 94/D3
Phumi Mlu Prey, Camb. 94/D3
Phumi O Pou, Camb. 94/D3
Phumi Phang, Camb. 94/C3
Phumi Phsa Romeas, Camb. 94/D3
Phumi Phsar, Camb. 94/D3
Phumi Prek Kak, Camb. 94/D3
Phumi Prek Preah, Camb. 94/D3
Phumi Samraong, Camb. 94/C3
Phumi Spoe Tbong, Camb. 94/D3
Phumi Sre Ta Chan, Camb. 94/D3
Phumi Ta Krei, Camb. 94/C3
Phumi Thma Pok, Camb. 94/C3
Phumi Toek Sok, Camb. 94/C3
Phumi Veal Renh, Camb. 94/C4
Phuntsholing, Bhu. 97/G2
Phutthaisong, Thai. 94/C3
Pi (riv.), China 78/H5
Pi Xian, China 86/D2
Pia, D.R. Congo 121/F2
Piaçabuçu, Braz. 187/F1
Piacenza, It. 62/C3
Piacenza (prov.), It. 62/C3
Piacoa, Ven. 181/F2
Piadena, It. 62/D3
Piaggine, It. 48/D2
Pian di Serra (peak), It. 63/F7
Pian-Upe Game Rsv., Ugan. 119/A1
Piancastagnaio, It. 48/B1
Pianella, It. 65/D3
Pianello val Tidone, It. 62/C4
Pianezza, It. 62/A2
Piangipane, It. 63/F5
Pianling, China 81/B2
Piano di Sorrento, It. 65/D6
Pianoro, It. 63/E5
Pianosa (isl.), It. 48/A1
Piaoli, China 87/F3
Piapot Ind. Res., Sk, Can. 156/B2
Piarco (int'l arpt.), Trin. 181/F2
Piasco, It. 64/D3
Piaseczno, Pol. 43/L2
Piatra Neamţ, Rom. 72/D4
Piauí (riv.), Braz. 183/F5
Piauí (state), Braz. 183/F4
Piave (riv.), It. 45/K3
Piazza, It. 62/D2
Piazza, It. 62/D2
Piazza al Serchio, It. 62/D5
Piazza Armerina, It. 48/D4
Piazza Brembana, It. 61/F6
Piazzola sul Brenta, It. 63/E2
Pibor (riv.), Sudan 117/G4
Pibor Post, Sudan 117/G4
Pic (isl.), On, Can. 157/L3
Pic (riv.), On, Can. 157/L3
Pica, Chile 188/B2
Picacho, Az, US 149/G4
Picacho del Centinela (peak), Mex. 150/C3
Picahos, Cerro Dos (peak), Mex. 174/B2
Picardie (pol. reg.), Fr. 44/E2
Picardy (reg.), Fr. 54/B4
Picatinny Arsenal, NJ, US 168/D2
Picauville, Fr. 56/D2
Picayune, Ms, US 164/D2
Piccaninny (cr.), Austl. 133/B3
Piccolo (lag.), It. 49/E2
Picentino (riv.), It. 65/D6
Pichacani, Peru 184/D5
Pichanal, Arg. 188/C2
Picher, Ok, US 153/G2
Pichidangui, Chile 190/C2
Pichidegua, Chile 190/N9
Pichilemu, Chile 190/B2
Pichincha (dept.), Ecu. 180/B4
Pichincha, Ecu. 180/B5
Pichkiryayevo, Rus. 71/G1
Pichl bei Wels, Aus. 59/G6
Pichor, India 96/B3
Pichucalco, Mex. 176/C2
Pickens, Ok, US 153/G3
Pickens, SC, US 163/F3
Pickens, Ms, US 162/C4
Pickering, Eng, UK 35/H3
Pickering, On, Can. 160/U8
Pickford, Mi, US 160/D1
Pickle Lake, On, Can. 157/J2
Pickton, Tx, US 153/G4
Pickwick (dam), Tn, US 162/C3
Pickwick (lake), Al,Ms, US 162/C3
Pickwick Dam, Tn, US 162/C3
Picnic Bay, Austl. 134/B2
Pico (isl.), Azor., Port. 47/S12
Pico da Neblina, PN do, Braz. 181/E4
Pico de Orizaba, PN, Mex. 175/M7
Pico de Salamanca, Arg. 190/D5
Pico Rivera, Ca, US 166/F8
Pico Truncado, Arg. 190/D5
Picos, Braz. 183/F4
Picota, Peru 184/B2
Picsi, Peru 184/B2
Picton, On, Can. 161/H3
Picton, NZ 135/C3
Picton, Austl. 133/E2
Pictou (isl.), NS, Can. 159/F3
Pictou, NS, Can. 159/F3
Picture Butte, Ab, Can. 145/H3
Picture Gorge (gorge), Or, US 146/D1
Picture Rock (pass), Or, US 146/C2
Picture Rocks, Pa, US 168/B1
Pictured Rocks Nat'l Lakeshore, Mi, US 157/L4
Picuí, Braz. 183/G4
Picuris Ind. Res., NM, US 149/K2
Pidcoke, Tx, US 150/F2
Piddle (riv.), Eng, UK 36/D5
Pidhorodne, Ukr. 73/H3
Pidi, D.R. Congo 121/F4
Pidurutagala (peak), SrL. 95/D5
Pidvolochys'k, Ukr. 72/D3
Pie (isl.), On, Can. 157/K3
Pie Town, NM, US 149/H3
Piedade, Port. 47/P10
Piedade do Rio Grande, Braz. 187/M6
Piedecuesta, Col. 180/C3
Piediluco (lake), It. 65/B2
Piedimulera, It. 61/E5
Piedmont, Al, US 162/E4
Piedmont, Ca, US 167/K11
Piedmont, Mo, US 162/B2
Piedmont, Ok, US 153/F3
Piedmont, SD, US 154/C1
Piedmont, SC, US 163/F3
Piedmont (upland), SC, US 163/G3
Piedmont NWR, Ga, US 162/F4
Piedra, Ca, US 148/C2
Piedra Grande, Ven. 180/D2
Piedra Sola, Uru. 189/E5
Piedrabuena, Sp. 46/C3
Piedrahita, Sp. 46/C2
Piedras (pt.), Arg. 191/K11
Piedras, Col. 183/L8
Piedras Coloradas, Uru. 191/K10
Piedras Negras, Mex. 175/N8
Piedras, Río de las (riv.), Peru 184/D3
Piedritas, Arg. 190/E2
Piekary Śląskie, Pol. 43/K3
Piekenierskloof (pass), SAfr. 124/L10
Pieksämäki, Fin. 68/E3
Pielinen (lake), Fin. 38/J3
Piemonte (pol.reg.), It. 45/G4
Pieniński NP, Pol. 43/L4
Piennes, Fr. 55/E5
Pieńsk, Pol. 43/H3
Piera, Sp. 47/K6
Pierce, Co, US 154/B3
Pierce (lake), Fl, US 164/M8
Pierce, Fl, US 164/M8
Pierce, Id, US 144/G4
Pierce, Ne, US 154/F2
Pierce (co.), Wi, US 157/Q7
Pierce City, Mo, US 153/G2
Pierceville, Ks, US 152/D2
Pieris, It. 63/G2
Piermont, NY, US 169/K7
Pierowall, Sc, UK 31/V14
Pierre (cap.), SD, US 154/D1
Pierre Menue (peak), It. 64/C2
Pierre Part, La, US 164/C3
Pierre Plate (peak), Fr. 64/D5
Pierre-de-Bresse, Fr. 60/B4
Pierre-Levée, Fr. 30/M5
Pierrefeu-du-Var, Fr. 64/C6
Pierrefitte-sur-Seine, Fr. 30/K5
Pierrefonds, Qu, Can. 159/N7
Pierrefontaine-les-Varans, Fr. 60/C3
Pierrelatte, Fr. 64/A4
Pierrelaye, Fr. 30/J4
Pierres, Fr. 57/G3
Pierrevert, Fr. 64/B5
Pierry, Fr. 54/C5
Pierson, Fl, US 165/H3
Piešťany, Slvk. 43/J4
Piesting (riv.), Aus. 51/P7
Piet Retief, SAfr. 125/E2
Pietarsaari (Jakobstad), Fin. 68/D3
Pieterlen, Swi. 60/D3
Pietermaritzburg, SAfr. 125/E3
Pietersburg, SAfr. 123/F4
Pietra Ligure, It. 62/B5
Pietracatella, It. 65/D4
Pietralunga, It. 63/F7
Pietramelara, It. 65/D5
Pietrasanta, It. 62/D6
Pietravairano, It. 65/D5
Pietravecchia (peak), It. 62/A5
Pietrosul (peak), Rom. 51/G2
Pieve del Cairo, It. 62/B3
Pieve di Cento, It. 63/E4
Pieve di Soligo, It. 63/F2
Pieve di Teco, It. 62/A4
Pieve Emanuele, It. 62/C3
Pieve Ligure, It. 62/C5
Pieve Porto Morone, It. 62/C3
Pieve Santo Stefano, It. 63/F6
Pieve Vergonte, It. 61/E6
Pievepelago, It. 62/D5
Pigum (isl.), SKor. 81/C5
Pigeon (riv.), Can.,US 157/J3
Pigeon, Mi, US 160/E3
Pigeon (riv.), On, Can. 140/G4
Pigeon (lake), Ab, Can. 145/H1
Pigeon House (mtn.), Austl. 133/E2
Piggott, Ar, US 162/B2
Piggs Peak, Swaz. 125/E2
Piglio, It. 65/C4
Pigna, It. 64/D5
Pignataro Maggiore, It. 65/D5
Pigs (bay), Cuba 172/E3
Pigu, Gha. 115/E4
Pigüé, Arg. 190/E3
Pihāni, India 96/C2
Pijáo, Col. 183/K8
Pijijiapan, Mex. 176/C3
Pijnacker, Neth. 52/B4
Pijol (peak), Hon. 176/E3
Pike (co.), Pa, US 168/C1
Pikelot (isl.), Micr. 136/D4
Pikes (peak), Co, US 152/B1
Pikes Creek (res.), Pa, US 168/B1
Pikesville, Md, US 168/B5
Piketberg, SAfr. 124/L10
Piketon, Oh, US 163/F1
Pikeville, Ky, US 163/F2
Pikeville, Tn, US 162/E3
Pikit, Phil. 88/D4
Pikou, China 81/B3
Piła, Pol. 43/J2
Pila, Arg. 191/J12
Pilane, Bots. 122/E5
Pilanesberg (range), SAfr. 124/P12
Pilani, India 98/C5
Pilão Arcado, Braz. 187/E1
Pilar, Arg. 190/E1
Pilar, Arg. 188/D4
Pilar, Braz. 187/G1
Pilar, Par. 188/E3
Pilar, Phil. 91/F1
Pilatus (peak), Swi. 61/E4
Pilaya (riv.), Bol. 188/C2
Pilchuck (riv.), Wa, US 167/D1
Pilcomayo (riv.), SAm. 179/C5
Pilgrims Hatch, Eng, UK 30/D2
Pili, Phil. 88/C2
Pīlībhīt, India 96/B1
Pilica (riv.), Pol. 70/B2
Pílion (peak), Gre. 49/H3
Pilis (mts.), Hun. 51/R9
Pilis (peak), Hun. 51/Q9
Pilis, Hun. 50/D2
Piliscsaba, Hun. 51/Q9
Pilisvörösvár, Hun. 51/Q9
Pilkhua, India 98/D5
Pillar (cape), Austl. 132/C4
Pillar (peak), Eng, UK 35/E3
Pillar (pt.), Ca, US 167/J12
Pillar (pt.), Wa, US 144/B3
Pilliga, Austl. 132/D1
Pillow, Pa, US 168/B2
Pilões, Serra dos (mtn.), Braz. 189/H1
Pilon du Roi (peak), Fr. 64/B6
Pílos, Gre. 49/G4
Pilot (peak), Id, US 144/G5
Pilot (peak), Nv, US 146/E4
Pilot (mtn.), Tn, US 162/E2
Pilot (peak), Tn, US 162/E2
Pilot Butte, Sk, Can. 156/B2
Pilot Grove, Mo, US 153/H1
Pilot Grove (cr.), Tx, US 150/L6
Pilot Knob, Mo, US 162/B2
Pilot Mound, Mb, Can. 156/E3
Pilot Mountain, NC, US 163/G2
Pilot Point, Ak, US 171/G4
Pilot Point, Tx, US 153/F4
Pilot Rock, Or, US 146/D1
Pilot Station, Ak, US 171/F3
Pilottown, La, US 164/D3
Pilsting, Ger. 59/F5
Piltene, Lat. 41/J3
Piltown, Ire. 32/C5
Pilyugino, Rus. 71/K1
Pima, Az, US 149/H4
Pimamga-Moke, D.R. Congo 120/D3
Pimenta Bueno, Braz. 185/F3
Pimpi, Indo. 91/F3
Pimpri-Chinchwad, India 95/B2
Piña (pt.), Pan. 177/G5
Pinacate, Cerro (peak), Mex. 149/F5
Pináculo (peak), Arg. 191/B6
Pinaleno (mts.), Az, US 149/G4
Pinamalayan, Phil. 88/C2
Pinamar, Arg. 191/F3
Pinang (isl.), Malay. 90/A2
Pinang (cape), Malay. 89/B1
Pinangah, Malay. 88/B4
Pinar del Río, Cuba 177/F1
Pınarbaşı, Turk. 102/D2
Pınarhisar, Turk. 51/H5
Piñas, Ecu. 184/B1
Pinatubo (mt.), Phil. 88/C2
Pinawa, Mb, Can. 156/G2
Pinchbeck, Eng, UK 35/H6
Pincher Creek, Ab, Can. 145/H3
Pinckney, Mi, US 160/E3
Pinckneyville, Il, US 162/C1
Pinconning, Mi, US 160/E3
Pîncota, Rom. 50/E2
Pincourt, Qu, Can. 159/N7
Pińczów, Pol. 43/L3
Pind Dādan Khān, Pak. 98/B3
Pinda, Ang. 120/C5
Pindall, Ar, US 153/H2
Pindamonhangaba, Braz. 187/L7
Pindaré (riv.), Braz. 183/E4
Pindaré-Mirim, Braz. 183/E3
Píndhos NP, Gre. 49/G3
Pindi Bhattiān, Pak. 98/B4
Pindi Gheb, Pak. 98/B3
Pindiu, PNG 129/G1
Pindobaçu, Braz. 187/E1
Pindobal, Braz. 182/D3
Pindus (mts.), Gre. 67/J2
Pindwāra, India 92/B3
Pine (cape), Nf, Can. 159/L2
Pine, Az, US 149/G3
Pine, Co, US 152/B1
Pine (isl.), Fl, US 165/G4
Pine (pt.), Fl, US 165/G3
Pine, Id, US 147/F2
Pine (riv.), Mi, US 160/D3
Pine (hills), Ms, US 164/C2
Pine (ridge), Ne, US 154/C2
Pine (cr.), Pa, US 168/A1
Pine, Tx, US 153/G4
Pine Apple, Al, US 164/E2
Pine Barrens (phys. reg.), NJ, US 168/D4
Pine Bluff, Ar, US 153/H3
Pine Bluff Arsenal, Ar, US 153/H3
Pine Bluffs, Wy, US 154/B3
Pine Bush, NY, US 161/J4
Pine Castle, Fl, US 164/N7
Pine City, Mn, US 157/H5
Pine Creek (lake), Ok, US 153/G3
Pine Creek, Austl. 128/C3
Pine Creek (pt.), Ct, US 169/E1
Pine Dock, Mb, Can. 156/F2
Pine Falls, Mb, Can. 156/F2
Pine Flat (res.), Ca, US 148/C2
Pine Grove, La, US 164/C2
Pine Grove, Pa, US 168/B2
Pine Hill, Al, US 164/E2
Pine Hill, NJ, US 168/D4
Pine Island, Fl, US 164/K6
Pine Island, Mn, US 155/H1
Pine Island Bay (flat), Ant. 192/S
Pine Island Nat'l Wild. Ref., Fl, US 165/G4
Pine Knot, Ky, US 162/E2
Pine Level, Al, US 165/E1
Pine Mills, Tx, US 151/G1
Pine Point, NW, Can. 140/E2
Pine Prairie, La, US 164/B2
Pine Ridge, SD, US 154/C2
Pine Ridge Ind. Res., SD, US 154/C2
Pine River, Mn, US 157/G4
Pine River, Mb, Can. 156/D2
Pine Springs, Tx, US 150/B2
Pine Stump Junction, Mi, US 160/D1
Pine Valley, Ut, US 149/F2
Pine Valley, Ca, US 148/D4
Pine, South Branch (riv.), Mi, US 167/G6
Pinebluff, NC, US 163/H3
Pinecliff (lake), NJ, US 169/H7
Pinecreek, Mn, US 156/G3
Pinedale, Wy, US 147/J2
Pinedale, Ca, US 148/C2
Pinedale, Az, US 149/G3
Pinega (riv.), Rus. 74/E3
Pinega, Rus. 68/J2
Pinehurst, Ga, US 162/F4
Pinehurst, Id, US 144/F4
Pinehurst, NC, US 163/H3
Pinehurst, Tx, US 151/G2
Pineland, Fl, US 165/G4
Pineland, SC, US 163/G4
Pineland, Tx, US 151/H2
Pinelands, SAfr. 124/L10
Pinellas (co.), Fl, US 164/K8
Pinellas (pt.), Fl, US 164/K8
Pinellas Park, Fl, US 164/K8
Pineola, Fl, US 164/L6
Piñera, Uru. 191/K10
Pinerolo, It. 64/D3
Pinesdale, Mt, US 145/G4
Pineto, It. 65/D2
Pinetop-Lakeside, Az, US 149/H3
Pinetops, NC, US 163/J3
Pinetown, SAfr. 125/E3
Pinetta, Fl, US 165/G2
Pineuilh, Fr. 44/D4
Pineview, Ga, US 165/G1
Pineville, Ky, US 162/F2
Pineville, La, US 164/B2
Pineville, Mo, US 153/G2
Pineville, SC, US 163/G4
Pineville, WV, US 163/G2
Piney, Ar, US 153/H3
Piney (isl.), Fl, US 165/F2
Piney Green, NC, US 163/J3
Piney Point, Fl, US 164/K8
Piney Point, Md, US 163/J1
Piney Point Village, Tx, US 151/M9
Piney River, Va, US 163/H2
Ping (riv.), Thai. 93/G4
Ping (riv.), Myan. 94/B2
Ping Chau (isl.), China 87/M6
Pingbian Miaozu Zizhixian, China 86/D4
Pingchang, China 87/E2
Pingchao, China 87/J1
Pingding, China 80/C3
Pingdingshan, China 80/C4
Pingdu, China 80/D3
Pingelap (isl.), Micr. 136/F4
Pingelly, Austl. 130/C5
Ping'erguan, China 94/D1
Pingfa, China 87/E3
Pinggu, China 80/H6
Pingguo, China 93/J3
Pinghai, China 87/H3
Pinghai, China 87/G4
Pinghu, China 80/L9
Pingjing (pass), China 80/C5
Pingjinpu, China 87/E2
Pingle, China 87/F3
Pinglu, China 80/C3
Pinglu, China 80/B4
Pingquan, China 80/D2
Pingree, Id, US 147/G2
Pingsha, China 87/G4
Pingshan, China 80/C3
Pingshi, China 87/G3
Pingshun, China 80/C3
Pingtang, China 93/J2
Pingtou, China 78/F5
P'ingtung, Tai. 87/J4
Pingwang, China 80/L9
Pingxiang, China 87/E4
Pingxiang, China 87/G3
Pingxiang, China 80/C3
Pingxing Guan (pass), China 80/C3
Pingyang, China 79/J4
Pingyao, China 80/C3
Pingyi, China 80/D4
Pingyin, China 94/E1
Pingyin, China 80/D3
Pingyong, China 87/F3
Pingyu, China 80/C4
Pingyuan, China 80/D3
Pinhal, Braz. 187/K7
Pinhal Novo, Port. 47/Q10
Pinheiro, Braz. 183/E3
Pinheiro Machado, Braz. 189/F4
Pinheiros, Braz. 187/E3
Pinhel, Port. 46/B2
Pinhook (swamp), Fl, US 165/G2
Pinhuã (riv.), Braz. 185/E2
Pini (isl.), Indo. 89/B2
Pinjar (lake), Austl. 130/K6
Pinjarra, Austl. 130/B5
Pink Hill, NC, US 163/J3
Pinkafeld, Aus. 50/C2
Pinkawillinie Consv. Park, Austl. 131/G5
Pinkegat (chan.), Neth. 52/C2
Pinlebu, Myan. 93/G3
Pinnacles Nat'l Mon., Ca, US 148/B2
Pinnån (riv.), Swe. 39/K6
Pinnaroo, Austl. 131/J5
Pinnau (riv.), Ger. 53/G1
Pinneberg, Ger. 53/G1
Pino Hachado, (pass), Arg. 190/C3

Pino To – Port Ap

Pino Torinese, It. 62/A2
Pinole, Ca, US 167/K10
Pinon, Co, US 152/B1
Piñon, NM, US 152/B4
Pinon, Az, US 149/G2
Pinon Hills, Ca, US 166/C2
Pinopolis, SC, US 163/G4
Pinopolis (dam), SC, US 163/H4
Pinos (mt.), Ca, US 148/C3
Pinos, Mex. 175/E4
Pinos, Isla de (Isla de la Juventud) (isl.), Cuba 172/E3
Pinos-Puente, Sp. 46/D4
Pinoso, Sp. 47/E3
Pinrang, Indo. 91/E4
Pinsdorf, Aus. 59/G7
Pinsk, Bela. 70/C1
Pinta, Isla (isl.), Ecu. 184/J6
Pintada Arroyo (cr.), NM, US 152/B3
Pintado, Uru. 191/K10
Pintados, Chile 188/B2
Pinto, Chile 190/C3
Pinto, Sp. 47/N9
Pintura, Ut, US 149/F2
Pintuyan, Phil. 88/D3
Pinzolo, It. 61/G5
Pio Xii, Braz. 183/E3
Piobbico, It. 63/F6
Pioche, Nv, US 148/E2
Piolenc, Fr. 64/A4
Piomba (riv.), It. 65/C2
Piombino, It. 48/B1
Piombino Dese, It. 63/F2
Pioneer, La, US 153/J4
Pioneer (mts.), Mt, US 147/G1
Pioneer World, Austl. 130/L7
Pioner (isl.), Rus. 74/J2
Pionerskiy, Rus. 41/J4
Pionki, Pol. 43/L3
Piopio, NZ 135/C2
Piopolis, Qu, Can. 158/B3
Piorini (lake), Braz. 181/F5
Piorini (riv.), Braz. 185/F1
Piossasco, It. 64/D3
Piota (riv.), It. 62/B3
Piotrków Trybunalski, Pol. 43/K3
Piove di Sacco, It. 63/F3
Piovene-Rocchette, It. 63/E2
Pīpār, India 92/B2
Pipariā, India 96/B4
Pipe Spring Nat'l Mon., Az, US 149/F2
Pipersville, Pa, US 168/C3
Pipestem (cr.), ND, US 156/E4
Pipestone (cr.), Sk, Can. 156/D3
Pipestone, Mb, Can. 156/D3
Pipestone (riv.), On, Can. 140/G3
Pipestone, Mn, US 155/F1
Pipestone Nat'l Mon., Mn, US 155/F1
Piplān, Pak. 98/A3
Pipmuacan (res.), Qu, Can. 141/J4
Pippingarra Abor. Land, Austl. 130/C2
Pipra, India 96/D3
Pipraich, India 96/D2
Pipriac, Fr. 56/D5
Piqanlik, China 99/D3
Piqua, Ks, US 153/G2
Piqua, Oh, US 160/D4
Piquet Carneiro, Braz. 183/G4
Piquete, Braz. 187/L7
Piquiri (riv.), Braz. 189/F3
Pīr Mahal, Pak. 98/B4
Pir Panjal (range), India 98/C3
Piracanjuba, Braz. 186/C3
Piracaua, Braz. 182/E3
Piracicaba, Braz. 189/H2
Piracuruca, Braz. 183/F3
Pirae-bong (peak), NKor. 81/C2
Piraí, Braz. 187/N7
Piraí do Sul, Braz. 189/G3
Piraiévs, Gre. 49/N9
Piraju, Braz. 189/G2
Pirajuí, Braz. 189/G2
Pirámide (peak), Chile 191/B6
Piran, Slov. 63/G2
Pirané, Arg. 188/E3
Piranga (riv.), Braz. 187/E4
Piranhas (riv.), Braz. 183/G4
Piranhas, Braz. 186/C3
Pirapemas, Braz. 183/E3
Pirapora, Braz. 186/D3
Pirarajá, Uru. 191/G2
Pirássununga, Braz. 189/H2
Piratini (riv.), Braz. 189/F4
Piray (riv.), Bol. 185/F5
Pircas (peak), Arg. 188/B4
Pirenópolis, Braz. 186/C2
Pires do Rio, Braz. 186/C3
Pīrganj, Bang. 97/G3
Pírgos, Gre. 49/J5
Pírgos, Gre. 49/G4
Piri, Ang. 120/C5
Piriac-sur-Mer, Fr. 56/C6
Piriápolis, Uru. 191/G2
Piribebuy, Par. 189/E3
Pirimapun, Indo. 129/E1
Pirin (peak), Bul. 49/H2
Pirin (mts.), Bul. 49/H2
Pirin NP, Bul. 49/H2
Pirinoa, NZ 135/J9
Piripiri, Braz. 183/F4
Piritiba, Braz. 187/E1
Píritu, Ven. 180/D2
Pirkkala, Fin. 41/K1
Pirmasens, Ger. 55/G5
Pirna, Ger. 43/G3
Piro, India 97/E3
Pirojpur, Bang. 97/G4
Pirot, Serb. 50/F4
Pirpirituba, Braz. 183/H4
Pirre (mtn.), Pan. 180/B3
Pirthīpur, India 96/B3
Pirttikoski, Fin. 39/D3
Pirttsaari (isl.), Fin. 39/F4
Piru, Ca, US 166/B2
Piru (cr.), Ca, US 166/B1
Piru (lake), Ca, US 166/B1
Piryíon, Gre. 49/J3
Pisa, It. 62/D6
Pisa (prov.), It. 63/D6
Pisac, Peru 184/D4
Pisagua, Chile 188/B1
Pisanino (peak), It. 62/D5
Pisau (cape), Malay. 88/B4
Pisba, PN, Col. 180/C3
Piscataway, NJ, US 168/D2
Piscataway, Md, US 168/B6
Pisco, Peru 184/B4
Pisco (riv.), Peru 184/C4
Piscobamba, Peru 184/B3
Pisek, ND, US 156/F3
Písek, Czh. 59/H4
Písek (peak), Czh. 59/H3
Pisgah, Oh, US 160/D5
Pishan, China 99/C4
Pishanka, Ukr. 72/E3
Pishīn, Pak. 101/J2
Pīshīn, Iran 101/H3
Pishnur, Rus. 69/K4
Pīshvā, Iran 103/G3
Piskavica, Bosn. 50/C3
Piskivka, Ukr. 72/E2
Piso Firme, Bol. 185/F4
Pisoc (peak), Swi. 61/G4
Pisogne, It. 62/D2
Pisoniano, It. 65/B4
Pissila, Burk. 115/E3
Pissis (peak), Arg. 188/B3
Pistakee (lake), Il, US 167/P15
Pisticci, It. 48/E2
Pistoia, It. 63/D6
Pistoia (prov.), It. 63/D5
Pistol River, Or, US 146/A2
Pisuerga (riv.), Sp. 46/C1
Pisz, Pol. 43/L2
Pit (riv.), Ca, US 146/C3
Pita, Gui. 114/B4
Pitalito, Col. 180/B4
Pitanga, Braz. 189/G3
Pitcairn (isl.), Pitc. 137/N7
Pitcairn Islands (dpcy.), UK 137/N7
Pitch Place, Eng, UK 30/B3
Piteå, Swe. 38/G2
Piteälven (riv.), Swe. 38/F2
Pitești, Rom. 51/G3
Pithāpuram, India 95/D2
Píthion, Gre. 51/H5
Pithiviers, Fr. 57/H4
Pithlachascotee (riv.), Fl, US 164/K7
Pithom (ruin), Egypt 113/D3
Pithoragarh, India 96/C1
Pitigliano, It. 48/B1
Pitimbu, Braz. 183/H4
Pitiquito, Mex. 174/B2
Pitjantjatjara Aboriginal Lands, Austl. 131/F3
Pitkas Point, Ak, US 171/F3
Pitkin, La, US 164/B2
Pitkin, Co, US 149/J1
Pitlochry, Sc, UK 33/C3
Pitman, NJ, US 168/C4
Pitmedden, Sc, UK 33/D2
Pitogo, Phil. 88/C2
Pitomača, Cro. 50/C3
Piton de la Fournaise (peak), Fr. 125/S15
Piton des Neiges (peak), Fr. 125/S15
Pitowa, Camr. 116/B3
Pîtres, Fr. 57/G2
Pitrufquén, Chile 190/B3
Pitsane, Bots. 122/E5
Pitsunda, Geo. 70/G4
Pitt, Mn, US 157/G3
Pitt (str.), NZ 135/E4
Pitt (isl.), NZ 135/E4
Pitt (riv.), BC, Can. 144/C3
Pitt Water (bay), Austl. 134/H8
Pittenweem, Sc, UK 33/D4
Pitts, Ga, US 165/G2
Pittsboro, Ms, US 162/C4
Pittsboro, NC, US 163/H3
Pittsburg, Ca, US 146/C4
Pittsburg, Ks, US 153/G2
Pittsburg, Mo, US 153/H2
Pittsburg, NH, US 161/L2
Pittsburg, Ok, US 153/G3
Pittsburgh, Pa, US 160/G4
Pittsburg, Tx, US 153/G4
Pittsfield, Ma, US 161/K3
Pittsfield, Il, US 155/J4
Pittsford, Vt, US 161/K3
Pittston, Pa, US 161/J4
Pittstown, NJ, US 168/D2
Pittsville, Va, US 163/H2
Pittsworth, Austl. 134/C4
Pitzbach (riv.), Aus. 61/G4
Piuí, Braz. 186/D4
Piumazzo, It. 63/E4
Piura (dept.), Peru 184/A2
Piura, Peru 184/A2
Piute (res.), Ut, US 147/G4
Pivan', Rus. 79/M1
Pivdenne, Ukr. 73/J3
Pivdenny Buh (riv.), Ukr. 74/C5
Pivijay, Col. 180/C2
Pivsko (lake), Serb. 49/F1
Pixoyal, Mex. 172/C4
Piz d'Err (peak), Swi. 61/F4
Pizacoma, Peru 184/D5
Pizarra, Sp. 46/C4
Pizhma (riv.), Rus. 69/K4
Pizol (peak), Swi. 61/F4
Pizzighettone, It. 62/C3
Pizzo, It. 48/E3
Pizzo dei Tre Signori (peak), It. 61/F6
Pizzo della Presolana (peak), It. 61/G6
Pizzo di Coca (peak), It. 61/G5
Pizzo di Vogorno (peak), Swi. 61/E5
Pizzoli, It. 65/C3
Pizzuto (peak), It. 65/B3
Plabennec, Fr. 56/A3
Placentia, Nf, Can. 159/L2
Placentia (bay), Nf, Can. 159/K2
Placentia, Ca, US 166/G8
Placer (co.), Ca, US 167/M9
Placer, Phil. 88/C3
Placer, Phil. 88/D3
Placerville, Co, US 149/H1
Placerville, Ca, US 146/C4
Placetas, Cuba 177/G1
Plachkovtsi, Bul. 51/G4
Plácido de Castro, Braz. 185/E3
Placilla de Caracoles, Chile 188/B2
Plaffeien, Swi. 60/D4
Plai Mat (riv.), Thai. 94/C3
Plaidt, Ger. 55/G3
Plailly, Fr. 30/K4
Plain Dealing, La, US 153/H4
Plain of Jars, Laos 86/D5
Plaine (riv.), Fr. 60/C1
Plainfield, In, US 160/C5
Plainfield, Il, US 167/P16
Plainfield, NJ, US 169/H9
Plainfield, Wi, US 155/K1
Plains, Tx, US 152/C4
Plains, Ga, US 165/F1
Plains, Mt, US 144/G4
Plains, Pa, US 168/C1
Plains (West Plains), Ks, US 152/D2
Plainsboro, NJ, US 168/D3
Plaintel, Fr. 56/C4
Plainview, Ar, US 153/H3
Plainview, Mn, US 155/H1
Plainview, Ne, US 154/F2
Plainview, NY, US 169/M8
Plainview, Tx, US 152/D3
Plainville, Ks, US 154/E4
Plainwell, Mi, US 160/D3
Plaisir, Fr. 30/H5
Plaju, Indo. 89/D3
Plampang, Indo. 91/E5
Plan-de-Cuques, Fr. 64/B6
Plan-de-la-Tour, Fr. 64/C6
Plan-d'Orgon, Fr. 64/A5
Plan-les-Ouates, Swi. 60/C5
Planá, Czh. 59/F3
Plana Cays (isls.), Bahm. 177/H1
Planada, Ca, US 148/B2
Planalto da Borborema (plat.), Braz. 183/G4
Planalto da Huíla (plat.), Ang. 122/B2
Planalto da Lichinga (plat.), Moz. 123/G2
Planalto do Bíe (plat.), Ang. 122/C2
Planalto do Chimoio (plat.), Moz. 123/G3
Planalto dos Macondes (plat.), Moz. 119/B4
Planchada, Chile 190/N8
Plancher-Bas, Fr. 60/C2
Plancher-les-Mines, Fr. 60/C2
Plancoët, Fr. 56/C3
Plandište, Serb. 50/E3
Planerskoye, Ukr. 73/H5
Planet Ocean, Fl, US 164/P11
Planeta Rica, Col. 180/C2
Plánice, Czh. 59/G4
Planken, Lcht. 61/F3
Plankinton, SD, US 154/E2
Plano, Il, US 155/K3
Plano, Tx, US 150/L6
Plant City, Fl, US 164/L7
Plantation, Fl, US 164/P10
Plantation Key, Fl, US 165/H5
Plantersville, Ms, US 162/C3
Plaquemine, La, US 164/C2
Plasencia, Sp. 46/B2
Plast, Rus. 69/P5
Plaster Rock, NB, Can. 158/D2
Plaster Rock-Renous Game Ref., NB, Can. 158/D2
Plastun, Rus. 79/M3
Plasy, Czh. 59/G3
Plata (riv.), Arg. 179/D6
Plata (est.), Arg.,Uru. 191/K11
Plata, Río de la (riv.), Uru. 191/F2
Platanal, Ven. 181/E4
Platani (riv.), It. 48/C4
Plateau, NS, Can. 159/G2
Plateau (state), Nga. 115/H4
Plateau Batéké (plat.), Congo 120/C3
Plateau de Mangueni (plat.), Niger 108/B4
Plateau de Tehiga'i (plat.), Niger 108/B4
Plateau de Valensole (plat.), Fr. 64/B5
Plateau des Bolovens (plat.), Laos 94/D3
Plateau du Tademaït (plat.), Alg. 111/E3
Plateau of Yorubaland (plat.), Nga. 115/F4
Plateaux (pol. reg.), Congo 120/C3
Platí, Gre. 49/H2
Platinum, Ak, US 171/F4
Platnirovskaya, Rus. 73/K5
Plato, Col. 180/C2
Platón Sánchez, Mex. 176/B1
Platte (riv.), US 139/G5
Platte, SD, US 154/E2
Platte City, Mo, US 155/G4
Platte, North (riv.), Ne,Wy, US 142/E3
Platte, South (riv.), Co, US 142/F3
Platteville, Co, US 154/B3
Platteville, Wi, US 155/J2
Plattling, Ger. 59/F5
Plattsburg, Mo, US 155/G4
Plattsburgh, NY, US 161/K2
Plattsmouth, Ne, US 155/G3
Plauen, Ger. 59/F1
Plav, Serb. 50/D4
Pļaviņas, Lat. 41/L3
Plavna Dadaint (peak), Swi. 61/G4
Plavsk, Rus. 70/F1
Playa de los Muertos (ruin), Hon. 176/E3
Playa del Carmen, Mex. 176/E1
Playa Noriega (lake), Mex. 174/C2
Playa Vicente, Mex. 176/C2
Playas, Ecu. 180/A5
Playas (lake), NM, US 149/H5
Pleak, Tx, US 151/G3
Pleasant (mtn.), NB, Can. 158/D3
Pleasant Bay, NS, Can. 159/G2
Pleasant Grove, Ut, US 147/H3
Pleasant Hill, Ca, US 167/K11
Pleasant Hill, La, US 164/B2
Pleasant Hill, Mo, US 153/G1
Pleasant Hills, Md, US 168/B5
Pleasant Hope, Mo, US 153/H2
Pleasant Point, NZ 135/B4
Pleasant Prairie, Wi, US 160/C3
Pleasant View, Ut, US 147/H3
Pleasant View, Tn, US 162/D2
Pleasantdale, Sk, Can. 145/M1
Pleasanton, Ca, US 167/L11
Pleasanton, Ks, US 153/G1
Pleasanton, NM, US 149/H4
Pleasanton, Ne, US 154/E3
Pleasanton, Tx, US 150/E3
Pleasantville, Ia, US 155/H3
Pleasantville, NJ, US 168/D5
Pleasantville, NY, US 169/K7
Pleasantville, Tn, US 162/D3
Pleasure Ridge Park, Ky, US 162/E1
Pleaux, Fr. 44/E4
Pléchâtel, Fr. 56/D5
Plédran, Fr. 56/C4
Plei Doch, Viet. 94/D3
Pleiku, Viet. 94/D3
Pleine-Fougères, Fr. 56/D3
Pleinfeld, Ger. 58/D4
Pleisse (riv.), Ger. 42/G3
Plélan-le-Grand, Fr. 56/C4
Plélan-le-Petit, Fr. 56/C4
Plémet, Fr. 56/C4
Pléneuf-Val-André, Fr. 56/C3
Pleniţa, Rom. 51/F3
Plenty (riv.), Austl. 132/G5
Plenty, Sk, Can. 145/K2
Plenty (bay), NZ 127/H6
Plentywood, Mt, US 156/B3
Plered, Indo. 89/D4
Plérin, Fr. 56/C3
Plesetsk, Rus. 68/J3
Pleshchenitsy, Bela. 41/M4
Plesná (riv.), Czh. 59/F2
Pleso (int'l arpt.), Cro. 50/C3
Plessé, Fr. 56/D5
Plessisville, Qu, Can. 158/B2
Plestan, Fr. 56/C4
Plestin-les-Grèves, Fr. 56/B3
Pleszew, Pol. 43/J3
Plettenberg, Ger. 53/E6
Pleubian, Fr. 56/B3
Pleurtuit, Fr. 56/C3
Pleurtuit (int'l arpt.), Fr. 56/C3
Pleven, Bul. 51/G4
Plevna, Mt, US 156/B4
Pleyben, Fr. 56/B4
Pleyber-Christ, Fr. 56/B3
Plibo, Libr. 114/D5
Plimmerton, NZ 135/H9
Pliska, Bul. 51/H4
Plitvice Lakes NP, Cro. 50/B3
Plitvička Jezera, NP, Cro. 45/L4
Pljevlja, Serb. 50/D4
Plobsheim, Fr. 60/D1
Ploča, Rt (pt.), Cro. 50/B4
Plöcckenstein (peak), Ger. 59/G5
Plŏce, Cro. 50/C4
Plochingen, Ger. 58/C5
Płock, Pol. 43/K2
Ploćno (peak), Bosn. 50/C4
Ploegsteert, Belg. 54/B2
Ploemeur, Fr. 56/B5
Ploërmel, Fr. 56/C5
Plogastel-Saint-Germain, Fr. 56/A5
Plogoff, Fr. 56/A4
Ploieşti, Rom. 51/H3
Plomárion, Gre. 49/K3
Plombières, Belg. 55/E2
Plombières-lès-Dijon, Fr. 60/A3
Plön, Ger. 40/D4
Plonéour-Lanvern, Fr. 56/A5
Płońsk, Pol. 43/L2
Plouagat, Fr. 56/B3
Plouaret, Fr. 56/B3
Plouay, Fr. 56/B5
Ploubalay, Fr. 56/C3
Ploubazlanec, Fr. 56/B3
Ploubezre, Fr. 56/B3
Plœuc-sur-Lié, Fr. 56/C4
Ploučnice (riv.), Czh. 43/H3
Ploudalmézeau, Fr. 56/A3
Ploudaniel, Fr. 56/A3
Plouescat, Fr. 56/A3
Ploufragan, Fr. 56/C4
Plougasnou, Fr. 56/B3
Plougastel-Daoulas, Fr. 56/A4
Plougonven, Fr. 56/B3
Plouguenast, Fr. 56/C4
Plouguerneau, Fr. 56/A3
Plouguernével, Fr. 56/B4
Plouguiel, Fr. 56/B3
Plouha, Fr. 56/C3
Plouhinec, Fr. 56/A4
Plouider, Fr. 56/A3
Plouigneau, Fr. 56/B3
Ploumagoar, Fr. 56/B3
Ploumilliau, Fr. 56/B3
Plounéour-Trez, Fr. 56/A3
Plouray, Fr. 56/B4
Plourin-lès-Morlaix, Fr. 56/B3
Plouvorn, Fr. 56/A3
Plouzané, Fr. 56/A4
Plouzévédé, Fr. 56/A3
Plovdiv (pol. reg.), Bul. 49/J2
Plovdiv, Bul. 51/G4
Plovdiv (prov.), Hun. 51/G5
Plover, Wi, US 155/K1
Plover Cove (res.), China 87/L7
Plozévet, Fr. 56/A5
Pluguffan, Fr. 56/A5
Pluguffan (int'l arpt.), Fr. 56/A5
Plum (isl.), NY, US 169/F1
Plum City, Wi, US 155/H1
Plum Coulee, Mb, Can. 156/F3
Plum Grove, Tx, US 151/G2
Plumas, Mb, Can. 156/E2
Plumaugat, Fr. 56/C4
Plumbridge, NI, UK 34/A2
Plumerville, Ar, US 153/H3
Plumieux, Fr. 56/C4
Plummer, Id, US 144/F4
Plumridge Lakes Nature Reserve, Austl. 130/E4
Plumsteadville, Pa, US 168/C3
Plumtree, Zim. 123/E4
Plungė, Lith. 41/J4
Plush, Or, US 146/D2
Pluvigner, Fr. 56/B5
Plymouth (cap.), Monts. 173/N8
Plymouth, Eng, UK 36/B6
Plymouth (co.), Eng, UK 36/B6
Plymouth (arpt.), Eng, UK 36/B6
Plymouth (sound), Eng, UK 36/B6
Plymouth, Ca, US 146/C4
Plymouth, Fl, US 164/M6
Plymouth, Il, US 155/J3
Plymouth, In, US 160/C4
Plymouth, Ma, US 161/L4
Plymouth, Mn, US 157/P7
Plymouth, NC, US 163/J3
Plymouth, Ne, US 155/F3
Plymouth, NH, US 161/L3
Plymouth, Oh, US 160/E4
Plymouth, Pa, US 168/C1
Plymouth, Wi, US 160/C3
Plymouth Rock, Ma, US 161/L4
Plynlimon (peak), Wal, UK 36/C2
Plzeň, Czh. 59/G3
Plzeňský (pol. reg.), Slvk. 59/G4
PNC Bank Arts Center, NJ, US 169/J10
Pniel, SAfr. 124/L10
Pniewy, Pol. 43/J2
Pô, Burk. 115/E4
Po (riv.), It. 29/F4
Po di Venezia (riv.), It. 63/F2
Po di Volano (riv.), It. 63/E3
Po Klong Garai Cham Towers, Viet. 94/E4
Po Toi Group (isls.), China 87/M8
Pô, PN de, Burk. 115/E4
Po (valley), It. 65/F1
Poa (riv.), Ven. 181/E2
Poá, Braz. 187/K8
Poabli, Libr. 114/C5
Poatina, Austl. 132/C4
Pobé, Ben. 115/F5
Pobedy (peak), Kyr. 99/D3
Pobiedziska, Pol. 43/J2
Pobla de Segur, Sp. 47/F1
Poca, WV, US 163/G1
Pocahontas, Ab, Can. 144/F1
Pocahontas, Ar, US 162/B2
Pocahontas, Ia, US 155/G2
Pocahontas, Il, US 155/K4
Poção de Pedra, Braz. 183/E4
Pocasse Nat'l Wild. Ref., SD, US 156/D5
Pocasset, Ok, US 153/F3
Pocatello, Id, US 147/G2
Pochayiv, Ukr. 72/C2
Pochep, Rus. 70/E1
Pochinok, Rus. 68/G5
Poch'ŏn, NKor. 81/E2
P'och'ŏn, SKor. 81/G6
Pochtovoye, Ukr. 73/G5
Pocinhos, Braz. 183/G4
Pöcking, Ger. 61/H2
Pöcking, Ger. 59/G6
Pocklington, Eng, UK 35/H4
Pocklington Reef (reef), PNG 136/E6
Poço Fundo, Braz. 187/L6
Pocoata, Bol. 188/C1
Poções, Braz. 187/E2
Pocola, Ok, US 153/G3
Pocomoke City, Md, US 163/K1
Pocona, Bol. 188/C1
Poconchile, Chile 188/B1
Poconé, Braz. 185/G5
Pocono (mts.), Pa, US 168/C1
Pocono (lake), Pa, US 168/C1
Pocono (cr.), Pa, US 168/C1
Pocono Lake, Pa, US 168/C1
Pocono Pines, Pa, US 168/C1
Poços de Caldas, Braz. 187/K6
Pocpo, Bol. 188/C1
Pocrí, Pan. 180/A2
Podberez'ye, Rus. 41/P3
Podbořany, Czh. 59/G2
Podborov'ye, Rus. 68/G4
Podcher'ye, Rus. 69/N3
Poddębice, Pol. 43/K3
Poddor'ye, Rus. 41/P3
Podenzano, It. 62/C4
Podgorenskiy, Rus. 73/K2
Podgorica, Serb. 50/D4
Podkarpackie (prov.), Pol. 43/L4
Podlasie (reg.), Bela.,Pol. 43/M3
Podlaskie (prov.), Pol. 43/M3
Podol'sk, Rus. 69/W9
Podor, Sen. 114/B2
Podporozh'ye, Rus. 68/G3
Podravska Slatina, Cro. 50/C3
Podujevo, Serb. 50/E4
Poenari Burchi, Rom. 51/H3
Pofadder, SAfr. 124/B3
Poggibonsi, It. 63/E7
Poggio di Chiesanuova, SMar. 63/F6
Poggio Mirteto, It. 65/B3
Poggio Moiano, It. 65/B3
Poggio Renatico, It. 63/E4
Poggio Rusco, It. 63/E4
Poggiola, It. 63/E7
Poggiomarino, It. 65/D6
Pogoso, D.R. Congo 120/D4
Pogradec, Alb. 49/G2
Pogranichnyy, Rus. 79/L3
Pogromni (mt.), Ak, US 171/F5
Pogromnoye, Rus. 71/K1
Poh, Indo. 91/F4
P'oha-ri, NKor. 81/E2
P'ohang, SKor. 84/A2
Pohatcong (cr.), NJ, US 168/C2
Pohénégamook, Qu, Can. 158/C2
Pohja (Pojo), Fin. 41/K1
Pohjanmaa (reg.), Fin. 38/G3
Pohjois-Karjala (prov.), Fin. 68/F3
Pohnpei (isl.), Micr. 136/E4
Pohong, China 87/E4
Pohopoco (cr.), Pa, US 168/C2
Pohopoco (mtn.), Pa, US 168/C2
Pohrebyshche, Ukr. 72/E3
Poiana Mare, Rom. 72/B6
Poigny-la-Forêt, Fr. 30/H5
Poikkipuoliainen (lake), Fin. 39/E4
Poing, Ger. 59/E6
Poinsett (cape), Ant. 192/H
Point, La, US 153/H4
Point (lake), NW, Can. 140/E2
Point a la Hache, La, US 164/D3
Point au Fer (pt.), La, US 164/C3
Point au Fer (isl.), La, US 164/C3
Point Baker, Ak, US 171/M4
Point Blank, Tx, US 151/G2
Point Comfort, Tx, US 150/F3
Point Edward, On, Can. 160/E3
Point Fortin, Trin. 181/F2
Point Hope, Ak, US 171/E2
Point Judith, RI, US 161/L4
Point Judith C. G. Station, RI, US 158/B5
Point Lance, Nf, Can. 159/K2
Point Lay, Ak, US 171/F2
Point Lookout (peak), Austl. 132/E1
Point Marion, Pa, US 161/G5
Point Mugu Naval Air Sta., Ca, US 166/A2
Point Mugu State Park, Ca, US 166/A2
Point Nepean NP, Austl. 133/B4
Point of Aire (pt.), Wal, UK 35/E5
Point of Ayre (pt.), IM, UK 34/D3
Point Pedro, SrL. 95/D4
Point Pelee NP, On, Can. 160/E4
Point Pleasant, NJ, US 168/D3
Point Pleasant, Oh, US 162/E1
Point Pleasant, Pa, US 168/C3
Point Pleasant, WV, US 163/F1
Point Pleasant Beach, NJ, US 168/D3
Point Reyes National Seashore, Ca, US 146/B4
Point Roberts, Wa, US 144/C3
Point Salines (int'l arpt.), Gren. 181/F1
Point Salvation Abor. Rsv., Austl. 130/D4
Pointe à Gravois (pt.), Haiti 177/H2
Pointe à Raquette, Haiti 177/H2
Pointe au Baril Station, On, Can. 160/F2
Pointe d'Arcachon (pt.), Fr. 44/C4
Pointe d'Archeboc (peak), Fr. 64/C1
Pointe de Calle-Rousse (pt.), Fr. 64/C6
Pointe de Charbonnel (peak), Fr. 64/D2
Pointe de Chassiron (pt.), Fr. 44/C3
Pointe de la Coubre (pt.), Fr. 44/C4
Pointe de la Grande Casse (peak), Fr. 64/C2
Pointe de la Sambury (peak), Fr. 64/C1
Pointe de la Sana (peak), Fr. 64/C2
Pointe de Saume (peak), Fr. 64/C3
Pointe des Issambres (pt.), Fr. 64/C6
Pointe des Verres (peak), Fr. 60/C6
Pointe du Bois, Mb, Can. 157/G2
Pointe du Cap Roux (pt.), Fr. 64/C6
Pointe du Cheval Blanc (pt.), Haiti 177/H2
Pointe du Déffend (pt.), Fr. 64/B6
Pointe du Hourdel (pt.), Fr. 54/A3
Pointe Noir (int'l arpt.), Congo 120/B4
Pointe-à-la-Croix, Qu, Can. 158/D1
Pointe-à-Pitre, Fr. 173/N8
Pointe-au-Pic, Qu, Can. 158/B2
Pointe-aux-Outardes, Qu, Can. 158/C1
Pointe-aux-Trembles, Qu, Can. 159/P6
Pointe-Calumet, Qu, Can. 159/N6
Pointe-Claire, Qu, Can. 159/N7
Pointe-du-Lac, Qu, Can. 161/K1
Pointe-Noire, Congo 120/B4
Pointe-Verte, NB, Can. 158/E2
Poirino, It. 62/A3
Poison (cr.), Wy, US 147/K2
Poisson Blanc (res.), Qu, Can. 161/J1
Poissonier (pt.), Austl. 130/C1
Poissy, Fr. 30/J5
Poitiers, Fr. 44/D3
Poitou (reg.), Fr. 66/C1
Poitou-Charentes (reg.), Fr. 44/C3
Poix-de-Picardie, Fr. 54/A4
Poix-Terron, Fr. 55/D4
Pojo, Bol. 188/C1
Pojo (Pohja), Fin. 41/K1
Pojoaque, NM, US 149/J3
Pok Liu Chau (isl.), China 87/L8
Pokaran, India 101/K3
Pokataroo, Austl. 132/D1
Pokegama (lake), Mn, US 157/H4
Pokharā, Nepal 96/D1
Pokhvistnevo, Rus. 71/K1
Poko, D.R. Congo 121/F2
Pokrovka, Rus. 71/K1
Pokrovsk, Rus. 75/N3
Pokrovs'ke, Ukr. 73/K3
Pokrovs'ke, Ukr. 73/J4
Pokrovskoye, Rus. 70/F1
Pokrovskoye, Rus. 73/K4
Pol'ana (peak), Slvk. 70/A2
Pol-e Khomrī, Afg. 101/J1
Pol-e Sefīd, Iran 103/H2
Pola, Rus. 41/P3
Pola de Laviana, Sp. 46/C1
Pola de Lena, Sp. 46/C1
Pola de Siero, Sp. 46/C1
Polabská Nižina (phys. reg.), Czh. 43/H3
Polacca, Az, US 149/G3
Polacca Wash (riv.), Az, US 149/G3
Polače, Cro. 50/C4
Polān, Iran 101/H3
Polanco del Yi, Uru. 191/K10
Poland (ctry.) 43/K2
Poland, Me, US 161/L2
Poland, NY, US 161/J3
Połaniec, Pol. 43/L3
Polatlı, Turk. 102/C2
Polatsk, Bela. 41/N4
Polch, Ger. 55/G3
Połczyn-Zdrój, Pol. 40/G5
Pole of Inaccessability, Ant. 192/E
Polesella, It. 63/E4
Polesine (reg.), It. 63/E3
Poleski NP, Pol. 43/M3
Polesworth, Eng, UK 37/E1
Poles'ye, Bela. 70/D1
Polevskoy, Rus. 69/P4
Polgár, Hun. 50/E2
Pŏlgyo, SKor. 81/D5
Poli, Camr. 116/B3
Políaigos (isl.), Gre. 49/J4
Policastro (gulf), It. 48/D3
Police, Pol. 40/F5
Policoro, It. 48/E2
Poligny, Fr. 60/B4
Políkastron, Gre. 49/H2
Políkhni, Gre. 49/H2
Polikhnítos, Gre. 49/K3
Polillo (str.), Phil. 88/C2
Polillo (isl.), Phil. 88/C2
Polillo (isls.), Phil. 88/C2
Polis, Cyp. 104/C2
Polis'ke, Ukr. 72/E2
Polistena, It. 48/E3
Políyiros, Gre. 49/H2
Polje, Slov. 45/L3
Polk (co.), Fl, US 164/M8
Polk, Ne, US 154/F3
Polk City, Fl, US 164/M7
Polkowice, Pol. 43/J3
Polkville, Ms, US 162/C4
Polkville, NC, US 163/G3
Polla, It. 48/D2
Pollāchi, India 95/C4
Pollar, Bol. 185/E3
Pollença, Sp. 47/G3
Pollock, Id, US 146/E1
Pollock, La, US 164/B2
Pollock, SD, US 156/D5
Pollock Pines, Ca, US 146/C4
Pollockville, Ab, Can. 145/J2
Polo, Il, US 155/K3
Polo, Mo, US 155/G4
Polochic (riv.), Guat. 176/D3
Polohy, Ukr. 73/J4
Polomolok, Phil. 88/D4
Polonia (cape), Uru. 191/G2
Polonia, Wi, US 155/K1
Polonia (int'l arpt.), Indo. 89/B2
Polonne, Ukr. 72/D2
Polperro, Eng, UK 36/B6
Polski Trŭmbesh, Bul. 51/G4
Polson, Mt, US 145/G4
Poltava, Ukr. 73/H3
Poltavs'ka Oblast, Ukr. 70/E2
Põltsamaa, Est. 41/L2
Poluška (peak), Czh. 59/H5
Põlva, Est. 41/M2
Polvadera, NM, US 149/J3
Polvaredas, Arg. 190/P8
Polvijärvi, Fin. 68/F3
Polyarnyy, Rus. 68/G1
Polyarnyy, Rus. 142/U12
Polynesia (reg.) 136/G6
Pomabamba, Peru 184/B3
Pomarance, It. 45/J5
Pomaria, SC, US 163/G3
Pomarico, It. 48/E2
Pomáz, Hun. 51/R9
Pombal, Port. 46/A3
Pombal, Braz. 183/G4
Pombas, CpV. 107/J9
Pomerania (reg.), Pol. 40/F4
Pomeranian (bay), Ger.,Pol. 40/F4
Pomerode, Braz. 189/G3
Pomeroon-Supenaam (pol. reg.), Guy. 181/G3
Pomeroy, NI, UK 34/B2
Pomeroy, Oh, US 163/F1
Pomeroy, Wa, US 144/F4
Pomezia, It. 65/B4
Pomichna, Ukr. 72/F3
Pomigliano d'Arco, It. 65/D6
Pomme de Terre (riv.), Mn, US 155/G1
Pommersfelden, Ger. 58/D3
Pomona, Ks, US 153/G1
Pomona, Mo, US 153/J2
Pomona, Ca, US 166/C2
Pomona (lake), Ks, US 155/G4
Pomona, Namb. 124/A2
Pomona, NJ, US 168/D5
Pomona, Md, US 168/B5
Pomorie, Bul. 51/H4
Pomorskie (prov.), Pol. 43/J1
Pomos (pt.), Cyp. 104/C2
Pomozdino, Rus. 69/M3
Pompano Beach, Fl, US 164/P10
Pompei, It. 65/D6
Pompei (ruin), It. 65/D6
Pompéia, Braz. 189/G2
Pompeu, Braz. 186/D3
Pompey, Fr. 55/F6
Pompeys Pillar Nat'l Mon., Mt, US 145/L5
Pompiano, It. 62/C3
Pompton (riv.), NJ, US 169/H8
Pompton Lakes, NJ, US 169/H8
Ponca (cr.), SD,Ne, US 154/E2
Ponca, Ne, US 155/F2
Ponca City, Ok, US 153/F2
Poncarale, It. 62/D3
Ponce, PR 173/M8
Ponce de Leon, Fl, US 165/F2
Ponce Inlet, Fl, US 165/H3
Poncha Springs, Co, US 149/J1
Ponchatoula, La, US 164/C2
Pond (inlet), Nun, Can. 141/J1
Pond (cr.), Co, US 154/C4
Pond (cape), Austl. 128/B3
Pond (riv.), Ky, US 162/D2
Pond (pt.), Ct, US 169/E1
Pond Creek, Ok, US 153/F2
Pond Inlet, Nun, Can. 141/J1
Ponder, Tx, US 150/K6
Pondera Coulee (riv.), Mt, US 145/J3
Ponderay, Id, US 144/F3
Ponderosa, NM, US 149/J3
Pondicherry (terr.), India 92/B5
Ponemah, Mn, US 157/G3
Ponente, Riveradi (coast), Fr. 62/B5
Ponferrada, Sp. 46/B1
Pong Nam Ron, Thai. 94/C3
Pongaí, Braz. 189/G2
Pongdong, SKor. 81/D5
Ponghwa, SKor. 84/A2
Pongo (riv.), Sudan 117/E4
Pongolo (riv.), SAfr. 125/E2
Pongsan, NKor. 81/C3
Pongwe, Tanz. 119/B3
Poni (prov.), Burk. 114/E4
Poniatowa, Pol. 43/M3
Ponnaiyar (riv.), India 92/C5
Ponnani, India 95/B4
Ponoka, Ab, Can. 145/H1
Ponomarevka, Rus. 71/K1
Ponorogo, Indo. 89/E4
Ponoy, Rus. 68/J2
Ponoy (riv.), Rus. 74/D3
Ponrang, Indo. 91/F4
Pons, Fr. 44/C4
Ponsacco, It. 62/D6
Ponsonby (nbrhd.), NZ 135/F6
Pont Canavese, It. 64/D2
Pont Yates, Wal, UK 36/B3
Pont-à-Celles, Belg. 55/D3
Pont-à-Marcq, Fr. 54/C2
Pont-à-Mousson, Fr. 55/F6
Pont-Audemer, Fr. 57/F2
Pont-Aven, Fr. 56/B5
Pont-Croix, Fr. 56/A4
Pont-D'Ain, Fr. 60/B5
Pont-de-Buis-Lès-Quimerch, Fr. 56/A4
Pont-de-Chéruy, Fr. 60/B6
Pont-de-L'Arche, Fr. 57/G2
Pont-de-L'Isére, Fr. 64/A3
Pont-de-Roide, Fr. 60/C3
Pont-de-Vaux, Fr. 60/A5
Pont-de-Veyle, Fr. 60/A5
Pont-du-Château, Fr. 44/E4
Pont-Évêque, Fr. 64/A1
Pont-Hébert, Fr. 57/D2
Pont-L'Abbé, Fr. 56/A5
Pont-L'Évêque, Fr. 57/F2
Pont-Remy, Fr. 54/A3
Pont-Saint-Esprit, Fr. 64/A4
Pont-Saint-Martin, It. 62/A1
Pont-Sainte-Maxence, Fr. 54/B5
Pont-Scorff, Fr. 56/B5
Pont-y-Cymmer, Wal, UK 36/C3
Ponta da Barra (pt.), Moz. 123/G4
Ponta da Barra Falsa (pt.), Moz. 123/G4
Ponta da Marca (pt.), Ang. 122/A3
Ponta das Palmeirinhas (pt.), Ang. 120/C5
Ponta das Salinas (pt.), Ang. 122/B2
Ponta de Juatinga (pt.), Braz. 187/M8
Ponta de Pedras, Braz. 182/D3
Ponta de Pelindã (pt.), GBis. 114/A4
Ponta de São José (pt.), Ang. 122/B2
Ponta Delgada, Azor., Port. 47/T13
Ponta do Camboriú (pt.), Braz. 189/H3
Ponta do Ouro (pt.), Moz. 125/F2
Ponta do Padrão (pt.), Ang. 120/C4
Ponta do Pico (peak), Azor., Port. 47/S12
Ponta Grossa, Braz. 189/G3
Ponta Porã, Braz. 189/F2
Ponta Ta'benghisa (pt.), Malta 48/L7
Pontardawe, Wal, UK 36/C3
Pontardulais, Wal, UK 36/B3
Pontarlier, Fr. 60/C4
Pontarmé, Fr. 30/K4
Pontassieve, It. 63/E6
Pontault-Combault, Fr. 30/K5
Pontcarré, Fr. 30/L5
Pontcharra, Fr. 64/C2
Pontchartrain (lake), La, US 143/H5
Pontchâteau, Fr. 56/C6
Ponte Alta do Bom Jesus, Braz. 186/D2
Ponte Alta do Tocantins, Braz. 186/D1
Ponte Buggianese, It. 63/D6
Ponte de Sor, Port. 46/A3
Ponte dell'Olio, It. 62/C4
Ponte di Legno, It. 61/G5
Ponte di Piave, It. 63/F2
Ponte do Lima, Port. 46/A2
Ponte Lambro, It. 62/C2
Ponte Nova, Braz. 187/E4
Ponte San Nicolò, It. 63/E3
Ponte Tresa, It. 61/E6
Pontecagnano, It. 65/D6
Pontecorvo, It. 65/C5
Pontecurone, It. 62/B4
Pontedera, It. 62/D6
Pontefract, Eng, UK 35/G4
Ponteix, Sk, Can. 145/L3
Ponteland, Eng, UK 35/G1
Pontelandolfo, It. 65/D5
Pontelongo, It. 63/F3
Pontenure, It. 62/C4
Ponterwyd, Wal, UK 36/C2
Pontes e Lacerda, Braz. 185/G4
Pontesbury, Eng, UK 36/D1
Pontestura, It. 62/B3
Pontevedra, Sp. 46/A1
Pontevedra, Phil. 88/C3
Pontevico, It. 62/D3
Pontgouin, Fr. 57/G4
Ponthévrard, Fr. 30/H6
Ponthieu (reg.), Fr. 54/A3
Pontiac, Mo, US 153/H2
Pontiac, Mi, US 160/E3
Pontiac (lake), Mi, US 167/E6
Pontiac, Il, US 155/K3
Pontian Kechil, Malay. 89/C2
Pontianak, Indo. 90/C4
Pontinia, It. 65/C5
Pontivy, Fr. 56/C4
Pontlevoy, Fr. 57/G4
Pontlevoy, Fr. 57/G6
Ponto da Divisão, Braz. 182/B5
Pontoise, Fr. 30/J4
Pontonnyy, Rus. 69/T7
Pontorson, Fr. 56/D3
Pontotoc, Ms, US 162/C3
Pontotoc, Ok, US 153/F3
Pontotoc, Tx, US 150/E2
Pontpoint, Fr. 54/B5
Pontremoli, It. 62/C5
Pontresina, Swi. 61/F5
Pontrhydfendigaid, Wal, UK 36/C2
Pontrilas, Eng, UK 36/D3
Pontrilas, Sk, Can. 145/M1
Pontvallain, Fr. 57/F5
Pontyclun, Wal, UK 36/C3
Pontypool, On, Can. 161/G2
Pontypool, Wal, UK 36/C3
Ponui (isl.), NZ 135/G6
Pony, Mt, US 147/H1
Ponyo, Myan. 93/G2
Ponza, It. 48/C2
Ponza (isl.), It. 65/B6
Ponzer, NC, US 163/J3
Ponziane (isls.), It. 65/C6
Ponziane (isl.), It. 65/B6
Pool (pol. reg.), Congo 120/C3
Poole, Eng, UK 36/D5
Poole (co.), Eng, UK 36/D5
Poole (bay), Eng, UK 37/E5
Poolewe, Sc, UK 31/R8
Poona (Pune), India 101/K5
Pooncarie, Austl. 132/B2
Poondarrie (peak), Austl. 130/C3
Poondinna (mt.), Austl. 131/F3
Poopó (lake), Bol. 179/C4
Poopó, Bol. 188/C1
Poor Man Ind. Res., Sk, Can. 156/B2
Poortugaal, Neth. 52/B5
Pöõsapää (pt.), Est. 41/K2
Poosepatuck Ind. Res., NY, US 169/F2
Popa (peak), Myan. 86/B4
Popasna, Ukr. 73/K3
Popayán, Col. 180/B4
Pope (A.F.B.), NC, US 163/H3
Poperinge, Belg. 54/B2
Popigochic (riv.), Mex. 174/C2
Popil'nya, Ukr. 72/E3
Popilta (lake), Austl. 131/J5
Popina, Bul. 51/H3
Popio (lake), Austl. 132/B2
Poplar (riv.), Mb,On, Can. 140/G3
Poplar (isl.), Md, US 168/B6
Poplar, Mt, US 156/B3
Poplar (riv.), Mt, US 145/M3
Poplar Bluff, Mo, US 162/B2
Poplar Creek, BC, Can. 144/F2
Poplar Hill, On, Can. 157/G1
Poplar Tent, NC, US 163/G3
Poplar, West Fork (riv.), Mt, US 156/B3
Poplar-Cotton Center, Ca, US 148/C2
Poplarfield, Mb, Can. 156/F2
Poplarville, Ms, US 164/D2
Popocatépetl (vol.), Mex. 175/L7
Popokabaka, CAfr. 116/C4
Popoli, It. 65/C3
Popondetta, PNG 129/H2
Popovo, Bul. 51/H4
Poppberg (peak), Ger. 59/E4
Poppel, Belg. 52/C6
Poppenhausen, Ger. 58/D2
Poppenhausen, Ger. 58/C2
Poppi, It. 63/E6
Poprad, Slvk. 43/L4
Poprad (riv.), Slvk. 43/L4
Pŏptong, NKor. 81/D3
Poquoson, Va, US 163/J2
Poranga, Braz. 183/F4
Porangahau, NZ 135/D3
Porangatu, Braz. 186/C2
Porbandar, India 101/J4
Porcari, It. 62/D6
Porce (riv.), Col. 180/C3
Porcheville, Fr. 30/H5
Porcia, It. 63/F2
Porco, Bol. 188/C1
Porcuna, Sp. 46/C4
Porcupine (riv.), Can.,US 171/K2
Porcupine (hills), Sk, Can. 156/C1
Porcupine (cr.), Mt, US 145/L3
Porcupine, SD, US 154/C2
Porcupine Gorge NP, Austl. 134/B3
Pordenone, It. 63/F2
Pordenone (prov.), It. 63/F2
Pordic, Fr. 56/C3
Pordim, Bul. 51/G4
Pore, Col. 180/D3
Poreč, Cro. 63/G3
Porecatu, Braz. 189/G2
Porech'ye, Bela. 41/L5
Porepunkah, Austl. 133/C3
Poretskoye, Rus. 69/K5
Poretta (int'l arpt.), Fr. 48/A1
Porgera, PNG 129/F1
Pori (int'l arpt.), Fin. 41/J1
Pori, Fin. 41/J1
Porirua (har.), NZ 135/H9
Porirua, NZ 135/H9
Porkhov, Rus. 41/N3
Porkkala, Fin. 39/E5
Porkkalanselkä (bay), Fin. 39/E5
Porlamar, Ven. 181/F2
Porlezza, It. 61/F5
Porlock, Eng, UK 36/C4
Pormpuraaw Abor. Land, Austl. 129/F3
Pornainen (Borgnäs), Fin. 39/F4
Pornic, Fr. 44/B3
Pornichet, Fr. 56/C6
Poronaysk, Rus. 79/N2
Porongo (peak), Arg. 188/C4
Porongurup NP, Austl. 130/C5
Póros, Gre. 49/H4
Porozhsk, Rus. 69/M3
Porpoise (bay), Ant. 192/J
Porrentruy, Swi. 60/D3
Porretta Terme, It. 63/D5
Porriño, Sp. 46/A1
Porsangen (inlet), Nor. 38/H1
Porsgrunn, Nor. 40/C2
Porsuk (riv.), Turk. 70/D5
Port (isl.), Japan 83/H6
Port Adelaide (nbrhd.), Austl. 131/M8
Port Albert, Austl. 133/C4
Port Alexander, Ak, US 171/M4
Port Alfred, SAfr. 124/D4
Port Allegany, Pa, US 161/G4
Port Allen, La, US 164/C2
Port Angeles, Wa, US 144/C3
Port Antonio, Jam. 177/G2
Port Appin, Sc, UK 33/A3

Port Ar – Puerto

Port Aransas, Tx, US 151/F4
Port Arthur, Tx, US 151/H3
Port Askaig, Sc, UK 31/Q9
Port au Port (pen.), Nf, Can. 159/H1
Port au Port (bay), Nf, Can. 159/H1
Port Augusta, Austl. 131/H5
Port Austin, Mi, US 160/E2
Port Bannatyne, Sc, UK 33/A5
Port Barre, La, US 164/C2
Port Blair, India 93/F5
Port Blakely, Wa, US 167/C2
Port Blandford, Nf, Can. 159/K1
Port Bolivar, Tx, US 151/N9
Port Bouet (Abidgan) (int'l arpt.), C.d'Iv. 114/E5
Port Broughton, Austl. 131/H5
Port Burwell, On, Can. 160/F3
Port Burwell, Qu, Can. 141/K2
Port Canning, India 97/G4
Port Carbon, Pa, US 168/B2
Port Carling, On, Can. 161/G2
Port Chalmers, NZ 135/B4
Port Charlotte, Fl, US 165/G4
Port Chester, NY, US 169/L8
Port Clements, BC, Can. 171/M5
Port Clinton, Oh, US 160/E4
Port Clinton, Pa, US 168/B2
Port Colborne, On, Can. 160/U10
Port Columbus (int'l arpt.), Oh, US 160/E5
Port Credit, On, Can. 160/T8
Port Darlington, On, Can. 160/V8
Port Davey (har.), Austl. 132/C4
Port Deposit, Md, US 168/B4
Port Dickson, Malay. 89/C2
Port Discovery (bay), Wa, US 167/B1
Port Douglas, Austl. 134/B2
Port Eads, La, US 164/D3
Port Edward, BC, Can. 171/M4
Port Edwards, Wi, US 155/K1
Port Elgin, On, Can. 158/E2
Port Elgin, On, Can. 160/F2
Port Elizabeth, SAfr. 124/D4
Port Elizabeth, NJ, US 168/D5
Port Ellen, Sc, UK 31/Q9
Port Elliot, Austl. 131/H5
Port Erin, IM, UK 34/D3
Port Fairy, Austl. 132/B3
Port Gamble, Wa, US 167/B2
Port Gamble Ind. Res., Wa, US 167/B2
Port Gibson, Ms, US 164/C2
Port Glasgow, Sc, UK 33/B5
Port Graham, Ak, US 171/H4
Port Harcourt (int'l arpt.), Nga. 115/G5
Port Harcourt, Nga. 115/G5
Port Hardy, BC, Can. 140/D3
Port Hawkesbury, NS, Can. 159/G3
Port Hedland (int'l arpt.), Austl. 130/C2
Port Hedland, Austl. 130/C2
Port Heiden, Ak, US 171/G4
Port Hood, NS, Can. 159/G2
Port Hope, Mi, US 160/E3
Port Hope, On, Can. 161/G3
Port Howard, UK 191/F6
Port Hueneme, Ca, US 166/A2
Port Huron, Mi, US 160/E3
Port İliç, Azer. 103/G2
Port Isaac (bay), Eng, UK 36/B5
Port Isaac, Eng, UK 36/B5
Port Isabel, Tx, US 150/F4
Port Jefferson, NY, US 169/E2
Port Jervis, NY, US 161/J4
Port Keats, Austl. 128/C3
Port Kembla, Austl. 133/E2
Port Kenny, Austl. 131/G5
Port Lambton, On, Can. 167/H6
Port Lavaca, Tx, US 150/F3
Port Leyden, NY, US 161/J3
Port Lincoln, Austl. 131/G5
Port Lions, Ak, US 171/H4
Port Loko, SLeo. 114/B4
Port Louis (cap.), Mrts. 125/T15
Port Ludlow, Wa, US 144/C4
Port Macdonnell, Austl. 132/B3
Port Macquarie, Austl. 132/E1
Port Madison Ind. Res., Wa, US 167/B2
Port Maria, Jam. 177/G2
Port Medway, NS, Can. 158/E3
Port Monmouth, NJ, US 169/J10
Port Moresby (cap.), PNG 129/G2
Port Neches, Tx, US 151/H3
Port Nicholson (bay), NZ 135/H9
Port Nolloth, SAfr. 124/B3
Port Norris, NJ, US 168/C5
Port O'Conner, Tx, US 150/F3
Port of Ness, Sc, UK 31/Q7
Port Orange, Fl, US 165/H3
Port Orchard, Wa, US 144/C4
Port Orford, Or, US 146/A2
Port Penn, De, US 168/C4
Port Phillip (bay), Austl. 132/C3
Port Pirie, Austl. 131/H5
Port Reading, NJ, US 169/J9
Port Renfrew, BC, Can. 144/B3
Port Republic, NJ, US 168/D4
Port Rexton, Nf, Can. 159/L1
Port Richey, Fl, US 164/K7
Port Richmond (nbrhd.), NY, US 169/J9
Port Rowan, On, Can. 160/F3
Port Royal, Pa, US 168/A2
Port Royal (sound), SC, US 163/G4
Port Said (Būr Sa'īd), Egypt 113/D2
Port Saint Joe, Fl, US 165/F3
Port Saint Johns, SAfr. 124/E3
Port Saint Lucie, Fl, US 165/H4
Port Saint Mary, IM, UK 34/D3
Port San Carlos, UK 191/F6
Port Seton, Sc, UK 33/D5
Port Shepstone, SAfr. 125/E3
Port Simpson, BC, Can. 171/M4
Port Stanley, On, Can. 160/F3
Port Stephens, UK 191/E7
Port Stevens (bay), Austl. 127/E4
Port Sudan (Būr Sūdān), Sudan 109/H5
Port Sulphur, La, US 164/D3
Port Townsend, Wa, US 144/C3
Port Union, Nf, Can. 159/L1
Port Victoria, Austl. 131/H5
Port Wakefield, Austl. 131/H5
Port Washington, Wi, US 160/C3
Port Washington, NY, US 169/L8
Port Weld, Malay. 89/C1
Port William, Sc, UK 34/D2
Port Williams, NS, Can. 158/E3
Port Wing, Wi, US 157/J4
Port-au-Prince (cap.), Haiti 177/H2
Port-Bergé, Madg. 125/H6
Port-Bouët, C.d'Iv. 114/E5
Port-Brillet, Fr. 57/E4
Port-Cartier, Qu, Can. 141/K3
Port-Cros Nat'l Park, Fr. 64/C7
Port-de-Bouc, Fr. 64/A6
Port-de-Paix, Haiti 177/H2
Port-en-Bessin-Huppain, Fr. 57/E2
Port-Eynon (pt.), Wal, UK 36/B3
Port-Gentil, Gabon 120/B3
Port-la-Nouvelle, Fr. 44/E5
Port-Louis, Fr. 56/B5
Port-Louis, Fr. 173/N8
Port-Menier, Qu, Can. 141/K4
Port-of-Spain (cap.), Trin. 181/F2
Port-Saint-Louis-du-Rhône, Fr. 64/A6
Port-sur-Saône, Fr. 60/C2
Port-Vila (cap.), Van. 136/F6
Porta Westfalica, Ger. 53/F4
Porta Westfalica (pass), Ger. 53/F4
Portachuelo, Bol. 185/F5
Portadown, NI, UK 34/B3
Portaferry, NI, UK 34/C3
Portage (bay), Mb, Can. 156/E2
Portage (lake), Mi, US 157/K4
Portage (pt.), Mi, US 160/C2
Portage, Mi, US 160/D3
Portage, Pa, US 161/G4
Portage, Wi, US 155/K2
Portage la Prairie, Mb, Can. 156/E3
Portage-du-Fort, Qu, Can. 161/H2
Portageville, Mo, US 162/C2
Portal, Az, US 149/H5
Portal, Ga, US 163/G4
Portal, ND, US 156/C3
Portalegre (dist.), Port. 46/B3
Portalegre, Port. 46/B3
Portales, NM, US 152/C3
Portarlington, Ire. 32/C3
Portarlington, Austl. 133/B4
Portavogie, NI, UK 34/C3
Portbail, Fr. 56/D2
Portbou, Sp. 44/E5
Portchester, Eng, UK 37/E5
Porteiras, Braz. 183/G4
Portel, Braz. 182/D3
Porteña, Arg. 188/D4
Porter, Ok, US 153/G3
Porter, Tx, US 151/M8
Porterdale, Ga, US 162/F4
Porters (lake), Pa, US 168/C1
Porters Lake, NS, Can. 158/F3
Porterville, SAfr. 124/L10
Porterville, Ca, US 148/C2
Portes d'Enfer, D.R. Congo 121/F4
Portes-lès-Valence, Fr. 64/A3
Portet-sur-Garonne, Fr. 44/D5
Portete (bay), Col. 177/J3
Portezuelo de Socompa (pass), Chile 188/B3
Portglenone, NI, UK 34/B2
Portgordon, Sc, UK 33/C1
Porth, Wal, UK 36/C3
Porthill, Id, US 144/F3
Porthleven, Eng, UK 36/A6
Portici, It. 65/D6
Portillo, Chile 190/N8
Portimão, Port. 46/A4
Portishead, Eng, UK 36/D4
Portknockie, Sc, UK 33/D1
Portland (cape), Austl. 132/C4
Portland, Austl. 133/E1
Portland, Austl. 132/B3
Portland, On, Can. 161/H2
Portland (pt.), Jam. 177/G2
Portland, NZ 135/C1
Portland, Eng, UK 36/D5
Portland, Ar, US 153/J4
Portland, Fl, US 165/E2
Portland, In, US 160/D4
Portland, Me, US 158/B4
Portland, ND, US 156/F4
Portland, Or, US 146/B1
Portland (int'l arpt.), Or, US 144/C5
Portland, Tn, US 162/D2
Portland, Tx, US 151/F4
Portland Canal (bay), BC, Can. 171/M4
Portland Jetport (int'l arpt.), Me, US 161/L3
Portlaoise, Ire. 32/C3
Portlaw, Ire. 32/C5
Portlethen, Sc, UK 33/D2
Portlock Reefs (reef), PNG 129/G2
Portmahomack, Sc, UK 33/C1
Portmarnock, Ire. 34/B5
Portmore, Jam. 177/G2
Portneuf (riv.), Qu, Can. 158/C1
Porto, Braz. 183/F3
Porto (gulf), Fr. 48/A1
Porto, Port. 46/A2
Porto (dist.), Port. 46/A2
Porto (int'l arpt.), Port. 46/A2
Porto Alegre, Braz. 189/G4
Porto Amboim, Ang. 120/C5
Porto Amboim (bay), Ang. 122/B1
Porto Azzurro, It. 48/B1
Porto Calvo, Braz. 183/H5
Porto Ceresio, It. 61/E6
Pôrto da Fôlha, Braz. 187/F1
Porto de Mós, Port. 46/A3
Porto de Moz, Braz. 182/C3
Porto de Pedras, Braz. 183/H5
Porto Empedocle, It. 48/C4
Porto Ercole, It. 48/B1
Porto Feliz, Braz. 189/H2
Porto Ferreira, Braz. 189/H2
Porto Franco, Braz. 183/E4
Porto Garibaldi, It. 63/F4
Porto Gole, GBis. 114/B4
Porto Inglês, CpV. 107/K10
Porto Moniz, Port. 110/A2
Porto Murtinho, Braz. 188/E2
Porto Nacional, Braz. 186/C1
Porto Novo, CpV. 107/J9
Porto Poet, Braz. 182/C2
Porto Potenza Picena, It. 63/G7
Porto Recanati, It. 63/G7
Porto Rico, Ang. 120/C4
Porto Rico, Braz. 189/F2
Porto San Giorgio, It. 65/C1
Porto Santo (isl.), Port. 110/A2
Porto Santo Stefano, It. 48/B1
Porto Seguro, Braz. 187/F3
Porto Tolle, It. 63/F4
Porto Torres, It. 48/A2
Porto União, Braz. 189/G3
Porto Valtravaglia, It. 61/E6
Porto Velho, Braz. 185/F3
Porto-Novo (cap.), Ben. 115/F5
Porto-Vecchio, Fr. 48/A2
Portobelo, PN, Pan. 177/G4
Portocannone, It. 65/D4
Portoferraio, It. 48/B1
Portofino, It. 62/C5
Portogruaro, It. 63/F2
Portola, Ca, US 146/C4
Portomaggiore, It. 63/E4
Portovenere, It. 62/C5
Portoviejo, Ecu. 180/A5
Portpatrick, Sc, UK 34/C2
Portree, Sc, UK 31/Q8
Portroe, Ire. 32/B4
Portrush, NI, UK 34/B1
Portsea (isl.), Eng, UK 37/E5
Portslade-by-Sea, Eng, UK 37/F5
Portsmouth, Dom. 173/N9
Portsmouth, Eng, UK 37/E5
Portsmouth (co.), Eng, UK 37/E5
Portsmouth (isl.), NC, US 163/J3
Portsmouth, Oh, US 163/F1
Portsmouth, Va, US 163/J2
Portsoy, Sc, UK 33/D1
Portstewart, NI, UK 34/B1
Portugal (ctry.) 46/A3
Portugalete, Bol. 188/C2
Portugalete, Sp. 44/B5
Portuguesa (riv.), Ven. 173/H6
Portuguesa (state), Ven. 180/D2
Portuguese Bend (nbrhd.), Ca, US 166/F8
Portumna, Ire. 32/B3
Porum, Ok, US 153/G3
Porvenir, Bol. 184/D3
Porvenir, Bol. 185/F4
Porvenir, Chile 191/C7
Porvenir, Peru 184/C2
Porvenir, Uru. 191/K10
Porvoo (Borgå), Fin. 41/L1
Porvoonjoki (riv.), Fin. 39/F4
Porz, Ger. 55/G2
Porzuna, Sp. 46/C3
Posada, It. 48/A2
Posadas, Sp. 46/C4
Posadas, Arg. 189/F3
Posavina (valley), Bosn.,Cro. 67/H1
Posavina (valley), Bosn. 50/C3
Poschiavo, Swi. 61/G5
Poseyville, In, US 162/D1
Poshnjë, Alb. 49/F2
Posht-e Bādām, Iran 103/H3
Posio, Fin. 68/F2
Positano, It. 65/D6
Poso (cr.), Ca, US 148/C3
Poso, Indo. 91/F4
Poso (lake), Indo. 91/F4
Posof, Turk. 71/G4
Posŏng (riv.), SKor. 81/D5
Posŏng, SKor. 81/D5
Posorja, Ecu. 180/A5
Pospelikha, Rus. 99/D1
Posse, Braz. 186/D2
Possel, CAfr. 116/C4
Possession (pt.), Wa, US 167/C2
Possession (sound), Wa, US 167/C2
Possum Kingdom (lake), Tx, US 151/E1
Post, Tx, US 152/D4
Post Falls, Id, US 144/F4
Postal (Burgstall), It. 61/H4
Poste Maurice Cortier (ruin), Alg. 111/F5
Postmasburg, SAfr. 124/C3
Postoak, Tx, US 153/E4
Postojna, Slov. 45/L4
Postolprty, Czh. 59/G2
Poston, Az, US 148/E4
Postrervalle, Bol. 188/D1
Postville, Ia, US 155/J2
Pot (mtn.), Id, US 144/G4
Pota, Indo. 91/F5
Potam, Mex. 174/C3
Potamós, Gre. 49/H5
Potaro (riv.), Guy. 182/B1
Potaro-Siparuni (pol. reg.), Guy. 181/G3
Potawatomi Ind. Res., Ks, US 155/F4
Potawatomi Ind. Res., Mi, US 157/L5
Potawatomi Ind. Res., Mi, US 160/C2
Potawatomi Ind. Res., Wi, US 157/K5
Potawatomi Ind. Res., Wi, US 155/K1
Potchefstroom, SAfr. 124/D2
Poteau, Ok, US 153/G3
Poteet, Tx, US 150/E3
Potengi, Braz. 183/G4
Potenza, It. 48/D2
Potenza (riv.), It. 48/C1
Potenza Picena, It. 63/G7
Potes, Sp. 46/C1
Potgietersrus, SAfr. 123/F5
Poth, Tx, US 151/E3
Potholes (res.), Wa, US 144/E4
P'ot'i, Geo. 71/G4
Poti (riv.), Braz. 183/F4
Potigny, Fr. 57/E3
Potlatch, Id, US 144/F4
Potomac, Il, US 160/C4
Potomac, Md, US 168/A5
Potomac (riv.), Md, US 163/J1
Potoru, SLeo. 114/C5
Potosi (mtn.), Nv, US 148/E3
Potosi, Mo, US 162/B2
Potosí (dept.), Bol. 188/C2
Potosí, Bol. 188/C1
Potosi, Tx, US 150/E1
Potrerillos, Chile 188/B3
Potrero, Ca, US 148/D4
Potro, Cerro del (peak), Arg.,Chile 188/B4
Potsdam, NY, US 161/J2
Potsdam, Ger. 42/Q7
Pottangi, India 95/D2
Pottenstein, Ger. 59/E3
Potter, Ne, US 154/C3
Potter Street, Eng, UK 30/D1
Potters Bar, Eng, UK 30/C1
Potterspury, Eng, UK 37/F2
Pottersville, Mo, US 153/H2
Pöttmes, Ger. 58/E5
Potton, Eng, UK 37/F2
Potts Camp, Ms, US 162/C3
Pottsboro, Tx, US 153/F4
Pottstown, Pa, US 168/C3
Pottsville, Pa, US 168/B2
Potwin, Ks, US 153/F2
Pouch Cove, Nf, Can. 159/L2
Poudre d'or, Mrts. 125/T15
Poughkeepsie, NY, US 161/K4
Pouilley-les-Vignes, Fr. 60/B3
Poulains (pt.), Fr. 56/B6
Poulan, Ga, US 165/G2
Poulaphouca (res.), Ire. 32/D3
Poulaphoucha (res.), Ire. 34/B5
Pouldreuzic, Fr. 56/A5
Poulsbo, Wa, US 144/C4
Poulter (riv.), Eng, UK 35/G5
Poultney, Vt, US 161/K3
Poulton-le-Fylde, Eng, UK 35/F4
Pouma, Camr. 120/B2
Poŭn, SKor. 81/D4
Pound, Wi, US 160/B2
Pounga-Nganda, Gabon 120/B3
Poungthak, Laos 94/D2
Poura, Burk. 114/E4
Pourri (peak), Fr. 64/C1
Pouru-Saint-Remy, Fr. 55/E4
Pouso Alegre, Braz. 187/L7
Pouss, Camr. 116/B3
Pouthisat, Camb. 94/C3
Pouthisat (riv.), Camb. 93/H5
Pouzauges, Fr. 44/C3
Považská Bystrica, Slvk. 43/K4
Povegliano Veronese, It. 63/D3
Povenets, Rus. 68/G3
Poverty Point Nat'l Mon., La, US 162/B4
Poviglio, It. 62/D4
Póvoa de Varzim, Port. 46/A2
Povoação, Azor., Port. 47/T13
Povorino, Rus. 73/M2
Povorotnyy, Mys (pt.), Rus. 79/L3
Povungnituk (riv.), Qu, Can. 141/J2
Povungnituk, Qu, Can. 141/J2
Powassan, On, Can. 161/G1
Poway, Ca, US 166/C5
Powder (riv.), Mt,Wy, US 142/E2
Powder River (pass), Wy, US 147/K1
Powder River, Wy, US 147/K2
Powder Springs, Ga, US 163/L7
Powder, North Fork (riv.), Wy, US 154/A2
Powder, South Fork (riv.), Wy, US 154/A2
Powderhorn, Co, US 149/J1
Powderly, Tx, US 153/G4
Powderville, Mt, US 156/B5
Powell (lake), Az,Ut, US 139/F6
Powell (cr.), Pa, US 168/B3
Powell, Tn, US 162/E2
Powell (riv.), Va, US 163/F2
Powell (mtn.), WV, US 163/G1
Powell, Wy, US 147/J1
Powell River, BC, Can. 144/B3
Powellton, WV, US 163/G1
Power (res.), NY, US 160/U9
Power, Mt, US 145/J4
Power Head (pt.), Ire. 32/B6
Powers (lake), Wi, US 167/P14
Powers, Or, US 146/A2
Powers Lake, ND, US 156/C3
Powhatan, Va, US 163/J2
Powhatan Point, Oh, US 160/F5
Powys (co.), Wal, UK 36/C2
Poxoreo, Braz. 186/B2
Poxoreu (riv.), Braz. 185/H5
Poy Sippi, Wi, US 155/K1
Poyang (lake), China 80/D5
Poygan (lake), Wi, US 155/K1
Poynette, Wi, US 155/K2
Poynor, Tx, US 151/G1
Poynton, Eng, UK 35/F5
Poyo, Sp. 46/A1
Poysdorf, Aus. 43/J4
Poza Rica, Mex. 175/M6
Požarevac, Serb. 50/E3
Požega, Serb. 50/E4
Pozhva, Rus. 69/N4
Poznań, Pol. 43/J2
Pozo Alcón, Sp. 46/D4
Pozo Almonte, Chile 188/B2
Pozo Colorado, Par. 188/E2
Pozo del Molle, Arg. 188/D5
Pozo del Tigre, Bol. 185/F5
Pozo Hondo, Arg. 188/C3
Pozoblanco, Sp. 46/C3
Pozohondo, Sp. 46/E3
Pozuelo de Alarcón, Sp. 47/N9
Pozuelos, Ven. 181/E2
Pozuelos (lag.), Arg. 188/C2
Pozuzo, Peru 184/C3
Pozza, It. 63/D4
Pozzallo, It. 48/D4
Pozzilli, It. 65/D4
Pozzolo Formigaro, It. 62/B4
Pozzoni (peak), It. 65/C2
Pozzonovo, It. 63/E3
Pozzuoli, It. 65/D6
Pozzuolo, It. 65/A1
Prabuty, Pol. 41/H5
Pracham Hiang (pt.), Thai. 94/B4
Prachatice, Czh. 59/H4
Prachin Buri, Thai. 94/C3
Prachin Buri (riv.), Thai. 94/C3
Prachuap Khiri Khan, Thai. 94/B4
Prad am Stilfserjoch (Prato allo Stelvio), It. 61/G4
Praděd (peak), Czh. 43/J3
Pradera, Col. 180/B4
Prado (dam), Ca, US 148/D4
Prado, Braz. 187/F3
Prado del Rey, Sp. 46/C4
Prado Flood Control (basin), Ca, US 166/C3
Pragelpass (pass), Swi. 61/E4
Prague, Ok, US 153/F3
Prague (Praha) (cap.), Czh. 59/H2
Praha (pol. reg.), Czh. 59/H2
Praha (peak), Czh. 59/G3
Prahova (prov.), Rom. 51/G3
Praia (int'l arpt.), CpV. 107/K11
Praia (cap.), CpV. 107/K11
Praia da Vitória, Azor., Port. 47/S12
Praia Grande, Braz. 187/K9
Prainha, Braz. 182/A4
Prainha, Braz. 182/C3
Prairie, Austl. 134/B3
Prairie (cr.), Ne, US 154/E3
Prairie City, SD, US 156/C5
Prairie Dog (cr.), Ks, US 154/D4
Prairie Dog Town Fk. (riv.), Tx, US 142/F4
Prairie du Chien, Wi, US 155/J2
Prairie Farm, Wi, US 157/J5
Prairie Grove, Il, US 167/P15
Prairie Island Ind. Res., Mn, US 155/H1
Prairie Point, Ms, US 162/C4
Prairie View, Tx, US 151/G2
Prairie, South (cr.), Wa, US 167/C3
Prairies (riv.), Qu, Can. 159/N6
Prairieville, Tx, US 151/F1
Prakhon Chai, Thai. 94/C3
Pralboino, It. 62/D3
Pralognan-la-Vanoise, Fr. 64/C2
Pralungo, It. 62/B2
Pram (riv.), Aus. 59/G6
Prambachkirchen, Aus. 59/G6
Prambanan (ruin), Indo. 89/E4
Pramort, Ger. 40/E4
Pran Buri (res.), Thai. 93/G5
Pran Buri, Thai. 94/B3
Prang, Gha. 115/E5
Prangins, Swi. 60/C5
Prānhita (riv.), India 92/C4
Prapat, Indo. 89/B2
Prasat Preah Vihear, Camb. 94/D3
Praskoveya, Rus. 71/H3
Præstø, Den. 40/E4
Praszka, Pol. 43/K3
Prat, Chile, Ant. 192/W
Prata, Braz. 183/G4
Prata di Pordenone, It. 63/F2
Prata di Principato Ultra, It. 65/D6
Prata do Piauí, Braz. 183/F4
Pratantico, It. 63/E7
Pratas (Dongsha) (isl.), China 87/H4
Pratas (reef), China 87/H4
Prätlgau (valley), Swi. 61/F4
Prato, It. 63/E6
Prato (Leventina), Swi. 61/E5
Prato allo Stelvio (Prad am Stilfserjoch), It. 61/G4
Pratola Peligna, It. 65/C3
Pratomagno (mts.), It. 63/E4
Pratovecchio, It. 63/E6
Pratt, Ks, US 153/E2
Pratt (isl.), Chile 191/B6
Pratteln, Swi. 60/D2
Prattsville, Ar, US 153/H3
Prattsville, NY, US 161/J3
Prattville, Al, US 162/D4
Prauthoy, Fr. 60/B2
Pravdinsk, Rus. 69/J4
Pravets, Bul. 49/H1
Pravia, Sp. 46/B1
Prawle (pt.), Eng, UK 36/C6
Praxedis G. Guerrero, Mex. 150/B2
Praya, Indo. 91/E5
Pré-en-Pail, Fr. 57/E4
Pré-Saint-Didier, It. 60/C6
Preah Vihear (ruin), Camb. 94/D3
Préalpes (upland), Fr. 64/B2
Précigné, Fr. 57/E5
Précy-sur-Oise, Fr. 54/B5
Predappio, It. 63/E5
Predazzo, It. 45/J3
Predeal, Rom. 51/G3
Predosa, It. 62/B4
Preeceville, Sk, Can. 156/C2
Prees, Eng, UK 35/F6
Preesall, Eng, UK 35/F4
Preetz, Ger. 40/D4
Preganziol, It. 63/F2
Pregarten, Aus. 59/H6
Pregolya (riv.), Pol. 41/J4
Pregolya (riv.), Rus. 43/L1
Pregonero, Ven. 180/D2
Preiļi, Lat. 41/M3
Prek Pouthi, Camb. 94/D4
Prelate, Sk, Can. 145/K2
Premana, It. 61/F5
Prémery, Fr. 44/E3
Premià de Mar, Sp. 47/L7
Premont, Tx, US 151/E4
Prenjas, Alb. 49/G2
Prentice, Wi, US 157/J5
Prentiss, Ms, US 164/D2
Prenzlau, Ger. 43/G2
Preobrazheniye, Rus. 79/L3
Přerov, Czh. 43/J4
Presanella (peak), It. 61/G5
Prescot, Eng, UK 35/F5
Prescott, On, Can. 161/J2
Prescott, Ar, US 153/H4
Prescott, Az, US 149/F3
Prescott, Ks, US 153/G1
Prescott, Ia, US 155/G3
Prescott, Wi, US 157/Q7
Prescott Valley, Az, US 149/F3
Preševo, Serb. 49/G1
Presidencia Roque Sáenz Peña, Arg. 188/D3
Presidente Bernardes, Braz. 186/C4
Presidente Dutra, Braz. 183/E4
Presidente Epitácio, Braz. 189/F2
Presidente Hayes (dept.), Par. 186/A4
Presidente Médici, Braz. 185/F3
Presidente Prudente, Braz. 189/G2
Presidente Venceslau, Braz. 189/G2
Presidential Lake Estates, NJ, US 168/D4
Presidio (riv.), Mex. 174/D4
Presidio, Tx, US 150/B3
Presidio La Bahia, Tx, US 151/F3
Preslav, Bul. 51/H4
Presles, Fr. 30/J4
Presles-en-Brie, Fr. 30/L5
Prešov, Slvk. 43/L4
Prešovský (pol. reg.), Slvk. 43/L4
Prespa (lake), Alb. 50/E5
Presqu'Île de Giens (pen.), Fr. 64/C6
Presque Isle, Wi, US 157/K4
Presque Isle (pt.), Mi, US 157/L4
Presque Isle, Mi, US 160/E2
Presque Isle, Me, US 141/K4
Presquile Nat'l Wild. Ref., Va, US 163/J2
Pressath, Ger. 59/E3
Pressbaum, Aus. 51/N7
Prestatyn, Wal, UK 35/E5
Prestea, Gha. 115/E5
Prestfoss, Nor. 40/C1
Přeštice, Czh. 59/G3
Preston (cape), Austl. 130/C2
Preston (nbrhd.), Austl. 132/G5
Preston, Eng, UK 36/D5
Preston, Eng, UK 35/F4
Preston, Ga, US 165/F1
Preston, Ia, US 155/J2
Preston, Id, US 147/H2
Preston, Ks, US 153/E2
Preston, Md, US 168/C6
Preston, Mn, US 155/H2
Preston, Ms, US 162/C4
Preston, Nv, US 147/F4
Preston, Ok, US 153/G3
Preston, Sc, UK 33/D5
Preston, Wa, US 167/D2
Prestonpans, Sc, UK 33/D5
Prestonsburg, Ky, US 163/F2
Prestwich, Eng, UK 35/F4
Prestwick, Sc, UK 33/B6
Prestwick (int'l arpt.), Sc, UK 33/B5
Prêto (riv.), Braz. 186/D3
Prêto do Igapó-Açu (riv.), Braz. 182/A4
Pretoria (cap.), SAfr. 124/E2
Pretoriuskop, SAfr. 123/F5
Pretty Boy (res.), Md, US 168/B4
Pretty Prairie, Ks, US 153/E2
Pretty Rock Nat'l Wild. Ref., ND, US 156/D4
Preussisch Olendorf, Ger. 53/F4
Prevalje, Slov. 45/L3
Préveza, Gre. 49/G3
Prévost, Qu, Can. 159/M6
Prewitt, NM, US 149/H3
Prey Veng, Camb. 94/D4
Priargunsk, Rus. 79/H1
Priazov Upland (upland), Ukr. 73/J4
Pribilof (isls.), Ak, US 171/D4
Priboj, Serb. 50/D4
Příbram, Czh. 59/H3
Price, Qu, Can. 158/C1
Price (falls), Ok, US 153/F3
Price (riv.), Ut, US 147/H4
Price, Ut, US 147/H4
Price, Md, US 168/C5
Pricedale, Ms, US 164/C2
Prichard, Al, US 164/D2
Prichsenstadt, Ger. 58/D3
Priddy, Tx, US 151/E2
Pridgen, Ga, US 165/G2
Priego, Sp. 46/D2
Priego de Córdoba, Sp. 46/C4
Priekulė, Lith. 41/J4
Priekule, Lat. 41/J3
Prien am Chiemsee, Ger. 59/F7
Prienai, Lith. 41/K4
Prieska, SAfr. 124/C3
Priest (riv.), Id, US 144/F3
Priest Rapids (dam), Wa, US 144/E4
Priest River, Id, US 144/F3
Prieta (mtn.), Sp. 46/C1
Prievidza, Slvk. 43/K4
Prignitz (reg.), Ger. 42/F2
Prijedor, Bosn. 50/C3
Prijepolje, Serb. 50/D4
Prikaspian (plain), Kaz.,Rus. 74/E5
Prikumsk, Rus. 71/H3
Prikumskiy, Rus. 71/H3
Prilep, FYROM 49/G2
Prilly, Swi. 60/C4
Prim, Ar, US 153/H3
Prima Porta, It. 65/B4
Primavera, Braz. 183/E3
Prime Hook NWR, De, US 168/C6
Primeira Cruz, Braz. 183/F3
Primero (cape), Chile 191/B6
Primero (riv.), Arg. 188/D4
Primero de Mayo, Mex. 150/D4
Primethorpe, Eng, UK 37/E1
Primghar, Ia, US 155/G2
Primorsk, Azer. 103/G1
Primorsk, Rus. 71/H2
Primorsk, Rus. 41/N1
Primorsk, Rus. 41/J4
Primorskiy Kray, Rus. 75/P5
Primorsko, Bul. 51/H4
Primorsko-Akhtarsk, Rus. 73/K4
Primorskoye, Ukr. 73/J4
Primorskoye, Ukr. 51/K3
Prims (riv.), Ger. 55/F4
Prince, Sk, Can. 145/K1
Prince Albert (sound), NW, Can. 140/E1
Prince Albert (pen.), NW, Can. 140/E1
Prince Albert, SAfr. 124/C4
Prince Albert NP, Sk, Can. 140/F3
Prince Alfred (cape), NW, Can. 141/Q7
Prince Charles (isl.), Nun, Can. 141/J2
Prince Edward (isls.), S.Afr. 27/L7
Prince Edward (isl.), Can. 139/L5
Prince Edward Island (prov.), Can. 158/F2
Prince Edward Island NP, PE, Can. 158/F2
Prince Frederick, Md, US 163/J1
Prince George, BC, Can. 140/D3
Prince George, Va, US 163/J2
Prince Georges (co.), Md, US 168/B6
Prince Gustav Adolf (sea), Nun, Can. 141/R7
Prince Leopold (isl.), Nun, Can. 140/G1
Prince of Wales (isl.), Austl. 129/F2
Prince of Wales (isl.), Nun, Can. 139/G2
Prince of Wales (str.), NW, Can. 140/E1
Prince of Wales (isl.), Ak, US 140/C3
Prince Olav (coast), Ant. 192/D
Prince Patrick (isl.), Can. 139/E2
Prince Regent (inlet), Nun, Can. 140/G1
Prince Regent Nature Rsv., Austl. 128/B3
Prince Rupert, BC, Can. 140/C3
Prince William, NB, Can. 158/D3
Prince William (sound), Ak, US 171/J3
Prince William Forest Park, Va, US 163/J1
Princenhof (lake), Neth. 52/C2
Princes Lake, In, US 160/C5
Princes Risborough, Eng, UK 37/F3
Princes Town, Trin. 173/J5
Princesa Isabel, Braz. 183/G4
Princess Anne, Md, US 163/K1
Princess Charlotte (bay), Austl. 127/D2
Princess Juliana (int'l arpt.), Neth. 173/N8
Princess Margaret (range), Nun, Can. 141/S6
Princess Royal (isl.), BC, Can. 140/C3
Princeton, BC, Can. 144/D3
Princeton, Il, US 155/K3
Princeton, In, US 162/D1
Princeton, Ks, US 153/G1
Princeton, Ky, US 162/D2
Princeton, La, US 153/H4
Princeton, Mi, US 157/L4
Princeton, Mn, US 157/H5
Princeton, Mo, US 155/H3
Princeton, NJ, US 168/D3
Princeton, Tx, US 150/L6
Princeton, WV, US 163/G2
Princeton Junction, NJ, US 168/D3
Princeville, Il, US 155/K3
Príncipe (isl.), SaoT. 120/A2
Prindle (mt.), Ak, US 171/K3
Prineville, Or, US 146/C1
Prineville (res.), Or, US 146/C1
Pringle, Tx, US 152/D3
Pringle, SD, US 154/C2
Pringsewu, Indo. 90/B5
Pringy, Fr. 60/C6
Prinsburg, Mn, US 155/G1
Prinsenbeek, Neth. 52/B5
Prinses Margriet (canal), Neth. 52/C3
Prinzapolka (riv.), Nic. 177/E3
Prinzapolka, Nic. 177/F3
Priolo di Gargallo, It. 48/D4
Prior (cape), Sp. 46/A1
Prior Lake, Mn, US 157/P7
Prior Lake Ind. Res., Mn, US 157/P7
Priore (peak), It. 65/C2
Priozernyy, Kaz. 99/D2
Priozersk, Rus. 41/P1
Pripet Marshes (swamp), Bela.,Ukr. 70/C1
Prlpyat' (riv.), Ukr. 70/C2
Prisdorf, Ger. 53/G1
Pristen', Rus. 73/J2
Priština, Serb. 50/E4
Pritchett, Co, US 152/C2
Prittriching, Ger. 61/G1
Pritzwalk, Ger. 42/G2
Privas, Fr. 64/A3
Priverno, It. 65/C5
Privokzal'nyy, Rus. 69/P4
Privolzhskiy, Rus. 71/H2
Privolzh'ye, Rus. 71/J1
Priyutnoye, Rus. 71/G3
Priyutovo, Rus. 71/K1
Prizren, Serb. 49/G1
Prnjavor, Serb. 50/D3
Prnjavor, Bosn. 50/C3
Probištip, FYROM 49/H1
Probolinggo, Indo. 89/F4
Probstzella, Ger. 59/E1
Procida, It. 65/D6
Proctor, Ok, US 153/G3
Proctor, Tx, US 150/E2
Proctor (lake), Tx, US 151/E1
Proctor, WV, US 160/F5
Proddatūr, India 95/C3
Proença-a-Nova, Port. 46/B3
Profondeville, Belg. 55/D3
Progreso, Mex. 150/D4
Progreso, Mex. 176/D1
Progreso, Mex. 175/K6
Progreso, Pan. 177/F4
Progreso, Uru. 191/K11
Progress, Rus. 79/K2
Progresso, It. 63/E4
Prokhladnyy, Rus. 71/G4
Prokhorovka, Rus. 73/J2
Prokop'yevsk, Rus. 99/E1
Prokuplje, Serb. 50/E4
Proletarsk, Rus. 73/L4
Proletarskiy, Rus. 73/H2
Promised Land (lake), Pa, US 168/C1
Promissão, Braz. 189/G2
Promissão (res.), Braz. 186/C4
Promontory, Ut, US 147/G3
Promyslovoye, Rus. 71/H3
Propriá, Braz. 187/F1
Propriano, Fr. 48/A2
Prorva, Kaz. 71/K3
Prosecco, It. 63/G2
Proserpine, Austl. 134/C3
Prosna (riv.), Pol. 43/J2
Prosotsáni, Gre. 49/H2
Prospect, Pa, US 160/F4
Prospect, Or, US 146/B2
Prospect (nbrhd.), Austl. 131/M8
Prospect Park, Pa, US 161/G4
Prospect Park, NJ, US 169/J8
Prospector (mt.), Yk, Can. 171/L3
Prosper, Tx, US 150/L6
Prosperidad, Phil. 88/D3
Prosperity, WV, US 163/G2
Prosperity, SC, US 163/G3
Prosperous, Ire. 32/D3
Prosser, Wa, US 144/E4
Prostějov, Czh. 43/J4
Proston, Austl. 134/C4
Proszowice, Pol. 43/L3
Protection, Ks, US 152/E2
Protivín, Czh. 59/H4
Protvino, Rus. 68/H5
Provadiya, Bul. 51/H4
Provencal, La, US 164/B2
Provence (int'l arpt.), Fr. 64/B6
Provence (reg.), Fr. 66/E2
Provence-Alpes-Côte D'Azur (pol. reg.), Fr. 47/H1
Provence-Alpes-Côte-D'Azur, Fr. 45/G4
Providence, Fl, US 164/M7
Providence (cape), NZ 135/A4
Providence, Ut, US 147/H3
Providence (mts.), Ca, US 148/E3
Providence, Ky, US 162/D2
Providence, Al, US 162/D4
Providence (cap.), RI, US 158/B5
Providence Bay, On, Can. 160/E2
Providencia, Isla de (isl.), Col. 172/E5
Providência, Serra de (mts.), Braz. 185/F3
Providenciales (isl.), Bahm. 177/H1
Provideniya, Rus. 171/D3
Provo, Ut, US 147/H3
Provo (riv.), Ut, US 147/H3
Provost, Ab, Can. 145/J1
Prozor, Bosn. 50/C4
Prudentópolis, Braz. 189/G3
Prudhoe, Eng, UK 35/G2
Prudhoe Bay, Ak, US 171/J1
Prudhoe (bay), Ak, US 171/J1
Prudnik, Pol. 43/J3
Prudyanka, Ukr. 73/J2
Prue, Ok, US 153/F2
Prüm, Ger. 55/F3
Prüm (riv.), Ger. 42/D4
Prunay-en-Yvelines, Fr. 30/H6
Prunedale, Ca, US 148/B2
Prunelli-di-Fiumorbo, Fr. 48/A1
Pruszcz Gdański, Pol. 40/H4
Pruszków, Pol. 43/L2
Prut (riv.), Eur. 74/C5
Prut (riv.), Rom. 67/K1
Prut (riv.), Ukr. 72/C3
Prutz, Aus. 61/G3
Pruzhany, Bela. 43/N2
Pryazovs'ke, Ukr. 73/H4
Prykolotne, Ukr. 73/J2
Pryluky, Ukr. 73/G1
Prymors'ke, Ukr. 73/J4
Prymors'kyy, Ukr. 73/H5
Pryor, Mt, US 147/J1
Pryor (cr.), Mt, US 147/J1
Pryor (Creek), Ok, US 153/G2
Prypyat', Ukr. 72/F2
Prypyats' (riv.), Bela. 74/C4
Przasnysz, Pol. 43/L2
Przemków, Pol. 43/H3
Przemyśl, Pol. 43/M4
Przeworsk, Pol. 43/M3
Przylądek Rozewie (cape), Pol. 40/H4
Przysucha, Pol. 43/L3
Psakhná, Gre. 49/H3
Psará (isl.), Gre. 49/J3
Psárion, Gre. 49/G4
Psebay, Rus. 71/G3
Psël (riv.), Ukr.,Rus. 70/E2
Psël (riv.), Ukr. 73/G3
Pskovskaya Oblast, Rus. 68/F4
Pskov (lake), Rus. 68/E5
Pskov, Rus. 41/N3
Pšovka (riv.), Czh. 59/H2
Pszczyna, Pol. 43/K4
Pt Morin (riv.), Fr. 44/E2
Pt. Reyes Nat'l Seashore, Ca, US 148/A1
Ptolemaís, Gre. 49/G2
Ptolemaïs (ruin), Libya 108/D1
Ptuj, Slov. 50/B2
Pu Xian, China 80/B3
Puan, SKor. 81/D5
Pu'an, China 86/E3
Puangue, Chile 190/N8
Puca Barranca, Peru 180/C5
Pucacaca, Peru 184/B2
Pucallpa, Peru 184/C3
Pucara, Bol. 188/C1
Pucará, Ecu. 184/B1
Pucará, Peru 184/D4
Pucará, Peru 184/B2
Pucarani, Bol. 188/B1
Pucaurco, Peru 180/D5
Puce, On, Can. 167/G7
Puchenau, Aus. 59/H6
Pucheng, China 80/B4
Puchheim, Ger. 59/E6
Puch'on, SKor. 81/F7
Puchuncaví, Chile 190/N8
Pucioasa, Rom. 51/G3
Puck, Pol. 40/H4
Puckaun, Ire. 32/B4
Puckaway (lake), Wi, US 155/K2
Puckeridge, Eng, UK 37/G3
Pucking, Aus. 59/H6
Pucón, Chile 190/C3
Pucusana, Peru 184/B4
Pudasjärvi, Fin. 68/E2
Puddletown, Eng, UK 36/D5
Pudem, Rus. 69/M4
Puderbach, Ger. 55/G2
Pudimoe, SAfr. 124/D2
Pudozh, Rus. 68/H3
Pudsey, Eng, UK 35/G4
Pudukkottai, India 95/C4
Puebla (state), Mex. 172/B4
Puebla, Mex. 175/L7
Puebla de Alcocer, Sp. 46/C3
Puebla de Don Fadrique, Sp. 46/D4
Puebla de la Calzada, Sp. 46/B3
Puebla de Sanabria, Sp. 46/B1
Puebla de Trives, Sp. 46/B1
Puebla del Caramiñal, Sp. 46/A1
Pueblillo, Mex. 175/M6
Pueblito, Col. 180/C2
Pueblo, Co, US 152/B1
Pueblo Army Depot, Co, US 154/B4
Pueblo de Taos Ind. Res., NM, US 152/B2
Pueblo de Taos Ind. Res., NM, US 149/K2
Pueblo Nuevo, Nic. 176/E3
Pueblo Nuevo, Ven. 180/D2
Pueblo West, Co, US 152/B1
Pueblo Yaqui, Mex. 174/C3
Puelches, Arg. 190/D3
Puelén, Arg. 190/D3
Puente (hills), Ca, US 166/G8
Puente Alto, Chile 190/N8
Puente Caldelas, Sp. 46/A1
Puente de Ixtla, Mex. 175/K8
Puente del Inca, Arg. 190/C2
Puente del Inca, Arg. 190/P8
Puente Nacional, Col. 180/C3
Puente Piedra, Peru 184/B3
Puente-Ceso, Sp. 46/A1
Puente-Genil, Sp. 46/C4
Puenteareas, Sp. 46/A1
Puentedeume, Sp. 46/A1
Puentes de García Rodríguez, Sp. 46/B1
Pu'er, China 86/D4
Puerco (riv.), Az,NM, US 149/H3
Puerto Abente, Par. 188/E2
Puerto Acosta, Bol. 184/D4
Puerto Aguirre, Chile 190/B5
Puerto Aisén, Chile 190/B5
Puerto Alegre, Bol. 185/F4
Puerto Almacen, Bol. 185/E4
Puerto América, Peru 184/B2
Puerto Ángel, Mex. 176/B3
Puerto Argentina, Col. 180/C4
Puerto Armuelles, Pan. 177/F4
Puerto Arturo, Bol. 185/F4
Puerto Arturo, Chile 191/C7
Puerto Arturo, Peru 180/C5
Puerto Asís, Col. 180/B4
Puerto Ayacucho, Ven. 181/E3
Puerto Ayora, Ecu. 184/J7
Puerto Bahía Negra, Par. 188/E2
Puerto Ballivián, Bol. 185/E4
Puerto Baquerizo Moreno, Ecu. 184/K7
Puerto Barrios, Guat. 176/D3
Puerto Bermúdez, Peru 184/C3
Puerto Berrío, Col. 180/C3
Puerto Bertrand, Chile 191/B5
Puerto Caballas, Peru 184/C4
Puerto Cabello, Ven. 180/D2
Puerto Cabezas, Nic. 177/F3
Puerto Calvimonte, Bol. 185/E4
Puerto Canoa, Bol. 185/E4
Puerto Carranza, Col. 180/D5
Puerto Carreño, Col. 181/E3
Puerto Casado, Par. 188/E2
Puerto Chacabuco, Chile 190/B5
Puerto Cisnes, Chile 190/B5
Puerto Coig, Arg. 191/C6
Puerto Colón, Par. 188/E2
Puerto Cortés, Hon. 176/E3
Puerto Cortés, Mex. 174/C3
Puerto Cumarebo, Ven. 180/D2
Puerto de la Cruz, Sp. 110/A3
Puerto de la Libertad, Mex. 174/B2
Puerto de Navacerrada (pass), Sp. 47/M8
Puerto del Rosario, Sp. 110/B3
Puerto del Son, Sp. 46/A1
Puerto Deseado, Arg. 191/D5
Puerto El Carmen, Ecu. 180/C4
Puerto Escondido, Col. 180/B2
Puerto Escondido, Mex. 176/B3
Puerto Esperanza, Arg. 189/F3
Puerto Esperanza, Par. 188/E2
Puerto Fonciere, Par. 188/E2
Puerto Frey, Bol. 185/F4
Puerto General Busch, Bol. 188/E1
Puerto General Ovando, Bol. 185/E3
Puerto Grether, Bol. 185/E5
Puerto Guadal, Chile 190/B5
Puerto Harberton, Arg. 191/D7
Puerto Heath, Bol. 184/D4
Puerto Huitoto, Col. 180/C4
Puerto Iguazú, Arg. 189/F3
Puerto Inca, Peru 184/C3
Puerto Ingeniero Ibáñez, Chile 190/C5
Puerto Inírida, Col. 180/E4
Puerto Isabel, Bol. 188/E1
Puerto Izozog, Bol. 188/D1
Puerto José Pardo, Peru 184/B1
Puerto La Cruz, Ven. 181/E2
Puerto Leda, Par. 188/E2
Puerto Leguía, Peru 184/D4
Puerto Leguízamo, Col. 180/C5
Puerto Leigue, Bol. 185/E4
Puerto Lempira, Hon. 177/F3
Puerto Lobos, Arg. 190/D4
Puerto López, Col. 180/C3
Puerto López, Col. 180/D2
Puerto Lumbreras, Sp. 46/E4
Puerto Madero, Mex. 176/C3
Puerto Madryn, Arg. 190/D4

Map Section
262
263

Puerto Magdalena, Mex. 174/B3
Puerto Maldonado, Peru 184/D4
Puerto Mamoré, Bol. 185/E5
Puerto María, Par. 188/E2
Puerto Mercedes, Col. 180/C4
Puerto Mihanovich, Par. 188/E2
Puerto Montt, Chile 190/B4
Puerto Morazán, Nic. 176/E3
Puerto Morelos, Mex. 172/D3
Puerto Morín, Peru 184/B3
Puerto Napo, Ecu. 180/B5
Puerto Natales, Chile 191/B6
Puerto Niño, Col. 183/L7
Puerto Nuevo, Col. 180/D3
Puerto Nuevo, Chile 191/C7
Puerto Obaldía, Pan. 180/B2
Puerto Ocopa, Peru 184/C3
Puerto Olaya, Col. 183/L6
Puerto Padre, Cuba 177/G1
Puerto Páez, Ven. 181/E3
Puerto Pando, Bol. 184/E4
Puerto Patiño, Bol. 185/E5
Puerto Peñasco, Mex. 149/F5
Puerto Pinasco, Par. 188/E2
Puerto Pirámides, Arg. 190/D4
Puerto Piray, Arg. 189/F3
Puerto Píritu, Ven. 181/E2
Puerto Pizarro, Col. 180/C4
Puerto Portillo, Peru 184/C3
Puerto Prado, Peru 184/C3
Puerto Prat, Chile 191/B6
Puerto Princesa, Phil. 88/B3
Puerto Puyuguapi, Chile 190/B5
Puerto Quellón, Chile 190/B4
Puerto Real, Sp. 46/B4
Puerto Rico, Bol. 185/E3
Puerto Rico, Col. 180/C4
Puerto Rico, Col. 180/C4
Puerto Rico (dpcy.), US 173/M7
Puerto Rico, Tx, US 151/E4
Puerto Rondón, Col. 180/D3
Puerto Ruiz, Arg. 191/J10
Puerto Saavedra, Chile 190/B3
Puerto Saíz, Col. 180/C4
Puerto Salgar, Col. 183/L7
Puerto Salinas, Bol. 185/E4
Puerto San Carlos, Mex. 174/B3
Puerto San Julián, Arg. 191/D6
Puerto Santa Cruz, Arg. 191/C6
Puerto Santa Maria, Phil. 88/C4
Puerto Sastre, Par. 188/E2
Puerto Saucedo, Bol. 185/F4
Puerto Serrano, Sp. 46/C4
Puerto Siles, Bol. 185/E4
Puerto Suárez, Bol. 188/E1
Puerto Supe, Peru 184/B3
Puerto Tacurú Pytá, Par. 189/E2
Puerto Tahuantinsuyo, Peru 184/D4
Puerto Tejada, Col. 180/B4
Puerto Toledo, Col. 180/C5
Puerto Torno, Bol. 185/E5
Puerto Tunigrama, Peru 180/B5
Puerto Vallarta, Mex. 174/D4
Puerto Varas, Chile 190/B4
Puerto Vargas, Bol. 185/E4
Puerto Velarde, Bol. 185/F5
Puerto Victoria, Peru 184/C3
Puerto Viejo, CR 177/E4
Puerto Villamil, Ecu. 184/J7
Puerto Villarroel, Bol. 185/E5
Puerto Villazón, Bol. 185/F4
Puerto Wilches, Col. 180/C3
Puerto Williams, Chile 191/D7
Puerto Yartou, Chile 191/C7
Puertollano, Sp. 46/C3
Puesto Cunambo, Peru 184/B1
Puesto de Pailas, Bol. 188/D1
Pueyrredón (lake), Arg. 190/C5
Puffin (isl.), Wal, UK 34/D5
Pugachev, Rus. 71/J1
Pūgal, India 98/B5
Puge, Tanz. 119/A3
Puger, Indo. 89/F5
Puget (sound), Wa, US 142/B2
Puget-sur-Argens, Fr. 64/C6
Puget-Théniers, Fr. 64/C5
Puget-Ville, Fr. 64/C6
Puglia (pol. reg.), It. 48/E2
Puglia (prov.), It. 50/C5
Pugwash, NS, Can. 158/F3
Puhja, Est. 41/M2
Puigcerdà, Sp. 44/D5
Puigmal (peak), Fr. 47/G1
Puina, Bol. 184/D4
Puiseux-en-France, Fr. 30/K4
Pujaut, Fr. 64/A5
Pujehun, SLeo. 114/C5
Pujiang, China 86/D2
Pujilí, Ecu. 180/B5
Pujŏn (lake), NKor. 81/D2
Pujut (cape), Indo. 89/D4
Pukaki (lake), NZ 135/B3
Puk'an-san (peak), SKor. 81/F6
Puk'an-san NP, SKor. 81/D4
Pukapuka (isl.), CookIs. 137/J6
Pukarua (isl.), FrPol. 137/M6
Pukaskwa NP, On, Can. 157/L3
Pukch'ang, NKor. 81/D3
Pukchin, NKor. 81/C2
Pukch'ŏng, NKor. 81/E2
Pukdae (riv.), NKor. 81/E2
Pukë, Alb. 49/F1
Pukerua Bay, NZ 135/H9
Pukhan (riv.), NKor.,SKor. 81/D3
Pukhan (riv.), SKor. 81/G6
Pukhovichi, Bela. 41/N5
Pukhrāyān, India 96/B2
Pukkila, Fin. 39/F4
Pukŭ-san, SKor. 81/F6
Pukou, China 87/H3
Pukovac, Serb. 50/E4
Pukp'ot'ae-san (peak), NKor. 81/E2
Puksoozero, Rus. 68/J3
Pukuatu (cape), Indo. 128/A2
Pula, Cro. 45/K4
Pulacayo, Bol. 188/C2
Pulandian (bay), China 81/A3
Pulanduta (pt.), Phil. 91/F1
Pulangi (riv.), Phil. 88/D3
Pulap (isl.), Micr. 136/D4
Pulāsar, India 98/C5
Pulaski, Ms, US 162/C4
Pulaski, NY, US 161/H3
Pulaski, Tn, US 162/D3
Pulaski, Wi, US 160/B2
Pulaski, Va, US 163/G2
Pulau (riv.), Indo. 91/J5
Pulau Ayer Chawan (isl.), Sing. 89/H6
Pulau Bukum (isl.), Sing. 89/J7
Pulau Pinang (state), Malay. 89/B1
Pulau Sudong (isl.), Sing. 89/H7
Pulau Tekong (isl.), Sing. 89/K6
Pulau Ubin (isl.), Sing. 89/J6
Pulaukijang, Indo. 89/C3
Puławy, Pol. 43/L3
Pulborough, Eng, UK 37/F5
Pulguk-sa, SKor. 84/A3
Pulheim, Ger. 55/F2
Pulí, Col. 183/L8
Pulisan (cape), Indo. 91/G3
Pulkovo (int'l arpt.), Rus. 69/T7
Pullach im Isartal, Ger. 61/H1
Pullman, Mi, US 160/C3
Pullman, Wa, US 144/F4
Pully, Swi. 60/C5
Pulog (mt.), Phil. 88/C1
Pulsnitz (riv.), Ger. 43/G3
Pułtusk, Pol. 43/L2
Pulu, China 99/D4
Pülümür, Turk. 102/D2
Puluwat (isl.), Micr. 136/D4
Pulversheim, Fr. 60/D2
Pulwama, India 98/C3
Pum (riv.), China 97/F1
Puma (lake), China 97/H1
Puma, Tanz. 119/A3
Pumpkin (cr.), Mt, US 145/M4
Pumpsaint, Wal, UK 36/C2
Pumpville, Tx, US 150/D3
Pumu (pass), China 93/F2
Puna de Atacama (plat.), Arg. 188/C3
Punaauia, FrPol. 137/X15
Punakaiki, NZ 135/B3
Punākha, Bhu. 97/G2
Punata, Bol. 188/C1
Pūnch, India 98/C3
Pūnch (riv.), India 98/C3
Punchaw, BC, Can. 144/C1
Püncogling, China 97/F1
Punda Maria, SAfr. 123/F4
Pūndri, India 98/D5
Pune (Poona), India 101/K5
Punelia (lake), Fin. 39/E4
Punggai (cape), Malay. 90/B3
P'unggi, SKor. 81/E4
Pungo (riv.), NC, US 163/J3
Pungo NWR, NC, US 163/J3
Púngoè (riv.), Moz. 123/G3
Pungoteague, Va, US 163/K2
P'ungsan, NKor. 81/E2
P'ungsŏ, NKor. 81/E2
Pungwe (falls), Zim. 123/G3
Punia, D.R. Congo 121/F3
Punitaqui, Chile 188/B4
Punjab (plain), Pak. 101/K2
Punjab (state), India 99/B5
Puno (dept.), Peru 188/B1
Puno, Peru 184/D4
Pūnpūn (riv.), India 97/E3
Punta, Ca, US 166/A2
Punta Allen, Mex. 172/D4
Punta Alta, Arg. 190/E3
Punta Arena, (pt.), Mex. 174/C4
Punta Arenas, Chile 191/C7
Punta Banda, (cape), Mex. 174/A2
Punta Cardón, Ven. 180/D2
Punta Celarain, (pt.), Mex. 176/E1
Punta Colnett, (pt.), Mex. 174/A2
Punta Colonet, Mex. 174/A2
Punta de Bombón, Peru 184/D5
Punta de Díaz, Chile 188/B4
Punta de Mata, Ven. 181/F2
Punta de Pietra (res.), Ven. 183/Q8
Punta del Este, Uru. 191/G2
Punta del Este (Capitán Curbelo) (int'l arpt.), Uru. 191/G2
Punta Gorda, Fl, US 165/G4
Punta Gorda (bay), Nic. 172/E5
Punta Gorda, Belz. 176/D2
Punta Marina, It. 63/F5
Punta Raisi (int'l arpt.), It. 48/C3
Punta Umbría, Sp. 46/B4
Puntarenas, CR 177/E4
Puntas de Maciel, Uru. 191/K10
Punxsutawney, Pa, US 161/G4
Pupiales, Col. 180/B4
Pupuya (peak), Bol. 184/D4
Puqi, China 87/G2
Puqian, China 93/K3
Puquio, Peru 184/C4
Puquios, Chile 184/D5
Pur (riv.), Rus. 74/H3
Pura, India 96/A3
Puracé (vol.), Col. 180/B4
Puracé, PN, Col. 180/B4
Pūranpur, India 96/C1
Purari (riv.), PNG 129/G1
Purbeck (isl.), Eng, UK 36/D5
Purbolinggo, Indo. 89/E4
Purcell, Ok, US 153/F3
Purcell (mts.), BC, Can. 144/F2
Purcell (mtn.), Wa, US 144/D4
Purdin, Mo, US 155/H4
Purdy, Mo, US 153/H2
Purdy, On, Can. 161/H2
Purdy, Va, US 163/J2
Puré (riv.), Col. 180/D5
Pure, Indo. 128/A1
Purén, Chile 190/B3
Purgatoire (riv.), Co, US 154/C5
Pürgen, Ger. 61/G1
Purgstall an der Erlauf, Aus. 45/L2
Purificación, Col. 180/C4
Purikari (pt.), Est. 41/L2
Purkersdorf, Aus. 51/N7
Purleigh, Eng, UK 30/F1
Purley (nbrhd.), Eng, UK 30/C3
Purmerend, Neth. 52/B3
Pūrna (riv.), India 92/C3
Pūrna, India 95/C2
Purnia, India 97/F3
Purple (mtn.), Ire. 32/A6
Purton, Eng, UK 37/E3
Puruê (riv.), Braz. 180/D5
Puruey, Ven. 181/E3
Purūlia, India 97/F4
Puruname, Ven. 181/E4
Puruni (riv.), Guy. 181/G3
Purús (riv.), Braz. 179/C3
Purushottampur, India 95/E2
Purutu (isl.), PNG 129/F2
Purvis, Ms, US 164/D2
Pŭrvomay, Bul. 51/G4
Purwa, India 96/C2
Purwakarta, Indo. 89/D4
Purwodadi, Indo. 89/E4
Purwokerto, Indo. 89/E4
Purworejo, Indo. 89/E4
Puryear, Tn, US 162/C2
Puryŏng, NKor. 79/K3
Pusad, India 95/C2
Pusan-jikhalsi (prov.), SKor. 84/A3
Pusat Gayo (mts.), Indo. 90/A3
Puschendorf, Ger. 58/D3
Pushchino, Rus. 68/H5
Pushkin, Rus. 69/T7
Pushkin (arpt.), Rus. 69/T7
Pushkino, Rus. 71/H2
Pushkino, Rus. 69/W8
Pushkinskiye Gory, Rus. 41/N3
Pushmataha, Al, US 162/C4
Püspökladány, Hun. 50/E2
Pussay, Fr. 57/H4
Püssi, Est. 41/M2
Pustomyty, Ukr. 72/B3
Pustoshka, Bela. 72/E1
Pusuga, Gha. 115/E4
Pusula, Fin. 39/D4
Pusur (riv.), Bang. 97/G4
Puta, Zam. 121/G5
Putaendo, Chile 190/C2
Putah (cr.), Ca, US 148/A1
Putai, Tai. 87/J4
Putana (vol.), Chile 188/C2
Putanges-Pont-Écrepin, Fr. 57/E3
Putao, Myan. 86/C3
Putaoxu, China 87/F3
Putaruru, NZ 135/C2
Puthia, Bang. 97/G3
Puthukkudiyiruppu, SrL. 95/D4
Putian, China 87/G2
Putina, Peru 184/D4
Puting (cape), Indo. 90/D4
Putintsevo, Kaz. 78/A2
Putla de Guerrero, Mex. 176/B2
Putnam, Al, US 164/D1
Putnam, Ct, US 161/L4
Putnam, Ok, US 152/E3
Putnam, Tx, US 150/E1
Putney, SD, US 156/E5
Putney, Ga, US 165/F2
Putney, Vt, US 161/K3
Putomayo (dept.), Col. 180/C4
Putorana (mts.), Rus. 74/K3
Putrachoique (peak), Arg. 190/C4
Putre, Chile 188/B1
Putte, Belg. 55/D1
Puttelange-aux-Lacs, Fr. 55/F5
Putten (isl.), Neth. 52/B5
Putten, Neth. 52/C4
Puttenham, Eng, UK 30/B3
Puttgarden, Ger. 40/D4
Püttlach (riv.), Ger. 59/E3
Püttlingen, Ger. 55/F5
Putu (range), Libr. 114/C5
Putula, Fin. 39/F4
Putumayo (riv.), Ecu. 180/B4
Putumayo (riv.), SAm. 179/B3
Putumayo (riv.), SAm. 180/C5
Putumayo (riv.), Col.,Peru 184/D1
Putussibau, Indo. 90/D3
Putyla, Ukr. 72/C3
Putyvl', Ukr. 73/G2
Puula (lake), Fin. 41/M1
Puurmani, Est. 41/M2
Puurs, Belg. 55/D1
Puwei, China 86/D3
Puxi, China 87/H3
Puxico, Mo, US 162/B2
Puy de Sancy (peak), Fr. 44/E4
Puy-Saint-Vincent, Fr. 64/C3
Puyallup (riv.), Wa, US 167/C3
Puyallup, Wa, US 144/C4
Puyallup Ind. Res., Wa, US 167/C3
Puyang, China 80/C4
Puye Cliff Dwellings, NM, US 149/J3
Puyehué (lake), Chile 190/B4
Puyehue (vol.), Chile 190/B4
Puylaurens, Fr. 44/E5
Puyŏ, SKor. 81/D4
Puyo, Ecu. 180/B5
Puysegur (pt.), NZ 135/A4
Puyun, NKor. 81/E2
Puzal, Sp. 47/E3
P'warwŏn, NKor. 81/C3
Pwawi (prov.), Tanz. 119/B3
Pweto, D.R. Congo 121/G5
Pwllheli, Wal, UK 34/D6
Pyalitsa, Rus. 68/H2
Pyal'ma, Rus. 68/G3
Pyamalaw (riv.), Myan. 86/B5
Pyandzh, Taj. 101/J1
Pyandzh (Panj) (riv.), Afg.,Taj. 99/B4
Pyaozero (lake), Rus. 38/J2
Pyapon, Myan. 93/G4
Pyasina (riv.), Rus. 74/J2
Pyatigorsk, Rus. 71/G3
P'yatykhatky, Ukr. 73/G3
Pye, Myan. 86/B5
Pyfara (peak), Fr. 44/F4
Pyhä-Häkin NP, Fin. 68/E3
Pyhäjärvi, Fin. 68/E3
Pyhäjärvi (lake), Fin. 41/K1
Pyhäntä, Fin. 68/E2
Pyhätunturi (peak), Fin. 68/E2
Pyingaing, Myan. 86/B4
Pyinmana, Myan. 86/C5
Pyle, Wal, UK 36/C3
Pyŏktong, NKor. 81/C2
P'yŏngan-namdo (prov.), NKor. 81/C3
P'yŏngch'ang, SKor. 81/E4
P'yŏnggang, NKor. 81/D3
P'yŏnghae, SKor. 81/E4
P'yŏngnamjin, NKor. 81/D2
P'yŏngsan, NKor. 81/D3
P'yŏngsong, NKor. 81/C3
Pyŏngt'aek, SKor. 81/D4
P'yŏngwŏn, NKor. 81/C3
P'yŏngyang (cap.), NKor. 81/C3
P'yŏngyang (int'l arpt.), NKor. 81/C3
P'yŏngyang-si (prov.), NKor. 81/C3
Pyŏnsanbando NP, SKor. 81/D5
Pyramid (mt.), BC, Can. 171/M4
Pyramid (lake), Ca, US 142/C3
Pyramid (peak), Id, US 147/G1
Pyramid (pt.), Mi, US 160/D2
Pyramid (peak), Wy, US 154/A2
Pyramid Lake Ind. Res., Nv, US 146/D3
Pyramids Of Jīzah, Egypt 113/C5
Pyrenees (range), Eur. 47/E1
Pyrenees (mts.), Fr.,Sp. 29/D4
Pyrénées Occidentales, PN, Fr. 47/E1
Pyryatyn, Ukr. 73/G1
Pyrzyce, Pol. 43/H2
Pyshchug, Rus. 69/K4
Pyshma (riv.), Rus. 69/Q4
Pys'menne, Ukr. 73/H3
Pytalovo, Rus. 41/M3
Pyu, Myan. 86/C5
Pyuntaza, Myan. 94/B2
Pyuthān, Nepal 96/D1

Q

Qā 'al Jafr (salt pan), Jor. 104/E4
Qabalān, WBnk. 105/C4
Qabātiyah, WBnk. 105/C4
Qabb Ilyās, Leb. 105/D1
Qābis (gov.), Tun. 111/H2
Qābis, Tun. 66/F4
Qabr Hūd, Yem. 100/E5
Qachas Nek, Les. 124/E3
Qaḑḑ al Qamḩ (well), Libya 108/D2
Qādiān, India 98/C4
Qadima, Isr. 105/B4
Qādirpur Rān, Pak. 98/A4
Qā'emshahr, Iran 103/H2
Qā'en, Iran 101/G2
Qafa e Malit (pass), Alb. 49/G1
Qaffīn, WBnk. 105/C4
Qāfilah, Egypt 113/B2
Qafşah (gov.), Tun. 111/H2
Qafşah, Tun. 66/F4
Qagan (lake), China 79/J2
Qagannur, China 99/E3
Qahā, Egypt 113/C4
Qahar Youyi Qianqi, China 80/C2
Qahar Youyi Zhongqi, China 80/C2
Qaidam (basin), China 78/C4
Qal at Bīshah, SAr. 100/D5
Qala'an Naḩl, Sudan 117/G2
Qalamshāh, Egypt 113/B6
Qalansuwa, Isr. 105/B4
Qal'at Al Andalus, Tun. 48/B4
Qal'at ar Rabaḑ (ruin), Jor. 105/D4
Qal'at Aş Şanam, Tun. 112/L7
Qal'at Dizah, Iraq 103/F2
Qal'at Jandal, Syria 105/D2
Qal'at Sukkar, Iraq 103/F4
Qal'eh-ye Deh-e Bārez, Iran 101/G3
Qallābāt, Sudan 117/H2
Qallīn, Egypt 113/B2
Qalqīlyah, WBnk. 105/B4
Qalyūb, Egypt 113/C4
Qamīnis, Libya 108/D2
Qanā, SAr. 102/E5
Qānā, Leb. 105/C2
Qanah (wadi), Isr. 105/C4
Qanat Junqoley (canal), Sudan 117/F4
Qandala, Som. 118/D3
Qanţarah (peak), Egypt 113/B4
Qanţarat Al Fahş, Tun. 112/L6
Qapshagay Bögeni (res.), Kaz. 99/C3
Qapshaghay, Kaz. 99/C3
Qarabutaq, Kaz. 71/M2
Qaraghandy, Kaz. 99/B2
Qaraghandy Oblast, Kaz. 99/A2
Qārah, SAr. 102/E4
Qarak, China 99/C4
Qarānqū (riv.), Iran 103/F2
Qarārat al Hayyirah (depr.), Libya 108/B3
Qārat ar Raml (peak), Egypt 113/B4
Qārat Jahannam (peak), Egypt 113/B6
Qarataū, Kaz. 99/B3
Qardho, Som. 118/D3
Qareh Chāy (riv.), Iran 100/E2
Qareh Sū (riv.), Iran 71/H5
Qareh Ẕīā' od Dīn, Iran 103/F2
Qarn (wadi), Libya 108/D1
Qarqan (riv.), China 99/E4
Qarqannah, Juzur (isls.), Tun. 67/F4
Qarqaraly, Kaz. 74/H5
Qarrit (pass), Alb. 49/G2
Qarshi, Uzb. 74/G6
Qarţājannah (Carthage) (ruin), Tun. 48/B4
Qārūn (lake), Egypt 109/F2
Qaryat abu Nujaym, Libya 108/B2
Qaryat Abū Qurayn, Libya 108/B2
Qaryat az Zuwaytīnah, Libya 108/D2
Qāsim, Syria 105/E3
Qāsimwāla, Pak. 98/B4
Qaşr al Ḩallābāt (ruin), Jor. 105/E4
Qaşr al Jady, Libya 67/K5
Qaşr al Kharānah, Jor. 105/E5
Qaşr al Khubbāz, Iraq 102/E3
Qaşr al Mushattá (ruin), Jor. 105/E5
Qaşr 'Amrah, Jor. 105/F5
Qaşr aş Şāghah (ruin), Egypt 113/B5
Qaşr Baghdād, Egypt 113/B3
Qaşr Farāfirah, Egypt 109/E3
Qaşr Hallāl, Tun. 48/B5
Qaşr Qārūn, Egypt 113/B6
Qaşr-e Qand, Iran 101/H3
Qaşr-e-Shīrīn, Iran 103/F3
Qa'ţabah, Yem. 118/C2
Qaţanā, Syria 105/E2
Qatar (ctry.) 100/F3
Qattara Depression (depr.), Egypt 102/A4
Qaţţīnah (lake), Syria 104/E2
Qawz Abū Dulū (dune), Sudan 117/G1
Qawz Rajab, Sudan 117/G1
Qaxi, China 99/D3
Qaysān, Sudan 117/G3
Qayü, China 86/B2
Qayyārah, Iraq 103/E3
Qazaqtyng Usaqshoqzlyghy, (uplands), Kaz. 74/H5
Qazax, Azer. 103/F1
Qāzi Ahmad, Pak. 92/A2
Qazimämmäd, Azer. 103/G1
Qazvīn, Iran 103/G2
Qedma, Isr. 105/B5
Qendrevica (peak), Alb. 49/F2
Qeqertarsuaq (Disko) (isl.), Grld. 141/L2
Qeshm, Iran 103/J5
Qeshm (isl.), Iran 103/H5
Qeydār, Iran 103/G2
Qezel Owzan (riv.), Iran 100/E1
Qi (riv.), China 93/J2
Qi Xian, China 80/C4
Qian (mts.), China 81/B2
Qian (riv.), China 80/D5
Qian Gorlos Mongolzu Zizhixian, China 79/J2
Qian'an, China 79/J3
Qianban, China 87/H3
Qiancun, China 87/J2
Qianfodong, China 99/D3
Qiange, China 87/H3
Qianjiang, China 87/G2
Qianning, China 86/D2
Qianqing, China 80/L9
Qianqiu (pass), China 87/H2
Qianshanlaoba, China 99/D2
Qianxi, China 80/J6
Qiaodong, China 87/G2
Qiaojia, China 86/D3
Qiaomaidi, China 94/C1
Qiaoshe, China 87/G2
Qiaosi, China 80/L9
Qiaotouhe, China 87/F3
Qiaoxu, China 87/F4
Qibilī, Tun. 66/F4
Qibyā, WBnk. 105/C5
Qidaogou, China 81/D2
Qidong, China 93/K2
Qidong, China 80/L8
Qidukou, China 78/D5
Qiemo, China 99/E4
Qifeng (pass), China 87/F2
Qigong, China 87/G3
Qihe, China 80/D3
Qikiqtarjuaq, Nun, Can. 141/K2
Qikou, China 79/H4
Qila Dīdār Singh, Pak. 98/C3
Qila Sobha Singh, Pak. 98/C3
Qilian (mts.), China 77/J6
Qilian (peak), China 78/D4
Qilihe, China 81/A2
Qiling, China 87/G3
Qilizhen, China 78/C3
Qilţ (wadi), Isr. 105/C5
Qimantag (mts.), China 78/C4
Qimen, China 87/H2
Qin (riv.), China 78/G4
Qin (mts.), China 80/B4
Qinā, Egypt 109/G3
Qinā (gov.), Egypt 109/G3
Qinā (wadi), Egypt 109/G3
Qing (riv.), China 80/B5
Qing'an, China 79/K2
Qingchengzi, China 81/B2
Qingdao, China 80/E3
Qingduizi, China 81/A2
Qingfeng, China 80/C4
Qingfu, China 86/E2
Qinggang, China 79/K2
Qinghai (lake), China 78/D4
Qinghai (mts.), China 78/D4
Qinghe, China 81/C2
Qinghe, China 80/C3
Qinghecheng, China 81/C2
Qinghemen, China 81/A2
Qinghua, China 87/H2
Qinglong, China 80/D2
Qingping, China 87/F4
Qingping, China 87/F2
Qingpu, China 80/L8
Qingshan, China 87/G2
Qingshen, China 86/D2
Qingshizui, China 78/E4
Qingshui (riv.), China 87/F3
Qingshuihe, China 78/D5
Qingshuihe, China 80/B3
Qingshuihezi, China 99/E3
Qingshuilang (mts.), China 86/C3
Qingxi, China 87/F3
Qingyang, China 87/H2
Qingyuan, China 81/C1
Qingyuan, China 93/K3
Qingyuan (mts.), China 87/G4
Qingyuan, China 87/H3
Qingyun, China 80/D3
Qingzhou, China 80/D3
Qinhuangdao, China 80/D3
Qinshui, China 80/C4
Qinyang, China 80/C4
Qinyuan, China 80/C3
Qinzhou, China 87/F4
Qionghai, China 93/K4
Qionglai, China 86/D2
Qionglai (mts.), China 78/E5
Qiongshan, China 93/K4
Qiongzhong, China 94/E2
Qipan (pass), China 87/E1
Qiqihar, China 79/J2
Qiquanhu, China 78/B3
Qiquanhu, China 99/E3
Qīr, Iran 103/H4
Qira, China 99/D4
Qiryat Ata, Isr. 105/C3
Qiryat Bialik, Isr. 105/C3
Qiryat Gat, Isr. 105/B5
Qiryat Mal'akhi, Isr. 105/B5
Qiryat Motzkin, Isr. 105/C3
Qiryat Shemona, Isr. 105/D2
Qiryat Tiv'on, Isr. 105/C3
Qiryat Yam, Isr. 105/C3
Qishn, Yem. 118/D2
Qishuyan, China 80/L8
Qitai, China 99/E3
Qitaihe, China 79/L2
Qiumuzhuang, China 81/B2
Qixia, China 80/E3
Qixing (riv.), China 75/P5
Qixing (pass), China 86/E3
Qixingpao, China 79/K2
Qixitian, China 87/H2
Qizhan, China 79/K1
Qiziqum (des.), Kaz. 74/G5
Qogir (peak), China 101/L1
Qom, Iran 103/G3
Qom (riv.), Iran 100/F2
Qomo, China 86/B2
Qomsheh, Iran 103/G3
Qondūz (riv.), Afg. 101/J1
Qonggyai, China 97/H1
Qoraqalpoghiston Aut. Rep., Uzb. 71/L3
Qormi, Malta 48/L7
Qorveh, Iran 103/F3
Qorveh, Iran 103/G3
Qoryooley, Som. 119/D1
Qostanay, Kaz. 69/P5
Qostanay (int'l arpt.), Kaz. 69/P5
Qostanay Oblast, Kaz. 69/P5
Qoţbābād, Iran 103/J5
Qoţbābād, Iran 103/H4
Qoţūr, Iran 103/F2
Qu (riv.), China 78/F5
Quabbin (res.), Ma, US 158/A4
Quainton, Eng, UK 37/F3
Quairading, Austl. 130/C5
Quakenbrück, Ger. 53/E3
Quakertown, Pa, US 168/C3
Qualiano, It. 65/D6
Qualicum Beach, BC, Can. 144/B3
Quamba, Mn, US 157/H5
Quambatook, Austl. 132/B2
Quambone, Austl. 132/C1
Quan (riv.), China 78/H5
Quanah, Tx, US 152/E3
Quanbao (mtn.), China 80/B4
Quandialla, Austl. 133/C2
Quang Ngai, Viet. 94/E3
Quang Trach, Viet. 94/D2
Quang Tri, Viet. 94/D2
Quangongting, China 80/L9
Quanjiao, China 80/D4
Quantico M.C. Res., Va, US 163/J1
Quanyang, China 81/D1
Quanzhou, China 87/H3
Quanzhou, China 87/F3
Quapaw, Ok, US 153/G2
Qu'Appelle, Sk, Can. 156/C2
Qu'Appelle (dam), Sk, Can. 156/A2
Qu'Appelle (riv.), Sk, Can. 156/C2
Quaqtaq, Qu, Can. 141/K2
Quaraí, Braz. 189/E4
Quaregnon, Belg. 54/C3
Quarles (mts.), Indo. 91/E4
Quarona, It. 62/B2
Quarrata, It. 63/D6
Quarryville, Pa, US 168/B4
Quarto, It. 65/D6
Quarto d'Altino, It. 63/F2
Quarto de Fevereiro (int'l arpt.), Ang. 120/C5
Quartu Sant'elena, It. 48/A3
Quartz (peak), Ca, US 148/E4
Quartz Hill, Ca, US 166/B1
Quartzsite, Az, US 148/E4
Quatre Bornes, Mrts. 125/T15
Quattervals (peak), Swi. 61/G4
Quay, NM, US 152/C3
Quba, Azer. 71/J4
Quballāţ, Tun. 112/L6
Qūchān, Iran 101/G1
Que Son, Viet. 94/E3
Queanbeyan, Austl. 133/D2
Québec (prov.), Can. 141/J3
Québec (cap.), Qu, Can. 158/B2
Québec (int'l arpt.), Qu, Can. 158/B2
Quebra-Cangalha (mts.), Braz. 187/L8
Quebracho, Uru. 188/E4
Quechisla, Bol. 188/C2
Quecholac, Mex. 175/M8
Quechutenango, Mex. 175/F5
Quedal (pt.), Chile 190/B4
Quedas do Iguaçu, Braz. 189/F3
Quedgeley, Eng, UK 36/D3
Queen Alia (int'l arpt.), Jor. 105/E5
Queen Anne, Md, US 168/C6
Queen Annes (co.), Md, US 168/C5
Queen Bess (mt.), BC, Can. 144/B2
Queen Charlotte, BC, Can. 171/M5
Queen Charlotte (isls.), BC, Can. 140/C3
Queen Charlotte (sound), BC, Can. 140/C3
Queen City, Tx, US 153/G4
Queen Creek, Az, US 149/G4
Queen Elizabeth (isls.), Can. 139/E2
Queen Mary (res.), Eng, UK 30/B2
Queen Mary (coast), Ant. 192/G
Queen Mary, Ca, US 166/F8
Queen Maud (mts.), Ant. 192/P
Queen Maud (gulf), Nun, Can. 140/F2
Queen Maud Land (phys. reg.), Ant. 192/Z
Queen Victoria Spring Nature Reserve, Austl. 130/D4
Queenborough, Eng, UK 37/G4
Queens (chan.), Austl. 128/C3
Queens (chan.), Nun, Can. 141/S7
Queens (co.), NY, US 169/E2
Queensberry (peak), Sc, UK 33/C6
Queensbury, Eng, UK 35/G4
Queenscliff, Austl. 133/B4
Queensferry, Wal, UK 35/E5
Queensferry, Sc, UK 33/C5
Queensland (state), Austl. 127/C3
Queenston, On, Can. 160/U9
Queenstown, NZ 135/B4
Queenstown, Austl. 132/C4
Queenstown, Guy. 181/G3
Queenstown (nbrhd.), Sing. 89/J6
Queenstown, SAfr. 124/D3
Queenstown, Md, US 168/B6
Queich (riv.), Ger. 55/H5
Queidersbach, Ger. 55/G5
Queilén, Chile 190/B4
Queimada (isl.), Braz. 182/D3
Queimadas, Braz. 183/H4
Queimadas, Braz. 187/F1
Quela, Ang. 120/D5
Quelimane, Moz. 123/H3
Queluz, Port. 47/P10
Quemado, Tx, US 150/D3
Quemado, Punta del (pt.), Cuba 177/H1
Quembo (riv.), Ang. 122/C2
Quémez, Bol. 188/B2
Quemú Quemú, Arg. 190/E3
Quenington, Eng, UK 37/E3
Quepos, CR 177/E4
Quequén, Arg. 190/F3
Quequén Grande (riv.), Arg. 190/F3
Querceta, It. 62/D6
Querecotillo, Peru 184/A2
Querétaro, Mex. 175/E4
Querétaro de Arteaga (state), Mex. 172/A5
Quero, It. 63/E2
Querobabi, Mex. 174/C2
Querqueville, Fr. 56/D1
Quesada, CR 177/E4
Quesada, Sp. 46/D4
Queshan, China 80/C4
Quesnel (lake), BC, Can. 140/D3
Quesnel, BC, Can. 144/C1
Quesnel (riv.), BC, Can. 144/D1
Quesnoy-sur-Deûle, Fr. 54/C2
Quessoy, Fr. 56/C4
Questa, NM, US 152/B2
Questembert, Fr. 56/C5
Quetame, Col. 183/M8
Quetigny, Fr. 60/B3
Quetta, Pak. 101/J2
Quettehou, Fr. 56/D1
Queulat, PN, Chile 190/B5
Queve Cangombe, Ang. 122/B1
Quevedo (riv.), Ecu. 180/B5
Quéven, Fr. 56/B5
Quévert, Fr. 56/C4
Quezaltenango, Guat. 176/D3
Quezon, Phil. 88/D4
Quezon, Phil. 88/B3
Quezon City, Phil. 88/E6
Quezon NP, Phil. 88/C2
Qufār, SAr. 102/E5
Qufu, China 80/D4
Qui Nhon, Viet. 94/E3
Qui Parle (lake), Mn, US 155/F1
Quibala, Ang. 120/C5
Quibaxe, Ang. 120/C5
Quibdó, Col. 180/B3
Quiberon (pen.), Fr. 56/B6
Quiberon, Fr. 56/B6
Quiberon (bay), Fr. 44/B3
Quibocolo, Ang. 120/C4
Quíbor, Ven. 180/D2
Quicacha, Peru 184/C4
Quiçama, PN da, Ang. 120/C5
Quickborn, Ger. 53/G1
Quicombo, Ang. 122/B1
Quidico, Chile 190/B3
Quiers, Fr. 30/L6
Quierschied, Ger. 55/G5
Quijotoa, Az, US 149/F4
Quila, Mex. 174/D3
Quilaco, Chile 190/B3
Quilán (cape), Chile 190/B4
Quilca, Peru 184/C5
Quilcene, Wa, US 167/B2
Quilengues, Ang. 122/B2
Quileute Ind. Res., Wa, US 144/B4
Quiliano, It. 62/B5
Quilicura, Chile 190/N8
Quilimarí, Chile 190/C2
Quilino, Arg. 188/C4
Quill Lake, Sk, Can. 156/B1
Quill Lakes, Sk, Can. 140/F3
Quill Lakes (lakes), Sk, Can. 145/M2
Quillabamba, Peru 184/C4
Quillacas, Bol. 188/C1
Quillacollo, Bol. 188/C1
Quillagua (pt.), Chile 190/B4
Quillebeuf-sur-Seine, Fr. 57/F2
Quilleco, Chile 190/C3
Quillota, Chile 190/N8
Quilmaná, Peru 184/B4
Quilmes (peak), Arg. 188/C3
Quilombo dos Dembos, Ang. 120/C5
Quilpie, Austl. 134/B4
Quilpué, Chile 190/N8
Quilty, Ire. 32/A4
Quimbata, Ang. 120/C4
Quimbele, Ang. 120/D4
Quime, Bol. 188/C1
Quimilí, Arg. 188/D3
Quimome, Bol. 188/D1
Quimone (riv.), Bol. 188/D1
Quimper, Fr. 56/A4
Quimperlé, Fr. 56/B5
Quin, Ire. 32/B4
Quinault (riv.), Wa, US 144/C4
Quinault Ind. Res., Wa, US 144/B4
Quincampoix, Fr. 57/G1
Quince Mil, Peru 184/D4
Quincey, Fr. 60/C2
Quincy, Fl, US 165/F2
Quincy, Il, US 155/J4
Quincy, Ma, US 161/L3
Quincy, Mi, US 160/D4
Quincy, Wa, US 144/E4
Quincy-East Quincy, Ca, US 146/C4
Quincy-sous-Sénart, Fr. 30/K5
Quincy-Voisins, Fr. 30/L5
Quindío (dept.), Col. 180/A4
Quines, Arg. 188/C5
Quinhagak, Ak, US 171/F4
Quinlan, Tx, US 153/F4
Quinn (riv.), Nv, US 146/D3
Quinns Rocks, Austl. 130/K6
Quintana de la Serena, Sp. 46/C3
Quintana Roo (state), Mex. 172/D4
Quintanar de la Orden, Sp. 46/D3
Quintanar del Rey, Sp. 46/E3
Quintay, Chile 190/N8
Quinte (bay), On, Can. 161/H2
Quintenas, Fr. 64/A2
Quinter, Ks, US 154/D4
Quintero, Chile 190/N8
Quintin, Fr. 56/C4
Quinto, Swi. 61/E4
Quinto, Sp. 47/E2
Quinto (riv.), Arg. 190/D2
Quinto di Treviso, It. 63/F2
Quinto di Valpantena, It. 63/E3
Quinton, Ok, US 153/G3
Quinton, NJ, US 168/C4
Quinwood, WV, US 163/G1
Quinzano d'Oglio, It. 62/C3
Quinzau, Ang. 120/C4
Quionga, Moz. 119/C4
Quipapá, Braz. 183/G5
Quipungo, Ang. 122/B2
Quirey, Col. 180/D3
Quirihue, Chile 190/B3
Quirimba (arch.), Moz. 119/C4
Quirindi, Austl. 132/D1
Quirinópolis, Braz. 186/C3
Quiriquire, Ven. 181/F2
Quiroga, Sp. 46/B1
Quiroga, Bol. 188/C1
Quiroga, Mex. 175/E5
Quirusillas, Bol. 188/D1
Quiruvilca, Peru 184/B3
Quisiro, Ven. 180/D2
Quispamsis, NB, Can. 158/E3
Quissanga, Moz. 123/J2
Quissico, Moz. 123/G5
Quistello, It. 63/D4
Quita Sueño (bank), Col. 177/F3
Quitapa, Ang. 120/D5
Quitaque, Tx, US 152/D3
Quiteve, Ang. 122/B3
Quitilipi, Arg. 188/D3
Quitman, Tx, US 153/G4
Quitman, La, US 153/H4
Quitman, Ga, US 165/G2
Quitman, Ms, US 164/D1
Quito (cap.), Ecu. 180/B5
Quitratúe, Chile 190/B3
Quivara Nat'l Wild. Ref., Ks, US 154/E4
Quivira Nat'l Wildlife Res., Ks, US 153/E1
Quixadá, Braz. 183/G4
Quixeramobim, Braz. 183/G4
Quixeré, Braz. 183/G4
Quizenga, Ang. 120/C5
Qujiang, China 87/G3
Qujie, China 87/F4
Qujing, China 86/D3
Qulaybīyah, Tun. 48/B4
Quli, China 87/E4
Qulin, Mo, US 162/B2
Qumar (riv.), China 78/C4
Qumarrabdün, China 78/C5
Qumaym, Jor. 105/D3
Qumbu, SAfr. 124/E3
Qŭnghirot, Uzb. 74/F5
Quogue, NY, US 169/F2
Quoich (lake), Sc, UK 33/A2
Quoich (riv.), Nun, Can. 140/G2
Quoile (riv.), NI, UK 34/C3
Quoin (pt.), SAfr. 124/L11
Quorn, Austl. 131/H5
Qŭqon, Uzb. 99/B3
Quranbāliyah, Tun. 48/B4
Qurbah, Tun. 48/B4
Qŭrghonteppa, Taj. 101/J1
Qurnat as Sawdā' (peak), Leb. 104/E2
Qūş, Egypt 109/G3
Qusar, Azer. 71/J4
Quşayr ad Daffah (ruin), Libya 108/D2
Qūshchī, Iran 103/F2
Qūsheh, Iran 103/H3
Qusmuryn, Kaz. 74/G4
Quşūr As Sāf, Tun. 48/B5
Quthing, Les. 124/D3
Quttinirpaaq Nat'l Park, Nun., Can 141/T6
Quţūr, Egypt 113/B3
Quwan, China 87/G1
Quwaysinā, Egypt 113/C3
Quwo, China 80/B4
Quwu (mts.), China 78/F4
Qūxū, China 97/H1
Quyang, China 80/C3
Quynh Nhai, Viet. 86/D4
Quzhou, China 87/H2
Quzhou, China 80/C3
Qvareli, Geo. 71/H4
Qyzylorda, Kaz. 74/G5
Qyzylorda Oblast, Kaz. 71/L3

R

Raab (riv.), Aus. 45/L3
Raab, Aus. 59/G6
Raabs an der Thaya, Aus. 43/H4
RAAF-Richmond (A.F.B.), Austl. 134/G8
Raahe, Fin. 68/E2
Raalte, Neth. 52/D4
Raamsdonk, Neth. 52/B5
Råån (riv.), Swe. 39/J7
Ra'ananna, Isr. 105/B4
Raanes (pen.), Nun, Can. 141/S7
Raas (isl.), Indo. 89/F4
Raas Jumbo, Som. 119/C2
Raasiku, Est. 41/L2
Rab (isl.), Cro. 67/G1
Rab, Cro. 45/L4
Rába (riv.), Hun. 50/C2
Rábafüzes, Hun. 50/C2
Rábahidvég, Hun. 50/C2
Rabai, Kenya 119/B2
Rabak, Sudan 117/G2
Rabastens, Fr. 47/F1
Rabat, Malta 48/L7
Rabat (cap.), Mor. 112/A2
Rabat (Sale) (int'l arpt.), Mor. 112/A2
Rabat (Victoria), Malta 48/L6
Rabbi (riv.), It. 45/K4
Rabbit (cr.), SD, US 154/C1
Rabbit Ear (mtn.), NM, US 152/C2
Rabbit Ears (pass), Co, US 147/K3
Rabbit Lake, Sk, Can. 145/L1
Rabgala (pass), China 97/F2
Rābigh, SAr. 100/C4
Rabil, CpV. 107/K10
Rabinal, Guat. 176/D3
Rabiusa (riv.), Swi. 61/F4
Rabka, Pol. 43/K4
Rabkavi-Banhatti, India 101/L5
Rabocheostrovsk, Rus. 68/G2
Raby (pt.), On, Can. 160/V8
Rabyānah (des.), Libya 108/C3
Raccoon (riv.), Oh, US 160/E5
Raccoon (pt.), La, US 164/C3
Raccoon (pt.), Fl, US 164/K6
Raceland, La, US 164/C3
Rach Gia (bay), Viet. 94/D4
Rach Gia, Viet. 94/D4
Rachel Carson Nat'l Wild. Ref., Me, US 161/L3
Racibórz, Pol. 43/K3
Racine (peak), Swi. 60/C3
Racine, Wi, US 160/C3
Racine (co.), Wi, US 167/P14
Racola, Mo, US 162/B1
Rada Tilly, Arg. 190/D5
Radaur, India 98/D4
Rădăuţi, Rom. 72/C4
Radbuza (riv.), Czh. 42/G4
Radchenskoye, Rus. 73/L3
Radcliff, Ky, US 162/E2
Radcliffe, Eng, UK 35/F4
Radcliffe on Trent, Eng, UK 35/G6
Raddestorf, Ger. 53/F4
Rade de Brest (har.), Fr. 56/A4
Radeč (peak), Czh. 59/G3
Radekhiv, Ukr. 72/C2
Radenthein, Aus. 45/K3
Radersburg, Mt, US 145/J4
Radevormwald, Ger. 53/E6
Radford, Va, US 163/G2
Rādhanpur, India 101/K4
Radisson, Wi, US 157/J5
Radisson, Sk, Can. 145/L1
Radium Hill, Austl. 131/J5
Radium Springs, NM, US 149/J4
Radlett, Eng, UK 30/C2
Rådmansö, Swe. 39/B1
Radnevo, Bul. 51/G4
Radnice, Czh. 59/G3
Radolfzell, Ger. 61/E2
Radom, Pol. 43/L3
Radom NP, Sudan 117/E3
Radomir, Bul. 50/F4
Radomsko, Pol. 43/K3
Radomyshl', Ukr. 72/E2
Radoviš, FYROM 49/H2
Radovljica, Slov. 45/L3
Radøy (isl.), Nor. 40/A1
Radstadt, Aus. 45/K3
Radstock, Eng, UK 36/D4
Radun', Bela. 41/L4
Radviliškis, Lith. 41/K4
Radville, Sk, Can. 156/B3
Radyr, Wal, UK 36/C3
Radziejów, Pol. 43/K2
Radzymin, Pol. 43/L2
Radzyń Podlaski, Pol. 43/M3
Rae (riv.), Nun, Can. 140/E2
Rae (isth.), Nun, Can. 141/H2
Rāe Bareli, India 96/C2
Rae-Edzo, NW, Can. 140/E2
Raeford, NC, US 163/H3
Raeren, Belg. 55/F2
Raesfeld, Ger. 52/D5
Raeside (lake), Austl. 130/D4
Raetihi, NZ 135/C2
Rafael J. Garcia, Mex. 175/M7
Rafael Núñez (int'l arpt.), Col. 180/C2
Rafaela, Arg. 188/D4
Rafaḩ, Isr. 105/A6
Rafai, CAfr. 116/D4
Rafḩā', SAr. 103/E4
Rafīdīyah, WBnk. 105/C4
Rafiganj, India 97/E3
Rafína, Gre. 49/P8
Rafrāf, Tun. 48/B4
Rafsanjān, Iran 103/J4
Raft (riv.), Id, US 147/G2
Raft (pt.), Austl. 128/B4
Rafz, Swi. 61/E2
Raga, Sudan 117/E3
Ragang (mt.), Phil. 88/D4
Ragay (gulf), Phil. 88/C2
Ragged (isl.), Me, US 158/C4
Ragged (mt.), Austl. 130/D5
Ragged (pt.), Chile 191/B7
Rāghugarh, India 96/A3
Raghunāthpur, India 97/F4
Raglan, NZ 135/C2
Raglan, Wal, UK 36/D3
Ragland, Al, US 162/D4
Rago NP, Nor. 38/E2
Ragstone (range), Eng, UK 30/D3
Raguli, Rus. 71/G3
Ragusa, It. 48/D4
Ra'gyagoinba, China 78/E5
Rahad al Bardī, Sudan 116/D3
Rahama, Nga. 115/H4
Rahan, Ire. 32/C3
Rāhatgarh, India 96/B4
Rahden, Ger. 53/F4
Rahīmyār Khān, Pak. 98/A5
Rahole Nat'l Rsv., Kenya 119/B1
Råholt, Nor. 40/D1
Rāhon, India 98/D4
Rahotu, NZ 135/C2
Rāhuri, India 95/B2
Rahway, NJ, US 169/H9
Rai, Fr. 57/F3
Raiano, It. 65/C3
Raiatea (isl.), FrPol. 137/K6
Raiganj, India 97/G3
Raigarh, India 96/D5
Raijua (isl.), Indo. 128/A2

Rāikera, India 97/E4
Raikot, India 98/C4
Railroad, Pa, US 168/B4
Railroad Canyon (res.), Ca, US 166/C3
Rain, Ger. 58/D5
Rainbach im Mühlkreis, Aus. 59/H5
Rainbow, Ca, US 166/C4
Rainbow, Austl. 132/B2
Rainbow Beach, Austl. 134/D4
Rainbow Bridge Nat'l Mon., Ut, US 149/G2
Rainbow City, Al, US 162/D4
Rainelle, WV, US 163/G2
Rainham (nbrhd.), Eng, UK 30/D2
Rainham, Eng, UK 30/E2
Rainier (mt.), Wa, US 144/D4
Rainier, Or, US 144/C4
Rainis, Indo. 91/G3
Rainsville, Al, US 162/E3
Rainworth, Eng, UK 35/G5
Rainy (riv.), Can.,US 157/H3
Rainy (lake), On, Can. 140/G4
Rainy River, On, Can. 157/G3
Rāipur, India 99/C5
Rairoa (atoll), FrPol. 137/L6
Ra'īs, SAr. 109/H4
Raisdorf, Ger. 40/D4
Raisen, India 96/A4
Rāisinghnagar, India 98/B5
Raisio, Fin. 41/K1
Raismes, Fr. 54/C3
Raith, On, Can. 157/K3
Raivavae (isl.), FrPol. 137/L7
Rāiwind, Pak. 98/C4
Raizeux, Fr. 30/H6
Rāj Gāngpur, India 97/E4
Raja (pt.), Indo. 89/B2
Rāja Jang, Pak. 98/C4
Rajabasa (peak), Indo. 89/D4
Rajamäki, Fin. 39/E4
Rājampet, India 95/C3
Rajang (riv.), Malay. 90/D3
Rājanpur, Pak. 98/A5
Rājaori, India 98/C3
Rājapālaiyam, India 95/C4
Rājāpur, India 96/C3
Rājasar, India 98/C5
Rājasthān (state), India 92/B2
Rajauli, India 97/E3
Rājawas, India 98/C5
Rājbāri, Bang. 97/G4
Rājbirāj, Nepal 97/F2
Rājendraganj, Bang. 97/G3
Rājgarh, India 98/C5
Rājgarh, India 96/A2
Rājgarh, India 92/C3
Rājgir, India 97/E3
Rājim, India 95/D1
Rajka, Hun. 50/C1
Rājkot, India 101/K4
Rājmahāl, India 97/F3
Rājmahal (hills), India 97/F3
Rājpur, India 97/G4
Rājpura, India 98/D4
Rājshāhi (pol. reg.), Bang. 97/G3
Rājshāhi, Bang. 97/G3
Rājshāhi (pol. div.), Bang. 97/G3
Rājula, India 101/K4
Raka, China 97/E1
Raka (riv.), China 97/F1
Rakahanga (isl.), Cookls. 137/J5
Rakaia, NZ 135/C3
Rakaia (riv.), NZ 135/B3
Rakamaz, Hun. 50/E1
Rakaposhi (peak), Pak. 98/C1
Rakhine (state), Myan. 93/F4
Rakhiv, Ukr. 72/C3
Rakhny-Lisovi, Ukr. 72/E3
Rakhshān (riv.), Pak. 101/H3
Rakino (isl.), NZ 135/F6
Rakitnoye, Rus. 73/H2
Rakke, Est. 41/M2
Rakkestad, Nor. 40/D2
Rakops, Bots. 122/E4
Rakos-patak (riv.), Hun. 51/R9
Rakovnicky Potok (riv.), Czh. 59/G2
Rakovník, Czh. 59/G2
Rakovski, Bul. 51/G4
Rakvere, Est. 41/M2
Rakwaro, Kenya 119/A2
Raldon, It. 63/E3
Raleigh, ND, US 156/D4
Raleigh, Ms, US 164/D1
Raleigh (cap.), NC, US 163/H3
Raleigh-Durham (int'l arpt.), NC, US 163/H3
Ralik Chain (isls.), Mrsh. 136/F4
Rælingen, Nor. 38/T8
Ralingen, Ger. 55/F4
Ralls, Tx, US 152/D4
Ralph, Mi, US 157/L4
Ralston, Wy, US 147/J1
Ralston, Ab, Can. 145/J2
Rām Allāh, WBnk. 105/C5
Ram Head (pt.), Ire. 32/C6
Rama, Isr. 105/C3
Rama Ind. Res., On, Can. 161/G2
Ramādah, Tun. 66/F4
Ramādah, Yem. 118/B2
Rāmagundam, India 95/C2
Ramah, NM, US 149/H3
Ramah Navajo Ind. Res., NM, US 149/H3
Ramalho, Serra do (mts.), Braz. 186/D2
Rāmanāthapuram, India 95/C4
Rāmannaguda, India 95/D2
Ramapo (mts.), NJ, US 169/H7
Ramapo (riv.), NJ, US 168/J7
Ramas (cape), India 95/B3
Ramat Gan, Isr. 105/B4
Ramat Ha Sharon, Isr. 105/B4
Ramatlabama, Bots. 122/E5
Ramatuelle, Fr. 64/C6
Rambervillers, Fr. 60/C1
Rambi (isl.), Fiji 137/Z17
Rambouillet, Fr. 57/G3
Rame (pt.), Eng, UK 36/B6
Rame Head (cape), Austl. 133/D3
Ramea, Nf, Can. 159/J2
Rāmechhāp, Nepal 97/F2
Ramenskoye, Rus. 69/X9
Ramer, Al, US 165/E1
Rāmeshwar, India 96/C1
Rāmeswaram, India 95/C4
Rāmgangā (riv.), India 96/B1
Rāmgarh, Bang. 97/H4
Rāmgarh, India 97/E4
Rāmhormoz, Iran 103/G4
Rāmīān, Iran 103/H2
Ramiere (peak), It. 64/C3
Ramingining, Austl. 129/D3
Ramírez, Mex. 175/M7
Ramīs Shet' (riv.), Eth. 118/B3
Ramiswil, Swi. 60/D3
Rāmjībanpur, India 97/F4
Ramkin Inlet (Kangiqcling), Nun, Can. 140/G2
Ramla, Isr. 105/B5
Ramløse, Den. 39/J6
Ramlu (peak), Erit. 118/B2
Ramme, Den. 40/C3
Rammūn, WBnk. 105/C5
Rāmnagar, India 98/C3
Rāmnagar, India 96/C3
Rāmnagar, India 96/D3
Rāmnagar, India 96/B1
Ramnäs, Swe. 40/G2
Ramokgwebana, Bots. 123/E4
Ramon', Rus. 73/K2
Ramona, Ok, US 153/G2
Ramona, Ca, US 148/D4
Ramonchamp, Fr. 60/C2
Ramor (lake), Ire. 34/A4
Ramosch, Swi. 61/G4
Ramotswa, Bots. 122/E5
Rāmpāl, Bang. 97/G4
Rampart, Ak, US 171/H2
Rampillon, Fr. 30/M6
Rāmpur, India 98/D4
Rāmpur, India 96/B1
Rāmpur, India 92/B3
Rāmpur Hāt, India 97/F3
Rampura, India 98/C5
Rāmpura Phūl, India 98/C4
Ramree (isl.), Myan. 93/F4
Rāmsanehīghāt, India 96/C2
Ramsar, India 92/B2
Ramsay, Mt, US 145/H5
Ramsbottom, Eng, UK 35/F4
Ramsbury, Eng, UK 37/E4
Ramsden Bellhouse, Eng, UK 30/E2
Ramsden Heath, Eng, UK 30/E2
Ramsen, Swi. 61/E2
Ramseur, NC, US 163/H3
Ramsey (isl.), Wal, UK 36/A3
Ramsey, Eng, UK 37/F2
Ramsey, IM, UK 34/D3
Ramsey (bay), IM, UK 34/D3
Ramsey, NJ, US 169/J7
Ramsey, Il, US 155/K4
Ramsey (co.), Mn, US 157/P7
Ramsgate, Eng, UK 37/H4
Rāmshīr, Iran 103/G4
Ramstadslettet (peak), Nor. 38/T8
Ramstein-Miesenbach, Ger. 55/G5
Ramu, Kenya 118/B5
Ramu (riv.), PNG 136/D5
Ramygala, Lith. 41/L4
Rana, Nor. 38/E2
Rānāghāt, India 97/G4
Ranai, Indo. 90/C3
Rånäs, Swe. 39/B1
Ranau, Malay. 88/B4
Ranbirpura, India 98/D2
Ranburne, Al, US 162/E4
Rancagua, Chile 190/N9
Rance (riv.), Fr. 44/E5
Rancheria (riv.), Col. 180/C2
Ranchester, Wy, US 147/K1
Rānchī, India 97/E4
Rancho Cordova, Ca, US 146/C4
Rancho Cucamonga (Cucamonga), Ca, US 166/C2
Rancho Palos Verdes, Ca, US 166/F8
Rancho Santa Fe, Ca, US 166/C4
Ranchos, Arg. 190/F2
Ranchos de Taos, NM, US 152/B2
Ranco (lake), Chile 190/B4
Rancocas, NJ, US 168/D4
Rancul, Arg. 190/D2
Randa, Djib. 118/B3
Randaberg, Nor. 40/A2
Randall, Mn, US 157/G4
Randallstown, Md, US 168/B5
Randalstown, NI, UK 34/B2
Randazzo, It. 48/D4
Randburg, SAfr. 124/P13
Randers, Den. 40/D3
Randi Ii, Gabon 120/B3
Randleman, NC, US 163/H3
Randlett, Ok, US 153/E3
Randlett, Ut, US 147/J3
Randolph, Az, US 149/G4
Randolph, Ne, US 155/F2
Randolph, NJ, US 168/D2
Randolph (A.F.B.), Tx, US 151/E3
Randolph, Ut, US 147/H3
Randolph, Vt, US 161/K3
Randolph, Wi, US 155/K2
Random (isl.), Nf, Can. 159/L1
Randow (riv.), Ger. 43/H2
Randowaya, Indo. 91/J4
Randsburg, Ca, US 148/D3
Randsfjorden (lake), Nor. 40/D1
Randwick (nbrhd.), Austl. 134/H8
Råneå, Swe. 68/D2
Ranérou, Sen. 114/B3
Rāneswar, India 97/F3
Ranfurly, NZ 135/B4
Rang (peak), Thai. 94/C2
Rang-du-Fliers, Fr. 54/A3
Rangae, Thai. 89/C1
Rāngāmāti (pol. reg.), Bang. 97/H4
Rāngāmāti, Bang. 93/F3
Rangāpāra, India 86/B3
Rangasa (cape), Indo. 91/E4
Rangeley, Me, US 161/L2
Rangely, Co, US 147/J3
Ranger, NC, US 162/E3
Ranger, Tx, US 151/E1
Rangia, India 97/H2
Rangiora, NZ 135/C3
Rangiroa (isl.), FrPol. 137/L6
Rangkasbitung, Indo. 89/D4
Rangoon (Yangon) (cap.), Myan. 86/C5
Rangoon (Yangon) (int'l arpt.), Myan. 86/C5
Rangpur, Bang. 97/G3
Rangpur (pol. reg.), Bang. 97/G3
Rangsdorf, Ger. 42/Q7
Rāni Tāl, India 96/D3
Rānia, India 98/C5
Rānībennur, India 95/B3
Ranier, Mn, US 157/H3
Rānīganj, India 97/E3
Rānīganj, India 97/F2
Rānīganj, India 97/F4
Rānīganj, India 96/D2
Rānīkhet, India 96/B1
Rānīpur, India 96/B3
Ranjitpura, India 101/K3
Ranken (riv.), Austl. 129/E5
Rankin, Il, US 160/C4
Rankin, Tx, US 150/D2
Rankins Springs, Austl. 133/C1
Rankūs, Syria 105/E1
Rankweil, Aus. 61/F3
Rannoch (lake), Sc, UK 33/B3
Rano, Nga. 115/H4
Ranohira, Madg. 125/H8
Ranomafana, Madg. 125/H8
Ranong, Thai. 94/B4
Ranotsara-Avaratra, Madg. 125/H8
Ranquil del Norte, Arg. 190/C3
Ransbach-Baumbach, Ger. 55/G3
Ransiki, Indo. 91/H4
Ransom, Ks, US 152/E1
Ransomville, NY, US 160/V9
Ranson, WV, US 163/J1
Ranst, Belg. 52/B6
Ranstadt, Ger. 58/B2
Rantabe, Madg. 125/J6
Rantaukampar, Indo. 89/C2
Rantaupanjang, Indo. 89/C3
Rantauprapat, Indo. 89/B2
Rantekombola (peak), Indo. 91/F4
Rantigny, Fr. 54/B5
Rantīs, WBnk. 105/C4
Rantoul, Il, US 160/B4
Rantsila, Fin. 68/E2
Ranzan, Japan 83/C1
Rao Co (peak), Laos 94/D2
Raon-L'Étape, Fr. 60/C1
Raoui, 'Erg er (des.), Alg. 110/E3
Raoul (isl.), NZ 136/H7
Raoyang (riv.), China 81/A2
Raoyang, China 80/C3
Rapa (isl.), FrPol. 137/L7
Rapallo, It. 62/C5
Rapel, Chile 190/N8
Rapel (lake), Chile 190/N9
Rapelje, Mt, US 145/K5
Raphine, Va, US 163/H2
Rapid (cr.), SD, US 154/C1
Rapid Bay, Austl. 131/H5
Rapid City, Mb, Can. 156/D2
Rapid City, Mi, US 160/D2
Rapid City, SD, US 154/C1
Rapid River, Mi, US 160/C2
Rapide-Blanc, Qu, Can. 158/A2
Rapides de Gozobangi (rapids), CAfr. 116/D4
Rapides de L'ELéphant (rapids), CAfr. 116/C4
Rapides de Yalala (falls), D.R. Congo 120/C4
Rapido (riv.), It. 65/C4
Räpina, Est. 41/M2
Rapirrán, Bol. 185/E3
Rapla, Est. 41/L2
Rappahannock (riv.), Va, US 163/J2
Rapper (cape), Chile 190/B5
Rāpti (zone), Nepal 96/D1
Rapti (riv.), India 92/D2
Rápulo (riv.), Bol. 185/E4
Rara NP, Nepal 96/D1
Raritan (bay), NJ, US 168/D3
Raritan (riv.), NJ, US 168/D2
Raritan, South Branch (riv.), NJ, US 168/D2
Raron, Swi. 60/D5
Rarotonga (isl.), Cookls. 137/J7
Ra's Abū Madd (pt.), SAr. 109/H3
Ra's Ajdīr, Libya 67/F4
Ra's al 'Ayn, Syria 102/E2
Ra's al Basīt (pt.), Syria 104/D2
Ra's al Ḥadd (pt.), Oman 101/G4
Ra's Al Jabal, Tun. 48/B4
Ra's al Khafjī, SAr. 103/G4
Ra's al Khalīj, Egypt 113/C2
Ra's al Khaymah, UAE 101/G3
Ra's al Madrakah (pt.), Oman 101/G5
Ra's al Mish'āb (pt.), SAr. 103/G4
Ra's al 'Ushsh, Egypt 113/D2
Ra's An Naqb, Jor. 104/D5
Ra's as Saffānīyah (pt.), SAr. 100/E3
Ra's ash Sharbatāt (pt.), Oman 101/G5
Ra's at Tīn (pt.), Libya 67/J4
Ra's Banās (pt.), Egypt 109/G4
Ra's Barīdī (pt.), SAr. 109/H3
Râs el Mâ, Mali 114/D2
Râs el Ma, Alg. 112/D2
Râs el Oued, Alg. 112/H5
Râs el-Barr, Egypt 113/C1
Ra's Fartak (pt.), Yem. 100/F5
Ras Gharib, Egypt 109/G2
Ra's Ḥāṭibah (pt.), SAr. 100/C4
Ras il-Qammieħ (pt.), Malta 48/L7
Ra's Jibsh (pt.), Oman 101/G4
Ra's Muḥammad (pt.), Egypt 109/G3
Ra's Nawṣ (pt.), Oman 101/G5
Ras San Dimitri (pt.), Malta 48/L6
Ra's Ṣawqirah (pt.), Oman 101/G5
Rasa (pt.), Arg. 190/E4
Raschau, Ger. 59/F1
Raseiniai, Lith. 41/K4
Rashaant, Mong. 78/C2
Rashād, Sudan 117/F3
Rasharkin, NI, UK 34/B2
Rāshayyā, Leb. 105/D1
Rashīd, Egypt 113/B2
Rashīd, Massabb (Rosetta) (mouth), Egypt 113/B1
Rasht, Iran 103/G2
Rasi Salai, Thai. 94/D3
Rāsk, Iran 101/H3
Raška, Serb. 50/E4
Rāsla, India 101/K3
Rasmussen (basin), Nun, Can. 140/G2
Raso (cape), Port. 47/P10
Rason (lake), Austl. 127/B3
Rasrā, India 96/D3
Rassina, It. 63/E6
Rasskazovo, Rus. 71/G1
Rassypnaya, Rus. 71/K2
Rastatt, Ger. 58/B5
Rastede, Ger. 53/F2
Rasūlnagar, Pak. 98/B3
Rat (isls.), Ak, US 171/B6
Rat Buri, Thai. 94/B3
Rata (cape), Indo. 89/D4
Ratahan, Indo. 91/F3
Ratak Chain (isls.), Mrsh. 136/F3
Ratanpur, India 96/D4
Ratcliff, Tx, US 151/G2
Rāth, India 96/B3
Rathangan, Ire. 32/C3
Rathbun (lake), Ia, US 155/H3
Rathcoole, Ire. 34/B5
Rathcormack, Ire. 32/B5
Rathdowney, Ire. 32/C4
Rathdrum, Ire. 34/B6
Rathdrum, Id, US 144/F4
Rathedaung, Myan. 93/F3
Rathenow, Ger. 42/G2
Rathfriland, NI, UK 34/B3
Rathgormuck, Ire. 32/C5
Rathkeale, Ire. 32/B4
Rathlin (isl.), NI, UK 34/B1
Rathlin (sound), NI, UK 34/B1
Rathluirc, Ire. 32/B5
Rathmore, Ire. 32/A5
Rathmore, Ire. 32/D3
Rathnew, Ire. 34/B6
Rathowen, Ire. 32/C2
Rathvilly, Ire. 32/D4
Rathwire, Ire. 32/C2
Ratia, India 98/C5
Ratingen, Ger. 52/D6
Ratlām, India 92/C3
Ratnapura, SrL. 95/D5
Ratne, Ukr. 72/C2
Ratoath, Ire. 34/B4
Raton, NM, US 152/B2
Rattaphum, Thai. 94/C5
Rattlesnake (cr.), Ks, US 154/E4
Rattray, Sc, UK 33/C3
Rattray (pt.), Sc, UK 33/E1
Rättvik, Swe. 40/F1
Rau, Indo. 89/C2
Raub, Malay. 89/C2
Rauch, Mn, US 157/H4
Rauch, Arg. 190/F3
Raudales Malpaso, Mex. 176/C2
Raudhinúpur (pt.), Ice. 38/P6
Raufarhöfn, Ice. 38/P6
Raufoss, Nor. 40/D1
Rauhe Ebrach (riv.), Ger. 58/D3
Raul Soares, Braz. 187/E4
Rauma, Fin. 41/J1
Rauna, Lat. 41/L3
Raunds, Eng, UK 37/F2
Raung (peak), Indo. 89/F5
Raunheim, Ger. 58/B2
Raupehu (vol.), NZ 135/C2
Raurkela, India 97/E4
Rausa Garhi, Nepal 97/E1
Rausu, Japan 82/D1
Rautjärvi, Fin. 41/N1
Rauzan, Bang. 97/H4
Rava-Rus'ka, Ukr. 72/B2
Ravanusa, It. 48/C4
Rāvar, Iran 103/J4
Ravarino, It. 63/E4
Ravels, Belg. 52/B6
Raven, Va, US 163/G2
Ravena, NY, US 161/K3
Ravendale, Ca, US 146/C3
Ravenglass, Eng, UK 35/E3
Ravenna, Oh, US 160/F4
Ravenna, Ca, US 166/B2
Ravenna, It. 63/F5
Ravenna (prov.), It. 63/E4
Ravenna, Ky, US 162/F2
Ravenna, Ne, US 154/E3
Ravensburg, Ger. 61/F2
Ravensdale, Wa, US 167/D3
Ravenshead, Eng, UK 35/G5
Ravenshoe, Austl. 134/B2
Ravensthorpe, Austl. 130/D5
Ravenswood, WV, US 163/G1
Rāvi (riv.), India 99/C5
Ravne na Koroškem, Slov. 45/L3
Ravnina, Trkm. 101/H1
Rawa Mazowiecka, Pol. 43/L3
Rāwah, Iraq 102/E3
Rawaki (Phoenix) (isl.), Kiri. 137/H5
Rāwalpindi, Pak. 98/B3
Rāwatsār, India 98/C5
Rawdon, Qu, Can. 161/K1
Rawene, NZ 135/C1
Rawḩah, SAr. 100/D5
Rawicz, Pol. 43/J3
Rawlinna, Austl. 130/E4
Rawlins, Wy, US 147/K3
Rawlinson (mt.), Austl. 131/E3
Rawmarsh, Eng, UK 35/G5
Rawson, Arg. 190/D4
Rawtenstall, Eng, UK 35/F4
Rawu, China 86/C2
Raxaul Bazar, India 97/E2
Ray, ND, US 156/C3
Ray (cape), Nf, Can. 159/H2
Ray Hubbard (lake), Tx, US 150/L7
Ray Roberts (lake), Tx, US 151/F1
Raya (peak), Indo. 90/D4
Rāyachoti, India 95/C3
Rāyadrug, India 95/C3
Raybon, Ga, US 165/H2
Raychikhinsk, Rus. 79/K2
Rāyen, Iran 103/J4
Rayevskiy, Rus. 69/M5
Rayleigh, Eng, UK 37/G3
Raymond, Wi, US 167/P14
Raymond, Ca, US 148/C2
Raymond, Ms, US 162/B4
Raymond, Mn, US 155/G1
Raymond, Il, US 155/K4
Raymond, Wa, US 144/C4
Raymond, Ab, Can. 145/H3
Raymond Terrace, Austl. 133/E1
Raymondville, Mo, US 153/J2
Raymondville, Tx, US 151/F4
Raymore, Sk, Can. 156/B2
Raymore, Mo, US 153/G1
Rayne, La, US 164/B2
Rayón, Mex. 175/Q10
Rayón, Mex. 174/C2
Rayón, Mex. 175/F4
Rayón, PN, Mex. 175/E5
Rayong, Thai. 94/C3
Raysūt, Oman 100/F5
Rayville, La, US 153/J4
Rāzām, India 95/D2
Razan, Iran 103/G3
Razelm (lake), Rom. 67/L1
Razgrad, Bul. 51/H4
Razlog, Bul. 49/H2
Razumnoye, Rus. 73/J2
Ré (isl.), Fr. 66/C1
Re di Castello (peak), It. 61/G5
Rea (lake), Ire. 32/B3
Rea (riv.), Eng, UK 36/D1
Reading, Eng, UK 37/F4
Reading (co.), Eng, UK 37/E4
Reading, Ks, US 153/G1
Reading, Mi, US 160/D4
Reading, Oh, US 162/E1
Reading, Pa, US 168/C3
Reading Regional/Carl A. Spaatz Field (arpt.), Pa, US 168/C3
Readlyn, Sk, Can. 145/M3
Readsville, Mo, US 153/J1
Reagan, Tx, US 151/F2
Real de San Carlos, Uru. 191/K11
Réal Martin (riv.), Fr. 64/C6
Realicó, Arg. 190/D2
Realitos, Tx, US 151/E4
Realp, Swi. 61/E4
Reamstown, Pa, US 168/B3
Reang Kesei, Camb. 94/C3
Reao (isl.), FrPol. 137/M6
Réau, Fr. 30/K6
Rebais, Fr. 54/C6
Rebecca, Ga, US 165/G2
Rebecca (lake), Austl. 127/B4
Rębiechowo (int'l arpt.), Pol. 40/H4
Rebstein, Swi. 61/F3
Rebun, Japan 82/B1
Rebun (isl.), Japan 79/N2
Recanati, It. 63/G7
Recco, It. 62/C5
Rēchah Lām, Afg. 98/A2
Recherche (arch.), Austl. 127/B4
Rechnitz, Aus. 45/M3
Rechthalten, Swi. 60/D4
Rechytsa, Bela. 70/D1
Recife, Braz. 183/H5
Recife (cape), SAfr. 124/D4
Recke, Ger. 53/E4
Reckingen, Swi. 61/E5
Recklinghausen, Ger. 53/E5
Recknitz (riv.), Ger. 42/G2
Réclère, Swi. 60/C3
Reclining Buddha (Shwethalyaung), Myan. 86/C5
Recluse, Wy, US 154/B1
Recoaro Terme, It. 63/E2
Reconquista, Arg. 188/E4
Reconvilier, Swi. 60/D3
Recreo, Arg. 188/C4
Recreo, Arg. 188/D4
Rector, Ar, US 162/B2
Recuay, Peru 184/B3
Red (lakes), China 77/H7
Red (sea), Afr.,Asia 77/C7
Red (riv.), Mb, Can. 156/F3
Red (bay), NI, UK 34/B1
Red (isl.), Nf, Can. 159/K2
Red (cr.), Ms, US 164/D2
Red (riv.), La, US 151/J2
Red (riv.), Mn, US 143/G2
Red (lake), Mn, US 143/H2
Red (riv.), Viet. 94/D1
Red (Yuan) (riv.), China 86/D4
Red Bank, Tn, US 162/E3
Red Bank, NJ, US 168/D3
Red Bank, SC, US 163/G4
Red Bay, Fl, US 165/F2
Red Bay, Al, US 162/C3
Red Bluff (res.), Tx, US 152/B5
Red Bluff, Ca, US 146/B3
Red Bluff, BC, Can. 144/C1
Red Boiling Springs, Tn, US 162/E2
Red Bud, Il, US 162/C1
Red Cliff Ind. Res., Wi, US 157/J4
Red Cliffs, Austl. 132/B2
Red Cloud, Ne, US 154/E3
Red Creek, NY, US 161/H3
Red Deer (riv.), Sk, Can. 140/E3
Red Deer, Ab, Can. 145/H1
Red Devil, Ak, US 171/G3
Red Feather Lakes, Co, US 154/B3
Red Fish (isl.), Tx, US 151/N9
Red Gate, Tx, US 151/E4
Red Hill, Pa, US 168/C3
Red Hill Patrick Henry Nat'l Mem., Va, US 163/H2
Red Indian (lake), Nf, Can. 159/J1
Red Lake, On, Can. 157/H2
Red Lake, Mn, US 157/G4
Red Lake Falls, Mn, US 156/F4
Red Lake Ind. Res., Mn, US 157/G3
Red Lake Road, On, Can. 157/H3
Red Level, Al, US 164/E2
Red Lion, Pa, US 168/B4
Red Lion, De, US 168/C4
Red Lodge, Mt, US 147/J1
Red Mountain, Ca, US 148/D3
Red Oak, Ia, US 155/G3
Red Oak, Ga, US 163/M7
Red Oak (cr.), Tx, US 150/L7
Red Oak, Tx, US 150/L7
Red River of the North (riv.), ND,Mn, US 156/F4
Red Pheasant Ind. Res., Sk, Can. 145/K1
Red River (valley), Mn, US 156/F3
Red River Army Depot, Tx, US 153/G4
Red Rock, On, Can. 157/K3
Red Rock (riv.), Mt, US 147/G1
Red Rock (plat.), Ut, US 149/G2
Red Rock (lake), Ia, US 155/H3
Red Rock, Tx, US 150/F3
Red Rock Lakes NWR, Mt, US 147/G1
Red Rocks (pt.), Austl. 131/E5
Red Scaffold, SD, US 154/D1
Red Sea (hills), Sudan 107/F2
Red Shirt, SD, US 154/C2
Red Springs, NC, US 163/H3
Red Volta (riv.), Burk. 115/E4
Red Willow (dam), Ne, US 154/D3
Red Willow (cr.), Ne, US 154/D3
Red Wing, Co, US 152/B2
Red Wing, Mn, US 155/H1
Red, North Fork (riv.), Tx,Ok, US 152/D3
Red, Salt Fork (riv.), Tx,Ok, US 152/D3
Reda, Pol. 40/H4
Redan, Ga, US 163/M7
Redang (isl.), Malay. 89/C1
Redange-sur-Attert, Lux. 55/E4
Redberry (lake), Sk, Can. 145/L1
Redbourn, Eng, UK 37/F3
Redbridge (bor.), Eng, UK 30/D2
Redby, Mn, US 157/G4
Redcar, Eng, UK 35/G2
Redcar and Cleveland (co.), Eng, UK 35/G2
Redcliff, Zim. 123/F3
Redcliff, Ab, Can. 145/J2
Redcliffe (mt.), Austl. 130/D4
Redcliffe (nbrhd.), Austl. 134/F6
Redden, De, US 168/C6
Reddersburg, SAfr. 124/D3
Reddick, Fl, US 165/G3
Redding, Ca, US 146/B3
Redding, Ct, US 169/E1
Reddish (peak), WV, US 163/H1
Redditch, Eng, UK 37/E2
Rede (riv.), Eng, UK 35/F1
Redenção, Braz. 182/D5
Redenção do Gurguéia, Braz. 183/E5
Redfield, Ar, US 153/H3
Redfield, SD, US 154/E1
Redford, Mi, US 167/F7
Redford, Mo, US 162/B2
Redford, Tx, US 150/B3
Redhill, Eng, UK 30/C3
Rédics, Hun. 50/C2
Redig, SD, US 156/C5
Redington Beach, Fl, US 164/K8
Redkey, In, US 160/D4
Redkino, Rus. 68/H4
Redland, Md, US 168/A5
Redland Bay, Austl. 134/F7
Redlands, Ca, US 166/C2
Redlands, Co, US 147/J4
Redlin, Ger. 42/G2
Redmond, Ut, US 149/G1
Redmond, Or, US 146/C1
Redmond (res.), Ks, US 155/F4
Redmond, Wa, US 144/C4
Rednitz (riv.), Ger. 58/D4
Redon, Fr. 56/C5
Redondela, Sp. 46/A1
Redondo, Wa, US 167/C3
Redondo, Port. 46/B3
Redondo (peak), NM, US 149/J3
Redondo Beach, Ca, US 166/F8
Redoubt (mt.), Ak, US 171/H3
Redrock, NM, US 149/H4
Redruth, Eng, UK 36/A6
Redstone (riv.), NW, Can. 140/D2
Redstone (cr.), SD, US 154/F1
Redstone Arsenal, Al, US 162/D3
Redvale, Co, US 149/H1
Redvers, Sk, Can. 156/D3
Redwater (riv.), Mt, US 145/M4
Redway, Ca, US 146/B3
Redwood (riv.), Mn, US 155/G1
Redwood Falls, Mn, US 155/G1
Redwood NP, Ca, US 146/A3
Ree, Lough (lake), Ire. 32/C3
Reece City, Al, US 162/D3
Reed, Ar, US 153/J4
Reed, Ok, US 152/E3
Reed City, Mi, US 160/D3
Reeder, ND, US 156/C4
Reedham, Eng, UK 37/H1
Reedley, Ca, US 148/C2
Reeds (bay), NJ, US 168/D5
Reeds Spring, Mo, US 153/H2
Reedsburg, Wi, US 155/J2
Reedsport, Or, US 146/A2
Reedy (cr.), Fl, US 164/N7
Reedy (lake), Fl, US 164/N8
Reedy Creek, Austl. 132/B3
Reef (isls.), Sol. 136/F6
Reef (pt.), Belz. 175/J5
Reefton, NZ 135/B3
Reelfoot Lake NWR, Tn, US 162/C2
Reepham, Eng, UK 37/H1
Rees, Ger. 52/D5
Reese, Mi, US 160/E3
Reese (riv.), Nv, US 142/C4
Reessum, Ger. 53/G2
Reest (riv.), Neth. 52/D3
Reeth, Eng, UK 35/G3
Reeuwijk, Neth. 52/B4
Refahiye, Turk. 102/D2
Reform, Al, US 162/C4
Reforma, Mex. 176/C2
Refugio, Tx, US 151/F3
Refugio Io Valdés, Chile 190/N8
Rega (riv.), Pol. 40/F5
Regen, Ger. 59/G5
Regen (riv.), Ger. 59/F4
Regência, Pontal da (pt.), Braz. 187/F3
Regeneração, Braz. 183/F4
Regensburg, Ger. 59/F4
Regensdorf, Swi. 61/E3
Regenstauf, Ger. 59/F4
Regent, ND, US 156/C4
Regents Park (nbrhd.), Austl. 134/H8
Reggane, Alg. 111/F4
Regge (riv.), Neth. 52/D4
Reggello, It. 63/E6
Reggio, La, US 164/D3
Reggio di Calabria, It. 48/D3
Reggio di Calabria (prov.), It. 48/D3
Reggio nell' Emilia (prov.), It. 62/D3
Reggio nell'Emilia, It. 62/D4
Reggiolo, It. 63/D4
Reghin, Rom. 51/G2
Regina (cap.), Sk, Can. 156/B2
Regina, NM, US 149/J2
Régina, FrG. 182/C1
Regina Beach, Sk, Can. 156/B2
Región Metropolitana Santiago (pol. reg.), Chile 190/B1
Registro, Braz. 189/H3
Regnitz (riv.), Ger. 45/J2
Regoledo, It. 61/F5
Reguengos de Monsaraz, Port. 46/B3
Regway, Sk, Can. 156/B3
Rehau, Ger. 59/F2
Rehburg-Loccum, Ger. 53/G4
Rehfelde, Ger. 42/Q6
Rehlī, India 96/B4
Rehling, Ger. 58/D6
Rehlingen-Siersburg, Ger. 55/F5
Rehoboth, Namb. 122/C4
Rehoboth, NM, US 149/H3
Réhon, Fr. 55/E4
Reḥovot, Isr. 105/B5
Rehrersburg, Pa, US 168/B3
Reichelsheim, Ger. 58/B3
Reichelsheim, Ger. 58/B2
Reichenbach, Ger. 59/F1
Reichenbach im Kandertal, Swi. 60/D4
Reichenbach-Steegen, Ger. 55/G4
Reichenberg, Ger. 58/C3
Reichertshausen, Ger. 59/E6
Reichshof, Ger. 55/G2
Reichshoffen, Fr. 55/G6
Reichstett, Fr. 55/G6
Reid, Austl. 131/F4
Reid (lake), Sk, Can. 145/L2
Reiden, Swi. 60/D3
Reidland, Ky, US 162/C2
Reidsville, Ga, US 163/F4
Reidsville, NC, US 163/H2
Reigate, Eng, UK 30/C3
Reignier, Fr. 60/C5
Reillanne, Fr. 64/B5
Reilly (hill), Ne, US 154/C3
Re'im, Isr. 105/A6
Reims, Fr. 54/D5
Reims (Champagne) (arpt.), Fr. 54/D5
Reina Adelaida (arch.), Chile 191/A6
Reina Beatrix (int'l arpt.), NAnt. 180/D1
Reinach, Swi. 60/D3
Reinach, Swi. 60/E3
Reinbeck, Ia, US 155/H2
Reinbek, Ger. 53/H1
Reindeer (isl.), Mb, Can. 156/F1
Reindeer (lake), Sk, Can. 139/G4
Reinerton-Orwin-Muir, Pa, US 168/B2
Reinheim, Ger. 58/B3
Reinickendorf, Ger. 42/Q6
Reinland, Mb, Can. 156/F3
Reinosa, Sp. 46/C1
Reinsfeld, Ger. 55/F4
Reischach, Ger. 59/F6
Reisdorf, Lux. 55/F4
Reisduoddarhal'di (peak), Nor. 38/G1
Reiskirchen, Ger. 58/B1
Reisterstown, Md, US 168/B5
Reitdiep (riv.), Neth. 52/D2
Reitz, SAfr. 124/E2
Rejaf, Sudan 117/F4
Rejón (int'l arpt.), Mex. 176/D1
Rekkam (plat.), Mor. 112/C2
Reliance, NW, Can. 140/F2
Reliance, Wy, US 147/J3
Reliance, SD, US 154/E2
Relizane (wilaya), Alg. 112/F5
Relizane, Alg. 112/F5
Rellingen, Ger. 53/G1
Remagen, Ger. 55/G2
Remanso, Bol. 185/F4
Remanso, Braz. 183/F5
Remanzacco, It. 63/G1
Remarde (riv.), Fr. 30/H6
Remarkable (mt.), Austl. 131/H5
Rembang, Indo. 89/E4
Rembau, Malay. 89/C2
Remchi, Alg. 112/D2
Remedios, Pan. 177/F4
Remer, Mn, US 157/H4
Remerton, Ga, US 165/G2
Remich, Lux. 55/F4
Remicourt, Belg. 55/E2
Remington, In, US 160/C4
Rémire, FrG. 182/C1
Remiremont, Fr. 60/C1
Remlap, Al, US 162/D4
Remlingen, Ger. 53/H4
Remontnoye, Rus. 71/G3
Rems (riv.), Ger. 45/H2
Remscheid, Ger. 53/E6
Remsen, NY, US 161/J3
Remsen, Ia, US 155/G2
Remy, Fr. 54/B5
Ren (riv.), China 78/F5
Rena, Nor. 40/D1
Rena Lara, Ms, US 162/B3
Renage, Fr. 64/B2
Renāla Khurd, Pak. 98/B4
Renan, Swi. 60/C3
Renarde (riv.), Fr. 30/J6
Renazé, Fr. 57/D5
Renazzo, It. 63/E4
Renca, Chile 190/N8
Rencēni, Lat. 41/L3
Rench (riv.), Ger. 58/A5
Renchen, Ger. 60/E1
Rencontre East, Nf, Can. 159/K2
Rend (lake), Il, US 162/C1
Renda, Lat. 41/K3
Rendeux, Belg. 55/E3
Rendsburg, Ger. 40/C4
Renens, Swi. 60/C4
Renews-Cappahayden, Nf, Can. 159/L2
Renfrew, Sc, UK 33/B5
Renfrewshire (co.), Sc, UK 33/B5
Renfrew, On, Can. 161/H2
Rengam, Malay. 89/C2
Rengat, Indo. 89/C3
Rengo, Chile 190/N9
Rengsdorf, Ger. 55/G3
Renhua, China 93/K2
Renhuai, China 87/E3
Reni, Ukr. 51/J3
Renish (pt.), Sc, UK 31/Q8
Renkajärvi (lake), Fin. 39/E4
Renko, Fin. 39/E4
Renkomäki, Fin. 39/F4
Renkum, Neth. 52/C5
Renmark, Austl. 131/J5
Rennell (isl.), Sol. 136/F6
Rennerod, Ger. 55/H2
Rennertshofen, Ger. 58/E5
Rennes, Fr. 56/D4
Rennie, Mb, Can. 157/G3
Renningen, Ger. 58/B5
Reno, Tx, US 153/G4
Reno (riv.), It. 67/F1
Reno, Nv, US 146/D4
Reno, Tx, US 150/K7
Renoster (riv.), SAfr. 124/C3
Renovo, Pa, US 161/H4
Renqiu, China 80/D3
Renshizhen, China 87/E2
Renshou, China 87/H3
Rensselaer, In, US 160/C4
Rentería, Sp. 44/C5
Renton, Sc, UK 33/B5
Renton, Wa, US 144/C4
Rentz, Ga, US 165/G1
Renville, Mn, US 155/G1
Renwer, Mb, Can. 156/D1
Renwez, Fr. 55/D4
Réo, Burk. 115/E3
Reo, Indo. 91/F5
Reoti, India 97/E3
Répcelak, Hun. 50/C2
Repelón, Col. 177/H4
Repentigny, Qu, Can. 159/P6
Repino, Rus. 69/S6
Replonges, Fr. 60/A5
Repton, Eng, UK 35/G6
Republic, Mi, US 157/L4
Republic, Mo, US 153/H2
Republic (arpt.), NY, US 169/M9
Republic, Ks, US 154/F4
Republic, Wa, US 144/E3
Republican (riv.), Ks,Ne, US 143/G3
Republican, South Fork (riv.), Co,Ks, US 152/C1
Republican, South Fork (riv.), Co, US 154/C4
Repulse (bay), Ausrl. 127/D3
Repulse Bay (isl.), Austl. 134/C3
Repulse Bay, Nun, Can. 141/H2
Rep'yëvka, Rus. 73/K2
Requena, Sp. 47/E3
Requena, Peru 184/C2
Requínoa, Chile 190/N9
Rera, Braz. 181/F3
Rerdell, Fl, US 164/L6
Reriutaba, Braz. 183/F4
Reşadiye, Turk. 102/D1
Resaro, Swe. 39/B1
Reschen (Resia), It. 61/G4
Reschensee (Resia) (lake), It. 61/G4
Rescue (pt.), Chile 190/B5
Reseda (nbrhd.), Ca, US 166/E7
Resegone (peak), It. 62/C2
Resen, FYROM 49/G2
Resende, Port. 46/B2
Resende, Braz. 187/M7
Reserve, Sk, Can. 156/C1
Reserve, Mt, US 156/B3
Reserve, Wi, US 157/J5
Reserve, NM, US 149/H4
Réserve de Campo, Camr. 120/B2
Réserve de Douala-Edéa, Camr. 120/B2
Réserve de Faune du Siniaka-Minia, Chad 116/C3
Réserve de Kenié-Baoulé, Mali 114/C3
Réserve de La Léfini, Congo 120/C3
Réserve Totale de Faune de l'Arly, Burk. 115/F4
Reshetylivka, Ukr. 73/H3
Resia (Reschen), It. 61/G4
Resia (Reschensee) (lake), It. 61/G4
Resia, Passo di (pass), It. 61/G4
Resistencia, Arg. 188/E3
Reşiţa, Rom. 50/E3
Resolution (isl.), Nun, Can. 141/K2
Resolven, Wal, UK 36/C3
Respenda de la Peña, Sp. 46/C1
Resplendor, Braz. 187/E3
Ressano Garcia, Moz. 123/G5
Restigné, Fr. 57/F6
Restigouche (riv.), NB, Can. 158/D2
Reston, Mb, Can. 156/D3
Reston, Va, US 168/A6
Reszel, Pol. 41/J4
Retalhuleu, Guat. 176/D3
Rethel, Fr. 55/D4
Rethem, Ger. 53/G3
Réthimnon, Gre. 49/J5
Retie, Belg. 52/C6
Retiers, Fr. 56/D5
Retrezap NP, Rom. 70/B3
Rétság, Hun. 50/D2
Rettenberg, Ger. 61/G2
Retz, Aus. 43/H4
Reugny, Fr. 57/F6
Réunion (dpcy.), Fr. 125/S15
Reus, Sp. 47/F2
Reusel, Neth. 52/C6
Reuss (riv.), Swi. 61/E3
Reuterstadt Stavenhagen, Ger. 40/E5
Reutlingen, Ger. 58/C6
Reutov, Rus. 69/W9
Reutte, Aus. 61/G3
Revadim, Isr. 105/B5
Revda, Rus. 68/G2
Revda, Rus. 69/N4
Reveille (peak), Nv, US 148/D2
Réveillon (riv.), Fr. 30/K5
Revel, Fr. 44/D5
Revelstoke, BC, Can. 144/E2
Reventazón, Peru 184/A2
Revenue, Sk, Can. 145/K1
Revere, It. 63/E3
Revesby (nbrhd.), Austl. 134/H8
Revfülöp, Hun. 50/C2
Revigny-sur-Ornain, Fr. 55/D6
Revillagigedo (isls.), Mex. 139/F8
Réville, Fr. 56/D1
Revillo, SD, US 155/F1
Revin, Fr. 55/D4
Revolyutsii (peak), Taj. 99/B4
Revsbotn (inlet), Nor. 38/G1
Revúboè (riv.), Moz. 123/G2
Revuè (riv.), Moz. 123/G3
Rewa, India 96/C3
Rewa (riv.), Guy. 181/G4
Rex, Ga, US 163/M7
Rex Dome (mt.), Ak, US 171/J3
Rexburg, Id, US 147/H2
Rexford, Mt, US 144/G3
Rexton, NB, Can. 158/E2
Rey (isl.), Pan. 173/F6
Rey Bouba, Camr. 116/B3
Reydell, Ar, US 153/J3
Reydon, Eng, UK 37/H2
Reyes, Bol. 185/E4
Reyhanlı, Turk. 104/E1
Reykjanestá (cape), Ice. 38/M7
Reykjavík (cap.), Ice. 38/N7
Reykjavik (int'l arpt.), Ice. 38/N7
Reynolds, Mo, US 153/J2
Reynolds, Ga, US 162/E4
Reynoldsburg, Oh, US 160/E5
Reynoldsville, Pa, US 161/G4
Reynosa, Mex. 151/E4
Reyran (riv.), Fr. 64/C5
Reyssouze (riv.), Fr. 60/B5
Rezé, Fr. 56/D6
Rēzekne, Lat. 41/M3
Rezina, Mol. 72/E4
Rezzato, It. 62/D2
Rhaetian Alps (mts.), Swi., Aus. 45/H3
Rhallamane (lake), Mrta. 110/C4
Rhallamane (reg.), Mrta. 110/C5
Rhame, ND, US 156/C4
Rhart (peak), Mor. 110/D3
Rhat (peak), Mor. 110/D3
Rhätikon (mts.), Swi.,Aus. 61/F3
Rhayader, Wal, UK 36/C2
Rheda-Wiedenbrück, Ger. 53/F5
Rhede, Ger. 52/D5
Rhede, Ger. 53/E2
Rheden, Neth. 52/D4
Rheidol (riv.), Wal, UK 36/C2
Rhein, Sk, Can. 156/C2
Rhein (Rhine) (riv.), Aus.,Ger. 42/D3
Rheinau, Swi. 61/E2
Rheinbach, Ger. 55/F2
Rheinberg, Ger. 52/D5
Rheinbreitbach, Ger. 55/G2
Rheinbrohl, Ger. 55/G3
Rheine, Ger. 53/E4
Rheinfall, Swi. 61/E2
Rheinfelden, Ger. 60/D2
Rheinland-Pfalz (state), Ger. 58/A3
Rheinwaldhorn (peak), Swi. 61/F5
Rheinzabern, Ger. 58/B4
Rhemiles (well), Alg. 110/D3
Rhenen, Neth. 52/C5
Rheris, Oued (riv.), Mor. 110/D3
Rhin (Rhine) (riv.), Fr. 55/H6
Rhinau, Fr. 60/D1
Rhine (riv.), Eur. 66/F1
Rhine-Herne (canal), Ger. 53/E5
Rhinebeck, NY, US 161/K4
Rhineland, Mo, US 155/J4
Rhineland, Sk, Can. 145/L2
Rhinelander, Wi, US 157/K5
Rhinns (pt.), Sc, UK 31/Q9
Rhino Camp, Ugan. 121/G2
Rhiou (riv.), Alg. 112/F5
Rhiou (riv.), Alg. 112/F5
Rhir (cape), Mor. 110/C3
Rhisnes, Belg. 55/D3
Rhiw (riv.), Wal, UK 36/C1
Rho, It. 62/C2
Rhode, Ire. 32/C3
Rhode Island (state), US 161/L4
Rhode Island (sound), RI, US 158/B5
Rhodes (isl.), Gre. 29/G5
Rhodes (Ródhos), Gre. 102/B2
Rhodope (mts.), Bul.,Gre. 67/J2
Rhome, Tx, US 150/K6
Rhön (mts.), Ger. 58/D1
Rhondda, Wal, UK 36/C3
Rhondda Cynon Taff (co.), Wal, UK 36/C3
Rhône (dept.), Fr. 60/A6
Rhone (glacier), Swi. 61/E4
Rhône (riv.), Fr. 29/E4
Rhône au Rhin (canal), Fr. 60/B3
Rhône-Alpes (pol. reg.), Fr. 60/B5
Rhonelle (riv.), Fr. 54/C3
Rhosllanerchrugog, Wal, UK 35/E6
Rhossili, Wal, UK 36/B3
Rhuddlan, Wal, UK 34/E5
Rhum (isl.), Sc, UK 31/Q8
Rhume (riv.), Ger. 53/H5
Rhumel, Oued el (riv.), Alg. 112/J4
Rhuys (pen.), Fr. 56/C6
Rhyddhywel (peak), Wal, UK 36/C2
Rhydowen, Wal, UK 36/B2

Rhyl, Wal, UK 34/E5
Rhynie, Sc, UK 33/D2
Rhyolite, Nv, US 148/D2
Riaba, EqG. 120/B2
Riachão, Braz. 183/E4
Riachão das Neves, Braz. 186/D1
Riachão do Jacuípe, Braz. 187/F1
Riacho de Santana, Braz. 187/E2
Riacho Monte Lindo (riv.), Arg. 188/E3
Riacho Pilagá (riv.), Arg. 188/E3
Riachuelo, Uru. 191/K11
Riachuelo, Braz. 183/H4
Riaillé, Fr. 56/D5
Riala, Swe. 39/B1
Rialto, Ca, US 166/C2
Riangnom, Sudan 117/F3
Rianjo, Sp. 46/A1
Riano, It. 65/B3
Riaño, Sp. 46/C1
Rians, Fr. 64/B5
Riāsi, India 98/C3
Riau (isls.), Indo. 90/B3
Riau (prov.), Indo. 89/C2
Riaza, Sp. 46/D2
Rib (mtn.), Wi, US 155/K1
Rib Lake, Wi, US 157/J5
Ribadeo, Sp. 46/B1
Ribadesella, Sp. 46/C1
Riban'i Manamby (mts.), Madg. 125/H9
Ribas do Rio Pardo, Braz. 189/F2
Ribauè, Moz. 123/H2
Ribble (riv.), Eng, UK 35/F4
Ribblesdale (valley), Eng, UK 35/F3
Ribe, Den. 40/C4
Ribe (co.), Den. 40/C4
Ribeauvillé, Fr. 60/D1
Ribécourt-Dreslincourt, Fr. 54/B4
Ribeira (riv.), Braz. 189/G3
Ribeira Brava, Port. 110/A2
Ribeira Brava, CpV. 107/J10
Ribeira de Pena, Port. 46/B2
Ribeira do Pombal, Braz. 187/F1
Ribeira Grande, CpV. 107/J9
Ribeira Grande, Azor., Port. 47/T13
Ribeirão, Braz. 183/H5
Ribeirão Preto, Braz. 189/H2
Ribeiro Gonçalves, Braz. 183/E4
Ribera, It. 48/C4
Ribera, NM, US 152/B3
Riberalta, Bol. 185/E3
Ribiers, Fr. 64/B4
Rîbniţa, Mol. 72/E4
Ribnitz-Damgarten, Ger. 40/E4
Ribstone, Ab, Can. 145/J1
Ribstone (cr.), Ab, Can. 145/J1
Říčany u Prahy, Czh. 59/H3
Ricaurte, Col. 180/B4
Riccia, It. 65/D5
Riccione, It. 63/F6
Ricco'del Golfo, It. 62/C5
Rice, Mn, US 157/G5
Rice (lake), On, Can. 161/G2
Rice, Ca, US 148/E3
Rice, Wa, US 144/E3
Rice, Tx, US 151/F1
Rice Lake, Wi, US 157/J5
Rice Lake NWR, Mn, US 157/H4
Riceboro, Ga, US 165/H2
Riceville, Ia, US 155/H2
Rich (mtn.), Ar, US 153/G3
Rich, Mor. 110/D2
Rich Hill, Mo, US 153/G1
Rich Square, NC, US 163/J2
Richard B. Russell (dam), SC, US 163/F3
Richard Toll, Sen. 114/B2
Richards, Mo, US 153/G2
Richards (isl.), NW, Can. 140/C2
Richard's Bay, SAfr. 125/F3
Richards Landing, On, Can. 160/D1
Richardson, Tx, US 150/L7
Richardson Lakes (lakes), NH, US 158/B3
Richardton, ND, US 156/C4
Richboro, Pa, US 168/C3
Riche (cape), Austl. 130/C5
Richebourg, Fr. 30/G5
Richel (isl.), Neth. 52/C2
Richelieu (riv.), Qu, Can. 161/K2
Richelieu, Qu, Can. 159/P7
Richey, Mt, US 156/B4
Richfield, Ut, US 149/F1
Richfield, Id, US 147/F2
Richfield, Mn, US 157/P7
Richfield, Pa, US 168/A2
Richford, Vt, US 161/K2
Richhill, NI, UK 34/B3
Richibucto, NB, Can. 158/E2
Richland, Mo, US 153/H2
Richland, Ga, US 165/F1
Richland, Ms, US 162/B4
Richland, Tx, US 151/F2
Richland, Wa, US 144/E4
Richland, Pa, US 168/B3
Richland, NJ, US 168/D5
Richland Balsam (peak), NC, US 163/F3
Richland Center, Wi, US 155/J2
Richland Creek (res.), Tx, US 151/F2
Richland Hills, Tx, US 150/K7
Richland Springs, Tx, US 150/E2
Richlands, Va, US 163/G2
Richlands, NC, US 163/J3
Richlandtown, Pa, US 168/C3
Richmond, Austl. 134/A3
Richmond, BC, Can. 144/C3
Richmond, Qu, Can. 161/K2
Richmond, NZ 135/C3
Richmond, SAfr. 124/C3
Richmond, SAfr. 125/E3
Richmond, Eng, UK 35/G3
Richmond, Ar, US 153/G4
Richmond, Ks, US 153/G1
Richmond, Mn, US 157/G5
Richmond, In, US 160/D5
Richmond, Mi, US 160/E3
Richmond, Il, US 167/P15
Richmond, Ut, US 147/H3
Richmond, Ky, US 162/E2
Richmond, Mo, US 155/H4
Richmond, Tx, US 151/M9
Richmond (cap.), Va, US 163/J2
Richmond (co.), NY, US 168/D2
Richmond Beach-Innis Arden, Wa, US 167/B2
Richmond Dale, Oh, US 163/F1
Richmond Heights, Fl, US 164/P11
Richmond Hill, On, Can. 160/U8
Richmond Nat'l Bfld. Park, Va, US 163/J2
Richmond Park (bor.), Eng, UK 30/C2
Richmond Town (nbrhd.), NY, US 169/J9
Richmond Upon Thames (bor.), Eng, UK 30/B2
Richmond-Windsor, Austl. 134/G8
Richmondville, NY, US 161/J3
Richmound, Sk, Can. 145/K2
Richtersveld NP, SAfr. 124/B3
Richterswil, Swi. 61/E3
Richthofen (mt.), Co, US 154/B3
Richton, Ms, US 164/D2
Richville, NY, US 161/J2
Richwiller, Fr. 60/D2
Richwood, Tx, US 150/G3
Richwood, La, US 153/H4
Richwood, Oh, US 160/E4
Richwood, WV, US 163/G1
Richwoods, Mo, US 162/B1
Rickenbach, Ger. 60/D2
Ricketts Glen St. Park, Pa, US 168/B1
Rickman, Tn, US 162/E2
Rickmansworth, Eng, UK 30/B2
Ricla, Sp. 46/E2
Rico, Ga, US 163/L7
Ricse, Hun. 43/L4
Ridā', Yem. 118/C2
Riddells Creek, Austl. 133/B3
Ridderkerk, Neth. 52/B5
Riddle, Id, US 146/E2
Riddle, Or, US 146/B2
Rideau (riv.), On, Can. 161/J2
Rideau (lake), On, Can. 161/H2
Ridge, Mt, US 154/B1
Ridge Farm, Il, US 160/C5
Ridge Manor, Fl, US 164/L6
Ridge Spring, SC, US 163/G4
Ridgecrest, La, US 164/C2
Ridgecrest, Ca, US 148/D3
Ridgefield, NJ, US 169/K8
Ridgefield, Wa, US 144/C5
Ridgefield, Ct, US 169/E1
Ridgefield NWR, Or, US 144/C5
Ridgefield Park, NJ, US 169/J8
Ridgeland, Ms, US 162/B4
Ridgeland, SC, US 163/G4
Ridgely, Tn, US 162/C2
Ridgely, Md, US 168/C6
Ridgetown, On, Can. 160/F3
Ridgeville, SC, US 163/G4
Ridgeway, Mo, US 155/H3
Ridgeway, Va, US 163/H2
Ridgewood (nbrhd.), NY, US 169/K9
Ridgewood, NJ, US 169/J8
Ridgewood State Park, NJ, US 168/D2
Ridgway, Pa, US 161/G4
Ridgway, Co, US 149/J1
Riding Mill, Eng, UK 35/G2
Riding Mountain NP, Mb, Can. 156/D2
Riding (mtn.), Mb, Can. 156/D2
Ridlees Cairn (hill), Eng, UK 33/D6
Ridley (cr.), Pa, US 168/C4
Riec-sur-Belon, Fr. 56/B5
Riecito (riv.), Col. 180/D3
Ried im Innkreis, Aus. 59/G6
Ried im Traunkreis, Aus. 59/H6
Riede, Ger. 53/F3
Riedenburg, Ger. 59/E5
Riedisheim, Fr. 60/D2
Riedlingen, Ger. 61/F1
Riegelsberg, Ger. 55/F5
Riegelsville, Pa, US 168/C2
Riegsee (lake), Ger. 61/H2
Riehen, Swi. 60/D2
Riemst, Belg. 55/E2
Rieneck, Ger. 58/C2
Rienzi, Ms, US 162/C3
Riesa, Ger. 43/G3
Rieschweiler-Mühlbach, Ger. 55/G5
Riesco (isl.), Chile 191/B7
Riese Pio X, It. 63/E2
Riet (riv.), SAfr. 124/D3
Rietavas, Lith. 41/J4
Rietberg, Ger. 53/F5
Rietbron, SAfr. 124/C4
Rietfontein, Namb. 122/D4
Rietfontein (riv.), Namb. 122/D4
Rieti, It. 65/B3
Rieti (prov.), It. 65/B3
Rievaulx, Eng, UK 35/G3
Riez, Fr. 64/C5
Riffe (lake), Wa, US 144/C4
Rifle, Co, US 147/K4
Rifsnes (pt.), Ice. 38/N6
Rift Valley (prov.), Kenya 119/A1
Rig-Rig, Chad 116/B2
Riga (gulf), Eur. 74/C4
Riga (Rīga) (cap.), Lat. 41/L3
Rigacikun, Nga. 115/G4
Rigby, Id, US 147/H2
Rīgestan (pol. reg.), Afg. 101/H2
Riggins, Id, US 146/E1
Rigi (peak), Swi. 61/E3
Rignano Flaminio, It. 65/B3
Rignano sull'Arno, It. 63/E6
Rigolet, Nf, Can. 141/L3
Rigside, Sc, UK 33/C5
Riguldi, Est. 41/K2
Riḩāb, Jor. 105/E4
Rihand (riv.), India 96/D3
Rihand (dam), India 96/D3
Rihand Sāgar (res.), India 92/D3
Riihimäki, Fin. 41/L1
Riiser-Larsen (pen.), Ant. 192/C
Riiser-Larsen Ice Shelf, Ant. 192/Y
Riisitunturin NP, Fin. 68/F2
Rijeka, Cro. 45/L4
Rijen, Neth. 52/B5
Rijksmuseum Kröller Müller, Neth. 52/C4
Rijnsburg, Neth. 52/B4
Rijsbergen, Neth. 52/B5
Rijssen, Neth. 52/D4
Rijswijk, Neth. 52/B4
Rikers (isl.), NY, US 169/K8
Rikitea, FrPol. 137/M7
Rikuchū-Kaigan NP, Japan 82/C4
Rikuzentakata, Japan 82/B4
Rila, Bul. 49/H1
Rila (mts.), Bul. 49/H1
Riley, Or, US 146/D2
Riley, Ks, US 155/F4
Riley Brook, NB, Can. 158/D2
Rillieux-la-Pape, Fr. 60/A6
Rillito, Az, US 149/G4
Rilski Manastir, Bul. 49/H1
Rīmah (wadi), SAr. 100/D3
Rimatara (isl.), FrPol. 137/K7
Rimavská Sobota, Slvk. 43/L4
Rimbach, Ger. 58/B3
Rimbey, Ab, Can. 145/G1
Rimbo, Swe. 39/B1
Rimé (riv.), Chad 116/C2
Rimersburg, Pa, US 161/G4
Rimforsa, Swe. 40/F2
Rimini, It. 63/F5
Rîmnicu Sărat, Rom. 51/H3
Rîmnicu Vîlcea, Rom. 51/G3
Rimogne, Fr. 55/D4
Rimouski, Qu, Can. 158/C1
Rimouski (riv.), Qu, Can. 158/C1
Rimouski-Est, Qu, Can. 158/C1
Rimpar, Ger. 58/C3
Rimpfischhorn (peak), Swi. 60/D5
Rimsting, Ger. 59/F7
Rimutaka (range), NZ 135/H9
Rimutaka Forrest Park, NZ 135/H9
Rinas (int'l arpt.), Alb. 49/F2
Rinbung, China 97/G1
Rinchnach, Ger. 59/G5
Rincon (peak), Az, US 149/G4
Rincón, Uru. 191/G2
Rincon, NM, US 149/J4
Rincón (peak), Arg.,Chile 188/C3
Rincon, Ga, US 163/G4
Rincón de la Vieja, PN, CR 172/D5
Rincón de Romos, Mex. 174/E4
Rinconada, Arg. 188/C2
Rindge, NH, US 161/K3
Ringarooma, Austl. 132/C4
Ringaskiddy, Ire. 32/B6
Ringboy (pt.), NI, UK 34/C3
Ringebu, Nor. 40/D1
Ringelspitz (peak), Swi. 61/F4
Ringgold, La, US 153/H4
Ringgold, Ga, US 162/E3
Ringim, Nga. 115/H3
Ringkøbing, Den. 40/C3
Ringkøbing (co.), Den. 40/B3
Ringkøbing (fjord), Den. 40/B3
Ringling, Mt, US 145/J4
Ringling, Ok, US 153/F3
Ringling Musuem of Art, Fl, US 165/G4
Ringmer, Eng, UK 37/G5
Ringoes, NJ, US 168/D3
Ringold, Ok, US 153/G3
Ringsend, NI, UK 34/B1
Ringsön (isl.), Swe. 39/A2
Ringsted, Den. 40/D4
Ringtown, Pa, US 168/B2
Ringvaart (riv.), Neth. 52/B4
Ringvassøy (isl.), Nor. 38/F1
Ringway (Manchester) (int'l arpt.), Eng, UK 35/F5
Ringwood, NJ, US 169/H7
Ringwood, Austl. 131/G2
Ringwood (nbrhd.), Austl. 132/G5
Ringwood, Eng, UK 37/E5
Ringwood State Park, NJ, US 168/D1
Rínia (isl.), Gre. 49/J4
Riñihue, Chile 190/B3
Rinteln, Ger. 53/G4
Rinxent, Fr. 54/A2
Rio, La, US 164/D2
Río Abiseo, PN, Peru 184/B2
Rio Azul, Braz. 189/G3
Rio Blanco, Co, US 147/K4
Río Blanco, Chile 190/N8
Río Blanco, Bol. 184/D5
Río Blanco, Mex. 175/M8
Rio Bonito, Braz. 187/P7
Rio Branco, Braz. 184/E3
Rio Branco, Uru. 189/F5
Rio Branco do Sul, Braz. 189/G3
Río Bravo, Mex. 151/E5
Rio Brilhante, Braz. 189/F2
Río Bueno, Chile 190/B4
Río Cauto, Cuba 177/G1
Río Ceballos, Arg. 188/C4
Río Chico, Arg. 191/C6
Río Clarillo, PN, Chile 190/N8
Rio Claro, Trin. 181/F2
Rio Claro, Braz. 187/M7
Rio Claro, Braz. 189/H2
Río Colorado, Arg. 190/D3
Río Cuarto, Arg. 190/D2
Río de Bavispe (riv.), Mex. 174/C2
Rio de Contas, Braz. 187/E2
Rio de Janeiro (int'l arpt.), Braz. 187/N7
Rio de Janeiro, Braz. 187/N7
Rio de Janeiro (state), Braz. 187/E4
Rio Dell, Ca, US 146/A3
Rio do Sul, Braz. 189/G3
Rio Frio, Port. 47/Q10
Río Gallegos, Arg. 191/C6
Río Grande, Arg. 191/D7
Rio Grande, Braz. 189/F5
Rio Grande (riv.), Mex.,US 142/G6
Rio Grande (canal), Co, US 152/A2
Rio Grande (plain), Tx, US 172/B2
Rio Grande, NJ, US 168/D5
Rio Grande, Oh, US 163/F1
Rio Grande City, Tx, US 151/E4
Rio Grande da Serra, Braz. 187/K8
Río Grande de Matagalpa (riv.), Nic. 172/D5
Río Grande de Santiago (riv.), Mex. 174/D4
Rio Grande do Norte (state), Braz. 183/G4
Rio Grande do Piauí, Braz. 183/F4
Rio Grande do Sul (state), Braz. 189/F4
Rio Grande Valley (int'l arpt.), Tx, US 151/F4
Rio Hondo, Tx, US 150/F4
Rio Jaú, PN do, Braz. 181/F5
Río Lagartos, Mex. 176/D1
Rio Largo, Braz. 183/H5
Rio Maior, Port. 46/A3
Río Mayo, Arg. 190/C5
Rio Muni (pol. reg.), EqG. 120/B2
Rio Negrinho, Braz. 189/G3
Río Negro, Chile 190/B4
Río Negro (prov.), Arg. 190/E3
Río Negro, Chile 190/B4
Río Negro (res.), Uru. 189/F5
Rio Negro, Braz. 189/F1
Rio Negro (dept.), Uru. 189/F5
Rio Pardo, Braz. 189/F4
Rio Rancho, NM, US 149/J3
Rio Real, Braz. 187/F1
Rio Saliceto, It. 63/D4
Río Segundo, Arg. 188/D4
Río Simpson, PN, Chile 190/B5
Río Tala, Arg. 191/J10
Río Tercero, Arg. 188/C5
Río Tigre, Ecu. 180/B5
Rio Tinto, Braz. 183/H4
Río Verde, Chile 191/C7
Rio Verde, Braz. 186/C3
Río Verde, Mex. 175/F4
Rio Verde de Mato Grosso, Braz. 189/F1
Rio Vista, Ca, US 167/L10
Rio Vista, Tx, US 151/F1
Riobamba, Ecu. 180/B5
Ríohacha, Col. 180/C2
Rioja, Peru 184/B2
Riolo Terme, It. 63/E5
Riom, Fr. 44/E4
Riom-ès-Montagne, Fr. 44/E4
Riomaggiore, It. 62/C5
Rion-des-Landes, Fr. 44/C5
Riondel, BC, Can. 144/F3
Ríonegro, Col. 180/C3
Ríonegro, Col. 183/K6
Rionero in Vulture, It. 48/D2
Rionero Sannitico, It. 65/D4
Riorges, Fr. 44/F3
Ríos, Sp. 46/B2
Ríos (lake), Chile 190/B5
Ríosucio, Col. 180/B3
Ríosucio, Col. 183/K7
Rioz, Fr. 60/C3
Riozinho (riv.), Braz. 185/E2
Ripa Sottile (lake), It. 65/B3
Ripalimosano, It. 65/D4
Ripalti, Punta dei (pt.), It. 48/B1
Ripanj, Serb. 50/E3
Riparbella, It. 62/D7
Ripatransone, It. 65/C2
Ripky, Ukr. 72/F2
Ripley, Eng, UK 35/G5
Ripley, Eng, UK 30/B3
Ripley, Ca, US 148/E4
Ripley, Ms, US 162/C3
Ripley, Oh, US 162/F1
Ripley, Ok, US 153/F2
Ripley, Tn, US 162/C3
Ripley, WV, US 163/G1
Ripoll, Sp. 47/G1
Ripoll (riv.), Sp. 47/L6
Ripollet, Sp. 47/L6
Ripon, Eng, UK 35/G3
Ripon, Qu, Can. 161/J2
Ripon, Ca, US 148/B2
Ripon, Wi, US 155/K2
Riposto, It. 48/D4
Ripples, NB, Can. 158/D2
Rippon, WV, US 161/H5
Ripponden, Eng, UK 35/G4
Rippowam (riv.), Ct, US 169/L7
Riri Bāzār, Nepal 96/D2
Ris-Orangis, Fr. 30/K6
Risaralda (dept.), Col. 180/A4
Risaralda, Col. 183/K7
Risasi, D.R. Congo 121/F3
Rîşcani, Mol. 72/D4
Rishiri, Japan 82/B1
Rishiri (isl.), Japan 79/N2
Rishiri-Rebun-Sarobetsu NP, Japan 82/B1
Rishon Leẕiyyon, Isr. 105/B5
Rishrāsh (wadi), Egypt 113/C6
Rising Star, Tx, US 150/E1
Rising Sun, In, US 162/E1
Rising Sun, Md, US 168/B4
Rising Sun-Lebanon, De, US 168/C5
Riske Creek, BC, Can. 144/C2
Risle (riv.), Fr. 44/D2
Risley (Estell Manor), NJ, US 168/D5
Risnjak (peak), Cro. 45/L4
Risnjak NP, Cro. 50/B3
Rîşnov, Rom. 51/G3
Rison, Ar, US 153/H4
Risør, Nor. 40/C2
Risoul, Fr. 64/C3
Riss (riv.), Ger. 61/F1
Risse (riv.), Fr. 60/C5
Rişşū (peak), Egypt 113/B5
Risti, Est. 41/L2
Ristiina, Fin. 41/M1
Rita Blanca (cr.), Tx, US 152/C2
Ritacuba (peak), Col. 180/C3
Ritaiō (isl.), Japan 136/D2
Rito (cr.), NM, US 149/H3
Ritoio (peak), It. 63/E6
Ritterhude, Ger. 53/F2
Rittman, Oh, US 160/F4
Rittō, Japan 83/J5
Ritzville, Wa, US 144/E4
Riva, It. 61/G6
Riva Ligure, It. 62/A5
Riva Presso Chieri, It. 62/A3
Riva San Vitale, Swi. 61/E6
Rivadavia, Arg. 190/E2
Rivadavia, Arg. 188/D3
Rivadavia, Arg. 188/B4
Rival (riv.), Fr. 64/B2
Rivalta, It. 62/D3
Rivalta di Torino, It. 62/A2
Rivanazzano, It. 62/C4
Rivanna (riv.), Va, US 163/H2
Rivara, It. 64/D2
Rivarolo Canavese, It. 62/A2
Rivarolo Mantovano, It. 62/D3
Rivas, Nic. 176/E4
Rīvash, Iran 101/G1
Rive-de-Gier, Fr. 64/A1
River Bourgeois, NS, Can. 159/G3
River Cess, Libr. 114/C5
River Denys, NS, Can. 159/G3
River Edge, NJ, US 169/J8
River Falls, Al, US 164/E2
River Falls, Wi, US 157/Q7
River Hébert, NS, Can. 158/E3
River John, NS, Can. 158/F3
River Kwai Bridge, Thai. 94/B3
River Oaks, Tx, US 150/K7
River Rouge, Mi, US 167/F7
River Vale, NJ, US 169/J8
Rivera, Swi. 61/E5
Rivera (isl.), Chile 190/B5
Rivera, Arg. 190/E3
Rivera (dept.), Uru. 189/F4
Rivera, Uru. 189/F4
Riverdale, ND, US 156/D4
Riverdale, NJ, US 169/H8
Riverdale (nbrhd.), NY, US 169/K8
Riverdale, Ca, US 148/C2
Riverdale, Ga, US 163/M7
Rivergaro, It. 62/C4
Riverhead, NY, US 169/F2
Riverhurst, Sk, Can. 145/L2
Riverport, NS, Can. 158/E3
Rivers, Mb, Can. 156/D2
Rivers (state), Nga. 115/G5
Riversdale, SAfr. 124/C4
Riverside, Tx, US 151/G2
Riverside (co.), Ca, US 166/C3
Riverside, Ca, US 166/C3
Riverside, Or, US 146/D2
Riverside (canal), Co, US 154/B3
Riverside, Pa, US 168/B2
Riverside, NJ, US 168/D3
Riverside-Albert, NB, Can. 158/E3
Riverstone (nbrhd.), Austl. 134/G8
Riverstown, Ire. 32/B6
Riverstown, Ire. 32/B1
Riverton, Mb, Can. 156/F2
Riverton, NS, Can. 159/F3
Riverton, Austl. 131/H5
Riverton, NZ 135/B4
Riverton, Wy, US 147/J2
Riverton, Ut, US 147/H3
Riverview, NB, Can. 158/E2
Riverview, Mi, US 160/E3
Riverview, Fl, US 164/L8
Riverwoods, Il, US 167/Q15
Rîves, Fr. 64/B2
Riviera, Az, US 148/E3
Riviera, Tx, US 151/F4
Riviera Beach, Fl, US 164/P9
Riviera Beach, Md, US 168/B5
Rivière-à-Pierre, Qu, Can. 158/A2
Rivière-au-Renard, Qu, Can. 158/E1
Rivière-Bleue, Qu, Can. 158/C2
Rivière-du-Loup, Qu, Can. 158/C2
Rivière-Éternité, Qu, Can. 158/B1
Riviersonderendreeks (mts.), SAfr. 124/L11
Rivignano, It. 63/G2
Rivne, Ukr. 72/D2
Rivnens'ka Oblast, Ukr. 70/C2
Rivoli, It. 64/D2
Rivolta d'Adda, It. 62/C3
Rixensart, Belg. 55/D2
Rixheim, Fr. 60/D2
Riyadh (Ar Riyāḑ) (cap.), SAr. 100/E4
Rīyāq, Leb. 105/D1
Rizal, Phil. 88/C2
Rizal (prov.), Phil. 88/F6
Rize, Turk. 71/G4
Rizhao, China 80/D4
Rizokarpasso, Cyp. 104/D2
Rizzuto (cape), It. 49/E3
Rjukan, Nor. 40/C2
Rkîz, Mrta. 114/B2
Rkîz (lake), Mrta. 114/B2
Rö, Swe. 39/B1
Roa, Nor. 40/D1
Roa, Sp. 46/D2
Road Town (cap.), BVI 173/M8
Roade, Eng, UK 37/F2
Roadside, Sc, UK 33/D3
Roan (plat.), Ut, US 147/J4
Roan Fell (hill), Sc, UK 35/F1
Roan High (peak), NC, US 163/F2
Roanne (riv.), Fr. 64/B3
Roanne, Fr. 44/F3
Roanoke, Al, US 162/E4
Roanoke, Tx, US 150/K6
Roanoke (riv.), Va, US 163/H2
Roanoke (pt.), NY, US 169/F2
Roanoke, Va, US 163/H2
Roanoke Rapids, NC, US 163/J2
Roans Prairie, Tx, US 151/G2
Roaring (cr.), Pa, US 168/B2
Roaring Fk. (riv.), Co, US 147/K4
Roaring Springs, Tx, US 152/D4
Roatán (isl.), Hon. 172/D4
Roatán, Hon. 176/E2
Robards, Ky, US 162/D2
Robassomero, It. 64/D2
Robāţ Karīm, Iran 103/G3
Robāţ-e Khān, Iran 103/J3
Robāţ-e Sang, Iran 101/G1
Robb, Ab, Can. 144/F1
Robbiate, It. 62/C2
Robbins (isl.), Austl. 132/C4
Robbins, NC, US 163/H3
Robbinsville, NC, US 162/F3
Robbio, It. 62/B3
Robe (riv.), Ire. 32/A2
Robē, Eth. 118/A4
Robe (mt.), Austl. 132/B1
Robe, Austl. 132/A3
Robecchetto con Induno, It. 62/B2
Röbel, Ger. 40/E4
Röbel, Ger. 42/G2
Robersonville, NC, US 163/J3
Robert (peak), Fr. 60/B5
Robert Lee, Tx, US 150/D2
Roberta, Ga, US 162/E4
Roberts (mt.), Ak, US 171/E4
Roberts, Id, US 147/G2
Roberts, Il, US 160/B4
Roberts, Mt, US 147/J1
Roberts (Monrovia) (int'l arpt.), Libr. 114/C5
Roberts Creek (mtn.), Nv, US 146/E4
Roberts Creek, BC, Can. 144/C3
Robertsbridge, Eng, UK 37/G5
Robertsfors, Swe. 38/G2
Robertsganj, India 96/D3
Robertson, SAfr. 124/L10
Robertson, Wy, US 147/H3
Robertsport, Libr. 114/C5
Robertstown, Ire. 32/D3
Roberval, Qu, Can. 158/A1
Robesonia, Pa, US 168/B3
Robilante, It. 64/D4
Robin Hood's Bay, Eng, UK 35/H3
Robins (A.F.B.), Ga, US 163/F4
Robinson, Il, US 162/D1
Robinson, Tx, US 151/F2
Robinson (mtn.), Mt, US 144/G3
Robinson . (range), Austl. 127/A3
Robinson Crusoe (isl.), Chile 179/B6
Robinson Gorge NP, Austl. 134/C4
Robinson River, Austl. 129/E4
Robinson River, PNG 129/H2
Robinson River Abor. Land, Austl. 129/E4
Robinson Springs, Al, US 162/D4
Robinvale, Austl. 132/B2
Robion, Fr. 64/B5
Robledo (mtn.), NM, US 149/J4
Roblin, Mb, Can. 156/D2
Roboré, Bol. 188/E1
Robsart, Sk, Can. 145/K3
Robson (mt.), BC, Can. 144/E1
Robstown, Tx, US 151/F4
Roby, Mo, US 153/H2
Roby, Tx, US 150/D1
Roc (pt.), Fr. 56/D3
Roc de France (peak), Fr. 47/G1
Roc du Haut du Faite (peak), Fr. 60/D1
Roca Partida (isl.), Mex. 174/B5
Roca Partida, Punta (pt.), Mex. 176/C2
Roca, Cabo da (cape), Port. 47/P10
Rocafuerte, Ecu. 180/A5
Rocanville, Sk, Can. 156/D2
Rocas (isl.), Braz. 183/H3
Rocca di Mezzo, It. 65/C3
Rocca di Papa, It. 65/B4
Rocca San Casciano, It. 63/E5
Roccabianca, It. 62/D3
Roccagorga, It. 65/C4
Roccamandolfi, It. 65/D5
Roccamonfina, It. 65/C5
Roccarainola, It. 65/D6
Roccasecca, It. 65/C4
Roccastrada, It. 48/B1
Roccavione, It. 64/D4
Rocciamelone (peak), It. 64/D2
Rocha, Uru. 191/G2
Rocha (dept.), Uru. 191/G2
Rochambeau (int'l arpt.), FrG. 182/C1
Rochdale, Eng, UK 35/F4
Rochdale (co.), Eng, UK 35/F4
Roche, Swi. 60/C5
Roche, Eng, UK 36/B6
Roche Bernaude (peak), Fr. 64/C2
Roche de la Muzelle (peak), Fr. 64/C3
Roche du Sapin Sec (peak), Fr. 60/C1
Roche Faurio (peak), Fr. 64/C3
Roche-lez-Beaupré, Fr. 60/C3
Rochebrune, Pic de (peak), Fr. 64/C3
Rochefort, Belg. 55/E3
Rochefort, Fr. 44/C4
Rochefort-en-Terre, Fr. 56/C5
Rochefort-sur-Loire, Fr. 57/E6
Rochelaire, Pic de (peak), Fr. 64/C3
Rochelle, Ga, US 165/G2
Rochelle, Il, US 155/K3
Rochelle, Tx, US 150/E2
Rochelle Park, NJ, US 169/J8
Rochemaure, Fr. 64/A3
Rochers de la Tude (peak), Fr. 47/G1
Rochers du Bourbet (peak), Fr. 60/C3
Roches Blanches (peak), Fr. 64/C6
Rochester, Austl. 133/B3
Rochester, Eng, UK 37/G4
Rochester, NY, US 161/H3
Rochester, In, US 160/C4
Rochester, NH, US 161/L3
Rochester, Vt, US 161/K3
Rochester, Wi, US 167/P14
Rochester, Mi, US 167/F6
Rochester, Mn, US 155/H1
Rochester, Ky, US 162/D2
Rochester, Il, US 155/K4
Rochester Hills, Mi, US 160/E3
Rochford, Eng, UK 30/F2
Rochfortbridge, Ire. 32/C3
Rock (riv.), Ia,Mn, US 155/F2
Rock (riv.), Il, US 143/J3
Rock, Mi, US 157/L4
Rock (cr.), Mt, US 147/J1
Rock (lake), ND, US 156/E3
Rock Bluff, Fl, US 165/F2
Rock Cave, WV, US 163/G1
Rock Creek, Yk, Can. 171/L3
Rock Falls, Wi, US 155/J1
Rock Falls, Il, US 155/K3
Rock Forest, Qu, Can. 161/L2
Rock Glen, Pa, US 168/B2
Rock Hall, Md, US 168/B5
Rock Hill, SC, US 163/G3
Rock Island, Il, US 155/J3
Rock Island, Tx, US 150/F3
Rock Mills, Al, US 162/E4
Rock Port, Mo, US 155/G3
Rock Rapids, Ia, US 155/F2
Rock River, Wy, US 154/B3
Rock Springs, Wy, US 147/J3
Rock Springs, Mt, US 145/L4
Rock Valley, Ia, US 155/F2
Rockall (isl.), UK 29/C3
Rockaway (pt.), NY, US 169/K9
Rockaway (inlet), NY, US 169/K9
Rockaway (riv.), NJ, US 168/D2
Rockaway, NJ, US 168/D2
Rockaway (Rockaway Beach), Or, US 144/C5
Rockaway Beach (Rockaway), Or, US 144/C5
Rockaway Park (nbrhd.), NY, US 169/K9
Rockcorry, Ire. 32/C1
Rockdale, Il, US 167/P17
Rockdale (nbrhd.), Austl. 134/H8
Rockdale (co.), Ga, US 163/M7
Rockdale, Tx, US 151/F2
Rockefeller (plat.), Ant. 192/R
Rockenhausen, Ger. 55/G4
Rockett, Tx, US 150/L7
Rockfield, Ky, US 162/D2
Rockford, Oh, US 160/D4
Rockford, Il, US 155/K2
Rockford, Al, US 162/D4
Rockford, Wa, US 144/F4
Rockglen, Sk, Can. 145/M3
Rockhampton, Austl. 134/C3
Rockhampton Downs, Austl. 129/D4
Rockhill, Tx, US 150/L6
Rockingham, Vt, US 161/K3
Rockingham, Austl. 130/K7
Rockingham, NC, US 163/H3
Rockland, Tx, US 151/G2
Rockland, On, Can. 161/J2
Rockland, Id, US 147/G2
Rockland (co.), NY, US 168/D1
Rockland Lake, NY, US 169/K7
Rocklands (res.), Austl. 132/B3
Rockledge, Fl, US 165/H3
Rockledge, Pa, US 168/C3
Rocklin, Ca, US 146/C4
Rockmart, Ga, US 162/E3
Rockport, Ar, US 153/H3
Rockport, Ca, US 146/B4
Rockport, In, US 162/D2
Rockport, Ky, US 162/D2
Rockport, Ms, US 164/C2
Rockport, Tx, US 150/F3
Rockport, Wa, US 144/D3
Rocks (pt.), NZ 135/C3
Rocks, Md, US 168/B4
Rocksprings, Tx, US 150/D2
Rockstone, Guy. 181/G3
Rockton, Il, US 160/B3
Rockvale, Co, US 152/B1
Rockville, NS, Can. 158/D4
Rockville, In, US 160/C5
Rockville, Md, US 163/J1
Rockville, Ut, US 149/F2
Rockville Centre, NY, US 169/L9
Rockwall, Tx, US 150/L7
Rockwall (co.), Tx, US 150/L7
Rockwell, Ia, US 155/H2
Rockwell City, Ia, US 155/G2
Rockwood, Me, US 161/M2
Rockwood, On, Can. 160/S8
Rockwood, Tn, US 162/E3
Rockwood, Tx, US 150/E2
Rocky (pt.), Austl. 128/C2
Rocky (mts.), Can.,US 139/E4
Rocky (pt.), Namb. 122/B3
Rocky (mtn.), Ky, US 162/F2
Rocky (pt.), NY, US 169/F1
Rocky (riv.), NC, US 163/G3
Rocky, Ok, US 152/E3
Rocky Boys Ind. Res., Mt, US 145/K3
Rocky Cape NP, Austl. 132/C4
Rocky Ford, Co, US 152/C1
Rocky Ford, Ga, US 163/G4
Rocky Fork (lake), Oh, US 160/E5
Rocky Island (lake), On, Can. 160/E1
Rocky Mount, Mo, US 153/H1
Rocky Mount, NC, US 163/J3
Rocky Mount, Va, US 163/H2
Rocky Mountain Arsenal, Co, US 152/B1
Rocky Mountain House, Ab, Can. 144/G1
Rocky Mountain NP, Co, US 154/A3
Rocky Point, NC, US 163/J3
Rocky Reach (dam), Wa, US 144/D4
Rockyford, Ab, Can. 145/H2
Rockypoint, Wy, US 154/B1
Rocroi, Fr. 55/D4
Roda, Sp. 66/C3
Rodach (riv.), Ger. 59/E2
Rodach bei Coburg, Ger. 58/D2
Rodalben, Ger. 55/G5
Rodanthe, NC, US 163/K3
Rødberg, Nor. 40/C1
Rødbyhavn, Den. 40/D4
Rødbyvatn (lake), Nor. 38/S9
Rødding, Den. 40/C4
Roden (riv.), Eng, UK 35/F6
Rodenbach, Ger. 58/C2
Rodeo, Ca, US 167/K10
Rodeo, NM, US 149/H5
Rodeo, Mex. 174/D3
Roderfield, WV, US 163/G2
Rödermark, Ger. 58/B3
Rodessa, La, US 153/H4
Rodewisch, Ger. 59/F1
Rodez, Fr. 44/E4
Rodholívos, Gre. 49/H2
Ródhos (ruin), Gre. 102/B2
Ródhos (Rhodes), Gre. 102/B2
Rodigo, It. 62/D3
Roding (riv.), Eng, UK 30/D2
Roding, Ger. 59/F4
Rodinga (mt.), Austl. 131/G3
Rödinghausen, Ger. 53/F4
Rodney (cape), NZ 135/C2
Rodoč, Bosn. 50/C4
Rodolfo Sánchez Toboada, Mex. 174/A2
Rødovre, Den. 39/J7
Rodrigues, Braz. 184/C2
Rodríguez, Uru. 191/K11
Rødvig, Den. 39/J7
Rodyns'ke, Ukr. 73/J3
Roe (riv.), NI, UK 34/B2
Roebourne, Austl. 130/C2
Roebuck (bay), Austl. 127/B2
Roebuck, SC, US 163/G3
Roebuck Plains, Austl. 128/A4
Roedtan, SAfr. 123/F5
Roen (peak), It. 61/H5
Roer (riv.), Neth. 52/D6
Roermond, Neth. 52/C6
Roes Welcome Sound (str.), Nun, Can. 141/H2
Roeselare, Belg. 54/C2
Roesiger (lake), Wa, US 167/D2
Roff, Ok, US 153/F3
Rogač, Cro. 50/C4
Rogachev, Bela. 70/D1
Rogachëvka, Rus. 73/K2
Rogagua (lake), Bol. 185/E4
Rogaland (co.), Nor. 38/C4
Rogaška Slatina, Slov. 45/L3
Rogatica, Bosn. 50/D4
Rogers, ND, US 156/E4
Rogers, Ar, US 153/G2
Rogers (mt.), Va, US 163/G2
Rogers, BC, Can. 144/F2
Rogers, Tx, US 150/F2
Rogers City, Mi, US 160/E2
Rogersville, NB, Can. 158/E2
Rogersville, Mo, US 153/H2
Rogersville, Tn, US 163/F2
Rogersville, Al, US 162/D3
Roggwil, Swi. 60/D3
Rogliano, Fr. 48/A1
Roglio (riv.), It. 63/D5
Rognac, Fr. 64/B6
Rognes, Fr. 64/B5
Rognon (riv.), Fr. 44/F2
Rognonas, Fr. 64/A5
Rogo, Nga. 115/G4
Rogoaguado (lake), Bol. 185/E4
Rogoźno, Pol. 43/J2
Rogue (riv.), Or, US 146/A2
Rogue River, Or, US 146/B2
Rohatyn, Ukr. 72/C3
Rohl (riv.), Sudan 117/F4
Rohnert Park, Ca, US 146/B4
Rohr, Ger. 59/E5
Rohrbach bei Mattersburg, Aus. 50/C2
Rohrbach in Oberösterreich, Aus. 59/G5
Rohrbach-lès-Bitche, Fr. 55/G5
Rohri, Pak. 101/J3
Röhrmoos, Ger. 59/E6
Rohtak, India 98/D5
Rohtās, India 96/D3
Rohwer, Ar, US 153/J4
Roi Et, Thai. 94/C2
Roia (riv.), It. 64/D5
Roiffieux, Fr. 64/A2
Roine (lake), Fin. 41/L1
Roissy, Fr. 30/K5
Roissy-en-France, Fr. 30/K4
Roja, Lat. 41/K3
Rojas, Arg. 190/E2
Rojo (cape), PR 173/M8
Rojo, Cabo (cape), Mex. 176/B1
Roka, Kenya 119/B2
Rokan, Indo. 89/C2
Rokan (river), Indo. 89/C2
Rokan (riv.), Indo. 90/B3
Rokeby Croll Creek NP, Austl. 134/A1
Rokel (riv.), SLeo. 114/C4
Rokiškis, Lith. 41/L4
Rokkasho, Japan 82/B3
Rokkō-san (peak), Japan 83/H6
Rokot (cape), Indo. 89/B3
Rokugō, Japan 83/A3
Rokycany, Czh. 59/G3
Rokytka (riv.), Czh. 59/H2
Rokytne, Ukr. 72/D2
Rokytne, Ukr. 72/F3
Rolampont, Fr. 60/B2
Roland, Mb, Can. 156/F3
Roland, Ia, US 155/H2
Rolândia, Braz. 186/C4
Rolava (riv.), Czh. 59/F2
Røldal, Nor. 40/B2
Rolde, Neth. 52/D3
Rolette, ND, US 156/E3
Rolfe, Ia, US 155/G2
Rolim de Moura, Braz. 185/F3
Roll, Az, US 149/F4
Rolla, ND, US 156/E3
Rolla, Mo, US 153/J2
Rolle, Swi. 60/C5
Rolle, SAfr. 123/F5
Rolling Fork, Ms, US 162/B4
Rolling Hills, Ab, Can. 145/J2
Rolling Hills Estates, Ca, US 166/F8
Rolling Meadows, Il, US 167/P15
Rolling Prairies (plain), Tx, US 152/D4
Rollingbay, Wa, US 167/B2
Rolo, It. 63/D4
Rom (peak), Ugan. 117/G5
Roma, Austl. 134/C4
Roma (Rome) (cap.), It. 65/B4
Roma (prov.), It. 65/B4
Roma, Swe. 40/H3
Roma, Tx, US 150/E4
Romagna (reg.), It. 67/F1
Romagnano Sesia, It. 62/B2
Romagnat, Fr. 44/E4
Romain (cape), SC, US 163/H4
Romaine (riv.), Fr. 60/B2
Romaine (riv.), Qu, Can. 141/K3
Roman, Bul. 51/F4
Roman, Rom. 72/D4
Roman Kosh (peak), Ukr. 73/H5
Romanche (riv.), Fr. 64/C2
Romang (isl.), Indo. 128/B1
Romang (str.), Indo. 128/B1
Romania (ctry.) 51/F3
Romano (cape), Fl, US 165/H5
Romano Canavese, It. 62/A2
Romano d'Ezzelino, It. 63/E2
Romano di Lombardia, It. 62/C2
Romanovka, Rus. 71/H2
Romanovka, Rus. 78/G1
Romans d'Isonzo, It. 63/G2
Romans-sur-Isère, Fr. 64/B2
Romanshorn, Swi. 61/F2
Romanzof (cape), Ak, US 171/E3
Romashki, Rus. 71/H2
Rombas, Fr. 55/F5
Romblon, Phil. 88/C2
Rome (Roma) (cap.), It. 65/B4
Rome, Ga, US 162/E3
Rome, Il, US 155/K3
Rome, NY, US 161/J3
Rome, Or, US 146/E2
Rome, Pa, US 161/H4
Rome, Wi, US 167/N14
Romenay, Fr. 60/B4
Romeo, Mi, US 160/E3
Romeo, Co, US 149/K2
Romeoville, Il, US 167/P16
Romford (nbrhd.), Eng, UK 30/D2
Römhild, Ger. 58/D2
Romillé, Fr. 56/D4
Romilly-sur-Andelle, Fr. 57/G2
Rommani, Mor. 110/D2
Rommerskirchen, Ger. 55/F1
Romney, WV, US 161/G5
Romney Marsh (phys. reg.), Eng, UK 37/G4
Romny, Ukr. 73/G2
Rømø (isl.), Den. 40/C4
Romodan, Ukr. 73/G3
Romodanovo, Rus. 71/H1
Romoland, Ca, US 166/C3
Romont, Swi. 60/C4
Romorantin-Lanthenay, Fr. 57/G6
Romsey, Eng, UK 37/E5
Romsey, Austl. 133/B3
Rømskog, Nor. 40/D2
Romulus, Mi, US 160/E3
Ron, Viet. 94/D2
Ron (cape), Viet. 87/E5
Ron Phibun, Thai. 94/B4
Ronaldsway (Isle of Man) (arpt.), IM, UK 34/D3
Ronan, Mt, US 145/G4
Roncade, It. 63/F2
Roncador, Braz. 189/F3
Roncador Cay (isl.), Col. 173/F5
Roncador, Serra do (mts.), Braz. 186/B2
Ronceverte, WV, US 163/G2
Ronchamp, Fr. 60/C2
Ronchi dei Legionari (int'l arpt.), It. 63/G2
Ronchi dei Legionari, It. 63/G2
Ronciglione, It. 65/B3
Ronco (riv.), It. 63/F5
Ronco All'Adige, It. 63/E3
Ronco Scrivia, It. 62/B4
Roncoferraro, It. 63/D3
Roncq, Fr. 54/C2
Ronda, Sp. 46/C4
Rondane NP, Nor. 38/D3
Rondo, Ar, US 162/B3
Rondônia (state), Braz. 182/A5
Rondonópolis, Braz. 186/B3
Rondu, Pak. 98/C2
Rong (riv.), China 93/J2
Rong Kwang, Thai. 94/C2
Rong Xian, China 93/K3
Rong'an, China 87/F3
Rongchang, China 86/E2
Rongcheng, China 81/B4
Rongcheng, China 80/G7
Ronge (lake), Sk, Can. 140/F3
Rongelap (isl.), Mrsh. 136/F3
Rongerik (isl.), Mrsh. 136/F3
Rongjiang, China 87/F3
Rongjiawan, China 87/G2
Rongkou, China 87/H2
Rongshui Miaozu Zizhixian, China 93/J2
Rõngu, Est. 41/M2
Roniu (peak), FrPol. 137/X15
Ronkonkoma, NY, US 169/E2
Rønne, Den. 40/F4
Rönne (riv.), Swe. 39/K6
Ronne Ice Shelf, Ant. 192/W
Ronneby, Swe. 40/F3
Rønnede, Den. 39/J7
Ronnenberg, Ger. 53/G4
Rönninge, Swe. 39/A1
Ronquerolles, Fr. 30/J4
Ronsard (cape), Austl. 130/B3
Ronsberg, Ger. 61/G2
Ronse, Belg. 54/C2
Ronuro (plat.), Braz. 185/H4
Roodeport, SAfr. 124/P13
Roodhouse, Il, US 155/J4
Rooiberg (peak), Namb. 124/B2
Roosendaal, Neth. 52/B5
Roosevelt (isl.), Ant. 192/N
Roosevelt (riv.), Braz. 179/C4
Roosevelt (mt.), BC, Can. 140/D3
Roosevelt, Az, US 149/G4
Roosevelt, NJ, US 168/D3
Roosevelt, NY, US 169/L9
Roosevelt (isl.), NY, US 169/K8
Roosevelt, Ok, US 152/E3
Roosevelt, Ut, US 147/J3
Roosville, BC, Can. 144/G3
Root (mt.), Ak, US 171/L4
Root (riv.), Wi, US 167/P14
Root, West Branch (riv.), Wi, US 167/P14
Roper (riv.), Austl. 128/D3
Roper, NC, US 163/J3
Roper Valley, Austl. 128/D3
Ropesville, Tx, US 152/C4
Roque Pérez, Arg. 191/J11
Roquebillière, Fr. 64/D4
Roquebrune-Cap-Martin, Fr. 64/D5
Roquebrune-sur-Argens, Fr. 64/C6
Roquefort-la-Bédoule, Fr. 64/B6
Roquemaure, Fr. 64/A4
Roquesteron, Fr. 64/D5
Roquetas de Mar, Sp. 46/D4
Roquevaire, Fr. 64/B6
Roraima (peak), Ven. 181/F3
Roraima (state), Braz. 181/F4
Rørby, Den. 39/H7
Rori, India 98/C5

Rorke's – Saint A

Map Section 266 267

Rorke's Drift, SAfr. 125/E3
Rorke's Drift Battlesite, SAfr. 125/E3
Rorketon, Mb, Can. 156/E2
Røros, Nor. 38/D3
Rorschach, Swi. 61/F3
Rosa (cape), Alg. 112/L6
Rosa (lake), Bahm. 177/H1
Rosà, It. 63/E2
Rosa, La, US 164/B2
Rosa Punta (pt.), Mex. 174/C3
Rosa Zárate, Ecu. 180/B4
Rosablanche (peak), Swi. 60/D5
Rosal, Sp. 46/A2
Rosales, Mex. 150/B3
Rosalia, Ks, US 153/F2
Rosalia, Wa, US 144/F4
Rosalie (lake), Fl, US 164/N8
Rosalina, Par. 189/F2
Rosamond, Ca, US 148/C3
Rosamorada, Mex. 174/D4
Rosanna (riv.), Aus. 61/G3
Rosans, Fr. 64/B4
Rosario, Arg. 190/E2
Rosario (riv.), Arg. 188/C3
Rosario, Bol. 185/E4
Rosário, Braz. 183/E3
Rosario, Mex. 174/D4
Rosario, Mex. 174/C3
Rosario, Par. 189/E3
Rosario, Phil. 88/C1
Rosario, Phil. 88/E7
Rosario, Uru. 191/K11
Rosario de la Frontera, Arg. 188/C3
Rosario de Lerma, Arg. 188/C3
Rosario del Tala, Arg. 191/J10
Rosário do Sul, Braz. 189/F4
Rosário Oeste, Braz. 185/G4
Rosarno, It. 48/D3
Rosas, Col. 180/B4
Rosas (gulf), Sp. 47/G1
Rosate, It. 62/C3
Rosay, Fr. 30/G5
Rosbach vor der Höhe, Ger. 58/B2
Rosche, Ger. 53/H3
Roscoe, Il, US 155/K2
Roscoe, Mo, US 153/H2
Roscoe, Tx, US 150/D1
Roscoff, Fr. 56/B3
Roscommon, Ire. 32/B2
Roscommon (co.), Ire. 32/B2
Roscommon, Mi, US 160/D2
Roscrea, Ire. 32/C4
Rosdorf, Ger. 53/G5
Rose (isl.), ASam. 137/J6
Rose (peak), Az, US 149/H4
Rose Belle, Mrts. 125/T15
Rose Bud, Ar, US 153/H3
Rose City, Mi, US 160/D2
Rose Hill, Ks, US 153/F2
Rose Hill, Ms, US 162/C4
Rose Hill, Va, US 163/F2
Rose Lodge, Or, US 146/B1
Rose Valley, Sk, Can. 156/C1
Roseau (cap.), Dom. 173/N9
Roseau, Mn, US 156/G3
Roseau (riv.), Mn, US 156/F3
Roseau River, Mb, Can. 156/F3
Roseaux, Haiti 177/H2
Rosebery, Austl. 132/C4
Roseboro, NC, US 163/H3
Rosebud, Ga, US 163/N7
Rosebud, Tx, US 151/F2
Rosebud (riv.), Ab, Can. 145/H2
Rosebud, Mt, US 145/L4
Rosebud (cr.), Mt, US 145/L4
Rosebud Ind. Res., SD, US 154/D2
Roseburg, Or, US 146/B2
Rosedale, Austl. 133/C4
Rosedale, Ca, US 148/C3
Rosedale, Md, US 168/B5
Rosedale, Ms, US 162/B4
Rosedale, Va, US 163/G2
Roseglen, ND, US 156/D4
Rosehearty, Sc, UK 33/D1
Roseira, Braz. 187/L7
Roseires (dam), Sudan 117/G3
Roseisle, Mb, Can. 156/E3
Roseland, La, US 164/C2
Roseland, NJ, US 169/H8
Roselette, Aiguille de (peak), Fr. 60/C6
Roselle, NJ, US 169/H9
Roselle, Il, US 167/P16
Roselle Park, NJ, US 169/H9
Rosemark, Tn, US 162/C3
Rosemead, Ca, US 166/F7
Rosemère, Qu, Can. 159/N6
Rosemount, Oh, US 163/F1
Rosemount, Mn, US 157/P7
Rosenberg, Tx, US 151/G3
Rosenberg, Ger. 58/D4
Rosenfeld, Ger. 61/E1
Rosenhayn, NJ, US 168/C5
Rosenhof, Sk, Can. 145/L2
Rosenort, Mb, Can. 156/F3
Rosepine, La, US 164/B2
Roses, Sp. 47/G1
Roseto, Pa, US 168/C2
Roseto degli Abruzzi, It. 65/D2
Rosetown, Sk, Can. 145/L2
Rosetta, Ms, US 164/C2
Rosetta (Massabb Rashīd) (mouth), Egypt 113/B1
Rosetta Branch (riv.), Egypt 104/B4
Roseville, Ca, US 146/C4
Roseville, Il, US 155/J3
Roseville, Mi, US 167/G6
Roseville, Mn, US 157/P6
Roseville, Oh, US 160/E5
Rosevine, Tx, US 151/H2
Rosewood, Austl. 128/C4
Rosh Ha'ayin, Isr. 105/B4
Rosh Hakarmel (pt.), Isr. 105/B3
Rosh Haniqra (pt.), Isr. 105/C2
Rosh Pina (arpt.), Isr. 105/D3
Rosh Pinah, Namb. 124/B2
Rosh Pinna, Isr. 105/D3
Rosharon, Tx, US 151/M9
Rosheim, Fr. 60/D1
Roshkhvār, Iran 101/G2
Rosholt, SD, US 156/F5
Rosholt, Wi, US 155/K1
Rosiclare, Il, US 162/C2
Rosières-en-Santerre, Fr. 54/B4
Rosignano Marittimo, It. 62/D7
Rosignano Solvay, It. 62/D7
Rosignol, Guy. 182/B1
Roșiori de Vede, Rom. 51/G3
Rositsa, Bul. 51/H4
Roskilde, Den. 40/E4
Roskilde (co.), Den. 40/D4
Roskilde (inlet), Den. 39/H7
Roslags-Bro, Swe. 39/B1
Roslags-Kulla, Swe. 39/B1
Roslags-Näsby, Swe. 39/B1
Roslavl', Rus. 70/E1
Roslev, Den. 40/C3
Roslyakova, Rus. 68/G1
Roslyatino, Rus. 69/K4
Roslyn, Wa, US 144/D4
Rosmalen, Neth. 52/C5
Rosmaninhal, Port. 46/B3
Rosneath, Sc, UK 33/B4
Rosny-sous-Bois, Fr. 30/K5
Rosny-sur-Seine, Fr. 57/G2
Rosolina, It. 63/F3
Rosolini, It. 48/D4
Rosporden, Fr. 56/B5
Rösrath, Ger. 55/G2
Ross (isl.), Ant. 192/M
Ross (sea), Ant. 192/P
Ross, Austl. 132/C4
Ross (pt.), On, Can. 160/V8
Ross, NZ 135/B3
Ross (mt.), NZ 135/C3
Ross (dist.), Sc, UK 33/C1
Ross, Tx, US 151/F2
Ross (lake), Wa, US 144/D3
Ross Barnett (res.), Ms, US 162/C4
Ross Carbery, Ire. 32/A6
Ross Ice Shelf, Ant. 192/N
Ross River, Yk, Can. 171/M3
Ross-on-Wye, Eng, UK 36/D3
Rossa, Swi. 61/F5
Rossa (peak), It. 45/K3
Rossall (pt.), Eng, UK 35/E4
Rossano Stazione, It. 48/E3
Rossano Veneto, It. 63/E2
Rossbach, Ger. 59/F5
Rossberg (peak), Fr. 60/D2
Rossburn, Mb, Can. 156/D2
Rossdorf, Ger. 58/B3
Rossel (isl.), PNG 136/E6
Rosselange, Fr. 55/F5
Rosser, Mb, Can. 156/F3
Rosser, Tx, US 150/L7
Rosshaupten, Ger. 61/G2
Rossie, NY, US 161/J2
Rossiglione, It. 62/B4
Rossignol (lake), NS, Can. 158/E3
Rössing, Namb. 122/B4
Rössjöholmsån (riv.), Swe. 39/J6
Rosskeeragh (pt.), Ire. 31/P9
Rossland, BC, Can. 144/F3
Rosslare, Ire. 32/D5
Rosslare (bay), Ire. 32/D5
Rosslare (pt.), Ire. 32/D5
Rosslea, NI, UK 32/C1
Rosslyn Village, On, Can. 157/K3
Rosso, Mrta. 114/B2
Rossosh', Rus. 73/K2
Rossport, On, Can. 157/L3
Rossstock (peak), Swi. 61/E4
Rosstal, Ger. 58/D4
Rosston, Ar, US 153/H4
Rossville, Il, US 160/C4
Røst, Nor. 38/E2
Rostāq, Iran 103/H5
Rostāq, Afg. 99/A4
Rostellan, Ire. 32/B6
Rosthern, Sk, Can. 145/L1
Rostock, Ger. 40/E4
Rostov, Rus. 68/H4
Rostov, Rus. 73/K4
Rostov (int'l arpt.), Rus. 73/K4
Rostovskaya Oblast, Rus. 71/G2
Rostrenen, Fr. 56/B4
Rostrevor, NI, UK 34/B3
Roswell, Ga, US 163/M6
Roswell, NM, US 152/B4
Rot (riv.), Ger. 42/E4
Rota (isl.), NMar. 136/D3
Rota, Sp. 46/B4
Rotan, Tx, US 152/D4
Rote Wand (peak), Aus. 61/F3
Rotebro, Swe. 39/A1
Rotenburg, Ger. 53/G2
Rotenburg an der Fulda, Ger. 53/G7
Roter Main (riv.), Ger. 42/F3
Rötgen, Ger. 55/F2
Roth (riv.), Ger. 61/G1
Roth bei Nürnberg, Ger. 58/E4
Rothaargebirge (mts.), Ger. 53/F6
Rothau, Fr. 60/D1
Rothbury, Eng, UK 33/E6
Röthenbach an der Pegnitz, Ger. 58/E4
Rothenberg, Ger. 58/B3
Rothenburg, Swi. 61/E3
Rothenburg ob der Tauber, Ger. 58/D4
Rothera, UK, Ant. 192/V
Rotherham, Eng, UK 35/G5
Rotherham (co.), Eng, UK 35/G5
Rothes, Sc, UK 33/C1
Rothesay, Sc, UK 33/A5
Rotheux-Rimière, Belg. 55/E2
Rothsay, Mn, US 156/F4
Rothschild, Wi, US 155/K1
Rothwell, Eng, UK 35/G4
Rothwell, Eng, UK 37/F2
Roti (isl.), Indo. 91/F6
Rotifunk, SLeo. 114/B4
Roto, Austl. 133/B1
Rotonda, Fl, US 165/G4
Rotondo (peak), It. 65/C2
Rotorua, NZ 135/D2
Rotselaar, Belg. 55/D2
Rott (riv.), Ger. 42/G4
Rott am Inn, Ger. 59/F7
Rottach-Egern, Ger. 42/F5
Rotte (riv.), Fr. 55/F6
Rotten (riv.), Swi. 60/E5
Rottenacker, Ger. 61/F1
Röttenbach, Ger. 58/E4
Rottenberg, Ger. 58/C2
Rottenburg am Neckar, Ger. 58/B6
Rottenburg an der Laaber, Ger. 59/F5
Rotterdam, Neth. 52/B5
Rotterdam (int'l arpt.), Neth. 52/B5
Rottershausen, Ger. 58/D2
Rotthalmünster, Ger. 59/G6
Rottingdean, Eng, UK 37/F5
Röttingen, Ger. 58/C3
Rottne, Swe. 40/F3
Rottnest (isl.), Austl. 130/B5
Rottofreno, It. 62/C3
Rottum (riv.), Ger. 61/F1
Rottumeroog (isl.), Neth. 52/D1
Rottumerplaat (isl.), Neth. 52/D1
Rottweil, Ger. 61/E1
Rotuma (isl.), Fiji 136/G6
Rötz, Ger. 59/F4
Roubaix, Fr. 54/C2
Roubion (riv.), Fr. 44/F4
Roudnice nad Labem, Czh. 59/H2
Rouen, Fr. 57/G2
Rouffach, Fr. 60/D2
Rougé, Fr. 56/D5
Rouge (riv.), Qu, Can. 141/J4
Rouge, Middle (riv.), Mi, US 167/F7
Rougemont, Fr. 60/C3
Rougemont-le-Château, Fr. 60/C2
Rough (riv.), Ky, US 162/D2
Rough River (lake), Ky, US 162/D2
Rouleau, Sk, Can. 156/B2
Roullet-Saint-Estèphe, Fr. 44/D4
Round (hill), In, US 162/E1
Round (hill), Ky, US 162/E2
Round (hill), Oh, US 160/F4
Round (hill), Pa, US 168/B3
Round Butte (dam), Or, US 146/C1
Round Hill (pt.), Austl. 134/C4
Round Lake, Il, US 167/P15
Round Lake Beach, Il, US 167/P15
Round Lake Park, Il, US 167/P15
Round Mountain, Nv, US 146/E4
Round Mountain, Tx, US 150/E2
Round Rock, Tx, US 151/F2
Round Spring, Mo, US 153/J2
Round Top, Tx, US 151/F2
Round Valley (res.), NJ, US 168/D2
Round Valley Ind. Res., Ca, US 146/B4
Roundup, Mt, US 145/K4
Roundway (hill), Eng, UK 36/E4
Rounthwaite, Mb, Can. 156/E3
Roura, FrG. 182/C1
Rousay (isl.), Sc, UK 31/V14
Rouse Hill (nbrhd.), Austl. 134/G8
Rouses Point, NY, US 161/K2
Rouseville, Pa, US 161/G4
Rousies, Fr. 54/D3
Rousínov, Czh. 43/J4
Rousset, Fr. 64/B6
Roussillon, Fr. 64/B5
Roussillon, Fr. 64/A2
Routhierville, Qu, Can. 158/D1
Rouvre (riv.), Fr. 57/E3
Rouvres, Fr. 30/M4
Rouvroy, Belg. 55/E4
Rouxmesnil-Bouteilles, Fr. 57/G1
Rouxville, SAfr. 124/D3
Rouyn-Noranda, Qu, Can. 141/J4
Rovaniemi (int'l arpt.), Fin. 68/E2
Rovaniemi, Fin. 68/E2
Rovasenda, It. 62/B2
Rovato, It. 62/C2
Roven'ki, Rus. 73/K3
Roven'ky, Ukr. 73/K3
Rover, Mo, US 153/J2
Rover, Ar, US 153/H3
Roverbella, It. 63/D3
Rovereto, It. 61/H6
Rovereto, It. 63/D4
Roviano, It. 65/C3
Rovieng Tbong, Camb. 94/D3
Rovigo, It. 63/E3
Rovigo (prov.), It. 63/E2
Rovinj, Cro. 63/G3
Rovira, Col. 183/K8
Rovnoye, Rus. 71/H2
Rovuma (riv.), Moz. 119/A4
Rowell, Ar, US 153/H4
Rowena, Austl. 132/D1
Rowena, Tx, US 150/D2
Rowland, NC, US 163/H3
Rowledge, Eng, UK 30/A3
Rowlett (cr.), Tx, US 150/L6
Rowlett, Tx, US 150/L7
Rowley (isl.), Nun, Can. 141/J2
Rowley Shoals (isl.), Austl. 127/A2
Rowta, India 97/J2
Roxa (isl.), GBis. 114/B4
Roxas, Phil. 88/C3
Roxas, Phil. 88/C1
Roxas, Phil. 88/B3
Roxboro, NC, US 163/H2
Roxborough, Trin. 181/F2
Roxburgh, NZ 135/B4
Roxbury, Ks, US 153/F1
Roxbury, NY, US 161/J3
Roxen (lake), Swe. 40/F2
Roxie, Ms, US 164/C2
Roxo (cape), Sen. 114/A3
Roxton, Tx, US 153/G4
Roxwell, Eng, UK 30/E1
Roy, NM, US 152/B3
Roy, Wa, US 167/B3
Roy, Ut, US 147/G3
Roy, Mt, US 145/K4
Roy Hill, Austl. 130/C2
Roya (riv.), Fr. 45/G5
Royal (canal), Ire. 35/B3
Royal Botanical Garden, On, Can. 160/T9
Royal Center, In, US 160/C4
Royal Chitwan NP, Nepal 97/E2
Royal City, Wa, US 144/E4
Royal (gorge), Co, US 152/B1
Royal Natal NP, SAfr. 124/E3
Royal NP, Austl. 132/D2
Royal Oak, Mi, US 167/F7
Royal Paekje Tombs, SKor. 81/D4
Royal Palm Beach, Fl, US 164/P9
Royal Pines, NC, US 163/F3
Royal Tombs, Viet. 94/D2
Royal Tunbridge Wells, Eng, UK 37/G4
Royalton, Mn, US 157/G5
Royalton, Vt, US 161/K3
Royalton, Pa, US 168/B3
Royalty, Tx, US 150/C2
Royan, Fr. 44/C4
Roydon, Eng, UK 30/D1
Roye, Fr. 60/C2
Roye, Fr. 54/B4
Royersford, Pa, US 168/C3
Røyken, Nor. 40/D2
Royse City, Tx, US 150/L7
Royston, Eng, UK 35/G4
Royston, Ga, US 163/F3
Royston, Eng, UK 37/F2
Royston, BC, Can. 144/B3
Royton, Eng, UK 35/F4
Rožaj, Serb. 50/E4
Rozay-en-Brie, Fr. 54/B6
Rozdil'na, Ukr. 72/F4
Rozdol'ne, Ukr. 73/G5
Rozel, Chl, UK 56/C2
Rozellville, Wi, US 155/J1
Rozenburg, Neth. 52/B5
Rozendo, Moz. 123/H3
Rozhaya (riv.), Rus. 69/W9
Rozhyshche, Ukr. 72/C2
Rozivka, Ukr. 73/J4
Rožmberk (lake), Czh. 59/H4
Rožmital pod Třemšínem, Czh. 59/G3
Rožňava, Slvk. 43/L4
Roztoczański PN, Pol. 72/B2
Roztoky, Czh. 59/H2
Rozzano, It. 62/C3
Rrëshen, Alb. 49/F2
Rrogozhinë, Alb. 49/F2
Rtishchevo, Rus. 71/G1
Ru (cape), Malay. 89/C2
Ruabon, Wal, UK 35/E6
Ruacana (falls), Ang. 122/B3
Ruacana, Namb. 122/B3
Ruaha NP, Tanz. 119/A3
Ruamahanga (riv.), NZ 135/J9
Ruapuke (isl.), NZ 135/B4
Ruatapu, NZ 135/B3
Ruawai, NZ 135/C2
Rub' al Khali (des.), SAr. 77/D7
Rubeho (mts.), Tanz. 119/B3
Rubelles, Fr. 30/L6
Rubeshibe, Japan 82/C2
Rubi (riv.), D.R. Congo 121/F2
Rubi, D.R. Congo 121/F2
Rubí, Sp. 47/L7
Rubiataba, Braz. 186/C2
Rubidoux, Ca, US 166/C3
Rubiera, It. 63/D4
Rubigen, Swi. 60/D4
Rubim, Braz. 187/E3
Rubizhne, Ukr. 73/K3
Rubondo NP, Tanz. 121/G3
Rubonia, Fl, US 164/K8
Rubottom, Ok, US 153/F4
Řubřina (riv.), Czh. 59/G4
Rubtsovsk, Rus. 99/D1
Rubuga, Tanz. 119/A3
Ruby, Ak, US 171/G3
Ruby, La, US 164/B2
Ruby (lake), Nv, US 146/F3
Ruby (mts.), Nv, US 146/F3
Ruby (riv.), Mt, US 147/G1
Ruby Lake NWR, Nv, US 146/F3
Ruby Valley, Nv, US 146/F3
Rubyvale, Austl. 134/B3
Rucava, Lat. 41/J3
Ruch'i, Rus. 68/J2
Rucphen, Neth. 52/B5
Ruda Woda (lake), Pol. 43/K2
Rudall River NP, Austl. 130/D2
Rūdarpur, India 96/D2
Rudauli, India 96/C2
Ruddell, Sk, Can. 145/L1
Ruddington, Eng, UK 35/G6
Rudensk, Bela. 41/M5
Rüdersdorf, Ger. 42/Q7
Rüdesheim, Ger. 55/G4
Rüdesheim, Ger. 55/G4
Rudewa, Tanz. 119/A4
Rudi, Tanz. 119/B3
Rudiano, It. 62/C3
Rūdiškės, Lith. 41/L4
Rudkøbing, Den. 40/D4
Rudky, Ukr. 72/B3
Rudnaya Pristan', Rus. 79/M3
Rudnik, Pol. 43/M3
Rudnya, Rus. 41/P4
Rudnytsya, Ukr. 72/E3
Rūdnyy, Kaz. 69/P5
Rudolf (isl.), Rus. 74/F1
Rudolf (Turkana) (lake), Kenya 107/F4
Rudolph, Wi, US 155/K1
Rudong, China 80/E4
Rudozem, Bul. 49/J2
Ruds-Vedby, Den. 39/H7
Rūdsar, Iran 103/G2
Rudston, Eng, UK 35/H3
Rudyard, Mi, US 160/D1
Rudyard, Mt, US 145/J3
Rue, Swi. 60/C4
Rue (pt.), NI, UK 34/B1
Rue, Fr. 54/A3
Rueda, Sp. 46/C2
Rueil-Malmaison, Fr. 30/J5
Ruell (riv.), Sc, UK 33/A4
Ruelle-sur-Touvre, Fr. 44/D4
Ruen (peak), Bul. 50/F4
Ruenya (riv.), Zim. 123/G3
Ruetzbach (riv.), Aus. 61/H3
Rufā'ah, Sudan 117/G2
Rufe, Ok, US 153/G3
Ruffano, It. 49/F3
Ruffec, Fr. 44/D3
Ruffin, SC, US 163/G4
Rufiji (riv.), Tanz. 107/F5
Rufina, It. 63/E6
Rufino, Arg. 190/E2
Rufisque, Sen. 114/A3
Rufunsa, Zam. 123/F2
Rufus Woods (lake), Wa, US 144/E3
Rugāji, Lat. 41/M3
Rugao, China 80/E4
Rugby, ND, US 156/E3
Rugby, Eng, UK 37/E2
Rugeley, Eng, UK 37/E1
Rügen (isl.), Ger. 40/E4
Ruggell, Lcht. 61/F3
Rugles, Fr. 57/F3
Ruḩama, Isr. 105/B5
Ruhmannsfelden, Ger. 59/F5
Ruhnu saar (isl.), Lat. 41/K3
Ruhr (reg.), Ger. 42/E3
Ruhr (riv.), Ger. 42/D3
Ruhrgebiet (phys. reg.), Ger. 52/D6
Ruhstorf an der Rott, Ger. 59/F5
Ruicheng, China 80/B4
Ruidosa, Tx, US 150/B3
Ruidoso, NM, US 152/B4
Ruihong, China 87/H2
Ruinen, Neth. 52/D3
Ruins of Cahabra, Al, US 162/D4
Ruipa, Tanz. 119/B4
Ruiru, Kenya 119/B2
Ruiselede, Belg. 54/C1
Ruislip (nbrhd.), Eng, UK 30/B2
Ruiz, Mex. 174/D4
Rujen (peak), FYROM 49/H1
Rūjiena, Lat. 41/L3
Ruki (riv.), D.R. Congo 107/D5
Rukua, Indo. 128/B1
Rukumkot, Nepal 96/D1
Rukuru, South (riv.), Tanz. 123/G1
Rukwa (prov.), Tanz. 119/A3
Rukwa (lake), Tanz. 107/F5
Rule, Tx, US 152/E4
Ruleville, Ms, US 162/B4
Rulhieres (cape), Austl. 128/B3
Rulles (riv.), Belg. 55/E4
Rülzheim, Ger. 58/B4
Rum, Aus. 61/H3
Rum (riv.), Mn, US 157/H5
Rum Cay (isl.), Bahm. 173/G3
Rum Jungle, Austl. 128/C3
Ruma, Serb. 50/D3
Ruma Bāzār, Bang. 86/B4
Ruma NP, Kenya 119/A2
Rumāḩ, SAr. 100/E3
Rumán, Ven. 181/F3
Rumaylah, Sudan 117/G2
Rumaysh, Leb. 105/C2
Rumbalara, Austl. 131/G3
Rumbek, Sudan 117/F4
Rumeli Hisar, Turk. 103/N6
Rumelifeneri, Turk. 103/N6
Rumes, Belg. 54/C2
Rumia, Pol. 40/H4
Rumilly, Fr. 60/B6
Rümlang, Swi. 61/E3
Rumley, Tx, US 151/E2
Rumney, NH, US 161/L3
Rumney, Wal, UK 36/C3
Rumoi, Japan 82/B2
Rumphi, Malw. 119/A4
Rumson, NJ, US 168/E3
Rumst, Belg. 55/D1
Rumuruti, Kenya 119/B1
Run (riv.), Mn, US 155/H1
Runabay (pt.), NI, UK 34/B1
Runan, China 80/C4
Runanga, NZ 135/B3
Runaway (cape), NZ 135/D2
Runcorn, Eng, UK 35/F5
Rundēni, Lat. 41/M3
Runding, Ger. 59/F4
Rundu, Namb. 122/C3
Runere, Tanz. 119/A2
Runge, Tx, US 151/F3
Rungsted, Den. 39/J7
Rungu, D.R. Congo 121/F2
Rungwa (riv.), Tanz. 119/A3
Rungwa, Tanz. 119/A3
Rungwa, Tanz. 121/G4
Rungwa Game Reserve, Tanz. 119/A3
Rungwe (peak), Tanz. 119/A4
Runio (riv.), Fr. 56/C5
Runkel, Ger. 58/B2
Runmarö (isl.), Swe. 39/B1
Runn (lake), Swe. 40/F1
Runnelstown, Ms, US 164/D2
Runnemede, NJ, US 168/C4
Running (cr.), Co, US 152/B1
Running Springs, Ca, US 166/C2
Running Water Draw (riv.), Tx,NM, US 152/C3
Runwell, Eng, UK 30/E2
Ruo (riv.), China 75/K5
Ruokolahti, Fin. 41/N1
Ruoqiang, China 99/E4
Rupat (isl.), Indo. 90/B3
Rupea, Rom. 51/G2
Rupel (riv.), Belg. 55/D1
Rupert, Id, US 147/G2
Rupert (riv.), Qu, Can. 141/J3
Rupert, Ga, US 162/E4
Rupert, WV, US 163/G2
Rupert House (Waskaganish), Qu, Can. 141/J3
Rūpnagar, India 98/D4
Ruppichteroth, Ger. 55/G2
Rupt-sur-Moselle, Fr. 60/C2
Rupununi (riv.), Guy. 181/G4
Rur (riv.), Ger. 42/D3
Rur-Strasse (lake), Ger. 55/F2
Rural Hall, NC, US 163/G2
Rural Retreat, Va, US 163/G2
Rurrenabaque, Bol. 185/E4
Rurutu (isl.), FrPol. 137/K7
Rusagonis, NB, Can. 158/D3
Rusape, Zim. 123/G3
Rüschegg, Swi. 60/D4
Rüschlikon, Swi. 61/E3
Ruscom (riv.), On, Can. 167/G7
Ruse (pol. reg.), Bul. 49/K1
Ruse, Bul. 51/G4
Rusera, India 97/F3
Rush, Co, US 152/B1
Rush, Ire. 34/B4
Rush (cr.), Co, US 154/C4
Rush City, Mn, US 157/H5
Rush Springs, Ok, US 153/F3
Rushall, Eng, UK 37/E4
Rushan, China 80/E3
Rushden, Eng, UK 37/F2
Rushford, Mn, US 155/J2
Rushoon, Nf, Can. 159/K2
Rushville, In, US 160/D5
Rushville, Il, US 155/J3
Rushville, Ne, US 154/C2
Rushworth, Austl. 133/B3
Rusk, Tx, US 150/G2
Ruskin, Fl, US 164/L8
Ruskington, Eng, UK 35/H5
Ruskovce, Slvk. 50/C1
Rusnė, Lith. 41/J4
Russ, Fr. 60/D1
Russas, Braz. 183/G4
Russbach (riv.), Aus. 51/N7
Russell, Ks, US 152/E1
Russell, Mb, Can. 156/D2
Russell, On, Can. 161/J2
Russell, NY, US 161/J2
Russell, NZ 135/C1
Russell (isls.), Austl. 134/F7
Russell (isl.), Nun, Can. 141/R7
Russell (res.), SC, US 163/F3
Russell Cave Nat'l Mon., Al, US 162/E3
Russell Springs, Ky, US 162/E2
Russells Point, Oh, US 160/E4
Russellville, Mo, US 153/H1
Russellville, Ar, US 153/H3
Russellville, Ky, US 162/D2
Russellville, Tn, US 163/F2
Russellville, Al, US 162/D3
Rüsselsheim, Ger. 58/B3
Russi, It. 63/F5
Russia (ctry.) 74/H3
Russian (riv.), Ca, US 146/B4
Russian Mission, Ak, US 171/F3
Russkaya, Rus., Ant. 192/Q
Russkiy Brod, Rus. 70/F1
Rust'avi, Geo. 71/H4
Rustburg, Va, US 163/H2
Rustenburg, SAfr. 123/E5
Ruston, La, US 153/H4
Ruston, Wa, US 167/C3
Rusutjärvi, Fin. 39/E4
Rutana, Buru. 121/G3
Rute, Sp. 46/C4
Rutenga, Zim. 123/F4
Ruth, Ms, US 164/C2
Ruth, Nv, US 147/F4
Rüthen, Ger. 53/F6
Rutherford, NJ, US 169/J8
Rutherford, Tn, US 162/C2
Rutherford, Al, US 162/E4
Rutherfordton, NC, US 163/G3
Rutherglen, Sc, UK 33/B5
Rutherglen, On, Can. 161/G1
Rutherglen, Austl. 133/C3
Rutheron, NM, US 149/J2
Rüthi, Swi. 61/F3
Ruthin, Wal, UK 35/E5
Ruthven, On, Can. 167/G7
Rüti, Swi. 61/F4
Rüti, Swi. 61/E3
Rutland, ND, US 156/F4
Rutland, Vt, US 161/K3
Rutland, Oh, US 163/F1
Rutland Plains, Austl. 134/A1
Rutland Water (res.), Eng, UK 37/F1
Rutledge, Mn, US 157/H4
Rutledge, Tn, US 163/F2
Rutog, China 99/C5
Rutshuru (riv.), D.R. Congo 121/G3
Rutshuru, D.R. Congo 121/G3
Rutten, Neth. 52/C3
Ruukki, Fin. 68/E2
Ruurlo, Neth. 52/D4
Ruvo di Puglia, It. 48/E2
Ruvu (riv.), Tanz. 119/B3
Ruvu, Tanz. 119/B3
Ruvu, Tanz. 119/B3
Ruvubu (riv.), Buru. 121/G3
Ruvuma (prov.), Tanz. 119/B4
Ruvuma (riv.), Tanz. 107/F6
Ruwa, Zim. 123/F3
Ruwāndūz, Iraq 103/F2
Ruwenzori (range), Ugan. 121/G2
Ruwī, Oman 101/G4
Ruxton, Co, US 152/C2
Ruy, Fr. 64/B1
Ruya (riv.), Zim. 123/F3
Ruyang, China 80/C4
Ruyigi, Buru. 121/G3
Ruyuan Yaozu Zizhixian, China 87/G3
Ruzayevka, Rus. 71/H1
Ruzhany, Bela. 43/N2
Ruzhyn, Ukr. 72/E3
Ruzizi (riv.), D.R. Congo 121/G3
Ružomberok, Slvk. 43/K4
Ruzyně (int'l arpt.), Czh. 59/H2
Ruzzah (peak), Egypt 113/B4
Rwanda (ctry.) 121/G3
Rwenjaza, Ugan. 121/G2
Rwenzori NP, Ugan. 121/G3
Ryabobskiy, Rus. 73/L2
Ryan, Ok, US 153/F3
Ryan (inlet), Sc, UK 34/C2
Ryan (mt.), Austl. 134/A1
Ryan (mt.), Austl. 133/D1
Ryazan', Rus. 68/H5
Ryazanskaya Oblast, Rus. 68/H5
Ryazhsk, Rus. 70/G1
Rybachiy (pen.), Rus. 38/K1
Rybinsk, Rus. 68/H4
Rybinsk (res.), Rus. 29/J2
Rybnik, Pol. 43/K3
Rybnoye, Rus. 68/H5
Ryd, Swe. 40/F3
Rydaholm, Swe. 40/F3
Ryde, Ca, US 167/L10
Ryde (nbrhd.), Austl. 134/H8
Ryde, Eng, UK 37/E5
Rydebäck, Swe. 39/J7
Rydet, Swe. 40/D3
Rye, Co, US 152/B2
Rye, Tx, US 151/G2
Rye, Ar, US 153/J4
Rye (riv.), Eng, UK 35/H3
Rye, NY, US 169/L8
Rye (bay), Eng, UK 37/G5
Rye, Eng, UK 37/G5
Rye Brook, NY, US 169/L7
Rye Patch (dam), Nv, US 146/D3
Rye Patch (res.), Nv, US 146/D3
Ryegate, Mt, US 145/K4
Rygge, Nor. 40/D2
Ryki, Pol. 43/L3
Ryley, Ab, Can. 145/H1
Ryl'sk, Rus. 73/H2
Rylstone, Austl. 133/D1
Ryn-Peski (plain), Kaz. 71/J2
Ryōkami, Japan 83/B2
Ryökkä, Fin. 39/E4
Ryōtsu, Japan 85/F1
Ryōzen-yama (peak), Japan 83/K5
Rypin, Pol. 43/K2
Rysy (peak), Pol. 43/L4
Ryton, Eng, UK 35/G2
Ryton-on-Dunsmore, Eng, UK 37/E2
Rytterknægten (peak), Den. 40/F4
Ryttylä, Fin. 39/E4
Ryūgasaki, Japan 85/G3
Ryukyu (isls.), Japan 77/M7
Ryūō, Japan 83/K5
Ryūō, Japan 83/B2
Rzeszów, Pol. 43/M3
Rzhev, Rus. 68/G4
Rzhyshchiv, Ukr. 72/F3

S

's-Graveland, Neth. 52/C4
's Gravendeel, Neth. 52/B5
's-Gravenhage (The Hague) (cap.), Neth. 52/B4
's Heerenberg, Neth. 52/D5
's Hertogenbosch, Neth. 52/C5
S'ør-Trøndelag (co.), Nor. 38/D3
Sa, Thai. 94/C2
Şā al Ḩajar (ruin), Egypt 113/B3
Sa Dec, Viet. 94/D4
Sa Pa, Viet. 94/C1
Saab (int'l arpt.), Swe. 40/F2
Sa'ad, Isr. 105/B6
Sääksjärvi (lake), Fin. 41/K1
Saal an der Donau, Ger. 59/E5
Saalbach (riv.), Ger. 58/B4
Saaldorf, Ger. 59/E2
Saale (riv.), Ger. 42/F3
Saalfelden am Steinernen Meer, Aus. 45/K3
Saâne (riv.), Fr. 57/F1
Saane (riv.), Swi. 60/D5
Saanen, Swi. 60/D5
Saanta (peak), Kenya 119/B1
Saar (riv.), Ger. 55/F5
Saarbrücken, Ger. 55/F5
Saarbrücken (Ensheim) (arpt.), Ger. 55/G5
Saarburg, Ger. 55/F4
Sääre, Est. 41/K3
Saaremaa (isl.), Est. 68/D4
Saarland (state), Ger. 45/G2
Saarlouis, Ger. 55/F5
Saas, Swi. 61/F4
Saas Fee, Swi. 60/D5
Saastal (valley), Swi. 60/D5
Sa'ata, Sudan 117/F2
Saatlı, Azer. 103/G2
Saatta, Erit. 117/H1
Sab (riv.), Camb. 94/D3
Saba (isl.), NAm. 173/J4
Saba (isl.), NAnt. 173/N8
Šabac, Serb. 50/D3
Sabadell, Sp. 47/L6
Sabae, Japan 84/E3
Sabah (reg.), Malay. 77/L9
Sabalgarh, India 96/A2
Sabana, Cuba 177/H1
Sabana (arch.), Bang. 177/F1
Sabana de Uchire, Ven. 181/E2
Sabanalarga, Col. 180/C2
Sabanalarga, Col. 180/C3
Sabancuy, Mex. 176/D2
Sabaneta, Ven. 180/D2
Sabang, Indo. 89/A1
Sabanita, Pan. 177/G4
Sabará, Braz. 186/E3
Sabaragamuwa (prov.), SrL. 95/D5
Sabasţīyah, WBnk. 105/C4
Sabat (riv.), Sudan 107/F4
Sabato (riv.), It. 65/D5
Sabaudia, It. 65/C5
Sabaudia (lake), It. 65/C5
Sabaya, Bol. 188/B1
Sabbio Chiese, It. 62/D2
Sabbioneta, It. 62/D4
Sabdê, China 86/D2
Sabetha, Ks, US 155/G4
Sabhā, Libya 108/B3
Sabie (riv.), Moz. 125/F2
Sabierivier (riv.), SAfr. 123/F5
Sabile, Lat. 41/K3
Sabin, Mn, US 156/F4
Sabinal, Tx, US 150/E3
Sabinal (riv.), Tx, US 150/E3
Sabiñánigo, Sp. 47/E1
Sabinas, Mex. 150/D4
Sabinas (riv.), Mex. 150/D4
Sabinas Hidalgo, Mex. 150/D4
Sabine (lake), La,Tx, US 151/H3
Sabine (riv.), La,Tx, US 151/H2
Sabine NWR, La, US 151/H3
Sabine Pass, Tx, US 151/H3
Sabini, Monti (mts.), It. 48/C1
Sabirabad, Azer. 103/G1
Sabkhat al Bardawīl (lag.), Egypt 104/C4
Sabkhat al Hayshah (swamp), Libya 108/B2
Sabkhat al Kabīyah (swamp), Tun. 48/A5
Sabkhat al Milḩ (swamp), Libya 108/C2
Sabkhat ash Shuwayrib (swamp), Libya 108/C2
Sabkhat Ghuzayyil (swamp), Libya 108/C2
Sabkhat Shunayn (swamp), Libya 108/D2
Sablayan, Phil. 88/C2
Sable (cape), NS, Can. 158/E4
Sable (isl.), NS, Can. 141/L4
Sable (cape), Fl, US 172/E2
Sablé-sur-Sarthe, Fr. 57/E5
Sables (riv.), Qu, Can. 158/B1
Saboeiro, Braz. 183/G4
Sabon Gida, Nga. 115/H5
Sabongidda, Nga. 115/G5
Sabor (riv.), Port. 46/B2
Sabou, Burk. 115/E3
Saboyá, Col. 183/M7
Sabra (cape), Indo. 91/H4
Şabrātah, Libya 67/G4
Sabratha (ruin), Libya 67/G4
Sabrina (coast), Ant. 192/J
Sabrūm, India 97/H4
Sabual, India 86/B4
Sabugal, Port. 46/B2
Sabula, Ia, US 155/J2
Sabulubek, Indo. 89/B3
Şabyā, SAr. 100/D5
Sabzevār, Iran 103/J2
Sac City, Ia, US 155/G2
Sacaca, Bol. 188/C1
Sacajawea (peak), Or, US 146/E1
Sacajawea (lake), Wa, US 144/E4
Sácama, Col. 180/C3
Sacandica, Ang. 120/C4
Sacanta, Arg. 188/D4
Sacarnoochee (riv.), Ms, US 162/C4
Sacaton, Az, US 149/G4
Sacavém, Port. 47/P10
Saccarel (peak), Fr. 64/D4
Saccarello (peak), It. 62/A4
Sacco (riv.), It. 48/C2
Sacedón, Sp. 46/D2
Săcele, Rom. 51/G3
Sachanga, Ang. 122/C2
Sachigo (riv.), On, Can. 140/G3
Sachojere, Bol. 185/E4
Sachs Harbour, NW, Can. 140/D1
Sachse, Tx, US 150/L7
Sachseln, Swi. 61/E4
Sachsen (state), Ger. 42/G3
Sachsen-Anhalt (state), Ger. 42/F3
Sachsenbrunn, Ger. 58/D2
Sachsenhagen, Ger. 53/G4
Sacile, It. 63/F2
Säckingen, Ger. 60/D2
Sackville, NB, Can. 158/E3
Saclay, Fr. 30/J5
Saco, Me, US 161/L3
Saco, Al, US 165/F2
Saco (bay), Me, US 158/B4
Saco (riv.), Me, US 161/L3
Saco, Mt, US 145/L3
Saco do Giraul, Ang. 122/B2
Sacra di San Michele, It. 64/D2
Sacramento, Mex. 150/D4
Sacramento (co.), Ca, US 167/M10
Sacramento (riv.), Ca, US 142/B4
Sacramento (cap.), Ca, US 146/C4
Sacramento, Ky, US 162/D2
Sacramento (mts.), NM, US 142/E5
Sacramento Metropolitan (arpt.), Ca, US 167/L9
Sacramento NWR, Ca, US 146/B4
Sacramento River Deep Water Ship Canal, Ca, US 167/L10
Sacratif (cape), Sp. 46/D4
Sacriston, Eng, UK 35/G2
Sacro (peak), It. 48/E2
Sacro Monte, It. 62/B2
Sada, May. 125/H6
Sada, SAfr. 124/D4
Sádaba, Sp. 46/E1
Sadābād, India 96/B2
Sa'dah, Yem. 100/D5
Sadani, Tanz. 119/B3
Sadasar, India 92/B2
Sādāt Maḩalleh, Iran 103/G2
Sadd al Qir'awn (dam), Leb. 105/D1
Saddam (int'l arpt.), Iraq 103/F3
Saddle (mtn.), Az, US 149/G2
Saddle (riv.), NJ, US 169/J8
Saddle (mtn.), Or, US 144/C5
Saddle Brook, NJ, US 169/J8
Saddle Mtn. NWR, Wa, US 144/E4
Saddle River, NJ, US 169/J7
Saddle Rock, NY, US 169/K8
Saddleback (mesa), NM, US 152/C3
Saddlestring, Wy, US 147/K1
Saddleworth, Eng, UK 35/G4
Saddleworth, Austl. 131/H5
Sadêng, China 86/B2
Sādhaura, India 98/D4
Sadi, Eth. 117/G3
Sadīch, Iran 101/G3
Sadiola, Mali 114/C3
Sadiya, India 86/B3
Sadjoavato, Madg. 125/J6
Sadler, Tx, US 153/F4
Sado (riv.), Port. 46/A3
Sado (isl.), Japan 79/M4
Sadovo, Bul. 51/G4
Sadovoye, Rus. 71/H3
Sadowara, Japan 84/B4
Sādri, India 92/B2
Sadripante (mt.), Phil. 88/D3
Sādullāpur, Bang. 97/G3
Sadulshahar, India 98/C5
Saerbeck, Ger. 53/E4
Saeul, Lux. 55/E4
Safané, Burk. 114/E3
Safāpur, India 98/C2
Safāqis (gov.), Tun. 111/H2
Safed Koh (range), Pak. 98/A3
Safety Harbor, Fl, US 164/K8
Saffig, Ger. 55/G3
Säffle, Swe. 40/E2
Safford, Az, US 149/H4
Saffron Walden, Eng, UK 37/G2
Safi, Mor. 110/C2
Safi (cape), Mor. 110/C2
Safīd (riv.), Afg. 101/J1
Safid Khers (mts.), Afg. 101/K1
Safid Kūh (mts.), Afg. 101/H2
Safidon, India 98/D5
Safien, Swi. 61/F4
Safīpur, India 96/C2
Şāfītā, Syria 104/E2
Safonovo, Rus. 68/G5
Safranbolu, Turk. 70/E4
Şaft al 'Inab, Egypt 113/B3
Şaft al Mulūk, Egypt 113/B3
Şaft Turāb, Egypt 113/C3
Sag Harbor, NY, US 169/F2
Saga, China 97/E1
Saga, Japan 84/B4
Saga (pref.), Japan 84/A4
Sagaba, Ang. 122/D1
Sagae, Japan 82/B4
Sagaing (state), Myan. 93/F3
Sagaing, Myan. 86/B4
Sagami (sea), Japan 85/F3
Sagami (riv.), Japan 83/C2
Sagami (lake), Japan 83/C2
Sagami (bay), Japan 83/C3
Sagamihara, Japan 85/F3
Sagamiko, Japan 83/C2
Sagamore Hill Nat'l Hist. Site, NY, US 169/M8
Sagan, Indo. 91/H4
Sagana, Kenya 119/B2
Saganaga (lake), Can.,US 157/J3
Sāgar, India 96/B4
Sāgar, India 95/B3
Sagard, Ger. 40/E4
Sagarejo, Geo. 71/H4
Sagarmatha (zone), Nepal 97/F2
Sagarmatha (Everest) (mtn.), China, Nepal 97/F2
Sagarmatha NP, Nepal 97/F2
Sagata, Sen. 114/A3
Sagauli, India 97/E2
Sagavanirktok (riv.), Ak, US 171/J2
Sagay, Phil. 88/C3
Sagay, Phil. 88/D3
Sage, Ar, US 153/J2
Sage (cr.), Mt, US 145/J3
Sagemace (bay), Mb, Can. 156/D1
Saggart, Ire. 34/B5
Şaghīr (canal), Egypt 113/C2
Saginaw, Mi, US 160/E3
Saginaw (bay), Mi, US 160/E3
Saginaw, Or, US 146/B2
Saginaw, Tx, US 150/K7
Sagittario (riv.), It. 65/C4
Sagiz, Kaz. 71/K2
Sagle, Id, US 144/F3
Saglek (bay), Nf, Can. 141/K3
Sagola, Mi, US 157/K4
Sagone (gulf), Fr. 48/A1
Sagsay (riv.), Mong. 99/E2
Sagter Ems (riv.), Ger. 53/E2
Sagu, Indo. 128/A2
Sagua de Tánamo, Cuba 177/H1
Sagua la Grande, Cuba 177/F1
Saguache, Co, US 149/J1
Saguache (cr.), Co, US 149/J1
Saguaro NP, Az, US 149/G4
Saguia el Hamra (riv.), WSah. 110/C4
Sagunto, Sp. 47/E3
Sagy, Fr. 30/H4
Sa'gya, China 97/G1
Sagyz (riv.), Kaz. 71/K2
Saḩāb, Jor. 105/D5
Sahaba, Sudan 109/F5
Sahagún, Col. 180/C2
Sahagún, Sp. 46/C1
Sahagún, Mex. 175/L7
Saḩam, Jor. 105/D3
Sahand (mtn.), Iran 103/F2
Sahara (des.), Afr. 107/B2
Sahāranpur, India 98/D5
Saharsa, India 97/F3
Sahaspur, India 96/B1
Sahaswān, India 96/B1
Sahavato, Madg. 125/J8
Sahāwar, India 96/B2
Sahel (riv.), Alg. 112/H4
Sāhibganj, India 97/F3
Şahin, Turk. 51/H5
Şahinli, Turk. 51/H5
Sāhīwāl, Pak. 98/B4
Sahiwal, Pak. 98/B4
Şaḩneh, Iran 103/F3
Sahoué, Gabon 120/B2
Şahrajat al Kubrá, Egypt 113/C3
Sahrho, Jebel (mts.), Mor. 110/D3
Sahu, Indo. 91/G3
Sahuaripa, Mex. 174/C2
Sahuarita, Az, US 149/G5
Sahuayo de Morelos, Mex. 174/E4
Šahy, Slvk. 43/K4
Sai (riv.), India 96/C2
Sai (chan.), India 92/D2
Sai (riv.), Japan 84/E2
Sai Buri, Thai. 94/C5
Sai Kung, China 87/M7
Sai Yok, Thai. 94/B3
Sai Yok NP, Thai. 94/B3
Saibai (isl.), Austl. 129/F2
Sa'id Bundas, Sudan 117/E3
Saïda, Alg. 112/F5
Saïdia, Mor. 112/C2
Saidor, PNG 129/G1
Saidpur, India 96/D3
Saidpur, Bang. 97/G3
Saidu, Pak. 98/B2
Saignelégier, Swi. 60/D3
Saignon, Fr. 64/B5
Saigō, Japan 84/C2
Saigon, Viet. 94/D4
Saijō, Japan 84/C4
Saikai NP, Japan 84/A4
Saiki, Japan 84/B4
Saillans, Fr. 64/B3
Sailly, Fr. 30/H4
Sailly-sur-la-Lys, Fr. 54/B2
Sailolof, Indo. 91/H4
Sailu, India 92/C4
Saima, China 81/C2
Saimaa (lake), Fin. 38/J3
Sain Alto, Mex. 174/E4
Şā'īn Dezh, Iran 103/F2
Sainghin-en-Weppes, Fr. 54/B2
Sains-du-Nord, Fr. 54/D3
Saint (swamp), Fl, US 165/H3
Saint Mary's (riv.), NS, Can. 159/F3
Saint Abb's (pt.), Sc, UK 33/D5
Saint Abbs, Sc, UK 33/D5
Saint Adolphe, Mb, Can. 156/F3
Saint Agnes (pt.), Eng, UK 36/A6
Saint Agnes, Eng, UK 36/A6
Saint Alban's, Nf, Can. 159/K2
Saint Albans, Eng, UK 30/C1
Saint Albans, Vt, US 161/K2
Saint Albans, WV, US 163/G1
Saint Albert, Ab, Can. 145/H1
Saint Ambroise, Mb, Can. 156/E2
Saint Andrews (bay), Sc, UK 33/D4
Saint Andrews, NB, Can. 158/D3
Saint Andrews, Sc, UK 33/D4

Saint A – Šal'a

Saint Andrew's, Nf, Can. 159/H2
Saint Ann (cape), SLeo. 114/B5
Saint Anne, Chl, UK 56/C1
Saint Ann's (pt.), Wal, UK 36/A3
Saint Anns, On, Can. 160/U9
Saint Ann's Bay, Jam. 173/F4
Saint Ansgar, Ia, US 155/H2
Saint Anthony, Id, US 147/H2
Saint Anthony, ND, US 156/D4
Saint Anthony, Nf, Can. 141/L3
Saint Arnaud, Austl. 132/B3
Saint Arthur, NB, Can. 158/D2
Saint Asaph, Wal, UK 34/E5
Saint Athan, Wal, UK 36/C4
Saint Aubin, Chl, UK 56/C2
Saint Aubin's (bay), UK 56/C2
Saint Augustine, Fl, US 165/H3
Saint Augustine Beach, Fl, US 165/H3
Saint Austell (bay), Eng, UK 36/B6
Saint Austell, Eng, UK 36/B6
Saint Barthélemy (int'l arpt.), Neth. 173/N8
Saint Bathans (mt.), NZ 135/B4
Saint Bees, Eng, UK 34/E3
Saint Bees (pt.), Eng, UK 34/E2
Saint Benedict, Sk, Can. 145/M1
Saint Blaize (cape), SAfr. 124/C4
Saint Boswells, Sc, UK 33/D5
Saint Briavels, Eng, UK 36/D3
Saint Bride's (bay), Wal, UK 36/A3
Saint Bride's, Nf, Can. 159/K2
Saint Brieux, Sk, Can. 145/M1
Saint Catharines, On, Can. 160/U9
Saint Catherine, Fl, US 164/L6
Saint Catherine (mt.), Gren. 181/F1
Saint Catherines (isl.), Ga, US 165/H2
Saint Catherine's (hill), Eng, UK 37/E5
Saint Catherine's (pt.), Eng, UK 37/E5
Saint Charles, Il, US 167/P16
Saint Charles, Mi, US 160/D3
Saint Charles, Mo, US 155/J4
Saint Charles, Mn, US 155/H2
Saint Charles, Md, US 163/J1
Saint Christoffel (peak), NAnt. 180/D1
Saint Clair (riv.), On, Can. 160/E3
Saint Clair (lake), Can.,US 167/G7
Saint Clair (co.), Mi, US 167/G6
Saint Clair, Mi, US 160/E3
Saint Clair, Mn, US 155/H1
Saint Clair, Pa, US 168/B2
Saint Clair Beach, On, Can. 167/G7
Saint Clair Shores, Mi, US 167/G6
Saint Clairsville, Oh, US 160/F4
Saint Cloud, Fl, US 164/N7
Saint Cloud, Mn, US 157/G5
Saint Columb Major, Eng, UK 36/B6
Saint Combs, Sc, UK 33/E1
Saint Croix, NB, Can. 158/D3
Saint Croix (riv.), Wi, US 157/H5
Saint Croix (riv.), Mn,Wi, US 155/H1
Saint Croix (co.), Wi, US 157/G6
Saint Croix (isl.), USVI 173/M8
Saint Croix Ind. Res., Wi, US 157/H5
Saint Cyr (mt.), Yk, Can. 171/M3
Saint Cyrus, Sc, UK 33/D3
Saint David, Az, US 149/G5
Saint David's, Wal, UK 36/A3
Saint David's (pt.), Wal, UK 36/A3
Saint Edward, PE, Can. 158/E2
Saint Edward, Ne, US 154/F3
Saint Eleanors, PE, Can. 158/F2
Saint Elias (mts.), Ak, US 171/K3
Saint Elias (mt.), Ak, US 171/K3
Saint Elias (cape), Ak, US 171/K3
Saint Eustatius (isl.), NAnt. 173/N8
Saint Fergus, Sc, UK 33/E1
Saint Francis (cape), SAfr. 124/D4
Saint Francis (riv.), Ar,Mo, US 162/B2
Saint Francis, Ks, US 154/D4
Saint Francis, SD, US 154/D2
Saint Francis, Wi, US 167/Q14
Saint Francisville, La, US 164/C2
Saint Francisville, Il, US 162/D1
Saint Francois (mts.), Mo, US 153/J2
Saint François (riv.), Qu, Can. 161/L2
Saint Gabriel, La, US 164/C2
Saint Gallen (canton), Swi. 61/F3
Saint Geoirs (arpt.), Fr. 64/B2
Saint George, Austl. 134/C5
Saint George, NB, Can. 158/D3
Saint George (cape), Nf, Can. 159/H1
Saint George, On, Can. 160/S9
Saint George, Ak, US 171/E4
Saint George (isl.), Ak, US 171/E4
Saint George (cape), Fl, US 165/F3
Saint George, Ga, US 165/G2
Saint George (nbrhd.), NY, US 169/J9
Saint George, SC, US 163/G4
Saint George, Ut, US 149/F2
Saint George's (chan.) 34/C6
Saint George's (bay), Nf, Can. 159/H1
Saint George's, Nf, Can. 159/H1
Saint George's (cap.), Gren. 181/F1
Saint Georges, De, US 168/C4
Saint Georges Head (pt.), Austl. 133/E2
Saint Govan's (pt.), Wal, UK 36/B3
Saint Gregory (cape), Nf, Can. 159/H1
Saint Helen, Mi, US 160/D2
Saint Helena (isl.), Austl. 134/F6
Saint Helena (isl.), UK 26/J6
Saint Helena (bay), SAfr. 124/B4
Saint Helena (mt.), Ca, US 146/B4
Saint Helena, Ca, US 146/B4
Saint Helena (sound), SC, US 163/G4
Saint Helens, Austl. 132/D4
Saint Helens (pt.), Austl. 132/D4
Saint Helens, Eng, UK 35/F5
Saint Helens (co.), Eng, UK 35/F5
Saint Helens, Or, US 144/C5
Saint Helens (mt.), Wa, US 144/C4
Saint Helier, Chl, UK 56/C2
Saint Henry, Oh, US 160/D4
Saint Hilaire, Mn, US 156/F3
Saint Ignace (isl.), On, Can. 157/L3
Saint Ignace, Mi, US 160/D2
Saint Ignatius, Mt, US 145/G4
Saint Ives (nbrhd.), Austl. 134/H8
Saint Ives, Eng, UK 37/F2
Saint Ives (bay), Eng, UK 36/A6
Saint Ives, Eng, UK 36/A6
Saint Jacques (int'l arpt.), Fr. 56/D4
Saint James, Mo, US 153/J2
Saint James, Ar, US 153/J3
Saint James, Mi, US 160/D2
Saint James (cape), BC, Can. 140/C3
Saint James, Mn, US 155/G2
Saint James, NY, US 169/E2
Saint James City, Fl, US 165/G4
Saint Jo, Tx, US 153/F4
Saint Joe, Ar, US 153/H2
Saint Joe (riv.), Id,Wa, US 142/C2
Saint John, Chl, UK 56/C2
Saint John, Ks, US 153/E1
Saint John, NB, Can. 158/D3
Saint John, ND, US 156/E3
Saint John (riv.), NB, Can. 158/D3
Saint John (lake), La, US 164/C2
Saint John (riv.), Me, US 141/K4
Saint John (isl.), USVI 173/M8
Saint John, Wa, US 144/F4
Saint John's (cap.), Anti. 173/N8
Saint John's (cap.), Nf, Can. 159/L2
Saint John's (pt.), NI, UK 34/C3
Saint Johns, Az, US 149/H3
Saint Johns (riv.), Fl, US 165/H3
Saint Johns, Mi, US 160/D3
Saint Johnsbury, Vt, US 161/K2
Saint Jones (riv.), De, US 168/C5
Saint Joseph (pen.), Fl, US 165/F3
Saint Joseph (lake), La, US 164/C1
Saint Joseph (isl.), On, Can. 160/E1
Saint Joseph, Mi, US 160/C3
Saint Joseph (riv.), Mi, US 160/D3
Saint Joseph (lake), On, Can. 140/G3
Saint Joseph (pt.), Fl, US 165/F3
Saint Joseph, Fl, US 164/L7
Saint Joseph, La, US 164/C2
Saint Joseph, Mo, US 155/G4
Saint Joseph, Tn, US 162/D3
Saint Just, Eng, UK 36/A6
Saint Just-in-Roseland, Eng, UK 36/A6
Saint Kilda (isl.), UK 31/P8
Saint Kilda (nbrhd.), Austl. 132/F5
Saint Kitts (isl.), StK. 173/N7
Saint Kitts and Nevis (ctry.) 173/N7
Saint Landry, La, US 164/B2
Saint Laurent, Mb, Can. 156/F2
Saint Lawrence, Nf, Can. 159/K2
Saint Lawrence (riv.), NAm. 161/J2
Saint Lawrence, Austl. 134/C3
Saint Lawrence, Eng, UK 37/E5
Saint Lawrence (riv.), Can.,US 139/K5
Saint Lawrence (gulf), Can. 139/L5
Saint Lawrence (isl.), Ak, US 171/D3
Saint Lawrence, Pa, US 168/C3
Saint Lawrence, Tx, US 150/D2
Saint Lawrence Islands NP, On, Can. 161/H2
Saint Leo, Fl, US 164/L7
Saint Leon, Mb, Can. 156/E3
Saint Leonard (mt.), Austl. 132/G5
Saint Leonards, Austl. 133/B4
Saint Llorenc del Munt, PN, Sp. 47/K6
Saint Louis (lake), Qu, Can. 159/N7
Saint Louis, Sk, Can. 145/M1
Saint Louis (riv.), Mn, US 157/H4
Saint Louis, Mi, US 160/D3
Saint Louis, Mo, US 155/J4
Saint Louis Park, Mn, US 157/P7
Saint Lucia (ctry.) 173/N8
Saint Lucia (cape), SAfr. 125/F3
Saint Lucia (lake), SAfr. 125/F3
Saint Lucia (chan.), Mart.,StL. 173/N9
Saint Lucia Estuary, SAfr. 125/F3
Saint Lucie, Fl, US 165/H4
Saint Lucie (canal), Fl, US 165/H4
Saint Lucie (inlet), Fl, US 165/H4
Saint Maarten (isl.), NAnt. 173/N8
Saint Magnus (bay), Sc, UK 31/W13
Saint Malo, Mb, Can. 156/F3
Saint Margaret's at Cliffe, Eng, UK 54/A1
Saint Margaret's Hope, Sc, UK 31/V14
Saint Maries, Id, US 144/F4
Saint Marks, Fl, US 165/F2
Saint Marks, SAfr. 124/D4
Saint Marks NWR, Fl, US 165/F2
Saint Martin (lake), Mb, Can. 156/E2
Saint Martin (isl.), Mi, US 157/L5
Saint Martins, NB, Can. 158/E3
Saint Martins (isl.), Bang. 86/A4
Saint Martinville, La, US 164/C2
Saint Mary (peak), Austl. 131/H4
Saint Mary (riv.), BC, Can. 144/F3
Saint Mary (cape), NS, Can. 158/D3
Saint Mary (cape), Gam. 114/A3
Saint Mary's (bay), Ns., Can. 158/D3
Saint Mary's, Nf, Can. 159/L2
Saint Mary's, On, Can. 160/F3
Saint Mary's, Sc, UK 31/V14
Saint Mary's, Ak, US 171/F3
Saint Mary's, Zam. 123/E2
Saint Marys, Austl. 132/D4
Saint Marys (nbrhd.), Austl. 134/G8
Saint Marys, Ga, US 165/H2
Saint Marys (riv.), In, US 160/D4
Saint Marys, Ks, US 155/F4
Saint Marys, Mo, US 162/C2
Saint Marys, Oh, US 160/D4
Saint Marys, Pa, US 161/G4
Saint Marys, WV, US 160/F5
Saint Mary's Entrance (inlet), Ga,Fl, US 165/H2
Saint Matthew (isl.), Ak, US 171/D3
Saint Matthews, SC, US 163/G4
Saint Matthias Group (isls.), PNG 136/E5
Saint Maurice, La, US 164/B2
Saint Mawes, Eng, UK 36/A6
Saint Meinrad, In, US 162/D1
Saint Mellons, Wal, UK 36/C3
Saint Michael, Ak, US 171/F3
Saint Michael, Mn, US 157/N6
Saint Michaels, Md, US 168/B6
Saint Monance, Sc, UK 33/D4
Saint Moritz (Sankt Moritz), Swi. 45/H3
Saint Neots, Eng, UK 37/F2
Saint Nicholas Greek Orthodox Church, Fl, US 164/K7
Saint Niklaus, Swi. 60/D5
Saint Onge (peak), SD, US 154/C1
Saint Ouen's (bay), Chi., UK 56/C2
Saint Paris, Oh, US 160/E4
Saint Patrickswell, Ire. 32/B4
Saint Paul, Ab, Can. 140/E3
Saint Paul, Fr. 125/S15
Saint Paul (isl.), Fr. 27/N7
Saint Paul (cape), Gha. 115/F5
Saint Paul (riv.), Libr. 114/C5
Saint Paul, Ak, US 171/D4
Saint Paul (isl.), Ak, US 171/D4
Saint Paul, Ar, US 153/H3
Saint Paul, In, US 160/D5
Saint Paul, Ks, US 153/G2
Saint Paul (cap.), Mn, US 157/P7
Saint Paul, Ne, US 154/E3
Saint Paul, SC, US 163/G4
Saint Pauls, NC, US 163/H3
Saint Paul's Church Nat'l Hist. Site, NY, US 169/K8
Saint Peter (isl.), Austl. 131/G5
Saint Peter, Il, US 162/C1
Saint Peter, Ks, US 154/D4
Saint Peter, Mn, US 155/H1
Saint Peter and Saint Paul Rocks, (isl.), Braz. 26/H5
Saint Peter Port, Chl, UK 56/C2
Saint Peters, PE, Can. 159/F2
Saint Peters, NS, Can. 159/G3
Saint Peter's, Eng, UK 37/H4
Saint Peters, Mo, US 155/J4
Saint Peter's Basilica, VatC. 65/G7
Saint Peter's Square, VatC. 65/G7
Saint Petersburg, Rus. 69/T7
Saint Petersburg, Fl, US 164/K8
Saint Petersburg Beach, Fl, US 164/K8
Saint Petersburg-Clearwater International (arpt.), Fl, US 164/K8
Saint Philips, Sk, Can. 156/D2
Saint Pierre and Miquelon (dpcy.), Fr. 139/M5
Saint Pierre-Jolys, Mb, Can. 156/F3
Saint Regis Ind. Res., NY, US 161/J2
Saint Sampson's, Chl, UK 56/C2
Saint Saviour, Chl, UK 56/C2
Saint Shotts, Nf, Can. 159/L2
Saint Simons (isl.), Ga, US 165/H2
Saint Simons Island, Ga, US 165/H2
Saint Stephen, NB, Can. 158/D3
Saint Stephen-in-Brannel, Eng, UK 36/B6
Saint Stephens, Al, US 164/D2
Saint Stephens, NC, US 163/G3
Saint Stephens Church, Va, US 163/J2
Saint Thomas, Mo, US 153/H1
Saint Thomas, ND, US 156/F3
Saint Thomas, On, Can. 160/F3
Saint Thomas (isl.), USVI 173/H4
Saint Victor, Sk, Can. 145/M3
Saint Vika, Swe. 39/A2
Saint Vincent (pt.), Austl. 132/C4
Saint Vincent, It. 62/A1
Saint Vincent (isl.), StV. 173/N9
Saint Vincent and the Grenadines (ctry.) 173/N8
Saint Vincent Nat'l Wild. Ref., Fl, US 165/F3
Saint Vincent Passage (chan.), StL.,StV. 173/N9
Saint Walburg, Sk, Can. 145/K1
Saint Xavier, Mt, US 147/K1
Saint-Affrique, Fr. 44/E5
Saint-Aignan, Fr. 57/G6
Saint-Alexis-de-Matapédia, Qu, Can. 158/D2
Saint-Alexis-des-Monts, Qu, Can. 161/K1
Saint-Amable, Qu, Can. 159/P6
Saint-Amand, Fr. 57/E2
Saint-Amand-les-Eaux, Fr. 54/C3
Saint-Amand-Longpré, Fr. 57/G5
Saint-Amand-Montrond, Fr. 44/E3
Saint-Amarin, Fr. 60/D2
Saint-Ambroise, Qu, Can. 158/B1
Saint-Amé, Fr. 60/C1
Saint-Andiol, Fr. 64/A5
Saint-André, NB, Can. 158/D2
Saint-André, Fr. 54/C2
Saint-André, Fr. 64/D5
Saint-André, Fr. 125/S15
Saint-André-de-Cubzac, Fr. 44/C4
Saint-André-de-l'Eure, Fr. 57/G3
Saint-André-le-Gaz, Fr. 64/B1
Saint-André-les-Alpes, Fr. 64/C5
Saint-André-les-Vergers, Fr. 44/F2
Saint-Anicet, Qu, Can. 161/J2
Saint-Antoine, NB, Can. 158/E2
Saint-Antoine, Qu, Can. 159/N6
Saint-Antonin, Qu, Can. 158/C2
Saint-Arnoult-en-Yvelines, Fr. 30/H6
Saint-Athanase, Qu, Can. 158/C2
Saint-Auban, Fr. 64/C5
Saint-Aubert, Qu, Can. 158/B2
Saint-Aubin, Fr. 60/B3
Saint-Aubin, Swi. 60/C4
Saint-Aubin-d'Aubigné, Fr. 56/D4
Saint-Aubin-du-Cormier, Fr. 56/D4
Saint-Aubin-lès-Elbeuf, Fr. 57/G2
Saint-Aubin-sur-Gaillon, Fr. 57/G2
Saint-Augustin, Madg. 125/G8
Saint-Augustin, Fr. 30/M5
Saint-Augustin, Qu, Can. 159/N6
Saint-Avé, Fr. 56/C5
Saint-Avertin, Fr. 57/F6
Saint-Avold, Fr. 55/F5
Saint-Baldoph, Fr. 64/B1
Saint-Barthélemy, Qu, Can. 161/K1
Saint-Barthélemy (isl.), Fr. 173/N8
Saint-Barthélemy, Pic de (peak), Fr. 44/D5
Saint-Barthélemy-d'Anjou, Fr. 57/E6
Saint-Basile, NB, Can. 158/C2
Saint-Benoît, Fr. 125/S15
Saint-Benoît, Fr. 44/D3
Saint-Benoît, Qu, Can. 159/M6
Saint-Berthevin, Fr. 57/E4
Saint-Blaise, Swi. 60/C3
Saint-Blaise, Qu, Can. 159/P7
Saint-Bonnet-de-Mure, Fr. 64/B1
Saint-Bonnet-en-Champsaur, Fr. 64/C3
Saint-Briac-sur-Mer, Fr. 56/C3
Saint-Brice-Courcelles, Fr. 54/C5
Saint-Brice-sous-Forêt, Fr. 30/K5
Saint-Brieuc, Fr. 56/C3
Saint-Brieuc (bay), Fr. 44/B2
Saint-Bruno (co.), Qu, Can. 159/P6
Saint-Bruno-de-Montarville, Qu, Can. 159/P6
Saint-Calais, Fr. 57/F5
Saint-Cannat, Fr. 64/B5
Saint-Canut, Qu, Can. 159/M6
Saint-Cassien (lake), Fr. 64/C5
Saint-Cast-le-Guildo, Fr. 56/C3
Saint-Céré, Fr. 44/D4
Saint-Cergue, Swi. 60/C5
Saint-Cergues, Fr. 60/C5
Saint-Chamas, Fr. 64/B5
Saint-Charles, NB, Can. 158/E2
Saint-Chef, Fr. 64/B1
Saint-Chély-d'Apcher, Fr. 44/E4
Saint-Chéron, Fr. 30/J6
Saint-Clair-de-la-Tour, Fr. 64/B1
Saint-Clair-du-Rhône, Fr. 64/A2
Saint-Claude, Fr. 60/B5
Saint-Cloud, Fr. 30/J5
Saint-Constant, Qu, Can. 159/N7
Saint-Cosme-de-Vair, Fr. 57/F4
Saint-Coulomb, Fr. 56/D3
Saint-Croix (lake), Fr. 64/C5
Saint-Cyprien, Qu, Can. 158/C2
Saint-Cyr-en-Val, Fr. 57/G5
Saint-Cyr-l'École, Fr. 30/J5
Saint-Cyr-sous-Dourdan, Fr. 30/J6
Saint-Cyr-sur-Loire, Fr. 57/F6
Saint-Cyr-sur-Mer, Fr. 64/B6
Saint-Cyr-sur-Morin, Fr. 30/M5
Saint-Cyrille, Qu, Can. 161/K2
Saint-Damase, Qu, Can. 158/D1
Saint-Damien-de-Buckland, Qu, Can. 158/B2
Saint-David-de-Falardeau, Qu, Can. 158/B1
Saint-Denis, Fr. 125/S15
Saint-Denis, Fr. 30/K5
Saint-Denis-en-Bugey, Fr. 60/B6
Saint-Denis-les-Ponts, Fr. 57/G4
Saint-Didier, Fr. 64/B5
Saint-Dié, Fr. 60/C1
Saint-Dizier, Fr. 55/D6
Saint-Donat, Qu, Can. 161/J1
Saint-Donat-sur-l'Herbasse, Fr. 64/A2
Saint-Doulchard, Fr. 44/E3
Saint-Édouard, Qu, Can. 159/N7
Saint-Égrève, Fr. 64/B2
Saint-Élie, FrG. 182/C1
Saint-Éloy-les-Mines, Fr. 44/E3
Saint-Esprit, Qu, Can. 159/N6
Saint-Estève, Fr. 44/E5
Saint-Étienne-au-Mont, Fr. 54/A2
Saint-Étienne-de-Baïgorry, Fr. 44/C5
Saint-Étienne-de-Cuines, Fr. 64/C2
Saint-Étienne-de-Montluc, Fr. 56/D6
Saint-Étienne-de-Tinée, Fr. 64/C4
Saint-Étienne-du-Grès, Fr. 64/A5
Saint-Étienne-du-Rouvray, Fr. 57/G2
Saint-Étienne-les-Orgues, Fr. 64/B4
Saint-Étienne-lès-Remiremont, Fr. 60/C1
Saint-Eusèbe, Qu, Can. 158/C2
Saint-Eustache, Qu, Can. 159/N6
Saint-Fabien, Qu, Can. 158/C1
Saint-Fargeau-Ponthierry, Fr. 30/K6
Saint-Félicien, Qu, Can. 158/A1
Saint-Félicien, Fr. 64/A2
Saint-Félix, Fr. 60/B6
Saint-Ferréol-les-Neiges, Qu, Can. 158/B2
Saint-Fidèle-de-Mont-Murray, Qu, Can. 158/C2
Saint-Firmin, Fr. 64/C3
Saint-Florent-le-Vieil, Fr. 57/D6
Saint-Florent-sur-Cher, Fr. 44/E3
Saint-Florentin, Fr. 44/E2
Saint-Fons, Fr. 64/A1
Saint-Four, Fr. 44/E4
Saint-François (riv.), Qu, Can. 158/A3
Saint-François-du-Lac, Qu, Can. 161/K1
Saint-Front, Sk, Can. 145/M1
Saint-Fulgence, Qu, Can. 158/B1
Saint-Gabriel, Qu, Can. 161/K1
Saint-Gaudens, Fr. 44/D5
Saint-Gaudens Nat'l Hist. Site, NH, US 161/K3
Saint-Gédéon, Qu, Can. 158/B3
Saint-Genis-Laval, Fr. 64/A1
Saint-Genis-Pouilly, Fr. 60/C5
Saint-Genix-sur-Guiers, Fr. 64/B1
Saint-Georges, Qu, Can. 158/B2
Saint-Georges, FrG. 182/D2
Saint-Georges-Buttavent, Fr. 57/E4
Saint-Georges-de-Cacouna, Qu, Can. 158/C2
Saint-Georges-des-Groseillers, Fr. 57/E3
Saint-Georges-du-Vièvre, Fr. 57/F2
Saint-Georges-sur-Cher, Fr. 57/G6
Saint-Georges-sur-Eure, Fr. 57/G4
Saint-Georges-sur-Loire, Fr. 57/E6
Saint-Géréon, Fr. 56/D6
Saint-Germain, Fr. 60/C2
Saint-Germain-de-la-Grange, Fr. 30/H5
Saint-Germain-du-Bois, Fr. 60/B4
Saint-Germain-du-Corbéis, Fr. 57/F4
Saint-Germain-du-Plain, Fr. 60/A4
Saint-Germain-en-Laye, Fr. 30/J5
Saint-Germain-lès-Corbeil, Fr. 30/K6
Saint-Germain-sous-Doue, Fr. 30/M5
Saint-Germain-sur-Morin, Fr. 30/L5
Saint-Germer-de-Fly, Fr. 54/A5
Saint-Gervais, Fr. 30/H4
Saint-Gervais-la-Forêt, Fr. 57/G5
Saint-Gervais-les-Bains, Fr. 60/C6
Saint-Ghislain, Belg. 54/C3
Saint-Gildas-des-Bois, Fr. 56/C5
Saint-Gilles-Croix-de-Vie, Fr. 44/C3
Saint-Gingolph, Swi. 60/C5
Saint-Girons, Fr. 44/D5
Saint-Gobain, Fr. 54/C4
Saint-Godefroi, Qu, Can. 158/E1
Saint-Gratien, Fr. 30/J5
Saint-Grégoire, Fr. 56/D4
Saint-Guillaume-Nord, Qu, Can. 161/J1
Saint-Herblain, Fr. 56/D6
Saint-Hermas, Qu, Can. 159/M6
Saint-Herménégilde, Qu, Can. 158/B3
Saint-Hilaire-du-Harcouët, Fr. 57/D3
Saint-Hilarion, Fr. 30/H6
Saint-Hippolyte, Fr. 60/C3
Saint-Honorat (peak), Fr. 64/C4
Saint-Honoré, Qu, Can. 158/B3
Saint-Honoré, Qu, Can. 158/B1
Saint-Hubert, Qu, Can. 158/C2
Saint-Hubert, Belg. 55/E3
Saint-Hubert (pond), Fr. 30/H5
Saint-Hubert, Qu, Can. 159/P6
Saint-Hugues, Qu, Can. 161/K2
Saint-Hyacinthe, Qu, Can. 161/K2
Saint-Imier, Swi. 60/D3
Saint-Irénée, Qu, Can. 158/B2
Saint-Isidore, NB, Can. 158/E2
Saint-Isidore-de-Laprairie, Qu, Can. 159/N7
Saint-Ismier, Fr. 64/B2
Saint-Jacques, NB, Can. 158/C2
Saint-Jacques-de-la-Lande, Fr. 56/D4
Saint-Jacques-le-Mineur, Qu, Can. 159/P7
Saint-James, Fr. 56/D3
Saint-Jean (riv.), Qu, Can. 158/E1
Saint-Jean (lake), Qu, Can. 141/J4
Saint-Jean, FrG. 182/C1
Saint-Jean-Cap-Ferrat, Fr. 64/D5
Saint-Jean-d'Angély, Fr. 44/C4
Saint-Jean-de-Bboiseau, Fr. 56/D6
Saint-Jean-de-Bournay, Fr. 64/B2
Saint-Jean-de-Braye, Fr. 57/G5
Saint-Jean-de-Dieu, Qu, Can. 158/C1
Saint-Jean-de-la-Ruelle, Fr. 57/G5
Saint-Jean-de-Losne, Fr. 60/B3
Saint-Jean-de-Luz, Fr. 44/C5
Saint-Jean-de-Matha, Qu, Can. 161/K1
Saint-Jean-de-Muzols, Fr. 64/A2
Saint-Jean-en-Royans, Fr. 64/B2
Saint-Jean-Port-Joli, Qu, Can. 158/B2
Saint-Jean-sur-Richelieu, Qu, Can. 161/K2
Saint-Jeannet, Fr. 64/D5
Saint-Jeoire, Fr. 60/C5
Saint-Jérôme, Qu, Can. 159/N6
Saint-Joachim, Fr. 56/C6
Saint-Joseph, NB, Can. 158/E3
Saint-Joseph, Fr. 125/S15
Saint-Joseph-de-Beauce, Qu, Can. 158/B2
Saint-Joseph-de-Madawaska, NB, Can. 158/C2
Saint-Joseph-de-Mékinac, Qu, Can. 158/A2
Saint-Jovite, Qu, Can. 161/J1
Saint-Juéry, Fr. 44/E5
Saint-Julien, Fr. 60/B3
Saint-Julien-de-Vouvantes, Fr. 56/D5
Saint-Julien-en-Genevois, Fr. 60/C5
Saint-Julien-les-Villas, Fr. 44/F2
Saint-Julien-Mont-Denis, Fr. 64/C2
Saint-Junien, Fr. 44/D4
Saint-Just-en-Chaussée, Fr. 54/B4
Saint-Juste-de-Bretenières, Qu, Can. 158/B2
Saint-Lambert, Qu, Can. 159/P6
Saint-Laurent, Qu, Can. 159/N6
Saint-Laurent du Maroni (dist.), FrG. 182/C1
Saint-Laurent du Maroni, FrG. 182/C1
Saint-Laurent-Blangy, Fr. 54/B3
Saint-Laurent-de-Cerdans, Fr. 44/E5
Saint-Laurent-de-Mure, Fr. 64/B1
Saint-Laurent-des-Arbres, Fr. 64/A4
Saint-Laurent-du-Pont, Fr. 64/B2
Saint-Laurent-du-Var, Fr. 64/D5
Saint-Laurent-en-Grandvaux, Fr. 60/B4
Saint-Laurent-Nouan, Fr. 57/G5
Saint-Laurent-sur-Saône, Fr. 60/A5
Saint-Lazare, Qu, Can. 158/B2
Saint-Lazare, Qu, Can. 159/M7
Saint-Léger, Belg. 55/E4
Saint-Léger-en-Yvelines, Fr. 30/H5
Saint-Léger-lès-Domart, Fr. 54/B3
Saint-Léonard, Fr. 54/A2
Saint-Léonard, Qu, Can. 159/N6
Saint-Leu, Fr. 125/S15
Saint-Leu-d'Esserent, Fr. 54/B5
Saint-Leu-la-Forêt, Fr. 30/J4
Saint-Liboire, Qu, Can. 158/A3
Saint-Lô, Fr. 57/D2
Saint-Louis, Fr. 60/D2
Saint-Louis (pol. reg.), Sen. 114/B3
Saint-Louis, Sen. 114/A2
Saint-Louis, Fr. 125/S15
Saint-Louis du Nord, Haiti 177/H2
Saint-Louis-de-Gonzague, Qu, Can. 159/N7
Saint-Louis-de-Kent, NB, Can. 158/E2
Saint-Loup-sur-Semouse, Fr. 60/C2
Saint-Lubin-des-Joncherets, Fr. 57/G3
Saint-Luc, Qu, Can. 159/P7
Saint-Lucien, Fr. 30/G6
Saint-Lunaire, Fr. 56/C3
Saint-Magloire-de-Bellechasse, Qu, Can. 158/B2
Saint-Maixent l'École, Fr. 44/C3
Saint-Malachie, Qu, Can. 158/B2
Saint-Malo, Fr. 56/C3
Saint-Malo (gulf), UK 44/B2
Saint-Malo-de-Guersac, Fr. 56/C6
Saint-Mandrier-sur-Mer, Fr. 64/B6
Saint-Marc, Haiti 177/H2
Saint-Marc-des-Carrières, Qu, Can. 158/A2
Saint-Marc-sur-Richelieu, Qu, Can. 159/P6
Saint-Marcel, Fr. 57/G2
Saint-Marcel, Fr. 60/A4
Saint-Marcel (peak), FrG. 182/C2
Saint-Marcel-d'Ardèche, Fr. 64/A4
Saint-Marcel-lès-Valence, Fr. 64/A3
Saint-Marcellin, Fr. 64/B2
Saint-Marcouf (isls.), Fr. 57/D1
Saint-Mard, Fr. 30/L4
Saint-Mars-la-Brière, Fr. 57/F4
Saint-Mars-la-Jaille, Fr. 57/D5
Saint-Martin, Swi. 60/D5
Saint-Martin (isl.), Fr. 173/J4
Saint-Martin-Boulogne, Fr. 54/A2
Saint-Martin-d'Ablois, Fr. 54/C6
Saint-Martin-de-Belleville, Fr. 64/C2
Saint-Martin-de-Crau, Fr. 64/A5
Saint-Martin-des-Champs, Fr. 56/B3
Saint-Martin-d'Hères, Fr. 64/B2
Saint-Martin-du-Tertre, Fr. 30/K4
Saint-Martin-du-Var, Fr. 64/D5
Saint-Martin-la-Garenne, Fr. 30/H4
Saint-Martin-Vésubie, Fr. 64/D4
Saint-Mathieu (pt.), Fr. 56/A4
Saint-Mathieu-de-Beloeil, Qu, Can. 159/N7
Saint-Maur-des-Fossés, Fr. 30/K5
Saint-Maurice, Swi. 60/D5
Saint-Maurice (riv.), Qu, Can. 158/A2
Saint-Maurice (riv.), Qu, Can. 141/J4
Saint-Maurice-L'Exil, Fr. 64/A2
Saint-Max, Fr. 55/F6
Saint-Maxime-du-Mont-Louis, Qu, Can. 158/E1
Saint-Maximin-la-Sainte-Baume, Fr. 64/B6
Saint-Méen-le-Grand, Fr. 56/C4
Saint-Memmie, Fr. 55/D6
Saint-Méry, Fr. 30/L6
Saint-Michel, Fr. 55/D4
Saint-Michel (mtn.), Fr. 56/B4
Saint-Michel-Chef-Chef, Fr. 56/C6
Saint-Michel-de-Maurienne, Fr. 64/C2
Saint-Michel-des-Saints, Qu, Can. 161/K1
Saint-Michel-sur-Meurthe, Fr. 60/C1
Saint-Michel-sur-Orge, Fr. 30/J6
Saint-Mihiel, Fr. 55/E6
Saint-Mitre-les-Remparts, Fr. 64/B6
Saint-Montant, Fr. 64/A4
Saint-Nabord, Fr. 60/C1
Saint-Nazaire, Fr. 56/C6
Saint-Nazaire, FrG. 182/C1
Saint-Nicolas, Belg. 55/E2
Saint-Nicolas-d'Aliermont, Fr. 57/G1
Saint-Nicolas-du-Pélem, Fr. 56/B4
Saint-Nom-la-Bretèche, Fr. 30/J5
Saint-Omer, Fr. 54/B2
Saint-Omer-en-Chaussée, Fr. 54/A4
Saint-Ouen, Fr. 57/G5
Saint-Ouen, Fr. 54/B3
Saint-Ouen-en-Brie, Fr. 30/L6
Saint-Ouen-L'Aumône, Fr. 30/J4
Saint-Pabu, Fr. 56/A3
Saint-Pacôme, Qu, Can. 158/C2
Saint-Pair-sur-Mer, Fr. 56/D3
Saint-Pamphile, Qu, Can. 158/C2
Saint-Pascal, Qu, Can. 158/C2
Saint-Paterne, Fr. 57/F4
Saint-Pathus, Fr. 30/L4
Saint-Paul, Fr. 64/D5
Saint-Paul, Fr. 64/C3
Saint-Paul-du-Nord, Qu, Can. 158/C1
Saint-Paul-en-Jarez, Fr. 64/A2
Saint-Paul-lès-Dax, Fr. 44/C5
Saint-Paul-Trois-Châteaux, Fr. 64/A4
Saint-Pé-de-Bigorre, Fr. 44/C5
Saint-Péray, Fr. 64/A3
Saint-Père-en-Retz, Fr. 56/C6
Saint-Philippe-de-Laprairie, Qu, Can. 159/P7
Saint-Pierre (pt.), Qu, Can. 158/E1
Saint-Pierre, Nf, Fr. 159/J2
Saint-Pierre (lake), Qu, Can. 158/A2
Saint-Pierre, It. 60/D6
Saint-Pierre, Fr. 125/S15
Saint-Pierre, Fr. 173/N9
Saint-Pierre-d'Albigny, Fr. 64/C1
Saint-Pierre-d'Allevard, Fr. 64/C2
Saint-Pierre-de-Bœuf, Fr. 64/A2
Saint-Pierre-des-Corps, Fr. 57/F6
Saint-Pierre-des-Fleurs, Fr. 57/F2
Saint-Pierre-du-Mont, Fr. 44/C5
Saint-Pierre-du-Perray, Fr. 30/K6
Saint-Pierre-Église, Fr. 56/D1
Saint-Pierre-en-Faucigny, Fr. 60/C5
Saint-Pierre-en-Port, Fr. 57/F1
Saint-Pierre-la-Cour, Fr. 57/D4
Saint-Pierre-lès-Elbeuf, Fr. 57/G2
Saint-Pierre-Montlimart, Fr. 57/D6
Saint-Pierre-Quiberon, Fr. 56/B5
Saint-Pierre-sur-Dives, Fr. 57/E2
Saint-Point (lake), Fr. 60/C4
Saint-Pol-de-Léon, Fr. 56/B3
Saint-Pol-sur-Mer, Fr. 54/B1
Saint-Pol-sur-Ternoise, Fr. 54/B3
Saint-Pourçain-sur-Sioule, Fr. 44/E3
Saint-Prex, Swi. 60/C5
Saint-Priest, Fr. 64/A1
Saint-Prime, Qu, Can. 158/A1
Saint-Prix, Fr. 30/J4
Saint-Prosper, Qu, Can. 158/B2
Saint-Quay-Portrieux, Fr. 56/C3
Saint-Quentin, Fr. 54/C4
Saint-Quentin (pond), Fr. 30/H5
Saint-Quentin, Canal de (canal), Fr. 54/C4
Saint-Rambert-d'Albon, Fr. 64/A2
Saint-Rambert-en-Bugey, Fr. 60/B6
Saint-Raphaël, Qu, Can. 158/B2
Saint-Raphaël, Fr. 64/C6
Saint-Raymond, Qu, Can. 158/B2
Saint-Rémi, Qu, Can. 159/N7
Saint-Rémy-de-Provence, Fr. 64/A5
Saint-Rémy-lès-Chevreuse, Fr. 30/J5
Saint-Rémy-l'Honoré, Fr. 30/H5
Saint-Rémy-sur-Avre, Fr. 57/G3
Saint-Renan, Fr. 56/A4
Saint-René-de-Matane, Qu, Can. 158/D1
Saint-Roch-de-L'Achigan, Qu, Can. 159/N6
Saint-Romain-de-Colbosc, Fr. 57/F1
Saint-Romans, Fr. 64/B2
Saint-Saëns, Fr. 57/G1
Saint-Saturnin-lès-Apt, Fr. 64/B5
Saint-Saturnin-lès-Avignon, Fr. 64/A5
Saint-Saulve, Fr. 54/C3
Saint-Sauveur, Fr. 60/C2
Saint-Sauveur-des-Monts, Qu, Can. 159/M6
Saint-Sauveur-le-Vicomte, Fr. 56/D2
Saint-Sauveur-Lendelin, Fr. 56/D2
Saint-Savin, Fr. 64/B1
Saint-Sébastien, Qu, Can. 158/B3
Saint-Sébastien-sur-Loire, Fr. 56/D6
Saint-Sever, Fr. 44/C5
Saint-Sever-Calvados, Fr. 57/D3
Saint-Siméon-de-Bressieux, Fr. 64/B2
Saint-Soupplets, Fr. 30/L4
Saint-Sulpice, Fr. 44/D5
Saint-Sylvain-d'Anjou, Fr. 57/E5
Saint-Symphorien (arpt.), Fr. 57/F6
Saint-Symphorien-d'Ozon, Fr. 64/A1
Saint-Théodore-d'Acton, Qu, Can. 161/K2
Saint-Théophile, Qu, Can. 158/B3
Saint-Timothée, Qu, Can. 159/M7
Saint-Trivier-de-Courtes, Fr. 60/B5
Saint-Tropez (gulf), Fr. 64/C6
Saint-Tropez, Fr. 64/C6
Saint-Ubalde, Qu, Can. 158/A2
Saint-Urbain, Fr. 60/B1
Saint-Urbain, Qu, Can. 158/B2
Saint-Urbain-Premier, Qu, Can. 159/N7
Saint-Ursanne, Swi. 60/D3
Saint-Uze, Fr. 64/A2
Saint-Vaast-la-Hougue, Fr. 56/D1
Saint-Valery-en-Caux, Fr. 57/F1
Saint-Valery-sur-Somme, Fr. 54/A3
Saint-Vallier, Fr. 64/A2
Saint-Vallier, Fr. 44/F3
Saint-Vallier-de-Thiey, Fr. 64/C5
Saint-Vaury, Fr. 44/D3
Saint-Viâtre, Fr. 57/G5
Saint-Vigor-le-Grand, Fr. 57/E2
Saint-Vincent-de-Tyrosse, Fr. 44/C5
Saint-Vincent-des-Landes, Fr. 56/D5
Saint-Vit, Fr. 60/B3
Saint-Vith, Belg. 55/F3
Saint-Vrain, Fr. 30/K6
Saint-Wandrille-Rançon, Fr. 57/F1
Saint-Witz, Fr. 30/K4
Saint-Yrieix-la-Perche, Fr. 44/D4
Saint-Yvy, Fr. 56/B5
Saint-Zacharie, Fr. 64/B6
Saintala, India 95/D1
Sainte Agathe, Mb, Can. 156/F3
Sainte Amélie, Mb, Can. 156/E3
Sainte Anne, Mb, Can. 156/F3
Sainte Genevieve, Mo, US 162/B2
Sainte Rose du Lac, Mb, Can. 156/E2
Sainte-Adèle, Qu, Can. 161/J2
Sainte-Adresse, Fr. 57/F1
Sainte-Agathe-des-Monts, Qu, Can. 161/J1
Sainte-Anne-D'Auray, Fr. 56/C5
Sainte-Anne-de-Beaupré, Qu, Can. 158/B2
Sainte-Anne-de-Madawaska, NB, Can. 158/C2
Sainte-Anne-des-Monts, Qu, Can. 158/D1
Sainte-Anne-des-Plaines, Qu, Can. 159/N6
Sainte-Anne-du-Lac, Qu, Can. 161/J1
Sainte-Aulde, Fr. 30/M5
Sainte-Blandine, Qu, Can. 158/C1
Sainte-Cécile-les-Vignes, Fr. 64/A4
Sainte-Croix, Swi. 60/C4
Sainte-Croix, Qu, Can. 158/B2
Sainte-Croix-aux-Mines, Fr. 60/D1
Sainte-Florence, Qu, Can. 158/D1
Sainte-Foy-lès-Lyon, Fr. 64/A1
Sainte-Françoise, Qu, Can. 158/C1
Sainte-Gemmes-sur-Loire, Fr. 57/E6
Sainte-Geneviève-de-Batiscan, Qu, Can. 158/A2
Sainte-Geneviève-des-Bois, Fr. 30/K6
Sainte-Hénédine, Qu, Can. 158/B2
Sainte-Jamme-sur-Sarthe, Fr. 57/F4
Sainte-Julie, Qu, Can. 159/P6
Sainte-Julienne, Qu, Can. 161/K2
Sainte-Luce-sur-Loire, Fr. 56/D6
Sainte-Marie, Qu, Can. 158/B2
Sainte-Marie, Fr. 173/N9
Sainte-Marie-aux-Chênes, Fr. 55/F5
Sainte-Martine, Qu, Can. 159/N7
Sainte-Maxime, Fr. 64/C6
Sainte-Menehould, Fr. 55/D5
Sainte-Mère-Église, Fr. 56/D2
Sainte-Mesme, Fr. 30/H6
Sainte-Reine-de-Bretagne, Fr. 56/C6
Sainte-Rose-de-Watford, Qu, Can. 158/B2
Sainte-Rose-du-Nord, Qu, Can. 158/B1
Sainte-Sigolène, Fr. 44/F4
Sainte-Suzanne, Fr. 57/E4
Sainte-Thècle, Qu, Can. 158/A2
Sainte-Thérèse, Qu, Can. 159/N6
Sainte-Tulle, Fr. 64/B5
Sainte-Véronique, Qu, Can. 161/J1
Saintes, Fr. 44/C4
Saintfield, NI, UK 34/C3
Sainthia, India 97/F4
Saipan (isl.), NMar. 136/D3
Saipina, Bol. 188/C1
Sairakkala, Fin. 39/F4
Saiss (Fez) (int'l arpt.), Mor. 112/B3
Saitama (pref.), Japan 85/F2
Saito, Japan 84/B4
Saiwa Swamp NP, Kenya 119/A1
Sajama, Bol. 184/D5
Sajama (peak), Bol. 188/B1
Sajama NP, Bol. 188/B1
Sajānan, Tun. 112/L6
Sajószentpéter, Hun. 43/L4
Sak (riv.), SAfr. 124/C3
Sakado, Japan 83/C2
Sakae, Japan 83/E2
Sakahogi, Japan 83/L5
Sakai, Japan 85/F2
Sakai, Japan 84/E2
Sakai (riv.), Japan 83/C3
Sakai, Japan 83/C1
Sakaide, Japan 84/C3
Sakaigawa, Japan 83/B2
Sakaiminato, Japan 84/C3
Sakākah, SAr. 102/E4
Sakakawea (lake), ND, US 156/C4
Sakami (lake), Qu, Can. 141/J3
Sakania, D.R. Congo 123/F2
Sakar (isl.), PNG 129/G1
Sakaraha, Madg. 125/H8
Sakarya (riv.), Turk. 70/D4
Sakarya (prov.), Turk. 70/D4
Sakata, Japan 82/A4
Sakauchi, Japan 83/K3
Sakawa, Japan 84/C4
Sakay (riv.), Madg. 125/H7
Sakçagöze, Turk. 102/D2
Sakchu, NKor. 81/C2
Sakden, Bhu. 93/F2
Sake, D.R. Congo 121/G3
Sakeny (riv.), Madg. 125/H7
Saketa, Indo. 91/G4
Sakété, Ben. 115/F5
Sakhā, Egypt 113/B2
Sakha, Resp., Rus. 77/N3
Sakhalin (isl.), Rus. 77/P4
Sakhalin (gulf), Rus. 75/Q4
Sakhalinskaya Oblast, Rus. 75/Q4
Sakhnīn, Isr. 105/C3
Sakhnovshchyna, Ukr. 73/H3
Sakht Sar, Iran 103/G2
Şäki, Azer. 71/H4
Šakiai, Lith. 41/K4
Sākib, Jor. 105/D4
Sakishima (isl.), Japan 77/M7
Sakmara (riv.), Rus. 71/L1
Sakon Nakhon, Thai. 94/D2
Sakrand, Pak. 101/J3
Sakrivier, SAfr. 124/C3
Saksaul'skiy, Kaz. 74/G5
Sakti, India 96/D4
Saku, Japan 85/F2
Saku, Japan 83/A1
Sakura, Japan 83/E2
Sakura, Japan 83/E1
Sakuragawa, Japan 83/E1
Sakurai, Japan 83/J6
Sakyk, Ukr. 73/G5
Sakya Monastery, China 97/G1
Säkylä, Fin. 41/K1
Sal (isl.), CpV. 107/K10
Sal (pt.), Hon. 176/E3
Sal (riv.), Rus. 71/G3
Sal Rei, CpV. 107/K10
Sala, Swe. 40/G2
Sala, It. 65/D6
Šal'a, Slvk. 50/C1

Sala Ba – San Mar

Sala Baganza, It. 62/D4
Sala Consilina, It. 48/D2
Sala Mok, Laos 94/C1
Sala Pac Thu, Laos 94/C2
Salabangka, Indo. 90/D4
Salacgrīva, Lat. 41/L3
Salada (lake), Mex. 174/B1
Salada, Laguna (dry lake), Mex. 148/E4
Saladas, Arg. 188/E4
Saladilio (riv.), Arg. 191/J11
Saladillo, Arg. 190/F2
Saladillo (riv.), Arg. 188/C4
Salado (riv.), Arg. 179/C6
Salado (riv.), Cuba 177/G1
Salado (riv.), NM, US 149/J3
Salado, Tx, US 150/F2
Salado del Norte (riv.), Arg. 179/C5
Salaga, Gha. 115/E4
Salagle, Som. 119/C1
Şalaḩ Ad Din (gov.), Iraq 103/E3
Sala'ilua, Sam. 137/R9
Salaise-sur-Sanne, Fr. 64/A2
Sălaj (co.), Rom. 43/M5
Sălaj (prov.), Rom. 51/F2
Salal, Chad 116/C2
Salala, Libr. 114/C5
Şalālah, Sudan 109/H4
Salālah, Oman 100/F5
Salamá, Guat. 176/D3
Salamajärven NP, Fin. 68/E3
Salamanca, NY, US 161/G3
Salamanca, Chile 188/B4
Salamanca, Mex. 175/E4
Salamanca, Sp. 46/C2
Salamat (pref.), Chad 116/D3
Salamatof, Ak, US 171/H3
Salamina, Col. 180/C2
Salamina, Col. 183/K7
Salamís, Gre. 49/H3
Salamís (isl.), Gre. 49/N9
Salamīyah, Syria 104/E2
Salāmūn, Egypt 113/C2
Salangen, Nor. 38/F1
Salantai, Lith. 41/J3
Salar de Arizaro, Arg. 188/B3
Salar de Ascotan, Bol. 188/B2
Salar de Atacama, Chile 188/B2
Salar de Coipasa, Bol. 188/B1
Salar de la Isla, Chile 188/B3
Salar de Pedernales, Chile 188/B3
Salar de Pipanaco, Arg. 188/C4
Salar de Punta Negra, Chile 188/B3
Salar de Uyuni, Bol. 188/B2
Salas, Sp. 46/B1
Salas, Peru 184/B2
Salas de los Infantes, Sp. 46/D1
Salat (riv.), Fr. 47/F1
Salatiga, Indo. 89/E4
Salavat, Rus. 71/K1
Salaverry, Peru 184/B3
Salbris, Fr. 57/H6
Salcantay (peak), Peru 184/C4
Salcedo, Phil. 88/D3
Šalčininkai, Lith. 41/L4
Salcombe, Eng, UK 36/C6
Saldaña, Sp. 46/C1
Saldanhabaai (bay), Safr. 124/K10
Saldus, Lat. 41/K3
Sale, Austl. 133/C4
Sale, Eng, UK 35/F5
Sale, It. 62/B4
Salé, Mor. 112/A2
Salé (prov.), Mor. 112/A3
Sale (Rabat) (int'l arpt.), Mor. 112/A2
Sale City, Ga, US 165/F2
Sale Marasino, It. 62/D2
Salebabu (isl.), Indo. 91/G3
Salebhatta, India 95/D1
Salekhard, Rus. 74/G3
Salem, Ger. 61/F2
Salem, India 95/C4
Salem, Namb. 122/B4
Salem, Swe. 39/A1
Salem, Ar, US 153/J2
Salem, Il, US 162/C1
Salem, In, US 162/D1
Salem, Ma, US 161/L3
Salem, Mi, US 167/E7
Salem, Mo, US 153/J2
Salem, NH, US 161/L3
Salem, NJ, US 168/C4
Salem (co.), NJ, US 168/C4
Salem (cr.), NJ, US 168/C4
Salem, NM, US 149/J4
Salem, Oh, US 160/F4
Salem (cap.), Or, US 146/B1
Salem, SD, US 154/F2
Salem, Va, US 163/G2
Salem, WV, US 160/F5
Salemi, It. 48/C4
Salentina (pen.), It. 67/H3
Salernes, Fr. 64/C5
Salerno, It. 65/D6
Salerno (gulf), It. 65/D6
Salerno (prov.), It. 65/D6
Sales (pt.), Eng, UK 37/G3
Saleux, Fr. 54/B4
Salfīt, WBnk. 105/C4
Salford, Eng, UK 35/F5
Salford (co.), Eng, UK 35/F5
Salgado Filho (int'l arpt.), Braz. 189/G4
Salgan, Rus. 69/K5
Salgar, Col. 180/C3
Salgesch, Swi. 60/D5
Salgótarján, Hun. 43/K4
Salgueiro, Braz. 183/G5
Salhus, Nor. 40/A1
Sali, Cro. 50/B4
Salida, Co, US 149/K1
Salies-de-Béarn, Fr. 44/C5
Salies-du-Salat, Fr. 44/D5
Şalīf, Yem. 118/B2
Salihli, Turk. 102/B2
Salima, Malw. 123/G2
Salīmah (oasis), Sudan 109/F4
Salims, Tanz. 119/B4
Salin, Myan. 86/B4
Salina (pt.), Bahm. 177/H1
Salina (isl.), It. 67/G3
Salina, Ks, US 153/F1
Salina, Ut, US 149/G1
Salina Cruz, Mex. 176/C2
Salina de Rincón, Chile 188/C2
Salinas, Ecu. 180/A5
Salinas (cape), Sp. 47/G3
Salinas, Ca, US 148/B2
Salinas (riv.), Ca, US 148/B2
Salinas de Ambargasta, Arg. 188/C4
Salinas de Garci Mendoza, Bol. 188/C1
Salinas de Hidalgo, Mex. 175/E4
Salinas Grande, Arg. 188/C2
Salinas Pueblo Missions Nat'l Mon., NM, US 149/J3
Salinas Victoria, Mex. 150/D5
Salinas Y Aguada Blanca, Res. Nacional, Peru 184/D4
Saline, It. 63/D7
Saline, Sc, UK 33/C4
Saline (riv.), Ks, US 155/E4
Saline, La, US 153/H4
Saline (lake), La, US 164/B2
Saline, Mi, US 160/E3
Saline Bayou (riv.), La, US 151/H1
Salinello (riv.), It. 65/C2
Salineno, Tx, US 150/E4
Salinópolis, Braz. 183/E3
Salins-les-Bains, Fr. 60/B4
Salins-les-Thermes, Fr. 64/C2
Salisbury (nbrhd.), Austl. 131/M8
Salisbury, NB, Can. 158/E2
Salisbury (isl.), Nun, Can. 141/J2
Salisbury, Eng, UK 37/E4
Salisbury (plain), Eng, UK 36/D4
Salisbury, Ct, US 161/K4
Salisbury, Md, US 163/K1
Salisbury, Mo, US 155/H4
Salisbury, NC, US 163/G3
Salisbury, NY, US 161/J3
Salisbury, NY, US 169/L9
Salisbury Downs, Austl. 132/B1
Salish (mts.), Mt, US 144/G3
Salitpa, Al, US 164/D2
Salitre, Ecu. 180/B5
Salitre (riv.), Braz. 187/E1
Salka, Slvk. 50/D2
Salkehatchie (riv.), SC, US 163/G4
Salla, Fin. 68/F2
Salladasburg, Pa, US 168/A1
Sallanches, Fr. 60/C6
Salland (phys. reg.), Neth. 52/D4
Sallatouk (pt.), Gui. 114/B4
Sallaumines, Fr. 54/B3
Sallent, Sp. 47/F2
Salles, Belg. 55/D3
Sallins, Ire. 32/D3
Salliqueló, Arg. 190/E3
Sallisaw, Ok, US 153/G3
Sallūm, Sudan 109/H5
Sally (pass), Ire. 34/B5
Salm (riv.), Ger. 55/F3
Salmān Pāk, Iraq 103/F3
Salmās, Iran 103/F2
Salme, Est. 41/K2
Salmo (riv.), BC, Can. 144/F3
Salmon (mts.), Ca, US 146/B3
Salmon, Id, US 147/G1
Salmon (dam), Id, US 147/F2
Salmon (riv.), Id, US 142/C2
Salmon (peak), Tx, US 150/D3
Salmon Arm, BC, Can. 144/E2
Salmon Cove, Nf, Can. 159/L2
Salmon Creek (res.), Id, US 147/F2
Salmon Creek, Wa, US 144/C5
Salmon Falls (cr.), Id, US 147/F2
Salmon Gums, Austl. 130/D5
Salmon River, NS, Can. 158/D3
Salmon River (mts.), Id, US 142/C2
Salmon Ruin, NM, US 149/H2
Salmon, Middle Fork (riv.), Id, US 147/F1
Salmon, South Fork (riv.), Id, US 146/F1
Salmtal, Ger. 55/F4
Salo, Fin. 41/K1
Salò, It. 62/D2
Salo, CAfr. 120/D2
Salole, Eth. 118/A4
Salome, Az, US 149/F4
Salon (riv.), Fr. 42/C5
Salon, India 96/C2
Salon-de-Provence, Fr. 64/B5
Salonga (riv.), D.R. Congo 121/E3
Salonga, PN de la, D.R. Congo 121/E3
Salonta, Rom. 50/E2
Salorno (Salurn), It. 61/H5
Salouël, Fr. 54/B4
Salpausselkä (mts.), Fin. 41/M1
Salpo, Peru 184/B3
Salses-le-Château, Fr. 44/E5
Sal'sk, Rus. 73/L4
Salso (riv.), It. 48/C4
Salsomaggiore Terme, It. 62/C4
Salt (range), Pak. 98/B3
Salt (riv.), SAfr. 124/C4
Salt, Sp. 47/G2
Salt (cr.), Il, US 155/K4
Salt (cr.), Mo, US 153/J1
Salt (lakes), Tx, US 150/B2
Salt (basin), Tx, US 152/B5
Salt Cay (isl.), UK 177/J1
Salt Draw (riv.), Tx, US 150/B2
Salt Fork (riv.), Ks,Ok, US 152/E2
Salt Lake City (cap.), Ut, US 147/H3
Salt Lake City (int'l arpt.), Ut, US 147/H3
Salt Meadow Nat'l Wild. Ref., Ct, US 169/F1
Salt Plains Nat'l Wildlife Res., Ok, US 153/E2
Salt, Middle Fork (riv.), Mo, US 155/H4
Salt, North (riv.), Mo, US 155/H4
Salta, Arg. 188/C3
Salta (int'l arpt.), Arg. 188/C3
Salta (prov.), Arg. 188/C3
Saltair, BC, Can. 144/C3
Saltaire, NY, US 169/E2
Saltash, Eng, UK 36/B6
Saltburn, Eng, UK 35/H2
Saltcoats, Sk, Can. 156/C2
Saltcoats, Sc, UK 33/B5
Saltdal, Nor. 38/E2
Saltee (isls.), Ire. 32/D5
Saltfjorden (inlet), Nor. 38/E2
Saltford, Eng, UK 36/D4
Saltholm (isl.), Den. 39/J7
Saltillo, Ms, US 162/C3
Saltillo, Tn, US 162/C3
Saltillo, Mex. 175/E3
Salto, Arg. 190/E2
Salto, Braz. 189/H2
Salto (lake), It. 65/C3
Salto (riv.), It. 65/B3
Salto, Uru. 188/E4
Salto (dept.), Uru. 189/E4
Salto da Divisa, Braz. 187/F3
Salto del Guairá, Par. 189/F3
Salto Grande (res.), Arg. 188/E4
Salto Santiago (res.), Braz. 189/F3
Salton Sea (lake), Ca, US 142/C5
Salton Sea Nat'l Wild. Ref., Ca, US 148/E4
Saltpond, Gha. 115/E5
Saltsjöbaden, Swe. 39/B1
Saltvik, Fin. 41/J1
Saltville, Va, US 163/G2
Saltykovka, Rus. 71/H1
Saluda (riv.), SC, US 163/G3
Saluda, SC, US 163/G3
Saluda, Va, US 163/J2
Salug, Phil. 88/C3
Saluggia, It. 62/B3
Salunga-Landisville, Pa, US 168/B3
Sālūr, India 95/D2
Salurn (Salorno), It. 61/H5
Salut (isls.), FrG. 182/C1
Saluta, Indo. 91/G3
Saluzzo, It. 64/D3
Salvación (bay), Chile 191/B6
Salvador (lake), La, US 164/C3
Salvador, Braz. 187/F2
Salvador, Sk, Can. 145/K1
Salvador Dali Museum, Fl, US 164/K8
Salvaleón de Higüey, DRep. 173/H4
Salvaterra, Braz. 182/D3
Salvaterra de Magos, Port. 46/A3
Salvatierra, Mex. 175/E4
Salvatierra de Miño, Sp. 46/A1
Salvisa, Ky, US 162/E2
Salween (riv.), Asia 77/J8
Salween (riv.), Myan.,Thai. 94/B2
Salween (Nu) (riv.), China 78/D5
Salyan, Azer. 103/G2
Salyān, Nepal 96/D1
Salyersville, Ky, US 163/F2
Salza (riv.), Aus. 43/H5
Salzach (riv.), Ger. 42/G5
Salzano, It. 63/F2
Salzbergen, Ger. 53/E4
Salzburg (prov.), Aus. 43/G5
Salzgitter, Ger. 53/H4
Salzhausen, Ger. 53/H2
Salzhemmendorf, Ger. 53/G4
Salzkotten, Ger. 53/F5
Salzwedel, Ger. 42/F2
Sam, Gabon 120/B2
Sam Houston Memorial Museum, Tx, US 151/G2
Sam Khok, Thai. 94/C3
Sam Ngao, Thai. 94/B2
Sam Rayburn (res.), Tx, US 151/G2
Sam Rayburn (dam), Tx, US 151/G2
Sam Sao (mts.), Laos,Viet. 94/C1
Sam Son, Viet. 94/D2
Sama, Sp. 46/C1
Samādūn, Egypt 113/B4
Samagaltay, Rus. 99/G1
Samaipata, Bol. 188/D1
Samak (cape), Indo. 89/D3
Samalayuca, Mex. 150/A2
Samales Group (isls.), Phil. 88/C4
Samālkha, India 98/D5
Samālūt, Egypt 109/F2
Samāna, India 98/D4
Samaná (cape), DRep. 173/H4
Samana (isl.), Bahm. 177/H1
Samaná, Col. 183/K7
Samanco, Peru 184/B3
Samandağı, Turk. 104/D1
Samandira, Turk. 103/N7
Samani, Japan 82/C2
Samaniego, Col. 180/B4
Samannūd, Egypt 113/C3
Samar (isl.), Phil. 77/M8
Samar (sea), Phil. 88/D3
Samar, Jor. 105/D3
Samara (int'l arpt.), Rus. 71/J1
Samara, Rus. 71/J1
Samara (riv.), Rus. 71/K1
Samaraskaya Oblast, Rus. 71/J1
Samarai, PNG 136/E6
Samarate, It. 62/B2
Samarga (riv.), Rus. 79/M2
Samaria (reg.), Isr. 105/C4
Samariapo, Ven. 180/E3
Samarinda, Indo. 91/E4
Samarqand, Uzb. 74/G6
Sāmarrā', Iraq 103/E3
Samarskoye, Rus. 71/L1
Samarskoye, Rus. 73/K4
Samasata, Pak. 98/A5
Samāstipur, India 97/E3
Samate, Indo. 91/H4
Samatigila, C.d'Iv. 114/D4
Şamaxi, Azer. 71/J4
Sāmba, India 98/C3
Samba, D.R. Congo 121/E2
Samba, D.R. Congo 121/F4
Samba Lucala, Ang. 120/C5
Sambaíba, Braz. 183/E4
Sambaïlo, Gui. 114/B3
Sambao (riv.), Madg. 125/H7
Sambar (cape), Indo. 90/D4
Sambas, Indo. 90/C3
Sambava, Madg. 125/J6
Samberbaba, Indo. 91/J4
Sambhal, India 96/B1
Sambili, D.R. Congo 116/D4
Sambir, Ukr. 43/M4
Sambo, Ang. 122/C2
Sambo, Indo. 91/E4
Sambong-ni, NKor. 81/E2
Sambor Prei Kuk (ruin), Camb. 94/D3
Samborobón (riv.), Arg. 191/K11
Samborombón (bay), Arg. 191/F2
Sambre (riv.), Fr. 42/C3
Sambre à l'Oise, Canal de (canal), Fr. 54/C4
Sambriāl, Pak. 98/C3
Sambro, NS, Can. 158/F3
Sambu, Japan 83/E2
Sambuceto, It. 65/D3
Samburu, Kenya 119/B2
Samburu Nat'l Rsv., Kenya 119/B1
Samchi, Bhu. 97/G2
Samch'ŏk, SKor. 84/A2
Samch'ŏnp'o, SKor. 81/E5
Samdrup Jongkhar, Bhu. 97/H2
Same, Tanz. 119/B3
Same, ETim. 128/B2
Samedan, Swi. 61/F4
Samer, Fr. 54/A2
Samfya Mission, Zam. 123/F1
Sámi, Gre. 49/G3
Sami, Myan. 86/B4
Saminskiy Pogost, Rus. 68/H3
Samiria (riv.), Peru 184/C2
Samit (cape), Camb. 94/C4
Samjiyŏn, NKor. 81/E2
Samka, Myan. 94/B1
Şämkir, Azer. 71/H4
Samkos (peak), Camb. 94/C3
Sammamish (lake), Wa, US 167/C2
Sammatti, Fin. 39/D4
Sammeron, Fr. 30/M5
Samnangjin, SKor. 84/A3
Samnaun, Swi. 61/G4
Samnorwood, Tx, US 152/D3
Samnū, Libya 108/B3
Samo Alto, Chile 188/B4
Samoa (ctry.) 137/R9
Samobor, Cro. 50/B3
Samoëns, Fr. 60/C5
Samoggia (riv.), It. 63/E4
Samokov, Bul. 51/F4
Samora (riv.), Port. 47/Q10
Samora Correia, Port. 47/Q10
Sámos, Gre. 102/A2
Sámos (isl.), Gre. 102/A2
Samothráki, Gre. 49/J2
Samouay, Laos 94/D2
Samoylovka, Rus. 71/G2
Sampacho, Arg. 190/D2
Sampang, Indo. 89/F4
Samper de Calanda, Sp. 47/E2
Sampeyre, It. 64/D3
Sampit (riv.), Indo. 90/D4
Sampit, Indo. 90/D4
Sampwe, D.R. Congo 121/F5
Samrāla, India 98/D4
Samrē, Eth. 118/A2
Samrong Thap, Thai. 94/C3
Sams, Co, US 149/J1
Samsang, China 99/D5
Samsø (isl.), Den. 40/D4
Samsø Bælt (chan.), Den. 40/D4
Samson, Al, US 165/E2
Samson (mt.), Austl. 134/E6
Samson Ind. Res., Ab, Can. 145/H1
Samsonvale (lake), Austl. 134/E6
Samsu, NKor. 81/E2
Samsun, Turk. 70/F4
Samsun (prov.), Turk. 70/E4
Samthar, India 96/B3
Samuel (mt.), Austl. 128/D4
Samuels, Id, US 144/F3
Samugheo, It. 48/A3
Samui (isl.), Thai. 93/H6
Samukawa, Japan 83/C3
Samundri, Pak. 98/B4
Samur (riv.), Azer.,Rus. 74/E5
Samur (riv.), Rus. 71/H4
Samut Prakan, Thai. 94/C3
Samut Sakhon, Thai. 94/C3
Samut Songkhram, Thai. 94/B3
Samye Monastery, China 97/H1
San (riv.), Pol. 70/B2
San, Mali 114/D3
San (riv.), Camb. 94/D3
San (riv.), China 79/H5
San Acacia, NM, US 149/J3
San Adrián, Cabo de (cape), Sp. 46/A1
San Agustín, Col. 180/B4
San Agustin (cape), Phil. 88/D4
San Agustín, Bol. 188/C2
San Agustín, Bol. 185/F5
San Agustin de Guadalix, Sp. 47/N8
San Agustín, Parque Arqeológico, Col. 180/B4
San Agustin, Plains of (plains), NM, US 149/H4
Şān al Ḩajar al Qiblīyah, Egypt 113/C3
San Ambrosio (isl.), Chile 179/B5
San Andreas (lake), Ca, US 167/J11
San Andreas, Ca, US 146/C4
San Andrés, Bol. 185/E4
San Andrés, Col. 177/F3
San Andrés, Col. 180/C3
San Andrés, Col. 180/C3
San Andrés (lake), Mex. 176/B1
San Andres, Phil. 88/D2
San Andres (mts.), NM, US 149/J4
San Andrés Cuexcontitlán, Mex. 175/Q10
San Andrés de Giles, Arg. 191/J11
San Andrés de Machaca, Bol. 184/D5
San Andrés del Rabanedo, Sp. 46/C1
San Andres Nat'l Wild Ref., NM, US 149/J4
San Andrés Tuxtla, Mex. 176/C2
San Andrés, Isla de (isl.), Col. 172/E5
San Angelo, Tx, US 150/D2
San Anselmo, Ca, US 167/J11
San Antonio (cape), Arg. 191/F3
San Antonio, Arg. 190/D2
San Antonio, Bol. 185/E4
San Antonio, Chile 190/N8
San Antonio, Ecu. 180/B4
San Antonio, Mex. 174/C4
San Antonio, Peru 184/B4
San Antonio, Phil. 88/C2
San Antonio, Uru. 191/K11
San Antonio, Ven. 181/E2
San Antonio, Ven. 181/F2
San Antonio (res.), Ca, US 148/B3
San Antonio (mt.), Ca, US 166/C2
San Antonio, Fl, US 164/L7
San Antonio, NM, US 149/J4
San Antonio (mtn.), NM, US 149/J2
San Antonio, Tx, US 151/E3
San Antonio (bay), Tx, US 151/F3
San Antonio (int'l arpt.), Tx, US 151/E3
San Antonio (riv.), Tx, US 151/F3
San Antonio Abad, Sp. 47/F3
San Antonio de Areco, Arg. 191/J11
San Antonio de Caparo, Ven. 180/D3
San Antonio de Lípez, Bol. 188/C2
San Antonio de los Cobres, Arg. 188/C3
San Antonio de Tabasca, Ven. 181/F2
San Antonio de Tamanaco, Ven. 183/P8
San Antonio del Golfo, Ven. 181/F2
San Antonio del Táchira, Ven. 180/C3
San Antonio Oeste, Arg. 190/D4
San Antonio, Punta (pt.), Mex. 174/B2
San Ardo, Ca, US 148/B2
San Augustin (pass), NM, US 149/J4
San Augustine, Tx, US 151/G2
San Bartolo, Peru 184/B4
San Bartolomé de Tirajana, Sp. 110/B4
San Bartolome Tlaltelulco, Mex. 175/Q10
San Bartolomeo in Bosco, It. 63/E4
San Bartolomeo in Galdo, It. 65/E5
San Bautista, Uru. 191/L11
San Benedetto (range), It. 63/E5
San Benedetto dei Marsi, It. 65/C3
San Benedetto del Tronto, It. 65/C2
San Benedetto in Alpe, It. 63/E6
San Benedetto Po, It. 63/D3
San Benedicto (isl.), Mex. 174/C5
San Benito (mtn.), Ca, US 148/B2
San Benito (riv.), Ca, US 148/B2
San Benito, Tx, US 150/F4
San Bernard (riv.), Tx, US 151/F3
San Bernard NWR, Tx, US 151/G3
San Bernardino, Swi. 61/F5
San Bernardino (mts.), Ca, US 166/C2
San Bernardino (co.), Ca, US 166/C2
San Bernardino, Ca, US 166/C2
San Bernardino (str.), Phil. 88/D2
San Bernardino Nat'l Forest, Ca, US 166/C2
San Bernardino Nat'l Wild. Ref., Az, US 149/H5
San Bernardo, Arg. 188/D3
San Bernardo (pt.), Col. 180/C2
San Bernardo, Chile 190/N8
San Bernardo, Col. 183/L8
San Blas, Mex. 150/D4
San Blas, Mex. 174/C3
San Blas, Mex. 174/D4
San Blas (cape), Fl, US 165/F3
San Bonifacio, It. 63/E3
San Borja, Bol. 185/E4
San Bruno, Ca, US 167/K11
San Bruno, Mex. 174/B3
San Buenaventura, Mex. 150/D4
San Buenaventura (Ventura), Ca, US 166/A2
San Candido (Innichen), It. 45/K3
San Carlos, Arg. 188/C3
San Carlos, Bol. 188/D1
San Carlos, Chile 190/C3
San Carlos, Col. 183/L6
San Carlos, Mex. 175/F3
San Carlos, Mex. 150/D3
San Carlos, Nic. 177/E4
San Carlos, Pan. 180/B2
San Carlos, Par. 189/E2
San Carlos, Phil. 88/C2
San Carlos, Ven. 180/D2
San Carlos, Uru. 191/G2
San Carlos, Az, US 149/G4
San Carlos, Ca, US 167/K11
San Carlos (lake), Az, US 149/G4
San Carlos de Bariloche, Arg. 190/C4
San Carlos de Bariloche (int'l arpt.), Arg. 190/C4
San Carlos de Río Negro, Ven. 181/E4
San Carlos del Zulia, Ven. 180/D2
San Carlos Ind. Res., Az, US 149/G4
San Casciano in Val di Pesa, It. 63/E6
San Casimiro, Ven. 183/N7
San Cataldo, It. 49/F2
San Cayetano, Arg. 190/F3
San Cayetano, Col. 183/L7
San Cesario sul Panaro, It. 63/E4
San Cipriano d'Aversa, It. 65/D5
San Ciro de Acosta, Mex. 175/F4
San Clemente, Ca, US 166/C4
San Clemente, Sp. 46/D3
San Clemente, Chile 190/C2
San Clemente (isl.), Ca, US 148/C4
San Clemente del Tuyú, Arg. 191/F3
San Clemente in Casauria, It. 65/C3
San Colombano al Lambro, It. 62/C3
San Cristóbal, Arg. 188/D4
San Cristóbal, Bol. 188/C2
San Cristóbal, Bol. 185/F4
San Cristóbal, Cuba 177/F1
San Cristóbal (isl.), Ecu. 184/K7
San Cristóbal (vol.), Nic. 176/E3
San Cristobal (isl.), Sol. 136/F6
San Cristobal, NM, US 152/B2
San Cristóbal, Ven. 180/C3
San Cristóbal de las Casas, Mex. 176/C2
San Cristobal Wash (riv.), Az, US 149/F4
San Damiano d'Asti, It. 62/B4
San Damiano Macra, It. 64/D4
San Demetrio ne'Vestini, It. 65/C3
San Diego (cape), Arg. 191/D7
San Diego, Bol. 185/F5
San Diego, Bol. 188/C2
San Diego (co.), Ca, US 166/C4
San Diego (bay), Ca, US 166/C5
San Diego (aqueduct), Ca, US 166/C4
San Diego, Ca, US 166/C5
San Diego (riv.), Ca, US 148/D4
San Diego, Tx, US 151/E4
San Diego International-Lindbergh Field (int'l arpt.), Ca, US 166/C5
San Diego Naval Station, Ca, US 166/C5
San Diego Wild Animal Park, Ca, US 166/C4
San Diego Zoo, Ca, US 166/C5
San Diequito (riv.), Ca, US 166/C5
San Dimas, Ca, US 166/C2
San Donà di Piave, It. 63/F2
San Donato Val di Comino, It. 65/C4
San Donnino, It. 63/E6
San Dorligo della Valle, It. 63/G2
San Elizario, Tx, US 150/A2
San Estanislao, Par. 189/E3
San Esteban de Gormaz, Sp. 46/D2
San Fabián de Alico, Chile 190/C3
San Felice a Cancello, It. 65/D6
San Felice Circeo, It. 65/C5
San Felice del Benaco, It. 62/D2
San Felice sul Panaro, It. 63/E4
San Felipe, Ven. 180/C2
San Felipe, Ven. 180/D2
San Felipe (cr.), Ca, US 148/D4
San Felipe, Chile 190/N8
San Felipe, Mex. 174/B2
San Felipe de Puerto Plata, DRep. 173/G4
San Felipe de Vichayal, Peru 184/A2
San Felipe Ind. Res., NM, US 149/J3
San Felipe Jalapa de Díaz, Mex. 175/F5
San Felipe Pueblo, NM, US 149/J3
San Felipe Torres Mochas, Mex. 175/E4
San Felix (isl.), Chile 179/A5
San Fernando, Arg. 191/J11
San Fernando, Arg. 188/C3
San Fernando, Chile 190/C2
San Fernando, Phil. 88/C2
San Fernando, Phil. 88/C1
San Fernando, Phil. 88/C2
San Fernando, Sp. 46/B4
San Fernando, Trin. 181/F2
San Fernando (valley), Ca, US 166/B2
San Fernando, Ca, US 166/F7
San Fernando de Apure, Ven. 181/E3
San Fernando de Atabapo, Ven. 180/E3
San Fernando de Henares, Sp. 47/N9
San Fernando de Presas, Mex. 175/F3
San Fidel, NM, US 149/J3
San Fior di Sopra, It. 63/F2
San Francesco al Campo, It. 62/A2
San Francisco (riv.), Arg. 188/C2
San Francisco, Arg. 188/D4
San Francisco, Bol. 185/E4
San Francisco, Bol. 188/E1
San Francisco, Col. 183/L8
San Francisco, Col. 180/B4
San Francisco, ESal. 176/D3
San Francisco, Phil. 88/C2
San Francisco, Phil. 88/D3
San Francisco (mts.), Az, US 149/G3
San Francisco (riv.), Az, US 149/H4
San Francisco (bay), Ca, US 148/A2
San Francisco (co.), Ca, US 167/K11
San Francisco (cr.), Tx, US 150/C3
San Francisco, Ven. 180/D2
San Francisco Acuautla, Mex. 175/R10
San Francisco Bay NWR, Ca, US 167/K11
San Francisco Chimalpa, Mex. 175/Q10
San Francisco de la Paz, Hon. 176/E3
San Francisco de Macorís, DRep. 173/G4
San Francisco de Mostazal, Chile 190/N8
San Francisco de Tiznados, Ven. 183/N8
San Francisco del Chañar, Arg. 188/D4
San Francisco del Mezquital, Mex. 174/D4
San Francisco del Monte de Oro, Arg. 190/D2
San Francisco del Oro, Mex. 174/D3
San Francisco del Rincón, Mex. 175/E4
San Francisco Telixtlahuaca, Mex. 172/B4
San Francisco, Cabo de (cape), Ecu. 180/A4
San Francisco, Paso de (pass), Arg.,Chile 188/B3
San Fratello, It. 48/D3
San Gabriel (riv.), Ca, US 166/C2
San Gabriel (res.), Ca, US 166/C2
San Gabriel, Ca, US 166/F7
San Gabriel, Ecu. 180/B4
San Gabriel (mts.), Ca, US 148/C3
San Gabriel, Chile 190/N8
San Gabriel, (pt.), Mex. 174/B2
San Gavino Monreale, It. 48/A3
San Gemini, It. 65/B2
San Genaro, Arg. 188/D5
San Germán, Cuba 177/G1
San Germano Vercellese, It. 62/B3
San Giacomo (Sankt Jakob), It. 61/H4
San Gil, Col. 180/C3
San Gimignano, It. 63/E7
San Ginesio, It. 65/C1
San Giorgio a Cremano, It. 65/D6
San Giorgio del Sannio, It. 65/D5
San Giorgio delle Pertiche, It. 63/E2
San Giorgio di Piano, It. 63/E4
San Giorgio Ionico, It. 49/E2
San Giorgio Piacentino, It. 62/C4
San Giovanni al Natisone, It. 63/G2
San Giovanni Bianco, It. 62/C2
San Giovanni Gemini, It. 48/C4
San Giovanni in Croce, It. 62/D3
San Giovanni in Fiore, It. 48/E3
San Giovanni in Marignano, It. 63/F6
San Giovanni in Persiceto, It. 63/E4
San Giovanni in Venere, It. 65/D3
San Giovanni Lupatoto, It. 63/E3
San Giovanni Rotondo, It. 48/D2
San Giovanni Valdarno, It. 63/E6
San Giuliano, It. 62/B4
San Giuliano Terme, It. 62/D6
San Giuseppe Vesuviano, It. 65/D6
San Giustino, It. 63/F6
San Giusto Canavese, It. 62/A2
San Gorgonio (mtn.), Ca, US 148/D3
San Gottardo, Passo del (pass), Swi. 61/E4
San Gregorio, Arg. 190/E2
San Gregorio, Uru. 191/L10
San Gregorio, Uru. 191/K10
San Gregorio, Ca, US 167/K12
San Guiliano Milanese, It. 62/C3
San Guillermo, Arg. 188/D4
San Hipólito Punta (pt.), Mex. 174/B3
San Ignacio, Belz. 176/D2
San Ignacio, Bol. 185/E4
San Ignacio, Bol. 185/F5
San Ignacio, Bol. 188/D1
San Ignacio, Chile 190/B3
San Ignacio, Par. 189/E3
San Ignacio, Peru 184/B2
San Ignacio (riv.), Mex. 174/B2
San Ignacio, Mex. 174/D4
San Ignacio, Mex. 174/B3
San Ildefonso, Sp. 46/D2
San Ildefonso (cape), Phil. 88/C1
San Isidro, Nic. 176/E3
San Isidro, CR 177/F4
San Isidro de Curuguaty, Par. 189/F3
San Jacinto, Col. 180/C2
San Jacinto, Nv, US 147/F3
San Jacinto, Ca, US 148/D4
San Jacinto, Phil. 88/C2
San Jacinto, Uru. 191/L11
San Jacinto (dam), Tx, US 151/M9
San Jacinto Battleground, Tx, US 151/M9
San Jaime, Arg. 188/E4
San Javier, Arg. 190/E4
San Javier, Arg. 188/E4
San Javier, Bol. 185/F5
San Javier, Bol. 185/E4
San Javier, Chile 190/C2
San Javier, Sp. 47/E4
San Javier, Uru. 191/J10
San Jerónimo, Col. 183/K6
San Jerónimo, Mex. 174/E3
San Joaquin (co.), Ca, US 167/L11
San Joaquin (hills), Ca, US 166/G8
San Joaquín, Col. 180/C3
San Joaquin, Ca, US 148/B2
San Joaquin (riv.), Ca, US 148/B2
San Joaquin (valley), Ca, US 148/B2
San Joaquín (peak), Ecu. 184/K7
San Joaquín (riv.), Bol. 185/F4
San Joaquín, Par. 189/E3
San Joaquín, Bol. 185/E4
San Joaquín, Ven. 183/N7
San Joaquin, South Fork (riv.), Ca, US 148/C2
San Jorge (gulf), Sp. 66/D2
San Jorge (riv.), Col. 177/H5
San Jorge (gulf), Arg. 179/C7
San Jorge (cape), Arg. 190/D5
San Jorge, Arg. 188/D4
San Jorge (bay), Mex. 174/B2
San José, Arg. 188/C4
San José (gulf), Arg. 190/D4
San José (cap.), CR 177/E4
San José, Col. 180/B4
San José (isl.), Mex. 174/C3
San José, Peru 184/B2
San José, Peru 184/D4
San Jose, Phil. 88/C2
San Jose, Phil. 88/C3
San José, Sp. 47/F3
San José (dept.), Uru. 191/K11
San José, Ven. 180/E3
San Jose (riv.), Uru. 191/K10
San Jose (hills), Ca, US 166/G7
San Jose, Il, US 155/K3
San Jose (riv.), NM, US 149/J3
San Jose (isl.), Tx, US 151/F4
San José de Amacuro, Ven. 181/F2
San José de Aura, Mex. 150/D4
San José de Chiquitos, Bol. 188/D1
San José de Feliciano, Arg. 188/E4
San José de Guanipa, Ven. 181/E2
San José de Guaribe, Ven. 181/E2
San José de Jáchal, Arg. 188/B4
San Jose de la Banda (int'l arpt.), Bol. 188/C1
San José de la Esquina, Arg. 190/E2
San Jose de Los Molinos, Peru 184/C4
San José de los Remates, Nic. 176/E3
San José de Maipo, Chile 190/N8
San José de Mayo, Uru. 191/K11
San José de Raíces, Mex. 175/E3
San José de Río Chico, Ven. 183/P7
San José de Seque, Ven. 180/D2
San José de Tiznados, Ven. 183/N8
San José del Cabo, Mex. 174/C4
San José del Guaviare, Col. 180/C4
San Jose del Monte, Phil. 88/F6
San José del Ocuné, Col. 180/D3
San José Iturbide, Mex. 175/E4
San José Viejo, Mex. 174/C4
San Juan (cape), Arg. 191/E7
San Juan (prov.), Arg. 188/B4
San Juan, Arg. 188/B4
San Juan (riv.), Bol. 188/C1
San Juan, Bol. 188/E1
San Juan (riv.), Col. 180/B3
San Juan (cape), EqG. 120/B2
San Juan (pt.), ESal. 176/D3
San Juan (riv.), Nic. 172/E5
San Juan, Peru 184/C4
San Juan, Peru 184/C4
San Juan, Phil. 88/C2
San Juan, Phil. 88/D3
San Juan, PR 173/M8
San Juan (cr.), Ca, US 166/C4
San Juan (mts.), Co, US 142/E4
San Juan (basin), NM, US 149/H2
San Juan, NM, US 149/J4
San Juan (isl.), Wa, US 144/C3
San Juan Abajo, Mex. 174/D4
San Juan Bautista, Ca, US 148/B2
San Juan Bautista, Par. 189/E3
San Juan Bautista Coixtlahuaca, Mex. 176/B2
San Juan Bautista de Ñeembucú, Par. 188/E3
San Juan Bautista Tuxtepec, Mex. 176/B2
San Juan Bautista Valle Nacional, Mex. 176/B2
San Juan Capistrano, Ca, US 166/C3
San Juan de Alicante, Sp. 47/E3
San Juan de Aznalfarache, Sp. 46/B4
San Juan de la Costa, Mex. 174/C3
San Juan de Lima, (pt.), Mex. 174/E5
San Juan de los Cayos, Ven. 180/D2
San Juan de los Lagos, Mex. 174/E4
San Juan de los Morros, Ven. 183/N8
San Juan de Manapiare, Ven. 181/E3
San Juan de Ríoseco, Col. 183/L8
San Juan del Norte, Nic. 177/F4
San Juan del Piray, Bol. 188/C2
San Juan del Potrero, Bol. 188/C1
San Juan del Río, Mex. 175/F4
San Juan Guichicovi, Mex. 172/B4
San Juan Hot Springs, Ca, US 166/C3
San Juan Ixcaquixtla, Mex. 175/M8
San Juan Juquila Mixes, Mex. 176/C2
San Juan Nat'l Wild. Ref., Wa, US 144/C3
San Juan Nepomuceno, Col. 180/C2
San Juan Nepomuceno, Par. 189/F3
San Juan Pueblo, NM, US 149/J2
San Juanico, Mex. 174/B3
San Juanico Punta (pt.), Mex. 174/B3
San Juanito, Mex. 174/D2
San Justo, Arg. 188/D4
San Lázaro, Par. 188/E2
San Lázaro (cape), Mex. 174/B3
San Lazzaro, It. 63/E5
San Leandro (res.), Ca, US 167/K11
San Leandro, Ca, US 167/K11
San Leon, Tx, US 151/N9
San Leonardo in Passiria (Sankt Leonhard in Passeier), It. 61/H4
San Lorenzo, Bol. 185/E4
San Lorenzo, Bol. 185/E3
San Lorenzo, Bol. 188/C2
San Lorenzo (peak), Chile 191/B5
San Lorenzo, Ecu. 180/B4
San Lorenzo, Hon. 176/E3
San Lorenzo (cape), It. 48/A3
San Lorenzo (riv.), Mex. 174/D3
San Lorenzo, Nic. 176/E3
San Lorenzo, Peru 184/D3
San Lorenzo, Ca, US 167/K11
San Lorenzo, NM, US 149/J4
San Lorenzo al Mare, It. 62/A5
San Lorenzo de El Escorial, Sp. 47/M8
San Lorenzo in Campo, It. 63/F6
San Lucas, Nic. 176/E3
San Lucas, Bol. 188/C2
San Lucas, Cabo (cape), Mex. 174/C4
San Luis, Arg. 190/D2
San Luis (prov.), Arg. 188/C5
San Lucas, Ca, US 148/B2
San Luis (lake), Bol. 185/E4
San Luis, Bol. 188/E1
San Luis, Col. 183/K8
San Luís, Col. 183/L6
San Luis, Cuba 177/H1
San Luis, Guat. 176/D2
San Luis, Peru 184/B4
San Luis, Ven. 180/D2
San Luis, Az, US 148/E4
San Luis (dam), Ca, US 148/B2
San Luis (res.), Ca, US 148/B2
San Luis (cr.), Co, US 149/K1
San Luis, Co, US 152/B2
San Luis (valley), Co, US 149/J2
San Luis Acatlán, Mex. 176/B2
San Luis al Medio, Uru. 191/G2
San Luis Archaeological Site, Fl, US 165/F2
San Luis de la Paz, Mex. 175/E4
San Luis NWR, Ca, US 148/B2
San Luis Obispo, Ca, US 148/B3
San Luis Potosí (state), Mex. 172/A3
San Luis Potosí, Mex. 175/E4
San Luis Rey (riv.), Ca, US 166/C4
San Luis Rey, Ca, US 166/C4
San Manuel, Az, US 149/G4
San Manuel, Chile 188/B3
San Marcello Pistoiese, It. 63/D5
San Marco (peak), It. 65/D5
San Marco dei Cavoti, It. 65/D5
San Marco la Catola, It. 65/D4
San Marcos, Col. 180/C2
San Marcos, CR 177/E4
San Marcos, Guat. 176/D3
San Marcos, Mex. 172/B4
San Marcos, Peru 184/B2
San Marcos, Peru 184/B3
San Marcos, Ca, US 166/C4
San Marcos (riv.), Tx, US 151/F3
San Marcos, Tx, US 151/F3
San Maria di Porto Novo, It. 63/G6
San Mariano, Phil. 88/C1
San Marino (ctry.) 63/F5
San Marino (cap.), SMar. 63/F5
San Marino, Ca, US 166/F7
San Martín, Arg. 190/C2
San Martín (lake), Arg. 179/B7
San Martín (riv.), Bol. 185/F4
San Martín, Col. 180/C4
San Martín, Mex. 175/R9
San Martín, Peru 180/C5
San Martín (dept.), Peru 184/B2
San Martin (cape), Ca, US 148/B3
San Martin, Ca, US 148/B2
San Martin Cuautlalpan, Mex. 175/R10
San Martín de los Andes, Arg. 190/C4
San Martín de Valdeiglesias, Sp. 46/C2
San Martín Número Dos, Arg. 188/E3
San Martino al Cimino, It. 65/B3

Map Section
268
269

San Mar – Santo D

San Martino Buon Albergo, It. 63/E3
San Martino di Lupari, It. 63/E2
San Martino di Venezze, It. 63/E3
San Martino in Passiria (Sankt Martin in Passieir), It. 61/H4
San Martino in Pensilis, It. 65/E4
San Martino in Rio, It. 63/D4
San Martino in Strada, It. 62/C3
San Martino Siccomario, It. 62/C3
San Martino-di-Lota, Fr. 48/A1
San Mateo, Phil. 88/F6
San Mateo, Peru 184/B3
San Mateo, Sp. 47/F2
San Mateo (cr.), Ca, US 166/C4
San Mateo (co.), Ca, US 167/K12
San Mateo, Fl, US 165/H3
San Mateo, NM, US 149/J3
San Mateo (mts.), NM, US 149/J3
San Mateo, Ven. 181/E2
San Mateo, Ven. 183/N7
San Mateo Atarasquillo, Mex. 175/Q10
San Mateo Xoloc, Mex. 175/Q9
San Matías (gulf), Arg. 179/C7
San Matías, Bol. 185/G5
San Mauricio, Ven. 181/E2
San Maurizio d'Opaglio, It. 62/B2
San Mauro Pascoli, It. 63/F5
San Mauro Torinese, It. 62/A2
San Michele al Tagliamento, It. 63/F2
San Miguel, Arg. 188/E4
San Miguel, Bol. 185/E4
San Miguel, Bol. 185/F5
San Miguel (riv.), Bol. 188/D1
San Miguel (riv.), Bol. 185/F4
San Miguel (riv.), Col. 180/B4
San Miguel, ESal. 176/D3
San Miguel, Mex. 150/C3
San Miguel (gulf), Pan. 177/G4
San Miguel, Pan. 180/B2
San Miguel, Peru 184/C4
San Miguel, Peru 184/B2
San Miguel (bay), Phil. 88/C2
San Miguel (isl.), Ca, US 148/B3
San Miguel (riv.), Co, US 149/H1
San Miguel, NM, US 149/J4
San Miguel (cr.), Tx, US 151/E3
San Miguel Coatlincham, Mex. 175/R10
San Miguel de Allende, Mex. 175/E4
San Miguel de Huachi, Bol. 185/E4
San Miguel de los Bancos, Ecu. 180/B4
San Miguel de Tucumán, Arg. 188/C3
San Miguel del Monte, Arg. 191/J11
San Miguel Tlaixpan, Mex. 175/R9
San Miguel Totolapan, Mex. 172/A4
San Miguelito, Bol. 184/D3
San Miguelito, Bol. 185/F5
San Miniato, It. 63/D6
San Nicola la Strada, It. 65/D5
San Nicolas (isl.), Ca, US 148/C4
San Nicolás de los Arroyos, Arg. 190/E2
San Nicolò, It. 62/C3
San Nicolò a Tordino, It. 65/C2
San Onofre, Col. 180/C2
San Onofre, Ca, US 166/C4
San Onofre (mtn.), Ca, US 166/C4
San Pablo, Bol. 184/D5
San Pablo, Bol. 185/F4
San Pablo, Chile 190/B4
San Pablo, Col. 180/B4
San Pablo, Peru 184/B2
San Pablo, Phil. 88/C2
San Pablo (int'l arpt.), Sp. 46/C4
San Pablo, Ven. 181/E2
San Pablo (res.), Ca, US 167/K11
San Pablo, Ca, US 167/K11
San Pablo (bay), Ca, US 146/B4
San Pablo, Co, US 152/B2
San Pablo Bay NWR, Ca, US 167/K10
San Pablo de Borbur, Col. 183/L7
San Pablo de las Salinas, Mex. 175/Q9
San Pablo de Lipez, Bol. 188/C2
San Pablo Huixtepec, Mex. 176/B2
San Paolo, It. 62/D3
San Pascual, Phil. 88/C2
San Pawl il-Baħar, Malta 48/L7
San Pédro, C.d'Iv. 114/D5
San Pedro, Arg. 191/J10
San Pedro, Arg. 188/C3
San Pedro, Belz. 176/E2
San Pedro, Bol. 188/C1
San Pedro, Bol. 185/E4
San Pedro, Bol. 185/E3
San Pedro, Bol. 185/F5
San Pedro, Bol. 184/E3
San Pedro, Chile 188/B2
San Pedro (pt.), Chile 188/B3
San Pedro, Chile 190/N8
San Pedro (vol.), Chile 188/B2
San Pedro, Col. 183/K6
San Pedro (riv.), Guat. 176/D2
San Pedro (riv.), Mex.,US 149/G4
San Pedro (dept.), Par. 186/A4
San Pedro, Par. 189/E3
San Pedro (mts.), Sp. 46/B3
San Pedro (riv.), Az, US 149/G4
San Pedro (nbrhd.), Ca, US 166/F8
San Pedro (chan.), Ca, US 148/C4
San Pedro Arriba, Mex. 175/Q10
San Pedro Carchá, Guat. 176/D3
San Pedro de Arimena, Col. 180/D3
San Pedro de Cajas, Peru 184/C3
San Pedro de Cururu, Bol. 185/F4
San Pedro de la Cueva, Mex. 174/C2
San Pedro de Las Bocas, Ven. 181/F3
San Pedro de Lloc, Peru 184/B2
San Pedro de Lóvago, Nic. 177/E3
San Pedro de Macorís, DRep. 173/H4
San Pedro del Paraná, Par. 189/E3
San Pedro del Pinatar, Sp. 47/E4
San Pedro Huamelula, Mex. 176/C2
San Pedro Pochutla, Mex. 176/B3
San Pedro Sula, Hon. 176/D3
San Pedro Tapanatepec, Mex. 176/C2
San Pedro Totoltepec, Mex. 175/Q10
San Pellegrino Terme, It. 62/C2
San Perlita, Tx, US 151/F4
San Piero a Sieve, It. 63/E6
San Piero in Bagno, It. 63/E6
San Pierre, In, US 160/C4
San Pietro (isl.), It. 66/E3
San Pietro in Casale, It. 63/E4
San Pietro in Gù, It. 63/E2
San Pietro in Vincoli, It. 63/F5
San Pietro in Volta, It. 63/F3
San Pitch (riv.), Ut, US 147/H4
San Polo d'Enza, It. 62/D4
San Polo di Piave, It. 63/F2
San Possidonio, It. 63/D4
San Prisco, It. 65/D5
San Quentin, Ca, US 167/K11
San Quintín, Mex. 174/B2
San Quintín (cape), Mex. 174/B2
San Rafael, Arg. 190/C2
San Rafael, Bol. 184/D4
San Rafael, Bol. 185/F5
San Rafael, Chile 190/C2
San Rafael, Col. 183/K6
San Rafael, Mex. 175/N6
San Rafael, Peru 184/B3
San Rafael, Peru 184/B2
San Rafael (mts.), Ca, US 148/C3
San Rafael (hills), Ca, US 166/F7
San Rafael (riv.), Ut, US 147/H4
San Rafael, Ca, US 146/B5
San Rafael (des.), Ut, US 147/H4
San Rafael, NM, US 149/J3
San Rafael de Orituco, Ven. 183/P8
San Rafael del Moján, Ven. 180/D2
San Rafael Swell (upland), Ut, US 147/H4
San Ramón, Bol. 185/E4
San Ramón, Bol. 185/F4
San Ramón, CR 177/E4
San Ramón, Peru 184/C3
San Ramón, Uru. 191/L11
San Ramon, Ca, US 167/L11
San Ramón de la Nueva Orán, Arg. 188/C2
San Remo, It. 62/A5
San Rocco al Porto, It. 62/C3
San Romano, It. 63/D6
San Roque, Sp. 46/C4
San Roque, Col. 183/K6
San Rosendo, Chile 190/B3
San Saba, Tx, US 151/E2
San Saba (riv.), Tx, US 175/F2
San Salvador (cap.), ESal. 176/D3
San Salvador (riv.), Uru. 191/J10
San Salvador (isl.), Ecu. 184/J7
San Salvador, Arg. 188/E4
San Salvador (Watling) (isl.), Bahm. 173/G3
San Salvador de Jujuy, Arg. 188/C3
San Salvador el Seco, Mex. 175/M7
San Salvador, Isla (isl.), Bahm. 173/G3
San Salvatore Monferrato, It. 62/B4
San Salvo, It. 65/D3
San Sebastián, Sp. 44/C5
San Sebastián, Arg. 191/C7
San Sebastián, Ven. 183/N8
San Sebastián de los Reyes, Sp. 47/N8
San Sebastián de Yalí, Nic. 176/E3
San Sebastiano, It. 62/D2
San Secondo Parmense, It. 62/D4
San Severino Marche, It. 65/C1
San Severo, It. 48/D2
San Simeon, Ca, US 148/B3
San Simon (riv.), Az, US 149/H4
San Simón, Bol. 185/F4
San Simon Wash (riv.), Az, US 149/F4
San Telmo, (pt.), Mex. 174/E5
San Timoteo, Ven. 180/D2
San Tomé, Ven. 181/E2
San Valentín (peak), Chile 190/B5
San Valentino, It. 63/G2
San Vicente, Arg. 188/D4
San Vicente, Chile 190/C2
San Vicente, Chile 190/N9
San Vicente, ESal. 176/D3
San Vicente, Mex. 174/A2
San Vicente (res.), Ca, US 166/D5
San Vicente, Ven. 180/E3
San Vicente de Alcántara, Sp. 46/B3
San Vicente de Cañete, Peru 184/B4
San Vicente del Caguán, Col. 180/C4
San Vicente del Raspeig, Sp. 47/E3
San Vincenzo, It. 45/J5
San Vito (cape), It. 48/C3
San Vito, CR 177/F4
San Vito al Tagliamento, It. 63/F2
San Vito Chietino, It. 65/D3
San Vito Romano, It. 65/B4
San Xavier Ind. Res., Az, US 149/G4
San Ygnacio, Tx, US 150/E4
San Ysidro, Ca, US 166/C5
San Ysidro, NM, US 149/J3
Sana (riv.), Bosn. 50/C3
Sanā', Yem. 118/D1
Saña, Peru 184/B2
Şan'ā (Sanaa) (cap.), Yem. 118/C2
Sanaa (int'l arpt.), Yem. 118/C2
Sanaa (Şan'ā) (cap.), Yem. 118/C2
Sanae IV, SAfr., Ant. 192/Z
Sanafā, Egypt 113/C3
Sanaga (riv.), Camr. 107/C4
Sanajärvi (lake), Fin. 39/F4
Sanak (isl.), Ak, US 171/F5
Sanām, SAr. 100/D4
Sanana (isl.), Indo. 91/G4
Sanandaj, Iran 103/F3
Sanandita, Bol. 188/D2
Sananduva, Braz. 189/G3
Sanankoroba, Mali 114/D3
Sanary-sur-Mer, Fr. 64/B6
Sanatorium, Ms, US 164/D2
Sanaur, India 98/D4
Sanāw, Yem. 100/F5
Sānāwad, India 92/C3
Sanborn, ND, US 156/E4
Sanborn, Mn, US 155/G1
Sanborn, NY, US 160/V9
Sanbu, China 78/E4
Sancha, China 87/F3
Sancha, China 78/E5
Sancha (riv.), China 86/E3
Sanchahe, China 81/B2
Sánchez Grande, Uru. 191/K10
Sanch'ŏng, SKor. 81/D5
Sanco, Tx, US 150/D1
Sancti Spíritu, Arg. 190/E2
Sancti Spíritus, Cuba 177/G1
Sand, Nor. 40/B2
Sand (hills), Ne, US 142/F3
Sand (cr.), SD, US 154/E1
Sand (pt.), Eng, UK 36/D4
Sand (riv.), SAfr. 124/D3
Sand am Main, Ger. 58/D3
Sand Arroyo (riv.), Ks,Co, US 152/D2
Sand Coulee, Mt, US 145/J4
Sand Draw (riv.), Ne,Co, US 154/D3
Sand Key (isl.), Fl, US 164/K8
Sand Lake, Tx, US 150/L7
Sand Lake NWR, SD, US 156/E5
Sand Lake NWR, SD, US 154/E1
Sand Patch (pt.), Austl. 133/D3
Sand Point, Ak, US 171/F4
Sandspit, BC, Can. 171/M5
Sand Springs, Mt, US 145/L4
Sanda (isl.), Sc, UK 34/C1
Sanda, Japan 83/H6
Sandakan, Malay. 88/B4
Sandan, Camb. 94/D3
Sandane, Nor. 38/C3
Sandanski, Bul. 75/H2
Sandaré, Mali 114/C3
Sandarne, Swe. 40/G1
Sanday (isl.), Sc, UK 31/V14
Sandbach, Eng, UK 35/F5
Sandberg, Ger. 58/C2
Sandborn, In, US 162/D1
Sande, Nor. 38/R9
Sande, Ger. 53/F1
Sandebukta (bay), Nor. 38/R9
Sandefjord, Nor. 40/D2
Sanderson, Tx, US 150/C2
Sandersville, Ms, US 164/D2
Sandersville, Ga, US 163/F4
Sandgate (nbrhd.), Austl. 134/F6
Sandhamn, Swe. 39/B1
Sandhead, Sc, UK 34/D2
Sandhill, On, Can. 160/T8
Sandhurst, Eng, UK 37/F4
Sandia, Peru 184/D4
Sandia Mil. Res., NM, US 149/J3
Sandia Park, NM, US 149/J3
Sandia Peak Tramway, NM, US 149/J3
Sandia Pueblo Ind. Res., NM, US 149/J3
Sandıklı, Turk. 102/B2
Sandīla, India 96/C2
Sandillon, Fr. 57/H5
Sanding (isl.), Indo. 89/C3
Sandino, Cuba 172/E3
Sandnes, Nor. 40/A2
Sandoa, D.R. Congo 121/E5
Sandomierz, Pol. 43/L3
Sandoná, Col. 180/B4
Sándorfalva, Hun. 50/E2
Sandougou (riv.), Sen. 114/B3
Sandoval, Il, US 162/C1
Sandover (riv.), Austl. 131/G2
Sandoway, Myan. 86/B5
Sandown, Eng, UK 37/E5
Sandpoint, Id, US 144/F3
Sandrakatsy, Madg. 125/J7
Sandrigo, It. 63/E2
Sandringham (nbrhd.), Austl. 132/G5
Sandrivier (riv.), SAfr. 123/F4
Sandrohy, Madg. 125/H8
Sands, Mi, US 157/L4
Sands (pt.), NY, US 169/L8
Sands Point, NY, US 169/L8
Sandstedt, Ger. 53/F2
Sandstone, Austl. 130/C3
Sandstone Nat'l Wild. Ref., Mn, US 157/H4
Sandu, China 87/G2
Sandu Shuizu Zizhixian, China 87/E3
Sandungen (lake), Nor. 38/S9
Sandusky, Mi, US 160/E3
Sandusky, Oh, US 160/E4
Sandusky (riv.), Oh, US 160/E4
Sandvika, Nor. 40/D2
Sandviken, Swe. 40/G1
Sandweiler, Lux. 55/F4
Sandwell (co.), Eng, UK 36/D2
Sandwich, Ma, US 161/L4
Sandwich, NH, US 161/L3
Sandwich (cape), Austl. 134/B2
Sandwich, Il, US 155/K3
Sandwich, Eng, UK 37/H4
Sandwīp (isl.), Bang. 97/H4
Sandy (lake), Nf., Can. 159/J1
Sandy (cape), Austl. 134/D4
Sandy, Ut, US 147/H3
Sandy (lake), On, Can. 140/G3
Sandy, Eng, UK 37/F2
Sandy (pt.), SC, US 163/G4
Sandy (pt.), RI, US 169/G1
Sandy Creek, NY, US 161/H3
Sandy Hook, Ky, US 163/F1
Sandy Hook (bay), NJ, US 168/D3
Sandy Hook (isl.), NJ, US 169/J10
Sandy Hook Lighthouse, NJ, US 169/J10
Sandy Lake, Mb, Can. 156/D2
Sandy Point, NS, Can. 158/E4
Sandy Springs, Ga, US 163/M7
Sandykachi, Trkm. 101/H1
Sandyville, WV, US 163/G1
Sanem, Lux. 55/E4
Sånfjällets NP, Swe. 38/E3
Sanford, Mb, Can. 156/F3
Sanford (mt.), Ak, US 171/K3
Sanford, Co, US 149/K2
Sanford, Fl, US 165/H3
Sanford, Me, US 161/L3
Sanford, Ms, US 164/D2
Sanford, NC, US 163/H3
Sanfront, It. 64/D3
Sanga, D.R. Congo 121/G4
Sanga, Ang. 122/B1
Sangachaly, Azer. 103/G1
Sangamon (riv.), Il, US 155/J3
Sangān (mtn.), Afg. 101/H2
Sangano, It. 64/D2
Sangar, Rus. 75/N3
Sangar Sarāy, Afg. 98/A2
Sangardo, Gui. 114/C4
Sangareddi, India 95/C2
Sangaréya, Gui. 114/B4
Sangaria, India 98/C5
Sangatte, Fr. 54/A2
Sangay (vol.), Ecu. 180/B5
Sangbé, Camr. 116/B4
Sange, D.R. Congo 121/G3
Sangejing, China 78/F3
Sangenjo, Sp. 46/A1
Sanger, Tx, US 153/F4
Sanger, Ca, US 148/C2
Sanggan (riv.), China 80/C2
Sanggarmai, China 86/D1
Sanggau, Indo. 90/D3
Sanggou (bay), China 81/B4
Sangha (pol. ref), Congo 120/C2
Sangha (pref.), CAfr. 116/B5
Sangha (riv.), D.R. Congo 116/C5
Sangha (riv.), CAfr. 107/D4
Sanghar, Pak. 101/J3
Sangihe (isl.), Phil. 77/M9
Sangihe (isl.), Indo. 91/G3
Sangiyn Dalay (lake), Mong. 78/D2
Sangiyn Dalay, Mong. 78/E2
Sangju, SKor. 81/E4
Sangkha, Thai. 94/C3
Sangkhla, Thai. 94/B3
Sangkulirang, Indo. 91/E3
Sāngla, Pak. 98/B4
Sangley Point Nav. Air Sta., Phil. 88/E7
Sangmélima, Camr. 120/C2
Sangō, Japan 83/J6
Sangpang (mts.), Myan. 86/B3
Sangre de Cristo (mts.), Co, US 154/B4
Sangre Grande, Trin. 181/F2
Sangri, China 97/J1
Sangro (riv.), It. 48/D2
Sangrūr, India 98/C4
Sangsang, China 97/F1
Sangster (int'l arpt.), Jam. 177/G2
Sangue, Rio do (riv.), Braz. 185/G3
Sangüesa, Sp. 44/C5
Sanguie (prov.), Burk. 115/E4
Sanguinetto, It. 63/E3
Sangwŏn, NKor. 81/D3
Sanha (pref), Afr. 120/C2
Sanhe, China 80/H7
Sanhuang, China 87/F3
Sanhūr, Egypt 113/B6
Sani (pass), Les. 124/E3
Sāni Bheri (riv.), Nepal 96/D1
Sanibel (isl.), Fl, US 165/G4
San'in Kaigin NP, Japan 84/D3
Saniquellie, Libr. 114/C5
Sanito, Phil. 88/C4
Sanjahā, Egypt 113/C3
Sanje, Zam. 123/E2
Sanjia, China 87/F4
Sanjiang, China 87/E2
Sanjō, Japan 85/F2
Sankanbiriwa (peak), SLeo. 114/C4
Sankeyushu, China 81/C2
Sankh (riv.), India 97/E4
Sānko, India 98/C2
Sankoroni (riv.), Gui. 114/C4
Sankosh (riv.), India 97/G2
Sānkra, India 101/K3
Sankt Aegyd am Neuwalde, Aus. 45/L3
Sankt Agatha, Aus. 59/G6
Sankt Andrä-Wördern, Aus. 51/N7
Sankt Andreasberg, Ger. 53/H5
Sankt Anton am Arlberg, Aus. 61/G3
Sankt Augustin, Ger. 55/G2
Sankt Blasien, Ger. 60/E2
Sankt Florian am Inn, Aus. 59/G6
Sankt Gallen, Swi. 61/F3
Sankt Gallenkirch, Aus. 61/F3
Sankt Georgen bei Salzburg, Aus. 59/F7
Sankt Georgen im Attergau, Aus. 59/G7
Sankt Georgen im Schwarzwald, Ger. 61/E1
Sankt Goar, Ger. 55/G3
Sankt Goarshausen, Ger. 55/G3
Sankt Ingbert, Ger. 55/G5
Sankt Jakob (San Giacomo), It. 61/H4
Sankt Johann am Walde, Aus. 59/G6
Sankt Johann im Pongau, Aus. 45/K3
Sankt Johann in Tirol, Aus. 45/K3
Sankt Leonhard im Pitztal, Aus. 61/G3
Sankt Leonhard in Passeier (San Leonardo in Passiria), It. 61/H4
Sankt Marien, Aus. 59/H6
Sankt Martin im Mühlkreis, Aus. 59/H6
Sankt Martin in Passeier (San Martino in Passiria), It. 61/H4
Sankt Michael in Obersteiermark, Aus. 45/L3
Sankt Moritz, Swi. 61/F5
Sankt Moritz (Saint Moritz), Swi. 45/H3
Sankt Oswald bei Freistadt, Aus. 59/H5
Sankt Pantaleon, Aus. 59/F6
Sankt Pauli, Ger. 53/G1
Sankt Peter am Hart, Aus. 59/G6
Sankt Peter in der Au, Aus. 59/H6
Sankt Peter-Ording, Ger. 40/C4
Sankt Pölten, Aus. 43/H4
Sankt Stephan, Swi. 60/D4
Sankt Ulrich bei Steyr, Aus. 59/H6
Sankt Valentin, Aus. 59/H6
Sankt Veit, Aus. 50/B1
Sankt Veit an der Glan, Aus. 45/L3
Sankt Wendel, Ger. 55/G5
Sankt Wolfgang, Ger. 59/F6
Sankuru (riv.), D.R. Congo 121/E4
Sanlong, China 79/J5
Sanlúcar de Barrameda, Sp. 46/B4
Sanmatenga (prov.), Burk. 115/E3
Sanmenxia, China 80/B4
Sanming, China 87/H3
Sannan, Japan 83/H5
Sannār, Sudan 116/G2
Sannazzaro de'Burgondi, It. 62/B3
Sannicandro Garganico, It. 48/D2
Sannikova (str.), Rus. 75/P2
Sannio (mts.), It. 65/D5
San'nohe, Japan 82/B3
Sannois, Fr. 30/J5
Sannūr (wadi), Egypt 113/C6
Sano, Japan 85/F2
Sañogasta, Arg. 188/C4
Sanok, Pol. 43/M4
Sanostee, NM, US 149/H2
Sanpoil (riv.), Wa, US 144/E3
Sanqiao, China 80/K9
Sanquhar, Sc, UK 33/C6
Sanquianga, PN, Col. 180/B4
Sans Bois (mts.), Ok, US 153/G3
Sansalé, Gui. 114/B4
Sansepolcro, It. 63/F6
Sansha, China 87/J3
Sanshilipu, China 78/F4
Sansui, China 87/F3
Sant Adrià de Besòs, Sp. 47/L7
Sant 'Antioco (isl.), It. 66/E3
Sant Boi de Llobregat, Sp. 47/L7
Sant Carles de la Ràpita, Sp. 47/F2
Sant Celoni, Sp. 47/L6
Sant Cugat del Vallès, Sp. 47/L7
Sant Eeufemia (gulf), It. 48/D3
Sant Feliu de Guíxols, Sp. 47/G2
Sant Feliu de Llobregat, Sp. 47/L7
Sant Julia, And. 44/D5
Sant Pere de Ribes, Sp. 47/K7
Sant Sadurní d'Anoia, Sp. 47/K7
Sant Vicenç de Castellet, Sp. 47/K6
Sant Vicenç dels Horts, Sp. 47/L7
Santa (riv.), Peru 184/B3
Santa, Peru 184/B3
Santa, Id, US 144/F4
Santa Ana, Bol. 188/E1
Santa Ana, Bol. 185/F5
Santa Ana, Bol. 185/E4
Santa Ana, Col. 180/D4
Santa Ana, Ecu. 180/A5
Santa Ana, ESal. 176/D3
Santa Ana (vol.), ESal. 176/D3
Santa Ana, Hon. 176/E3
Santa Ana, Mex. 174/C2
Santa Ana (riv.), Ca, US 166/C3
Santa Ana (riv.), Ca, US 166/C3
Santa Ana (mts.), Ca, US 166/C3
Santa Ana, Ca, US 166/G8
Santa Ana (mts.), Ca, US 148/D4
Santa Ana, Ven. 180/C3
Santa Ana, Ven. 180/D2
Santa Ana, Ven. 182/A1
Santa Ana del Alto Beni, Bol. 185/E4
Santa Ana Ind. Res., NM, US 152/A3
Santa Ana Ind. Res., NM, US 149/J3
Santa Ana Nat'l Wild. Ref., Tx, US 151/E4
Santa Anna, Tx, US 150/E2
Santa Bárbara, Braz. 187/E3
Santa Bárbara, Chile 190/B3
Santa Bárbara, Col. 183/K7
Santa Bárbara, Hon. 176/D3
Santa Bárbara, Mex. 174/D3
Santa Barbara, Phil. 88/C1
Santa Barbara, Ca, US 166/A2
Santa Barbara (chan.), Ca, US 148/B3
Santa Barbara (isl.), Ca, US 148/C4
Santa Barbara (co.), Ca, US 166/A1
Santa Bárbara, Ven. 181/E4
Santa Bárbara, Ven. 180/D2
Santa Bárbara, Ven. 180/D3
Santa Bárbara d'Oeste, Braz. 189/H2
Santa Barbara Mountains NRA, Ca, US 166/E7
Santa Catalina, Ven. 180/D3
Santa Catalina, Pan. 177/F4
Santa Catalina (isl.), CA, US 142/B5
Santa Catalina (gulf), Ca, US 148/D4
Santa Catalina, Phil. 88/C3
Santa Catarina (isl.), Braz. 189/G3
Santa Catarina (state), Braz. 189/G3
Santa Catarina, Mex. 175/E3
Santa Clara, Cuba 177/G1
Santa Clara, Mex. 174/E3
Santa Clara (res.), Port. 46/A4
Santa Clara (riv.), Ca, US 166/B2
Santa Clara, Ca, US 167/L12
Santa Clara (co.), Ca, US 167/L12
Santa Clara, Ca, US 148/B2
Santa Clara, Ut, US 149/F2
Santa Clara, Ven. 181/E2
Santa Clara de Olimar, Uru. 191/G2
Santa Clarita, Ca, US 166/B2
Santa Claus, In, US 162/D1
Santa Clotilde, Peru 180/C5
Santa Coloma de Farners, Sp. 47/G2
Santa Coloma de Gramanet, Sp. 47/L7
Santa Comba, Sp. 46/A1
Santa Croce (peak), It. 65/C5
Santa Croce di Magliano, It. 65/D4
Santa Croce sull'Arno, It. 63/D6
Santa Cruz, Ang. 120/D4
Santa Cruz (prov.), Arg. 190/C5
Santa Cruz (riv.), Arg. 179/B8
Santa Cruz (riv.), Bol. 185/F5
Santa Cruz, Braz. 183/G4
Santa Cruz, Chile 190/C2
Santa Cruz, CR 176/E4
Santa Cruz (isl.), Ecu. 184/J7
Santa Cruz (mts.), Guat. 176/D3
Santa Cruz, Mex. 149/G5
Santa Cruz (riv.), Mex.,US 149/G5
Santa Cruz, Peru 184/C2
Santa Cruz, Phil. 88/D4
Santa Cruz, Phil. 88/B2
Santa Cruz, Phil. 88/C1
Santa Cruz, Phil. 88/C2
Santa Cruz, SaoT. 120/A2
Santa Cruz (isls.), Sol. 136/F6
Santa Cruz (isl.), Ca, US 148/C4
Santa Cruz da Graciosa, Azor., Port. 47/S12
Santa Cruz das Flores, Azor., Port. 47/R12
Santa Cruz de Bucaral, Ven. 180/D2
Santa Cruz de El Seibo, DRep. 173/H4
Santa Cruz de la Palma, Sp. 110/A3
Santa Cruz de la Sierra, Bol. 188/D1
Santa Cruz de la Zarza, Sp. 46/D3
Santa Cruz de Mudela, Sp. 46/D3
Santa Cruz de Orinoco, Ven. 181/E2
Santa Cruz de Tenerife, Sp. 110/A3
Santa Cruz del Quiché, Guat. 176/D3
Santa Cruz del Sur, Cuba 177/G1
Santa Cruz do Capibaribe, Braz. 183/G4
Santa Cruz do Cuando, Ang. 122/D3
Santa Cruz do Piauí, Braz. 183/F4
Santa Cruz do Rio Pardo, Braz. 189/G2
Santa Cruz do Sul, Braz. 189/F4
Santa Elena, Arg. 188/D4
Santa Elena, Arg. 188/E4
Santa Elena, Bol. 188/C2
Santa Elena, Hon. 176/E2
Santa Elena (bay), CR 176/E4
Santa Elena, Ecu. 180/A5
Santa Elena (cape), CR 176/E4
Santa Elena (peak), Arg. 190/D5
Santa Elena, Peru 184/C2
Santa Elena de Turuchipa, Bol. 188/C1
Santa Elena de Uairén, Ven. 181/F3
Santa Eugenia de Ribeira, Sp. 46/A1
Santa Eulalia del Río, Sp. 47/F3
Santa Fe, Arg. 188/D4
Santa Fe (prov.), Arg. 188/D4
Santa Fe, Bol. 185/E3
Santa Fe, Cuba 177/F1
Santa Fé, Sp. 46/D4
Santa Fe (riv.), Fl, US 165/G3
Santa Fe (lake), Fl, US 165/G3
Santa Fe (cap.), NM, US 149/K3
Santa Fe (mts.), NM, US 152/B3
Santa Fe, Tx, US 151/M9
Santa Fé do Sul, Braz. 189/G2
Santa Fe Springs, Ca, US 166/F8
Santa Felicia (dam), Ca, US 166/B2
Santa Filomena, Braz. 183/E5
Santa Giustina (lake), It. 61/H5
Santa Helena, Braz. 183/E3
Santa Helena, Braz. 189/F3
Santa Helena de Goiás, Braz. 186/C3
Santa Inés (isl.), Chile 191/B7
Santa Inês, Braz. 187/F2
Santa Inês, Braz. 183/E3
Santa Isabel, Arg. 190/E2
Santa Isabel, Arg. 190/D3
Santa Isabel, Braz. 187/K8
Santa Isabel, Bol. 188/C2
Santa Isabel, Col. 177/F3
Santa Isabel, Ecu. 184/B1
Santa Isabel (riv.), Guat. 176/D2
Santa Isabel (isl.), Sol. 136/E5
Santa Isabel, Ven. 181/E4
Santa Isabel de Sihuas, Peru 184/C5
Santa Isabel do Ivaí, Braz. 189/F2
Santa Isabel do Pará, Braz. 182/D3
Santa Isabel, Pico de (peak), EqG. 120/B2
Santa Juliana, Braz. 186/D3
Santa Lucía, Arg. 188/E4
Santa Lucia (riv.), Arg. 189/E4
Santa Lucía, Ecu. 180/B5
Santa Lucía, Peru 184/D4
Santa Lucía, Uru. 191/K11
Santa Lucía, Sp. 110/B4
Santa Lucía, Ven. 183/P7
Santa Lucia (range), Ca, US 148/B2
Santa Lucía, Ven. 180/D2
Santa Lucia di Piave, It. 63/F2
Santa Luz, Braz. 187/F1
Santa Luzia (isl.), CpV. 107/J10
Santa Luzia, Braz. 183/G4
Santa Luzia, Braz. 183/E3
Santa Magdalena, Arg. 190/E2
Santa Magdalena (isl.), Mex. 174/B3
Santa Margarita (isl.), Mex. 174/B3
Santa Margarita (riv.), Ca, US 166/C4
Santa Margarita (riv.), Ca, US 148/D4
Santa Margherita Ligure, It. 62/C5
Santa María, Arg. 188/C3
Santa María, Bol. 188/D1
Santa María, Bol. 185/F4
Santa María, Chile 190/N8
Santa María, Ecu. 184/J7
Santa María (isl.), Ecu. 184/J7
Santa Mariá, Mex. 175/L7
Santa María (riv.), Mex. 174/D2
Santa María (bay), Mex. 174/C3
Santa Maria (cape), Port. 46/B4
Santa María, Ven. 181/E3
Santa Maria, Braz. 189/F4
Santa Maria (riv.), Braz. 189/F4
Santa Maria (isl.), Chile 190/B3
Santa Maria, CpV. 107/K10
Santa Maria, Phil. 88/D4
Santa Maria, Phil. 88/C1
Santa Maria, Phil. 88/E6
Santa Maria (isl.), Azor., Port. 47/T13
Santa Maria, Ca, US 148/B3
Santa Maria a Monte, It. 63/D6
Santa Maria a Vico, It. 65/D5
Santa Maria Capua Vetere, It. 65/D5
Santa Maria da Boa Vista, Braz. 183/G5
Santa Maria da Vitória, Braz. 186/D2
Santa María de Cayón, Sp. 46/D1
Santa María de Erebató, Ven. 181/E3
Santa María de Ipire, Ven. 181/E2
Santa María de Nanay, Peru 184/C1
Santa Maria degli Angeli, It. 65/B1
Santa María del Oro, Mex. 174/D3
Santa Maria della Versa, It. 62/C4
Santa Maria di Leuca (cape), It. 67/H3
Santa Maria di Leuca, Capo (cape), It. 75/F3
Santa Maria do Pará, Braz. 183/E3
Santa Maria do Suaçui, Braz. 187/E3
Santa Maria la Carità, It. 65/D6
Santa Maria la Fossa, It. 65/D5
Santa Maria Maddalena, It. 63/E4
Santa Maria Maggiore, It. 61/E5
Santa Maria Nuova, It. 63/G7
Santa María Xadani, Mex. 172/B4
Santa Maria, Cabo de (cape), Moz. 125/F2
Santa Marta, Col. 180/C2
Santa Marta Grande, Cabo de (cape), Braz. 189/G4
Santa Marta, Sierra Nevada de (mts.), Col. 180/C2
Santa Monica (bay), Ca, US 166/B3
Santa Monica (mts.), Ca, US 166/B2
Santa Monica, Ca, US 166/F7
Santa Monica Mountains NRA, Ca, US 166/B2
Santa Olalla del Cala, Sp. 46/B4
Santa Paula (peak), Ca, US 166/A2
Santa Paula, Ca, US 166/A2
Santa Pola, Sp. 47/E3
Santa Pola, Cabo de (cape), Sp. 47/E3
Santa Quitéria, Braz. 183/F4
Santa Quitéria do Maranhão, Braz. 183/F3
Santa Rita, Braz. 183/H4
Santa Rita, Braz. 183/E3
Santa Rita, NM, US 149/H4
Santa Rita, Ven. 181/E2
Santa Rita, Ven. 180/D2
Santa Rita de Cássia, Braz. 186/D1
Santa Rita do Sapucaí, Braz. 187/L7
Santa Rosa, Arg. 188/C5
Santa Rosa, Arg. 188/C2
Santa Rosa, Arg. 190/D3
Santa Rosa, Braz. 189/F3
Santa Rosa, Bol. 185/E4
Santa Rosa, CR 176/E4
Santa Rosa, Uru. 191/K11
Santa Rosa, Bol. 185/E3
Santa Rosa, Bol. 188/C1
Santa Rosa, Braz. 182/C4
Santa Rosa, Par. 189/E3
Santa Rosa, Ecu. 184/B1
Santa Rosa, Peru 184/D4
Santa Rosa, Ca, US 146/B4
Santa Rosa (range), Nv, US 146/E3
Santa Rosa (isl.), Ca, US 148/C4
Santa Rosa, NM, US 152/B3
Santa Rosa (mts.), Nv, US 142/C3
Santa Rosa, Ven. 180/D3
Santa Rosa, Ven. 180/D2
Santa Rosa, Ven. 180/E3
Santa Rosa and San Jacinto Mountains NM, Ca, US 148/D4
Santa Rosa de Aguán, Hon. 176/E3
Santa Rosa de Amanadona, Ven. 181/E4
Santa Rosa de Cabal, Col. 183/K8
Santa Rosa de Calamuchita, Arg. 188/C5
Santa Rosa de Copán, Hon. 176/D3
Santa Rosa de la Roca, Bol. 185/F5
Santa Rosa de Osos, Col. 180/C3
Santa Rosa de Viterbo, Braz. 189/H2
Santa Rosa del Palmar, Bol. 185/F5
Santa Rosa del Sara, Bol. 188/D1
Santa Rosa Wash (riv.), Az, US 149/F4
Santa Rosa, PN 172/C5
Santa Rosalía (pt.), Mex. 174/B2
Santa Rosalía, Mex. 174/B3
Santa Rosalía, Ven. 180/D2
Santa Rosalía, Ven. 181/E3
Santa Sofia, It. 63/E6
Santa Susana (mts.), Ca, US 166/B2
Santa Teresa, Austl. 131/G3
Santa Teresa, Braz. 187/E3
Santa Teresa (riv.), Braz. 186/C2
Santa Teresa, Braz. 186/C2
Santa Teresa, Ven. 183/P7
Santa Teresa Abor. Land, Austl. 131/G2
Santa Teresa, PN, Uru. 191/G2
Santa Teresinha, Braz. 186/C1
Santa Teresita, Arg. 191/F3
Santa Victoria, Arg. 188/D2
Santa Vitória, Braz. 186/C3
Santa Vitória do Palmar, Braz. 191/G2
Santa Ynez (mts.), Ca, US 166/A2
Santa Ynez (riv.), Ca, US 148/C3
Santa Ynez Ind. Res., Ca, US 148/B3
Santa Ysabel Ind. Res., Ca, US 148/D4
Santaella, Sp. 46/C4
Sant'Agata Bolognese, It. 63/E4
Sant'Agata di Militello, It. 48/D3
Sant'Agata Feltria, It. 63/F6
Sant'Agnello, It. 65/D6
Sant'Agostino, It. 63/E4
Sāntāhār, Bang. 97/G3
Sant'Alberto, It. 63/F4
Santana, Braz. 186/D2
Santana (isl.), Braz. 183/F3
Santana, Port. 110/A2
Santana, Port. 47/P11
Santana da Boa Vista, Braz. 189/F4
Santana do Acaraú, Braz. 183/F3
Santana do Cariri, Braz. 183/G4
Santana do Ipanema, Braz. 183/G5
Santana do Livramento, Braz. 189/F4
Sant'Anastasia, It. 65/D6
Santander (dept.), Col. 177/H5
Santander, Sp. 46/D1
Santander, Phil. 88/C3
Santander de Quilichao, Col. 180/B4
Santander Jiménez, Mex. 175/F3
Sant'Andrea del Pizzone, It. 65/D5
Sant'Angelo in Formis, It. 65/D5
Sant'Angelo in Vado, It. 63/F6
Sant'Angelo Lodigiano, It. 62/C3
Sant'Antioco, It. 66/F3
Sant'Antioco (isl.), It. 48/A3
Sant'Antonino di Susa, It. 64/D2
Sant'Antonio, It. 63/D3
Sant'Antonio Abate, It. 65/D6
Santañy, Sp. 47/G3
Sant'Apollinare in Classe, It. 63/F5
Santaquin, Ut, US 147/H4
Santarcángelo, It. 63/F5
Santarém (dist.), Port. 46/A3
Santarém, Port. 46/A3
Santarém, Braz. 182/C3
Santarém Novo, Braz. 183/E3
Sant'Arsenio, It. 48/D2
Santee, Ca, US 166/D5
Santee (pt.), SC, US 163/H4
Santee (dam), SC, US 163/G4
Santee (riv.), SC, US 163/H4
Santee Ind. Res., Ne, US 154/F2
Santee Nat'l Wild. Ref., SC, US 163/G4
Sant'Egidio alla Vibrata, It. 65/C2
Sant'Elia a Pianisi, It. 65/D4
Sant'Elia Fiumerapido, It. 65/C4
Sant'Elpidio a Mare, It. 65/C1
Santena, It. 62/A3
Santerno (riv.), It. 45/J4
Santeuil, Fr. 30/H4
Santhia, It. 62/B3
Santiago, Bol. 188/D1
Santiago, Braz. 189/F4
Santiago (cape), Chile 191/B6
Santiago (cap.), Chile 190/N8
Santiago (riv.), Ecu. 184/B1
Santiago (pt.), EqG. 120/B2
Santiago (mtn.), Pan. 177/F4
Santiago, Pan. 180/A2
Santiago, Par. 189/E3
Santiago (riv.), Peru 180/B5
Santiago, Peru 184/C4
Santiago, Phil. 88/C1
Santiago (int'l arpt.), Sp. 46/A1
Santiago (peak), Ca, US 166/C3
Santiago (res.), Ca, US 166/C3
Santiago (mts.), Tx, US 150/C3
Santiago (peak), Tx, US 150/C3
Santiago (Arturo Merino Benitez) (int'l arpt.), Chile 190/N8
Santiago Cuautlalpan, Mex. 175/Q9
Santiago Cuautlalpan, Mex. 175/R10
Santiago de Cao, Peru 184/B2
Santiago de Chocorvos, Peru 184/C4
Santiago de Chuco, Peru 184/B3
Santiago de Compostela, Sp. 46/A1
Santiago de Cuba, Cuba 177/H1
Santiago de los Caballeros, DRep. 173/G4
Santiago de Machaca, Bol. 184/D5
Santiago de Pacaguaras, Bol. 184/D4
Santiago del Estero (prov.), Arg. 188/D3
Santiago del Estero, Arg. 188/C3
Santiago do Cacém, Port. 46/A3
Santiago Ixcuintla, Mex. 174/D4
Santiago Jamiltepec, Mex. 176/B2
Santiago Juxtlahuaca, Mex. 176/B2
Santiago Miahuatlán, Mex. 175/M8
Santiago Papasquiaro, Mex. 174/D3
Santiago Pinotepa Nacional, Mex. 176/B2
Santiago Tilapa, Mex. 175/Q10
Santiago Tolman, Mex. 175/R9
Santiago Vázquez, Uru. 191/K11
Santiago Zacatepec, Mex. 176/C2
Santiam, North (riv.), Or, US 146/B1
Santiam, South (riv.), Or, US 146/B1
Santigi, Indo. 91/F3
Sant'Ilario d'Enza, It. 62/D4
Sāntipur, India 97/G4
Säntis (peak), Swi. 61/F3
Santisteban del Puerto, Sp. 46/D3
Santō, Japan 83/K5
Santō, Japan 83/G5
Santo, Tx, US 151/E1
Santo Amaro, Braz. 187/F2
Santo Amara (isl.), Braz. 187/K8
Santo Amaro (isl.), Braz. 187/K8
Santo Amaro das Brotas, Braz. 187/F1
Santo Anastácio, Braz. 189/G2
Santo André, Braz. 187/K8
Santo Ângelo, Braz. 189/F4
Santo Antão (isl.), CpV. 107/J9
Santo António, SaoT. 120/A2
Santo Antônio do Içá, Braz. 180/E5
Santo Antônio do Leverger, Braz. 186/A2
Santo Antônio do Sudoeste, Braz. 189/F3
Santo Antônio dos Lopes, Braz. 183/E4
Santo Augusto, Braz. 189/F3
Santo Corazón, Bol. 188/E1
Santo Domingo, Bol. 185/E3
Santo Domingo, Cuba 177/F1
Santo Domingo, Chile 190/N8
Santo Domingo (cap.), DRep. 173/H4
Santo Domingo (pt.), Mex. 174/B3
Santo Domingo, Mex. 175/E4

Santo D – Seabro

Santo Domingo de la Calzada, Sp. 44/B5
Santo Domingo de los Colorados, Ecu. 180/B5
Santo Domingo Petapa, Mex. 176/C2
Santo Domingo Pueblo, NM, US 149/J3
Santo Domingo Tehuantepec, Mex. 176/C2
Santo Domingo Zanatepec, Mex. 176/C2
Santo Stefano (isl.), It. 65/C6
Santo Stefano Belbo, It. 62/B4
Santo Stefano d'Aveto, It. 62/C4
Santo Stefano di Magra, It. 62/C5
Santo Stino di Livenza, It. 63/F2
Santo Tomás (vol.), Ecu. 184/J7
Santo Tomás, Mex. 174/A2
Santo Tomás, (pt.), Mex. 174/A2
Santo Tomas (mt.), Phil. 88/C1
Santo Tomás, Peru 184/B2
Santo Tomás, Peru 184/C4
Santo Tomé, Arg. 189/E4
Santo Tomé, Arg. 188/D4
Santoña, Sp. 44/B5
Sant'Onofrio, It. 65/G8
Sant'Oreste, It. 65/B3
Santorso, It. 63/E2
Santos, Braz. 187/K8
Santos Dumont (int'l arpt.), Braz. 187/N7
Santos Dumont, Braz. 187/N6
Santos Mercado, Bol. 185/E3
Santos Reyes Nopala, Mex. 176/B2
Santuario, Col. 183/K7
Santuario, Col. 183/K6
Santuario di Crea, It. 62/B3
Santuario di Monte Vergine, It. 65/D6
Santuario di Oropa, It. 62/A1
Santunying, China 80/J6
Šānūr, WBnk. 105/C4
Sanwa, Japan 83/D1
Sanxing, China 80/L8
Sanya, China 87/F5
Sanyang, China 87/H2
Sanyati (riv.), Zim. 123/F3
Sanyuanba, China 87/E1
Sanyuanpu, China 81/C1
Sanza Pombo, Ang. 120/C4
São Bartolomeu (riv.), Braz. 186/D3
São Benedito, Braz. 183/F4
São Benedito do Rio Prêto, Braz. 183/F3
São Bento, Braz. 183/G4
São Bento, Braz. 183/E3
São Bento do Sapucaí, Braz. 187/L7
São Bento do Sul, Braz. 189/G3
São Bento do Una, Braz. 183/G5
São Bernardo do Campo, Braz. 187/K8
São Borja, Braz. 189/F4
São Braz, Cabo de (cape), Ang. 120/C5
São Carlos, Braz. 189/H2
São Cristóvão, Braz. 187/F1
São Desidério, Braz. 186/D2
São Domingos, Braz. 186/D2
São Domingos (riv.), Braz. 186/D2
São Domingos, GBis. 114/A3
São Domingos do Capim, Braz. 182/E3
São Domingos do Maranhão, Braz. 183/E4
São Félix do Araguaia, Braz. 186/C1
São Félix do Piauí, Braz. 183/F4
São Félix do Xingu, Braz. 182/D4
São Fidélis, Braz. 187/E4
São Filipe, CpV. 107/J11
São Francisco (riv.), Braz. 179/F3
São Francisco (isl.), Braz. 189/G3
São Francisco, Braz. 186/D2
São Francisco do Sul, Braz. 189/G3
São Fransisco de Assis, Braz. 189/F4
São Fransisco de Paula, Braz. 189/G4
São Gabriel, Braz. 189/F4
São Gabriel da Palha, Braz. 187/E3
São Gonçalo, Braz. 187/N7
São Gonçalo do Sapuçaí, Braz. 187/L6
São Gotardo, Braz. 189/H1
São Hill, Tanz. 119/A4
São Joachim da Barra, Braz. 189/H2
São João Batista, Braz. 183/E3
São João Batista, Braz. 189/G3
São João da Aliança, Braz. 186/D2
São João da Boa Vista, Braz. 187/K6
São João da Madeira, Port. 46/A2
São João da Pesqueira, Port. 46/B2
São João da Ponte, Braz. 186/D2
São João das Lampas, Port. 47/P10
São João de Meriti, Braz. 187/N7
São João del Rei, Braz. 186/D4
São João do Araguaia, Braz. 182/D4
São João do Jaguaribe, Braz. 183/G4
São João do Paraíso, Braz. 187/E2
São João do Piauí, Braz. 183/F5
São João dos Patos, Braz. 183/F4
São João Evangelista, Braz. 187/E3
São João Nepomuceno, Braz. 187/N6
São João, Serra de (mts.), Braz. 185/F3
São Joaquim, Braz. 189/G4
São Joaquim, PN de, Braz. 189/G4
São Jorge (isl.), Azor., Port. 47/S12
São José, Braz. 189/G3
São José da Laje, Braz. 183/G5
São José de Mipibu, Braz. 183/H4
São José de Ribamar, Braz. 183/E3
São José do Belmonte, Braz. 183/G4
São José do Campestre, Braz. 183/H4
São José do Egito, Braz. 183/G4
São José do Gurupi, Braz. 183/E3
São José do Norte, Braz. 189/F5
São José do Peixe, Braz. 183/F4
São José do Rio Pardo, Braz. 187/K6
São José do Rio Prêto, Braz. 189/G2
São José dos Campos, Braz. 187/L8
São José dos Pinhais, Braz. 189/G3
São Julião, Braz. 183/F4
São Lourenço, Port. 47/P11
São Lourenço, Braz. 187/L7
São Lourenço (riv.), Braz. 185/G5
São Lourenço da Mata, Braz. 183/H5
São Lourenço do Sul, Braz. 189/G4
São Lourenço d'Oeste, Braz. 189/F3
São Lucas, Ang. 120/D5
São Luís, Braz. 183/E3
São Luís de Montes Belos, Braz. 186/C3
São Luís do Curu, Braz. 183/G3
São Luís do Quitunde, Braz. 183/H5
São Luís Gonzaga, Braz. 189/F4
São Mamede, Braz. 183/G4
São Marcos (bay), Braz. 179/E3
São Marcos (riv.), Braz. 186/D3
São Martinho do Porto, Port. 46/A3
São Mateus, Braz. 187/F3
São Mateus (riv.), Braz. 187/E3
São Mateus do Maranhão, Braz. 183/E4
São Mateus do Sul, Braz. 189/G3
São Miguel (isl.), Azor., Port. 47/T13
São Miguel, Braz. 183/G4
São Miguel do Araguaia, Braz. 186/C2
São Miguel do Guamá, Braz. 183/E3
São Miguel do Tapuio, Braz. 183/F4
São Miguel d'Oeste, Braz. 189/F3
São Miguel dos Campos, Braz. 187/F1
São Nicolau (isl.), CpV. 107/J10
São Paulo, Braz. 187/K8
São Paulo (state), Braz. 186/C4
São Paulo de Olivença, Braz. 184/D1
São Paulo do Potengi, Braz. 183/H4
São Pedro do Piauí, Braz. 183/F4
São Pedro do Sul, Port. 46/A2
São Pedro do Sul, Braz. 189/F4
São Rafael, Braz. 183/G4
São Raimundo das Mangabeiras, Braz. 183/E4
São Raimundo Nonato, Braz. 183/F5
São Romão, Braz. 186/D3
São Roque (cape), Braz. 183/H4
São Roque do Pico, Azor., Port. 47/S12
São Sebastião, Braz. 187/L8
São Sebastião (isl.), Braz. 187/E3
São Sebastião (pt.), Moz. 123/G4
São Sebastião da Boa Vista, Braz. 182/D3
São Sebastião do Paraíso, Braz. 189/H2
São Sebastião do Tocantins, Braz. 182/D4
São Sebastião do Umbuzeiro, Braz. 183/G5
São Simão, Braz. 186/C3
São Simão (riv.), Braz. 185/F4
São Simão (res.), Braz. 186/C3
São Teotónio, Port. 46/A4
São Tiago (isl.), CpV. 107/K10
São Tomé (cap.), SaoT. 120/A2
São Tomé (int'l arpt.), SaoT. 120/A2
São Tomé (isl.), SaoT. 120/A2
São Tomé and Príncipe (ctry.) 120/A2
São Tomé, Cabo de (cape), Braz. 187/E4
São Vicente (cape), Port. 46/A4
São Vicente, Braz. 187/K8
São Vicente (isl.), CpV. 107/J10
São Vicente Ferrer, Braz. 183/E3
Saône (riv.), Fr. 66/E1
Saône-et-Loire (dept.), Fr. 60/B4
Saori, Japan 83/L5
Saouru, Oued (riv.), Alg. 111/E3
Sapāhār, Bang. 97/G3
Sápai, Gre. 75/J2
Sapallanga, Peru 184/C4
Sapanca, Turk. 51/K5
Saparua, Indo. 91/G4
Sapatgrām, India 97/H2
Sapawe, On, Can. 157/J3
Sapé, Braz. 183/H4
Sapele, Nga. 115/G5
Sapelo (isl.), Ga, US 165/H2
Saphane, Turk. 70/D5
Sapiéndza (isl.), Gre. 75/G4
Sapkyo, SKor. 81/D4
Sapo (mts.), Pan. 177/G5
Sapo NP, Libr. 114/C5
Sapo-Sapo, D.R. Congo 121/E4
Saponé, Burk. 115/E3
Saposoa, Peru 184/B2
Sapozhok, Rus. 71/G1
Sappa (cr.), Ks, US 154/D4
Sappa, Middle Fork (cr.), Ks, US 152/D1
Sappa, South Fork (cr.), Ks, US 152/D1
Sappemeer, Neth. 52/D2
Sapphire, Austl. 134/B3
Sapporo, Japan 82/B2
Sapri, It. 48/D2
Sapsi (isl.), SKor. 81/D3
Sapt Kosi (riv.), Nepal 97/F2
Sapucai (riv.), Braz. 187/L7
Sapucai (riv.), Braz. 189/H2
Sapucaia, Braz. 187/P6
Sapudi (isl.), Indo. 89/F4
Sapulpa, Ok, US 153/F3
Sapulut, Malay. 88/B4
Sāqiyat Sīdī Yūsuf, Tun. 112/L6
Saqqez, Iran 103/F2
Saquena, Peru 184/C2
Saquisilí, Ecu. 180/B5
Šar (mts.), Serb. 50/E4
Sar Dasht, Iran 103/F2
Sara, Phil. 88/C3
Sara Buri, Thai. 94/C3
Sarāb, Iran 103/F2
Sarābiyūm, Egypt 113/D3
Saraceno (peak), It. 65/D5
Saraf Doungous, Chad 116/C2
Sarafjagān, Iran 103/G3
Saragosa, Tx, US 150/C2
Saragossa (Zaragoza), Sp. 47/E2
Saraguro, Ecu. 184/B1
Sarāi Alamgīr, Pak. 98/B3
Sarāi Sidhu, Pak. 98/A4
Saraikela, India 97/E4
Sarāil, Bang. 97/H3
Saraipāli, India 95/D1
Sarajevo (cap.), Bosn. 50/D4
Saraktash, Rus. 71/L2
Saraland, Al, US 164/D2
Saramabila, D.R. Congo 121/F4
Saramacca (dist.), Sur. 181/H3
Saramati (peak), India 86/B3
Sarampiuni, Bol. 184/D4
Saran, Fr. 57/G5
Saran (peak), Indo. 90/D4
Saran', Kaz. 99/B2
Saranac Lake, NY, US 161/J2
Saranda, Tanz. 119/A3
Sarandapótamos (riv.), Gre. 75/N8
Sarandë, Alb. 75/G3
Sarandi, Braz. 189/F3
Sarandí de Navarro, Uru. 191/K10
Sarandí del Yí, Uru. 191/G2
Sarandí Grande, Uru. 191/K10
Sārangagada, India 95/E1
Sarangani (isls.), Phil. 91/G2
Sarangani (isl.), Phil. 88/D4
Sārangarh, India 95/D1
Sārangpur, India 92/C3
Saranley, Som. 119/C1
Saransk, Rus. 71/H1
Sarapul, Rus. 69/M4
Sarare (riv.), Ven. 180/D3
Saraskheri, India 96/A3
Sarasota, Fl, US 165/G4
Sarata, Ukr. 51/J2
Saratoga, Ca, US 167/K12
Saratoga, Wy, US 147/K3
Saratoga Nat'l Hist. Park, NY, US 161/K3
Saratoga Springs, NY, US 161/K3
Saratok, Malay. 90/D3
Saratov (res.), Rus. 71/J1
Saratov, Rus. 71/H2
Saratovskaya Oblast, Rus. 71/H2
Saravan, Laos 94/D3
Sarawaget (range), PNG 129/G1
Sarawak (reg.), Malay. 77/L9
Saray, Turk. 51/H5
Sarayacu, Ecu. 180/B5
Sarāyān (riv.), India 96/C2
Sarayköy, Turk. 102/B2
Sarayönü, Turk. 102/C2
Sarbāz, Iran 101/H3
Sarbhāng, Bhu. 97/H2
Sárbogárd, Hun. 50/D2
Sarcari, Bol. 188/C2
Sarcelles, Fr. 30/K5
Sarco, Chile 188/B4
Sarcoxie, Mo, US 153/G2
Sārda (riv.), India 96/C1
Sārda (canal), India 96/C2
Sārda (riv.), India 92/D2
Sardara, It. 48/A3
Sardārpura, India 98/B5
Sardārshahar, India 98/C5
Sardegna (prov.), It. 48/A2
Sardhana, India 98/D5
Sardinata, Col. 180/C2
Sardinia (isl.), It. 48/A2
Sardinia, Oh, US 162/F1
Sardis (dam), Ms, US 162/C3
Sardis, Ms, US 162/C3
Sardis, Tx, US 150/L7
Sardis, Ga, US 163/G4
Sardis (lake), Ms, US 162/C3
Sareks NP, Swe. 38/F2
Sarektjåkko (peak), Swe. 38/F2
Sarempaka (peak), Indo. 91/E4
Sarenga, India 97/E4
Sarentino, It. 61/H4
Sarepta, La, US 153/H4
Sarezzo, It. 62/D2
Sargans, Swi. 61/F3
Sargents, Co, US 149/J1
Sargodha, Pak. 98/B3
Sarh, Chad 116/C3
Sārī, Iran 103/H2
Sari (cape), Malay. 89/C2
Sari-Solenzara, Fr. 48/A2
Saria, India 98/C3
Saribi (cape), Indo. 91/J4
Sarigan (isl.), NMar. 136/D3
Sarigazi (arpt.), Turk. 103/N7
Sarıgöl, Turk. 102/B2
Sarıkamış, Turk. 102/E1
Sarıkaya (prov.), Turk. 70/E5
Sarıkaya, Turk. 70/E5
Sarikei, Malay. 90/D3
Sarina, Austl. 134/C3
Sarine (riv.), Swi. 45/G3
Sariñena, Sp. 47/E2
Sarīr Kalanshiyū (des.), Libya 134/D3
Sarīr Kalanshiyū ar Ramlī al Kabīr (des.), Libya 134/D2
Sarīr Tibasti (des.), Libya 134/C4
Sarita, Tx, US 151/F4
Sariwŏn, NKor. 81/C3
Sarju (riv.), India 96/C1
Sark (isl.), Fr. 56/C2
Sark (isl.), Chl, UK 44/B2
Sarkad, Hun. 50/E2
Sarkant, Kaz. 74/H5
Särkijärvi (lake), Fin. 39/D4
Şarkikaraağaç, Turk. 102/B2
Şarkışla, Turk. 102/D2
Şarköy, Turk. 51/H5
Sarlat-la-Canéda, Fr. 44/D4
Sarleinsbach, Aus. 59/G5
Sarmato, It. 62/C3
Sarmeola, It. 63/E3
Sarmi, Indo. 91/J4
Sarmiento, Arg. 190/C5
Sarmiento (peak), Chile 191/C7
Särna, Swe. 40/E1
Sarnano, It. 65/C1
Sarnen, Swi. 61/E4
Sarnia, On, Can. 160/E3
Sarnico, It. 62/C2
Sarno, It. 65/D6
Sarny, Ukr. 72/D2
Saroako, Indo. 91/F4
Sarolangun, Indo. 89/C3
Saroma (lake), Japan 82/C1
Saronic (gulf), Gre. 67/J3
Sarono, It. 62/C2
Saros (gulf), Turk. 70/C4
Sárospatak, Hun. 43/L4
Sarpsborg, Nor. 40/D2
Sarralbe, Fr. 55/G6
Sarras, Fr. 64/A2
Sarratt, Eng, UK 30/B1
Sarre (riv.), Fr. 54/F6
Sarre-Union, Fr. 55/G6
Sarrebourg, Fr. 55/G6
Sarreguemines, Fr. 55/G5
Sarria, Sp. 46/B1
Sarrians, Fr. 64/A4
Sarroch, It. 48/A3
Sarry, Fr. 55/D6
Sarsāwa, India 98/D4
Sarsina, It. 63/F6
Särsö (isl.), Swe. 39/B1
Sarstedt, Ger. 53/G4
Sarstún (riv.), Guat. 176/D3
Sartang (riv.), Rus. 75/P3
Sarteano, It. 48/B1
Sartell, Mn, US 157/G5
Sartène, Fr. 48/A2
Sarthe (dept.), Fr. 57/F4
Sarthe (riv.), Fr. 44/C3
Sarthon (riv.), Fr. 56/D3
Sartilly, Fr. 56/D3
Sartrouville, Fr. 30/J5
Sarufutsu, Japan 82/C1
Saruhanlı, Turk. 70/C5
Şārūr, Azer. 103/F2
Sárvár, Hun. 50/C2
Sarvestān, Iran 103/H4
Sárviz (riv.), Hun. 50/D2
Sary Ishikotrau (des.), Kaz. 99/C2
Saryagach, Kaz. 99/A3
Sarybasat, Kaz. 71/M3
Sarych (cape), Ukr. 73/G5
Saryg-Sep, Rus. 99/G1
Sarygamysh Köli (lake), Trkm. 71/L4
Saryshaghan, Kaz. 99/B2
Sarysu (riv.), Kaz. 74/G5
Sarzana, It. 62/C5
Sarzeau, Fr. 56/C5
Sas Van Gent, Neth. 54/C1
Sa'sa', Syria 105/E2
Sasabe, Az, US 149/G5
Sasaginnigack (lake), Mb, Can. 157/G2
Sasak, Indo. 89/B2
Sasarām, India 97/E3
Sasayama, Japan 83/H5
Sasayama (riv.), Japan 83/H5
Sásd, Hun. 50/D2
Sasebo, Japan 84/A4
Sashima, Japan 83/D1
Saskatchewan (riv.), Can. 139/G4
Saskatchewan (prov.), Can. 140/F3
Saskatoon, Sk, Can. 145/L1
Saslaya (mtn.), Nic. 176/E3
Saslaya, PN, Nic. 176/E3
Sāsni, India 96/B2
Sasolburg, SAfr. 124/D2
Sasoma, India 98/D2
Sasovo, Rus. 71/G1
Sassafras (peak), Tn, US 162/E3
Sassafras (mtn.), SC, US 163/F3
Sassafras, Md, US 168/C5
Sassafras (riv.), Md, US 168/B5
Sassandra, C.d'Iv. 114/D5
Sassandra (riv.), C.d'Iv. 114/D5
Sassari, It. 48/A2
Sasse (riv.), Fr. 64/C4
Sassello, It. 62/B5
Sassenage, Fr. 64/B2
Sassenberg, Ger. 53/F4
Sassenheim, Neth. 52/B4
Sasser, Ga, US 165/F2
Sassnitz, Ger. 40/E4
Sasso Marconi, It. 63/E5
Sassocorvaro, It. 63/F6
Sassoferrato, It. 63/F7
Sassoumbouroum, Niger 115/H3
Sasstown, Libr. 114/C5
Sassuolo, It. 63/D4
Sástago, Sp. 47/E2
Sastre, Arg. 188/D4
Sasykkol (lake), Kaz. 99/D2
Sata-misaki (cape), Japan 84/B5
Satadougou Tintiba, Mali 114/C3
Satara, SAfr. 123/F5
Satawan (isl.), Micr. 136/E4
Satellite Beach, Fl, US 165/H3
Satema, CAfr. 116/D4
Säter, Swe. 40/F1
Saticoy, Ca, US 166/A2
Satilla (riv.), Ga, US 165/G2
Satillieu, Fr. 64/A2
Satipo, Peru 184/C3
Satis, Rus. 69/J5
Sātkānia, Bang. 97/J4
Sātkhira, Bang. 97/G4
Satley, Eng, UK 35/G2
Satna, India 96/C3
Satolas (Lyon) (int'l arpt.), Fr. 60/B6
Sátoraljaújhely, Hun. 43/L4
Satpayev, Kaz. 99/A2
Satpura (range), India 92/C3
Sætre, Nor. 38/S8
Satsuma, Al, US 164/D2
Satsuma, Tx, US 151/M9
Sattahip, Thai. 94/C3
Satte, Japan 83/D1
Satteins, Aus. 61/F3
Satteldorf, Ger. 58/D4
Sattelberg, PNG 129/G1
Sättra, Swe. 39/A1
Satu Mare, Rom. 43/M5
Satu Mare (co.), Rom. 43/M5
Satuk, Thai. 94/C3
Satun, Thai. 94/C5
Satupaitea, Sam. 137/R9
Saturna, BC, Can. 144/C3
Sauce, Arg. 188/E4
Sauce, Peru 184/B2
Sauce de Luna, Arg. 188/E4
Sauce Grande (riv.), Arg. 190/E3
Saucedo, Uru. 188/E4
Saucier, Ms, US 164/D2
Saucillo, Mex. 174/D2
Sauda, Nor. 40/B2
Saudhárkrókur, Ice. 38/N6
Saudi Arabia (ctry.) 100/D4
Sauer (riv.), Ger. 53/F5
Sauerlach, Ger. 61/H2
Sauerland (reg.), Ger. 42/D3
Sauêruiná (riv.), Braz. 185/G4
Saugatuck, Mi, US 160/C3
Saugatuck (riv.), Ct, US 169/E1
Saugeen (riv.), On, Can. 160/F2
Saugeen Ind. Res., On, Can. 160/F2
Saugerties, NY, US 161/K3
Sauiá, Braz. 182/B3
Saujon, Fr. 44/C4
Sauk (riv.), Mn, US 155/G1
Sauk Centre, Mn, US 157/G5
Sauk City, Wi, US 155/K2
Sauk Rapids, Mn, US 157/G5
Saukkola, Fin. 39/D4
Saül, FrG. 182/C2
Sauland, Nor. 40/C2
Saulce-sur-Rhône, Fr. 64/A3
Sauldre (riv.), Fr. 44/D3
Saulgau, Ger. 61/F1
Saulheim, Ger. 58/B3
Saulieu, Fr. 44/F3
Saulkrasti, Lat. 41/L3
Saulnierville, NS, Can. 158/D3
Sault, Fr. 64/B4
Sault aux Cochons (riv.), Qu, Can. 158/C1
Sault Sainte Marie, On, Can. 160/D1
Sault Sainte Marie, Mi, US 160/D1
Sault-lès-Rethel, Fr. 55/D5
Saulx, Fr. 60/C2
Saulx (riv.), Fr. 42/C4
Saulxures-sur-Moselotte, Fr. 60/C2
Saumlaki, Indo. 128/C1
Saumur, Fr. 57/E6
Saunders (cape), NZ 135/B4
Saunders (peak), Austl. 130/E3
Saundersfoot, Wal, UK 36/B3
Saura (riv.), India 97/F3
Saurimo, Ang. 121/E5
Sausalito, Ca, US 167/J11
Sausseron (riv.), Fr. 30/J4
Sausset-les-Pins, Fr. 64/B6
Sausu, Indo. 91/F4
Saut-Tigre, FrG. 182/C1
Sautatá, Col. 180/B3
Sautet (lake), Fr. 64/B3
Sauteurs, Gren. 181/F1
Sautron, Fr. 56/D6
Sauzon, Fr. 56/B6
Sava, It. 75/E2
Sava (riv.), Eur. 67/J1
Savá, Hon. 176/E3
Savage, Mt, US 156/B4
Savage (mtn.), Md, US 161/G5
Savage (dam), Ca, US 166/D5
Savage, Mn, US 157/P7
Savage River, Austl. 132/C4
Savai'i (isl.), Sam. 137/H6
Savalou, Ben. 115/F5
Savanna, Ok, US 153/G3
Savanna, Il, US 155/J2
Savanna-la-Mar, Jam. 177/G2
Savannah (riv.), US 139/J6
Savannah, Mo, US 155/G4
Savannah, Tn, US 162/C3
Savannah (brook), Austl. 130/L6
Savannah, Ga, US 165/G1
Savannah NWR, Ga, US 165/H1
Savannah River Plant, SC, US 163/G4
Savannakhet, Laos 94/D2
Savant (lake), On, Can. 157/J2
Savant Lake, On, Can. 157/J2
Sävar, Swe. 38/G3
Savaştepe, Turk. 70/C5
Savate, Ang. 122/C3
Savé, Ben. 115/F4
Save (riv.), Moz. 107/F7
Save (riv.), Zim. 123/G4
Sāveh, Iran 103/G3
Savena (riv.), It. 63/E4
Savenay, Fr. 56/D6
Savéni, Rom. 72/D4
Saverdun, Fr. 44/D5
Saverne, Fr. 55/G6
Savièse, Swi. 60/D5
Savigliano, It. 64/D3
Savignano sul Panaro, It. 63/E5
Savignano sul Rubicone, It. 63/F5
Savigné-l'Évêque, Fr. 57/F4
Savigny-le-Temple, Fr. 30/K6
Savigny-sur-Braye, Fr. 57/F5
Savigny-sur-Orge, Fr. 30/K5
Savines-le-Lac, Fr. 64/C3
Saviniemi, Fin. 39/E3
Sävja, Swe. 40/G2
Savognin, Swi. 61/F4
Savoie (dept.), Fr. 60/C6
Savona, It. 62/B5
Savona (prov.), It. 62/B4
Savona, BC, Can. 144/D2
Savonburg, Ks, US 153/G2
Savoonga, Ak, US 171/D3
Savoy, Tx, US 153/F4
Savoy, Il, US 160/B4
Savoy (reg.), Fr. 66/E1
Savoy, SD, US 154/C1
Savoy, Ma, US 145/K3
Savoy Alps (mts.), Fr. 60/C6
Saxman, Ak, US 171/M4
Şavşat, Turk. 71/G4
Sävsjö, Swe. 40/F3
Savu (sea), Phil. 77/M10
Savusavu, Fiji 137/Z17
Sawahlunto, Indo. 89/C3
Sawākin, Sudan 109/H5
Sawang Daeh Din, Thai. 94/C2
Sawankhalok, Thai. 94/B2
Sawara, Japan 85/G3
Sawasaki-bana (pt.), Japan 85/F2
Sawatch (range), Co, US 154/A4
Sawbridgeworth, Eng, UK 37/G3
Sawdā', Jabal (peak), SAr. 100/D5
Sawdirī, Sudan 116/F2
Saweba (cape), Indo. 91/H4
Sawel (mtn.), NI, UK 34/A2
Sawena, Eth. 118/B4
Sawi, India 93/F6
Sawkanah, Libya 134/B2
Sawmills, Zim. 123/F3
Sawpit, Co, US 149/H2
Sawston, Eng, UK 37/G2
Sawtell, Austl. 132/E1
Sawtooth (range), Id, US 147/F1
Sawtooth (mtn.), Mt, US 145/K3
Sawtooth Nat'l Rec. Area, Id, US 147/F1
Sawu, Indo. 128/A2
Sawu (isl.), Indo. 128/A2
Sawu (isls.), Indo. 91/F6
Sawyer, ND, US 156/D3
Sawyer, Ks, US 153/E2
Sawyers Bar, Ca, US 146/B3
Sax, Sp. 47/E3
Saxån (riv.), Swe. 39/K7
Saxarfjärden (sound), Swe. 39/B1
Saxilby, Eng, UK 35/H5
Saxis, Va, US 163/K2
Saxmundham, Eng, UK 37/H2
Saxon, Swi. 60/D5
Say, Niger 115/F3
Say-Utes, Kaz. 71/K3
Saya, Japan 83/L5
Saya, Bol. 188/C1
Sayabec, Qu, Can. 158/D1
Sayak, Kaz. 74/H5
Sayama, Japan 83/C1
Sayama, Japan 83/J6
Sayán, Peru 184/B3
Sayansk, Rus. 78/E1
Şaydā (Sidon), Leb. 105/C1
Şaydnāyā, Syria 105/E1
Sayhūt, Yem. 118/D2
Sayil (ruin), Mex. 176/D1
Sayingpan, China 86/D3
Saykhin, Kaz. 71/H2
Saylah, Egypt 113/B6
Saynbach (riv.), Ger. 55/G2
Sayner, Wi, US 157/K5
Sayram (lake), China 99/D3
Sayre, Ok, US 152/E3
Sayre, Pa, US 161/H3
Sayreville, NJ, US 169/H10
Saysu, China 99/F3
Sayula, Mex. 174/E5
Sayville, NY, US 169/E2
Saywūn, Yem. 118/D2
Sazan (isl.), Alb. 75/F2
Sazan (isl.), Gre. 50/D5
Sazdy, Kaz. 71/J3
Sazīn, Pak. 98/B2
Sazli Dere (riv.), Turk. 103/M6
Sbaa, Alg. 111/E3
Scaër, Fr. 56/B4
Scafati, It. 65/D6
Scafell Pikes (peak), Eng, UK 35/E3
Scalasaig, Sc, UK 31/Q8
Scalby, Eng, UK 35/H3
Scald Law (peak), Sc, UK 33/C5
Scalea, It. 48/D3
Scalino (peak), It. 61/F5
Scalloway, Sc, UK 31/W13
Scammon Bay, Ak, US 171/E3
Scandia, Ab, Can. 145/H2
Scandia, Ks, US 153/E2
Scandia, Mn, US 157/Q6
Scandia, Wa, US 167/B2
Scandiano, It. 63/D4
Scandicci, It. 63/E6
Scanlon, Mn, US 157/H4
Scanno, It. 65/C4
Scapa Flow (chan.), Sc, UK 31/V14
Scar Water (riv.), Sc, UK 34/E1
Scarborough, Eng, UK 35/H3
Scarborough, Trin. 181/F2
Scarborough (nbrhd.), Austl. 130/K6
Scarborough (co.), On, Can. 160/U8
Scarborough Shoal (isl.), Phil. 88/B2
Scardovari, It. 63/F4
Scarinish, Sc, UK 31/Q8
Scarpe (riv.), Fr. 42/B3
Scarperia, It. 63/E6
Scarriff, Ire. 32/B4
Scarsdale, NY, US 169/K7
Scatarie (isl.), Ns., Can. 159/H3
Scattery (isl.), Ire. 32/A4
Scauri, It. 65/C5
Sceaux, Fr. 30/J5
Scerni, It. 65/D3
Scey-sur-Saône-et-St-Albin, Fr. 60/B2
Schaefferstown, Pa, US 168/B3
Schaerbeek, Belg. 55/D2
Schaffer, Mi, US 157/L5
Schaffhausen, Swi. 61/E2
Schaffhausen (canton), Swi. 61/E2
Schäftlarn, Ger. 61/H2
Schagen, Neth. 52/B3
Schaijk, Neth. 52/C5
Schalchen, Aus. 59/G6
Schalkau, Ger. 58/E2
Schalksmühle, Ger. 53/E6
Schaller, Ia, US 155/G2
Schanck (cape), Austl. 133/B4
Schangnau, Swi. 60/D4
Scharans, Swi. 61/F4
Schardenberg, Aus. 59/G5
Schärding, Aus. 59/G6
Scharfreiter (peak), Aus. 61/H3
Scharhorn (isl.), Ger. 53/F1
Scharnebeck, Ger. 53/H2
Scharnhorst (pt.), PNG 129/G1
Scharnitz (pass), Ger. 61/H3
Scharnstein, Aus. 59/G7
Schashagen, Ger. 42/F1
Schattdorf, Swi. 61/E4
Schauenstein, Ger. 59/E2
Schaumburg, Il, US 167/P15
Scheemda, Neth. 52/D2
Scheer, Ger. 61/F1
Scheessel, Ger. 53/G2
Schefferville, Qu, Can. 141/K3
Scheibbs, Aus. 43/H4
Scheidegg, Ger. 61/F2
Scheinfeld, Ger. 58/D3
Schelde (riv.), Belg. 54/C2
Scheldt (riv.), Belg. 44/E1
Schelklingen, Ger. 58/C6
Schell City, Mo, US 153/G1
Schell Creek (range), Nv, US 147/F4
Schellerten, Ger. 53/H4
Schellville, Ca, US 167/K10
Schenectady, NY, US 161/K3
Schenefeld, Ger. 53/G1
Schererville, In, US 160/C4
Schermbeck, Ger. 52/D5
Scherpenzeel, Neth. 52/C3
Schertz, Tx, US 151/E3
Schesaplana (peak), Aus. 61/F3
Schesslitz, Ger. 58/E3
Scheveningen, Neth. 52/B4
Scheyern, Ger. 59/E5
Schiedam, Neth. 52/B5
Schieder-Schwalenberg, Ger. 53/G5
Schiehallion (peak), Sc, UK 33/B3
Schier Monnikoog (isl.), Neth. 42/D2
Schierling, Ger. 59/F5
Schiermonnikoog (isl.), Neth. 52/D1
Schiermonnikoog, Neth. 52/D2
Schiers, Swi. 61/F4
Schifferstadt, Ger. 58/B4
Schiffweiler, Ger. 55/G5
Schijndel, Neth. 52/C5
Schilde, Belg. 52/B6
Schildmeer (lake), Neth. 52/D2
Schillighörn (cape), Ger. 53/E2
Schillingsfürst, Ger. 58/D4
Schiltach, Ger. 61/E1
Schiltigheim, Fr. 60/D1
Schinnen, Neth. 55/E2
Schinznach-Dorf, Swi. 60/E3
Schio, It. 62/E2
Schipbeek (riv.), Neth. 52/D4
Schiphol (Amsterdam) (int'l arpt.), Neth. 52/B4
Schirmeck, Fr. 60/D1
Schkumbin (riv.), Alb. 75/G2
Schladen, Ger. 53/H4
Schladming, Aus. 45/K3
Schlanders (Silandro), It. 61/G4
Schlangen, Ger. 53/F5
Schlangenbad, Ger. 58/B2
Schlater, Ms, US 162/B4
Schleiden, Ger. 55/F2
Schleitheim, Swi. 61/E2
Schleiz, Ger. 59/E1
Schlema, Ger. 59/F1
Schleswig, Ger. 40/C4
Schleswig, Ia, US 155/G2
Schleswig-Holstein (state), Ger. 40/B4
Schleswig-Holsteinisches Wattenmeer NP, Ger. 40/C4
Schleuse (riv.), Ger. 58/D2
Schleusingen, Ger. 58/D2
Schliengen, Ger. 60/D2
Schlierbach, Aus. 59/H7
Schlieren, Swi. 61/E3
Schloss Herrenchiemsee, Ger. 59/F7
Schloss Holte-Stukenbrock, Ger. 53/F5
Schloss Sanssouci, Ger. 42/Q7
Schloss Wilhelmstein, Ger. 53/G4
Schlotheim, Ger. 53/H6
Schluchsee, Ger. 60/E2
Schlüchtern, Ger. 58/C2
Schluderns (Sluderno), It. 61/G4
Schlüsselfeld, Ger. 58/D3
Schlüsslberg, Aus. 59/G6
Schmallenberg, Ger. 53/F6
Schmeich (riv.), Ger. 58/C6
Schmelz, Ger. 55/F5
Schmiech (riv.), Ger. 61/F1
Schmitten, Swi. 60/D4
Schmitten, Ger. 58/B2
Schmutter (riv.), Ger. 58/D5
Schnaitsee, Ger. 59/F6
Schnaittach, Ger. 59/E3
Schnaittenbach, Ger. 59/F3
Schnarrtanne, Ger. 59/F1
Schnecksville, Pa, US 168/C2
Schneeberg (peak), Ger. 59/E2
Schneeberg, Ger. 59/F1
Schneeberg, Ger. 58/C3
Schneifel (upland), Ger. 42/D3
Schneverdingen, Ger. 53/G2
Schoenchen, Ks, US 152/E1
Schofield, Wi, US 155/K1
Schoharie, NY, US 161/J3
Scholle, NM, US 149/J3
Schollene, Ger. 42/G2
Schöllkrippen, Ger. 58/C2
Schömberg, Ger. 61/E1
Schömberg, Ger. 58/B5
Schönaich, Ger. 58/C5
Schönau im Schwarzwald, Ger. 60/D2
Schönberg, Ger. 40/D4
Schönberg, Ger. 59/G5
Schönbrunn, Ger. 58/D1
Schondorf am Ammersee, Ger. 61/H1
Schondra (riv.), Ger. 58/C2
Schönebeck, Ger. 42/F2
Schöneck, Ger. 58/B2
Schöneck, Ger. 59/F2
Schönecken, Ger. 55/F3
Schönefeld (int'l arpt.), Ger. 42/Q7
Schöneiche, Ger. 42/Q7
Schongau, Ger. 61/G2
Schöningen, Ger. 42/F2
Schönow, Ger. 42/Q6
Schönsee, Ger. 59/F3
Schönungen, Ger. 58/D2
Schönwald, Ger. 58/E2
Schoolcraft, Mi, US 160/D3
Schoonebeek, Neth. 52/D3
Schoonhoven, Neth. 52/B5
Schoorl, Neth. 52/B3
Schopfheim, Ger. 60/D2
Schopfheim, Ger. 55/G4
Schopfloch, Ger. 58/D4
Schöppenstedt, Ger. 53/H4
Schörfling, Aus. 59/G7
Schorndorf, Ger. 58/C5
Schortens, Ger. 53/E1
Schoten, Belg. 52/B6
Schotten, Ger. 58/C1
Schouten (isls.), Indo. 136/C5
Schouten (isl.), Austl. 132/D4
Schouwen (isl.), Neth. 52/A5
Schramberg, Ger. 61/E1
Schrankogel (peak), Aus. 61/H3
Schreckhorn (peak), Swi. 60/E4
Schreiber, On, Can. 157/L3
Schriesheim, Ger. 58/B4
Schriever, La, US 164/C3
Schrobenhausen, Ger. 58/E5
Schroeder, Mn, US 157/J4
Schroffenstein (peak), Namb. 124/B2
Schrozberg, Ger. 58/C4
Schruns, Aus. 61/F3
Schübelbach, Swi. 61/E3
Schuby, Ger. 40/C4
Schulenburg, Tx, US 151/F3
Schuler, Ab, Can. 145/J2
Schulter, Ok, US 153/G3
Schulzendorf, Ger. 42/Q7
Schunter (riv.), Ger. 53/H4
Schüpfheim, Swi. 60/E4
Schurz, Nv, US 146/D4
Schussen (riv.), Ger. 61/F2
Schussenried, Ger. 61/F1
Schutter (riv.), Ger. 60/D1
Schutterwald, Ger. 60/D1
Schüttorf, Ger. 53/E4
Schuyler, Ne, US 155/F3
Schuylkill (riv.), Pa, US 168/C3
Schuylkill (co.), Pa, US 168/B2
Schuylkill Haven, Pa, US 168/B2
Schwabach, Ger. 58/D4
Schwabhausen bei Dachau, Ger. 59/E6
Schwäbisch Gmünd, Ger. 58/C5
Schwäbisch Hall, Ger. 58/C4
Schwäbische Alb (range), Ger. 42/E4
Schwabmünchen, Ger. 61/G1
Schwaig bei Nürnberg, Ger. 58/E4
Schwaigern, Ger. 58/C4
Schwalbach, Ger. 55/F5
Schwalbach am Taunus, Ger. 58/B2
Schwalm (riv.), Ger. 42/E3
Schwalmtal, Ger. 52/D6
Schwanden, Swi. 61/F4
Schwandorf im Bayern, Ger. 59/F4
Schwanebeck, Ger. 42/Q6
Schwanenstadt, Aus. 59/G6
Schwaner (mts.), Indo. 90/D4
Schwanewede, Ger. 53/F2
Schwanfeld, Ger. 58/D3
Schwangau, Ger. 61/G2
Schwarmstedt, Ger. 53/G3
Schwartz Elster (riv.), Ger. 43/G3
Schwarzerberg (peak), Namb. 124/B2
Schwarza (riv.), Ger. 58/E1
Schwarzach, Ger. 59/F5
Schwarzach (riv.), Ger. 59/E4
Schwarzach im Pongau, Aus. 45/K3
Schwarze Laber (riv.), Ger. 59/E4
Schwarzenbach am Wald, Ger. 59/E2
Schwarzenbek, Ger. 53/H1
Schwarzenberg, Ger. 59/F1
Schwarzenbruck, Ger. 58/E4
Schwarzenburg, Swi. 60/D4
Schwarzenfeld, Ger. 59/F4
Schwarzer Mann (peak), Ger. 55/F3
Schwarzhorn (peak), Aus. 61/H3
Schwarzrand (mts.), Namb. 122/C5
Schwarzwald (Black Forest) (for.), Ger. 58/B6
Schwaz, Aus. 45/J3
Schwebheim, Ger. 58/D3
Schwechat, Aus. 51/N7
Schwechat (int'l arpt.), Aus. 51/P7
Schwedt, Ger. 43/H2
Schwegenheim, Ger. 58/B4
Schweich, Ger. 55/F4
Schweighouse-sur-Moder, Fr. 55/G6
Schweinfurt, Ger. 58/D2
Schweitenkirchen, Ger. 59/E5
Schweizer-Reneke, SAfr. 124/D2
Schwelm, Ger. 53/E6
Schwendi, Ger. 61/F1
Schwenksville, Pa, US 168/C3
Schwerin, Ger. 40/D5
Schweriner (lake), Ger. 42/F2
Schwertberg, Aus. 59/H6
Schwerte, Ger. 53/E6
Schwetzingen, Ger. 58/B4
Schwinge (riv.), Ger. 53/G1
Schwörstadt, Ger. 60/D2
Schwülme (riv.), Ger. 53/G5
Schwülper, Ger. 53/H4
Schwyz (canton), Swi. 61/E3
Schwyz, Swi. 61/E3
Sciacca, It. 48/C4
Scicli, It. 48/D4
Science Hill, Ky, US 162/E2
Science Museum of Minnesota, Mn, US 157/P7
Scilly (isls.), Eng, UK 31/Q11
Ścinawa, Pol. 43/J3
Scio, Or, US 146/B1
Scionzier, Fr. 60/C5
Sciota, Pa, US 168/C2
Scioto (riv.), Oh, US 163/F1
Sclater, Mb, Can. 156/D2
Scobey, Mt, US 145/M3
Scofield (res.), Ut, US 147/H4
Scolt (pt.), Eng, UK 37/G1
Scone, Austl. 132/D2
Scooba, Ms, US 162/C4
Scopello, It. 62/B2
Scordia, It. 48/D4
Scorff (riv.), Fr. 56/B5
Scorzè, It. 63/F2
Scotch Corner, Eng, UK 35/G3
Scotch Creek, BC, Can. 144/E2
Scotch Plains, NJ, US 169/H9
Scotchman (peak), Id, US 144/F3
Scotia (sea) 192/W
Scotia, Ca, US 146/A3
Scotland, UK 34/D1
Scotland, Tx, US 153/E4
Scotland Neck, NC, US 163/J2
Scots Bay, NS, Can. 158/E3
Scotstown, Ire. 32/C1
Scott (cape), Austl. 128/C3
Scott (cape), BC, Can. 140/D3
Scott (cape), NW, Can. 141/R7
Scott (lake), NW, Can. 140/F2
Scott, Sk, Can. 145/K1
Scott, NZ, Ant. 192/M
Scott (riv.), Ca, US 146/B3
Scott (A.F.B.), Il, US 155/K4
Scott (co.), Mn, US 157/N7
Scott (mt.), Ok, US 153/E3
Scott City, Ks, US 152/D1
Scott City, Mo, US 162/C2
Scott NP, Austl. 130/B5
Scott (reef), Austl. 128/A3
Scottburgh, SAfr. 125/E3
Scottdale, Pa, US 161/G4
Scottdale, Ga, US 163/M7
Scottish Borders (co.), Sc, UK 33/C5
Scotts (cr.), Austl. 131/M9
Scotts Bluff Nat'l Mon., Ne, US 154/C3
Scotts Hill, Tn, US 162/C3
Scotts Peak (dam), Austl. 132/C4
Scottsbluff, Ne, US 154/C3
Scottsboro, Al, US 162/D3
Scottsburg, In, US 162/E1
Scottsdale, Austl. 132/C4
Scottsdale, Az, US 149/G4
Scottsmoor, Fl, US 165/H3
Scottsville, Ky, US 162/D2
Scottville, Mi, US 160/C3
Scotty's Castle, Ca, US 148/D2
Scoudouc, NB, Can. 158/E2
Scourie, Sc, UK 31/R7
Scranton, ND, US 156/C4
Scranton, Pa, US 161/J4
Scranton, SC, US 163/H4
Scraper, Ok, US 153/G2
Screven, Ga, US 165/G2
Scribner, Ne, US 155/F3
Scripps Aquarium/Museum, Ca, US 166/C5
Scrivia (riv.), It. 62/B3
Scunthorpe, Eng, UK 35/H4
Scuol, Swi. 61/G4
Scuppernong (riv.), Wi, US 167/N14
Scurdie Ness (pt.), Sc, UK 33/D3
Scurry, Tx, US 150/L7
Scutari (lake), Serb. 75/F1
Scye (riv.), Fr. 56/D2
Sea (isls.), Ga, SC, US 163/G5
Sea Cliff, Ca, US 166/A2
Sea Cliff, NY, US 169/L8
Sea Girt, NJ, US 168/D3
Sea Isle City, NJ, US 168/D5
Sea Lake, Austl. 132/B2
Sea Pines, SC, US 163/G5
Sea Ranch Lakes, Fl, US 164/P10
Sea World of Florida, Fl, US 164/N7
Sea-Tac, Wa, US 167/C3
Seabeck, Wa, US 167/B2
Seaboard, NC, US 163/J2
Seabold, Wa, US 167/B2
Seabra, Braz. 187/E2
Seabrook, NH, US 161/L3
Seabrook, NJ, US 168/C5
Seabrook, SC, US 163/G4
Seabrook, Tx, US 151/M9

Map Section
270
271

Seadri – Sheffi

Seadrift, Tx, US 150/F3
Seaford, Eng, UK 37/G5
Seaford, NY, US 169/M9
Seaford, De, US 163/K1
Seaforde, NI, UK 34/C3
Seaforth, On, Can. 160/F3
Seaforth, Austl. 134/C3
Seagoville, Tx, US 150/L7
Seagraves, Tx, US 152/C4
Seaham, Eng, UK 35/G2
Seahorse (pt.), Nun, Can. 141/J2
Seahurst, Wa, US 167/C3
Seal (isl.), Me, US 158/C4
Seal, Eng, UK 30/D3
Seal (riv.), MB, Can. 140/G3
Seal (pt.), Chile 190/B5
Seal (cape), SAfr. 124/C4
Seal Beach, Ca, US 166/F8
Seal Beach NWR, Ca, US 166/F8
Seal Cove, NS, Can. 158/D3
Seal Cove, Nf, Can. 159/J2
Seale, Eng, UK 30/A3
Seale, Al, US 162/E4
Sealy, Tx, US 150/F3
Seaman, Oh, US 162/F1
Seamer, Eng, UK 35/H3
Seano, It. 63/E6
Searchlight, Nv, US 148/E3
Searchmont, On, Can. 160/D1
Searcy, Ar, US 153/J3
Seascale, Eng, UK 34/E3
Seaside, Ca, US 148/B2
Seaside, Or, US 144/C5
Seaside Heights, NJ, US 168/D4
Seaside Park, NJ, US 168/D4
Seaton, Eng, UK 36/C5
Seaton (riv.), Eng, UK 36/B6
Seaton Carew, Eng, UK 35/G2
Seattle, Wa, US 144/C4
Seattle Art Museum, Wa, US 167/C2
Seattle Center, Wa, US 167/C2
Seattle-Tacoma (int'l arpt.), Wa, US 144/C4
Seatuck Nat'l Wild. Ref., NY, US 169/E2
Seba, Indo. 128/A2
Sébaco, Nic. 176/E3
Sebago (lake), Me, US 161/L3
Sebaou (riv.), Alg. 112/H4
Sebastian, Fl, US 165/H4
Sebastian, Tx, US 151/F4
Sebastián Vizcaíno (bay), Mex. 174/B2
Sebastopol, Austl. 133/A3
Sebastopol, Ca, US 146/B4
Sebastopol, Ms, US 162/C4
Sebastopol, Tx, US 151/G2
Sebatik (isl.), Malay. 88/B4
Sebayan (peak), Indo. 90/D4
Sebderat, Erit. 116/H2
Sebdou, Alg. 112/D2
Sébé (riv.), Gabon 120/C3
Sebec (lake), Me, US 158/C3
Sebeka, Mn, US 157/G4
Sébékoro, Mali 114/C3
Seben, Turk. 51/K5
Sebeş, Rom. 51/F3
Sebeta, Eth. 118/A3
Sebewaing, Mi, US 160/E3
Sebezh, Rus. 41/N3
Sebina, Bots. 123/E4
Şebinkarahisar, Turk. 102/D1
Sebiş, Rom. 50/F2
Sebkhet al Kalīyah (drylake), Alg. 112/M7
Seblat, Indo. 89/C3
Sebnitz, Ger. 43/H3
Seboruco, Ven. 180/C2
Seboto (pt.), Phil. 88/C4
Sebou (riv.), Mor. 112/B2
Sebou, Oued (riv.), Mor. 110/D2
Seboyeta, NM, US 149/J3
Sebree, Ky, US 162/D2
Sebring, Fl, US 165/H4
Sebuku (isl.), Indo. 91/E4
Sebuku (bay), Indo. 88/B5
Secaucus, NJ, US 169/J8
Secchia (riv.), It. 45/J4
Sechelt, BC, Can. 144/C3
Sechura, Peru 184/A2
Sechura (bay), Peru 184/A2
Sechura, Desierto de (des.), Peru 184/A2
Seclin, Fr. 54/C2
Seco (riv.), Arg. 191/D6
Seco (riv.), Mex.,US 149/G5
Seco (cr.), Tx, US 150/E3
Second Cataract (falls), Sudan 109/F4
Second Mesa, Az, US 149/G3
Second Mountain (mtn.), Pa, US 168/B3
Second San Diego Aqueduct (riv.), Ca, US 166/C4
Second Watchung (mtn.), NJ, US 169/H9
Section, Al, US 162/E3
Secunda, SAfr. 124/E2
Secure (riv.), Bol. 185/E4
Security-Widefield, Co, US 152/B1
Seda, Lith. 41/K3
Sedalia, Mo, US 153/H1
Sedalia, Ab, Can. 145/J2
Sedan, Ks, US 153/F2
Sedan, NM, US 152/C2
Sedan, Fr. 55/D4
Sedano, Sp. 46/D1
Sedaung (mtn.), Myan. 94/B3
Sedayu, Indo. 89/F4
Sedbergh, Eng, UK 35/F3
Seddenga Temple (ruin), Sudan 109/F4
Seddon, NZ 135/C3
Seddonville, NZ 135/B3
Seddülbahir, Turk. 75/K2
Sedeh, Iran 101/G2
Sederot, Isr. 105/B5
Sedgefield, Eng, UK 35/G2
Sedgewick, Ab, Can. 145/J1
Sedgwick (mt.), Yk, Can. 171/L2
Sedgwick, Ks, US 153/F2
Sedhiou, Sen. 114/B3
Sedlčany, Czh. 59/H3
Sedlo (peak), Czh. 59/H1
Sedona, Az, US 149/G3
Sedot Yam, Isr. 105/B4
Sedrata, Alg. 112/K6
Sedro-Woolley, Wa, US 144/C3
Šeduva, Lith. 41/K4
Sędziszów, Pol. 43/L3
Sędziszów Małopolski, Pol. 72/A2
Sée (riv.), Fr. 44/C2
Seeb (int'l arpt.), Oman 101/G4
Seebe, Ab, Can. 144/G2
Seeboden, Aus. 45/K3
Seedskadee NWR, Wy, US 147/J3
Seefeld in Tirol, Aus. 61/H3
Seefin (peak), Ire. 32/A6
Seefin (peak), Ire. 32/C5
Seeg, Ger. 61/G2
Seehausen, Ger. 42/F2
Seeheim, Namb. 124/B2
Seeheim-Jugenheim, Ger. 58/B3
Seeis, Namb. 122/C4
Seekirchen Markt, Aus. 59/G7
Seekooi (riv.), SAfr. 124/D3
Seeley, Ca, US 148/E4
Seeley Lake, Mt, US 145/H4
Seelow, Ger. 43/H2
Seeon-Seebruck, Ger. 59/F7
Seer Green, Eng, UK 30/B2
Sées, Fr. 57/F3
Seesen, Ger. 53/H5
Seeshaupt, Ger. 61/H2
Seeve (riv.), Ger. 53/G2
Seewalchen, Aus. 59/G7
Seewis im Prättigau, Swi. 61/F4
Séez, Fr. 64/C1
Şefaatlı, Turk. 102/C2
Seffner, Fl, US 164/L8
Sefhare, Bots. 123/E4
Sefīd Rūd (riv.), Iran 103/G2
Sefrou, Mor. 112/B3
Sefton (mt.), NZ 135/B3
Sefton (co.), Eng, UK 35/E4
Segag, Eth. 118/B4
Segama (riv.), Malay. 88/B4
Segamat, Malay. 89/C2
Segarcea, Rom. 51/F3
Ségbana, Ben. 115/F4
Ségélo-Koro, C.d'Iv. 114/D4
Segelstad Bru, Nor. 40/D1
Segen Wenz (riv.), Eth. 116/H4
Seget, Indo. 91/H4
Segezha, Rus. 68/G3
Segni, It. 65/C4
Segorbe, Sp. 47/E3
Ségou, Mali 114/D3
Ségou (pol. reg.), Mali 114/D3
Segovia, Col. 180/C3
Segovia, Sp. 46/C2
Segovia, Tx, US 150/E2
Segozero (lake), Rus. 68/G3
Segrate, It. 62/C3
Segré, Fr. 57/E5
Segre (riv.), Sp. 47/F2
Seguam (isl.), Ak, US 171/D5
Seguam Pass (Str.), Ak, US 171/D5
Séguédine, Niger 134/B4
Séguéla, C.d'Iv. 114/D5
Séguénéga, Burk. 115/E3
Seguin, Tx, US 151/F3
Segundo (riv.), Arg. 188/D4
Segura (riv.), Sp. 66/C3
Segusino, It. 63/E2
Sehithwa, Bots. 122/D4
Sehnde, Ger. 53/G4
Sehonghong, Les. 124/E3
Sehore, India 92/C3
Sehwān, Pak. 101/J3
Seibersbach, Ger. 55/G4
Seiche (riv.), Fr. 56/D5
Seiches-sur-le-Loir, Fr. 57/E5
Seiersberg, Aus. 50/B2
Seika, Japan 83/J6
Seiling, Ok, US 152/E2
Seille (riv.), Fr. 42/C5
Seinäjoki, Fin. 68/D3
Seine (riv.), On, Can. 157/J3
Seine (bay), Fr. 44/C2
Seine (riv.), On, Can. 140/G4
Seine (riv.), Fr. 29/E4
Seine-et-Marne (dept.), Fr. 54/B5
Seine-Maritime (dept.), Fr. 54/A4
Seine-St-Denis (dept.), Fr. 54/B6
Seitenstetten, Aus. 59/H6
Seiwa, Japan 83/K7
Seix, Fr. 44/D5
Seixal, Port. 47/P10
Seixas (pt.), Braz. 183/H4
Sejaka, Indo. 91/E4
Sejerø (isl.), Den. 40/D4
Sejero (flat), Den. 39/H7
Sejny, Pol. 41/K4
Sekayu, Indo. 89/C3
Seke, Tanz. 119/A2
Seke-Banza, D.R. Congo 120/C4
Sekenke, Tanz. 119/A3
Seki (riv.), Turk. 104/A1
Seki, Japan 83/L5
Seki, Japan 83/K6
Sekigahara, Japan 83/K5
Sekijo, Japan 83/D1
Sekiyado, Japan 83/D1
Sekoma, Bots. 122/D5
Sekondi, Gha. 115/E5
Sek'ot'a, Eth. 118/A2
Sel, Nor. 38/D3
Selah, Wa, US 144/D4
Selama, Malay. 89/C1
Selangor (state), Malay. 89/C2
Selaön (isl.), Swe. 39/A1
Selaphum, Thai. 94/C2
Selargius, It. 48/A3
Selaru (isl.), Indo. 91/H5
Selatan (cape), Indo. 90/D4
Selawik, Ak, US 171/F2
Selawik (lake), Ak, US 171/F2
Selayar (isl.), Indo. 91/F5
Selb, Ger. 59/F2
Selbitz, Ger. 59/E2
Selbitz (riv.), Ger. 59/E2
Selbu, Nor. 38/D3
Selby, SD, US 156/D5
Selby, Eng, UK 35/G4
Selby-On-The-Bay, Md, US 168/B6
Selci, It. 63/F6
Selçuk, Turk. 102/A2
Selden, Ks, US 154/D4
Selden, NY, US 169/E2
Seldovia, Ak, US 171/H4
Sele (riv.), It. 48/D2
Selebi-Phikwe, Bots. 123/E4
Seleka, Bots. 123/E4
Selela (pt.), Moz. 123/J2
Seleli (hill), Tanz. 121/H5
Selemdzha (riv.), Rus. 75/N4
Selenča, Serb. 50/D3
Selenduma, Rus. 78/F1
Selenga (riv.), Rus. 78/F1
Selenge (prov.), Mong. 78/F2
Selenge (riv.), Mong. 78/F2
Selenginsk, Rus. 78/F1
Selenicë, Alb. 75/F2
Sélestat, Fr. 60/D1
Seletar (res.), Sing. 89/J6
Selety (riv.), Kaz. 99/B1
Seletyteniz (lake), Kaz. 99/B1
Seleznëvo, Rus. 41/N1
Selfoss, Ice. 38/N7
Selfridge, ND, US 156/D4
Sélia (well), Chad 116/C2
Sélibabi, Mrta. 114/B3
Seligenstadt, Ger. 58/B2
Seliger (lake), Rus. 68/G4
Seligman, Mo, US 153/H2
Seligman, Az, US 149/F3
Selim River, Malay. 89/C2
Selimbau, Indo. 90/D3
Selimiye, Turk. 102/A2
Selinsgrove, Pa, US 168/B2
Seljord, Nor. 40/C2
Selkan (tun.), Japan 82/B3
Selkirk, Sc, UK 33/D5
Selkirk, Mb, Can. 140/G3
Selkirk (mts.), BC, Can. 144/E2
Selleck, Wa, US 167/D3
Sellers, Al, US 165/E1
Sellersville, Pa, US 168/C3
Selles-sur-Cher, Fr. 57/G6
Sellières, Fr. 60/B4
Sells, Az, US 149/G5
Selly Oak, Eng, UK 36/E2
Sellye, Hun. 50/C3
Selm, Ger. 53/E5
Selma, Al, US 162/D4
Selma, Ar, US 153/J4
Selma, Ca, US 148/C2
Selma, NC, US 163/H3
Selman, Ok, US 152/E2
Selmer, Tn, US 162/C3
Selommes, Fr. 57/G5
Selongey, Fr. 60/B2
Selouma, Gui. 114/C4
Selous (mt.), Yk, Can. 171/M3
Selous, Zim. 123/F3
Selous Game Reserve, Tanz. 119/B4
Selsey, Eng, UK 37/F5
Selsey Bill (pt.), Eng, UK 37/F5
Selsingen, Ger. 53/G2
Sel'tso, Rus. 70/E1
Seltz, Fr. 58/B5
Selu (isl.), Indo. 128/C1
Sélune (riv.), Fr. 44/C2
Selvas (for.), Braz. 179/C3
Selvik, Nor. 38/R9
Selway (riv.), Id, US 147/F1
Selway (falls), Id, US 144/G4
Selwyn, Austl. 134/A3
Selwyn (range), Austl. 129/F5
Selydove, Ukr. 73/J3
Selz (riv.), Ger. 45/H2
Semara, WSah. 110/C4
Semarang, Indo. 89/E4
Semarsot, India 96/D4
Semau (isl.), Indo. 128/A2
Sembakung (riv.), Indo. 88/B4
Sembawang (nbrhd.), Sing. 89/J6
Sembé, Congo 120/C2
Sembehun, SLeo. 114/B5
Sembera (riv.), Czh. 59/H2
Semberong (riv.), Malay. 89/C2
Şemdinli, Turk. 103/F2
Séméac, Fr. 44/D5
Semelle (riv.), Fr. 57/F4
Semendua, D.R. Congo 120/D3
Semenivka, Ukr. 72/G1
Semenivka, Ukr. 73/G3
Semenov, Rus. 69/K4
Semeru (peak), Indo. 89/F5
Semey, Kaz. 99/D1
Semidi (isls.), Ak, US 171/G4
Semikarakorsk, Rus. 73/L4
Semilovo, Rus. 68/J5
Semiluki, Rus. 73/K2
Seminole, Fl, US 164/K8
Seminole (lake), Ga, US 165/F2
Seminole, Ok, US 153/F3
Seminole, Tx, US 150/C1
Seminoe (dam), Wy, US 147/K2
Seminoe (res.), Wy, US 147/K2
Seminole Draw (riv.), Tx, US 150/C1
Seminole Ind. Res., Fl, US 165/H4
Semipalatinsk (int'l arpt.), Kaz. 99/D1
Semirara (isl.), Phil. 88/C3
Semīrom, Iran 103/G4
Semisopochnoi (isl.), Ak, US 171/B5
Semitau, Indo. 90/D4
Semliki (riv.), D.R. Congo 121/G2
Semnān, Iran 103/H3
Semnān (gov.), Iran 103/H3
Semnon (riv.), Fr. 44/C3
Semois (riv.), Belg. 44/F2
Semouse (riv.), Fr. 60/C2
Semoy, Fr. 57/G5
Semoy (riv.), Fr. 55/D4
Sempach, Swi. 60/E3
Sempacher (lake), Swi. 60/D3
Semporna, Malay. 88/B4
Semprevisa (peak), It. 65/C4
Semsales, Swi. 60/C4
Semskefjellet (peak), Nor. 38/E2
Sen (riv.), Camb. 93/H5
Sen-san (peak), Japan 83/G7
Sena, Thai. 94/C3
Sena, Bol. 185/E3
Sena Madureira, Braz. 182/E5
Senador Pompeu, Braz. 183/G4
Senador Sá, Braz. 183/F3
Sen'afē, Erit. 118/A2
Senai, Malay. 89/C2
Senaja, Malay. 88/B4
Senaki, Geo. 71/G4
Senanga, Zam. 122/D3
Sénas, Fr. 64/B5
Senate, Sk, Can. 145/K3
Senath, Mo, US 162/B2
Senatobia, Ms, US 162/C3
Sence (riv.), Eng, UK 37/E1
Send, Eng, UK 30/B3
Sendafa, Eth. 118/A3
Sendai (riv.), Japan 84/D3
Sendai, Japan 85/G1
Sendai (int'l arpt.), Japan 85/G1
Sendai, Japan 84/B5
Sendai (bay), Japan 82/B4
Sendal (riv.), Japan 84/B5
Senden, Ger. 58/D6
Senden, Ger. 53/E5
Sendenhorst, Ger. 53/E5
Sendhwa, India 95/B1
Senebui, Indo. 89/C2
Senebui (cape), Indo. 89/C2
Senec, Slvk. 43/J4
Seneca, Mo, US 153/G2
Seneca (lake), NY, US 161/H3
Seneca, Or, US 146/D1
Seneca, SC, US 163/F3
Seneca, Ks, US 155/F4
Seneca Creek State Park, Md, US 168/A5
Seneca Falls, NY, US 161/H3
Seneca Rocks NRA, WV, US 163/H1
Senecaville (lake), Oh, US 160/F5
Seneffe, Belg. 55/D2
Senegal (ctry.) 114/B3
Sénégal (riv.), Afr. 114/B2
Senekal, SAfr. 124/D3
Seney, Mi, US 160/D1
Seney NWR, Mi, US 157/L4
Senezhskoye (lake), Rus. 69/W8
Senfi, Gha. 115/E5
Senftenberg, Ger. 43/H3
Senga Hill Mission, Zam. 121/G5
Sengenthal, Ger. 59/E4
Sênggê (riv.), China 99/D5
Sengilev, Rus. 71/J1
Sengor, Bhu. 97/H2
Senguer (riv.), Arg. 190/D3
Sengwe (riv.), Zim. 123/F3
Senhor do Bonfim, Braz. 187/E1
Senica, Slvk. 43/J4
Senirkent, Turk. 102/B2
Senise, It. 48/E2
Senj, Cro. 45/L4
Senja (isl.), Nor. 38/F1
Senkaku-Shotō (isl.), Japan 85/G8
Şenkaya, Turk. 102/E1
Senkevychivka, Ukr. 72/C2
Şenköy, Turk. 104/E1
Senlac, Sk, Can. 145/K1
Senlis, Fr. 54/B5
Senmonoron, Camb. 94/D3
Sennan, Japan 83/H7
Sennar (dam), Sudan 116/G2
Senne (riv.), Belg. 55/D2
Sennecey-le-Grand, Fr. 60/A4
Sennfeld, Ger. 58/D2
Senno, Bela. 41/N4
Sennoy, Rus. 71/G2
Sennoy, Rus. 71/H1
Sennwald, Swi. 61/F3
Sennybridge, Wal, UK 36/C3
Séno (prov.), Burk. 115/F3
Senonches, Fr. 57/G3
Senones, Fr. 60/C1
Senorbì, It. 48/A3
Senovo, Bul. 51/H4
Sens, Fr. 44/E2
Sens-de-Bretagne, Fr. 56/D4
Sensuntepeque, ESal. 176/D3
Senta, Serb. 50/E3
Sentani, Indo. 91/K4
Sentery, D.R. Congo 121/F4
Sentinel, Ok, US 152/E3
Sentinel, Az, US 149/F4
Sentosa (isl.), Sing. 89/J6
Sentrum, SAfr. 123/E5
Senya Beraku, Gha. 115/E5
Senyavin (isls.), Micr. 136/E4
Senzig, Ger. 42/Q7
Seohārā, India 96/B1
Seon, Swi. 60/E3
Seondha, India 96/B2
Seoni, India 96/B4
Seonī Mālwā, India 96/A4
Seoul (Sŏul) (cap.), SKor. 79/K4
Seoul Grand Park, SKor. 81/G7
Seoul Jikhalsi (prov.), SKor. 81/D4
Sepang (pt.), Malay. 89/D2
Sepanjang (isl.), Indo. 89/F4
Separ, NM, US 149/H4
Separation (pt.), NZ 135/C3
Sepatini (riv.), Braz. 185/E3
Sepetiba (bay), Braz. 187/M8
Sepik (riv.), PNG 136/D5
Sepino, It. 65/D5
Sep'o, NKor. 81/D3
Sepo, Indo. 91/G3
Sępólno Krajeńskie, Pol. 43/J2
Sepopa, Bots. 122/D3
Sept-Îles, Qu, Can. 141/K3
Septèmes-les-Vallons, Fr. 64/B6
Septemvri, Bul. 75/J1
Septeuil, Fr. 57/G3
Sepulveda (dam), Ca, US 166/F7
Sequeros, Sp. 46/B2
Sequim (bay), Wa, US 167/A1
Sequim, Wa, US 144/C3
Sequoia NP, Ca, US 148/C2
Sequoyah Nat'l Wildlife Res., Ok, US 153/G3
Sera (isl.), Indo. 128/C1
Serafimovich, Rus. 73/M3
Seraincourt, Fr. 30/H4
Seraing, Belg. 55/E2
Serambe, Sudan 117/E2
Serampore, India 97/G4
Sèran (riv.), Fr. 60/B6
Serang, Indo. 89/D4
Serangoon (nbrhd.), Sing. 89/J6
Serasan (str.), Indo.,Malay. 90/C3
Serasan, Indo. 90/C3
Seravezza, It. 62/D6
Serbeulangit (mts.), Indo. 89/B2
Serbia (reg.), Serb. 50/E3
Serbia and Montenegro (Yugoslavia) (ctry.) 50/D3
Serbin, Tx, US 151/F2
Serchhīp, India 86/B4
Serchio (riv.), It. 62/D4
Serdang (cape), Indo. 89/D4
Serdo, Eth. 118/B3
Serdobsk, Rus. 71/H1
Serebryansk, Kaz. 74/J5
Serednikovo, Rus. 68/H5
Seredžius, Lith. 41/K4
Seregno, It. 62/C2
Serein (riv.), Fr. 42/D4
Serémange-Erzange, Fr. 55/F5
Seremban, Malay. 89/C2
Serengeti (plain), Tanz. 119/A2
Serengeti NP, Tanz. 119/A2
Serenje, Zam. 123/F2
Serere, Ugan. 119/A1
Sergach, Rus. 69/K5
Sergeantsville, NJ, US 168/D3
Sergen, Turk. 51/H5
Sergeya Kirova (isls.), Rus. 74/J2
Sergeyevka, Kaz. 69/Q5
Sergipe (state), Braz. 187/F1
Sergiyev Posad, Rus. 68/H4
Sergnano, It. 62/C3
Seria, Bru. 90/D3
Seriate, It. 62/C2
Sérifontaine, Fr. 54/A5
Sérifos, Gre. 75/J4
Sérifos (isl.), Gre. 75/J4
Sérignan, Fr. 44/E5
Serik, Turk. 104/B1
Serikbuya, China 99/C4
Seringa, Serra da (mts.), Braz. 182/D4
Serinyol, Turk. 104/E1
Serio (riv.), It. 62/C2
Serkout (peak), Alg. 111/G5
Sermaises, Fr. 57/H4
Sermaize-les-Bains, Fr. 55/D6
Sermata (isls.), Indo. 128/C2
Sermide, It. 63/E4
Sermoneta, It. 65/B4
Sernaglia della Battaglia, It. 63/F2
Sernovodsk, Rus. 71/J1
Sernur, Rus. 69/L4
Serón, Sp. 46/D4
Serós, Sp. 47/F2
Serottini (peak), It. 61/G5
Serov, Rus. 74/G4
Serowe, Bots. 123/E4
Serpa, Port. 46/B4
Serpeddi (peak), It. 48/A3
Serpent Mound, Oh, US 163/F1
Serpent's Mouth (str.), Trin.,Ven. 181/F2
Serpentine (dam), Austl. 132/C4
Serpentine Lakes, Austl. 131/F4
Serpukhov, Rus. 68/H5
Serquigny, Fr. 57/F2
Serra (peak), It. 62/D6
Serra, Braz. 187/E4
Serra Branca, Braz. 183/G4
Serra da Bocaina, PN, Braz. 189/H2
Serra da Bocaína, PN da, Braz. 186/D4
Serra da Canastra, PN, Braz. 189/H2
Serra da Canastra, PN da, Braz. 186/D4
Serra da Capivara, PN da, Braz. 187/E1
Serra da Capivara, PN da, Braz. 183/F5
Serra da Chela (mts.), Ang. 122/B3
Serra da Estrela (peak), Port. 46/B2
Serra da Estrela (mts.), Port. 46/A3
Serra do Cipó, PN da, Braz. 187/E3
Serra do Congo (mts.), Ang. 120/C4
Serra do Navio, Braz. 182/C2
Serra dos Órgãos, PN da, Braz. 187/N7
Serra Negra do Norte, Braz. 183/G4
Serra San Bruno, It. 48/E3
Serra San Quirico, It. 63/G7
Serra Talhada, Braz. 183/G4
Sérrai, Gre. 75/H2
Serralta di San Vito (peak), It. 48/E3
Serramanna, It. 48/A3
Serramazzoni, It. 63/D5
Serrana Bank (isl.), Col. 173/F5
Serranía de la Cerbatana (mts.), Ven. 181/E3
Serranía de la Neblina, PN, Ven. 181/E4
Serranías del Burro (mts.), Mex. 174/E2
Serranilla Bank (isl.), Col. 173/F4
Serrano, Arg. 190/E2
Serranópolis, Braz. 186/B3
Serrat (cape), Tun. 48/A4
Serravalle, It. 63/F4
Serravalle, SMar. 63/F6
Serravalle di Chienti, It. 65/B1
Serravalle Scrivia, It. 62/B4
Serravalle Sesia, It. 62/B2
Serre (riv.), Fr. 42/B4
Serre Chevalier (peak), Fr. 64/C3
Serre-Ponçon (lake), Fr. 64/C3
Serrenti, It. 48/A3
Serres, Fr. 64/B4
Serrières, Fr. 64/A2
Serrinha, Braz. 187/F1
Serris, Fr. 30/L5
Serrita, Braz. 183/G4
Sêrro, Braz. 189/J1
Sersale, It. 48/E3
Sertã, Port. 46/A3
Sertânia, Braz. 183/G5
Sertãozinho, Braz. 189/H2
Sertavul (pass), Turk. 104/C1
Serteng (mts.), China 78/C4
Sēru, Eth. 118/B4
Serui, Indo. 91/J4
Serule, Bots. 123/E4
Serurumi (riv.), Bots. 122/E4
Seruwai, Indo. 89/B1
Seruyan (riv.), Indo. 90/D4
Servance, Fr. 60/C2
Servel (Lannion) (arpt.), Fr. 56/B3
Servi, Turk. 102/E2
Sérvia, Gre. 75/G2
Serviceton, Austl. 132/B3
Servigliano, It. 65/C1
Serwaru, Indo. 128/B2
Sesayap (riv.), Indo. 88/B5
Sese (isls.), Ugan. 121/G3
Sesebi (ruin), Sudan 109/F4
Sesepe, Indo. 91/G4
Sesfontein, Namb. 122/B3
Sesheke, Zam. 122/E3
Sesia (riv.), It. 45/H4
Sesimbra, Port. 47/P11
Seskar (isl.), Rus. 41/N1
Sespe, Ca, US 166/B2
Sespe (cr.), Ca, US 166/A1
Sespe Condor Sanctuary, Ca, US 148/C3
Sessa Aurunca, It. 65/C5
Sesser, Il, US 162/C1
Sesslach, Ger. 58/D2
Sesto Calende, It. 62/B2
Sesto Campano, It. 65/D5
Sesto Fiorentino, It. 63/E6
Sesto San Giovanni, It. 62/C2
Sesto Ulteriano, It. 62/C3
Sestola, It. 63/D5
Sestra (riv.), Rus. 69/W8
Sestri Levante, It. 62/C5
Sestroretsk, Rus. 69/S6
Sestroretskiy (lake), Rus. 69/T6
Sestu, It. 48/A3
Sesvenna (peak), It. 61/G4
Sesvete, Cro. 50/C3
Šeta, Lith. 41/L4
Setana, Japan 82/A2
Sète, Fr. 44/E5
Sete Cidades, PN de, Braz. 183/F4
Sete Lagoas, Braz. 186/D3
Seth, WV, US 163/G1
Sethārja, Pak. 101/J3
Seti (riv.), Nepal 96/C1
Seti (zone), Nepal 96/C1
Sétif, Alg. 112/H4
Sétif (wilaya), Alg. 112/H4
Seto, Japan 83/M5
Seto-Naikai NP, Japan 84/C4
Setouchi, Japan 85/K6
Settat, Mor. 110/D2
Setté-Cama, Gabon 120/B3
Settecamini, It. 65/B4
Settepani (peak), It. 62/B5
Settimo Torinese, It. 62/A2
Settimo Vittone, It. 62/A1
Settle, Eng, UK 35/F3
Settsu, Japan 83/J6
Setúbal (dist.), Port. 46/A3
Setúbal (bay), Port. 46/A3
Setúbal, Port. 47/Q10
Seubersdorf, Ger. 59/E4
Seudre (riv.), Fr. 44/C4
Seugne (riv.), Fr. 44/C4
Seuil-D'Argonne, Fr. 55/E6
Seul (lake), On, Can. 140/G3
Seulimeum, Indo. 89/A1
Seulles (riv.), Fr. 57/E2
Seurre, Fr. 60/B4
Seuzach, Swi. 61/E2
Sevan, Arm. 103/F1
Sevana (lake), Arm. 74/E5
Sevastopol', Ukr. 73/G5
Sevelen, Swi. 61/F3
Seven (riv.), Eng, UK 35/H3
Seven (cr.), Ab, Can. 145/J3
Seven Heads (pt.), Ire. 32/B6
Seven Oaks, Tx, US 151/G2
Seven Sisters Falls, Mb, Can. 156/F2
Seven Valleys, Pa, US 168/B4
Sevenmile (hill), Ne, US 154/D2
Sevenoaks, Eng, UK 30/D3
Sevenoaks Weald, Eng, UK 30/D3
Seventy Mile House, BC, Can. 144/D2
Séveraisse (riv.), Fr. 64/C3
Severn (riv.), Wal, UK 35/F6
Severn (riv.), On, Can. 140/G3
Severn (riv.), Md, US 168/B5
Severn, Md, US 168/B5
Severna Park, Md, US 168/B5
Severnaya Osetiya-Alaniy, Resp., Rus. 75/Q6
Severnaya Sos'va (riv.), Rus. 69/N3
Severnaya Zemlya (isls.), Rus. 74/J2
Severnyy, Rus. 69/P2
Severo-Kuril'sk, Rus. 75/R4
Severo-Yeniseyskiy, Rus. 74/K3
Severobaykal'sk, Rus. 75/L4
Severočeský (pol. reg.), Czh. 45/L1
Severodvinsk, Rus. 68/H2
Severomoravský (pol. reg.), Czh. 45/M1
Severomorsk, Rus. 68/G1
Severomuysk, Rus. 75/M4
Severoural'sk, Rus. 69/N3
Seversk, Ukr. 73/K3
Severskaya, Rus. 73/K5
Severukha, Rus. 69/P4
Severy, Ks, US 153/F2
Seveso, It. 62/C2
Sevier (lake), Ut, US 147/G4
Sevier (des.), Ut, US 147/G4
Sevier, Ut, US 149/F1
Sevier (riv.), Ut, US 142/D4
Sevier (plat.), Ut, US 149/F1
Sevier, East Fork (riv.), Ut, US 149/F2
Sevierville, Tn, US 163/F3
Sevilla, Col. 183/K8
Seville, Sp. 46/C4
Seville, Austl. 132/G5
Sevilleta Nat'l Wild. Ref., NM, US 149/J3
Sevlievo, Bul. 51/G4
Sevnica, Slov. 50/B2
Sevojno, Serb. 50/D4
Sevran, Fr. 30/K5
Sevsk, Rus. 73/H1
Sewa (riv.), SLeo. 114/C5
Sewall, BC, Can. 171/M5
Sewanee, Tn, US 162/E3
Seward (pen.), Ak, US 171/E2
Seward, Ak, US 171/J3
Seward, Ne, US 155/F3
Sewaren, NJ, US 169/J9
Sewell, Chile 190/N9
Sewell Inlet, BC, Can. 171/M5
Sextons Creek, Ky, US 162/F2
Seyah Cheshmeh, Iran 103/F2
Seybaplaya, Mex. 176/D2
Seybouse, Oued (riv.), Alg. 112/K6
Seydhisfjördhur, Ice. 38/Q6
Seydişehir, Turk. 102/B2
Seyhan (dam), Turk. 104/D1
Seyhan (riv.), Turk. 104/D1
Seyitgazi, Turk. 102/B2
Seylac, Som. 118/B3
Seym (riv.), Rus. 70/E2
Seymour, Austl. 133/B3
Seymour, Ia, US 155/H3
Seymour, In, US 162/E1
Seymour, Mo, US 153/H2
Seymour, Tx, US 152/E4
Seymour, Wi, US 160/B2
Seymour Arm, BC, Can. 144/E2
Seymour Johnson (A.F.B.), NC, US 163/J3
Seyne, Fr. 64/C4
Seynod, Fr. 60/C6
Seyssel, Fr. 60/B6
Seyssinet-Pariset, Fr. 64/B2
Şeytan (riv.), Turk. 103/M6
Sežana, Slov. 45/K4
Sézanne, Fr. 54/C6
Sezimovo Ústí, Czh. 59/H4
Sezze, It. 65/C5
Sfîntu Gheorghe, Rom. 51/J3
Sfîntu Gheorghe, Rom. 51/G3
Sfîntu Gheorghe Branch (riv.), Rom. 51/J3
Sfizef, Alg. 112/E5
Sgurr a' Chaorachain (peak), Sc, UK 33/A2
Sgurr a' Choire Ghlais (peak), Sc, UK 33/B2
Sgurr a' Mhuilinn (peak), Sc, UK 33/B1
Sgurr Mór (peak), Sc, UK 33/A1
Sgurr na Ciche (peak), Sc, UK 33/A2
Sgurr na Lapaich (peak), Sc, UK 33/A2
Sha (riv.), China 80/C4
Sha Tau Kok, China 87/L6
Sha Tin, China 87/L7
Shaanxi (prov.), China 78/F5
Shab'ā, Leb. 105/D2
Shaba Nat'l Rsv., Kenya 119/B1
Shābah, Egypt 113/B2
Shabās al Milḩ, Egypt 113/B2
Shabās ash Shuhadā', Egypt 113/B2
Shabās 'Umayr, Egypt 113/B2
Shabashah, Sudan 116/G2
Shābāzpur (riv.), Bang. 97/H4
Shabla, Bul. 51/J4
Shabo, Ukr. 72/F4
Shabqadar, Pak. 98/A2
Shabunda, D.R. Congo 121/F3
Shabwah, Yem. 118/C2
Shache, China 99/C4
Shackan Ind. Res., BC, Can. 144/D2
Shackleford, Eng, UK 30/B3
Shadaogou, China 87/F2
Shade (mtn.), Pa, US 168/A2
Shadehill (dam), SD, US 156/C5
Shadehill, SD, US 156/C5
Shadeland, In, US 160/C4
Shadrinsk, Rus. 69/P4
Shaduzup, Myan. 86/C3
Shady Cove, Or, US 146/B2
Shady Grove, Fl, US 165/G2
Shady Spring, WV, US 163/G2
Shadyside, Oh, US 160/F5
Shafer (lake), In, US 160/C4
Shafranovo, Rus. 69/M5
Shafter, Ca, US 148/C3
Shafter, Nv, US 147/F3
Shafter, Tx, US 150/B3
Shaftesbury, Eng, UK 36/D4
Shaftsbury, Vt, US 161/K3
Shag Harbour, NS, Can. 158/E4
Shagamu, Nga. 115/F5
Shagan (riv.), Kaz. 99/C2
Shagang, China 81/B2
Shagany (lake), Urk. 72/E5
Shagany (lake), Rom. 51/J3
Shageluk, Ak, US 171/G3
Shagonar, Rus. 78/C1
Shah Alam, Malay. 89/C2
Shāh Kot, Pak. 98/B4
Shāhābād, India 98/D4
Shāhābād, India 96/B2
Shāhābād, India 96/B1
Shāhābād, India 96/A3
Shahbā', Syria 105/F3
Shāhbandar, Pak. 101/J4
Shahdād, Iran 101/G2
Shāhdādkot, Pak. 101/J3
Shāhdādpur, Pak. 101/J3
Shāhdara, Pak. 98/C4
Shāhdasht, Iran 103/F4
Shahdol, India 96/C4
Shahekan, China 78/F5
Shāhganj, India 96/D2
Shaḩḩāt, Libya 67/J4
Shāhjahānpur, India 96/B2
Shāhpur, Pak. 98/B3
Shāhpur, India 98/D3
Shāhpur, India 96/A4
Shāhpur Chākar, Pak. 92/A2
Shāhpura, India 96/C4
Shahr Sultān, Pak. 98/A5
Shahr-e Bābak, Iran 103/H4
Shahr-e Kord, Iran 103/G3
Shahr-e Monjān, Afg. 98/A1
Shahrak, Iran 103/G3
Shāhrūd, Iran 103/G3
Shahryār, Iran 103/G3
Shāhzādpur, India 98/D4
Shāhzādpur, Bang. 97/G3
Shā'ib al Banāt (peak), Egypt 109/G3
Shaikhpura, India 97/E3
Shāistāganj, Bang. 97/H3
Shājāpur, India 92/C3
Shaji, China 78/F4
Shajian, China 87/H3
Shajianzi, China 81/C2
Shakargarh, Pak. 98/C3
Shakaskraal, SAfr. 125/E3
Shakawe, Bots. 122/D3
Shakespeare (isl.), On, Can. 157/K3
Shakhbuz, Azer. 71/H5
Shakhtars'k, Ukr. 73/K3
Shakhtërsk, Rus. 79/N2
Shakhtinsk, Kaz. 74/H5
Shakhty, Rus. 73/L4
Shakhun'ya, Rus. 69/K4
Shaki, Nga. 115/F4
Shakīso, Eth. 118/A4
Shakopee, Mn, US 157/N7
Shakotan (pen.), Japan 82/B2
Shaksha, Rus. 69/N5
Shaktoolik, Ak, US 171/F3
Shāl, Iran 103/G3
Shala (lake), Eth. 118/A4
Shalaanbood, Som. 119/D1
Shalbuzdag (peak), Rus. 71/H4
Shaldon, Eng, UK 36/C5
Shalford, Eng, UK 30/B3
Shali, Rus. 71/H4
Shaling, China 81/B2
Shallotte, NC, US 163/H4
Shallow Reach (inlet), Austl. 131/M8
Shallowater, Tx, US 152/D4
Shalqar, Kaz. 71/L3
Shal'skiy, Rus. 68/H3
Shaluli (mts.), China 78/D5
Shalyhyne, Ukr. 73/H2
Shama (riv.), Tanz. 119/A3
Shamary, Rus. 69/N4
Shamattawa (riv.), On, Can. 141/H3
Shambe, Sudan 116/F4
Shambu, Eth. 116/H3
Shambungu, D.R. Congo 120/D4
Shāmgarh, India 92/C3
Shamīl, Iran 103/J5
Shāmli, India 98/D5
Shammar, Jabal (mts.), SAr. 100/D3
Shamokin (cr.), Pa, US 168/B2
Shamokin, Pa, US 168/B2
Shamokin Dam, Pa, US 168/B2
Shāmpur, India 96/A2
Shamrock, Tx, US 152/D3
Shamrock Dome (mt.), Yk, Can. 171/L3
Shamsābād, India 96/A4
Shamsābād, India 96/B2
Shamva, Zim. 123/F3
Shan (state), Myan. 93/G3
Shan (plat.), Myan. 93/G3
Shan (pass), China 87/H3
Shan-Ngaw (range), Myan. 86/C3
Shanagolden, Ire. 32/A4
Shanchengzhen, China 81/C1
Shandī, Sudan 116/G1
Shandon, Ca, US 148/B3
Shandong (prov.), China 79/H4
Shandong (pen.), China 79/H4
Shandong (isl.), China 80/E3
Shangani, Zim. 123/F3
Shangani (riv.), Zim. 123/F3
Shangcai, China 80/C4
Shangcheng, China 80/C5
Shangchuan (isl.), China 87/G4
Shangdu, China 87/G3
Shangdu, China 78/G3
Shangfang, China 87/H2
Shanghai (prov.), China 79/J5
Shanghai, China 80/L8
Shanghe, China 80/D3
Shanghekou, China 81/C2
Shangjiahe, China 81/C2
Shangjiaodao, China 87/H2
Shangjing, China 87/H3
Shangliang, China 78/F5
Shanglin, China 93/J3
Shangolume, D.R. Congo 121/F5
Shangombo, Zam. 122/D3
Shangping, China 87/G3
Shangqiu, China 80/C4
Shangrao, China 87/H2
Shangshui, China 80/C4
Shangsi, China 94/D1
Shangyi, China 80/C2
Shangyou (riv.), China 87/G3
Shanhua, Tai. 87/J4
Shani, Nga. 116/B3
Shanklin, Eng, UK 37/E5
Shankou, China 87/F2
Shanks, WV, US 161/G5
Shanmatang (mtn.), China 87/F3
Shanmen, China 87/F3
Shannawona (peak), Ire. 32/A3
Shannon, Qu, Can. 158/B2
Shannon (int'l arpt.), Ire. 32/B4
Shannon (riv.), Ire. 32/B4
Shannon, NZ 135/C3
Shannon, Ga, US 162/E3
Shannon, Ms, US 162/C3
Shannon (lake), Wa, US 144/C3
Shannon Hills, Ar, US 153/H3
Shannonbridge, Ire. 32/B3
Shanshan, China 78/C3
Shanshūr, Egypt 113/C4
Shantangyi, China 87/F3
Shanṭanūf, Egypt 113/C4
Shantar (isl.), Rus. 77/N4
Shantar (isls.), Rus. 75/P4
Shantou, China 87/H4
Shanty Bay, On, Can. 161/G2
Shanwa, Tanz. 119/A2
Shanxi (prov.), China 78/G4
Shanyang, China 87/H3
Shanyao, China 87/H3
Shanyin, China 80/C3
Shaodong, China 87/F3
Shaoguan, China 87/G3
Shaoshan, China 87/G3
Shaoxing, China 87/J2
Shaoyang, China 87/F3
Shap, Eng, UK 35/F2
Shapa, China 87/F4
Shapki, Rus. 41/P2
Shapkina (riv.), Rus. 69/M2
Shaqiuhe, China 99/E2
Shaqlāwah, Iraq 103/F2
Shaqrā', SAr. 100/E3
Shaqrā', Yem. 118/C2
Sharafkhāneh, Iran 103/F2
Sharan, Rus. 69/M5
Sharanga, Rus. 69/K4
Sharbot Lake, On, Can. 161/H2
Sharga, Mong. 78/D2
Sharhorod, Ukr. 72/E3
Shari, Japan 82/D2
Sharïngol, Mong. 78/F2
Sharjah (int'l arpt.), UAE 101/G3
Shark (bay), Austl. 127/A3
Shark River (inlet), NJ, US 168/D3
Sharkovshchina, Bela. 41/M4
Sharlyk, Rus. 71/K1
Sharm ash Shaykh, Egypt 109/G3
Sharnbrook, Eng, UK 37/F2
Sharnūb, Egypt 113/B2
Sharon, Ct, US 161/K4
Sharon, Pa, US 160/F4
Sharon, Tn, US 162/C2
Sharon, Vt, US 161/K3
Sharon Springs, Ks, US 152/D1
Sharonville, Oh, US 160/D5
Sharovka, Ukr. 73/H2
Sharpe (lake), SD, US 154/E1
Sharpes, Fl, US 165/H3
Sharpsburg, Ky, US 162/F1
Sharqpur, Pak. 98/C4
Sharquī, Jazīrat ash (isl.), Tun. 67/F4
Shar'ya, Rus. 69/K4
Shasha, Eth. 116/G4
Shashe, Bots. 123/E4
Shashe (riv.), Bots. 123/F4
Shashemenē, Eth. 118/A4
Shashi, China 87/G2
Shasta (lake), Ca, US 146/B3
Shasta (mt.), Ca, US 146/B3
Shasta (dam), Ca, US 146/B3
Shatalovo, Rus. 68/G5
Shāţi (wadi), Libya 134/B3
Shatsk, Rus. 71/G1
Shatsk, Bela. 41/M5
Shatskiy NP, Ukr. 43/M3
Shatt al Arab (riv.), Iraq 100/E2
Shattāy, Sudan 116/D2
Shattuck, Ok, US 152/E2
Shaughnessy, Ab, Can. 145/H3
Shaunavon, Sk, Can. 145/K3
Shavano Park, Tx, US 151/E3
Shave Ẕiyyon, Isr. 105/C3
Shaver Lake, Ca, US 148/C2
Shaw, La, US 164/C2
Shaw, Ms, US 162/B4
Shaw, Eng, UK 37/E4
Shaw (A.F.B.), SC, US 163/G4
Shawan, China 87/H3
Shawano, Wi, US 155/K1
Shawbury, Eng, UK 36/D1
Shawnee, Co, US 152/B1
Shawnee, Oh, US 160/E5
Shawnee, Ok, US 153/F3
Shawneetown, Il, US 162/C2
Shawnī, Egypt 113/B3
Shawville, Qu, Can. 161/H2
Shaxi, China 87/F3
Shay Gap, Austl. 130/D2
Shaykh Miskīn, Syria 105/E3
Shaykh Sa'd, Iraq 103/F3
Shaykh 'Uthmān, Yem. 118/C2
Shaykhān, Iraq 103/E2
Shaymak, Taj. 99/B4
Shazaoyuan, China 78/C4
Shazipo, China 87/F2
Shchara (riv.), Bela. 70/C1
Shchastya, Ukr. 73/K3
Shchedok, Rus. 71/G3
Shchekino, Rus. 70/F1
Shchelkovo, Rus. 69/W9
Shchel'yabozh, Rus. 69/N2
Shchel'yayur, Rus. 69/M2
Shcherbakty, Kaz. 74/H4
Shcherbinka, Rus. 69/W9
Shchigry, Rus. 73/J2
Shchors, Ukr. 72/F2
Shchuchin, Bela. 41/L5
Shchūchīnsk, Kaz. 99/B1
Shchuch'ye, Rus. 69/P5
She Xian, China 87/H2
Shea Stadium, NY, US 169/K9
Sheaville, Or, US 146/E2
Shebē, Eth. 116/H4
Shebekino, Rus. 73/J2
Sheberghān, Afg. 101/J1
Sheboygan, Wi, US 160/C3
Sheboygan Falls, Wi, US 160/C3
Shebunino, Rus. 79/N2
Shedd, Or, US 146/B1
Shediac, NB, Can. 158/E2
Shee (riv.), Sc, UK 33/C3
Sheelin (lake), Ire. 34/A4
Sheep (mt.), Ak, US 171/F2
Sheep (cr.), Id, US 146/F2
Sheep (mts.), Nv, US 148/E2
Sheep (riv.), Ab, Can. 144/G2
Sheep Mountain (peak), SD, US 154/C2
Sheepshead Bay (nbrhd.), NY, US 169/K9
Sheerness, Eng, UK 37/G4
Sheerness, Ab, Can. 145/J2
Sheet Harbour, NS, Can. 159/F3
Shefar'am, Isr. 105/C3
Shefayim, Isr. 105/B4
Sheffield, Austl. 132/C4
Sheffield, Eng, UK 35/G5

Sosúa, DRep. 173/G4
Sos'va (riv.), Rus. 74/G3
Sot (riv.), India 96/B1
Sotik, Kenya 119/A2
Sotkajärvi (lake), Fin. 39/E4
Soto del Real, Sp. 47/N8
Soto la Marina, Mex. 175/F4
Sotouboua, Togo 115/F4
Sotteville-lès-Rouen, Fr. 57/G2
Sottrum, Ger. 53/G2
Sotuta, Mex. 176/D1
Souanké, Congo 120/C2
Soubre, C.d'Iv. 114/D5
Soudan, Austl. 129/E5
Soudan, Fr. 56/D5
Soudan, Ar, US 162/B3
Soudan, Mn, US 157/H4
Soude (riv.), Fr. 55/D6
Souderton, Pa, US 168/C3
Soúdha, Gre. 75/J5
Souellaba (pt.), Camr. 120/B2
Souesmes, Fr. 57/H6
Souffelweyersheim, Fr. 55/G6
Soufflenheim, Fr. 55/G6
Souffles, Pic des (peak), Fr. 64/C3
Souflíon, Gre. 51/H5
Soufrière (peak), StV. 173/N9
Soufrière (peak), Guad. 173/N8
Sougéta, Gui. 114/B4
Souillac, Mrts. 125/T15
Souillac, Fr. 44/D4
Souk Ahras (wilaya), Alg. 112/K6
Souk Ahras, Alg. 112/K6
Souk el Arba du Rharb, Mor. 112/A2
Sŏul (Seoul) (cap.), SKor. 79/K4
Soulanges (co.), Qu, Can. 159/M7
Soulijärvi (lake), Fin. 39/E4
Soulles (riv.), Fr. 56/D2
Soultz-Haut-Rhin, Fr. 60/D2
Soultz-sous-Forêts, Fr. 58/A5
Soum (prov.), Burk. 115/E3
Soumagne, Belg. 55/E2
Sound of Bute (sound), Sc, UK 33/A5
Sounding (lake), Ab, Can. 145/J1
Sounding (cr.), Ab, Can. 145/J2
Souppes-sur-Loing, Fr. 44/E2
Sour El Ghozlane, Alg. 112/G4
Sour Lake, Tx, US 151/G2
Sourbaral (peak), Chad 116/D2
Sources, Mont aux (peak), Les. 124/E3
Sourdeval, Fr. 57/E3
Sourdough (peak), Id, US 146/F1
Soure, Port. 46/A2
Soure, Braz. 182/D3
Souris (riv.), Can.,US 140/F4
Souris, Mb, Can. 156/D3
Souris, PE, Can. 159/F2
Souris (riv.), Sk, Can. 145/N3
Souris, ND, US 156/D3
Souris (riv.), ND, US 156/D3
Sourou (prov.), Burk. 114/E3
Sours, Fr. 57/G4
Sous, Oued (riv.), Mor. 110/C3
Sousa, Braz. 183/G4
Sout (riv.), SAfr. 124/C3
South (cr.), Austl. 134/G8
South (mts.), NS, Can. 158/E3
South (bay), Nun, Can. 167/H2
South (sound), Ire. 32/A4
South (isl.), NZ 127/H7
South (cape), NZ 135/A4
South (pt.), La, US 164/C3
South (riv.), NC, US 163/H3
South (mtn.), Pa, US 168/A3
South Africa (ctry.) 107/E7
South Alligator (riv.), Austl. 128/D3
South Amboy, NJ, US 169/H10
South America (cont.) 202/*
South Anna (riv.), Va, US 163/H2
South Augusta, Ga, US 163/F4
South Australia (state), Austl. 127/C3
South Ayrshire (co.), Sc, UK 33/B6
South Bay, Fl, US 165/H4
South Baymouth, On, Can. 160/E2
South Beloit, Il, US 155/K2
South Bend, In, US 160/C4
South Bend, Tx, US 153/E4
South Bend, Wa, US 144/C4
South Benfleet, Eng, UK 37/G3
South Berwick, Me, US 161/L3
South Boston, Va, US 163/H2
South Branch, Nf, Can. 159/H2
South Brent, Eng, UK 36/C6
South Brook, Nf, Can. 159/J1
South Burlington, Vt, US 161/K2
South Caicos (isl.), UK 177/J1
South Carolina (state), US 163/G3
South Charleston, WV, US 163/G1
South China (sea), Asia 77/L8
South Cle Elum, Wa, US 144/D4
South Coffeyville, Ok, US 153/G2
South Colby, Wa, US 167/B2
South Colton, NY, US 161/J2
South Dakota (state), US 154/D1
South Dorset Downs (uplands), Eng, UK 36/D5
South Dos Palos, Ca, US 148/B2
South Downs (hills), Eng, UK 37/F5
South Dum Dum, India 97/G4
South East (pt.), Austl. 133/C4
South East (cape), Austl. 127/D5
South Elgin, Il, US 167/P16
South Elmsall, Eng, UK 35/G4
South Entrance (inlet), PNG 129/F2
South Esk (riv.), Sc, UK 33/C3
South Fallsburg, NY, US 161/J4
South Farmingdale, NY, US 169/M9
South Foreland (pt.), UK 54/A1
South Fork, Co, US 149/J2
South Fork Ind. Res., Nv, US 146/F3
South Fork Koyukuk (riv.), Ak, US 171/H2
South Fork Kuskokwim (riv.), Ak, US 171/H3
South Fox (isl.), Mi, US 157/M5
South Fulton, Tn, US 162/C2
South Gate, Ca, US 166/F8
South Gate, Md, US 168/B5
South Georgia (isl.), UK 26/H8
South Glamorgan (co.), Wal, UK 36/C4
South Gloucestershire (co.), Eng, UK 36/D3
South Grand (riv.), Mo, US 153/G1
South Grand (riv.), Mo, US 155/G4
South Hams (plain), Eng, UK 36/C6
South Haven, Mi, US 160/C3
South Heart, ND, US 156/C4
South Hill, Va, US 163/H2
South Holland, Il, US 167/Q16
South Holmwood, Eng, UK 30/C3
South Horr, Kenya 119/B1
South Houston, Tx, US 151/M9
South Hutchinson, Ks, US 153/F1
South Island NP, Kenya 119/B1
South Kinangop, Kenya 119/B2
South Kirkby, Eng, UK 35/G4
South Kitui Nat'l Rsv., Kenya 119/B2
South Koel (riv.), India 97/E4
South Korea (ctry.) 81/D4
South Lake Tahoe, Ca, US 146/D4
South Lanarkshire (co.), Sc, UK 33/C5
South Llano (riv.), Tx, US 150/D2
South Loup (riv.), Ne, US 154/E3
South Luangwa NP, Zam. 123/F2
South Lyon, Mi, US 167/E7
South Magnetic Pole, Ant. 192/K
South Manitou (isl.), Mi, US 160/C2
South Miami, Fl, US 164/P11
South Mills, NC, US 163/J2
South Milwaukee, Wi, US 160/C3
South Molton, Eng, UK 36/C4
South Monroe, Mi, US 160/E4
South Naknek, Ak, US 171/G4
South Nation (riv.), On, Can. 161/J2
South New River (canal), Fl, US 164/P10
South Normanton, Eng, UK 35/G5
South Nyack, NY, US 169/K7
South Ockenden, Eng, UK 30/D2
South Ogden, Ut, US 147/H3
South Ohio, NS, Can. 158/D4
South Orange, NJ, US 169/H9
South Orkney (isls.), UK 192/X
South Ossetia (reg.), Geo. 71/G4
South Oxhey, Eng, UK 30/B2
South Oyster (bay), NY, US 169/M9
South Pacific (ocean) 26/B7
South Padre Island, Tx, US 150/F4
South Palm Beach, Fl, US 164/P9
South Para (res.), Austl. 131/M8
South Paris, Me, US 161/L2
South Pasadena, Fl, US 164/K8
South Pasadena, Ca, US 166/F7
South Pekin, Il, US 155/K3
South Perth (nbrhd.), Austl. 130/K6
South Petherton, Eng, UK 36/D5
South Pine (riv.), Austl. 134/E6
South Plainfield, NJ, US 169/H9
South Plains, Tx, US 152/D3
South Platte (riv.), Co, Ne, US 154/C3
South Platte (riv.), Co, US 154/B4
South Platte, Middle Fork (riv.), Co, US 152/A1
South Polar (plat.), Ant. 192/Y
South Pole, Ant. 192/A
South Portland, Me, US 161/L3
South Prairie, Wa, US 167/C3
South Prong South Alafia (riv.), Fl, US 164/L8
South Pugwash, NS, Can. 158/F3
South Range Refuge, Ut, US 147/G4
South River, On, Can. 161/G2
South River, NJ, US 169/H10
South Rockwood, Mi, US 167/F7
South Ronaldsay (isl.), Sc, UK 31/V14
South Saint Paul, Mn, US 157/P7
South San Francisco, Ca, US 167/K11
South Sandwich (isls.), UK 26/H8
South Saskatchewan (riv.), Sk, Can. 140/E3
South Seaville, NJ, US 168/D5
South Shetland (isls.), UK 192/W
South Shields, Eng, UK 35/G2
South Shore, SD, US 155/F1
South Shore, Ky, US 163/F1
South Sioux City, Ne, US 155/F2
South Sister (peak), Or, US 146/C1
South Skunk (riv.), Ia, US 155/H2
South Sulphur (riv.), Tx, US 151/G1
South Sulphur (riv.), Tx, US 153/G4
South Taranaki Bight (bay), NZ 135/C2
South Tucson, Az, US 149/G4
South Tyne (riv.), Eng, UK 35/F2
South Ubian, Phil. 88/C4
South Uist (isl.), Sc, UK 31/Q8
South Umpqua (riv.), Or, US 146/B2
South Valley Stream, NY, US 169/L9
South West (cape), Austl. 132/C4
South West (cape), NZ 135/A4
South West City, Mo, US 153/G2
South West NP, Austl. 132/C4
South West Port Mouton, NS, Can. 158/E4
South West Rocks, Austl. 132/E1
South Whittier, Ca, US 166/F8
South Wichita (riv.), Tx, US 152/D4
South Williamsport, Pa, US 168/B1
South Woodham Ferrers, Eng, UK 30/E2
South Yorkshire (co.), Eng, UK 35/G5
South Zanesville, Oh, US 160/E5
Southall (nbrhd.), Eng, UK 30/B2
Southam, Eng, UK 37/E2
Southampton, On, Can. 160/F2
Southampton (isl.), Nun, Can. 167/H2
Southampton (cape), Nun, Can. 167/H2
Southampton (isl.), Can. 139/J3
Southampton, Eng, UK 37/E5
Southampton (co.), Eng, UK 37/E5
Southampton, NY, US 169/F2
Southampton Water (inlet), Eng, UK 37/E5
Southaven, Ms, US 162/B3
Southborough, Eng, UK 37/G4
Southbourne, Eng, UK 37/F5
Southbridge, Ma, US 161/K3
Southbridge, NZ 135/C3
Southbury, Ct, US 161/K4
Southeast (pt.), Bahm. 177/H1
Southeast (dist.), Bots. 122/E5
Southeast (pt.), Jam. 177/G2
Southeast (cape), Ak, US 171/E3
Southend, Sc, UK 34/C1
Southend (int'l arpt.), Eng, UK 37/G3
Southend-on-Sea, Eng, UK 37/G3
Southend-on-Sea (co.), Eng, UK 37/G3
Southern (riv.), Austl. 130/K7
Southern (dist.), Bots. 122/E5
Southern (dist.), Isr. 104/D4
Southern, Malw. 123/G2
Southern (mts.), NZ 127/G7
Southern (prov.), SLeo. 114/B5
Southern (prov.), SrL. 95/D5
Southern (prov.), Zam. 123/E3
Southern Cook (isls.), CookIs. 137/J6
Southern Cross, Austl. 130/C4
Southern Harbour, Nf, Can. 159/L2
Southern Highlands (prov.), PNG 129/F1
Southern Indian (lake), Mb, Can. 140/G3
Southern NP, Sudan 116/F4
Southern Pines, NC, US 163/H3
Southern Shores, NC, US 163/K2
Southern Uplands (hills), Sc, UK 35/D1
Southern Ural (mts.), Rus. 69/N5
Southern Ute Ind. Res., Co, US 149/H2
Southery, Eng, UK 37/G1
Southesk Tablelands (plat.), Austl. 127/B2
Southey, Sk, Can. 156/B2
Southfield, Mi, US 160/E3
Southgate, Mi, US 160/E3
Southgate (nbrhd.), Eng, UK 30/C2
Southgate (riv.), BC, Can. 144/B2
Southlake, Tx, US 150/K7
Southland, Tx, US 152/D4
Southminster, Eng, UK 37/G3
Southold, NY, US 169/F1
Southport, Eng, UK 35/E4
Southport, Fl, US 165/F2
Southport, NY, US 161/H3
Southport, NC, US 163/H4
Southside, Al, US 162/D4
Southside, Tn, US 162/D2
Southside Place, Tx, US 151/M9
South Tyneside (co.), Eng, UK 35/G2
Southwark (bor.), Eng, UK 30/A1
Southwell, Eng, UK 35/H5
Southwold, Eng, UK 37/H2
Southwood NP, Austl. 134/C4
Southworth, Wa, US 167/C3
Soutpansberg (mts.), SAfr. 123/F4
Sovata, Rom. 51/G2
Soverato Marina, It. 48/E3
Sovere, It. 62/D2
Sovetsk, Rus. 69/L4
Sovetsk, Rus. 41/J4
Sovetskaya, Rus. 73/L5
Sovetskaya Gavan', Rus. 79/N2
Sovetskiy, Rus. 69/L4
Sovetskoye, Rus. 71/H3
Sovets'kyy, Ukr. 73/H5
Sōwa, Japan 83/D1
Sowa Pan (salt pan), Bots. 122/E4
Sowerby Bridge, Eng, UK 35/G4
Soweto, SAfr. 124/D2
Sōya-misaki (cape), Japan 82/B1
Soyana (riv.), Rus. 68/J2
Soyang (lake), SKor. 84/A2
Soyaux, Fr. 44/D4
Soyen, Ger. 59/F6
Soyhières, Swi. 60/D3
Soyo, Ang. 120/C4
Sozh (riv.), Bela. 70/D1
Sozopol, Bul. 51/H4
Spa, Belg. 55/E3
Spaceport USA, Fl, US 165/H3
Spada (lake), Wa, US 167/D2
Spaichingen, Ger. 61/E1
Spain (ctry.) 46/C2
Spakenburg, Neth. 52/C4
Spalding, Austl. 131/H5
Spalding, Sk, Can. 145/M1
Spalding, Eng, UK 35/H6
Spalding, Mi, US 160/C2
Spallumcheen, BC, Can. 144/E2
Spalt, Ger. 58/D4
Spanaway, Wa, US 144/C4
Spangenberg, Ger. 53/G6
Spangle, Wa, US 144/F4
Spangler, Pa, US 161/G4
Spanish (pt.), Ire. 32/A4
Spanish Fork, Ut, US 147/H3
Spanish Fort, Al, US 164/E2
Spanish River Ind. Res., On, Can. 160/E1
Spanish Town, Jam. 177/G2
Spannort (peak), Swi. 61/E4
Spar City, Co, US 149/J2
Sparanise, It. 65/D5
Sparkman, Ar, US 153/H4
Sparks, Ga, US 165/G2
Sparks, Nv, US 146/D4
Sparks, Tx, US 150/F2
Sparlingville, Mi, US 167/G6
Sparreholm, Swe. 40/G2
Sparta, Ga, US 163/F4
Sparta, Il, US 162/C1
Sparta, Mo, US 153/H2
Sparta, Mi, US 160/D3
Sparta, NJ, US 168/D1
Sparta, NC, US 163/G2
Sparta, Tn, US 162/E3
Sparta, Wi, US 155/J2
Sparta (Spárti), Gre. 75/H4
Spartanburg, SC, US 163/G3
Spartel (cape), Mor. 112/B2
Spárti (Sparta), Gre. 75/H4
Spartivento (cape), It. 48/E4
Sparwood, BC, Can. 144/G3
Spas-Demensk, Rus. 68/G5
Spassk-Dal'niy, Rus. 79/L3
Spasskaya Guba, Rus. 68/G3
Spáta, Gre. 75/N9
Spátha (cape), Gre. 75/H5
Spavinaw, Ok, US 153/G2
Spay, Ger. 55/G3
Spean (riv.), Sc, UK 33/B3
Spean Bridge, Sc, UK 33/B3
Spearfish, SD, US 154/C1
Spearman, Tx, US 152/D2
Spearville, Ks, US 152/E2
Speculator, NY, US 161/J3
Speedway, In, US 160/C5
Speer (peak), Swi. 61/F3
Speers, Sk, Can. 145/L1
Speicher, Swi. 61/F3
Speicher, Ger. 55/F4
Speichersdorf, Ger. 59/E3
Speke, Eng, UK 35/F5
Speke (int'l arpt.), Eng, UK 35/F5
Speke (gulf), Tanz. 119/A2
Spelle, Ger. 53/E4
Spello, It. 65/B2
Spence Bay, Nun, Can. 140/G2
Spencer (cape), Austl. 131/H5
Spencer (gulf), Austl. 127/C4
Spencer (cape), Ak, US 171/E2
Spencer, In, US 160/C5
Spencer, Ia, US 155/G2
Spencer, NC, US 163/G3
Spencer, Tn, US 162/E3
Spencer, Wi, US 155/J1
Spencer, WV, US 163/G1
Spencerville, Ok, US 153/G3
Spencerville, Oh, US 160/D4
Spences Bridge, BC, Can. 144/D2
Spenge, Ger. 53/F4
Spennymoor, Eng, UK 35/G2
Spentrup, Den. 40/D3
Sperkhiás, Gre. 75/H3
Sperkhíos (riv.), Gre. 75/H3
Sperlonga, It. 65/C5
Sperrin (mts.), NI, UK 34/A2
Spessart (range), Ger. 58/C3
Spétsai, Gre. 75/H4
Spey (bay), Sc, UK 33/C1
Spey (riv.), Sc, UK 33/B2
Speyer, Ger. 58/B4
Speyerbsch (riv.), Ger. 58/B4
Speyside, On, Can. 160/T8
Spezzano Albanese, It. 48/E3
Špičák (peak), Czh. 59/F2
Spicer (isls.), Nun, Can. 167/H2
Spicer, Mn, US 155/G1
Spicewood, Tx, US 150/E2
Spickard, Mo, US 155/H3
Spiddle, Ire. 32/A3
Spiekeroog (isl.), Ger. 53/E1
Spiez, Swi. 60/D4
Spigno Monferrato, It. 62/B4
Spijkenisse, Neth. 52/B5
Spike (mt.), Ak, US 171/K2
Spilamberto, It. 63/E4
Spílion, Gre. 75/J5
Spillersboda, Swe. 39/B1
Spillimacheen (riv.), BC, Can. 144/F2
Spillimacheen, BC, Can. 144/F2
Spilsby, Eng, UK 35/J5
Spilve (int'l arpt.), Lat. 41/L3
Spina (peak), It. 48/A2
Spinea, It. 63/F3
Spinetta Marengo, It. 62/B4
Spino d'Adda, It. 62/C3
Spirano, It. 62/C2
Spirit, Wi, US 157/J5
Spirit (lake), Ia, US 155/G2
Spirit Lake, Ia, US 155/G2
Spirit Lake, Id, US 144/F4
Spirit, North (lake), On, Can. 157/H1
Spiritwood, Sk, Can. 145/L1
Spiro, Ok, US 153/G3
Spišská Nová Ves, Slvk. 43/L4
Spitak, Arm. 71/H4
Spiti (riv.), India 98/D3
Spitsbergen (isl.), Sval. 74/B2
Spittal an der Drau, Aus. 45/K3
Spivey, Ks, US 153/E2
Spivey (lake), Ga, US 163/M7
Splendora, Tx, US 151/G2
Split, Cro. 50/C4
Split (int'l arpt.), Cro. 50/C4
Split (lake), Mb, Can. 140/G3
Split (mtn.), Ca, US 148/C2
Splitrock (res.), NJ, US 169/H8
Spluga, Passo dello (pass), Swi. 61/F5
Splügen, Swi. 61/F4
Špoği, Lat. 41/M3
Spokane, Mo, US 153/H2
Spokane, Wa, US 144/F4
Spokane Ind. Res., Wa, US 144/E4
Spokoynaya, Rus. 73/L5
Spöl (riv.), It. 61/G5
Spoleto, It. 65/B2
Spoltore, It. 65/D3
Spook Cave, Ia, US 155/J2
Spoon (riv.), Il, US 155/K3
Spooner, Wi, US 157/J5
Spotorno, It. 62/B5
Spotswood, NJ, US 169/H10
Spotsylvania Courthouse, Va, US 163/J1
Sprague, Mb, Can. 157/G3
Sprague (riv.), Or, US 146/C2
Sprague, Wa, US 144/F4
Sprang, Neth. 52/C5
Spranger (mt.), BC, Can. 144/D1
Spratly (isls.) 90/D2
Spray, Or, US 146/D1
Spree (riv.), Ger. 43/H2
Sprendlingen, Ger. 55/G4
Spresiano, It. 63/F2
Sprimont, Belg. 55/E3
Spring (riv.), Ar, US 162/B2
Spring (lake), Ca, US 148/D3
Spring (cr.), Nv, US 146/E3
Spring (cr.), Ne, US 154/D3
Spring (mts.), Nv, US 148/E2
Spring, Tx, US 151/M8
Spring City, Pa, US 168/C3
Spring City, Tn, US 162/E3
Spring City, Ut, US 147/H4
Spring Grove, Il, US 167/P15
Spring Grove, Mn, US 155/J2
Spring Grove, Pa, US 168/B4
Spring Hill, Ar, US 153/H4
Spring Hill, Fl, US 164/K7
Spring Hill, Ks, US 153/G1
Spring Hill, Tn, US 162/D3
Spring Lake, Fl, US 164/L7
Spring Lake, NJ, US 168/D3
Spring Lake, NC, US 163/H3
Spring Valley, Ca, US 166/D5
Spring Valley, NY, US 169/J7
Spring Valley, Mn, US 155/H2
Spring Valley, Tx, US 151/M9
Springbok, SAfr. 124/B3
Springbokvlatke (valley), SAfr. 123/F5
Springboro, Oh, US 160/D5
Springdale, Ar, US 153/G2
Springdale, Ut, US 149/F2
Springdale, Wa, US 144/F3
Springdale, SC, US 163/G3
Springe, Ger. 53/G4
Springer, Ok, US 153/F3
Springer, NM, US 152/B2
Springerville, Az, US 149/H3
Springfield, Co, US 152/C2
Springfield, Fl, US 165/F2
Springfield, Ga, US 163/G4
Springfield, Ky, US 162/E2
Springfield, Ma, US 161/K3
Springfield, Mi, US 160/D3
Springfield, Mo, US 153/H2
Springfield, Oh, US 160/E5
Springfield, NJ, US 169/H9
Springfield, Or, US 146/B1
Springfield, SD, US 154/F2
Springfield, Mn, US 155/G1
Springfield (cap.), Il, US 155/K4
Springfield, Tn, US 162/D2
Springfield, Va, US 168/A6
Springfield, Vt, US 161/K3
Springfontein, SAfr. 124/D3
Springhill, NS, Can. 158/E3
Springhill, La, US 153/H4
Springs, SAfr. 124/E2
Springs, NY, US 169/F1
Springside, Sk, Can. 156/C2
Springsure, Austl. 134/C4
Springtown, Tx, US 150/K7
Springvale, Me, US 161/L3
Springvale (nbrhd.), Austl. 132/G5
Springview, Ne, US 154/E2
Springville, NY, US 161/G3
Springville, Ut, US 147/H3
Springville, Al, US 162/D4
Springville, Ia, US 155/J2
Springwater, NY, US 161/H3
Springwater, Sk, Can. 145/K2
Springwater Nat'l Wild. Ref., ND, US 156/D4
Sprockhövel, Ger. 53/E6
Sprowston, Eng, UK 37/H1
Spruce (mtn.), Nv, US 147/F3
Spruce (peak), WV, US 163/H1
Spruce Knob NRA, WV, US 163/H1
Spruce Lake, Sk, Can. 145/K1
Spruce Pine, NC, US 163/F3
Spruce Run (res.), NJ, US 168/C2
Sprucewoods, Mb, Can. 156/E3
Spui (riv.), Neth. 52/B5
Spur, Tx, US 152/D4
Spurn (pt.), Eng, UK 35/J4
Spuzzum, BC, Can. 144/D3
Spydeberg, Nor. 38/T9
Spydeberg (peak), Nor. 38/S9
Squa Pan (lake), Me, US 158/C2
Squamish (riv.), BC, Can. 144/C3
Squamish, BC, Can. 144/C3
Square Butte, Mt, US 145/J4
Squaw Creek Nat'l Wild. Ref., Mo, US 155/G3
Squaw Harbor, Ak, US 171/F4
Squaw Lake, Mn, US 157/G4
Squaw Valley, Ca, US 148/C2
Squaxin Island Ind. Res., Wa, US 167/A3
Squinzano, It. 75/F2
Squire, WV, US 163/G2
Squires (mt.), Austl. 131/E3
Squires, Mo, US 153/H2
Srbobran, Serb. 50/D3
Sre Ambel, Camb. 94/C4
Sre Khtum, Camb. 94/D3
Sre Noy, Camb. 94/D3
Srebrenica, Bosn. 50/D3
Sredna (mts.), Bul. 75/J1
Srednebelaya, Rus. 79/K1
Srednekolymsk, Rus. 75/R3
Sredniy Ikorets, Rus. 73/K2
Srednogorie, Bul. 51/G4
Srednyaya Akhtuba, Rus. 71/H2
Śrem, Pol. 43/J2
Sremčica, Serb. 50/E3
Sremska Mitrovica, Serb. 50/D3
Sreng (riv.), Camb. 94/C3
Srepok (riv.), Camb. 94/D3
Sretensk, Rus. 79/H1
Sri Dungargarh, India 101/K3
Sri Gangānagar, India 98/B5
Sri Jayewardenepura Kotte (cap.), SrL. 95/C5
Sri Kshetra (ruin), Myan. 86/B5
Sri Lanka (ctry.) 92/D6
Srikākulam, India 95/D2
Srimangal, Bang. 97/H3
Srīnagar, India 98/C2
Srīrampur, India 95/B2
Srīvardhan, India 95/B2
Środa Śląska, Pol. 43/J3
Środa Wielkopolska, Pol. 43/J2
St-Floris, PN de, CAfr. 116/D3
Staaten (riv.), Austl. 129/F4
Staaten River NP, Austl. 129/F4
Stabbursdalen NP, Nor. 38/H1
Staberhuk (pt.), Ger. 40/D4
Stabroek, Belg. 52/B6
Stacyville, Ia, US 155/H2
Stadbroke, North (isl.), Austl. 127/E3
Stade, Ger. 53/G1
Staden, Belg. 54/C2
Stadl-Paura, Aus. 59/G6
Stadskanaal, Neth. 52/D3
Stadtbergen, Ger. 58/D6
Stadthagen, Ger. 53/G4
Stadtlauringen, Ger. 58/D2
Stadtlohn, Ger. 52/D5
Stadtoldendorf, Ger. 53/G5
Stadtsteinach, Ger. 59/E2
Stäfa, Swi. 61/E3
Staffanstorp, Swe. 40/E4
Staffelberg (peak), Ger. 58/E2
Staffelegg (pass), Swi. 60/E3
Staffelsee (lake), Ger. 61/H2
Staffelstein, Ger. 58/D2
Staffhorst, Ger. 53/F3
Staffora (riv.), It. 62/C3
Stafford, Eng, UK 35/F6
Stafford, Ct, US 161/K4
Stafford, Tx, US 151/M9
Stafford, Va, US 163/J1
Stagno, It. 62/D6
Stagnone, Isole della (isl.), It. 48/B4
Stahnsdorf, Ger. 42/Q7
Staicele, Lat. 41/L3
Staindrop, Eng, UK 35/G2
Staines, Eng, UK 30/B2
Stains, Fr. 30/K5
Stakes (mt.), Ca, US 167/M12
Stäket, Swe. 39/A1
Stakhanov, Ukr. 73/K3
Stalbridge, Eng, UK 36/D5
Stalden, Swi. 60/D5
Stalham, Eng, UK 37/H1
Stallarholmen, Swe. 39/A1
Stallworthy (cape), Nun, Can. 167/S6
Stalowa Wola, Pol. 43/M3
Stalwart, Sk, Can. 145/M2
Stalybridge, Eng, UK 35/F5
Stambaugh, Mi, US 157/K4
Stamboliyski, Bul. 75/J1
Stamford, Austl. 134/A3
Stamford, Eng, UK 37/F1
Stamford, Ct, US 169/L7
Stamford, NY, US 161/J3
Stamford, Tx, US 152/E4
Stamford (lake), Tx, US 150/E1
Stamford Bridge, Eng, UK 35/H4
Stampa, Swi. 61/F5
Stampede (res.), Ca, US 146/C4
Stampriet, Namb. 122/C5
Stamps, Ar, US 153/H4
Stamullen, Ire. 34/B4
Stanardsville, Va, US 163/H1
Stanberry, Mo, US 155/G3
Stanchfield, Mn, US 157/H5
Standard, Ab, Can. 145/H2
Standerton, SAfr. 124/E2
Standing Indian (peak), NC, US 163/F3
Standing Rock, Al, US 162/E4
Standing Rock Ind. Res., SD, US 154/D1
Standish, Mi, US 160/E3
Standish, Me, US 161/L3
Standish-with-Langtree, Eng, UK 35/F4
Stanfield, Az, US 149/G4
Stanfield, Or, US 144/E5
Stanford, Ky, US 162/E2
Stanford, Mt, US 145/J4
Stanford Rivers, Eng, UK 30/D1
Stanford-le-Hope, Eng, UK 37/G3
Stange, Nor. 40/D1
Stangelville, Wi, US 160/C2
Stanger, SAfr. 125/E3
Stanghella, It. 63/E3
Stanhope, Eng, UK 35/F2
Stanhope, NJ, US 168/D2
Stanišić, Serb. 50/D3
Stanislaus (co.), Ca, US 167/M12
Stanislaus (riv.), Ca, US 146/C4
Stanke Dimitrov, Bul. 75/H1
Stanley, NB, Can. 158/D2
Stanley, ND, US 156/C3
Stanley, Sc, UK 33/C4
Stanley, Eng, UK 35/G2
Stanley, Austl. 132/C4
Stanley, NM, US 149/K3
Stanley, Wi, US 155/J1
Stanley (mt.), Austl. 131/F2
Stanley (res.), India 92/C5
Stanley (cap.), Falk. 191/F6
Stanley, China 87/L8
Stanley (mt.), Austl. 133/B5
Stanleytown, Va, US 163/H2
Stanleyville, NC, US 163/G2
Stanovo, Serb. 50/E4
Stanovoy (range), Rus. 77/M4
Stans, Swi. 61/E4
Stanstead Plain, Qu, Can. 161/K2
Stansted, Eng, UK 30/D3
Stansted (int'l arpt.), Eng, UK 37/G3
Stansted Mountfitchet, Eng, UK 37/G3
Stanthorpe, Austl. 134/C5
Stanton, Eng, UK 37/G2
Stanton, Al, US 162/D4
Stanton, Ca, US 166/G8
Stanton, De, US 168/C4
Stanton, Ky, US 162/F2
Stanton, Ia, US 155/G3
Stanton, Mi, US 160/D3
Stanton, ND, US 156/D4
Stanton, Ne, US 155/F3
Stanton, NJ, US 168/D2
Stanton, Tn, US 162/C3
Stanton, Tx, US 150/D1
Stanwell, Eng, UK 30/B2
Stanwood, Wa, US 144/C3
Stanychno-Luhans'ke, Ukr. 73/K3
Staphorst, Neth. 52/D3
Stapleford, Eng, UK 37/E4
Stapleford Abbotts, Eng, UK 30/D2
Staplehurst, Ne, US 155/F3
Staplehurst, Eng, UK 37/G4
Staples, Mn, US 157/G4
Staples, On, Can. 167/G7
Stapleton, Al, US 164/E2
Stapleton, Ga, US 163/F4
Stapleton, Ne, US 154/D3
Stąporków, Pol. 43/L3
Star', Rus. 70/E1
Star, Tx, US 151/E2
Star City, Sk, Can. 145/M1
Star City, Ar, US 153/J4
Star Lake, NY, US 161/J2
Stara Pazova, Serb. 50/E3
Stara Planina (mts.), Serb. 50/F3
Stara Vyzhivka, Ukr. 72/C2
Stara Zagora, Bul. 51/G4
Starachowice, Pol. 43/L3
Staranzano, It. 63/G2
Staraya Racheyka, Rus. 71/J1
Staraya Russa, Rus. 41/P2
Starbuck, Mb, Can. 156/F3
Starbuck, Mn, US 157/G5
Starbuck (isl.), Kiri. 137/K5
Starcke NP, Austl. 134/B1
Stargard Szczeciński, Pol. 40/F5
Stari Grad, Cro. 50/C4
Stark, Ks, US 153/G2
Starke, Fl, US 165/G3
Starkey, Or, US 146/D1
Starkville, Ms, US 162/C4
Starkweather, ND, US 156/E3
Starnberg, Ger. 59/E6
Starnbergersee (lake), Ger. 61/H2
Starobil's'k, Ukr. 73/K3
Staroderevyankovskaya, Rus. 73/K4
Starodub, Rus. 70/E1
Starogard Gdański, Pol. 40/H5
Starokostyantyniv, Ukr. 72/D3
Starominskaya, Rus. 73/K4
Staronizhestebliyevskaya, Rus. 73/K5
Staroshcherbinovskaya, Rus. 73/K4
Starotitarovskaya, Rus. 73/J5
Starovelichkovskaya, Rus. 73/K5
Start (bay), Eng, UK 36/C6
Start (pt.), Eng, UK 36/C6
Start (pt.), Sc, UK 31/V14
Start, La, US 153/J4
Startup, Wa, US 167/D2
Staryy Kistruss, Rus. 68/J5
Staryy Krym, Ukr. 73/H5
Staryy Oskol`, Rus. 73/J2
Staryy Studenets, Rus. 69/L5
Staryye Dorogi, Bela. 70/D1
Staszów, Pol. 43/L3
State College, Pa, US 161/H4
State Fair Park (Cotton Bowl), Tx, US 150/L7
State Fairgrounds, De, US 168/C6
State Line, Ms, US 164/D2
Staten (isl.), NY, US 168/D2
Statenville, Ga, US 165/G2
States (int'l arpt.), Chl, UK 56/C2
Statesboro, Ga, US 163/G4
Statesville, NC, US 163/G3
Statham, Ga, US 162/F4
Statts Mills, WV, US 163/G1
Statue of Liberty Nat'l Mon., NY, US 169/J9
Staufen im Breisgau, Ger. 60/D2
Staufenberg, Ger. 42/E3
Staunton, Il, US 155/K4
Staunton, Eng, UK 36/D3
Staunton, Va, US 163/H1
Staunton on Wye, Eng, UK 36/D2
Stavanger, Nor. 40/A2
Staveley, Eng, UK 35/F3
Staveley, Eng, UK 35/G5
Stavelot, Belg. 55/E3
Stavely, Ab, Can. 145/H2
Staveren, Neth. 52/C3
Stavern, Nor. 40/D2
Stavropol', Rus. 73/M5
Stavropol'skiy Kray, Rus. 74/E5
Stavrós, Gre. 75/H2
Stavsnäs, Swe. 39/B1
Stavyshche, Ukr. 72/F3
Stawell, Austl. 132/B3
Stayner, On, Can. 160/F2
Stayton, Or, US 146/B1
Steamboat Slough (riv.), Ca, US 167/L10
Steamboat Springs, Co, US 147/K3
Stearns, Ky, US 162/E2
Stebbins, Ak, US 171/F3
Stebnyk, Ukr. 72/B3
Steckborn, Swi. 61/E2
Stederau (riv.), Ger. 53/H3
Steeg, Aus. 61/G3
Steel (mtn.), Id, US 147/F2
Steele, ND, US 156/E4
Steele, Mo, US 162/C2
Steele (cr.), Austl. 132/F5
Steele's Knowe (hill), Sc, UK 33/C4
Steeleville, Il, US 162/C1
Steelpoortrivier (riv.), SAfr. 125/E2
Steelton, Pa, US 168/B3
Steelville, Mo, US 153/J2
Steenbergen, Neth. 52/B5
Steenkool, Indo. 91/H4
Steens Mtn. Recreation Lands, Or, US 146/D2
Steensby (inlet), Nun, Can. 167/J1
Steenvoorde, Fr. 54/B2
Steenwijk, Neth. 52/D3
Steep (pt.), Austl. 130/B3
Steep Holm (isl.), Eng, UK 36/C4
Steep Rock, Mb, Can. 156/E2
Steeping (riv.), Eng, UK 35/J5
Ştefăneşti, Rom. 72/D4
Stefansson (isl.), Nun, Can. 140/F1
Steffen (peak), Chile 190/C5
Steffisburg, Swi. 60/D4
Steg, Swi. 60/D5
Stege, Den. 40/E4
Steglitz, Ger. 42/Q7
Steiermark (prov.), Aus. 43/H5
Steigerwald (for.), Ger. 45/J2
Steilacoom, Wa, US 167/B3
Steilloopbrug, SAfr. 123/F4
Steimbke, Ger. 53/G3
Stein, Neth. 55/E2
Stein (riv.), BC, Can. 144/D2
Stein am Rhein, Swi. 61/E2
Stein bei Nünnberg, Ger. 58/E4
Steina (riv.), Ger. 61/E2
Steinach, Ger. 58/E2
Steinach (riv.), Ger. 58/E2
Steinach, Ger. 59/F5
Steinach am Brenner, Aus. 61/H3
Steinau an der Strasse, Ger. 58/C2
Steinbach, Mb, Can. 156/F3
Steinbach an der Steyr, Aus. 59/H7
Steinbourg, Fr. 55/G6
Steinen, Ger. 60/D2
Steinen (riv.), Braz. 185/H4
Steinerkirchen an der Traun, Aus. 59/G6
Steinfeld, Ger. 58/B4
Steinfeld, Ger. 58/C3
Steinfeld, Ger. 53/F3
Steinfort, Lux. 55/E4
Steingaden, Ger. 61/G2
Steinhagen, Ger. 53/F4
Steinhatchee, Fl, US 165/G3
Steinhausen, Swi. 61/E3
Steinhausen, Namb. 122/C4
Steinhausen an der Rottum, Ger. 61/F1
Steinheid, Ger. 58/D2
Steinheim, Ger. 53/G5
Steinheim am Albuch, Ger. 58/D5
Steinheim an der Murr, Ger. 58/C5
Steinhorst, Ger. 53/H3
Steinhuder (lake), Ger. 53/G4
Steinkjer, Nor. 38/D2
Steinsland, Nor. 40/A1
Steinstücken, Ger. 42/Q7
Steinweiler, Ger. 58/B4
Stekene, Belg. 52/B6
Steklyanka, Rus. 68/J4
Stella (peak), It. 61/F5
Stella, SAfr. 124/D2
Stella, Ne, US 155/G3
Stellarton, NS, Can. 159/F3
Stelle, Ger. 53/H2
Stellenbosch, SAfr. 124/L10
Stello (peak), Fr. 48/A1
Stelvio, Passo di (pass), It. 61/G4
Stelvio, PN dello (nat'l park), It. 45/J3
Stenay, Fr. 55/E5
Stendal, Ger. 42/F2
Stende, Lat. 41/K3
Steneto NP, Bul. 51/G4
Stenhamra, Swe. 39/A1
Stenhousemuir, Sc, UK 33/C4
Stenlille, Den. 39/H7
Stenløse, Den. 39/J7
Stensån (riv.), Swe. 39/K6
Stenungsund, Swe. 40/D2
Step'anavan, Arm. 71/H4
Stepaside, Ire. 34/B5
Stephan, SD, US 154/E1
Stephansposching, Ger. 59/F5
Stephens, Ar, US 153/H4
Stephens City, Va, US 163/H1
Stephens Creek, Austl. 132/B1
Stephensburg, Ky, US 162/D2
Stephenson, Mi, US 160/C2
Stephenville, Nf, Can. 159/H1
Stephenville, Tx, US 151/E1
Stephenville Crossing, Nf, Can. 159/H1
Stepnoy, Rus. 69/P5
Stepnoye, Rus. 71/H3
Stepnoye, Rus. 71/H2
Steptoe (valley), Nv, US 147/F4
Steptoe, Wa, US 144/F4
Sterkspruit, SAfr. 124/D3
Sterkstroom, SAfr. 124/D3
Sterling, Ak, US 171/H3
Sterling, Co, US 154/C3
Sterling, Ga, US 165/H2
Sterling, Il, US 155/K3
Sterling, Ks, US 153/E1
Sterling, Mi, US 160/D2
Sterling City, Tx, US 150/D2
Sterling Heights, Mi, US 160/E3
Sterlington, La, US 153/H4
Sterlitamak, Rus. 71/K1
Sternstein (peak), Aus. 59/H5
Sterzing (Vipiteno), It. 61/H4
Stęszew, Pol. 43/J2
Štěti, Czh. 59/H2
Stetsonville, Wi, US 155/J1
Stettler, Ab, Can. 145/H1
Steubenville, Oh, US 160/F4
Stevenage, Eng, UK 37/F3
Stevens Point, Wi, US 155/K1
Stevens Village, Ak, US 171/J2
Stevenson (cr.), Austl. 131/G3
Stevenson, Al, US 162/E3
Stevenson, Wa, US 144/D5
Stevenson Entrance (Str.), Ak, US 171/H4
Stevenston, Sc, UK 33/B5
Stevensville, Mi, US 160/C3
Stevensville, Mt, US 145/G4
Stevensville, Md, US 168/B6
Stevinsluizen (dam), Neth. 52/C3
Stewardson, Il, US 162/C1
Stewart (mt.), Ab, Can. 144/F1
Stewart, BC, Can. 171/N4
Stewart (riv.), Yk, Can. 140/C2
Stewart (isl.), NZ 127/G7
Stewart, Al, US 162/D4
Stewart, Ms, US 162/C4
Stewart Crossing, Yk, Can. 171/L3
Stewart Lake Nat'l Wild. Ref., ND, US 156/C4
Stewart River, Yk, Can. 171/L3
Stewart Valley, Sk, Can. 145/L2
Stewarton, Sc, UK 33/B5
Stewartstown, NI, UK 34/B2
Stewartstown, Pa, US 168/B4
Stewartville, Mn, US 155/H2
Stewiacke, NS, Can. 158/F3
Steyning, Eng, UK 37/F5
Steynrus, SAfr. 124/D2
Steynsburg, SAfr. 124/D3
Steyr (riv.), Aus. 43/H5
Steyr, Aus. 59/H6
Steyregg, Aus. 59/H6
Steytlerville, SAfr. 124/D4
Stia, It. 63/E6
Stiava, It. 62/D6
Stickney (mt.), Wa, US 167/D2
Stiens, Neth. 52/C2
Stigler, Ok, US 153/G3
Stigtomta, Swe. 40/G2
Stikine, BC, Can. 171/M4
Stikine (riv.), BC, Can. 171/M4
Stilbaai, SAfr. 124/C4
Stiles, Tx, US 150/D2
Stiles, Wi, US 160/B2
Stilfontein, SAfr. 124/D2
Stilís, Gre. 75/H3
Still Creek (res.), Pa, US 168/C2
Still Pond, Md, US 168/B5
Stilling, Den. 40/D3
Stillmore, Ga, US 163/F4
Stillwater, Ok, US 153/F2
Stillwater (res.), NY, US 161/J3
Stillwater (riv.), Mt, US 147/J1
Stillwater (range), Nv, US 146/D4
Stillwater, Mn, US 157/Q6
Stillwater (lake), Pa, US 168/C1
Stillwater, Pa, US 168/B1
Stillwater NWR, Nv, US 146/D4
Stilo (cape), It. 48/E3
Stilwell, Ok, US 153/G3
Štimlje, Serb. 50/E4
Stimpfach, Ger. 58/D4
Stimson (mt.), Mt, US 145/H3
Stinchar (riv.), Sc, UK 34/D1
Stinking Water (cr.), Ne, US 154/D3
Stinnett, Tx, US 152/D3
Štip, FYROM 75/H2
Stiring-Wendel, Fr. 55/F5
Stírka (peak), Czh. 59/G4
Stirling, Austl. 131/G2
Stirling (mt.), Austl. 130/C4
Stirling (nbrhd.), Austl. 131/M9
Stirling (nbrhd.), Austl. 130/K6
Stirling, Ab, Can. 145/H3
Stirling, On, Can. 161/H2
Stirling, Sc, UK 33/C4
Stirling (co.), Sc, UK 33/B4
Stirling Range NP, Austl. 130/C5
Stirone (riv.), It. 62/C3
Stites, Id, US 144/G4
Stjørdal, Nor. 38/D3
Stob a' Choin (peak), Sc, UK 33/B4
Stob Choire Claurigh (peak), Sc, UK 33/B3
Stochov, Czh. 59/G2
Stock (lake), Fr. 55/F6
Stock, Eng, UK 30/E2
Stockach, Ger. 61/F2
Stockbridge, Mi, US 160/D3
Stockbridge, Ma, US 161/K3
Stockbridge, Ga, US 163/M7
Stockbridge, Eng, UK 37/E4
Stockbridge Ind. Res., Wi, US 155/K1
Stockbury, Eng, UK 30/E3
Stockdale, Tx, US 151/F3
Stockerau, Aus. 51/N7
Stockertown, Pa, US 168/C2
Stockett, Mt, US 145/J4
Stockheim, Ger. 58/E2
Stockholm, Sk, Can. 156/C2

Swanse – Tarpor

Swansea, Austl. 132/D4
Swansea (bay), Eng, UK 36/C3
Swansea, Wal, UK 36/C3
Swansea (co.), Wal, UK 36/B3
Swanson (res.), Ne, US 154/D3
Swanton, Oh, US 160/E4
Swanton, Vt, US 161/K2
Swanville, Mn, US 157/G5
Swart Kei (riv.), SAfr. 124/D3
Swarthmore, Pa, US 168/C4
Swartruggens, SAfr. 123/E5
Swartswood (lake), NJ, US 168/D1
Swartz (cr.), Mi, US 167/E6
Swartz Creek, Mi, US 160/E3
Swarzędz, Pol. 43/J2
Swarzenbach an der Sächsischen Saale, Ger. 59/E2
Swarzrand (mts.), Namb. 124/B2
Swāt (riv.), Pak. 98/B2
Swatara, Mn, US 157/H4
Swatara (cr.), Pa, US 168/B3
Swatragh, NI, UK 34/B2
Swauk (pass), Wa, US 144/D4
Sway, Eng, UK 37/E5
Swayambhunath, Nepal 97/E2
Swaziland (ctry.) 125/E2
Sweden (ctry.) 38/E3
Swedesboro, NJ, US 168/C4
Swedru, Gha. 115/E5
Sweeden, Ky, US 162/D2
Sweeny, Tx, US 150/G3
Sweers (isl.), Austl. 129/E4
Sweet Grass Ind. Res., Sk, Can. 145/K1
Sweet Home, Or, US 146/B1
Sweet Home, Tx, US 151/F3
Sweet Springs, Mo, US 155/H4
Sweet Water, Al, US 164/E1
Sweetwater (res.), Ca, US 166/D5
Sweetwater, Fl, US 164/P11
Sweetwater (lake), ND, US 156/E3
Sweetwater, Ok, US 152/E3
Sweetwater, Tn, US 162/E3
Sweetwater, Tx, US 150/D1
Sweetwater (riv.), Wy, US 147/J2
Swellendam, SAfr. 124/C4
Świdnica, Pol. 43/J3
Świdnik, Pol. 43/M3
Świdwin, Pol. 40/F5
Świebodzice, Pol. 43/J3
Świebozin, Pol. 43/H2
Świecie, Pol. 43/K2
Świętokrzyskie (prov.), Pol. 43/K3
Świętokrzysky NP, Pol. 43/L3
Swift (riv.), BC, Can. 144/C1
Swift Current, Sk, Can. 145/L2
Swifterbant, Neth. 52/C3
Swifton, Ar, US 162/B3
Swiftown, Ms, US 162/B4
Swifts Creek, Austl. 133/C3
Swilly, Lough (inlet), Ire. 31/Q9
Swimming River (res.), NJ, US 168/D3
Swindmish Ind. Res., Wa, US 144/C3
Swindon, Eng, UK 37/E3
Swindon (co.), Eng, UK 37/E3
Swineford, Ire. 32/B2
Swineshead, Eng, UK 35/H6
Świnoujście, Pol. 40/F5
Swinton, Eng, UK 35/G5
Swisshome, Or, US 146/B1
Swist Bach (riv.), Ger. 55/F2
Switzerland (ctry.) 60/D4
Sword Beach, Fr. 57/E2
Swords, Ire. 34/B5
Swoyersville, Pa, US 168/C1
Syābru, Nepal 97/E1
Syamozero (lake), Rus. 68/G3
Syas'stroy, Rus. 41/Q1
Syava, Rus. 69/K4
Sycamore, Al, US 162/D4
Sycamore, Ga, US 165/G2
Sycamore, Il, US 155/K3
Sycan (riv.), Or, US 146/C2
Syców, Pol. 43/J3
Sydney, Austl. 134/H8
Sydney, NS, Can. 159/G2
Sydney (Manra) (isl.), Kiri. 137/H5
Sydney, Fl, US 164/L8
Sydney, ND, US 156/E4
Sydney-Kingsford Smith (int'l arpt.), Austl. 134/H8
Syeverodonets'k, Ukr. 73/K3
Sykäri (lake), Fin. 39/F4
Syke, Ger. 53/F3
Sykeston, ND, US 156/E4
Sykesville, Md, US 168/B5
Sykkylven, Nor. 38/C3
Syktyvkar, Rus. 69/L3
Sylacauga, Al, US 162/D4
Sylarna (peak), Swe. 38/E3
Sylhet (pol. reg.), Bang. 97/H3
Sylhet, Bang. 93/F3
Sylling, Nor. 38/R8
Sylva (riv.), Rus. 69/N4
Sylva, NC, US 163/F3
Sylvan Grove, Ks, US 153/E1
Sylvan Lake, Ab, Can. 145/G1
Sylvan Lake, Mi, US 167/F6
Sylvania, Sk, Can. 145/M1
Sylvania, Al, US 162/E3
Sylvania, Ga, US 163/G4
Sylvania, Oh, US 160/E4
Sylvenstein-Stausee (lake), Ger. 61/H2
Sylvester (lake), Austl. 129/E4
Sylvester, Ga, US 165/G2
Sylvester, Tx, US 150/D1
Sylvia, Ks, US 153/E2
Synel'nykove, Ukr. 73/H3
Synnott (range), Austl. 128/B4
Syntagma, Gre. 75/N8
Synya, Rus. 69/N2
Syosset, NY, US 169/L8
Syowa, Japan, Ant. 192/C
Syracuse, In, US 160/D4
Syracuse, Ks, US 152/D2
Syracuse, Ne, US 155/F3
Syracuse, NY, US 161/H3
Syracuse (Siracusa), It. 48/D4
Syracuse Hancock (int'l arpt.), NY, US 161/H3
Syrdarīya (riv.), Kaz. 77/F5
Syria (ctry.) 102/D3
Syriam, Myan. 93/G4
Syrian (des.), Jor. 100/C2
Syrskiy, Rus. 70/F1
Sysmä, Fin. 41/L1
Sysola (riv.), Rus. 69/L3
Syston, Eng, UK 37/E1
Sytkivtsi, Ukr. 72/E3
Syzran', Rus. 71/J1
Szabolcs-Szatmár-Bereg (co.), Hun. 43/L4
Szamotuły, Pol. 43/J2
Szarvas, Hun. 50/E2
Százhalombatta, Hun. 51/Q10
Szczebrzeszyn, Pol. 43/M3
Szczecin, Pol. 40/F5
Szczecinek, Pol. 40/G5
Szczytna, Pol. 43/J3
Szczytno, Pol. 43/L2
Szeged, Hun. 50/E2
Szeghalom, Hun. 50/E2
Székesfehérvár, Hun. 50/D2
Szekszárd, Hun. 50/D2
Szendro, Hun. 50/E1
Szent László-Vize (riv.), Hun. 51/Q10
Szentendre, Hun. 51/R9
Szentes, Hun. 50/E2
Szentlorinc, Hun. 50/C2
Szerencs, Hun. 43/L4
Szeskie (peak), Pol. 41/K4
Sziget-Szentmiklós, Hun. 51/R10
Szigetvár, Hun. 50/C2
Szirák, Hun. 43/K5
Szolnok, Hun. 50/E2
Szombathely, Hun. 50/C2
Szprotawa, Pol. 43/H3
Sztum, Pol. 41/H5
Szubin, Pol. 43/J2
Szydłowiec, Pol. 43/L3

T

T'aipei (cap.), Tai. 87/J3
Ta Fou San, Laos 94/C1
Ta Khmau, Camb. 94/D4
Ta Phraya, Thai. 94/C3
Ta Seng, Camb. 94/D3
Ta Waewae (bay), NZ 135/A4
Tabaco, Phil. 88/C2
Tabanan, Indo. 89/F5
Tabango, Phil. 88/D3
Tabaquite, Trin. 181/F2
Ţabarqah, Tun. 112/L6
Ţabas, Iran 103/J3
Tabasará (mts.), Pan. 177/F4
Tabasco (state), Mex. 172/C4
Tabatinga, Serra da (mts.), Braz. 186/D1
Tabayama, Japan 83/B2
Tabbs (bay), Tx, US 151/M9
Tabda, Som. 119/C1
Tabelbala, Alg. 110/E3
Tabelbalet (well), Alg. 111/G4
Taber, Ab, Can. 145/H3
Tabernes de Valldigna, Sp. 47/E3
Tabiang, Kiri. 136/F5
Tabibuga, PNG 129/G1
Tabing (int'l arpt.), Indo. 89/C3
Tabio, Col. 183/L8
Tabira, Braz. 183/G4
Tabiteuea (isl.), Kiri. 136/G5
Tabitta, Austl. 133/B2
Tablas (isl.), Phil. 91/F1
Tablas (str.), Phil. 88/C2
Tablas de Daimiel, PN, Sp. 46/D3
Table (mtn.), Ire. 32/D3
Table (bay), SAfr. 124/B4
Table (mtn.), SAfr. 124/L10
Table (cape), NZ 135/D2
Table (mtn.), Wa, US 144/D4
Table Rock (dam), Mo, US 153/H2
Table Rock (lake), Mo, US 153/G2
Tableland Station, Austl. 128/B4
Tabletop (mt.), PNG 129/G1
Tabligbo, Togo 115/F5
Tábor, Czh. 59/H4
Tabor City, NC, US 163/H3
Tabora, Tanz. 121/H4
Tabora, Tanz. 119/B4
Tabora (prov.), Tanz. 119/A3
Tabory, Rus. 69/P4
Tabou, C.d'Iv. 114/D5
Tabrīz, Iran 103/F2
Tabuaeran (Fanning) (isl.), Kiri. 137/K4
Tabubil, PNG 91/K5
Tabūk, SAr. 109/H2
Tabuk, Phil. 88/C1
Tabuleiro do Norte, Braz. 183/G4
Ţaburbah, Tun. 48/A4
Taburno (peak), It. 65/D5
Tabursuq, Tun. 112/L6
Tabuyung, Indo. 89/B2
Tabwemasana (peak), Van. 136/F6
Täby, Swe. 39/B1
Tacabamba, Peru 184/B2
Tacámbaro de Codallos, Mex. 175/E5
Tacaná (vol.), Mex. 176/C3
Tacaratu, Braz. 183/G5
Tacarcuna (mtn.), Pan. 180/B2
Tacheng, China 99/D2
Tachia (riv.), Tai. 87/J3
Tachibana (bay), Japan 84/A4
Tachikawa, Japan 85/F3
Tachinger (lake), Ger. 59/F7
Tachira (state), Ven. 177/H5
Tachoshui, Tai. 87/J3
Tachov, Czh. 59/F3
Tacipi, Indo. 91/F4
Tacloban, Phil. 88/D3
Tacna, Az, US 149/F4
Tacna, Peru 188/B1
Tacna (dept.), Peru 184/D5
Tacobamba, Bol. 188/C1
Tacoma, Wa, US 144/C4
Tacopaya, Bol. 188/C1
Tacora (vol.), Chile 188/B1
Tacotalpa, Mex. 176/C2
Tacuarembó (dept.), Uru. 191/G2
Tacuarembó, Uru. 189/F4
Tacuarembo (dept.), Uru. 189/F5
Tacurong, Phil. 88/D4
Tacutu (riv.), Braz. 181/F4
Tadaoka, Japan 83/H7
Tadcaster, Eng, UK 35/G4
Ta'Delimara (pt.), Malta 48/M7
Tādepallegūdem, India 95/D2
Tadine, NCal. 137/V12
Tadjoura, Djib. 118/B3
Tadley, Eng, UK 37/E4
Tadmur, Syria 102/D3
Tadmur (Palmyra) (ruin), Syria 102/D3
Tadó, Col. 180/B3
Tado, Japan 83/L5
Tadohae Hasang NP, SKor. 81/C5
Tadotsu, Japan 84/C3
Tadoussac, Qu, Can. 158/C1
Tādpatri, India 95/C3
Tadrart (mts.), Alg. ,Libya 108/H4
Taduno, Indo. 91/F4
Tadworth, Eng, UK 30/C3
Tadzewu, Gha. 115/F5
T'aean, SKor. 81/D4
T'aebaek, SKor. 81/E4
T'aebaek (mts.), NKor.,SKor. 79/K4
Taebudo (isl.), SKor. 81/F7
Taech'ŏng (isl.), SKor. 81/C4
Taech'ŏn, SKor. 81/D4
T'aech'ŏn, NKor. 81/C3
Taedŏk, SKor. 81/D5
Taedong (riv.), NKor. 81/D3
Taedong, NKor. 81/C3
Taegang-got (pt.), NKor. 81/D3
Taegu, SKor. 81/E5
Taegu-jikhalsi (prov.), SKor. 84/A3
Taegwan, NKor. 81/C2
Taehŭksan (isl.), SKor. 81/C5
Taehŭng, NKor. 81/D2
Taehwa (isl.), NKor. 81/C3
T'aein, SKor. 81/D5
Taejŏn, SKor. 81/D4
Taejŏn-jikhalsi (prov.), SKor. 81/D4
Taeryŏng (riv.), NKor. 81/C2
T'aet'an, NKor. 81/C3
Tafalla, Sp. 44/C5
Ţafas, Syria 105/E3
Tafassasset, Oued (riv.), Alg. 111/H4
Taff (riv.), Wal, UK 36/C3
Tafí Viejo, Arg. 188/C3
Tafiré, C.d'Iv. 114/D4
Tafraout, Mor. 110/C3
Tafresh, Iran 103/G3
Taft, Iran 103/H4
Taft, Ok, US 153/G3
Taft, Fl, US 164/N7
Taft, Ca, US 148/C3
Taft, Phil. 88/D3
Taft, Tx, US 151/F4
Taftān (mtn.), Iran 101/H3
Taga, Japan 83/K5
Taga Dzong, Bhu. 97/G2
Taganrog, Rus. 73/K4
Tagant (pol. reg.), Mrta. 114/C2
Tagarav (peak), Trkm. 103/J2
Tagawa, Japan 84/B4
Tagbilaran, Phil. 88/C3
Taggia, It. 62/A5
Taghit, Alg. 111/E3
Taghmon, Ire. 32/D5
Tagish, Yk, Can. 171/M3
Tagliacozzo, It. 65/C3
Tagliamento (riv.), It. 45/K3
Taglio di Po, It. 63/F4
Tagolo (pt.), Phil. 88/C3
Tagoloan, Phil. 88/D3
Tagounit, Mor. 110/D3
Taguasco, Cuba 177/G1
Taguatinga, Braz. 186/D2
Taguatinga, Braz. 186/C2
Tagudin, Phil. 88/C1
Taguig, Phil. 88/F6
Tagula (isl.), PNG 136/E6
Tagum, Phil. 88/D4
Tagun (riv.), Rus. 69/P4
Tagus (riv.), Port.,Sp. 66/B3
Tagus (riv.), Sp. 29/D5
Tagus (Tajo) (riv.), Sp. 46/C3
Tagus Rio Tejo (lake), Port. 47/P10
Tahakopa, NZ 135/B4
Tahan (peak), Malay. 89/C1
Tahanea (isl.), FrPol. 137/L6
Tahanroz'ka (gulf), Ukr.,Rus. 70/F3
Tahar-Souk, Mor. 112/B3
Tahara, Japan 83/M6
Tahat (peak), Alg. 111/G5
Tahat, Oued et (riv.), Alg. 112/F5
Tahe, China 79/J1
Tahilt, Mong. 78/D2
Tahir (pass), Turk. 102/E2
Tahiti (isl.), FrPol. 137/L6
Tahkuna (pt.), Est. 41/K2
Tahlequah, Ok, US 153/G3
Tahmoor, Austl. 133/E2
Tahnaout, Mor. 110/D3
Tahoe (lake), Ca,Nv, US 140/D5
Tahoka, Tx, US 152/D4
Taholah, Wa, US 144/B4
Tahoua, Niger 115/G3
Tahoua (dept.), Niger 115/G3
Tahquamenon (falls), Mi, US 160/D1
Taḩtā, Egypt 109/F3
Tahua, Bol. 184/E4
Tahuamanu (riv.), Peru 184/D3
Tahuamanú, Peru 184/D3
Tahuata (isl.), FrPol. 137/L6
Tahulandang (isl.), Indo. 91/G3
Tahuna, Indo. 91/G3
Tahuya (riv.), Wa, US 167/B3
Tahuya, Wa, US 167/A3
Ţahwāy, Egypt 113/B4
Taï, C.d'Iv. 114/D5
Tai (lake), China 79/J5
Tai Long Wan (bay), China 87/M7
Tai Mo Shan (peak), China 87/L7
Tai O, China 87/K8
Tai Po, China 87/L7
Tai Xian, China 80/E4
Taï, PN de, C.d'Iv. 114/D5
Taiama, SLeo. 114/B4
Tai'an, China 81/B2
Tai'an, China 80/D3
Tai'angang, China 80/L8
Taiarapu (pen.), FrPol. 137/X15
Taiaret (well), Mor. 110/B5
Taibai (peak), China 78/F5
Taibus, China 78/H3
Taicang, China 80/L8
T'aichung, Tai. 87/J3
Taiei, Japan 83/E2
Taigu, China 80/C3
Taihang (mts.), China 80/C3
Taihape, NZ 135/C2
Taihe, China 80/C4
Taihsi, Tai. 87/J4
Taihu, China 87/H2
Taikang, China 80/C4
Taiki, Japan 82/C2
Tailai, China 79/J2
Taileleo, Indo. 89/B3
Tailem Bend, Austl. 131/H5
Tailfingen, Ger. 58/B5
Taima, Japan 83/J6
Tain, Sc, UK 33/B1
Tain-L'Hermitage, Fr. 64/A2
T'ainan, Tai. 87/J4
Taínaron (cape), Gre. 75/H4
Taingainony, Madg. 125/H8
Taino, It. 62/B2
Taió, Braz. 189/G3
Taiobeiras, Braz. 187/E2
Taiohae, FrPol. 137/L5
Taiping, China 94/D1
Taiping, Malay. 89/C1
Taiping, China 87/F4
Taiping, China 87/H2
Taiping, China 87/G1
Taiping (peak), China 79/J2
Taipinggou, China 79/L2
Taipingshao, China 81/C2
Taipu, Braz. 183/H4
Tais, Indo. 89/C4
Taisha, Japan 84/C3
Taishan, China 87/G4
Taishi, Japan 83/J6
Taishun, China 87/H3
Taiskirchen im Innkreis, Aus. 59/G6
Taissy, Fr. 55/D5
Taitao (pen.), Chile 179/B7
Taiti (peak), Kenya 119/A1
T'aitung, Tai. 87/J4
Taiwan (ctry.) 87/J3
Taiwan (str.), China,Tai 87/H3
Taixing, China 80/E4
Taíyetos (mts.), Gre. 75/H4
Taiyuan, China 80/C3
Taizhao, China 86/B2
Taizhou, China 80/D4
Taizi (riv.), China 80/F2
Ta'izz, Yem. 118/C2
Tāj Mahal, India 96/B2
Tajarhī, Libya 134/B3
Tajikistan (ctry.) 74/H6
Tajima, Japan 85/F2
Tajimi, Japan 83/M5
Tajique, NM, US 149/J3
Tajiri, Japan 83/H7
Tājirwīn, Tun. 112/L7
Tajo (Tagus) (riv.), Sp. 46/C3
Tājpur, India 96/B1
Tajrīsh, Iran 103/G3
Tajumulco (vol.), Guat. 176/D3
Tajuña (riv.), Sp. 46/D2
Tājūrā, Libya 67/G4
Tak, Thai. 94/B2
Takāb, Iran 103/F2
Takahagi, Japan 85/G2
Takahama, Japan 83/J5
Takahama, Japan 83/L6
Takahashi (riv.), Japan 84/C3
Takahashi, Japan 84/C3
Takahata, Japan 85/G1
Takaishi, Japan 83/H6
Takajärvi (lake), Fin. 39/E3
Takaka, NZ 135/C3
Takama, Guy. 182/B1
Takamatsu, Japan 84/D3
Takami-yama (peak), Japan 83/K7
Takanabe, Japan 84/B4
Takane, Japan 83/A2
Takanosu, Japan 82/B3
Takanosu-yama (peak), Japan 83/C2
Takaoka, Japan 85/E2
Takapau, NZ 135/D3
Takapuna, NZ 135/F6
Takarazuka, Japan 83/H6
Takaroa (isl.), FrPol. 137/L6
Takasaki, Japan 85/F2
Takashima, Japan 83/K5
Takatomi, Japan 83/L5
Takatori, Japan 83/J7
Takatsuki, Japan 83/K5
Takatsuki, Japan 83/J6
Takaungu, Kenya 119/B2
Takayama, Japan 85/E2
Takefu, Japan 84/E3
Takehara, Japan 84/C3
Tākestān, Iran 103/G2
Taketa, Japan 84/B4
Taketoyo, Japan 83/L6
Takev, Camb. 94/D4
Takh, India 98/D3
Takhatgarh, India 92/B2
Takhatpur, India 96/C4
Takhli, Thai. 94/C3
Takht-i-Bhāi, Pak. 98/A2
Takhta, Rus. 73/M5
Takhta-Bazar, Trkm. 74/G6
Takhtamygda, Rus. 79/J1
Taki, Japan 83/L7
Takiéta, Niger 115/H3
Takijuq (lake), Nun, Can. 140/E2
Takikawa, Japan 82/B2
Takingeun, Indo. 89/B1
Takino, Japan 83/G6
Takla Makan (des.), China 77/H6
Tāknis, Libya 67/J4
Tako, Japan 83/E2
Takoradi, Gha. 115/E5
Takouch (cape), Alg. 112/K6
Takoukout, Niger 115/H3
Taksimo, Rus. 75/M4
Taksony, Hun. 51/R10
Takum, Nga. 115/H5
Takundi, D.R. Congo 120/D4
Tala, Kenya 119/B2
Talā, Egypt 113/B3
Tala, Uru. 191/L11
Tala, Mex. 174/E4
Tala Mugongo, Ang. 120/D5
Talacasto, Arg. 188/B4
Talacre, Wal, UK 35/E5
Talagang, Pak. 98/B3
Talagante, Chile 190/N8
Tālah, Tun. 112/L7
Talaimannar, SrL. 95/C4
Talāja, India 101/K4
Talak (phys. reg.), Niger 115/G2
Talala, Ok, US 153/G2
Talalayivka, Ukr. 73/G2
Talamanca (mts.), CR 177/F4
Talamba, Pak. 98/B4
Talamona, It. 61/F5
Talang (peak), Indo. 89/C3
Talanga, Hon. 176/E3
Talangbatu, Indo. 89/D4
Talangbetutu, Indo. 89/D3
Talange, Fr. 55/F5
Talant, Fr. 60/A3
Talara, Peru 184/A2
Talas, Turk. 102/C2
Talas (riv.), Kaz. 99/B3
Talas, Kyr. 99/B3
Talata Ampano, Madg. 125/H8
Talata Mafara, Nga. 115/G3
Talaud (isl.), Phil. 77/M9
Talavera de la Reina, Sp. 46/C3
Talawakele, SrL. 95/D5
Talawdī, Sudan 116/F3
Talawgyi, Myan. 86/C3
Talayuela, Sp. 46/C3
Talbingo (dam), Austl. 133/D2
Talbingo (res.), Austl. 133/D2
Talbingo, Austl. 133/D2
Talbot (mt.), Austl. 130/E3
Talbot, Ab, Can. 145/J1
Talbot (co.), Md, US 168/B6
Talbotton, Ga, US 162/E4
Talca, Chile 190/C2
Talcahuano, Chile 190/B3
Tālcher, India 95/E1
Talcho, Niger 115/F3
Talco, Tx, US 153/G4
Talcott, WV, US 163/G2
Taldan, Rus. 79/J1
Taldykuduk, Kaz. 71/J2
Taldyqorghan, Kaz. 99/C3
Taleex, Som. 118/D3
Talence, Fr. 44/C4
Talent (riv.), Swi. 60/C4
Talent, Or, US 146/B2
Tālesh, Iran 103/G2
Talfer (Talvera) (riv.), It. 61/H4
Talgar, Kaz. 74/H5
Tali Post, Sudan 116/F4
Taliabu (isl.), Indo. 91/F4
Tālibwāla, Pak. 98/B4
Talihina, Ok, US 153/G3
T'alin, Arm. 103/E1
Talinay, PN, Chile 188/B4
Taliouine, Mor. 110/D3
Talipaw, Phil. 88/C4
Talisayan, Indo. 91/E3
Talisayan, Phil. 88/D3
Talitsa, Rus. 69/P4
Taliwang, Indo. 91/E5
Tal'ka, Bela. 41/N5
Talkeetna, Ak, US 171/H3
Ţalkhā, Egypt 113/C2
Tall 'Afar, Iraq 102/E2
Tall al Muqayyar (ruin), Iraq 100/E2
Tall ar Rub' (ruin), Egypt 113/C3
Tall 'Āsūr (peak), WBnk. 105/C5
Tall Kayf, Iraq 103/E2
Tall Kūjik, Syria 102/E2
Tall Rāk, Egypt 113/C3
Tall Timay (ruin), Egypt 113/C3
Talladega, Al, US 162/D4
Tallaght, Ire. 34/B5
Tallahala (cr.), Ms, US 164/D1
Tallahassee (cap.), Fl, US 165/F2
Tallahatchie (riv.), Ms, US 162/B3
Tallangatta, Austl. 133/C3
Tallanstown, Ire. 34/B4
Tallapoosa (riv.), Al, US 162/E4
Tallapoosa, Ga, US 162/E4
Tallard, Fr. 64/C4
Tallassee, Al, US 162/E4
Tallering (peak), Austl. 130/B4
Talleyville, De, US 168/C4
Tallgrass Prairie Nat'l Prsv., Ks, US 155/F4
Tallinn (cap.), Est. 41/L2
Tallmadge, Oh, US 160/F4
Tallman Mountain State Park, NY, US 169/K7
Talloires, Fr. 60/C6
Tallow, Ire. 32/B5
Tallowa (dam), Austl. 133/E2
Talmage, Ut, US 147/H3
Talmassons, It. 63/G2
Talmoon, Mn, US 157/H4
Tal'ne, Ukr. 72/F3
Talo (peak), Eth. 116/H3
Taloda, India 95/B1
Taloga, Ok, US 152/E2
Tāloqān, Afg. 101/J1
Talovaya, Rus. 73/L2
Talpa, Tx, US 150/E2
Talpa de Allende, Mex. 174/D4
Talshand, Mong. 78/D2
Talsi, Lat. 41/K3
Talsperre Pöhl (res.), Ger. 59/F1
Taltal, Chile 188/B3
Taltson (riv.), NW, Can. 140/E2
Talty, Tx, US 150/L7
Taluk, Indo. 89/C3
Talukbayur, Indo. 91/E3
Talumphuk (pt.), Thai. 94/C4
Talut (pt.), Fr. 56/B5
Talvera (Talfer) (riv.), It. 61/H4
Talwandi Bhāi, India 98/C4
Talwandi Sābo, India 98/C5
Talwāra, India 98/C4
Taly, Rus. 73/L3
Ţalyā, Egypt 113/C4
Tam Ky, Viet. 94/E3
Tam Le, Viet. 94/D2
Tam Quan, Viet. 94/E3
Tama (riv.), Japan 83/D2
Tama, Japan 83/C2
Tama Abu (range), Malay. 88/A5
Tamagawa, Japan 83/C2
Tamaha, Ok, US 153/G3
Tamaho, Japan 83/B2
Tamaki (str.), NZ 135/F6
Tamaki, Japan 83/L7
Tamalameque, Col. 180/C2
Ţamalāy, Egypt 113/B3
Tamale, Gha. 115/E4
Tamamura, Japan 83/C1
Taman', Rus. 73/J5
Taman (bay), Rus. 73/J5
Taman, Indo. 90/D5
Taman Negara NP, Malay. 89/C1
Taman-Rasset, Oued (riv.), Alg. 111/F5
Tamaná (peak), Col. 180/B3
Tamana (isl.), Kiri. 136/G5
Tamanaco (riv.), Ven. 183/P8
Tamanar, Mor. 110/C3
Tamanghasset (pol. reg.), Alg. 115/F1
Tamanghasset, Oued (riv.), Alg. 111/F5
Tamanhint, Libya 134/B3
Tamanrasset, Alg. 111/G5
Tamanrasset (wilaya), Alg. 111/F4
Tamanthi, Myan. 86/B3
Tamaqua, Pa, US 168/C2
Tamar (riv.), Eng, UK 36/B5
Tamara (isl.), Japan 85/H8
Tamarac, Fl, US 164/P10
Tamarack, Mn, US 157/H4
Tamarak NWR, Mn, US 157/G4
Tamari, Japan 83/E1
Tamarike, Indo. 129/F2
Tamarindo Nat'l Wild. Ref., CR 176/E4
Tamarite de Litera, Sp. 47/F2
Tamaro (peak), Swi. 61/E5
Tamási, Hun. 50/D2
Tamassoumît, Mrta. 114/B2
Tamatama, Ven. 181/E4
Tamatsukuri, Japan 83/E1
Tamaulipas (state), Mex. 172/B3
Tamazula de Gordiano, Mex. 174/E5
Tamazunchale, Mex. 176/B1
Tamba, Japan 83/H5
Tamba (uplands), Japan 83/H5
Tambach, Kenya 119/A1
Tambacounda (pol. reg.), Sen. 114/B3
Tambacounda, Sen. 114/B3
Tambakara, Mali 114/C3
Tambaoura, Falaise de (cliff), Mali 114/C3
Tambar Springs, Austl. 132/D1
Tambara, Moz. 123/G3
Tambawel, Nga. 115/G3
Tambea, Indo. 91/F4
Tambelan (isls.), Indo. 90/C3
Tambellup, Austl. 130/C5
Tambey, Rus. 74/H2
Tambisan, Malay. 88/B4
Tambo (peak), Swi. 61/F5
Tambo, Austl. 134/B4
Tambo (riv.), Peru 184/C3
Tambo (riv.), Austl. 133/C3
Tambo Colorado (ruin), Peru 184/C4
Tambo de Mora, Peru 184/B4
Tambo Grande, Peru 184/A2
Tambobamba, Peru 184/C4
Tambohorano, Madg. 125/G7
Tambopata (riv.), Peru 184/D4
Tambora (peak), Indo. 91/E5
Tambores, Uru. 189/E4
Tamboril, Braz. 183/F4
Tamboritha (mt.), Austl. 133/C3
Tambov, Rus. 71/G1
Tambovskaya Oblast, Rus. 71/G1
Tambre (riv.), Sp. 46/A1
Tambu, Indo. 91/E4
Tambul, PNG 129/F1
Tambunan, Malay. 88/B4
Tambura, Sudan 117/E4
Tamchaket, Mrta. 114/C2
Tame, Col. 180/D3
Tame (riv.), Eng, UK 37/E1
Tameside (co.), Eng, UK 35/F5
Támega (riv.), Port. 46/B2
Tamel Aike, Arg. 191/C6
Tamentit, Alg. 111/E4
Támesis, Col. 183/K7
Tamgak (peak), Niger 115/H2
Tamghas, Nepal 96/D1
Tamiahua, Mex. 176/B1
Tamiahua (lag.), Mex. 176/B1
Tamiami (canal), Fl, US 165/H5
Tamiami, Fl, US 164/P11
Tamiang (pt.), Indo. 89/B1
Tamil Nādu (state), India 92/C5
Taminango, Col. 180/B4
Tamines, Belg. 55/D3
Ţāmiyah, Egypt 113/B6
Tamkuhi, India 97/E2
Tamlūk, India 97/F4
Tāmma, India 86/B3
Tammany (mt.), NJ, US 168/C2
Tammaro (riv.), It. 65/D5
Tammela, Fin. 41/K1
Tammisaari (Ekenäs), Fin. 41/K2
Ţammūn, WBnk. 105/C4
Tamo, Ar, US 153/J3
Tampa, Ks, US 153/F1
Tampa, Fl, US 164/L8
Tampa (bay), Fl, US 164/K8
Tampa (int'l arpt.), Fl, US 164/K8
Tampalakamam, SrL. 95/D4
Tampang, Indo. 89/D4
Tampere, Fin. 41/K1
Tampere-Pirkkala (int'l arpt.), Fin. 41/K1
Tampico, Mex. 176/B1
Tampin, Malay. 89/C2
Tampines (nbrhd.), Sing. 89/J6
Tampoc (riv.), FrG. 181/H4
Tampon Ambohitra (peak), Madg. 125/J6
Tampulonanjing (peak), Indo. 89/B2
Tamra, Isr. 105/C3
Tamrah, SAr. 100/E4
Tamsalu, Est. 41/M2
Tamshiyacu, Peru 184/C2
Tamuín, Mex. 176/B1
Tamuín (riv.), Mex. 176/B1
Tāmulpur, India 97/H2
Tamur (riv.), Nepal 97/F2
Tamworth, Austl. 132/D1
Tamworth, Eng, UK 37/E1
Tamyang, SKor. 81/D5
Tan (riv.), China 93/K3
Tan An, Viet. 94/D4
Tan-Tan, Mor. 110/C3
Tana (riv.), Fin. 74/C3
Tana (riv.), Nor. 38/H1
Tana, Nor. 38/J1
Tana (lake), Eth. 107/F3
Tana (riv.), Kenya 107/G5
Tana River Primate Nat'l Rsv., Kenya 119/C2
Tanabe, Japan 84/D4
Tanabe, Japan 83/J6
Tanabi, Braz. 189/G2
Tanacross, Ak, US 171/K3
Tanafjorden (estu.), Nor. 38/J1
Tanaga (isl.), Ak, US 171/C6
Tanaga (mt.), Ak, US 171/C6
Tanagura, Japan 85/G2
Tanahbala (isl.), Indo. 90/A4
Tanahmasa (isl.), Indo. 89/B3
Tanahmerah, Indo. 129/F1
Tanahputih, Indo. 89/C2
Tanakpur, India 96/C1
Tanambe, Madg. 125/J7
Tanami, Austl. 128/C4
Tanami (des.), Austl. 127/C2
Tanami Desert Wildlife Sanctuary, Austl. 128/C5
Tanana, Ak, US 171/H2
Tanana (riv.), Ak, US 171/J3
Tanandava, Madg. 125/G8
Tanangozi, Tanz. 119/A3
Tanaro (riv.), It. 45/G4
Tancacha, Arg. 188/D5
Tancarville, Fr. 57/F2
Tancheng, China 80/D4
Tanch'ŏn, NKor. 81/E2
Tancítaro, Pico de (peak), Mex. 174/E5
Tancitaro, PN de, Mex. 172/A4
Tandā, India 96/D2
Tanda, C.d'Iv. 114/E5
Tanda (lake), Mali 114/D3
Tānda, India 96/B1
Tandag, Phil. 88/D3
Tandaltī, Sudan 116/F2
Ţăndărei, Rom. 51/H3
Tāndi, India 98/D3
Tandian, China 81/C2
Tandil, Arg. 190/F3
Tandjilé (pref.), Chad 116/C3
Tandjoaré, Togo 115/F4
Tāndliānwāla, Pak. 98/B4
Tando Ādam, Pak. 101/J3
Tando Allāhyār, Pak. 101/J3
Tando Muhammad Khān, Pak. 101/J3
Tandou (lake), Austl. 127/D4
Tandragee, NI, UK 34/B3
Tandrano, Madg. 125/H8
Taneatua, NZ 135/D2
Tanega (isl.), Japan 79/L5
Tanem (range), Myan.,Thai. 93/G4
Taneytown, Md, US 161/H5
Taneyville, Mo, US 153/H2
Tanezrouft (des.), Alg. 107/B2
Tanezrouft-n-Ahenet (des), Alg. 111/F5
Tang (riv.), China 80/C4
Tanga (prov.), Tanz. 119/B3
Tanga, Tanz. 119/B3
Tangail, Bang. 97/G3
Tangail (pol. reg.), Bang. 97/G3
Tangalī, Iran 103/H2
Tangali, Gui. 114/C4
Tangang, China 87/G2
Tanganyika (lake), D.R. Congo 107/F5
Tangará da Serra, Braz. 185/G4
Tangdan, China 86/D3
Tangent (pt.), Ak, US 171/G1
Tanger, Mor. 112/B2
Tanger (prov.), Mor. 112/A2
Tangerang, Indo. 89/D4
Tangerhütte, Ger. 42/F2
Tangerine, Fl, US 164/M6
Tangermünde, Ger. 42/F2
Tangfang, China 80/J7
Tanggula (pass), China 99/F5
Tanggula (mts.), China 99/E5
Tanghe, China 80/C4
Tangi, Pak. 98/A2
Tangier, Va, US 163/K2
Tangier (sound), Md, US 163/J1
Tangier (Boukhalf) (int'l arpt.), Mor. 112/B2
Tangipahoa (riv.), Ms, US 164/C2
Tangipahoa, La, US 164/C2
Tangjin, SKor. 81/D4
Tangkak, Malay. 89/C2
Tanglewilde-Thompson Place, Wa, US 167/B3
Tangmai, China 86/B2
Tango, Ang. 120/C5
Tangqi, China 80/L9
Tangra (lake), China 99/E5
Tangshan, China 80/J7
Tangtou, China 87/F3
Tangub, Phil. 88/C3
Tanguiéta, Ben. 115/F4
Tangwan, China 87/F3
Tangxi, China 87/H2
Tangyan (riv.), China 87/F2
Tangyin, China 80/C4
Tangyuan, China 79/K2
Tanhaçu, Braz. 187/E2
Taniantaweng (mts.), China 86/C2
Tanigumi, Japan 83/L4
Tanimbar (isl.), Indo. 77/N10
Taninges, Fr. 60/C5
Tanintharyi (state), Myan. 93/G5
Tanis (ruin), Egypt 113/C3
Taniwel, Indo. 91/G4
Tanjay, Phil. 88/C3
Tanjiachang, China 87/F2
Tanjong Malim, Malay. 89/C2
Tanjung, Indo. 90/E4
Tanjung Sedano (pt.), Indo. 89/F4
Tanjungbalai, Indo. 89/B2
Tanjungbatu, Indo. 89/C2
Tanjungenim, Indo. 89/C3
Tanjungkarang-Telukbetung, Indo. 89/D4
Tanjungpandan, Indo. 90/C4
Tanjungpinang, Indo. 89/D2
Tanjungpura, Indo. 89/B2
Tanjunguban, Indo. 89/D2
Tānk, Pak. 98/A3
Tankersley, Tx, US 150/D2
Tankwa Karoo NP, SAfr. 124/B4
Tann, Ger. 59/F6
Tanna (isl.), Van. 136/F6
Tanna, Ger. 59/E1
Tannan, Japan 83/H5
Tannersville, Pa, US 168/C1
Tannheim, Aus. 61/G3
Tannu-Ola (mts.), Rus. 78/C1
Tano (riv.), Gha. 115/E5
Tânout, Niger 115/H3
Tanqiu, China 87/G3
Tanque Verde, Az, US 149/G4
Tanquián de Escobedo, Mex. 176/B1
Tansen, Nepal 96/D2
Tānsing, Nepal 96/D2
Ţanţā, Egypt 113/B3
Tantabin, Myan. 86/C5
Tantallon, Sk, Can. 156/D2
Tantallon, Md, US 168/A6
Tantangara (dam), Austl. 133/D2
Tantō, Japan 83/G5
Tantou, China 87/H2
Tantoyuca, Mex. 176/B1
Tantu, China 79/J2
Tanuku, India 95/D2
Tanumshede, Swe. 40/D2
Tanunda, Austl. 132/A2
Tanxu, China 94/E1
Tanyang, SKor. 81/E4
Tanza, Phil. 88/E7
Tanzania (ctry.) 107/F5
Tanzawa-yama (peak), Japan 83/C3
Tanzishan, China 87/G3
Tao (riv.), China 78/E5
Tao (isl.), Myan. 94/B4
Taochuan, China 87/F3
Tao'er (riv.), China 79/J2
Taolañaro, Madg. 125/H9
Taole, China 78/F4
Taolin, China 87/G3
Taonan, China 79/J2
Taormina, It. 48/D4
Tāoru, India 98/D5
Taos, NM, US 152/B2
Taos, Mo, US 153/H1
Taoudenni, Mali 110/E5
Taounate, Mor. 112/B2
Taounate (town), Mor. 112/B2
Taourirt, Alg. 111/F4
Taourirt, Mor. 112/C2
Taoxi, China 87/H2
Taoyuan, China 93/K2
T'aoyüan, Tai. 87/J3
Tap Mun Chau (isl.), China 87/M7
Tap O'Noth (hill), Sc, UK 33/D2
Tapa, Est. 41/L2
Tapacarí, Bol. 188/C1
Tapachula, Mex. 176/C3
Tapah, Malay. 89/C1
Tapajós (riv.), Braz. 179/D3
Tapajós (Amazônia), PN de, Braz. 185/G2
Tapaktuan, Indo. 89/B2
Tapan, Indo. 89/C3
Tapanahoni (riv.), Sur. 181/H4
Tapanti Nat'l Wild. Ref., CR 177/F4
Tapanui, NZ 135/B4
Tapará, Serra da (mts.), Braz. 182/C3
Tapauá (riv.), Braz. 185/E2
Tapauá, Braz. 185/E2
Tapaz, Phil. 88/C3
Tapenagá (riv.), Arg. 188/E3
Taperoá, Braz. 183/G4
Tapeta, Libr. 114/C5
Taphan Hin, Thai. 94/C2
Tapi Aike, Arg. 191/C6
Tapia de Casariego, Sp. 46/B1
Tapiche (riv.), Peru 184/C2
Tapili, D.R. Congo 121/F2
Tapilula, Mex. 176/C2
Taping (riv.), Myan. 86/C3
Tapini, PNG 129/G2
Tapis (peak), Malay. 89/C1
Tāplejun, Nepal 97/F2
Tapo, Peru 184/C3
Tapoa (prov.), Burk. 115/F3
Tapolca, Hun. 50/C2
Tappahannock, Va, US 163/J2
Tappan (lake), Oh, US 160/F4
Tappan, NY, US 169/K7
Tappan Zee (riv.), NY, US 169/K7
Tappan Zee (lake), NY, US 169/E1
Tappanahoni (riv.), Sur. 182/C2
Tappen, ND, US 156/E4
Tappi-zaki (pt.), Japan 82/B3
Tappino (riv.), It. 65/D4
Tapps (lake), Wa, US 167/C3
Tāpti (riv.), India 92/B3
Tapul Group (isls.), Phil. 88/C4
Tapun, India 86/C3
Taqab, Sudan 109/F5
Taqātu' Hayyā, Sudan 100/C5
Taqian, China 87/H2
Taquari, Braz. 189/G4
Taquari (riv.), Braz. 186/A3
Taquari (riv.), Braz. 189/F1
Taquaritinga, Braz. 189/G2
Taquarituba, Braz. 189/G2
Taquaruçu (res.), Braz. 186/B4
Taquil, Ecu. 184/B1
Tar (riv.), Ire. 32/B5
Tar (riv.), Kyr. 99/B3
Tar (riv.), NC, US 163/J3
Tara, Austl. 134/C4
Tara, Rus. 74/H4
Tara (riv.), Serb. 50/D4
Tara, Zam. 123/E3
Taraba (state), Nga. 115/H5
Taraba (riv.), Nga. 115/H4
Tarabuco, Bol. 188/C1
Ţarābulus, Leb. 104/D2
Ţarābulus (Tripoli) (cap.), Libya 67/G4
Taraclia, Mol. 51/J3
Taradale, NZ 135/D2
Tarairí, Bol. 188/D2
Tarakan (int'l arpt.), Indo. 91/E3
Tarakan, Indo. 91/E3
Tarakit (peak), Kenya 119/A1
Taraklı, Turk. 51/K5
Tārākot, Nepal 96/D1
Taraku (isl.), Rus. 82/E2
Taralga, Austl. 133/D2
Taramana, Indo. 128/B2
Taranagar, India 98/C5
Tarancón, Sp. 46/D2
Tarangire NP, Tanz. 119/A2
Taranna, Austl. 132/C4
Taranto, It. 75/E2
Taranto (gulf), It. 67/H2
Tarapacá, Col. 180/D5
Tarapacá (pol. reg.), Chile 188/B1
Tarapoa, Ecu. 180/B5
Tarapoto, Peru 184/B2
Tarare, Fr. 44/F4
Tarariras, Uru. 191/K11
Tararua (range), NZ 135/J9
Tarascon, Fr. 64/A5
Tarascon-sur-Ariège, Fr. 44/D5
Tarashcha, Ukr. 72/F3
Tarata, Bol. 188/C1
Tarata, Peru 188/B1
Tarauacá, Braz. 184/D3
Tarauacá (riv.), Braz. 184/D2
Taravai (isl.), FrPol. 137/M7
Tarawa (isl.), Kiri. 136/G4
Tarawa (cap.), Kiri. 136/G4
Tarawera (vol.), NZ 135/D2
Tarazona, Sp. 46/E2
Tarazona, Sp. 46/E3
Tarbagatay (mts.), Kaz. 99/D2
Tarbaj, Kenya 119/C1
Tarbat Ness (pt.), Sc, UK 33/C1
Tarbela (res.), Pak. 98/B2
Tarbela (dam), Pak. 98/B2
Tarbela (res.), India 99/B5
Tarbert, Sc, UK 31/Q8
Tarbert, Ire. 32/A4
Tarbes, Fr. 44/D5
Tarbolton, Sc, UK 33/B5
Tarboro, Ga, US 165/H2
Tarboro, NC, US 163/J3
Tarbûl Abu Khashîrât (peak), Egypt 113/C6
Tarcento, It. 45/K3
Tarcoola, Austl. 131/G4
Tarcutta, Austl. 133/C2
Tardes (riv.), Fr. 44/E3
Tardienta, Sp. 47/E2
Tardoire (riv.), Fr. 44/D4
Tardoki-Jani (peak), Rus. 79/M2
Taree, Austl. 132/E1
Tarf Water (riv.), Sc, UK 34/D2
Ţarfā' (wadi), Egypt 109/F2
Tarfaya, Mor. 110/B4
Target Rock Nat'l Wild. Ref., NY, US 169/M8
Targuist, Mor. 112/B2
Tarhūnah, Libya 67/G4
Tari, PNG 129/F1
Tariana, Col. 180/D4
Tarīf, UAE 100/F4
Tarifa, Sp. 46/C4
Tarifa, Ecu. 184/B1
Tarija (dept.), Bol. 188/C2
Tarija (int'l arpt.), Bol. 188/C2
Tarija, Bol. 188/C2
Tariku (riv.), Indo. 91/J4
Tariku-Taritatu (plain), Indo. 91/J4
Tarim (riv.), China 74/J5
Tarim (basin), China 74/J6
Tarīm, Yem. 118/D1
Tarim Liuchang, China 99/E3
Tarime, Tanz. 119/A2
Tarin (riv.), Afg. 101/J2
Tarin (Torino), It. 45/G4
Taring, Indo. 89/B2
Taritatu (riv.), Indo. 91/J4
Tarkastad, SAfr. 124/D4
Tarkhankut (cape), Ukr. 73/G5
Tarkio, Mo, US 155/G3
Tarkio (cr.), Mo, Ia, US 155/G3
Tarko-Sale, Rus. 74/H3
Tarkwa, Gha. 115/E5
Tarlac, Phil. 88/C2
Tarland, Sc, UK 33/D2
Tarlton Downs, Austl. 131/H2
Tarma, Peru 184/C3
Tarmstedt, Ger. 53/G2
Tarn (riv.), Fr. 67/D2
Tarn Tāran, India 98/C4
Tarna (riv.), Mong. 78/E2
Tarnak (riv.), Afg. 101/J2
Tårnby, Den. 39/J7
Tarnobrzeg, Pol. 43/L3
Tarnogskiy Gorodok, Rus. 69/J3
Tarnów, Pol. 43/L3
Tärnsjö, Swe. 40/G1
Tärnskär (isl.), Swe. 39/B1
Taro (riv.), It. 45/J4
Taro (lake), China 99/D5
Tarō, Japan 82/B4
Taroko NP, Tai. 87/J3
Ţārom, Iran 103/H4
Taroms'ke, Ukr. 73/H3
Taroom, Austl. 134/C4
Tarouca, Port. 46/B2
Taroudannt, Mor. 110/C3
Tarp, Ger. 40/C4
Tarpa, Hun. 50/F1
Tarpon (lake), Fl, US 165/G3
Tarpon Springs, Fl, US 164/K7
Tarporley, Eng, UK 35/F5

Map Section 276 277

Tarqui – Thoiry

Tarqui, Peru 180/C5
Tarquinia, It. 48/B1
Tarqūmiyah, WBnk. 105/C5
Tarrafal, CpV. 107/K10
Tarragona, Sp. 47/F2
Tarraleah, Austl. 132/C4
Tarrant, Al, US 162/D4
Tarrant (co.), Tx, US 150/K7
Tàrrega, Sp. 47/F2
Tarrenz, Aus. 61/G3
Tarryall (mts.), Co, US 152/B1
Tarrytown, Fl, US 164/L6
Tarrytown, NY, US 169/K7
Tarshīhā, Isr. 105/C2
Tarsus, Turk. 104/D1
Tarsus (riv.), Turk. 104/D1
Tartagal, Arg. 188/E4
Tartagal, Arg. 188/D2
Tärtär, Azer. 103/F1
Tartaro (riv.), It. 63/E2
Tartas, Fr. 44/C5
Tartu, Est. 41/M2
Ţarţūs, Syria 104/D2
Ţarţus (dist.), Syria 104/D2
Tarui, Japan 83/L5
Tarumizu, Japan 84/B5
Tarusa, Rus. 68/H5
Ţārūţ, Egypt 113/C3
Tarutao NP, Thai. 94/B5
Tarutung, Indo. 89/B2
Tarutyne, Ukr. 51/J2
Tarvagatay (mts.), Mong. 78/D2
Tarvin, Eng, UK 35/F5
Tarzan, Tx, US 150/D1
Tarzana (nbrhd.), Ca, US 166/E7
Taşağıl, Turk. 104/B1
Tasawáh, Libya 134/B3
Täsch, Swi. 60/D5
Taşçı, Turk. 102/C2
Taseko (mtn.), BC, Can. 144/C2
Taseko (riv.), BC, Can. 144/C2
Tash-Kömür, Kyr. 99/B3
Tashanta, Rus. 99/E2
Tashi Gang, Bhu. 97/H2
Ţashk (lake), Iran 103/H4
Tashkent (cap.), Uzb. 99/A3
Tashkent (int'l arpt.), Uzb. 99/A3
Tashkepri, Trkm. 101/H1
Tashtagol, Rus. 99/E1
Tasikmalaya, Indo. 89/E4
Taşkent, Turk. 102/C2
Taşköprü, Turk. 70/E4
Taşlıçay, Turk. 103/E2
Tasman (bay), NZ 127/H7
Tasman (cape), Austl. 132/C4
Tasman (pt.), Austl. 129/E3
Tasman (pen.), Austl. 127/D5
Tasman (sea) 136/E8
Tasman NP, NZ 135/C3
Tasmania (state), Austl. 127/D5
Tăşnad, Rom. 50/F2
Taşova, Turk. 70/F4
Tasquillo, Mex. 175/K6
Tassara, Niger 115/G2
Tassili Oua-n Ahaggar (mts.), Alg. 111/G5
Tassili-n-Ajjer (mts.), Alg. 111/G4
Tastrup, Den. 39/J7
Tastuba, Rus. 69/N5
Taşucu, Turk. 104/C1
Tasu, BC, Can. 171/M5
Tasudi, Myan. 94/B2
Tata, Mor. 110/D3
Tata, Hun. 50/D2
Tata, D.R. Congo 116/F5
Tata Mailau (peak), ETim. 128/B2
Tataba, Indo. 91/F4
Tatabánya, Hun. 50/D2
Tatakoto (isl.), FrPol. 137/L6
Tatalin (riv.), China 78/D4
Tatamy, Pa, US 168/C2
Tatar (str.), Rus. 77/P5
Tatarbunary, Ukr. 51/J3
Tatarlar, Turk. 51/H5
Tatarsk, Rus. 74/H4
Tatarstan, Resp., Rus. 74/E4
Tatau, Malay. 90/D3
Tataurovo, Rus. 69/L4
Taţāwīn (gov.), Tun. 111/H2
Taţāwīn, Tun. 66/F4
Tate, Ga, US 162/E3
Tate-yama (peak), Japan 85/E2
Tatebayashi, Japan 83/D1
Tatéma, Gui. 114/B4
Tateshina, Japan 83/A1
Tateville, Ky, US 162/E2
Tateyama, Japan 85/F3
Tathlina (lake), NW, Can. 140/E2
Tathlīth, SAr. 100/D5
Tathra, Austl. 133/D3
Tatilt (well), Mrta. 114/B2
Tatitlek, Ak, US 171/J3
Tatkon, Myan. 94/B1
Tatlayoko Lake, BC, Can. 144/B2
Tatlikbulak, China 99/E4
Tatnam (cape), Mb, Can. 140/G3
Tatomi, Japan 83/B2
Tatranský NP, Slvk. 43/K4
Tatsfield, Eng, UK 30/D3
Tatsinskiy, Rus. 73/L3
Tatsuno, Japan 85/E3
Tatsuta, Japan 83/L5
Tattershall, Eng, UK 35/H5
Tatuí, Braz. 189/H2
Tatum, Tx, US 151/G1
Tatura, Austl. 133/B3
Tatvan, Turk. 102/E2
Tauá, Braz. 183/F4
Taubaté, Braz. 187/L8
Tauber (riv.), Ger. 42/E4
Tauberbischofsheim, Ger. 58/C3
Tauca, Peru 184/B3
Tauchik, Kaz. 71/J3
Taufkirchen, Ger. 59/F6
Taufkirchen an der Pram, Aus. 59/G6
Taufstein (peak), Ger. 58/C1
Tauherenikau (riv.), NZ 135/J9
Taulignan, Fr. 64/A4
Taulihawa, Nepal 96/D2
Taum Sauk (mtn.), Mo, US 162/B2
Taumarunui, NZ 135/C2
Taung, SAfr. 124/D2
Taungdwingyi, Myan. 86/B4
Taunggyi, Myan. 86/C4
Taungthonlon (peak), Myan. 86/B3
Taungup (pass), Myan. 86/B5
Taungup, Myan. 86/B5
Taungzun, Myan. 94/B3
Taunsa, Pak. 98/A4
Taunton, Ma, US 161/L4
Taunton, Eng, UK 36/C4
Taunton, On, Can. 160/V8
Taunus (range), Ger. 58/A2
Taunusstein, Ger. 58/B2
Taupo (lake), NZ 127/H6
Taupo, NZ 135/D2
Tauragė, Lith. 41/K4
Tauranga, NZ 135/D2
Taurion (riv.), Fr. 44/D3
Taurisano, It. 75/F3
Tauroa (pt.), NZ 135/C1
Taurus (mts.), Turk. 102/C2
Tauste, Sp. 46/E2
Tauta, PNG 129/G1
Taute (riv.), Fr. 44/C2
Tautira, FrPol. 137/X15
Tauu (isls.), PNG 136/E5
Tavanbulag, Mong. 78/E2
Tavannes, Swi. 60/D3
Tavänti (lake), Fin. 39/F3
Tavares, Fl, US 164/M6
Tavarnelle, It. 63/E6
Tavarnuzze, It. 63/E6
Tavas, Turk. 102/B2
Tavaux, Fr. 60/B3
Tavazzano, It. 62/C3
Tavda (riv.), Rus. 74/G4
Tavda, Rus. 69/Q4
Tavel, Fr. 64/A4
Taverham, Eng, UK 37/H1
Tavernerio, It. 62/C2
Tavernes, Fr. 64/C5
Taverny, Fr. 30/J4
Taveta, Kenya 119/B2
Taveuni (isl.), Fiji 137/Y18
Taviano, It. 75/F3
Tavin, Mong. 78/F2
Tavira, Port. 46/B4
Tavistock, Eng, UK 36/B5
Tavo (riv.), It. 65/D3
Tavoy (pt.), Myan. 94/B3
Tavoy (Dawei), Myan. 94/B3
Tavrichanka, Rus. 79/L3
Tavşanlı, Turk. 102/B2
Tavy (riv.), Eng, UK 36/B6
Taw (riv.), Eng, UK 36/C5
Tawa, NZ 135/H9
Tawaeli, Indo. 91/E4
Tawakoni (lake), Tx, US 151/F1
Tawaramoto, Japan 83/J6
Tawas City, Mi, US 160/E2
Tawau, Malay. 88/B4
Tawau (int'l arpt.), Malay. 88/B4
Tawe (riv.), Wal, UK 36/C3
Tawern, Ger. 55/F4
Tāwi (riv.), India 98/C3
Tawi, Tanz. 119/B4
Tawi-tawi (isl.), Phil. 88/B4
Tawo, China 87/F2
Ţāwūq, Iraq 103/F3
Tāwurghā', Libya 67/G4
Tāwurghā, Sabkhat (swamp), Libya 67/G4
Tawzar (gov.), Tun. 111/G2
Tawzar, Tun. 66/F4
Taxco, Mex. 175/K8
Taxila, Pak. 98/B3
Taxila (ruin), Pak. 98/B3
Taxkorgan Tajik Zizhixian, China 99/C4
Tay (riv.), Sc, UK 33/C3
Tay (lake), Sc, UK 33/B3
Tay Ninh, Viet. 94/D4
Tayabamba, Peru 184/B3
Tayandu (isls.), Indo. 128/C1
Taybola, Rus. 68/G1
Tayeegle, Som. 118/C4
Taylor, Ar, US 153/H4
Taylor, Pa, US 161/J4
Taylor, Al, US 165/F2
Taylor, Mi, US 167/F7
Taylor (riv.), Co, US 147/K4
Taylor, Az, US 149/G3
Taylor (mt.), NM, US 149/J3
Taylor, Ne, US 154/E3
Taylor, Tx, US 151/F2
Taylor Town, Tx, US 153/G4
Taylors, SC, US 163/F3
Taylorsville, Ms, US 164/D2
Taylorsville, In, US 160/D5
Taylorsville, Ca, US 146/C3
Taylorsville, Ky, US 162/E1
Taylorsville, NC, US 163/G3
Taylorsville-Bennion, Ut, US 147/H3
Taylortown, La, US 153/H4
Taylorville, Il, US 155/K4
Taymā', SAr. 102/D5
Taymouth, NB, Can. 158/D2
Taymyr (pen.), Rus. 77/H2
Taymyr (isl.), Rus. 75/L2
Taymyr (riv.), Rus. 74/K2
Taymyrskiy Aut. Okrug, Rus. 74/J2
Tayoltita, Mex. 174/D3
Tayport, Sc, UK 33/D4
Tayrona, PN, Col. 180/C2
Tayshet, Rus. 75/K4
Taytay, Phil. 88/B3
Taytay, Phil. 88/F6
Tayu, Indo. 89/E4
Taz (riv.), Rus. 77/H3
Taza (prov.), Mor. 112/C2
Taza, Mor. 112/B2
Tazawako, Japan 82/B4
Tazekka (peak), Mor. 112/B2
Tazenakht, Mor. 110/D3
Tazewell, Va, US 163/G2
Tazewell, Tn, US 163/F2
Tazicheng, China 79/J2
Tāzirbū (oasis), Libya 134/D3
Tazovskiy, Rus. 74/H3
Tazrouk, Alg. 111/G5
Tāzughrān, Tun. 48/B4
Tazumal (ruin), ESal. 176/D3
T'bilisi (cap.), Geo. 71/H4
Tbilisskaya, Rus. 73/L5
Tchamba, Camr. 116/B3
Tchamba, Togo 115/F4
Tchaourou, Ben. 115/F4
Tchetti, Ben. 115/F5
Tchibanga, Gabon 120/B3
Tchikala-Tcholohanga, Ang. 122/C2
Tchin Tabaradene, Niger 115/G3
Tchindjenje, Ang. 122/B2
Tcholliré, Camr. 116/B3
Tchula, Ms, US 162/B4
Tczew, Pol. 41/H4
Te Anau, NZ 135/A4
Te Anu (lake), NZ 135/A4
Te Araroa, NZ 135/D2
Te Aroha, NZ 135/C2
Te Awamutu, NZ 135/C2
Te Kao, NZ 135/C1
Te Karaka, NZ 135/D2
Te Kauwhata, NZ 135/C2
Te Kopuru, NZ 135/C2
Te Kuiti, NZ 135/C2
Te Teko, NZ 135/D2
Tea (riv.), Braz. 181/E5
Teacapán, Mex. 174/D4
Teague, Tx, US 151/F2
Tealby, Eng, UK 35/H5
Teaneck, NJ, US 169/J8
Teano, It. 65/D5
Teapa, Mex. 176/C2
Teapot Dome Nav. Petroleum Rsv., Wy, US 154/A2
Teapot Dome Naval Res., Wy, US 147/K2
Tearce, FYROM 75/G1
Teasdale, Ut, US 149/G1
Tebak (peak), Indo. 89/D4
Teberda, Rus. 71/G4
Tébessa (wilaya), Alg. 111/G2
Tebessa (mts.), Alg. 112/L7
Tébessa, Alg. 112/L7
Tebesselamane (well), Mali 115/F2
Tebicuary (riv.), Par. 188/E3
Tebingtinggi, Indo. 89/C3
Tebingtinggi, Indo. 89/B2
Tebingtinggi (isl.), Indo. 89/C2
Tebtunis (ruin), Egypt 113/B6
Tebulos-Mta (peak), Rus. 71/H4
Tecalitlán, Mex. 174/E5
Tecamac, Mex. 175/R9
Tecamachalco, Mex. 175/M8
Tech (riv.), Fr. 47/G1
Techirghiol, Rom. 51/J3
Tecirli, Turk. 102/D2
Tecka, Arg. 190/C4
Tecka (riv.), Arg. 190/C4
Teckla, Wy, US 154/B2
Tecklenberg, Ger. 53/E4
Teckomatorp, Swe. 39/K7
Tecolutla, Mex. 175/M6
Tecomán, Mex. 174/E5
Tecopa, Ca, US 148/D3
Tecozautla, Mex. 175/K6
Tecpan de Galeana, Mex. 175/E5
Tecuala, Mex. 174/D4
Tecuci, Rom. 51/H3
Tecumseh, Ok, US 153/F3
Tecumseh, Mi, US 160/E3
Tecumseh, On, Can. 167/G7
Tecumseh, Ne, US 155/F3
Ted Ceidaar Dabole, Som. 118/B4
Tedjert (well), Alg. 111/H1
Tedodita Sakan, Myan. 86/C5
Tedzhen (riv.), Trkm. 74/G6
Tees (bay), Eng, Uk 35/G2
Tees (riv.), Eng, UK 35/G3
Teesside (int'l arpt.), Eng, UK 35/G3
Tefé (riv.), Braz. 185/E2
Tefé, Braz. 185/E1
Tefé (int'l arpt.), Braz. 185/E1
Tefé (lake), Braz. 185/E1
Teferič, Serb. 50/E4
Tega (lake), Japan 83/E2
Tega Cay, SC, US 163/G3
Tegal, Indo. 89/E4
Tegel (int'l arpt.), Ger. 42/Q6
Tegelen, Neth. 52/D6
Tegeler (lake), Ger. 42/Q6
Tegheri (well), Libya 111/H4
Teghra, India 97/E3
Tegina, Nga. 115/G4
Tegineneng, Indo. 89/D4
Teglio, It. 61/G5
Tégouma (riv.), Niger 115/H3
Tegouma (riv.), Niger 116/A2
Tegsh, Mong. 78/D2
Tegualda, Chile 190/B4
Tegucigalpa (cap.), Hon. 176/E3
Tehachapi, Ca, US 148/C3
Tehachapi (mts.), Ca, US 148/C3
Tehamiyam, Sudan 100/C5
Tehek (lake), Nun, Can. 140/G2
Tehoru, Indo. 91/G4
Tehrān (cap.), Iran 103/G3
Tehrān (gov.), Iran 103/G2
Tehri, India 99/C5
Tehuacán, Mex. 175/M8
Tehuacana, Tx, US 151/F2
Tehuantepec (riv.), Mex. 176/C2
Tehuantepec (gulf), Mex. 139/H8
Tehuantepec (isth.), Mex. 175/G5
Teide, Pico de (peak), Sp. 110/A3
Teifi (riv.), Wal, UK 36/B2
Teifiside (valley), Wal, UK 36/B2
Teiga (plat.), Sudan 117/E2
Teign (riv.), Eng, UK 36/C5
Teignmouth, Eng, UK 36/C5
Teignousse (str.), Fr. 56/B6
Teisendorf, Ger. 59/F7
Teith (riv.), Sc, UK 33/B4
Teixeira Pinto, GBis. 114/A3
Tejakula, Indo. 89/F5
Tejen, Trkm. 101/H1
Tejn, Den. 40/F4
Tejupilco de Hidalgo, Mex. 175/E5
Tekamah, Ne, US 155/F3
Tékane, Mrta. 114/B2
Tekapo (lake), NZ 135/B3
Tekāri, India 97/E3
Tekax de Álvaro Obregón, Mex. 176/D1
Teke, Turk. 51/J5
Tekeli, Kaz. 99/C3
Tekes (riv.), China 74/J5
Tekezē Wenz (riv.), Eth. 100/C6
Tekiliktag (peak), China 99/D4
Tekirdağ (prov.), Turk. 51/H5
Tekirdağ, Turk. 51/H5
Tekit, Mex. 176/D1
Tekkali, India 95/E2
Tekke, Turk. 102/D1
Tekkeköy, Turk. 70/F4
Tekman, Turk. 102/E2
Tekoa, Wa, US 144/F4
Teksneslia, Nor. 38/S9
Teku, Indo. 91/F4
Tel 'Akko (ruin), Isr. 105/C3
Tel Aviv (dist.), Isr. 104/D3
Tel Aviv-Yafo, Isr. 105/B4
Tel Hazor NP, Isr. 105/D2
Tel Megiddo (ruin), Isr. 105/C3
Tela, Hon. 176/E3
Télagh, Alg. 112/D2
Télataï, Mali 115/F2
T'elavi, Geo. 71/H4
Telde, Sp. 110/B3
Télé (lake), Mali 114/D2
Telefomin, PNG 91/K5
Telegraph, Tx, US 150/E2
Telegraph Creek, BC, Can. 171/M4
Telekhany, Bela. 70/C1
Telêmaco Borba, Braz. 189/G3
Telemark (co.), Nor. 38/D4
Telen (riv.), Indo. 91/E3
Teleorman (prov.), Rom. 51/G4
Telephone, Tx, US 153/F4
Telertheba (peak), Alg. 111/G4
Teles Pires (riv.), Braz. 179/D3
Telescope (peak), Ca, US 148/D2
Telese, It. 65/D5
Telford, Pa, US 168/C3
Telford Dawley, Eng, UK 36/D1
Telfs, Aus. 61/H3
Telgate, It. 62/C2
Telgruc-sur-Mer, Fr. 56/A4
Telgte, Ger. 53/E5
Telica, Nic. 176/E3
Télig (well), Mali 110/E5
Télimélé, Gui. 114/B4
Telipok, Malay. 88/B4
Teljo (peak), Sudan 117/E2
Tell, Tx, US 152/D3
Tell Atlas (mts.), Alg. 66/D3
Tell City, In, US 162/D2
Teller, Ak, US 171/E2
Tellī (lake), Mrta. 110/C4
Tellico (lake), Tn, US 162/E3
Tellico Plains, Tn, US 162/E3
Tellier, Arg. 191/D5
Tellin, Belg. 55/E3
Telluride, Co, US 149/J2
Telmen (lake), Mong. 78/D2
Telok Anson, Malay. 89/C1
Teloloapan, Mex. 175/F5
Telotskoye (lake), Rus. 99/E1
Telsen, Arg. 190/D4
Telšiai, Lith. 41/K4
Teltow (reg.), Ger. 43/G2
Teltow, Ger. 42/Q7
Teluk Punggur (pt.), Indo. 89/C3
Telukbayur, Indo. 89/C3
Telukdalem, Indo. 89/B2
Telukmelano, Indo. 90/C4
Telukmerbau, Indo. 89/C2
Tema, Gha. 115/E5
Temacine, Alg. 111/G2
Temagami (lake), On, Can. 160/F1
Temanggung, Indo. 89/E4
Temax, Mex. 176/D1
Tembagapura, Indo. 91/J4
Tembesi (riv.), Indo. 89/C3
Tembilahan, Indo. 89/C3
Tembisa, SAfr. 124/E2
Temblador, Ven. 181/F2
Tembo, D.R. Congo 120/D4
Tembo Aluma, Ang. 120/D4
Tembue, Moz. 123/G2
Teme (riv.), Eng, UK 36/C2
Temecula, Ca, US 166/C4
Temelkovo, Bul. 51/F4
Temerin, Serb. 50/D3
Temerloh, Malay. 90/B3
Teminabuan, Indo. 91/H4
Temir, Kaz. 71/L2
Temirtaū, Kaz. 99/B1
Témiscaming, Qu, Can. 161/G1
Temma, Austl. 132/C4
Temnik (riv.), Rus. 78/E1
Temoaya, Mex. 175/Q10
Temoe (isl.), FrPol. 137/M7
Temora, Austl. 133/C2
Tempe, Az, US 149/G4
Tempe Downs, Austl. 131/G3
Tempelhof (arpt.), Ger. 42/Q7
Tempelhof, Ger. 42/Q7
Temperance, Mi, US 160/E4
Temperanceville, Va, US 163/K2
Tempio Pausania, It. 48/A2
Temple, Ok, US 153/E3
Temple, La, US 164/B2
Temple (bay), Austl. 129/F3
Temple (mt.), Ab., Can. 144/F2
Temple, Tx, US 150/F2
Temple, Pa, US 168/C3
Temple City, Ca, US 166/F7
Temple of Lady Chua Xu, Viet. 94/D4
Temple Terrace, Fl, US 164/L7
Templemore, Ire. 32/C4
Templepatrick, NI, UK 34/B2
Templestowe (nbrhd.), Austl. 132/G5
Templetouhy, Ire. 32/C4
Templeuve, Fr. 54/C2
Templeville, Md, US 168/C5
Templin, Ger. 43/G2
Templiner (lake), Ger. 42/Q7
Tempoal de Sánchez, Mex. 176/B1
Têmpung, China 78/D4
Temryuk, Rus. 73/J5
Temryuk (gulf), Rus. 73/J5
Temse, Belg. 55/D1
Temuco, Chile 190/B3
Temuka, NZ 135/B4
Temyasovo, Rus. 71/L1
Ten Boer, Neth. 52/D2
Ten Mile, Tn, US 162/E3
Ten Sleep, Wy, US 147/K1
Ten Thousand (isls.), Fl, US 165/H5
Tena, Ecu. 180/B5
Tenabo, Mex. 176/D1
Ténado, Burk. 115/E3
Tenafly, NJ, US 169/K8
Tenaha, Tx, US 151/G2
Tenakee Springs, Ak, US 171/L4
Tenāli, India 95/D2
Tenancingo, Mex. 175/K8
Tenango, Mex. 175/R10
Tenango de Arista, Mex. 175/Q10
Tenasserim (range), Myan. 94/B3
Tenasserim, Myan. 94/B3
Tenay, Fr. 60/B6
Tenbury, Eng, UK 36/D2
Tenby, Wal, UK 36/B3
Tencarola, It. 63/E3
Tendaho, Eth. 118/B3
Tende, Fr. 64/D4
Tenderovsk (bay), Ukr. 51/K2
Tenderovsk Spit (isl.), Mol. 51/K2
Tendō, Japan 82/B4
Tendoy, Id, US 147/G1
Tendrara, Mor. 111/E2
Tendre (peak), Swi. 60/C4
Ténenkou, Mali 114/D3
Tenente Portela, Braz. 189/F3
Ténéré (des.), Niger 115/H1
Ténéré du Tafassasset (des.), Niger 111/H5
Tenerife, Col. 180/C2
Tenerife (isl.), Sp. 107/A2
Tenes (riv.), Sp. 47/L6
Ténès, Alg. 112/F4
Teng (riv.), Myan. 93/G3
Teng Xian, China 80/D4
Teng'aopu, China 81/B2
Tengchong, China 86/C3
Tenggarong, Indo. 91/E4
Tengger (des.), China 78/E4
Tengiz (lake), Kaz. 74/G4
Tengqiao, China 94/E2
Tenguel, Ecu. 180/B5
Tenibre (peak), Fr. 64/C4
Tenibres (peak), It. 64/C4
Teniente Enciso, PN, Par. 188/D2
Tenigerbad, Swi. 61/E4
Teningen, Ger. 60/D1
Tenino, Wa, US 144/C4
Tenja, Cro. 50/D3
Tenjo, Col. 183/L8
Tenkāsi, India 95/C4
Tenke, D.R. Congo 121/F5
Tenkiller (lake), Ok, US 153/G3
Tenkodogo, Burk. 115/E4
Tenmile (cr.), Tx, US 150/L7
Tenmile Wash (riv.), Az, US 149/F4
Tenna (riv.), It. 65/C1
Tennant Creek, Austl. 128/D4
Tennessee (riv.), US 162/E2
Tennessee (state), US 162/D3
Tennessee Ridge, Tn, US 162/D2
Tennessee-Tombigbee Waterway (canal), Ms, US 162/C3
Tenneville, Belg. 55/E3
Tennille, Al, US 165/F2
Tennille, Ga, US 163/F4
Tennuaca (well), Mor. 110/B5
Teno, Chile 190/C2
Tenojoki (riv.), Fin. 38/H1
Tenom, Malay. 88/A4
Tenosique de Pino Suárez, Mex. 176/D2
Tenri, Japan 83/J6
Tenryū, Japan 85/E3
Tenryū (riv.), Japan 85/E3
Tensas (basin), La, US 151/J2
Tensas (riv.), La, US 153/J5
Tensas River NWR, La, US 151/J1
Tensift (pol. reg.), Mor. 110/C3
Tensift, Oued (riv.), Mor. 110/C3
Tenstrike, Mn, US 157/G4
Tenta, Eth. 118/A3
Tentena, Indo. 91/F4
Tenterden, Eng, UK 37/G4
Tenterfield, Austl. 132/E1
Tentolomatinan (peak), Indo. 91/F3
Tenus (peak), Kenya 119/A1
Teo, Sp. 46/A1
Teocaltiche, Mex. 172/A3
Teocelo, Mex. 175/N7
Teodelina, Arg. 190/E2
Teodoro Sampaio, Braz. 189/F2
Teófilo Otoni, Braz. 187/E3
Teopisca, Mex. 176/C2
Teotihuacán (ruin), Mex. 175/R9
Teotihuacán, Mex. 175/R9
Teotitlán del Camino, Mex. 176/B2
Tepa, Indo. 128/C1
Tepache, Mex. 174/C2
Tepalcatepec, Mex. 174/E5
Tepalcingo, Mex. 175/L8
Tepatitlán de Morelos, Mex. 172/A3
Tepatlaxco, Mex. 175/M7
Tepeapulco, Mex. 175/L7
Tepebaşı, Turk. 104/C1
Tepee (mtn.), Ok, US 152/E3
Tepehuaje, Mex. 175/F4
Tepehuanes, Mex. 174/D3
Tepeji del Río de Ocampo, Mex. 175/K7
Tepelenë, Alb. 75/G2
Tepelská Plošina (mts.), Czh. 59/F2
Tepetlaoxtoc, Mex. 175/R9
Tepexi, Mex. 175/M8
Tepexpan, Mex. 175/R9
Tepī, Eth. 116/G4
Tepic, Mex. 174/D4
Teplá (riv.), Czh. 42/G3
Teplá Vltava (riv.), Czh. 59/G5
Teplice, Czh. 43/G3
Tepoca (cape), Mex. 174/B2
Tepoca, Cabo (cape), Mex. 174/B2
Tepoto (isl.), FrPol. 137/L6
Tepotzotlán, Mex. 175/Q9
Tepoztlán, Mex. 175/K8
Tequila, Mex. 174/E4
Tequisquiapan, Mex. 175/F4
Tequixquiac, Mex. 175/K7
Ter (riv.), Sp. 47/G1
Ter Aar, Neth. 52/B4
Ter Apel, Neth. 53/E3
Téra, Niger 115/F3
Tera (riv.), Sp. 46/B1
Teraina (Washington) (isl.), Kiri. 137/J4
Terakeka, Sudan 116/F4
Teramo, It. 65/C2
Teramo (prov.), It. 65/C2
Terang, Austl. 132/B3
Terborg, Neth. 52/D5
Terbuny, Rus. 70/F1
Tercan, Turk. 102/E2
Terceira (isl.), Azor., Port. 47/S12
Tercero (riv.), Arg. 188/D5
Terebovlya, Ukr. 72/C3
Terek (riv.), Rus. 71/H4
Terek, Rus. 71/H4
Terekhovka, Bela. 72/F1
Terekli-Mekteb, Rus. 71/H3
Terempa, Indo. 89/D2
Terengganu (riv.), Malay. 89/C1
Terengganu (state), Malay. 89/C1
Terenuthis (ruin), Egypt 113/B4
Terenzano, It. 63/G2
Terepaima, PN, Ven. 180/D2
Teresina, Braz. 183/F4
Teresópolis, Braz. 187/P7
Terespol, Pol. 43/M2
Terevinto, Bol. 188/D1
Tergnier, Fr. 54/C4
Tergun Daba (mts.), China 78/D4
Terhathum, Nepal 97/F2
Terheijden, Neth. 52/B5
Teriberka, Rus. 68/G1
Teriberskiy (pt.), Rus. 68/G1
Terkaplesterpoelen (lake), Neth. 52/C2
Terlan (Terlano), It. 61/H4
Terlano (Terlan), It. 61/H4
Terlingua, Tx, US 150/C3
Termas del Arapey, Uru. 188/E4
Termeno (Tramin), It. 61/H5
Termessos (Güllükdağı) NP, Turk. 102/B2
Termini Imerese, It. 48/C4
Terminiers, Fr. 57/G4
Terminillo (peak), It. 65/B3
Terminio (peak), It. 65/D6
Términos (lag.), Mex. 176/D2
Terminus (dam), Ca, US 148/C2
Termit-Kaoboul, Niger 116/A2
Termiz, Uzb. 101/J1
Termo, Ca, US 146/C3
Termoli, It. 65/D4
Termonfeckin, Ire. 34/B4
Termunten, Neth. 52/E2
Ternate, Indo. 91/G3
Ternay, Fr. 64/A1
Ternberg, Aus. 59/H7
Terneuzen, Neth. 52/A6
Terney, Rus. 79/M2
Terni (prov.), It. 65/B2
Terni, It. 65/B2
Ternin (riv.), Fr. 44/F3
Ternivka, Ukr. 73/J3
Ternoise (riv.), Fr. 54/B3
Ternopil', Ukr. 72/C3
Ternopil's'ka Oblast, Ukr. 70/C2
Ternovka, Rus. 73/L2
Terowie, Austl. 132/C2
Terpeniya (bay), Rus. 75/Q5
Terpeniya (cape), Rus. 79/N2
Terpní, Gre. 75/H2
Terra Ceia, Fl, US 164/K8
Terra Cotta, On, Can. 160/T8
Terra del Sole, It. 63/E5
Terra Nova, Braz. 183/G5
Terra Nova NP, Nf, Can. 159/K1
Terra Rica, Braz. 189/F2
Terrabonne (bay), La, US 164/C3
Terrace, BC, Can. 140/D3
Terrace Bay, On, Can. 157/L3
Terrace Heights, Wa, US 144/D4
Terracina, It. 65/C5
Terråk, Nor. 38/E2
Terral, Ok, US 153/F4
Terralba, It. 48/A3
Terranuova Bracciolini, It. 63/E6
Terrassa, Sp. 47/L6
Terrasson-la-Villedieu, Fr. 44/D4
Terre Haute, In, US 160/C5
Terre Hill, Pa, US 168/B3
Terrebonne (co.), Qu, Can. 159/N6
Terrebonne, Qu, Can. 159/N6
Terrell, Tx, US 151/F1
Terrenceville, Nf, Can. 159/K2
Terreton, Id, US 147/G2
Terrey Hills (nbrhd.), Austl. 134/H8
Terri (peak), Swi. 61/F4
Terrigal, Austl. 133/E1
Terrington Saint Clement, Eng, UK 37/G1
Terry, Mt, US 145/M4
Tersakan, Trkm. 103/H2
Tersakkan (riv.), Kaz. 99/A1
Terschelling (isl.), Neth. 52/C2
Tertenia, It. 48/A3
Teruel, Sp. 47/E2
Terutao (isl.), Thai. 93/G6
Tervakoski, Fin. 39/E4
Tervel, Bul. 51/H4
Terza Grande (peak), It. 45/K3
Terzo d'Aquileia, It. 63/G2
Tes-Khem (riv.), Rus. 78/C1
Tešanj, Bosn. 50/C3
Tescott, Ks, US 153/F1
Tescou (riv.), Fr. 44/D5
Teseney (Tessenie), Erit. 116/H2
Tesero, It. 61/H5
Teshekpuk (lake), Ak, US 171/G1
Teshi, Gha. 115/E5
Teshikaga, Japan 82/D2
Teshio, Japan 82/B1
Teshio (riv.), Japan 82/C1
Teshio-dake (peak), Japan 82/C2
Tesiyn (riv.), Mong. 78/D2
Teslić, Bosn. 50/C3
Teslin (riv.), Yk, Can. 140/C2
Teslin (lake), BC, Can. 140/C3
Teslin, Yk, Can. 171/M3
Tësovo-Netyl'skiy, Rus. 41/P2
Tessalit, Mali 115/F1
Tessaoua, Niger 115/G3
Tessé-la-Madeleine, Fr. 57/E3
Tessenderlo, Belg. 55/E1
Tessenie (Teseney), Erit. 116/H2
Tessy-sur-Vire, Fr. 57/D3
Test (riv.), Eng, UK 37/E4
Testa del Gargano (pt.), It. 48/E2
Testa del Rutor (peak), It. 64/D1
Tét, Hun. 50/C2
Têt (riv.), Fr. 47/G1
Tetas (pt.), Chile 188/B2
Tete, Moz. 123/G3
Tete (prov.), Moz. 123/G2
Tête d'Alpe (peak), Fr. 64/D5
Tête de Faux (peak), Fr. 60/D1
Tête de l'Enchastraye (peak), Fr. 64/C4
Tête de l'Estrop (peak), Fr. 64/C4
Tête de Moïse (peak), Fr. 64/C4
Tête de Siguret (peak), Fr. 64/C4
Tête de Soulaure (peak), Fr. 64/C3
Tête du Torraz (peak), Fr. 60/C6
Tête Jaune Cache, BC, Can. 144/E1
Tête Nord des Fours (peak), Fr. 64/C1
Tête Ronde (peak), Swi. 60/D5
Tetela, Mex. 175/M7
Teterow, Ger. 40/E5
Teteven, Bul. 51/G4
Tetford, Eng, UK 35/H5
Tetiaroa (isl.), FrPol. 137/L6
Tetiyiv, Ukr. 72/E3
Tëtkino, Rus. 73/H2
Tetlin, Ak, US 171/K3
Teton (riv.), Id, US 147/H2
Teton (range), Wy, US 147/H2
Teton, Id, US 147/H2
Tetonia, Id, US 147/H2
Tétouan, Mor. 112/B2
Tétouan (prov.), Mor. 112/B2
Tetovo, FYROM 75/G1
T'et'ritsqaro, Geo. 71/H4
Tettnang, Ger. 61/F2
Tetulia, Bang. 97/G2
Tetulia (riv.), Bang. 97/H4
Teublitz, Ger. 59/F4
Teuchezhsk, Rus. 73/K5
Teuco (riv.), Arg. 188/D3
Teufen, Swi. 61/F3
Teúl de González Ortega, Mex. 174/E4
Teulada (cape), It. 48/A3
Teulon, Mb, Can. 156/F2
Teupasenti, Hon. 176/E3
Teuri (isl.), Japan 82/B1
Teuschnitz, Ger. 59/E2
Teutoburger Wald (for.), Ger. 53/F4
Teutopolis, Il, US 162/C1
Tevere (Tiber) (riv.), It. 45/K5
Teverya, Isr. 105/D3
Teviot (riv.), Sc, UK 33/D6
Teviotdale (valley), Sc, UK 33/D6
Tevli, Bela. 43/N2
Tewantin-Noosa, Austl. 134/D4
Tewaukon Nat'l Wild. Ref., ND, US 156/F5
Tewkesbury, Eng, UK 36/D3
Texada (isl.), BC, Can. 144/B3
Texana (lake), Tx, US 151/F3
Texarkana, Ar, US 153/G4
Texarkana, Tx, US 153/G4
Texas, Austl. 132/D1
Texas (state), US 142/G5
Texas City, Tx, US 151/N9
Texas Point NWR, La, US 151/H3
Texas Safari Wildlife Park, Tx, US 151/F2
Texas Stadium, Tx, US 150/L7
Texcoco, Mex. 175/R9
Texel (isl.), Neth. 42/C2
Texhoma, Ok, US 152/D2
Texmelucan, Mex. 175/L7
Texoma (lake), Ok, US 143/G5
Teyateyaneng, Les. 124/D3
Teykovo, Rus. 68/J4
Tezio (peak), It. 65/B1
Teziutlán, Mex. 175/M7
Tezonapa, Mex. 175/N8
Tezontepec, Mex. 175/L7
Tezontepec de Aldama, Mex. 175/K6
Tezoyuca, Mex. 175/R9
Tezpur, India 86/B3
Tezu, India 86/C3
Tezze, It. 63/E2
Tha (riv.), Laos 86/D4
Tha Chin (riv.), Thai. 94/B3
Tha Mai, Thai. 94/C3
Tha Rua, Thai. 94/C3
Tha Sala, Thai. 94/B4
Tha Tum, Thai. 94/C3
Tha Wang Pha, Thai. 94/C2
Tha-Anne (riv.), Nun, Can. 140/G2
Thaba Nchu, SAfr. 124/D3
Thabana-Ntlenyana (peak), Les. 124/E3
Thabankulu (peak), SAfr. 125/E2
Thabazimbi, SAfr. 123/E5
Thabor (peak), Fr. 64/C2
Thādiq, SAr. 100/E3
Thaen (pt.), Thai. 94/B4
Thagaya, Myan. 94/B2
Thai Binh, Viet. 87/E4
Thai Nguyen, Viet. 86/E4
Thailand (ctry.) 94/C3
Thailand (gulf), Asia 94/C4
Thākurdwāra, India 96/B1
Thākurgaon, Bang. 97/G2
Thākurmunda, India 95/E1
Thal, Pak. 98/A3
Thal (des.), Pak. 98/A4
Tha'l (mtn.), Sudan 116/E2
Thal (des.), India 99/B5
Thalang, Thai. 94/B4
Thaleban NP, Thai. 94/C5
Thaleischweiler-Fröschen, Ger. 55/G5
Thalerhof (int'l arpt.), Aus. 50/B2
Thalgau, Aus. 59/G7
Thalheim bei Wels, Aus. 59/H6
Thalmann, Ga, US 165/H2
Thalmässing, Ger. 58/E4
Thalwil, Swi. 61/E3
Thame (riv.), Eng, UK 37/F3
Thame, Eng, UK 37/F3
Thames (riv.), Eng., UK 37/G4
Thames (riv.), On, Can. 160/F3
Thames, NZ 135/C2
Thames Barrier, Eng, UK 30/D2
Thāna, India 95/B2
Thāna Bhawan, India 98/D5
Thāna Kasbā, India 96/A3
Thanatpin, Myan. 86/C5
Thanbyuzayat, Myan. 94/B3
Thānesar, India 98/D5
Thāneswar, Bang. 97/H3
Thang Duc, Viet. 94/D3
Thanggu, India 97/G2
Thangool, Austl. 134/C4
Thanh Hoa, Viet. 86/E5
Thanh Lang Xa, Viet. 93/J4
Thanh Phu, Viet. 94/D4
Thanh Tri, Viet. 94/D4
Thānkot, Nepal 97/E2
Thann, Fr. 60/D2
Thannhausen, Ger. 61/G1
Thanya Buri, Thai. 94/C3
Thaoge (riv.), Bots. 122/D3
Thaon-les-Vosges, Fr. 60/C1
Thap Put, Thai. 94/B4
Thap Sakae, Thai. 94/B4
Thar (riv.), Fr. 56/D3
Thar (des.), Pak. 98/A5
Tharād, India 101/K4
Thargomindah, Austl. 134/A5
Tharrawaddy, Myan. 86/B5
Thásos, Gre. 75/J2
Thásos (isl.), Gre. 70/C4
That Khe, Viet. 87/E4
That Phanom, Thai. 94/D2
Thatcham, Eng, UK 37/E4
Thatcher, Id, US 147/H2
Thatcher, Az, US 149/H4
Thaton, Myan. 94/B2
Thaungdut, Myan. 86/B3
Thaur, Aus. 61/H3
Thaxted, Eng, UK 37/G3
Thaxton, Ms, US 162/C3
Thaya (riv.), Aus. 43/H4
Thayer, Mo, US 153/J2
Thayer, Ks, US 153/G2
Thayetmyo, Myan. 86/B5
Thayngen, Swi. 61/E2
Thazi, Myan. 86/C4
The Alamo, Tx, US 151/E3
The Atomium, Belg. 55/D2
The Ballpark, Tx, US 150/K7
The Bourne (riv.), Eng, UK 30/B3
The Broads NP, Eng, UK 37/H1
The Buck (peak), Sc, UK 33/D2
The Burren (reg.), Ire. 32/A3
The Calf (peak), Eng, UK 35/F3
The Caprock (cliff), NM, US 152/C3
The Cheviot (peak), Eng, UK 33/D6
The Colony, Tx, US 150/L6
The Curragh, Ire. 32/D3
The Dalles (dam), Or, US 146/C1
The Dalles, Or, US 146/C1
The English Companys (isls.), Austl. 129/E2
The Entrance, Austl. 133/E1
The Everglades (swamp), Fl, US 165/H5
The Fens (phys. reg.), Eng, UK 35/H6
The Fens (phys. reg.), Eng, UK 37/G1
The Flat Tops (mts.), Co, US 147/K4
The Gap (pass), Ire. 32/C5
The Gap, Austl. 132/B1
The Grampians (range), Austl. 132/B3
The Granites (peak), Austl. 131/F2
The Hague ('s-Gravenhage) (cap.), Neth. 52/B4
The Hermitage, NZ 135/B3
The Key Ind. Res., Sk, Can. 156/C2
The Lakes NP, Austl. 133/C3
The Lizard (pen.), Eng, UK 36/A6
The Loup, NI, UK 34/B2
The Machars (pen.), Sc, UK 34/D2
The Malpais (lava flow), NM, US 149/H3
The Malpais (lava flow), NM, US 149/J4
The Naze (pt.), Eng, UK 37/H3
The Oaks, Ca, US 166/B1
The Oaks, Austl. 133/E2
The Paps (peak), Ire. 32/A5
The Pas, Mb, Can. 140/F3
The Peak (peak), NC, US 163/G2
The Pilot (mtn.), Austl. 133/D3
The Pine (hills), Mt, US 145/M4
The Pinnacles (peak), BC, Can. 144/E2
The Plains, Oh, US 160/E5
The Quantocks (hills), Eng, UK 36/C4
The Range, Zim. 123/F3
The Raven (pt.), Ire. 32/D5
The Rhinns (pt.), Sc, UK 34/C2
The Rock, Austl. 133/C2
The Royal NP, Austl. 134/H9
The Saddle (peak), Sc, UK 33/A2
The Seven Hogs (isl.), Ire. 30/N10
The Sisters (isl.), NZ 135/E3
The Solent (chan.), Eng, UK 37/E5
The Storr (peak), Sc, UK 31/Q8
The Swale (riv.), Eng, Ire. 37/G4
The Twins (peak), Ab, Can. 144/F1
The Valley (cap.), Angu. 173/N8
The Woodlands, Tx, US 151/G2
The Wrekin (co.), Eng, UK 36/D1
The Wrekin (hill), Eng, UK 36/D1
The Yellow (mtn.), Austl. 133/C1
Theale, Eng, UK 37/E4
Thebes (ruin), Egypt 109/G3
Thedaw, Myan. 94/B1
Thedford, Ne, US 154/D3
Theilheim, Ger. 58/D3
Thelepte, Tun. 66/F4
Thelon (riv.), NW,Nun, Can. 140/F2
Thelon (riv.), Can. 139/G3
Themar, Ger. 58/D1
Thémericourt, Fr. 30/H4
Theo (mt.), Austl. 131/F2
Theodore, Sk, Can. 156/C2
Theodore, Al, US 164/D2
Theodore, Austl. 134/C4
Theodore Roosevelt (dam), Az, US 149/G4
Theodore Roosevelt (lake), Az, US 149/G4
Theodore Roosevelt NP, ND, US 156/C4
Theodosia, Mo, US 153/H2
Théoule-sur-Mer, Fr. 64/C6
Thérain (riv.), Fr. 44/D2
Thermaic (gulf), Gre. 70/B4
Thermal, Ca, US 148/D4
Thermalito, Ca, US 146/C4
Thérmi, Gre. 75/H2
Thermopílai (Thermopylae) (pass), Gre. 75/H3
Thermopolis, Wy, US 147/J2
Thermopylae (Thermopílai) (pass), Gre. 75/H3
Thérouanne (riv.), Fr. 30/L4
Thésée, Fr. 57/G6
Thesprotikón, Gre. 75/G3
Thessalon, On, Can. 160/E1
Thessaloníki, Gre. 75/H2
Thessaly (reg.), Gre. 67/J3
Thet (riv.), Eng, UK 37/G2
Thetford, Eng, UK 37/G2
Thetford Mines, Qu, Can. 158/B2
Thetkala, Myan. 86/C5
Theunissen, SAfr. 124/D3
Theux, Belg. 55/E2
Thève (riv.), Fr. 30/K4
Theydon Bois, Eng, UK 30/D2
Thiais, Fr. 30/K5
Thíamis (riv.), Gre. 75/G3
Thiant, Fr. 54/C3
Thiaucourt-Regniéville, Fr. 55/E6
Thiberville, Fr. 57/F2
Thibodaux, La, US 164/C3
Thick (mtn.), Pa, US 161/H4
Thickwood (hills), Sk, Can. 145/L1
Thief River Falls, Mn, US 156/F3
Thielle (riv.), Swi. 60/C4
Thielsen (mt.), Or, US 146/B2
Thien Ngon, Viet. 94/D4
Thiene, It. 63/E2
Thiérache (reg.), Fr. 54/C4
Thierhaupten, Ger. 58/D5
Thiers, Fr. 44/E4
Thiers-sur-Thève, Fr. 30/K4
Thierville-sur-Meuse, Fr. 55/E5
Thiès, Sen. 114/A3
Thiès (pol. reg.), Sen. 114/A3
Thiet Tra, Viet. 86/E4
Thika, Kenya 119/B2
Thimād al Khuwaymah (well), Libya 134/C2
Thimphu (cap.), Bhu. 97/G2
Thingvellir NP, Ice. 38/N7
Thio, NCal. 137/V12
Thionville, Fr. 55/F5
Thiou, Burk. 115/E3
Thíra, Gre. 75/J4
Thíra (isl.), Gre. 67/K3
Third Cataract (falls), Sudan 109/F5
Third Lake, Il, US 167/Q15
Thirlmere (lake), Eng, UK 35/E2
Thirlmere, Austl. 133/E2
Thiron Gardais, Fr. 57/G4
Thironne (riv.), Fr. 57/G4
Thirsk, Eng, UK 35/G3
Thirsty (mt.), Austl. 130/D5
Thirtymile (pt.), NY, US 160/W9
Thiruvananthapuram, India 95/C4
Thise, Fr. 60/C3
Thisted, Den. 40/C3
Thistilfjördhur (estu.), Ice. 38/P6
Thistle (isl.), Austl. 131/H5
Thistle (mt.), Yk, Can. 171/L3
Thithia (isl.), Fiji 137/Y18
Thívai, Gre. 75/H3
Thiverval-Grignon, Fr. 30/H5
Thjósa (riv.), Ice. 38/N7
Thlanship, India 86/B3
Thlewiaza (riv.), Nun, Can. 140/G2
Thoen, Thai. 94/B2
Thoeng, Thai. 94/C2
Thohoyandou, SAfr. 123/F4
Thoi Binh, Viet. 94/D4
Thoiry, Fr. 30/H5

Tholen – Torii-t

Tholen (isl.), Neth. 52/B5
Tholen, Neth. 52/B5
Tholey, Ger. 55/G5
Thomas, Ok, US 153/E3
Thomas, WV, US 163/H1
Thomasboro, Il, US 160/B4
Thomaston, Al, US 162/D4
Thomaston, Ga, US 162/E4
Thomastown, Ire. 32/C4
Thomastown, Ms, US 162/C4
Thomasville, Al, US 164/E2
Thomasville, Ga, US 165/G2
Thomasville, Mo, US 153/J2
Thomasville, NC, US 163/G3
Thomasville, Pa, US 168/B4
Thomes (cr.), Ca, US 146/B4
Thompson (peak), NM, US 152/B3
Thompson, ND, US 156/F4
Thompson, Mi, US 160/C2
Thompson, Ct, US 161/L4
Thompson, Ut, US 149/H1
Thompson, Mb, Can. 140/G3
Thompson (peak), Ca, US 146/B3
Thompson (riv.), Ia,Mo, US 155/G3
Thompson (lake), Austl. 130/K7
Thompson (riv.), BC, Can. 144/D2
Thompson Falls, Mt, US 144/G4
Thompsonville, Mi, US 160/D2
Thompsonville, Il, US 162/C2
Thomsen (riv.), NW, Can. 140/E1
Thomson, Ga, US 163/F4
Thomson, Il, US 155/J3
Thomson (riv.), Austl. 127/D3
Thon Lac Nghiep, Viet. 94/E4
Thon Song Pha, Viet. 94/E4
Thongwa, Myan. 94/B2
Thonnance-lès-Joinville, Fr. 60/B1
Thonon-les-Bains, Fr. 60/C5
Thonotosassa, Fl, US 164/L7
Thonotosassa (lake), Fl, US 164/L7
Thoreau, NM, US 149/H3
Thorens-Glières, Fr. 60/C6
Thorigny-sur-Marne, Fr. 30/L5
Thorlákshöfn, Ice. 38/N7
Thorn (cr.), Il, US 167/Q16
Thornaby-on-Tees, Eng, UK 35/G2
Thornbury, On, Can. 160/F2
Thornbury, Eng, UK 36/D3
Thorndale, Tx, US 151/F2
Thorndale, Pa, US 168/C4
Thorne, Eng, UK 35/H4
Thorne, On, Can. 161/G1
Thorne Bay, Ak, US 171/M4
Thornfield, Mo, US 153/H2
Thornhill, Sc, UK 34/E1
Thornhill, Sc, UK 33/B4
Thornhurst, Pa, US 168/C1
Thornley, Eng, UK 35/G2
Thornthwaite, Eng, UK 35/G3
Thornton, Ar, US 153/H4
Thornton, Ca, US 167/M10
Thornton, Co, US 154/B4
Thornton, Tx, US 151/F2
Thornton Cleveleys, Eng, UK 35/E4
Thornton Dale, Eng, UK 35/H3
Thorntonville, Tx, US 150/C2
Thorntown, In, US 160/C4
Thornwood Common, Eng, UK 30/D1
Thorold, On, Can. 160/U9
Thorold South, On, Can. 160/U9
Thorp, Wi, US 155/J1
Thorp, Wa, US 144/D4
Thorpe, Eng, UK 30/B2
Thorpe Thewles, Eng, UK 35/G2
Thorpe-le-Soken, Eng, UK 37/H3
Thorsby, Al, US 162/D4
Thorsby, Ab, Can. 145/G1
Thórshöfn, Ice. 38/P6
Thouarcé, Fr. 57/E6
Thouaré-sur-Loire, Fr. 56/D6
Thoubāl, India 86/B3
Thouet (riv.), Fr. 44/C3
Thourotte, Fr. 54/B5
Thousand (isl.), On, Can. 161/H2
Thousand Oaks, Ca, US 166/B2
Thousand Springs (cr.), Nv, US 147/F3
Thowa (riv.), Kenya 119/B2
Thrace (reg.), Bul.,Gre. 67/K2
Thracian (sea), Gre. 70/C4
Thread (cr.), Mi, US 167/E6
Thredbo Village, Austl. 133/D3
Three Bridges, NJ, US 168/D2
Three Creek, Id, US 147/F2
Three Forks, Mt, US 145/J5
Three Guardsmen (mt.), Yk, Can. 171/L3
Three Hills, Ab, Can. 145/H2
Three Kings (isls.), NZ 135/B1
Three Lakes, Wi, US 157/K5
Three Mile (isl.), Pa, US 168/B3
Three Mile Plains, NS, Can. 158/E3
Three Notch, Al, US 165/F1
Three Oaks, Mi, US 160/C4
Three Pagodas (pass), Myan. 94/B3
Three Points (cape), Gha. 115/E5
Three Rivers, Mi, US 160/D4
Three Rivers, NM, US 149/J4
Three Rivers, Austl. 130/C3
Three Springs, Austl. 130/B4
Three Valley, BC, Can. 144/E2
Threehills (cr.), Ab, Can. 145/H2
Thrifty, Tx, US 150/E2
Throckmorton, Tx, US 152/E4
Throssel (lake), Austl. 127/B3
Thrums, BC, Can. 144/F3
Thrumster, Sc, UK 31/S7
Thrushel (riv.), Eng, UK 36/B5
Thu Dau Mot, Viet. 94/D4
Thu Duc, Viet. 94/D4
Thud (pt.), Austl. 129/F3
Thuin, Belg. 55/D3
Thuir, Fr. 44/E5
Thulba (riv.), Ger. 58/C2
Thule Air Base, Den. 141/T7
Thun, Swi. 60/D4
Thunder (bay), On, Can. 157/K3
Thunder (mtn.), Wi, US 157/K5
Thunder Bay, On, Can. 157/K3
Thunder Butte (cr.), SD, US 154/C1
Thundersley, Eng, UK 30/E2
Thuner (lake), Swi. 45/G3
Thung Chang, Thai. 94/C2
Thung Salaeng Luang NP, Thai. 94/C2
Thung Song, Thai. 94/B4
Thüngersheim, Ger. 58/C3
Thunkar, Bhu. 97/H2
Thur (riv.), Swi. 45/H3
Thurgau (canton), Swi. 61/E2
Thüringen, Aus. 61/F3
Thüringen (state), Ger. 45/J1
Thüringer Schiefergebirge (mts.), Ger. 58/E2
Thüringer Wald (for.), Ger. 42/F3
Thurlaston, Eng, UK 37/E2
Thurles, Ire. 32/C4
Thurloo Downs, Austl. 132/B1
Thurlow, Mt, US 145/L4
Thurmont, Md, US 161/H5
Thurnau, Ger. 59/E2
Thurø By, Den. 40/D4
Thurrock (co.), Eng, UK 37/G3
Thursday Island, Austl. 129/F2
Thursley, Eng, UK 30/A3
Thurso, Qu, Can. 161/J2
Thurso, Sc, UK 31/V14
Thurston (co.), Wa, US 167/A3
Thurston (isl.), Ant. 192/T
Thury-en-Valois, Fr. 30/M4
Thury-Harcourt, Fr. 57/E3
Thusis, Swi. 61/F4
Thyez, Fr. 60/C5
Thyolo, Malw. 123/G3
Ti-m-Merhsoï (riv.), Niger 115/G2
Ti-n-Essako, Mali 115/F2
Ti-n-Jedane, Oued (riv.), Alg. 111/G4
Ti-n-Toumma (reg.), Niger 116/A1
Ti-n-Zaouâtene, Mali 115/F2
Ti-Tree Abor. Land, Austl. 131/G2
Tia, Austl. 132/D1
Tiahuanco (ruin), Bol. 188/B1
Tian Shan (mts.), China 77/H5
Tianbao, China 87/H3
Tiancang, China 78/D3
Tianchang, China 80/D4
Tiandeng, China 87/E4
Tian'e, China 93/J2
Tianguá, Braz. 183/F3
Tianguistenco, Mex. 175/Q10
Tianhua, China 87/G3
Tianjin (prov.), China 79/H4
Tianjin, China 80/H7
Tianlin, China 93/J3
Tianmen, China 87/G2
Tianmu (mts.), China 80/K9
Tianping, China 87/F3
Tianqiao, China 87/F2
Tianshifu, China 81/C2
Tianshui, China 78/F5
Tianshuihai, China 99/C4
Tianzhen, China 80/C2
Tianzhu, China 87/F3
Tianzhuangtai, China 81/B2
Tiaret, Alg. 112/F5
Tiassalé, C.d'Iv. 114/D5
Tiatucurá, Uru. 191/K10
Tiavea, Sam. 137/S9
Tibagi (riv.), Braz. 186/C4
Tibagi, Braz. 189/G3
Tibaná, Col. 180/C3
Tibati, Camr. 116/B4
Tibba, Pak. 98/A5
Tibbee (cr.), Ms, US 162/C4
Tibberton, Eng, UK 36/D1
Tibbie, Al, US 164/D2
Tibble, Swe. 39/A1
Tibé, Pic de (peak), Gui. 114/C4
Tiber (riv.), It. 67/G2
Tiber (dam), Mt, US 145/J3
Tiber (Tevere) (riv.), It. 45/K5
Tiberias (lake), Isr. 104/D3
Tiberias, Isr. 105/D3
Tibert (peak), It. 64/D4
Tibesti (mts.), Chad 107/D3
Tibet (reg.), China 77/H6
Tibet (Xizang) (aut. reg.), China 78/C5
Tibiri, Niger 115/G3
Tibnīn, Leb. 105/C2
Tibooburra, Austl. 131/J4
Tibro, Swe. 40/F2
Tibshelf, Eng, UK 35/G5
Tiburon (cape), Haiti 173/G4
Tiburon, Ca, US 167/K11
Tiburón, Isla (isl.), Mex. 174/B2
Ticaco, Peru 184/D5
Ticehurst, Eng, UK 37/G4
Tichigan (lake), Wi, US 167/P14
Tîchît, Mrta. 114/C2
Tichla, Mor. 110/B5
Tichnor, Ar, US 153/J3
T'īcho, Eth. 118/A4
Ticino (canton), Swi. 61/E5
Ticino (riv.), Swi. 61/E6
Tickfaw, La, US 164/C2
Ţicleni, Rom. 51/F3
Ticllos, Peru 184/B3
Ticonderoga, NY, US 161/K3
Ticul, Mex. 176/D1
Tīdah, Egypt 113/B2
Tidaholm, Swe. 40/E2
Tiddim, Myan. 86/B4
Tideswell, Eng, UK 35/G5
Tidikelt (plain), Alg. 111/F4
Tidioute, Pa, US 161/G4
Tidjikdja, Mrta. 114/C2
Tidone (riv.), It. 62/C3
Tidore (isl.), Indo. 91/G3
Tidsit (lake), WSah. 110/B5
Tie Plant, Ms, US 162/C4
Tiébélé Corabie, Burk. 115/E4
Tiébissou, C.d'Iv. 114/D5
Tiéboro, Chad 134/C4
Tiechang, China 81/D2
Tiede, PN del, Sp. 110/A3
Tiefencastel, Swi. 61/F4
Tiefensee, Ger. 42/Q6
Tiéfinzo, C.d'Iv. 114/D4
Tiège, Belg. 55/E2
Tiel, Neth. 52/C5
Tieli, China 79/K2
Tieling, China 80/E2
Tielt, Belg. 54/C2
Tielt-Winge, Belg. 55/D2
Tiemba (riv.), C.d'Iv. 114/D4
Tiemen (pass), China 99/E3
Tien Yen, Viet. 94/D1
Tien Yen, Viet. 94/D2
Tienen, Belg. 55/D2
Tiénigbe, C.d'Iv. 114/D4
Tieniu (pass), China 87/H3
Tiercé, Fr. 57/E5
Tieri, Austl. 134/C3
Tieroko (peak), Chad 134/C4
Tierp, Swe. 40/G1
Tierra Amarilla, NM, US 149/J2
Tierra Amarilla, Chile 188/B3
Tierra Blanca (cr.), Tx,NM, US 152/C3
Tierra Blanca, Mex. 175/N8
Tierra Colorada, Mex. 175/F5
Tierra del Fuego (isl.), Arg. 179/C8
Tierra del Fuego, Antártida e Islas del Atlántico Sur, Arg. 191/C7
Tierra del Fuego, PN, Chile 191/C7
Tierradentro, Col. 180/B4
Tierranueva, Mex. 175/E4
Tiétar (riv.), Sp. 46/C2
Tietê (riv.), Braz. 179/D5
Tieton, Wa, US 144/D4
Tieton (peak), Wa, US 144/D4
Tieyon, Austl. 131/G3
Tifariti, WSah. 110/C4
Tiffany, Co, US 149/J2
Tiffany (mtn.), Wa, US 144/E3
Tiffin (riv.), Oh, US 160/D4
Tiffin, Oh, US 160/E4
Tiflet, Mor. 112/A3
Tifton, Ga, US 165/G2
Tigapuluh (mts.), Indo. 89/C3
Tigeaux, Fr. 30/L5
Tiger (hills), Mb, Can. 156/D3
Tiger (lake), Fl, US 164/N8
Tigerton, Wi, US 155/K1
Tighina (Bendery), Mol. 72/E4
Tighvein (hill), Sc, UK 33/A6
Tigil', Rus. 75/R4
Tignall, Ga, US 163/F4
Tignère, Camr. 116/B4
Tignieu-Jameyzieu, Fr. 60/B6
Tignish, PE, Can. 158/E2
Tigray (prov.), Eth. 116/H2
Tigre (riv.), Ven. 173/J6
Tigre (riv.), Ven. 181/F2
Tigre, Arg. 191/J11
Tigres (bay), Ang. 122/A3
Tigris (riv.), Iraq 77/C6
Tiguent, Mrta. 114/A2
Tigui (well), Chad 134/C5
Tiguidit, Falaise de (cliff), Niger 115/G2
Tigy, Fr. 57/H5
Tigzirt, Alg. 112/H4
Tihamat al Yaman (valley), Yem. 118/B1
Tihosuco, Mex. 176/D1
Tihuatlán, Mex. 176/B1
Tiilikkajärven NP, Fin. 68/F3
Tijāra, India 96/A2
Tijger (falls), Sur. 182/B2
Tījī, Libya 134/A1
Tijuana, Mex. 166/C5
Tijuca, PN da, Braz. 187/N7
Tijucas, Braz. 189/G3
Tijuco (riv.), Braz. 186/C3
Tikal (ruin), Guat. 176/D2
Tikal, Guat. 175/H5
Tīkamgarh, India 96/B3
Tikanlik, China 99/E3
Tikarapāra, India 95/D1
Tikaré, Burk. 115/E3
Tikchik Lakes, Ak, US 171/G3
Tikehau (isl.), FrPol. 137/L6
Tikhoretsk, Rus. 73/L5
Tikhvin, Rus. 68/G4
Tiko, Camr. 120/B1
Tikrīt, Iraq 103/E3
Tiksi, Rus. 75/N2
Tikveš (lake), FYROM 75/H2
Tila, Mex. 176/C2
Tiläänjärvi (lake), Fin. 39/F4
Tilburg, Neth. 52/C5
Tilbury, On, Can. 160/E3
Tilbury, Eng, UK 30/E2
Tilcha, Austl. 131/J4
Tilden, Il, US 162/C1
Tilden, Tx, US 151/E3
Tilford, Eng, UK 30/A3
Tilford, SD, US 154/C1
Tilghman, Md, US 168/B6
Tilghman (isl.), Md, US 168/B6
Tilhar, India 96/B2
Tilin, Myan. 86/B4
Tilisarao, Arg. 190/D2
Till (riv.), Eng, UK 33/D5
Tillabéry, Niger 115/F3
Tillamook (bay), Or, US 146/A1
Tillamook, Or, US 144/C5
Tillar, Ar, US 153/J4
Tille (riv.), Fr. 42/C5
Tillery (lake), NC, US 163/G3
Tilley, Sk, Can. 145/J2
Tillicoultry, Sc, UK 33/C4
Tillières-sur-Avre, Fr. 57/G3
Tillmans Corner, Al, US 164/D2
Tillsonburg, On, Can. 160/F3
Tilly-sur-Seulles, Fr. 57/E2
Tilomar, ETim. 128/B2
Tilomonte, Chile 188/B2
Tilopozo, Chile 188/B2
Tilpa, Austl. 132/C1
Tilst, Den. 40/D3
Tilston, Mb, Can. 156/D3
Tilt (riv.), Sc, UK 33/C3
Tiltagara, Austl. 132/C1
Tiltil, Chile 190/N8
Tilton, Il, US 160/C4
Tim, Den. 40/C3
Tim, Rus. 73/J2
Ţimā, Egypt 102/B5
Timan (ridge), Rus. 74/F3
Timaná, Col. 180/C4
Timane (riv.), Par. 188/D2
Timanfaya, PN de, Sp. 110/B3
Timaru, NZ 135/B4
Timashevo, Rus. 71/J1
Timashevsk, Rus. 73/K5
Timbákion, Gre. 75/J5
Timbalier (bay), La, US 164/C3
Timbaúba, Braz. 183/H4
Timbédra, Mrta. 114/C2
Timber (mtn.), Tx, US 150/C2
Timber Lake, SD, US 156/D5
Timberlake, Va, US 163/H2
Timberville, Va, US 163/H1
Timbiquí, Col. 180/B4
Timbiras, Braz. 183/F4
Timbo, Gui. 114/C4
Timbó, Braz. 189/G3
Timboon, Austl. 132/B3
Timbué (pt.), Moz. 123/H3
Timbuni (riv.), Indo. 91/H4
Timehri (int'l arpt.), Guy. 181/G3
Timelkam, Aus. 59/G6
Timenocalin (well), Libya 134/A3
Timetrine, Mali 115/E2
Timetrout (peak), Mor. 66/B4
Timfristós (peak), Gre. 75/G3
Timgad (ruin), Alg. 66/E4
Tîmia, Niger 115/H2
Timimoun, Alg. 111/F3
Timiris (cape), Mrta. 114/A2
Timiş (riv.), Rom. 70/B3
Timiş (prov.), Rom. 50/E3
Timişoara (int'l arpt.), Rom. 50/E3
Timişoara, Rom. 50/E3
Timmins, On, Can. 167/H4
Timmonsville, SC, US 163/H3
Timms (hill), Wi, US 157/J5
Timoleague, Ire. 32/B6
Timon, Braz. 183/F4
Timonium, Md, US 168/B5
Timor (isl.), Indo. 77/M10
Timor (sea), Asia,Austl. 77/M11
Timor Timur (prov.), Indo. 128/A2
Timóteo, Braz. 187/E3
Timpas, Co, US 152/C2
Timpson, Tx, US 151/G2
Timpton (riv.), Rus. 75/N4
Tims Ford (dam), Tn, US 162/D3
Tims Ford (lake), Tn, US 162/D3
Timsāḩ (lake), Egypt 113/D3
Timsher, Rus. 69/M3
Timucuan Nat'l Prsv., Fl, US 165/H2
Timurnī, India 96/A4
Tin Can Bay, Austl. 134/D4
Tin Shui Wai, China 87/K7
Tina (riv.), SAfr. 124/B1
Tinaca (pt.), Phil. 88/D4
Tinaco, Ven. 180/D2
Tinahely, Ire. 32/D4
Tinca, Rom. 50/E2
Tinchebray, Fr. 57/E3
Tincup, Co, US 149/J1
Tinderry (mtn.), Austl. 133/D2
Tindivanam, India 95/C3
Tindouf (wilaya), Alg. 110/D3
Tindouf, Alg. 110/C4
Tiné, Oued (riv.), Chad 116/D2
Tinée (riv.), Fr. 64/C4
Tineo, Sp. 46/B1
Ting (riv.), China 87/H3
Tinga (peak), CAfr. 116/D3
Tingalpa (res.), Austl. 134/F7
Tingaringy NP, Austl. 132/D3
Tingha, Austl. 132/D1
Tingi (mts.), SLeo. 114/C4
Tingjegaon, Nepal 96/D1
Tinglin, China 80/L9
Tingmerkpuk (mt.), Ak, US 171/F2
Tingo María, Peru 184/C3
Tingping, China 87/F3
Tingréla, C.d'Iv. 114/D4
Tingri, China 97/F1
Tingsryd, Swe. 40/F3
Tinguiririca (vol.), Chile 190/C2
Tinh Gia, Viet. 94/D2
Tinharé (isl.), Braz. 187/F2
Tinian (isl.), NMar. 136/D3
Tinicum Nat'l Consv. Area, Pa, US 168/C4
Tinker (A.F.B.), Ok, US 153/F3
Tinkisso (riv.), Gui. 114/C4
Tinley Park, Il, US 167/Q16
Tinogasta, Arg. 188/C4
Tínos, Gre. 75/J4
Tínos (isl.), Gre. 67/K3
Tinqueux, Fr. 54/C5
Tinrhir, Mor. 110/D3
Tinsman, Ar, US 153/H4
Tinsukia, India 86/B3
Tinta, Peru 184/D4
Tintagel (pt.), Eng, UK 36/B5
Tintagel, Eng, UK 36/B5
Tîntâne, Mrta. 114/C2
Tinténiac, Fr. 56/D4
Tintern Abbey, Eng, UK 36/D3
Tintigny, Belg. 55/E4
Tintina, Arg. 188/D3
Tintinara, Austl. 132/B2
Tinto (peak), Sc, UK 33/C5
Tinto (riv.), Sp. 46/B4
Tinton Falls (New Shrewsbury), NJ, US 168/D3
Tintwistle, Eng, UK 35/G5
Tinui, NZ 135/D3
Tinyahuarco, Peru 184/B3
T'i'o, Erit. 118/B2
Tioga, Tx, US 153/F4
Tioga, ND, US 156/C3
Tioga (peak), Ca, US 148/C2
Tioga, WV, US 163/G1
Tiom, Indo. 91/J4
Tioman (isl.), Malay. 90/B3
Tione di Trento, It. 61/G5
Tionesta, Pa, US 161/G4
Tip Top (mt.), On, Can. 157/L3
Tipac (hill), Braz. 182/D2
Tipasa, Alg. 112/G4
Tipasa (wilaya), Alg. 112/F4
Tipp City, Oh, US 160/D5
Tipperary, Ire. 32/B5
Tipperary (co.), Ire. 32/C4
Tippettville, Ga, US 165/G1
Tipton, Ok, US 152/E3
Tipton, Mo, US 153/H1
Tipton, Pa, US 161/G4
Tipton, In, US 160/C4
Tipton, Ks, US 154/E4
Tipton, Ia, US 155/J3
Tiptonville, Tn, US 162/C2
Tiptree, Eng, UK 37/G3
Tiptūr, India 95/C3
Tiputa, FrPol. 137/L6
Tir Rhiwiog (peak), Wal, UK 36/C1
Tira, Tx, US 153/G4
Tīra Sujānpur, India 98/D4
Tiracambu, Serra do (mts.), Braz. 183/E4
Tiran (isl.), SAr. 109/G3
Tiran (str.), Egypt, SAr. 109/G3
Tiran Sinafir (isl.), SAr. 102/C5
Tiranë (cap.), Alb. 75/F2
Tirano, It. 61/G5
Tiraque, Bol. 188/C1
T'irarē Shet' (riv.), Eth. 118/A2
Tirari (des.), Austl. 131/H4
Tiraspol, Mol. 72/E4
Tirat Karmel, Isr. 105/B3
Tirat Ẕevi, Isr. 105/D4
Tire, Turk. 102/A2
Tirebolu, Turk. 70/F4
Tiree (isl.), Sc, UK 31/Q8
Tirest (well), Mali 115/F1
Tirgol, Eth. 116/G4
Tîrgovişte, Rom. 51/G3
Tîrgu Bujor, Rom. 51/H3
Tîrgu Cărbuneşti, Rom. 51/F3
Tîrgu Frumos, Rom. 72/D4
Tîrgu Jiu, Rom. 51/F3
Tîrgu Lăpuş, Rom. 51/F2
Tîrgu Mureş, Rom. 51/G2
Tîrgu Neamţ, Rom. 72/D4
Tîrgu Ocna, Rom. 51/H2
Tîrgu Secuiesc, Rom. 51/H2
Tiris (reg.), WSah. 110/B5
Tiris Zemmour (pol. reg.), Mrta. 110/C4
Tiritiri Matangi (isl.), NZ 135/F6
Tirlyanskiy, Rus. 69/N5
Tîrnava Mare (riv.), Rom. 51/G2
Tîrnava Mică (riv.), Rom. 51/F2
Tîrnăveni, Rom. 51/G2
Tírnavos, Gre. 75/H3
Tiro, Gui. 114/C4
Tirol (prov.), Aus. 42/F5
Tirrenia, It. 62/D6
Tirschenreuth, Ger. 59/F3
Tirso (riv.), It. 66/F2
Tirstup (int'l arpt.), Den. 40/D3
Tirúa, Chile 190/B3
Tiruchendūr, India 95/C4
Tiruntán, Peru 184/C2
Tirupati (int'l arpt.), India 95/C3
Tirūr, India 95/B4
Tiruttani, India 92/C3
Tiruvalla, India 95/C4
Tiruvannāmalai, India 95/C3
Tisa (riv.), Serb. 67/K1
Tisbury, Eng, UK 36/D4
Tisdale, Sk, Can. 145/M1
Tishkovo, Rus. 71/J3
Tishomingo, Ok, US 153/F3
Tishomingo, Ms, US 162/C3
Tishomingo Nat'l Wildlife Res., Ok, US 153/F3
Ţīsīyah, Syria 105/E4
Tissa, Mor. 112/B2
Tissemsilt, Alg. 112/F5
Tissemsilt (wilaya), Alg. 112/F5
Tissø (lake), Den. 39/H7
Tista (riv.), Bang. 97/G2
Tisvilde, Den. 39/J6
Tisza (riv.), Hun. 70/B3
Tiszaföldvár, Hun. 50/E2
Tiszafüred, Hun. 50/E2
Tiszakécske, Hun. 50/E2
Tiszalök, Hun. 50/E1
Tiszavasvári, Hun. 43/L5
Tit, Alg. 111/F4
Titano (peak), SMar. 63/F6
Titao, Burk. 115/E3
Titay, Phil. 88/C4
Titel, Serb. 50/E3
Titerno (riv.), It. 65/D5
Titi, Congo 120/C3
Titicaca (lake), Bol.,Peru 179/B4
Titistee-Neustadt, Ger. 60/E2
Titlagarh, India 95/D1
Titlis (peak), Swi. 61/E4
Tito, It. 48/D2
Titov Veles, FYROM 75/G2
Titov vrh (peak), FYROM 75/G2
Titsey, Eng, UK 30/D3
Titting, Ger. 58/E5
Tittmoning, Ger. 59/F6
Titu, Rom. 51/G3
Titule, D.R. Congo 121/F2
Titusville, Pa, US 161/G4
Titusville, Fl, US 165/H3
Titusville, NJ, US 168/D3
Tiuni, India 98/D4
Tiva (riv.), Kenya 119/B2
Tivaouane, Sen. 114/A3
Tivat, Serb. 50/D4
Tiverton, On, Can. 160/F2
Tiverton, Eng, UK 36/C5
Tivoli, It. 65/B4
Tivoli, Tx, US 151/F3
Tiwanacu, Bol. 188/B1
Ţīwī, Oman 101/G4
Tixán, Ecu. 184/B1
Tixtla de Guerrero, Mex. 175/F5
Tizayuca, Mex. 175/L7
Tizi Ouzou (wilaya), Alg. 112/H4
Tizi Ouzou, Alg. 112/H4
Tizimín, Mex. 176/D1
Tizmant ash Sharqīyah, Egypt 113/C6
Tiznados (riv.), Ven. 183/N8
Tiznap (riv.), China 101/L1
Tiznit, Mor. 110/C3
Tjæreborg, Den. 40/C4
Tjeldstø, Nor. 40/A1
Tjeukemeer (lake), Neth. 52/C3
Tjøme, Nor. 40/D2
Tjorn (isl.), Den. 40/D3
Tkhab (peak), Rus. 73/K5
Tkibuli, Geo. 71/G4
Tlachichuca, Mex. 175/M7
Tlacolula de Matamoros, Mex. 176/B2
Tlacotalpan, Mex. 175/P8
Tlacotepec, Mex. 175/F5
Tlalixcoyan, Mex. 175/N8
Tlalmanalco, Mex. 175/Q10
Tlalnepantla, Mex. 175/Q9
Tláloc (vol.), Mex. 175/Q10
Tlalpan (nbrhd.), Mex. 175/Q10
Tlaltenango de Sánchez Román, Mex. 174/E4
Tlaltizapan, Mex. 175/K8
Tlapa de Comonfort, Mex. 176/B2
Tlapacoya (ruin), Mex. 175/Q10
Tlapacoyan, Mex. 175/M7
Tlapehuala, Mex. 175/E5
Tlaquepaque, Mex. 174/E4
Tlaquiltenango, Mex. 175/K8
Tlatlauquitepec, Mex. 175/M7
Tlaxcala (state), Mex. 172/A5
Tlaxcala, Mex. 175/L7
Tlaxco, Mex. 175/L7
Tlaxcoapan, Mex. 175/K6
Tlell, BC, Can. 171/M5
Tlemcen, Alg. 112/D2
Tlokweng, Bots. 122/E5
Tmassah, Libya 134/B3
To-grenda, Nor. 38/S8
Toa Payoh (nbrhd.), Sing. 89/J6
Toabré, Pan. 180/A2
Toaca (peak), Rom. 51/G2
Toachi (riv.), Ecu. 180/B4
Toadlena, NM, US 149/H2
Toamasina, Madg. 125/J7
Toamasina (prov.), Madg. 125/J7
Toandos (pen.), Wa, US 167/B2
Toasi, Gha. 115/E5
Toast, NC, US 163/G2
Toau (isl.), FrPol. 137/L6
Toay, Arg. 190/D3
Toba (lake), Indo. 90/A3
Toba, China 78/D5
Toba, Japan 83/L7
Toba (inlet), BC, Can. 144/B2
Toba (riv.), BC, Can. 144/B2
Toba Kākar (range), Pak. 101/J2
Toba Tek Singh, Pak. 98/B4
Tobago (isl.), Trin. 173/J5
Tobarra, Sp. 46/E3
Tobbio (peak), It. 62/B4
Tobeatic Game Sanct., NS, Can. 158/E3
Tobercurry, Ire. 32/B1
Tobermore, NI, UK 34/B2
Tobermorey, Austl. 131/H2
Tobermory, On, Can. 160/F2
Tōbetsu, Japan 82/B2
Tobias, Ang. 120/C5
Tobias Barreto, Braz. 187/F1
Tobin (lake), Austl. 127/B3
Tobique (riv.), NB, Can. 158/D2
Tobishima, Japan 83/L5
Toblol (riv.), Kaz.,Rus. 77/F4
Toboali, Indo. 89/D3
Tobol (riv.), Rus. 69/Q5
Tobol, Kaz. 71/M1
Tobruk (Ţubruq), Libya 67/J4
Tobseda, Rus. 69/M1
Tobu, Japan 83/A1
Toburdanovo, Rus. 69/K5
Tobyhanna (lake), Pa, US 168/C1
Tobyhanna (riv.), Pa, US 168/C1
Tobyhanna, Pa, US 168/C1
Tobyhanna St. Park, Pa, US 168/C1
Tobyl (riv.), Rus.,Kaz. 74/G4
Tobysh (riv.), Rus. 69/L2
Tocache, Peru 184/B3
Tocaima, Col. 183/L8
Tocantínia, Braz. 182/D5
Tocantinópolis, Braz. 183/E4
Tocantins (riv.), Braz. 179/E4
Tocantins (state), Braz. 182/D5
Tocco da Casauria, It. 65/C3
Toccoa, Ga, US 163/F3
Toccoa (riv.), Ga, US 162/E3
Toce (riv.), It. 45/H3
Tochigi (pref.), Japan 85/F2
Tochigi, Japan 85/F2
Tochimilco, Mex. 175/L8
Tochio, Japan 85/F2
Tocina, Sp. 46/C4
Töcksfors, Swe. 40/D2
Toco, Tx, US 153/G4
Toco, Trin. 181/F2
Tocomechi, Bol. 188/D1
Tocopilla, Chile 188/B2
Tocumen, Pan. 180/B2
Tocumwal, Austl. 133/B2
Tocuyito, Ven. 180/D2
Tocuyo (riv.), Ven. 173/H5
Toda, Japan 83/D2
Toda Bhīm, India 92/C2
Toddington, Eng, UK 37/F3
Todenyang, Kenya 116/G4
Tödi (peak), Swi. 61/E4
Todi, It. 65/B2
Todmorden, Eng, UK 35/F4
Todos os Santos (bay), Braz. 187/F2
Todos Santos, Bol. 188/B1
Todos Santos, Bol. 185/E4
Todos Santos, Bol. 188/C1
Todos Santos, Mex. 174/C4
Todt Hill (nbrhd.), NY, US 169/J9
Todtmoos, Ger. 60/E2
Todtnau, Ger. 60/D2
Toe (pt.), Ire. 32/A7
T'oejo, NKor. 81/D3
Toffal (hill), Mrta. 110/C5
Toffo, Ben. 115/F5
Tofield, Ab, Can. 145/H1
Tofte, Nor. 38/S9
Tofua (isl.), Tonga 137/H6
Tōgane, Japan 83/E2
Togatax, China 99/D4
Togba (well), Mrta. 114/C2
Toggenburg (valley), Swi. 61/F3
Togher, Ire. 34/B5
Togiak, Ak, US 171/F4
Töging am Inn, Ger. 59/F6
Togo (ctry.) 115/F4
Togo, Sk, Can. 156/D2
Tōgō, Japan 83/M5
Tögrög, Mong. 78/C2
Togtoh, China 80/B2
Tōgyu-san NP, SKor. 81/D5
Togyz, Kaz. 71/M3
Tohāna, India 98/C5
Tohatchi, NM, US 149/H3
Tohickon (cr.), Pa, US 168/C3
Tohivea (peak), FrPol. 137/X15
Tōhoku (prov.), Japan 85/F1
Tohom, China 78/F3
Tohopekaliga (lake), Fl, US 165/H3
Tohopekaliga, East (lake), Fl, US 164/N7
Tohor (cape), Malay. 89/C2
Tohoun, Togo 115/F5
Toi, Japan 85/F3
Toibalawe, India 93/F5
Toijala, Fin. 39/D3
Tōin, Japan 83/L5
Toiyabe (range), Nv, US 146/E4
Tojō, Japan 84/C3
Tōjō, Japan 83/H6
Tok, Ak, US 171/K3
Tokachi (riv.), Japan 82/C2
Tōkai, Japan 83/L5
Tokaj, Hun. 43/L4
Tōkamachi, Japan 85/F2
Tokanui, NZ 135/B4
Tokar, Sudan 109/H5
Tokar Game Reserve, Sudan 109/H5
Tokar Nat'l Rsv., Sudan 109/F4
Tokara (isls.), Japan 136/B1
Tokarevka, Rus. 71/G2
Tokat, Turk. 102/D1
Tokat (prov.), Turk. 70/F4
Tŏkchŏk (arch.), NKor. 81/C4
Tŏkchŏk (isl.), NKor. 81/C4
Tŏkch'ŏn, NKor. 81/D3
Tokeen, Ak, US 171/M4
Tokeland, Wa, US 144/C4
Tokelau (terr.), NZ 137/H5
Toki (riv.), Japan 83/M5
Toki, Japan 83/M5
Tokigawa, Japan 83/C2
Tokio, ND, US 156/E4
Tokkya Chaung, Myan. 94/B3
Tokmak, Ukr. 73/H4
Tokmok, Kyr. 74/H5
Tokomaru Bay, NZ 135/D2
Tokoname, Japan 83/L6
Tokonou, Gui. 114/C4
Tokoro, Japan 82/D1
Tokoro (riv.), Japan 82/C2
Tokoroa, NZ 135/C2
Tokorozawa, Japan 85/F3
Tŏksŏng, NKor. 79/K3
Toksook Bay, Ak, US 171/E3
Toksovo, Rus. 69/T6
Toksun, China 99/E3
Toktogul (res.), Kyr. 99/B3
Toktogul, Kyr. 99/B3
Tokuno (isl.), Japan 85/K7
Tokunoshima, Japan 85/K7
Tokur, Rus. 79/L1
Tokushima, Japan 84/D3
Tokushima (pref.), Japan 84/C4
Tokuyama, Japan 84/B3
Tokwe (riv.), Zim. 123/F3
Tōkyō (pref.), Japan 85/F3
Tōkyō (cap.), Japan 85/F3
Tōkyō (bay), Japan 83/D2
Tōkyō Disneyland, Japan 83/D2
Tola, Nic. 176/E4
Tolaga Bay, NZ 135/D2
Tolar, Tx, US 151/F1
Tolar Grande, Arg. 188/C3
Tolbazy, Rus. 69/M5
Tolbo, Mong. 78/C2
Toledo, Oh, US 160/E4
Toledo, Col. 180/C3
Toledo, Sp. 46/C3
Toledo, Or, US 146/B1
Toledo, Il, US 162/C1
Toledo, Ia, US 155/H3
Toledo, Phil. 88/C3
Toledo, Uru. 191/K11
Toledo, Braz. 189/F3
Toledo, Bol. 188/C1
Toledo, Wa, US 144/C4
Toledo Bend (dam), Tx, US 151/H2
Toledo Bend (res.), Tx, US 151/H2
Toledo, Montes de (mts.), Sp. 46/C3
Tolentino, It. 65/C1
Tolfa, It. 65/A3
Tolfaccia (peak), It. 65/A3
Tolhuaca, PN, Chile 190/C3
Toli, China 99/D2
Toliara, Madg. 125/G8
Toliara (prov.), Madg. 125/G8
Tolima, Col. 180/C5
Tolima (dept.), Col. 180/C4
Tolitoli, Indo. 91/F3
Tolka (riv.), Ire. 34/B5
Tolkis (Tolkkinen), Fin. 39/F4
Tolkkinen (Tolkis), Fin. 39/F4
Tolland, Ab, Can. 145/J1
Tollarp, Swe. 39/K7
Tollette, Ar, US 153/H4
Tolley, ND, US 156/D3
Tollo, It. 65/D3
Tølløse, Den. 39/H7
Tolmezzo, It. 45/K3
Tolna, ND, US 156/E4
Tolna (prov.), Hun. 50/D2
Tolna, Hun. 50/D2
Tolo, D.R. Congo 120/D3
Tolo (gulf), Indo. 91/F4
Tolo (chan.), China 87/L7
Tolochin, Bela. 41/N4
Tolokiwa (isl.), PNG 129/G1
Tolongoina, Madg. 125/H8
Tolono, Il, US 160/B5
Tolosa, Sp. 44/B5
Tolsan (isl.), SKor. 81/D5
Tolstoy, SD, US 154/E1
Tolt (riv.), Wa, US 167/D2
Tolt (res.), Wa, US 167/D2
Tolt, North Fork (riv.), Wa, US 167/D2
Tolt, South Fork (riv.), Wa, US 167/D2
Toltén, Chile 190/B3
Toltén (riv.), Chile 190/B3
Tolú, Col. 180/C2
Toluca, Il, US 155/K3
Toluca, Mex. 175/Q10
Tolúviejo, Col. 180/C2
Tol'yatti, Rus. 71/J1
Tolybay, Kaz. 71/M2
Tom' (riv.), Rus. 74/J4
Tom, Ok, US 153/G4
Tom Price, Austl. 130/C2
Tom White (mt.), Ak, US 171/K3
Toma, Burk. 114/E3
Toma, PNG 129/G2
Tomah, Wi, US 155/J2
Tomahawk, Wi, US 157/K5
Tomahawk, Ab, Can. 144/G1
Tomakin, Austl. 133/E2
Tomakivka, Ukr. 73/H4
Tomakomai, Japan 82/B2
Tomamae, Japan 82/B1
Tomanao, Phil. 88/D4
Tomanivi (peak), Fiji 137/Y18
Tomar, Port. 46/A3
Tomari, Rus. 79/N2
Tómaros (peak), Gre. 75/G3
Tomarpaån (riv.), Swe. 39/L7
Tomarza, Turk. 102/C2
Tomás, Peru 184/C4
Tomás Barrón, Bol. 188/C1
Tomás de Berlanga, Ecu. 184/J7
Tomashëvka, Bela. 43/M3
Tomaszów Lubelski, Pol. 43/M3
Tomaszów Mazowiecki, Pol. 43/L3
Tomat, Sudan 117/E3
Tomatin, Sc, UK 33/C2
Tomatlán, Mex. 174/D5
Tomave, Bol. 188/C2
Tomb of Qinshihuang, China 80/B4
Tombador, Serra do (mts.), Braz. 185/G3
Tomball, Tx, US 151/M8
Tombe, Sudan 116/F4
Tombigbee (riv.), Al, Ms, US 143/J5
Tomboco, Ang. 120/C4
Tombolo, It. 63/E2
Tombouctou (pol. reg.), Mali 110/D5
Tombouctou, Mali 114/E2
Tombstone, Az, US 149/G5
Tombua, Ang. 122/A2
Tomé (isl.), Fr. 44/B2
Tomé, Chile 190/B3
Tome, NM, US 149/J3
Tomé-Açu, Braz. 182/D3
Tomea (isl.), Indo. 128/A1
Tomelilla, Swe. 40/E4
Tomelloso, Sp. 46/D3
Tomika, Japan 83/L5
Tomina, Bol. 188/C1
Tomingley, Austl. 133/D1
Tomini (gulf), Indo. 77/M10
Tominian, Mali 114/D3
Tomiño, Sp. 46/A2
Tomintoul, Sc, UK 33/C2
Tomioka, Japan 83/B1
Tomisato, Japan 83/E2
Tomiura, Japan 83/D3
Tomiyama, Japan 85/F3
Tomizawa, Japan 83/A3
Tommot, Rus. 75/N4
Tomo (riv.), Col. 180/D3
Tomorlog, China 99/F4
Tompa, Hun. 50/D2
Tompe, Indo. 91/E4
Tompkins, Sk, Can. 145/K2
Tompkinsville, Ky, US 162/E2
Tompo, Indo. 91/F3
Toms (riv.), NJ, US 168/D3
Toms River, NJ, US 168/D4
Tomsk, Rus. 74/J4
Tomskaya Oblast, Rus. 74/J4
Tömük, Turk. 104/D1
Tonalá, Mex. 176/C2
Tonale, Passo del (pass), It. 61/G5
Tonalea, Az, US 149/G2
Tonasket, Wa, US 144/E3
Tonate, FrG. 182/C1
Tonawanda (cr.), NY, US 160/V9
Tonawanda (res.), NY, US 160/V9
Tonawanda, NY, US 160/V9
Tonbridge, Eng, UK 30/D3
Tonckens (falls), Sur. 182/B1
Toncontín (int'l arpt.), Hon. 176/E3
Tondabayashi, Japan 83/J7
Tondano, Indo. 91/F3
Tondi Kiwindi, Niger 115/F3
Tondo, D.R. Congo 120/D3
Tondon, Gui. 114/B4
Tondoro, Namb. 122/C3
Tondu (peak), Fr. 60/C6
Tone (riv.), Japan 85/G3
Tone, Japan 83/E2
Tone (riv.), Eng, UK 36/C5
Tonekābon, Iran 103/G2
Tonelagee (peak), Ire. 34/B5
Tong (riv.), China 78/F5
Tong Fuk, China 87/K8
Tong Xian, China 80/H7
Tonga, Sudan 116/F3
Tonga (ctry.) 137/H7
Tongaat, SAfr. 125/E3
Tongala, Austl. 133/B3
Tong'an, China 87/H3
Tongareva (Penrhyn) (isl.), CookIs. 137/J5
Tongariro (vol.), NZ 135/C2
Tongariro NP, NZ 135/C2
Tongatapu (isl.), Tonga 137/H7
Tongbai, China 80/C4
Tongbei, China 79/K2
Tongbu, SKor. 81/G6
Tongbu (nbrhd.), SKor. 81/G6
Tongch'ang, NKor. 81/C2
Tongcheng, China 80/D5
Tongcheng, China 87/G2
T'ongch'ŏn, NKor. 81/D3
Tongchuan, China 80/B4
Tongdaemun (nbrhd.), SKor. 81/G6
Tongdao Dongzu Zizhixian, China 87/F3
Tongduch'on, SKor. 81/G6
Tongeren, Belg. 55/E2
Tonggou, China 81/C2
Tonggu, China 93/K2
Tonggu (peak), China 87/H3
Tonghae, SKor. 81/E4
Tongham, Eng, UK 30/A3
Tonghua, China 81/C2
Tonghua, China 81/C2
Tongjiadian, China 79/J3
Tongliao, China 80/E2
Tongling, China 87/H2
Tongmu, China 87/G3
Tongnae, SKor. 81/E5
Tongnan, China 86/E2
Tongnim, NKor. 81/C3
Tongno (riv.), NKor. 81/D2
Tongo, Austl. 132/B1
Tongo (peak), Indo. 91/E5
Tongobory, Madg. 125/H8
Tongren, China 87/F3
Tongsa (riv.), Bhu. 97/H2
Tongsa Dzong, Bhu. 97/H2
Tongshan, China 87/G2
Tongsin, NKor. 81/D2
Tongtian (riv.), China 78/D5
Tongue, Sc, UK 31/R7
Tongue (riv.), Mt, US 142/E2
Tongxu, China 80/C4
Tongyu, China 79/J3
Tongyuan, China 87/H2
Tongyuanpu, China 81/B2
Tonino-Anivskiy (pen.), Rus. 82/C1
Tönisvorst, Ger. 52/D6
Tonj (riv.), Sudan 116/F4
Tonj, Sudan 116/F4
Tonk, India 92/C2
Tonkawa, Ok, US 153/F2
Tonkin (gulf), China,Viet. 77/K7
Tonkoui (peak), C.d'Iv. 114/D5
Tonle Sap (lake), Camb. 93/H5
Tonneins, Fr. 44/D4
Tonnerre, Fr. 44/E3
Tönning, Ger. 40/C4
Tōno, Japan 82/B4
Tonopah, Az, US 149/F4
Tonoshō, Japan 84/D3
Tonosí, Pan. 180/A3
Tonota, Bots. 123/E4
Tons (riv.), India 96/C3
Tønsberg, Nor. 40/D2
Tonstad, Nor. 40/B2
Tonsina, Ak, US 171/J3
Tonto Nat'l Mon., Az, US 149/G4
Tontouta (Noumea) (int'l arpt.), NCal. 137/V13
Tonya, Turk. 70/F4
Toodyay, Austl. 130/C4
Tooele, Ut, US 147/G3
Tooele Army Dep., Ut, US 147/G3
Tooke (lake), Fl, US 164/K6
Tool, Tx, US 151/F1
Tooleybuc, Austl. 132/B2
Toomsboro, Ga, US 163/F4
Toomuc (cr.), Austl. 132/G6
Toomyvara, Ire. 32/B4
Tooradin, Austl. 132/C3
Tooraweenah, Austl. 132/D1
Tooromt, Mong. 78/C1
Toosey Ind. Res., BC, Can. 144/C2
Toot Hill, Eng, UK 30/D1
Tootsi, Est. 41/L2
Toowoomba, Austl. 134/C4
Top (mt.), Austl. 131/G2
Top of the World (peak), Wy, US 154/B2
Top Springs, Austl. 128/C4
Topaipí, Col. 183/L7
Topanaga State Park, Ca, US 166/B2
Topanga, Ca, US 166/B2
Topanga Beach, Ca, US 166/E7
Topawa, Az, US 149/G5
Tope de Coroa (mtn.), CpV. 107/J10
Topeka, In, US 160/D4
Topeka (cap.), Ks, US 155/G4
Topia, Mex. 174/D3
Topkapi Palace, Turk. 103/M6
Topliţa, Rom. 72/C4
Topock, Az, US 148/E3
Topohoco, Bol. 184/D5
Topol'čany, Slvk. 43/K4
Topol'níky, Slvk. 50/C2
Topolobampo, Mex. 174/C3
Topoloveni, Rom. 51/G3
Topolovgrad, Bul. 51/H4
Topozero (lake), Rus. 38/J2
Toppenish, Wa, US 144/D4
Toppenish (cr.), Wa, US 144/D4
Toprakkale, Turk. 104/E1
Topsham, Eng, UK 36/C5
Topton, Pa, US 168/C3
Toquepala, Peru 184/D5
Toquerville, Ut, US 149/F2
Toquima (range), Nv, US 146/E4
Tor, Eth. 116/G4
Tor (bay), Eng, UK 36/C6
Tor Lupara, It. 65/B4
Tora, D.R. Congo 121/G2
Torahime, Japan 83/K5
Torata, Peru 184/D5
Torawitan (cape), Indo. 91/G3
Torbalı, Turk. 102/A2
Torbat-e Ḩeydarīyeh, Iran 101/G1
Torbay, Nf, Can. 159/L2
Torbay (co.), Eng, UK 36/C6
Torbeck, Haiti 177/H2
Torbert (mt.), Ak, US 171/H3
Torbeyevo, Rus. 71/G1
Torch (lake), Mi, US 160/D2
Torcy, Fr. 30/K5
Tordera (riv.), Sp. 47/L6
Tordesillas, Sp. 46/C2
Tordino (riv.), It. 65/C2
Töreboda, Swe. 40/F2
Torekov, Swe. 39/J6
Torelló, Sp. 47/G1
Torez, Ukr. 73/K3
Torfaen (co.), Wal, UK 36/C3
Torgelow, Ger. 40/E5
Torghay, Kaz. 74/G4
Torghay, Kaz. 74/G5
Torhamnsudde (pt.), Swe. 40/F3
Torhout, Belg. 54/C1
Tori, India 97/E4
Tori-shima (isl.), Japan 136/D1
Toride, Japan 83/E2
Torigni-sur-Vire, Fr. 57/E2
Torii-tōge (pass), Japan 85/E3

Map Section
278
279

Tunda Chissococua, Ang. 122/C1
Tundazi (hill), Zim. 123/F3
Tundla, India 96/B2
Tunduma, Tanz. 121/H5
Tunduru, Tanz. 119/B4
Tundyk (riv.), Kaz. 99/C1
Tundzha (riv.), Bul. 67/K2
Tune, Den. 39/J7
Tung Chung, China 87/K7
Tung Lung (riv.), China 87/M8
Tungabhadra (riv.), India 92/C4
Tungabhadra (res.), India 92/C4
Tungamah, Austl. 132/C3
Tungaru, Sudan 116/F3
Tungawan, Phil. 88/C4
Tungelsta, Swe. 39/B1
Tungku, Malay. 88/B4
Tŭngsan-got (pt.), NKor. 81/C4
Tungshih, Tai. 87/J3
Tungsten, NW, Can. 140/D2
Tungurahua (prov.), Ecu. 180/B5
Tünhel, Mong. 78/F2
Tuni, India 95/D2
Tunica, La, US 164/C2
Tunica, Ms, US 162/B3
Tūnis (cap.), Tun. 48/B4
Tūnis (gov.), Tun. 48/B4
Tunisia (ctry.) 111/H2
Tunjá, Col. 180/C3
Tunkhannock, Pa, US 161/J4
Tunku Abdul Rahman NP, Malay. 88/B4
Tunliu, China 80/C3
Tunnel Creek NP, Austl. 128/B4
Tunnels of Vinh Moc, Viet. 94/D2
Tuntum, Braz. 183/E4
Tuntutuliak, Ak, US 171/F3
Tunungayualuk (isl.), Nf, Can. 141/K3
Tunuyán (riv.), Arg. 190/C2
Tunuyán, Arg. 190/C2
Tuo (riv.), China 78/E5
Tuokou, China 87/F3
Tuolu, China 87/E4
Tuolumne (riv.), Ca, US 146/D5
Tuolumne Grove, Ca, US 148/C2
Tuong Duong, Viet. 94/D2
Tuoniang (riv.), China 93/J3
Tuoro sul Trasimeno, It. 65/B1
Tuotuo (riv.), China 99/F5
Tuotuoheyan, China 78/C5
Tūp Āghāj, Iran 103/F2
Tupã, Braz. 189/G2
Tupaciguara, Braz. 189/G1
Tupai (isl.), FrPol. 137/K6
Tupambaé, Uru. 191/G2
Tupanatinga, Braz. 183/G5
Tupanciretã, Braz. 189/F4
Tuparro (riv.), Col. 180/D3
Tupelo, Ok, US 153/F3
Tupelo, Ms, US 162/C3
Tupelo Nat'l Bfld., Ms, US 162/C3
Tupi Paulista, Braz. 189/G2
Tupik, Rus. 68/G5
Tupinambarana (isl.), Braz. 182/B3
Tupiza, Bol. 188/C2
Tupman, Ca, US 148/C3
Tupper Lake, NY, US 161/J2
Tupungato, Arg. 190/C2
Tupungato (peak), Arg. 190/P8
Tuquan, China 79/J2
Tura (riv.), Rus. 74/G4
Tura, Rus. 75/L3
Tura, India 97/H3
Tura, China 99/E4
Ţurá, Egypt 113/C5
Turabah, SAr. 100/D4
Turakina, NZ 135/C3
Turan, Rus. 78/C1
Tur'ān, Isr. 105/C3
Turan Lowland (plain), Uzb. 74/G5
Turana (mts.), Rus. 79/L1
Turanganui (riv.), NZ 135/J9
Turangi, NZ 135/C2
Turano (riv.), It. 65/B3
Ţurayf, SAr. 102/D4
Turbaco, Col. 180/C2
Turbat, Pak. 101/H3
Turbenthal, Swi. 61/E3
Turbeville, SC, US 163/G4
Turbo, Col. 180/B2
Turbotville, Pa, US 168/B1
Turckheim, Fr. 60/D1
Turda, Rom. 51/F2
Tureia (isl.), FrPol. 137/M7
Turek, Pol. 43/K2
Turenki, Fin. 39/E4
Tŭrgovishte, Bul. 51/H4
Turgutlu, Turk. 102/A2
Turhal, Turk. 102/D1
Türi, Est. 41/L2
Turiaçu (bay), Braz. 183/E3
Turiaçu, Braz. 183/E3
Turiamo, Ven. 183/N7
Turin (Torino), It. 62/A2
Turiys'k, Ukr. 72/C2
Turka, Ukr. 43/M4
Turka, Rus. 78/F1
Turkana (Rudolf) (lake), Kenya 107/F4
Turkana Nat'l Rsv., Kenya 119/A1
Türkeli, Turk. 70/E4
Túrkeve, Hun. 50/E2
Turkey (ctry.) 102/C2
Turkey (riv.), Ia, US 155/J2
Turkey (cr.), Tx, US 150/E3
Turkey Creek (lake), La, US 164/C2
Turkey Creek, Austl. 128/C4
Türkheim, Ger. 61/G1
Turki, Rus. 73/M2
Türkistan, Kaz. 99/A3
Türkmenabat, Trkm. 74/G6
Türkmen-Kala, Trkm. 101/H1
Türkmenistan (ctry.) 74/F6
Türkoğlu, Turk. 102/D2
Turks (isls.), Haiti 173/G3
Turks and Caicos (isls.), UK 139/K7
Turks Island Passage (chan.), UK 177/J1
Turku (int'l arpt.), Fin. 41/K1
Turku (Åbo), Fin. 41/K1
Turku Ja Pori (prov.), Fin. 38/G3
Turkwel (riv.), Kenya 119/A1
Turley, Ok, US 153/G2
Turlingua (cr.), Tx, US 150/C3
Turlock, Ca, US 148/B2
Turmalina, Braz. 187/E3
Turmantas, Lith. 41/M4
Turmero, Ven. 183/N7
Turnagain (cape), NZ 135/D3
Turnberry, Sc, UK 33/B6
Turnbull (dry lake), Or, US 146/E2
Turnbull (mt.), Az, US 149/G4
Turnbull NWR, Wa, US 144/F4
Turneffe (isls.), Belz. 172/D4
Turner (mt.), Austl. 130/C2
Turner, Me, US 161/L2
Turner, Mt, US 145/K3
Turner Valley, Ab, Can. 144/G2
Turnersville, NJ, US 168/C4
Turnersville, Tx, US 150/F2
Turnhouse (int'l arpt.), Sc, UK 33/C5
Turnhout, Belg. 52/B6
Turnov, Czh. 43/H3
Turnu Măgurele, Rom. 51/G4
Turon, Ks, US 153/E2
Turon (riv.), Austl. 133/D1
Tuross Head, Austl. 133/E3
Turov, Bela. 72/D1
Turpan, China 99/E3
Turquino (peak), Cuba 177/G2
Turrell, Ar, US 162/B3
Turretot, Fr. 57/F1
Turriaco, It. 63/G2
Turriers, Fr. 64/C4
Turriff, Sc, UK 33/D1
Tursunzoda, Taj. 74/G6
Turt, Mong. 78/E1
Turtle (riv.), ND, US 156/F3
Turtle (isls.), SLeo. 114/B5
Turtle (cr.), SD, US 154/E1
Turtle (pt.), Austl. 128/C3
Turtle Lake, ND, US 156/D4
Turtle Mountain Ind. Res., ND, US 156/E3
Turtle River, Mn, US 157/G4
Turtleford, Sk, Can. 145/K1
Turton, Eng, UK 35/F4
Turton, SD, US 154/E1
Turukhansk, Rus. 74/J3
Turvo (riv.), Braz. 186/C4
Tuscaloosa, Al, US 162/D4
Tuscaloosa (lake), Al, US 162/D4
Tuscano (arch.), Fr. 48/B1
Tuscano (arch.), It. 66/F2
Tuscany (reg.), It. 67/F2
Tuscarawas (riv.), Oh, US 160/F4
Tuscarora, Nv, US 146/E3
Tuscarora (mtn.), Pa, US 168/A3
Tuscola, Il, US 160/B5
Tuscola, Tx, US 150/E1
Tuscumbia, Mo, US 153/H1
Tuscumbia, Al, US 162/D3
Tushar (mts.), Ut, US 149/F1
Tushino (nbrhd.), Rus. 69/W9
Tushka, Ok, US 153/F3
Tuskahoma, Ok, US 153/G3
Tuskegee, Al, US 162/E4
Tuskegee Institute Nat'l Hist. Site, Al, US 162/E4
Tusket, NS, Can. 158/E4
Tussy, Ok, US 153/F3
Tustin, Ca, US 166/G8
Tuszyn, Pol. 43/K3
Tutak, Turk. 103/E2
Tutayev, Rus. 68/H4
Tutbury, Eng, UK 35/G6
Tutin, Serb. 50/E4
Tutóia, Braz. 183/F3
Tutong, Bru. 88/A4
Tutrakan, Bul. 51/H3
Tuttle, ND, US 156/E4
Tuttle, Ok, US 153/F3
Tuttle Creek (res.), Ks, US 153/F1
Tuttlingen, Ger. 61/E2
Tutuala, ETim. 128/B2
Tutubu, Tanz. 121/H4
Tutuila (isl.), ASam. 137/T10
Tuţūn, Egypt 113/B6
Tutupaca (vol.), Peru 184/D5
Tututalak (mt.), Ak, US 171/F2
Tutwiler, Ms, US 162/B3
Tutzing, Ger. 61/H2
Tuul (riv.), Mong. 78/F2
Tuulos, Fin. 39/E3
Tuusula, Fin. 41/L1
Tuusulajärvi (lake), Fin. 39/E4
Tuvalu (ctry.) 136/G5
Ţuwayq, Jabal (mts.), SAr. 100/E3
Tuxford, Sk, Can. 145/M2
Tuxford, Eng, UK 35/H5
Tuxpan, Mex. 174/D4
Tuxpan, Mex. 174/E5
Tuxpan de Rodríguez Cano, Mex. 176/B1
Tuxtla Gutiérrez, Mex. 176/C2
Túy, Sp. 46/A1
Tuy (riv.), Ven. 183/P7
Tuy An, Viet. 94/E3
Tuy Hoa, Viet. 94/E3
Tuyen Hoa, Viet. 94/D2
Tuyen Quang, Viet. 94/D1
Tuymazy, Rus. 69/M5
Tūysarkān, Iran 103/G3
Tuyuk, Kaz. 99/C3
Tuz (lake), Turk. 102/C2
Ţūz Khurmātū, Iraq 103/F3
Tuzha, Rus. 69/K4
Tuzigoot Nat'l Mon., Az, US 149/F3
Tuzla, Turk. 104/D1
Tuzla, Bosn. 50/D3
Tuzla, Turk. 103/N7
Tuzluca, Turk. 103/E1
Tuzlukçu, Turk. 102/B2
Tuzly, Ukr. 51/K3
Tuzule, D.R. Congo 121/E4
Tvååker, Swe. 40/E3
Tvedestrand, Nor. 40/C2
Tver', Rus. 68/G4
Tverskaya Oblast, Rus. 41/P3
Tvertsa (riv.), Rus. 68/G4
Tvŭrditsa, Bul. 51/G4
Twapia, Zam. 123/F2
Twardogóra, Pol. 43/J3
Tway, Sk, Can. 145/M1
Tweed (riv.), Sc, UK 33/C5
Tweed, On, Can. 161/H2
Tweed Heads, Austl. 134/D5
Tweed-New Haven (arpt.), Ct, US 169/F1
Tweedmouth, Eng, UK 33/D5
Tweedsmuir, Sc, UK 33/C5
Twello, Neth. 52/D4
Twente (pol. reg.), Neth. 52/D4
Twente (canal), Neth. 52/D4
Twenty Mile (cr.), On, Can. 160/T9
Twentynine Palms, Ca, US 148/D3
Twentynine Palms Marine Corps Base, Ca, US 148/D3
Twig, Mn, US 157/H4
Twin (falls), Id, US 147/F2
Twin Bridges, Mt, US 147/G1
Twin Buttes (res.), Tx, US 150/D2
Twin City, Ga, US 163/F4
Twin Falls, Id, US 147/F2
Twin Hills, Ak, US 171/F4
Twin Lake, Mi, US 160/C3
Twin Lakes, Wi, US 167/P14
Twin Rivers, NJ, US 168/D3
Twin Rocks, Or, US 144/C5
Twin Valley, Mn, US 156/F4
Twin, North (lake), Wi, US 157/K4
Twingi, Zam. 123/F1
Twist, Ger. 52/E3
Twiste (riv.), Ger. 53/G6
Twistringen, Ger. 53/F3
Twitchell (res.), Ca, US 148/B3
Two Butte (cr.), Co, US 152/C2
Two Harbors, Mn, US 157/J4
Two Hills, Ab, Can. 145/J1
Two Medicine (riv.), Mt, US 145/H3
Two Rivers (res.), NM, US 152/B4
Two Rivers, Wi, US 160/C2
Twodot, Mt, US 145/J4
Twycross, Eng, UK 37/E1
Twyfelfontein Rock Engravings, Namb. 122/B4
Twyford, Eng, UK 37/F4
Twymyn (riv.), Wal, UK 36/C1
Twynholm, Sc, UK 34/D2
Tyachiv, Ukr. 72/B3
Tyao (riv.), India 86/B4
Tyatya (vol.), Rus. 82/E1
Tybee Nat'l Wild. Ref., Ga, US 165/H1
Tychy, Pol. 43/K3
Tydd Saint Giles, Eng, UK 37/G1
Tye, Tx, US 150/E1
Tyémé, C.d'Iv. 114/D4
Tyendinaga, On, Can. 161/H2
Tygart (lake), WV, US 163/H1
Tygda, Rus. 79/K1
Tyger (riv.), SC, US 163/G3
Tygh Valley, Or, US 146/C1
Tyi Grounto (plat.), Niger 134/B4
Tyldesley, Eng, UK 35/F4
Tyler, Mn, US 155/F1
Tyler, Tx, US 151/G1
Tylers Green, Eng, UK 30/A2
Tylersville, Pa, US 168/A2
Tylertown, Ms, US 164/C2
Tymovskoye, Rus. 79/N1
Týn, Czh. 43/H4
Tynagh, Ire. 32/B3
Tynan, Tx, US 150/F3
Tynda, Rus. 75/N4
Tyndall, Mb, Can. 156/F2
Tyndall (A.F.B.), Fl, US 165/F2
Tyndall, SD, US 154/F2
Tyndrum, Sc, UK 33/B4
Tyne (riv.), Sc, UK 33/D5
Tyne and Wear (co.), Eng, UK 35/G2
Tyne Valley, PE, Can. 158/F2
Tynemouth, Eng, UK 35/G1
Tyner, Ky, US 162/F2
Tynset, Nor. 38/D3
Tyonek, Ak, US 171/H3
Tyre (Şūr), Leb. 105/C2
Tyresö, Swe. 39/B1
Tyrifjorden (lake), Nor. 40/C1
Tyringe, Swe. 40/E3
Tyrma (riv.), Rus. 79/L2
Tyrnyauz, Rus. 71/G4
Tyro, Ks, US 153/G2
Tyrone, Ok, US 152/D2
Tyrone, Pa, US 161/G4
Tyrone, NM, US 149/H4
Tyrone, Ga, US 163/L8
Tyronza, Ar, US 162/B3
Tyrrell (cr.), Austl. 132/B2
Tyrrellspass, Ire. 32/C3
Tyrrhenian (sea), It. 29/F4
Tyshkivka, Ukr. 72/F3
Tysnes, Nor. 40/A1
Tysnesøy (isl.), Nor. 40/A2
Tysons Corner, Va, US 168/A6
Tysse, Nor. 40/A1
Tystberga, Swe. 40/G2
Tytuvėnai, Lith. 41/K4
Tyub-Karagan (pt.), Kaz. 71/J3
Tyulen'i (isls.), Rus. 71/J3
Tyuleniy (isl.), Rus. 71/H3
Tyumenskaya Oblast, Rus. 69/Q4
Tyumen', Rus. 69/Q4
Tyumen (int'l arpt.), Rus. 69/Q4
Tyup, Kyr. 99/C3
Tyva Resp., Rus. 74/K4
Tywi (riv.), Wal, UK 36/B3
Tywyn, Wal, UK 36/B1
Tzaneen, SAfr. 123/F4
Tzucacab, Mex. 176/D1

U

U S Army Ammunition Plant, Ok, US 153/F3
U. S. Naval Weapons Station, Ca, US 166/F8
U.C.-Irvine, Ca, US 166/G8
U.K. Sovereign Base Area (gov.), Cyp. 104/C2
U.S.S. Alabama Battleship Park, Al, US 164/E2
Ua Huka (isl.), FrPol. 137/M5
Ua Pou (isl.), FrPol. 137/L5
Uad Assag (riv.), WSah. 110/B4
Uad Atui (riv.), WSah. 110/B5
Uad el Jat (riv.), WSah. 110/B4
Uad Tenuaiur (riv.), WSah. 110/A5
Uadi Uadaimo (wadi), Som. 118/D3
Uamba (riv.), D.R. Congo 120/D4
Uamh Bheag (peak), Sc, UK 33/B4
Uanda, Austl. 134/B3
Uato-Lari, ETim. 128/B2
Uatuma (riv.), Braz. 182/B3
Uatumã (riv.), Braz. 181/G5
Uauá, Braz. 187/F1
Uaupés (riv.), Braz. 180/D4
Uaxactún (ruin), Guat. 176/D2
Ub, Serb. 50/E3
Ubá, Braz. 187/E4
Uba, Nga. 116/B3
Ubach over Worms, Neth. 55/F2
Übach-Palenberg, Ger. 55/F2
Ubagan (riv.), Kaz. 69/Q5
Ubaitaba, Braz. 187/F2
Ubajara, Braz. 183/F3
Ubajara, PN de, Braz. 183/F3
Ubangi (riv.), D.R. Congo 107/D4
Ubatã, Braz. 187/F2
Ubaté, Col. 183/M7
Ubatuba, Braz. 187/L8
Ubay, Phil. 88/D3
Ubaye (riv.), Fr. 45/G4
Ubbergen, Neth. 52/C5
Ube, Japan 84/B4
Úbeda, Sp. 46/D3
Uberaba, Braz. 189/H1
Uberaba (lake), Braz. 185/G5
Überherrn, Ger. 55/F5
Uberlândia, Braz. 186/C3
Überlingen, Ger. 61/F2
Überlingersee (lake), Ger. 61/E2
Ubia (peak), Indo. 91/J4
Ubiaja, Nga. 115/G5
Ubina, Bol. 188/C2
Ubinas, Peru 184/D5
Ubly, Mi, US 160/E3
Ubombo, SAfr. 125/F2
Ubon Ratchathani, Thai. 94/D3
Ubrique, Sp. 46/C4
Ubundu, D.R. Congo 121/F3
Ubute, D.R. Congo 121/F3
Ucar, Azer. 103/F1
Ucayali (riv.), Peru 179/B3
Ucayali (dept.), Peru 184/C3
Uccle, Belg. 55/D2
Uch, Pak. 98/A5
Uch-Adzhi, Trkm. 101/H1
Uch-Aral, Kaz. 74/J5
Ucha (riv.), Rus. 69/W8
Uchab, Namb. 122/C3
Uchaly, Rus. 69/N5
Uchāna, India 98/D5
Ucharonidge, Austl. 128/D4
Uchinskoye (res.), Rus. 69/W8
Uchiura (bay), Japan 79/N3
Uchiza, Peru 184/B3
Uchkeken, Rus. 73/M6
Uchquduq, Uzb. 74/G5
Uchte (riv.), Ger. 42/F2
Uchte, Ger. 53/F3
Uchumarca, Peru 184/B2
Uchumayo, Peru 184/D5
Uchur (riv.), Rus. 75/P4
Ücker (riv.), Ger. 40/E5
Uckermark (reg.), Ger. 43/G2
Uckfield, Eng, UK 37/G5
Ucluelet, BC, Can. 144/B3
Ucon, Id, US 147/H2
Üçpınar, Turk. 104/C1
Ucross, Wy, US 147/K1
Ucua, Ang. 120/C5
Ucumasi, Bol. 188/C1
Uda (riv.), Rus. 75/M4
Udaipur, India 92/B3
Udaipur Garhi, Nepal 97/F2
Udaipura, India 96/B4
Udamalpet, India 95/C4
Udara, Nga. 115/G4
Uddevalla, Swe. 40/D2
Uddingston, Sc, UK 33/B5
Uddjaure (lake), Swe. 38/F2
Üdem, Ger. 52/D5
Uden, Neth. 52/C5
Udenhout, Neth. 52/C5
Uder, Ger. 53/H6
Udgīr, India 95/C2
Udhampur, India 98/C3
Udi, Nga. 115/G5
Udimskiy, Rus. 69/K3
Udine (prov.), It. 63/G1
Udine, It. 45/K3
Udmurtiya Resp., Rus. 74/F4
Udomlya, Rus. 68/G4
Udon (riv.), Fr. 57/E3
Udon Thani, Thai. 94/C2
Ueckermünde, Ger. 40/F5
Ueda, Japan 85/F2
Uele (riv.), D.R. Congo 107/E4
Uelen, Rus. 171/D2
Uelsen, Ger. 52/D3
Uelzen, Ger. 53/H3
Ueno, Japan 83/K6
Ueno, Japan 83/B1
Uenohara, Japan 85/F3
Uere (riv.), D.R. Congo 117/E4
Uetendorf, Swi. 60/D4
Uetersen, Ger. 53/G1
Uetze, Ger. 53/H4
Ufa, Rus. 69/M5
Ufa (riv.), Rus. 69/N5
Uffenheim, Ger. 58/D3
Uffing, Ger. 61/H2
Uffington, Eng, UK 37/E3
Ufra, Trkm. 103/H2
Ugab (riv.), Namb. 122/B4
Ugāle, Lat. 41/K3
Ugalla (riv.), Tanz. 121/G4
Ugalla, Tanz. 121/G4
Ugalla River Game Rsv., Tanz. 121/G4
Uganda (ctry.) 107/F4
Ugbobo Ani, Nga. 115/G5
Ugento, It. 75/F3
Ugep, Nga. 115/H5
Ughelli, Nga. 115/G5
Ugie (riv.), Sc, UK 33/E1
Ugine, Fr. 60/C6
Uglegorsk, Ukr. 73/K3
Uglegorsk, Rus. 79/N2
Ugleural'skiy, Rus. 69/N4
Uglich, Rus. 68/H4
Ugljan (isl.), Cro. 45/L4
Uglovoye, Rus. 79/L3
Ugod, Hun. 50/C2
Ugol'nyye Kopi, Rus. 75/T3
Ugra (riv.), Rus. 68/G5
Ugŭrchin, Bul. 51/G4
Ugweno, Tanz. 119/B2
Uherské Hradiště, Czh. 43/J4
Uhingen, Ger. 58/C5
Uhland, Tx, US 150/F3
Úhlava (riv.), Czh. 43/G4
Úhlavka (riv.), Czh. 59/F3
Uhrichsville, Oh, US 160/F4
Uia di Ciamarella (peak), It. 64/D2
Uiangombe, Ang. 120/C5
Uig, Sc, UK 31/Q7
Uig, Sc, UK 31/Q8
Uíge, Ang. 120/C4
Uíge (prov.), Ang. 120/C4
Ŭihŭng, SKor. 81/E4
Ŭijŏngbu, SKor. 81/G6
Ŭiju, NKor. 81/C2
Uil, Kaz. 71/K2
Uil (riv.), Kaz. 71/K2
Uilkraal (riv.), SAfr. 124/L11
Uilpata (Gora Peak), Rus. 71/G4
Uinta (basin), Ut, US 147/H3
Uinta (mts.), Ut, US 147/H3
Uinta and Ouray Ind. Res., Ut, US 147/H3
Uiraúna, Braz. 183/G4
Ŭiryŏng, SKor. 81/E5
Ŭisŏng, SKor. 84/A2
Uitenhage, SAfr. 124/D4
Uitgeest, Neth. 52/B3
Uithoorn, Neth. 52/B4
Uithuizen, Neth. 52/D2
Uiwang, SKor. 81/F7
Ujae (isl.), Mrsh. 136/F4
Ujelang (isl.), Mrsh. 136/F4
Újfehértó, Hun. 43/L5
Ujhāni, India 96/B1
Uji (riv.), Japan 84/D3
Uji, Japan 83/J6
Ujiji, Tanz. 121/G4
Ujitawara, Japan 83/J6
Ujjain, India 92/C3
Ujohbilang, Indo. 90/E3
Ujung Pandang, Indo. 91/E5
Ujunggading, Indo. 89/B2
Ujunggenteng, Indo. 89/D4
Ukara (isl.), Tanz. 119/A2
Ukata, Nga. 115/G4
Ukerewe (isl.), Tanz. 119/A2
Ukhiya, Bang. 93/F3
Ukhta, Rus. 69/M3
Ukiah, Ca, US 146/B4
Ukiah, Or, US 146/D1
Uklāna, India 98/C5
Ukmergė, Lith. 41/L4
Ukraine (ctry.) 72/F4
Ukwama, Tanz. 119/A4
Ukwatutu, D.R. Congo 117/E4
Ul Bend NWR, Mt, US 145/L4
Ula, Turk. 67/L3
Ulaan-Uul, Mong. 78/G3
Ulaanbaatar (cap.), Mong. 78/F2
Ulaanbaatar (int'l arpt.), Mong. 78/F2
Ulaandel, Mong. 78/G2
Ulaangom, Mong. 99/F2
Ulaanjirem, Mong. 78/F2
Ulan Erge, Rus. 71/H3
Ulan Ul (lake), China 99/F5
Ulan-Burgasy (mts.), Rus. 78/F1
Ulan-Kholl, Rus. 71/H3
Ulan-Ude, Rus. 78/F1
Ulangati, D.R. Congo 121/F3
Ulanhot, China 79/J2
Ulatis (cr.), Ca, US 167/L10
Ulaya, Tanz. 119/B3
Ulchin, SKor. 84/A2
Ulcinj, Serb. 75/F2
Ulcumayo, Peru 184/C3
Uldz (riv.), Mong. 78/G2
Ulefoss, Nor. 40/C2
Ulemiste (int'l arpt.), Est. 41/L2
Ulen, Mn, US 156/F4
Ulgain (riv.), China 79/H2
Ulhāsnagar, India 95/B2
Uliastay, Mong. 78/D2
Ulindi (riv.), D.R. Congo 121/F3
Ulithi (isl.), Micr. 136/C3
Uljma, Serb. 50/E3
Ulla, Bela. 41/N4
Ulla (riv.), Sp. 46/A1
Ulla Ulla, Bol. 184/D4
Ulla Ulla, Res. Nacional, Bol. 184/D4
Ulladulla, Austl. 133/E2
Ullāpāra, Bang. 97/G3
Ullapool, Sc, UK 31/R8
Ullared, Swe. 40/E3
Ulldecona, Sp. 47/F2
Ullensvang, Nor. 40/B1
Ullerslev, Den. 39/G7
Üllő, Hun. 51/R10
Ulloma, Bol. 188/B1
Ullsfjorden (estu.), Nor. 38/F1
Ullswater (lake), Eng, UK 35/F2
Ullŭng (isl.), SKor. 79/L4
Ŭllyul, NKor. 81/C3
Ulm, Ger. 58/C6
Ulm, Ar, US 153/J3
Ulman, Mo, US 153/H1
Ulmarra, Austl. 132/E1
Ulmen, Ger. 55/F3
Ulonguè, Moz. 123/G2
Ulricehamn, Swe. 40/E3
Ulrichen, Swi. 61/E5
Ulrichsberg, Aus. 59/G5
Ulrichstein, Ger. 58/C1
Ulrum, Neth. 52/D2
Ulsan, SKor. 84/A3
Ulstein, Nor. 38/C3
Ulster (reg.), Ire. 34/A3
Ulster, Pa, US 161/H4
Ulster (riv.), Ger. 58/C1
Ulster American Folk Park, NI, UK 34/A2
Ulu, Indo. 91/G3
Ulu, Sudan 116/G3
Ulúa (riv.), Hon. 172/D4
Ulua (riv.), Hon. 176/E3
Uluçınar, Turk. 104/D1
Uludağ (peak), Turk. 102/B1
Uludoruk (peak), Turk. 103/F2
Uluguru (mts.), Tanz. 119/B3
Ulukışla, Turk. 102/C2
Ulundi, SAfr. 125/E3
Ulungur (riv.), China 78/B2
Ulungur (lake), China 78/B2
Uluru (Ayers Rock) (peak), Austl. 131/F3
Uluru NP, Austl. 131/F3
Ulutau (peak), Kaz. 99/A2
Ulverston, Eng, UK 35/E3
Ulverstone, Austl. 132/C4
Ulvik, Nor. 40/B1
Ulvila, Fin. 41/J1
Ul'yanovka, Rus. 41/P2
Ul'yanovka, Ukr. 72/F3
Ul'yanovo, Rus. 70/E1
Ul'yanovsk, Rus. 69/L5
Ul'yanovskaya Oblast, Rus. 71/H1
Ulysses, Ks, US 152/D2
Ulysses, Pa, US 161/H4
Ulysses, Ne, US 155/F3
Um Dafuq, Sudan 116/D3
Umala, Bol. 188/C1
Uman', Ukr. 72/F3
Umán, Mex. 176/D1
Umanum (pt.), Phil. 88/D3
Umari, Braz. 183/G4
Umarizal, Braz. 183/G4
Umarkot, India 95/D2
Umāsi La (pass), India 98/D3
Umatilla, Fl, US 165/H3
Umatilla, Or, US 144/E5
Umatilla (riv.), Or, US 146/D1
Umatilla Ind. Res., Or, US 146/D1
Umatilla NWR, Or, US 146/D1
Umba, Rus. 68/G2
Umbakumba, Austl. 129/E3
Umbeara, Austl. 131/G3
Umberto I, Arg. 188/D4
Umbogintwini, SAfr. 125/E3
Umboi (isl.), PNG 136/D5
Umbrail (peak), Swi. 61/G4
Umbrailpass (pass), Swi. 61/G4
Umbria (pol. reg.), It. 63/F6
Umbria (prov.), It. 45/K5
Umbuluze (riv.), Afr. 123/F5
Ume (riv.), Swe. 74/B3
Ume (riv.), Zim. 123/F3
Umeå, Swe. 38/G3
Umeälven (riv.), Swe. 38/F2
Umedpur, Bang. 97/G4
Umët, Rus. 71/G1
Umfolozi (riv.), SAfr. 125/E3
Umfreville (lake), On, Can. 157/G2
Umfuli (riv.), Zim. 123/F3
Umgeni (riv.), SAfr. 125/E3
Umhausen, Aus. 61/G3
Umiat, Ak, US 171/H2
Umkirch, Ger. 60/D1
Umkomaas, SAfr. 125/E3
Umm al Abīd, Libya 134/B3
Umm al Arānib, Libya 134/B3
Umm al Birak, SAr. 100/C4
Umm al Ghirbāl (well), Libya 134/B2
Umm al Khashab, SAr. 100/D5
Umm al Qaywayn, UAE 101/G3
Umm Buru, Sudan 116/D2
Umm Dam, Sudan 116/F2
Umm Dhibbān, Sudan 116/G2
Umm Dhibbān, Sudan 116/F2
Umm Durmān (Omdurman), Sudan 116/G2
Umm el Faḩm, Isr. 105/C3
Umm Inderaba, Sudan 116/F2
Umm Jawzah, Jor. 105/D4
Umm Kaddādah, Sudan 117/E2
Umm Lajj, SAr. 109/H3
Umm Qaşr, Iraq 103/F4
Umm Qawzayn, Sudan 117/E2
Umm Qays (Gedara) (ruin), Jor. 105/D3
Umm Ruwābah, Sudan 116/F2
Umm Sayyālah, Sudan 116/F2
Ummendorf, Ger. 61/F1
Umnak (isl.), Ak, US 171/E5
Umnak Pass (str.), Ak, US 171/E5
Umniati, Zim. 123/F3
Umniati (riv.), Zim. 123/F3
Umphang, Thai. 94/B2
Umpqua (riv.), Or, US 142/B3
Umpqua, Or, US 146/B2
Umpulo, Ang. 122/C2
Umraniye, Turk. 102/B2
Umred, India 95/C1
Ŭmsŏng, SKor. 81/D4
Umtata, SAfr. 124/E3
Umu Duru, Nga. 115/G5
Umuahia, Nga. 115/G5
Umuarama, Braz. 189/F2
Umuda (isl.), PNG 129/F2
Umunede, Nga. 115/G5
Umurbey, Turk. 75/K2
Umzimvubu (riv.), SAfr. 124/E3
Umzingwani (riv.), Zim. 123/F4
Umzinto, SAfr. 125/E3
Una, Braz. 187/F2
Una (riv.), Bosn.,Cro. 50/B3
Una, India 98/D4
Una (mt.), NZ 135/C3
Unadilla, Ga, US 162/F4
Unadilla, NY, US 161/J3
Unaí, Braz. 186/D3
Unaka (mts.), Tn, US 163/F2
Unalakleet, Ak, US 171/F3
Unalaska, Ak, US 171/E5
Unalaska (isl.), Ak, US 171/E5
Unas (isl.), Fin. 39/F4
'Unayzah, SAr. 100/D3
Uncastillo, Sp. 47/E1
Unchahra, India 96/C3
Uncompaghre (riv.), Co, US 147/K4
Uncompaghre (plat.), Co, US 147/J4
Uncompahgre (peak), Co, US 149/J1
Undaunda, Zam. 123/F2
Unden (lake), Swe. 40/F2
Undenheim, Ger. 58/B3
Underberg, SAfr. 124/E3
Underbool, Austl. 132/B2
Underwood, ND, US 156/D4
Underwood-Petersville, Al, US 162/D3
UNDOF Zone, Syria 105/D2
Undu (pt.), Fiji 137/Z17
Unduavi, Bol. 184/E5
Une, Col. 183/L8
Unecha, Rus. 70/E1
Unga (isl.), Ak, US 171/F4
Ungama (bay), Kenya 119/C2
Ungarie, Austl. 133/C1
Ungava (bay), Can. 141/K3
Ungava (pen.), Qu, Can. 141/J2
Unggi, NKor. 79/L3
Ungheni, Mol. 72/D4
Ungwariba (pt.), Austl. 129/E3
Unhošt, Czh. 59/H2
Unhŭng, NKor. 81/E2
União, Braz. 183/F4
União da Vitória, Braz. 189/G3
União dos Palmares, Braz. 183/G5
Unimak (isl.), Ak, US 171/E5
Unimak (str.), Ak, US 171/E5
Unini (riv.), Braz. 181/F5
Unini, Peru 184/C3
Unión, Arg. 190/D2
Unión, Par. 189/E3
Union (canal), Sc, UK 33/C5
Union, Al, US 162/D4
Union (mt.), Az, US 149/F3
Union, Mo, US 162/B1
Union, Ms, US 162/C4
Union, NJ, US 169/H9
Union (lake), NJ, US 168/C5
Union, Oh, US 160/D5
Union, Or, US 146/E1
Union, SC, US 163/G3
Union, WV, US 163/G2
Union Beach, NJ, US 169/J10
Union Bridge, Md, US 168/A4
Union Center, SD, US 154/C1
Union City, Ca, US 167/K11
Union City, Ga, US 163/L7
Union City, In, US 160/D4
Union City, Mi, US 160/D3
Union City, NJ, US 169/J8
Union City, Ok, US 153/F3
Union City, Pa, US 161/G4
Union City, Tn, US 162/C2
Union Creek, Or, US 146/B2
Unión de Reyes, Cuba 177/F1
Unión de Tula, Mex. 174/D5
Union Flat (cr.), Wa, US 144/F4
Union Grove, Wi, US 160/B3
Unión Hidalgo, Mex. 176/C2
Union Mills, Md, US 168/A4
Union Park, Fl, US 164/N6
Union Pier, Mi, US 160/C4
Union Point, Ga, US 163/F4
Union Springs, Al, US 162/E4
Union Springs, NY, US 161/H3
Uniondale, SAfr. 124/C4
Uniondale, NY, US 169/L9
Unionhall, Ire. 32/A6
Uniontown, Al, US 162/D4
Uniontown, Ar, US 153/G3
Uniontown, Ky, US 162/D2
Uniontown, Md, US 168/A4
Uniontown, Pa, US 161/G5
Unionville, Ga, US 165/G2
Unionville, In, US 160/C5
Unionville, Mi, US 160/E3
Unionville, Mo, US 155/H3
Unionville, Nv, US 146/D3
Unionville, On, Can. 160/U8
Unionville, Va, US 163/J1
Unita (riv.), Ut, US 147/J3
United Arab Emirates (ctry.) 100/F4
United Kingdom (ctry.) 31/*
United Nations, NY, US 169/K9
United Nations Mem. Cemetery, SKor. 84/A3
United States (ctry.) 142/*
United States (range), Nun, Can. 141/T6
United States Coast Guard Receiving Center, NJ, US 168/D6
United States Department of Energy, Md, US 168/A5
United States Naval Academy, Md, US 168/B6
United States Naval Reservation Mil. Res., PR 173/M8
Unitsa, Rus. 68/G3
Unity, Sk, Can. 145/K1
Unity (pond), Me, US 158/C3
Unity, Or, US 146/D1
Unity, Wi, US 155/J1
Universal City, Tx, US 150/E3
Universal Studios Florida, Fl, US 164/M7
University of Minnesota Landscape Arboretum, Mn, US 157/N7
University Park, NM, US 149/J4
University Park, Tx, US 150/L7
University Place, Wa, US 167/B3
Unjha, India 101/K4
Unjŏn, NKor. 81/C3
Unkel, Ger. 55/G2
Unkurda, Rus. 69/N5
Unley (nbrhd.), Austl. 131/M8
Unna, Ger. 53/E5
Unnão, India 96/C2
Ŭnp'a, NKor. 81/C3
Unsan, NKor. 81/C2
Ŭnsan-ŭp, NKor. 81/D3
Unshin (riv.), Ire. 32/B1
Unst (isl.), Sc, UK 31/W13
Unsu-Nodongjagu, NKor. 81/D2
Unter Pleichfeld, Ger. 58/D3
Unterägeri, Swi. 61/E3
Unterargen (riv.), Ger. 61/F2
Untergriesbach, Ger. 59/G5
Unterhaching, Ger. 59/E6
Unteriberg, Swi. 61/E3
Unterkulm, Swi. 60/E3
Unterlüss, Ger. 53/H3
Unterschleissheim, Ger. 59/E6
Untersee (lake), Swi. 61/E2
Unterseen, Swi. 60/D4
Untersiggenthal, Swi. 61/E3
Unterthingau, Ger. 61/G2
Untervaz, Swi. 61/F4
Unterweissenbach, Aus. 59/H6
Unuli Horog, China 99/F4
Unverre, Fr. 57/G4
Ünye, Turk. 70/F4
Unzen-Amakusa NP, Japan 84/A4
Unzen-dake (peak), Japan 84/B4
Unzha (riv.), Rus. 74/E4
Unzimkulu, SAfr. 125/E3
Uonquén, Ven. 181/F3
Uozu, Japan 85/E2
Upala, CR 177/E4
Upalco, Ut, US 147/H3
Upanema, Braz. 183/G4
Upata, Ven. 181/F2
Upemba (lake), D.R. Congo 121/F5
Upemba, PN de l', D.R. Congo 121/F5
Uphall, Sc, UK 33/C5
Upi, Phil. 88/D4
Upington, SAfr. 124/C3
Upinniemi (Obbnäs), Fin. 39/E4
Upiriwombe, Zam. 119/A4
Upland, In, US 160/D4
Upland, Pa, US 168/C4
Upleta, India 101/K4
Upminster (nbrhd.), Eng, UK 30/D2
Upolu (isl.), Sam. 137/S9
Upolu (pt.), Hi, US 142/S9
Upper (falls), Wy, US 147/H1
Upper (pen.), Mi, US 143/J2
Upper (lake), Ca, US 146/C3
Upper (bay), NY, US 168/D2
Upper Arlington, Oh, US 160/E4
Upper Arrow (lake), BC, Can. 144/F2
Upper Blackville, NB, Can. 158/E2
Upper Darby, Pa, US 168/C4
Upper Demerara-Berbice (pol. reg.), Guy. 181/G3
Upper Dicker, Eng, UK 37/G5
Upper East (pol. reg.), Gha. 115/E4
Upper Engadine (valley), Swi. 61/F5
Upper Fairmount, Md, US 163/K1
Upper Falls, Md, US 168/B5
Upper Ganges (canal), India 96/A1
Upper Hale, Eng, UK 30/A3
Upper Hutt, NZ 135/J9
Upper Iowa (riv.), Ia, US 155/J2
Upper Klamath (lake), Or, US 146/B2
Upper Klamath NWR, Or, US 146/C2
Upper Lake, Ca, US 146/B4
Upper Lough Erne (lake), NI, UK 31/Q9
Upper Marlboro (Marlboro), Md, US 168/B6
Upper Mesa (falls), Id, US 147/H1
Upper Missouri River Breaks Nat'l Mon., Mt, US 145/K4
Upper Ouachita NWR, La, US 151/H1
Upper Peoria (lake), Il, US 155/K3
Upper Red (lake), Mn, US 157/G3
Upper Rouge (riv.), Mi, US 167/F7
Upper Saddle River, NJ, US 169/J7
Upper Sandusky, Oh, US 160/E4
Upper Sioux Ind. Res., Mn, US 155/G1
Upper Souris NWR, ND, US 156/D3
Upper Takutu-Upper Essequibo (pol. reg.), Guy. 181/G4
Upper Thames (valley), Eng, UK 37/E3
Upper Trajan's Wall (wall), Mol. 70/D3
Upper Vaughan, NS, Can. 158/E3
Upper West (pol. reg.), Gha. 115/E4
Upper Yarra (res.), Austl. 133/B3
Upperglade, WV, US 163/G1
Upperlands, NI, UK 34/B2
Uppingham, Eng, UK 37/F1
Upplands-Bro, Swe. 39/A1
Upplands-Väsby, Swe. 40/G2
Uppsala (co.), Swe. 38/F3
Uppsala, Swe. 40/G2
Upsala, On, Can. 157/J3
Upshi, India 98/D3
Upson, Wi, US 157/J4
Upstart (cape), Austl. 134/B2
Upstart (bay), Austl. 129/G4
Upton, Wy, US 154/B1
Upton, Ky, US 162/E2
Upton upon Severn, Eng, UK 36/D2
Urabá (gulf), Col. 177/G4
Uracoa, Ven. 181/F2
Urad Qianqi, China 80/B2
Uraga (chan.), Japan 83/D3
Urahoro, Japan 82/C2
Urajärvi (lake), Fin. 39/F3
Urakawa, Japan 82/C2
Ural (riv.), Kaz.,Rus. 71/J2
Ural (mts.), Rus. 74/F3
Ural (Zhāyya) (riv.), Kaz.,Rus. 71/J2
Uralla, Austl. 132/D1
Ural'skiy, Rus. 71/J2
Ural'skoye, Rus. 71/L1
Urambo, Tanz. 121/H4
Urana (lake), Austl. 133/C2
Urana, Austl. 133/C2
Urangeline (cr.), Austl. 133/C2
Urania, La, US 164/B2
Uranium City, Sk, Can. 140/F3
Uranquinty, Austl. 133/C2
Urapunga, Austl. 128/D3
Uraras, Namb. 122/B4
Uraricoera (riv.), Braz. 181/F4
Uraricoera, Braz. 181/F4
Urasoe, Japan 85/J7
Uravan, Co, US 149/H1
Urawa, Japan 85/F3
Uray, Rus. 74/G3
Urayasu, Japan 83/D2
Urazovka, Rus. 69/K5
Urazovo, Rus. 73/K2
Urbach, Ger. 58/C5
Urbana, Mo, US 153/H2
Urbana, Il, US 160/B4
Urbana, Md, US 168/A5
Urbana, Oh, US 160/E4
Urbandale, Ia, US 155/H3
Urbania, It. 63/F6
Urbano Santos, Braz. 183/F3
Urbenville, Austl. 134/D5
Urbino, It. 63/F6
Urcos, Peru 184/D4
Urda, Kaz. 71/H2
Urda, Sp. 46/D3
Urdinarrain, Arg. 191/J10
Urdorf, Swi. 61/E3
Urdzhar, Kaz. 99/D2
Ure (riv.), Eng, UK 35/G3
Urein, Egypt 113/B3
Ureki, Geo. 71/G4
Urengoy, Rus. 74/H3
Ures, Mex. 174/C2
Ureshino, Japan 83/K6
Ureterp, Neth. 52/D2
Urewera NP, NZ 135/D2
Urfa, Turk. 102/D2
Urfa (prov.), Turk. 102/D2
Urft (lake), Ger. 55/F2
Urft (riv.), Ger. 53/G6
Urgal, Rus. 79/L1
Urganch, Uzb. 74/G5
Urgnano, It. 62/C2
Urho Kekkosen NP, Fin. 38/H1
Uri, India 98/C2
Uri-Rotstock (peak), Swi. 61/E4
Uriah, Al, US 164/E2
Uriangato, Mex. 175/E4
Uribante (riv.), Ven. 180/D3
Uribia, Col. 180/C2
Uricani, Rom. 72/B5
Urich, Mo, US 153/G1
Urie (riv.), Sc, UK 33/D2
Urim, Isr. 105/B6
Urimán, Ven. 181/F3
Uriménil, Fr. 60/C1
Uriondo, Bol. 188/C2
Urique (riv.), Mex. 174/D3
Uriranteriña, Ven. 181/F3
Uritskiy, Kaz. 74/G4
Urjala, Fin. 41/K1
Urk, Neth. 52/C3
Urla, Turk. 70/C5
Urlaţi, Rom. 51/H3
Urlingford, Ire. 32/C4
Urman, Rus. 69/N5
Urmar, India 98/C4
Urmi (riv.), Rus. 78/L2
Urmia (lake), Iran 103/F2
Urmitz, Ger. 55/G3
Urmston, Eng, UK 35/F5
Urnäsch, Swi. 61/F3
Urnersee (lake), Swi. 61/E4
Uroševac, Serb. 50/E4
Urr Water (riv.), Sc, UK 34/E1
Urrin (riv.), Ire. 32/D4
Ursensollen, Ger. 59/E4
Ursulo Galván, Mex. 175/N7
Urtazym, Rus. 71/L1
Uru Uru (lake), Bol. 188/C1
Uruaçu, Braz. 186/C2
Uruapan, Mex. 148/D5
Uruapan, Mex. 174/E5
Urubamba, Peru 184/C4
Urubamba (riv.), Peru 184/C3
Urubichá, Bol. 185/F4
Urubu (riv.), Braz. 181/G5
Urubuquara (hill), Braz. 182/C3
Uruburetama, Braz. 183/G3
Urucará, Braz. 182/B3
Urucu (riv.), Braz. 185/E2
Uruçuí, Braz. 183/E4
Uruçuí Preto (riv.), Braz. 183/E5
Uruçuí, Serra do (mts.), Braz. 183/E5
Urucuia (riv.), Braz. 186/D3
Urucurituba, Braz. 182/B3
Uruguai (riv.), Braz. 189/F3
Uruguaiana, Braz. 189/E4
Uruguay (ctry.) 179/D6
Uruguay (riv.), SAm. 179/D5
Urumaco, Ven. 180/D2
Ürümqi (int'l arpt.), China 99/E3
Ürümqi, China 99/E3
Urunga, Austl. 132/E1
Uruoca, Braz. 183/F3
Urup (isl.), Rus. 77/Q5
Ururi, It. 65/E4
Urus-Martan, Rus. 71/H4
Urussanga, Braz. 189/G4
Urussu, Rus. 71/K1
Uruwira, Tanz. 121/G4
Uruyén, Ven. 181/F3
Uryumkan (riv.), Rus. 79/H1
Uryupinsk, Rus. 73/M2
Urzhum, Rus. 69/L4
Urziceni, Rom. 51/H3
Us, Fr. 30/H4
Us (riv.), Rus. 78/C1
Usa (riv.), Rus. 74/F3
Usa, Japan 84/B4
USAF Academy, Co, US 154/B4
USAF Res., Tn, US 162/D3
Usagara, Tanz. 119/A2
Uşak, Turk. 102/B2
Uşak (prov.), Turk. 102/B2
Usakos, Namb. 122/B4
Usborne (mt.), UK 191/F6
Uscio, It. 62/C5
Usedom (isl.), Ger. 40/E4
Usedom, Ger. 40/E5
Useldange, Lux. 55/E4
Useless Loop, Austl. 130/B3

Usevia, Tanz. 121/G4
'Usfān, SAr. 100/C4
Ushachi, Bela. 41/N4
Ushaki, Rus. 41/P2
Ushashi, Tanz. 119/A2
'Ushayrah, SAr. 100/D4
Ushetu, Tanz. 121/H4
Ushibori, Japan 83/F2
Ushibuka, Japan 84/B4
Ushiku, Japan 83/E2
Ushirombo, Tanz. 121/G3
Ushkovo, Rus. 69/S6
Ushtobe, Kaz. 99/C2
Ushuaia, Arg. 191/C7
Ushumun, Rus. 79/K1
Usi, NKor. 81/C2
Usibelli, Ak, US 171/J3
Usicayos, Peru 184/D4
Usilampatti, India 92/C6
Usinge, Tanz. 121/G4
Usingen, Ger. 58/B2
Usino, PNG 129/G1
Usinsk, Rus. 74/E4
Üsküdar (nbrhd.), Turk. 103/N7
Üsküp, Turk. 51/H5
Uslar, Ger. 53/G5
Usman', Rus. 70/F1
Usoke, Tanz. 121/H4
Usol'ye-Sibirskoye, Rus. 78/E1
Uson, Phil. 88/C2
Uspallata, Arg. 190/C2
Uspallata, Paso de (pass), Chile 190/N8
Uspenka, Ukr. 73/K3
Usquil, Peru 184/B2
Ussel, Fr. 44/E4
Ussel (riv.), Ger. 58/D5
Usses (riv.), Fr. 60/C5
Ussoque, Ang. 122/B2
Ussure, Tanz. 119/A3
Ussuri (riv.), China,Rus. 75/P5
Ussuriysk, Rus. 79/L3
Ussy-sur-Marne, Fr. 30/M5
Ust'-Barguzin, Rus. 78/F1
Ust'-Ilimsk, Rus. 75/L4
Ust'-Ishim, Rus. 74/H4
Ust'-Kamchatsk, Rus. 75/S4
Ust'-Karsk, Rus. 79/H1
Ust'-Kulom, Rus. 69/M3
Ust'-Kut, Rus. 75/L4
Ust'-Kuyga, Rus. 75/P2
Ust'-Labinsk, Rus. 73/K5
Ust'-Luga, Rus. 41/N2
Ust'-Man'ya, Rus. 69/P3
Ust'-Maya, Rus. 75/P3
Ust'-Nera, Rus. 75/Q3
Ust'-Ocheya, Rus. 69/L3
Ust'-Olenëk, Rus. 75/M2
Ust'-Omchug, Rus. 75/Q3
Ust'-Ordynskiy, Rus. 78/E1
Ust'-Ordynskiy Buryatskiy Aut. Okrug, Rus. 75/Q6
Ust'-Pinega, Rus. 68/J2
Ust'-Port, Rus. 74/J3
Ust'-Pozhva, Rus. 69/N4
Ust'-Tsil'ma, Rus. 69/M2
Ust'-Uda, Rus. 78/E1
Ústecký (pol. reg.), Czh. 43/G3
Úštěk, Czh. 59/H1
Uster, Swi. 61/E3
Ustica, It. 48/C3
Ustica (isl.), It. 67/G3
Ustka, Pol. 40/G4
Ustrzyki Dolne, Pol. 43/M4
Ust'ya (riv.), Rus. 69/K3
Ustyurt (plat.), Kaz. 77/D5
Ustyuzhna, Rus. 68/H4
Usu, China 99/D3
Usuda, Japan 83/A1
Usuki, Japan 84/B4
Usulután, ESal. 176/D3
Usuma, D.R. Congo 117/E4
Usumacinta (riv.), Mex. 172/C4
Uta, Indo. 91/J4
Utah (state), US 142/D4
Utah (lake), Ut, US 147/G3
Utah Beach, Fr. 56/D2
Utah Test and Training Range, Ut, US 147/G3
Utale, Malw. 123/G2
Utangan (riv.), India 96/A2
Utano, Japan 83/J7
Utashinai, Japan 82/C2
'Utaybah (lake), Syria 105/F1
Ute (cr.), NM, US 152/C2
Ute Mountain Ind. Res., Co, US 149/H2
Utembo (riv.), Ang. 122/D3
Utena, Lith. 41/L4
Utengule, Tanz. 119/A4
Utero (peak), It. 65/C2
Uterský (riv.), Czh. 59/G3
Utete, Tanz. 119/B3
Uthai Thani, Thai. 94/C3
Utica, NY, US 161/J3
Utica, Oh, US 160/E4
Utica, Mi, US 167/F6
Utica, Mo, US 155/H4
Utica, Ne, US 155/F3
Utica, Ms, US 162/B4
Utiel, Sp. 46/E3
Utila (isl.), Hon. 176/E2
Utinga, Braz. 187/E2
Utirik (isl.), Mrsh. 136/G3
Utiroa, Kiri. 136/G5
Utlyukskiy Estuary (estu.), Ukr. 73/H4
Utmānzai, Pak. 98/A2
Utnūr, India 95/C2
Utö (isl.), Swe. 39/B2
Utö, Swe. 39/B2
Utopia, Austl. 131/G2
Utopia, Tx, US 150/E3
Utopia Abor. Land, Austl. 131/G2
Utorgosh, Rus. 41/P2
Utraulā, India 96/D2
Utrecht (prov.), Neth. 52/C4
Utrecht, Neth. 52/C4
Utrecht, SAfr. 125/E2
Utrera, Sp. 46/C4
Utsunomiya, Japan 85/F2
Utta, Rus. 71/H3
Uttar Patiata, Bang. 97/G3
Uttar Pradesh (state), India 99/C6
Uttaradit, Thai. 94/C2
Uttaranchal (state), India 96/B1
Uttendorf, Aus. 59/G6
Uttenweiler, Ger. 61/F1
Uttoxeter, Eng, UK 35/G6
Utuado, PR 173/M8
Utupua (isl.), Sol. 136/F6
Uturoa, FrPol. 137/K6
Utzenstorf, Swi. 60/D3
Uulu, Est. 41/L2
Üür (riv.), Mong. 78/E1
Üüreg (lake), Mong. 78/C1
Uusikaupunki, Fin. 41/J1
Uusimaa (prov.), Fin. 38/H3
Uva (riv.), Col. 180/D4
Uva (prov.), SrL. 95/D5
Uvalda, Ga, US 165/G1
Uvalde, Tx, US 150/E3
Uvarovo, Rus. 71/G2
Uvel'skiy, Rus. 69/P5
Uverito, Ven. 181/E2
Uvinza, Tanz. 121/G4
Uvira, D.R. Congo 121/G3
Uvongo, SAfr. 125/E3
Uvs (lake), Mong. 78/C1
Uvs (prov.), Mong. 78/C2
Uvs Nuur (lake), Mong. 99/F1
Uwajima, Japan 84/C4
'Uwaybid (peak), Egypt 113/D4
Uwayl, Sudan 117/E3
Uwekuli, Indo. 91/F4
Uwimmerah (riv.), Indo. 91/K5
Uxbridge (nbrhd.), Eng, UK 30/B2
Uxin Qi, China 80/B3
Uxmal (ruin), Mex. 176/D1
Üydzin, Mong. 78/F3
Uyo, Nga. 115/G5
Üyönch, Mong. 78/C2
Uyu (riv.), Myan. 86/B3
Uyuni, Bol. 188/C2
Uzbekistan (ctry.) 74/G5
Uzcudún, Arg. 190/D5
Uzein (int'l arpt.), Fr. 44/C5
Uzel, Fr. 56/C4
Uzen', Kaz. 71/K4
Uzerche, Fr. 44/D4
Uzès, Fr. 44/F4
Uzhhorod, Ukr. 43/M4
Uzhok (pass), Ukr. 43/M4
Užice, Serb. 50/D4
Uzlovaya, Rus. 70/F1
Uznach, Swi. 61/E3
Üzümlü, Turk. 102/D2
Uzunköprü, Turk. 51/H5
Užventis, Lith. 41/K4
Uzwil, Swi. 61/F3
Uzyn, Ukr. 72/F3

V

V.C. Bird (int'l arpt.), Anti. 173/N8
V.P. Rosales, PN, Chile 190/B4
Vääksy, Fin. 39/F3
Vaal (riv.), SAfr. 107/E7
Vaala, Fin. 38/H2
Vaalbos NP, SAfr. 124/D3
Vaaldam (res.), SAfr. 124/D2
Vaals, Neth. 55/F2
Vaalserberg (hill), Neth. 55/E2
Vaalwater, SAfr. 123/F5
Vaas, Fr. 57/F5
Vaasa (int'l arpt.), Fin. 38/G3
Vaasa (prov.), Fin. 38/G3
Vaasa (Vasa), Fin. 38/G3
Vaassen, Neth. 52/C4
Vabalninkas, Lith. 41/L4
Vác, Hun. 50/D2
Vaca (mt.), Ca, US 167/K10
Vaca (mts.), Ca, US 167/K10
Vacacai (riv.), Braz. 189/F4
Vacaria, Braz. 189/G4
Vacaria (riv.), Braz. 186/B4
Vacaville, Ca, US 146/C4
Vaccares (swamp), Fr. 64/A6
Vachères (peak), Fr. 64/B3
Vachères (riv.), Fr. 64/C3
Vachi, Rus. 71/H4
Vachon (riv.), Qu, Can. 141/J2
Vacov, Czh. 59/G4
Vad, Rus. 69/K5
Vada, It. 62/D7
Vaden, Ar, US 153/H4
Vadheim, Nor. 40/A1
Vado, NM, US 150/A1
Vado Ligure, It. 62/B5
Vadodara (Baroda), India 92/B3
Vadret (peak), Swi. 61/F4
Vadsø, Nor. 38/J1
Vadstena, Swe. 40/F2
Vadul lui Voda, Mol. 72/E4
Vaduz (cap.), Lcht. 61/F3
Vaernes (int'l arpt.), Nor. 38/D3
Vaga (riv.), Rus. 68/J3
Vågå, Nor. 38/D3
Vågan, Nor. 38/E1
Vaganski Vrh (peak), Cro. 50/B3
Vagay (riv.), Rus. 69/R4
Vaggeryd, Swe. 40/F3
Vagney, Fr. 60/C1
Vagnhärad, Swe. 39/A2
Vagos, Port. 46/A2
Vågsøy, Nor. 38/C3
Vah (riv.), Slvk. 43/J4
Vahermanjärvi (lake), Fin. 39/E4
Vahitahi (isl.), FrPol. 137/M6
Vaiano, It. 63/E6
Vaiano Cremasco, It. 62/C3
Vaich (lake), Sc, UK 33/B1
Vaiden, Ms, US 162/C4
Vaige (riv.), Fr. 57/E5
Vaiges, Fr. 57/E4
Vaihingen an der Enz, Ger. 58/B5
Vaijāpur, India 101/K5
Väike-Maarja, Est. 41/M2
Vail, Az, US 149/G4
Vailate, It. 62/C3
Vailsburg (nbrhd.), NJ, US 169/J9
Vaiņode, Lat. 41/J3
Vair (riv.), Fr. 60/B1
Vairano Patenora, It. 65/D5
Vaire (riv.), Fr. 64/C4
Vaisali (riv.), India 96/B2
Vaison-la-Romaine, Fr. 64/B4
Vaitupu (isl.), Tuv. 136/G5
Vaivre-et-Montoille, Fr. 60/C2
Vakaga (pref.), CAfr. 116/D3
Vakfıkebir, Turk. 70/F4
Vakh (riv.), Rus. 74/J3
Vākhān (mts.), Afg. 101/K1
Vakhrushev, Rus. 79/N2
Vakhrushi, Rus. 69/L4
Vakhsh (riv.), Taj. 101/J1
Vakhtan, Rus. 69/K4
Vál, Hun. 50/D2
Val de Cans (int'l arpt.), Braz. 182/D3
Val Lagarina (valley), It. 63/D1
Val Marie, Sk, Can. 145/L3
Val Venosta (valley), It. 61/G4
Val Verde, Ca, US 166/B2
Val-Brillant, Qu, Can. 158/D1
Val-d'Oise (dept.), Fr. 57/G2
Val-David, Qu, Can. 161/J1
Val-de-Marne (dept.), Fr. 54/B6
Val-de-Reuil, Fr. 57/G2
Val-des-Monts, Qu, Can. 161/J2
Val-d'Isère, Fr. 64/C2
Val-d'Or, Qu, Can. 141/J4
Valais (canton), Swi. 60/D5
Valajärvi (lake), Fin. 39/E4
Valaská Belá, Slvk. 43/K4
Valbo, Swe. 40/G1
Valburg, Neth. 52/C5
Valcheta, Arg. 190/D4
Valcourt, Qu, Can. 161/K2
Valdagno, It. 63/E2
Valdahon, Fr. 60/C3
Valdai (hills), Rus. 68/G4
Valdarno (valley), It. 63/E5
Valday, Rus. 68/G4
Valdecañas (res.), Sp. 46/C3
Valdemarpils, Lat. 41/K3
Valdemarsvik, Swe. 40/G2
Valdemorillo, Sp. 47/M8
Valdense, Uru. 191/K11
Valdepeñas, Sp. 46/D3
Valderas, Sp. 46/C1
Valderrobres, Sp. 47/F2
Valdés (pen.), Arg. 179/C7
Valdeverdeja, Sp. 46/C3
Valdez, Ecu. 180/B4
Valdez, Ak, US 171/J3
Valdivia, Col. 180/C3
Valdivia, Chile 190/B3
Valdobbiadene, It. 63/F2
Valdoie, Fr. 60/C2
Valdosta, Ga, US 165/G2
Valdoviño, Sp. 46/A1
Vale, Chl, UK 56/C2
Vale, Geo. 71/G4
Vale, Or, US 146/E2
Vale of Conwy (valley), Wal, UK 34/E5
Vale of Evesham (valley), Eng, UK 36/D2
Vale of Glamorgan (co.), Wal, UK 36/C4
Vale of Pickering (valley), Eng, UK 35/H3
Vale of Powys (valley), Wal, UK 36/C1
Vale of St. Albans (valley), Eng, UK 30/B1
Vale of Sussex (valley), Eng, UK 37/F4
Vale of York (valley), Eng, UK 35/G3
Valea lui Mihai, Rom. 43/M5
Valeggio sul Mincio, It. 63/D3
Valemount, BC, Can. 144/E1
Valença, Port. 46/A1
Valença, Braz. 187/N7
Valença, Braz. 187/F2
Valença do Piauí, Braz. 183/F4
Valence, Fr. 64/A3
Valence, Fr. 44/D4
Valence-sur-Baïse, Fr. 44/D5
Valencia (isl.), Ire. 30/P11
Valencia, Ecu. 180/B5
Valencia (state), Sp. 46/E2
Valencia (int'l arpt.), Sp. 47/E3
Valencia, Sp. 47/E3
Valencia, NM, US 149/J3
Valencia, Phil. 88/D4
Valencia, Phil. 88/D3
Valencia (lake), Ven. 183/N7
Valencia (int'l arpt.), Ven. 183/N7
Valencia, Ven. 183/M7
Valencia de Alcántara, Sp. 46/B3
Valencia de Don Juan, Sp. 46/C1
Valenciennes, Fr. 54/C3
Valendas, Swi. 61/F4
Vălenii de Munte, Rom. 51/H3
Valensole, Fr. 64/B5
Valentigney, Fr. 60/C3
Valentin, Rus. 79/L3
Valentine, Az, US 149/F3
Valentine, Ne, US 154/D2
Valentine, Tx, US 150/B2
Valentine Nat'l Wild. Ref., Ne, US 154/D2
Valentines, Uru. 191/G2
Valentines, Va, US 163/J2
Valenton, Fr. 30/K5
Valenza, It. 62/B3
Valenzuela, Phil. 88/E6
Våler, Nor. 40/D2
Våler, Nor. 40/D1
Valera, Ven. 180/D2
Valfabbrica, It. 65/B1
Valff, Fr. 60/D1
Valga, Est. 41/M3
Valhalla, NY, US 169/K7
Valier (peak), Fr. 47/F1
Valier, Il, US 162/C1
Valier, Mt, US 145/H3
Valinco (gulf), Fr. 48/A2
Valinhos, Braz. 187/J7
Valjevo, Serb. 50/D3
Valka, Lat. 41/M3
Valkeakoski, Fin. 41/K1
Valkeala, Fin. 41/M1
Valkenburg, Neth. 55/E2
Valkenswaard, Neth. 52/C6
Valkininkai, Lith. 41/L4
Valky, Ukr. 73/H3
Vall de Uxó, Sp. 47/E3
Valladolid, Mex. 176/D1
Valladolid, Sp. 46/C2
Valladolid (int'l arpt.), Sp. 46/C2
Vallangoujard, Fr. 30/J4
Vallauris, Fr. 64/D5
Valle, Nor. 40/B2
Valle, Ecu. 180/B5
Valle d Aosta (pol.reg.), It. 45/G4
Valle D'Aosta (pol. reg.), It. 64/D1
Valle d'Aosta (valley), It. 64/D1
Valle de Bravo, Mex. 175/E5
Valle de Cauca (dept.), Col. 180/B4
Valle de Encantado, PN, Chile 188/B4
Valle de Guanape, Ven. 181/E2
Valle de La Pascua, Ven. 183/P8
Valle de Santiago, Mex. 175/E4
Valle Fértil (valley), Arg. 188/C4
Valle Hermoso, Mex. 175/F3
Valle Lomellina, It. 62/B3
Valle, Río del (riv.), Arg. 188/C4
Valle Mosso, It. 62/B2
Vallecas (nbrhd.), Sp. 47/N9
Vallecillo, Mex. 150/E4
Vallecitos, NM, US 149/J2
Vallecitos de Zaragoza, Mex. 175/E5
Vallecorsa, It. 65/C5
Vallecrosia, It. 64/D5
Valledupar, Col. 180/C2
Valleé de l'Azaouak (riv.), Mali 115/G2
Vallée du Ferlo (riv.), Sen. 114/B3
Valleé du Mboune (riv.), Sen. 114/B3
Valleé du Saloum (riv.), Sen. 114/B3
Valleé du Serpent (riv.), Mali 114/C3
Vallée-Jonction, Qu, Can. 158/B2
Vallegrande, Bol. 188/C1
Vallehermoso, Sp. 110/A3
Vallejo, Ca, US 146/B4
Vallenar, Chile 188/B4
Vallendar, Ger. 55/G3
Vallentuna, Swe. 39/B1
Vallerano, It. 65/B3
Valleroy, Fr. 55/E5
Valles Mines, Mo, US 162/B1
Valletta (cap.), Malta 48/M7
Valley, Al, US 162/E4
Valley, Wa, US 144/F3
Valley Center, Ca, US 166/C4
Valley Centre, Sk, Can. 145/L2
Valley City, ND, US 156/E4
Valley Cottage, NY, US 169/K7
Valley East, On, Can. 160/F1
Valley Falls, Or, US 146/C2
Valley Falls, Ks, US 155/G4
Valley Farms, Az, US 149/G4
Valley Forge Nat'l Hist. Park, Pa, US 168/C3
Valley Head, Al, US 162/E3
Valley Head, WV, US 163/G1
Valley Mills, Tx, US 150/F2
Valley of Desolation, SAfr. 124/D4
Valley of the Kings, Egypt 109/G3
Valley Park, Ms, US 162/B4
Valley River, Mb, Can. 156/D2
Valley Spring, Tx, US 151/E2
Valley Springs, Ar, US 153/H2
Valley Stream, NY, US 169/L9
Valley View, Tx, US 153/F4
Valleyfair, Mn, US 157/N7
Valleyford, Wa, US 144/F4
Valleyview, Ab, Can. 140/E3
Vallière (riv.), Fr. 60/B4
Vallimanca, Arroyo (stream), Arg. 190/E3
Vallo della Lucania, It. 48/D2
Valloire, Fr. 64/C2
Vallorbe, Swi. 60/C4
Valls, Sp. 47/F2
Valluga (peak), Aus. 61/G3
Valmayor (res.), Sp. 47/M8
Valme (riv.), Ger. 53/F6
Valmiera, Lat. 41/L3
Valmondois, Fr. 30/J4
Valmont, NM, US 150/B1
Valmontone, It. 65/B4
Valmy, Wi, US 160/C2
Valmy, Nv, US 146/E3
Valognes, Fr. 56/D2
Valois (reg.), Fr. 54/B5
Valona (bay), Gre. 75/F2
Valona, Ga, US 165/H2
Valpaços, Port. 46/B2
Vālpārai, India 95/C4
Valparaiso, In, US 160/C4
Valparaiso, Fl, US 165/E2
Valparaíso (pol. reg.), Chile 190/C2
Valparaiso, Ne, US 155/F3
Valparaíso, Col. 183/K7
Valparaíso, Chile 190/N8
Valparaíso, Mex. 174/E4
Valperga, It. 64/D2
Valpovo, Cro. 50/D3
Valréas, Fr. 64/A4
Valrico, Fl, US 164/L8
Vals, Swi. 61/F4
Vals (cape), Indo. 129/E2
Vals (riv.), SAfr. 124/D2
Vals-les-Bains, Fr. 44/F4
Valsaquillo (res.), Mex. 175/L8
Valsbaai (bay), SAfr. 124/B4
Valserine (riv.), Fr. 60/B5
Valserrhein (riv.), Swi. 61/F4
Valsura (riv.), It. 61/G4
Valtellina (valley), It. 61/F5
Valuyki, Rus. 73/K2
Valverde, Sp. 110/A4
Valverde del Camino, Sp. 46/B4
Valyermo, Ca, US 166/C2
Våmhus, Swe. 40/F1
Vamizi (isl.), Moz. 123/J1
Vammala, Fin. 41/K1
Vamori Wash (riv.), Az, US 149/F5
Vámos, Gre. 75/J5
Vámosmikola, Hun. 50/D2
Vámospércs, Hun. 50/E2
Van, Turk. 103/E2
Van (lake), Turk. 74/E6
Van (pt.), Fr. 56/A4
Van, Or, US 146/D2
Van, WV, US 163/G2
Van (prov.), Turk. 103/E2
Van, Tx, US 151/G1
Van Alstyne, Tx, US 153/F4
Van Buren, Ar, US 153/G3
Van Buren, Mo, US 162/B2
Van Cortlandt Park, NY, US 169/K8
Van Diemen (cape), Austl. 129/E4
Van Diemen (cape), Austl. 128/C2
Van Diemen (gulf), Austl. 127/C2
Van Harinxmakanaal (riv.), Neth. 52/C2
Van Hoa, Viet. 94/D1
Van Horn, Tx, US 150/B2
Van Lear, Ky, US 163/F2
Van Ninh, Viet. 94/E3
Van Norman Lakes, Ca, US 166/B2
Van Nuys (nbrhd.), Ca, US 166/F7
Van Rees (mts.), Indo. 91/J4
Van Vleck, Tx, US 151/G3
Van Wert, Oh, US 160/D4
Van Wert, Ia, US 155/H3
Van Yen, Viet. 94/D1
Vana-Javesi (lake), Fin. 41/K1
Vanadzor, Arm. 71/H4
Vananda, Mt, US 145/L4
Vanavara, Rus. 75/L3
Vanavaro (isl.), FrPol. 137/L7
Vance (A.F.B.), Ok, US 153/F2
Vanceboro, NC, US 163/J3
Vanceburg, Ky, US 163/F1
Vancon (riv.), Fr. 64/C4
Vancourt, Tx, US 150/D2
Vancouver (cape), Austl. 130/C5
Vancouver, BC, Can. 144/C3
Vancouver (isl.), BC, Can. 140/D4
Vancouver (int'l arpt.), BC, Can. 144/C3
Vancouver (mt.), Yk, Can. 171/L3
Vancouver, Wa, US 144/C5
Vandalia, Oh, US 160/D5
Vandalia, Il, US 162/C1
Vandalia, Mo, US 155/J4
Vandalia, Mt, US 145/L3
Vandans, Aus. 61/F3
Vandenberg (A.F.B.), Ca, US 148/B3
Vanderbijlpark, SAfr. 124/D2
Vanderbilt, Tx, US 151/F3
Vanderbilt Museum, NY, US 169/E2
Vanderhoof, BC, Can. 140/D3
Vanderlin (isl.), Austl. 129/E3
Vanderlin Abor. Land, Austl. 129/E3
Vandervoort, Ar, US 153/G3
Vandœuvre-Lès-Nancy, Fr. 55/F6
Vändra, Est. 41/L2
Vandra (riv.), It. 65/D4
Vandysh, Rus. 68/J3
Vandžiogala, Lith. 41/K4
Vanegas, Mex. 175/E4
Vänern (lake), Swe. 74/B4
Vänersborg, Swe. 40/E2
Vanga, Kenya 119/B3
Vangaindrano, Madg. 125/H8
Vanguard, Sk, Can. 145/L3
Vanier, On, Can. 161/J2
Vanier (isl.), Nun, Can. 141/R7
Vanikolo (isl.), Sol. 136/F6
Vanil Noir (peak), Swi. 60/D4
Vanimo, PNG 136/D5
Vanino, Rus. 79/N2
Vännäs, Swe. 38/F3
Vanndale, Ar, US 162/B3
Vanne (riv.), Fr. 44/E2
Vannes, Fr. 56/C5
Vanoise, PN, Fr. 45/G4
Vanreenenpas (pass), SAfr. 124/E3
Vanrhynsdorp, SAfr. 124/B3
Vanrook, Austl. 134/A2
Vansant, Va, US 163/F2
Vansbro, Swe. 40/F1
Vanscoy, Sk, Can. 145/L1
Vanse, Nor. 40/B2
Vansittart (isl.), Nun, Can. 141/H2
Vansittart (bay), Austl. 128/B3
Vantaa, Fin. 41/L1
Vantage, Sk, Can. 145/L3
Vantage, Wa, US 144/E4
Vanua Levu (isl.), Fiji 136/G6
Vanuatu (ctry.) 136/F6
Vanwyksvlei, SAfr. 124/C3
Vanzant, Mo, US 153/H2
Vapnyarka, Ukr. 72/E3
Var (dept.), Fr. 64/C5
Var (riv.), Fr. 45/G5
Vara, Swe. 40/E2
Vara (riv.), It. 62/C4
Varadero, Cuba 177/F1
Varades, Fr. 57/D6
Varaita (riv.), It. 62/A3
Varaita (riv.), Fr. 64/D3
Varakļāni, Lat. 41/M3
Varalé, C.d'Iv. 114/E4
Varallo, It. 62/B2
Varāmīn, Iran 103/G3
Vārānāsi, India 96/D3
Varandey, Rus. 69/N1
Varanger-Halvøya (pen.), Nor. 38/J1
Varangerfjorden (estu.), Nor. 38/J1
Varangéville, Fr. 55/F6
Varano (lake), It. 48/D2
Varano Borghi, It. 62/B2
Varaždin, Cro. 50/C2
Varazze, It. 62/B5
Varberg, Swe. 40/E3
Varces-Allières-et-Risset, Fr. 64/B2
Vardaman, Ms, US 162/C4
Vardar (riv.), FYROM 67/J2
Varde, Den. 40/C4
Vardenis, Arm. 103/F1
Várdha, Gre. 75/G3
Vardø, Nor. 38/J1
Varel, Ger. 53/F2
Varėna, Lith. 41/L4
Varengeville-sur-Mer, Fr. 57/F1
Varenikovskaya, Rus. 73/J5
Varenne (riv.), Fr. 44/C2
Varennes, Qu, Can. 159/P6
Varennes-Jarcy, Fr. 30/K5
Varennes-Vauzelles, Fr. 44/E3
Vareš, Bosn. 50/D3
Varese (prov.), It. 61/E6
Varese, It. 62/B2
Varese Ligure, It. 62/C5
Varèze (riv.), Fr. 64/A2
Vårgårda, Swe. 40/E2
Vargem Grande, Braz. 183/F3
Vargem Grande do Sul, Braz. 187/K6
Varginha, Braz. 187/L6
Varik, Neth. 52/C5
Varilhes, Fr. 44/D5
Varillas, Chile 188/B3
Varkala, India 95/C4
Värmdö, Swe. 39/B1
Värmdölandet (isl.), Swe. 39/B1
Värmeln (lake), Swe. 40/E2
Värmland (co.), Swe. 38/E3
Varna (pol. reg.), Bul. 75/K1
Varna, Rus. 69/P5
Varna, Bul. 51/H4
Varna (int'l arpt.), Bul. 51/H4
Varna (prov.), Rom. 51/H4
Värnamo, Swe. 40/F3
Varnek, Rus. 69/N1
Varniai, Lith. 41/K4
Varnville, SC, US 163/G4
Varois-et-Chaignot, Fr. 60/B3
Varoška Rijeka, Bosn. 50/C3
Várpalota, Hun. 50/D2
Varraddes, Fr. 30/L5
Vars, Fr. 64/C3
Varsi, It. 62/C4
Värska, Est. 41/M3
Vårsta, Swe. 40/G2
Vartashen, Azer. 71/H4
Vartholomión, Gre. 75/G4
Varto, Turk. 102/E2
Vartry (res.), Ire. 34/B5
Vartry (riv.), Ire. 34/B5
Varva, Ukr. 73/G1
Varzaneh, Iran 103/H3
Várzea Alegre, Braz. 183/G4
Várzea da Palma, Braz. 186/D3
Várzea Grande, Braz. 186/A2
Várzea Grande, Braz. 183/F4
Varzi, It. 62/C4
Varzo, It. 61/E5
Varzuga (riv.), Rus. 68/H2
Vas (prov.), Hun. 50/C2
Vasa (Vaasa), Fin. 38/G3
Vasa Barris (riv.), Braz. 187/F1
Vasai (Bassein), India 101/K5
Vasanello, It. 65/B3
Vásárosnamény, Hun. 43/M4
Vaşcău, Rom. 50/F2
Vashka (riv.), Rus. 69/K2
Vashon (isl.), Wa, US 167/C3
Vashon, Wa, US 167/C3
Vasile Roaită, Rom. 51/J3
Vasilevichi, Bela. 72/E1
Vasiliká, Gre. 75/H2
Vasil'yevskiy (isl.), Rus. 69/T7
Vaslui, Rom. 72/D4
Vaslui (prov.), Rom. 51/H2
Vassar, Mb, Can. 156/G3
Vassar, Mi, US 160/E3
Vassdalsegga (peak), Nor. 40/B2
Vassés (Bassae) (ruin), Gre. 75/G4
Vassouras, Braz. 187/N7
Vassy, Fr. 57/E3
Västerås, Swe. 40/G2
Västerbotten (co.), Swe. 38/F2
Västerdalälven (riv.), Swe. 40/E1
Västerhaninge, Swe. 39/B1
Västerljung, Swe. 39/A2
Västernorrland (co.), Swe. 38/F3
Västervik, Swe. 40/G3
Västmanland (co.), Swe. 38/E3
Vasto, It. 65/D3
Västra Silen (lake), Swe. 40/E2
Vasvár, Hun. 50/C2
Vasylivka, Ukr. 73/H4
Vasyl'kiv, Ukr. 72/F2
Vasyl'kivka, Ukr. 73/J3
Vasyurinskaya, Rus. 73/K5
Vaterstetten, Ger. 59/E6
Vatican City (ctry.) 65/F7
Vatican Gardens, VatC. 65/G7
Vatican Museums, VatC. 65/G7
Vatnajökull (glacier), Ice. 38/P7
Vatneyri, Ice. 38/M6
Vatö (isl.), Swe. 39/B1
Vatomandry, Madg. 125/J7
Vatra Dornei, Rom. 72/C4
Vättern (lake), Swe. 38/E4
Vatukoula, Fiji 137/Y18
Vatutine, Ukr. 72/F3
Vaucluse (dept.), Fr. 64/A4
Vaucluse, SC, US 163/G4
Vaucluse, Monts de (mts.), Fr. 64/B5
Vaucouleurs (riv.), Fr. 30/H5
Vaud (canton), Swi. 60/C4
Vaudelle (riv.), Fr. 57/E4
Vaudoy-en-Brie, Fr. 30/M5
Vaudreuil (co.), Qu, Can. 159/M7
Vaudreuil-Dorion, Qu, Can. 159/M7
Vaughan, Ms, US 162/B4
Vaughan, On, Can. 160/T8
Vaughn, NM, US 152/B3
Vaughn, Mt, US 145/J4
Vaughn, Wa, US 167/B3
Vaulruz, Swi. 60/C4
Vaulx-en-Velin, Fr. 60/A6
Vaunoise (riv.), Fr. 56/D4
Vaupés (dept.), Col. 180/D4
Vaupés (riv.), Col. 179/B2
Vauréal, Fr. 30/J4
Vauvert, Fr. 44/F5
Vauvillers, Fr. 60/C2
Vaux (riv.), Fr. 42/C4
Vaux-sur-Seine, Fr. 30/H4
Vaux-sur-Sûre, Belg. 55/E4
Vauxhall, Ab, Can. 145/H2
Vavatenina, Madg. 125/J7
Vava'u Group (isls.), Tonga 137/H6
Vavenby, BC, Can. 144/E2
Vavoua, C.d'Iv. 114/D5
Vawkavysk, Bela. 43/N2
Vawn, Sk, Can. 145/K1
Vaxholm, Swe. 39/B1
Vaxjo (int'l arpt.), Swe. 40/F3
Växjö, Swe. 40/F3
Vay, Fr. 56/D5
Vaygach (isl.), Rus. 74/F3
Vazante, Braz. 186/D3
Vázea Paulista, Braz. 187/K8
Vazhgort, Rus. 69/K2
Vazuza (res.), Rus. 68/G5
Vazzola, It. 63/F2
Veberöd, Swe. 39/K7
Veblen, SD, US 156/F5
Vecchiano, It. 62/D6
Vechelde, Ger. 53/H4
Vechigen, Swi. 60/D4
Vecht (riv.), Neth. 52/D3
Vechta, Ger. 53/F3
Vechte (riv.), Ger. 52/D3
Veckholm, Swe. 39/A1
Vecpiebalga, Lat. 41/L3
Vecsés, Hun. 50/D2
Vecumnieki, Lat. 41/L3
Vedano Olona, It. 62/B2
Veddige, Swe. 40/E3
Vedelago, It. 63/F2
Vedène, Fr. 64/A5
Vedia, Arg. 190/E2
Vedra, Sp. 46/A1
Veedersburg, In, US 160/C4
Veendam, Neth. 52/D2
Veenendaal, Neth. 52/C4
Veenhuizen, Neth. 52/D2
Veere, Neth. 52/A5
Veerse Meer (res.), Neth. 52/A5
Vefsn, Nor. 38/E2
Vega, Tx, US 152/C3
Vega (isl.), Nor. 38/D2
Véga (riv.), Fr. 64/A1
Vega, Swe. 39/B1
Vega (pt.), Ak, US 171/B6
Vega de Alatorre, Mex. 175/N6
Vegafjorden (estu.), Nor. 38/D2
Vegeån (riv.), Swe. 39/J6
Vegesack, Ger. 53/F2
Veghel, Neth. 52/C5
Vegorítis (lake), Gre. 75/G2
Vègre (riv.), Fr. 57/E4
Vègreville, Ab, Can. 145/H1
Végueta, Peru 184/B3
Veguita, NM, US 149/J3
Vehkalahti, Fin. 41/M1
Vehne (riv.), Ger. 53/F2
Veigné, Fr. 57/F6
Veikkola, Fin. 39/E4
Veilsdorf, Ger. 58/D2
Veinticinco de Mayo, Arg. 190/E2
Veinticinco de Mayo, Arg. 190/D3
Veinticinco de Mayo, Uru. 191/K11
Veintiocho de Mayo, Ecu. 184/B1
Veintiocho de Noviembre, Arg. 191/B6
Veio (ruin), It. 65/B3
Veisiejai, Lith. 41/K4
Veitsch, Aus. 50/B2
Veitshöchheim, Ger. 58/C3
Vejen, Den. 40/C4
Vejer de la Frontera, Sp. 46/C4
Vejle, Den. 40/C4
Vejle (co.), Den. 40/C4
Vejprnice, Czh. 59/G3
Vejprty, Czh. 59/G2
Vejrø (isl.), Den. 39/G7
Vela Luka, Cro. 50/C4
Vela, Cabo de la (pt.), Col. 180/C1
Velaines, Fr. 55/E6
Vélan (peak), Swi. 60/D6
Velarde, NM, US 149/K2
Velardeña, Mex. 174/E3
Velas, Azor., Port. 47/S12
Velasco Ibarra, Ecu. 180/B5
Velaux, Fr. 64/B5
Velázquez, Uru. 191/G2
Velbert, Ger. 52/E6
Velburg, Ger. 59/E4
Velddrif, SAfr. 124/L10
Velden, Ger. 59/F6
Velden, Neth. 52/D6
Velden am Wörthersee, Aus. 45/L3
Veldhoven, Neth. 52/C6
Velen, Ger. 52/D5
Velenje, Slov. 50/B2
Velešta, FYROM 75/G2
Velestínon, Gre. 75/H3
Vélez, Col. 180/C3
Vélez-Blanco, Sp. 46/D4
Vélez-Málaga, Sp. 46/C4
Vélez-Rubio, Sp. 46/D4
Velhas, Rio das (riv.), Braz. 186/D3
Velika Gorica, Cro. 50/C3
Velika Kladuša, Bosn. 50/B3
Velika Lepetykha, Ukr. 73/G4
Velika Novosilka, Ukr. 73/J4
Velika Plana, Serb. 50/E3
Velikaya (riv.), Rus. 68/F4
Veliki Birky, Ukr. 72/C3
Velikiy Ustyug, Rus. 69/K3
Velikiye Luki, Rus. 41/P3
Veliko Tŭrnovo, Bul. 51/G4
Velikodvorskiy, Rus. 68/J5
Velikovisochnoye, Rus. 69/M2
Velille, Peru 184/D4
Vélingara, Sen. 114/B3
Vélingara, Sen. 114/B3
Velingrad, Bul. 75/J1
Velino (peak), It. 65/C3
Velino (riv.), It. 65/C3
Velizh, Rus. 41/P4
Vélizy-Villacoublay, Fr. 30/J5
Velké Meziříčí, Czh. 43/J4
Velké Žernoseky, Czh. 59/H1
Vel'ký Krtíš, Slvk. 43/K4
Velký Zvon (peak), Czh. 59/F3
Vellberg, Ger. 58/C4
Velleron, Fr. 64/B5
Velletri, It. 65/B4
Vellinge, Swe. 40/E4
Vellinge, Swe. 39/K7
Vellmar, Ger. 53/G6
Vellón (res.), Sp. 47/N8
Velma, Ok, US 153/F3
Vélon, Gre. 75/H4
Velp, Neth. 52/C5
Velsen-Noord, Neth. 52/B4
Vel'sk, Rus. 68/J3
Velten, Ger. 42/Q6
Veluwe (phys. reg.), Neth. 52/C4
Veluwemeer (lake), Neth. 52/C4
Veluwezoom, NP, Neth. 52/C4
Velva, ND, US 156/D3
Velvary, Czh. 59/H2
Velvendós, Gre. 75/H2
Velykodolyns'ke, Ukr. 72/F4
Velykyy Bereznyy, Ukr. 43/M4
Velykyy Burluk, Ukr. 73/J2
Velykyy Lyubin', Ukr. 72/B3
Vémars, Fr. 30/K4
Vemb, Den. 40/C3
Vembādi Shola (peak), India 95/C4
Vémend, Hun. 50/D2
Ven (isl.), Swe. 39/J7
Vena Park, Austl. 134/A2
Venachar (lake), Sc, UK 33/B4
Venadillo, Col. 183/L8
Venado Tuerto, Arg. 190/E2
Venados, Mex. 175/L6
Venafro, It. 65/D5
Venamo (peak), Ven. 181/F3
Venâncio Aires, Braz. 189/F4
Venango, Ne, US 154/C3
Venaria, It. 64/D2
Venarotta, It. 65/C2
Vence, Fr. 64/D5
Venceslau Brás, Braz. 189/G2
Vendas Novas, Port. 46/A3
Vendelsö, Swe. 39/B1
Vendôme, Fr. 57/G5
Vendrell, Sp. 47/F2
Vendrest, Fr. 30/M4
Venecia, Col. 183/K7
Venelles, Fr. 64/B5
Vénéon (riv.), Fr. 64/C2
Veneta (lake), It. 63/F2
Veneta, Or, US 146/B1
Venetie, Ak, US 171/J2
Veneto (pol. reg.), It. 45/J4
Venëv, Rus. 70/F1
Venezia (gulf), Eur. 67/G1
Venezia (prov.), It. 63/F1
Venezia (Venice), It. 63/F3
Venezuela (ctry.) 181/E3
Venezuela (gulf), Col.,Ven. 179/B1
Veniaminof (mt.), Ak, US 171/G4
Venice (Venezia), It. 63/F3
Venice (nbrhd.), Ca, US 166/F8
Venice, Fl, US 165/G4
Venice, Ut, US 149/F1
Vénissieux, Fr. 64/A1
Venjan, Swe. 40/E1
Venjansjön (lake), Swe. 40/E1
Venkatāpuram, India 95/D2
Venlo, Neth. 52/D6
Venn, Sk, Can. 145/M2
Vennesla, Nor. 40/B2
Veno (bay), Den. 40/C3
Venoge (riv.), Swi. 60/C4
Venosa, It. 48/D2
Venray, Neth. 52/C5
Venta (riv.), Lat.,Lith. 41/J3
Venta de Baños, Sp. 46/C2
Ventabren, Fr. 64/B5
Ventersburg, SAfr. 124/D3
Ventersdorp, SAfr. 124/D2
Venterspos, SAfr. 124/P13
Venterstad, SAfr. 124/D3
Ventimiglia, It. 64/D5
Ventiseri, Fr. 48/A2
Ventnor, Eng, UK 37/E5
Ventnor City, NJ, US 168/D5
Ventotene (isl.), It. 65/C6
Ventoux (peak), Fr. 64/B4
Ventspils, Lat. 41/J3
Ventuari (riv.), Ven. 181/E3
Ventura (co.), Ca, US 166/A2
Ventura (riv.), Ca, US 166/A2
Ventura (San Buenaventura), Ca, US 166/A2
Venturina, It. 48/B1
Venturosa, Braz. 183/G5
Vénus (pt.), FrPol. 137/X15
Venus, Tx, US 150/K7
Venustiano Carranza, Mex. 172/C4
Venustiano Carranza (res.), Mex. 175/E3
Véore (riv.), Fr. 64/B3
Vép, Hun. 50/C2
Ver-sur-Launette, Fr. 30/L4
Vera, Arg. 188/D4
Vera, Sp. 46/E4
Vera, Tx, US 152/E4
Vera Cruz, Pan. 180/B2
Veracruz, Mex. 175/N7
Veracruz-Llave (state), Mex. 172/B3
Veranópolis, Braz. 189/G4
Verāval, India 101/K4
Verbania, It. 61/E6
Verbena, Al, US 162/D4
Verberie, Fr. 54/B5
Verbicaro, It. 48/D3
Verbovskiy, Rus. 68/J5
Vercelli (prov.), It. 60/E6
Vercelli, It. 62/B3
Verchères (co.), Qu, Can. 159/P6
Verchères, Qu, Can. 159/P6
Vercors (upland), Fr. 64/B3
Verda, Ky, US 163/F2
Verdal, Nor. 38/D3
Verde (cape), It. 62/A5
Verde (coast), Sp. 46/B1
Verde (bay), Arg. 190/E3
Verde (riv.), Az, US 149/F3
Verde (riv.), Braz. 189/F2
Verde (riv.), Braz. 185/F4
Verde (riv.), Braz. 189/G1
Verde (riv.), Mex. 175/F4
Verde Grande (riv.), Braz. 187/E2
Verde Island Passage (chan.), Phil. 88/C2
Verden, Ger. 53/G3
Verdhikoússa, Gre. 75/G3
Verdigris (riv.), Ks, US 153/G2
Verdon (riv.), Fr. 44/F5
Verdugo (mts.), Ca, US 166/F7
Verdun, Qu, Can. 159/N7
Verdun, Fr. 55/E5
Verdunville, WV, US 163/F2
Vereeniging, SAfr. 124/D2
Veregin, Sk, Can. 156/C2
Verena (peak), It. 61/H6
Vereshchagino, Rus. 69/M4
Veretskiy (pass), Ukr. 43/M4
Verga (cape), Gui. 114/B4
Vergara, Uru. 191/G2
Vergara, Arg. 191/K11
Vergas, Mn, US 156/G4
Vergato, It. 63/E5
Vergennes, Vt, US 161/K2
Vergiate, It. 62/B2
Vergína (ruin), Gre. 75/H2
Verhknyaya Toyma, Rus. 69/K3
Veribest, Tx, US 150/D2
Verigenstadt, Ger. 61/F1
Verín, Sp. 46/B2
Veriora, Est. 41/M3
Verkaån (riv.), Swe. 39/K7
Verkhazovka, Rus. 71/J2
Verkhivtseve, Ukr. 73/H3
Verkhnebakanskiy, Rus. 73/J5
Verkhnedneprovskiy, Rus. 68/G5
Verkhnedvinsk, Bela. 41/M4
Verkhnetulomskiy (res.), Rus. 68/F1
Verkhneural'sk, Rus. 69/N5
Verkhni Rohachyk, Ukr. 73/H4
Verkhniy At Uryakh, Rus. 75/R3
Verkhniy Baskunchak, Rus. 71/H2
Verkhniy Mamon, Rus. 73/L2
Verkhniy Tagil, Rus. 69/N4
Verkhniy Ufaley, Rus. 69/N4
Verkhniye Kigi, Rus. 69/N5
Verkhniye Osel'ki, Rus. 69/T6
Verkhn'odniprovs'k, Ukr. 73/H3
Verkhnyaya Orlyanka, Rus. 71/J1
Verkhnyaya Pyshma, Rus. 69/P4
Verkhnyaya Salda, Rus. 69/P4
Verkhnyaya Sinyachikha, Rus. 69/P4
Verkhnyaya Tura, Rus. 69/N4
Verkhnyaya Zolotitsa, Rus. 68/J2
Verkhoyansk, Rus. 75/P3
Verkhoyansk (range), Rus. 77/M2
Verl, Ger. 53/F5
Verlo, Sk, Can. 145/K2
Vermenagna (riv.), It. 62/A4
Vermenagna (riv.), Fr. 64/D4
Vermilion, Ab, Can. 145/J1
Vermilion (riv.), Ab, Can. 145/J1
Vermilion (hills), Sk, Can. 145/L2
Vermilion (bay), La, US 151/H3
Vermilion (lake), Mn, US 157/H4
Vermilion (range), Mn, US 157/H4
Vermilion Bay, On, Can. 157/H3
Vermilion Lake Ind. Res., Mn, US 157/H4
Vermillion (riv.), Il, US 155/F2
Vermillion, SD, US 155/F2
Vermillion (cr.), Wy, US 147/J3
Vermillion Cliffs Nat'l Mon., Az, US 149/F2
Vermillion, East Fork (riv.), SD, US 155/F2
Vermillion, West Fork (riv.), SD, US 155/F2
Vermont (state), US 161/K3
Vermont, Il, US 155/J3
Vermontville, Mi, US 160/D3
Vern-sur-Saiche, Fr. 56/D4
Vernāg, India 98/C3
Vernaison (riv.), Fr. 64/B3
Vernal, Ut, US 147/J3
Vernante, It. 64/D4
Vernantes, Fr. 57/F6
Vernayaz, Swi. 60/D5
Vernazza, It. 62/C5
Verndale, Mn, US 157/G4
Verneuil-sur-Avre, Fr. 57/F3
Verneuil-sur-Seine, Fr. 30/H5
Verneukpan (salt pan), SAfr. 124/C3
Vernier, Swi. 60/C5
Vernon, BC, Can. 144/E2
Vernon, Fr. 57/G2
Vernon, Al, US 162/C4
Vernon, Ct, US 161/K4
Vernon, Fl, US 165/F2
Vernon, In, US 162/E1
Vernon (lake), La, US 164/B2
Vernon, Tx, US 152/E3
Vernon Hills, Il, US 167/Q15
Vernon Valley, NJ, US 168/D1
Vernonia, Or, US 144/C5
Vernouillet, Fr. 57/G3
Vernouillet, Fr. 30/H5
Vernoux-en-Vivarais, Fr. 64/A3
Vero Beach, Fl, US 165/H4
Véroia, Gre. 75/H2
Verolanuova, It. 62/D3
Verolavecchia, It. 62/D3
Verolengo, It. 62/A2
Veroli, It. 65/C4
Verona, ND, US 156/E4
Verona, On, Can. 161/H2
Verona (int'l arpt.), It. 63/D3
Verona, It. 63/D3
Verona (prov.), It. 63/D1
Verona, NJ, US 169/J8
Verona, Ms, US 162/C3
Verona, Va, US 163/H1
Verónica, Arg. 191/K11
Verrès, It. 62/A1
Verret (lake), La, US 164/C3
Verrières-le-Buisson, Fr. 30/J5
Verrino (riv.), It. 65/D4
Versa (riv.), It. 62/B3
Versalles, Bol. 185/F4
Versailles, Fr. 30/J5
Versailles, Il, US 155/J4
Versailles, In, US 162/E1
Versailles, Ky, US 162/E1
Versailles, Mo, US 153/H1
Versailles, Oh, US 160/D4
Vershino-Darasunskiy, Rus. 78/H1

Vershi – Vyazem

Vershino-Shakhtaminskiy, Rus. 79/H1
Versigny, Fr. 30/L4
Verskla (riv.), Ukr.,Rus. 74/D4
Versmold, Ger. 53/F4
Versoix, Swi. 60/C5
Vert-le-Grand, Fr. 30/K6
Vert-le-Petit, Fr. 30/K6
Vert-Saint-Denis, Fr. 30/K6
Vertana (peak), It. 61/G4
Verte (peak), Fr. 60/C6
Vertemate, It. 62/C2
Vertientes, Cuba 177/G1
Vertiyivka, Ukr. 72/F2
Vertou, Fr. 44/C3
Vertova, It. 62/C2
Vertus, Fr. 54/D6
Verviers, Belg. 55/E2
Vervins, Fr. 54/C4
Verwoerdburg, SAfr. 124/Q12
Verwood, Eng, UK 37/E5
Veryan (bay), Eng, UK 36/B6
Verzasca (riv.), Swi. 61/E5
Verzasca (Gerra), Swi. 61/E5
Verzée (riv.), Fr. 57/D5
Verzel (peak), It. 64/D2
Verzenay, Fr. 55/D5
Verzuolo, It. 64/D3
Verzy, Fr. 55/D5
Vescovato, Fr. 48/A1
Vescovato, It. 62/D3
Vesdre (riv.), Belg. 44/F1
Vesele, Ukr. 73/H4
Veselí nad Lužnicí, Czh. 59/H4
Veselynove, Ukr. 72/F4
Veselyy (res.), Rus. 71/G3
Vesgre (riv.), Fr. 54/A6
Veshenskaya, Rus. 73/L3
Veshkayma, Rus. 71/H1
Vesijärvi (lake), Fin. 41/L1
Vesle (riv.), Fr. 42/C4
Vesoul, Fr. 60/C2
Vespolate, It. 62/B3
Vest-Agder (co.), Nor. 38/C4
Vest-Sjælland (prov.), Den. 40/D4
Vest-Vlaanderen (prov.), Belg. 54/B2
Vestbjerg, Den. 40/C3
Vestby, Nor. 40/D2
Vestbygd, Nor. 40/B2
Vester Ringsjön (lake), Swe. 39/K7
Vesterålen (isls.), Nor. 38/E1
Vestfjorden (inlet), Nor. 68/B2
Vestfold (co.), Nor. 38/D4
Vestmannaeyjar, Ice. 38/N7
Vestmarka (reg.), Nor. 38/S8
Vestone, It. 62/D2
Vestvågøy, Nor. 38/E1
Vestvågøya (isl.), Nor. 38/E1
Vésubie (riv.), Fr. 64/D5
Vesuvio (Vesuvius) (vol.), It. 65/D6
Vesuvius, Va, US 163/H2
Vesuvius (Vesuvio) (vol.), It. 65/D6
Ves'yegonsk, Rus. 68/H4
Veszprém, Hun. 50/C2
Veszprém (prov.), Hun. 50/C2
Vészto, Hun. 50/E2
Vet (riv.), SAfr. 124/D3
Veteran, Ab, Can. 145/J1
Vétheuil, Fr. 30/H4
Vetka, Bela. 70/D1
Vetlanda, Swe. 40/F3
Vetluga (riv.), Rus. 74/E4
Vetluzhskiy, Rus. 69/K4
Vetralla, It. 65/B3
Vétraz, Fr. 60/C5
Vetrino, Bela. 41/N4
Větřni, Czh. 59/H5
Vettore (peak), It. 65/C2
Veude (riv.), Fr. 44/D3
Veulettes-sur-Mer, Fr. 57/F1
Veurne, Belg. 54/B1
Veuve (riv.), Fr. 57/F5
Vevay, In, US 162/E1
Vevey, Swi. 60/C5
Vex, Swi. 60/D5
Veybach (riv.), Ger. 55/F2
Veyle (riv.), Fr. 60/B5
Veynes, Fr. 64/B3
Veyo, Ut, US 149/F2
Veyrier-du-Lac, Fr. 60/C6
Vézelise, Fr. 60/C1
Vézère (riv.), Fr. 44/D4
Vezin-le-Coquet, Fr. 56/D4
Vezirköprü, Turk. 70/E4
Vezza (riv.), It. 65/B3
Vezza d'Oglio, It. 61/G5
Vezzano Ligure, It. 62/C5
Vi Thanh, Viet. 94/D4
Viacha, Bol. 188/B1
Viadana, It. 62/D4
Viale, Arg. 188/D4
Vian, Ok, US 153/G3
Viana, Ang. 120/C5
Viana, Braz. 183/E3
Viana del Bollo, Sp. 46/B1
Viana do Alentejo, Port. 46/A3
Viana do Castelo, Port. 46/A2
Viana do Castelo (dist.), Port. 46/A2
Vianden, Lux. 55/F4
Vianen, Neth. 52/C4
Viangchan (Vientiane) (cap.), Laos 94/C2
Viangphoukha, Laos 86/D4
Viar (riv.), Sp. 46/C4
Viareggio, It. 62/D6
Viarmes, Fr. 30/K4
Viaur (riv.), Fr. 44/E4
Vibank, Sk, Can. 156/C2
Vibo Valentia, It. 48/E3
Viborg, Den. 40/C3
Viborg (co.), Den. 40/C3
Viborg, SD, US 155/F2
Viburnum, Mo, US 162/B2
Viby, Swe. 39/L6
Viby, Den. 39/J7
Vic, Sp. 47/G2
Vic-en-Bigorre, Fr. 44/D5
Vic-Fezensac, Fr. 44/D5
Vicam, Mex. 174/C3
Vícar, Sp. 46/D4
Vicarello, It. 62/D6
Vicchio, It. 63/E6
Vice, Peru 184/A2
Vicente (pt.), Ca, US 166/F8
Vicente Guerrero, Mex. 148/E4
Vicente Guerrero, Mex. 174/A2
Vicente Guerrero, Mex. 174/E4
Vicente López, Arg. 191/J11
Vicenza (prov.), It. 61/H6
Vicenza, It. 63/E2
Viceroy, Sk, Can. 145/M3
Vichada (riv.), Col. 180/D3
Vichada (dept.), Col. 180/D3
Vichadero, Uru. 189/F4
Vichaya, Bol. 188/B1
Vichuga, Rus. 68/J4
Vichy, Mo, US 153/J1
Vichy, Fr. 44/E3
Vici, Ok, US 152/E2
Vick, La, US 164/B2
Vickham (cape), Austl. 133/A4
Vicksburg, Mi, US 160/D3
Vicksburg, Az, US 149/F4
Vicksburg, Ms, US 162/B4
Vicksburg Nat'l Military Park, Ms, US 153/J4
Vico, Fr. 48/A1
Vico (lake), It. 48/C1
Vico del Gargano, It. 50/B5
Vico Equense, It. 65/D6
Vicopisano, It. 62/D6
Viçosa, Braz. 183/G5
Viçosa, Braz. 187/E4
Viçosa do Ceará, Braz. 183/F3
Vicosoprano, Swi. 61/F5
Vicou Gorge NP, Gre. 75/G3
Vicovaro, It. 65/B3
Vicq, Fr. 30/H5
Victoire, Sk, Can. 145/L1
Victor, Co, US 152/B1
Victor, Ca, US 146/C4
Victor, Ia, US 155/H3
Victor Harbor, Austl. 131/H5
Víctor Rosales, Mex. 174/E4
Victoria, Arg. 188/D5
Victoria (lake), Austl. 133/C3
Victoria (riv.), Austl. 128/C3
Victoria (state), Austl. 127/D4
Victoria (peak), Belz. 176/D2
Victoria (isl.), Can. 139/F2
Victoria (cap.), BC, Can. 144/C3
Victoria (str.), Nun, Can. 140/F2
Victoria (isl.), NW,Nun, Can. 140/E1
Victoria, On, Can. 160/T8
Victoria, Chile 190/B3
Victoria, China 87/L7
Victoria, Col. 183/L7
Victoria, Gui. 114/B4
Victoria, Gren. 181/F1
Victoria, Hon. 176/E3
Victoria, Malay. 88/A4
Victoria (mt.), Myan. 86/B4
Victoria, Phil. 88/C2
Victoria (peak), Phil. 88/B3
Victoria, Rom. 51/G3
Victoria (lake), Ugan. 107/F5
Victoria (falls), Zim. 122/E3
Victoria, Ks, US 152/E1
Victoria, Mn, US 157/N7
Victoria, Mo, US 162/B1
Victoria, Ms, US 162/C3
Victoria, Tx, US 151/F3
Victoria, Tx, US 151/F2
Victoria, Va, US 163/H2
Victoria (Rabat), Malta 48/L6
Victoria Beach, Mb, Can. 156/F2
Victoria de las Tunas, Cuba 177/G1
Victoria Falls (int'l arpt.), Zim. 122/E3
Victoria Falls, Zim. 122/E3
Victoria Land (pol. reg.), Ant. 192/M
Victoria Nile (riv.), Ugan. 121/G2
Victoria River Downs, Austl. 128/C4
Victoria West, SAfr. 124/C3
Victorias, Phil. 88/C3
Victoriaville, Qu, Can. 161/L1
Victorica, Arg. 190/D3
Victorino, Ven. 180/E4
Victorville, Ca, US 166/C1
Vicuña, Chile 188/B4
Vicuña Mackenna, Arg. 190/D2
Vida, Mt, US 145/M4
Vidal, Ca, US 148/E3
Vidal (cape), SAfr. 125/F3
Vidalia, La, US 164/C2
Vidalia, Ga, US 163/F4
Vidauban, Fr. 64/C6
Videira, Braz. 189/G3
Videla, Arg. 188/D4
Videle, Rom. 51/G3
Vidhošt (peak), Czh. 59/G4
Vidigueira, Port. 46/B3
Vidigulfo, It. 62/C3
Vidin, Bul. 51/F4
Vidisha, India 96/A4
Vidlitsa, Rus. 41/Q1
Vidnoye, Rus. 69/W9
Vidor, Tx, US 151/G2
Vidor, It. 63/F2
Vidöstern (lake), Swe. 40/F3
Vidourle (riv.), Fr. 44/E5
Vie (riv.), Fr. 44/D2
Viechtach, Ger. 59/F4
Viedma, Arg. 190/E4
Viedma (lake), Arg. 191/B6
Viehberg (peak), Aus. 59/H5
Vieille-Eglise-en-Yvelines, Fr. 30/H6
Vieira Grande (riv.), Braz. 182/D3
Vieja (peak), Tx, US 150/B2
Vieja Palestina, Mex. 150/D3
Viejo (peak), Peru 184/B2
Viekšniai, Lith. 41/K3
Viella, Sp. 44/D5
Vielsalm, Belg. 55/E3
Vienenburg, Ger. 53/H5
Vienna, Mo, US 153/J1
Vienna, WV, US 160/F5
Vienna, Ga, US 165/G1
Vienna, Il, US 162/C2
Vienna, Va, US 168/A6
Vienna (Wien) (cap.), Aus. 51/N7
Vienne, Fr. 64/A1
Vienne (riv.), Fr. 66/D1
Vientiane (int'l arpt.), Laos 94/C2
Vientiane (Viangchan) (cap.), Laos 94/C2
Vieques (isl.), PR 173/M8
Viére (riv.), Fr. 55/D6
Vierlingsbeek, Neth. 52/D5
Viernheim, Ger. 58/B3
Vierre (riv.), Belg. 55/E4
Viersen, Ger. 52/D6
Vierwaldstättersee (Lucerne) (lake), Swi. 61/E3
Vierzon, Fr. 57/H6
Viesca, Mex. 174/E3
Viesīte, Lat. 41/L3
Vieste, It. 48/E2
Viet Tri, Viet. 86/E4
Vietnam (ctry.) 94/D2
Vietri sul Mare, It. 65/D6
Vieux Chaillol (peak), Fr. 64/C3
Vieux Fort, StL. 173/N9
Vieux-Boucau-les-Bains, Fr. 44/C5
Vieux-Charmont, Fr. 60/C2
Vieux-Condé, Fr. 54/C3
Vieux-Thann, Fr. 60/D2
Vievis, Lith. 41/L4
Viewpark, Sc, UK 33/B5
Vieytes, Arg. 191/K11
Vieze (riv.), Swi. 60/C5
Vif, Fr. 64/B2
Vig, Den. 39/H7
Viga, Phil. 88/D2
Vigan, Phil. 88/C1
Vigarano Mainarda, It. 63/E4
Vigasio, It. 63/D3
Vigevano, It. 62/B3
Viggiù, It. 61/E6
Vigia, Braz. 182/D3
Vigie (int'l arpt.), StL. 173/N9
Vigliano Biellese, It. 62/B2
Viglio (peak), It. 65/C4
Vignacourt, Fr. 54/B3
Vignanello, It. 65/B3
Vignemale (peak), Fr. 44/C5
Vigneulles-lès-Hattonchâtel, Fr. 55/E6
Vigneux-sur-Seine, Fr. 30/K5
Vignola, It. 63/D5
Vignot, Fr. 55/E6
Vigny, Fr. 57/G4
Vigo, Sp. 46/A1
Vigodarzere, It. 63/E3
Vigone, It. 64/D3
Vigonovo, It. 63/F3
Vigonza, It. 63/E3
Vigrestad, Nor. 40/A2
Viguzzolo, It. 62/B4
Vihanti, Fin. 68/E2
Vihāri, Pak. 98/B4
Vihti, Fin. 41/L1
Vihtijärvi (lake), Fin. 39/E4
Viiala, Fin. 39/D3
Viitasaari, Fin. 68/E3
Viivikonna, Est. 41/M2
Vijayanagar, India 86/C3
Vijosë (riv.), Eur. 67/H2
Vik, Nor. 40/B1
Vík, Ice. 38/N7
Vikajärvi, Fin. 68/E2
Vikedal, Nor. 40/A2
Vikeke, ETim. 128/B2
Viken, Swe. 39/J6
Vikersund, Nor. 40/C2
Vikeså, Nor. 40/B2
Vikevåg, Nor. 40/A2
Vikhren (peak), Bul. 75/H2
Viking, Ab, Can. 145/J1
Vikmanshyttan, Swe. 40/F1
Vila Bela da Santíssima Trindade, Braz. 185/G4
Vila Bittencourt, Braz. 180/D5
Vila da Maganja, Moz. 123/H3
Vila de Porto Santo, Port. 110/A2
Vila de Sena, Moz. 123/G3
Vila do Bispo, Port. 46/A4
Vila do Conde, Port. 46/A2
Vila do Porto, Azor., Port. 47/T13
Vila Franca de Xira, Port. 47/P10
Vila Franca do Campo, Azor., Port. 47/T13
Vila Nova de Fozcoa, Port. 46/B2
Vila Nova de Gaia, Port. 46/A2
Vila Nova de Milfontes, Port. 46/A4
Vila Nova do Seles, Ang. 122/B1
Vila Pouca de Aguiar, Port. 46/B2
Vila Real, Port. 46/B2
Vila Real (dist.), Port. 46/B2
Vila Velha, Braz. 182/D2
Vila Velha Argolas, Braz. 187/E4
Vila Velha de Ródão, Port. 46/B3
Vila Verde, Port. 46/A2
Vila Viçosa, Port. 46/B3
Vila-Vila, Chile 188/B1
Vilacaya, Bol. 188/C1
Viladecans, Sp. 47/K7
Vilafranca del Penedès, Sp. 47/K7
Vilaine (riv.), Fr. 44/B3
Viļaka, Lat. 41/M3
Vilama (lake), Arg. 188/C2
Vilanandro (cape), Madg. 125/H7
Vilanculos, Moz. 123/G4
Viļāni, Lat. 41/M3
Vilanova i la Geltrù, Sp. 47/K7
Vilar Formoso, Port. 46/B2
Vilcabamba, Peru 184/B3
Vîlcea (prov.), Rom. 51/F3
Vil'cha, Ukr. 72/E2
Vilches, Sp. 46/D3
Vilcún, Chile 190/B4
Vileyka, Bela. 41/M4
Vilhelmina, Swe. 38/F2
Vilhena, Braz. 185/F4
Viliya (riv.), Bela. 68/E5
Viljandi, Est. 41/L2
Viljoenskroon, SAfr. 124/D2
Vilkaviškis, Lith. 41/K4
Vilkija, Lith. 41/K4
Vil'kitsogo (str.), Rus. 75/K2
Villa Abecia, Bol. 188/C2
Villa Aberastain, Arg. 188/B4
Villa Adriana (ruin), It. 65/B4
Villa Alemana, Chile 190/N8
Villa Alhué, Chile 190/N9
Villa Ana, Arg. 188/E4
Villa Ángela, Arg. 188/D3
Villa Aroma, Bol. 188/C1
Villa Atamisqui, Arg. 188/D4
Villa Atuel, Arg. 190/D2
Villa Bartolomea, It. 63/E3
Villa Bella, Bol. 185/E3
Villa Berthet, Arg. 188/D3
Villa Bruzual, Ven. 180/D2
Villa Cañás, Arg. 190/E2
Villa Carcina, It. 62/D2
Villa Carlos Paz, Arg. 188/C4
Villa Chañar Ladeado, Arg. 190/E2
Villa Constitución, Arg. 190/E2
Villa Corzo, Mex. 176/C2
Villa Cuauhtemoc, Mex. 175/Q10
Villa d'Almè, It. 62/C2
Villa de Arista, Mex. 175/E4
Villa de Cos, Mex. 174/E4
Villa de Costa Rica, Mex. 174/D3
Villa de Cura, Ven. 183/N7
Villa de La Paz, Mex. 175/E4
Villa de Reyes, Mex. 175/E4
Villa de Soto, Arg. 188/C4
Villa del Carbón, Mex. 175/Q9
Villa del Carmen, Uru. 191/K10
Villa del Río, Sp. 46/C4
Villa del Rosario, Arg. 188/D4
Villa di Serio, It. 62/C2
Villa Dolores, Arg. 190/D1
Villa Flores, Mex. 176/C2
Villa Florida, Par. 189/E3
Villa Gesell, Arg. 191/F3
Villa Grove, Il, US 160/B5
Villa Grove, Co, US 149/K1
Villa Guardia, It. 62/C2
Villa Guillermina, Arg. 188/E4
Villa Hayes, Par. 188/E3
Villa Hernandarias, Arg. 188/E4
Villa Hidalgo, Mex. 174/C2
Villa Hidalgo, Mex. 174/D4
Villa Huidobro, Arg. 190/D2
Villa Industrial, Chile 184/D5
Villa Iris, Arg. 190/E3
Villa Isabela, DRep. 177/J2
Villa Jaragua, DRep. 177/J2
Villa Juárez, Mex. 174/C3
Villa Juárez, Mex. 174/D3
Villa La Angostura, Arg. 190/C4
Villa Lázaro Cárdenas, Mex. 175/M6
Villa Literno, It. 65/D6
Villa López, Mex. 174/D3
Villa Mantero, Arg. 191/J10
Villa María, Arg. 188/D5
Villa María Grande, Arg. 188/E4
Villa Martín, Bol. 188/C2
Villa Mazán, Arg. 188/C4
Villa Minetti, Arg. 188/D4
Villa Minozzo, It. 62/D5
Villa Montes, Bol. 188/D2
Villa Nueva, Nic. 176/E3
Villa Nueva, Guat. 176/D3
Villa Nueva, Arg. 190/C2
Villa Ocampo, Arg. 188/E4
Villa Ojo de Agua, Arg. 188/D4
Villa Opicina, It. 63/G2
Villa Oropeza, Bol. 188/C1
Villa Park, Ca, US 166/G8
Villa Park, Il, US 167/Q16
Villa Regina, Arg. 190/D3
Villa Rica, Ga, US 162/E4
Villa Rica, Peru 184/C3
Villa Rosario, Col. 180/C3
Villa San José, Arg. 188/E5
Villa Sandino, Nic. 177/E3
Villa Santa Maria, It. 65/D4
Villa Sarmiento, Arg. 190/D2
Villa Serrano, Bol. 188/C1
Villa Talavera, Bol. 188/C1
Villa Tunari, Bol. 188/C1
Villa Unión, Mex. 150/D3
Villa Unión, Mex. 176/C2
Villa Unión, Arg. 188/B4
Villa Unión, Mex. 174/D4
Villa Valeria, Arg. 190/D2
Villa Verucchio, It. 63/F6
Villa Viscarra, Bol. 188/C1
Villaba, Sp. 44/C5
Villaba, Phil. 88/D3
Villablino, Sp. 46/B1
Villacañas, Sp. 46/D3
Villacarrillo, Sp. 46/D3
Villada, Sp. 46/C1
Villadiego, Sp. 46/C1
Villadose, It. 63/E3
Villadossola, It. 61/E5
Villafamés, Sp. 47/E2
Villafranca, Sp. 46/E1
Villafranca d'Asti, It. 62/B4
Villafranca de los Barros, Sp. 46/B3
Villafranca del Bierzo, Sp. 46/B1
Villafranca del Cid, Sp. 47/E2
Villafranca di Verona, It. 63/D3
Villafranca in Lunigiana, It. 62/C5
Villafranca Piemonte, It. 64/D3
Villagarcía, Sp. 46/A1
Village, Ar, US 153/H4
Village (cr.), Tx, US 150/K7
Village (cr.), Ar, US 162/B2
Village Mills, Tx, US 151/G2
Villagrán, Mex. 175/F3
Villaguay, Arg. 188/E4
Villahermosa, Mex. 176/C2
Villahermosa, Sp. 46/D3
Villahermosa, Col. 183/K8
Villaines-la-Juhel, Fr. 57/E4
Villajoyosa, Sp. 47/E3
Villalba, Sp. 46/B1
Villalcampo (res.), Sp. 46/B2
Villaldama, Mex. 150/D4
Villalón de Campos, Sp. 46/C1
Villalonga, Arg. 190/E3
Villalpando, Sp. 46/C2
Villamartín, Sp. 46/C4
Villandro (peak), It. 61/H4
Villanova, It. 63/F5
Villanova, It. 63/E5
Villanova d'Asti, It. 62/A3
Villanova Mondovì, It. 62/A4
Villanterio, It. 62/C3
Villanueva, Hon. 176/E3
Villanueva, Col. 180/C2
Villanueva, Mex. 174/E4
Villanueva de Arosa, Sp. 46/A1
Villanueva de Córdoba, Sp. 46/C3
Villanueva de la Serena, Sp. 46/C3
Villanueva de los Infantes, Sp. 46/D3
Villanueva de Oscos, Sp. 46/B1
Villanueva del Arzobispo, Sp. 46/D3
Villanuova sul Clisi, It. 62/D2
Villány, Hun. 50/D3
Villar, Bol. 188/C1
Villar del Arzobispo, Sp. 47/E3
Villar Perosa, It. 64/D3
Villar-Saint-Pancrace, Fr. 64/C3
Villarcayo, Sp. 44/B5
Villard, Mn, US 157/G5
Villard-Bonnot, Fr. 64/B2
Villard-de-Lans, Fr. 64/B2
Villardevós, Sp. 46/B2
Villaret (cape), Austl. 128/A4
Villarreal de los Infantes, Sp. 47/E3
Villarrica (lake), Chile 190/B3
Villarrica, Chile 190/B3
Villarrica (vol.), Chile 190/C3
Villarrica, Par. 189/E3
Villarrica, PN, Chile 190/C3
Villarrobledo, Sp. 46/D3
Villarrubia de los Ojos, Sp. 46/D3
Villars-les-Dombes, Fr. 60/B6
Villars-sur-Glâne, Swi. 60/D4
Villars-sur-Var, Fr. 64/D5
Villas, NJ, US 168/D5
Villasana de Mena, Sp. 44/B5
Villasanta, It. 62/C2
Villastellone, It. 62/A3
Villaverde (nbrhd.), Sp. 47/N9
Villaverde del Río, Sp. 46/C4
Villaverla, It. 63/E2
Villavicencio, Col. 180/C3
Villaviciosa, Sp. 46/C1
Villaviciosa de Odón, Sp. 47/N9
Villazón, Bol. 188/C2
Ville Platte, La, US 164/B2
Villebarou, Fr. 57/G5
Villecresnes, Fr. 30/K5
Villedieu-les-Poêles, Fr. 56/D3
Villefermoy (pond), Fr. 30/L6
Villefontaine, Fr. 64/B1
Villefranche-de-Rouergue, Fr. 44/E4
Villefranche-sur-Cher, Fr. 57/G6
Villefranche-sur-Mer, Fr. 64/D5
Villejuif, Fr. 30/K5
Villelaure, Fr. 64/B5
Villemur-sur-Tarn, Fr. 44/D5
Villena, Sp. 47/E3
Villeneuve, Swi. 60/C5
Villeneuve-D'Ascq, Fr. 54/C2
Villeneuve-le-Comte, Fr. 30/L5
Villeneuve-le-Roi, Fr. 30/K5
Villeneuve-lès-Avignon, Fr. 64/A5
Villeneuve-Loubet, Fr. 64/D5
Villeneuve-Saint-Denis, Fr. 30/L5
Villeneuve-Saint-Georges, Fr. 30/K5
Villeneuve-Saint-Germain, Fr. 54/C5
Villeneuve-sur-Lot, Fr. 44/D4
Villeneuve-sur-Yonne, Fr. 44/E2
Villeneuve-Tolosane, Fr. 44/D5
Villennes-sur-Seine, Fr. 30/H5
Villeparisis, Fr. 30/K5
Villepinte, Fr. 30/K5
Villepreux, Fr. 30/J5
Villeroy, Fr. 30/L4
Villers-Bocage, Fr. 57/E2
Villers-Bretonneux, Fr. 54/B4
Villers-Cotterêts, Fr. 54/C5
Villers-en-Arthies, Fr. 30/H4
Villers-le-Bouillet, Belg. 55/E2
Villers-le-Lac, Fr. 60/C3
Villers-lès-Nancy, Fr. 55/F6
Villers-Saint-Genest, Fr. 30/L4
Villers-Saint-Paul, Fr. 54/B5
Villers-Semeuse, Fr. 55/D4
Villers-sur-Mer, Fr. 57/E2
Villersexel, Fr. 60/C2
Villerupt, Fr. 55/E5
Villeta, Col. 183/L7
Villette, Fr. 30/H5
Villeurbanne, Fr. 60/A6
Villevaudé, Fr. 30/K5
Villiers, SAfr. 124/E2
Villiers-en-Lieu, Fr. 55/D6
Villiers-le-Bel, Fr. 30/K4
Villiers-Saint-Georges, Fr. 54/C6
Villiers-sur-Marne, Fr. 30/K5
Villiers-sur-Morin, Fr. 30/L5
Villiersdorp, SAfr. 124/L10
Villieu-Loyes-Mollon, Fr. 60/B6
Villingen-Schwenningen, Ger. 61/E1
Villisca, Ia, US 155/G3
Villmar, Ger. 58/B2
Villongo, It. 62/C2
Villorba, It. 63/F2
Villupuram, India 95/C4
Vilnius (int'l arpt.), Lith. 41/L4
Vilnius (cap.), Lith. 41/L4
Vilonia, Ar, US 153/H3
Vils, Aus. 61/G2
Vils (riv.), Ger. 42/F4
Vilsbiburg, Ger. 59/F6
Vilseck, Ger. 59/E3
Vil'shanka, Ukr. 72/F3
Vilshofen, Ger. 59/G5
Vilters, Swi. 61/F3
Vilvoorde, Belg. 55/D2
Vilyuy (riv.), Rus. 77/L3
Vilyuy (range), Rus. 75/M3
Vilyuysk, Rus. 75/N3
Vimercate, It. 62/C2
Vimeu (reg.), Fr. 54/A3
Vimioso, Port. 46/B2
Vimmerby, Swe. 40/F3
Vimodrone, It. 62/C3
Vimoutiers, Fr. 57/F3
Vimperk, Czh. 59/G4
Vina (riv.), Camr. 116/B4
Viña del Mar, Chile 190/N8
Vinadio, It. 64/D4
Vinaigre (peak), Fr. 64/C6
Vinanivao, Madg. 125/J6
Vinaroz, Sp. 47/F2
Vinay, Fr. 64/B2
Vincennes (lake), Fr. 30/L5
Vincennes, Fr. 30/K5
Vincennes (bay), Ant. 192/H
Vincennes, In, US 162/D1
Vincent, Ca, US 166/B1
Vincent, Al, US 162/D4
Vincent, Tx, US 150/D1
Vincentown, NJ, US 168/D4
Vinces, Ecu. 180/B5
Vincey, Fr. 60/C1
Vinchiaturo, It. 65/D5
Vinchina, Arg. 188/B4
Vinchina (riv.), Arg. 188/B4
Vinchos, Peru 184/C4
Vinci, It. 63/D6
Vindeby, Den. 40/D4
Vindeln, Swe. 38/F2
Vindhya (range), India 96/A4
Vine Grove, Ky, US 162/E2
Vineland, Mn, US 157/H4
Vineland, On, Can. 160/U9
Vineland, NJ, US 168/C5
Vineland Station, On, Can. 160/U9
Vineta, Namb. 122/B4
Vineuil, Fr. 57/G5
Vingåker, Swe. 40/F2
Vingerklip, Namb. 122/B4
Vinh, Viet. 94/D2
Vinh Long, Viet. 94/D4
Vinh Quoi, Viet. 94/D4
Vinh Thanh, Viet. 94/E3
Vinh Yen, Viet. 94/D1
Vinhais, Port. 46/B2
Vinhedo, Braz. 187/K8
Vinica, FYROM 49/H2
Vinings, Ga, US 163/M7
Vinita, Ok, US 153/G2
Vînju Mare, Rom. 50/F3
Vinkeveen, Neth. 52/B4
Vinkovci, Cro. 50/D3
Vinningen, Ger. 55/G5
Vinnyts'ka Oblast, Ukr. 70/D2
Vinnyts'ka (prov.), Bul. 51/J1
Vinnytsya, Ukr. 72/E3
Vinon-sur-Verdon, Fr. 64/B5
Vinovo, It. 64/D3
Vinslöv, Swe. 39/K6
Vinson Massif (peak), Ant. 192/U
Vinsulla, BC, Can. 144/D2
Vintar, Phil. 88/C1
Vinton, Ia, US 155/H2
Viny, Rus. 41/Q2
Viola, Ar, US 153/J2
Viola, NY, US 169/J7
Viola, Il, US 155/J3
Viola, De, US 168/C5
Violet Grove, Ab, Can. 144/G1
Violet Town, Austl. 133/B3
Violet Valley Abor. Land, Austl. 128/B4
Viosne (riv.), Fr. 54/A5
Viotá, Col. 183/L8
Vipiteno (Sterzing), It. 61/H4
Virac, Phil. 88/D2
Viracopos (int'l arpt.), Braz. 189/H2
Viranşehir, Turk. 102/D2
Virār, India 95/B2
Virbalis, Lith. 41/K4
Virden, Mb, Can. 156/D3
Virden, NM, US 149/H4
Virden, Il, US 155/K4
Vire, Fr. 57/E3
Vire (riv.), Fr. 44/C2
Virei, Ang. 122/B2
Viren (lake), Swe. 40/F2
Vireux-Wallerand, Fr. 55/D3
Virgelle, Mt, US 145/J3
Virgil, On, Can. 160/U9
Virgin (isls.), UK,US 173/M8
Virgin (riv.), Az, Ut, US 149/F2
Virgin Gorda (isl.), UK 173/M8
Virgin Gourda (int'l arpt.), UK 173/M8
Virgin Islands NP, USVI 173/M8
Virginia, Mn, US 157/H4
Virginia, Ire. 32/C2
Virginia (state), US 163/H2
Virginia, Il, US 155/J4
Virginia, SAfr. 124/D3
Virginia Beach, Va, US 163/K2
Virginia City, Mt, US 147/H1
Virginia City, Nv, US 146/D4
Virginia Dale, Co, US 154/B3
Virginia Water, Eng, UK 30/B2
Virgolândia, Braz. 187/E3
Viriat, Fr. 60/B5
Virieu-le-Grand, Fr. 60/B6
Virkkala, Fin. 39/E4
Virochey, Camb. 94/D3
Viroflay, Fr. 30/J5
Viroin (riv.), Belg. 55/D3
Viroqua, Wi, US 155/J2
Virovitica, Cro. 50/C3
Virserum, Swe. 40/F3
Virton, Belg. 55/E4
Virtsu, Est. 41/K2
Virú, Peru 184/B3
Viru Viru (int'l arpt.), Bol. 188/D1
Viru-Jaagupi, Est. 41/M2
Virudunagar, India 95/C4
Virunga, D.R. Congo 121/G3
Virunga, PN des, D.R. Congo 121/G3
Viry-Châtillon, Fr. 30/K6
Vis (isl.), Cro. 67/H2
Vis, Cro. 50/C4
Visaginas, Lith. 41/M4
Visalia, Ca, US 148/C2
Visan, Fr. 64/A4
Visandre (riv.), Fr. 30/M5
Visayan (sea), Phil. 91/F1
Visbek, Ger. 53/F3
Visby, Swe. 40/H3
Visciano, It. 65/D6
Visconde do Rio Branco, Braz. 187/E4
Viscount Melville (sound), NW,Nun, Can. 141/R7
Visé, Belg. 55/E2
Višegrad, Bosn. 50/D4
Viseu, Port. 46/B2
Viseu (dist.), Port. 46/B2
Viseu, Braz. 183/E3
Vişeu de Sus, Rom. 72/C4
Vishera (riv.), Rus. 69/L3
Vishnëvoye, Ukr. 72/F2
Vishoek, SAfr. 124/L11
Visinesti, Mol. 72/E4
Viskafors, Swe. 40/E3
Vislanda, Swe. 40/F3
Visnagar, India 101/K4
Višnjevac, Cro. 50/D3
Viso (peak), It. 64/D3
Visoko, Bosn. 50/D4
Visp, Swi. 60/D5
Visperterminen, Swi. 60/D5
Visselhövede, Ger. 53/G3
Vissenbjerg, Den. 40/D4
Vissoie, Swi. 60/D5
Vista, Ca, US 166/C4
Vistonís (lake), Gre. 49/J2
Vistula (riv.), Pol. 29/H3
Visviri, Chile 184/D5
Vit (riv.), Bul. 49/J1
Vita, Mb, Can. 156/F3
Viterbo (prov.), It. 65/B3
Viterbo, It. 65/B3
Vitez, Bosn. 50/C3
Viti Levu (isl.), Fiji 136/G6
Vitiaz (str.), PNG 129/G1
Vitichi, Bol. 188/C2
Vitigudino, Sp. 46/B2
Vitim (plat.), Rus. 75/M4
Vitim (riv.), Rus. 77/L4
Vitim, Rus. 75/M4
Vitimskiy, Rus. 75/M4
Vitinia, It. 65/B4
Vítkuv Kamen (peak), Czh. 59/H5
Vitomirica, Serb. 50/E4
Vitor, Peru 184/D5
Vitoria, Sp. 44/B5
Vitória, Braz. 187/E4
Vitoría, Braz. 182/C3
Vitória da Conquista, Braz. 187/E2
Vitória de Santo Antão, Braz. 183/H5
Vitória do Mearim, Braz. 183/E3
Vitorino Freire, Braz. 183/E4
Vitosha NP, Bul. 51/F4
Vitré, Fr. 56/D4
Vitrey-sur-Mance, Fr. 60/B2
Vitrolles, Fr. 64/B6
Vitry-en-Artois, Fr. 54/B3
Vitry-le-François, Fr. 55/D6
Vitry-sur-Seine, Fr. 30/K5
Vitshumbi, D.R. Congo 121/G3
Vitsyebsk, Bela. 41/P4
Vitsyebskaya Voblasts, Bela. 68/E5
Vittangi, Swe. 38/G2
Vittel, Fr. 60/B1
Vittoria, It. 48/D4
Vittorio Veneto, It. 45/K4
Vitträsk (lake), Fin. 39/E4
Vittsjö, Swe. 39/K6
Vitulano, It. 65/D5
Vitulazio, It. 65/D5
Viu, It. 64/D2
Vivarais (mts.), Fr. 44/F4
Viveiro, Sp. 46/B1
Viverone (lake), It. 62/B2
Viverone, It. 62/B3
Vivian, La, US 153/H4
Viviers, Fr. 64/A4
Vivonne, Fr. 44/D3
Vizcachilla, Bol. 188/C2
Vizcaya Museum, Fl, US 164/P11
Vize, Turk. 51/H5
Vizhas (riv.), Rus. 69/K2
Vizhas, Rus. 69/K2
Vizianagaram, India 95/D2
Vizille, Fr. 64/B2
Vizinga, Rus. 69/L3
Viziru, Rom. 51/H3
Vlaardingen, Neth. 52/B5
Vlădeasa (peak), Rom. 51/F2
Vladikavkaz, Rus. 71/H4
Vladimirskaya Oblast, Rus. 68/J5
Vladimir, Rus. 68/J4
Vladivostok, Rus. 79/L3
Vlagtwedde, Neth. 53/E2
Vlăhiţa, Rom. 51/G2
Vlajna (peak), Serb. 50/E4
Vlasenica, Bosn. 50/D3
Vlasotince, Serb. 50/F4
Vleuten, Neth. 52/C4
Vlieland (isl.), Neth. 42/C2
Vliestroom (chan.), Neth. 52/C2
Vlijmen, Neth. 52/C5
Vlissingen, Neth. 52/A6
Vlorë, Alb. 49/F2
Vlotho, Ger. 53/F4
Vltava (riv.), Czh. 43/H4
Vnukovo (int'l arpt.), Rus. 69/W9
Vobarno, It. 62/D2
Voca, Tx, US 150/E2
Vöcklabruck, Aus. 59/G6
Vöcklamarkt, Aus. 59/G6
Vodice, Cro. 45/L4
Vodlozero (lake), Rus. 68/H3
Vodňany, Czh. 59/H4
Vodskov, Den. 40/D3
Voerde, Ger. 52/D5
Vogan, Togo 115/F5
Vogar, Mb, Can. 156/E2
Vogelsberg (mts.), Ger. 45/H1
Voghera, It. 62/C4
Vogogna, It. 61/E6
Vogorno (lake), Swi. 61/E5
Vogtareuth, Ger. 59/F7
Vogtland (reg.), Ger. 42/F3
Voh, NCal. 137/U12
Vohburg an der Donau, Ger. 59/E5
Vohenstrauss, Ger. 59/F3
Vohilava, Madg. 125/J8
Vohilava, Madg. 125/H8
Vohimena (cape), Madg. 125/H9
Vohimena, Madg. 125/J7
Vohipeno, Madg. 125/H8
Vohiposa, Madg. 125/H8
Vohitrambo, Madg. 125/H8
Võhma, Est. 41/L2
Voi, Kenya 119/B2
Void-Vacon, Fr. 55/E6
Voight (cr.), Wa, US 167/C3
Voil (lake), Sc, UK 33/B4
Voinjama, Libr. 114/C4
Voinsles, Fr. 30/M5
Voiron, Fr. 64/B2
Voise (riv.), Fr. 44/D2
Voisey (bay), Nf, Can. 141/K3
Voiteur, Fr. 60/B4
Vojakkala, Fin. 39/E4
Vojosë (riv.), Alb. 50/D5
Vojvodina (prov.), Serb. 50/D3
Voka, Congo 120/C4
Vokhma, Rus. 69/K4
Völklingen, Ger. 55/F5
Volano, It. 61/H6
Volary, Czh. 59/G5
Volborg, Mt, US 145/M5
Volcán Barú, PN, Pan. 177/F4
Volcán Poás, PN, CR 177/E4
Volcano (isls.), Japan 136/C2
Volcans, PN des, Rwa. 121/G3
Volchiy Nos (cape), Rus. 41/Q1
Volda, Nor. 38/C3
Volendam, Neth. 52/C3
Volga, SD, US 155/F1
Volga (riv.), Rus. 29/J3
Volga-Baltic Waterway (canal), Rus. 68/H3
Volgelsheim, Fr. 60/D1
Volgodonsk, Rus. 73/M4
Volgograd (res.), Rus. 71/H2
Volgograd, Rus. 71/H2
Volgograd (int'l arpt.), Rus. 71/H2
Volgogradskaya Oblast, Rus. 71/G2
Volimbos, Gre. 67/K4
Volkach, Ger. 58/D3
Volkach (riv.), Ger. 58/D3
Volkeradam (dam), Neth. 52/B5
Völkermarkt, Aus. 45/L3
Volketswil, Swi. 61/E3
Volkhov (riv.), Rus. 68/F4
Volkhov, Rus. 41/Q2
Volkmarsen, Ger. 53/G6
Volksrust, SAfr. 125/E2
Vollenhove, Neth. 52/C3
Volnovakha, Ukr. 73/J4
Volochanka, Rus. 74/K2
Volochayevka, Rus. 79/L2
Volochys'k, Ukr. 72/D3
Volodars'ke, Ukr. 73/J4
Volodarsky (nbrhd.), Rus. 69/T7
Volodymyr-Volyns'kyy, Ukr. 72/C2
Vologda, Rus. 68/H4
Vologodskaya Oblast, Rus. 68/J3
Vologne (riv.), Fr. 42/D4
Volokolamsk, Rus. 68/G4
Volokonovka, Rus. 73/J2
Volonne, Fr. 64/C4
Vólos, Gre. 49/H3
Volos (gulf), Gre. 49/H3
Volosovo, Rus. 41/N2
Volot, Rus. 41/P3
Volovets', Ukr. 43/M4
Volovo, Rus. 70/F1
Volozhin, Bela. 41/M4
Volpago del Montello, It. 63/F2
Volpiano, It. 62/A2
Völs, Aus. 61/H3
Vols, Fin. 39/E4
Vol'sk, Rus. 71/H1
Volta (pol. reg.), Gha. 115/F5
Volta (riv.), Gha. 115/F5
Volta (lake), Gha. 107/B4
Volta Mantovana, It. 62/D3
Volta Redonda, Braz. 187/M7
Voltaire (cape), Austl. 128/B3
Voltana, It. 63/E4
Volterra, It. 63/D7
Voltlage, Ger. 53/E4
Voltri, It. 62/B5
Volturara Irpina, It. 65/D6
Volturino (peak), It. 48/D2
Volturno (riv.), It. 48/D2
Volubilis (ruin), Mor. 112/B2
Volvera, It. 64/D3
Vólvi (lake), Gre. 49/H2
Vólvi (lake), Serb. 51/F5
Volx, Fr. 64/B5
Volyně, Czh. 59/G4
Volyňka (riv.), Czh. 59/G4
Volyno-Podol'sk Upland (upland), Ukr. 72/D3
Volyns'ka Oblast, Ukr. 70/C2
Volzhsk, Rus. 69/L5
Volzhskiy, Rus. 71/H2
Vom, Nga. 115/H4
Vomano (riv.), It. 65/C2
Vombsjön (lake), Swe. 39/K7
Vonda, Sk, Can. 145/L1
Vondrozo, Madg. 125/H8
Vonêche, Belg. 55/D3
Von Frank (mt.), Ak, US 171/H3
Vónitsa, Gre. 49/G3
Vonne (riv.), Fr. 44/D3
Võnnu, Est. 41/M2
Voorburg, Neth. 52/B4
Voorne (isl.), Neth. 52/B5
Voorschoten, Neth. 52/B4
Voorst, Neth. 52/D4
Vopnafjördhur, Ice. 38/P6
Vorab (peak), Swi. 61/F4
Vorarlberg (prov.), Aus. 42/E5
Vorbach (riv.), Ger. 58/C4
Vorchdorf, Aus. 59/G6
Vorden, Neth. 52/D4
Vorderrhein (riv.), Swi. 45/H3
Vorderweissenbach, Aus. 59/H5
Vordingborg, Den. 40/D4
Vorë, Alb. 49/F2
Voreppe, Fr. 64/B2
Vorkuta, Rus. 69/P2
Vorkuta (int'l arpt.), Rus. 69/Q2
Vormsi (isl.), Est. 41/K2
Vóroi, Gre. 49/J5
Vorokhta, Ukr. 72/C3
Vorona (riv.), Rus. 71/G1
Voronezh (riv.), Rus. 70/F1
Voronezh, Rus. 73/K2
Voronezh (int'l arpt.), Rus. 73/K2
Voronezhskaya Oblast, Rus. 71/G2
Voronovo, Bela. 41/L4
Voronovytsya, Ukr. 72/E3
Vorontsovka, Rus. 73/L2
Voron'ya (riv.), Rus. 68/G1
Voropayevo, Bela. 41/M4
Vorozhba, Ukr. 73/H2
Vorskla (riv.), Ukr. 70/E2
Vorst, Belg. 55/E1
Vorstershoop, SAfr. 124/C2
Võrts (lake), Est. 68/E4
Võru, Est. 41/M3
Vorya (riv.), Rus. 69/X8
Vorzel', Ukr. 72/F2
Vosburg, SAfr. 124/C3
Vösendorf, Aus. 51/N7
Vosges (dept.), Fr. 60/C1
Vosges (mts.), Fr. 42/D5
Voskresenka, Rus. 71/H2
Voskresensk, Rus. 68/H5
Voskresenskoye, Rus. 69/K4
Voskresenskoye, Rus. 68/H4
Voss, Nor. 40/B1
Vossburg, Ms, US 164/D2
Vostochnyy, Rus. 79/L3
Vostok (cape), Ant. 192/V
Vostok, Rus., Ant. 192/H
Vostok (isl.), Kiri. 137/K6
Votice, Czh. 59/H3
Votkinsk (res.), Rus. 69/M4
Votkinsk, Rus. 69/M4
Votorantim, Braz. 189/H2
Votuporanga, Braz. 189/G2
Vouga (riv.), Port. 46/A2
Vougba, CAfr. 116/D4
Vouglans (lake), Fr. 60/B5
Voujeaucourt, Fr. 60/C3
Voúla, Gre. 49/N9
Voulangis, Fr. 30/L5
Voutinainen, Fin. 39/E4
Vouvray, Fr. 57/F6
Vouvry, Swi. 60/C5
Voúxa (cape), Gre. 49/H5
Vouziers, Fr. 55/D5
Vouzon, Fr. 57/H5
Vovchans'k, Ukr. 73/J2
Voves, Fr. 57/G4
Vovodo (riv.), CAfr. 117/E4
Voy-Vozh, Rus. 69/M3
Voyageurs NP, Mn, US 157/H3
Voyeykov Ice Shelf, Ant. 192/J
Voytolovka (riv.), Rus. 69/T7
Vozhe (lake), Rus. 68/H3
Vozhega, Rus. 68/J3
Vozherovo, Rus. 69/K4
Voznesens'k, Ukr. 72/F4
Vrå, Den. 40/C3
Vradiyivka, Ukr. 72/F4
Vraine (riv.), Fr. 60/B1
Vramsån (riv.), Swe. 39/K6
Vrancea (prov.), Rom. 51/H3
Vrangelya (isl.), Rus. 77/T2
Vranje, Serb. 50/E4
Vranjska Banja, Serb. 50/E4
Vranov nad Teplou, Slvk. 43/L4
Vrapčište, FYROM 49/G2
Vratsa, Bul. 51/F4
Vrbas (riv.), Bosn. 67/H1
Vrbas, Serb. 50/D3
Vrchy (peak), Czh. 59/H4
Vrede, SAfr. 124/E2
Vredefort, SAfr. 124/D2
Vreden, Ger. 52/D4
Vredenburg-Saldanha, SAfr. 124/K10
Vredendal, SAfr. 124/B3
Vresse-sur-Semois, Belg. 55/D4
Vrhnika, Slov. 45/L4
Vriddhāchalam, India 95/C4
Vries, Neth. 52/D2
Vriezenveen, Neth. 52/D4
Vrigstad, Swe. 40/F3
Vrin (riv.), Fr. 42/B5
Vrindāban, India 96/A2
Vrnjačka Banja, Serb. 50/E4
Vrondádhos, Gre. 49/K3
Vroomshoop, Neth. 52/D4
Vršac, Serb. 50/E3
Vryburg, SAfr. 124/D2
Vryheid, SAfr. 125/E2
Vsetín, Czh. 43/K4
Vsevidof (mt.), Ak, US 171/E5
Vsevolozhsk, Rus. 69/T6
Vtáčnik (peak), Slvk. 43/K4
Vu Liet, Viet. 94/D2
Vuca, Eth. 117/G4
Vučitrn, Serb. 50/E4
Vught, Neth. 52/C5
Vukovar, Cro. 50/D3
Vulcan, Ab, Can. 145/H2
Vulcan, Rom. 51/F3
Vulcan, Mo, US 153/J2
Vulcăneşti, Mol. 51/J3
Vulcano (isl.), It. 48/D3
Vŭlchedrŭm, Bul. 51/F4
Vŭlchi Dol, Bul. 51/H4
Vulci (ruin), It. 48/B1
Vung Tau, Viet. 94/D4
Vunisea, Fiji 136/G6
Vuntut NP, Yk., Can. 171/K2
Vuoggatjålme, Swe. 38/F2
Vuohijärvi (lake), Fin. 41/M1
Vuollerim, Swe. 38/G2
Vuoska (lake), Rus. 41/N1
Vuotso, Fin. 68/E1
Vŭrbitsa, Bul. 51/H4
Vuria (peak), Kenya 119/B2
Vurnary, Rus. 69/K5
Vŭrshets, Bul. 51/F4
Vuruena, Res. Florestal do, Braz. 186/A1
Vuyyūru, India 95/D2
Vvedenka, Kaz. 69/P5
Vwawa, Tanz. 121/H5
Vyāra, India 92/B3
Vyatka (riv.), Rus. 74/E4
Vyatskiye Polyany, Rus. 69/L4
Vyatskoye, Rus. 68/J4
Vyazemskiy, Rus. 79/L2

Map Section
282
283

Weilhe – Willin

Map Section 284 285

Weilheim an der Teck, Ger. 58/C5
Weilmünster, Ger. 58/B2
Weimar, Ger. 42/F3
Weimar, Tx, US 150/F3
Weinan, China 80/B4
Weiner, Ar, US 162/B3
Weinfelden, Swi. 61/F2
Weingarten, Ger. 61/F2
Weingarten, Ger. 58/B4
Weinheim, Ger. 58/B3
Weinsberg, Ger. 58/C4
Weinstadt, Ger. 58/C5
Weinviertel (reg.), Aus. 45/M2
Weipa, Austl. 129/F3
Weipa Abor. Rsv., Austl. 129/F3
Weipa South, Austl. 129/F3
Weir, Ks, US 153/G2
Weir, Tx, US 151/F2
Weirsdale, Fl, US 165/H3
Weirton, WV, US 160/F4
Weischlitz, Ger. 59/F2
Weisendorf, Ger. 58/D3
Weisenheim am Berg, Ger. 58/B3
Weiser, Id, US 146/E1
Weiser (riv.), Id, US 146/E1
Weishan, China 80/D4
Weishan (lake), China 79/H5
Weishi, China 80/C4
Weiskirchen, Ger. 55/F4
Weismain, Ger. 58/E2
Weiss (dam), Al, US 162/E3
Weiss (lake), Al, US 162/E3
Weissach, Ger. 58/B5
Weisse Elster (riv.), Ger. 42/G3
Weisse Laber (riv.), Ger. 59/E4
Weissenbach am Lech, Aus. 61/G3
Weissenburg im Bayern, Ger. 58/D4
Weissenfels, Ger. 42/F3
Weissenhorn, Ger. 61/G1
Weissensee, Ger. 42/Q6
Weissenstadt, Ger. 59/E2
Weissenthurm, Ger. 55/G3
Weisser (peak), Ger. 55/F3
Weisser Main (riv.), Ger. 59/E2
Weisshorn (peak), Swi. 60/D5
Weissmies (peak), Swi. 60/D5
Weisswasser, Ger. 43/H3
Weistrach, Aus. 59/H6
Weitefeld, Ger. 55/G2
Weiterstadt, Ger. 58/B3
Weitian, China 87/H3
Weitra, Aus. 43/H4
Weixi, China 93/G2
Weiyuan, China 78/E4
Weiyuan (riv.), China 86/D4
Weiz, Aus. 50/B2
Weizhou (isl.), China 93/J3
Weizhou (isl.), Viet. 87/F4
Weiziyu, China 81/C2
Wejherowo, Pol. 40/H4
Wekame, Myan. 94/B3
Wekiva (riv.), Fl, US 164/N6
Welātām, Myan. 93/G2
Welbekend, SAfr. 124/E2
Welch, Ok, US 153/G2
Welch, WV, US 163/G2
Welch (hill), Pa, US 168/A3
Welcome, NC, US 163/G3
Welda, Ks, US 153/G1
Welden, Ger. 58/D6
Weldiya, Eth. 118/A3
Weldon, Tx, US 151/G2
Weldon (riv.), Ia, Mo, US 155/H3
Weldon, Eng, UK 37/F2
Weleetka, Ok, US 153/F3
Welega (pol. reg.), Eth. 117/G3
Welel (peak), Eth. 117/G3
Welford, Austl. 134/A4
Welford, Eng, UK 37/F4
Welham Green, Eng, UK 30/C1
Welkenraedt, Belg. 55/E2
Welk'īt'ē, Eth. 117/H3
Welkom, SAfr. 124/D3
Welland (riv.), Eng, UK 35/H6
Welland (canal), On, US 160/U10
Welland, On, Can. 160/U10
Wellandport, On, Can. 160/U9
Wellborn, Fl, US 165/G2
Wellen, Belg. 55/E2
Wellesley (isls.), Austl. 129/E4
Wellford, SC, US 163/F3
Wellin, Belg. 55/E3
Wellingborough, Eng, UK 37/F2
Wellington, Austl. 133/D1
Wellington (lake), Austl. 132/C3
Wellington, On, Can. 161/H3
Wellington (isl.), Chile 179/B7
Wellington (chan.), Nun, Can. 141/S7
Wellington, SAfr. 124/L10
Wellington (int'l arpt.), NZ 135/H9
Wellington (cap.), NZ 135/H9
Wellington, Ks, US 153/F2
Wellington, Tx, US 152/D3
Wellington, Nv, US 146/D4
Wellington, Co, US 154/B3
Wellington, Eng, UK 36/D2
Wellington, Eng, UK 36/C5
Wellington (co.), On, Can. 160/S8
Wellman, Tx, US 152/C4
Wellman, Ia, US 155/J3
Wells (lake), Austl. 127/B3
Wells, BC, Can. 144/D1
Wells, Eng, UK 36/D4
Wells, Tx, US 150/G2
Wells, NY, US 161/J3
Wells, Me, US 161/L3
Wells, Nv, US 147/F3
Wells, Mn, US 155/H2
Wells-next-the-Sea, Eng, UK 37/G1
Wellsboro, Pa, US 161/H4
Wellsburg, WV, US 160/F4
Wellsford, NZ 135/C2
Wellston, Ok, US 153/F3
Wellston, Mi, US 160/D2
Wellston, Oh, US 163/F1
Wellsville, Ks, US 153/G1
Wellsville, NY, US 161/H3
Wellsville, Ut, US 147/H3
Wellsville, Mo, US 155/J4
Wellsville, Pa, US 168/B3
Wellwood, Mb, Can. 156/E2
Welo (prov.), Eth. 118/A3
Wels, Aus. 59/H6
Welschbillig, Ger. 55/F4
Welsh, La, US 164/B2
Welshnofen (Nova Levante), It. 61/H5
Welshpool, Wal, UK 36/C1
Welty, Ok, US 153/F3
Welver, Ger. 53/E5
Welwel, Eth. 118/C4
Welwyn, Sk, Can. 156/D2
Welzheim, Ger. 58/C5
Wem, Eng, UK 35/F6
Wembere (riv.), Tanz. 119/A3
Wembley Stadium, Eng, UK 30/C2
Wemding, Ger. 58/D5
Wemindji, Qu, Can. 141/J3
Wemmel, Belg. 55/D2
Wemyss Bay, Sc, UK 33/B5
Wen Xian, China 80/C4
Wenago, Eth. 118/A4
Wen'an, China 80/H7
Wenatchee, Wa, US 144/D4
Wenatchee (mts.), Wa, US 144/D4
Wenchang, China 87/F5
Wencheng, China 87/J3
Wenchi, Gha. 115/E5
Wendeburg, Ger. 53/H4
Wendell, Mn, US 156/F4
Wenden, Ger. 55/G2
Wenden, Az, US 149/F4
Wendeng, China 81/B4
Wendi, China 87/F4
Wendji, D.R. Congo 120/D3
Wendlingen am Neckar, Ger. 58/C5
Wendo, Eth. 118/A4
Wendou Borou, Gui. 114/B4
Wendover, Nv, US 147/F3
Wendover, Eng, UK 37/F3
Wendron, Eng, UK 36/A6
Wendte, SD, US 154/D1
Wengdong, China 87/F3
Wengjiang, China 87/G2
Wengshui, China 93/G2
Wengyang, China 87/J2
Wengyuan, China 93/K3
Wenlock Edge (ridge), Eng, UK 36/D2
Wenne (riv.), Ger. 53/F6
Wenningsen, Ger. 53/G4
Wennington, Eng, UK 35/F3
Wenona, Il, US 155/K3
Wenonah, NJ, US 168/C4
Wenquan, China 87/E2
Wenquan, China 86/D2
Wenquan, China 99/F5
Wenquanzhen, China 87/G3
Wenshan, China 93/H3
Wenshang, China 80/D4
Wenshui, China 80/C3
Wensleydale (valley), Eng, UK 35/F3
Went (riv.), Eng, UK 35/G4
Wentang, China 87/G2
Wentworth, Austl. 132/B2
Wentworth, NC, US 163/H2
Wenxi, China 80/B4
Wenzhou, China 87/J3
Weohyakapka (lake), Fl, US 164/N8
Weott, Ca, US 146/B3
Wepener, SAfr. 124/D3
Wépion, Belg. 55/D3
Wer, India 96/A2
Werda, Bots. 122/D5
Werdēr, Eth. 118/C4
Werder, Ger. 42/P7
Werdohl, Ger. 53/E6
Were Īlu, Eth. 118/A3
Werinama, Indo. 91/G4
Werkendam, Neth. 52/B5
Werl, Ger. 53/E5
Werlte, Ger. 53/E3
Wermelskirchen, Ger. 55/G1
Wern (riv.), Ger. 58/C3
Wernau, Ger. 58/C5
Wernberg-Köblitz, Ger. 59/F3
Werne an der Lippe, Ger. 53/E5
Werneck, Ger. 58/D3
Werner Lake, On, Can. 157/G2
Werneuchen, Ger. 42/Q6
Wernigerode, Ger. 53/H5
Werong (mt.), Austl. 133/D2
Werra (riv.), Ger. 42/E3
Werre (riv.), Ger. 42/E2
Werrikimbe NP, Austl. 132/E1
Werrimull, Austl. 132/B2
Werrington, Eng, UK 35/F5
Werris Creek, Austl. 132/D1
Werse (riv.), Ger. 53/E5
Wertach (riv.), Ger. 58/D6
Wertheim, Ger. 58/C3
Wertheim Nat'l Wild. Ref., NY, US 169/F2
Werther, Ger. 53/F4
Werther, Ger. 53/H6
Wertingen, Ger. 58/D5
Wervershoof, Neth. 52/C3
Wervik, Belg. 54/C2
Weschnitz (riv.), Ger. 58/B3
Wesergebirge (mts.), Ger. 53/F4
Wesel, Ger. 52/D5
Wesel-Datteln (canal), Ger. 53/E5
Wesely E. Seale (dam), Tx, US 151/F3
Wesenberg, Ger. 42/G2
Weser (riv.), Ger. 42/E2
Weslaco, Tx, US 151/F4
Wesley, Ia, US 155/H2
Wesley Hills, NY, US 169/J7
Wessel (cape), Austl. 129/E2
Wessel (isls.), Austl. 127/C2
Wesselburen, Ger. 40/C4
Wesseling, Ger. 55/F2
Wesselsbron, SAfr. 124/D2
Wessex (reg.), Eng, UK 36/D4
Wessington, SD, US 154/E1
Wessington Springs, SD, US 154/E1
Wesson, Ar, US 153/H4
Wesson, Ms, US 164/C2
West (isl.), Austl. 129/E3
West (pt.), Austl. 132/C4
West (cape), NZ 135/A4
West (bay), La, US 164/D3
West, Tx, US 151/F2
West (pt.), Wa, US 167/C2
West Abor. Land, Austl. 129/E3
West Allis, Wi, US 160/B3
West Arichat, NS, Can. 159/G3
West Augusta, Ga, US 163/F4
West Augusta, Va, US 163/H1
West Babylon, NY, US 169/E2
West Bank 105/C4
West Baraboo, Wi, US 155/K2
West Barns, Sc, UK 33/D5
West Bay, NS, Can. 159/G3
West Bend, Sk, Can. 156/C2
West Bend, Wi, US 160/B3
West Bend, Ia, US 155/G2
West Bengal (state), India 92/E3
West Bergholt, Eng, UK 37/G3
West Berkshire (co.), Eng, UK 37/E4
West Bijou (cr.), Co, US 154/B4
West Blocton, Al, US 162/D4
West Branch, Mi, US 160/D2
West Branch Devers (canal), Tx, US 151/N9
West Brattleboro, Vt, US 161/K3
West Bridgford, Eng, UK 35/G6
West Bromwich, Eng, UK 36/E1
West Byfleet, Eng, UK 30/B3
West Caicos (isl.), UK 177/H3
West Calder, Sc, UK 33/C5
West Caldwell, NJ, US 169/H8
West Cap Howe NP, Austl. 130/C5
West Carthage, NY, US 161/J3
West Chester, Pa, US 168/C4
West Chicago, Il, US 167/P16
West Chyulu Game Consv. Area, Kenya 119/B2
West Clandon, Eng, UK 30/B3
West Coast NP, SAfr. 124/L10
West Columbia, Tx, US 150/G3
West Columbia, SC, US 163/G4
West Cornforth, Eng, UK 35/G2
West Covina, Ca, US 166/G7
West Creek, NJ, US 168/D4
West Crossett, Ar, US 153/J4
West Des Moines, Ia, US 155/H3
West Dover, NS, Can. 158/F3
West Dunbartonshire (co.), Sc, UK 33/B4
West Elk (mts.), Co, US 147/K4
West Elmira, NY, US 161/H3
West End, Eng, UK 30/B3
West Falkland (isl.), UK 191/E6
West Fargo, ND, US 156/F4
West Farleigh, Eng, UK 30/E4
West Fayu (isl.), Micr. 136/D4
West Flamborough, On, Can. 160/S9
West Fork, Ar, US 153/G3
West Frankfort, Il, US 162/C2
West Frisian (isls.), Neth. 42/C2
West Frostproof, Fl, US 164/M8
West Glamorgan (co.), Wal, UK 36/C3
West Glen (riv.), Eng, UK 35/H6
West Green, Ga, US 165/G2
West Grove, Pa, US 168/C4
West Ham (nbrhd.), Eng, UK 30/D2
West Hanningfield, Eng, UK 30/E2
West Haven, Ct, US 169/F1
West Haverstraw, NY, US 168/E1
West Hawk Lake, Mb, Can. 157/G3
West Helena, Ar, US 162/B3
West Hempstead, NY, US 169/L9
West Hills, NY, US 169/M8
West Hollywood, Ca, US 166/F7
West Horndon, Eng, UK 30/E2
West Horseley, Eng, UK 30/B3
West Ice Shelf, Ant. 192/F
West Indies (isls.), NAm. 139/L7
West Islet (isl.), Austl. 127/E3
West Islip, NY, US 169/E2
West Jefferson, NC, US 163/G2
West Jordan, Ut, US 147/H3
West Kennebago (mtn.), Me, US 161/L2
West Kilbride, Sc, UK 33/B5
West Kingsdown, Eng, UK 30/D3
West Kirby, Eng, UK 35/E5
West Knock (peak), Sc, UK 33/D3
West Lafayette, Oh, US 160/F4
West Lafayette, In, US 160/C4
West Lake Hills, Tx, US 151/F2
West Lamma (chan.), China 87/L8
West Lebanon, In, US 160/C4
West Liberty, Oh, US 160/E4
West Liberty, Ky, US 163/F2
West Liberty, Ia, US 155/J3
West Linn, Or, US 146/B1
West Lorne, On, Can. 160/F3
West Lothian (co.), Sc, UK 33/C5
West Lunga NP, Afr. 122/E2
West Malling, Eng, UK 30/E3
West Melbourne, Fl, US 165/H3
West Memphis, Ar, US 162/B3
West Mersea, Eng, UK 37/G3
West Miami, Fl, US 164/P11
West Midlands (co.), Eng, UK 37/E1
West Milford, NJ, US 169/H7
West Milford, WV, US 163/G1
West Milton, Pa, US 168/B1
West Monroe, La, US 153/H4
West Monroe, Mi, US 160/E4
West New Britain (prov.), PNG 129/H1
West New York, NJ, US 169/J8
West Nicholson, Zim. 123/F4
West Nishnabotna (riv.), Ia, US 155/G3
West Nodaway (riv.), Ia, US 155/G3
West Nueces (riv.), Tx, US 150/D3
West Nyack, NY, US 169/K7
West Olive, Mi, US 160/C3
West Orange, Tx, US 151/H2
West Orange, NJ, US 169/J8
West Palm Beach (canal), Fl, US 164/P9
West Palm Beach, Fl, US 164/P9
West Paterson, NJ, US 169/J8
West Pensacola, Fl, US 164/E2
West Plains, Mo, US 153/J2
West Plains (Plains), Ks, US 152/D2
West Point, Ca, US 146/C4
West Point, Il, US 155/J3
West Point, Ia, US 155/J3
West Point, Ga, US 162/E4
West Point (dam), Ga, US 162/E4
West Point, Ms, US 162/C4
West Point, Ne, US 155/F3
West Point (res.), Ga, US 162/E4
West Point Mil. Acad, NY, US 161/J4
West Poplar, Sk, Can. 145/L3
West Reading, Pa, US 168/C3
West Redding, Ct, US 169/E1
West Richland, Wa, US 144/E4
West Road (riv.), BC, Can. 144/B1
West Sacramento, Ca, US 167/L9
West Saint Paul, Mn, US 157/P7
West Salem, Il, US 162/C1
West Sayville, NY, US 169/E2
West Seneca, NY, US 160/V10
West Siberian (plain), Rus. 74/H3
West Sister Island Nat'l Wild. Ref., Oh, US 160/E4
West Sussex (co.), Eng, UK 37/F4
West Tawakoni, Tx, US 153/F4
West Thurrock, Eng, UK 30/D2
West Tisbury, Ma, US 158/B5
West Union, WV, US 160/F5
West Union, Il, US 160/C5
West Union, Ia, US 155/J2
West Union, Oh, US 163/F1
West Unity, Oh, US 160/D4
West University Place, Tx, US 151/M9
West Valley City, Ut, US 147/H3
West Vancouver, BC, Can. 144/C3
West Virginia (state), US 143/K4
West Walker (riv.), Ca,Nv, US 148/C1
West Warwick, RI, US 161/L4
West Water (riv.), Sc, UK 33/D3
West Winfield, NY, US 161/J3
West Wyalong, Austl. 133/C1
West Yellowstone, Mt, US 147/H1
West York, Pa, US 168/B4
West Yorkshire (co.), Eng, UK 35/G4
West-Nieuwland, Neth. 52/A5
West-Terschelling, Neth. 52/C2
Westall (pt.), Austl. 131/G5
Westboro, Wi, US 157/J5
Westbourne, Mb, Can. 156/E2
Westbrook, Mn, US 155/G1
Westbrook, Ct, US 169/F1
Westbury, NY, US 169/L9
Westbury, Eng, UK 36/D4
Westby, Wi, US 155/J2
Westchester (co.), NY, US 169/E1
Westchester County (arpt.), NY, US 169/L7
Westcliffe, Co, US 152/B1
Westcott, Eng, UK 30/B3
Westdorpe, Neth. 54/C1
Westend, Ca, US 148/D3
Westerblokker, Neth. 52/C3
Westerbork, Neth. 52/D3
Westerburg, Ger. 55/G2
Westerham, Eng, UK 30/D3
Westerheim, Ger. 61/G1
Westerholt, Ger. 53/E1
Westerkappeln, Ger. 53/E4
Westerland, Ger. 40/C4
Westerlo, Belg. 55/D1
Westerly, RI, US 161/L4
Western (des.), Egypt 109/F3
Western (pol. reg.), Gha. 115/E5
Western (chan.), SKor. 84/A3
Western (prov.), Kenya 119/A1
Western (prov.), PNG 129/F1
Western (prov.), SrL. 95/C5
Western Area (prov.), SLeo. 114/B4
Western Australia (state), Austl. 127/B3
Western Cape (prov.), SAfr. 124/C4
Western Caprivi Game Park, Namb. 122/D3
Western Ghats (mts.), India 92/B4
Western Highlands (uplands), PNG 129/G1
Western Run (riv.), Md, US 168/B4
Western Sahara 107/A2
Western Sayan (mts.), Rus. 78/C1
Western Sayans (mts.), Rus. 74/J4
Western Springs (nbrhd.), NZ 135/F6
Westernport, Md, US 161/G5
Westerschelde (chan.), Belg. 52/A6
Westerstede, Ger. 53/E2
Westervoort, Neth. 52/C5
Westerwald (mts.), Ger. 42/D3
Westfield, NB, Can. 158/D3
Westfield, Ma, US 161/K3
Westfield, NY, US 161/G3
Westfield, NJ, US 169/H9
Westfield, Wi, US 155/K2
Westgat (chan.), Neth. 52/D2
Westhampton, NY, US 169/F2
Westhampton Beach, NY, US 169/F2
Westhausen, Ger. 58/D5
Westheim, Ger. 58/B4
Westhill, Sc, UK 33/D2
Westhofen, Ger. 58/B3
Westhoff, Tx, US 151/F3
Westhope, ND, US 156/D3
Westhoughton, Eng, UK 35/F4
Westkapelle, Neth. 52/A5
Westlake, La, US 164/B2
Westlake Village, Ca, US 166/B2
Westland, Mi, US 167/F7
Westland NP, NZ 135/B3
Westlock, Ab, Can. 140/E3
Westmalle, Belg. 52/B6
Westminster, Ca, US 166/F8
Westminster, SC, US 163/F3
Westminster, Co, US 154/B4
Westminster, Md, US 168/B4
Westminster, City of (bor.), Eng, UK 30/A1
Westmont, Pa, US 161/G4
Westmont, Il, US 167/P16
Westmont (Haddon), NJ, US 168/C4
Westmoreland, Ks, US 155/F4
Westmoreland, Austl. 129/E4
Westmorland (reg.), Eng, UK 35/F3
Westmorland, Ca, US 148/E4
Westmount, Qu, Can. 159/N7
Westmuir, Sc, UK 33/C3
Westoak, Ga, US 163/L7
Weston, Co, US 152/B2
Weston, Oh, US 160/E4
Weston, Ga, US 165/F2
Weston, Id, US 147/H2
Weston, WV, US 163/G1
Weston, Wi, US 155/H1
Weston, Wy, US 154/B1
Weston, Malay. 88/A4
Weston, Ct, US 169/E1
Weston Zoyland, Eng, UK 36/D4
Weston-super-Mare, Eng, UK 36/D4
Westonaria, SAfr. 124/P13
Westover, WV, US 160/G5
Westover (A.F.B.), Ma, US 161/K3
Westover, SD, US 154/D2
Westphalia, Ks, US 153/G1
Westport, NS, Can. 158/D3
Westport, Ire. 32/A2
Westport, On, Can. 161/H2
Westport, NZ 135/B3
Westport, In, US 162/E1
Westport, Wa, US 144/B4
Westport, Ct, US 169/E1
Westray (isl.), Sc, UK 31/V14
Westside, Ga, US 162/F3
Westview, Sk, Can. 156/C2
Westville, Ok, US 153/G3
Westville, Ga, US 165/F1
Westville, In, US 160/C4
Westville, Il, US 160/C4
Westville, NS, Can. 159/F3
Westville, SC, US 163/G3
Westward Ho!, Eng, UK 36/B4
Westwold, BC, Can. 144/E2
Westwood, NJ, US 169/J8
Westwood, Zam. 123/F2
Westwood, Ca, US 146/C3
Westwood, Ky, US 163/F1
Westwood Lakes, Fl, US 164/P11
Westworth Village, Tx, US 150/K7
Westzaan, Neth. 52/B4
Wet (mts.), Co, US 154/B4
Wetan (isl.), Indo. 128/C1
Wetar (isl.), Indo. 128/B1
Wetar (str.), ETim.,Indo. 128/B2
Wetaskiwin, Ab, Can. 145/H1
Wete, D.R. Congo 121/F4
Wete, Tanz. 119/B3
Wetheral, Eng, UK 35/F2
Wetherby, Eng, UK 35/G4
Wetlet, Myan. 94/A1
Wetmore, Ks, US 155/G4
Wetter (riv.), Ger. 58/B2
Wetter, Ger. 53/E6
Wetterau (reg.), Ger. 58/C2
Wetteren, Belg. 54/C2
Wetterhorn (peak), Swi. 60/E4
Wettingen, Swi. 61/E3
Wettringen, Ger. 53/E4
Wetumka, Ok, US 153/F3
Wetumpka, Al, US 162/D4
Wetuppa, Austl. 132/B2
Wetzikon, Swi. 61/E3
Wetzlar, Ger. 58/B1
Wetzstein (peak), Ger. 59/E2
Wevelgem, Belg. 54/C2
Wewahitchka, Fl, US 165/F2
Wewak, PNG 136/D5
Wewoka, Ok, US 153/F3
Wexford, Ire. 32/D5
Wexford (co.), Ire. 32/D5
Wexford (har.), Ire. 32/D5
Wey (riv.), Eng, UK 30/A3
Weyanoke, La, US 164/C2
Weyauwega, Wi, US 155/K1
Weybourne, Eng, UK 37/H1
Weybridge, Eng, UK 30/B2
Weyburn, Sk, Can. 156/C3
Weygand (ruin), Alg. 111/F4
Weyhausen, Ger. 53/H4
Weyland (pt.), Austl. 131/G5
Weymouth, NS, Can. 158/D3
Weymouth (cape), Austl. 129/F3
Weymouth, Eng, UK 36/D5
Weymouth (bay), Eng, UK 36/D5
Weymouth North, NS, Can. 158/E3
Wezep, Neth. 52/D4
Whakatane, NZ 135/D2
Whale Cove, Nun, Can. 140/G2
Whaletown, BC, Can. 144/B2
Whaley Bridge, Eng, UK 35/G5
Whalsey (isl.), Sc, UK 31/W13
Whangamata, NZ 135/C2
Whangaparaoa (head), NZ 135/F6
Whangarei, NZ 135/C1
Wharfe (riv.), Eng, UK 35/G3
Wharncliffe, WV, US 163/G2
Wharton, Tx, US 151/F3
Whataroa, NZ 135/B3
Whatatutu, NZ 135/D2
Whatley, Al, US 164/E2
Wheatland, Mo, US 153/H2
Wheatland, Wy, US 154/B2
Wheatland No. 2 (res.), Wy, US 154/B3
Wheatley, On, Can. 160/E3
Wheatley, Ar, US 162/B3
Wheatley, Eng, UK 37/E3
Wheaton, Mn, US 156/F5
Wheaton, Mo, US 153/G2
Wheaton, Il, US 160/B4
Wheaton Aston, Eng, UK 36/D1
Wheaton Village, NJ, US 168/C5
Wheaton-Glenmont, Md, US 168/A5
Wheeler (peak), NM, US 152/B2
Wheeler, Tx, US 152/D3
Wheeler (peak), Nv, US 147/F4
Wheeler, Ms, US 162/C3
Wheeler, Or, US 144/C5
Wheeler (lake), Al, US 162/D3
Wheeler NWR, Al, US 162/D3
Wheeler Springs, Ca, US 166/A1
Wheelersburg, Oh, US 163/F1
Wheeless, Ok, US 152/C2
Wheeling, WV, US 160/F4
Wheeling, Il, US 167/Q15
Wheeling, Mo, US 155/H4
Wheelock, Tx, US 151/F2
Wheelwright, Arg. 190/E2
Whelen Springs, Ar, US 153/H4
Whenuapai (arpt.), NZ 135/F6
Whernside (peak), Eng, UK 35/F3
Whickham, Eng, UK 35/G2
Whidbey (pt.), Austl. 131/G5
Whidbey (isl.), Wa, US 144/C4
Whiddy (isl.), Ire. 32/A6
Whigham, Ga, US 165/F2
Whinham (mt.), Austl. 131/F3
Whiskeytown-Shasta-Trinity Nat'l Rec. Area, Ca, US 146/B3
Whistler, BC, Can. 144/C2
Whitakers, NC, US 163/J2
Whitbourne, Nf, Can. 159/L2
Whitburn, Sc, UK 33/C5
Whitburn, Eng, UK 35/G2
Whitby, Eng, UK 35/H3
Whitby, On, Can. 160/V8
Whitchurch, Eng, UK 35/F6
Whitchurch, Eng, UK 37/E4
Whitchurch, Wal, UK 36/C3
Whitchurch, Eng, UK 37/F3
Whitchurch-Stouffville, On, Can. 161/G3
Whitcombe (mt.), NZ 135/B3
White (sea), Swe. 68/B3
White, Ar, US 153/J4
White (lake), On, Can. 157/M3
White (bay), Nf, Can. 141/L3
White (riv.), Co, US 147/J3
White (pass), Va, US 163/G2
White, Ga, US 162/E3
White, SD, US 155/F1
White (pass), Wa, US 144/D4
White (lake), Austl. 127/B3
White, Vernon Fork (riv.), In, US 162/E1
White Bear (riv.), Nf, Can. 159/J1
White Bear, Sk, Can. 145/K2
White Bear Lake, Mn, US 157/P6
White Bird, Id, US 146/E1
White Bluff, Tn, US 162/D2
White Butte, SD, US 156/C5
White Castle, La, US 164/C2
White City, Ks, US 153/F1
White City, Sk, Can. 156/B2
White City, Fl, US 165/H4
White City, Fl, US 165/F3
White Cliffs, Austl. 132/B1
White Cloud, Mi, US 160/D3
White Coomb (peak), Sc, UK 33/C6
White Deer (cr.), Pa, US 168/A1
White Earth, Mn, US 156/G4
White Earth, ND, US 156/C3
White Earth (riv.), ND, US 156/C3
White Earth Indian (res.), Mn, US 157/G4
White Esk (riv.), Sc, UK 33/C6
White Hall, Ar, US 153/H3
White Hall, Al, US 162/D4
White Hall, Md, US 168/B4
White Haven, Pa, US 168/C1
White Horse Draw (riv.), Tx, US 150/B2
White House, Tn, US 162/D2
White Lake, Wi, US 157/K5
White Lake, On, Can. 161/H2
White Lake Nat'l Wild. Ref., ND, US 156/C4
White Marsh, Md, US 168/B5
White Mills, Ky, US 162/D2
White Mountain, Ak, US 171/F3
White Mountain (peak), Ca, US 148/C2
White Nile (riv.), Sudan 107/F4
White Oak, Ga, US 165/H2
White Oak, Oh, US 162/E1
White Oak (bayou), Tx, US 151/M9
White Oak, Tx, US 151/G1
White Oak, Md, US 168/B5
White Otter (lake), On, Can. 157/J3
White Pigeon, Mi, US 160/D4
White Pine, Tn, US 163/F2
White Plains, NY, US 169/K7
White Plains, NC, US 163/G2
White Rapids (dam), Mi, US 160/C2
White River, SD, US 154/D2
White River NWR, Ar, US 162/B3
White Rock, Tx, US 153/F4
White Rock (cr.), Ks, US 155/E4
White Rock, NM, US 149/J3
White Rock (lake), Tx, US 150/L7
White Salmon, Wa, US 144/D5
White Sands (des.), NM, US 149/J4
White Sands, NM, US 149/J4
White Sands Missile Range, NM, US 149/J4
White Sands Nat'l Mon., NM, US 150/A1
White Sands Space Harbor, NM, US 149/J4
White Settlement, Tx, US 150/K7
White Shield, ND, US 156/D4
White Springs, Fl, US 165/G2
White Sulphur Springs, Mt, US 145/J4
White Sulphur Springs, WV, US 163/G2
White Swan, Wa, US 144/D4
White Volta (riv.), Gha. 107/B4
White Waltham, Eng, UK 30/A2
White Woman (cr.), Co,Ks, US 154/D4
White, East Fork (riv.), In, US 162/D1
White, West Fork (riv.), Wa, US 167/D3
Whiteadder Water (riv.), Sc, UK 33/D5
Whitecourt, Ab, Can. 140/E3
Whiteface (riv.), Mn, US 157/H4
Whiteface, Tx, US 152/C4
Whiteface (res.), Mn, US 157/H4
Whiteface (mtn.), NY, US 161/K2
Whitefield, Eng, UK 35/F4
Whitefield, NH, US 161/L2
Whitefish (lake), Mn, US 157/G4
Whitefish (pt.), Wi, US 160/C2
Whitefish (bay), Mi, US 160/D1
Whitefish, Mt, US 144/G3
Whitefish Point, Mi, US 160/D1
Whitefish Station, Yk, Can. 171/L2
Whiteford (pt.), Wal, UK 36/B3
Whiteford, Md, US 168/B4
Whitegate, Ire. 32/B6
Whitegate, Ire. 32/B4
Whitehall, NY, US 161/K3
Whitehall, Oh, US 160/E5
Whitehall, Mi, US 160/C3
Whitehall, Wi, US 155/J1
Whitehall, Mt, US 145/H5
Whitehall (Fullerton), Pa, US 168/C2
Whitehaven, Eng, UK 34/E2
Whitehead, NI, UK 34/C2
Whitehills, Sc, UK 33/D1
Whitehorse (cap.), Yk, Can. 171/L3
Whitehorse (hill), Eng, UK 37/E3
Whitehorse, SD, US 156/D5
Whitehouse, Ga, US 163/M7
Whitehouse, Oh, US 160/E4
Whitehouse, Tx, US 151/G1
Whiteland, In, US 160/C5
Whiteman (A.F.B.), Mo, US 153/H1
Whitemark, Austl. 133/D5
Whitemouth (lake), Mb, Can. 157/G3
Whitemouth, Mb, Can. 156/G3
Whitemouth (riv.), Mb, Can. 156/G3
Whitepine, Co, US 149/J1
Whiteriver, Az, US 149/H4
Whites City, NM, US 150/B1
Whites Lake, NS, Can. 158/F3
Whitesboro, Ok, US 153/G3
Whitesboro, Tx, US 153/F4
Whitesburg, Ky, US 163/F2
Whiteside (chan.), Chile 191/C7
Whitestone Hill Bfld. Hist. Site, ND, US 156/E4
Whitesunday NP, Austl. 129/H5
Whitesville, Ky, US 162/D2
Whitesville, NJ, US 168/D3
Whitesville, NY, US 161/H3
Whitetail, NM, US 152/B4
Whitetail, Mt, US 156/B3
Whitetop, Va, US 163/G2
Whiteville, Tn, US 162/C3
Whiteville, NC, US 163/H3
Whitewater, Ks, US 153/F2
Whitewater (lake), On, Can. 157/K2
Whitewater (bay), Fl, US 165/H5
Whitewater, Co, US 147/J4
Whitewater, Wi, US 155/K2
Whitewater, Mt, US 145/L3
Whitewater Baldy (peak), NM, US 149/H4
Whitewood, Sk, Can. 156/C2
Whitewright, Tx, US 153/F4
Whithorn, Sc, UK 34/D2
Whitianga, NZ 135/C2
Whiting, In, US 167/R16
Whiting, Ia, US 155/F2
Whiting, Ks, US 155/G4
Whiting, Wi, US 155/K1
Whiting Bay, Sc, UK 33/A6
Whiting Field Nav. Air Sta., Fl, US 164/E2
Whitland, Wal, UK 36/B3
Whitlash, Mt, US 145/J3
Whitley Bay, Eng, UK 35/G1
Whitley City, Ky, US 162/E2
Whitmore Lake, Mi, US 160/E3
Whitney, On, Can. 161/G2
Whitney (mt.), Ca, US 142/C4
Whitney, Tx, US 151/F2
Whitney Point, NY, US 161/J3
Whitsand (bay), Eng, UK 36/B6
Whitsett, Tx, US 151/E3
Whitstable, Eng, UK 37/H4
Whitsunday (isl.), Austl. 127/D3
Whitsunday Island NP, Austl. 134/C3
Whitt, Tx, US 153/E4
Whittaker, Mi, US 167/E7
Whittier, Ak, US 171/J3
Whittier, Ca, US 166/F8
Whittington, Eng, UK 35/F6
Whittlesea, Austl. 132/G5
Whittlesey (mt.), Wi, US 157/J4
Whittlesey, Eng, UK 37/F1
Whitton, Austl. 133/C2
Whitwell, Eng, UK 35/G5
Whitwell, Tn, US 162/E3
Whitworth, Eng, UK 35/F4
Wholdaia (lake), NW, Can. 140/F2
Why, Az, US 149/F4
Whyalla, Austl. 131/H5
Whycocomagh, NS, Can. 159/G3
Whyjonta, Austl. 132/B1
Wi (isl.), SKor. 81/D5
Wiang Kosai NP, Thai. 94/B2
Wiarton, On, Can. 160/F2
Wiawer, Ugan. 119/A1
Wiawso, Gha. 115/E5
Wibaux, Mt, US 156/B4
Wichabai, Guy. 181/G4
Wich'alē, Eth. 118/A3
Wichelen, Belg. 54/C2
Wichian Buri, Thai. 94/C3
Wichita (riv.), Tx, US 152/E4
Wichita (mts.), Ok, US 153/E3
Wichita, Ks, US 153/F2
Wichita Falls, Tx, US 153/E4
Wichita Mountains NWR, Ok, US 153/E3
Wick, Sc, UK 31/S7
Wick Hill, Eng, UK 30/A2
Wickede, Ger. 53/E6
Wickede (Dortmund) (int'l arpt.), Ger. 53/E5
Wickenburg, Az, US 149/F4
Wickepin, Austl. 130/C5
Wickes, Ar, US 153/G3
Wickford, Eng, UK 30/E2
Wickham, Austl. 130/C2
Wickham Market, Eng, UK 37/H2
Wickiup (res.), Or, US 146/B2
Wickliffe, Ky, US 162/C2
Wicklow (pt.), Ire. 34/B6
Wicklow (mts.), Ire. 32/D4
Wicklow, Ire. 34/B6
Wicklow (pass), Ire. 34/B5
Wicklow (co.), Ire. 32/D4
Wickriede (riv.), Ger. 53/F4
Wid (riv.), Eng, UK 30/E2
Widgiemooltha, Austl. 130/D4
Widnau, Swi. 61/F3
Widnes, Eng, UK 35/F5
Więcbork, Pol. 43/J2
Wied (riv.), Ger. 45/G1
Wiedau (riv.), Ger. 53/G2
Wiefelstede, Ger. 53/F2
Wiehengebirge (ridge), Ger. 53/F4
Wiehl, Ger. 55/G2
Wielenbach, Ger. 61/H2
Wieliczka, Pol. 43/L4
Wielkopolski NP, Pol. 43/J2
Wielkopolskie (prov.), Pol. 43/J2
Wielsbeke, Belg. 54/C2
Wieluń, Pol. 43/K3
Wien (prov.), Aus. 43/J4
Wien (riv.), Aus. 51/N7
Wien (Vienna) (cap.), Aus. 51/N7
Wiener Neudorf, Aus. 51/N7
Wiener Neustadt, Aus. 50/C2
Wienerwald (reg.), Aus. 51/N7
Wienwald (reg.), Aus. 45/L2
Wieprz (riv.), Pol. 70/B2
Wierden, Neth. 52/D4
Wieren, Ger. 53/H3
Wieringermeerpolder (polder), Neth. 52/B3
Wieringerwerf, Neth. 52/C3
Wierum, Neth. 52/D2
Wieruszów, Pol. 43/K3
Wiesbaden, Ger. 58/B2
Wiese (riv.), Ger. 45/G3
Wiese (isl.), Rus. 74/H2
Wieseck (riv.), Ger. 58/B1
Wiesendangen, Swi. 61/E2
Wiesensteig, Ger. 58/C5
Wiesent (riv.), Ger. 58/E4
Wiesentheid, Ger. 58/D3
Wiesloch, Ger. 58/B4
Wiesmoor, Ger. 53/E2
Wietmarschen, Ger. 53/D4
Wietze (riv.), Ger. 53/G3
Wietze, Ger. 53/G3
Wietzendorf, Ger. 53/G3
Wiezyca (peak), Pol. 40/H4
Wigan, Eng, UK 35/F4
Wigan (co.), Eng, UK 35/F4
Wiggins, Ms, US 164/D2
Wight, Isle of (isl.), UK 44/C1
Wigierski NP, Pol. 43/M1
Wigmore, Eng, UK 30/E3
Wignehies, Fr. 54/D3
Wigry (lake), Pol. 41/K5
Wigston, Eng, UK 37/E1
Wigton, Eng, UK 35/E2
Wigtown, Sc, UK 34/D2
Wigtown (bay), Sc, UK 34/D2
Wijchen, Neth. 52/C5
Wijhe, Neth. 52/D4
Wijk bij Duurstede, Neth. 52/C5
Wijk en Aalburg, Neth. 52/C5
Wikieup, Az, US 149/F3
Wik'ro, Eth. 118/A2
Wikwemikong, On, Can. 160/F2
Wikwemikong Ind. Res., On, Can. 160/F2
Wil, Swi. 61/F3
Wilber, Ne, US 155/F3
Wilberforce (cape), Austl. 129/E2
Wilberforce, Austl. 134/G8
Wilberfoss, Eng, UK 35/H4
Wilbur, Wa, US 144/E4
Wilburgstetten, Ger. 58/D4
Wilburton, Ok, US 153/G3
Wilcannia, Austl. 132/B1
Wilchingen, Swi. 61/E2
Wilcox, Sk, Can. 156/B2
Wilcox, Pa, US 161/G4
Wilczek (isl.), Rus. 74/G1
Wild (coast), SAfr. 124/E4
Wild Creek (res.), Pa, US 168/C2
Wild Horse (hill), Ne, US 154/D3
Wild Rice (riv.), Mn, US 156/F4
Wild Rose, Wi, US 155/K1
Wild World, Md, US 168/B6
Wildau, Ger. 42/Q7
Wildbad im Schwarzwald, Ger. 58/B5
Wildberg, Ger. 58/B5
Wilder, Id, US 146/E2
Wildersville, Tn, US 162/C3
Wilderswil, Swi. 60/D4
Wildervank, Neth. 52/D2
Wildeshausen, Ger. 53/F3
Wildfield, On, Can. 160/T8
Wildflecken, Ger. 58/C2
Wildgrat (peak), Aus. 61/G3
Wildhaus, Swi. 61/F3
Wildhay (riv.), Ab, Can. 144/E1
Wildhorn (peak), Swi. 60/D5
Wildomar, Ca, US 166/C3
Wildrose, ND, US 156/C3
Wildspitze (peak), Aus. 61/G4
Wildstrubel (peak), Swi. 60/D5
Wildsville, La, US 164/C2
Wildwood, Mn, US 157/H4
Wildwood, Fl, US 165/G3
Wildwood, Ab, Can. 144/G1
Wildwood, NJ, US 168/D6
Wildwood Crest, NJ, US 168/D6
Wiley, Co, US 152/C1
Wilge (riv.), SAfr. 124/E2
Wilhelm (mt.), PNG 129/G1
Wilhelm II (coast), Ant. 192/F
Wilhelmina (mts.), Sur. 181/G4
Wilhelminakanaal (canal), Neth. 52/C5
Wilhelmsburg, Ger. 53/G1
Wilhelmshaven, Ger. 53/F1
Wilhelmshorst, Ger. 42/Q7
Wilhelmstal, Namb. 122/C4
Wilhering, Aus. 59/H6
Wilkes Land (phys. reg.), Ant. 192/J
Wilkes-Barre, Pa, US 168/C1
Wilkes-Barre/Scranton Int'l (arpt.), Pa, US 168/C1
Wilkesboro, NC, US 163/G2
Wilkeson, Wa, US 167/C3
Wilkie, Sk, Can. 145/K1
Wilkins (sound), Ant. 192/U
Wilkinson Heights, SC, US 163/G4
Will (mt.), BC, Can. 171/N4
Will (co.), Il, US 167/P16
Will Rogers World (int'l arpt.), Ok, US 153/F3
Willa Cather Memorial, Ne, US 154/E3
Willacoochee, Ga, US 165/G2
Willamette (riv.), Or, US 146/B1
Willandra Billabong (cr.), Austl. 133/B1
Willandra NP, Austl. 132/C2
Willandra NP, Austl. 133/B1
Willapa (bay), Wa, US 144/C4
Willapa NWR, Wa, US 144/C4
Willard, Mt, US 156/B4
Willard, Ok, US 152/E2
Willard, Mo, US 153/H2
Willard, Oh, US 160/E4
Willard, Ut, US 147/G3
Willard, NM, US 149/J3
Willaston, Eng, UK 35/F5
Willaura, Austl. 132/B3
Willcox, Az, US 149/H4
Willcox Playa (dry lake), Az, US 149/G4
Willebadessen, Ger. 53/G5
Willebroek, Belg. 55/D1
Willemstad (cap.), NAnt. 180/D1
Willemstad, Neth. 52/B5
Willernie, Mn, US 157/Q6
Willeroo, Austl. 128/C3
Willerzie, Belg. 55/D4
Willesden (nbrhd.), Eng, UK 30/C2
William (mt.), Austl. 132/B3
William Bay NP, Austl. 130/C5
William Bill Dannely (res.), Al, US 164/E1
William Creek, Austl. 131/H4
William P. Hobby (arpt.), Tx, US 151/M9
Williams, Mn, US 157/G3
Williams (A.F.B.), Az, US 149/G4
Williams, Az, US 149/F3
Williams, Austl. 130/C5
Williams, SC, US 163/G4
Williams Bay, Wi, US 155/K2
Williams Lake, BC, Can. 144/C1
Williams Lake Ind. Res., BC, Can. 144/C1
Williamsburg (nbrhd.), NY, US 169/K9
Williamsburg, Ky, US 162/E2
Williamsburg, NM, US 149/J4
Williamsburg, Ia, US 155/H3
Williamsburg, Va, US 163/J2
Williamsfield, Oh, US 160/F4
Williamson (riv.), Or, US 146/C2
Williamson, WV, US 163/F2
Williamsport, In, US 160/C4
Williamsport, Pa, US 168/A1
Williamsport-Lycoming County (arpt.), Pa, US 168/B1
Williamston, SC, US 163/F3
Williamston, NC, US 163/J3
Williamstown, NY, US 161/J3
Williamstown, WV, US 160/F5
Williamstown, Vt, US 161/K2
Williamstown, Ky, US 162/E1
Williamstown, Mo, US 155/J3
Williamstown (nbrhd.), Austl. 132/F5
Williamstown, Pa, US 168/B2
Williamstown, NJ, US 168/D4
Williamsville, Mo, US 162/B2
Williamsville, NY, US 160/V10
Willich, Ger. 52/D6
Willimantic, Ct, US 161/K4
Willingboro, NJ, US 168/D3
Willingen, Ger. 53/F6
Willington, Eng, UK 35/G2

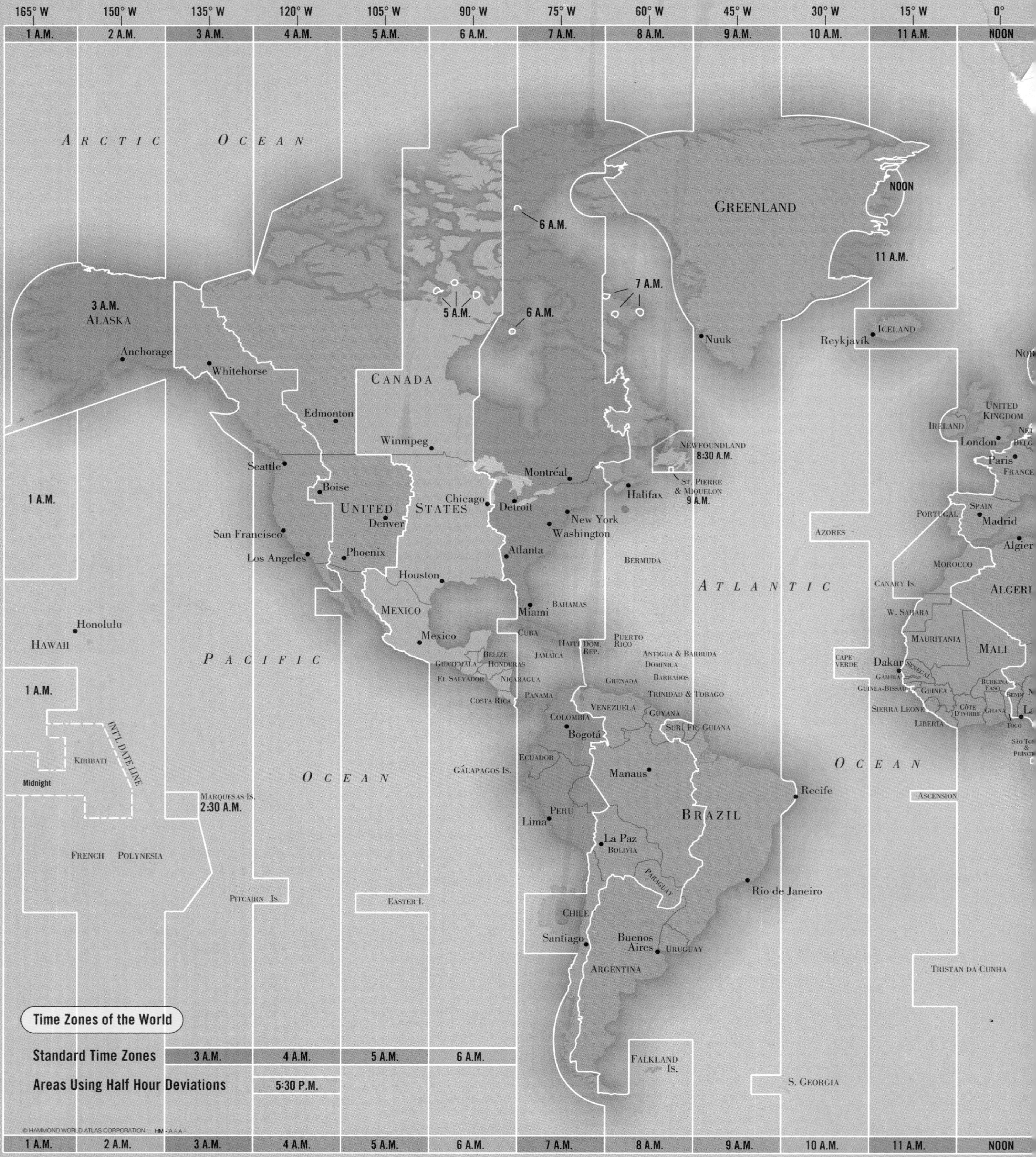

Time Zones of the World
Standard Time Zones
3 A.M.
4 A.M.
5 A.M.
6 A.M.
Areas Using Half Hour Deviations
5:30 P.M.
165° W
150° W
135° W
120° W
105° W
90° W
75° W
60° W
45° W
30° W
15° W
0°
1 A.M.
2 A.M.
3 A.M.
4 A.M.
5 A.M.
6 A.M.
7 A.M.
8 A.M.
9 A.M.
10 A.M.
11 A.M.
NOON
ARCTIC OCEAN
PACIFIC OCEAN
ATLANTIC OCEAN
GREENLAND
NOON
11 A.M.
6 A.M.
7 A.M.
5 A.M.
6 A.M.
3 A.M.
ALASKA
Anchorage
Whitehorse
CANADA
Edmonton
Winnipeg
Nuuk
Reykjavík
ICELAND
NEWFOUNDLAND
8:30 A.M.
ST. PIERRE & MIQUELON
9 A.M.
Halifax
Montréal
Seattle
Boise
UNITED STATES
Chicago
Detroit
Denver
New York
Washington
San Francisco
Los Angeles
Phoenix
Atlanta
Houston
BERMUDA
AZORES
MEXICO
Mexico
Miami
BAHAMAS
CUBA
HAITI
DOM. REP.
PUERTO RICO
JAMAICA
BELIZE
HONDURAS
GUATEMALA
EL SALVADOR
NICARAGUA
COSTA RICA
PANAMA
ANTIGUA & BARBUDA
DOMINICA
BARBADOS
GRENADA
TRINIDAD & TOBAGO
VENEZUELA
GUYANA
SURI.
FR. GUIANA
COLOMBIA
Bogotá
ECUADOR
GÁLAPAGOS IS.
Manaus
PERU
Lima
BRAZIL
Recife
La Paz
BOLIVIA
PARAGUAY
Rio de Janeiro
CHILE
Santiago
Buenos Aires
URUGUAY
ARGENTINA
FALKLAND IS.
S. GEORGIA
1 A.M.
Honolulu
HAWAII
1 A.M.
INT'L DATE LINE
KIRIBATI
Midnight
MARQUESAS IS.
2:30 A.M.
FRENCH POLYNESIA
PITCAIRN IS.
EASTER I.
UNITED KINGDOM
IRELAND
London
Paris
FRANCE
PORTUGAL
SPAIN
Madrid
Algier
MOROCCO
CANARY IS.
ALGERI
W. SAHARA
MAURITANIA
MALI
CAPE VERDE
Dakar
SENEGAL
GAMBIA
GUINEA-BISSAU
GUINEA
BURKINA FASO
SIERRA LEONE
CÔTE D'IVOIRE
GHANA
LIBERIA
TOGO
SÃO TOMÉ & PRÍNCIPE
ASCENSION
TRISTAN DA CUNHA
© HAMMOND WORLD ATLAS CORPORATION